The Hotel Guide 2001

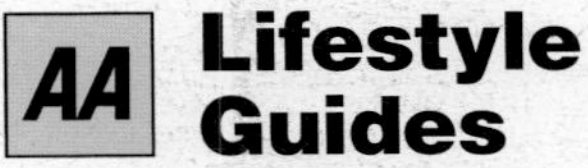

34th edition October 2000

First published by the Automobile Association as the Hotel and Restaurant Guide, 1967

Mapping is produced by the Cartographic Department of the Automobile Association.

Maps © The Automobile Association 2000
Cover design by Sue Climpson, Whitchurch, England
Design by Nautilus Design UK Ltd, Basingstoke, Hampshire

The main cover photograph shows Bindon Country House Hotel & Restaurant, Wellington, Somerset. Image courtesy of the proprietors.

Typesetting and colour repro by Microset Graphics Ltd, Basingstoke, England

Printed and bound in Italy by Amilcare Pizzi SpA, Milan

Advertisement Production: Karen Weeks, telephone 01256 491545

Directory compiled by the AA Hotel Services Department and generated from the AA establishment database.

A CIP catalogue record for this book is available from the British Library
ISBN 0 7495 2532 0

Published by AA Publishing, a trading name of Automobile Association Developments Limited, whose registered office is Norfolk House, Priestley Road, Basingstoke, Hampshire RG24 9NY. Registered number 1878835

Contents

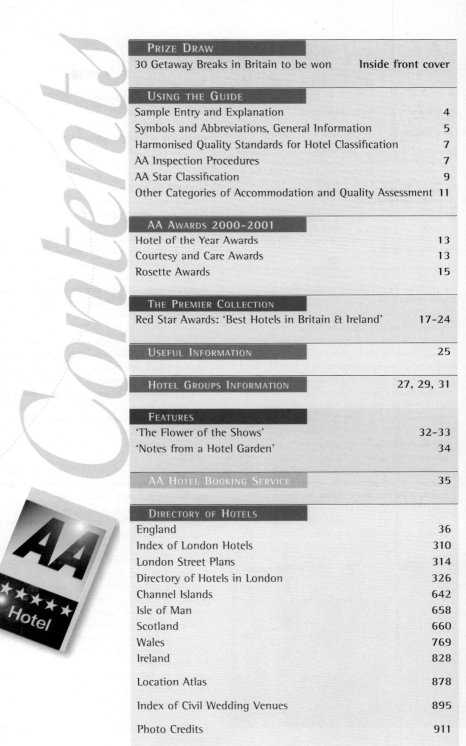

AA ★★★★★ Hotel

Using the Guide

1 ANYTOWN, Anyshire Map 4 SU46

2 ★★★★71% The Example Hotel
Any Road XX1 XX11.
☎ 0022 001122 0022 001122
e-mail: sendto@isp.co.uk

3 *Dir: 2m north of Any Town - Any Road signed turn left at Business Park.*
A purpose-built modern complex with a well equipped leisure and conference centre in a separate, linked building. Bedrooms are generously planned to give working space and adequate power points and lighting. Reception rooms consist of a bar lounge and carvery-style dining room.

4 **ROOMS:** 50 en suite (6 fmly) s fr £68; d fr £125 (incl. bkfst) * LB

5 **FACILITIES:** STV air con. Indoor swimming(H) Squash Snooker Gym Sauna
CONF: Thtr 80 Class 30 Board 40 **PARKING:** 30 **NOTES:** No dogs
No children 14 yrs No smoking in restaurant Civ Wed 80 7

8 **CARDS:**

6

Sample Entry

Explanation of entries and notes on abbreviations

(see also the key opposite)

1. Town Listed alphabetically within each country section: England, Channel Islands, Isle of Man, Scotland, Wales, Ireland. The administrative county or region follows the town name. Towns on islands are listed under the island (e.g. Wight, Isle of). The map reference gives the map page number, then the National Grid Reference. Read the first figure across and the second figure vertically within the lettered square.

2. Hotel Name Preceded by the star rating, quality percentage score (see page 11) and rosette award, followed by address, phone/fax numbers and e-mail address where applicable. (E-mail addresses are believed correct at the time of printing but may change during the currency of the guide.) Listed in star and quality percentage score order within each location. If the hotel name is in italic type the information that follows has not been confirmed by the hotel management. A company or consortium name or logo may appear (hotel groups are listed on pages 27-31); for those with a central reservation number specify the name and location of the hotel when booking.

The Lanesborough, London

3. Dir: Directions to the hotel.

4. ROOMS The first figure shows the number of en suite letting bedrooms, or total number of bedrooms, then the number with en suite or family facilities. Bedrooms in an annexe or extension are only noted if they are at least equivalent to those in the main building, but facilities and prices may differ. In some hotels all bedrooms are in an annexe/extension. **Prices** (per room per night) are provided by hoteliers in good faith and are indications not firm quotations. Most hotels only accept cheques if notice is given and a cheque card produced. Not all hotels take travellers cheques.

5. FACILITIES Colour TV is provided in all bedrooms unless otherwise indicated. Weekly live **entertainment** should be available at least once a week all year. Some hotels provide entertainment only in summer or on special occasions, check when booking. **Leisure facilities** are as stated. **Child facilities** may include: baby intercom, baby-sitting service, playroom, playground, laundry, drying/ironing facilities, cots, high chairs, special meals. In some hotels children can sleep in parents' rooms at no extra cost; check all details when booking.

6. PARKING Shows number of spaces available for guests' use. May include covered, charged spaces.

7. NOTES No dogs Where hotels allow dogs, some breeds may be forbidden and dogs may be excluded from areas of the hotel, especially the dining room. It is essential to check when booking. **No children** A minimum age may be given, e.g. 'No children 4 yrs'. Where neither 'ch fac' (see FACILITIES) nor 'no children' appears, hotels accept children but may not have special facilities (e.g. high chairs). It is essential to check when booking. **RS** Some hotels have a restricted service during quieter months, e.g. for the restaurant or leisure facilities; check when booking. **Civ Wed 50** The establishment is licensed for civil weddings and can accommodate up to 50 guests for the ceremony. An index of establishments holding civil wedding licences can be found on pages 895-910. N.B. All establishments in Scotland are licensed for civil weddings; check details with the hotel.

8. CARDS Credit cards may be subject to a surcharge; check when booking.

Key to Symbols *and Abbreviations*

★ Star Classification (see page 9)
% Quality Percentage Score (see page 11)
★ Red stars denote the AA's highest quality award (see pages 17-23)
❀ Rosette Award for quality of food (see page 15)
Country House Hotel
○ Hotel has applied for recognition, subject to inspection, or is due to open during currency of guide
* 2000 prices

Different accommodation categories (see page 11 for explanation)

Townhouse Accommodation
Travel Accommodation

ROOMS

fmly	Family rooms (and number)
s	Single room
d	Double room
incl bkfst.	Breakfast included
LB	Special leisure breaks available
Off Peak	Lower prices/concessions may be available; check when booking

FACILITIES

STV	Satellite television
air con	Air conditioning
indoor swimming(H)	Heated indoor swimming pool
outdoor swimming(H)	Heated outdoor swimming pool
ch fac	Special facilities for children
Xmas	Special programme for Christmas/New Year

Leisure facilities are as stated, e.g. indoor swimming (H).

CONF

Conference facilities available

Thtr	Seats theatre style (and number)
Class	Seats classroom style (and number)
Board	Seats boardroom style (and number)
Del	Typical overnight delegate rate

NOTES

No dogs	No dogs allowed in bedrooms (guide dogs for the blind may be excepted)
No children	Indicates that children cannot be accommodated
RS	Restricted opening, e.g. RS Jan-Mar, Closed Xmas/New Year
Civ Wed	Licensed for civil weddings (and maximum number of guests)

Other restrictions as stated, e.g. no smoking in restaurant.

CARDS

Cards accepted where symbols are shown

General Information

Booking

Book as early as possible, particularly for peak periods (June to September inclusive), public holidays and, in some parts of Scotland, during the ski season. Some hotels ask for a deposit or full payment in advance, especially for one-night bookings from chance callers. Not all hotels will take advance bookings for bed and breakfast, overnight or short stays. Some will not make reservations from mid week. Some hotels charge half-board (bed, breakfast and dinner) whether you eat the meals or not. Some hotels only accept full-board bookings.

Cancellation

Once a booking is confirmed, notify the hotel immediately if you are unable to keep your reservation. If the hotel cannot relet your room you may be liable to pay about two-thirds of the room price (a deposit will count towards this payment). In Britain a legally binding contract is made when an intending guest accepts an offer of accommodation, either in writing or by telephone. Illness is not accepted as a release from this contract. You are advised to effect insurance cover against possible cancellation, for example AA Travelsure (Telephone 0870 606 1612 for details).

Complaints

If you have a complaint about hotel food, services or facilities, we strongly advise you to take it up with the management there and then, in order to give the hotelier a chance to put things right straight away. If this personal approach fails, you can write to AA Hotel Services, Fanum House, Basing View, Basingstoke, Hampshire RG21 4EA. The AA does not undertake to obtain compensation for complaints, or to enter into any correspondence.

See page 25 for Useful Information on fire regulations, licensing and prices.

MACDONALD
HOTELS
★★★★

Harmonised Quality Standards *for Hotel Classification*

Everyone is familiar with the distinctive yellow signs outside hotels showing AA star classification to denote the levels of service, accommodation and facilities a hotel guest can expect. The internationally recognised star symbol is used by the AA, the RAC and the English Tourist Board.

Swynford Paddocks, Six Mile Bottom

An establishment may approach any of the above organisations for classification, in the knowledge that their hotel will be inspected according to the same harmonised quality standards, agreed by the Chief Inspectors of the organisations concerned. Hotel guests can choose between hotels regardless of which organisation has carried out the inspection: the quality, facilities and services will meet the same standards.

Scotland and Wales

The Scottish and Welsh Tourist Boards act independently and have their own criteria for a classification scheme, although they still use stars as their symbol. The AA also offers hotels in Scotland and Wales a classification under the new quality standards.

All the hotels featured in the Scotland and Wales sections of the AA Hotel Guide, as well as those in England, the Channel Islands and the Isle of Man, have been inspected and classified by the AA Inspectorate according to the same harmonised quality standards, and only this classification is shown.

Lainston House, Winchester

AA INSPECTION PROCEDURES

How does the AA assess an hotel?

Hotels applying for AA recognition are visited on a 'mystery guest' basis by one of the AA's team of qualified hotel and restaurant inspectors. The inspector stays overnight to make a thorough test of the accommodation, food and hospitality offered and as many of the hotel facilities as possible. After settling the bill the following morning they declare their identity and ask to be shown round the entire premises. The inspector completes a full report, making a recommendation for the appropriate star classification and quality percentage score.

After this first inspection, the hotel receives an annual unannounced visit to check that standards are maintained. If the hotel changes hands, the new owners must reapply for classification as AA recognition is not transferable.

Establishments featured pay an annual fee for AA inspection, recognition and rating. One of the benefits of such recognition is a basic text entry in the AA Hotel Guide. The annual fee varies according to the star classification and the number of rooms. AA inspectors pay as a guest for their inspection visit. In addition to the text entry in the guide, hotels may purchase additional advertising such as a photograph or display advertisement.

AA Star Classification

What you can expect from an AA recognised hotel

All hotels recognised by the AA should have the highest standards of cleanliness, proper records of booking, give prompt and professional service to guests, assist with luggage on request, accept and deliver messages, provide a designated area for breakfast and dinner with drinks available in a bar or lounge, provide an early morning call on request, good quality furniture and fittings, adequate heating and lighting and proper maintenance.

What you can expect from a one star hotel

★

Polite, courteous staff providing a relatively informal yet competent style of service, available during the day and evening to receive guests. At least one designated eating area open to residents for breakfast and dinner. Last orders for dinner no earlier than 6.30pm, a reasonable choice of hot and cold dishes and a short range of wines available. Television in lounge or bedroom. Majority of rooms en suite, bath or shower room available at all times.

What you can expect from a two star hotel

★★

Smartly and professionally presented management and staff providing competent, often informal service, available throughout the day and evening to greet guests. At least one restaurant or dining room open to residents for breakfast and dinner. Last orders for dinner no earlier than 7pm, a choice of substantial hot and cold dishes and a short range of wines available. Television in bedroom. En suite or private bath or shower and WC.

What you can expect from a three star hotel

★★★

Management and staff smartly and professionally presented and usually uniformed. Technical and social skills of a good standard in responding to guests' needs and requests. A dedicated receptionist on duty, clear direction to rooms and some explanation of hotel facilities. At least one restaurant or dining room open to residents and non-residents for breakfast and dinner whenever the hotel is open. A wide selection of drinks served in a bar or lounge, available to residents and their guests throughout the day and evening. Last orders for dinner no earlier than 8pm, full dinner service provided. Remote control television, direct dial telephone. En suite bath or shower and WC.

What you can expect from a four star hotel

★★★★

A formal, professional staffing structure with smartly presented, uniformed staff, anticipating and responding to guests' needs and requests. Usually spacious, well appointed public areas. Bedrooms offering superior quality and comfort than at three star. A strong emphasis on food and beverages and a serious approach to cuisine. Reception staffed 24 hours per day by well trained staff. Express checkout facilities where appropriate. Porterage available on request and readily provided by uniformed staff. Night porter available. Newspapers can be ordered and delivered to rooms, additional services and concierge as appropriate to the style and location of the hotel. At least one restaurant open to residents and non-residents for all meals seven days per week. Drinks available to residents and their guests throughout the day and evening, table service available. Last orders for dinner no earlier than 9pm, an extensive choice of hot and cold dishes and a comprehensive list of wines. Remote control television, direct dial telephone, a range of high quality toiletries. En suite bath with fixed overhead shower and WC.

What you can expect from a five star hotel

★★★★★

Flawless guest services, professional, attentive staff, technical and social skills of the highest order. Spacious and luxurious accommodation and public areas with a range of extra facilities. First-time guests, as a minimum, escorted by reception staff or management to their bedroom. Multilingual service consistent with the needs of the hotel's normal clientele. Guest accounts well explained and presented, perhaps in an envelope or folder. Porterage offered and provided by uniformed staff. Luggage handling on arrival and departure with systems in place to ensure the minimum delay. Doorman or means of greeting guests at the hotel entrance. Full concierge service provided. At least one restaurant open to residents and non-residents for all meals seven days per week. Staff showing evidence of a serious commitment to and enthusiasm for food and wine. A wide selection of drinks, including cocktails, available in a bar or lounge, table service provided. Last orders for dinner no earlier than 10pm. High quality menu and wine list properly reflecting and complementing the style of cooking and providing exceptional quality. Evening turn-down service. Remote control television, direct dial telephone at bedside and desk, a range of luxury toiletries, bath sheets and robes. En suite bath with fixed overhead shower and WC.

Other Categories *of Accommodation*

Capital, London

FURTHER AA QUALITY ASSESSMENTS

In addition to the star classification, the AA makes a further quality assessment to help intending guests in their choice of hotel, the Quality Percentage Score. The highest achievers in this assessment are awarded Red Stars and can be easily identified in the guide, appearing first in their location with a highlighted entry. The Quality Percentage Score and Red Star awards are assessed as follows:

Quality Percentage Score - making hotel choice easier

AA inspectors supplement their general report with an additional quality assessment of everything the hotel offers, including hospitality, based on what they experience as the 'mystery guest'. This enables them to award an overall Quality Percentage Score.

The Quality Percentage Score offers a comparison of quality within the star classification, so a one star hotel may receive as high a Quality Percentage Score within its classification as a four or five star hotel.

When using the guide, intending guests can see at a glance that, for example, a two star hotel with a percentage score of 69 offers a higher quality experience within its star classification than a two star hotel with a percentage score of 59.

To gain AA recognition in the first place, a hotel must achieve a minimum quality score of 50 per cent. The Quality Percentage Score for ordinary star classification effectively runs between 50 and 80 per cent.

Red Star Awards - 'Best Hotels in Britain and Ireland'

At each of the five classification levels, the AA recognises exceptional quality of accommodation and hospitality by awarding Red Stars for excellence. A hotel with Red Stars is judged to be the best in its star classification and this award recognises that the hotel offers outstanding levels of comfort, hospitality and customer care. As a general rule, Red Star hotels achieve a Quality Percentage Score between 81 and 100 per cent; the actual percentage score is not shown in the guide.

★ **Red Star hotels are listed on pages 17-23**

Country House Hotels

Country House Hotels offer a relaxed, informal atmosphere, with an emphasis on personal welcome. They are usually, but not always, in a secluded or rural setting and should offer peace and quiet regardless of location.

Townhouse Accommodation

This classification denotes small, individual town-centre hotels which afford a high degree of privacy and concentrate on luxuriously furnished bedrooms and suites with high-quality room service, rather than the public rooms or formal dining rooms usually associated with hotels. They are usually in areas well served by restaurants. All fall broadly within the four or five star classification, though no Quality Percentage Score is shown in the guide.

Travel Accommodation

This classification denotes budget or lodge accommodation suitable for an overnight stay, usually in purpose-built units close to main roads and motorways, often forming part of motorway service areas. They provide consistent levels of accommodation and service, matching today's expectations.

○ Hotels with no star classification

Hotels with this symbol ○ have no star classification as they are due to open during the currency of the guide, or because due to a late entry to the scheme, it was impossible to make a final overnight inspection before our press date.

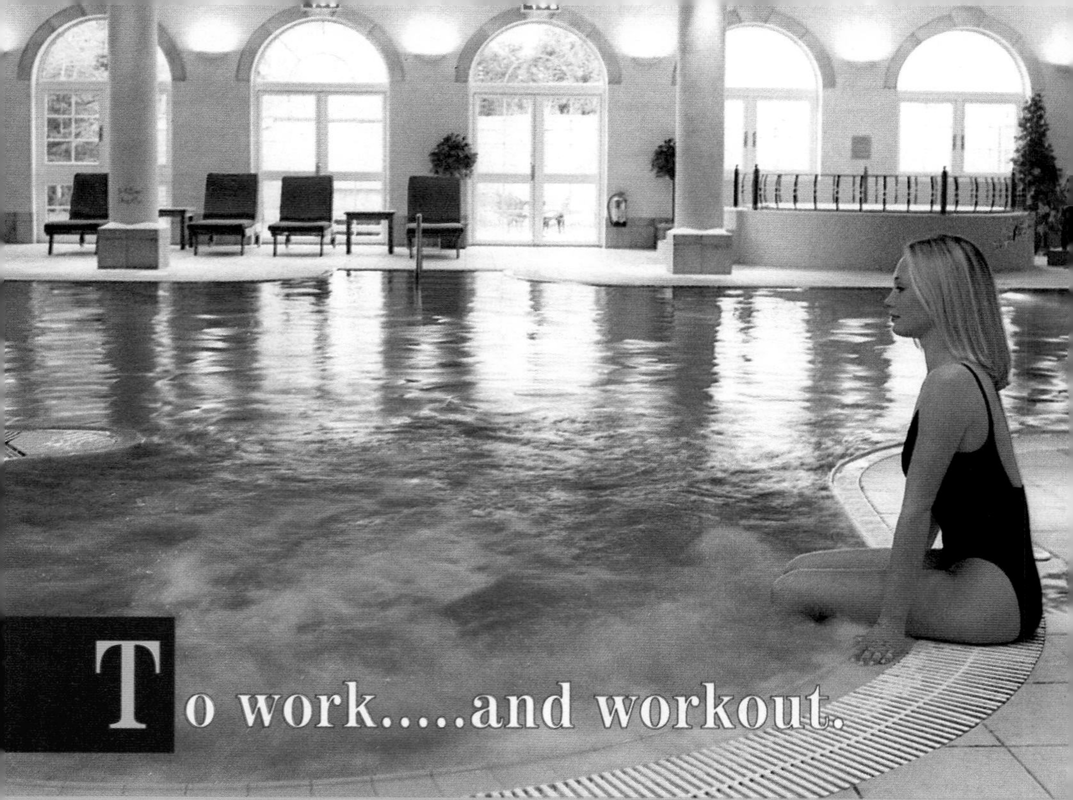

AA Awards 2000-2001

Hotel of the Year Award

Hotel of the Year is the AA's most prestigious award. Winning hotels receive a specially commissioned, framed watercolour of the hotel by artist Duncan Palmar. National awards are made for England, Scotland, Wales and Ireland; a photograph of the hotel appears at the beginning of the relevant country section in the guide. Awards for 2000-2001 are as follows:

Hotel of the Year, England

★★★★ | Castle House Hotel, Hereford
Proprietor: Dr A Heijn
General Manager: Mr Ben Jager

Hotel of the Year, Scotland

★★★★ 77% | The Macdonald Holyrood Hotel, Edinburgh
General Manager: Mr W. Gorol

Hotel of the Year, Wales

★★★★★ 77% | The Celtic Manor Resort, Newport
Proprietor: Dr T. H. Matthews OBE
Chief Executive: Kay Dawes

Hotel of the Year, Ireland

★★★★★ 79% | The Merrion Hotel, Dublin
General Manager: Mr P. McCann

Courtesy and Care Awards 2000-2001

This award is made to hotels where staff offer exceptionally high standards of courtesy and care. National awards are made for England, Scotland, Wales and Ireland. Members of staff receive a specially designed lapel badge to wear on duty. In addition, a large framed certificate is commissioned for display by the hotels and they have a highlighted entry with photograph in the guide. Awards for 2000-2001 are as follows:

Courtesy and Care Award, England

★★★ 81% | Linthwaite House Hotel & Restaurant, Windermere
Proprietor: Mr Mike Bevans

Courtesy and Care Award, Scotland

★★ 80% | Kilcamb Lodge Hotel, Strontian
Proprietors: Mr & Mrs P. Blakeway

Courtesy and Care Award, Wales

★★★ 76% | Coed-y-Mwstwr Hotel, Bridgend
Proprietor: Mr J. Hitchcock

Courtesy and Care Award, Ireland

★★★ 77% | Rock Glen Country House Hotel, Clifden
Proprietors: Mr & Mrs J. Roche

AA Rosette Awards

How the AA assesses restaurants for Rosette Awards

The AA's rosette award scheme was the first nation-wide scheme for assessing the quality of food served by restaurants and hotels. The rosette scheme is an award scheme, not a classification scheme and although there is necessarily an element of subjectivity when it comes to assessing taste, we aim for a consistent approach to our awards throughout the UK. It is important, however, to remember that many places serve enjoyable food but do not qualify for an AA award.

Our awards are made solely on the basis of a meal visit or visits by one or more of our hotel and restaurant inspectors who have an unrivalled breadth and depth of experience in assessing quality. They award rosettes annually on a rising scale of one to five.

So what makes a restaurant worthy of a Rosette Award?

For our inspectors the top and bottom line is the food. The taste of the food is what counts for them, and whether the dish successfully delivers to the diner what the menu promises. A restaurant is only as good as its worst meal. Although presentation and competent service should be appropriate to the style of the restaurant and the quality of the food, they cannot affect the rosette assessment as such, either up or down.

The following summaries attempt to explain what our inspectors look for, but are intended only as guidelines. The AA is constantly reviewing its award criteria and competition usually results in an all-round improvement in standards, so it becomes increasingly difficult for restaurants to reach award level.

One rosette 

At the simplest level, one rosette, the chef should display a mastery of basic techniques and be able to produce dishes of sound quality and clarity of flavours, using good, fresh ingredients

Two rosettes 

To gain two rosettes, the chef must show greater technical skill, more consistency and judgement in combining and balancing ingredients and a clear ambition to achieve high standards. Inspectors will look for evidence of innovation to test the dedication of the kitchen brigade, and the use of seasonal ingredients sourced from quality suppliers.

Three rosettes  

This award takes a restaurant into the big league, and, in a typical year, fewer than 10 per cent of restaurants in our scheme achieve this distinction. Expectations of the kitchen are high, and inspectors find little room for inconsistencies. Exact technique, flair and imagination will come through in every dish, and balance and depth of flavour are all-important.

Four rosettes   

This is an exciting award because, at this level, not only should all technical skills be exemplary, but there should also be daring ideas, and they must work. There is no room for disappointment. Flavours should be accurate and vibrant.

Five rosettes    

This award is the ultimate awarded only when the cooking is at the pinnacle of achievement. Technique should be of such perfection that flavours, combinations and textures show a faultless sense of balance, giving each dish an extra dimension. The sort of cooking that never falters and always strives to give diners a truly memorable taste experience.

Further details of all restaurants with AA rosette awards can be found in The Restaurant Guide published annually by the AA and available from bookshops.

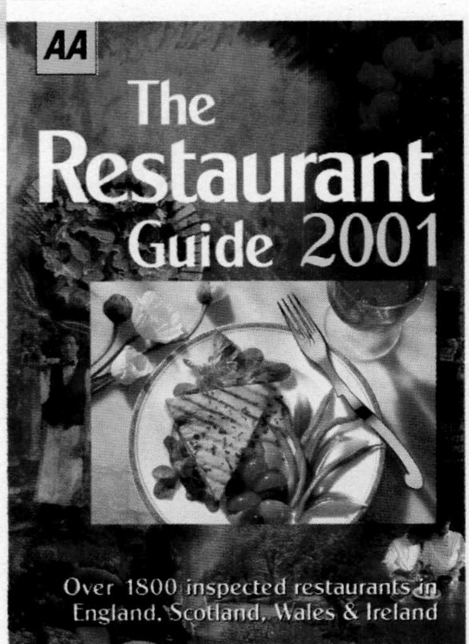

AA

Red Star Awards 2000 - 2001

Best Hotels

In Britain and Ireland

AA Red Star Awards for hotels are made annually in recognition of excellence within each star rating.
The Red Star Award demands consistently outstanding levels of hospitality, service, food and comfort.

Red Star Hotels Map

Red Star Hotels
Regional Index

The number shown against each hotel in the index corresponds with the number given on the Red Star Hotels Map. Hotels are listed in Country and County order, showing their star classification, rosettes and telephone number.

ENGLAND

BERKSHIRE

1	★★★★	❀❀❀	MAIDENHEAD	Fredrick's Hotel	☎ 01628 581000
2	★★★★	❀❀❀	NEWBURY	The Vineyard at Stockcross	☎ 01635 528770

BUCKINGHAMSHIRE

3	★★★★	❀❀❀	AYLESBURY	Hartwell House	☎ 01296 747444
4	★★★★★	❀❀❀	TAPLOW	Cliveden Hotel	☎ 01628 668561

CHESHIRE

5	★★★	❀❀	SANDIWAY	Nunsmere Hall Country House Hotel	☎ 01606 889100

CORNWALL & ISLES OF SCILLY

6	★★	❀❀❀	LISKEARD	Well House Hotel	☎ 01579 342001
7	★★★	❀❀❀	ST MARTIN'S	St Martin's on the Isle	☎ 01720 422090

CUMBRIA

8	★★★	❀❀	BRAMPTON	Farlam Hall Hotel	☎ 016977 46234
9	★★★	❀❀❀❀	GRASMERE	Michael's Nook Country House Hotel & Restaurant	☎ 015394 35496
10	★	❀❀	GRASMERE	White Moss House	☎ 015394 35295
11	★★★	❀❀❀	HOWTOWN	Sharrow Bay Country House Hotel	☎ 017684 86301
12	★	❀	KIRKBY LONSDALE	Hipping Hall	☎ 015242 71187
13	★	❀	WATERMILLOCK	Old Church Hotel	☎ 017684 86204
14	★★★	❀❀❀	WINDERMERE	Holbeck Ghyll Country House Hotel	☎ 015394 32375
15	★★	❀❀	WINDERMERE	Miller Howe Hotel	☎ 015394 42536
16	★★★	❀❀❀	WINDERMERE	Gilpin Lodge Country House Hotel & Restaurant	☎ 015394 88818

DERBYSHIRE

17	★★★	❀	BASLOW	Cavendish Hotel	☎ 01246 582311
18	★★	❀❀❀	BASLOW	Fischer's Baslow Hall	☎ 01246 583259

The Savoy, London

DEVON

19	★★	❀❀	BARNSTAPLE	Halmpstone Manor	☎ 01271 830321
20	★★★	❀❀❀❀❀	CHAGFORD	Gidleigh Park	☎ 01647 432367
21	★★★	❀❀	LEWDOWN	Lewtrenchard Manor	☎ 01566 783256 & 783222

DORSET

22	★★★	❀❀❀	EVERSHOT	Summer Lodge	☎ 01935 83424
23	★★★	❀❀	WAREHAM	Priory Hotel	☎ 01929 551666

ESSEX

24	★★★	❀❀	DEDHAM	Maison Talbooth	☎ 01206 322367

GLOUCESTERSHIRE

25	★★★	❀❀❀	BUCKLAND	Buckland Manor	☎ 01386 852626
26	★★★	❀❀❀	CHELTENHAM	The Greenway	☎ 01242 862352
27	★★★	❀❀❀	CHELTENHAM	Hotel On the Park	☎ 01242 518898
28	★★★	❀❀	CHIPPING CAMPDEN	Cotswold House	☎ 01386 840330
29	★★	❀❀	COLN ST-ALDWYNS	The New Inn At Coln	☎ 01285 750651
30	★★★	❀❀❀	LOWER SLAUGHTER	Lower Slaughter Manor	☎ 01451 820456

No.	Stars	Rosettes	Location	Hotel	Telephone
31	★★★	❁❁	TETBURY	Calcot Manor	☎ 01666 890391
32	★★★	❁❁	THORNBURY	Thornbury Castle	☎ 01454 281182
33	★★★	❁❁❁❁	UPPER SLAUGHTER	Lords of the Manor	☎ 01451 820243
HAMPSHIRE					
34	★★★★★	❁❁❁	NEW MILTON	Chewton Glen Hotel	☎ 01425 275341
35	★★★★	❁❁	ROTHERWICK	Tylney Hall Hotel	☎ 01256 764881
ISLE OF WIGHT					
36	★★★	❁❁❁	YARMOUTH	George Hotel	☎ 01983 760331
KENT					
37	★★	❁❁	CRANBROOK	Kennel Holt Hotel	☎ 01580 712032
LEICESTERSHIRE					
38	★★★★	❁❁	MELTON MOWBRAY	Stapleford Park	☎ 01572 787522
LINCOLNSHIRE					
39	★★	❁❁❁❁	WINTERINGHAM	Winteringham Fields	☎ 01724 733096
CENTRAL LONDON					
40	★★★★★	*	LONDON NW1	Landmark Hotel	☎ 020 7631 8000
41	★★★★★	❁❁❁❁❁	LONDON SW1	The Berkeley	☎ 020 7235 6000
42	★★★★★	❁❁❁❁	LONDON SW1	Mandarin Oriental Hyde Park	☎ 020 7235 2000
43	★★★★	❁❁	LONDON SW1	Goring Hotel	☎ 020 7396 9000
44	★★★★	❁❁	LONDON SW1	The Stafford	☎ 020 7493 0111
45	★★★★	❁❁❁	LONDON SW1	The Halkin Hotel	☎ 020 7333 1000
46	★★★★★	❁❁❁	LONDON SW1	The Lanesborough	☎ 020 7259 5599
47	★★★★	❁❁❁	LONDON SW3	The Capital	☎ 020 7589 5171
48	★★★★★	❁❁	LONDON W1	Claridge's	☎ 020 7629 8860
49	★★★★★	❁❁	LONDON W1	The Connaught	☎ 020 7499 7070
50	★★★★★	❁❁❁	LONDON W1	The Dorchester	☎ 020 7629 8888
51	★★★★★	❁❁	LONDON W1	Four Seasons Hotel	☎ 020 7499 0888
52	★★★★	❁	LONDON W1	Athenaeum Hotel & Apartments	☎ 020 7499 3464
53	★★★★★	❁	LONDON W8	Milestone Hotel & Apartments	☎ 020 7917 1000
54	★★★★★	❁❁❁	LONDON WC2	The Savoy	☎ 020 7836 4343
NORFOLK					
55	★★	❁❁❁	BLAKENEY	Morston Hall	☎ 01263 741041
56	★★★	❁❁	GRIMSTON	Congham Hall Country House Hotel	☎ 01485 600250
OXFORDSHIRE					
57	★★★★	❁❁❁❁❁	GREAT MILTON	Le Manoir Aux Quat' Saisons	☎ 01844 278881
RUTLAND					
58	★★★	❁❁❁❁	OAKHAM	Hambleton Hall	☎ 01572 756991
SHROPSHIRE					
59	★★★	❁❁❁	WORFIELD	Old Vicarage Hotel	☎ 01746 716497
SOMERSET					
60	★★★	❁❁	BATH	The Queensberry Hotel	☎ 01225 447928
61	★★	❁	DULVERTON	Ashwick House Hotel	☎ 01398 323868
62	★★★	❁❁❁	HINTON CHARTERHOUSE	Homewood Park Hotel	☎ 01225 723731
63	★★	❁❁	PORLOCK	The Oaks Hotel	☎ 01643 862265
64	★★★	❁❁❁	SHEPTON MALLET	Charlton House	☎ 01749 342008
65	★★★★	❁❁	STON EASTON	Ston Easton Park	☎ 01761 241631
66	★★★	❁❁❁	TAUNTON	Castle Hotel	☎ 01823 272671
67	★★	❁❁	WIVELISCOMBE	Langley House Hotel & Restaurant	☎ 01984 623318

* *At our press date rosettes for food were not yet confirmed.*

Thornbury Castle, Thornbury

No.	Stars	Rosettes	Location	Hotel	Telephone
68	★	❀❀❀	YEOVIL	Little Barwick House	☎ 01935 423902
STAFFORDSHIRE					
69	★★	❀❀❀	WATERHOUSES	Old Beams Restaurant with Rooms	☎ 01538 308254
SUFFOLK					
70	★★★★	❀❀❀	HINTLESHAM	Hintlesham Hall Hotel	☎ 01473 652334
SURREY					
71	★★	❀❀	HORLEY	Langshott Manor	☎ 01293 786680
SUSSEX EAST					
72	★★★★	❀❀	FOREST ROW	Ashdown Park Hotel	☎ 01342 824988
SUSSEX WEST					
73	★★★	❀❀	AMBERLEY	Amberley Castle	☎ 01798 831992
74	★★★	❀❀❀	EAST GRINSTEAD	Gravetye Manor Hotel	☎ 01342 810567
75	★★★★	❀❀❀	LOWER BEEDING	South Lodge Hotel	☎ 01403 891711
76	★★★	❀❀❀	TURNERS HILL	Alexander House	☎ 01342 714914
WARWICKSHIRE					
77	★★★	❀❀❀	ROYAL LEAMINGTON SPA	Mallory Court Hotel	☎ 01926 330214
78	★	❀	ROYAL LEAMINGTON SPA	Lansdowne Hotel	☎ 01926 450505
WEST MIDLANDS					
79	★★★	❀❀	HOCKLEY HEATH	Nuthurst Grange Country House Hotel	☎ 01564 783972
80	★★★★	❀❀	SUTTON COLDFIELD	New Hall	☎ 0121 378 2442
WILTSHIRE					
81	★★★★	❀❀❀	CASTLE COMBE	Manor House Hotel	☎ 01249 782206
82	★★★★	❀❀	COLERNE	Lucknam Park	☎ 01225 742777
83	★★	❀❀❀	SALISBURY	Howard's House Hotel	☎ 01722 716392
WORCESTERSHIRE					
84	★★★★	❀❀	BROADWAY	The Lygon Arms	☎ 01386 852255
85	★★★	❀❀❀	CHADDESLEY CORBETT	Brockencote Hall Country House Hotel	☎ 01562 777876
YORKSHIRE NORTH					
86	★★★	❀❀	BOLTON ABBEY	The Devonshire Arms Country House Hotel	☎ 01756 710441
87	★★★	❀❀❀	YORK	Middlethorpe Hall Hotel	☎ 01904 641241
88	★★★	❀❀	YORK	The Grange Hotel	☎ 01904 644744

CHANNEL ISLANDS

No.	Stars	Rosettes	Location	Hotel	Telephone
JERSEY					
89	★★★	❀❀	ROZEL BAY	Château La Chaire	☎ 01534 863354
90	★★★★	❀❀❀	ST SAVIOUR	Longueville Manor Hotel	☎ 01534 725501

SCOTLAND

No.	Stars	Rosettes	Location	Hotel	Telephone
ABERDEENSHIRE					
91	★★	❀❀	BALLATER	Balgonie Country House Hotel	☎ 013397 55482
ARGYLL & BUTE					
92	★★★★	❀❀❀	ERISKA	Isle of Eriska	☎ 01631 720371
93	★★	❀	KILLIECHRONAN	Killiechronan House	☎ 01680 300403
94	★★★	❀❀❀	PORT APPIN	Airds Hotel	☎ 01631 730236
CITY OF EDINBURGH					
95	★★★★	❀❀	EDINBURGH	The Howard	☎ 0131 315 2220
CITY OF GLASGOW					
96	★★★	❀❀❀	GLASGOW	One Devonshire Gardens Hotel	☎ 0141 339 2001
DUMFRIES & GALLOWAY					
97	★	❀❀	MOFFAT	Well View Hotel	☎ 01683 220184
98	★★★	❀❀❀	NEWTON STEWART	Kirroughtree House	☎ 01671 402141
99	★★	❀❀❀	PORTPATRICK	Knockinaam Lodge Hotel	☎ 01776 810471
EAST LOTHIAN					
100	★★★	❀❀	GULLANE	Greywalls Hotel	☎ 01620 842144
FIFE					
101	★★★★	❀❀	MARKINCH	Balbirnie House	☎ 01592 610066
102	★★	❀❀❀	PEAT INN	The Peat Inn	☎ 01334 840206
103	★★★	❀❀	ST ANDREWS	Rufflets Country House & Garden Restaurant	☎ 01334 472594
HIGHLAND					
104	★★★	❀❀❀	ARISAIG	Arisaig House	01687 450622
105	★★	❀❀❀	COLBOST	Three Chimneys Restaurant & House Over-By	☎ 01470 511258
106	★★★★	❀❀❀	FORT WILLIAM	Inverlochy Castle Hotel	☎ 01397 702177
107	★★	❀❀❀	KINGUSSIE	The Cross	☎ 01540 661166

Inverlochy Castle, Fort William

108 ★ ❀❀ The Dower House
MUIR OF ORD ☎ 01463 870090

109 ★★ ❀❀ Knockie Lodge Hotel
WHITEBRIDGE ☎ 01456 486276

NORTH AYRSHIRE

110 ★★ ❀ Kilmichael Country House Hotel
BRODICK ☎ 01770 302219

PERTH & KINROSS

111 ★★★★★ ❀❀ The Gleneagles Hotel
AUCHTERARDER ☎ 01764 662231

112 ★★★ ❀❀❀ Kinloch House Hotel
BLAIRGOWRIE ☎ 01250 884237

113 ★★★ ❀❀❀ Kinnaird
DUNKELD ☎ 01796 482440

SOUTH AYRSHIRE

114 ★★ ❀ Ladyburn
MAYBOLE ☎ 01655 740585

115 ★★★ ❀❀❀ Lochgreen House
TROON ☎ 01292 313343

116 ★★★★★ ❀❀ Turnberry Hotel, Golf Courses & Spa
TURNBERRY 01655 331000

STIRLING

117 ★★★ ❀❀ Cromlix House Hotel
DUNBLANE ☎ 01786 822125

118 ★ ❀❀ Creagan House
STRATHYRE ☎ 01877 384638

WALES

CEREDIGION

119 ★★★ ❀❀❀ Ynyshir Hall
EGLWYSFACH ☎ 01654 781209

CONWY

120 ★★ ❀❀❀ Tan-y-Foel Country House Hotel
BETWS-Y-COED ☎ 01690 710507

121 ★★ ❀❀❀ The Old Rectory Country House
CONWY ☎ 01492 580611

122 ★★★ ❀❀❀ Bodysgallen Hall Hotel
LLANDUDNO ☎ 01492 584466

123 ★★ ❀❀❀ St Tudno Hotel
LLANDUDNO ☎ 01492 874411

DENBIGHSHIRE

124 ★★ ❀❀ Tyddyn Llan Country Hotel & Restaurant
LLANDRILLO ☎ 01490 440264

GWYNEDD

125 ★★ ❀❀❀ Hotel Maes y Neuadd
TALSARNAU ☎ 01766 780200

POWYS

126 ★★★ ❀❀ Lake Country House Hotel
LLANGAMMARCH WELLS ☎ 01591 620202

127 ★★★★ ❀❀ Llangoed Hall
LLYSWEN 01874 754525

SWANSEA

128 ★★ ❀❀❀ Fairyhill
REYNOLDSTON ☎ 01792 390139

IRELAND

CLARE

129 ★★★ ❀❀ Gregans Castle
BALLYVAUGHAN ☎ 065 7077 005

CORK

130 ★★★★ ❀ Hayfield Manor
CORK ☎ 021 315600

131 ★★★ ❀❀❀ Longueville House Hotel
MALLOW ☎ 022 47156

DUBLIN

132 ★★★★ ❀❀❀ The Clarence
DUBLIN ☎ 01 4070800

GALWAY

133 ★★★ ❀❀ Cashel House Hotel
CASHEL ☎ 095 31001

134 ★★★★ ❀❀ Glenlo Abbey Hotel
GALWAY ☎ 091 526666

KERRY

135 ★★★★ ❀❀❀ Park Hotel Kenmare
KENMARE ☎ 064 41200

136 ★★★★ ❀❀ Sheen Falls Lodge
KENMARE ☎ 064 41600

KILDARE

137 ★★★★★ ❀❀❀ The Kildare Hotel & Country Club
STRAFFAN ☎ 01 6017200

KILKENNY

138 ★★★★ ❀❀ Mount Juliet Hotel
THOMASTOWN ☎ 056 73000

WEXFORD

139 ★★★ ❀❀ Marlfield House Hotel
GOREY ☎ 055 21124

WICKLOW

140 ★★★ ❀❀ Tinakilly Country House & Restaurant
RATHNEW ☎ 0404 69274

Red Star Awards 2000-2001

Red Star Hotels are listed here in star order, from five stars to one star. The number corresponds with the map index and regional listing. * *At our press date rosettes for food were not yet confirmed.*

5 star
★★★★★

41	The Berkeley	❀❀❀❀❀
42	Mandarin Oriental Hyde Park	❀❀❀❀
34	Chewton Glen Hotel	❀❀❀
4	Cliveden Hotel	❀❀❀
50	The Dorchester	❀❀❀
137	The Kildare Hotel & Country Club	❀❀❀
46	The Lanesborough	❀❀❀
54	The Savoy	❀❀❀
48	Claridge's	❀❀
51	Four Seasons Hotel	❀❀
49	The Connaught	❀❀
111	The Gleneagles Hotel	❀❀
116	Turnberry Hotel, Golf Courses & Spa	❀❀
53	Milestone Hotel & Apartments	❀
40	Landmark Hotel *	

4 star
★★★★

57	Le Manoir Aux Quat' Saisons	❀❀❀❀❀
1	Fredrick's Hotel	❀❀❀
3	Hartwell House	❀❀❀
70	Hintlesham Hall Hotel	❀❀❀
106	Inverlochy Castle Hotel	❀❀❀
92	Isle of Eriska	❀❀❀
90	Longueville Manor Hotel	❀❀❀
81	Manor House Hotel	❀❀❀
135	Park Hotel Kenmare	❀❀❀
75	South Lodge Hotel	❀❀❀
47	The Capital	❀❀❀
132	The Clarence	❀❀❀
45	The Halkin Hotel	❀❀❀
2	The Vineyard at Stockcross	❀❀❀
72	Ashdown Park Hotel	❀❀
101	Balbirnie House	❀❀
134	Glenlo Abbey Hotel	❀❀
43	Goring Hotel	❀❀
127	Llangoed Hall	❀❀
82	Lucknam Park	❀❀
138	Mount Juliet Hotel	❀❀
80	New Hall	❀❀
136	Sheen Falls Lodge	❀❀
38	Stapleford Park	❀❀
65	Ston Easton Park	❀❀
95	The Howard	❀❀
84	The Lygon Arms	❀❀
44	The Stafford	❀❀
35	Tylney Hall Hotel	❀❀
52	Athenaeum Hotel & Apartments	❀
130	Hayfield Manor	❀

3 star
★★★

20	Gidleigh Park	❀❀❀❀❀
58	Hambleton Hall	❀❀❀❀
33	Lords of the Manor	❀❀❀❀
9	Michael's Nook Country House	❀❀❀❀
94	Airds Hotel	❀❀❀
76	Alexander House	❀❀❀
104	Arisaig House	❀❀❀
122	Bodysgallen Hall Hotel	❀❀❀
85	Brockencote Hall Country House	❀❀❀
25	Buckland Manor	❀❀❀
66	Castle Hotel	❀❀❀
64	Charlton House	❀❀❀
36	George Hotel	❀❀❀
16	Gilpin Lodge Country House	❀❀❀
74	Gravetye Manor Hotel	❀❀❀
14	Holbeck Ghyll Country House Hotel	❀❀❀
62	Homewood Park Hotel	❀❀❀
27	Hotel On the Park	❀❀❀
112	Kinloch House Hotel	❀❀❀
113	Kinnaird	❀❀❀
98	Kirroughtree House	❀❀❀
115	Lochgreen House	❀❀❀
131	Longueville House Hotel	❀❀❀
30	Lower Slaughter Manor	❀❀❀
77	Mallory Court Hotel	❀❀❀
87	Middlethorpe Hall Hotel	❀❀❀
59	Old Vicarage Hotel	❀❀❀
96	One Devonshire Gardens Hotel	❀❀❀
11	Sharrow Bay Country House Hotel	❀❀❀
7	St Martin's on the Isle	❀❀❀
22	Summer Lodge	❀❀❀
26	The Greenway	❀❀❀
119	Ynyshir Hall	❀❀❀
73	Amberley Castle	❀❀
31	Calcot Manor	❀❀
133	Cashel House Hotel	❀❀
89	Chateau La Chaire	❀❀
56	Congham Hall Country House Hotel	❀❀
28	Cotswold House	❀❀
117	Cromlix House Hotel	❀❀
8	Farlam Hall Hotel	❀❀
129	Gregans Castle	❀❀
100	Greywalls Hotel	❀❀
126	Lake Country House Hotel	❀❀
21	Lewtrenchard Manor	❀❀
24	Maison Talbooth	❀❀
139	Marlfield House Hotel	❀❀
5	Nunsmere Hall Country House Hotel	❀❀
79	Nuthurst Grange Country House Hotel	❀❀
23	Priory Hotel	❀❀
103	Rufflets Country House	❀❀
86	The Devonshire Arms Country House	❀❀
88	The Grange Hotel	❀❀
60	The Queensberry Hotel	❀❀
32	Thornbury Castle	❀❀
140	Tinakilly Country House & Restaurant	❀❀
17	Cavendish Hotel	❀

2 star
★★

39	Winteringham Fields	❀❀❀❀
128	Fairyhill	❀❀❀
18	Fischer's Baslow Hall	❀❀❀
125	Hotel Maes y Neuadd	❀❀❀
83	Howard's House Hotel	❀❀❀
99	Knockinaam Lodge Hotel	❀❀❀
55	Morston Hall	❀❀❀
69	Old Beams Restaurant with Rooms	❀❀❀
123	St Tudno Hotel	❀❀❀
120	Tan-y-Foel Country House Hotel	❀❀❀
107	The Cross	❀❀❀
121	The Old Rectory Country House	❀❀❀
102	The Peat Inn	❀❀❀
105	Three Chimneys Restaurant	❀❀❀
6	Well House Hotel	❀❀❀
91	Balgonie Country House Hotel	❀❀
19	Halmpstone Manor	❀❀
37	Kennel Holt Hotel	❀❀
109	Knockie Lodge Hotel	❀❀
67	Langley House Hotel & Restaurant	❀❀
71	Langshott Manor	❀❀
15	Miller Howe Hotel	❀❀
29	The New Inn At Coln	❀❀
63	The Oaks Hotel	❀❀
124	Tyddyn Llan Country Hotel & Restaurant	❀❀
61	Ashwick House Hotel	❀
93	Killiechronan House	❀
110	Kilmichael Country House Hotel	❀
114	Ladyburn	❀

1 star
★

68	Little Barwick House	❀❀❀
118	Creagan House	❀❀
108	The Dower House	❀❀
97	Well View Hotel	❀❀
10	White Moss House	❀❀
12	Hipping Hall	❀
78	Lansdowne Hotel	❀
13	Old Church Hotel	❀

Useful Information

BRITAIN

The Fire Precautions Act does not apply to the Channel Islands, Republic of Ireland, or the Isle of Man, which have their own rules. As far as we are aware, all hotels listed in Great Britain have applied for and not been refused a fire certificate.

Licensing laws differ in England, Wales, Scotland, the Republic of Ireland, the Isle of Man, the Isles of Scilly and the Channel Islands. Public houses are generally open from mid morning to early afternoon, and from about 6 or 7pm until 11pm, closing times may be earlier or later, some are open all afternoon. Unless otherwise stated, establishments listed are licensed. Hotel residents can obtain alcoholic drinks at all times, if the licensee is prepared to serve them. Non-residents eating at the hotel restaurant can have drinks with meals. Children under 14 (or 18 in Scotland) may be excluded from bars where no food is served. Those under 18 may not purchase or consume alcoholic drinks. Club licence means that drinks are served to club members only, 48 hours must elapse between joining and ordering. Please note that at the time of going to press licensing laws were under review and may well change during the currency of this guide.

Prices The AA encourages the use of the Hotel Industry Voluntary Code of Booking Practice, which aims to ensure that guests know how much they will have to pay and what services and facilities that includes, before entering a financially binding agreement. If the price has not previously been confirmed in writing, guests should be given a card stipulating the total obligatory charge when they register at reception.

The Tourism (Sleeping Accommodation Price Display) **Order of 1977** compels hotels, travel accommodation, guest houses, farmhouses, inns and self-catering accommodation with four or more letting bedrooms, to display in entrance halls the minimum and maximum prices charged for each category of room. Tariffs shown are the minimum and maximum for one or two persons but they may vary without warning.

NORTHERN IRELAND & REPUBLIC OF IRELAND

Prices for the Republic of Ireland are shown in Irish Punts (IR£), hotels may also display prices in Euros. As this guide went to press IR£1 = 1.27 Euros.

Rookery Hall, Nantwich

The Fire Services (NI) Order 1984 covers establishments accommodating more than six people, which must have a certificate from the Northern Ireland Fire Authority. Places accommodating fewer than six persons need adequate exits. AA officials inspect emergency notices, fire-fighting equipment and fire exits here. Republic of Ireland safety regulations are a matter for local authority regulations. For your own and others' safety, read the emergency notices and be sure you understand them.

Licensing Regulations

Northern Ireland: public houses open Mon-Sat 11.30-23.00 and Sun 12.30-14.30 and 19.00-22.00. Hotels can serve residents without restriction. Non-residents can be served from 12.30-22.00 on Christmas Day. Children under 18 are not allowed in the bar area and may neither buy nor consume liquor in hotels.

Republic of Ireland: General licensing hours are Mon-Sat 10.30-23.00 (23.30 in summer). Sun and St Patrick's Day (17th Mar), 12.30-14.00 and 16.00-23.00. Hotels can serve residents without restriction. There is no service on Christmas Day (except for hotel residents) or Good Friday.

Telephone Numbers Area codes for numbers in the Republic of Ireland apply only within the Republic. If dialling from outside check the telephone directory. Area codes for numbers in Britain and Northern Ireland cannot be used directly from the Republic.

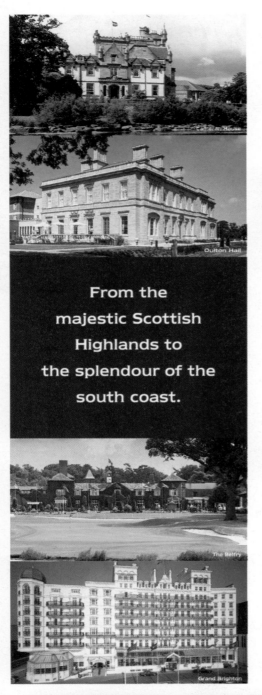

Hotel Groups *Information*

The following hotel groups have at least five hotels and 400 rooms or are part of an internationally significant brand with a central reservations number.

Brand Logo	Company Statement	Central Reservations/ Contact Number
	A group of three and four star hotels, many are rurally based, all of which have at least one rosette	020 7340 4800 (Head Office)
Best Western	Great Britain's largest group has around 400 independently owned hotels, modern and traditional, mainly in the three and four star markets. Many have leisure facilities and over 150 have rosette awards	0345 73 73 73
Brend Hotels	A privately owned group of eleven three and four star hotels in Devon and Cornwall	01271 34 44 9
Campanile	Campanile offers modern accommodation for the budget market	020 8569 6969
CHOICE HOTELS EUROPE	Choice offers mainly two brands in the UK: Quality Hotels in the three star market, and Comfort Inns at two star	0800 44 44 44
corus	A growing brand of three star hotels, representing the best of Regal Hotel Group	0345 33 44 00
COURTYARD	There are ten hotels in the UK, part of the international brand of modern three star hotels	0800 221 222
CROWNE PLAZA	These modern hotels offer four star level accommodation around the country. They often have leisure facilities	0800 897121
DAYS I	A new brand of good quality modern budget accommodation at motorway services	0800 02 80 400
De Vere Hotels	De Vere comprises around sixteen four and five star hotels, which specialise in leisure, golf and conferences	01925 639499
Express by Holiday Inn	Holiday Inn's most recent development in the UK, which reaches the superior budget marketplace	0800 89 71 21
	A privately owned group of about a dozen three star hotels across the south of England	0500 276440
	Half a dozen three and four star hotels based in the Oxfordshire area	01993 700100
	A small group of three and four star hotels located mainly in the central counties of England	0345 444 123
	A group of provincial hotels across the UK, mainly three star, including many well known former coaching inns	0800 40 40 40

	These modern hotels offer four star level accommodation. They often have leisure facilities	0800 89 71 21
ibis hotel	Ibis is a chain of modern travel accommodation	020 8283 4550
	A consortium of independently owned mainly two and three star hotels across Britain	0800 88 55 44
INTER-CONTINENTAL	This internationally known group is primarily represented in the UK with three five star hotels in central London	0345 581444
	An association of owner-managed establishments across Ireland	00 353 1 0462 3416
	This Irish company has a range of three and four star hotels in the UK and the Republic of Ireland	00 353 1 0607 5000
LONDON SIGNATU	A collection of mainly four star hotels in and near London	0800 40 40 40
	A large number of hotels in the three and four star markets, traditional and modern	01506 815215
Malmaison	A growing brand of three star city centre hotels, all rated over 70%	01737 780 200 (Head Office)
MANOR HOUSE HOTELS	Manor House Hotels of Ireland are country house hotels; they include castles, stately homes and Georgian manors	0990 300 200 00 353 1 295 8900
Marriott HOTELS · RESORTS · SUITES	This international brand operates four star hotels in primary locations; most are modern and have leisure facilities. Some have a focus on golf	0800 221 222
MARSTON HOTELS	A small group of three and four star hotels in the southern half of England	0845 700 1300
	A group of three and four star hotels across Britain	0870 600 3013
MERIDIE	An international brand of four and five star hotels, represented mainly in and around London	0800 40 40 40
	Modern four star hotels in primary provincial locations and central London	0845 30 20 001
	A consortium of independently owned mainly two and three star hotels across Britain	01253 292000
	Part of French group Accor, Novotel provides modern three star hotels	020 8283 4500
	A large collection of former coaching inns, mainly in the two and three star markets	0800 917 3085
PARAMOUNT GROUP OF HOTELS	Over 16 mainly four and five star hotels across the UK	0500 342 543
PEEL HOTELS	A group of mainly three star hotels located across the UK	0845 601 7335
Posthouse	Over 80 modern three star hotels. Often situated on the edge of towns, many have leisure facilities	0800 40 40 40
PREMIER LODGE	A new brand of modern travel accommodation across the UK. Every lodge features an adjacent licensed popular restaurant, such as Millers Kitchen, Outside Inn, Chef & Brewer	08702 01 02 03

	A consortium of privately owned British hotels, often in the country house style	01264 324400 (Head Office)
	A small group of three and four star hotels in various locations across the country	0800 454 454
	There are ten hotels at three, four and five star levels, almost entirely in central London	0800 37 44 11
	A large national hotel company with almost 100 three star hotels in both town centre and country locations	0345 33 44 00
	An international consortium of rural privately owned hotels, mainly in the country house style.	00 33 1 457 296 50
	Five red star hotels, four in London, one in the Cotswolds	020 7872 8080 (General Enquiries)
	A consortium of independent Scottish hotels, in the three and four star market	01333 360 888
	Two star hotels across the country generally based round a busy restaurant operation	0990 39 38 39
	Sheraton is represented in the UK by a small number of four and five star hotels in London and Edinburgh	0800 35 35 35
	A small group of mostly four star hotels across the country	01282 416987 (Head Office)
	Part of an international consortium of mainly privately owned hotels, often in the country house style	0800 964470
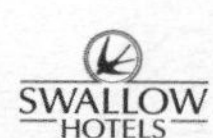	In most cases modern four star hotels in primary provincial locations and London; most have indoor leisure facilities	0191 419 4666
	A consortium of independently owned mainly two and three star hotels across Britain	01865 875888
	A group of mainly four star hotels across the UK, with many in London and some country house properties	0800 18 17 16
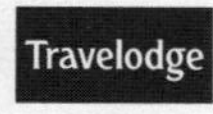	Good quality modern budget accommodation across the UK. Almost every lodge has an adjacent family restaurant, often a Little Chef, Harry Ramsden's or Burger King	0800 850 950
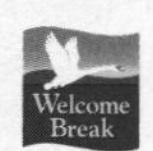	Lodge accommodation at motorway services	0800 731 4466
	A small group of three star hotels, mainly in the southern half of England	01635 35494 (Head Office)

The Flower of the Shows

by Julia Hynard

'The Garden' has been chosen as the theme for this year's AA Lifestyle Guides. In the Hotel Guide, 'The Flower of the Shows' pays a fleeting visit to the best of Britain and Ireland's flower shows, while 'Notes from a Hotel Garden' details just some of the horticultural highlights to be found in hotel gardens, as described by hoteliers in response to our Garden Survey.

The flower show is one of the greatest treats of the growing season, pretty much the perfect day out for sensory delight, inspiration and the chance to see the latest ideas, plants and equipment - everything you ever needed to know about gardening, and more you'd never even imagined. Take your time, a sensible pair of shoes, and prepare to be enthralled.

If all the flower festivals held across the country, the Chelsea Flower Show is the choicest bloom. The statistics surrounding the show are impressive in themselves, but the sheer impact of the space, the heady perfume and the dazzling colour is impossible to quantify - it must be experienced.

The Chelsea site covers 21 acres, centred on the 3.5-acre Grand Marquee - the largest tent in the world - but numbers are limited and tickets greatly prized. There is little doubt that this is the premier show for garden innovation, setting the scene for the summer to

. . . continued

come. Exhibitors from around the world create fantastic floral arrangements and high-profile companies sponsor stunning show gardens, giving form to the most fabulous designs.

The show, organised by the Royal Horticultural Society, is held annually at the Royal Hospital, Chelsea, London SW3. Dates for 2001 are 22nd-25th May, though the 22nd and 23rd are for members only. The ticket hotline is 0870 906 3781.

Chelsea is a key event in the social as well as the horticultural calendar, but it is not the biggest; that position goes to the Royal Horticultural Society's show at Hampton Court Palace, East Mosley, Surrey. The Hampton Court Show, in the spacious surroundings of the palace, is the largest annual gardening event in the world, both in area and attendance. Like Chelsea, it has show gardens created by cutting edge designers, and incorporates the British Rose Festival, specialist society exhibits and many competitions. Plants and gardening equipment are also available to buy. The show will be held on the 3rd to the 8th of July 2001, and the 3rd and 4th will be members' privilege days; for booking details telephone 0870 906 3791.

The RHS's Tatton Park Show, near Knutsford, Cheshire, is a relative newcomer, inaugurated in 1999, held in parkland surrounding the National Trust's stately home Tatton Hall. The show has a regional emphasis, rooted in the horticultural traditions of the Northwest of England. It

includes show gardens and various marquees filled with magnificent floral displays, and seems set to become a popular fixture. The dates for 2001 are 18th-22nd July, ticket hotline 0870 906 3811.

The RHS's Scottish National Gardening Show didn't happen in 2000, and at the time of writing no plans have been confirmed for 2001. Another Scottish show, new for 2000, has proved such a success that it has been confirmed a perennial. This is Gardening Scotland at the Royal Highland Centre, Ingliston, organised by the Royal Caledonian Horticultural Society together with Rural Projects. The new show attracted 300 exhibits from throughout the UK and Europe, and visitors flocked from all over Scotland. Dates for 2001 are 1st-3rd June, for booking details telephone 0131 333 0964 or 0131 333 0969.

In Ireland, check out the Dun Laoghaire and Rathdown Flower Show, run in conjunction with the South Co Dublin Horticultural Society, established in the late 1920s. There is a huge interest in flowers in this area, which boasts some of the finest gardens in Ireland, and the show attracts some 6,000-10,000 visitors to admire the exquisite floral arrangements, participate in competitions and visit the trade stands. Dates for 2001 will probably be 11th-12th August, telephone 00 353 1 2841864 for further details.

Notes from a Hotel Garden

Notes from a Hotel Garden

Tregenna Castle Hotel, St. Ives

Beeches Hotel, Norwich

Guests have access to a three acre Grade II listed Victorian Garden created from an old chalk quarry. With Gothic fountain, Italianate steps and ornate walls, the 'Secret Garden' was rediscovered in 1980 and is being restored by the Plantation Garden Preservation Trust.

Berryhead Hotel, Brixham

The Revd H Lyte wrote the hymn *Abide with me* in the garden at Berryhead, which was actually laid out by French prisoners of war when the house was a military hospital.

Dale Head Hall, Keswick

A Keswick in Bloom award-winner, the hotel gardens include a gnome home and an arboretum of trees from all over the world, originally planted by the Manchester Corporation.

Derwentwater Hotel, Keswick

The grounds of this hotel are designated as an SSSI and a European Area of Special Conservation. They include three wildlife ponds, a lake and river frontage, and are home to deer, foxes, red squirrels, ducks, pheasants and over 115 bird species.

Holne Chase Hotel, Ashburton

The 70-acre gardens have won several awards. The River Dart encircles the property, which is on an Iron Age hill fort estate, designated as an SSSI and Nature Reserve.

Kinfauns Castle, Perth

The 26 acres of gardens at Kinfauns Castle feature two seven-foot statues dating from 1850, one of Robert the Bruce and the other of William Wallace.

Lainston House, Winchester

The beautiful 63 acres at Lainston include a walled garden, 12th-century chapel and a three-quarter mile avenue of lime trees.

Meudon Hotel, Mawnan Smith

Laid out 200 years ago by Robert Were Fox, these sub-tropical gardens feature a wealth of ancient specimens including banana trees and Australian tree ferns. There is an Italian sunken garden and a freshwater spring provides a stream running down to the sea.

Tregenna Castle Hotel, St Ives

The hotel has 72 acres of gardens, employing five full-time gardeners, and featuring a subtropical walled garden designed by Chelsea Gold Medal-winner, John Moreland of Penzance.

Sheen Falls Lodge, Kenmare

The 300 acres of grounds here, including ponds, waterfalls and subtropical garden, have won a landscape design award from the Association of Landscape Contractors of Ireland.

Swynford Paddocks Hotel, Six Mile Bottom

Lord Byron wrote poetry in the grounds of Swynford Paddocks (the home of his half sister). It is also the burial place of legendary racehorse Brigadier Gerard.

Waterton Park Hotel, Wakefield

The hotel is set on an island surrounded by a 26-acre lake with access via a picturesque iron footbridge.

Ynyshir Hall, Eglwysfach

The 14 acres at Ynyshir Hall, surrounded by an RSPB nature reserve, include a waterfall, pond and stream, and a lovely old parrotia (ironstone) tree, apparently planted by Queen Victoria.

Ynyshir Hall, Eglwysfach

Hotel of the Year, England

Castle House Hotel,
Hereford

ABBERLEY, Worcestershire Map 07 SO76

★★★78% *The Elms*

Stockton Rd WR6 6AT
☎ 01299 896666 01299 896804
Dir: *on A443 between Worcester and Tenbury Wells 2m beyond Great Witley*

A fine Queen Anne mansion built over 250 years ago. The spacious public rooms and the generously proportioned bedrooms are full of character. The restaurant, overlooking the landscaped gardens, serves imaginative and seasonal dishes.
ROOMS: 16 en suite **FACILITIES:** Tennis (hard) Croquet lawn **CONF:** Thtr 60 Class 30 Board 24 **PARKING:** 61 **NOTES:** No dogs (ex guide dogs) No smoking in restaurant **CARDS:**

ABBOT'S SALFORD, Warwickshire Map 04 SP05

★★★75% Salford Hall

WR11 5UT
☎ 01386 871300 01386 871301
e-mail: reception@salfordhall.co.uk
Dir: *from A46 take road signed Salford Priors, Abbot's Salford & Harvington. Hotel 1.5m on left*

Salford Hall is a beautifully restored 15th-century manor house which retains many of its period features. Public rooms include a cosy bar, a conservatory courtyard and an oak-panelled restaurant. Bedrooms are superbly equipped and feature a wealth of thoughtful extras.
ROOMS: 14 en suite 19 annexe en suite s £80-£150; d £115-£150 (incl. bkfst) * LB **FACILITIES:** Tennis (hard) Snooker Sauna Solarium **CONF:** Thtr 50 Class 35 Board 25 Del from £130 * **PARKING:** 51 **NOTES:** No dogs (ex guide dogs) No smoking in restaurant Closed 24-30 Dec Civ Wed 50 **CARDS:**

See advert under STRATFORD-UPON-AVON

ABINGDON, Oxfordshire Map 04 SU49

★★★66% Upper Reaches

Thames St OX14 3JA
☎ 0870 400 8101 01235 555182
Dir: *on A415 in Abingdon follow signs for Dorchester and turn left just before the bridge over the Thames*
Dating back to the 17th-century this hotel was once a water mill. Ideally set on the banks of the Thames with moorings for boats, it is within walking distance of the town. The spacious bedrooms offer a high standard of comfort.
ROOMS: 31 en suite (4 fmly) No smoking in 15 bedrooms s £105-£125; d £135-£150 * **FACILITIES:** STV Fishing Xmas **CONF:** Thtr 25 Class 15 Board 18 Del from £135 * **PARKING:** 60 **NOTES:** No smoking in restaurant **CARDS:**

★★★65% Abingdon Four Pillars Hotel

FOUR PILLARS HOTELS

Marcham Rd OX14 1TZ
☎ 01235 553456 01235 554117
e-mail: enquiries@four-pillars.co.uk
Dir: *turn off A34 at junct with A415, on entry into Abingdon, turn right at rdbt, hotel on right*
This modern hotel is particularly appealing to the business guest, due to its fine range of meeting rooms and spacious bedrooms with good desk space. The friendly team of staff is typical of this small group of hotels.
ROOMS: 62 en suite (7 fmly) No smoking in 40 bedrooms s £79-£85; d £89-£95 (incl. bkfst) * LB **FACILITIES:** STV entertainment Xmas **CONF:** Thtr 140 Class 80 Board 48 Del from £80 * **PARKING:** 85 **NOTES:** No smoking in restaurant Civ Wed 60
CARDS:

★★62% *Crown & Thistle*

SCOTTISH NEWCASTLE

Bridge St OX14 3HS
☎ 01235 522556 01235 553281
Dir: *follow A415 towards Dorchester into the centre of Abingdon*
A warm welcome awaits at this charming old coaching inn, built in 1605, whose name signifies the union of England and Scotland under James I. With its quaint cobbled courtyard, this listed building is in a lovely location near to the Abbey grounds and the River Thames. The attractive bedrooms retain much of their original character.
ROOMS: 21 rms (16 en suite) (3 fmly) **FACILITIES:** Snooker Pool table Bar Billards entertainment **CONF:** Thtr 30 Class 16 Board 12 **PARKING:** 36 **NOTES:** No dogs (ex guide dogs)
CARDS:

ACCRINGTON, Lancashire Map 07 SD72

★★★★62% *Dunkenhalgh*

MACDONALD HOTELS

Blackburn Rd, Clayton-le-Moors BB5 5JP
☎ 01254 398021 01254 872230
Dir: *adj to M65, junct 7*
This historic country house, set in attractive grounds, has been considerably extended. It boasts a new wing of executive rooms, all providing a high standard of comfort. There are good meeting, banqueting and leisure facilities available.

continued

ACCRINGTON, continued

Dunkenhalgh, Accrington

ROOMS: 37 en suite 42 annexe en suite (13 fmly) No smoking in 10 bedrooms **FACILITIES:** STV Indoor swimming (H) Snooker Sauna Solarium Gym Steam room entertainment **CONF:** Thtr 400 Class 200 Board 100 **PARKING:** 400 **CARDS:**

★★★63% **Sparth House Hotel**
Whalley Rd, Clayton Le Moors BB5 5RP
☎ 01254 872263 01254 872263
Dir: *take A6185 to Clitheroe along Dunkenhalgh Way, right at lights onto A678, left at next lights - A680 to Whalley. Hotel on left after 2 lights*

This 18th-century listed building is set in three acres of mature grounds and gardens. Bedrooms are individually styled and those in the main section are particularly spacious, including one with original furnishings from one of the great liners. The panelled restaurant is a peaceful setting in which to enjoy a wide range of dishes.
ROOMS: 16 en suite (3 fmly) s £54-£64; d £75-£87 (incl. bkfst) * LB **CONF:** Thtr 100 Class 75 Board 60 Del from £75 * **PARKING:** 50 **NOTES:** No smoking in restaurant Civ Wed 100
CARDS:

ACLE, Norfolk Map 05 TG41

Travelodge
NR13 3BE
☎ 01493 751970 01493 751970
Dir: *junc A47 & Acle Bypass*

Travelodge

This modern building offers accommodation in smart, spacious and well equipped bedrooms, all with en suite bathrooms. Refreshments may be taken at the nearby family restaurant. For further details and the Travelodge phone number, consult the Hotel Groups page.
ROOMS: 40 en suite

ACTON TRUSSELL, Staffordshire Map 07 SJ91

★★★★70% **The Moat House**
Lower Penkridge Rd ST17 0RJ
☎ 01785 712217 01785 715344
e-mail: info@moathouse.co.uk
Dir: *off M6 junct 13 onto the A449 through the village of Acton Trussell. The hotel is on the right hand side on the way out of the village*

This 17th-century timbered building, with a peaceful canal-side setting, has been skilfully extended. Bedrooms are attractively decorated, well equipped and comfortable. The bar offers a wide range of snacks, which supplement the interesting carte served in the main restaurant.
ROOMS: 32 en suite (4 fmly) No smoking in 22 bedrooms s fr £99; d fr £115 (incl. bkfst) * LB **FACILITIES:** STV Fishing **CONF:** Thtr 200 Class 60 Board 60 Del from £135 * **PARKING:** 200 **NOTES:** No dogs (ex guide dogs) No smoking in restaurant Closed 25-26 Dec & 1 Jan Civ Wed 150 **CARDS:**

See advert under STAFFORD

ALBRIGHTON, Shropshire Map 07 SJ80

★★★63% **Lea Manor Hotel**
Holyhead Rd WV1 3BX
☎ 01902 373266 01902 372853
e-mail: hotel@leamanor.co.uk
Dir: *junct 3 of M54, follow A41 towards Wolverhampton then A464 towards Shifnal for approx. 2m, hotel on the left*

MINOTEL Great Britain

This hotel offers well equipped bedrooms. Greatly extended, half of the bedrooms are in the original building and half are on the ground floor of a nearby modern building. The restaurant and lounge bar serve a good range of popular dishes. There is also a large function room.
ROOMS: 6 en suite 8 annexe en suite No smoking in 6 bedrooms s £55-£65; d £65-£75 (incl. bkfst) * LB **CONF:** Thtr 200 Class 60 Board 40 Del from £80 * **PARKING:** 200 **NOTES:** No dogs (ex guide dogs) No smoking in restaurant Civ Wed 60 **CARDS:**

A

ALCESTER, Warwickshire Map 04 SP05

★★★66% Kings Court
Kings Coughton B49 5QQ
☎ 01789 763111 01789 400242
e-mail: info@kingscourthotel.co.uk
Dir: *1m N on A435*
This privately-owned hotel and grounds partly dates back to Tudor times. Many of the well equipped bedrooms are in a modern wing, some on the ground floor and some suitable for disabled guests. Bedrooms in the original house boast oak beams and rustic appeal. A choice of menus is served in the smart restaurant and quaint bar.
ROOMS: 4 en suite 38 annexe en suite (3 fmly) No smoking in 15 bedrooms s fr £56; d fr £80 (incl. bkfst) * LB **CONF:** Thtr 120 Class 40 Board 30 Del £82 * **PARKING:** 120 **NOTES:** Closed 24-30 Dec
CARDS:

Travelodge
A435 Birmingham Rd, Oversley Mill Roundabout B49 6AA
☎ 0800 850 950
Dir: *at junc A46/A435*
This modern building offers accommodation in smart, spacious and well equipped bedrooms, all with en suite bathrooms. Refreshments may be taken at the nearby family restaurant. For further details and the Travelodge phone number, consult the Hotel Groups page.
ROOMS: 40 en suite

Travelodge

ALDEBURGH, Suffolk Map 05 TM45

★★★73% White Lion
Market Cross Place IP15 5BJ
☎ 01728 452720 01728 452986
e-mail: whitelionaldeburgh@btinternet.com
Dir: *from A12 at Saxmundham take A1094 approx 5m, on seafront*

Best Western

Excellent customer care continues to charm guests back to this popular seaside hotel. Fresh shellfish and seafood are the speciality of the beamed restaurant in the evenings and there is a modern brasserie for lunch. Comfortable public areas include a smart air-conditioned conference room and two lounges with open fires.
ROOMS: 38 en suite (1 fmly) No smoking in 15 bedrooms
FACILITIES: STV **CONF:** Thtr 120 Class 50 Board 50 **PARKING:** 15
NOTES: No smoking in restaurant **CARDS:**

See advert on this page

Bad hair day? Hairdryers in all rooms three stars and above.

ALDEBURGH, continued

★★★72% ❀ Wentworth
Wentworth Rd IP15 5BD
☎ 01728 452312 ▯ 01728 454343
e-mail: wentworth.hotel@anglianet.co.uk
Dir: *turn off A12 onto A1094, 6m to Aldeburgh, leave church on left and turn left at bottom of hill*

This popular hotel near the seafront has a loyal following. Public areas, featuring log fires, are welcoming, spacious and comfortably furnished. Bedrooms are well equipped and attractively decorated. Some very spacious bedrooms with a charming Mediterranean feel are located in Darfield House across the road.
ROOMS: 30 rms (28 en suite) 7 annexe en suite No smoking in all bedrooms s £66-£72; d £106-£126 (incl. bkfst) * LB **FACILITIES:** Xmas **CONF:** Thtr 15 Class 8 Board 14 Del from £98 * **PARKING:** 30 **NOTES:** No smoking in restaurant Closed 27 Dec-5 Jan
CARDS:

See advert on page 39

★★★68% The Brudenell
The Parade IP15 5BU
☎ 01728 452071 ▯ 01728 454082
Dir: *on seafront, adjoining Fort Green car park*

This popular seafront hotel has been greatly refurbished and offers bedrooms which are comfortable and attractively decorated, many enjoying lovely sea views. The smart restaurant offers an interesting choice of dishes and specialises in locally caught fish.
ROOMS: 47 en suite (1 fmly) No smoking in 11 bedrooms s £60-£65; d £96-£116 * LB **FACILITIES:** Xmas **CONF:** Thtr 50 Class 25 Board 35 **SERVICES:** Lift **PARKING:** 22 **NOTES:** No smoking in restaurant
CARDS:

★★67% Uplands
Victoria Rd IP15 5DX
☎ 01728 452420 ▯ 01728 454872
Dir: *turn off A12 onto A1094, Aldeburgh 6m, Parish Church on left, hotel is opposite*
This hotel, situated on the edge of town beside the church, has an attractive walled garden. Spacious public rooms include an airy conservatory, two lounges with open fires, an elegant dining room and an intimate bar. Bedrooms vary in size and style, with period furnishings in the main house and a contemporary look in the chalet-style garden cottages.

ROOMS: 10 en suite 7 annexe en suite (4 fmly) s £50; d £70 (incl. bkfst) * LB **PARKING:** 22 **NOTES:** No smoking in restaurant Closed 23 Dec-3 Jan **CARDS:**

ALDERLEY EDGE, Cheshire Map 07 SJ87

★★★71% ❀❀ Alderley Edge
Macclesfield Rd SK9 7BJ
☎ 01625 583033 ▯ 01625 586343
e-mail: sales@alderley-edge-hotel.co.uk
Dir: *turn off A34 in Alderley Edge onto B5087 towards Macclesfield. Hotel 200yds on right*
Alderley Edge with its charming grounds was originally a country house built for one of the region's cotton kings. The bedrooms and suites are attractively furnished, offering excellent quality and comfort. The welcoming bar and adjacent lounge lead into the split-level restaurant, which offers freshly prepared meals.
ROOMS: 46 en suite s £99.50-£400; d £115-£400 * LB **FACILITIES:** STV entertainment Xmas **CONF:** Thtr 120 Class 80 Board 40 Del from £100 * **SERVICES:** Lift **PARKING:** 90 **NOTES:** No dogs (ex guide dogs) Civ Wed 100 **CARDS:**

⌂ Premier Lodge (Wilmslow South)
London Rd, Alderley Edge SK9 7AA
☎ 0870 700 1576 ▯ 0870 700 1577

PREMIER LODGE
THE BEST. REST ASSURED.

Premier Lodge offers modern, well equipped, en suite accommodation suitable for both business and leisure travellers. Meals can be taken at the adjacent popular restaurant and bar which is fully licensed. For further details, consult the Hotel Groups page.
ROOMS: 37 en suite d £46 *

ALDERMINSTER, Warwickshire Map 04 SP24

★★★★75% ❀❀ Ettington Park
CV37 8BU
☎ 01789 450123 ▯ 01789 450472

ARCADIAN HOTELS
Distinctly Different

Dir: *off A3400, 5m S of Stratford just outside the village of Alderminster*
A magnificent Grade I listed Victorian mansion with superb architectural features, set in 40 acres of attractive parkland on the banks of the Stour. Bedrooms are elegantly furnished and have stylish bathrooms; many have views of the gardens and the 12th-century chapel. Service is attentive yet discreet.
ROOMS: 48 en suite (5 fmly) s fr £125; d £185-£350 (incl. bkfst) * LB **FACILITIES:** STV Indoor swimming (H) Tennis (hard) Fishing Riding Sauna Solarium Croquet lawn Jacuzzi/spa Clay pigeon shooting Archery

continued

Croquet Hot Air Ballooning Health & Beauty salon entertainment Xmas **CONF:** Thtr 75 Class 40 Board 48 Del £195 * **SERVICES:** Lift **PARKING:** 150 **NOTES:** No smoking in restaurant
CARDS:

See advert under STRATFORD-UPON-AVON

ALDERSHOT, Hampshire Map 04 SU85

★★★69% Potters International

1 Fleet Rd GU11 2ET
☎ 01252 344000 01252 311611
Dir: *access via A325 and A321 towards Fleet*
This modern hotel and leisure complex stands on the site of a former army officers' mess building. Spacious, well equipped bedrooms are attractively decorated and furnished. Extensive air conditioned public areas include a pub and a more formal restaurant; there is also a business centre and good leisure club.
ROOMS: 97 en suite (6 fmly) No smoking in 10 bedrooms s fr £105; d fr £125 (incl. bkfst) * **FACILITIES:** STV Indoor swimming (H) Sauna Solarium Gym Pool table Jacuzzi/spa **CONF:** Thtr 400 Class 150 Board 40 Del from £165 * **SERVICES:** Lift **PARKING:** 120 **NOTES:** No dogs (ex guide dogs) No smoking in restaurant
CARDS:

ALDWARK, North Yorkshire Map 08 SE46

★★★69% Aldwark Manor Hotel, Golf & Country Club

YO61 1UF
☎ 01347 838146 & 838251 01347 838867
e-mail: reception@aldwarkmanor.co.uk
Dir: *from A1, A59 towards Green Hammerton, B6265 Little Ouseburn & follow signs Aldwark Bridge/Manor. A19 through Linton on Ouse*
Surrounded by a well designed golf course, this 19th-century manor house offers spacious bedrooms and public rooms furnished in period style. The brasserie serves light meals and snacks. The restaurant offers imaginative dishes in a more formal setting.
ROOMS: 25 en suite 3 annexe rms (2 en suite) (2 fmly) s fr £65; d £100-£120 (incl. bkfst) * LB **FACILITIES:** STV Indoor swimming (H) Golf 18 Fishing Sauna Solarium Gym Putting green Jacuzzi/spa Coarse fishing Xmas **CONF:** Thtr 80 Class 40 Board 30 **PARKING:** 150 **NOTES:** No smoking in restaurant Civ Wed 100
CARDS:

ALFRETON, Derbyshire Map 08 SK45

Travelodge

Travelodge

Old Swanwick Colliery Rd DE55 1HJ
☎ 01773 520040 01773 520040
Dir: *3m from junc 28 M1 where the A38 joins the A61*
This modern building offers accommodation in smart, spacious and well equipped bedrooms, all with en suite bathrooms. Refreshments may be taken at the nearby family restaurant. For further details and the Travelodge phone number, consult the Hotel Groups page. **ROOMS:** 60 en suite

ALFRISTON, East Sussex Map 05 TQ50

★★★69% *White Lodge Country House*

Sloe Ln BN26 5UR
☎ 01323 870265 01323 870284
Dir: *turn off A27 at rdbt take road to Alfriston. After 1.5m note hotel sign and 250yds on turn sharp right into narrow lane, hotel 60yds on left*
Set in five acres, overlooking the River Cuckmere Valley, this hotel is an extended Edwardian house offering comfort in a tranquil atmosphere. Day rooms have a sumptuous Victorian feel. Bedrooms are individually decorated and well equipped.
ROOMS: 17 en suite (1 fmly) No smoking in 2 bedrooms
FACILITIES: STV Snooker **CONF:** Thtr 25 Class 25 Board 16 Del £105 * **SERVICES:** Lift **PARKING:** 30 **NOTES:** No smoking in restaurant
CARDS:

See advert on this page

★★★68% Deans Place

Best Western

Seaford Rd BN26 5TW
☎ 01323 870248 01323 870918
Dir: *turn off A27 signposted Alfriston & Drusillas Zoo Park. Pass through village towards south side*
This creeper-clad hotel stands on the southern fringes of the village. Bedrooms vary in size, all have benefited from refurbishment. A wide range of food is offered including an extensive bar menu.
ROOMS: 36 en suite (2 fmly) No smoking in 4 bedrooms s £90-£105; d £115-£125 (incl. bkfst) * LB **FACILITIES:** STV Outdoor swimming (H) Croquet lawn Putting green Xmas **CONF:** Thtr 170 Class 70 Board 45 Del from £90 * **PARKING:** 100 **NOTES:** No smoking in restaurant Civ Wed 150 **CARDS:**

ALFRISTON, continued

★★★67% The Star Inn
BN26 5TA
☎ 0870 400 8102 📠 01323 870922
Dir: *2m off A27 at Drusillas roundabout*
This 14th-century hotel combines modern comforts with original character. Bedrooms are divided between the main building and the newer extension, all are well equipped and traditionally furnished. There are two beamed lounges with open fires and a bar with a flagstone floor.
ROOMS: 37 en suite (1 fmly) No smoking in 10 bedrooms s £69-£86; d £98-£132 (incl. bkfst) * LB **FACILITIES:** Xmas **CONF:** Thtr 35 Class 15 Board 25 Del £99 * **PARKING:** 27 **NOTES:** No smoking in restaurant **CARDS:**

ALNWICK, Northumberland — Map 12 NU11
see also Embleton

★★★60% White Swan
Bondgate Within NE66 1TD
☎ 01665 602109 📠 01665 510400
Dir: *from A1 follow town centre. Through Bondgate Tower archway on right*

Located in the heart of this market town, this popular hotel offers thoughtfully equipped bedrooms in a variety of styles. The Olympic Suite features the hand-carved panelling from the SS Olympic, sister ship to the ill-fated Titanic.
ROOMS: 58 en suite (4 fmly) No smoking in 15 bedrooms **CONF:** Thtr 200 Class 80 Board 15 Del from £79 * **PARKING:** 30 **NOTES:** No smoking in restaurant Civ Wed 120 **CARDS:**

ALRESFORD, Hampshire — Map 04 SU53

★★63% Swan
11 West St SO24 9AD
☎ 01962 732302 & 734427 📠 01962 735274
e-mail: swanhotel@btinternet.com
Dir: *turn off A31 onto B3047*
Located in the centre of this pretty town, there has been an inn on this site for 300 years. Bedrooms are in the old main building or the more modern wing. The lounge bar is open all day. There is also a separate restaurant.
ROOMS: 11 rms (10 en suite) 12 annexe en suite (3 fmly) s fr £37.50; d fr £50 (incl. bkfst) * **CONF:** Thtr 90 Class 60 Board 40 Del from £55 * **PARKING:** 75 **NOTES:** No dogs (ex guide dogs) RS 25-26 Dec
CARDS:

See advert on opposite page

ALREWAS, Staffordshire — Map 07 SK11

★★62% *Claymar Hotel*
118A Main St DE13 7AE
☎ 01283 790202
This hotel sits in the centre of the village, just off the A38. Personal and friendly service ensures a welcoming environment. There is a lounge bar and restaurant with carte, vegetarian and special diet meals available. Bedrooms are well equipped.
ROOMS: 20 en suite **PARKING:** 35

ALSAGER, Cheshire — Map 07 SJ75

★★★73% ❀❀ Manor House
Audley Rd ST7 2QQ
☎ 01270 884000 📠 01270 882483
e-mail: manres@compasshotels.co.uk
Dir: *from M6 junct 16 take A500 toward Stoke. In approx 0.5m take 1st slip road, Alsager, turn left at top & continue, hotel on left approaching village*
This modern hotel has been developed around an old farmhouse. The original oak beams still feature in the bars and restaurant, which serves imaginative and satisfying cuisine. Bedrooms are well equipped and include family and ground floor rooms. There is a pleasant patio garden and staff are helpful and caring.
ROOMS: 57 en suite (4 fmly) No smoking in 12 bedrooms s £89-£99; d £99-£109 (incl. bkfst) LB **FACILITIES:** STV Indoor swimming (H) Jacuzzi/spa entertainment Xmas **CONF:** Thtr 200 Class 108 Board 82 Del £115 * **PARKING:** 200 **NOTES:** No smoking in restaurant Civ Wed 50 **CARDS:**

See advert under STOKE ON TRENT

ALSTON, Cumbria — Map 12 NY74

★★73% ❀❀ Lovelady Shield Country House
CA9 3LF
☎ 01434 381203 & 381305 📠 01434 381515
e-mail: enquiries@lovelady.co.uk
Dir: *2m E, signposted off A689 where it joins the B6294*

This delightful hotel, in two acres of grounds high on the Pennines, offers bedrooms varying in style, most with moorland views. The stylish restaurant serves accomplished cuisine and the menu makes good use of seasonal local produce. The inviting bar, lounge and library capture the rural charm of the house.
ROOMS: 10 en suite (1 fmly) s £87.50-£107.50; d £175-£215 (incl. bkfst & dinner) * LB **FACILITIES:** Xmas **CONF:** Class 12 Board 12 Del £95 * **PARKING:** 20 **NOTES:** No smoking in restaurant Civ Wed 100
CARDS:

★★68% Lowbyer Manor Country House
CA9 3JX
☎ 01434 381230 📠 01434 382937
Dir: *on the edge of town on A686 towards Newcastle*
A 17th-century manor house situated in mature, well tended gardens on the edge of the town. This friendly hotel, under the personal supervision of the resident proprietors, offers comfortable accommodation and a warm and relaxing atmosphere. Home cooked dishes feature on the dinner menu which also includes a vegetarian section.
ROOMS: 8 en suite 4 annexe en suite s £36; d £72 (incl. bkfst) * LB **FACILITIES:** Xmas **CONF:** Thtr 40 Class 14 Board 10 Del £80 * **PARKING:** 14 **CARDS:**

★★68% Nent Hall Country House Hotel
CA9 3LQ
☎ 01434 381584 📠 01434 382668
Dir: *2m SE of Alston, on the A689 heading towards Nenthend, Stanhope & Durham*
A smartly presented hotel, nestling in delightful gardens, south east of Alston. The bedrooms are well equipped, stylish and modern. Public areas have a relaxed country house atmosphere and enjoyable dinners are served in the spacious dining room.
ROOMS: 8 en suite 9 annexe en suite (2 fmly) No smoking in all bedrooms s fr £42; d fr £60 (incl. bkfst) * LB **FACILITIES:** Golf **CONF:** Thtr 25 Class 25 Board 50 **PARKING:** 37 **NOTES:** No smoking in restaurant Closed 24-26 Dec **CARDS:**

ALTARNUN, Cornwall & Isles of Scilly Map 02 SX28

★★75% Penhallow Manor Country House
PL15 7SJ
☎ 01566 86206 📠 01566 86179
e-mail: penhallow@ukonline.co.uk
Dir: *8m W of Launceston towards Bodmin village, 1m N of A30. Hotel is next to church*

Located on the edge of Bodmin Moor, this Grade II listed building is situated beside the village church. Bedrooms are individually decorated, well equipped and include many thoughtful extras. The menu offers a wide choice of dishes, featuring local produce and a carefully selected wine list. Breakfast is served in the conservatory.
ROOMS: 6 en suite No smoking in all bedrooms s £55-£60; d £100 (incl. bkfst) * LB **FACILITIES:** Croquet lawn Art courses Hawking Bird Watching Xmas **CONF:** Thtr 30 Class 16 Board 12 Del from £75 * **PARKING:** 10 **NOTES:** No children 12yrs No smoking in restaurant Closed 3 Jan-14 Feb **CARDS:**

Early start? Hotels at all star levels should provide in-room alarm clocks and/or alarm calls.

A

ALTHORPE, Lincolnshire Map 08 SE80

★★60% The Lansdowne House Hotel
1 Main St DN17 3HJ
☎ 01724 783369 📠 01724 783369
A Victorian house situated in two acres of grounds and gardens only a short distance from both Scunthorpe and the M180 motorway. The River Trent runs close by. Most of the bedrooms are spacious, several have antique furnishings and one has a four-poster bed. There is a comfortable lounge with a small bar in one corner and an open fire on chilly days. The restaurant is attractively decorated in period style. A large lawn, capable of taking a marquee, is an ideal setting for wedding receptions.
ROOMS: 8 rms (7 en suite) 2 annexe en suite No smoking in 2 bedrooms s £59.50-£62.50; d £69.50-£72.50 (incl. bkfst) * **PARKING:** 30 **NOTES:** No dogs (ex guide dogs) No smoking in restaurant Closed 25-31 Dec **CARDS:**

ALTON, Hampshire Map 04 SU73

★★★67% Alton House
Normandy St GU34 1DW
☎ 01420 80033 📠 01420 89222
e-mail: mail@altonhouse.com
Dir: *turn off A31, close to railway station*
Conveniently located on the edge of the town, this popular, friendly hotel offers comfortably furnished and well equipped bedrooms. The restaurant serves carte and daily set menus. There is also an attractive garden.
ROOMS: 39 en suite (3 fmly) No smoking in 2 bedrooms d £70-£80 * LB **FACILITIES:** STV Outdoor swimming (H) Tennis (hard) Snooker Sauna Solarium Gym Croquet lawn Jacuzzi/spa **CONF:** Thtr 150 Class 80 Board 50 Del from £100 * **PARKING:** 94 **NOTES:** No dogs (ex guide dogs) Closed 25-26 Dec RS 27-29 Dec Civ Wed 75
CARDS:

See advert on page 43

★★★66% Alton Grange
London Rd GU34 4EG
☎ 01420 86565 📠 01420 541346
e-mail: info@altongrange.co.uk
Dir: *from A31 take first right at rdbt signed Alton/Holybourne/Bordon B3004, hotel will be found 300yds on left*
This friendly hotel, on the edge of the town, provides well equipped accommodation. Bedrooms, including some on the ground floor, are spacious and individually decorated. Guests can dine in Truffles Restaurant or more informally at the bar. The beautiful two acre garden is designed in an Oriental style.
ROOMS: 26 en suite 4 annexe en suite (4 fmly) No smoking in 2 bedrooms s £71-£87.50; d £87.50-£100 (incl. bkfst) * **FACILITIES:** STV Hot air ballooning **CONF:** Thtr 80 Class 30 Board 40 Del from £129 * **PARKING:** 48 **NOTES:** No children 3yrs No smoking in restaurant Closed 24 Dec-2 Jan Civ Wed 100
CARDS:

ALTRINCHAM, Greater Manchester Map 07 SJ78

★★★72% Woodland Park
Wellington Rd, Timperley WA15 7RG
☎ 0161 928 8631 📠 0161 941 2821
e-mail: info@woodlandpark.co.uk
Dir: *off the A560*
This private, friendly hotel is situated in a quiet residential area, yet near to the motorways. Bedrooms are individually furnished and the lounges are elegant. Carefully prepared meals are served in the Terrace Restaurant. Air-conditioned function rooms are available.

continued

ROOMS: 46 en suite (2 fmly) No smoking in 20 bedrooms s £77.50-£90; d £120-£135 (incl. bkfst) * LB **CONF:** Thtr 150 Class 100 Board 50 Del £120 * **PARKING:** 151 **NOTES:** No dogs (ex guide dogs) No smoking in restaurant Civ Wed 80 **CARDS:**

★★★67% Quality Hotel Altrincham
Langham Rd, Bowdon WA14 2HT
☎ 0161 928 7121 📠 0161 927 7560
e-mail: admin@gb064.u-net.com
Dir: *M6 leave junct 19 to airport, join A556, cross M56 rdbt onto A56, right at lights onto B5161, hotel 1m on right*
Located within easy reach of the motorways and Manchester airport, this popular hotel provides comfortable and well equipped bedrooms. There are two styles of eating options: the modern Cafe Continental which serves drinks and light snacks or the main restaurant offering more formal dining.
ROOMS: 89 en suite (4 fmly) No smoking in 19 bedrooms s £45-£83; d £70-£99 * LB **FACILITIES:** Indoor swimming (H) Sauna Solarium Gym Jacuzzi/spa Beauty treatments Xmas **CONF:** Thtr 130 Class 60 Board 48 Del from £90 * **PARKING:** 160
CARDS:

★★★65% *Cresta Court*
Church St WA14 4DP
☎ 0161 927 7272 📠 0161 926 9194
e-mail: info@cresta-court.co.uk
Dir: *on the A56 town centre Altrincham. Courtesy transport available from Manchester Airport*
Accommodation at this large, town centre hotel has been refurbished and now includes a number of four-poster suites with spa baths. Meals are available all day in the popular bar and there is also a restaurant.
ROOMS: 138 en suite (5 fmly) No smoking in 40 bedrooms **FACILITIES:** STV Solarium Gym **CONF:** Thtr 320 Class 140 Board 50 **SERVICES:** Lift **PARKING:** 200 **NOTES:** No smoking in restaurant
CARDS:

⌂ Premier Lodge (Altrincham North)
Manchester Rd, West Timperley WA14 5NH
☎ 0870 700 1308 📠 0870 700 1309
Premier Lodge offers modern, well equipped, en suite accommodation suitable for both business and leisure travellers. Meals can be taken at the adjacent popular restaurant and bar which is fully licensed. For further details, consult the Hotel Groups page.
ROOMS: 48 en suite d £46 *

⌂ Premier Lodge (Altrincham South)
Manchester Rd WA14 4PH
☎ 0870 700 1306 📠 0870 700 1307
Premier Lodge offers modern, well equipped, en suite accommodation suitable for both business and leisure travellers. Meals can be taken at the adjacent popular restaurant and bar which is fully licensed. For further details, consult the Hotel Groups page.
ROOMS: 46 en suite d £46 *

ALVELEY, Shropshire Map 07 SO78

★★★★66% Mill Hotel & Restaurant
WV15 6HL
☎ 01746 780437 📠 01746 780850
Dir: *between Kidderminster/Bridgnorth, turn off A442 signposted Enville/Turley Green*
Built around a 17th-century flour mill, with the original water wheel still on display, this modern hotel is set in eight acres of

continued

landscaped grounds. Bedrooms are pleasant and include some superior rooms, which have sitting areas, and some rooms with four-poster beds. The restaurant provides carefully prepared dishes.
ROOMS: 21 en suite (3 fmly) No smoking in 18 bedrooms s £64-£95; d £77-£110 (incl. cont bkfst) * LB **FACILITIES:** STV Gym **CONF:** Thtr 200 Class 200 Board 100 Del from £105 * **SERVICES:** Lift **PARKING:** 200 **NOTES:** No dogs No smoking in restaurant Civ Wed 200 **CARDS:**

See advert under BRIDGNORTH

ALVESTON, Gloucestershire Map 03 ST68

★★★74% Alveston House

Davids Ln BS35 2LA
☎ 01454 415050 01454 415425
e-mail: info@alvestonhousehotel.co.uk
Dir: *near A38, between juncts 14 & 16 of M5*
This popular hotel provides well maintained, modern bedrooms. The restaurant and bar are open-plan and extend into a conservatory. Menus offer a good choice and service is efficient.
ROOMS: 30 en suite (1 fmly) s £84.50-£94.50; d £94.50-£104.50 (incl. bkfst) * LB **FACILITIES:** STV **CONF:** Thtr 85 Class 48 Board 50 Del from £125 * **PARKING:** 75 **NOTES:** No smoking in restaurant Civ Wed 75 **CARDS:**

Premier Lodge (Bristol North)

PREMIER LODGE

Thornbury Rd BS35 3LL
☎ 0870 700 1338 0870 7001339
Premier Lodge offers modern, well equipped, en suite accommodation suitable for both business and leisure travellers. Meals can be taken at the adjacent popular restaurant and bar which is fully licensed. For further details, consult the Hotel Groups page.
ROOMS: 74 en suite d £49.50 *

AMBERLEY, West Sussex Map 04 TQ01

Premier Collection

★★★ Amberley Castle

BN18 9ND
☎ 01798 831992 01798 831998
e-mail: info@amberleycastle.co.uk
Dir: *SW of village, off B2139*
Few hotels boast the status of being a listed monument and fewer, if any, have enjoyed the honour of having a Royal Navy frigate named after it. This 11th-century luxury hotel is certainly unique, a treasure trove of history featuring a massive gate-house, portcullis and delightful gardens. Bedrooms are charming and individually decorated, some with direct access to the battlements and ramparts. The antique-dotted day rooms are cosy and stacked full of interesting books and historic bijouterie. The Queens Room restaurant offers accomplished cooking.
ROOMS: 15 en suite 5 annexe en suite d £145-£300 * LB **FACILITIES:** Croquet lawn Jacuzzi/spa Xmas **CONF:** Thtr 60 Class 24 Board 32 Del from £190 * **PARKING:** 50 **NOTES:** No dogs (ex guide dogs) No children 12yrs No smoking in restaurant Civ Wed 48 **CARDS:**

AMBLESIDE, Cumbria Map 07 NY30

see also Elterwater

★★★75% Nanny Brow Country House

Clappersgate LA22 9NF
☎ 015394 32036 015394 32450
e-mail: reservations@nannybrowhotel.demon.co.uk
Dir: *on A593, 1.5m from Ambleside*
Set in several acres of grounds and gardens, this country house has beautiful views over the River Brathey. The bedrooms are well equipped, with some four-poster rooms and garden suites available. A drawing room, bar and restaurant are provided for guests.
ROOMS: 17 en suite (3 fmly) No smoking in all bedrooms s £55-£105; d £110-£210 (incl. bkfst & dinner) * LB **FACILITIES:** STV Fishing Solarium Croquet lawn Putting green Jacuzzi/spa Free use of private leisure club Xmas **CONF:** Thtr 30 Class 30 Board 20 Del from £120 * **PARKING:** 20 **NOTES:** No smoking in restaurant **CARDS:**

See advert on this page

AMBLESIDE, continued

A

★★★75% Rothay Manor

Rothay Bridge LA22 0EH
☎ 015394 33605 015394 33607
e-mail: hotel@rothaymanor.co.uk
Dir: *in Ambleside follow signs for Coniston. Hotel is 0.25m SW on the road to Coniston opposite rugby pitch*

A Regency-style hotel in landscaped gardens, within walking distance of the town centre. Public rooms are relaxing and the bedrooms, all with personal touches such as fruit and flowers, are spacious and stylish. Some family rooms and rooms with balconies are available.

ROOMS: 15 en suite 3 annexe en suite (7 fmly) s £65-£75; d £110-£135 (incl. bkfst) * LB **FACILITIES:** Nearby leisure centre free to guests Xmas **CONF:** Thtr 22 Board 18 Del from £125 * **PARKING:** 45 **NOTES:** No dogs (ex guide dogs) No smoking in restaurant Closed 3 Jan-9 Feb **CARDS:**

See advert on opposite page

★★★74% Regent

Waterhead Bay LA22 0ES
☎ 015394 32254 015394 31474
e-mail: info@regentlakes.co.uk
Dir: *1m S A591*

This comfortable holiday hotel, situated close to Waterhead Bay, offers a warm welcome. Bedrooms are comfortably furnished including three suites and five bedrooms in the Garden wing. There is a choice of relaxing lounges, one of which contains a bar, and the elegant restaurant offers a fine dining experience using quality fresh ingredients.

ROOMS: 30 en suite (7 fmly) No smoking in 4 bedrooms s £59-£79; d £99-£109 (incl. bkfst) * LB **FACILITIES:** Indoor swimming (H) Jacuzzi/spa entertainment **PARKING:** 38 **NOTES:** No smoking in restaurant **CARDS:**

See advert on opposite page

★★★72% Wateredge

Borrans Rd, Waterhead LA22 0EP
☎ 015394 32332 015394 31878
e-mail: info-a@wateredgehotel.co.uk
Dir: *on A591, at Waterhead Bay, adj Steamer Pier*

Idyllically situated on the shores of Windermere, this delightful hotel, converted from two fishermen's cottages, retains oak beams and original charm. The elegant lounges overlook the gardens and lake. Bedrooms include impressive studio suites, each with their own patio or balcony. Freshly prepared dinners, lunches and home-made afternoon teas are available.

continued

ROOMS: 17 en suite 6 annexe en suite (1 fmly) No smoking in 1 bedroom s fr £64; d £110-£156 (incl. bkfst) * LB **FACILITIES:** Rowing boat Free use of Leisure Club Private jetty, Boat Launching **PARKING:** 25 **NOTES:** No children 7yrs No smoking in restaurant Closed mid Dec-early Jan **CARDS:**

★★★71% Ambleside Salutation Hotel

Best Western

Lake Rd LA22 9BX
☎ 015394 32244 015394 34157
e-mail: enquiries@hotelambleside.uk.com
Dir: *take A591 to Ambleside and follow one way system down Wansfell Road into Compston Road. At traffic lights take right hand lane back into village*

This former coaching inn has been tastefully transformed into a comfortable, stylish hotel. The well equipped bedrooms vary in size, with many enjoying open patios and delightful views. There is a spacious air-conditioned lounge and a restaurant offering an ambitious menu. A range of snacks is also available in the bar.

ROOMS: 38 en suite 4 annexe en suite (4 fmly) No smoking in 9 bedrooms s £44-£52; d £88-£104 (incl. bkfst) **FACILITIES:** STV Jacuzzi/spa Free membership of nearby leisure club Xmas **CONF:** Thtr 150 Board 16 Del from £78 * **PARKING:** 41 **NOTES:** No smoking in restaurant **CARDS:**

See advert on opposite page

★★73% *Fisherbeck*

Lake Rd LA22 0DH
☎ 015394 33215 015394 33600
Dir: *S of Ambleside on A591*

A welcoming, family-run hotel offering friendly and attentive service. Bedrooms vary in style and include several on the ground floor and some smart rooms with balconies. There is a split-level restaurant and lounge bar, both serving creative dishes.

continued on p48

AMBLESIDE, continued

Fisherbeck, Ambleside

ROOMS: 18 en suite (2 fmly) No smoking in 4 bedrooms
FACILITIES: Free use of nearby Leisure Complex **PARKING:** 24
NOTES: No dogs No smoking in restaurant Closed 26 Dec-15 Jan
CARDS:

★★70% Skelwith Bridge

Skelwith Bridge LA22 9NJ
☎ 015394 32115 015394 34254
e-mail: skelwithbr@aol.com
Dir: *2.5m W on the A593 at junction of B5343 to Langdale*

Lying at the heart of the Lake District National Park, this is a welcoming family-run hotel. There is a good choice of lounges and contrasting bars, and the restaurant offers carefully prepared fare. Bedrooms are comfortable and modern in style.
ROOMS: 23 en suite 6 annexe en suite (3 fmly) No smoking in 6 bedrooms s £33-£53; d £61-£104 (incl. bkfst) * LB **FACILITIES:** Fishing Pool table Jacuzzi/spa ch fac Xmas **CONF:** Thtr 45 Class 25 Board 25 Del from £52 * **PARKING:** 60 **NOTES:** No smoking in restaurant Closed 15-24 Dec **CARDS:**

See advert on opposite page

★★66% Waterhead

Lake Rd LA22 0ER
☎ 015394 32566 015394 31255
e-mail: waterhead@elh.co.uk
Dir: *A591 into Ambleside, hotel is opposite Waterhead Pier*
Situated opposite the bay, this holiday hotel boasts views of the lakeside and gardens where guests can sit and enjoy the surroundings. In addition to the main restaurant there is also a Mediterranean-style café bar and an Irish theme bar. Bedrooms, all well equipped, vary in style.
ROOMS: 28 en suite (3 fmly) No smoking in 14 bedrooms s £42.50; d £85-£120 (incl. bkfst) * LB **FACILITIES:** STV Use of sister hotel's leisure facilities entertainment Xmas **CONF:** Thtr 40 Class 30 Board 25 Del from £87 * **PARKING:** 50 **NOTES:** No smoking in restaurant
CARDS:

AMERSHAM, Buckinghamshire Map 04 SU99

★★★66% The Crown

High St HP7 0DH
☎ 0870 400 8103 01494 431283
e-mail: heritagehotelsamersham.crown@forte-hotels.com
Dir: *access to car park immediately next to Nags Head pub*
A convenient base for antique shopping and walks in the Chilterns. This 16th-century coaching inn combines the charm of the period with modern comforts. The attractive bedrooms vary in style, some featuring original hand painted murals. The hotel was featured in the hit film *Four Weddings and a Funeral.*
ROOMS: 19 en suite 18 annexe en suite No smoking in 7 bedrooms s £125-£145; d £145-£165 * LB **FACILITIES:** Xmas **PARKING:** 32
NOTES: No smoking in restaurant **CARDS:**

AMESBURY, Wiltshire Map 04 SU14

★★60% Antrobus Arms

MINOTEL Great Britain

15 Church St SP4 7EU
☎ 01980 623163 01980 622112
e-mail: reception@antrobushotel.co.uk
Dir: *from rdbt on A303 proceed through town on one way system to T junct, turn left hotel on left*

The Antrobus Arms, advertised as the nearest hotel to Stonehenge, offers individually furnished bedrooms, some overlooking the walled Victorian garden. Bar meals are available as an alternative to the main restaurant.
ROOMS: 16 en suite (2 fmly) s £50.50-£75; d £80-£110 (incl. bkfst) * LB **FACILITIES:** STV Tennis (hard) Xmas **CONF:** Thtr 40 Class 40 Board 20 **PARKING:** 15 **NOTES:** No smoking in restaurant
CARDS:

Travelodge

Travelodge

Countess Services SP4 7AS
☎ 01980 624966 01980 624966
Dir: *junc A345 & A303 eastbound*
This modern building offers accommodation in smart, spacious and well equipped bedrooms, all with en suite bathrooms. Refreshments may be taken at the nearby family restaurant. For further details and the Travelodge phone number, consult the Hotel Groups page.
ROOMS: 32 en suite

Late for dinner? Quality Standards star rating means that last orders for dinner should be no earlier than:
★ 6.30pm ★★ 7.00pm ★★★ 8.00pm
★★★★ 9.00pm ★★★★★ 10.00pm

ANDOVER, Hampshire Map 04 SU34

★★★73% ❀❀ Esseborne Manor

Hurstbourne Tarrant SP11 0ER
☎ 01264 736444 📠 01264 736725
e-mail: esseborne_manor@compuserve.com
Dir: *halfway between Andover and Newbury on A343*

An attractive manor house, set in two acres of well tended gardens, surrounded by open countryside. The individually furnished, spacious bedrooms, including many thoughtful extras, are split between the main house, adjoining courtyard and a separate garden cottage. There are also comfortable public rooms.

ROOMS: 6 en suite 8 annexe en suite s £95-£105; d £100-£160 (incl. bkfst) * LB **FACILITIES:** STV Tennis (hard) Croquet lawn Putting green Jacuzzi/spa **CONF:** Thtr 40 Class 35 Board 30 Del £140 * **PARKING:** 50 **NOTES:** No dogs (ex guide dogs) No smoking in restaurant Civ Wed 120 **CARDS:**

See advert on this page

ANDOVER, continued

A

★★★67% White Hart
Bridge St SP10 1BH
☎ 01264 352266 📠 01264 323767
Dir: *from A303 follow signs to town centre, then signs for London St, Bridge St and High St, hotel is on left hand side halfway along Bridge St*
This 17th-century former coaching inn offers well equipped bedrooms. The restaurant serves fixed price and carte menus and Simon's Wine Bar provides an alternative eating option in an informal atmosphere.
ROOMS: 27 en suite (2 fmly) No smoking in 6 bedrooms s fr £80; d fr £90 * **FACILITIES:** STV Sauna Solarium Gym **CONF:** Thtr 70 Class 30 Board 30 **PARKING:** 30 **NOTES:** No smoking in restaurant
CARDS:

Best Western

★★★63% Quality Hotel Andover
Micheldever Rd SP11 6LA
☎ 01264 369111 📠 01264 369000
e-mail: andover@quality-hotels.co.uk
Dir: *turn off A303 at A3091. 1st rdbt take 1st exit, 2nd rdbt take 1st exit. Turn left immediately before BP petrol station, then left*
This peaceful hotel is set in grounds on the outskirts of the town. Bedrooms are comfortable and well equipped, with extras such as modem points and satellite TV. The range of conference and meeting rooms makes this hotel a popular venue for functions and weddings.
ROOMS: 9 en suite 26 annexe en suite No smoking in 7 bedrooms s £50-£69; d £74-£125 * LB **FACILITIES:** STV **CONF:** Thtr 180 Class 40 Board 60 Del from £90 * **PARKING:** 100 **NOTES:** No dogs (ex guide dogs) No smoking in restaurant Civ Wed 85
CARDS:

CHOICE HOTELS EUROPE

APPLEBY-IN-WESTMORLAND, Cumbria
Map 12 NY62

★★★77% Appleby Manor Country House
Roman Rd CA16 6JB
☎ 017683 51571 📠 017683 52888
e-mail: reception@applebymanor.co.uk
Dir: *from M6 junct 40, take A66 towards Brough. Take Appleby turn off, then immediately right and continue for 0.5m*

Best Western

This family-run Victorian mansion, set in open countryside, enjoys scenic views. There are three styles of bedroom - modern garden rooms, main house rooms and coach house rooms across the courtyard. There is a delightful lounge and a bright conservatory. An imaginative carte dinner menu is offered and the hotel stocks an impressive range of whiskies.
ROOMS: 23 en suite 7 annexe en suite (9 fmly) No smoking in 6 bedrooms s £80-£100; d £120-£140 (incl. bkfst) LB **FACILITIES:** STV Indoor swimming (H) Sauna Solarium Pool table Putting green Jacuzzi/spa Steam room Table tennis **CONF:** Thtr 38 Class 25 Board 28 Del from £109.95 * **PARKING:** 53 **NOTES:** No smoking in restaurant Closed 24-26 Dec **CARDS:**

See advert on opposite page

★★★70% Tufton Arms
Market Square CA16 6XA
☎ 017683 51593 📠 017683 52761
e-mail: info@fishing-shooting.co.uk
Dir: *in the centre of Appleby, by-passed by the A66, on B6260*
Situated in the centre of this popular market town, this hotel is stylishly furnished to reflect its grand Victorian character. Bedrooms include lavish suites, studio rooms, and mews rooms. The smart conservatory restaurant features some ambitious cooking and offers fixed price and carte menus.
ROOMS: 21 en suite (4 fmly) s £55-£95; d £90-£145 (incl. bkfst) * LB **FACILITIES:** STV Fishing Shooting **CONF:** Thtr 100 Class 60 Board 50 Del from £99 * **PARKING:** 17 **NOTES:** Civ Wed 100
CARDS:

Best Western

★★71% Royal Oak Inn
Bongate CA16 6UN
☎ 017683 51463 📠 017683 52300
e-mail: m.m.royaloak@btinternet.com
Dir: *from M6 junct 38 follow B6260, hotel is 0.5m from Appleby centre on old A66 in direction of Scotch Corner*
A comfortable inn providing well equipped accommodation. The traditional bars are packed full of history and include beamed ceilings, open fires and real ales. A commendable selection of food is served from varied and imaginative menus.
ROOMS: 9 rms (7 en suite) (1 fmly) s £38-£53; d £76-£90 (incl. bkfst) * LB **FACILITIES:** Xmas **CONF:** Class 20 Board 15 **PARKING:** 13
CARDS:

APPLETON-LE-MOORS, North Yorkshire
Map 08 SE78

★★68% Appleton Hall Country House Hotel
YO62 6TF
☎ 01751 417227 📠 01751 417540
Dir: *off A170 to Appleton-le-Moors*

Set in delightful gardens, this well maintained gracious Victorian country house offers a comfortable lounge, with a real fire in a marble fireplace and an elegant dining room, where good home-cooking is served. Bedrooms, all individually and attractively decorated, are well equipped, two have their own sitting room.
ROOMS: 9 en suite No smoking in all bedrooms s £60-£70; d £120-£156 (incl. bkfst & dinner) * **FACILITIES:** Croquet lawn **SERVICES:** Lift **PARKING:** 12 **NOTES:** No dogs (ex guide dogs) No children 14yrs No smoking in restaurant **CARDS:**

ARNCLIFFE, North Yorkshire
Map 07 SD97

★★75% Amerdale House
BD23 5QE
☎ 01756 770250 📠 01756 770266
Dir: *fork left off Threshfield-Kettlewell road 0.5m past Kilnsey Crag*
There are fine views of the dale and fells from every bedroom in this delightful former manor house. There is a choice of

continued

welcoming lounges looking out over the gardens and in the dining room a hand-written menu of carefully prepared dishes is offered. The comfortable bedrooms are decorated with style and elegance.

ROOMS: 10 en suite 1 annexe en suite (3 fmly) s £79.50-£81.50; d £139-£143 (incl. bkfst & dinner) * LB **PARKING:** 30 **NOTES:** No dogs (ex guide dogs) No smoking in restaurant Closed mid Nov-mid Mar
CARDS:

ARUNDEL, West Sussex Map 04 TQ00

★★★70% Burpham Country House & Restaurant

Old Down, Burpham BN18 9RJ
☎ 01903 882160 01903 884627
Dir: *3m NE off A27 turning by Arundel Railway Station clearly signed to hotel, Warningcamp & Burpham, continue for 2.5m along lane, hotel on right*

Set in a peaceful rural location just outside the historic town of Arundel, this hotel offers tastefully furnished bedrooms with a range of modern facilities. The restaurant has a daily changing menu and the conservatory enjoys superb views of the beautiful countryside.
ROOMS: 10 en suite No smoking in all bedrooms s £45-£60; d £90-£110 (incl. bkfst) * LB **FACILITIES:** Croquet lawn Xmas **PARKING:** 12
NOTES: No dogs No children 10yrs No smoking in restaurant RS Mon
CARDS:

★★★67% Norfolk Arms

Forestdale Hotels

High St BN18 9AD
☎ 01903 882101 01903 884275
Dir: *in centre of High Street*
Originally built as a Georgian coaching inn over 200 years ago, the Norfolk Arms stands in the heart of the town. Bedrooms, including some in a separate courtyard building, are comfortably furnished. The public areas consist of two bars and an attractively decorated lounge.
ROOMS: 21 en suite 13 annexe en suite (4 fmly) No smoking in 3 bedrooms s fr £60; d fr £120 (incl. bkfst & dinner) * LB
FACILITIES: Xmas **CONF:** Thtr 100 Class 40 Board 40 Del from £100 *
PARKING: 34 **NOTES:** Civ Wed **CARDS:**

★★★65% *The Arundel Swan Hotel*

27-29 High St BN18 9AG
☎ 01903 882314 01903 883759
Dir: *off A27*

Situated in the heart of Arundel, this well presented Victorian hotel offers smart and well equipped accommodation. There is a lively tap room bar, a small combined reception and lounge and a pleasant restaurant, serving an inviting range of dishes. Room service, light snacks and bar meals are also available.
ROOMS: 15 en suite (5 fmly) No smoking in all bedrooms
PARKING: 15 **NOTES:** No dogs (ex guide dogs) No smoking in restaurant **CARDS:**

Popped the question? Hotels with Civ Wed in their entry are licensed for civil wedding ceremonies. Maximum numbers for the ceremony only are shown, e.g. Civ Wed 50

ARUNDEL, continued

★★68% Comfort Inn

Junction A27/A284, Crossbush BN17 7QQ
☎ 01903 840840 01903 849849
e-mail: admin@gb642.u-net.com
Dir: *from Worthing on the A27 towards Arundel, turn left on the A284 towards Littlehampton and straight right, hotel next to McDonalds restaurant*
This modern, purpose-built hotel provides a good base for exploring the nearby historic town of Arundel and the ancient walled city of Chichester. Good access to local road networks and a range of meeting rooms also make this an ideal venue for business guests. Bedrooms are spacious, smartly decorated and very well equipped.
ROOMS: 53 en suite (4 fmly) No smoking in 39 bedrooms d £44-£55 * LB **FACILITIES:** STV Gym Xmas **CONF:** Thtr 30 Class 12 Board 24 Del from £72 * **PARKING:** 50 **CARDS:**

ASCOT, Berkshire — Map 04 SU96

★★★★68% The Royal Berkshire
London Rd, Sunninghill SL5 0PP
☎ 01344 623322 01344 627100
Dir: *from A30 then toward Bagshot turn right opposite Wentworth Club onto A329, continue for 2m hotel entrance on right*

Originally built for the Churchill family, the Royal Berkshire Hotel enjoys a peaceful location, set in 14 acres of grounds and gardens. Bedrooms are generally spacious and well equipped. There is also an elegant lounge and a smart restaurant.
ROOMS: 63 en suite (1 fmly) No smoking in 34 bedrooms s £175-£195; d £200-£220 * LB **FACILITIES:** STV Indoor swimming (H) Tennis (hard) Squash Sauna Gym Croquet lawn Putting green Jacuzzi/spa Xmas **CONF:** Thtr 70 Class 45 Board 32 Del from £229 * **PARKING:** 250 **NOTES:** No smoking in restaurant **CARDS:**

★★★★62% The Berystede

Bagshot Rd, Sunninghill SL5 9JH
☎ 0870 400 8111 01344 872301
e-mail: brianshanahan@forte-hotels.com
Dir: *turn off A30 onto B3020 (Windmill Pub). Continue for approx. 1.25m to hotel on left just before junct with A330*
This impressive Victorian mansion, close to Ascot Racecourse, is set in nine acres of wooded grounds. Spacious bedrooms have comfortable armchairs and facilities for business guests. There is a cosy bar and a restaurant which overlooks the heated outdoor swimming pool and gardens.
ROOMS: 90 en suite (6 fmly) No smoking in 36 bedrooms s £145-£200; d £165-£200 * LB **FACILITIES:** STV Outdoor swimming (H) Croquet lawn Putting green Xmas **CONF:** Thtr 120 Class 55 Board 50 Del from £205 * **SERVICES:** Lift **PARKING:** 240 **NOTES:** No smoking in restaurant Civ Wed 60 **CARDS:**

★★74% *Highclere*
19 Kings Rd, Sunninghill SL5 9AD
☎ 01344 625220 01344 872528
Dir: *opposite Sunninghill Post Office*
This welcoming hotel, in a quiet side street location, provides easy access to the Ascot and Windsor areas. Bedrooms are well equipped and include thoughtful extras. There is a lounge, bar and dining room and these are all enhanced with fresh floral displays.
ROOMS: 11 en suite (1 fmly) No smoking in 3 bedrooms **FACILITIES:** STV **PARKING:** 11 **NOTES:** No dogs (ex guide dogs) No smoking in restaurant **CARDS:**

★★66% Brockenhurst
Brockenhurst Rd SL5 9HA
☎ 01344 621912 01344 873252
Dir: *on A330*
This attractive former Edwardian home is situated south of the town and offers easy access to the race course, the historic town of Windsor and several local golf courses. Bedrooms are spacious and feature a range of extra facilities, some even have whirlpool baths.
ROOMS: 11 en suite 4 annexe en suite (2 fmly) s £79-£89; d £89-£100 (incl. cont bkfst) * **FACILITIES:** STV Xmas **CONF:** Thtr 50 Class 25 Board 30 Del from £159 * **PARKING:** 32 **NOTES:** No dogs (ex guide dogs) **CARDS:**

ASHBOURNE, Derbyshire — Map 07 SK14

★★★75% Callow Hall
Mappleton Rd DE6 2AA
☎ 01335 300900 01335 300512
e-mail: reservations@callowhall.demon.co.uk
Dir: *take A515 through Ashbourne toward Buxton, turn left at Bowling Green pub on left, then first right*

This delightful creeper-clad, early Victorian house, set in a 44 acre estate, enjoys views over Bentley Brook and the Dove Valley. The atmosphere is relaxed and welcoming and the bedrooms vary in style. Some spacious main house bedrooms have comfortable sitting areas. Public rooms feature high ceilings, ornate plasterwork and antique furniture. There is a good range of dishes available from the fixed price and carte menus.
ROOMS: 16 en suite (2 fmly) No smoking in 8 bedrooms s £85-£110; d £130-£190 (incl. bkfst) * LB **FACILITIES:** Fishing **CONF:** Thtr 30 Board 16 Del from £136.50 * **PARKING:** 21 **NOTES:** No dogs (ex guide dogs) No smoking in restaurant Closed 25-26 Dec
CARDS:

See advert on opposite page

Arriving late? Four and five star hotels have night porters to assist with your luggage; and 24hr room service.

★★★66% **Hanover International**
Derby Rd DE6 1XH
☎ 01335 346666 01335 346549
Dir: *on A52 to Ashbourne at rdbt take right turn to Airfield Ind Est, hotel is 400yds on right*

This modern, purpose-built hotel, just a short drive from the town, offers comfortable, well equipped bedrooms, with some rooms designed especially for disabled visitors. A choice of eating options includes the Milldale restaurant or, as a more informal alternative, the brasserie. Several function suites and meeting rooms are also available.
ROOMS: 50 en suite (5 fmly) No smoking in 10 bedrooms s £47-£80; d £60-£95 (incl. bkfst) * LB **FACILITIES:** STV Indoor swimming (H) Sauna Gym Pool table Steam room entertainment **CONF:** Thtr 200 Class 100 Board 80 Del from £95 * **SERVICES:** Lift **PARKING:** 130 **NOTES:** No dogs (ex guide dogs) No smoking in restaurant Civ Wed
CARDS:

★★61% ***The Dog & Partridge***
Swinscoe DE6 2HS
☎ 01335 343183
This 17th-century inn sits in the hamlet of Swinscoe, within easy reach of Alton Towers. Accommodation styles vary, most are separate weather boarded rooms within the grounds. Well presented self-catering units are sometimes used during quieter periods. Meals are available every evening until late.
ROOMS: 25 en suite No smoking in 3 bedrooms LB **FACILITIES:** ch fac **PARKING:** 90

ASHBURTON, Devon — Map 03 SX77

★★★74% ❀❀❀ **Holne Chase**
Two Bridges Rd TQ13 7NS
☎ 01364 631471 01364 631453
e-mail: info@holne-chase.co.uk
Dir: *3m N on Two Bridges/Tavistock road (unclass)*
Set in idyllic woodland, this former hunting lodge provides a peaceful, charming hideaway. Bedrooms, decorated and furnished to a very high standard, vary in style, some have original fireplaces and four-poster beds. There are also delightful split-level suites situated in the converted stables. The daily changing menu makes good use of local produce.
ROOMS: 11 en suite 6 annexe en suite (8 fmly) s fr £95; d £125-£165 (incl. bkfst) * LB **FACILITIES:** Fishing Croquet lawn Putting green Fly fishing Xmas **CONF:** Thtr 20 Class 20 Board 20 Del from £150 * **PARKING:** 40 **NOTES:** No smoking in restaurant
CARDS:

See advert on this page

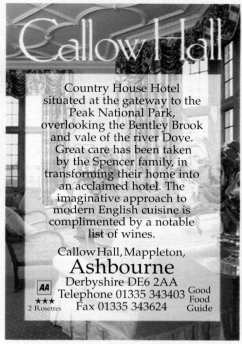

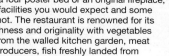

ASHBURTON, continued

★★67% The Lavender House
Knowle Hill TQ13 7QY
☎ 01364 652697 🖷 01364 654325
Dir: *turn off A38 at Peartree, go uphill & after approx 400yds look for hotel sign on right, hotel within 100yds*
Much renovation has taken place here over the last few years to create a hotel with pretty, stylish, individual bedrooms, a very comfortable lounge, welcoming bar and more intimate restaurant. Set in approximately three acres, views are lovely and peace and quiet prevail. The hotel is only a few minutes from the M5 and is also close to the Dartmoor Country Park.
ROOMS: 11 en suite (2 fmly) **FACILITIES:** entertainment ch fac **PARKING:** 100 **NOTES:** Closed Jan **CARDS:**

★★65% *Dartmoor Lodge*
Peartree Cross TQ13 7JW
☎ 01364 652232 🖷 01364 653990
Dir: *turn off A38 at Peartree Junction and follow 'Hotel & Services' signs*
Situated between Plymouth and Exeter, this popular hotel is close to Dartmoor and the South Devon coast. Bedrooms, including two with four-poster beds, are well equipped. The bar and some of the function rooms display old beams and open fireplaces. There is also an attractive restaurant.
ROOMS: 30 en suite (5 fmly) No smoking in 5 bedrooms **FACILITIES:** STV **CONF:** Thtr 100 Board 32 **SERVICES:** Lift **PARKING:** 80 **CARDS:**

ASHFORD, Kent Map 05 TR04

★★★★78% Eastwell Manor
Eastwell Park, Boughton Lees TN25 4HR
☎ 01233 213000 🖷 01233 635530
e-mail: eastwell@btinternet.com
Dir: *on A251, 200 yds on left when entering Boughton Aluph*

A fine hotel, set in 62 acres of beautiful grounds and gardens. Its rich history is reflected in the architecture - stonework, open fires, antiques and wood panelling feature throughout. Spacious, individually decorated bedrooms include many thoughtful extras. A high standard of cuisine is served in the elegant dining room.
ROOMS: 23 en suite 39 annexe en suite (2 fmly) No smoking in 4 bedrooms s £150-£310; d £180-£340 (incl. bkfst) * **FACILITIES:** STV Indoor swimming (H) Outdoor swimming (H) Tennis (hard) Sauna Solarium Gym Croquet lawn Putting green Jacuzzi/spa Boule Hairdressing salon entertainment Xmas **CONF:** Thtr 200 Class 60 Board 48 Del £180 * **SERVICES:** Lift **PARKING:** 80 **NOTES:** No smoking in restaurant Civ Wed 250 **CARDS:**

★★★★62% *Ashford International*
Simone Weil Av TN24 8UX
☎ 01233 219988 🖷 01233 647743
Dir: *off junct 9, M20*
A modern, purpose-built hotel, within easy reach of the M20. As a central feature it boasts a long mall containing boutiques and several places to eat, including a popular brasserie and The Alhambra, a more formal restaurant. Bedrooms are spacious and well equipped.
ROOMS: 200 en suite (4 fmly) No smoking in 57 bedrooms **FACILITIES:** Indoor swimming (H) Snooker Sauna Solarium Gym Jacuzzi/spa **CONF:** Thtr 400 Class 160 Board 100 **SERVICES:** Lift **PARKING:** 400 **CARDS:**

★★★64% Pilgrims Rest
Canterbury Rd, Kennington TN24 9QR
☎ 01233 636863 🖷 01233 610119
e-mail: pilgrimsrest@fullers.demon.co.uk
Dir: *on A28 1m N of town centre, and 1m from junct 9/10 on M20*
Set in five acres of mature grounds, this hotel overlooks the South Downs. The focal point is the informal bar which leads into the restaurant. Meeting rooms and a small first floor lounge are also provided.
ROOMS: 34 en suite (1 fmly) No smoking in 12 bedrooms d £46 * LB **FACILITIES:** STV **CONF:** Thtr 75 Class 40 Board 40 **PARKING:** 60 **CARDS:**

★★★64% *Posthouse Ashford*
Canterbury Rd TN24 8QQ
☎ 0870 400 9001 🖷 01233 643176
Dir: *off A28*
Suitable for both the business and leisure traveller, this bright hotel provides modern accommodation in well equipped bedrooms with en suite bathrooms.
ROOMS: 103 en suite (45 fmly) No smoking in 60 bedrooms **FACILITIES:** ch fac **CONF:** Thtr 120 Class 65 Board 40 **PARKING:** 130 **CARDS:**

ASHFORD-IN-THE-WATER, Derbyshire Map 07 SK17

★★★79% Riverside House
Fennel St DE45 1QF
☎ 01629 814275 🖷 01629 812873
e-mail: riversidehouse@enta.net
Dir: *turn right off A6 Bakewell/Buxton road 2m from Bakewell village, hotel at end of main street*
Partly dating back to 1630 this delightful hotel, in the centre of the village, is surrounded by gardens beside the River Wye. It offers individually decorated bedrooms, and public rooms include a conservatory, an oak panelled lounge with inglenook fireplace, a drawing room and two dining rooms. Good quality cuisine is served and service is attentive.
ROOMS: 15 en suite No smoking in all bedrooms s £95-£135; d £115-£155 (incl. bkfst) * **FACILITIES:** Croquet lawn Xmas **CONF:** Thtr 15 Class 15 Board 15 Del from £145 * **PARKING:** 24 **NOTES:** No dogs (ex guide dogs) No children 10yrs No smoking in restaurant Civ Wed 30 **CARDS:**

See advert on opposite page

ASHTON-UNDER-LYNE, Greater Manchester Map 07 SJ99

★★69% York House

York Place, Richmond St OL6 7TT
☎ 0161 330 9000 🖷 0161 343 1613
Dir: *close to junct A635/A6017*
Developed from a cluster of Victorian houses and set around a

continued

courtyard with award-winning gardens, this welcoming hotel offers comfortable, well equipped bedrooms. Carefully prepared meals are served in the elegant restaurant and service is professional and friendly.
ROOMS: 24 en suite 10 annexe en suite (2 fmly) s £62; d £80 (incl. bkfst) * LB **FACILITIES:** STV Reduced cost at local gym/pool **CONF:** Thtr 50 Class 20 Board 22 Del £88 * **PARKING:** 34 **NOTES:** Closed 26 Dec RS Sun Civ Wed 50
CARDS:

ASPLEY GUISE, Bedfordshire — Map 04 SP93

★★★66% Moore Place

Best Western

The Square MK17 8DW
☎ 01908 282000 Fax 01908 281888
e-mail: info@mooreplace.co.uk
Dir: *from junct 13 of M1, take A507 and then follow signs for Aspley Guise and Woburn Sands. Hotel is on left hand side of village square*
This impressive Georgian house, set in delightful gardens in the centre of the village, is very conveniently located for access to the M1. Public rooms include a foyer lounge, a cosy bar and a smart conservatory restaurant. The comfortable, well equipped bedrooms vary in size and style.
ROOMS: 39 en suite 15 annexe en suite s £80; d £99-£189 (incl. bkfst) * LB **FACILITIES:** STV Xmas **CONF:** Thtr 40 Class 24 Board 20 Del from £155 * **PARKING:** 70 **NOTES:** No smoking in restaurant Civ Wed 80 **CARDS:**

ATHERSTONE, Warwickshire — Map 04 SP39

★★75% ❀❀ Chapel House

Friar's Gate CV9 1EY
☎ 01827 718949 Fax 01827 717702
Dir: *next to St Marys Church in Market Square*
Nestling beside the church, this hotel offers warm hospitality and good cooking. There are pleasant dining rooms and a comfortable conservatory lounge, overlooking the attractive walled garden. Bedrooms are all individual in size and style. The interesting monthly changing carte is supplemented by daily dishes and specialities.
ROOMS: 14 en suite s £52-£70; d £70-£85 (incl. bkfst) * LB **CONF:** Thtr 15 Board 20 Del from £78 * **NOTES:** No dogs (ex guide dogs) No smoking in restaurant Closed 24-26 Dec RS BH
CARDS:

See advert on this page

AUSTWICK, North Yorkshire — Map 07 SD76

★★66% The Austwick Country House

LA2 8BY
☎ 015242 51224 Fax 015242 51796
e-mail: austwick@cs.com
Dir: *4m N of Settle, off A65*
A Georgian country house, previously known as The Traddock, with pleasant gardens. Most of the bedrooms are spacious and comfortably furnished, all include thoughtful extras such as fruit and a decanter of sherry. Open fires in the lounge and bar enhance the warm atmosphere. Much emphasis is placed on the high quality dinner menu.
ROOMS: 9 en suite (3 fmly) No smoking in all bedrooms s £57-£60; d £114-£120 (incl. bkfst & dinner) * LB **FACILITIES:** Croquet lawn Putting green Xmas **CONF:** Thtr 70 Class 30 Board 20 **PARKING:** 15 **NOTES:** No dogs (ex guide dogs) No smoking in restaurant
CARDS:

AXBRIDGE, Somerset Map 03 ST45

★★61% The Oak House
The Square BS26 2AP
☎ 01934 732444 01934 733112
Dir: *2m E of Cheddar, 0.25m off A371*

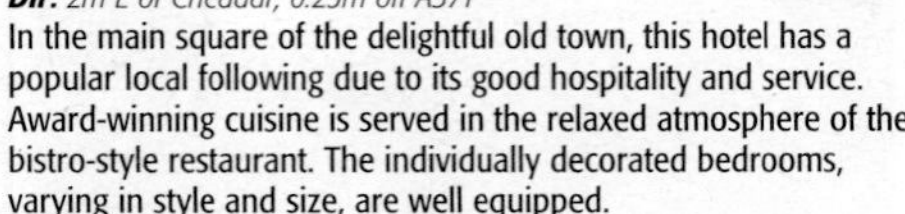

In the main square of the delightful old town, this hotel has a popular local following due to its good hospitality and service. Award-winning cuisine is served in the relaxed atmosphere of the bistro-style restaurant. The individually decorated bedrooms, varying in style and size, are well equipped.
ROOMS: 11 en suite (2 fmly) **CONF:** Thtr 40 Class 40 Board 22
CARDS:

AXMINSTER, Devon Map 03 SY29

★★★74% Fairwater Head
Hawkchurch EX13 5TX
☎ 01297 678349 01297 678459
e-mail: reception@fairwater.demon.co.uk
Dir: *turn off B3165 (Crewkerne to Lyme Regis Road) hotel signposted to Hawkchurch*
A delightful Edwardian house, set in landscaped gardens and rolling countryside. Bedrooms are attractively decorated and furnished, several are in a separate modern house in the grounds. Public areas include comfortable sitting rooms and a spacious dining room, where freshly prepared meals using local produce are served.
ROOMS: 14 en suite 7 annexe en suite s £95-£98; d £170-£176 (incl. bkfst & dinner) * LB **FACILITIES:** Croquet lawn Xmas **CONF:** Thtr 20 Class 20 Board 12 **PARKING:** 30 **NOTES:** No smoking in restaurant Closed mid Dec-mid Feb (ex Xmas pakages)
CARDS:

★★79% Lea Hill
Membury EX13 7AQ
☎ 01404 881881 & 881388 01404 881890
Dir: *from George Hotel in Axminster take Membury road and cross railway. In Membury continue through village past Trout Farm. Hotel 0.5m on right*
A delightful thatched Devon longhouse, partly dating back to the 1300s, set in unspoilt countryside. Bedrooms are mostly situated in thatched cottages and converted barns around the main house. Rooms are decorated to enhance their cottage style and there is a lounge bar, a study and a meeting room. The flagstoned, beamed restaurant serves an imaginative fixed-price menu, prepared from fresh produce, often featuring local fish.
ROOMS: 2 en suite 9 annexe en suite (2 fmly) No smoking in all bedrooms s £59-£68; d £98-£116 (incl. bkfst) * LB
FACILITIES: Croquet lawn Jacuzzi/spa Par 3 6-hole golf course ch fac Xmas **PARKING:** 25 **NOTES:** No children 16yrs No smoking in restaurant Closed 1st week Mar **CARDS:**

AYLESBURY, Buckinghamshire Map 04 SP81

Premier Collection

★★★★ Hartwell House
Oxford Rd HP17 8NL
☎ 01296 747444 01296 747450
e-mail: info@hartwell-house.com
Dir: *signposted 2m SW on A418 towards Oxford*
This hotel, set in 90 acres of grounds, has truly magnificent reception rooms. Bedrooms are spacious with great consideration paid to guest comfort. The health centre houses the Buttery coffee shop and the cuisine served in the main dining room is consistently good. Function rooms are available and service is friendly.

ROOMS: 30 en suite 16 annexe en suite No smoking in 12 bedrooms s £135; d £215-£375 * LB **FACILITIES:** Indoor swimming (H) Tennis (hard) Fishing Sauna Solarium Gym Croquet lawn Jacuzzi/spa Treatment room Xmas **CONF:** Thtr 100 Class 40 Board 40 Del from £245 * **SERVICES:** Lift **PARKING:** 91
NOTES: No children 8yrs No smoking in restaurant
CARDS:

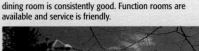

★★★69% *Posthouse Aylesbury*
Aston Clinton Rd HP22 5AA
Posthouse
☎ 0870 400 9002 01296 392211
Dir: *on A41*
This modern hotel offers spacious accommodation, furnished and decorated in a contemporary style. Public areas include the Junction dining room and a selection of well equipped meeting rooms. Leisure facilities are also available.
ROOMS: 94 en suite (6 fmly) No smoking in 47 bedrooms
FACILITIES: Indoor swimming (H) Sauna Solarium Gym Jacuzzi/spa
CONF: Thtr 110 Class 80 Board 40 **PARKING:** 150
CARDS:

BABBACOMBE See Torquay

BADMINTON, Gloucestershire Map 03 ST88

★★68% *Bodkin House*
Petty France GL9 1AF
☎ 01454 238310 01454 238422
e-mail: hotel@bodkin-house.freeserve.co.uk
Dir: *on A46, 6m N of junct 18 on M4*

This charming 17th-century inn is full of historic character, featuring open fires, flagstone floors and oak panelling. Comfortable bedrooms combine traditional style with modern facilities. The restaurant and lounge are attractively decorated and meals can also be taken in the bar.

continued

ROOMS: 9 en suite (2 fmly) **FACILITIES:** Hot air ballooning **CONF:** Thtr 20 Class 12 Board 12 **PARKING:** 35 **NOTES:** No dogs (ex guide dogs) No smoking in restaurant **CARDS:**

See advert under BATH

BAGINTON, Warwickshire — Map 04 SP37

★★66% Old Mill

Mill Hill CV8 3AH
☎ 024 76302241 Fax 024 76307070
Dir: *in village 0.25m from junction A45 & A46*

Situated in the village of Baginton on the outskirts of Coventry, this friendly riverside hotel offers comfortable accommodation within easy access of the motorway networks. Public areas include a popular restaurant and bar.

ROOMS: 28 en suite (6 fmly) d £80 * LB **CONF:** Class 16 Board 20 **PARKING:** 200 **NOTES:** No dogs (ex guide dogs) No smoking in restaurant **CARDS:**

BAGSHOT, Surrey — Map 04 SU96

★★★★★72% Pennyhill Park

London Rd GU19 5EU
☎ 01276 471774 Fax 01276 473217
e-mail: pennyhillpark@msn.com
Dir: *on A30 between Bagshot and Camberley opposite Texaco garage*

A Victorian country house hotel set in 120 acres of grounds. Public areas include a bar and a choice of several restaurants, one of which serves food with a strong French influence. Individually decorated bedrooms are particularly impressive and feature many antique pieces.

continued

ROOMS: 31 en suite 92 annexe en suite (1 fmly) No smoking in 20 bedrooms s £150-£350; d £165-£350 * LB **FACILITIES:** Outdoor swimming (H) Golf 9 Tennis (hard) Fishing Gym Croquet lawn Jacuzzi/spa Archery Clay pigeon shooting Volleyball Half size snooker table entertainment Xmas **CONF:** Thtr 160 Class 80 Board 60 Del from £260 * **SERVICES:** Lift **PARKING:** 460 **NOTES:** No children 5yrs No smoking in restaurant Civ Wed 160 **CARDS:**

See advert on this page

BAINBRIDGE, North Yorkshire — Map 07 SD99

★★61% Rose & Crown

DL8 3EE
☎ 01969 650225 Fax 01969 650735
e-mail: stay@rose-and-crown.freeserve.co.uk
Dir: *on A684 in centre of village*

For almost 700 years this appealing coaching inn has warmly welcomed guests crossing the Pennines. There is a strong flavour

continued

BAINBRIDGE, continued

of heritage and character in the bars, featuring roaring open fires. Bedrooms, modern in style, are well equipped. There is also a cosy lounge and a wide range of food is served in the bars or in the spacious restaurant.
ROOMS: 12 rms (11 en suite) (1 fmly) No smoking in 2 bedrooms s £26-£36; d £52-£64 (incl. bkfst) * LB **FACILITIES:** Pool table **CONF:** Class 30 Board 30 **PARKING:** 65 **CARDS:**

BAKEWELL, Derbyshire Map 08 SK26

★★★73% Hassop Hall
Hassop DE45 1NS
☎ 01629 640488 📠 01629 640577
e-mail: hassophallhotel@btinternet.com
Dir: *take B6001 from Bakewell for approx. 2m into Hassop, hotel opposite church*
This magnificent stately home combines charm with all modern comforts. Bedrooms are tastefully furnished and well equipped, most have lovely views of the grounds. There is a choice of comfortable lounges and dinner is served in the elegant, pleasantly furnished dining room.
ROOMS: 13 en suite (2 fmly) d £79-£139 * LB **FACILITIES:** Tennis (hard) entertainment **SERVICES:** Lift **PARKING:** 80 **NOTES:** Closed 24-25 Dec RS 26 Dec Civ Wed 120 **CARDS:**

★★★69% *Rutland Arms*
The Square DE45 1BT
☎ 01629 812812 📠 01629 812309
e-mail: rutland@bakewell.demon.co.uk
Dir: *on main A6 between Matlock/Manchester. In main square opposite War Memorial*

This historic hotel lies at the very centre of Bakewell. There is a wide range of quality accommodation. The friendly staff are attentive and welcoming, both in the adjacent Tavern bar and in the main hotel. The Four Seasons restaurant offers an interesting menu and fine dining.
ROOMS: 18 en suite 17 annexe en suite (1 fmly) No smoking in 10 bedrooms **FACILITIES:** STV Pool table **CONF:** Thtr 100 Class 60 Board 40 **PARKING:** 25 **NOTES:** No smoking in restaurant
CARDS:

★★73% Croft Country House
Great Longstone DE45 1TF
☎ 01629 640278
Dir: *from Bakewell follow A6 towards Buxton, turn right on to A6020, turn left at sign to Great Longstone, entrance on right 0.25m into village*
Hidden away in mature gardens and grounds, this delightful Victorian house exudes charm. Public rooms leading off from the central galleried lounge include a cosy bar and a restaurant. Freshly prepared evening meals are served from an interesting four-course set menu. Bedrooms have modern comforts and some fine period pieces.
continued

ROOMS: 9 en suite s £50-£55; d £75-£99 (incl. bkfst) * LB **FACILITIES:** Xmas **SERVICES:** Lift **PARKING:** 40 **NOTES:** No dogs (ex guide dogs) No smoking in restaurant Closed 28 Dec-7 Feb
CARDS:
See advert on opposite page

BALDOCK, Hertfordshire Map 04 TL23

⌂ *Travelodge*
Travelodge
Great North Rd, Hinxworth SG7 5EX
☎ 01462 835329 📠 01462 835329
Dir: *on A1, southbound*
This modern building offers accommodation in smart, spacious and well equipped bedrooms, all with en suite bathrooms. Refreshments may be taken at the nearby family restaurant. For further details and the Travelodge phone number, consult the Hotel Groups page.
ROOMS: 40 en suite

BALSALL COMMON, West Midlands Map 04 SP27

★★★★67% Nailcote Hall
Nailcote Ln, Berkswell CV7 7DE
☎ 024 7646 6174 📠 024 7647 0720
e-mail: info@nailcotehall.co.uk
Dir: *on B4101*

This charming, historic Elizabethan manor house remains largely unspoilt, with heavy timbers and open fires. The intimate restaurant serves an exciting menu and the Mediterranean-style bistro offers more informal dining. The modern bedroom wing has a variety of styles; the more traditional bedrooms are in the main house. Service is efficient and courteous.
ROOMS: 21 en suite 17 annexe en suite (2 fmly) s fr £140; d fr £150 (incl. bkfst) * LB **FACILITIES:** Indoor swimming (H) Golf 9 Tennis (hard) Snooker Solarium Gym Croquet lawn Putting green Jacuzzi/spa entertainment Xmas **CONF:** Thtr 100 Class 80 Board 45 Del from £135 * **SERVICES:** Lift **PARKING:** 200 **NOTES:** No smoking in restaurant Civ Wed 120 **CARDS:**
See advert under SOLIHULL

B

★★75% Haigs

Kenilworth Rd CV7 7EL
☎ 01676 533004 📠 01676 535132
Dir: *on A452 4m N of Kenilworth and 6m S of junct 4 of M6. 5m S of M42 junct 6. 8m N of M40 junct 15*

Set in residential surroundings this charming, stylish hotel offers a warm welcome and attentive service. The newer bedrooms are particularly attractive and comfortable. Public areas include the lounge bar, a meeting room and The Poppies restaurant, where an interesting and varied range of carefully prepared dishes is offered.
ROOMS: 23 en suite No smoking in 8 bedrooms s £55-£63; d £75-£85 (incl. bkfst) * **CONF:** Thtr 35 Class 20 Board 20 Del from £85 * **PARKING:** 22 **NOTES:** No dogs (ex guide dogs) No smoking in restaurant Closed 26 Dec-3 Jan & Etr **CARDS:**

BAMBURGH, Northumberland — Map 12 NU13

★★★68% Waren House

Waren Mill NE70 7EE
☎ 01668 214581 📠 01668 214484
e-mail: enquiries@warenhousehotel.co.uk
Dir: *2m E of A1 turn off on B1342 to Waren Mill, at T-junct turn right, hotel 100yds on right*
A delightfully restored Georgian country house with themed bedrooms (Victorian, Edwardian, Nursery or Oriental) providing good levels of comfort. Public rooms are attractively furnished, with an elegant dining room, welcoming drawing room and adjoining library. Many rooms enjoy fine views over gardens and the coastline.
ROOMS: 10 en suite No smoking in 9 bedrooms s £85-£105; d £115-£185 (incl. bkfst) * LB **FACILITIES:** STV Croquet lawn Xmas **CONF:** Class 24 Board 24 Del from £98 * **PARKING:** 20 **NOTES:** No children 14yrs No smoking in restaurant
CARDS:

★★71% *Victoria*

Best Western

Front St NE69 7BP
☎ 01668 214431 📠 01668 214404
Dir: *turn off the A1 north of Alnwick onto the B1342, near Belford & follow signs to Bamburgh. Hotel in centre of Bamburgh opposite the village green.*
Friendly and attentive service is just one feature of this hotel, which has been stylishly refurbished. The ground floor areas include a modern Brasserie with conservatory roof, a popular bar and an indoor children's playden. Bedrooms are cheerful and well equipped.

continued

BAMBURGH, continued

Victoria, Bamburgh

ROOMS: 29 en suite (2 fmly) No smoking in 18 bedrooms **FACILITIES:** Pool table Games room ch fac **CONF:** Thtr 50 Class 30 Board 20 **PARKING:** 12 **CARDS:**

★★65% Lord Crewe Arms

Front St NE69 7BL
☎ 01668 214243 🖷 01668 214273
e-mail: lca@tinyonline.co.uk
Dir: *just below the castle*

Developed from an old country inn, this inviting hotel lies in the centre of the village, where the impressive Bamburgh Castle dominates the skyline. Guests can relax in either of the two comfortable lounges, and there is a choice of eating options.
ROOMS: 12 rms (11 en suite) s £40-£50; d £75-£98 (incl. bkfst) * LB **PARKING:** 10 **NOTES:** No dogs (ex guide dogs) No children 5yrs No smoking in restaurant Closed Nov-Etr **CARDS:**

★★63% The Mizen Head

Lucker Rd NE69 7BS
☎ 01668 214254 🖷 01668 214104
Dir: *turn off the A1 onto the B1341 for Bamburgh, the hotel is the first building on the left as you enter the village*

Set in gardens, on the western edge of the village, this family-run hotel offers a relaxed and friendly atmosphere. A range of good value meals is served in both the dining room and the bar.
ROOMS: 13 rms (12 en suite) (2 fmly) s £37.50; d £75 (incl. bkfst) * LB **FACILITIES:** Pool table Darts ch fac Xmas **CONF:** Class 45 Del from £39.50 * **PARKING:** 30 **NOTES:** No smoking in restaurant
CARDS:

BAMFORD, Derbyshire — Map 08 SK28

★★69% Yorkshire Bridge Inn

Ashopton Rd, Hope Valley S33 0AZ
☎ 01433 651361 🖷 01433 651361
e-mail: mr@ybridge.force9.co.uk
Dir: *A57 Sheffield/Glossop Road, at Ladybower Reservoir take A6013 Bamford Road, Yorkshire Bridge Inn is on the right hand side in 1m*

A well established country inn, ideally located within reach of the Peak Park's many attractions and beauty spots. The hotel offers a wide range of excellent dishes in both the bar and dining area, along with a good selection of real ales. Bedrooms are attractively furnished, comfortable and well equipped.

ROOMS: 14 en suite (3 fmly) No smoking in 10 bedrooms s £38-£40 (incl. bkfst) * LB **FACILITIES:** Xmas **CONF:** Class 12 **PARKING:** 40
CARDS:

BAMPTON, Devon — Map 03 SS92

★★77% ❀❀ Bark House

Oakford Bridge EX16 9HZ
☎ 01398 351236
Dir: *9m N of Tiverton on the A396*

Set in a peaceful location in the beautiful Exe Valley, this cottage-style hotel has a tiered garden. There is a low beamed dining room and a lounge with log fire. Bedrooms include thoughtful extras such as flowers. Imaginative meals are served in the restaurant, making use of the best fresh ingredients.
ROOMS: 5 rms (4 en suite) (1 fmly) s £35-£45; d £65-£85 (incl. bkfst) * LB **FACILITIES:** Croquet lawn Xmas **PARKING:** 15 **NOTES:** No smoking in restaurant RS Nov-Mar

BANBURY, Oxfordshire — Map 04 SP44

★★★70% Banbury House

Best Western

Oxford Rd OX16 9AH
☎ 01295 259361 🖷 01295 270954
e-mail: banburyhouse@compuserve.com
Dir: *approx 200yds from Banbury Cross on the A423 towards Oxford*

An attractive Georgian property, Banbury House is smart and comfortable with modern facilities. Friendly and attentive staff help to create a welcoming atmosphere. Public areas include a lounge, cellar bar and a restaurant. A bar menu is available.
ROOMS: 63 en suite (4 fmly) No smoking in 24 bedrooms s £83; d £93 * LB **FACILITIES:** STV **CONF:** Thtr 70 Class 35 Board 28 Del £127.50 * **PARKING:** 60 **NOTES:** No dogs (ex guide dogs) Closed 24-30 Dec
CARDS:

★★★70% ❀ Wroxton House

Best Western

Wroxton St Mary OX15 6QB
☎ 01295 730777 🖷 01295 730800
e-mail: wroxtonhse@aol.com
Dir: *follow A422 from Banbury, 2.5m to Wroxton, hotel on right on entering village*

Converted from three 17th-century cottages, this charming hotel is situated just two miles west of Banbury. Guests will find this a pleasant retreat. Bedrooms are well equipped and vary in style from the more traditionally furnished in the older wing to modern rooms. The elegant restaurant offers a range of dishes, making good use of local produce.
ROOMS: 29 en suite 3 annexe en suite (1 fmly) No smoking in 14 bedrooms s fr £39.55; d £79.10-£99 * LB **FACILITIES:** STV Xmas

continued

CONF: Thtr 45 Class 20 Board 28 Del from £140 * **PARKING:** 50 **NOTES:** No dogs (ex guide dogs) No smoking in restaurant Closed 28-30 Dec RS 31 Dec & 1 Jan Civ Wed 60
CARDS:

★★★68% Whately Hall

Banbury Cross OX16 0AN
☎ 0870 400 8104 📠 01295 271736
Dir: *from M40 junct 11. Straight over 2 rdbts, turn left at 3rd, carry on to Banbury Cross about 1/4m & hotel on right*
This hotel, originally a 17th-century coaching inn, is close to Banbury Cross. The bedrooms, varying in size and style, are well equipped. Spacious and very comfortable public areas include cosy lounges and an informal bar. Some of the original oak panelling and the black beams are still intact and service is attentive and friendly.
ROOMS: 72 en suite (1 fmly) No smoking in 24 bedrooms d £55-£100 * LB **FACILITIES:** Croquet lawn Xmas **CONF:** Thtr 150 Class 80 Board 40 Del from £120 * **SERVICES:** Lift **PARKING:** 80 **NOTES:** Civ Wed 100 **CARDS:**

⌂ Premier Lodge

Warwick Rd, Warmington OX17 1JJ
☎ 0870 700 1310 📠 0870 7001311
Premier Lodge offers modern, well equipped, en suite accommodation suitable for both business and leisure travellers. Meals can be taken at the adjacent popular restaurant and bar which is fully licensed. For further details, consult the Hotel Groups page.
ROOMS: 15 en suite d £46 *

BARFORD, Warwickshire — Map 04 SP26

★★★69% The Glebe at Barford

Church St CV35 8BS
☎ 01926 624218 📠 01926 624625
Dir: *leave M40 at junct 15, take exit A429 Barford/Wellesbourne, at mini island turn left, hotel 500mtrs on right*
This former rectory offers a friendly atmosphere and modern accommodation. Public rooms include a lounge area, bar and an inviting conservatory restaurant. Bedrooms have a range of useful facilities and are individually furnished with cheerful, co-ordinated decor.
ROOMS: 39 en suite (3 fmly) s fr £95; d fr £115 (incl. bkfst) * **FACILITIES:** STV Indoor swimming (H) Sauna Gym Croquet lawn Jacuzzi/spa Beauty salon Xmas **CONF:** Thtr 120 Class 60 Board 60 Del from £145 * **SERVICES:** Lift **PARKING:** 60
CARDS:

BARKING, Greater London — Map 05 TQ48

⌂ Hotel Ibis

Highbridge Rd IG11 7BA
☎ 020 8477 4100
e-mail: H2042@accor-hotels.com
Dir: *exit Barking on A406*
Modern, budget hotel offering comfortable accommodation in bright and practical bedrooms. Breakfast is self-service and dinner is available in the restaurant. For further details, consult the Hotel Groups page.
ROOMS: 86 en suite d £55 *

○ Premier Lodge

Highbridge Rd IG11 7BA
☎ 0870 700 1444 📠 0870 700 1445

BARLBOROUGH, Derbyshire — Map 08 SK47

⌂ Express by Holiday Inn Sheffield

Tally's End, Barlborough Links S43 4TX
☎ 01246 813222 📠 813444
e-mail: barlborough@premierhotels.co.uk
Dir: *leave M1 at junct 30. Head towards A619. Right at rdbt towards Chesterfield. Hotel is immediately left*

A modern budget hotel offering comfortable accommodation in refreshing, spacious and comprehensively-equipped bedrooms, en suite bathrooms with power showers and continental buffet breakfast included in the room rate. Suitable for business travellers or families. For further details and the Express by Holiday Inn phone number, consult the Hotel Groups page.
ROOMS: 86 en suite (incl. cont bkfst) d £49.50 * **CONF:** Thtr 35 Board 20 Del £79 *

BARNARD CASTLE, Co Durham Map 12 NZ01

★★★66% Morritt Arms Hotel & Restaurant

Greta Bridge DL12 9SE
☎ 01833 627232 🖷 01833 627392
e-mail: relax@themorritt.co.uk
Dir: *A1 Scotch Corner, turn onto A66 in direction of Penrith and after 9m turn off at Greta Bridge. Hotel just over the bridge on left*

This delightful 17th-century coaching house offers comfortable public rooms, including an open-plan lounge and a bar with an interesting Dickensian mural. The well equipped bedrooms come in a variety of shapes and sizes and the wood-panelled dining room serves a selection of appetizing meals. Service is friendly and professional.

ROOMS: 23 en suite No smoking in 16 bedrooms s £59.50-£75; d £79.50-£99.50 (incl. bkfst) * LB **FACILITIES:** Pool table Membership of nearby leisure facility Xmas **CONF:** Thtr 200 Class 100 Board 125 Del from £85.50 * **PARKING:** 103 **NOTES:** No smoking in restaurant Civ Wed **CARDS:**

BARNBY MOOR, Nottinghamshire Map 08 SK68

★★★62% Ye Olde Bell Hotel

DN22 8QS
☎ 01777 705121 🖷 01777 860424
Dir: *S on A1, take A634 & turn right on A638, hotel is on left*

This historic coaching inn, close to Sherwood Forest, is convenient for the A1. It provides comfortable lounges and a lovely oak panelled restaurant where a good range of dishes is served. Bedrooms offer all modern comforts and service is friendly and polite.

ROOMS: 65 en suite s £35-£60; d £50-£95 (incl. bkfst) * LB **FACILITIES:** Xmas **CONF:** Thtr 250 Class 100 Board 50 **PARKING:** 50 **NOTES:** No smoking in restaurant **CARDS:**

BARNHAM BROOM, Norfolk Map 05 TG00

★★★74% Barnham Broom

NR9 4DD
☎ 01603 759393 🖷 01603 758224
e-mail: enquiry@barnhambroomhotel.co.uk
Dir: *signposted from A11 and A47, follow brown tourist signs with Barnham Broom and golf flag*

This hotel, set in a rural location, is about 15 miles from Norwich city centre. Extensive public areas include the Sports bar, where a range of meals is available all day, and the smart, more formal restaurant serving carte and set choice menus. Bedrooms are modern, attractive and well equipped. There is also a golf simulator and two 18-hole courses.

ROOMS: 52 en suite (8 fmly) s fr £75; d fr £99 (incl. bkfst) * LB **FACILITIES:** Indoor swimming (H) Golf 36 Tennis (hard) Squash Sauna Solarium Gym Pool table Putting green Jacuzzi/spa Hairdressing salon Beautician Indoor golf simulator Xmas **CONF:** Thtr 150 Class 90 Board 70 Del from £78 * **PARKING:** 200 **NOTES:** No dogs (ex guide dogs) No smoking in restaurant Civ Wed 200
CARDS:

See advert under NORWICH

BARNSDALE BAR SERVICE AREA, North Yorkshire Map 08 SE51

⌂ *Travelodge*

Wentbridge WF8 3JB
☎ 01977 620711 🖷 01977 620711
Dir: *on A1, southbound*

This modern building offers accommodation in smart, spacious and well equipped bedrooms, all with en suite bathrooms. Refreshments may be taken at the nearby family restaurant. For further details and the Travelodge phone number, consult the Hotel Groups page.

ROOMS: 56 en suite

BARNSLEY, South Yorkshire Map 08 SE30
see also Tankersley

★★★71% Ardsley House

Doncaster Rd, Ardsley S71 5EH
☎ 01226 309955 🖷 01226 205374
e-mail: sales@ardsley-house.co.uk
Dir: *on A635, 0.75m from Stainfoot Rdbt*

Quietly situated two miles east of Barnsley, this extended Georgian house offers modern bedrooms that are well equipped. Public rooms include a choice of bars and a pleasant restaurant, where diners can choose from a good range of carefully prepared dishes. A useful range of meeting rooms and function suites are also available.

ROOMS: 74 en suite (12 fmly) No smoking in 35 bedrooms s fr £76; d fr £92 * LB **FACILITIES:** STV Indoor swimming (H) Sauna Solarium Gym Pool table Jacuzzi/spa entertainment Xmas **CONF:** Thtr 350 Class 250 Board 40 Del from £100 * **PARKING:** 200
CARDS:

See advert on opposite page

⌂ *Travelodge*

520 Doncaster Rd S70 3PE
☎ 01226 298799 🖷 01226 298799
Dir: *at Stairfoot roundabout A633/A635*

This modern building offers accommodation in smart, spacious and well equipped bedrooms, all with en suite bathrooms. Refreshments may be taken at the nearby family restaurant. For further details and the Travelodge phone number, consult the Hotel Groups page.

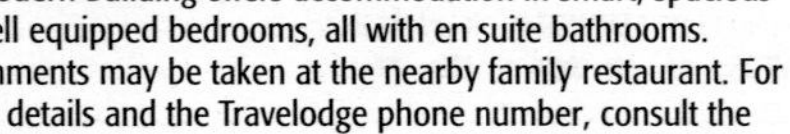

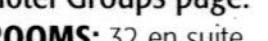

ROOMS: 32 en suite

BARNSTAPLE, Devon Map 02 SS53

★★★★70% The Imperial

Taw Vale Pde EX32 8NB
☎ 01271 345861 🖷 01271 324448
e-mail: info@brend-imperial.co.uk
Dir: *from M5, take junct 27, A361 Barnstaple. Follow signs for town centre, passing Tescos. Straight ahead at next 2 rdbts. Hotel is on the right*

Overlooking the river and an easy stroll away from the town centre, this hotel offers the warm hospitality associated with the Brend group of hotels. Bedrooms are richly decorated and the sumptuously furnished reception rooms have a peaceful, relaxing atmosphere.

continued on p64

IN THE HEART OF NORTH DEVON

The luxurious Imperial Hotel, stands in its own manicured grounds on the banks of the River Taw. Boasting all the elegance and style of a beautiful hotel it provides first class service with the finest of wines and superb cuisine, with ensuite bedrooms, satellite TV and a lift to all floors.

In a central location with free resident parking, The Imperial is the perfect base from which to explore the historic market town of Barnstaple, Englands oldest borough and many time 'Britain in Bloom' winner, or the idyllic surroundings of places like Clovelly, Lynmouth and Saunton.

FOR A FREE COLOUR BROCHURE, PLEASE CONTACT:

THE IMPERIAL HOTEL

AA ★★★★

TAW VALE PARADE, BARNSTAPLE, NORTH DEVON EX32 8NB.
TEL: (01271) 345861 FAX: (01271) 324448
www.brend-imperial.co.uk e-mail: info@brend-imperial.co.uk

The Westcountry's Leading Hotel Group

B

NORTHCOTE MANOR

country house hotel

Stay awhile in timeless tranquillity

Step free from the stresses of life and enjoy the uniquely peaceful and relaxing atmosphere of Northcote Manor Country House Hotel. Twenty acres of mature woodlands, lawns and gardens, including an outstanding view over the Taw River Valley, set the scene for healthy relaxation and gentle leisure.

Each of the 11 bedrooms and suites has been individually designed and luxuriously furnished, providing a wonderful level of comfort and elegance in which to rest.

Dining at Northcote is an experience to savour. The spacious and harmonious Manor House Restaurant makes the ideal setting for a relaxing meal freshly prepared to the highest standards.

Northcote Manor Country House Hotel, Burrington, Umberleigh, North Devon EX37 9LZ
Telephone: 01769 560501 Fax: 01769 560770 E-mail: rest@northcotemanor.co.uk

BARNSTAPLE, continued

The Imperial, Barnstaple

ROOMS: 65 en suite (15 fmly) s £59-£69; d £78-£138 (incl. bkfst) * LB **FACILITIES:** STV Xmas **SERVICES:** Lift **PARKING:** 80 **CARDS:**

See advert on page 63

★★★71% Royal & Fortescue

Boutport St EX31 1HG
☎ 01271 342289 01271 342289
e-mail: sales@royalfortescue.co.uk
Dir: *follow A361 along Barbican Rd signposted town centre, turn right into Queen St & left (oneway) Boutport St, hotel on left*

Originally a coaching inn this hotel, situated in the centre of this delightful market town, offers a friendly atmosphere. Bedrooms vary in size, all are decorated and furnished to a high standard. In addition to the formal restaurant, guests can take snacks in the coffee shop or dine more informally in The Bank, a bistro and cafe bar.

ROOMS: 50 en suite (5 fmly) s £49-£59; d £50-£70 * LB **FACILITIES:** STV entertainment Xmas **CONF:** Thtr 50 Class 50 Board 50 **SERVICES:** Lift **PARKING:** 40 **CARDS:**

★★★70% Barnstaple Hotel

Braunton Rd EX31 1LE
☎ 01271 376221 01271 324101
e-mail: info@barnstaplehotel.co.uk
Dir: *on the outskirts of Barnstaple on A361*

Situated on the edge of the town, this purpose-built hotel offers an excellent range of facilities. The restaurant serves a wide range of dishes and an extensive snack menu is available in the lounge bar. There is also a pool-side cafe. Bedrooms are set around the outdoor pool and sun terrace, many with direct access. Meeting rooms and an impressive function suite are also available.

ROOMS: 60 en suite (6 fmly) s £59; d £84-£94 (incl. bkfst) * LB **FACILITIES:** STV Indoor swimming (H) Outdoor swimming (H) Snooker Sauna Solarium Gym Jacuzzi/spa ch fac Xmas **CONF:** Thtr 250 Class 250 Board 250 **PARKING:** 250 **NOTES:** Civ Wed **CARDS:**

★★★66% Park

Taw Vale EX32 9AE
☎ 01271 372166 01271 323157
e-mail: info@parkhotel.co.uk
Dir: *opposite Rock Park, 0.5m from town centre*

Situated opposite the park, within easy walking distance of the town centre, this modern hotel has bedrooms in both the main building and the Garden Court, which is just across the car park. Public rooms are open-plan in style and the friendly staff offer attentive service in a relaxed atmosphere.

ROOMS: 25 en suite 17 annexe en suite (7 fmly) s £49-£59; d £50-£70 * LB **FACILITIES:** STV entertainment Xmas **CONF:** Thtr 150 Class 150 Board 150 **PARKING:** 80 **CARDS:**

Premier Collection

★★ Halmpstone Manor

Bishop's Tawton EX32 0EA
☎ 01271 830321 01271 830826
e-mail: jane@halmpstonemanor.co.uk
Dir: *5m S of Barnstaple, leave A377 at Bishop's Tawton opposite petrol station and follow unclassified road 2m then right at Halmpstone Manor sign*

This historic manor house is surrounded by rich farmlands. Bedrooms, including two with four-poster beds, have many useful extras and thoughtful touches. The comfortable, spacious and relaxing lounge has a log fire. Dinner, which is expertly cooked from quality local produce, is served in the panelled dining room.

ROOMS: 5 en suite No smoking in 1 bedroom s fr £70; d £100-£140 (incl. bkfst) * **PARKING:** 12 **NOTES:** No children 12yrs No smoking in restaurant Closed Nov & Jan **CARDS:**

BARROW-IN-FURNESS, Cumbria — Map 07 SD16

★★60% *Lisdoonie*

307/309 Abbey Rd LA14 5LF
☎ 01229 827312 01229 820944
Dir: *on A590, first set of traffic lights in town (Strawberry pub on left), continue for 100yds, hotel on right. Car park right in Furness Park Rd*

This popular and friendly hotel, conveniently located close to the centre of the town, features two lounges, one of which has a bar. There is also a traditionally-styled dining room and comfortable bedrooms which vary in size and style.

ROOMS: 12 en suite (2 fmly) **CONF:** Class 255 **PARKING:** 30 **NOTES:** Closed Xmas & New Year **CARDS:**

BARTON, Lancashire — Map 07 SD53

★★★70% Barton Grange

Garstang Rd PR3 5AA
☎ 01772 862551 01772 861267
e-mail: stay@bartongrangehotel.com
Dir: *from M6 junct 32 follow A6, signed Garstang, for two and half miles, hotel on the right*

Situated next to the A6, by its own garden centre, a unique feature of this hotel is the Walled Garden restaurant which is based on plans for an original walled garden attached to the early 20th-century residence. Bedrooms are very well equipped, including one with a four-poster bed. Some rooms are in an adjacent cottage.

continued

ROOMS: 42 en suite 8 annexe en suite (4 fmly) **FACILITIES:** STV Indoor swimming (H) Sauna Gym Pool table Jacuzzi/spa Garden Centre Beauty salon **CONF:** Thtr 300 Class 100 Board 80 Del £110 * **SERVICES:** Lift **PARKING:** 250 **NOTES:** No dogs (ex guide dogs) Civ Wed 120 **CARDS:**

BARTON MILLS, Suffolk — Map 05 TL77

Travelodge

IP28 6AE
☎ 01638 717675 Fax 01638 717675
Dir: *on A11*
This modern building offers accommodation in smart, spacious and well equipped bedrooms, all with en suite bathrooms. Refreshments may be taken at the nearby family restaurant. For further details and the Travelodge phone number, consult the Hotel Groups page.
ROOMS: 40 en suite

BARTON-ON-SEA, Hampshire — Map 04 SZ29

★★75% *The Cliff House*

Marine Dr West BH25 7QL
☎ 01425 619333 Fax 01425 612462
Dir: *turn off A337 on to Sea Road at Barton-on-Sea. Hotel at end of road on cliff top*
In a superb clifftop location overlooking the sea, this charming family-run hotel has a warm and welcoming atmosphere. Bedrooms are prettily decorated and many have panoramic sea views. Popular with both locals and visitors, the restaurant serves a variety of menus.
ROOMS: 9 en suite No smoking in all bedrooms **FACILITIES:** STV **PARKING:** 50 **NOTES:** No dogs (ex guide dogs) No children 10yrs No smoking in restaurant **CARDS:**

BARTON STACEY, Hampshire — Map 04 SU44

Travelodge

SP21 3NP
☎ 01264 720260 Fax 01264 720260
Dir: *on A303*
This modern building offers accommodation in smart, spacious and well equipped bedrooms, all with en suite bathrooms. Refreshments may be taken at the nearby family restaurant. For further details and the Travelodge phone number, consult the Hotel Groups page.
ROOMS: 20 en suite

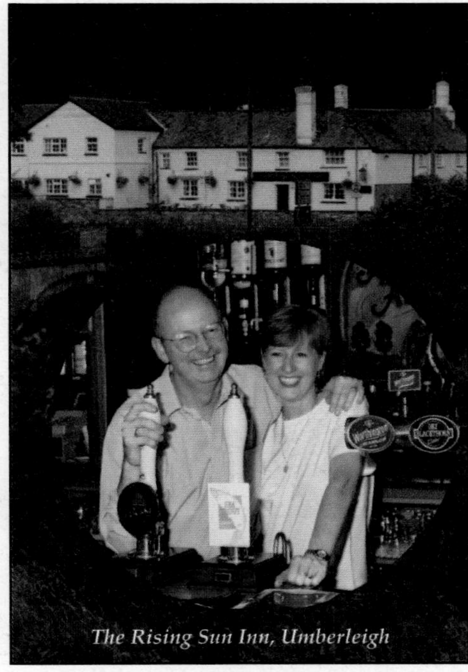

The Rising Sun Inn, Umberleigh

BARTON-UNDER-NEEDWOOD, Staffordshire — Map 07 SK11

Travelodge (Northbound)

DE13 8EG
☎ 01283 716343 Fax 01283 716343
Dir: *on A38,northbound*
This modern building offers accommodation in smart, spacious and well equipped bedrooms, all with en suite bathrooms. Refreshments may be taken at the nearby family restaurant. For further details and the Travelodge phone number, consult the Hotel Groups page.
ROOMS: 20 en suite

Travelodge (Southbound)

Rykneld St DE13 8EH
☎ 01283 716784 Fax 01283 716784
Dir: *on A38, southbound*
This modern building offers accommodation in smart, spacious and well equipped bedrooms, all with en suite bathrooms. Refreshments may be taken at the nearby family restaurant. For further details and the Travelodge phone number, consult the Hotel Groups page.
ROOMS: 40 en suite

BARTON-UPON-HUMBER, Lincolnshire — Map 08 TA02

★★★70% *Reeds Hotel*

Westfield Lakes, Far-ings Rd DN18 5RG
☎ 01652 632313 Fax 01652 636361
Nestling beside the Humber, between a couple of freshwater lakes, this hotel enjoys splendid views of the Humber Bridge - the world's largest single span suspension bridge. Public rooms

continued

B

BARTON-UPON-HUMBER, continued

include an attractive restaurant, foyer lounge and Clippers Tea Room, with panoramic views. Bedrooms vary in size, all are well equipped and nicely presented.

Reeds Hotel, Barton-Upon-Humber

ROOMS: 6 en suite (1 fmly) No smoking in all bedrooms **FACILITIES:** Alternative therapy centre entertainment **CONF:** Thtr 100 Class 40 Board 35 **NOTES:** No dogs (ex guide dogs) No smoking in restaurant **CARDS:**

BASILDON, Essex

Map 05 TQ78

★★★67% Chichester

Old London Rd, Wickford SS11 8UE
☎ 01268 560555 ▯ 01268 560580
Dir: *off A129*
Situated just off the A120 near Basildon, this family-run hotel boasts its own landscaped grounds and is surrounded by open farmland. The spacious and comfortable bedrooms are located around an attractive courtyard. Meals may be taken in the restaurant or in the more informal bar area.
ROOMS: 2 en suite 32 annexe en suite s £58-£68; d £68 * LB **PARKING:** 150 **NOTES:** No dogs (ex guide dogs) No children 5yrs No smoking in restaurant **CARDS:**

★★★64% *Posthouse Basildon*

Posthouse

Cranes Farm Rd SS14 3DG
☎ 0870 400 9003 ▯ 01268 530119
Dir: *off A1235, via A127*
Suitable for both the business and leisure traveller, this bright hotel provides modern accommodation in well equipped bedrooms.
ROOMS: 149 en suite (30 fmly) No smoking in 70 bedrooms **FACILITIES:** Use of nearby Leisure Club (David Lloyd) **CONF:** Thtr 300 Class 80 Board 80 **SERVICES:** Lift **PARKING:** 200 **CARDS:**

⌂ Premier Lodge

PREMIER LODGE

Pipps Hill Rd South, Festival Leisure Park SS14 3DG
☎ 0870 700 1376 ▯ 0870 700 1377
Premier Lodge offers modern, well equipped, en suite accommodation suitable for both business and leisure travellers. Meals can be taken at the adjacent popular restaurant and bar which is fully licensed. For further details, consult the Hotel Groups page.
ROOMS: 64 en suite d £46 *

⌂ Campanile

Campanile

Pipps Hill, Southend Arterial Rd SS14 3AE
☎ 01268 530810 ▯ 01268 286710
Dir: *M25 junct29 exit in direction of Basildon take first exit to Basildon, go back under A127 then at roundabout go left*
This modern building offers accommodation in smart well equipped bedrooms, all with en suite bathrooms. Refreshments may be taken at the informal Bistro. For further details and the Campanile phone number, consult the Hotel Groups page.

ROOMS: 98 annexe en suite **CONF:** Thtr 35 Class 18 Board 20

BASINGSTOKE, Hampshire

Map 04 SU65

see also North Waltham, Odiham & Stratfield Turgis

★★★★ Tylney Hall Hotel

Tylney Hall RG27 9AZ
☎ 01256 764881 ▯ 01256 768141
e-mail: sales@tylneyhall.com
(For full entry see Rotherwick)

★★★★68% Audleys Wood

THISTLE HOTELS

Alton Rd RG25 2JT
☎ 01256 817555 ▯ 01256 817500
e-mail: audleys.wood@thistle.co.uk
Dir: *1.5m S of Basingstoke on A339*
A Gothic Renaissance style residence set in seven acres of woodland, offering contemporary, spacious bedrooms and bathrooms fitted in marble. The bar and lounges retain much of their original character.
ROOMS: 71 en suite (6 fmly) No smoking in 35 bedrooms d fr £145 * LB **FACILITIES:** STV Croquet lawn Putting green Archery Bicycles Xmas **CONF:** Thtr 50 Class 20 Board 26 Del from £195 * **PARKING:** 100 **NOTES:** No smoking in restaurant **CARDS:**

★★★74% Romans

Little London Rd RG7 2PN
☎ 0118 970 0421 ▯ 0118 970 0691
e-mail: romanhotel@hotmail.com
(For full entry see Silchester)

★★★71% The Hampshire Centrecourt Hotel

MARSTON HOTELS

Centre Dr, Chineham RG24 8FY
☎ 01256 816664 ▯ 01256 816727
e-mail: hampshire@marstonhotels.co.uk
Dir: *off A33 Reading Road behind the Chineham Shopping Centre via Great Binfields Road*
This modern single storey hotel, with an established leisure and tennis club, has easy access to the M3, M4 and business areas. Weekend breaks include coaching and lessons. Bedrooms are spacious and well equipped, some with balconies overlooking the tennis courts. Public areas have a relaxed and friendly atmosphere.
ROOMS: 50 en suite (6 fmly) No smoking in 25 bedrooms s £116-£126; d £137-£157 (incl. bkfst) * LB **FACILITIES:** STV Indoor swimming (H) Tennis (hard) Sauna Solarium Gym Pool table Jacuzzi/spa Steam room Beauty salon **CONF:** Thtr 100 Class 40 Board 40 Del from £145 * **SERVICES:** Lift **PARKING:** 120 **NOTES:** No dogs (ex guide dogs) Closed 24 Dec-31 Jan **CARDS:**

Tylney Hall

★★★★

Set in 66 acres of the rich rolling Hampshire countryside, Tylney Hall with its luxurious four poster bedrooms, gourmet restaurant, excellent leisure facilities and beautiful manicured gardens provides the perfect retreat.

Rotherwick, Hook, Hampshire RG27 9AZ
Telephone +44 (0)1256 764881
Facsimile +44 (0)1256 768141
E-mail reservations@tylneyhall.com
Website www.tylneyhall.com
SEE FULL ENTRY UNDER BASINGSTOKE

ROMANS

COUNTRY HOUSE HOTEL

★★★

LITTLE LONDON ROAD, SILCHESTER
BASINGSTOKE RG7 2PN
TEL: 01189 700421 FAX: 01189 700691

ONLY AN HOUR'S DRIVE FROM LONDON.

A PRIVATELY OWNED HOTEL, SET IN THE HISTORIC VILLAGE OF SILCHESTER, THE HOUSE, BUILT IN THE STYLE OF LUTYENS, HAS BEEN SYMPATHETICALLY CONVERTED TO OFFER GUESTS THE BEST IN MODERN FACILITIES, WHILE RETAINING THE ATMOSPHERE AND PERIOD DETAILS OF AN EDWARDIAN COUNTRY RESIDENCE.

DELIGHTFUL RESTAURANT. INNOVATIVE FRENCH CUISINE.

HEALTH AND LEISURE CENTRE WITH GYMNASIUM, SAUNA, TENNIS AND OUTDOOR POOL, HEATED TO A STEAMING 30°c ALL YEAR ROUND.

BASINGSTOKE, continued

★★★70% Basingstoke Country

Scures Hill, Nately Scures, Hook RG27 9JS
☎ 01256 764161 01256 768341
e-mail: maxine.butler@hotels.com
Dir: *leave M3 junct 5 take turning on roundabout to Newnham/Basingstoke, proceed 0.5m until reaching T junct, turn left onto A30, hotel is 200yds on right*

A wide range of facilities, including extensive meeting rooms, two eating options and a well equipped leisure club, is offered at this popular hotel. Bedrooms and suites provide all modern comforts. A range of delicious and well prepared dishes is served in the Winchester restaurant.
ROOMS: 100 en suite (8 fmly) No smoking in 35 bedrooms s £115; d £125 * LB **FACILITIES:** STV Indoor swimming (H) Sauna Solarium Gym Jacuzzi/spa Beauty salon Dance studio **CONF:** Thtr 200 Class 95 Board 80 Del from £145 * **SERVICES:** Lift **PARKING:** 164 **NOTES:** Civ Wed **CARDS:**

See advert under HOOK

★★★65% Ringway

Popley Way, Aldermaston Roundabout, Ringway North (A339) RG24 9NU
☎ 01256 796700 01256 796701
e-mail: ringwayhotel@aol.com
Dir: *situated off M3 junct 6. Follow ringroad N to exit A340 (Aldermaston), hotel on rdbt take 5th exit into Popley Way for access*

The Ringway is conveniently located for access to major routes and remains a popular venue for both business and leisure guests. Bedrooms are modern and pay great attention to comfort and quality.
ROOMS: 128 en suite No smoking in 100 bedrooms s £98-£120; d £135-£145 * LB **FACILITIES:** STV Indoor swimming (H) Sauna Solarium Gym **CONF:** Thtr 140 Class 70 Board 40 Del from £60 * **SERVICES:** Lift **PARKING:** 200 **NOTES:** No dogs (ex guide dogs) No smoking in restaurant Civ Wed 200 **CARDS:**

See advert on opposite page

★★★63% *Posthouse Basingstoke*

Posthouse

Grove Rd RG21 3EE
☎ 0870 400 9004 01256 840081
Dir: *on A339 Alton road S of Basingstoke*
This modern, purpose-built hotel, situated on the outskirts of Basingstoke, is ideally located for easy access to the M3. It offers a good standard of accommodation in well equipped rooms. There is also a popular restaurant and function rooms are available.
ROOMS: 84 en suite (3 fmly) No smoking in 42 bedrooms
FACILITIES: Pool table Childrens indoor/outdoor play areas ch fac
CONF: Thtr 150 Class 80 Board 80 **PARKING:** 150
CARDS:

★★★63% Red Lion

ZOFFANY

24 London St RG21 7NY
☎ 01256 328525 01256 844056
e-mail: redlion@zoffanyhotels.co.uk
Central to Basingstoke town, the Red Lion is an ideal choice for business guests. Bedrooms, mostly spacious, are pleasant. The restaurant and bar have a relaxed atmosphere. There is also an attractive lounge.
ROOMS: 59 en suite (2 fmly) No smoking in 6 bedrooms s £94.50; d fr £104.50 (incl. bkfst) * **FACILITIES:** STV Pool table entertainment Xmas **CONF:** Thtr 40 Class 40 Board 20 Del £117.50 * **SERVICES:** Lift **PARKING:** 62 **NOTES:** No smoking in restaurant
CARDS:

See advert on opposite page

⇧ *Travelodge*

Travelodge

Stag and Hounds, Winchester Rd RG22 5HN
☎ 01256 843566 01256 843566
Dir: *off A30*
This modern building offers accommodation in smart, spacious and well equipped bedrooms, all with en suite bathrooms. Refreshments may be taken at the nearby family restaurant. For further details and the Travelodge phone number, consult the Hotel Groups page.
ROOMS: 32 en suite

BASLOW, Derbyshire Map 08 SK27

Premier Collection

★★★ Cavendish

DE45 1SP
☎ 01246 582311 01246 582312
e-mail: info@cavendish-hotel.net
Dir: *on A619*
A country house hotel on the edge of the Chatsworth estate, offering comfortable bedrooms with many thoughtful extras. Adorning the walls are works of art, loaned by the Duke and Duchess of Devonshire. There is a relaxing lounge and light

continued

meals are served in the Garden Room conservatory. More formal cuisine, using fresh local produce where possible, is served in the restaurant.
ROOMS: 24 en suite No smoking in 2 bedrooms s £95-£115; d £125-£145 * LB **FACILITIES:** STV Fishing Putting green Xmas
CONF: Thtr 25 Board 18 Del from £174 * **PARKING:** 50
NOTES: No dogs (ex guide dogs) No smoking in restaurant
CARDS:

Premier Collection

★★ **Fischer's Baslow Hall**
Calver Rd DE45 1RR
☎ 01246 583259 ▤ 01246 583818
Dir: *on the A623 between Baslow & Calver*
A cosy country house hotel. This welcoming manor house has sumptuous bedrooms, several with period bathroom fittings.

continued on p70

BASLOW, continued

Public rooms centre around the restaurant and slightly more casual Café-Max, with its brasserie-style menu. The cuisine is worth travelling for and the staff are efficient and friendly.
ROOMS: 6 en suite No smoking in all bedrooms s £80-£95; d £95-£130 (incl. cont bkfst) * LB **FACILITIES:** Xmas **CONF:** Thtr 40 Board 18 Del from £130 * **PARKING:** 40 **NOTES:** No dogs (ex guide dogs) No smoking in restaurant Closed 25-26 Dec Civ Wed 40
CARDS:

BASSENTHWAITE, Cumbria Map 11 NY23

★★★★70% Armathwaite Hall

CA12 4RE
☎ 017687 76551 017687 76220
e-mail: reservations@armathwaite-hall.com
Dir: *M6 junct40, A66 to Keswick roundabout then A591 signposted Carlisle. 8m to Castle Inn junction, turn left hotel 300yds ahead*

A 17th-century stately mansion, standing in 400 acres of woodland and open meadows. Impressive public rooms have superb woodwork and grand fireplaces, while the bedrooms offer a variety of styles. A six-course dinner menu is served in the panelled dining room. Extensive leisure facilities are also available.
ROOMS: 43 en suite (4 fmly) s £110-£130; d £130-£230 (incl. bkfst) * LB **FACILITIES:** STV Indoor swimming (H) Tennis (hard) Fishing Riding Snooker Sauna Solarium Gym Croquet lawn Putting green Jacuzzi/spa Archery Beauty salon Clay shooting Quad bikes ch fac Xmas **CONF:** Thtr 120 Class 50 Board 60 Del from £110 * **SERVICES:** Lift **PARKING:** 100 **NOTES:** No smoking in restaurant Civ Wed 100
CARDS:

See advert under KESWICK

★★★65% Castle Inn

REGAL

CA12 4RG
☎ 017687 76401 017687 76604
Dir: *leave A66 at Keswick and take A591 towards Carlisle, pass Bassenthwaite village on right and hotel is 6m on the left*

continued

Located to the north of the Lake, enjoying distant mountain views, this traditionally styled hotel is best known for its leisure facilities. Bedrooms are well equipped and some 'superior' rooms are available. Public areas are spacious and the staff are cheerful and friendly.
ROOMS: 48 en suite (6 fmly) No smoking in 14 bedrooms s £47-£75; d £94-£115 (incl. bkfst) * LB **FACILITIES:** STV Indoor swimming (H) Tennis (grass) Snooker Sauna Solarium Gym Pool table Putting green Jacuzzi/spa Badminton Table tennis Health & beauty spa Xmas **CONF:** Thtr 120 Class 35 Board 40 Del from £89 * **PARKING:** 100 **NOTES:** No smoking in restaurant Civ Wed 120
CARDS:

★★72% Overwater Hall

Ireby CA5 1HH
☎ 017687 76566 017687 76566
e-mail: welcome@overwaterhall.co.uk
Dir: *from Keswick on A591, turn right at Castle Inn crossroads, 2m along this road, turn right at sign in wall*

This splendid mansion lies in 18 acres of woodland near the Overwater Tarn. Spacious public rooms include a cosy bar, where the counter - a baby grand piano – is an unusual feature. Bedrooms are comfortable and thoughtfully furnished. The restaurant serves an excellent five-course dinner.
ROOMS: 12 en suite (4 fmly) s £68.50; d £117 (incl. bkfst & dinner) * LB **FACILITIES:** Fishing Putting green Xmas **PARKING:** 25 **NOTES:** No smoking in restaurant **CARDS:**

★★66% Ravenstone

CA12 4QG
☎ 017687 76240 017687 76733
e-mail: info@ravenstone-hotel.co.uk
Dir: *4.5m N of Keswick on Carlisle road A591*

A popular hotel with panoramic views across the valley towards Bassenthwaite Lake. The house retains its original character with oak panelling, antiques and pictures. There is a comfortable lounge, dining room, bar and games room. Bedrooms are well presented and feature superb hand-carved furniture. There are two four-poster rooms available.

continued

ROOMS: 20 en suite (2 fmly) No smoking in all bedrooms s £25-£35; d £50-£70 (incl. bkfst) * LB **FACILITIES:** Snooker Pool table Table tennis Xmas **PARKING:** 25 **NOTES:** No dogs No smoking in restaurant **CARDS:**

BATH, Somerset Map 03 ST76
see also Chelwood, Colerne & Hinton Charterhouse

★★★★★70% The Royal Crescent

16 Royal Crescent BA1 2LS
☎ 01225 823333 01225 339401
e-mail: reservations@royalcrescent.co.uk
Dir: *cont along A4. R at traffic lights. 2nd L onto Bennett St. Cont into the Circus, 2nd exit onto Brock St, proceed ahead to cobbled street & No.16.*

In the centre of John Wood's masterpiece of fine Georgian architecture, The Royal Crescent Hotel offers high levels of hospitality, service and cuisine. The Brasserie and Bar, situated in the Dower House, offer menus with a Mediterranean touch in a friendly atmosphere. The bedrooms, in different period buildings around a spacious central garden, vary in size and outlook; all are tastefully furnished and equipped with modern comforts. A stunning leisure facility has been cleverly designed to give the feel of Roman baths.

ROOMS: 45 en suite (8 fmly) No smoking in 8 bedrooms d £195-£750 * **FACILITIES:** Indoor swimming (H) Sauna Croquet lawn Outdoor heated plunge pool, Hot air ballooning, 1920s river launch entertainment ch fac Xmas **CONF:** Thtr 100 Class 45 Del £245 * **SERVICES:** Lift air con **PARKING:** 27 **NOTES:** No smoking in restaurant Civ Wed 90 **CARDS:**

★★★★★63% The Bath Spa

Sydney Rd BA2 6JF
☎ 0870 400 8222 01225 444006
e-mail: fivestar@bathspa.u-net.com
Dir: *M4 junct 18 to A46 for Bath. Right at rdbt for A4 city centre. Left for A36 at first lights. Right at mini rdbt then left into Sydney Place*

An imposing hotel set in immaculately maintained gardens, overlooking the city. Bedrooms are thoughtfully equipped and public areas include an elegant drawing room and an inviting front hall. The popular Alfresco Restaurant serves light meals in an airy colonnade, looking out on to the gardens. An alternative eating option is the Vellore Restaurant, a former ballroom, where the quality of the food has been awarded two Rosettes.

ROOMS: 98 en suite (2 fmly) No smoking in 31 bedrooms s £160-£239; d £179-£359 * LB **FACILITIES:** STV Indoor swimming (H) Tennis (hard) Sauna Gym Croquet lawn Jacuzzi/spa Beauty treatment Hair salon entertainment Xmas **CONF:** Thtr 140 Class 72 Board 55 Del from £179 * **SERVICES:** Lift **PARKING:** 156 **NOTES:** No smoking in restaurant Civ Wed 140 **CARDS:**

Bad hair day? Hairdryers in all rooms three stars and above.

B

BATH, continued

★★★★78% Bath Priory
Weston Rd BA1 2XT
☎ 01225 331922 01225 448276
e-mail: 106076.1265@compuserve.com
This delightful Georgian house contains a smart leisure centre themed on the Roman Baths. The individually styled bedrooms display unique charm and are furnished with antiques. There are two elegant sitting rooms and a dining room overlooking beautiful gardens. Accomplished cuisine, using the finest fresh ingredients, is served in the restaurant.
ROOMS: 28 en suite (6 fmly) **FACILITIES:** STV Indoor swimming (H) Outdoor swimming (H) Sauna Solarium Gym Croquet lawn Jacuzzi/spa **CONF:** Thtr 60 Class 30 Board 24 **PARKING:** 28 **NOTES:** No dogs (ex guide dogs) No smoking in restaurant
CARDS:

★★★★66% Combe Grove Manor Hotel & Country Club
Brassknocker Hill, Monkton Combe BA2 7HS
☎ 01225 834644 01225 834961
e-mail: james.parker@combegrovemanor.com
Dir: *exit at junct 18 of the M4, follow A46 to City Centre. Next follow signs for University and American Museum, hotel is 2m past University on left*
Based around a Georgian manor house, this hotel commands stunning views. Stylishly furnished, the main house boasts two restaurants. Most bedrooms are in the Garden Lodge, with balconies and garden furniture. There is also a superb leisure centre.
ROOMS: 9 en suite 31 annexe en suite (11 fmly) d £99-£275 (incl. bkfst) * LB **FACILITIES:** STV Indoor swimming (H) Outdoor swimming (H) Golf 5 Tennis (hard) Sauna Solarium Gym Croquet lawn Putting green Jacuzzi/spa Aerobics Beauty salon ch fac Xmas **CONF:** Thtr 100 Class 40 Board 36 Del £149 * **PARKING:** 150 **NOTES:** No dogs No smoking in restaurant Civ Wed 50
CARDS:

Premier Collection

★★★ Queensberry
Russel St BA1 2QF
☎ 01225 447928 01225 446065
e-mail: queensberry@dial.pipex.com
Dir: *100mtrs from the Assembly Rooms*
This carefully restored Bath-stone town house is conveniently located within walking distance of the city centre. Bedrooms are individually decorated and tastefully furnished with sofas, fresh flowers and marble bathrooms. A lounge and bar open onto a courtyard garden. The Olive Tree Restaurant offers freshly cooked cuisine, with a Mediterranean influence.
ROOMS: 29 en suite s £100-£140; d £120-£210 (incl. cont bkfst) * LB **CONF:** Thtr 35 Board 25 Del £145 * **SERVICES:** Lift **PARKING:** 5 **NOTES:** No dogs (ex guide dogs) No smoking in restaurant Closed 24-28 Dec RS Sun **CARDS:**

★★★73% Cliffe
Crowe Hill, Limpley Stoke BA3 6HY
☎ 01225 723226 01225 723871
e-mail: cliffe.hotel@virgin.net
Dir: *A36 S from Bath, in approx 3m at traffic lights take B3108 to Lower Limpley Stoke. At sharp left hand bend take minor road to village*

Best Western

A short drive from Bath, this attractive country house benefits from hill top views and a tranquil setting. Several bedrooms are particularly spacious and all are well equipped. A number of rooms are situated on the ground floor of an adjacent wing. The restaurant overlooks the outdoor pool and surrounding garden.
ROOMS: 11 en suite (4 fmly) s £75-£95; d £95-£115 (incl. bkfst) * LB **FACILITIES:** STV Outdoor swimming (H) ch fac Xmas **CONF:** Thtr 20 Board 10 Del £110 * **PARKING:** 40 **NOTES:** No smoking in restaurant Civ Wed 50 **CARDS:**

See advert on opposite page

★★★72% Lansdown Grove Hotel
Lansdown Rd BA1 5EH
☎ 01225 483888 01225 483838
e-mail: lansdown@marstonhotels.co.uk
Dir: *follow signs to Lansdown Park & Ride and continue towards town centre. Hotel on left*

MARSTON HOTELS

A well established hotel, an uphill walk from the city centre, offering a relaxed atmosphere and comfortable accommodation. The well equipped, tastefully decorated bedrooms, some with access to an ornate veranda, vary in size. There is a reception lounge, bar and peaceful drawing room. Innovative dishes are served in the elegant dining room.
ROOMS: 50 en suite (3 fmly) No smoking in 9 bedrooms s £90-£116; d £121-£161 (incl. bkfst) * LB **FACILITIES:** Gym Xmas **CONF:** Thtr 100 Class 45 Board 40 Del from £110 * **SERVICES:** Lift **PARKING:** 44
CARDS:

★★★70% The Francis
Queen Square BA1 2HH
☎ 0870 400 8223 01225 319715
Dir: *M4 junct 18, follow A46 until Bath junct. 3rd exit onto A4. Right fork into George St, sharp left into Gay St onto Queen Sq and hotel on left*
Situated in a central location, this well established hotel offers a warm welcome and a feeling of tradition. The lounge is a popular venue for afternoon tea and snacks are available in the contemporary coffee bar. A more formal dining experience is provided in the restaurant. Bedrooms are comfortable and well decorated.
ROOMS: 94 en suite (1 fmly) No smoking in 38 bedrooms s £104-£109; d £129-£149 * LB **FACILITIES:** Xmas **CONF:** Thtr 80 Class 40 Board 30 Del from £126 * **SERVICES:** Lift **PARKING:** 42 **NOTES:** No smoking in restaurant **CARDS:**

THE GEORGE at Nunney

★★

Church Street, Nunney
Somerset BA11 4LW

Tel: 01373 836458

Beside the historic and moated Nunney Castle is the equally famous George which embodies traditional high standards of English hospitality. The extremely well equipped rooms offer every convenience for both the businessman and holidaymaker alike. Off road parking in the pretty conservation area village centre. Close by are many **golf courses - the Georgian splendour of Bath - Longleat Safari Park - The Royal Bath and West Showground** - each within a short drive. Good value Bargain Breaks - including Christmas and New Year - are a feature at the George as is the cuisine which specialises in the best of local produce.

Telephone or write for a brochure and tariff

THE CLIFFE HOTEL

Limpley Stoke, BATH BA3 6HY

AA ★★★ 73%

Situated in over 3 acres of wooded grounds, this elegant Country House Hotel offers one of the finest views over the Avon Valley. The hotel is actively run by the resident owners who pride themselves on attention to detail, and good service. All rooms are tastefully and individually decorated to the highest standards. Each room has full en-suite facilities, and most have commanding Valley views. The hotel has an outdoor heated swimming pool and more than adequate parking space.

AA Red Rosette award for à la carte Restaurant

TELEPHONE 01225 723226 FAX 01225 723871

★★★ 63%

DUKES HOTEL

Great Pulteney Street
Bath, Avon
BA2 4DN

Tel: (01225) 463512 Fax: (01225) 483733

This Grade II Listed Townhouse is situated on Europe's most elegant Georgian boulevard – just a short stroll from the Roman Baths and Abbey.

Our 24 bedrooms are all equipped with tea and coffee-making facilities, hairdryer, satellite TV and direct-dial telephone.

We offer a peaceful and relaxed atmosphere with emphasis on personal service and excellent food. Dinner is prepared from the finest local produce complemented by our reasonably priced wines.

The Abbey Hotel

Situated in the very heart of Bath close to the Abbey, Roman Baths and Pump Rooms.
The Abbey Hotel is your ideal base for exploring this historic city of World Heritage importance.
The attractive, elegant restaurant offers first class food with warm friendly service.

A member of Best Western Hotels.
The world's largest group of fine independent hotels.

North Parade, Bath BA1 1LF
Tel: 01225 461603 Fax: 01225 447758

B

BATH, continued

★★★67% The Abbey Hotel

North Pde BA1 1LF
☎ 01225 461603 🖷 01225 447758
e-mail: ahres@compasshotels.co.uk
Dir: *close to the Abbey in city centre*

Originally built as a wealthy merchant's house in the 1740s and forming part of a handsome Georgian terrace, this welcoming hotel is ideally situated in the heart of the city. The thoughtfully equipped bedrooms vary in size and style. Public areas include a smart lounge bar and a formal restaurant.
ROOMS: 60 en suite (4 fmly) No smoking in 13 bedrooms s £75-£85; d £115-£125 (incl. bkfst) * LB **FACILITIES:** STV Xmas **SERVICES:** Lift **NOTES:** No smoking in restaurant **CARDS:**

See advert on previous page

★★★66% Pratts

Forestdale Hotels

South Pde BA2 4AB
☎ 01225 460441 🖷 01225 448807
Dir: *take A46 into Bath City Centre*
Part of an attractive Georgian terrace, this long established and popular hotel stands at the heart of the city centre. Public rooms retain a traditional atmosphere, with an intimate writing room, two lounges and a modern bar. Bedrooms vary in size and all are well equipped; some rooms are cosy with low ceilings and small windows.
ROOMS: 46 en suite (2 fmly) No smoking in 2 bedrooms s fr £60; d fr £120 (incl. bkfst & dinner) * LB **FACILITIES:** Xmas **CONF:** Thtr 50 Class 12 Board 30 Del from £115 * **SERVICES:** Lift **NOTES:** No smoking in restaurant **CARDS:**

★★★63% Dukes' Hotel

Great Pulteney St BA2 4DN
☎ 01225 463512 🖷 01225 483733

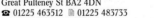

This stylish hotel offers modern facilities combined with the elegance and charm of a fine listed Georgian building. Bedrooms are comfortable and attractively decorated. In addition to the cosy bar and lounge, there is a restaurant serving a tempting selection of freshly prepared dishes.
ROOMS: 24 en suite (1 fmly) s £55-£70; d £70-£110 (incl. bkfst) * **FACILITIES:** STV **CONF:** Thtr 20 Class 14 Board 14 Del from £80 * **NOTES:** No dogs (ex guide dogs) No smoking in restaurant
CARDS:

See advert on previous page

★★74% Haringtons

8/10 Queen St BA1 1HE
☎ 01225 461728 🖷 01225 444804
e-mail: post@haringtonshotel.co.uk
Dir: *from A4 go to George St and turn into Milsom St. 1st right into Quiet St and 1st left into Queen St*
Located in the centre of Bath, this hotel dates back to the 18th century. The cafe-bar is open throughout the day for light meals and refreshments. Bedrooms are all of a good standard and offer modern comforts.
ROOMS: 13 en suite (3 fmly) No smoking in all bedrooms s £60-£88; d £78-£115 (incl. bkfst) * LB **FACILITIES:** STV **NOTES:** No dogs (ex guide dogs) No smoking in restaurant Closed 24-26 Dec
CARDS:

★★72% The Bath Tasburgh

Warminster Rd BA2 6SH
☎ 01225 425096 🖷 01225 463842
e-mail: hotel@bathtasburgh.demon.co.uk
Dir: *follow signs for A36. Hotel stands on N side of A36 - adjacent to Bathampton Ln junct - approx. 0.5m from Bathwick St rdbt and Sydney Gardens*
Set in beautiful gardens and meadowland leading down to the Kennet and Avon Canal, this charming Victorian house offers a variety of bedrooms, including four-posters. The dining room serves an imaginative fixed-price menu, complemented by an interesting selection of wines. The bright and airy conservatory opens onto a garden terrace.
ROOMS: 12 en suite (3 fmly) No smoking in all bedrooms s £52-£65; d £75-£98 (incl. bkfst) * **FACILITIES:** Croquet lawn **CONF:** Thtr 15 Class 15 Board 15 **PARKING:** 16 **NOTES:** No dogs No smoking in restaurant **CARDS:**

See advert on opposite page

★★68% Avondale Hotel & Duck & Punt Restaurant

London Rd East, Bathford BA1 7RB
☎ 01225 859847 & 852207 🖷 01225 859847
Dir: *from A46/A4 junct follow signs Chippenham/Batheaston/Bathford. Continue through Batheaston towards large rdbt & hotel on right just before rdbt*
In a pleasant riverside location, this hotel offers a good standard of accommodation. The restaurant serves an imaginative range of dishes, together with a selection of real ales and malt whiskies. Staff work hard to create a relaxed atmosphere so guests can enjoy the peaceful surroundings.
ROOMS: 15 rms (13 en suite) (3 fmly) s £38-£65; d £65-£95 (incl. bkfst) * **FACILITIES:** Fishing Boating **PARKING:** 26 **NOTES:** No dogs (ex guide dogs) **CARDS:**

★★68% The Old Mill

Tollbridge Rd, Batheaston BA1 7DE
☎ 01225 858476 🖷 01225 852600
e-mail: info@oldmillbath.co.uk
Dir: *take A46 for 8m, turn left for Bath at large rdbt turn left towards Batheaston in 0.5m turn right after Waggon & Horses to Bathampton Toll Bridge*
This attractive, creeper-clad hotel was formerly a flour mill. The original waterwheel can be seen from the restaurant which

continued on p76

The Old Mill

"Bath's most beautifully located hotel"

In a picturesque position on the banks of the river Avon just 1.4 miles from the centre of Bath. All bedrooms are en suite and have been totally refurbished in 1999 with the majority having river views, there are some with 4-poster beds. Dine in the Waterwheel Restaurant with views of the historic toll bridge, revolving water wheel, pretty gardens and the river and its wild life. Free private parking.

Tollbridge Road, Batheaston, Bath BA1 7DE
Tel: 01225 858476 Fax: 01225 852600
E-mail: info@oldmillbath.co.uk
www.oldmillbath.co.uk

AA ★★

Tel:
01225 425096
Fax:
01225 463842
WARMINSTER ROAD
BATH BA2 6SH
Website: www.bathtasburgh.co.uk
Email: reservations@bathtasburgh.co.uk

A Victorian mansion standing in seven acres of beautiful gardens and meadowpark stretching down to the Kennet & Avon canal. With spectacular views the hotel provides ideal country comfort in a city setting and is convenient for central Bath. The adjacent canal towpath provides an idyllic walk into Bath. Individually decorated en-suite bedrooms (including 4-posters and family). Elegant Drawing Room and stunning Conservatory. Evening meals. Licensed. Ample parking. Caring and friendly service.

Wentworth House Hotel

AA ★★ 67%

106 Bloomfield Road, Bath, BA2 2AP **Tel: 01225 339193 · Fax: 01225 310460**
E-mail: stay@wentworthhouse.co.uk **Website: www.wentworthhouse.co.uk**

An imposing Victorian Mansion set on the hillside in a peaceful location but just a 15 minute walk to the city centre.

Guests can enjoy a refreshing swim in our heated outdoor swimming pool or take a quiet drink or snack on one of the garden terraces.

The elegant drawing room has complimentary newspapers and a well stocked cocktail bar. Our sunny Conservatory Restaurant serves a generous English breakfast and in the evenings a delicious table d'hôte menu. The bedrooms are individually styled, many with antique and four-poster beds. Large car park. Short breaks offers and hotel gift vouchers available.

BATH, continued

overlooks the gardens, lying alongside the River Avon. Bedrooms vary in size, all offering good levels of decor and comfort, particularly in the main house. The varied menus offer something for everyone.
ROOMS: 17 en suite 10 annexe en suite (5 fmly) s £49-£65; d £65-£115 (incl. bkfst) * LB **FACILITIES:** STV Fishing entertainment Xmas **CONF:** Thtr 100 Class 80 Board 80 Del from £85 * **PARKING:** 50 **NOTES:** Civ Wed 40 **CARDS:**

See advert on previous page

★★67% Wentworth House Hotel
106 Bloomfield Rd BA2 2AP
☎ 01225 339193 📠 01225 310460
e-mail: stay@wentworthhouse.co.uk

An imposing Victorian mansion built in 1887, enjoying a peaceful location overlooking the city of Bath, yet only a fifteen minute walk to the centre. Bedrooms are individually furnished and include many thoughtful extras. Enjoyable home-cooked dinners and hearty breakfasts are served in the conservatory restaurant.
ROOMS: 18 en suite (3 fmly) No smoking in 5 bedrooms s £50-£70; d £65-£95 (incl. bkfst) * LB **FACILITIES:** Outdoor swimming (H) **PARKING:** 18 **NOTES:** No dogs No children 5yrs No smoking in restaurant Closed Xmas & New Year weeks
CARDS:

See advert on previous page

★★63% Old Malt House
MINOTEL Great Britain
Radford, Timsbury BA3 1QF
☎ 01761 470106 📠 01761 472726
e-mail: hotel@oldmalthouse.co.uk
Dir: *from Bath take A367 south for 1.5m then right onto B3115 towards Timsbury. Continue down hill to Camerton Inn then second left and second left again*
This former brewery malt house is peacefully located just outside Bath and provides a good base from which to explore the local area. Bedrooms, including some on the ground floor, are well equipped and include thoughtful extras. There is a wood-burning stove in the bar and a varied choice of home-cooked meals is served in the pleasant restaurant.
ROOMS: 12 en suite (2 fmly) s £36-£45.50; d £72-£75 (incl. bkfst) * LB **PARKING:** 40 **NOTES:** No smoking in restaurant Closed 24-27 Dec
CARDS:

○ The Windsor Hotel
69 Great Pulteney St BA2 4DL
☎ 01225 422100
NOTES: Open

BATLEY, West Yorkshire
Map 08 SE22

★★70% Alder House
Towngate Rd, Healey Ln WF17 7HR
☎ 01924 444777 📠 01924 442644
e-mail: info@alderhousehotel.co.uk
An attractive Georgian house tucked away in leafy grounds. Bedrooms are pleasantly furnished and extremely well equipped. There is a cosy dining room offering a selection of interesting dishes. There is also a bar and a separate lounge area.
ROOMS: 20 en suite (1 fmly) s £47.50-£55; d £62-£100 (incl. bkfst) * LB **FACILITIES:** STV **CONF:** Thtr 80 Class 40 Board 35 Del from £64 * **PARKING:** 52 **NOTES:** No smoking in restaurant Civ Wed 100
CARDS:

BATTLE, East Sussex
Map 05 TQ71

★★★70% Powder Mills
Powdermill Ln TN33 0SP
☎ 01424 775511 📠 01424 774540
e-mail: powdc@aol.com
Dir: *through town in direction of Hastings, past abbey on A2100, 1st turning on right and hotel on right after a mile*
An 18th-century wisteria-clad mansion set in 150 acres of grounds with lakes and woodlands. The particularly well furnished bedrooms are in The Mill, others are in a separate building. Extensive day rooms are filled with antiques and provide a relaxing setting.
ROOMS: 25 en suite 10 annexe en suite s £70-£95; d £95-£160 (incl. bkfst) * LB **FACILITIES:** STV Outdoor swimming Fishing Xmas **CONF:** Thtr 250 Class 50 Board 16 Del £125 * **PARKING:** 101 **NOTES:** No smoking in restaurant Civ Wed 100
CARDS:

See advert on opposite page

○ Leeford Place Hotel
Mill Ln, Whatlington TN33 0ND
☎ 01424 772863
NOTES: Open

BAWTRY, South Yorkshire
Map 08 SK69

★★★61% The Crown
REGAL
High St DN10 6JW
☎ 01302 710341 📠 01302 711798
Dir: *leave A1 at Blyth Service Station, taking A614 to Bawtry. The Crown is on the left hand side in the town centre*

Situated in the centre of the town, this 17th-century coaching inn retains much of its original charm. Public areas include an oak-panelled bar and a cosy restaurant. Well equipped bedrooms come in a variety of styles and sizes and some have been refurbished to the new 'Corus' brand standard.

continued

ROOMS: 57 en suite No smoking in 18 bedrooms s fr £62; d fr £75 * LB **CONF:** Thtr 150 Class 80 Board 60 Del from £85 * **PARKING:** 50 **NOTES:** No smoking in restaurant Civ Wed 100
CARDS:

BEACONSFIELD, Buckinghamshire — Map 04 SU99

★★★★67% Bellhouse

Oxford Rd HP9 2XE
☎ 01753 887211 🖷 01753 888231
e-mail: bellhouse@devere-hotels.com
Dir: *leave M40 at junct 2, exit signed Gerrards Cross/Beaconsfield. At rdbt take A40 to Gerrards Cross. Hotel is 1m on right hand side*

This smart Mediterranean-style hotel is conveniently located close to the M40 and M25. The cosy bedrooms are well equipped. There is a casual brasserie and also a more formal restaurant. A range of conference and leisure facilities is available.

ROOMS: 136 en suite (11 fmly) No smoking in 86 bedrooms s fr £145; d fr £165 * LB **FACILITIES:** STV Indoor swimming (H) Squash Snooker Sauna Solarium Gym Jacuzzi/spa Beauty therapy room Xmas **CONF:** Thtr 400 Class 200 Board 40 Del £190 * **SERVICES:** Lift **PARKING:** 405 **NOTES:** No dogs No smoking in restaurant
CARDS:

BEAMINSTER, Dorset — Map 03 ST40

★★★71% Bridge House

3 Prout Bridge DT8 3AY
☎ 01308 862200 🖷 01308 863700
e-mail: enquiries@bridge-house.co.uk
Dir: *off A3066, 100yds from Town Square*

This family-owned 13th-century property has an attractive walled garden. Bedrooms are divided between the main house and the coach house. All are tastefully decorated and offer modern comforts. Public rooms are smartly furnished and there is a Georgian dining room.

ROOMS: 9 en suite 5 annexe en suite (1 fmly) No smoking in all bedrooms s £70-£88; d £97-£124 (incl. bkfst) * LB **FACILITIES:** Tennis (hard) Xmas **CONF:** Thtr 20 Class 16 Board 16 Del from £115 * **PARKING:** 22 **NOTES:** No smoking in restaurant Closed 27-29 Dec
CARDS:

BEAMISH, Co Durham — Map 12 NZ25

★★★67% Beamish Park

Beamish Burn Rd NE16 5EG
☎ 01207 230666 🖷 01207 281260
e-mail: beamishparkhotel@btclick.com
Dir: *from A1(M) take A692 towards Consett, then A6076 towards Stanley. Hotel on left behind Causey Arch Inn*

This modern hotel is within easy reach of the main north-east commercial and heritage centres and offers bedrooms that come in a variety of styles. Public areas include a dining room, lounge bar and conservatory brasserie. There is also an outside pub.

ROOMS: 47 en suite (7 fmly) No smoking in 20 bedrooms s £44.50-£53.50; d £61.50-£65.50 * LB **FACILITIES:** STV Golf 9 Putting green 20 bay floodlit golf driving range Golf tuition by PGA professional **CONF:** Thtr 30 Class 10 Board 25 Del from £74 * **PARKING:** 100
CARDS:

Read all about it! Newspapers delivered to bedrooms in four and five star hotels.

BEAULIEU, Hampshire — Map 04 SU30

★★★78% Master Builders House Hotel

Bucklers Hard SO42 7XB
☎ 01590 616253 🖷 01590 616297
e-mail: res@themasterbuilders.co.uk
Dir: *turn off M27, junct2, follow signs Beaulieu, at T junct left onto B3056 1st left to Bucklers Hard, hotel is 2m on left just before village entrance*

This 18th-century house, beside the marina at Bucklers Hard, has its own boat operating between the hotel and the Isle of Wight. Many rooms have riverside views and all offer a high standard of comfort. Meals are served in either the Riverview Restaurant or the Yachtsman's Bar and spacious lounges filled with plump sofas complete the picture.

ROOMS: 8 en suite 17 annexe en suite (2 fmly) No smoking in 12 bedrooms s fr £110; d £145-£195 (incl. bkfst) * LB **FACILITIES:** STV Fishing Xmas **CONF:** Thtr 50 Class 50 Board 25 Del from £165 * **PARKING:** 70 **NOTES:** Civ Wed **CARDS:**

★★★70% *Montagu Arms*

Palace Ln SO42 7ZL
☎ 01590 612324 🖷 01590 612188
e-mail: enquires@montagu-arms.co.uk
Dir: *leave M27 at junct 2, turn left at rdbt, then follow tourist signs for Beaulieu, continue to Dibden Purlieu, then right at rdbt, hotel is on left*

This attractive, creeper-clad hotel stands in the centre of picturesque Beaulieu. Bedrooms are tastefully decorated and thoughtfully equipped. Public rooms include a cosy bar, an elegant lounge and adjoining conservatory, which overlooks the pretty walled garden. Guests can dine in either the restaurant or the more informal Monty's.

continued

B

BEAULIEU, continued

Montagu Arms, Beaulieu

ROOMS: 24 en suite **FACILITIES:** Pool table Use of health club facilities in Brockenhurst **CONF:** Thtr 50 Class 30 Board 30 **PARKING:** 86 **NOTES:** No smoking in restaurant **CARDS:**

See advert on opposite page

★★★63% Beaulieu

Beaulieu Rd SO42 7YQ
☎ 023 8029 3344 📠 023 8029 2729
e-mail: information@carehotels.co.uk

Dir: *M27 junct 1 follow signs onto A337 towards Lyndhurst. Left at traffic lights in Lyndhurst through village turn right onto B3056 & continue for 3m*

Conveniently located in the heart of the New Forest and close to Beaulieu Road railway station. This popular, small hotel provides an ideal base for exploring the surrounding area. Facilities include an indoor swimming pool, an outdoor children's play area and an adjoining pub. A daily changing menu is offered in the restaurant, which has excellent views.

ROOMS: 15 en suite 3 annexe en suite (2 fmly) s £70-£77.50; d £110-£125 (incl. bkfst) * LB **FACILITIES:** Indoor swimming (H) Steam room Xmas **CONF:** Thtr 60 Class 40 Board 30 Del from £95 * **PARKING:** 60 **NOTES:** Civ Wed 80 **CARDS:**

BEBINGTON, Merseyside

Map 07 SJ38

Travelodge

Travelodge

New Chester Rd L62 9AQ
☎ 0151 327 2489 📠 0151 327 2489

Dir: *on A41, northbound off, junct 5 on M53*

This modern building offers accommodation in smart, spacious and well equipped bedrooms, all with en suite bathrooms. Refreshments may be taken at the nearby family restaurant. For further details and the Travelodge phone number, consult the Hotel Groups page.

ROOMS: 31 en suite

BECKINGTON, Somerset

Map 03 ST85

★★69% Woolpack Inn

Old English Inns & Hotels

BA3 6SP
☎ 01373 831244 📠 01373 831223

Dir: *on A36*

This charming coaching inn dates back to the 16th century and retains many original features including flagstone floors, open fireplaces and exposed beams. There is a cosy lounge and a choice of places to eat: the bar for light snacks and for more substantial meals the Oak Room, or the Garden Room, which leads onto an inner courtyard.

ROOMS: 12 en suite No smoking in 1 bedroom **FACILITIES:** STV **CONF:** Thtr 30 Class 20 Board 20 **PARKING:** 16 **NOTES:** No children 5yrs **CARDS:**

Travelodge

Travelodge

BA3 6SF
☎ 01373 830251 📠 01373 830251

Dir: *on A36*

This modern building offers accommodation in smart, spacious and well equipped bedrooms, all with en suite bathrooms. Refreshments may be taken at the nearby family restaurant. For further details and the Travelodge phone number, consult the Hotel Groups page.

ROOMS: 40 en suite

BEDFORD, Bedfordshire

Map 04 TL04

★★★74% Woodlands Manor

Green Ln, Clapham MK41 6EP
☎ 01234 363281 📠 01234 272390
e-mail: woodlands.manor@pageant.co.uk

Dir: *A6 from Bedford, towards Kettering. Clapham is 1st village N of town centre, on entering village first right into Green Lane, Manor 200mtrs on right*

A country house hotel set in wooded grounds on the outskirts of the village. The drawing room, with its rich colour scheme, wood panelled walls and large sofas, is very comfortable. Bedrooms are pleasantly decorated with cherry wood furniture and co-ordinated colour schemes. The elegant restaurant offers imaginative cooking.

ROOMS: 30 en suite 3 annexe en suite (4 fmly) No smoking in 6 bedrooms s £59.50-£77.50; d £87.50-£95 (incl. bkfst) * LB **FACILITIES:** STV Xmas **CONF:** Thtr 80 Class 28 Board 40 Del from £105 * **PARKING:** 100 **NOTES:** No smoking in restaurant Civ Wed 50 **CARDS:**

★★★72% The Barns

corus

Cardington Rd MK44 3SA
☎ 01234 270044 📠 01234 273102

Dir: *take A421 from M1 and turn off at A603 Sandy, turn left to Bedford on A603*

With the Great Ouse flowing behind and a delightful medieval tithe barn, this 17th-century manor house still has many original features. Modern, well equipped bedrooms are found in the

continued

extension wings, all are smartly decorated. The relaxing riverside public areas include a country pub, a cocktail bar and the Anglers restaurant.
ROOMS: 48 en suite No smoking in 16 bedrooms s fr £90; d fr £100 * LB **FACILITIES:** STV Free use of local leisure centre (1mile) Xmas **CONF:** Thtr 120 Class 40 Board 40 Del £128 * **PARKING:** 90 **NOTES:** No smoking in restaurant Civ Wed 100
CARDS:

BELFORD, Northumberland Map 12 NU13

★★★68% Blue Bell
Market Place NE70 7NE
☎ 01668 213543 ▤ 01668 213787
e-mail: bluebel@globalnet.co.uk
Dir: *centre of village on left of St Mary's church*
This long-established, creeper-clad former coaching inn is located in the centre of Belford just off the A1. It has a friendly atmosphere and retains much of its original character. Bedrooms are all individual in style. A variety of menus provide an extensive choice of food in the bar, bistro and main restaurant.
ROOMS: 17 en suite (1 fmly) No smoking in 4 bedrooms s £34-£44; d £68-£96 (incl. bkfst) * LB **FACILITIES:** Pool table Xmas **CONF:** Thtr 140 Class 120 Board 30 Del from £66 * **PARKING:** 17 **NOTES:** No smoking in restaurant **CARDS:**

Purdy Lodge
Adderstone Services NE70 7JU
☎ 01668 213000 ▤ 01668 213111
Dir: *between Alnwick & Berwick turn off A1 to B1341*
Conveniently situated on the A1, this family-owned lodge provides practical accommodation. All the bedrooms look out over fields to the rear and are insulated from road noise. As well as a 24-hour café there is a restaurant open for dinners and a cosy lounge bar, also serving food.
ROOMS: 20 en suite d £39.95-£41.50 *

BELLINGHAM, Northumberland Map 12 NY88

★★68% Riverdale Hall
NE48 2JT
☎ 01434 220254 ▤ 01434 220457
e-mail: iben@riverdalehall.demon.co.uk
Dir: *turn off B6320, after bridge, hotel on left*

Standing in grounds overlooking its own cricket pitch and the North Tyne river, this hotel offers well equipped bedrooms in a variety of sizes, the larger ones with their own balconies. The menus in the restaurant feature freshly cooked dishes, including seafood and vegetarian specialities, all complemented by a tempting wine list.
ROOMS: 20 en suite (11 fmly) s £46-£48; d £69-£84 (incl. bkfst) * LB **FACILITIES:** Indoor swimming (H) Fishing Sauna Croquet lawn Putting green Cricket field Petanque Xmas **CONF:** Thtr 40 Class 40 Board 20 Del from £69 * **PARKING:** 60 **CARDS:**

BELPER, Derbyshire Map 08 SK34

★★★70% Makeney Hall Country House
corus
Makeney, Milford DE56 0RS
☎ 01332 842999 ▤ 01332 842777
e-mail: reservations@corushotels.com
Dir: *turn off A6 between Belper and Duffield at Milford, signposted Makeney. Hotel is 0.25m further along on left*

A beautiful Victorian mansion, set in six acres of delightful grounds, above the River Derwent. The main house bedrooms offer particularly high standards of comfort. There are nine ground floor courtyard rooms, two have been designed for disabled access. Lavinia's restaurant, an oak-panelled room overlooking the garden, serves a range of interesting dishes.
ROOMS: 27 en suite 18 annexe en suite No smoking in 6 bedrooms s £85; d £95-£150 * LB **FACILITIES:** STV Xmas **CONF:** Thtr 180 Class 80 Board 50 Del from £110 * **SERVICES:** Lift **PARKING:** 150 **NOTES:** No smoking in restaurant Civ Wed 150
CARDS:

B

BELPER, continued

★★68% *Lion*
Bridge St DE56 1AX
☎ 01773 824033 📠 01773 880321
Dir: *on A6*
On the border of the Peak District, yet close to the M1, this 18th-century hotel provides an ideal base for exploring local attractions. The tasteful bedrooms are well equipped. There are two cosy bars and a function room.
ROOMS: 20 rms (14 en suite) (1 fmly) No smoking in 6 bedrooms **CONF:** Thtr 130 Class 60 Board 50 **PARKING:** 25 **NOTES:** No smoking in restaurant **CARDS:**

BELTON, Lincolnshire — Map 08 SK93

★★★★73% ❀ Belton Woods
NG32 2LN
DE VERE HOTELS
☎ 01476 593200 📠 01476 574547
e-mail: devere.belton@airtime.co.uk
Dir: *from A1 turn onto B1174, follow signs to Belton House. Turn left towards Great Gonerby. Then left onto A607. Hotel 0.5m on left*
Enjoying an idyllic location in 475 acres of rolling countryside this hotel is within easy access of major routes. This stylish complex is a major leisure and golf resort combined with extensive meeting suites, attractive public areas and a choice of restaurants and bars. Smartly appointed bedrooms are spacious and well equipped, many overlook the golf courses. A range of carefully prepared dishes is available in the Manor restaurant. Staff are welcoming and attentive.
ROOMS: 136 en suite No smoking in 48 bedrooms s fr £125; d fr £150 * LB **FACILITIES:** STV Indoor swimming (H) Golf 45 Tennis (hard) Squash Snooker Sauna Solarium Gym Croquet lawn Putting green Jacuzzi/spa Hair & beauty salon Steamroom Xmas **CONF:** Thtr 245 Class 130 Board 80 Del £175 * **SERVICES:** Lift **PARKING:** 500 **NOTES:** No smoking in restaurant Civ Wed 60 **CARDS:**

BERKELEY, Gloucestershire — Map 03 ST69

★★76% The Old Schoolhouse
Canonbury St GL13 9BG
☎ 01453 811711 📠 01453 511761
e-mail: schoolhouse@btinternet.com
Dir: *1.5m off A38 next to Berkeley Castle. Follow brown tourist signs*
Situated next to Berkeley Castle, this fine old building was formerly a school. Bedrooms, all of a generous size, have extensive modern facilities. Cooking is of a high standard and a varied menu is served. The owners are renowned for their excellent hospitality.
ROOMS: 8 en suite (1 fmly) No smoking in 5 bedrooms s £52.50-£62.50; d £62.50-£72.50 (incl. bkfst) * LB **PARKING:** 20 **NOTES:** No dogs (ex guide dogs) No smoking in restaurant
CARDS:

BERKELEY ROAD, Gloucestershire — Map 03 ST79

★★★66% *Prince of Wales*
Berkeley Rd GL13 9HD
☎ 01453 810474 📠 01453 511370
Dir: *on A38, 6m S of M5 junc 13 and 6m N of junc 14*
A comfortable hotel with modern amenities, offering attractively furnished, bright, modern bedrooms. There is an informal bar and a restaurant which serves food with an Italian influence.
ROOMS: 43 en suite (2 fmly) No smoking in 10 bedrooms **FACILITIES:** STV Pool table **CONF:** Thtr 200 Class 60 Board 60 **PARKING:** 150 **CARDS:**

BERWICK-UPON-TWEED, Northumberland — Map 12 NT95

★★★71% ❀ Marshall Meadows Country House
TD15 1UT
☎ 01289 331133 📠 01289 331438
e-mail: stay@marshallmeadows.co.uk
Dir: *signposted directly off A1, 200 yds from Scottish Border*
This stylish Georgian mansion, set in wooded grounds flanked by farmland, is a popular venue for weddings and conferences. Bedrooms are comfortable and well equipped. Public rooms include a cosy bar, an inviting lounge and a two-tier restaurant, serving imaginative dishes.
ROOMS: 19 en suite (2 fmly) No smoking in 15 bedrooms s fr £75; d fr £85 (incl. bkfst) * LB **FACILITIES:** STV Tennis (hard) Croquet lawn Petanque Xmas **CONF:** Thtr 120 Class 180 Board 60 Del £120 * **PARKING:** 87 **NOTES:** No smoking in restaurant
CARDS:

See advert on opposite page

★63% Queens Head
Sandgate TD15 1EP
☎ 01289 307852 📠 01289 307858
Dir: *in town centre adjacent to town walls*
Set in the centre, close to the old walls of this garrison town, this small hotel provides mainly spacious bedrooms. Good value meals are served in either the lounge area or the dining room.
ROOMS: 6 en suite (5 fmly) s £35-£40; d £55-£60 (incl. bkfst) * LB
CARDS:

BEVERLEY, East Riding of Yorkshire — Map 08 TA03

★★★68% ❀ Tickton Grange
Tickton HU17 9SH
☎ 01964 543666 📠 01964 542556
e-mail: maggy@tickton-grange.demon.co.uk
Dir: *3m NE on A1035*
Set in four acres, this charming Georgian house retains much charm and character. The well equipped bedrooms are individually decorated. Public rooms, including a comfortable lounge bar, are smartly presented. Skilfully prepared dinners are served in the restaurant.
ROOMS: 18 en suite (2 fmly) s £65; d £85 LB **FACILITIES:** STV **CONF:** Thtr 200 Class 100 Board 80 Del from £105 * **PARKING:** 65 **NOTES:** No dogs (ex guide dogs) No smoking in restaurant RS 25-29 Dec Civ Wed 150 **CARDS:**

★★★67% Beverley Arms
North Bar Within HU17 8DD
REGAL
☎ 01482 869241 📠 01482 870907
Dir: *opposite St Marys Church, just before North Bar*

History links this hotel with the highwayman Dick Turpin. Today a feature of the hotel is the spacious, flagstoned, Shires Lounge.
continued

There are also two bars and an attractively appointed restaurant. Bedrooms, in the older part of the building, are particularly charming. All rooms are equipped with modern comforts. Staff are friendly and helpful.
ROOMS: 56 en suite (4 fmly) No smoking in 30 bedrooms s £75-£80; d £95 * LB **FACILITIES:** Xmas **CONF:** Thtr 60 Class 40 Board 30 Del £95 * **SERVICES:** Lift **PARKING:** 50 **NOTES:** No smoking in restaurant **CARDS:**

★★73% The Manor House

Northlands, Walkington HU17 8RT
☎ 01482 881645 01482 866501
e-mail: the-manor-house@fsbusiness.co.uk
Dir: *4m SW off B1230. Follow brown 'Walkington' signs from junct 38 on M62*
This delightful country house hotel is set in beautiful, well tended gardens. The spacious bedrooms have been attractively decorated and thoughtfully equipped. Public rooms include a conservatory restaurant and an inviting lounge. A good range of dishes is available from two menus, with an emphasis on local produce.
ROOMS: 6 en suite 1 annexe en suite (1 fmly) s £65-£80; d £75-£100 * LB **CONF:** Thtr 20 **PARKING:** 40 **CARDS:**

BEWDLEY, Worcestershire — Map 07 SO77

★★62% The George

Load St DY12 2AW
☎ 01299 402117 01299 401269
Dir: *in town centre opposite town hall*
Situated in the heart of Bewdley, this friendly 16th-century inn features large oak beams, panelling, slate tiles and traditional fireplaces. Bedrooms are individually decorated and furnished to a good standard. Public areas include a coffee shop, function rooms, bars and a restaurant serving a wide-ranging menu.
ROOMS: 11 en suite s £42-£45; d £59-£69 (incl. bkfst) * LB
CONF: Thtr 50 Class 50 Board 40 **PARKING:** 50 **NOTES:** No dogs (ex guide dogs) No smoking in restaurant **CARDS:**

★★60% Black Boy

Kidderminster Rd DY12 1AG
☎ 01299 402119 01299 403250
e-mail: rc@midnet.co.uk
This 18th-century inn stands on the A456 close to both the River Severn and the centre of this lovely old town. The bedrooms are simple but comfortable. There are pleasant bar facilities and a small, cosy restaurant.
ROOMS: 17 rms (5 en suite) 8 annexe rms (2 en suite) (2 fmly)
PARKING: 28 **NOTES:** Closed 25 Dec **CARDS:**

BEXLEY, Greater London — Map 05 TQ47

★★★★69% Bexleyheath Marriott

1 Broadway DA6 7JZ
☎ 020 8298 1000 020 8298 1234
Marriott HOTELS · RESORTS · SUITES
Dir: *take A2 (London Bound) from junct 2 of M25 exit Black Prince interchange onto A220, follow signs Bexleyheath, 3rd rdbt turn left into*
This very modern hotel is located on the fringes of the town centre and is linked to a covered municipal car park. The bedrooms are smart, comfortable and well laid out. There are two restaurants, as well as full room service. Staff create a warm and welcoming atmosphere.

continued

B

BEXLEY, continued

ROOMS: 142 en suite (16 fmly) No smoking in 53 bedrooms s £120; d £140-£170 (incl. bkfst) * LB **FACILITIES:** STV Indoor swimming (H) Solarium Gym Jacuzzi/spa Steam room entertainment Xmas **CONF:** Thtr 250 Class 120 Board 40 Del from £114 * **SERVICES:** Lift air con **PARKING:** 100 **NOTES:** Civ Wed 50 **CARDS:**

★★★65% ***Posthouse Bexley***

Posthouse

Black Prince Interchange, Southwold Rd DA5 1ND
☎ 0870 400 9006 🖹 01322 526113
Dir: *follow A2 to exit signposted A220/A223 Black Prince interchange Bexley, Bexleyheath & Crayford*
A purpose built hotel with well equipped bedrooms, all smartly appointed in a modern style. Public areas include a choice of bars and the Junction restaurant, offering a range of popular dishes. The hotel offers meeting rooms and a business centre.
ROOMS: 105 en suite (10 fmly) No smoking in 50 bedrooms **FACILITIES:** ch fac **CONF:** Thtr 70 Class 30 Board 30 **SERVICES:** Lift **PARKING:** 200 **CARDS:**

BIBURY, Gloucestershire Map 04 SP10

★★★79% ❀❀ ***Swan***
GL7 5NW
☎ 01285 740695 🖹 01285 740473
e-mail: swanhot1@swanhotel-cotswolds.co.uk
Dir: *off B4425, by bridge over the River Coln*
The Swan hotel, originally built as a 17th-century coaching inn, is set in peaceful, picturesque and beautiful surroundings. It now provides well equipped and smartly presented accommodation, and public areas that are comfortable and elegant. There is a choice of dining options to suit all tastes.
ROOMS: 18 en suite (1 fmly) **FACILITIES:** Fishing **CONF:** Thtr 85 Class 60 Board 10 **SERVICES:** Lift **PARKING:** 16 **NOTES:** No dogs (ex guide dogs) No smoking in restaurant **CARDS:**

See advert on opposite page

★★★71% ❀❀ **Bibury Court**
GL7 5NT
☎ 01285 740337 🖹 01285 740660
e-mail: aj@biburycourt.co.uk
Dir: *on B4425 beside the River Coln, behind St Marys Church*
Standing in extensive grounds beside the River Coln, this elegant manor house dates back to Tudor times. Spacious public areas have a wealth of charm and character, the bedrooms are furnished in keeping with the style of the building and enjoyable food is served in the restaurant.
ROOMS: 18 en suite (3 fmly) s £75-£95; d £105-£150 (incl. cont bkfst) * LB **FACILITIES:** Fishing Pool table Croquet lawn **CONF:** Thtr 20 Board 12 Del £160 * **PARKING:** 100 **NOTES:** No smoking in restaurant **CARDS:**

See advert on opposite page

BICESTER, Oxfordshire Map 04 SP52

★★60% ❀ **Bignell Park Hotel & Restaurant**
Chesterton OX6 8UE
☎ 01869 241444 & 241192 🖹 01869 241444
Dir: *on A4095 Witney road*
This charming hotel near Bicester features a dramatic galleried restaurant with fine artwork, a fireplace and exposed beams. The cuisine is imaginative and many of the dishes use fresh local produce. Bedrooms are stylish and comfortably furnished with some unusual pieces of furniture, the newer rooms are particularly spacious.

ROOMS: 23 en suite s £65-£80; d £85-£150 (incl. bkfst) * **FACILITIES:** STV **CONF:** Thtr 30 Class 20 Board 18 Del from £110 * **PARKING:** 40 **NOTES:** No dogs (ex guide dogs) No children 6yrs No smoking in restaurant RS Sun **CARDS:**

⌂ ***Travelodge***

Travelodge

Northampton Rd, Ardley OX6 9RD
☎ 01869 346060 🖹 01869 345030
Dir: *M40 junct 10*
This modern building offers accommodation in smart, spacious and well equipped bedrooms, all with en suite bathrooms. Refreshments may be taken at the nearby family restaurant. For further details and the Travelodge phone number, consult the Hotel Groups page.
ROOMS: 98 en suite **CONF:** Thtr 40 Class 20 Board 20

BIDEFORD, Devon Map 02 SS42

★★★67% **Royal**

Brend Hotels

Barnstaple St EX39 4AE
☎ 01237 472005 🖹 01237 478957
e-mail: info@royalbideford.co.uk
Dir: *at eastern end of Bideford Bridge*
Attractive and well equipped bedrooms are offered at this late 16th-century hotel, conveniently situated near the town centre and the quay. Freshly prepared meals are served in the spacious restaurant, while in the bar, a range of lighter meals is available. The wood panelled Kingsley suite is ideal for functions or meetings. Service is friendly and attentive.
ROOMS: 31 en suite (3 fmly) s £49-£59; d £50-£70 * LB **FACILITIES:** STV entertainment Xmas **CONF:** Thtr 100 Class 100 Board 100 **SERVICES:** Lift **PARKING:** 70 **NOTES:** Civ Wed 100 **CARDS:**

★★75% ❀ **Yeoldon Country House**

THE CIRCLE
Selected Individual Hotels
GREAT BRITAIN

Durrant Ln, Northam EX39 2RL
☎ 01237 474400 🖹 01237 476618
e-mail: yeoldonhouse@aol.com
Dir: *from Barnstaple follow A39 over River Torridge Bridge, at rdbt turn right onto A386 towards Northam then 3rd right into Durrant Ln*
A Victorian country house hotel in a peaceful location, overlooking the River Torridge. Individually decorated bedrooms are well equipped with modern facilities. In the attractive dining room imaginative menus are offered, featuring fresh local produce. In addition to the comfortable lounge bar, there is also a cosy lounge.

continued

ROOMS: 10 en suite No smoking in all bedrooms s £50-£55; d £80-£90 (incl. bkfst) * LB **PARKING:** 15 **NOTES:** No smoking in restaurant Closed 24-26 Dec **CARDS:**

BIGBURY-ON-SEA, Devon Map 03 SX64

★★67% Henley
TQ7 4AR
☎ 01548 810240 📠 01548 810240
Dir: *through Bigbury village, pass Golf Centre into Bigbury-on-Sea. Hotel on left as road slopes towards the shore*

Overlooking Bigbury Bay, this family-run holiday hotel provides comfortable accommodation with modern facilities and friendly service. A sandy beach can be reached by a private cliff path descending through the hotel's pretty gardens. The menu offers dishes cooked with care and imagination.

ROOMS: 7 en suite (1 fmly) No smoking in all bedrooms s £35-£50; d £69-£80 (incl. bkfst) * LB **FACILITIES:** STV **PARKING:** 9 **NOTES:** No smoking in restaurant Closed Dec-Feb **CARDS:**

BIGGLESWADE, Bedfordshire Map 04 TL14

★★66% Stratton House Hotel
London Rd SG18 8ED
☎ 01767 312442 📠 01767 600416
e-mail: reception@strattonhouse.demon.co.uk
Dir: *Nthbound; A1 1st turning to Biggleswade, hotel before town centre. Sthbound; A1 leave at Sainsburys rdbt through town on right opposite Red Lion PH*

Ideally situated just a few minutes from the A1, this small hotel offers comfortable accommodation. Bedrooms are well presented and public areas include a cosy lounge, with a fire and a popular bar.

ROOMS: 31 en suite (1 fmly) No smoking in 6 bedrooms s fr £58; d fr £68 (incl. bkfst) * LB **CONF:** Thtr 50 Class 30 Board 28 Del from £85 * **PARKING:** 40 **CARDS:**

BILBROUGH, North Yorkshire Map 08 SE54

Travelodge
Tadcaster LS24 8EG
☎ 01937 531823 📠 01937 531823
Dir: *A64 eastbound*

This modern building offers accommodation in smart, spacious and well equipped bedrooms, all with en suite bathrooms. Refreshments may be taken at the nearby family restaurant. For further details and the Travelodge phone number, consult the Hotel Groups page.

ROOMS: 62 en suite

BILLINGHAM See Stockton-on-Tees

BILLINGSHURST, West Sussex
Map 04 TQ02

★★62% *Newstead Hall Hotel*
THE CIRCLE Selected Individual Hotels GREAT BRITAIN

Adversane RH14 9JH
☎ 01403 783196 📠 01403 784228
This Tudor-style hotel is situated just a couple of miles south of Billingshurst. Five bedrooms are in the older part of the building, while the remainder are located in an extension. Public rooms include a comfortable bar with open fireplace and a popular restaurant.
ROOMS: 15 en suite **PARKING:** 60

BILSBORROW, Lancashire
Map 07 SD53

○ *Premier Lodge (Preston North)*
PREMIER LODGE THE BEST. REST ASSURED.

Garstang Rd PR3 0RN
☎ 0870 700 1516 📠 0870 700 1517

BINFIELD, Berkshire
Map 04 SU87

⌂ *Travelodge*
Travelodge

London Rd RG42 4AA
☎ 01344 485940
Dir: *exit junct 10 on M4(Bracknell) take 1st exit towards Binfield*
This modern building offers accommodation in smart, spacious and well equipped bedrooms, all with en suite bathrooms. Refreshments may be taken at the nearby family restaurant. For further details and the Travelodge phone number, consult the Hotel Groups page.
ROOMS: 35 en suite

BIRCH MOTORWAY SERVICE AREA (M62), Greater Manchester
Map 07 SD80

⌂ *Travelodge (East)*
Travelodge

M62 Service Area East Bound OL10 2HQ
☎ Central Res 0800 850950 📠 01525 878450
This modern building offers accommodation in smart, spacious and well equipped bedrooms, all with en suite bathrooms. Refreshments may be taken at the nearby family restaurant. For further details and the Travelodge phone number, consult the Hotel Groups page.
ROOMS: 55 en suite

⌂ *Travelodge (West)*
Travelodge

M62 Service Area West Bound OL10 2HQ
This modern building offers accommodation in smart, spacious and well equipped bedrooms, all with en suite bathrooms. Refreshments may be taken at the nearby family restaurant. For further details and the Travelodge phone number, consult the Hotel Groups page.
ROOMS: 35 en suite

BIRKENHEAD, Merseyside
Map 07 SJ38

★★★69% Bowler Hat
corus

2 Talbot Rd, Prenton CH43 2HH
☎ 0151 652 4931 📠 0151 653 8127
Dir: *1m from junct 3 of M53*
This friendly hotel is situated in a quiet, leafy area on the edge of town. Extensive function facilities are provided and the hotel is popular for wedding receptions. Bedrooms are well equipped with modern facilities. There is a popular restaurant and a selection of lighter meals are available in the bar.

ROOMS: 32 en suite No smoking in 18 bedrooms **FACILITIES:** STV **CONF:** Thtr 150 Class 80 Board 40 Del £100 * **PARKING:** 85 **NOTES:** No smoking in restaurant Civ Wed 90
CARDS:

★★★67% Riverhill
MINOTEL Great Britain

Talbot Rd, Prenton CH43 2HJ
☎ 0151 653 3773 📠 0151 653 7162
e-mail: riverhill@tinyonline.co.uk
Dir: *1m from M53 junct 3, along the A552 turn left onto B5151 at traffic lights hotel 0.5m on right*
Pretty lawns and gardens provide the setting for this friendly hotel, conveniently situated about a mile from the M53. Attractively furnished, well equipped bedrooms include ground floor, family, and four-poster rooms. Business meetings and weddings can be catered for. A wide choice of dishes is available in the restaurant, overlooking the garden.
ROOMS: 14 en suite (1 fmly) d £54.50 * LB **FACILITIES:** Free use of local leisure facilities **PARKING:** 30 **NOTES:** No dogs (ex guide dogs)
CARDS:

⌂ Premier Lodge (Wirral)
PREMIER LODGE THE BEST. REST ASSURED.

1 Greasby Rd L49 2PP
☎ 0870 700 1582 📠 0870 700 1583
Premier Lodge offers modern, well equipped, en suite accommodation suitable for both business and leisure travellers. Meals can be taken at the adjacent popular restaurant and bar which is fully licensed. For further details, consult the Hotel Groups page.
ROOMS: 30 en suite d £42 *

BIRMINGHAM, West Midlands
Map 07 SP08

see also Bromsgrove, Lea Marston, Oldbury & Sutton Coldfield

★★★★★72% ❀❀❀ Birmingham Marriott
Marriott HOTELS·RESORTS·SUITES

12 Hagley Rd, Five Ways B16 8SJ
☎ 0121 452 1144 📠 0121 456 3442
On the edge of the city centre stands the Birmingham Marriot, a listed building and a hotel of real character and quality. The two restaurants, Langtry's and for fine dining the Sir Edward Elgar, are at the hub of the hotel. The bedrooms and public areas are stylishly furnished. Staff are professional and friendly.

continued

ROOMS: 98 en suite No smoking in 54 bedrooms s fr £170; d fr £195 * LB **FACILITIES:** STV Indoor swimming (H) Solarium Gym Jacuzzi/spa Hair & beauty salon Steam room entertainment Xmas **CONF:** Thtr 25 Board 20 Del from £160 * **SERVICES:** Lift air con **PARKING:** 70 **CARDS:**

★★★★69% The Burlington
Burlington Arcade, 126 New St B2 4JQ
☎ 0121 643 9191 📠 0121 628 5005
e-mail: mail@burlingtonhotel.com
Dir: *exit M6 junct 6 and follow signs for City Centre, then onto A38*

The Burlington's original Victorian design, much of it still in evidence, has been blended together with modern facilities. Bedrooms are furnished and equipped to a good standard. Carefully prepared meals are served in the Berlioz Restaurant.
ROOMS: 112 en suite (6 fmly) No smoking in 49 bedrooms s £40-£135; d £80-£157 * LB **FACILITIES:** STV Sauna Solarium Gym Jacuzzi/spa Xmas **CONF:** Thtr 400 Class 175 Board 60 Del from £125 * **SERVICES:** Lift **CARDS:**

★★★★68% Crowne Plaza Birmingham
Central Square B1 1HH
☎ 0121 631 2000 📠 0121 643 9018
Dir: *from A38, follow City Centre signs, go over flyover & through 2 tunnels. After 2nd tunnel-Suffolk Queensway-join left slip road*
Located in the city centre, this smart hotel offers spacious, very well equipped bedrooms with air-conditioning. Additional facilities include a good range of conference and meeting rooms and a leisure club. Service is professional and efficient.
ROOMS: 284 en suite (188 fmly) No smoking in 159 bedrooms s £109-£136; d £119-£146 * LB **FACILITIES:** STV Indoor swimming (H) Sauna Solarium Gym Jacuzzi/spa Children's pool, steam room. Xmas **CONF:** Thtr 150 Class 75 Board 50 Del from £135 * **SERVICES:** Lift air con **CARDS:**

Arriving late? Four and five star hotels have night porters to assist with your luggage; and 24hr room service.

★★★★65% Copthorne Birmingham

Paradise Circus B3 3HJ
☎ 0121 200 2727 📠 0121 200 1197

Dir: *follow signs to 'International Convention Centre, then bear right for hotel entrance*
Situated in the heart of Birmingham, this hotel offers spacious bedrooms with attractive colour schemes and excellent facilities. Guests can enjoy a variety of food and drinks in a choice of bars and restaurants, catering for all tastes. Additional features include a wide range of function rooms, a business centre, and a leisure complex.
ROOMS: 212 en suite No smoking in 108 bedrooms s £140-£160; d £160-£180 * LB **FACILITIES:** STV Indoor swimming (H) Sauna Gym Jacuzzi/spa **CONF:** Thtr 180 Class 120 Board 30 Del from £140 * **SERVICES:** Lift **PARKING:** 88 **NOTES:** No dogs (ex guide dogs) **CARDS:**

★★★71% The Westley
80-90 Westley Rd, Acocks Green B27 7UJ
☎ 0121 706 4312 📠 0121 706 2824
e-mail: reservations@westeyhotel.co.uk
Dir: *take A41 signed Birmingham on Solihull By-Pass and continue to Acocks Green. At roundabout take second exit B4146 Westley Rd, hotel 200 yds on left*
The Westley is a long established hotel, set in the city suburbs, conveniently located for the N.E.C and airport. The atmosphere is friendly and relaxed. Bedrooms are well equipped and smartly presented. In addition to the main restaurant, there is also a lively bar and brasserie.
ROOMS: 27 en suite 9 annexe en suite (1 fmly) s fr £73; d £83-£95 * LB **FACILITIES:** STV **CONF:** Thtr 200 Class 80 Board 50 Del from £75 * **PARKING:** 150 **NOTES:** Civ Wed 70
CARDS:

B

BIRMINGHAM, continued

★★★67% *Posthouse Birmingham Great Barr*

Posthouse

Chapel Ln, Great Barr B43 7BG
☎ 0870 400 9009 🖷 0121 357 7503
Dir: *take Jct7 M6. Turn onto A34 signposted Walsall. Hotel located 200yds on the right hand side across the carriage-way in Chapel Lane*
Situated in pleasant surroundings, this modern hotel offers well equipped and comfortable bedrooms. In addition to the popular restaurant there is an all-day lounge menu and 24-hour room service. There is also a courtyard patio and garden.
ROOMS: 192 en suite (36 fmly) No smoking in 108 bedrooms **FACILITIES:** Indoor swimming (H) Sauna Solarium Gym Pool table Jacuzzi/spa Aerobics studio Beauty treatments **CONF:** Thtr 120 Class 70 Board 50 **PARKING:** 400 **CARDS:**

★★★65% Novotel

NOVOTEL

70 Broad St B1 2HT
☎ 0121 643 2000 🖷 0121 643 9796
e-mail: h1077@accor-hotels.com
Dir: *2mins from the International Conference Centre*

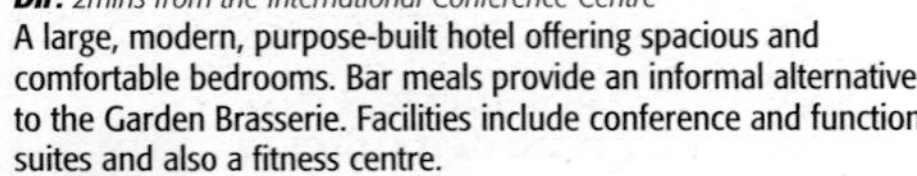

A large, modern, purpose-built hotel offering spacious and comfortable bedrooms. Bar meals provide an informal alternative to the Garden Brasserie. Facilities include conference and function suites and also a fitness centre.
ROOMS: 148 en suite (148 fmly) No smoking in 98 bedrooms d £90-£120 * LB **FACILITIES:** STV Sauna Gym Jacuzzi/spa **CONF:** Thtr 300 Class 120 Board 90 Del from £95 * **SERVICES:** Lift air con **PARKING:** 50 **CARDS:**

★★★65% Westmead

corus

Redditch Rd, Hopwood B48 7AL
☎ 0121 445 1202 🖷 0121 445 6163
Dir: *M42 junct 2 head towards Birmingham on A441 upto rdbt and turn right, follow A441 for 1m and hotel is on right hand side*
This hotel, set in a rural location on the edge of the city, has easy access to the motorway network. All bedrooms are attractive, spacious and well equipped. In addition to the Colonial restaurant, snacks are served in the Hopwood bar and a carvery is available at weekends. There are also meeting rooms and function suites.
ROOMS: 58 en suite (2 fmly) No smoking in 28 bedrooms s £95; d £105 * LB **FACILITIES:** STV Sauna Solarium **CONF:** Thtr 300 Class 120 Board 80 Del from £120 * **PARKING:** 155 **NOTES:** No dogs (ex guide dogs) No smoking in restaurant Civ Wed 120
CARDS:

★★★64% Plough & Harrow

REGAL

135 Hagley Rd B16 8LS
☎ 0121 454 4111 🖷 0121 454 1868
e-mail: reservations@plough.co.uk
Dir: *along A456 (Hagley Rd), hotel on right after 5 ways rdbt*

continued

A well established hotel, approximately a mile west of the city centre, with a relaxed and friendly atmosphere. Bedrooms come in a variety of styles and sizes. The restaurant serves a good selection of dishes.
ROOMS: 44 en suite No smoking in 11 bedrooms s fr £105; d fr £115 * LB **FACILITIES:** Xmas **CONF:** Thtr 100 Class 60 Board 50 Del from £90 * **SERVICES:** Lift **PARKING:** 80 **NOTES:** No smoking in restaurant
CARDS:

★★★64% Portland

313 Hagley Rd B16 9LQ
☎ 0121 455 0535 🖷 0121 456 1841
e-mail: sales@portland-hotel.demon.co.uk
Dir: *2m from city centre on A456*
A large, purpose-built, privately-owned hotel just west of the city centre. It provides well equipped, modern accommodation including some ground floor rooms. There is an attractive restaurant, a pleasant lounge bar and a choice of function suites and meeting rooms.
ROOMS: 63 en suite No smoking in 7 bedrooms s £53-£65; d £65-£80 (incl. bkfst) * LB **FACILITIES:** STV **CONF:** Thtr 80 Class 40 Board 40 Del from £79.95 * **SERVICES:** Lift **PARKING:** 80 **NOTES:** No dogs (ex guide dogs) **CARDS:**

★★★64% *Posthouse Birmingham City*

Posthouse

Smallbrook Queensway B5 4EW
☎ 0870 400 9008 🖷 0121 631 2528
e-mail: gm1841@forte-hotels.com
Dir: *from M6 junct 6 follow signs on A38 for 'City Centre' through two tunnels. Take second slip road off, then 1st left to hotel in 100yds*
A large, modern hotel in the city centre. Bedrooms are comfortable and well designed. Facilities include extensive meeting rooms, a business centre and a leisure club. There is a lounge bar with a terrace and an all-day menu. 24-hour room service is also available.
ROOMS: 251 en suite No smoking in 174 bedrooms **FACILITIES:** STV Indoor swimming (H) Squash Sauna Solarium Gym Pool table Health & fitness club Beauty treatment **CONF:** Thtr 630 Class 380 Board 50 **SERVICES:** Lift air con **CARDS:**

★★★62% Quality Inn & Suites

257/267 Hagley Rd, Edgbaston B16 9NA
☎ 0121 454 8071 🖷 0121 455 6149
e-mail: admin@gb606.u-net.com
Dir: *M6-A38 onto ringroad towards Kidderminster, after 4m right at rdbt, hotel on right*
Close to the city centre, this large hotel is particularly popular with business travellers. Bedrooms vary in size and style. Guests have the benefit of using the leisure facilities at a nearby sister hotel.
ROOMS: 166 en suite No smoking in 40 bedrooms s fr £71; d fr £96 * LB **FACILITIES:** STV entertainment **CONF:** Thtr 100 Class 40 Board 30 Del from £60 * **SERVICES:** Lift **PARKING:** 120 **NOTES:** No smoking in restaurant **CARDS:**

★★★61% Great Barr Hotel & Conference Centre

Pear Tree Dr, Newton Rd, Great Barr B43 6HS
☎ 0121 357 1141 🖷 0121 357 7557
e-mail: sales@thegreatbarrhotel.co.uk
Dir: *1m W of junc A34/A4041*
This busy hotel, situated in a residential area just off the A4041, is particularly popular with conference delegates and business people. Bedrooms are well equipped and modern in style.
ROOMS: 105 en suite (1 fmly) s fr £69; d £85-£111 * LB **FACILITIES:** STV Xmas **CONF:** Thtr 120 Class 50 Board 50 Del from £105 * **PARKING:** 175 **NOTES:** No dogs (ex guide dogs) RS BH (restaurant may be closed) **CARDS:**

★★70% **Copperfield House**
60 Upland Rd, Selly Park B29 7JS
☎ 0121 472 8344 Fax 0121 415 5655
e-mail: info@copperfieldhousehotel.fsnet.co.uk
Dir: *exit M6 at junct 6, take A38 through city centre, at second set of traffic lights turn left, at next traffic lights turn right (A441), third right*
Copperfield House is a delightful Victorian house, built in 1868. Situated within easy reach of the centre of Birmingham and close to the BBC's Pebble Mill Studios. The hotel provides smartly presented and well equipped accommodation.
ROOMS: 17 en suite (1 fmly) s £58-£68; d £69-£79 (incl. bkfst) * LB **PARKING:** 11 **NOTES:** No dogs (ex guide dogs) No smoking in restaurant **CARDS:**

★★70% **Norwood**
87-89 Bunbury Rd, Northfield B31 2ET
☎ 0121 411 2202 Fax 0121 411 2202
Dir: *turn left on A38 at Grosvenor shopping centre, 5m S of city centre*
This comfortable, tastefully appointed hotel provides well equipped, modern accommodation. Pleasant public rooms include a conservatory. Carefully prepared home-cooking is served in the attractive dining room and the service is both friendly and attentive.
ROOMS: 18 en suite s £62.50-£77.50; d £67.50-£82.50 (incl. bkfst) * LB **FACILITIES:** STV **CONF:** Thtr 40 Class 24 Board 20 **PARKING:** 11 **NOTES:** Closed 23-26 Dec RS 27-31 Dec
CARDS:

★★68% **Oxford Hotel**
21 Oxford Rd B13 9EH
Best Western
☎ 0121 449 3298 Fax 0121 442 4212
e-mail: oxford@bestwestern.co.uk
Dir: *3m S of Birmingham A435, on entering Moseley village turn R at traffic lights, then R again at Ford Garage. Hotel is situated 50yds on the L.*
Situated three miles south of Birmingham, this privately-owned hotel offers a comfortable and relaxed atmosphere. Bedrooms are spacious, attractively decorated and well equipped. Additional features include a dining room, a cosy lounge and a bar. Meeting rooms are also available.
ROOMS: 15 en suite 9 annexe en suite (5 fmly) No smoking in 7 bedrooms s £60-£76; d £70-£86 (incl. bkfst) * LB **FACILITIES:** STV Snooker Pool table **CONF:** Thtr 70 Class 70 Board 40 Del from £99.95 * **SERVICES:** air con **PARKING:** 60 **NOTES:** No smoking in restaurant RS Bank holidays **CARDS:**

★★66% ***Westbourne Lodge***
27/29 Fountain Rd, Edgbaston B17 8NJ
☎ 0121 429 1003 Fax 0121 429 7436
e-mail: westbourne@lodgehotel.co.uk
Dir: *off A456, 3m from junct 3 of the M5, 1.25 m from city*
This friendly, privately-run hotel, located just two miles west of the city centre, is within easy reach of the motorway. Bedrooms are well equipped and comfortable. Other facilities include a cosy lounge, a small bar and a pleasant dining room overlooking the terrace and garden.
ROOMS: 22 en suite (5 fmly) No smoking in all bedrooms **FACILITIES:** Private garden and Patio Area **PARKING:** 22 **NOTES:** No smoking in restaurant **CARDS:**

★★65% **Heath Lodge**
117 Coleshill Rd, Marston Green B37 7HT
☎ 0121 779 2218 Fax 0121 779 2218
e-mail: reception@heathlodgehotel.freeserve.co.uk
Dir: *join A446 from M6 J4 travelling nothwards to Coleshill, after 0.5m turn left into Coleshill Heath Rd, signposted to Marston Green. Hotel on right*
This privately-owned and personally-run hotel is within easy reach of the the N.E.C, Birmingham Airport and the M6 and M42

motorways. The modern bedrooms are well equipped and comfortable. Day rooms consist of a small bar, a lounge and a dining room overlooking the garden.
ROOMS: 17 rms (16 en suite) (1 fmly) s £45-£49; d £59-£64 (incl. bkfst) * **CONF:** Thtr 36 Class 30 Del from £79 * **PARKING:** 22 **NOTES:** No smoking in restaurant **CARDS:**

★★65% **Hotel Clarine**
229 Hagley Rd, Edgbaston B16 9RP
☎ 0121 454 6514 Fax 0121 456 2722
Dir: *on A456*
This extended Regency property stands on the A456, one and a half miles west of the city centre. It provides modernly furnished, well equipped accommodation, including some bedrooms on the ground floor. A good variety of dishes is served in the pleasant brasserie style restaurant. There is also a bright, attractive bar, a conference/meeting room and a lounge.
ROOMS: 27 en suite (2 fmly) No smoking in 18 bedrooms s £35-£45; d £48-£58 (incl. bkfst) * LB **FACILITIES:** Xmas **CONF:** Thtr 20 Class 12 Board 12 Del from £65 * **PARKING:** 28 **NOTES:** No dogs (ex guide dogs) No smoking in restaurant **CARDS:**

★★64% **Astoria**
311 Hagley Rd B16 9LQ
☎ 0121 454 0795 Fax 0121 456 3537
e-mail: anne@astoriahotel.uk.com
Dir: *on A456 2m from city centre*
This Victorian property stands between the city centre and the M5 motorway. Personally run, it provides modern accommodation which includes some family and ground floor rooms. There is a
continued

BIRMINGHAM, continued

choice of lounges and a homely bar. The traditionally furnished dining room serves a selection of grill-type dishes.
ROOMS: 26 en suite (6 fmly) No smoking in 2 bedrooms s fr £40; d £50-£55 (incl. bkfst) * **FACILITIES:** STV **PARKING:** 27 **NOTES:** No dogs (ex guide dogs) No smoking in restaurant
CARDS:

★★64% Fountain Court
339-343 Fountain Court Hotel B17 8NH
☎ 0121 429 1754 📠 0121 429 1209
e-mail: fountain-court@excite.co.uk
Dir: *on A456, towards Birmingham*
This family-owned hotel is on the A456, near to the M5 and Birmingham. Bedrooms include a family suite and some rooms on the ground floor. There is a brightly decorated dining room, a choice of sitting areas and a bar.
ROOMS: 23 en suite (4 fmly) s £39.50-£48.50; d £60-£65 (incl. bkfst) * **PARKING:** 20 **CARDS:**

★★63% Sheriden House
82 Handsworth Wood Rd, Handsworth Wood B20 2PL
☎ 0121 554 2185 & 0121 523 5960 📠 0121 551 4761
e-mail: g.f.harmon@btinternet.com
Dir: *at junct 7 of M6 turn onto A34, through traffic lights at A4041 next right filter onto B4124, straight through to hotel approx 1.5m on left*
This privately owned and personally-run hotel provides well equipped accommodation. Facilities include a pleasant bar, a cosy lounge and a restaurant.
ROOMS: 11 en suite No smoking in 3 bedrooms s £39-£48; d £56 (incl. bkfst) * LB **CONF:** Thtr 40 Class 25 Board 20 Del from £45.95 * **PARKING:** 30 **NOTES:** No dogs (ex guide dogs) No smoking in restaurant **CARDS:**

See advert on opposite page

★★62% *Edgbaston Palace*
198 Hagley Rd B16 9PQ
☎ 0121 452 1577 📠 0121 452 1577
This fine Georgian property provides a variety of well equipped, modern bedrooms, including some family and ground floor rooms. In addition to the cosy dining room, spacious breakfast room and bar, there is also a separate TV lounge and conference room. A shuttle service to the city centre and the airport is available for guests.
ROOMS: 30 rms (29 en suite) (4 fmly) **FACILITIES:** STV **CONF:** Thtr 150 Class 50 Board 50 **PARKING:** 53 **NOTES:** Closed 24-30 Dec
CARDS:

⇧ Hotel Ibis
55 Irving St B1 1DH
☎ 0121 622 4925 📠 0121 622 4195
Dir: *150yds from Dome Night Club, just off Bristol Street*
Modern, budget hotel offering comfortable accommodation in bright and practical bedrooms. Breakfast is self-service and dinner is available in the restaurant. For further details, consult the Hotel Groups page.
ROOMS: 51 en suite s £42-£52; d £42-£52 * **CONF:** Thtr 35 Class 18 Board 20

Fancy a Singapore Sling? Bar staff in five star hotels should be skilled cocktail mixers.

⇧ Campanile

Aston Locks, Chester St B6 4BE
☎ 0121 359 3330 📠 0121 359 1223
Dir: *next to rdbt at junct of A4540/A38*

This modern building offers accommodation in smart well equipped bedrooms, all with en suite bathrooms. Refreshments may be taken at the informal Bistro. For further details and the Campanile phone number, consult the Hotel Groups page.
ROOMS: 111 en suite **CONF:** Thtr 245 Class 105 Board 122

⇧ Express by Holiday Inn Birmingham North

Birmingham Rd, Great Barr B43 7AG
☎ 0121 3584044 📠 0121 358 4644
Dir: *M6 junct7 onto A34 towards Walsall*

A modern budget hotel offering comfortable accommodation in refreshing, spacious and comprehensively-equipped bedrooms, en suite bathrooms with power showers and continental buffet breakfast included in the room rate. Suitable for business travellers or families. For further details and the Express by Holiday Inn phone number, consult the Hotel Groups page.
ROOMS: 32 en suite (incl. cont bkfst) d £49.95 * **CONF:** Thtr 25 Class 20 Board 16

⇧ Express by Holiday Inn Castle Bromwich
Express by Holiday Inn
1200 Chester Rd, Castle Bromwich B35 7AF
☎ 0121 747 6633 📠 747 6644
Dir: *travelling N, off at jct5. Follow Fort Shopping Park signs. Travelling S, off at jct6. Take A38 for Tyburn, right into Chester Rd, follow Park signs*
A modern budget hotel offering comfortable accommodation in refreshing, spacious and comprehensively-equipped bedrooms, en suite bathrooms with power showers and continental buffet breakfast included in the room rate. Suitable for business

continued

travellers or families. For further details and the Express by Holiday Inn phone number, consult the Hotel Groups page.
ROOMS: 98 en suite (incl. cont bkfst) d £52.75-£55 * **CONF:** Thtr 25 Class 10 Board 15 Del from £110 *

Hotel Ibis Birmingham Bordesley

1 Bordesley Park Rd, Bordesley B10 0PD
☎ 0121 506 2600 📠 0121 506 2610
Modern, budget hotel offering comfortable accommodation in bright and practical bedrooms. Breakfast is self-service and dinner is available in the restaurant. For further details, consult the Hotel Groups page.
ROOMS: 87 en suite

Premier Lodge (Birmingham City Centre)

PREMIER LODGE
THE BEST. REST ASSURED.

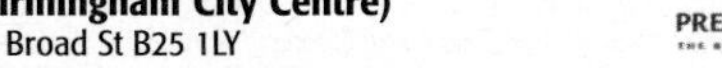

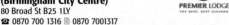

80 Broad St B25 1LY
☎ 0870 700 1316 📠 0870 7001317
Premier Lodge offers modern, well equipped, en suite accommodation suitable for both business and leisure travellers. Meals can be taken at the adjacent popular restaurant and bar which is fully licensed. For further details, consult the Hotel Groups page.
ROOMS: 60 en suite d £46 *

Premier Lodge (Birmingham South)

PREMIER LODGE
THE BEST. REST ASSURED.

Birmingham Great Park, Bristol Rd South, Ruberry B45 9PA
☎ 0870 700 1324 📠 0870 700 1325
Premier Lodge offers modern, well equipped, en suite accommodation suitable for both business and leisure travellers. Meals can be taken at the adjacent popular restaurant and bar which is fully licensed. For further details, consult the Hotel Groups page.
ROOMS: 62 en suite d £46 *

Travelodge (Birmingham Central)

230 Broad St B15 1AY
☎ 0121 644 5266
This modern building offers accommodation in smart, spacious and well equipped bedrooms, all with en suite bathrooms. Refreshments may be taken at the nearby family restaurant. For further details and the Travelodge phone number, consult the Hotel Groups page.
ROOMS: 136 en suite

Travelodge (Birmingham East)

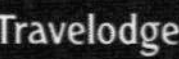

A45 Coventry Rd, Acocks Green B26 1DS
☎ 0800 850950
This modern building offers accommodation in smart, spacious and well equipped bedrooms, all with en suite bathrooms. Refreshments may be taken at the nearby family restaurant. For further details and the Travelodge phone number, consult the Hotel Groups page.
ROOMS: 40 en suite

Hotel Ibis

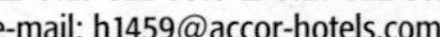

Arcadian Centre, Ladywell Walk B5 4ST
☎ 0121 622 6010 📠 0121 622 6020
e-mail: h1459@accor-hotels.com

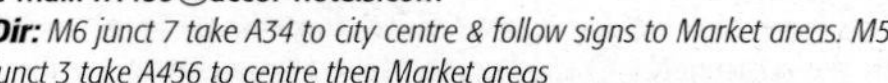

Dir: *M6 junct 7 take A34 to city centre & follow signs to Market areas. M5 junct 3 take A456 to centre then Market areas*
Modern, budget hotel offering comfortable accommodation in bright and practical bedrooms. Breakfast is self-service and dinner is available in the restaurant. For further details, consult the Hotel Groups page.
ROOMS: 159 en suite **CONF:** Thtr 100 Class 60 Board 40

BIRMINGHAM AIRPORT, West Midlands — Map 07 SP18

★★★65% *Posthouse Birmingham Airport*

Posthouse

Coventry Rd B26 3QW
☎ 0870 400 9007 📠 0121 782 2476
Dir: *from junct 6 of M42 take A45 towards Birmingham for 1.5m*
Conveniently located for the airport and the N.E.C, this hotel offers well equipped bedrooms, including all modern comforts. Guests can dine in the Junction restaurant. Conference and meeting facilities are also available.
ROOMS: 141 en suite (3 fmly) No smoking in 84 bedrooms **CONF:** Thtr 130 Class 100 Board 70 **PARKING:** 250
CARDS:

> Packed in a hurry? Ironing facilities should be available at all star levels, either in rooms or on request.

BIRMINGHAM AIRPORT, continued

★★★64% Novotel
B26 3QL
☎ 0121 782 7000 🖷 0121 782 0445
e-mail: H1158@accor-hotels.com
***Dir:** junct 6 M42, A45 direction Birmingham, follow signs to airport, hotel opp. main terminal*
This modern hotel is opposite the main passenger terminal and is linked with the monorail to Birmingham International station and the N.E.C. Food service is flexible and extensive - meals are available from early morning until midnight.
ROOMS: 195 en suite (20 fmly) No smoking in 130 bedrooms d £99-£110 * **FACILITIES:** STV Pool table **CONF:** Thtr 35 Class 20 Board 22 Del from £125 * **SERVICES:** Lift air con
CARDS:

BIRMINGHAM (NATIONAL EXHIBITION CENTRE), West Midlands Map 07 SP18
see also Sutton Coldfield

★★★★67% Nailcote Hall
Nailcote Ln, Berkswell CV7 7DE
☎ 024 7646 6174 🖷 024 7647 0720
e-mail: info@nailcotehall.co.uk
(For full entry see Balsall Common)

★★★64% Sutton Court
60-66 Lichfield Rd B74 2NA
☎ 0121 354 4991 🖷 0121 355 0083
e-mail: reservations@sutton-court-hotel.co.uk
(For full entry see Sutton Coldfield)

★★★63% *Arden Hotel & Leisure Club*
Coventry Rd, Bickenhill B92 0EH
☎ 01675 443221 🖷 01675 443221
***Dir:** from junc 6 of M42 take A45 towards Birmingham, hotel 0.25m on right hand side, just off B'ham Airport Island*
This successful, family-run hotel thrives from the business created by the adjacent N.E.C. The bedrooms are all modern and well equipped. Facilities here include a coffee shop, a formal restaurant and terraced water gardens.
ROOMS: 146 en suite (6 fmly) **FACILITIES:** STV Indoor swimming (H) Snooker Sauna Solarium Gym Jacuzzi/spa entertainment **CONF:** Thtr 220 Class 60 Board 40 **SERVICES:** Lift **PARKING:** 300
CARDS:

See advert under SOLIHULL

★★75% Haigs
Kenilworth Rd CV7 7EL
☎ 01676 533004 🖷 01676 535132
(For full entry see Balsall Common)

⇧ Express by Holiday Inn
Bickenhill Parkway B40 1QA
☎ 0121 782 3222 🖷 780 4224
e-mail: sales_nec@ingramhotels.co.uk
***Dir:** follow signs for National Exhibition Centre (NEC) from junct6 of M42*
A modern budget hotel offering comfortable accommodation in refreshing, spacious and comprehensively-equipped bedrooms, en suite bathrooms with power showers and continental buffet breakfast included in the room rate. Suitable for business

travellers or families. For further details and the Express by Holiday Inn phone number, consult the Hotel Groups page.
ROOMS: 179 en suite (incl. cont bkfst) d £69.95 * **CONF:** Thtr 100 Del £99 *

○ *Premier Lodge (NEC/Airport)*
Northway, National Exhibition Centre
☎ 0870 700 1328 🖷 0870 700 1329

BISHOP'S STORTFORD, Hertfordshire Map 05 TL42

★★★★67% *Down Hall Country House*
Hatfield Heath CM22 7AS
☎ 01279 731441 🖷 01279 730416
e-mail: reservations@downhall.demon.co.uk
***Dir:** follow A1060, at Hatfield Heath keep left, turn right into lane opposite Hunters Meet restaurant & left at the end following signpost*
This country house hotel, an impressive Victorian mansion set in 100 acres of grounds, is within easy reach of the M11 and Stansted Airport. Bedrooms, varying in size, are situated either in the main building or newer wing. All are nicely decorated and comfortable. The Downham and Lambourne restaurants offer a choice of dining, alternatively snacks are available in the bar or lounge.
ROOMS: 103 en suite **FACILITIES:** STV Indoor swimming (H) Tennis (hard) Snooker Sauna Gym Croquet lawn Putting green Jacuzzi/spa Petanque Giant chess Whirlpool **CONF:** Thtr 290 Class 154 Board 84 **SERVICES:** Lift **PARKING:** 150 **NOTES:** No smoking in restaurant
CARDS:

BLACKBURN, Lancashire Map 07 SD62
see also Langho

★★★★64% Clarion Hotel & Suites Foxfields
Whalley Rd, Billington BB7 9HY
☎ 01254 822556 🖷 01254 824613
e-mail: admin@gb065.u-net.com
***Dir:** turn off A59 at signpost for Billington/Whalley & hotel after 0.5m on right*
A modern hotel with particularly good bedrooms, including many with separate sitting and dressing rooms, situated in a rural location just off the A59. Expressions Restaurant and cocktail bar offers mainly English dishes, cooked in a modern style. There is also a smart Leisure Club.
ROOMS: 44 en suite (27 fmly) No smoking in 20 bedrooms s £45-£97; d £70-£117 * LB **FACILITIES:** STV Indoor swimming (H) Sauna Gym Steam room entertainment Xmas **CONF:** Thtr 180 Class 60 Board 60 Del from £90 * **PARKING:** 170 **NOTES:** No dogs (ex guide dogs) No smoking in restaurant Civ Wed 200
CARDS:

★★★ 63% County Hotel Blackburn

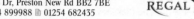

Yew Tree Dr, Preston New Rd BB2 7BE
☎ 01254 899988 📠 01254 682435
Dir: *on A667/A6119 junct W of town*

This hotel offers well appointed bedrooms and bright and modern public areas. Meeting, conference and banqueting facilities are also available. Service is friendly and willing.

ROOMS: 101 en suite (1 fmly) No smoking in 70 bedrooms s £85; d £95 * LB **FACILITIES:** Pool table Xmas **CONF:** Thtr 350 Class 150 Board 100 Del from £65 * **SERVICES:** Lift **PARKING:** 200
CARDS:

★★ 76% Millstone

Church Ln, Mellor BB2 7JR
☎ 01254 813333 📠 01254 812628
e-mail: millstone@shireinns.co.uk
Dir: *3m NW off A59*

This inviting stone-built former coaching inn provides a very high standard of accommodation, professional and friendly service and food of a good quality. Bedrooms, some in an adjacent house, have been tastefully furnished. All are very well equipped. Rooms on the ground floor and a room for disabled guests are also available. There is a choice of charming bars.

ROOMS: 18 en suite 6 annexe en suite (1 fmly) No smoking in 4 bedrooms s fr £88 (incl. bkfst) * LB **FACILITIES:** STV Xmas **CONF:** Thtr 25 Class 15 Board 16 Del from £75 * **PARKING:** 40 **NOTES:** No smoking in restaurant **CARDS:**

⌂ Premier Lodge

Myerscough Rd, Balderstone BB2 7LE
☎ 0870 700 1330 📠 0870 7001331

Premier Lodge offers modern, well equipped, en suite accommodation suitable for both business and leisure travellers. Meals can be taken at the adjacent popular restaurant and bar which is fully licensed. For further details, consult the Hotel Groups page.

ROOMS: 20 en suite d £46 *

BLACKPOOL, Lancashire — Map 07 SD33

★★★★ 64% De Vere

East Park Dr FY3 8LL
☎ 01253 838866 📠 01253 798800
Dir: *M6 junct 32/M55 junct 4, A583, at 4th set of traffic lights turn right into South Park Drive & follow signs for zoo. Hotel on right*

This popular, modern hotel, conveniently located on the quieter edge of town, offers excellent indoor and outdoor leisure facilities, including a championship golf course. There is a choice of smart bars and dining options. Many of the bedrooms enjoy views over the golf course.

ROOMS: 164 en suite (8 fmly) No smoking in 95 bedrooms s fr £120; d fr £130 (incl. bkfst) * LB **FACILITIES:** STV Indoor swimming (H) Golf 18 Tennis (hard) Squash Snooker Sauna Solarium Gym Pool table Jacuzzi/spa Aerobic studio Beauty room Xmas **CONF:** Thtr 600 Class 310 Board 30 Del from £110 * **SERVICES:** Lift **PARKING:** 500 **NOTES:** Civ Wed 600 **CARDS:**

Late for dinner? Quality Standards star rating means that last orders for dinner should be no earlier than:
★ 6.30pm ★★ 7.00pm ★★★ 8.00pm
★★★★ 9.00pm ★★★★★ 10.00pm

★★★ 60% Savoy

Queens Promenade, North Shore FY2 9SJ
☎ 01253 352561 📠 01253 595549
Dir: *located along the seafront at Queens Promenade, 0.75m N of Blackpool Tower*

Enjoying panoramic sea views, on the North Promenade, this hotel offers modern accommodation. In addition to the stylish open-plan bar and lounge, there is an attractive wood-panelled restaurant with an interesting stained glass ceiling. A variety of meeting and function suites is also available.

ROOMS: 131 en suite (14 fmly) No smoking in 58 bedrooms s £37.50-£90; d £75-£120 (incl. bkfst) * LB **FACILITIES:** Xmas **CONF:** Thtr 400 Class 250 Board 50 Del from £95 * **SERVICES:** Lift **PARKING:** 40 **NOTES:** No dogs (ex guide dogs) No smoking in restaurant Civ Wed 200 **CARDS:**

★★ 68% Hotel Sheraton

54-62 Queens Promenade FY2 9RP
☎ 01253 352723 📠 01253 595499
e-mail: hotelsheraton@aol.com
Dir: *1m N from Blackpool Tower on promenade towards Fleetwood*

This family-friendly seafront hotel offers many child facilities including a games room, swimming pool, baby listening service and children's entertainment. Bedrooms are modern and well equipped and the spacious lounge area, and separate non-smoking lounge, overlook the promenade. The hotel offers a good choice of cuisine.

ROOMS: 108 en suite (44 fmly) s £45-£55; d £80-£108 (incl. bkfst & dinner) * LB **FACILITIES:** Indoor swimming (H) Sauna Pool table Table tennis Darts entertainment Xmas **CONF:** Thtr 200 Class 100 Board 150 Del from £35 * **SERVICES:** Lift **PARKING:** 20 **NOTES:** No dogs (ex guide dogs) **CARDS:**

See advert on this page

BLACKPOOL, continued

★★66% Brabyns
1-3 Shaftesbury Av, North Shore FY2 9QQ
☎ 01253 354263 01253 352915
e-mail: brabynshotel@netscapeonline.co.uk
In a residential area close to the seafront, this privately owned hotel is a popular venue. Freshly decorated bedrooms are comfortable and thoughtfully equipped. There is a cosy lounge bar and an attractive, wood-panelled dining room. Service is friendly and hospitable.
ROOMS: 22 en suite 3 annexe en suite s £25-£40; d £50-£65 (incl. bkfst) * LB **FACILITIES:** STV Xmas **PARKING:** 12 **NOTES:** No children No smoking in restaurant **CARDS:**

★★61% Belgrave
272 Queens Promenade FY2 9HD
☎ 01253 351570 01253 353335
This family run hotel is located on the north shore at the quieter end of town and offers a variety of bedrooms including a four poster and rooms suitable for families, some of which have sea views. There is a spacious lounge bar often offering live entertainment. The bright restaurant and television lounge both have views across the promenade to the sea.
ROOMS: 33 en suite (7 fmly) **FACILITIES:** STV Pool table **SERVICES:** Lift **PARKING:** 16 **NOTES:** No dogs No smoking in restaurant Closed Jan RS Feb-Mar & Nov-Dec **CARDS:**

★★61% Warwick
603-609 New South Promenade FY4 1NG
☎ 01253 342192 01253 405776
***Dir:** from M55 junct 4 take A5230 for South Shore then rt on A584, Promenade South*
Standing on the south shore, close to the famous Pleasure Beach, this popular hotel offers comfortable well furnished bedrooms, the largest being on the first floor. Rafferty's Bar has frequent live entertainment, and there is a separate restaurant.
ROOMS: 50 en suite (11 fmly) s £20-£35; d £40-£70 (incl. bkfst & dinner) * LB **FACILITIES:** Indoor swimming (H) Solarium Pool table Table tennis entertainment Xmas **CONF:** Thtr 50 Class 24 Board 30 Del from £45.75 * **SERVICES:** Lift **PARKING:** 30 **NOTES:** No smoking in restaurant Closed Jan-13 Feb **CARDS:**

★★60% Revill's
190-194 North Promenade FY1 1RJ
☎ 01253 625768 01253 624736
e-mail: revills.hotel@blackpool.net
***Dir:** just N of Blackpool Tower, almost opposite the North Pier*
This family-run hotel enjoys a seafront location close to the North Pier. There is a choice of bars and a good value evening meal is offered in the attractively decorated restaurant. Bedrooms are comfortable and those to the front boast fine sea views.
ROOMS: 47 en suite (10 fmly) s £22.50-£33; d £45-£56 (incl. bkfst) * LB **FACILITIES:** Snooker Xmas **SERVICES:** Lift **PARKING:** 23 **NOTES:** No dogs No smoking in restaurant
CARDS:

○ Premier Lodge
Whitehills Park, Preston New Rd
☎ 0870 700 1514 0870 700 1515

Popped the question? Hotels with Civ Wed in their entry are licensed for civil wedding ceremonies. Maximum numbers for the ceremony only are shown, e.g. Civ Wed 50

BLAKENEY, Norfolk Map 09 TG04

★★★71% The Blakeney
The Quay NR25 7NE
☎ 01263 740797 01263 740795
***Dir:** off A149*
A charming setting and traditional hospitality are hallmarks of this typically English hotel. The elegant restaurant serves freshly prepared meals, while the refurbished sun lounge has delightful views overlooking the marshes. The thoughtfully laid out bedrooms vary in size and style, and all are well furnished.
ROOMS: 49 en suite 10 annexe en suite (11 fmly) s £56-£112; d £112-£224 (incl. bkfst & dinner) * LB **FACILITIES:** Indoor swimming (H) Snooker Sauna Gym Pool table Jacuzzi/spa Table tennis Xmas **CONF:** Thtr 70 Class 40 Board 32 Del from £86 * **SERVICES:** Lift **PARKING:** 60 **NOTES:** No smoking in restaurant
CARDS:

Premier Collection

★★ Morston Hall
Morston NR25 7AA
☎ 01263 741041 01263 740419
e-mail: reception@morstonhall.com.uk
***Dir:** 1m W of Blakeney on A149 Kings Lynn/Cromer Rd coastal road*
Morston Hall is situated in a quiet setting in a small Norfolk coastal village and dates back to the 17th century. It is surrounded by well tended gardens and offers lovely views across Morston creek. The public rooms are superbly comfortable with a choice of smart lounges and a sunny conservatory. The elegant dining room is an ideal place to relax and enjoy the excellent set dinners, which are complemented by an extensive wine list. The bedrooms are spacious and individually decorated, with plush furnishings and thoughtful extra little touches.
ROOMS: 6 en suite s fr £110; d fr £200 (incl. bkfst & dinner) * LB **PARKING:** 40 **NOTES:** No smoking in restaurant Closed 25-26 Dec
CARDS:

★★73% The Pheasant
Coast Rd, Kelling NR25 7EG
☎ 01263 588382 01263 588101
e-mail: enquiries@pheasanthotelnorfolk.co.uk
***Dir:** on A419 coast road, mid-way between Sheringham & Blakeney*
Set well back from the coast road amidst landscaped grounds, this popular hotel offers traditional-style bedrooms in the main house and more modern and spacious rooms in a newer wing. The restaurant serves a wide ranging selection of appetising dishes and guests also have the use of a lounge and bar area.
ROOMS: 27 en suite No smoking in 16 bedrooms s £38-£48; d £76 (incl. bkfst) * LB **FACILITIES:** Xmas **CONF:** Thtr 80 Class 50 Board 50 **PARKING:** 80 **NOTES:** No smoking in restaurant
CARDS:

★★66% *Manor*
Blakeney NR25 7ND
☎ 01263 740376 🖷 01263 741116
Dir: *turn off A149 at St Mary's church*
This popular hotel is situated just a short walk from the quayside. The bedrooms, located in courtyards adjacent to the main building, were converted from flint face barns and come in a variety of styles. The spacious public rooms offer guests a choice of dining options, informal bar fare or imaginative restaurant cuisine.
ROOMS: 8 en suite 30 annexe en suite **PARKING:** 40 **NOTES:** No children 14yrs No smoking in restaurant Closed 31 Dec-21 Jan
CARDS:

BLANCHLAND, Northumberland — Map 12 NY95

★★68% Lord Crewe Arms
DH8 9SP
☎ 01434 675251 🖷 01434 675337
e-mail: lord@crewearms.freeserve.co.uk
Dir: *10m S of Hexham via B6306*
This historic hotel dates from medieval times and features flagstone floors, vaulted ceilings and original stonework. The restaurant serves an interesting range of dishes, and the menu in the crypt bar is equally appetising. Bedrooms are split between the main hotel and a former estate building across the road. All are well equipped and retain a period style.
ROOMS: 9 en suite 10 annexe en suite (2 fmly) s fr £80; d fr £110 (incl. bkfst) * LB **FACILITIES:** Xmas **CONF:** Thtr 20 Class 20 Board 16
NOTES: Civ Wed 65 **CARDS:**

BLANDFORD FORUM, Dorset — Map 03 ST80

★★★67% Crown
West St DT11 7AJ
☎ 01258 456626 🖷 01258 451084
Dir: *100mtrs from town bridge*

An attractive former coaching house in the centre of Blandford. Bedrooms are well equipped, comfortable and spacious. Snacks are served in the bar and library bar. A choice of menus is available in the wood-panelled dining room and the comfortable lounge is heated by a real fire.
ROOMS: 32 en suite (2 fmly) No smoking in 11 bedrooms s £65-£70; d £78-£85 (incl. bkfst) * LB **FACILITIES:** STV Fishing Shooting ch fac **CONF:** Thtr 250 Class 200 Board 60 Del from £80 * **SERVICES:** Lift **PARKING:** 144 **NOTES:** Closed 25-28 Dec Civ Wed 140
CARDS:

See advert on this page

Arriving late? Four and five star hotels have night porters to assist with your luggage; and 24hr room service.

BLOCKLEY, Gloucestershire — Map 04 SP13

★★★67% *Crown Inn*
High St GL56 9EX
☎ 01386 700245 🖷 01386 700247
This charming 16th-century former coaching inn has much appeal and character, with exposed stone walls and open fires. There is a choice of eating options including one of the best fish and grill menus in the area. The accommodation features rooms in the main house and separate wing, all of which are well equipped and attractively decorated.
ROOMS: 13 en suite 8 annexe en suite (2 fmly)
FACILITIES: entertainment **CONF:** Board 18 **PARKING:** 50
CARDS:

BLUNDELLSANDS, Merseyside — Map 07 SJ39

★★★64% The Blundellsands
Blundellsands Rd West L23 6TN
☎ 0151 924 6515 🖷 0151 931 5364
e-mail: simon.cowie@blundellsands-hotel.co.uk
Dir: *from A565 from Liverpool turn left at College Rd (Merchant Taylors School) to roundabout. Turn left & take third right into Agnes Rd*
This elegant Victorian hotel is conveniently located opposite the station in a quiet, residential area of Crosby. Bedrooms are attractively furnished and well equipped. Dining options include the formal Mauretania Restaurant; alternatively light meals and snacks are available in the popular bar.
ROOMS: 30 en suite (4 fmly) No smoking in 6 bedrooms s £45-£85; d £70-£110 (incl. bkfst) * LB **FACILITIES:** STV Xmas **CONF:** Thtr 640 Class 350 Board 320 Del from £90 * **SERVICES:** Lift **PARKING:** 150
NOTES: Civ Wed 80 **CARDS:**

B

BLYTH, Nottinghamshire Map 08 SK68

★★★69% Charnwood
Sheffield Rd S81 8HF
☎ 01909 591610 📠 01909 591429
e-mail: info@charnwoodhotel.com
Dir: *A614 into Blyth village, turn right past church onto A634 Sheffield road. Hotel 0.5m on right past humpback bridge*
This hotel enjoys a rural setting, surrounded by attractive gardens. Bedrooms are comfortably furnished and attractively decorated. A range of carefully prepared meals and snacks is offered in the restaurant, or in the modern restyled lounge bar overlooking the gardens. Service is both friendly and attentive.
ROOMS: 34 en suite (1 fmly) No smoking in 6 bedrooms s £50-£65; d £70-£90 (incl. bkfst) * LB **FACILITIES:** STV Mini-gym **CONF:** Thtr 135 Class 60 Board 45 Del £99.95 * **PARKING:** 70 **NOTES:** No dogs (ex guide dogs) No smoking in restaurant Civ Wed 120
CARDS:

⇧ *Travelodge*
Hilltop Roundabout S81 8HG
☎ 01909 591841
Dir: *at junct of A1M/A614*
This modern building offers accommodation in smart, spacious and well equipped bedrooms, all with en suite bathrooms. Refreshments may be taken at the nearby family restaurant. For further details and the Travelodge phone number, consult the Hotel Groups page.
ROOMS: 39 en suite

BODMIN, Cornwall & Isles of Scilly Map 02 SX06

★★74% Trehellas House
Washaway PL30 3AD
☎ 01208 72700 📠 01208 73336
Dir: *3.5m N of Bodmin on A389. On right opposite a Celtic Cross*
This early 18th-century former posting inn retains many original features, cleverly interwoven with contemporary additions, to create appealing accommodation. Bedrooms are located in the main house and adjacent coach house; all have been refurbished to the same high standard. Authentic Malaysian cuisine is served in the slate-floored Memories of Malaya Restaurant.
ROOMS: 5 en suite 7 annexe en suite No smoking in all bedrooms s £30-£37; d £60 (incl. bkfst) * **FACILITIES:** Outdoor swimming (H) **PARKING:** 30 **NOTES:** No smoking in restaurant Closed Jan
CARDS:

★66% Westberry
Rhind St PL31 2EL
☎ 01208 72772 📠 01208 72212
Dir: *on ring road directly off A30 & A38*
This popular hotel is convenient for Bodmin town centre and the A30. Bedrooms are comfortably furnished and equipped with a range of facilities. A spacious bar-lounge is provided, plus a billiard room. The restaurant serves both fixed-price and carte menus, and an extensive bar menu is available for lunch.
ROOMS: 10 en suite 8 annexe en suite (1 fmly) s £45; d £60 (incl. bkfst) * LB **FACILITIES:** STV Snooker Gym **CONF:** Thtr 60 Class 20 Board 30 **PARKING:** 30 **NOTES:** Closed 5 days Xmas/New Year
CARDS:

Early start? Hotels at all star levels should provide in-room alarm clocks and/or alarm calls.

BOGNOR REGIS, West Sussex Map 04 SZ99

★★★61% The Inglenook
255 Pagham Rd, Nyetimber PO21 3QB
☎ 01243 262495 & 265411 📠 01243 262668
e-mail: inglenook@btinternet.com
This friendly 16th-century inn retains much of its original charm with exposed beams throughout. Bedrooms, which vary in shape and size, are all individually decorated and well equipped. Public areas include a cosy lounge, and the bar is full of character. The spacious restaurant overlooks the garden, and serves pleasing cuisine.
ROOMS: 18 en suite (1 fmly) No smoking in all bedrooms s £50-£70; d £90-£150 (incl. bkfst) * LB **FACILITIES:** Xmas **CONF:** Thtr 100 Class 50 Board 50 Del from £80 * **PARKING:** 35 **NOTES:** Civ Wed 120
CARDS:

★★71% Beachcroft
Clyde Rd, Felpham Village PO22 7AH
☎ 01243 827142 📠 01243 827142
e-mail: reservations@beachcroft-hotel.co.uk
Dir: *turn off A259 at Butlins rdbt into Felpham Village, in 800mtrs turn right into Sea Rd then 2nd left into Clyde Rd*

This welcoming family-run hotel offers bright, airy and spacious accommodation located in a quiet area next to the seafront. Guests enjoy the informal atmosphere and the traditional cuisine. There is a heated indoor swimming pool and plenty of lounge space.
ROOMS: 38 en suite (4 fmly) No smoking in 3 bedrooms s £27.50-£43; d £47-£66.50 (incl. bkfst) * LB **FACILITIES:** STV Indoor swimming (H) **CONF:** Thtr 50 Class 30 Board 30 **PARKING:** 27 **NOTES:** No dogs Closed 24 Dec-10 Jan **CARDS:**

★★69% Aldwick Hotel
Aldwick Rd, Aldwick PO21 2QU
☎ 01243 821945 📠 01243 821316
Dir: *at rbt junct with A259/A29 take Victoria Drive, signed Aldwick. At traffic lights turn rt into Aldwick Road. Hotel 250yds on left-1km W of Pier*
This friendly, refurbished hotel has the benefit of a quiet residential location, close to Marine Park Gardens and the beach. All the bedrooms are freshly decorated and well equipped. Public areas include a spacious dining room, smart bar and lounges.
ROOMS: 20 en suite No smoking in all bedrooms **CONF:** Thtr 50 Class 20 Board 24 **SERVICES:** Lift **PARKING:** 10 **NOTES:** No smoking in restaurant **CARDS:**

⇧ Premier Lodge
Main Rd, Shripney PO22 9PA
☎ 0870 700 1332 📠 0870 7001333
Dir: *on A29*
Premier Lodge offers modern, well equipped, en suite accommodation suitable for both business and leisure travellers.

continued

Meals can be taken at the adjacent popular restaurant and bar which is fully licensed. For further details, consult the Hotel Groups page.
ROOMS: 28 en suite d £42 * **CONF:** Thtr 50 Class 40 Board 30

BOLTON, Greater Manchester Map 07 SD70

★★★★ 63% Last Drop Hotel

The Last Drop Village & Hotel, Bromley Cross BL7 9PZ
☎ 01204 591131 🖷 01204 304122
e-mail: info@lastdrop.macdonald-hotels.co.uk
Dir: *3m N of Bolton off B5472*

Formerly a farm complex, the buildings were transformed into an hotel in the 1960s. There are excellent leisure and conference facilities, and the well appointed bedrooms are either in the main building, or in the courtyard and separate cottages. A cobbled way leads from reception to the restaurant and a variety of shops.
ROOMS: 118 en suite 10 annexe en suite (72 fmly) No smoking in 60 bedrooms s £60-£75; d £70-£95 (incl. bkfst) * LB **FACILITIES:** STV Indoor swimming (H) Squash Snooker Sauna Solarium Gym Pool table Jacuzzi/spa Craft shops entertainment Xmas **CONF:** Thtr 700 Class 300 Board 95 **SERVICES:** Lift **PARKING:** 400 **NOTES:** No smoking in restaurant **CARDS:**

★★★ 59% *Posthouse Bolton*

Posthouse

Beaumont Rd BL3 4TA
☎ 08704 400 9011 🖷 01204 61064
Dir: *on A58 W of town*
A modern hotel conveniently situated close to junction 5 of the M61 motorway. Bedrooms are designed to modern standards and upgrading is planned for the near future. Public areas include 'Seasons' restaurant and bar, a banqueting suite and conference facilities. Staff are friendly and helpful and there is an all day lounge menu and 24 hour room service.
ROOMS: 101 en suite No smoking in 50 bedrooms **FACILITIES:** Pool table ch fac **CONF:** Thtr 130 Class 100 Board 50 **PARKING:** 150 **CARDS:**

⇧ *Comfort Inn Bolton*

CHOICE HOTELS EUROPE

Bolton West Service Area, Horwich BL6 5UZ
☎ 01204 468641 🖷 01204 668585
ROOMS: 32 en suite **CONF:** Thtr 60 Class 60 Board 30

⇧ Express by Holiday Inn Bolton

Express by Holiday Inn

Arena Approach 3, Horwich BL6 6LB
☎ 01204 469111 🖷 469222
Dir: *turn off M61 junct6 onto slip road, turn right at rdbt & left at 2nd*
A modern budget hotel offering comfortable accommodation in refreshing, spacious and comprehensively-equipped bedrooms, en

suite bathrooms with power showers and continental buffet breakfast included in the room rate. Suitable for business travellers or families. For further details and the Express by Holiday Inn phone number, consult the Hotel Groups page.
ROOMS: 74 en suite (incl. cont bkfst) d £49.95 * **CONF:** Thtr 30 Class 20 Board 20

BOLTON ABBEY, North Yorkshire Map 07 SE05

Premier Collection

★★★ *The Devonshire Arms Country House*

SLH

BD23 6AJ
☎ 01756 710441 🖷 01756 710564
e-mail: dev.arms@legend.co.uk
Dir: *on B6160, 250yds N of junct with A59*
Owned by the Duke and Duchess of Devonshire, this fine country house hotel stands by the River Wharfe in the heart of the Yorkshire Dales. Rooms are furnished with many fine antiques and the walls are adorned with pictures lent by the owners. The Burlington Restaurant offers a traditional style of cooking, but the brasserie follows a lighter, more modern style. Both restaurants use local produce, some grown in the hotel's own gardens. There is a well equipped leisure club.
ROOMS: 41 en suite No smoking in 12 bedrooms
FACILITIES: Indoor swimming (H) Tennis (hard) Fishing Sauna Solarium Gym Croquet lawn Putting green Jacuzzi/spa Laser pigeon shooting Falconry **CONF:** Thtr 120 Class 80 Board 40
PARKING: 150 **NOTES:** No smoking in restaurant
CARDS:

BONCHURCH See Wight, Isle of

B

BOROUGHBRIDGE, North Yorkshire
Map 08 SE36

★★★70% Crown
Horsefair YO51 9LB
☎ 01423 322328 🖷 01423 324512
e-mail: emmalee.crown@barclays.net

Best Western

Dir: *take junct 48 off A1(M). Hotel 1m towards town centre at T-junct*

Situated just off the A1, The Crown provides well appointed bedrooms and a range of comfortable public rooms, including a delightful restaurant which serves a wide range of well prepared food; service is relaxed and friendly. Several modern conference rooms are available, as well as a leisure complex.

ROOMS: 37 en suite (2 fmly) s fr £60; d fr £75 (incl. bkfst) * LB **FACILITIES:** STV Indoor swimming (H) Sauna Gym Jacuzzi/spa Xmas **CONF:** Thtr 200 Class 120 Board 120 Del from £85 * **SERVICES:** Lift **PARKING:** 60 **NOTES:** No smoking in restaurant Civ Wed 70
CARDS:

★★★69% Rose Manor
Horsefair YO51 9LL
☎ 01423 322245 🖷 01423 324920
e-mail: rosemanorhotel@ukf.net

Dir: *turn off A1(M) at exit 48 onto B6265, hotel within 1m*

Rose Manor is a country mansion lying on the south side of Boroughbridge with a friendly and relaxing atmosphere. It has an inviting lounge and a split level dining room. Bedrooms are comfortable and well equipped with modern facilities. The large self-contained conference suite is particularly popular.

ROOMS: 19 en suite 2 annexe en suite (1 fmly) No smoking in 11 bedrooms s fr £78.50; d fr £103 (incl. bkfst) * LB **FACILITIES:** STV **CONF:** Thtr 250 Class 250 Board 25 Del from £99 * **PARKING:** 100 **NOTES:** No dogs **CARDS:**

BORROWDALE, Cumbria
Map 11 NY21

see also Keswick & Rosthwaite

★★★77% Borrowdale Gates Country House
CA12 5UQ
☎ 017687 77204 🖷 017687 77254
e-mail: hotel@borrowdale-gates.com

Dir: *from Keswick follow Borrowdale signs on B5289, after approx 4m turn right at sign for Grange, hotel is on right approx 0.25m through village*

In a sedate woodland setting, this family-run hotel commands stunning views of the Borrowdale valley. Inviting public rooms include lounges, a cosy bar and an attractive restaurant. The recently completed wing of bedrooms provides a high standard of facilities.

ROOMS: 31 en suite (2 fmly) s £82-£92.50; d £155-£175 (incl. bkfst & dinner) LB **FACILITIES:** ch fac Xmas **PARKING:** 40 **NOTES:** No dogs (ex guide dogs) No smoking in restaurant Closed Jan
CARDS:

See advert under KESWICK

★★★70% Borrowdale
CA12 5UY
☎ 017687 77224 🖷 017687 77338
e-mail: theborrowdalehotel@yahoo.com

Dir: *on B5289 at south end of Lake Derwentwater*

A traditional holiday hotel in the beautiful Borrowdale Valley overlooking Derwentwater and 15 minutes drive from Keswick. Extensive public areas include a choice of lounges, a stylish dining room, and a lounge bar and conservatory serving hearty bar meals. There is a wide choice of bedroom size, the larger rooms are best.

ROOMS: 33 en suite (9 fmly) s £60-£65; d £114-£152 (incl. bkfst & dinner) * LB **FACILITIES:** Free use of nearby Health Club Xmas **CONF:** Class 30 **PARKING:** 100 **NOTES:** No smoking in restaurant
CARDS:

BOSCASTLE, Cornwall & Isles of Scilly
Map 02 SX09

★★64% *The Wellington Hotel*
The Harbour PL35 0AQ
☎ 01840 250202 🖷 01840 250621
e-mail: vtobutt@enterprise.net

THE CIRCLE
Selected Individual Hotels
GREAT BRITAIN

The 'Welly', as it is known locally, dates back 400 years and has connections with Thomas Hardy and, more recently, Guy Gibson of 'Dambusters' fame. Stone built with a crenellated tower on one corner and comfortable rooms of varying sizes, the hotel offers comfortable lounges and a cheery beamed bar where local folk singers gather every Monday night. The appetising dinner menu of home-cooked dishes has a strong French influence.

ROOMS: 16 en suite (1 fmly) **FACILITIES:** Pool table Games room entertainment **CONF:** Board 24 **PARKING:** 20 **NOTES:** No children 7yrs RS 29 Nov-16 Dec & 10 Jan-10 Feb
CARDS:

BOSHAM, West Sussex
Map 04 SU80

★★★72% The Millstream
Bosham Ln PO18 8HL
☎ 01243 573234 🖷 01243 573459
e-mail: info@millstream-hotel.co.uk

Dir: *4m W of Chichester on A259, turn left at Bosham roundabout, 1m turn right at T junction follow signs to church & quay hotel 0.5m on right*

Lying in the idyllic village of Bosham, this attractive hotel provides comfortable and tastefully decorated bedrooms, each with an individual theme. Public rooms include a cocktail bar, which opens out onto the garden, a lounge and a well appointed restaurant.

ROOMS: 33 en suite (2 fmly) No smoking in 14 bedrooms s £72-£85; d £115-£120 (incl. bkfst) * LB **FACILITIES:** Sailing breaks Bridge breaks entertainment Xmas **CONF:** Thtr 45 Class 20 Board 24 Del from £99 * **PARKING:** 44 **NOTES:** No smoking in restaurant Civ Wed 90
CARDS:

See advert under CHICHESTER

BOSTON, Lincolnshire
Map 08 TF34

★★★59% *New England*
49 Wide Bargate PE21 6SH
☎ 01205 365255 🖷 01773 880321
Dir: *E side of town off John Adams Way*
Situated close to the town centre, this popular hotel continues to be improved. Morning coffee and afternoon tea are served in its open-plan public areas, and the restaurant serves a brasserie-style menu.
ROOMS: 25 en suite (2 fmly) No smoking in 5 bedrooms **FACILITIES:** STV **CONF:** Thtr 40 Class 18 Board 25 **NOTES:** No smoking in restaurant **CARDS:**

★★67% Comfort Friendly Inn
Donnington Rd, Bicker Bar PE20 3AN
☎ 01205 820118 🖷 01205 820228
e-mail: admin@gb607.u-net.com
Dir: *at junct of A17/A52*
A purpose-built hotel with well equipped bedrooms offering good levels of comfort and value for money. Facilities include two meeting rooms, a small open plan lounge bar with TV and adjacent restaurant. Reasonably priced meals are available all day. Public areas are air-conditioned.
ROOMS: 55 en suite (30 fmly) No smoking in 27 bedrooms d £44 * LB **FACILITIES:** STV Gym Xmas **CONF:** Thtr 70 Class 28 Board 35 Del £72 * **SERVICES:** air con **PARKING:** 50 **CARDS:**

BOSTON SPA, West Yorkshire
Map 08 SE44

★★62% *Royal Hotel*
182 High St LS23 6BT
☎ 01937 842142
Situated in the centre of the town, this old coaching inn dates back to 1768 and offers well equipped and modern bedrooms. Harts restaurant provides a wide range of interesting dishes while food is also served in the bars. Conference facilities are also available.
ROOMS: 13 en suite

BOTLEY, Hampshire
Map 04 SU51

★★★★69% *Botley Park Hotel Golf & Country Club*

Winchester Rd, Boorley Green SO32 2UA
☎ 01489 780888 🖷 01489 789242
Dir: *on B3354, approx 2m from village*

Set in 176 acres of landscaped park and golf course, Botley Park boasts extensive sports and leisure facilities. These include squash courts, dance studio, fitness centre and pool with steam room. Bedrooms are spacious and quiet. Guests have a choice of dining options; in the restaurant or more casually in the Swing and Divot bar.

continued

ROOMS: 100 en suite No smoking in 52 bedrooms **FACILITIES:** STV Indoor swimming (H) Golf 18 Tennis (hard) Squash Snooker Sauna Solarium Gym Croquet lawn Jacuzzi/spa Aerobics studio Beauty salon entertainment **CONF:** Thtr 240 Class 100 Board 60 **PARKING:** 250 **NOTES:** No smoking in restaurant **CARDS:**

See advert under SOUTHAMPTON

BOUGHTON STREET, Kent
Map 05 TR05

★★★68% *The Garden Hotel & Restaurant*
167-169 The Street, Boughton ME13 9BH
☎ 01227 751411 🖷 01227 751801
e-mail: gardenhotel@lineone.net
Dir: *from M2 junct 7 follow signs Canterbury/Dove (A2). Take first left signposted Boughton/Dunkirk*
In the centre of the pretty village of Boughton on the Canterbury road, The Garden Hotel offers comfortable accommodation. Bedrooms are fresh and modern and are thoughtfully equipped for guests' every need. The airy conservatory restaurant looks out over the eponymous garden and serves carefully prepared dishes in a modern style.
ROOMS: 10 en suite No smoking in 5 bedrooms **CONF:** Thtr 30 Class 20 Board 16 Del £99 * **PARKING:** 70 **NOTES:** No smoking in restaurant RS Rest closed Sun evening **CARDS:**

BOURNE, Lincolnshire
Map 08 TF02

★★69% ❀❀ Black Horse Inn
Grimsthorpe PE10 0LY
☎ 01778 591247 🖷 01778 591373
e-mail: blackhorseinn@saqnet.co.uk
Dir: *turn off A1 onto A151, hotel 9m on left 0.5m after entrance to Grimsthorpe Castle*
Set around three sides of a courtyard, this 18th century inn is peacefully situated in a small village. Attractively furnished bedrooms include one with a four poster bed and a suite is also available. Good quality English cooking is featured on the menus, served in either the welcoming bar or the nicely appointed Buttery.
ROOMS: 6 en suite s £45-£55; d £65-£95 (incl. bkfst) * **FACILITIES:** Jacuzzi/spa Xmas **CONF:** Class 40 Board 12 **PARKING:** 41 **NOTES:** No dogs (ex guide dogs) No smoking in restaurant **CARDS:**

BOURNEMOUTH, Dorset
Map 04 SZ09

see also Christchurch

★★★★71% ❀ Swallow Highcliff
St Michaels Rd, West Cliff BH2 5DU
☎ 01202 557702 🖷 01202 292734
e-mail: info@swallowhotels.com
Dir: *take A338 dual carriageway through Bournemouth, then follow signs for Bournemouth International Centre to West Cliff Rd, then 2nd turning right*
Enjoying panoramic sea views, this hotel is close to the BIC, yet within easy walking distance of the town centre. Bedrooms are traditionally furnished and well equipped. The Robert Wild Room Restaurant is popular.

continued

B

BOURNEMOUTH, continued

Swallow Highcliff, Bournemouth

ROOMS: 143 en suite 14 annexe en suite (26 fmly) No smoking in 65 bedrooms s £85-£195; d £140-£250 (incl. bkfst) * LB **FACILITIES:** STV Indoor swimming (H) Outdoor swimming (H) Tennis (hard) Sauna Solarium Gym Croquet lawn Putting green Jacuzzi/spa Golf driving net Beautician Volleyball Xmas **CONF:** Thtr 400 Class 180 Board 90 Del from £145 * **SERVICES:** Lift **PARKING:** 130 **NOTES:** No smoking in restaurant Civ Wed 100 **CARDS:**

★★★★71% Menzies East Cliff Court

East Overcliff Dr BH1 3AN

MENZIES HOTELS

☎ 0500 636943 (Central Res) 🖷 01773 880321

e-mail: info@menzies-hotels.co.uk

Dir: *from A338 follow signs to East Cliff*

Enjoying panoramic views across the bay, this popular hotel offers accommodation of high quality, with many rooms benefiting from balconies and sea views. Stylish public areas provide both comfort and tasteful vibrancy with a choice of lounges available. Additional facilities include south-facing terraces leading down to a heated swimming pool.

ROOMS: 70 en suite (10 fmly) s £95-£160; d £130-£160 (incl. bkfst) * LB **FACILITIES:** STV Outdoor swimming (H) Leisure facilities available at neighbouring hotels Xmas **CONF:** Thtr 150 Class 40 Board 45 Del from £95 * **SERVICES:** Lift **PARKING:** 70 **NOTES:** No smoking in restaurant Civ Wed 150 **CARDS:**

★★★★70% Menzies Carlton

East Overcliff BH1 3DN

MENZIES HOTELS

☎ 0500 636943 (Central Res) 🖷 01773 880321

e-mail: info@menzies-hotels.co.uk

Dir: *take A338 to the East Cliff*

Enjoying a prime location on the East Cliff, and with views of the Isle of Wight and Dorset coastline, the Carlton is set in attractive gardens and offers good leisure and meeting facilities. Most of the spacious bedrooms enjoy sea views, and all are well equipped. Guests can enjoy an interesting range of carefully prepared dishes in the Fredericks restaurant.

ROOMS: 74 en suite s £115-£155; d £155-£195 (incl. bkfst) * LB **FACILITIES:** STV Indoor swimming (H) Outdoor swimming (H) Sauna Solarium Gym Jacuzzi/spa Xmas **CONF:** Thtr 140 Class 90 Board 45 Del from £100 * **SERVICES:** Lift **PARKING:** 70 **NOTES:** No smoking in restaurant Civ Wed 140 **CARDS:**

★★★★68% ***Royal Bath***

Bath Rd BH1 2EW

De Vere Hotels

☎ 01202 555555 🖷 01202 554158

e-mail: devere.royalbath@airtime.co.uk

Dir: *from A338 follow tourist signs for Pier and Beaches. The hotel is on Bath Rd just before Lansdowne rdbt and the Pier*

This longstanding and very popular hotel, surrounded by well tended gardens, enjoys an enviable position overlooking Bournemouth Bay. Significant investment has been made in the public rooms which include spacious lounges, a choice of restaurants and state of the art leisure facilities. Valet parking is provided for a small charge.

ROOMS: 140 en suite **FACILITIES:** STV Indoor swimming (H) Sauna Solarium Gym Jacuzzi/spa Beauty salon Hairdressing entertainment **CONF:** Thtr 400 Class 220 Board 100 **SERVICES:** Lift **PARKING:** 70 **NOTES:** No dogs (ex guide dogs) **CARDS:**

★★★75% Chine

Boscombe Spa Rd BH5 1AX

☎ 01202 396234 🖷 01202 391737

e-mail: reservations@chinehotel.co.uk

Set in delightful gardens with private access to the seafront and beach, this traditionally-run hotel benefits from superb views. An excellent range of facilities is provided, including both an indoor and outdoor pool. Attractively decorated and thoughtfully equipped bedrooms are comfortable, some have balconies. Staff are friendly and unfailingly helpful.

ROOMS: 69 en suite 23 annexe en suite (13 fmly) No smoking in 14 bedrooms s £58-£68; d £116-£136 (incl. bkfst) * LB **FACILITIES:** STV Indoor swimming (H) Outdoor swimming (H) Sauna Solarium Croquet lawn Putting green Games room Outdoor & indoor childrens play area Xmas **CONF:** Thtr 140 Class 70 Board 30 Del from £85 * **SERVICES:** Lift **PARKING:** 50 **NOTES:** No dogs (ex guide dogs) No smoking in restaurant **CARDS:**

See advert on opposite page

★★★72% Elstead

Knyveton Rd BH1 3QP

☎ 01202 293071 🖷 01202 293827

e-mail: info@the-elstead.co.uk

The hotel is well situated close to the heart of Bournemouth, just a short stroll from the beach and convenient for all the major transport networks. Guests are assured of a friendly welcome and comfortable, well equipped accommodation. The hotel also has a

continued

bar, restaurant and excellent leisure facilities, as well as convenient parking.
ROOMS: 50 en suite (4 fmly) No smoking in 5 bedrooms s £51-£82; d £82-£114 (incl. bkfst) * LB **FACILITIES:** STV Indoor swimming (H) Snooker Sauna Solarium Gym Pool table Jacuzzi/spa **CONF:** Thtr 80 Class 60 Board 40 Del from £79.50 * **SERVICES:** Lift **PARKING:** 40 **NOTES:** No smoking in restaurant **CARDS:**

See advert on this page

★★★72% *Langtry Manor*
26 Derby Rd, East Cliff BH1 3QB
☎ 01202 553887 01202 290115
e-mail: lillie@langtrymanor.com
Dir: *from A31 onto A338 at 1st rdbt by rail station turn left over next rdbt 1st left into Knyveton Rd, hotel on opposite corner of small rdbt*
Built in 1877 by Edward VII as a rendezvous for he and his mistress Lillie Langtry, the house retains a stately atmosphere. The stylish bedrooms are individually furnished and several boast four-poster beds. The high ceilinged dining hall has several large Tudor tapestries.
ROOMS: 14 en suite 14 annexe en suite (3 fmly) No smoking in 2 bedrooms **FACILITIES:** Sports Centre 2min walk **CONF:** Thtr 100 Class 100 Board 50 **PARKING:** 30 **NOTES:** No smoking in restaurant **CARDS:**

★★★70% Hotel Miramar
East Overcliff Dr, East Cliff BH1 3AL
☎ 01202 556581 01202 291242
e-mail: sales@miramar-bournemouth.com
On the East Cliff, close to the town centre, this smart hotel sits in landscaped gardens with super views of the sea. All areas offer a high standard of decoration, quality and comfort and a number of thoughtful extras.

continued on p100

B

BOURNEMOUTH, continued

Hotel Miramar, Bournemouth

ROOMS: 45 en suite (6 fmly) No smoking in 10 bedrooms s £65-£85; d £130-£160 (incl. bkfst & dinner) * LB **FACILITIES:** STV Croquet lawn entertainment Xmas **CONF:** Thtr 200 Class 50 Board 50 Del from £65 * **SERVICES:** Lift **PARKING:** 80 **NOTES:** No smoking in restaurant Civ Wed 130 **CARDS:**

★★★70% Queens

Meyrick Rd, East Cliff BH1 3DL
☎ 01202 554415 01202 294810
e-mail: hotels@arthuryoung.co.uk

Only yards from the seafront, the hotel enjoys a good location and is popular for conferences and functions. The public areas include a bar lounge and a restaurant. There is also the Queensbury Leisure Club. Bedrooms range in size and style.

ROOMS: 113 en suite (15 fmly) s £56.50-£62.50; d £113-£125 (incl. bkfst) * LB **FACILITIES:** Indoor swimming (H) Snooker Sauna Solarium Gym Pool table Jacuzzi/spa Beauty salon Games Room entertainment Xmas **CONF:** Thtr 220 Class 120 Board 50 Del from £67.50 * **SERVICES:** Lift **PARKING:** 80 **NOTES:** No smoking in restaurant **CARDS:**

★★★69% Durley Hall

Durley Chine Rd, West Cliff BH2 5JS
☎ 01202 751000 01202 757585
e-mail: Sales@durleyhall.co.uk
Dir: *from A338 follow signs to the West Cliff & Bournemouth International Centre*

Equally suitable for leisure and business guests, this hotel is well situated on the West Cliff. Bedrooms are smartly decorated and furnished. There are several executive and honeymoon rooms, some with feature beds and baths. As well as the Starlight restaurant there is a café overlooking the outdoor pool. In addition, the range of leisure facilities is very good and the hotel can cater for conferences and functions.

ROOMS: 70 en suite 11 annexe en suite (27 fmly) s £42-£58; d £84-£116 (incl. bkfst & dinner) * LB **FACILITIES:** STV Indoor swimming (H) Outdoor swimming (H) Sauna Solarium Gym Pool table Jacuzzi/spa Beauty therapist Hairdresser Steam room Table tennis Toning table entertainment Xmas **CONF:** Thtr 200 Class 80 Board 35 Del from £65 * **SERVICES:** Lift **PARKING:** 150 **NOTES:** No dogs (ex guide dogs) No smoking in restaurant Civ Wed 85
CARDS:

★★★69% East Anglia

6 Poole Rd BH2 5QX
☎ 01202 765163 01202 752949
Dir: *leave A338 at Bournemouth West rdbt, follow signs for B.I.C. and West Cliff, at next rdbt turn right into Poole Rd, hotel on right hand side*

Best Western

Attractive bedrooms provide comfortable accommodation at this well managed hotel. This is enhanced by the friendly team of staff who ensure a warm welcome and pleasant service throughout. Public areas include a number of function/conference rooms, ample lounges and an air conditioned restaurant.

ROOMS: 46 en suite 24 annexe en suite (18 fmly) No smoking in 2 bedrooms s £49-£53; d £90-£106 (incl. bkfst) LB **FACILITIES:** STV Outdoor swimming (H) Sauna Pool table Jacuzzi/spa Xmas **CONF:** Thtr 150 Class 75 Board 60 Del from £80 * **SERVICES:** Lift **PARKING:** 70 **NOTES:** No dogs (ex guide dogs) No smoking in restaurant Closed 2-8 Jan **CARDS:**

★★★69% Hermitage

Exeter Rd BH2 5AH
☎ 01202 557363 01202 559173
e-mail: info@hermitage-hotel.co.uk
Dir: *follow signs for Bournemouth International Centre or pier, hotel opposite both*

Situated in the heart of Bournemouth's town centre, the Hermitage has direct access to the shops, beaches and Pavilion gardens. Bedrooms and bathrooms are all very smart, well coordinated with good quality furnishing and many useful extra facilities. Public areas are attractive and very comfortable.

ROOMS: 63 en suite 12 annexe en suite (10 fmly) No smoking in 52 bedrooms s £42-£64; d £84-£128 (incl. bkfst) * LB **FACILITIES:** Free swimming at Bournemouth International Centre Xmas **CONF:** Thtr 180 Class 60 Board 60 Del from £58 * **SERVICES:** Lift **PARKING:** 58 **NOTES:** No dogs (ex guide dogs) No smoking in restaurant
CARDS:

See advert on opposite page

★★★69% Menzies Anglo-Swiss

16 Gervis Rd, East Cliff BH1 3EQ
☎ 0500 636943 (Central Res) 01773 880321
e-mail: info@menzies-hotels.co.uk
Dir: *follow signs to East Cliff from A338*

MENZIES HOTELS

A short walk from the town centre and East Cliff, this attractive hotel goes from strength to strength. Bedrooms are comfortable, many offer balconies, and some family suites are available. The relaxing lounges and bar make ideal locations to unwind and enjoy the service provided by the attentive staff.

ROOMS: 57 en suite 8 annexe en suite (16 fmly) s £80-£110; d £110-£135 (incl. bkfst) * LB **FACILITIES:** STV Indoor swimming (H) Sauna Solarium Gym Jacuzzi/spa entertainment Xmas **CONF:** Thtr 75 Class 30 Board 30 Del from £70 * **SERVICES:** Lift **PARKING:** 70 **NOTES:** Civ Wed 150 **CARDS:**

★★★69% Piccadilly

Bath Rd BH1 2NN
☎ 01202 552559 01202 298235
Dir: *follow signs for 'Lansdowne'*

This personally-run hotel prides itself on its friendly atmosphere and superb ballroom. Bedrooms are comfortably furnished,

continued

pleasantly decorated and well equipped. There is a spacious open-plan lounge and bar and an attractive dining room where the table d'hôte choice is popular at dinner. A carte menu is also available.
ROOMS: 45 en suite (2 fmly) s £50-£66; d £80-£92 (incl. bkfst) * LB **FACILITIES:** STV Ballroom dancing Xmas **CONF:** Thtr 100 Class 50 Board 40 **SERVICES:** Lift **PARKING:** 30 **NOTES:** No dogs (ex guide dogs) No smoking in restaurant **CARDS:**

★★★69% Wessex

Forestdale Hotels

West Cliff Rd BH2 5EU
☎ 01202 551911 🖷 01202 297354
Dir: *via M27/A35 through New Forest. A338 from Dorchester and A347 to the North. Hotel on West Cliff side of the town*
This well presented hotel is centrally located for both the town centre and the beach. Bedrooms vary in size but are smartly appointed with comfortable furnishings and a range of modern facilities. There is a super leisure club and an open-plan bar and lounge. The hotel has a relaxing atmosphere with attentive service provided by the friendly young team.
ROOMS: 109 en suite (22 fmly) No smoking in 3 bedrooms s fr £60; d fr £120 (incl. bkfst & dinner) * LB **FACILITIES:** STV Indoor swimming (H) Outdoor swimming (H) Snooker Sauna Solarium Gym Table tennis Xmas **CONF:** Thtr 400 Class 160 Board 160 Del from £100 * **SERVICES:** Lift **PARKING:** 250 **CARDS:**

★★★68% *The Connaught*

Best Western

West Hill Rd, West Cliff BH2 5PH
☎ 01202 298020 🖷 01202 298028
e-mail: sales@theconnaught.co.uk
Dir: *follow signs 'Town Centre West & BIC'*
An attractive hotel on Bournemouth's West Cliff. Bedrooms are neatly decorated and equipped with modern facilities. There is a choice of lounges and a smart leisure centre. Extensive meeting facilities are available. Professional staff are attentive and friendly.
ROOMS: 60 en suite (15 fmly) No smoking in 4 bedrooms
FACILITIES: STV Indoor swimming (H) Snooker Sauna Solarium Gym Pool table Jacuzzi/spa Cardio-vascular suite Table tennis entertainment **CONF:** Thtr 200 Class 70 Board 70 **SERVICES:** Lift **PARKING:** 45 **NOTES:** No smoking in restaurant **CARDS:**

★★★68% Cumberland

East Overcliff Dr BH1 3AF
☎ 01202 290722 🖷 01202 311394
e-mail: hotels@arthuryoung.co.uk
Many of the well equipped and attractively decorated bedrooms benefit from sea views and balconies here. The public areas are spacious and comfortable. The restaurant offers a daily changing fixed price menu. Guests have use of the leisure club at the sister hotel, The Queens.
ROOMS: 102 en suite (12 fmly) s £46-£56; d £92-£112 (incl. bkfst) * LB **FACILITIES:** Outdoor swimming (H) Pool table Free membership of nearby Leisure Club entertainment Xmas **CONF:** Thtr 120 Class 70 Board 45 Del from £59.50 * **SERVICES:** Lift **PARKING:** 51 **NOTES:** No smoking in restaurant **CARDS:**

★★★67% *Hotel Collingwood*

11 Priory Rd, West Cliff BH2 5DF
☎ 01202 557575 🖷 01202 293219
Dir: *from A338 left at West cliff sign across 1st rdbt left at 2nd rdbt, hotel 500yds on left in Priory Rd*
Privately owned and well managed, this hotel is ideally located for the BIC, the town centre and the seafront, and offers good leisure facilities. Public areas are spacious and each evening in Pinks Restaurant, a fixed-price menu is available.

continued

B

BOURNEMOUTH, continued

Hotel Collingwood, Bournemouth

ROOMS: 53 en suite (16 fmly) **FACILITIES:** STV Indoor swimming (H) Snooker Sauna Solarium Pool table Jacuzzi/spa Mini gym Steam room Games room Pool table entertainment **SERVICES:** Lift **PARKING:** 55 **NOTES:** No smoking in restaurant **CARDS:**

See advert on page 101

★★★67% Hinton Firs

Manor Rd, East Cliff BH1 3HB
☎ 01202 555409 01202 299607
e-mail: hintonfirs@bournemouth.co.uk
Dir: *from A338 turn west at St Paul's Rdbt across next 2 rdbts then immediately fork left to side of church, hotel on next corner*

A friendly team of staff welcome guests old and new to this hotel, conveniently situated on the East Cliff. Bedrooms, six of which are in a separate wing, are pleasantly decorated and comfortable. Included in the facilities are indoor and outdoor pools, a games room, bar and lounges. Dinner offers a good choice and dishes are well cooked.

ROOMS: 46 en suite 6 annexe en suite (12 fmly) s £40-£48; d £65-£85 (incl. bkfst) LB **FACILITIES:** Indoor swimming (H) Outdoor swimming (H) Sauna Jacuzzi/spa Games room entertainment Xmas **CONF:** Thtr 60 Class 40 Board 30 Del from £60 * **SERVICES:** Lift **PARKING:** 40 **NOTES:** No dogs No smoking in restaurant
CARDS:

★★★67% Trouville

Priory Rd BH2 5DH
☎ 01202 552262 01202 293324
e-mail: hotels@arthuryoung.co.uk
Dir: *close to International Centre*

Close to Bournemouth's International Centre and the seafront, this large privately-owned hotel is situated on the West Cliff. The bedrooms are attractively decorated and well co-ordinated. In addition to a smart leisure suite, there is a comfortable bar and separate lounge.

continued

ROOMS: 77 en suite (21 fmly) s £49.50-£56; d £99-£112 (incl. bkfst & dinner) * LB **FACILITIES:** Indoor swimming (H) Sauna Solarium Gym Jacuzzi/spa entertainment Xmas **CONF:** Thtr 100 Class 45 Board 50 Del from £65 * **SERVICES:** Lift **PARKING:** 60 **NOTES:** No smoking in restaurant **CARDS:**

★★★66% Bay View Court

35 East Overcliff Dr BH1 3AH
☎ 01202 294449 01202 292883
e-mail: enquiry@bayviewcourt.co.uk
Dir: *on A338 left at St Pauls roundabout. Go straight over St Swithuns roundabout. Left down Manor Rd, bear left onto Manor Rd, 1st right, next right*

This friendly family-run hotel enjoys splendid views across the bay. Bedrooms vary in size but are all attractively furnished. The lounges are comfortable and south-facing and leisure facilities are lovely.

ROOMS: 64 en suite (11 fmly) s fr £50; d fr £100 (incl. bkfst & dinner) * LB **FACILITIES:** STV Indoor swimming (H) Snooker Gym Pool table Jacuzzi/spa Steam room entertainment Xmas **CONF:** Thtr 170 Class 85 Board 50 Del from £50 * **SERVICES:** Lift **PARKING:** 58 **NOTES:** No smoking in restaurant **CARDS:**

★★★66% Carrington House

ZOFFANY HOTELS

Knyveton Rd BH1 3QQ
☎ 01202 369988 01202 292221
e-mail: carrington@zoffanyhotels.co.uk

This hotel, situated in a quiet tree-lined avenue, within easy reach of local amenities, offers excellent conference rooms and award-winning facilities for disabled guests. Children are especially well catered for, with their own play rooms and menu.

ROOMS: 104 en suite No smoking in 50 bedrooms s £77-£85; d £94-£105 (incl. bkfst) * **FACILITIES:** STV **PARKING:** 110 **NOTES:** No smoking in restaurant **CARDS:**

★★★66% Cliffeside

East Overcliff Dr BH1 3AQ
☎ 01202 555724 01202 314534
e-mail: hotels@arthuryoung.co.uk
Dir: *from M27 to Ringwood A338. From Ringwood approximately 7m, then first rdbt left into East Cliff*

Many of the public areas and bedrooms benefit from bay views at this popular hotel. The friendly staff create a good rapport with guests and a relaxed atmosphere prevails. The bedrooms are attractively decorated. A set price menu is offered in the restaurant.

ROOMS: 62 en suite (10 fmly) **FACILITIES:** Outdoor swimming (H) Pool table Table tennis **CONF:** Thtr 180 Class 140 Board 60 Del from £65 * **SERVICES:** Lift **PARKING:** 45 **NOTES:** No smoking in restaurant **CARDS:**

★★★66% *Hotel Courtlands*

Best Western

16 Boscombe Spa Rd, East Cliff BH5 1BB
☎ 01202 302442 01202 309880
Dir: *from A338 towards Bournemouth, then East Cliff, then Boscombe. Turn left over 1st rdbt left at 2nd & next right after Boscombe Gdns*

A popular hotel close to Boscome Pier. Bedrooms, some with sea views, are neatly decorated and furnished. Two smart and comfortable lounges overlook the south facing gardens. The outdoor pool is well used in summer. Traditional meals are served in the spacious dining room and there is also room for functions and meetings.

ROOMS: 58 en suite (8 fmly) **FACILITIES:** STV Outdoor swimming (H) Sauna Solarium Pool table Jacuzzi/spa Free use of nearby Health Club **CONF:** Thtr 120 Class 85 Board 20 **SERVICES:** Lift **PARKING:** 50 **NOTES:** No smoking in restaurant **CARDS:**

B

★★★66% Marsham Court
Russell Cotes Rd, East Cliff BH1 3AB
☎ 01202 552111 ⎙ 01202 294744
e-mail: reservations@marshamcourt.co.uk
With splendid views over the sea and town, this hotel is conveniently located on the East Cliff, only a short walk from the town centre. Public areas include a comfortable bar and lounge, a range of conference/function rooms, and a spacious restaurant. The bedrooms vary in size and style, the front facing rooms always proving popular.
ROOMS: 86 en suite (15 fmly) s £53-£60; d £86-£100 (incl. bkfst) * LB **FACILITIES:** STV Outdoor swimming (H) Pool table Free swimming at BIC Xmas **CONF:** Thtr 200 Class 120 Board 80 Del from £70 * **SERVICES:** Lift **PARKING:** 100 **NOTES:** No dogs (ex guide dogs) No smoking in restaurant Civ Wed 200
CARDS:

★★★66% Quality Hotel Bournemouth
8 Poole Rd BH2 5QU
CHOICE HOTELS EUROPE
☎ 01202 763006 ⎙ 01202 766168
e-mail: admin@gb641.u-net.com
Dir: *0.5m from A338 road and by-pass. Follow signs B.I.C. from by-pass then right at rbt into Poole Road*
A modern popular hotel on the West Cliff, a good base for visiting the attractions and beach. Bedrooms are attractively decorated and well equipped. Public areas, although not extensive, are bright and comfortable with a relaxed, friendly atmosphere.
ROOMS: 54 en suite (3 fmly) No smoking in 17 bedrooms s £64; d £76 * LB **FACILITIES:** STV Xmas **CONF:** Thtr 70 Class 36 Board 32 Del from £58 * **SERVICES:** Lift **PARKING:** 55 **NOTES:** No smoking in restaurant **CARDS:**

★★★65% Belvedere
Bath Rd BH1 2EU
☎ 01202 297556 & 293336 ⎙ 01202 294699
e-mail: belvedere_hotel@msn.com
Dir: *from A338 keep railway station & ASDA on left at rdbt take 1st left then 3rd exit at next 2 rdbts. Hotel on Bath Hill just after 4th rdbt*
Spacious public areas and comfortable bedrooms are on offer at this friendly hotel, found close to the town centre and seafront. There is a lively bar, and the attractive restaurant is popular with locals.
ROOMS: 61 en suite (12 fmly) s £39-£55; d £64-£98 (incl. bkfst) LB **FACILITIES:** STV entertainment ch fac Xmas **CONF:** Thtr 80 Class 30 Board 30 Del from £61.50 **SERVICES:** Lift **PARKING:** 55 **NOTES:** No dogs (ex guide dogs) No smoking in restaurant
CARDS:

★★★65% Durlston Court
47 Gervis Rd, East Cliff BH1 3DD
☎ 01202 316316 ⎙ 01202 316999
e-mail: dch@seaviews.co.uk
Dir: *on A338 10m from M27/A338 junct left large rdbt, right next rdbt, 3rd junct next rdbt (Meyrick Rd) next rdbt right into Gervis Rd. Hotel on left*
This hotel, located on the East Cliff, is close to the town's attractions and beaches. Comfortable bedrooms vary in size with one room specifically for disabled guests. The bright and airy bar and lounge overlook the sheltered pool and terrace. A fixed price menu is available in the spacious restaurant.

continued

ROOMS: 56 en suite (16 fmly) No smoking in 10 bedrooms s £41-£51.50; d £82-£103 (incl. bkfst & dinner) * LB **FACILITIES:** STV Outdoor swimming (H) Sauna Gym Pool table Jacuzzi/spa entertainment Xmas **CONF:** Thtr 120 Class 60 Board 35 **SERVICES:** Lift **PARKING:** 50 **NOTES:** No dogs (ex guide dogs)
CARDS:

★★★65% Pavilion
22 Bath Rd BH1 2NS
☎ 01202 291266 ⎙ 01202 559264
A friendly team of staff ensure a warm welcome for all guests. The requirements of both the leisure and business guest are catered for, with well equipped bedrooms which vary in size, spacious and comfortable public areas and good conference facilities. The hotel is located close to the town centre with easy access to the seafront and attractions.
ROOMS: 44 en suite (6 fmly) s fr £25; d £50-£74 (incl. bkfst) * LB **FACILITIES:** Special rates for International Centre entertainment Xmas **CONF:** Thtr 100 Class 50 Board 50 Del from £50 * **SERVICES:** Lift **PARKING:** 40 **NOTES:** No smoking in restaurant
CARDS:

★★★65% *Tralee Hotel*
West Hill Rd, West Cliff BH2 5EQ
☎ 01202 556246
The Tralee Hotel, situated on the West Cliff, is within easy reach of the town centre and its many attractions. Bedrooms are equipped to a high standard and a choice of bars and lounges is available, including the fourth floor Solarium lounge, with its spectacular views.
ROOMS: 68 en suite

★★★64% Burley Court
Bath Rd BH1 2NP
☎ 01202 552824 & 556704 ⎙ 01202 298514
e-mail: burleycourt@btclick.com
Dir: *leave A338 at St Pauls roundabout, take 3rd exit at next roundabout (Holdenhurst Rd), 3rd exit at next roundabout (Bath Rd), overcrossing, 1st left*
This personally owned and managed hotel is within easy walking distance of the town centre, attracting many loyal guests. Bedrooms vary in style and standard. Public areas are spacious and comfortable. A daily changing table d'hote menu is served in the dining room.
ROOMS: 38 en suite (8 fmly) No smoking in 8 bedrooms s £31-£42; d £62-£82 (incl. bkfst) * LB **FACILITIES:** Outdoor swimming (H) Solarium Pool table Free use of local indoor leisure pool **CONF:** Thtr 30 Class 15 Board 15 **SERVICES:** Lift **PARKING:** 35 **NOTES:** No smoking in restaurant Closed 30 Dec-14 Jan **CARDS:**

BOURNEMOUTH, continued

★★★64% Heathlands Hotel
12 Grove Rd, East Cliff BH1 3AY
☎ 01202 553336 01202 555937
e-mail: info@heathlandshotel.com
Dir: *from A338 St Pauls rdbt take Holdenhurst Road, then take 2nd exit off Lansdowne rdbt, into Meyrick Rd. Left into Gervis Rd. Hotel on R*
A large hotel on the East Cliff, Bournemouth Heathlands is popular with groups. Public areas are bright and spacious. The coffee shop is open all day and there is regular live entertainment.
ROOMS: 115 en suite (13 fmly) No smoking in 15 bedrooms s £35-£86; d £70-£172 (incl. bkfst) * LB **FACILITIES:** STV Outdoor swimming (H) Sauna Gym Jacuzzi/spa Health suite entertainment ch fac Xmas **CONF:** Thtr 270 Class 102 Board 54 Del from £75 * **SERVICES:** Lift **PARKING:** 100 **NOTES:** No smoking in restaurant Civ Wed
CARDS:

★★★63% Chesterwood
East Overcliff Dr BH1 3AR
☎ 01202 558057 01202 556285
e-mail: chesterwood@aol.com
All of the public rooms enjoy splendid sea views from this hotel on the East Cliff. In the spacious restaurant a fixed price menu is available each evening and Sunday lunches are provided. A comfortable bar lounge offers an informal seating alternative to the drawing room. The bedrooms are pleasing and well equipped.
ROOMS: 49 en suite (13 fmly) s £30-£45; d £60-£90 (incl. bkfst) * LB **FACILITIES:** Outdoor swimming (H) Pool table entertainment Xmas **CONF:** Thtr 150 Class 100 Board 30 Del from £39.50 * **SERVICES:** Lift **PARKING:** 47 **NOTES:** No smoking in restaurant
CARDS:

★★★63% New Durley Dean
West Cliff Rd BH2 5HE
☎ 01202 557711 01202 292815
Dir: *off A338*
Conveniently located on the West Cliff, this large hotel is equally suited to both business and leisure guests. At the time of our last inspection, bedrooms were being upgraded to a good standard. Facilities include a leisure centre with pool and night club where entertainment is provided some evenings.
ROOMS: 122 en suite (27 fmly) s £30-£73; d £60-£146 (incl. bkfst & dinner) * LB **FACILITIES:** STV Indoor swimming (H) Sauna Solarium Gym Pool table Jacuzzi/spa Table tennis Steam room entertainment Xmas **CONF:** Thtr 150 Class 70 Board 40 **SERVICES:** Lift **PARKING:** 45 **NOTES:** No smoking in restaurant **CARDS:**

★★★63% *Suncliff*
29 East Overcliff Dr BH1 3AG
☎ 01202 291711 01202 293788
Dir: *A338 to Bournemouth. 1st left at rdbt into St Pauls Rd, follow signs for East Cliff*
A large privately owned hotel on the East Cliff with glorious views from the public rooms and many bedrooms. Rooms are equipped with modern facilities, and are spacious and comfortably furnished. Public rooms include a pleasant conservatory.
ROOMS: 94 en suite (29 fmly) **FACILITIES:** Indoor swimming (H) Squash Sauna Solarium Gym Pool table Jacuzzi/spa Table tennis entertainment **CONF:** Thtr 100 Class 70 Board 60 **SERVICES:** Lift **PARKING:** 60 **CARDS:**

★★★62% Grosvenor
Bath Rd, East Cliff BH1 2EX
☎ 01202 558858 01202 298332
e-mail: grosvenor@post.bournemouth-net.co.uk.
Within a short walk of the seafront and conveniently close to the shops, this hotel offers a range of comfortable bedrooms. Guests can relax in the well furnished lounge bar and a separate sitting room is available. A popular indoor leisure suite is provided.
ROOMS: 40 en suite (12 fmly) s £38-£48; d £76-£96 (incl. bkfst) * LB **FACILITIES:** STV Indoor swimming (H) Sauna Solarium Pool table Jacuzzi/spa entertainment Xmas **CONF:** Thtr 30 Class 50 Board 20 **SERVICES:** Lift **PARKING:** 40 **NOTES:** No dogs (ex guide dogs) No smoking in restaurant **CARDS:**

★★71% *Sun Court*
West Hill Rd, West Cliff BH2 5PH
☎ 01202 551343 01202 316747
Standing on the West Cliff, this hotel is family-owned and run by friendly staff. Bedrooms vary in size and style, but are all well equipped, and several have lounge areas. Public areas include the Palm Court Bar and a spacious dining room where a fixed price menu is served each evening.
ROOMS: 33 en suite (7 fmly) **FACILITIES:** Outdoor swimming (H) Solarium Gym Facilities at sister hotel **SERVICES:** Lift **PARKING:** 50 **NOTES:** No smoking in restaurant **CARDS:**

★★70% Arlington
Exeter Park Rd BH2 5BD
☎ 01202 552879 & 553012 01202 298317
Dir: *follow signs to Bournemouth International Centre through Priory Rd, onto rdbt and exit at Royal Exeter Hotel sign. Hotel is along Exeter Park Rd*
The Arlington has a relaxed, friendly atmosphere and a superb location midway between the Square and Bournemouth Pier. The attractive bar/lounge overlooks the main Bournemouth Flower Gardens and bandstand. Well equipped bedrooms are decorated to a good standard and downstairs home cooked dishes are served in Impressions Restaurant.
ROOMS: 27 en suite 1 annexe en suite (6 fmly) s £36.50-£44.50; d £73-£89 (incl. bkfst & dinner) * LB **FACILITIES:** STV Xmas **SERVICES:** Lift **PARKING:** 21 **NOTES:** No dogs No children 2yrs Closed 4-15 Jan
CARDS:

★★70% Durley Grange
6 Durley Rd, West Cliff BH2 5JL
☎ 01202 554473 & 290743 01202 293774
Dir: *turn left off Wessex Way-A338 on St Michaels rdbt, through next rdbt, 1st left into Sommerville Rd, turn right into Durley Rd*
This friendly hotel is located in a quiet area, within easy walking distance of the pier and town centre. Bedrooms are simply decorated, comfortable and well equipped. Home-cooked meals are served in the dining room and there is a lounge bar.
ROOMS: 52 en suite (4 fmly) No smoking in 2 bedrooms s £34-£47; d £68-£94 (incl. bkfst & dinner) * LB **FACILITIES:** STV Indoor swimming (H) Sauna Solarium Jacuzzi/spa entertainment Xmas **SERVICES:** Lift **PARKING:** 35 **NOTES:** No children 5yrs No smoking in restaurant Closed 2 Jan-1 Feb **CARDS:**

★★70% *Whitehall*
Exeter Park Rd BH2 5AX
☎ 01202 554682 01202 554682
e-mail: whitehallhotel@lineone.net
Dir: *follow signs B.I.C. then turn into Exeter Park Road off Exeter Road*
The warmest of welcomes awaits guests at this comfortable hotel. Bedrooms are bright and attractively decorated in co-ordinating fabrics. There is a small, well stocked bar and two attractive lounges, one of which overlooks the garden.
ROOMS: 47 rms (44 en suite) (5 fmly) **SERVICES:** Lift **PARKING:** 25 **NOTES:** No smoking in restaurant Closed Nov-Feb
CARDS:

B

★★69% Chinehurst
Alum Chine, 18-20 Studland Rd, Westbourne BH4 8JA
☎ 01202 764583 🖷 01202 762854
Dir: *turn off A338, second junction off Frizzel roundabout, follow signs for Alum Chine*
A warm welcome is assured at this family run hotel, peacefully situated on the west side of town. Bedrooms are bright and attractive, some with sea views, including the honeymoon suite which has a super outlook. There is a path leading to the beach and regular buses run to the town centre if required.
ROOMS: 30 en suite (4 fmly) No smoking in 4 bedrooms s £30-£45; d £60-£80 (incl. bkfst) * LB **FACILITIES:** Pool table Games room entertainment Xmas **CONF:** Thtr 60 Class 40 Board 40 Del from £45 * **PARKING:** 14 **NOTES:** No children 3yrs No smoking in restaurant **CARDS:**

★★68% *Royal Exeter*
Exeter Rd BH2 5AG
☎ 01202 290566 🖷 01202 297963
Scottish Newcastle
Dir: *opposite the Bournemouth International Centre*
This smart hotel is situated opposite the Bournemouth International Centre, only a short walk from the town centre. The bedrooms are well maintained and provide good facilities. There is a spacious bar and restaurant where guests can choose from a good selection of well cooked meals. There is also a relaxing patio and the Lighthouse Coffee Shop.
ROOMS: 46 en suite (12 fmly) **FACILITIES:** Childrens indoor play area **CONF:** Thtr 40 Class 25 Board 25 **SERVICES:** Lift **PARKING:** 56 **NOTES:** No dogs (ex guide dogs) **CARDS:**

★★67% *Croham Hurst*
9 Durley Rd South, West Cliff BH2 5JH
☎ 01202 552353 🖷 01202 311484
Dir: *off A35 at Cambridge Rd roundabout, follow signs to BIC, hotel on the right just before Durley roundabout*

Enjoying high levels of repeat business from loyal customers, this popular family-run hotel is convenient for both the beach and town centre. Rooms are a mixture of traditional and modern styles but all are spacious and well equipped. The lounge doubles as an entertainment venue and the spacious restaurant offers traditional home-cooked dishes.
ROOMS: 40 en suite (10 fmly) **FACILITIES:** STV entertainment **SERVICES:** Lift **PARKING:** 30 **NOTES:** No dogs (ex guide dogs) No smoking in restaurant Closed 2 Jan-10 Feb **CARDS:**

★★67% *Mansfield*
West Cliff Gardens BH2 5HL
☎ 01202 552659
Dir: *from A338 follow signs for West Cliff, straight on at two rdbts via Cambridge & Durley Chine Rd*
Located in a quiet crescent on the West Cliff, Mansfield Hotel is convenient for access to the seafront and town centre. The bedrooms are comfortably furnished. Staff make every effort to ensure that guests have an enjoyable stay. Two lounges adjoin the cosy bar.
ROOMS: 30 en suite (7 fmly) **PARKING:** 12 **NOTES:** No dogs No smoking in restaurant Closed 29 Dec-17 Jan **CARDS:**

★★66% *New Westcliff*
29 Chine Crescent, West Cliff BH2 5LB
☎ 01202 551926 🖷 01202 310671
Dir: *follow signs for Bournemouth International Centre, West Cliff and Town Centre pass Durley Hall Hotel on right, Durley Chine hotel is 50yds on right*
Ideally located for town and beach, a warm welcome awaits guests at this family run hotel. While varied in size, the bedrooms are attractively decorated and well equipped. There is a lovely garden and three lounges. All-weather leisure facilities, including a small cinema, are a definite plus.
ROOMS: 23 en suite 17 annexe en suite (7 fmly) **PARKING:** 40 **NOTES:** No smoking in restaurant Closed 2-16 Jan **CARDS:**

★★65% Cliff Court
15 Westcliff Rd BH2 5EX
☎ 01202 555994 🖷 01202 780954
Dir: *A338 (Wessex Way) into Cambridge Road, follow Durley Chine Road into West Cliff Road*
This hotel is on the West Cliff within easy reach of the town centre, local attractions and the beach. A range of comfortable bedrooms is available. Public rooms include a bar and lounge.
ROOMS: 40 en suite (4 fmly) No smoking in 5 bedrooms s £25-£38 (incl. bkfst) * LB **FACILITIES:** STV entertainment Xmas **SERVICES:** Lift **PARKING:** 39 **NOTES:** No smoking in restaurant **CARDS:**

★★65% Fircroft
4 Owls Rd BH5 1AE
☎ 01202 309771 🖷 01202 395644
Dir: *off A338 signposted Boscombe Pier, hotel is 400yds from pier close to Christchurch Road*
Guests will find a warm welcome at this hotel which is popular with tour groups, and well situated close to Boscombe Pier. Bedrooms are well equipped and comfortable. In addition to a separate cocktail bar, there are a number of lounge areas for guests' use.
ROOMS: 51 en suite (20 fmly) s £24-£30; d £48-£60 (incl. bkfst) * LB **FACILITIES:** Indoor swimming (H) Squash Sauna Solarium Gym Pool table Jacuzzi/spa Sports at health club owned by hotel Xmas **CONF:** Thtr 200 Class 100 Board 40 **SERVICES:** Lift **PARKING:** 50 **NOTES:** No smoking in restaurant **CARDS:**

★★65% Ullswater
West Cliff Gardens BH2 5HW
☎ 01202 555181 🖷 01202 317896
e-mail: ullswaterhotel@talk21.com
Dir: *on entering Bournemouth follow signs to Westcliff, hotel just off Westcliff Road*
Situated on the West Cliff, this hotel attracts a loyal following. Bedrooms vary in size but all are decorated in fresh colours and furnished to a good standard. Downstairs there is a spacious and comfortable lounge-bar and a very attractive dining room, where a good choice of dishes are on offer.
ROOMS: 42 en suite (7 fmly) s £27-£32; d £54-£64 (incl. bkfst) * LB **FACILITIES:** Snooker Table tennis entertainment Xmas **CONF:** Thtr 40 Class 30 Board 24 Del from £47.50 * **SERVICES:** Lift **PARKING:** 10 **NOTES:** No dogs (ex guide dogs) No smoking in restaurant **CARDS:**

B

BOURNEMOUTH, continued

★★65% West Cliff Towers
12 Priory Rd BH2 5DG
☎ 01202 553319 🖹 01202 553313
Dir: *exit A338 (A35) onto B3066 (Cambridge Road) straight across 1st rdbt, left at 2nd rdbt through traffic lights, hotel 2nd road on right*
This friendly private hotel is situated within 150 yards of the beach and the International Centre. A comfortable lounge and well stocked bar are available. Bedrooms are light, airy and soundly furnished. Daily changing fixed-price menus, which use fresh local ingredients wherever possible, are served in the dining room.
ROOMS: 28 en suite (7 fmly) No smoking in 3 bedrooms s £35-£45; d £70-£90 (incl. bkfst) * LB **FACILITIES:** STV Xmas **SERVICES:** Lift **PARKING:** 26 **NOTES:** No smoking in restaurant
CARDS:

★★62% Diplomat Hotel
6/8 Durley Chine Rd, West Cliff BH2 5JY
☎ 01202 555025 🖹 01202 559019
Dir: *in Bournemouth follow Town Centre/West Cliff sign. Cross St Michaels rdbt and hotel on left*

The Diplomat is ideally placed to benefit from all of the town's attractions. Bedrooms have all the expected amenities and are decorated in warm colours. The refurbished Chine Inn is open for drinks all day and for dinner, guests can choose from the table d'hôte menu in the main dining room or a bar snack.
ROOMS: 58 en suite (10 fmly) **FACILITIES:** STV entertainment **SERVICES:** Lift **PARKING:** 40 **NOTES:** No smoking in restaurant
CARDS:

★★61% *Bourne Hall Hotel*
14 Priory Rd, West Cliff BH2 5DN
☎ 01202 299715 🖹 01202 552669
e-mail: info@bournehall.co.uk
Dir: *A31 & M27 from Ringwood into Bournemouth on A338 (Wessex Way) - pick up signs to B.I.C. onto West Cliff - Hotel on right*

This spacious hotel is a short stroll from the town centre, seafront and theatres. The well equipped bedrooms are furnished for comfort. Downstairs there is a large lounge bar and the lower bar can also provide a useful area for meetings. The atmosphere throughout is relaxed and welcoming.
ROOMS: 48 en suite (9 fmly) No smoking in 12 bedrooms **FACILITIES:** STV Pool table **CONF:** Thtr 70 Class 70 **SERVICES:** Lift **PARKING:** 35 **NOTES:** No smoking in restaurant
CARDS:

★★61% Lynden Court
8 Durley Rd, West Cliff BH2 5JL
☎ 01202 553894 🖹 01202 317711
Dir: *A338 from Ringwood, left at Town Centre West rdbt to St Michaels rdbt, straight across and second left, hotel facing*
This hotel is well situated on the West Cliff. Bedrooms vary in size; some are suited for family occupation and some conveniently located on the ground floor. The public areas include a comfortable lounge and bar, and an attractive restaurant. A choice from the English menu is offered at dinner and breakfast.
ROOMS: 32 en suite (10 fmly) s £24-£35; d £48-£80 (incl. bkfst) * **FACILITIES:** STV Pool table entertainment Xmas **SERVICES:** Lift **PARKING:** 20 **CARDS:**

★★61% *Taurus Park*
16 Knyveton Rd BH1 3QN
☎ 01202 557374 🖹 01202 557374
Guests are assured a pleasant stay at Taurus Park. Situated in a quiet residential area, only a short walk from the town centre, it offers comfortable accommodation with modern facilities. There is a large dining room and bar.
ROOMS: 43 rms (38 en suite) (7 fmly) **FACILITIES:** Pool table **SERVICES:** Lift **PARKING:** 20 **NOTES:** No dogs No children 5yrs No smoking in restaurant **CARDS:**

★★60% *County*
Westover Rd BH1 2BT
☎ 01202 552385 & 0500 141401 🖹 01202 297255
The central location of this hotel is a real plus and secure parking is also provided. Bedroom facilities are good and the majority of rooms are spacious. There is an attractive lounge bar, dining room and super, newly refurbished Piano Bar where entertainment is provided every evening during the main season.
ROOMS: 48 en suite (11 fmly) **FACILITIES:** STV Use of Bournemouth International Pool **CONF:** Thtr 25 Board 25 **SERVICES:** Lift **PARKING:** 6
CARDS:

★★60% St George
West Cliff Gardens BH2 5HL
☎ 01202 556075 🖹 01202 557330
Set in its own gardens with direct access to the cliff-top and the sea below, this popular and informal hotel has a relaxed and friendly atmosphere. The bedrooms are tidy with modern facilities. Public areas include a spacious, well furnished lounge and well stocked bar. A fixed-price menu is offered in the dining room at garden level.
ROOMS: 22 rms (20 en suite) (5 fmly) s £24.50-£31; d £49-£62 (incl. bkfst) LB **FACILITIES:** STV Xmas **SERVICES:** Lift **PARKING:** 4 **NOTES:** No smoking in restaurant Closed mid Nov-mid Dec & 3 Jan-Mar
CARDS:

★★56% *Russell Court*
Bath Rd BH1 2EP
☎ 01202 295819 🖹 01202 293457
Bright, well maintained bedrooms are provided at this popular coaching hotel, several benefiting from sea views. Live entertainment features on some evenings in the spacious and comfortable public rooms. Informal and friendly service is provided by the young staff.

continued

ROOMS: 62 rms (58 en suite) (6 fmly) **FACILITIES:** entertainment **CONF:** Thtr 20 **SERVICES:** Lift **PARKING:** 60 **NOTES:** No dogs (ex guide dogs) No smoking in restaurant **CARDS:**

○ Gresham Court Hotel

4 Grove Rd, East Cliff BH1 3AX
☎ 01202 551732 01202 551559
This friendly, personally run East Cliff hotel enjoys a high level of repeat business. It is particularly popular with groups, and sequence dancing is a speciality, although individuals are well looked after. The traditionally furnished bedrooms are bright and well equipped, and there is a choice of lounges in which to relax.
NOTES: Open

BOURTON-ON-THE-WATER, Gloucestershire Map 04 SP12

★★74% Dial House

The Chestnuts, High St GL54 2AN
☎ 01451 822244 01451 810126
e-mail: info@dialhousehotel.com
Dir: *off A429, 0.5m to village centre*

This charming hotel built of mellow Cotswold stone dates back to 1698. Public rooms are tastefully appointed and include a cosy bar and adjoining lounge and two small dining rooms. Bedrooms vary in size and style, all are comfortably furnished and well equipped. Guests appreciate the high standard of cooking.
ROOMS: 14 en suite No smoking in 3 bedrooms s £52-£64.50; d £104-£129 (incl. bkfst) * LB **FACILITIES:** STV Croquet lawn Putting green Xmas **PARKING:** 20 **NOTES:** No dogs (ex guide dogs) No children 10yrs No smoking in restaurant **CARDS:**

See advert on this page

★★68% *Old New Inn*

High St GL54 2AF
☎ 01451 820467 01451 810236
e-mail: 106206.2571@compuserve.com
Dir: *off A429*

Situated near the famous model village, the inn offers a variety of styles of bedroom, some in a nearby cottage. Public areas are full of character and staff offer a warm and friendly welcome.
ROOMS: 16 rms (8 en suite) 4 annexe rms **PARKING:** 31 **NOTES:** No smoking in restaurant Closed 25 Dec **CARDS:**

★★66% *Chester House Hotel & Motel*

MINOTEL Great Britain

Victoria St GL54 2BU
☎ 01451 820286 01451 820471
e-mail: juliand@chesterhouse.u-net.com
Chester House occupies a secluded but central location in this delightful Cotswold village. Rooms are comfortable and thoughtfully equipped. Public areas include an attractive restaurant and separate breakfast room. The family and ground floor rooms and 'pets welcome' philosophy appeal to many visitors. The car park is also a bonus.
ROOMS: 13 en suite 10 annexe en suite (8 fmly) **CONF:** Board 121 **PARKING:** 20 **NOTES:** Closed mid Dec-Jan
CARDS:

BOVEY TRACEY, Devon Map 03 SX87

★★★73% Edgemoor

Haytor Rd, Lowerdown Cross TQ13 9LE
☎ 01626 832466 01626 834760
e-mail: edgemoor@btinternet.com
Dir: *from A382 follow signs for Haytor and Widecombe*
This peaceful country house hotel lies in two acres of gardens on the edge of Dartmoor. The individual bedrooms are well equipped; some ground floor rooms are available. The relaxed ambience is enhanced by the pleasant, spacious lounge and

continued on p108

BOVEY TRACEY, continued

beamed bar, both with welcoming open fires. A tempting selection of award-winning cooking is served in the elegant dining room.

Edgemoor Hotel, Bovey Tracey

ROOMS: 12 en suite 5 annexe en suite (3 fmly) s £57.50-£72.50; d £95-£100 (incl. bkfst) * LB **FACILITIES:** STV **CONF:** Thtr 60 Class 40 Board 25 Del from £65 * **PARKING:** 45 **NOTES:** No smoking in restaurant **CARDS:**

See advert on opposite page

★★66% Coombe Cross

THE CIRCLE Selected Individual Hotels

Coombe Cross TQ13 9EY
☎ 01626 832476 📠 01626 835298
Dir: *from A38 follow signs for Bovey Tracey and town centre, along High St & up the hill 400yds beyond the Parish Church, hotel on the left*

Set on the hill, a minute's walk from town, Coombe Cross enjoys views over the surrounding countryside and its own pretty gardens. Decor throughout is smart and bedrooms offer a good level of comfort and some useful extras. There is an elegant dining room, two lounges, a small bar and some lovely leisure facilities.

ROOMS: 24 en suite (2 fmly) s £45; d £70 (incl. bkfst) * LB **FACILITIES:** Indoor swimming (H) Sauna Solarium Gym Jacuzzi/spa ch fac **CONF:** Thtr 40 Class 60 Board 30 **PARKING:** 26 **NOTES:** No smoking in restaurant **CARDS:**

★★62% Riverside Inn

Fore St TQ13 9AF
☎ 01626 832293 📠 01626 833880
e-mail: riversideinn@boveytracey.freeserve.co.uk
Dir: *hotel by bridge in town centre*

The Inn enjoys fishing rights on the River Bovey which flows beside the property. Bedrooms are well decorated and equipped, and downstairs a good range of dishes is available in the Tracey Bar or Buttery Restaurant. Other facilities include The River Room and a lovely garden.

ROOMS: 10 en suite s £29.50; d £39.50 (incl. bkfst) * LB **FACILITIES:** STV Fishing **CONF:** Thtr 100 Class 80 Board 50 **PARKING:** 100 **CARDS:**

BOWNESS ON WINDERMERE See Windermere

BRACKLEY, Northamptonshire

Map 04 SP53

○ *Premier Lodge (Silverstone)*

Brackley Hatch, Syresham NN13 5TX
☎ 0870 700 1588 📠 0870 700 1589

Bad hair day? Hairdryers in all rooms three stars and above.

BRACKNELL, Berkshire

Map 04 SU86

see also Wokingham

★★★★76% Coppid Beech

John Nike Way RG12 8TF
☎ 01344 303333 📠 01344 301200
e-mail: welcome@coppid-beech-hotel.co.uk
Dir: *from junct 10 on M4 take Wokingham/Bracknell option on to A329, in 2 miles at roundabout take B3408 to Binfield, hotel 200yds on the right hand side*

The chalet-style Coppid Beech complex includes health club, ski slope and ice rink. Other amenities include a night-club, bierkeller and conference facilities. Bedrooms are spacious and all beds have feather duvets. Rowan's restaurant serves award-winning cuisine.

ROOMS: 205 en suite (6 fmly) No smoking in 138 bedrooms s fr £155; d fr £175 (incl. bkfst) * LB **FACILITIES:** STV Indoor swimming (H) Sauna Solarium Gym Jacuzzi/spa entertainment Xmas **CONF:** Thtr 400 Class 240 Board 24 Del from £195 * **SERVICES:** Lift air con **PARKING:** 350 **NOTES:** Civ Wed 150 **CARDS:**

★★★72% Stirrups Country House

Best Western

Maidens Green RG42 6LD
☎ 01344 882284 📠 01344 882300
e-mail: reception@stirrupshotel.co.uk
Dir: *3m N on B3022 towards Windsor*

Situated in a peaceful location between Maidenhead, Bracknell and Windsor, this hotel has high standards of comfort in the bedrooms, with newer rooms boasting a small sitting room area. Bathrooms all have power showers. There is a popular bar and refurbished restaurant.

ROOMS: 29 en suite (4 fmly) No smoking in 16 bedrooms s £100-£125; d £105-£125 * LB **FACILITIES:** STV **CONF:** Thtr 100 Class 50 Board 40 Del from £125 * **SERVICES:** Lift **PARKING:** 100 **NOTES:** No dogs (ex guide dogs) No smoking in restaurant
CARDS:

BRADFORD, West Yorkshire

Map 07 SE13

see also Gomersal & Shipley

★★★★64% Cedar Court Hotel Bradford

Mayo Av, Off Rooley Ln BD5 8HZ
☎ 01274 406606 & 406601 📠 01274 406600
e-mail: sales@cedarcourt-hotel-bradford.co.uk
Dir: *leave M62 at junct 26, then follow M606. At the end take 3rd exit off rdbt onto A6177 toward Bradford, take 1st sharp right at lights*

Convenient for Bradford and the M606, this hotel offers nicely furnished, comfortable bedrooms. There is an elegant Four Seasons restaurant and a spacious central bar lounge. Meeting and function suites are impressive, as is the manned business centre.

ROOMS: 131 en suite (7 fmly) No smoking in 75 bedrooms d £59-£99 * LB **FACILITIES:** Indoor swimming (H) Sauna Solarium Gym Pool table Jacuzzi/spa Beauty treatments Xmas **CONF:** Thtr 800 Class 500 Board 100 Del from £70 * **SERVICES:** Lift **PARKING:** 350 **NOTES:** RS Xmas & New Year Civ Wed 600 **CARDS:**

★★★69% Midland Hotel

Peel Hotels

Forster Square BD1 4HU
☎ 01274 735735 📠 01274 720003
e-mail: info@peelhotel.com

Centrally located with the added advantage of secure parking, this hotel has a pleasing mix of features, including a Victorian passage that led directly to the station platform. By contrast, bedrooms have smart modern decor and are equipped with every modern convenience. The extensive public areas provide good comforts.

continued

ROOMS: 90 en suite (10 fmly) No smoking in 9 bedrooms s fr £75; d fr £85 (incl. bkfst) * LB **FACILITIES:** STV Pool table Free use of local health club entertainment **CONF:** Thtr 500 Class 150 Board 100 Del from £100 * **SERVICES:** Lift **PARKING:** 200 **NOTES:** No dogs **CARDS:**

★★★67% Apperley Manor

Apperley Ln, Apperley Bridge BD10 0PQ
☎ 0113 250 5626 📠 0113 250 0075
e-mail: janette@apperley-manor.co.uk

Dir: *on A658 Bradford to Harrogate road, 2m from Leeds/Bradford Int Airport*

This friendly hotel lies between Leeds and Bradford, with easy access to the airport. Spacious bedrooms are well furnished and equipped with modern facilities. Carefully prepared meals are served in the candlelit restaurant by courteous and welcoming staff; the newly added Brasserie provides an interesting alternative choice of dishes.

ROOMS: 13 en suite (2 fmly) s £59.50-£75; d £69.50-£80 * **FACILITIES:** Jacuzzi in 2 bedrooms **CONF:** Thtr 80 Class 40 Board 30 Del from £82.50 * **SERVICES:** Lift **PARKING:** 100 **NOTES:** No dogs (ex guide dogs) **CARDS:**

★★★66% Courtyard by Marriott Leeds/Bradford

COURTYARD

The Pastures, Tong Ln BD4 0RP
☎ 0113 285 4646 📠 0113 285 3661

Dir: *from junct 27 M62, take A650 towards Bradford. 3rd rdbt, take 3rd exit 'Tong Village & Pudsey'. Turn left Tong Lane. Hotel 0.5m on right*

This former 18th-century vicarage with modern but sympathetically designed bedroom wings is situated in a rural location just near the M62 motorway. The spacious and well equipped bedrooms are particularly well appointed and several have separate sitting rooms.

ROOMS: 53 en suite (5 fmly) No smoking in 28 bedrooms d £79-£81 * LB **FACILITIES:** STV Gym **CONF:** Thtr 300 Class 150 Board 100 **SERVICES:** Lift **PARKING:** 300 **NOTES:** No dogs (ex guide dogs) Civ Wed **CARDS:**

★★★65% Guide Post Hotel

Common Rd, Low Moor BD12 0ST
☎ 01274 607866 📠 01274 671085

Dir: *follow A638 towards Oakenshaw/Low Moor, pass large factory (CIBA), pass petrol station on left, take 2nd left into Common Road*

Just two miles from the junction of the M606 and M62, this hotel offers attractively furnished and spacious bedrooms. An extensive range of dishes, often including a daily list of fresh fish, is offered in the bright restaurant, with lighter meals served in the bar. The hotel has two well maintained function suites.

ROOMS: 43 en suite (3 fmly) No smoking in 7 bedrooms s £65-£75; d £75-£85 (incl. bkfst) * LB **FACILITIES:** STV **CONF:** Thtr 120 Class 80 Board 60 **PARKING:** 100 **NOTES:** No dogs (ex guide dogs) Civ Wed 100 **CARDS:**

See advert on this page

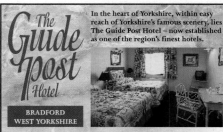

BRADFORD, continued

★★★64% Quality Hotel Bradford
Bridge St BD1 1JX
☎ 01274 728706 📠 01274 736358
e-mail: admin@gb654.u-net.com
Dir: *behind Bradford Interchange Station, next to St Georges Concert Hall*
This Victorian hotel, which is ideally situated right in the city centre and has the benefit of its own car park, provides modern thoughtfully equipped bedrooms and suites. Extensive public areas include a choice of eating and drinking options in the form of a brasserie and a lively bar.
ROOMS: 60 en suite (3 fmly) No smoking in 40 bedrooms
FACILITIES: STV Sauna Gym entertainment **CONF:** Thtr 150 Class 90 Board 60 **SERVICES:** Lift **PARKING:** 69
CARDS:

★★★62% Novotel
Merrydale Rd BD4 6SA
☎ 01274 683683 📠 01274 651342
e-mail: h0510@accor-hotels.com
Dir: *adjacent to M606 junct 2, 3m from city centre*
On the outskirts of the city, close to the motorway, this was one of the first Novotels built in this country. The bedrooms are spacious and public areas include a newly refurbished bar and a lounge leading into the Garden Brasserie. Several function rooms are also available.
ROOMS: 127 en suite (127 fmly) No smoking in 74 bedrooms d £37-£60 * **FACILITIES:** STV Outdoor swimming (H) Pool table **CONF:** Thtr 300 Class 150 Board 100 **SERVICES:** Lift **PARKING:** 180
CARDS:

★★68% Park Drive
12 Park Dr BD9 4DR
☎ 01274 480194 📠 01274 484869
e-mail: sales@parkdrivehotel.co.uk
Dir: *turn off A650 Keighley Road into Emm Lane, at Lister Park, then turn 2nd right*

This hotel stands in a quiet residential area, close to Lister Park. Spacious bedrooms have attractive soft furnishings and comfortable seating. Wholesome home cooking is a feature of the neatly presented dining room and there is also a welcoming lounge.
ROOMS: 11 en suite (1 fmly) s £47-£52; d £57-£62 (incl. bkfst) LB
CONF: Thtr 20 Class 8 Board 12 Del from £72 * **PARKING:** 10
NOTES: No smoking in restaurant **CARDS:**

See advert on opposite page

★★67% Park Grove
28 Park Grove, Frizinghall BD9 4JY
☎ 01274 543444 📠 01274 495619
e-mail: enquiry@parkgrovehotel.co.uk
Dir: *off A650 Keighley road, turn right after the Park Pub*
A welcoming hotel offering spacious and comfortable accommodation. Friendly service is provided, with a small lounge next to the attractively decorated restaurant, where a mix of Punjabi and English dishes is available.
ROOMS: 15 en suite (3 fmly) s £35-£47; d £45-£60 (incl. bkfst) * LB
FACILITIES: STV **PARKING:** 8 **NOTES:** No dogs No smoking in restaurant **CARDS:**

BRADFORD-ON-AVON, Wiltshire — Map 03 ST86

★★★74% ❀❀ Woolley Grange
Woolley Green BA15 1TX
☎ 01225 864705 📠 01225 864059
e-mail: woolley@luxury-hotel.demon.co.uk
Dir: *on B3105, 0.5m NE at Woolley Green*

A splendid Cotswold manor house set in beautiful countryside. Children are made welcome; there is a trained nanny on duty in the nursery. Bedrooms and public areas are charmingly furnished and decorated in true country house style with many thoughtful touches and luxurious extras. The hotel's well balanced menus continue to gain praise.
ROOMS: 14 en suite 9 annexe en suite (8 fmly) **FACILITIES:** STV Outdoor swimming (H) Tennis (grass) Pool table Croquet lawn Putting green Badminton Games room ch fac **CONF:** Thtr 40 Class 12 Board 22 Del from £150 * **PARKING:** 40 **NOTES:** No smoking in restaurant
CARDS:

See advert on opposite page

★★★67% *Leigh Park Hotel*
Leigh Park West BA15 2RA
☎ 01225 864885 📠 01225 862315
Dir: *A363 Bath/Frome road, take B3105 signed Holt/Woolley Green) hotel 0.25m on right on crossroads of B3105/B3109, N side of Bradford-on-Avon*
Set in five acres of well tended grounds, complete with a vineyard, this relaxing Georgian hotel enjoys splendid views and combines charm and character with modern facilities. The restaurant serves dishes cooked to order, using home-grown fruit and vegetables, and wine from the vineyard.
ROOMS: 21 en suite (4 fmly) No smoking in 7 bedrooms
FACILITIES: Tennis (hard) Snooker **CONF:** Thtr 120 Class 60 Board 60
PARKING: 80 **NOTES:** No smoking in restaurant
CARDS:

BRAINTREE, Essex — Map 05 TL72

★★★61% White Hart
Bocking End CM7 9AB
☎ 01376 321401 📠 01376 552628
e-mail: reservations
@thewhitearthotel.freeserve.co.uk
Dir: *turn off A120. Head into Town Centre. Hotel at junct B1256 & Bocking Causeway*
Parts of this former coaching inn date back to the 16th century,

continued

giving the hotel old world charm. There are a small number of character rooms in the original part of the building as well as some more modern rooms to the rear of the property. The hotel has a very loyal local following and its charm and location make it popular with guests.
ROOMS: 31 en suite (8 fmly) No smoking in 9 bedrooms s £56; d £65 (incl. bkfst) * LB **FACILITIES:** STV Sauna Solarium Gym **CONF:** Thtr 40 Class 16 Board 24 **PARKING:** 52 **NOTES:** No dogs (ex guide dogs) Civ Wed 60 **CARDS:**

Express by Holiday Inn Braintree

Galley's Corner, Cressing Rd CM7 8DJ
☎ 01376 551141 01376 551142
Dir: *turn off A120 onto B1018 at Galley's Corner. Hotel is situated next door to Wyevale Garden Centre*

A modern budget hotel offering comfortable accommodation in refreshing, spacious and comprehensively-equipped bedrooms, en suite bathrooms with power showers and continental buffet

continued on p112

BRADFORD

Park Drive Hotel

AA ★★

12 Park Drive, Bradford
West Yorkshire BD9 4DR
Tel: 01274 480194 Fax: 01274 484869

Just 1·5 miles from the city centre you will discover this elegant Victorian residence in its fine woodland setting.
Experience the delicious home cooking, a peaceful night's sleep, safe parking inside the grounds and the friendly personal service.

"It's like staying in the country!"

Hotel & Restaurant

17th century stone manor house set in open countryside, within walking distance of Bradford on Avon and eight miles from Bath. Offers a warm welcome to families, with award winning child facilities, a wide range of good food and an outdoor swimming pool.

Meeting facilities for up to 24 people

Woolley Grange, Bradford on Avon
Wiltshire BA15 1TX
Tel: 01225 864705 Fax: 01225 864059
Email: info@woolleygrange.com
Website: www.woolleygrange.com

★ ★

OLD WHITE LION HOTEL

HAWORTH, KEIGHLEY, **BRADFORD**, WEST YORKSHIRE
Tel: (01535) 642313 Email: enquiries@oldwhitelionhotel.com
Fax: (01535) 646222 Website: www.oldwhitelionhotel.com

This family run hotel is situated at the centre of this famous village close to the Brontë museum, church and parsonage. Catering for the discriminating businessman as well as tourists from all over the world. Fourteen comfortable bedrooms, all with en-suite facilities, colour TV, radio/direct dial telephone, tea making facilities, some with magnificent views. Fax and e-mail facilities also available. Central heating throughout. Residents' Lounge, Cocktail and Lounge Bars. Beamed candlelit restaurant open 7 days a week – Table D'Hôte and À La Carte. Sunday lunch a speciality. Open to non-residents. Hot and cold bar snacks prepared by our chefs at all meal times. Special weekend rates available.

BRAINTREE, continued

breakfast included in the room rate. Suitable for business travellers or families. For further details and the Express by Holiday Inn phone number, consult the Hotel Groups page.
ROOMS: 47 en suite (incl. cont bkfst) d £49.95 * **CONF:** Thtr 30 Class 20 Board 20

B

BRAITHWAITE, Cumbria Map 11 NY22

★★68% *Ivy House*
CA12 5SY
☎ 017687 78338 📠 017687 78113
Dir: *in the middle of the village turn left immediately after the Royal Oak pub*
Dating from the 17th century, this fine period house is conveniently situated in the village centre. The cosy lounge features ancient timbers and open fires. The galleried restaurant, candlelit by night, serves a skilfully prepared daily-changing menu.
ROOMS: 12 en suite **PARKING:** 17 **NOTES:** No children No smoking in restaurant Closed Jan **CARDS:**

BRAMHALL, Greater Manchester Map 07 SJ88

★★★64% County Hotel Bramhall
REGAL
Bramhall Ln South SK7 2EB
☎ 0161 455 9988 📠 0161 440 8071
Dir: *M56 junct6 to Wilmslow A34 bypass towards Manchester, A5102 to Bramhall. From M60 junct3, A34 bypass to Congleton - A5102 to Bramhall*

This modern hotel in a pleasant suburban area offers accommodation in comfortable and well equipped bedrooms. The restaurant serves a wide range of dishes, and there is also the Shires Pub.
ROOMS: 65 en suite (3 fmly) No smoking in 20 bedrooms s £83-£97; d £85-£115 * LB **FACILITIES:** Xmas **CONF:** Thtr 200 Class 80 Board 60 Del from £95 * **PARKING:** 120 **NOTES:** No smoking in restaurant Civ Wed 140 **CARDS:**

BRAMHOPE, West Yorkshire Map 08 SE24

★★★70% *Posthouse Bramhope*
Posthouse
Leeds Rd LS16 9JJ
☎ 0113 284 2911 📠 0113 284 3451
Dir: *on A660 6m N of Leeds city centre. Follow signs 'Leeds/Bradford Airport'*
This modern hotel is peacefully situated in 16 acres of grounds. Bedrooms offer a good range of facilities and are comfortably appointed. Public areas are smartly presented and include a restaurant, conference rooms and a training centre. An all-day lounge service is available, in addition to the 24-hour room service.
ROOMS: 124 en suite No smoking in 40 bedrooms **FACILITIES:** STV Indoor swimming (H) Sauna Solarium Gym Pool table Jacuzzi/spa **CONF:** Thtr 160 Class 80 Board 40 **SERVICES:** Lift air con **PARKING:** 126 **NOTES:** No smoking in restaurant **CARDS:**

BRAMPTON, Cumbria Map 12 NY56

Premier Collection

★★★ Farlam Hall
RELAIS & CHATEAUX
Hallbankgate CA8 2NG
☎ 016977 46234 📠 016977 46683
e-mail: farlamhall@dial.pipex.com
Dir: *from A69 take A689 to Alston, the hotel is approx 2m on the left, not in Farlam village*
A delightful 16th-century house in extensive landscaped gardens, Farlam Hall has a warm and welcoming atmosphere. Bedrooms are furnished to the highest standards as guest comfort is paramount. Public areas too are elegantly decorated. Service is attentive throughout.
ROOMS: 11 en suite 1 annexe en suite s £120-£135; d £220-£250 (incl. bkfst & dinner) * LB **FACILITIES:** Croquet lawn **PARKING:** 35 **NOTES:** No children 5yrs Closed 25-30 Dec
CARDS:

★★65% Tarn End House
Talkin Tarn CA8 1LS
☎ 016977 2340 📠 016977 2089
Dir: *from A69 take B6413 for 2m and turn off towards Talkin Village*
There is a warm and relaxed atmosphere at this farmhouse, which enjoys an idyllic location. The hotel provides an ideal retreat and is also popular with golfers, the local course being on its doorstep. Dinner is a treat, with an extremely imaginative and daily changing menu.
ROOMS: 7 en suite (1 fmly) s £37.50-£52.50; d £55-£74.50 (incl. bkfst) LB **FACILITIES:** Xmas **CONF:** Board 20 Del from £85 * **PARKING:** 40 **NOTES:** No smoking in restaurant Closed 27-29 Dec & 3-25 Jan
CARDS:

BRANDESBURTON, East Riding of Yorkshire Map 08 TA14

★★68% Burton Lodge
YO25 8RU
☎ 01964 542847 📠 01964 544771
e-mail: burton@lodge5755freeserve.co.uk
Dir: *7m from Beverley off A165, adjoining Hainsworth Park Golf Club*
Surrounded by landscaped gardens next to a golf course, this friendly, modern hotel offers very pleasant accommodation. An open fire is a welcoming feature of the lounge and the attractive dining room serves well produced home cooking.
ROOMS: 7 en suite 2 annexe en suite (2 fmly) s £35-£37; d £46-£52 (incl. bkfst) * LB **FACILITIES:** Golf 18 Tennis (grass) Putting green Pitch and putt **PARKING:** 14 **NOTES:** No smoking in restaurant
CARDS:

B

BRANDON, Suffolk

Map 05 TL78

★★70% Brandon House

MINOTEL Great Britain

High St IP27 0AX
☎ 01842 810171 🖷 01842 814859
e-mail: reservationa@brandonhouse.co.uk
Dir: *in Brandon town centre take left at traffic lights into High Street. Hotel 400yds on right just beyond small bridge over the Ouse*

Strikingly built in red brick, this manor house dates back to the 18th century. The bedrooms vary in size and style, but all are well equipped. The spacious public rooms include the traditional Conifers English Restaurant for serious dining, a more informal bistro, and a large comfortable lounge bar. Friendly staff provide a warm welcome.

ROOMS: 15 en suite (3 fmly) **FACILITIES:** STV **CONF:** Thtr 70 Class 25 Board 20 **PARKING:** 40 **NOTES:** No smoking in restaurant Closed 25-26 Dec & 1 Jan **CARDS:**

BRANDON, Warwickshire

Map 04 SP47

★★★64% The Brandon Hall

Main St CV8 3FW
☎ 0870 400 8105 🖷 024 7654 4909
Dir: *off A428 to Rugby*

Peacefully located in 17 acres of lawns and woodland, this former shooting lodge is found by following signs for the village centre of Brandon. Many bedrooms have been refurbished to a very high standard, providing a good range of modern facilities and very smart bathrooms.

ROOMS: 60 en suite No smoking in 29 bedrooms d £99-£120 * LB **FACILITIES:** STV Squash Croquet lawn Putting green Xmas **CONF:** Thtr 90 Class 40 Board 40 Del £139 * **PARKING:** 250 **NOTES:** No smoking in restaurant Civ Wed 90 **CARDS:**

BRANDS HATCH, Kent

Map 05 TQ56

★★★66% Brandshatch Place

ARCADIAN HOTELS distinctly different

Fawkham DA3 8NQ
☎ 01474 872239 🖷 01474 879652
e-mail: bhplace@aol.com
Dir: *from A20 follow signs Fawkham. Tourist sign Brandshatch Place Hotel. After 1 mile follow tourist sign, take third turn left under motorway bridge*

This delightful Georgian country house in extensive gardens is peaceful despite being close to the famous racing circuit. The hotel has excellent leisure facilities and a range of meeting rooms. Bedrooms are spacious, comfortable and equipped with extra amenities. The kitchen takes pride in its cuisine.

ROOMS: 29 en suite 12 annexe en suite (2 fmly) No smoking in 12 bedrooms s fr £77; d fr £97 (incl. bkfst) * LB **FACILITIES:** STV Indoor swimming (H) Tennis (hard) Squash Snooker Sauna Solarium Gym Jacuzzi/spa Beauty therapy Steam room Xmas **CONF:** Thtr 120 Class 60 Board 75 Del from £125 * **PARKING:** 100 **NOTES:** No smoking in restaurant Civ Wed 80 **CARDS:**

BRANKSOME See Poole

BRANSCOMBE, Devon

Map 03 SY18

★★67% The Masons Arms

EX12 3DJ
☎ 01297 680300 🖷 01297 680500
e-mail: reception@masonsarms.co.uk
Dir: *turn off A3052 towards Branscombe, head down hill, hotel in the valley at the bottom of the hill*

This charming 14th-century inn is only half a mile from the sea in the picturesque village of Branscombe. There is a choice of bedrooms offering cottage rooms or comfortable berths in the main house. There is a cosy first floor lounge, and the bar is built around a central fireplace, serving fine ales and food. Oak beams feature in the restaurant.

ROOMS: 6 rms (5 en suite) 16 annexe en suite (2 fmly) s £24-£100; d £44-£120 (incl. bkfst) * LB **FACILITIES:** Xmas **CONF:** Thtr 60 Class 20 Board 20 Del from £95 * **PARKING:** 43 **NOTES:** No smoking in restaurant **CARDS:**

BRANSTON, Lincolnshire

Map 08 TF06

★★★65% Moor Lodge

Best Western

Sleaford Rd LN4 1HU
☎ 01522 791366 🖷 01522 794389
e-mail: moorlodge@bestwestern.co.uk
Dir: *3m S of Lincoln on B1188*

To the south east of Lincoln, this friendly and welcoming hotel features a restaurant named 'Arnhem', after the history of the wartime paratroopers who trained locally. A menu featuring lighter fare is offered in the relaxed bar and lounge. Bedrooms are modern and comfortable.

ROOMS: 24 en suite (2 fmly) No smoking in 2 bedrooms s fr £52.50; d fr £70 (incl. bkfst) * LB **CONF:** Thtr 200 Class 80 Board 60 Del from £85 * **PARKING:** 150 **CARDS:**

★★★64% Branston Hall

Branston Park LN4 1PD
☎ 01522 793305 🖷 01522 790549
e-mail: brahal@enterprise.net
Dir: *3m from Lincoln city centre along B1188 towards Woodhall Spa. On entering Branston village, hotel is located directly opposite the village hall*

Set in picturesque parkland with a lake in its grounds, this imposing house still has many of its original architectural features. The well equipped and furnished bedrooms come in a variety of sizes and styles. In the restaurant an ambitious menu covers most tastes. There is also a bar, lounge, conference rooms and gym.

ROOMS: 37 en suite 6 annexe en suite (3 fmly) s fr £59.50; d fr £79.50 (incl. bkfst) * LB **FACILITIES:** Indoor swimming (H) Sauna Gym Croquet lawn Jacuzzi/spa Jogging circuit Xmas **CONF:** Thtr 200 Class 70 Board 60 Del £90 * **SERVICES:** Lift **PARKING:** 150 **NOTES:** Civ Wed 120 **CARDS:**

See advert under LINCOLN

BRAY, Berkshire

Map 04 SU97

★★★★63% Monkey Island

Old Mill Ln SL6 2EE
☎ 01628 623400 01628 784732
e-mail: monkeyisland@btconnect.com
Dir: *exit M4 at junct 8/9 and take A308 signposted Windsor, take 1st left into Bray then 1st right into Old Mill Lane, which is opposite the Crown pub*

A charming feature of this riverside hotel is its island setting. Access is by footbridge or boat but there is a large carpark nearby. The hotel comprises two buildings, one for accommodation and the other for dining and drinking. Ample grounds provide a peaceful haven for wildlife.

ROOMS: 26 en suite (1 fmly) No smoking in 12 bedrooms **FACILITIES:** STV Fishing Gym Croquet lawn Clay pigeon shooting Boating by request **CONF:** Thtr 150 Class 60 Board 70 **PARKING:** 120 **NOTES:** No dogs **CARDS:**

See advert under MAIDENHEAD

★★★68% Chauntry House Hotel & Restaurant

SL6 2AB
☎ 01628 673991 01628 773089
e-mail: res@chauntryhouse.com
Dir: *from M4 junct 8/9 take A308(M) towards Windsor then B3028 to Bray village. Hotel on left*

Located in an attractive Berkshire village, this smart, traditional country house hotel features spacious and stylish bedrooms, each individually appointed and decorated. The lounge bar and restaurant provide a tranquil environment for guests to relax and the standard of cuisine is high.

ROOMS: 11 en suite 4 annexe en suite s fr £108; d £140-£145 (incl. bkfst) * **FACILITIES:** STV **CONF:** Board 22 Del from £140 * **PARKING:** 35 **NOTES:** No smoking in restaurant Closed 24 Dec-2 Jan RS Sun & BH Civ Wed 55 **CARDS:**

BREADSALL, Derbyshire

Map 08 SK33

★★★★62% Marriott Breadsall Priory Hotel, Country Club

Marriott HOTELS·RESORTS·SUITES

Moor Rd DE7 6DL
☎ 01332 832235 01332 833509
Dir: *take A52 to Derby, then signs to Chesterfield. Right at 1st rndbt, left at next following A608 to Heanor road, after 3m left then left again*

This extended mansion house is set in 400 acres of parkland. The smart bedrooms are mostly contained within modern wings. There is a vibrant café-bar, a more formal restaurant and extensive room service.

continued

ROOMS: 12 en suite 100 annexe en suite (35 fmly) No smoking in 56 bedrooms d £89-£109 * LB **FACILITIES:** STV Indoor swimming (H) Golf 36 Tennis (hard) Sauna Solarium Gym Croquet lawn Putting green Jacuzzi/spa Health/beauty/hair salon Dance studio Xmas **CONF:** Thtr 120 Class 50 Board 36 Del from £135 * **SERVICES:** Lift **PARKING:** 300 **NOTES:** No dogs (ex guide dogs) No smoking in restaurant Civ Wed 100 **CARDS:**

BRENT KNOLL, Somerset

Map 03 ST35

★★68% Woodlands Country House

Hill Ln TA9 4DF
☎ 01278 760232 01278 769090
e-mail: cjllapage@aol.com
Dir: *from A38 take first left into village, then fifth right and first left*

Set in four acres of grounds, this family-run hotel offers tasteful, well equipped bedrooms. An imaginative dinner menu is served in elegant surroundings, and on cooler evenings, guests can enjoy a log fire in the lounge-bar.

ROOMS: 8 en suite No smoking in all bedrooms s £50-£80; d £60-£115 (incl. bkfst) * LB **FACILITIES:** Outdoor swimming Xmas **CONF:** Thtr 80 Class 40 Board 30 Del £90 * **PARKING:** 12 **NOTES:** No children 8yrs No smoking in restaurant **CARDS:**

See advert under WESTON-SUPER-MARE

★★66% Battleborough Grange Hotel

Bristol Rd TA9 4HJ
☎ 01278 760208 01278 760208
e-mail: battleborough@hotel1999.freeserve.co.uk
Dir: *on A38 Weston-Super-Mare Rd, opposite the Goat House*

This popular hotel is conveniently located for easy access to the M5 and is surrounded by mellow Somerset countryside. Bedrooms are well equipped; some benefit from extensive views of the historic Iron Age fort of Brent Knoll. In addition to the convivial bar and conservatory restaurant, extensive function facilities are available.

ROOMS: 16 rms (14 en suite) s fr £49; d fr £63 (incl. bkfst) * LB **FACILITIES:** Jacuzzi/spa **CONF:** Thtr 80 Class 40 Board 40 Del from £65 * **PARKING:** 50 **NOTES:** No dogs (ex guide dogs) No smoking in restaurant Civ Wed 80 **CARDS:**

BRENTWOOD, Essex

Map 05 TQ59

★★★★70% Marygreen Manor

London Rd CM14 4NR
☎ 01277 225252 01277 262809
Dir: *on A1023*

A 16th-century local nobleman originally named this house 'Manor of Mary Green' for his bride. Beamed ceilings and carved wood panelling are features of the public areas; the baronial hall restaurant is particularly impressive. There are three bedrooms in

continued

the main house, the majority are more recent additions and face onto an attractive courtyard garden.

ROOMS: 3 en suite 40 annexe en suite No smoking in 8 bedrooms s £115.50-£141; d £134-£211 **FACILITIES:** STV **CONF:** Thtr 60 Class 20 Board 25 Del £180 * **PARKING:** 100 **NOTES:** No dogs (ex guide dogs) No smoking in restaurant Civ Wed 60
CARDS:

See advert on this page

★★★69% *Posthouse Brentwood*
Brook St CM14 5NF **Posthouse**
☎ 0870 400 9012 🖷 01277 264264
Dir: *close to M25/A12 interchange*
This modern hotel is conveniently located for access to the motorway and London. Bedrooms are smartly decorated and offer a range of extra facilities. Guests have a choice of dining options with Garfunkles and Café Express open all day and Atrio Restaurant open evenings only. There is a well appointed health club and a range of meeting rooms.
ROOMS: 145 en suite (30 fmly) No smoking in 80 bedrooms
FACILITIES: Indoor swimming (H) Sauna Solarium Gym Health & fitness club **CONF:** Thtr 120 Class 60 Board 50 **SERVICES:** Lift **PARKING:** 190
CARDS:

BRIDGNORTH, Shropshire — Map 07 SO79

see also Alveley

★★★★66% Mill Hotel & Restaurant
WV15 6HL
☎ 01746 780437 🖷 01746 780850
(For full entry see Alveley)

★★★ 🏵🏵🏵 Old Vicarage Hotel
WV15 5JZ
☎ 01746 716497 & 0800 0968010
🖷 01746 716552
e-mail: admin@the-old-vicarage.demon.co.uk
(For full entry see Worfield)

PRIDE OF BRITAIN MEMBER

★★61% Parlors Hall
Mill St WV15 5AL
☎ 01746 761931 🖷 01746 767058
Dir: *turn left off A454 then right and right again for 200yds*
Parlors Hall has been a hotel since 1929 and retains many original features, such as oak panelling and magnificent fireplaces. Named after the family who lived here between 1419 and 1539, the property now features well equipped bedrooms, some with four-poster beds, restaurant and charming bar.
ROOMS: 15 en suite (2 fmly) s £42; d £54-£60 (incl. bkfst) *
FACILITIES: Xmas **CONF:** Thtr 50 Class 25 Board 25 **PARKING:** 24
NOTES: No dogs (ex guide dogs) **CARDS:**

See advert on page 117

BRIDGNORTH, continued

★★60% Falcon Hotel

Saint John St, Lowtown WV15 6AG
☎ 01746 763134 01746 765401
Dir: *from A442 Telford-Kidderminster follow Bridgnorth town centre signs. Hotel 100yds on left before bridge over the River Severn*

This 17th-century former coaching inn stands near the River Severn in the Lowtown area of Bridgnorth. Bedrooms are equipped to modern standards, and a good selection of dishes is served in the open-plan bar with its beamed restaurant.
ROOMS: 12 rms (11 en suite) s £39-£42; d £46-£49 (incl. bkfst) LB **CONF:** Thtr 40 Class 20 Board 25 Del from £70 * **PARKING:** 100 **CARDS:**

★67% Croft

Saint Mary's St WV16 4DW
☎ 01746 762416 01746 767431
Dir: *follow signs for town centre and turn right immediately after Town Hall*
This 400-year old, grade II listed building lies just off the High Street. The traditionally furnished accommodation has modern equipment and facilities, and includes family rooms plus a bedroom on ground floor level. Other facilities here include a bar, a lounge and a dining room.
ROOMS: 12 rms (10 en suite) (3 fmly) s £25-£41; d £46-£50 (incl. bkfst) * LB **FACILITIES:** ch fac **CONF:** Thtr 30 Class 20 Board 12 **NOTES:** No smoking in restaurant **CARDS:**

BRIDGWATER, Somerset Map 03 ST33

see also Holford

★★★73% Walnut Tree Hotel

Best Western

North Petherton TA6 6QA
☎ 01278 662255 01278 663946
e-mail: sales.walnuttree@btinternet.com
Dir: *on A38, 1m S of exit 24 on M5*
This 18th-century former coaching inn is a popular choice. The majority of bedrooms are furnished and decorated to an executive standard, all are equipped with a range of facilities. In addition to the formal Dukes restaurant with its interesting carte, the Cottage Room bistro serves a range of meals and snacks in informal surroundings.
ROOMS: 32 en suite (5 fmly) No smoking in 3 bedrooms s £45-£95; d £60-£125 (incl. bkfst) * LB **FACILITIES:** STV Solarium ch fac Xmas **CONF:** Thtr 130 Class 76 Board 70 **PARKING:** 70 **NOTES:** No dogs (ex guide dogs) **CARDS:**

★★66% Friarn Court

37 St Mary St TA6 3LX
☎ 01278 452859 01278 452988
Dir: *at junct of A38 & A39 turn into St Mary St*
Service at this popular town centre hotel is friendly and relaxed. Guests have a choice of bedrooms, either executive or standard; all are comfortably furnished and tastefully appointed. In the spacious restaurant a full carte menu is served. There is also a cosy bar and separate lounge.
ROOMS: 16 en suite (3 fmly) No smoking in 4 bedrooms s £40-£60; d £60-£70 (incl. bkfst) * LB **CONF:** Thtr 60 Class 40 Board 30 **PARKING:** 14 **CARDS:**

BRIDLINGTON, East Riding of Yorkshire Map 08 TA16

★★★67% Revelstoke

1-3 Flamborough Rd YO15 2HU
☎ 01262 672362 01262 672362
e-mail: info@revelstokehotel.co.uk
Dir: *take B1255 Flamborough Head rd & in 0.5m turn right at mini rdbt to junct of the Promenade & Flamborough Rd. Hotel across from Holy Trinty*

This family owned and run hotel, near the town centre and seafront, is a popular place to stay. Bedrooms offer a good standard of comfort and are well equipped. Public rooms are well furnished and the restaurant serves a wide range of well produced dishes.
ROOMS: 25 en suite (5 fmly) **FACILITIES:** STV entertainment **CONF:** Thtr 250 Class 200 Board 100 **PARKING:** 14 **NOTES:** No dogs (ex guide dogs) No smoking in restaurant
CARDS:

See advert on opposite page

★★★66% Expanse

North Marine Dr YO15 2LS
☎ 01262 675347 01262 604928
e-mail: expanse@brid.demon.co.uk
Dir: *follow signs North Beach P, pass under railway arch for North Marine Drive. Hotel at bottom of hill*

This traditional seaside hotel overlooks the bay and has been in the same family's ownership for many years. Comfortable public areas include a large bar and inviting lounge. The modern bedrooms are well equipped. Service is relaxed and friendly.
ROOMS: 48 en suite (4 fmly) s £33-£46; d £62-£84 (incl. bkfst) * LB **FACILITIES:** entertainment Xmas **CONF:** Thtr 200 Class 90 Board 40 Del from £50 * **SERVICES:** Lift **PARKING:** 23 **NOTES:** No dogs (ex guide dogs) **CARDS:**

See advert on opposite page

THE

EXPANSE

HOTEL

A haven of peace and comfort overlooking the Beach and Flamborough Head Heritage Coast, where the beach and cliff walks beckon. The Expanse is a place to relax, with a feel all of its own – built to capture those unique views, where friendly old world courtesy and modern facilities combine for a special break.

North Marine Drive
Bridlington · YO15 2LS
Tel 01262 675347
Fax 01262 604928

Parlors Hall Hotel ★★

Mill Street, Bridgnorth
Shropshire WV15 5AL
Tel: (01746) 761931 Fax: (01746) 767058

The original Parlors Hall which dates back to the 12th century became an hotel in 1929. Since then it has been carefully refurbished but keeping many of the ancient features, including the fireplaces and oak panelling. Today the hotel offers fifteen luxury en suite bedrooms, each individually decorated in keeping with the character of the building. The attractive restaurant offers an à la carte and carvery menus. Ideally located for business visitors or visiting the many tourist attractions of the area.

1-3 Flamborough Road
Bridlington
East Yorkshire YO15 2HU

Telephone: (01262) 672362 · Fax: (01262) 672362
E-mail: info@revelstokehotel.co.uk · Website: revelstokehotel.co.uk

The Revelstoke Hotel is one of the finest hotels in the Bridlington area.

Ideally located on north side of the town and only two minutes walk away from the sea-front and the town centre.

Our English and Continental restaurant is renowned for its high standards.
Function and conference facilities are available to accommodate up to 250 covers.
Our fully licensed lounge and public bar offer a host of popular beers and lager.
Sky Digital TV installed in all our rooms.
A comprehensive wine list is available with reasonable prices.

For more information about our hotel, visit our website, e-mail or telephone for one of our brochures or information packs.

B

BRIDPORT, Dorset

Map 03 SY49

★★★58% Haddon House
West Bay DT6 4EL
☎ 01308 423626 & 425323 🖷 01308 427348
Dir: *0.5m off the A35 Crown Inn rdbt signposted to West Bay*

This is an attractive hotel a few minutes from the quay and seafront. Bedrooms offer good standards of accommodation. There is a comfortable lounge and popular bar that serves a wide range of food. The restaurant offers an interesting menu of carefully prepared dishes.
ROOMS: 12 en suite (2 fmly) s £49.50-£59.50; d £55-£85 (incl. bkfst) * LB **FACILITIES:** STV Solarium Xmas **CONF:** Thtr 50 Class 30 Board 20 **PARKING:** 74 **NOTES:** No dogs (ex guide dogs) No smoking in restaurant **CARDS:**

★★66% *Roundham House*
Roundham Gardens, West Bay Rd DT6 4BD
☎ 01308 422753 & 425779 🖷 01308 421500
Dir: *take A35 Bridport road, do not take left turn to Bridport follow A35 to rdbt Crown Inn, follow signs for West Bay along West Bay Rd hotel signed*
This small hotel is located on the edge of the town and benefits from wonderful views across the Dorset countryside. Bedrooms vary in size, but all offer good levels of comfort and equipment.
ROOMS: 8 rms (7 en suite) (2 fmly) **PARKING:** 13 **NOTES:** No smoking in restaurant Closed Jan-Feb **CARDS:**

★64% Bridge House
115 East St DT6 3LB
☎ 01308 423371 🖷 01308 423371
Dir: *turn off at rdbt with A35 & A3066, hotel 150yds on right next to River Asker bridge*
This 18th-century hotel is a short stroll from the town centre. The well equipped bedrooms vary in size. In addition to the main lounge, there is a small bar-lounge and a separate breakfast room. Good home-cooked meals that use top quality produce are provided in the lower ground floor restaurant.
ROOMS: 10 en suite (2 fmly) s £30-£38; d £42-£52 (incl. bkfst) * LB **CONF:** Thtr 20 Board 12 Del £70 * **PARKING:** 12 **NOTES:** No dogs (ex guide dogs) No smoking in restaurant **CARDS:**

BRIGHOUSE, West Yorkshire

Map 07 SE12

★★★67% *Posthouse Brighouse*
Posthouse
Clifton Village HD6 4HW
☎ 0870 400 9013 🖷 01484 400068
Dir: *on A644 just off junct 25 of M62*
Bedrooms at this modern hotel are spacious and comfortably furnished, and include rooms suitable for disabled guests and family rooms. Public areas are also spacious and include an attractively appointed Junction restaurant, several versatile conference and meeting rooms and a leisure club. Service includes the provision of an all-day lounge menu and 24 hour room service.
ROOMS: 94 en suite (20 fmly) No smoking in 62 bedrooms **FACILITIES:** STV Indoor swimming (H) Sauna Solarium Gym Croquet lawn Jacuzzi/spa **CONF:** Thtr 200 Class 120 Board 60 **PARKING:** 155 **CARDS:**

BRIGHTON & HOVE, East Sussex

Map 04 TQ30

★★★★★66% Grand
De Vere Hotels
King's Rd BN1 2FW
☎ 01273 224300 🖷 01273 224321
e-mail: reservations@grandbrighton.co.uk
Dir: *next to Brighton Centre facing Palace Pier & seafront, turn right along Grand Junction Rd into King's Rd.*
This landmark hotel has graced the Brighton seafront since 1864 and continues to be a popular choice. Bedrooms, many of which enjoy sea views, are smart and equipped to a very high standard. Features include a bar with adjoining conservatory, an attractive restaurant, a leisure club, and extensive conference facilities.
ROOMS: 200 en suite (70 fmly) s fr £155; d fr £210 (incl. bkfst) * LB **FACILITIES:** STV Indoor swimming (H) Sauna Solarium Gym Jacuzzi/spa Hairdresser Masseur Steam room entertainment Xmas **CONF:** Thtr 800 Class 420 **SERVICES:** Lift **PARKING:** 65 **NOTES:** Civ Wed 400 **CARDS:**

★★★71% *The Granville*
124 King's Rd BN1 2FA
☎ 01273 326302 🖷 01273 728294
e-mail: granville@brighton.co.uk
Dir: *On seafront opposite West Pier*

This stylish hotel is located on Brighton's busy seafront. Bedrooms are carefully furnished and decorated with great style. Trogs vegetarian restaurant and the adjoining bar are busy and bright and great care has been taken to source high quality organic foods. Breakfasts allow a concession to the carnivorous guest but quality is never compromised.
ROOMS: 24 en suite No smoking in all bedrooms **SERVICES:** Lift **NOTES:** No smoking in restaurant **CARDS:**

★★★67% Queens Hotel
1-5 King's Rd BN1 1NS
☎ 01273 321222 🖷 01273 203059
Dir: *follow signs to the seafront, at the seafront turn right, the hotel is approx 400yds on right*
This grand old lady on Brighton's seafront has been totally refurbished and has been rescued from decline in a most impressive manner. All the bedrooms are now bright, modern and well equipped and many have wonderful sea views. Guests benefit from a modern leisure suite and extensive meeting facilities that are now available.

continued

ROOMS: 90 en suite (8 fmly) No smoking in 46 bedrooms s £70-£95; d £115-£135 (incl. bkfst) * LB **FACILITIES:** STV Indoor swimming (H) Sauna Gym Jacuzzi/spa Xmas **CONF:** Thtr 75 Class 50 Board 34 Del £105 * **SERVICES:** Lift **NOTES:** No dogs (ex guide dogs) No smoking in restaurant Civ Wed **CARDS:**

★★★ 66% Courtlands

21-27 The Drive BN3 3JE
☎ 01273 731055 01273 328295
e-mail: courtlands@pavilion.co.uk
Dir: *A23 junct A27 Worthing-take 1st exit to Hove, 2nd exit at rdbt, then right at 1st junct and turn left at shops. Straight on at junct, hotel on left*
This popular hotel benefits from continued improvements. Bedrooms tend to be spacious and are tastefully decorated. Friendly staff are positive and attentive. Guests have the use of a comfortable lounge, cosy bar, a well appointed restaurant and, for those with a little more energy, there is also a covered swimming pool.
ROOMS: 75 en suite No smoking in 12 bedrooms s fr £65; d fr £85 (incl. bkfst) * LB **FACILITIES:** Indoor swimming (H) Solarium Xmas **CONF:** Thtr 100 Board 70 Del from £75 * **SERVICES:** Lift air con **PARKING:** 24 **CARDS:**

★★★ 66% Princes Marine

153 Kingsway BN3 4GR
☎ 01273 207660 01273 325913
e-mail: princesmarine@bestwestern.co.uk
Dir: *turn right at Palace Pier and follow seafront for approx 2m, hotel is approx 200yds from King Alfred sports & leisure centre*
Enjoying a seafront location to the west of town, this friendly hotel offers spacious, comfortable bedrooms equipped with a good range of facilities. There is a cosy restaurant, bar and a useful meeting room.
ROOMS: 48 en suite (4 fmly) No smoking in 6 bedrooms s £45-£60; d £75-£95 (incl. bkfst) * LB **FACILITIES:** Xmas **CONF:** Thtr 80 Class 40 Board 40 Del from £60 * **SERVICES:** Lift **PARKING:** 30 **NOTES:** Civ Wed **CARDS:**

★★★ 65% Imperial

First Av BN3 2GU
☎ 01273 777320 01273 777310
e-mail: imperialhotel@pavilion.co.uk
Dir: *M23 to Brighton seafront, right at roundabout to Hove, 1.5 miles to First Avenue turn right*

On First Avenue, in elegant Regency Hove, this hotel is close to the seafront and a short distance from the town centre at Brighton. Bedrooms are generally spacious, tastefully decorated and have benefited from recent improvements. The public areas include a quiet lounge and an informal bar and restaurant.
ROOMS: 76 en suite (4 fmly) No smoking in 10 bedrooms s £45-£78; d £70-£100 (incl. bkfst) * LB **FACILITIES:** STV Xmas **CONF:** Thtr 110 Class 50 Board 32 Del from £79.50 * **SERVICES:** Lift **NOTES:** No dogs (ex guide dogs) **CARDS:**

See advert on this page

★★★ 64% *Brighton Hotel*

143/145 King's Rd BN1 2PQ
☎ 01273 820555 01273 821555
e-mail: bthotel@pavilion.co.uk
Dir: *follow signs to Palace Pier, turn right and hotel is 100yds past West Pier*
Enjoying a prime seafront location close to the historic West Pier, this friendly family run hotel is well placed. All rooms are bright and well equipped and the smart public areas are a popular meeting place. Limited car parking facilities are a real bonus in Brighton.
ROOMS: 52 en suite **FACILITIES:** STV Sauna Solarium Gym Jacuzzi/spa **CONF:** Thtr 90 Board 40 **SERVICES:** Lift **PARKING:** 18 **CARDS:**

★★★ 64% Quality Hotel Brighton

West St BN1 2RQ
☎ 01273 220033 01273 778000
e-mail: admin@gb057.u-net.com
Dir: *follow A23 into Brighton. Follow signs for Town Centre & seafront. Take A259 to Hove & Worthing. Hotel situated next door to Brighton Centre*
Conveniently located for the seafront and close to the town centre, this purpose built hotel offers modern and well equipped bedrooms. Public areas include a spacious, open plan lobby area, a feature staircase, smoking and non smoking areas in the lounge/bar and Spinnakers restaurant which serves a range of international dishes.
ROOMS: 138 en suite No smoking in 60 bedrooms s fr £76; d fr £92 * LB **FACILITIES:** STV **CONF:** Thtr 200 Class 80 Board 60 Del from £95 * **SERVICES:** Lift air con **NOTES:** No smoking in restaurant **CARDS:**

B

BRIGHTON & HOVE, continued

★★63% St Catherines Lodge

Seafront, Kingsway BN3 2RZ
☎ 01273 778181 ▯ 01273 774949
Dir: *opposite King Alfred Leisure Centre on main A259*

Privately owned and family-run, this hotel is located by the seafront at Hove. Bedrooms are neatly decorated and comfortably appointed. Public areas retain many original features including Adam-style ceilings and antique Delft tiling in the restaurant.
ROOMS: 50 rms (40 en suite) (4 fmly) s £45-£55; d £65-£75 (incl. bkfst) * LB **FACILITIES:** Games room Xmas **CONF:** Thtr 40 Class 24 Board 24 Del from £65 * **SERVICES:** Lift **PARKING:** 9 **NOTES:** No dogs (ex guide dogs) **CARDS:**

See advert on opposite page

⇧ Premier Lodge

144 North St BN1 1DN
☎ 0870 700 1334 ▯ 0870 700 1335

PREMIER LODGE
THE BEST. REST ASSURED.

Premier Lodge offers modern, well equipped, en suite accommodation suitable for both business and leisure travellers. Meals can be taken at the adjacent popular restaurant and bar which is fully licensed. For further details, consult the Hotel Groups page.
ROOMS: 160 en suite d £46 *

○ The Dudley

Lansdowne Place BN3 1HQ
☎ 01273 736266 ▯ 01273 729802
Just a few yards from the sea front, the Dudley offers well-appointed public areas and extensive, well-decorated function rooms behind its Regency façade. Bedrooms vary in style, and the best feature 1920s fitted furniture or traditional free-standing pieces. Some parking is available.
ROOMS: (3 fmly) **NOTES:** Open

BRISTOL, Bristol — Map 03 ST57

★★★★75% ❀❀ *Bristol Marriott Royal*

College Green BS1 5TA
☎ 0117 925 5100 ▯ 0117 925 1515

Marriott
HOTELS · RESORTS · SUITES

Dir: *in the city centre next to the cathedral*
Next to the cathedral, this landmark hotel offers plenty of lounges and an impressive leisure club. Dining options include the casual Terrace restaurant and the splendid Palm Court restaurant with its three-storey-high ceiling. A harpist plays here three nights a week. Charming bedrooms have good quality furnishings, comfortable armchairs, luxurious marbled bathrooms and air conditioning.

continued

ROOMS: 242 en suite (14 fmly) No smoking in 100 bedrooms **FACILITIES:** STV Indoor swimming (H) Sauna Solarium Gym Jacuzzi/spa **CONF:** Thtr 300 Class 140 Board 30 **SERVICES:** Lift air con **PARKING:** 200 **CARDS:**

★★★★70% ❀ Aztec

SHIRE INNS

Aztec West Business Park,
Almondsbury BS32 4TS
☎ 01454 201090 ▯ 01454 201593
e-mail: aztec@shireinns.co.uk
Dir: *access via M5 (junct 16) & M4*
This impressive, modern hotel offers smart, well equipped bedrooms and bright public areas. Situated close to the M4/M5 junction, guests can make use of a good range of meeting rooms. Quarterjacks restaurant offers a good standard of well executed modern cooking, and the cosy bar serves a range of light meals.
ROOMS: 128 en suite (13 fmly) No smoking in 55 bedrooms s £144-£164 (incl. bkfst) * LB **FACILITIES:** STV Indoor swimming (H) Squash Snooker Sauna Solarium Gym Jacuzzi/spa Steam room Childrens splash pool Health & beauty Xmas **CONF:** Thtr 250 Class 120 Board 48 Del from £89 * **SERVICES:** Lift **PARKING:** 240 **NOTES:** No smoking in restaurant Civ Wed 250 **CARDS:**

★★★★67% ❀ Bristol Marriott City Centre

Marriott
HOTELS · RESORTS · SUITES

Lower Castle St BS1 3AD
☎ 0117 929 4281 ▯ 0117 927 6377
Dir: *from M32 follow signs to Broadmead, taking slip road to large rdbt. Take 3rd exit. Hotel located on right hand side*
A modern hotel with high standards of comfort in a central location. The Brasserie restaurant is popular for casual dining and the more formal restaurant, Le Chateau, is reopening as a new concept serving British cuisine. Bedrooms have air conditioning and power showers. The executive floor has its own lounge and extra luxuries. Parking is adjacent to the hotel with valet service on request.
ROOMS: 289 en suite (136 fmly) No smoking in 221 bedrooms s £109-£119; d £119-£129 (incl. bkfst) * LB **FACILITIES:** STV Indoor swimming (H) Sauna Solarium Gym Jacuzzi/spa Steam room **CONF:** Thtr 600 Class 280 Board 40 Del from £135 * **SERVICES:** Lift air con **NOTES:** No dogs (ex guide dogs) Civ Wed 500
CARDS:

Popped the question? Hotels with Civ Wed in their entry are licensed for civil wedding ceremonies. Maximum numbers for the ceremony only are shown, e.g. Civ Wed 50

BRISTOL, continued

★★★★64% Jurys Bristol Hotel
Prince St BS1 4QF
☎ 0117 923 0333 📠 0117 923 0300
e-mail: con_ring@jurys.com
Dir: *from Temple Meads turn right at 1st rdbt into Victoria St. At Bristol Bridge traffic lights left Baldwil St, 2nd left Marsh St, right at rdbt*
This popular hotel is centrally located on the waterside, close to Bristol's Millennium development. Bedrooms are spacious and well equipped with modern amenities. There is a range of eating options including a Quayside pub. Residents have free overnight parking in the adjacent multi-storey.

ROOMS: 191 en suite (22 fmly) No smoking in 53 bedrooms d £120 * LB **FACILITIES:** STV **50%** Discount at local Gym entertainment Xmas **CONF:** Thtr 350 Class 140 Board 80 Del from £120 * **SERVICES:** Lift **NOTES:** No dogs (ex guide dogs) **CARDS:**

See advert on page 121

★★★70% Redwood Lodge Hotel
Beggar Bush Ln, Failand BS8 3TG
☎ 01275 393901 📠 01275 392104
e-mail: redwood.lodge@virgin.net
Dir: *M5 junct 19, A369 for 3m then right at lights, hotel is 1m on left*

This popular modern hotel offers friendly service and well equipped accommodation. Steps cafe bar is ideal for casual dining, and the attractive restaurant provides more formal surroundings.
ROOMS: 112 en suite No smoking in 81 bedrooms s fr £95; d fr £110 * LB **FACILITIES:** STV Indoor swimming (H) Outdoor swimming Tennis (hard) Squash Sauna Solarium Gym Pool table 175 seater Cinema Aerobics/Dance studios Xmas **CONF:** Thtr 175 Class 80 Board 30 Del from £105 * **PARKING:** 1000 **NOTES:** No dogs (ex guide dogs) No smoking in restaurant **CARDS:**

★★★69% *Berkeley Square*
15 Berkeley Square, Clifton BS8 1HB
☎ 0117 925 4000 📠 0117 925 2970
Dir: *from M32 follow signs for Clifton, take first turn left at traffic lights by Willis Memorial Tower (University) into Berkeley Sq*
Set in a peaceful square close to the university, art gallery and Clifton Village, this smart Georgian hotel has thoughtfully furnished and tastefully decorated bedrooms. There is a busy bar in the basement, and the restaurant serves interesting dishes.
ROOMS: 42 en suite No smoking in 12 bedrooms **FACILITIES:** STV **CONF:** Thtr 15 Class 12 Board 12 **SERVICES:** Lift **PARKING:** 20 **CARDS:**

★★★69% *Posthouse Bristol*
Filton Rd, Hambrook BS16 1QX
☎ 0870 400 9014 📠 0117 956 9735
Dir: *M4 junct 19 onto M32. Take junct 1 off M32 onto A4174 towards Filton, Bristol and Parkway Station. Hotel 800yds on the left*
This popular, modern hotel is adjacent to the Frenchay Campus of UWE. Conferences are attracted by the range of meeting rooms and business and leisure facilities. Bedrooms have been completely restyled. Meals are served in the Junction brasserie, and snacks are available in the lounge.
ROOMS: 198 en suite (21 fmly) No smoking in 131 bedrooms **FACILITIES:** STV Indoor swimming (H) Sauna Solarium Gym Pool table Outdoor badminton **CONF:** Thtr 250 Class 130 Board 60 **SERVICES:** Lift **PARKING:** 400 **CARDS:**

★★★65% The Avon Gorge
Sion Hill, Clifton BS8 4LD
☎ 0117 973 8955 📠 0117 923 8125
Dir: *from M5 S junct 19/A369 to Clifton via toll bridge then Sion Hill. From M5 N junct 18/A4 to Bristol left at lights under suspension bridge*
Overlooking Avon Gorge and Brunel's famous suspension bridge, this popular hotel is situated in the heart of fashionable Clifton. Bedrooms, many of which have glorious views, are well equipped with such extras as additional telephone points and ceiling fans. Two rooms have four-poster beds. There is a choice of bars (one with a popular terrace) and an attractive restaurant.
ROOMS: 76 en suite (6 fmly) No smoking in 30 bedrooms s £99-£109; d £109-£160 (incl. bkfst) * LB **FACILITIES:** STV Childrens activity play area entertainment Xmas **CONF:** Thtr 100 Class 50 Board 26 Del from £120 * **SERVICES:** Lift **PARKING:** 23 **NOTES:** Civ Wed 100 **CARDS:**

★★★63% Henbury Lodge
Station Rd, Henbury BS10 7QQ
☎ 0117 950 2615 📠 0117 950 9532
Dir: *4.5m NW of City centre off A4018, 1m from M5 junct 17*
This comfortable former country house, built in 1760, is conveniently situated in a quiet suburb within easy access of the M5. Bedrooms are within the main house and in the adjoining stable conversion; all are attractively decorated and well equipped. The dining room offers a range of freshly-cooked dishes.
ROOMS: 12 en suite 9 annexe en suite (4 fmly) No smoking in 6 bedrooms s £89.50-£97.50; d £99.50-£107.50 (incl. bkfst) * LB **FACILITIES:** STV Sauna Solarium Gym Xmas **CONF:** Thtr 32 Board 20 Del from £105 * **PARKING:** 24 **NOTES:** No smoking in restaurant **CARDS:**

★★70% Seeley's
17-27 St Paul's Rd, Clifton BS8 1LX
☎ 0117 973 8544 0117 973 2406
e-mail: admin@seeleys.demon.co.uk
Dir: *M5 junct17, follow A4018 for 4.5 m to BBC studios, turn right at lights and hotel is on the left*
A privately owned hotel with easy access to Clifton village, the university and city centre. Comfortable public areas are spacious. A wide selection of dishes is offered in Le Chasseur Restaurant, lighter meals and snacks are served in the bar. The bedrooms, some in adjacent properties, are all pleasing and well equipped.
ROOMS: 37 en suite 18 annexe en suite (10 fmly) s £65-£85; d £80-£95 (incl. bkfst) * LB **FACILITIES:** STV Sauna Solarium Gym Jacuzzi/spa **CONF:** Thtr 70 Class 30 Board 25 Del from £87.50 * **PARKING:** 25 **NOTES:** No dogs (ex guide dogs) Closed 24 Dec-2 Jan
CARDS:

★★66% The Bowl Inn
16 Church Rd, Lower Almondsbury BS32 4DT
☎ 01454 612757 01454 619910
e-mail: thebowl@3wa.co.uk
Dir: *from M5 junct 6 on Gloucester road turn left Over Lane by Almondsbury Garden Centre. Hotel next to St Mary's Church on right*
This inn offers all the comforts of modern life housed within the character and architecture of a 16th-century hostelry. Each bedroom has been individually furnished to complement the many original features. Huge ceiling beams, stonework niches and fireplaces abound. Dining options include an extensive bar menu with cask ales, or a more intimate restaurant.
ROOMS: 11 en suite 2 annexe en suite No smoking in 5 bedrooms s £79.50-£87.50; d £99.50-£109.50 (incl. bkfst) * LB **FACILITIES:** STV **CONF:** Board 25 **PARKING:** 30 **NOTES:** RS 25 Dec
CARDS:

★★65% Clifton
St Pauls Rd, Clifton BS8 1LX
☎ 0117 973 6882 0117 974 1082
MINOTEL Great Britain
Dir: *take M32 into Bristol & follow signs for Clifton. Go up Park St (very steep hill) follow road ahead & turn left at traffic lights into St Pauls Rd*
This popular hotel offers well equipped bedrooms. There is a smart lounge at reception, during summer months drinks can be taken on the terrace. Racks Bar and Restaurant offers an interesting selection of modern dishes from an imaginative menu. Street parking is unrestricted, secure parking is available for a small charge.
ROOMS: 60 rms (48 en suite) (2 fmly) No smoking in 15 bedrooms **FACILITIES:** STV **SERVICES:** Lift **PARKING:** 20 **NOTES:** Closed 23-29 Dec **CARDS:**

★★65% Glenroy
Victoria Square, Clifton BS8 4EW
Best Western
☎ 0117 973 9058 0117 973 9058
e-mail: admin@glenroyhotel.demon.co.uk
Dir: *junct 19 of M5, follow signs for Clifton come over suspension bridge and turn left after the bakery, hotel around corner on right*
Convenient for the university and city centre, this hotel is geared to the short stay business guest. Bedrooms, in the main house and an adjacent property, are varied in size, some quite compact, but all well equipped. Facilities include a congenial open-plan bar, carvery restaurant, and the Victoria and Albert conference rooms.
ROOMS: 25 en suite 19 annexe en suite (9 fmly) s £47-£60; d £57-£90 (incl. bkfst) * **FACILITIES:** STV **CONF:** Thtr 45 Class 16 Board 25 Del from £90 * **PARKING:** 16 **NOTES:** Closed 24-31 Dec
CARDS:

★★64% Rodney Hotel
4 Rodney Place, Clifton BS8 4HY
☎ 0117 973 5422 0117 946 7092
Dir: *off Clifton Down Road*
With easy access from the M5, this attractive, listed building in Clifton is conveniently close to the city centre. The individually decorated bedrooms provide a useful range of extra facilities for the business traveller. Snacks are served in the bar-lounge or by way of room service and the more formal restaurant offers an appealing selection of dishes.
ROOMS: 31 en suite No smoking in 9 bedrooms **FACILITIES:** STV **CONF:** Thtr 30 Class 20 Board 15 **NOTES:** Closed 22 Dec-3 Jan RS Sun
CARDS:

Town House

★★★★ Hotel du Vin & Bistro
The Sugar House, Narrow Lewins BS1 2NU
☎ 0117 925 5577 0117 925 1199
The third property in what must be among Britain's most exciting and innovative hotel groups maintains and extends the high standards Hotel du Vin is renowned for. Situated in a converted 18th-century sugar refinery the hotel is Grade II listed. The 40 bedrooms are named after some of the world's great wine and spirit producers and all are exceptionally well designed. Great facilities are provided and the modern minimalist feel is a welcome change from chintz. The bistro offers an excellent menu of simply constructed dishes.
ROOMS: 40 en suite

BRISTOL, continued

⌂ *Travelodge*
Cribbs Causeway BS10 7TL
☎ 0117 950 1530 🖹 0117 950 1530
Dir: *A4018, just off junc17 M5*
This modern building offers accommodation in smart, spacious and well equipped bedrooms, all with en suite bathrooms. Refreshments may be taken at the nearby family restaurant. For further details and the Travelodge phone number, consult the Hotel Groups page.
ROOMS: 56 en suite

⌂ Express by Holiday Inn Bristol
Temple Gate BS1 6PL
☎ 0117 9304800 🖹 9304900
Dir: *M4 junct 19 leads to M32 into Bristol. Keep left & follow signs to Temple Meads Train Station. Hotel directly opposite on Temple Gate*

A modern budget hotel offering comfortable accommodation in refreshing, spacious and comprehensively-equipped bedrooms, en suite bathrooms with power showers and continental buffet breakfast included in the room rate. Suitable for business travellers or families. For further details and the Express by Holiday Inn phone number, consult the Hotel Groups page.
ROOMS: 94 en suite (incl. cont bkfst) d £59.50 * **CONF:** Thtr 35 Class 16 Board 20

⌂ Premier Lodge (Bristol City East)
Shield Retail Park, Gloucester Rd North, Filton BS12 7AA
☎ 0870 700 1336 🖹 0870 7001337
Premier Lodge offers modern, well equipped, en suite accommodation suitable for both business and leisure travellers. Meals can be taken at the adjacent popular restaurant and bar which is fully licensed. For further details, consult the Hotel Groups page.
ROOMS: 66 en suite d £49.50 *

○ *Premier Lodge (City Centre)*
Landoger Trow, Kings St
☎ 0870 700 1342 🖹 0870 700 1343

Fancy a Singapore Sling? Bar staff in five star hotels should be skilled cocktail mixers.

Read all about it! Newspapers delivered to bedrooms in four and five star hotels.

BRIXHAM, Devon Map 03 SX95

★★★66% Berryhead
Berryhead Rd TQ5 9AJ
☎ 01803 853225 🖹 01803 882084
e-mail: berryhd@aol.com
Dir: *to Brixham Harbour turn right past statue & then left to Marina; straight on another quarter of a mile past Marina*
Enjoying glorious views from a stunning clifftop position, this imposing property dates back to 1809 and was the former residence of Rev. Henry Lyte, who wrote many hymns including 'Abide With Me'. The hotel offers individually designed accommodation, some rooms are newer additions. Public areas include popular bars and all-day eating options.
ROOMS: 32 en suite (7 fmly) **FACILITIES:** Indoor swimming (H) Croquet lawn Jacuzzi/spa Petanque Sailing Deep sea fishing **CONF:** Thtr 350 Class 250 Board 40 Del from £65 * **PARKING:** 200 **NOTES:** No smoking in restaurant Civ Wed 200 **CARDS:**

See advert on opposite page

★★★66% ❀ Quayside
41-49 King St TQ5 9TJ
☎ 01803 855751 🖹 01803 882733
e-mail: quayside.hotel@virgin.net
Dir: *from Exeter follow signs for Torquay on A380, at the 2nd rdbt at Kinkerswell follow signs for Brixham on A3022, hotel overlooks the harbour*

Created from six cottages and enjoying panoramic views, the Quayside Hotel offers friendly and attentive service. There is a cosy lounge, a snug residents' bar and the busier Ernie Lister's public bar. An extensive range of enjoyable dishes is available in the intimate restaurant, including fresh fish landed directly from the boats. Bedrooms are modern and well equipped.
ROOMS: 29 en suite (2 fmly) No smoking in 6 bedrooms s £48-£58; d £60-£84 (incl. bkfst) * LB **FACILITIES:** entertainment Xmas **CONF:** Thtr 25 Class 18 Board 18 **PARKING:** 30 **NOTES:** No smoking in restaurant **CARDS:**

★★73% ❀ Maypool Park
Maypool, Galmpton TQ5 0ET
☎ 01803 842442 🖹 01803 845782
e-mail: peacock@maypoolpark.co.uk
Dir: *at Churston (A3022) turn SW signed Maypool/Passenger ferry/ Greenway Quay to Manor Vale Rd. Follow signs through village to hotel*
These converted cottages offer stunning views across a wooded valley and the River Dart. Now run as a country hotel, they provide bedrooms equipped with every modern comfort, a choice of comfortable lounges, and an intimate bar. The attractive dining room serves beautifully presented cuisine. An interesting wine list complements the innovative menus.

continued

ROOMS: 10 en suite No smoking in all bedrooms s £39-£48; d £61-£104 (incl. bkfst) * LB **FACILITIES:** Xmas **CONF:** Thtr 30 Class 20 Board 20 **PARKING:** 15 **NOTES:** No dogs No children 12yrs No smoking in restaurant **CARDS:**

★58% Smuggler's Haunt

Church Hill East TQ5 8HH
☎ 01803 853050 & 859416 ℻ 01803 858738
e-mail: enquires@smugglershaunt-hotel-devon.co.uk

This 300-year-old hotel in the centre of the historic fishing town, offers straightforward accommodation, with all the local amenities just a short stroll away. The restaurant and bar menus provide a wide selection of carefully cooked dishes from around the world.
ROOMS: 14 en suite (4 fmly) s £25-£32 (incl. bkfst) * LB **FACILITIES:** Xmas **CARDS:**

BROADSTAIRS, Kent — Map 05 TR36

★★★61% Royal Albion

Albion St CT10 1AN
☎ 01843 868071 ℻ 01843 861509
e-mail: enquiries@albion-bstairs.demon.co.uk
Dir: *on entering the town follow signs for seafront*

A seafront hotel with delightful views. Bedrooms are attractive and well equipped with modern furnishings. The hotel houses reception, public bar, lounge and breakfast room, and the restaurant is two doors down the street in Marchesi's. Staff are friendly and the atmosphere is very relaxed and informal.
ROOMS: 19 en suite (3 fmly) No smoking in 3 bedrooms s £55-£95; d £85-£105 (incl. bkfst) * LB **FACILITIES:** STV Xmas **CONF:** Thtr 40 Class 30 Board 30 **PARKING:** 22 **NOTES:** No dogs (ex guide dogs) RS Sun **CARDS:**

BROADWAY, Worcestershire — Map 04 SP03

see also Buckland

Premier Collection

★★★★ The Lygon Arms

High St WR12 7DU
☎ 01386 852255 ℻ 01386 858611
e-mail: info@the-lygon-arms.co.uk
Dir: *in centre of village*

The Savoy Group

This 16th-century coaching inn commands a prime location in the heart of Broadway and features a wealth of historical charm and character. Bedrooms vary in style and layout, offering comfort, modern facilities and some fine antique furniture. Public rooms include a variety of lounge areas, some with open fires.

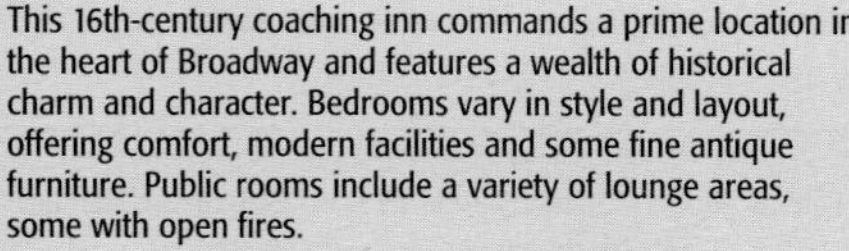

continued

ROOMS: 65 rms (62 en suite) (3 fmly) s £110-£150; d £150-£425 (incl. cont bkfst) * LB **FACILITIES:** STV Indoor swimming (H) Tennis (hard) Snooker Sauna Gym Pool table Croquet lawn Jacuzzi/spa Beauty treatments Steam Room Bike Hire Xmas **CONF:** Thtr 80 Class 48 Board 30 Del from £198 * **PARKING:** 152 **NOTES:** No smoking in restaurant Civ Wed 80 **CARDS:**

★★★74% Dormy House

Willersey Hill WR12 7LF
☎ 01386 852711 ℻ 01386 858636
e-mail: reservations@dormyhouse.co.uk.
Dir: *2m E off A44, at top of Fish Hill 1.5m from Broadway village, take turn signposted Saintbury/Picnic area. After 0.5m fork left Dormy House on left*

A 17th-century farmhouse converted into a large complex in extensive grounds. Rooms are traditionally furnished and well equipped, some with four-poster beds. Many are in separate

continued on p126

BROADWAY, continued

cottage-style buildings. There are comfortable lounges and a pleasant bar. The attractive restaurant serves tempting and imaginative cuisine. The Barn Owl pub offers a less formal eating option.

ROOMS: 25 en suite 23 annexe en suite (3 fmly) s £75-£100; d £150-£180 (incl. bkfst) * LB **FACILITIES:** Sauna Gym Pool table Croquet lawn Putting green Games room Nature/jogging trail **CONF:** Thtr 200 Class 100 Board 25 Del from £175 * **PARKING:** 80 **NOTES:** Closed 25 & 26 Dec RS Sat (restaurant closed for lunch) Civ Wed 170 **CARDS:**

See advert on opposite page

★★★65% Broadway

The Green, High St WR12 7AA
☎ 01386 852401 01386 853879
e-mail: bookings@cotswold-inns-hotels.co.uk
Dir: *set back from the High Street, behind the village green*

The Broadway Hotel is a 15th-century property built as a retreat for the Abbots of Pershore. Following refurbishment the hotel now combines modern and attractive decor with original charm and character. Bedroom are tastefully furnished, well equipped and public rooms include relaxing lounge, cosy bar and charming restaurant.

ROOMS: 20 en suite (1 fmly) No smoking in 4 bedrooms s £68.50-£75; d £110-£125 (incl. bkfst) * LB **FACILITIES:** Xmas **CONF:** Thtr 20 Board 16 Del from £110 * **PARKING:** 20 **NOTES:** No smoking in restaurant Civ Wed 50 **CARDS:**

★★73% Collin House

Collin Ln WR12 7PB
☎ 01386 858354 01386 858697
e-mail: collin.house@virgin.net
Dir: *1 mile NW of Broadway - the hotel is clearly marked at the roundabout at the junction of the A44 and is 40 metres from the roundabout*

This charming 17th-century country house, built from mellow Cotswold stone, is set in several acres of orchards and gardens. It provides tastefully furnished accommodation, which includes rooms with four-poster beds. The public areas have a wealth of charm and character, enhanced by features such as flagstone floors, oak beams and an inglenook fireplace in the bar.

ROOMS: 6 en suite No smoking in all bedrooms s £69; d £92 (incl. bkfst) * LB **FACILITIES:** Croquet lawn **PARKING:** 25 **NOTES:** No dogs (ex guide dogs) No smoking in restaurant Closed 24-28 Dec **CARDS:**

BROCKENHURST, Hampshire — Map 04 SU30

★★★76% Rhinefield House

Rhinefield Rd SO42 7QB
☎ 01590 622922 01590 622800
Dir: *take A35 towards Chistchurch. 3m from Lyndhurst turn left to Rhinefield, 1.5m to hotel*

This splendid 19th-century, mock-Elizabethan mansion is set in 40 acres of beautifully landscaped gardens. Bedrooms are spacious with great consideration given to guest comfort. The open-plan lounge and bar overlook an ornamental pond and the elegant restaurant is impressive, with antique features such as carved panelled walls.

ROOMS: 34 en suite No smoking in 12 bedrooms s fr £110; d fr £145 (incl. bkfst) * LB **FACILITIES:** STV Indoor swimming (H) Outdoor swimming (H) Tennis (hard) Sauna Gym Pool table Croquet lawn Putting green Jacuzzi/spa Xmas **CONF:** Thtr 100 Class 30 Board 40 Del £150 * **PARKING:** 80 **NOTES:** No dogs (ex guide dogs) No smoking in restaurant Civ Wed 80 **CARDS:**

★★★75% New Park Manor

Lyndhurst Rd SO42 7QH
☎ 01590 623467 01590 622268
e-mail: enquires@newparkmanorhotel.co.uk
Dir: *on A337 1.5m from Lyndhurst between Brockenhurst and Lyndhust*

Once a favoured hunting lodge of King Charles II, this hotel enjoys a tranquil setting and its own equestrian centre. Fully modernised, it boasts a conference wing and bedrooms refurbished to a high standard. The comfortable public areas include the Stag restaurant and Rufus bar, both with log fires and historic features.

ROOMS: 24 en suite (4 fmly) No smoking in 8 bedrooms s £80; d £110-£190 (incl. bkfst) * **FACILITIES:** STV Outdoor swimming (H) Tennis (hard) Riding Xmas **CONF:** Thtr 120 Class 120 Board 80 Del from £89 * **PARKING:** 50 **NOTES:** No smoking in restaurant Civ Wed 50 **CARDS:**

See advert on opposite page

★★★74% Whitley Ridge Country House

Beaulieu Rd SO42 7QL
☎ 01590 622354 01590 622856
e-mail: whitleyridge@brockenhurst.co.uk
Dir: *access via B3055 towards Beaulieu*

This charming hotel enjoys a picturesque setting in the heart of the New Forest. Day rooms include two relaxing lounges and large dining room, all with lovely views of the forest. Each bedroom has an individual style, all are very comfortable.

ROOMS: 14 rms (13 en suite) No smoking in all bedrooms s £76-£80; d £128-£130 (incl. bkfst & dinner) * LB **FACILITIES:** Tennis (hard) Xmas **CONF:** Thtr 40 Class 40 Board 20 Del from £96 * **PARKING:** 32 **NOTES:** No smoking in restaurant **CARDS:**

Late for dinner? Quality Standards star rating means that last orders for dinner should be no earlier than:
★ 6.30pm ★★ 7.00pm ★★★ 8.00pm
★★★★ 9.00pm ★★★★★ 10.00pm

B

★★★73% ❁ Careys Manor

SO42 7RH
☎ 01590 623551 🖷 01590 622799
e-mail: info@careysmanor.com
Dir: *follow signs for Lyndhurst & Lymington A337, enter Brockenhurst, hotel after 30mph sign*

Careys Manor was one of the first buildings in the village. Public areas include the large naturally lit lounge with massive log fire. The leisure centre is definitely worth a visit, as it includes a good sized pool and gym. Le Blaireau Cafe provides an informal French style dining option, and the main restaurant enjoys a good local reputation.

ROOMS: 15 en suite 64 annexe en suite No smoking in 28 bedrooms s £79; d £129-£159 (incl. bkfst) * LB **FACILITIES:** STV Indoor swimming (H) Sauna Gym Croquet lawn Jacuzzi/spa Steam room Beauty therapists Xmas **CONF:** Thtr 120 Class 70 Board 40 Del from £125 * **PARKING:** 180 **NOTES:** No smoking in restaurant Civ Wed 110
CARDS:

See advert on this page

BROCKENHURST, continued

★★★69% Balmer Lawn
Lyndhurst Rd SO42 7ZB
☎ 01590 623116 01590 623864
e-mail: blh@btinternet.com
Dir: *take A337 towards Lymington, hotel on left hand side behind village cricket green*

One of the best locations in the heart of the New Forest, this historic house provides comfortable public rooms and a good range of bedrooms. The terrace is ideal for watching the world go by. Extensive function and leisure facilities skirt the hotel and make it a popular conference venue.
ROOMS: 55 en suite (4 fmly) No smoking in 45 bedrooms
FACILITIES: Indoor swimming (H) Outdoor swimming (H) Tennis (hard) Squash Sauna Gym Jacuzzi/spa **CONF:** Thtr 150 Class 50 Board 50
SERVICES: Lift **PARKING:** 80 **NOTES:** No smoking in restaurant
CARDS:

See advert on opposite page

★★★67% Forest Park
Forestdale Hotels

Rhinefield Rd SO42 7ZG
☎ 01590 622844 01590 623948
Dir: *from A337 to Brockenhurst turn into Meerut Rd, follow winding road through Waters Green, 0.5m to a T junct, turn right into Rhinefield Road*
This friendly hotel in the heart of the New Forest is popular for weekend breaks and quieter midweek stays. There are splendid walks and riding stables next door. The well equipped, comfortable bedrooms vary in size and style, and there is a choice of lounge areas.
ROOMS: 38 en suite (2 fmly) No smoking in 2 bedrooms s fr £65; d fr £130 (incl. bkfst & dinner) * LB **FACILITIES:** Outdoor swimming (H) Tennis (hard) Riding Sauna Xmas **CONF:** Thtr 50 Class 20 Board 24 Del from £110 * **PARKING:** 80 **NOTES:** No smoking in restaurant Civ Wed **CARDS:**

★★72% Cloud
Meerut Rd SO42 7TD
☎ 01590 622165 01590 622818
e-mail: enquires@cloudhotel.co.uk
Dir: *first turning right off A337 approaching Brockenhurst from Lyndhurst. Follow brown tourist signs*
This charming hotel enjoys a peaceful location on the edge of the village. The bedrooms are bright and comfortably furnished, with smart en suite facilities. The public rooms include a restaurant specialising in wholesome English food and several cosy lounges with log fires for the winter months.
ROOMS: 18 en suite (3 fmly) s fr £55; d fr £84 (incl. bkfst) * LB **FACILITIES:** Xmas **CONF:** Thtr 40 Class 12 Board 12 **PARKING:** 20 **NOTES:** No smoking in restaurant Civ Wed 40 **CARDS:**

★★67% Watersplash
The Rise SO42 7ZP
☎ 01590 622344 01590 624047
e-mail: waterob@aol.com
This popular Victorian hotel has been in the same family for 40 years. Upgraded bedrooms have co-ordinated decor and good facilities. The restaurant overlooks the pretty garden. There is also a comfortable residents' lounge, separate bar and outdoor pool.
ROOMS: 23 en suite (6 fmly) **FACILITIES:** Outdoor swimming (H) Motor cruiser **CONF:** Thtr 80 Class 20 Board 20 **PARKING:** 29
CARDS:

BROME, Suffolk Map 05 TM17

★★★70% Cornwallis Country Hotel & Restaurant
IP23 8AJ
☎ 01379 870326 01379 870051
Dir: *off B1077, 50yds from junct with A140 in direction of Eye*

A striking 16th-century dower house approached down a long tree-lined avenue and set amidst attractive well tended grounds. There is a Tudor bar, an elegant open-plan restaurant which runs into a relaxing lounge area and a vine-laden conservatory. The bedrooms, some of which have exposed beams, are furnished in baronial style, yet with modern facilities.
ROOMS: 11 en suite 5 annexe en suite (2 fmly) **FACILITIES:** STV Archery Hot air ballooning **CONF:** Thtr 40 Class 30 Board 20
NOTES: No smoking in restaurant **CARDS:**

BROMLEY, Greater London
See LONDON SECTION plan 1 *G1*

★★★70% Bromley Court
Best Western

Bromley Hill BR1 4JD
☎ 020 8464 5011 020 8460 0899
e-mail: bromleyhotel@btinternet.com
Dir: *N, signposted off A21. Opposite Mercedes Benz garage on Bromley Hill*
A grand mansion with modern extensions standing amid three acres of grounds. Accommodation is spread among several buildings, rooms vary in character, all are exceptionally well designed. The restaurant features dinner dancing and live entertainment on Friday and Saturday nights. Other facilities include a leisure club and good meeting rooms.
ROOMS: 115 en suite (3 fmly) No smoking in 24 bedrooms s £89-£92; d £90-£98 (incl. bkfst) * **FACILITIES:** STV Sauna Gym Croquet lawn Putting green Jacuzzi/spa Xmas **CONF:** Thtr 150 Class 80 Board 45 Del from £125 * **SERVICES:** Lift **PARKING:** 100 **NOTES:** Civ Wed 50
CARDS:

BROMSGROVE, Worcestershire
Map 07 SO97

★★★★69% Pine Lodge
Kidderminster Rd B61 9AB
☎ 01527 576600 01527 878981
e-mail: enquiries@pine-lodge-hotel.co.uk
Dir: *on A448 Bromsgrove to Kidderminster road, 1m W of Bromsgrove town centre*

This modern hotel, with its Mediterranean architecture and wealth of features appeals to all its visitors. A good choice of well equipped accommodation includes full suites, family-bedded rooms, ladies' rooms, and a room for disabled guests. There is a choice of formal and informal restaurants where the cuisine delivers upon its good reputation.
ROOMS: 114 en suite (18 fmly) No smoking in 18 bedrooms **FACILITIES:** STV Indoor swimming (H) Snooker Sauna Solarium Gym Jacuzzi/spa Childrens play area **CONF:** Thtr 200 Class 140 Board 30 **SERVICES:** Lift **PARKING:** 250 **CARDS:**

Premier Lodge
Worcester Rd, Upton Warren B61 7ET
☎ 0870 700 1314 0870 700 1315
Premier Lodge offers modern, well equipped, en suite accommodation suitable for both business and leisure travellers. Meals can be taken at the adjacent popular restaurant and bar which is fully licensed. For further details, consult the Hotel Groups page.
ROOMS: 27 en suite d £46 *

BROOK (NEAR CADNAM), Hampshire
Map 04 SU21

★★★66% Bell Inn
SO43 7HE
☎ 023 8081 2214 023 8081 3958
e-mail: bell@bramshaw.co.uk
Dir: *leave M27 junct 1 onto B3079, hotel a mile and a half on right*

The Inn is part of the Bramshaw Golf Club and has tailored its style to suit this market, but it is also an ideal base from which to visit the New Forest. Bedrooms are comfortable and attractively furnished, and the public areas have a cosy and friendly atmosphere.
ROOMS: 25 en suite No smoking in 11 bedrooms s £55-£65; d £80-£85 (incl. bkfst) * LB **FACILITIES:** Golf 36 Putting green Xmas **CONF:** Thtr 50 Class 20 Board 30 Del from £75 * **PARKING:** 150 **NOTES:** No dogs (ex guide dogs) No smoking in restaurant
CARDS:

BROXTON, Cheshire
Map 07 SJ45

★★★★72% De Vere Carden Park
Carden Park CH3 9DQ
☎ 01829 731000 01829 731032
e-mail: reservation@carden-park.co.uk
Dir: *leave M56 junct 15 for M53 Chester, take A41 for Whitchurch for approx 8m, at Broxton rdbt turn right on to A534 Wrexham continue 1.5m hotel on left*
This fine modern hotel provides a full range of leisure, conference and function facilities. A choice of golf courses is available, including one designed by Jack Nicklaus. A brasserie serves light meals and snacks and the more formal Garden Restaurant offers fixed-price and carte menus. Bedrooms are spacious and well equipped, many located in nearby buildings with views over the courses.
ROOMS: 115 en suite 77 annexe en suite (24 fmly) No smoking in 134 bedrooms s £110-£250; d £125-£250 * LB **FACILITIES:** STV Indoor swimming (H) Golf 45 Tennis (hard) Snooker Sauna Solarium Gym Pool table Croquet lawn Putting green Jacuzzi/spa Archery Quad bikes Jack Nicklaus Golf School Xmas **CONF:** Thtr 400 Class 240 Board 125 Del from £140 * **SERVICES:** Lift **PARKING:** 500 **NOTES:** No dogs (ex guide dogs) No smoking in restaurant Civ Wed 100
CARDS:

BROXTON, continued

★★★64% Broxton Hall Country House
Whitchurch Rd CH3 9JS
☎ 01829 782321 01829 782330
Dir: *on A41 S of Chester at Broxton Rdbt A534, halfway between Whitchurch & Chester*
Set in its own beautiful grounds, this impressive half-timbered Tudor hall offers public areas elegantly equipped with antique and period furnishings. Bedrooms are all individually furnished to a high standard, some with beautiful antique four-poster beds . The popular restaurant overlooks the well tended gardens.
ROOMS: 10 en suite s £65-£80; d £75-£120 (incl. bkfst) * LB **FACILITIES:** Croquet lawn entertainment **CONF:** Thtr 23 Board 12 **PARKING:** 30 **NOTES:** No children 12yrs Closed 25 Dec & 1 Jan
CARDS:

★★73% Frogg Manor
Fullersmoor, Nantwich Rd CH3 9JH
☎ 01829 782629 & 782280 01829 782238
Dir: *from Chester take A41 towards Whitchurch, then left on A534 towards Nantwich. Hotel 0.75m on right*

This delightful Georgian house, set in eight acres of grounds and beautiful gardens which include a tennis court, is situated on the A534 about three quarters of a mile east of its junction with the A41. The house has been tastefully refurbished to create this small, personally run hotel with well equipped accommodation.
ROOMS: 6 en suite s £50-£110; d £70-£140 * LB **FACILITIES:** STV Tennis (hard) **CONF:** Thtr 25 Class 15 Board 10 Del from £115 * **PARKING:** 37 **NOTES:** No children 4yrs No smoking in restaurant RS Restaurant must be pre-booked Civ Wed 60
CARDS:

BRYHER See Scilly, Isles of

BUCKDEN, North Yorkshire Map 07 SD97

★★67% Buck Inn
BD23 5JA
☎ 01756 760228 & 760416 01756 760227
e-mail: thebuckinn@yorks.net
Dir: *from A59 take B6265 to Threshfield, then B6160 to Buckden passing through Kettlewell & Starbotton*
This Georgian inn is situated amidst glorious Dales scenery, with fine views from many of the rooms. Bedrooms are attractively furnished and there is a cosy lounge area for visitors. A wide range of interesting snacks and meals is served in the welcoming lounge bar. The Courtyard restaurant offers a more formal menu using fresh quality produce.
ROOMS: 14 en suite (2 fmly) s £33-£36; d £66-£72 (incl. bkfst) * LB **FACILITIES:** Xmas **CONF:** Class 30 **PARKING:** 30 **NOTES:** No smoking in restaurant Closed 2 wks early Jan **CARDS:**

BUCKHURST HILL, Essex Map 05 TQ49

★★★63% Roebuck
North End IG9 5QY
☎ 020 8505 4636 020 8504 7826

corus

The pleasant rural appeal of the climber-clad exterior belies the modern style of the interior here. The new restaurant features a bold colour scheme which also extends to the bar.
ROOMS: 28 en suite No smoking in 10 bedrooms s fr £89; d fr £100 * LB **FACILITIES:** Xmas **CONF:** Thtr 200 Class 60 Board 14 Del £125 * **PARKING:** 40 **NOTES:** Civ Wed 120
CARDS:

○ Express by Holiday Inn
High Rd IG9 5HT
☎ 0800 897121
ROOMS: 49 rms **NOTES:** Opening September 2000

Express by Holiday Inn

BUCKINGHAM, Buckinghamshire Map 04 SP63

★★★72% *Villiers*
3 Castle St MK18 1BS
☎ 01280 822444 01280 822113
e-mail: villiers@villiers-hotels.demon.co.uk

Built around a cobbled courtyard, this comfortable, welcoming hotel boasts a state-of-the-art conference facility. The roomy bedrooms provide high levels of comfort and are very well equipped. Split-level suites and new purpose-designed Executive rooms are also available. There are relaxing sitting areas and a choice of contrasting bars, while Henry's Restaurant offers a fine dining experience.
ROOMS: 38 en suite (25 fmly) **FACILITIES:** STV Free membership of nearby leisure club entertainment **CONF:** Thtr 250 Class 100 Board 60 **SERVICES:** Lift **PARKING:** 53 **NOTES:** No dogs (ex guide dogs)
CARDS:

See advert on opposite page

B

★★★66% Buckingham Four Pillars Hotel
Buckingham Ring Rd South MK18 1RY
☎ 01280 822622 🖷 01280 823074
e-mail: buckingham@four-pillars.co.uk
Dir: *on A421 near junct with A413*

FOUR PILLARS HOTELS

A purpose-built hotel providing extensive conference facilities and large, well appointed bedrooms with plenty of desk space. There is a well equipped leisure suite with pool, spa and fitness room; also a snooker table for the less energetic. The open-plan restaurant and bar offers a good range of dishes including a carvery on selected days.
ROOMS: 70 en suite (6 fmly) No smoking in 24 bedrooms s £49-£90; d £55-£100 * LB **FACILITIES:** STV Indoor swimming (H) Sauna Solarium Gym Pool table Jacuzzi/spa Steam room Games room entertainment Xmas **CONF:** Thtr 160 Class 90 Board 50 Del from £110 * **PARKING:** 120 **NOTES:** Closed 28 Dec-4 Jan
CARDS:

BUCKLAND (NEAR BROADWAY), Gloucestershire — Map 04 SP03

Premier Collection

★★★ Buckland Manor
WR12 7LY
☎ 01386 852626 🖷 01386 853557
e-mail: buckland-manor-uk@msn.com
Dir: *off B4632*

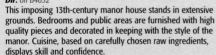

RELAIS & CHATEAUX.

This imposing 13th-century manor house stands in extensive grounds. Bedrooms and public areas are furnished with high quality pieces and decorated in keeping with the style of the manor. Cuisine, based on carefully chosen raw ingredients, displays skill and confidence.
ROOMS: 13 en suite (2 fmly) s £195-£335; d £205-£345 (incl. bkfst) **FACILITIES:** STV Outdoor swimming (H) Tennis (hard) Croquet lawn Putting green Xmas **PARKING:** 30 **NOTES:** No dogs No children 12yrs No smoking in restaurant
CARDS:

BUCKLOW HILL, Cheshire — Map 07 SJ78

Premier Lodge (Knutsford North)
Bucklow Hill WA16 6RD
☎ 0870 700 1480 🖷 0870 700 1481

PREMIER LODGE

Premier Lodge offers modern, well equipped, en suite accommodation suitable for both business and leisure travellers. Meals can be taken at the adjacent popular restaurant and bar which is fully licensed. For further details, consult the Hotel Groups page.
ROOMS: 66 en suite d £46 *

BUDE, Cornwall & Isles of Scilly — Map 02 SS20

★★★70% *Falcon*
Breakwater Rd EX23 8SD
☎ 01288 352005 🖷 01288 356359
Dir: *turn off A39 into Bude and follow road to Widemouth bay. Hotel is on right as you cross over canal bridge.*

The Falcon Hotel is located on the edge of the town in delightful gardens. An extensive range of menus, including a selection of locally caught fish and a range of vegetarian options, is offered in the elegant restaurant. A wide selection of bar meals is also available.
ROOMS: 26 en suite (5 fmly) **FACILITIES:** STV Sauna Solarium Gym Croquet lawn Jacuzzi/spa **CONF:** Thtr 60 Class 30 Board 30 **PARKING:** 40 **NOTES:** No smoking in restaurant
CARDS:

See advert on page 133

BUDE, continued

★★★70% Hartland
Hartland Ter EX23 8JY
☎ 01288 355661 ▤ 01288 355664
Conveniently located between the town centre and the beaches, the long established Hartland Hotel has a loyal following. In the comfortably furnished restaurant, an interesting fixed-price menu is offered. During the season, entertainment is provided in the ballroom on certain evenings.
ROOMS: 28 en suite (2 fmly) No smoking in 8 bedrooms s £38-£49; d £68-£82 (incl. bkfst) * LB **FACILITIES:** Outdoor swimming (H) entertainment Xmas **SERVICES:** Lift **PARKING:** 30 **NOTES:** No smoking in restaurant Closed mid Nov-Etr (ex Xmas & New Year)

★★66% Atlantic House
17-18 Summerleaze Crescent EX23 8HJ
☎ 01288 352451 ▤ 01288 356666
e-mail: ahbude@aol.com
Dir: *leave M5 junct 31, follow A30 dual carriageway to bypass Okehampton, follow signs to Bude via Halwill and Holsworthy*
This relaxed and personally-run hotel is set in a quiet area overlooking the beach. Bedrooms are comfortable and well maintained; some face the sea and there are some 'teenager rooms'. An imaginative, well balanced fixed-price menu is served in the restaurant. The hotel is renowned for well supervised, activity holidays.
ROOMS: 13 en suite (3 fmly) No smoking in 1 bedroom s £33.90-£43.20; d £45.20-£57.60 (incl. bkfst) * LB **FACILITIES:** Pool table Games room Multi-activity outdoor sports **PARKING:** 10 **NOTES:** No dogs (ex guide dogs) No smoking in restaurant Closed 11 Nov-2 Mar
CARDS:

★★65% *Maer Lodge*
MINOTEL Great Britain
Crooklets Beach EX23 8NG
☎ 01288 353306 ▤ 01288 354005
e-mail: maerlodgehotel@btinternet.com
Dir: *leave A39 at Stratton to Bude 1m. Go right into The Strand and up Belle Vue past shops. Bear left at Somerfield to Crooklets Beach, hotel to right*
With views over the Downs and surrounding countryside, this long established, family-run hotel is quietly located. Traditionally furnished public areas are comfortable and include a cosy bar and spacious lounge. In the dining room a choice from a short fixed-price menu is offered. The bedrooms are soundly furnished and appointed.
ROOMS: 19 en suite (4 fmly) No smoking in all bedrooms **FACILITIES:** STV Putting green **CONF:** Class 60 Board 15 **PARKING:** 15 **NOTES:** No smoking in restaurant **CARDS:**

★★65% *Stamford Hill Hotel*
Stratton EX23 9AY
☎ 01288 352709 ▤ 01288 352709
Dir: *on the edge of the village of Stratton, just off A39, brown tourist signs direct to the hotel*
Built on the site of the Battle of Stamford Hill, this Georgian manor is set in beautiful woodland and gardens, only a mile from Bude's sandy beaches. The hotel offers comfortable, well equipped bedrooms, many with views over the surrounding countryside. There is a spacious lounge, a relaxing bar and a restaurant serving carefully prepared meals.
ROOMS: 14 en suite (5 fmly) No smoking in 1 bedroom **FACILITIES:** Outdoor swimming (H) Tennis (grass) Sauna Pool table Badminton court **PARKING:** 20 **NOTES:** No smoking in restaurant Closed 18 Dec-18 Jan **CARDS:**

★★64% *Penarvor*
Crooklets Beach EX23 8NE
☎ 01288 352036 ▤ 01288 355027
e-mail: hotel.penarvor@mcmail.com
There is a relaxed and friendly atmosphere at this family-owned hotel overlooking Crooklets Beach. Particularly popular with golfers, the hotel is adjacent to the golf course and a short walk from the town centre. Bedrooms vary in size but are all equipped to a similar standard. In the restaurant an interesting selection of dishes uses fresh local produce.
ROOMS: 16 en suite (3 fmly) **FACILITIES:** STV Pool table **PARKING:** 20 **NOTES:** No smoking in restaurant
CARDS:

★★61% Camelot
Downs View EX23 8RE
☎ 01288 352361 ▤ 01288 355470
e-mail: stay@camelot-hotel.co.uk
Dir: *turn off A39 into Bude, right at rdbt, through one-way system keep left, hotel on left overlooking golf course*

Overlooking Bude and Cornwall Golf Club, this Edwardian property has an enviable reputation among the golfing fraternity. Comfortable public areas include a well furnished lounge and bar, the latter featuring golfing ties from around the world. Bedrooms are light, airy and furnished in a contemporary style.
ROOMS: 24 en suite (3 fmly) s £25-£32; d £50-£64 (incl. bkfst) * LB **FACILITIES:** Pool table Darts Table tennis **PARKING:** 21 **NOTES:** No dogs (ex guide dogs) No smoking in restaurant
CARDS:

★★60% Inn On The Green
Crooklets Beach EX23 8NF
☎ 01288 356013 ▤ 01288 356244
e-mail: bude@innonthegreen46.freeserve.co.uk
Dir: *A39 to Bude, through High Street, fork left at supermarket to Crooklets Beach*
Overlooking the golf course and adjacent to Crooklets Beach, the Inn on the Green offers comfortable accommodation and a friendly, relaxed service. Bedrooms vary in size and style, with several single rooms available. In addition to the menus provided in the restaurant, an extensive range of bar meals is served.
ROOMS: 17 en suite (2 fmly) **FACILITIES:** Pool table **PARKING:** 3 **NOTES:** Closed Xmas **CARDS:**

BURFORD, Oxfordshire
Map 04 SP21

★★★73% The Lamb Inn
Sheep St OX18 4LR
☎ 01993 823155 ▤ 01993 822228
Dir: *off Burford High Street*
A wonderful old inn set in a cottage garden in a pretty Cotswold village. Bedrooms retain the character of the building and are well equipped with tasteful furnishings and fabrics. Flagstone floors

continued

and log fires set the tone in the three comfortable lounges, furnished with sumptuous sofas and fireside chairs. Meals are taken in the formal dining room, where guests can savour the fine cuisine.
ROOMS: 15 en suite s £65-£80; d £100-£120 (incl. bkfst) * LB
PARKING: 6 **NOTES:** No smoking in restaurant Closed 25-26 Dec
CARDS:

★★★65% The Bay Tree
12-14 Sheep St OX18 4LW
☎ 01993 822791 01993 823008
e-mail: bookins@cotswold-inns-hotels.co.uk
Dir: *off A40, down hill onto A361 towards Burford, Sheep St 1st left*
This historic inn retains many original features; the main staircase with its heraldic decor is particularly impressive. The bedrooms are individually decorated with traditional and modern furnishings, and equipped to a high standard. A number of rooms feature four-poster and half-tester beds, and the cottage rooms overlook an attractive walled garden.
ROOMS: 7 en suite 14 annexe en suite s fr £90; d £135-£210 (incl. bkfst) * LB **FACILITIES:** Croquet lawn Xmas **CONF:** Thtr 40 Class 12 Board 25 Del from £140 * **PARKING:** 50 **NOTES:** No smoking in restaurant Civ Wed 70 **CARDS:**

★★★65% Cotswold Gateway
Cheltenham Rd OX18 4HX
☎ 01993 822695 01993 823600
e-mail: cotswold.gateway@dial.pipex.com
Dir: *situated at the roundabout on the A40 Oxford/Cheltenham at junct with A361*
Situated on the A40 route to Cheltenham, this friendly hotel is a convenient base from which to explore the Cotswolds. Bedrooms are decorated with pleasant fabrics and attractive furnishings, the two four-poster rooms are particularly good. There is a separate coffee shop and an elegant restaurant where traditional and modern dishes are served.
ROOMS: 13 en suite 8 annexe en suite (2 fmly) No smoking in all bedrooms s fr £70; d £95-£125 (incl. bkfst) * LB **FACILITIES:** Xmas **CONF:** Thtr 40 Class 20 Board 24 **PARKING:** 60 **NOTES:** No dogs (ex guide dogs) No smoking in restaurant **CARDS:**

★★★61% The Inn For All Seasons
The Barringtons OX18 4TN
☎ 01451 844324 01451 844375
e-mail: sharp@innforallseasons.com
Dir: *3m W of Burford on A40*
A warm, friendly welcome awaits at this 16th-century, family-run coaching inn. Comfortable rooms are steadily being upgraded with bright, attractive decor. The interior of the hotel, whilst providing modern amenities, retains original fireplaces, oak beams and period furniture. A good selection of bar meals is available at lunchtime, in addition to a full evening restaurant menu.
ROOMS: 9 en suite 1 annexe en suite (2 fmly) s £35-£49; d £70-£90 (incl. bkfst) * LB **FACILITIES:** STV Clay pigeon shooting Xmas **CONF:** Thtr 25 Class 30 Board 30 Del from £127 * **PARKING:** 62 **NOTES:** No smoking in restaurant **CARDS:**

★★63% Golden Pheasant
Old English Inns & Hotels
91 High St OX18 4QA
☎ 01993 823223 01993 822621
Dir: *leave M40 at junct 8 and follow signs A40 Cheltenham into Burford*
This attractive old inn on Burford's main street has parts that date back to the 16th century. Bedrooms can be a little compact but all are well furnished; attractive fabrics and period furniture are combined with useful extras. Meals can either be taken in the bar or in the restaurant with its solid-fuel stove.
ROOMS: 12 rms (11 en suite) (1 fmly) **PARKING:** 12 **NOTES:** No smoking in restaurant **CARDS:**

⌂ *Travelodge*
Travelodge
Bury Barn OX7 5TB
☎ 01993 822699 01993 822699
Dir: *A40*
This modern building offers accommodation in smart, spacious and well equipped bedrooms, all with en suite bathrooms. Refreshments may be taken at the nearby family restaurant. For further details and the Travelodge phone number, consult the Hotel Groups page.
ROOMS: 40 en suite

BURLEY, Hampshire — Map 04 SU20

★★★67% Burley Manor
Forestdale Hotels
Ringwood Rd BH24 4BS
☎ 01425 403522 01425 403227
Dir: *leave A31 at Burley signpost, hotel 3m on left*
Set in extensive grounds, this 18th-century hotel enjoys a relaxed ambience and a peaceful setting. Half of the well equipped, comfortable bedrooms, including several with four-posters, are located in the main house and the remainder, many of which have balconies, in the adjacent converted stable block and new wing. Riding can be arranged. Cosy public rooms are warmed by log fires in winter.

continued on p134

BURLEY, continued

ROOMS: 21 en suite 17 annexe en suite (3 fmly) No smoking in 4 bedrooms s fr £65; d fr £130 (incl. bkfst & dinner) * LB
FACILITIES: Outdoor swimming (H) Fishing Riding Croquet lawn Xmas
CONF: Thtr 60 Class 40 Board 40 Del from £115 * **PARKING:** 60
NOTES: No smoking in restaurant Civ Wed
CARDS:

★★★63% Moorhill House

BH24 4AG
☎ 01425 403285 01425 403715
e-mail: info@carehotels.co.uk
Dir: *follow A31 for approx 5m pass two shell gardens on either side of the road & sign for Burley, into village. Road opposite Queens Head then 1st left*

Situated in the heart of the New Forest, this hotel has two lounges overlooking the garden. Service is friendly and relaxed and bedrooms vary in size.

ROOMS: 24 en suite (7 fmly) s £70-£77.50; d £110-£125 (incl. bkfst) * LB **FACILITIES:** Indoor swimming (H) Sauna Croquet lawn Putting green Jacuzzi/spa Xmas **CONF:** Thtr 54 Class 48 Board 28 Del from £95 * **PARKING:** 40 **CARDS:**

BURNHAM, Buckinghamshire Map 04 SU98

★★★71% ❀ Grovefield

Taplow Common Rd SL1 8LP
☎ 01628 603131 01628 668078

Grovefield is set in spacious grounds, and is situated conveniently close to Heathrow and Gatwick. Bedrooms are spacious and attractively decorated. The restaurant is a comfortable place to eat rosette worthy cuisine and the bar lounge has been refurbished. Its location near the golf course makes it ideal for weekend breaks.

ROOMS: 40 en suite (5 fmly) No smoking in 24 bedrooms s fr £140; d fr £150 (incl. bkfst) * LB **FACILITIES:** STV Fishing Croquet lawn Putting green Xmas **CONF:** Thtr 250 Class 80 Board 80 Del from £180 * **SERVICES:** Lift **PARKING:** 155 **NOTES:** No smoking in restaurant Civ Wed 200 **CARDS:**

★★★68% ❀ Burnham Beeches

REGAL

Grove Rd SL1 8DP
☎ 01628 429955 01628 603994
Dir: *follow A355 towards Slough. Straight on at 1st rbt, right at 2nd and right at 3rd then follow signs to hotel*

In its own grounds, this extended Georgian manor house stands on the fringes of woodland convenient for the M4 and M40. Spacious bedrooms are comfortable, quiet and well equipped. Facilities include a fitness centre with pool and a cosy lounge bar where all-day snacks are available.

continued

ROOMS: 82 en suite (19 fmly) No smoking in 18 bedrooms s £120-£140; d £140-£160 * LB **FACILITIES:** STV Indoor swimming (H) Tennis (hard) Snooker Sauna Solarium Gym Croquet lawn Jacuzzi/spa Beauty Treatments by prior arrangement Xmas **CONF:** Thtr 180 Class 100 Board 60 Del from £160 * **SERVICES:** Lift **PARKING:** 200 **NOTES:** No dogs (ex guide dogs) Civ Wed 120 **CARDS:**

BURNHAM MARKET, Norfolk Map 09 TF84

★★71% ❀❀ Hoste Arms

The Green PE31 8HD
☎ 01328 738777 01328 730103
e-mail: 106504.2472@compuserve.com
Dir: *signposted on B1155, 5m W of Wells-Next-the-Sea*

This stylish, atmospheric hotel has an excellent restaurant and traditional pub. Bedrooms, in a range of styles, are all charming and richly decorated and furnished.

ROOMS: (1 fmly) s fr £64; d fr £86 (incl. bkfst) LB **FACILITIES:** Xmas **CONF:** Thtr 30 Class 22 Board 24 **PARKING:** 60 **NOTES:** No children 5yrs **CARDS:**

BURNLEY, Lancashire Map 07 SD83

★★★73% Oaks

SHIRE INNS

Colne Rd, Reedley BB10 2LF
☎ 01282 414141 01282 433401
e-mail: oaks@shireinns.co.uk
Dir: *on A56 between Burnley and Nelson*

The panelled hall of this hotel leads to a gallery lounge with a splendid stained glass window. Other public areas include a leisure club, Quills restaurant and, at lunchtime, the more informal Archives brasserie. Comfortable bedrooms are well equipped to suit visitors' every need.

ROOMS: 50 en suite (10 fmly) No smoking in 20 bedrooms s £96 (incl. bkfst) * LB **FACILITIES:** STV Indoor swimming (H) Sauna Solarium Gym Jacuzzi/spa Steam room Xmas **CONF:** Thtr 120 Class 48 Board 60 Del from £85 * **PARKING:** 110 **NOTES:** No smoking in restaurant Civ Wed 150 **CARDS:**

★★★69% Sparrow Hawk

Church St BB11 2DN
☎ 01282 421551 01282 456506
Dir: *on Inner Ring Road (A682), opposite St Peters Church*

This well maintained Victorian hotel provides comfortable, modern bedrooms which are well equipped with many thoughtful extras. There is a choice between a cocktail bar and a popular lounge bar, where a range of real ales is served. A full carte menu is available in the restaurant during the week, changing to a grill menu at weekends.

ROOMS: 36 en suite (2 fmly) No smoking in 18 bedrooms s fr £49.50; d fr £57 (incl. bkfst) * LB **FACILITIES:** STV Pool table entertainment Xmas **CONF:** Thtr 80 Class 40 Board 30 Del from £68 * **PARKING:** 24 **NOTES:** No dogs (ex guide dogs) **CARDS:**

★★★65% Rosehill House
Rosehill Av BB11 2PW
☎ 01282 453931 01282 455628
e-mail: rhhotel@provider.co.uk
Dir: *0.5m S of Burnley town centre, off the A682*
Many original features of this Grade II listed building remain, including some fine ornate ceilings. Public areas include a choice of function rooms, comfortable bar lounge and a well appointed restaurant and conservatory, where a selection of carefully prepared dishes is offered. Bedrooms are individually furnished and thoughtfully equipped.
ROOMS: 30 en suite (2 fmly) No smoking in 1 bedroom s £40-£50; d £50-£75 (incl. bkfst) * LB **FACILITIES:** STV Snooker Gym **CONF:** Thtr 50 Class 30 Board 30 **PARKING:** 52 **NOTES:** No dogs (ex guide dogs) Civ Wed 100 **CARDS:**

★★65% Alexander
2 Tarleton Av, Todmorden Rd BB11 3ET
☎ 01282 422684 01282 424094
Dir: *leave M65 at junct 10 and follow signs for 'Towneley Hall' to Tarleton Avenue. Hotel 100yds from Towneley Hall main entrance*
Close to the town centre, this hotel takes pride in its dining facilities, and an extensive range of dishes can be enjoyed in the Gourmet Restaurant or in the more informal surrounds of the attractive café bar. Bedrooms are well equipped and include family rooms. Staff are helpful.
ROOMS: 11 en suite 5 annexe en suite (2 fmly) s £35-£42; d £53 (incl. bkfst) * LB **FACILITIES:** STV Xmas **CONF:** Thtr 120 Class 40 Board 45 **PARKING:** 18 **NOTES:** No dogs (ex guide dogs)
CARDS:

★★60% Comfort Friendly Inn
Keirby Walk BB11 2DH
☎ 01282 427611 01282 436370
e-mail: admin@gb608.u-net.com
Dir: *follow Burnley Town Centre signs, on approaching Town Centre there is a rdbt with Sainsburys & Gala Bingo. Hotel on opposite side of rdbt*
Situated in the centre of the town this hotel offers value-for-money accommodation in a friendly and informal atmosphere. Bedrooms, although compact, are particularly well equipped. Public areas include a popular bar and a restaurant.
ROOMS: 50 en suite (1 fmly) No smoking in 18 bedrooms d £46.75 * LB **FACILITIES:** STV Xmas **CONF:** Thtr 300 Class 130 Board 35 Del from £49.50 * **SERVICES:** Lift **PARKING:** 75
CARDS:

Travelodge
Cavalry Barracks, Barracks Rd BB11 4AS
☎ 01282 416039 01282 416039
Dir: *junc A671/A679*
This modern building offers accommodation in smart, spacious and well equipped bedrooms, all with en suite bathrooms. Refreshments may be taken at the nearby family restaurant. For further details and the Travelodge phone number, consult the Hotel Groups page.
ROOMS: 32 en suite

BURNSALL, North Yorkshire Map 07 SE06

★★67% Red Lion Hotel
By the Bridge BD23 6BU
☎ 01756 720204 01756 720292
e-mail: redlion@daelnet.co.uk
Dir: *on B6160 between Grassington and Bolton Abbey*
This charming 16th-century Dales inn stands by a bridge over the River Wharfe - guests are free to fish the hotel's own stretch of water. Attractive bedrooms are comfortable, and the homely lounge is complemented by a traditional bar. The intimate restaurant makes excellent use of fresh local ingredients; breakfast is especially recommended.
ROOMS: 7 en suite 4 annexe en suite (2 fmly) s £58-£63; d £90-£116 (incl. bkfst) * LB **FACILITIES:** Fishing Xmas **CONF:** Thtr 30 Class 10 Board 20 Del from £90 * **PARKING:** 80 **NOTES:** No dogs No smoking in restaurant Civ Wed 50 **CARDS:**

BURRINGTON (NEAR PORTSMOUTH ARMS STATION), Devon Map 03 SS61

★★★81% Northcote Manor
EX37 9LZ
☎ 01769 560501 01769 560770
e-mail: rest@northcotemanor.co.uk
Dir: *turn off A377 opposite Portsmouth Arms Pub, into hotel's own drive marked Northcote Manor. Do not enter Burrington village*

This beautiful stone-built, gabled manor house has views over the peaceful Devon countryside. Restored to its former glory, rooms are extremely comfortable and modern facilities have been cleverly provided without compromising the elegance of the architecture. Award-winning cuisine can be enjoyed in the Manor House Restaurant.
ROOMS: 11 en suite s £90-£200; d £120-£290 (incl. bkfst & dinner) * LB **FACILITIES:** STV Tennis (hard) Croquet lawn Xmas **PARKING:** 20 **NOTES:** No smoking in restaurant Civ Wed 40
CARDS:

See advert under BARNSTAPLE

BURTON MOTORWAY SERVICE AREA (M6), Cumbria Map 07 SD57

Travelodge
Burton in Kendal LA6 1JF
☎ 01524 781234
Dir: *between junct35/36 southbound M6*
This modern building offers accommodation in smart, spacious and well equipped bedrooms, all with en suite bathrooms. Refreshments may be taken at the nearby family restaurant. For further details and the Travelodge phone number, consult the Hotel Groups page.
ROOMS: 40 en suite

Late for dinner? Quality Standards star rating means that last orders for dinner should be no earlier than:
★ 6.30pm ★★ 7.00pm ★★★ 8.00pm
★★★★ 9.00pm ★★★★★ 10.00pm

B

BURTON UPON TRENT, Staffordshire Map 08 SK22

⇧ Express by Holiday Inn
2nd Av, Centrum 100 DE14 2WF
☎ 01283 504300 📠 504301
Dir: *take A38 Branston exit. Follow signs A5121 Town Centre. At rdbt of McDonalds, turn left into 2nd Avenue. Hotel on left*

A modern budget hotel offering comfortable accommodation in refreshing, spacious and comprehensively-equipped bedrooms, en suite bathrooms with power showers and continental buffet breakfast included in the room rate. Suitable for business travellers or families. For further details and the Express by Holiday Inn phone number, consult the Hotel Groups page.
ROOMS: 82 en suite (incl. cont bkfst) d £45-£59.50 * **CONF:** Thtr 60 Class 30 Board 30 Del from £95 *

BURTONWOOD MOTORWAY SERVICE AREA (M62), Cheshire Map 07 SJ59

⇧ Days Inn

Burtonwood Services, M62, Great Sankey WA5 3AX
☎ 01925 710376 📠 01925 710378
Dir: *between junc 7 & 9 M62 westbound*
Fully refurbished, Days Inn offers well equipped, brightly appointed, modern accommodation with smart en suite bathrooms. There is a fully staffed reception; continental breakfast is available and other refreshments may be taken at the nearby family restaurant.
ROOMS: 40 en suite d fr £45 *

BURWARDSLEY, Cheshire Map 07 SJ55

★★66% Pheasant Inn

Higher Burwardsley CH3 9PF
☎ 01829 770434 📠 01829 771097
e-mail: the pheasantinn@aol.com
Dir: *from A41 left for Tattenhall, once there right at 1st junct & left at 2nd to Higher Burwardsley, as far as post office then left, hotel is signposted*
This 300-year-old inn is set high in the Peckforton Hills, with spectacular views over the Cheshire plain. Well equipped, comfortable bedrooms are housed in an adjacent converted barn. Food is served either in the restaurant or in the traditional beamed bar. Real fires are lit in the winter months.
ROOMS: 2 en suite 8 annexe en suite (2 fmly) No smoking in 4 bedrooms s fr £49.50; d £70-£80 (incl. bkfst) * LB **CONF:** Thtr 30 Board 18 Del from £105 * **PARKING:** 35 **NOTES:** Closed 26 Dec & 1 Jan RS 25 Dec bar only open **CARDS:**

Packed in a hurry? Ironing facilities should be available at all star levels, either in rooms or on request.

BURY, Greater Manchester Map 07 SD81

★★★65% *Bolholt Country Park*
Walshaw Rd BL8 1PU
☎ 0161 762 4000 📠 0161 762 4100
Dir: *from M66 take turn-off for Bury Town Centre and after 50yds fork right and at 4-lane filter system take right hand lanes and signpost for Walshaw*
Quietly situated but within easy access of the town centre, this former mill owner's house, set in 50 acres of parkland, has been extended to include modern, comfortable bedrooms. There is a choice of lounges and, separate from the hotel, a well equipped fitness and leisure centre. Service is friendly and attentive.
ROOMS: 66 en suite (13 fmly) No smoking in 4 bedrooms **FACILITIES:** STV Indoor swimming (H) Fishing Sauna Solarium Gym Pool table Jacuzzi/spa Fitness & leisure centre entertainment **CONF:** Thtr 300 Class 120 Board 40 **PARKING:** 300 **NOTES:** No smoking in restaurant **CARDS:**

BURY ST EDMUNDS, Suffolk Map 05 TL86

★★★72% ❀ Angel
Angel Hill IP33 1LT
☎ 01284 741000 📠 01284 741001
e-mail: reception@theangel.co.uk
Dir: *from A134 turn left at rdbt into Northgate St, straight on to T junct with traffic lights right into Mustow St left onto Angel Hill on right*
Charles Dickens once stayed in this delightful 15th-century hotel. A number of smart new air-conditioned bedrooms were being added at the time of our last inspection. A choice of two restaurants, a popular bar, plenty of comfortable lounge space and supervised parking are further attractions.
ROOMS: 66 en suite (4 fmly) No smoking in 6 bedrooms s £69-£99; d £81-£150 * LB **FACILITIES:** STV entertainment Xmas **CONF:** Thtr 80 Class 20 Board 30 Del from £115 * **SERVICES:** Lift **PARKING:** 54 **NOTES:** No smoking in restaurant Civ Wed 100
CARDS:

★★★70% Ravenwood Hall
Rougham IP30 9JA
☎ 01359 270345 📠 01359 270788
Dir: *3m E off A14*
Amidst seven acres of lawns and woodland, Ravenwood Hall dates back to the 15th century and retains much original character with carved timbers and inglenook fireplaces. Spacious bedrooms are individually decorated, furnished with period pieces and well equipped. There is an attractive restaurant offering an appealing menu.
ROOMS: 7 en suite 7 annexe en suite No smoking in all bedrooms s £69-£92; d £90-£125 (incl. bkfst) * LB **FACILITIES:** Outdoor swimming (H) Tennis (hard) Riding Croquet lawn Shooting & fishing parties Free membership of local healthclub Xmas **CONF:** Thtr 200 Class 80 Board 40 **PARKING:** 150 **NOTES:** No smoking in restaurant Civ Wed 200 **CARDS:**

★★★69% *The Priory*
Tollgate IP32 6EH
☎ 01284 766181 📠 01284 767604
e-mail: reservations@prioryhotel.co.uk
Dir: *off A1101 towards Mildenhall*
This delightful hotel has a country house atmosphere. There are two restaurant areas, a conservatory, dining room and a bustling bar. The restaurant serves a range of appetising dishes from the carte and fixed-priced menus. Attractively furnished bedrooms are available in the main house and the garden wings.

continued

ROOMS: 9 en suite 18 annexe en suite (3 fmly) No smoking in 14 bedrooms **CONF:** Thtr 40 Class 20 Board 20 **PARKING:** 60 **NOTES:** Closed 27 Dec-3 Jan RS Sat & Sun **CARDS:**

★★★65% Butterfly

Moreton Hall IP32 7BW
☎ 01284 760884 01284 755476
e-mail: burybutterfly@lineone.net
Dir: *from A14 take Bury East exit and at rndbt take exit for Moreton Hall. Left at next rndbt*

On the town's outskirts the Butterfly offers comfortable bedrooms and accommodation well suited to business travellers. The hotel provides ground floor, ladies and studio rooms, and rooms for the disabled. Walt's Restaurant and Bar offers a comprehensive carte and daily-changing menus, in addition to room and lounge service selections.
ROOMS: 65 en suite (2 fmly) No smoking in 10 bedrooms d £67.50 * LB **CONF:** Thtr 40 Class 21 Board 22 **PARKING:** 85 **NOTES:** No dogs (ex guide dogs) **CARDS:**

BUTTERMERE, Cumbria — Map 11 NY11

★★70% Bridge

CA13 9UZ
☎ 017687 70252 017687 70215
e-mail: enquires@bridge-hotel.com
Dir: *take A66 around town centre, turn off at Braithwaite & head over the Newlands pass. Follow signs for Buttermere. Hotel in village*
This long-established family-run hotel lies by a stream in the centre of the village in the beautiful Buttermere Valley. Bar meals and real ales can be enjoyed in the traditional beamed bar, and there is also a separate restaurant. Afternoon tea is served to residents in the lounge. There are no televisions in the bedrooms, but all have stunning views and some have balconies.
ROOMS: 21 en suite No smoking in 10 bedrooms s £60-£68; d £120-£136 (incl. bkfst & dinner) * LB **FACILITIES:** Xmas **PARKING:** 60 **NOTES:** No smoking in restaurant **CARDS:**

BUXTON, Derbyshire — Map 07 SK07

★★★★64% Palace Hotel

PARAMOUNT GROUP OF HOTELS

Palace Rd SK17 6AG
☎ 01298 22001 01298 72131
e-mail: palace@paramount-hotels.co.uk
Dir: *in town centre adjacent to railway station*
There are fine views over the town and surrounding hills from this landmark Victorian hotel. The bedrooms are spacious and comfortable. Public rooms include a choice of bars, a library lounge and a spacious and elegant restaurant.

continued

ROOMS: 122 en suite (12 fmly) No smoking in 33 bedrooms s £99; d £116 (incl. bkfst) * LB **FACILITIES:** STV Indoor swimming (H) Sauna Solarium Gym Pool table Croquet lawn Putting green Xmas **CONF:** Thtr 375 Class 125 Board 60 **SERVICES:** Lift **PARKING:** 200 **NOTES:** No smoking in restaurant **CARDS:**

★★★75% ❀❀ Best Western Lee Wood

Best Western

The Park SK17 6TQ
☎ 01298 23002 01298 23228
e-mail: leewoodhotel@btinternet.com
Dir: *NE on A5004, 300mtrs beyond the Devonshire Royal Hospital*
This elegant Georgian hotel offers high standards of comfort and hospitality. Individually furnished bedrooms are generally spacious, with all the expected modern conveniences. There is a choice of two bars, two comfortable lounges and a conservatory restaurant. Quality cooking is a feature of the hotel, as is good service and fine hospitality.

continued on p138

B

BUXTON, continued

ROOMS: 35 en suite 5 annexe en suite (4 fmly) No smoking in 14 bedrooms s £78-£83; d £85-£90 * LB **FACILITIES:** Xmas **CONF:** Thtr 120 Class 65 Board 40 Del from £115 * **SERVICES:** Lift **PARKING:** 50 **NOTES:** Civ Wed 160 **CARDS:**

★★★65% Buckingham Hotel
1 Burlington Rd SK17 9AS
☎ 01298 70481 📠 01298 72186
e-mail: frontdesk@buckinghamhotel.co.uk
Dir: *follow signs for Pavilion Gardens/Pavilion Gardens Car Park. Hotel opposite car park*
A welcoming hotel close to the Pavilion Gardens, the Buckingham offers pleasant, modern public areas which include Ramsay's Bar, serving bar meals and real ales, and the popular carvery, serving grills and other dishes. Bedrooms are spacious and comfortable, many overlook the Pavilion Gardens.
ROOMS: 31 en suite (11 fmly) No smoking in 22 bedrooms s £50-£70; d £70-£90 (incl. bkfst) * LB **FACILITIES:** STV Xmas **CONF:** Thtr 40 Class 20 Board 16 Del from £75 * **SERVICES:** Lift **PARKING:** 25 **NOTES:** No smoking in restaurant **CARDS:**

★★64% Hartington
18 Broad Walk SK17 6JR
☎ 01298 22638 📠 01298 22638
e-mail: harthot@globalnet.co.uk
This welcoming hotel is in an ideal position opposite the lake and gardens, a short walk from Buxton town centre. Bedrooms are attractively furnished, and the lounge is a comfortable area in which to relax. Good home cooking is provided, service is both friendly and attentive.
ROOMS: 12 rms (9 en suite) (2 fmly) No smoking in 6 bedrooms s £50-£60; d £60-£70 (incl. bkfst) * LB **PARKING:** 15 **NOTES:** No dogs (ex guide dogs) Closed 17 Dec-2 Jan RS Nov-Mar **CARDS:**

★★62% Portland Hotel & Park Restaurant
32 St John's Rd SK17 6XQ
☎ 01298 71493 📠 01298 27464
e-mail: brian@portland_hotel.freeserve.co.uk
Dir: *on A53 opposite the Pavilion and Gardens*
This popular hotel is situated near the famous Opera House and the Pavilion Gardens. Lounge and bar provide comfortable and relaxing areas, and the Park Restaurant, housed in the conservatory, specialises in traditional English dishes.
ROOMS: 22 en suite (3 fmly) No smoking in 3 bedrooms s £45-£60; d £65-£80 (incl. bkfst) * LB **FACILITIES:** STV Xmas **CONF:** Thtr 50 Class 30 Board 25 Del from £60 * **PARKING:** 18 **NOTES:** No smoking in restaurant **CARDS:**

CADNAM, Hampshire — Map 04 SU21

★★★69% Bartley Lodge
Lyndhurst Rd SO40 2NR
☎ 023 80812248 📠 023 80812075
e-mail: info@carehotels.co.uk
Dir: *leave M27 junct 1, at 1st rndbt take 1st exit, at 2nd rdbt take 3rd exit onto A337. On joining this road hotel sign is on left*
This 18th-century former hunting lodge is quietly situated, yet just minutes from the M27/A35 junction. Rooms vary in size but all are well equipped. There is a grand entrance hall, cosy bar and an indoor pool with sauna and fitness suite. The Crystal dining room serves very good cuisine.
ROOMS: 31 en suite (14 fmly) s £70-£77.50; d £110-£125 (incl. bkfst) * LB **FACILITIES:** Indoor swimming (H) Tennis (hard) Sauna Gym Croquet lawn ch fac Xmas **CONF:** Thtr 60 Class 40 Board 40 Del from £95 * **PARKING:** 60 **NOTES:** No smoking in restaurant Civ Wed 100 **CARDS:**

CALNE, Wiltshire — Map 03 ST97

★★★64% Lansdowne Strand

The Strand SN11 0EH
☎ 01249 812488 📠 01249 815323
e-mail: reservations@lansdownestrand.co.uk
Dir: *on A4*
In the centre of the market town, this former 16th-century coaching inn still retains many period features. Individually decorated bedrooms vary in size. There are two friendly bars, one offers a wide selection of ales and a cosy fireplace. Carriages Restaurant serves a carte and a fixed-price menu.
ROOMS: 21 en suite 5 annexe en suite (3 fmly) No smoking in 4 bedrooms s fr £65; d fr £86 (incl. bkfst) * LB **FACILITIES:** Xmas **CONF:** Thtr 90 Class 28 Board 30 Del £100 * **PARKING:** 21 **CARDS:**

CAMBERLEY, Surrey — Map 04 SU86

★★★69% Frimley Hall
Portsmouth Rd GU15 2BG
☎ 0870 400 8224 📠 01276 691253
e-mail: heritagehotels_camberley.frimley_hall@forte-hotels.com
A handsome Victorian manor retaining many original features. Public rooms comprise the elegant Wellington restaurant, a comfortable lounge and the beamed Sandhurst bar. Wood panels and stained glass add to the style of the grand staircase and wide corridors lead to the fine original bedrooms. The more modern rooms are smart and offer good facilities.
ROOMS: 86 en suite (20 fmly) No smoking in 25 bedrooms d £165-£195 * LB **FACILITIES:** Croquet lawn Putting green entertainment **CONF:** Thtr 60 Class 30 Board 40 Del from £140 * **PARKING:** 100 **NOTES:** No smoking in restaurant Civ Wed 120 **CARDS:**

★★★63% *Lakeside International*
Wharf Rd, Frimley Green GU16 6JR
☎ 01252 838000 & 838808 📠 01252 837857
Dir: *off A321*
Chiefly geared to conferences and the corporate market, the hotel offers well equipped facilities and bedrooms, some with lakeside views. The complex includes a renowned night club and a health and fitness club.
ROOMS: 98 en suite (1 fmly) No smoking in 18 bedrooms **FACILITIES:** STV Indoor swimming (H) Squash Snooker Sauna Solarium Gym Pool table Jacuzzi/spa **CONF:** Thtr 100 Class 100 Board 36 **SERVICES:** Lift **PARKING:** 250 **NOTES:** No dogs (ex guide dogs) No smoking in restaurant **CARDS:**

CAMBORNE, Cornwall & Isles of Scilly — Map 02 SW64

★★★68% Tyacks
27 Commercial St TR14 8LD
☎ 01209 612424 📠 01209 612435
Dir: *town centre opposite town clock*
This 18th-century former coaching inn has spacious, well furnished public areas which include a smart lounge and bar, a popular public bar and a refurbished restaurant serving fixed-price and carte menus. The comfortable bedrooms are attractively decorated and well equipped; two have separate sitting areas.
ROOMS: 15 en suite (2 fmly) No smoking in 3 bedrooms s fr £45; d fr £60 (incl. bkfst) * LB **FACILITIES:** STV Pool table entertainment Xmas **PARKING:** 28 **CARDS:**

CAMBRIDGE, Cambridgeshire

Map 05 TL45

★★★★60% University Arms

Regent St CB2 1AD

DE VERE HOTELS

☎ 01223 351241 ▯ 01223 461319

e-mail: dua.sales@devere-hotels.com

With a 160-year heritage and an imposing position on the edge of Parker's Piece, this striking Victorian-style building embodies much of the elegance of Cambridge. Public areas include the quaintly-domed lounge, traditional-styled restaurant and bar. Bedrooms, which vary in size and outlook, have benefited from refurbishment.

ROOMS: 115 en suite (5 fmly) No smoking in 38 bedrooms s £90-£118; d £135-£170 * LB **FACILITIES:** STV Xmas **CONF:** Thtr 350 Class 100 Board 60 Del from £140 * **SERVICES:** Lift **PARKING:** 88 **NOTES:** No smoking in restaurant Civ Wed 200 **CARDS:**

★★★70% Gonville

Gonville Place CB1 1LY

Best Western

☎ 01223 366611 & 221111 ▯ 01223 315470

e-mail: all@gonvillehotel.co.uk

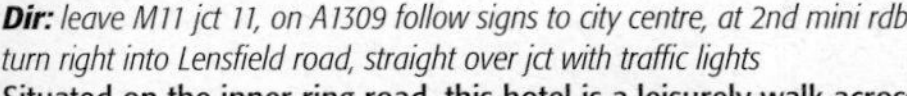

Dir: *leave M11 jct 11, on A1309 follow signs to city centre, at 2nd mini rdbt turn right into Lensfield road, straight over jct with traffic lights*

Situated on the inner ring road, this hotel is a leisurely walk across the green to the city centre. Well established, with regular guests and very experienced staff, the Gonville is popular for its relaxing, informal atmosphere. The air-conditioned public areas are cheerfully furnished, and bedrooms are well appointed and appealing.

ROOMS: 64 en suite (1 fmly) No smoking in 12 bedrooms s fr £89.50; d fr £112 LB **FACILITIES:** Arrangement with nearby gym & swimming pool Xmas **CONF:** Thtr 200 Class 100 Board 50 Del from £125 * **SERVICES:** Lift **PARKING:** 80 **NOTES:** No smoking in restaurant **CARDS:**

★★★70% Royal Cambridge

Trumpington St CB2 1PY

ZOFFANY HOTELS

☎ 01223 351631 ▯ 01223 352972

e-mail: royalcambridge@zoffanyhotels.co.uk

Dir: *leave M11 junct 11, follow signs for city centre. At 1st mini rdbt turn left into Fen Causeway, then first right for hotel*

This attractive, friendly Georgian townhouse offers a wide range of comfortable bedrooms, all of which are well equipped and pleasingly decorated. Relaxing public rooms are intimate and include an elegant split-level restaurant serving modern British cuisine; bar snacks and hot room service meals are also available.

ROOMS: 49 en suite (8 fmly) No smoking in 28 bedrooms s £99-£115; d £135-£175 (incl. bkfst) * LB **FACILITIES:** STV **CONF:** Thtr 120 Class 40 Board 40 Del from £135 * **SERVICES:** Lift **PARKING:** 80 **NOTES:** No smoking in restaurant Civ Wed 100 **CARDS:**

★★★68% *Posthouse Cambridge*

Lakeview, Bridge Rd, Impington CB4 9PH

Posthouse

☎ 0870 400 9015 ▯ 01223 233426

Dir: *2.5m N, on N side of rdbt jct A14/B1049*

In a rural location at the junction of the A14 and B1049, this hotel offers spacious, well appointed bedrooms, which include the new Millennium rooms. There are also facilities for disabled guests. There is a well equipped health club as well as a secluded courtyard garden with a children's play area. The Junction restaurant offers a range of dishes.

ROOMS: 165 en suite (14 fmly) No smoking in 105 bedrooms **FACILITIES:** Indoor swimming (H) Sauna Gym Jacuzzi/spa **CONF:** Thtr 60 Class 30 Board 30 **PARKING:** 200 **NOTES:** RS 24-27 Dec & 31 Dec **CARDS:**

★★71% Arundel House

Chesterton Rd CB4 3AN

☎ 01223 367701 ▯ 01223 367721

e-mail: info@arundelhousehotels.co.uk

Dir: *on A1303, overlooking the River Cam*

Overlooking the Cam and enjoying views over open parkland, this popular hotel was originally a row of Victorian townhouses. The smart public areas feature a conservatory for informal snacks, a spacious bar and an elegant restaurant for serious dining. Bedrooms are attractive and have a special character.

ROOMS: 83 rms (80 en suite) 22 annexe en suite (6 fmly) No smoking in 89 bedrooms s £55-£75; d £71-£99 (incl. cont bkfst) * LB **CONF:** Thtr 50 Class 34 Board 32 **PARKING:** 70 **NOTES:** No dogs No smoking in restaurant Closed 25-26 Dec **CARDS:**

CAMBRIDGE, continued

★★68% *Centennial*
63-71 Hills Rd CB2 1PG
☎ 01223 314652 🖷 01223 315443
Dir: *from M11 junct 11 take A1309 to Cambridge. Turn right onto Brooklands Av, at the end of Av turn left, hotel in 100yds on right*
Close to the town centre but easily accessed by the ring road, this pleasant hotel offers a relaxing bar, welcoming lounge and a friendly restaurant. The bedrooms are well maintained and equipped, including several easy-access rooms on the ground floor.
ROOMS: 39 en suite (1 fmly) No smoking in 20 bedrooms **CONF:** Thtr 35 Class 26 Board 26 **PARKING:** 30 **NOTES:** No dogs Closed 23 Dec-1 Jan **CARDS:**

See advert on opposite page

★★68% Sorrento
190-196 Cherry Hinton Rd CB1 7AN
☎ 01223 243533 🖷 01223 213463
e-mail: sorrento-hotel@cb17an.freeserve.co.uk
Situated within easy striking distance of the city centre, this friendly, family-run hotel has an Italian feel in its comfortable public rooms. The bedrooms vary in size and style, and are all attractively decorated and equipped with many useful extras.
ROOMS: 30 en suite No smoking in 15 bedrooms s fr £59.50; d £99-£129.50 (incl. bkfst) * **FACILITIES:** STV **PARKING:** 25
CARDS:

⌂ *Travelodge*
Travelodge
Fourwentways
☎ 01223 839479
Dir: *adjacent to Little Chef at junct A11/A1307, 5m S of Cambridge*
This modern building offers accommodation in smart, spacious and well equipped bedrooms, all with en suite bathrooms. Refreshments may be taken at the nearby family restaurant. For further details and the Travelodge phone number, consult the Hotel Groups page.
ROOMS: 40 en suite

CANNOCK, Staffordshire — Map 07 SJ91

★★★62% Roman Way
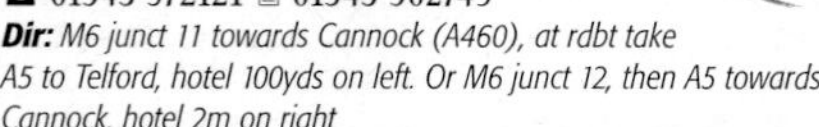

Watling St, Hatherton WS11 1SH
☎ 01543 572121 🖷 01543 502749
Dir: *M6 junct 11 towards Cannock (A460), at rdbt take A5 to Telford, hotel 100yds on left. Or M6 junct 12, then A5 towards Cannock, hotel 2m on right*

Named after the Roman road on which it stands, this modern hotel provides a good standard of accommodation. Doric columns and marble floors feature in the reception area and Nero's Restaurant and Gilpin's Lounge provide formal or informal eating options.

continued

ROOMS: 56 en suite (17 fmly) No smoking in 23 bedrooms s £75-£79; d £95-£100 * LB **FACILITIES:** STV Xmas **CONF:** Thtr 150 Class 100 Board 50 **PARKING:** 150 **NOTES:** No smoking in restaurant Civ Wed
CARDS:

CANTERBURY, Kent — Map 05 TR15

★★★67% Falstaff
corus
St Dunstans St, Westgate CT2 8AF
☎ 01227 462138 🖷 01227 463525
Dir: *turn into St Peters Place off the A2, pass Westgate Towers into St Dunstans Street, hotel on right*

Many original features testify to the 16th-century origins of this historic old coaching inn. It stands next to the Westgate Tower and offers easy access to the city centre and motorway network. Bedrooms vary in size and all have very smart bathrooms.
ROOMS: 26 en suite 22 annexe en suite (1 fmly) No smoking in 14 bedrooms s £91-£100; d £100-£115 * LB **FACILITIES:** STV **PARKING:** 41 **NOTES:** No smoking in restaurant
CARDS:

See advert on opposite page

★★★65% Howfield Manor
Chartham Hatch CT4 7HQ
☎ 01227 738294 🖷 01227 731535
e-mail: enquiries@howfield.invictanet.co.uk
Dir: *from A2, follow signs for Chartham Hatch after Gate Service Station, continue for 2.25 miles. Hotel is on left at junct with A28*
This charming family run hotel on the outskirts of historic Canterbury sits in several acres of well manicured grounds. Bedrooms are comfortable and are traditionally styled. The restaurant, with its feature working well used by former occupants of the house, serves confident modern cuisine.
ROOMS: 15 en suite s £75; d £95 (incl. bkfst) * LB **FACILITIES:** Xmas **CONF:** Thtr 100 Class 45 Board 45 Del £105.50 * **PARKING:** 80 **NOTES:** No dogs (ex guide dogs) No children 10yrs
CARDS:

★★★62% The Chaucer
Ivy Ln CT1 1TU
☎ 0870 400 8106 🖷 01227 450397
e-mail: heritagehotels_canterbury.chaucer_hotel@forte-hotels.com
Dir: *approaching city on A2, follow signs for Dover. Turn right at fifth rdbt, then 1st left*
Located just outside the old city walls and within easy walking distance of the city centre and cathedral, this Georgian residence offers comfortably furnished bedrooms. The lounge and bar area has a traditional charm and the restaurant offers a range of cuisine.
ROOMS: 42 en suite (5 fmly) No smoking in 19 bedrooms s £85-£105; d £105-£150 * LB **FACILITIES:** Xmas **CONF:** Thtr 120 Class 45 Board 45 Del £125 * **PARKING:** 45 **NOTES:** No smoking in restaurant Civ Wed 100 **CARDS:**

★★75% Ebury
65/67 New Dover Rd CT1 3DX
☎ 01227 768433 🖹 01227 459187
e-mail: info@ebury-hotel.co.uk
Dir: *follow A2, take Canterbury turn off, then ring road around Canterbury follow Dover signs at 5th rdbt signs to Dover in 1m on left is Ebury Hotel*
A delightful family-run hotel in two acres of pretty gardens. Bedrooms are attractively furnished and well equipped. Public areas include a spacious restaurant, with an interesting menu of skilfully prepared dishes. Room service is available, including continental breakfast.
ROOMS: 15 en suite (2 fmly) s £50-£65; d £65-£79 (incl. bkfst) * LB
FACILITIES: Indoor swimming (H) Jacuzzi/spa Exercise equipment
PARKING: 30 **NOTES:** No smoking in restaurant Closed 19 Dec-11 Jan
CARDS:

★★68% ❀ Canterbury
71 New Dover Rd CT1 3DZ
☎ 01227 450551 🖹 01227 780145
e-mail: canterbury.hotel@btinternet.com
Dir: *on A2, Dover road*
This Georgian-style hotel close to the city centre offers two styles of comfortable, well equipped bedroom accommodation: standard and superior. Public areas are attractively furnished and include a reception/bar, and a separate TV lounge which can be used for private meetings. The bright, attractive restaurant has a Continental feel, with French staff and a classic French menu.
ROOMS: 23 en suite (1 fmly) s £55-£85; d £75-£105 (incl. bkfst) * LB
FACILITIES: STV **CONF:** Thtr 25 Board 12 Del from £70 *
SERVICES: Lift **PARKING:** 50 **NOTES:** No smoking in restaurant
CARDS:

CANTERBURY, continued

★★66% *Victoria*

59 London Rd CT2 8JY
☎ 01227 459333 📠 01227 781552
Dir: *accessible via main London/Dover M2/A2 onto main A2052, hotel on left off the 1st rdbt*
Fifteen minutes' walk from the city centre, the Victoria has attractively decorated bedrooms varying in size and comfort; all are well maintained and have excellent facilities. The public areas include a bustling bar with satellite TV, and a restaurant where guests can choose to eat from a short menu or the carvery. Staff are friendly and willing.
ROOMS: 34 en suite (12 fmly) No smoking in 4 bedrooms **CONF:** Thtr 20 Class 20 Board 20 **PARKING:** 70 **NOTES:** No dogs (ex guide dogs)
CARDS:

★★65% Pointers Hotel
1 London Rd CT2 8LR
☎ 01227 456846 📠 01227 452786
e-mail: pointers.hotel@dial.pipex.com
Dir: *Canterbury exit off A2, follow signposts for university. Opposite St Dunstans Church*
This small, family-run hotel is centrally located in historic Canterbury and is an ideal base for visiting the cathedral. Rooms are compact but comfortable and dinners are freshly prepared from quality raw ingredients.
ROOMS: 12 en suite (3 fmly) s £45-£50; d £60-£75 (incl. bkfst) * LB **PARKING:** 10 **NOTES:** Closed 23 Dec-14 Jan
CARDS:

See advert on page 141

⇧ *Travelodge*
Travelodge
A2 Gate Services, Dunkirk ME13 9LN
☎ 01227 752781 📠 01227 752781
Dir: *5m W on A2 northbound*
This modern building offers accommodation in smart, spacious and well equipped bedrooms, all with en suite bathrooms. Refreshments may be taken at the nearby family restaurant. For further details and the Travelodge phone number, consult the Hotel Groups page.
ROOMS: 40 en suite

⇧ Express by Holiday Inn Canterbury

Upper Harbledown CT2 9HX
☎ 01227 865000 📠 01227 865100
Dir: *on A2, 4m from city centre*

A modern budget hotel offering comfortable accommodation in refreshing, spacious and comprehensively-equipped bedrooms, en suite bathrooms with power showers and continental buffet breakfast included in the room rate. Suitable for business travellers or families. For further details and the Express by Holiday Inn phone number, consult the Hotel Groups page.
ROOMS: 89 en suite (incl. cont bkfst) d £45-£56 * **CONF:** Thtr 35 Class 15 Board 20 Del from £75 *

CARBIS BAY — Map 02 SW53
See St Ives

CARCROFT, South Yorkshire — Map 08 SE50

⇧ *Travelodge*
Travelodge
Great North Rd DN6 9LF
☎ 01302 330841 📠 01302 330841
Dir: *on A1 northbound*
This modern building offers accommodation in smart, spacious and well equipped bedrooms, all with en suite bathrooms. Refreshments may be taken at the nearby family restaurant. For further details and the Travelodge phone number, consult the Hotel Groups page.
ROOMS: 40 en suite

CARLISLE, Cumbria — Map 11 NY45
see also Brampton

★★★77% Crosby Lodge Country House
High Crosby, Crosby-on-Eden CA6 4QZ
☎ 01228 573618 📠 01228 573428
e-mail: crosbylodge@crosby-eden.demon.co.uk
Dir: *leave M6 at junc 44, 3.5m from motorway off A689*
An Aladdin's cave of antiques and period furnishings, this hotel offers a relaxing atmosphere with elegant and efficient service. Freshly-made food and delicious home baking are popular features. The opulent bedrooms are all individual, and provide thoughtful little touches; two are in a tastefully converted stable block.
ROOMS: 9 en suite 2 annexe en suite (3 fmly) s £80-£85; d £110-£150 (incl. bkfst) * LB **CONF:** Thtr 25 Board 12 **PARKING:** 40 **NOTES:** No smoking in restaurant Closed 24 Dec-20 Jan RS Sun evening (restaurant-residents only) **CARDS:**

★★★71% Crown
SHIRE INNS
Wetheral CA4 8ES
☎ 01228 561888 📠 01228 561637
e-mail: crown@shireinns.co.uk
Situated in the charming village of Wetheral, this 19th-century hotel has a good range of conference rooms and leisure facilities. It has two contrasting bars, one a cocktail bar and the other a traditional 'pub' serving snacks. The separate conservatory restaurant offers a choice of well prepared dishes. The well appointed rooms provide comfortable accommodation.
ROOMS: 49 en suite 2 annexe en suite (3 fmly) No smoking in 10 bedrooms s fr £102; d fr £122 (incl. bkfst) * LB **FACILITIES:** STV Indoor swimming (H) Squash Sauna Solarium Gym Jacuzzi/spa Children's splash pool Steam room **CONF:** Thtr 175 Class 90 Board 50 Del from £88 * **PARKING:** 80 **NOTES:** Civ Wed
CARDS:

★★★67% Cumbria Park
Best Western
32 Scotland Rd, Stanwix CA3 9DG
☎ 01228 522887 📠 01228 514796
Dir: *1.5m N on A7*
Situated to the north of the city within easy access of the M6 and central amenities, this family-run hotel provides a comfortable base for the visiting businessman and tourist alike. Public areas are smartly presented, and the tasteful bedrooms offer mixed styles of furnishings along with all the expected facilities.
ROOMS: 47 en suite (3 fmly) No smoking in 13 bedrooms s £74-£87.50; d £95-£120 (incl. bkfst) * LB **FACILITIES:** STV **CONF:** Thtr 190 Class 50 Board 50 Del from £105 * **SERVICES:** Lift **PARKING:** 40 **NOTES:** No dogs (ex guide dogs) Closed 25-26 Dec
CARDS:

See advert on opposite page

★★★67% *Posthouse Carlisle*

Posthouse

Parkhouse Rd CA3 0HR
☎ 0870 400 9018 🖹 01228 543178
e-mail: fcmail@fphcarlisle.com
Dir: *junc 44/M6 take A7 signposted Carlisle, hotel on right at first set of traffic lights*

This refurbished hotel offers smart bedrooms; the stylish Millennium rooms provide a host of thoughtful extras. As well as comprehensive leisure facilities, the hotel boasts an informal restaurant that provides wide-ranging, multicultural menus.

ROOMS: 127 en suite (34 fmly) No smoking in 85 bedrooms
FACILITIES: Indoor swimming (H) Sauna Gym Pool table Jacuzzi/spa
CONF: Thtr 120 Class 64 Board 60 **PARKING:** 150
CARDS:

★★★64% Swallow Hilltop

SWALLOW HOTELS

London Rd CA1 2PQ
☎ 01228 529255 🖹 01228 525238
e-mail: info@swallowhotels.com
Dir: *from M6 junct 42 take A6 to Carlisle. In 1m hotel on left on hill*

This hotel offers a variety of meeting rooms and well equipped leisure facilities. Most of the bedrooms have been refurbished to a good standard. Spacious public rooms include a comfortable open-plan lounge bar leading into a stylishly furnished restaurant that overlooks the surrounding area from the hotel's elevated position.

ROOMS: 92 en suite (6 fmly) No smoking in 24 bedrooms s £85-£95; d £105-£110 (incl. bkfst) * LB **FACILITIES:** STV Indoor swimming (H) Sauna Solarium Gym Pool table Jacuzzi/spa Massage Steam room Xmas **CONF:** Thtr 500 Class 250 Board 90 Del from £95 *
SERVICES: Lift **PARKING:** 350 **NOTES:** Civ Wed 300
CARDS:

★★★60% Central Plaza

Victoria Viaduct CA3 8AL
☎ 01228 520256 🖹 01228 514657
e-mail: info@centralplazahotel.co.uk
Dir: *in city centre, just N of main BR station on A6*

Offering accommodation in a variety of styles, this grand hotel lies in the city centre close to the station. At the time of our last inspection, a refurbishment programme was coming to completion, with all public areas and bedrooms being upgraded to a good standard.

ROOMS: 84 en suite (3 fmly) No smoking in 4 bedrooms s £45-£65; d £65-£75 (incl. bkfst) * LB **FACILITIES:** STV Pool table Xmas **CONF:** Thtr 100 Class 54 Board 40 Del from £70 * **SERVICES:** Lift **PARKING:** 17 **NOTES:** No smoking in restaurant
CARDS:

See advert on this page

CARLISLE, continued

★★★60% The Crown & Mitre

4 English St CA3 8HZ
☎ 01228 525491 🖷 01228 514553
Dir: *A6 into city centre, pass station on left then left past Woolworths. Sharp right into Blackfriars St. Hotel car park and rear entrance at end*
This handsome, town-centre, Edwardian hotel is being restored to its original splendour. Bedrooms have been decorated and furnished to a very high standard and public rooms display many original architectural features.
ROOMS: 74 en suite 20 annexe en suite (4 fmly) No smoking in 10 bedrooms s £84-£95; d £109-£110 (incl. bkfst) * LB **FACILITIES:** STV Indoor swimming (H) Pool table Jacuzzi/spa Xmas **CONF:** Thtr 400 Class 250 Board 50 Del from £90 * **SERVICES:** Lift **PARKING:** 42
CARDS:

★★★59% Cumbrian

Court Square CA1 1QY
☎ 01228 531951 🖷 01228 547799
Dir: *leave M6 at junct43. Follow signs for city centre & railway station. The Hotel is adjacent to the railway station*
This well preserved Victorian hotel, next to the railway station, offers bedrooms equipped with all modern comforts. The inviting public rooms include a restaurant as well as an attractive lounge bar. The hotel has good conference and function suites.
ROOMS: 70 en suite (4 fmly) No smoking in 22 bedrooms s £60-£71; d £80-£98 (incl. bkfst) * LB **FACILITIES:** STV Xmas **CONF:** Thtr 300 Class 80 Board 60 Del from £75 * **SERVICES:** Lift **PARKING:** 35 **NOTES:** No smoking in restaurant **CARDS:**

★★64% *Pinegrove*

262 London Rd CA1 2QS
☎ 01228 524828 🖷 01228 810941
Dir: *on A6*
The Pinegrove is a late-Victorian mansion which lies on the south side of the city. Public rooms include a comfortable bar, spacious restaurant and a room for pool and darts. Guests have free access to a local leisure club. A friendly atmosphere prevails throughout the hotel.
ROOMS: 27 rms (26 en suite) 18 annexe rms (16 en suite) (8 fmly) **FACILITIES:** STV Pool table Darts **CONF:** Thtr 120 Class 100 Board 100 **PARKING:** 50 **NOTES:** Closed 25 Dec
CARDS:

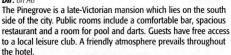

★★59% County

9 Botchergate CA1 1QP
☎ 01228 531316 🖷 01228 401805
e-mail: countyh@cairn-hotels.co.uk
Conveniently positioned in the heart of the city opposite the railway station, this long established hotel remains a popular base for visiting tour groups. Public areas include a choice of bars and eating options where good value meals are served. Bedrooms come in varying sizes and styles and offer a good range of amenities.
ROOMS: 84 en suite (4 fmly) s £50-£60; d £60-£70 * LB **FACILITIES:** Xmas **CONF:** Thtr 150 Class 75 Board 50 Del from £75 * **SERVICES:** Lift **PARKING:** 35 **NOTES:** No smoking in restaurant
CARDS:

See advert on opposite page

⇧ Premier Lodge

Kingstown Rd CA3 0AT
☎ 0870 700 1348 🖷 0870 7001349
Premier Lodge offers modern, well equipped, en suite accommodation suitable for both business and leisure travellers. Meals can be taken at the adjacent popular restaurant and bar which is fully licensed. For further details, consult the Hotel Groups page.
ROOMS: 49 en suite d £46 *

CARNFORTH, Lancashire — Map 07 SD47

★66% Royal Station

Market St LA5 9BT
☎ 01524 732033 & 733636 🖷 01524 720267
Dir: *leave M6 junct 35 join A6 signed Carnforth & Morecambe, in 1m at x-rds in centre of Carnforth turn rt into Market St. Hotel opposite railway station*
Situated close to the railway station, this commercial hotel provides modern well equipped bedrooms. There is a choice of bars and a good range of food is served both there and in the restaurant.
ROOMS: 13 en suite (1 fmly) s £99; d £145-£295 (incl. bkfst) * LB **FACILITIES:** Pool table Xmas **CONF:** Thtr 150 Class 100 Board 100 Del from £150 * **PARKING:** 8 **NOTES:** No smoking in restaurant Civ Wed 50 **CARDS:**

CARPERBY, North Yorkshire — Map 07 SE08

★62% *Wheatsheaf*

DL8 4DF
☎ 01969 663216 🖷 01969 663019
e-mail: wheatsheaf@paulmit.globalnet.co.uk
Dir: *from A1 take west route on A684 to Wensley, turn right signposted Castle Bolton next village is Carperby*
The Wheatsheaf is a typical Dales hotel offering comfortable accommodation. The bedrooms are pleasantly furnished and include two attractive four-poster beds. The lounge features a 17th-century stone fireplace, and guests can eat from the extensive menus either in the cosy pub or the dining room.
ROOMS: 8 en suite (1 fmly) **FACILITIES:** Trout fishing can be arranged **PARKING:** 42 **NOTES:** No smoking in restaurant
CARDS:

CARTMEL, Cumbria — Map 07 SD37

★★76% ❀ Aynsome Manor

LA11 6HH
☎ 015395 36653 🖷 015395 36016
e-mail: info@aynsomemanorhotel.co.uk
Dir: *from M6 junc 36, follow A590 signed Barrow in Furness. Continue towards Cartmel turn left at end of dual carriageway, hotel just before village*
A lovely old manor house standing peacefully in its own well tended gardens on the edge of the village, offering wonderful hospitality, good food and a relaxing atmosphere. Inviting public areas include a cosy bar, choice of lounges and an elegant panelled restaurant, where the honest home-cooking is carefully prepared and very rewarding.
ROOMS: 10 en suite 2 annexe en suite (2 fmly) s £52.65-£72; d £92-£125 (incl. bkfst & dinner) LB **FACILITIES:** Xmas **PARKING:** 20 **NOTES:** No smoking in restaurant Closed 2 Jan-1 Feb
CARDS:

CASTLE ASHBY, Northamptonshire — Map 04 SP85

★★72% ❀ Falcon

NN7 1LF
☎ 01604 696200 🖷 01604 696673
e-mail: falcon@castleashby.co.uk
Dir: *follow signs to Castle Ashby, opposite war memorial*
This hotel occupies two separate village properties, each with its

continued

own character; bedrooms throughout are individually decorated and feature a wealth of extras and stylish bold furnishings and decor. Public rooms, in the main house, include a first-floor sitting area, a choice of bars and a separate restaurant where an interesting selection of dishes is offered from the menus.
ROOMS: 6 rms (5 en suite) 11 annexe en suite s £79.50; d £95.50 (incl. bkfst) * LB **FACILITIES:** STV Xmas **CONF:** Thtr 30 Class 30 Board 20 Del from £105 * **PARKING:** 75 **NOTES:** Civ Wed 60
CARDS:

CASTLE CARY, Somerset — Map 03 ST63

★★68% The George

Market Place BA7 7AH
☎ 01963 350761 📠 01963 350035
Dir: *from M5 junct 23 follow A39 to Shepton Mallet then A371 to Castle Cary. From A303 to Wincanton, then A371 to Castle Cary*

OLD ENGLISH INNS & HOTELS

A 15th-century coaching inn with a distinctive thatched roof and bay windows. Rooms are generally spacious, offering a good standard of accommodation and comfort. Guests can choose to eat in the formal dining room, with its imaginative range of dishes, or in one of the two cosy bars. An attractive lounge with a real log fire is also available.
ROOMS: 14 en suite (1 fmly) No smoking in 4 bedrooms **PARKING:** 10 **NOTES:** No dogs (ex guide dogs) No smoking in restaurant
CARDS:

CASTLE COMBE, Wiltshire — Map 03 ST87

Premier Collection

★★★★ 🏵🏵🏵 Manor House

SN14 7HR
☎ 01249 782206 📠 01249 782159
e-mail: enquiries@manor-house.co.uk
Dir: *follow Chippenham signs from M4 junc17, onto A420 signed Bristol, then right onto B4039. Go through village, turn rt after crossing river bridge*
Set in 26 acres of grounds with a romantic Italian style garden, this 14th-century country house offers superbly furnished rooms. Public areas include a number of cosy lounge areas with roaring fires. The bedrooms stand in a row of original stone cottages within the grounds and reflect the quality of the main house.
ROOMS: 21 en suite 24 annexe en suite (8 fmly) d £120-£350 * LB **FACILITIES:** STV Outdoor swimming (H) Golf 18 Tennis (hard) Fishing Snooker Sauna Pool table Croquet lawn Jogging track Xmas **CONF:** Thtr 60 Class 36 Board 36 Del from £170 * **PARKING:** 100 **NOTES:** No dogs (ex guide dogs) No smoking in restaurant Civ Wed 90 **CARDS:**

★★★68% 🏵 Castle Inn

SN14 7HN
☎ 01249 783030 📠 01249 782315
e-mail: res@castle-inn.co.uk
Dir: *take A420 to Chippenham follow signs for Castle Combe. Hotel is situated in the heart of the village*
This famous 12th-century hostelry is set in the market place of the historic village of Castle Combe. Bedrooms, many with old beams, are individually decorated, and have many thoughtful extras. Guests can dine in the restaurant or bar where the food is interesting and well cooked.
ROOMS: 11 en suite s £68-£80; d £90-£110 (incl. bkfst) * LB **FACILITIES:** STV N Xmas **CONF:** Thtr 22 Class 19 Board 16 Del from £110 * **NOTES:** No dogs (ex guide dogs) No smoking in restaurant
CARDS:

CASTLE DONINGTON See East Midlands Airport

CASTLEFORD, West Yorkshire — Map 08 SE42

⌂ Premier Lodge

Pioneer Way WF10 5TG
☎ 0870 700 1412 📠 0870 700 1413

PREMIER LODGE

Premier Lodge offers modern, well equipped, en suite accommodation suitable for both business and leisure travellers. Meals can be taken at the adjacent popular restaurant and bar which is fully licensed. For further details, consult the Hotel Groups page.
ROOMS: 76 en suite d £46 *

CATTERICK BRIDGE, North Yorkshire Map 08 SE29

★★63% Bridge House
DL10 7PE
☎ 01748 818331 Fax 01748 818331
Dir: *4m S of Scotch Corner, on bridge opp Catterick Racecourse*
Formerly a coaching inn, this commercial hotel sits by the River Swale close to the racecourse. There is a wide choice of bedroom size, all of the rooms are well furnished and equipped. A good range of freshly prepared meals is served in the bar and the restaurant.
ROOMS: 15 en suite (2 fmly) s £40-£50; d £60-£70 (incl. bkfst) * LB **FACILITIES:** STV Fishing Pool table **CONF:** Thtr 100 Class 50 Board 40 Del from £65 * **PARKING:** 71 **CARDS:**

CHADDESLEY CORBETT, Worcestershire Map 07 SO87

Premier Collection

★★★ Brockencote Hall Country House
DY10 4PY
☎ 01562 777876 Fax 01562 777872
e-mail: info@brockencotehall.com
Dir: *0.5m W, off A448, opposite St Cassians Church*
A magnificent Victorian mansion in extensive parkland, with a Tudor dovecote, lake and fine trees. Spacious bedrooms are appointed to a high standard, with many thoughtful extras. Comfortable lounges and an elegant dining room overlook the landscaped grounds.
ROOMS: 17 en suite (2 fmly) s £110-£130; d £135-£170 (incl. bkfst) * LB **FACILITIES:** STV Tennis (hard) Croquet lawn Jacuzzi/spa Xmas **CONF:** Thtr 30 Class 20 Board 20 Del from £155 * **SERVICES:** Lift **PARKING:** 45 **NOTES:** No dogs (ex guide dogs) No smoking in restaurant **CARDS:**

CHAGFORD, Devon Map 03 SX78

Premier Collection

★★★ Gidleigh Park
TQ13 8HH
☎ 01647 432367 Fax 01647 432574
e-mail: gidleighpark@gidleigh.co.uk
Dir: *approach from Chagford, turn right at Lloyds Bank into Mill St. After 150 yds fork right, follow lane 2 miles to end*
Gidleigh Park is a now a legend in hotel keeping. It is the epitome of relaxed luxury, set in pretty gardens and surrounded by 45 acres of the Dartmoor National Park. Bedrooms vary in size and outlook but all guarantee excellent levels of comfort. Outstanding dishes, many using local ingredients, are offered in the restaurant and there is an excellent wine list.
continued

ROOMS: 12 en suite 3 annexe en suite s £250-£410; d £370-£460 (incl. bkfst & dinner) * LB **FACILITIES:** STV Tennis (hard) Fishing Croquet lawn Putting green Bowls **CONF:** Board 22 Del from £300 * **PARKING:** 25 **NOTES:** No smoking in restaurant
CARDS:

★★★73% Mill End
Dartmoor National Park, Sandy Park TQ13 8JN
☎ 01647 432282 Fax 01647 433106
e-mail: millendhotel@talk21.com
Dir: *from A30 at Whiddon Down follow A382 to Moretonhampstead. After 3.5 miles a hump back bridge at Sandy Park, hotel on right by river*

Peace and relaxation are keynotes of this charming hotel, within the beauty of Dartmoor National Park. Bedrooms have countryside views and each offers a high standard of decoration. There are very comfortable lounges and an elegant dining room which makes optimum use of fresh local produce. The hotel benefits from six miles of fishing on the Teign.
ROOMS: 17 rms (15 en suite) (2 fmly) s £47-£79; d £64-£100 (incl. bkfst) * LB **FACILITIES:** Fishing Croquet lawn Xmas **CONF:** Thtr 40 Class 20 Board 30 Del from £87 * **PARKING:** 21 **NOTES:** No smoking in restaurant Civ Wed 60 **CARDS:**

★★72% *Easton Court*
Easton Cross TQ13 8JL
☎ 01647 433469 Fax 01647 433654
e-mail: stay@easton.co.uk
Dir: *turn off A30 onto A382, hotel 4m on left near turning to Chagford*
This Grade II listed, thatched Tudor house offers a wealth of character and charm, with granite walls, oak beams and an inglenook fireplace complete with bread oven. Bedrooms offer a combination of pretty fabrics, tasteful furnishings and modern facilities. A short fixed-price menu is available in the candlelit dining room.
ROOMS: 8 en suite **PARKING:** 20 **NOTES:** No children 12yrs No smoking in restaurant Closed Jan **CARDS:**

★★65% **Three Crowns Hotel**
High St TQ13 8AJ
☎ 01647 433441 & 433444 📠 01647 433117
e-mail: threecrowns@msn.com
Dir: *turn left off A30 at Whiddon Down, in Chagford town centre opposite church*

Dating back to the 13th century and situated in the heart of the village, this hotel retains many original architectural features, such as open fires, exposed beams and mullioned windows. Many of the bedrooms offer four-poster beds. Public areas include a choice of bars, small lounge and intimate restaurant as well as a function room with separate bar.
ROOMS: 14 en suite (1 fmly) **FACILITIES:** STV Pool table **CONF:** Board 90 **PARKING:** 14 **NOTES:** No smoking in restaurant
CARDS:

CHALE See Wight, Isle of

CHARD, Somerset Map 03 ST30

★★★68% **Lordleaze**
Henderson Dr, Forton Rd TA20 2HW
☎ 01460 61066 📠 01460 66468
e-mail: lordleaze@fsbdial.co.uk
Dir: *from centre of Chard take A358 towards Axminster, pass St Mary's Church on your right then turn left to Forton & Winsham, 3rd left to hotel*

The Lordleaze is an excellent base from which to explore the West Country. The comfortable bedrooms are well equipped, with rooms available on the ground floor. A focal point is the relaxed and friendly lounge bar. In addition to the carte served in the restaurant, a tempting selection of bar meals is available.
ROOMS: 16 en suite (1 fmly) No smoking in 4 bedrooms s £49.50-£55; d £69.50-£80 (incl. bkfst) * LB **FACILITIES:** Xmas **CONF:** Thtr 180 Class 60 Board 40 Del from £75 * **PARKING:** 55 **NOTES:** No smoking in restaurant Civ Wed 110 **CARDS:**

See advert on this page

CHARINGWORTH, Gloucestershire Map 04 SP13

★★★75% ❀ **Charingworth Manor**
GL55 6NS

☎ 01386 593555 📠 01386 593353
e-mail: charingworthmanor @englishrosehotels.co.uk
Dir: *on B4035 3m E of Chipping Campden*
This 14th-century manor house retains many original features including flagstone floors, exposed beams and open fireplaces. The house has a beautiful setting in 50 acres of grounds and has been carefully expanded to provide high quality accommodation. The bedrooms are furnished with period pieces and modern amenities; four-poster rooms and suites are available.
ROOMS: 26 en suite s £95-£150; d £150-£180 (incl. bkfst) * LB **FACILITIES:** STV Indoor swimming (H) Tennis (hard) Sauna Solarium Gym Croquet lawn Steam room Xmas **CONF:** Thtr 36 Class 16 Board 30 Del from £150 * **PARKING:** 50 **NOTES:** No dogs (ex guide dogs) No smoking in restaurant Civ Wed 50
CARDS:

See advert under CHIPPING CAMPDEN

CHARMOUTH, Dorset Map 03 SY39

★★76% **White House**
2 Hillside, The Street DT6 6PJ
☎ 01297 560411 📠 01297 560702
e-mail: white-house@lineone.net
Dir: *turn off A35-signed Charmouth, hotel opposite the church*
This friendly hotel offers comfortable accommodation in a charming Regency property. The interesting beach, famous for its fossils and cliff top walks, is nearby. Individually styled bedrooms

continued on p148

CHARMOUTH, continued

are equipped with modern facilities. A five course menu is offered at night, cooked using fresh produce.
ROOMS: 7 en suite 3 annexe en suite No smoking in all bedrooms s £49.50-£54.50; d £79-£89 (incl. bkfst) * LB **PARKING:** 12
NOTES: No children 14yrs No smoking in restaurant Closed mid Nov-mid Feb **CARDS:**

★★67% ***Hensleigh Hotel***
Lower Sea Ln DT6 6LW
☎ 01297 560830 01297 560830
This family-run hotel is set midway between the beach and the village. Bedrooms are neatly decorated and furnished. There is a large conservatory leading to a smaller dining room and a cosy lounge bar. For dinner, guests can choose from the menu or specials; breakfast offers a good choice too.
ROOMS: 10 en suite (1 fmly) No smoking in all bedrooms
PARKING: 19 **NOTES:** No smoking in restaurant RS mid-end Feb & 3 Nov-4 Dec **CARDS:**

CHATHAM, Kent — Map 05 TQ76

★★★★77% **Bridgewood Manor Hotel**
MARSTON HOTELS
Bridgewood Roundabout, Walderslade Woods ME5 9AX
☎ 01634 201333 01634 201330
e-mail: bridgewoodmanor@marstonhotels.co.uk
Dir: *adjacent to Bridgewood rdbt on A229. Take third exit signed 'Walderslade/Lordswood'. Hotel 50mtrs on left*
Although relatively modern in style, this hotel takes a serious approach to the traditional values of service and hospitality. The hotel offers quality, well equipped accommodation, augmented by a full complement of leisure facilities. Seriously good cuisine is served in the elegant surroundings of Squires Restaurant. Try the Terrace for a lighter bite.
ROOMS: 100 en suite (12 fmly) No smoking in 63 bedrooms s £69-£97; d £85-£115 * LB **FACILITIES:** STV Indoor swimming (H) Tennis (hard) Snooker Sauna Solarium Gym Putting green Jacuzzi/spa Hairdressing Beauty treatments Xmas **CONF:** Thtr 200 Class 110 Board 80
SERVICES: Lift **PARKING:** 178 **NOTES:** No smoking in restaurant Civ Wed 120 **CARDS:**

CHATTERIS, Cambridgeshire — Map 05 TL38

★73% **Cross Keys**
16 Market Hill PE16 6BA
☎ 01354 693036 & 692644 01354 694454
Dir: *at junct A141/142, opposite parish church*

Dating back to Elizabethan times, this small inn with a big character has been tastefully extended. The spacious restaurant, cosy bar, dining area and residents' lounge are pleasant and relaxing. The older bedrooms offer a wide variety of room sizes and styles, and the rooms in the newer wing are well equipped and spacious.
ROOMS: 12 rms (10 en suite) (1 fmly) No smoking in 5 bedrooms s £21-£40; d £32.50-£68 (incl. bkfst) * LB **CONF:** Class 40
PARKING: 12 **NOTES:** No dogs (ex guide dogs) No smoking in restaurant Closed 26-28 Dec **CARDS:**

CHEDDAR See Axbridge

CHELMSFORD, Essex — Map 05 TL70

★★★69% ***Pontlands Park Country***
West Hanningfield Rd, Great Baddow CM2 8HR
☎ 01245 476444 01245 478393
e-mail: sales@pontlandsparkhotel.co.uk
Dir: *leave A12 at junct A130. Take A1116 to Chelmsford. 1st exit at rdbt, 1st slip road on left. Left towards Gt Baddow, 1st left into West Hanningfield rd*
Quietly located in the village of Great Baddow on the outskirts of Chelmsford, Pontlands Park offers spacious, comfortable accommodation. Leisure facilities include outdoor and indoor swimming pools, and a leisure club.
ROOMS: 17 en suite (1 fmly) **FACILITIES:** Indoor swimming (H) Outdoor swimming (H) Sauna Solarium Gym Jacuzzi/spa Beauty salon
CONF: Thtr 40 Class 30 Board 20 Del from £125 * **PARKING:** 100
NOTES: No dogs (ex guide dogs) Closed 24 Dec-7 Jan (ex 31 Dec)
CARDS:

★★★68% ***County***
Rainsford Rd CM1 2QA
☎ 01245 491911 01245 492762
e-mail: sales@countyhotel-essex.co.uk
Dir: *from town centre continue past railway and bus station to hotel 300yds on left beyond traffic lights*
Located in the very centre of town, this hotel benefits from an extensive car park and a range of popular meeting rooms. Bedrooms vary in size and offer a range of useful facilities and there are now one or two feature rooms which have been decorated with a very individual style.
ROOMS: 28 en suite 8 annexe en suite **CONF:** Thtr 200 Class 60 Board 40 **PARKING:** 80 **NOTES:** Closed 27-30 Dec
CARDS:

CHELTENHAM, Gloucestershire — Map 03 SO92

★★★★67% **Cheltenham Park**
PARAMOUNT GROUP OF HOTELS
Cirencester Rd, Charlton Kings GL53 8EA
☎ 01242 222021 01242 254880
e-mail: cheltenhampark@paramount-hotels.co.uk
Dir: *on the A435, 2m SE of Cheltenham near the Lilley Brook Golf Course*

A smart modern hotel that is located on the edge of Cheltenham, but is convenient for the town centre. Amongst the attractions are extensive leisure facilities, and tranquil gardens at the rear of the hotel.

continued

ROOMS: 144 en suite (2 fmly) No smoking in 70 bedrooms s £89-£99; d £115-£128 * LB **FACILITIES:** STV Indoor swimming (H) Sauna Solarium Gym Jacuzzi/spa Steam room Xmas **CONF:** Thtr 370 Class 222 Board 144 Del from £115 * **PARKING:** 200 **NOTES:** No smoking in restaurant Civ Wed 300 **CARDS:**

★★★★58% The Queen's

The Promenade GL50 1NN
☎ 0870 400 8107 🖷 01242 224145
e-mail: gm1050@forte-hotels.com
Dir: *follow signs to Town Centre. Left at Montpellier Walk rdbt. Approx 500mtrs on right entrance after Le Petit Blane restaurant*

The Queen's Hotel is situated in the centre of town overlooking the Regency Gardens. This elegant and traditional hotel provides well equipped and comfortable accommodation. The attractive lobby and lounge area is a popular place to meet and take refreshments.

ROOMS: 79 en suite (8 fmly) No smoking in 20 bedrooms **FACILITIES:** STV **CONF:** Thtr 100 Class 60 Board 40 Del £135 * **SERVICES:** Lift **PARKING:** 85 **NOTES:** No smoking in restaurant Civ Wed 50 **CARDS:**

Premier Collection

★★★ The Greenway

Shurdington GL51 5UG
☎ 01242 862352 🖷 01242 862780
e-mail: greenway@btconnect.com
Dir: *2.5m SW on A46*

The Greenway is a charming Elizabethan manor house dating back to 1587. The dining room offers high standards of cuisine, taking full advantage of fresh local produce. The spacious, individually decorated bedrooms are divided between the main house and the smartly refurbished Georgian coach house. Rooms retain many original features and offer thoughtful extras.

ROOMS: 11 en suite 8 annexe en suite (1 fmly) No smoking in 8 bedrooms s £99-£130; d £165-£240 (incl. bkfst) * LB **FACILITIES:** STV Croquet lawn Clay pigeon shooting Horse riding Mountain biking Guided walks Xmas **CONF:** Thtr 35 Class 25 Board 22 Del £150 * **PARKING:** 50 **NOTES:** No dogs No children 7yrs No smoking in restaurant Civ Wed 45 **CARDS:**

Premier Collection

★★★ Hotel On the Park

38 Evesham Rd GL52 2AH
☎ 01242 518898 🖷 01242 511526
e-mail: stay@hotelonthepark.co.uk
Dir: *opposite Pittville Park. Join one-way system and turn off A435 towards Evesham*

A beautiful hotel close to the centre of town and brimming with style. The bar, restaurant and drawing room are decorated in Regency style and fine soft furnishings provide a note of opulence. Bedrooms are stunningly furnished and many little extras are offered. Cuisine is distinctive and accomplished.

ROOMS: 12 en suite No smoking in 4 bedrooms s £78.50-£141.50; d £96.50-£156.50 * LB **FACILITIES:** STV **PARKING:** 9 **NOTES:** No children 8yrs No smoking in restaurant
CARDS:

★★★68% Charlton Kings

London Rd, Charlton Kings GL52 6UU
☎ 01242 231061 🖷 01242 241900
Dir: *2.5m SE on A40 1st property on left entering Cheltenham from Oxford on the A40*

On the outskirts of Cheltenham, the Charlton Kings is an attractive and friendly hotel providing comfortable, modern accommodation. Bedrooms are well equipped and tastefully furnished. The restaurant serves well cooked food from a varied menu based on quality ingredients.

ROOMS: 14 en suite (2 fmly) No smoking in 5 bedrooms s £53-£80; d £68-£104 (incl. bkfst) * LB **CONF:** Thtr 30 Class 30 Board 20 Del from £85 * **PARKING:** 20 **NOTES:** No smoking in restaurant
CARDS:

★★★67% Carlton

Parabola Rd GL50 3AQ
☎ 01242 514453 🖷 01242 226487

This well presented Regency property is conveniently situated close to the town centre. Family owned and run, it provides spacious and comfortable accommodation. An annexe provides rooms with a more luxurious feel and other features include a choice of bars, lounge and conference facilities.

ROOMS: 62 en suite 13 annexe en suite (2 fmly) No smoking in 20 bedrooms s £62.50-£65; d £83.50-£87.50 (incl. bkfst) * LB **FACILITIES:** STV Xmas **CONF:** Thtr 225 Class 150 Board 100 Del from £75 * **SERVICES:** Lift **PARKING:** 85
CARDS:

★★★66% *Royal George*

Birdlip GL4 8JH
☎ 01452 862506 🖷 01452 862277
Dir: *on the B4070, off the A417*

Situated in an idyllic village, this mellow stone building has been sympathetically converted and extended into a pleasant hotel. Bedrooms are comfortably furnished with modern facilities. Open-plan public areas are informally designed around the bar and restaurant. A path links the hotel to the Cotswold Way.

ROOMS: 34 en suite (4 fmly) No smoking in 6 bedrooms **FACILITIES:** STV Putting green **CONF:** Thtr 100 Class 50 Board 40 **PARKING:** 120 **NOTES:** No dogs (ex guide dogs)
CARDS:

CHELTENHAM, continued

★★★66% White House

Gloucester Rd GL51 0ST
☎ 01452 713226 🖷 01452 857590
e-mail: felicity@whitehousehotel.freeserve.uk
Dir: *leave M5 junc 11 onto A40 to Cheltenham, then left at roundabout hotel half a mile on left*

Situated on the edge of town, the White House Hotel provides comfortable and modern accommodation. The lounge bar and restaurant are attractively presented and staff offer a warm welcome.
ROOMS: 49 en suite (4 fmly) No smoking in 13 bedrooms **FACILITIES:** STV Pool table entertainment **CONF:** Thtr 180 Class 80 Board 45 **PARKING:** 150 **NOTES:** No smoking in restaurant RS 13-16 Mar, 17-28 Jul, 10-12 Nov Civ Wed 180
CARDS:

See advert on opposite page

★★★64% George Hotel

St Georges Rd GL50 3DZ
☎ 01242 235751 🖷 01242 224359
e-mail: hotel@stayatthegeorge.co.uk
Dir: *head to Town Centre, follow one way system to Bath Rd. Right into Oriel Road at junct next to Theatre, then across The Promenade & into St George St*

The George Hotel is privately owned, and part of a terraced row of Regency properties situated close to the centre of town. Bedrooms are well equipped and tastefully furnished with additional facilities including a lounge bar, dining room and convenient car park.
ROOMS: 38 en suite (2 fmly) No smoking in 3 bedrooms s fr £60; d fr £80 (incl. bkfst) * LB **FACILITIES:** STV Xmas **CONF:** Thtr 40 Class 24 Board 20 Del from £85 * **PARKING:** 30 **NOTES:** No dogs (ex guide dogs) No smoking in restaurant **CARDS:**

★★★63% The Prestbury House Hotel & Restaurant

The Burgage, Prestbury GL52 3DN
☎ 01242 529533 🖷 01242 227076
Dir: *2m NE A46 from Cheltenham racecourse follow signs for Prestbury hotel is 2nd on the left half a mile from racecouse*

The Prestbury House hotel retains much of its historical charm and is well situated for the town centre and racecourse. Well equipped accommodation is divided between spacious rooms in the main house and those in a converted coach house. The owners also run a management training company, and team-building activities sometimes take place in the hotel grounds.

ROOMS: 8 en suite 9 annexe en suite (3 fmly) No smoking in 6 bedrooms s £66; d £85 (incl. bkfst) * LB **FACILITIES:** STV Riding Croquet lawn Clay pigeon shooting Archery Mountain bike hire Xmas **CONF:** Thtr 70 Class 30 Board 25 Del from £108 * **PARKING:** 50 **NOTES:** No dogs (ex guide dogs) Civ Wed 60
CARDS:

★★71% *Wyastone*

Parabola Rd, Montpellier GL50 3BG
☎ 01242 245549 🖷 01242 522659
e-mail: reservations@wyastonehotel.co.uk
Dir: *from junct 11 M5, travel 3m to end of Lansdown Rd, at Montpellier (rdbt with ornate lampstand) 2nd left around Bank of Scotland into Parabola Rd*

This charming period hotel, situated in the elegant Montpellier district, is run with great personal care. Day rooms are furnished in keeping with the style of the building. Bedrooms are comfortable and well equipped, and some ground floor and family rooms are available.
ROOMS: 13 en suite (2 fmly) No smoking in all bedrooms **FACILITIES:** STV Secluded patio garden **CONF:** Thtr 25 Board 15 **PARKING:** 12 **NOTES:** No dogs (ex guide dogs) No smoking in restaurant Closed Xmas & New Year **CARDS:**

★★68% Cotswold Grange

Pittville Circus Rd GL52 2QH
☎ 01242 515119 🖷 01242 241537
e-mail: paul@cotswold-grange.fsnet.co.uk
Dir: *from town centre follow signs 'Prestbury'. Turn right at first roundabout, hotel 200yds on left*

Cotswold Grange is an attractive Georgian property built from mellow Cotswold limestone. Situated conveniently close to the centre of Cheltenham the hotel offers well equipped and comfortable accommodation. Facilities include busy bar, spacious restaurant, cosy lounge and convenient car park.
ROOMS: 25 en suite (4 fmly) s £50; d £75 (incl. bkfst) * LB **CONF:** Thtr 20 Class 15 Board 15 Del from £80 * **PARKING:** 20 **NOTES:** No smoking in restaurant Closed 24 Dec-1 Jan RS Sat & Sun evening (food by arrangement) **CARDS:**

★★64% North Hall

Pittville Circus Rd GL52 2PZ
☎ 01242 520589 🖷 01242 261953
e-mail: northhallhotel@btinternet.com
Dir: *head towards Cheltenham Town Centre, following directions for Pittville. At Pittville Circus take 1st left into Pittville Circus Rd. Hotel on right*

This large Victorian house, now a privately owned and personally

continued

run hotel, is within easy reach of the town centre. It provides well equipped accommodation, which is equally suitable for tourists and business people. Facilities include a small bar and a comfortable lounge.

ROOMS: 20 en suite (2 fmly) No smoking in 8 bedrooms s £40-£55; d £60-£90 (incl. bkfst) * LB **FACILITIES:** Xmas **CONF:** Thtr 30 Class 20 Board 16 Del from £65 * **PARKING:** 25 **NOTES:** No smoking in restaurant **CARDS:**

Town House

★★★★ **Kandinsky**
Bayshill Rd, Montpellier GL50 3AS
☎ 01242 527788 01242 226412
e-mail: info@hotelkandinsky.com

Dir: *exit M5 Junct 11 follow A40 Town centre. Turn right at 2nd rdbt. At 3rd, take 2nd exit into Bayshill Rd. Hotel on corner of Bayshill/Parabola Rds*

The former Savoy Hotel has been transformed and has reopened under a new name. Bedrooms are stylish and modern in design, all equipped to a high standard with CD and video players. Public areas have a quirky appeal, decorated with an unusual array of trinkets. Cafe Paradiso is bright and buzzy, and hidden in the cellars is U-bahn, a 1950s club.

ROOMS: 48 en suite (3 fmly) No smoking in 4 bedrooms s £75; d £105 (incl. bkfst) * LB **FACILITIES:** STV entertainment **CONF:** Thtr 20 Del £120 * **SERVICES:** Lift **PARKING:** 32 **NOTES:** No dogs (ex guide dogs) No smoking in restaurant **CARDS:**

See advert on this page

Early start? Hotels at all star levels should provide in-room alarm clocks and/or alarm calls.

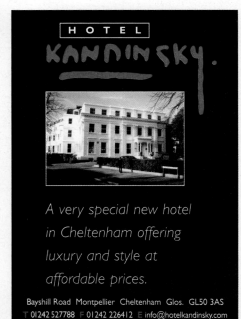

C

CHELWOOD, Somerset
Map 03 ST66

★★69% Chelwood House
BS39 4NH
☎ 01761 490730 🖷 01761 490072
Dir: *on A37 200yds S of junct with A368*
This imposing 300-year-old country house is convenient for both Bath and Bristol. Spacious bedrooms are well equipped and include four-poster and ground floor rooms. The elegant lounge reflects similar high standards of quality and comfort, and the conservatory restaurant is refreshingly attractive.
ROOMS: 12 en suite (1 fmly) s £55-£65; d £89.50-£100 (incl. bkfst) * LB **FACILITIES:** Croquet lawn **CONF:** Thtr 30 Class 12 Board 12 **PARKING:** 30 **NOTES:** No smoking in restaurant RS Sun
CARDS:

CHENIES, Buckinghamshire
Map 04 TQ09

★★★69% Bedford Arms Chenies
WD3 6EQ
☎ 01923 283301 🖷 01923 284825
Dir: *off A404, signposted*
PEEL HOTELS
This attractive, 19th-century country inn enjoys a peaceful rural setting. Attractive bedrooms are decorated in traditional style and feature a range of thoughtful extras. Each room is named after a relation of the Duke of Bedford, whose family has an historic association with the hotel. There are two bars and a popular restaurant.
ROOMS: 10 en suite No smoking in 3 bedrooms s fr £145; d £145-£160 * **FACILITIES:** STV **CONF:** Thtr 25 Class 10 Board 15 Del £185 * **PARKING:** 60 **NOTES:** No dogs (ex guide dogs)
CARDS:

CHERTSEY, Surrey
Map 04 TQ06

★★★65% The Crown
7 London St KT16 8AP
☎ 01932 564657 🖷 01932 570839
Dir: *adjacent to Old Town Hall, located in the Town Centre*
Situated in the centre of historic Chertsey, the Crown offers spacious, comfortable accommodation with good business facilities. The popular public bar and conservatory offer a good selection of house wines by the glass.
ROOMS: 30 annexe en suite (4 fmly) No smoking in 13 bedrooms s £94; d £106 (incl. bkfst) * LB **FACILITIES:** STV Xmas **CONF:** Thtr 100 Class 40 Board 35 **PARKING:** 50
CARDS:

CHESHUNT, Hertfordshire
Map 05 TL30

★★★★65% Cheshunt Marriott
Halfhide Ln, Turnford EN10 6NG
☎ 01992 451245 🖷 01992 440120
Marriott HOTELS · RESORTS · SUITES
Dir: *take Turnford/Wormley exit from A10, turn right at Beefeater, New River Arms rdbt, take 3rd exit from next rdbt. Hotel on 3rd exit*
Conveniently located off the A10, this purpose built hotel offers spacious, air-conditioned accommodation, some of which overlooks a pretty, central courtyard. Guests may eat in either the busy Washington Bar or the restaurant. Ask for directions when you book.
ROOMS: 143 en suite (37 fmly) No smoking in 92 bedrooms d £85-£164 (incl. bkfst) * LB **FACILITIES:** STV Indoor swimming (H) Gym Jacuzzi/spa Xmas **CONF:** Thtr 180 Class 100 Board 90 Del from £166 * **SERVICES:** Lift air con **PARKING:** 200 **NOTES:** No dogs (ex guide dogs) No smoking in restaurant Civ Wed 120
CARDS:

CHESTER, Cheshire
Map 07 SJ46
see also Puddington

★★★★★78% ❀❀❀ The Chester Grosvenor

Eastgate CH1 1LT
☎ 01244 324024 🖷 01244 313246
e-mail: chesgnov@chestergrosvenor.co.uk
Dir: *turn off M56 for M53 Chester, then A56 Chester - follow signs for city centre hotels*
Found within the Roman walls of the city, this popular hotel is the essence of Englishness. The Brasserie is bustling and the Library has a discreet club-like feel. In the Arkle restaurant, guests are offered imaginative cuisine using seasonal ingredients in the modern British style. Suites and bedrooms are designed for guest comfort and are of the highest standard.
ROOMS: 85 en suite No smoking in 21 bedrooms s £152.75-£176.25; d £229.13-£270.25 * LB **FACILITIES:** STV Sauna Solarium Gym Membership of Country Club - 2m from hotel with complimentary transport entertainment **CONF:** Thtr 250 Class 120 Board 48 Del £211.50 * **SERVICES:** Lift air con **NOTES:** No dogs (ex guide dogs) Closed 25-26 Dec RS 27-30 Dec & 1-23 Jan Civ Wed
CARDS:

★★★★77% ❀❀ Crabwall Manor
Parkgate Rd, Mollington CH1 6NE
☎ 01244 851666 🖷 01244 851400
e-mail: sales@crabwall.com
Dir: *NW off A540*
First mentioned in the Domesday Book, this re-built manor house hotel dates from the 17th-century. Spacious bedrooms and suites are attractively decorated and include useful extra features, such as luxuriously large bathtubs. There are a number of small, comfortable lounge areas, in addition to a billiard room, and the conservatory restaurant.
ROOMS: 48 en suite No smoking in 2 bedrooms s £125; d £135-£150 (incl. bkfst) * LB **FACILITIES:** STV Indoor swimming (H) Snooker Sauna Solarium Gym Croquet lawn Jacuzzi/spa Heli pad Xmas **CONF:** Thtr 100 Class 60 Board 36 Del from £152.75 * **PARKING:** 120 **NOTES:** No dogs (ex guide dogs) No smoking in restaurant Civ Wed 90
CARDS:
See advert on opposite page

★★★★72% De Vere Carden Park
Carden Park CH3 9DQ
DE VERE HOTELS Hotels of character, run with pride.
☎ 01829 731000 🖷 01829 731032
e-mail: reservation@carden-park.co.uk
(For full entry see Broxton)

★★★★66% ❀ Mollington Banastre
Parkgate Rd CH1 6NN
ARCADIAN HOTELS Distinctly Different
☎ 01244 851471 🖷 01244 851165
Dir: *M56 to junct 16 at next rdbt turn left for Chester A540. Hotel is 2m down the A540 on right*
This hotel, situated between the city and the M56, has its own attractive gardens. Bedrooms vary in size and include family suites. There are meeting and function rooms and also a leisure centre. Stylish public areas include a comfortable bar, the Garden Room restaurant and the less formal Place Apart.
ROOMS: 63 en suite (8 fmly) No smoking in 12 bedrooms s £75-£90; d £95-£110 (incl. bkfst) * LB **FACILITIES:** STV Indoor swimming (H) Squash Sauna Solarium Gym Croquet lawn Jacuzzi/spa Hairdressing Health & beauty salon Xmas **CONF:** Thtr 260 Class 60 Board 50 Del from £115 * **SERVICES:** Lift **PARKING:** 200 **NOTES:** No smoking in restaurant Civ Wed **CARDS:**

★★★★64% Queen
City Rd CH1 3AH
☎ 01244 305000 01244 318483
Dir: *follow signs for railway station, hotel is opposite*
Centrally located, this elegant 19th-century hotel with its own private garden stands opposite the railway station. Bedrooms are brightly decorated and equipped with all modern facilities. The reception area, graced by an impressive central gallery staircase, gives access to the public areas, which include two lounges, two bars and a restaurant.
ROOMS: 128 en suite (6 fmly) No smoking in 24 bedrooms s £60-£95; d £70-£120 (incl. bkfst) * LB **FACILITIES:** STV Croquet lawn entertainment Xmas **CONF:** Thtr 280 Class 100 Board 50 Del from £110 * **SERVICES:** Lift **PARKING:** 100 **NOTES:** No smoking in restaurant Civ Wed 250 **CARDS:**

★★★69% Hoole Hall
Warrington Rd, Hoole Village CH2 3PD
☎ 01244 408800 01244 320251
Dir: *from junct 12 on M53 continue 0.5m on A56 towards city centre*
This hotel, dating from the 18th century, is two miles from the city centre and stands in extensive grounds. The hotel is now much extended and modernised, and refurbishment has considerably enhanced the bedroom accommodation. There is a wide range of facilities for meetings, banquets and conferences, and ample car parking to cater for all events.

continued on p154

CHESTER, continued

Hoole Hall, Chester

ROOMS: 97 en suite (4 fmly) No smoking in 48 bedrooms s fr £80; d fr £95 * LB **FACILITIES:** STV Xmas **CONF:** Thtr 150 Class 40 Board 50 Del from £112.50 * **SERVICES:** Lift **PARKING:** 200 **NOTES:** No smoking in restaurant Civ Wed 140
CARDS:

★★★68% *Rowton Hall Country House Hotel*
Whitchurch Rd, Rowton CH3 6AD
☎ 01244 335262 01244 335464
e-mail: rowtonhall@rowtonhall.co.uk
Dir: *2m SE A41 towards Whitchurch*
This impressive creeper-clad 18th-century country house lies in several acres of mature grounds. Original features include a superb carved staircase and several fireplaces. The modern extensions house a leisure centre and extensive function facilities. The rooms in the manor house are luxuriously spacious. Modern rooms are available in the courtyard.
ROOMS: 42 en suite (4 fmly) **FACILITIES:** STV Indoor swimming (H) Tennis (hard) Sauna Solarium Gym Croquet lawn Jacuzzi/spa **CONF:** Thtr 200 Class 48 Board 50 **PARKING:** 120 **NOTES:** No smoking in restaurant **CARDS:**

★★★66% *The Gateway To Wales*
Welsh Rd, Sealand, Deeside CH5 2HX
☎ 01244 830332 01244 836190
Dir: *4m NW via A548 towards Sealand and Queensferry*
Aptly named, this modern hotel is well located for exploring the area with easy access to Chester and the arterial route. Public areas include The Louis XVI lounge bar, The Regency Room restaurant and good leisure facilities. Bedrooms are comfortable and offer modern amenities.
ROOMS: 39 en suite (4 fmly) No smoking in 10 bedrooms **FACILITIES:** STV Indoor swimming (H) Sauna Solarium Gym Jacuzzi/spa Use of Indoor Bowls & Snooker Club **CONF:** Thtr 110 Class 50 Board 50 **SERVICES:** Lift **PARKING:** 51 **NOTES:** No dogs (ex guide dogs) No smoking in restaurant **CARDS:**

★★★66% Grosvenor Pulford
Wrexham Rd, Pulford CH4 9DG
☎ 01244 570560 01244 570809
e-mail: enquiries@grosvenorpulfordhotel.co.uk
Dir: *exit M53/A55 at junct signposted A483 Chester, Wrexham & North Wales. Turn onto B5445, hotel is 2m on right*
Set in rural surrounds, this hotel features a magnificent leisure club with a large Roman-style swimming pool. A choice of rooms includes several executive suites and others contain spiral staircases leading to the bedroom sections. A Victorian-style, beamed restaurant and bar provide a wide range of imaginative dishes in a relaxed atmosphere.

continued

ROOMS: 68 en suite (4 fmly) No smoking in 3 bedrooms s £67.50-£77.50; d £85-£95 (incl. bkfst) * LB **FACILITIES:** STV Indoor swimming (H) Snooker Sauna Solarium Gym Jacuzzi/spa Hairdressing & Beauty salon with latest treatments Xmas **CONF:** Thtr 200 Class 100 Board 50 Del from £94 * **PARKING:** 160 **NOTES:** Civ Wed 250
CARDS:

See advert on opposite page

★★★66% *Posthouse Chester*
Posthouse

Wrexham Rd CH4 9DL
☎ 0870 400 9019 01244 674100
Dir: *near Wrexham junct on A483, off A55*
This modern, child-friendly hotel has a spacious restaurant, a leisure club and a children's play area. A variety of bedrooms are available, all are well equipped, particularly the impressive newer Millennium-style and superior rooms. An all-day lounge menu and 24-hour room service are offered.
ROOMS: 145 en suite (44 fmly) No smoking in 99 bedrooms **FACILITIES:** Indoor swimming (H) Sauna Solarium Gym Pool table Jacuzzi/spa **CONF:** Thtr 100 Class 50 Board 40 **PARKING:** 220
CARDS:

★★★64% Broxton Hall Country House
Whitchurch Rd CH3 9JS
☎ 01829 782321 01829 782330
(For full entry see Broxton)

★★★62% Blossoms
St John St CH1 1HL
☎ 0870 400 8108
01244 346433
e-mail: heritagehotels-chester.blossoms@forte-hotels.com
Dir: *in city centre, around the corner from the Eastgate Clock*
This well established hotel is ideally situated right in the heart of the city and offers smart, refurbished accommodation. The public areas retain some of their Victorian charm and the atmosphere is enhanced at dinner, on occasions, with live piano music in the lobby. Free parking is available nearby in Newgate Street, close to the hotel.
ROOMS: 64 en suite (2 fmly) No smoking in 43 bedrooms s £85; d £105 * LB **FACILITIES:** entertainment Xmas **CONF:** Thtr 80 Class 60 Board 60 Del £105 * **SERVICES:** Lift **NOTES:** No smoking in restaurant
CARDS:

★★68% *Westminster*
Best Western

City Rd CH1 3AF
☎ 01244 317341 01244 325369
Dir: *from A56 approx. 3 miles to Chester City Centre, turn left when signposted rail station, hotel directly opposite station*
The Westminster has long been established as a hotel and is close to the railway station and city centre. It has an attractive, Tudor-style exterior but bedrooms are brightly decorated with a modern theme. There is a choice of bars and a large dining room serving a good range of dishes.
ROOMS: 75 en suite (5 fmly) No smoking in 20 bedrooms **FACILITIES:** STV entertainment **CONF:** Thtr 30 Class 20 Board 20 **SERVICES:** Lift **CARDS:**

★★67% *Curzon*
52/54 Hough Green CH4 8JQ
☎ 01244 678581 01244 680866
Dir: *on A5104*
Just one mile from the city centre and close to the racecourse, this is an ideal spot for both business and leisure guests. Bedrooms are large, some have four-poster beds and some family rooms are available. The bar has a friendly atmosphere, and the dinner menu offers a good choice, including some traditional Swiss

continued

dishes inspired by the owners. Pretty gardens lead to a car park at the rear of the hotel.

ROOMS: 16 en suite (7 fmly) No smoking in 7 bedrooms **FACILITIES:** Pool table **PARKING:** 20 **NOTES:** No smoking in restaurant Closed 20-29 Dec **CARDS:**

See advert on this page

★★ 66% Brookside

Brook Ln CH2 2AN
☎ 01244 381943 📠 01244 379701
e-mail: info@hotel-chester.com
Dir: *0.5m from city, turn off A5116 into Brook Lane, hotel 300yds on left*

The Brookside is a friendly hotel located just north of the city centre. The attractive public areas consist of a foyer lounge, a small bar and a split-level restaurant. Bedrooms are brightly decorated, and well equipped.

ROOMS: 24 en suite (7 fmly) s £40-£45; d £55-£60 (incl. bkfst) * LB **FACILITIES:** STV Xmas **PARKING:** 20 **NOTES:** No smoking in restaurant **CARDS:**

CHESTER, continued

★★66% Cavendish
42-44 Hough Green CH4 8JQ
☎ 01244 675100 📠 01244 678844
e-mail: brooksid@globalnet.co.uk
Dir: *S of Chester, from the A483 take A5104 signposted Saltney. Hotel is approx 350yds on the right, next to Youth hostel*
Conveniently located less than a mile from the city centre, this Georgian house offers spacious, well-equipped bedrooms, including some with four poster beds and a garden room with a private patio. There is a comfortable lounge and a small bar beside the restaurant that overlooks the garden.
ROOMS: 19 en suite (4 fmly) s £45-£55; d £55-£80 (incl. bkfst) * LB **FACILITIES:** STV Xmas **PARKING:** 35 **NOTES:** No dogs (ex guide dogs) No smoking in restaurant **CARDS:**

★★66% Dene
95 Hoole Rd CH2 3ND
☎ 01244 321165 📠 01244 350277
e-mail: denehotel@btconnect.com
Dir: *0.75m E of city centre, from junct 12 of M53 take A56 towards Chester, hotel just after Alexander Park*
Conveniently close to the city centre and motorway network, The Dene provides comfortable accommodation. Bedrooms, split between the main house and an adjacent block, vary in size but all are suitably equipped. As well as bar meals an interesting choice of dishes is offered in the welcoming Franc's Brasserie.
ROOMS: 44 en suite 8 annexe en suite (5 fmly) No smoking in 16 bedrooms s £45; d £57 (incl. bkfst) * LB **FACILITIES:** STV Pool table **CONF:** Thtr 30 Class 12 Board 16 Del from £70 * **PARKING:** 55 **NOTES:** No smoking in restaurant **CARDS:**

★★62% *Chester Court*
Hoole Rd CH2 3NL
☎ 01244 320779 📠 01244 344795
e-mail: chestercourthotel@classic.msn.com
Dir: *approach city centre on A56 Hoole Road. Hotel on right opposite All Saints Church*
This hotel lies on the leafy outskirts of Chester. Bedrooms are well equipped with modern facilities and many are located at ground level in a peaceful courtyard. Several rooms have four-poster beds, and family accommodation is available. The hotel has a lounge and a bar, and a well appointed restaurant featuring a pleasing conservatory.
ROOMS: 8 en suite 12 annexe en suite (2 fmly) **FACILITIES:** STV **CONF:** Thtr 20 Class 9 Board 12 **PARKING:** 20 **NOTES:** No smoking in restaurant **CARDS:**

★★62% Eaton
29/31 City Rd CH1 3AE
☎ 01244 320840 📠 01244 320850
e-mail: welcome@eatonhotelchester.co.uk
Dir: *400 metres from the station, towards the city centre, adjacent to the canal*
This privately owned hotel is a short walk from the city centre and conveniently placed for the railway station. There is an attractive cane-furnished bar and a wood-panelled dining room with a small daily fixed-price menu. Enclosed car parking is also available.
ROOMS: 16 en suite (3 fmly) s fr £49.50; d fr £65.50 (incl. bkfst) * LB **PARKING:** 10 **NOTES:** No smoking in restaurant
CARDS:

Fancy a Singapore Sling? Bar staff in five star hotels should be skilled cocktail mixers.

⌂ Premier Lodge
76 Liverpool Rd CH2 1AU
☎ 0870 700 1350 📠 0870 700 1351
Premier Lodge offers modern, well equipped, en suite accommodation suitable for both business and leisure travellers. Meals can be taken at the adjacent popular restaurant and bar which is fully licensed. For further details, consult the Hotel Groups page.
ROOMS: 31 en suite d £42 *

CHESTERFIELD, Derbyshire Map 08 SK37

★★★62% *Sandpiper*
Sheffield Rd, Sheepbridge S41 9EH
☎ 01246 450550 📠 01246 452805
Dir: *leave M1 junct 29 follow A617 to Chesterfield. Follow A61 to Sheffield then at 1st exit take Dronfield Rd. Hotel 0.5m on left*
Conveniently situated for the A61 and M1, just three miles from Chesterfield, this modern hotel offers comfortable and well furnished bedrooms. Public areas are situated in a separate building across the car park and include a cosy bar and open plan restaurant, serving a range of interesting and popular dishes.
ROOMS: 28 annexe en suite (4 fmly) No smoking in 14 bedrooms **FACILITIES:** STV **CONF:** Thtr 60 Class 30 Board 40 **PARKING:** 220 **NOTES:** No dogs (ex guide dogs) **CARDS:**

★★68% Portland
West Bars S40 1AY
☎ 01246 234502 & 234211 📠 01246 550915
Dir: *in town centre overlooking Market Place*
This popular Victorian hotel is close to the market place, and has the benefit of private car parking. Public areas include meeting and function rooms, a popular bar and a quieter lounge bar, aswell as a pleasant restaurant offering a carvery and traditional dishes. Bedrooms are well equipped and nicely decorated with colourful soft furnishings.
ROOMS: 24 en suite (6 fmly) s £49; d £55 (incl. bkfst) * LB **CONF:** Thtr 50 Class 50 Board 20 **PARKING:** 30 **NOTES:** No dogs (ex guide dogs) **CARDS:**

★★67% Abbeydale
Cross St S40 4TD
☎ 01246 277849 📠 01246 558223
e-mail: elaine@abbey.66.freeserve.co.uk
Dir: *A617 to Chesterfield, A619 to Buxton & Bakewell, at B&Q rdbt 3rd turning off to Foljambe Rd across lights into West St, right at T junct of Cross St*
Situated in a quiet residential area of the town, this friendly hotel offers excellent service and warm hospitality. Bedrooms, two of which are on the ground floor, are bright, fresh and well equipped. A short selection of freshly prepared dishes are served in the dining room, adjacent to the cosy lounge and bar.
ROOMS: 12 rms (11 en suite) (1 fmly) No smoking in 6 bedrooms s £38-£45; d £55-£60 (incl. bkfst) * **PARKING:** 18 **NOTES:** No smoking in restaurant Closed 23 Dec-2 Jan **CARDS:**

⌂ *Travelodge*
Brimmington Rd, Inner Ring Rd, Wittington Moor S41 9BE
☎ 01246 455411 📠 01246 455411
Dir: *A61, N of town centre*
This modern building offers accommodation in smart, spacious and well equipped bedrooms, all with en suite bathrooms. Refreshments may be taken at the nearby family restaurant. For further details and the Travelodge phone number, consult the Hotel Groups page.
ROOMS: 20 en suite

⇧ Express by Holiday Inn Chesterfield
Lords Mill St S41 7RW
☎ 01246 221333 📠 221444
e-mail: chesterfield@premierhotels.co.uk
Dir: *M1 junct29, take A617 to Chesterfield. Straight over main rdbt. Hotel is located on the next rdbt*

A modern budget hotel offering comfortable accommodation in refreshing, spacious and comprehensively-equipped bedrooms, en suite bathrooms with power showers and continental buffet breakfast included in the room rate. Suitable for business travellers or families. For further details and the Express by Holiday Inn phone number, consult the Hotel Groups page.
ROOMS: 86 en suite (incl. cont bkfst) d fr £55 * **CONF:** Thtr 35 Class 20 Board 22 Del from £80 *

CHICHESTER, West Sussex — Map 04 SU80

★★★★69% ❀❀ Marriott Goodwood Park
PO18 0QB
☎ 01243 775537 📠 01243 520120
(For full entry see Goodwood)

★★★72% ❀ The Millstream
Bosham Ln PO18 8HL
☎ 01243 573234 📠 01243 573459
e-mail: info@millstream-hotel.co.uk
(For full entry see Bosham)

★★★69% ❀ Crouchers Bottom Country Hotel
Birdham Rd PO20 7EH
☎ 01243 784995 📠 01243 539797
e-mail: crouchers_bottom@btconnect.com
Dir: *turn off A27 to the A286, 1.5m from Chichester centre opposite the Black Horse pub*
Close to the harbour, this family-run hotel provides attractive coach house rooms, all of which are well equipped. Public areas are spacious, and in addition to a comfortable lounge and separate bar, there is a smart, beamed restaurant.
ROOMS: 15 en suite (1 fmly) No smoking in 9 bedrooms s £52-£59; d £85-£105 (incl. bkfst) * LB **PARKING:** 40 **NOTES:** No smoking in restaurant **CARDS:**

★★★67% ❀ Ship
North St PO19 1NH
☎ 01243 778000 📠 01243 788000
e-mail: booking@shophotel.com
Dir: *enter Chichester from A27, go round the inner ring road to Northgate, at large Northgate rdbt turn left into North St, hotel is on left*
This well presented and friendly Georgian hotel has a prime position at the top of North Street. Popular with non-residents, the bar and restaurant offer a comfortable venue for refreshments

continued on p158

CHICHESTER, continued

and meals. Bedrooms have been refurbished to a high standard, all are well equipped. A subtle nautical theme runs through the hotel, once the home of Admiral George Murray.

Ship, Chichester

ROOMS: 34 en suite (4 fmly) s £67-£75; d £92-£155 (incl. bkfst) * LB **FACILITIES:** STV Xmas **CONF:** Thtr 70 Class 35 Board 30 Del from £99.50 * **SERVICES:** Lift **PARKING:** 38 **NOTES:** No smoking in restaurant **CARDS:**

See advert on page 157

★★69% Suffolk House

3 East Row PO19 1PD
☎ 01243 778899 01243 787282
e-mail: info@suffolkhshotel.co.uk
Dir: *turn right off East St into Little London, follow into East Row, hotel on left*
A warm welcome is assured at this Georgian hotel just a couple of minutes' walk from the city centre. Bedrooms vary in shape and size, all are comfortably furnished and feature many thoughtful touches. There is a cosy lounge, small bar, pleasant patio and a restaurant offering an interesting menu. Telephone beforehand about parking.
ROOMS: 11 en suite (2 fmly) No smoking in 3 bedrooms s £62-£86; d £94-£128 (incl. bkfst) * LB **FACILITIES:** STV **CONF:** Thtr 25 Class 12 Board 16 **NOTES:** No dogs (ex guide dogs) No smoking in restaurant **CARDS:**

★★67% Bedford

Southgate PO19 1DP
☎ 01243 785766 01243 533175
e-mail: bedford@win-ship.demon.co.uk
Dir: *from A27 (Chichester Bypass) continue N past level crossing at Chichester Station. Hotel 400yds on right*
Close to the centre of Chichester and near the station, this well presented hotel dates back to the 1700s. Bedrooms are attractively decorated, comfortably furnished and well equipped. Public areas include a cosy bar, separate lounges (one non smoking) and dining room which overlooks the rear patio. Service is friendly and guests are assured a warm welcome.
ROOMS: 19 rms (16 en suite) (2 fmly) No smoking in 11 bedrooms s £45-£72; d £88-£110 (incl. bkfst) * LB **PARKING:** 8 **NOTES:** No smoking in restaurant Closed 24 Dec-5 Jan
CARDS:

CHIDEOCK, Dorset — Map 03 SY49

★★69% Chideock House

Main St DT6 6JN
☎ 01297 489242 01297 489184
e-mail: enquiries@chideockhousehotel.com
Dir: *on A35 between Lyme Regis and Bridport*
This delightful, part-thatched house dates back to the 15th century. It is full of character and retains many original beams and fireplaces. Thoughtful touches abound in the bedrooms, and there is a choice of lounges. An interesting menu is offered in the restaurant.
ROOMS: 9 rms (8 en suite) d £60-£80 (incl. bkfst) * LB **FACILITIES:** Xmas **PARKING:** 20 **NOTES:** Closed 2 Jan-mid Feb RS mid Feb-Mar **CARDS:**

CHIPPENHAM, Wiltshire — Map 03 ST9

★★★70% Angel Hotel

Market Place SN15 3HD
☎ 01249 652615 01249 443210
Dir: *follow brown tourist signs for Bowood House. Pass under railway arch, then follow signs for 'Borough Parade Parking'. Hotel next to car park*
Dating back many centuries, this impressive building is home to a smart, comfortable hotel. Bedrooms vary from the main house where character is the key, to smart executive style courtyard rooms; both have modern facilities and are of a good size. There are two popular bars and a lovely panelled Dining room.
ROOMS: 15 en suite 35 annexe en suite (3 fmly) s £82.50-£85.50; d £92.50-£95.50 * LB **FACILITIES:** Indoor swimming (H) Gym **CONF:** Thtr 120 Class 50 Board 50 Del from £85 * **PARKING:** 50 **NOTES:** Civ Wed 100 **CARDS:**

★★★68% Stanton Manor Country House Hotel

SN14 6DQ
☎ 01666 837552 01666 837022
e-mail: reception@stantonmanor.co.uk
(For full entry see Stanton St Quintin)

CHIPPERFIELD, Hertfordshire — Map 04 TL0

★★72% *The Two Brewers*

The Common WD4 9BS
☎ 01923 265266 01923 261884
Dir: *turn left in centre of village, hotel overlooks common*
This 16th-century inn retains much of its old world charm while providing modern comforts and amenities. The spacious bedrooms are tastefully furnished and decorated, offering a comprehensive range of in-room facilities. The focal point of the hotel is the bar which serves an enjoyable pub-style meal and has a loyal local following.
ROOMS: 20 en suite No smoking in 10 bedrooms **FACILITIES:** STV **CONF:** Board 16 **PARKING:** 25 **NOTES:** No dogs (ex guide dogs) **CARDS:**

CHIPPING, Lancashire — Map 07 SD6

★★★★69% The Gibbon Bridge

Forest of Bowland PR3 2TQ
☎ 01995 61456 01995 61277
e-mail: reception@gibbon-bridge.co.uk
Dir: *at T-junct in Chipping turn right towards Clitheroe. Hotel 1m on right*
This fine hotel offers high levels of comfort for visitors. Bedrooms, including four-poster rooms and split-level suites, are a delight; public areas include a conservatory and a welcoming restaurant that provides enjoyable and carefully prepared meals.
ROOMS: 14 en suite 15 annexe en suite s £70-£100; d £100-£225 (incl. bkfst) * LB **FACILITIES:** STV Tennis (grass) Fishing Sauna Solarium Gym Beauty studio entertainment Xmas **CONF:** Thtr 70 Class 30 Board 35 Del from £110 * **SERVICES:** Lift **PARKING:** 252 **NOTES:** No dogs (ex guide dogs) No smoking in restaurant Civ Wed 180
CARDS:

CHIPPING CAMPDEN, Gloucestershire Map 04 SP13

Premier Collection

★★★ **Cotswold House**
The Square GL55 6AN
☎ 01386 840330 📠 01386 840310
e-mail: reception@cotswold-house.com
Dir: *from A44 take B4081 signposted to Chipping Campden village. Turn right into High St at T junct. Cotswold House is located at the Square*

Overlooking the town square, this elegant 17th-century house offers individually decorated, comfortable bedrooms with many thoughtful extra touches. A choice of eating options is available.

ROOMS: 15 en suite No smoking in all bedrooms s £110-£140; d £130-£180 (incl. bkfst) * LB **FACILITIES:** STV Gym Croquet lawn Access to local Sports Centre entertainment Xmas **CONF:** Thtr 30 Board 20 Del from £150 * **PARKING:** 15 **NOTES:** No smoking in restaurant Civ Wed 40 **CARDS:**

★★★73% **Noel Arms**
High St GL55 6AT
☎ 01386 840317 📠 01386 841136
e-mail: bookings@cotswold-inns-hotels.co.uk
Dir: *turn off A44 onto B4081 to Chipping Campden, take 1st right down hill into town. Hotel on right opposite Market Hall.*

Situated right in the heart of the town, this 14th-century hotel retains much of its original character, yet has been extensively refurbished. Bedrooms are well co-ordinated and have smart modern en suites. Public areas include a popular bar, conservatory lounge and bright restaurant offering high standards of cuisine.

ROOMS: 26 en suite (1 fmly) s fr £75; d £110-£125 (incl. bkfst) * LB **FACILITIES:** Xmas **CONF:** Thtr 50 Board 25 Del from £110 * **PARKING:** 30 **NOTES:** No smoking in restaurant Civ Wed 70 **CARDS:**

★★★73% **Seymour House**
High St GL55 6AH
☎ 01386 840429 📠 01386 840369
e-mail: enquiry@seymourhousehotel.com
Dir: *Hotel in middle of High St opposite Lloyds Bank, Chipping Campden at centre of road links A34/46/44*

Centrally located in one of the most idyllic villages in England, this lovely Cotswold property dates back to the early 18th century. Bedrooms vary in size and style, and all offer good levels of comfort. Public rooms, including a drawing room, the Vinery restaurant and separate bar, reflect the house's original charm and character.

continued

ROOMS: 11 en suite 4 annexe en suite s fr £72.50; d £95-£180 (incl. bkfst) * LB **FACILITIES:** STV Xmas **CONF:** Thtr 65 Class 26 Board 30 Del from £125 * **PARKING:** 28 **NOTES:** No dogs (ex guide dogs) No smoking in restaurant Civ Wed 65 **CARDS:**

★★★72% **Three Ways House**
Mickleton GL55 6SB
☎ 01386 438429 📠 01386 438118
e-mail: threeways@puddingclub.com
Dir: *situated on B4632 Stratford upon Avon to Broadway Road, hotel in centre of Mickleton Village*

THE CIRCLE
Selected Individual Hotels

This charming hotel was built in 1870, and is now the home of the famous Pudding Club. An extensive refurbishment programme has seen improvements to the now stylish and air-conditioned restaurant and Randalls bar/bistro, along with lounges and meeting rooms. Bedrooms are spacious and attractively furnished with some reflecting the pudding theme.

continued on p160

CHIPPING CAMPDEN, continued

ROOMS: 41 en suite (5 fmly) s £67-£82; d £97-£125 (incl. bkfst) * LB **FACILITIES:** entertainment Xmas **CONF:** Thtr 100 Class 40 Board 35 Del from £120 * **PARKING:** 37 **NOTES:** No smoking in restaurant Civ Wed 80 **CARDS:**

See advert on opposite page

CHITTLEHAMHOLT, Devon Map 03 SS62

★★★69% Highbullen

EX37 9HD
☎ 01769 540561 01769 540492
e-mail: highbullen@sosi.net
Dir: *leave M5 junct 27 onto A361 to South Molton, then B3226 Crediton Rd after 5.2m turn right up hill to Chittlehamholt, hotel 0.5m beyond village*

Highbullen is a Victorian gothic mansion, set in parkland with its own 18-hole golf course. An imaginative, fixed-price menu is served in the cellar restaurant. Light lunches are served in the bar or pleasing courtyard, while breakfast is served in a room with magnificent views of the valley. There is a wide choice of bedroom, spread between the mansion and fully converted buildings in the grounds.

ROOMS: 12 en suite 25 annexe en suite **FACILITIES:** Indoor swimming (H) Outdoor swimming (H) Golf 18 Tennis (hard) Fishing Squash Snooker Sauna Solarium Gym Croquet lawn Putting green Hairdressing Beauty treatment Massage Indoor tennis **CONF:** Board 20 **PARKING:** 60 **NOTES:** No dogs (ex guide dogs) No children 8yrs No smoking in restaurant **CARDS:**

CHOLLERFORD, Northumberland Map 12 NY97

★★★73% Swallow George Hotel

SWALLOW HOTELS

NE46 4EW
☎ 01434 681611 01434 681727
e-mail: info@swallowhotels.com
Dir: *0.25m W of Hexham turn off A69 onto A6079, follow road NW for 4m until crossroads, turn left onto B6318, hotel 0.25m on right hand side over bridge*

This hotel is situated where the old Roman road crosses the Tyne, in terraced gardens running down to the river. Comfort and hospitality are strong features. Accommodation is stylish and well equipped; some rooms overlook the river and gardens. The Riverside restaurant serves fine food and there is also a cocktail lounge.

ROOMS: 47 en suite (5 fmly) No smoking in 19 bedrooms s £85-£110; d £120-£150 (incl. bkfst) * LB **FACILITIES:** STV Indoor swimming (H) Fishing Sauna Solarium Gym Putting green Jacuzzi/spa Jogging track Exercise equipment Xmas **CONF:** Thtr 60 Class 30 Board 32 Del from £99 * **PARKING:** 70 **NOTES:** No smoking in restaurant Civ Wed 80 **CARDS:**

CHORLEY, Lancashire Map 07 SD5

★★★70% Shaw Hill Hotel Golf & Country Club

Preston Rd, Whittle-le-Woods PR6 7PP
☎ 01257 269221 01257 261223
e-mail: info@shaw-hill.co.uk
Dir: *from Chorley on A6, then signs for A49, at lights turn left past golf course, left to Dawson Ln. At T-junct go right. Hotel 50yds on right*

A championship golf course is just one of the attractions at this privately owned hotel. The Georgian mansion has been sympathetically extended and bedrooms are categorised accordin to their size and view. Two are full suites. Facilities include a choic of bars and a well appointed restaurant, overlooking the golf course.

ROOMS: 26 en suite 4 annexe en suite (1 fmly) s £68-£100; d £88-£12 (incl. bkfst) * LB **FACILITIES:** STV Indoor swimming (H) Golf 18 Snooker Sauna Solarium Gym Putting green Jacuzzi/spa Beauty salon Hairdresser **CONF:** Thtr 350 Class 100 Board 150 Del from £95 * **PARKING:** 200 **NOTES:** No dogs (ex guide dogs) Closed 24-27 Dec Civ Wed 200 **CARDS:**

See advert on opposite pa

★★★69% *Park Hall*

Best Western

Park Hall Rd, Charnock Richard PR7 5LP
☎ 01257 452090 01257 451838
Dir: *off A49 W of village. Follow brown tourist signs from M6/M61*

Situated beside the Camelot Theme Park, the hotel provides a choice of well equipped bedrooms ranging from modern contemporary rooms to themed and cottage style accommodation Guests have the choice of eating in the Park View Restaurant or less formally in the American themed Sam's Diner.

ROOMS: 54 en suite 84 annexe en suite (59 fmly) No smoking in 11 bedrooms **FACILITIES:** STV Indoor swimming (H) Sauna Solarium Gy Pool table Jacuzzi/spa Steam room Weights room **CONF:** Thtr 700 Clas 230 Board 50 **SERVICES:** Lift **PARKING:** 2600 **NOTES:** No dogs (ex guide dogs) **CARDS:**

See advert under PRESTO

Welcome Lodge

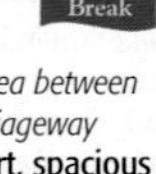

Welcome Break, Charnock Richard - M6, Mill Ln PR7 5LR
☎ 01257 791746 01257 793596
Dir: *on north-bound side of the Welcome Break service area between junct 27 & 28 of the M6. Accessible from south-bound carriageway*

This modern building offers accommodation in smart, spacious and well equipped bedrooms, suitable for families and businessmen, and all with en suite bathrooms. Refreshments may be taken at the nearby family restaurant. For further details and the Welcome Break phone number, consult the Hotel Groups page

ROOMS: 100 en suite d fr £45 * **CONF:** Thtr 30 Board 20

Premier Lodge

PREMIER LODG

Malt House farm, Moss Ln,
Whittle le Woods PR6 8AB
☎ 0870 700 1354 0870 700 1355

Premier Lodge offers modern, well equipped, en suite accommodation suitable for both business and leisure travellers. Meals can be taken at the adjacent popular restaurant and bar which is fully licensed. For further details, consult the Hotel Groups page.

ROOMS: 60 en suite d £42 *

Premier Lodge (Chorley South)

Bolton Rd PR7 4AB
☎ 0870 700 1352 Fax 0870 700 1353
Premier Lodge offers modern, well equipped, en suite accommodation suitable for both business and leisure travellers. Meals can be taken at the adjacent popular restaurant and bar which is fully licensed. For further details, consult the Hotel Groups page.
ROOMS: 29 en suite d £42 *

Travelodge

Preston Rd, Clayton-le-Woods PR6 7JB
☎ 01772 311963
Dir: *from M6 junc28 take B5256 for approx 2m, next to Halfway House public house*
This modern building offers accommodation in smart, spacious and well equipped bedrooms, all with en suite bathrooms. Refreshments may be taken at the nearby family restaurant. For further details and the Travelodge phone number, consult the Hotel Groups page.
ROOMS: 40 en suite

CHRISTCHURCH, Dorset — Map 04 SZ19

★★★ 74% Waterford Lodge

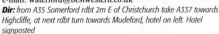

87 Bure Ln, Friars Cliff, Mudeford BH23 4DN
☎ 01425 272948 & 278801 Fax 01425 279130
e-mail: waterford@bestwestern.co.uk
Dir: *from A35 Somerford rdbt 2m E of Christchurch take A337 towards Highcliffe, at next rdbt turn towards Mudeford, hotel on left. Hotel signposted*

Situated within easy reach of Christchurch, the hotel is popular with business guests as well as holiday makers. It offers attractive, spacious bedrooms, a comfortable bar lounge overlooking the gardens and a well appointed restaurant.
ROOMS: 18 en suite (1 fmly) s fr £82; d fr £95 * LB **FACILITIES:** STV **CONF:** Thtr 100 Class 48 Board 36 Del from £105.75 * **PARKING:** 38 **NOTES:** No smoking in restaurant Closed 27 Dec-02 Jan **CARDS:**

★★★ 67% The Avonmouth

95 Mudeford BH23 3NT
☎ 0870 400 8120 Fax 01202 479004
e-mail: heritagehotels-mudeford_christchurch.avonmouth@forte-hotels.com
Dir: *approaching Christchurch on A35 from Lyndhurst, left at rdbt on A337 to Highcliffe, right at next rdbt, follow road for approx 1.5m, hotel on left*
In a superb location alongside Mudeford Quay, this friendly hotel offers smart garden rooms with their own small patios. A number of bedrooms in the main house overlook the Quay. Modern facilities and decor enhance overall comfort. Traditional public

continued on p162

CHRISTCHURCH, continued

areas are comfortable and very well cooked meals are served in the lovely restaurant.
ROOMS: 26 en suite 14 annexe en suite No smoking in 14 bedrooms s £70-£90; d £110-£130 * LB **FACILITIES:** Outdoor swimming (H) Croquet lawn Putting green Golf practice net entertainment Xmas **CONF:** Thtr 60 Class 25 Board 24 Del from £110 * **PARKING:** 80 **NOTES:** No smoking in restaurant Civ Wed 70
CARDS:

★★68% Fisherman's Haunt
Sailsbury Rd, Winkton BH23 7AS
☎ 01202 477283 & 484071 📠 01202 478883
Dir: *2.5m N on B3347*
The bedrooms, two with four-poster beds, offer exceptional standards of comfort, decor and furnishing. A few rooms are in the main house, but most are in two attractive cottages. The public areas include a lively bar and a restaurant.
ROOMS: 4 en suite 14 annexe en suite (3 fmly) No smoking in 6 bedrooms s £48; d £64 (incl. bkfst) * LB **FACILITIES:** STV **PARKING:** 75 **NOTES:** No smoking in restaurant Closed 25 Dec
CARDS:

CHURCHILL, Somerset — Map 03 ST45

★★62% Winston Manor
Bristol Rd BS25 5NL
☎ 01934 852348 📠 01934 852033
Dir: *On A38 100yds N of junction with A368 Bath to Weston-Super-Mare*
This small hotel is run in a friendly and relaxed manner by the resident proprietors. It is conveniently located for both Bristol International airport and the many local attractions. Bedrooms, including many on the ground floor, are neatly decorated and well equipped. The dinner menu includes an interesting selection of well prepared fresh home cooking.
ROOMS: 14 en suite (1 fmly) No smoking in 4 bedrooms s fr £45; d £55-£75 (incl. bkfst) * LB **CONF:** Thtr 40 Class 30 Board 30 **PARKING:** 24 **NOTES:** No smoking in restaurant
CARDS:

CHURCH STRETTON, Shropshire — Map 07 SO49

★★★66% Stretton Hall Hotel
All Stretton SY6 6HG
☎ 01694 723224 📠 01694 724365
e-mail: charlie@strettonhall.freeserve.co.uk
Dir: *from Shrewsbury, travelling along the A49, turn right onto B4370 signed to All Stretton, hotel in 1m on left opposite The Yew Tree PH*

A fine 18th-century country house standing in spacious gardens. Original oak panelling features throughout the lounge bar, lounge and halls. Bedrooms are traditionally furnished yet have modern facilities. Family and four-poster rooms are available and the restaurant has been tastefully refurbished.
ROOMS: 12 en suite (1 fmly) s £40-£70; d £55-£80 (incl. bkfst) * LB **FACILITIES:** Xmas **CONF:** Thtr 60 Class 24 Board 18 Del from £69 * **PARKING:** 70 **NOTES:** No smoking in restaurant
CARDS:

★★69% Mynd House
Ludlow Rd, Little Stretton SY6 6RB
☎ 01694 722212 📠 01694 724180
e-mail: myndhouse@go2.co.uk
Dir: *off A49 onto B4370 and follow signs for Little Stretton, hotel 0.75m on left just beyond Raglett Inn*
A large Edwardian house reached via a steep driveway. The attractive bedrooms have many thoughtful extras and are well equipped. Two suites are available. Day rooms comprise a comfortable lounge, pleasant bar and attractive, traditional dining room.
ROOMS: 7 en suite (2 fmly) No smoking in all bedrooms s £40-£70; d £60-£120 (incl. bkfst) * LB **FACILITIES:** Jacuzzi/spa **CONF:** Board 20 **PARKING:** 8 **NOTES:** No children 10yrs No smoking in restaurant
CARDS:

CHURT, Surrey — Map 04 SU83

★★★68% Frensham Pond Hotel

Bacon Ln GU10 2QD
☎ 01252 795161 📠 01252 792631
Dir: *from A3 turn right onto A287. After 4m turn left at 'Beware Horses' sign to hotel 0.25m along Pond Lane*

The hotel has a picturesque setting overlooking Frensham Pond with its ducks, swans and geese. Built in the 15th century as a private residence, it offers modern facilities including a leisure club, quality dining and 24-hour room service. All rooms are doubles, garden suites offer family accommodation overlooking the lawns.
ROOMS: 39 en suite 12 annexe en suite s £75-£95; d £85-£110 (incl. cont bkfst) * LB **FACILITIES:** Indoor swimming (H) Squash Sauna Solarium Gym Pool table Jacuzzi/spa Steam room Xmas **CONF:** Thtr 120 Class 45 Board 40 Del from £110 * **PARKING:** 120 **NOTES:** No dogs (ex guide dogs) **CARDS:**

See advert under FARNHAM

★★70% Pride of the Valley
Jumps Rd GU10 2LE
☎ 01428 605799 📠 01428 605875
This friendly hotel has been totally refurbished in an eclectic style. Bedrooms are all individually decorated with such themes as nautical or Far Eastern. Contrasting in style, the bar and restaurant both offer a good menu and high levels of comfort.
ROOMS: 13 en suite 3 annexe en suite (1 fmly) No smoking in all bedrooms s £75; d £95 (incl. bkfst) * LB **FACILITIES:** Xmas **PARKING:** 85 **NOTES:** No dogs No smoking in restaurant
CARDS:

CIRENCESTER, Gloucestershire Map 04 SP00

★★★69% ❀ The Crown of Crucis
Ampney Crucis GL7 5RS
☎ 01285 851806 📠 01285 851735
e-mail: info@thecrownofcrucis.co.uk
Dir: *take A417 to Fairford, hotel is approx 2.5m on left hand side of road*
This delightful hotel consists of two buildings, one a 16th-century coaching inn, which now houses the bar and restaurant, and a more modern bedroom block which surrounds a courtyard. Rooms are attractively appointed and offer modern facilities, and the restaurant serves good imaginative food.
ROOMS: 25 en suite (2 fmly) No smoking in 10 bedrooms s fr £62; d fr £88 (incl. bkfst) LB **FACILITIES:** Free membership of local leisure centre **CONF:** Thtr 80 Class 40 Board 25 Del from £89.50 * **PARKING:** 82 **NOTES:** No smoking in restaurant Closed 24-30 Dec
CARDS:

★★★68% ❀ Stratton House

Gloucester Rd GL7 2LE
☎ 01285 651761 📠 01285 640024
Dir: *M4 junct 15, A419 to Cirencester, hotel on left on A417. M5 exit 11 to Cheltenham, follow B4070 to A417, hotel on right*
This attractive 17th-century manor house offers a wing of spacious 'premier' rooms and well equipped standard rooms in the main house. Day rooms include a split-level drawing room and a traditional restaurant overlooking the garden. Food is well prepared and menus offer a wide choice of dishes.
ROOMS: 41 en suite No smoking in 19 bedrooms s fr £60; d fr £120 (incl. bkfst & dinner) * LB **FACILITIES:** Xmas **CONF:** Thtr 150 Class 50 Board 40 Del from £115 * **PARKING:** 100 **NOTES:** No smoking in restaurant **CARDS:**

★★❀❀ The New Inn At Coln
GL7 5AN
☎ 01285 750651 📠 01285 750657
e-mail: stay@new-inn.co.uk
(For full entry see Coln St-Aldwyns)

CLACTON-ON-SEA, Essex Map 05 TM11

★★68% Esplanade Hotel
27-29 Marine Pde East CO15 1UU
☎ 01255 220450 📠 01255 221800
Dir: *enter Clacton on Sea on the A133 follow sign to Sea Front (Carnarvon Rd) at sea front turn right, hotel on right in 50yds*
In a seafront location, the hotel is an easy walk from the pier, the town centre and local attractions. Bedrooms are furnished and decorated to a high standard and many have sea views. There is a comfortable lounge bar and Coasters restaurant also offers sea views.
ROOMS: 29 en suite (2 fmly) s £28-£40; d £56-£76 (incl. bkfst) * LB **FACILITIES:** Xmas **CONF:** Class 50 Del from £45 * **PARKING:** 13 **NOTES:** No dogs (ex guide dogs) No smoking in restaurant Civ Wed 70
CARDS:

★73% Chudleigh
13 Agate Rd, Marine Pde West CO15 1RA
☎ 01255 425407 📠 01255 425407
Dir: *follow signs to Town Centre, Seafront and Pier. Turn right at seafront and then right again into Agate Rd after crossing traffic lights at Pier*
This family run hotel is a relaxing oasis close to the pier and the bustling seafront. It offers spruced and tidy accommodation. There is a comfortable lounge where drinks are served and home cooked meals are served in the spacious restaurant.
ROOMS: 10 en suite (2 fmly) No smoking in 2 bedrooms s £37-£39; d £50-£52 (incl. bkfst) * **PARKING:** 7 **NOTES:** No smoking in restaurant RS Oct-Mar **CARDS:**

CLANFIELD, Oxfordshire Map 04 SP20

★★★71% ❀❀ Plough at Clanfield
Bourton Rd OX18 2RB
☎ 01367 810222 📠 01367 810596
e-mail: ploughatclanfield@hotmail.com
Dir: *on edge of village at junct of A4095/B4020*
An archetypal stone-built Elizabethan manor house retaining many original features. The cosy bar has two log-burning fires and each of the individually-styled bedrooms is well equipped with extra touches such as decanters of sherry and bathrobes. Food is taken seriously and the kitchen brigade cooks with flair. A friendly yet unstuffy professional atmosphere prevails.
ROOMS: 6 en suite s £75-£95; d £95-£125 (incl. bkfst) * LB **FACILITIES:** Xmas **PARKING:** 30 **NOTES:** No dogs (ex guide dogs) No children 12yrs No smoking in restaurant Closed 25-30 December
CARDS:

CLAVERDON, Warwickshire Map 04 SP16

★★★68% ❀ Ardencote Manor Hotel & Country Club
Lye Green Rd CV35 8LS
☎ 01926 843111 📠 01926 842646
e-mail: hotel@ardencote.com
Dir: *follow sign post direction towards Shrewley off A4189 in centre of Claverdon, Hotel 0.5m on right*
The range of public areas and leisure facilities available at Ardencote are unsurpassed in a hotel of this size. Bedrooms are well equipped and decorated with pretty fabrics and smart furnishings. There is a varied choice of eating options; the Oak Room offers an imaginative modern menu with formal service.

continued on p164

CLAVERDON, continued

Informal snacks and meals are served in the members' bar and at the lakeside sports lodge.

Ardencote Manor Hotel & Country Club, Claverdon

ROOMS: 18 en suite (1 fmly) No smoking in 2 bedrooms s £87.50; d £135 (incl. bkfst) * LB **FACILITIES:** STV Indoor swimming (H) Tennis (hard) Fishing Squash Sauna Solarium Gym Putting green Jacuzzi/spa Trout fishing 9 hole golf from mid 2001 Xmas **CONF:** Thtr 120 Class 60 Board 50 Del from £100 * **PARKING:** 120 **NOTES:** No dogs (ex guide dogs) No smoking in restaurant Civ Wed 150

CARDS:

See advert under WARWICK

CLEARWELL, Gloucestershire — Map 03 SO50

★★★67% Wyndham Arms

GL16 8JT

☎ 01594 833666 📠 01594 836450

Dir: *in centre of village on the B4231*

This charming village inn traces its history back over 600 years. Exposed stone walls, original beams and an impressive inglenook fireplace in the bar, add to its character. Most of the bedrooms are in a modern extension close to the main entrance and a new suite has been added to the main house. There are both bar and restaurant menus.

ROOMS: 6 en suite 12 annexe en suite (4 fmly) s £50.50; d £100 (incl. bkfst) * LB **CONF:** Thtr 56 Class 30 Board 22 Del from £57.50 * **PARKING:** 54 **NOTES:** No smoking in restaurant

CARDS:

★★71% ® *Tudor Farmhouse Hotel & Restaurant*

GL16 8JS

☎ 01594 833046 📠 01594 837093

This idyllic and charming house conceals a host of original characteristics including exposed stonework, oak beams, wall panelling and open inglenook fireplaces. Good quality food is served in the delightful restaurant. Bedrooms are individually styled and thoughtfully equipped, located in the main house and two converted cottages.

ROOMS: 6 en suite 7 annexe en suite (3 fmly) No smoking in 6 bedrooms **PARKING:** 20 **NOTES:** No smoking in restaurant Closed 24-30 Dec **CARDS:**

CLEATOR, Cumbria — Map 11 NY01

★★★76% *Ennerdale Country House*

CA23 3DT

☎ 01946 813907 📠 01946 815260

Best Western

Dir: *take A5086 towards Egremont after approximately 14m arrive at Cleator Moor. Stay on the A5086 for a further mile until village of Cleator*

This popular hotel provides stylish, well equipped bedrooms that come in a variety of sizes and include split-level rooms with four-posters. The smart restaurant offers an appealing menu of both classical and contemporary cuisine. There is also a comfortable cocktail lounge and a less formal bar.

ROOMS: 30 en suite (4 fmly) No smoking in 4 bedrooms **FACILITIES:** STV **CONF:** Thtr 150 Class 100 Board 40 **PARKING:** 65 **NOTES:** No smoking in restaurant **CARDS:**

CLECKHEATON, West Yorkshire — Map 07 SE12

★★★64% The Whitcliffe

Prospect Rd BD19 3HD

☎ 01274 873022 📠 01274 870376

e-mail: info@thewhitcliffehotel.co.uk

Dir: *M62 junct 26, follow A638 towards Dewsbury, through 1st set of lights then right into Mount Street, up to 'T' junction, turn right then 1st left*

This popular commercial hotel in Cleckheaton is close to junction 26 of the M62. All rooms are en suite and well equipped; public areas offer a variety of amenities, including the Tudor Conference Room. In addition to the main restaurant there is a public bar. Hospitality is a major strength here.

ROOMS: 34 en suite 6 annexe en suite (1 fmly) No smoking in 17 bedrooms s £35-£49.50; d £49.50-£59.50 (incl. bkfst) * LB **FACILITIES:** STV Pool table ch fac Xmas **CONF:** Thtr 90 Class 60 Board 35 Del from £75 * **PARKING:** 150 **NOTES:** No dogs (ex guide dogs) No smoking in restaurant **CARDS:**

CLEETHORPES, Lincolnshire — Map 08 TA30

★★★70% ® Kingsway

Kingsway DN35 0AE

☎ 01472 601122 📠 01472 601381

Dir: *leave A180 at Grimsby, head to Cleethorpes seafront. The hotel is at jct of The Kingsway and Queen Parade (A1098)*

This seafront hotel has been in the same family for four generations and continues to provide traditional comfort and professional friendly service. The lounges are comfortable and good food is served in the pleasant dining room. Most of the bedrooms are of good comfortable proportions, and all are bright and pleasantly furnished.

ROOMS: 50 en suite s £58-£75; d £84-£90 (incl. bkfst) * LB **FACILITIES:** STV **CONF:** Thtr 22 Board 18 Del from £85 * **SERVICES:** Lift **PARKING:** 50 **NOTES:** No dogs (ex guide dogs) No children 5yrs Closed 25-26 December **CARDS:**

CLEOBURY MORTIMER, Shropshire — Map 07 SO67

★★★71% ® Redfern

DY14 8AA

☎ 01299 270395 📠 01299 271011

e-mail: info@redferon-hotel.co.uk

Dir: *on A4117 midway between Kidderminster & Ludlow*

This delightful hotel offers warm hospitality and excellent cuisine to its guests. Well equipped accommodation includes six rooms in a purpose-built cottage-style annexe. Other facilities include a restaurant, a pleasant bar and a roof-top conservatory doubling as a coffee shop, which serves breakfast.

ROOMS: 5 en suite 6 annexe en suite (4 fmly) s £53-£65; d £80-£101 (incl. bkfst) * LB **FACILITIES:** Clay pigeon shooting Pheasant shooting Xmas **CONF:** Thtr 30 Class 30 Board 20 Del from £70 * **PARKING:** 20 **NOTES:** No smoking in restaurant **CARDS:**

Fancy a Singapore Sling? Bar staff in five star hotels should be skilled cocktail mixers.

CLEVEDON, Somerset
Map 03 ST47

★★★65% *Walton Park*
Wellington Ter BS21 7BL
☎ 01275 874253 🖷 01275 343577
Quietly located, this popular Victorian hotel enjoys glorious views across the Bristol Channel towards Wales. A friendly and relaxed style of service is offered from the long-serving staff. Bedrooms are well decorated and equipped including many extra facilities. A high standard of home-cooked food is served in the comfortable restaurant.
ROOMS: 40 en suite (4 fmly) **FACILITIES:** STV **CONF:** Thtr 150 Class 80 Board 80 **SERVICES:** Lift **PARKING:** 50
CARDS:

CLIMPING, West Sussex
Map 04 SU90

★★★76% Bailiffscourt
BN17 5RW
☎ 01903 723511 🖷 01903 723107
e-mail: bailiffscourt@hshotels.co.uk
Dir: *turn off A259 Littlehampton to Bognor road marked Climping Beach & Bailiffscourt. The hotel is 0.5 of a mile on right.*
A truly unique 'medieval' hotel created in the 1930s from original 13th-century building materials and other salvaged antique features. Inside, a number of inter-connecting rooms provide comfortable lounges. The antique theme is carried through to the beamed restaurant which serves a consistently good standard of food. Bedrooms come with antique oak furniture and embroidered fabrics that are very much in sympathy with the hotel's style.
ROOMS: 9 en suite 22 annexe en suite s £130-£295; d £145-£315 (incl. bkfst) * LB **FACILITIES:** STV Outdoor swimming (H) Tennis (hard) Pool table Croquet lawn Golf practice area Clay pigeon Xmas **CONF:** Thtr 50 Class 20 Board 22 Del £180 * **PARKING:** 60 **NOTES:** No smoking in restaurant Civ Wed 70 **CARDS:**

CLITHEROE, Lancashire
Map 07 SD74

★★★67% Stirk House
BB7 4LJ
☎ 01200 445581 🖷 01200 445744
Dir: *W of village, on A59. Hotel 0.5m on left*
In secluded grounds, well back from the A59, this hotel offers bedrooms in a variety of styles, with delegate rooms providing especially good value. The main house has comfortable lounges and sitting areas. In the restaurant guests will be tempted by the imaginative menu. Staff throughout are friendly and attentive.
ROOMS: 40 en suite 10 annexe en suite (2 fmly) No smoking in 25 bedrooms **FACILITIES:** STV Indoor swimming (H) Squash Sauna Solarium Gym Jacuzzi/spa entertainment **CONF:** Thtr 300 Class 150 Board 50 Del from £75 * **PARKING:** 130 **NOTES:** No dogs (ex guide dogs) Civ Wed 150 **CARDS:**

★★68% Shireburn Arms
Whalley Rd, Hurst Green BB7 9QJ
☎ 01254 826518 🖷 01254 826208
Dir: *on B6243 at the entrance to Hurst Green village*
This family run inn is peacefully situated in the Ribble valley, just a short drive from Clitheroe. Attractively decorated bedrooms are spacious, well equipped and comfortably furnished. The airy restaurant has fine views over open fields and guests can choose between dining there or in one of the inviting bar lounges.
ROOMS: 18 en suite (3 fmly) s £45-£55; d £65-£80 (incl. bkfst) * LB **FACILITIES:** Xmas **CONF:** Thtr 100 Class 50 Board 50 **PARKING:** 71 **NOTES:** No smoking in restaurant Civ Wed 80
CARDS:

CLOVELLY, Devon
Map 02 SS32

★★72% Red Lion
The Quay EX39 5TF
☎ 01237 431237 🖷 01237 431044
e-mail: redlion@clovelly.co.uk
Dir: *turn off A39 at Clovelly Cross on to B3237. Proceed to bottom of hill and take first turning on left by white rails to harbour*
This quaint 18th-century inn is a tranquil haven that is regularly frequented by local villagers. In the restaurant, an imaginative fixed price menu is offered each evening, using the best fresh local ingredients where ever possible, the fish coming straight from the sea. Bedrooms offer high levels of comfort and many have glorious views.
ROOMS: 11 en suite (2 fmly) s £76.75-£86.75; d £123.50-£143.50 (incl. bkfst & dinner) * LB **FACILITIES:** Xmas **PARKING:** 11 **NOTES:** No dogs (ex guide dogs) No smoking in restaurant
CARDS:

★★71% New Inn
High St EX39 5TQ
☎ 01237 431303 🖷 01237 431636
e-mail: newinn@clovelly.co.uk
Dir: *at Clovelly Cross, turn off A39 onto B3237. Follow road down hill for 1.5m. Turn right at sign "All vehicles for Clovelly" and park in main car park*
In the heart of this historic fishing village, overlooking the beauty of Barnstaple Bay, the New Inn sits on the cobbled High Street. Carefully renovated and retaining much of its original character, both bedrooms and public areas are smartly presented with quality furnishings. Meals may be taken in the elegant restaurant or the popular Upalongs bar.

continued on p166

CLOVELLY, continued

ROOMS: 8 en suite (2 fmly) s £56; d £82 (incl. bkfst) * LB **FACILITIES:** Xmas **NOTES:** No dogs (ex guide dogs) No smoking in restaurant **CARDS:**

COALVILLE, Leicestershire Map 08 SK41

★★65% Charnwood Arms

Beveridge Ln, Bardon Hill LE67 2TB
☎ 01530 813644 01530 815425
Dir: *1m W of junct 22 of M1, on A511*
Conveniently located for access to the M1, this popular inn offers pleasant well furnished courtyard accommodation. Public areas in the main building include a spacious lounge bar and dining areas in which hearty fare and cask conditioned ales are served.
ROOMS: 34 en suite No smoking in 4 bedrooms s £34.70-£44.45; d £39.65-£49.40 (incl. bkfst) * **CONF:** Thtr 200 Class 100 Board 60 **PARKING:** 150 **NOTES:** No dogs (ex guide dogs) No smoking in restaurant Civ Wed **CARDS:**

See advert on page 165

COBHAM, Surrey Map 04 TQ16

Premier Lodge

Portsmouth Rd, Fairmile KT11 1BW
☎ 0870 700 1432 0870 7001433
Premier Lodge offers modern, well equipped, en suite accommodation suitable for both business and leisure travellers. Meals can be taken at the adjacent popular restaurant and bar which is fully licensed. For further details, consult the Hotel Groups page.
ROOMS: 48 en suite d £49.50 *

COCKERMOUTH, Cumbria Map 11 NY13

★★★71% The Trout

Crown St CA13 0EJ
☎ 01900 823591 01900 827514
e-mail: enquires@trouthotel.co.uk
Dir: *next to Wordsworth House and Mineral Museum*
This smart hotel lies by the banks of the River Derwent, next to Wordsworth's birthplace. Public areas, which include an attractive restaurant, are traditionally styled, while bedrooms in the original building come in a variety of sizes. Dinner provides an ample choice with creative dishes found on both the carte and table d'hôte menus.
ROOMS: 30 en suite (4 fmly) No smoking in 12 bedrooms s £60-£105; d £85-£140 (incl. bkfst) * LB **FACILITIES:** STV Fishing Xmas **CONF:** Thtr 50 Class 30 Board 25 Del from £109.95 * **PARKING:** 60 **NOTES:** No smoking in restaurant Civ Wed 60 **CARDS:**

★★★64% *The Manor House Hotel*

Crown St CA13 0EH
☎ 01900 828663 01900 828679
Dir: *turn off A66 at Cockermouth junct, continue 0.75m to T junct to hotel 700yds on left*
This is a lovely old stone house set back from the road and situated on the edge of the town centre. The lounge is warmly decorated, and is furnished with deep winged armchairs and sofas. The first floor bedrooms are large, and have additional in-room facilities.
ROOMS: 13 en suite (1 fmly) **PARKING:** 20 **NOTES:** No smoking in restaurant **CARDS:**

★★64% Broughton Craggs

Great Broughton CA13 0XW
☎ 01900 824400 01900 825350
e-mail: peter_john.caddy@virgin.net
Dir: *leave A66 2m W of town, signposted Great Broughton. Over River Derwent and up Little Brow to T-junction. Turn right.*
Tucked away in its own landscaped grounds, this hotel enjoys splendid views across the Derwent valley to the distant fells. Well equipped, comfortable bedrooms together with good hospitality and versatile public areas make for an enjoyable stay.
ROOMS: 14 en suite (1 fmly) s fr £52.50; d fr £70 (incl. bkfst) * LB **FACILITIES:** STV **CONF:** Thtr 120 Class 80 Board 60 **PARKING:** 80 **NOTES:** No dogs (ex guide dogs) Civ Wed 150 **CARDS:**

COGGESHALL, Essex Map 05 TL82

★★★69% White Hart

Market End CO6 1NH
☎ 01376 561654 01376 561789
e-mail: wharthotel@ndirect.co.uk
Dir: *from A12 follow through Kelvedon & then take B1024 to Coggeshall*
Parts of this former coaching inn date back to the early 15th century. The whole hotel has since been modernised and now offers spacious, comfortable and stylish bedrooms. The bar is the centre point of the hotel and is popular with locals and residents. A wide selection of bar food is available. The restaurant is brimming with character and offers an authentic Italian menu.
ROOMS: 18 en suite (1 fmly) s £61.50-£66.50; d fr £97 (incl. bkfst) * LB **FACILITIES:** STV **CONF:** Thtr 30 Class 10 Board 22 Del from £97.50 * **PARKING:** 47 **NOTES:** No dogs **CARDS:**

See advert on opposite page

COLCHESTER, Essex Map 05 TL92

★★★72% George

116 High St CO1 1JD
☎ 01206 578494 01206 761732
Dir: *200yds beyond Town Hall on the High Street*
An elegant 15th-century coaching inn located in the centre of town. Individually decorated bedrooms offer a high level of comfort with quality furnishings and fabrics. The decor in the lounge and bar areas is stylishly modern yet blends harmoniously with the character of the building. Guests have a wide choice of dishes and daily specials served in the attractive restaurant, or a more simple bar snacks menu served in the lounge.
ROOMS: 47 en suite No smoking in 32 bedrooms s £52.50-£92.50; d £52.50-£102.50 * **FACILITIES:** STV **CONF:** Thtr 70 Class 30 Board 30 Del from £118.95 * **PARKING:** 46
CARDS:

★★★68% Butterfly

Old Ipswich Rd CO7 7QY
☎ 01206 230900 01206 231095
e-mail: colbutterfly@lineone.net
Dir: *A12/A120 Ardleigh Junction*
Conveniently located for major routes to London, the Port of Harwich and near two major business parks, this hotel is well situated for the business traveller. There are a variety of spacious bedrooms, each featuring a useful range of extra facilities, and a number of function rooms.
ROOMS: 50 en suite (2 fmly) No smoking in 11 bedrooms d fr £67.50 * LB **FACILITIES:** STV **CONF:** Thtr 80 Class 40 Board 40 **PARKING:** 85 **NOTES:** No dogs (ex guide dogs) **CARDS:**

★★★68% **Marks Tey**
London Rd, Marks Tey CO6 1DU
☎ 01206 210001 Fax 01206 212167
e-mail: sales@patenhotels.freeserve.co.uk
Dir: *off A12/A120 junction*
This modern, well kept hotel is situated just off the A12, close to the historic town of Colchester. The bedrooms are comfortable and furnished to a high standard. There is a wide range of function rooms and a new leisure centre.
ROOMS: 110 en suite (12 fmly) No smoking in 42 bedrooms s £72; d £80 * LB **FACILITIES:** STV Indoor swimming (H) Tennis (hard) Sauna Solarium Gym Pool table Jacuzzi/spa entertainment **CONF:** Thtr 200 Class 100 Board 60 Del from £95 * **PARKING:** 200 **NOTES:** No dogs (ex guide dogs) Civ Wed 160 **CARDS:**

★★★65% ***Posthouse Colchester***
Posthouse
Abbotts Ln, Eight Ash Green CO6 3QL
☎ 0870 400 9020 Fax 01206 766577
Dir: *junct A1124 of A12 signposted to Halstead*
This modern, purpose built hotel is conveniently located on the outskirts of Britain's oldest recorded town. Bedrooms are practically furnished and equipped with a useful range of in-room facilities. The public areas consist of a bar, restaurant, a range of meeting rooms and a well equipped health club.
ROOMS: 110 en suite (30 fmly) No smoking in 58 bedrooms **FACILITIES:** Indoor swimming (H) Sauna Solarium Gym Jacuzzi/spa Steam room Treatment rooms **CONF:** Thtr 150 Class 70 Board 60 **PARKING:** 150 **CARDS:**

★★★64% **The Stoke by Nayland Club Hotel**
Keepers Ln, Leavenheath CO6 4PZ
☎ 01206 262836 Fax 01206 263356
e-mail: info@golf-club.co.uk
Dir: *Turn off A134 onto B1068, hotel 0.75 miles on right*
Located in the heart of Constable country and within easy reach of local places of interest, this hotel is surrounded by 300 acres of wooded golf courses and lakes. Well served by road and rail networks, it is also ideal for the business traveller.
ROOMS: 30 en suite (4 fmly) No smoking in 15 bedrooms s £69; d £89 * LB **FACILITIES:** STV Indoor swimming (H) Golf 18 Fishing Squash Snooker Sauna Solarium Gym Putting green Jacuzzi/spa steam room **CONF:** Thtr 30 Class 15 Board 24 Del from £90 * **SERVICES:** Lift **PARKING:** 300 **NOTES:** No dogs (ex guide dogs) No smoking in restaurant **CARDS:**

★★★63% **Quality Hotel**
CHOICE HOTELS EUROPE
East St CO1 2TS
☎ 01206 865022 Fax 01206 792884
e-mail: qhotel@netscapeonline.co.uk
The hotel is a converted flour mill set alongside the river Colne and within walking distance of the town centre. Much of the original character of the building has been retained, although the style today is fairly modern. Bedrooms are tastefully decorated and offer all the modern conveniences. Public areas include a lounge, residents' bar and the conservatory Quayside restaurant.
ROOMS: 58 en suite No smoking in 6 bedrooms s £39.95; d £39.95-£95 (incl. bkfst) * **FACILITIES:** Xmas **CONF:** Thtr 80 Class 20 Board 35 Del from £85 * **SERVICES:** Lift **PARKING:** 100 **NOTES:** No smoking in restaurant **CARDS:**

Popped the question? Hotels with Civ Wed in their entry are licensed for civil wedding ceremonies. Maximum numbers for the ceremony only are shown, e.g. Civ Wed 50

COLEFORD, Gloucestershire — Map 03 SO51

★★★71% **The Speech House**

GL16 7EL
☎ 01594 822607 Fax 01594 823658
e-mail: relax@thespeechhouse.co.uk
Dir: *on B4226 between Cinderford and Coleford*

Dating back to 1676, this former hunting lodge is tucked away in the Forest of Dean. Bedrooms, some with impressive four-poster beds, combine modern amenities with period charm. The beamed restaurant serves good, imaginative food. Additional features include a mini gym, aquaspa and conference facilities.
ROOMS: 15 en suite 17 annexe rms (10 en suite) (4 fmly) No smoking in 6 bedrooms s £42.75-£72.50; d £81.50-£179 (incl. bkfst) * LB **FACILITIES:** Golf 18 Sauna Solarium Gym Jacuzzi/spa Cricket Bridge Health Spa Xmas **CONF:** Thtr 70 Class 40 Board 40 Del £105 * **PARKING:** 70 **NOTES:** No smoking in restaurant Civ Wed **CARDS:**

COLEFORD, continued

★★62% The Angel Hotel
Market Place GL16 8AE
☎ 01594 833113 🖷 01594 832413
Dir: *access to hotel via A48 or A40*
Centrally located and close to many attractions stands this 17th-century coaching Inn. Bedrooms are all spacious and well equipped. Additional features include a bar and restaurant with a traditional feel, and 'Magnums' night club.
ROOMS: 7 en suite (1 fmly) s £32-£39; d £45-£55 (incl. bkfst) * LB **FACILITIES:** STV entertainment Xmas **PARKING:** 4
CARDS:

COLERNE, Wiltshire Map 03 ST87

Premier Collection

★★★★ Lucknam Park
SN14 8AZ
☎ 01225 742777 🖷 01225 743536
e-mail: reservations@lucknampark.co.uk
Dir: *leave M4 at junct 17, A350 to Chippenham, then A420 towards Bristol for 3m. At Ford village, turn left towards Colerne, after 3m right at crossroads*
Dating back to 1720, this magnificent Palladian mansion is set within 500 acres of glorious parkland. Style and grace are evident throughout both the elegant day rooms and the individually presented bedrooms and suites. A choice of menus offers a balanced selection of accomplished cuisine. Leisure facilities include an indoor pool, beauty salon and even an equestrian centre.
ROOMS: 23 en suite 18 annexe en suite s £150-£670; d £190-£670 * LB **FACILITIES:** STV Indoor swimming (H) Tennis (hard) Riding Snooker Sauna Solarium Gym Croquet lawn Jacuzzi/spa Whirlpool Beauty salon Steam room Hair salon Cross country course entertainment Xmas **CONF:** Thtr 24 Class 30 Board 64 Del from £230 * **PARKING:** 90 **NOTES:** No dogs (ex guide dogs) No smoking in restaurant Civ Wed 64 **CARDS:**

COLESHILL, Warwickshire Map 04 SP28

★★★65% Grimstock Country House
Gilson Rd, Gilson B46 1LJ
☎ 01675 462121 & 462161 🖷 01675 467646
e-mail: enquiries@grimstockhotel.co.uk
Dir: *turn off A446 onto B4117 to Gilson, hotel 100yds on right*
This privately owned, friendly hotel stands in its own grounds, convenient for the motorway network, Birmingham International Airport and the NEC. It provides modern well equipped bedrooms and the public rooms include a choice of restaurants. Good conference facilities are also available.

continued

ROOMS: 44 en suite (1 fmly) **FACILITIES:** STV Solarium Gym **CONF:** Thtr 100 Class 60 Board 50 Del from £105 * **PARKING:** 100 **NOTES:** No smoking in restaurant Civ Wed 90
CARDS:

COLN ST-ALDWYNS, Gloucestershire Map 04 SP10

Premier Collection

★★ The New Inn At Coln
GL7 5AN
☎ 01285 750651 🖷 01285 750657
e-mail: stay@new-inn.co.uk
Dir: *8m E of Cirencester, between Bibury and Fairford*
In a peaceful setting this delightful inn, dating back to the reign of Elizabeth I, offers genuine hospitality and enchanting bedrooms, divided between the main building and the Dovecote. Features include flagstone floors, wooden beams and inglenook fireplaces. The popular bar and restaurant serve enjoyable food prepared to a high standard.
ROOMS: 8 en suite 6 annexe en suite (1 fmly) s £68-£99; d £96-£115 (incl. bkfst) * LB **CONF:** Thtr 20 Board 12 Del from £119.50 * **PARKING:** 22 **NOTES:** No children 10 yrs No smoking in restaurant **CARDS:**

COLSTERWORTH, Lincolnshire Map 08 SK92

Travelodge
NG33 5JR
☎ 01476 861077 🖷 01476 861078
Dir: *on A1/A151 southbound at junct with B151/B676*
This modern building offers accommodation in smart, spacious and well equipped bedrooms, all with en suite bathrooms. Refreshments may be taken at the nearby family restaurant. For further details and the Travelodge phone number, consult the Hotel Groups page.
ROOMS: 31 en suite

Travelodge

COLTISHALL, Norfolk Map 09 TG21

★★77% *Norfolk Mead*
Church Ln NR12 7DN
☎ 01603 737531 🖷 01603 737521
e-mail: norfolkmead@aol.com
Dir: *from Norwich take B1150. In Coltishall turn right just beyond hump backed bridge. Hotel 600yds on right just before church*
On a quiet edge of the Norfolk Broads leading down to the River Bure lies this attractive Georgian manor house. The bedrooms are individually furnished in a mixture of designs from Edwardian to French and have lovely views of the gardens. Dinner is served in the candlelit restaurant which offers a constantly changing menu featuring local produce.

continued

ROOMS: 9 en suite (1 fmly) No smoking in all bedrooms **FACILITIES:** Outdoor swimming (H) Fishing Croquet lawn Jacuzzi/spa Beauty salon **CONF:** Thtr 30 Board 30 Del from £110 * **PARKING:** 50 **NOTES:** No smoking in restaurant **CARDS:**

COLYFORD, Devon Map 03 SY29

★★77% Swallows Eaves

EX24 6QJ
☎ 01297 553184 01297 553574
Dir: *on A3052, in centre of village, opposite village store*

This delightful hotel has built up a well deserved reputation for excellent service, food and hospitality. The bedrooms are very comfortable and attractively decorated with many thoughtful extras. The restaurant serves a daily menu of carefully prepared dishes which often use fresh local ingredients.

ROOMS: 8 en suite No smoking in all bedrooms s £40-£54; d £68-£88 (incl. bkfst) * LB **FACILITIES:** Free use of nearby Swimming Club Xmas **PARKING:** 10 **NOTES:** No dogs (ex guide dogs) No children 14yrs No smoking in restaurant RS Dec-Jan **CARDS:**

CONGLETON, Cheshire Map 07 SJ86

★★★61% Lion & Swan

Swan Bank CW12 1JR
☎ 01260 273115 01260 299270
Dir: *M6 junct 17, signed Congleton to roundabout, straight over and follow one way system round to right, hotel at top*

OLD ENGLISH INNS & HOTELS

Centrally located, this black and white half-timbered coaching inn dates back to the 16th century. It retains many original features, with numerous exposed beams and a fine carved fireplace in the lounge bar. Bedrooms vary in size and include one with a magnificent carved four poster bed.

ROOMS: 21 en suite (1 fmly) No smoking in 3 bedrooms **CONF:** Thtr 130 Class 70 Board 40 **PARKING:** 49 **NOTES:** No smoking in restaurant **CARDS:**

CONSETT, Co Durham Map 12 NZ15

★★★62% The Raven Hotel

Broomhill, Ebchester DH8 6RY
☎ 01207 562562 01207 560262
e-mail: enquiries@ravenhotel.co.uk
Dir: *on B6309, overlooking village*

Spacious, well equipped bedrooms are a feature of this modern and stylishly furnished hotel, which stands on a hillside overlooking the village. Well prepared dinners are served in the attractive conservatory restaurant and a good range of popular bar meals is available along with a range of hand pulled real ales.

ROOMS: 28 en suite (7 fmly) s fr £52; d fr £69 (incl. bkfst) * LB **FACILITIES:** STV Xmas **CONF:** Thtr 150 Class 80 Board 40 **SERVICES:** air con **PARKING:** 100 **NOTES:** No dogs (ex guide dogs) Civ Wed 140 **CARDS:**

CONSTANTINE, Cornwall & Isles of Scilly Map 02 SW72

★★70% Trengilly Wartha Inn

Nancenoy TR11 5RP
☎ 01326 340332 01326 340332
e-mail: trengilly@compuserve.com
Dir: *take A39 to Falmouth, at rdbt by Asda store in Penryn follow signs to Constantine then direction Gweek, hotel signposted to the left in 1m*

THE CIRCLE *Selected Individual Hotels* GREAT BRITAIN

A popular and busy country inn hotel, peacefully located in a designated area of outstanding natural beauty. The smart restaurant and busy bar serve fresh Cornish produce, complemented by a comprehensive wine list. Bedrooms are individual in character, two are purpose built family rooms overlooking the lake. The lounge, with its easy chairs and ample reading matter, is the place to relax in front of an open log fire.

ROOMS: 6 rms (5 en suite) 2 annexe en suite (2 fmly) No smoking in 2 bedrooms s £45; d £60-£87 (incl. bkfst) * LB **FACILITIES:** Pool table **PARKING:** 50 **NOTES:** RS 25 Dec (breakfast only) **CARDS:**

CONSTANTINE BAY, Cornwall & Isles of Scilly Map 02 SW87

★★★77% Treglos

PL28 8JH
☎ 01841 520727 01841 521163
e-mail: enquires@treglos-hotel.co.uk
Dir: *turn right at Constantine Bay stores, hotel 50yds on left*

This fine hotel has high standards of hospitality and service. A choice of comfortable lounges is available, one specifically for guests wishing to play bridge. Bedrooms vary in size, those with splendid views are always popular. The restaurant continues to provide imaginative and interesting dishes.

ROOMS: 44 en suite (12 fmly) s £70-£81; d £140-£162 (incl. bkfst & dinner) * LB **FACILITIES:** Indoor swimming (H) Snooker Pool table Croquet lawn Jacuzzi/spa Converted 'boat house' for table tennis ch fac **CONF:** Board 20 **SERVICES:** Lift **PARKING:** 58 **NOTES:** No smoking in restaurant Closed 4 Nov-16 Mar **CARDS:**

See advert under PADSTOW

COPTHORNE See Gatwick Airport

CORBRIDGE, Northumberland Map 12 NY96

★★66% *Angel Inn*

Main St NE45 5LA
☎ 01434 632119 01434 632119
Dir: *half a mile off A69, signed Corbridge*

Corbridge's oldest inn provides accommodation of modern quality and yet retains much of its original character. Guests can relax in the lounge or enjoy a drink in the snug bar. Diners are offered an excellent choice, whether in the restaurant or the lounge bar which is set up for meals. Bedrooms vary in size, but all are well equipped and smart. Staff are willing and efficient.

ROOMS: 5 en suite (2 fmly) **FACILITIES:** STV **PARKING:** 20 **NOTES:** No dogs (ex guide dogs) No smoking in restaurant **CARDS:**

CORFE CASTLE, Dorset Map 03 SY98

★★★69% Mortons House

East St BH20 5EE
☎ 01929 480988 01929 480820
e-mail: stay@mortonshouse.co.uk
Dir: *on A351 between Wareham/Swanage*

A charming hotel, Mortons House has been sensitively improved

continued on p170

CORFE CASTLE, continued

over recent years. Traditional features include an oak panelled drawing room and carved wooden friezes. Bedrooms are decorated with style, individuality and taste. Some accomplished cuisine is on offer.
ROOMS: 14 en suite 3 annexe en suite (1 fmly) No smoking in 3 bedrooms d £111-£116 (incl. bkfst) * LB **FACILITIES:** Jacuzzi/spa Xmas **CONF:** Thtr 45 Board 20 Del from £100 * **PARKING:** 40 **NOTES:** No smoking in restaurant **CARDS:**

C

CORNHILL-ON-TWEED, Northumberland Map 12 NT83

★★★71% Tillmouth Park Country House
TD12 4UU
☎ 01890 882255 01890 882540
e-mail: reception@tillmouthpark.force9.co.uk
Dir: *turn off A1(M) at East Ord rdbt at Berwick-upon-Tweed and follow A698 towards Cornhill and Coldstream. Hotel 9m along A698 on left*
Built in 1882, this stunning 'folly' is set in mature grounds by the banks of the River Till. The house retains all of its period charm, with gracious public rooms and a choice of spacious relaxing lounges. The refined dining room offers a range of imaginatively created dishes, while more informal dining is available in the bistro. Bedrooms combine the traditional and the modern with great success. The hotel is popular for fishing and shooting.
ROOMS: 12 en suite 2 annexe en suite (1 fmly) s £90-£120; d £160-£190 (incl. bkfst) * LB **FACILITIES:** STV Croquet lawn Clay pigeon shooting Snooker table 3/4 size Xmas **CONF:** Thtr 50 Class 20 Board 20 Del from £100 * **PARKING:** 50 **NOTES:** Civ Wed
CARDS:

CORSE LAWN, Gloucestershire Map 03 SO83

★★★75% Corse Lawn House
GL19 4LZ
☎ 01452 780479 & 780771 01452 780840
e-mail: hotel@corselawnhouse.u-net.com
Dir: *on B4211 5m SW of Tewkesbury*
A Queen Anne country house standing in extensive grounds. The public rooms feature a bistro and bar in addition to the main restaurant; a drawing room and other seating areas are also provided. The bedrooms are elegantly decorated, and feature many extra touches. Cooking is of a high standard with good use made of top quality ingredients.
ROOMS: 19 en suite (2 fmly) s £75; d £120 (incl. bkfst) * LB **FACILITIES:** STV Indoor swimming (H) Tennis (hard) Croquet lawn Badminton **CONF:** Thtr 50 Class 30 Board 25 Del from £130 * **PARKING:** 62 **NOTES:** No smoking in restaurant Closed 24-25 Dec Civ Wed 75 **CARDS:**

COVENTRY, West Midlands Map 04 SP37
see also Brandon, Meriden & Nuneaton

★★★73% Brooklands Grange Hotel & Restaurant
Holyhead Rd CV5 8HX
☎ 024 7660 1601 024 7660 1277
e-mail: enquiries@brooklands-grange.co.uk
Dir: *leave A45 at roundabout marked city centre onto A4114 go to next roundabout & stay on A4114, hotel 100yds on left*
Behind the Jacobean façade of Brooklands Grange is a modern and comfortable business hotel. The food is worthy of note, with an interesting carte offering carefully presented dishes, and service is both friendly and attentive. Bedrooms are well equipped and thoughtfully laid-out.

continued

ROOMS: 30 en suite (1 fmly) No smoking in 15 bedrooms s £90-£110; d £105-£125 (incl. bkfst) * **CONF:** Thtr 20 Class 20 Board 18 Del £140 * **PARKING:** 52 **NOTES:** No dogs (ex guide dogs) No smoking in restaurant Closed 26-28 Dec & 1-2 Jan
CARDS:

★★★70% *Posthouse Coventry*
Posthouse
Hinckley Rd, Walsgrave CV2 2HP
☎ 0870 400 9021 024 7662 1736
e-mail: gm1412@forte-hotels.com
Dir: *on A4600*
This hotel offers bright, modern accommodation. Half the rooms are in the new Millennium style, the others are more traditional but equally comfortable and well equipped. The Academy has its own reception, lounge and air-conditioned meeting rooms. Other facilities include the Rotisserie and coffee lounge.
ROOMS: 160 en suite (15 fmly) No smoking in 112 bedrooms **FACILITIES:** Indoor swimming (H) Sauna Gym Jacuzzi/spa Steam room Childrens play areas entertainment ch fac **CONF:** Thtr 250 Class 150 Board 50 **SERVICES:** Lift **PARKING:** 300 **NOTES:** No smoking in restaurant **CARDS:**

★★★69% Hylands
Best Western
Warwick Rd CV3 6AU
☎ 024 7650 1600 024 7650 1027
e-mail: accomm@hylands-hotel.co.uk
Dir: *on A429, 500 yds from J6 town centre ring road, opp Memorial Park*
This hotel is convenient for the station and the city centre, yet overlooks an attractive park. Restaurant 153 offers good standards of food and service. Bedroom styles may vary, yet each room is well equipped and fully en suite; most recent additions are smart with bold colour schemes.
ROOMS: 61 en suite (4 fmly) No smoking in 54 bedrooms s £75-£88; d £85-£95 (incl. bkfst) * LB **FACILITIES:** STV **CONF:** Thtr 60 Class 40 Board 30 Del from £85 * **PARKING:** 60 **NOTES:** No smoking in restaurant **CARDS:**

★★★68% Aston Court
80-90 Holyhead Rd CV1 3AS
☎ 024 7625 8585 024 7622 5547
e-mail: astoncourtcoventry@hotelres.co.uk
Bedrooms at this hotel are smartly decorated, comfortable and well equipped for the business guest. Public areas include a restaurant where a daily set menu and a carte are offered.
ROOMS: 82 en suite (6 fmly) No smoking in 43 bedrooms s £75-£95; d £85-£105 * LB **FACILITIES:** Xmas **CONF:** Thtr 260 Class 150 Board 80 Del from £105 * **SERVICES:** Lift **PARKING:** 40 **NOTES:** No smoking in restaurant Civ Wed 60
CARDS:

★★★68% Courtyard by Marriott Coventry
COURTYARD
London Rd, Ryton on Dunsmore CV8 3DY
☎ 024 7630 1585 024 7630 1610
Dir: *M6 junct 2, take A46 towards Warwick, take turning towards A45 London at Coventry Airport*
This modern hotel is conveniently situated on the outskirts of the city and provides very comfortable and spacious accommodation. Public areas are particularly well designed and include a lounge bar, foyer lounge and an informal restaurant. There are versatile meeting and conference facilities.
ROOMS: 49 en suite (2 fmly) No smoking in 25 bedrooms s fr £79; d fr £88.50 (incl. bkfst) * LB **FACILITIES:** STV Xmas **CONF:** Thtr 300 Class 100 Board 24 Del from £119 * **PARKING:** 120 **NOTES:** No dogs (ex guide dogs) Civ Wed 112 **CARDS:**

C

★★★66% Menzies Leofric

Broadgate CV1 1LZ

MENZIES HOTELS

☎ 0500 636943 (Central Res) 📠 01773 880321

e-mail: info@menzies-hotels.co.uk

Dir: *opposite West Orchards Car Park*

Reputedly the first hotel to be built in Britain after the Second World War, the Leofric is near the cathedral and the shopping centre. Open plan public areas include a choice of bars and a brasserie. The West Orchards car park gives direct access to the hotel.

ROOMS: 94 en suite (5 fmly) No smoking in 20 bedrooms s £95-£105; d £105-£130 * LB **FACILITIES:** STV Xmas **CONF:** Thtr 500 Class 200 Board 80 Del from £80 * **SERVICES:** Lift **NOTES:** No dogs (ex guide dogs) Civ Wed 500 **CARDS:**

★★★64% The Chace

London Rd, Toll Bar End CV3 4EQ

corus

☎ 024 7630 3398 📠 024 7630 1816

e-mail: chacehotel@corushotels.com

Dir: *from S M40, exit junct 15, A46 to Coventry, right onto A45 & follow to 1st rdbt, turn left onto B4110, straight on at next mini rdbt, hotel on left*

This rapidly growing hotel retains many of its original Victorian features. Characterful public rooms have stained glass windows and oak panelling, within a large open plan lounge bar and separate restaurant. The bedrooms have been recently upgraded offering bright attractive decor and comfortable furnishings.

ROOMS: 66 en suite (23 fmly) No smoking in 34 bedrooms s £80-£95; d £90-£115 * LB **FACILITIES:** STV Pool table Croquet lawn entertainment Xmas **CONF:** Thtr 65 Class 40 Board 36 Del from £90 * **PARKING:** 120 **NOTES:** No dogs (ex guide dogs) No smoking in restaurant Civ Wed 60 **CARDS:**

★★★63% Allesley

Birmingham Rd, Allesley Village CV5 9GP

☎ 024 7640 3272 📠 024 7640 5190

e-mail: rita@allesleyhotel.freeserve.co.uk

Dir: *from the A45. Turn off slip road A4114 Brownshill Green/City Centre. 4th exit, at next rndbt 1st exit Allesley Village. Hotel is 150yds on left*

The Allesley provides well appointed accommodation that is light and inviting. All rooms are well equipped for today's corporate guest. Public areas are split over two levels and include a spacious reception foyer, a restaurant, and bar. Extensive conference and function facilities are readily available and have dedicated audio-visual and secretarial support.

ROOMS: 75 en suite 15 annexe en suite (2 fmly) No smoking in 31 bedrooms s £80-£100; d £102-£125 (incl. bkfst) * LB **FACILITIES:** Pool table entertainment **CONF:** Thtr 450 Class 150 Board 80 Del from £145 * **SERVICES:** Lift **PARKING:** 500 **NOTES:** No smoking in restaurant Civ Wed 350 **CARDS:**

★★★62% Novotel

Wilsons Ln CV6 6HL

NOVOTEL

☎ 024 7636 5000 📠 024 7636 2422

e-mail: h0506@accor-hotels.com

Dir: *exit M6 junct 3, follow signs for B4113 towards Longford, Bedworth. Take 3rd exit on large rdbt*

The first Novotel built in the UK, this modern hotel offers bedrooms which include family as well as disabled rooms. There is also a useful range of meeting rooms. Guests can dine until midnight in the cheerfully redecorated brasserie, or take meals from the extensive room service menu. The hotel has a children's play area.

ROOMS: 98 en suite (98 fmly) No smoking in 26 bedrooms d £65-£75 * LB **FACILITIES:** STV Outdoor swimming (H) Pool table Petanque **CONF:** Thtr 200 Class 100 Board 40 Del from £85 * **SERVICES:** Lift air con **PARKING:** 120 **CARDS:**

⌂ *Hotel Ibis*

Abbey Rd, Whitley CV3 4BJ

☎ 024 7663 9922 📠 024 7630 6898

e-mail: H2094@accor-hotels.com

Dir: *signposted from A46/A423 roundabout, take A423 towards A45 & London stay in left hand lane. Follow signs for the Racquet Centre.*

Modern, budget hotel offering comfortable accommodation in bright and practical bedrooms. Breakfast is self-service and dinner is available in the restaurant. For further details, consult the Hotel Groups page.

ROOMS: 51 en suite **CONF:** Thtr 35 Class 18 Board 20

COVENTRY, continued

Campanile
4 Wigston Rd, Walsgrave CV2 2SD
☎ 024 7662 2311 📠 024 7660 2362
Dir: *exit 2 of M6, at 2nd roundabout turn right*
This modern building offers accommodation in smart well equipped bedrooms, all with en suite bathrooms. Refreshments

may be taken at the informal Bistro. For further details and the Campanile phone number, consult the Hotel Groups page.
ROOMS: 50 en suite **CONF:** Thtr 35 Class 18 Board 20

Express by Holiday Inn Coventry
Kempass Highway CV3 6PB
☎ 024 7641 7555 📠 024 7641 3388
A modern budget hotel offering comfortable accommodation in refreshing, spacious and comprehensively-equipped bedrooms, en suite bathrooms with power showers and continental buffet breakfast included in the room rate. Suitable for business travellers or families. For further details and the Express by Holiday Inn phone number, consult the Hotel Groups page.

ROOMS: 37 en suite (incl. cont bkfst) d £49.95 * **CONF:** Thtr 24 Class 16 Board 16

Hotel Ibis Coventry Ringway
Mill Ln, St John's Ringway CV1 2LN
☎ 024 7625 0500
Modern, budget hotel offering comfortable accommodation in bright and practical bedrooms. Breakfast is self-service and dinner is available in the restaurant. For further details, consult the Hotel Groups page.
ROOMS: 88 en suite

Premier Lodge
Combe Fields Rd, Ansty CV7 9JP
☎ 0870 700 1356 📠 0870 700 1357
Premier Lodge offers modern, well equipped, en suite accommodation suitable for both business and leisure travellers. Meals can be taken at the adjacent popular restaurant and bar which is fully licensed. For further details, consult the Hotel Groups page.
ROOMS: 28 en suite d £42 *

COWES See Wight, Isle of

CRANBROOK, Kent — Map 05 TQ73

Premier Collection

★★ Kennel Holt
Goudhurst Rd TN17 2PT
☎ 01580 712032 📠 01580 715495
e-mail: hotel@kennelholt.demon.co.uk
Dir: *between Goudhurst and Cranbrook on A262*
This Elizabethan manor house is a charming retreat with immaculately kept gardens. The relaxing public rooms are full of original features. Individually-styled bedrooms, some including four-poster beds, are traditionally comfortable and are furnished in keeping with the style of the property. The food is good and the wine list is a real treat.
ROOMS: 10 en suite s £90-£120; d £145-£175 (incl. bkfst) * LB **FACILITIES:** Croquet lawn Putting green **PARKING:** 20 **NOTES:** No dogs No smoking in restaurant Closed middle 2 wks Jan
CARDS:

CRATHORNE, North Yorkshire — Map 08 NZ40

★★★★70% Crathorne Hall
TS15 0AR
☎ 01642 700398 📠 01642 700814
Dir: *off A19, take slip road marked Teeside Airport and Kirklevington, then a right turn signposted Crathorne leads straight to the hotel*
This fine Edwardian hall, which enjoys fabulous views over the Leven Valley, provides magnificent public rooms and very thoughtfully equipped bedrooms. A number of rooms retain some splendid original features. Service, whilst attentive, is friendly and relaxed.
ROOMS: 37 en suite (4 fmly) No smoking in 15 bedrooms s fr £90; d £160-£234 (incl. bkfst & dinner) * LB **FACILITIES:** STV Fishing Croquet lawn Jogging track Clay pigeon shooting Xmas **CONF:** Thtr 140 Class 80 Board 60 Del £155 * **PARKING:** 120 **NOTES:** No smoking in restaurant Civ Wed 132 **CARDS:**

See advert on opposite page

CRAWLEY See Gatwick Airport

CREDITON, Devon — Map 03 SS80

★★★69% Coombe House Country Hotel
Coleford EX17 5BY
☎ 01363 84487 📠 01363 84722
e-mail: relax@coombehouse.com
Dir: *turn left off A377 Exeter/Barnstaple road 1m NW of Crediton signposted, hotel 1m on left*
This Georgian manor house offers a relaxed and friendly

continued

atmosphere. The bedrooms reflect two styles with bright modern rooms and traditionally appointed rooms with period furniture. Impressive cuisine makes good use of the excellent local produce.
ROOMS: 15 en suite (2 fmly) s £57.50-£67.50; d £82-£102 (incl. bkfst) * LB **FACILITIES:** Tennis (hard) Croquet lawn Gymnasium equipment Xmas **CONF:** Thtr 80 Board 25 Del from £92.25 * **PARKING:** 70 **NOTES:** No smoking in restaurant Civ Wed 80 **CARDS:**

CREWE, Cheshire — Map 07 SJ75

★★★★68% Crewe Hall
Weston Rd CW1 6UZ
☎ 01270 253333 Fax 01270 253322
e-mail: reservations@crewehall.com
Proudly standing in 500 acres of mature grounds, this historic Hall, converted into a very comfortable hotel, dates back to the 17th century. It retains a very elaborate and comfortable interior which is a true reflection of Victorian style. Bedrooms are spacious and offer high levels of comfort. Quality modern cooking is served in the elegant Ranulph restaurant.
ROOMS: 25 en suite (4 fmly) No smoking in 10 bedrooms s £125-£310; d £150-£350 (incl. bkfst) * LB **FACILITIES:** STV Tennis (hard) Croquet lawn Xmas **CONF:** Thtr 260 Class 110 Board 100 Del from £185 * **SERVICES:** Lift **PARKING:** 140 **NOTES:** No smoking in restaurant Civ Wed 220 **CARDS:**

★★★66% White Lion
Weston CW2 5NA
☎ 01270 587011 & 500303 Fax 01270 500303
Dir: *from M6 junct 16 follow A500 signposted 'Crewe, Nantwich, Chester' to 2nd rdbt then right into Weston village. Hotel in centre on left*
Parts of this privately owned hotel were once a Tudor farmhouse. Now it provides well equipped modern accommodation and offers a choice of bars and eating options. Facilities here include a conference room and the hotel is also licensed for civil wedding ceremonies.
ROOMS: 16 en suite (2 fmly) s fr £58; d fr £68 (incl. bkfst) * LB **FACILITIES:** Crown Green bowling **CONF:** Thtr 50 Class 28 Board 20 Del from £90 * **PARKING:** 100 **NOTES:** No smoking in restaurant Closed Xmas & New Year Civ Wed 65
CARDS:

★★★64% Hunters Lodge
Sydney Rd, Sydney CW1 5LU
☎ 01270 583440 Fax 01270 500553
e-mail: info@hunterslodge.co.uk
Dir: *1m from Crewe station, off A534*
This hotel has a purpose-built, modern bedroom wing, with several family rooms and a select number of rooms with four poster beds. Imaginative dishes are served in the spacious restaurant, and the popular bar also offers a wide choice of tempting meals.
ROOMS: 47 en suite (2 fmly) No smoking in 21 bedrooms s £30-£64; d £55-£79 (incl. bkfst) LB **FACILITIES:** STV Sauna Solarium Gym Jacuzzi/spa Xmas **CONF:** Thtr 160 Class 100 Board 80 Del from £82.50 * **PARKING:** 240 **NOTES:** No dogs (ex guide dogs) No smoking in restaurant Civ Wed 130 **CARDS:**

⌂ *Travelodge*
Travelodge
Alsager Rd, Barthomley CW2 5PT
☎ 01270 883157 Fax 01270 883157
Dir: *5m E, at junc 16 M6/A500*
This modern building offers accommodation in smart, spacious and well equipped bedrooms, all with en suite bathrooms. Refreshments may be taken at the nearby family restaurant. For further details and the Travelodge phone number, consult the Hotel Groups page.
ROOMS: 42 en suite

CRICK, Northamptonshire — Map 04 SP57

★★★66% *Posthouse Northampton/Rugby*
Posthouse
NN6 7XR
☎ 0870 400 9059 Fax 01788 823955
Dir: *at junct 18 of M1*
A modern hotel just off the M1, whose spacious grounds include a children's play area. Bedrooms, in various styles, include several family rooms and some have pleasant country views. There is a restaurant, a lounge serving refreshments all day, and 24-hour room service. There are good leisure facilities and ample parking space.
ROOMS: 88 en suite (17 fmly) No smoking in 51 bedrooms **FACILITIES:** Indoor swimming (H) Sauna Solarium Gym Pool table Jacuzzi/spa ch fac **CONF:** Thtr 200 Class 100 Board 142 **PARKING:** 200 **CARDS:**

CRICKLADE, Wiltshire — Map 04 SU09

★★★68% Cricklade Hotel
Common Hill SN6 6HA
☎ 01793 750751 Fax 01793 751767
Dir: *turn off A419 onto B4040. Turn left at clock tower. Right at rdbt. Hotel 0.5m up hill on left*
Surounded by over 30 acres of Wiltshire countryside, the hotel offers a peaceful and tranquil venue for guests. Bedrooms all offer high levels of comfort and quality. In addition to the elegant lounge and dining room, a Victorian style conservatory runs the full length of the building, from which wonderful views can be enjoyed.

continued

CRICKLADE, continued

Cricklade Hotel, Cricklade

ROOMS: 25 en suite 21 annexe en suite (1 fmly) s £90-£100; d £115-£125 (incl. bkfst) * LB **FACILITIES:** Indoor swimming (H) Golf 9 Tennis (hard) Snooker Sauna Solarium Gym Pool table Croquet lawn Jacuzzi/spa Aromatherapy Beautician entertainment **CONF:** Thtr 130 Class 50 Board 60 Del from £135 * **PARKING:** 100 **NOTES:** No dogs (ex guide dogs) No children 14yrs Civ Wed 120 **CARDS:**

CROFT-ON-TEES, North Yorkshire Map 08 NZ20

★★★63% *Croft Spa*
DL2 2ST
☎ 01325 720319 📠 01325 721252
Dir: *from Darlington take A167 Northallerton road. Hotel 3m S*
This large hotel stands beside the River Tees and offers mainly spacious and well equipped bedrooms. The public rooms consist of a large bar lounge together with the pleasant Alices Restaurant. A fitness centre is also provided as are good conference facilities.
ROOMS: 37 en suite (4 fmly) **FACILITIES:** STV Snooker Sauna Solarium Gym **CONF:** Thtr 400 Class 130 Board 35 Del from £50 * **PARKING:** 200 **NOTES:** No dogs (ex guide dogs) No smoking in restaurant **CARDS:**

CROMER, Norfolk Map 09 TG24

★★66% Red Lion
Brook St NR27 9HD
☎ 01263 514964 📠 01263 512834
Dir: *from town centre take first left after church*
A focal point for the area, the Red Lion dates from Victorian times. Public areas are comfortable, and the snooker room is a popular feature. Locals and residents mingle in the bars, which are Edwardian in style. Bedrooms offer a good standard of comfort and come in a variety of attractive styles and sizes.
ROOMS: 12 en suite (1 fmly) s £46-£50; d £76-£84 (incl. bkfst) * **FACILITIES:** Snooker Sauna Solarium Discount for local leisure centre **CONF:** Thtr 60 Class 50 Board 40 **PARKING:** 12 **NOTES:** No dogs No smoking in restaurant **CARDS:**

CROOKLANDS, Cumbria Map 07 SD58

★★★67% ❀ Crooklands
LA7 7NW
☎ 015395 67432 📠 015395 67525
e-mail: crooklands_hotel@postmaster.co.uk
Dir: *on A65, 1.5m from junct 36 of M6*
Best Western
Situated close to the M6, Lake District and Yorkshire Dales, this welcoming family-run hotel is convenient for all guests' purposes. Public areas, which have natural stone walls and heavy beams, include a choice of bars and eating options. Bedrooms, all located in the wing extension, vary in size with mixed styles of furnishings.
ROOMS: 30 en suite No smoking in 12 bedrooms s £52.50-£55; d £52.50-£60 * LB **FACILITIES:** Pool table **CONF:** Thtr 100 Class 60 Board 50 Del from £99.50 * **PARKING:** 150 **NOTES:** No dogs Closed 24-26 Dec Civ Wed **CARDS:**

CROSTHWAITE, Cumbria Map 07 SD49

★★★59% *Damson Dene*
LA8 8JE
☎ 015395 68676 📠 015395 68227
Dir: *on A5074, approx 6m from Bowness on right*
Owned by Methodist Holiday Hotels, the spirit of Christian fellowship is evident throughout this hotel but attendance at services in the hotel chapel is entirely voluntary. The modern leisure centre is especially popular with family visitors. Bedrooms, some of which are more compact, are benefiting from an extensive programme of refurbishment. Public areas include a traditional foyer lounge, well-stocked bar and a spacious restaurant.
ROOMS: 37 en suite (3 fmly) No smoking in 8 bedrooms **FACILITIES:** Indoor swimming (H) Squash Snooker Sauna Solarium Gym Pool table Putting green Jacuzzi/spa Steam Room Turkish Bath **CONF:** Thtr 140 Class 60 Board 40 **PARKING:** 40 **NOTES:** No smoking in restaurant **CARDS:**

CROWBOROUGH, East Sussex Map 05 TQ53

★★★70% ❀❀ Winston Manor Hotel
Beacon Rd TN6 1AD
☎ 01892 652772 📠 01892 665537
e-mail: welcome@winstonmanor.fsnet.co.uk
Dir: *on the A26 Tunbridge Wells to Brighton*
CHOICE HOTELS EUROPE
On the main A26 between Tunbridge Wells and Lewes, Winston Manor is now a privately owned hotel. Some of the bedrooms are particularly suitable for families and there are extensive leisure facilities.
ROOMS: 45 en suite (5 fmly) s £50-£65; d £70-£95 (incl. bkfst) * LB **FACILITIES:** STV Indoor swimming (H) Sauna Solarium Gym Jacuzzi/spa **CONF:** Thtr 300 Class 70 Board 50 Del from £90 * **SERVICES:** Lift **PARKING:** 100 **NOTES:** No smoking in restaurant RS 24-30 Dec Civ Wed 45 **CARDS:**

See advert on opposite page

CROWTHORNE, Berkshire Map 04 SU86

★★★69% Waterloo
Duke's Ride RG45 6DW
☎ 01344 777711 📠 01344 778913
Dir: *M3 junct 3 towards Bracknell follow A322 then follow signs for Crowthorne, once in village follow sign for Hotel & Conference centre*
corus
This much extended Victorian property is conveniently located for both the M3 and M4 motorways. The modern equipped bedrooms are attractively appointed. No smoking bedrooms and interconnecting pairs of rooms are both available. Public areas include a pleasant brasserie style restaurant and a choice of bar areas. Conference rooms are available.
ROOMS: 58 en suite No smoking in 22 bedrooms s £109-£123; d fr £135 * LB **FACILITIES:** Xmas **CONF:** Thtr 50 Class 24 Board 20 Del from £148 * **PARKING:** 70 **CARDS:**

CROYDE, Devon Map 02 SS43

★★69% ***Kittiwell House***
St Mary's Rd EX33 1PG
☎ 01271 890247 📠 01271 890460
e-mail: kittiwell@aol.com
Dir: *0.5m from village centre in direction of Georgeham*
The comfortable bedrooms in this delightfully cosy, thatched hotel are individually decorated and furnished, reflecting the character of the property. Beamed ceilings, open fires and an interesting collection of bric-a-brac create a relaxing environment. Popular locally, the attractive restaurant offers both carte and fixed-price menus.
ROOMS: 12 en suite (2 fmly) No smoking in 4 bedrooms **PARKING:** 21
NOTES: No smoking in restaurant Closed mid Jan-mid Feb
CARDS:

See advert on this page

CROYDON, Greater London Map 04 TQ36

★★★★77% ❀❀ **Coulsdon Manor**
Coulsdon Court Rd, Coulsdon CR5 2LL
☎ 020 8668 0414 📠 020 8668 3118
e-mail: coulsdonmanor@marstonhotels.co.uk

MARSTON HOTELS

Dir: *A23 turn right into Stoats Nest Road. Hotel at top of hill on left*
Extended in keeping with its original style to provide modern, well equipped bedrooms, this fine Victorian manor house is set within 140 acres of parkland. Attentive service and hospitality are provided by a dedicated staff. There is a comfortable lounge bar with separate dining area, a formal restaurant and cocktail bar. The innovative carte and set-priced menus demonstrate a

continued on p176

C

CROYDON, continued

dedicated approach to enjoyable cooking. Leisure facilities are excellent and include a professional 18-hole golf course.
ROOMS: 35 en suite No smoking in 2 bedrooms s £97-£107; d £115-£135 * LB **FACILITIES:** STV Golf 18 Tennis (hard) Squash Sauna Solarium Gym Putting green ch fac Xmas **CONF:** Thtr 180 Class 90 Board 70 Del from £145 * **SERVICES:** Lift **PARKING:** 200 **NOTES:** No dogs (ex guide dogs) No smoking in restaurant Civ Wed 60
CARDS:

★★★★ 69% Selsdon Park

PRINCIPAL HOTELS

Addington Rd, Sanderstead CR2 8YA
☎ 020 8657 8811 020 8651 6171
e-mail: selsdonpark@principalhotels.co.uk
Dir: *3m SE off A2022*
The extensive well kept grounds of this imposing Jacobean mansion include a professional 18-hole golf course. Popular for weddings and conferences, guests will find smart bedrooms equipped to a high standard. There is a grand restaurant where interesting rosette worthy food is served. There are also good leisure facilities.
ROOMS: 204 en suite (12 fmly) s £120; d £155 * LB **FACILITIES:** STV Indoor swimming (H) Outdoor swimming (H) Golf 18 Tennis (hard & grass) Squash Sauna Solarium Gym Croquet lawn Putting green Jacuzzi/spa Boules Jogging track entertainment Xmas **CONF:** Thtr 400 Class 100 Board 60 Del from £189 * **SERVICES:** Lift **PARKING:** 300 **NOTES:** No dogs (ex guide dogs) No smoking in restaurant Civ Wed 100
CARDS:

See advert on page 175

★★★ 65% *Posthouse Croydon*

Posthouse

Purley Way CR9 4LT
☎ 0870 400 9022 020 8681 6438
Dir: *off A23*
Suitable for both the business and leisure traveller, this bright hotel provides modern accommodation in well equipped bedrooms with en suite bathrooms.
ROOMS: 83 en suite No smoking in 40 bedrooms **CONF:** Thtr 100 Class 50 Board 40 **PARKING:** 70 **CARDS:**

★★★ 64% Dukes Head

6 Manor Rd, The Green, Wallington SM6 0AA
☎ 020 8401 7410 020 8401 7420
Located between Croydon and Sutton, this brewery owned hotel has undergone substantial investment. Spacious bedrooms have been furnished to a high standard, and public areas include a characterful bar and a brightly appointed restaurant.
ROOMS: 24 en suite (4 fmly) No smoking in 15 bedrooms s fr £92; d fr £102 (incl. bkfst) * LB **FACILITIES:** STV Xmas **CONF:** Thtr 28 Class 30 Board 28 **PARKING:** 35 **NOTES:** No dogs (ex guide dogs)
CARDS:

★★ 68% Markington Hotel & Conference Centre

9 Haling Park Rd CR2 6NG
☎ 020 8681 6494 020 8688 6530
e-mail: rooms@markingtonhotel.com
Dir: *travelling N from Purley, Haling Park Rd is 1st on left after bus garage. Hotel on left*
This popular hotel is close to Croydon's centre, but is peaceful and relaxing. Bedrooms are comfortable, smart and well equipped; public areas comprise a smart bar/lounge and attractive dining room.
ROOMS: 29 en suite (3 fmly) No smoking in 5 bedrooms s £50.50-£79; d £65-£79 (incl. bkfst) * **FACILITIES:** STV Guests may visit nearby gym which has full facilities (pool/sauna) for £1 **CONF:** Thtr 30 Class 20 Board 25 **PARKING:** 17 **NOTES:** No dogs (ex guide dogs) No smoking in restaurant Closed 23 Dec-2 Jan **CARDS:**

★★ 66% The South Park Hotel

3-5 South Park Hill Rd, South Croydon CR2 7DY
☎ 020 8688 5644 & 020 8688 0840 020 8760 0861
e-mail: reception@southprkhotel.co.uk
Dir: *from A235 to Croydon town centre, take A212 towards Addington, continue for 1.5m to rdbt. Take 3rd exit off onto South Park Hill Rd*
Under an owner committed to high standards, the hotel offers refurbished bedrooms with good beds and soft furnishings. The small lounge is furnished with comfortable Chesterfields, there is a reception-bar and a terrace overlooking the attractive rear garden.
ROOMS: 19 en suite (2 fmly) No smoking in 8 bedrooms s fr £50; d fr £65 (incl. bkfst) * **PARKING:** 15 **NOTES:** No dogs (ex guide dogs) No smoking in restaurant **CARDS:**

Premier Lodge

PREMIER LODGE

619 Purley Way RH0 4RJ
☎ 0870 700 1434 0870 700 1435
Premier Lodge offers modern, well equipped, en suite accommodation suitable for both business and leisure travellers. Meals can be taken at the adjacent popular restaurant and bar which is fully licensed. For further details, consult the Hotel Groups page.
ROOMS: 81 en suite d £46 *

CUCKFIELD, West Sussex

Map 04 TQ32

★★★ 75% Ockenden Manor

Ockenden Ln RH17 5LD
☎ 01444 416111 01444 415549
e-mail: ockenden@hshotels.co.uk
Dir: *turn off A23 in direction of Brighton onto B2115 signed Cuckfield Village. Follow signs into village, take first right into Ockendon Lane, at end*
This charming 16th-century hotel enjoys fine views of the South Downs. Public rooms retain much of the original character, such as stained glass windows and oak-panelled walls. The elegant sitting room has all the elements for a relaxing afternoon in front of the fire. Bedrooms are divided between the main building and a new wing, offering high standards of accommodation. The cuisine is impressive.
ROOMS: 22 en suite (1 fmly) s £108-£155; d £127-£265 (incl. cont bkfst) * **FACILITIES:** STV Croquet lawn Xmas **CONF:** Thtr 50 Class 25 Board 25 Del £170 * **PARKING:** 45 **NOTES:** No dogs No smoking in restaurant Civ Wed 75 **CARDS:**

★★ 70% Hilton Park Hotel

Tylers Green RH17 5EG
☎ 01444 454555 01444 457222
e-mail: hiltonpark@janus-systems.com
Dir: *halfway between Cuckfield and Haywards Heath on the A272*
Enjoying panoramic views, this delightful, family-run Victorian country house enjoys a peaceful setting in three acres of grounds. The attractive bedrooms are comfortably furnished and public areas include an elegant drawing room, smart dining room and conservatory bar.
ROOMS: 11 en suite (2 fmly) s £75-£90; d £100-£115 (incl. bkfst) * LB **FACILITIES:** STV ch fac **CONF:** Thtr 30 Board 12 Del £110 * **PARKING:** 50 **NOTES:** No dogs (ex guide dogs) No smoking in restaurant **CARDS:**

Late for dinner? Quality Standards star rating means that last orders for dinner should be no earlier than:
★ 6.30pm ★★ 7.00pm ★★★ 8.00pm
★★★★ 9.00pm ★★★★★ 10.00pm

DALTON-IN-FURNESS, Cumbria Map 07 SD27

★★★65% Clarence House Country Hotel & Restaurant

LA15 8BQ
☎ 01229 462508 01229 4677177
Dir: *from A590 in Lindal take Dalton-in-Furness Bypass road signed Barrow. At 2nd rdbt take first junct into Dalton. Hotel on right at top of hill*
This hotel hides discretely in a peaceful location, bordering open countryside and rolling hills. The bedrooms offer a high standard of facilities and stylish interior design. The public rooms are spacious and also furnished to a high standard. The conservatory restaurant provides impressive dinners and hearty breakfasts.
ROOMS: 7 en suite 10 annexe en suite (2 fmly) s fr £68; d fr £85 (incl. bkfst) * LB **CONF:** Thtr 45 Class 20 Board 20 Del from £85 *
PARKING: 40 **NOTES:** Closed 25-26 Dec
CARDS:

DARLINGTON, Co Durham Map 08 NZ21

see also Tees-Side Airport

★★★74% Hall Garth Golf & Country Club

CORUS
Coatham Mundeville DL1 3LU
☎ 01325 300400 01325 310083
Dir: *at junct 59 A1(M) take A167 towards Darlington, after 600yds turn left at top of hill, hotel is on right*

This tastefully extended 16th-century house stands in delightful gardens. The facilities include a nine-hole golf course, leisure centre, Stables Pub, and Hugo's Restaurant, which offers imaginatively prepared dishes. Bedrooms in the original house are traditional in style, but have every modern facility and include some with four-posters. Rooms in the newer wings are also well equipped and furnished.
ROOMS: 30 en suite 11 annexe en suite (4 fmly) No smoking in 21 bedrooms s £85-£114; d £95-£140 * LB **FACILITIES:** STV Indoor swimming (H) Golf 9 Sauna Solarium Gym Putting green Jacuzzi/spa Steam room **CONF:** Thtr 300 Class 120 Board 80 Del from £110 *
PARKING: 150 **NOTES:** No smoking in restaurant Civ Wed 170
CARDS:

★★★68% Headlam Hall

Headlam, Gainford DL2 3HA
☎ 01325 730238 01325 730790
e-mail: admin@headlamhall.co.uk
Dir: *2m N of A67 between Piercebridge and Gainford*
Previously the ancestral home of Lord Brocket and then Lord Gainford, this impressive Jacobean hall exudes a warm, relaxing atmosphere. The hotel has successfully moved with the times to provide a wide range of modern amenities. Bedrooms in the manor house are traditionally styled while bedrooms in the converted coach house are pine furnished in cottage style.
Attractive banqueting facilities make this hotel a popular venue for weddings.
ROOMS: 19 en suite 17 annexe en suite (4 fmly) No smoking in 19 bedrooms s £65-£90; d £80-£105 (incl. bkfst) * LB **FACILITIES:** STV Indoor swimming (H) Tennis (hard) Fishing Sauna Gym Croquet lawn ch fac **CONF:** Thtr 150 Class 40 Board 40 Del from £99 *
PARKING: 60 **NOTES:** No dogs (ex guide dogs) No smoking in restaurant Closed 24-25 Dec Civ Wed 150
CARDS:

★★★67% Blackwell Grange

Blackwell Grange DL3 8QH
REGAL
☎ 01325 509955 01325 380899
Dir: *on A167, 1.5m from central ring road*

This 17th-century mansion is set in attractive parkland, surrounded by an eighteen hole golf course. Many of the bedrooms are in modern extensions, although more spacious rooms are situated in the original building.
ROOMS: 99 en suite 11 annexe en suite (3 fmly) No smoking in 14 bedrooms s £89-£110; d £110-£150 * LB **FACILITIES:** STV Indoor swimming (H) Golf 18 Tennis Sauna Solarium Gym Pool table Croquet lawn Jacuzzi/spa Boules Xmas **CONF:** Thtr 300 Class 110 Board 50 Del from £110 * **SERVICES:** Lift **PARKING:** 250 **NOTES:** No smoking in restaurant Civ Wed 200 **CARDS:**

★★★66% Kings Head

Priest Gate DL1 1NW
☎ 01325 380222 01325 382006
e-mail: admin@gb076.u-net.com
Dir: *A1 northbound follow signs to Darlington. 3rd exit off next rdbt, 2nd off next, 1st exit off next, 1st right then 1st left. Hotel on right*
Situated next to the Cornmill Shopping Centre, this modern hotel provides a sound standard of accommodation in well equipped bedrooms. Public areas include the Priestgate foyer lounge, open all day for light snacks, and a traditional restaurant on the second floor. The hotel has the advantage of a secure car park, and extensive function facilities.
ROOMS: 85 en suite (3 fmly) No smoking in 51 bedrooms s £75-£90; d £85-£110 (incl. bkfst) * LB **FACILITIES:** STV Xmas **CONF:** Thtr 250 Class 180 Board 180 Del from £88 * **SERVICES:** Lift **PARKING:** 24
CARDS:

★★★63% White Horse Hotel

Harrogate Hill DL1 3AD
☎ 01325 382121 01325 355953
e-mail: reservations@whitehorse.co.uk
Dir: *on A167 between A1(M) and town centre*
Situated just outside Darlington, and within very easy reach of the A1, this well positioned business hotel provides identically equipped bedrooms, including a number of family rooms. Guests may chose to eat less formally in one of the smartly presented bars.

continued

DARLINGTON, continued

ROOMS: 40 en suite (3 fmly) No smoking in 20 bedrooms s £39-£59; d £39-£74 * LB **FACILITIES:** Pool table **CONF:** Thtr 70 Class 25 Board 30 **SERVICES:** Lift **PARKING:** 200
CARDS:

★★64% *Devonport*

16-18 The Front, Middleton-one-Row DL2 1AS
☎ 01325 332255 ▯ 01325 333242
Delightfully situated in a former spa village this historic hotel enjoys fine views across the River Ouse. Originally a 300-year old inn, the hotel has been completely upgraded to offer smart public areas which include a pub and restaurant offering a contemporary bistro-style menu. Bedrooms are well equipped, comfortable, and many are particularly spacious.
ROOMS: 16 en suite (1 fmly) No smoking in 5 bedrooms **CONF:** Thtr 50 Class 30 Board 40 **PARKING:** 30
CARDS:

○ Walworth Castle

Walworth DL2 2LY
☎ 01325 485470
This 12th-century castle lies in 18 acres amidst farmland yet only three miles from the motorway. Specialising in weddings and conferences, it is also well suited to the business market. Accommodation ranges from standard rooms in an adjoining wing to rather grand rooms in the castle itself. The restaurant and Farmers Bar give a choice of eating options.
ROOMS: 36 rms **NOTES:** Open

DARRINGTON, West Yorkshire Map 08 SE42

★★60% *The Darrington Hotel*

Great North Rd WF8 3BL
☎ 01977 791458 ▯ 01977 602286
Dir: *off A1, 2m S of A1/M62 interchange (junct 33). Signposted*
Conveniently close to the A1 and on the edge of the village of Darrington, this popular hotel offers modern bedrooms which include hair dryers and trouser presses. There are lively bars and a Homespreads restaurant. Service is relaxed and friendly.
ROOMS: 27 en suite (1 fmly) **FACILITIES:** STV entertainment **CONF:** Thtr 24 Class 12 Board 12 **PARKING:** 90 **NOTES:** No dogs (ex guide dogs) **CARDS:**

DARTFORD, Kent Map 05 TQ57

★★★★75% Rowhill Grange Hotel & Spa

DA2 7QH
☎ 01322 615136 ▯ 01322 615137
e-mail: admin@rowhillgrange.com
Dir: *on B258 opposite Texaco Garage*

This magnificent country house hotel has nine acres of woodland and gardens. Bedrooms are individually decorated with great style and taste and have elegant bathrooms. Guests may eat in the more formal Garden Restaurant or in the Topiary Brasserie. All guests have membership of the hotel's superb Utopia health and leisure spa.
ROOMS: 30 en suite (1 fmly) No smoking in 24 bedrooms s £129-£169; d £154-£199 * LB **FACILITIES:** STV Indoor swimming (H) Sauna Solarium Gym Croquet lawn Jacuzzi/spa Beauty treatment Hair salon Aerobic studio Therapy pool Xmas **CONF:** Thtr 100 Class 50 Board 30 Del from £165 * **SERVICES:** Lift **PARKING:** 100 **NOTES:** No dogs (ex guide dogs) No smoking in restaurant Civ Wed 60
CARDS:

See advert on opposite page

⌂ Campanile

Clipper Boulevard West, Business Park, Crossways DA2 6QN
☎ 01322 278925 ▯ 01322 278948
Dir: *follow signs for Ferry Terminal from Dartford Bridge*

This modern building offers accommodation in smart well equipped bedrooms, all with en suite bathrooms. Refreshments may be taken at the informal Bistro. For further details and the Campanile phone number, consult the Hotel Groups page.
ROOMS: 125 en suite **CONF:** Thtr 50 Class 20 Board 25

⌂ Express by Holiday Inn Dartford

University Way DA1 5PA
☎ 01322 290333 ▯ 290444
e-mail: dartford@premierhotels-7.demon.co.uk
Dir: *follow A206 to Erith. Hotel located off University Way via signposted sliproad*

A modern budget hotel offering comfortable accommodation in refreshing, spacious and comprehensively-equipped bedrooms, en suite bathrooms with power showers and continental buffet breakfast included in the room rate. Suitable for business travellers or families. For further details and the Express by Holiday Inn phone number, consult the Hotel Groups page.
ROOMS: 126 en suite (incl. cont bkfst) d £59.50 * **CONF:** Thtr 35 Board 20 Del from £93.50 *

DARTMOUTH, Devon Map 03 SX85

★★★72% The Dart Marina

Sandquay TQ6 9PH
☎ 0870 400 8134 🖷 01803 835040
e-mail: heritagehotels_dartmouth.dart_marina
@forte-hotels.com
Dir: *A3122 from Totnes to Dartmouth, follow road which becomes College Way, just before the Higher Ferry, The Dart Marina is sharp left in Sandquay Rd*

A fine hotel in an unrivalled position by the marina, with direct access to the water. Public rooms are comfortable and inviting with a nautical theme. Bedrooms, each enjoying the view, have extras such as fresh flowers and home made fudge. Locally caught fish are served in the smart restaurant.

ROOMS: 46 en suite 4 annexe en suite No smoking in 23 bedrooms s £80-£87.50; d £110-£125 * LB **FACILITIES:** Xmas **PARKING:** 50 **NOTES:** No smoking in restaurant **CARDS:**

★★★71% Royal Castle

11 The Quay TQ6 9PS
☎ 01803 833033 🖷 01803 835445
e-mail: enquiry@y-castle-hotel.co.uk
Dir: *in the centre of the town, overlooking Boat float Inner Harbour*

This 17th-century coaching inn stands right on Dartmouth harbour. Its two bars serve traditional ales and a range of locally popular bar meals. Upstairs, there are several quiet lounges and the more formal Adams Restaurant. The attractive, individual bedrooms, several with four-poster beds, offer modern facilities and many personal touches.

ROOMS: 25 en suite (4 fmly) s £66.95-£77; d £115-£145 (incl. bkfst) * LB **FACILITIES:** STV entertainment Xmas **CONF:** Thtr 70 Class 40 Board 40 Del from £75 * **PARKING:** 17 **NOTES:** No smoking in restaurant **CARDS:**

★★★67% Stoke Lodge

Stoke Fleming TQ6 0RA
☎ 01803 770523 🖷 01803 770851
e-mail: mail@stokelodge.co.uk
Dir: *2m S A379*

Stoke Lodge is a popular hotel with many guests returning year upon year. All bedrooms are comfortably furnished with modern facilities. The spacious restaurant offers an extensive wine list and both carte and fixed-price menus. A large range of indoor and outdoor leisure facilities are available depending upon the season.

ROOMS: 25 en suite (5 fmly) s £47-£53; d £78-£99 (incl. bkfst) * LB **FACILITIES:** Indoor swimming (H) Outdoor swimming (H) Tennis (hard) Snooker Sauna Pool table Putting green Jacuzzi/spa Table tennis Xmas **CONF:** Thtr 80 Class 60 Board 30 Del from £60 * **PARKING:** 50 **NOTES:** No smoking in restaurant **CARDS:**

D

DARTMOUTH, continued

★★66% Townstal Farmhouse
Townstal Rd TQ6 9HY
☎ 01803 832300 📠 01803 835428
Dir: *on A3122 opposite Royal Naval College gate*
A former 16th-century farmhouse, just half a mile from the town centre and ideal for visitors to the Royal Naval College opposite. Rooms in the original building contain many original features, while the spacious annexe rooms, one of which is designed for disabled access, are very popular. Guests enjoy good home-cooked meals in the beamed dining room, and relax in front of the cosy lounge's log fire.
ROOMS: 9 en suite 8 annexe en suite (5 fmly) **PARKING:** 17
NOTES: No smoking in restaurant **CARDS:**

○ The Little Admiral
27-29 Victoria Rd TQ6 9RT
☎ 01803 832572
NOTES: Open

DARWEN, Lancashire — Map 07 SD62

★★★67% Whitehall
Springbank, Whitehall BB3 2JU
☎ 01254 701595 📠 01254 773426
e-mail: hotel@thewhitehallhotel.freeserve.co.uk
Dir: *off A666 S of town*
A friendly hotel, set in attractive grounds on the edge of town, offering spacious accommodation. A wide range of dishes is served in the elegant restaurant, and lighter meals are available in the bar and lounge. Leisure facilities include a snooker room.
ROOMS: 17 en suite (2 fmly) **FACILITIES:** STV Indoor swimming (H) Sauna Solarium Pool table 3/4 size snooker table **CONF:** Thtr 50 Class 50 Board 25 **PARKING:** 60 **NOTES:** No smoking in restaurant Civ Wed 120 **CARDS:**

★★★65% The Old Rosins Inn
Pickup Bank, Hoddlesden BB3 3QD
☎ 01254 771264 📠 01254 873894
Dir: *leave M65 at junct 5, follow signs for Haslingdon then right after 2m signed Egworth, then right after 0.5m and continue 0.5m*
Most bedrooms at this hotel have fine countryside views, all offer attractive decor and comfort. Public areas, including a popular lounge bar and nicely appointed restaurant, are situated on the first floor to take full advantage of the views.
ROOMS: 15 en suite (3 fmly) s £43-£53; d £55-£65 (incl. bkfst) * LB **FACILITIES:** STV **CONF:** Thtr 30 Class 24 Board 70 Del from £79.95 * **PARKING:** 200 **NOTES:** No dogs (ex guide dogs)
CARDS:

DAVENTRY, Northamptonshire — Map 04 SP56

★★★★75% Fawsley Hall
Fawsley NN11 3BA
☎ 01327 892000 📠 01327 892001
e-mail: fawsley@compuserve.com
Dir: *signed 'Fawsley Hall' follow this single track road for 1.5m until you reach wrought iron gates of Fawsley Hall*
This fine 15th-century manor house has been sympathetically converted into a comfortable and welcoming hotel. It is set in peaceful open countryside, surrounded by gardens designed by Capability Brown. Bedrooms, including suites and interconnecting rooms, are comfortably furnished. Public areas are set around the courtyard and feature an impressive Great Hall with vaulted roof. An excellent menu is served in what was once a Tudor kitchen.
continued

PRIDE OF BRITAIN MEMBER

ROOMS: 30 en suite (1 fmly) No smoking in 2 bedrooms s £135-£195; d £175-£295 (incl. bkfst) * LB **FACILITIES:** STV Tennis (hard) Croquet lawn Putting green Jacuzzi/spa Xmas **CONF:** Thtr 70 Class 36 Board 22 Del from £160 * **PARKING:** 100 **NOTES:** Civ Wed 140
CARDS:

★★★★62% Hanover International Hotel & Club Daventry
Sedgemoor Way, off Ashby Rd NN11 5SG
☎ 01327 301777 📠 01327 706313
Dir: *N of Daventry on the A361 Ring Road*

This imposing modern hotel, set in its own grounds, overlooking Drayton Water, is within easy reach of both the M1 and the M40. The spacious public areas include a good range of banqueting, meeting and leisure facilities. Also boasting a fully equipped business centre, the hotel is a popular venue for conferences. The comfortable bedrooms all have double beds.
ROOMS: 138 en suite No smoking in 73 bedrooms d £105-£110 * LB **FACILITIES:** STV Indoor swimming (H) Sauna Solarium Gym Pool table Jacuzzi/spa Steam room Health & beauty salon **CONF:** Thtr 600 Class 200 Board 30 Del from £120 * **SERVICES:** Lift **PARKING:** 350 **NOTES:** No dogs (ex guide dogs) No smoking in restaurant RS 26-30 Dec Civ Wed 200 **CARDS:**

⇧ Express By Holiday Inn Daventry
Park Lands, Crick NN6 7EX
☎ 01788 824331 📠 01788 824332
e-mail: crick@premierhotels.co.uk
Dir: *M1 junct18. Take A428 to Daventry. Immediately on right*

A modern budget hotel offering comfortable accommodation in refreshing, spacious and comprehensively-equipped bedrooms, en suite bathrooms with power showers and continental buffet breakfast included in the room rate. Suitable for business travellers or families. For further details and the Express by Holiday Inn phone number, consult the Hotel Groups page.
ROOMS: 111 en suite (incl. cont bkfst) d fr £55 * **CONF:** Thtr 35 Class 20 Board 20

DAWLISH, Devon Map 03 SX97

★★★68% Langstone Cliff

Dawlish Warren EX7 0NA
☎ 01626 868000 🖷 01626 868006
e-mail: reception@langstone-hotel.co.uk
Dir: *1.5m NE off A379 Exeter road*

This charming, family owned and run hotel, stands in wooded grounds overlooking the sea and the Exe Estuary. Lounges and bars are spacious and comfortable, with a carvery operation usually offered in the restaurant. Bedrooms vary in size and style, some benefiting from seaward facing balconies. During the winter months, special cabaret weekends attract a regular following.
ROOMS: 64 en suite 4 annexe en suite (52 fmly) s £53-£63; d £90-£136 (incl. bkfst) * LB **FACILITIES:** STV Indoor swimming (H) Outdoor swimming (H) Tennis (hard) Snooker Gym Table tennis Golf practice area entertainment ch fac Xmas **CONF:** Thtr 400 Class 200 Board 80 Del £78 * **SERVICES:** Lift **PARKING:** 200 **NOTES:** Civ Wed 400
CARDS:

See advert on this page

DEAL, Kent Map 05 TR35

★★★66% Dunkerleys Hotel & Restaurant

19 Beach St CT14 7AH
☎ 01304 375016 🖷 01304 380187
e-mail: Dunkerleysofdeal@btinternet.com
Dir: *from M20 or M2 follow signs for A258 Deal. Hotel is situated on the seafront close to Deal Pier.*
Almost opposite the pier, Dunkerleys can be identified by the bright array of summertime window boxes. Bedrooms are furnished to a high standard with a good range of amenities; principal rooms feature jacuzzis. The restaurant and bar have views of the Channel and are a popular venue for locals and residents alike. Menus make good use of fresh local seafood; diners can choose to eat in the restaurant or more informal bistro. The hotel caters for private dinner parties in the Ship's Hold function suite.
ROOMS: 16 en suite (2 fmly) s £50-£70; d £80-£110 (incl. bkfst) * LB **FACILITIES:** STV Jacuzzi/spa Xmas **NOTES:** No dogs (ex guide dogs) RS Mon **CARDS:**

★★70% Royal Hotel

Beach St CT14 6JD
☎ 01304 375555 🖷 01304 372270
e-mail: royalhotel@theroyalhotel.com
Dir: *turn off A2 onto the A258. Follow the road for 5m into Deal. Follow the one-way system onto the seafront. The Royal is 100yds from the pier*
A spacious imposing hotel on the seafront. The focus is the vibrant brasserie, where an appealing selection of dishes can be enjoyed.

continued on p182

DEAL, continued

Comfortable bedrooms feature smart colour schemes, and there is also a conference/function suite.
ROOMS: 22 en suite (4 fmly) No smoking in 2 bedrooms s £40-£75; d £75-£130 (incl. bkfst) * LB **FACILITIES:** STV **CONF:** Thtr 50 Class 20 Board 20 Del from £75 * **NOTES:** No dogs (ex guide dogs) Civ Wed 30
CARDS:

See advert on page 181

D

DEDDINGTON, Oxfordshire

Map 04 SP43

★★★71% Holcombe Hotel & Restaurant

Best Western

High St OX15 0SL
☎ 01869 338274 01869 337167
e-mail: reception@holcombehotel.freeserve.co.uk
Dir: *on the A4260 between Oxford & Banbury, at traffic lights in Deddington*

This charming privately owned hotel offers good accommodation and warm hospitality. The bedrooms are attractively decorated, well maintained and equipped with many useful extras. There is a convivial air in the bar, where informal meals and snacks are available and, for the more serious diner, there is a separate restaurant.
ROOMS: 17 en suite (3 fmly) s £65.50-£78.50; d £95-£110 (incl. bkfst) * LB **FACILITIES:** STV Xmas **CONF:** Thtr 25 Class 14 Board 18 Del from £120 * **PARKING:** 40 **NOTES:** Closed 2-10 Jan Civ Wed
CARDS:

See advert on opposite page

★★★66% Deddington Arms

Horsefair OX15 0SH
☎ 01869 338364 01869 337010
e-mail: deddarms@aol.com

There has been an inn on this site for over 400 years and the Deddington Arms retains much of its past character. Accommodation, upgraded and extended, offers smart, modern rooms. In the heart of this historic village the bar has a busy local trade and the delightful restaurant enjoys a good reputation.
ROOMS: 27 en suite (4 fmly) s £65-£80; d £75-£120 (incl. bkfst) * LB **FACILITIES:** STV Xmas **CONF:** Thtr 40 Class 30 Board 30 Del from £99 * **PARKING:** 35 **CARDS:**

See advert under BANBURY

DEDHAM, Essex

Map 05 TM03

Premier Collection

★★★ Maison Talbooth

Pride of Britain Member

Stratford Rd CO7 6HN
☎ 01206 322367 01206 322752
e-mail: mtreception@talbooth.co.uk
Dir: *A12 towards Ipswich, 1st turning signed Dedham, follow road until nasty left hand bend, take right hand turn, hotel 1m on right*
Overlooking the tranquil Dedham Vale, this pretty Georgian hotel offers a warm welcome. There is a comfortable drawing room where guests may take afternoon tea or snacks. Excellent breakfasts are served in the spacious bedrooms. Residents are chauffeured to the popular Le Talbooth Restaurant just half a mile away for dinner.
ROOMS: 10 en suite (1 fmly) s £120-£150; d £155-£195 (incl. cont bkfst) * LB **FACILITIES:** Croquet lawn Garden chess Xmas **CONF:** Thtr 30 Class 20 Board 16 Del from £140 * **PARKING:** 20 **NOTES:** No dogs (ex guide dogs) Civ Wed
CARDS:

DERBY, Derbyshire

Map 08 SK33

★★★★74% Menzies Mickleover Court

MENZIES HOTELS

Etwall Rd, Mickleover DE3 5XX
☎ 0500 636943 01773 880321
e-mail: info@menzies-hotels.co.uk
Dir: *take first exit off A516 signposted Mickleover*
Situated on the outskirts of Derby, this impressive modern hotel offers smartly appointed, thoughtfully equipped, air-conditioned bedrooms, each with a balcony. Smart public areas include open-plan circular lounges and an internal glass lift. There is a choice of two restaurants; the Stelline Italian restaurant or the Avesbury brasserie.
ROOMS: 99 en suite (20 fmly) No smoking in 45 bedrooms s £125-£150; d £150-£170 * LB **FACILITIES:** STV Indoor swimming (H) Sauna Solarium Gym Jacuzzi/spa Beauty salon Steam room entertainment Xmas **CONF:** Thtr 200 Class 80 Board 40 Del from £120 * **SERVICES:** Lift air con **PARKING:** 270 **NOTES:** No dogs (ex guide dogs) Civ Wed 200 **CARDS:**

★★★★62% Marriott Breadsall Priory Hotel, Country Club

Moor Rd DE7 6DL
☎ 01332 832235 01332 833509
(For full entry see Breadsall)

Arriving late? Four and five star hotels have night porters to assist with your luggage; and 24hr room service.

★★★74% **Midland**
Midland Rd DE1 2SQ
☎ 01332 345894 🖷 01332 293522
e-mail: res@midland-derby.co.uk
Dir: *situated opposite Derby central railway station*

This early Victorian hotel situated opposite Derby Midland Station provides good modern accommodation. The executive rooms are ideal for business travellers, equipped with writing desks, fax/computer points and first class bathrooms. Public rooms have been traditionally decorated and provide a comfortable lounge and a popular restaurant. Service is both professional and friendly. There is also a walled garden and a private car parking.
ROOMS: 100 en suite No smoking in 41 bedrooms s £77.50-£129; d £84-£139 * LB **FACILITIES:** entertainment **CONF:** Thtr 150 Class 50 Board 40 Del from £95 * **SERVICES:** Lift **PARKING:** 120 **NOTES:** No dogs (ex guide dogs) No smoking in restaurant Closed 24-26 Dec & 1 Jan Civ Wed 100 **CARDS:**

See advert on this page

DERBY, continued

★★★65% Hotel Ristorante La Gondola
220 Osmaston Rd DE23 8JX
☎ 01332 332895 🖷 01332 384512
Dir: *on A514 towards Melbourne*
Imaginatively designed and well equipped bedrooms, including a spacious family suite, are offered at this elegant Georgian house, situated between the inner and outer ring roads. There are two small comfortable lounges and a well established Italian restaurant. Extensive conference and banqueting rooms are also available.
ROOMS: 20 rms (19 en suite) (7 fmly) s £51-£58; d £54-£61 (incl. bkfst) * LB **FACILITIES:** STV entertainment Xmas **CONF:** Thtr 80 Class 50 Board 80 Del from £72.50 * **PARKING:** 70 **NOTES:** No dogs (ex guide dogs) **CARDS:**

★★★64% *Posthouse Derby*
Posthouse
Pastures Hill, Littleover DE23 7BA
☎ 0870 400 9023 🖷 01332 518668
Dir: *from M1/A52 head towards Derby. Take A5111 ringroad following signs to Littleover, hotel located through Littleover on rdbt opp Derby High School*
The hotel is situated in well tended gardens, about 3 miles south west of the city centre. The Junction Restaurant and Bar, reception, meeting and function facilities, are situated in the former manor house. The well equipped bedrooms are in a modern extension at the rear. Both lounge and room service are extensive and the atmosphere is warm and relaxed.
ROOMS: 63 en suite No smoking in 29 bedrooms
FACILITIES: Pitch'n'Putt **CONF:** Thtr 85 Class 60 Board 25
PARKING: 150 **CARDS:**

★★★63% International
288 Burton Rd DE23 6AD
☎ 01332 369321 🖷 01332 294430
Dir: *0.5m from city centre on A5250*
Within easy reach of the city centre, this hotel offers comfortable, modern public rooms. An extensive range of dishes is offered in the pleasant restaurant. There is a wide range of bedroom sizes and styles, and each room is very well equipped; some suites are also available.
ROOMS: 41 en suite 21 annexe en suite (4 fmly) No smoking in 5 bedrooms s £54-£75; d £65-£75 (incl. bkfst) * LB **FACILITIES:** STV entertainment Xmas **CONF:** Thtr 70 Class 40 Board 30 Del from £60 * **SERVICES:** Lift **PARKING:** 100 **NOTES:** Civ Wed 100
CARDS:

★★61% Aston Court
Midland Rd DE1 2SL
☎ 01332 342716 🖷 01332 293503
e-mail: astoncourtderby@hotelres.co.uk
Dir: *Midland Road opposite entrance of the Derby Railway Station*
Situated just a few minutes from the city centre this hotel offers comfortable accommodation. Bedrooms are being steadily upgraded and public areas include an open plan bar and traditional restaurant.
ROOMS: 58 en suite (3 fmly) s £65-£100; d £75-£100 * LB **FACILITIES:** Jacuzzi/spa **CONF:** Thtr 150 Class 80 Board 50 Del from £99 * **SERVICES:** Lift **PARKING:** 40 **NOTES:** No smoking in restaurant Civ Wed 60 **CARDS:**

TV dinner? Room service at three stars and above.

European Inn
Midland Rd DE1 2SL
☎ 01332 292000 🖷 01332 293940
e-mail: admin@euro-derby.co.uk
Dir: *200yds from railway station*
Excellent value accommodation is provided at this modern lodge, along with secure car parking and conference facilities. Bedrooms are well appointed and equipped with a range of modern facilities. Shops form part of the complex, including an Italian pizza restaurant. A good choice English breakfast is served buffet-style in the breakfast room, which may also be used for consumption of take-away meals.
ROOMS: 88 en suite d £46.50 * **CONF:** Thtr 80 Class 30 Board 25 Del from £83 *

Express by Holiday Inn Derby
Express by Holiday Inn
Roundhouse Rd, Off Pride Parkway DE24 8HX
☎ 01332 388000 🖷 388038
Dir: *A52 towards Derby, follow for 6m, taking exit signed Pride Park. Straight over 1st three rdbt. Right at 4th, left at next. Take 1st left & hotel on right*

A modern budget hotel offering comfortable accommodation in refreshing, spacious and comprehensively-equipped bedrooms, en suite bathrooms with power showers and continental buffet breakfast included in the room rate. Suitable for business travellers or families. For further details and the Express by Holiday Inn phone number, consult the Hotel Groups page.
ROOMS: 103 en suite (incl. cont bkfst) d £41-£49.50 * **CONF:** Thtr 28 Class 20 Board 16

Premier Lodge

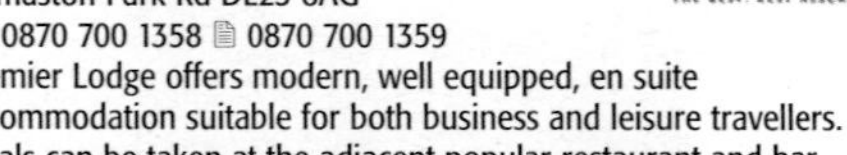

Foresters Leisure Park,
Oamaston Park Rd DE23 8AG
☎ 0870 700 1358 🖷 0870 700 1359
Premier Lodge offers modern, well equipped, en suite accommodation suitable for both business and leisure travellers. Meals can be taken at the adjacent popular restaurant and bar which is fully licensed. For further details, consult the Hotel Groups page.
ROOMS: 26 en suite d £46 *

DESBOROUGH, Northamptonshire — Map 04 SP88

Travelodge
Travelodge
Harborough Rd NN14 2UG
☎ 01536 762034 🖷 01536 762034
Dir: *on A6, southbound*
This modern building offers accommodation in smart, spacious and well equipped bedrooms, all with en suite bathrooms. Refreshments may be taken at the nearby family restaurant. For further details and the Travelodge phone number, consult the Hotel Groups page.
ROOMS: 32 en suite

DEVIZES, Wiltshire
Map 04 SU06

★★★64% *Bear*
Market Place SN10 1HS
☎ 01380 722444 🖷 01380 722450
Dating back to 1599, this attractive building sits to one side of the Market Place. Bedrooms vary between the older part of the inn to newer rooms but all are comfortable, and in addition there is a lovely lounge and two bars where beams and open fires add to the character. Home-made cakes are available throughout the day and lunch and dinner are complemented by a varied and interesting choice of wines.
ROOMS: 24 en suite (5 fmly) **FACILITIES:** Solarium **CONF:** Thtr 150 Board 50 **PARKING:** 25 **NOTES:** Closed 25-26 Dec
CARDS:

DEWSBURY, West Yorkshire
Map 08 SE22

★★★65% Heath Cottage Hotel & Restaurant
Wakefield Rd WF12 8ET
☎ 01924 465399 🖷 01924 459405
Dir: *from M1 junct 40 take A638 for 2.5m towards Dewsbury. Hotel just before traffic lights*
Standing in approximately an acre of grounds, Heath Cottage is 2.5 miles from the M1. It has ample parking, and well appointed modern bedrooms. A converted stable building houses some ground-floor rooms. The lounge bar and restaurant are air-conditioned and service is professional.
ROOMS: 23 en suite 6 annexe en suite (3 fmly) No smoking in 18 bedrooms s £52-£59; d £70-£75 (incl. bkfst) * LB **CONF:** Thtr 80 Class 50 Board 30 Del from £84 * **SERVICES:** air con **PARKING:** 70 **NOTES:** No dogs (ex guide dogs) No smoking in restaurant Civ Wed 100
CARDS:

See advert on this page

★★70% Healds Hall
Leeds Rd, Liversedge WF15 6JA
☎ 01924 409112 🖷 01924 401895
Dir: *on A62 between Leeds and Huddersfield*
This 18th-century house in the heart of West Yorkshire offers comfortable and well equipped accommodation. The hotel has earned a good local reputation for the quality of its food, and offers both a fixed-price menu and a full carte.
ROOMS: 24 en suite (3 fmly) No smoking in 9 bedrooms s £57-£60; d £60-£80 (incl. bkfst) * LB **FACILITIES:** STV **CONF:** Thtr 100 Class 60 Board 80 Del from £82 * **PARKING:** 80 **NOTES:** No smoking in restaurant Closed New Years Day **CARDS:**

DONCASTER, South Yorkshire
Map 08 SE50

★★★72% Mount Pleasant

Great North Rd DN11 0HW
☎ 01302 868696 & 868219 🖷 01302 865130
e-mail: mountpleasant@fax.co.uk
(For full entry see Rossington)

★★★67% Regent
Regent Square DN1 2DS
☎ 01302 364180 🖷 01302 322331
e-mail: admin@theregenthotel.co.uk
Dir: *on the corner of the A630 & A638, 1m from racecourse*
The Regent is located within the town centre, overlooking a delightful small square. Bedrooms have been furnished along modern lines, most with co-ordinated colour schemes. The public rooms include a choice of bars (Library and O'Gradys) and the refurbished restaurant offers an interesting range of dishes.
continued

ROOMS: 50 en suite (4 fmly) s £58-£78; d £65-£75 (incl. bkfst) * LB **FACILITIES:** STV Sauna entertainment **CONF:** Thtr 80 Class 50 Board 40 Del £99.50 * **SERVICES:** Lift **PARKING:** 20 **NOTES:** Closed New Year's Day Xmas Day RS Bank Hols
CARDS:

★★★65% Grand St Leger
Bennetthorpe DN2 6AX
☎ 01302 364111 🖷 01302 329865
Dir: *follow signs for Doncaster Racecourse, at Racecourse rdbt hotel on corner*
Conveniently situated opposite the racecourse, this hotel offers comfortable accommodation in two styles, standard and superior, including some rooms with four poster beds. Public areas include a lounge bar and restaurant, appropriately, both sport a horse racing theme. Service is both attentive and friendly, delivered in a helpful manner by a small team.
ROOMS: 20 en suite No smoking in all bedrooms s fr £75; d fr £95 (incl. bkfst) * LB **FACILITIES:** STV Xmas **CONF:** Thtr 65 Class 40 Board 40 Del £85 * **PARKING:** 28 **NOTES:** No dogs (ex guide dogs) No smoking in restaurant RS Christmas Day (lunch only) Civ Wed 60
CARDS:

★★★62% Danum
High St DN1 1DN
☎ 01302 342261 🖷 01302 329034
e-mail: admin@danumhotel.sagehost.co.uk
Dir: *from M18 juct3 A6182 to Doncaster. Cross rdbt, & right at next rdbt. Turn right at give way sign, left at mini rdbt, & hotel straight ahead*
Situated in the centre of the town, this Edwardian hotel offers spacious public rooms together with soundly equipped
continued on p186

DONCASTER, continued

accommodation. A very pleasant restaurant on the first floor serves adventurous dishes. There are good conference facilities.
ROOMS: 66 en suite (3 fmly) No smoking in 24 bedrooms s £59-£75; d £79-£90 (incl. bkfst) * LB **FACILITIES:** STV Free entry to local Leisure Centre entertainment Xmas **CONF:** Thtr 350 Class 160 Board 100 Del from £94 * **SERVICES:** Lift **PARKING:** 68 **NOTES:** Civ Wed 250
CARDS:

⌂ Campanile

Doncaster Leisure Park, Bawtry Rd DN4 7PD
☎ 01302 370770 📠 01302 370813
Dir: *follow signs to Dome Leisure Centre and turn left at entrance to Dome complex*

This modern building offers accommodation in smart well equipped bedrooms, all with en suite bathrooms. Refreshments may be taken at the informal Bistro. For further details and the Campanile phone number, consult the Hotel Groups page.
ROOMS: 50 en suite **CONF:** Thtr 35 Class 18 Board 20

⌂ Travelodge Doncaster North

DN8 5GS
☎ 01302 351221 📠 01302 847711
Dir: *M18 junct 5*
This modern building offers accommodation in smart, spacious and well equipped bedrooms, all with en suite bathrooms. Refreshments may be taken at the nearby family restaurant. For further details and the Travelodge phone number, consult the Hotel Groups page.
ROOMS: 39 en suite s fr £39.95 *

DONNINGTON See Telford

DORCHESTER, Dorset — Map 03 SY69

★★★62% The Wessex Royale

32 High St DT1 1UP
☎ 01305 262660 📠 01305 251941
Dir: *On the main high street in the centre of Dorchester*
Formally the family home of the Earl of Ilchester, this period property is situated near the centre of Dorchester. Equally suited to both the business and leisure traveller, the bedrooms vary in size and offer modern facilities. Each evening an interesting selection of dishes is available in the hotel's restaurant, while at lunch time a range of lighter meals is provided.

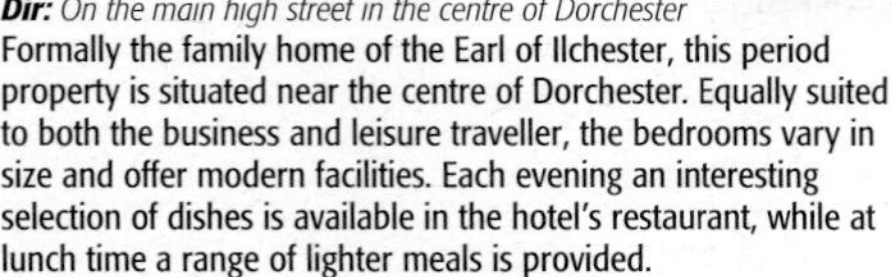

ROOMS: 25 en suite (2 fmly) No smoking in 10 bedrooms s fr £49; d fr £69 (incl. bkfst) * **PARKING:** 6 **NOTES:** No dogs (ex guide dogs)
CARDS:

DORCHESTER-ON-THAMES, Oxfordshire — Map 04 SU59

★★★68% 🏵 George

25 High St OX10 7HH
☎ 01865 340404 📠 01865 341620

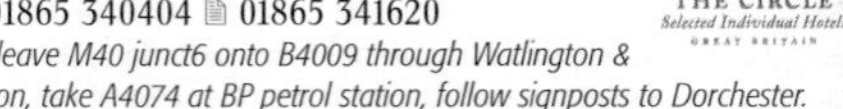

Dir: *leave M40 junct6 onto B4009 through Watlington & Benson, take A4074 at BP petrol station, follow signposts to Dorchester. Hotel on left.*
The George dates back to the 15th century with historic features throughout such as a vaulted ceiling in the restaurant. Bedrooms retain the character of the building with beams and furnishings to suit the period. Diners have two options for meals as the hotel has a busy bar and offers a full menu in the restaurant with an excellent wine list.
ROOMS: 9 en suite 9 annexe en suite (1 fmly) No smoking in 4 bedrooms s fr £65; d fr £85 (incl. cont bkfst) * LB **CONF:** Thtr 35 Class 25 Board 26 Del from £120 * **PARKING:** 75 **NOTES:** No smoking in restaurant **CARDS:**

★★64% 🏵 White Hart

High St OX10 7HN
☎ 01865 340074 📠 01865 341082
e-mail: whitehart.dorchester@virgin.net
Dir: *just off A415/A4074*
This historic inn, situated on a Thameside village high street, offers good modern cooking in a charming setting. The village is known for its abbey and antique shops. The bar and restaurant are across a courtyard, and the well equipped bedrooms are available in a variety of shapes and sizes.
ROOMS: 19 en suite (3 fmly) s £65-£85; d £75-£95 (incl. bkfst) * LB **FACILITIES:** Xmas **CONF:** Thtr 50 Class 20 Board 20 Del £115 * **PARKING:** 25 **CARDS:**

DORKING, Surrey — Map 04 TQ14

★★★★67% The Burford Bridge

Burford Bridge, Box Hill RH5 6BX
☎ 0870 400 8283 📠 01306 880386
Dir: *from M25 junct 9 follow signs for Dorking on A24. Hotel is located on this road on the left hand side*
This hotel nestles at the bottom of Box Hill, a landscape feature that was a source of inspiration for poets Keats and Wordsworth. Some of the bedrooms have balconies overlooking the well-tended gardens. There are extensive conference and banqueting facilities, for which a fine 16th-century tithe barn may be used.
ROOMS: 57 en suite No smoking in 17 bedrooms s £165; d £165-£175 * LB **FACILITIES:** Outdoor swimming (H) Croquet lawn Putting green Xmas **CONF:** Thtr 300 Class 100 Board 60 Del from £170 * **PARKING:** 80 **CARDS:**

★★★67% The White Horse

High St RH4 1BE
☎ 0870 400 8282 📠 01306 887241
Dir: *from M25 junct 9 take A24 S towards Dorking.Hotel is situated in the centre of the town*
Former guests at this old coaching inn include Charles Dickens who apparently wrote whilst here. With its oak beams, open fires and lounge, complete with quiet nooks, there is a definite Dickensian flavour to the hotel. Bedrooms provide all the expected modern comforts and amenities, yet have all the character of a bygone age. Additional accommodation is provided in the more modern wing.
ROOMS: 37 en suite 32 annexe en suite (2 fmly) No smoking in 20 bedrooms d £135-£145 * LB **FACILITIES:** Xmas **CONF:** Thtr 50 Class 30 Board 30 Del from £140 * **PARKING:** 73
CARDS:

★★★63% **Gatton Manor Hotel Golf & Country Club**
Standon Ln RH5 5PQ
☎ 01306 627555 01306 627713
e-mail: gattonmanor@enterprise.net
(For full entry see Ockley)

Travelodge
Reigate Rd RH4 1QB
☎ 01306 740361 01306 740361
Dir: *0.5m E, on A25*
This modern building offers accommodation in smart, spacious and well equipped bedrooms, all with en suite bathrooms. Refreshments may be taken at the nearby family restaurant. For further details and the Travelodge phone number, consult the Hotel Groups page.
ROOMS: 54 en suite

DORRIDGE, West Midlands Map 07 SP17

★★65% **Forest Hotel**
25 Station Approach B93 8JA
☎ 01564 772120 01564 770677
Dir: *take junct 5 off M42, follow A4141 for 2m, after Knowle village turn right (signed Dorridge) in 1.5m left just before rail bridge, hotel 200yds*
This well established privately run hotel is situated in the heart of Dorridge village thirty minutes from Stratford upon Avon and the Cotswolds. Rooms have been refurbished throughout and are very well equipped with modern facilities. Downstairs there is a choice of bars where meals are available and there is also a hotel restaurant.
ROOMS: 12 en suite (1 fmly) s £55; d £70 (incl. bkfst) * **SERVICES:** air con **PARKING:** 70 **NOTES:** No dogs (ex guide dogs) **CARDS:**

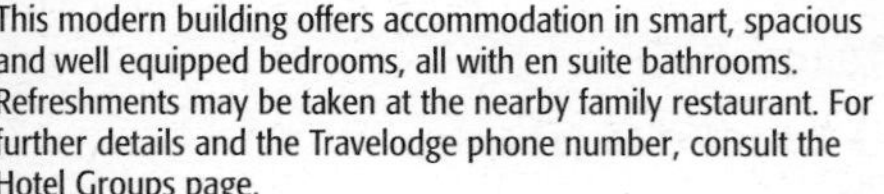

DOVER, Kent Map 05 TR34

★★★75% **Wallett's Court**
West Cliffe, St Margarets-at-Cliffe CT15 6EW
☎ 01304 852424 01304 853430
e-mail: wallettscourt@compuserve.com
Dir: *take A258 towards Deal; 1st right to St Margarets-at-Cliffe & West Cliffe, 1m on right opposite West Cliffe church*
This country house hotel has at its core a lovely Jacobean manor. Bedrooms in the original house are traditionally furnished and rooms in the courtyard buildings are more modern, all are equipped to a high standard. The restaurant offers well prepared traditional food.
ROOMS: 3 en suite 12 annexe en suite (2 fmly) **FACILITIES:** Indoor swimming (H) Tennis (hard) Riding Sauna Solarium Gym Croquet lawn Putting green Jacuzzi/spa **CONF:** Thtr 25 Class 25 Board 16 Del from £110 * **PARKING:** 32 **NOTES:** No dogs (ex guide dogs) No smoking in restaurant **CARDS:**

★★★69% **The Churchill**
Dover Waterfront CT17 9BP
☎ 01304 203633 01304 216320
e-mail: enquiries@churchill-hotel.com
Dir: *from A20 follow signs for Hoverport, turn left onto seafront, hotel 800yds along*
Located on Dover's waterfront overlooking the harbour, this completely refurbished hotel forms part of a listed Regency terrace. Bedrooms are furnished to a comfortable standard; executive rooms have mini bars and there are ten with balconies. Winston's Restaurant serves enjoyable cooking and there is a well appointed bar lounge, sun lounge and front terrace.
continued

ROOMS: 66 rms (65 en suite) (6 fmly) No smoking in 12 bedrooms s £59; d £79 * **FACILITIES:** STV Sauna Solarium Gym Health Club Aeorbics Studio Steam Aromatherapy Xmas **CONF:** Thtr 110 Class 60 Board 50 Del £89 * **SERVICES:** Lift **PARKING:** 32 **NOTES:** No smoking in restaurant Civ Wed 80
CARDS:

See advert on this page

★★★60% **County Hotel Dover**
Townwall St CT16 1SZ
☎ 01304 509955 01304 213230
Dir: *follow A20 over 3 rdbts, then at 4th stay left signed 'Eastern Docks' and take 2nd slip road on left*
Conveniently located for the ferry terminal, this hotel offers spacious well equipped rooms with air-conditioning. A refurbishment programme is under way and the newly completed
continued on p188

DOVER, continued

rooms are bright and modern. The indoor swimming pool is popular.

County Hotel, Dover

ROOMS: 79 en suite (32 fmly) No smoking in 31 bedrooms s £40-£60; d £40-£70 * LB **FACILITIES:** Indoor swimming (H) Xmas **CONF:** Thtr 80 Class 46 Board 40 Del £85 * **SERVICES:** Lift **PARKING:** 48
CARDS:

★★★ *Posthouse Dover*

Posthouse

Singledge Ln, Whitfield CT16 3LF
☎ 0870 400 9024 ▯ 01304 825576
Dir: *from M2, take A2 towards Dover, turn left immediately before Esso garage or from M20, at Eastern Docks rdbt turn right, over 2 rdbts then turn right*
Suitable for both the business and leisure traveller, this bright hotel provides accommodation in well equipped bedrooms. It is located to the north of town.
ROOMS: 68 en suite (19 fmly) No smoking in 37 bedrooms
FACILITIES: ch fac **CONF:** Thtr 60 Class 20 Board 24 **PARKING:** 80
CARDS:

○ *Premier Lodge*

Marine Court, Marine Parage
☎ 0870 700 1364 ▯ 0870 700 1365

DOWNHAM MARKET, Norfolk Map 05 TF60

★★69% Castle

High St PE38 9HF
☎ 01366 384311 ▯ 01366 384311
e-mail: howards@castle-hotel.com
Dir: *from M11 take A10 for Ely into Downham Market, on reaching town hotel opposite traffic lights, on corner of High St*
Situated close to the centre of town, this coaching inn has been welcoming guests for over 300 years. Well maintained public areas include a cosy lounge bar and two smartly appointed restaurants offering a choice of carte and set menus. Inviting bedrooms, some with four-poster beds, are thoughtfully equipped and have co-ordinated soft furnishings.
ROOMS: 12 en suite s £54-£64; d £69-£95 (incl. bkfst) * LB
FACILITIES: Xmas **CONF:** Thtr 60 Class 30 Board 40 Del from £79 *
PARKING: 26 **NOTES:** No smoking in restaurant **CARDS:**

DRIFFIELD (GREAT), East Riding of Yorkshire Map 08 TA05

★★★70% Bell

Best Western

46 Market Place YO25 6AN
☎ 01377 256661 ▯ 01377 253228
Dir: *enter town from A164, turn right at traffic lights. Car park 50yds on left behind black railings*
This 250-year-old hotel is furnished with many antique and period pieces. The bedrooms vary in shape and size; all have modern facilities and some have their own sitting rooms. There is a good leisure and natural health centre across the courtyard. The hotel has a relaxed, friendly atmosphere.
ROOMS: 16 en suite No smoking in 4 bedrooms s £76-£90; d £105-£120 (incl. bkfst) * LB **FACILITIES:** Indoor swimming (H) Squash Snooker Sauna Solarium Gym Jacuzzi/spa Masseur entertainment **CONF:** Thtr 250 Class 200 Board 50 **SERVICES:** Lift **PARKING:** 18 **NOTES:** No children 12yrs No smoking in restaurant Civ Wed 100
CARDS:

DROITWICH, Worcestershire Map 03 SO86

★★★★67% Château Impney

WR9 0BN
☎ 01905 774411 ▯ 01905 772371
e-mail: chateau@impney.demon.co.uk
Dir: *on A38, 1m from M5 junct 5 towards Droitwich/Worcester*
Overlooking 120 acres of beautiful parkland, this elegant and imposing French-style chateau dates back to the 1800s. All bedrooms are furnished and equipped to modern standards, and come in a variety of sizes. The hotel has excellent conference, function and leisure facilities.
ROOMS: 67 en suite 53 annexe en suite (10 fmly) s £69.95-£109.95; d £79.95-£129.95 (incl. bkfst) * **FACILITIES:** Tennis (hard) Sauna Solarium Gym Pool table **CONF:** Thtr 1000 Class 550 Board 160 Del from £79.95 * **SERVICES:** Lift **PARKING:** 1000 **NOTES:** No dogs (ex guide dogs) No smoking in restaurant Closed Xmas
CARDS:

★★★★65% Raven

Victoria Square WR9 8DQ
☎ 01905 772224 ▯ 01905 797100
e-mail: sales@ravenhotel.demon.co.uk
Dir: *in town centre on A38, 1.5m from M5 junct 5 towards Droitwich/Worcester*
Situated in the heart of this spa town this unique timber framed property dates back to the early 16th century. Considerably extended over the centuries, it now provides modern, well equipped accommodation. Public areas include a spacious lounge, pleasant lounge bar with pianist, and charming restaurant with exposed beams and wall timbers.
ROOMS: 72 en suite (1 fmly) s £69.95-£109.95; d £79.95-£129.95 (incl. bkfst) * **CONF:** Thtr 150 Class 70 Board 40 Del from £146.85 *
SERVICES: Lift **PARKING:** 250 **NOTES:** No dogs (ex guide dogs) No smoking in restaurant Closed Xmas
CARDS:

★★65% The Hadley Bowling Green Inn

Hadley Heath WR9 0AR
☎ 01905 620294 ▯ 01905 620771
e-mail: hbginn@backissues.freeserve.co.uk
Dir: *from M5 junct 5 A38 towards Droitwich. Follow Ring Road (A38) towards Worcester. Take next left signed Ombersley/Tenbury and follow hotel signs*
This 16th-century inn claims to have one of the country's oldest crown greens. Guy Fawkes and his confederates reputedly planned the Gunpowder Plot here. There is a choice of bars and a pleasant restaurant. A wide range of food is available. The well equipped accommodation includes two rooms with four-poster beds, family rooms and bedrooms on the ground floor of a separate building.

continued

ROOMS: 11 en suite 3 annexe en suite (2 fmly) s £53-£58; d £69-£85 (incl. bkfst) * LB **FACILITIES:** Pool table Clay pigeon shooting Crown bowling Craft weekends Xmas **PARKING:** 100 **NOTES:** Closed 26 Dec pm **CARDS:**

Travelodge

Rashwood Hill WR9 8DA
☎ 01527 861545 📠 01527 861545
Dir: *2m N, on A38 from junc 5 at M5*
This modern building offers accommodation in smart, spacious and well equipped bedrooms, all with en suite bathrooms. Refreshments may be taken at the nearby family restaurant. For further details and the Travelodge phone number, consult the Hotel Groups page.
ROOMS: 32 en suite

DRONFIELD, Derbyshire — Map 08 SK37

★★66% Chantry

Church St S18 1QB
☎ 01246 413014 📠 01246 413014
Dir: *6m from Sheffield and Chesterfield on A61. Opposite church with spire*
Next to an attractive church, this hotel has award-winning gardens and friendly service. Day rooms include a pleasant conservatory coffee shop, and a spacious restaurant and a bar. Bedrooms are thoughtfully designed and relatively spacious.
ROOMS: 7 en suite s £48; d £65 (incl. bkfst) * **PARKING:** 28
CARDS:

DUDLEY, West Midlands — Map 07 SO99

see also Himley

★★★★68% The Copthorne Merry Hill-Dudley

COPTHORNE

The Waterfront, Level St, Brierley Hill DY5 1UR
☎ 01384 482882 📠 01384 482773
Dir: *follow signs for Merry Hill Centre*
Situated to the west of the city, this new hotel has a scenic position overlooking the Merry Hill development and marina. Polished marbled floors, rich fabrics and striking interior design are features of the stylish public areas which include the informal Faradays bar and restaurant. Bedrooms are spacious and well equipped.
ROOMS: 138 en suite (14 fmly) No smoking in 90 bedrooms s £130; d £140 * LB **FACILITIES:** STV Indoor swimming (H) Sauna Solarium Gym Jacuzzi/spa Aerobics studio Beauty & massage therapists
CONF: Thtr 570 Class 240 Board 60 Del £165 * **SERVICES:** Lift
PARKING: 100 **NOTES:** No dogs (ex guide dogs)
CARDS:

★★★65% Ward Arms

corus

Birmingham Rd DY1 4RN
☎ 01384 458070 📠 01384 457502
e-mail: 113566.1360@compuserve.com
Dir: *on A461. At M5 junct 2 1st left at rdbt, then 3rd exit from next rdbt, proceed for 1.5m. Take 1st exit at 3rd rdbt, hotel 500yds on left*

This busy and popular, modern hotel is conveniently located within easy reach of the M5 motorway. The bedrooms are well equipped and have recently benefited from refurbishment work. Rooms on ground floor level are available. Public areas include the traditionally furnished conservatory restaurant and bar, where popular dishes are served. There is also Morriseys, a very popular Irish theme bar. Rooms for functions and conferences are available.
ROOMS: 72 en suite No smoking in 14 bedrooms d fr £80 * LB
FACILITIES: STV Pool table Xmas **CONF:** Thtr 60 Class 50 Board 60 Del from £85 * **PARKING:** 150 **CARDS:**

Travelodge

Dudley Rd, Brierley Hill DY5 1LQ
☎ 01384 481579 📠 01384 481579
Dir: *3m W, on A461*
This modern building offers accommodation in smart, spacious and well equipped bedrooms, all with en suite bathrooms. Refreshments may be taken at the nearby family restaurant. For further details and the Travelodge phone number, consult the Hotel Groups page.
ROOMS: 32 en suite

DULVERTON, Somerset — Map 03 SS92

★★★71% Carnarvon Arms

TA22 9AE
☎ 01398 323302 📠 01398 324022
e-mail: carnarvon.arms@virgin.net
Dir: *leave A396 at Exbridge onto B3222, hotel 1m on right*
All that is best in the English country house hotel, including cosy public rooms with open fires and fresh flowers. The restaurant offers a choice of menus, and meals are also served in the informal Buttery Bar. Look out for the old railway buildings which are a feature of the delightful grounds.
ROOMS: 25 rms (23 en suite) (2 fmly) s £45-£70; d fr £80 (incl. bkfst) * LB **FACILITIES:** Outdoor swimming (H) Tennis (hard) Fishing Snooker Croquet lawn Clay pigeon shooting **CONF:** Thtr 100 Class 25 Board 40 **PARKING:** 121 **NOTES:** No smoking in restaurant Civ Wed
CARDS:

> Packed in a hurry? Ironing facilities should be available at all star levels, either in rooms or on request.

DULVERTON, continued

Premier Collection

★★ Ashwick House
TA22 9QD
☎ 01398 323868 01398 323868
e-mail: ashwickhouse@talk21.com
Dir: *turn left at post office, 3m NW on B3223, over two cattlegrids, signposted on left*
A small Edwardian hotel, peacefully set in six acres on the edge of Exmoor. Public areas are extensive, the main feature being the galleried hall with its welcoming log fire. Bedrooms are spacious and comfortable, with every conceivable facility. Each evening a set menu is served, with a choice of starter and pudding, using the finest local produce.
ROOMS: 6 en suite No smoking in 1 bedroom s £79-£86; d £138-£152 (incl. bkfst & dinner) * LB **FACILITIES:** Solarium Xmas **PARKING:** 27 **NOTES:** No dogs No children 8yrs No smoking in restaurant

★★63% Lion
Bank Square TA22 9BU
☎ 01398 323444 01398 323980
Dir: *turn right from A361 at Tiverton rdbt on to A396. Turn left at Exbridge onto B3223. Over bridge in Dulverton, hotel is in Bank Sq*
A charming traditional inn, The Lion is situated in the centre of Dulverton. The bar is popular for real ales and a range of quality meals is available at lunch times and during the evening. Well equipped bedrooms are comfortable, and are undergoing a programme of improvements. The Lion is a great place from which to explore Exmoor National Park.
ROOMS: 13 en suite (1 fmly) s £29.50; d £55 (incl. bkfst) * **FACILITIES:** Xmas **PARKING:** 6 **NOTES:** No smoking in restaurant
CARDS:

DUNCHURCH, Warwickshire — Map 04 SP47

Travelodge
London Rd, Thurlaston CV23 9LG
☎ 01788 521538 01788 521538
Dir: *A45, westbound*
This modern building offers accommodation in smart, spacious and well equipped bedrooms, all with en suite bathrooms. Refreshments may be taken at the nearby family restaurant. For further details and the Travelodge phone number, consult the Hotel Groups page.
ROOMS: 40 en suite

DUNSTABLE, Bedfordshire — Map 04 TL02

★★★67% *Old Palace Lodge*
Church St LU5 4RT
☎ 01582 662201 01582 696422
Dir: *exit M1 at junct 11 and take A505. Hotel 2m on right opposite Priory church*

Well positioned between the town centre and the motorway, this ivy-clad Grade II listed building offers comfortable bedrooms in either period or modern style. Public areas include a comfortably furnished bar lounge and an attractive restaurant serving a daily menu and a varied carte.
ROOMS: 68 en suite (7 fmly) No smoking in 21 bedrooms **FACILITIES:** STV **CONF:** Thtr 40 Class 18 Board 25 **SERVICES:** Lift **PARKING:** 70 **CARDS:**

See advert on opposite page

Travelodge
Watling St LU7 9LZ
☎ 01525 211177 01525 211177
Dir: *3m N, on A5*
This modern building offers accommodation in smart, spacious and well equipped bedrooms, all with en suite bathrooms. Refreshments may be taken at the nearby family restaurant. For further details and the Travelodge phone number, consult the Hotel Groups page.
ROOMS: 28 en suite

DUNSTER, Somerset — Map 03 SS94

★★★64% The Luttrell Arms
High St TA24 6SG
☎ 0870 400 8110 01643 821567
Dir: *20m beyond the Exmoor Visitor Centre on A396, opposite the Yarn Market*
The Luttrell Arms dates back to the 15th century and was formerly the guest house to Cleeve Abbey. Bedrooms vary in size and style, ranging from spacious four poster rooms to more compact rooms. The smart split-level restaurant serves home cooked meals. The bar also serves meals and there is a comfortable, beamed lounge on the first floor.
ROOMS: 27 en suite (4 fmly) No smoking in 9 bedrooms s £79-£104; d £138-£163 (incl. bkfst & dinner) * LB **FACILITIES:** Xmas **CONF:** Thtr 25 Board 15 **PARKING:** 3 **NOTES:** No smoking in restaurant
CARDS:

Bad hair day? Hairdryers in all rooms three stars and above.

DURHAM, Co Durham

Map 12 NZ24

see also Rushyford

★★★★72% ❀❀ Swallow Royal County

Old Elvet DH1 3JN
☎ 0191 386 6821 🖷 0191 386 0704
e-mail: royal.county@swallow-hotels.co.uk
Dir: *from A1(M) take junct 62 towards Durham, over 1st rdbt, turn left at 2nd rdbt over the bridge. Turn left at traffic lights, hotel on left*

This long established hotel sits by the river in the heart of the city. Bedrooms are split between three different buildings. Public areas include a cocktail bar and foyer and two restaurants, the elegant County serving rosette-worthy cuisine.
ROOMS: 151 en suite (4 fmly) No smoking in 99 bedrooms s £110-£135; d £145-£225 (incl. bkfst) * LB **FACILITIES:** STV Indoor swimming (H) Sauna Solarium Gym Jacuzzi/spa Steam room Plunge pool Impulse showers Xmas **CONF:** Thtr 140 Class 50 Board 45 Del from £145 * **SERVICES:** Lift **PARKING:** 80 **CARDS:**

★★★70% *Ramside Hall*

Carrville DH1 1TD
☎ 0191 386 5282 🖷 0191 386 0399
Dir: *take A690 towards Sunderland from A1M/A690 interchange, 200mtrs after going under railway bridge*

Ramside Hall is set in attractive parkland with its own golf course, a driving range and a new conference centre. Facilities include a choice of eating options and a mix of public areas which include an elegant foyer and lounge, plus various bar lounge areas. The majority of bedrooms are spacious, located in an extension of the original building.
ROOMS: 80 en suite (10 fmly) No smoking in 36 bedrooms
FACILITIES: STV Golf 27 Snooker Sauna Putting green entertainment
CONF: Thtr 400 Class 160 Board 40 **SERVICES:** Lift air con
PARKING: 500 **CARDS:**

★★★69% Swallow Three Tuns

New Elvet DH1 3AQ
☎ 0191 386 4326 🖷 0191 386 1406
e-mail: info@swallowhotels.com
Dir: *from A1 follow A690 for city. At 1st rdbt take 2nd exit at 2nd rdbt take 1st exit. Hotel 100yds on left over bridge and through traffic lights*

Dating in part from the 16th century, this city-centre hotel preserves its individuality, and its friendly, attentive staff are the key to its popularity. Bedrooms are well equipped, the executive rooms being particularly spacious. Guests have use of the leisure facilities at the Swallow County Hotel, a few yards away.
ROOMS: 50 en suite (2 fmly) No smoking in 30 bedrooms s fr £99; d fr £115 (incl. bkfst) * LB **FACILITIES:** STV Complimentary use of leisure facilities at Royal County Hotel entertainment Xmas **CONF:** Thtr 350 Class 200 Board 160 **PARKING:** 60
CARDS:

DURHAM, continued

★★★ 60% *Bowburn Hall*
Bowburn DH6 5NH
☎ 0191 377 0311 📠 0191 377 3459
***Dir:** head towards Bowburn, go right at Cooperage Pub, then 0.5 miles along country road to left junct signposted Durham. Hotel on immediate left*
This hotel, in five acres of grounds, lies in a quiet residential area, yet with easy access to the A1 just south of the city. Cosy bedrooms are attractively decorated, and the spacious lounge bar and conservatory overlook the gardens. Bar meals are popular with locals and visitors alike, more formal dining also being available in the restaurant.
ROOMS: 19 en suite **FACILITIES:** STV **CONF:** Thtr 150 Class 80 Board 60 **PARKING:** 100 **CARDS:**

★★ 62% Rainton Lodge
West Rainton DH4 6QY
☎ 0191 512 0540 & 512 0534 📠 0191 584 1221
***Dir:** 1.5m from junct 62 A1(M) on A690 towards Sunderland*
Enjoying a fine outlook across the valley, this hotel has an attractive interior. The bar and restaurant feature a good range of dishes, the fixed price dinner is excellent value. Bedrooms vary in style and size, some furnished in a contemporary style, the others with traditional pine.
ROOMS: 27 en suite (3 fmly) s £34-£38; d £44-£48 (incl. bkfst) * LB **FACILITIES:** STV Riding entertainment Xmas **CONF:** Thtr 100 Class 70 Board 50 **PARKING:** 80 **NOTES:** No dogs (ex guide dogs)
CARDS:

DUXFORD, Cambridgeshire — Map 05 TL44

★★★ 72% ❀❀ Duxford Lodge
Ickleton Rd CB2 4RU
☎ 01223 836444 📠 01223 832271
e-mail: duxford@btclick.com
***Dir:** at M11 junct 10, turn onto A505 to Duxford. Take first turn right at 'T' junction, hotel on left*

A warm welcome is assured at this attractive red brick hotel in the heart of this delightful village. Public areas include a bar, separate lounge, and an attractive restaurant where an excellent and imaginative menu is offered. The bedrooms are comfortable and smartly appointed.
ROOMS: 11 en suite 4 annexe en suite s £50-£83; d £89-£110 (incl. bkfst) * LB **FACILITIES:** Xmas **CONF:** Thtr 30 Class 20 Board 20 Del from £120 * **PARKING:** 34 **NOTES:** Closed 26-30 Dec & 1 Jan RS Saturday lunch **CARDS:**

See advert under CAMBRIDGE

Arriving late? Four and five star hotels have night porters to assist with your luggage; and 24hr room service.

EASINGTON, North Yorkshire — Map 08 NZ71

★★★ 71% ❀ Grinkle Park
TS13 4UB
☎ 01287 640515 📠 01287 641278
e-mail: hotels@leeds.taverns.bass.co.uk
***Dir:** 9m from Guisborough, signed left off the main A171 Guisborough/Whitby Road*
Standing in extensive grounds, this elegant Victorian house has an attentive and friendly staff and delightfully furnished bedrooms. There are comfortable lounges and a gracious restaurant which serves well presented dishes using the best of local produce.
ROOMS: 20 en suite s fr £79; d fr £115.65 (incl. bkfst & dinner) * LB **FACILITIES:** Tennis (hard) Snooker Croquet lawn Xmas **CONF:** Thtr 70 Class 20 Board 25 Del from £100.95 * **PARKING:** 122
CARDS:

EASINGWOLD, North Yorkshire — Map 08 SE56

★★ 67% George
Market Place YO61 3AD
☎ 01347 821698 📠 01347 823448
e-mail: info@the-george-hotel.co.uk
***Dir:** off A19 midway between York & Thirsk, in Market Place*
An old coaching inn overlooking the cobbled market square. Bedrooms to the rear have been decorated and furnished to a very good standard. An extensive range of well produced food is available either in the bar or candlelit restaurant. A cosy and comfortable lounge is also provided, along with friendly and attentive service.
ROOMS: 14 en suite (2 fmly) s £45-£55; d £60-£75 (incl. bkfst) LB **PARKING:** 10 **NOTES:** No dogs (ex guide dogs) No smoking in restaurant **CARDS:**

EAST AYTON, North Yorkshire — Map 08 SE98

★★★ 63% East Ayton Lodge
Moor Ln, Forge Valley YO13 9EW
☎ 01723 864227 📠 01723 862680
***Dir:** 400 yds off A170*
This family-run hotel stands in three acres of grounds close to the River Derwent, off a quiet lane on the edge of East Ayton. Bedrooms are well equipped and those in the courtyard are particularly spacious. A good range of food is available and there are plans to add a leisure centre.
ROOMS: 11 en suite 20 annexe en suite (3 fmly) s £39.50-£49.50; d £50-£99 (incl. bkfst) * LB **FACILITIES:** Xmas **CONF:** Thtr 46 Class 74 Board 32 **PARKING:** 50 **NOTES:** No smoking in restaurant
CARDS:

EASTBOURNE, East Sussex — Map 05 TV69

★★★★★ 73% ❀❀ Grand
King Edward's Pde BN21 4EQ
☎ 01323 412345 📠 01323 412233
e-mail: Reservations@GrandEastbourne.co.uk
***Dir:** on seafront west of Eastbourne 1m from railway station*
Huge investment has returned this famous Victorian hotel back to its former glory. Extensive public rooms, dominated by the Great Hall with its marble columns and high ceiling, are especially spacious and comfortable. The thoughtfully equipped bedrooms and suites, some of which enjoy the most stunning sea views and have their own balconies, provide the expected levels of comfort. Guests have a choice of two restaurants and the Mirabelle is well deserving of its Rosette award. Service throughout is attentive and the atmosphere relaxed.

continued

ROOMS: 152 en suite (20 fmly) s £120-£360; d £152-£400 (incl. bkfst) * LB **FACILITIES:** Indoor swimming (H) Outdoor swimming (H) Snooker Sauna Solarium Gym Putting green Jacuzzi/spa Hairdressing beauty & massage entertainment ch fac Xmas **CONF:** Thtr 300 Class 200 Board 60 Del from £215 * **SERVICES:** Lift **PARKING:** 64 **NOTES:** No smoking in restaurant Civ Wed 200 **CARDS:**

See advert on this page

★★★73% Lansdowne

King Edward's Pde BN21 4EE

☎ 01323 725174 📠 01323 739721

e-mail: thelansdowne@btinternet.com

Dir: *hotel situated at west end of seafront (B2103) facing Western Lawns*

This hotel has both a prime seafront location and range of meeting rooms, making it an ideal location for all visitors. Bedrooms are attractively furnished and decorated, many offering

continued on p194

EASTBOURNE, continued

sea views. There are a range of lounges, a well appointed cocktail bar and a games room available for guests to enjoy.
ROOMS: 115 en suite (8 fmly) s £55-£63; d £87-£109 (incl. bkfst) * LB **FACILITIES:** STV Snooker Pool table Darts Table tennis pool table **CONF:** Thtr 120 Class 50 Board 50 Del from £75 * **SERVICES:** Lift **PARKING:** 22 **NOTES:** No smoking in restaurant Closed 1-18 Jan **CARDS:**

See advert on page 193

★★★71% Hydro
Mount Rd BN20 7HZ
☎ 01323 720643 01323 641167
Dir: *proceed to pier/seafront, turn right along Grand Parade, at Grand Hotel you will see a road with the sign Hydro Hotel, proceed up South Cliff 200yds*
This well established hotel has been owned by the same family for over a century. It enjoys an elevated position and offers some lovely views of its attractive gardens and the sea beyond. The spacious bedrooms are attractively furnished and decorated. In addition to the lounges, guests also have access to fitness facilities and a hairdressing salon.
ROOMS: 83 en suite (1 fmly) s £35-£58; d £64-£110 (incl. bkfst) * LB **FACILITIES:** STV Outdoor swimming (H) Sauna Gym Pool table Croquet lawn Putting green Beauty room Hairdressing Xmas **CONF:** Thtr 140 Class 90 Board 40 Del from £55 * **SERVICES:** Lift **PARKING:** 50 **NOTES:** No smoking in restaurant Civ Wed 100 **CARDS:**

★★★61% Chatsworth
Grand Pde BN21 3YR
☎ 01323 411016 01323 643270
e-mail: sales@chatsworth-hotel.demon.co.uk
Dir: *on seafront between the pier and the bandstand*

Within minutes of the town centre and the pier, this attractive Edwardian hotel enjoys one of the best positions on the seafront. Bedrooms, many of which have sea views, are traditional in style and offer a useful range of in room facilities. The public areas consist of the cosy Dukes Bar, spacious lounge and the Devonshire Restaurant.
ROOMS: 47 en suite (2 fmly) No smoking in 10 bedrooms s £41-£56; d £72-£112 (incl. bkfst) * LB **FACILITIES:** STV entertainment Xmas **CONF:** Thtr 100 Class 60 Board 30 Del from £97.50 * **SERVICES:** Lift **NOTES:** No smoking in restaurant Civ Wed 140 **CARDS:**

See advert on opposite page

★★★61% Quality Hotel Eastbourne
Grand Pde BN21 3YS
☎ 01323 727411 01323 720665
e-mail: admin@gb610.u-net.com
Dir: *take A22 to Eastbourne and follow through to seafront where the hotel is located between the pier and the bandstand*

CHOICE HOTELS EUROPE

This hotel benefits from an ideal location on the seafront, a short distance from the pier. Bedrooms vary in size and shape, but all are well equipped and practically furnished. The public areas include a spacious restaurant and a lounge/bar area with sun terrace. There is regular entertainment including bingo and live music.
ROOMS: 95 en suite (6 fmly) No smoking in 47 bedrooms s £64; d £76 * LB **FACILITIES:** STV Gym Xmas **CONF:** Thtr 150 Class 80 Board 20 Del £74.75 * **SERVICES:** Lift **NOTES:** No smoking in restaurant **CARDS:**

★★★61% Wish Tower
King Edward's Pde BN21 4EB
☎ 01323 722676 01323 721474
Dir: *opposite Wish Tower on seafront, W of the pier*

An established seafront hotel, located opposite the Martello tower. It is convenient for local theatres, amenities and the well known winter gardens. Bedrooms vary, all are practically furnished and most have sea views. Public areas consist of a spacious lounge/bar and downstairs dining room.
ROOMS: 56 en suite No smoking in 3 bedrooms s £35-£60; d £50-£95 (incl. bkfst) * LB **CONF:** Thtr 60 Class 20 Board 30 **SERVICES:** Lift **PARKING:** 3 **CARDS:**

★★69% New Wilmington
25 Compton St BN21 4DU
☎ 01323 721219 01323 728900
e-mail: reservations@new-wilmington.sagehost.co.uk
Dir: *A22 to Eastbourne along the seafront, turn right along promenade until Wishtower. Turn right off Promenade and hotel is on the first left*
This family run hotel is conveniently located close to the town centre and to the seafront. Bedrooms are comfortably appointed and tastefully decorated with some suitable for family accommodation. Public areas include a cosy bar, non smoking lounge and a spacious, informal restaurant.
ROOMS: 40 en suite (8 fmly) s fr £42; d fr £74 (incl. bkfst & dinner) * LB **FACILITIES:** entertainment Xmas **SERVICES:** Lift **PARKING:** 2 **NOTES:** No smoking in restaurant Closed Jan & Feb **CARDS:**

★★69% *West Rocks*
Grand Pde BN21 4DL
☎ 01323 725217 01323 720421
Dir: *on seafront western end*
Set mid-way along the Grand Parade, this family run hotel is convenient for the seafront, local attractions and only a short walk from the town centre shops. Bedrooms vary with many offering sea views, all are furnished and decorated to a good standard. Guests have the choice of two comfortable lounges and a bar in which to relax.
ROOMS: 45 en suite (4 fmly) **FACILITIES:** entertainment **CONF:** Thtr 50 Class 26 Board 20 **SERVICES:** Lift **NOTES:** No dogs No children 3yrs Closed mid Nov-end Feb **CARDS:**

★★68% The Downland Hotel & Restaurant
37 Lewes Rd BN21 2BU
☎ 01323 732689 🖷 01323 720321
Dir: *on A22, take 1st exit at Willingdon rdbt, follow sign to seafront, go past college and hospital straight over rdbt. Hotel in 0.5m*
This well maintained hotel is set just out of the town centre. Bedrooms are comfortable and equipped with a range of quality extras. The dining room offers a short menu of dishes, all cooked to order.
ROOMS: 12 en suite (2 fmly) No smoking in 4 bedrooms s £25-£35; d £55-£75 (incl. bkfst) * LB **PARKING:** 10 **NOTES:** No dogs (ex guide dogs) No children 10yrs No smoking in restaurant **CARDS:**

★★68% *Stanley House Hotel*
9/10 Howard Square BN21 4BQ
☎ 01323 731393 🖷 01323 738823
This friendly hotel close to the bandstand and pier continues to be popular for holidays. The good value accommodation offers all the expected modern comforts in an attractive setting. Public areas include a well stocked bar, choice of lounges and spacious dining room which offers a daily changing selection of traditional fare.
ROOMS: 25 en suite (3 fmly) **FACILITIES:** entertainment
SERVICES: Lift **NOTES:** No dogs No smoking in restaurant Closed Jan-Feb **CARDS:**

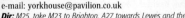

★★68% York House
14/22 Royal Pde BN22 7AP
☎ 01323 412918 🖷 01323 646238
e-mail: yorkhouse@pavilion.co.uk
Dir: *M25, take M23 to Brighton, A27 towards Lewes and then Eastbourne. York House is on the sea front 0.25m east of the pier*

Owned by the Williamson family since 1896, the York House enjoys an enviable location almost on the beach. Bedrooms and facilities continue to be upgraded. An open verandah makes the best of the seafront location, other public areas include a spacious reception hall, cosy bar and separate lounge plus a games room and indoor swimming pool.
ROOMS: 93 en suite (8 fmly) s £39; d £78 (incl. bkfst) * LB
FACILITIES: STV Indoor swimming (H) Pool table Games room
CONF: Thtr 100 Class 30 Board 24 Del from £65 * **SERVICES:** Lift
NOTES: No smoking in restaurant Closed 23-29 Dec Civ Wed 40
CARDS:

See advert on this page

★★66% Farrar's Hotel
Wilmington Gardens BN21 4JN
☎ 01323 723737 🖷 01323 732902
Dir: *turn off seafront by Wish Tower, hotel opposite Congress Theatre*
This small, privately owned hotel is located just opposite Devonshire Park and is only minutes away from the seafront. Bedrooms are furnished and decorated to a good standard and feature a good range of facilities. Public areas have been

continued

EASTBOURNE, continued

redecorated to a high standard and include a cosy bar, separate lounge areas and an attractive downstairs dining room.
ROOMS: 45 en suite (3 fmly) **CONF:** Thtr 80 **SERVICES:** Lift **PARKING:** 35 **NOTES:** No smoking in restaurant Closed Jan
CARDS:

★★66% Langham

MINOTEL Great Britain

Royal Pde BN22 7AH
☎ 01323 731451 01323 646623
e-mail: langhamhotel@mistral.co.uk
Dir: *from A22, A27 or A259 to Eastbourne follow signs for the seafront, hotel half a mile E of the pier, near the Redoubt Fortress*
This friendly hotel enjoys a prime seafront location. Bedrooms are neatly appointed with modern facilities. Spacious public areas include a sea-facing terrace restaurant and the Westdene Suite (with live entertainment four nights a week from May to September) in addition to the ground floor lounges and bar. There is a main dining room and an à la carte conservatory restaurant.
ROOMS: 87 en suite (5 fmly) s £42-£50; d £84-£100 (incl. bkfst) LB **FACILITIES:** Temporary membership of Sovereign Club Xmas **CONF:** Thtr 80 Class 40 Board 24 Del from £50.50 * **SERVICES:** Lift **PARKING:** 4 **NOTES:** No smoking in restaurant Closed 2 Jan-15 Feb
CARDS:

★★65% Ashley Grange Hotel

THE CIRCLE Selected Individual Hotels GREAT BRITAIN

Lewes Rd BN21 2BY
☎ 01323 721550 01323 721550
e-mail: ashleygrange@hotmail.com
Dir: *on A22 turn left at Willingdon rdbt, go past Hospital on King's Drive, pass School on left, Hotel is approx. 100 mtrs on left*
Located on the edge of town, this small friendly hotel offers comfortably furnished, well equipped bedrooms. Smartly appointed public areas include a cosy bar and attractive dining room with access to a large rear garden.
ROOMS: 6 rms (4 en suite) s fr £34; d fr £58.80 (incl. bkfst) * LB **FACILITIES:** Fun pool **CONF:** Thtr 16 Class 16 Board 12 **PARKING:** 6 **NOTES:** No dogs Closed 24-27 Dec
CARDS:

★★64% *Oban*

King Edward's Pde BN21 4DS
☎ 01323 731581 01323 721994
Dir: *opposite Wish Tower seafront area*
This privately owned, friendly hotel is located on the seafront and overlooks well kept lawns. Bedrooms are well cared for, cheerfully decorated and offer a good range of in room facilities. Public areas include a spacious lounge/bar overlooking the seafront and an attractively decorated downstairs dining room retaining many period features.
ROOMS: 31 en suite (2 fmly) **FACILITIES:** Lounge bar activities entertainment **SERVICES:** Lift **NOTES:** No smoking in restaurant Closed Dec-Feb (ex Xmas) **CARDS:**

★★60% Lathom

4-6 Howard Square, Grand Pde BN21 4BG
☎ 01323 720985 & 641986 01323 416405
This friendly hotel continues to cater successfully for large parties. The brightly decorated bedrooms vary in size. There is a lounge and a small bar. A set price menu is offered at dinner, and there is a good choice at breakfast.
ROOMS: 45 en suite (5 fmly) s £27-£32; d £54-£64 (incl. bkfst) * LB **FACILITIES:** entertainment Xmas **SERVICES:** Lift **PARKING:** 6 **NOTES:** No dogs (ex guide dogs) Closed Nov-Feb (ex Xmas & New Year)
CARDS:

EAST GRINSTEAD, West Sussex — Map 05 TQ33

Premier Collection

★★★ Gravetye Manor

RELAIS & CHATEAUX.

RH19 4LJ
☎ 01342 810567 01342 810080
e-mail: gravetye@relaischateaux.fr
Dir: *B2028 towards Haywards Heath. 1m after Turners Hill, take left fork towards Sharpthorne, then 1st left into Vowels Lane*
Gravetye, built in 1598, was one of the first country house hotels and remains a shining example in its class. The day rooms are comfortably furnished, and the bedrooms are decorated in traditional English style: furnished with antiques, including many thoughtful extras. The cuisine uses home grown fruit and vegetables as well as local spring water.
ROOMS: 18 en suite s £135-£150; d £180-£310 * **FACILITIES:** Fishing Croquet lawn **PARKING:** 35 **NOTES:** No dogs No children 7yrs No smoking in restaurant RS 25 Dec
CARDS:

★★★64% Woodbury House

Best Western

Lewes Rd RH19 3UD
☎ 01342 313657 01342 314801
e-mail: stay@woodbury-house.demon.co.uk
Dir: *0.5m S of town on A22*
This cosy hotel offers smart accommodation in well equipped bedrooms. Guests are provided with a choice of eating options in the hotel restaurant or the more informal bistro. Service is both friendly and attentive from the dedicated team of staff.
ROOMS: 14 en suite (1 fmly) No smoking in 2 bedrooms s fr £80; d fr £95 (incl. bkfst) * LB **FACILITIES:** STV Xmas **CONF:** Thtr 40 Class 30 Board 24 **PARKING:** 52 **NOTES:** No smoking in restaurant Civ Wed 80 **CARDS:**

See advert on opposite page

EAST HORNDON, Essex — Map 05 TQ68

Travelodge

CM13 3LL
☎ 01277 810819 01277 810819
Dir: *on A127, eastbound 4m off junc 29 M25*
This modern building offers accommodation in smart, spacious and well equipped bedrooms, all with en suite bathrooms. Refreshments may be taken at the nearby family restaurant. For further details and the Travelodge phone number, consult the Hotel Groups page.
ROOMS: 22 en suite

EASTLEIGH, Hampshire — Map 04 SU41

★★★64% *Posthouse Eastleigh/ Southampton*

Posthouse

Leigh Rd SO50 9PG
☎ 0870 400 9075 Fax 023 8064 3945
Dir: *follow A335 to Eastleigh, hotel on right*

Located close to junction 13 of the M3 motorway, this well sited hotel is suitable for both business and leisure traveller. It is bright and provides modern accommodation in well equipped and well laid-out bedrooms. It has a leisure centre with a decent-sized swimming pool and welcomes children.

ROOMS: 116 en suite (3 fmly) No smoking in 86 bedrooms
FACILITIES: Indoor swimming (H) Sauna Gym Pool table Jacuzzi/spa Beauty treatment Leisure club **CONF:** Thtr 250 Class 90 Board 90
SERVICES: Lift **PARKING:** 160 **CARDS:**

Travelodge

Travelodge

Twyford Rd SO50 4LF
☎ 023 8061 6813 Fax 023 8061 6813
Dir: *off junct 12 on M3 on A335*

This modern building offers accommodation in smart, spacious and well equipped bedrooms, all with en suite bathrooms. Refreshments may be taken at the nearby family restaurant. For further details and the Travelodge phone number, consult the Hotel Groups page.

ROOMS: 32 en suite

EAST MIDLANDS AIRPORT, Leicestershire — Map 08 SK42

★★★73% Rosette **Yew Lodge Hotel & Conference Centre**

Best Western

Packington Hill DE74 2DF
☎ 01509 672518 Fax 01509 674730
Dir: *leave M1 at junc 24, then follow signs to Loughborough & Kegworth on the A6. At the bottom of the hill, first right, 400yds Yew Lodge on right*

Significant investment has been made in this smart, family-owned hotel, which is very conveniently and peacefully located. Bedrooms and public areas are very well appointed and thoughtfully equipped. At the time of our inspection, fellow guests were full of praise for the food which is well deserving of its Rosette award.

ROOMS: 64 en suite (3 fmly) No smoking in 18 bedrooms s £45-£75; d £60-£85 * LB **FACILITIES:** STV Xmas **CONF:** Thtr 150 Class 60 Board 36 Del from £90 * **SERVICES:** Lift **PARKING:** 120
NOTES: Civ Wed 150 **CARDS:**

★★★70% **Donington Manor**

High St DE74 2PP
☎ 01332 810253 Fax 01332 850330
e-mail: cngrist@dmhgrist.demon.co.uk
Dir: *1m into village on B5430 situated on left at traffic lights*

A graceful Georgian building just off the village centre offers high standards of hospitality and a professional service. Many of the original architectural features have been preserved through public rooms and some bedrooms, the elegant dining room is particularly appealing. Bedrooms are individually designed, with the most recently created suites offering a good range of facilities, comforts and decorative bathrooms; among the luxurious bathrooms is one formerly belonging to Elvis Presley.

ROOMS: 25 en suite 1 annexe en suite (1 fmly) s £66-£84; d £84-£100 (incl. bkfst) * LB **FACILITIES:** STV **CONF:** Thtr 80 Class 50 Board 20 Del £95 * **PARKING:** 40 **NOTES:** No dogs (ex guide dogs) Closed 24-30 Dec RS Sat Civ Wed 120 **CARDS:**

EAST MIDLANDS AIRPORT, continued

★★★69% The Priest House on the River
Kings Mills DE74 2RR
☎ 01332 810649 01332 811141
Dir: *M1 junct 23A towards airport, pass airport entrance, after 1.5m turn right into Castle Donington. At 1st traffic lights turn left & follow road*

An historic hotel nestling peacefully in a picturesque riverside setting. The hotel itself is now mostly contemporary in style, with bedrooms in converted cottages and the main building; bedrooms in the main building offer superior comfort. The restaurant serves excellent dishes with an imaginative modern British flair.
ROOMS: 25 en suite 20 annexe en suite (1 fmly) s fr £90; d fr £110 (incl. bkfst) * LB **FACILITIES:** STV Fishing Archery Clay pigeon shooting entertainment Xmas **CONF:** Thtr 140 Class 45 Board 36 Del from £115 * **PARKING:** 150 **NOTES:** No smoking in restaurant Civ Wed
CARDS:

See advert on page 197

★★66% *Kegworth*
Packington Hill DE74 2DF
☎ 01509 672427 01509 674664
Dir: *0.5m from junct 24 of the M1/A42 on the A6 towards Loughborough*
This modern hotel offers good accommodation, ranging from 'standard' to 'executive' rooms. Public areas include an open-plan lounge bar, where refreshments and simple meals are served, and a full-scale restaurant with a choice of menus and a hot buffet. The hotel was formerly a squash club and has kept a few of the courts as part of its leisure centre. There is also a range of conference rooms.
ROOMS: 60 en suite (3 fmly) No smoking in 24 bedrooms **FACILITIES:** STV Indoor swimming (H) Sauna Solarium Gym Jacuzzi/spa Aromatherapy & massage **CONF:** Thtr 300 Class 110 Board 120 **PARKING:** 150 **CARDS:**

⇧ *Travelodge*

This modern building offers accommodation in smart, spacious and well equipped bedrooms, all with en suite bathrooms. Refreshments may be taken at the nearby family restaurant. For further details and the Travelodge phone number, consult the Hotel Groups page.

○ Express by Holiday Inn
DE74 2TQ
☎ 01509 678000 01509 670954
ROOMS: 90 rms **NOTES:** Open August 2000

EAST RETFORD, Nottinghamshire Map 08 SK78

★★★64% West Retford
24 North Rd DN22 7XG
☎ 01777 706333 01777 709951
Dir: *on A638 on outskirts of East Retford*
Set in attractive grounds close to the town centre, this 18th-century manor house offers a good range of well equipped meeting facilities. The spacious, well laid out bedrooms and suites are located in a separate building.
ROOMS: 62 annexe en suite (37 fmly) No smoking in 36 bedrooms s £68; d £80 * LB **FACILITIES:** STV Croquet lawn Xmas **CONF:** Thtr 150 Class 40 Board 43 Del from £80 * **PARKING:** 100 **NOTES:** No smoking in restaurant **CARDS:**

EDGWARE, Greater London
See LONDON SECTION plan 1 C6

○ *Premier Lodge (London Edgware)*
Burnt Oak Broadway
☎ 0870 700 1454 0870 700 1455

EGHAM, Surrey Map 04 TQ07

★★★★73% Runnymede Hotel & Spa
Windsor Rd TW20 0AG
☎ 01784 436171 01784 436340
e-mail: info@runnymedehotel.com
Dir: *off junc 13 of M25, on A308 towards Windsor*

Within easy reach of Heathrow and the motorways, and enjoying a river side location, there is no wonder that this hotel is so popular. Bedrooms and conference facilities have undergone a full refurbishment programme, and all are air conditioned. Two dining options and riverside terrace are some of the features of the public areas.
ROOMS: 180 en suite (19 fmly) No smoking in 116 bedrooms s £152-£215; d £189-£255 * LB **FACILITIES:** STV Indoor swimming (H) Tennis (hard & grass) Snooker Sauna Solarium Gym Croquet lawn Putting green Jacuzzi/spa Steam room Beauty Salon Dance studio Hairdressers **CONF:** Thtr 300 Class 250 Board 76 Del from £235 * **SERVICES:** Lift air con **PARKING:** 280 **NOTES:** No dogs (ex guide dogs) RS Restaurant closed Sat lunch/Sun dinner Civ Wed 150
CARDS:

See advert under WINDSOR

ELLESMERE PORT, Cheshire Map 07 SJ47

★★★65% Quality Hotel Chester
Welsh Road/Berwick Rd, Little Sutton L66 4PS
☎ 0151 339 5121 0151 339 3214
e-mail: admin@gb066.u-net.com
Dir: *M53 junct 5 turn left at rdbt at 2nd set of traffic lights, turn right onto A550 over the hump back bridge turn left into Berwick Road*
Conveniently located close to the M53, yet in an attractive and tranquil setting this friendly hotel offers modern, well equipped accommodation. The refurbished public areas are popular for large parties. There is a good range of facilities including a leisure complex and versatile banqueting and conference suites.

continued

ROOMS: 53 en suite (8 fmly) No smoking in 18 bedrooms s £38-£76; d £46-£92 * LB **FACILITIES:** STV Indoor swimming (H) Sauna Steam room Exercise equipment entertainment Xmas **CONF:** Thtr 300 Class 150 Board 100 Del from £95 * **PARKING:** 200 **NOTES:** No smoking in restaurant Civ Wed **CARDS:**

★★61% *Woodcore Hotel & Restaurant*

3 Hooton Rd L66 1QU
☎ 0151 327 1542 📠 0151 328 1328
Dir: *M53 junc 5, take A41 towards Chester, first traffic lights turn right towards Willaston. Hotel 300 yards on left*

This popular commercial hotel offers generally spacious, well equipped rooms, many of which are located in a separate building. The bars and restaurant are attractively decorated and there is a separate breakfast room. A range of popular, reasonably priced dishes are on offer.

ROOMS: 7 en suite 13 annexe en suite (1 fmly) **FACILITIES:** entertainment **CONF:** Thtr 90 Class 50 Board 48 **PARKING:** 35 **NOTES:** No dogs (ex guide dogs) **CARDS:**

ELSTREE, Hertfordshire — Map 04 TQ19

★★★70% Edgwarebury

corus

Barnet Ln WD6 3RE
☎ 020 8953 8227 📠 020 8207 3668
e-mail: edgwarebury@corushotels.com
Dir: *M1 junct 5 follow A41 to Harrow, turn left onto A411 into Elstree cont through crossroads into Barnet Ln, hotel entrance is on the right*

Within easy reach of the M1 and M25, this delightful Tudor revivalist residence is set in 10 acres of manicured grounds. Comfortable modern bedrooms have been added to the main building, which has retained many original features including stone fireplaces and oak panelling. A creative dinner menu is served in the stately dining room.

ROOMS: 47 en suite (1 fmly) No smoking in 19 bedrooms s fr £115; d fr £135 * LB **FACILITIES:** STV **CONF:** Thtr 80 Class 50 Board 10 Del from £115 * **PARKING:** 100 **NOTES:** No smoking in restaurant Civ Wed **CARDS:**

ELTERWATER, Cumbria — Map 07 NY30

★★★72% Langdale Hotel & Country Club

LA22 9JD
☎ 01539 437302 📠 01539 437694
e-mail: itsgreat@langdale.co.uk
Dir: *follow road into Langdale, hotel part of private estate on left in the bottom of the valley*

An extensive modern hotel offering a wide range of comfortable and well equipped bedrooms,of which five rooms are in the main hotel and others in attractive buildings within the grounds. Leisure facilities feature an indoor pool and a well equipped gym. A wide range of dishes is served within either of the two stylish restaurants.

ROOMS: 5 en suite 60 annexe en suite (8 fmly) s £70-£130; d £110-£210 (incl. bkfst) * LB **FACILITIES:** STV Indoor swimming (H) Tennis (hard) Fishing Squash Sauna Solarium Gym Pool table Jacuzzi/spa Steam room Hair & beauty salon Cycle hire entertainment ch fac Xmas **CONF:** Thtr 100 Class 66 Board 50 Del from £100 * **PARKING:** 65 **NOTES:** No dogs No smoking in restaurant RS Oct-Dec & Jan-Apr **CARDS:**

See advert under AMBLESIDE

★★68% Eltermere Country House

LA22 9HY
☎ 01539 437207 📠 01539 437540
e-mail: colin@hensington.demon.co.uk
Dir: *on unclass road between A593 & B5343, turn left after cattle grid through village of Elterwater, cross bridge 100mtrs on left*

This well established hotel is in a quiet location with colourful landscaped gardens giving views over Elterwater Tarn. Well maintained throughout, it offers comfortable, inviting public rooms and enjoyable food. Most bedrooms and the public rooms offer fine views.

ROOMS: 19 rms (14 en suite) (4 fmly) s £41.50-£60.50; d £83-£121 (incl. bkfst & dinner) * LB **FACILITIES:** Fishing Putting green Use of leisure facilties at nearby Langdale Hotel Xmas **PARKING:** 20 **NOTES:** No smoking in restaurant **CARDS:**

★66% Britannia Inn

LA22 9HP
☎ 01539 437210 📠 01539 437311
e-mail: info@britinn.co.uk
Dir: *from A593 at Skelwith Bridge Hotel turn right onto B5343 after crossing cattle grid on main road take left turn into village of Elterwater*

A delightful country inn overlooking the village green and surrounded by majestic Lakeland scenery. Bedrooms have modern features, are particularly well equipped and are tastefully furnished. Public areas, which include popular oak beamed bars and a residents lounge and dining room, are furnished with antiques. The Inn is renowned for its home cooking.

ROOMS: 9 rms (8 en suite) 4 annexe rms (1 en suite) s £27; d £54-£70 (incl. bkfst) * LB **PARKING:** 10 **NOTES:** Closed 25 & 26 Dec **CARDS:**

ELY, Cambridgeshire — Map 05 TL58

★★★68% ❀ Lamb

OLD ENGLISH INNS & HOTELS

2 Lynn Rd CB7 4EJ
☎ 01353 663574 📠 01353 662023
Dir: *enter Ely on A10, hotel in centre of city near Cathedral on the corner of Lynn Rd & the High St*

This pleasant 15th-century coaching inn has been sympathetically developed to provide many creature comforts. Informal snacks are

continued

ELY, continued

served in the smart bars, modern British cooking features on the appealing menus in the Octagon Restaurant. Bedrooms offer co-ordinated soft furnishings, decor and modern light wood furniture.
ROOMS: 32 en suite (6 fmly) s fr £67; d fr £90 (incl. bkfst) * LB **FACILITIES:** STV Xmas **CONF:** Thtr 45 Class 28 Board 30 Del from £80 * **PARKING:** 20 **NOTES:** No smoking in restaurant
CARDS:

★★60% Nyton
7 Barton Rd CB7 4HZ
☎ 01353 662459 📠 01353 666217
e-mail: nytonhotel@yahoo.co.uk
Dir: *from S A10 into Ely. Pass golf course on right, then first right after passing two garages. Hotel 200yds on right*
Set in two-acre gardens, this family-run hotel offers comfortable bedrooms in a variety of sizes and styles. Informal meals are served in the bar with more serious dining in the wood-panelled restaurant; there is also a conservatory lounge.
ROOMS: 10 en suite (3 fmly) s £40-£45; d fr £65 (incl. bkfst) * LB **PARKING:** 25 **NOTES:** No dogs (ex guide dogs)
CARDS:

⇧ *Travelodge*
Travelodge
Witchford Rd CB6 3NN
☎ 01353 668499 📠 01353 668499
Dir: *at roundabout A10/A142*
This modern building offers accommodation in smart, spacious and well equipped bedrooms, all with en suite bathrooms. Refreshments may be taken at the nearby family restaurant. For further details and the Travelodge phone number, consult the Hotel Groups page.
ROOMS: 39 en suite

EMBLETON, Northumberland
Map 12 NU22

★★70% Dunstanburgh Castle Hotel
NE66 3UN
☎ 01665 576111
e-mail: duncashot@compuserve.com
Dir: *from A1, take B1240 to Denwick then 3m past Rennington & Masons Arms. Next right signed Embleton & continue into village*

Spotlessly maintained, this family hotel stands in rural surroundings within easy reach of the sea. Comfortable public rooms include a choice of lounges, both with open fires in season. There is also a choice of eating options, with a residents dining room and the grill room next to the bar.
ROOMS: 17 en suite (4 fmly) s £29.90-£32.50; d £59.80-£65 (incl. bkfst) * LB **PARKING:** 16 **NOTES:** No smoking in restaurant Closed Nov-Feb
CARDS:

EMPINGHAM, Rutland
Map 04 SK90

★★67% The White Horse Inn
Main St LE15 8PR
☎ 01780 460221 & 460521 📠 01780 460521
e-mail: info@the-white-horse.co.uk
Dir: *on A606, Oakham-Stamford road*
This attractive stone-built inn has bright and well equipped bedrooms that are located either across the courtyard or inside the inn, where the rooms are en suite. A wide range of meals is served in the various rooms that make up the bar, and a full menu is available in the comfortable restaurant; service is relaxed and friendly.
ROOMS: 4 en suite 9 annexe en suite (4 fmly) No smoking in 1 bedroom s fr £50; d fr £63 (incl. bkfst) * LB **FACILITIES:** Xmas **CONF:** Thtr 60 Class 60 Board 34 Del from £60 * **PARKING:** 60 **NOTES:** No smoking in restaurant **CARDS:**

EMSWORTH, Hampshire
Map 04 SU70

★★★68% Brookfield
Havant Rd PO10 7LF
☎ 01243 373363 & 376383 📠 01243 376342
Dir: *Emsworth junct off A27, turn onto B529, hotel is 0.5m on the left on the way into Emsworth*
This well established hotel is run by the Gibson family, who provide friendly, attentive service. Bedrooms are in a modern style, and comfortably furnished. The popular Hermitage Restaurant offers a seasonally changing menu and an award-winning wine list.
ROOMS: 40 en suite (4 fmly) No smoking in 20 bedrooms s £62-£69.50; d £85-£110 (incl. bkfst) * LB **FACILITIES:** STV **CONF:** Thtr 100 Class 50 Board 40 Del £110 * **PARKING:** 80 **NOTES:** No dogs (ex guide dogs) Closed 25 Dec-1 Jan **CARDS:**

⇧ *Travelodge*
Travelodge
PO10 7RB
☎ 01243 370877 📠 01243 370877
Dir: *A27*
This modern building offers accommodation in smart, spacious and well equipped bedrooms, all with en suite bathrooms. Refreshments may be taken at the nearby family restaurant. For further details and the Travelodge phone number, consult the Hotel Groups page.
ROOMS: 36 en suite

ENFIELD, Greater London
Map 04 TQ39

★★★70% Royal Chace
The Ridgeway EN2 8AR
☎ 020 8884 8181 📠 020 8884 8150
e-mail: royal.chace@dial.pipex.com
Dir: *from junct 24 on M25 take A1005 towards Enfield. Hotel 3m on right*
Although only a few minutes from the M25 motorway, this privately owned hotel enjoys a peaceful North London location with open fields to the rear. Bedrooms are tastefully decorated and furnished and there are a good range of in room facilities. The spacious public areas include a variety of versatile function rooms.
ROOMS: 92 en suite (2 fmly) No smoking in 34 bedrooms s fr £99; d fr £115 (incl. bkfst) * **FACILITIES:** STV Outdoor swimming (H) Free access to local gym swimming pool jacuzzi & steam room **CONF:** Thtr 250 Class 100 Board 40 Del from £125 * **PARKING:** 300 **NOTES:** No dogs (ex guide dogs) No smoking in restaurant Closed 24-30 Dec RS Restaurant closed lunchtime/Sun eve Civ Wed 220
CARDS:

See advert under LONDON E1

★★71% Oak Lodge

80 Village Rd, Bush Hill Park EN1 2EU
☎ 020 8360 7082

Dir: *turn right at 11th set of lights from M25, exit 25. Turn right at next lights onto A105. Hotel is located 0.25m on the right*

This charming, privately-run hotel is located in a leafy, suburban area. Both the service and hospitality continue to be particularly noteworthy and a warm welcome is offered to all guests. Public areas are comfortable and the availability of car parking is an added bonus.

ROOMS: 7 en suite (1 fmly) No smoking in 6 bedrooms s £69-£93; d £90-£130 (incl. bkfst) * **FACILITIES:** Special arrangement with David Lloyd Sports Centre entertainment Xmas **CONF:** Board 16 **PARKING:** 4 **NOTES:** No dogs (ex guide dogs) No smoking in restaurant
CARDS:

EPPING, Essex — Map 05 TL40

★★★62% *Posthouse Epping*

Posthouse

High Rd, Bell Common CM16 4DG
☎ 0870 400 9027 🖷 01992 560402

Dir: *on B1393*

Bedrooms, which are spacious and well equipped, are being upgraded to the new company standard. Public areas include a small popular bar and the Junction restaurant which offers a range of modern dishes. There are good parking facilities, meeting rooms are available.

ROOMS: 79 annexe en suite (22 fmly) No smoking in 32 bedrooms **CONF:** Thtr 85 Class 50 Board 32 **PARKING:** 95
CARDS:

EPSOM, Surrey — Map 04 TQ26

⌂ Premier Lodge (Epsom)

PREMIER LODGE — THE BEST. REST ASSURED.

272 Kingston Rd, Ewell KT19 0SH
☎ 0870 700 1436 🖷 0870 700 1437

Premier Lodge offers modern, well equipped, en suite accommodation suitable for both business and leisure travellers. Meals can be taken at the adjacent popular restaurant and bar which is fully licensed. For further details, consult the Hotel Groups page.

ROOMS: 29 en suite d £46 *

ESCRICK, North Yorkshire — Map 08 SE64

★★★75% ❀❀ Parsonage Country House

York Rd YO19 6LF
☎ 01904 728111 🖷 01904 728151
e-mail: reservations@parsonagehotel.co.uk

Dir: *next to St Helens Church on A19*

An early 19th-century parsonage with a charming country house atmosphere, standing in well tended grounds. Lounges are comfortable and now include a spacious conservatory. The bedrooms are well equipped and attractive while staff are caring and professional. Good conference facilities are available.

ROOMS: 12 en suite 9 annexe en suite (3 fmly) No smoking in 13 bedrooms s fr £95; d fr £110 (incl. bkfst) * LB **FACILITIES:** STV Xmas **CONF:** Thtr 160 Class 80 Board 80 Del from £120 * **PARKING:** 100 **NOTES:** No dogs (ex guide dogs) No smoking in restaurant Civ Wed 50
CARDS:

ESHER, Surrey See LONDON SECTION plan 1 *B1*

★★64% Haven

Best Western

Portsmouth Rd KT10 9AR
☎ 020 8398 0023 🖷 020 8398 9463

Dir: *1m NE on A307*

With its distinctive black and white timbered facade, the Haven is convenient for visitors to Sandown Racecourse. Bedrooms vary in size and style and are generally well equipped and quiet, four rooms are in a separate Lodge. There is a residential-licensed bar with television.

ROOMS: 16 en suite 4 annexe en suite (3 fmly) s £67-£79; d £79-£110 (incl. bkfst) * **FACILITIES:** STV **CONF:** Thtr 40 Class 24 Board 20 Del from £85 * **PARKING:** 20 **NOTES:** No dogs (ex guide dogs) No smoking in restaurant **CARDS:**

ESKDALE GREEN, Cumbria — Map 06 NY10

★★62% Bower House Inn

CA19 1TD
☎ 019467 23244 🖷 019467 23308
e-mail: bowerhouseinn@compuserve.com

Dir: *4m off A595 1/2 mile west of Eskdale Green*

This former farmhouse nestles in idyllic countryside and enjoys stunning mountain views, offering true peace and relaxation, and combining the charm of a coaching inn, with the stylish appointments of a country house. Dinner provides the highlight of any visit and the menus available in the bar or restaurant provide excellent choice and variety. Bedrooms are housed in a smartly converted barn, a secluded garden house, and inside the original inn; all rooms are well appointed and comfortable.

ROOMS: 5 en suite 19 annexe en suite (3 fmly) s £53.50; d £74 (incl. bkfst) * LB **FACILITIES:** Xmas **CONF:** Thtr 50 Class 50 Board 40 Del £85 * **PARKING:** 60 **NOTES:** No dogs No smoking in restaurant Civ Wed 60 **CARDS:**

> Popped the question? Hotels with Civ Wed in their entry are licensed for civil wedding ceremonies. Maximum numbers for the ceremony only are shown, e.g. Civ Wed 50

EVERSHOT, Dorset Map 03 ST50

Premier Collection

★★★ **Summer Lodge**

DT2 0JR

☎ 01935 83424 01935 83005

e-mail: sumlodge@sumlodge.demon.co.uk

RELAIS & CHATEAUX.

Dir: *1m W of A37 halfway between Dorchester & Yeovil*

Surrounded by beautiful countryside, this delightful hotel enjoys a peaceful village setting. Quality and comfort feature in public rooms and in the individually decorated bedrooms. Floral arrangements, log fires and watercolours add to the charm. An imaginative, daily set menu draws upon the strength of local produce.

ROOMS: 11 en suite 6 annexe en suite (1 fmly) **FACILITIES:** Outdoor swimming (H) Tennis (hard & grass) Croquet lawn **CONF:** Thtr 20 Board 20 **PARKING:** 40 **NOTES:** No smoking in restaurant **CARDS:**

EVESHAM, Worcestershire Map 04 SP04

see also Fladbury

★★★★73% **Wood Norton Hall**

Wood Norton WR11 4YB

☎ 01386 420007 01386 420190

e-mail: woodnorton.hall@bbc.co.uk

Dir: *2m from Evesham on the A4538, after the village of Chadbury travelling westwards or 4m after Wyre Piddle travelling eastwards*

This impressive Victorian hall stands in a 170-acre estate just north-west of Evesham. At the start of WWII, after it was purchased by the BBC, it became the largest broadcasting centre in Europe. Since then it has become a training centre for the BBC and provides excellent business and conference facilities. The Hall itself retains much of its bygone splendour, including carved oak panelling and ornate fireplaces. Bedrooms are comfortably furnished, well equipped and spacious.

ROOMS: 15 en suite 30 annexe en suite No smoking in 40 bedrooms **FACILITIES:** STV Tennis (hard) Fishing Squash Snooker Gym Pool table Croquet lawn **CONF:** Thtr 70 Class 35 Board 32 Del £160 * **PARKING:** 300 **NOTES:** No dogs (ex guide dogs) No smoking in restaurant Closed 26 Dec-4 Jan Civ Wed 60

CARDS:

★★★71% **The Evesham**

Coopers Ln, Off Waterside WR11 6DA

☎ 01386 765566 & 0800 716969 (Res) 01386 765443

e-mail: reception@eveshamhotel.com

Dir: *Coopers lane is off the road alongside the River Avon*

Originally built in 1540, the property was considerably altered and extended in 1810, which accounts for its Georgian appearance. The grounds feature mulberry trees reputed to be 500 years old. Well equipped bedrooms include family suites. The hotel has a well deserved reputation for its food, complemented by an extensive wine list. There are lots of things to keep children amused, making the hotel ideal for families.

ROOMS: 39 en suite 1 annexe en suite (3 fmly) No smoking in 5 bedrooms s £63-£71; d £98 (incl. bkfst) * LB **FACILITIES:** Indoor swimming (H) Croquet lawn Putting green ch fac **PARKING:** 50 **NOTES:** No smoking in restaurant Closed 25 & 26 Dec

CARDS:

★★★69% **Waterside**

56 Waterside WR11 6JZ

☎ 01386 442420 01386 446272

Dir: *A44/A435 junc 40yds on right alongside river*

This friendly hotel stands in a prominent position overlooking the River Avon and is within easy reach of the town centre. Bedrooms are attractively furnished and well equipped. Public areas include the popular Strollers restaurant and bar, which has an American theme and provides a wide variety of dishes. Cream teas are served in the riverside gardens on sunny days.

ROOMS: 14 en suite 4 annexe en suite (2 fmly) s £57-£64; d £68-£80 (incl. bkfst) * LB **FACILITIES:** Fishing **PARKING:** 30

CARDS:

★★★68% ***Northwick Hotel***

Waterside WR11 6BT

☎ 01386 40322 01386 41070

Best Western

Dir: *turn off A46 onto A44 over traffic lights to next set turn right along B4035 past hospital hotel on right side opposite river*

Standing opposite the River Avon this, former coaching inn is within easy walking distance of the centre of Evesham's market Town. Bedrooms are tastefully decorated and well equipped, with one specially adapted for disabled guests. The recently refurbished public areas offer a choice of bars, meeting rooms and restaurant.

ROOMS: 31 en suite (4 fmly) No smoking in 10 bedrooms **FACILITIES:** Hot air ballooning Clay pigeon shooting Archery Paint balling **CONF:** Thtr 240 Class 150 Board 80 **PARKING:** 200 **NOTES:** No smoking in restaurant **CARDS:**

★★80% **The Mill at Harvington**

Anchor Ln, Harvington WR11 5NR

☎ 01386 870688 01386 870688

Dir: *Harvington is 4m NE of Evesham. The hotel is on the banks of the Avon, reached by a bridge over the new A46 and not in village*

A former Georgian house and mill in extensive grounds on the banks of the River Avon. The comfortable lounge has fine views; there is a conservatory bar and elegant restaurant; cuisine is of a high standard. Bedrooms are generally spacious and thoughtfully equipped.

ROOMS: 15 en suite 6 annexe en suite s £63-£75; d £89-£125 (incl. bkfst) * LB **FACILITIES:** Outdoor swimming (H) Fishing Croquet lawn **PARKING:** 50 **NOTES:** No dogs (ex guide dogs) No children 10yrs No smoking in restaurant Closed 24-27 Dec

CARDS:

★★73% **Riverside**

The Parks, Offenham Rd WR11 5JP

☎ 01386 446200 01386 40021

e-mail: riversidehotel@theparksoffenhamfreeserve.co.uk

Dir: *off the A46 follow signs for Offenham. Take turning on right B4510 (Offenham) 1/2 mile turn left along private drive called The Parks to end*

Standing in three acres of gardens sloping down to the River Avon, this family-owned and run hotel offers comfortable bedrooms, many of which overlook the river, as do the lounge and restaurant. Cooking remains a strength here, with a menu of imaginative dishes based on really good produce.

continued

ROOMS: 7 en suite s £60; d £90 (incl. bkfst) * LB **FACILITIES:** Fishing **PARKING:** 40 **NOTES:** No dogs (ex guide dogs) No smoking in restaurant Closed 25 Dec, Sun night & Mon RS 2-20 Jan (wknds only) **CARDS:**

EWEN, Gloucestershire — Map 04 SU09

★★70% Wild Duck Inn

Drakes Island GL7 6BY
☎ 01285 770310 Fax 01285 770924
e-mail: wduckinn@aol.com
Dir: *from Cirencester take A429 on reaching Kemble take left turn to Ewen keep driving to the centre of the village*

A bustling, ever popular inn dating back to the early 16th century. Open fires, old beams and rustic pine tables lend character to the bar and restaurant, where imaginative, robust cooking and cheerful service are further strengths.
ROOMS: 11 en suite s fr £55; d £75-£90 (incl. cont bkfst) * **PARKING:** 50 **NOTES:** RS 25 Dec **CARDS:**

See advert under CIRENCESTER

EXETER, Devon — Map 03 SX99

★★★★67% The Southgate

Southernhay East EX1 1QF
☎ 0870 400 8333 Fax 01392 413549
e-mail: heritagehotels-exeter.southgate@forte-hotels.com
Dir: *on Southernhay roundabout near cathedral*
This attractive modern hotel, situated close to the town centre, and across from the quay, is popular with business, conference and leisure guests alike. The smart bedrooms offer a good level of comfort and are equipped with such extra facilities as trouser press and mini bar. The elegant public rooms are richly furnished, giving a real country house ambience.
ROOMS: 110 en suite (6 fmly) No smoking in 55 bedrooms d £110 * LB **FACILITIES:** STV Indoor swimming (H) Sauna Solarium Gym Jacuzzi/spa Xmas **CONF:** Thtr 100 Class 70 Board 50 Del from £99 * **SERVICES:** Lift **PARKING:** 115 **NOTES:** No smoking in restaurant RS Sat (restaurant closed for lunch) Civ Wed 80 **CARDS:**

★★★73% *Barton Cross Hotel & Restaurant*

Huxham, Stoke Canon EX5 4EJ
☎ 01392 841245 Fax 01392 841942
Dir: *0.5m off A396 at Stoke Canon just 3 miles north of Exeter*
'Seventeenth century charm with 20th century luxury' perfectly sums up this lovely countryside hotel. The eight bedrooms are tastefully decorated and well maintained. Public areas include the cosy first floor lounge, in addition to the lounge/bar with its warming log fire. The restaurant offers a seasonally changing menu and fine cuisine.

continued

EXETER, continued

ROOMS: 9 en suite (2 fmly) No smoking in 2 bedrooms
FACILITIES: STV **CONF:** Board 12 **PARKING:** 35 **NOTES:** No smoking in restaurant **CARDS:**

See advert on page 203

★★★71% Royal Clarence

Cathedral Yard EX1 1HD
☎ 01392 319955 🖹 01392 439423
Dir: *facing cathedral*

This historic, 14th-century building is a landmark in Exeter, situated opposite the Cathedral. Smart dining areas serve light lunches, excellent carte dinners and afternoon cream teas. There is a quiet residents' lounge and a stylish cafe bar. Bedrooms are well equipped, attractively furnished and individually decorated.
ROOMS: 57 en suite (6 fmly) No smoking in 16 bedrooms s £99; d £125-£155 * LB **FACILITIES:** Xmas **CONF:** Thtr 120 Class 50 Board 50 **SERVICES:** Lift **PARKING:** 15 **NOTES:** No dogs (ex guide dogs) No smoking in restaurant Civ Wed 50
CARDS:

★★★70% Devon

Exeter Bypass, Matford EX2 8XU
☎ 01392 259268 🖹 01392 413142
e-mail: info@devonhotel.co.uk
Dir: *leave M5 at junct 30, follow signpost to Marsh Barton Ind Est A379, hotel is on main A38 rdbt*
Conveniently situated for the city centre and with easy access to the M5, this hotel offers modern accommodation. The Carriages brasserie is popular with locals and visitors alike, offering a wide range of dishes from around the world as well as a more traditional carvery. Service is efficient, and extensive meeting and function rooms are also available.
ROOMS: 41 annexe en suite (3 fmly) s £54-£59; d £72-£82 * LB **FACILITIES:** STV entertainment Xmas **CONF:** Thtr 150 Class 150 Board 150 **PARKING:** 250 **NOTES:** Civ Wed 100
CARDS:

★★★68% Buckerell Lodge

Topsham Rd EX2 4SQ
☎ 01392 221111 🖹 01392 491111
Dir: *M5 junct 30 follow signs for City Centre, hotel is located on the main Topsham Rd approx 0.5m from Exeter*
Very popular for wedding parties, and conveniently situated for the city centre, this hotel offers comfortable accommodation in a relaxed atmosphere. Public areas include a smart cocktail bar and a range of meeting rooms. Fine dining is a feature of Raffles Restaurant where fixed-price and carte menus are offered; call in advance to check dining arrangements at weekends. For snacks and a more informal experience the Lodge Bar makes an ideal alternative.

continued

ROOMS: 53 en suite (2 fmly) No smoking in 15 bedrooms s £94; d £120 * LB **FACILITIES:** STV Jacuzzi/spa Xmas **CONF:** Thtr 50 Class 35 Board 30 **PARKING:** 100 **NOTES:** No smoking in restaurant
CARDS:

★★★68% Queens Court

Bystock Ter EX4 4HY
☎ 01392 272709 🖹 01392 491390
e-mail: sales@queenscourt-hotel.co.uk
Located just a short walk from the City centre, this totally refurbished hotel provides every service that the modern traveller could need. Both public areas and the well appointed bedrooms are furnished in contemporary style. The adjacent 'Olive Tree' restaurant offers an interesting selection of Mediterranean influenced dishes.
ROOMS: 18 en suite No smoking in 4 bedrooms s £59-£69; d £69-£79 * LB **FACILITIES:** STV **CONF:** Thtr 80 Class 30 Board 40 Del from £79 * **SERVICES:** Lift **PARKING:** 6 **NOTES:** No dogs (ex guide dogs)
CARDS:

★★★66% Gipsy Hill

Gipsy Hill Ln, Pinn Ln, Monkerton EX1 3RN
☎ 01392 465252 🖹 01392 464302
e-mail: gipsyhill@bestwestern.co.uk

Dir: *3m E on B3181, leave M5 at junct 30, follow signs to Sowton Ind Est, turn right on roundabout then first left (Pinn Lane)*
A popular hotel just outside Exeter and close to the M5 and the airport. Set in attractive, well tended gardens with country views, the hotel offers conference and function rooms with comfortable bedroom accommodation and modern facilities. An intimate bar and lounge are next to the elegant restaurant, daily and carte menus are available.
ROOMS: 20 en suite 17 annexe en suite (5 fmly) No smoking in 6 bedrooms **CONF:** Thtr 120 Class 55 Board 36 Del £97.50 * **PARKING:** 100 **NOTES:** No smoking in restaurant Closed 25-30 Dec Civ Wed 120 **CARDS:**

See advert on opposite page

★★★66% *Lord Haldon*

Dunchideock EX6 7YF
☎ 01392 832483 🖹 01392 833765
e-mail: lordhaldon@eclipse.co.uk
Dir: *from A30 follow signs to Ide then continue through village for 2.5m. After telephone box turn left. In 0.5m pass under stone bridge turn left*
Situated in some of Devon's most picturesque countryside, the Lord Haldon is a family owned establishment, offering a warm welcome and comfortable accommodation. It is a spacious hotel, proud of its reputation and ideally suited to the needs of both business and leisure travellers. Bedrooms are individual in style and well equipped, many enjoying wonderful views across the peaceful landscape.

continued on p206

EXETER, continued

ROOMS: 19 en suite (3 fmly) No smoking in 10 bedrooms
FACILITIES: STV ch fac **CONF:** Thtr 200 Class 140 Board 100
PARKING: 60 **NOTES:** No smoking in restaurant
CARDS:

See advert on page 205

★★★65% St Olaves Court
Mary Arches St EX4 3AZ
☎ 01392 217736 01392 413054
e-mail: info@olaves.co.uk
Dir: *drive to City centre, follow signs to Mary Arches Parking. Hotel entrance is directly opposite car park entrance*
This hotel is just a short stroll from the cathedral, shops and medieval centre of Exeter. Bedrooms are smart and include thoughtful extras such as a complimentary decanter of sherry. The intimate Golsworthy's Restaurant offers a high standard of cuisine with an imaginative carte.
ROOMS: 11 en suite 4 annexe en suite (4 fmly) s £80-£95; d £90-£120 (incl. cont bkfst) * LB **FACILITIES:** Jacuzzi/spa Xmas **CONF:** Thtr 45 Class 35 Board 35 **PARKING:** 15 **NOTES:** No smoking in restaurant
CARDS:

★★★64% *White Hart*
66 South St EX1 1EE
☎ 01392 279897 01392 250159
The White Hart is over 400 years old and an important city-centre landmark in Exeter. Comfortable bedrooms offer all modern comforts. Meals are available in both the bar and the dining room.
ROOMS: 57 en suite (6 fmly) No smoking in 11 bedrooms
FACILITIES: STV Reduced entry to neighbouring gym **CONF:** Thtr 60 Class 24 Board 22 **SERVICES:** Lift **PARKING:** 55 **NOTES:** No dogs (ex guide dogs) Closed 24-26 Dec **CARDS:**

See advert on page 205

★★73% St Andrews
28 Alphington Rd EX2 8HN
☎ 01392 276784 01392 250249
Dir: *M5 junct 31 signed Okehampton. Follow sign for Exeter city centre/ Marsh Barton along Alphington Rd. A377 A main route into City, hotel on left*
This welcoming family-run hotel, within walking distance of the city centre, offers brightly decorated, spotless and well equipped bedrooms. There is a comfortable lounge with separate bar, whilst the restaurant menu offers an extensive choice of dishes using the best local meat and vegetables. A room is available for disabled guests.
ROOMS: 17 en suite (2 fmly) No smoking in 5 bedrooms s £45-£49; d £60-£65 (incl. bkfst) * LB **FACILITIES:** STV **PARKING:** 21
NOTES: No dogs (ex guide dogs) No smoking in restaurant Closed 24 Dec-2 Jan **CARDS:**

★★69% Fairwinds Hotel
Kennford EX6 7UD
☎ 01392 832911 01392 832911
Dir: *4m S of Exeter, from M5 junct 31, continue along A38, after 2m turn left at sign for Kennford. First hotel on the left*
A warm and genuine welcome is assured at this conveniently situated hotel, which lies within easy reach of Exeter, Torbay and Plymouth. Being a strictly non-smoking hotel throughout, guests are therefore assured of a pleasant environment in which to relax and unwind. A small bar-lounge is available adjacent to the restaurant, where enjoyable and interesting home-made dishes are served. Bedrooms are well maintained, combining comfort with useful facilities, four rooms being available on the ground floor.
ROOMS: 6 en suite (1 fmly) No smoking in all bedrooms s £35-£37; d £45-£52 (incl. bkfst) * LB **PARKING:** 8 **NOTES:** No dogs No smoking in restaurant Closed 19 Nov-31 Dec **CARDS:**

★★66% Comfort Inn
A38 (Kennford) EX6 7UX
☎ 01392 832121 01392 833590
e-mail: admin@gb056.u-net.com
Dir: *on A38 turn off for Kennford Services follow hotel signs*
Conveniently located for both the city and the M5, this hotel is popular with all types of guest. Bedrooms, all located in adjacent motel style buildings, are comfortably appointed and well equipped. Public areas include an open plan bar and restaurant, and conference facilities.
ROOMS: 63 en suite (5 fmly) No smoking in 37 bedrooms s £43.75-£64; d £54.50-£87.75 (incl. bkfst) * LB **FACILITIES:** STV **CONF:** Thtr 120 Class 80 Board 60 Del from £58 * **PARKING:** 250 **NOTES:** No smoking in restaurant **CARDS:**

CHOICE HOTELS EUROPE

★★65% *Ebford House*
Exmouth Rd EX3 0QH
☎ 01392 877658 01392 874424
e-mail: ebford@eclipse.co.uk
Dir: *1m E of Topsham on A376*
This charming Georgian house lies between Exeter and Exmouth and has is popular with both business and leisure guests alike. A choice of dining options is available with the elegant surroundings of Hortons or the informality of Frisco's Bistro, offering interesting home-cooked dishes and other blackboard specials. Bedrooms are individual in style and size and include many modern facilities.
ROOMS: 16 en suite No smoking in 6 bedrooms **FACILITIES:** STV Sauna Gym Jacuzzi/spa **CONF:** Thtr 25 Class 10 Board 18
PARKING: 45 **NOTES:** No dogs (ex guide dogs) No smoking in restaurant Closed 23 Dec-28 Dec **CARDS:**

★★62% Red House
2 Whipton Village Rd EX4 8AR
☎ 01392 256104 01392 666145
e-mail: 505431@eclipse.co.uk
Dir: *jct 30 off M5, left before services signed Middlemoor, right at rdbt towards Pinhoe & University, in 0.75m left to Whipton/University, hotel 1m on right*

MINOTEL Great Britain

This family-owned hotel is located on the edge of the city, and offers an extensive menu, including a carvery, served either in the popular bar or in the adjacent dining room. The bedrooms are modern and well equipped offering accommodation that is suitable all types of guest.
ROOMS: 12 en suite (2 fmly) No smoking in 8 bedrooms s £35-£40; d £52-£56 (incl. bkfst) * LB **FACILITIES:** STV **CONF:** Class 50 Board 20
PARKING: 28 **CARDS:**

Fancy a Singapore Sling? Bar staff in five star hotels should be skilled cocktail mixers.

⇧ Express by Holiday Inn Exeter

Guardian Way EX1 3PE
☎ 01392 261000 📠 01392 261061
Dir: *turn off M5 at junct 29 and follow signs for Exeter City Centre. Hotel located on 1st rdbt*

A modern budget hotel offering comfortable accommodation in refreshing, spacious and comprehensively-equipped bedrooms, en suite bathrooms with power showers and continental buffet breakfast included in the room rate. Suitable for business travellers or families. For further details and the Express by Holiday Inn phone number, consult the Hotel Groups page.
ROOMS: 122 en suite d £49.50 (incl. cont bkfst) * **CONF:** Thtr 32 Class 30 Board 24

⇧ *Travelodge*

Travelodge

Moor Ln, Sandygate EX2 4AR
☎ 01392 74044 📠 01392 410406
Dir: *M5 jnct 30*
This modern building offers accommodation in smart, spacious and well equipped bedrooms, all with en suite bathrooms. Refreshments may be taken at the nearby family restaurant. For further details and the Travelodge phone number, consult the Hotel Groups page.
ROOMS: 74 en suite **CONF:** Thtr 80 Class 18 Board 25

○ *Premier Lodge (Exeter)*

PREMIER LODGE

Nutwell Lodge, Exmouth Rd EX8 5AJ
☎ 0870 700 1586 📠 0870 700 1587

EXFORD, Somerset

Map 03 SS83

★★★72% ❀❀ Crown

Park St TA24 7PP
☎ 01643 831554 📠 01643 831665
e-mail: bradleyhotelsexmoor@easynet.co.uk
Dir: *leave M5 junct 25 and follow signs for Taunton. Take the A358 out of Taunton, then the B3224 via Wheddon Cross into Exford*
Guest comfort is paramount in this corner of Somerset and it shines through the Crown Hotel. Afternoon teas served in the lounge beside a roaring fire and tempting menus in the bar and restaurant are all part of the charm of this delightful old coaching inn. Bedrooms offer space, comfort and modern facilities, many with views of the pretty moorland village.
ROOMS: 17 en suite s fr £47.50; d £80-£116 (incl. bkfst) * LB
FACILITIES: Fishing Riding Shooting Xmas **PARKING:** 30
CARDS:

Early start? Hotels at all star levels should provide in-room alarm clocks and/or alarm calls.

EXMOUTH, Devon Map 03 SY08

★★★67% Royal Beacon

The Beacon EX8 2AF
☎ 01395 264886 🖹 01395 268890
e-mail: reception@royalbeaconhotel.co.uk
Dir: *in Exmouth follow seafront signs to the Beacon. Hotel on left*

A welcoming hotel, the Royal Beacon is an elegant Georgian property overlooking both the town of Exmouth and the beautiful Devon coastline. The hotel enjoys fine views, an inviting bar and restaurant, well appointed rooms and an impressive function suite.
ROOMS: 23 en suite (2 fmly) No smoking in 4 bedrooms s £40-£45; d £70-£85 (incl. bkfst) * LB **FACILITIES:** Xmas **CONF:** Thtr 150 Class 100 Board 40 Del from £67 * **SERVICES:** Lift **PARKING:** 10 **NOTES:** Civ Wed 150 **CARDS:**

See advert on page 207

★★★62% The Imperial

The Esplanade EX8 2SW
☎ 01395 274761 🖹 01395 265161
Dir: *M5 junct 30 A376 to Exmouth follow signs for seafront. Over 1st rdbt left at next, hotel at end of T-junction*
A traditional hotel set in grounds with an outdoor swimming pool and tennis court, close to the town centre and facing the sea front. A well chosen menu of British dishes can be enjoyed in the spacious restaurant. Bedrooms vary in style and size but are all equipped with modern facilities.
ROOMS: 57 en suite (3 fmly) No smoking in 18 bedrooms **FACILITIES:** Outdoor swimming (H) Tennis (hard) entertainment **CONF:** Thtr 120 Class 30 Board 36 Del from £78 * **SERVICES:** Lift **PARKING:** 70 **NOTES:** No smoking in restaurant
CARDS:

★★68% Barn

Foxholes Hill, Marine Dr EX8 2DF
☎ 01395 224411 🖹 01395 225445
e-mail: david@barnhotel.co.uk
Dir: *M5 junct 30 follow signs for Exmouth A376, to seafront in an easterly direction, next rdbt last exit into Foxholes Hill. Hotel on right*
The Barn is a unique Grade II listed, butterfly-shaped property. The hotel has a real homely feel and sees guests returning year after year. Bedrooms are comfortable with modern facilities. Additional features include beautiful grounds, cosy lounge, bar, car park and lovely sea views.
ROOMS: 11 en suite (4 fmly) No smoking in all bedrooms s £30-£34; d £60-£68 (incl. bkfst) * LB **FACILITIES:** Outdoor swimming Putting green **CONF:** Class 40 Board 20 **PARKING:** 24 **NOTES:** No dogs No smoking in restaurant Closed 23 Dec-10 Jan
CARDS:

★★62% Manor

The Beacon EX8 2AG
☎ 01395 272549 & 274477 🖹 01395 225519
Dir: *M5 junct 30 take A376 to Exmouth take signs for seafront, hotel 300yds from seafront by Tourist Information Office*
Traditional hospitality is the hallmark of this friendly, family-run hotel. The convenience of the location, overlooking the town centre and the sea, is a factor which brings back guests year after year. The well equipped bedrooms vary in style and size, with many offering the added bonus of far reaching views. The table d'hôte menu offers a selection of traditional dishes, after which a drink can be enjoyed in the convivial surroundings of the lounge bar.
ROOMS: 38 en suite (3 fmly) s £27.50-£32.50; d £50-£60 (incl. bkfst) * LB **FACILITIES:** Xmas **CONF:** Thtr 100 **SERVICES:** Lift **PARKING:** 15 **NOTES:** No dogs (ex guide dogs) No smoking in restaurant
CARDS:

FAIRFORD, Gloucestershire Map 04 SP10

★★64% Bull Hotel

The Market Place GL7 4AA
☎ 01285 712535 & 712217 🖹 01285 713782
e-mail: mashd@markdudley.freeserve.co.uk
Dir: *on the A417 in the market square adjacent to the post office*

A family-run inn on the picturesque market square offers neatly furnished, well equipped bedrooms. The bar is a popular meeting place, and has kept its original character. There is a good choice of food, either in the bar or in the separate restaurant.
ROOMS: 22 rms (20 en suite) (1 fmly) s £47.50-£69.50; d £69.50-£89.50 (incl. bkfst) * LB **FACILITIES:** Fishing **CONF:** Thtr 60 Class 40 Board 40 Del £72.50 * **PARKING:** 10 **NOTES:** No smoking in restaurant
CARDS:

See advert on opposite page

FAKENHAM, Norfolk Map 09 TF92

★★66% *Crown*

Market Place NR21 9BP
☎ 01328 851418 🖹 01328 862433
Dir: *in town centre*
Originally a coaching inn and focal point of this old market town, parts of The Crown date back to the 16th century. Bedrooms are attractively decorated and well equipped. The bar menu and blackboard offer a range of snacks whilst the restaurant has a carte menu.
ROOMS: 12 en suite (2 fmly) No smoking in 1 bedroom **FACILITIES:** Garage lock up for bicycles **PARKING:** 25 **NOTES:** No dogs (ex guide dogs) Closed 25 Dec **CARDS:**

★★66% Sculthorpe Mill
Lynn Rd, Sculthorpe NR21 9QG
☎ 01328 856161 🖷 01328 856651
Dir: *turn off A148 from Fakenham to Kings Lynn, just beyond village of Sculthorpe*

An 18th-century watermill situated within easy striking distance of the town centre in an idyllic and tranquil position. With its open fires, low beams and nooks and crannies, it is popular both as a watering hole for locals and a fine dining venue. The bedrooms are spacious and well equipped; one has a four-poster bed.
ROOMS: 6 en suite (1 fmly) No smoking in all bedrooms s fr £50; d fr £75 (incl. bkfst) * LB **FACILITIES:** ch fac Xmas **CONF:** Thtr 25 Class 16 Board 16 **PARKING:** 60 **NOTES:** No smoking in restaurant RS Oct-Good Fri Mon-Fri closed 3-6pm Civ Wed 120
CARDS:

FALMOUTH, Cornwall & Isles of Scilly — Map 02 SW83
see also Mawnan Smith

★★★★70% ❀❀ Royal Duchy
Cliff Rd TR11 4NX
☎ 01326 313042 🖷 01326 319420
e-mail: info@royalduchy.co.uk
Dir: *located on Cliff Rd, along Falmouth Sea Front*

Situated on the sea front, just a short walk from the town centre, this hotel continues to attract a regular clientele. The lounges enjoy spectacular views, as does the restaurant, where carefully prepared dishes are served. Bedrooms vary in size and aspect, with sea facing rooms always being in demand.
ROOMS: 43 en suite (6 fmly) s £60-£86; d £112-£192 (incl. bkfst) * LB **FACILITIES:** STV Indoor swimming (H) Sauna Solarium Pool table Jacuzzi/spa Table tennis entertainment ch fac Xmas **CONF:** Thtr 50 Class 50 Board 50 **SERVICES:** Lift **PARKING:** 50 **NOTES:** No dogs (ex guide dogs) Civ Wed **CARDS:**

See advert on this page

★★★75% Penmere Manor
Mongleath Rd TR11 4PN
☎ 01326 211411 🖷 01326 317588
e-mail: reservations@penmere.demon.co.uk
Dir: *turn right off Hillhead roundabout and follow road for approx 1m then turn left into Mongleath Road*

Best Western

Quitely located within five acres of gardens and woodlands, this family-owned hotel is a popular choice. A wide range of bedrooms are offered with the spacious garden wing rooms being furnished and equipped to a particularly high standard. Imaginative dishes using local produce are served in Bolitho's Restaurant. Fountains Bar, part of the leisure club, offers light meals and snacks in a more informal setting.

continued on p210

FALMOUTH, continued

Penmere Manor, Falmouth

ROOMS: 37 en suite (14 fmly) No smoking in 29 bedrooms s £55.50-£95.50; d £85-£119 (incl. bkfst) * LB **FACILITIES:** STV Indoor swimming (H) Outdoor swimming (H) Sauna Solarium Gym Pool table Croquet lawn Jacuzzi/spa Table tennis Boules entertainment Xmas **CONF:** Thtr 40 Class 30 Board 30 Del from £75 * **PARKING:** 50 **NOTES:** No smoking in restaurant Closed 24-28 Dec Civ Wed 80 **CARDS:**

See advert on opposite page

★★★72% Falmouth Beach Resort Hotel

Gyllyngvase Beach, Seafront TR11 4NA
☎ 01326 318084 📠 01326 319147
e-mail: info@falmouthbeachhotel.co.uk
Dir: *from A39 to Falmouth follow signs to seafront & Gyllyngvase Beach, hotel opposite Gyllyngvase Beach, near tennis courts*

This large, popular hotel has a 250-seater restaurant, Sandpipers, as well as the more formal Ospreys. The Feathers Bar has been enlarged and there is also the Features lounge. Bedrooms vary in style and all are nicely decorated and have modern amenities. There are good leisure facilities at The Beach Club.
ROOMS: 111 en suite 7 annexe en suite (20 fmly) No smoking in 94 bedrooms s £59; d £69-£73 * LB **FACILITIES:** STV Indoor swimming (H) Tennis (hard) Sauna Solarium Gym Pool table Jacuzzi/spa Steam room entertainment Xmas **CONF:** Thtr 300 Class 200 Board 150 Del from £72 * **SERVICES:** Lift **PARKING:** 95 **NOTES:** No smoking in restaurant Civ Wed 300 **CARDS:**

See advert on opposite page

★★★69% Falmouth

Castle Beach TR11 4NZ
☎ 01326 312671 & Freephone 0800 0193121 📠 01326 319533
e-mail: info@falmouthhotel.com
Dir: *from Exeter take A30 to Truro then A390 to Falmouth. Hotel on the seafront near Pendennis Castle*
This Victorian hotel is set in five acres of gardens overlooking Castle Beach and just a short walk from the town centre. All bedrooms offer good levels of comfort and facilities and include family, non-smoking and balconied rooms. A choice of lounges, looking out across the bay, an elegant restaurant, large ballroom and leisure club complete the amenities. There are also self-catering apartments in the grounds.

ROOMS: 69 en suite 34 annexe en suite (13 fmly) No smoking in 18 bedrooms s £50-£102; d £80-£180 (incl. bkfst) * LB **FACILITIES:** STV Indoor swimming (H) Snooker Sauna Solarium Gym Pool table Croquet lawn Putting green Jacuzzi/spa Membership of local tennis & squash club free to all guests ch fac **CONF:** Thtr 300 Class 150 Board 100 Del from £59 * **SERVICES:** Lift **PARKING:** 175 **NOTES:** Closed 24 Dec-3 Jan Civ Wed 250 **CARDS:**

See advert on opposite page

★★★68% The Greenbank

Harbourside TR11 2SR
☎ 01326 312440 📠 01326 211362
e-mail: sales@greenbank-hotel.com
Dir: *200yds past Falmouth Marina*
History abounds at this gracious harbourside hotel which boasts its own private 17th-century quay. Refurbishment has sensitively combined contemporary expectations with the charm and elegance of yesteryear. Bedrooms are spacious and well equipped, many having sea views. A choice of dining options is available.
ROOMS: 59 en suite (4 fmly) No smoking in 2 bedrooms s £57-£72; d £98-£145 (incl. bkfst) * LB **FACILITIES:** Sauna Solarium Gym Xmas **CONF:** Thtr 80 Class 45 Board 20 Del from £79.50 * **SERVICES:** Lift **PARKING:** 68 **NOTES:** No smoking in restaurant
CARDS:

★★★67% Green Lawns

Western Ter TR11 4QJ
☎ 01326 312734 📠 01326 211427
e-mail: info@greenlawnshotel.com
Dir: *on A39*
Popular with both business and leisure guests, this established hotel offers extensive facilities, including a spacious function room and an attractive split-level restaurant where both a table d'hôte and a carte menu is available to guests and non-residents alike. Bedrooms vary in size and style, although all offer many modern facilities and comforts.
ROOMS: 39 en suite (8 fmly) No smoking in 8 bedrooms **FACILITIES:** STV Indoor swimming (H) Tennis (hard & grass) Squash Sauna Solarium Gym Jacuzzi/spa entertainment **CONF:** Thtr 200 Class 80 Board 100 Del £85 * **PARKING:** 69 **NOTES:** No smoking in restaurant Closed 24-30 Dec **CARDS:**

★★★67% Penmorvah Manor

Budock Water TR11 5ED
☎ 01326 250277 📠 01326 250509
e-mail: enquiries@penmorvah.force9.co.uk
Dir: *take A39 to Hillhead roundabout take 2nd exit. At Falmouth Football Club turn right, through Budock, hotel opposite Penjerrick Gardens*
Situated within two miles of central Falmouth, this extended

continued on p212

Best Western

Penmere MANOR

FALMOUTH, CORNWALL UK

A beautiful 3 star Country House hotel in 5 acres of gardens and woodland offering the last word in comfort, friendliness and attentive service, Penmere is everything you want in a hotel.

Mongleath Road, Falmouth,
Cornwall TR11 4PN

FREEPHONE 0800 980 4611
web: www.penmere.co.uk
email: reservations@penmere.co.uk

A PLACE OF PEACE AND BEAUTY

...where the gardens sweep down to the sea

Family run Country House Hotel specialists in local seafood, traditional service, cosseted comforts, antiques, log fires and fresh flowers.

Meudon

AA ★★★ 78% **GOLF IS FREE**

Please see full entry under Mawnan Smith

Tel 01 326 250541 • Fax 250543

www.meudon.co.uk

CASTLE BEACH
FALMOUTH
CORNWALL
TR11 4NZ
Tel: 01326 312671
Fax: 01326 319533

AA ★★★ **Website: www.falmouthhotel.com**

A beautiful hotel commanding an unrivalled seafront position. 100 luxurious bedrooms, apartments and cottages, some with balconies and jacuzzis, you can choose between B&B, HB or SC.

Delightful restaurants, bars and lounges with stunning views and a wonderfully relaxing ambience. Superb leisure complex with pool, sauna, jacuzzi, solarium and gymnasium. The perfect location for a holiday or short break as well as a delightful venue for weddings, conferences and all functions.

Please call for a brochure and tariff.

What a position to be in!

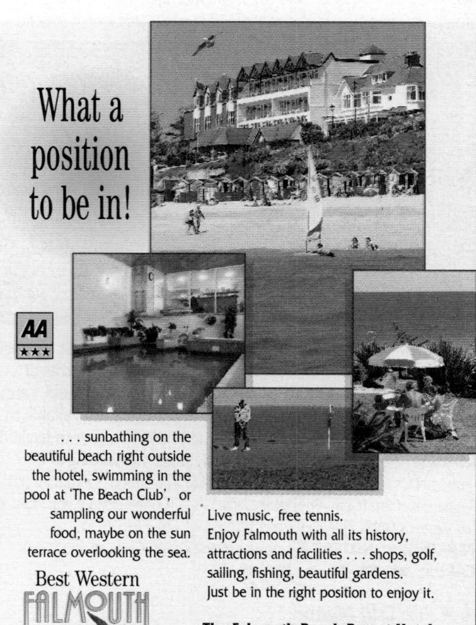

AA ★★★

. . . sunbathing on the beautiful beach right outside the hotel, swimming in the pool at 'The Beach Club', or sampling our wonderful food, maybe on the sun terrace overlooking the sea.

Live music, free tennis.
Enjoy Falmouth with all its history, attractions and facilities . . . shops, golf, sailing, fishing, beautiful gardens.
Just be in the right position to enjoy it.

Best Western
FALMOUTH BEACH
RESORT HOTEL & Conference Centre

The Falmouth Beach Resort Hotel.
Gyllyngvase Beach, Falmouth, Cornwall.
Tel: 01326 312999 Fax: 319147
Email: info@falmouthbeachhotel.co.uk
Website: www.famouthbeachhotel.co.uk

FALMOUTH, continued

Victorian manor house is peacefully set in six acres of private woodland and gardens. Activity holidays and leisure breaks are available, including a painters' workshop, and garden and golfing holidays. Most of the rooms are located in a modern wing, with half the rooms on the ground floor. In the candlelit restaurant an interesting fixed-price menu is offered.
ROOMS: 27 en suite (1 fmly) No smoking in all bedrooms s fr £55; d £77.50-£120 (incl. bkfst) * LB **FACILITIES:** Pool table Croquet lawn ch fac Xmas **CONF:** Thtr 250 Class 100 Board 56 Del from £93.50 * **PARKING:** 150 **NOTES:** No smoking in restaurant
CARDS:

★★★61% Gyllyngdune Manor
Melvill Rd TR11 4AR
☎ 01326 312978 🖷 01326 211881
Dir: *from A39 follow signs for beaches and docks. Hotel 200yds beyond Pavilion and Beer Garden on right*
This imposing Georgian manor house, situated above the town in its own mature grounds, has fine views of Falmouth Bay. The hotel has friendly staff and comfortable public areas in addition to an indoor swimming pool, games room and gymnasium. Bedrooms include ground floor, four-poster, and family options.
ROOMS: 30 en suite (3 fmly) s £46-£50; d £92-£100 (incl. bkfst & dinner) * LB **FACILITIES:** Indoor swimming (H) Sauna Solarium Gym Pool table Table tennis entertainment Xmas **PARKING:** 27 **NOTES:** No smoking in restaurant Closed 27 Dec-11 Jan
CARDS:

★★★60% St Michaels of Falmouth
REGAL
Gyllyngvase Beach, Seafront TR11 4NB
☎ 01326 312707 🖷 01326 211772
Dir: *follow the A39 into Falmouth, at 2nd rdbt, take Melville Rd, then take the 3rd right turn and right again into Stracey Rd*

Conveniently situated for the beaches and town centre, St Michael's Hotel benefits from spacious public areas and its four acres of gardens. A popular leisure centre, including an indoor pool, sauna, solarium and well equipped gym add to the facilities available to guests. Bedrooms vary in size and style and offer modern facilities.
ROOMS: 57 en suite 8 annexe en suite (2 fmly) No smoking in 4 bedrooms s £57; d £75 * LB **FACILITIES:** STV Indoor swimming (H) Sauna Solarium Gym Pool table Jacuzzi/spa Concessionary golf rates ch fac Xmas **CONF:** Thtr 200 Class 150 Board 120 Del £75 * **PARKING:** 30 **NOTES:** No smoking in restaurant Civ Wed 100
CARDS:

★★70% *Crill Manor*
Maen Valley, Budock Water TR11 5BL
☎ 01326 211880 🖷 01326 211229
Dir: *2.5m W on unclass rd*
This delightful family-run hotel lies in an idyllic spot two miles from Falmouth, set in attractive gardens, surrounded by an area of outstanding natural beauty. Bedrooms are stylishly decorated, well equipped with modern facilities, and two are located in an adjoining building. The open-plan lounge and bar look out over the swimming pool and gardens.
ROOMS: 12 en suite 2 annexe en suite (2 fmly) No smoking in all bedrooms **FACILITIES:** Outdoor swimming (H) **PARKING:** 14 **NOTES:** No dogs No children 10yrs No smoking in restaurant
CARDS:

★★67% Carthion
Cliff Rd TR11 4AP
☎ 01326 313669 🖷 01326 212828
e-mail: info@carthion.f9.co.uk
Dir: *from A39 follow signs to sea-front*
The Carthion excels at catering for smaller functions and private parties. The lounges, bar and marvellous conservatory, where guests take breakfast, offer stunning views over Falmouth Bay. The bedrooms are generally spacious and comfortably furnished, many with sea views. Consistently good traditional cuisine is available on two menus.
ROOMS: 18 en suite (4 fmly) s £43-£51; d £74-£88 (incl. bkfst) * LB **FACILITIES:** STV **PARKING:** 18 **NOTES:** No dogs (ex guide dogs) No children 10yrs No smoking in restaurant RS Nov-Feb
CARDS:

★★66% Park Grove
Kimberley Park Rd TR11 2DD
☎ 01326 313276 🖷 01326 211926
e-mail: reception@parkgrovehotel.com
Dir: *turn off A39 at traffic lights by Riders Garage, towards harbour. Hotel is 400yds on left opposite the park*
A long established family-run hotel, conveniently situated opposite Kimberley Gardens within walking distance of Falmouth town centre. Relaxed, friendly service is provided by a small team of loyal staff. Bedrooms are neat and comfortably furnished with many modern facilities. Each evening a four-course meal is served in the dining room, next to the bar.
ROOMS: 17 en suite (6 fmly) s £25-£27; d £50-£54 (incl. bkfst) * LB **FACILITIES:** STV **PARKING:** 28 **NOTES:** No smoking in restaurant
CARDS:

★★64% Broadmead
THE CIRCLE Selected Individual Hotels GREAT BRITAIN
66-68 Kimberley Park Rd TR11 2DD
☎ 01326 315704 & 318036 🖷 01326 311048
Dir: *turn off A39 at traffic lights by Riders Garage, towards town centre, hotel 150yds on left*
This informal, family-run hotel overlooks the attractive Kimberley Park and is within easy walking distance of Falmouth town centre. Bedrooms are well appointed and ideally suited to both business and leisure guests. A choice of comfortable lounges is available, together with a small bar and smart dining room where a fixed price menu is offered.
ROOMS: 12 rms (11 en suite) (1 fmly) s fr £28; d £54-£60 (incl. bkfst) * LB **PARKING:** 8 **NOTES:** No dogs No smoking in restaurant Closed 20 Dec-3 Jan **CARDS:**

★★63% *Rosslyn*
110 Kimberley Park Rd TR11 2JJ
☎ 01326 312699 🖷 01326 312699
On the northern edge of Falmouth, this family-run hotel is popular with tour groups. Public areas are spacious and comfortable with a choice of lounges, one specifically for non-smokers. The attractive gardens at the rear of the property are well tended and peaceful. Bedrooms vary in size and are freshly decorated.
ROOMS: 27 rms (21 en suite) (2 fmly) No smoking in all bedrooms **FACILITIES:** Pool table Putting green Table tennis Darts **CONF:** Class 60 **PARKING:** 10 **NOTES:** No smoking in restaurant RS 24 Dec-28 Feb
CARDS:

★★62% Membly Hall
Sea Front, Cliff Rd TR11 4NT
☎ 01326 312869 & 311115 📠 01326 211751
e-mail: memblyhallhotel@netscapeonline.co.uk
Dir: *from A30 turn onto A3076 for Truro then follow A39 to Falmouth. At Falmouth follow signs for seafront and beaches. Hotel located middle of seafront*

This holiday hotel lies on the seafront with superb views over Falmouth Bay. Bedrooms are decorated with pretty wallpapers and are well equipped. Several rooms are located at ground-floor level and many are suitable for families. Public areas are spacious and live entertainment is held regularly.
ROOMS: 37 en suite (3 fmly) s £24-£40; d £48-£80 (incl. bkfst) * LB **FACILITIES:** STV Pool table Putting green Indoor short bowls Table tennis Darts ch fac **CONF:** Thtr 150 Class 130 Board 60 Del from £40 * **SERVICES:** Lift **PARKING:** 30 **NOTES:** No smoking in restaurant Closed Xmas week RS Dec to Feb

FAREHAM, Hampshire

Map 04 SU50

★★★★74% ❀ Solent
Rookery Av, Whiteley PO15 7AJ
☎ 01489 880000 📠 01489 880007
e-mail: solent@shireinns.co.uk
Dir: *on Solent Business Park just off junct 9 on M27*

SHIRE INNS

Although close to the M27, this smart, purpose-built hotel enjoys a peaceful location. Bedrooms are well appointed and public areas include a good range of meeting and leisure facilities. There is a pub in the grounds which serves real ale and home-cooked food, and the hotel also has a more formal restaurant, Woodlands. Staff are friendly and helpful.
ROOMS: 111 en suite (9 fmly) No smoking in 30 bedrooms s fr £122 (incl. bkfst) * LB **FACILITIES:** STV Indoor swimming (H) Tennis (hard) Squash Sauna Solarium Gym Pool table Jacuzzi/spa Steam room Childrens splash pool Xmas **CONF:** Thtr 250 Class 120 Board 80 Del from £98 * **SERVICES:** Lift **PARKING:** 200 **NOTES:** No smoking in restaurant Civ Wed 250 **CARDS:**

★★★68% *Posthouse Fareham*
Cartwright Dr, Titchfield PO15 5RJ
☎ 0870 400 9028 📠 01329 844666
Dir: *exit M27 at junct 9 and follow signs for A27. Continue across Segensworth roundabout following road for 1.5m, turn left at next roundabout*

Posthouse

This well established Posthouse continues to attract both business and leisure markets. Bedrooms are modern and well equipped, including a mini-bar. Spacious public areas include several conference rooms, newly refurbished leisure centre with pool and large restaurant.

continued on p214

FARRHAM, continued

ROOMS: 125 en suite (25 fmly) No smoking in 78 bedrooms **FACILITIES:** Indoor swimming (H) Sauna Solarium Gym Pool table Jacuzzi/spa Childrens play area **CONF:** Thtr 160 Class 80 Board 50 **PARKING:** 130 **NOTES:** No smoking in restaurant **CARDS:**

See advert on page 213

★★★62% Lysses House

51 High St PO16 7BQ
☎ 01329 822622 01329 822762
e-mail: lysses@lysses.co.uk
Dir: *take M27 junct 11 and stay in left hand lane till rdbt, take third exit in to East St and follow into High St. Hotel is at top on right*

A Georgian hotel in a quiet location on the edge of the town centre. Rooms are well equipped, appealing particularly to the business traveller. There are conference facilities, a lounge and bar, serving a range of snacks. The Richmond Restaurant has an interesting selection of dishes on set and carte menus.

ROOMS: 21 en suite s fr £65; d fr £80 (incl. bkfst) * **CONF:** Thtr 95 Class 42 Board 28 Del from £90 * **SERVICES:** Lift **PARKING:** 30 **NOTES:** No dogs (ex guide dogs) No smoking in restaurant Closed 25 Dec-1 Jan RS 24 Dec Civ Wed 95 **CARDS:**

FARINGDON, Oxfordshire — Map 04 SU29

★★★73% Sudbury House Hotel & Conference Centre

London St SN7 8AA
☎ 01367 241272 01367 242346
e-mail: sudburyhouse@cix.co.uk
Dir: *off A420, signposted Folly Hill*

Sudbury House lies on the edge of the Cotswolds between Oxford and Swindon. Bedrooms are attractive, decorated in warm colour schemes, spacious and well equipped. Dining options include the restaurant and bar and a comprehensive room service menu. Conference facilities and private dining rooms are also available.

ROOMS: 49 en suite (2 fmly) No smoking in 22 bedrooms s £62-£85; d £65-£95 (incl. bkfst) * LB **FACILITIES:** STV Croquet lawn Putting green Pitch & Putt Badminton Xmas **CONF:** Thtr 90 Class 90 Board 40 Del from £139.50 * **SERVICES:** Lift **PARKING:** 100 **CARDS:**

See advert on opposite page

★★62% Faringdon

1 Market Place SN7 7HL
☎ 01367 240536 01367 243250
Dir: *M4 junct 15 A419 take A420 signposted to Oxford for 10m follow signs for Faringdon, hotel next to All Saints Church*

Opposite the 12th Century parish church, Faringdon Hotel occupies a lovely spot in the Market Place of this small town. The hotel itself has much history and it is believed that it stands on what was the site of the Royal Palace of Alfred the Great. Bedrooms offer good facilities and are spacious, with some four poster rooms available. Ideal for business or pleasure guests can relax after a hard day and enjoy the hotel bar and dinner in the Surin Thai Restaurant.

ROOMS: 15 en suite 5 annexe en suite (3 fmly) s £55-£65; d £65-£75 (incl. bkfst) * LB **CONF:** Thtr 30 Class 15 Board 20 **CARDS:**

FARNBOROUGH, Hampshire — Map 04 SU85

★★★67% *Posthouse Farnborough*

Posthouse

Lynchford Rd GU14 6AZ
☎ 0870 400 9029 01252 377210
Dir: *from M3 junct 4, follow A325 for Farnborough. Take A325 through Farnborough town centre towards Aldershot. Hotel on the left at The Queen's rdbt*

Combining a mix of traditional and modern style, and very conveniently placed for the bi-annual air show, this smart hotel continues to improve, with extensive refurbishment work carried out this year. Well equipped bedrooms are a feature, in addition to a range of meeting rooms, and good leisure facilities.

ROOMS: 143 en suite (39 fmly) No smoking in 80 bedrooms **FACILITIES:** Indoor swimming (H) Sauna Solarium Gym Jacuzzi/spa Health & fitness centre ch fac **CONF:** Thtr 120 Class 60 Board 60 **PARKING:** 175 **CARDS:**

★★★60% *Falcon*

68 Farnborough Rd GU14 6TH
☎ 01252 545378 01252 522539
Dir: *on A325 opposite Aerospace Centre airfield*

This hotel is conveniently placed for the town centre and access to major roads. Popular with an international business clientele, the bedrooms are modern and well equipped. There is a pleasant club-like atmosphere in the public areas, which include a small bar and open-plan lounge.

ROOMS: 30 en suite (1 fmly) **FACILITIES:** STV **CONF:** Thtr 25 Class 10 Board 16 **PARKING:** 30 **NOTES:** No dogs (ex guide dogs) RS Xmas & New Year **CARDS:**

FARNHAM, Surrey — Map 04 SU84

see also Churt

★★★72% Bishop's Table

Best Western

27 West St GU9 7DR
☎ 01252 710222 01252 733494
e-mail: bishops.table@btinternet.com
Dir: *take the A331 (from M3 J4), or A31 (from A3) and follow signs for town centre, hotel is located next to the library*

Guests can expect a warm welcome at this charming Georgian townhouse hotel. Bedrooms some of which occupy a restored coach house, are all individual in style and tastefully appointed. Public areas include a relaxing bar, and a smart restaurant offering

continued

an interesting range of carefully prepared dishes. Service is both friendly and attentive.

ROOMS: 9 en suite 8 annexe en suite s fr £90; d fr £110 (incl. bkfst) * LB **CONF:** Thtr 26 Class 36 Board 15 Del from £150 * **NOTES:** No dogs (ex guide dogs) No children 16yrs No smoking in restaurant Closed 25 Dec-3 Jan RS Closed for lunch Sat **CARDS:**

See advert on this page

★★★64% The Bush

The Borough GU9 7NN
☎ 0870 400 8225 📠 01252 733530
Dir: *join A31 Farnham follow signs for town centre. At crossroads left and hotel on the right*

Situated in the centre of town, this ivy-clad 17th-century coaching inn offers a range of different styles of bedroom, some in the original building, some in an extension. Day rooms include a bar, a separate lounge with frescoes depicting historical scenes, and the Georgian-style Thackeray restaurant.

ROOMS: 83 en suite No smoking in 48 bedrooms d £145 * LB **FACILITIES:** Croquet lawn Xmas **CONF:** Thtr 60 Class 30 Board 30 Del from £135 * **PARKING:** 60 **NOTES:** Civ Wed 90
CARDS:

★★★61% Farnham House

Alton Rd GU10 5ER
☎ 01252 716908 📠 01252 722583
e-mail: mail@farnhamhousehotel.com
Dir: *1m from town, off A31 Alton road*

Popular for conferences and weddings, Farnham House is surrounded by five acres of grounds. The Victorian architecture is part Tudor, part baronial in style, and features an oak-panelled bar

continued

FARNHAM, continued

with an inglenook fireplace. Comfortable, well appointed bedrooms enjoy views over tranquil countryside.
ROOMS: 25 en suite (1 fmly) No smoking in 5 bedrooms s fr £70; d fr £75 * **FACILITIES:** STV Outdoor swimming (H) Tennis (hard) **CONF:** Thtr 65 Class 15 Board 24 Del £130 * **PARKING:** 75 **NOTES:** No dogs (ex guide dogs) RS 25 & 26 Dec Civ Wed 70
CARDS:

FAVERSHAM, Kent — Map 05 TR06

Travelodge
Thanet Way ME8 9EL
☎ 01227 770980
Dir: *from junc 7 M2, take A299*
This modern building offers accommodation in smart, spacious and well equipped bedrooms, all with en suite bathrooms. Refreshments may be taken at the nearby family restaurant. For further details and the Travelodge phone number, consult the Hotel Groups page.
ROOMS: 40 en suite

FEERING, Essex — Map 05 TL82

Travelodge
A12 London Rd Northbound CO5 9EL
☎ 0800 850950
This modern building offers accommodation in smart, spacious and well equipped bedrooms, all with en suite bathrooms. Refreshments may be taken at the nearby family restaurant. For further details and the Travelodge phone number, consult the Hotel Groups page.
ROOMS: 39 en suite

FELIXSTOWE, Suffolk — Map 05 TM33

★★★67% Orwell
Hamilton Rd IP11 7DX
☎ 01394 285511 📠 01394 670687
Dir: *approaching on A45, straight across Dock Roundabout, straight across next roundabout, 4th exit off third roundabout*
An imposing building, the Orwell's interior decor gives the feel of a grand hotel. Bedrooms are smartly decorated, and it is worth requesting one of the spacious 'Superior' rooms. Guests have a choice of two bars, and for meals, an informal buttery or the spacious restaurant.
ROOMS: 58 en suite (8 fmly) No smoking in 4 bedrooms s fr £60; d fr £70 * LB **FACILITIES:** STV entertainment Xmas **CONF:** Thtr 200 Class 100 Board 60 **SERVICES:** Lift **PARKING:** 70 **NOTES:** No dogs (ex guide dogs) No smoking in restaurant
CARDS:

★★70% Waverley
2 Wolsey Gardens IP11 7DF
☎ 01394 282811 📠 01394 670185
This attractive Victorian hotel provides well equipped, spacious accommodation throughout, and some rooms have balconies and views over the promenade. Public areas include Gladstone's bar where hot and cold snacks are available. For more formal surroundings there is the Wolsey restaurant which offers an extensive menu.
ROOMS: 19 en suite (4 fmly) s £50-£56.95; d £60-£74.95 * LB **FACILITIES:** entertainment Xmas **CONF:** Thtr 85 Class 35 Board 25 Del from £69.95 * **PARKING:** 30 **NOTES:** No smoking in restaurant
CARDS:

★★61% Marlborough
Sea Front IP11 8BJ
☎ 01394 285621 📠 01394 670724
Dir: *from A14 follow for Docks. Go straight on at Dock rdbt, over railway crossing & traffic lights. Turn left at 'T' junc, Hotel 400mtrs on left*
Situated on the seafront within easy walking distance of the pier leisure complex is this traditional seaside hotel. The public areas feature the smart Rattan Restaurant, the well appointed Flying Boat Bar and L'Aperitif lounge bar. Many of the well equipped bedrooms have lovely sea views.
ROOMS: 47 en suite s £47-£52; d £52-£62 (incl. bkfst) * LB **FACILITIES:** STV Pool table Xmas **CONF:** Thtr 80 Class 60 Board 40 Del from £60 * **SERVICES:** Lift **PARKING:** 16 **NOTES:** No dogs (ex guide dogs) No smoking in restaurant **CARDS:**

FENNY BENTLEY, Derbyshire — Map 07 SK14

★66% The Bentley Brook Inn & Fenny's Restaurant
DE6 1LF
☎ 01335 350278 📠 01335 350422
e-mail: bentleybrookinn@btinternet.com
Dir: *on B5056*
This busy, family-run country inn lies within the Peak District National Park. It is a charming half-timbered building with an attractive terrace and sweeping lawns. Trout fishing is available. The ground floor is dominated by a well appointed restaurant, and the character bar is open throughout the day for informal dining. Bedrooms, which vary in styles and sizes, are well equipped. An on-site brewery, Leatherbritches, supplies award-winning real ales to the bar.
ROOMS: 9 rms (6 en suite) 1 annexe en suite (1 fmly) No smoking in 1 bedroom s £35-£45; d £50-£65 (incl. bkfst) * LB **FACILITIES:** Fishing Boules Skittles Xmas **CONF:** Thtr 28 Board 18 **PARKING:** 60 **NOTES:** No smoking in restaurant **CARDS:**

FENSTANTON, Cambridgeshire — Map 04 TL36

Travelodge
PE18 9JG
☎ 01954 230919 📠 01954 230919
Dir: *4m SE of Huntingdon, on A14 eastbound*
This modern building offers accommodation in smart, spacious and well equipped bedrooms, all with en suite bathrooms. Refreshments may be taken at the nearby family restaurant. For further details and the Travelodge phone number, consult the Hotel Groups page.
ROOMS: 40 en suite

FERNDOWN, Dorset — Map 04 SU00

★★★★69% Dormy
New Rd BH22 8ES
☎ 01202 872121 📠 01202 895388
Dir: *off A347 from Bournemouth*
Set in attractive grounds, this well established hotel remains popular. Bedrooms are located in both the main building and in several nearby cottage wings. Public rooms feature traditional wood panelling and open fires. There are several eating options including Hennessys the hotel's new fine dining restaurant which offers a high standard of cuisine and service.

continued

ROOMS: 115 en suite (15 fmly) No smoking in 28 bedrooms
FACILITIES: STV Indoor swimming (H) Tennis (hard) Squash Snooker Sauna Solarium Gym Pool table Putting green Jacuzzi/spa Beauty salon entertainment ch fac **CONF:** Thtr 250 Class 150 Board 60
SERVICES: Lift **PARKING:** 220 **CARDS:**

FERRYBRIDGE SERVICE AREA, West Yorkshire Map 08 SE42

Travelodge

Travelodge

WF11 0AF
☎ 01977 672767
Dir: *A1/M62 jnct 33*
This modern building offers accommodation in smart, spacious and well equipped bedrooms, all with en suite bathrooms. Refreshments may be taken at the nearby family restaurant. For further details and the Travelodge phone number, consult the Hotel Groups page.
ROOMS: 36 en suite

FILEY, North Yorkshire Map 08 TA18

★★72% Downcliffe House Hotel

The Beach YO14 9LA
☎ 01723 513310 01723 513773
e-mail: paulmanners@onyxnet.co.uk
Dir: *leave A165 & join A1039 into centre of Filey, continue through centre along Cargate Hill & turn right. Hotel is approx 200yds along sea front*
Standing beside the sea, this delightful hotel has been furnished to a very high standard. There is a pleasant ground floor bar together with a first floor lounge while a good range of dishes is available in the attractive restaurant. Service is provided in a friendly and courteous manner and all bedrooms are well equipped and attractively furnished.
ROOMS: 10 en suite (2 fmly) s £35-£37 (incl. bkfst) * LB
FACILITIES: Xmas **PARKING:** 7 **NOTES:** No smoking in restaurant Closed 2-31 Jan **CARDS:**

★★65% *Sea Brink*

3 The Beach YO14 9LA
☎ 01723 513257 01723 514139
Dir: *Leave A165 following A1039 into Filey town centre and to beach. Turn right, hotel is 300yds along seafront*
A friendly sea front hotel with superb views over the bay, offering good value and fine hospitality. The bright, fresh bedrooms are well equipped and the short dining room menu offers an adequate choice of home-cooked food. A newly furnished, cosy lounge enjoys fine sea views.
ROOMS: 9 en suite (3 fmly) **NOTES:** No smoking in restaurant Closed Jan & Nov/Dec **CARDS:**

Bad hair day? Hairdryers in all rooms three stars and above.

FINDON, West Sussex Map 04 TQ10

★★★65% *Findon Manor*

High St BN14 0TA
☎ 01903 872733 01903 877473
e-mail: findon@dircon.co.uk
Dir: *500yds off A24 at the sign for Findon*
Findon Manor is a former rectory situated in the centre the village. A beamed lounge doubles as reception, a cosy bar offering a very good range of bar food and is popular with locals. Bedrooms, several with four-posters, are prettily decorated. The restaurant overlooks a garden and offers modern and traditional dishes.
ROOMS: 11 en suite (2 fmly) **CONF:** Thtr 45 Class 25 Board 20
PARKING: 28 **CARDS:**

FIR TREE, Co Durham Map 12 NZ13

★★★62% Helme Park Hall Hotel

DL13 4NW
☎ 01388 730970 01388 730970
Dir: *1m N of roundabout at A689/A68 intersection between Darlington and Corbridge*
Dating back to the 13th century, this hospitable family-owned hotel commands super views over the Wear Valley. The lounge bar, warmed by roaring fires in winter, is extremely popular for its comprehensive selection of bar meals. The bedrooms are modern in style and vary in size.
ROOMS: 13 en suite (1 fmly) **CONF:** Thtr 200 Class 100 Board 120 Del £72.50 * **PARKING:** 70 **NOTES:** No dogs (ex guide dogs) Civ Wed 150
CARDS:

FIVE OAKS, West Sussex Map 04 TQ02

Travelodge

Travelodge

Staines St RH14 9AE
☎ 01403 782711 01403 782711
Dir: *on A29, northbound, 1m N of Billingshurst*
This modern building offers accommodation in smart, spacious and well equipped bedrooms, all with en suite bathrooms. Refreshments may be taken at the nearby family restaurant. For further details and the Travelodge phone number, consult the Hotel Groups page.
ROOMS: 26 en suite

FLADBURY, Worcestershire Map 03 SO94

★★66% The Chequers Inn

Chequers Ln WR10 2PZ
☎ 01386 860276 & 860527 01386 861286
Dir: *off A4538 between Evesham & Pershore. Once in village pass the church, right at War Memorial into Chequers Lane*
This charming old inn, which dates from the 14th Century, stands in the centre of this rural village. Features include a bar with beamed ceiling and real open fires. Meals can be ordered in the bar or in the restaurant, which also offers a carvery buffet. The bedrooms include one suitable for families, and all are equipped with modern facilities.
ROOMS: 8 en suite (2 fmly) s £40-£49.50; d £60-£72.50 (incl. bkfst) * LB **FACILITIES:** Fishing Xmas **PARKING:** 24
CARDS:

See advert under EVESHAM

Early start? Hotels at all star levels should provide in-room alarm clocks and/or alarm calls.

FLAMBOROUGH, East Riding of Yorkshire Map 08 TA26

★★70% North Star
North Marine Dr YO15 1BL
☎ 01262 850379
Dir: *in town follow signs for 'North Landing'. Hotel 100yds from the sea*
Standing close to the North Landing of Flamborough Head, this family-run hotel overlooks delightful countryside. The hotel has been tastefully furnished and provides excellent bedrooms together with a busy bar. A good range of well produced food is available in both the bar and the spacious dining room.
ROOMS: 7 en suite s fr £40; d fr £60 (incl. bkfst) * LB **PARKING:** 30 **NOTES:** No dogs (ex guide dogs) No smoking in restaurant Closed Xmas **CARDS:**

F

★★64% Flaneburg
North Marine Rd YO15 1LF
☎ 01262 850284 ▯ 01262 850284
Dir: *from the centre of Flamborough, follow the signs for "hotel" & "North Landing". The hotel is situated on the very edge of the village on the left*
This friendly good-value hotel, on the North Landing of Flamborough Head, is popular with bird watchers and golfers. The traditional-style bedrooms are pleasantly furnished and the public rooms are comfortable and cosy. A good range of well prepared dishes is provided in the bar and dining room. Hotel service is friendly and attentive.
ROOMS: 13 en suite (3 fmly) s £36.50; d £55 (incl. bkfst) * LB **FACILITIES:** Xmas **CONF:** Thtr 30 Class 20 Board 20 **PARKING:** 50 **NOTES:** No smoking in restaurant **CARDS:**

FLEET, Hampshire Map 04 SU85

★★★62% Lismoyne
Church Rd GU13 8NA
☎ 01252 628555 ▯ 01252 811761
e-mail: mvanhagen@btconnect.com
Dir: *approach town on B3013, cross over railway bridge and continue to town centre. Pass through traffic lights & take fourth right. Hotel 0.25m on left*
The Lismoyne is popular with commercial guests who appreciate the spacious, quiet rooms. Situated in a residential area in its own extensive grounds but close to Fleet centre. The restaurant serves a good range of dishes, room service is also an option. The newly refurbished lounge and bar are comfortable.
ROOMS: 44 en suite (3 fmly) No smoking in 13 bedrooms s £71-£79; d £103-£114 * LB **FACILITIES:** ch fac Xmas **CONF:** Thtr 150 Class 105 Board 50 Del from £135 * **PARKING:** 120 **NOTES:** No smoking in restaurant Civ Wed 200 **CARDS:**

FLEET MOTORWAY SERVICE AREA (M3), Hampshire Map 04 SU75

⇧ Days Inn
DAYS INN
Fleet Services, M3 RG27 8BN
☎ 01252 815587 ▯ 01252 815587
Dir: *between junct 4a & 5 southbound M3*
Fully refurbished, Days Inn offers well equipped, brightly appointed, modern accommodation with smart en suite bathrooms. There is a fully staffed reception; continental breakfast is available and other refreshments may be taken at the nearby family restaurant.
ROOMS: 58 en suite d fr £49 *

FLITWICK, Bedfordshire Map 04 TL03

★★★80% ❀❀ Menzies Flitwick Manor
MENZIES HOTELS
Church Rd MK45 1AE
☎ 0500 636943 (Central Res) ▯ 01773 880321
e-mail: info@menzies-hotels.co.uk
Dir: *on A5120, 2m from M1 exit 12 towards Ampthill*
This delightful Georgian house is peacefully set within extensive parkland and gardens. The individually decorated bedrooms are extremely comfortable and provided with a host of very useful, and thoughtful extras. The public rooms are equally as spoiling. Guests are warmly received and very well cared by the small team of long standing staff and the highlight of any stay has to be Richard Salt's cooking, which is very well deserving of its Two Rosette award.
ROOMS: 17 en suite s £120-£145; d £145-£175 * LB **FACILITIES:** Tennis (hard) Croquet lawn Putting green Xmas **CONF:** Thtr 40 Class 30 Board 24 **PARKING:** 50 **NOTES:** No smoking in restaurant Civ Wed 50 **CARDS:**

FLORE, Northamptonshire Map 04 SP66

★★★72% Courtyard by Marriott Daventry
COURTYARD
The High St NN7 4LP
☎ 01327 349022 ▯ 01327 349017
Dir: *from junct 16 on M1, follow A45 towards Daventry. Hotel 1m on right between and Upper Heyford and Flore*
Just off the M1 motorway in rural surroundings, this modern hotel is particularly suited to the business guest. Bedrooms provide smart, soft furnishings, together with good beds and useful workspaces. Public rooms are bright and pleasant. The friendly team of staff provide a warm welcome and helpfull service.
ROOMS: 53 en suite (7 fmly) No smoking in 19 bedrooms d £72-£75 * LB **FACILITIES:** STV Gym Xmas **CONF:** Thtr 80 Class 40 Board 48 Del £125 * **PARKING:** 120 **NOTES:** No dogs (ex guide dogs) Civ Wed 100 **CARDS:**

FOLKESTONE, Kent Map 05 TR23

★★★70% Clifton
Best Western
The Leas CT20 2EB
☎ 01303 851231 ▯ 01303 851231
e-mail: reservations@thecliftonhotel.com
Dir: *from M20 junct 13, quarter mile W of town centre on A259*

This privately owned Victorian-style hotel occupies a prime location with far reaching views across the English Channel. The bedrooms are all comfortable and most have views of the sea. The public areas include a comfortable, traditionally furnished lounge, a popular bar with a good range of beers and several well appointed coference rooms.

continued

ROOMS: 80 en suite (5 fmly) No smoking in 13 bedrooms s £58-£59; d £78 (incl. bkfst) * LB **FACILITIES:** STV Solarium Games room Xmas **CONF:** Thtr 80 Class 72 Board 32 **SERVICES:** Lift
CARDS:

See advert on this page

★★ 78% Sandgate Hotel et Restaurant La Terrasse

The Esplanade, Sandgate CT20 3DY
☎ 01303 220444 01303 220496
Dir: *exit M20 junct 12 (Cheriton/Tunnel) and follow Sandgate, go through Sandgate on A249 towards Hythe, hotel on right facing sea*
A pebble's throw from the beach, this smart French country house style hotel offers comfortable bedrooms, some with balconies overlooking the sea. The restaurant is the focal point and the tiered terrace is perfect for breakfast, tea and pre-dinner drinks.
ROOMS: 14 en suite s £45-£71; d £58-£76 (incl. bkfst) *
FACILITIES: Xmas **SERVICES:** Lift **PARKING:** 4 **NOTES:** No dogs (ex guide dogs) No smoking in restaurant Closed January, 2nd wk Oct, Sun evng **CARDS:**

FONTWELL, West Sussex — Map 04 SU90

Travelodge

Travelodge

BN18 0SB
☎ 01243 543973 01243 543973
Dir: *on A27/A29 roundabout*
This modern building offers accommodation in smart, spacious and well equipped bedrooms, all with en suite bathrooms. Refreshments may be taken at the nearby family restaurant. For further details and the Travelodge phone number, consult the Hotel Groups page.
ROOMS: 63 en suite

FORDINGBRIDGE, Hampshire — Map 04 SU11

★★ 70% Ashburn Hotel & Restaurant

MINOTEL Great Britain

Station Rd SP6 1JP
☎ 01425 652060 01425 652150
e-mail: ashburn@mistral.co.uk
Dir: *from Fordingbridge High St follow road signposted Damerham. Pass police and fire station and hotel is 400yds on left-hand side*
Located on the edge of the village, this traditional family-run hotel provides a range of comfortable, well equipped bedrooms, many looking out over the New Forest. In addition to the attractive dining room and residents' lounge, the pool is a bonus.
ROOMS: 20 en suite (3 fmly) No smoking in 10 bedrooms s £39.50-£49.50; d £74-£84 (incl. bkfst) * LB **FACILITIES:** Outdoor swimming (H) Xmas **CONF:** Thtr 150 Class 80 Board 50 Del from £70 *
PARKING: 60 **NOTES:** No smoking in restaurant Civ Wed 180
CARDS:

FOREST ROW, East Sussex — Map 05 TQ43

Premier Collection

★★★★ Ashdown Park

Wych Cross RH18 5JR
☎ 01342 824988 01342 826206
e-mail: reservations@ashdownpark.co.uk
Dir: *take A264 to East Grinstead, then A22 to Eastbourne, 2m S of Forest Row at Wych Cross, turn left to Hartfield, hotel situated on right*
An extended country house overlooking a lake and set in unrivalled grounds, Ashdown Park has some magnificent features such as the converted chapel with stained glass windows, working organ and wonderful acoustics for conferences. Bedrooms are spacious and decorated in traditional style. The kitchen provides classically based dishes with light touches.

ROOMS: 107 en suite s £120-£299; d £152-£330 (incl. bkfst) * LB
FACILITIES: STV Indoor swimming (H) Golf 18 Tennis (hard) Snooker Sauna Solarium Gym Croquet lawn Putting green Jacuzzi/spa Indoor & outdoor golf Beauty therapy Hair salon Aerobics studio Treatment rooms Xmas **CONF:** Thtr 150 Class 60 Board 60 Del from £215 * **SERVICES:** Lift **PARKING:** 200 **NOTES:** No dogs (ex guide dogs) No smoking in restaurant Civ Wed 140
CARDS:

See advert under GATWICK AIRPORT (LONDON)

FORMBY, Merseyside Map 07 SD30

★★★62% *Tree Tops*
Southport Old Rd L37 0AB
☎ 01704 572430 01704 572430
Dir: *off A565 Southport to Liverpool road*
This privately owned hotel offers chalet-style accommodation and an outdoor swimming pool in its five acres of wooded grounds. Bedrooms are well equipped, with the larger ones being particularly suitable for families. There is a lounge bar and a restaurant with conservatory extension that provides carefully prepared meals.
ROOMS: 11 en suite (2 fmly) **FACILITIES:** Outdoor swimming (H) **CONF:** Thtr 200 Class 80 Board 40 **PARKING:** 100 **NOTES:** No dogs **CARDS:**

See advert under SOUTHPORT

FORTON MOTORWAY SERVICE AREA (M6), Lancashire Map 07 SD55

Travelodge
Travelodge
White Carr Ln, Bay Horse LA2 9DU
☎ 01524 792227 01524 791703
Dir: *between juncts 32 & 33 M6*
This modern building offers accommodation in smart, spacious and well equipped bedrooms, all with en suite bathrooms. Refreshments may be taken at the nearby family restaurant. For further details and the Travelodge phone number, consult the Hotel Groups page.
ROOMS: 53 en suite

FOSSEBRIDGE, Gloucestershire Map 04 SP01

★★67% Fossebridge Inn
GL54 3JS
☎ 01285 720721 01285 720793
e-mail: fossebridgeinn@compuserve.com
Dir: *from M4 junct 15 take A419 towards Cirencester, then take A429 towards Stow. Hotel approx 7m on left.*
The Bridge Bar dates from the 15th century, and has kept features such as its old beams, Yorkstone floors and inglenook fireplace. There are good bar meals, and the restaurant offers an enjoyable fixed-price menu. Bedrooms are divided between the main inn and a converted stable block.
ROOMS: 11 en suite (1 fmly) No smoking in all bedrooms s fr £52; d fr £79 (incl. bkfst) * LB **FACILITIES:** Fishing Xmas **CONF:** Thtr 60 Class 30 Board 30 Del from £99.50 * **PARKING:** 60 **NOTES:** No smoking in restaurant RS 24-26 Dec Civ Wed 75
CARDS:

FOUR MARKS, Hampshire Map 04 SU63

Travelodge
Travelodge
156 Winchester Rd GU34 5HZ
☎ 01420 562659 01420 562659
Dir: *5m S of Alton on the A31, northbound*
This modern building offers accommodation in smart, spacious and well equipped bedrooms, all with en suite bathrooms. Refreshments may be taken at the nearby family restaurant. For further details and the Travelodge phone number, consult the Hotel Groups page.
ROOMS: 31 en suite

Arriving late? Four and five star hotels have night porters to assist with your luggage; and 24hr room service.

FOWEY, Cornwall & Isles of Scilly Map 02 SX15

★★★73% Fowey
Best Western
The Esplanade PL23 1HX
☎ 01726 832551 01726 832125
e-mail: fowey@richardsonhotels.co.uk
Dir: *from M5 follow for A38 Fowey for 7m. Continue through Fowey for 1m then left in to Hansons Dv, left into Daglands Rd & left turn to Hotel*

This attractive hotel stands proudly above the estuary, with marvellous views of the river from the public areas and the majority of the bedrooms. High standards of appointment and decor are evident throughout, combined with a warm and welcoming atmosphere. Public areas include a spacious bar, elegant restaurant and smart new drawing room. Imaginative dinners make good use of local ingredients, much enjoyed by the many regular visitors.
ROOMS: 24 en suite No smoking in 1 bedroom **FACILITIES:** Fishing Jacuzzi/spa ch fac **CONF:** Thtr 100 Class 60 Board 20 **SERVICES:** Lift **PARKING:** 20 **NOTES:** No smoking in restaurant
CARDS:

★★★ Fowey Hall
Hanson Dr PL23 1ET
☎ 01726 833866 01726 834100
Dir: *on arriving in Fowey cross mini rdbt continue until you descend into town centre. Pass school on right after 400mtrs right into Hanson Drive*

Built in 1899, this listed mansion above the estuary looks out into the English Channel. Imaginatively designed bedrooms offer charm and sumptuous comfort. Beautifully appointed public rooms include the wood panelled dining room where accomplished cuisine is served. Families are a priority with a range of facilities to entertain children of all ages. The grounds have a covered pool and sunbathing area.
ROOMS: 17 en suite 8 annexe en suite (18 fmly) d £145-£230 (incl. bkfst) * LB **FACILITIES:** STV Indoor swimming (H) Pool table Croquet lawn Childrens play area Table tennis Bicycle hire Xmas **CONF:** Thtr 35 Class 12 Board 18 Del £130 * **PARKING:** 40 **NOTES:** No smoking in restaurant Civ Wed 40 **CARDS:**

See advert on opposite page

★★73% ❀ Marina
Esplanade PL23 1HY
☎ 01726 833315 ▤ 01726 832779
e-mail: marina.hotel@dial.pipex.com
Dir: *drive into town down Lostwithiel Street, near bottom of hill turn right into Esplanade*

A charming Georgian property of great character and retaining many original features. Bedrooms are well equipped and some have balconies from which lovely sea views can be enjoyed. Public rooms include a choice of lounges, bar and Waterside Restaurant.
ROOMS: 12 en suite s £54-£62; d £76-£108 (incl. bkfst) * LB
FACILITIES: Fishing Sailing **NOTES:** No dogs (ex guide dogs) No smoking in restaurant Closed 15 Dec-28 Feb
CARDS:

See advert on this page

FOWNHOPE, Herefordshire — Map 03 SO53

★★67% Green Man Inn
HR1 4PE
☎ 01432 860243 ▤ 01432 860207
Dir: *on B4224 midway between Ross-on-Wye and Hereford*
This charming 15th-century village inn has a wealth of character. Well equipped accommodation includes bedrooms on ground-floor level and one room with a four-poster bed. Some bedrooms are located in two separate cottage-style buildings. There are two lounges, a choice of bars, and a restaurant with a beamed ceiling. Other facilities include a beer garden and a play area for children.
ROOMS: 10 en suite 9 annexe en suite (3 fmly) **FACILITIES:** STV Indoor swimming (H) Fishing Sauna Solarium Gym Jacuzzi/spa
CONF: Thtr 40 Class 60 Board 30 **PARKING:** 75 **NOTES:** No smoking in restaurant **CARDS:**

FRANKLEY MOTORWAY SERVICE AREA (M5), West Midlands — Map 07 SO98

⇧ *Travelodge*
Illey Ln, Frankley Motorway Service Area, Frankley B32 4AR
☎ 0121 550 3131

Travelodge

Dir: *between junc 3 and 4 on southbound carriageway of M5*
This modern building offers accommodation in smart, spacious and well equipped bedrooms, all with en suite bathrooms. Refreshments may be taken at the nearby family restaurant. For further details and the Travelodge phone number, consult the Hotel Groups page.
ROOMS: 62 en suite

Read all about it! Newspapers delivered to bedrooms in four and five star hotels.

F

FRINTON-ON-SEA, Essex — Map 05 TM21

★★71% Maplin

THE CIRCLE *Selected Individual Hotels* GREAT BRITAIN

Esplanade CO13 9EL
☎ 01255 673832 🖷 01255 673832
e-mail: maplin@globalnet.co.uk
Dir: *from A133 towards Clacton, follow local signs to Frinton B1033. Turn at level crossing on to Connaught Av at end turn right onto Esplanade*

An impressive house, Maplin Hotel was built in 1911, at the quiet end of the esplanade. Bedrooms are attractively furnished to a high standard, and some have spa baths. Public areas feature beautiful oak panelling and leaded windows.

ROOMS: 11 rms (10 en suite) (2 fmly) s £52.50-£85; d £70-£110 (incl. bkfst) * LB **FACILITIES:** Outdoor swimming (H) Xmas **CONF:** Thtr 35 Class 20 Board 30 Del from £69.50 * **PARKING:** 12 **NOTES:** No smoking in restaurant Closed Jan **CARDS:**

FRITTON, Norfolk — Map 05 TG40

★★★71% Caldecott Hall Golf & Leisure

Caldecott Hall, Beccles Rd NR31 9EY
☎ 01493 488488 🖷 01493 488561

Close to Fritton Lake in its own landscaped grounds is this small privately owned hotel. The spacious bedrooms are individually decorated with bright fabrics and have quality furniture as well as many useful extras. Public areas include a smart sitting room, a lounge bar, restaurant and leisure facilities. There is also an 18 hole golf course with a clubhouse as well as banqueting and conference facilities.

ROOMS: 8 en suite (6 fmly) No smoking in all bedrooms s £50-£65; d £70-£95 * LB **FACILITIES:** Golf 27 Driving range Pitch & Putt Xmas **CONF:** Thtr 100 Class 80 Board 20 Del from £70 * **PARKING:** 100 **NOTES:** No dogs (ex guide dogs) No smoking in restaurant **CARDS:**

FRODSHAM, Cheshire — Map 07 SJ57

★★★67% Forest Hill Hotel & Leisure Complex

Bellemonte Rd, Overton Hill WA6 6HH
☎ 01928 735255 🖷 01928 735517
e-mail: info@foresthillshotel.com
Dir: *at Frodsham turn onto B5151 after 1m turn right into Manley Rd after 0.5m turn right into Simons Ln. Hotel 0.5m along road past Frodsham golf course*

Situated high on Overton Hill, enjoying panoramic views across the Cheshire plain and over to the distant Welsh hills, this modern hotel offers spacious and well equipped bedrooms, many of which have been redecorated and refurbished. There is a choice of bars for guests to relax in.

ROOMS: 57 en suite (4 fmly) No smoking in 5 bedrooms **FACILITIES:** STV Indoor swimming (H) Squash Snooker Sauna Solarium Gym Jacuzzi/spa Nightclub entertainment ch fac **CONF:** Thtr 200 Class 80 Board 48 **PARKING:** 350 **NOTES:** No smoking in restaurant **CARDS:**

FROME, Somerset — Map 03 ST74

★★67% The George at Nunney

11 Church St BA11 4LW
☎ 01373 836458 🖷 01373 836565
e-mail: georgenunney@aol.com
(For full entry see Nunney)

GARFORTH, West Yorkshire — Map 08 SE43

★★★69% Milford Lodge

Best Western

A1 Great North Rd, Peckfield LS25 5LQ
☎ 01977 681800 🖷 01977 681245
e-mail: enquires@mlh.co.uk
Dir: *on the southbound carriageway of the A1, E of Leeds where A63 joins A1 from Leeds*

Milford Lodge stands on the A1, north of the M62 interchange. There is a good range of well furnished and equipped bedrooms, some of which accommodate families. Public rooms include an open plan bar and restaurant with an attractive waterwheel centrepiece. Helpful and relaxed service is provided, and there is a cosmopolitan ambience in the restaurant with a variety of imaginative dishes.

ROOMS: 47 en suite (10 fmly) No smoking in 19 bedrooms d £49-£59 * LB **FACILITIES:** STV Xmas **CONF:** Thtr 70 Class 35 Board 30 Del £95 * **SERVICES:** air con **PARKING:** 80 **CARDS:**

See advert under LEEDS

GARSTANG, Lancashire — Map 07 SD44

★★★68% Pickering Park Country House

MINOTEL *Great Britain*

Garstang Rd, Catterall PR3 0HD
☎ 01995 600999 🖷 01995 602100
e-mail: hotel@pickeringpark.demon.co.uk
Dir: *from S M6 junct 32 take A6 N. After Esso garage turn right onto B6430 then right after bus shelter*

A former vicarage dating from the 17th century which is today a very comfortable hotel. Bedrooms are well presented and generally quite spacious. The lounges are attractively presented, and there is a wide range of carefully prepared dishes offered in the restaurant. The rear gardens are delightful.

ROOMS: 14 en suite 2 annexe en suite (1 fmly) s fr £60; d fr £76 (incl. bkfst) * LB **FACILITIES:** Xmas **CONF:** Thtr 65 Class 50 Board 35 Del £94 * **PARKING:** 50 **NOTES:** No dogs (ex guide dogs) No smoking in restaurant Civ Wed 60 **CARDS:**

★★★65% Crofters

Cabus PR3 1PH
☎ 01995 604128 🖷 01995 601646
Dir: *on A6, midway between junc 32 & 33 of M6*

This friendly, family run hotel, is conveniently situated on the A6, near the market town of Garstang. Comfortable accommodation includes a number of executive rooms with additional facilities. Crofters Tavern provides an alternative eating and drinking option to the more formal restaurant and cocktail bar.

ROOMS: 19 en suite (4 fmly) s £38-£45; d £44-£65 * **FACILITIES:** STV Pool table entertainment Xmas **CONF:** Thtr 200 Class 120 Board 50 **PARKING:** 200 **CARDS:**

GATESHEAD, Tyne & Wear Map 12 NZ26
see also Beamish & Whickham

★★★★68% Newcastle Marriott City Centre

Metro Centre NE11 9XF
☎ 0191 493 2233 📠 0191 493 2030
Dir: *on A1 follow signs for Metro Centre & then signs for Marriott Hotel*
Conveniently situated just off the A1, this smart modern hotel is close to the Metro Centre. Bedrooms are comprehensively equipped and provide either one or two double beds. In addition to the main restaurant, the café bar serves popular dishes. There is an impressive range of banqueting and leisure facilities.
ROOMS: 148 en suite (136 fmly) No smoking in 75 bedrooms d fr £89 * LB **FACILITIES:** STV Indoor swimming (H) Sauna Solarium Gym Jacuzzi/spa Health & beauty clinic Dance studio Xmas **CONF:** Thtr 450 Class 190 Board 40 Del from £135 * **SERVICES:** Lift air con **PARKING:** 300 **NOTES:** No dogs (ex guide dogs) Civ Wed 100
CARDS:

★★★67% Swallow

High West St NE8 1PE
☎ 0191 477 1105 📠 0191 478 7214
e-mail: info@swallowhotels.com
Dir: *A1, A184 to Gateshead, follow signs for centre. At mini rdbt turn right, pass bus stn, lights, and two rdbts. Take 3rd left, hotel at bottom of road*
Just across the Tyne from Newcastle city centre, this purpose-built hotel offers a good range of services. The attractive, modern bedrooms come in a variety of sizes. Guests wishing to relax can enjoy the pool and leisure facilities, or alternatively work off some of the good food found in the restaurant in the smartly converted gym.
ROOMS: 103 en suite (12 fmly) No smoking in 60 bedrooms s £85-£95; d £105-£115 (incl. bkfst) * LB **FACILITIES:** STV Indoor swimming (H) Sauna Solarium Gym Jacuzzi/spa Xmas **CONF:** Thtr 350 Class 150 Board 100 Del from £90 * **SERVICES:** Lift **PARKING:** 190 **NOTES:** No smoking in restaurant **CARDS:**

★★72% ❁ Eslington Villa
8 Station Rd, Low Fell NE9 6DR
☎ 0191 487 6017 & 420 0666 📠 0191 420 0667
Dir: *turn off A1 onto Team Valley Trading Estate, take 2nd rdbt turn right along Eastern Av then turn left just past Belle Vue Motors, hotel on left*
Situated in a quiet residential area, with easy access to the A1, this hotel's lounge and dining room have been been refurbished in keeping with the period building. Bedrooms offer good levels of comfort and space. Service is friendly and attentive, and a wide range of dishes is available in the dining room, overlooking well maintained grounds.
ROOMS: 17 en suite (2 fmly) s £45-£65; d £54-£75 (incl. bkfst) * **CONF:** Thtr 36 Class 30 Board 25 Del from £110 * **PARKING:** 15 **NOTES:** No dogs No smoking in restaurant Closed 25-26 Dec RS Sun/BHs (restricted restaurant service) Civ Wed
CARDS:

⇧ Premier Lodge

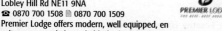

Lobley Hill Rd NE11 9NA
☎ 0870 700 1508 📠 0870 700 1509
Premier Lodge offers modern, well equipped, en suite accommodation suitable for both business and leisure travellers. Meals can be taken at the adjacent popular restaurant and bar which is fully licensed. For further details, consult the Hotel Groups page.
ROOMS: 40 en suite d £42 *

○ Express by Holiday Inn

Riverside Way, Derwenthaugh NE39 1EJ
☎ 0800 897121
ROOMS: 100 rms **NOTES:** Open Autumn 2000

GATWICK AIRPORT (LONDON), West Sussex Map 04 TQ24
see also Dorking, East Grinstead & Reigate

★★★★70% ❁❁ Copthorne London Gatwick

COPTHORNE

Copthorne Way RH10 3PG
☎ 01342 348800 & 348888 📠 01342 348833
e-mail: coplgw@mill-cop.com
Dir: *on A264, 2m E of A264/B2036 roundabout*
This well-run hotel is set in 100 acres of wooded, landscaped gardens which contain jogging tracks, a putting green and even a petanque pit. The sprawling building is built around a 16th-century farmhouse and has comfortable, well maintained bedrooms divided into three categories. In addition to the brasserie there is a more formal restaurant, the Lion D'Or, where carefully prepared meals are served. There is a wide choice from the main menu as well as a set price menu.
ROOMS: 227 en suite (10 fmly) No smoking in 136 bedrooms s fr £130; d fr £140 * LB **FACILITIES:** STV Indoor swimming (H) Tennis (hard) Squash Solarium Gym Pool table Cróquet lawn Putting green Jacuzzi/spa Petanque pit entertainment **CONF:** Thtr 150 Class 65 Board 40 Del £160 * **SERVICES:** Lift **PARKING:** 300 **NOTES:** No smoking in restaurant RS 24 Dec-4 Jan Civ Wed **CARDS:**

★★★★67% Le Meridien London Gatwick

LE MERIDIEN

North Terminal RH6 0PH
☎ 0870 4008494 📠 01293 567739
e-mail: gm1096@forte-hotels.com
Dir: *M23 junct 9, follow dual carriageway to second rdbt, hotel is large white building straight ahead*
This modern hotel, moments from the terminals, has been refurbished to become part of Le Meridien brand. Smart rooms boast a range of facilities and high standards of guest comfort. Visitors have a range of eating options, including the Brasserie, a French-style café and an Oriental restaurant. There is a useful business centre and both corporate and leisure guests will appreciate the health and fitness facilities. The North terminal is accessed via a covered walkway.
ROOMS: 494 en suite (36 fmly) No smoking in 228 bedrooms s £180; d £190 * **FACILITIES:** STV Indoor swimming (H) Sauna Solarium Gym Pool table Xmas **CONF:** Thtr 250 Class 100 Board 40 Del from £170 * **SERVICES:** Lift air con **NOTES:** Civ Wed 250
CARDS:

★★★★66% Renaissance London Gatwick
Povey Cross Rd RH6 0BE
☎ 01293 820169 📠 01293 820259
e-mail: alex.holmes@renaissancehotels.com
Dir: *from M23 exit 9 follow signs to South Terminal & continue to next rdbt. Join dual carriageway and at next rdbt turn left. Hotel 500yds on right*
Newly refurbished public areas in this hotel have added a smart look to the ground floor. Bedrooms are well maintained and equipped with up-to-date amenities. In addition to an informal coffee shop there is the Pavilion Restaurânt where the kitchen makes a keen effort at creating tasty, freshly prepared dishes.
ROOMS: 255 en suite (5 fmly) No smoking in 203 bedrooms d £105-£120 * **FACILITIES:** STV Indoor swimming (H) Squash Snooker Sauna Solarium Gym Pool table Jacuzzi/spa Beautician service Aerobic studio **CONF:** Thtr 200 Class 100 Board 75 Del from £110 * **SERVICES:** Lift air con **PARKING:** 364 **CARDS:**

G

GATWICK AIRPORT, continued

★★★★64% Copthorne Effingham Park

West Park Rd RH10 3EU
☎ 01342 714994 📠 01342 716039
e-mail: reservations.effingham@mill-cop.com

COPTHORNE

***Dir:** from M23 junct 10, take A264 towards East Grinstead. Go straight over rdbt, at 2nd rdbt turn left along B2028. Effingham Park is on right*

Set in 40 acres of grounds, this hotel is popular with conference organisers and for weekend functions. The main restaurant is an open-plan, Mediterranean-themed brasserie, and snacks are also available in the bar. Both categories of bedroom are spacious and well cared for.

ROOMS: 122 en suite (6 fmly) No smoking in 48 bedrooms s fr £130; d fr £140 * LB **FACILITIES:** STV Indoor swimming (H) Golf 9 Tennis (hard) Sauna Solarium Gym Croquet lawn Putting green Jacuzzi/spa Dance studio Bowls **CONF:** Thtr 600 Class 250 Board 30 Del £160 * **SERVICES:** Lift **PARKING:** 500 **NOTES:** No dogs (ex guide dogs) No smoking in restaurant Civ Wed **CARDS:**

G

★★★66% Stanhill Court

Stanhill Rd, Charlwood RH6 0EP
☎ 01293 862166 📠 01293 862773
e-mail: enquiries@stanhillcourthotel.co.uk

***Dir:** N of Charlwood towards Newdigate*

With 35 acres of grounds, this baronial style hotel built in 1881 has authenic features such as stained glass panels. Many rooms have four-poster beds, all are individually decorated and well equipped. There is a cosy lounge, enclosed conservatory patio bar and wood-panelled restaurant, an extensive range of dishes are offered.

ROOMS: 12 en suite (3 fmly) No smoking in 2 bedrooms s fr £110; d fr £125 * LB **FACILITIES:** STV Tennis (hard) Fishing Croquet lawn ch fac **CONF:** Thtr 250 Class 100 Board 60 Del from £145 * **PARKING:** 100 **NOTES:** No dogs (ex guide dogs) No smoking in restaurant Civ Wed 160 **CARDS:**

★★★63% *Posthouse Gatwick Airport*

Povey Cross Rd RH6 0BA
☎ 0870 400 9030 📠 01293 771054

Posthouse

***Dir:** from M23 junct 9 follow signs for Gatwick, then Reigate. Hotel on left after 3rd rdbt*

Suitable for both the business and leisure traveller, this bright hotel provides modern accommodation in well equipped bedrooms with en suite bathrooms.

ROOMS: 210 en suite (19 fmly) No smoking in 105 bedrooms **CONF:** Thtr 160 Class 90 Board 60 **SERVICES:** Lift **PARKING:** 300 **CARDS:**

Premier Collection

★★ Langshott Manor

Langshott Ln RH6 9LN
☎ 01293 786680 📠 01293 783905
e-mail: admin@langshottmanor.com

***Dir:** from A23 take Ladbroke Rd, turn off the Chequers rdbt to Langshott, proceed for 0.75 miles, entrance to hotel on right*

This small wood framed Elizabethan manor house is set in its own beautiful gardens. The cosy day rooms include a morning room/bar and a gallery sitting room. Bedrooms combine the most up to date modern comforts with flair, individuality and traditional elegance. The restaurant offers good cooking.

continued

ROOMS: 7 en suite 8 annexe en suite No smoking in all bedrooms s £145-£220; d £165-£250 (incl. bkfst) * LB **FACILITIES:** Croquet lawn Xmas **CONF:** Thtr 40 Class 20 Board 22 Del from £166 * **PARKING:** 25 **NOTES:** No dogs (ex guide dogs) No smoking in restaurant Civ Wed 60 **CARDS:**

Express by Holiday Inn Crawley

Haslett Av East RH10 1UG
☎ 01293 525523 📠 01293 525529

Express by Holiday Inn

A modern budget hotel offering comfortable accommodation in refreshing, spacious and comprehensively-equipped bedrooms, en suite bathrooms with power showers and continental buffet breakfast included in the room rate. Suitable for business travellers or families. For further details and the Express by Holiday Inn phone number, consult the Hotel Groups page.

ROOMS: 74 en suite (incl. cont bkfst) d £52.50 * **CONF:** Thtr 30 Class 20 Board 16

See advert under CRAWLEY

Premier Lodge

London Rd, Lowfield Heath RH10 2ST
☎ 0870 700 1388 📠 0870 700 1389

PREMIER LODGE THE BEST. REST ASSURED.

Premier Lodge offers modern, well equipped, en suite accommodation suitable for both business and leisure travellers. Meals can be taken at the adjacent popular restaurant and bar which is fully licensed. For further details, consult the Hotel Groups page.

ROOMS: 100 en suite d £46 *

Premier Lodge (Gatwick)

Goffs Park Rd RH11 8AX
☎ 0870 700 1390 📠 0870 700 1391

PREMIER LODGE THE BEST. REST ASSURED.

Premier Lodge offers modern, well equipped, en suite accommodation suitable for both business and leisure travellers. Meals can be taken at the adjacent popular restaurant and bar which is fully licensed. For further details, consult the Hotel Groups page.

ROOMS: 56 en suite d £49.50 * **CONF:** Thtr 120 Class 70 Board 40

⇧ *Travelodge*

Travelodge

Church Rd, Lowfield Heath RH11 0PQ
☎ 01293 533441 ▯ 01293 535369
Dir: *1m S, off A23 junc 10 M23*
This modern building offers accommodation in smart, spacious and well equipped bedrooms, all with en suite bathrooms. Refreshments may be taken at the nearby family restaurant. For further details and the Travelodge phone number, consult the Hotel Groups page.
ROOMS: 126 en suite **CONF:** Thtr 60 Class 25 Board 25

○ Hotel Ibis

ibis hotel

London Rd, County Oak RH11 0PF
☎ 020 8283 4550
Modern, budget hotel offering comfortable accommodation in bright and practical bedrooms. Breakfast is self-service and dinner is available in the restaurant. For further details, consult the Hotel Groups page.
ROOMS: 130 rms **NOTES:** Open July 2000

GERRARDS CROSS, Buckinghamshire — Map 04 TQ08

★★★70% Bull

Oxford Rd SL9 7PA
☎ 01753 885995 ▯ 01753 885504
e-mail: bull@sarova.co.uk
Dir: *from M40 junct 2 follow signs for Beaconsfield (A355). After 0.5m at rdbt take 2nd exit signed A40 Gerrards Cross for 2m to The Bull on right*
This 17th-century Inn, once the haunt of highwaymen, has been sympathetically been refurbished to a high standard. The Inn is well located for the M40 and M25 motorways and enjoys a quiet location overlooking the common. Spacious bedrooms are

continued

GERRARDS CROSS, continued

tastefully furnished and provide an excellent range of facilities. Guests have the use of the popular Jack Shrimpton bar or the attractive cocktail bar and meals are served in the comfortable restaurant.
ROOMS: 109 en suite (3 fmly) No smoking in 72 bedrooms s fr £150; d fr £170 * LB **FACILITIES:** STV Leisure facilities available nearby entertainment **CONF:** Thtr 200 Class 88 Board 50 Del from £150 * **SERVICES:** Lift **PARKING:** 200 **NOTES:** No dogs (ex guide dogs) No smoking in restaurant Civ Wed 200
CARDS:

See advert on opposite page

★★65% *Ethorpe*

Packhorse Rd SL9 8HY
☎ 01753 882039 01753 887012

Scottish Newcastle hotels

This attractive hotel is located in the centre of town and is within easy reach of the motorway network and Heathrow Airport. Bedrooms are well equipped and offer a good range of extra facilities. Meals may be taken in the bar or restaurant.
ROOMS: 34 rms (31 en suite) (2 fmly) **FACILITIES:** STV **CONF:** Thtr 30 Board 18 **PARKING:** 80 **NOTES:** No dogs (ex guide dogs)
CARDS:

G

GILLAN, Cornwall & Isles of Scilly — Map 02 SW72

★★80% Tregildry

TR12 6HG
☎ 01326 231378 01326 231561
e-mail: trgildry@globalnet.co.uk
***Dir:** from Helston join the A3083 Lizard road and take first turning left for St Keverne and follow signs for Manaccan and Gillan*
From its unspoilt and peaceful location Tregildry is blessed with both sea and river views. The tastefully furnished bedrooms and lounges make the most of the wonderful views. The dining room provides the perfect environment to enjoy the imaginative and innovative menus. There is direct access to the beach and adjacent coastal footpath.
ROOMS: 10 en suite No smoking in all bedrooms s £76; d £150-£160 (incl. bkfst & dinner) * LB **FACILITIES:** Boat hire Windsurfing **PARKING:** 15 **NOTES:** No children 8yrs No smoking in restaurant Closed Nov-Feb **CARDS:**

GILLINGHAM, Kent — Map 05 TQ76

Travelodge

Medway Motorway Service Area, Rainham ME8 8PQ
☎ 01634 233343 01634 360848

Travelodge

***Dir:** between juncts 4 & 5 M2*
This modern building offers accommodation in smart, spacious and well equipped bedrooms, all with en suite bathrooms. Refreshments may be taken at the nearby family restaurant. For further details and the Travelodge phone number, consult the Hotel Groups page.
ROOMS: 58 en suite

GLENRIDDING, Cumbria — Map 11 NY31

★★★70% Glenridding

CA11 0PB
☎ 017684 82228 017684 82555

Best Western

***Dir:** on A592 in village*
A friendly village hotel with views of the lake. There is a wide choice of accommodation, with a newly furbished wing offering very good quality. The smart new leisure club has a heated indoor pool, kiddies pool and sauna. Well equipped conference facilities are available. The hotel has a formal carte restaurant, a friendly pub with traditional hearty dishes and a cosy coffee shop.
ROOMS: 36 en suite (6 fmly) s fr £78; d fr £106 (incl. bkfst) * LB **FACILITIES:** STV Indoor swimming (H) Sauna Pool table Jacuzzi/spa Billiards 3/4 Snooker table Xmas **CONF:** Thtr 30 Class 30 Board 20 Del from £85 * **SERVICES:** Lift **PARKING:** 38 **NOTES:** No smoking in restaurant Civ Wed 60 **CARDS:**

GLOSSOP, Derbyshire — Map 07 SK09

★★77% Wind in the Willows

Derbyshire Level, Sheffield Rd SK13 7PT
☎ 01457 868001 01457 853354
e-mail: info@windinthewillows.co.uk
***Dir:** 1m E on A57 opposite the Royal Oak*
A warm relaxed atmosphere prevails at this small hotel. Bedrooms are comfortable and individually decorated, and offer many thoughtful extras. There are two comfortable lounges and a dining room that overlooks the pretty garden.
ROOMS: 12 en suite s £74-£92; d £99-£119 (incl. bkfst) LB **FACILITIES:** Fishing **CONF:** Thtr 20 Class 12 Board 12 Del from £134 * **PARKING:** 16 **NOTES:** No dogs No children 10yrs No smoking in restaurant **CARDS:**

GLOUCESTER, Gloucestershire — Map 03 SO81

★★★69% Hatton Court

Upton Hill, Upton St Leonards GL4 8DE
☎ 01452 617412 01452 612945
e-mail: res@hatton-court.co.uk
***Dir:** leave Gloucester on B4073 Painswick road. Hotel at top of hill on right*
This beautifully preserved 17th-century Cotswold manor house is set in seven acres of well kept gardens. It stands at the top of Upton Hill and commands spectacular views of the Severn Valley. Bedrooms are comfortable, tastefully furnished with many extras. The elegant Carringtons Restaurant offers a varied choice of menus, there is a traditionally furnished bar, as well as a very comfortable foyer lounge.
ROOMS: 17 en suite 28 annexe en suite No smoking in 11 bedrooms s £79-£119; d £99-£129 (incl. bkfst) * LB **FACILITIES:** STV Outdoor swimming (H) Sauna Gym Croquet lawn Jacuzzi/spa Xmas **CONF:** Thtr 60 Class 30 Board 30 Del from £99 * **PARKING:** 80 **NOTES:** No dogs (ex guide dogs) No smoking in restaurant Civ Wed 80
CARDS:

★★★68% *Posthouse Gloucester*

Crest Way, Barnwood GL4 7RX
☎ 0870 400 9034 01452 371036

Posthouse

***Dir:** on A417 ring road to Barnwood, next to Cheltenham & Gloucester building*
This modern hotel is conveniently located close to many local attractions. Bedrooms are all spacious, attractively designed and benefit from a number of first rate features. Guests can enjoy a varied range of food and drinks in the stylish bar or 'Seasons' restaurant, and there is an excellent range of leisure facilities.
ROOMS: 122 en suite (25 fmly) No smoking in 60 bedrooms **FACILITIES:** STV Indoor swimming (H) Sauna Solarium Gym Pool table Jacuzzi/spa Spa pool Sauna Dance Studio **CONF:** Thtr 100 Class 45 Board 40 **PARKING:** 135 **NOTES:** No smoking in restaurant
CARDS:

Arriving late? Four and five star hotels have night porters to assist with your luggage; and 24hr room service.

★★★67% New County
44 Southgate St GL1 2DU
☎ 01452 307000 Fax 01452 500487
e-mail: newcounty@meridianleisure.com
Dir: *follow signs for City & Docks along A38. Along Bristol road for 2m, turn left after docks and then left at Black Swan Inn. Hotel on left, opp Priory*
This character hotel in the heart of the city has been refurbished to offer modern comforts and bright well furnished bedrooms with good facilities. Public rooms include a bistro-style restaurant, a bar and a ballroom/function suite.
ROOMS: 39 en suite (3 fmly) No smoking in 3 bedrooms s £50-£55; d £60-£65 (incl. bkfst) * LB **CONF:** Thtr 130 Class 60 Board 60 Del from £75 * **NOTES:** No smoking in restaurant
CARDS:

See advert on this page

★★★63% Hatherley Manor
Down Hatherley Ln GL2 9QA
☎ 01452 730217 Fax 01452 731032
Dir: *from Gloucester, go through the village of Twigworth on the A38 & take turning for Down Hatherley, hotel 0.25m on left*
This stylish 17th-century manor is conveniently located within 3 miles of the M5 and on the edge of the Cotswolds. Hatherley Manor has both bedrooms in the original building, as well as purpose built rooms. The restaurant offers both fixed price and carte menus, featuring an imaginative selection of dishes using predominantly fresh ingredients.
ROOMS: 56 en suite No smoking in 6 bedrooms s fr £85; d fr £105 (incl. bkfst) * LB **FACILITIES:** In-house movies Xmas **CONF:** Thtr 300 Class 90 Board 70 Del from £145 * **PARKING:** 350 **NOTES:** No smoking in restaurant Civ Wed 300 **CARDS:**

GLOUCESTER, continued

★63% Rotherfield House
5 Horton Rd GL1 3PX
☎ 01452 410500 01452 381922
Dir: *adjacent to Royal Hospital*
Close to the Royal Hospital and only a mile from the city centre, this large Victorian house is privately owned and personally run. It provides well equipped bedrooms and attractive public rooms.
ROOMS: 13 rms (8 en suite) (2 fmly) s £24-£36; d £50 (incl. bkfst) * LB **PARKING:** 9 **NOTES:** No smoking in restaurant
CARDS:

Express by Holiday Inn Gloucester South
Waterwells Business Park, Quedgeley GL2 4SA
☎ 01452 726400 722922

A modern budget hotel offering comfortable accommodation in refreshing, spacious and comprehensively-equipped bedrooms, en suite bathrooms with power showers and continental buffet breakfast included in the room rate. Suitable for business travellers or families. For further details and the Express by Holiday Inn phone number, consult the Hotel Groups page.
ROOMS: 106 en suite (incl. cont bkfst) d £52.50-£56 * **CONF:** Thtr 35 Class 15 Board 20

Premier Lodge (Gloucester North)
Tewkesbury Rd, Twigworth GL2 9PG
☎ 0870 700 1404 0870 700 1405
Premier Lodge offers modern, well equipped, en suite accommodation suitable for both business and leisure travellers. Meals can be taken at the adjacent popular restaurant and bar which is fully licensed. For further details, consult the Hotel Groups page.
ROOMS: 52 en suite d £42 *

GOATHLAND, North Yorkshire Map 08 NZ80

★★71% Mallyan Spout
YO22 5AN
☎ 01947 896486 01947 896327
e-mail: mallyan@ukgateway.net
Dir: *off A169*
This welcoming, personally run hotel on the edge of a delightful moorland village offers good service, good food and attractive bedrooms. There is a choice of lounges and bars, where snacks and light meals are available. The pleasant, spacious restaurant serves well prepared evening meals.
ROOMS: 20 en suite 4 annexe en suite s £50-£80; d £70-£130 (incl. bkfst) * LB **FACILITIES:** Xmas **CONF:** Thtr 70 Class 70 Board 40 **PARKING:** 50 **NOTES:** Closed 25 & 26 Dec
CARDS:

See advert on opposite page

GOLANT, Cornwall & Isles of Scilly Map 02 SX15

★★70% Cormorant
PL23 1LL
☎ 01726 833426 01726 833426
e-mail: cormorant@eclipse.co.uk
Dir: *in village bear right on approaching the estuary and follow the coastline to hotel via a steep drive on right*
This delightful hotel lies above the fishing village of Golant with unforgettable views over the Fowey Estuary. The bedrooms are equipped with period furnishings and all have full length picture windows that take full advantage of the views. An interesting menu is offered in the restaurant, with an emphasis on local fish.
ROOMS: 11 en suite s £38-£57.50; d £76-£90 (incl. bkfst) * LB **FACILITIES:** Indoor swimming (H) Boating Xmas **PARKING:** 20
CARDS:

GOMERSAL, West Yorkshire Map 08 SE22

★★★67% Gomersal Park
Moor Ln BD19 4LJ
☎ 01274 869386 01274 861042
Dir: *take A62 towards Huddersfield, at junct with A651 (by Greyhound Pub) turn right, after approx 1m take first right after Oakwell Hall*
Built around a 19th century house, this modern hotel enjoys a peaceful location and pleasant grounds. A comfortable lounge is provided, and imaginative meals are served in the Harlequin restaurant. Bedrooms are well equipped and comfortable.
ROOMS: 52 en suite (4 fmly) No smoking in 14 bedrooms s fr £83; d fr £94 * LB **FACILITIES:** STV Indoor swimming (H) Sauna Solarium Gym Jacuzzi/spa 5 a side football pitch Xmas **CONF:** Thtr 220 Class 130 Board 60 Del from £110 * **PARKING:** 220 **NOTES:** No smoking in restaurant Civ Wed 200 **CARDS:**

★★63% Gomersal Lodge
Spen Ln BD19 4PJ
☎ 01274 861111 01274 861111
Dir: *M62 junct 26, take A638 to Cleckheaton, 2nd lights turn left along Peg Lane leading to Spen Lane. Hotel on left just after Old Saw Pub on right*
Standing in five acres of grounds this 19th-century house offers well furnished bedrooms together with a cosy bar and a pleasant restaurant. A good range of dishes is available and service is polite and friendly.
ROOMS: 9 en suite (1 fmly) No smoking in 4 bedrooms s fr £46.50; d fr £55 (incl. bkfst) * **CONF:** Thtr 20 Class 12 Board 12 Del from £63 * **PARKING:** 70 **NOTES:** No dogs (ex guide dogs) No smoking in restaurant **CARDS:**

GOODRICH, Herefordshire Map 03 SO51

★★69% Ye Hostelrie
HR9 6HX
☎ 01600 890241 01600 890838
e-mail: ye_hostelrie@lineone.net
Dir: *1m off the A40, between Ross-on-Wye & Monmouth, within 100yds of Goodrich Castle*
Parts of this unusual building are reputed to date back to 1625. Considerable improvements have been made to both the accommodation and public areas, and there is a pleasant garden and patio area.

continued

ROOMS: 6 en suite (2 fmly) s £31.50-£33; d £48-£50 (incl. bkfst) * **FACILITIES:** Xmas **CONF:** Thtr 60 Class 40 Board 30 **PARKING:** 32 **NOTES:** No smoking in restaurant **CARDS:**

See advert under ROSS-ON-WYE

GOODRINGTON See Paignton

GOODWOOD, West Sussex Map 04 SU80

★★★★69% Marriott Goodwood Park
PO18 0QB
☎ 01243 775537 01243 520120
Dir: *off the A285, 3m NE of Chichester*

This popular hotel, which is part of the Goodwood estate, is ideally located close to the racecourse. Bedrooms and public areas are smartly appointed. Excellent leisure facilities and a choice of eating options are available to guests.
ROOMS: 94 en suite (1 fmly) No smoking in 66 bedrooms s £79-£89; d £88-£118 (incl. bkfst) * LB **FACILITIES:** STV Indoor swimming (H) Golf 18 Tennis (hard) Sauna Solarium Gym Putting green Jacuzzi/spa Beauty salons Xmas **CONF:** Thtr 150 Class 60 Board 60 Del from £130 * **PARKING:** 250 **NOTES:** No dogs (ex guide dogs) No smoking in restaurant Civ Wed 120 **CARDS:**

GOOLE, East Riding of Yorkshire Map 08 SE72

★★70% Clifton
155 Boothferry Rd DN14 6AL
☎ 01405 761336 01405 762350
e-mail: cliftonhotel@teline.co.uk
Dir: *leave M62 junct 36 & follow town centre signs. At 2nd set of traffic lights turn right into Boothferry Rd. Hotel is on left*
Convenient for the town centre, this comfortable small hotel offers well eqipped bedrooms and inviting day rooms. A cosy lounge and a small bar complement an attractive restaurant, which offers a good choice of dishes. Service is friendly and attentive.

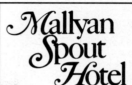

continued

ROOMS: 9 rms (8 en suite) (1 fmly) s fr £42; d fr £49 (incl. bkfst) * LB **CONF:** Thtr 40 Class 20 Board 20 **PARKING:** 8 **NOTES:** No smoking in restaurant **CARDS:**

GORDANO MOTORWAY SERVICE AREA (M5), Somerset Map 03 ST57

Days Inn
M5 Motorway BS20 9XG
☎ 01275 373709 01275 374104
Dir: *M5 junct 19*
Fully refurbished, Days Inn offers well equipped, brightly appointed, modern accommodation with smart en suite bathrooms. There is a fully staffed reception; continental breakfast is available and other refreshments may be taken at the nearby family restaurant.
ROOMS: 60 en suite d fr £45 *

GORLESTON-ON-SEA See Great Yarmouth

GOSFORTH, Cumbria Map 11 NY00

★★71% Westlakes
CA20 1HP
☎ 019467 25221 019467 25099
e-mail: westlakeshotel@compuserve.com
Dir: *junc of A595 and B5344*
Guests are advised to book well in advance at this very popular hotel. There is a compact lounge bar, and the attractive dining room comprises three rooms, one of which is ideal for private parties. Bedrooms in the original house are traditional in character, and those in the extension follow a modern theme.

continued

GOSFORTH, continued

ROOMS: 9 en suite (1 fmly) s £49.50-£51; d £66.50-£68 (incl. bkfst) * **FACILITIES:** STV **PARKING:** 25 **NOTES:** No dogs (ex guide dogs) No smoking in restaurant RS Christmas & New Year
CARDS:

GRANGE-OVER-SANDS, Cumbria Map 07 SD47

★★★69% Netherwood

Lindale Rd LA11 6ET
☎ 015395 32552 015395 34121
e-mail: blawith@aol.com
Dir: *on B5277 just before the station*
This stylish Georgian mansion commands panoramic views across Morecambe Bay. It has been tastefully extended to provide many facilities but retains many original features, such as magnificent oak pannelling and open fires. Bedrooms vary in size; all have Italian furniture and smart, modern bathrooms.
ROOMS: 28 en suite (5 fmly) No smoking in 14 bedrooms s £55-£65; d £110-£130 (incl. bkfst) * LB **FACILITIES:** Indoor swimming (H) Solarium Gym Croquet lawn Jacuzzi/spa Beauty salon Steam room ch fac **CONF:** Thtr 150 Class 30 Board 40 Del from £92 * **SERVICES:** Lift **PARKING:** 160 **NOTES:** No smoking in restaurant Civ Wed 150
CARDS:

★★★64% Graythwaite Manor

Fernhill Rd LA11 7JE
☎ 015395 32001 & 33755 015395 35549
e-mail: enquiries@graythwaitemanor.co.uk
Dir: *follow B5277 through Grange, Fernhill Road opposite fire station behind small traffic island, hotel first left*

In superb gardens above the town, this hotel enjoys lovely views. The comfortable bedrooms vary in size and style, and there is a choice of lounges and a restaurant. The ambitious cooking remains a real highlight.
ROOMS: 21 en suite (2 fmly) s £55-£65; d £99-£130 (incl. bkfst) * LB **FACILITIES:** Tennis (hard) Fishing Putting green 3/4 size billiard table Xmas **SERVICES:** Lift **PARKING:** 32 **NOTES:** No dogs (ex guide dogs) No smoking in restaurant Closed 8-29 Jan
CARDS:

★★67% Hampsfell House

Hampsfell Rd LA11 6BG
☎ 015395 32567 015395 35995
e-mail: hampsfellhotel@msn.com
Dir: *M6 junct 36, take exit A590 signed Barrow-in-Furness. Continue to junct with B5277 and follow to Grange-over-Sands*
Handy for the town and local amenities, this friendly hotel is situated in its own gardens off a quiet wooded lane. There are two cosy lounges served by one bar, and the well maintained bedrooms are bright and cheerful.

continued

ROOMS: 9 en suite (1 fmly) No smoking in 3 bedrooms s £31-£39; d £62-£70 (incl. bkfst) * LB **FACILITIES:** Xmas **PARKING:** 12 **NOTES:** No children 5yrs No smoking in restaurant
CARDS:

★76% Clare House

Park Rd LA11 7HQ
☎ 015395 33026 & 34253
e-mail: ajread@clarehouse.fsbusiness.co.uk
Dir: *turn off A590 onto B5277, through Lindale into Grange, keep left, hotel 0.5m on left past Crown Hill/St Paul's Church*
Standing in secluded gardens, this family-run hotel offers bedrooms furnished to a high standard of comfort. Some rooms have balconies, and most enjoy delightful views across Morecambe Bay. There is a choice of lounges, and very good food is served in the dining room. Breakfast is a speciality.
ROOMS: 17 rms (16 en suite) (1 fmly) s £52; d £104 (incl. bkfst & dinner) * LB **FACILITIES:** Croquet lawn Putting green **PARKING:** 18 **NOTES:** No dogs (ex guide dogs) No children 5yrs No smoking in restaurant Closed Dec-Mar

GRANTHAM, Lincolnshire Map 08 SK93

★★★74% Swallow

Swingbridge Rd NG31 7XT
☎ 01476 593000 01476 592592
e-mail: info@swallowhotels.com
Dir: *junc of A1 southbound with A607*
SWALLOW HOTELS
This smart, modern hotel offers comfortable and spacious public rooms; in the summer they extend into a pretty courtyard. Bedrooms are roomy, attractively furnished and well equipped. There is also a full range of conference and leisure facilities and good car parking.
ROOMS: 90 en suite (6 fmly) No smoking in 55 bedrooms s fr £95; d fr £105 (incl. bkfst) * LB **FACILITIES:** STV Indoor swimming (H) Sauna Gym Jacuzzi/spa Steam room Xmas **CONF:** Thtr 200 Class 90 Board 50 Del from £130 * **PARKING:** 150 **NOTES:** No smoking in restaurant **CARDS:**

★★★67% Kings

North Pde NG31 8AU
☎ 01476 590800 01476 590800
e-mail: kingshotel@compuserve.com
Dir: *turn off A1 at rdbt northern end of Grantham onto B1174, follow road for 2m. Hotel on left by rail bridge*
An extended Georgian house, set back from the main road. Bedrooms are attractively decorated and furnished in modern light oak. A popular alternative to the more formal Victorian restaurant, the Orangery serves as both coffee shop and breakfast room. There is also a smart open-plan foyer lounge and bar.
ROOMS: 21 en suite (1 fmly) s £48-£60; d £58-£75 (incl. bkfst) * LB **FACILITIES:** STV Tennis (hard) **CONF:** Thtr 100 Class 50 Board 40 Del from £65 * **PARKING:** 36 **NOTES:** No smoking in restaurant
CARDS:

⇧ *Travelodge*

Grantham Service Area, Grantham North, Gonerby Moor NG32 2AB
Travelodge
☎ 01476 577500
Dir: *4m N on A1*
This modern building offers accommodation in smart, spacious and well equipped bedrooms, all with en suite bathrooms. Refreshments may be taken at the nearby family restaurant. For further details and the Travelodge phone number, consult the Hotel Groups page.
ROOMS: 40 en suite

GRASMERE, Cumbria

Map 11 NY30

★★★★67% Wordsworth

LA22 9SW
☎ 015394 35592 Fax 015394 35765
e-mail: enquiry@wordsworth-grasmere.co.uk
Dir: *in centre of village adjacent to St Oswalds Church*

With fells rising in the background, The Wordsworth is a busy hotel in the heart of Grasmere village. There are a host of leisure facilities, a pub and plenty of spacious lounge areas. Bedrooms are individually and traditionally styled.

ROOMS: 37 en suite (3 fmly) s £82-£124; d £84-£168 (incl. bkfst) * LB **FACILITIES:** STV Indoor swimming (H) Sauna Solarium Gym Pool table Croquet lawn Jacuzzi/spa Table tennis entertainment Xmas **CONF:** Thtr 130 Class 50 Board 40 Del from £115 * **SERVICES:** Lift **PARKING:** 60 **NOTES:** No dogs (ex guide dogs) No smoking in restaurant Civ Wed 120 **CARDS:**

See advert on this page

Premier Collection

★★★ Michael's Nook Country House

LA22 9RP
☎ 015394 35496 Fax 015394 35645
e-mail: m-nook@wordsworth-grasmere.co.uk
Dir: *turn off A591 between The Swan Hotel and its car park just N of village. Hotel 400yds on right*

This fine Victorian house has been transformed into a country house hotel of the highest standard. Public areas are elegant, comfortable and retain a homely feel. Bedrooms have interesting features: one is on two levels and another has a private patio. Dinner sets a standard for others to follow.

ROOMS: 14 en suite s £145-£160; d £180-£290 (incl. bkfst & dinner) * LB **FACILITIES:** Croquet lawn Use of leisure facilities at Wordsworth Hotel Xmas **CONF:** Thtr 24 Board 20 Del from £165 * **PARKING:** 20 **NOTES:** No dogs (ex guide dogs) No smoking in restaurant Civ Wed 30 **CARDS:**

GRASMERE, continued

★★★72% Gold Rill Country House

Red Bank Rd LA22 9PU
☎ 015394 35486 015394 35486
e-mail: enquiries@gold-rill.co.uk
Dir: *turn off A591 into village centre, turn into road opposite St Oswalds Church. Hotel 300yds on left*

This relaxed and friendly hotel enjoys fine views of the lake and fells. There are comfortable lounges and an attractive restaurant, where steamed puddings are an irresistible speciality. Most of the pleasantly decorated bedrooms take advantage of the impressive view.

ROOMS: 25 en suite 3 annexe en suite (2 fmly) s £35-£59; d £70-£118 (incl. bkfst & dinner) * LB **FACILITIES:** STV Outdoor swimming (H) Croquet lawn Putting green Xmas **PARKING:** 35 **NOTES:** No dogs No smoking in restaurant Closed mid Dec-mid Jan (open Xmas & New Year) **CARDS:**

See advert on page 231

★★★70% Red Lion

Red Lion Square LA22 9SS
☎ 015394 35456 015394 35579
e-mail: enquires@hotelgrasmere.uk.com
Dir: *turn off A591, signposted Grasmere Village, hotel is in centre of the village*

Best Western

In the heart of the village, this former coaching inn, now a spacious hotel, provides smart, modern bedrooms and comfortable multi-purpose public areas. These include a lively pub and buttery as well as the main restaurant, and an attractive conservatory extension to the foyer bar.

ROOMS: 47 en suite (4 fmly) No smoking in 12 bedrooms s £46-£55.50; d £90-£111 (incl. bkfst) * **FACILITIES:** STV Sauna Solarium Gym Pool table Jacuzzi/spa Hairdressing Xmas **CONF:** Thtr 60 Class 30 Board 30 Del from £80 * **SERVICES:** Lift **PARKING:** 38 **NOTES:** No smoking in restaurant **CARDS:**

See advert on opposite page

★★★70% Rothay Garden

Broadgate LA22 9RJ
☎ 015394 35334 015394 35723
e-mail: rothay@grasmere.com
Dir: *turn off A591, opposite Swan Hotel, into Grasmere village, 300 yds on left*

Located on the northern approach to this unspoilt Cumbrian village, the Rothay Garden offers comfortable bedrooms, including some with four-posters and whirlpool baths. There is a choice of relaxing lounges and a cosy cocktail bar, as well as a conservatory restaurant.

continued

ROOMS: 25 en suite (2 fmly) s £65-£90; d £130-£170 (incl. bkfst & dinner) * LB **FACILITIES:** STV Fishing Jacuzzi/spa use of local leisure club Xmas **CONF:** Thtr 25 Class 16 Board 12 Del from £90 * **PARKING:** 38 **NOTES:** No smoking in restaurant **CARDS:**

★★★69% The Swan

LA22 9RF
☎ 0870 400 8132 015394 35741
Dir: *M6 junct 36, take A590 past Windermere, follow signs for Grasmere and Keswick. The Swan Hotel is located on outskirts of village*

A 300-year-old inn mentioned in Wordsworth's poem 'The Waggoner'. Stylish bedrooms have modern facilities; many enjoy views of the surrounding fells. Fresh flowers decorate comfortable lounges, which include one of Wordsworth's chairs. The Waggoners Restaurant is renowned for its fine cuisine; less formal meals are taken in the bar or Cygnet lounge.

ROOMS: 38 en suite No smoking in 20 bedrooms s £72-£89; d £144-£179 (incl. bkfst & dinner) * LB **FACILITIES:** Xmas **PARKING:** 40 **NOTES:** No smoking in restaurant **CARDS:**

★★73% Grasmere

Broadgate LA22 9TA
☎ 015394 35277 015394 35277
e-mail: grashotel@aol.com
Dir: *take A591 from Ambleside, then second turning left into town centre. Follow road over humpbacked bridge, past playing field. Hotel on left*

Service is attentive at this hospitable, family-run hotel. There are two cosy lounges (one with residents' bar) and the attractive dining room looks onto the garden, which stretches down to the River Rothay. The thoughtfully chosen dinner menu makes careful use of fresh ingredients. Most of the cheerful bedrooms are furnished in pine.

ROOMS: 12 en suite s £35-£60; d £80-£124 (incl. bkfst) * LB **FACILITIES:** STV Croquet lawn Putting green Xmas **PARKING:** 16 **NOTES:** No children 6yrs No smoking in restaurant Closed Jan-8 Feb **CARDS:**

★★73% Oak Bank
Broadgate LA22 9TA
☎ 015394 35217 015394 35685
e-mail: oakbankhotel@btinternet.com
Dir: *in centre of village just off A591*
A very welcoming lake district hotel. The open plan restaurant with conservatory extension serves traditional lakeland four-course dinners. There are stylish lounges with log fires. Bedrooms vary in size, with attractive decor and antique pine furniture.
ROOMS: 15 en suite (1 fmly) s £30-£55; d £60-£110 (incl. bkfst & dinner) * LB **FACILITIES:** Jacuzzi/spa **PARKING:** 15 **NOTES:** No smoking in restaurant Closed Jan **CARDS:**

Premier Collection

★ White Moss House
Rydal Water LA22 9SE
☎ 015394 35295 015394 35516
e-mail: dixon@whitemoss.demon.co.uk
Dir: *on A591, 1m S of Grasmere*
This traditional Lakeland house, once owned by Wordsworth, is a friendly, intimate country hotel with a loyal following. Bedrooms are individually decorated, and there is a two-room suite in a cottage on the hillside above the hotel. The set five-course dinner uses local ingredients. There is no bar; pre-dinner drinks are served in the lounge.
ROOMS: 7 en suite 2 annexe en suite **FACILITIES:** Free use of local leisure club Free fishing at all local waters **PARKING:** 10 **NOTES:** No dogs No smoking in restaurant Closed early Dec-early Mar RS Sun
CARDS:

GRASSINGTON, North Yorkshire — Map 07 SE06

★★63% Grassington House
5 The Square BD23 5AQ
☎ 01756 752406 01756 752135
Dir: *Take B6265 from Skipton, on right hand side of village square*
Located in the main square, this popular, family-owned hotel offers homely and welcoming bedrooms. Day rooms are spacious and pleasant to relax in. Service is willing and friendly, and a good range of dishes is available either in the bar or the elegant dining room.
ROOMS: 9 en suite (1 fmly) s £29-£35; d £58 (incl. bkfst) * LB **FACILITIES:** Xmas **PARKING:** 20 **NOTES:** No smoking in restaurant Closed 25 & 26 Dec **CARDS:**

Late for dinner? Quality Standards star rating means that last orders for dinner should be no earlier than:
★ 6.30pm ★★ 7.00pm ★★★ 8.00pm
★★★★ 9.00pm ★★★★★ 10.00pm

GRAVESEND, Kent — Map 05 TQ67

★★★60% Overcliffe
15-16 The Overcliffe DA11 0EF
☎ 01474 322131 01474 536737
Dir: *outside town centre, to the west on the A226*
This family-run hotel, consisting of the main house and a nearby Victorian lodge, is just a short distance from the town centre. It provides comfortable, well equipped accommodation. Live piano entertainment is provided most evenings in the bar/lounge and restaurant.
ROOMS: 19 en suite 10 annexe en suite s £65-£75; d £75-£85 (incl. bkfst) * **FACILITIES:** STV entertainment **PARKING:** 35
CARDS:

★★66% *Clarendon Royal Hotel*
Royal Pier Rd DA12 2BD
☎ 01474 63151
This grand old riverside hotel has been updated and transformed into a friendly, modern hotel. Bedrooms are very smart and equipped with an excellent range of facilities. The popular family-style restaurant is lively and staff really make an effort to welcome their guests.
ROOMS: 24 rms (14 en suite) **PARKING:** 100

Premier Lodge
Hevercourt Rd, Singlewell DA12 5UQ

☎ 0870 700 1382 0870 700 1383
Premier Lodge offers modern, well equipped, en suite accommodation suitable for both business and leisure travellers. Meals can be taken at the adjacent popular restaurant and bar which is fully licensed. For further details, consult the Hotel Groups page.
ROOMS: 31 en suite d £42 *

GREAT CHESTERFORD, Essex

Map 05 TL54

★★ 67% The Crown House

CB10 1NY

☎ 01799 530515 01799 530683

Dir: *on B1383 1m from junct 9 on M11*

This small listed hotel dates back to Tudor times. The bedrooms in the main house have much character and those in the courtyard annexe are popular with guests who want peace and quiet. Cosy public rooms include a comfortable lounge bar, a dining room and a conservatory where breakfast is served.

ROOMS: 8 en suite 10 annexe en suite (1 fmly) s fr £62.50; d £85-£89.50 (incl. bkfst) * LB **CONF:** Thtr 50 Class 30 Board 25 Del from £86 * **PARKING:** 30 **NOTES:** Civ Wed 40

CARDS:

GREAT DUNMOW, Essex

Map 05 TL62

★★ 63% The Saracen's Head

REGAL

High St CM6 1AG

☎ 01371 873901 01371 875743

Dir: *take A120 towards Colchester turn left at 2nd rndbt, hotel 0.50m downhill*

Situated at the heart of an attractive market town, this former coaching inn is conveniently located for Stanstead Airport. Much of the original character of the building has been preserved in the beamed public rooms. The spacious bedrooms are decorated in traditional style and equipped with a useful range of extras.

ROOMS: 4 en suite 20 annexe en suite (3 fmly) No smoking in 5 bedrooms s £75-£85; d £90-£105 * LB **CONF:** Thtr 50 Class 30 Board 34 Del from £95 * **PARKING:** 50 **NOTES:** No smoking in restaurant

CARDS:

GREAT LANGDALE See Elterwater

GREAT MILTON, Oxfordshire

Map 04 SP60

Premier Collection

★★★★ Le Manoir Aux Quat' Saisons

RELAIS & CHATEAUX

OX44 7PD

☎ 01844 278881 01844 278847

e-mail: lemanoir@blanc.co

Dir: *from A329 take 2nd right turn to Great Milton Manor, hotel 200yds on right*

This delightful mellow stone 15th-century manor house lies peacefully in immaculate gardens, complete with sculptures, kitchen garden, and a traditional Japanese tea house. Bedrooms and suites are quite stunning and offer a superb level of comfort in both period and contemporary styles. The public rooms are furnished and decorated with immaculate taste, and offer high standards of comfort and luxury. The highlight of any stay has to be the outstanding quality of cuisine which continues to earn our supreme accolade of Five Rosettes, completing a perfect combination of cuisine, accommodation and service.

ROOMS: 32 rms (9 en suite) d £230-£550 (incl. cont bkfst) * LB **FACILITIES:** STV Croquet lawn Cookery School Water Gardens Xmas **CONF:** Thtr 24 Board 20 Del £310 * **PARKING:** 60 **NOTES:** No dogs (ex guide dogs) No smoking in restaurant Civ Wed 55 **CARDS:**

GREAT YARMOUTH, Norfolk

Map 05 TG50

★★★ 73% Cliff

Best Western

Gorleston NR31 6DH

☎ 01493 662179 01493 653617

e-mail: cliffhotel@aol.com

Dir: *2m S A12*

This hotel offers excellent accommodation, a smart restaurant, a choice of bars and an attractive lounge, all conducive to relaxation. Guests can eat in the bar as well as in the restaurant. Bedrooms vary in style; all are furnished to a good standard, with well matched furnishings.

ROOMS: 39 en suite (5 fmly) No smoking in 2 bedrooms s £69-£84; d fr £97 (incl. bkfst) * LB **FACILITIES:** STV Xmas **CONF:** Thtr 170 Class 150 Board 80 Del from £84.50 * **PARKING:** 70 **NOTES:** Civ Wed

CARDS:

★★★ 67% Star

Hall Quay NR30 1HG

☎ 01493 842294 01493 330215

e-mail: StarHotel@rjt.co.uk

Dir: *from Norwich A47 continue straight over 1st rdbt onto 2nd rdbt and take 3rd exit. Continue & hotel on left*

In the town centre, overlooking the quayside, the Star is a well furnished and friendly hotel with a fascinating history. The intimate public rooms are richly decorated and welcoming. The bedrooms are freshly furbished and have vibrant interior design and good facilities.

ROOMS: 40 en suite (1 fmly) No smoking in 13 bedrooms s £66-£75; d £82-£94 (incl. bkfst) * LB **FACILITIES:** STV Xmas **CONF:** Thtr 75 Class 30 Board 30 Del from £45 * **SERVICES:** Lift **PARKING:** 20

CARDS:

★★★ 66% Imperial

North Dr NR30 1EQ

☎ 01493 851113 01493 852229

e-mail: imperiale@scs-datacom.co.uk

Dir: *follow signs to seafront and turn left, Hotel opposite tennis courts*

Hospitable proprietors lead a professional staff at this spacious hotel. The extensive public areas include banqueting rooms, the

continued

comfortable Savoie Lounge Bar, and the Rambouillet Restaurant and Brasserie. The colour-coordinated accommodation is attractive and well equipped.
ROOMS: 39 en suite (4 fmly) No smoking in 12 bedrooms s £50-£67; d £59.80-£84 (incl. bkfst) * LB **FACILITIES:** STV Xmas **CONF:** Thtr 120 Class 30 Board 30 Del from £65 * **SERVICES:** Lift **PARKING:** 50
CARDS:

★★★65% Regency Dolphin

Albert Square NR30 3JH
☎ 01493 855070 Fax 01493 853798
e-mail: regency@meridianleisure.com
Dir: *proceed along seafront and turn right at Wellington Pier, turn right into Kimberley Terr, follow and turn left into Albert Sq, hotel is on left*
This smart hotel is set back from the beach and close to the local attractions. The bedrooms come in a variety of styles and sizes, and each one is well appointed with colour-coordinated decor and soft furnishings. An all-day menu is available in the lounge and on room service.
ROOMS: 48 en suite (6 fmly) No smoking in 8 bedrooms s £45-£65; d £60-£75 (incl. bkfst) * LB **FACILITIES:** STV Outdoor swimming (H) Xmas **CONF:** Thtr 140 Class 50 Board 40 Del £75 * **PARKING:** 30
NOTES: No smoking in restaurant Civ Wed 140
CARDS:

See advert on this page

★★66% Knights Court Hotel

22 North Dr NR30 4EW
☎ 01493 843089 Fax 01493 850780
Dir: *follow seafront signs. Hotel opposite Venetian Waterways & Gardens*
Overlooking the Venetian waterways and the sea beyond, this small hotel is immaculately maintained. The spacious bedrooms, many of which have sea views, are smartly decorated and well equipped. There is a neat lounge bar and an attractive restaurant where guests can choose from a set or carte menu.
ROOMS: 14 en suite (3 fmly) s £35-£40; d £56-£60 (incl. bkfst)
CONF: Class 20 Del from £50 * **PARKING:** 18 **NOTES:** No smoking in restaurant Closed mid Oct-mid Mar Civ Wed **CARDS:**

★★65% Regency

5 North Dr NR30 1ED
☎ 01493 843759 Fax 01493 330411
Dir: *on sea front*
On the wide seafront road at the quieter end of town, this traditional hotel has a friendly ambience and many regular guests, who appreciate the high standards. There is a variety of bedroom sizes and styles, but all rooms offer good facilities.
ROOMS: 14 en suite (2 fmly) s £35; d £46-£52 (incl. bkfst) * LB
FACILITIES: Xmas **PARKING:** 10 **NOTES:** No dogs (ex guide dogs) No children 7yrs No smoking in restaurant Closed Jan
CARDS:

★★64% Burlington Palm Court

11 North Dr NR30 1EG
☎ 01493 844568 & 842095 Fax 01493 331848
e-mail: enquiries@burlington-hotel.co.uk
Dir: *A12 to sea front, turn left at Britannia Pier. Hotel close to tennis courts*
Sitting at the more tranquil end of the seafront, the sister properties, Burlington and Palm Court, provide joint facilities for all residents. A well run, traditional resort hotel, the pleasant bedrooms are well equipped, whilst the public areas offer a spacious bar and lounge.

continued

Burlington Palm Court
Great Yarmouth

GREAT YARMOUTH, continued

ROOMS: 71 en suite (9 fmly) No smoking in 14 bedrooms s £50-£70; d £70-£80 (incl. bkfst) * LB **FACILITIES:** STV Indoor swimming (H) Pool table Jacuzzi/spa Turkish steam room entertainment Xmas **CONF:** Thtr 120 Class 40 Board 20 Del from £50 * **SERVICES:** Lift **PARKING:** 70 **NOTES:** No dogs (ex guide dogs) No smoking in restaurant Closed Jan-Feb RS Dec (group bookings only) **CARDS:**

See advert on page 235

★★62% **Furzedown**
19-20 North Dr NR30 4EW
☎ 01493 844138 01493 844138
e-mail: PaulG@Furzedownhotel.freeserve.co.uk
Dir: *At end of A47 or A12, head for seafront, turn left, hotel is opposite Waterways*

This private, family-run hotel at the north end of the seafront overlooks the beaches and Venetian Waterways. Well equipped bedrooms are brightly decorated and represent good value for money. Fresh floral displays feature in the day rooms, which include a bar and a TV lounge. Set price and carte menus are offered for dinner.
ROOMS: 23 rms (19 en suite) (11 fmly) s £31.50-£36.50; d £45-£53 (incl. bkfst) * LB **FACILITIES:** STV **CONF:** Class 60 Board 30 Del from £45 * **PARKING:** 15 **CARDS:**

GREENFORD, Greater London See LONDON SECTION plan 1 *B4*

★★★69% **The Bridge**
Western Av UB6 8ST
☎ 020 8566 6246 020 8566 6140
Ideally located for access to and from central London, this hotel remains a popular choice. Spacious bedrooms offer a good range of facilities and some have four-poster beds. There is a popular bar and bistro-style restaurant. Secure car parking is an added bonus for car users.
ROOMS: 68 en suite (4 fmly) No smoking in 44 bedrooms s fr £92; d fr £105 (incl. bkfst) * **FACILITIES:** STV Arrangement with local leisure centre **CONF:** Thtr 130 Class 60 Board 60 **SERVICES:** Lift **PARKING:** 68 **NOTES:** No dogs (ex guide dogs) No smoking in restaurant **CARDS:**

GRIMSBY, Lincolnshire Map 08 TA20

★★★64% **Beeches**
42 Waltham Rd, Scartho DN33 2LX
☎ 01472 278830 01472 278830
In the suburb of Scartho, a short distance from the town centre, this contemporary hotel offers good modern accommodation and pleasing public rooms. Bedrooms are inviting and nicely equipped with a thoughtful range of facilities. There is a popular brasserie and a comfortable lounge bar.

continued

ROOMS: 10 en suite No smoking in all bedrooms s £42.50-£47.50; d £59.50-£64 * LB **CONF:** Thtr 30 Class 20 Board 20 Del from £90 * **SERVICES:** Lift **PARKING:** 70 **NOTES:** No dogs (ex guide dogs) No smoking in restaurant **CARDS:**

★★★63% ***Humber Royal***
Littlecoates Rd DN34 4LX
☎ 01472 350311 01472 241354
Dir: *take A1136 signed Greatcoates, left at first rdbt right at second rdbt. Hotel is on right 200 metres down*
Bedrooms at this pleasantly situated hotel are equipped with all modern comforts and many have large windows and balconies overlooking the adjoining golf course; this view is also shared by the popular restaurant. There is a large banqueting suite in addition to the smaller meeting and conference rooms.
ROOMS: 52 en suite (2 fmly) No smoking in 27 bedrooms **FACILITIES:** Pool table **CONF:** Thtr 300 Class 100 Board 60 **SERVICES:** Lift **PARKING:** 250 **CARDS:**

GRIMSTON, Norfolk Map 09 TF72

Premier Collection

★★★ **Congham Hall Country House**
Lynn Rd PE32 1AH
☎ 01485 600250 01485 601191
e-mail: reception@conghamhallhotel.com
Dir: *A149/A148 interchange north east of King's Lynn, follow A148 to Sandringham/Fakenham/Cromer for 100yds. Turn right to Grimston, hotel 2.5m on left*
Attractive landscaped grounds and 30 acres of parkland surround this Georgian country house. Inside, the elegant reception rooms provide a range of beautifully furnished and comfortable areas in which to sit and relax. Quality cuisine is provided in the Orangery Restaurant, through a choice of interesting menus; service is both attentive and friendly. Many of the bedrooms, mostly furnished in period style, look out over the attractive gardens and grounds.
ROOMS: 14 en suite No smoking in all bedrooms s £85-£145; d £130-£230 (incl. bkfst) * LB **FACILITIES:** Outdoor swimming (H) Tennis (hard) Croquet lawn Putting green Jacuzzi/spa Cricket Xmas **CONF:** Thtr 50 Class 20 Board 30 Del from £155 * **PARKING:** 50 **NOTES:** No dogs No children 7yrs No smoking in restaurant Civ Wed 40 **CARDS:**

PRIDE OF BRITAIN MEMBER

Early start? Hotels at all star levels should provide in-room alarm clocks and/or alarm calls.

GRINDLEFORD, Derbyshire

Map 08 SK27

★★★68% Maynard Arms

Main Rd S32 2HE

☎ 01433 630321 🖷 01433 630445

Dir: *leave Sheffield on the A625 towards Castleton. Turn left into Grindleford on the B6521 after the Fox House. Hotel is on left*

Enjoying fine views, this country mansion is a good base from which to explore the northern Peak District. Attractive bedrooms include some larger 'superior' rooms and two suites. For dinner, guests can choose either the lounge bar or Padley's Restaurant, which overlooks the garden. There is a comfortable lounge on the first floor.

ROOMS: 10 en suite s £69-£89; d £79-£99 (incl. bkfst) * LB **FACILITIES:** STV Xmas **CONF:** Thtr 140 Class 80 Board 60 Del from £86.50 * **PARKING:** 80 **NOTES:** No smoking in restaurant Civ Wed 120 **CARDS:**

GUILDFORD, Surrey

Map 04 SU94

★★★78% ❀❀ The Angel Posting House and Livery

91 High St GU1 3DP

☎ 01483 564555 🖷 01483 533770

e-mail: angelhotel@hotmail.com

This historic coaching inn offers excellent, friendly service. Many of the bedroom suites are beamed; all are equipped with thoughtful extras. Cosy public areas retain original features such as a Jacobean fireplace and 17th-century parliament clock. The 13th-century, stone-vaulted Crypt Restaurant serves tempting dishes based on high quality ingredients.

ROOMS: 11 en suite 10 annexe en suite (4 fmly) d £135-£200 * LB **FACILITIES:** STV **CONF:** Thtr 80 Class 20 Board 40 Del from £221 * **SERVICES:** Lift **NOTES:** No smoking in restaurant **CARDS:**

See advert on this page

★★★70% The Manor

Newlands Corner GU4 8SE

☎ 01483 222624 🖷 01483 211389

Dir: *3.5m on A25 to Dorking*

Built in the 1890s and set in nine acres of well kept grounds, the Manor is a popular venue for meetings, conferences and weddings. Bedrooms are attractively decorated, and there are good lounge facilities as well as an air-conditioned function room.

ROOMS: 45 en suite (4 fmly) No smoking in 4 bedrooms s fr £75; d fr £90 * LB **FACILITIES:** Croquet lawn entertainment **CONF:** Thtr 200 Class 80 Board 80 Del from £145 * **PARKING:** 100 **NOTES:** Civ Wed 120 **CARDS:**

GUILDFORD, continued

★★★ 69% *Posthouse Guildford*

Posthouse

Egerton Rd GU2 5XZ
☎ 0870 400 9036 🖷 01483 302960
Dir: *exit A3 for Hospital and Cathedral, take third exit at rdbt then second exit at next*
Located near the cathedral and university, this large, modern hotel has smartly appointed bedrooms, all of which are spacious and well equipped. Public areas include a large, comfortable bar lounge and a health club.
ROOMS: 162 en suite (100 fmly) No smoking in 71 bedrooms
FACILITIES: STV Indoor swimming (H) Sauna Solarium Gym
CONF: Thtr 200 Class 100 Board 45 **PARKING:** 220
CARDS:

GUISBOROUGH, North Yorkshire — Map 08 NZ61

★★ 63% Cross Keys

Scottish Newcastle hotels

Upsall TS14 6RW
☎ 01287 610035 🖷 01287 639037
This large, stone-built property is in open countryside in a main road location. There are extensive dining areas offering a wide range of dishes. Lodge-style bedrooms are modern and well equipped.
ROOMS: 20 en suite (2 fmly) No smoking in 10 bedrooms s £40; d £40 * LB **FACILITIES:** entertainment Xmas **PARKING:** 300 **NOTES:** No dogs (ex guide dogs) No smoking in restaurant
CARDS:

GULWORTHY, Devon — Map 02 SX47

★★★ 75% Horn of Plenty

PL19 8JD
☎ 01822 832528 🖷 01822 832528
e-mail: enquiries@thehornofplenty.co.uk
Dir: *from Tavistock take A390 W for 3m and turn right at Gulworthy Cross. After 400yds turn left and continue for a further 400yds to hotel on right*
Set above the Tamar Valley, this beautiful country house enjoys stunning views across to Bodmin Moor. All bedrooms are well equipped and have many thoughtful extras. The elegantly furnished public rooms are comfortable and the renowned restaurant benefits from excellent views. The cuisine has flair and imagination. There is a well tended, walled garden.
ROOMS: 4 en suite 6 annexe en suite (3 fmly) No smoking in 1 bedroom s £105-£190; d £115-£200 (incl. bkfst) * LB **FACILITIES:** Xmas **CONF:** Thtr 20 Class 20 Board 12 **PARKING:** 25 **NOTES:** No smoking in restaurant Closed 24-26 Dec Civ Wed 120
CARDS:

GUNTHORPE, Nottinghamshire — Map 08 SK64

★★ 68% *Unicorn*

Gunthorpe Bridge NG14 7FB
☎ 0115 966 3612 🖷 0115 966 4801
Dir: *on A6097, between Lowdham and Bingham*
This popular riverside inn of great character offers a spacious restaurant and bars featuring exposed timbers and brickwork. A good range of snacks and meals is offered during the day, and a carte menu during the evening. Cheerful bedrooms are well proportioned and thoughtfully equipped.
ROOMS: 16 en suite (3 fmly) **FACILITIES:** STV Fishing **PARKING:** 200 **NOTES:** No dogs (ex guide dogs) **CARDS:**

HACKNESS, North Yorkshire — Map 08 SE99

★★★ 70% Hackness Grange Country House

Best Western

North York National Park YO13 0JW
☎ 01723 882345 🖷 01723 882391
Dir: *A64 to Scarborough and then A171 to Whitby/Scalby, follow signs to Hackness/Forge Valley National Park, through Hackness village on left hand side*
Close to Scarborough and the North Yorkshire Moors National Park, Hackness Grange is surrounded by well tended gardens with tennis courts and a pitch and putt course. Comfortable bedrooms have views of the countryside; those in the cottages are ideally suited to families. Lounges and the restaurant are spacious and relaxing.
ROOMS: 33 en suite (5 fmly) s £67.50-£77.50; d £95-£180 (incl. bkfst) * LB **FACILITIES:** STV Indoor swimming (H) Tennis (hard) Croquet lawn Putting green Jacuzzi/spa 9 hole pitch & putt Xmas **CONF:** Thtr 15 Class 8 Board 8 Del from £95 * **PARKING:** 60 **NOTES:** No dogs (ex guide dogs) No smoking in restaurant **CARDS:**

HADLEY WOOD, Greater London — Map 04 TQ29

★★★★ 71% West Lodge Park

Cockfosters Rd EN4 0PY
☎ 020 8216 3900 🖷 020 8216 3937
e-mail: beales_westlodgepark@compuserve.com
Dir: *on A111, 1m S of exit 24 on M25*
An impressive country house hotel set in parkland and gardens, yet only 12 miles from London's West End. Bedrooms are individually furnished and decorated, offering a comprehensive range of in-room facilities. The Cedar Restaurant offers a range of interesting dishes and currently holds our Two Rosette award.
ROOMS: 46 en suite 9 annexe en suite (1 fmly) No smoking in 19 bedrooms s £98; d £130-£205 * LB **FACILITIES:** STV Croquet lawn Putting green Fitness trail Free membership of David Lloyd Club Xmas **CONF:** Thtr 80 Class 24 Board 30 Del from £160 * **SERVICES:** Lift **PARKING:** 200 **NOTES:** No dogs (ex guide dogs) No smoking in restaurant Civ Wed 40 **CARDS:**

HAILSHAM, East Sussex — Map 05 TQ50

★★★ 65% Boship Farm

Forestdale Hotels

Lower Dicker BN27 4AT
☎ 01323 844826 🖷 01323 843945
Dir: *on A22 at Boship roundabout, junct of A22/A267/A271*
Dating back to 1652, this lovely old farmhouse forms the hub of the hotel. Set in 17 acres of well tended grounds, guests have the use of an all-weather tennis court and outdoor pool; croquet is available for the less energetic. Bedrooms are smartly appointed and well equipped; most have views across the fields and countryside beyond.
ROOMS: 47 annexe en suite (5 fmly) No smoking in 17 bedrooms s fr £60; d fr £120 (incl. bkfst) * LB **FACILITIES:** Outdoor swimming (H) Tennis (hard) Gym Croquet lawn Jacuzzi/spa Xmas **CONF:** Thtr 175 Class 40 Board 46 Del from £95 * **PARKING:** 100 **NOTES:** No smoking in restaurant Civ Wed **CARDS:**

★★ 68% The Olde Forge Hotel & Restaurant

Magham Down BN27 1PN
☎ 01323 842893 🖷 01323 842893
e-mail: theoldeforgehotelandrestaurant@tesco.net
Dir: *off Boship rdbt on A271 to Bexhill. 3m on left, opposite The Red Lion Public House*
In the heart of the lovely Wealdon countryside, this family-run

continued

hotel offers a warm welcome, a friendly, informal atmosphere and tastefully decorated, comfortable accommodation. The restaurant, with its timbered beams and log fires, once the home of a 16th-century forge, is gaining a growing reputation for its cuisine and service.
ROOMS: 7 rms (6 en suite) (1 fmly) s £44; d £58-£68 (incl. bkfst) * LB
PARKING: 11 **NOTES:** No smoking in restaurant
CARDS:

⌂ *Travelodge*
Boship Roundabout, Hellingly BN27 4DT
☎ 01323 844556 📠 01323 844556
Dir: *on A22 at Boship roundabout*
This modern building offers accommodation in smart, spacious and well equipped bedrooms, all with en suite bathrooms. Refreshments may be taken at the nearby family restaurant. For further details and the Travelodge phone number, consult the Hotel Groups page.
ROOMS: 40 en suite

HALIFAX, West Yorkshire — Map 07 SE02

★★★75% ❀❀ Holdsworth House
Holdsworth HX2 9TG
☎ 01422 240024 📠 01422 245174
e-mail: info@holdsworthhouse.co.uk
Dir: *3m NW off A629 Keighley Road*

This beautiful 17th-century Jacobean manor house is set in pretty gardens and has been extended to provide individually decorated, thoughtfully equipped rooms. Guests can relax in front of a real fire in one of the many cosy lounges. The cuisine is not to be missed.
ROOMS: 40 en suite (2 fmly) No smoking in 15 bedrooms s £85-£118; d £104-£134 (incl. cont bkfst) * LB **FACILITIES:** STV **CONF:** Thtr 150 Class 75 Board 50 Del £122.50 * **PARKING:** 60 **NOTES:** No smoking in restaurant Civ Wed 118 **CARDS:**

★★★67% Rock Inn Hotel & Churchills
Holywell Green HX4 9BS
☎ 01422 379721 📠 01422 379110
e-mail: therock@dial.pipex.com
Dir: *junct 24 off M62, signs for Blackley, left at crossroads approx 1/2m on left*
Quietly situated, this privately-owned hotel offers attractively furnished bedrooms. The bar and brasserie are popular with locals and visitors alike; meals can also be taken in Churchills restaurant. The hotel is a popular venue for functions.
ROOMS: 30 en suite (5 fmly) No smoking in 15 bedrooms d £64-£110 (incl. bkfst) * LB **FACILITIES:** STV Games room Xmas **CONF:** Thtr 200 Class 100 Board 100 Del £99 * **PARKING:** 122 **NOTES:** No smoking in restaurant Civ Wed 200 **CARDS:**

★★★63% The Imperial Crown
42/46 Horton St HX1 1QE
☎ 01422 342342 📠 01422 349866
e-mail: imperialcrown@corushotels.com
Dir: *opposite Railway Station*

Bedrooms at this hotel are split between the imposing main building and a lodge across the road, where there is also an American-style diner. The Wallis Simpson restaurant offers a more formal dining option.
ROOMS: 41 en suite 15 annexe en suite (3 fmly) No smoking in 10 bedrooms s £85; d £95 * LB **FACILITIES:** STV entertainment **CONF:** Thtr 150 Class 120 Board 70 Del from £90 * **PARKING:** 63 **NOTES:** Civ Wed 200 **CARDS:**

⌂ Premier Lodge
Salterhebble Hill, Huddersfield Rd HX3 0QT
☎ 0870 700 1410 📠 0870 700 1411
Premier Lodge offers modern, well equipped, en suite accommodation suitable for both business and leisure travellers. Meals can be taken at the adjacent popular restaurant and bar which is fully licensed. For further details, consult the Hotel Groups page.
ROOMS: 31 en suite d £46 *

HALLAND, East Sussex — Map 05 TQ41

★★★61% *Halland Forge*
BN8 6PW
☎ 01825 840456 📠 01825 840773
e-mail: hallandforge@pavilion.co.uk
Dir: *on A22 at junct with B2192, 4m S of Uckfield*
Conveniently located on the A22, this popular hotel offers good sized bedrooms in an adjoining two-storey, motel-style block. Public areas include a spacious lounge bar, a popular coffee shop and a traditional restaurant.
ROOMS: 20 annexe en suite (2 fmly) **CONF:** Thtr 70 Class 50 Board 50 **PARKING:** 70 **NOTES:** No children 5yrs
CARDS:

HAMBLETON, North Yorkshire — Map 08 SE53

★★64% *Owl*
Main Rd YO8 9JH
☎ 01757 228374 📠 01757 228125
Dir: *4m W on A63*
In the centre of the village, this modern and very well equipped hotel offers a very extensive range of popular food. Bedrooms, located in the main building and in a nearby wing, have been pleasantly decorated and thoughtfully furnished.
ROOMS: 7 en suite 15 annexe en suite (2 fmly) **FACILITIES:** STV **CONF:** Thtr 80 Class 40 Board 50 **PARKING:** 101 **NOTES:** No dogs (ex guide dogs) **CARDS:**

HAMPSON GREEN, Lancashire Map 07 SD45

★★63% Hampson House
Hampson Ln LA2 0JB
☎ 01524 751158 📠 01524 751779
Dir: *leave Junc 33 M6, follow for Garstang 1st left into Hampson Lane, the Hotel is 400yds on the left*
Conveniently situated close to the M6, this traditional hotel nestles in over an acre of mature gardens, and part of the building dates back to 1666. An imaginative choice of dishes is offered in the open-plan restaurant, and the bedrooms are bright and well equipped.
ROOMS: 12 en suite 2 annexe en suite (4 fmly) s fr £42; d fr £54 (incl. bkfst) * LB **FACILITIES:** Xmas **CONF:** Thtr 90 Class 40 Board 26 Del from £56 * **PARKING:** 60 **NOTES:** Civ Wed 70 **CARDS:**

HAMPTON COURT, Greater London
See LONDON SECTION plan 1 *B1*

★★★★67% The Carlton Mitre
Hampton Court Rd KT8 9BN
☎ 020 8979 9988 📠 020 8979 9777
e-mail: mitre@carltonhotels.co.uk
Dir: *from M3 junct 1 follow signs to Sunbury & Hampton Court Palace, continue until Hampton Court Palace rdbt, turn right & The Mitre is on the right*
Dating back in parts to 1665 and located on the Thames, this hotel originally served as lodging for courtiers who could not be accommodated at Hampton Court Palace opposite. The riverside terrace, restaurant and brasserie all command good views. Bedrooms are generally spacious with good facilities, some also with views. Parking is limited.
ROOMS: 36 en suite (2 fmly) No smoking in 16 bedrooms d £160-£195 * LB **FACILITIES:** STV Jacuzzi/spa entertainment Xmas **CONF:** Thtr 30 Class 15 Board 20 Del from £195 * **SERVICES:** Lift **PARKING:** 13
CARDS:

★★★64% Menzies Liongate
MENZIES HOTELS
Hampton Court Rd KT8 9DD
☎ 0500 636943 (Central Res)
📠 01773 880321
e-mail: info@menzies-hotels.co.uk
Dir: *from London approach via A3 and A308. From SW leave M3 at junct 1 and follow A308*
Well situated opposite the Lion Gate entrance to Hampton Court and beside the entrance to Bushy Park, this hotel has well equipped bedrooms and friendly staff. In addition to those in the main house there are rooms in a small mews across the road. The hotel also has a modern open-plan restaurant and bar.
ROOMS: 29 en suite s £110-£130; d £130-£140 * LB **FACILITIES:** STV Xmas **CONF:** Thtr 60 Class 30 Board 30 Del from £95 * **PARKING:** 30 **NOTES:** No smoking in restaurant Civ Wed 60
CARDS:

HANDFORTH See Manchester Airport

HARLESTON, Norfolk Map 05 TM28

★★62% The Swan Hotel
The Thoroughfare IP20 9AS
☎ 01379 852221 📠 01379 854817
e-mail: swan@norfolk-hotels.co.uk
Dir: *turn off A140 onto B1134 signed 'The Pulhams'. Through Pulham villages to Starston, then Harleston. Hotel at end of Swan Lane on left*
In the heart of this pleasant town, The Swan is a focal point with its locals' bar and warm, homely atmosphere. The attractive, well equipped bedrooms come in a variety of sizes. Downstairs the bar and restaurant are full of character with lots of original woodwork.
ROOMS: 15 en suite (2 fmly) s fr £35; d fr £54 (incl. bkfst) * LB **FACILITIES:** entertainment **CONF:** Thtr 60 Class 30 Board 10 **PARKING:** 30 **NOTES:** No smoking in restaurant
CARDS:

HARLOW, Essex Map 05 TL41

★★★73% *Swallow Churchgate Hotel*
SWALLOW HOTELS
Churchgate St Village, Old Harlow CM17 0JT
☎ 01279 420246 📠 01279 420246
e-mail: info@swallowhotels.com
Dir: *on B183, NE of Old Harlow. Exit M11 Junc 7 for Harlow. At 4th rdbt turn right on B183 follow signs for Churchgate Street*

The Swallow Churchgate is a Jacobean house in a quiet village north-east of Old Harlow. 'Executive' rooms are the best of the high quality bedrooms and there is extensive room service as well as the elegant Manor Restaurant.
ROOMS: 85 en suite (6 fmly) No smoking in 41 bedrooms **FACILITIES:** STV Indoor swimming (H) Sauna Solarium Gym Jacuzzi/spa **CONF:** Thtr 180 Class 70 Board 40 Del from £135 * **PARKING:** 120 **NOTES:** No smoking in restaurant Closed 27-29 Dec Civ Wed **CARDS:**

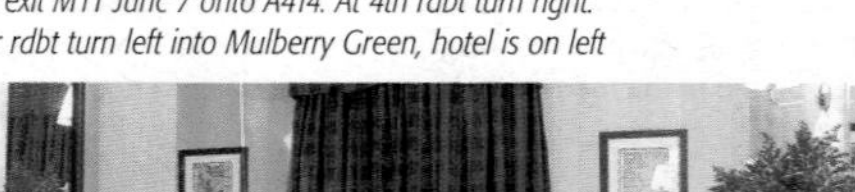

★★★65% Green Man
corus
Mulberry Green, Old Harlow CM17 0ET
☎ 01279 442521 📠 01279 626113
Dir: *exit M11 Junc 7 onto A414. At 4th rdbt turn right. After rdbt turn left into Mulberry Green, hotel is on left*

This original coaching inn, which has been welcoming guests since the 14th century, houses a popular bar with a separate modern restaurant, and several function rooms. The smart refurbished bedrooms are housed in a modern purpose-built extension and come in a range of styles with smart coordinated colours.
ROOMS: 55 annexe en suite No smoking in 27 bedrooms s £89; d £99 * LB **FACILITIES:** Xmas **CONF:** Thtr 60 Class 26 Board 30 Del £120 * **PARKING:** 75 **NOTES:** No smoking in restaurant
CARDS:

HARLYN BAY, Cornwall & Isles of Scilly Map 02 SW87

★66% *Polmark*
PL28 8SB
☎ 01841 520206 01841 520206
Dir: *A39 to Padstow, then Padstow to Harlyn Bay*
Friendly service is offered at this 1920s Cornish stone property. Bedrooms are well equipped, ranging from rooms in the original house to new bedrooms in a purpose-built wing. On cooler evenings, log fires burn in the lounge bar. Imaginative menus are offered each evening and Thai specialities are a feature.
ROOMS: 13 en suite (3 fmly) **FACILITIES:** Outdoor swimming (H)
PARKING: 20 **NOTES:** No smoking in restaurant Closed Nov-Mar
CARDS:

HAROME See Helmsley

HARPENDEN, Hertfordshire Map 04 TL11

★★★73% Glen Eagle
1 Luton Rd AL5 2PX
☎ 01582 760271 01582 460819
e-mail: davidhunter9@virgin.net
Dir: *in town centre just beyond Oggelsby's Garage*
A smart, well established hotel, located near the centre of this prosperous commuter town. Sheldon's Brasserie provides a modern and informal dining menu. The bedrooms are furnished and decorated to a high standard and offer a very good range of extra facilities.
ROOMS: 60 en suite (12 fmly) No smoking in 25 bedrooms s fr £95; d £110-£150 * LB **FACILITIES:** STV Free membership of local leisure club **CONF:** Thtr 150 Class 60 Board 44 Del from £125 *
SERVICES: Lift **PARKING:** 100 **NOTES:** Civ Wed 120
CARDS:

See advert on this page

★★★69% Harpenden House
18 Southdown Rd AL5 1PE
REGAL
☎ 01582 449955 01582 769858
Dir: *from M1 junct 10a, right onto A1081. Continue until just before town. On reaching 3rd mini rdbt turn left into Bull Rd. Hotel 200 yds on the left*

This attractive grade II listed Georgian building is situated in the town centre. Accommodation is located in the main building or adjacent wing, which includes two self-contained apartments. The public rooms provide a smart, comfortable environment for guests to relax in.
ROOMS: 17 en suite 59 annexe en suite (13 fmly) No smoking in 49 bedrooms s £120-£130; d £150-£200 * LB **FACILITIES:** STV
CONF: Thtr 150 Class 60 Board 70 Del from £90 * **PARKING:** 80
NOTES: RS Weekends & Bank Holiday
CARDS:

HARROGATE, North Yorkshire Map 08 SE35
see also Hazlewood & Knaresborough

★★★★76% Rudding Park House & Hotel
Rudding Park, Follifoot HG3 1JH
☎ 01423 871350 01423 872286
e-mail: sales@rudding-park.co.uk
Dir: *from A61, at rdbt with A658 take exit for York and follow brown signs to Rudding Park*

Part of a 230 acre estate, this hotel is elegant and welcoming. The well equipped and very comfortable bedrooms are stylish yet simple. Public areas include the contemporary Clocktower Restaurant and Bar, a sunny atrium and a separate residents' drawing room.

continued

HARROGATE, continued

ROOMS: 50 en suite No smoking in 31 bedrooms s £115; d £145 (incl. bkfst) * LB **FACILITIES:** STV Golf 18 Croquet lawn Jogging trail Membership of local gym Xmas **CONF:** Thtr 350 Class 170 Board 40 Del from £170 * **SERVICES:** Lift **PARKING:** 150 **NOTES:** No dogs (ex guide dogs) Civ Wed **CARDS:**

See advert on opposite page

★★★★67% The Majestic

Ripon Rd HG1 2HU

☎ 01423 700300 01423 502283

e-mail: majestic@paramount-hotels.co.uk

PARAMOUNT GROUP OF HOTELS

Dir: *from M1 continue on A1(M) link road, on leaving A1 at Wetherby take A661 to Harrogate. Hotel in town centre opposite The Royal Hall*

This elegant Edwardian hotel is convienently situated within easy walking distance of the conference centre. The impressive public rooms feature chandeliers, murals, paintings and beautiful wood panelling. The bedrooms are comfortable, well equipped and include several spacious suites with separate sitting rooms.

ROOMS: 156 en suite (10 fmly) No smoking in 46 bedrooms s £70-£99; d £90-£136 * LB **FACILITIES:** STV Indoor swimming (H) Tennis (hard) Squash Snooker Sauna Solarium Gym Jacuzzi/spa Health & beauty salon entertainment Xmas **CONF:** Thtr 500 Class 250 Board 66 Del from £135 * **SERVICES:** Lift **PARKING:** 240 **NOTES:** Civ Wed 450 **CARDS:**

★★★★61% Old Swan

Swan Rd HG1 2SR

☎ 01423 500055 01423 501154

e-mail: info@oldswan.macdonald-hotels.co.uk

Dir: *follow Town Centre & Harrogate International Centre signs onto the Ripon Rd, through traffic lights, 2nd left turning into Swan Rd, 300yrds on right*

One of the town's oldest hotels, The Old Swan was made famous in 1926 when Agatha Christie 'disappeared'. The public rooms include an impressive Wedgwood Room and the Library Restaurant. Bedrooms are well equipped. There are a number of spacious suites with their own sitting rooms.

ROOMS: 124 en suite (10 fmly) No smoking in 38 bedrooms s fr £105; d fr £120 * LB **FACILITIES:** STV Croquet lawn Xmas **CONF:** Thtr 450 Class 150 Board 100 Del from £125 * **SERVICES:** Lift **PARKING:** 200 **NOTES:** No smoking in restaurant RS Xmas/New Year Civ Wed 450 **CARDS:**

★★★75% ❀❀ The Boar's Head Hotel

Ripley Castle Estate HG3 3AY

☎ 01423 771888 01423 771509

e-mail: boarshead@ripleycastle.co.uk

Dir: *on the A61 Harrogate/Ripon road, the hotel is in the centre of Ripley Village*

In the private village of Ripley Castle estate, this charming hotel overlooks the market square. It is renowned for its warm hospitality, traditional hostelry and the restaurant with its mix of modern dishes and traditional classics. Bedrooms offer many creature comforts, and the opulent day rooms feature works of art from the nearby castle. Guests have free admission to the deer park, the lakeside and the walled gardens.

ROOMS: 13 en suite 12 annexe en suite (2 fmly) No smoking in 3 bedrooms s £95-£115; d £115-£135 (incl. bkfst) * LB **FACILITIES:** STV Tennis (hard) Fishing Croquet lawn Clay pigeon shooting entertainment Xmas **CONF:** Thtr 60 Class 35 Board 30 Del £145 * **PARKING:** 53 **CARDS:**

★★★71% Grants

3-13 Swan Rd HG1 2SS

☎ 01423 560666 01423 502550

e-mail: enquires@grantshotel-harrogate.com

Dir: *off A61*

A welcoming hotel a short walk from the town centre. Individually styled bedrooms are comfortable, attractively furnished and thoughtfully equipped. Freshly prepared meals are served in the smart bistro restaurant where the walls display interesting pictures.

ROOMS: 42 en suite (2 fmly) s £60-£110; d £110-£165 (incl. bkfst) * LB **FACILITIES:** Use of local Health & Leisure Club Xmas **CONF:** Thtr 70 Class 20 Board 30 **SERVICES:** Lift **PARKING:** 26 **CARDS:**

See advert on opposite page

★★★69% Imperial

Prospect Place HG1 1LA

☎ 01423 565071 01423 500082

Dir: *follow A61 into town centre. Hotel opposite Betty's Tea Rooms*

This town-centre hotel provides attractive, comfortable accommodation. Day rooms include a cocktail bar and the spacious Ambassadors Restaurant, as well as relaxing lounge areas.

ROOMS: 83 en suite s £35-£60; d £50-£95 (incl. bkfst) * LB **FACILITIES:** Xmas **CONF:** Thtr 200 Class 80 Board 40 **SERVICES:** Lift **PARKING:** 12 **NOTES:** No smoking in restaurant **CARDS:**

H

HARROGATE, continued

★★★66% Studley
Swan Rd HG1 2SE
☎ 01423 560425 01423 530967
Dir: *Adjacent to the Valley Gardens on Swan Rd*
This welcoming hotel, close to the town centre and Valley Gardens, is renowned for its friendly and attentive service. Le Breton Restaurant boasts a genuine charcoal grill, and both the carte and table d'hote menus are excellent value for money. Bedrooms are well equipped and vary in size. Sizeable day rooms are comfortably furnished.
ROOMS: 36 en suite (2 fmly) s £68-£92; d £88-£110 (incl. bkfst) * LB **FACILITIES:** STV Xmas **CONF:** Thtr 15 Class 15 Board 12 **SERVICES:** Lift **PARKING:** 15 **CARDS:**

★★★66% Swallow St George
1 Ripon Rd HG1 2SY
☎ 01423 561431 01423 530037
e-mail: info@swallowhotels.com
Dir: *on A61 opposite the Royal Hall, Conference Centre*

Situated close to the conference centre, this well furnished hotel offers comfortable, thoughtfully equipped accommodation. Bedrooms, which include a superb ground-floor suite and a number of family rooms, vary in size and outlook. There are excellent facilities for meetings and smart lounge areas.
ROOMS: 90 en suite (14 fmly) No smoking in 35 bedrooms s fr £95; d fr £120 (incl. bkfst) * LB **FACILITIES:** STV Indoor swimming (H) Sauna Solarium Gym Jacuzzi/spa Boutique Beautician Masseuse Steamroom Cardio-vascular room ch fac Xmas **CONF:** Thtr 200 Class 80 Board 50 Del from £107 * **SERVICES:** Lift **PARKING:** 60 **NOTES:** No smoking in restaurant Civ Wed 140
CARDS:

★★★66% White House
10 Park Pde HG1 5AF
☎ 01423 501388 01423 527973
e-mail: info@whitehouse-hotel.demon.co.uk
Dir: *at rdbt junct of A59/A6040, take Skipton direction, first turn left (Church Sq) at bottom turn left and house on right*
This hotel, overlooking the famous Stray, is a firm favourite. The imaginative dinners served in the elegant dining room are excellent. Two lounges are also provided. The thoughtfully equipped bedrooms are stylishly furnished in keeping with the hotel's Victorian character.
ROOMS: 10 en suite (1 fmly) No smoking in all bedrooms **CONF:** Thtr 40 Class 30 Board 20 Del from £100 * **NOTES:** No dogs (ex guide dogs) No smoking in restaurant Civ Wed 60
CARDS:

★★★62% The Harrogate Spa Hotel
Prospect Place, West Park HG1 1LB
☎ 01423 564601 01423 507508
Dir: *from A61 Leeds/Ripon Road, continue along West Park towards City Centre. Right at traffic lights into Albert St & 1st right to hotel*

PEEL HOTELS

Overlooking the Stray, this Georgian terrace property is a short walk from the main shopping area. Drinks can be enjoyed in the warm atmosphere of the David Copperfield bar where lighter meals are also served. Bedrooms are comfortable and well equipped. Service is friendly and professional.
ROOMS: 71 en suite (5 fmly) No smoking in 9 bedrooms s £70-£97; d £80-£108 (incl. bkfst) * LB **FACILITIES:** STV Xmas **CONF:** Thtr 150 Class 75 Board 58 Del from £80 * **SERVICES:** Lift **PARKING:** 40 **NOTES:** No smoking in restaurant **CARDS:**

★★★59% The Crown
Crown Place HG1 2RZ
☎ 01423 567755 01423 502284
Dir: *take A61 into Harrogate continue down Parliament St to traffic lights by Royal Hall, left towards Valley Gardens, 1st left to rdbt, hotel on right*

REGAL

An imposing 18th-century coaching inn, situated next to the Royal Pump Room and near the shops and conference centre. The entrance hall, lounge, bar and panelled Ripley Restaurant are quite impressive and reminiscent of the period, although much modernisation has taken place. The majority of the bedrooms are generously proportioned.
ROOMS: 121 en suite (8 fmly) No smoking in 61 bedrooms s £70-£85; d £90-£115 * LB **FACILITIES:** free use of local sports club Xmas **CONF:** Thtr 400 Class 200 Board 80 Del £135 * **SERVICES:** Lift **PARKING:** 60 **NOTES:** No smoking in restaurant Civ Wed 400
CARDS:

★★71% Ascot House
53 Kings Rd HG1 5HJ
☎ 01423 531005 01423 503523
e-mail: admin@ascothouse.com
Dir: *follow signs to town centre/conference and exhibition centre. At Kings Rd, drive past conference centre, Ascot House on left immediately after park*

MINOTEL Great Britain

Attentive service is assured at this friendly, family-owned hotel. Bedrooms are neatly decorated and thoughtfully equipped. There is a smart lounge and spacious lounge bar. A range of freshly prepared meals are served from the daily menu and short carte in the attractive restaurant.

continued

ROOMS: 19 en suite (2 fmly) s £49.50-£59.50; d £74-£86 (incl. bkfst) * LB **FACILITIES:** Xmas **CONF:** Thtr 80 Class 36 Board 36 Del from £75 * **PARKING:** 14 **NOTES:** Closed 27 Dec-2 Jan & 19 Jan-4 Feb
CARDS:

★★68% Grafton

1-3 Franklin Mount HG1 5EJ
☎ 01423 508491 📠 01423 523168
e-mail: enquiries@graftonhotel.co.uk
Dir: *500yds from Conference Centre*

Convenient for both the town and the conference centre, this friendly hotel offers pleasant, good value accommodation. The bedrooms are comfortable and the public rooms consist of a cosy lounge bar and a dining room overlooking the well tended front garden.

ROOMS: 17 en suite (3 fmly) No smoking in all bedrooms s £45-£65; d £60.50-£74 (incl. bkfst) * LB **PARKING:** 3 **NOTES:** No dogs (ex guide dogs) No smoking in restaurant Closed 16 Dec-5 Jan
CARDS:

★★68% ❀ Harrogate Brasserie Hotel & Bar

28-30 Cheltenham Pde HG1 1DB
☎ 01423 505041 📠 01423 722300
e-mail: brasserie@zoom.co.uk
Dir: *on A61 Town Centre behind Theatre*

This town centre hotel is distinctly continental in style. The popular brasserie features live jazz at weekends. Bedrooms are individual in style and offer a varied standard of appointment. There is also a comfortable residents' lounge on the first floor.

ROOMS: 13 en suite (3 fmly) s £45-£55; d £65-£75 (incl. bkfst) * LB **FACILITIES:** STV entertainment Xmas **PARKING:** 12
CARDS:

See advert on this page

★★66% The Croft

THE CIRCLE
Selected Individual Hotels
GREAT BRITAIN

42-46 Franklin Rd HG1 5EE
☎ 01423 563326 📠 01423 530733
e-mail: reservations@crofthotel.demon.co.uk
Dir: *proceed to Conference Centre, opposite turn into Strawberry Dale Av, first left into Franklin Road*

Located in a quiet residential road within easy walking distance of the town and conference centre. Bright, fresh bedrooms are thoughtfully equipped, and the lounge and bar are inviting and comfortable. Quality home-cooked food is available in the cosy rear dining room.

ROOMS: 13 en suite s £40-£52; d £60-£65 (incl. bkfst) * LB **FACILITIES:** Pool table **PARKING:** 10 **NOTES:** No dogs No smoking in restaurant **CARDS:**

Fancy a Singapore Sling? Bar staff in five star hotels should be skilled cocktail mixers.

★★66% *Low Hall*

Ripon Rd, Killinghall HG3 2AY
☎ 01423 508598 📠 01423 560848
Dir: *exit Harrogate on A61 northbound in the direction of Ripon in 2m on exiting the village of Killinghall, Low Hall is 300mtrs on the right*

On the edge of Killinghall village, to the north of Harrogate, this 17th-century, grade II listed building has great charm and character. Beams and stone walls are much in evidence in the public rooms and the galleried dining area is very attractive. Bedrooms vary in size but are well equipped.

ROOMS: 7 en suite No smoking in all bedrooms **FACILITIES:** STV **CONF:** Thtr 90 Class 70 Board 70 **PARKING:** 40 **NOTES:** No dogs (ex guide dogs) No smoking in restaurant **CARDS:**

★★65% *Bay Horse Inn & Motel*

Burnt Yates HG3 3EJ
☎ 01423 770230 📠 01423 771894
e-mail: enquiry@bayhorseinn.co.uk
Dir: *W on B6165 next to village church*

This 18th-century inn is surrounded by rolling countryside, north west of Harrogate. Set in a small village, the inn provides well equipped, comfortable bedrooms. Very good food is offered, prepared from fresh ingredients, and can be taken either in the restaurant or the cosy bar.

ROOMS: 6 en suite 10 annexe en suite (2 fmly) No smoking in 4 bedrooms **CONF:** Board 35 **PARKING:** 75 **NOTES:** No dogs (ex guide dogs) No smoking in restaurant **CARDS:**

Read all about it! Newspapers delivered to bedrooms in four and five star hotels.

HARROW, Greater London
See LONDON SECTION plan 1 *B5*

★★★67% Cumberland
1 St Johns Rd HA1 2EF
☎ 020 8863 4111 020 8861 5668
This town centre hotel offers modern, practical bedrooms with a good range of in-room facilities, located in the main house and in two other separate wings. Public areas include a range of meeting rooms, a popular bar, quiet lounge and an attractive, modern restaurant.

ROOMS: 31 en suite 53 annexe en suite (5 fmly) No smoking in 51 bedrooms s £90-£95; d £98-£103 (incl. bkfst) * LB **FACILITIES:** STV Sauna Gym Small Fitness Room **CONF:** Thtr 140 Class 50 Board 40 Del £115 * **PARKING:** 57 **NOTES:** No dogs (ex guide dogs)
CARDS:

See advert on opposite page

★★★67% Quality Harrow Hotel
Roxborough Bridge, 12-22 Pinner Rd HA1 4HZ
☎ 020 8427 3435 020 8861 1370
e-mail: info@harrowhotel.co.uk
Dir: *off rdbt on A404 at junction with A312*
A privately-owned, commercial hotel consisting of three interlinked houses dating back to the early 20th century. Bedrooms are smart, comfortable and practically furnished. Public areas comprise a bar, conservatory lounge, meeting rooms and a smart conservatory restaurant. Ample off road parking is available for car users.
ROOMS: 53 en suite 23 annexe en suite (2 fmly) No smoking in 28 bedrooms s fr £90; d fr £105 (incl. bkfst) * **FACILITIES:** STV **CONF:** Thtr 160 Class 60 Board 60 Del from £130 * **PARKING:** 70 **NOTES:** No smoking in restaurant RS Xmas (limited service) Civ Wed 120 **CARDS:**

See advert on opposite page

★★★65% Menzies Northwick Park
2-12 Northwick Park Rd HA1 2NT
☎ 0500 636943 (Central Res) 01773 880321
e-mail: info@menzies-hotels.co.uk
Dir: *off A4006*
This north-London hotel is only 20 minutes from the city centre and conveniently situated for access to the M1 and A41. There are a variety of rooms, located either in the main building or in the adjacent wing. There is a large function room, a relaxing bar and a modern restaurant.
ROOMS: 75 en suite (3 fmly) No smoking in 30 bedrooms s £95; d £95-£110 * **FACILITIES:** STV Xmas **CONF:** Thtr 180 Class 80 Board 50 Del from £80 * **PARKING:** 65 **CARDS:**

HARROW WEALD, Greater London
See LONDON SECTION plan 1 *B6*

★★★68% Grim's Dyke
Old Redding HA3 6SH
☎ 020 8385 3100 020 8954 4560
e-mail: enquiries@grimsdyke.com
Formerly the home of Sir William Gilbert, of Gilbert and Sullivan fame, this impressive grade II listed building is set in 40 acres of gardens and woodland. Sir William wrote much of his music in the library, now the bar and the music room with its impressive alabaster fireplace and minstrels gallery is now a very attractive dining room. The smart, well equipped bedrooms are located in the main house or the adjacent garden lodge.
ROOMS: 9 en suite 34 annexe en suite s fr £119; d fr £145 (incl. bkfst) * LB **FACILITIES:** STV Croquet lawn entertainment Xmas **CONF:** Thtr 300 Class 60 Board 200 Del £149 * **PARKING:** 97
CARDS:

HARTLEBURY, Worcestershire — Map 07 SO87

⌂ *Travelodge*
Shorthill Nurseries DY13 9SH
☎ 01299 250553 01299 250553
Dir: *A449 southbound*
This modern building offers accommodation in smart, spacious and well equipped bedrooms, all with en suite bathrooms. Refreshments may be taken at the nearby family restaurant. For further details and the Travelodge phone number, consult the Hotel Groups page.
ROOMS: 32 en suite

HARTLEPOOL, Co Durham — Map 08 NZ53

★★★64% The Grand
Swainson St TS24 8AA
☎ 01429 266345 01429 265217
Dir: *opposite shopping centre, adjacent to Civic Centre*
In the centre of the town this splendid Victorian building, with its impressive facade, offers spacious, well equipped bedrooms. Public rooms are extensive and include a pleasant restaurant, a bar and a ballroom. A good range of food is available in the bar or the restaurant.
ROOMS: 47 en suite (4 fmly) No smoking in 1 bedroom s £54.50-£100; d £65.50-£100 (incl. bkfst) * LB **FACILITIES:** STV Free use of adjacent local leisure centre **CONF:** Thtr 200 Class 150 Board 35 Del from £85 * **SERVICES:** Lift **PARKING:** 50 **NOTES:** No dogs (ex guide dogs) Civ Wed 200 **CARDS:**

HARTSHEAD MOOR SERVICE AREA, West Yorkshire — Map 07 SE12

⌂ Days Inn
Hartshead Moor Service Area, Clifton HD6 4JX
☎ 01274 851706 01274 855169
Dir: *M62 eastbound between junct 25 & 26*
Fully refurbished, Days Inn offers well equipped, brightly appointed, modern accommodation with smart en suite bathrooms. There is a fully staffed reception; continental breakfast is available and other refreshments may be taken at the nearby family restaurant.
ROOMS: 38 en suite d fr £45 *

HARVINGTON (NEAR EVESHAM), Worcestershire Map 04 SP04

★★ 80% The Mill At Harvington

Anchor Ln, Harvington WR11 5NR
☎ 01386 870688 01386 870688
Dir: *Harvington is 4m NE of Evesham. The hotel is on the banks of the Avon, reached by a bridge over the new A46 and not in village*

A former Georgian house and mill in extensive grounds on the banks of the River Avon. The comfortable lounge has fine views; there is a conservatory bar and elegant restaurant; cuisine is of a high standard. Bedrooms are generally spacious and thoughtfully equipped.

ROOMS: 15 en suite 6 annexe en suite s £63-£75; d £89-£125 (incl. bkfst) * LB **FACILITIES:** Outdoor swimming (H) Fishing Croquet lawn **PARKING:** 50 **NOTES:** No dogs (ex guide dogs) No children 10yrs No smoking in restaurant Closed 24-27 Dec
CARDS:

HARWICH, Essex Map 05 TM23

★★★ 70% The Pier at Harwich

The Quay CO12 3HH
☎ 01255 241212 01255 551922
e-mail: leslie@thepieratharwich.co.uk
Dir: *from A12, take A120 to the Quay, hotel is opposite the Lifeboat Station*

Just across the road from the harbourside, most rooms at this lovely hotel offer a sea view. The Harbourside Restaurant specialises in seafood and currently holds two AA rosettes. There is also a second, less formal, bistro-style restaurant and an attractive modern bar.

ROOMS: 6 en suite 7 annexe en suite (3 fmly) s £67.50-£100; d £90-£150 (incl. cont bkfst) * **FACILITIES:** STV **CONF:** Thtr 50 Class 50 Board 24 **PARKING:** 10 **NOTES:** No dogs (ex guide dogs) Civ Wed
CARDS:

★★ 64% Cliff

Marine Pde, Dovercourt CO12 3RE
☎ 01255 503345 & 507373 01255 240358
Dir: *A120 to Parkeston rdbt, take road to Dovercourt, on seafront after Dovercourt town centre*

In a central position on the cliff overlooking Dovercourt Bay, this hotel is within five minutes' drive of the ferry terminals and railway station. There is a lounge, restaurant and two bars: the Marine with its sea views, or the more 'youthful' Shade Bar. Bedrooms vary in style and size but are modern and offer a good range of facilities.

ROOMS: 26 en suite (3 fmly) No smoking in 1 bedroom s £50; d £60 (incl. bkfst) * LB **FACILITIES:** STV Pool table **CONF:** Thtr 200 Class 150 Board 40 Del from £78.50 * **PARKING:** 50 **NOTES:** RS Xmas & New Year **CARDS:**

HARWICH, continued

★★63% Hotel Continental
28/29 Marine Pde, Dovercourt CO12 3RG
☎ 01255 551298 01255 551698
e-mail: hotconti@aol.com
Dir: *turn off A120 at Ramsay rdbt onto B1352 continue until reaching a pedestrain crossing & Co-op store on right, turn right here into Fronks Rd*

This hotel benefits from its seafront location and easy access to ferry terminals. Many of the comfortable rooms have sea views; some feature innovative decorative touches such as round glass sinks. The bar is popular with residents and locals alike. There is also a comfortable non-smoking residents lounge.
ROOMS: 13 en suite (2 fmly) No smoking in 1 bedroom s fr £30; d fr £60 (incl. bkfst) * LB **FACILITIES:** STV **CONF:** Thtr 30 Board 20 **PARKING:** 4 **NOTES:** No smoking in restaurant
CARDS:

HASLEMERE, Surrey Map 04 SU93

★★★★65% Lythe Hill
Petworth Rd GU27 3BQ
☎ 01428 651251 01428 644131
e-mail: lythe@lythehill.co.uk
Dir: *turn left from Haslemere High St onto B2131. Lythe Hill 1.25m on right*

Set in 20 acres of grounds including a bluebell wood and several lakes, this hotel is a cluster of 15th-century buildings. Many of the individually styled bedrooms are designed around the original features. There are separate garden suites and five rooms in the original timbered house with its jetted upper storey. There are two restaurants and the oak-panelled Auberge de France serves consistently rewarding cuisine.
ROOMS: 41 en suite (8 fmly) s £98-£225; d £120-£225 * LB **FACILITIES:** STV Tennis (hard) Fishing Pool table Croquet lawn Boules Games Room Xmas **CONF:** Thtr 60 Class 40 Board 30 Del from £108 * **PARKING:** 202 **NOTES:** No smoking in restaurant Civ Wed 128
CARDS:

HASTINGS & ST LEONARDS, East Sussex Map 05 TQ80

★★★69% Beauport Park
Battle Rd TN38 8EA
☎ 01424 851222 01424 852465
e-mail: reservations@beauportparkhotel.demon.co.uk
Dir: *3m N off A2100*

An elegant Georgian manor house set in 40 acres just outside Hastings. The bedrooms are tastefully decorated and well equipped. Public rooms convey much of the original character of the building and the Garden restaurant offers an extensive range of dishes.
ROOMS: 25 en suite (2 fmly) No smoking in 11 bedrooms s £88; d £115 (incl. bkfst) * LB **FACILITIES:** STV Outdoor swimming (H) Golf 18 Tennis (hard) Riding Croquet lawn Putting green entertainment Xmas **CONF:** Thtr 70 Class 25 Board 30 Del from £105 * **PARKING:** 60 **NOTES:** No smoking in restaurant Civ Wed 65
CARDS:

See advert on opposite page

★★★66% Cinque Ports Hotel
Bohemia Rd TN34 1ET
☎ 01424 439222 01424 437277
e-mail: enquires@cinqueports.co.uk
Dir: *follow A21 into Hastings as far as Police HQ and courts on left. Hotel next left before ambulance HQ*
This popular and conveniently situated hotel offers smart modern bedrooms and comfortable public areas. The bar and foyer areas have real log fires, tapestry wall hangings, stone floors and attractive oriental rugs. There is all-day room service, including early morning tea.
ROOMS: 40 en suite (4 fmly) No smoking in 6 bedrooms s £50-£60; d £70-£80 (incl. bkfst) * LB **FACILITIES:** STV Pool table Free swimming at next door leisure centre Xmas **CONF:** Thtr 200 Class 130 Board 60 Del from £60 * **PARKING:** 80 **CARDS:**

★★★65% High Beech
Battle Rd TN37 7BS
☎ 01424 851383 01424 854265
Dir: *400yds from A2100 between Hastings and Battle*
Bedrooms at this privately-owned hotel are generally of a good size and come with complimentary wine and fresh fruit. The Mountbatten Bar doubles as the lounge area and the attractive Wedgwood Restaurant serves a good cooked breakfast. Self-catering suites are available.

continued

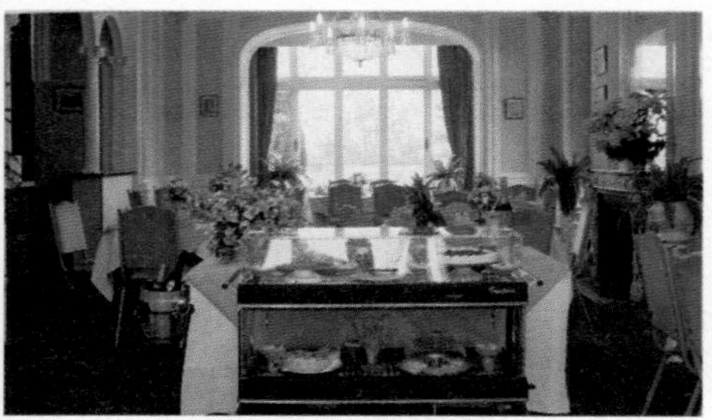

ROOMS: 17 en suite (3 fmly) s fr £55; d £85-£95 (incl. bkfst) * LB **FACILITIES:** STV Xmas **CONF:** Thtr 250 Class 192 Board 146 Del from £65 * **PARKING:** 65 **NOTES:** No dogs (ex guide dogs)
CARDS: 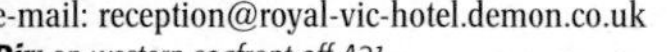

See advert on this page

★★★64% ***Royal Victoria***

Marina, St Leonards-on-Sea TN38 0BD
☎ 01424 445544 📠 01424 721995
e-mail: reception@royal-vic-hotel.demon.co.uk
Dir: *on western seafront off A21*

Purpose built as a hotel in 1828, and numbering the eponymous Queen among its famous guests, the Royal Victoria is an imposing presence on the seafront at St Leonards. A fine marble staircase leads up from the lobby to the main public areas on the first floor which are gradually being refurbished. Bedrooms are unusually spacious and include a number of duplex and family suites. Staff are attentive and friendly.

continued

HASTINGS & ST LEONARDS, continued

Royal Victoria, Hastings & St Leonards

ROOMS: 50 en suite (15 fmly) **FACILITIES:** entertainment **CONF:** Thtr 100 Class 50 Board 250 **SERVICES:** Lift **PARKING:** 6 **NOTES:** No smoking in restaurant **CARDS:**

See advert on page 249

HATFIELD, Hertfordshire Map 04 TL20

★★★64% Quality Hotel Hatfield

Roehyde Way AL10 9AF
☎ 01707 275701 01707 266033
e-mail: admin@gb059.u-net.com
Dir: *M25 junct 23 take A1(M) northbound to junct 2, at rdbt take exit left, hotel in 0.5m on right*

CHOICE HOTELS EUROPE

This is a modern hotel with a strong business market, located within minutes of the A1(M). Well equipped rooms feature extras such as trouser presses and modem access. Executive rooms are more spacious. There is 24-hour room service and guests can dine in the bar/brasserie or main restaurant.

ROOMS: 76 en suite (14 fmly) No smoking in 39 bedrooms s £80-£101; d £95-£111 * **FACILITIES:** STV Xmas **CONF:** Thtr 120 Class 60 Board 50 Del from £105 * **PARKING:** 120 **NOTES:** No smoking in restaurant **CARDS:**

HATHERSAGE, Derbyshire Map 08 SK28

★★★70% The George at Hathersage

Main Rd S32 1BB
☎ 01433 650436 01433 650099
e-mail: info@george-hotel.net
Dir: *in village centre on A625 from Sheffield*

The George is a relaxing historic hostelry in the heart of this picturesque town. The beamed bar lounge has much character, and the partitioned restaurant is full of antique charm. Upstairs the decor is simpler with lots of light hues; the split-level and four-poster rooms are especially appealing.

ROOMS: 19 en suite (2 fmly) s £69.50-£79.50; d £99.50-£119.50 (incl. bkfst) * LB **CONF:** Thtr 30 Class 15 Board 20 Del from £115 * **PARKING:** 40 **NOTES:** No dogs (ex guide dogs) No smoking in restaurant **CARDS:**

★★★66% *Hathersage Inn*

Main Rd S32 1BB
☎ 01433 650259 01433 651199
Dir: *in village centre on A625*

Best Western

A 200 year old stone built inn situated in the centre of the village with well equipped bedrooms, including some with four poster beds. Ground floor rooms are available in Morley Lodge, next door. A feature of the hotel is its smart and recently refurbished restaurant in which Head Chef Simon Hollings provides an imaginative range of delectable dishes well worthy of the One Rosette award. The Cricketers Bar, which offers real ale, is popular with locals and visitors alike and staff throughout are attentive.

ROOMS: 11 en suite 4 annexe en suite **CONF:** Thtr 18 Class 12 Board 12 **PARKING:** 20 **CARDS:**

HAWES, North Yorkshire Map 07 SD88

★★73% Simonstone Hall

Simonstone DL8 3LY
☎ 01969 667255 01969 667741
e-mail: simonstonehall@demon.co.uk
Dir: *1.5m N on road signed to Muker and Buttertubs*

This former hunting lodge provides professional, friendly service in a relaxed atmosphere. There is an inviting drawing room, stylish restaurant and character bar serving value-for-money pub food. Bedrooms reflect the style of the house and are generally spacious. The creative dinner menu makes excellent use of local game, fish and delicious cheeses.

ROOMS: 18 en suite (10 fmly) No smoking in all bedrooms s £45-£80; d £90-£160 (incl. bkfst) * LB **FACILITIES:** Fishing Xmas **CONF:** Thtr 30 Class 20 Board 20 Del from £130 * **PARKING:** 40 **NOTES:** No smoking in restaurant Civ Wed 120 **CARDS:**

★★71% Stone House

Sedbusk DL8 3PT
☎ 01969 667571 01969 667720
e-mail: daleshotel@aol.com
Dir: *from Hawes take road signposted 'Muker & The Buttertubs' to T-junct then right towards Sedbusk & Askrigg. Hotel 500yds on left*

With panoramic views across luscious green fields, this stylish Edwardian hotel retains the charm and character of a bygone age. Carefully prepared Yorkshire dinners are served each evening in the restaurant. Bedrooms are well equipped and attractively furnished.

ROOMS: 18 rms (17 en suite) 4 annexe en suite (1 fmly) No smoking in all bedrooms s £38-£89; d £66-£89 (incl. bkfst) * LB
FACILITIES: Tennis (grass) Croquet lawn Billiards table Xmas
CONF: Thtr 35 Class 35 Board 35 **PARKING:** 30 **NOTES:** No smoking in restaurant Closed Jan RS mid Nov-Dec & Feb
CARDS:

HAWKHURST, Kent Map 05 TQ73

★★★70% Tudor Court

Rye Rd TN18 5DA
☎ 01580 752312 01580 753966
e-mail: tudor-court@kentindex.com
Dir: *approx 1m from Hawkhurst on the Rye A268 road*

This welcoming small hotel offers comfortably furnished bedrooms equipped with modern facilities. The public areas include bars, a comfortable lounge and an attractive restaurant

continued

overlooking the garden, children's play area, croquet lawn, clock golf and hard tennis courts.
ROOMS: 18 en suite (2 fmly) No smoking in 2 bedrooms s £40-£65; d £60-£80 (incl. bkfst) * LB **FACILITIES:** Tennis (hard) Croquet lawn Putting green Clock golf Childrens play area Xmas **CONF:** Thtr 60 Class 40 Board 32 Del £75 * **PARKING:** 50 **NOTES:** No dogs (ex guide dogs) No smoking in restaurant **CARDS:**

HAWKSHEAD (NEAR AMBLESIDE), Cumbria Map 07 SD39

★★75% Highfield House Country Hotel

Hawkshead Hill LA22 0PN
☎ 015394 36344 015394 36793
e-mail: Highfield.Hawkshead@btinternet.com
Dir: *on B5285 towards Coniston three quarters of a mile from Hawkshead village*
This comfortable country house hotel enjoys one of the most stunning panoramas in the Lake District, across rolling hills and valleys. Bedrooms, which combine both the traditional and the contemporary, enjoy these views. Inviting day rooms include a lounge, cosy bar and cheerful dining room, serving good food and excellent breakfasts.
ROOMS: 11 en suite (2 fmly) No smoking in 1 bedroom s £44; d £84-£95 (incl. bkfst) * LB **FACILITIES:** ch fac **PARKING:** 15 **NOTES:** No smoking in restaurant Closed 20-27 Dec & 3-31 Jan
CARDS:

★★66% *Queen's Head*

Main St LA22 0NS
☎ 015394 36271 015394 36722
Dir: *leave M6 at junct 36, then A590 to Newby Bridge. Take 2nd right and continue 8m into Hawkshead*

This 16th-century inn features a wood-pannelled bar with low, oak-beamed ceilings and an open log fire. Substantial, carefully prepared meals are served in the bar and in the pretty dining room. The bedrooms, three of which are in an adjacent cottage, are attractively furnished and include some four-poster rooms.
ROOMS: 10 rms (8 en suite) 3 annexe en suite (2 fmly) No smoking in all bedrooms **NOTES:** No dogs (ex guide dogs) No smoking in restaurant
CARDS:

See advert on this page

HAWORTH, West Yorkshire Map 07 SE03

★★66% Old White Lion

6 West Ln BD22 8DU
☎ 01535 642313 01535 646222
e-mail: enquires@oldwhitelionhotel.com
Dir: *turn off A629 onto B6142, hotel 0.5m past Haworth Station*
Almost 300 years old, this historic hotel is situated at the top of an old cobbled street. There is a choice of bars, in addition to the oak-panelled lounge, serving a range of snacks and meals. More formal dining is available in the popular restaurant. Comfortably furnished bedrooms vary in size and style.

continued

ROOMS: 15 en suite (3 fmly) s fr £46; d fr £62 (incl. bkfst) * LB **FACILITIES:** Xmas **CONF:** Thtr 70 Class 40 Board 30 **PARKING:** 10 **NOTES:** No dogs (ex guide dogs) **CARDS:**

See advert under BRADFORD

★★65% Three Sisters

Brow Top Rd BD22 9PH
☎ 01535 643458 01535 646842
Dir: *from A629 Keighley/Halifax road take B6144 at Flappit Corner. Hotel 0.75m on right*
Once a Victorian farmhouse, this popular hotel and inn now offers modern, spacious bedrooms. A wide selection of freshly prepared meals and snacks is served, in generous portions, in either the bar or the restaurant, which enjoys fine views over Haworth and the surrounding area.

continued

HAWORTH, continued

ROOMS: 9 en suite (1 fmly) s £33-£38; d £45-£50 (incl. bkfst) * LB **FACILITIES:** STV Pool table entertainment Xmas **CONF:** Thtr 250 Class 200 Board 100 Del £55 * **PARKING:** 300 **NOTES:** No dogs (ex guide dogs) No smoking in restaurant **CARDS:**

HAYDOCK, Merseyside Map 07 SJ59

★★★66% ***Posthouse Haydock***
Lodge Ln WA12 0JG
☎ 0870 400 9039 🖷 01942 718419
Dir: *adj to M6 junct 23, on A49*

Posthouse

A modern hotel, convenient for the M6 and Haydock Park racecourse. Comfortable bedrooms, with 24-hour room service, are well appointed and public areas, including the popular Seasons restaurant, are similarly relaxing. There is an excellent leisure club. An all-day menu is served in the lounge.
ROOMS: 138 en suite (41 fmly) No smoking in 74 bedrooms **FACILITIES:** Indoor swimming (H) Sauna Solarium Gym Pool table Jacuzzi/spa ch fac **CONF:** Thtr 180 Class 100 Board 60 **SERVICES:** Lift **PARKING:** 197 **CARDS:**

H

⌂ ***Travelodge***
Piele Rd WA11 9TL
☎ 01942 272055 🖷 01942 272055
Dir: *2m W of junct 23 on M6, on A580 westbound*

Travelodge

This modern building offers accommodation in smart, spacious and well equipped bedrooms, all with en suite bathrooms. Refreshments may be taken at the nearby family restaurant. For further details and the Travelodge phone number, consult the Hotel Groups page.
ROOMS: 40 en suite

HAYES Hotels are listed under Heathrow Airport

HAYLING ISLAND, Hampshire Map 04 SU70

★★★63% ***Posthouse Havant***
Northney Rd PO11 0NQ
☎ 0870 400 9038 🖷 023 9246 6468
Dir: *from A27 signposted Havant/Hayling Island follow A3023 across roadbridge onto Hayling Island and take sharp left on leaving bridge*
This purpose-built hotel, just south of the A27, overlooks Langstone harbour. Bedrooms are well equipped and benefit from 24-hour room service. The refurbished leisure centre includes a pool, steam room and gym.
ROOMS: 92 en suite (10 fmly) No smoking in 44 bedrooms **FACILITIES:** Indoor swimming (H) Sauna Gym Pool table Jacuzzi/spa Massage & beauty therapy, Steam Room **CONF:** Thtr 180 Class 80 Board 50 **PARKING:** 150 **NOTES:** No smoking in restaurant
CARDS:

HAYTOR VALE, Devon Map 03 SX77

★★★78% ❀ **Bel Alp House**
TQ13 9XX
☎ 01364 661217 🖷 01364 661292
Dir: *2.5m W of Bovey Tracey, A38 onto A382*
This delightful Edwardian house offers spacious, well equipped bedrooms and has outstanding views of Dartmoor. Stained glass windows and open fires are features of the public rooms, and the set six-course dinner should not be missed.
ROOMS: 8 en suite (2 fmly) No smoking in 1 bedroom s £60-£75; d £120-£150 (incl. bkfst) * **FACILITIES:** Snooker Croquet lawn **PARKING:** 20 **NOTES:** No smoking in restaurant
CARDS:

★★74% ❀ **Rock Inn**
TQ13 9XP
☎ 01364 661305 & 661465 🖷 01364 661242
e-mail: rockinn@eclipse.co.uk
Dir: *turn off A38 onto A382 to Bovey Tracey, approx 0.5m turn left and join B3387 to Haytor*
Set in a pretty hamlet on the edge of Dartmoor, the Rock Inn has been a coaching inn since 1750. Individually decorated bedrooms have good facilities and some nice extra touches; each is named after a Grand National winner. A wide range of dishes is served in a variety of dining areas. The bars are full of character, with flagstone floors and old beams.
ROOMS: 9 en suite (2 fmly) No smoking in 2 bedrooms s £50.50-£60; d £66.95 (incl. bkfst) * LB **FACILITIES:** STV **PARKING:** 20 **NOTES:** No dogs (ex guide dogs) No smoking in restaurant Closed 25-26 Dec
CARDS:

HEATHROW AIRPORT (LONDON), Greater London Map 04 TQ07
see also Slough & Staines

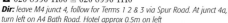

★★★★76% ❀❀ **London Heathrow Marriott Hotel**
Bath Rd UB3 5AN
☎ 020 8990 1100 🖷 020 8990 1110
Dir: *leave M4 junct 4, follow for Terms 1 2 & 3 via Spur Road. At junct 4a, turn left on A4 Bath Road. Hotel approx 0.5m on left*

Marriott HOTELS · RESORTS · SUITES

This smart hotel meets all expectations of a modern airport hotel. The spacious atrium offers several eating and drinking options, including the excellent Tuscany restaurant. Spacious bedrooms are very well sound-proofed and feature many useful amenities. The hotel has secure car parking space.
ROOMS: 390 en suite (20 fmly) No smoking in 320 bedrooms d £125-£205 * LB **FACILITIES:** STV Indoor swimming (H) Sauna Solarium Gym Jacuzzi/spa Steam Room **CONF:** Thtr 540 Class 214 Board 50 Del from £175 * **SERVICES:** Lift air con **PARKING:** 290
CARDS:

★★★★75% ❀ **Crowne Plaza London - Heathrow**
Stockley Rd UB7 9NA
☎ 01895 445555 🖷 01895 445122
e-mail: cplhr@netscapeonline.co.uk
Dir: *leave M4 junct 4 follow signs to Uxbridge on A408, hotel entrance approx 400yds on left*

CROWNE PLAZA HOTELS & RESORTS

This modern hotel is conveniently located for access to Heathrow Airport and the motorway network. A very good range of facilities is available for guests including versatile conference and meeting rooms, golfing and a 24-hour leisure complex. Guests have the choice of two bars, both serving food, and two restaurants. Air-conditioned bedrooms are furnished and decorated to a high standard and feature a comprehensive range of extra facilities.
ROOMS: 458 en suite (220 fmly) No smoking in 187 bedrooms d fr £175 * LB **FACILITIES:** STV Indoor swimming (H) Golf 9 Sauna Solarium Gym Jacuzzi/spa Beauty therapy room Helipad Xmas **CONF:** Thtr 200 Class 120 Board 75 **SERVICES:** Lift air con **PARKING:** 410 **CARDS:**

★★★★70% ❀ **Sheraton Skyline**
Bath Rd UB3 5BP
☎ 020 8759 2535 🖷 020 8750 9150
e-mail: mary_casey@sheraton.com

Sheraton HOTELS & RESORTS

Dir: *leave M4 junct 4 for Heathrow, follow for Terminals 1,2 & 3. Before Airport entrance take slip road to left for 0.25m signed A4 Cen London*
Within easy access of all terminals, this hotel offers spacious, air-conditioned bedrooms and a freeform pool within a leafy atrium
continued

complex. Eating options include snacks in the lobby lounge, the popular sports bar or the more formal Colony Room restaurant which earns an AA Rosette. An extensive room service menu is also available.
ROOMS: 351 rms (343 en suite) (12 fmly) No smoking in 177 bedrooms s £85-£190; d £85-£200 * LB **FACILITIES:** STV Indoor swimming (H) Gym Xmas **CONF:** Thtr 380 Class 325 Board 16 Del from £175 * **SERVICES:** Lift air con **PARKING:** 300 **NOTES:** RS Restaurant closed Bank Holidays Civ Wed 360 **CARDS:**

★★★★68% Slough/Windsor Marriott
Ditton Rd, Langley SL3 8PT
☎ 01753 544244 01753 540272
Dir: *from junct 5 of M4/A4, follow 'Langley' signs and turn left at traffic lights into Ditton Road*
A busy commercial hotel, convenient for access to the local motorway network and Heathrow Airport. Bedrooms are spacious and well geared to the needs of the business traveller. The excellent range of facilities includes several meeting rooms, a shop and a well equipped leisure centre.
ROOMS: 380 en suite (149 fmly) No smoking in 231 bedrooms d £125-£175 * LB **FACILITIES:** STV Indoor swimming (H) Tennis (hard) Sauna Solarium Gym Beautician entertainment Xmas **CONF:** Thtr 300 Class 150 Board 10 Del from £165 * **SERVICES:** Lift air con **PARKING:** 600 **NOTES:** No dogs (ex guide dogs) **CARDS:**

★★★★67% *Forte Crest Heathrow*
Sipson Rd UB7 0JU
☎ 020 8759 2323 020 8897 8659
Dir: *M4 junct4, keep left, take first left into Holloway Lane, left at mini rdbt then immediately left through hotel gates*
This modern hotel is the largest in the Heathrow area, catering well for the needs of the international traveller. Facilities include several meeting rooms, four restaurants, two bars and business services. There is a range of bedroom types, all equipped with useful extras.
ROOMS: 610 en suite (284 fmly) No smoking in 359 bedrooms **FACILITIES:** STV **CONF:** Thtr 130 Class 60 Board 60 **SERVICES:** Lift **PARKING:** 478 **NOTES:** No dogs (ex guide dogs)
CARDS:

★★★★65% The Renaissance London Heathrow Hotel

Bath Rd TW6 2AQ
☎ 020 8897 6363 020 8897 1113
e-mail: 106047.3556@compuserve.com
Dir: *leave M4 junct 4 follow spur road towards airport, take 2nd turning left & follow road to rdbt take 2nd exit, signposted 'Renaissance Hotel'*
This large, busy hotel is well placed and offers views of one of Heathrow's main runways. Air-conditioned bedrooms are steadily being upgraded through a major refurbishment programme. There is a wide range of conference facilities and a new club lounge.
ROOMS: 649 en suite No smoking in 168 bedrooms d £98-£149 * LB **FACILITIES:** STV Sauna Solarium Gym Steam Room Dance Studio entertainment Xmas **CONF:** Thtr 450 Class 280 Board 60 Del from £185 * **SERVICES:** Lift air con **PARKING:** 675 **NOTES:** No dogs (ex guide dogs) Civ Wed 400 **CARDS:**

★★★★62% Le Meridien Excelsior
Bath Rd UB7 0DU
☎ 0870 400 8899 020 8759 3421
e-mail: excelsior@lemeridien.co.uk
Dir: *adjacent to M4 spur at junct with A4*
This convenient, large corporate hotel offers a wide range of facilities including two bars, two restaurants, a health club and hotel shop. Bedrooms vary - Crown Club rooms in particular are of a high standard and offer added extras such as free airport transfers.
ROOMS: 537 en suite (43 fmly) No smoking in 259 bedrooms d fr £141 * LB **FACILITIES:** STV Indoor swimming (H) Sauna Solarium Gym Jacuzzi/spa Xmas **CONF:** Thtr 700 Class 310 Board 60 Del from £169 * **SERVICES:** Lift air con **PARKING:** 500 **NOTES:** No dogs (ex guide dogs) Civ Wed **CARDS:**

★★★70% Novotel

Junction 4 M4, Cherry Ln UB7 9HB
☎ 01895 431431 01895 431221
e-mail: h1551@accor-hotels.com
Dir: *leave M4 junct 4 follow signs for Uxbridge(A408), keep left & take 2nd exit off traffic island into Cherry Ln signed West Drayton. Hotel on left*
This modern hotel is conveniently located for the airport and motorway network. Bedrooms feature a good range of the latest facilities, such as game TV. The huge indoor atrium is stunning and creates a sense of space in the public areas, which include a cocktail bar, meeting rooms, fitness centre and indoor swimming pool.
ROOMS: 178 en suite (34 fmly) No smoking in 112 bedrooms d £112 * LB **FACILITIES:** STV Indoor swimming (H) Gym **CONF:** Thtr 250 Class 100 Board 90 Del from £149 * **SERVICES:** Lift **PARKING:** 150 **CARDS:**

H

★★★68% *Posthouse Heathrow Airport*
118 Bath Rd UB3 5AJ
☎ 0870 400 9040 020 8564 9265
Dir: *leave M4 junct 4, take spur road to Heathrow Airport, 1st left off towards A4, on to A4 Bath Road, through 3 traffic lights, hotel on left*
This hotel benefits from an extensive refurbishment programme. The bar/lounge and Rotisserie Restaurant are particularly smart and well appointed, as are the new Millennium rooms. For the conference delegate, the Academy meeting rooms fulfil a range of needs.
ROOMS: 186 en suite No smoking in 100 bedrooms **CONF:** Thtr 50 Class 20 Board 24 **SERVICES:** Lift air con **PARKING:** 105 **NOTES:** No dogs (ex guide dogs) **CARDS:**

★★★65% *Master Robert*
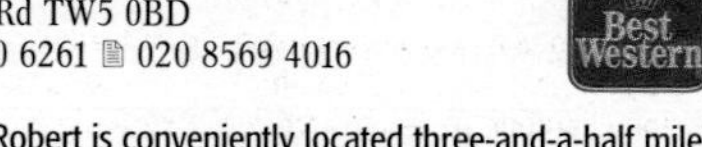
Great West Rd TW5 0BD
☎ 020 8570 6261 020 8569 4016
Dir: *A4*
The Master Robert is conveniently located three-and-a-half miles from Heathrow on the A4 towards London. The well equipped bedrooms are modern in style and are set in motel-style buildings behind the main hotel. There is a residents' lounge bar, a restaurant and a popular pub.
ROOMS: 94 en suite (8 fmly) No smoking in 33 bedrooms **FACILITIES:** STV **CONF:** Thtr 130 Class 48 Board 40 **PARKING:** 135 **NOTES:** No dogs (ex guide dogs) **CARDS:**

★★★65% Osterley Four Pillars Hotel

764 Great West Rd TW7 5NA
☎ 020 8568 9981 020 8569 7819
e-mail: enquires@four-pillars.co.uk
(For full entry see Osterley)

Fancy a Singapore Sling? Bar staff in five star hotels should be skilled cocktail mixers.

HEATHROW AIRPORT, continued

Hotel Ibis

112/114 Bath Rd UB3 5AL
☎ 020 8759 4888 020 8564 7894
e-mail: H0794@accor-hotels.com
Dir: *follow signs for Heathrow terminals 1,2,3. Take the spur road, turn off at sign for A4 Central London, hotel 0.5m on left*
Modern, budget hotel offering comfortable accommodation in bright and practical bedrooms. Breakfast is self-service and dinner is available in the restaurant. For further details, consult the Hotel Groups page.
ROOMS: 354 en suite (incl. cont bkfst) s £67.25; d £72.50 *

HEBDEN BRIDGE, West Yorkshire Map 07 SD92

★★★ 66% Carlton

Albert St HX7 8ES
☎ 01422 844400 01422 843117
e-mail: ctonhotel@aol.com
Dir: *turn right at cinema for hotel at top of Hope St*
Formerly the general store of Hebden Bridge, a collection of shops remains on the ground floor of this Victorian building. Individually designed bedrooms are attractively furnished, whilst public areas are peaceful and comfortable. Diners can choose between snacks served in the bar or more extensive meals in the dining room.
ROOMS: 16 en suite s £56-£67; d £75-£85 (incl. bkfst) * LB
FACILITIES: STV **CONF:** Thtr 120 Class 40 Board 40 Del from £90 *
SERVICES: Lift **NOTES:** No smoking in restaurant Civ Wed 90
CARDS:

★★ 68% Hebden Lodge Hotel

6-10 New Rd HX7 8AD
☎ 01422 845272 01422 842959
Dir: *on A646 opposite Hebden Bridge Marina*
Opposite the Rochdale canal marina, this hospitable, family-owned hotel offers a range of bedrooms equipped with all modern facilities. Restyled public rooms are light and modern. Square One Café-bar and Bistro serves modern cuisine, ranging from light snacks and tapas to a full carte menu. Staff are friendly and attentive.
ROOMS: 13 en suite (1 fmly) No smoking in 9 bedrooms s £25-£35; d £50 (incl. bkfst) * LB **FACILITIES:** Xmas **NOTES:** No dogs (ex guide dogs) No smoking in restaurant **CARDS:**

HECKFIELD, Hampshire Map 04 SU76

★★ 68% New Inn

RG27 0LE
☎ 0118 932 6374 0118 932 6550
Dir: *turn off A33 onto B3349, turn right at island and continue on B3349 to hotel 0.5m on left*
Partly dating back to the 15th century, this well maintained inn is within easy reach of major business centres. It features low, beamed ceilings and two roaring log fires in the bar which create a cosy atmosphere. Bedrooms are spacious, well equipped and comfortable.
ROOMS: 16 en suite (1 fmly) s £70; d £80 (incl. bkfst) * LB
FACILITIES: STV **CONF:** Thtr 25 Class 14 Board 16 Del from £85 *
PARKING: 80 **NOTES:** Closed 25 Dec Civ Wed
CARDS:

TV dinner? Room service at three stars and above.

HEDDON'S MOUTH, Devon Map 03 SS64

★★ 76% Heddon's Gate Hotel

EX31 4PZ
☎ 01598 763313 01598 763363
e-mail: info@hgate.co.uk
Dir: *3.5m W of Lynton on A39 turn R, signs Martinhoe & Woody Bay. Follow signs for Hunter's Inn & Heddon's Mouth, hotel on R 0.25m before Hunter's Inn*

Breathtaking countryside surrounds this friendly hotel, which takes great pride in the quality of its food - do not miss afternoon tea. Bedrooms are individually designed and comfortable day rooms include a bar, a Victorian morning room/library and an Edwardian sitting room with superb views.
ROOMS: 11 en suite 3 annexe en suite **PARKING:** 20 **NOTES:** No children No smoking in restaurant Closed Nov-Etr
CARDS:

See advert on opposite page

HELLIDON, Northamptonshire Map 04 SP55

★★★★ 69% Hellidon Lakes Hotel & Country Club

NN11 6GG
☎ 01327 262550 01327 262559
e-mail: stay@hellidon.demon.co.uk
Dir: *signposted, off A361 between Daventry and Banbury*
Set in grounds including 12 lakes and an 18-and nine-hole golf course, this hotel offers spacious, well equipped bedrooms furnished in striking tulip wood. Facilities include a beauty salon and bowling alley. There are two restaurants, one serving modern British cuisine and the other, the spectacular new Four Seasons, showing great promise.
ROOMS: 71 en suite **FACILITIES:** STV Indoor swimming (H) Golf 27 Tennis (hard) Fishing Solarium Gym Putting green Jacuzzi/spa Beautician Ten Pin Bowling Golf simulator Steam room **CONF:** Thtr 150 Class 70 Board 50 **PARKING:** 140 **NOTES:** No dogs (ex guide dogs) No smoking in restaurant **CARDS:**

HELMSLEY, North Yorkshire Map 08 SE68

★★★ 75% The Black Swan

Market Place YO62 5BJ
☎ 0870 400 8112 01439 770174
e-mail: HeritageHotels_Helmsley.BlackSwan@Forte-hotels.com
Dir: *follow A170 towards Scarborough into Helmsley and hotel at top of Market Square*
In a prime position overlooking the square, the Black Swan is made up of a Tudor rectory, an Elizabethan coaching inn and a Georgian house. It offers attractively decorated and thoughtfully equipped accommodation. The many lounges are pleasant and comfortable.

continued

ROOMS: 45 en suite (4 fmly) No smoking in 13 bedrooms s £120-£135; d £145-£160 * LB **FACILITIES:** Croquet lawn Xmas **CONF:** Thtr 60 Class 16 Board 22 Del £135 * **PARKING:** 50 **NOTES:** No smoking in restaurant **CARDS:**

★★★70% **Feversham Arms**
High St YO62 5AG
☎ 01439 770766 📠 01439 770346
e-mail: recption@feversham-helmsley.fsnet.co.uk
Dir: take A168 'Thirsk' from A1 then A170. Alternative: Take A64 'York' from A1 to York North & then B1363 to Helmsley. Hotel 125mtrs from Mkt Pl

This well-furnished, comfortable hotel has been popular with guests for many years. Each summer a colourful display of roses adorns the façade. Both the restaurant and bar menus offer a good selection of dishes. The comfortable bedrooms are well equipped and hospitality is very good.
ROOMS: 18 en suite (4 fmly) s £55-£60; d £80-£90 (incl. bkfst) * LB **FACILITIES:** STV Outdoor swimming (H) Tennis (hard) **CONF:** Thtr 30 Class 30 Board 24 Del from £98 * **PARKING:** 30 **NOTES:** No smoking in restaurant **CARDS:**

★★★70% **Pheasant**
Harome YO62 5JG
☎ 01439 771241 📠 01439 771744
Dir: 2.5m SE, leave A170 after 0.25m, turn right signposted Harome for further 2m
Enjoying a charming setting next to the village pond, this welcoming hotel has attractive, comfortable bedrooms. The beamed, stone-flagged bar leads into the extended conservatory dining room, where wholesome English food is served. There is a comfortable lounge in which to relax.
ROOMS: 12 en suite 2 annexe en suite s £60-£66; d £120-£132 (incl. bkfst & dinner) * LB **FACILITIES:** Indoor swimming (H) **PARKING:** 20 **NOTES:** No children 12yrs No smoking in restaurant Closed Xmas & Jan-Feb **CARDS:**

★★68% **Carlton Lodge**
Bondgate YO62 5EY
☎ 01439 770557 📠 01439 770623
e-mail: carlton.lodge@dial.pipex.com
Dir: on the A170 Scarborough road, close to Market Sq
A friendly, welcoming hotel on the edge of the town and offering comfortable, well furnished bedrooms. Public areas include an inviting lounge with an open fire, and a well appointed dining room where good quality, home-cooked evening meals are served.
ROOMS: 7 rms (6 en suite) 4 annexe en suite (1 fmly) s £29.50-£40; d £55-£75 (incl. bkfst) * LB **FACILITIES:** Xmas **CONF:** Thtr 150 Class 0 Board 50 Del from £49.95 * **PARKING:** 45 **NOTES:** No smoking in restaurant Civ Wed 160 **CARDS:**

★★68% **Crown**
Market Square YO62 5BJ
☎ 01439 770297 📠 01439 771595
Dir: on A170
A 16th-century inn with lots of character, standing in the market square and noted for its colourful flower arrangements. Bedrooms are individual and thoughtfully equipped. Public areas are pleasantly traditional and include cosy bars, a residents' lounge and a dining room serving wholesome dishes in generous portions.
ROOMS: 12 en suite (1 fmly) s £30-£35; d £60-£70 (incl. bkfst) * LB **FACILITIES:** Xmas **PARKING:** 20 **CARDS:**

★★64% ***Feathers***
Market Place YO62 5BH
☎ 01439 770275 📠 01439 771101
Dir: in Helmsley market place on A170
This 15th-century, creeper-clad hotel and inn offers very pleasantly furnished and well equipped bedrooms. An extensive range of food is available in either the bar or the dining room. The bars are particularly popular, especially with the friendly locals.
ROOMS: 14 en suite **PARKING:** 24 **NOTES:** No dogs (ex guide dogs) No children 12yrs No smoking in restaurant
CARDS:

Early start? Hotels at all star levels should provide in-room alarm clocks and/or alarm calls.

H

HELSTON, Cornwall & Isles of Scilly Map 02 SW62

★★79% Nansloe Manor
Meneage Rd TR13 0SB
☎ 01326 574691 01326 564680
e-mail: info@nansloe.co.uk
Dir: *300yds on the left from Helston/Lizard roundabout A394/A3083*

Built in 1735, this grade II Georgian house is a haven of tranquillity and understated elegance, complemented by attentive, thoughtful service. Bedrooms retain character and are equipped with many personal touches, and the gracious lounge and dining room typify the high standards of presentation. The imaginative cuisine is a high priority. Guests can wander the grounds, which include a wonderful walled garden.
ROOMS: 7 rms (6 en suite) s £59-£80; d £110-£140 (incl. bkfst) * LB **FACILITIES:** Croquet lawn Xmas **PARKING:** 40 **NOTES:** No dogs No children 10yrs No smoking in restaurant **CARDS:**

★★66% The Gwealdues
Falmouth Rd TR13 8JX
☎ 01326 572808 01326 561388
e-mail: gwealdves@hotel44.freeserve.co.uk
Dir: *Hotel is on approach into Helston on A394, coming from Truro or Falmouth*
On the outskirts of town, this friendly hotel is much in demand for its smart function room. Most bedrooms offer modern accommodation and many useful facilities, in addition to complimentary newspapers. Guests can choose from the main menu in the homely dining room or sample one of the many bar snacks.
ROOMS: 17 en suite (5 fmly) s £35-£45; d £50-£60 (incl. bkfst) * LB **CONF:** Board 100 **PARKING:** 60 **NOTES:** No smoking in restaurant
CARDS:

HEMEL HEMPSTEAD, Hertfordshire Map 04 TL00

★★★66% *Posthouse Hemel Hempstead*
Posthouse
Breakspear Way HP2 4UA
☎ 0870 400 9041 01442 211812
Dir: *exit junct 8 of M1, straight over roundabout and 1st left after BP garage*
Within easy access of the motorway network, this modern hotel is well suited to its largely business clientele. The bedrooms are practically furnished and decorated, offering many in-room facilities. There is a well equipped health club and a range of meeting rooms.
ROOMS: 145 en suite (33 fmly) No smoking in 76 bedrooms **FACILITIES:** Indoor swimming (H) Sauna Solarium Gym Pool table Jacuzzi/spa Children's playroom/play area at weekends ch fac **CONF:** Thtr 60 Class 22 Board 30 **SERVICES:** Lift **PARKING:** 195
CARDS:

★★★64% Watermill
London Rd, Bourne End HP1 2RJ
☎ 01442 349955 01442 866130
e-mail: watermill@sarova.co.uk
Dir: *from M1 junct 8 or M25 junct 20 follow signs to & join A41 for Aylesbury then A4251 to Bourne End*
Built around a former flour mill adjacent to the Grand Union Canal, the Watermill is a peaceful countryside retreat. The various annexe wings feature modern, well equipped rooms, some overlooking the river. A large bar with superb river views serves snacks throughout the day.
ROOMS: 75 annexe en suite (9 fmly) No smoking in 26 bedrooms s fr £90; d fr £99 * LB **FACILITIES:** STV Fishing **CONF:** Thtr 100 Class 70 Board 48 Del from £139 * **PARKING:** 100 **NOTES:** No dogs (ex guide dogs) No smoking in restaurant Civ Wed 100
CARDS:

○ Boxmoor Lodge
London Rd HP1 2RA
☎ 01442 230770 01442 252230
Dir: *M25-A41 to Aylesbury,2nd exit for Boxmoor,follow signs for Boxmoor on A4251,hotel on right*
ROOMS: 23 en suite (3 fmly) No smoking in 10 bedrooms **FACILITIES:** STV **CONF:** Thtr 36 Class 15 Board 18 **PARKING:** 40 **NOTES:** No dogs (ex guide dogs) No smoking in restaurant Closed 25 Dec-4 Jan **CARDS:**

HENLEY-ON-THAMES, Oxfordshire Map 04 SU7
see also Stonor

★★★71% Red Lion
Hart St RG9 2AR
☎ 01491 572161 01491 410039
e-mail: reservations@redlionhenley.co.uk
Dir: *adjacent to Henley Bridge*
The front rooms of this 16th-century Thames-side hotel offer fabulous views of the river. Bedrooms and public areas retain original features such as wood panelling, flagstone floors and beams. Bedrooms, decorated to a high standard, feature period furniture. Beds are new and extremely comfortable.
ROOMS: 27 en suite (1 fmly) s £90-£115; d £130-£150 * **CONF:** Thtr 60 Class 20 Board 30 Del from £165 * **PARKING:** 25 **NOTES:** No do
CARDS:

HEREFORD, Herefordshire Map 03 SO5
see also Much Birch

★★★67% Three Counties Hotel
Belmont Rd HR2 7BP
☎ 01432 299955 01432 275114
e-mail: threecountieshotel@hotmail.com
Dir: *on A465 Abergavveny Rd*
A mile west of the city centre, this large, modern complex has we equipped, spacious bedrooms, many of which are located in separate single-storey buildings around the extensive car park. There is a spacious, comfortable lounge, a traditional bar and an attractive restaurant.
ROOMS: 28 en suite 32 annexe en suite (4 fmly) No smoking in 23 bedrooms s £37.50-£59.25; d £55-£74.50 (incl. bkfst) * LB **FACILITIES:** STV Xmas **CONF:** Thtr 300 Class 100 Board 60 Del from £75 * **PARKING:** 250 **NOTES:** Civ Wed
CARDS:

THE 'HOTEL OF THE YEAR' IS THE MOST ELEGANT HOTEL IN HEREFORD

In Castle House we set out to create a gracious and hospitable town mansion in the heart of the beautiful and historic city of Hereford, with quiet garden views over the tranquil moat and barely one hundred metres from the Cathedral and its world famous Chained Library and Mappa Mundi.

All the rooms are different with each one individually designed and furnished to create an atmosphere that's charming and hospitable.
Dining in the award winning restaurant is an experience not to be missed.
The menus are designed by internationally renowned chef, Stuart McLeod best known for his individual style of modern English cooking.

For further information and brochure contact us today

Castle House . Castle Street . Hereford . England . HR1 2NW
Tel: +44(0)1432 356321 . Fax: +44(0)1432 365909
Email: info@castlehse.co.uk

H

HEREFORD, continued

★★★64% *Graftonbury Garden Hotel*

Grafton Ln HR2 8BN
☎ 01432 268826 📠 01432 354633
Dir: *2m S of Hereford, 0.5m off A49 to Ross-on-Wye*

In a secluded location to the south of Hereford, this hotel is conveniently located for the city. It benefits from bright public areas, including a bar, lounge and bistro, as well as extensive function/ conference rooms. Bedrooms are comfortable and well equipped.
ROOMS: 25 en suite 4 annexe en suite (3 fmly)
FACILITIES: entertainment **CONF:** Thtr 150 Class 100 Board 80
PARKING: 100 **NOTES:** No smoking in restaurant
CARDS:

★★★63% The Green Dragon

Broad St HR4 9BG
☎ 0870 400 8113 📠 01432 352139
e-mail: HeritageHotels_HerefordGreenDragon@Forte-Hotels.com
Dir: *follow signs for Cathedral and Mappa Mundi to rdbt. First exit, then 2nd left into West St, then 2nd right into Aubrey St and hotel garage*
Close to the cathedral, this landmark hotel is on the one-way city-centre road system. Impressive public areas have the appealing charm of an elegant bygone era. The comfortable lounges are popular for leisurely afternoon tea, and there is a choice of bars, a large function room and a secure car park.
ROOMS: 83 en suite (22 fmly) No smoking in 29 bedrooms s £75; d fr £94 (incl. bkfst) * LB **FACILITIES:** N Xmas **CONF:** Thtr 200 Class 60 Board 40 Del from £92 * **SERVICES:** Lift **PARKING:** 110
CARDS:

★★★62% Belmont Lodge & Golf Course

Belmont HR2 9SA
☎ 01432 352666 📠 01432 358090
e-mail: info@belmontlodge.co.uk
Dir: *from city centre turn off A465 to Abergavenny into Ruckhall Lane, hotel located on right in approx 0.5m*
This hotel and golfing complex occupies a superb location above the River Wye. The modern, well equipped bedrooms are in a purpose-built lodge, and the restaurant and bar are located in the clubhouse, in the grade II listed Belmont House.
ROOMS: 30 en suite (4 fmly) No smoking in 15 bedrooms s fr £49.50; d fr £67.50 (incl. bkfst) * LB **FACILITIES:** Golf 18 Tennis (hard) Fishing Snooker Putting green Bowls Darts **CONF:** Thtr 60 Class 14 Board 25 Del from £67.50 * **PARKING:** 150 **NOTES:** Civ Wed
CARDS:

★★71% ❀❀ *Ancient Camp Inn*

Ruckhall HR2 9QX
☎ 01981 250449 📠 01981 251581
Dir: *A465, turn right to Belmont Abbey, 2.5m to hotel*
In a superb location above the River Wye enjoying stunning views, the inn is named after a nearby Iron Age fort. It features flagstone floors, exposed beams and real fires in the quaint bar and dining room. The well crafted cuisine is rustic in style and proving a genuine success.
ROOMS: 5 en suite (1 fmly) **FACILITIES:** Fishing **PARKING:** 30
NOTES: No dogs (ex guide dogs) No children 12 No smoking in restaurant Closed 1-14 Jan RS Mon **CARDS:**

★★63% Merton Hotel & Governors Restaurant

28 Commercial Rd HR1 2BD
☎ 01432 265925 📠 01432 354983
e-mail: sales@mertonhotel.co.uk
Dir: *on main A4103, close to rail station, opposite the cinema*
A privately-owned hotel close to the bus station (with its public car park) and in walking distance of the railway station. The modern bedrooms are well equipped; two have four-poster beds. The cosy lounge has real fires in cold weather. There is a pleasant restaurant and a lounge bar with adjacent eating area.
ROOMS: 19 en suite (2 fmly) s £45-£50; d £60-£65 (incl. bkfst) * LB
FACILITIES: Fishing Sauna Solarium Gym Shooting fishing (by arrangement) entertainment **CONF:** Thtr 30 Class 20 Board 20
PARKING: 4 **CARDS:**

Hotel of the Year

★★★★ ❀❀❀❀ Castle House

Castle St HR1 2NW
☎ 01432 356321 📠 01432 365909
e-mail: info@castlehse.co.uk
Dir: *follow signs for city centre & city centre east, pass town hall, where St Owen's St narrows turn sharp right twice into St Ethelbert St*
This riverside Victorian town mansion has been chosen as Hotel of the Year for England. Once the home of the Bishop of Hereford, the hotel provides superb accommodation and elegant public rooms of the highest quality. Excellent service is offered by welcoming, smartly attired staff. The restaurant serves some exceptionally good cuisine.
ROOMS: 15 en suite s £90-£210; d £155-£210 (incl. cont bkfst) * LB **FACILITIES:** STV Xmas **SERVICES:** Lift **PARKING:** 15
CARDS:

See advert on page 257

HERTFORD, Hertfordshire Map 04 TL31

★★★66% The White Horse

Hertingfordbury SG14 2LB
☎ 0870 400 8114 📠 01992 550809
e-mail: heritagehotelshertingfordbury.whitehorse @forte-hotels.com
Dir: *1m W of Hertford on A414*
Situated in a quaint village, this former coaching inn has a Georgian façade but a much older interior. Most of the

continued

comfortable bedrooms are in the modern extension and are attractively decorated. The restaurant looks onto a lovely garden, and the relaxing lounge features open beams.
ROOMS: 42 en suite No smoking in 14 bedrooms s £100; d £110 * LB **FACILITIES:** Xmas **CONF:** Thtr 60 Class 30 Board 30 Del £138 * **PARKING:** 60 **CARDS:**

HESTON MOTORWAY SERVICE AREA (M4), Greater London See LONDON SECTION plan 1 *A3*

Travelodge

Travelodge

Phoenix Way TW5 9NB
☎ 0800 850950 📠 01384 78578
Dir: *M4 junc 2&3 westbound*
This modern building offers accommodation in smart, spacious and well equipped bedrooms, all with en suite bathrooms. Refreshments may be taken at the nearby family restaurant. For further details and the Travelodge phone number, consult the Hotel Groups page.
ROOMS: 95 en suite

HETHERSETT, Norfolk — Map 05 TG10

★★★72% **Park Farm**

NR9 3DL
☎ 01603 810264 📠 01603 812104
e-mail: enq@parkfarm-hotel.co.uk
Dir: *5m S of Norwich, off A11 on B1172*

This attractive Georgian farmhouse sits in landscaped grounds at the end of a long lane. The public rooms have been restyled and look very smart. Bedrooms, available in the main house or garden wings, are thoughtfully equipped and most have rich colour schemes.
ROOMS: 6 en suite 42 annexe en suite (20 fmly) s £80-£105; d £110-£140 (incl. bkfst) * LB **FACILITIES:** Indoor swimming (H) Sauna Solarium Gym Jacuzzi/spa Beauty salon Hairdressing Xmas **CONF:** Thtr 120 Class 50 Board 50 Del £112.50 * **PARKING:** 151 **NOTES:** No dogs (ex guide dogs) No smoking in restaurant
CARDS:

See advert under NORWICH

HEVERSHAM, Cumbria — Map 07 SD48

★★★68% ***Blue Bell***

Prince's Way LA7 7EE
☎ 015395 62018 📠 015395 62455
Dir: *1m N of Milnthorpe, on A6*
This comfortable old Jacobean coaching inn provides well equipped, modern bedrooms. There is a spacious restaurant, cosy lounge and traditional bar complete with oak-beamed ceilings. The good range of skilfully prepared food includes afternoon tea and an early diners' menu. Staff throughout are considerate and obliging.
ROOMS: 21 en suite (4 fmly) **FACILITIES:** Pool table **CONF:** Thtr 85 Class 35 Board 25 **PARKING:** 100 **NOTES:** No smoking in restaurant
CARDS:

HEXHAM, Northumberland — Map 12 NY96

★★★★71% **De Vere Slaley Hall**

De Vere Hotels

Slaley NE47 0BY
☎ 01434 673350 📠 01434 673050
e-mail: slaley.hall@devere-hotels.com
Dir: *from the A69 take the A68 turn off towards Darlington. Slaley Hall is signposted all the way*
Superbly situated in 1000 acres which includes two championship golf courses, this smart hotel offers thoughtfully equipped air-conditioned bedrooms and suites. There is an excellent health spa and leisure club. The food served in Fairways Brasserie is well deserving of its Rosette award.
ROOMS: 139 en suite (23 fmly) No smoking in 17 bedrooms s £95-£125; d £150-£170 (incl. bkfst) * **FACILITIES:** STV Indoor swimming (H) Golf 18 Snooker Sauna Solarium Gym Jacuzzi/spa Quad bikes Honda pilots 4x4 driving Hot air ballooning Archery Clay shooting Xmas **CONF:** Thtr 250 Class 220 Board 150 Del from £125 * **SERVICES:** Lift air con **PARKING:** 500 **NOTES:** No smoking in restaurant
CARDS:

★★★69% **Langley Castle**

Langley on Tyne NE47 5LU
☎ 01434 688888 📠 01434 684019
e-mail: manager@langleycastle.com
Dir: *from A69 S on A686 for 2m. Castle on right*
Langley is a magnificent 14th-century fortified castle in ten acres of parkland. There is a restaurant, a comfortable drawing room and cosy bar. The bedrooms are furnished with period pieces and most feature window seats set into thick, exposed stone walls. Restored

continued

HEXHAM, continued

buildings in the grounds have been converted into very smart bedrooms.

Langley Castle, Hexham

ROOMS: 8 en suite 10 annexe en suite (4 fmly) s £89.50-£109.50; d £111-£165 (incl. bkfst) * LB **FACILITIES:** STV Xmas **CONF:** Thtr 100 Class 50 Board 30 Del from £135 * **PARKING:** 60 **NOTES:** No smoking in restaurant Civ Wed 120 **CARDS:**

See advert on page 259

★★★68% Beaumont

Beaumont St NE46 3LT
☎ 01434 602331 📠 01434 606184
e-mail: beaumont.hotel@btinternet.com
Dir: *on A69 towards Hexham*

The Beaumont overlooks the park in Hexham town centre. Its bright attractive bedrooms are well equipped. There are two bars, a relaxing foyer lounge and a first-floor restaurant featuring well presented, innovative dishes.
ROOMS: 25 en suite (3 fmly) No smoking in 18 bedrooms s £63-£73; d £92-£102 * LB **FACILITIES:** STV Snooker Solarium **CONF:** Thtr 100 Class 60 Board 40 Del from £69 * **SERVICES:** Lift **PARKING:** 8 **NOTES:** No dogs No smoking in restaurant Closed 25-26 Dec & 1 Jan **CARDS:**

See advert on opposite page

HICKSTEAD, West Sussex — Map 04 TQ22

★★★62% *The Hickstead Hotel*

Jobs Ln, Bolney RH17 5PA
☎ 01444 248023 📠 01444 245280
Dir: *0.25m E of A23 turn off at Hickstead village towards Burgess Hill*
Set in the heart of West Sussex this hotel enjoys a peaceful location not far from the A23. The bedrooms are modern in style and comfortably furnished. Lounge and bar areas are compact but the hotel benefits from an indoor leisure centre, conference rooms and ample car parking.

continued

ROOMS: 50 en suite (8 fmly) No smoking in 25 bedrooms **FACILITIES:** STV Indoor swimming (H) Sauna Solarium Gym Jacuzzi/spa **CONF:** Thtr 120 Class 60 Board 40 **PARKING:** 150 **NOTES:** No smoking in restaurant **CARDS:**

⌂ *Travelodge*

Travelodge

Jobs Ln RH17 5NX
☎ 01444 881377 📠 01444 881377
Dir: *A23 southbound*
This modern building offers accommodation in smart, spacious and well equipped bedrooms, all with en suite bathrooms. Refreshments may be taken at the nearby family restaurant. For further details and the Travelodge phone number, consult the Hotel Groups page.
ROOMS: 40 en suite

HIGHBRIDGE, Somerset — Map 03 ST34

★★62% Sundowner

74 Main Rd, West Huntspill TA9 3QU
☎ 01278 784766 📠 01278 794133
e-mail: runnalls@msn.com
Dir: *3m south on A38 from M5 junct 22 or 3m N on A38 from M5 junct 23*
The friendly service and informal atmosphere of this cosy hotel make the Sundowner a particularly pleasant place to stay. The open-plan lounge/bar is a comfortable area in which to relax, and an extensive menu is offered in the popular restaurant.
ROOMS: 8 en suite (1 fmly) s £40; d £54 (incl. bkfst) * **CONF:** Thtr 40 Board 24 Del from £59.95 * **PARKING:** 18 **NOTES:** No smoking in restaurant **CARDS:**

HIGHCLERE, Hampshire — Map 04 SU45

Premier Collection

★★★ Hollington Country House

Woolton Hill RG20 9XA
☎ 01635 255100 📠 01635 255075
e-mail: hollington.house@newbury.net
Dir: *take A343 from Newbury towards Andover, after 3m turn right & follow signs to hotel & Hollington Herb Garden*
This charming country house is a peaceful retreat. Public rooms are architecturally interesting and overlook the delightful gardens and parkland. Spacious bedrooms are decorated with taste and an eye for detail. The cuisine is of a high standard, and the fine wine list offers a superb Australian selection.
ROOMS: 20 en suite (1 fmly) No smoking in 2 bedrooms **FACILITIES:** Indoor swimming (H) Outdoor swimming (H) Tennis (hard) Snooker Pool table Croquet lawn Putting green Jacuzzi/spa Free bicycle hire **CONF:** Thtr 60 Class 25 Board 30 **SERVICES:** Lift **PARKING:** 39 **NOTES:** No dogs (ex guide dogs) No smoking in restaurant Civ Wed 50 **CARDS:**

HIGH WYCOMBE, Buckinghamshire Map 04 SU89

★★★66% *Posthouse High Wycombe*

Posthouse

Handy Cross HP11 1TL
☎ 0870 400 9042 🖷 01494 439071
Dir: *intersection of M40 and A4010*

A modern, purpose-built hotel, convenient for the motorway network. Bedrooms are spacious and well equipped for the business traveller, featuring a comprehensive range of extra facilities. Guests have a choice of eating options, including the Junction Restaurant and the more informal Mongolian Barbecue.

ROOMS: 106 en suite (4 fmly) No smoking in 55 bedrooms **FACILITIES:** Pool table **CONF:** Thtr 200 Class 100 Board 40 **PARKING:** 173 **NOTES:** No dogs (ex guide dogs) **CARDS:**

HILLINGTON, Norfolk Map 09 TF72

★★67% Ffolkes Arms

Lynn Rd PE31 6BJ
☎ 01485 600210 🖷 01485 601196
e-mail: ffolkespub@aol.com
Dir: *on main A148 turn right towards Cromer at roundabout hotel 6m along A148 at Hillington*

This popular 17th-century coaching inn, ideally situated for many of west Norfolk's attractions, has been sympathetically adapted. Facilities include a bar, restaurant and lounge area. The courtyard boasts a popular function suite and social club. The spacious bedrooms are situated in a modern wing.

ROOMS: 20 annexe en suite (2 fmly) No smoking in all bedrooms s £35-£50; d £50-£70 (incl. bkfst) * LB **FACILITIES:** Snooker Pool table Xmas **CONF:** Thtr 250 Class 80 Board 50 Del from £60 * **PARKING:** 200 **NOTES:** No dogs (ex guide dogs) No smoking in restaurant **CARDS:**

HILTON PARK MOTORWAY SERVICE AREA (M6), West Midlands Map 07 SJ90

⌂ *Travelodge*

Travelodge

Hilton Park Services (M6), Essington WV11 2DR
☎ Cen Res 0800 850950 🖷 01922 701967
Dir: *on M6 between juncts 10a & 11*

This modern building offers accommodation in smart, spacious and well equipped bedrooms, all with en suite bathrooms. Refreshments may be taken at the nearby family restaurant. For further details and the Travelodge phone number, consult the Hotel Groups page.

ROOMS: 64 en suite

HIMLEY, Staffordshire Map 07 SO89

★★★63% Himley Country Hotel

corus

School Rd DY3 4LG
☎ 01902 896716 🖷 01902 896668
Dir: *100yds off A449*

This modern hotel on the Shropshire border has been built around a 19th-century village schoolhouse. Bedrooms feature all modern comforts and the restaurant has a wide range of eating options, as well as a pleasant bar with open fire.

continued

ROOMS: 73 en suite (1 fmly) No smoking in 38 bedrooms s £60-£85; d £70-£95 * LB **FACILITIES:** STV entertainment **CONF:** Thtr 150 Class 80 Board 50 Del from £85 * **PARKING:** 100 **NOTES:** No smoking in restaurant **CARDS:**

★★65% *Himley House Hotel*

Scottish Newcastle hotels

Stourbridge Rd DY3 4LD
☎ 01902 892468 🖷 01902 892604
Dir: *on A449 N of Stourbridge*

Dating back to the 17th century, this one-time lodge house for the nearby Himley Hall offers spacious, well equipped and attractive accommodation. Bedrooms are located in the main house and separate buildings around the hotel, and the busy restaurant offer a wide selection of dishes.

ROOMS: 24 en suite (2 fmly) **FACILITIES:** entertainment **CONF:** Thtr 50 Class 30 Board 22 **PARKING:** 162 **NOTES:** No dogs (ex guide dogs) **CARDS:**

HINCKLEY, Leicestershire

Map 04 SP49

★★★★57% Hanover International Hotel & Club Hinckley

Watling St LE10 3JA
☎ 01455 631122 01455 251865
e-mail: hisland@webleicester.co.uk
Dir: *on A5, S of junct 1 on M69*

Convenient for the motorways and airports, this large hotel offers smart, comfortable bedrooms. The Club Floor is well designed for business visitors; each bedroom has a desk, fax and PC. Dinner is served in the Brasserie and lighter meals and snacks are available in the Snooty Fox pub.

ROOMS: 348 en suite (47 fmly) No smoking in 197 bedrooms d £90-£130 * LB **FACILITIES:** STV Indoor swimming (H) Snooker Sauna Solarium Gym Jacuzzi/spa Xmas **CONF:** Thtr 400 Class 190 Board 40 Del from £130 * **SERVICES:** Lift air con **PARKING:** 500 **NOTES:** No dogs (ex guide dogs) No smoking in restaurant Civ Wed 250
CARDS:

★★★74% Sketchley Grange

Sketchley Ln, Burbage LE10 3HU
☎ 01455 251133 01455 631384
e-mail: sketchleygrange@btinternet.com
Dir: *SE of town, off A5, take B4109 (Hinckley) turn left at mini rdbt. First right onto Sketchley Lane*

Set in its own landscaped gardens on the edge of town, Sketchley Grange is a sympathetically yet dramatically renovated country house. There is a good choice of bars and eating options, which include the Willows Restaurant and the lively Terrace Bistro Bar. Bedrooms are smart, modern and spacious.

ROOMS: 55 en suite (9 fmly) No smoking in 15 bedrooms d £99 * LB **FACILITIES:** STV Indoor swimming (H) Sauna Solarium Gym Jacuzzi/spa Steam room Hairdressing Creche ch fac **CONF:** Thtr 300 Class 150 Board 50 Del from £99 * **SERVICES:** Lift **PARKING:** 200 **NOTES:** No smoking in restaurant Civ Wed 250
CARDS:

See advert on opposite page

★★71% Kings Hotel & Restaurant

13/19 Mount Rd LE10 1AD
☎ 01455 637193 01455 636201
e-mail: kingshinck@aol.com
Dir: *follow A447 signposted to Hinckley. Under railway bridge and turn right at rdbt. First road left opposite railway station and then third right*

In a quiet part of town, this friendly hotel is convenient for the centre and the station. Decor is striking, varying from Chinese-style wallpaper in the bar to Victoriana in the restaurant, where cooking is personally supervised by the proprietor. Bedrooms are individual, well equipped and vary in size.

ROOMS: 7 en suite No smoking in all bedrooms s fr £64.90; d fr £74.90 (incl. bkfst) * LB **FACILITIES:** STV **CONF:** Thtr 30 Class 40 Board 20 Del from £80 * **PARKING:** 20 **NOTES:** No dogs No smoking in restaurant Civ Wed 60 **CARDS:**

HINDHEAD, Surrey

Map 04 SU83

★★★64% Devils Punch Bowl Hotel

London Rd GU26 6AG
☎ 01428 606565 01428 605713
Dir: *on A3*

This local landmark hotel has been completely transformed by a major programme of refurbishment. The freshly decorated bedrooms are suitable for both business and leisure travellers. The hub of the operation is the large bar area with its informal, welcoming atmosphere.

ROOMS: 36 en suite (1 fmly) **FACILITIES:** Pool table entertainment **CONF:** Thtr 100 Class 60 Board 60 **PARKING:** 80
CARDS:

See advert under GUILDFORD

HINDON, Wiltshire

Map 03 ST93

★★74% The Grosvenor Arms

High St SP3 6DJ
☎ 01747 820696 01747 820869
Dir: *village centre 1.5m from A303 & A350, through village B3089 to Salisbury*

This small hotel has been decorated to a high standard: bedrooms are smartly appointed with co-ordinating furnishings and fabrics. Public areas include a cosy lounge, spacious bar, with log fire and attractive dining room where guests can watch the chefs work in the open plan kitchen.

continued

ROOMS: 7 en suite (2 fmly) No smoking in all bedrooms s £45-£55; d £75-£90 (incl. bkfst) * **FACILITIES:** Fishing Xmas **PARKING:** 18
NOTES: No children 5yrs No smoking in restaurant
CARDS:

★★70% ❀ *Lamb at Hindon*

SP3 6DP
☎ 01747 820573 🖷 01747 820605
Dir: *1m from A303 & A350, on B3089 in the centre of the village*

This popular free house offers a warm welcome and good levels of comfort. Bedrooms are spacious and well decorated. Public areas have beamed ceilings and log fires. Tempting dishes are featured on the fixed-price menu, and the bar has a sophisticated choice of daily specials. Both dining options offer an excellent wine list.

ROOMS: 12 en suite **FACILITIES:** Fishing Shooting Mountain bikes
CONF: Thtr 35 Class 30 Board 20 **PARKING:** 26 **NOTES:** No smoking in restaurant **CARDS:**

HINTLESHAM, Suffolk Map 05 TM04

Premier Collection

★★★★❀❀❀ Hintlesham Hall

IP8 3NS
☎ 01473 652334 & 652268
🖷 01473 652463
e-mail: reservations@hintlesham-hall.co.uk
Dir: *4m W of Ipswich on A1071 to Sudbury*

Hintlesham Hall is a fine country house hotel, with polished yet friendly service. The magnificent Georgian façade belies the Tudor origins of the house. The parlour is sometimes used as a second dining room but the main dining room, The Salon, is a grand, elegant room serving classical cuisine. Bedrooms vary in style and design, each with individual decor and furniture. Guests may take advantage of the 18-hole golf facilities for a fee, or enjoy the smart new health and leisure complex in the Orangery.

continued

ROOMS: 33 en suite (1 fmly) s £84-£112; d £120-£350 (incl. cont bkfst) * LB **FACILITIES:** Outdoor swimming (H) Golf 18 Tennis (hard) Riding Snooker Sauna Gym Croquet lawn Putting green Jacuzzi/spa Clay & game shooting Health & beauty suite Xmas
CONF: Thtr 80 Class 50 Board 32 Del from £175 * **PARKING:** 100
NOTES: No smoking in restaurant RS Sat Civ Wed 120
CARDS:

Late for dinner? Quality Standards star rating means that last orders for dinner should be no earlier than:
★ 6.30pm ★★ 7.00pm ★★★ 8.00pm
★★★★ 9.00pm ★★★★★ 10.00pm

HINTON CHARTERHOUSE, Somerset Map 03 ST75

Premier Collection

★★★ Homewood Park

BA3 6BB

☎ 01225 723731 📠 01225 723820

e-mail: res@homewoodpark.com

Dir: *6m SE of Bath on A36, turn left at 2nd sign for Freshford*

Set in delightful grounds, Homewood Park offers relaxed surroundings and maintains high standards of quality and comfort throughout. Bedrooms, all individually decorated, include thoughtful extras to ensure a comfortable stay. The hotel has a reputation for its excellent standard of cuisine - with an imaginative interpretation of classical dishes featuring an impressive, not to be missed, eight-course tasting dinner.

ROOMS: 19 en suite s fr £109; d £139-£249 (incl. bkfst) * LB **FACILITIES:** STV Outdoor swimming (H) Tennis (hard) Croquet lawn Xmas **CONF:** Thtr 40 Class 30 Board 25 Del from £160 * **PARKING:** 30 **NOTES:** No dogs No smoking in restaurant Civ Wed 80 **CARDS:**

HITCHIN, Hertfordshire Map 04 TL12

★63% **Firs**

83 Bedford Rd SG5 2TY

☎ 01462 422322 📠 01462 432051

e-mail: firshotel@freewayuk.com

Dir: *turn off A505 onto A600. Hotel 1m on left next to Shell petrol Station*

On the northern outskirts, this pleasant hotel is well suited to the needs of its mainly business clientele. Originally it was a manor house and the comfortable public areas include a lounge bar, conference room and Italian-styled restaurant. The bedrooms come in an array of sizes and styles, all are well equipped.

ROOMS: 31 rms (25 en suite) (3 fmly) No smoking in 7 bedrooms s £37-£47; d £52-£57 (incl. bkfst) * **CONF:** Thtr 30 Class 24 Board 20 Del £95 * **PARKING:** 30 **NOTES:** No smoking in restaurant **CARDS:**

HOCKLEY HEATH, West Midlands Map 07 SP17

Premier Collection

★★★ **Nuthurst Grange Country House**

Nuthurst Grange Ln B94 5NL

☎ 01564 783972 📠 01564 783919

e-mail: info@nuthurst-grange.com

Dir: *0.5m S on A3400*

This charming country house, set in an idyllic landscaped environment, provides excellent accommodation and fine cuisine. Bedrooms, thoughtfully furnished, include a wealth of extras. The restaurant offers accomplished cooking and an imaginative selection of dishes. Staff are committed to providing a warm and relaxing atmosphere.

ROOMS: 15 en suite (2 fmly) s fr £135; d fr £155 (incl. bkfst) * LB **FACILITIES:** STV Croquet lawn Helipad **CONF:** Thtr 100 Class 50 Board 45 Del £169 * **PARKING:** 86 **NOTES:** No smoking in restaurant Civ Wed 100 **CARDS:**

HODNET, Shropshire Map 07 SJ62

★★65% **Bear**

TF9 3NH

☎ 01630 685214 📠 01630 685787

Dir: *junct of A53 & A442 on sharp corner in middle of small village*

This 16th-century former coaching inn provides bedrooms equipped with all modern comforts. The public areas have a wealth of charm and character, enhanced by features such as exposed beams. There is a large baronial-style function room and medieval banquets are something of a speciality here.

ROOMS: 6 en suite 2 annexe en suite s £40.50-£42.50; d £60-£70 (incl. bkfst) * LB **FACILITIES:** Ten-pin & Skittles to order Xmas **CONF:** Thtr 100 Class 50 Board 40 **PARKING:** 70 **NOTES:** No dogs (ex guide dogs) Civ Wed 70 **CARDS:**

HOLFORD, Somerset Map 03 ST14

★★71% **Combe House**

TA5 1RZ

☎ 01278 741382 📠 01278 741322

e-mail: enquires@combehouse.co.uk

Dir: *from A39 in Holford take lane between garage and Plough Inn, bear left at fork and continue for 0.25m to Holford Combe*

A friendly welcome awaits guests at this 17th-century former tannery, deep in the heart of the Quantock Hills. Many original features have been retained, including a water wheel (non-operational), and the comfortable bedrooms are equipped with all the expected modern facilities. The good honest cooking uses fresh produce, local wherever possible.

ROOMS: 16 en suite (2 fmly) s £34-£38; d £68-£87 (incl. bkfst) * LB **FACILITIES:** Indoor swimming (H) Tennis (hard) Xmas **PARKING:** 17 **NOTES:** No smoking in restaurant Closed Jan **CARDS:**

HOLMES CHAPEL, Cheshire Map 07 SJ76

★★★65% **Holly Lodge Hotel & "Truffles" Restaurant**

70 London Rd CW4 7AS

☎ 01477 537033 📠 01477 535823

e-mail: sales@hollylodgehotel.co.uk

Dir: *A50/A54 crossroads, 1m from junct 18 of M6*

A popular venue near the centre of Holmes Chapel. A number of

continued

the comfortably furnished bedrooms are located around a courtyard overflowing with hanging baskets. A carefully prepared menu is served in Truffles Restaurant.
ROOMS: 17 en suite 25 annexe en suite (3 fmly) No smoking in 17 bedrooms s fr £75; d fr £87.50 (incl. bkfst) * LB **FACILITIES:** STV Pool table Xmas **CONF:** Thtr 120 Class 60 Board 60 Del from £99.95 * **PARKING:** 90 **NOTES:** No smoking in restaurant Civ Wed 140 **CARDS:**

★★★65% Old Vicarage

Knutsford Rd CW4 8EF
☎ 01477 532041 01477 535728
e-mail: oldvichotel@aol.com
Dir: *on the A50, 1m from junct 18 on the M6*
Parts of this grade II listed building date back to the 17th century. Most bedrooms are in the newer wing, overlooking the River Dane and open fields beyond. An atmospheric beamed bar leads into the restaurant, which offers a wide range of freshly prepared dishes. There is also a light and airy lounge for guests to relax in after dinner.
ROOMS: 29 en suite No smoking in 4 bedrooms s fr £70.50; d fr £82.50 (incl. bkfst) * LB **FACILITIES:** STV **CONF:** Thtr 36 Class 14 Board 22 Del from £110 * **PARKING:** 70 **NOTES:** No dogs (ex guide dogs) No smoking in restaurant **CARDS:**

HOLMFIRTH, West Yorkshire — Map 07 SE10

○ Old Bridge

Market Walk HD7 1DA
☎ 01484 681212 01484 687978
e-mail: oldbridgehotel@enterprise.net
Dir: *At lights on A6024/A635 in the centre of Holmfirth,turn into Victoria St for 20m,left immediately after bank and shops into hotel car park*
Situated right in the centre of town and with good parking facilities, this stone built hotel offers well equipped bedrooms and spacious public rooms. There is a wide range of food available.
ROOMS: 20 en suite **CONF:** Thtr 80 Class 50 Board 40 **PARKING:** 30 **CARDS:**

HONILEY, Warwickshire — Map 04 SP27

★★★67% Honiley Court

corus

CV8 1NP
☎ 01926 484234 01926 484474
Dir: *from M40 junc 15, take A46 then A4177 to Solihull, at 1st main rdbt turn right to hotel approx 2m on left*

An extension of the Old Boot Inn, this modern hotel is within easy reach of the motorways and airport. Restyled open-plan public areas are smart and modern with vibrant colour schemes and comfortable furnishings. A range of meeting rooms is served by a dedicated conference team. Bedrooms are spacious, comfortable and well equipped.

continued

ROOMS: 62 en suite (4 fmly) No smoking in 31 bedrooms s fr £90; d fr £100 * LB **FACILITIES:** STV Xmas **CONF:** Thtr 170 Class 60 Board 45 **SERVICES:** Lift **PARKING:** 250 **NOTES:** No smoking in restaurant Civ Wed 146 **CARDS:**

HONITON, Devon — Map 03 ST10

see also Yarcombe

★★★73% Combe House at Gittisham

Gittisham EX14 3AD
☎ 01404 540400 01404 46004
e-mail: stay@thishotel.com
Dir: *turn off A30 1m S of Honiton, follow Gittisham Heathpark signs*

Set within thousands of acres of woodland, meadows and pasture, this historic Elizabethan mansion exudes a sense of serene splendour. Bedrooms are individually styled, many offer wonderful views across the countryside. The menu changes daily and features local produce, complemented by a choice of interesting wines.
ROOMS: 15 en suite s £80-£165; d £108-£186 (incl. bkfst) * LB **FACILITIES:** Fishing Croquet lawn Jacuzzi/spa ch fac Xmas **CONF:** Thtr 60 Class 40 Board 26 Del from £120 * **PARKING:** 51 **NOTES:** No smoking in restaurant Civ Wed 100 **CARDS:**

★★69% Home Farm

Wilmington EX14 9JR
☎ 01404 831278
Dir: *3m E on A35 in village of Wilmington*
This thatched, 16th-century former farmhouse retains many original features. All rooms, both in the main house and in the 'Stable Block' around the cobbled courtyard, are traditionally furnished and comfortably equipped. Guests can dine in the character bar, or in the more intimate restaurant; the standard of cooking is high in both.
ROOMS: 6 en suite 7 annexe en suite (3 fmly) s £34.50; d £65-£70 (incl. bkfst) * LB **PARKING:** 25 **NOTES:** No smoking in restaurant **CARDS:**

★★65% Monkton Court

Monkton EX14 9QH
☎ 01404 42309 01404 46861
e-mail: tony@thosking.freeserve.co.uk
Dir: *2m E of Honiton on A30 towards Illminster, opposite Monkton Church*
A 17th-century manor house set in five acres of grounds. Much of its historical character has been retained and the comfortable, beamed lounge bar is dominated by a large log fire. Bedrooms have been restyled and the dining room offers an array of imaginative dishes plus some old favourites.
ROOMS: 6 en suite (2 fmly) s £50-£60; d £65-£75 (incl. bkfst) * LB **FACILITIES:** Beauty therapy Xmas **CONF:** Thtr 30 Class 30 Board 20 **PARKING:** 60 **NOTES:** No dogs (ex guide dogs) No smoking in restaurant **CARDS:**

H

HONITON, continued

★★63% *Honiton Motel*
Turks Head Corner, Exeter Rd EX14 8BL
☎ 01404 43440 📠 01404 47767
Dir: *off A35*

The Honiton Motel offers well maintained budget accommodation with modern facilities. All rooms have their own access and are set around the large car park. In the main building, additional features include bars, restaurant, function suite and fast-food bar.
ROOMS: 15 annexe en suite (3 fmly) **FACILITIES:** Pool table **CONF:** Thtr 150 Class 100 Board 50 **PARKING:** 50
CARDS:

HOOK, Hampshire
Map 04 SU75

★★71% *Hook House*
London Rd RG27 9EQ
☎ 01256 762630 📠 01256 760232
Dir: *1m E of Hook on A30*
This charming, family-run hotel in several acres of landscaped grounds has a reputation for warmth and good service. Bedrooms are quiet, attractive and well equipped; the refurbished rooms are exceptionally well presented.
ROOMS: 13 en suite **FACILITIES:** Croquet lawn **CONF:** Thtr 20 Class 20 Board 20 **PARKING:** 20 **NOTES:** No dogs No children 13yrs No smoking in restaurant Closed Xmas **CARDS:**

HOPE COVE, Devon
Map 03 SX64

★★66% Lantern Lodge
TQ7 3HE
☎ 01548 561280 📠 01548 561736
Dir: *turn right off A381 Kingsbridge-Salcombe road, take first right after passing Hope Cove sign then first left along Grand View Rd*
A friendly team welcomes guests to this attractive small hotel close to the South Devon coastal path. Bedrooms are well furnished and the home-cooked meals are particularly good. There is a choice of lounges and a pretty, enclosed garden with putting green. The indoor pool has large doors opening to the garden.
ROOMS: 14 en suite (1 fmly) s £64-£82; d £106-£136 (incl. bkfst & dinner) * LB **FACILITIES:** Indoor swimming (H) Sauna Putting green Multi-gym **PARKING:** 15 **NOTES:** No dogs (ex guide dogs) No children 12yrs No smoking in restaurant Closed Dec-Feb
CARDS:

★★65% Cottage
TQ7 3HJ
☎ 01548 561555 📠 01548 561455
e-mail: info@hopecove.com
Dir: *from Kingsbridge A381 towards Salcombe, it is suggested you take 2nd right at village of Marlborough continue & turn left for Inner Hope*
This friendly, family-owned hotel has a homely feel, and stunning coastal views. Bedrooms include deluxe balcony rooms with extras such as videos. There are three lounges and a delightful cabin bar, built from original timbers from the Herzogin Cecilie. The menu offers a good choice of home-cooked dishes and is complemented by a varied wine list.
ROOMS: 35 rms (25 en suite) (5 fmly) s £46.50-£67.25; d £93-£114.50 (incl. bkfst & dinner) * LB **FACILITIES:** STV Xmas **CONF:** Thtr 50 Class 20 Board 24 Del from £35 * **PARKING:** 50 **NOTES:** No smoking in restaurant Closed 3-30 Jan **CARDS:**

HORLEY Hotels are listed under Gatwick Airport

HORNCASTLE, Lincolnshire
Map 08 TF26

★★71% Admiral Rodney
North St LN9 5DX
☎ 01507 523131 📠 01507 523104
e-mail: admiralrodney@bestwestern.co.uk
Dir: *off A153*
Best Western
This smart, well furnished hotel stands in the centre of this popular town. The Rodney bar is in the style of an old galleon and the informal Courtyard restaurant serves a wide range of food and snacks. Modern bedrooms are well appointed, thoughtfully equipped and generally quite spacious.
ROOMS: 31 en suite (3 fmly) No smoking in 6 bedrooms s £45-£54; d £58-£76 (incl. bkfst) * LB **FACILITIES:** STV Xmas **CONF:** Thtr 140 Class 60 Board 50 Del £64 * **SERVICES:** Lift **PARKING:** 60 **NOTES:** No dogs (ex guide dogs) **CARDS:**

HORNING, Norfolk
Map 09 TG31

★★★64% Petersfield House
Lower St NR12 8PF
☎ 01692 630741 📠 01692 630745
e-mail: reception@petersfieldhotel.co.uk
Dir: *from Wroxham take A1062 follow for two and a half miles then turn right into Horning Village, hotel in centre of village on left*
Near the Norfolk Broads in the centre of this delightful riverside village, Petersfield House lies in attractive landscaped gardens. The property was built in the 1920s as a large private residence. Bedrooms vary in size and are furnished in a modern style with most rooms enjoying pretty views over the gardens.
ROOMS: 18 en suite (1 fmly) s £58-£63; d £75-£85 (incl. bkfst) * LB **FACILITIES:** Fishing Putting green Boating entertainment Xmas **CONF:** Thtr 50 Class 40 Board 30 Del from £88 * **PARKING:** 70
CARDS:

HORNINGSHAM, Wiltshire

★★63% The Bath Arms
Longleat Estate BA12 7LY
☎ 01985 844308 📠 01985 844150
Situated at the driveway to Longleat House, the Bath Arms is located in the picturesque village of Horningsham, an ideal centre from which to explore the many attractions the area has to offer. An imaginative menu is available in the restaurant and the bar menu extends the option for guests. Popular during the summer months, families are welcome in the beer garden. Bedrooms vary in size and all are well appointed and comfortable. A two bedroomed, self catering cottage adjoins the hotel and is especially suitable for families.
ROOMS: 6 en suite 2 annexe en suite (1 fmly) **PARKING:** 15
NOTES: No smoking in restaurant RS Xmas & New Year
CARDS:

HORRABRIDGE, Devon

Map 02 SX56

★★65% *Overcombe*
PL20 7RA
☎ 01822 853501 01822 85351
Dir: *on A386, 4m S of Tavistock*

With views over Walkham Valley to the granite tors of Dartmoor beyond, this friendly small hotel has a relaxed atmosphere. The individually decorated bedrooms are comfortable and well equipped; two rooms are on the ground floor, and one is specifically suited to disabled guests. An ideal base from which to explore this beautiful area.

ROOMS: 8 en suite (3 fmly) No smoking in all bedrooms
FACILITIES: Croquet lawn Walking with professional guide **PARKING:** 8
NOTES: No smoking in restaurant **CARDS:**

HORSHAM, West Sussex

Map 04 TQ13

★★★★ South Lodge
Brighton Rd RH13 6PS
☎ 01403 891711 01403 891766
e-mail: enqiuries@southlodgehotel.co.uk
(For full entry see Lower Beeding)

★★★71% Random Hall
Stane St, Slinfold RH13 7QX
☎ 01403 790558 01403 791046
Dir: *on A29 0.5m from village of Slinfold*

This 16th-century former farmhouse has beams and timbers, polished flagstones and open fireplaces. The bedrooms are furnished and decorated in keeping with the rest of the hotel. Guests can enjoy modern British cooking in the Tapestry restaurant and professional service from the friendly staff.

ROOMS: 15 en suite (2 fmly) s fr £80; d fr £90 (incl. bkfst) * LB
PARKING: 50 **NOTES:** No dogs No smoking in restaurant Closed Dec 28-Jan 11 **CARDS:**

★★67% Ye Olde King's Head
Carfax RH12 1EG
☎ 01403 253126 01403 242291
Dir: *close to town hall, 0.5m from railway station, at junction of Carfax & East St*

In the centre of Horsham, this 14th-century former coaching inn retains many original features. The smart, well equipped bedrooms vary in size and there is an attractive restaurant, cosy bar and wine cellar and a popular coffee shop, a buzz of activity throughout the day.

ROOMS: 42 rms (41 en suite) (1 fmly) No smoking in 12 bedrooms s £77-£87; d £92-£112 (incl. bkfst) * LB **FACILITIES:** STV **CONF:** Thtr 45 Class 40 Board 30 **PARKING:** 40 **NOTES:** No smoking in restaurant
CARDS:

HORSHAM, continued

★★64% ***Brookfield Farm Hotel***
Winterpit Ln, Lower Beeding RH13 6LY
☎ 01403 891191 01403 891499
In the heart of the countryside a few miles from Horsham, this hotel offers attractively furnished bedrooms. There is a comfortable lounge, and the bar and dining room overlook a pond and the golf course. Guests may enjoy the terrace on sunny days.
ROOMS: 19 en suite (3 fmly) **FACILITIES:** STV Golf Fishing Putting green **CONF:** Thtr 30 Class 30 Board 20 Del from £97.50 * **PARKING:** 90 **NOTES:** No dogs (ex guide dogs)
CARDS:

HORTON-CUM-STUDLEY, Oxfordshire Map 04 SP51

★★★77% **Studley Priory**
OX33 1AZ
☎ 01865 351203 & 351254 01865 351613
e-mail: res@studley-priory.co.uk
Dir: *2.5m off B4027 between Wheatley and Islip*
Set in extensive grounds and enjoying beautiful countryside views, this very special hotel is just six miles from the centre of Oxford. The former Benedictine nunnery was founded in the 12th century and extended by the Croke family, who acquired the property when Henry VIII dissolved the monasteries. A professional, friendly welcome awaits, and lattice-windowed bedrooms are tastefully decorated with lots of thoughtful extras. Cuisine is imaginative and skilfully prepared.
ROOMS: 18 en suite No smoking in 4 bedrooms s £105-£115; d £140-£145 (incl. cont bkfst) * LB **FACILITIES:** STV Tennis (hard & grass) Croquet lawn Xmas **CONF:** Thtr 40 Class 25 Board 25 Del from £165 * **PARKING:** 101 **NOTES:** No dogs No smoking in restaurant Civ Wed 50
CARDS:

HORWICH, Greater Manchester Map 07 SD61

○ **De Vere Whites**
De Havilland Way BL6 6SF
☎ 01204 667788
ROOMS: 125 rms **NOTES:** Open October 2000

HOUGHTON-LE-SPRING, Tyne & Wear Map 12 NZ34

★★61% **Chilton Lodge**
Black Boy Rd, Chilton Moor, Fencehouses DH4 6LX
☎ 0191 385 2694 0191 385 6762
Dir: *leave A1(M) at junct 62, then A690 towards Sunderland. Turn left at Rainton Bridge/Fencehouses sign, cross rdbt and take 1st left*
Set in open countryside near the village of Fencehouses, this complex evolved from original farm cottages, and now provides a country pub and spacious ballroom catering for functions and weddings. There is a wide choice of bar and dining room meals. Accommodation is modern and comfortable.
ROOMS: 25 en suite (7 fmly) No smoking in 7 bedrooms s £34-£48; d £44-£58 (incl. bkfst) * LB **FACILITIES:** STV Horse riding available at British Horse Society Approved centre entertainment Xmas **CONF:** Thtr 60 Class 50 Board 30 **PARKING:** 100 **NOTES:** No dogs (ex guide dogs)
CARDS:

Fancy a Singapore Sling? Bar staff in five star hotels should be skilled cocktail mixers.

HOUNSLOW Hotels are listed under Heathrow Airport

HOVE See Brighton & Hove

HOVINGHAM, North Yorkshire Map 08 SE67

★★★67% **Worsley Arms**
High St YO62 4LA
☎ 01653 628234 01653 628130
e-mail: worsleyarms@aol.com
Dir: *situated on the main street through Hovingham*
The focal point of the village, this hotel has comfortable and attractive lounges with welcoming open fires. The restaurant provides good quality cooking, with less formal dining in the Cricketers Bar and Bistro to the rear. Several bedrooms are contained in cottages across the green.
ROOMS: 10 en suite 8 annexe en suite s £60; d £80 (incl. bkfst) * LB **FACILITIES:** Tennis (hard) Squash Shooting Xmas **CONF:** Thtr 40 Class 40 Board 20 Del from £120 * **PARKING:** 2 **NOTES:** No smoking in restaurant Civ Wed 90 **CARDS:**

HOWTOWN (NEAR POOLEY BRIDGE), Cumbria Map 12 NY41

Premier Collection

★★★ **Sharrow Bay Country House**
Sharrow Bay CA10 2LZ
☎ 017684 86301 & 86483 017684 86349
e-mail: enquiries@sharrow-bay.com
Dir: *at Pooley Bridge take right hand fork by church towards Howtown. At cross road turn right and follow Lakeside Road for 2m.*
Standing at the water's edge, with views across the lake to the mountains, Sharrow Bay is often described as the first country house hotel. Individually furnished bedrooms are split between the main house and the Elizabethan farmhouse, complete with its own service staff, lounges and breakfast room. There is a choice of inviting lounges to relax in after the six-course meal.
ROOMS: 10 rms (8 en suite) 16 annexe en suite s £125-£145; d £150-£200 (incl. bkfst & dinner) * LB **PARKING:** 35 **NOTES:** No dogs No children 13yrs No smoking in restaurant Closed 4 Dec-2 March Civ Wed 35 **CARDS:**

Read all about it! Newspapers delivered to bedrooms in four and five star hotels.

HUCKNALL, Nottinghamshire
Map 08 SK54

Premier Lodge (Nottingham North West)
PREMIER LODGE

Nottingham Rd NG15 7PY

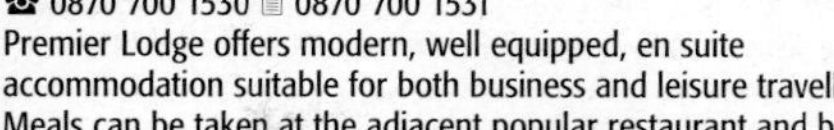

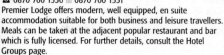

☎ 0870 700 1530 📠 0870 700 1531

Premier Lodge offers modern, well equipped, en suite accommodation suitable for both business and leisure travellers. Meals can be taken at the adjacent popular restaurant and bar which is fully licensed. For further details, consult the Hotel Groups page.

ROOMS: 34 en suite d £42 *

HUDDERSFIELD, West Yorkshire
Map 07 SE11

★★★69% Old Golf House Hotel
corus

New Hey Rd, Outlane HD3 3YP

☎ 01422 379311 📠 01422 372694

Dir: *leave M62 at junct 23 (Eastbound only), or junct 24 & follow A640 towards Rochdale. Hotel on A640 (New Hey Rd) at Outlane*

Close to the M62, this hotel offers well insulated bedrooms equipped to a good modern standard. A wide choice of dishes is served in the restaurant, and lighter meals are availablein the comfortable lounge bar.

ROOMS: 52 en suite (4 fmly) No smoking in 30 bedrooms s £85-£100; d £95-£110 * LB **FACILITIES:** STV Putting green 5 Hole pitch & putt Xmas **CONF:** Thtr 100 Class 50 Board 40 Del from £60 * **PARKING:** 100 **NOTES:** No smoking in restaurant Civ Wed 180 **CARDS:**

★★★68% Bagden Hall
Wakefield Rd, Scissett HD8 9LE

☎ 01484 865330 📠 01484 861001

e-mail: info@bagdenhall.demon.co.uk

Dir: *on A636, between Scissett and Denby Dale*

Set in grounds, with a par three nine-hole golf course, this elegant mansion house is close to the village of Scissett. The public rooms include a bright conservatory where light meals are served, and a good conference/function room. Bedrooms vary in size, all are well equipped and pleasantly furnished.

continued

ROOMS: 17 en suite (3 fmly) No smoking in 2 bedrooms s £56-£60; d £80-£100 (incl. bkfst) * LB **FACILITIES:** STV Golf 9 Putting green **CONF:** Thtr 80 Class 40 Board 30 Del £99 * **PARKING:** 96 **NOTES:** No dogs (ex guide dogs) RS 24-25 Dec Civ Wed 76 **CARDS:**

★★★66% George
PRINCIPAL HOTELS

St George's Square HD1 1JA

☎ 01484 515444 📠 01484 435056

e-mail: StuartMcManus@Principalhotels.co.uk

Dir: *M62 Junc 24 follow signs Huddersfield Town Centre, adjacent to railway station*

This Victorian hotel, the venue for the first meeting of the Rugby League back in 1895, is conveniently sited adjacent to the railway station. Generally spacious bedrooms are equipped to a good standard. The pleasant restaurant serves a wide range of dishes, and there is a comfortable lounge bar.

ROOMS: 60 en suite (1 fmly) No smoking in 15 bedrooms s £55-£80; d £65-£90 * LB **FACILITIES:** STV Free use of local Sports Centre Xmas **CONF:** Thtr 200 Class 60 Board 60 Del from £75 * **SERVICES:** Lift **PARKING:** 23 **NOTES:** No smoking in restaurant Civ Wed 150 **CARDS:**

★★★64% Huddersfield
33-47 Kirkgate HD1 1QT

☎ 01484 512111 📠 01484 435262

e-mail: enquiries@huddersfieldhotel.com

Dir: *on A62 ring road, below parish church, opposite sports centre*

This popular town centre hotel offers comfortable and attractively furnished bedrooms, including some with four-posters. A choice of bars and dining areas is available, with an all-day brasserie and evening bistro for meals and snacks. The car park reaches award winning standards for high security.

ROOMS: 50 en suite (6 fmly) s £52; d £70 (incl. bkfst) * LB **FACILITIES:** STV Pool table entertainment Xmas **SERVICES:** Lift **PARKING:** 70 **CARDS:**

★★★63% *Briar Court*
Halifax Rd, Birchencliffe HD3 3NT

☎ 01484 519902 📠 01484 431812

e-mail: briarcourthotel@btconnect.com

Dir: *on A629, 300yds S of junc 24 on M62*

Close to J24 of the M62, this modern hotel offers well equipped bedrooms. Diners can choose from the main restaurant or the popular, lively Da Sandro Restaurant, with its range of Italian dishes. Public rooms have been upgraded and extended and now include the Zanzibar wine and coffee lounge.

continued

HUDDERSFIELD, continued

Briar Court, Huddersfield

ROOMS: 48 en suite (3 fmly) No smoking in 20 bedrooms
FACILITIES: STV **CONF:** Thtr 150 Class 50 Board 60 **PARKING:** 140
NOTES: No dogs (ex guide dogs) No smoking in restaurant
CARDS:

★★71% Lodge
48 Birkby Lodge Rd, Birkby HD2 2BG
☎ 01484 431001 01484 421590
Dir: *junct 24 of M62, then exit A629 for Birkby. Turn right at Nuffield Hospital down Birkby Lodge Road, hotel 200yds on left*
This quiet, family-run hotel offers attractively furnished bedrooms. Public areas include two comfortable lounges and an inviting restaurant, where carefully prepared meals are served. A wood-panelled meeting room is available; service is friendly and efficient.
ROOMS: 12 en suite (2 fmly) No smoking in all bedrooms s £55-£60; d £70-£80 (incl. bkfst) * **CONF:** Thtr 40 Class 20 Board 20 Del from £85 * **PARKING:** 41 **NOTES:** No smoking in restaurant Closed 25-27 Dec **CARDS:**

★★67% Pennine Manor
Nettleton Hill Rd, Scapegoat Hill HD7 4NY
☎ 01484 642368 01484 642866
Dir: *junct 24 M62 follow signs for Rochdale-Outlane Village-left after Highlander onto Round Ings Rd-top of Hill turn left onto Nettleton Hill Rd*
This attractive stone-built hotel offers well equipped and modern bedrooms. There is a popular bar serving a good selection of snacks and meals, with more formal dining in the spacious and well appointed restaurant which overlooks the surrounding countryside.
ROOMS: 31 en suite (4 fmly) No smoking in 6 bedrooms s fr £62; d fr £72 (incl. bkfst) * LB **FACILITIES:** STV **CONF:** Thtr 132 Class 56 Board 30 **PARKING:** 115 **NOTES:** Civ Wed 100
CARDS:

★67% Elm Crest
2 Queens Rd, Edgerton HD2 2AG
☎ 01484 530990 01484 516227
e-mail: elmcresthotel@talk21.com
Dir: *1.5m from M62 (J24), 1m from the town centre on A629*
The attractively furnished bedrooms at this small hotel are generally spacious, and the lounge, on the lower ground floor, is comfortable and cosy. Freshly-prepared evening meals and hearty breakfasts are served in the adjacent dining room. Hospitality is very good.
ROOMS: 8 rms (5 en suite) (2 fmly) No smoking in all bedrooms s £38-£40; d £55-£60 (incl. bkfst) * LB **CONF:** Thtr 15 Class 15 Board 12 Del from £40 * **PARKING:** 12 **NOTES:** No dogs No smoking in restaurant
CARDS:

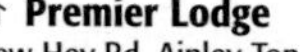

Premier Lodge
New Hey Rd, Ainley Top HD2 2EA
☎ 0870 700 1408 0870 700 1409

Premier Lodge offers modern, well equipped, en suite accommodation suitable for both business and leisure travellers. Meals can be taken at the adjacent popular restaurant and bar which is fully licensed. For further details, consult the Hotel Groups page.
ROOMS: 40 en suite d £42 *

HULL, East Riding of Yorkshire — Map 08 TA02
see also Little Weighton

★★★71% Willerby Manor
Well Ln HU10 6ER
☎ 01482 652616 01482 653901
e-mail: info@willerbymanor.co.uk
(For full entry see Willerby)

★★★68% Posthouse Hull Marina
The Marina, Castle St HU1 2BX
☎ 0870 400 9043 01482 213299
Dir: *from M62 join A63 to Hull. Follow signs for 'Marina and Ice Arena'. Hotel on left next to Ice Arena*
This modern hotel occupies a prime position overlooking Hull Marina. Bedrooms are particularly well appointed and include family and executive rooms. The waterside restaurant serves international and British dishes. Secretarial services can be provided and there is a well equipped health and fitness club.
ROOMS: 99 en suite (12 fmly) No smoking in 66 bedrooms
FACILITIES: Indoor swimming (H) Sauna Solarium Gym **CONF:** Thtr 150 Class 60 Board 50 **SERVICES:** Lift **PARKING:** 130 **NOTES:** No smoking in restaurant **CARDS:**

★★★67% Portland
Paragon St HU1 3JP
☎ 01482 326462 01482 213460
e-mail: info@portland.co.uk
Dir: *leave M62 onto A63 to 1st main rdbt at 2nd set of lights turn left at x-roads across next junct turn right onto Carr Ln follow 1-way system*
This tall, modern hotel is right in the heart of the city and offers well equipped accommodation. Public rooms include a spacious bar-lounge and an elegant restaurant serving a good range of well produced dishes. There is also an all-day coffee shop on the ground floor.
ROOMS: 106 en suite (4 fmly) No smoking in 9 bedrooms
FACILITIES: STV **CONF:** Thtr 240 Class 70 Board 100 **SERVICES:** Lift
PARKING: 2 **CARDS:**

★★★65% Quality Hotel Hull
170 Ferensway HU1 3UF
☎ 01482 325087 01482 323172
e-mail: admin@gb611.u-net.com
Dir: *follow signs for Railway Station*
This Victorian railway hotel has been renovated to provide modern, well equipped bedrooms. The spacious and practical public areas are well designed and comfortably furnished. The restaurant overlooks the station concourse, and guests have free use of an adjacent leisure centre.
ROOMS: 155 en suite No smoking in 85 bedrooms d £59-£90 * LB
FACILITIES: STV Indoor swimming (H) Sauna Solarium Gym Pool table Jacuzzi/spa Spa pool Steamroom Xmas **CONF:** Thtr 450 Class 150 Board 105 Del from £85 * **SERVICES:** Lift **PARKING:** 130
NOTES: Civ Wed 450 **CARDS:**

★★★63% ***Humber Crown***
Ferriby High Rd HU14 3LG
☎ 01482 645212 📠 01482 643332
(For full entry see North Ferriby)

★★68% **The Rowley Manor**
Rowley Rd HU20 3XR
☎ 01482 848248 📠 01482 849900
(For full entry see Little Weighton)

★★58% **Comfort Inn**
11 Anlaby Rd HU1 2PJ
☎ 01482 323299 📠 01482 214730
e-mail: admin@gb631.u-net.com
Dir: *follow signs to Railway Station*
Centrally located, this city centre hotel offers modern, well equipped accommodation, with open-plan lounge, bar and restaurant on the first floor. Bedrooms are comfortable and provide all expected facilities.
ROOMS: 59 en suite (5 fmly) No smoking in 29 bedrooms d £47 * LB
FACILITIES: STV Full leisure facilities at sister Hotel next door Xmas
CONF: Thtr 140 Class 80 Board 45 **SERVICES:** Lift **PARKING:** 100
CARDS:

CHOICE HOTELS EUROPE

⌂ ***Travelodge***
Beacon Service Area HU15 1RZ
☎ 01430 424455 📠 01430 424455
(For full entry see South Cave)

⌂ **Campanile**
Beverley Rd, Freetown Way HU2 9AN
☎ 01482 325530 📠 01482 587538
Dir: *pass station and first right after crossroads*

Campanile

This modern building offers accommodation in smart well equipped bedrooms, all with en suite bathrooms. Refreshments may be taken at the informal Bistro. For further details and the Campanile phone number, consult the Hotel Groups page.
ROOMS: 50 annexe en suite **CONF:** Thtr 35 Class 18 Board 20

HUNMANBY, North Yorkshire — Map 08 TA07

★★68% **Wrangham House Hotel**
10 Stonegate YO14 0NS
☎ 01723 891333 📠 01723 892973
e-mail: mervynpoulter@lineone.net
Dir: *from main A64 road, follow the A1039 to Filey, turning right onto Hunmanby road, the hotel is behind All Saints Church in Hunmanby village*
Standing in delightful gardens next to the church, this former vicarage is now a comfortable, well furnished hotel. The attractive bedrooms are thoughtfully equipped. Two comfortable lounges are available, and a good selection of well produced dishes is served in the elegant dining room.

continued

ROOMS: 8 en suite 4 annexe en suite No smoking in all bedrooms s £38.50-£48.50; d £67-£77 (incl. bkfst) * LB **FACILITIES:** Croquet lawn Xmas **CONF:** Thtr 50 Class 20 Board 20 Del from £60 * **PARKING:** 20
NOTES: No children 12yrs No smoking in restaurant
CARDS:

HUNSTANTON, Norfolk — Map 09 TF64

★★★67% **Le Strange Arms**
Golf Course Rd, Old Hunstanton PE36 6JJ
☎ 01485 534411 📠 01485 534724
e-mail: lestrangearms@netmatters.co.uk
Dir: *turn off A149 1m N of Hunstanton town. Road bends sharply right and access road to hotel is on bend*
This hotel enjoys magnificent views from the wide lawns down to the sandy beach and across the wash. A choice of menus is served in the attractive restaurant. Bedrooms come in a range of styles,

Best Western

continued

HUNSTANTON, continued

from original rooms in the main house with period furnishings, to more contemporary rooms in the new wing.
ROOMS: 36 en suite (4 fmly) s £57.50-£65; d £85-£105 (incl. bkfst) * LB **FACILITIES:** Tennis Snooker Xmas **CONF:** Thtr 180 Class 150 Board 50 Del from £98 * **PARKING:** 80 **NOTES:** No smoking in restaurant Civ Wed 150 **CARDS:**

See advert on page 271

★★74% Caley Hall
Old Hunstanton Rd PE36 6HH
☎ 01485 533486 01485 533348
Dir: *1m from Hunstanton, on A149*
This 17th-century manor house, originally part of a working farm, offers relaxing public areas including a cosy bar, an open-plan lounge, a billiard room and a spacious restaurant serving a daily-changing menu. The pleasantly furnished bedrooms are in courtyard style blocks, tastefully converted from the authentic buildings.
ROOMS: 33 annexe en suite (5 fmly) s £29-£45; d £58-£70 (incl. bkfst) * LB **FACILITIES:** STV Snooker Xmas **CONF:** Board 40 **PARKING:** 70 **NOTES:** No smoking in restaurant Closed Jan-Feb
CARDS:

★★70% The Lodge Hotel & Restaurant
Old Hunstanton Rd PE36 6HX
☎ 01485 532896 01485 535007
e-mail: reception@thelodgehotel.co.uk
Dir: *1m E of Hunstanton on A149*
A friendly hotel within easy reach of the beach and town centre. The attractive bedrooms are generally spacious, well maintained and offer good facilities. Six new bedrooms have been added to the rear. There is a large garden in which to enjoy cream teas, a popular restaurant, food-serving bar and a comfortable lounge.
ROOMS: 16 en suite 6 annexe en suite (3 fmly) No smoking in 6 bedrooms s £35-£50; d £68-£92 (incl. bkfst) * LB **FACILITIES:** Snooker Pool table Games room Xmas **CONF:** Thtr 30 Class 20 Board 20
PARKING: 70 **NOTES:** No smoking in restaurant
CARDS:

See advert on opposite page

HUNSTRETE, Somerset
Map 03 ST66

★★★78% ❀❀❀ Hunstrete House
BS39 4NS
☎ 01761 490490 01761 490732
e-mail: user@hunstretehouse.co.uk
Dir: *from Bath A4 to Bristol, take A39 through Marksbury, A368 turn off Hunstrete Village*

Set in 92 acres of deer park and woodland on the edge of the Mendip Hills, this 18th-century house exudes a timeless elegance. The individual bedrooms have modern facilities and enjoy tranquil views. Public areas feature antiques, paintings and fine china. The creative cooking uses the finest ingredients prepared with great skill and imagination.
ROOMS: 23 en suite (2 fmly) s £98-£155; d £130-£325 (incl. bkfst) * LB **FACILITIES:** Outdoor swimming (H) Tennis (hard) Croquet lawn Xmas **CONF:** Thtr 50 Class 40 Board 30 Del from £155 *
PARKING: 75 **NOTES:** No dogs (ex guide dogs) No smoking in restaurant Civ Wed 50 **CARDS:**

HUNTINGDON, Cambridgeshire
Map 04 TL27

★★★★72% Huntingdon Marriott
Kingfisher Way, Hinchingbrooke Business Park PE18 8FL
☎ 01480 446000 01480 451111
Dir: *situated 1m from the centre of Huntington on the A14*
This hotel has all the trappings of a modern, well designed operation. The first-class, air-conditioned bedrooms are most comfortable and there is an open-plan lounge and quiet drawing room. A good range of services is provided by a smartly uniformed team of staff.
ROOMS: 150 en suite No smoking in 60 bedrooms s £75-£130; d £90-£150 (incl. bkfst) * LB **FACILITIES:** STV Indoor swimming (H) Gym Jacuzzi/spa Xmas **CONF:** Thtr 300 Class 150 Board 100 Del from £110 *
SERVICES: Lift air con **PARKING:** 250 **NOTES:** No smoking in restaurant Civ Wed 250 **CARDS:**

★★★75% ❀❀ The Old Bridge
1 High St PE29 3TQ
☎ 01480 424300 01480 411017
e-mail: oldbridge@huntsbridge.co.uk
Dir: *from A14 or A1 follow signs for 'Huntingdon'. The Old Bridge is clearly visible from the inner ring road*

A delightful 18th-century hotel combining classical architecture with modern facilities. The two eating areas, the convivial terrace and the more formal restaurant, offer the same appealing menu. Individual rooms are designed with style and include many useful extras. There is a particularly good business centre with secretarial services.
ROOMS: 24 en suite (3 fmly) s £79.50-£110; d £95-£139 (incl. bkfst) * LB **FACILITIES:** STV Fishing Private mooring for boats Xmas
CONF: Thtr 50 Class 20 Board 24 Del from £129.50 * **PARKING:** 50
NOTES: No smoking in restaurant Civ Wed 80
CARDS:

★★66% The Stukeleys Country Hotel
Ermine St, Great Stukeley PE17 5AL
☎ 01480 456927 01480 450260
Dir: *on B1043, off A1/A14 junction*
This attractive 16th-century coaching inn offers comfortable accommodation with exposed beams and open fireplaces. The spacious bedrooms are individually decorated and tastefully

continued

furnished in pine. There is a cosy lounge bar and dining area as well as a smart restaurant.
ROOMS: 8 en suite (1 fmly) s fr £69; d fr £80 (incl. cont bkfst) * LB
FACILITIES: Xmas **PARKING:** 30 **NOTES:** No dogs (ex guide dogs)
CARDS:

HYDE, Cheshire Map 07 SJ99

Premier Lodge (Manchester East)

Stockport Rd, Mottram SK14 3AU
☎ 0870 700 1478 📠 0870 700 1479

PREMIER LODGE

Premier Lodge offers modern, well equipped, en suite accommodation suitable for both business and leisure travellers. Meals can be taken at the adjacent popular restaurant and bar which is fully licensed. For further details, consult the Hotel Groups page.
ROOMS: 84 en suite d £42 *

HYTHE, Kent Map 05 TR13

★★★★77% The Hythe Imperial

Princes Pde CT21 6AE
☎ 01303 267441 📠 01303 264610
e-mail: hytheimperial@marstonhotels.co.uk

MARSTON HOTELS

Dir: *M20, junct 11 take A261*
In a 50 acre seafront estate, this magnificent building, evocative of a bygone era, is surrounded by a golf course and beautiful gardens. Spacious, well equipped bedrooms have lovely views of the grounds or the sea. Professional, friendly staff serve a wide range of carefully prepared dishes in the restaurant. Lighter dishes are available in the sunny Bistro Bar. Leisure facilities are excellent.
ROOMS: 100 en suite (5 fmly) No smoking in 38 bedrooms s £85-£95; d £115-£155 * LB **FACILITIES:** STV Indoor swimming (H) Golf 9 Tennis (hard & grass) Squash Snooker Sauna Solarium Gym Croquet lawn Putting green Jacuzzi/spa Beauty salon Fitness assessments ch fac Xmas
CONF: Thtr 250 Class 120 Board 80 Del £145 * **SERVICES:** Lift
PARKING: 201 **NOTES:** No dogs (ex guide dogs) No smoking in restaurant Civ Wed 200 **CARDS:**

★★★73% Stade Court

West Pde CT21 6DT
☎ 01303 268263 📠 01303 261803
e-mail: stadecourt@marstonhotels.co.uk

MARSTON HOTELS

Dir: *M20, junc 11 on A261*
A comfortable base from which to explore the local area. Attractive bedrooms are well equipped and a number have additional seating overlooking the channel. The committed team offer smooth service and genuine hospitality. Leisure facilities are available at the sister hotel, the Hythe Imperial.
ROOMS: 42 en suite (5 fmly) No smoking in 7 bedrooms s £75; d £105 (incl. bkfst) * LB **FACILITIES:** STV Indoor swimming (H) Golf 9 Tennis (hard & grass) Squash Snooker Sauna Solarium Gym Croquet lawn Putting green Jacuzzi/spa All leisure facilities at sister hotel Xmas
CONF: Thtr 60 Class 50 Board 30 Del from £99 * **SERVICES:** Lift
PARKING: 13 **NOTES:** No smoking in restaurant
CARDS:

ILFORD, Greater London
See LONDON SECTION plan 1 *H5*

Travelodge

Beehive Ln, Gants Hill IG4 5DR
☎ 020 8550 4248 📠 020 8550 4248

Travelodge

This modern building offers accommodation in smart, spacious and well equipped bedrooms, all with en suite bathrooms. Refreshments may be taken at the nearby family

continued

ILFORD, continued

restaurant. For further details and the Travelodge phone number, consult the Hotel Groups page.
ROOMS: 32 en suite

ILFRACOMBE, Devon Map 02 SS54

★★71% Elmfield
Torrs Park EX34 8AZ
☎ 01271 863377 🖹 01271 866828
Dir: *take A361 to Ilfracombe left at 1st traffic lights, left again at 2nd traffic lights, after 10yds left again hotel near top of hill on left*
Set in pleasant terraced gardens, this Victorian house is immaculately maintained. There is a choice of deluxe or standard bedrooms; two of the former have four-poster beds. Good home-cooked meals are served in the traditional dining room, and there is also a bar and lounge leading to a small games room.
ROOMS: 11 en suite 2 annexe en suite s £36; d £72 (incl. bkfst) * LB **FACILITIES:** Indoor swimming (H) Sauna Solarium Gym Pool table Jacuzzi/spa Darts Xmas **PARKING:** 14 **NOTES:** No dogs No children 8yrs No smoking in restaurant Closed Nov-Mar ex Xmas
CARDS:

See advert on opposite page

★★66% Ilfracombe Carlton
Runnacleave Rd EX34 8AR
☎ 01271 862446 & 863711 🖹 01271 865379
Dir: *take A361 to Ilfracombe left at traffic lights, left at next lights follow brown sign 'tunnels, beaches'*

This well maintained hotel in the centre of town has a loyal clientele. Bedrooms are attractively decorated, and the dining room is bright and airy.
ROOMS: 48 en suite (8 fmly) No smoking in all bedrooms s £27.50-£29.50; d £45-£50 (incl. bkfst) * LB **FACILITIES:** entertainment Xmas **CONF:** Thtr 50 Class 50 Board 50 Del from £45 * **SERVICES:** Lift **PARKING:** 25 **NOTES:** No dogs (ex guide dogs) No smoking in restaurant Closed Jan-Feb RS Mar **CARDS:**

See advert on opposite page

★★65% St Helier
Hillsborough Rd EX34 9QQ
☎ 01271 864906 🖹 01271 864906
e-mail: st_helier_hotel@yahoo.co.uk
Dir: *leave M5 junct 27 onto A361 continue to Ilfracombe, then take Combe Martin road through High St hotel opposite 'Old Thatched Inn'*
This small, family-run hotel is in walking distance of the centre and the harbour. Bedrooms have well chosen colour schemes and from some there are views to the sea. The public areas include a comfortable reception/lounge, a convivial Cellar Bar and separate dining room.
ROOMS: 10 en suite (2 fmly) **PARKING:** 29 **NOTES:** No smoking in restaurant Closed Nov to Apr **CARDS:**

★69% Westwell Hall Hotel
Torrs Park EX34 8AZ
☎ 01271 862792 🖹 01271 862792
e-mail: colin.lomas@westwellhall.freeserve.co.uk
Dir: *along Ilfracombe High Street, onto Worthfield road at lights, then L up Torrs Park. Turn R (Upper Torrs). Westwell Hall is 3rd drive on the left*
Set in large gardens and overlooking the town, this fine Victorian hotel is convenient for both beaches and shops. Well equipped bedrooms are individually decorated and day rooms include a bar, a lounge and a restaurant looking out on the patio.
ROOMS: 10 en suite s £22-£26; d £44-£52 (incl. bkfst) * **PARKING:** 10 **NOTES:** No smoking in restaurant Closed Nov to Easter
CARDS:

★65% Torrs
Torrs Park EX34 8AY
☎ 01271 862334 🖹 01271 862334
Dir: *from Barnstaple (A361), 1st set of lights in Ilfracombe L into Wilder Road. Next set of lights, turn L then L again. Hotel 320yds on right*
Standing in its own gardens, this personally run, detached hotel, benefits from views over both the town and surrounding countryside. The light and airy bedrooms are comfortable and equipped with the expected modern amenities.
ROOMS: 14 en suite (5 fmly) s £25; d £50 (incl. bkfst) * LB **PARKING:** 14 **NOTES:** No children 5yrs No smoking in restaurant Closed mid Nov-mid Feb **CARDS:**

ILKLEY, West Yorkshire Map 07 SE14

★★★71% Rombalds
11 West View, Wells Rd LS29 9JG
☎ 01943 603201 🖹 01943 816586
e-mail: reception@rombalds.demon.co.uk
Best Western
Dir: *on Leeds/Skipton road A65, left at 2nd lights, follow signs Ilkley Moor. Right at Midland Bank onto Wells Road. Hotel is 600yds on left*

Standing between the town and the moors, this elegantly furnished hotel provides comfortable lounges, well equipped bedrooms and an attractive restaurant serving well produced meals. Hospitality is good, and the whole atmosphere of the hotel is inviting.
ROOMS: 15 en suite (2 fmly) No smoking in 4 bedrooms s £69.50-£99.50; d £89-£119 (incl. bkfst) * LB **FACILITIES:** STV Xmas **CONF:** Thtr 70 Class 40 Board 25 Del from £107.50 * **PARKING:** 28 **NOTES:** No smoking in restaurant Civ Wed 70
CARDS:

★★★68% *The Craiglands*
Cowpasture Rd LS29 8RQ
☎ 01943 430001 🖹 01943 430002
e-mail: reservations@craiglandshotel.co.uk
A magnificent Victorian hotel in mature, landscaped grounds, close to the town centre. Public rooms are light and airy, and include an

continued

elegant restaurant and comfortable bar and lounge. Bedroom styles vary; each room is comfortably furnished and suitably equipped, many enjoying splendid views of the moor.
ROOMS: 73 rms (53 en suite) No smoking in 4 bedrooms
FACILITIES: Tennis (hard) putting croquet **CONF:** Thtr 250 Class 100 Board 450 Del from £105 * **SERVICES:** Lift **PARKING:** 200
CARDS:

★65% *Moorview*
104 Skipton Rd LS29 9HE
☎ 01943 600156 📠 01943 817313
Dir: *travelling west on A65 through Ilkley hotel on right just on western side of town*
The public rooms of this large Victorian house are furnished to a good standard. There is an inviting, comfortable lounge with a cosy real fire. Good home-cooking is provided in the small dining room. There is a wide choice of bedroom sizes and styles.
ROOMS: 12 en suite (3 fmly) **PARKING:** 15 **NOTES:** No smoking in restaurant **CARDS:**

ILMINSTER, Somerset
Map 03 ST31

★★★67% Pheasant Hotel & Restaurant
Water St, Seavington St Mary TA19 0QH
☎ 01460 240502 📠 01460 242388
Dir: *3m E of Ilminster, off B3168*
A delightful, part thatched former farmhouse in well tended gardens, close to the Dorset-Devon border. It is full of character, with oak beams and splendid inglenook fireplaces. Individually styled bedrooms, some in stone-built cottages around the main house, are equipped with modern comforts and thoughtful extras.
ROOMS: 2 en suite 6 annexe en suite s £70-£100; d £90-£120 (incl. bkfst) * LB **FACILITIES:** STV ch fac **CONF:** Thtr 28 Board 12
PARKING: 30 **NOTES:** No smoking in restaurant Closed 24 Dec, 26 Dec & 1 Jan RS BH's (bed & breakfast only)
CARDS:

★★★66% Shrubbery
Best Western
TA19 9AR
☎ 01460 52108 📠 01460 53660
e-mail: stuart@shrubberyhotel.demon.co.uk
Dir: *half a mile from A303 towards Ilminster town centre*
Set in attractive terraced gardens, this Victorian hotel offers well equipped bedrooms of various sizes, including three on the ground floor. A carte is offered at dinner, along with a selection of fish dishes. Less formal bar meals are available at lunch. Guests can take a dip in the heated outdoor pool on warmer days.
ROOMS: 14 en suite (3 fmly) **FACILITIES:** STV Outdoor swimming (H) Tennis (grass) **CONF:** Thtr 250 Class 100 Board 60 **PARKING:** 100
NOTES: Civ Wed 200 **CARDS:**

⇧ *Travelodge*
Travelodge
Southfields Roundabout, Horton Cross TA19 9PT
☎ 01460 53748 📠 01460 53748
Dir: *on A303*
This modern building offers accommodation in smart, spacious and well equipped bedrooms, all with en suite bathrooms. Refreshments may be taken at the nearby family restaurant. For further details and the Travelodge phone number, consult the Hotel Groups page.
ROOMS: 32 en suite

Read all about it! Newspapers delivered to bedrooms in four and five star hotels.

ILSINGTON, Devon

Map 03 SX77

★★★70% ❀ The Ilsington Country

Ilsington Village TQ13 9RR
☎ 01364 661452 📠 01364 661307
e-mail: hotel@ilsington.co.uk
Dir: *from M5 take A38 to Plymouth. Exit at Newton Abbot turn, then 3rd exit from rdbt to 'Islington',then 1st right and Hotel 5m on by P.Office*

This friendly, peaceful hotel on the southern slopes of Dartmoor is approached along four miles of winding country roads. Bedrooms are individually furnished, some are on the ground floor. The daily changing menu offers innovative dishes using local fish, meat and game. Leisure facilities are good.
ROOMS: 25 en suite (2 fmly) s £62.50-£67.50; d £95-£100 (incl. bkfst & dinner) * LB **FACILITIES:** STV Indoor swimming (H) Tennis (hard) Sauna Solarium Gym Croquet lawn Jacuzzi/spa Beautician Xmas **CONF:** Thtr 35 Class 30 Board 30 Del from £110 * **SERVICES:** Lift **PARKING:** 100 **NOTES:** No smoking in restaurant
CARDS:

IMMINGHAM, Lincolnshire

Map 08 TA11

★★65% Old Chapel Hotel & Restaurant

50 Station Rd, Habrough DN40 3AY
☎ 01469 572377 📠 01469 577883
e-mail: bewick18@aol.com
Dir: *M180/A180 turn off A180 onto A160 (Killingholme/Immingham) right at 1st rdbt to Harbrough. Straight over mini rdbt, 500mtrs on right after flyover*
This converted early 19th-century chapel offers comfortable, well equipped bedrooms and a friendly atmosphere. Day rooms include a small bar, a bright conservatory lounge and a cosy beamed restaurant where a range of popular dishes is served.
ROOMS: 14 en suite (1 fmly) s £45-£50; d £55 (incl. bkfst) * **PARKING:** 20 **NOTES:** No smoking in restaurant
CARDS:

INGATESTONE, Essex

Map 05 TQ69

★★★66% The Heybridge

Roman Rd CM4 9AB
☎ 01277 355355 📠 01277 353288
Dir: *follow M25/A12. Take B1002 exit (Ingatestone). Through Mountnessing and bridge over A12, 1st right (A12 London & Heybridge). Hotel 200yds on left*
With parts of the building dating back to the 15th-century, this family-run hotel offers plenty of character along with all modern comforts. Bedrooms are spacious and offer a very good range of in-room facilities. Guests have a choice of two bars and there is an attractive, traditional restaurant.

continued

ROOMS: 22 en suite (3 fmly) No smoking in 2 bedrooms s £92-£129; d £112-£149 * **FACILITIES:** STV entertainment Xmas **CONF:** Thtr 600 Class 400 Board 70 Del £132.50 * **PARKING:** 220 **NOTES:** No dogs Civ Wed 200 **CARDS:**

INSTOW, Devon

Map 02 SS43

★★★74% Commodore

Marine Pde EX39 4JN
☎ 01271 860347 📠 01271 861233
e-mail: di@the-commodore.freeserve.co.uk
Dir: *leave M5 junct 27 follow N Devon link road to Bideford. Turn right before bridge to Instow hotel 3m from bridge*
The majority of this hotel's well equipped bedrooms have balconies that take advantage of its delightful location overlooking the sandy beach at the mouth of the Taw and Torridge Estuaries. An extensive range of bar meals is served in the Quarter Deck Bar, and the restaurant offers a fixed-price menu and seasonally changed carte.
ROOMS: 20 en suite s £59.50-£73; d £115.50-£130 (incl. bkfst & dinner) * LB **CONF:** Thtr 250 Class 250 Board 80 Del from £74 * **PARKING:** 200 **NOTES:** No dogs No smoking in restaurant Closed 22-27 Dec **CARDS:**

IPPLEPEN, Devon

Map 03 SX86

★★★60% *Old Church House Inn*

Torbryan TQ12 5UR
☎ 01803 812372 📠 01803 812180
Dir: *take A381 from Newton Abbot after 5m turn right into Ipplepen continue a further one & a quarter miles to Torbryan. Hotel opposite the church*
This charming 13th-century thatched inn is an ideal retreat, successfully combining old-world character with modern comforts. Guests have a choice of rooms and bars in which to eat, and there is also a cosy lounge. Newton Abbot and Totnes are a short drive away and the area is good for country walks.
ROOMS: 12 en suite (5 fmly) **CONF:** Thtr 30 Class 30 Board 20 **PARKING:** 30 **NOTES:** No dogs **CARDS:**

IPSWICH, Suffolk

Map 05 TM14

★★★★❀❀❀ Hintlesham Hall

IP8 3NS
☎ 01473 652334 & 652268 📠 01473 652463
e-mail: reservations@hintlesham-hall.co.uk
(For full entry see Hintlesham)

Arriving late? Four and five star hotels have night porters to assist with your luggage; and 24hr room service.

★★★73% Swallow Belstead Brook

Belstead Rd IP2 9HB

☎ 01473 684241 🖷 01473 681249

e-mail: info@swallowhotels.com

Dir: *take A1214 from A12/A14 interchange rdbt & follow signs to hotel*

Standing in eight acres of landscaped grounds, this leisure-orientated hotel provides comfortable bedrooms equipped with modern facilities and many thoughtful touches. Public areas include a lounge area, bar and wood-panelled restaurant, in addition to a leisure club.

ROOMS: 76 en suite 12 annexe en suite (2 fmly) No smoking in 65 bedrooms s £90-£130; d £109-£149 (incl. bkfst) * LB **FACILITIES:** STV Indoor swimming (H) Sauna Solarium Gym Croquet lawn Steam Room entertainment Xmas **CONF:** Thtr 180 Class 75 Board 50 Del from £130 * **SERVICES:** Lift **PARKING:** 120 **NOTES:** No smoking in restaurant Civ Wed 130 **CARDS:**

★★★71% ❀❀ Marlborough

Henley Rd IP1 3SP

☎ 01473 257677 🖷 01473 226927

e-mail: reception@themarlborough.co.uk

Dir: *take A1156 from A14 or A1214 from A12 turn right at Henley Rd/ A1214 x-rds*

This delightful hotel with a country house atmosphere sits in quiet residential surroundings. Bedrooms are thoughtfully equipped and attractively decorated. Drinks are served in the contemporary bar, and the smart restaurant overlooks the well tended gardens. The adventurous cooking makes excellent use of good local produce.

ROOMS: 22 en suite (3 fmly) s £59-£72; d £82-£89 * LB **FACILITIES:** STV Xmas **CONF:** Thtr 40 Class 20 Board 26 **PARKING:** 60 **NOTES:** No smoking in restaurant Civ Wed 120 **CARDS:**

See advert on this page

★★★69% Courtyard by Marriott Ipswich

The Havens, Ransomes Europark IP3 9SJ

☎ 01473 272244 🖷 01473 272484

Dir: *just off A14 Ipswich By Pass at 1st jnct after Orwell Bridge signed Ransomes Europark when travelling towards Felixstowe, hotel faces the slip road*

This modern, well maintained hotel offers stylish accommodation with attractive, spacious bedrooms. Public rooms include an open-plan restaurant and bar, and a suite of popular conference rooms. The small fitness studio is an added bonus.

ROOMS: 60 en suite (26 fmly) No smoking in 45 bedrooms d £45-£95 * LB **FACILITIES:** STV Gym Pool table Xmas **CONF:** Thtr 180 Class 80 Board 60 Del from £90 * **SERVICES:** Lift **PARKING:** 150 **NOTES:** No dogs (ex guide dogs) Civ Wed **CARDS:**

Packed in a hurry? Ironing facilities should be available at all star levels, either in rooms or on request.

★★★66% County Hotel Ipswich

London Rd, Copdock IP8 3JD

☎ 01473 209988 🖷 01473 730801

REGAL

Dir: *close to the A12/A14 interchange S of Ipswich. Exit A12 at junct signposted Washbrook/Copdock. Hotel on old A12 1m on left*

Located close the main Colchester road, this modern hotel is popular with both business and leisure guests. The bar and restaurant have an informal atmosphere and room service is actively promoted.

ROOMS: 76 en suite (3 fmly) No smoking in 27 bedrooms d fr £70 * LB **FACILITIES:** Indoor swimming (H) Sauna Solarium Gym Jacuzzi/spa Xmas **CONF:** Thtr 500 Class 200 Board 35 Del from £80 * **SERVICES:** Lift **PARKING:** 360 **NOTES:** No smoking in restaurant Civ Wed 120 **CARDS:**

Bad hair day? Hairdryers in all rooms three stars and above.

IPSWICH, continued

★★★64% *Novotel*

Greyfriars Rd IP1 1UP
☎ 01473 232400 🖷 01473 232414
Dir: *from A14 towards Felixstowe turn left onto A137 & follow for 2m into centre of town, hotel on double rdbt by Stoke Bridge*
This continental style modern red brick hotel features open plan public areas, including a Mediterranean style restaurant and a bar with a games area. It is a popular business and meeting venue. Smart bedrooms are simple in decor, well designed and equipped to a modern standard.
ROOMS: 100 en suite (6 fmly) No smoking in 76 bedrooms
FACILITIES: STV Pool table **CONF:** Thtr 180 Class 75 Board 45
SERVICES: Lift air con **PARKING:** 50 **CARDS:**

★★★63% *Posthouse Ipswich*

London Rd IP2 0UA
☎ 0870 400 9045 🖷 01473 680412
Dir: *from A12/A45, go on A1214. At Tesco's go straight over 1st rndbt and hotel is 200yds on left*
This pleasant modern hotel is located to the west of the town centre. Bedrooms and public areas are suited to the needs of both business and leisure guests, and the leisure club is a useful feature.
ROOMS: 109 en suite (48 fmly) No smoking in 66 bedrooms
FACILITIES: Indoor swimming (H) ch fac **CONF:** Thtr 120 Class 50 Board 40 **PARKING:** 200 **CARDS:**

★★69% Claydon Country House

16-18 Ipswich Rd, Claydon IP6 0AR
☎ 01473 830382 🖷 01473 832476
e-mail: kayshotels@aol.com
Dir: *from A14, north west of Ipswich 4m take Great Blakenham road, B1113 then turn off to Claydon, hotel on left*
A range of modern, well equipped accommodation is offered, including a spacious, attractively furnished four poster-room. The smart restaurant offers a wide choice of appealing dishes. On the lower floor there is a relaxing lounge bar.
ROOMS: 14 en suite (2 fmly) s fr £59; d fr £69 (incl. bkfst) * LB
FACILITIES: STV ch fac Xmas **CONF:** Thtr 40 Class 30 Board 20
PARKING: 60 **NOTES:** No dogs (ex guide dogs) No smoking in restaurant **CARDS:**

⌂ Express by Holiday Inn Ipswich

Old Hadleigh Rd, Sproughton IP8 3AR
☎ 01473 222279
A modern budget hotel offering comfortable accommodation in refreshing, spacious and comprehensively-equipped bedrooms, en suite bathrooms with power showers and continental buffet breakfast included in the room rate. Suitable for business travellers or families. For further details and the Express by Holiday Inn phone number, consult the Hotel Groups page.

ROOMS: 49 en suite (incl. cont bkfst) d £49.95 * **CONF:** Thtr 30 Class 16 Board 16

⌂ *Travelodge*

Capel St Mary IP9 2JP
☎ 01473 312157 🖷 01473 312157
Dir: *5m S on A12*
This modern building offers accommodation in smart, spacious and well equipped bedrooms, all with en suite bathrooms. Refreshments may be taken at the nearby family restaurant. For further details and the Travelodge phone number, consult the Hotel Groups page.
ROOMS: 32 en suite

ISLE OF Places incorporating the words 'Isle of' or 'Isle' will be found under the actual name - eg Isle of Wight is listed under Wight, Isle of.

IVYBRIDGE, Devon Map 02 SX65

★★74% *Glazebrook House Hotel & Restaurant*

TQ10 9JE
☎ 01364 73322 🖷 01364 72350
Dir: *turn off A38 at Avonwick, South Brent jct. proceed 1.5m to South Brent. Pass the London Inn, in 100yds the jct for Glazebrook is on the right*

An elegant mid-Victorian country house surrounded by four acres of gardens standing on the southern slopes of the Dartmoor National Park. Bedrooms are decorated in pleasing colour schemes, and extra little touches add to a feeling of comfort.
ROOMS: 11 en suite (3 fmly) **FACILITIES:** ch fac **CONF:** Thtr 100 Class 80 Board 60 **PARKING:** 50 **NOTES:** No dogs (ex guide dogs) No smoking in restaurant **CARDS:**

See advert under PLYMOUTH

★★64% *Sportsmans Inn Hotel & Restaurant*

Exeter Rd PL21 0BQ
☎ 01752 892280 🖷 01752 690714
Dir: *turn off A38 Devon expressway at Ivybridge exit, follow main road through town, hotel on the main road*
Popular with both locals and visitors, the Sportsmans offers a wide choice of meals and snacks in its open-plan bar and restaurant, and there are well equipped bedrooms, including one on the ground floor.
ROOMS: 10 en suite **FACILITIES:** STV entertainment **PARKING:** 40
NOTES: No dogs (ex guide dogs) **CARDS:**

KEGWORTH See East Midlands Airport

Popped the question? Hotels with Civ Wed in their entry are licensed for civil wedding ceremonies. Maximum numbers for the ceremony only are shown, e.g. Civ Wed 50

KEIGHLEY, West Yorkshire — Map 07 SE04

★★66% Dalesgate
406 Skipton Rd, Utley BD20 6HP
☎ 01535 664930 Fax 01535 611253
e-mail: Stephen.E.Atha@btinternet.com
Dir: *from Town centre follow A629 over rdbt. After 3/4 mile turn tight into St. John's Road and 1st right into Hotel car park*
Originally the residence of a local chapel minister, this modern hotel has been expanded with the addition of a new wing to provide well furnished bedrooms. The hotel also has a cosy bar and a comfortable restaurant serving a good range of well produced dishes.
ROOMS: 20 en suite (2 fmly) s fr £45; d fr £65 (incl. bkfst) * LB **FACILITIES:** ch fac **PARKING:** 25 **CARDS:**

KENDAL, Cumbria — Map 07 SD59

see also Crooklands

★★★73%
The Castle Green Hotel in Kendal

LA9 6BH
☎ 01539 734000 Fax 01539 735522
e-mail: reception@castlegreen.co.uk
Dir: *from M6 junc 36, head for Kendal. Right at 1st traffic lights, left at rdbt to "K" Village then right for 0.75m to hotel at T-junct*
Commanding views of the distant fells, this new hotel has been created from former offices. Bedrooms are stylish and well equipped, and many enjoy fine views. The Greenhouse Restaurant provides imaginative and skilfully prepared dishes, and a business centre offers conference facilities.
ROOMS: 100 en suite (3 fmly) s £65-£71; d £75-£89 (incl. bkfst) * LB **FACILITIES:** STV Indoor swimming (H) Tennis (grass) Solarium Gym Croquet lawn Steam Room Aerobics Yoga Beauty Salon Hairdressing entertainment **CONF:** Thtr 400 Class 200 Board 100 Del £99 * **SERVICES:** Lift **PARKING:** 230 **NOTES:** No dogs (ex guide dogs) No smoking in restaurant Civ Wed 300 **CARDS:**

★★64% Garden House
Fowl-ing Ln LA9 6PH
☎ 01539 731131 Fax 01539 740064
e-mail: gardenhouse.hotel@virgin.net
Dir: *leave M6 junct 36 follow signs for A6 north & turn right at Duke of Cumberland after 200yds take 2nd right, next to secondhand car show room*
An early 19th-century country house situated in wooded grounds and formal gardens. Bedrooms are well equipped and individually furnished and some have four-posters. The conservatory restaurant, with a mural of the hotel on one wall, looks out over the garden.
ROOMS: 11 en suite (2 fmly) No smoking in 4 bedrooms s £49.50-£57; d £75-£79 (incl. bkfst) * LB **FACILITIES:** Croquet lawn Putting green **CONF:** Thtr 60 Class 40 Board 30 **PARKING:** 30 **NOTES:** No smoking in restaurant RS 26-30 Dec **CARDS:**

KENILWORTH, Warwickshire — Map 04 SP27

★★★★63% De Montfort
The Square CV8 1ED
MACDONALD HOTELS ★★★★
☎ 01926 855944 Fax 01926 855952
Dir: *take A452 into Kenilworth, hotel at top end of main street by rdbt*
Located in the heart of Shakespeare country the De Montfort Hotel offers accommodation of a high standard. Its public areas include a smart café bar and a restaurant.

continued

ROOMS: 104 en suite (15 fmly) No smoking in 50 bedrooms **FACILITIES:** STV Pool table entertainment **CONF:** Thtr 250 Class 90 Board 60 **SERVICES:** Lift **PARKING:** 85 **NOTES:** No smoking in restaurant **CARDS:**

★★★★63% Chesford Grange
Chesford Bridge CV8 2LD
PRINCIPAL HOTELS
☎ 01926 859331 Fax 01926 859075
e-mail: sales.chesford@btinternet.com
Dir: *0.5m SE junct A46/A452 at rdbt take right exit signed Leamington Spa. After approx 250yds at x-rds turn right hotel on left*
With good access to major road links, this successful business and conference hotel offers bedrooms ranging in style from standard to 'executive'. All are well equipped and comfortable.
ROOMS: 145 en suite 9 annexe en suite (12 fmly) No smoking in 55 bedrooms s £115-£130; d £130-£145 (incl. bkfst) * LB **FACILITIES:** STV Indoor swimming (H) Fishing Sauna Solarium Gym Jacuzzi/spa entertainment Xmas **CONF:** Thtr 860 Class 300 Board 50 Del from £110 * **SERVICES:** Lift **PARKING:** 550 **NOTES:** No smoking in restaurant Civ Wed 80 **CARDS:**

★★68% Clarendon House
Old High St CV8 1LZ
☎ 01926 857668 Fax 01926 850669
e-mail: clarendon@nuthurst-grange.com
Dir: *from A452 pass castle, then left and continue into High Street*
Situated in the conservation area, this building incorporates the original 15th-century timber-framed Castle Tavern, which was supported by an oak tree. The public rooms have been totally transformed with modern appointments tastefully introduced through a lounge bar and brasserie. Bedroom styles and sizes vary, but all are equipped with modern facilities.

continued

K

KENILWORTH, continued

ROOMS: 30 en suite (1 fmly) No smoking in 6 bedrooms s £49.50-£55; d £75-£90 (incl. bkfst) * LB **CONF:** Thtr 150 Class 100 Board 70 Del £99 * **PARKING:** 30 **NOTES:** Closed 1 week Xmas Civ Wed 150 **CARDS:**

KESWICK, Cumbria Map 11 NY22

★★★72% Dale Head Hall Lakeside

Lake Thirlmere CA12 4TN
☎ 017687 72478 017687 71070
e-mail: onthelakeside@dale-head-hall.co.uk
Dir: *mid-way between Keswick & Grasmere, off A591, onto private drive to shores of Lake Thirlmere*

Dated from the 16th-century, the house features inviting lounges and tastefully decorated bedrooms. Dinner offers good British cooking, along with a recommended wine list.
ROOMS: 12 en suite (1 fmly) No smoking in all bedrooms d £80-£100 (incl. bkfst) * LB **FACILITIES:** Tennis Fishing Croquet lawn Xmas **PARKING:** 21 **NOTES:** No dogs No smoking in restaurant Closed 31 Dec-3 Feb **CARDS:**

See advert on opposite page

★★★72% Derwentwater

Portinscale CA12 5RE
☎ 017687 72538 017687 71002
e-mail: derwentwater.hotel@dial.pipex.com
Dir: *off A66 turn into village of Portinscale, follow signs*

With gardens that stretch down to the shores of Derwentwater, this pretty hotel offers bedrooms with many thoughtful extras and some with good views of the lake. The conservatory, also with lake views, is a popular place for taking afternoon tea and snacks. There is also a small shop selling local specialities and souvenirs.
ROOMS: 46 en suite (1 fmly) s £79-£89; d £130-£180 (incl. bkfst) * LB **FACILITIES:** Fishing Pool table Putting green entertainment Xmas **SERVICES:** Lift **PARKING:** 120 **NOTES:** No smoking in restaurant **CARDS:**

See advert on page 283

★★★66% Skiddaw

Main St CA12 5BN
☎ 017687 72071 017687 74850
Dir: *A66 to Keswick follow signs for town centre. Hotel in the Market Square in heart of the town*

Overlooking the market square, some of the rooms from this hotel boast views of the famous Skiddaw. A major refurbishment programme has resulted in some stylish 'summit' rooms, in addition to a contemporary restaurant. The lounge bar is popular for coffee, lunch and afternoon tea, and there is also the quieter private residents' lounge.
ROOMS: 40 en suite (7 fmly) No smoking in 10 bedrooms **FACILITIES:** STV Sauna Free use of out of town leisure fac **CONF:** Thtr 70 Class 60 Board 40 **SERVICES:** Lift **PARKING:** 22 **NOTES:** No dogs (ex guide dogs) No smoking in restaurant **CARDS:**

See advert on opposite page

★★★61% Keswick Country House

PRINCIPAL HOTELS

Station Rd CA12 4NQ
☎ 017687 72020 017687 71300
Dir: *adjacent to Keswick Leisure Pool*
Country house hotel surrounded by gardens which nestle under Latrigg and Skiddaw fells just a short stroll across Fitz Park from the town's market place. The former railway station is contained by the hotel and connected by a Victorian conservatory.
ROOMS: 74 en suite (10 fmly) s £88; d £120 (incl. bkfst) * LB **FACILITIES:** STV Snooker Croquet lawn Putting green Pitch & putt entertainment Xmas **CONF:** Thtr 80 Class 35 Board 35 Del from £80 * **SERVICES:** Lift **PARKING:** 70 **NOTES:** No smoking in restaurant Civ Wed 130 **CARDS:**

See advert on opposite page

★★73% Highfield

The Heads CA12 5ER
☎ 017687 72508
Dir: *M6, J40 – A66 take 2nd exit at rdbt, turn left follow road to T-junc left again & right at mini rdbt, The Heads is 4th turning on right*
This attractive hotel enjoys a peaceful setting, overlooking the park with stunning views of the mountains beyond. Bedrooms are stylishly furnished to a high standard and thoughtfully equipped. Guests can relax in a choice of homely lounges which look out onto the well tended gardens. Hotel cuisine is of a high standard with an interesting range of carefully prepared dishes.
ROOMS: 18 en suite (1 fmly) No smoking in all bedrooms s £33-£40; d £54-£80 (incl. bkfst) * LB **PARKING:** 19 **NOTES:** No dogs No children 8yrs No smoking in restaurant Closed Dec-Jan excl. Xmas & New Year **CARDS:**

> TV dinner? Room service at three stars and above.

PH

T H E

KESWICK

COUNTRY HOUSE HOTEL

KESWICK ON DERWENTWATER

AA ★★★ AA

A splendid fully refurbished Victorian hotel set in four acres of landscaped gardens in the heart of the Lake District, minutes walk from the centre of Keswick.

Bygone Breakaways

Enjoy a luxury break inclusive of dinner, bed, breakfast and free entrance to several of the Lake District's major attractions. THEATRE, GOLF AND WALKING BREAKS ALSO AVAILABLE. **From £60.00 per person per night.**

Conferences and Meetings

A superb range of character function rooms are available for conferences for up to 100 delegates and private dinners.

The hotel has a large car park and the lakeland towns of Windermere and Penrith are only a 20 minute drive away.

The Keswick Country House Hotel
Station Road, Keswick, Cumbria CA12 4NQ
Tel: 0800 454454 www.principalhotels.co.uk

AA
★★★
THE
Skiddaw
HOTEL
Keswick's Premier Hotel
Main Street
Keswick
Cumbria

Telephone: (017687) 72071 Fax: (017687) 74850
Web: www.skiddawhotel.co.uk
Email: info@skiddawhotel.co.uk

Stay in comfort in the centre of Keswick. Enjoy true hospitality and excellent cuisine in this family run hotel. All rooms are ensuite with colour TV and SKY channels, hair dryer, tea/coffee maker and telephone. Lovely cuisine with many Cumbrian specialities.

Superb Summit Rooms and Family Suites

GOLF breaks and champagne luxury breaks available. FREE entrance to nearby exclusive leisure club. Special Breaks always available.

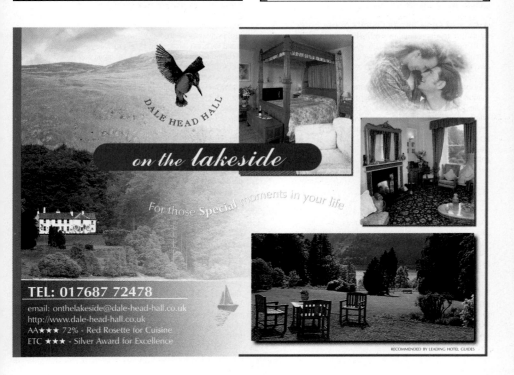

DALE HEAD HALL

on the lakeside

For those Special moments in your life

TEL: 017687 72478

email: onthelakeside@dale-head-hall.co.uk
http://www.dale-head-hall.co.uk
AA★★★ 72% - Red Rosette for Cuisine
ETC ★★★ - Silver Award for Excellence

RECOMMENDED BY LEADING HOTEL GUIDES

K

KESWICK, continued

★★72% Lyzzick Hall Country House
Under Skiddaw CA12 4PY
☎ 017687 72277 017687 72278
e-mail: lyzzickhall@netscapeonline.co.uk
Dir: *from M6 junct 40, A66 Keswick do not enter town keep to Keswick by-pass, 3rd exit off rdbt onto A591 to Carlisle, hotel is 1.5m on right*
Nestling in the foothills of Skiddaw, this fine country house has lovely views across the valley. There are two spacious lounges, a small bar area and an attractive restaurant that offers a wide range of dishes plus an interesting wine list. Bedrooms are well equipped and thoughtfully decorated.
ROOMS: 28 en suite 1 annexe en suite (3 fmly) s £45-£48; d £90-£96 (incl. bkfst) * LB **FACILITIES:** Indoor swimming (H) Sauna Jacuzzi/spa ch fac **PARKING:** 40 **NOTES:** No dogs No smoking in restaurant Closed 24-26 Dec & mid Jan-mid Feb **CARDS:**

★★70% Lairbeck
Vicarage Hill CA12 5QB
☎ 017687 73373 017687 73144
e-mail: info@lairbeck.demon.co.uk
Dir: *follow A66 to rdbt with A591 turn left then immediately right onto Vicarage Hill, hotel 150 yds on right*
Situated close to the town but peacefully set amidst attractive gardens, this inviting Victorian country house provides a range of furnished bedrooms in a variety of sizes and styles. There is a welcoming residents' bar and a smart dining room in which a range of freshly prepared dishes are served each day.
ROOMS: 14 en suite (1 fmly) No smoking in all bedrooms s £38; d £76 (incl. bkfst) * LB **PARKING:** 16 **NOTES:** No dogs No children 5yrs No smoking in restaurant Closed Jan & Feb RS Dec
CARDS:

★★69% *Applethwaite Country House Hotel*
Applethwaite, Underskiddaw CA12 4PL
☎ 017687 72413 017687 75706
e-mail: ryan@applethwaite.freeserve.co.uk
Dir: *from M6 follow A66 to Keswick. Do not take left turn into Keswick but continue to rdbt then right A591 to Carlisle and 1st right signed Underscar*
A Victorian residence built of local stone and standing in the shadow of Skiddaw. Traditional public rooms enjoy stunning views of the Borrowdale Valley and include comfortable non-smoking sitting rooms. Home cooking is served in the dining room. Bedrooms offer both traditional and modern furnishings.
ROOMS: 12 en suite (2 fmly) No smoking in all bedrooms
FACILITIES: Pool table Croquet lawn Putting green Bowling green
PARKING: 10 **NOTES:** No dogs (ex guide dogs) No children 5yrs No smoking in restaurant Closed Dec-10 Feb **CARDS:**

★★69% Chaucer House
Derwentwater Place CA12 4DR
☎ 017687 72318 & 73223 017687 75551
e-mail: enquiries@chaucer-house.demon.co.uk

THE CIRCLE
Selected Individual Hotels
GREAT BRITAIN

Dir: *turn right off A591 into Manor Brow, continue down hill, past Castlerigg Catholic Training Centre and sharp double bend, hotel on right*
This friendly hotel enjoys a quiet residential location close to the town centre. Bedrooms are neatly appointed and well equipped. Public areas include a range of lounges, a well stocked bar and an attractive dining room where guests are offered a wide range of imaginative dishes.
ROOMS: 33 rms (31 en suite) (4 fmly) s £20-£25; d £62-£74.50 (incl. bkfst) * LB **FACILITIES:** STV **SERVICES:** Lift **PARKING:** 25
NOTES: No smoking in restaurant Closed Dec-Jan
CARDS:

★★69% Thwaite Howe
Thornthwaite CA12 5SA
☎ 017687 78281 017687 78529
Dir: *follow signs to Thornthwaite Gallery from A66 approx 3 miles from Keswick. Hotel is signposted from outside Gallery*

This Victorian country house enjoys an idyllic setting and magnificent views across the valley and distant hills. Public rooms feature a cosy residents' bar, comfortable lounge with a real fire, and an attractive dining room. Bedrooms are all individually furnished and well equipped.
ROOMS: 8 en suite No smoking in all bedrooms s £32-£57; d £66-£72 (incl. bkfst) * LB **FACILITIES:** entertainment Xmas **PARKING:** 12
NOTES: No children 12yrs No smoking in restaurant
CARDS:

★★68% Edwardene
26 Southey St CA12 4EF
☎ 017687 73586 017687 73824
e-mail: haveabreak@edwardenehotel.fsnet.co.uk
Dir: *take A591 towards Keswick town centre. At pedestrian traffic lights turn left into Southey St*
Just a stones throw from the town centre and forming part of a grand Victorian terrace, this hotel provides well equipped accommodation. The stylish, well equipped bedrooms vary in size and style and are all nicely furnished in pine. There are two cosy lounges, and a delightfully decorated dining room.
ROOMS: 11 en suite (1 fmly) No smoking in all bedrooms s £25; d £50 (incl. bkfst) * **FACILITIES:** Xmas **NOTES:** No smoking in restaurant
CARDS:

★★65% Crow Park
The Heads CA12 5ER
☎ 017687 72208 017687 74776
A welcoming atmosphere prevails at this holiday hotel which enjoys views over the lake to the Borrowdale Valley. Attractive public areas include a lounge, a cosy bar and a dining room. Bedrooms are variable in size with practical appointments and a good range of amenities.
ROOMS: 26 en suite (1 fmly) No smoking in 1 bedroom s fr £30.50; d fr £61 (incl. bkfst) * LB **FACILITIES:** STV Xmas **PARKING:** 27
NOTES: No smoking in restaurant **CARDS:**

★★64% Horse & Farrier Inn
Threlkeld CA12 4SQ
☎ 017687 79688 017687 79824
Dir: *12m from Penrith M6, just off A66 4m from Keswick*
This attractive traditional inn offers good value accommodation. Bedrooms are smartly appointed. Open plan public areas retain much original character and guests can enjoy an interesting range of carefully prepared dishes offered in the dining rooms.
ROOMS: 9 en suite No smoking in all bedrooms s fr £30.50; d fr £61 (incl. bkfst) * LB **PARKING:** 60 **CARDS:**

AA ★★★
77% ❀❀ food

The Borrowdale Gates

Country House Hotel

Grange in Borrowdale
Keswick, Cumbria CA12 5UQ
Telephone: 017687 77204 Fax: 017687 77254

The hotel is surrounded by two acres of wooded gardens and is situated on the edge of the ancient hamlet of Grange amidst breathtaking scenery. Comfortable lounges with log fires and antiques. 28 tastefully furnished en-suite bedrooms including 13 new Premier rooms. Indulge yourself in excellent rosette award food complemented by a fine wine list.

ARMATHWAITE HALL HOTEL

★ ★ ★ ★

English Lake District

Armathwaite Hall, 4-star Country House Hotel, set in 400 acres of parkland with lake frontage. Log fires, wood panelled rooms and superb food. Leisure Club & Beauty Salon. Our own Equestrian Centre and Trotters World of Animals. Families welcome – excellent childrens programme. Perfect for holidays or conferences and team-building courses.

Bassenthwaite Lake, Keswick, Cumbria, CA12 4RE
Tel: 017687 76551 Fax: 017687 76220
Web Site: www.armathwaite-hall.com
E Mail: reservations@armathwaite-hall.com

Keswick – Unrivalled Lakeshore Location – Lake District

★★★

The Derwentwater Hotel

Remaining in private hands The Derwentwater is the epitome of a Lakeland Country House Hotel without being the least pretentious. A relaxing haven on the shores of Lake Derwentwater in 16 acres of conservation grounds (designated European area of special conservation). Fabulous lake and fell views from our conservatory and many bedrooms.

Be pampered in our Deluxe Rooms, which come complete with Fridge, CD and Video player, Slippers and Bathrobe, Sherry Decanter, lounge area and much much more.

Quality local produce is prepared with skill and care in our Deers Leap Restaurant.

Award Winning Hospitality, Customer Care and Environmental Policy.

Dedicated to realising the true art of RELAXATION.

Telephone 017687 72538

Visit our website: www.derwentwater-hotel.@.uk

K

KESWICK, continued

★★64% Ladstock Country House
Thornthwaite CA12 5RZ
☎ 017687 78210 017687 78088
e-mail: enquiries@keswickhotel.co.uk
This traditional country house hotel is set in pretty gardens overlooking Bassenthwaite and the valley towards Skiddaw. Once the local parsonage, the house contains splendid oak panelling and mullioned windows designed by Sir Edwin Lutyens.
ROOMS: 18 en suite d £70-£90 (incl. bkfst) * **NOTES:** No dogs
CARDS:

KETTERING, Northamptonshire Map 04 SP87

★★★★72% Kettering Park

Kettering Parkway NN15 6XT
☎ 01536 416666 01536 416171
e-mail: kpark@shireinns.co.uk
***Dir:** just off junct 9 of A14, M1 to A1 link, on the Kettering Venture Park*
This smart, purpose-built hotel is situated just outside Kettering and offers spacious, thoughtfully designed bedrooms and suites. Langberrys Restaurant serves an imaginative menu. Guests will appreciate the excellent leisure facilities, and the well supervised staff are friendly and helpful.
ROOMS: 119 en suite (28 fmly) No smoking in 60 bedrooms s fr £125 (incl. bkfst) * LB **FACILITIES:** STV Indoor swimming (H) Squash Snooker Sauna Solarium Gym Jacuzzi/spa Steam rooms Childrens splash pool Xmas **CONF:** Thtr 260 Class 120 Board 40 Del from £105 * **SERVICES:** Lift **PARKING:** 200 **NOTES:** No smoking in restaurant Civ Wed 200 **CARDS:**

⇧ *Travelodge*
Travelodge
On the A14
☎ 0800 850950
This modern building offers accommodation in smart, spacious and well equipped bedrooms, all with en suite bathrooms. Refreshments may be taken at the nearby family restaurant. For further details and the Travelodge phone number, consult the Hotel Groups page.

KIDDERMINSTER, Worcestershire Map 07 SO87

★★★★67% Stone Manor
Stone DY10 4PJ
☎ 01562 777555 01562 777834
***Dir:** 2m SE on A448*
This former Manor House stands in 25 acres of beautiful grounds and gardens. Bedrooms are well equipped, spacious and tastefully decorated in a variety of styles. An excellent range of facilities include function rooms, lounges and a convenient car park.
ROOMS: 52 en suite No smoking in 6 bedrooms d £70-£135 * LB **FACILITIES:** STV Outdoor swimming Tennis (hard) Pool table Croquet lawn Putting green Xmas **CONF:** Thtr 150 Class 48 Board 60 Del £135 * **PARKING:** 400 **NOTES:** No smoking in restaurant Civ Wed 50
CARDS:

★★★63% Gainsborough House
Bewdley Hill DY11 6BS
☎ 01562 820041 01562 66179
e-mail: reservations@gainsboroughhotel.co.uk
***Dir:** on A456 Kidderminster/Bewdley road, at General Hospital, straight over at traffic lights, hotel 200yds on right-hand side*
This Listed Georgian building, situated on the edge of the town, has benefited from substantial improvements to public areas. Bedrooms are well equipped and comfortable. Additional features include a bar lounge, carvery and attractive function rooms.
continued

ROOMS: 43 en suite (8 fmly) No smoking in 12 bedrooms s fr £65; d fr £80 * LB **FACILITIES:** Xmas **CONF:** Thtr 250 Class 80 Board 60 Del from £95 * **PARKING:** 130 **NOTES:** No smoking in restaurant
CARDS:

★★64% Cedars
MINOTEL Great Britain
Mason Rd DY11 6AG
☎ 01562 515595 01562 751103
e-mail: reservations@cedars-hotel.co.uk
***Dir:** on ring road follow signs to Bridgnorth (A442) take left turn from last rdbt signed Habberley, 400 metres on left opposite Police Station*
The Cedars is a privately owned, detached house situated in a residential area close to the centre of Kidderminster. Bedrooms are comfortable and attractively furnished. Additional facilities include a lounge bar, an adjacent conservatory lounge, dining room, and a delightful garden.
ROOMS: 21 en suite (3 fmly) No smoking in 7 bedrooms s £48-£58; d £58-£72 (incl. bkfst) * LB **FACILITIES:** STV ch fac **CONF:** Thtr 25 Class 15 Board 12 **PARKING:** 21 **NOTES:** No dogs (ex guide dogs) No smoking in restaurant Closed 24 Dec-2 Jan
CARDS:

KINGHAM, Oxfordshire Map 04 SP22

★★★73% Mill House Hotel & Restaurant
OX7 6UH
☎ 01608 658188 01608 658492
e-mail: stay@millhousehotel.co.uk
***Dir:** turn off A44 at Chipping Norton or Stow-on-the-Wold onto B4450, hotel on outskirts of Kingham village signposted by brown tourist signs*

This Cotswold stone hotel is set in extensive well kept grounds, bordered by its own trout stream. Bedrooms are individually decorated and thoughtfully equipped. Guests may relax in the lounge or in the bar with its log burning fire. The restaurant is popular with locals and guests alike.
ROOMS: 21 en suite 2 annexe en suite (1 fmly) **FACILITIES:** STV Fishing Croquet lawn **CONF:** Thtr 70 Class 24 Board 20 Del from £125 * **PARKING:** 62 **NOTES:** No smoking in restaurant
CARDS:

KINGSBRIDGE, Devon Map 03 SX74

★★★79% Buckland-Tout-Saints
Goveton TQ7 2DS
☎ 01548 853055 01548 856261
e-mail: buckland@tout-saints.co.uk
***Dir:** turn off A381 Totnes/Kingsbridge Rd towards Goveton, left into Goveton and up hill towards St Peters Church, hotel 2nd right after church*
This Queen Anne manor house stands in seven acres of grounds. Bedrooms are individual in style and size and day rooms include
continued

an intimate restaurant, a choice of lounges, and a bar-lounge. There is also a function room and the hotel has a license for Civil Weddings.

ROOMS: 15 en suite (1 fmly) No smoking in 1 bedroom s £75-£120; d £130-£240 (incl. bkfst) * **FACILITIES:** Croquet lawn Putting green Xmas **CONF:** Thtr 150 Class 100 Board 70 Del from £95 * **PARKING:** 42 **NOTES:** No smoking in restaurant Civ Wed 130 **CARDS:**

See advert on this page

★★70% White House

Chillington TQ7 2JX
☎ 01548 580580 📠 01548 581124
e-mail: tinawhthse@cs.com
Dir: *on the A379 at the eastern end of the village*

Set in an acre of gardens, this listed building has a relaxed ambience enhanced by professional service. Bedrooms are spacious and well furnished and many enjoy views of the garden and surrounding hills. The Garden Room Restaurant has a lovely outlook and there is a choice of comfortable lounges.
ROOMS: 7 en suite (1 fmly) No smoking in all bedrooms s £60-£72; d £92-£112 (incl. bkfst) * LB **FACILITIES:** Croquet lawn Xmas **PARKING:** 8 **NOTES:** No dogs (ex guide dogs) No smoking in restaurant **CARDS:**

KINGS LANGLEY, Hertfordshire — Map 04 TL00

Premier Lodge

Hempstead Rd WD4 8BR
☎ 0870 700 1568 📠 0870 700 1569
Premier Lodge offers modern, well equipped, en suite accommodation suitable for both business and leisure travellers. Meals can be taken at the adjacent popular restaurant and bar which is fully licensed. For further details, consult the Hotel Groups page.
ROOMS: 60 en suite d £42 *

KING'S LYNN, Norfolk — Map 09 TF62

★★★ Congham Hall Country House

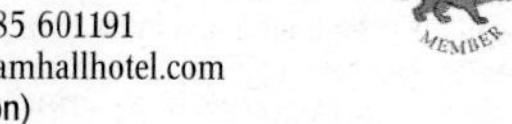

Lynn Rd PE32 1AH
☎ 01485 600250 📠 01485 601191
e-mail: reception@conghamhallhotel.com
(For full entry see Grimston)

★★★68% Knights Hill

Knights Hill Village, South Wootton PE30 3HQ
☎ 01553 675566 📠 01553 675568
e-mail: reception@knightshill.co.uk
Dir: *junct A148/A149*

Knights Hill is a hotel village complex, set around a 16th-century site. In the main house and the surrounding buildings, historical charm has been combined with modern facilities such as conference and banqueting suites and an indoor leisure centre. The accommodation is mainly in extensions to the original hunting lodge. Dining options include formal meals in the Garden Restaurant, or informal choices in the Farmers Arms pub.
ROOMS: 43 en suite 18 annexe en suite No smoking in 16 bedrooms s £85-£110; d £90-£125 * LB **FACILITIES:** STV Indoor swimming (H) Tennis (hard) Sauna Solarium Gym Croquet lawn Jacuzzi/spa Heli-pad Xmas **CONF:** Thtr 350 Class 150 Board 30 **PARKING:** 350 **NOTES:** No smoking in restaurant Civ Wed 75 **CARDS:**

Read all about it! Newspapers delivered to bedrooms in four and five star hotels.

KINGS LYNN, continued

★★★66% Butterfly

Beveridge Way, Hardwick Narrows PE30 4NB
☎ 01553 771707 🖹 01553 768027
e-mail: kingsbutterfly@linone.net
Dir: *on A10/A47 roundabout, exit for Hardwick Narrows Ind Est*
This popular modern hotel is ideal for business travellers. A variety of bedroom types are available; ladies', studio and ground floor rooms are all provided. The lounge areas and Walt's Restaurant and Bar are both popular venues.
ROOMS: 50 en suite (2 fmly) No smoking in 10 bedrooms d fr £67.50 * LB **FACILITIES:** STV **CONF:** Thtr 40 Class 21 Board 22 **PARKING:** 70 **NOTES:** No dogs (ex guide dogs) **CARDS:**

★★★64% The Duke's Head

REGAL

Tuesday Market Place PE30 1JS
☎ 01553 774996 🖹 01553 763556
Dir: *in town centre one-way system go left when road splits then left at lights, along St Anns St into Chapel St, hotel just past carpark on right*

The Dukes Head is a 16th-century coaching inn which overlooks the Tuesday Market Place. Bedrooms are smartly furnished, well equipped and have a modern appearance. Public areas include a lounge, a non smoking bar and a public bar. In addition there is the Griffins restaurant and a more traditional main restaurant.
ROOMS: 71 en suite (2 fmly) No smoking in 33 bedrooms s £69-£79; d £85-£95 * LB **FACILITIES:** Xmas **CONF:** Thtr 240 Class 120 Board 60 Del from £80 * **SERVICES:** Lift **PARKING:** 41 **NOTES:** No smoking in restaurant Civ Wed 100 **CARDS:**

★★70% *Globe Hotel*

Tuesday Market Place PE30 1EZ
☎ 01553 772617 🖹 01553 761315
Dir: *from A10 or A1/A47 follow signs for King's Lynn centre (Old Town). Hotel overlooks the market place*
A relaxed pub-restaurant with rooms, the focal point of the hotel is the busy popular family style restaurant, offering a wide variety of dishes. The Globe is located on a corner of Tuesday Market Square in the 'Old Town' of Kings Lynn. Bedrooms are equipped with a range of useful facilities.
ROOMS: 38 en suite (4 fmly) No smoking in 18 bedrooms **FACILITIES:** STV Pool table entertainment **CONF:** Thtr 60 Class 40 Board 30 **PARKING:** 20 **NOTES:** No dogs (ex guide dogs) **CARDS:**

★★67% *Russet House*

53 Goodwins Rd PE30 5PE
☎ 01553 773098 🖹 01553 773098
Dir: *follow town centre signs along Hardwick Rd at small rdbt just before Southgates turn right into Vancouver Av after short drive hotel on left*
Russet House dates back to 1890, and is just a short walk from the River Ouse and Kings Lynn town centre. Bedrooms are neatly decorated, have a bright airy feel and offer a good degree of comfort. The public rooms feature a lounge with open fire and French doors which open onto the gardens.
ROOMS: 13 en suite (2 fmly) No smoking in 1 bedroom **PARKING:** 14 **NOTES:** No smoking in restaurant Closed 22 Dec-1 Jan RS Sun (restaurant closed) **CARDS:**

See advert on opposite page

★★67% Stuart House

35 Goodwins Rd PE30 5QX
☎ 01553 772169 🖹 01553 774788
e-mail: stuarthousehotel@btinternet.com
Dir: *A47/A10/A149 rdbt follow signs for King Lynn Town Centre. Pass under the Southgate Arch right into Guanock Ter. Right Goodwins Rd*
In a quiet area close to the town, this comfortable hotel offers informal public rooms, and guests may choose between meals in the popular bar, or the carte menu and daily specials on offer in the elegant restaurant. The accommodation is in a variety of sizes and attractively appointed.
ROOMS: 18 en suite (2 fmly) No smoking in 4 bedrooms s £52; d £72-£100 (incl. bkfst) * LB **FACILITIES:** STV Jacuzzi/spa entertainment Xmas **CONF:** Thtr 40 Class 40 Board 30 Del from £68 * **PARKING:** 30 **NOTES:** No dogs (ex guide dogs) No smoking in restaurant **CARDS:**

★★65% The Tudor Rose

St Nicholas St, Tuesday Market Place PE30 1LR
☎ 01553 762824 🖹 01553 764894
e-mail: KLTudorRose@aol.com
Dir: *Hotel is off Tuesday Market Place in the centre of Kings Lynn*
A Grade II listed building dating back to before the 14th century. There are exposed beams in the restaurant, and the entire hotel has a pleasant atmosphere. Public rooms include a small reception lounge and two bars, where real ales and informal fare are served. Bedroom styles and sizes vary and each room is well equipped.
ROOMS: 13 rms (11 en suite) s fr £45; d fr £60 (incl. bkfst) * LB **NOTES:** No smoking in restaurant **CARDS:**

★★63% Grange

Willow Park, South Wootton Ln PE30 3BP
☎ 01553 673777 & 671222 🖹 01553 673777
e-mail: grange@btinternet.com
Dir: *take A148 towards King's Lynn for 1.5m at traffic lights turn left into Wootton Rd 400yds on right South Wootton Ln hotel 1st on left*
This imposing yet welcoming Edwardian house sits in a quiet residential area, surrounded by its own gardens. Most of the bedrooms are in the main house, with some in an adjacent courtyard-style annexe. All the accommodation is comfortably appointed.
ROOMS: 5 en suite 4 annexe en suite (2 fmly) **CONF:** Thtr 20 Class 15 Board 12 **PARKING:** 15 **NOTES:** No smoking in restaurant **CARDS:**

KINGSTON UPON THAMES, Greater London
See LONDON SECTION plan 1 *C1*

★★★70% Kingston Lodge

Kingston Hill KT2 7NP
☎ 0870 400 8115 🖹 020 8547 1013
Dir: *A3 Robin Hood intersection A308 towards Kingston. Hotel 1.5m on left*
The location of this friendly hotel and the quality of many of the bedrooms contribute to its all round popularity. Overlooking the peaceful courtyard there is now a smart, new brasserie, Burnt Orange, which provides a modern style of eating in an informal atmosphere.

continued

ROOMS: 64 en suite No smoking in 25 bedrooms d £150-£170 * LB **FACILITIES:** STV entertainment **CONF:** Thtr 80 Class 50 Board 35 Del from £155 * **PARKING:** 74 **CARDS:**

★★61% Chase Lodge
10 Park Rd, Hampton Wick KT1 4AS
☎ 020 8943 1862 020 8943 9363
e-mail: chaselodgehotel@aol.com
***Dir:** from M3 take 1st exit right for Hampton Court. After 4m left at rdbt & then left onto A308. After 1.5 miles turn left A310 & left again*
Close to the centre of Kingston in Hampton Wick, Chase Lodge offers high standards of comfort and individually fashioned bedrooms, three with four-poster beds and one with fabric-covered walls. Public areas comprise an open-plan conservatory restaurant and bar.
ROOMS: 6 en suite 4 annexe en suite (1 fmly) No smoking in 2 bedrooms s £65-£95; d £95-£125 (incl. bkfst) * LB **FACILITIES:** STV Xmas **CONF:** Class 60 Board 35 **PARKING:** 20
CARDS:

KINGTON, Herefordshire — Map 03 SO25

★★66% Burton
Mill St HR5 3BQ
☎ 01544 230323 01544 230323
e-mail: burton@hotelkington.kc31td.co.uk
***Dir:** at rdbt of A44/A411 interchange take road signed town centre*
This privately owned and friendly hotel is located in the town centre. It provides spacious bedrooms, which are well equipped and suitable for both business people and tourists. Facilities include a lounge bar, a small lounge and a restaurant. There is also a meeting room and a large ballroom.
ROOMS: 16 en suite (5 fmly) s £40; d £59-£65 (incl. bkfst) * LB **FACILITIES:** Xmas **CONF:** Thtr 150 Class 100 Board 20 Del from £55 * **PARKING:** 50 **CARDS:**

KIRKBURTON, West Yorkshire — Map 07 SE11

★★★69% Hanover International
Penistone Rd HD8 0PE
☎ 01484 607788 01484 607961
***Dir:** 3m S of Huddersfield town centre, on A629, close to M1 and M62*

This converted former Victorian textile mill lies just a few miles to the south of Huddersfield. Modern bedrooms are generally quite spacious and are nicely furnished. A wide range of dishes is offered in the comfortable restaurant, and a variety of meeting and function suites is also available.
ROOMS: 47 en suite (2 fmly) No smoking in 20 bedrooms s fr £45; d fr £55 * LB **FACILITIES:** STV Pool table Xmas **CONF:** Thtr 150 Class 30 Board 42 Del from £70 * **PARKING:** 100 **NOTES:** No smoking in restaurant Closed 26 to 30 Dec Civ Wed 80
CARDS:

KIRKBY LONSDALE, Cumbria — Map 07 SD67

★★69% Pheasant Inn
LA6 2RX
☎ 015242 71230 015242 71230
e-mail: pheasant.casterton@eggconnect.net
***Dir:** leave M6 junc36 onto A65, turn left at A683 1m onwards in centre of village*

A family run inn, located in the village of Casterton north of Kirby Lonsdale. Public areas include a choice of cosy bars and a panelled restaurant, where a range of home-cooked fare is offered at competitive prices. Bedrooms are variable in size with both modern and traditional furnishings.
ROOMS: 11 en suite s fr £40; d fr £72 (incl. bkfst) * LB **FACILITIES:** Xmas **PARKING:** 40 **NOTES:** No smoking in restaurant Closed 4-6 Jan **CARDS:**

KIRBY LONSDALE, continued

★★56% ***Plough Hotel***
Cow Brow LA6 1PJ
☎ 015395 67227 015395 67848
Dir: *turn off junc 36 M6, head for Skipton/Kirkby Lonsdale, 1m from M6*

This coaching inn combines the best of traditional values with many modern amenities. Bedrooms vary in size, but all are soundly furnished and suitably equipped. Guests can enjoy a wide range of bar snacks, or more serious fare from the daily-changing fixed-price menu in the dining room.
ROOMS: 12 en suite (2 fmly) **FACILITIES:** STV Fishing ch fac **CONF:** Thtr 100 Class 100 Board 60 **PARKING:** 72 **NOTES:** No smoking in restaurant **CARDS:**

K

Premier Collection

★ **Hipping Hall**
Cowan Bridge LA6 2JJ
☎ 015242 71187 015242 72452
e-mail: hippinghal@aol.com
Dir: *0.5m E of Cowan Bridge on A65*
This delightful country house provides comfortable, attractively furnished bedrooms, including two cottage suites with spiral staircases. Breakfast is taken in the morning room; other meals are served in the baronial hall, complete with minstrel's gallery.
ROOMS: 4 en suite 2 annexe en suite No smoking in 4 bedrooms s fr £74; d fr £92 (incl. bkfst) * LB **FACILITIES:** Croquet lawn **PARKING:** 20 **NOTES:** No children 12yrs No smoking in restaurant Closed Dec-Feb **CARDS:**

KIRKBYMOORSIDE, North Yorkshire Map 08 SE68

★★65% **George & Dragon Hotel**
17 Market Place YO62 6AA
☎ 01751 433334 01751 432933
Dir: *off A170 between Thirsk/Scarborough, in centre of market town*
A 17th-century coaching inn set in the centre of a pleasant market town. The pub, with its blazing fire and sporting theme has a great atmosphere. A wide range of hearty dishes is offered from the carte and the blackboard. Spacious bedrooms are individually furnished and housed in two nearby annexes.
ROOMS: 11 en suite 7 annexe en suite (2 fmly) s £45-£49; d £79-£90 (incl. bkfst) * LB **FACILITIES:** Gym Xmas **CONF:** Thtr 50 Class 20 Board 20 **PARKING:** 20 **CARDS:**

KIRKBY STEPHEN, See advert on opposite page

KIRKHAM, Lancashire Map 07 SD43

Premier Lodge (Blackpool East)
Fleetwood Rd, Greenhalgh PR4 3HE
☎ 0870 700 1510 0870 700 1511
PREMIER LODGE
Premier Lodge offers modern, well equipped, en suite accommodation suitable for both business and leisure travellers. Meals can be taken at the adjacent popular restaurant and bar which is fully licensed. For further details, consult the Hotel Groups page.
ROOMS: 28 en suite d £42 *

KNARESBOROUGH, North Yorkshire Map 08 SE35

★★★70% **Dower House**
Bond End HG5 9AL
☎ 01423 863302 01423 867665
e-mail: enquiries@bwdowerhouse.co.uk
Best Western
Dir: *A1M to A59 Harrogate through Knaresborough hotel on right after lights at end of High Street*

Dower House is delightfully furnished and offers well equipped bedrooms and inviting public rooms. The Terrace Restaurant is a perfect setting for quality British cooking, which features much local produce. Conferences and business meetings are catered for and there is also an excellent leisure and health club available.
ROOMS: 28 en suite 3 annexe en suite (2 fmly) No smoking in 20 bedrooms s £60-£88; d £84-£96 (incl. bkfst) * LB **FACILITIES:** Indoor swimming (H) Sauna Gym Jacuzzi/spa Xmas **CONF:** Thtr 65 Class 35 Board 40 Del from £90 * **PARKING:** 80 **NOTES:** No smoking in restaurant **CARDS:**

★★★64% **General Tarleton Inn**
Boroughbridge Rd, Ferrensby HG5 0QB
☎ 01423 340284 01423 340288
e-mail: gti@generaltarleton.co.uk
Dir: *on A6055, on cross road in Ferrensby*
This hotel is renowned for its high standard of cooking not only in its formal restaurant, but also in its bars in which a wide range of dishes are available. Once an 18th-century coaching inn, 14 modern bedrooms have been added in a sympathetic extension and a covered courtyard has been completed.
ROOMS: 14 en suite d £65 * LB **FACILITIES:** Xmas **CONF:** Thtr 60 Class 35 Board 28 Del from £100 * **PARKING:** 80 **NOTES:** No smoking in restaurant Closed 25 Dec only **CARDS:**

KNUTSFORD, Cheshire

Map 07 SJ77

★★★★69% ❀ Mere Court Hotel & Conference Centre

Warrington Rd, Mere WA16 0RW
☎ 01565 831000 🖷 01565 831001
e-mail: sales@merecourt.co.uk

Conveniently located, yet set in its own well tended grounds, Mere Court combines a high standard of accommodation with extensive conference facilities. Bedrooms are especially impressive both in terms of high quality decoration and excellent facilities.

ROOMS: 34 en suite (24 fmly) No smoking in 5 bedrooms s £70-£110; d £80-£130 * **FACILITIES:** STV Croquet lawn Jacuzzi/spa **CONF:** Thtr 120 Class 40 Board 40 Del from £135 * **SERVICES:** Lift **PARKING:** 150 **NOTES:** No smoking in restaurant **CARDS:**

See advert on this page

★★★★66% ❀ Cottons

SHIRE INNS

Manchester Rd WA16 0SU
☎ 01565 650333 🖷 01565 755351
e-mail: cottons@shireinns.co.uk

Dir: *on A50 1m from junct 19 of M6*

Just a short distance from Manchester Airport, this smartly appointed hotel provides an excellent range of facilities, for both business and leisure guests. Bedrooms are thoughtfully equipped and there are superb leisure facilities.

ROOMS: 99 en suite (4 fmly) No smoking in 44 bedrooms d £120-£140 (incl. bkfst) * LB **FACILITIES:** STV Indoor swimming (H) Tennis (hard) Squash Sauna Solarium Gym Jacuzzi/spa Fitness and beauty rooms Steam room Childrens splash pool Xmas **CONF:** Thtr 200 Class 120 Board 30 Del from £110 * **SERVICES:** Lift **PARKING:** 180 **NOTES:** No smoking in restaurant Civ Wed **CARDS:**

★★

Ponder the thought of a few days away from it all.

❀❀

The Black Swan

Proprietors Gordon and Norma Stuart

AT RAVENSTONEDALE

Kirkby Stephen, Cumbria CA17 4NG

Tel: (015396) 23204 Fax: (015396) 23604

A Country Hotel in a delightful village in the Eden Valley, adjacent to the Yorkshire Dales and the English Lakes. Close to the M6 and J38.
Proprietor run, guaranteeing excellent cuisine, attentive service and comfortable accommodation.
All rooms en-suite, TV and telephone.
Superb country walking, private fishing on the river and nearby tarn.

Telephone for brochure and details of our TWO & THREE DAY BREAKS

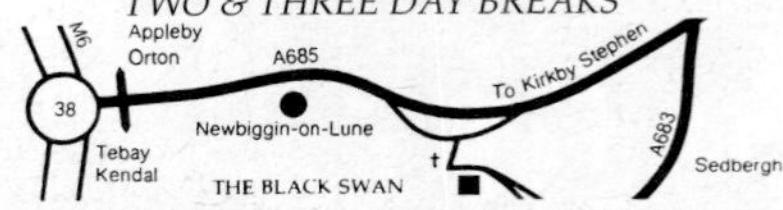

Mere Court – a fine sophisticated country house hotel standing in 7 acres of mature gardens and parkland with an ornamental lake in the most desirable part of the Cheshire countryside, offering a harmonious blend of the historic, modern and luxury. The main house offers four poster suites half tester beds some with double jacuzzi spa baths, all rooms are individually designed and tastefully furnished offering luxury accommodation.

The Lakeside rooms standing at the top of the lake offers king-size bedrooms but is furnished to the same standard as the original house. Extensive Conference and Banqueting facilities, with first class dining facilities in unique surroundings with lakeside views. *Ten minutes from Manchester Airport, M6/M56/M62/M60 motorway networks.*

WARRINGTON ROAD · MERE
KNUTSFORD · CHESHIRE · WA16 0RW · Telephone: 01565 831000
Fax: 01565 831001 · www.merecourt.co.uk · Email: sales@merecourt.co.uk

KNUTSFORD, continued

★★★67% Cottage Restaurant & Lodge
London Rd, Allostock WA16 9LU
☎ 01565 722470 📠 01565 722749
Dir: *on A50 between Holmes Chapel and Knutsford*
Much enlarged over the years, this modern hotel retains the character of the original cottage restaurant. The bedrooms, some of them at ground level, are all in adjacent buildings and are comfortably furnished.
ROOMS: 12 en suite (4 fmly) No smoking in 4 bedrooms s £50-£70; d £50-£80 (incl. bkfst) * **FACILITIES:** STV Xmas **CONF:** Thtr 40 Class 40 Board 40 Del from £65 * **PARKING:** 60 **NOTES:** No dogs (ex guide dogs) No smoking in restaurant **CARDS:**

★★74% The Longview Hotel & Restaurant
55 Manchester Rd WA16 0LX
☎ 01565 632119 📠 01565 652402
e-mail: longview_hotel@compuserve.com
Dir: *from M6 junct 19 take A556 W towards Chester. Left at lights onto A5033 1.5m to rdbt then left. Hotel 200yds on right*

A friendly Victorian hotel with high standards of service. Attractive public areas include a cellar bar and foyer lounge. The restaurant has a Victorian feel and offers an imaginative selection of dishes. Bedrooms offer a great range of thoughtful amenities.
ROOMS: 13 en suite 13 annexe en suite (1 fmly) s £67-£100; d £80-£120 (incl. bkfst) * LB **FACILITIES:** Free use of local fitness club **PARKING:** 29 **NOTES:** No smoking in restaurant Closed 24 Dec-8 Jan **CARDS:**

★★63% *Royal George*
King St WA16 6EE
☎ 01565 634151 📠 01565 634955
Dir: *exit M6 junct 19 and take A556. Follow signs to town centre. Follow one way system into Princess St and turn left before Midland Bank*
Conveniently situated in the town centre, this former 14th-century coaching inn is reputed to have been visited by Queen Victoria, Winston Churchill and General Patton. Bedrooms are well equipped, and some have four-poster beds. The Café Bar serves innovative cuisine.
ROOMS: 31 rms (25 en suite) (6 fmly) No smoking in 20 bedrooms **FACILITIES:** entertainment **CONF:** Thtr 160 Class 120 Board 60 **SERVICES:** Lift **PARKING:** 50 **NOTES:** No dogs (ex guide dogs) No smoking in restaurant **CARDS:**

⌂ Premier Lodge (Knutsford North West)
Warrington Rd, Hoo Green, Mere WA16 0PZ
☎ 0870 700 1482 📠 0870 700 1483

Premier Lodge offers modern, well equipped, en suite accommodation suitable for both business and leisure travellers. Meals can be taken at the adjacent popular restaurant and bar which is fully licensed. For further details, consult the Hotel Groups page.
ROOMS: 28 en suite d £46 *

⌂ *Travelodge*
Chester Rd, Tabley WA16 0PP
☎ 01565 652187 📠 01565 652187
Dir: *on A556, northbound just E of junct 19 on M6*
This modern building offers accommodation in smart, spacious and well equipped bedrooms, all with en suite bathrooms. Refreshments may be taken at the nearby family restaurant. For further details and the Travelodge phone number, consult the Hotel Groups page.
ROOMS: 32 en suite

LANCASTER, Lancashire — Map 07 SD46
see also Hampson Green

★★★★67% Lancaster House
Green Ln, Ellel LA1 4GJ
☎ 01524 844822 📠 01524 844766
e-mail: lanchouse@elh.co.uk
Dir: *M6 junct 33 N towards Lancaster. Through Galgate village, into Green Lane. Hotel just before University entrance on right*
This modern hotel is discreetly situated in open countryside. The bedrooms are spacious and particularly well designed and equipped. The Gressingham Restaurant provides an extensive carte menu of mainly British dishes. There is also a self-contained management development centre which provides the latest technology.
ROOMS: 80 en suite (10 fmly) No smoking in 36 bedrooms d £72-£124 * LB **FACILITIES:** STV Indoor swimming (H) Sauna Gym Jacuzzi/spa Activity centre 1 mile Xmas **CONF:** Thtr 180 Class 50 Board 60 Del from £109 * **PARKING:** 100 **NOTES:** No smoking in restaurant
CARDS:

★★★67% *Posthouse Lancaster*
Waterside Park, Caton Rd LA1 3RA
☎ 0870 400 9047 📠 01524 841265
Dir: *take junct 34 off M6, turn towards Lancaster, hotel first on right*
Situated alongside the River Lune, this modern hotel provides comfortable bedrooms and stylish lounges. The Traders Bar and Grill serves a varied menu and there is an all-day eating option. The smart leisure and conferencing facilities make this hotel popular with both the business and leisure guest.
ROOMS: 157 en suite (82 fmly) No smoking in 73 bedrooms **FACILITIES:** Indoor swimming (H) Sauna Gym Jacuzzi/spa Health & fitness centre **CONF:** Thtr 120 Class 60 Board 60 **SERVICES:** Lift **PARKING:** 300 **NOTES:** No smoking in restaurant **CARDS:**

★★★65% Menzies Royal Kings Arms
Market St LA1 1HP
☎ 0500 636943 (Central Res) 📠 01773 880321
e-mail: info@menzies-hotels.co.uk
Dir: *follow 'City Centre' signs from M6, then 'Castle & Railway Station', turn off before traffic lights next to Waterstones bookshop*
This traditional, city-centre hotel, with its own small car park, is also close to the station. It has kept many of its 19th-century features, including a fine galleried restaurant. Bedrooms come in a variety of styles, but all have modern facilities. Staff are friendly and welcoming.
ROOMS: 55 en suite (2 fmly) No smoking in 15 bedrooms s £65-£85; d £85-£95 * LB **FACILITIES:** STV entertainment Xmas **CONF:** Thtr 100 Class 50 Board 60 Del from £75 * **SERVICES:** Lift **PARKING:** 20 **NOTES:** No smoking in restaurant Civ Wed 100
CARDS:

★★63% Hampson House
Hampson Ln LA2 0JB
☎ 01524 751158 📠 01524 751779
(For full entry see Hampson Green)

★63% *Scarthwaite Country House*
Crook O Lune, Caton LA2 9HR
☎ 01524 770267 📠 01524 770711
Dir: *leave M6 at junct 34 onto A683 towards Caton hotel 1.5m on right*
This attractive stone house sits back from the road in a peaceful woodland setting. Recently refurbished bedrooms provide pretty co-ordinated themes. There is a cosy bar, small television lounge and spacious function room. The hotel is a popular wedding reception venue.
ROOMS: 10 en suite (1 fmly) No smoking in 2 bedrooms **CONF:** Thtr 150 Class 90 Board 50 **PARKING:** 75
CARDS:

LANCING, West Sussex — Map 04 TQ10

★★70% *Sussex Pad*
Old Shoreham Rd BN15 0RH
☎ 01273 454647 📠 01273 453010
Dir: *situated on the main A27 oposite Shoreham Airport and by Lancing College*
Bedrooms, all named after champagne houses, are comfortably furnished and well equipped. Public areas centre around a spacious conservatory including a bar. Bar meals and light refreshments are available throughout the day and a more formal menu is available in Ladywells Restaurant.
ROOMS: 19 en suite **FACILITIES:** STV **CONF:** Thtr 20 Board 20 **PARKING:** 60 **NOTES:** No smoking in restaurant
CARDS:

LAND'S END, Cornwall & Isles of Scilly — Map 02 SW32

see also Sennen

★★★65% *The Land's End Hotel*
TR19 7AA
☎ 01736 871844 📠 01736 871599
e-mail: info@landsend-landmark.co.uk
Dir: *from Penzance follow A30 & signs to Land's End. After Sennen continue for 1m to Land's End*
With its famous clifftop location the hotel commands views across the Atlantic and over to the Longships lighthouse. Recently opened is 'Longships' Restaurant and Bar, here fresh local produce is used and fish dishes are a speciality. All bedrooms are comfortably furnished with modern facilities.
ROOMS: 33 en suite (2 fmly) **FACILITIES:** Free entry to Lands End visitor centre & exhibitions entertainment **CONF:** Thtr 200 Class 100 Board 50 **PARKING:** 1000 **NOTES:** No smoking in restaurant
CARDS:

LANGAR, Nottinghamshire — Map 08 SK73

★★70% ❀ Langar Hall
NG13 9HG
☎ 01949 860559 📠 01949 861045
e-mail: langarhall-hotel@ndirect.co.uk
Dir: *accessible via Bingham on the A52 or Cropwell Bishop from the A46, both signposted, the house adjoins the church*
At this country house hotel the majority of the bedrooms have fine antique furniture, paintings and quality soft furnishings. Drinks are served in the elegant white room, and dinner in the pillared hall dining room. There are also two private dining rooms leading out on to the garden.

continued

ROOMS: 10 en suite (1 fmly) No smoking in all bedrooms
FACILITIES: Fishing Croquet lawn **CONF:** Thtr 20 Class 20 Board 20
PARKING: 20 **NOTES:** No smoking in restaurant Civ Wed 40
CARDS:

LANGHO, Lancashire — Map 07 SD73

★★★71% ❀❀❀ Northcote Manor
Northcote Rd BB6 8BE
☎ 01254 240555 📠 01254 246568
e-mail: admin@northcotemanor.com
Dir: *M6 junct 31, 8m to Northcote, follow signs to Clitheroe, Hotel is set back on the left just before the rdbt*
Northcote Manor provides a very comfortable environment in which to sample the delights of its famous restaurant. Bedrooms have been individually furnished and thoughtfully equipped. Enjoy a drink in one of the lounges while browsing the tempting menus, which include much of Lancashire's finest fare.
ROOMS: 14 en suite s £75-£90; d £90-£110 (incl. bkfst) * LB
FACILITIES: STV Croquet lawn Xmas **CONF:** Thtr 40 Class 20 Board 26 Del from £125 * **PARKING:** 50 **NOTES:** No dogs (ex guide dogs) No smoking in restaurant Closed 1 Jan Civ Wed 40
CARDS:

LANGTOFT, East Riding of Yorkshire — Map 08 TA06

★★70% Old Mill Hotel & Restaurant
MINOTEL Great Britain
Mill Ln YO25 3BQ
☎ 01377 267383 📠 01377 267383
Dir: *6m N of Driffield, on B1249, through village of Langtoft on B1249 approx 1m N, turn left at hotel sign hotel straight ahead*
Standing in open countryside, this modern hotel has been very well furnished throughout. It provides thoughtfully equipped bedrooms, and a popular bar-lounge where a good range of well produced food is available. There is also a charming restaurant.
ROOMS: 9 en suite (1 fmly) s £45.50-£54; d £55.50-£64 (incl. bkfst) * LB **CONF:** Thtr 40 Class 20 Board 20 **PARKING:** 30 **NOTES:** No dogs (ex guide dogs) No children 12yrs No smoking in restaurant
CARDS:

LASTINGHAM, North Yorkshire — Map 08 SE79

★★★72% Lastingham Grange
YO62 6TH
☎ 01751 417345 & 417402 📠 01751 417358
e-mail: lastinghamgrange@aol.com
Dir: *2m E on A170 towards Scarborough, onto Lastingham, in village turn left uphill towards Moors. Hotel can be found on right*

This charming hotel dating from the 17th century remains a very popular place to stay. Fine antiques are displayed, both in the attractively decorated bedrooms, and in the public areas. Quality

continued

L

LASTINGHAM, continued

home cooking is offered and there is a welcoming lounge. The colourful grounds feature a sunken rose garden.
ROOMS: 12 en suite (2 fmly) s £82-£85; d £155-£160 (incl. bkfst) * LB **FACILITIES:** Large adventure playground ch fac **PARKING:** 32 **NOTES:** No smoking in restaurant Closed Dec-Feb

LAUNCESTON, Cornwall & Isles of Scilly — Map 02 SX38

see also Lifton

★★75% Penhallow Manor Country House

PL15 7SJ
☎ 01566 86206 🖷 01566 86179
e-mail: penhallow@ukonline.co.uk
(For full entry see Altarnun)

★★64% *Eagle House*

Castle St PL15 8BA
☎ 01566 772036 🖷 01566 772036
Next to the castle, this elegant Georgian house dating back to 1767 is within walking distance of all local amenities. Many of the bedrooms have views over the Cornish countryside. A fixed-price menu is served in the restaurant, and on Sunday evenings a more modest menu is available.
ROOMS: 14 en suite (1 fmly) **FACILITIES:** STV **CONF:** Thtr 190 Class 190 Board 190 **PARKING:** 100 **NOTES:** No dogs (ex guide dogs) **CARDS:**

LAVENHAM, Suffolk — Map 05 TL94

★★★★66% The Swan

High St CO10 9QA
☎ 0870 400 8116 🖷 01787 248286
e-mail: HeritageHotels_Lavenham.Swan@forte-hotels.com
Dir: *in centre of village on A134 Bury St Edmunds/Hadleigh*
The Swan has been impressively upgraded whilst retaining much of its original character. Bedrooms have been furnished to a high standard and feature thoughtful touches such as CD players and mini bars. Public areas offer open fire places and a choice of bars. Guests can enjoy modern cooking in the beamed restaurant.
ROOMS: 51 en suite No smoking in 15 bedrooms s £100; d £145 * LB **FACILITIES:** STV entertainment Xmas **CONF:** Thtr 60 Class 35 Board 25 Del from £175 * **PARKING:** 60 **NOTES:** No smoking in restaurant Civ Wed 40 **CARDS:**

★★68% Angel

Market Place CO10 9QZ
☎ 01787 247388 🖷 01787 248344
e-mail: angellav@aol.com
Dir: *from A14 take Bury East/Sudbury turn off A143, after 4m take A1141 to Lavenham, Angel is off the High Street*
This charming 15th-century inn is situated in the centre of this historic wool town. The restaurant is very popular with locals and guests alike and offers a wide choice of meals made from fresh ingredients. Each bedroom is individually furnished and decorated. Guests also have a spacious and comfortable lounge in which to relax.
ROOMS: 8 en suite (1 fmly) s £45; d £70 (incl. bkfst) * LB **FACILITIES:** Use of Lavenham Tennis Club facilities entertainment **PARKING:** 5 **NOTES:** Closed 25-26 Dec **CARDS:**

Bad hair day? Hairdryers in all rooms three stars and above.

LEA MARSTON, Warwickshire — Map 04 SP29

★★★71% *Lea Marston Hotel & Leisure Complex*

Haunch Ln B76 0BY
☎ 01675 470468 🖷 01675 470871
e-mail: info@leamarstonhotel.co.uk
Dir: *leave M42 at junct 9 and take A4097 towards Kingsbury. Hotel signposted 1.5m on right*

Conveniently positioned for Birmingham and the M42 this hotel is not only popular with the leisure market, but also with the conference delegates. Bedrooms are comfortable, spacious and have excellent facilities. A good range of bars, eating options, function rooms, a business centre, leisure complex and secure car park are additional features.
ROOMS: 83 en suite (6 fmly) No smoking in 34 bedrooms **FACILITIES:** STV Indoor swimming (H) Golf 9 Tennis (hard) Sauna Solarium Gym Pool table Croquet lawn Putting green Jacuzzi/spa Golf driving range entertainment ch fac **CONF:** Thtr 110 Class 60 Board 40 **PARKING:** 220 **NOTES:** No dogs (ex guide dogs) No smoking in restaurant **CARDS:**

LEAMINGTON SPA (ROYAL), Warwickshire — Map 04 SP36

Premier Collection

★★★ Mallory Court

Harbury Ln, Bishop's Tachbrook CV33 9QB
☎ 01926 330214 🖷 01926 451714
e-mail: reception@mallory.co.uk
Dir: *2m S off B4087 towards Harbury*
English country house set amidst ten acres of beautifully landscaped grounds. Most of the tastefully appointed bedrooms enjoy views over the gardens, and each one is individually styled. Public areas include two elegant and comfortable lounges, a drawing room, conservatory, private dining room and an impressive panelled restaurant.

continued

ROOMS: 18 en suite (1 fmly) s £165-£225; d £175-£275 (incl. cont bkfst) * LB **FACILITIES:** STV Outdoor swimming Tennis (hard) Croquet lawn entertainment Xmas **CONF:** Thtr 20 Board 20 Del from £175 * **PARKING:** 52 **NOTES:** No children 9yrs No smoking in restaurant Civ Wed 35 **CARDS:**

★★★67% The Leamington Hotel & Bistro

Best Western

64 Upper Holly Walk CV32 4JL
☎ 01926 883777 Fax 01926 330467
e-mail: leamington@bestwestern.co.uk
Dir: *exit M40 junct 13 take Leamington Spa road A452*

Public rooms include a welcoming residents' lounge with a high ceiling and ornate plasterwork. The modern bistro-style menu combines traditional English and French cuisine with a modern twist. Bedrooms are generally spacious, each with a range of thoughtful extras and modern facilities.

ROOMS: 30 en suite (6 fmly) No smoking in 4 bedrooms s £68-£78; d £78-£88 (incl. cont bkfst) * LB **FACILITIES:** Xmas **CONF:** Thtr 45 Class 32 Board 24 Del from £125 * **PARKING:** 22 **NOTES:** No dogs (ex guide dogs) Civ Wed 40 **CARDS:**

★★★66% Falstaff

16-20 Warwick New Rd CV32 5JQ
☎ 01926 312044 Fax 01926 450574
e-mail: falstaff@meridianleisure.com
Dir: *from M40 junct 13/14 follow signs for Leamington Spa over 4 rdbts then under bridge. Left into Princes Drive, then right at mini-rdbt*

Bedrooms come in a variety of styles and sizes, and are all well equipped. The lounge bar and restaurant are smartly appointed; an interesting range of dishes from daily and carte menus are offered. There are also conference and banqueting facilities available.

ROOMS: 63 en suite (2 fmly) No smoking in 5 bedrooms s £70; d £80 (incl. bkfst) * LB **FACILITIES:** STV Arrangement with local Health Club Xmas **CONF:** Thtr 60 Class 40 Board 32 Del from £90 * **PARKING:** 50 **NOTES:** No smoking in restaurant Civ Wed **CARDS:**

See advert on this page

★★★65% Courtyard by Marriott Leamington Spa

COURTYARD

Olympus Av, Tachbrook Park CV34 6RJ
☎ 01926 425522 Fax 01926 881322
Dir: *located on the A452, 1m S of the town centre, 3m from the M40*

This modern hotel is situated in Tachbrook Park, a business development on the edge of the town and within easy reach of the M40. Bedrooms are well equipped with good-sized beds, and although the public areas are compact, they are bright and relaxing.

continued

ROOMS: 95 en suite (15 fmly) No smoking in 48 bedrooms d £79-£89 * LB **FACILITIES:** STV Gym **CONF:** Thtr 70 Class 35 Board 30 Del from £120 * **SERVICES:** Lift **PARKING:** 120 **CARDS:**

★★★61% Angel

143 Regent St CV32 4NZ
☎ 01926 881296 Fax 01926 881296
Dir: *in the town centre at junct of Regent Street and Holly Walk*

This well established hotel comes in two parts - the original inn and a modern extension. Public rooms include a comfortable foyer lounge area, a smart restaurant and an informal bar. Bedrooms are individual in style, and, whether modern or traditional, have all the expected facilities.

ROOMS: 50 en suite (3 fmly) s £35-£55; d £50-£65 (incl. bkfst) * LB **FACILITIES:** STV Xmas **CONF:** Thtr 70 Class 40 Board 40 **SERVICES:** Lift **PARKING:** 38 **CARDS:**

★★★60% Manor House

REGAL

Avenue Rd CV31 3NJ
☎ 01926 423251 Fax 01926 425933
Dir: *from M40 follow signs for A452. At rdbt take 3rd exit for Leamington. Follow signs for station. Hotel directly behind station*

Near the town centre, this Victorian hotel offers well equipped bedrooms which vary in style and size. The spacious lounge and bar and the atmospheric restaurant all add to the character of the building. Service is friendly and welcoming.

continued

LEAMINGTON SPA, continued

Manor House, Leamington Spa

ROOMS: 53 en suite (2 fmly) No smoking in 19 bedrooms s fr £80; d fr £95 * LB **FACILITIES:** Reduced price at nearby leisure club Xmas **CONF:** Thtr 200 Class 60 Board 50 Del from £115 * **SERVICES:** Lift **PARKING:** 70 **NOTES:** No smoking in restaurant Civ Wed 96 **CARDS:**

★★70% Adams

22 Avenue Rd CV31 3PQ
☎ 01926 450742 01926 313110
Dir: *situated near Library on A452*

A welcoming, family-run hotel, a converted Regency house just south of the town centre and close to the railway station. The public areas include a relaxing lounge with comfortable leather chairs and a residents bar. Adjacent is the elegant dining room where enjoyable home cooked fare is served. Bedrooms are tastefully furnished and offer a good range of accessories.

ROOMS: 12 en suite **PARKING:** 14 **NOTES:** No dogs (ex guide dogs) No smoking in restaurant **CARDS:**

Premier Collection

★ Lansdowne

87 Clarendon St CV32 4PF
☎ 01926 450505 01926 421313
Dir: *town centre at junct of Clarendon St & Warwick St*

THE CIRCLE
Selected Individual Hotels
GREAT BRITAIN

A cosy Regency hotel, just a minute's walk from the City Centre, with a charming, friendly atmosphere. Bedrooms are individual in style and offer a good range of facilities. Day rooms include a small, quiet lounge and a bar for pre-dinner drinks. The dining room offers well chosen menus and dishes are attractively presented.

ROOMS: 14 en suite (1 fmly) s fr £58.95; d fr £68 (incl. bkfst) * LB **PARKING:** 11 **NOTES:** No dogs (ex guide dogs) No children 5yrs No smoking in restaurant RS 26 Dec-2 Jan **CARDS:**

LEATHERHEAD, Surrey — Map 04 TQ15

★★61% Bookham Grange

Little Bookham Common, Bookham KT23 3HS
☎ 01372 452742 01372 450080
e-mail: bookhamgrange@easynet.co.uk
Dir: *off A246 at Bookham High Street, carry on into Church Road, take first turning right after Bookham railway station*

Quietly situated in 2.5 acres, this family-run hotel has the style of an English country house. As well as two function and meeting rooms, there is a beamed bar, central sitting area and Restaurant. The bedrooms are well equipped.

ROOMS: 21 en suite (3 fmly) s £65-£75; d £85-£90 (incl. bkfst) * LB **FACILITIES:** Xmas **CONF:** Thtr 80 Class 24 Board 24 **PARKING:** 100 **NOTES:** Civ Wed 100 **CARDS:**

LEDBURY, Herefordshire — Map 03 SO73

★★★72% Feathers

High St HR8 1DS
☎ 01531 635266 01531 638955
e-mail: mary@feathers-ledbury.co.uk
Dir: *S from Worcester A449, E from HerefordA438, N from Gloucester A417, hotel is situated in the High Street*

Standing in the centre of town, this timber-framed coaching inn has a wealth of charm and character. There is a comfortable lounge and "Fuggles" bar/bistro, where a wide range of dishes is available. Recent improvements include a leisure centre and function suite. Bedrooms are individually styled and well equipped.

ROOMS: 19 en suite (2 fmly) No smoking in 2 bedrooms s £69.50-£77; d £89-£125 (incl. bkfst) * LB **FACILITIES:** STV Indoor swimming (H) Solarium Gym Jacuzzi/spa Steam room entertainment Xmas **CONF:** Thtr 140 Class 80 Board 40 Del £130 * **PARKING:** 30 **NOTES:** Civ Wed 90 **CARDS:**

See advert on opposite page

★★65% *The Verzons Country House*

Trumpet HR8 2PZ
☎ 01531 670381 01531 670830
Dir: *3m W of Ledbury A438*

This large country house dates back to 1790, and stands in extensive gardens near Ledbury. Bedrooms are well equipped, and many have views of the Malvern Hills. Public areas include a bar, a lounge, an adjacent bistro-style restaurant, and a larger traditionally furnished dining room, which is also available for functions and meetings.

ROOMS: 9 en suite (2 fmly) **CONF:** Thtr 50 Class 25 Board 20 **PARKING:** 60 **NOTES:** Closed 25 Dec **CARDS:**

Packed in a hurry? Ironing facilities should be available at all star levels, either in rooms or on request.

LEEDS, West Yorkshire

see also Gomersal & Shipley

Map 08 SE33

★★★★★63% Oulton Hall

Rothwell Ln, Oulton LS26 8HN

☎ 0113 282 1000 ▯ 0113 282 8066

e-mail: oulton.hall@devere-hotels.com

Dir: *2m from M62 junct 30/A639 on the left hand side, or 1m from M1 junct 44 then follow signs to Castleford/Pontefract A639*

This elegant 19th-century house is set in gardens and parkland, within easy reach of the city centre. The graceful public rooms in the original house include the impressive galleried Great Hall, to which meeting and leisure facilities have been added. A well rounded hotel, which proves popular with both business and leisure guests.

ROOMS: 152 en suite No smoking in 128 bedrooms s £95-£140; d £105-£160 (incl. bkfst) * LB **FACILITIES:** STV Indoor swimming (H) Golf 27 Squash Snooker Sauna Solarium Gym Croquet lawn Jacuzzi/spa Beauty therapy Aerobics Xmas **CONF:** Thtr 350 Class 150 Board 40 Del from £140 * **SERVICES:** Lift **PARKING:** 260 **NOTES:** No smoking in restaurant **CARDS:**

★★★★71% Crowne Plaza Leeds

Wellington St LS1 4DL

☎ 0113 244 2200 ▯ 0113 244 0460

e-mail: riches.angela@hiw.com

Dir: *from M1 follow signs to City Centre, at City Square left into Wellington Street*

This modern hotel within walking distance of the city centre, provides an excellent standard of well appointed and thoughtfully equipped accommodation. Secure parking, leisure facilities and extensive meeting rooms are also available.

ROOMS: 135 en suite (38 fmly) No smoking in 90 bedrooms s £50-£175; d £50-£195 (incl. bkfst) * LB **FACILITIES:** STV Indoor swimming (H) Sauna Solarium Gym Jacuzzi/spa Steam room Childrens playroom Xmas **CONF:** Thtr 200 Class 100 Board 60 **SERVICES:** Lift air con **PARKING:** 125 **NOTES:** No dogs (ex guide dogs) Civ Wed 150 **CARDS:**

★★★★70% Leeds Marriott

4 Trevelyan Square, Boar Ln LS1 6ET

☎ 0113 236 6366 ▯ 0113 236 6367

Dir: *take A653 to City Centre. Follow signs for station, right Gt Wilson St, left at lights, over bridge, through next lights & under brige & 2 lefts*

A large, modern hotel in the city centre, offering spacious bedrooms comfortably furnished and equipped. John T's bar and restaurant serves a wide range of dishes. A variety of function rooms and leisure centre are available.

continued

ROOMS: 244 en suite (26 fmly) No smoking in 194 bedrooms d £105-£117 * LB **FACILITIES:** STV Indoor swimming (H) Sauna Solarium Gym Jacuzzi/spa Subsidised use of NCP car park Xmas **CONF:** Thtr 280 Class 120 Board 80 Del from £140 * **SERVICES:** Lift air con **NOTES:** Civ Wed 280 **CARDS:**

★★★★69% Queen's

City Square LS1 1PL

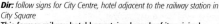

☎ 0113 243 1323 & 0870 4008696 ▯ 0113 242 5154

Dir: *follow signs for City Centre, hotel adjacent to the railway station in City Square*

This former railway hotel has retained much of its original splendour. Public rooms include the comfortable Palm Court Lounge, the elegant Harewood Restaurant, the Carvery Restaurant and the popular Piano Bar. Bedrooms are mostly spacious and well furnished. A good variety of banqueting and meeting rooms are available.

ROOMS: 199 en suite No smoking in 72 bedrooms s fr £115; d fr £125 * LB **FACILITIES:** STV Xmas **CONF:** Thtr 600 Class 160 Board 40 Del from £120 * **SERVICES:** Lift **PARKING:** 88 **NOTES:** Civ Wed 400 **CARDS:**

★★★★63% Metropole

King St LS1 2HQ

☎ 0113 245 0841 ▯ 0113 242 5156

Dir: *from M1/M62/M621 follow signs for City Centre. Take A65 Airport into Wellington St, at first traffic Island turn right into King St Hotel on right*

This splendid terracotta-fronted hotel stands in the heart of the city. Well equipped bedrooms range in style from standard to spacious executive rooms. Public areas include a very smart foyer

continued

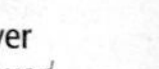

LEEDS, continued

and lounge. Staff are cheerful and helpful; valet parking is provided.
ROOMS: 118 en suite No smoking in 98 bedrooms s fr £102; d fr £122 * LB **FACILITIES:** STV **CONF:** Thtr 250 Class 100 Board 80 Del from £150 * **SERVICES:** Lift **PARKING:** 40 **NOTES:** No dogs (ex guide dogs) No smoking in restaurant RS 26 Dec-1 Jan Civ Wed
CARDS:

★★★80% Haley's Hotel & Restaurant
Shire Oak Rd, Headingley LS6 2DE
☎ 0113 278 4446 0113 275 3342
e-mail: info@haleys.co.uk
Dir: *from city centre follow local signs to University on A660, 1.5m turn right in Headingley between HSBC and Yorkshire Banks*

Two elegant Victorian houses set in a quiet tree-lined cul-de-sac, convenient for the county cricket ground. Individually styled bedrooms and spacious public areas are furnished to a high standard with some fine antiques. Good modern British cooking continues to excel.
ROOMS: 22 en suite 7 annexe en suite (3 fmly) No smoking in 10 bedrooms s £90-£120; d £125-£165 (incl. bkfst) * LB **FACILITIES:** STV **CONF:** Thtr 30 Class 20 Board 25 Del from £115 * **PARKING:** 25 **NOTES:** No dogs (ex guide dogs) No smoking in restaurant Closed 26-30 Dec RS Sun evening Civ Wed 136
CARDS:

See advert on opposite page

★★★75% Hazlewood Castle
Paradise Ln, Hazlewood LS24 9NJ
☎ 01937 535353 01937 530630
e-mail: info@hazlewood-castle.co.uk
(For full entry see Tadcaster)

★★★73% Malmaison Hotel
Sovereign Quay LS1 1DQ
☎ 0113 398 1000 0113 398 1002
e-mail: leeds@malmaison.com
Dir: *follow signs for 'City Centre', turn into Sovereign Street, go past the KPMG office. Hotel is at end of street on right*
Close to the waterfront, this stylish property offers striking bedrooms with CD players and air conditioning. The bar leads into a brasserie, where guests can choose between a full three course meal or a substantial snack. Service is both willing and friendly. A small fitness centre and impressive meeting rooms complete the package.
ROOMS: 100 en suite No smoking in 70 bedrooms d £105 * LB **FACILITIES:** STV Gym **CONF:** Thtr 40 Class 20 Board 28 Del £155 * **SERVICES:** Lift air con **NOTES:** No dogs (ex guide dogs)
CARDS:

★★★69% The Merrion
Merrion Centre LS2 8NH
☎ 0113 243 9191 0113 242 3527
Dir: *from the M1/M62/A61 join city loop road to junct 7, the Hotel is situated on Wade Lane adjoining the Merrion Centre*
Situated to the north of the city centre, this modern hotel can be entered from the next-door car park. There are comfortable, well equipped bedrooms, and the public rooms include a restaurant and bar with an art deco theme, an open-plan lounge and a conference suite. It is wise to phone for directions.
ROOMS: 109 en suite No smoking in 76 bedrooms s £109; d £119 * LB **FACILITIES:** STV Xmas **CONF:** Thtr 80 Class 25 Board 25 Del from £85 * **SERVICES:** Lift **NOTES:** No smoking in restaurant
CARDS:

★★★69% Milford Lodge Hotel
A1 Great North Rd, Peckfield LS25 5LQ
☎ 01977 681800 01977 681245
e-mail: enquires@mlh.co.uk
(For full entry see Garforth)

★★★65% Golden Lion
2 Lower Briggate LS1 4AE
☎ 0113 243 6454 0113 242 9327
Dir: *between junct 16 (Bridge End) and 17 (Sovereign Street). Hotel situated on junct of Lower Briggate & Swinegate*
This centrally situated hotel is one of Leeds oldest, but the accommodation provided has every modern facility. Staff are friendly and helpful and the atmosphere is warm and informal. Meeting and conference facilities are available and free parking is provided in a modern 24-hour multi-storey car park close to the hotel.
ROOMS: 89 en suite (5 fmly) No smoking in 46 bedrooms s fr £99; d fr £109 (incl. bkfst) * LB **FACILITIES:** STV Xmas **CONF:** Thtr 120 Class 65 Board 45 Del from £80 * **SERVICES:** Lift **PARKING:**
CARDS:

★★★56% *Posthouse Leeds/Selby*
LS25 5LF
☎ 0870 400 9050 01977 685462
(For full entry see Lumby)

★★69% Aragon
250 Stainbeck Ln LS7 2PS
☎ 0113 275 9306 0113 275 7166
Dir: *from A61 Harrogate follow from City Centre this turns into Scott Hall Road at 2nd rdbt turn left into Stainbeck Lane half mile on right*
This attractive stone building stands in a relatively quiet leafy part of north Leeds. Public rooms include a separate comfortable lounge and a small bar. Freshly produced meals are available in

continued

the dining room. Modern bedrooms are smartly furnished with soft furnishings and co-ordinated furniture.
ROOMS: 12 en suite (2 fmly) No smoking in all bedrooms s £39.90-£43.90; d £49.90-£53.90 (incl. bkfst) * **PARKING:** 20 **NOTES:** No smoking in restaurant Closed 25 Dec-1 Jan
CARDS:

Town House

★★★★ 42 The Calls

LS2 7EW
☎ 0113 244 0099 ▤ 0113 234 4100
e-mail: hotel@42thecalls.co.uk
Dir: *leave city centre loop road at junct 15 (The Calls). Hotel next to Calls Landing*
This wonderful conversion of a canal side warehouse provides luxury bedrooms complete with many thoughtful extras and comforts. Breakfast may be taken either in the bedrooms or in the breakfast room which overlooks the canal. There are many good restaurants nearby, one of these is located next door.
ROOMS: 41 en suite No smoking in 6 bedrooms s £98-£250; d £128-£250 * LB **FACILITIES:** STV Fishing **CONF:** Thtr 70 Class 40 Board 42 Del from £165 * **SERVICES:** Lift **PARKING:** 28
NOTES: Closed 5 days Xmas **CARDS:**

Express by Holiday Inn Leeds

Express by Holiday Inn
Cavendish St LS3 1LY
☎ 0113 242 6200 ▤ 242 6300
e-mail: leeds@premierhotels.co.uk
Dir: *M621 junct2 follow signs for City Centre, turning left onto A65. Hotel situated opposite MD Foods*

A modern budget hotel offering comfortable accommodation in refreshing, spacious and comprehensively-equipped bedrooms, en suite bathrooms with power showers and continental buffet breakfast included in the room rate. Suitable for business

continued

travellers or families. For further details and the Express by Holiday Inn phone number, consult the Hotel Groups page.
ROOMS: 112 en suite (incl. cont bkfst) d £55 * **CONF:** Thtr 45 Class 20 Board 25 Del £99 *

Premier Lodge (Leeds City West)

City West One Office Park, Gelderd Rd LS12 6SN
☎ 0870 700 1414 ▤ 0870 700 1415
Premier Lodge offers modern, well equipped, en suite accommodation suitable for both business and leisure travellers. Meals can be taken at the adjacent popular restaurant and bar which is fully licensed. For further details, consult the Hotel Groups page.
ROOMS: 125 en suite d £46 *

Travelodge

Travelodge
Blaydes Court, Blaydes Yard, off Swinegate LS1 4AD
This modern building offers accommodation in smart, spacious and well equipped bedrooms, all with en suite bathrooms. Refreshments may be taken at the nearby family restaurant. For further details and the Travelodge phone number, consult the Hotel Groups page.

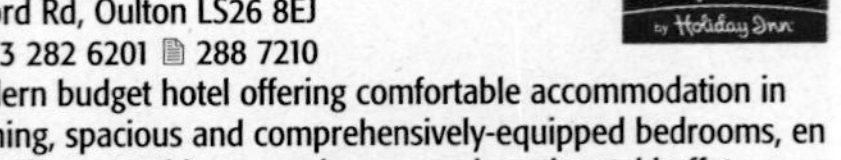

Express by Holiday Inn Leeds East

Express by Holiday Inn
Aberford Rd, Oulton LS26 8EJ
☎ 0113 282 6201 ▤ 288 7210
A modern budget hotel offering comfortable accommodation in refreshing, spacious and comprehensively-equipped bedrooms, en suite bathrooms with power showers and continental buffet breakfast included in the room rate. Suitable for business

continued

LEEDS, continued

Express by Holiday Inn, Leeds East

travellers or families. For further details and the Express by Holiday Inn phone number, consult the Hotel Groups page.
ROOMS: 77 en suite (incl. cont bkfst) s £49.95 * **CONF:** Thtr 30 Class 20 Board 16

○ Hotel Ibis

Vicar Ln
☎ 020 8283 4550
Modern, budget hotel offering comfortable accommodation in bright and practical bedrooms. Breakfast is self-service and dinner is available in the restaurant. For further details, consult the Hotel Groups page.
ROOMS: 143 rms **NOTES:** Due to open Spring 2001

LEEK, Staffordshire — Map 07 SJ95

★★★64% Hotel Rudyard

Lake Rd, Rudyard ST13 8RN
☎ 01538 306208 🖷 01538 306208
A large stone-built Victorian property, now a private hotel, set in extensive wooded grounds in the centre of Rudyard village. It provides modern and well equipped accommodation, a room with a four-poster bed is available. There is a function room, a large carvery restaurant and a traditionally furnished bar.
ROOMS: 15 en suite (2 fmly) No smoking in 2 bedrooms s £35-£45; d £55-£65 (incl. bkfst) * LB **CONF:** Thtr 80 Class 60 Board 40 **PARKING:** 100 **NOTES:** No smoking in restaurant
CARDS:

★★68% ❀ Three Horseshoes Inn & Restaurant

Buxton Rd, Blackshaw Moor ST13 8TW

☎ 01538 300296 🖷 01538 300320
***Dir:** 2m N of Leek on the A53 Leek/Buxton Road*

A family owned hostelry in spacious grounds, which include a beer garden and children's play area. The no smoking bedrooms are tastefully appointed and furnished in style with the character of the hotel. The public areas are traditional in style and include a choice of bars and eating options.
ROOMS: 6 en suite No smoking in all bedrooms s £45-£55; d £55-£65 (incl. bkfst) * LB **FACILITIES:** entertainment **PARKING:** 80 **NOTES:** No dogs (ex guide dogs) No smoking in restaurant Closed 24 Dec-1 Jan
CARDS:

LEE-ON-THE-SOLENT, Hampshire — Map 04 SU50

★★★60% Belle Vue

39 Marine Pde East PO13 9BW
☎ 023 9255 0258 🖷 023 9255 2624
e-mail: information@bellevue-hotel.co.uk
***Dir:** M27 junct9/11 to Fareham follow signs to Lee-on-Solent, hotel is on seafront*
Almost as close as one can get to the sea, the views from public areas and front facing bedrooms are impressive. Bedrooms are well decorated and are comfortably furnished. Public rooms include a spacious bar and an attractive restaurant offering a wide range of popular dishes.
ROOMS: 24 en suite 3 annexe en suite (4 fmly) s £49.50-£77.50; d £71.50-£77.50 * LB **FACILITIES:** STV entertainment **CONF:** Thtr 150 Class 60 Board 40 Del from £89.50 * **PARKING:** 55 **NOTES:** Closed 25-26 Dec RS 24 Dec **CARDS:**

LEICESTER, Leicestershire — Map 04 SK50

★★★72% ❀ Belmont House

Best Western

De Montfort St LE1 7GR
☎ 0116 254 4773 🖷 0116 247 0804
e-mail: info@belmonthotel.co.uk
***Dir:** from A6 in S direction, take first right after BR station, 200yds on right*

Close to the station and town centre, Belmont House is well suited to the needs of the midweek business user or the weekend leisure guest. There are a choice of dining options, the lower-ground floor Bistro providing informal meals, or the more formal Cherries Restaurant. The bedrooms are thoughtfully designed and well equipped.
ROOMS: 75 en suite (7 fmly) No smoking in 40 bedrooms s £85-£95; d £93-£103 * LB **FACILITIES:** entertainment **CONF:** Thtr 120 Class 60 Board 50 Del from £109.79 * **SERVICES:** Lift **PARKING:** 60 **NOTES:** Closed 24 Dec-2 Jan Civ Wed 100 **CARDS:**

See advert on opposite page

★★★68% Hermitage

REGAL

Wigston Rd, Oadby LE2 5QE
☎ 0116 256 9955 🖷 0116 272 0559/272 0686
***Dir:** from city centre follow A6 Market Harborough. After 4m pass ASDA on left turn right at lights for Oadby Village and over rdbt to hotel on left*
Located in a residential area, this modern hotel appeals to business guests. Bedrooms are well equipped and there is a good

continued

range of meeting and function suites. Public areas have recently been refurbished, these include a comfortable foyer lounge and a carvery restaurant.

ROOMS: 56 en suite (3 fmly) No smoking in 24 bedrooms s fr £75; d fr £85 (incl. bkfst) * LB **FACILITIES:** Xmas **CONF:** Thtr 250 Class 100 Board 60 Del from £110 * **SERVICES:** Lift **PARKING:** 160 **NOTES:** No smoking in restaurant Civ Wed 200
CARDS:

★★★68% *Posthouse Leicester*

Braunstone Ln East LE3 2FW **Posthouse**
☎ 0870 400 9051 🖷 0116 282 3623
Dir: *from junct 21 of M1 at M69 interchange take A5460 and continue towards city to hotel 1m on right*
A feature of this recently refurbished hotel is the warmth and friendliness reflected by staff throughout. Additional services include 24-hour room service and an all day lounge menu. Meeting and conference facilities are available.
ROOMS: 172 en suite (35 fmly) No smoking in 110 bedrooms
CONF: Thtr 85 Class 54 Board 45 **SERVICES:** Lift **PARKING:** 300
CARDS:

★★★66% Regency

360 London Rd LE2 2PL
☎ 0116 270 9634 🖷 0116 270 1375
Dir: *on the A6 London Road 1.5m from the city centre, near outer ring road which leads to the M1 & M9 approx 4m away*

Originally a convent, this modernised hotel provides bright and well equipped accommodation. The pleasantly appointed bedrooms are attractively decorated. A conservatory brasserie, next to the lounge bar, is an informal alternative to the restaurant which offers more formal dining.
ROOMS: 32 en suite (4 fmly) s £46-£52; d fr £62 (incl. bkfst) *
FACILITIES: STV entertainment Xmas **CONF:** Thtr 70 Class 50 Board 30
PARKING: 40 **NOTES:** No dogs (ex guide dogs)
CARDS:

LEICESTER, continued

★★★66% Time Out Hotel & Leisure

corus

Enderby Rd, Blaby LE8 4GD
☎ 0116 278 7898 🖷 0116 278 1974
Dir: *M1 junct.21, A5460 Leicester take 4th exit at 1st rdbt, ahead at 2nd, left at 3rd follow signs to Blaby, over 4th rdbt Hotel on left*

Adjacent to the link road on the outskirts of the city, this pleasant hotel provides spacious and comfortable bedrooms, a bustling open plan restaurant and two bars; executive and superior rooms are particularly desirable. The modern leisure complex is a popular attraction for both corporate and weekend guests.
ROOMS: 48 en suite (2 fmly) No smoking in 26 bedrooms s £84; d £95-£100 * LB **FACILITIES:** STV Indoor swimming (H) Sauna Solarium Gym Jacuzzi/spa Steam room Xmas **CONF:** Thtr 70 Class 30 Board 36 Del from £110 * **PARKING:** 110 **NOTES:** Civ Wed 90
CARDS:

L

★★★65% Leicester Stage Hotel

Leicester Rd, Wigston LE18 1JW
☎ 0116 288 6161 🖷 0116 281 1874
e-mail: reservations@stagehotel.co.uk
Dir: *from M69/M1 junct 21 take ring road South Leicester. Follow signs for Oadby & Wigston,turn right onto A50 towards Northampton. Hotel on left*
An imposing glass fronted building to the south of the city centre, the Stage's smart public areas are impressive. Recent investment has dramatically upgraded the conference, leisure and downstairs areas. Bedrooms offer all the expected amenities and comfort.
ROOMS: 75 en suite (10 fmly) No smoking in 30 bedrooms s £85-£95; d £99-£109 (incl. bkfst) * LB **FACILITIES:** STV Indoor swimming (H) Sauna Gym Jacuzzi/spa Xmas **CONF:** Thtr 450 Class 200 Board 100 Del from £75 * **PARKING:** 200 **NOTES:** No dogs (ex guide dogs) Civ Wed 300 **CARDS:**

★★65% Charnwood

48 Leicester Rd, Narborough LE9 5DF
☎ 0116 286 2218 🖷 0116 275 0119
e-mail: info@thecharnwood.co.uk
Dir: *junct 21 of M1 follow B4114 to Narborough*
The public rooms are smart and cheerful. An attractive restaurant with small dispense bar, separate bar and comfortable seating overlooks gardens. Bar meals supplement a carte offering traditional and international dishes. Bedroom refurbishment is underway, completed rooms are equipped with useful facilities. The hotel is a popular venue for weddings.
ROOMS: 20 en suite s £48; d £66 (incl. bkfst) * **CONF:** Thtr 50 Class 20 Board 30 Del £83.50 * **PARKING:** 30 **NOTES:** No children Closed 26 Dec-3 Jan Civ Wed 150 **CARDS:**

★★65% Red Cow

Hinckley Rd, Leicester Forest East LE3 3PG
☎ 0116 238 7878 🖷 0116 238 6539
Dir: *follow A47 out of Leicester towards Hinckley, hotel is on right approx 4m from city centre*
To the west of Leicester this is a modern and popular pub restaurant with an adjacent bedroom block. A good range of food is available in the bar, restaurant and conservatory; the latter overlooks a rear garden and is set aside for families. The accommodation is modern and well equipped.
ROOMS: 31 en suite (26 fmly) No smoking in 23 bedrooms d £40 *
PARKING: 120 **NOTES:** No dogs (ex guide dogs)
CARDS:

See advert on opposite page

★★56% *Gables*

368 London Rd LE2 2PN
☎ 0116 270 6969 🖷 0116 270 6969
Dir: *0.5m city side of junction A563 (South East) and A6*
This privately owned commercial hotel is located south of the city centre and conveniently placed for the university. The public rooms include a restaurant and a cosy lounge bar; an adjoining room serves as a popular venue for business meetings and local functions.
ROOMS: 30 en suite (9 fmly) **CONF:** Thtr 60 Class 12 Board 28
PARKING: 29 **NOTES:** No dogs (ex guide dogs) No smoking in restaurant **CARDS:**

⇧ Hotel Ibis

ibis hotel

Constitution Hill, St Georges Way LE1 1PL
☎ 0116 248 7200 🖷 0116 262 0880
e-mail: H3061@accor-hotels.com
Dir: *Take A5460, follow signs for railway station, turn left at Mercedes garage*
Modern, budget hotel offering comfortable accommodation in bright and practical bedrooms. Breakfast is self-service and dinner is available in the restaurant. For further details, consult the Hotel Groups page.
ROOMS: 94 en suite s fr £42; d fr £42 *

⇧ Premier Lodge (Leciester West)

PREMIER LODGE

Leicester Rd, Glenfield LE3 8HB
☎ 0870 700 1416 🖷 0870 700 1417
Premier Lodge offers modern, well equipped, en suite accommodation suitable for both business and leisure travellers. Meals can be taken at the adjacent popular restaurant and bar which is fully licensed. For further details, consult the Hotel Groups page.
ROOMS: 43 en suite d £46 *

⇧ Premier Lodge (Leicester South)

PREMIER LODGE

Glen Rise, Oadby LE2 4RG
☎ 0870 700 1418 🖷 0870 700 1419
Premier Lodge offers modern, well equipped, en suite accommodation suitable for both business and leisure travellers. Meals can be taken at the adjacent popular restaurant and bar which is fully licensed. For further details, consult the Hotel Groups page.
ROOMS: 30 en suite d £46 *

○ *Premier Lodge (Leicester Central)*

Groby Rd
☎ 0870 700 1420 🖷 0870 700 1421

LEICESTER FOREST SERVICE AREA (M1), Leicestershire Map 04 SK50

Days Inn

Leicester Forest East, Junction 21 M1 LE3 3GB
☎ 0116 239 0534 ▤ 0116 239 0546
Dir: *situated on M1 motorway N/bound between junct 21 & 21A*
Fully refurbished, Days Inn offers well equipped, brightly appointed, modern accommodation with smart en suite bathrooms. There is a fully staffed reception; continental breakfast is available and other refreshments may be taken at the nearby family restaurant.
ROOMS: 93 en suite d fr £45 *

LEIGH DELAMERE MOTORWAY SERVICE AREA (M4), Wiltshire Map 03 ST87

Travelodge

Travelodge

SN14 6LB
☎ Central Res 0800 850950 ▤ 01666 837112
Dir: *Between junc 17 & 18 on the M4*
This modern building offers accommodation in smart, spacious and well equipped bedrooms, all with en suite bathrooms. Refreshments may be taken at the nearby family restaurant. For further details and the Travelodge phone number, consult the Hotel Groups page.
ROOMS: 70 en suite

LEISTON, Suffolk Map 05 TM46

★60% ***White Horse***
Station Rd IP16 4HD
☎ 01728 830694 ▤ 01728 833105
e-mail: whihorse@globalnet.co.uk
Dir: *on B1119, signposted Leiston, 4m to hotel*
Dating back to the 1700s, this convivial inn is located on a major junction in the centre of town. There are two bars to choose from as well as a cosy beamed restaurant. For children there is an adventure play area to the rear, where barbecues are also put on during the summer months. There is a range of comfortable bedrooms in mixed styles.
ROOMS: 10 rms (9 en suite) 3 annexe en suite (1 fmly)
FACILITIES: Pool table ch fac **PARKING:** 17
CARDS:

LENHAM, Kent Map 05 TQ85

★★★★73% ❀❀ **Chilston Park**
Sandway ME17 2BE

ARCADIAN HOTELS Distinctly Different

☎ 01622 859803 ▤ 01622 858588
Dir: *turn right at x-roads in Lenham. Then left after 0.5m into Boughton Road. Straight over x-roads, and hotel is on left*
Standing in extensive well cared for grounds,this antique-filled country house is of somewhat eccentric but lovingly constructed and thoroughly stylish taste. Many of the bedrooms have four-poster beds and all are furnished in unique style. Public areas include meeting rooms and lounges that are comfortable and smart. Stylish modern European food is served in a candle-lit cavernous dining room.
ROOMS: 30 en suite 23 annexe en suite (2 fmly) s £85-£312; d £115-£325 (incl. bkfst) * LB **FACILITIES:** STV Tennis (hard) Fishing Snooker Croquet lawn Xmas **CONF:** Thtr 120 Class 40 Board 44 Del from £115 * **SERVICES:** Lift **PARKING:** 100 **NOTES:** No smoking in restaurant Civ Wed 80 **CARDS:**

LEOMINSTER, Herefordshire Map 03 SO45

★★★65% **Talbot**

Best Western

West St HR6 8EP
☎ 01568 616347 ▤ 01568 614880
Dir: *approach either from A49, A44 or A4112, the Hotel can be found at the centre of the town*
The charm and character of this former coaching inn is enhanced by exposed ceiling beams, antique furniture in the bars and welcoming fires. Bedrooms are well equipped and many have recently been refurbished. Facilities are available for private functions and conferences.
ROOMS: 20 en suite (3 fmly) s fr £46; d fr £62 * LB
FACILITIES: Xmas **CONF:** Thtr 150 Class 35 Board 28 Del from £80 *
PARKING: 20 **NOTES:** No smoking in restaurant Civ Wed 150
CARDS:

★★60% **Royal Oak**
South St HR6 8JA
☎ 01568 612610 ▤ 01568 612710
Dir: *junct A44/A49*
This privately owned hotel is conveniently located in the town centre. It is personally run in an informal manner and provides warm and friendly hospitality. The recently refurbished public ares have charm and character and they include a bistro style restaurant.
ROOMS: 17 en suite 1 annexe en suite (2 fmly) No smoking in 2 bedrooms s £35-£39; d £48-£58 (incl. bkfst) * LB **CONF:** Thtr 220 Class 100 Board 50 Del £87.25 * **PARKING:** 25 **NOTES:** No smoking in restaurant **CARDS:**

LEWDOWN, Devon Map 02 SX48

Premier Collection

★★★ Lewtrenchard Manor

EX20 4PN
☎ 01566 783256 & 783222 01566 783332
e-mail: s&j@lewtrenchard.co.uk
Dir: *A30 from Exeter turn on to Plymouth/Tavistock road. T-junct right and immediately left onto Old A30 Lewdown 6m turn left signposted Lewtrenchard*

This delightful Jacobean manor house enjoys an elevated position beautifully kept gardens. Spacious well-equipped bedrooms have extensive views. The public rooms have ornate ceilings, oak panelling, large open fireplaces and rich furnishings. Imaginative and innovative dishes are complemented by an extensive and carefully considered wine cellar.

ROOMS: 9 en suite s £85-£110; d £115-£170 (incl. bkfst) * LB **FACILITIES:** Fishing Croquet lawn Clay pigeon shooting Xmas **CONF:** Thtr 50 Class 40 Board 30 **PARKING:** 50 **NOTES:** No children 7yrs No smoking in restaurant Civ Wed 100
CARDS:

LEWES, East Sussex Map 05 TQ41

★★★76% Shelleys Hotel

High St BN7 1XS
☎ 01273 472361 01273 483152
Dir: *follow A23 to Brighton, turn onto A27 to Lewes. At 1st rdbt turn left for Town centre, after crossroads hotel is located on left*

Previous owners of this 16th-century inn include the Earl of Dorset and the family of the poet Shelley. Today, Shelleys boasts beautifully appointed bedrooms, furnished and decorated in a traditional style. The restaurant, overlooking a lovely garden, serves a variety of interesting dishes from a well conceived menu.

ROOMS: 19 en suite (2 fmly) No smoking in 4 bedrooms s £126-£140; d £165-£250 * LB **FACILITIES:** STV entertainment Xmas **CONF:** Thtr 50 Class 20 Board 28 Del from £160 * **PARKING:** 25 **NOTES:** No smoking in restaurant Civ Wed 50
CARDS:

★★★65% White Hart

55 High St BN7 1XE
☎ 01273 476694 01273 476695
Dir: *from A27 follow signs for town centre. Hotel opposite County Court*

This historic hotel was where the first draft of the American constitution was written. Today the hotel combines the old and the new. A leisure centre, patio and conservatory have been added to the Tudor bar, lounge and restaurant. Bedrooms vary between the character of the original inn and the more modern annexe rooms.

continued

ROOMS: 23 en suite 29 annexe en suite (3 fmly) s £58-£61; d £82-£86 * LB **FACILITIES:** STV Indoor swimming (H) Sauna Solarium Gym Jacuzzi/spa entertainment Xmas **CONF:** Thtr 250 Class 120 Board 90 Del from £73.50 * **PARKING:** 40
CARDS:

See advert on opposite page

LEYBURN, North Yorkshire Map 07 SE19

★65% Golden Lion

Market Place DL8 5AS
☎ 01969 22161 01969 23836
e-mail: AnneGoldenLion@aol.com
Dir: *set on the A684 in Market Square*

Enjoying a prominent location in the market square, this popular Georgian inn provides well equipped, comfortable bedrooms. There is a good range of value for money food in both the bar and the cosy dining room and they serve their own beer called Oliver John. Staff are friendly and keen to please.

ROOMS: 15 rms (14 en suite) (5 fmly) s £22-£32; d £44-£64 (incl. bkfst) * LB **SERVICES:** Lift **NOTES:** Closed 25 & 26 Dec
CARDS:

LICHFIELD, Staffordshire Map 07 SK10

★★★68% Little Barrow

Beacon St WS13 7AR
☎ 01543 414500 01543 415734
Dir: *200 yds from cathedral on right*

Conveniently situated for the cathedral and the city, this friendly hotel offers well equipped accommodation. The cosy lounge bar, popular with locals and visitors alike, has a range of real ales and a choice of bar meals. More formal meals are available in the pleasantly appointed restaurant; service is relaxed and attentive.

ROOMS: 24 en suite (2 fmly) s £57.50-£67.50; d £75-£85 (incl. bkfst) * LB **CONF:** Thtr 80 Class 30 Board 30 Del from £95 * **PARKING:** 70 **NOTES:** No dogs (ex guide dogs) No smoking in restaurant Closed 24-26 Dec Civ Wed 80 **CARDS:**

★★66% The Olde Corner House

Walsall Rd, Muckley Corner WS14 OBG
☎ 01543 372182 01543 372211
Dir: *at junct of A5/A461 5 mins from A38*

This coaching inn dates back to the 17th century in parts and retains much of its character. Two dining rooms offer a range of well prepared dishes, and there is a popular bar and a separate comfortable lounge. Bedrooms all are attractively furnished and well equipped, including rooms in the newer wing. Service is informal and welcoming.

ROOMS: 23 en suite No smoking in all bedrooms s fr £39.95; d £55.95-£75 (incl. bkfst) * **FACILITIES:** Pool table **CONF:** Thtr 24 Class 18 Del from £58 * **PARKING:** 65 **NOTES:** No dogs
CARDS:

★★63% Angel Croft
Beacon St WS13 7AA
☎ 01543 258737 🖹 01543 415605
Dir: *situated opposite main west gate entrance to Lichfield Cathedral*
This family run traditional Georgian hotel is close to the cathedral and city centre. A comfortable lounge leads into a nicely appointed dining room; there is also a cosy bar on lower ground floor. Bedrooms vary but most are generally spacious, particularly those in the adjacent Westgate House.
ROOMS: 10 rms (8 en suite) 8 annexe en suite (1 fmly) s fr £62; d fr £75 (incl. bkfst) * **CONF:** Thtr 30 Board 20 **PARKING:** 60
NOTES: No dogs (ex guide dogs) No smoking in restaurant Closed 25 & 26 Dec RS Sun evenings **CARDS:**

⌂ Premier Lodge
Rykneld St, Fradley ws13 8rd
☎ 0870 700 1318 🖹 0870 700 1319

Premier Lodge offers modern, well equipped, en suite accommodation suitable for both business and leisure travellers. Meals can be taken at the adjacent popular restaurant and bar which is fully licensed. For further details, consult the Hotel Groups page.
ROOMS: 30 en suite d £46 *

○ Express by Holiday Inn
Wall Island, Shenstone WS16
☎ 0800 897121

ROOMS: 102 rms **NOTES:** Open Autumn 2000

LIFTON, Devon Map 02 SX38

★★★75% ❀❀❀ Arundell Arms
PL16 0AA
☎ 01566 784666 🖹 01566 784494
e-mail: arundellarms@btinternet.com
Dir: *40m West of Exeter and M5, 1m off A30 in Lifton Village*

This delightful 18th-century,former coaching inn has been run by Anne Voss-Bark for 40 years.The hotel offers 20 miles of salmon and trout fishing and other country pursuits. A relaxed and friendly atmosphere is created by the experienced, efficient team of staff. Highly rated, the hotel's cooking deserves its good reputation for a wide range of natural but vibrant recipes.
ROOMS: 23 en suite 5 annexe en suite s £45-£74; d £90-£113 (incl. bkfst) * LB **FACILITIES:** STV Fishing Skittle alley Games room
CONF: Thtr 100 Class 36 Board 46 Del from £104 * **PARKING:** 80
NOTES: No smoking in restaurant Closed 3 days Xmas Civ Wed 100
CARDS:

See advert on this page

L

LIFTON, continued

★★71% Lifton Hall Country House
PL16 0DR
☎ 01566 784863 & 784263 🖷 01566 784770
Dir: off A30 at Lifton village exit into village, down hill on left handside
This small hotel is traditionally English in style, particularly in the bar. Each of the bedrooms has character and charm. One room is located on the ground floor and is ideal for the less able.
ROOMS: 11 en suite (2 fmly) s £25-£45; d £50-£65 (incl. bkfst) * LB **FACILITIES:** Fishing Falconry & hawking Xmas **CONF:** Thtr 30 Class 20 Board 22 Del £72.50 * **PARKING:** 30
CARDS:

LINCOLN, Lincolnshire Map 08 SK97

★★★★59% The White Hart
Bailgate LN1 3AR
☎ 0870 400 8117 🖷 01522 531798
e-mail: HeritageHotels_Lincoln.White-Hart@forte-hotels.com
Dir: from A15 rdbt on north side of city follow historic Lincoln signs go through Newport Arch continue along Bailgate, hotel on corner at bend of road
A centrally located hotel, with convenient car parking, between the castle and imposing cathedral. Bedrooms are attractively decorated and comfortably furnished, many have lovely views over the city. Public areas are traditional in style and furnished with some impressive antique pieces.
ROOMS: 48 en suite (4 fmly) No smoking in 18 bedrooms s fr £60; d fr £120 (incl. bkfst) * LB **FACILITIES:** entertainment Xmas **CONF:** Thtr 90 Class 40 Board 30 Del £130 * **SERVICES:** Lift **PARKING:** 57 **NOTES:** No smoking in restaurant Civ Wed 120
CARDS:

★★★72% The Bentley Hotel & Leisure Club
Newark Rd, South Hykeham LN6 9NH
☎ 01522 878000 🖷 01522 878001
Dir: from A1 take A46 E towards Lincoln for 10m. Cross 1st rdbt on Lincoln Bypass to hotel 50yds on left
This smart, conveniently located, new hotel offers bright, attractive accommodation. The bedrooms are spacious and well equipped. There is a stylish leisure suite with gymnasium, sauna, steam room and a large pool with disabled access. For the less energetic there is a beauty salon. Air-conditioned.
ROOMS: 53 en suite (3 fmly) s £60-£76; d £75-£100 (incl. bkfst) * LB **FACILITIES:** STV Indoor swimming (H) Sauna Gym Jacuzzi/spa Beauty salon Xmas **CONF:** Thtr 350 Class 150 Board 30 Del from £94 * **SERVICES:** Lift **PARKING:** 140 **NOTES:** No dogs (ex guide dogs) No smoking in restaurant Civ Wed 120 **CARDS:**

★★★71% Washingborough Hall
Church Hill, Washingborough LN4 1BE
☎ 01522 790340 🖷 01522 792936
e-mail: washingborough.hall@btinternet.com
Dir: from B1188 onto B1190 Church Hill, 2m turn right opposite Methodist Church
This Georgian manor stands on the edge of the village and is set in attractive gardens with an outdoor swimming pool. Public rooms are pleasantly furnished and comfortable. The restaurant offers interesting menus and the bedrooms are individually designed, most looking out to the grounds or countryside.
ROOMS: 14 en suite No smoking in 3 bedrooms s £65-£80; d £80-£99.50 (incl. bkfst) * LB **FACILITIES:** Outdoor swimming (H) Pool table Croquet lawn Jacuzzi/spa **CONF:** Thtr 50 Class 18 Board 24 Del £115 * **PARKING:** 50 **NOTES:** No children 15yrs No smoking in restaurant
CARDS:

★★★69% Courtyard by Marriott Lincoln
Brayford Wharf North LN1 1YW
☎ 01522 544244 🖷 01522 560805
Dir: from A46 take A57-Lincoln Central,after Tanvics go straight ahead at the lights hotel on the left
Within easy walking distance of the city centre, overlooking Bayford Pool, this smart modern hotel offers spacious bedrooms, many of which look out over the waterfront. The public areas are comfortable and inviting, one of the main features is the restaurant with a gallery which overlooks the lounge bar.
ROOMS: 95 en suite (20 fmly) No smoking in 44 bedrooms d £61-£73 * LB **FACILITIES:** STV Gym **CONF:** Thtr 30 Class 20 Board 20 Del £92 * **SERVICES:** Lift air con **PARKING:** 100 **NOTES:** No dogs (ex guide dogs) **CARDS:**

★★★68% Grand Hotel
Saint Mary's St LN5 7EP
☎ 01522 524211 🖷 01522 537661
Dir: from A1 take A46, follow signs for Lincoln Central and then railway station

Close to the railway station, this friendly family-owned hotel is ideal for exploring the city and it's many attractions. The tastefully decorated bedrooms include a number of smart executive rooms, and some four-poster beds. Staff are willing and helpful, and the hotel benefits from two restaurants and bars.
ROOMS: 46 en suite (2 fmly) s £52-£67; d £67-£77 (incl. bkfst) * LB **FACILITIES:** STV Xmas **CONF:** Thtr 80 Class 50 Board 30 Del from £85 * **PARKING:** 30 **NOTES:** No dogs (ex guide dogs)
CARDS:

★★★65% Moor Lodge
Sleaford Rd LN4 1HU
☎ 01522 791366 🖷 01522 794389
e-mail: moorlodge@bestwestern.co.uk
(For full entry see Branston)

★★★65% Posthouse Lincoln
Eastgate LN2 1PN
☎ 0870 400 9052 🖷 01522 510780
Dir: adjacent to cathedral

This modern and friendly hotel is opposite Lincoln Cathedral and its grounds contain ruins of the Roman wall and Eastgate. Bedrooms have every modern facility and those facing the cathedral have balconies. Those on the ground floor have patio doors opening to a secluded garden. Facilities include the 'Seasons' restaurant and bar.
ROOMS: 70 en suite (7 fmly) No smoking in 46 bedrooms **CONF:** Thtr 90 Class 50 Board 40 **SERVICES:** Lift **PARKING:** 110
CARDS:

★★71% ❀ Castle
Westgate LN1 3AS
☎ 01522 538801 🖷 01522 575457
e-mail: castlehotel@ukcomplete.co.uk
Dir: *follow signs for 'Historic Lincoln' Hotel is at NE corner of the Castle*
This hotel offers delightful bedrooms named after British castles; the Lincoln suite has a comfortable bedroom with a lounge area. There is a cosy first-floor lounge and a small bar with an attractive open-plan restaurant, where a wide selection of dishes is offered, featuring quality seafood and local game.
ROOMS: 17 en suite 3 annexe en suite (1 fmly) No smoking in 11 bedrooms s £62-£79; d £79-£89 (incl. bkfst) * LB **FACILITIES:** Xmas **CONF:** Thtr 50 Class 18 Board 22 **PARKING:** 20 **NOTES:** No children 10yrs No smoking in restaurant **CARDS:**

See advert on this page

★★71% Hillcrest
15 Lindum Ter LN2 5RT
☎ 01522 510182 🖷 01522 510182
e-mail: jennifer@hillcresthotel.freeserve.co.uk
Dir: *from A15/Wragby Road, turn into Upper Lindium Road at brown tourist sign. Continue and turn left at bottom. Hotel 200mtrs on right*

The hospitality offered by Jenny Bennett and her staff is one of the strengths of Hillcrest, which sits in a quiet location not far from the town centre. The well-equipped bedrooms come in a variety of sizes, and a cosy dining room offers a good range of freshly prepared food and the pleasant conservatory overlooks the adjacent park.
ROOMS: 16 en suite (4 fmly) No smoking in 6 bedrooms s fr £52; d fr £79 (incl. bkfst) * LB **PARKING:** 8 **NOTES:** No smoking in restaurant Closed 23 Dec-3 Jan **CARDS:**

★★65% Loudor
37 Newark Rd, North Hykeham LN6 8RB
☎ 01522 680333 & 500474 🖷 01522 680403
Dir: *turn off A1 10m on A46 A1434 2m hotel on left opposite shopping forum*
Three miles from the city, this hotel offers soundly furnished, suitably equipped bedrooms with a good level of facilities. The relaxing public rooms include a cosy lounge, small bar and welcoming restaurant.
ROOMS: 9 en suite 1 annexe en suite (1 fmly) s £29.50-£33; d £39.50-£45 (incl. bkfst) * **FACILITIES:** STV **PARKING:** 12 **NOTES:** No dogs **CARDS:**

⌂ Express by Holiday Inn Lincoln
Runcorn Rd, off Whisby Rd LN6 3QZ
☎ 01522 698333 🖷 698444
e-mail: lincoln@premierhotels-9.demon.co.uk
Dir: *turn off A46 ringroad onto the Whisby Road. Take 1st turning on the left*
A modern budget hotel offering comfortable accommodation in refreshing, spacious and comprehensively-equipped bedrooms, en

continued on p306

LINCOLN, continued

Express by Holiday Inn, Lincoln

suite bathrooms with power showers and continental buffet breakfast included in the room rate. Suitable for business travellers or families. For further details and the Express by Holiday Inn phone number, consult the Hotel Groups page.
ROOMS: 86 en suite (incl. cont bkfst) d £49.50 * **CONF:** Thtr 35 Board 25 Del £85 *

⌂ *Travelodge*

Travelodge

Thorpe on the Hill LN6 9AJ
☎ 0800 850950
Dir: *on A46*
This modern building offers accommodation in smart, spacious and well equipped bedrooms, all with en suite bathrooms. Refreshments may be taken at the nearby family restaurant. For further details and the Travelodge phone number, consult the Hotel Groups page.
ROOMS: 32 en suite

LIPHOOK, Hampshire Map 04 SU83

★★★73% Old Thorns Hotel, Golf & Country Club

Longmoor Rd, Griggs Green GU30 7PE
☎ 01428 724555 01428 725036
e-mail: generalmanager@oldthorns.freeserve.co.uk
Dir: *A3 Guildford to Portsmouth, take Griggs Green exit (first after Liphook). Signposted*
This smartly presented hotel has many attractions: an 18-hole golf course with golf shop, an indoor pool with sauna and solarium, spacious bedrooms, some with balconies, and two restaurants, one of which, the Nippon Kan, is Japanese and specialises in Teppan-Yaki cuisine.
ROOMS: 28 en suite 4 annexe en suite s £100-£125; d £130-£145 (incl. bkfst) * LB **FACILITIES:** STV Indoor swimming (H) Golf 18 Tennis (hard) Sauna Solarium Gym Pool table Putting green Steam room Beauty treatment rooms Xmas **CONF:** Thtr 100 Class 50 Board 30 Del from £130 * **PARKING:** 120 **NOTES:** Civ Wed 80
CARDS:

⌂ *Travelodge*

Travelodge

GU30 7TT
☎ 0800 850950
Dir: *on northbound carriageway of A3, 1m from Griggs Green exit at Shell services*
This modern building offers accommodation in smart, spacious and well equipped bedrooms, all with en suite bathrooms. Refreshments may be taken at the nearby family restaurant. For further details and the Travelodge phone number, consult the Hotel Groups page.
ROOMS: 40 en suite

LISKEARD, Cornwall & Isles of Scilly Map 02 SX26

Premier Collection

★★ Well House

St Keyne PL14 4RN
☎ 01579 342001 01579 343891
e-mail: wellhse@aol.com
Dir: *from Liskeard A38 take B3254 to St Keyne, at church take left fork signed St Keynewell, hotel 0.5m from church*
This charming small hotel offers tastefully furnished, spacious and very well equipped bedrooms. There is an elegant sitting room with log fire, and an intimate bar. Guests can relax over afternoon tea on the terrace overlooking the splendid grounds. Carefully prepared, award-winning cuisine is served in the comfortable dining room.
ROOMS: 9 en suite (1 fmly) s £75-£90; d £110-£160 (incl. bkfst) * LB **FACILITIES:** Outdoor swimming (H) Tennis (hard) Croquet lawn Xmas **PARKING:** 30 **NOTES:** No smoking in restaurant
CARDS:

★★64% Lord Eliot

Castle St PL14 3AU
☎ 01579 342717 01579 347593
Dir: *take A38 into Liskeard, hotel 0.5m on left past St Martins Church*
A friendly team is on hand to welcome guests at the Lord Eliot Hotel. Bedrooms are comfortable and have been decorated smartly. An extensive range of bar meals is available in the traditional bar, which is a popular meeting place for locals; a separate TV lounge across the hall.
ROOMS: 15 rms (14 en suite) (1 fmly) No smoking in 2 bedrooms s fr £49; d fr £55 (incl. bkfst) * LB **FACILITIES:** Xmas **CONF:** Thtr 180 Class 180 Board 180 **PARKING:** 60 **NOTES:** No smoking in restaurant RS 25 Dec, closed evening **CARDS:**

LITTLEBOURNE, Kent Map 05 TR25

★★69% Bow Window Inn

50 High St CT3 1ST
☎ 01227 721264 01227 721250
e-mail: bow@windowhotel.freeserve.co.uk
A 300-year-old country cottage offering warm comfortable accommodation. Bedrooms are furnished in keeping with the style of the house and are well equipped. Public areas are limited, the restaurant offers attractive surroundings with exposed oak beams and a large Kentish fireplace.
ROOMS: 10 en suite (1 fmly) No smoking in 3 bedrooms s £42-£45; d £55-£60 (incl. bkfst) * LB **PARKING:** 16 **NOTES:** No smoking in restaurant **CARDS:**

LITTLE HALLINGBURY See Bishop's Stortford

LITTLE LANGDALE, Cumbria Map 07 NY30

★★67% Three Shires Inn
LA22 9NZ
☎ 015394 37215 🖷 015394 37127
e-mail: Ian@threeshiresinn.co.uk
Dir: *turn off A593, 2.5m from Ambleside at 2nd junct signposted for the Langdales. 1st left 0.5m, then hotel 1m up lane*

This delightful country hotel and inn lies in a small village amidst dramatic mountain scenery. One can eat from an extensive menu in either the dining room or the bar. The cooking reflects the high skill of the chef. There is a cosy, quiet foyer lounge with a log fire on cooler days.
ROOMS: 10 en suite (1 fmly) No smoking in all bedrooms s £38-£51; d £76-£86 (incl. bkfst) * LB **FACILITIES:** Xmas **PARKING:** 22 **NOTES:** No dogs No smoking in restaurant Closed Jan (ex New Year) RS Dec **CARDS:**

LITTLE WEIGHTON, East Riding of Yorkshire Map 08 SE93

★★68% The Rowley Manor
Rowley Rd HU20 3XR
☎ 01482 848248 🖷 01482 849900
Dir: *leave A63 at South Cave/Market Weighton sign into South Cave, turn right into Beverley Rd at the clock tower & follow signs for Rowley*
Rowley Manor is a Georgian country house set in lovely gardens and parkland. Bedrooms are traditionally furnished and decorated, and many have pleasant views. Some master rooms are particularly spacious. The cosy public rooms feature a magnificent pine-panelled study.
ROOMS: 16 en suite (2 fmly) s £70-£75; d £80-£95 (incl. bkfst) * LB **FACILITIES:** STV Riding Croquet lawn Xmas **CONF:** Thtr 90 Class 30 Board 50 Del from £90 * **PARKING:** 120 **NOTES:** Civ Wed 100 **CARDS:**

LIVERPOOL, Merseyside Map 07 SJ39
see also Blundellsands

★★★★68% ❀ Liverpool Marriott City Centre
Marriott HOTELS·RESORTS·SUITES
1 Queen Square L1 1RH
☎ 0151 476 8000 🖷 0151 474 5000
Dir: *from City Centre follow signs for Queen Square Parking. Hotel adjacent*
This impressive modern hotel is in the newly developed Queen Square area. The interior is rich and elegant and large bedrooms, including three suites, are comfortably furnished. Olivier's Restaurant on the first floor provides a high standard of cuisine in stylish surrounds.

continued

ROOMS: 146 en suite (29 fmly) No smoking in 90 bedrooms s £110-£230; d £130-£230 (incl. bkfst) * LB **FACILITIES:** STV Indoor swimming (H) Sauna Solarium Gym Jacuzzi/spa entertainment Xmas **CONF:** Thtr 250 Class 90 Board 30 Del from £115 * **SERVICES:** Lift air con **PARKING:** 158 **NOTES:** No smoking in restaurant Civ Wed 250 **CARDS:**

★★★63% The Royal
Marine Ter, Waterloo L22 5PR
☎ 0151 928 2332 🖷 0151 949 0320
e-mail: royalhotel@compuserve.com
Dir: *6.50m NW of city centre, turn left off A565 Liverpool/Southport road at monument, hotel at bottom of this road*
On the outskirts of the city, beside the Marine Gardens, this hotel, dated 1815, commands views of the Wirral and North Wales. Bedrooms are modern and spacious public areas include a conservatory adjacent to the brightly decorated restaurant, a split level bar where meals can be taken.
ROOMS: 25 en suite (5 fmly) s £45-£55; d £65 (incl. bkfst) * LB **FACILITIES:** STV **CONF:** Thtr 120 Class 70 Board 40 **PARKING:** 25 **NOTES:** No dogs (ex guide dogs) **CARDS:**

⌂ Express by Holiday Inn Liverpool
Express by Holiday Inn
Brittania Pavilion, Albert Dock L3 4AD
☎ 0151 709 1133 🖷 709 1144
e-mail: liverpool@premierhotels.co.uk
Dir: *follow signs for Liverpool City Centre & Albert Dock*
A modern budget hotel offering comfortable accommodation in refreshing, spacious and comprehensively-equipped bedrooms, en suite bathrooms with power showers and continental buffet breakfast included in the room rate. Suitable for business

continued

LIVERPOOL, continued

Express by Holiday Inn, Liverpool

travellers or families. For further details and the Express by Holiday Inn phone number, consult the Hotel Groups page.
ROOMS: 117 en suite (incl. cont bkfst) d £59.50 **CONF:** Thtr 35 Class 30 Board 25 Del from £95 *

⇧ Premier Lodge (Liverpool City Centre)

45 Victoria St L1 6JB
☎ 0870 700 1422 ▤ 0870 700 1423
PREMIER LODGE THE BEST. REST ASSURED.
Premier Lodge offers modern, well equipped, en suite accommodation suitable for both business and leisure travellers. Meals can be taken at the adjacent popular restaurant and bar which is fully licensed. For further details, consult the Hotel Groups page.
ROOMS: 39 en suite d £46 *

⇧ Premier Lodge (Liverpool North)

Dunningsbridge Rd L30 6YN
☎ 0870 700 1428 ▤ 0870 700 1429
PREMIER LODGE THE BEST. REST ASSURED.
Premier Lodge offers modern, well equipped, en suite accommodation suitable for both business and leisure travellers. Meals can be taken at the adjacent popular restaurant and bar which is fully licensed. For further details, consult the Hotel Groups page.
ROOMS: 62 en suite d £42 *

⇧ Premier Lodge (Liverpool South East)

Roby Rd, Huyton L36 4HD
☎ 0870 700 1426 ▤ 0870 700 1427
PREMIER LODGE THE BEST. REST ASSURED.
Premier Lodge offers modern, well equipped, en suite accommodation suitable for both business and leisure travellers. Meals can be taken at the adjacent popular restaurant and bar which is fully licensed. For further details, consult the Hotel Groups page.
ROOMS: 53 en suite d £46 *

⇧ Campanile

Chaloner St, Queens Dock L3 4AJ
☎ 0151 709 8104 ▤ 0151 709 8725
***Dir:** follow brown tourist signs marked "Albert Dock" Hotel is situated south on the waterfront*

This modern building offers accommodation in smart well equipped bedrooms, all with en suite bathrooms. Refreshments may be taken at the informal Bistro. For further details and the Campanile phone number, consult the Hotel Groups page.
ROOMS: 103 en suite **CONF:** Thtr 35 Class 18 Board 20

LIZARD, THE, Cornwall & Isles of Scilly — Map 02 SW71

★★★68% Housel Bay

Housel Cove TR12 7PG
☎ 01326 290417 & 290917 ▤ 01326 290359
e-mail: hotel@houselbay.com
***Dir:** follow A39/A394 to Helston, take the A3083 to the Lizard, at Lizard sign bear left, at school turn left and proceed down Lane to Hotel*
This hotel has stunning views over the sea to The Lizard, enjoyed from the sunny lounge and many bedrooms. Most bedrooms have high standards of comfort with modern facilities and extras. Highly enjoyable home-made cuisine is available in the elegant dining room.
ROOMS: 21 en suite (1 fmly) No smoking in 2 bedrooms s £30.50-£112; d £61-£112 (incl. bkfst) * LB **FACILITIES:** STV Xmas **SERVICES:** Lift **PARKING:** 37 **NOTES:** No dogs (ex guide dogs) No smoking in restaurant RS Winter **CARDS:**

★★80% ❀❀ Tregildry

TR12 6HG
☎ 01326 231378 ▤ 01326 231561
e-mail: trgildry@globalnet.co.uk
(For full entry see Gillan)

LOCKINGTON — Map 08 SK42

Hotels are listed under East Midlands Airport

LOLWORTH, Cambridgeshire — Map 05 TL36

⇧ *Travelodge*

Travelodge
Huntingdon Rd CB3 8DR
☎ 01954 781335 ▤ 01954 781335
***Dir:** on A14 northbound, 3m N of junct 14 on M11*
This modern building offers accommodation in smart, spacious and well equipped bedrooms, all with en suite bathrooms. Refreshments may be taken at the nearby family restaurant. For further details and the Travelodge phone number, consult the Hotel Groups page.
ROOMS: 20 en suite

London

AA London Hotels

Index of London Hotels

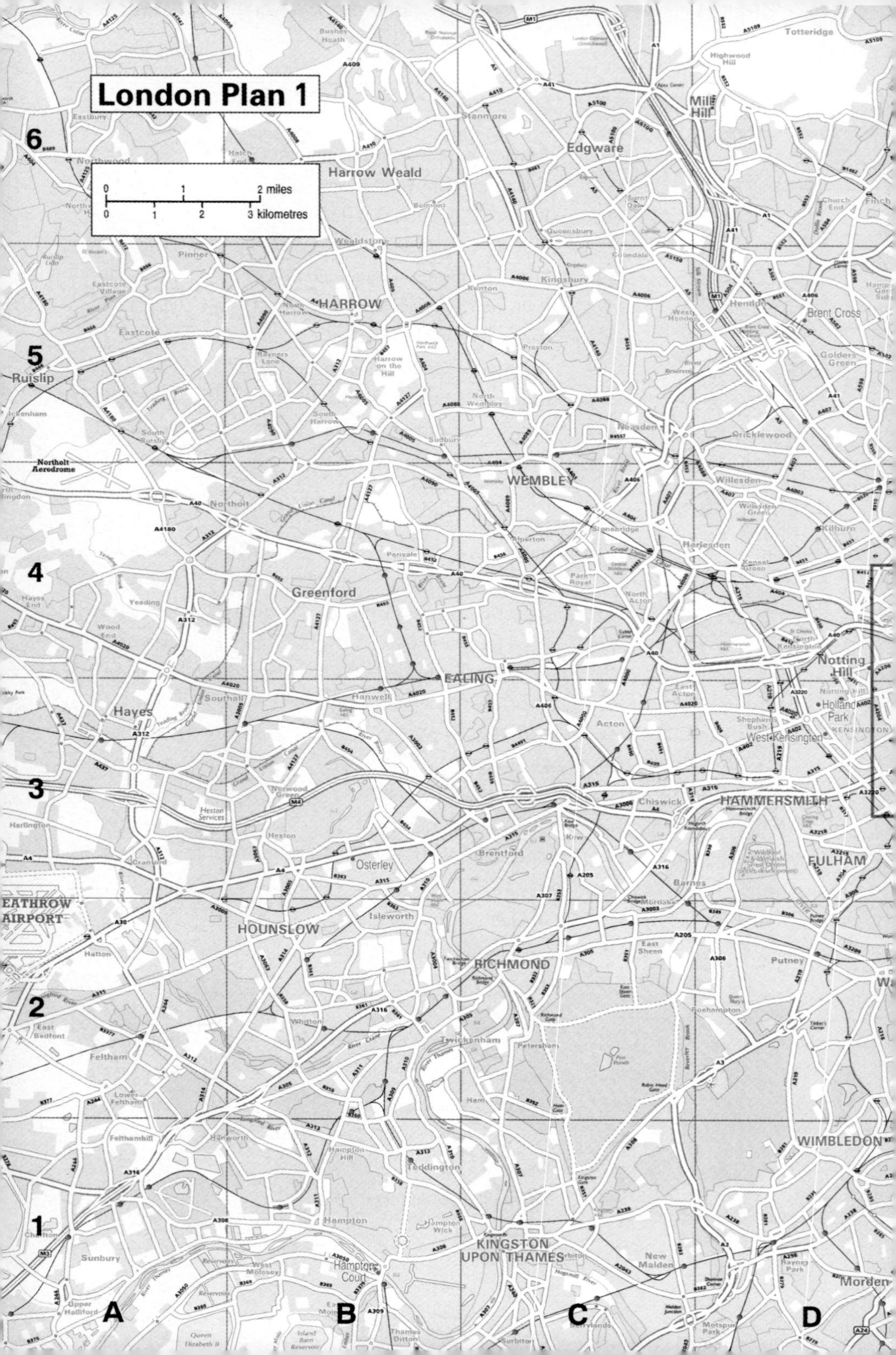
London Plan 1
0
1
2 miles
0
1
2
3 kilometres
A
B
C
D
1
2
3
4
5
6
Harrow Weald
Edgware
Mill Hill
HARROW
WEMBLEY
Greenford
EALING
Hayes
HOUNSLOW
RICHMOND
HAMMERSMITH
FULHAM
Notting Hill
Holland Park
WIMBLEDON
KINGSTON UPON THAMES
Brent Cross
Ruislip
Northolt Aerodrome
Osterley
Acton
Hampton Court
Teddington
Twickenham
Feltham
Sunbury
Putney
Barnes
Chiswick
Brentford
Isleworth
Hampton
Morden
New Malden
Totteridge
Stanmore
Pinner
Harlesden
Kilburn
Willesden
Cricklewood

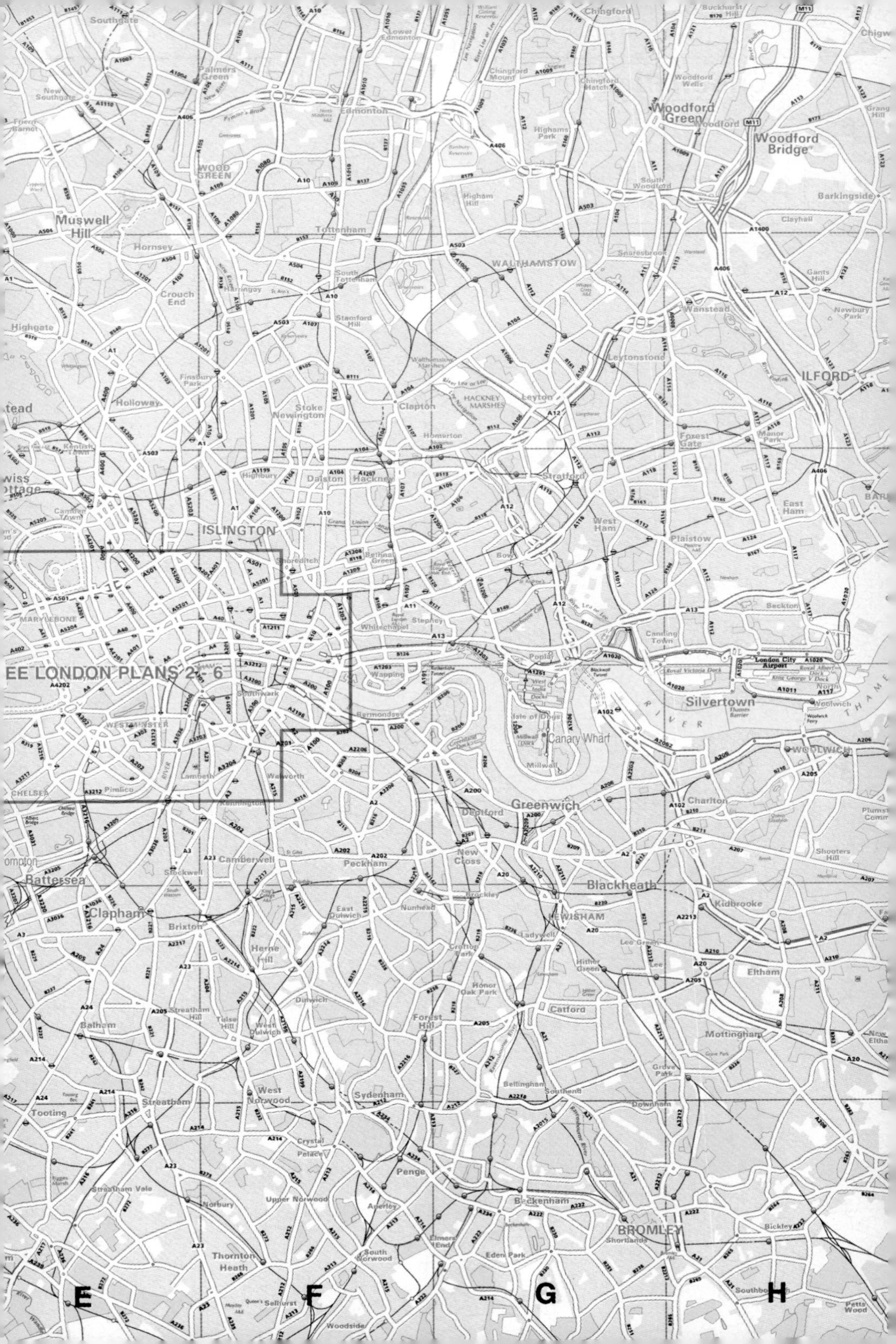
SEE LONDON PLANS 2–6
Southgate
Palmers Green
New Southgate
Edmonton
Lower Edmonton
Chingford
Chingford Mount
Chingford Hatch
Buckhurst Hill
Woodford Wells
Woodford Green
Woodford
Woodford Bridge
Friern Barnet
Wood Green
Highams Park
Higham Hill
South Woodford
Barkingside
Clayhall
Muswell Hill
Hornsey
Tottenham
South Tottenham
Walthamstow
Snaresbrook
Wanstead
Gants Hill
Newbury Park
Crouch End
Harringay
Highgate
Stamford Hill
Leytonstone
Ilford
Holloway
Finsbury Park
Stoke Newington
Clapton
Hackney Marshes
Leyton
Kentish Town
Homerton
Forest Gate
Manor Park
Highbury
Dalston
Hackney
Stratford
Swiss Cottage
Camden Town
Islington
West Ham
East Ham
Plaistow
Shoreditch
Bethnal Green
Bow
Marylebone
Stepney
Whitechapel
Beckton
Canning Town
Poplar
London City Airport
Royal Victoria Dock
Royal Albert Dock
King George V Dock
Wapping
West India Docks
Southwark
Bermondsey
Westminster
Isle of Dogs
Canary Wharf
Millwall
Silvertown
River Thames
North Woolwich
Woolwich
Lambeth
Walworth
Chelsea
Pimlico
Kennington
Deptford
Greenwich
Charlton
Camberwell
Peckham
New Cross
Stockwell
Battersea
Blackheath
Lewisham
Kidbrooke
Shooters Hill
Clapham
Brixton
East Dulwich
Nunhead
Brockley
Ladywell
Lee Green
Herne Hill
Crofton Park
Hither Green
Lee
Eltham
Honor Oak Park
Dulwich
Catford
Streatham Hill
Tulse Hill
West Dulwich
Balham
Forest Hill
Mottingham
Grove Park
Bellingham
Southend
Downham
Streatham
West Norwood
Sydenham
Tooting
Crystal Palace
Penge
Streatham Vale
Upper Norwood
Norbury
Beckenham
Anerley
Bromley
Shortlands
Bickley
Thornton Heath
Elmers End
Eden Park
South Norwood
Selhurst
Woodside
Southborough
Petts Wood
E
F
G
H

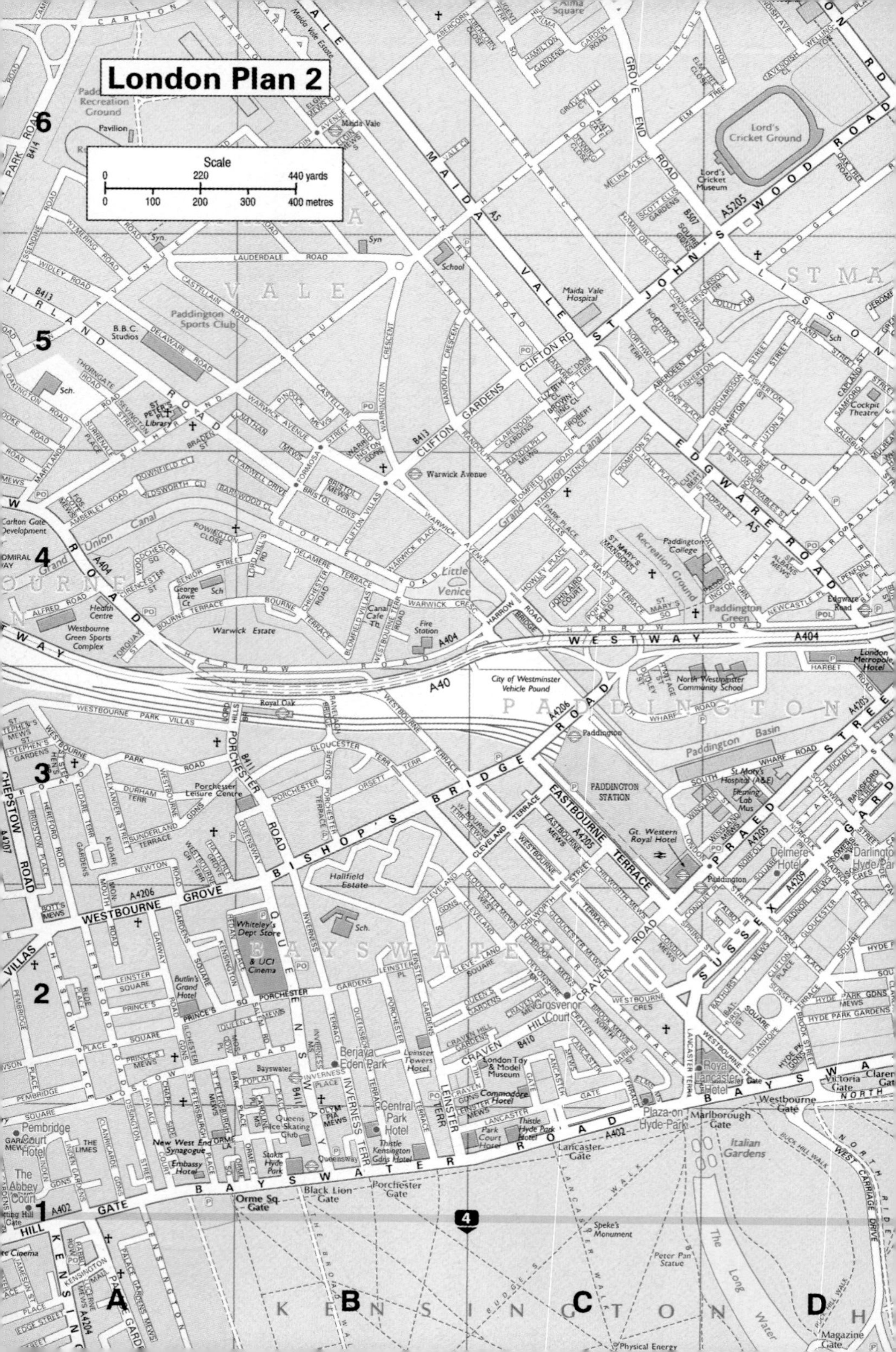
London Plan 2
Scale
0
220
440 yards
0
100
200
300
400 metres
6
5
4
3
2
1
A
B
C
D
4
Paddington Recreation Ground
Pavilion
Maida Vale
Maida Vale Estate
Lord's Cricket Ground
Lord's Cricket Museum
ST JOHN'S WOOD ROAD
A5205
GROVE END ROAD
MAIDA VALE
A5
EDGWARE ROAD
Maida Vale Hospital
School
Syn
LAUDERDALE ROAD
VALE
Paddington Sports Club
B.B.C. Studios
DELAWARE ROAD
CASTELLAIN ROAD
WARWICK AVENUE
Warwick Avenue
CLIFTON GARDENS
CLIFTON RD
RANDOLPH AVENUE
RANDOLPH CRESCENT
WARRINGTON CRESCENT
ELGIN AVENUE
SUTHERLAND AVENUE
B413
HIRLAND ROAD
Sch.
ST PETER'S PL Library
FORMOSA STREET
BRISTOL GDNS
BRISTOL MEWS
CLIFTON VILLAS
BLOMFIELD ROAD
Grand Union Canal
Little Venice
Canal Cafe Th
Fire Station
WARWICK CRESC
DELAMERE TERRACE
WESTBOURNE TERR ROAD
CHICHESTER ROAD
BOURNE TERRACE
George Lowe Ct
Warwick Estate
Health Centre
Westbourne Green Sports Complex
ALFRED ROAD
HARROW ROAD
A404
Carlton Gate Development
WESTWAY
A40
City of Westminster Vehicle Pound
North Westminster Community School
PADDINGTON
Royal Oak
WESTBOURNE PARK VILLAS
Paddington Recreation Ground
Paddington College
ST MARY'S MANSIONS
ST MARY'S TERRACE
Paddington Green
Edgware Road
London Metropole Hotel
Paddington Basin
Paddington
PADDINGTON STATION
EASTBOURNE TERRACE
A4206
BISHOP'S BRIDGE ROAD
PORCHESTER ROAD
B411
Porchester Leisure Centre
Hallfield Estate
St Mary's Hospital (A&E)
Fleming Lab Mus
Gt. Western Royal Hotel
PRAED STREET
A4205
SUSSEX GARDENS
A4209
Delmere Hotel
Darlington Hyde Park
WESTBOURNE GROVE
Whiteley's Dept Store & UCI Cinema
BAYSWATER
QUEENSWAY
Butlin's Grand Hotel
LEINSTER SQUARE
PRINCE'S SQUARE
Grosvenor Court
CRAVEN HILL
CRAVEN ROAD
B410
London Toy & Model Museum
Commodore Hotel
Berjaya Eden Park
Leinster Towers Hotel
Central Park Hotel
Queens Ice Skating Club
Bayswater
New West End Synagogue
Embassy Hotel
Stakis Hyde Park
Queensway
Thistle Kensington Gdns Hotel
Park Court Hotel
Thistle Hyde Park Hotel
Plaza-on Hyde-Park
Royal Lancaster Hotel
Lancaster Gate
BAYSWATER ROAD
A402
Marlborough Gate
Italian Gardens
Victoria Gate
Westbourne Gate
Pembridge Court Hotel
The Abbey Court
NOTTING HILL GATE
CHEPSTOW ROAD
A4207
Black Lion Gate
Porchester Gate
Orme Sq. Gate
Speke's Monument
Peter Pan Statue
The Long Water
KENSINGTON
Physical Energy
Magazine Gate
NORTH CARRIAGE DRIVE
WEST CARRIAGE DRIVE
KENSINGTON PALACE GARDENS
A4204
Cockpit Theatre
Sch
LISSON GROVE
ST MARYLEBONE

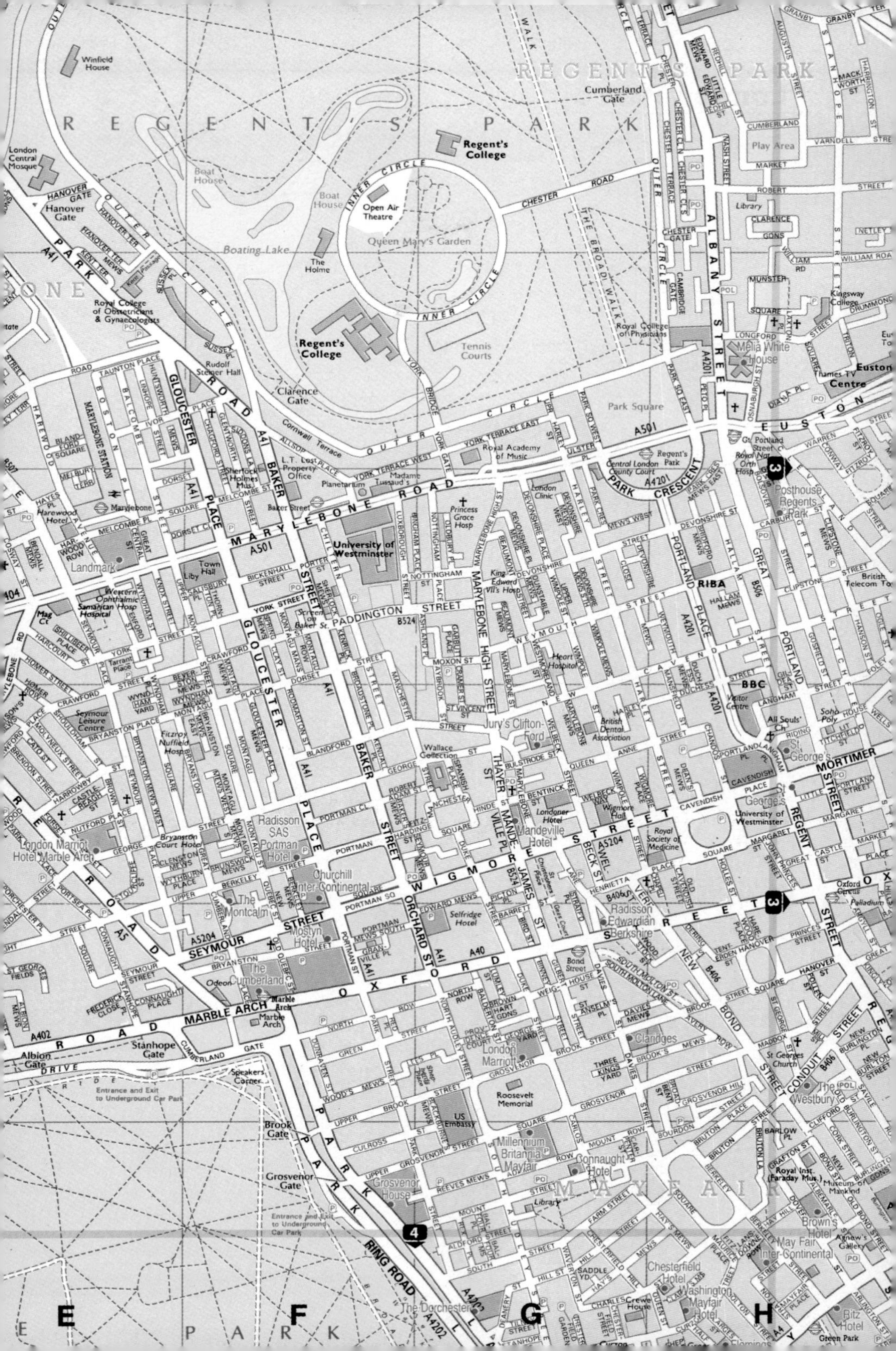

REGENTS PARK
Winfield House
London Central Mosque
Hanover Gate
Boat House
Boating Lake
Regent's College
Inner Circle
Open Air Theatre
Queen Mary's Garden
The Holme
Tennis Courts
Chester Road
Cumberland Gate
The Broad Walk
Royal College of Physicians
Royal College of Obstetricians & Gynaecologists
Outer Circle
Park Road
Sussex Place
Rudolf Steiner Hall
Clarence Gate
Cornwall Terrace
York Bridge
Park Square
Royal Academy of Music
Madame Tussaud's
Planetarium
L.T. Lost Property Office
Sherlock Holmes Mus.
Baker Street
Marylebone
Marylebone Station
Marylebone Road
A501
University of Westminster
Princess Grace Hosp
Central London County Court
Regent's Park
Park Crescent
Euston Road
Albany Street
Cumberland Market
Play Area
Library
Kingsway College
Melia White House
Thames TV Centre
Euston
Great Portland Street
Posthouse Regents Park
London Clinic
King Edward VII's Hosp
Heart Hospital
RIBA
Portland Place
BBC
All Souls' Ch
St George's
University of Westminster
Cavendish Square
Mortimer Street
Regent Street
Oxford Circus
Oxford Street
Harewood Hotel
Landmark
Town Hall
Liby
Western Ophthalmic Hosp
Samaritan Hospital
Gloucester Place
Baker Street
Paddington Street
Marylebone High Street
Wigmore Street
Wigmore Hall
Seymour Leisure Centre
Fitzroy Nuffield Hosp
Wallace Collection
Jury's Clifton-Ford
British Dental Association
Royal Society of Medicine
Mandeville Hotel
Londoner Hotel
London Marriott Hotel Marble Arch
Bryanston Court Hotel
Radisson SAS Portman Hotel
Churchill Inter-Continental
The Montcalm
Mostyn Hotel
Selfridge Hotel
Radisson Edwardian Berkshire
Bond Street
Seymour Street
The Cumberland
Odeon
Marble Arch
Edgware Road
Bayswater Road
Albion Gate
Stanhope Gate
Speakers' Corner
Entrance and Exit to Underground Car Park
Brook Gate
Grosvenor Gate
Park Lane
Ring Road
Oxford Street
North Audley Street
London Marriott
Roosevelt Memorial
US Embassy
Grosvenor Square
Claridges
Brook Street
Grosvenor Street
Millennium Britannia Mayfair
Connaught Hotel
Grosvenor House
MAYFAIR
New Bond Street
St Georges Church
Conduit Street
The Westbury
Royal Inst. (Faraday Mus.)
Museum of Mankind
Brown's Hotel
Agnew's Gallery
May Fair Inter-Continental
Chesterfield Hotel
Washington Mayfair Hotel
Crewe House
The Dorchester
Ritz Hotel
Green Park
Hyde Park
E
F
G
H
3
4

London Plan 3
6
5
4
3
2
1
A
B
C
D
SOMERS TOWN
ST PANCRAS
BLOOMSBURY
SOHO
ST GILES
ST JAMES'S
British Library
St Pancras Station
King's Cross St Pancras
Great Northern
Euston Station
National Temperance Hospital
Kennedy Hotel
Play Area
Library
Ibis Euston
Euston
Euston Square
Friends House
Wellcome Inst
Euston Tower
Thames TV Centre
Kingsway College
Melia White House
Camden Town Hall & St Pancras Liby
St Pancras International Youth Hostel
London Euston Travel Inn
New Ambassadors Hotel
County Hotel
Euston Plaza Hotel
Elizabeth Garrett Anderson Hosp.
Fire Sta
British Medical Assoc
St George's Gardens
Thomas Coram Foundation
Coram's Fields Playground
University College
University College Hosp
Bloomsbury Theatre
Percival David Foundation of Chinese Arts
Tavistock Hotel
Royal National Hotel
Brunswick Housing & Shopping Centre
Renoir Cinema
Posthouse Bloomsbury
Hotel Russell
President Hotel
National Hosp
Royal London Homeopathic Hospital
Imperial Hotel
Waverley House Hotel
Bloomsbury Park Hotel
The Bonnington in Bloomsbury
Radisson Edwardian Grafton
Warren Street
Great Portland Street
Royal Nat Orth Hosp
Posthouse Regents Park
Regent's Park
RIBA
BBC
All Souls'
London Foot Hosp
Middlesex Hospital
British Telecom Tower
Pollock's Toy Museum
Goodge Street
Drill Hall
Building Centre
R.A.D.A.
Vanbrugh Th.
Academy Hotel
University of London
Montague on the Gardens
British Museum and Library
Blooms Hotel
Bedford Hotel
Myhotel
Rathbone Hotel
ABC
Radisson Edwardian Kenilworth
Radisson Edwardian Mountbatten
YMCA
Dominion
St Giles Circus
Tottenham Court Road
Astoria
Centre Pt
Princes Circus
Shaftesbury Th
Oasis Sports Centre
Drury Lane Moat House
Kingsway Hall
Holborn Town Hall
New London Theatre
Freemason's Hall
Cochrane Theatre
Kingsley Hotel
Mag Court
St George's
University of Westminster
Cavendish Square
Oxford Circus
Palladium
Marshall Street Leisure Centre
House of St Barnabas
Soho Theatre
Prince Edward Th
Palace Th
Curzon (Soho)
Phoenix Th
Shaftesbury Hosp
Contemp Applied Arts
Donmar Th
New Ambass Th
Cambridge Th
Royal Opera House
Theatre Mus
London Transport Mus
Covent Garden
Africa Centre
St Paul's
Jubilee Mkt
Gielgud Th
Queens Th
Apollo Th
Lyric Th
Trocadero Centre
Prince Charles
St John's Hosp
Hippodrome
Warner
Empire
MGM (Swiss Centre)
Leicester Square
County Ct
Wyndhams Th
Albery Th
Duke of York Th
Radisson Edwardian Hampshire
Coliseum
Leicester Square Theatre Booking Off
Odeon
Radisson Edwardian Pastoria
Prince of Wales Th
Comedy Th
Criterion Th
Piccadilly Circus
London Pavilion
Le Meridien Piccadilly
Royal Academy of Arts
Royal Inst (Faraday Mus.)
Museum of Mankind
Brown's Hotel
The Westbury
St Georges Church
May Fair Inter-Continental
Agnew's Gallery
22 Jermyn Street
St James's Church
Cavendish St James
Britain Centre
Her Majesty's Th
Theatre Royal Haymarket
National Portrait Gallery
National Gallery
St Martin-in-the-Fields
Trafalgar Sq Hotel
Nelson's Column
Canada Hse
Africa House
Charing Cross
Charing Cross Hotel
Charing Cross Sta
Players Th
York Watergate
Embankment
Embankment Pier
Victoria Embankment Gardens
Royal Society of Arts
Adelphi Th
Vaudeville Th
Savoy Th
Strand Palace
Government Offices
Min of Agriculture
Mall Gallery
Ritz Hotel
Green Park
Washington Mayfair Hotel
Chesterfield Hotel
Euston Road
Tottenham Court Road
Gower Street
Oxford Street
New Oxford Street
Regent Street
Piccadilly
Shaftesbury Avenue
Charing Cross Road
Trafalgar Square
Strand
Haymarket
Pall Mall
Long Acre
High Holborn
Southampton Row
Russell Square
Bedford Square
Bloomsbury Street
Great Portland Street
Portland Place
Albany Street
Mortimer Street
Goodge Street
Northumberland Avenue
The Mall
A501
A400
A40
A4
A4200

Scale
0
220
440 yards
0
100
200
300
400 metres
PENTONVILLE
FINSBURY
CLERKENWELL
ST LUKE'S
PENTON RISE
Kingsway College
Magistrates Court
London Ryan Hotel
Holiday Inn
Mount Pleasant (Postal Sorting Office)
Lilian Baylis Theatre
Sadlers Wells Theatre
Town Hall
London Records Office
House of Detention
Kingsway College
Clerkenwell Heritage Centre
Museum of the Order of St John
St Bartholomew's Medical School
Charterhouse
Barbican Hotel
Finsbury Leisure Complex
Moorfields Eye Hosp
Exhibition Halls
Barbican Centre
The Barbican
Guildhall School of Music & Drama
St Giles
Gray's Inn
St Alban's
St Etheldreda's Ch
Farringdon
Barbican
Central London Markets
Founders' Hall
Butcher's Hall
St Bart the Great
St Bartholomew's Hospital
Holy Sepulchre
Ironmongers Hall
Barber Surgeons' Hall
Mus of London
Salters' Hall
Brewers' Hall
Girdlers' Hall
Plaisterers' Hall
Pewterers' Hall
Clock Museum
Haberdashers' Hall
Guildhall
St Botolph's
St Anne & St Agnes Ch
Goldsmiths' Hall
Waxchandlers' Hall
Saddlers Hall
BT Centre
Stationery Office
Chancery Lane
Staple Inn
London Silver Vaults
Daily Mirror Offices
Patent Office
Science Ref. Lib.
Lincoln's Inn
Public Record Office
Dr Johnson's House
City Temple
Central Criminal Court
Cutters' Hall
St Paul's
St Paul's Cathedral
Bank of England Extension
St Mary le Bow
Mercers' Hall
St Mary Aldermary
Temple of Mithras
Royal Courts of Justice
London School of Economics
St Clement Danes
Australia House
St Mary-le-Strand
Prince Henry's Room
Temple Church
Inns of Court and Chancery
Middle Temple Hall
Inner Temple
Middle Temple
Roman Bath
Howard Hotel
King's College
Temple
St Brides
The Bridewell Th
Stationers Hall
St Martin's
Youth Hostel
Apothecaries' Hall
Faraday Building
College of Arms
Mansion House
Painters' Hall
St Benet's
Mermaid Theatre
City of London School
Vintners' Hall
Innholders' Hall
Livery Halls
Blackfriars
BLACKFRIARS STATION
HMS President
Blackfriars Millennium Pier
Blackfriars Pier
HQS Wellington (Master Mariners)
Thames Police Station
Millennium Bridge
Queenhithe Stairs
Southwark Br Stairs
Old Barge House Stairs
Oxo Tower Wharf
Bankside Gallery
Bankside Jetty
Globe Th Shakespeare Globe Exhibition
Tate Gallery of Modern Art
Financial Times
Clink Exhibition
Vinopolis City of Wine
Golden Hinde
The London Television Centre (LWT)
Royal National Theatre
National Film Th.
Queen Elizabeth Hall
Purcell Room
London Nautical Sch
Express by Holiday Inn Southwark
Premier Lodge (London Southwark)
St Christopher House
CLERKENWELL ROAD
ROSEBERY AVENUE
FARRINGDON ROAD
GRAY'S INN ROAD
HOLBORN
HOLBORN VIADUCT
NEWGATE STREET
FLEET STREET
LUDGATE HILL
CHEAPSIDE
POULTRY
CANNON STREET
QUEEN VICTORIA STREET
UPPER THAMES STREET
VICTORIA EMBANKMENT
STRAND
GOSWELL ROAD
ALDERSGATE STREET
OLD STREET
CITY ROAD
LONDON WALL
CHISWELL STREET
BEECH STREET
BLACKFRIARS BRIDGE
SOUTHWARK BRIDGE
SOUTHWARK STREET
STAMFORD STREET
WATERLOO BRIDGE
RIVER
NORTH SOUTHWARK
E
F
G
H
5
9

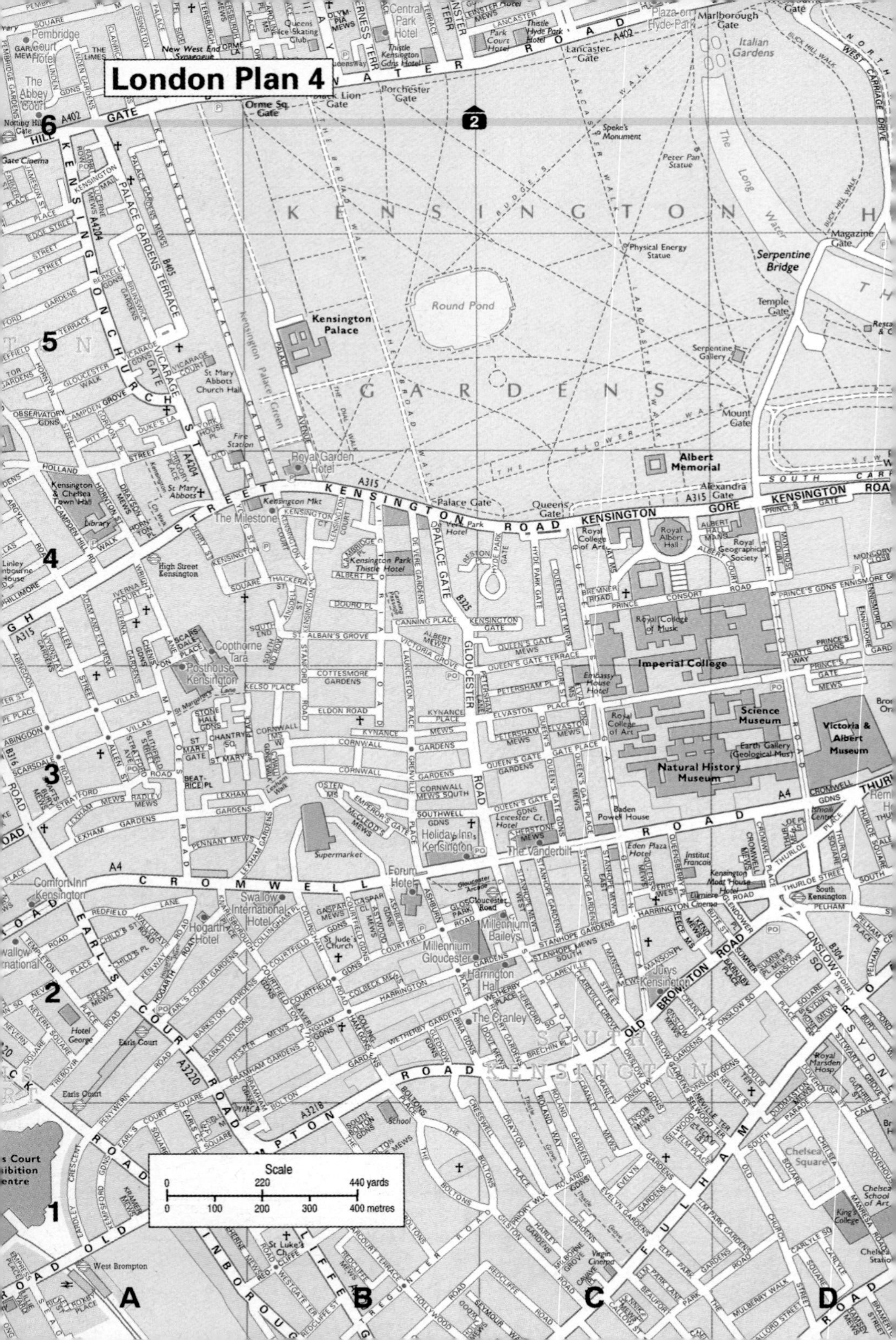

London Plan 4
Kensington Gardens
Kensington Palace
Round Pond
Serpentine Bridge
Serpentine Gallery
Italian Gardens
The Long Water
Speke's Monument
Peter Pan Statue
Physical Energy Statue
Albert Memorial
Royal Albert Hall
Royal College of Art
Royal Geographical Society
Royal College of Music
Imperial College
Science Museum
Natural History Museum
Victoria & Albert Museum
Earth Gallery (Geological Mus)
Baden Powell House
Kensington Road
Kensington Gore
Bayswater Road
Notting Hill Gate
Kensington Church St
Kensington High Street
Cromwell Road
Old Brompton Road
Fulham Road
Earl's Court Road
Gloucester Road
Queen's Gate
Exhibition Road
Palace Gate
Lancaster Gate
Marlborough Gate
Black Lion Gate
Orme Sq. Gate
Queens Gate
Alexandra Gate
Palace Gate
Mount Gate
Temple Gate
Magazine Gate
High Street Kensington
Gloucester Road
South Kensington
Earls Court
West Brompton
Kensington & Chelsea Town Hall
Library
Copthorne Tara
Posthouse Kensington
Royal Garden Hotel
Holiday Inn Kensington
Forum Hotel
Swallow International Hotel
Hogarth Hotel
Millennium Gloucester
Millennium Baileys
Harrington Hall
Jurys Kensington
The Cranley
The Vanderbilt
Comfort Inn Kensington
Hotel George
Chelsea Square
Chelsea School of Art
King's College
Royal Marsden Hosp
Institut Français
Lumière Cinema
Virgin Cinema
St Mary Abbots
St Jude's Church
St Luke's Ch.
The Boltons
South Kensington
Supermarket
Scale
0 220 440 yards
0 100 200 300 400 metres
A B C D
1 2 3 4 5 6
A4 A315 A402 A4204 A3220 A3218 B325 B304 B405 B316

Memorial
US Embassy
Brook Gate
Grosvenor Gate
Entrance and Exit to Underground Car Park
PARK LANE
RING ROAD
A4202
Grosvenor House
Millennium Britannia Mayfair
Connaught Hotel
MAYFAIR
Library
Royal Inst. (Faraday Mus.)
Museum of Mankind
Brown's Hotel
May Fair Inter-Continental
Agnew's Gallery
Chesterfield Hotel
Washington Mayfair Hotel
Crewe House
The Dorchester
Curzon (Mayfair)
Green Park Hotel
Flemings Mayfair
Ritz Hotel
Green Park
PICCADILLY
A4
PARK
Boat House
Pier
SERPENTINE
SERPENTINE ROAD
ROTTEN ROW
Curzon Gate
Metropolitan Hotel
Park Lane Hotel
Four Seasons Hotel
Athenaeum Hotel
GREEN PARK
Queen Mother Gate
Inter-Continental Hotel
Apsley House (Wellington Mus)
Hyde Park Corner
HYDE PARK CORNER
Wellington Arch
POL
Albert Gate
SOUTH CARRIAGE DRIVE
Edinburgh Gate
Mandarin Oriental Hyde Park
Knightsbridge Barracks
Bowater House
KNIGHTSBRIDGE
The Berkeley
The Lanesborough
CONSTITUTION HILL (CLOSED TO TRAFFIC ON SUNDAYS)
Buckingham Palace Gardens
Buckingham Palace
Queen's Gallery
A315
Sheraton Park Tower
Basil Street Hotel
Knightsbridge Fire Sta
Capital Hotel
The Millennium Knightsbridge
The Halkin Hotel
GROSVENOR CRES
GROSVENOR PL
A302
RING ROAD
BELGRAVE SQUARE
Lowndes Hyatt Hotel
Hyatt Carlton Tower Hotel
Harrods Store
BROMPTON ROAD
The Parkes Hotel
The Beaufort
SLOANE STREET
A3216
The Royal Mews
Rubens at the Palace
BUCKINGHAM GATE
A3214
Westminster Th.
The Goring Hotel
Royal Westminster Thistle Hotel
GROSVENOR GDNS
HOBART PL
A3217
London Tourist Board & Convention Bureau
Victoria Palace
Victoria Bus Sta
Thistle Victoria Hotel
VICTORIA STATION
Apollo Victoria
Victoria Place Shopping Centre
Victoria Rail/Air Terminal
BROMPTON
Cadogan Hotel
PONT STREET
B319
EATON SQUARE
ECCLESTON STREET
RING ROAD
EATON SQ
Ebury Court Hotel
BELGRAVIA
The Cadogan
Wilbraham Hotel
Royal Ct Hotel
The Cliveden Town House
Royal Court Th
Sloane Square
Coach Sta Arrivals
Victoria Coach Sta.
BUCKINGHAM PALACE ROAD
The Colonnades Shopping Centre
Quality Hotel Westminster
B310
School
Guinness Trust Estate
Duke of York's H.Q.
LOWER SLOANE STREET
PIMLICO ROAD
EBURY BRIDGE
B324
Abbots Manor Estate
WARWICK WAY
KING'S ROAD
A3217
Burtons Court
Chelsea Barracks
CHELSEA BRIDGE ROAD
EBURY BRIDGE ROAD
B313
Ranelagh Gardens
Royal Hospital
Museum
ROYAL HOSPITAL ROAD
B302
National Army Museum
Lister Hosp
GROSVENOR ROAD
A3212
Churchill Gardens
PIMLICO
E
F
G
H

London Plan 5
6
5
4
3
2
1
A
B
C
D
PICCADILLY
GREEN PARK
ST JAMES'S PARK
St James's Park Lake
Duck Island
Queen Victoria Memorial
Buckingham Palace
Queen's Gallery
Wellington Barracks
Guards' Chapel & Museum
Home Office
Horse Guards Parade
Old Admiralty
Admiralty Arch
Foreign & Commonwealth Office
Treasury
Cabinet War Rooms
Ministry of Defence
Banqueting House
Royal Horseguards
Cenotaph
Norman Shaw Building (MPs Offices)
Westminster Pier
Big Ben
Houses of Parliament
Westminster Abbey
Westminster School
Jewel Tower
Victoria Tower Gardens
Lambeth Pier
LAMBETH BRIDGE
WESTMINSTER BRIDGE
Thames House
Millbank Tower
Tate Gallery of British Art
Clore Gallery
Royal Army Medical College
Millbank Estate
Westminster Cathedral
Westminster City Hall
New Scotland Yard
Dept of Trade and Industry
Queen Elizabeth II Conf. Centre
Middx. Guildhall
Central Hall
VICTORIA STATION
Victoria Place Shopping Centre
Victoria Rail/Air Terminal
The Colonnades Shopping Centre
Goring Hotel
The Royal Mews
Rubens at the Palace
Westminster School Playing Field
Greycoat Hosp School
Royal Hort. Society New Hall
Royal Hort. Society Old Hall
Queen Mother Sports Centre
Quality Hotel Westminster
Lillington Gardens Estate
Holiday Inn Express Hotel
Pimlico
PIMLICO
WESTMINSTER
Churchill Gardens
Pimlico Gardens
St George Wharf Development (under construction)
VAUXHALL STATION
VAUXHALL BRIDGE (RING ROAD)
National Gallery
National Portrait Gallery
St Martin-in-the-Fields
Nelson's Column
TRAFALGAR SQUARE
Charing Cross
CHARING CROSS STA
Embankment
Hungerford
Hispaniola
Royal Society of Arts
Leicester Square
Piccadilly Circus
Trocadero Centre
Le Meridien Piccadilly
Royal Academy of Arts
Brown's Hotel
May Fair Inter-Continental
Ritz Hotel
Green Park
Stafford Hotel
Duke's Hotel
Spencer House
St James's Palace
Clarence House
Lancaster House
Marlborough House
Schomberg House
Carlton House
Duke of York Column
Inst. of Contemporary Arts
Mall Gallery
Her Majesty's Th
Britain Visitor Centre
HAYMARKET
PALL MALL
ST JAMES'S STREET
WHITEHALL
PARLIAMENT ST
NORTHUMBERLAND AVE
VICTORIA EMBANKMENT
VICTORIA STREET
VAUXHALL BRIDGE ROAD
MILLBANK
HORSEFERRY ROAD
GROSVENOR ROAD
BELGRAVE ROAD
ALBERT EMBANKMENT
Fire Brigade Headquarters
A302
A3212
A202
A4
B310

London Plan 6
Scale
0 220 440 yards
0 100 200 300 400 metres
A
B
C
D
1
2
3
4
5
6

LONDON
Greater London Plans 1-5, pages 314-324. (Small scale maps 4 & 5 at back of book.) Hotels are listed below in postal district order, commencing East, then North, South and West, with a brief indication of the area covered. Detailed plans 2-5 show the locations of AA-appointed hotels within the Central London postal districts. If you do not know the postal district of the hotel you want, please refer to the index preceding the street plans for the entry and map pages.

E1 STEPNEY AND EAST OF THE TOWER OF LONDON
See advert on opposite page

E14 CANARY WHARF & LIMEHOUSE
See LONDON plan 1 *G3*

★★★★★74% Four Seasons Hotel Canary Wharf
Westferry Circus, Canary Wharf E14 8RS
☎ 0207 5101999 🖹 0207 5101998
e-mail: andrew.peart@fourseasons.com
Dir: *Leave A13 and follow signs to Canary Wharf/Isle of Dogs/Westferry Circus.Hotel is located off the 3rd exit of Westferry Circus r/about*
This stylish, modern hotel commands a superb riverside location and enjoys stunning views of the sky line of London. The well equipped bedrooms provide top quality finishes and are thoughtfully designed to meet the demands of both the international leisure and business guest. Extensive leisure facilities include a large heated pool and a four floor exercise complex. Staff throughout are friendly and provide impeccable service.
ROOMS: 142 en suite No smoking in 99 bedrooms s £240; d £260 *
FACILITIES: STV Indoor swimming (H) Tennis (hard) Sauna Solarium Gym Jacuzzi/spa entertainment Xmas **CONF:** Thtr 200 Class 120 Board 56 **SERVICES:** Lift air con **PARKING:** 29
CARDS:

⇧ Hotel Ibis London Docklands
1 Baffin Way E14 9PE
☎ 020 7517 1100 🖹 020 7987 5916
e-mail: H2177@accor-hotels.com
Modern, budget hotel offering comfortable accommodation in bright and practical bedrooms. Breakfast is self-service and dinner is available in the restaurant. For further details, consult the Hotel Groups page.
ROOMS: 87 en suite (incl. cont bkfst) s fr £62.25; d fr £66.50 *

⇧ *Travelodge*
Coriander Av, East India Dock Rd E14 2AA
☎ 020 7531 9705
Dir: *fronts A13 at East India Dock Road*
This modern building offers accommodation in smart, spacious and well equipped bedrooms, all with en suite bathrooms. Refreshments may be taken at the nearby family restaurant. For further details and the Travelodge phone number, consult the Hotel Groups page.
ROOMS: 132 en suite

E16 See LONDON plan 1 *H4*

○ Express by Holiday Inn

1 Silvertown Way, Silvertown E16 1EA
☎ 020 7540 4040 🖹 020 7540 4050
ROOMS: 88 rms **NOTES:** Opening August 2000

EC1 CITY OF LONDON

⇧ Express by Holiday Inn London City

275 Old St EC1V 9LN
☎ 020 7300 4300 🖹 7300 4400
e-mail: reservationsfc
@holidayinnlondon.demon.co.uk

A modern budget hotel offering comfortable accommodation in refreshing, spacious and comprehensively-equipped bedrooms, en suite bathrooms with power showers and continental buffet breakfast included in the room rate. Suitable for business travellers or families. For further details and the Express by Holiday Inn phone number, consult the Hotel Groups page.
ROOMS: 224 en suite (incl. cont bkfst) d £95 * **CONF:** Thtr 90 Class 40 Board 36 Del £155 *

EC2

★★★★★69% Great Eastern Hotel
Liverpool St EC2M 7QN
☎ 020 7618 5000 🖹 020 7618 5001
e-mail: sales@great-eastern-hotel.co.uk
Recently opened as we went to press (with more bedrooms to come) the stylish, rejuvenated Liverpool Street hotel is a striking new addition to the capital. The hotel is skirted by a selection of eating options (the Rosettes are for Aurora)and bars, including Japanese food and a take on the traditional English pub.
ROOMS: 267 en suite s £229-£264; d £264-£299 * LB
FACILITIES: STV Gym steam room **CONF:** Thtr 300 Class 180 Board 34 **SERVICES:** Lift air con **NOTES:** No dogs (ex guide dogs)
CARDS:

EC3

○ Novotel London Tower Bridge
10 Pepys St EC3
☎ 020 7265 6000
ROOMS: 203 en suite **NOTES:** Opening August 2000

N1 ISLINGTON See LONDON plan 1 *F4*

★★★66% *Great Northern*
Kings Cross N1 9AN
☎ 020 7837 5454 🖹 020 7278 5270
Dir: *entrance faces side of Kings Cross station*
This mainly commercial hotel is very well located close to Kings Cross and Euston stations. Bedrooms are spacious and offer a very good range of extra facilities. Laundry and 24 hour room service are also available. Meals are taken in the Coffee House which is open all day.
ROOMS: 82 en suite (16 fmly) No smoking in 22 bedrooms
FACILITIES: STV **CONF:** Thtr 100 Class 60 Board 45 **SERVICES:** Lift
PARKING: 12 **NOTES:** No dogs **CARDS:**

★★★ 62% Jurys Inn London
60 Pentonville Rd, Islington N1 9LA
☎ 020 7282 5500 ▤ 020 7282 5511
e-mail: enquiry@jurys.com
Dir: *from A1 turn right onto A501, turn right and continue onto Pentonville Road*
The Jury's Inn concept is based on good value rooms, that can easily be adapted to family use. All the rooms have a double bed and air-conditioning. Other facilities and services are fairly low-key. The Angel Tube station is nearby and there are several car parks in the neighbourhood.
ROOMS: 229 en suite (116 fmly) No smoking in 135 bedrooms d £84-£110 * **FACILITIES:** STV **CONF:** Thtr 30 Class 10 Board 15 **SERVICES:** Lift air con **NOTES:** No dogs (ex guide dogs) Closed 24-27 Dec **CARDS:**

See advert on this page

N10 MUSWELL HILL See LONDON plan 1 *E6*

★★★ 68% Raglan Hall
8-12 Queens Ave, Muswell Hill N10 3NR
☎ 020 8883 9836 ▤ 020 8883 5002
e-mail: raglanhall@aol.com
Dir: *North Circ B550 for Muswell Hill. At roundabout take last exit to Queens Avenue. Hotel is 75yds on the right.*
Located on an elegant tree lined avenue in North London, this hotel is well situated for access to major road and rail networks. Bedrooms vary, with some suitable for family accommodation, all are thoughtfully. Limited off street parking is available.
ROOMS: 46 en suite (8 fmly) No smoking in 12 bedrooms s £79-£104; d £79-£109 * **FACILITIES:** STV **CONF:** Thtr 120 Class 40 Board 50 Del from £110 * **PARKING:** 12 **NOTES:** No dogs (ex guide dogs) Civ Wed 100 **CARDS:**

London

NW1 REGENT'S PARK See LONDON plan 1 *E4*

Premier Collection

★★★★★ Landmark

222 Marylebone Rd NW1 6JQ
☎ 020 7631 8000 📠 020 7631 8080
e-mail: reservations@thelandmark.co.uk
Dir: *located on Marylebone Road in front of Marylebone Railway Station*

This spectacular hotel has an eight storey central atrium which offers light meals and teas. The Cellars restaurant offers a clubby atmosphere, and the main dining room offers impressive European cuisine. Bedrooms are extremely stylish, generously proportioned and air-conditioned, with marble bathrooms offering deep tubs and separate showers. At our press date rosettes for food were not yet confirmed. Check the AA website for current information.

ROOMS: 299 en suite (60 fmly) No smoking in 147 bedrooms s fr £334.88; d fr £358.38 * LB **FACILITIES:** STV Indoor swimming (H) Sauna Gym Health club Massage Steam room Whirlpool Armatherapy Reflexology Therapeutic Xmas **CONF:** Thtr 500 Class 180 Board 80 **SERVICES:** Lift air con **PARKING:** 90 **NOTES:** No dogs (ex guide dogs) Civ Wed 300
CARDS:

★★★★73% ❀❀ Melia· White House Regents Park

Albany St, Regents Park NW1 3UP
☎ 020 7387 1200 📠 020 7388 0091
e-mail: melia.white.house@solmelia.es
Dir: *opposite Gt Portland St Underground and set slightly back from Marylebone & Euston Rd*

This delightful hotel began life as an apartment building in 1936 and offers high standards of comfort and service. Bedrooms on the 'Reserve' floor are the most spacious and have their own dedicated lounge. The café bar has a brasserie-style menu. There is also a formal dining room and The Wine Press, often used for private parties. *continued*

ROOMS: 582 en suite (1 fmly) No smoking in 166 bedrooms d £180-£230 * **FACILITIES:** STV Sauna Gym Xmas **CONF:** Thtr 120 Class 45 Board 40 Del from £195 * **SERVICES:** Lift air con **PARKING:** 7 **NOTES:** No dogs (ex guide dogs) **CARDS:**

See advert on page 327

⌂ *Hotel Ibis Euston*

ibis hotel

3 Cardington St NW1 2LW
☎ 020 7388 7777 📠 020 7388 0001
e-mail: h0921@accor-hotels.com
Dir: *from Euston station or Euston Rd, turn right to Melton St leading to Cardington St*

Modern, budget hotel offering comfortable accommodation in bright and practical bedrooms. Breakfast is self-service and dinner is available in the restaurant. For further details, consult the Hotel Groups page.

ROOMS: 300 en suite **CONF:** Thtr 100 Class 50 Board 50

NW3 HAMPSTEAD AND SWISS COTTAGE See LONDON plan 1 *E5/E4*

★★★★68% London Marriott Hotel Regents Park

Marriott HOTELS · RESORTS · SUITES

128 King Henry's Rd NW3 3ST
☎ 020 7722 7711 📠 020 7586 5822
Dir: *at the junct of Adelaide Rd and King Henry's Rd. Approximately 200yds off Finchley Rd, A41*

Close to Swiss Cottage, this large, modern hotel boasts very good standards. A massive refit should be completed by November 2000; this will include all bedrooms and public areas. Smart public areas comprise an open plan marbled lobby and bar-lounge, gym, pool and leisure centre, free parking and a shop.

ROOMS: 303 en suite (157 fmly) No smoking in 190 bedrooms d £120-£160 * LB **FACILITIES:** STV Indoor swimming (H) Sauna Solarium Gym Hair & Beauty salon entertainment **CONF:** Thtr 300 Class 150 Board 90 Del from £190 * **SERVICES:** Lift air con **PARKING:** 150 **NOTES:** No dogs (ex guide dogs) Civ Wed 250
CARDS:

★★★64% *Posthouse Hampstead*

Posthouse

215 Haverstock Hill NW3 4RB
☎ 0870 400 9037 📠 020 7435 5586
Dir: *take A41 to Swiss Cottage just before this junction take feeder road left into Buckland Cres onto Belsize Av left into Haverstock Hill*

Suitable for business and leisure travellers, this bright hotel provides modern accommodation in well equipped bedrooms. A recent refurbishment has completed two floors of smart 'Millennium' rooms. The Traders bar and restaurant is open for lunch and dinner.

ROOMS: 140 en suite No smoking in 70 bedrooms **CONF:** Thtr 35 Board 20 **SERVICES:** Lift **PARKING:** 70
CARDS:

○ Swiss Cottage Hotel

Best Western

4 Adamson Rd, Swiss Cottage NW3 3HP
☎ 020 7722 2281
NOTES: Open

> Late for dinner? Quality Standards star rating means that last orders for dinner should be no earlier than:
> ★ 6.30pm ★★ 7.00pm ★★★ 8.00pm
> ★★★★ 9.00pm ★★★★★ 10.00pm

NW6 MAIDA VALE

★★★★66% London Marriott West Hampstead

Plaza Pde, Maida Vale NW6 5RP
☎ 020 7543 6000 Fax 020 7543 2100
e-mail: regentsplaza@btinternet.com

Situated at Maida Vale, this large, modern hotel has spacious bedrooms, air conditioning and excellent facilities. Smart public areas comprise a marbled lobby and a choice of restaurants. The hotel also offers valet parking, an impressive leisure club and a range of conference rooms.
ROOMS: 221 en suite (6 fmly) No smoking in 110 bedrooms d £185-£205 * LB **FACILITIES:** Indoor swimming (H) Sauna Gym **CONF:** Thtr 200 Class 90 Board 40 Del from £195 * **SERVICES:** Lift air con **PARKING:** 26 **NOTES:** No dogs (ex guide dogs)
CARDS:

NW7 MILL HILL
See LONDON plan 1 *D6*

⌂ *Welcome Lodge*
Welcome Break Service Area, London Gateway, M1, Mill Hill NW7 3HB
☎ 020 8906 0611 Fax 020 8906 3654
Dir: *on M1, between junct 2 & 3 - northbound. Accessible from southbound carriageway*
This modern building offers accommodation in smart, spacious and well equipped bedrooms, suitable for families and businessmen, and all with en suite bathrooms. Refreshments may be taken at the nearby family restaurant. For further details and the Welcome Break phone number, consult the Hotel Groups page.
ROOMS: 101 en suite **CONF:** Thtr 40 Board 20

SE1 SOUTHWARK AND WATERLOO

★★★★★69% ❀❀ London Marriott County Hall
County Hall SE1 7PB
☎ 020 7928 5200 Fax 020 7928 5300
Dir: *located on River Thames opposite The Houses of Parliament & next to Westminster Bridge & The London Eye*
The London Marriott occupies the majority of the historic County Hall building, just over Westminster Bridge and adjacent to the new London Eye. Notable features are very smart, well laid-out bedrooms and first class leisure facilities, including a superb 25m swimming pool. Staff are extremely efficient and friendly.
ROOMS: 200 en suite (60 fmly) No smoking in 147 bedrooms d £200-£276 * LB **FACILITIES:** STV Indoor swimming (H) Sauna Solarium Gym Jacuzzi/spa Xmas **CONF:** Thtr 72 Class 34 Board 30 Del from £280 * **SERVICES:** Lift air con **PARKING:** 120 **NOTES:** No dogs (ex guide dogs) Civ Wed 85 **CARDS:**

★★★69% Novotel London Waterloo
113 Lambeth Rd SE1 7LS
☎ 020 7793 1010 Fax 020 7793 0202
e-mail: h1785@accor-hotels.com
Dir: *opposite Houses of Parliament on the S bank of the River Thames, situated just off Lambeth Bridge, opposite Lambeth Palace on Lambeth Road*
This modern young hotel, close to Waterloo station, benefits from its own secure car park. Bedrooms are spacious and include air conditioning. The open plan public areas include a garden brasserie, the "Flag and Whistle Pub", a small shop, and leisure facilities.
ROOMS: 187 en suite (80 fmly) No smoking in 158 bedrooms s fr £130; d fr £150 * LB **FACILITIES:** STV Sauna Gym Pool table Steam room **CONF:** Thtr 40 Class 25 Board 24 Del from £172 * **SERVICES:** Lift air con **PARKING:** 40 **CARDS:**

⌂ *Days Inn Waterloo*
54 Kennington Rd SE1 7BJ
☎ 020 792 21331
Fully refurbished, Days Inn offers well equipped, brightly appointed, modern accommodation with smart en suite bathrooms. There is a fully staffed reception; continental breakfast is available and other refreshments may be taken at the nearby family restaurant.

⌂ Express by Holiday Inn Southwark
103-109 Southwark St SE1 0JQ
☎ 020 7401 2525 Fax 020 7401 3322
e-mail: stay@expresssouthwark.co.uk
Dir: *Follow A20 changing into the A2 to City Centre. Head towards Elephant & Castle. Right before Blackfriars bridge at 1st large t/light intersection*

A modern budget hotel offering comfortable accommodation in refreshing, spacious and comprehensively-equipped bedrooms, en suite bathrooms with power showers and continental buffet breakfast included in the room rate. Suitable for business travellers or families. For further details and the Express by Holiday Inn phone number, consult the Hotel Groups page.
ROOMS: 88 en suite (incl. cont bkfst) d £81-£87 *

○ Hotel Mercure
Skyline House, 200 Union St SE1 0LX
NOTES: Open

○ *Premier Lodge (London Southwark)*
Anchor, Bankside, 34 Park St SE1
☎ 0870 700 1456 Fax 0870 700 1457

Bad hair day? Hairdryers in all rooms three stars and above.

London

SE3 BLACKHEATHSee LONDON plan 1 *G3*

★★★ 64% Bardon Lodge

15-17 Stratheden Rd, Blackheath SE3 7TH
☎ 020 8853 7000 ▯ 020 8858 7387
e-mail: bardonlodge@btclick.com

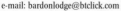

On the edge of the pretty village of Blackheath, this is a friendly hotel, popular for small conferences during the week and equally in demand by weekend visitors to Greenwich. The Vanbrugh Hotel across the road is under the same ownership and offers budget accommodation.

ROOMS: 32 en suite (4 fmly) s fr £85; d fr £110 (incl. bkfst) * LB **FACILITIES:** STV Xmas **CONF:** Thtr 45 Class 20 Board 20 Del from £95 * **PARKING:** 16 **NOTES:** No smoking in restaurant
CARDS:

★★ 61% Clarendon

8-16 Montpelier Row, Blackheath SE3 0RW
☎ 020 8318 4321 ▯ 020 8318 4378
Dir: *A2, turn off at Blackheath junct, hotel on left just before village overlooking Blackheath & Greenwich Royal Park*

This imposing Georgian building stands on the edge of the Royal Hundred of Blackheath with commanding views over open countryside. Bedrooms are neat and well equipped. Function and meeting rooms are available. The Chart Bar is an attractive feature of the hotel.

ROOMS: 193 en suite (3 fmly) No smoking in 22 bedrooms s fr £65; d fr £79 (incl. bkfst) * LB **FACILITIES:** STV Pool table Xmas **CONF:** Thtr 200 Class 50 Board 120 Del from £99 * **SERVICES:** Lift **PARKING:** 80 **NOTES:** Civ Wed 50
CARDS:

See advert on opposite page

SE10 GREENWICH See LONDON plan 1 *G3*

★★ 69% *Hamilton House*

14 West Grove, Greenwich SE10 8QT
☎ 020 8694 9899

⌂ Express by Holiday Inn Greenwich

Bugsby's Way, Greenwich SE10 0GD
☎ 020 826 95000 ▯ 020 826 95069
e-mail: greenwich@stannifer-hotels.com
Dir: *just S of Blackwell Tunnel off A102, on Greenwich Peninsula, near The Millennium Dome*

A modern budget hotel offering comfortable accommodation in refreshing, spacious and comprehensively-equipped bedrooms, en suite bathrooms with power showers and continental buffet breakfast included in the room rate. Suitable for business travellers or families. For further details and the Express by Holiday Inn phone number, consult the Hotel Groups page.

ROOMS: 162 en suite (incl. cont bkfst) d £72.50-£89.50 * **CONF:** Thtr 75 Class 45 Board 45 Del from £110 *

⌂ Hotel Ibis

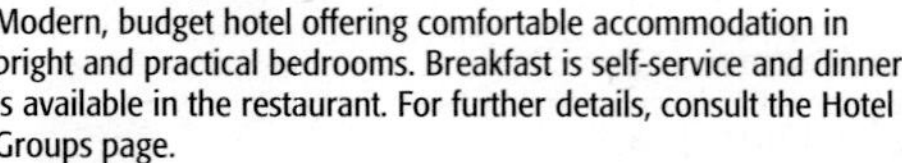

30 Stockwell St SE10 9JN
☎ 020 8305 1177 ▯ 020 8858 7139
e-mail: H0975@accor-hotels.com

Modern, budget hotel offering comfortable accommodation in bright and practical bedrooms. Breakfast is self-service and dinner is available in the restaurant. For further details, consult the Hotel Groups page.

ROOMS: 82 en suite s fr £58; d fr £58 *

SW1 WESTMINSTER

Premier Collection

★★★★★ ❀❀❀❀❀ The Berkeley

Wilton Place, Knightsbridge SW1X 7RL
☎ 020 7235 6000 ▯ 020 7235 4330
e-mail: info@the-berkeley.co.uk
Dir: *300mtrs along Knightsbridge from Hyde Park Corner*

The Savoy Group

Considered to be the bench-mark for the very best in hotel-keeping and service, the Berkeley has an excellent range of bedrooms, some with sizeable balconies, furnished with care and attention to detail. Reception rooms, including the Lutyens Writing Room, are adorned with magnificent flower arrangements, and there are superb leisure facilities. The two restaurants offer a complete contrast of style: modern, influenced by South East Asia at Vong and French cuisine at La Tante Claire.

ROOMS: 168 en suite No smoking in 28 bedrooms s £329-£376; d £400-£3055 * LB **FACILITIES:** STV Indoor swimming (H) Sauna Solarium Gym Beauty/therapy treatments Xmas **CONF:** Thtr 220 Class 100 Board 50 **SERVICES:** Lift air con **PARKING:** 50 **NOTES:** No dogs (ex guide dogs) Civ Wed 160
CARDS:

See advert on page 325

Premier Collection

★★★★★ 🏵🏵🏵 ***Lanesborough***
Hyde Park Corner SW1X 7TA
☎ 020 7259 5599 📠 020 7259 5606
e-mail: info@lanesborough.co.uk
Dir: *follow signs to central London and Hyde Park Corner*
Occupying an enviable position on Hyde Park Corner, the Lanesborough offers the highest levels of comfort in its range of bedrooms and suites. Twenty-four-hour service from a personal butler ensures that guests are well catered for, and the reception rooms, with their lavish furnishings and magnificent flower arrangements, are a delight to use. The popular cocktail bar has a wonderful supply of vintage cognac, whiskies and ports, and the conservatory restaurant offers an attractive atmosphere for dining.

continued

ROOMS: 95 en suite No smoking in 24 bedrooms **FACILITIES:** STV Gym Jacuzzi/spa Fitness studio entertainment **CONF:** Thtr 90 Class 60 Board 50 **SERVICES:** Lift air con **PARKING:** 38
CARDS:

Late for dinner? Quality Standards star rating means that last orders for dinner should be no earlier than:
★ 6.30pm ★★ 7.00pm ★★★ 8.00pm
★★★★ 9.00pm ★★★★★ 10.00pm

London

SW1 WESTMINSTER, continued

Premier Collection

★★★★★ Mandarin Oriental Hyde Park
66 Knightsbridge SW1X 7LA
☎ 020 7235 2000 020 7235 4552
e-mail: reserve-molon@mohg.com
Dir: *after passing Harrods, on the righthand side, the hotel is 0.5m on the left opposite Harvey Nichols department store*
Situated between the fashionable shopping district of Knightsbridge and the peaceful green expanse of Hyde Park, this famous hotel offers a luxurious atmosphere. Marble is used to elegant effect in the reception areas, which include a popular cocktail lounge and the princpal restaurant, The Park, where dishes exemplify subtle flavours and high quality ingredients. The standard of food, accommodation and service are all excellent.
ROOMS: 200 en suite No smoking in 72 bedrooms s fr £245; d £295-£375 * LB **FACILITIES:** STV Gym Fitness centre entertainment Xmas **CONF:** Thtr 250 Class 130 Board 60 **SERVICES:** Lift air con **NOTES:** No dogs (ex guide dogs) Civ Wed 400 **CARDS:**

★★★★★70% **Hyatt Carlton Tower**
Cadogan Place SW1X 9PY
☎ 020 7235 1234 020 7235 9129
e-mail: ctower@hytlondon.co.uk
Dir: *turn down Sloane St, Cadogan Place is the second turning on the left immediately before Pont St*
In the heart of Knightsbridge, the Hyatt Carlton Tower offers modern bedrooms and bright public areas. Extra facilities are impressive. The ground floor houses the Chinoiserie lounge and Rib Room restaurant with its clubby bar. Modern Italian cooking, awarded two AA rosettes, is on offer in the friendly Grissini restaurant.
ROOMS: 220 en suite No smoking in 61 bedrooms s fr £280; d fr £305 * LB **FACILITIES:** STV Indoor swimming (H) Tennis (hard) Sauna Solarium Gym Jacuzzi/spa Beauty treatment Hair salon Health club Massage & Spa treatments entertainment Xmas **CONF:** Thtr 400 Class 250 Board 80 **SERVICES:** Lift air con **PARKING:** 80 **NOTES:** No dogs (ex guide dogs) Civ Wed 360 **CARDS:**

★★★★★69%
Sheraton Park Tower
THE LUXURY COLLECTION
101 Knightsbridge SW1X 7RN
☎ 020 7235 8050 & 7235 3368 Res
020 7235 3368
e-mail: morten_ebbesen@sheraton.com
Dir: *close to Knightsbridge Underground Station*
This unique, circular, modern hotel has good standard-sized bedrooms; higher tariffs have better views and facilities, up to full butler service. Public areas have a lively atmosphere; the main bar off the lobby has a 'clubby' feel with tasteful polo prints. Afternoon tea can be taken in the Rotunda Lounge. Restaurant One-O-One serves cuisine de la mer, meeting a very high standard of cooking.
ROOMS: 289 en suite (289 fmly) No smoking in 80 bedrooms s £351-£469; d £375-£492 * **FACILITIES:** STV Health facilities at affiliated club entertainment Xmas **CONF:** Thtr 60 Class 50 Board 30 Del from £255 * **SERVICES:** Lift air con **PARKING:** 90 **NOTES:** No dogs (ex guide dogs) **CARDS:**

Premier Collection

★★★★ **Goring**

Beeston Place, Grosvenor Gardens SW1W 0JW
☎ 020 7396 9000 020 7834 4393
e-mail: reception@goringhotel.co.uk
Dir: *behind Buckingham Palace, right off Lower Grosvenor Place, just prior to the Royal Mews on the left*
This hotel, run by the Goring family since 1910, is an excellent example of the British tradition of hotel keeping. The well equipped bedrooms are traditionally furnished and boast high levels of comfort and quality. Stylish reception rooms include the garden bar and the drawing room, both popular for afternoon tea and cocktails. The restaurant menu has a classic repertoire but also has a well deserved reputation for delivering contemporary British cuisine.
ROOMS: 74 en suite s £213; d £258-£320 * LB **FACILITIES:** STV Free membership of nearby Health Club entertainment Xmas **CONF:** Thtr 60 Class 30 Board 30 **SERVICES:** Lift air con **PARKING:** 8 **NOTES:** No dogs Civ Wed 50 **CARDS:**

Premier Collection

★★★★ **The Halkin Hotel**
Halkin St, Belgravia SW1X 7DJ
☎ 020 7333 1000 020 7333 1100
e-mail: sales@halkin.co.uk
Dir: *Hotel located between Belgrave Sq & Grosvenor Place. Access via Chapel St into Headfort Pl & turn left into Halkin St*
Modern in design, this individual hotel also offers high levels of professional service. Bedrooms, fully air-conditioned, combine comfort with practicality and include state of the art communications for business visitors. Stefano Cavallini cooks in a contemporary light style, modifying Italian dishes to suit today's tastes.

ROOMS: 41 en suite No smoking in 9 bedrooms d £270-£345 * LB **FACILITIES:** STV Gym entertainment **CONF:** Thtr 30 Class 15 Board 26 **SERVICES:** Lift air con **NOTES:** No dogs (ex guide dogs) **CARDS:**

Premier Collection

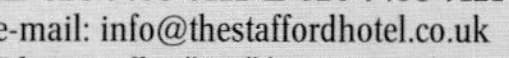

★★★★ The Stafford

16-18 St James's Place SW1A 1NJ
☎ 020 7493 0111 🖷 020 7493 7121
e-mail: info@thestaffordhotel.co.uk
Dir: *turn off Pall Mall into St James's Street, take second left turn into St James's Place*

Quietly located in exclusive St James, this charming hotel retains the friendly formality and understated luxury that have been its trademark for decades. Elegant, individually designed bedrooms include carriage houses. Afternoon tea is a long-standing tradition in the comfortable drawing room and the American Bar is famous for its collection of celebrity photos, caps and ties. In the restaurant, menus balance traditional grills with more creative dishes. There are several private dining rooms, including the 350 year old wine cellars. Service and hospitality throughout the hotel demonstrates a serious commitment to customer care.

ROOMS: 81 en suite s £234-£305; d £258-£305 * **FACILITIES:** STV Membership of Fitness Club available Xmas **CONF:** Thtr 40 Board 24 **SERVICES:** Lift air con **NOTES:** No dogs Civ Wed 60 **CARDS:**

★★★★77% ✿✿ *The Cadogan Hotel*

75 Sloane St SW1X 9SG
☎ 020 7235 7141 🖷 020 7245 0994
e-mail: info@cadogan.com

This elegant Victorian hotel, set discreetly on Sloane St, lists Lillie Langtry and Oscar Wilde as two of its most celebrated visitors. Bedrooms, mostly air-conditioned, are traditionally furnished and feature a host of modern facilities. The sumptuous drawing room is popular for afternoon tea and the dining room enjoys a well deserved reputation for fine food.

ROOMS: 65 en suite (1 fmly) No smoking in 16 bedrooms **FACILITIES:** STV **CONF:** Thtr 50 Class 12 Board 20 **SERVICES:** Lift **NOTES:** No dogs (ex guide dogs) RS Sat **CARDS:**

★★★★70% ✿ The Royal Horseguards

THISTLE HOTELS

Whitehall Court SW1A 2EJ
☎ 020 7839 3400 🖷 020 7925 2263
e-mail: royal.horseguards@thistle.co.uk

In a quiet area of Whitehall, overlooking the Thames, the Royal Horseguards provides tastefully furnished, air-conditioned bedrooms offering a high level of comfort and facilities. Public areas include an impressive front foyer, a smart bar and restaurant which earns a Rosette for its cuisine. There is an alliance with the magnificent meeting facilities of the adjacent One Whitehall, owned by the same company.

ROOMS: 280 en suite No smoking in 180 bedrooms d £155-£295 * **FACILITIES:** STV Gym **CONF:** Thtr 60 Class 30 Board 24 **SERVICES:** Lift air con **NOTES:** No dogs **CARDS:**

★★★★70% The Rubens at the Palace

39 Buckingham Palace Rd SW1W 0PS
☎ 020 7834 6600 🖷 020 7233 6037
e-mail: reservations@rubens.redcarnationhotels.com
Dir: *opposite the Royal Mews*

Overlooking the Royal Mews, behind Buckingham Palace and close to Victoria Station, the Rubens offers very comfortable, well appointed accommodation. The two restaurants offer a good choice of menus; there is also an extensive lounge menu. Room service provides hot dishes throughout the night.

ROOMS: 173 en suite No smoking in 80 bedrooms s £125-£135; d £139-£169 * **FACILITIES:** STV entertainment Xmas **CONF:** Thtr 60 Class 30 Board 25 Del from £220 * **SERVICES:** Lift air con **NOTES:** No dogs (ex guide dogs) No smoking in restaurant **CARDS:**

★★★★69% ✿✿ The Millennium Knightsbridge

MILLENNIUM HOTELS AND RESORTS

17 Sloane St, Knightsbridge SW1X 9NU
☎ 020 7235 4377 🖷 020 7235 3705
e-mail: reservations.chelsea@mill-cop.com
Dir: *from A4, Sloane St is located on the right, just past Harrods. Vehicle access to the hotel via Pavilion Road*

This modern, stylish hotel is located just a short walk from Harrods and Harvey Nichols. Bedrooms are decorated to a high standard and offer an excellent range of modern facilities. The lounge is popular for coffee or snacks and the open-plan Chelsea restaurant is the ideal venue for the modern, skilled cooking.

ROOMS: 222 en suite No smoking in 70 bedrooms d £253 * LB **FACILITIES:** STV **CONF:** Thtr 120 Class 80 Board 50 Del from £190 * **SERVICES:** Lift air con **PARKING:** 10 **NOTES:** No dogs **CARDS:**

★★★★66% ✿ The Cavendish St James's

LONDON SIGNATURE HOTELS

81 Jermyn St SW1Y 6JF
☎ 0870 400 8706 🖷 020 7839 2125
e-mail: rm1248@forte-hotels.com
Dir: *follow signs for Marble Arch along Park Lane to Hyde Park Corner left to Piccadilly. Past Ritz hotel right down Dukes St Behind Fortnum and Mason*

Close to Piccadilly and Green Park, this busy hotel is particularly popular with business guests. The Sub Rosa Bar is a cosy, club-like venue next to the lobby, and there is a spacious lounge on the first floor. '81' Restaurant offers a European-style menu with hints of Spanish influence.

continued

London

SW1 WESTMINSTER, continued

ROOMS: 251 en suite No smoking in 195 bedrooms s fr £194; d fr £229 * LB **FACILITIES:** STV entertainment Xmas **CONF:** Thtr 100 Class 50 Board 40 **SERVICES:** Lift **PARKING:** 65
CARDS:

★★★★ 69% Crowne Plaza London St James
Buckingham Gate SW1E 6AF
☎ 020 7834 6655
e-mail: sales@cponsj.co.uk
ROOMS: 342 en suite d £235 * **NOTES:** Open

★★★★ 65% Sheraton Belgravia
Sheraton HOTELS & RESORTS
20 Chesham Place SW1X 8HQ
☎ 020 7235 6040 🖹 7259 6243
e-mail: paul_james@sheraton.com
Dir: *follow A4 Brompton Rd into Central London. After Brompton Oratory right into Beauchamp Place. Follow into Pont St. Cross Sloane St & hotel on corner*
Situated in the heart of Belgravia, the shops of Knightsbridge, Kings Road and Sloan Street are just a short walk away. The facade is modern, the interiors very elegant. Accommodation features textured fabrics ranging from rich russets to warm yellows and there is a comprehensive range of in-room facilities.
ROOMS: 89 en suite No smoking in 37 bedrooms s £270.25-£575.75; d £346.63-£599.25 * **FACILITIES:** STV complimentary membership to local healthspa entertainment **CONF:** Thtr 35 Class 14 Board 20 **SERVICES:** Lift air con **NOTES:** No dogs (ex guide dogs)
CARDS:

London

★★★ 65% Quality Hotel Westminster

82-83 Eccleston Square SW1V 1PS
☎ 020 7834 8042 🖹 020 7630 8942
e-mail: admin@gb614.u-net.com
Popular with both leisure and business guests, this hotel is conveniently close to Victoria Station. Bedrooms, which vary in shape and size, are all comfortably furnished. Public areas include a small foyer bar, a range of meeting rooms and a brasserie-style restaurant.
ROOMS: 107 en suite (3 fmly) No smoking in 23 bedrooms s £85-£98; d £98-£111 * LB **FACILITIES:** STV **CONF:** Thtr 150 Class 65 Board 40 Del from £142 * **SERVICES:** Lift **NOTES:** No smoking in restaurant
CARDS:

Town House

★★★★ The Lowndes Hyatt Hotel
21 Lowndes St SW1X 9ES
☎ 020 7823 1234 🖹 020 7235 1154
e-mail: lowndes@hyattintl.com
Dir: *follow A4 from M4 into London,turn left from Brompton Road into Sloane Street.Then left into Pont Street,Lowndes Street is next left, Hotel on right*
This small, intimately run hotel is discreetly located in a very smart part of the city. Its size allows for a personal level of service, whether by the concierge, in the modern brasserie restaurant or via 24-hour room service.
ROOMS: 78 en suite No smoking in 31 bedrooms s £202.10-£267.90; d £213.85-£279.65 * **FACILITIES:** STV Indoor swimming (H) Tennis (hard) Sauna Gym Jacuzzi/spa Xmas **CONF:** Thtr 25 Board 18 **SERVICES:** Lift air con **NOTES:** No dogs (ex guide dogs)
CARDS:

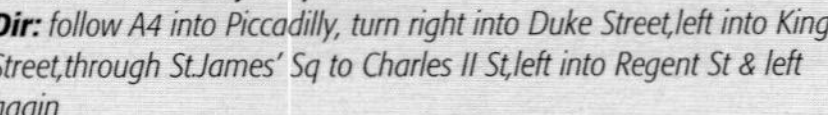

★★★★★ 22 Jermyn Street
St James's SW1Y 6HL
☎ 020 7734 2353 🖹 020 7734 0750
e-mail: office@22jermyn.com
Dir: *follow A4 into Piccadilly, turn right into Duke Street,left into King Street,through St.James' Sq to Charles II St,left into Regent St & left again*
An elegant town house, in a street renowned for its exclusivity. Bedrooms and suites offer very high standards of comfort and include thoughtful extras. There is a wide range of secretarial and business services, 24-hour room service and a mini-bar. Restaurants abound in the area.
ROOMS: 18 en suite (13 fmly) s £205-£290; d £205-£325 * **FACILITIES:** STV Membership of nearby Health Club (£10 per day) (2 minutes away) **SERVICES:** Lift air con **NOTES:** No smoking in restaurant **CARDS:**

⇧ Express by Holiday Inn London Victoria

106 - 110 Belgrave Rd, Victoria SW1V 2BJ
☎ 020 7630 8888 🖹 020 7828 0441
e-mail: ligatom@expressvictoria.co.uk
Dir: *from A13 (Tilbury Road) turn onto A1011 towards Airport. Immediately turn off Canning Town. Underground on right, hotel 20metres further on left*

A modern budget hotel offering comfortable accommodation in refreshing, spacious and comprehensively-equipped bedrooms, en suite bathrooms with power showers and continental buffet breakfast included in the room rate. Suitable for business travellers or families. For further details and the Express by Holiday Inn phone number, consult the Hotel Groups page.
ROOMS: 52 en suite (incl. cont bkfst) d £89 *

Late for dinner? Quality Standards star rating means that last orders for dinner should be no earlier than:
★ 6.30pm ★★ 7.00pm ★★★ 8.00pm
★★★★ 9.00pm ★★★★★ 10.00pm

SW3 CHELSEA, BROMPTON

Premier Collection

★★★★ Capital
Basil St, Knightsbridge SW3 1AT
☎ 020 7589 5171 020 7225 0011
e-mail: reservations@capitalhotel.co.uk
Located in the heart of Knightsbridge, this small and exclusive hotel is the epitome of excellence. Individually designed bedrooms are of the highest quality using the likes of handmade furniture, Egyptian cotton sheets and marble-lined bathrooms. One of the highlights of staying at this charming hotel is dinner in the restaurant where some exquisite dishes are served.
ROOMS: 48 en suite s fr £180; d fr £235 * **FACILITIES:** STV **CONF:** Thtr 30 Del from £310 * **SERVICES:** Lift air con **PARKING:** 15 **CARDS:**

★★★70% Basil Street
Basil St, Knightsbridge SW3 1AH
☎ 020 7581 3311 020 7581 3693
e-mail: info@TheBasil.com
Dir: *from M4 & A4 Brompton Road, turn right immediately before Harrods, the left into Basil Street. Hotel is on left hand side*
Built in Edwardian times, the Basil Street Hotel aims to recreate the gentle atmosphere of those bygone days. Day rooms, with antiques, parquet floors and comfortable armchairs suggest more of a country-house setting than a city hotel. Bedrooms follow a similar, traditional style of furnishings but have up-to-date facilities.
ROOMS: 80 en suite (4 fmly) No smoking in 40 bedrooms s £146.88-£150.40; d £217.38-£223.25 * LB **FACILITIES:** STV entertainment Xmas **CONF:** Thtr 30 Class 16 Board 20 Del from £210 * **SERVICES:** Lift **PARKING:** 2 **CARDS:**

Town House

★★★★ The Beaufort
33 Beaufort Gardens SW3 1PP
☎ 020 7584 5252 020 7589 2834
e-mail: thebeaufort@nol.co.uk
Dir: *100yds from Harrods*
In a tranquil, leafy location, yet just 100 yards from Harrods, the Beaufort offers the highest levels of hospitality. Luxurious bedrooms provide many extras such as chocolates, fresh flowers, videos and CD players. The attentive service leaves guests feeling relaxed and pampered.

ROOMS: 28 en suite (7 fmly) No smoking in 6 bedrooms s fr £155; d fr £180 (incl. cont bkfst) * **FACILITIES:** STV Complimentary entry to local health club **SERVICES:** Lift air con **NOTES:** No dogs (ex guide dogs) **CARDS:**

See advert on this page

SW3 CHELSEA, BROMPTON, continued

Town House

★★★★★ **Cliveden Townhouse**
26 Cadogan Gardens SW3 2RP
☎ 020 7730 6466 020 7730 0236
Only yards from Sloane Square, this townhouse bears all the hallmarks of quality and style. Luxurious bedrooms are beautifully furnished and day rooms comprise two lounges, where refreshments are served. There is also a sheltered garden. A complimentary executive car chauffeurs guests to the City twice each morning.
ROOMS: 35 en suite (9 fmly) No smoking in 30 bedrooms
FACILITIES: STV Gym Beauty treatment Massage **CONF:** Board 12
SERVICES: Lift air con **CARDS:**

Town House

★★★★ **Parkes**
41 Beaufort Gardens, Knightsbridge SW3 1PW
☎ 020 7581 9944 020 7581 1999
e-mail: receiption@parkeshotel.com
Dir: *off Brompton Road, 150yds from Harrods*
Only five minutes from Knightsbridge, this charming little hotel, situated in the oasis of a peaceful square, offers every modern comfort yet retains the atmosphere of an elegant home. Its well equipped suites come in a range of sizes, and many have a kitchenette. Breakfast is served in an attractive dining room and there is a small lounge.
ROOMS: 33 en suite (16 fmly) **FACILITIES:** STV **SERVICES:** Lift air con **NOTES:** No dogs (ex guide dogs)
CARDS:

SW4 CLAPHAM See LONDON plan 1 *E2*

★★★68% **The Windmill on The Common**
Southside, Clapham Common SW4 9DE
☎ 020 8673 4578 020 8675 1486
A traditional 18th-century pub forms the nucleus of this comfortable hotel, which has been skilfully extended to provide modern accommodation. There are three large bars, a bistro counter, a small lounge and a separate wood-panelled restaurant.
ROOMS: 29 en suite No smoking in 15 bedrooms **FACILITIES:** STV **CONF:** Thtr 40 Class 25 Board 20 **PARKING:** 16
CARDS:

SW5 EARLS COURT

★★★★67% **Swallow International**
Cromwell Rd SW5 0TH
☎ 020 7973 1000 020 7244 8194
e-mail: international@swallow-hotels.co.uk
Dir: *on the A4, within minutes of the M4*
One of the few London hotels with its own car park. The modern bedrooms, if a little compact, are thoughtfully equipped. In addition to an all-day eating option, there is the more formal Blayneys restaurant where some interesting dishes are offered. The hotel has an indoor leisure facility.

SWALLOW HOTELS

continued

ROOMS: 421 en suite (36 fmly) No smoking in 76 bedrooms s fr £155; d fr £170 * LB **FACILITIES:** STV Indoor swimming (H) Sauna Solarium Gym Jacuzzi/spa Whirlpool spa Turkish Steamroom entertainment
CONF: Thtr 200 Class 100 Board 60 **SERVICES:** Lift air con
PARKING: 80 **NOTES:** Closed 23-26 Dec
CARDS:

★★★73% **The Hogarth**
33 Hogarth Rd, Kensington SW5 0QQ
☎ 020 7370 6831 020 7373 6179
e-mail: hogarth@marstonhotels.co.uk

MARSTON HOTELS

Dir: *turn into Earls Court Rd from Cromwell Rd (A4), take 3rd turning left into Hogarth Rd. Hotel is at the end of the rd on the left*
This friendly, purpose-built hotel offers a good standard of accommodation. Bedrooms vary in size but are well equipped with such extras as safes and trouser presses; some have balconies. Room service is available. The popular restaurant/bar, The Terrace, serves a range of freshly prepared dishes throughout the day. The hotel benefits from its own secure car park.
ROOMS: 85 en suite (12 fmly) No smoking in 18 bedrooms s £108-£118; d £137-£157 (incl. bkfst) * LB **FACILITIES:** STV **CONF:** Thtr 50 Class 20 Board 24 Del from £125 * **SERVICES:** Lift **PARKING:** 20 **NOTES:** No smoking in restaurant **CARDS:**

★★67% **Comfort Inn Kensington**
22-32 West Cromwell Rd, Kensington SW5 9QJ
☎ 020 7373 3300 020 7835 2040
e-mail: admin@gb043.u-net.com

CHOICE HOTELS EUROPE

Dir: *on the Northern side of West Cromwell Rd, between juncts of Cromwell Rd, Earls Court Rd & Warwick Rd*
Convenient for Earl's Court, this cheerful, modern hotel offers smartly-kept bedrooms of varying sizes, with a range of amenities including air-conditioning. The welcoming public areas are bright and comfortable.
ROOMS: 125 en suite (2 fmly) No smoking in 48 bedrooms s £85-£98; d £98-£111 * LB **FACILITIES:** STV **CONF:** Thtr 70 Class 50 Board 45 Del from £115.50 * **SERVICES:** Lift air con **NOTES:** No dogs (ex guide dogs) No smoking in restaurant **CARDS:**

Town House

★★★★ **Cranley Hotel**
10-12 Bina Gardens, South Kensington SW5 0LA
☎ 020 7373 0123 020 7373 9497
A charming town house in a residential area of South Kensington, the Cranley provides a haven of peace away from the city bustle. Staff are welcoming and attentive to every need. The bedrooms, including five suites, are attractively decorated and well furnished, with many thoughtful extras. Complimentary afternoon tea is served each day.
ROOMS: 37 en suite (2 fmly) **FACILITIES:** STV **SERVICES:** Lift air con **CARDS:**

London

SW6 FULHAM See LONDON plan 1 *D3*

★★★★71% *Chelsea Village*
Stamford Bridge, Fulham Rd SW6 1HS
☎ 020 7565 1400 🖷 020 7565 1450
e-mail: reservation@chelseavillage.co.uk
This stylish eye-catching hotel forms part of the ambitious development at Chelsea Football Club and is a bold modern structure adjacent to the ground. The spacious bedrooms are well equipped and the range of public areas includes five different styles of eating option that will satisfy the many varied markets of the hotel.
ROOMS: 160 en suite (64 fmly) No smoking in 56 bedrooms **FACILITIES:** STV **CONF:** Thtr 50 Class 25 Board 30 **SERVICES:** Lift air con **PARKING:** 250 **NOTES:** No dogs (ex guide dogs)
CARDS:

★★★63% *Paragon Hotel*
47 Lillie Rd SW6 1UD
☎ 020 7385 1255 🖷 020 7381 0215
e-mail: sales@paragonhotel.co.uk
Dir: *A4 to central London,0.5m after Hammersmith flyover turn right at traffic lights into North End Rd follow for 0.5m to mini rdbt left into Lillie Rd*
Conveniently located for the Earls Court Exhibition Centre, this large, modern hotel is gradually being upgraded. Bedrooms are comfortable and well equipped. Two restaurants offer a choice of light meals and pizzas or more formal traditional menus. There are also extensive conference facilities and an underground car park.
ROOMS: 501 en suite No smoking in 96 bedrooms **FACILITIES:** STV **CONF:** Thtr 1750 Class 900 Board 50 **SERVICES:** Lift **PARKING:** 130 **NOTES:** No dogs (ex guide dogs) **CARDS:**

SW7 SOUTH KENSINGTON

★★★★77% The Millennium Gloucester Hotel
MILLENNIUM HOTELS AND RESORTS
4-18 Harrington Gardens SW7 4LJ
☎ 020 7373 6030 🖷 020 7373 0409
e-mail: gloucester@mill-cop.com
Dir: *opposite Gloucester Road underground station*
Bedrooms in this smart, cosmopolitan hotel are furnished in contemporary styles with marble bathrooms and air conditioning systems. Club rooms have additional facilities including a dedicated lounge with extra services. Eating options range from informal snacks to Singaporean cuisine in Bugis and the showcase Southwest 17, an evening restaurant awarded one AA Rosette for its Italian fare.
ROOMS: 610 en suite (4 fmly) No smoking in 232 bedrooms s £225-£275 * LB **FACILITIES:** STV Gym **CONF:** Thtr 800 Class 500 Del £305 * **SERVICES:** Lift air con **PARKING:** 100 **NOTES:** Civ Wed 300
CARDS:

★★★★72% Harrington Hall
5-25 Harrington Gardens SW7 4JW
☎ 020 7396 9696 🖷 020 7396 9090
e-mail: harringtonsales@compuserve.com
Dir: *head towards Knightsbridge into Gloucester Rd. Take 2nd right into Harrington Gdns hotel on the left*
Popular with both the international business and leisure guest, this modern, air-conditioned hotel provides well equipped, spacious bedrooms and comfortable, stylish reception rooms. The open-plan restaurant offers a choice of a hot buffet or a traditional carte from which an imaginative choice of dishes are cooked to order.

ROOMS: 200 en suite No smoking in 132 bedrooms d £180 * LB **FACILITIES:** STV Sauna Gym entertainment Xmas **CONF:** Thtr 260 Class 150 Board 50 Del from £205 * **SERVICES:** Lift air con **NOTES:** No dogs (ex guide dogs) **CARDS:**

See advert on this page

★★★★67% The Millennium Baileys Hotel
MILLENNIUM HOTELS AND RESORTS
140 Gloucester Rd SW7 4QH
☎ 020 7373 6000 🖷 020 7370 3760
e-mail: baileys@mill-cop.com
Dir: *M4, take A4 which turns into Cromwell Road, turn right onto Gloucester Road, hotel on the right opposite tube station*
Purpose built in 1876 and given a new lease of life by its current owners, this friendly hotel has modern bedrooms with useful facilities such as air-conditioning and TV guest-link system. Public

continued

London

SW7 SOUTH KENSINGTON, continued

areas are shared with its large sister hotel. The modern restaurant, Olives, produces enjoyable food in contemporary style.
ROOMS: 212 en suite No smoking in 80 bedrooms s £125-£250; d £225-£250 * **FACILITIES:** STV Fitness room **CONF:** Thtr 500 Class 300 Board 16 Del from £195 * **SERVICES:** Lift air con **PARKING:** 70 **NOTES:** No dogs (ex guide dogs) **CARDS:**

★★★★65% Radisson Edwardian Vanderbilt

Radisson Edwardian

68/86 Cromwell Rd SW7 5BT
☎ 020 7761 9000 🖷 020 7761 9001
e-mail: resvand@radisson.com
Dir: *A4 into Central London, past the junc with Gloucester Rd, hotel on left 100m beyond the traffic lights*
A terraced Victorian property with a difference. The interior is both cheerful and contemporary. As well as the main bar and restaurant, there is also Cleo's brasserie in the basement which serves food all day. Room facilities are superb - all have air conditioning, modems, several telephone lines, safes and mini-bars.
ROOMS: 215 en suite (15 fmly) No smoking in 90 bedrooms s £116-£215; d £123-£233 * **FACILITIES:** STV Gym Xmas **CONF:** Thtr 120 Class 36 Board 40 Del £225 * **SERVICES:** Lift air con **NOTES:** No dogs (ex guide dogs) **CARDS:**

★★★★63% Forum

INTER-CONTINENTAL. HOTELS AND RESORTS

97 Cromwell Rd SW7 4DN
☎ 020 7370 5757 🖷 020 7373 1448
e-mail: forumlondon@interconti.com
Dir: *from South Circular onto North Circular at Chiswick Flyover, join A4 Cromwell Rd as far as the Gloucseter Rd*
London's tallest hotel enjoys panoramic views over the city from most of its smartly decorated and well equipped bedrooms. Facilities include a business centre, a large shop and several eating outlets. A variety of useful conference and function suites are also available.
ROOMS: 910 en suite (36 fmly) No smoking in 176 bedrooms s fr £170; d fr £190 * LB **FACILITIES:** STV Fitness room entertainment Xmas **CONF:** Thtr 400 Class 200 Board 35 **SERVICES:** Lift **PARKING:** 75 **NOTES:** No dogs (ex guide dogs) **CARDS:**

★★★★62% Jurys Kensington Hotel

JURYS HOTEL GROUP

109-113 Queensgate, South Kensington SW7 5LR
☎ 020 7589 6300 🖷 020 7581 1492
Dir: *from A3218 (Old Bromton Rd), hotel is approx 300 yards on left at junction with Queensgate*
This fine hotel offers a traditional Irish welcome. The attractive lobby/bar and library lounge areas are popular. Kavanagh's bar is lively, Copplestones restaurant more sedate. Bedrooms range from stylish fifth-floor cottage rooms with floral fabrics, to smart executive suites.
ROOMS: 172 en suite (4 fmly) No smoking in 36 bedrooms s £180; d £180-£200 * LB **FACILITIES:** STV entertainment **CONF:** Thtr 80 Class 42 Board 40 Del £199 * **SERVICES:** Lift air con **NOTES:** No dogs (ex guide dogs) No smoking in restaurant Closed 24-27 Dec
CARDS:

★★★★62% *Rembrandt*

11 Thurloe Place SW7 2RS
☎ 020 7589 8100 🖷 020 7225 3363
e-mail: rembrandt@sarova.co.uk
Dir: *opp Victoria & Albert Museum*
The ornate architecture of the Rembrandt connects it stylistically to nearby Harrods. A strength of this plush, comfortable hotel is the leisure centre, designed in a style reminiscent of ancient Rome.
continued

ROOMS: 195 en suite (25 fmly) No smoking in 28 bedrooms **FACILITIES:** STV Indoor swimming (H) Sauna Solarium Gym Jacuzzi/spa Health, fitness & beauty centre entertainment **CONF:** Thtr 200 Class 90 Board 60 **SERVICES:** Lift **NOTES:** No dogs (ex guide dogs) **CARDS:**

SW10 WEST BROMPTON See LONDON plan 1 *E3*

★★★★★66% ❀ Conrad International London

Chelsea Harbour SW10 0XG
☎ 020 7823 3000 🖷 020 7351 6525
Dir: *A4 Earls Court Rd south towards river. Right into Kings Rd left down Lots Rd Chelsea Harbour is in front of you*
This modern hotel is in a smart development overlooking a small marina at Chelsea Harbour. Accommodation takes the form of superbly equipped private suites. There is an excellent range of leisure facilities and meeting rooms. The restaurant is informal and has a modern menu with fusion influences.
ROOMS: 160 en suite (41 fmly) No smoking in 62 bedrooms s £200-£350; d £225-£375 * LB **FACILITIES:** STV Indoor swimming (H) Sauna Solarium Gym Steam room Massage therapist entertainment Xmas **CONF:** Thtr 200 Class 120 Board 50 Del from £299 * **SERVICES:** Lift air con **PARKING:** 88 **CARDS:**

SW11 BATTERSEA See LONDON plan 1 *E3*

⌂ *Travelodge*

Travelodge

200 York Rd, Battersea SW11 3SA
☎ 020 7228 5508
Dir: *from Wandsworth Bridge southern rdbt, take York Road A3205 towards Battersea. Travelodge 0.5m on left*
This modern building offers accommodation in smart, spacious and well equipped bedrooms, all with en suite bathrooms. Refreshments may be taken at the nearby family restaurant. For further details and the Travelodge phone number, consult the Hotel Groups page.
ROOMS: 80 en suite

SW18 WANDSWORTH

○ Express by Holiday Inn

Express by Holiday Inn

Smugglers Way, Wandsworth SW18 1EG
☎ 0800 897121
ROOMS: 148 rms **NOTES:** Opening Autumn 2000

SW19 WIMBLEDON See LONDON plan 1 *D1*

★★★★75% ❀❀ Cannizaro House

THISTLE HOTELS

West Side, Wimbledon Common SW19 4UE
☎ 020 8879 1464 🖷 020 8879 7338
e-mail: cannizaro.house@thistle.co.uk
Dir: *approaching from A3 follow A219 signed Wimbledon into Parkside and past old fountain sharp right then 2nd on right*

continued

London

This impressive, 18th-century house has a long tradition of hosting the rich and famous of London society. A few miles from the city centre, the landscaped grounds provide a peaceful haven. Oil paintings, murals and stunning fireplaces feature throughout. Spacious bedrooms are decorated in a country house style. The restaurant has earned the accolade of two AA Rosettes.
ROOMS: 45 en suite No smoking in 19 bedrooms d £199-£288 * **FACILITIES:** STV Croquet lawn Massage treatments entertainment Xmas **CONF:** Thtr 80 Class 34 Board 40 Del from £230 * **SERVICES:** Lift **PARKING:** 60 **NOTES:** No dogs (ex guide dogs) Civ Wed 60 **CARDS:**

Express by Holiday Inn Wimbledon

200 High St, Colliers Wood, Wimbledon SW19 2BH
☎ 020 8545 7300 8545 7301
***Dir:** M25 junct10. A3 to Central London, follow to Merton turn off at A238, past S Wimbledon underground on right. Proceed through t/lights, hotel on left*

Express by Holiday Inn

A modern budget hotel offering comfortable accommodation in refreshing, spacious and comprehensively-equipped bedrooms, en suite bathrooms with power showers and continental buffet breakfast included in the room rate. Suitable for business travellers or families. For further details and the Express by Holiday Inn phone number, consult the Hotel Groups page.
ROOMS: 83 en suite (incl. cont bkfst) d £81.25-£85 * **CONF:** Thtr 60 Class 25 Board 25

Late for dinner? Quality Standards star rating means that last orders for dinner should be no earlier than:
★ 6.30pm ★★ 7.00pm ★★★ 8.00pm
★★★★ 9.00pm ★★★★★ 10.00pm

W1 WEST END

Premier Collection

★★★★★ Claridge's

Brook St W1A 2JQ
☎ 020 7629 8860 020 7499 2210
e-mail: info@claridges.co.uk
***Dir:** between Grosvenor Square and New Bond Street parallel with Oxford Street*

The Savoy Group

This renowned hotel has blended state-of-the-art modern design and technology into a traditional setting. Reception rooms and public areas are best described as opulent and immaculate, giving an overall impression that is simply majestic. In addition to the famous restaurant, refreshments are also served in the lounge and reading room. The bar restyling has increased floor space.
ROOMS: 197 en suite No smoking in 18 bedrooms s fr £340.75; d fr £393.60 * LB **FACILITIES:** STV Sauna Gym Tennis at the Vanderbilt Club entertainment Xmas **CONF:** Thtr 260 Class 130 Board 50 **SERVICES:** Lift air con **NOTES:** No dogs (ex guide dogs) Civ Wed 240 **CARDS:**

Premier Collection

★★★★★ Connaught

Carlos Place W1Y 6AL
☎ 020 7499 7070 020 7495 3262
e-mail: info@the-connaught.co.uk
***Dir:** situated between Grosvenor Square and Berkeley Square in Mayfair*

The Savoy Group

The Connaught is a bastion of tradition, offering superb attention to its guests in quiet comfort. Butlers and valets respond at the touch of a button. The Restaurant and The Grill Room share the same impeccable service and exhaustive menu of classical cuisine.
ROOMS: 90 en suite s fr £290; d fr £370 * LB **FACILITIES:** STV Health & beauty facilities available at sister hotels **SERVICES:** Lift air con **NOTES:** No dogs **CARDS:**

London

W1 WEST END, continued

Premier Collection

★★★★★ ❀❀❀ **The Dorchester**
Park Ln W1A 2HJ
☎ 020 7629 8888 ▤ 020 7409 0114
e-mail: reservations@dorchesterhotel.com
Dir: *half way along Park Lane between Hyde Park Corner & Marble Arch, overlooking Hyde Park on corner of Park Lane & Deanery St*
One of London's finest hotels, the Dorchester is sumptuously decorated in every department. Bedrooms have individual design schemes, are beautifully furnished, and their luxurious bathrooms have huge baths which have become a Dorchester hallmark. Leading off from the foyer, the Promenade is the perfect setting for afternoon tea or drinks, and in the evenings there is live jazz in the famous bar which specialises in Italian dishes and cocktails. The Grill is a restaurant in the traditional style and there is also an acclaimed Cantonese restaurant, the Oriental.
ROOMS: 248 en suite No smoking in 24 bedrooms s £323.13-£346.63; d £358.38-£393.63 * LB **FACILITIES:** STV Sauna Solarium Gym Jacuzzi/spa The Dorchester Spa Health club entertainment ch fac Xmas **CONF:** Thtr 500 Class 300 Board 42 Del from £376 * **SERVICES:** Lift air con **PARKING:** 21 **NOTES:** No dogs (ex guide dogs) Civ Wed 500
CARDS:

Premier Collection

★★★★★ ❀❀ **Four Seasons**
Hamilton Place, Park Ln W1A 1AZ
☎ 020 7499 0888 ▤ 020 7493 6629
Set back from Park Lane, the Four Seasons Hotel offers the highest standards of attentive, friendly service. Bedrooms and their bathrooms are more spacious and better designed than most. The Lanes restaurant is contemporary in style; it has its

continued

own cocktail bar and lounge adjacent. Room and business services are operated around the clock.
ROOMS: 220 en suite No smoking in 72 bedrooms s £270-£280; d £315-£325 * LB **FACILITIES:** STV Gym Fitness club entertainment Xmas **CONF:** Thtr 500 Class 180 Board 90 **SERVICES:** Lift air con **PARKING:** 55 **NOTES:** No dogs (ex guide dogs) Civ Wed 500 **CARDS:**

★★★★★ 72% ❀❀
Hotel Inter-Continental
1 Hamilton Place, Hyde Park Corner W1V 0QY
☎ 020 7409 3131 ▤ 020 7493 3476
e-mail: london@interconti.com
Dir: *situated at Hyde Park Corner, on the corner of Park Lane & Piccadilly*
Situated in a prominent position on Hyde Park Corner, this fine hotel has excellent views of the surrounding area from the upper floors. Bedrooms vary from inner courtyard rooms to spacious suites. The smart, marbled foyer houses the Observatory lounge for light meals and afternoon teas, and the Coffee House for breakfast and all-day dining. The jewel in the hotel's crown is Le Soufflé Restaurant.
ROOMS: 458 en suite No smoking in 312 bedrooms d fr £340.75 * LB **FACILITIES:** STV Sauna Gym Jacuzzi/spa Beauty treatments entertainment Xmas **CONF:** Thtr 750 Class 340 Board 66 **SERVICES:** Lift air con **PARKING:** 100 **NOTES:** No dogs (ex guide dogs) Civ Wed 750 **CARDS:**

★★★★★ 81% ❀❀ **The Ritz**
150 Piccadilly W1V 9DG
☎ 020 7493 8181 ▤ 020 7493 2687
e-mail: enquire@theritzhotel.co.uk.
Dir: *from Hyde Park Corner travel E on Piccadilly. The Ritz is the first building on the right immediately after Green Park*
This hotel continues its stately progress into the third millennium, having recaptured much of its former glory. Bedrooms are furnished in Louis XVI style and have fine marble bathrooms and every imaginable guest comfort. Elegant reception rooms include the Palm Court with its famous afternoon teas, and the sumptuous Ritz Restaurant with its gold chandeliers and extraordinary trompe l'oeil decoration.
ROOMS: 131 en suite No smoking in 20 bedrooms s fr £335; d £382.75-£1410 * LB **FACILITIES:** STV Gym entertainment Xmas **CONF:** Thtr 60 Class 25 Board 30 **SERVICES:** Lift air con **NOTES:** No dogs (ex guide dogs) Civ Wed 50 **CARDS:**

★★★★★ 75% ❀❀❀
Le Meridien Piccadilly
21 Piccadilly W1V 0BH
☎ 0870 400 8400 ▤ 020 7437 3574
e-mail: lmpiccres@forte-hotels.com
Dir: *100mtrs from Piccadilly Circus*
Within whistling distance of Piccadilly Circus, this well established hotel can justifiably lay claim to be the closest to the capital's hub. It has traditionally decorated and well equipped bedrooms and smartly appointed public rooms, including a new Mezzanine Lounge and Cigar Club. The Oak Room restaurant is run as a separate entity to the hotel's own La Terrace restaurant. Champney's health club provides first class health and leisure facilities.
ROOMS: 267 en suite (19 fmly) No smoking in 91 bedrooms s £265; d £305 * LB **FACILITIES:** STV Indoor swimming (H) Squash Sauna Solarium Gym Jacuzzi/spa Beauty treatments Aerobics Massage Xmas **CONF:** Thtr 250 Class 160 Board 80 Del from £70 * **SERVICES:** Lift air con **NOTES:** No dogs (ex guide dogs) Civ Wed 200
CARDS:

London

★★★★★73% Grosvenor House
Park Ln W1A 3AA
☎ 0870 400 8500 020 7493 3341
e-mail: gros.house@virgin.net
Dir: *Marble Arch, halfway down Park Lane*
Majestically positioned on Park Lane, this internationally recognised hotel offers thoughtfully equipped accommodation including a number of impressive suites. Executive Crown Club rooms boast a range of extra services and facilities. Guests have the choice between the award-winning Chez Nico restaurant or, within the hotel, La Terrazza, which offers a more informal dining experience, with an Italian theme.
ROOMS: 453 en suite (140 fmly) No smoking in 154 bedrooms d fr £341 * LB **FACILITIES:** STV Indoor swimming (H) Sauna Solarium Gym Jacuzzi/spa Health & Fitness centre entertainment Xmas **CONF:** Thtr 110 Class 60 Board 36 **SERVICES:** Lift air con **PARKING:** 95 **NOTES:** No dogs (ex guide dogs) Civ Wed 100
CARDS:

★★★★★72%
Churchill Inter-Continental
30 Portman Square W1A 4ZX
☎ 020 7486 5800 020 7486 1255
e-mail: churchill@interconti.com
Overlooking Portman Square, The Churchill boasts excellent in-room business amenities and services. Club and deluxe rooms entitle occupants to many additional facilities and services. Public areas display a wealth of marble, pillars and chandeliers, and afternoon teas in the relaxed surroundings of The Terrace lounge are really special. By contrast, the Cigar Divan bar has a club atmosphere and an impressive selection of Cuban cigars and fine whiskies. Clementine's Restaurant is the setting for Mediterranean-inspired cooking.
ROOMS: 441 en suite No smoking in 135 bedrooms d £352.50 * LB **FACILITIES:** STV Tennis (hard) entertainment ch fac Xmas **CONF:** Thtr 250 Class 150 Board 54 **SERVICES:** Lift air con **PARKING:** 50 **NOTES:** No dogs (ex guide dogs) Civ Wed 180
CARDS:

★★★★★64%
May Fair Inter-Continental London
Stratton St W1A 2AN
☎ 020 7629 7777 020 7629 1459
e-mail: mayfair@interconti.com
Dir: *from Hyde Park Corner/Piccadilly turn left onto Stratton St & hotel is on left*
This well established hotel in congenial surroundings has an intimate atmosphere. Air-conditioned bedrooms of varying sizes include good suites and business-dedicated rooms with a useful range of amenities. The choice of bars and restaurants includes the Opus 70 restaurant, the showcase for the hotel's modern British cuisine. There is also a manned business centre and a conference auditorium.
ROOMS: 290 en suite (14 fmly) No smoking in 148 bedrooms d £305-£365 * LB **FACILITIES:** STV Indoor swimming (H) Sauna Solarium Gym Hair & Beauty salon entertainment Xmas **CONF:** Thtr 292 Class 108 Board 60 **SERVICES:** Lift air con **NOTES:** No dogs (ex guide dogs) Civ Wed 250 **CARDS:**

★★★★★59% Sheraton Park Lane
Piccadilly W1Y 8BX
☎ 020 7499 6321 020 7499 1965
Dir: *On Piccadilly opposite Green Park*
This hotel, featuring a magnificent art deco ballroom and Citrus restaurant, has benefitted from much refurbishment. The period-style Palm Court is the perfect setting for afternoon tea with harp accompaniment. There are a large number of suites and the remaining rooms vary in size.
ROOMS: 307 en suite (20 fmly) No smoking in 116 bedrooms s fr £323.13; d fr £346.63 * LB **FACILITIES:** STV Gym entertainment Xmas **CONF:** Thtr 450 Class 240 Board 52 **SERVICES:** Lift **PARKING:** 120 **NOTES:** No dogs (ex guide dogs) Civ Wed 600
CARDS:

Premier Collection

★★★★ Athenaeum
116 Piccadilly W1V 0BJ
☎ 020 7499 3464 020 7493 1860
e-mail: info@athenaeumhotel.com
Dir: *located on Piccadily, overlooking Green Park*
Overlooking Green Park, this well loved hotel attracts a loyal clientele who enjoy the genuine hospitality and efficient service. The superb bedrooms have air conditioning and many quality features. Bullochs Restaurant offers brasserie-style dining in contemporary surroundings. Afternoon tea and other refreshments are served in the Windsor Lounge and there is also a clubby, panelled cocktail bar.
ROOMS: 157 en suite No smoking in 58 bedrooms s £195-£320; d £195-£695 * LB **FACILITIES:** STV Sauna Gym Jacuzzi/spa Massage & treatment rooms ch fac **CONF:** Thtr 55 Class 35 Board 36 Del from £260 * **SERVICES:** Lift air con **NOTES:** No dogs (ex guide dogs) Civ Wed 55 **CARDS:**

★★★★77% The Montcalm-Hotel Nikko London
Great Cumberland Place W1A 2LF
☎ 020 7402 4288 020 7724 9180
e-mail: reservations@montcalm.co.uk
Dir: *by Marble Arch*
Originally named after the 18th-century French General Montcalm, this Japanese-owned hotel offers extremely comfortable accommodation, ranging from standard to duplex 'junior' and penthouse suites. Japanese guests appreciate 'the best Japanese breakfast outside Japan'. Staff are charming and the Crescent Restaurant has a reputation for good modern cooking. Lunch is particularly good value for money.
ROOMS: 120 en suite No smoking in 28 bedrooms s fr £258.50; d £282-£705 * LB **FACILITIES:** STV **CONF:** Thtr 80 Class 36 Board 36 **SERVICES:** Lift air con **PARKING:** 10 **NOTES:** No dogs (ex guide dogs) Civ Wed 100 **CARDS:**

Popped the question? Hotels with Civ Wed in their entry are licensed for civil wedding ceremonies. Maximum numbers for the ceremony only are shown, e.g. Civ Wed 50

London

W1 WEST END, continued

★★★★76% Brown's
Albemarle St, Mayfair W1X 4BP
☎ 020 7493 6020 020 7493 9381
e-mail: brownshotel@brownshotel.com
Dir: *from Green Park Underground Station on Piccadilly, take third left into Albemarle Street*
Brown's is famous for its English country-house style and emphasis on comfortable furnishings and quality decor. Accommodation is excellent and rooms are particularly spacious for the Mayfair setting. There is a smartly decorated restaurant, the oldest hotel restaurant in London, with an imaginative menu. The hotel is a popular refuge for afternoon tea.
ROOMS: 118 en suite (15 fmly) **FACILITIES:** STV entertainment **CONF:** Thtr 70 Class 30 Board 35 **SERVICES:** Lift **NOTES:** No dogs (ex guide dogs) **CARDS:**

★★★★ Radisson Edwardian Berkshire
350 Oxford St W1N 0BY
☎ 020 7629 7474 020 7629 8156
e-mail: resberk@radisson.com
Dir: *central London, on Oxford Street opposite Bond Street Underground Station*
Sandwiched between Oxford St's department stores, this is an ideal hotel for grand-scale shopping. Intimate, warm and friendly, the hotel attracts an international business clientele. Bedrooms, though not over-large, are stylishly decorated. Public rooms include an elegant drawing room, the Ascot cocktail bar and a first-floor restaurant.
ROOMS: 147 en suite (2 fmly) No smoking in 44 bedrooms s £240; d £287 * **FACILITIES:** STV **CONF:** Thtr 45 Class 20 Board 26 Del from £220 * **SERVICES:** Lift air con **NOTES:** No dogs (ex guide dogs) **CARDS:**

★★★★74% The Washington Mayfair Hotel
5-7 Curzon St, Mayfair W1Y 8DT
☎ 020 7499 7000 020 7495 6172
e-mail: general@washington-mayfair.co.uk
Dir: *From Green Park station take Picadilly exit and turn right,3rd street on right Charles St leads to Curzon St and hotel*
This smart, modern hotel offers a very high standard of accommodation. Bedrooms, furnished in burred oak, range from state rooms and suites with spa baths to equally comfortable twins and doubles. Light refreshments are served in the marbled and wood-panelled public areas. There is a concierge desk and help with car parking.
ROOMS: 173 en suite No smoking in 94 bedrooms d fr £223.25 * LB **FACILITIES:** entertainment Xmas **CONF:** Thtr 90 Class 40 Board 36 Del from £250 * **SERVICES:** Lift air con **NOTES:** No dogs (ex guide dogs) **CARDS:**

See advert on opposite page

★★★★73% London Marriott Grosvenor Square
Grosvenor Square W1A 4AW
☎ 020 7493 1232 020 7491 3201
e-mail: businesscentrre@londonmarriott.co.uk
Dir: *M4 east to Cromwell Rd through Knightsbridge to Hyde Park Corner, Park Lane right at Brook Gate onto upper Brook St to Grosvenor Sq/Duke St*
Superbly situated in the heart of Mayfair, this is a smartly appointed and extremely popular hotel. Friendly staff remain unfailingly helpful and willing to please. Excellent food is served in the Diplomat Restaurant overlooking the gardens of Grosvenor Square.

continued

ROOMS: 221 en suite (26 fmly) No smoking in 120 bedrooms s fr £195; d fr £245 * LB **FACILITIES:** STV Gym Exercise & fitness centre Xmas **CONF:** Thtr 1000 Class 550 Board 120 **SERVICES:** Lift air con **PARKING:** 80 **NOTES:** No dogs (ex guide dogs) **CARDS:**

★★★★72% Jurys Clifton-Ford
47 Welbeck St W1M 8DN
☎ 020 7486 6600 020 7486 7492
e-mail: sales@cliftonf.itsnet.co.uk
Dir: *from Portland Place, turn into New Cavendish Street. Welbeck Street is last turning on the left.*
This well managed, friendly hotel is popular for business use, as well as keeping its appeal for holidaymakers. The standard of accommodation is high, especially in the private suites. A marbled lobby, where guests may enjoy complimentary sherry and canapés during the cocktail hour, leads into an intimate lounge. There is also a cocktail bar and brasserie.
ROOMS: 255 en suite (7 fmly) d £195-£250 * LB **FACILITIES:** STV Indoor swimming (H) Sauna Solarium Gym Jacuzzi/spa Fully equipped leisure club **CONF:** Thtr 200 Class 70 Board 40 Del from £242 * **SERVICES:** Lift air con **PARKING:** 9 **CARDS:**

★★★★72% Radisson SAS Portman
22 Portman Square W1H 9FL
☎ 020 7208 6000 020 7208 6001
e-mail: portman@lonza.rdsas.com
Dir: *100mtrs N of Oxford St and 500mtrs E of Edgware Rd*
Situated in London's West End, the hotel is just a short stroll from Oxford St, Marble Arch and Hyde Park. All rooms are well equipped, including air conditioning, mini-bar and satellite TV. The Library restaurant provides a formal menu and an intimate atmosphere. For a more informal meal, the Portman Corner restaurant is a popular choice.
ROOMS: 272 en suite (21 fmly) No smoking in 129 bedrooms s £195-£249; d £215-£275 * LB **FACILITIES:** STV Tennis (hard) Sauna Solarium Gym entertainment Xmas **CONF:** Thtr 700 Class 350 Board 65 **SERVICES:** Lift air con **PARKING:** 400 **NOTES:** No dogs (ex guide dogs) Civ Wed 450 **CARDS:**

★★★★72% The Westbury
New Bond St W1A 4UH
☎ 020 7629 7755 020 7495 1163
e-mail: westburyhotel@compuserve.com
Dir: *from Oxford Circus south down Regent St turn right onto Conduit St, hotel at junct of Conduit St & Bond St*

In the heart of London's shopping district, this distinctive hotel benefits from an unhurried, relaxing atmosphere. Standards of accommodation are high throughout, attracting an international clientele. Reception rooms include the Polo Lounge and The

continued

London

Restaurant, serving traditional dishes at lunchtime and a more adventurous evening menu.
ROOMS: 254 en suite No smoking in 150 bedrooms d fr £252.62 * LB **FACILITIES:** STV Complimentary access to nearby Health Club entertainment Xmas **CONF:** Thtr 120 Class 65 Board 36 **SERVICES:** Lift air con **NOTES:** No dogs (ex guide dogs)
CARDS:

See advert on this page

★★★★ 71% The Chesterfield
35 Charles St, Mayfair W1X 8LX
☎ 020 7491 2622 020 7491 4793
e-mail: reservations@chesterfield.redcarnationhotels.com
Dir: *Hyde Park corner along Picadilly, turn right into Half Moon St. At the end turn left and first right into Queens St, then turn right onto Charles St*
Quiet elegance and an atmosphere of exclusivity characterise this privately-owned hotel. The lobby, with its marble floor, glittering chandelier and fluted pillars, leads into a library lounge and clubby bar. The restaurant is traditional in decor and provides a modern menu. Stylish bedrooms have direct Internet access via the TV.
ROOMS: 110 en suite (7 fmly) No smoking in 34 bedrooms s fr £229; d fr £270 * LB **FACILITIES:** STV entertainment Xmas **CONF:** Thtr 90 Class 50 Board 45 Del from £215 * **SERVICES:** Lift air con
NOTES: Civ Wed 100 **CARDS:**

★★★★ 71% Millennium Britannia Mayfair

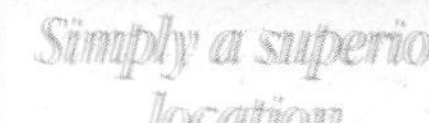

Grosvenor Square W1A 3AN
☎ 020 7629 9400 020 7629 7736
e-mail: britannia.sales@mill-cop.com
The hotel offers a wide range of facilities including a cocktail bar, piano bar, restaurant and the popular Shogun restaurant, which merits two Rosettes for its Japanese fare. Bedrooms vary in size, but all are smartly appointed and well equipped. Deluxe rooms on the new Club floor benefit from their own lounge and extra services.
ROOMS: 348 en suite No smoking in 145 bedrooms s £199.75-£287.87; d £264.31-£287.87 * LB **FACILITIES:** STV Gym entertainment Xmas **CONF:** Thtr 460 Class 310 Board 40 Del from £240 * **SERVICES:** Lift air con **NOTES:** No dogs (ex guide dogs) Civ Wed 400
CARDS:

★★★★ 68% London Marriott Hotel Marble Arch

Marriott HOTELS·RESORTS·SUITES

134 George St W1H 6DN
☎ 020 7723 1277 020 7402 0666
Dir: *from Marble Arch turn into the Edgware Road then take 4th turning on right into George St. Turn immediate left into Forset Street for main entrance*
This modern hotel, conveniently situated just off the Edgware Road, and close to Oxford St shops, offers a good standard of accommodation. Bedrooms are well equipped and furnished with quality fittings. Public lounge and bar areas, although not spacious, are comfortable. The hotel also benefits from car parking.
ROOMS: 240 en suite (100 fmly) No smoking in 120 bedrooms **FACILITIES:** STV Indoor swimming (H) Sauna Solarium Gym Jacuzzi/spa **CONF:** Thtr 150 Class 75 Board 80 **SERVICES:** Lift air con **PARKING:** 80 **NOTES:** No dogs (ex guide dogs)
CARDS:

> Fancy a Singapore Sling? Bar staff in five star hotels should be skilled cocktail mixers.

London

W1 WEST END, continued

★★★★67% The Cumberland

Marble Arch W1H 8DP
LONDON SIGNATURE HOTELS
☎ 0870 400 8701 🖷 020 7724 4621
Dir: *M4 to central London. At Hyde Park Corner take Park Lane to Marble Arch. Hotel is above Marble Arch tube station*
In an unrivalled location near Hyde Park, the hotel provides a range of eating and drinking options, including cafés, oriental dining in Sampans, the ever popular Carvery, and Callaghan's bar and restaurant for fresh Irish fare and nightly live music. The excellent, manned business complex has 17 conference rooms. Bedrooms are comfortable and modern; Premier Club rooms provide extra comfort and amenities.
ROOMS: 917 en suite (21 fmly) No smoking in 480 bedrooms s fr £176; d fr £223 * LB **FACILITIES:** STV entertainment Xmas **CONF:** Thtr 750 Class 350 Board 80 Del from £198 * **SERVICES:** Lift **NOTES:** No dogs (ex guide dogs) **CARDS:**

★★★★65% The Berners Hotel

Berners St W1A 3BE
☎ 020 7666 2000 🖷 020 7666 2001
e-mail: berners@berners.co.uk
Dir: *head towards Central London. At Baker Street turn left into Oxford Street*
Well positioned in the heart of London's West End, just off Oxford St, this traditional hotel has an elegant, classical marble-columned foyer with a comfortable lounge - popular for afternoon tea - and attractive restaurant. Bedrooms are all equipped with modern comforts.
ROOMS: 217 en suite No smoking in 100 bedrooms s £170-£240; d £205-£250 * **FACILITIES:** STV **CONF:** Thtr 180 Class 80 Board 36 Del from £242.50 * **SERVICES:** Lift **NOTES:** Civ Wed
CARDS:

★★★★63% *Flemings Mayfair*

7-12 Half Moon St, Mayfair W1Y 7RA
☎ 020 7499 2964 🖷 202 7491 8866
e-mail: sales@flemings-mayfair.co.uk
Town house in style and character, this property has a certain charm. The nature of the building has created a range of bedroom sizes but all are similarly equipped with modern amenities. There are similar restrictions to public areas but this lends a cosy atmosphere.
ROOMS: 121 en suite (11 fmly) No smoking in 25 bedrooms
FACILITIES: STV **CONF:** Thtr 55 Class 30 Board 30 **SERVICES:** Lift air con **NOTES:** No dogs (ex guide dogs)
CARDS:

★★★74% Radisson Edwardian Grafton

130 Tottenham Court Rd W1P 9HP
Radisson Edwardian
☎ 020 7388 4131 🖷 020 7387 7394
e-mail: resgrafton@radisson.com
Dir: *central London, along Euston Road, turn into Tottenham Court Road. Past Warren Street Tube*
Ongoing investment and a commitment to provide excellent levels of hospitality and service sees The Grafton going from strength to strength. Public areas are smart and, whilst bedrooms come in a variety of size and styles, all are very thoughtfully equipped. The hotel is well placed just opposite Warren Street Tube station.
ROOMS: 324 en suite (8 fmly) No smoking in 163 bedrooms s fr £182.13; d fr £211.50 * **FACILITIES:** Gym **CONF:** Thtr 100 Class 50 Board 30 Del from £200 * **SERVICES:** Lift **NOTES:** No dogs (ex guide dogs) **CARDS:**

★★★68% *Mostyn*

4 Bryanston St W1H 8DE
Best Western
☎ 020 7935 2361 🖷 020 7487 2759
e-mail: mostynhotel@btinternet.com

Close to Oxford St and Marble Arch, this Georgian hotel has well equipped bedrooms with good quality furnishings and smart marble bathrooms. All 121 bedrooms are fully air-conditioned. There are two car parks a short walk away.
ROOMS: 121 en suite (15 fmly) No smoking in 54 bedrooms
FACILITIES: STV **CONF:** Thtr 140 Class 80 Board 60 **SERVICES:** Lift
NOTES: No dogs (ex guide dogs) **CARDS:**

See advert on opposite page

★★★68% *Posthouse Regents Park*

Carburton St, Regents Park W1P 8EE
Posthouse
☎ 0870 400 9111 🖷 020 7387 2806
This modern hotel with its own car park is undergoing significant improvements. The smart public areas are modern in design and air-conditioned. The bedrooms are comfortable and well designed. There is 24-hour room service and an all-day lounge menu.
ROOMS: 326 en suite No smoking in 184 bedrooms **FACILITIES:** STV entertainment **CONF:** Thtr 350 Class 180 Board 50 **SERVICES:** Lift **PARKING:** 85 **NOTES:** No dogs (ex guide dogs)
CARDS:

★★★65% Mandeville

Mandeville Place W1M 6BE
☎ 020 7935 5599 🖷 020 7935 9588
e-mail: info@mandeville.co.uk
Dir: *off Oxford Street & Wigmore St near Bond St underground station*
This quiet hotel is only a short walk from Oxford St. The language skills of reception staff, plus the helpful concierge desk, have made it popular with foreign visitors. There are good business and conference facilities. The Oceana Restaurant offers inventive, up-market cooking, and there is another all-day restaurant and a pub serving bar food.
ROOMS: 165 en suite No smoking in 30 bedrooms s fr £128; d fr £169 (incl. cont bkfst) * LB **FACILITIES:** STV **CONF:** Thtr 35 Class 30 Board 20 Del from £169 * **SERVICES:** Lift **NOTES:** No dogs (ex guide dogs)
CARDS:

See advert on opposite page

★★★63% St George's

Langham Place, Regent St W1N 8QS
☎ 020 7580 0111 🖷 020 7436 7997
e-mail: stgeorgeshotel@talk21.com
Dir: *Located in Langham Place at the intersection of Regent St and Portland Place*
This unique hotel is situated within Henry Wood House, shared by the BBC. The reception lobby is on the ground floor but there are

continued

London

no further public areas until the 15th floor, which has superb views across the city. Here there is a contemporary bar area, a restaurant and several meeting rooms.
ROOMS: 86 en suite No smoking in 30 bedrooms s £99-£168; d £99-£193 * **FACILITIES:** STV Xmas **CONF:** Thtr 32 Class 24 Board 20 Del £220 * **SERVICES:** Lift **CARDS:**

W2 BAYSWATER, PADDINGTON

★★★★73% Royal Lancaster

Lancaster Ter W2 2TY
☎ 020 7262 6737 020 7724 3191
e-mail: book@royallancaster.com
Dir: *directly above Lancaster Gate Underground Station*

Overlooking Hyde Park and Kensington Gardens, the Royal Lancaster's upper storeys offer fine views across London. There is 24-hour room service and efficient porterage. The choice of eating ranges from the lounge, the Pavement Café, the smart Park Restaurant or the exotic and authentic Nipa Thai.
ROOMS: 416 en suite (9 fmly) No smoking in 51 bedrooms d £259-£347 * LB **FACILITIES:** STV entertainment Xmas **CONF:** Thtr 1500 Class 650 Board 40 Del from £199 * **SERVICES:** Lift air con **PARKING:** 100 **NOTES:** No dogs (ex guide dogs) **CARDS:**

★★★64% Plaza on Hyde Park

corus

1-7 Lancaster Gate W2 3LG
☎ 020 7262 5022 020 7724 8666
e-mail: plazaonhydepark@corushotels.com
Dir: *200yds from Lancaster Gate Underground Station. 0.25m from Paddington Station*

Conveniently situated opposite Hyde Park and only a few minutes' walk from Marble Arch, this busy hotel is gradually being upgraded. Public areas are particularly smart and modern in style. Bedrooms are well equipped with refurbished ones featuring air conditioning.
ROOMS: 402 en suite (10 fmly) No smoking in 200 bedrooms s £110-£130; d £130-£150 * LB **FACILITIES:** STV **CONF:** Thtr 20 Class 12 Board 20 Del from £150 * **SERVICES:** Lift **NOTES:** No dogs (ex guide dogs) **CARDS:**

★★★63% Berjaya Eden Park Hotel

35-39 Inverness Ter, Bayswater W2 3JS
☎ 020 7221 2220 020 7221 2286
e-mail: edenpark@dircon.co.uk
Dir: *from Marble Arch, straight across main rdbt onto Bayswater Rd, turn right into Queensway,the first turn left into Inverness Terrace*

This friendly hotel close to Queensway offers attractively furnished and well equipped bedrooms. The restaurant is locally popular and the comfortable and stylish bar serves complimentary coffee to residents during the afternoon.
ROOMS: 75 rms (67 en suite) 62 annexe en suite (8 fmly) s £102; d £120 * **FACILITIES:** STV **SERVICES:** Lift **NOTES:** No dogs (ex guide dogs) **CARDS:**

London

W2 BAYSWATER, PADDINGTON, continued

★★★ 63% *Grosvenor Court*
27 Devonshire Ter W2 3DP
☎ 020 7262 2204 020 7402 9351
e-mail: info@grosvenor-court.co.uk
Dir: *from A40 take exit signed Paddington Station, at station turn into Craven Road hotel on right*

This hotel is less than five minutes' walk from Hyde Park and Kensington Gardens and offers easy access to the West End. There is a variety of smart and tastefully decorated bedrooms suitable for the single traveller, couples or families. Guests may relax in the attractive lounge or meet to discuss the day's events in the popular Historian Bar.
ROOMS: 157 en suite (34 fmly) **FACILITIES:** STV **SERVICES:** Lift **NOTES:** No dogs (ex guide dogs) **CARDS:**

★★★ 62% Central Park
Queensborough Ter W2 3SS
☎ 020 7229 2424 020 7229 2904
e-mail: cpn@centralpark.london
Central Park is a popular hotel just off the Bayswater Road and close to London's West End. Bedrooms offer all the expected modern comforts, and there are spacious public areas. Garage parking is available.
ROOMS: 255 en suite **CONF:** Thtr 800 Class 50 Board 50 **SERVICES:** Lift **PARKING:** 30 **CARDS:**
See advert on opposite page

★★ 70% Delmere
130 Sussex Gardens, Hyde Park W2 1UB
☎ 020 7706 3344 020 7262 1863
e-mail: delmerehotel@compuserve.com
Dir: *From M25 take A40 to London and exit at Paddington. Drive along Westbourne Terrace which turns into Sussex Gardens*
Well positioned on historic Sussex Gardens for Hyde Park and the West End, this hotel provides well equipped bedrooms designed to make the best use of available space. Public rooms include a jazz-themed bar and a particularly comfortable lounge that is provided with books, up-to-date magazines and newspapers.
ROOMS: 36 en suite (1 fmly) s £78-£92; d £98-£113 (incl. cont bkfst) * LB **SERVICES:** Lift **PARKING:** 2 **NOTES:** No dogs **CARDS:**

Town House

★★★★ The Abbey Court
20 Pembridge Gardens, Kensington W2 4DU
☎ 020 7221 7518 020 7792 0858
e-mail: info@abbeycourthotel.co.uk
Dir: *2 minute walk from Nottinghill Gate Underground station*
Situated in Notting Hill and close to Kensington, this elegant, five-storey town house is in a quiet side road. Rooms are individually decorated and furnished to a high standard and there is room service of light snacks. Breakfast is taken in the conservatory.
ROOMS: 22 en suite (1 fmly) No smoking in 10 bedrooms s £99-£135; d £145-£195 (incl. cont bkfst) * **FACILITIES:** STV
NOTES: No dogs (ex guide dogs)
CARDS:

Town House

★★★★ The Darlington Hyde Park
111-117 Sussex Gardens W2 2RU
☎ 020 7460 8800 020 7460 8828
e-mail: darlinghp@aol.com
Dir: *just off Edgware Road*
Although not offering the full range of hotel services, this comfortable town house provides smart, well maintained rooms with excellent facilities, including good desk space. Breakfast is served in an airy dining room, which also offers drinks and snacks in the early evening.
ROOMS: 40 en suite (2 fmly) No smoking in 5 bedrooms s £90-£145; d £120-£145 (incl. cont bkfst) * **FACILITIES:** STV **SERVICES:** Lift **NOTES:** No dogs (ex guide dogs) No smoking in restaurant **CARDS:**

Town House

★★★★ Pembridge Court
34 Pembridge Gardens W2 4DX
☎ 020 7229 9977 020 7727 4982
e-mail: reservations@pemct.co.uk
Dir: *off the Bayswater Rd at Nottinghill Gate by underground Station*
Just minutes from Portobello Market and in Notting Hill Gate, this Victorian town house provides very well appointed, smart, stylish bedrooms with 24-hour room service. Staff are friendly and clearly enjoy having guests to stay.
ROOMS: 20 en suite (4 fmly) s fr £120; d fr £150 (incl. bkfst) * **FACILITIES:** STV Membership of local Health Club **SERVICES:** Lift air con **PARKING:** 2 **CARDS:**

W6 HAMMERSMITH See LONDON plan 1 *D3*

★★★ 68% Novotel London West
Hammersmith Int. Centre, 1 Shortlands W6 8DR
☎ 020 8741 1555 020 8741 2120
e-mail: h0737@accor-hotels.com
Dir: *turn off A4 onto Hammersmith Broadway, then follow signs for City Centre, take first left and hotel is on the left*
This large, purpose-built hotel, close to Hammersmith underground station, is easily accessible from the M4 and Heathrow Airport. Practical, spacious bedrooms are equipped with a range of modern facilities including air conditioning. Open-plan public areas include a brasserie, a choice of bars and a useful shop. Secure parking is available.
ROOMS: 629 en suite (73 fmly) No smoking in 421 bedrooms s fr £145; d fr £165 * LB **FACILITIES:** STV Pool table entertainment **CONF:** Thtr 900 Class 600 Board 300 Del from £174 * **SERVICES:** Lift air con **PARKING:** 250 **CARDS:**

Bad hair day? Hairdryers in all rooms three stars and above.

London

★★★66% Vencourt

255 King St, Hammersmith W6 9LU
☎ 020 8563 8855 Fax 020 8563 9988

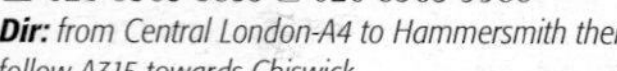

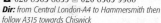

Dir: *from Central London-A4 to Hammersmith then follow A315 towards Chiswick*

This modern hotel is close to the centre of Hammersmith where there is good public transport. Rooms have the expected modern comforts and most have good views over London, especially on the upper of the 12 storeys. The open-plan public areas include a lounge bar, where snacks are served all day, and a small restaurant for more substantial meals.

ROOMS: 120 en suite (25 fmly) No smoking in 18 bedrooms s £89-£109; d £99-£109 * LB **FACILITIES:** STV Xmas **CONF:** Thtr 50 Class 45 Board 32 Del from £99 * **SERVICES:** Lift **PARKING:** 27
CARDS:

W8 KENSINGTON See LONDON plan 1 *D3*

★★★★★74% Royal Garden Hotel

2-24 Kensington High St W8 4PT
☎ 020 7937 8000 Fax 020 7361 1991
e-mail: sales@royalgdn.co.uk

Dir: *next to Kensington Palace*

With views over Kensington Gardens and Hyde Park, this tall, modern hotel provides guests with the expected international levels of comfort and service. The Tenth is the hotel's showcase restaurant - contemporary, bright and smart with great views. Cooking style has its base in the classical repertoire but grabs modern ideas.

ROOMS: 398 en suite (19 fmly) No smoking in 164 bedrooms s fr £246.75; d £305.50-£333.25 * **FACILITIES:** STV Sauna Solarium Gym Health & fitness centre entertainment Xmas **CONF:** Thtr 550 Class 280 Board 80 **SERVICES:** Lift air con **NOTES:** No dogs (ex guide dogs) Civ Wed 400 **CARDS:**

See advert on this page

★★★★63% Copthorne Tara

Scarsdale Place, Wrights Ln W8 5SR
☎ 020 7937 7211 Fax 020 7937 7100
e-mail: tara.sales@mill-cop.com

Dir: *located just off Kensington High Street*

One of the city's larger hotels, located in a residential area off Kensington High Street. Public areas have a bustling and smart atmosphere and include the relaxing setting of Café Mozart or Jerome's Restaurant. Bedrooms are bright and equipped with a useful range of facilities.

ROOMS: 834 en suite No smoking in 265 bedrooms d £185-£210 * LB **FACILITIES:** STV Xmas **CONF:** Thtr 400 Class 160 Board 92 Del £205 * **SERVICES:** Lift air con **PARKING:** 86 **NOTES:** No dogs (ex guide dogs) **CARDS:**

★★★70% *Posthouse Kensington*

Posthouse

Wright's Ln, Kensington W8 5SP
☎ 0870 400 9000 Fax 020 7937 8289

Dir: *off Kensington High Street*

Positioned close to Kensington High Street, this hotel offers well equipped bedrooms and an extensive range of facilities; these include an impressive new leisure club, dedicated conference rooms and several eating outlets, including an all day conservatory coffee shop and two restaurants. A refurbishment programme has enhanced the quality and decor of the public areas. Bedrooms are benefiting from a stylish re-vamp, and although some rooms are quite compact, they all offer good facilities.

ROOMS: 550 en suite No smoking in 150 bedrooms **FACILITIES:** STV Indoor swimming (H) Squash Sauna Solarium Gym Pool table Jacuzzi/spa Health & Fitness centre with Beauty room Steam room **CONF:** Thtr 180 Class 80 Board 60 **SERVICES:** Lift **PARKING:** 70
CARDS:

London

W8 KENSINGTON, continued

Premier Collection

★★★★★ Milestone Hotel & Apartments

1 Kensington Court W8 5DL
020 7917 1000 020 7917 1010
e-mail: guestservices@milestone.redcarnationhotels.com
Dir: *from M4 follow into Central London. Turn into Warwick Road and then right into Kensington High St. Hotel 400yds past Kensington Underground*

Much care has been lavished on this town house property. Themed bedrooms are individually decorated to a high standard and their wide range of facilities includes DVD players. There are superb suites and some duplex such as the Safari, complete with colonial fan, safari print fabrics, tiger soaps and tented ceiling. Staff are very friendly and the bar and kitchen produce fresh, enjoyable cocktails and meals. In addition to a luxurious lounge, there is a snug bar with a conservatory extension. Office facilities are available.

ROOMS: 57 en suite No smoking in 10 bedrooms d £250-£800 * **FACILITIES:** STV Sauna Gym Jacuzzi/spa entertainment Xmas **CONF:** Thtr 28 Class 12 Board 16 **SERVICES:** Lift air con **CARDS:**

W11 HOLLAND PARK, NOTTING HILL
See LONDON plan 1 *D3/D4*

★★★★78% Halcyon

81 Holland Park W11 3RZ
020 7727 7288 020 7229 8516
e-mail: information@thehalcyon.com

Faithfully restored and situated in the fashionable Holland Park area, this elegant hotel provides amply proportioned bedrooms equipped with every comfort. Staff provide round-the-clock attentive and friendly service. The restaurant is a well known dinner venue.

ROOMS: 43 en suite s £176; d £282 * **FACILITIES:** STV Xmas **CONF:** Class 20 Board 10 **SERVICES:** Lift air con **NOTES:** No dogs (ex guide dogs) Civ Wed 120 **CARDS:**

WC1 BLOOMSBURY, HOLBORN

★★★★69% *The Montague on the Gardens*

15 Montague St, Bloomsbury WC1B 5BJ
020 7637 1001 020 7637 2516
e-mail: reservations@montaque.redcarnationshotels.com

A stylish, privately-owned hotel in the centre of London. The public areas are decorated with a sense of individuality and a great deal of attention to detail. Bedrooms are a little compact, but feature furnishings of good quality with bold and original decor.

ROOMS: 104 en suite No smoking in 20 bedrooms **FACILITIES:** STV Sauna Gym Jacuzzi/spa entertainment **CONF:** Thtr 120 Class 50 Board 50 **SERVICES:** Lift **NOTES:** No dogs (ex guide dogs) **CARDS:**

★★★★68% Radisson Edwardian Marlborough

Bloomsbury St WC1B 3QD
020 7636 5601 020 7636 0532
e-mail: resmarl@radisson.com
Dir: *continue past Oxford Street and down New Oxford Street turn into Bloomsbury Street*

This stylish period hotel offers a wide range of services and a choice of eating options. Bedrooms are individually furnished and fully equipped with modern facilities. Refurbished public areas feature a choice of bars and a smart restaurant.

ROOMS: 173 en suite (3 fmly) No smoking in 57 bedrooms s £183-£215; d £199-£215 * LB **CONF:** Thtr 250 Class 90 Board 50 **SERVICES:** Lift **CARDS:**

★★★★66% *Holiday Inn Kings Cross/ Bloomsbury*

1 Kings Cross Rd WC1X 9HX
020 7833 3900 020 7917 6163
e-mail: peterstubbs@axford.com
Dir: *0.50m from Kings Cross station on the corner of King Cross Rd and Calthorpe St*

Conveniently located for Kings Cross station and the City, this modern hotel offers smart accommodation with a range of useful facilities. The hotel has two restaurants, one of which is Indian, limited lounge seating, versatile meeting rooms, a cosy bar and a small, well equipped fitness centre.

ROOMS: 405 en suite (163 fmly) No smoking in 160 bedrooms **FACILITIES:** STV Indoor swimming (H) Sauna Solarium Gym Jacuzzi/spa Hair & Beauty salon **CONF:** Thtr 220 Class 120 Board 30 **SERVICES:** Lift air con **PARKING:** 12 **NOTES:** No dogs (ex guide dogs) **CARDS:**

★★★★61% Hotel Russell

Russell Square WC1B 5BE
020 7837 6470 020 7837 2857

This wonderful Victorian building has undergone much restoration, retaining its original character. Bedrooms are spacious, smart and well equipped. Restyled public areas include two restaurants and bars, a business centre and a magnificent and popular ballroom.

ROOMS: 329 en suite No smoking in 56 bedrooms s £168-£218; d £188-£238 * LB **FACILITIES:** STV Xmas **CONF:** Thtr 450 Class 200 Board 35 Del from £210 * **SERVICES:** Lift air con **CARDS:**

See advert on opposite page

★★★71% The Bonnington in Bloomsbury

92 Southampton Row WC1B 4BH
020 7242 2828 020 7831 9170
e-mail: sales@bonnington.com
Dir: *from M40 Euston Rd opposite Stn turn south into Upper Woburn Place past Russell Sq into Southampton Row. Bonnington on left*

Within easy access of the City and West End, this hotel offers traditional service and modern comfort. Bedrooms are well laid out with many extras. The attractive Waterfalls Restaurant serves a range of dishes, or guests can choose from the bar menu.

ROOMS: 215 en suite (4 fmly) No smoking in 87 bedrooms s £111; d £140 (incl. bkfst) * **FACILITIES:** STV **CONF:** Thtr 250 Class 80 Board 100 Del from £110 * **SERVICES:** Lift **CARDS:**

London

continued

★★★68% Radisson Edwardian Kenilworth

Radisson Edwardian

Great Russell St WC1B 3LB
☎ 020 7637 3477 📠 020 7631 3133
e-mail: resmarl@radisson.com
Dir: *continue past Oxford Street and down New Oxford Street. Turn into Bloomsbury Street*

This stylish, Edwardian hotel offers friendly service and a choice of dining options. Smart bedrooms are individually furnished and fully equipped with modern facilities.

ROOMS: 187 en suite No smoking in 20 bedrooms s £145-£175; d £175-£199 * LB **FACILITIES:** STV **CONF:** Thtr 150 Class 50 Board 50 **SERVICES:** Lift **CARDS:**

★★★61% Posthouse Bloomsbury

Posthouse

Coram St WC1N 1HT
☎ 0870 400 9222 📠 020 7837 5374
Dir: *off Upper Woburn Place near to Russell Square*

Designed with the business traveller in mind, this large hotel offers a wide range of services and facilities. Refurbished rooms are smart, comfortable and well equipped. An Irish-themed bar has been added, and there is a car park nearby.

ROOMS: 284 en suite (29 fmly) No smoking in 211 bedrooms **FACILITIES:** STV **CONF:** Thtr 200 Class 140 Board 22 **SERVICES:** Lift **PARKING:** 80 **NOTES:** No dogs (ex guide dogs) **CARDS:**

Town House

★★★★ Blooms

7 Montague St WC1B 5BP
☎ 020 7323 1717 📠 020 7636 6498
e-mail: blooms@mermaid.co.uk
Dir: *off Russell Square*

Part of an 18th-century terrace, this elegant town house is just around the corner from the British Museum. Bedrooms are furnished in Regency style and day rooms consist of a lobby lounge, a garden terrace, a breakfast room and cocktail bar, all graced with antique pieces, paintings and flowers. The lounge menu is also available as room service, and meals can be delivered from some of the local restaurants.

ROOMS: 27 en suite s fr £130; d £195-£205 (incl. bkfst) * LB **FACILITIES:** STV Xmas **CONF:** Thtr 20 Class 10 Board 18 Del £200 * **SERVICES:** Lift **NOTES:** No dogs (ex guide dogs) **CARDS:**

See advert on this page

Packed in a hurry? Ironing facilities should be available at all star levels, either in rooms or on request.

London

WC2 SOHO, STRAND

Premier Collection

★★★★★ ❀❀❀ The Savoy
Strand WC2R 0EU
☎ 020 7836 4343 🖷 020 7240 6040
e-mail: info@the-savoy.co.uk
The Savoy Group
Dir: *situated halfway along The Strand between Trafalgar Square and Aldwych*

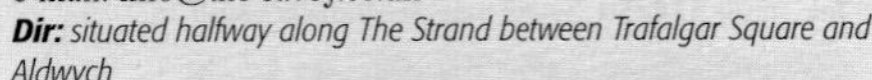

This splendid hotel of international repute retains its enviable position as one of the best. Bedrooms provide very high standards of comfort, with quality linens and fabrics throughout. The marble bathrooms with their celebrated thunderstorm showers are superb, and guests will find all the luxurious extras one would expect in a hotel of this calibre. The American bar is an excellent watering-hole for the discerning, the Grill is a popular choice for dining, and the River Room is renowned for the flavours and precision of its menu. Afternoon tea remains a highlight for both residents and visitors, and Saturday night 'Stomping at the Savoy' is a real treat.
ROOMS: 228 en suite (6 fmly) No smoking in 55 bedrooms s £280-£395; d £330-£370 * LB **FACILITIES:** STV Indoor swimming (H) Sauna Gym Tennis at the Vanderbilt Club entertainment Xmas **CONF:** Thtr 500 Class 200 Board 32 **SERVICES:** Lift air con **PARKING:** 65 **NOTES:** No dogs (ex guide dogs) **CARDS:**

★★★★★ 75% ❀❀ One Aldwych
1 Aldwych WC2B 4BZ
☎ 020 7300 1000 🖷 020 7300 1001
e-mail: sales@onealdwych.co.uk
Dir: *at the point where the Aldwych meets the Strand, near Waterloo Bridge*
From its position on the corner of the Aldwych, within easy access of Theatreland, this magnificent hotel enjoys commanding views across Waterloo Bridge and Covent Garden. Once the home of the Morning Post newspaper, the building has been carefully restored and now combines all the expected modern comforts with the charm of the original architecture. Accommodation is bright, stylish and fully air-conditioned. All rooms are equipped with CD player and voicemail. The Axis and Indigo restaurants provide quality dining, and the cocktail bar is a popular meeting place.
ROOMS: 105 en suite No smoking in 39 bedrooms s fr £299.63; d fr £323.13 * LB **FACILITIES:** STV Indoor swimming (H) Sauna Gym Steam room 2 Treatment rooms Xmas **CONF:** Thtr 60 Board 40 **SERVICES:** Lift air con **NOTES:** No dogs (ex guide dogs) Civ Wed 60 **CARDS:**

★★★★★ 72% ❀❀ Le Meridien Waldorf
Aldwych WC2B 4DD
☎ 0870 400 8484 🖷 020 7836 7244
Dir: *from Trafalgar Sq follow The Strand all the way to the end, when the one way system brings you into Aldwych*
This famous hotel, which has a very special atmosphere, goes from strength to strength with continued investment and upgrading, enthusiastic and committed management and friendly, helpful staff. The Palm Court remains an institution with weekend afternoon tea dances as popular as ever, and regular jazz evenings. Luxurious bedrooms are tastefully styled and air conditioned. In addition to the Palm Court, where guests can enjoy a wide range of dishes, there is a smart brasserie.
ROOMS: 292 en suite (6 fmly) No smoking in 150 bedrooms s £240-£340; d £270-£560 * LB **FACILITIES:** STV Complimentary use of nearby Health club entertainment Xmas **CONF:** Thtr 250 Class 120 Board 70 Del from £150 * **SERVICES:** Lift air con **NOTES:** No dogs (ex guide dogs) **CARDS:**

★★★★ 76% ❀❀ Radisson Edwardian Mountbatten
Monmouth St, Seven Dials, Covent Garden WC2H 9HD
☎ 020 7836 4300 🖷 020 7240 3540
e-mail: resmoun@radisson.com
Dir: *just off Shaftesbury Av, on the corner of Seven Dials rdbt*
Situated in the heart of Theatreland, this popular hotel provides excellent levels of service. The smart, air-conditioned bedrooms are not over-large but are very comfortable. At the time of our last inspection, the restaurant was about to be restyled and renamed The Dial.
ROOMS: 128 en suite No smoking in 64 bedrooms s fr £225; d fr £260 (incl. bkfst) * LB **FACILITIES:** STV Gym entertainment Xmas **CONF:** Thtr 90 Class 45 Board 32 **SERVICES:** Lift air con **CARDS:**

★★★★ 73% ❀ Radisson Edwardian Hampshire
Leicester Square WC2H 7LH
☎ 020 7839 9399 🖷 020 7930 8122
e-mail: reshamp@radisson.com
Dir: *situated on Leicester Square*
This popular hotel is superbly situated in Leicester Square. Public areas have been smartly refurbished and the air-conditioned bedrooms are both comfortable and very thoughtfully equipped. Good food can be enjoyed in the stylish Apex restaurant.
ROOMS: 124 en suite No smoking in 20 bedrooms d £341-£447 * **FACILITIES:** STV Gym **CONF:** Thtr 100 Class 40 Board 34 **SERVICES:** Lift air con **CARDS:**

★★★★ 70% Kingsway Hall
Great Queen St, Covent Garden WC2B 5BZ
☎ 020 7309 0909 🖷 020 7309 9696
e-mail: kingswayhall@compuserve.com
Dir: *from Holborn Underground Station follow Kingsway towards Aldwych. At first lights turn right. Hotel 50mtrs on left*
Situated in Covent Garden, this smart new hotel offers a high standard of accommodation. Air-conditioned bedrooms have been well designed and feature excellent facilities. There is a spacious restaurant, lounge bar and a selection of conference rooms.

continued

ROOMS: 170 en suite No smoking in 112 bedrooms s £185; d £198 * **FACILITIES:** STV Sauna Gym Jacuzzi/spa Xmas **CONF:** Thtr 150 Class 70 Board 45 Del £205 * **SERVICES:** Lift air con **NOTES:** No dogs (ex guide dogs) **CARDS:**

See advert on this page

★★★66% *Strand Palace*

LONDON SIGNATURE HOTELS

Strand WC2R 0JJ
☎ 0870 400 8702 🖷 020 7836 2077

This busy hotel has a range of restaurants and bars that offer guests a wide choice of eating options. The Academy provides state-of-the-art conference and banqueting suites. Rooms vary in size and style; a supplement buys a room on the smart Club floor where bedrooms have added luxuries and guests can use the exclusive lounge.

ROOMS: 783 en suite No smoking in 305 bedrooms **FACILITIES:** STV Discount at nearby Health Club **CONF:** Thtr 160 Class 85 Board 40 **SERVICES:** Lift **NOTES:** No dogs (ex guide dogs)
CARDS:

★★★65% Radisson Edwardian Pastoria

Radisson Edwardian

3-6 St Martins St WC2H 7HL
☎ 020 7930 8641 🖷 020 7925 0551
e-mail: reshamp@radisson.com
Dir: *S side of Leicester Square*

In a discreet side street off Leicester Square, this small hotel has smart public areas and an informal restaurant. The bedrooms are tastefully furnished and comfortable, and offer room service. Those on the top floor are more spacious and have marble bathrooms. Staff go out of their way to ensure guests are well looked after.

ROOMS: 58 en suite No smoking in 16 bedrooms **FACILITIES:** STV **CONF:** Thtr 60 Class 28 Board 26 **SERVICES:** Lift **NOTES:** No dogs (ex guide dogs) **CARDS:**

LONDON AIRPORTS See under Gatwick & Heathrow

LONG EATON, Derbyshire
Map 08 SK43

see also Sandiacre

★★★65% *Novotel*
Bostock Ln NG10 4EP
☎ 0115 946 5111 📠 0115 946 5900

Dir: *M1 junct 25. Take B6002 to Long Eaton, hotel is 400 yds on left*

A purpose-built hotel, close to J25 of the M1. Bedrooms are uniform in size and layout, offering the range of facilities and comfort associated with this international brand. Services are efficiently provided by a young, friendly team.

ROOMS: 108 en suite (31 fmly) No smoking in 58 bedrooms **FACILITIES:** STV Outdoor swimming (H) Pool table **CONF:** Thtr 220 Class 100 Board 100 **SERVICES:** Lift **PARKING:** 180 **CARDS:**

★★64% Europa
20-22 Derby Rd NG10 1LW
☎ 0115 972 8481 📠 0115 946 0229

Dir: *on A6005, in the centre of Long Eaton*

Convenient for the town centre and the M1, this commercial hotel offers clean, brightly furnished bedrooms. In addition to the restaurant, light refreshments are available throughout the day in the conservatory. Cheerful, informal service is provided by friendly staff.

ROOMS: 15 en suite (2 fmly) s fr £39.95; d fr £47.95 (incl. bkfst) * **CONF:** Thtr 35 Class 35 Board 28 **PARKING:** 24 **NOTES:** No dogs (ex guide dogs) No smoking in restaurant **CARDS:**

LONGHORSLEY, Northumberland
Map 12 NZ19

★★★★65% *Linden Hall*
NE65 8XF
☎ 01670 516611 📠 01670 788544

Dir: *1m N on A697*

Standing in 400 acres of park and woodlands, this impressive Georgian mansion boasts extensive leisure and conference facilities. The hotel is an impressive complex; public areas lead off a grand inner hall and include a stately drawing room, smart cocktail lounge and an elegant restaurant serving imaginative lunches and dinners. Bedrooms vary in size but all are smartly furnished and equipped with thoughtful extras.

ROOMS: 50 en suite (4 fmly) **FACILITIES:** STV Indoor swimming (H) Golf 18 Tennis (hard) Snooker Sauna Solarium Gym Pool table Croquet lawn Putting green Jacuzzi/spa Hairdressing Health & beauty spa **CONF:** Thtr 300 Class 100 Board 40 **SERVICES:** Lift **PARKING:** 260 **NOTES:** No smoking in restaurant **CARDS:**

See advert on opposite page

LONG MELFORD, Suffolk
Map 05 TL84

★★★67% The Bull
Hall St CO10 9JG
☎ 01787 378494 📠 01787 880307

Dir: *3m N of Sudbury on the A134*

Parts of this building date back to the 15th century and some features still remain such as carvings in a beam in one of the lounges and heraldic markings on the wall. The individual bedrooms vary in size, and are comfortable and full of character. There is a bar and two lounges, one non-smoking, in which guests can relax.

ROOMS: 25 en suite (3 fmly) No smoking in 11 bedrooms s fr £65; d fr £100 (incl. bkfst) * LB **FACILITIES:** Xmas **CONF:** Thtr 60 Class 30 Board 35 Del £100 * **PARKING:** 30 **NOTES:** No smoking in restaurant Civ Wed 50 **CARDS:**

★★72% The Black Lion
The Green CO10 9DN
☎ 01787 312356 📠 01787 374557

Dir: *at junct of A134/A1092*

This 15th-century hotel offers a great deal of charm and character. Each bedroom is individually decorated, all are spacious and comfortable with a number of thoughtful extras. Guests may choose to dine in the bar or opt for the more formal environment of the restaurant.

ROOMS: 9 en suite (3 fmly) s £70; d £90 (incl. bkfst) * LB **CONF:** Thtr 15 Class 20 Board 20 **PARKING:** 10 **NOTES:** No smoking in restaurant **CARDS:**

LONGRIDGE, Lancashire
Map 07 SD63

★★64% Ferrari's Country House
Chipping Rd, Thornley PR3 2TB
☎ 01772 783148 📠 01772 786174

Dir: *from Longridge centre follow signs for Chipping past Safeway, along Chipping Lane for 1m, past Derby Arms to hotel 50yds on left*

A privately-owned country house hotel set in attractive grounds. Part of the house was rebuilt early this century following a fire, but there are reminders of the original house in the beamed Coach Room banqueting suite. Bedrooms are traditional in style, some extremely spacious; most look out onto the splendid garden. There is a comfortable lounge bar and dining room.

ROOMS: 11 en suite (2 fmly) s £35; d £50-£75 (incl. bkfst) * LB **FACILITIES:** Xmas **CONF:** Thtr 60 Class 30 Board 30 Del from £55 * **PARKING:** 50 **NOTES:** Civ Wed 120 **CARDS:**

LONG SUTTON, Lincolnshire
Map 09 TF42

Travelodge
Wisbech Rd PE12 9AG
☎ 01406 362230 📠 01406 362230

Dir: *on junct A17/A1101 roundabout*

This modern building offers accommodation in smart, spacious and well equipped bedrooms, all with en suite bathrooms. Refreshments may be taken at the nearby family restaurant. For further details and the Travelodge phone number, consult the Hotel Groups page.

ROOMS: 40 en suite

LOOE, Cornwall & Isles of Scilly
Map 02 SX25

★★★65% Hannafore Point
Marine Dr, West Looe PL13 2DG
☎ 01503 263273 📠 01503 263272

Dir: *on A38 Plymouth road turn left onto A385 to Looe across bridge and take immediate left. Hotel is half mile on left*

Panoramic coastal views are enjoyed at this warm and welcoming hotel. The spacious restaurant shares the view, where a short fixed-price menu is offered, served by a friendly team of staff. All the accommodation is equipped to a good standard.

ROOMS: 37 en suite (2 fmly) s £45-£63; d £90-£132 (incl. bkfst) * LB **FACILITIES:** Indoor swimming (H) Squash Sauna Solarium Gym Pool table Jacuzzi/spa 3/4 billiard table Xmas **CONF:** Thtr 100 Class 120 Board 40 Del from £60 * **SERVICES:** Lift **PARKING:** 37 **NOTES:** No smoking in restaurant Civ Wed 160 **CARDS:**

See advert on opposite page

> Early start? Hotels at all star levels should provide in-room alarm clocks and/or alarm calls.

★★74% Fieldhead
Portuan Rd, Hannafore PL13 2DR
☎ 01503 262689 01503 264114
e-mail: field.head@virgin.net

Dir: *from West Looe and follow road alongside estuary left signposted 'Hannafore' around headland, onto promenade then right and right again*
This charming hotel assures a warm welcome and offers commanding views of the bay and St George's Island. Bedrooms are individually furnished and decorated with modern equipment and facilities. Public areas include a relaxed bar and a smart restaurant. The fixed-price menu changes daily and features fresh ingredients, including local seafood.
ROOMS: 14 en suite (2 fmly) s £50-£60; d £70-£80 (incl. bkfst) * LB **FACILITIES:** Outdoor swimming (H) Xmas **PARKING:** 15 **NOTES:** No smoking in restaurant **CARDS:**

See advert on this page

★★62% *Rivercroft Hotel*
Station Rd PL13 1HL
☎ 01503 262251
e-mail: rivercroft.hotel@virgin.net
Dir: *from A38, B387 to Looe. On left nr bridge*
Standing high above the river, this family run hotel is conveniently located, just a short walk from the town centre and beach. Bedrooms are comfortably furnished and well equipped, many enjoying wonderful views of the varied activity below. An extensive menu is offered in the Croft Restaurant, or alternatively, meals can be enjoyed in the convivial atmosphere of the bar.
ROOMS: 15 en suite (8 fmly) s £25-£28; d £50-£70 (incl. bkfst) LB **NOTES:** No smoking in restaurant **CARDS:**

Linden Hall Hotel, Longhorsley

LOSTWITHIEL, Cornwall & Isles of Scilly — Map 02 SX15

★★★64% Restormel Lodge
Hillside Gardens PL22 0DD
☎ 01208 872223 📠 01208 873568
e-mail: restlodge@aol.com
Dir: *on A390 in Lostwithiel*
This friendly and relaxed hotel has been owned by the same family for over 30 years. The original building, housing the bar, restaurant and lounges, has kept much of its original character. Bedrooms are located in modern blocks.
ROOMS: 21 en suite 12 annexe en suite (3 fmly) s £55-£74; d £77-£90 (incl. bkfst) * LB **FACILITIES:** STV Outdoor swimming (H) Xmas **CONF:** Thtr 100 Class 80 Board 60 Del from £80 * **PARKING:** 40 **NOTES:** No smoking in restaurant **CARDS:**

★★66% Lostwithiel Hotel Golf & Country Club
Lower Polscoe PL22 0HQ
☎ 01208 873550 📠 01208 873479
e-mail: info@golf-hotel.co.uk
Dir: *turn off A38 at Dobwalls onto the A390, on entering Lostwithiel turn right - signposted from main road*
Established as a leisure resort in its own right, Lostwithiel offers a wide range of activities in addition to its challenging 18-hole golf course. The well equipped bedrooms are housed in attractive Cornish stone buildings. A range of interesting meals are served in the Sportsman's Bar and the Black Prince restaurant.
ROOMS: 19 en suite **FACILITIES:** Indoor swimming (H) Golf 18 Tennis (hard) Fishing Snooker Gym Pool table Putting green Undercover floodlit driving range **CONF:** Thtr 200 Class 60 Board 40 **PARKING:** 120 **CARDS:**

LOUGHBOROUGH, Leicestershire — Map 08 SK51

★★★★70% Quorn Country Hotel
Charnwood House, 66 Leicester Rd LE12 8BB
☎ 01509 415050 📠 01509 415557
e-mail: quorncountry.hotel@virgin.net
(For full entry see Quorn)

★★★64% The Quality Hotel
New Ashby Rd LE11 0EX
☎ 01509 211800 📠 01509 211868
e-mail: admin@gb613.u-net.com
Dir: *leave M1 at junct 23 and take A512 towards Loughborough. Hotel 1m on left*
Close to J23 of the M1, this popular, modern hotel offers comfortable, well equipped accommodation. All the bedrooms offer a spacious work area, and some rooms have small lounges and kitchenettes, ideal for the longer stay or families. There is a small leisure centre and versatile conference facilities.
ROOMS: 94 en suite (12 fmly) No smoking in 47 bedrooms s fr £83; d fr £105 * LB **FACILITIES:** STV Indoor swimming (H) Sauna Solarium Gym Jacuzzi/spa Xmas **CONF:** Thtr 225 Class 120 Board 80 Del from £100 * **PARKING:** 160 **NOTES:** Civ Wed 80 **CARDS:**

★★67% *Cedars Hotel*
Cedar Rd LE11 2AB
☎ 01509 214459 📠 01509 233573
e-mail: goodman@cedars01.freeserve.co.uk
Dir: *leaving Loughborough for Leicester on the A6, Cedar Road is last road on the left opposite Crematorium*
South of the town centre, this well established hotel is popular with local businessmen and diners. Modest bedrooms and relaxing open-plan public areas with partitioned restaurant and banqueting rooms are well suited to the needs of the varied business, leisure and function clientele.

ROOMS: 36 en suite (4 fmly) **FACILITIES:** Outdoor swimming (H) Sauna Solarium **CONF:** Thtr 40 Class 24 Board 25 **PARKING:** 50 **NOTES:** No smoking in restaurant **CARDS:**

★★66% The Falcon
Main St, Long Whatton LE12 5DG
☎ 01509 842416 📠 01509 646802
Located in the village of Long Whatton, approximately 7 miles from Loughborough and 4 miles from East Midlands Airport and Donnington Park race circuit. This village inn offers good accommodation within tastefully converted courtyard bedrooms, formerly the school house and stables. Attractive bedrooms, which vary in size, have been sympathetically furnished and very well equipped; modern en-suite bathrooms to each room. Ground floor public areas of the inn are dominated by a successful food and beverage operation, with plans to introduce a first floor lounge.
ROOMS: 11 annexe en suite No smoking in 3 bedrooms s £54-£62.50; d £58-£62.50 * **PARKING:** 42 **NOTES:** No dogs (ex guide dogs) **CARDS:**

★★61% Great Central
Great Central Rd LE11 1RW
☎ 01509 263405 📠 01509 264130
e-mail: reception@greatcentralhotel.co.uk
Dir: *from town centre take A60 towards Nottingham then first right. Hotel on left*
This aptly-named hotel is near the Great Central Steam Railway. Its high-ceilinged, Victorian-style bar has a convivial atmosphere and is decorated with railway memorabilia. Most of the attractive bedrooms have pine furniture and cheerful colour schemes; several four-poster bedrooms are also available.
ROOMS: 22 en suite (5 fmly) s £34; d £48 (incl. bkfst) * LB **FACILITIES:** STV Xmas **CONF:** Thtr 100 Class 100 Board 40 **PARKING:** 40 **CARDS:**

LOUTH, Lincolnshire — Map 08 TF38

★★★71% Brackenborough Arms Hotel
Cordeaux Corner, Brackenborough LN11 0SZ
☎ 01507 609169 📠 01507 609413
e-mail: ashley@brackenborough.force9.co.uk
Dir: *off A16 2m N of Louth*
Set amidst landscaped grounds, this hotel offers attractive bedrooms individually decorated with coordinated furnishings and many extras. There is a cocktail bar, and the Tippler's Retreat lounge bar, famous for its fish and chips. For the more serious diner, the Brackens Restaurant offers an interesting carte menu.

continued

ROOMS: 24 en suite (1 fmly) No smoking in 6 bedrooms s £59-£62; d £70-£75 (incl. bkfst) * LB **FACILITIES:** STV **CONF:** Thtr 34 Class 24 Board 32 **PARKING:** 90 **NOTES:** No dogs (ex guide dogs) Closed 25-26 Dec **CARDS:**

★★★69% Beaumont

66 Victoria Rd LN11 0BX
☎ 01507 605005 01507 607768
e-mail: enquiries@thebeaumont.freeserve.co.uk

In a peaceful residential street close to the town centre, this personally-run private hotel provides spacious, individually decorated bedrooms. A couple of small single rooms are also available. The lounge is comfortable and the restaurant offers set-priced and carte menus that include Italian specialities.

ROOMS: 16 en suite (2 fmly) s £40-£55; d £60-£85 (incl. bkfst) * LB **FACILITIES:** STV Xmas **CONF:** Thtr 80 Class 50 Board 46 **SERVICES:** Lift **PARKING:** 70 **NOTES:** RS Sun **CARDS:**

★★★64% Kenwick Park

Kenwick Park LN11 8NR
☎ 01507 608806 01507 608027
e-mail: enquiries@kenwick-park.co.uk

***Dir:** follow A16 from Grimsby, then A157 Mablethorpe/Manby road. Hotel is 400mtrs down hill on right*

An elegant Georgian-style house with modern extensions, on the 500 acre Kenwick Park Estate. Bedrooms are of comfortable proportions with every modern facility. The Fairway Restaurant has an imaginative carte and house menus. The conservatory-style Keepers Bar overlooks Kenwick Park Golf Course. There is an excellent leisure centre.

ROOMS: 19 en suite 5 annexe en suite (3 fmly) s fr £79.50; d fr £98 (incl. bkfst) * LB **FACILITIES:** STV Indoor swimming (H) Golf 18 Tennis (hard) Squash Snooker Sauna Solarium Gym Pool table Putting green Jacuzzi/spa Health & Beauty Centre ch fac Xmas **CONF:** Thtr 100 Class 40 Board 40 Del from £120 * **PARKING:** 50 **NOTES:** No smoking in restaurant Civ Wed 92 **CARDS:**

See advert on this page

LOWER BEEDING, West Sussex — Map 04 TQ22

Premier Collection

★★★★ South Lodge

Brighton Rd RH13 6PS
☎ 01403 891711 01403 891766
e-mail: enqiuries@southlodgehotel.co.uk

***Dir:** on A23 left onto B2110 'Handcross'. Turn right through Handcross and follow B2110, until A281 junct. Turn left and Hotel entrance on right*

Enjoying splendid views over the Downs, this Victorian mansion stands in 90 acres of gardens. Bedrooms are individually furnished and have lots of personal touches. Dishes such as duck confit with pumpkin risotto characterise the excellent cuisine served in the elegant restaurant, where traditional Sunday lunch is also very popular.

ROOMS: 41 en suite s £150; d £175 * LB **FACILITIES:** STV Golf 36 Tennis (hard) Snooker Croquet lawn Putting green Xmas **CONF:** Thtr 85 Class 40 Board 30 Del from £180 * **PARKING:** 80 **NOTES:** No dogs (ex guide dogs) No smoking in restaurant Civ Wed 65 **CARDS:**

See advert under HORSHAM

Fancy a Singapore Sling? Bar staff in five star hotels should be skilled cocktail mixers.

LOWER SLAUGHTER, Gloucestershire Map 04 SP12

Premier Collection

★★★ Lower Slaughter Manor

GL54 2HP
☎ 01451 820456 📠 01451 822150
e-mail: lowsmanor@aol.com
Dir: *off A429 signposted "The Slaughters", the manor is 0.5m on right entering village*

This charming grade II listed manor dates mainly from the 17th century and enjoys a tranquil location at the heart of one of the Cotswolds' most famous villages. Spacious bedrooms are tastefully furnished and thoughtfully equipped. The appealing public areas include an inviting lounge and drawing room with log fires in season.

ROOMS: 11 en suite 5 annexe en suite **FACILITIES:** Indoor swimming (H) Tennis (hard) Croquet lawn Putting green **CONF:** Thtr 30 Board 14 **PARKING:** 35 **NOTES:** No dogs (ex guide dogs) No children 8yrs No smoking in restaurant
CARDS:

★★★76% Washbourne Court

GL54 2HS
☎ 01451 822143 📠 01451 821045
e-mail: washbourne@classic.msn.com
Dir: *turn off A429 at signpost 'The Slaughters', between Stow-on-the-Wold and Bourton-on-the-Water. Hotel is in the centre of village*

Beamed ceilings, log fires and flagstone floors are features of this 17th-century hotel, set in four acres of grounds beside the River Eye. Bedrooms, in the main house and self-contained cottages, are smartly decorated. There are traditionally furnished sitting areas, a character bar and an elegant dining room serving an interesting menu and a comprehensive list of wines.

ROOMS: 15 en suite 13 annexe en suite **FACILITIES:** Tennis (hard) **CONF:** Thtr 30 Board 20 Del from £160 * **PARKING:** 40 **NOTES:** No dogs No children 7yrs No smoking in restaurant
CARDS:

See advert on opposite page

LOWESTOFT, Suffolk Map 05 TM59

★★★71% Ivy House Farm

Ivy Ln, Beccles Rd, Oulton Broad NR33 8HY
☎ 01502 501353 & 588144 📠 01502 501539
e-mail: admin@ivyhousefarm.co.uk
Dir: *on A146 SW of Oulton Broad turn into Ivy Ln beside Esso petrol station, over small railway bridge & follow private driveway into car park*

The skilfully restored Crooked Barn restaurant is the focal point of this popular venue, which offers some delightful meals. Attractive bedrooms are spacious and comfortably furnished, with bright modern bathrooms. All rooms enjoy views of the garden or neighbouring fields, home to a variety of wildfowl.

ROOMS: 19 annexe en suite (1 fmly) No smoking in 6 bedrooms s £69-£79; d £89-£95 (incl. bkfst) * LB **FACILITIES:** Arrangement with neighbouring leisure club for reduced rates Xmas **CONF:** Thtr 50 Board 24 **PARKING:** 50 **NOTES:** No smoking in restaurant
CARDS:

See advert on opposite page

★★★67% Wherry Hotel

Bridge Rd, Oulton Broad NR32 3LN
☎ 01502 516845 & 516846 📠 01502 501350
e-mail: wherry@wherry.force9.net
Dir: *Hotel is situated just north of the bridge in the centre of Oulton Broad on A146*

Built around 1900, the Wherry is named after the sailing barges typical of the Norfolk Broads area. Many original features can be seen in the bustling public areas which overlook the waterfront. Well equipped bedrooms come in a variety of sizes and styles, and there is a carvery-style restaurant, as well as public and lounge bars.

ROOMS: 29 en suite (4 fmly) s £48-£58; d £68-£82 (incl. bkfst) * LB **FACILITIES:** STV Pool table **CONF:** Thtr 250 Class 150 Board 80 Del from £70 * **SERVICES:** Lift **PARKING:** 185 **NOTES:** No smoking in restaurant Closed 24-26 Dec **CARDS:**

★★★65% Hotel Hatfield

Best Western

The Esplanade NR33 0QP
☎ 01502 565337 📠 01502 511885
Dir: *from town centre follow signs for 'South Beach' (A12 Ipswich). Hotel 200yds on left*

This hotel is situated on the esplanade overlooking the sea and has retained many of its original architectural features. The bedrooms are spacious and well equipped. There is a lively bar, which serves a range of snacks and a choice of real ales, and the sea-facing Chaplins restaurant offers international dishes to suit most tastes.

ROOMS: 33 en suite (1 fmly) s £42-£49; d £75-£85 (incl. bkfst) * LB **FACILITIES:** STV Xmas **CONF:** Thtr 100 Class 50 Board 40 Del from £70 * **SERVICES:** Lift **PARKING:** 26 **NOTES:** No dogs (ex guide dogs) No smoking in restaurant Civ Wed 200
CARDS:

LOWESWATER, Cumbria Map 11 NY12

★69% Grange Country House

CA13 0SU
☎ 01946 861211 & 861570
Dir: *turn left off A5086 for Mockerkin, through village and after 2m turn left for Loweswater Lake. Hotel at bottom of hill on left*

This delightful country hotel rests in a quiet valley at the north-western end of Loweswater. It has a friendly and relaxed

continued

atmosphere, cosy public areas and very friendly staff. There is a small bar, a residents' lounge and an attractive dining room. Bedrooms are comfortable and well equipped.

ROOMS: 8 rms (7 en suite) 2 annexe en suite (2 fmly)
FACILITIES: National Trust boats & fishing **CONF:** Thtr 25 Class 25 Board 25 **PARKING:** 22 **NOTES:** No smoking in restaurant RS Jan-Feb

LUDLOW, Shropshire Map 07 SO57

★★★78% ❀❀❀ **Overton Grange**
Hereford Rd SY8 4AD
☎ 01584 873500 🖷 01584 873524
Dir: *turn off A49 at B4361 Richards Castle, Ludlow and hotel is 200yds on left*

An Edwardian mansion situated above Ludlow with lovely views across the Shropshire countryside. Well manicured gardens and abundant fresh flowers create a pleasant appearance. There is a

continued on p358

Ivy House Farm, Lowestoft

LUDLOW, continued

comfortable lounge and bar, and the restaurant offers a high standard of cuisine with classic French flair.
ROOMS: 14 en suite (2 fmly) No smoking in 3 bedrooms s £57-£88; d £88-£120 (incl. bkfst) * LB **FACILITIES:** Croquet lawn Xmas **CONF:** Thtr 160 Class 80 Board 50 **PARKING:** 80 **NOTES:** No dogs (ex guide dogs) No smoking in restaurant 2nd & 3rd week in January
CARDS:

See advert on page 357

★★★71% Dinham Hall
By the Castle SY8 1EJ
☎ 01584 876464 01584 876019
Dir: *opposite the castle*
Built in 1792, this lovely old house in attractive gardens stands immediately opposite Ludlow Castle. It has a well deserved reputation for warm hospitality and fine cuisine. Well equipped bedrooms include two in a converted cottage and some four-posters. The comfortable public rooms are elegantly appointed.
ROOMS: 14 en suite (3 fmly) s £65-£95; d £110-£160 (incl. bkfst) * LB **FACILITIES:** Xmas **CONF:** Thtr 28 Class 28 Board 24 Del from £130 * **PARKING:** 16 **NOTES:** No smoking in restaurant
CARDS:

★★★64% The Feathers at Ludlow
Bull Ring SY8 1AA
REGAL
☎ 01584 875261 01584 876030
Dir: *in the centre of Ludlow*

Famous for the carved woodwork outside and in, this picturesque 17th-century hotel is one of the town's best known landmarks. Bedrooms are decorated in traditional style. The lounge and the Prince of Wales function suite are especially noteworthy for their decor.
ROOMS: 40 en suite (3 fmly) No smoking in 15 bedrooms s £65-£75; d £85-£115 * LB **FACILITIES:** Jacuzzi/spa Xmas **CONF:** Thtr 80 Class 40 Board 40 Del from £90 * **SERVICES:** Lift **PARKING:** 39
NOTES: No smoking in restaurant Civ Wed 80
CARDS:

★★64% Cliffe
Dinham SY8 2JE
☎ 01584 872063 01584 873991
e-mail: cliffhotel@lineone.net
Dir: *through Ludlow town centre to Castle turn left at castle gates to Dinham, follow road beneath castle over bridge, hotel sign 100yds from bridge*
Built in the last century and standing in extensive grounds and gardens, this hotel is quietly located close to the castle and the river. It provides well equipped accommodation, and facilities include a lounge bar, a pleasant restaurant and a patio overlooking the garden.
ROOMS: 9 en suite (2 fmly) No smoking in all bedrooms s £35-£40; d £60-£70 (incl. bkfst) * LB **PARKING:** 22 **NOTES:** No smoking in restaurant **CARDS:**

Travelodge
Travelodge
Woofferton SY8 4AL
☎ 01584 711695 01584 711695
Dir: *on A49 at junct A456/B4362*
This modern building offers accommodation in smart, spacious and well equipped bedrooms, all with en suite bathrooms. Refreshments may be taken at the nearby family restaurant. For further details and the Travelodge phone number, consult the Hotel Groups page.
ROOMS: 32 en suite

LULWORTH COVE See West Lulworth

LUMBY, North Yorkshire Map 08 SE43

★★★56% *Posthouse Leeds/Selby*
LS25 5LF
Posthouse
☎ 0870 400 9050 01977 685462
Dir: *leave A1 at A63 signposted Selby, hotel on A63 on left*
A modern hotel situated in extensive grounds near the A1/A63 junction. Attractive day rooms include the Seasons Restaurant and the Spa Leisure Club is a popular feature. Service, provided by friendly staff, includes an all-day lounge menu and 24-hour room service.
ROOMS: 97 en suite (18 fmly) No smoking in 50 bedrooms
FACILITIES: Indoor swimming (H) Tennis (hard) Sauna Putting green 9 Hole pitch & putt **CONF:** Thtr 160 Class 50 Board 40 **PARKING:** 330
CARDS:

LUTON, Bedfordshire Map 04 TL02

★★★56% The Chiltern
Waller Av LU4 9RU
REGAL
☎ 01582 575911 01582 581859
Dir: *M1 junct 11 take A505 to Luton go past two sets of lights over rdbt left filter lane left at lights hotel on right*

Conveniently close to the M1, this hotel is geared towards the business guest, having a range of conference and meeting rooms. Bedrooms offer good desk space, and room service is a bonus. The busy bar is at the hub of the hotel.
ROOMS: 91 en suite (6 fmly) No smoking in 63 bedrooms d fr £85 * LB **FACILITIES:** STV Xmas **CONF:** Thtr 180 Class 180 Board 30 Del £135 * **SERVICES:** Lift **PARKING:** 150 **NOTES:** No smoking in restaurant **CARDS:**

Late for dinner? Quality Standards star rating means that last orders for dinner should be no earlier than:
★ 6.30pm ★★ 7.00pm ★★★ 8.00pm
★★★★ 9.00pm ★★★★★ 10.00pm

LUTON AIRPORT, Bedfordshire Map 04 TL12

⇧ Hotel Ibis

Spittlesea Rd LU2 9NH
☎ 01582 424488 📠 01582 455511
e-mail: H1040@accor-hotels.com
Dir: *from junct 10 on M1 follow signs to Airport,hotel is 1km before airport*
Modern, budget hotel offering comfortable accommodation in bright and practical bedrooms. Breakfast is self-service and dinner is available in the restaurant. For further details, consult the Hotel Groups page.
ROOMS: 98 en suite d £53 * **CONF:** Thtr 80 Class 40 Board 40

LYDFORD, Devon Map 02 SX58

★★71% Lydford House

EX20 4AU
☎ 01822 820347 📠 01822 820442
e-mail: relax@lydfordhouse.co.uk
Dir: *turn off A386 halfway between Okehampton and Tavistock, signpost Lydford, 0.25m on right hand side*

This impressive Victorian country house is located on the edge of Dartmoor. The comfortable bedrooms are attractively decorated and, in addition to the conservatory lounge, a separate lounge is available. There are riding stables adjacent to the hotel which are run by the proprietors, so guests can take lessons or accompanied rides over the moors.
ROOMS: 12 rms (11 en suite) (4 fmly) s £34.20-£39.50; d £67.07-£79 (incl. bkfst) * LB **FACILITIES:** Riding **CONF:** Thtr 25 Board 20 Del from £55.50 * **PARKING:** 30 **NOTES:** No children 5yrs No smoking in restaurant **CARDS:**

LYME REGIS, Dorset Map 03 SY39

★★★70% Alexandra

Pound St DT7 3HZ
☎ 01297 442010 📠 01297 443229
e-mail: enquiries@hotelalexandra.co.uk
Dir: *from A30 turn onto A35 and then follow A358. Turn off onto A3052 to Lyme Regis*
Built in 1735 and grade II listed, this hotel features an elegant restaurant with picture windows taking in the magnificent views. Bedrooms have pretty chintz fabrics and attractive furniture. The south-facing conservatory opens onto gardens. During winter log fires burn in the lounge.
ROOMS: 26 en suite 1 annexe en suite (8 fmly) s £50-£65; d £115-£152 (incl. bkfst & dinner) * LB **PARKING:** 18 **NOTES:** No smoking in restaurant Closed Xmas & Jan **CARDS:**

★★74% Mariners Hotel

Silver St DT7 3HS
☎ 01297 442753 📠 01297 442431
Dir: *W of town on A3052, turn right on B3070*
A small, friendly hotel with a happy, relaxed atmosphere. The cosy, comfortable bedrooms are individually decorated with good quality furnishings and fabrics and good facilities. Some rooms have lovely sea views. There is a spacious lounge overlooking the bay, a bar and bright restaurant serving table d'hôte and carte menus.
ROOMS: 12 en suite No smoking in 6 bedrooms s £39-£42; d £78-£84 (incl. bkfst) * LB **PARKING:** 20 **NOTES:** No smoking in restaurant Closed Xmas & New Year **CARDS:**

★★68% Orchard Country

Rousdon DT7 3XW
☎ 01297 442972 📠 01297 443670
Dir: *off A3052 in Rousdon, Devon between Lyme Regis & Seaton, brown signposted from the centre of the village*
This small country hotel offers comfortable accommodation and a relaxed atmosphere. This is somewhere to unwind whilst enjoying the proprietors' warm hospitality and personal attention. The short, fixed-price menu focuses on careful preparation of fresh local produce.
ROOMS: 12 rms (9 en suite) No smoking in all bedrooms s £31-£46; d £50-£74 (incl. bkfst) * LB **PARKING:** 15 **NOTES:** No dogs (ex guide dogs) No children 8yrs No smoking in restaurant Closed Mid Dec-Feb **CARDS:**

LYME REGIS, continued

★★67% *Buena Vista*
Pound St DT7 3HZ
☎ 01297 442494 🖷 01297 444670
Dir: *W on A3052 out of town*

In attractive gardens overlooking the harbour and Cobb, this relaxed hotel offers comfortable accommodation. Parts of the hotel date back to the Regency period with original features still in evidence. Wonderful views can be enjoyed from many of the bedrooms. There is a choice of lounges and a south-facing sun terrace.
ROOMS: 18 rms (17 en suite) (1 fmly) **PARKING:** 18 **NOTES:** No smoking in restaurant Closed Dec-Jan **CARDS:**

L

★★64% Bay
Marine Pde DT7 3JQ
☎ 01297 442059
Dir: *on the seafront in the centre of Lyme Regis*
A relaxed and friendly atmosphere is guaranteed at this sea front hotel. Bedrooms are stylish and comfortable and the brightly decorated dining room offers an interesting menu that incorporates local seafood. The spacious lounge has its own billiard table.
ROOMS: 19 en suite (2 fmly) s £42-£55; d £84-£90 (incl. bkfst) * LB **FACILITIES:** Snooker Pool table Xmas **CONF:** Del from £60 * **PARKING:** 20 **NOTES:** No smoking in restaurant
CARDS:

See advert on page 359

★★64% Royal Lion
Broad St DT7 3QF
☎ 01297 445622 🖷 01297 445859
Built as a coaching inn in 1601, the Royal Lion retains much character. Bedrooms in the newer wing are more spacious, some have balconies, sea views or a private terrace. There are a number of lounge areas. The dining room provides an extensive range of dishes.
ROOMS: 30 en suite (4 fmly) s £40; d £80-£112 (incl. bkfst) * LB **FACILITIES:** Indoor swimming (H) Snooker Sauna Gym Pool table Jacuzzi/spa Games room Table tennis Xmas **PARKING:** 36 **NOTES:** Closed 3 days Xmas **CARDS:**

LYMINGTON, Hampshire
Map 04 SZ39

★★★72% Passford House
Mount Pleasant Ln SO41 8LS
☎ 01590 682398 🖷 01590 683494
Dir: *from A337 at Lymington straight on at mini rdbt, then first right at Tollhouse public house, then after 1m right into Mount Pleasant Lane*
A peaceful hotel set in attractive grounds on the edge of town. Bedrooms vary in size but all are comfortably furnished and well equipped. Extensive public areas include lounges, a smartly appointed bar and restaurant and leisure facilities. Attentive service is provided by a friendly and well motivated team.
ROOMS: 53 en suite 2 annexe en suite (2 fmly) No smoking in 5 bedrooms s £60-£90; d £90-£130 (incl. bkfst) * LB **FACILITIES:** Indoor swimming (H) Outdoor swimming (H) Tennis (hard) Sauna Solarium Gym Pool table Croquet lawn Putting green Jacuzzi/spa Petanque Table tennis Helicopter landing area Xmas **CONF:** Thtr 80 Class 30 Board 30 Del from £130 * **PARKING:** 100 **NOTES:** No smoking in restaurant
CARDS:

★★★72% Stanwell House
High St SO41 9AA
☎ 01590 677123 🖷 01590 677756
e-mail: sales@stanwellhousehotel.com
Dir: *A337 to town centre, on right hand side of High St before it descends to quay*
A privately-owned Georgian hotel in the heart of Lymington. Bedrooms are attractively decorated with quality fabrics and furnishings; deluxe rooms have four-posters and power showers. Guests can relax in the conservatory lounge and enjoy modern brasserie-style cuisine in the main bistro, or a lighter meal in the more informal bar.
ROOMS: 29 en suite (1 fmly) No smoking in 4 bedrooms d £105-£155 (incl. bkfst) * LB **FACILITIES:** Xmas **CONF:** Thtr 30 Class 20 Board 22 Del from £125 * **NOTES:** No smoking in restaurant Civ Wed 60
CARDS:

See advert on opposite page

★★★65% String of Horses
Mead End Rd SO41 6EH
☎ 01590 682631 🖷 01590 682911
e-mail: relax@stringofhorses.co.uk
(For full entry see Sway)

★★69% Gordleton Mill Hotel & Restaurant
Silver St, Hordle SO41 6DJ
☎ 01590 682219 🖷 01590 683073
Dir: *on Sway Rd which becomes Silver St*

A delightful 17th-century watermill on the banks of the River Avon. The restaurant takes full advantage of the hotel's position and serves an extensive range of dishes at lunch and dinner. The picturesque gardens are popular for al fresco dining during the warmer months and the attractive bedrooms are equipped with whirlpool baths.
ROOMS: 9 en suite (1 fmly) No smoking in 5 bedrooms s £50-£60; d £65-£100 (incl. bkfst) * LB **PARKING:** 60 **NOTES:** No dogs (ex guide dogs) No children 8yrs No smoking in restaurant
CARDS:

LYMPSHAM, Somerset Map 03 ST35

★★70% Batch Country Hotel

Batch Ln BS24 0EX
☎ 01934 750371 01934 750501
Dir: *off A370. Follow Tourist Board signs for 1.5m through village to hotel*

Midway between the resorts of Weston-super-Mare and Burnham-on-Sea, this attractive property offers relaxed and friendly service in a tranquil environment. The comfortable bedrooms have countryside views to the Mendip and Quantock Hills. Spacious lounges overlook the gardens and an extensive range of dishes is served in the beamed dining room.
ROOMS: 10 en suite (6 fmly) No smoking in 2 bedrooms
FACILITIES: Fishing **CONF:** Thtr 80 Class 60 Board 100 **PARKING:** 70
NOTES: No dogs No smoking in restaurant Closed Xmas
CARDS:

See advert under WESTON-SUPER-MARE

LYNDHURST, Hampshire Map 04 SU30

★★★77% Le Poussin at Parkhill

Beaulieu Rd SO43 7FZ
☎ 023 8028 2944 023 8028 3268
e-mail: lepoussin@parkhill.co.uk
Dir: *turn off A35 onto B3056 Beaulieu, Hotel 1m on left*
A Georgian country house set amidst unspoilt woodland. Elegant public rooms contain open fires and antiques. Large bedrooms are individual in style; most have super views over the forest. Dining is the high point of any stay here, with priority given to local seasonal ingredients such as New Forest wild mushrooms and wood pigeon. Service is professional.
ROOMS: 15 en suite 5 annexe en suite (2 fmly) No smoking in 16 bedrooms d £85-£95 (incl. cont bkfst) * **FACILITIES:** Outdoor swimming (H) Fishing Croquet lawn Putting green Outdoor chess Xmas
CONF: Thtr 40 Class 40 Board 30 Del from £125 * **PARKING:** 75
NOTES: No smoking in restaurant Civ Wed
CARDS:

★★★69% Crown

MARSTON HOTELS

High St SO43 7NF
☎ 023 8028 2922 023 8028 2751
e-mail: crown@marstonhotels.co.uk
Dir: *in the centre of the village, opposite the church*
In the heart of the village, this historic hotel has been welcoming visitors to the New Forest for generations. Bedrooms are attractively furnished and well equipped. The restaurant offers an interestiange of seasonal dishes, and the popular pannelled bar provides a less formal meal option. There are two comfortable lounges.

continued on p362

L

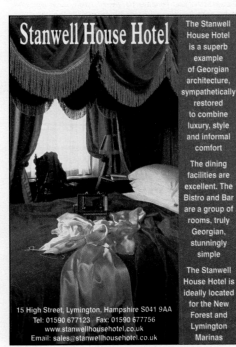

LYNDHURST, continued

Crown, Lyndhurst

ROOMS: 39 en suite (8 fmly) s £75-£100; d £120-£170 (incl. bkfst) * LB **FACILITIES:** STV Xmas **CONF:** Thtr 70 Class 30 Board 45 Del from £85 * **SERVICES:** Lift **PARKING:** 60 **NOTES:** No smoking in restaurant Civ Wed 30 **CARDS:**

See advert on opposite page

★★★66% Bell Inn

SO43 7HE
☎ 023 8081 2214 023 8081 3958
e-mail: bell@bramshaw.co.uk
(For full entry see Brook (Near Cadnam))

L

★★★64% Forest Lodge

Best Western

Pikes Hill, Romsey Rd SO43 7AS
☎ 023 8028 3677 023 8028 2940
e-mail: info@carehotels.co.uk
Dir: *exit M27 at junct 1 and join A337 towards Lyndhurst. On approaching village, police station/courts on right, take first right into Pikes Hill*
Situated on the edge of Lyndhurst, this well maintained hotel has comfortable bedrooms, many ideal for families, and attractively decorated public areas, which include two lounges, a bar and a restaurant. Service is friendly and attentive.
ROOMS: 28 en suite (7 fmly) s £70-£77.50; d £110-£125 (incl. bkfst) * LB **FACILITIES:** Indoor swimming (H) Sauna Gym ch fac Xmas **CONF:** Thtr 100 Class 70 Board 50 Del from £98 * **PARKING:** 50 **NOTES:** No smoking in restaurant Civ Wed 100
CARDS:

★★★64% Lyndhurst Park

Forestdale Hotels

High St SO43 7NL
☎ 023 8028 3923 023 8028 3019
Dir: *M27 Junct 1-3 to A35 to Lyndhurst. Hotel is situated at bottom of High Street*
A short walk from the high street, this extended Georgian house, set in five acres of mature grounds, is ideally placed for exploring the New Forest. There are two bars and a cosy oak-panelled restaurant with a sunny conservatory addition. Bedrooms vary in size and style and include several with four-posters.
ROOMS: 59 en suite (3 fmly) No smoking in 3 bedrooms s fr £60; d fr £120 (incl. bkfst & dinner) * LB **FACILITIES:** Outdoor swimming (H) Tennis (hard) Snooker Sauna Table tennis ch fac Xmas **CONF:** Thtr 300 Class 120 Board 80 Del from £100 * **SERVICES:** Lift **PARKING:** 100 **NOTES:** No smoking in restaurant Civ Wed
CARDS:

★★68% *Mill House Hotel*

Romsey Rd SO43 7AR
☎ 023 8028 2814 023 8028 2815
Dir: *leave junct 1 of M27 on to A31, turn right at rdbt onto A337 hotel 4m on left*
On the edge of the village, the Mill House provides brightly decorated, comfortably furnished bedrooms. Public areas include a very popular bar and restaurant operation which serves food all day.
ROOMS: 11 en suite (3 fmly) **PARKING:** 56 **NOTES:** No dogs (ex guide dogs) **CARDS:**

★71% Knightwood Lodge

MINOTEL Great Britain

Southampton Rd SO43 7BU
☎ 023 8028 2502 023 8028 3730
Dir: *on A35*
This friendly, family-run hotel is situated on the outskirts of Lyndhurst. Comfortable bedrooms are modern in style and well equipped with many useful extras. The hotel offers an excellent range of facilities which are free to residents.
ROOMS: 14 en suite 4 annexe en suite (2 fmly) s £45-£55; d £70-£90 (incl. bkfst) * LB **FACILITIES:** STV Indoor swimming (H) Sauna Solarium Gym Jacuzzi/spa Steam room **PARKING:** 15 **NOTES:** No smoking in restaurant **CARDS:**

LYNMOUTH, Devon Map 03 SS74
see also Lynton

★★★66% Tors

EX35 6NA
☎ 01598 753236 01598 752544
e-mail: torshotel@torslynmouth.co.uk
Dir: *adjacent to A39 on Countisbury Hill just before you enter Lynmouth*
In an elevated position overlooking Lynmouth Bay, this friendly hotel is set in five acres of woodland. The majority of the soundly furnished bedrooms benefit from the superb views, as do the public areas. A choice of comfortable, well presented lounges is provided. Both fixed-price and short carte menus are offered in the restaurant.
ROOMS: 33 en suite (7 fmly) s £40-£85; d £70-£110 (incl. bkfst) * LB **FACILITIES:** Outdoor swimming (H) Pool table Table tennis ch fac Xmas **CONF:** Thtr 60 Class 40 Board 25 Del from £57.50 * **SERVICES:** Lift **PARKING:** 40 **NOTES:** No smoking in restaurant Closed 4-31 Jan RS Feb (wknds only) **CARDS:**

★★76% Rising Sun

Harbourside EX35 6EQ
☎ 01598 753223 01598 753480
e-mail: risingsunlynmouth@easynet.co.uk
Dir: *leave M5 at junct 23 (Minehead), follow A39 to Lynmouth. Hotel is located on Harbourside*
This historic former smugglers' inn nestles on the harbour front and benefits from a popular bar and a good restaurant. The individually designed bedrooms with modern facilities are located within the inn or in the adjoining cottage rooms. In addition to the convivial bar, there is a comfortable, quiet lounge.
ROOMS: 11 en suite 5 annexe en suite No smoking in 11 bedrooms s £60; d £98-£140 (incl. bkfst) * LB **FACILITIES:** Fishing Xmas **NOTES:** No dogs (ex guide dogs) No children 8yrs No smoking in restaurant **CARDS:**

★★67% **Bath**
Sea Front EX35 6EL
☎ 01598 752238 01598 752544
e-mail: bathhotel@torslynmouth.co.uk
Dir: *M5 junct 25 follow A39 to Minehead then Porlock and Lynmouth*
This well established hotel stands near the harbour, and its sea-facing bedrooms are particularly attractive. Local fish in season features on the restaurant menu and cream teas are served in the sun lounge.
ROOMS: 24 en suite (9 fmly) s £29-£45; d £58-£80 (incl. bkfst) * LB **FACILITIES:** Pool table **PARKING:** 13 **NOTES:** No smoking in restaurant Closed Jan & Dec RS Nov-Mar **CARDS:**

LYNTON, Devon Map 03 SS74
see also Lynmouth

★★★72% **Hewitts**
North Walk EX35 6HJ
☎ 01598 752293 01598 752489
e-mail: hewitts.hotel@talk21.com
Dir: *North Walk runs off the Lee Road, entrance between St Mary's Church and Valley of Rocks hotel*
Built as a gentleman's country house in the late 1880s, Hewitts is perched on the hillside with splendid views over the Bristol Channel. The spacious, comfortable public areas feature unique stained glass windows and carved fireplaces. Each of the individually designed and decorated bedrooms benefits from views.
ROOMS: 9 en suite (1 fmly) No smoking in 8 bedrooms s £45-£70; d £100-£140 (incl. bkfst) * **FACILITIES:** STV Jacuzzi/spa entertainment **CONF:** Thtr 20 Class 16 Board 16 Del from £70 * **PARKING:** 12 **NOTES:** No children 10yrs No smoking in restaurant Closed 23 Dec-6 Jan RS 10 Nov-10 Feb **CARDS:**

★★★65% **Lynton Cottage**
North Walk EX35 6ED
☎ 01598 752342 01598 752597
e-mail: lyntoncot@aol.com
Dir: *turn into North Walk by St Mary's Church, hotel is 100mtrs on right*
This 17th-century hotel enjoys stunning views over the Lyn Valley and Lynmouth Bay and retains much of its period character. The fixed-priced menu offers a balanced selection of tempting dishes and delicious desserts. There is a spacious lounge and separate bar. The terrace overlooks the idyllic scenery and is very popular with guests.
ROOMS: 17 en suite No smoking in 2 bedrooms s £41-£57; d £82-£114 (incl. bkfst) * LB **PARKING:** 17 **NOTES:** No dogs No children 15yrs No smoking in restaurant Closed Jan & Dec
CARDS:

★★63% **Sandrock**
Longmead EX35 6DH
☎ 01598 753307 01598 752665
Dir: *follow signs to 'The Valley of the Rocks'*
Situated at the head of the Valley of the Rocks, on the edge of the village, this family-run hotel offers light, airy, modern bedrooms. It has a popular public bar, with a comfortable residents' lounge on the first floor.
ROOMS: 8 rms (6 en suite) (3 fmly) s £23.50-£25; d £47-£52 (incl. bkfst) * LB **FACILITIES:** Pool table **PARKING:** 9 **NOTES:** Closed Nov-Jan **CARDS:**

★73% **Seawood**
North Walk EX35 6HJ
☎ 01598 752272 01598 752272
e-mail: seawoodhotel@tinyworld.com
This charming hotel, nestling on wooded cliffs some 400 ft above the sea, provides spectacular views across Lynmouth Bay. Bedrooms are individually furnished and decorated, and some have four-poster beds. The menu changes daily.
ROOMS: 12 en suite s £27-£29; d £54-£58 (incl. bkfst) * LB **PARKING:** 10 **NOTES:** No children 11yrs No smoking in restaurant Closed Nov-Easter

★69% ***Chough's Nest***
North Walk EX35 6HJ
☎ 01598 753315 01598 763529
Dir: *turn onto North Walk by Parish Church in the centre of the High St. Chough's Nest last building on the left*
This lovely stone house was originally built as a home by a wealthy Dutchman and has fabulous views over the bay. Bedrooms are individually designed and offer a high standard of comfort. The restaurant offers a carefully chosen range of dishes and an interesting wine list.
ROOMS: 12 en suite (2 fmly) No smoking in all bedrooms **FACILITIES:** Beauty Therapist, Reflexology & Aromatherapy **PARKING:** 10 **NOTES:** No dogs No smoking in restaurant Closed Nov-Jan RS Feb & Early March **CARDS:**

LYNTON, continued

★67% North Cliff

North Walk EX35 6HJ
☎ 01598 752357
e-mail: northcliff@ukmax.co.uk
Dir: *from Lynton main street Lee Road take North Walk Hill Hotel on left*

With spectacular views over Lynmouth Bay, this small hotel offers guests a genuine welcome. Home-cooked meals are served in the dining room, which enjoys fine views, as does the lounge and many of the spacious, comfortable bedrooms.

ROOMS: 14 en suite (3 fmly) No smoking in all bedrooms s £30-£34; d £60-£68 (incl. bkfst) * LB **FACILITIES:** Snooker Pool table Table tennis ch fac **PARKING:** 15 **NOTES:** No smoking in restaurant Closed Nov-28 Feb **CARDS:**

LYTHAM ST ANNES, Lancashire — Map 07 SD32

★★★★64% Clifton Arms

West Beach, Lytham FY8 5QJ
☎ 01253 739898 01253 730657
e-mail: info@cliftonarms.demon.co.uk
Dir: *on the A584 along the seafront*

This long established hotel commands fine views over Lytham green and the Ribble estuary beyond. Bedrooms are particularly large and comfortable and include one room with a four-poster bed. The elegant restaurant offers a wide choice of delectable dishes and a selection of fine wines.

ROOMS: 48 en suite No smoking in 4 bedrooms s £89.50-£98.50; d £110-£120 (incl. bkfst) * LB **FACILITIES:** STV Xmas **CONF:** Thtr 300 Class 200 Board 100 Del £120 * **SERVICES:** Lift **PARKING:** 50 **NOTES:** No dogs (ex guide dogs) **CARDS:**

See advert on opposite page

★★★67% Chadwick

South Promenade FY8 1NP
☎ 01253 720061 01253 714455
e-mail: sales@chadwickhotel.com
Dir: *M6 Junct 32 take M55 Blackpool A5230 South Shore and follow signs for St Annes*

continued

In the same family for over 50 years, this traditional, friendly seafront hotel attracts regular visitors. Comfortably furnished bedrooms include some with sea views, as well as some with four-poster beds. Public areas are spacious and well maintained and include excellent swimming and fitness facilities as well as a children's play area.

ROOMS: 75 en suite (28 fmly) s £42-£46; d £60-£68 (incl. bkfst) * LB **FACILITIES:** STV Indoor swimming (H) Sauna Solarium Gym Pool table Jacuzzi/spa Turkish bath Games room Soft play adventure area entertainment ch fac Xmas **CONF:** Thtr 72 Class 24 Board 28 Del from £62 * **SERVICES:** Lift **PARKING:** 40 **NOTES:** No dogs (ex guide dogs) No smoking in restaurant **CARDS:**

See advert on opposite page

★★★63% Bedford

307-311 Clifton Dr South FY8 1HN
☎ 01253 724636 01253 729244
e-mail: reservations@bedford-hotel.com
Dir: *from M55 follow signs for airport to last set of lights. Turn left, through 2 sets of lights hotel is 300yds on left*

This family-run hotel is close to the town centre and the sea front. Bedrooms, varying in size, are attractively furnished and well equipped. Facilities include a conference and function suite, the Cartland Restaurant, a popular coffee shop and Kitty's public bar offering regular entertainment.

ROOMS: 36 en suite (6 fmly) s fr £45; d fr £65 (incl. bkfst) * LB **FACILITIES:** STV Sauna Solarium Gym Jacuzzi/spa Steam room entertainment Xmas **CONF:** Thtr 150 Class 100 Board 40 Del from £55 * **SERVICES:** Lift **PARKING:** 20 **NOTES:** No dogs (ex guide dogs) No smoking in restaurant Civ Wed 120
CARDS:

See advert on opposite page

★★68% Glendower

Best Western

North Promenade FY8 2NQ
☎ 01253 723241 01253 640069
e-mail: glendowerhotel@bestwestern.co.uk
Dir: *M55 follow airport signs turn left at Promenade to St Annes. Hotel situated on St Annes promenade 500yds from the pier*

On the seafront and close to the town centre, this popular, friendly hotel benefits from fine sea views. Rooms are comfortably furnished and well equipped, and include some four-poster and family rooms. There is a choice of smart, comfortable lounges and an indoor swimming pool.

ROOMS: 60 en suite (17 fmly) s £39-£49; d £75-£89 (incl. bkfst) * LB **FACILITIES:** STV Indoor swimming (H) Snooker Sauna Gym Jacuzzi/spa Table tennis Fitness room Childrens playroom ch fac Xmas **CONF:** Thtr 150 Class 120 Board 40 Del from £69 * **SERVICES:** Lift **PARKING:** 45 **NOTES:** No smoking in restaurant
CARDS:

See advert on opposite page

Bedford Hotel

BH

AA ★★★

307-311 CLIFTON DRIVE SOUTH
LYTHAM ST ANNES · FY8 1HN

Exclusive family run hotel with a reputation for fine cuisine complimented by an excellent standard of personal, caring service • All bedrooms are tastefully decorated with matching fabrics that please the eye and provide every facility and comfort • For that special occasion we have three beautiful Four-Poster bedrooms to make you feel truly pampered.

All Year Round Mini Breaks Available

TEL: 01253 724636 · FAX: 01253 729244
Email: bedford@cyberscape.co.uk

Clifton Arms Hotel

AA ★★★★

WEST BEACH
LYTHAM
LANCASHIRE
FY8 5QJ

Telephone: 01253 739898 Fax: 01253 730657
Email: info@cliftonarms.demon.co.uk
Reservations: Freephone 0800 0284372

The historic Clifton Arms Hotel is set in the picturesque Lancashire coastal town of Lytham with a fascinating heritage dating back over 300 years. Overlooking Lytham green and the beautiful seafront, the Clifton Arms offers a truly warm welcome and pleasant stay, whether you are here for business or pleasure. Our 48 bedrooms are stylishly furnished to make you feel comfortable and relaxed, or if you prefer something special, why not stay in one of our executive rooms or the Churchill Suite where Winston Churchill once stayed.

L

Best Western Glendower HOTEL

A family owned hotel offering an elegant yet relaxed atmosphere. Imaginative menus with quality dishes to suit all tastes. Visit our newly refurbished health and leisure club, now boasting a heated indoor pool, jacuzzi, sauna, steam room and gymnasium. Bedrooms are all tastefully decorated, some enjoying breathtaking sea views. The ideal venue for both business or pleasure, situated just three miles from Blackpool.

North Promenade, St. Annes on Sea
Lancashire FY8 2NQ
Tel: 01253 723241 Fax: 01253 640069
glendower@bestwestern.co.uk

The Chadwick Hotel

South Promenade
Lytham St Annes
FY8 1NP AA ★★★
Tel: (01253) 720061
Email: sales@chadwickhotel.com

TOURISM AWARDS 1999
SILVER

Modern family run hotel and leisure complex.
Renowned for good food, personal service, comfortable en suite bedrooms and spacious lounges.
The Health complex features an indoor swimming pool, sauna, Turkish bath, jacuzzi, solarium and gymnasium.
Daily rates for dinner, room and breakfast from £39.50 per person.

LYTHAM ST ANNES, continued

★★68% Lindum
63-67 South Promenade FY8 1LZ
☎ 01253 721534 & 722516 🖹 01253 721364
e-mail: info@lindumhotel.co.uk
Dir: *from airport, continue to seafront lights and turn left. Continue onto 2nd set of lights & turn right, then left at jct. Hotel on left*

THE CIRCLE Selected Individual Hotels GREAT BRITAIN

This friendly seafront hotel has been run by the same family for over 40 years. Bedrooms are generally spacious, comfortable and well equipped, with some enjoying fine sea views. There are several lounges, one with a large screen TV, a games room and a health suite. The airy restaurant offers a wide choice of dishes.
ROOMS: 76 en suite (25 fmly) No smoking in 4 bedrooms s £28-£40; d £50-£65 (incl. bkfst) * LB **FACILITIES:** Sauna Solarium Jacuzzi/spa Xmas **CONF:** Thtr 80 Class 30 Board 25 **SERVICES:** Lift air con **PARKING:** 20 **NOTES:** No smoking in restaurant
CARDS:

★★67% New England
314 Clifton Dr North, St Annes on Sea FY8 2PB
☎ 01253 722355 🖹 01253 726122
Dir: *200 yards from pier*
Between the promenade and the town centre, this smart, modern hotel offers spacious, well equipped accommodation. The focal point is Jay D's Bistro, a popular American-style restaurant. Residents also have access to the hotel's private members sports bar which houses an American pool table.
ROOMS: 10 en suite (5 fmly) s £35; d £50 (incl. bkfst) *
FACILITIES: Pool table Xmas **PARKING:** 14 **NOTES:** No dogs
CARDS:

L

⇧ Premier Lodge
Church Rd FY8 5LH
☎ 0870 700 1424 🖹 0870 700 1425

PREMIER LODGE THE BEST. REST ASSURED.

Premier Lodge offers modern, well equipped, en suite accommodation suitable for both business and leisure travellers. Meals can be taken at the adjacent popular restaurant and bar which is fully licensed. For further details, consult the Hotel Groups page.
ROOMS: 21 en suite d £46 *

MACCLESFIELD, Cheshire — Map 07 SJ97

★★★★63% Shrigley Hall Hotel Golf & Country Club
Shrigley Park, Pott Shrigley SK10 5SB
☎ 01625 575757 🖹 01625 573323
e-mail: shrigleyhall@paramount-hotels.co.uk
Dir: *turn off A523 at Legh Arms, towards Pott Shrigley, hotel is 2m on left just before village*

PARAMOUNT GROUP OF HOTELS

Set in 262 acres of mature parkland, this hotel and leisure complex offers a championship golf course and fishing by arrangement. There is a wide choice of room size and style. An extensive range of dishes is served in the restaurant, and lighter meals and snacks are available in the Courtyard lounge.
ROOMS: 150 en suite (8 fmly) No smoking in 28 bedrooms
FACILITIES: STV Indoor swimming (H) Golf 18 Tennis (hard) Fishing Sauna Solarium Gym Putting green Jacuzzi/spa Beauty salon Steam spa Tennis courts entertainment **CONF:** Thtr 280 Class 140 Board 50 Del from £165 * **SERVICES:** Lift **PARKING:** 300 **NOTES:** No smoking in restaurant Civ Wed 220 **CARDS:**

★★★67% Belgrade Hotel & Restaurant
Jackson Ln, Kerridge, Bollington SK10 5BG
☎ 01625 573246 🖹 01625 574791
e-mail: belgradehotel@btinternet.com
Dir: *off A523, 2m along B5090*

Best Western

Set in the peaceful Cheshire countryside, this hotel is convenient for Manchester Airport (courtesy transport available). The main building has an impressive carved staircase, high ceilings, a restaurant and a lounge. Attractively furnished accommodation is situated in a modern extension.
ROOMS: 54 en suite (2 fmly) No smoking in 36 bedrooms d £60-£70 * LB **FACILITIES:** STV Pool table Free use of neighbouring Leisure Club (5 minutes drive) **CONF:** Thtr 80 Class 50 Board 50 Del from £95 *
PARKING: 200 **NOTES:** No dogs (ex guide dogs) Civ Wed 50
CARDS:

⇧ Premier Lodge
Congleton Rd, Gawsworth SK11 7XD
☎ 0870 700 1466 🖹 0870 700 1467

PREMIER LODGE THE BEST. REST ASSURED.

Premier Lodge offers modern, well equipped, en suite accommodation suitable for both business and leisure travellers. Meals can be taken at the adjacent popular restaurant and bar which is fully licensed. For further details, consult the Hotel Groups page.
ROOMS: 28 en suite d £46 *

MAIDENCOMBE See Torquay

MAIDENHEAD, Berkshire — Map 04 SU88
see also Bray

Premier Collection

★★★★ ❀❀❀ Fredrick's
Shoppenhangers Rd SL6 2PZ
☎ 01628 581000 🖹 01628 771054
e-mail: reservations@fredricks-hotel.co.uk
Dir: *M4, A404 for Henley to Cox Green/White Waltham head to Maindenhead*
Quietly located, this delightful hotel provides individually decorated, well equipped bedrooms. The enthusiastic staff are

continued

friendly and efficient, and a highlight of any visit is a meal in the restaurant, which serves memorable modern dishes.
ROOMS: 37 en suite s £178-£198; d £210-£230 (incl. bkfst) * LB **FACILITIES:** STV Croquet lawn **CONF:** Thtr 120 Class 80 Board 60 Del from £250 * **PARKING:** 90 **NOTES:** No dogs (ex guide dogs) Closed 24 Dec-3 Jan Civ Wed 120 **CARDS:**

★★★69% Thames Riviera

At the Bridge SL6 8DW
☎ 01628 674057 01628 776586
e-mail: thamesriv.sales@dial.pipex.com
Dir: *turn off A4 by Maidenhead Historic Bridge, the hotel is situated by the bridge*
This refurbished hotel enjoys an enviable location on the river next to the historic bridge. Bedrooms are divided between the main building and the more modern wing to the rear of the hotel. There are extensive conference and banqueting facilities, a restaurant with views of the river and a coffee shop.
ROOMS: 34 en suite 18 annexe en suite (1 fmly) No smoking in 4 bedrooms s £70-£105; d £100-£120 * LB **FACILITIES:** STV entertainment **CONF:** Thtr 50 Class 30 Board 20 Del from £140 * **PARKING:** 60 **NOTES:** No dogs (ex guide dogs) Closed 26-30 Dec **CARDS:**

★★★68% Walton Cottage

Marlow Rd SL6 7LT
☎ 01628 624394 01628 773851
e-mail: res@walcothotel.co.uk
Dir: *A308 towards Marlow, hotel on right after passing town centre*
This family-run hotel, close to the town centre, provides high quality accommodation. Bedrooms are situated in adjacent units and some have separate lounges and kitchenettes. Service in the restaurant is restricted at weekends, when meals are available by prior arrangement only.
ROOMS: 25 en suite 45 annexe en suite s £109-£150; d £129-£179 (incl. bkfst) * **FACILITIES:** STV **CONF:** Thtr 70 Class 40 Board 30 **SERVICES:** Lift **PARKING:** 60 **NOTES:** No dogs (ex guide dogs) No smoking in restaurant Closed 24 Dec-3 Jan
CARDS:

★★★66% *Ye Olde Bell Hotel*

Hurley SL6 5LX
☎ 01628 825881 01628 825939
Dir: *take A4130 to Henley look for East Arms public house, High St is on the right just before the pub*
A deceptively large hotel, expanded from the original 17th-century inn to incorporate outbuildings next door and opposite. Situated in an idyllic village near Maidenhead with its own well tended gardens, this hotel offers good quality accommodation and food.
ROOMS: 11 en suite 31 annexe en suite (3 fmly) No smoking in 5 bedrooms **FACILITIES:** STV Tennis (hard) Croquet lawn Badminton Petanque **CONF:** Thtr 140 Class 60 Board 40 **PARKING:** 85
CARDS:

★69% Elva Lodge

Castle Hill SL6 4AD
☎ 01628 622948 01628 778954
e-mail: reservations@elvalodgehotel.demon.co.uk
Dir: *take A4 out of Maidenhead towards Reading. Hotel at top of hill on left*
Located on the A4, just minutes from the town centre, this family-run hotel offers a warm welcome. Bedrooms are comfortable and well equipped. Spacious public areas include a lounge bar and the Lion's Brasserie, which offers a wide range of popular dishes.

continued on p368

M

MAIDENHEAD, continued

Elva Lodge, Maidenhead

ROOMS: 26 rms (23 en suite) (2 fmly) No smoking in 3 bedrooms s £50-£90; d £85-£100 (incl. bkfst) * **FACILITIES:** Pool table Reduced rates at local Leisure Centre **CONF:** Thtr 50 Class 30 Board 30 **PARKING:** 32 **NOTES:** No smoking in restaurant Closed 24-30 Dec Civ Wed 60 **CARDS:**

MAIDSTONE, Kent Map 05 TQ75

★★★★70% Marriott Tudor Park Hotel & Country Club

Ashford Rd, Bearsted ME14 4NQ
☎ 01622 734334 🖹 01622 735360
***Dir:** leave M20 at junct 8 Lenham. At rdbt turn right and head to Bearsted and Maidstone. Hotel is situated 1m on the left hand side*

This fine country hotel provides good levels of comfort. Guests can dine in the main restaurant, Fairviews, which offers uncomplicated dishes, or the more relaxed environment of the Long Weekend Brasserie.
ROOMS: 120 en suite (48 fmly) No smoking in 65 bedrooms s £90-£105; d £105-£115 (incl. bkfst) * LB **FACILITIES:** STV Indoor swimming (H) Golf 18 Tennis (hard) Sauna Solarium Gym Putting green Jacuzzi/spa Driving range Beauty salon Steam room entertainment ch fac Xmas **CONF:** Thtr 250 Class 120 Board 60 Del from £135 * **SERVICES:** Lift **PARKING:** 250 **NOTES:** No dogs (ex guide dogs) No smoking in restaurant Civ Wed 180 **CARDS:**

★★★66% *Russell*

136 Boxley Rd ME14 2AE
☎ 01622 692221 🖹 01622 762084
This attractive former Carmelite convent is set in two acres of grounds on the edge of Maidstone. Bedrooms have modern facilities and the attractive restaurant offers good home-cooked food, attracting a strong local following. The hotel is a popular venue for wedding receptions and meetings. Service is enthusiastic and attentive.

continued

ROOMS: 42 en suite (5 fmly) **FACILITIES:** Jacuzzi/spa ch fac **CONF:** Thtr 300 Class 100 Board 90 **PARKING:** 100 **NOTES:** No dogs (ex guide dogs) **CARDS:**

See advert on opposite page

★★★63% Larkfield Priory

London Rd, Larkfield ME20 6HJ
☎ 01732 846858 🖹 01732 846786
***Dir:** M20 junct 4 take A228 to W Malling at traffic lights turn left signposted to Maidstone (A20), after 1m hotel on left*

Built in 1890, this hotel has been extended and upgraded to provide good levels of comfort. Many of the bedrooms have been restyled to offer smart, bright accommodation. The restaurant has a conservatory annexe, and the lounge bar is a pleasant alternative for lighter meals and snacks.
ROOMS: 52 en suite No smoking in 24 bedrooms s fr £70; d fr £80 * LB **FACILITIES:** Xmas **CONF:** Thtr 80 Class 36 Board 30 Del £105 * **PARKING:** 80 **NOTES:** No smoking in restaurant
CARDS:

★★66% Grange Moor

St Michael's Rd ME16 8BS
☎ 01622 677623 🖹 01622 678246
e-mail: reservations@grangemoor.co.uk
***Dir:** off A26, Tonbridge Road. Church on lft, turn left hotel on right*
A friendly, family-run hotel just off the A26. Bedrooms, some in a nearby building, are well equipped and modern in style, though some have four-poster beds. The popular bar serves a good range of bar meals, there is a small lounge and several dining and function rooms.
ROOMS: 51 en suite (6 fmly) s £40-£48; d £50-£52 (incl. bkfst) * LB **CONF:** Thtr 100 Class 60 Board 40 Del £80 * **PARKING:** 60 **NOTES:** Closed last week Dec **CARDS:**

MALDON See Tolleshunt Knights

MALHAM, North Yorkshire Map 07 SD96

★★65% *The Buck Inn*
BD23 4DA
☎ 01729 830317 📠 01729 830670
***Dir:** from Skipton, take A65 to Gargrave, signposted in village centre, Malham is 7 miles further along*
In the centre of the village, this stone-built inn provides attractively furnished and decorated bedrooms. In addition to the menus offered in the comfortable dining room, a wide choice of homemade dishes is available in the two bars.
ROOMS: 10 en suite (2 fmly) **PARKING:** 20 **NOTES:** No dogs (ex guide dogs) **CARDS:**

MALMESBURY, Wiltshire Map 03 ST98

★★★74% *Old Bell*
Abbey Row SN16 0AG
☎ 01666 822344 📠 01666 825145
***Dir:** off A429, in centre of Malmesbury, adjacent to the Abbey*

This hotel is reputed to be the oldest in England. Many original features have been retained and are combined with modern facilities. There is a choice of comfortable lounges in which to relax. Bedrooms are varied in size and style, ranging from character rooms to stylish Japanese-inspired rooms.
ROOMS: 31 en suite (3 fmly) **FACILITIES:** STV **CONF:** Thtr 40 Class 20 Board 26 **PARKING:** 30 **NOTES:** No smoking in restaurant
CARDS:

See advert on this page

★★★67% Knoll House
Swindon Rd SN16 9LU
MINOTEL Great Britain
☎ 01666 823114 📠 01666 823897
e-mail: knollhotel@malmesbury64.freeserve.co.uk
***Dir:** from M4 junct 17 follow A429 towards Cirencester, at first rdbt after 5m turn right, 3rd exit. Hotel is on left at top of hill along B4042*

Well tended gardens surround this small hotel, just outside Malmesbury, with views over the Wiltshire countryside. Whether

continued on p370

M

MALMESBURY, continued

in the main house or separate wing, bedrooms are well decorated and fitted. There is a comfortable lounge and bar. The Restaurant menu offers modern European cuisine.
ROOMS: 12 en suite 10 annexe en suite (1 fmly) s fr £70; d fr £95 (incl. bkfst) * LB **FACILITIES:** Outdoor swimming (H) Croquet lawn Xmas **CONF:** Thtr 50 Board 30 Del £120 * **PARKING:** 40 **NOTES:** No smoking in restaurant **CARDS:**

★★ 74% Mayfield House

Crudwell SN16 9EW
☎ 01666 577409 & 577198 01666 577977
e-mail: mayfield@callnetuk.com
Dir: *3m N on A429*
The owners, together with their attentive team offer a warm welcome at this charming hotel on the edge of the Cotswolds. A loyal group of guests return regularly to enjoy the relaxed atmosphere and sample the food. There is a foyer lounge, a bar offering a wide range of dishes and a restaurant with an imaginative menu. Bedrooms, some on the ground floor, are all equipped with modern facilities.
ROOMS: 21 en suite 3 annexe en suite (2 fmly) s £54-£56; d £76-£78 (incl. bkfst) * LB **FACILITIES:** Xmas **CONF:** Thtr 40 Class 30 Board 25 Del from £84 * **PARKING:** 50 **NOTES:** No smoking in restaurant
CARDS:

See advert on opposite page

MALTON, North Yorkshire Map 08 SE77

★★★ 71% *Burythorpe House*

Burythorpe YO17 9LB
☎ 01653 658200 01653 658204
Dir: *4m S of Malton, just outside the village of Burythorpe and 4m from A64 York to Scarborough*
This charming house is set in its own grounds on the edge of a village south of Malton. Bedrooms are generally spacious and individually furnished with five rooms in a rear courtyard. There is a comfortable lounge with a conservatory off and a wood-panelled dining room.
ROOMS: 11 en suite 5 annexe en suite (2 fmly) **FACILITIES:** Indoor swimming (H) Tennis (hard) Snooker Sauna Solarium Gym
PARKING: 50 **NOTES:** No smoking in restaurant
CARDS:

★★★ 61% Green Man

15 Market St YO17 7LY
☎ 01653 600370 01653 696006
e-mail: greenman@englishrosehotels.co.uk
Dir: *from A64 follow signs fo Malton town centre, turn left into Market St, hotel on left*
This charming hotel set in the centre of town has an inviting reception lounge where a log fire burns in winter. There is a choice of bars and dining options, and bedrooms are thoughtfully equipped.
ROOMS: 24 en suite (4 fmly) s £30-£55; d £60-£90 (incl. bkfst) * LB **FACILITIES:** Xmas **CONF:** Thtr 40 Class 20 Board 40 Del from £55 * **PARKING:** 40 **NOTES:** No dogs (ex guide dogs) No smoking in restaurant **CARDS:**

See advert on opposite page

★★ 67% Talbot

Yorkersgate YO17 7AJ
☎ 01653 694031 01653 693355
Dir: *off A64 towards Malton. The Talbot is on the right*
This well established, ivy-clad hotel overlooks the River Derwent and open countryside and offers friendly and attentive service. Attractive bedrooms are well equipped, and day rooms are traditional and comfortable.
ROOMS: 31 en suite (3 fmly) s £40-£60.50; d £75-£110 (incl. bkfst) * LB **FACILITIES:** Xmas **CONF:** Thtr 80 Class 40 Board 40 **PARKING:** 30 **NOTES:** No dogs (ex guide dogs) No smoking in restaurant
CARDS:

See advert on opposite page

★ 63% Wentworth Arms

Town St, Old Malton YO17 7HD
☎ 01653 692618 01653 692618
Dir: *turn off A64 onto A169 to Malton. Hotel 400yds on right*
This friendly inn has a 'home from home' atmosphere and neatly maintained, comfortable bedrooms. Generous meals can be taken either in the dining room, with its exposed stone walls and old beams, or in the bar. The inn has been owned by the same family for many years.
ROOMS: 5 rms (4 en suite) s fr £23; d fr £46 (incl. bkfst) *
PARKING: 30 **NOTES:** No dogs No children 6yrs Closed 25 Dec
CARDS:

MALVERN, Worcestershire Map 03 SO74

★★★ 76% Colwall Park

Walwyn Rd, Colwall WR13 6QG
☎ 01684 540206 01684 540847
e-mail: hotel@colwall.com
Dir: *3m SW on B4218*
Colwall Park is situated in extensive gardens in the picturesque Malvern Hills. Originally built to serve the local railway station, the hotel now provides well equipped and smartly presented accommodation. Public rooms include the elegant Edwardian restaurant.
ROOMS: 23 en suite (6 fmly) No smoking in 2 bedrooms s £64.50-£70; d £105-£150 (incl. bkfst) * LB **FACILITIES:** STV Croquet lawn Boule entertainment Xmas **CONF:** Thtr 120 Class 80 Board 50 Del from £100 * **PARKING:** 40 **NOTES:** No smoking in restaurant
CARDS:

See advert on opposite page

★★★ 73% Cottage in the Wood

Holywell Rd, Malvern Wells WR14 4LG
☎ 01684 575859 01684 560662
e-mail: proprietor@thecottageinthewood.co.uk
Dir: *3m S of Great Malvern off A449 500yds N of B4209 turning on opposite side of road*

This delightful hotel enjoys magnificent views and was once the haunt of Sir Edward Elgar. The cosy bedrooms are divided between the main house, Beech Cottage and the Coach House; all are well equipped with lots of thoughtful extras. Day rooms feature real fires, deep-cushioned sofas and fresh flowers.

continued on p372

MALVERN, continued

ROOMS: 8 en suite 12 annexe en suite s £75-£85; d £89.50-£145 (incl. bkfst) * LB **FACILITIES:** Xmas **CONF:** Thtr 20 Board 14 Del from £135 * **PARKING:** 40 **NOTES:** No smoking in restaurant
CARDS:

See advert on opposite page

★★★70% Foley Arms
14 Worcester Rd WR14 4QS
☎ 01684 573397 01684 569665
e-mail: reservations@foleyarmshotel.com
Dir: *M5 exit 7 north or 8 south, M50 exit 1, proceed to Great Malvern on A449*

The oldest hotel in Malvern, the Foley Arms is situated in the heart of town overlooking the Severn Valley. The bedrooms are comfortable and tastefully decorated with period furnishings and modern facilities. Elgar's Restaurant serves fine food, and there is a popular bar and a choice of comfortable lounges.
ROOMS: 28 en suite (2 fmly) No smoking in 5 bedrooms s £72-£80; d £92-£140 (incl. bkfst) * LB **FACILITIES:** STV Free use of leisure centre pool, gym & sauna entertainment Xmas **CONF:** Thtr 150 Class 40 Board 45 Del from £95 * **PARKING:** 64 **NOTES:** No smoking in restaurant
CARDS:

See advert on opposite page

★★★64% Abbey
Abbey Rd WR14 3ET
☎ 01684 892332 01684 892662
e-mail: abbey@sarova.co.uk
Dir: *leave M5 junct7, take A449 into Malvern, left hand turn (by Barclays bank) into Church St, turn right at traffic lighs and first right into Abbey Rd*
This large, impressive hotel is in the centre of Great Malvern. It provides well equipped, modern accommodation. A popular venue for conferences, the hotel has a very good range of function rooms.
ROOMS: 105 en suite (5 fmly) No smoking in 24 bedrooms s £85; d £95 (incl. bkfst) * LB **FACILITIES:** STV Free entry to Malvern Leisure Complex Xmas **CONF:** Thtr 300 Class 140 Board 70 Del £115 * **SERVICES:** Lift **PARKING:** 90 **NOTES:** No smoking in restaurant Civ Wed 300 **CARDS:**

★★76% Holdfast Cottage
Little Malvern WR13 6NA
☎ 01684 310288 01684 311117
Dir: *on A4104 midway between Welland and Little Malvern*
This charming cottage lies in extensive grounds with impressive views of the Malvern Hills. Accommodation is full of charm and character, with all the expected comforts. A Victorian-style bar, a lounge and a dining room furnished in period make pleasant day rooms. The hotel has a well deserved reputation for its cuisine.

continued

ROOMS: 8 en suite (1 fmly) No smoking in all bedrooms s £48-£62; d £82-£90 (incl. bkfst) * LB **FACILITIES:** Croquet lawn **PARKING:** 15 **NOTES:** No smoking in restaurant Closed Xmas & 3 wks in Jan
CARDS:

See advert on opposite page

★★66% Cotford
51 Graham Rd WR14 2HU
☎ 01684 572427 01684 572952
Dir: *from Worcester follow signs to Malvern on A449. Left into Graham Rd signed town centre hotel on right*
This delightful house, built in 1851 for the Bishop of Worcester, stands in spacious gardens within easy reach of Malvern. All rooms are tastefully decorated with modern facilities. Additional features include a bar, a cosy lounge and a pleasant restaurant.
ROOMS: 17 en suite (4 fmly) s fr £50; d fr £70 (incl. bkfst) * LB **FACILITIES:** STV **CONF:** Thtr 26 Class 26 Del from £65 * **PARKING:** 18 **NOTES:** No smoking in restaurant
CARDS:

★★66% Great Malvern
Graham Rd WR14 2HN
☎ 01684 563411 01684 560514
e-mail: sutton@great-malvern-hotel.co.uk
Dir: *from Worcester on A449, turn left just beyond the fire station into Graham Rd. Hotel is at the end of Graham Rd on the right*
This town-centre hotel is close to many cultural and scenic attractions. Popular with both business and leisure travellers, the hotel features well equipped and comfortable accommodation, a busy bar, a brasserie and meeting rooms.
ROOMS: 14 rms (13 en suite) (3 fmly) s fr £55; d fr £80 (incl. bkfst) * LB **CONF:** Thtr 60 Class 20 Board 30 Del from £69.45 * **SERVICES:** Lift **PARKING:** 9 **NOTES:** No dogs (ex guide dogs) No smoking in restaurant **CARDS:**

★★66% Mount Pleasant
THE CIRCLE
Selected Individual Hotels
GREAT BRITAIN

Belle Vue Ter WR14 4PZ
☎ 01684 561837 01684 569968
Dir: *on A449, 0.5m from Great Malvern station*
This attractive Georgian house overlooks the picturesque Severn Valley and the Priory Church. Well presented bedrooms vary in style and provide comfortable accommodation. There is a quiet lounge for residents, a lounge bar and the pleasant Café el Sol restaurant, which doubles as a coffee shop during the day.

continued on p374

Cottage in the Wood, Malvern

MALVERN, continued

Mount Pleasant, Malvern

ROOMS: 15 rms (14 en suite) s £49.50-£58; d £76-£88 (incl. bkfst) * LB **CONF:** Thtr 80 Class 40 Board 45 Del from £80 * **PARKING:** 20 **NOTES:** No dogs (ex guide dogs) Closed 25 & 26 Dec
CARDS:

See advert on opposite page

★★63% The Malvern Hills
Wynds Point WR13 6DW
☎ 01684 540690 🖷 01684 540327
e-mail: malhilhotl@aol.com
Dir: *4m S, at junct of A449 with B4232*

This popular 19th-century hotel stands in the heart of the Malvern Hills. Bedrooms are spacious and comfortable with most enjoying pleasant views. Public rooms include an oak-panelled bar with open fire and a friendly restaurant.
ROOMS: 15 rms (14 en suite) (2 fmly) No smoking in 4 bedrooms s £40-£50; d £75-£85 (incl. bkfst) * LB **FACILITIES:** Pool table entertainment Xmas **CONF:** Thtr 40 Class 40 Board 30 Del from £58.50 * **PARKING:** 35 **NOTES:** No smoking in restaurant
CARDS:

MANCHESTER, Greater Manchester — Map 07 SJ89
see also Manchester Airport & Salford

★★★★75% Le Meridien Victoria & Albert
Water St M3 4JQ
☎ 0870 400 8585 🖷 0161 834 2484
e-mail: gm1452@forte-hotels.com
Dir: *M602 to A57 through lights on Regent Rd pass Sainsbury's then left at lights into Water St go over lights and hotel is on the left*
Created from former warehouses on the banks of the Irwell, opposite Granada Studios, this hotel provides bedrooms named after Granada productions. The interior features exposed brick walls, iron pillars and wooden beams. There is an all-day brasserie, Cafe Maigret, and a more formal restaurant.

continued

ROOMS: 156 en suite (2 fmly) No smoking in 60 bedrooms d fr £165 * LB **FACILITIES:** STV Access to Livingwell Health Club - 2 mins walk from Hotel entertainment ch fac Xmas **CONF:** Thtr 250 Class 120 Board 72 Del from £159 * **SERVICES:** Lift air con **PARKING:** 120 **NOTES:** No dogs (ex guide dogs) Civ Wed 200
CARDS:

See advert on opposite page

★★★★74% Crowne Plaza Manchester-The Midland
Peter St M60 2DS
☎ 0161 236 3333 🖷 0161 932 4100
e-mail: sales@mhccl.demon.co.uk
Dir: *M62 towards Liverpool junct 12 to M602 City Centre. Follow Granada Studios signs and turn left into Water St past studios hotels on right*
A touch of Edwardian elegance in the heart of the city. Day rooms have a classical feel, and well equipped bedrooms are generally spacious. The three restaurants include the bright simplicity of Nico Central (one Rosette) and The French, at which the accomplished cooking has earned three Rosettes.
ROOMS: 303 en suite (62 fmly) No smoking in 180 bedrooms **FACILITIES:** STV Indoor swimming (H) Squash Sauna Solarium Gym Jacuzzi/spa Hairdressing Beauty salon entertainment **CONF:** Thtr 500 Class 360 Board 40 **SERVICES:** Lift air con
CARDS:

★★★★71% Palace
Oxford St M60 7HA
☎ 0161 288 1111 🖷 0161 288 2222
Dir: *Hotel is adjacent to Palace Theatre on corner of Oxford St & Whitworth St and opposite Oxford Road railway station*
This striking Victorian building was once the headquarters of the Refuge Assurance Company, the grandeur of the age reflected in the brass and marble staircase, ornately tiled pillars and overall spaciousness. Bedrooms in the newer Excalibur wing display the highest levels of quality and comfort. The stylish dining room serves enjoyable meals.
ROOMS: 252 en suite (59 fmly) No smoking in 30 bedrooms d £110-£144 * LB **FACILITIES:** STV entertainment **CONF:** Thtr 1000 Class 450 Board 100 Del from £140 * **SERVICES:** Lift **NOTES:** No dogs (ex guide dogs) Civ Wed 100 **CARDS:**

See advert on opposite page

★★★★67% Marriott Manchester Hotel & Country Club
Worsley Park, Worsley M28 2QT
☎ 0161 975 2000 🖷 0161 799 6341
e-mail: worsleypark@cs.com
Dir: *leave junct 13 M60, go straight on at 1st rdbt take A575 hotel 400yds on left*

This new hotel was developed from an old farm and offers modern, attractively furnished accommodation while preserving

continued

some interesting original features. There are extensive indoor leisure facilities.
ROOMS: 159 en suite (5 fmly) No smoking in 116 bedrooms d £94-£109 * LB **FACILITIES:** STV Indoor swimming (H) Golf 18 Sauna Solarium Gym Putting green Jacuzzi/spa Steam room Health & Beauty salon Xmas **CONF:** Thtr 200 Class 150 Board 100 Del from £135 * **SERVICES:** Lift **PARKING:** 400 **NOTES:** No dogs (ex guide dogs) Civ Wed
CARDS:

★★★★66% Copthorne Manchester

Clippers Quay, Salford Quays M5 2XP
☎ 0161 873 7321 0161 873 7318
COPTHORNE
e-mail: manchester@mill-cop.com
Dir: *from M602 follow signs for Salford Quays/Trafford Park (A5063)-Trafford Road, hotel is 3/4 mile along road on right*
Situated within the redeveloped Salford Quays, this modern hotel is connected to the city by the Metro Link. Bedrooms are very well appointed especially the Connoisseur rooms, many of which overlook the quay. Comfortably furnished public areas include the formal Chandlers restaurant and the informal Clippers restaurant.
ROOMS: 166 en suite (6 fmly) No smoking in 80 bedrooms d £145-£170 * LB **FACILITIES:** STV Indoor swimming (H) Sauna Gym Jacuzzi/spa Steam room **CONF:** Thtr 150 Class 70 Board 70 Del from £123 * **SERVICES:** Lift **PARKING:** 120 **NOTES:** No dogs (ex guide dogs)
CARDS:

Late for dinner? Quality Standards star rating means that last orders for dinner should be no earlier than:
★ 6.30pm ★★ 7.00pm ★★★ 8.00pm
★★★★ 9.00pm ★★★★★ 10.00pm

MANCHESTER, continued

★★★74% Malmaison

Piccadilly M1 3AQ
☎ 0161 278 1000 🖷 0161 278 1002
e-mail: manchester@malmaison.com
Dir: *follow city centre then railway station, hotel opposite station*
The Malmaison brand is chic and modern with a refreshing style. Furnishings and decor are distinctively bold throughout. Smart bedrooms are a particular strength, and all have CD players. The busy bar and French-style brasserie are well worth a visit.
ROOMS: 112 en suite **FACILITIES:** STV Sauna Solarium Gym Jacuzzi/spa **CONF:** Thtr 40 Class 32 Board 25 **SERVICES:** Lift air con
CARDS:

★★★70% ❀❀ *Quality Hotel Manchester*

Waters Reach, Old Trafford M17 1NS
☎ 01765 658911 🖷 0161 872 6556
e-mail: info@qualitymanchester.co.uk

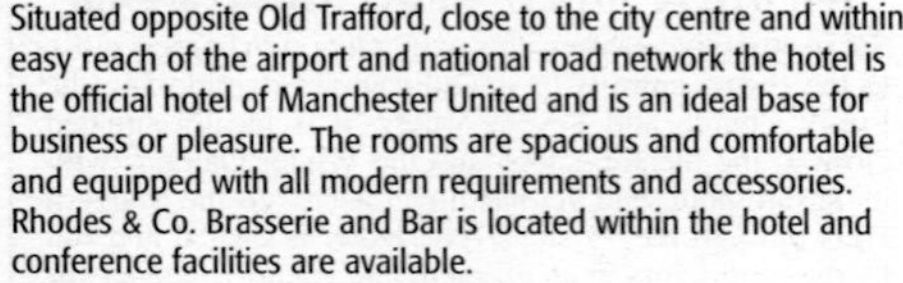

Situated opposite Old Trafford, close to the city centre and within easy reach of the airport and national road network the hotel is the official hotel of Manchester United and is an ideal base for business or pleasure. The rooms are spacious and comfortable and equipped with all modern requirements and accessories. Rhodes & Co. Brasserie and Bar is located within the hotel and conference facilities are available.
ROOMS: 111 en suite No smoking in 70 bedrooms

★★★67% Old Rectory Hotel

Meadow Ln, Haughton Green, Denton M34 7GD
☎ 0161 336 7516 🖷 0161 320 3212
e-mail: reservations@oldrectoryhotelmanchester.co.uk
This former Victorian rectory is peacefully situated and just a short drive from Manchester Airport. Bedrooms are very well appointed and staff throughout are friendly and helpful. There is a small enclosed garden, a games room and an attractively appointed restaurant with a good local reputation.
ROOMS: 30 en suite 6 annexe en suite (1 fmly) No smoking in 3 bedrooms s £62-£69; d £72-£79 (incl. bkfst) * LB **FACILITIES:** STV Pool table Games room Xmas **CONF:** Thtr 100 Class 45 Board 50 Del from £80 * **PARKING:** 50 **NOTES:** No smoking in restaurant
CARDS:

★★★66% Novotel

Worsley Brow M28 4YA
☎ 0161 799 3535 🖷 0161 703 8207
e-mail: h0907@accor-hotels.com
(For full entry see Worsley)

★★★64% *Posthouse Manchester*

Posthouse

Palatine Rd, Northenden M22 4FH
☎ 0870 400 9056 🖷 0161 946 0139
Dir: *at end of M56 follow B5166 Northenden right at lights Posthouse on left*
A modern hotel convenient for the city and the international airport. Services include an all-day lounge menu and 24-hour room service. Seasons Restaurant provides traditional British and international dishes. Many of the modern bedrooms enjoy panoramic views over the city and the hills beyond. Transport to the airport can be arranged.
ROOMS: 190 en suite (5 fmly) No smoking in 67 bedrooms **FACILITIES:** Free admittance to local Leisure Centre **CONF:** Thtr 120 Class 60 Board 80 **SERVICES:** Lift **PARKING:** 370 **NOTES:** Closed 22 Dec-5 Jan **CARDS:**

★★★64% Waterside

Wilmslow Rd, Didsbury M20 5WZ
☎ 0161 445 0225 🖷 0161 446 2090
e-mail: office@watersidehotel.co.uk
Dir: *M60 junct 3, A34 Disbury, at 3rd set of lights turn left, then left again on B5095 towards Cheadle. Hotel 2nd turning on right*
Conveniently situated for both the motorway network and the city centre, this modern hotel has a well equipped leisure centre. The brasserie and adjacent café bar, overlooking the river, offer a wide choice of meals and snacks.
ROOMS: 46 en suite (1 fmly) No smoking in 18 bedrooms s £79-£89; d £96-£106 * **FACILITIES:** STV Indoor swimming (H) Tennis (hard) Sauna Solarium Gym Jacuzzi/spa Beauty salon Xmas **CONF:** Thtr 160 Class 90 Board 56 Del from £125 * **PARKING:** 250 **NOTES:** No dogs (ex guide dogs) **CARDS:**

★★★60% Trafford Hall

23 Talbot Rd, Old Trafford M16 0PE
☎ 0161 848 7791 🖷 0161 848 0219
e-mail: info@traffordhallhotel.co.uk
Dir: *heading towards Manchester, turn off A56 onto Talbot Road. Continue until Old Trafford Cricket Ground & hotel is 700yds further on right hand side*
A Victorian building retaining some original features, including a splendid central staircase. The hotel is conveniently located for the city and Old Trafford. Spacious bedrooms are well equipped and a number are suitable for families.
ROOMS: 31 en suite 3 annexe en suite (7 fmly) s £39.50-£47.50; d £59.50-£63.50 * LB **FACILITIES:** STV Pool table **CONF:** Thtr 40 Class 20 Board 20 **PARKING:** 60 **NOTES:** No dogs (ex guide dogs)
CARDS:

★★68% *Chester Court*

728-730 Chester Rd, Old Trafford M32 0RS
☎ 0161 877 5375 🖷 0161 877 5431
e-mail: chestercourthotel@btinternet.com
Dir: *on A56 immediately in front of Manchester United football ground*
This prominently located hotel is close to Manchester United football ground and Lancashire Cricket Club. Bedrooms are tastefully decorated and all very well equipped. There is an attractive, comfortable bar and a wide range of meals is available in the elegant dining room.
ROOMS: 23 en suite No smoking in 9 bedrooms **FACILITIES:** STV **SERVICES:** Lift **NOTES:** No dogs (ex guide dogs)
CARDS:

★★65% Albany

21 Albany Rd, Chorlton-c-Hardy M21 0AY
☎ 0161 881 6774 🖷 0161 862 9405
Dir: *turn off A5103 onto A6010 follow for approx 1m turn right at Safeways store into Albany Road, hotel 100mtrs on left*

This small, early Victorian property has a very good reputation for its friendly hospitality and attractively appointed rooms. Traditional

continued

English cuisine is served in the elegant restaurant, next to the cosy bar and comfortable lounge. The hotel is tastefully decorated in period style throughout with all modern amenities.
ROOMS: 2 en suite 15 annexe rms (13 en suite) (4 fmly) s £39.50-£79.50; d £69.50-£89.50 (incl. bkfst) * **FACILITIES:** Pool table **CONF:** Thtr 40 Class 20 Board 25 Del from £65 * **PARKING:** 5 **NOTES:** RS 25 Dec-2 Jan **CARDS:**

★★64% Comfort Friendly Inn

Hyde Rd, Birch St, West Gorton M12 5NT
☎ 0161 220 8700 📠 0161 220 8848
e-mail: admin@gb615.u-net.com
Dir: *3m SE on A57*

A warm welcome is offered by the friendly and attentive staff of this hotel, just 3 miles from the city centre. The modest yet practical bedrooms offer value-for-money accommodation and every modern facility. Public areas include a lounge bar and attractive restaurant serving good value meals.
ROOMS: 90 en suite (5 fmly) No smoking in 45 bedrooms d £47.75 * LB **FACILITIES:** STV Gym entertainment Xmas **CONF:** Thtr 100 Class 50 Board 50 Del from £75 * **PARKING:** 70 **NOTES:** No smoking in restaurant **CARDS:**

★★64% Willow Bank

340-342 Wilmslow Rd, Fallowfield M14 6AF
☎ 0161 224 0461 📠 0161 257 2561
e-mail: reservations@willowbankhotel.co.uk
Dir: *situated 3m S of Manchester City Centre on B5093*

A conveniently located hotel, just three miles from the city centre and close to the universities. At the time of our last inspection, the hotel was undergoing a major refurbishment programme to upgrade bedrooms to an attractive new standard and to improve the restaurant and public areas.
ROOMS: 117 en suite (4 fmly) s fr £50; d fr £70 (incl. bkfst) * LB **FACILITIES:** entertainment Xmas **CONF:** Thtr 50 Class 28 Board 28 Del from £65 * **PARKING:** 100 **NOTES:** No dogs (ex guide dogs) **CARDS:**

★★62% Royals

Altrincham Rd M22 4BJ
☎ 0161 998 9011 📠 0161 998 4641
Dir: *head for Manchester International Airport, take junct 3a signposted A560*

Conveniently situated for the city and motorway, this hotel offers parking for guests using Manchester International Airport. The bedrooms vary in size and standard, and the conservatory restaurant is an informal dining venue. The bar is bright and inviting.
ROOMS: 32 en suite (6 fmly) No smoking in 6 bedrooms s £55-£65; d £68-£76 (incl. bkfst) * LB **FACILITIES:** Childrens Dungeons and Dragons play centre entertainment Xmas **CONF:** Thtr 100 Class 50 Board 40 Del from £70 * **PARKING:** 150 **NOTES:** No dogs (ex guide dogs) Civ Wed 100 **CARDS:**

⌂ Express by Holiday Inn Manchester

Express by Holiday Inn

Waterfront Quay, Salford Quays M5 2XW
☎ 0161 868 1000 📠 868 1068
Dir: *from M62 take M602 to Manchester. End of M602 take left lane towards A5063 Trafford Park. At 2nd t/lights on A5063 turn right. Hotel straight ahead*

A modern budget hotel offering comfortable accommodation in refreshing, spacious and comprehensively-equipped bedrooms, en suite bathrooms with power showers and continental buffet breakfast included in the room rate. Suitable for business travellers or families. For further details and the Express by Holiday Inn phone number, consult the Hotel Groups page.

ROOMS: 120 en suite (incl. cont bkfst) d £36.50-£56 * **CONF:** Thtr 25 Class 15 Board 10

⌂ Express by Holiday Inn Manchester East

Express by Holiday Inn

Debdale Park, Hyde Rd M18 7LS

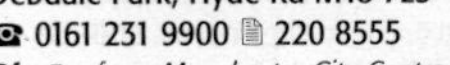

☎ 0161 231 9900 📠 220 8555
Dir: *3m from Manchester City Centre on left hand side of A57 at Debdale Park*

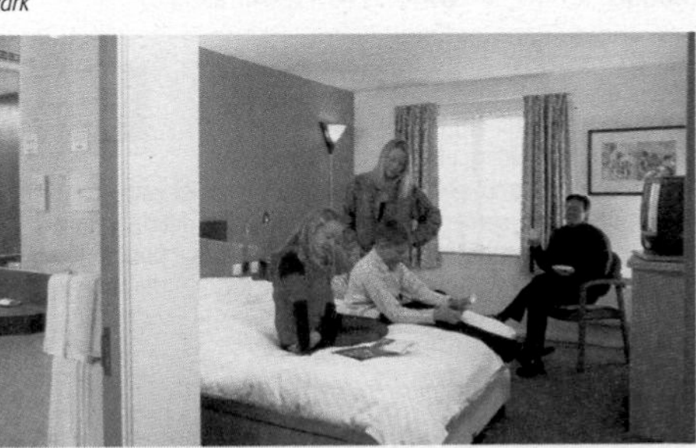

A modern budget hotel offering comfortable accommodation in refreshing, spacious and comprehensively-equipped bedrooms, en suite bathrooms with power showers and continental buffet breakfast included in the room rate. Suitable for business travellers or families. For further details and the Express by Holiday Inn phone number, consult the Hotel Groups page.
ROOMS: 97 en suite (incl. cont bkfst) d £52.50-£56 * **CONF:** Thtr 35 Class 15 Board 20

⌂ Premier Lodge (City Centre GMEX)

PREMIER LODGE
THE BEST. REST ASSURED.

7-11 Lower Mosley St M2 3DW
☎ 0870 700 1476 📠 0870 700 1477

Premier Lodge offers modern, well equipped, en suite accommodation suitable for both business and leisure travellers. Meals can be taken at the adjacent popular restaurant and bar which is fully licensed. For further details, consult the Hotel Groups page.
ROOMS: 147 en suite d £46 *

> Popped the question? Hotels with Civ Wed in their entry are licensed for civil wedding ceremonies. Maximum numbers for the ceremony only are shown, e.g. Civ Wed 50

M

MANCHESTER, continued

⇧ Campanile

55 Ordsall Ln, Salford M5 4RS
☎ 0161 833 1845 🖷 0161 833 1847
Dir: *take M602 towards Manchester, then A57, after large rdbt Sainsbury's on left turn left at next traffic lights, hotel on right*

This modern building offers accommodation in smart well equipped bedrooms, all with en suite bathrooms. Refreshments may be taken at the informal Bistro. For further details and the Campanile phone number, consult the Hotel Groups page.
ROOMS: 105 en suite **CONF:** Thtr 50 Class 40 Board 30

⇧ *Travelodge*

Townbury House, Blackfriars St
☎ 0800 850950
This modern building offers accommodation in smart, spacious and well equipped bedrooms, all with en suite bathrooms. Refreshments may be taken at the nearby family restaurant. For further details and the Travelodge phone number, consult the Hotel Groups page.

○ Manchester Conference Centre

Weston Building M1 3BB
☎ 0161 955 8000
NOTES: Open

○ *Premier Lodge (City South)*

Gaythorne, River St M15 5JF
☎ 0870 700 1490 🖷 0870 700 1491

○ *Premier Lodge (Manchester City Centre)*

North Tower, Victoria Bridge St, Salford M3 5AS
☎ 0870 700 1488 🖷 0870 700 1489

MANCHESTER AIRPORT, Greater Manchester Map 07 SJ88
see also Altrincham

★★★★68% ❀❀ Radisson SAS Hotel Manchester Airport

Chicago Av M90 3RA
☎ 0161 490 5000 🖷 0161 490 5100
e-mail: sales@manzq.rdscs.com
Dir: *from M56 junct 5, follow signs for Airport Terminal 2. At rdbt, take 2nd left and follow signs for railway station. Hotel next to station*
This hotel offers an excellent range of facilities for the travelling guest. The soundproofed building encompasses a central atrium, off which lead extensive meeting and leisure facilities, as well as the main eateries. The superbly designed, air-conditioned bedrooms are equipped with every extra.

continued

ROOMS: 360 en suite No smoking in 220 bedrooms s £155; d £170 * LB **FACILITIES:** STV Indoor swimming (H) Sauna Solarium Gym Steam room Xmas **CONF:** Thtr 350 Class 180 Board 50 Del from £150 * **SERVICES:** Lift air con **PARKING:** 150 **NOTES:** No dogs (ex guide dogs) **CARDS:**

See advert on opposite page

★★★★65% ❀ Belfry

Stanley Rd SK9 3LD
☎ 0161 437 0511 🖷 0161 499 0597
Dir: *off A34, approx 4m S of junct 3 M60*
Belfry House offers high standards of service and hospitality. A new café-bar has opened, serving light meals during the day and evening. Bedrooms are well equipped and traditionally furnished. There are conference and function facilities.
ROOMS: 80 en suite (2 fmly) No smoking in 40 bedrooms s £85-£95; d £96-£106 * LB **FACILITIES:** STV entertainment ch fac Xmas **CONF:** Thtr 120 Class 70 Board 50 Del from £120 * **SERVICES:** Lift **PARKING:** 150 **NOTES:** No dogs (ex guide dogs) Civ Wed 60 **CARDS:**

★★★★64% Swallow Four Seasons

Hale Rd, Hale Barns WA15 8XW
☎ 0161 904 0301 🖷 0161 980 1787
e-mail: info@swallowhotels.com
A modern hotel with good airport links, noteworthy leisure and business facilities and secure parking arrangements. Bedrooms are situated around open courtyards and offer comfortable acommodation. There is a good choice of bars and restaurants.
ROOMS: 147 en suite (16 fmly) No smoking in 64 bedrooms s £105-£250; d fr £120 * LB **FACILITIES:** STV Indoor swimming (H) Sauna Gym Jacuzzi/spa **CONF:** Thtr 200 Class 90 Board 50 Del from £99 * **SERVICES:** Lift **PARKING:** 480 **NOTES:** No dogs (ex guide dogs) Civ Wed 100 **CARDS:**

★★★73% ❀ Etrop Grange

Thorley Ln M90 4EG
☎ 0161 499 0500 🖷 0161 499 0790
e-mail: etropgrange@corushotels.com
Dir: *M56 junct 5 follow signs for terminal 2, go up slip rd to rdbt take 1st exit, take immediate left, hotel is 400yds ahead*

This impressive Georgian country house-style hotel is close to the airport but noise is minimal. Smart bedrooms offer all modern comforts. Some have four-poster beds, others have iron bedsteads and two have sitting rooms. Comfortable, elegant day rooms include the Coach House Restaurant, serving a high standard of cuisine. A chauffeured limousine is available for airport passengers.
ROOMS: 64 en suite No smoking in 10 bedrooms s £70-£125; d £90-£145 * LB **FACILITIES:** STV **CONF:** Thtr 80 Class 30 Board 36 Del from £105 * **PARKING:** 80 **NOTES:** No smoking in restaurant Civ Wed 90 **CARDS:**

★★★ 73% ❀❀ Stanneylands
Stanneylands Rd SK9 4EY
☎ 01625 525225 🖷 01625 537282
e-mail: reservations@stanneylands.co.uk
Dir: *leave M56 at Airport turn off, follow signs to Wilmslow, turn left into Station Rd, onto Stanneylands Rd, hotel is on the right*
This privately-owned hotel stands in delightful grounds. Public rooms feature fine wood panelling and real fires. Bedrooms, which vary in style, are attractively presented and well equipped. The cuisine on offer in the restaurant is of a high standard and ranges from traditional favourites to more imaginative contemporary dishes.
ROOMS: 31 en suite (2 fmly) No smoking in 10 bedrooms s £88; d £98-£118 * LB **FACILITIES:** STV entertainment **CONF:** Thtr 100 Class 50 Board 40 Del from £135 * **PARKING:** 80 **NOTES:** No dogs (ex guide dogs) Civ Wed 80 **CARDS:**

See advert on this page

★★★ 66% *Posthouse Manchester Airport*
Ringway Rd, Wythenshawe M90 3NS
Posthouse
☎ 0870 400 9055 🖷 0161 436 2340
A large, modern hotel set within the airport complex, providing transport to the various terminals. Modern bedrooms include several in the new Millennium design. Gazingi's Brasserie offers a varied menu and the Expresso lounge is open during the day. An all-day lounge menu and 24-hour room service are available.
ROOMS: 290 en suite (6 fmly) No smoking in 80 bedrooms **FACILITIES:** STV Indoor swimming (H) Sauna Solarium Gym Health & fitness centre **CONF:** Thtr 80 Class 26 Board 30 **SERVICES:** Lift air con **PARKING:** 290 **CARDS:**

M

MANCHESTER AIRPORT, continued

Premier Lodge (Manchester Airport)
30 Wilmslow Rd SK9 3EW
☎ 0870 700 1488 Fax 0870 700 1487
Premier Lodge offers modern, well equipped, en suite accommodation suitable for both business and leisure travellers. Meals can be taken at the adjacent popular restaurant and bar which is fully licensed. For further details, consult the Hotel Groups page.
ROOMS: 35 en suite d £46 *

MANSFIELD, Nottinghamshire Map 08 SK56

★★66% Pine Lodge
281-283 Nottingham Rd NG18 4SE
☎ 01623 622308 Fax 01623 656819
e-mail: plhotel@aol.com
Dir: *on A60 Nottingham to Mansfield road*
Located on the edge of Mansfield, this hotel offers welcoming and personal service to its many repeat guests. Day rooms include a comfortable lounge bar, a small restaurant and a choice of meeting and function rooms. Bedrooms are attractively furnished.
ROOMS: 20 en suite (2 fmly) s £35-£55; d £50-£65 (incl. bkfst) * LB **FACILITIES:** STV Sauna **CONF:** Thtr 50 Class 30 Board 35 **PARKING:** 40 **NOTES:** No dogs No smoking in restaurant Closed 25-26 Dec **CARDS:**

★★63% Portland Hall
Carr Bank Park, Windmill Ln NG18 2AL
☎ 01623 452525 Fax 01623 452550
Dir: *from town centre take A60 towards Worksop for 100yds then right at Pelican Crossing into Nursery Street - Carr Bank Park 50yds on right*
Portland Hall, a former Georgian mansion, sits in 15 acres of parkland. The house retains some fine examples of its past, with original plasterwork and friezes in the cosy lounge bar, and around the magnificent domed skylight over the spiral stairs. There is an attractive restaurant in which carvery and carte menus offer a flexible choice to diners.
ROOMS: 11 en suite (1 fmly) No smoking in 7 bedrooms s £50-£55; d £60-£65 (incl. bkfst) * LB **FACILITIES:** Bowls entertainment Xmas **CONF:** Thtr 60 Class 60 Board 30 Del from £50 * **PARKING:** 150 **NOTES:** No smoking in restaurant Civ Wed 150 **CARDS:**

M

MARAZION, Cornwall & Isles of Scilly Map 02 SW53

★★72% Mount Haven
Turnpike Rd TR17 0DQ
☎ 01736 710249 Fax 01736 711658
e-mail: mounthaven@compuserve.com
Dir: *approaching Penzance from A30 (E), at rdbt take Helston exit (A394). At next rdbt take right hand exit into Marazion, Hotel on left*

continued

A former coaching inn set on the outskirts of Marazion offering bright and cheerful bedrooms with modern facilities. Those at the front enjoy views of St Michael's Mount. The split-level restaurant serves a fixed-price menu and a short carte.
ROOMS: 17 en suite (5 fmly) s £41-£62; d £74-£86 (incl. bkfst) * LB **PARKING:** 30 **NOTES:** No smoking in restaurant Closed 15 Dec-31 Jan RS Oct-May **CARDS:**

See advert under PENZANCE

★★69% Godolphin Arms
TR17 0EN
☎ 01736 710202 Fax 01736 710171
e-mail: enquires@godolphinarms.co.uk
Dir: *from A30 follow Marazion signs for 1m to hotel at the end of the causeway to St Michael's Mount*
This 170-year-old waterside hotel is in a prime location. Stunning views of St Michael's Mount provide a backdrop for the restaurant and lounge bar. Bedrooms are colourful, comfortable and spacious. A choice of menu is offered in the main restaurant and the Gig Bar, with an emphasis on local seafood.
ROOMS: 10 en suite (2 fmly) s £37.50-£55; d £90 (incl. bkfst) * LB **FACILITIES:** STV entertainment **PARKING:** 48 **NOTES:** No smoking in restaurant **CARDS:**

See advert under PENZANCE

MARCH, Cambridgeshire Map 05 TL49

★★64% Olde Griffin
High St PE15 9JS
☎ 01354 652517 Fax 01354 650086
Dir: *March is on A141/142 north of Ely Cambs and off A47 east of Peterborough towards Norwich*
Situated overlooking the town square, this former coaching inn dates back to the 16th century. Bedrooms vary in size and style and all are fully equipped with creature comforts. Meals are available in the lounge and bar areas and there is a restaurant for more formal dining.
ROOMS: 20 rms (19 en suite) (1 fmly) s £45; d £59.50-£92.50 (incl. bkfst) * LB **CONF:** Thtr 100 Class 50 Board 36 **PARKING:** 50 **NOTES:** No dogs (ex guide dogs) **CARDS:**

MARKET DRAYTON, Shropshire Map 07 SJ63

★★★72% Goldstone Hall
Goldstone TF9 2NA
☎ 01630 661202 & 661487 Fax 01630 661585
e-mail: enquiries@GoldstoneHall.com
Dir: *4m S of Market Drayton off A529 signposted Goldstone Hall Gardens. 4m N of Newport signed off A41*
Situated in extensive grounds, this charming old house is now a family-run hotel. It provides traditionally furnished, well equipped accommodation. Public rooms include a choice of lounges, a snooker room and a conservatory. The hotel has a well deserved reputation for good food.
ROOMS: 8 en suite s fr £65; d £87.50-£100 (incl. bkfst) * LB **FACILITIES:** Fishing Snooker **CONF:** Thtr 50 Board 30 Del from £95 * **PARKING:** 60 **NOTES:** No dogs (ex guide dogs) Civ Wed 60 **CARDS:**

★★68% Rosehill Manor
Rosehill, Ternhill TF9 2JF
☎ 01630 638532 Fax 01630 637008
Dir: *from the rdbt at Ternhill A53/41 head towards Newport or M54 hotel 2m on right*
Parts of this charming, privately-owned house set in mature gardens date back to the 16th century. The well equipped

continued

accommodation includes family rooms. Public areas comprise a pleasant restaurant, a bar and a comfortable lounge, where a welcoming stove is lit in cold weather. The hotel has a well deserved reputation for its food.
ROOMS: 9 en suite s fr £50; d fr £70 (incl. bkfst) * LB **PARKING:** 80
NOTES: No smoking in restaurant Civ Wed 90
CARDS:

MARKET HARBOROUGH, Leicestershire Map 04 SP78

★★★72% Three Swans

21 High St LE16 7NJ
☎ 01858 466644 🖹 01858 433101
e-mail: sales@threeswans.co.uk
Dir: *at junct 20 take A4304 to Market Harborough. Passing through town centre on A6, the Hotel is on right*
This former coaching inn has been refurbished and extended to improve guests' comfort. Bold, warm colour schemes are used throughout the bars, reception and lounge area. The formal restaurant serves good food in a professional, attentive manner. A new bedroom wing houses modern executive rooms, which are well equipped and comfortably appointed.
ROOMS: 18 en suite 31 annexe en suite (7 fmly) No smoking in 20 bedrooms s £75-£85; d £85-£115 (incl. bkfst) * LB **FACILITIES:** STV **CONF:** Thtr 100 Class 60 Board 50 Del from £108 * **SERVICES:** Lift **PARKING:** 100 **NOTES:** No dogs (ex guide dogs) No smoking in restaurant Civ Wed 200 **CARDS:**

Best Western

★★★67% Menzies Angel

37 High St LE16 7NL
☎ 0500 636943 (Central Res) 🖹 01773 880321
e-mail: info@menzies-hotels.co.uk
Dir: *on A6*
A former coaching inn on the town's main street. The comfortably furnished public rooms are cheerful and decorative. Bedroom styles and sizes vary, but all rooms have a useful range of facilities. The newer bedrooms are particularly appealing and comfortably appointed.
ROOMS: 37 en suite s £75-£85; d £85-£105 * LB
FACILITIES: Jacuzzi/spa Xmas **CONF:** Thtr 24 Class 12 Board 14 Del from £75 * **PARKING:** 30 **NOTES:** No smoking in restaurant Civ Wed 75 **CARDS:**

MENZIES HOTELS

MARKET WEIGHTON, East Riding of Yorkshire Map 08 SE84

★★★68% *Londesborough Arms Hotel*

High St YO43 3AH
☎ 01430 872214 🖹 01430 872219
Dir: *Follow signs into Market Weighton from Shiptonthorpe rdbt at intersection of A1079 & A614, hotel on north side of High St, next to All Saints Church*
Carefully restored, this Georgian hotel in the town centre features high standards of interior design. The thoughtfully equipped bedrooms are spacious by design and include several regal four-posters. Lounges are comfortable.
ROOMS: 19 en suite **CONF:** Thtr 100 Class 100 Board 50 **PARKING:** 25
CARDS:

MARKFIELD, Leicestershire Map 08 SK41

⌂ *Travelodge*

Littleshaw Ln LE67 0PP
☎ Central Res 0800 850950
Dir: *on A50 fom junct22 with M1*
This modern building offers accommodation in smart, spacious and well equipped bedrooms, all with en suite bathrooms.

Travelodge

Refreshments may be taken at the nearby family restaurant. For further details and the Travelodge phone number, consult the Hotel Groups page.
ROOMS: 40 en suite

MARKHAM MOOR, Nottinghamshire Map 08 SK77

⌂ *Travelodge*

DN22 0QU
☎ 01777 838091 🖹 01777 838091
Dir: *on A1 northbound*
This modern building offers accommodation in smart, spacious and well equipped bedrooms, all with en suite bathrooms. Refreshments may be taken at the nearby family restaurant. For further details and the Travelodge phone number, consult the Hotel Groups page.
ROOMS: 40 en suite

Travelodge

MARKINGTON, North Yorkshire Map 08 SE26

★★★76% Hob Green

HG3 3PJ
☎ 01423 770031 🖹 01423 771589
Dir: *exit A61 4m after Harrogate and turn left at Wormald Green and follow brown hotel signs*
A charming 18th-century country house hotel set amidst 800 acres of beautiful rolling countryside, not far from Harrogate and Ripon. Comfortable lounges have open fires in winter. Bedrooms are furnished with antiques and retain many original features. The restaurant enjoys a fine reputation. Staff are friendly and helpful.
ROOMS: 12 en suite **FACILITIES:** Croquet lawn **PARKING:** 40
CARDS:

Best Western

See advert under HARROGATE

MARLBOROUGH, Wiltshire Map 04 SU16

★★★72% ❀❀ Ivy House Hotel

High St SN8 1HJ
☎ 01672 515333 🖷 01672 515338
e-mail: ivyhouse@btconnect.com
Dir: *M4 junct 15 take A346 to Marlborough, hotel is situated on High St*

A grade II listed Georgian property, built for the Earl of Aylesbury in 1707. The well equipped bedrooms are individually decorated. Facilities include the Beeches conference suite, lounges and the elegant Scott's restaurant, serving both fixed price and carte menus, offering a mix of traditional and more contemporary cuisine.

ROOMS: 28 en suite (3 fmly) No smoking in 21 bedrooms s £69-£85; d £84-£110 (incl. bkfst) * LB **FACILITIES:** STV Xmas **CONF:** Thtr 100 Class 40 Board 30 Del from £115 * **PARKING:** 36 **NOTES:** No dogs (ex guide dogs) No smoking in restaurant **CARDS:**

See advert on page 381

★★★61% The Castle & Ball

High St SN8 1LZ
☎ 01672 515201 🖷 01672 515895
Dir: *both the A338 and A4 lead into Marlborough and eventually into the High St*

This traditional town-centre coaching inn is right in the centre of Marlborough market square. The open-plan lounge and bar is a popular meeting place for locals and guests. Meeting rooms have been upgraded and bedrooms are spacious.

ROOMS: 34 en suite (1 fmly) No smoking in 13 bedrooms s fr £59; d fr £65 * LB **FACILITIES:** STV Xmas **CONF:** Thtr 45 Class 20 Board 30 **PARKING:** 48 **NOTES:** No smoking in restaurant
CARDS:

MARLOW, Buckinghamshire Map 04 SU88

★★★★75% ❀❀ Danesfield House

Henley Rd SL7 2EY
☎ 01628 891010 🖷 01628 890408
e-mail: sales@danesfieldhouse.co.uk
Dir: *2m from Marlow on A4155 towards Henley*

This impressive hotel boasts sixty five acres of mature landscaped grounds. Bedrooms are spacious, furnished and decorated to a high standard and boast a comprehensive range of facilities. The public areas are no less impressive, the Great Hall is almost Cathedral-like and the panelled Oak Room Restaurant is a good setting for more formal dining. The Orangery Restaurant, offers a less formal dining option with lovely views over the Thames.

continued

ROOMS: 87 en suite (3 fmly) No smoking in 5 bedrooms s £145-£155; d £185-£250 (incl. bkfst) * LB **FACILITIES:** STV Outdoor swimming (H) Tennis (hard) Snooker Croquet lawn Putting green Jacuzzi/spa Jogging trail entertainment Xmas **CONF:** Thtr 80 Class 60 Board 65 Del from £245 * **SERVICES:** Lift **PARKING:** 100 **NOTES:** No dogs (ex guide dogs) No smoking in restaurant Civ Wed 170
CARDS:

See advert on opposite page

★★★★73% ❀❀ The Compleat Angler

Marlow Bridge SL7 1RG
☎ 0870 400 8100 🖷 01628 486388
Dir: *from M40 junct 4 follow A404 to Bisham rdbt, right through Bisham Village. Hotel is on right before Marlow Bridge*

Enjoying an enviable position on the Thames overlooking Marlow Weir, this internationally famous hotel has kept a very pleasing and traditional atmosphere. Bedrooms, suites and public rooms are all very smartly appointed. The Riverside Restaurant serves award-winning cuisine.

ROOMS: 65 en suite (20 fmly) No smoking in 24 bedrooms s £205-£240; d £225-£260 * LB **FACILITIES:** STV Fishing Croquet lawn Boating entertainment Xmas **CONF:** Thtr 120 Class 60 Board 45 Del £233.82 * **SERVICES:** Lift **PARKING:** 100 **NOTES:** Civ Wed
CARDS:

See advert on opposite page

MARPLE, Greater Manchester Map 07 SJ98

★★70% Springfield

Station Rd SK6 6PA
☎ 0161 449 0721 🖷 0161 449 0766
Dir: *beside A626*

This well maintained hotel is on the edge of the Peak District, conveniently placed for both Stockport and Manchester. It offers comfortable and well equipped bedrooms. There are two lounges and a Victorian-style dining room serving good home-cooked dinners.

ROOMS: 8 en suite No smoking in 7 bedrooms s fr £40; d fr £55 (incl. bkfst) * LB **FACILITIES:** STV **PARKING:** 10 **NOTES:** No dogs (ex guide dogs) No children 6yrs No smoking in restaurant **CARDS:**

MARSTON MORETAINE, Bedfordshire Map 04 SP94

⌂ *Travelodge*

Travelodge

Beancroft Rd Junction MK43 0PZ
☎ 01234 766755 🖷 01234 766755
Dir: *on A421, northbound*

This modern building offers accommodation in smart, spacious and well equipped bedrooms, all with en suite bathrooms. Refreshments may be taken at the nearby family restaurant. For further details and the Travelodge phone number, consult the Hotel Groups page.

ROOMS: 32 en suite

MARSTON TRUSSELL, Northamptonshire Map 04 SP68

★★66% The Sun Inn
Main St LE16 9TY
☎ 01858 465531 01858 433155
e-mail: manager@suninn.com
Dir: *from M1 junct 20 take A4304. After Theddingworth, right to Marston Trussell (looks like a layby). Hotel on right of Main St*

This pleasant inn successfully combines a mixture of modern facilities and accommodation with the classical traditions of the rural English inn. There are two separate dining areas, including a popular restaurant, and a locally popular bar. Bedrooms are comfortable and well appointed.

ROOMS: 20 en suite (3 fmly) s fr £59; d fr £69 (incl. bkfst) * LB
FACILITIES: Fishing Xmas **CONF:** Thtr 60 Class 40 Board 28
PARKING: 60 **CARDS:**

MARTINHOE, Devon Map 03 SS64

★★73% Old Rectory
EX31 4QT
☎ 01598 763368 01598 763567
e-mail: reception@oldrectoryhotel.co.uk
Dir: *exit M5 jcnct 27 onto A361, right onto A399 Blackmoor Gate, right onto A39 bypass Parracombe, take 2nd left to Martinhoe & follow signs*

An ideal base for exploring Exmoor, within 500 yards of the coastal footpath. In addition to the comfortable lounge, guests can relax in the vinery, overlooking the delightful gardens. Interesting menus are served in the spacious dining room. Each bedroom is tastefully decorated, two are on the ground floor and there are also two self-catering cottages.

ROOMS: 9 en suite No smoking in all bedrooms s £79; d £138 (incl. bkfst & dinner) * LB **PARKING:** 10 **NOTES:** No dogs No children 14yrs No smoking in restaurant Closed Dec-Feb RS March & November (weekends only) **CARDS:**

MARTOCK, Somerset Map 03 ST41

★★★70% The Hollies
Bower Hinton TA12 6LG
☎ 01935 822232 01935 822249
e-mail: thehollieshotel@ukonline.co.uk
Dir: *on B3165 S of town centre just off A303*

Within easy access of the A303, the bar and restaurant of this popular venue are housed in an attractive 17th-century farmhouse. Located at the rear of the property in a purpose-built wing, the spacious, well equipped bedrooms include both suites and mini-suites. Bar meals are available in addition to the interesting carte menu.

ROOMS: 32 annexe en suite (2 fmly) No smoking in 4 bedrooms s £67.50-£90; d £85-£110 (incl. bkfst) * LB **FACILITIES:** STV
CONF: Thtr 150 Class 80 Board 60 Del from £103.99 * **PARKING:** 80
NOTES: No dogs (ex guide dogs) No smoking in restaurant RS Xmas & New Year **CARDS:**

MASHAM, North Yorkshire Map 08 SE28

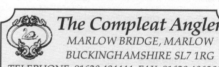

★★60% The Kings Head
Market Place HG4 4EF
☎ 01765 689295 01765 689070
Dir: *off the A6108 Ripon to Leyburn Rd in centre of village*

This historic, stone-built hotel, with its uneven floors, beamed bars and attractive window boxes, looks out over the large market square. Bedrooms are well decorated and comfortable, the bar is full of character and there is good food in the separate restaurant.

ROOMS: 10 en suite **CONF:** Thtr 40 Class 20 Board 20 **NOTES:** No dogs (ex guide dogs) **CARDS:**

MATFEN, Northumberland Map 12 NZ07

★★★70% Matfen Hall

NE20 0RH
☎ 01661 886500 🖷 01661 886055
e-mail: info@matfenhall.com

This fine mansion house is set amidst landscaped parkland and the public rooms and many of the bedrooms overlook the 18 hole golf course. Bedrooms vary from the standard to the luxurious and comfortable superior rooms. Apart from the golfers' bar, there is a splendid drawing room and library restaurant, both boasting carved wood fire surrounds and interesting plaster relief ceilings. There are a number of meeting and banqueting rooms, including the magnificent Great Hall.

ROOMS: 30 en suite (4 fmly) No smoking in 18 bedrooms s fr £80; d fr £120 (incl. bkfst) * **FACILITIES:** STV Golf 18 Putting green beauty room Xmas **CONF:** Thtr 120 Class 60 Board 40 Del from £95 * **PARKING:** 150 **NOTES:** No smoking in restaurant
CARDS:

MATLOCK, Derbyshire Map 08 SK36

★★★73% Riber Hall

DE4 5JU
☎ 01629 582795 🖷 01629 580475
e-mail: info@riber-hall.co.uk
Dir: *1m off A615 at Tansley*

This charming Elizabethan manor house has a walled garden with a number of rare plants and a peaceful conservatory. Highly individual, beautifully furnished bedrooms have carved four-poster beds and comfortable sitting areas. The lounge, with glowing log fire, is the perfect place to relax. The restaurant serves carefully prepared dishes and excellent wines.

ROOMS: 3 en suite 11 annexe en suite No smoking in 4 bedrooms s £95-£109; d £123-£168 (incl. cont bkfst) * LB **FACILITIES:** STV Tennis (hard) Croquet lawn **CONF:** Thtr 20 Class 20 Board 20 Del from £144 * **PARKING:** 50 **NOTES:** No children 10yrs Civ Wed 45
CARDS:

★★★65% New Bath

New Bath Rd DE4 3PX
☎ 0870 400 8119 🖷 01629 580268
e-mail: HeritageHotels_Bath.Matlock.New_Bath@ForteHotels.com
Dir: *M1 junct 28 to Alfreton follow signs for Matlock and then Matlock Bath. Hotel is on the A6 just after Matlock Bath on the right*

Built in 1802, this comfortable and traditional hotel is set in five acres of grounds at one of Derbyshire's finest locations. Two of the bedrooms have four-poster beds and others have half-testers; balconied rooms are also available.

ROOMS: 55 en suite (5 fmly) No smoking in 11 bedrooms s £85; d £105 * LB **FACILITIES:** Indoor swimming (H) Outdoor swimming Tennis (hard) Sauna Solarium Xmas **CONF:** Thtr 180 Class 60 Board 50 Del from £95 * **PARKING:** 200 **NOTES:** No smoking in restaurant Civ Wed **CARDS:**

★★73% Red House

Old Rd, Darley Dale DE4 2ER
☎ 01629 734854 🖷 01629 734885
e-mail: redhoose@aol.com
Dir: *just off A6 onto Old Road signposted Carriage Museum, 2.5m N of Matlock*

A peaceful country retreat set in lovely gardens just outside Matlock. Rich colour schemes are used to excellent effect throughout. Well equipped bedrooms include three ground floor rooms in the adjacent coach house. A comfortable lounge with delightful rural views is available for refreshments and pre-dinner drinks; service is friendly and attentive. Carefully presented meals are served in separate breakfast and dining rooms.

ROOMS: 7 en suite 3 annexe en suite No smoking in 54 bedrooms s fr £60; d fr £80 (incl. bkfst) * LB **FACILITIES:** Riding Xmas **CONF:** Class 60 Board 12 Del from £95 * **PARKING:** 15 **NOTES:** No dogs (ex guide dogs) No smoking in restaurant
CARDS:

MAWGAN PORTH, Cornwall & Isles of Scilly Map 02 SW86

★★68% Tredragon

TR8 4DQ
☎ 01637 860213 🖷 01637 860269
e-mail: tredragon@btinternet.com

The Tredragon enjoys panoramic views over the sea to the hills beyond, and has been run by the same family for many years. Bedrooms vary in size and style, and in the hotel's dining room, guests can enjoy a variety of home-cooked dishes. Special residential courses are arranged, including lace-making, cooking and painting.

ROOMS: 26 en suite (15 fmly) s £24-£47.50; d £48-£95 (incl. bkfst) * LB **FACILITIES:** Indoor swimming (H) Sauna Solarium Pool table ch fac Xmas **CONF:** Thtr 50 Class 40 Board 30 **PARKING:** 30 **NOTES:** No smoking in restaurant **CARDS:**

MAWNAN SMITH, Cornwall & Isles of Scilly Map 02 SW72

★★★★73% Budock Vean-The Hotel on the River

TR11 5LG
☎ 01326 252100 & Freephone 0800 833927 🖷 01326 250892
e-mail: relax@budockvean.co.uk
Dir: *from A39 Truro/Falmouth road follow the brown tourist info signs to Trebah Gdns, then continue for 0.5m to the hotel*

In 65 acres of mature grounds beside the River Helford, this impressive hotel has the advantage of a modern health spa centre in addition to extensive leisure facilities. Most bedrooms benefit from views over the valley and golf course.

continued

ROOMS: 58 en suite (4 fmly) No smoking in 6 bedrooms s £59-£97; d £118-£194 (incl. bkfst & dinner) * LB **FACILITIES:** STV Indoor swimming (H) Golf 9 Tennis (hard) Fishing Snooker Putting green Natual health spa entertainment Xmas **CONF:** Thtr 100 Class 100 Board 80 **SERVICES:** Lift **PARKING:** 100 **NOTES:** No smoking in restaurant Civ Wed 100 **CARDS:**

★★★ 78% Meudon

TR11 5HT
☎ 01326 250541 01326 250543
e-mail: info@meudon.co.uk
Dir: *leave A39 at Hillhead rdbt and follow signs to Maenporth beach, Meudon on left one mile after beach*

Surrounded by National Trust land, in nine acres of subtropical gardens leading down to Bream Cove and its own beach, this late-Victorian mansion has a very elegant drawing room and bar. Two modern wings provide beautifully furbished, well equipped bedrooms. An attractive conservatory restaurant serves a fixed-price dinner, with local seafood a speciality.
ROOMS: 29 en suite (1 fmly) s £49.50-£105; d £99-£200 (incl. bkfst & dinner) * LB **FACILITIES:** Fishing Riding Pool table Private beach Hair salon Subtropical gardens Xmas **CONF:** Thtr 30 Class 20 Board 15 Del from £64.50 * **SERVICES:** Lift **PARKING:** 52 **NOTES:** No smoking in restaurant Closed 2 Jan-9 Feb **CARDS:**

See advert under FALMOUTH

★★★ 67% Trelawne

TR11 5HS
☎ 01326 250226 01326 250909
Dir: *A39 towards Falmouth, turn right at Hillhead rdbt take exit signed Maenporth past beach and up the hill, hotel on left overlooking Falmouth Bay*

The Trelawne is surrounded by attractive lawns and gardens and commands superb views over the coastline from St Mawes to the Lizard. It provides neat, well equipped bedrooms and comfortable public areas. At dinner, award-winning cuisine brings many guests back year after year.

ROOMS: 14 en suite (2 fmly) s £39-£59; d £69-£108 (incl. bkfst) * LB **FACILITIES:** Indoor swimming (H) **PARKING:** 20 **NOTES:** No smoking in restaurant Closed 23 Dec-12 Feb
CARDS:

See advert under FALMOUTH

MELKSHAM, Wiltshire — Map 03 ST96

★★ 69% Shaw Country

Bath Rd, Shaw SN12 8EF
☎ 01225 702836 & 790321 01225 790275
e-mail: shawcountryhotel@ukbusiness.com
Dir: *1m from Melksham, 9m from Bath on A365*

Situated in an Area of Outstanding Natural Beauty, within easy driving distance of Bath and the M4, Shaw Country Hotel provides a warm welcome and very well equipped, comfortable bedrooms. There is a residents' lounge and bar and the Mulberry Restaurant offers a good choice of well cooked dishes. Friendly staff are always on hand to help.
ROOMS: 13 en suite (2 fmly) d fr £65 (incl. bkfst) * LB
FACILITIES: Jacuzzi/spa **CONF:** Thtr 30 Class 20 Board 30
PARKING: 30 **NOTES:** No smoking in restaurant Closed 26-27 Dec
CARDS:

See advert under BATH

M

MELKSHAM, continued

★★63% *Conigre Farm Hotel*
Semington Rd SN12 6BZ
☎ 01225 702229

All the bedrooms at this stone-built 17th-century former farmhouse are named after Dickens' characters, and the theme is carried through to the Mr Bumbles restaurant. The bedrooms, some in a wing across the car park, are well equipped. Lounges include one with a bar and one in a Victorian conservatory.
CONF: Class 40 Board 40

MELTON MOWBRAY, Leicestershire
Map 08 SK71

Premier Collection

★★★★ *Stapleford Park*
Stapleford LE14 2EF
☎ 01572 787522 01572 787651
e-mail: reservations@stapleford.telme.com
Dir: *1m SW of B676 4m E of Melton Mowbray and 9m W of Colsterworth*
Set in a 500-acre estate, this delightful stately home is surrounded by woods and parkland, originally laid out by Capability Brown. The main reception rooms are sumptuously decorated and furnished in grand country-house style. The dining room features carvings by Grinling Gibbons, and makes a fine setting for the daily-changing menu. Each of the bedrooms has been designed by a sponsor, such as Turnbull & Asser and David Hicks, and those in a cottage in the grounds by companies such as IBM and Coca-Cola.
ROOMS: 44 en suite 7 annexe en suite No smoking in 44 bedrooms **FACILITIES:** STV Indoor swimming (H) Golf 3 Tennis (hard) Fishing Riding Sauna Solarium Gym Pool table Croquet lawn Putting green Jacuzzi/spa Shooting Falconry Off road driving Archery Petanque entertainment **CONF:** Thtr 200 Class 140 Board 80 **SERVICES:** Lift **PARKING:** 120 **NOTES:** No children 9yrs No smoking in restaurant **CARDS:**

★★★67% *Sysonby Knoll*
Asfordby Rd LE13 0HP
☎ 01664 563563 01664 410364
e-mail: sysonby.knoll@btinternet.com
Dir: *0.5m from town centre beside A6006*
Situated just on the outskirts of Melton Mowbray, this Edwardian country house is set in beautiful grounds leading to the River Eye. Bedrooms are attractively furnished with a good range of facilities. The charming bar, restaurant and conservatory are the focal point, serving good food.
ROOMS: 23 en suite 1 annexe en suite (2 fmly) **FACILITIES:** STV Outdoor swimming Fishing Croquet lawn **CONF:** Thtr 30 Class 16 Board 24 **PARKING:** 40 **NOTES:** No smoking in restaurant Closed 25 Dec-1 Jan **CARDS:**

See advert on opposite page

★★73% Quorn Lodge
46 Asfordby Rd LE13 0HR
☎ 01664 566660 & 562590 01664 480660
e-mail: quornlodge@aol.com
Dir: *from town centre take A6006, hotel 300 yds from junct of A606/A607 on right*
Popular for its friendly and welcoming atmosphere, this appealing hotel was originally a hunting lodge. Bedrooms are individually decorated and thoughtfully designed. The public rooms offer an elegant restaurant, a cosy lounge bar and a modern function suite. High standards are maintained throughout.
ROOMS: 19 en suite (2 fmly) No smoking in 11 bedrooms s £49.50-£55; d £65-£75 (incl. bkfst) * LB **FACILITIES:** STV **CONF:** Thtr 90 Class 60 Board 85 Del £75 * **PARKING:** 33 **NOTES:** No dogs No smoking in restaurant **CARDS:**

★★62% Harboro Hotel
49 Burton St LE13 1AF
☎ 01664 560121 01664 564296
Dir: *in town centre between church and railway station on A606 Oakham road*

Just a short walk from the town centre, this well established hotel provides quality accommodation. Bedrooms vary in size and style, with a good selection of furnishings and facilities. The public rooms have a relaxed and informal atmosphere, with a range of meals available in the lounge bar or the more formal restaurant.
ROOMS: 27 en suite (3 fmly) No smoking in 4 bedrooms s fr £49.50; d fr £59.50 (incl. bkfst) * LB **FACILITIES:** Xmas **CONF:** Thtr 30 Class 30 Board 20 **PARKING:** 50 **CARDS:**

Early start? Hotels at all star levels should provide in-room alarm clocks and/or alarm calls.

MEMBURY MOTORWAY SERVICE AREA (M4), Berkshire — Map 04 SU37

⌂ Days Inn

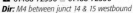

Membury Service Area RG17 7TZ
☎ 01488 72336 ▯ 01488 72336
Dir: *M4 between junct 14 & 15 westbound*

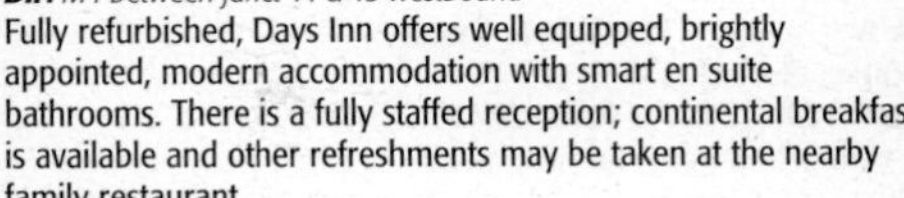

Fully refurbished, Days Inn offers well equipped, brightly appointed, modern accommodation with smart en suite bathrooms. There is a fully staffed reception; continental breakfast is available and other refreshments may be taken at the nearby family restaurant.
ROOMS: 38 en suite d fr £45 *

MERIDEN, West Midlands — Map 04 SP28

★★★★71% Marriott Forest of Arden

Maxstoke Ln CV7 7HR
☎ 01676 522335 ▯ 01676 523711
Dir: *M42 junct 6 onto A45 towards Coventry straight on at Stonebridge flyover, after 0.75m turn left into Shepherds Lane, hotel 1.5m on left*

This impressive modern hotel is surrounded by lakes, gardens, two golf courses and a driving range. One can enjoy a drink, snack or meal in an informal family setting. Alternatively, the hotel has a cocktail lounge and a split-level restaurant. The bedrooms boast a range of facilities.

> Fancy a Singapore Sling? Bar staff in five star hotels should be skilled cocktail mixers.

ROOMS: 214 en suite (4 fmly) No smoking in 135 bedrooms s £109-£152; d £109-£152 * LB **FACILITIES:** STV Indoor swimming (H) Golf 18 Tennis (hard) Fishing Sauna Solarium Gym Croquet lawn Putting green Jacuzzi/spa Health & Beauty salon Xmas **CONF:** Thtr 360 Class 200 Board 40 Del from £159 * **SERVICES:** Lift air con **PARKING:** 300 **NOTES:** No smoking in restaurant Civ Wed 150
CARDS:

★★★74% Manor

Main Rd CV7 7NH
☎ 01676 522735 ▯ 01676 522186
Dir: *from M42 junct 6, take A45 towards Coventry, after approx 2m cross dual carriageway onto B4104 for Meriden. Straight ahead at mini-rdbt*

A Georgian manor in a quiet village, within easy reach of the NEC and motorway network. The Regency Restaurant offers good food through a modern interesting carte, while the Triumph Buttery serves lighter meals and snacks. Bedroom styles vary

continued

MERIDEN, continued

considerably; the delightful Executive rooms are very smart and well equipped. Service is professional, friendly and attentive.
ROOMS: 114 en suite No smoking in 54 bedrooms s £75-£145; d £85-£155 (incl. bkfst) * LB **FACILITIES:** STV **CONF:** Thtr 250 Class 150 Board 60 Del from £95 * **SERVICES:** Lift **PARKING:** 200 **NOTES:** No smoking in restaurant **CARDS:**

MEVAGISSEY, Cornwall & Isles of Scilly Map 02 SX04

★★71% Tremarne
Polkirt PL26 6UY
☎ 01726 842213 📠 01726 843420
e-mail: tremarne@talk21.com
Dir: *from A390 at St Austell take B3273 to Mevagissey, follow Portmellon signs through Mevagissey, at top of Polkirt Hill turn right*
On the edge of the village, this relaxing, comfortable hotel is an ideal choice for those looking to unwind. Many of the thoughtfully equipped bedrooms have extensive views across the countryside to the sea beyond. Enjoy a drink in the lounge beside the flickering wood burner before moving through to sample the accomplished cuisine in the tasteful restaurant.
ROOMS: 14 en suite (2 fmly) No smoking in all bedrooms s £30-£36; d £58-£72 (incl. bkfst) * LB **FACILITIES:** Outdoor swimming (H) Xmas **PARKING:** 14 **NOTES:** No smoking in restaurant Closed 28-29 Dec
CARDS:

★★68% Spa Hotel
Polkirt Hill PL26 6UY
☎ 01726 842244 📠 01726 842244
e-mail: spahotelmevagissy@talk21.com
Dir: *from Mevagissey take Portmellion Rd. At the top of Polkirt Hill, turning on right, Hotel sign at this turning*

In an elevated position, the Spa enjoys wonderful coastal views. There is a wide choice of bedroom size; all are light, airy and colourful, and some have patio areas leading onto well tended gardens. A comfortable, cane-furnished lounge and a cosy bar are provided. A short fixed-price menu uses fresh local produce.
ROOMS: 11 en suite (4 fmly) No smoking in 7 bedrooms s £30; d £60 (incl. bkfst) * LB **FACILITIES:** Putting green **PARKING:** 12 **NOTES:** No smoking in restaurant **CARDS:**

MICHAEL WOOD MOTORWAY SERVICE AREA (M5), Gloucestershire Map 03 ST79

Days Inn
Lower Wick GL11 6DD
☎ 01454 261513 📠 01454 261513
Dir: *M5 northbound between junct 13 & 14*
Fully refurbished, Days Inn offers well equipped, brightly appointed, modern accommodation with smart en suite bathrooms. There is a fully staffed reception; continental breakfast is available and other refreshments may be taken at the nearby family restaurant.
ROOMS: 40 en suite d fr £45 *

MIDDLEHAM, North Yorkshire Map 07 SE18

★★76% The White Swan
Market Place DL8 4PE
☎ 01969 622093 📠 01969 624551
e-mail: whiteswan@easynet.co.uk
Dir: *exit A1 at Leeming Bar, take A684 to Leyburn, before Leyburn Centre take A6108 to Ripon, Middleham is 1.5m from this junct, in the Market Place*
This charming country inn has a growing reputation for its cosmopolitan cuisine and endearing, traditional values. Appealing bedrooms are smartly decorated and contain many thoughtful touches. Service throughout the hotel is especially friendly.
ROOMS: 11 en suite (2 fmly) s £38-£50; d £28-£40 (incl. bkfst) * LB **FACILITIES:** Xmas **PARKING:** 5 **CARDS:**

★★72% Millers House
DL8 4NR
☎ 01969 622630 📠 01969 623570
e-mail: millershouse@demon.co.uk
Dir: *from A1 onto A684 to Leyburn. Turn left to Middleham, hotel set back from market square*
This stylish Georgian house lies just off the market square and provides a welcoming atmosphere for the discerning traveller. There is a cosy lounge bar for residents and diners, and a stylish dining room with a conservatory extension. The elegant, comfortable bedrooms are thoughtfully equipped.
ROOMS: 7 rms (6 en suite) s £61-£122; d £122-£136 (incl. bkfst & dinner) LB **FACILITIES:** Xmas **PARKING:** 8 **NOTES:** No dogs (ex guide dogs) No children 10yrs No smoking in restaurant Closed Jan
CARDS:

★79% Waterford House
Kirkgate DL8 4PG
☎ 01969 622090 📠 01969 624020
Dir: *A1 to B6267 via Masham to Middleham. Hotel in right corner of Market Sq or A1 to Scotch Corner via Richmond & Leyburn to Middleham, Hotel at hilltop*
This delightful restaurant with rooms, furnished with antiques, china and silver, has a warm, restful atmosphere. Bedrooms also have antique furnishings, modern facilities and extras such as complimentary sherry and home-made shortbread. The fine cooking fully merits two Rosettes, and the owner's wine expertise can be confirmed from more than 800 selections.
ROOMS: 5 en suite s £50-£60; d £75-£95 (incl. bkfst) * LB **FACILITIES:** ch fac **PARKING:** 8 **NOTES:** No smoking in restaurant Civ Wed 24 **CARDS:**

MIDDLESBROUGH, North Yorkshire Map 08 NZ42

★★65% *Highfield*
358 Marton Rd TS4 2PA
☎ 01642 817638 📠 01642 821219
Dir: *off A172. From A1 (M) Darlington exit follow A1085 towards town centre*
This popular hotel has been refurbished throughout and provides friendly and attentive service. The pleasant restaurant is popular with families, as a play area is provided. The modern bedrooms are well equipped and pleasantly decorated.
ROOMS: 23 en suite (1 fmly) **FACILITIES:** STV Indoor childrens play area **CONF:** Thtr 200 Class 100 Board 50 **PARKING:** 100 **NOTES:** No dogs (ex guide dogs) **CARDS:**

MIDDLETON, Greater Manchester — Map 07 SD80

Premier Lodge (Manchester North)

818 Manchester Old Rd, Rhodes M24 4RF
☎ 0870 700 1474 📠 0870 700 1475

Premier Lodge offers modern, well equipped, en suite accommodation suitable for both business and leisure travellers. Meals can be taken at the adjacent popular restaurant and bar which is fully licensed. For further details, consult the Hotel Groups page.

ROOMS: 42 en suite d £42 *

MIDDLETON STONEY, Oxfordshire — Map 04 SP52

★★68% Jersey Arms

OX6 8SE
☎ 01869 343234 & 343505 📠 01869 343565
e-mail: jerseyarms@bestwestern.co.uk
Dir: *on the B430 10m N of Oxford, between junct 9 & 10 of M40*

This family-run hotel close to Bicester and the M40 is a former coaching inn with a long tradition of hospitality. Bedrooms are either in the main house or in buildings round the courtyard. The cosy bar is full of village atmosphere and meals may be taken here or in the more formal setting of the restaurant.

ROOMS: 6 en suite 10 annexe en suite (3 fmly) s fr £79; d fr £95 (incl. bkfst) * LB **FACILITIES:** Xmas **PARKING:** 55 **NOTES:** No dogs (ex guide dogs) No smoking in restaurant **CARDS:**

MIDDLE WALLOP, Hampshire — Map 04 SU23

★★★73% *Fifehead Manor*

SO20 8EG
☎ 01264 781565 📠 01264 781400
Dir: *from M3 exit at junct 8 onto A303 to Andover, then take A343 S for 6m to Middle Wallop*

This 11th-century manor house retains many of its original features. Bedrooms are comfortably furnished, well equipped and feature many thoughtful touches. Public areas include a well stocked bar, elegant lounge and charming restaurant which offers a high standard of cuisine. Service is attentive from the friendly team of staff.

ROOMS: 10 en suite 6 annexe en suite **FACILITIES:** STV Croquet lawn **CONF:** Thtr 30 Class 18 Board 12 **PARKING:** 40 **NOTES:** No dogs (ex guide dogs) No smoking in restaurant **CARDS:**

See advert under ANDOVER

MIDDLEWICH, Cheshire — Map 07 SJ76

Travelodge

M6 Junction 18, A54
☎ 0800 850 950

This modern building offers accommodation in smart, spacious and well equipped bedrooms, all with en suite bathrooms. Refreshments may be taken at the nearby family restaurant. For further details and the Travelodge phone number, consult the Hotel Groups page.

ROOMS: 32 en suite

MIDHURST, West Sussex — Map 04 SU82

★★★77% Spread Eagle

South St GU29 9NH
☎ 01730 816911 📠 01730 815668
e-mail: spreadeagle@hshotels.co.uk
Dir: *situated on South Street, A286*

Full of character with sloping floors, ancient beams and inglenook fireplaces. Individually-decorated bedrooms, furnished with antique and reproduction pieces, provide modern comforts. The leisure centre with pool, gym and beauty treatments is popular. The hotel cuisine is modern and satisfying.

ROOMS: 35 en suite 4 annexe en suite No smoking in 6 bedrooms s £95-£140; d £125-£205 (incl. bkfst) * LB **FACILITIES:** STV Indoor swimming (H) Sauna Gym Jacuzzi/spa Health & beauty treatment rooms Steam room Fitness trainer Xmas **CONF:** Thtr 70 Class 40 Board 35 Del from £150 * **PARKING:** 70 **NOTES:** No smoking in restaurant Civ Wed 120 **CARDS:**

★★★76% Angel

North St GU29 9DN
☎ 01730 812421 📠 01730 815928
Dir: *on S side of A272 in centre of Midhurst*

Now under the same ownership as the Spread Eagle also located in the town, this stylish hotel continues to offer high standards of hospitality and cuisine. Bedrooms many of which have been refurbished are individual in style and tastefully appointed. Public areas include a spacious, elegant lounge, and a popular bar and brasserie.

ROOMS: 24 en suite 4 annexe en suite s fr £90; d fr £125 (incl. cont bkfst) * LB **FACILITIES:** STV entertainment Xmas **CONF:** Thtr 45 Class 32 Board 32 **PARKING:** 32 **NOTES:** No dogs (ex guide dogs) No smoking in restaurant Civ Wed 40
CARDS:

★★★72% Southdowns Country

Dumpford Ln, Trotton GU31 5JN
☎ 01730 821521 📠 01730 821790
e-mail: reception@southdownshotel.freeserve.co.uk
Dir: *on A272, after town turn left at Keepers Arms*

This attractive hotel in peaceful surroundings offers good facilities for conferences, wedding receptions and country breaks. Most bedrooms have countryside views; all are attractively furnished and well equipped. The beamed Tudor bar has a roaring log fire in winter and serves drinks and light meals. The Country Restaurant offers more substantial fare, focusing on seasonal, quality produce.

ROOMS: 20 en suite (3 fmly) No smoking in 4 bedrooms s £60-£90; d £90-£150 (incl. bkfst) * LB **FACILITIES:** Indoor swimming (H) Tennis (hard) Sauna Solarium Croquet lawn Exercise equipment Xmas **CONF:** Thtr 120 Class 30 Board 30 Del from £90 * **PARKING:** 70 **NOTES:** No children 10yrs No smoking in restaurant Civ Wed 100
CARDS:

See advert under PETERSFIELD

> Fancy a Singapore Sling? Bar staff in five star hotels should be skilled cocktail mixers.

M

MIDSOMER NORTON, Somerset
Map 03 ST65

★★★70% Centurion
Charlton Ln BA3 4BD
☎ 01761 417711 01761 418357
Dir: *off A367, 10m S of Bath*
This family-run hotel incorporates the adjacent Fosseway Country Club with its nine-hole golf course and other extensive leisure amenities. Comfortable bedrooms are equipped and furnished to a high standard with coordinating fabrics. Public areas include a choice of bars, an attractive lounge and a range of meeting/function rooms.
ROOMS: 44 en suite (4 fmly) s fr £62; d fr £72 (incl. bkfst & dinner) * LB **FACILITIES:** STV Indoor swimming (H) Golf 9 Squash Sauna Gym Jacuzzi/spa Bowling green Sports field **CONF:** Thtr 180 Class 70 Board 50 Del from £90 * **PARKING:** 100 **NOTES:** No dogs (ex guide dogs) No smoking in restaurant Closed 24-26 Dec Civ Wed 80
CARDS:

MILDENHALL, Suffolk
Map 05 TL77

★★★76% Riverside
Mill St IP28 7DP
☎ 01638 717274 01638 715997
e-mail: cameronhotels@riversidehotel.freeserve.co.uk
Dir: *from A11 at fiveways rdbt take A1101 in Mildenhall Town turn left at mini-rdbt along High St, hotel is last building on left before bridge*
An imposing 18th-century red brick building situated on the banks of the River Lark, on the outskirts of this busy market town. The public rooms feature a restaurant which overlooks the river and attractive gardens to the rear. Although the bedrooms vary in size and style the more recently refurbished rooms are finished to a good standard.
ROOMS: 17 en suite 4 annexe en suite (4 fmly) s £62-£68; d £88-£92 (incl. bkfst) * LB **FACILITIES:** Fishing Xmas **CONF:** Thtr 150 Class 60 Board 40 Del from £79 * **SERVICES:** Lift **PARKING:** 60
CARDS:

★★★64% The Smoke House
Best Western
Beck Row IP28 8DH
☎ 01638 713223 01638 712202
Dir: *A1101 into Mildenhall, follow Beck Row signs. Hotel located immediately after mini-rdbt through Beck Row on right-hand side*

This busy complex is popular with visitors to the nearby airbases and tour parties, it has a shopping mall and conference centre. Public areas owe their character to 16th century origins, with open log fires, beams and exposed brickwork. There are two bars and a choice of dining options. The refurbished accommodation is mainly based around modern wings of well proportioned, comfortably appointed bedrooms.

continued

ROOMS: 94 en suite s £90-£135; d £110-£150 (incl. bkfst) * LB **FACILITIES:** Tennis Pool table entertainment Xmas **CONF:** Thtr 120 Class 80 Board 50 Del from £95 * **PARKING:** 200 **NOTES:** No dogs (ex guide dogs) No smoking in restaurant
CARDS:

See advert on opposite page

MILFORD ON SEA, Hampshire
Map 04 SZ29

★★★80% Westover Hall
Park Ln SO41 0PT
☎ 01590 643044 01590 644490
e-mail: westover@barclays.net
Dir: *M3/M27 W and the A337 to Lymington. Follow signs from Lymington fro Milford-on-Sea B3058 hotel is situated just outside village centre towards cliff*

An Arts and Crafts Victorian mansion in a truly spectacular location. The architecture of the building is impressive, boasting ceiling moulds, stained glass windows and original wood panelling. Accommodation is spacious with contemporary decor and fabrics accentuating period features with thoughtful extras such as fresh flowers and bathrobes.
ROOMS: 14 en suite (1 fmly) s £65-£80; d £110-£140 (incl. bkfst) * LB **FACILITIES:** Xmas **CONF:** Thtr 50 Class 30 Board 25 **PARKING:** 50 **NOTES:** No smoking in restaurant Civ Wed 100
CARDS:

See advert under LYMINGTON

★★★72% South Lawn
Lymington Rd SO41 0RF
☎ 01590 643911 01590 644820
e-mail: enquiries@southlawn.co.uk
Dir: *turn left off A337 at Everton onto B3058. Hotel approx 1m on right*

Owned by the same family since 1970, this former dower house offers good service provided by friendly staff. The hotel is situated close to the sea in four acres of grounds. Bedrooms are spacious and attractively decorated. The bright dining room serves a good range of local produce prepared with care.

continued

ROOMS: 24 en suite No smoking in all bedrooms s £65; d £110-£130 (incl. bkfst & dinner) * LB **FACILITIES:** STV **PARKING:** 60 **NOTES:** No dogs No children 7yrs No smoking in restaurant Closed 20 Dec-18 Jan **CARDS:**

See advert on this page

MILTON COMMON, Oxfordshire Map 04 SP60

★★★★72% The Oxford Belfry

MARSTON HOTELS

OX9 2JW
☎ 01844 279381 Fax 01844 279624
e-mail: oxfordbelfry@marstonhotels.co.uk
Dir: *M40 junct 7 - A329 to Thame. Turn left onto A40 by 3 Pigeons Pub. Hotel 300yds on right*

Set in extensive grounds yet conveniently placed for the M40, the Oxford Belfry offers an impressive choice of well appointed accommodation. Public areas are both smart and inviting and include conference rooms and a leisure club. The spacious restaurant offers an interesting range of carefully prepared dishes.
ROOMS: 130 en suite (10 fmly) No smoking in 68 bedrooms s £108-£128; d £137-£177 (incl. bkfst) * LB **FACILITIES:** STV Indoor swimming (H) Tennis (hard) Sauna Solarium Gym Xmas **CONF:** Thtr 370 Class 220 Board 120 Del from £149 * **SERVICES:** Lift **PARKING:** 200 **NOTES:** No smoking in restaurant Civ Wed 250
CARDS:

MILTON KEYNES, Buckinghamshire Map 04 SP83
see also Flitwick

★★★69% Courtyard by Marriott Milton Keynes

COURTYARD

London Rd, Newport Pagnell MK16 0JA
☎ 01908 613688 Fax 01908 617335
Dir: *0.5m from junct 14 of M1 on the A509*

Conveniently positioned for the M1, yet in a quiet spot, this popular hotel is designed around a handsome three-story Georgian House and a pretty courtyard. Public rooms are pleasantly appointed and inviting. Bedrooms are smartly decorated, thoughtfully designed and offer a good range of facilities.
ROOMS: 49 en suite (1 fmly) No smoking in 26 bedrooms d £89-£95 * LB **FACILITIES:** STV Gym entertainment **CONF:** Thtr 200 Class 90 Board 50 Del from £105 * **PARKING:** 160 **NOTES:** No dogs (ex guide dogs) No smoking in restaurant **CARDS:**

★★★66% *Posthouse Milton Keynes*

Posthouse

500 Saxon Gate West MK9 2HQ
☎ 0870 400 9057 Fax 01908 674714
Dir: *M1 junct 14 over 7 roundabouts right at 8th hotel on left*

This large modern hotel is situated in the city centre, and offers opulent public areas, with glass-sided lifts overlooking the lounges and restaurants. Bedrooms are comfortably appointed and include several designed for women.
ROOMS: 150 en suite No smoking in 79 bedrooms **FACILITIES:** STV Indoor swimming (H) Sauna Solarium Gym Health & fitness centre entertainment **CONF:** Thtr 150 Class 85 Board 35 **SERVICES:** Lift **PARKING:** 80 **CARDS:**

★★★65% Quality Hotel & Suites Milton Keynes

CHOICE HOTELS EUROPE

Monks Way, Two Mile Ash MK8 8LY
☎ 01908 561666 Fax 01908 568303
e-mail: admin@gb616.u-net.com
Dir: *junct A5/A422*

Bedrooms at this purpose built hotel are particularly well equipped, having extra phones and mini bars; there are also a

continued on p392

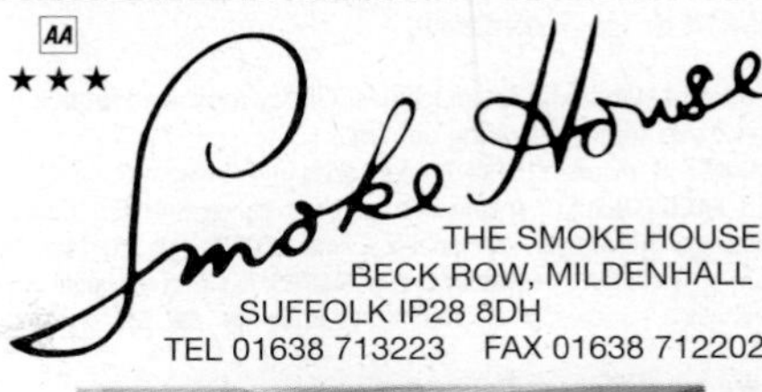

MILTON KEYNES, continued

number of suites with fax machines. All day room and lounge service are additional eating options.
ROOMS: 88 en suite (15 fmly) No smoking in 44 bedrooms d £115-£125 * LB **FACILITIES:** STV Indoor swimming (H) Sauna Solarium Gym Jacuzzi/spa Steam room Whirlpool spa Xmas **CONF:** Thtr 120 Class 70 Board 50 Del £120 * **PARKING:** 200 **NOTES:** No dogs (ex guide dogs) No smoking in restaurant Civ Wed 90 **CARDS:**

★★67% *Different Drummer*
94 High St, Stony Stratford MK11 1AH
☎ 01908 564733 📠 01908 260646
This attractive hotel on historic Stony Stratford's High Street offers a warm welcome to its guests. The smart Italian restaurant, Al Tamborista, is a popular dining spot and enjoys a good local reputation. Bedrooms are generally spacious, whilst the hotel lounge incorporates a bar and is particularly comfortable.
ROOMS: 8 en suite 4 annexe en suite (2 fmly) **NOTES:** No dogs (ex guide dogs) **CARDS:**

★★65% Swan Revived
High St, Newport Pagnell MK16 8AR
☎ 01908 610565 📠 01908 210995
e-mail: swanrevived@btinternet.com

Dir: *leave M1 junct 14, take A509 (B526) into Newport Pagnell (2m) the Hotel is on the High Street*
This charming coaching inn has stood in the heart of Newport Pagnell for centuries. Service is friendly, and bedrooms well equipped and spacious. The restaurant serves a wide variety of enjoyable dishes, and there is a cosy hotel bar, as well as a pub to the rear of the building, popular with locals.
ROOMS: 42 en suite (2 fmly) s fr £74; d fr £80 (incl. bkfst) * LB **FACILITIES:** STV **CONF:** Thtr 70 Class 30 Board 28 Del from £109 * **SERVICES:** Lift **PARKING:** 18 **NOTES:** RS 25 Dec-1 Jan Civ Wed 75 **CARDS:**

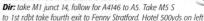

⌂ Campanile
40 Penn Rd, Fenny Stratford, Bletchley MK2 2AU
☎ 01908 649819 📠 01908 649818
Dir: *take M1 junct 14, follow for A4146 to A5. Take M5 S to 1st rdbt take fourth exit to Fenny Stratford. Hotel 500yds on left*

This modern building offers accommodation in smart well equipped bedrooms, all with en suite bathrooms. Refreshments may be taken at the informal Bistro. For further details and the Campanile phone number, consult the Hotel Groups page.
ROOMS: 80 en suite **CONF:** Thtr 40 Class 30 Board 25 Del from £68 *

⌂ Premier Lodge (Central)
Shirwell Crescent, Furzton MK4 1GA
☎ 0870 700 1494 📠 0870 700 1495

Premier Lodge offers modern, well equipped, en suite accommodation suitable for both business and leisure travellers. Meals can be taken at the adjacent popular restaurant and bar which is fully licensed. For further details, consult the Hotel Groups page.
ROOMS: 120 en suite d £49.50 *

⌂ Premier Lodge (Milton Keynes South)
Bletcham Way, Caldecotte MK7 8HP
☎ 0870 700 1492 📠 0870 700 1493
Premier Lodge offers modern, well equipped, en suite accommodation suitable for both business and leisure travellers. Meals can be taken at the adjacent popular restaurant and bar which is fully licensed. For further details, consult the Hotel Groups page.
ROOMS: 40 en suite d £49.50 *

⌂ *Travelodge*
109 Grafton Gate MK9 1AL
☎ 0800 850950
This modern building offers accommodation in smart, spacious and well equipped bedrooms, all with en suite bathrooms. Refreshments may be taken at the nearby family restaurant. For further details and the Travelodge phone number, consult the Hotel Groups page.
ROOMS: 80 en suite

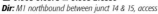

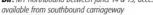

⌂ Welcome Lodge
Newport Pagnell Service Area MK16 8DS
☎ 01908 610878 📠 01908 216539
Dir: *M1 northbound between junct 14 & 15, access available from southbound carriageway*
This modern building offers accommodation in smart, spacious and well equipped bedrooms, suitable for families and businessmen, and all with en suite bathrooms. Refreshments may be taken at the nearby family restaurant. For further details and the Welcome Break phone number, consult the Hotel Groups page.
ROOMS: 92 en suite d fr £45 * **CONF:** Thtr 20 Class 10 Board 15

MINEHEAD, Somerset — Map 03 SS94

★★★71% *Benares*
Northfield Rd TA24 5PT
☎ 01643 704911 📠 01643 706373

Dir: *along sea front 75yds before harbour turn left into Blenheim Rd then right into Northfield Rd*

Set in an acre of beautiful gardens, this extended Edwardian house has views over the Bristol Channel. The resident proprietor and his smiling team provide friendly, attentive service. Italian fireplaces and stained glass windows feature in the comfortable day rooms. In the dining room, a fixed-price, five-course dinner is served.
ROOMS: 19 en suite (3 fmly) **PARKING:** 22 **NOTES:** No smoking in restaurant Closed 9 Nov-25 Mar (ex Xmas)
CARDS:

See advert on opposite page

★★★67% Northfield
Northfield Rd TA24 5PU
☎ 01643 705155 01643 707715
e-mail: reservations@northfield-hotel.co.uk
Dir: *exit M5 junct 23, follow A38 to Bridgwater & join A39 to Minehead.*
Set in delightfully maintained gardens, this hotel is located near the town centre and seafront. A range of comfortable sitting rooms and leisure facilities are provided. A fixed-price menu is served every evening in the oak-panelled dining room. The attractively co-ordinated bedrooms vary in size and are equipped to a good standard.
ROOMS: 25 en suite (7 fmly) d £56 (incl. bkfst & dinner) * LB
FACILITIES: Indoor swimming (H) Gym Putting green Jacuzzi/spa Steam room Xmas **CONF:** Thtr 70 Class 45 Board 30 Del from £70 *
SERVICES: Lift **PARKING:** 44 **NOTES:** No smoking in restaurant
CARDS:

★★76% Channel House Hotel
Church Path TA24 5QG
☎ 01643 703229 01643 708925
e-mail: channel.house@virgin.net
Dir: *from A39, at rdbt turn right to seafront, then left onto promenade, 1st right, then 1st left to Blenheim Gardens 1st right Northfield Road*

Set in two acres of well tended, colourful gardens, this charming and well-run hotel offers relaxing and tranquil surroundings. Many of the exceptionally well equipped bedrooms have wonderful views, while the dining room serves an imaginative menu using the best local produce. The South West coastal path starts from the hotel garden.
ROOMS: 8 en suite (1 fmly) s £69-£82; d £108-£134 (incl. bkfst & dinner) * LB **FACILITIES:** Xmas **SERVICES:** air con **PARKING:** 10
NOTES: No dogs No children 10yrs No smoking in restaurant Closed 6 Nov-16 Mar (ex Xmas) **CARDS:**

See advert on this page

★★75% Periton Park
Middlecombe TA24 8SN
☎ 01643 706885 01643 706885
Dir: *on S side of A39 from Minehead*
In wooded grounds on the edge of Exmoor, this delightful country house offers genuine hospitality and relaxed, competent service. Bedrooms are decorated in rich fabrics and there are deeps sofas in the comfortable lounges. The seasonally changing menu offers interesting dishes based on fresh local produce.
ROOMS: 8 en suite No smoking in 3 bedrooms s £54-£59; d £88-£99 (incl. bkfst) * LB **FACILITIES:** Riding Croquet lawn Xmas **CONF:** Thtr 24 Board 16 Del from £95 * **PARKING:** 12 **NOTES:** No children 12yrs No smoking in restaurant Closed Jan **CARDS:**

> Arriving late? Four and five star hotels have night porters to assist with your luggage; and 24hr room service.

MINEHEAD, continued

★★ 73% Wyndcott Hotel
Martlet Rd TA24 5QE
☎ 01643 704522 📠 01643 707577
e-mail: mineheadhotel@msn.com
Dir: *from Minehead town centre follow signs for North Hill. Hotel third of a mile on left*
In beautiful gardens above the town, this charming family-run hotel offers excellent hospitality. There are wonderful views from the dining room and some bedrooms, which are of a high standard. A ground floor garden room is also available. A choice of home-cooked dishes, prepared from fresh, often local, ingredients make up the dinner menu.
ROOMS: 9 en suite (1 fmly) No smoking in 7 bedrooms s £34-£50; d £68-£80 (incl. bkfst) * LB **FACILITIES:** Xmas **PARKING:** 15 **NOTES:** No smoking in restaurant **CARDS:**

MONK FRYSTON, North Yorkshire Map 08 SE52

★★★ 68% *Monk Fryston Hall*
LS25 5DU
☎ 01977 682369 📠 01977 683544
e-mail: monkfryston.hall@virgin.net
Dir: *A1/A63 junct towards Selby. Left-hand side in centre of Monk Fryston*
This historic mansion stands in attractive grounds in the centre of the village. Warming fires, oak panelling and large paintings are features, whilst service is attentive and the cooking is traditional in style. The bedrooms have been well equipped, and make thoughtful provision for business travellers.
ROOMS: 30 en suite (2 fmly) No smoking in 10 bedrooms **FACILITIES:** STV Riding Croquet lawn Putting green **CONF:** Thtr 100 Class 40 Board 30 **PARKING:** 100 **NOTES:** No smoking in restaurant **CARDS:**

See advert on opposite page

M

MORCOTT, Rutland Map 04 SK90

Travelodge
Uppingham LE15 9DL
☎ 01572 747719 📠 01572 747719
Dir: *on A47, eastbound*
Travelodge
This modern building offers accommodation in smart, spacious and well equipped bedrooms, all with en suite bathrooms. Refreshments may be taken at the nearby family restaurant. For further details and the Travelodge phone number, consult the Hotel Groups page.
ROOMS: 40 en suite

MORDEN, Greater London
See LONDON SECTION plan 1 *D1*

Travelodge
Epsom Rd SM4 5PH
☎ 020 8640 8227 📠 020 8640 8227
Dir: *on A24*
Travelodge
This modern building offers accommodation in smart, spacious and well equipped bedrooms, all with en suite bathrooms. Refreshments may be taken at the nearby family restaurant. For further details and the Travelodge phone number, consult the Hotel Groups page.
ROOMS: 32 en suite

Bad hair day? Hairdryers in all rooms three stars and above.

MORECAMBE, Lancashire Map 07 SD46

★★★ 64% Elms
Bare Village LA4 6DD
☎ 01524 411501 📠 01524 831979
This well established hotel stands in pleasant gardens, just off the North Promenade. The bedrooms are smartly presented and there are a number with four-poster beds. Public rooms include a refurbished lounge bar and an elegant Victorian-style restaurant.
ROOMS: 40 en suite (3 fmly) s £43-£61; d £55-£90 (incl. bkfst) * LB **FACILITIES:** Xmas **CONF:** Thtr 200 Class 72 Board 60 Del from £59 * **SERVICES:** Lift **PARKING:** 80 **NOTES:** No smoking in restaurant Civ Wed 100 **CARDS:**

★★★ 62% Strathmore
Marine Rd East LA4 5AP
☎ 01524 421234 📠 01524 414242
e-mail: info@strathmore-hotel.co.uk
Dir: *from Lancaster A589 to Morecambe 3rd rdbt follow signs for the Promenade on reaching coast road turn left and hotel on the left*
Situated on the promenade, this friendly hotel provides spacious and comfortable public rooms. At the time of going to press, an extensive refurbishment plan was sweeping through the smart bedrooms and stylish public areas. A skilfully prepared range of food is available.
ROOMS: 50 en suite (5 fmly) No smoking in 15 bedrooms s £45-£55; d £75-£85 (incl. bkfst) * LB **FACILITIES:** STV entertainment Xmas **CONF:** Thtr 180 Class 100 Board 50 Del £75 * **SERVICES:** Lift **PARKING:** 19 **NOTES:** No dogs (ex guide dogs) No smoking in restaurant Civ Wed 100 **CARDS:**

★ 57% *Clarendon*
Marine Rd West, West End Promenade LA4 4EP
☎ 01524 410180 📠 01524 421616
This popular resort hotel overlooking the promenade is just a short walk from the local attractions. The public rooms include a stylish dining room, a residents' lounge and a popular lounge bar where a good range of food is served. Bedrooms come in a range of sizes and styles.
ROOMS: 31 rms (28 en suite) (2 fmly) **FACILITIES:** Pool table **CONF:** Thtr 60 Class 50 Board 50 **SERVICES:** Lift **PARKING:** 21 **CARDS:**

MORETON, Merseyside Map 07 SJ28

★★★ 65% Leasowe Castle
Leasowe Rd CH46 3RF
☎ 0151 606 9191 📠 0151 678 5551
e-mail: leasowe.castle@mail.cybase.co.uk
Dir: *leave M53 junct 1 take 1st exit from rdbt at 1st slip road join A551 hotel three quarters of a mile on right*

continued

Partly dating back to 1592, this hotel was built to allow the owner to watch horseracing on the sands. Many impressive features remain, including ornately carved wall panels and a ceiling brought from the Palace of Westminster. Bedrooms are well equipped and comfortable. The beamed bar offers a range of meals and there is also a more formal restaurant.
ROOMS: 47 en suite (3 fmly) No smoking in 3 bedrooms s £49.50-£59.50; d £66.50-£76.50 (incl. bkfst) * LB **FACILITIES:** STV Sauna Gym Water sports Sea Fishing Sailing ch fac **CONF:** Thtr 220 Board 40 Del from £72.50 * **SERVICES:** Lift **PARKING:** 200 **NOTES:** No dogs (ex guide dogs) Civ Wed 120 **CARDS:**

MORETONHAMPSTEAD, Devon — Map 03 SX78

★★★★67% ❀ Manor House

TQ13 8RE
☎ 01647 440355 🖷 01647 440961
e-mail: manorhouse@principalhotels.co.uk
Dir: *2m from Moretonhampstead towards Princetown on B3212*
A substantial Victorian manor house set in quiet grounds in a tranquil location, which includes a championship golf course and a lake. The inviting bedrooms are decorated in keeping with the age and style of the building and are well equipped. The Hambledon Restaurant serves an interesting choice of dishes that are presented with considerable flair.
ROOMS: 90 en suite (5 fmly) s fr £78; d fr £136 (incl. bkfst & dinner) * LB **FACILITIES:** STV Golf 18 Tennis (hard) Fishing Snooker Croquet lawn Putting green Xmas **CONF:** Thtr 100 Class 50 Board 40 **SERVICES:** Lift **PARKING:** 100 **NOTES:** No smoking in restaurant Civ Wed 100 **CARDS:**

MORETON-IN-MARSH, Gloucestershire — Map 04 SP23

★★★72% ❀❀ *Manor House Hotel*

High St GL56 0LJ
☎ 01608 650501 🖷 01608 651481
e-mail: themanor2@aol.com
Dir: *off A429 at south end of the town*
Dating back to the 16th century, this charming Cotswold coaching inn retains much of its original character. Bedrooms vary in size, but all are well equipped and some are particularly opulent. Public rooms are comfortable and smartly presented.
ROOMS: 38 en suite (2 fmly) **FACILITIES:** Indoor swimming (H) Sauna Jacuzzi/spa **CONF:** Thtr 100 Class 55 Board 50 **SERVICES:** Lift **PARKING:** 30 **NOTES:** No dogs (ex guide dogs) No smoking in restaurant **CARDS:**

MORLEY, West Yorkshire — Map 08 SE22

★★65% The Old Vicarage

Bruntcliffe Rd LS27 0JZ
☎ 0113 253 2174 🖷 0113 253 3549
e-mail: oldvicarage@btinternet.com
Dir: *follow signs for A650, go through traffic lights and pass two garages on the left. Hotel is located just before St Andrew's Church*
This elegant stone building provides modern, well equipped bedrooms. The interesting public rooms have a delightful Victorian theme. A good range of well produced food is available and service is both friendly and attentive.

continued

The Old Vicarage, Morley

ROOMS: 21 en suite (1 fmly) No smoking in 14 bedrooms s £48; d £62 (incl. bkfst) * LB **PARKING:** 21 **NOTES:** No dogs (ex guide dogs) No smoking in restaurant **CARDS:**

MORPETH, Northumberland — Map 12 NZ28

★★★★65% *Linden Hall*

NE65 8XF
☎ 01670 516611 🖷 01670 788544
(For full entry see Longhorsley)

★★62% *Waterford Lodge*

Castle Square NE61 1YD
☎ 01670 512004
Modern, well equipped bedrooms are a feature of this hotel, whose public areas focus on an open plan bar which, along with the adjoining restaurant, offer an environment for informal dining.
ROOMS:: 16 en suite

MORTEHOE, Devon
Map 02 SS44

★ 70% Lundy House Hotel
Chapel Hill EX34 7DZ
☎ 01271 870372 01271 871001
e-mail: tibido.london@virgin.net
Dir: *take A361 to Braunton/Ilfracombe. Then Woolacombe exit at rdbt. In village right along esplanade and uphill towards Mortehoe, hotel on left*
Facing south across the rugged North Devon coastline to Lundy Island in the distance, this personally-run hotel offers a warm, friendly welcome. In the dining room, honest home cooking is served; vegetarians are particularly welcome. There is direct access to the coastal path from the hotel's terraced gardens.
ROOMS: 8 en suite (3 fmly) No smoking in all bedrooms s £32.50-£39; d £45-£58 (incl. bkfst) * LB **FACILITIES:** STV **PARKING:** 8 **NOTES:** No smoking in restaurant Closed Jan **CARDS:**

MOUSEHOLE, Cornwall & Isles of Scilly
Map 02 SW42

★★ 66% Old Coastguard Hotel
The Parade TR19 6PR
☎ 01736 731222 01736 731720
e-mail: bookings@oldcoastguardhotel.co.uk
Dir: *take A30 to Penzance, keep to waterfront & drive to Newlyn, turn left at bridge & follow coastal road 2m to village, hotel 1st building on left*
Situated on the edge of Mousehole, this charming hotel offers comfortable accommodation and modern facilities, and many rooms have sea views. An imaginative menu is offered, many dishes based on fresh fish from nearby Newlyn. The stylish bar, restaurant and sun lounge have wonderful views of the sea.
ROOMS: 14 rms (12 en suite) 8 annexe rms (7 en suite) (2 fmly) No smoking in all bedrooms s £44-£58; d £68-£80 (incl. bkfst) * LB **PARKING:** 12 **NOTES:** No smoking in restaurant RS Nov-Apr1
CARDS:

M

MUCH BIRCH, Herefordshire
Map 03 SO53

★★★ 63% Pilgrim
Ross Rd HR2 8HJ
☎ 01981 540742 01981 540620
e-mail: pilgrim540@aol.com
Dir: *midway between Hereford and Ross-on-Wye off A49*
This much extended former rectory, surrounded by extensive grounds, provides bedrooms equipped with modern comforts. There is a pleasant character bar, a traditionally furnished restaurant and a comfortable lounge. Other facilities include a small function room and a pitch and putt course.
ROOMS: 20 en suite (3 fmly) No smoking in 5 bedrooms s £49.50-£69.50; d £59.50-£90 (incl. bkfst) * LB **FACILITIES:** Croquet lawn Putting green Pitch & putt Badminton Xmas **CONF:** Thtr 45 Class 45 Board 25 **PARKING:** 40 **CARDS:**

MUCH WENLOCK, Shropshire
Map 07 SO69

★★★ 73% *Raven*
Barrow St TF13 6EN
☎ 01952 727251 01952 728416
Dir: *M54 junct 4 or 5, take the A442 S, then A4169 to Much Wenlock*
This town centre hotel is spread across several historic buildings with a 17th-century coaching inn at its centre. Accommodation is well furnished and equipped to offer modern comfort, with some ground floor rooms available. Public areas feature an interesting collection of prints and other memorabilia connected with the Olympic Games.
ROOMS: 8 en suite 7 annexe en suite **FACILITIES:** STV **CONF:** Thtr 16 Board 14 **PARKING:** 30 **NOTES:** No dogs (ex guide dogs) No smoking in restaurant **CARDS:**

★★ 67% Wheatland Fox
TF13 6AD
☎ 01952 727292 01952 727301
e-mail: wheatlandfox@muchwenlock42.freeserve.co.uk
Dir: *just off A458 Shrewsbury/Bridgnorth road turn into High Street Much Wenlock*
The original part of this Grade II listed building dates back to 1669. The modern, smartly equipped accommodation includes rooms with four-poster beds and a family bedded room. Service at the privately owned and personally run hotel is friendly and courteous.
ROOMS: 7 en suite s £40-£45; d £55-£60 (incl. bkfst) * LB
PARKING: 12 **NOTES:** No smoking in restaurant
CARDS:

MUDEFORD See Christchurch

MULLION, Cornwall & Isles of Scilly
Map 02 SW61

★★★ 71% Polurrian
TR12 7EN
☎ 01326 240421 01326 240083
e-mail: polurotel@aol.com
Dir: *exit A30 onto A3076 to Truro. Then follow signs for Helston A39 then A394 to The Lizard & Mullion*
Situated with marvellous views over Mullion Cove and the sea, this impressive Edwardian hotel has spacious and comfortable public areas and a well equipped leisure centre. Bedrooms, all individual in style and decor, are pleasing and comfortable, many have sea views.
ROOMS: 39 en suite (22 fmly) s £30-£100; d £60-£200 (incl. bkfst & dinner) * LB **FACILITIES:** STV Indoor swimming (H) Outdoor swimming (H) Tennis (hard) Squash Snooker Sauna Solarium Gym Croquet lawn Putting green Jacuzzi/spa Cricket net Whirlpool Mountain bikes & Wet suit hire entertainment ch fac Xmas **CONF:** Thtr 100 Class 60 Board 30 Del from £65 * **PARKING:** 80 **NOTES:** No smoking in restaurant **CARDS:**

See advert on opposite page

★★ 71% Mullion Cove Hotel
TR12 7EP
☎ 01326 240328 01326 240998
e-mail: mullion.cove@btinternet.com
Dir: *in Helston follow signs to The Lizard, turn right at Mullion Holiday Park. Through village & turn left for Cove & Hotel*

Enjoying a spectacular elevated position, the views from this imposing hotel will remain long in the memory. The elegant restaurant serves freshly prepared dishes, and lighter bites are offered in the informal setting of the conservatory bar. Bedrooms are furnished to a high standard and include many modern facilities.

continued

ROOMS: 28 en suite (9 fmly) s £40-£140; d £88-£158 (incl. bkfst & dinner) * LB **FACILITIES:** Outdoor swimming (H) Sauna Solarium Xmas **PARKING:** 60 **NOTES:** No smoking in restaurant
CARDS:

MUNDFORD, Norfolk Map 05 TL89

★★★68% Lynford Hall

Lynford Hall IP26 5HW
☎ 01842 878351 📠 01842 878252

Situated in a peaceful location at the end of a long drive, amidst attractive well tended gardens, is this delightful country hotel. The public rooms are very elegant and feature a large open plan hallway with leather chesterfields. In addition there is a comfortable well stocked lounge bar and the Duvernay restaurant where guests can choose from an interesting menu featuring organic food and wines. The spacious bedrooms are tastefully decorated and equipped with many useful extras.

ROOMS: 26 en suite (3 fmly) No smoking in all bedrooms s £79-£99; d £99-£115 (incl. bkfst) * LB **FACILITIES:** Riding Xmas **CONF:** Thtr 350 Class 150 Board 100 Del £135 * **PARKING:** 150 **NOTES:** No dogs No smoking in restaurant Civ Wed 550
CARDS:

MUNGRISDALE, Cumbria Map 11 NY33

★73% The Mill

CA11 0XR
☎ 01768 779659 📠 01768 779155
Dir: *exit M6 at junct 40, 2m N of A66*

Formerly a mill cottage dating from 1651, this charming hotel and restaurant lies beside a tranquil stream. Inside there are cosy lounges, low ceilings and a wealth of antiques, paintings and period pieces. Dinner is something of a special occasion. The menu is short but extends to five courses and will satisfy the heartiest of Lakeland appetites.

ROOMS: 7 rms (5 en suite) d £108-£148 (incl. bkfst & dinner) * **FACILITIES:** Fishing Games room **PARKING:** 15 **NOTES:** No smoking in restaurant Closed Nov-Feb

NAILSWORTH, Gloucestershire Map 03 ST89

★★70% Egypt Mill

GL6 0AE
☎ 01453 833449 📠 01453 836098
Dir: *on A46*

This former corn mill dates back to the 17th century. It offers a restaurant with adjoining bar, and a cellar bar with a popular bistro. The millstones and lifting equipment are still in evidence, as well as working waterwheels. There is also a riverside patio and gardens. Bedrooms are well equipped and tastefully furnished.

ROOMS: 8 en suite 10 annexe en suite (2 fmly) s fr £45.50; d £75-£95 (incl. bkfst) * LB **FACILITIES:** STV entertainment ch fac Xmas **CONF:** Thtr 100 Class 80 Del from £65 * **PARKING:** 120 **NOTES:** No dogs (ex guide dogs) No smoking in restaurant
CARDS:

NANTWICH, Cheshire Map 07 SJ65

★★★74% Rookery Hall

Main Rd, Worleston CW5 6DQ
☎ 01270 610016 📠 01270 626027
e-mail: rookery@aol.com
Dir: *take B5074 off the 4th rdbt on the Nantwich by-pass. Rookery Hall is 1.5m on the right*

Partly dating back to 1816, this fine mansion has been extended over the years. Spacious bedrooms, some in an adjacent coach

house, are comfortable. There is a light and airy salon and a bar leading out on to the patio. Dinner is served in the mahogany-panelled dining room, overlooking gardens and pastureland.

ROOMS: 30 en suite 15 annexe en suite s £95-£155; d £110-£170 (incl. bkfst) * LB **FACILITIES:** STV Tennis (hard) Croquet lawn Xmas **CONF:** Thtr 90 Class 40 Board 40 Del from £140 * **SERVICES:** Lift **PARKING:** 80 **NOTES:** No smoking in restaurant
CARDS:

★★69% Crown

High St CW5 5AS
☎ 01270 625283 📠 01270 628047
e-mail:
crownhotel@highstnantwich.freeserve.co.uk
Dir: *take A52 to Nantwich hotel in centre of town*

A grade I listed building and 16th-century coaching inn, this hotel is centrally situated within the pedestrianised main street. The

continued

NANTWICH, continued

hotel has much original character with exposed beams, uneven floors and narrow corridors. Rooms vary in size but all are neatly furnished and well equipped. The popular restaurant offers an extensive Italian menu.
ROOMS: 18 en suite (2 fmly) No smoking in 2 bedrooms s fr £59; d fr £69 * LB **CONF:** Thtr 200 Class 150 Board 70 **PARKING:** 18 **NOTES:** Closed 25 Dec Civ Wed 150 **CARDS:**

Premier Lodge

221 Crewe Rd CW5 6NE
☎ 0870 700 1496 📠 0870 700 1497
Premier Lodge offers modern, well equipped, en suite accommodation suitable for both business and leisure travellers. Meals can be taken at the adjacent popular restaurant and bar which is fully licensed. For further details, consult the Hotel Groups page.
ROOMS: 37 en suite d £46 *

NEEDHAM MARKET, Suffolk — Map 05 TM05

Travelodge

Beacon Hill IP6 8NY
☎ 01449 721640 📠 01449 721640
Dir: *A14/A140*

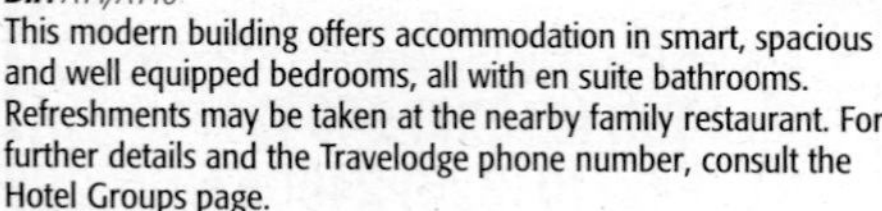

This modern building offers accommodation in smart, spacious and well equipped bedrooms, all with en suite bathrooms. Refreshments may be taken at the nearby family restaurant. For further details and the Travelodge phone number, consult the Hotel Groups page.
ROOMS: 40 en suite

NESSCLIFFE, Shropshire — Map 07 SJ31

★★ 70% Nesscliffe

Nesscliffe SY4 1DB
☎ 01743 741430 📠 01743 741104
e-mail: mike@wright70.co.uk
Dir: *on A5 between Shrewsbury/Oswestry*
This grade II listed property, which dates back to the early 19th century, provides good quality, tastefully appointed and well equipped accommodation, including two rooms with four-poster beds. The open plan public areas comprise an attractive lounge bar and a very pleasant restaurant area, where a wide range of dishes is available.
ROOMS: 8 en suite (1 fmly) s fr £45; d fr £55 (incl. bkfst) * LB **FACILITIES:** STV ch fac **PARKING:** 50 **NOTES:** No dogs (ex guide dogs) No smoking in restaurant **CARDS:**

NETHER STOWEY, Somerset — Map 03 ST13

★★ 66% Apple Tree

Keenthorne TA5 1HZ
☎ 01278 733238 📠 01278 732693
Dir: *on A39 approx. 7m W of Bridgwater and 2m E of Nether Stowey*
This attractive, roadside inn provides comfortable accommodation. Bedrooms are well equipped and smartly presented; several are located in an adjoining wing overlooking the garden. The bar, attractive conservatory and lounge offer areas in which to enjoy a quiet drink and home-cooked meal.
ROOMS: 15 en suite (1 fmly) No smoking in 3 bedrooms s fr £37.50; d fr £47.50 (incl. bkfst) * LB **PARKING:** 60 **NOTES:** No dogs (ex guide dogs) No smoking in restaurant **CARDS:**

NETHER WASDALE, Cumbria — Map 06 NY10

★★ 71% Low Wood Hall Hotel & Restaurant

CA20 1ET
☎ 019467 26111 📠 019467 26111
e-mail: lowwoodhallhotel@btinternet.com
Dir: *turn off A595 at Gosforth and bear left for Wasdale, after 3m turn right for Nether Wasdale*
This delightful country house hotel provides comfortable, modern accommodation. Some of the bedrooms in the main house have been stylishly refurbished. There is a sumptuous lounge and two smart and very individual restaurants, plus a sauna for those seeking true relaxation. Excellent dinners are the highlight of any visit.
ROOMS: 6 en suite 6 annexe en suite (1 fmly) No smoking in all bedrooms s £60-£80; d £75-£100 (incl. bkfst) * LB **FACILITIES:** Sauna Xmas **CONF:** Thtr 30 Class 30 Board 16 Del from £125 * **PARKING:** 20 **NOTES:** No dogs No smoking in restaurant Closed Jan RS Sun **CARDS:**

NEWARK-ON-TRENT, Nottinghamshire — Map 08 SK75

★★ 73% South Parade

117-119 Baldertongate NG24 1RY
☎ 01636 703008 & 703030 📠 01636 605593
e-mail: thesouthparadehotel@tesco.net
Dir: *from B6326 follow Newark signs drive into Newark turn right at lights on x-rds then right again hotel on left opposite Fountain Gardens*
This welcoming hotel is situated just a few minutes walk from the town centre and is a Grade II Listed Georgian building. Bedrooms offer attractively decorated and comfortably appointed accommodation, that has a good range of useful facilities. In addition to the homely lounge, there is a bar and restaurant on the lower ground floor.
ROOMS: 13 en suite (3 fmly) No smoking in 11 bedrooms s £39.50-£54; d £54-£74.50 (incl. bkfst) * LB **CONF:** Thtr 20 Class 20 Board 20 **PARKING:** 14 **NOTES:** No smoking in restaurant
CARDS:

NEWBURY, Berkshire — Map 04 SU46

Premier Collection

★★★★

The Vineyard at Stockcross

Stockcross RG20 8JU
☎ 01635 528770 📠 01635 528398
e-mail: general@the-vinyard.co.uk
Dir: *2.5m W of Newbury on B4000 north of the A4 Newbury to Hungerford road*
Guests can enjoy first class service and food at this outstanding hotel and restaurant, which has a very special atmosphere created by the well drilled, discreet and friendly staff. The grounds, public rooms and bedrooms are all artistically designed, and accurate, seasonal cooking is complemented by an outstanding wine list.

continued

ROOMS: 33 en suite No smoking in 10 bedrooms s £139-£195; d £165-£345 (incl. bkfst) * LB **FACILITIES:** STV Indoor swimming (H) Sauna Gym Jacuzzi/spa Treatment rooms entertainment **CONF:** Thtr 50 Class 32 Board 20 Del from £220 * **SERVICES:** Lift air con **PARKING:** 60 **NOTES:** No dogs (ex guide dogs) Closed Xmas Civ Wed **CARDS:**

★★★★79% Donnington Valley
Old Oxford Rd, Donnington RG14 3AG
☎ 01635 551199 01635 551123
e-mail: general@donningtonvalley.co.uk
Dir: *exit M4 junct 13, take A34 southbound and exit at Donnington Castle. Turn right over bridge then left hotel is 1m on right*

Public areas offer a high standard of comfort throughout. The well equipped meeting rooms, much in demand for conferences, have been decorated and furnished to give character to the striking modern structure of the building. The hotel also benefits from being situated on its own 18 hole golf course.
ROOMS: 58 en suite (11 fmly) No smoking in 30 bedrooms s £129; d £129-£200 * LB **FACILITIES:** STV Golf 18 Putting green entertainment Xmas **CONF:** Thtr 140 Class 60 Board 40 Del from £130 * **SERVICES:** Lift **PARKING:** 160 **NOTES:** No dogs (ex guide dogs) Civ Wed 85 **CARDS:**

★★★★75% Regency Park Hotel
Bowling Green Rd, Thatcham RG18 3RP
☎ 01635 871555 01635 871571
e-mail: regencypark@bestwestern.co.uk
Dir: *from Newbury take A4 signed Thatcham/Reading. At 2nd rdbt follow signs to Cold Ash. Hotel 1m on the left*
Peacefully situated in five acres of grounds, within easy reach of the M3 and M4, this hotel has been extended to add a smart leisure club, a further 36 bedrooms and a state-of-the-art function suite. Accommodation is spacious, modern and well equipped; the new executive rooms are particularly impressive. Day rooms include the stylish Watermark restaurant.

ROOMS: 45 en suite (7 fmly) s £115-£240; d £145-£280 * LB **FACILITIES:** STV Tennis (hard) entertainment Xmas **CONF:** Thtr 190 Class 75 Board 65 Del £145 * **SERVICES:** Lift **PARKING:** 160 **NOTES:** No smoking in restaurant **CARDS:**

See advert on this page

★★★64% The Chequers
Oxford St RG14 1JB
REGAL
☎ 01635 38000 01635 37170
Dir: *M4 junct 13 follow signs Newbury town centre. At rdbt with A4 take 4th exit. Over mini rdbt & right at Clocktower rdbt. Hotel on right*
In an enviable town centre location, this hotel offers bedrooms of varying sizes and outlook; most are in the original buildings but

continued

NEWBURY, continued

some are in modern wings. All have good facilities and offer high levels of comfort.

The Chequers, Newbury

ROOMS: 45 en suite 11 annexe en suite (3 fmly) No smoking in 40 bedrooms s £125-£140; d £135-£180 * LB **FACILITIES:** STV **CONF:** Thtr 200 Class 100 Board 50 Del from £140 * **PARKING:** 60 **NOTES:** No dogs (ex guide dogs) No smoking in restaurant Closed 24 Dec-4 Jan **CARDS:**

Premier Lodge

Bath Rd, Midgham RG7 5UX

☎ 0870 700 1498 0870 700 1499

Premier Lodge offers modern, well equipped, en suite accommodation suitable for both business and leisure travellers. Meals can be taken at the adjacent popular restaurant and bar which is fully licensed. For further details, consult the Hotel Groups page.

ROOMS: 29 en suite d £49.50 *

Travelodge

Chieveley, Oxford Rd RG18 9XX

☎ 01635 248024

Dir: *on A34/off junc 13 M4*

This modern building offers accommodation in smart, spacious and well equipped bedrooms, all with en suite bathrooms. Refreshments may be taken at the nearby family restaurant. For further details and the Travelodge phone number, consult the Hotel Groups page.

ROOMS: 64 en suite

NEWBY BRIDGE, Cumbria Map 07 SD38

★★★★ 75% Lakeside

Lakeside LA12 8AT

☎ 015395 31207 015395 31699

e-mail: sales@Lakesidehotel.co.uk

Dir: *from M6 junct 36 join A590 to Barrow and follow signs to Newby Bridge. Turn right over the bridge, the hotel is 1m along on the right*

On the southern shore of Lake Windermere, this grand hotel provides comfort and quality throughout. There is a delightful conservatory lounge and the elegant restaurant serves some imaginatively presented British and European cooking. Ruskin's Brasserie is more informal. Spacious bedrooms are thoughtfully equipped, some have furnished patios.

ROOMS: 80 en suite (7 fmly) No smoking in 34 bedrooms s £99.87-£210; d £120-£230 (incl. bkfst) * LB **FACILITIES:** STV Indoor swimming (H) Fishing Pool table Croquet lawn Jacuzzi/spa Private jetty Use of Health club entertainment Xmas **CONF:** Thtr 100 Class 50 Board 40 Del from £141 * **SERVICES:** Lift **PARKING:** 200 **NOTES:** No smoking in restaurant Civ Wed 140 **CARDS:**

★★★ 69% The Swan

LA12 8NB

☎ 015395 31681 015395 31917

e-mail: swanhotel@aol.com

Dir: *leave M6 junct 36 follow A590 sigposted Barrow for 16m, hotel on right of the old 5 arch bridge, in Newby Bridge*

This long-established hotel is set on the banks of the River Leven at the southern end of Lake Windermere, with riverside walks past all the moorings. The main restaurant, occupying an old barn with lofted ceiling and stone walls, is adjoined by a cocktail lounge. There is also a lounge bar and less formal restaurant. Bedrooms are traditionally furnished, well equipped and include some excellent family units.

ROOMS: 55 en suite (4 fmly) No smoking in 16 bedrooms s £85-£115; d £140-£180 (incl. bkfst) * LB **FACILITIES:** STV Indoor swimming (H) Fishing Sauna Solarium Gym Jacuzzi/spa Beauty treatment rooms Xmas **CONF:** Thtr 90 Class 60 Board 50 Del from £90 * **SERVICES:** Lift **PARKING:** 100 **NOTES:** No dogs (ex guide dogs) No smoking in restaurant Civ Wed 80 **CARDS:**

★★★ 65% Whitewater

The Lakeland Village LA12 8PX

☎ 015395 31133 015395 31881

Dir: *leave M6 junct 36 follow signs for A590 Barrow 1m through Newby Bridge, turn right at signpost for Lakeland Village, hotel on left*

On the banks of the spectacular River Leven, this smart hotel is a stylish conversion of an old mill. Public areas include a choice of bars and a restaurant offering meals prepared from fresh local produce. Bedrooms, with exposed natural stone, are especially spacious, modern, and comfortable.

ROOMS: 35 en suite (10 fmly) s £72-£87; d £120-£150 (incl. bkfst) * LB **FACILITIES:** STV Indoor swimming (H) Tennis (hard) Squash Sauna Solarium Gym Putting green Jacuzzi/spa Beauty treatment spa steam room table tennis golf driving net entertainment Xmas **CONF:** Thtr 80 Class 32 Board 40 Del from £90 * **SERVICES:** Lift **PARKING:** 50 **NOTES:** No dogs (ex guide dogs) No smoking in restaurant Civ Wed 100 **CARDS:**

See advert on opposite page

NEWCASTLE-UNDER-LYME, Staffordshire Map 07 SJ84

★★★ *Posthouse Stoke-on-Trent*

Clayton Rd ST5 4DL

☎ 0870 400 9077 01782 717138

Dir: *on A519 at junct 15 of M6*

This modern hotel is situated in spacious grounds. Facilities include a Spa leisure centre and popular Traders restaurant. Bedrooms are comfortably furnished and include interactive TV, hairdryers and trouser presses. Extended room service and all-day lounge service are available. Staff are professional, friendly and willing.

continued

ROOMS: 119 en suite (41 fmly) No smoking in 54 bedrooms **FACILITIES:** Indoor swimming (H) Sauna Solarium Gym Pool table Jacuzzi/spa Childrens play areas Beauty & therapy room **CONF:** Thtr 70 Class 40 Board 34 **PARKING:** 128 **CARDS:**

★★ 63% Comfort Inn

CHOICE HOTELS EUROPE

Liverpool Rd, Cross Heath ST5 9DX
☎ 01782 717000 🖷 01782 713669
e-mail: admin@gb617.u-net.com
Dir: *M6 junct 16 onto A500 towards Stoke-on-Trent. Take A34 to Newcastle-under-Lyme, hotel on right after 1.5m*

Some of the well equipped bedrooms at this purpose built hotel are in a separate block at the rear. There is a large lounge bar, an attractively appointed restaurant and a small gymnasium.

ROOMS: 43 en suite 24 annexe en suite (6 fmly) No smoking in 25 bedrooms d £42-£46.75 * LB **FACILITIES:** STV Xmas **CONF:** Thtr 130 Class 80 Board 50 Del from £72 * **PARKING:** 160 **NOTES:** No smoking in restaurant Civ Wed **CARDS:**

NEWCASTLE UPON TYNE, Tyne & Wear — Map 12 NZ26

see also Seaton Burn & Whickham

★★★★ 74% ❀❀ Vermont

Castle Garth NE1 1RQ
☎ 0191 233 1010 🖷 0191 233 1234
e-mail: info@vermont-hotel.co.uk
Dir: *city centre by the high level bridge & Castle Keep*

The Vermont presents a striking facade and sits next to Castle Keep and the Tyne Bridge in the city centre. Accommodation is comfortable and spacious with every expected facility. There are a number of dining and drinking options, from the lively Martha's bar and an all day Brasserie to the sedate Blue Room where ambitious cuisine is served.

ROOMS: 101 en suite (12 fmly) No smoking in 20 bedrooms s fr £145; d fr £165 * LB **FACILITIES:** STV Solarium Gym entertainment Xmas **CONF:** Thtr 210 Class 60 Board 36 Del £155 * **SERVICES:** Lift **PARKING:** 100 **CARDS:**

★★★★ 69% Copthorne Newcastle

COPTHORNE

The Close, Quayside NE1 3RT
☎ 0191 222 0333 🖷 0191 230 1111
e-mail: sales.newcastle@mill-cop.com
Dir: *east of A189 off B1600*

Set right on the banks of the River Tyne close to the city centre, this hotel provides a range of conference facilities and a leisure centre. First-floor bedrooms have balconies overlooking the river and there is a floor of 'Connoisseur' rooms with their own exclusive lounge.

ROOMS: 156 en suite (16 fmly) No smoking in 85 bedrooms s £145; d £170 * LB **FACILITIES:** STV Indoor swimming (H) Sauna Solarium Gym Jacuzzi/spa Steam room Xmas **CONF:** Thtr 200 Class 85 Board 60 Del from £145 * **SERVICES:** Lift air con **PARKING:** 180 **CARDS:**

★★★★ 68% Newcastle Marriott City Centre

Metro Centre NE11 9XF
☎ 0191 493 2233 🖷 0191 493 2030
(For full entry see Gateshead)

★★★★ 63% *Holiday Inn*

Great North Rd NE13 6BF
☎ 0191 201 9988 🖷 0191 236 8091
(For full entry see Seaton Burn)

Whitewater Hotel, Newby Bridge

★★★ 77% ❀ Malmaison

Malmaison HOTELS

Quayside NE1 3DX
☎ 0191 245 5000 🖷 0191 245 4545
e-mail: newcastle@malmaison.com
Dir: *follow signs for Newcastle city centre. Take road for Quayside/Law Courts. Hotel is approx 100yds past the Law Courts overlooking the river*

Overlooking the river in the redeveloped quayside, this old building has been transformed in the unique Malmaison style into an interesting modern hotel, popular with guests looking for a change from traditional accommodation. All bedrooms have good desk space, music and communications systems, as well as large beds. The busy riverside brasserie is a popular venue.

ROOMS: 116 en suite (10 fmly) d £105 * LB **FACILITIES:** STV Sauna Solarium Gym **CONF:** Thtr 60 Class 10 Board 22 **SERVICES:** Lift **PARKING:** 50 **NOTES:** No dogs (ex guide dogs) **CARDS:**

★★★ 67% *Posthouse Newcastle upon Tyne*

Posthouse

New Bridge St NE1 8BS
☎ 0870 400 9058 🖷 0191 261 8529
Dir: *follow signs for Gateshead/Newcastle A167M over Tyne Bridge take A193 Wallsend and City Centre left to Carliol Sq hotel on corner infront of junct*

This city centre hotel offers both traditional and 'Millennium' bedrooms and a choice of bars, together with the attractively furnished Junction restaurant. Other facilities include a manned business centre, wide choice of meeting and function rooms and an impressive leisure club. Secure parking is provided in the adjacent multistorey car park.

ROOMS: 166 en suite (2 fmly) No smoking in 108 bedrooms **FACILITIES:** Indoor swimming (H) Sauna Solarium Gym Jacuzzi/spa adjoning leisure club **CONF:** Thtr 600 Class 350 Board 50 **SERVICES:** Lift **PARKING:** 132 **CARDS:**

NEWCASTLE UPON TYNE, continued

★★★67% *Posthouse Washington*
Emerson District 5 NE37 1LB
☎ 0870 400 9084 🖷 0191 415 3371
(For full entry see Washington)

Posthouse

★★★67% Swallow
High West St NE8 1PE
☎ 0191 477 1105 🖷 0191 478 7214
e-mail: info@swallowhotels.com
(For full entry see Gateshead)

★★★66% Novotel
Ponteland Rd, Kenton NE3 3HZ
☎ 0191 214 0303 🖷 0191 214 0633
e-mail: H1118@accor-hotels.com

***Dir:** off A1(M) Airport junct - A696, take Kingston Park exit*

Convenient for the airport, this bright, modern hotel offers stylish public areas and spacious, well equipped accommodation. The Garden Brasserie is open for meals until late.

ROOMS: 126 en suite (126 fmly) No smoking in 82 bedrooms d £50-£75 * LB **FACILITIES:** STV Indoor swimming (H) Sauna Exercise equipment **CONF:** Thtr 220 Class 100 Board 25 Del from £99 * **SERVICES:** Lift **PARKING:** 260 **CARDS:**

★★★65% George Washington County Hotel
Stone Cellar Rd, District 12, High Usworth NE37 1PH
☎ 0191 402 9988 🖷 0191 415 1166
e-mail: reservations@corushotels.com
(For full entry see Washington)

REGAL

★★★64% The Caledonian Hotel, Newcastle
64 Osborne Rd, Jesmond NE2 2AT
☎ 0191 281 7881 🖷 0191 281 6241

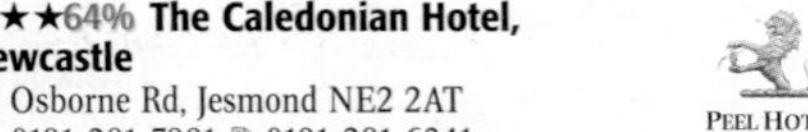

PEEL HOTELS

***Dir:** take B1318 through Gosforth to large rdbt turn left onto A189 to 2nd set of lights B1600/A1058 turn right hotel beyond St George's Church*

Situated on the east side of the city, this business and conference hotel provides comfortable well equipped bedrooms along with a relaxed informal atmosphere.

ROOMS: 89 en suite (6 fmly) No smoking in 17 bedrooms s £65-£89; d £75-£99 (incl. bkfst) * LB **FACILITIES:** STV Xmas **CONF:** Thtr 100 Class 60 Board 46 Del from £95 * **SERVICES:** Lift **PARKING:** 52 **CARDS:**

★★★64% New Kent Hotel
127 Osborne Rd NE2 2TB
☎ 0191 281 7711 🖷 0191 281 3369

Best Western

***Dir:** beside B1600, opposite St Georges Church*

This business hotel is situated in Jesmond and provides generously portioned meals in its attractive restaurant. The well equipped bedrooms come in a variety of sizes.

ROOMS: 32 en suite (4 fmly) s £48-£69; d £69-£79 (incl. bkfst) * LB **FACILITIES:** STV Xmas **CONF:** Thtr 90 Class 50 Board 24 **PARKING:** 22 **NOTES:** No smoking in restaurant **CARDS:**

★★★63% Swallow Imperial
Jesmond Rd NE2 1PR
☎ 0191 281 5511 🖷 0191 281 8472
e-mail: jesmond@swallow-hotels.co.uk

SWALLOW HOTELS

***Dir:** turn off A167(M) onto A1058 (Tynemouth/East Coast). Hotel 0.25m on left just after second mini rdbt*

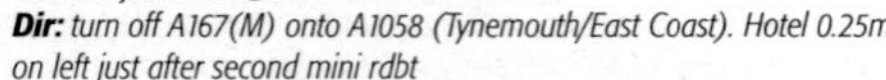

To the east of the city centre, the hotel is popular for conferences and seminars and has the added benefits of an undercover car park with the Metro only a few minutes walk away. Public areas include a comfortable club-style lounge and leisure facilities.

ROOMS: 122 en suite (6 fmly) No smoking in 77 bedrooms s fr £90; d fr £125 (incl. bkfst) * LB **FACILITIES:** STV Indoor swimming (H) Sauna Solarium Gym Jacuzzi/spa Steam room entertainment Xmas **CONF:** Thtr 150 Class 60 Board 50 Del from £95 * **SERVICES:** Lift **PARKING:** 100 **NOTES:** No smoking in restaurant Civ Wed 135 **CARDS:**

★★★61% *Chasley Hotel*
Newgate St NE1 5SX
☎ 0191 232 5025 🖷 0191 232 8428
e-mail: admin@gb077.u-net.com

***Dir:** from A6082 cross Redhuegh Bridge. Turn rightt 1st set of lights, then left, continue to Bingo hall & straight on, right*

Situated in the city centre and having the advantage of secure car parking, this hotel offers a rooftop restaurant and bar with fine views over the city. Bedrooms vary in standard, those more recently refurbished being the more comfortable.

ROOMS: 93 en suite No smoking in 41 bedrooms **FACILITIES:** STV entertainment **CONF:** Thtr 154 **SERVICES:** Lift **PARKING:** 120 **CARDS:**

★★72% Eslington Villa
8 Station Rd, Low Fell NE9 6DR
☎ 0191 487 6017 & 420 0666 🖷 0191 420 0667
(For full entry see Gateshead)

★★64% *Whites*
38-42 Osborne Rd, Jesmond NE2 2AL
☎ 0191 281 5126 🖷 0191 281 9953
e-mail: apuri80741@aol.com

***Dir:** 1m N, travelling from N or S follow A1058 signs for coast and turn left into Osborne Road at first rdbt*

This commercial hotel in Jesmond has the benefit of a secure car park and good transport links. Service is cheery, and the bedrooms are well equipped. Good value meals are offered in the restaurant.

ROOMS: 39 rms (38 en suite) (3 fmly) No smoking in 3 bedrooms **FACILITIES:** STV **CONF:** Thtr 75 Class 50 Board 40 **PARKING:** 40 **CARDS:**

★★60% Cairn
97/103 Osborne Rd, Jesmond NE2 2TJ
☎ 0191 281 1358 🖷 0191 281 9031

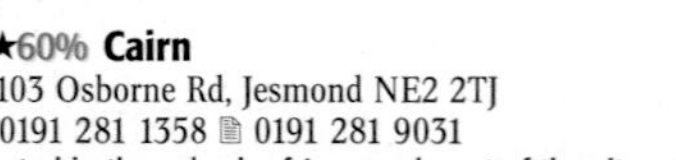

Situated in the suburb of Jesmond, east of the city centre, this commercial hotel offers friendly informal service and bright, well equipped bedrooms. Public areas feature a colonial-style restaurant and smart, trendy bar.

ROOMS: 50 en suite (2 fmly) **FACILITIES:** STV **CONF:** Thtr 150 Class 110 Board 100 **PARKING:** 22 **NOTES:** Civ Wed **CARDS:**

See advert on opposite page

★65% Hadrian Lodge Hotel

Hadrian Rd, Wallsend NE28 6HH
☎ 0191 262 7733 📠 0191 263 0714
Dir: *from Tyne tunnel (A19) take A187 to Wallsend follow this route for 1.5m, hotel on left opposite Hadrian Road Metro Station*

Conveniently situated near the metro system with easy access to the city centre, airport and railway station, this hotel offers modern accommodation, ground floor bedrooms tending to be somewhat larger. Service is friendly and a wide range of English and Italian dishes is available either in the spacious bar or in Pino's restaurant.
ROOMS: 25 en suite (1 fmly) No smoking in 2 bedrooms s fr £45; d fr £59.50 (incl. bkfst) * LB **FACILITIES:** STV Xmas **PARKING:** 60 **NOTES:** No dogs (ex guide dogs) **CARDS:**

⌂ Premier Lodge

PREMIER LODGE
THE BEST. REST ASSURED.

The Quayside NE1 3DW
☎ 0870 700 1504 📠 0870 700 1505
Premier Lodge offers modern, well equipped, en suite accommodation suitable for both business and leisure travellers. Meals can be taken at the adjacent popular restaurant and bar which is fully licensed. For further details, consult the Hotel Groups page.
ROOMS: 143 en suite d £49.50 *

○ Waterside Hotel

48-52 Sandhill, Quayside NE1 3JF
☎ 0191 2300 111
ROOMS: 11 rms **NOTES:** Open

NEWCASTLE UPON TYNE AIRPORT, Tyne & Wear — Map 12 NZ17

⌂ Premier Lodge

Callerton Ln Ends, Woolsington NE13 8DF
☎ 0870 700 1506 📠 0870 700 1507
Premier Lodge offers modern, well equipped, en suite accommodation suitable for both business and leisure travellers. Meals can be taken at the adjacent popular restaurant and bar which is fully licensed. For further details, consult the Hotel Groups page.
ROOMS: 52 en suite d £42 *

NEWICK, East Sussex — Map 05 TQ42

★★★80% ❀❀ Newick Park Country Estate

BN8 4SB
☎ 01825 723633 📠 01825 723969
e-mail: newick-park@msn.com
Dir: *turn S off A272 in Newick between Haywards Heath and Uckfield, pass the church and turn left at junct, entrance to Newick Park is 0.25m on right*
With views over expansive parkland, this Grade II listed Georgian

continued on p404

N

NEWICK, continued

house is set in 250 acres of tranquillity. Bedrooms are beautifully decorated and combine period charm with modern comforts. The restaurant provides dining in very elegant surroundings.
ROOMS: 13 en suite 3 annexe en suite (5 fmly) No smoking in 12 bedrooms **FACILITIES:** STV Outdoor swimming (H) Tennis (hard) Fishing Croquet lawn Badminton **CONF:** Thtr 80 Class 80 Board 25 Del £170 * **PARKING:** 52 **NOTES:** No smoking in restaurant Civ Wed 70
CARDS:

See advert on page 403

NEWMARKET, Suffolk Map 05 TL66

★★★74% Bedford Lodge
Bury Rd CB8 7BX
☎ 01638 663175 01638 667391
e-mail: info@bedfordlodgehotel.co.uk
Dir: *take Bury St Edmunds road from town centre, hotel 0.5m on left*
In three acres of secluded gardens a short drive from Newmarket race track, this 18th-century Georgian hunting lodge was originally built for the Duke of Bedford. The tasteful bedrooms are named after racecourses. Guests can dine in the bar or in the restyled restaurant which offers a wide variety of freshly prepared dishes.
ROOMS: 56 en suite (3 fmly) **FACILITIES:** Indoor swimming (H) Sauna Solarium Gym Jacuzzi/spa Steam room & beauty salon **CONF:** Thtr 200 Class 80 Board 60 Del from £134 * **SERVICES:** Lift **PARKING:** 90
CARDS:

★★★73% Swynford Paddocks Hotel
CB8 0UE
☎ 01638 570234 01638 570283
e-mail: info@swynfordpaddocks.com
(For full entry see Six Mile Bottom and advert opposite)

★★★69% Heath Court
Moulton Rd CB8 8DY
☎ 01638 667171 01638 666533
e-mail: quality@heathcourt-hotel.co.uk
Dir: *from A14 leave at Newmarket/Ely exit (A142) follow town centre signs through mini-rdbt at clocktower turn immediately left into Moulton Rd*
Close to the famed Newmarket Heath, this modern red-brick hotel is popular for its pleasant facilities. The bedrooms are spacious and smartly presented. Meals are served in the carvery which offers an a la carte menu in addition to the roasts.
ROOMS: 41 en suite (2 fmly) No smoking in 10 bedrooms s £78-£98; d £98-£118 (incl. bkfst) * LB **FACILITIES:** STV **CONF:** Thtr 150 Class 40 Board 40 Del from £100 * **SERVICES:** Lift **PARKING:** 60
NOTES: Civ Wed 80 **CARDS:**

NEW MILTON, Hampshire Map 04 SZ29

Premier Collection

★★★★★ Chewton Glen
Christchurch Rd BH25 6QS
☎ 01425 275341 01425 272310
e-mail: reservations@chewtonglen.com
Dir: *on A35 from Lyndhurst, drive 10 miles and turn left at staggered junct. Following brown tourist sign for hotel through Walkford, take second left*
Sumptuous accommodation and an abundance of thoughtful touches are provided at this internationally recognised hotel. A delightful haven of peace and tranquillity, the dedicated and professional team ensure a memorable stay for guests crossing its threshold. The restaurant serves imaginative and innovative dishes which make good use of excellent raw ingredients. The extensive wine list is another must for the wine enthusiast. Service and hospitality is of the highest standard.

ROOMS: 53 en suite 2 annexe en suite d £255-£665 * LB
FACILITIES: STV Indoor swimming (H) Outdoor swimming (H) Golf 9 Tennis (hard) Snooker Sauna Gym Pool table Croquet lawn Putting green Jacuzzi/spa Steam room Treatment rooms Hairdresser Indoor tennis courts entertainment Xmas **CONF:** Thtr 150 Class 70 Board 40 Del from £200 * **PARKING:** 100 **NOTES:** No dogs (ex guide dogs) No children 6yrs No smoking in restaurant Civ Wed 120
CARDS:

NEWPORT, Shropshire Map 07 SJ71

★★64% Royal Victoria
St Mary's St TF10 7AB
☎ 01952 820331 01952 820209
e-mail: info@royal-victoria.com.uk
Dir: *turn off A41 at 2nd Newport by-pass rdbt towards town centre turn right at 1st traffic lights. Hotel car park 150 metres on left*
This town centre hotel stands behind St Nicholas church. It dates back to Georgian times and its name derives from a visit by Princess Victoria, in 1832. The hotel provides well equipped, modern accommodation. Facilities here include an attractively appointed restaurant, a choice of bars and a large function/conference suite.
ROOMS: 24 en suite (2 fmly) s fr £44; d fr £59 (incl. bkfst) * LB
CONF: Thtr 140 Class 80 Del £90 * **PARKING:** 57
CARDS:

See advert on opposite page

NEWQUAY, Cornwall & Isles of Scilly Map 02 SW86

★★★71% Headland
Fistral Beach TR7 1EW
☎ 01637 872211 01637 872212
e-mail: office@headland.hotel.co.uk
Dir: *turn off A30 onto A392 at Indian Queens, on approaching Newquay follow signs for Fistral Beach*
Standing alone and surrounded on three sides by the sea, this unique Victorian hotel is built in one of the most marvellous settings in Cornwall. Most of the bedrooms benefit from the splendid views and all offer modern facilities. In addition to the formal dining options, the 'Garden Room' offers lighter meals throughout the day and evening.
ROOMS: 108 en suite (56 fmly) s £55-£75; d £78-£150 (incl. bkfst) * LB **FACILITIES:** STV Indoor swimming (H) Outdoor swimming (H) Golf 9 Tennis (hard) Snooker Sauna Gym Pool table Croquet lawn Putting green Jacuzzi/spa Surfing Children's indoor/outdoor play area entertainment ch fac **CONF:** Thtr 250 Class 120 Board 50 Del from £85 * **SERVICES:** Lift **PARKING:** 400 **NOTES:** No smoking in restaurant Closed 23-27 Dec Civ Wed 250 **CARDS:**

★★★ 70% Barrowfield
Hilgrove Rd TR7 2QY
☎ 01637 878878 🖷 01637 879490
e-mail: booking@barrowfield.prestel.co.uk
Dir: *take A3058 to Newquay towards Quintrell Downs, turn right at rdbt continue into town and turn left at Shell garage*
Conveniently located close to the town centre and the beaches, this popular hotel is equally suited for all guests needs. Public areas include an elegant restaurant, spacious foyer lounge, attractive coffee shop and intimate 'Piano Bar'. Some of the comfortable bedrooms have the benefit of sea views, all offer modern facilities.
ROOMS: 81 en suite 2 annexe en suite (18 fmly) s fr £60; d fr £120 (incl. bkfst & dinner) * LB **FACILITIES:** STV Indoor swimming (H) Outdoor swimming (H) Snooker Sauna Solarium Gym Pool table Jacuzzi/spa Table tennis Xmas **CONF:** Thtr 150 Class 60 Board 40 **SERVICES:** Lift **PARKING:** 70 **NOTES:** No smoking in restaurant Civ Wed 150 **CARDS:**

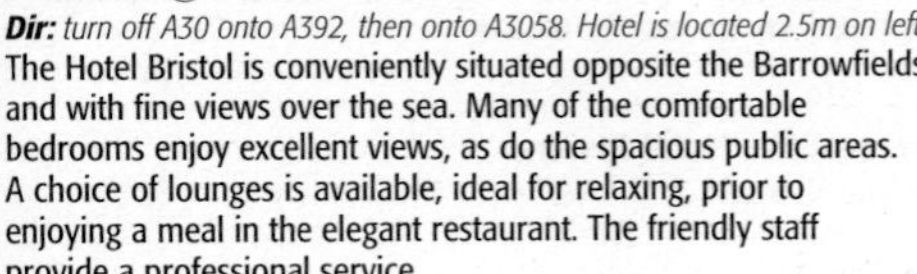

See advert on this page

★★★ 69% Hotel Bristol

Narrowcliff TR7 2PQ
☎ 01637 875181 🖷 01637 879347
e-mail: info@hotelbristol.co.uk
Dir: *turn off A30 onto A392, then onto A3058. Hotel is located 2.5m on left*
The Hotel Bristol is conveniently situated opposite the Barrowfields and with fine views over the sea. Many of the comfortable bedrooms enjoy excellent views, as do the spacious public areas. A choice of lounges is available, ideal for relaxing, prior to enjoying a meal in the elegant restaurant. The friendly staff provide a professional service.

continued on p406

N

NEWQUAY, continued

Hotel Bristol, Newquay

ROOMS: 74 en suite (23 fmly) s £52-£67; d £84-£94 * LB **FACILITIES:** Indoor swimming (H) Snooker Sauna Solarium Pool table Table tennis ch fac Xmas **CONF:** Thtr 200 Class 80 Board 20 Del from £75 * **SERVICES:** Lift **PARKING:** 105 **NOTES:** No smoking in restaurant **CARDS:**

See advert on opposite page

★★★67% Trebarwith

Trebarwith Crescent TR7 1BZ
☎ 01637 872288 📠 01637 875431
e-mail: trebahotel@aol.com
Dir: *from A3058 forward until Mount Wise Rd then 3rd right down Marcus Hill and across East St into Trebarwith Crescent. Hotel at end*

Set in its own grounds, with a path leading to the beach, this hotel is close to the town centre. Public rooms are spacious, including a lounge, a ballroom, and The Wedgwood Restaurant. The comfortable bedrooms include both four-poster and family rooms.
ROOMS: 41 en suite (8 fmly) s £36-£59; d £72-£118 (incl. bkfst & dinner) * LB **FACILITIES:** Indoor swimming (H) Fishing Snooker Sauna Solarium Pool table Jacuzzi/spa Video theatre Games room entertainment **CONF:** Thtr 45 **PARKING:** 41 **NOTES:** No dogs (ex guide dogs) No smoking in restaurant Closed Nov-8 Apr
CARDS:

See advert on opposite page

★★★66% Esplanade Hotel

Esplanade Rd, Pentire TR7 1PS
☎ 01637 873333 📠 01637 851413
e-mail: info@newquay-hotels.co.uk
Dir: *from A30 take A392 at Indian Queens towards Newquay, follow holiday route until rdbt, take left to Pentire, then right hand fork towards beach*
Overlooking Fistral Beach, this hotel offers warm hospitality. There is a choice of bedroom sizes; all have modern facilities and the most popular rooms benefit from stunning sea views. There are a number of bars, a continental-style coffee shop and the more formal surroundings of the Ocean View restaurant.

continued

ROOMS: 83 en suite (44 fmly) s £22-£35; d £44-£70 (incl. bkfst) * LB **FACILITIES:** STV Indoor swimming (H) Outdoor swimming (H) Sauna Solarium Pool table Jacuzzi/spa Table tennis Play area entertainment Xmas **CONF:** Thtr 300 Class 180 Board 150 Del from £45 * **SERVICES:** Lift **PARKING:** 40 **NOTES:** No smoking in restaurant
CARDS:

See advert on opposite page

★★★63% Glendorgal

Lusty Glaze Rd, Porth TR7 3AB
☎ 01637 874937 📠 01637 851341
e-mail: newquay@dircon.co.uk
Dir: *from A392 at Quintrell Downs rdbt turn right towards the sea do not turn towards Porth. Straight ahead of road & turn right at Hotel Riviera*
Enjoying direct access to the beach and dramatic views out to sea, the Glendorgal has a popular following. Sea-facing bedrooms are always in demand, and all rooms are equipped with modern facilities. There is a spacious, comfortable lounge and bar. Freshly prepared meals are served in the well appointed restaurant.
ROOMS: 39 en suite (16 fmly) s £40-£65; d £40-£52 (incl. bkfst & dinner) * LB **FACILITIES:** STV Indoor swimming (H) Outdoor swimming (H) Tennis (hard) Fishing Snooker Solarium Gym Jacuzzi/spa Steam Room entertainment Xmas **CONF:** Class 48 Board 25 Del from £60 * **PARKING:** 60 **NOTES:** No smoking in restaurant Civ Wed 100
CARDS:

See advert on opposite page

★★★62% Hotel Riviera

Lusty Glaze Rd TR7 3AA
☎ 01637 874251 📠 01637 850823
e-mail: a.newton@btinternet.com
Dir: *approaching Newquay from Porth turn right at The Barrowfields. Hotel on right overlooking the sea*
This popular cliff-top hotel enjoys panoramic views across the gardens to the sea beyond. Bedrooms are well equipped, although varied in terms of size and style. Comfortable lounges are provided for rest and relaxation; the more energetic may wish to use the squash court, followed by a dip in the heated outdoor pool.
ROOMS: 48 en suite (6 fmly) s £35-£45; d £70-£90 (incl. bkfst) * LB **FACILITIES:** STV Outdoor swimming (H) Tennis (hard & grass) Squash Snooker Sauna ch fac Xmas **CONF:** Thtr 200 Class 150 Board 50 Del from £54.95 * **SERVICES:** Lift **PARKING:** 70 **NOTES:** No dogs (ex guide dogs) No smoking in restaurant Civ Wed 200
CARDS:

★★★56% Kilbirnie

Narrowcliff TR7 2RS
☎ 01637 875155 📠 01637 850769
e-mail: enquirykilbirnie@aol.com
Dir: *on A392*
Overlooking the Barrowfields and the Atlantic Ocean, this family owned hotel has spacious reception rooms, including a ballroom, cocktail bar and a comfortable foyer lounge. Bedrooms vary in size and style and the hotel offers a good range of indoor facilities; the restaurant offers a fixed-price menu.
ROOMS: 66 en suite (3 fmly) s £30-£36; d £60-£72 (incl. bkfst & dinner) * LB **FACILITIES:** Indoor swimming (H) Outdoor swimming (H) Snooker Sauna Solarium Pool table Jacuzzi/spa Table tennis Xmas **CONF:** Thtr 80 Class 40 Board 20 Del from £50 * **SERVICES:** Lift air con **PARKING:** 68 **NOTES:** No smoking in restaurant Civ Wed
CARDS:

See advert on page 409

Bad hair day? Hairdryers in all rooms three stars and above.

The Esplanade Hotel

Esplanade Road · Pentire · Newquay
Cornwall TR7 1PS · Tel: (01637) 873333
Fax: (01637) 851413 · www.newquay-hotels.co.uk
Freephone 0500 900950

A warm welcome awaits you at this modern spacious hotel, directly overlooking the magnificent Fistral beach.

• INDOOR AND OUTDOOR HEATED POOLS •
• SAUNA, SOLARIUM AND SPA BATH • TWO LIFTS •
• BALLROOM BAR • CABARET BAR • FUNCTION SUITE •
• GAMES ROOM • COFFEE SHOP •
• CONCESSIONARY GOLF • PARKING •

All 83 rooms are attractively furnished, all front facing rooms enjoy a sea view. We also offer some business class rooms. A wide range of facilities, excellent cuisine and wine list combined with friendly yet professional service ensure that the Esplanade is an ideal base, whatever the nature of your visit to Newquay.

The HOTEL BRISTOL

Owned and managed since 1927 by four generations of the Young family The Bristol continues to be one of Newquay's leading hotels. Enjoy traditional hospitality by the sea. We are an excellent centre from which to explore Cornwall.

www.hotelbristol.co.uk

NARROWCLIFF
• NEWQUAY •
CORNWALL
TR7 2PQ

☆☆☆ AA

Best Western

TEL: 01637 875181

GLENDORGAL HOTEL

Lusty Glaze, Porth, Newquay, Cornwall TR7 3AB

Enjoy the relaxed seclusion of a 19th century, former gentleman's residence, situated in 17 acres of private headland with access to Porth beach · A peaceful location, yet only a mile from Newquay centre and station • Glendorgal is ideally situated for exploring Cornwall, or for walking the coastal path which runs close by · Our facilities include heated indoor and outdoor pools, spa, steam room, gym, solarium, snooker and tennis court, plus a poolside licensed bistro, so you may be happy just to while away your days within the peaceful setting of Glendorgal • See us online at **cornwall-online.co.uk/glandorgal** • Why not contact our friendly staff to discuss your requirements

Tel: 01637 874937 Fax: 01637 851341
Email: Newquay@dircon.co.uk

TREBARWITH HOTEL

★★★

NEWQUAY CORNWALL

Brochure Hotline Freephone 0800 387520

◆ Right on sea edge ◆ Large indoor pool ◆ Sauna, spa bath, solarium ◆ Secluded sun garden and patio ◆ No passing traffic ◆ Dancing and entertainments ◆ Film theatre ◆ Large games room ◆ Guest launderette ◆ Delightful Wedgewood Restaurant serving table d'hôte and à la carte ◆ 41 luxury bedrooms ◆ Family and four-poster suites ◆ Owned and managed by the Tarrant family for over 35 years ◆

SEND NOW FOR YOUR
SOUVENIR FULL COLOUR BROCHURE

N

NEWQUAY, continued

★★76% Corisande Manor
Riverside Av, Pentire TR7 1PL
☎ 01637 872042 01637 874557
e-mail: relax@corisande.com
Dir: *from A392 Newquay road follow signs for Pentire*
A Victorian hotel situated in three acres of grounds, with easy access to the town centre. Each evening a short menu offers an innovative choice of dishes, supported by an extensive and well chosen wine list. The bedrooms offer modern facilities and are decorated and furnished with great care and imagination.
ROOMS: 12 en suite s £75-£89; d £130-£160 (incl. bkfst & dinner) LB **FACILITIES:** Croquet lawn Putting green Xmas **PARKING:** 19 **NOTES:** No smoking in restaurant **CARDS:**

★★71% Whipsiderry
Trevelgue Rd, Porth TR7 3LY
☎ 01637 874777 01637 874777
e-mail: whipsiderry@cornwall.net
Dir: *turn right onto Padstow road B3276 out of Newquay, in half a mile turn right at Trevelgue Rd*
Benefitting from superb views over Newquay's Porth Beach, this long established, friendly family-run hotel continues to prove popular. Bedrooms vary in size and style; many enjoy superb scenery. Each evening in the dining room, an imaginative, well balanced menu is provided with the emphasis on fresh, local produce wherever possible. As dusk draws on, badger watching has become a special pastime for guests.
ROOMS: 24 rms (19 en suite) (5 fmly) s £23-£34; d £46-£68 (incl. bkfst) * LB **FACILITIES:** Outdoor swimming (H) Sauna Pool table entertainment ch fac Xmas **PARKING:** 30 **NOTES:** No smoking in restaurant Closed Nov-Etr (ex Xmas) **CARDS:**

N

★★68% Porth Veor Manor
Porth Way TR7 3LW
☎ 01637 873274 01637 851690
e-mail: booking@porthveor.co.uk
Dir: *on B3276 quarter of a mile from junct with A3058*
Standing in two acres of gardens and grounds, this stone house overlooks Porth Beach. It is a family-run hotel, with a friendly relaxed atmosphere. There is a variety of rooms available. The dining room, which benefits from splendid coastal views, serves a fixed-price menu.
ROOMS: 22 en suite (7 fmly) No smoking in 6 bedrooms s £40-£50; d £75-£95 (incl. bkfst & dinner) * LB **FACILITIES:** Croquet lawn Putting green Xmas **CONF:** Thtr 36 Class 24 Board 24 Del from £40 * **PARKING:** 40 **NOTES:** No smoking in restaurant RS Nov-Feb
CARDS:

★★67% Philema
1 Esplanade Rd, Pentire TR7 1PY
☎ 01637 872571 01637 873188
e-mail: info@philema.demon.co.uk
Dir: *from A30 follow A392 signs then signs for Fistral Beach & Pentire, turn left at rdbt for Pentire. Hotel at bottom of Pentire Rd*
Overlooking Fistral Beach, this family-run hotel prides itself on its hospitality and is situated close to the town centre and shops. With modern facilities, all of the bedrooms are comfortably furnished and some benefit from views of the beach. Public areas are spacious and leisure facilities are provided. Evening meals are served in the pleasant dining room.
ROOMS: 29 en suite (16 fmly) s £25-£40; d £50-£80 (incl. bkfst & dinner) * LB **FACILITIES:** STV Indoor swimming (H) Snooker Sauna Solarium Pool table Jacuzzi/spa Table tennis ch fac **PARKING:** 37 **NOTES:** No smoking in restaurant Closed Nov-Feb
CARDS:

★★66% Beachcroft
Cliff Rd TR7 1SW
☎ 01637 873022 01637 873022
e-mail: enquiries@beachcroft-newquay.co.uk
Dir: *turn off A30 towards St Mawgan RAF camp then onto Newquay opposite railway station*
Located in the centre of the town, this long established, family-run hotel continues to have a loyal following. In addition to the popular entertainment provided nightly in the ball room, a varied range of both indoor and outdoor leisure facilities is available. The spacious public areas include, several lounge areas, a bar serving real ales, and a small coffee shop.
ROOMS: 69 en suite (13 fmly) s £23-£39; d £46-£78 (incl. bkfst & dinner) * LB **FACILITIES:** Indoor swimming (H) Outdoor swimming (H) Tennis (hard) Sauna Solarium Pool table Putting green Games room Table tennis entertainment ch fac **SERVICES:** Lift **PARKING:** 80 **NOTES:** Closed early Oct-early Apr **CARDS:**

★★63% Cedars
Mount Wise TR7 2BA
☎ 01637 874225 01637 850421
Dir: *enter Newquay via Narrowcliff follow one way system into Berry Rd & Mountwise approx 500yds on right from Mountwise public car park*
With superb distant views of the coastline, this family-run hotel remains popular with holidaymakers. Friendly and enthusiastic staff serve in the dining room, while in the spacious lounge/bar, entertainment is provided during the season. Bedrooms vary in size, shape and style, and some are especially suitable for families.
ROOMS: 42 rms (31 en suite) (8 fmly) s £28-£36; d £56-£72 (incl. bkfst & dinner) * LB **FACILITIES:** Outdoor swimming (H) Sauna Solarium Gym Pool table Jacuzzi/spa entertainment Xmas **PARKING:** 42 **NOTES:** No smoking in restaurant Closed Nov-Mar (ex Xmas & New Year) **CARDS:**

★★63% Tremont
Pentire Av TR7 1PB
☎ 01637 872984 01637 851984
Dir: *from A30 onto B3902 into Newquay and follow Pentire signs*
Within walking distance of both Fistral Beach and the town centre, this popular hotel continues to have a loyal customer base. Entertainment is held on a regular basis during the summer months in the spacious lounges, and in addition a cosy bar is available for guests. Sensibly furnished, the bedrooms are all equipped with modern facilities.
ROOMS: 54 en suite (26 fmly) s £24-£35; d £48-£70 (incl. bkfst & dinner) * LB **FACILITIES:** Indoor swimming (H) Tennis (hard) Squash Sauna Solarium Gym Pool table Putting green Table tennis entertainment Xmas **CONF:** Thtr 160 **SERVICES:** Lift **PARKING:** 60 **NOTES:** No smoking in restaurant **CARDS:**

NEWTON ABBOT, Devon — Map 03 SX87
see also Ilsington

★★★71% Passage House
Hackney Ln, Kingsteignton TQ12 3QH
☎ 01626 355515 01626 363336
e-mail: mail@passagehousehotel.co.uk
Dir: *leave the A380 for the A381 and follow racecourse signs*
Enjoying a lovely location on the Teign estuary, this hotel provides smart modern bedrooms, meeting rooms and good health and leisure facilities. The restaurant offers a choice of menus and a well known historic inn, also called the Passage House, stands next door.
ROOMS: 38 en suite (32 fmly) No smoking in 3 bedrooms s £68-£78; d £80-£90 (incl. bkfst) * LB **FACILITIES:** STV Indoor swimming (H) Sauna Solarium Gym Pool table Jacuzzi/spa Xmas **CONF:** Thtr 120 Class 30 Board 40 Del from £80 * **SERVICES:** Lift **PARKING:** 300 **NOTES:** No smoking in restaurant **CARDS:**

★★65% Queens
Queen St TQ12 2EZ
☎ 01626 363133 & 354106 📠 01626 364922

Best Western

Dir: *Opposite the railway station, beside Courtenay Park*
A busy hotel near the railway station, attracting a local business clientele and younger customers at weekends in Azarats, the hotel's wine bar. Guests have the choice of dining in the Regency Restaurant or from the extensive bar or room service menus. Bedrooms offer comfortable accommodation with modern facilities.
ROOMS: 22 rms (20 en suite) (3 fmly) No smoking in 4 bedrooms
FACILITIES: Pool table **CONF:** Thtr 80 Class 40 Board 40 **PARKING:** 8
CARDS:

★65% Hazelwood Hotel
33a Torquay Rd TQ12 2LW
☎ 01626 366130 📠 01626 365021
Dir: *join A380 until reaching Newton Abbot. At main rdbt right past McDonalds. Keep left through 2 sets of lights. Hotel located on top of hill on right*
Set close to the town centre, this small hotel offers a friendly welcome, warm ambience and home-cooked dinners. Bedrooms are pleasantly decorated and well kept. There is a small, newly panelled dining room and comfy sofas in the lounge where guests can relax and enjoy a drink from the bar after a hard day working or exploring.
ROOMS: 7 en suite s £36-£40; d £49-£55 (incl. bkfst) * LB
PARKING: 7 **NOTES:** No dogs (ex guide dogs) No smoking in restaurant
CARDS:

> Packed in a hurry? Ironing facilities should be available at all star levels, either in rooms or on request.

NEWTON-LE-WILLOWS, Merseyside
Map 07 SJ59

★★65% Kirkfield Hotel
2/4 Church St WA12 9SU
☎ 01925 228196 📠 01925 291540
Dir: *on A49 Newton-le-Willows opposite St Peter's Church*
Situated directly opposite the church, this hotel offers accommodation with straightforward furnishings. A good range of meals is available in the bar or dining room, and the staff create a relaxing and informal atmosphere.
ROOMS: 15 en suite (3 fmly) No smoking in 5 bedrooms
FACILITIES: Pool table **CONF:** Thtr 70 Class 60 Board 20 **PARKING:** 50
NOTES: No dogs (ex guide dogs) Closed 25 Dec
CARDS:

NORMAN CROSS, Cambridgeshire
Map 04 TL19

★★★62% Posthouse Peterborough
Great North Rd PE7 3TB

Posthouse

☎ 0870 400 9063 📠 01733 244455
Dir: *on southbound A1(M) take A15 junct to Yaxley. On northbound A1(M take A15 junct to Yaxley*
Situated at the junction of the A1(M) and A15, approximately 6 miles from the town centre, this hotel offers a mixture of traditionally furnished and modern styled bedrooms, which are all well-equipped. A health club is a feature of the hotel together with Seasons restaurant which serves British and international dishes.
ROOMS: 93 en suite No smoking in 47 bedrooms **FACILITIES:** Indoor swimming (H) Sauna Gym Pool table Jacuzzi/spa Steam room
CONF: Thtr 50 Class 16 Board 24 **PARKING:** 150
CARDS:

N

NORTHALLERTON, North Yorkshire
Map 08 SE39

★★★68% Solberge Hall
Newby Wiske DL7 9ER
☎ 01609 779191 🖷 01609 780472
e-mail: jholl597@aol.com
Dir: *3.25kms S of Northallerton on the A167. Hotel is located on the right as you pass through North Otterington*
Standing proudly in its own extensive grounds, with fine views over surrounding countryside, this attractive Victorian hotel provides well equipped bedrooms. Public rooms are stylishly comfortable and a good choice of food is available in the elegant Garden Room Restaurant. Staff are professional and friendly.
ROOMS: 24 en suite (2 fmly) s £60-£85; d £80-£110 (incl. bkfst) * LB **FACILITIES:** STV Croquet lawn Xmas **CONF:** Thtr 100 Class 50 Board 40 Del from £72.95 * **PARKING:** 100 **NOTES:** No smoking in restaurant Civ Wed 100 **CARDS:**

★★68% The Golden Lion
High St DL7 8PP
☎ 01609 777411 🖷 01609 773250
Dir: *take A684 travel approx 5m onto A167 through built-up area 3rd exit at next rdbt to town centre at 3rd rdbt turn left into High St*
A popular town centre coaching inn offering a warm welcome. Lounges are stylish and comfortable, and there is a spacious bar containing a recently discovered well. The ambitious cooking served in the restaurant shows great flair and creativity. Bedrooms are available in a variety of sizes and are well equipped and comfortable.
ROOMS: 25 en suite (2 fmly) No smoking in 18 bedrooms s fr £65; d fr £85 (incl. bkfst) * LB **FACILITIES:** Xmas **CONF:** Thtr 150 Class 80 Board 40 Del from £95 * **PARKING:** 100 **NOTES:** No smoking in restaurant Civ Wed 70 **CARDS:**

N

NORTHAMPTON, Northamptonshire
Map 04 SP76
see also Flore

★★★★67% Northampton Marriott
Eagle Dr NN4 7HW
☎ 01604 768700 🖷 01604 769011
Dir: *off A45, between A428 & A508*
This hotel is ideal for conferences and even has its own self-contained management centre. Public areas are bright and inviting, and bedrooms are equally appealing, equipped with all modern comforts. Dining options include Spires, an elegant room overlooking the lake, and La Fontana, an Italian restaurant with a less formal atmosphere.
ROOMS: 120 en suite (12 fmly) No smoking in 82 bedrooms s £45-£125; d £72-£150 (incl. bkfst) * LB **FACILITIES:** STV Indoor swimming (H) Sauna Solarium Gym Jacuzzi/spa Steam room entertainment Xmas **CONF:** Thtr 220 Class 100 Board 36 Del from £146 * **PARKING:** 187 **NOTES:** Civ Wed 80 **CARDS:**

★★★71% Lime Trees
8 Langham Place, Barrack Rd NN2 6AA
☎ 01604 632188 🖷 01604 233012
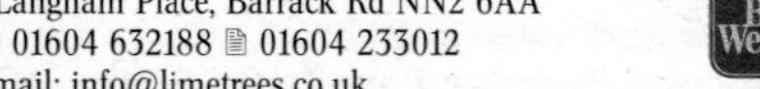
e-mail: info@limetrees.co.uk
Dir: *from city centre 0.5m N on A508 Leicester near racecourse park & cathedral*
This charming hotel remains ever popular. Bedrooms are well equipped and very comfortable. The hotel is popular with business guests throughout the week, who appreciate the efficient and friendly service; the weekends see more leisure guests. The smart restaurant offers a range of carefully prepared and popular dishes. Hospitality is excellent.

continued

ROOMS: 27 en suite (2 fmly) s £62-£67; d £67-£82 (incl. bkfst) * LB **CONF:** Thtr 50 Class 30 Board 30 Del from £91 * **PARKING:** 24 **NOTES:** No dogs (ex guide dogs) RS 27 Dec-New Year **CARDS:**

★★★69% Courtyard by Marriott Northampton
Bedford Rd NN4 7YF
☎ 01604 622777 🖷 01604 635454
Dir: *from M1 junct 15 follow A508 towards Northampton. Follow A45 towards Wellingborough for 2m then A428 towards Bedford, hotel on left*
On the eastern edge of the town centre and easily accessible for the business traveller, this modern, purpose-built hotel offers a good standard of facilities and spacious accommodation. The open-plan public areas offer an informal atmosphere and have been extended to give more space. Friendly staff provide a good range of services.
ROOMS: 104 en suite (55 fmly) No smoking in 50 bedrooms d £80-£100 * LB **FACILITIES:** STV Gym Xmas **CONF:** Thtr 40 Class 30 Board 30 Del from £135 * **SERVICES:** Lift air con **PARKING:** 150 **NOTES:** No dogs (ex guide dogs) No smoking in restaurant **CARDS:**

★★★64% Quality Hotel Northampton
Ashley Way, Weston Favell NN3 3EA
☎ 01604 739955 🖷 01604 415023
e-mail: admin@gb070.u-net.com
Dir: *leave A45 at junct with A43, towards Weston Favell. After 0.5m bear left to town centre. Turn left at top of slip road, hotel signposted off A4500*
Quietly situated, this established hotel offers smartly presented, well equipped accommodation. Attractive public rooms include comfortable lounge areas and an elegant restaurant, where interesting, well prepared dishes are available. The hotel has a number of excellent meeting rooms.
ROOMS: 31 en suite 35 annexe en suite (4 fmly) No smoking in 21 bedrooms s £39-£91.75; d £64-£125.50 * LB **FACILITIES:** STV Croquet lawn Putting green entertainment Xmas **CONF:** Thtr 150 Class 65 Board 60 Del from £75 * **SERVICES:** Lift **PARKING:** 100 **NOTES:** No smoking in restaurant Civ Wed 150 **CARDS:**

★★★63% Grand
15 Gold St NN1 1RE
☎ 01604 250511 🖷 01604 234534
e-mail: grand@zoffanyhotels.co.uk
Dir: *follow A508 to town centre, over traffic lights at the Carlsberg Brewery, take the road to left, hotel car park is 300m on left*
This impressive town centre hotel offers bright and attractive accommodation. The bedrooms are comfortably furnished and well equipped. Public areas include the Kasbah bar which offers a range of hot and cold snacks, and the lower ground floor dining room offering a daily set menu and small grill menu.
ROOMS: 56 en suite (2 fmly) No smoking in 21 bedrooms s £69-£89.50; d £99 (incl. bkfst) * LB **FACILITIES:** STV Pool table **CONF:** Thtr 120 Class 50 Board 40 Del from £100 * **SERVICES:** Lift **PARKING:** 72 **NOTES:** No smoking in restaurant **CARDS:**

⇧ Premier Lodge (Northampton East)
Crown Ln, Great Billing NN3 9DA
☎ 0870 700 1522 🖷 0870 700 1523

Premier Lodge offers modern, well equipped, en suite accommodation suitable for both business and leisure travellers. Meals can be taken at the adjacent popular restaurant and bar which is fully licensed. For further details, consult the Hotel Groups page.
ROOMS: 60 en suite d £46 *

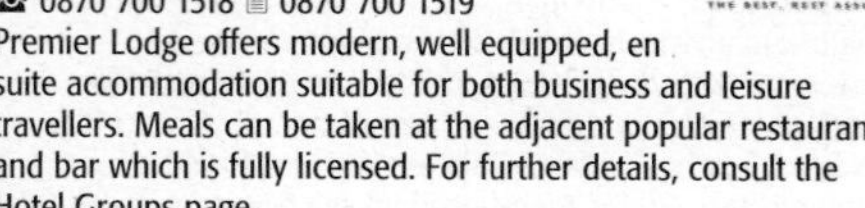

Premier Lodge (Northampton South)

London Rd West, Wootton NN4 7JN
☎ 0870 700 1518 ▤ 0870 700 1519
Premier Lodge offers modern, well equipped, en suite accommodation suitable for both business and leisure travellers. Meals can be taken at the adjacent popular restaurant and bar which is fully licensed. For further details, consult the Hotel Groups page.
ROOMS: 19 en suite d £42 *

Travelodge

Upton Way NN5 6EG
☎ 01604 758395 ▤ 01604 758395
Dir: *A45, towards M1 junct 16*
This modern building offers accommodation in smart, spacious and well equipped bedrooms, all with en suite bathrooms. Refreshments may be taken at the nearby family restaurant. For further details and the Travelodge phone number, consult the Hotel Groups page.
ROOMS: 62 en suite

NORTH FERRIBY, East Riding of Yorkshire — Map 08 SE92

★★★63% *Humber Crown*

Ferriby High Rd HU14 3LG
☎ 01482 645212 ▤ 01482 643332
Dir: *from M62 join A63 to Hull. Take exit for Humber Bridge. At rdbt follow signs for North Ferriby. Hotel is 0.5m on left*
This hotel commands fine views of the Humber Bridge and offers well maintained bedrooms with every modern facility. The popular restaurant overlooks the river, and there is a children's play area at the rear.
ROOMS: 95 en suite No smoking in 66 bedrooms **FACILITIES:** Pool table ch fac **CONF:** Thtr 100 Class 40 Board 40 **PARKING:** 140
CARDS:

NORTHLEACH, Gloucestershire — Map 04 SP11

★★65% *Wheatsheaf*

West End GL54 3EZ
☎ 01451 860244 ▤ 01451 861037
e-mail: whtshfhtl@aol.com
Dir: *junct A40/A429, take A429 for Cirencester. After 0.5m turn left at traffic lights, hotel 300yds on left*
The historic town of Northleach is the setting for this period coaching inn, built from Cotswold stone. Bedrooms are well equipped and smartly presented with public rooms featuring a comfortable restaurant and two adjoining bars where welcoming log fires burn during the winter.
ROOMS: 9 en suite (1 fmly) **PARKING:** 15 **NOTES:** No smoking in restaurant Closed 25 Dec **CARDS:**

NORTH MUSKHAM, Nottinghamshire — Map 08 SK75

Travelodge

NG23 6HT
☎ 01636 703635 ▤ 01636 703635
Dir: *3m N, on A1 southbound*
This modern building offers accommodation in smart, spacious and well equipped bedrooms, all with en suite bathrooms. Refreshments may be taken at the nearby family restaurant. For further details and the Travelodge phone number, consult the Hotel Groups page.
ROOMS: 30 en suite

NORTH WALSHAM, Norfolk — Map 09 TG23

★★79% Beechwood

Cromer Rd NR28 0HD
☎ 01692 403231 ▤ 01692 407284
Dir: *take B1150 from Norwich, at North Walsham turn left at first set of traffic lights then right at the next*

Situated close to the Norfolk coast, this delightful house provides comfortable public areas, attentive service and warm hospitality. Bedrooms are attractively decorated and well equipped, unique furnishings and antiques give them a feel of luxury. Good quality home cooked food is served in the pretty dining room.
ROOMS: 10 en suite No smoking in 7 bedrooms s £49-£60; d £68-£90 (incl. bkfst) * LB **CONF:** Thtr 20 Class 20 Board 20 **PARKING:** 17
NOTES: No children 10yrs No smoking in restaurant
CARDS:

See advert on this page

NORTH WALSHAM, continued

★★70% Scarborough Hill Country House
Old Yarmouth Rd NR28 9NA
☎ 01692 402151 🖷 01692 406686
Dir: *From B1150, proceed under railway bridge. At 1st t/lights follow ahead to rdbt. Right into Grammar School Rd. Right again, proceed 1m.Hotel on right*
Situated on the outskirts of town amidst lovely well tended gardens is this charming privately owned hotel. The spacious bedrooms are individually decorated, equipped with many useful extras and have attractive soft furnishings. Public rooms include a lounge bar with an adjacent dining area and a smart conservatory restaurant serving imaginative home cooked fare.
ROOMS: 8 en suite s £49.50-£65; d £75-£90 (incl. bkfst) * LB
CONF: Thtr 70 Class 70 Board 70 Del from £69 * **PARKING:** 50
NOTES: No smoking in restaurant **CARDS:**

NORTH WALTHAM, Hampshire Map 04 SU54

Premier Lodge (Basingstoke)
RG25 2BB
☎ 0870 700 1312 🖷 0870 700 1313
Dir: *on A30 one & a half miles from junc7 M3 follow signs for Basingstoke, then Kings Worthy & Popham*
Premier Lodge offers modern, well equipped, en suite accommodation suitable for both business and leisure travellers. Meals can be taken at the adjacent popular restaurant and bar which is fully licensed. For further details, consult the Hotel Groups page.
ROOMS: 28 en suite d £46 * **CONF:** Thtr 80 Class 30 Board 35

NORTHWICH, Cheshire Map 07 SJ67

★★★66% Quality Hotel Northwich
London Rd CW9 5HD
☎ 01606 44443 🖷 01606 42596
e-mail: admin@gb618.u-net.com
Dir: *from M6 junct 19 take A556 to Northwich. Follow signs for Chester & 'Salt Museum'. At 2nd rdbt take A553 London Road*
A first in the UK! This floating hotel has been built over the river and a very successful concept it is. The bedrooms are modern and well equipped and there is a carvery restaurant which, not surprisingly, overlooks the river.
ROOMS: 60 en suite (2 fmly) No smoking in 30 bedrooms s £40-£70; d £50-£81.50 * LB **FACILITIES:** Sauna Solarium Gym Xmas
CONF: Thtr 80 Class 40 Board 30 Del from £60.50 * **SERVICES:** Lift
PARKING: 110 **NOTES:** No smoking in restaurant Civ Wed 80
CARDS:

★★66% *Hartford Hall*
School Ln, Hartford CW8 1PW
☎ 01606 75711 🖷 01606 782285
Dir: *in village of Hartford, between Northwich and Chester on the A556*
This 17th-century former manor house is situated in four acres of gardens and grounds. The bedrooms are very well equipped. Public areas are characteristic of the period and feature the heavily beamed Nunn's Room in which civil weddings and other functions are held.
ROOMS: 20 en suite (2 fmly) **FACILITIES:** STV Croquet lawn
CONF: Thtr 40 Class 12 Board 25 **PARKING:** 50 **NOTES:** No dogs (ex guide dogs) **CARDS:**

★★66% *Wincham Hall*
Hall Ln, Wincham CW9 6DG
☎ 01606 43453 🖷 01606 40128
e-mail: sarah@wincham-hall.demon.co.uk
Dir: *leave M6 junct 19 take A556 to Chester. Turn right onto A559 to Northwich. At lights turn right. Hotel 0.5m on left*
This family run hotel offers well presented pine furnished bedrooms. Many of the rooms overlook the five acres of grounds, which include a walled garden and lily pond. Guests can relax in the lounge bar before enjoying a meal.
ROOMS: 10 rms (9 en suite) (1 fmly) **FACILITIES:** Croquet lawn
CONF: Thtr 100 Class 50 Board 20 **PARKING:** 200
CARDS:

Premier Lodge
520 Chester Rd, Sandiway CW8 2DN
☎ 0870 700 1524 🖷 0870 700 1525
Premier Lodge offers modern, well equipped, en suite accommodation suitable for both business and leisure travellers. Meals can be taken at the adjacent popular restaurant and bar which is fully licensed. For further details, consult the Hotel Groups page.
ROOMS: 52 en suite d £42 *

Premier Lodge (Northwich South)
London Rd, Leftwich CW9 8EG
☎ 0870 700 1526 🖷 0870 700 1527
Premier Lodge offers modern, well equipped, en suite accommodation suitable for both business and leisure travellers. Meals can be taken at the adjacent popular restaurant and bar which is fully licensed. For further details, consult the Hotel Groups page.
ROOMS: 32 en suite d £42 *

NORTHWOLD, Norfolk Map 05 TL79

★★67% Comfort Inn Thetford
Thetford Rd IP26 5LQ
☎ 01366 728888 🖷 01366 727121
e-mail: admin@gb632.u-net.com
Dir: *W of Mundford on A134*
Set in a rural location, this hotel consists of a cluster of attractive buildings. The spacious bedrooms are set around a courtyard and are ideal for families. The beamed Woodland Inn combines the roles of country pub and hotel restaurant.
ROOMS: 34 en suite (12 fmly) No smoking in 17 bedrooms s £50.75-£67.50; d £59-£85.50 * LB **FACILITIES:** STV Gym Xmas **CONF:** Thtr 150 Class 55 Board 60 Del £75.50 * **PARKING:** 250 **NOTES:** Civ Wed
CARDS:

NORTON, Shropshire Map 07 SJ70

★★76% ❀❀ Hundred House Hotel
Bridgnorth Rd TF11 9EE
☎ 01952 730353 🖷 01952 730355
e-mail: hphundredhouse@compuserve.com
Dir: *midway between Telford & Bridgnorth on A442. In centre of Norton village*
Primarily Georgian, but with parts dating back to the 14th century, this friendly hotel offers individually styled, well equipped bedrooms. Period furniture and attractive soft furnishings are used. Unusually, some rooms have romantic swings hanging from the ceiling. Public areas include cosy bars and intimate dining areas where memorable meals are served.

continued

ROOMS: 10 en suite (5 fmly) s £69-£85; d £95-£120 (incl. bkfst) * LB
FACILITIES: Xmas **CONF:** Class 20 Board 15 **PARKING:** 30
NOTES: Closed 25 Dec RS Sunday evenings
CARDS:

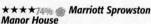

NORWICH, Norfolk — Map 05 TG20
see also South Walsham

★★★★74% Marriott Sprowston Manor House

Sprowston Park, Wroxham Rd, Sprowston NR7 8RP
☎ 01603 410871 01603 423911
Dir: 2m NE A1151-from A11 take the Wroxham road (A1151 and follow signs to Sprowston Park

Sprowston Manor, surrounded by parkland, stands within easy striking distance of Norwich city centre. Conference, banqueting and leisure facilities are its strength, and there is a golf course next to it. There are a number of different styles of bedroom and the restaurant serves an interesting range of dishes.

ROOMS: 94 en suite (3 fmly) No smoking in 68 bedrooms
FACILITIES: STV Indoor swimming (H) Golf 18 Sauna Solarium Gym Croquet lawn Jacuzzi/spa Beauty salon Health spa Steam room entertainment **CONF:** Thtr 160 Class 80 Board 50 **SERVICES:** Lift
PARKING: 150 **NOTES:** No smoking in restaurant
CARDS:

★★★★66% De Vere Dunston Hall

Ipswich Rd, Dunston NR14 8PQ
☎ 01508 470444 01508 471499
Dir: from A47 , take A140 Ipswich Road, hotel directly off this road on left after approx 0.25m

Set in 170 acres of landscaped grounds this Grade II listed building stands just two miles south of the city. The extensive range of outdoor facilities includes an 18 hole PGA golf course, two floodlit tennis courts and a floodlit driving range. Indoor facilities include a swimming pool, gym and hairdressing salon. Bedrooms are spacious, comfortably furnished and equipped to a high standard.

ROOMS: 130 en suite No smoking in 58 bedrooms **FACILITIES:** STV Indoor swimming (H) Golf 18 Snooker Sauna Solarium Gym Pool table Putting green Jacuzzi/spa Bowling green **CONF:** Thtr 299 Class 140 Board 90 **SERVICES:** Lift **PARKING:** 500 **NOTES:** No smoking in restaurant **CARDS:**

See advert on this page

★★★68% The George Hotel

10 Arlington Ln, Newmarket Rd NR2 2DA
☎ 01603 617841 01603 663708
e-mail: reservations@georgehotel.co.uk
Dir: approach on A11, follow City Ctr signs across outer ring road, large rdbt and inner ring road smaller rdbt. 3rd turning on left, Hotel on right

Guests will find a warm welcome from the friendly team at the

continued on p414

NORWICH, continued

George Hotel, situated in a residential area and within easy walking distance of the city centre. This well maintained hotel offers a good standard of accommodation in well decorated bedrooms. Public areas include an attractive and comfortable lounge bar and small grill-restaurant serving home cooked meals.
ROOMS: 36 en suite 4 annexe en suite (3 fmly) No smoking in 9 bedrooms s £63.50-£74.50; d £86-£103 (incl. bkfst) * LB
FACILITIES: STV Xmas **CONF:** Thtr 60 Class 25 Board 32 Del from £85 * **PARKING:** 40 **NOTES:** No smoking in restaurant
CARDS:

★★★ 67% *Posthouse Norwich*
Ipswich Rd NR4 6EP
Posthouse
☎ 0870 400 9060 🖷 01603 506400
Dir: *take A47, southern bypass, until sign for A140, then turn N into Norwich. Hotel 0.5m on right*
A modern hotel just out of the city. Public areas, including Seasons restaurant, are comfortably appointed, the well equipped Spa leisure club is a prominent feature. Bedrooms have every modern facility including mini bars and in-house movies. Staff are friendly and helpful, there is an all day lounge menu and 24 hour room service
ROOMS: 116 en suite (54 fmly) No smoking in 44 bedrooms
FACILITIES: Indoor swimming (H) Sauna Gym Jacuzzi/spa Health & fitness centre ch fac **CONF:** Thtr 100 Class 48 Board 40 **PARKING:** 200
CARDS:

★★★ 67% Swallow Nelson Hotel
Prince of Wales Rd NR1 1DX
SWALLOW HOTELS
☎ 01603 760260 🖷 01603 620008
e-mail: nelson@swallow-hotels.co.uk
Dir: *follow signs for city centre & football ground & railway station. Hotel is on riverside opposite station*

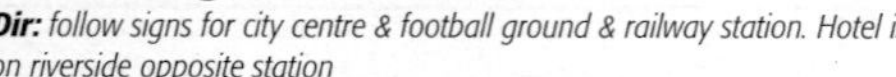

Overlooking the River Wensum and close by the station, this pleasant hotel has a nautical theme, featuring many references to its namesake. Public areas are well designed in a variety of styles, and the well appointed bedrooms have refrigerators; 24-hour room service is on offer. The choice of eating options, the leisure complex and conference suites make this a popular hotel.
ROOMS: 132 en suite s £95-£110; d £110-£130 (incl. bkfst) * LB
FACILITIES: STV Indoor swimming (H) Sauna Solarium Gym Steam room Beauty & hair salon Xmas **CONF:** Thtr 90 Board 44 Del from £115 * **SERVICES:** Lift **PARKING:** 210
CARDS:

★★★ 66% Quality Hotel
2 Barnard Rd, Bowthorpe NR5 9JB
CHOICE HOTELS EUROPE
☎ 01603 741161 🖷 01603 741500
e-mail: admin@gb619.u-net.com
Dir: *take A1074 to Norwich/Cromer. Hotel is situated off A47 Southern Bypass 4m from City Centre*
Close to the western side of the city centre and near the bypass, this modern hotel gives easy access to routes around Norwich. The atmosphere is friendly, and bedrooms are well equipped. There is a good leisure centre and a wide choice of meeting rooms.
ROOMS: 80 en suite (14 fmly) No smoking in 40 bedrooms s £65-£74.70; d £88.50-£97.20 * LB **FACILITIES:** STV Indoor swimming (H) Sauna Solarium Gym Jacuzzi/spa Steamroom Xmas **CONF:** Thtr 200 Class 80 Board 60 Del from £75 * **PARKING:** 140 **NOTES:** No smoking in restaurant Civ Wed 70 **CARDS:**

★★★ 60% Maids Head
Tombland NR3 1LB
REGAL
☎ 01603 209955 🖷 01603 613688
Dir: *follow city centre signs, continue past Norwich Castle, 3rd turning after castle into Upper King St, hotel opposite Norman cathedral*

This historic hotel, which dates back to the 13th century, is located in the heart of the city centre, close to the impressive Norman cathedral. The bedrooms, several of which have exposed oak beams, are well equipped and smartly furnished. The public rooms feature a Jacobean panelled bar, a range of seating areas and the Courtyard restaurant. There is a private car park to the rear of the building which is locked at night.
ROOMS: 84 en suite (7 fmly) No smoking in 30 bedrooms s £85-£105; d £105-£145 * LB **FACILITIES:** Xmas **CONF:** Thtr 300 Class 120 Board 40 Del from £95 * **SERVICES:** Lift **PARKING:** 60 **NOTES:** No smoking in restaurant Civ Wed 100 **CARDS:**

★★ 79% ❀ The Old Rectory
103 Yarmouth Rd, Thorpe St Andrew NR7 0HF
☎ 01603 700772 🖷 01603 300772
e-mail: RectoryH@aol.com
Dir: *from A47 Norwich Southern Bypass, take A1042 towards Norwich N & E. At mini-rdbt bear left (A1242), straight over at lights, hotel 100mtrs on right*

This delightful privately owned hotel is situated in quiet residential area amidst lovely well tended gardens. The combination of classical style and elegance together with a modern touch make

continued

this an ideal place to visit. An imaginative daily changing menu is offered in the attractive dining room and guests also have the use of a conservatory as well as a comfortable lounge with plush furnishings.
ROOMS: 5 en suite 3 annexe en suite No smoking in all bedrooms s £60-£70; d £78-£88 (incl. bkfst) * LB **FACILITIES:** STV Outdoor swimming (H) **CONF:** Thtr 25 Class 18 Board 18 Del from £95 * **PARKING:** 17 **NOTES:** No dogs (ex guide dogs) No smoking in restaurant Closed 23 Dec-11 Jan **CARDS:**

See advert on this page

★★76% ❀ Annesley House
6 Newmarket Rd NR2 2LA
☎ 01603 624553 01603 621577
Dir: *on A11 half a mile before city centre*
A lovely Georgian property situated close to the city centre in three acres of landscaped gardens. The accommodation is located in three separate houses two of which are linked by a glass walkway. Bedrooms are attractively decorated, tastefully furnished and equipped with many useful extras. The public rooms feature a smart conservatory restaurant which overlooks the gardens and guests also have the use of a comfortable lounge bar.

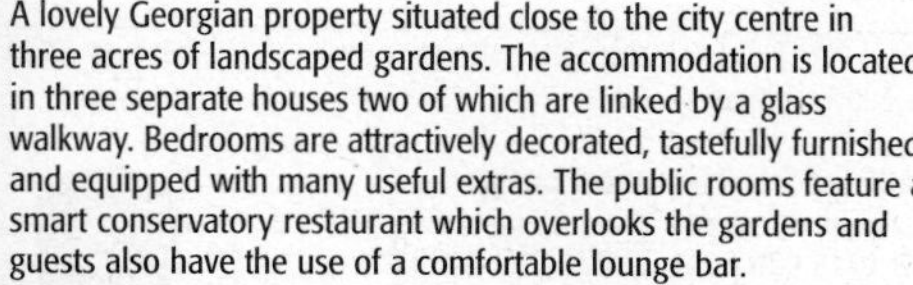

ROOMS: 18 en suite 8 annexe en suite (3 fmly) s £67.50-£80; d £80-£92.50 (incl. bkfst) * LB **FACILITIES:** STV **PARKING:** 25 **NOTES:** No dogs (ex guide dogs) No smoking in restaurant Closed 24-27 & 30-31 Dec **CARDS:**

Popped the question? Hotels with Civ Wed in their entry are licensed for civil wedding ceremonies. Maximum numbers for the ceremony only are shown, e.g. Civ Wed 50

N

NORWICH, continued

★★72% ❁ Beeches Hotel & Victorian Gardens
2-6 Earlham Rd NR2 3DB
☎ 01603 621167 📠 01603 620151
e-mail: reception@beeches.co.uk
Dir: *to the W of the City Centre on B1108, behind St Johns RC Cathedral just off inner ring road*
This grade II listed building is renowned for its sunken Victorian gardens and spacious landscaped grounds. The hotel offers charming, well maintained bedrooms with a good standard of facilities. Guests can use the smart bar with its all day snack menu and the bistro style restaurant tempts diners with appealing, freshly prepared dishes.
ROOMS: 16 en suite 20 annexe en suite No smoking in all bedrooms s £59-£64; d £76-£88 (incl. bkfst) * LB **FACILITIES:** STV English Heritage Grade 2 listed Victorian garden of 3 acres **CONF:** Class 20 **PARKING:** 34 **NOTES:** No dogs (ex guide dogs) No children 12yrs No smoking in restaurant Closed 22-31 Dec RS 31 Dec
CARDS:
See advert on opposite page

★★69% The Georgian House
32-34 Unthank Rd NR2 2RB
☎ 01603 615655 📠 01603 765689
e-mail: reception@georgian-hotel.co.uk
Dir: *follow signs for Roman Catholic Cathedral from city centre*

Close to the Catholic Cathedral and within easy walking distance of the city centre, this attractive hotel was originally two Victorian houses. Bedrooms come in a variety of styles, and public areas include a cosy bar, a television lounge and an elegant restaurant offering a choice of menus.
ROOMS: 27 en suite (4 fmly) No smoking in 6 bedrooms s £51.50; d £72 (incl. bkfst) * LB **CONF:** Class 20 **PARKING:** 40 **NOTES:** No dogs No smoking in restaurant **CARDS:**
See advert on opposite page

★★68% ❁ Cumberland
212-216 Thorpe Rd NR1 1TJ
☎ 01603 434550 & 434560 📠 01603 433355
e-mail: cumberland@paston.co.uk
Dir: *on A1242, 1m from railway station*
The exterior of this small hotel belies the hospitality and jovial warmth offered within by the owner and his friendly team. An interesting choice of dishes are offered in the vibrant restaurant and the welcoming public rooms include a smart lounge bar and a cosy sitting room. Bedroom sizes vary, but all are individually furnished and well equipped.
ROOMS: 22 en suite 3 annexe en suite No smoking in 10 bedrooms s £49.95-£69.95; d £55-£75 (incl. bkfst) * LB **CONF:** Thtr 75 Class 75 Board 40 Del from £74.95 * **PARKING:** 60 **NOTES:** No dogs (ex guide dogs) No children 12yrs No smoking in restaurant Closed 26 Dec-2 Jan
CARDS:

⌂ Travelodge
Thickthorn Service Area, Norwich Southern Bypass NR9 3AU
☎ 01603 457549 📠 01603 457549
Dir: *A11/A47 interchange*
This modern building offers accommodation in smart, spacious and well equipped bedrooms, all with en suite bathrooms. Refreshments may be taken at the nearby family restaurant. For further details and the Travelodge phone number, consult the Hotel Groups page.
ROOMS: 40 en suite

○ Premier Lodge
Hold Rd
☎ 0870 700 1528 📠 0870 700 1528

NOTTINGHAM, Nottinghamshire Map 08 SK54
see also Langar

★★★65% Bestwood Lodge
Bestwood Country Park, Arnold NG5 8NE
☎ 0115 920 3011 📠 0115 967 0409
Dir: *3m N off A60 at lights turn left into Oxclose Lane, at next lights, turn right onto Queens Bower Rd then 1st right, where road forks keep right*
A Victorian hunting lodge in 700 acres of parkland that provides contemporary bedrooms that vary in size and style. A refurbishment programme is on-going. The interior architecture includes Gothic features and high vaulted ceilings in the lounge bar and the gallery. The restaurant offers a choice of menus that have a good range of dishes. This is a popular venue for weddings and conferences.
ROOMS: 40 en suite (5 fmly) s £38-£75; d £76-£90 (incl. bkfst) * LB **FACILITIES:** Riding Guided walking Xmas **CONF:** Thtr 200 Class 65 Board 50 Del from £85 * **PARKING:** 120 **NOTES:** No smoking in restaurant RS Acc. unavailable Xmas Day/New Year's Day
CARDS:
See advert on opposite page

★★★65% *Posthouse Nottingham City*
St James's St NG1 6BN
☎ 0870 400 9061 📠 0115 948 4366
Dir: *from M1 junct 24,25,26 follow signs to city centre, then brown tourist signs to Nottingham Castle & Tales of Robin Hood, hotel is located next door*
This modern city centre hotel is close to all the main attractions of the city. There is a business centre, and good conference and function facilities. Behan's Irish Bar is a popular feature and there is also a separate restaurant.
ROOMS: 130 en suite (17 fmly) No smoking in 88 bedrooms **FACILITIES:** entertainment **CONF:** Thtr 600 Class 350 Board 120 **SERVICES:** Lift air con **CARDS:**

★★★64% Nottingham Gateway
Nuthall Rd, Cinderhill NG8 6AZ
☎ 0115 979 4949 📠 0115 979 4744
e-mail: nottingateway@btconnect.com
Dir: *take A610 from junct 26 of M1*
A modern hotel, convenient for the city and the motorway network. Well-equipped bedrooms are comfortable and there is a choice of restaurants, with a carvery and the Tum-Nuk Thai restaurant. With a number of meeting rooms leading off the glass atrium, this hotel offers a flexible range of facilities.
continued on p418

NOTTINGHAM, continued

Nottingham Gateway, Nottingham

ROOMS: 107 en suite (18 fmly) No smoking in 54 bedrooms s £42-£78; d £50-£95 * LB **FACILITIES:** STV Discounted entrance to nearby David Lloyd Health Club Xmas **CONF:** Thtr 300 Class 100 Board 50 Del from £100 * **SERVICES:** Lift **PARKING:** 250 **NOTES:** No dogs (ex guide dogs) **CARDS:**

See advert on page 416

★★★64% Westminster Hotel

312 Mansfield Rd, Carrington NG5 2EF
☎ 0115 955 5000 Fax 0115 955 5005
e-mail: mail@westminster-hotel.co.uk
Dir: *on A60 1m N of town centre*

This family run hotel offers well presented accommodation, including spacious superior rooms. Other bedrooms vary in size, reflecting the Victorian origins of the building, though all are equipped to the same high standard. There is a lounge bar and a beamed restaurant.

ROOMS: 72 en suite No smoking in 40 bedrooms s £72-£90; d £87-£105 * LB **FACILITIES:** STV **CONF:** Thtr 60 Class 30 Board 30 Del from £95 * **SERVICES:** Lift **PARKING:** 66 **NOTES:** No dogs (ex guide dogs) No smoking in restaurant Closed 25 Dec-2 Jan
CARDS:

See advert on opposite page

★★★63% Rutland Square Hotel by the Castle

ZOFFANY

St James St NG1 6FJ
☎ 0115 941 1114 Fax 0115 941 0014
e-mail: Rutlandsquare@zoffanyhotels.co.uk
Dir: *on entering the city follow brown signs to the castle, hotel on right 50yds on from the castle*

As the name suggests, this hotel is situated adjacent to the castle, and is close to the heart of the city centre. Behind its Regency facade the hotel is modern and comfortable with particularly good business facilities; there is a conference centre on the opposite side of the square with a smart new Terrace Café Bar in the floors below. Bedrooms vary considerably in size, each room is decorated in appealing warm colour schemes and offers a good range of facilities.

ROOMS: 105 en suite (3 fmly) No smoking in 38 bedrooms s £50-£87; d £70-£100 * LB **FACILITIES:** STV Free use of nearby Fitness Club Xmas **CONF:** Thtr 200 Class 70 Board 45 Del from £120 * **SERVICES:** Lift
CARDS:

See advert on opposite page

★★★63% The Strathdon

PEEL HOTELS

Derby Rd NG1 5FT
☎ 0115 941 8501 Fax 0115 948 3725
Dir: *from M1 junct 25, follow A52 into city centre. Hotel is situated on the right on Wollaton Street*

Situated close to the city centre, opposite the Albert Hall Conference and Exhibition Centre, this popular hotel provides modern accommodation for a predominantly business clientele. Public areas include a conservatory lounge, the Boston Bean bar, a comfortable cocktail bar and the attractive Bobbins restaurant. A variety of conference rooms, including boardroom facilities, are available.

ROOMS: 68 en suite (4 fmly) No smoking in 37 bedrooms s £68-£95; d £85-£125 * LB **FACILITIES:** STV **CONF:** Thtr 150 Class 65 Board 40 Del from £90 * **SERVICES:** Lift **PARKING:** 14
CARDS:

★★★60% Windsor Lodge

116 Radcliffe Rd, West Bridgford NG2 5HG
☎ 0115 952 8528 Fax 0115 952 0020
e-mail: windsor@btinternet.com
Dir: *A6011 & A52 Grantham, 0.5m Trent Bridge Cricket Ground*

Situated close to Trent Bridge cricket ground, Windsor Lodge offers well maintained bedrooms, including a number of ground floor rooms. Executive rooms offer extra comfort, and public areas include a comfortable bar lounge and a separate billiards room.

ROOMS: 47 en suite (8 fmly) **FACILITIES:** STV Snooker **CONF:** Thtr 40 Class 25 Board 24 **PARKING:** 50 **NOTES:** No dogs (ex guide dogs) Closed 25-26 Dec **CARDS:**

See advert on opposite page

★★★58% Swans Hotel & Restaurant

84-90 Radcliffe Rd, West Bridgford NG2 5HH
☎ 0115 981 4042 Fax 0115 945 5745
e-mail: swanshotel@aol.com
Dir: *on A6011, approached from either A60 or A52 close to Trent Bridge*

This privately owned hotel is conveniently located for the city centre. A welcoming atmosphere is generated in the cosy lounge bar while an interesting and varied choice of freshly prepared dishes is served in the restaurant. Bedrooms vary in size and style, all are well equipped.

ROOMS: 30 en suite (4 fmly) s £53-£58; d £63-£68 (incl. bkfst) * LB **FACILITIES:** STV **CONF:** Thtr 50 Class 10 Board 15 Del from £65 * **SERVICES:** Lift **PARKING:** 31 **NOTES:** No dogs (ex guide dogs) No smoking in restaurant Closed 24-28 Dec
CARDS:

See advert on page 421

Late for dinner? Quality Standards star rating means that last orders for dinner should be no earlier than:
★ 6.30pm ★★ 7.00pm ★★★ 8.00pm
★★★★ 9.00pm ★★★★★ 10.00pm

NOTTINGHAM, continued

★★65% Balmoral
55-57 Loughborough Rd, West Bridgford NG2 7LA
☎ 0115 955 2992 & 0800 952 2992 📠 0115 955 2991
e-mail: balmoralhotel55@hotmail.com
Dir: *beside A60 Loughborough Road, cross Trent Bridge, past cricket ground, hotel 200mtrs on left*
Ideally placed for the major sporting venues of the city, this popular hotel offers comfortable well equipped accommodation, including some bedrooms on the ground floor. Service is both friendly and helpful, creating a relaxed atmosphere within the public rooms, that are dominated by a lounge bar and open-plan dining area. Private car parking to the rear of the property.
ROOMS: 35 en suite (5 fmly) No smoking in 6 bedrooms s £29-£37.50; d £45-£47.50 (incl. bkfst) * **FACILITIES:** Pool table **CONF:** Thtr 20 Class 20 Board 20 Del from £55 * **PARKING:** 40 **NOTES:** No dogs (ex guide dogs) **CARDS:**

See advert on opposite page

★★65% *Rufford*
53 Melton Rd, West Bridgford NG2 7NE
☎ 0115 981 4202 📠 0115 945 5801
Dir: *on A606, near junct A60 Loughborough Road*

Conveniently situated for all the major sporting arenas, this family run hotel offers a bright conservatory bar and wood panelled restaurant. There is a wide choice of bedroom size and layout, with all rooms being comfortably furnished and thoughtfully designed to make full use of the space available.
ROOMS: 34 en suite No smoking in 3 bedrooms **FACILITIES:** STV Pool table **PARKING:** 35 **NOTES:** No dogs (ex guide dogs) Closed Xmas **CARDS:**

See advert on opposite page

★★60% The Stage
Gregory Boulevard NG7 6LB
☎ 0115 960 3261 📠 0115 969 1040
e-mail: reservations@stagenottingham.fsnet.co.uk

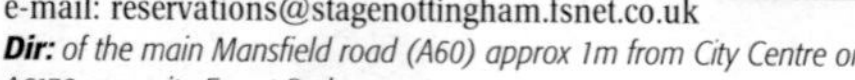

Dir: *of the main Mansfield road (A60) approx 1m from City Centre on A6130, opposite Forest Park*
Situated opposite Forest Park, where the famous Goose Fair is held, this commercial hotel is just a mile from the city centre. Public rooms include a spacious lounge bar, restaurant and various function rooms; a menu of popular dishes is offered within the restaurant. Bedroom sizes and styles vary, ranging from executive to standard rooms, but all are well equipped and generally of comfortable proportions.
ROOMS: 52 en suite (5 fmly) No smoking in 4 bedrooms s £40-£45; d £45-£55 (incl. bkfst) * LB **FACILITIES:** Xmas **CONF:** Thtr 100 Class 50 Board 35 Del £69.50 * **PARKING:** 80 **NOTES:** No dogs (ex guide dogs) **CARDS:**

Town House

★★★★ Lace Market
29-31 High Pavement NG1 1HE
☎ 0115 852 3232
e-mail: reservations@lacemarkethotel.co.uk
A smart, stylish hotel with quality décor and furnishings. Bedrooms have been equipped to a high standard and have many thoughtful extras. An extensive menu is available in the bar area, but guests wishing a more formal style of dining can take advantage of the full carte menu in the popular Merchants Restaurant.
ROOMS: 29 en suite s fr £89; d fr £99 * **FACILITIES:** STV
CARDS:

Premier Lodge (Nottingham North)
101 Mansfield Rd, Daybrook NG5 6BH
☎ 0870 700 1532 📠 0870 700 1533
Premier Lodge offers modern, well equipped, en suite accommodation suitable for both business and leisure travellers. Meals can be taken at the adjacent popular restaurant and bar which is fully licensed. For further details, consult the Hotel Groups page.
ROOMS: 64 en suite d £42 *

Premier Lodge (Nottingham South)
Loughborough Rd, Ruddington NG11 6LS

☎ 0870 700 1534 📠 0870 700 1535
Premier Lodge offers modern, well equipped, en suite accommodation suitable for both business and leisure travellers. Meals can be taken at the adjacent popular restaurant and bar which is fully licensed. For further details, consult the Hotel Groups page.
ROOMS: 42 en suite d £42 *

Travelodge (Nottingham Riverside)
Riverside Retail Park NG2 1RT
☎ 0115 985 0934
Dir: *on Riverside Retail Park*
This modern building offers accommodation in smart, spacious and well equipped bedrooms, all with en suite bathrooms. Refreshments may be taken at the nearby family restaurant. For further details and the Travelodge phone number, consult the Hotel Groups page.
ROOMS: 61 en suite

○ Hotel des Clos
Old Lenton Ln NG7 2SA
☎ 0115 986 6566 📠 0115 986 0343
This small riverside hotel is a careful conversion of Victorian farm buildings. Many of the thoughtfully furnished bedrooms are

continued on p422

NOTTINGHAM, continued

situated around a courtyard garden. Recent additions are two tastefully appointed spacious suites. The restaurant is the focal point where classic French menus are offered.
ROOMS: 17 rms **NOTES:** Open

○ ***Premier Lodge (Nottingham City Centre)***
Island Site, London Rd
☎ 0870 700 1536 📠 0870 700 1537

NUNEATON, Warwickshire — Map 04 SP39

★★★62% **Weston Hall**
Weston Ln, Weston in Arden, Bulkington CV12 9RU
☎ 024 76312989 📠 024 76640846

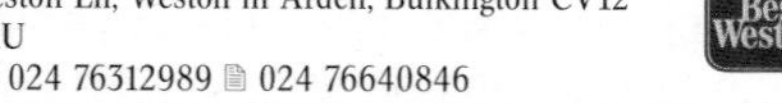

Dir: *M6 junct 2 follow B4065 through Ansty turn left in Shilton, follow Nuneaton signs out of Bulkington, turn into Weston Ln at 30mph sign*

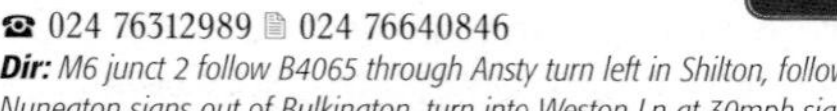

Close to Coventry, M6/M69 and the NEC this former dower house, dating from 1580, is set in seven acres of peaceful grounds. Bedrooms whilst thoughtfully equipped, do vary in size. The hotel has extensive conference facilities.
ROOMS: 40 en suite (7 fmly) No smoking in 6 bedrooms s £69.50-£95; d £85-£105 (incl. bkfst) * LB **FACILITIES:** Fishing Riding Sauna Gym Croquet lawn Jacuzzi/spa Steam room entertainment ch fac Xmas **CONF:** Thtr 200 Class 100 Board 80 **PARKING:** 300 **NOTES:** No smoking in restaurant **CARDS:**

See advert under COVENTRY

Travelodge
Bedworth CV10 7TF
☎ 024 76382541 📠 024 76382541
Dir: *2m S, on A444*
This modern building offers accommodation in smart, spacious and well equipped bedrooms, all with en suite bathrooms. Refreshments may be taken at the nearby family restaurant. For further details and the Travelodge phone number, consult the Hotel Groups page.
ROOMS: 40 en suite

Travelodge
St Nicholas Park Dr CV11 6EN
☎ 024 76353885 📠 024 76353885
Dir: *on A47*
This modern building offers accommodation in smart, spacious and well equipped bedrooms, all with en suite bathrooms. Refreshments may be taken at the nearby family restaurant. For further details and the Travelodge phone number, consult the Hotel Groups page.
ROOMS: 30 en suite

NUNNEY, Somerset — Map 03 ST74

★★67% **The George at Nunney**
11 Church St BA11 4LW
☎ 01373 836458 📠 01373 836565
e-mail: georgenunney@aol.com
Dir: *0.5m N off A361 Frome/Shepton Mallet*

Situated in the centre of Nunney, opposite the castle, The George dates back to the 17th century. Guests may choose from an extensive range of bar meals or a selection of dishes offered in the more intimate restaurant. A commendable selection of whiskies is also available. The cosy bedrooms are neatly furnished and particularly well equipped.
ROOMS: 9 rms (8 en suite) (2 fmly) No smoking in 2 bedrooms s £46-£48; d £62-£78 (incl. bkfst) * LB **FACILITIES:** STV Pool table Xmas **PARKING:** 30 **NOTES:** No dogs (ex guide dogs) **CARDS:**

See advert under BATH

OAKHAM, Rutland — Map 04 SK80

Premier Collection

★★★ **Hambleton Hall**
Hambleton LE15 8TH
☎ 01572 756991 📠 01572 724721
e-mail: hotel@hambletonhall.com
Dir: *3m E off A606*
Hambleton Hall in its landscaped grounds edging Rutland Water is the epitome of the English country hotel. Public rooms are stunning and include the bar and elegant drawing room. The restaurant showcases the inspired cuisine with its superb seasonal and locally sourced menu. The bedrooms are stylish and each room is individually decorated.
ROOMS: 15 en suite 2 annexe en suite s £140-£165; d £170-£195 (incl. cont bkfst) * **FACILITIES:** STV Outdoor swimming (H) Tennis (hard) Xmas **CONF:** Thtr 40 Class 40 Board 24 Del from £220 * **SERVICES:** Lift **PARKING:** 40 **NOTES:** No smoking in restaurant Civ Wed 60 **CARDS:**

★★★72% Barnsdale Lodge
The Avenue, Rutland Water, North Shore LE15 8AH
☎ 01572 724678 01572 724961
e-mail: barnsdale.lodge@btconnect.com
Dir: *turn off A1 onto A606. Hotel is located 5m on right hand side, 2m E of Oakham*
A very popular hotel overlooking Rutland Water. Bedrooms are comfortably appointed with excellent beds and period furnishings, enhanced by contemporary, stylish soft furnishings and thoughtful extras. The restaurant, which is a series of three intimate dining rooms, offers a good range of internationally appealing freshly cooked dishes.
ROOMS: 45 en suite (4 fmly) No smoking in 12 bedrooms s fr £65; d fr £89 (incl. bkfst) * LB **FACILITIES:** STV Fishing Shooting Archery Golf arranged Pitch'n'Putt ch fac Xmas **CONF:** Thtr 330 Class 120 Board 76 Del from £99.50 * **PARKING:** 200 **NOTES:** Civ Wed 100
CARDS:

★★★66% Barnsdale Hall Hotel & Country Club
Barnsdale LE15 8AB
☎ 01572 757901 01572 756235
e-mail: barnsdale@webleicester.co.uk
Dir: *from A1 take A606 towards Oakham, travel through the villages of Empingham then Whitwell, after approx 1m hotel on left overlooking Rutland Water*
Overlooking Rutland Water, this complex offers extensive leisure facilities and is set in attractive gardens. Spacious modern bedrooms in separate buildings in the grounds are comfortable and well equipped; many have the added benefit of a balcony and views. Public rooms offer a choice of modern dining options and a new lounge area.
ROOMS: 60 annexe en suite (9 fmly) No smoking in 8 bedrooms s £70; d £90 (incl. bkfst) * LB **FACILITIES:** STV Indoor swimming (H) Tennis (hard) Squash Snooker Sauna Solarium Gym Pool table Croquet lawn Putting green Jacuzzi/spa Boule Bowls Xmas **CONF:** Thtr 200 Class 80 Board 50 Del £125 * **SERVICES:** Lift **PARKING:** 100 **NOTES:** No dogs (ex guide dogs) Civ Wed 120 **CARDS:**

★★★60% Whipper-in Hotel
Market Place LE15 6DT
☎ 01572 756971 01572 757759
e-mail: umesh@brook-hotels.co.uk
Dir: *from A1 take B668 for Oakham and head for the Market Square*
A fashionable market town inn furnished with English country house style. An open fire warms the lounge bar, a popular meeting place for locals, whilst in the candlelit restaurant an interesting carte of modern British dishes is presented. Each bedroom is individually designed, four-poster and executive rooms are available.
ROOMS: 24 en suite No smoking in 4 bedrooms s £65-£69; d £75-£89 (incl. bkfst) * LB **FACILITIES:** Xmas **CONF:** Thtr 80 Class 25 Board 30 Del from £95 * **PARKING:** 40 **NOTES:** No smoking in restaurant Civ Wed 65 **CARDS:**

OCKLEY, Surrey — Map 04 TQ14

★★★63% Gatton Manor Hotel Golf & Country Club
Standon Ln RH5 5PQ
☎ 01306 627555 01306 627713
e-mail: gattonmanor@enterprise.net
Dir: *off A29 at Ockley turn into Cat Hill Lane, signposted for 2m hotel entrance on the right*
Enjoying a peaceful setting, this popular golf and country club offers a range of comfortable, modern bedrooms. Public areas feature the main club bar, small restaurant and attractive drawing room. Other facilities include a health club and the 18 hole professional golf course.

ROOMS: 18 en suite (2 fmly) No smoking in 6 bedrooms s £67.50-£82.50; d £105-£135 (incl. bkfst) * LB **FACILITIES:** STV Golf 18 Fishing Sauna Solarium Gym Putting green Jacuzzi/spa Bowling green entertainment Xmas **CONF:** Thtr 50 Class 40 Board 30 Del from £120 * **PARKING:** 250 **NOTES:** No dogs (ex guide dogs) No smoking in restaurant Civ Wed 50 **CARDS:**

ODIHAM, Hampshire — Map 04 SU75

★★71% George
High St RG29 1LP
☎ 01256 702081 01256 704213
Dir: *from M3 junct 5 follow signs to Alton/Odiham. In Odiham left at mini-rdbt, hotel is on left*
A focal point of this small town, the hotel boasts both a Seafood restaurant and brasserie style café bar which are popular with

continued

ODIHAM, continued

both locals and residents. Bedrooms come in a number of styles, the older part of the property having old beams and period features, newer rooms having a more contemporary feel.
ROOMS: 19 en suite 9 annexe en suite (1 fmly) No smoking in 14 bedrooms s £80-£85; d £90-£95 (incl. bkfst) * LB **FACILITIES:** STV **CONF:** Thtr 30 Class 20 Board 26 Del from £105 * **PARKING:** 20 **CARDS:**

OKEHAMPTON, Devon — Map 02 SX59

★★66% White Hart
Fore St EX20 1HD
☎ 01837 52730 & 54514 Fax 01837 53979
e-mail: graham@whitehartthotel.telme.com
Dir: *located in town centre, adjacent to the traffic lights, car park at rear of hotel*
This 17th-century, former coaching inn is equally suited for both the leisure and business users, also catering well for local functions. Bedrooms vary in size, all are well equipped and furnished in similar style. The public areas retain the original character and charm of the building, a choice of bars is provided with a range of meals being served, while in the restaurant both fixed price and carte menus are offered.
ROOMS: 19 en suite (2 fmly) No smoking in 4 bedrooms s £35-£40; d £50-£60 (incl. bkfst) * **FACILITIES:** Games room Skittle alley Xmas **CONF:** Thtr 100 Class 80 Board 40 **PARKING:** 22 **NOTES:** No dogs (ex guide dogs) **CARDS:**

See advert on page 423

★★65% Ashbury Hotel
Higher Maddaford, Southcott EX20 4NL
☎ 01837 55453 Fax 01837 55468
Dir: *turn off A30 at Sourton Cross onto A386. Turn left onto A3079 to Bude at Fowley Cross. After 1m turn right to Ashbury. Hotel 0.5m on right*
The Ashbury has three golf courses and a clubhouse with lounge, bar and dining facilities. The majority of the well equipped bedrooms are located in the adjacent farmhouse and courtyard-style development around the putting green. Guests can enjoy the many on-site leisure facilities or join in the multitude of activities available at the adjacent sister hotel.
ROOMS: 26 en suite 29 annexe en suite (21 fmly) s £28-£49; d £56-£98 (incl. bkfst & dinner) * LB **FACILITIES:** Indoor swimming (H) Golf 18 Tennis (hard) Snooker Sauna Pool table Putting green Jacuzzi/spa Driving range Indoor bowls Ten-pin bowling Xmas **PARKING:** 100 **NOTES:** No dogs (ex guide dogs) **CARDS:**

★★65% Manor House Hotel
Fowley Cross EX20 4NA
☎ 01837 53053 Fax 01837 55027
Dir: *turn off A30 at Sourton Cross flyover, take right onto A386, hotel is located 1.5m on right*
This popular hotel, set in 17 acres of grounds and about three miles from the town, enjoys stunning views of Dartmoor. It offers an extensive range of amenities and activities, catering exclusively for breaks. Guests can use the golfing facilities at the adjacent sister hotel. Many of the comfortable, well equipped bedrooms benefit from the views.
ROOMS: 161 en suite (66 fmly) s £33-£55; d £66-£110 (incl. bkfst & dinner) * LB **FACILITIES:** Indoor swimming (H) Tennis (hard) Squash Snooker Sauna Gym Pool table Croquet lawn Putting green Jacuzzi/spa Craft centre Indoor bowls Shooting range Laser clay pigeon shooting Aerobics ch fac Xmas **PARKING:** 200 **NOTES:** No dogs (ex guide dogs) **CARDS:**

See advert on opposite page

⌂ *Travelodge*
Whiddon Down EX20 2QT
☎ 01647 231626 Fax 01647 231626
Dir: *at Merrymeet rdbt on A30/A382*
This modern building offers accommodation in smart, spacious and well equipped bedrooms, all with en suite bathrooms. Refreshments may be taken at the nearby family restaurant. For further details and the Travelodge phone number, consult the Hotel Groups page.
ROOMS: 40 en suite

OLDBURY, West Midlands — Map 07 SO98

⌂ Express by Holiday Inn Oldbury
Bickley Park B69 2BD
☎ 0121 511 0000
e-mail: debbiehorton/shl@shl
Dir: *hotel is located off junct2 of the M5, behind ELF garage on the Wolverhampton Rd*

A modern budget hotel offering comfortable accommodation in refreshing, spacious and comprehensively-equipped bedrooms, en suite bathrooms with power showers and continental buffet breakfast included in the room rate. Suitable for business travellers or families. For further details and the Express by Holiday Inn phone number, consult the Hotel Groups page.
ROOMS: 109 en suite (incl. cont bkfst) d £53.50-£56.50 * **CONF:** Thtr 40 Class 25 Board 25

⌂ *Travelodge*
Wolverhampton Rd B69 2BH
☎ 0121 552 2967 Fax 0121 552 2967
Dir: *on A4123, northbound off junct 2 of M5*
This modern building offers accommodation in smart, spacious and well equipped bedrooms, all with en suite bathrooms. Refreshments may be taken at the nearby family restaurant. For further details and the Travelodge phone number, consult the Hotel Groups page.
ROOMS: 33 en suite

OLDHAM, Greater Manchester — Map 07 SD90

★★★★64% Menzies Avant
Windsor Rd, Manchester St OL8 4AS
☎ 0500 636943 (Central Res) Fax 01773 880321
e-mail: info@menzies-hotels.co.uk
Dir: *from junct 20 of M62 (East or West) follow Oldham town centre signs A627(M) then A62 Manchester St, hotel is on left*
This modern hotel offers smart well equipped accommodation. There is a variety of bedrooms sizes; all rooms are very attractive. A covered walkway leads to the public areas which include a bright and comfortable restaurant serving quality cuisine, and a

continued on p426

GOLF • CRAFT • INDOOR SPORT

Manor House Hotel

Unique Craft Centre - Pottery + 9 other crafts. Short courses daily. Indoor/Outdoor Tennis + Bowls, Badminton, Squash, Archery, Laser Clays, Snooker - ALL FREE. Heated Indoor Pools, Spa, Sauna. Guided Walks. Aromatherapy, etc.

2001 Bargain Breaks:-Full Board

March	**- 4nts £212, 3nts £180**
June	**- 4 nts £210, 3 nts £166**
August	**- 4 nts £268, 3 nts £201**
November	**- 4 nts £164, 3 nts £139**

AA ★★ AA ★★

Manor House and Ashbury Hotels, West Devon.

Two Country House Hotels, 2 miles apart. Courtesy mini-bus. All facilities freely available to guests at both hotels. Superb views, service and food. Full board. Child Rates. Party Discounts. Bargain Breaks all year. Enquiries - F'phone - 0800 389 9894. Bookings - 01837 53053. www.manorhousehotel.co.uk

The Ashbury Hotel

18 Hole Oakwood Course
27 Hole Ashbury Course - choice of three 18 hole Courses
18 Hole Par 3, Driving Range
Low cost Golf Cars - £3 - £12
Indoor Bowls, Snooker, Tennis
Heated Indoor Pool, Spa, Sauna
2001 Bargain Breaks:- Full Bd
March- 4 nts £159, 3nts £135
June- 4nts £210, 3nts £166
August- 4nts £246, 3nts £185
November- 4nts £149, 3nts £127

FREE GOLF AND WHOLE IN ONE

OLDHAM, continued

spacious bar. Conference and banqueting suites are also available. A leisure facility is planned.
ROOMS: 103 en suite (2 fmly) No smoking in 16 bedrooms d £85-£95 * LB **FACILITIES:** STV Xmas **CONF:** Thtr 200 Class 100 Board 60 Del from £80 * **SERVICES:** Lift **PARKING:** 120 **NOTES:** Civ Wed 200
CARDS:

★★★71% Hotel Smokies Park

Ashton Rd, Bardsley OL8 3HX
☎ 0161 785 5000 0161 785 5010
Dir: *on A627 between Oldham and Ashton-under-Lyne*

Best Western

This modern hotel offers smart, comfortable bedrooms and suites, with many amenities. An extensive range of Italian and English dishes are offered in the airy restaurant and there is a welcoming lounge bar where live entertainment is offered at weekends. A small but well equipped fitness centre is available for use by residents only. There is also a night-club on site, to which residents gain free admission.
ROOMS: 73 en suite (2 fmly) No smoking in 36 bedrooms s £70-£140; d £80-£150 (incl. bkfst) * LB **FACILITIES:** STV Sauna Solarium Gym Night club Cabaret lounge entertainment **CONF:** Thtr 200 Class 125 Board 50 Del from £95 * **SERVICES:** Lift **PARKING:** 120 **NOTES:** No dogs (ex guide dogs) **CARDS:**

★★★61% Pennine Way Hotel

Manchester St OL8 1UZ
☎ 0161 624 0555 0161 627 2031
Dir: *exit M62 junct 20 and follow signs for town centre*

This large purpose built hotel is close to the centre of town. Bedrooms are well equipped and staff are friendly and helpful. The fixed price dinner menu is good value and there is a special children's menu. The ballroom, accommodating up to 350, is one of a choice of rooms for functions and conferences. The hotel is a popular venue for coach tours.
ROOMS: 130 en suite (50 fmly) No smoking in 70 bedrooms s £55-£85; d £65-£95 (incl. bkfst) * LB **FACILITIES:** STV Gym Pool table Xmas **CONF:** Thtr 320 Class 70 Board 70 Del from £95 * **SERVICES:** Lift **PARKING:** 250 **NOTES:** No smoking in restaurant
CARDS:

★★68% High Point

64 Napier St East OL8 1TR
☎ 0161 624 4130 0161 627 2757
Dir: *M62 junct 20 to M627 Oldham onto A627 off at A62 (Manchester) under "Glass Bridge". Turn left onto Lee Street right at T-junct onto Napier St East*

MINOTEL Great Britain

A friendly welcome awaits at this privately owned town centre hotel, just a short drive from junction 20 of the M62. Bedrooms are attractively furnished and the conservatory restaurant, which enjoys fine views, serves an extensive range of dishes.
continued

ROOMS: 19 en suite (3 fmly) No smoking in 2 bedrooms s £42-£50; d £53-£70 (incl. bkfst) * LB **FACILITIES:** STV **CONF:** Thtr 40 Class 25 Board 25 Del from £69 * **PARKING:** 42 **NOTES:** No dogs (ex guide dogs) **CARDS:**

ONNELEY, Staffordshire — Map 07 SJ74

★★69% *Wheatsheaf Inn at Onneley*

Barhill Rd CW3 9QF
☎ 01782 751581 01782 751499
e-mail: wheatsheaf@pernickety.co.uk
Dir: *on A525 between Madeley/Woore, 6.5m W of Newcastle-under-Lyme*

This 18th century inn is situated next to Onneley golf club and opposite the new cricket field. It is convenient for access to The Potteries and the M6. It re-opened in July 1999 after extensive restructuring and refurbishment, during which no expense was spared in recreating an authentic Victorian ambience in the delightful public areas. The bedrooms whilst traditional in style and furnished with antiques, have the best of modern equipment and facilities.
ROOMS: 6 en suite **FACILITIES:** STV ch fac **CONF:** Thtr 60 Class 30 Board 30 **PARKING:** 150 **NOTES:** No dogs (ex guide dogs) No smoking in restaurant **CARDS:**

ORFORD, Suffolk — Map 05 TM45

★★67% Crown & Castle

IP12 2LJ
☎ 01394 450205 01394 450176
e-mail: info@crownandcastlehotel.co.uk
Dir: *turn right from B1084 on entering village*

Situated in a picturesque village overlooking the market square is this popular hotel which dates back to Tudor times. With commanding views of the castle and across the marshes it's an ideal place to visit when touring the Suffolk countryside. Bedrooms are located in the main house or the purpose-built wing; these are more spacious and have a patio with direct access to the gardens.
ROOMS: 9 en suite 10 annexe en suite (1 fmly) s £60; d £75-£90 (incl. bkfst) * LB **FACILITIES:** Xmas **PARKING:** 25
CARDS:

ORMSKIRK, Lancashire — Map 07 SD40

★★★67% Beaufort

High Ln, Burscough L40 7SN
☎ 01704 892655 01704 895135
e-mail: info@beaufort.uk.com
Dir: *from M58 junct 3 follow signs for Ormskirk which is 7m. Hotel is situated between Ormskirk and Burscough on A59*

A smart, modern, privately owned hotel with good open-plan lounge, bar and restaurant areas. A wide choice of food is
continued

available all day. Bedrooms are well equipped and comfortable, conference facilities are available.
ROOMS: 20 en suite s £60-£65; d £90-£95 (incl. bkfst) * LB
FACILITIES: STV Free use of sister Hotel's (Stutelea Hotel, Southport -8m) facilities Xmas **CONF:** Thtr 50 Class 30 Board 30 Del from £95 *
PARKING: 126 **NOTES:** No dogs (ex guide dogs) No smoking in restaurant Civ Wed 50 **CARDS:**

See advert on this page

OSTERLEY, Greater London
See LONDON SECTION plan 1 *B3*

★★★65% Osterley Four Pillars Hotel

FOUR PILLARS HOTELS

764 Great West Rd TW7 5NA
☎ 020 8568 9981 📠 020 8569 7819
e-mail: enquires@four-pillars.co.uk

Dir: *hotel at junct of A4 and Wood Lane. 1m past Osterley Tube Station, Eastbound on A4. 0.5m past Gillette, Westbound on A4*

This well situated hotel has good access to both central London and Heathrow Airport. Bedrooms are well designed, tastefully decorated and feature a useful range of extra facilities. Public areas include the Gresham's restaurant and bar, as well as a free house pub which is equally popular with locals.
ROOMS: 61 en suite (9 fmly) No smoking in 21 bedrooms s £47-£90; d £54-£100 * LB **FACILITIES:** STV Pool table entertainment
CONF: Thtr 250 Class 126 Board 80 Del from £110 * **PARKING:** 98
NOTES: Closed 26-27 Dec **CARDS:**

OSWESTRY, Shropshire — Map 07 SJ22

★★★74% Pen-y-Dyffryn Hall Country Hotel

Rhydycroesau SY10 7JD
☎ 01691 653700 📠 01691 650066
e-mail: stay@peny.co.uk
Dir: *from A5 into Oswestry town centre, follow signs to Llansilin on B4580, hotel is 3m W of Oswestry just before Rhydycroesau village*

A charming old house built as a rectory in 1840 and set in five acres of grounds. The accommodation is well equipped; comfortable public rooms are tastefully appointed and welcoming open fires flicker in the lounge on the chilly evenings. The hotel has an excellent reputation for the high quality of its food.
ROOMS: 8 en suite 2 annexe en suite (1 fmly) s £60-£64; d £78-£90 (incl. bkfst) * LB **FACILITIES:** Fishing Guided walks **PARKING:** 14
NOTES: No smoking in restaurant Closed 24 Dec-19 Jan
CARDS:

★★★68% Wynnstay

Best Western

Church St SY11 2SZ
☎ 01691 655261 📠 01691 670606
Dir: *take B4083 to town, then fork left at Honda Garage and right at lights. Hotel opposite parish church*

This Georgian property surrounds a unique 200 year old Crown Bowling Green. The hotel offers extensive function facilities and a

health, beauty and leisure centre. Well equipped bedrooms are individually styled and decorated, there are several suites and four-poster beds. The restaurant has an Italian theme and there is also a full range of bar food.
ROOMS: 29 en suite (4 fmly) No smoking in 14 bedrooms s £72-£92; d £92-£118 * LB **FACILITIES:** Indoor swimming (H) Sauna Solarium Gym Jacuzzi/spa Crown green bowling Beauty suite **CONF:** Thtr 290 Class 150 Board 50 Del from £95 * **PARKING:** 70 **NOTES:** Civ Wed 90
CARDS:

⌂ *Travelodge*

Travelodge

Mile End Service Area SY11 4JA
☎ 01691 658178 📠 01691 658178
Dir: *junct A5/A483*

This modern building offers accommodation in smart, spacious and well equipped bedrooms, all with en suite bathrooms. Refreshments may be taken at the nearby family restaurant. For further details and the Travelodge phone number, consult the Hotel Groups page.
ROOMS: 40 en suite

OTTERBURN, Northumberland — Map 12 NY89

★★64% Percy Arms

Best Western

NE19 1NR
☎ 01830 520261 📠 01830 520567
Dir: *centre of Otterburn village on A696*

This 17th-century coaching inn stands in the centre of the village surrounded by beautiful Northumberland moors. Public areas offer a good range and one has a choice of either the restaurant or the brasserie.

continued

O

OTTERBURN, continued

ROOMS: 28 en suite (2 fmly) No smoking in 2 bedrooms s £64-£80; d £80-£100 (incl. bkfst) * LB **FACILITIES:** Fishing Pool table Xmas **CONF:** Thtr 100 Class 60 Board 40 Del from £75 * **PARKING:** 74 **NOTES:** No smoking in restaurant **CARDS:**

○ Tower Hotel
NE19 1NP
☎ 01830 520620
Standing in its own grounds beside the A696 on the edge of the village, this old castellated building is now a family-owned hotel offering characterful accommodation. Bedrooms are spacious and pleasantly furnished. Welcoming fires burn in the hall and public rooms, which include a panelled restaurant. Staff provide friendly service.
ROOMS: 11 rms **NOTES:** Open

OTTERSHAW, Surrey — Map 04 TQ06

★★★★71% Foxhills
Stonehill Rd KT16 0EL
☎ 01932 872050 01932 874762
e-mail: mhayton@ibm.net
Dir: *A320 to Woking from M25. At 2nd rdbt take last exit Chobham Road, right into Foxhills Rd, right at T-junct, then left into Stonehill Rd*
Although close to the M25 and Heathrow, Foxhills is in a world of its own due to the vast expanse of grounds. Leisure is a primary attraction, golf courses, three pools, gym and weights room. Bedrooms are built around a courtyard, are spacious and designed with great consideration to comfort. Public areas in the Manor house include lounge, restaurant and conference facilities.
ROOMS: 38 en suite (1 fmly) d £135-£250 * LB **FACILITIES:** STV Indoor swimming (H) Outdoor swimming (H) Golf 45 Tennis (hard) Squash Snooker Sauna Solarium Gym Croquet lawn Putting green Boules Adventure playground for younger children ch fac Xmas **CONF:** Thtr 100 Class 52 Board 56 Del from £195 * **PARKING:** 500 **NOTES:** No dogs (ex guide dogs) **CARDS:**

See advert under WEYBRIDGE

OTTERY ST MARY, Devon — Map 03 SY19

★★70% Tumbling Weir Hotel & Restaurant
EX11 1AQ
☎ 01404 812752 01404 812752
e-mail: 106120.2702@compuserve.com
Dir: *turn off A30, take B3177 into Ottery St Mary, hotel adjoining 'Land of Canaan/long stay carpark'*
Situated between the River Otter and its millstream, this 17th-century cottage has old-world charm and attractive bedrooms. Original character has been retained with beams and candles helping to create an intimate atmosphere in the dining room and cosy lounge. Parking is available.
ROOMS: 11 en suite s £46; d £71 (incl. bkfst) LB **FACILITIES:** STV Fishing Xmas **CONF:** Thtr 95 Class 95 Board 95 **PARKING:** 10 **NOTES:** No smoking in restaurant **CARDS:**

OUNDLE, Northamptonshire — Map 04 TL08

★★★67% *The Talbot*
New St PE8 4EA
☎ 01832 273621 01832 274545
In the heart of this historic town, the Talbot dates from the 1600s. It has kept many of its original features and an atmosphere of old-world charm. Bedrooms are attractively furnished and public rooms display ancient beams. Ruined Fotheringhay Castle, where Mary, Queen of Scots spent her final, tragic days, provided some of the original building materials.
ROOMS: 39 en suite No smoking in 10 bedrooms **CONF:** Thtr 100 Class 40 Board 40 **PARKING:** 50 **NOTES:** No smoking in restaurant **CARDS:**

OXFORD, Oxfordshire — Map 04 SP50
see also Milton Common

★★★★ Le Manoir Aux Quat' Saisons
OX44 7PD
☎ 01844 278881 01844 278847
e-mail: lemanoir@blanc.co
(For full entry see Great Milton)

★★★★67% Oxford Spires Four Pillars Hotel
Abingdon Rd OX1 4PS
☎ 01865 324324 01865 324325
e-mail: enquiries@four-pillars.co.uk
Dir: *from A4142 over flyover and continue following 'City Centre (A4144)' Abingdon Road. Hotel 0.75m on right*
This brand new, purpose built hotel is surrounded by extensive parkland, yet is only a short walk to the city centre. Bedrooms are attractively furnished, well equipped and include several apartments. Smartly appointed public areas include a spacious restaurant, open plan bar/lounge, leisure club and extensive conference facilities.
ROOMS: 115 en suite (8 fmly) No smoking in 44 bedrooms s £79-£125; d £99-£160 * LB **FACILITIES:** STV Indoor swimming (H) Sauna Gym Pool table Jacuzzi/spa Private launch for hire Beauty room entertainment Xmas **CONF:** Thtr 266 Class 96 Board 76 Del from £149 * **SERVICES:** Lift **PARKING:** 95 **NOTES:** No dogs (ex guide dogs) **CARDS:**

★★★★67% Oxford Thames Four Pillars Hotel
Henley Rd, Sandford-on-Thames OX4 4GX
☎ 01865 334444 334400
e-mail: enquiries@four-pillars.co.uk
Dir: *turn off Eastern Bypass A4142 at rdbt onto A4074. Take first exit and follow signs to Sandford (1m)*
An impressive Victorian mansion in extensive grounds. The main house retains its galleried staircase leading to the bedrooms, individually decorated and with views of the river and gardens. Many rooms in the new wing have balconies, all are well equipped. Public areas include a comfortable lounge, open plan bar and a leisure suite.
ROOMS: 60 en suite (4 fmly) No smoking in 34 bedrooms s £79-£125; d £99-£160 * LB **FACILITIES:** STV Indoor swimming (H) Tennis (hard) Fishing Sauna Gym Croquet lawn Jacuzzi/spa Private launch for hire entertainment Xmas **CONF:** Thtr 160 Class 80 Board 60 Del from £149 * **PARKING:** 120 **NOTES:** No dogs (ex guide dogs) Civ Wed 140 **CARDS:**

★★★★67% The Randolph
Beaumont St OX1 2LN
☎ 0870 400 8200 01865 791678
e-mail: HeritageHotels_Oxford.Randolph@forte-hotels.com
Dir: *from M40 head for A40 Northern Bypass and at Pear Tree rdbt take exit S towards city centre into St Giles. Hotel on corner of Beaumont St*
This fine landmark hotel has an excellent location across from the Ashmolean Museum and is fortunate to have an adjoining garage. Built in 1864 in a Neo-Gothic style, the Randolph's public areas boast superb architectural features together with tasteful interior

continued

design. The elegant drawing room is known for its traditional afternoon teas. Spires restaurant is the place to watch the world go by from the huge picture windows. Bedrooms are attractively furnished with restful colour schemes and beautiful fabrics.
ROOMS: 119 en suite No smoking in 60 bedrooms s £140; d £170 * LB **FACILITIES:** STV Xmas **CONF:** Thtr 300 Class 120 Board 35 Del from £150 * **SERVICES:** Lift **PARKING:** 64 **NOTES:** No smoking in restaurant **CARDS:**

★★★77% Studley Priory
OX33 1AZ
☎ 01865 351203 & 351254 01865 351613
e-mail: res@studley-priory.co.uk
(For full entry see Horton-cum-Studley)

★★★70% Cotswold Lodge
66a Banbury Rd OX2 6JP
☎ 01865 512121 01865 512490
Dir: *turn off the A40 Oxford ring road onto the A4165, Banbury Road - signposted City centre/Summertown. Hotel 1.5m on left*
This family run hotel is set in a Victorian building close to the centre of Oxford and has undergone a total refurbishment. Bedrooms are smartly presented and well equipped, the comfortable public areas now offer an elegant country house charm. The hotel is popular with business guests and caters for conferences and banquets.
ROOMS: 49 en suite No smoking in 40 bedrooms s £125-£145; d £165-£220 (incl. bkfst) * LB **FACILITIES:** STV **CONF:** Thtr 100 Class 48 Board 30 Del from £140 * **PARKING:** 60 **NOTES:** No smoking in restaurant **CARDS:**

★★★70% Hawkwell House
Church Way, Iffley Village OX4 4DZ
☎ 01865 749988 01865 748525
Enjoying a quiet residential location, Hawkwell House is only minutes from the Oxford ring road. One of the strengths of this extended hotel is its smart and well designed new accommodation, upgrading is ongoing to modernise the older bedrooms to a similar high standard. A lively menu is offered in the bright and attractive Orangery restaurant whilst the recently enlarged conference and function suites are both popular and flexible.

ROOMS: 51 rms (50 en suite) (2 fmly) No smoking in 13 bedrooms s £90-£100; d £105-£115 * LB **FACILITIES:** STV Croquet lawn Xmas **CONF:** Thtr 200 Class 100 Board 200 Del from £130 * **SERVICES:** Lift **PARKING:** 60 **NOTES:** No dogs (ex guide dogs) No smoking in restaurant Civ Wed 200 **CARDS:**

Read all about it! Newspapers delivered to bedrooms in four and five star hotels.

★★★69% Fallowfields Country House Hotel
Faringdon Rd, Kingston Bagpuize, Southmoor OX13 5BH
☎ 01865 820416 01865 821275
e-mail: stay@fallowfields.com
Dir: *from A420, take A415 towards Abingdon for 100yds. Right at mini-rdbt, then through Kingston Bagpuize, Southmoor & Longworth and follow signs*

Once the home to Begum Aga Khan, this delightful hotel, set in its own grounds and gardens, is personally run by friendly proprietors. Spacious bedrooms are tastefully appointed and feature many thoughtful touches. Public rooms include an elegant drawing room and attractive conservatory restaurant which overlook the grounds. The hotel has a well deserved reputation for its food and makes much use of produce from its kitchen garden.
ROOMS: 10 en suite (2 fmly) No smoking in all bedrooms s £92.50-£99.50; d £115-£155 (incl. bkfst) * **FACILITIES:** STV Tennis (hard) Croquet lawn **CONF:** Thtr 70 Class 40 Board 35 Del from £150 * **PARKING:** 21 **NOTES:** No children 8yrs No smoking in restaurant Civ Wed 100 **CARDS:**

★★★67% *Weston Manor Hotel*
OX6 8QL
☎ 01869 350621 01869 350901
(For full entry see Weston-on-the-Green)

★★★66% Eastgate
The High, Merton St OX1 4BE
☎ 0870 400 8201 01865 791681
e-mail: HeritageHotels_Oxford.Eastgate@forte-hotels.com
Dir: *follow signs to Headington and Oxford City centre. Hotel is on corner of High St and Merton St after Magdalen Bridge and a set of traffic lights*

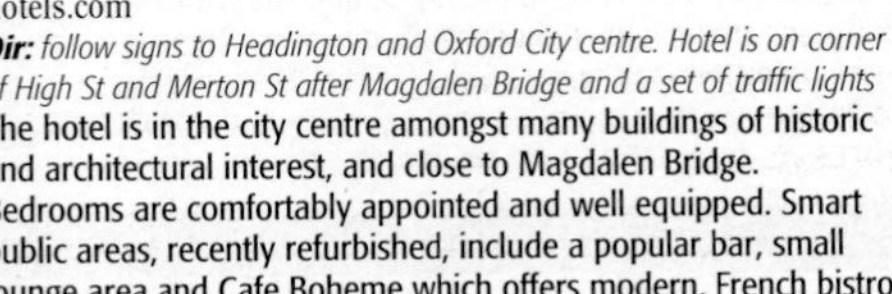

The hotel is in the city centre amongst many buildings of historic and architectural interest, and close to Magdalen Bridge. Bedrooms are comfortably appointed and well equipped. Smart public areas, recently refurbished, include a popular bar, small lounge area and Cafe Boheme which offers modern, French bistro style cuisine.
ROOMS: 64 en suite (3 fmly) No smoking in 25 bedrooms s £115; d £145 * LB **FACILITIES:** entertainment Xmas **SERVICES:** Lift **PARKING:** 27 **CARDS:**

★★★65% Linton Lodge
Linton Rd OX2 6UJ
☎ 01865 553461 01865 310365
e-mail: LintonLodge@vienna-group.co.uk
Dir: *take Banbury Rd leading out of Oxford City centre. Turn right into Linton Rd after approx 0.5m. Hotel is located opposite St Andrews Church*
Located in a side road of a residential area, Linton Lodge is within walking distance of the town centre. Bedrooms are well equipped
continued

O

OXFORD, continued

and comfortable. There are some quaint period features such as the wood-panelled restaurant and a bar overlooking the croquet lawn.
ROOMS: 71 en suite (2 fmly) No smoking in 20 bedrooms s £95-£105; d £112-£125 (incl. bkfst) * LB **FACILITIES:** STV Croquet lawn Putting green Bowls Area **CONF:** Thtr 120 Class 50 Board 35 Del from £100 * **SERVICES:** Lift **PARKING:** 40 **NOTES:** No smoking in restaurant Civ Wed 80 **CARDS:**

See advert on opposite page

★★65% The Balkan Lodge Hotel
315 Iffley Rd OX4 4AG
☎ 01865 244524 📠 01865 251090
Situated to the east of the city, Balkan Lodge offers easy access to the ring road and centre. Now family owned, the property has undergone extensive refurbishment. The bright, attractive bedrooms, have modern en suite facilities, and one room has a four-poster bed and a jacuzzi. There is a comfortable guest lounge and a smartly furnished dining room. Parking availability is also a real advantage.
ROOMS: 13 en suite No smoking in all bedrooms s £55.50-£62.50; d £68.50-£72.50 (incl. bkfst) * LB **FACILITIES:** STV **PARKING:** 13 **NOTES:** No smoking in restaurant Closed 12 Dec-20 Jan
CARDS:

★★64% Victoria
180 Abingdon Rd OX1 4RA
☎ 01865 724536 📠 01865 794909
Dir: *from M40/A40 take South bypass and head into the city*
The Victoria is a friendly hotel about fifteen minutes from the city centre and is a convenient base for touring the area. Meals have a Southern European flavour. Bedrooms have been recently refurbished to a high standard, and there is a new conservatory bar which will be at its best in the summer months.
ROOMS: 15 en suite 5 annexe en suite (1 fmly) s £55.50-£62.50; d £68.50-£78.50 (incl. bkfst) * LB **CONF:** Board 20 Del from £110 * **PARKING:** 20 **NOTES:** No smoking in restaurant
CARDS:

O

★★63% Palace
250 Iffley Rd OX4 1SE
☎ 01865 727627 📠 01865 200478
Dir: *on A4158 1m from City Centre*
A small family hotel close to the city centre. The attractive bedrooms are bright and thoughtfully equipped. There is a comfortable lounge and bar/dining facilities are available.
ROOMS: 8 en suite (2 fmly) No smoking in all bedrooms **PARKING:** 6 **NOTES:** No dogs **CARDS:**

Town House

★★★★ Old Bank
92-94 High St OX1 4BN
☎ 01865 799599 📠 01865 799598
e-mail: info@oldbank-hotel.co.uk
Dir: *Approach city centre via Headington over Magdalen Bridge into High St, hotel 50yds on left*
The tranquility of this hotel provides a contrast to the bustle of the High Street, just a few minutes away. This skilfully restored former bank offers smart, well equipped bedrooms, all with thoughtful extras and air conditioning. The Quod brasserie serves meals all day and there is also a peaceful courtyard.
ROOMS: 43 en suite (10 fmly) s fr £135; d £155-£300 * **FACILITIES:** STV ch fac **SERVICES:** Lift air con **PARKING:** 40 **NOTES:** No dogs (ex guide dogs) Closed 25-27 Dec
CARDS:

Town House

★★★★ Old Parsonage
1 Banbury Rd OX2 6NN
☎ 01865 310210 📠 01865 311262
e-mail: info@oldparsonage-hotel.co.uk
Dir: *from Oxford ring-road, approach city centre via Summertown, last building on right next to St Giles Church before entering city centre*
This charming, elegant hotel stands in a pretty street to the north of the city centre. Interior design cleverly reflects the architectural features of the building, and the focal point is the bar-cum-restaurant, open all day, which serves a wide-ranging menu and an interesting selection of wine. There is a small, peaceful lounge.
ROOMS: 30 en suite (4 fmly) s £130; d £150-£200 (incl. bkfst) * **FACILITIES:** STV ch fac **PARKING:** 16 **NOTES:** No dogs (ex guide dogs) Closed 24-27 Dec **CARDS:**

⌂ *Travelodge*
London Rd, Wheatley OX33 1JH
☎ 01865 875705 📠 01865 875905
Dir: *off A40 next to The Harvester on the outskirts of Wheatley*
This modern building offers accommodation in smart, spacious and well equipped bedrooms, all with en suite bathrooms. Refreshments may be taken at the nearby family restaurant. For further details and the Travelodge phone number, consult the Hotel Groups page.
ROOMS: 36 en suite

Travelodge

⌂ *Travelodge*
Peartree Roundabout, Woodstock Rd OX2 8JZ
☎ 01865 554301 📠 01865 513474
Dir: *junc A34/A43*
This modern building offers accommodation in smart, spacious and well equipped bedrooms, all with en suite bathrooms. Refreshments may be taken at the nearby family restaurant. For further details and the Travelodge phone number, consult the Hotel Groups page.
ROOMS: 98 en suite

Travelodge

⌂ Days Inn
OX33 1JN
☎ 01865 877000 📠 01865 877016
Dir: *situated at the Welcome Break service area of M40 junct 8A. Access available from both Southbound & northbound carriageways*
Fully refurbished, Days Inn offers well equipped, brightly appointed, modern accommodation with smart en suite bathrooms. There is a fully staffed reception; continental breakfast is available and other refreshments may be taken at the nearby family restaurant.
ROOMS: 59 en suite d fr £49 *

DAYS INN

PADSTOW, Cornwall & Isles of Scilly — Map 02 SW97
see also Constantine Bay

★★★70% The Metropole
Station Rd PL28 8DB
☎ 0870 400 8122 📠 01841 532867
e-mail: heritagehotels_padstow.metropole@forte-hotels.com
Dir: *leave M5 junct 31. Take A3 until it joins the A39 then the A389 following signs for Padstow*
Enjoying splendid views across the Camel Estuary, The Metropole provides comfortable public areas in which to relax. The smart lounge and veranda are popular for light lunches and afternoon

continued

teas. Bedrooms vary in size and aspect, but all are well equipped; the smart new Garden rooms are particularly spacious and attractively decorated.
ROOMS: 50 en suite (5 fmly) No smoking in 19 bedrooms s £85-£90; d £110-£160 * LB **FACILITIES:** Outdoor swimming (H) Swimming pool open Jul & Aug Xmas **SERVICES:** Lift **PARKING:** 38 **NOTES:** No smoking in restaurant **CARDS:**

★★★66% *Old Custom House Inn*

South Quay PL28 8ED
☎ 01841 532359 📠 01841 533372
Dir: *A359 from Wadebridge take 2nd right, once in Padstow follow road round hairpin bend at bottom of hill & cont, hotel is 2nd building*
Situated by the harbour, this charming inn continues to be a popular choice for locals and visitors alike. The lively bar serves real ales and good bar meals at lunch-time and in the evening. In the Restaurant locally caught fish and other captivating dishes are featured on the fixed price menu.
ROOMS: 27 en suite (8 fmly) **FACILITIES:** STV Pool table **CONF:** Board 85 **PARKING:** 9 **CARDS:**

★★66% Green Waves

West View Rd, Trevone Bay PL28 8RD
☎ 01841 520114 📠 01841 520568
The Green Waves is a friendly, family-run, and neatly kept hotel. Many of the tastefully furnished bedrooms are located on the ground floor, and all are comfortable and well equipped. Public areas include a spacious lounge, a separate bar and small snooker room. In the dining room a choice of home-cooked dishes is available.
ROOMS: 19 en suite s £26-£29; d £52-£58 (incl. bkfst) * LB **FACILITIES:** Half size snooker table **PARKING:** 16 **NOTES:** No children 4yrs No smoking in restaurant Closed mid Oct-Apr **CARDS:**

See advert on this page

PAIGNTON, Devon Map 03 SX86

★★★70% Redcliffe

Marine Dr TQ3 2NL
☎ 01803 526397 📠 01803 528030
e-mail: redclfe@aol.com
Dir: *follow signs for Paignton & sea front, hotel on sea front at Torquay end of Paignton Green*

Standing in three acres of grounds, this well-established hotel enjoys uninterrupted views across Tor Bay. Service is friendly and attentive and all bedrooms are comfortably furnished, with modern facilities. Spacious public rooms include the 'Dick Francis' suite and a leisure centre.
ROOMS: 65 en suite (8 fmly) s £45-£55; d £90-£110 (incl. bkfst) * LB **FACILITIES:** STV Indoor swimming (H) Outdoor swimming (H) Fishing Sauna Solarium Gym Pool table Putting green Jacuzzi/spa Table tennis Carpet Bowls entertainment ch fac Xmas **CONF:** Thtr 150 Class 50 Board 50 Del from £58 * **SERVICES:** Lift **PARKING:** 80 **NOTES:** No dogs (ex guide dogs) No smoking in restaurant Civ Wed 150
CARDS:

★★69% Preston Sands

10/12 Marine Pde TQ3 2NU
☎ 01803 558718 📠 01803 522875
Dir: *approx 1.5m from Paignton rail station, situated on Preston Beach*
Many of the bedrooms in this small, family-run hotel, situated right on the seafront, benefit from fine sea views. The owners take pains to ensure that guests enjoy their stay and the good, home-cooked meals.
ROOMS: 31 en suite (3 fmly) s £23-£28; d £46-£56 (incl. bkfst) * LB **FACILITIES:** Xmas **PARKING:** 24 **NOTES:** No children 8yrs No smoking in restaurant **CARDS:**

★★67% Clennon Valley Hotel

Clennon Rise, Goodrington TQ4 5HG
☎ 01803 550304 📠 01803 550304
Dir: *400yds N of Quay West Water Park*
Pleasantly renovated, this Victorian house stands between the town centre and beaches. Accommodation is well equipped and facilities include an attractive lounge, small bar and traditionally furnished dining room.
ROOMS: 9 en suite No smoking in all bedrooms s fr £32; d fr £54 (incl. bkfst) * **FACILITIES:** STV **PARKING:** 8 **NOTES:** No dogs No children 12yrs No smoking in restaurant Closed Nov-Feb **CARDS:**

★★66% *Tor Sands*

8 Sands Rd TQ4 6EH
☎ 01803 559695 📠 01803 526786
e-mail: torsands.hotel@dial.pipex.com
Continuing the family tradition, brother and sister Sally and Andrew Linskey run a comfortable and friendly hotel, providing regular entertainment and themed events for their guests. Attractive bedrooms all have modern facilities and enjoyable food is served in the dining room.
ROOMS: 29 rms (26 en suite) 5 annexe en suite No smoking in all bedrooms **FACILITIES:** entertainment **PARKING:** 15 **NOTES:** No smoking in restaurant Closed Jan-Feb

★★65% Dainton

95 Dartmouth Rd, Three Beaches, Goodrington TQ4 6NA
☎ 01803 550067 & 525901 📠 01803 666339
e-mail: Dave@Dainton-hotel.co.uk
Dir: *located on the A379 at Goodrington*
Situated at Goodrington, this pleasant Tudor-style property is in easy walking distance of the beach and leisure park. Bedrooms and bathrooms are very well furnished and have all been well designed. Guests have the option to eat in the bar or choose between a fixed-price menu or the full carte, available in the attractive restaurant later in the evening.
ROOMS: 11 en suite (2 fmly) No smoking in all bedrooms s fr £35; d fr £60 (incl. bkfst) * LB **FACILITIES:** entertainment Xmas **PARKING:** 20 **NOTES:** No smoking in restaurant
CARDS:

★★64% Torbay Holiday Motel

Totnes Rd TQ4 7PP
☎ 01803 558226 📠 01803 663375
e-mail: enquiries@thm.co.uk
Dir: *on A385 Totnes/Paignton road, 2.5m from Paignton*
Situated between Paignton and Totnes, this purpose-built complex houses a motel, self-catering apartments and leisure facilities. The comfortable bedrooms are very spacious and nicely decorated. The dining room serves traditional food, whilst a less formal menu is available in the bar-lounge.
ROOMS: 16 en suite s £32.50-£35.50; d £51-£57 (incl. bkfst) * **FACILITIES:** STV Indoor swimming (H) Outdoor swimming (H) Sauna Solarium Gym Pool table Putting green Crazy golf Adventure playground **PARKING:** 150 **NOTES:** Closed 24-31 Dec
CARDS:

See advert on opposite page

★68% The Commodore Hotel

14 Esplanade Rd TQ4 6EB
☎ 01803 553107
Dir: *follow A3022 stay in left lane to sea front, just past multiplex cinema complex, hotel on right*

This family run hotel enjoys a prime position on the seafront with the added bonus of lovely views across the bay. Bedrooms are neatly presented, bright and comfortable, whilst public areas include a spacious lounge, bar and smart dining room.
ROOMS: 12 en suite (4 fmly) s £18.50-£20.50; d £35-£41 (incl. bkfst) * **FACILITIES:** Xmas **PARKING:** 10 **NOTES:** No dogs (ex guide dogs) Closed Nov-Feb

★61% **Sattva**
Esplanade TQ4 6BL
☎ 01803 557820 📠 01803 557820
Dir: *hotel located on the seafront by the pier*
The Sattva Hotel is ideally situated on the sea-front being close to all the resort's beaches, shops and theatres and to Paignton Green. A strong feature here is the lively bar, with regular entertainment and the traditional English cooking served in the dining room. Some of the sea facing bedrooms also benefit from private balconies.
ROOMS: 20 en suite (2 fmly) No smoking in 3 bedrooms **FACILITIES:** **SERVICES:** Lift **PARKING:** 10 **NOTES:** No smoking in restaurant Closed Jan-Feb **CARDS:**

PAINSWICK, Gloucestershire Map 03 SO80

★★★78% **Painswick**
Kemps Ln GL6 6YB
☎ 01452 812160 📠 01452 814059
e-mail: reservations@painswickhotel.com
Dir: *turn off A46 in centre of village by the church. Hotel is located off 2nd road behind church off Tibbiwell Lane*

This hotel, formerly a rectory built in 1790, is set in beautiful rolling countryside. Bedrooms, all well equipped, are in the main house and adjacent building. Elegant day rooms feature antiques and high quality furnishings. The restaurant offers fine wines and noteworthy cuisine.
ROOMS: 19 en suite (4 fmly) s £85-£145; d £120-£185 (incl. bkfst) * LB **FACILITIES:** Croquet lawn Xmas **CONF:** Thtr 40 Class 20 Board 20 Del from £111.63 * **PARKING:** 25 **NOTES:** No smoking in restaurant Civ Wed 100 **CARDS:**

See advert on this page

PANGBOURNE, Berkshire Map 04 SU67

★★★76% **The Copper Inn**
RG8 7AR
☎ 0118 984 2244 📠 0118 984 5542
e-mail: reservations@copper-inn.co.uk
Dir: *from M4 junct 12 take A4 west then A340 to Pangbourne. Hotel located next to Pangbourne parish church at the junction of A329/A340*
Well known for its high standards of hotel keeping, the Copper Inn is a great place to stay, either on business or pleasure. Individually decorated bedrooms are comfortable and well equipped. The lovely restaurant has a Mediterranean feel and is a local dining destination.
ROOMS: 14 en suite 8 annexe en suite (1 fmly) No smoking in all bedrooms s £85-£110; d £130-£145 LB **FACILITIES:** STV Xmas **CONF:** Thtr 60 Class 24 Board 30 Del from £140 * **PARKING:** 20 **NOTES:** Civ Wed 80 **CARDS:**

PANGBOURNE, continued

★★★69% George Hotel
The Square RG8 7AJ
☎ 0118 984 2237 📠 0118 984 4354
e-mail: info@georgehotelpangbourne.co.uk
Dir: *leave M4/junct12 towards Newbury, at 2nd rdbt turn right onto A340, continue for 3m into Pangbourne. Right at rdbt, hotel 50yds on left*
Parts of this historic building date back to 1295. Well thought out spacious bedrooms are equipped with modern facilities and furnishings, three rooms have been specially fitted with bunk beds and play stations to attract younger visitors.
ROOMS: 26 en suite (3 fmly) No smoking in 9 bedrooms s £80-£90; d £85-£95 * LB **FACILITIES:** STV **CONF:** Thtr 80 Class 60 Board 50 Del from £120 * **PARKING:** 30 **NOTES:** RS Bank Holidays
CARDS:

PARBOLD, Lancashire Map 07 SD41

★★67% Lindley
Lancaster Ln WN8 7AB
☎ 01257 462804 📠 01257 464628
Dir: *exit M6 at junct 27 and take A5209 signposted Burscough. Turn right onto B5246, signposted Rufford, 500yds right hand side*
This hotel offers attractively furnished bedrooms with a range of facilities. The restaurant, popular with locals and visitors alike, offers a wide selection of dishes.
ROOMS: 8 en suite (1 fmly) s £45; d £55 (incl. bkfst) *
FACILITIES: STV **PARKING:** 46 **NOTES:** No dogs (ex guide dogs) No smoking in restaurant **CARDS:**

PARKHAM, Devon Map 02 SS32

★★★73% Penhaven Country House
Rectory Ln EX39 5PL
☎ 01237 451388 & 451711 📠 01237 451878
e-mail: reservations@penhaven.co.uk
Dir: *turn off A39 at Horns Cross and follow signs to Parkham, turn second left after Church into Rectory Lane*
With distant views of Exmoor, this 17th century hotel offers comfortable accommodation in a friendly and relaxed atmosphere. Bedrooms are either in the main building or in cottage suites in the grounds; two ground floor rooms are available for the less able. Local produce features on the interesting restaurant menu, with vegetarians being especially welcomed. Many guests visit this hotel specifically to see the badgers during the evening.
ROOMS: 12 en suite s £70-£75; d £140-£150 (incl. bkfst & dinner) * LB
FACILITIES: Xmas **PARKING:** 50 **NOTES:** No children 10yrs No smoking in restaurant **CARDS:**

PATELEY BRIDGE, North Yorkshire Map 07 SE16

★★68% Grassfields Country House
Low Wath Rd HG3 5HL
☎ 01423 711412 📠 01423 712844
e-mail: grassfields@nidderdale.co.uk
Dir: *turn off A59 onto B6451 and turn left at Summerbridge onto B6165. Cross bridge and take first right at petrol pumps*
A peaceful atmosphere prevails at this elegant Georgian house. There is a comfortable drawing room and a cosy bar. Bedrooms are mainly spacious and have been furnished in a country house style. Good home cooking is served in the elegant dining room.

continued

ROOMS: 9 en suite (3 fmly) s £31-£44.50; d £59-£75 (incl. bkfst) * LB
FACILITIES: Xmas **CONF:** Thtr 100 Class 70 Board 50 Del from £87.95 * **PARKING:** 30 **NOTES:** No smoking in restaurant
CARDS:

PATTERDALE, Cumbria Map 11 NY31

★★60% Patterdale
CA11 0NN
☎ 017684 82231 📠 017684 82440
Dir: *M6 junct 40, take A592 towards Ullsware, then 10m up Lakeside Rd to Patterdale*
Patterdale is a real tourist destination and this hotel enjoys fine views of the valley and fells being located at southern end of Ullswater. The hotel's core business is touring and accordingly it offers practical and functional accommodation.
ROOMS: 63 en suite (4 fmly) s fr £30; d fr £60 (incl. bkfst) * LB
FACILITIES: Tennis (hard) Fishing Pool table entertainment
CONF: Class 20 **SERVICES:** Lift **PARKING:** 31 **NOTES:** No smoking in restaurant Closed Jan-Feb Civ Wed 110 **CARDS:**

PATTINGHAM, Staffordshire Map 07 SO89

★★★66% Patshull Park Hotel Golf & Country Club
Patshull Park WV6 7HR
☎ 01902 700100 📠 01902 700874
e-mail: sales@patshull-park.co.uk
Dir: *1.5m W of Pattingham at Pattingham Church take the Patshull Rd hotel 1.5m on right*

There has been a manor house here since before the Norman Conquest. The present house, dating back to the 1730s, and its 280 acres of parkland now provide a hotel with golf, fishing, leisure and conference complex. Facilities include a coffee shop, golf shop, leisure club and swimming pool, along with extensive conference and banqueting suites. Bedrooms are well equipped.

continued

ROOMS: 49 en suite (2 fmly) s £85-£95; d £90-£110 (incl. bkfst) * LB **FACILITIES:** STV Indoor swimming (H) Golf 18 Fishing Sauna Solarium Gym Pool table Putting green Jacuzzi/spa Beauty therapist entertainment Xmas **CONF:** Thtr 250 Class 75 Board 44 Del from £99 * **PARKING:** 200 **NOTES:** No smoking in restaurant Civ Wed 100 **CARDS:**

See advert under WOLVERHAMPTON

PEASLAKE, Surrey — Map 04 TQ04

★★★67% Hurtwood Inn Hotel

Walking Bottom GU5 9RR
☎ 01306 730851 01306 731390
e-mail: sales@hurtwoodinnhotel.com
***Dir:** turn off A25 at Gomshall opposite Jet Filling Station towards Peaslake. After 2.5 turn right at village shop, hotel in village centre*

Situated in the peaceful village of Peaslake between Guildford and Dorking, this well presented hotel offers a warm and friendly atmosphere. The brightly appointed bedrooms, some located in an adjacent annexe overlooking the hotel garden, have benefited from refurbishment. Public areas include a small cosy bar/lounge and the oak-panelled Oscars restaurant where guests can enjoy a fine standard of cuisine.

ROOMS: 9 en suite 8 annexe en suite s fr £70; d £75-£85 * **CONF:** Thtr 40 Class 15 Board 20 **PARKING:** 40 **CARDS:**

PEASMARSH, East Sussex — Map 05 TQ82

★★★74% Flackley Ash

MARSTON HOTELS

TN31 6YH
☎ 01797 230651 01797 230510
e-mail: flackleyash@marstonhotels.co.uk
***Dir:** 3m from Rye, beside A268*

This attractive Georgian country house enjoys a peaceful setting in well kept grounds just a short distance to the north of Rye. Spacious bedrooms are individually furnished and feature a full range of modern facilities. The hotel is also equipped with conference facilities and an indoor leisure suite offering various health treatments. Guests can expect efficient, attentive service from a friendly young team.

ROOMS: 42 en suite (3 fmly) s £79-£94; d £119-£169 (incl. bkfst) * LB **FACILITIES:** Indoor swimming (H) Sauna Gym Croquet lawn Putting green Jacuzzi/spa Beautician Xmas **CONF:** Thtr 100 Class 50 Board 40 Del from £105 * **PARKING:** 70 **NOTES:** No smoking in restaurant Civ Wed 120 **CARDS:**

See advert on page 475

> Early start? Hotels at all star levels should provide in-room alarm clocks and/or alarm calls.

PELYNT, Cornwall & Isles of Scilly — Map 02 SX25

★★62% Jubilee Inn

PL13 2JZ
☎ 01503 220312 01503 220920
e-mail: rickard@jubilleinn.freeserve.co.uk
***Dir:** take A390 signposted St Austell at village of East Taphouse turn left onto B3359 signposted Looe & Polperro. Jubilee Inn on left on leaving Pelynt.*

A popular 16th-Century inn with flagstone floors and charming old-fashioned rooms. A choice of bars is available, whilst the menus have an emphasis on fresh local produce served in the bar or dining room. Bedrooms are individual in size and decor and provide comfortable accommodation with modern facilities.

ROOMS: 11 en suite (3 fmly) s fr £38.50; d fr £65 (incl. bkfst) * **FACILITIES:** Pool table Xmas **PARKING:** 80 **CARDS:**

PENDLEBURY, Greater Manchester

Premier Lodge (Manchester North West)

PREMIER LODGE
THE BEST. REST ASSURED.

219 Bolton Rd M27 8TG
☎ 0870 700 1470 0870 700 1471

Premier Lodge offers modern, well equipped, en suite accommodation suitable for both business and leisure travellers. Meals can be taken at the adjacent popular restaurant and bar which is fully licensed. For further details, consult the Hotel Groups page.

ROOMS: 31 en suite d £46 *

PENKRIDGE, Staffordshire — Map 07 SJ91

★★★65% Quality Hotel Stafford

Sleep Comfort Quality Clarion
CHOICE HOTELS EUROPE

Pinfold Ln ST19 5QP
☎ 01785 712459 01785 715532
e-mail: admin@gb067.u-net.com
***Dir:** from M6 junct 12 A5 towards Telford at 1st rdbt turn right onto A449, 2m into Penkridge turn left just beyond Ford garage, opposite White Hart*

In a quiet backwater of Staffordshire and surrounded by countryside, this hotel is just a few minutes drive from the M6. Bedrooms are spacious and well presented with good facilities. Bedrooms on ground floor level and no smoking bedrooms are both available. There is an attractive lounge and a smart restaurant offering an interesting menu.

ROOMS: 47 en suite (1 fmly) No smoking in 10 bedrooms s fr £76; d fr £97 * LB **FACILITIES:** STV Indoor swimming (H) Squash Sauna Solarium Gym Pool table entertainment Xmas **CONF:** Thtr 300 Class 120 Board 90 Del from £80 * **PARKING:** 160 **NOTES:** No smoking in restaurant Civ Wed 70 **CARDS:**

PENRITH, Cumbria — Map 12 NY53

see also Shap & Temple Sowerby

★★★★65% North Lakes

SHIRE INNS

Ullswater Rd CA11 8QT
☎ 01768 868111 01768 868291
e-mail: nlakes@shireinns.co.uk
***Dir:** M6 junct 40 at intersection with A66*

With a prime location just off junction 40 of the M6, this smartly appointed modern hotel is perfectly located for both business and leisure guests and offers a good standard of accommodation. Amenities include a good range of meeting and function rooms and an extensive range of excellent health and leisure facilities.

ROOMS: 84 en suite (6 fmly) No smoking in 25 bedrooms s fr £102; d fr £122 (incl. bkfst) * LB **FACILITIES:** STV Indoor swimming (H) Squash Sauna Solarium Gym Jacuzzi/spa Spa pool Childrens pool Childrens Club room Health & Beauty treatment rooms Xmas **CONF:** Thtr 200 Class 140 Board 24 Del from £95 * **SERVICES:** Lift **PARKING:** 150 **NOTES:** No smoking in restaurant Civ Wed 200 **CARDS:**

P

PENRITH, continued

★★★71% Westmorland Hotel

Orton CA10 3SB
☎ 015396 24351 015396 24354
(For full entry see Tebay)

★★★62% The George

Devonshire St CA11 7SU
☎ 01768 862696 01768 868223
Dir: *leave M6 junct 40 & follow route for town centre continue for approx 1m. If travelling from A6/A66 follow route for Penrith town centre*

Experienced new owners are committed to a total upgrade of this long-established town centre hotel which remains as friendly and as popular as ever. Already many bedrooms have been upgraded to a high standard, whilst public areas retain their old fashioned charm, the lounges being a venue for morning coffees and afternoon teas.
ROOMS: 34 en suite (3 fmly) No smoking in 9 bedrooms s £45; d £70-£80 (incl. bkfst) * LB **FACILITIES:** Free use of local pool and gym Xmas **CONF:** Thtr 140 Class 50 Board 400 Del from £68 * **PARKING:** 34 **NOTES:** No smoking in restaurant **CARDS:**

See advert on opposite page

P

★★66% Brantwood Country Hotel

Stainton CA11 0EP
☎ 01768 862748 01768 890164
e-mail: brantwood2@aol.com
Dir: *From M6 junct 40 join A66 Keswick road and in 0.5 mile turn left then right signposted Stainton*

Just two minutes drive from the M6, this family run hotel enjoys an open outlook to the rear. The bedroom decor is individual and cheerful in colour; five rooms are in a converted courtyard building. Good meals are served both in the bar and the restaurant.
ROOMS: 6 en suite 5 annexe en suite (3 fmly) No smoking in 5 bedrooms s £39.50-£48.50; d £59-£73 (incl. bkfst) * LB
FACILITIES: Croquet lawn Putting green **CONF:** Thtr 60 Class 30 Board 30 **PARKING:** 35 **NOTES:** No dogs No smoking in restaurant
CARDS:

See advert on opposite page

Travelodge

Travelodge

Redhills CA11 0DT
☎ 01768 866958 01768 866958
Dir: *on A66*
This modern building offers accommodation in smart, spacious and well equipped bedrooms, all with en suite bathrooms. Refreshments may be taken at the nearby family restaurant. For further details and the Travelodge phone number, consult the Hotel Groups page.
ROOMS: 40 en suite

PENZANCE, Cornwall & Isles of Scilly Map 02 SW43

★★★67% Mount Prospect

THE CIRCLE Selected Individual Hotels

Britons Hill TR18 3AE
☎ 01736 363117 01736 350970
e-mail: mtpros2000@aol.com
Dir: *from A30 pass heliport on right straight onto next rdbt, bear left for town centre take 3rd right by Pirates Hotel, hotel is on right*
This Elegant Edwardian house is set within sub-tropical gardens and boasts spectacular views across the splendour of Mounts Bay. A warm welcome is assured from the resident proprietors, who make every effort to ensure guests have an enjoyable stay. Bedrooms vary in style, many offering the added bonus of wonderful sea views, two rooms are available on the ground floor. An interesting menu makes full use of the excellent local produce.
ROOMS: 21 en suite (1 fmly) No smoking in 17 bedrooms s £45-£54; d £70-£90 (incl. bkfst) * LB **FACILITIES:** STV Outdoor swimming (H) Pool table **CONF:** Thtr 80 Class 50 Board 12 **PARKING:** 14 **NOTES:** No smoking in restaurant Closed 23 Dec-3 Jan
CARDS:

★★★66% Queen's

The Promenade TR18 4HG
☎ 01736 362371 01736 350033
e-mail: enquiries@queens-hotel.com
Dir: *A30 to Penzance, follow signs for seafront pass harbour & into promenade, hotel half a mile on right*

Overlooking the impressive sweep of Mount's Bay, this large Victorian hotel has a distinguished history. Bedrooms are individually styled and provide all modern comforts, many benefiting from wonderful views. The dining room provides an elegant venue in which to enjoy the daily changing menu.
ROOMS: 70 en suite (10 fmly) s £49-£55; d £85-£107 (incl. bkfst) * LB **FACILITIES:** STV Sauna Solarium Gym Xmas **CONF:** Thtr 200 Class 100 Board 80 Del from £65 * **SERVICES:** Lift **PARKING:** 50 **NOTES:** No smoking in restaurant Civ Wed 180
CARDS:

See advert on opposite page

Bad hair day? Hairdryers in all rooms three stars and above.

AA ★★★ 66%

THE QUEENS HOTEL PENZANCE

The Promenade, Penzance, Cornwall TR18 4HG
Tel 01736 362371 · Fax 01736 350033

Elegant Victorian hotel on the promenade at Penzance with majestic views over Mounts Bay and St. Michael's Mount. All 70 bedrooms are en-suite with satellite TV. Award winning seaview restaurant providing local Newlyn fish and produce. Ideal centre for Lands End, Minack Theatre and Tate Gallery.

Weekend and Special Breaks available.

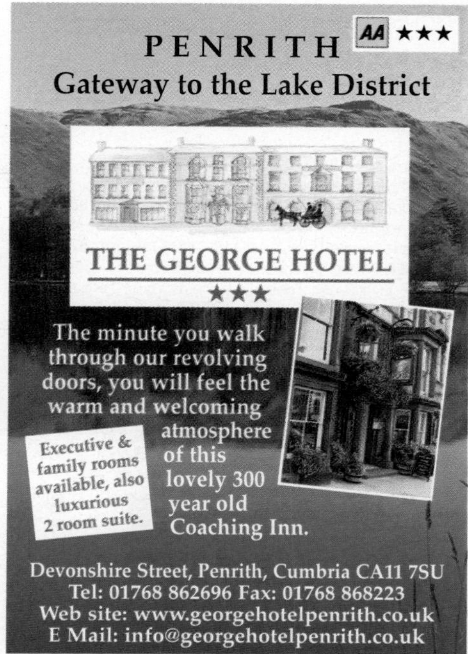

THE GODOLPHIN ARMS

Marazion · Cornwall ★★ 69%

Tel: 01736 710202 Fax: 01736 710171
www.godolphinarms.co.uk
Email: enquiries@godolphinarms.co.uk

On the edge of the sand at Marazion, the Godolphin Arms faces St Michael's Mount in the beautiful Mounts Bay. The view is breathtaking whatever the time of year. Relax in our refurbished bars or enjoy a fabulous meal in our restaurant overlooking the bay • We have ten individually designed en suite rooms most offering sea views, two with disabled access and two family rooms • Well situated for many attractions including Lands End, The Tate at St Ives and the Isles of Scilly just 28 nautical miles away.

Brantwood Country Hotel

STAINTON · PENRITH · CUMBRIA · CA11 0EP
Telephone: (01768) 862748 · Fax: (01768) 890164
Web: http://www.smoothhound.co.uk/hotels/brant.html
Email: brantwood2@aol.com

Pleasant rural country hotel in 3½ acres of secluded gardens. Relaxed and friendly atmosphere, personally run for the last 15 years by Susan and John Harvey with their sons Stephen and Mark. Comfortable en-suite rooms with colour television, tea and coffee making facilities, central heating and direct dial telephone. Enjoy a formal dinner in the Restaurant or choose from an extensive Bar menu.

Fully licensed. Open all year. Open to non residents. Large secure car park at rear of Hotel.

'Brantwood' is 1½ miles from junction 40, M6 motorway, off the A66 west from Penrith, 3 miles beautiful lake Ullswater.

P

PENZANCE, continued

★★★65% Higher Faugan
Newlyn TR18 5NS
☎ 01736 362076 01736 351648
e-mail: hfhotel@aol.com
Dir: *off B3115, 0.75m from Newlyn crossroads*
This gracious turn-of-the-century hotel is surrounded by acres of well kept gardens. Personal touches, including needlepoint cushions in the comfortable lounges, make it a real home from home. Bedrooms are generally spacious and some have luxurious corner-baths.
ROOMS: 11 en suite (2 fmly) s £60-£65; d £95-£115 (incl. bkfst) * LB
FACILITIES: Outdoor swimming (H) Tennis (hard) Snooker Solarium Pool table Croquet lawn Putting green Exercise equipment available
PARKING: 20 **NOTES:** No smoking in restaurant RS Nov-Mar
CARDS:

★★66% Tarbert
11-12 Clarence St TR18 2NU
☎ 01736 363758 & 364317 01736 331336
e-mail: reception@tarbert-hotel.co.uk
Dir: *take Land's End turning at town approach. At 2nd rdbt turn left, continue past next mini rdbt - 100yds turn right into Clarence St*

P

Formerly a sea captain's house, dating back to the 1830s, this family-run hotel is located just a short walk from the town centre and promenade. Bedrooms vary in size but all provide good levels of comfort and character. An interesting menu is offered with good use of local seafood. The bar provides a relaxing venue for guests to have a drink in.
ROOMS: 12 en suite No smoking in all bedrooms s £32-£35; d £54-£60 (incl. bkfst) * LB **PARKING:** 5 **NOTES:** No dogs No smoking in restaurant Closed Dec 23-Feb 2 **CARDS:**

★★65% *Union Hotel*
Chapel St TR18 4AE
☎ 01736 362319 01726 362319
Located in the centre of the town amidst many interesting shops, parts of this charming hotel date back to Tudor times. The Nelson bar is popular with locals and visitors alike, and offers a range of traditional bar meals. The Hamilton Restaurant offers a more formal dining option, with both fixed price and a la carte menus available. There is a variety of sizes and styles of accommodation, with all bedrooms having modern facilities.
ROOMS: 28 rms (22 en suite) (4 fmly) **PARKING:** 15 **NOTES:** No dogs
CARDS:

★67% *Estoril*
46 Morrab Rd TR18 4EX
☎ 01736 362468 & 367471 01736 367471
Dir: *from bus/train station keep left along promenade towards Newlyn, take 1st turning past "The Lugger", Estoril is 300yds along on left*
Ideally situated in a quiet location midway between the town centre and seafront, this is an ideal base for exploring the local area. Great attention is given to the care and well being of guests, with all the well-equipped bedrooms offering good levels of comfort. Fresh produce is frequently used for meals, which are served in the well-appointed dining room.
ROOMS: 9 en suite (2 fmly) No smoking in all bedrooms **PARKING:** 4
NOTES: No dogs No smoking in restaurant Closed 24 Dec-6 Jan
CARDS:

PERRANPORTH, Cornwall & Isles of Scilly Map 02 SW75

★★63% Beach Dunes
Ramoth Way, Reen Sands TR6 0BY
☎ 01872 572263 01872 573824
e-mail: beachdunes@thenet.co.uk
Dir: *turn off A30 onto B3075 at Goonhavern continue onto B3285 at 30mph sign private road on right Ramoth Way, Beach Dunes at end of road*
With stunning views over Perran Bay, the village and surrounding countryside, this small hotel is situated at the end of a private road adjoining the local 18-hole Golf Course. The well equipped bedrooms are neatly furnished and decorated. Guests enjoy the home-cooking served in the dining room.
ROOMS: 6 rms (5 en suite) 3 annexe en suite (2 fmly) No smoking in all bedrooms s £27.50-£56; d £55-£79 (incl. bkfst) * LB
FACILITIES: Indoor swimming (H) Squash Bar billiards **PARKING:** 15
NOTES: No children 3yrs No smoking in restaurant Closed Nov & Dec
CARDS:

PETERBOROUGH, Cambridgeshire Map 04 TL19
see also Wansford

★★★★68% Swallow
Peterborough Business Park,
Lynchwood PE2 6GB
☎ 01733 371111 01733 236725
e-mail: info@swallowhotels.com
Dir: *opposite East of England Showground at Alwalton*

SWALLOW HOTELS

Opposite the East of England showground, and next to the Peterborough Business Park, this modern hotel is commercially popular. Bedrooms are well equipped and comfortable. The fully air-conditioned public rooms include lounge and cocktail bars. The brasserie offers a variety of dishes to suit all tastes, and the formal restaurant is ideal for more serious dining. There is also a wide range of conference and banqueting facilities. The leisure club includes a children's pool and beautician.
ROOMS: 163 en suite (8 fmly) No smoking in 108 bedrooms s £125; d £150 (incl. bkfst) * LB **FACILITIES:** STV Indoor swimming (H) Sauna Solarium Gym Putting green Jacuzzi/spa Beauty therapist Hairdressing entertainment Xmas **CONF:** Thtr 300 Class 160 Board 45 Del £140 *
PARKING: 200 **NOTES:** No smoking in restaurant
CARDS:

★★★69% ❀❀ Bell Inn
Great North Rd PE7 3RA
☎ 01733 241066 01733 245173
e-mail: reception@thebellstitton.co.uk
(For full entry see Stilton)

★★★68% Bull
Westgate PE1 1RB
☎ 01733 561364 01733 557304
Dir: *turn off A1 follow signs to city centre, hotel in heart of city opposite Queensgate shopping centre. Car park is on Broadway next to Library*

PEEL HOTELS

An enthusiastic management team are achieving good results at this very pleasant city centre hotel, offering well equipped modern accommodation; a new wing of deluxe bedrooms is scheduled to

continued

be completed during mid 2000. The public rooms are extensive and include a good range of meeting rooms and conference facilities, which have been further complemented by a new dedicated conference centre. An interesting range of dishes are served in the elegant restaurant, alternative informal dining is available within the lounge.
ROOMS: 103 en suite (3 fmly) **CONF:** Thtr 200 Class 80 Board 60 **PARKING:** 100 **CARDS:**

★★★66% Butterfly
Thorpe Meadows, Longthorpe Parkway PE3 6GA
☎ 01733 64240 📠 01733 65538
e-mail: peterbutterfly@lineone.net
Dir: *from A1179 take exit for Thorpe Meadows and city centre, turn right at next two roundabouts*
Sitting in a pretty location beside the international rowing course in Thorpe Meadows, this hotel is near park, lake and river walks, as well as the local steam railway. The refurbished bedrooms are well designed and properly equipped, with paticular consideration for the needs of corporate guests; ground floor, studio and ladies' rooms are also available.
ROOMS: 70 en suite (2 fmly) No smoking in 10 bedrooms d fr £69.50 * LB **FACILITIES:** STV **CONF:** Thtr 80 Class 50 Board 50 **PARKING:** 85 **NOTES:** No dogs (ex guide dogs) **CARDS:**

★★★66% Orton Hall
Orton Longueville PE2 7DN
☎ 01733 391111 📠 01733 231912
e-mail: reception@ortonhall.co.uk
Dir: *off A605 (East) opposite Orton Mere*
Best Western
Set in 20 acres of woodland grounds, this impressive country house has been skilfully converted to a commendable hotel. Public areas are spacious and relaxing, with extra facilities dotted around the grounds. Original features include oak panelling in the Huntly Restaurant, the Grand Hall which is a popular banqueting venue, and some 16th-century terracotta floors. Across the courtyard is the Ramblewood Inn.
ROOMS: 65 en suite (2 fmly) No smoking in 42 bedrooms s £75-£104; d £101.50-£130 * LB **FACILITIES:** Three quarter size snooker table Xmas **CONF:** Thtr 120 Class 48 Board 42 **PARKING:** 200 **NOTES:** No smoking in restaurant Closed 27 Dec-4 Jan
CARDS:

★★★62% Posthouse Peterborough
Great North Rd PE7 3TB
☎ 0870 400 9063 📠 01733 244455
(For full entry see Norman Cross)
Posthouse

Travelodge
Great North Rd, Alwalton PE7 3UR
☎ 01733 231109 📠 01733 231109
Dir: *on A1, southbound*
Travelodge
This modern building offers accommodation in smart, spacious and well equipped bedrooms, all with en suite bathrooms. Refreshments may be taken at the nearby family restaurant. For further details and the Travelodge phone number, consult the Hotel Groups page.
ROOMS: 32 en suite

Popped the question? Hotels with Civ Wed in their entry are licensed for civil wedding ceremonies. Maximum numbers for the ceremony only are shown, e.g. Civ Wed 50

P

PETERBOROUGH, continued

⇧ Express by Holiday Inn Peterborough

East of England Way, Alwalton PE2 6HE
☎ 01733 284450 📠 01733 284451
Dir: 1m E of the A1 and 4m from city centre on the A605 Oundle Road, adjacent to East of England Showground

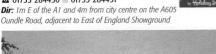

A modern budget hotel offering comfortable accommodation in refreshing, spacious and comprehensively-equipped bedrooms, en suite bathrooms with power showers and continental buffet breakfast included in the room rate. Suitable for business travellers or families. For further details and the Express by Holiday Inn phone number, consult the Hotel Groups page.
ROOMS: 80 en suite (incl. cont bkfst) d £52.50-£56 * **CONF:** Thtr 25 Class 20 Board 16

PETERLEE, Co Durham — Map 08 NZ44

★★69% Hardwicke Hall Manor

Hesleden TS27 4PA
☎ 01429 836326 📠 01429 837676
Dir: NE on B1281, off A19 at the sign for Durham/Blackhall
This comfortable creeper-clad mansion house is a family owned and run hotel and offers well furnished and thoughtfully equipped bedrooms. It is very popular for its food and the public rooms are inviting and cosy.
ROOMS: 15 en suite (2 fmly) s £49.50-£59.50; d £59.50-£69.50 (incl. bkfst) * LB **CONF:** Thtr 60 Board 20 **PARKING:** 100 **NOTES:** No smoking in restaurant Civ Wed 110
CARDS:

PETERSFIELD, Hampshire — Map 04 SU72

★★68% Langrish House

Langrish GU32 1RN
☎ 01730 266941 📠 01730 260543
Dir: turn off A3 onto A272 towards Winchester. Hotel signposted 3m on left
Dating back to the 17th century Langrish House is located in quiet grounds, a mile or so from the centre of Petersfield. Rooms vary in size, some very spacious, all have a good levels of comfort and views over the countryside. Conference and banqueting rooms are popular for weddings and have a separate entrance.
ROOMS: 14 en suite (1 fmly) s fr £72; d £95-£120 (incl. bkfst) * LB **FACILITIES:** Fishing Xmas **CONF:** Thtr 60 Class 18 Board 25 Del £95 * **PARKING:** 80 **NOTES:** No smoking in restaurant Civ Wed 60
CARDS:

Read all about it! Newspapers delivered to bedrooms in four and five star hotels.

PETTY FRANCE, Gloucestershire — Map 03 ST78

★★★68% Petty France

GL9 1AF
☎ 01454 238361 📠 01454 238768
e-mail: hotel@pettyfrance.telme.com
Dir: on A46 S of junct with A433, 6m N of M4 junction 18, A46
Surrounded by historical sights and the Cotswold countryside lies Petty France. This privately owned hotel features elegant rooms, pretty walled gardens, and a courtyard stable block converted into comfortable, modern bedrooms. Rooms in the main hotel reflect country house style. The attractive bar, lounge and restaurant have open fires which add to the atmosphere of this friendly country home.
ROOMS: 8 en suite 12 annexe en suite (1 fmly) No smoking in 1 bedroom s £69-£99; d £89-£125 (incl. cont bkfst) * LB **FACILITIES:** Croquet lawn Bicycle hire Xmas **CONF:** Thtr 55 Class 20 Board 24 Del from £90 * **PARKING:** 70 **NOTES:** No smoking in restaurant Civ Wed **CARDS:**

PEVENSEY, East Sussex — Map 05 TQ60

★★64% Priory Court

Castle Rd BN24 5LG
☎ 01323 763150 📠 01323 769030
e-mail: prioryct@easynet.co.uk
Dir: turn left from A22 look for Historic Pevensey Castle

The castle at Pevensey is an attractive backdrop for this charming, privately owned Inn. The public areas have recently been redecorated and include a character bar, tastefully decorated dining room and a cosy lounge. Bedrooms are spacious and equipped with a useful range of extras.
ROOMS: 9 rms (7 en suite) (1 fmly) s £45-£55; d £62-£82 (incl. bkfst) * LB **FACILITIES:** Xmas **CONF:** Class 25 Board 15 **PARKING:** 50
CARDS:

PICKERING, North Yorkshire — Map 08 SE78

★★★69% Forest & Vale

Malton Rd YO18 7DL
☎ 01751 472722 📠 01751 472972
Dir: on A169 between York & Pickering at a rdbt on the outskirts of Pickering
A warm welcome is assured at this pleasantly appointed hotel, which is professionally managed by the owners, and an attentive service provided by a friendly staff. The newly refurbished bedrooms are comfortable and include some spacious superior rooms, one with a four-poster bed. A good range of food is available, served either in the bar or within the restaurant, whilst room service is another alternative.

continued

ROOMS: 14 en suite 5 annexe en suite (5 fmly) No smoking in 6 bedrooms s £55; d £68-£90 (incl. bkfst) * LB **FACILITIES:** STV Xmas **CONF:** Thtr 120 Class 50 Board 50 **PARKING:** 70 **NOTES:** No dogs (ex guide dogs) No smoking in restaurant Civ Wed 100
CARDS:

★★72% Fox & Hounds Country Inn
Main St, Sinnington YO62 6SQ
☎ 01751 431577 01751 432791
e-mail: foxhoundsinn@easynet.co.uk
Dir: *3m W of Pickering, off A170*
This attractive inn lies in the quiet village of Sinnington just off the main road. It offers attractive well equipped bedrooms together with a cosy residents lounge. The restaurant provides a good selection of modern British dishes; there is also a good range of bar meals. Service throughout is friendly and attentive.
ROOMS: 10 en suite (1 fmly) No smoking in all bedrooms s £44; d £60-£75 (incl. bkfst) * LB **PARKING:** 40 **NOTES:** No smoking in restaurant
CARDS:

★★70% White Swan
Market Place YO18 7AA
☎ 01751 472288 01751 475554
e-mail: welcome@white-swan.co.uk
Dir: *in the market place between the Church and the Steam Railway Station*
The White Swan is in the town centre and combines traditional character with the best of modern hotel-keeping. The stylish bedrooms are particularly appealing and comfortable, while downstairs, the restaurant provides an interesting carte and a large wine list. The cosy bar also offers good food and service is friendly and helpful.
ROOMS: 12 en suite (3 fmly) No smoking in all bedrooms s £60-£65; d £90-£100 (incl. bkfst) * LB **FACILITIES:** Jacuzzi/spa Motorised Treasure hunt Mountain bike hire Horseriding Golf Micro-Lyte Xmas **CONF:** Thtr 15 Class 12 Board 20 **PARKING:** 35 **NOTES:** No smoking in restaurant **CARDS:**

★★68% Appleton Hall Country House Hotel
YO62 6TF
☎ 01751 417227 01751 417540
Dir: *off A170 to Appleton-le-Moors*
Set in delightful gardens, this well maintained gracious Victorian country house offers a comfortable lounge, with a real fire in a marble fireplace and an elegant dining room, where good home-cooking is served. Bedrooms, all individually and attractively decorated, are well equipped, two have their own sitting room.
ROOMS: 9 en suite No smoking in all bedrooms s £60-£70; d £120-£156 (incl. bkfst & dinner) * **FACILITIES:** Croquet lawn **SERVICES:** Lift **PARKING:** 12 **NOTES:** No dogs (ex guide dogs) No children 14yrs No smoking in restaurant **CARDS:**

PICKHILL, North Yorkshire Map 08 SE38

★★67% Nags Head Country Inn
YO7 4JG
☎ 01845 567391 & 567570 01845 567212
e-mail: reservations@nagsheadpickhill.freeserve.co.uk
Dir: *6m SE of Leeming Bar, 1.25m E of A1*
Convenient for the A1, this country inn offers an extensive range of food either in the bar or the newly refurbished and attractive restaurant. The bars are full of character and include an extensive collection of ties. Bedrooms are well equipped and modern while service is friendly and attentive.
ROOMS: 8 en suite 7 annexe en suite s £40; d £60 (incl. bkfst) * LB **FACILITIES:** Putting green Quoits pitch ch fac **CONF:** Thtr 36 Class 18 Board 24 Del from £60 * **PARKING:** 50 **CARDS:**

PINNER, Greater London
See LONDON SECTION plan 1 *A5*

★★72% Tudor Lodge
50 Field End Rd, Eastcote HA5 2QN
☎ 020 8429 0585 020 429 0117
e-mail: tudorlodge@meridianleisure.com

This friendly hotel, in its own grounds, is located a short walk from Eastcote station, convenient for Heathrow Airport and many local golf courses. Bedrooms vary in size, all are well equipped and some are suitable for families. As an alternative to the main restaurant a good range of bar snacks is offered.
ROOMS: 24 en suite s £74-£89; d £79-£89 (incl. bkfst) * LB

PLYMOUTH, Devon Map 02 SX45
see also St Mellion

★★★★63% Copthorne Plymouth
COPTHORNE
Armada Way PL1 1AR
☎ 01752 224161 01752 670688
e-mail: sales.plymouth@mill-cop.com
Dir: *from M5, follow A38 to Plymouth city centre. Follow continental ferryport signs over 3 rdbts. Hotel visible on first exit left before 4th rdbt*
This modern, centrally-located hotel provides well equipped, comfortable bedrooms. Public areas, which are divided over two floors, include a choice of restaurants, a modern leisure complex and a wide range of function rooms. The hotel has an arrangement with an adjacent multi-storey car park.
ROOMS: 135 en suite (29 fmly) No smoking in 38 bedrooms d fr £110 * LB **FACILITIES:** STV Indoor swimming (H) Gym Steam room **CONF:** Thtr 140 Class 60 Board 60 Del £130 * **SERVICES:** Lift **PARKING:** 50 **NOTES:** Civ Wed 100 **CARDS:**

Bad hair day? Hairdryers in all rooms three stars and above.

★★★73% Kitley House Hotel
Yealmpton PL8 2NW
☎ 01752 881555 01752 881667
e-mail: reservations@kitleyhousehotel.com
Dir: *from Plymouth take A379 to Kingsbridge. Hotel on right after Brixton & before Yealmpton.*

A mile long tree-lined drive leads to this fine Grade I Tudor-revival house built of Devonshire granite, set in 300 acres of peaceful wooded parkland along the Yealm estuary. Large bedrooms and suites are traditionally furnished to a high standard. The impressive entrance boasts a grand piano. Other public rooms include a striking book-lined dining room and a cosy bar.
ROOMS: 20 en suite (8 fmly) s £75-£115; d £90-£145 (incl. bkfst) * LB **FACILITIES:** STV Fishing Gym Croquet lawn Beauty salon ch fac Xmas **CONF:** Thtr 100 Class 80 Board 40 Del from £95 * **PARKING:** 100 **NOTES:** No smoking in restaurant Civ Wed 80
CARDS:

See advert on page 441

★★★70% New Continental
Millbay Rd PL1 3LD
☎ 01752 220782 01752 227013
e-mail: newconti@aol.com
Dir: *from A38 expressway follow City Centre signs for the Pavilions which are adjacent to hotel*
Within easy reach of the town centre and the Hoe, this privately owned hotel offers high standards of service and hospitality. Bedrooms vary in size and style, but all share the same levels of equipment and are suitable for all types of guests. There is a choice of restaurants for guests to dine in.
ROOMS: 99 en suite (20 fmly) No smoking in 28 bedrooms s £78-£83; d £88-£160 (incl. bkfst) * LB **FACILITIES:** STV Indoor swimming (H) Sauna Solarium Gym Steam Room Beautician **CONF:** Thtr 400 Class 100 Board 70 Del from £65 * **SERVICES:** Lift **PARKING:** 100 **NOTES:** Closed 24 Dec-2 Jan Civ Wed 130
CARDS:

See advert on opposite page

★★★69% Duke of Cornwall
Best Western
Millbay Rd PL1 3LG
☎ 01752 275850 01752 275854
e-mail: duke@heritagehotels.co.uk
Dir: *follow signs to city centre then to Plymouth Pavilions Conference & Leisure Centre which leads you past hotel*
This Grade II listed Victorian building, built in 1863, is an infamous landmark in this vibrant maritime city. Bedrooms and suites, including a number that have been refurbished, are smartly appointed and thoughtfully equipped. Interesting and carefully prepared dishes are available in the hotel's restaurant. Public rooms include a wide range of conference and banqueting suites.
continued

ROOMS: 71 en suite (6 fmly) No smoking in 20 bedrooms s £84.50-£89.50; d £99.50-£110 (incl. bkfst) * LB **FACILITIES:** Games room Xmas **CONF:** Thtr 300 Class 125 Board 84 Del from £85 * **SERVICES:** Lift **PARKING:** 50 **NOTES:** No smoking in restaurant Civ Wed 120 **CARDS:**

★★★66% ***Posthouse Plymouth***

Posthouse

Cliff Rd, The Hoe PL1 3DL

☎ 0870 400 9064 📠 01752 660974

Dir: *turn off A38 at Plymouth follow signs for City Centre, then follow signs for Hoe, the Hotel is situated on Cliff Road West Hoe*

This purpose built hotel, which commands superb views over Plymouth Sound, is equally suited to business and leisure travellers. The bedrooms are comfortable and well equipped. Lounge service is available throughout the day, and dinner is served in the Mayflower Restaurant.

continued on p444

PLYMOUTH, continued

ROOMS: 106 en suite No smoking in 65 bedrooms **FACILITIES:** Outdoor swimming (H) Pool table Childrens play area **CONF:** Thtr 90 Class 60 Board 40 **SERVICES:** Lift **PARKING:** 149
CARDS:

★★★65% Boringdon Hall

Colebrook, Plympton PL7 4DP
☎ 01752 344455 01752 346578
***Dir:** A38 at Marsh Mills rdbt follow signs for Plympton along dual carriageway to small island turn left over bridge and follow brown tourist signs*

Set in ten acres of grounds, this historic, listed property is only six miles from the city centre and retains much character. Most of the comfortable bedrooms, some with four-poster beds, are set round a central courtyard. Meals using local produce are served in the Gallery Restaurant overlooking the Great Hall.

ROOMS: 41 en suite (5 fmly) No smoking in 16 bedrooms **FACILITIES:** STV Indoor swimming (H) Tennis (hard) Sauna Gym pitch & putt 9 hole **CONF:** Thtr 120 Class 40 Board 50 **PARKING:** 200 **NOTES:** No smoking in restaurant **CARDS:**

★★★65% Novotel

Marsh Mills PL6 8NH
☎ 01752 221422 01752 223922
e-mail: h0508@accor-hotels.com
***Dir:** take 1st exit off A38 Plymouth/Kingsbridge, onto Marsh Mills rdbt, follow signs for Plympton the Hotel is straight ahead*

Located on the outskirts of the city, this modern hotel offers good value accommodation that caters for all types of guest. All rooms are spacious and adapted for family use. Public areas are open-plan and meals are available throughout the day in either the Garden Brasserie, the bar, or from room service. There is a heated outdoor swimming pool.

ROOMS: 100 en suite (15 fmly) No smoking in 50 bedrooms s £69-£73; d £82-£87 (incl. bkfst) * LB **FACILITIES:** STV Outdoor swimming (H) ch fac Xmas **CONF:** Thtr 300 Class 120 Board 100 Del from £85 * **SERVICES:** Lift **PARKING:** 140 **CARDS:**

★★★64% Grand

Elliot St, The Hoe PL1 2PT
☎ 01752 661195 01752 600653
e-mail: info@plymouthgrand.com
***Dir:** A38 to city centre, turn left at "Barbican" sign, follow road until 3rd set traffic lights, turn left, over crossroads, hotel is at top on right*

Spectacular views over The Hoe and Plymouth Sound are an attractive feature of the Grand. Public areas include a restaurant, bar and small lounge. Front-facing bedrooms, some with balconies, are always in high demand.

continued

ROOMS: 77 en suite (6 fmly) No smoking in 45 bedrooms s £82-£122; d £92-£142 (incl. bkfst) * LB **FACILITIES:** STV entertainment Xmas **CONF:** Thtr 70 Class 35 Board 30 Del from £65 * **SERVICES:** Lift **PARKING:** 70 **NOTES:** No smoking in restaurant
CARDS:

See advert on opposite page

★★★60% Strathmore

Elliot St, The Hoe PL1 2PR
☎ 01752 662101 01752 223690
***Dir:** off A38 at Marsh Mills and head for city centre, when you come to Exeter St, follow signs to the 'HOE', hotel is at end opposite the 'Grand Hotel'*

The city centre and The Hoe are in easy walking distance of this hotel. Bedrooms come in a variety of shapes and sizes, but all are equipped to a similar standard. The smartly decorated restaurant offers a sensible menu, often featuring locally caught fish.

ROOMS: 54 en suite (6 fmly) s £37-£42; d £49-£54 (incl. bkfst) * **FACILITIES:** STV **CONF:** Thtr 60 Class 40 Board 20 Del from £56 * **SERVICES:** Lift **CARDS:**

★★69% Invicta

11-12 Osborne Place, Lockyer St, The Hoe PL1 2PU
☎ 01752 664997 01752 664994
***Dir:** approaching Plymouth from A38, follow signs for City Centre, then look for the HOE park, the hotel is situated opposite the park entrance*

An elegant Victorian building, opposite the famous bowling green, and just a short stroll from the city centre and Barbican. The atmosphere is relaxed and friendly and every effort is made to ensure an enjoyable and relaxing stay. Bedrooms are well equipped and attractively decorated, ideally suited for both business and leisure guests. An extensive menu is offered in the dining room, with grills a popular feature.

ROOMS: 23 en suite (6 fmly) s £48-£52; d £58-£62 (incl. bkfst) * LB **CONF:** Thtr 35 Class 40 Board 60 Del from £57 * **PARKING:** 10 **NOTES:** No dogs (ex guide dogs) No children 12yrs No smoking in restaurant Closed 24 Dec-3 Jan **CARDS:**

★★68% Camelot

5 Elliot St, The Hoe PL1 2PP
☎ 01752 221255 & 669667 01752 603660
***Dir:** from the A38 follow signs fot the city centre, The Hoe, Citadel Rd and then onto Elliot St*

Located within easy walking distance of the city centre and the Barbican, the Camelot Hotel offers a friendly atmosphere. Bedrooms are comfortable and equipped with modern facilities. There is a well stocked bar and separate lounge for guests, with the restaurant offering both fixed-price and à la carte menus.

ROOMS: 17 en suite (4 fmly) s £39; d £50 (incl. bkfst) * LB **CONF:** Thtr 60 Class 40 Board 20 **NOTES:** No dogs (ex guide dogs) No smoking in restaurant **CARDS:**

★★68% Langdon Court

Down Thomas PL9 0DY
☎ 01752 862358 01752 863428
e-mail: langdon@eurobell.co.uk
***Dir:** follow HMS Cambridge signs from Elburton and brown tourist signs on A379*

Surrounded by seven acres of lush countryside, private woodland and gardens, Langdon Court is the perfect choice for a peaceful break. Once owned by Henry VIII, there is history at every turn. The convivial bar is very popular and a good range of bar meals is offered. For more formal dining, both fixed-price and carte menus are available in the elegant restaurant. The well-equipped bedrooms are individual in style and some have lovely views.

ROOMS: 18 en suite (4 fmly) s £56; d £79 (incl. bkfst) * LB **CONF:** Thtr 60 Board 20 Del £77 * **PARKING:** 100 **NOTES:** No smoking in restaurant Civ Wed 75 **CARDS:**

★★63% Grosvenor
7-9 Elliot St, The Hoe PL1 2PP
☎ 01752 260411 📠 01752 668878
Dir: *when approaching city centre turn left marked "Barbican", follow this road until the Walrus Pub, turn left, go over crossroads, hotel is on the left*
Converted from two adjoining Victorian buildings, the Grosvenor offers easy access to the city centre, the Hoe and the Barbican. Staff provide friendly service and meals are served in a smart modern bistro.
ROOMS: 28 en suite (2 fmly) s £35; d £45 (incl. bkfst) LB
FACILITIES: STV **PARKING:** 3 **NOTES:** Closed 24 Dec-1 Jan
CARDS:

★72% Victoria Court
62/64 North Rd East PL4 6AL
☎ 01752 668133 📠 01752 668133
e-mail: victoria.court@btinternet.com
Dir: *from A38 follow signs for city centre, past railway station follow North Road East for approx 200yds hotel on left*
Situated within walking distance of the city centre and railway station, this family run hotel offers comfortable accommodation. The public areas retain the Victorian character of the building, and include a comfortable lounge, bar and dining area. The attractively decorated bedrooms are well maintained with modern facilities.
ROOMS: 13 en suite (4 fmly) s £39-£42; d £49-£55 (incl. bkfst) * LB
PARKING: 6 **NOTES:** No dogs Closed 22 Dec-1 Jan
CARDS:

★68% Imperial
Lockyer St, The Hoe PL1 2QD
☎ 01752 227311 📠 01752 674986
Dir: *centrally located between Hoe Promenade & City Centre*
Close to the city centre, this Grade II listed hotel is suitable for both commercial and leisure travellers. The Jones family offer old fashioned hospitality in a friendly and convivial atmosphere. Guests can relax in either the cosy bar or TV lounge, both before and after sampling a menu offering a varied selection of dishes.
ROOMS: 22 rms (18 en suite) (4 fmly) s £35-£46; d £48-£59 (incl. bkfst) LB **CONF:** Thtr 25 Class 25 Board 16 **PARKING:** 14 **NOTES:** No dogs (ex guide dogs) Closed 25-31 Dec
CARDS:

★66% Grosvenor Park
114-116 North Rd East PL4 6AH
☎ 01752 229312 📠 01752 252777
Dir: *nearest hotel to Plymouth Station, approx 150yds from the main entrance in the heart of the city*
This friendly, small hotel is conveniently situated for both the city centre and the railway station. Public areas comprise a comfortable lounge, separate bar and dining room where a range of popular dishes is on offer.
ROOMS: 14 rms (11 en suite) (1 fmly) No smoking in 3 bedrooms s £20-£33; d £40-£44 (incl. bkfst) * **FACILITIES:** STV **PARKING:** 6
NOTES: No dogs (ex guide dogs) No smoking in restaurant
CARDS:

★65% Drake
1 & 2 Windsor Villas, Lockyer St, The Hoe PL1 2QD
THE CIRCLE Selected Individual Hotels
☎ 01752 229730 📠 01752 255092
e-mail: drakehotel@themutual.net
Dir: *follow City Centre signs, left at Theatre Royal, last left, first right*
Two adjoining Victorian houses have been linked to form this family run hotel. Bedrooms are well equipped, and public areas offer a lounge, bar and spacious dining room. The convenient

continued on p446

P

PLYMOUTH, continued

location, just a short walk from the city centre and the Hoe, make this a popular choice for both business and leisure guests.
ROOMS: 35 rms (30 en suite) (3 fmly) s £42; d £52 (incl. bkfst) * LB **PARKING:** 25 **NOTES:** No dogs (ex guide dogs) Closed 24 Dec-3 Jan
CARDS:

⇧ Hotel Ibis

Marsh Mills, Longbridge Rd, Forder Valley PL6 8LD
☎ 01752 601087 🖷 01752 223213
e-mail: H2093@accor-hotels.com

Dir: A38 towards Plymouth, 1st exit over the fly over toward Estover, Leigham and Parkway industrial estate. At rdbt, hotel on 4th exit
Modern, budget hotel offering comfortable accommodation in bright and practical bedrooms. Breakfast is self-service and dinner is available in the restaurant. For further details, consult the Hotel Groups page.
ROOMS: 51 en suite s fr £42; d fr £46 * **CONF:** Thtr 20 Class 20 Board 20

POCKLINGTON, East Riding of Yorkshire — Map 08 SE84

★★65% *Feathers*

Market Place YO42 2AH
☎ 01759 303155 🖷 01759 304382
Dir: from York, take B1246 signposted Pocklington. Hotel just off A1079
A busy hotel which has been fully modernised to provide comfortable accommodation, with some bedrooms in a separate rear building. Public areas are busy and enjoyable meals are served in the bar or in the conservatory restaurant. A wide choice of dishes are available.
ROOMS: 6 en suite 6 annexe en suite (1 fmly) **CONF:** Thtr 20 Class 8 Board 12 **PARKING:** 56 **NOTES:** No dogs (ex guide dogs)
CARDS:

★★65% *Yorkway Motel*

Hull-York Rd YO42 2NX
☎ 01759 303071 🖷 01759 305215
Dir: between Beverley & York on the A1079 with the junc of B1247
This family owned and run motel and diner is close to the village of Pocklington and offers value-for-money accommodation. Bedrooms are thoughtfully equipped and public rooms include a bar and cosy dining room, where a good range of food is served all day.
ROOMS: 15 annexe en suite (6 fmly) **FACILITIES:** Pool table **CONF:** Thtr 30 Class 12 Board 16 **PARKING:** 40 **NOTES:** No dogs (ex guide dogs) No smoking in restaurant
CARDS:

PODIMORE, Somerset — Map 03 ST52

⇧ *Travelodge*

BA22 8JG
☎ 01935 840074 🖷 01935 840074
Dir: on A303, near junct with A37
This modern building offers accommodation in smart, spacious and well equipped bedrooms, all with en suite bathrooms. Refreshments may be taken at the nearby family restaurant. For further details and the Travelodge phone number, consult the Hotel Groups page.
ROOMS: 31 en suite

Packed in a hurry? Ironing facilities should be available at all star levels, either in rooms or on request.

POLPERRO, Cornwall & Isles of Scilly — Map 02 SX25

★★★75% Talland Bay

PL13 2JB
☎ 01503 272667 🖷 01503 272940
e-mail: tallandbay@aol.com
Dir: signposted from crossroads on A387 Looe/Polperro road
Dating back to the 16th century, this Cornish stone manor house has a tropical influence, with delightful views over the gardens to the sea beyond. Public areas have been upgraded, while the menu incorporates the finest regional produce, with seafood featuring strongly. Bedrooms are charmingly furnished and decorated, each having its own character; several are located in cottages in the garden.
ROOMS: 16 en suite 6 annexe en suite (2 fmly) s £67-£96; d £134-£192 (incl. bkfst & dinner) * LB **FACILITIES:** Outdoor swimming (H) Sauna Pool table Croquet lawn Putting green Games room Xmas **CONF:** Thtr 30 Board 30 Del from £70 * **PARKING:** 20 **NOTES:** No smoking in restaurant Closed 2 Jan-late Feb **CARDS:**

★72% *Claremont*

The Coombes PL13 2RG
☎ 01503 272241 🖷 01503 272241
Dir: on Polperro's main street
This cosy and intimate hotel is situated in the picturesque village of Polperro. There is an à la carte menu with various interesting, home made dishes served in the bistro style restaurant and a small comfortable lounge and bar. Bedrooms vary in size and style and have wonderful character, along with modern amenities and facilities.
ROOMS: 12 en suite (2 fmly) **FACILITIES:** STV **PARKING:** 16 **NOTES:** No smoking in restaurant RS Oct-Mar
CARDS:

PONTEFRACT, West Yorkshire — Map 08 SE42

★★★65% Rogerthorpe Manor Hotel

Thorpe Ln, Badsworth WF9 1AB
☎ 01977 643839 🖷 01977 641571
e-mail: ops@rogerthorpemanor.co.uk
Dir: take A639 S from Pontefract, in approx 3m turn right at Fox & Hounds PH, Rogerthorpe Manor 1m on left

Rogerthorpe Manor has a lengthy and fascinating history, and today houses a friendly and comfortable hotel. It provides well equipped bedrooms, ample lounges, and a popular Jacobean bar serving real ale and good bar food. The hotel caters for weddings and other functions.
ROOMS: 24 en suite (2 fmly) No smoking in 6 bedrooms s £80-£110; d £95-£120 (incl. bkfst) * LB **FACILITIES:** STV Croquet lawn Xmas **CONF:** Thtr 300 Class 125 Board 50 Del from £110 * **PARKING:** 120 **NOTES:** No dogs (ex guide dogs) No smoking in restaurant Civ Wed 300
CARDS:

POOLE, Dorset

Map 04 SZ09

★★★★73% Haven

Banks Rd, Sandbanks BH13 7QL
☎ 01202 707333 📠 01202 708796
e-mail: reservations@havenhotel.co.uk
Dir: *take the B3965 towards Poole Bay and turn left onto the Peninsula. Hotel 1.5m on left next to the Swanage Toll Ferry point*

Overlooking Poole Bay and the Sandbanks ferry, this attractive hotel has enviable views. There are ample lounge areas, a waterside restaurant and a brasserie. Bedrooms vary in style and size, some have sea views and balconies. The restaurant and La Roche fish cafe serve carefully prepared dishes, and lighter meals are available in the conservatory.

ROOMS: 94 en suite (4 fmly) s £82-£132; d £164-£300 (incl. bkfst) LB **FACILITIES:** STV Indoor swimming (H) Outdoor swimming (H) Tennis (hard) Sauna Solarium Gym Jacuzzi/spa Steam room Spa pool Hair and Beauty salon Xmas **CONF:** Thtr 150 Class 40 Board 25 Del from £131 * **SERVICES:** Lift **PARKING:** 150 **NOTES:** No dogs (ex guide dogs) No smoking in restaurant Civ Wed 80
CARDS:

★★★80% Mansion House

Thames St BH15 1JN
☎ 01202 685666 📠 01202 665709
e-mail: enquiries@themansionhouse.co.uk
Dir: *A31 to Poole, follow signs to channel ferry, turn left at Pool bridge onto Poole Quay, take first left (Thames St), hotel is opposite church*

Tucked away off the Old Quay, this sophisticated hotel provides individually designed bedrooms and pleasant public areas that include a flagstoned entrance and a quiet drawing room. Guest care and comfort is of particular importance at this efficiently run hotel. The comfortable restaurant and the bistro serve a selection of award winning cuisine.

continued

POOLE, continued

ROOMS: 32 en suite (2 fmly) No smoking in 4 bedrooms s £65-£90; d £100-£128 (incl. bkfst) * LB **FACILITIES:** STV All facilities available locally Watersports Xmas **CONF:** Thtr 40 Class 18 Board 20 Del from £110 * **PARKING:** 46 **NOTES:** No dogs No smoking in restaurant Civ Wed 35 **CARDS:**

★★★80% Salterns

38 Salterns Way, Lilliput BH14 8JR
☎ 01202 707321 01202 707488
e-mail: reception@salterns.co.uk
Dir: *in Poole follow B3369 Sandbanks road. In 1m at Lilliput shops turn into Salterns Way by Barclays Bank*

Best Western

Situated beside its own marina and enjoying views across to Brownsea Island, this hotel has an enviable repuation. The bedrooms are mostly spacious and comfortably furnished. In the restaurant an interesting menu makes good use of local game and fish, there is also a bistro.

ROOMS: 20 en suite (4 fmly) No smoking in 3 bedrooms s £86; d £106-£126 * LB **FACILITIES:** STV Fishing Leisure facilities available at sister hotel Xmas **CONF:** Thtr 100 Class 50 Board 50 Del from £110 * **PARKING:** 300 **NOTES:** Civ Wed 120
CARDS:

See advert on page 447

★★★74% Sandbanks

15 Banks Rd, Sandbanks BH13 7PS
☎ 01202 707377 01202 708885
e-mail: reservations@sandbankshotel.co.uk
Dir: *follow A338 from Bournemouth onto Wessex Way to Liverpool Victoria rdbt. Keep left & take 2nd exit - B3965 to Sandbanks Bay. Hotel on left*

Popular with both leisure and business guests, this large hotel has direct access to a blue flag beach and stunning views across Poole Harbour. In addition to the main restaurant, Sands Brasserie serves an imaginative selection of dishes. Many of the well equipped bedrooms have balconies and there is an extensive range of leisure facilities ideal for entertaining families.

ROOMS: 116 en suite (31 fmly) No smoking in 33 bedrooms s £58-£85; d £116-£170 (incl. bkfst) * LB **FACILITIES:** STV Indoor swimming (H) Sauna Solarium Gym Pool table Putting green Jacuzzi/spa Hobie Cat Sailing Mountain bike hire Indoor children's play area entertainment ch fac Xmas **CONF:** Thtr 150 Class 40 Board 25 Del from £99.88 * **SERVICES:** Lift **PARKING:** 200 **NOTES:** No dogs (ex guide dogs) No smoking in restaurant **CARDS:**

★★★65% Harbour Heights

73 Haven Rd, Sandbanks BH13 7LW
☎ 01202 707272 01202 708594
Dir: *from M27 to Ringwood, follow signs to Poole and then to Sandbanks*

This pleasant hotel, with magnificent views of Brownsea Island and Studland Bay, caters admirably for its mix of business and leisure guests. The bedrooms are smartly furnished and comfortable and most have sea views. There is a choice of menus in the two popular restaurants.

ROOMS: 48 en suite (5 fmly) s fr £48; d fr £80 (incl. bkfst) * LB **FACILITIES:** STV ch fac **SERVICES:** Lift **PARKING:** 84 **NOTES:** Closed 24 Dec-8 Jan **CARDS:**

★★★64% *Arndale Court*

62/66 Wimborne Rd BH15 2BY
☎ 01202 683746 01202 668838
Dir: *on A349 close to Town Centre, opposite Poole Stadium entrance*

Well decorated bedrooms are popular with business guests during the week, but being close to the Town Centre and ferry terminal, the hotel is equally suited to leisure guests. Attractive public areas include the lounge, bar and restaurant where well cooked and interesting dishes are served. Ample parking is available.

ROOMS: 39 en suite (7 fmly) **FACILITIES:** STV **CONF:** Thtr 50 Class 35 Board 35 **PARKING:** 32 **NOTES:** No smoking in restaurant
CARDS:

★★62% Norfolk Lodge

1 Flaghead Rd, Canford Cliffs BH13 7JL
☎ 01202 708614 01202 708661
e-mail: allnmartin@aol.com
Dir: *between Poole & Bournemouth hotel on corner of Haven & Flaghead Rd*

Located in a quiet residential area, the Norfolk Lodge is just a few minutes' walk from the beach. The bedrooms are pleasantly decorated. A short, fixed price menu is offered each evening in the restaurant, overlooking the garden and its aviaries full of exotic birds.

ROOMS: 19 rms (17 en suite) (4 fmly) s £45-£50; d £60-£65 (incl. bkfst) * LB **FACILITIES:** ch fac **PARKING:** 16 **NOTES:** No smoking in restaurant **CARDS:**

★63% Harmony Hotel

19 St Peter's Rd, Parkstone BH14 0NZ
☎ 01202 747510 01202 747510
e-mail: david.madley@virgin.net
Dir: *at Ashley Cross on A35 Poole-Bournemouth road, turn into Parr St at Contral Hotel. Continue past church & into St Peters Rd. Hotel 100metres on left*

Quietly located mid-way between Poole and Bournemouth, this hotel is convenient for many of the nearby attractions. A relaxed and friendly style of service and hospitality is provided by the resident proprietors. Guests are encouraged to use the comfortably furnished lounge or bar before enjoying the tempting home cooking.

ROOMS: 11 rms (8 en suite) (3 fmly) No smoking in all bedrooms s £21-£25; d £40-£45 (incl. bkfst) * LB **PARKING:** 10
CARDS:

PORLOCK, Somerset

Map 03 SS84

★★★67% Anchor Hotel & Ship Inn

Porlock Harbour TA24 8PB
☎ 01643 862753 01643 862843
e-mail: anchorhotel@clara.net
Dir: *from A39 take the B3225 Porlock Weir road. Hotel is located after 1.5m in a cul-de-sac*

This long established hotel overlooks the harbour, the Bristol Channel and, in the distance, Wales. Two types of bedrooms are available: rooms full of original character in the 16th-century Ship inn; and more spacious rooms in the main hotel. The Harbour Restaurant offers fixed price and carte menus and the Ship Inn provides a range of bar meals.

ROOMS: 14 en suite 6 annexe en suite (2 fmly) s £140.16-£174.36; d £120.16-£154.36 (incl. bkfst & dinner) * LB **FACILITIES:** Xmas **CONF:** Thtr 20 Board 12 Del from £71.75 * **NOTES:** No smoking in restaurant RS Jan & Feb **CARDS:**

See advert on this page

Premier Collection

★★ The Oaks

TA24 8ES
☎ 01643 862265 01643 863131
e-mail: oakshotel@aol.com

This relaxing Edwardian country house offers distant views of Porlock Bay and Exmoor. Bedrooms are comfortably furnished, vary in size and have many thoughtful extras. Public rooms are attractively furnished with period pieces. In winter real coal fires can be enjoyed, while during the summer, the garden is the perfect place to enjoy a drink before sampling the mouth-watering cuisine.

ROOMS: 9 en suite No smoking in all bedrooms s fr £60; d fr £100 (incl. bkfst) * LB **FACILITIES:** Xmas **PARKING:** 12 **NOTES:** No children 8yrs No smoking in restaurant Closed Nov-Mar (excl. Xmas) **CARDS:**

★★71% Porlock Vale House

TA24 8NY
☎ 01643 862338 01643 863338
e-mail: info@porlockvale.co.uk
Dir: *off A39 at end of village, then right fork along the lower Porlock Weir coast road*

Originally a hunting lodge, this delightful Edwardian house stands on the edge of Exmoor and has splendid views of Porlock Bay. It has its own stables and riding instruction is available. There are two indoor schools and a varied cross-country course. Bedrooms vary in style, with the best having extensive views of the countryside, as far as distant Wales. There is a choice of lounges and an attractive, beamed dining room.

continued

ROOMS: 15 en suite No smoking in all bedrooms s £55-£70; d £80-£120 (incl. bkfst) * LB **FACILITIES:** Riding Xmas **PARKING:** 20 **NOTES:** No dogs (ex guide dogs) No children 14yrs No smoking in restaurant Closed 1st 2 weeks Jan **CARDS:**

PORT GAVERNE, Cornwall & Isles of Scilly

Map 02 SX08

★★70% *Port Gaverne*

PL29 3SQ
☎ 01208 880244 01208 880151
Dir: *signposted from B3314*

Half a mile from the old fishing village of Port Isaac and set back from a spectacular small cove, this traditional coastal inn retains its flagged floors, beamed ceilings and steep stairways and yet the bedrooms have modern facilities. Local produce often features on the hotel menus, including bar meals. Staff provide friendly and relaxed service.

ROOMS: 17 en suite **PARKING:** 30 **NOTES:** No smoking in restaurant Closed 5 Jan-11 Feb **CARDS:**

PORT GAVERNE, continued

★★66% Headlands
PL29 3SH
☎ 01208 880260 01208 880885
e-mail: headlandpg@aol.com
Dir: on cliff top, 0.50m E of Port Isaac
From its unrivalled position overlooking the tiny cove of Port Gaverne, the Headlands Hotel has spectacular views over the North Cornish coastline. The majority of bedrooms benefit from the views. In the relaxed restaurant a choice of menus is available.
ROOMS: 11 en suite (1 fmly) s £40-£47; d £65-£79 (incl. bkfst) * LB **FACILITIES:** Sauna Xmas **CONF:** Class 20 Board 12 **PARKING:** 40 **NOTES:** No smoking in restaurant **CARDS:**

MINOTEL Great Britain

PORT ISAAC, Cornwall & Isles of Scilly Map 02 SW98
see also Port Gaverne

★★68% Castle Rock
4 New Rd PL29 3SB
☎ 01208 880300 01208 880219
e-mail: castlerock@btclick.com
Dir: from A30 turn off after Launceston onto A395. Turn left at junction with A39 then take first right signposted Port Isaac, follow signs to village
With spectacular views of the rugged Cornish coastline, this friendly hotel is an ideal base for holidaymakers wishing to explore the many attractions the area has to offer. The hotel has comfortable and spacious accommodation, with all the public areas benefiting from the wonderful panoramic views over the cliffs and sea. In addition to the carte and fixed price menu, an extensive range of skilfully cooked and imaginative dishes is served in the bar or on the terrace during the summer months.
ROOMS: 14 en suite 4 annexe en suite (2 fmly) s £20-£37; d £40-£74 (incl. bkfst) * LB **PARKING:** 18 **NOTES:** No smoking in restaurant
CARDS:

See advert on opposite page

PORTSCATHO, Cornwall & Isles of Scilly Map 02 SW83

★★★79% Rosevine
TR2 5EW
☎ 01872 580206 01872 580230
e-mail: info@makepeacehotels.co.uk
Dir: from St Austell take A390 for Truro and turn left onto B3287 to Tregony. Leave Tregony by A3078 through Ruan High Lanes. Hotel third turning left

Sitauted in the heart of the spectacular Roseland peninsula, this Georgian country house is now under the close personal supervision of the Makepeace family. Completely refurbished, the hotel offers high standards of comfort combined with polished service and caring hospitality. Bedrooms are tastefully furnished and well equipped, many having the benefit of lovely views across the garden to the sparkling sea beyond. Extensive public rooms include a choice of lounges and the spacious dining room in which the accomplished cuisine is enjoyed. A heated indoor pool is also available with an adjacent paddling pool for the younger members of the family!
ROOMS: 11 en suite 6 annexe en suite (7 fmly) s £90-£130; d £150-£200 (incl. bkfst) LB **FACILITIES:** Indoor swimming (H) Table tennis Childrens playroom ch fac **PARKING:** 20 **NOTES:** No smoking in restaurant Closed Nov-11 Feb (ex Xmas)
CARDS:

See advert under ST MAWES

★★★67% *Roseland House*
Rosevine TR2 5EW
☎ 01872 580644 01872 580801
e-mail: anthony.hindley@btinternet.com
Dir: A3078 for St Mawes. Pass through Ruan-High-Lanes and signposted after 2m
Roseland House manages to attract many of its guests back each year, due to its natural friendliness and high level of informal yet professional service. The spacious, comfortable bedrooms have modern facilities, many personal touches and luxurious bathrooms. Fine cuisine is served in the smart restaurant with lovely views over the Peninsula.
ROOMS: 10 en suite (2 fmly) No smoking in all bedrooms
FACILITIES: Fishing Private beach with safe bathing ch fac **PARKING:** 25 **NOTES:** No dogs (ex guide dogs) No smoking in restaurant Closed Xmas & New Year **CARDS:**

PORTSMOUTH & SOUTHSEA, Hampshire Map 04 SZ69

★★★★65% Portsmouth Marriott
North Harbour PO6 4SH
☎ 023 9238 3151 023 9238 8701
Dir: from M27 junct 12-keep left, hotel on left
This large, busy hotel is on the north side of the city. Well equipped bedrooms offer a high standard of comfort. Open plan public areas include a modern bar and restaurant, shop and extensive leisure facilities.
ROOMS: 172 en suite (76 fmly) No smoking in 122 bedrooms s £60-£92; d £90-£112 (incl. bkfst) * LB **FACILITIES:** STV Indoor swimming (H) Sauna Solarium Gym Jacuzzi/spa Sunbed & exercise studio Xmas **CONF:** Thtr 350 Class 180 Board 36 Del from £135 * **SERVICES:** Lift air con **PARKING:** 300 **NOTES:** Civ Wed 100
CARDS:

Marriott HOTELS·RESORTS·SUITES

★★★67% Queen's Hotel
Clarence Pde PO5 3LJ
☎ 023 9282 2466 023 9282 1901
e-mail: reservations@queenshotel-southsea.co.uk
Dir: from M27 take junct 12 onto M275 and follow signs for Southsea seafront. Hotel is located opp. Hovercraft terminal
This elegant Edwardian hotel has dominated the Southsea seafront for over 100 years, and enjoys magnificent views over the Solent and Isle of Wight. Bedrooms are currently being gradually refurbished. There are family rooms available and many have sea views. Public areas include restaurant garden and pool, two comfortable bars and nightclub.
ROOMS: 73 en suite (3 fmly) No smoking in 51 bedrooms s £50-£75; d £75-£125 * LB **FACILITIES:** STV Outdoor swimming (H) Private garden Xmas **CONF:** Thtr 150 Class 120 Del from £89.50 * **SERVICES:** Lift **PARKING:** 70 **NOTES:** No dogs (ex guide dogs)
CARDS:

Best Western

See advert on opposite page

TV dinner? Room service at three stars and above.

★★★65% Innlodge Hotel

Burrfields Rd PO3 5HH
☎ 023 9265 0510 023 9269 3458
Dir: *from A3(M) & M27 follow A27, take Southsea exit and follow A2030. At 3rd set of traffic lights. Turn right into Burrfields Rd-hotel 2nd car-park on*

Situated on the eastern fringe of the city, the hotel is ideally placed for all major routes. The spacious bedrooms are modern in style, comfortable and well appointed. Guests are offered a choice of two eating options: the Farmhouse Inn or the American-style Beiderbecks restaurant and bar.

ROOMS: 73 en suite (10 fmly) No smoking in 9 bedrooms d £52.50-£62.50 * LB **FACILITIES:** STV Pool table Indoor fun factory & outdoor children's play area entertainment Xmas **CONF:** Thtr 150 Class 72 Board 40 Del from £80 * **PARKING:** 200 **NOTES:** No dogs (ex guide dogs) **CARDS:**

★★★61% *Posthouse Portsmouth*

Pembroke Rd PO1 2TA
Posthouse
☎ 0870 400 9065 023 9275 6715
e-mail: crown@marstonhotels.co.uk
Dir: *from M275, follow signs for Southsea and I.O.W Hovercroft for 1 mile, at Southsea Common the Hotel can be found on the right*

Conveniently located for the seafront, local shops and city centre, the hotel is a popular venue for functions at weekends. Bedrooms are gradually being refurbished, and are all well equipped. Guests can take advantage of the hotel's leisure facilities, including an indoor swimming pool and gym. The hotel also has a range of meeting rooms and a business centre.

ROOMS: 167 en suite (12 fmly) No smoking in 82 bedrooms **FACILITIES:** Indoor swimming (H) Sauna Solarium Gym Pool table Jacuzzi/spa Turkish steam room,Beauty Room, Pool room, Play room **CONF:** Thtr 220 Class 120 Board 80 **SERVICES:** Lift **PARKING:** 80 **NOTES:** No smoking in restaurant **CARDS:**

★★★61% Royal Beach

South Pde PO4 0RN
☎ 023 9273 1281 023 9281 7572
Dir: *follow M27 to M275, then follow signs to seafront, hotel is situated on seafront*

This well established hotel occupies a prime seafront location directly opposite Southsea Pier. Bedrooms are spacious, and many have views across the Solent. Public areas include bar/lounge and the Ark Royal Restaurant. Service is well supervised and friendly.

ROOMS: 115 en suite No smoking in 30 bedrooms s £49-£75; d £74-£145 (incl. bkfst) * LB **FACILITIES:** STV Xmas **CONF:** Thtr 250 Class 160 Board 30 **SERVICES:** Lift **PARKING:** 62 **NOTES:** No smoking in restaurant **CARDS:**

Arriving late? Four and five star hotels have night porters to assist with your luggage; and 24hr room service.

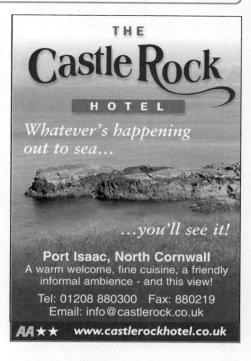

PORTSMOUTH & SOUTHSEA, continued

★★71% ***The Beaufort***
71 Festing Rd PO4 0NQ
☎ 023 9282 3707 📠 023 9287 0270
e-mail: res/enq@beauforthotel.co.uk
Dir: *follow signs for seafront at South Parade Pier take left fork, Festing Rd is fourth turning on left*
This friendly hotel is ideally situated for both the seafront and town centre. Bedrooms are equipped to a high standard and attractively furnished. Well presented public areas include the basement restaurant/bar, and an elegant lounge.
ROOMS: 19 en suite (1 fmly) No smoking in 10 bedrooms **FACILITIES:** STV **CONF:** Class 20 **PARKING:** 10 **NOTES:** No dogs No smoking in restaurant **CARDS:**

★★71% **Seacrest**
11/12 South Pde PO5 2JB
☎ 023 9273 3192 📠 023 9283 2523
e-mail: seacrest@mccail.com
Dir: *from M27 follow signs for Southsea seafront or the Pyramids. Hotel opposite Rock Gardens and the Pyramids*

In a premier seafront location, this friendly hotel provides the ideal base for exploring the historic maritime resort. Bedrooms, many benefiting from sea views, are all en suite and decorated to a high standard. All rooms are well equipped with the usual modern amenities. Guests can relax in either the South facing lounge furnished with comfortable leather chesterfields or the adjacent cosy bar, before enjoying a home-cooked meal in the downstairs dining room.
ROOMS: 28 en suite (3 fmly) No smoking in 10 bedrooms s £40-£55; d £45-£75 (incl. bkfst) * LB **FACILITIES:** STV Xmas **SERVICES:** Lift **PARKING:** 12 **NOTES:** No smoking in restaurant
CARDS:

★★71% ***Westfield Hall***
65 Festing Rd PO4 0NQ
☎ 023 9282 6971 📠 023 9287 0200
e-mail: jdanie@westfield-hall-hotel.co.uk
Dir: *follow signs Seafront, bear left at South Parade Pier then 3rd turning left*
Close to the seafront and town, this popular, family-run hotel provides a warm welcome to guests. Split between two houses, all the rooms offer en suite facilities and comfortable furnishings. Evening meals and breakfasts are served in the downstairs dining room.
ROOMS: 16 en suite 11 annexe en suite (5 fmly) No smoking in 14 bedrooms **FACILITIES:** STV **PARKING:** 18 **NOTES:** No dogs No smoking in restaurant **CARDS:**

Packed in a hurry? Ironing facilities should be available at all star levels, either in rooms or on request.

★★69% ***St Margarets***
3 Craneswater Gate PO4 0NZ
☎ 023 92820097 📠 023 92820097
Dir: *follow signs for D Day Museum/Sea Life Centre through city to sea front, head for South Parade Pier, at pier take left fork then 2nd left*
Enjoying a quiet residential location close to both the seafront and the town centre, St Margarets offers a warm and friendly atmosphere. Bedrooms are well presented with comfortable, co-ordinated furnishings. Guests have the option of quiet lounge or bar, meals are served in the spacious dining room.
ROOMS: 13 en suite (1 fmly) No smoking in 2 bedrooms **PARKING:** 5 **NOTES:** No dogs No smoking in restaurant Closed 21 Dec-2 Jan
CARDS:

★★61% **Sandringham**
7 Osborne Rd, Clarence Pde PO5 3LR
☎ 023 9282 6969 & 92822914 📠 023 9282 2330
Dir: *turn off M275 at Portsmouth junct, follow signs to historic ships, then to Southsea, along seafront, hotel on left, opposite council car park*
This well established hotel continues to be a popular venue for tourists because it is ideally located for the seafront, Southsea Common and the town centre. Bedrooms are comfortably furnished and well decorated. The lower ground floor dining room offers hearty meals and good cooking.
ROOMS: 44 en suite (7 fmly) s £45-£50; d £56-£76 (incl. bkfst) * LB **FACILITIES:** Xmas **CONF:** Thtr 150 Class 100 Board 40 Del from £75 * **SERVICES:** Lift **NOTES:** No dogs (ex guide dogs) No smoking in restaurant Civ Wed 130 **CARDS:**

⌂ **Hotel Ibis**
Winston Churchill Av PO1 2LX
☎ 023 9264 0000 📠 023 9264 1000
e-mail: h1461@accor-hotels.com
Dir: *M27 junct 2 onto M275 and follow signs first for city centre, then sealife centre, then Guildhall. Turn right at rdbt into Winston Churchill Ave*
Modern, budget hotel offering comfortable accommodation in bright and practical bedrooms. Breakfast is self-service and dinner is available in the restaurant. For further details, consult the Hotel Groups page.
ROOMS: 144 en suite **CONF:** Thtr 40 Class 30 Board 30 Del from £75 *

PRESTBURY, Cheshire Map 07 SJ97

★★★69% **Bridge**
The Village SK10 4DQ
☎ 01625 829326 📠 01625 827557
e-mail: info@bridge-hotel.co.uk
Dir: *off A538 through village, hotel next to church*

Dating in parts from the 17th century, this delightful hotel stands sideways to the village street, between the River Bollin and the ancient church. The cocktail bar provides the ideal place to relax

continued

before a satisfying meal in the restaurant. A wide range of bedrooms are available in the original building and a rear extension.
ROOMS: 23 en suite (1 fmly) s £85-£90; d £90-£100 * LB **FACILITIES:** entertainment **CONF:** Thtr 100 Class 56 Board 48 Del £107.50 * **PARKING:** 52 **NOTES:** No dogs (ex guide dogs) Civ Wed 100 **CARDS:**

Town House

★★★★ White House Manor
New Rd SK10 4HP
☎ 01625 829376 🖷 01625 828627
e-mail: stay@cheshire-white-house.com
Dir: *on the A538 Macclesfield Road*
This elegant Georgian house, situated in attractive gardens on the edge of the village, offers charming individually styled bedrooms, many with four-poster beds. Meals can be ordered from the room service menu and breakfast is served in the conservatory. The White House restaurant, under the same ownership, is just a short walk away but guests may be driven there if needed.
ROOMS: 11 en suite No smoking in all bedrooms s £70-£98; d £100-£120 * **FACILITIES:** STV Jacuzzi/spa **CONF:** Thtr 60 Class 40 Board 26 **PARKING:** 11 **NOTES:** No dogs (ex guide dogs) No children 10yrs Closed 25 Dec **CARDS:**

PRESTON, Lancashire — Map 07 SD52
see also Barton

★★★★67% Preston Marriott
Garstang Rd, Broughton PR3 5JB
☎ 01772 864087 🖷 01772 861728
Marriott HOTELS·RESORTS·SUITES
Dir: *M6 junct 32 onto M55 junct 1, follow A6 towards Garstang, the Hotel is 0.05m on the right*
Originally a farmhouse, this building has been greatly extended with much sympathy, retaining a good deal of character. It is quietly situated in its own grounds and within easy reach of the motorway network. The larger bedrooms are located in the original house, with all rooms being comfortably furnished and equipped to suit both the business and leisure visitor. A good standard of cooking is offered in the Broughton Park restaurant, with snacks and lighter meals also available in the Poolside Grill, adjacent to an impressive up-to-the-minute leisure complex.
ROOMS: 150 en suite (40 fmly) No smoking in 75 bedrooms s fr £89; d fr £97 (incl. bkfst) * LB **FACILITIES:** STV Indoor swimming (H) Sauna Solarium Gym Croquet lawn Jacuzzi/spa Steam room Beauty salon entertainment Xmas **CONF:** Thtr 200 Class 120 Board 40 Del £135 * **SERVICES:** Lift **PARKING:** 250 **NOTES:** No dogs (ex guide dogs) No smoking in restaurant Civ Wed 180 **CARDS:**

★★★★63% Tickled Trout
Preston New Rd, Samlesbury PR5 0UJ
☎ 01772 877671 🖷 01772 877463
MACDONALD HOTELS ★★★★
Dir: *close to M6 junct 31*
Popular with business guests, bedrooms are well equipped with good standards of quality and comfort. In addition to an open plan lounge, there are facilities for meetings and conferences, and a small leisure club.

continued

Tickled Trout, Preston

ROOMS: 72 en suite (56 fmly) No smoking in 40 bedrooms s £79-£85; d £90-£100 (incl. bkfst) * LB **FACILITIES:** STV Fishing Sauna Solarium Plunge pool Xmas **CONF:** Thtr 150 Class 60 Board 50 Del from £90 * **PARKING:** 150 **NOTES:** No smoking in restaurant Civ Wed 120 **CARDS:**

★★★66% Mill Hotel
Moor Rd, Croston PR5 7HP
☎ 01772 600110 🖷 01772 601623
e-mail: reception@themillhotel.co.uk
Dir: *M6 junct 28 exit for Wigan. After 2.5m turn right at mini- rdbt A581 Southport/Croston. The Hotel is 3.5m on right*
A well furnished and modern hotel that retains a rustic charm in the spacious public rooms which include two bars and a pleasant restaurant. A good range of family-style cooking is offered and the mainly spacious bedrooms have been well equipped. A playhouse is provided for younger guests.

continued

P

PRESTON, continued

ROOMS: 46 en suite (3 fmly) No smoking in 4 bedrooms s fr £49.50; d fr £65 (incl. bkfst) * **FACILITIES:** Pool table Xmas **CONF:** Thtr 150 Class 50 Board 30 Del from £60 * **PARKING:** 130 **NOTES:** Civ Wed 70 **CARDS:**

★★★66% Pines

570 Preston Rd, Clayton-Le-Wolds PR6 7ED
☎ 01772 338551 🖷 01772 629002
Dir: *on A6, 1m S of M6 junc 29*

Convenient for the motorway network, this privately owned hotel is set in four acres of mature gardens. Thoughtfully equipped bedrooms are comfortable, whilst public areas include a nicely furnished lounge. Haworths restaurant and bistro offers an interesting choice of dishes from traditional meals to light snacks. Meeting and function suites are available; service throughout is friendly and attentive.
ROOMS: 37 en suite (12 fmly) No smoking in 11 bedrooms s fr £70; d fr £80 (incl. bkfst) * LB **FACILITIES:** STV Jacuzzi/spa Xmas **CONF:** Thtr 150 Class 800 Board 60 Del from £96.50 * **PARKING:** 120 **NOTES:** No dogs (ex guide dogs) Civ Wed 150
CARDS:

★★★64% Novotel

NOVOTEL

Reedfield Place, Walton Summit PR6 8AA
☎ 01772 313331 🖷 01772 627868
e-mail: h10838@accor-hotels.com

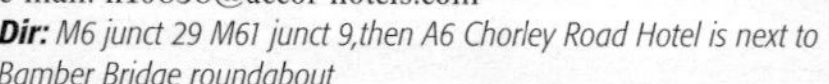

Dir: *M6 junct 29 M61 junct 9,then A6 Chorley Road Hotel is next to Bamber Bridge roundabout*
A modern, friendly hotel, conveniently located close to the M6 and M61 motorway networks. Bedrooms are spacious and the brightly decorated restaurant is open all day from early morning until late at night. There is also a good range of meeting and conference rooms.
ROOMS: 98 en suite (22 fmly) No smoking in 49 bedrooms d £49.50 * LB **FACILITIES:** STV Outdoor swimming (H) Pool table **CONF:** Thtr 180 Class 80 Board 52 **SERVICES:** Lift **PARKING:** 140
CARDS:

★★★64% Swallow

SWALLOW HOTELS

Preston New Rd, Samlesbury PR5 0UL
☎ 01772 877351 🖷 01772 877424
e-mail: info@swallowhotelseurope.com
Dir: *1m from M6, on A59/A677 junct*
Well suited to the business, conference and leisure guest alike, this hotel is easily accessible from the M6. The modern bedrooms are equipped to a high standard, and there is a good range of leisure facilities and spacious reception areas.
ROOMS: 78 en suite No smoking in 24 bedrooms s £85-£95; d £115-£120 (incl. bkfst) * LB **FACILITIES:** STV Indoor swimming (H) Sauna Solarium Gym Jacuzzi/spa Steam room Xmas **CONF:** Thtr 250 Class 100 Board 60 Del from £115 * **SERVICES:** Lift **PARKING:** 190 **NOTES:** No smoking in restaurant **CARDS:**

★★★59% *Posthouse Preston*

Posthouse

Ringway PR1 3AU
☎ 0870 400 9066 🖷 01772 201923
Dir: *M6 junct 31 follow A59 signs for the Town Centre right at T junct, Forte Posthouse is on the left*
A modern, town-centre hotel, where many of the well equipped bedrooms have panoramic views over the town. Public rooms, including the restaurant and bar are located on the first floor. There is an all-day lounge menu and 24 hour room service.
ROOMS: 119 en suite (11 fmly) No smoking in 73 bedrooms **FACILITIES:** Pool table **CONF:** Thtr 120 Class 50 Board 40 **SERVICES:** Lift **PARKING:** 30 **NOTES:** No smoking in restaurant
CARDS:

★★66% Claremont

516 Blackpool Rd, Ashton-on-Ribble PR2 1HY
☎ 01772 729738 🖷 01772 726274
Dir: *from M6 junct 31 take A59 towards Preston. At hilltop rdbt turn right onto A583. Hotel can be seen on the right just past pub and over bridge*
This friendly hotel is convenient for both the town centre and the motorways. Freshly decorated bedrooms are bright and thoughtfully equipped, and the public areas include a cosy lounge, as well as a comfortable bar and adjacent dining room. The self-contained function room is nicely presented and the rear garden is very attractive.
ROOMS: 14 en suite s fr £38.50; d fr £55 (incl. bkfst) * **CONF:** Thtr 85 Class 45 Board 50 **PARKING:** 27 **NOTES:** No dogs (ex guide dogs) No smoking in restaurant **CARDS:**

★★59% *Vineyard*

SCOTTISH NEWCASTLE hotels

Cinnamon Hill, Chorley Rd, Walton-Le-Dale PR5 4JN
☎ 01772 254646 🖷 01772 258967
Dir: *from M6 junct 29 take A6 to Preston. Then B6230 to Walton-le-Dale. Right at rdbt. Hotel up hill on left*
The exterior of this hotel has an Alpine look and public rooms include an extensive split level restaurant together with a cosy bar in the same style as well as a conference/function room. Bedrooms are well equipped and service is both friendly and attentive.
ROOMS: 16 en suite (1 fmly) **CONF:** Thtr 100 Class 40 Board 50 **PARKING:** 150 **NOTES:** No dogs (ex guide dogs)
CARDS:

⇧ Express by Holiday Inn Preston
Garstang Rd, Broughton PR3 5JE
☎ 01772 861800 🖹 01772 861900
e-mail: preston@premierhotels-25.demon.co.uk
Dir: *M6 junct32, then M55. Take left lane & pick up A6 sign. At slip road turn left, left again at mini-rdbt. Take 2nd turning. Hotel on right past pub*

A modern budget hotel offering comfortable accommodation in refreshing, spacious and comprehensively-equipped bedrooms, en suite bathrooms with power showers and continental buffet breakfast included in the room rate. Suitable for business travellers or families. For further details and the Express by Holiday Inn phone number, consult the Hotel Groups page.
ROOMS: 82 en suite (incl. cont bkfst) d £52.50 * **CONF:** Thtr 30 Class 20 Board 20 Del £75 *

⇧ Premier Lodge

Lostock Ln, Bamber Bridge PR5 6BA
☎ 0870 700 1512 🖹 0870 700 1513
Premier Lodge offers modern, well equipped, en suite accommodation suitable for both business and leisure travellers. Meals can be taken at the adjacent popular restaurant and bar which is fully licensed. For further details, consult the Hotel Groups page.
ROOMS: 40 en suite d £42 *

PUDDINGTON, Cheshire — Map 07 SJ37

★★★★66% ❀❀ Craxton Wood
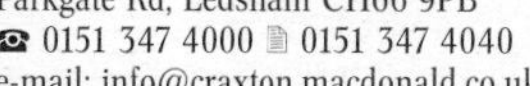
Parkgate Rd, Ledsham CH66 9PB
☎ 0151 347 4000 🖹 0151 347 4040
e-mail: info@craxton.macdonald.co.uk
Dir: *leave M6 take M56 direction North Wales, take A5117, A540 direction Hoylake, hotel is 200yds past the traffic lights*
Significant investment in the form of smart new bedrooms, which are both spacious and very thoughtfully equipped, as well as the addition of extensive meeting and leisure facilities make for a well rounded hotel. A bit of theatre is available in the restaurant, where traditional favourites such as Crepe Suzette are available.
ROOMS: 73 en suite (8 fmly) No smoking in 40 bedrooms s £75-£85; d £85.50-£95.50 (incl. bkfst) * LB **FACILITIES:** STV Indoor swimming (H) Sauna Gym Beauty spa Xmas **CONF:** Thtr 300 Class 150 Board 60 Del from £125 * **SERVICES:** Lift **PARKING:** 220 **NOTES:** No dogs (ex guide dogs) No smoking in restaurant Civ Wed 400
CARDS:

⇧ Premier Lodge (Wirral South)

Parkgate Rd, Two Mills L66 9PD
☎ 0870 700 1580 🖹 0870 700 1581
Premier Lodge offers modern, well equipped, en suite accommodation suitable for both business and leisure travellers. Meals can be taken at the adjacent popular restaurant and bar which is fully licensed. For further details, consult the Hotel Groups page.
ROOMS: 31 en suite d £42 *

PULBOROUGH, West Sussex — Map 04 TQ01

★★73% Chequers
Old Rectory Ln RH20 1AD
☎ 01798 872486 🖹 01798 872715
Dir: *100m mtrs N of junct of A283/A29 opposite church in Pulborough*
Personally run by friendly new owners, this charming Grade II listed hotel is located just north of Pulborough overlooking the South Downs. All rooms are individual in style, comfortably furnished and well equipped. Public areas include two cosy lounges where drinks are served and also a conservatory coffee shop. The attractive restaurant serves carefully prepared dishes using quality fresh produce.
ROOMS: 11 en suite (3 fmly) No smoking in all bedrooms s fr £49.50; d fr £85 (incl. bkfst) * LB **FACILITIES:** Xmas **CONF:** Thtr 20 Class 20 Board 20 **PARKING:** 15 **NOTES:** No smoking in restaurant
CARDS:

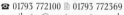

PURTON, Wiltshire — Map 04 SU08

★★★78% ❀❀ The Pear Tree at Purton
Church End SN5 9ED
☎ 01793 772100 🖹 01793 772369
e-mail: stay@peartreepurton.co.uk
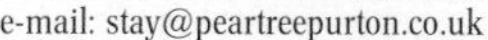
Dir: *from junct 16 of M4 follow signs to Purton, at Spar grocers turn right hotel is 0.25m on left*
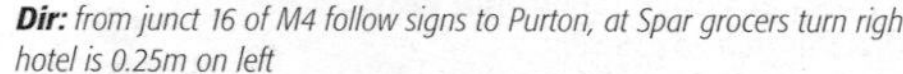
Originally a vicarage, this charming Cotswold stone house has been transformed into an elegant country retreat by its proprietors Francis and Anne Young. Bedrooms all individual in style, feature some super touches such as fresh fruit and sherry. The conservatory restaurant overlooking the delightful gardens, continues to offer a high standard of cooking. Service is most attentive from a friendly young team.
ROOMS: 18 en suite (2 fmly) s £100-£120; d £100-£140 (incl. bkfst) * **FACILITIES:** STV Croquet lawn **CONF:** Thtr 70 Class 30 Board 30 Del from £145 * **PARKING:** 60 **NOTES:** Civ Wed 50
CARDS:

QUORN, Leicestershire — Map 08 SK51

★★★★70% ❀❀ Quorn Country
Charnwood House, 66 Leicester Rd LE12 8BB
☎ 01509 415050 🖹 01509 415557
e-mail: quorncountry.hotel@virgin.net
Dir: *M1 junct 23-A512 into Loughborough and follow A6 signs. At 1st rdbt after town follow signs for Quorn, through lights-hotel 500yds from 2nd rdbt*

This pleasant hotel is set in four acres of landscaped grounds. There are two restaurants: the Shires and the conservatory style Orangery. Bedrooms are divided between the main house and appealing new suites. There are plans for expansion and refurbishment.

continued

QUORN, continued

ROOMS: 23 en suite (1 fmly) No smoking in 3 bedrooms s fr £102; d fr £115 * LB **FACILITIES:** STV Fishing **CONF:** Thtr 100 Class 32 Board 26 Del from £150 * **SERVICES:** air con **PARKING:** 100 **NOTES:** No dogs (ex guide dogs) Civ Wed 100 **CARDS:**

See advert under LEICESTER

RAINHILL, Merseyside

Map 07 SJ49

★62% Rockland

View Rd L35 0LG
☎ 0151 426 4603 📠 0151 426 0107
Dir: *leave M62 junc 7, take A57 towards Rainhill,after 1m turn left into View Rd, hotel 0.25m on left*

A former Victorian residence situated within attractive grounds and gardens, in a quite residential area, only a short distance from Junction 7 of the M62. A friendly family run hotel, with spacious and well equipped bedrooms, which provides good value for money in pleasant informal surrounds.

ROOMS: 11 rms (10 en suite) (2 fmly) s £32.50-£34.50; d £42-£45 (incl. bkfst) * LB **PARKING:** 30 **CARDS:**

⇧ Premier Lodge (Liverpool East)

804 Warrington Rd L35 6PE
☎ 0870 700 1430 📠 0870 700 1431

Premier Lodge offers modern, well equipped, en suite accommodation suitable for both business and leisure travellers. Meals can be taken at the adjacent popular restaurant and bar which is fully licensed. For further details, consult the Hotel Groups page.

ROOMS: 34 en suite d £46 *

RAMSGATE, Kent

Map 05 TR36

★★★66% *San Clu*

Victoria Pde, East Cliff CT11 8DT
☎ 01843 592345 📠 01843 580157
e-mail: sancluhotel@lineone.net
Dir: *opposite Granville Theatre*

This Victorian hotel stands on the seafront, close to the ferry and the town. Bedrooms, some with balconies, are generously sized and well equipped. Meals are served both in the bar lounge and in the restaurant.

ROOMS: 44 en suite (14 fmly) **CONF:** Thtr 180 Class 100 Board 100 **SERVICES:** Lift **PARKING:** 16 **CARDS:**

RAMSGILL, North Yorkshire

Map 07 SE17

★★73% ❀❀ Yorke Arms

HG3 5RL
☎ 01423 755243 📠 01423 755330
e-mail: enquiries@yorkearms.co.uk
Dir: *turn off B6265 at Pateley Bridge at the Nidderdale filling station onto Low Wath road, signed to Ramsgill, continue for 3.5m*

This smartly presented hotel stands in peaceful Upper Nidderdale, close to Gouthwaite reservoir and provides comfortable and well furnished bedrooms. The highlight of any stay here is the ambitious, skilled cooking, that makes excellent use of local produce. Staff are friendly and nothing is too much trouble.

ROOMS: 13 en suite (1 fmly) s £90-£100; d £170-£200 (incl. bkfst & dinner) * LB **FACILITIES:** Xmas **CONF:** Class 20 Del from £85 * **PARKING:** 20 **NOTES:** No dogs (ex guide dogs) No smoking in restaurant RS Sun **CARDS:**

See advert on opposite page

RANGEWORTHY, Gloucestershire

Map 03 ST68

★★72% ❀ Rangeworthy Court

Church Ln, Wotton Rd BS37 7ND
☎ 01454 228347 📠 01454 228945
e-mail: hotel@rangeworthy.demon.co.uk
Dir: *signposted off B4058*

This welcoming manor house hotel is within easy reach of the motorway network. It offers a choice of comfortable lounges, and bedrooms equipped to modern standards. Its restaurant provides a varied and interesting menu.

ROOMS: 13 en suite (4 fmly) s £65-£72; d £70-£82 (incl. bkfst) * LB **FACILITIES:** STV Outdoor swimming (H) Xmas **CONF:** Thtr 22 Class 14 Board 16 Del £98 * **PARKING:** 40 **NOTES:** No smoking in restaurant Civ Wed 60 **CARDS:**

RAVENSCAR, North Yorkshire

Map 08 NZ90

★★★64% *Raven Hall Country House*

YO13 0ET
☎ 01723 870353 📠 01723 870072
Dir: *from Scarborough take A171 to Whitby Rd, go through Cloughton Village turn right to Ravenscar*

Raven Hall Hotel occupies a dramatic location in 100 acres of grounds and gardens 600 feet above sea level, with views towards Robin Hood's Bay. The bedrooms are traditional in style as is the dining room where a satisfying range of food is available. Public areas are in keeping with a country mansion flavour while good leisure facilities and a function suite are provided.

ROOMS: 53 en suite (22 fmly) No smoking in 1 bedroom **FACILITIES:** Indoor swimming (H) Outdoor swimming Golf 9 Tennis (hard) Snooker Sauna Pool table Croquet lawn Putting green Crown green bowls Giant chess entertainment **CONF:** Thtr 160 Class 100 Board 60 **PARKING:** 200 **NOTES:** No dogs (ex guide dogs) No smoking in restaurant **CARDS:**

See advert under SCARBOROUGH

RAVENSTONEDALE, Cumbria

Map 07 NY70

★★68% ❀❀ Black Swan

CA17 4NG
☎ 015396 23204 📠 015396 23604
e-mail: reservations@blackswanhotel.com
Dir: *Ravenstondale is less than ten minutes from junct 38 on M6*

This friendly hotel is the focal point of a picturesque village less than ten minutes drive from the M6. Popular for its imaginative menus and real ales, dinner is served in the dining room with its antique furniture, or in the cosy bar where log fires welcome guests on cooler evenings. Bedrooms are well equipped and include ground floor chalet-style rooms with their own entrances.

continued

ROOMS: 13 en suite 4 annexe en suite (1 fmly) s £45-£50; d £70-£80 (incl. bkfst) * LB **FACILITIES:** Tennis (hard) Fishing Xmas **PARKING:** 30 **NOTES:** No smoking in restaurant **CARDS:**

See advert under KIRKBY STEPHEN

★★63% *The Fat Lamb*

Crossbank CA17 4LL
☎ 01539 623242 01539 623285
e-mail: fatlamb@cumbria.com
Dir: *on A683, between Kirkby Stephen/Sedbergh*

Formerly a 17th century farmhouse, the Fat Lamb is now a roadside country inn. The bar features an old range, and paintings and prints of the area adorn the walls. Bedrooms are in the house and a ground-floor extension which includes facilities for the disabled. An extensive bar menu, plus blackboard specials, complement the fixed-price dinner menu.

ROOMS: 12 en suite (4 fmly) No smoking in all bedrooms **FACILITIES:** Fishing Private 5 acre nature reserve **PARKING:** 60 **NOTES:** No smoking in restaurant **CARDS:**

READING, Berkshire

Map 04 SU77

see also Swallowfield & Wokingham

★★★★58% Holiday Inn

Caversham Bridge, Richfield Av RG1 8BD
☎ 0118 925 9988 0118 939 1665
e-mail: gmrhi@queensmoat.co.uk
Dir: *M4 junct 10/A329M to Reading. Join A4 follow signs to Caversham*

Close to the town centre and next to Caversham Bridge, this modern hotel provides a good range of facilities and well equipped, comfortable bedrooms. The open-plan bar and restaurant is topped with an eye-catching atrium roof and there is also a popular riverside bar.

ROOMS: 112 en suite No smoking in 40 bedrooms d £140-£160 * LB **FACILITIES:** STV Indoor swimming (H) Sauna Solarium Gym Pool table Aromatherapy Beauty treatment Xmas **CONF:** Thtr 200 Class 140 Board 60 Del from £158 * **SERVICES:** Lift **PARKING:** 200 **NOTES:** Civ Wed 35 **CARDS:**

★★★69% *Posthouse Reading*

Posthouse

Basingstoke Rd RG2 0SL
☎ 0870 400 9067 0118 931 1958
Dir: *from junct 11 on M4 follow A33 towards Reading. Hotel 0.5m on left*

Suitable for both the business and leisure traveller, this bright hotel provides very modern accommodation in well equipped bedrooms. Meals are served in the Rotisserie restaurant, or snacks are on offer in the lounge, which is also popular for informal one-to-one business meetings. The leisure centre is a bonus. The hotel offers easy access to both Reading and the M4.

ROOMS: 202 en suite (56 fmly) No smoking in 94 bedrooms **FACILITIES:** Indoor swimming (H) Sauna Solarium Gym Jacuzzi/spa Health & fitness centre ch fac **CONF:** Thtr 100 Class 50 Board 45 **PARKING:** 450 **CARDS:**

★★★68% Courtyard by Marriott Reading

COURTYARD

Bath Rd, Padworth RG7 5HT
☎ 0118 971 4411 0118 971 4442
Dir: *leave the M4 at junct 12 and follow A4 towards Newbury, hotel is 3.5m on left*

A modern purpose-built hotel, air-conditioned bedrooms are comfortably furnished, well equipped and suitable for business guests. The reception area features an attractive gallery lounge and there is a small gym. In the conservatory-style dining room dishes from the branded menu are supplemented by a small choice of daily specials.

continued

ROOMS: 50 en suite No smoking in 30 bedrooms s £96-£99; d £106-£110 (incl. bkfst) * LB **FACILITIES:** STV Gym Fitness room Xmas **CONF:** Thtr 200 Class 100 Board 80 Del from £125 * **SERVICES:** air con **PARKING:** 200 **NOTES:** No dogs (ex guide dogs) No smoking in restaurant Civ Wed 120 **CARDS:**

★★★67% Hanover International

Pingewood RG30 3UN
☎ 0118 950 0885 0118 939 1996
e-mail: hihreading.sales@virgin-net
Dir: *A33 towards Basingstoke, 3m cross rdbt, turn right signposted Burghfield, continue 300m, 2nd right, over M4, cross lights, hotel on left*

Quietly located a short distance south of Reading, with convenient access to the major routes, this modern hotel has the attractive feature of being built around a man-made lake, occasionally used for water sports. All rooms are spacious with good facilities and have balconies overlooking the lake. Leisure facilities include indoor pool and well equipped gym.

continued

R

READING, continued

ROOMS: 81 en suite (61 fmly) No smoking in 39 bedrooms d £125-£160 * LB **FACILITIES:** STV Indoor swimming (H) Tennis (hard) Squash Sauna Gym Pool table Jacuzzi/spa Beauty treatment Hairdresser Xmas **CONF:** Thtr 110 Class 50 Board 45 Del £136.30 * **SERVICES:** Lift **PARKING:** 200 **NOTES:** No dogs (ex guide dogs) No smoking in restaurant **CARDS:**

★★★64% Royal County Hotel
4-8 Duke St RG1 4RY
☎ 0118 958 3455 🖹 0118 950 4450
e-mail: shiphotel@aol.com
Situated in the city centre with handy parking, the hotel has a strong commercial following. The bedrooms are smart, well appointed and comfortable. The public rooms are all decorated in a modern style. The new Fusion Brasserie is already proving a popular venue.
ROOMS: 52 en suite (2 fmly) No smoking in 13 bedrooms s £90-£95; d £100-£105 * LB **FACILITIES:** STV **CONF:** Thtr 90 Class 40 Board 40 Del from £133.50 * **PARKING:** 20 **NOTES:** No dogs (ex guide dogs)
CARDS:

★★68% The Mill House
Old Basingstoke Rd, Swallowfield RG7 1PY
☎ 0118 988 3124 🖹 0118 988 5550
e-mail: info@themillhousehotel.co.uk
(For full entry see Swallowfield)

★★67% Rainbow Corner
132-138 Caversham Rd RG1 8AY
☎ 0118 955 6902 & 958 8140 🖹 0118 958 6500
e-mail: info@rainbowhotel.co.uk
Dir: *from junct 11 of M4 take A327 to town centre then follow signs to Caversham*
Close to city centre and station and with private parking. Staff are friendly and welcoming, creating a home from home atmosphere. The cosy bar is a focus of activity in the evenings. Spacious, comfortable, well equipped bedrooms all have usefull extra facilities.
ROOMS: 24 en suite (1 fmly) s £39-£70; d £49-£90 * LB
FACILITIES: STV **CONF:** Thtr 30 Class 30 Board 20 **PARKING:** 15
NOTES: No smoking in restaurant **CARDS:**

R

★★66% *Abbey House*
118 Connaught Rd RG30 2UF
☎ 0118 959 0549 🖹 0118 956 9299
e-mail: abbey.house@btinternet.com
Dir: *from town centre take A329 towards Pangborne after Reading West Railway bridge take 3rd left*
Personally run by proprietors Mr and Mrs Peck, this well presented hotel is conveniently placed for Reading centre yet situated in a quiet residential location. Spacious bedrooms (including four in a separate building) are well appointed and thoughtfully equipped. Public areas include a cosy dining room, bar and comfortable lounge.
ROOMS: 14 en suite 4 annexe en suite (1 fmly) No smoking in 6 bedrooms **FACILITIES:** STV **PARKING:** 14 **NOTES:** No dogs (ex guide dogs) No smoking in restaurant Closed Xmas-New Year
CARDS:

★★65% *George Hotel*
10-12 King St RG1 2HE
☎ 0118 957 3445 🖹 0118 950 8614
Dir: *leave M4 junct 11/12 (Newbury & West) or junct 10/11 (London & East). The hotel is located at the junct of Broad St & King St*
This traditionally styled coaching inn is located right in the centre of the city - ask for directions if arriving for the first time. Great progress has been made with a new Café Bar and an attractive brasserie-style restaurant. Alternatively, Albert's serves a traditional fish and chips option. The bar is very relaxing, and the bedrooms are comfortable.
ROOMS: 64 en suite (2 fmly) **FACILITIES:** entertainment **CONF:** Thtr 50 Class 36 Board 24 **NOTES:** No dogs (ex guide dogs)
CARDS:

⌂ *Travelodge (Eastbound)*
Burghfield RG30 3UQ
☎ 0118 9566966 🖹 01734 595444
Dir: *M4 between junc 11&12*
This modern building offers accommodation in smart, spacious and well equipped bedrooms, all with en suite bathrooms. Refreshments may be taken at the nearby family restaurant. For further details and the Travelodge phone number, consult the Hotel Groups page.
ROOMS: 45 en suite **CONF:** Thtr 20 Class 20 Board 20

⌂ *Travelodge*
387 Basingstoke Rd RG2 0JE
☎ 01734 750618 🖹 01734 750618
Dir: *on A33, southbound*
This modern building offers accommodation in smart, spacious and well equipped bedrooms, all with en suite bathrooms. Refreshments may be taken at the nearby family restaurant. For further details and the Travelodge phone number, consult the Hotel Groups page.
ROOMS: 36 en suite

⌂ Premier Lodge
Grazeley Rd RG7 1LS
☎ 0870 700 1500 🖹 0870 700 1501
Premier Lodge offers modern, well equipped, en suite accommodation suitable for both business and leisure travellers. Meals can be taken at the adjacent popular restaurant and bar which is fully licensed. For further details, consult the Hotel Groups page.
ROOMS: 32 en suite d £49.50 *

○ Comfort Inn Reading
Bath Rd, Padworth
☎ 0118 971 3282
ROOMS: 34 rms
NOTES: Open

○ Millennium Madejski Reading
Madejski Stadium RG2 0FL
☎ 0118 925 3500
Dir: *M4 junct 11*
ROOMS: 140 rms **NOTES:** Open

○ Quality Hotel Reading
648-654 Oxford Rd RG30 1EH
☎ 0118 950 0541
This purpose-built modern hotel is within easy reach of the city centre and is an excellent choice for the business traveller. Bedrooms are bright, spacious and well equipped with plenty of desk space. The comfortable lounge bar is furnished with leather sofas and is a relaxing place to have a drink. Whilst the current kitchen operation is rather limited, plans are afoot to improve this aspect of the hotel.
ROOMS: 95 rms **NOTES:** Open

REDDITCH, Worcestershire

Map 07 SP06

★★★69% *The Abbey Hotel Golf & Country Club*

Hither Green Ln, Dagnel End Rd, Bordesley B98 7BD
☎ 01527 63918 📠 01527 584112
Dir: *from M42 junct 2 take A441 to Redditch, at end dual carriage way turn left still on A441, Dagnell End Rd is on the left*

This large modern hotel complex is close to junction two of the M42, with access via the A411. Rooms are well equipped, spacious and attractively decorated. Public areas include a cosy restaurant with adjacent cocktail bar as well as a public bar. There are good leisure facilities and parking.
ROOMS: 38 en suite **FACILITIES:** Indoor swimming (H) Golf 18 Fishing Sauna Solarium Gym Putting green Jacuzzi/spa Steam room & Health Club **CONF:** Thtr 40 Class 24 Board 24 **PARKING:** 150 **NOTES:** No dogs (ex guide dogs) No smoking in restaurant **CARDS:**

★★★64% Quality Hotel

Pool Bank, Southcrest B97 4JS
☎ 01527 541511 📠 01527 402600
e-mail: admin@gb646.u-net.com
Dir: *follow signs to hotel, 2nd on right after B & Q DIY store*
Set in extensive wooded grounds, with delightful views and gardens, stands this former country house. Bedrooms vary in size and style, but all are tastefully furnished and well equipped. A varied choice of meals can be enjoyed in the refurbished restaurant or with a less formal feel, the bar/conservatory.
ROOMS: 73 en suite (2 fmly) No smoking in 16 bedrooms s £45-£105; d £58-£105 * LB **FACILITIES:** STV **CONF:** Thtr 100 Class 25 Board 50 Del from £105 * **PARKING:** 100 **NOTES:** No smoking in restaurant Civ Wed 100 **CARDS:**

★★62% *Montville*

101 Mount Pleasant, Southcrest B97 4JE
☎ 01527 544411 & 402566 📠 01527 544341
e-mail: hotelmontville@compuserve.com
Dir: *off M42 at junct 3 (A435) follow signs towards Redditch centre, then signs towards Southcrest (A441)*
This small and privately owned hotel lies less than half a mile from the town centre. It provides modern furnished and well equipped accommodation suitable for both business and leisure guests. Public areas include the pleasant 'Granny's' restaurant, a quaint bar and a homely lounge.
ROOMS: 16 en suite (2 fmly) No smoking in 5 bedrooms **CONF:** Thtr 60 Class 30 Board 24 **PARKING:** 12
CARDS:

⌂ Premier Lodge

Birchfield Rd B97 6PX
☎ 0870 700 1320 📠 0870 700 1321
Premier Lodge offers modern, well equipped, en suite accommodation suitable for both business and leisure travellers. Meals can be taken at the adjacent popular restaurant and bar which is fully licensed. For further details, consult the Hotel Groups page.
ROOMS: 33 en suite d £46 *

⌂ Campanile

Far Moor Ln, Winyates Green B98 0SD
☎ 01527 510710 📠 01527 517269
Dir: *A435 towards Redditch, then A4023 Redditch/Bromsgrove*

This modern building offers accommodation in smart well equipped bedrooms, all with en suite bathrooms. Refreshments may be taken at the informal Bistro. For further details and the Campanile phone number, consult the Hotel Groups page.
ROOMS: 50 annexe en suite **CONF:** Thtr 35 Class 18 Board 20

REDHILL, Surrey

Map 04 TQ25

★★★★70% ❀ Nutfield Priory

Nutfield RH1 4EL
☎ 01737 824400 📠 01737 823321
e-mail: nutpriory@aol.com
Dir: *exit M25 junct 6 & follow signs to Redhill via Godstone on A25. Hotel 1m on left after Nutfield Village*

Built in 1872 as an extravagant folly, this Victorian country house is set in forty acres of grounds and has wonderful views over the Surrey and Sussex countryside. Bedrooms are individually styled and equipped with a comprehensive range of in room facilities. Public areas include the impressive grand hall, Cloisters restaurant, the library, and a cosy lounge bar area.

continued

REDHILL, continued

ROOMS: 60 en suite (4 fmly) No smoking in 12 bedrooms s £115-£140; d £140-£240 (incl. bkfst) * LB **FACILITIES:** STV Indoor swimming (H) Squash Sauna Solarium Gym Jacuzzi/spa Steam room Creche Beauty therapy Hairdressing Xmas **CONF:** Thtr 80 Class 45 Board 40 Del from £193 * **SERVICES:** Lift **PARKING:** 130 **NOTES:** No smoking in restaurant Civ Wed 60 **CARDS:**

REDRUTH, Cornwall & Isles of Scilly Map 02 SW64

★★★65% Penventon

TR15 1TE
☎ 01209 203000 📠 01209 203001
e-mail: penventon@bigfoot.com
Dir: *turn off A30 at Redruth, hotel is 1m S*

This Georgian mansion is conveniently located for the A30 and a short walk from Redruth town centre. Public areas are luxurious, and additional facilities include a health spa and the lively Spice of Life bar. There is a wide choice of bedrooms, with the largest incorporating separate sitting areas. The restaurant, featuring a pianist, offers extensive menus of Italian, French, British and Cornish dishes.
ROOMS: 50 en suite (3 fmly) No smoking in 6 bedrooms s £30-£50; d £58-£99 (incl. bkfst) * LB **FACILITIES:** Indoor swimming (H) Sauna Solarium Gym Pool table Jacuzzi/spa Leisure spa Masseuse Steam bath entertainment Xmas **CONF:** Thtr 200 Class 100 Board 60 Del from £38 * **PARKING:** 100 **NOTES:** Civ Wed 200 **CARDS:**

R

★★69% Aviary Court

Mary's Well, Illogan TR16 4QZ
☎ 01209 842256 📠 01209 843744
e-mail: aviarycourt@connexions.co.uk
Dir: *turn off A30 at sign A3047 Camborne, Pool & Portreath. Follow Portreath & Illogan signs for approx 2m to Alexandra Rd*
Peace and tranquillity are assured at this charming property set in well tended gardens on the edge of Illogan Woods. The bedrooms are individually furnished and decorated and provide many thoughtful extras. The generous meals make full use of Cornish produce - Sunday lunches are a speciality and booking is essential.
ROOMS: 6 en suite (1 fmly) s £43; d £62 (incl. bkfst) * **FACILITIES:** Tennis (hard) **PARKING:** 25 **NOTES:** No dogs No children 3yrs No smoking in restaurant **CARDS:**

★★67% Crossroads

Scorrier TR16 5BP
☎ 01209 820551 📠 01209 820392
e-mail: crossroads.hotel@talk21.com
Dir: *off A30, Scorrier/Helston exit*
A purpose-built hotel, bedrooms differ in style and decor, nine executive rooms offer extra space and facilities. Twenty-four hour room service is available. The intimate restaurant serves a choice of menus, there is a separate breakfast room, a convivial red-plush bar and a comfortable lounge area.
ROOMS: 36 en suite (4 fmly) No smoking in 4 bedrooms s £35-£44; d £42-£54 (incl. bkfst) * LB **FACILITIES:** Pool table **CONF:** Thtr 100 Class 30 Board 30 **SERVICES:** Lift **PARKING:** 140 **CARDS:**

REDWORTH, Co Durham Map 08 NZ22

★★★★71% Redworth Hall Hotel & Country Club

PARAMOUNT GROUP OF HOTELS

DL5 6NL
☎ 01388 770600 📠 01388 770654
e-mail: redworthhall@paramount-hotels.co.uk
Dir: *from A1(M) junct 68 take A68 'Corbridge'. Follow brown Hotel signs*

This grand Elizabethan styled hotel and health club makes a fine impression. There are several spacious, comfortable lounges, and two restaurants, of which the Blue Room is the best showcase for the chef's talents. Bedrooms are comfortable, stylish and well equipped and have benefited from refurbishment. Leisure, conference and banqueting facilities are also popular.
ROOMS: 100 en suite (8 fmly) No smoking in 48 bedrooms s fr £105; d fr £135 (incl. bkfst) * LB **FACILITIES:** STV Indoor swimming (H) Tennis (hard) Sauna Solarium Gym Croquet lawn Jacuzzi/spa Spa pool Health club Childrens indoor & outdoor play area Hair & beauty salon ch fac Xmas **CONF:** Thtr 300 Class 150 Board 100 Del from £125 * **SERVICES:** Lift **PARKING:** 300 **NOTES:** Civ Wed 220 **CARDS:**

REEPHAM, Norfolk Map 09 TG12

★★69% The Old Brewery House Hotel

Market Place NR10 4JJ
☎ 01603 870881 📠 01603 870969
e-mail: oldbrewery@norfolk-hotels.co.uk
Dir: *off A1067 Norwich-Fakenham. Take B1145 sigposted Aylsham*
In a market square location, the Old Brewery House is the focal point of Reepham, where both guests and locals enjoy its relaxed atmosphere. The friendly staff offer a warm welcome and helpful service is readily given. The attractive bedrooms are spacious and a wide range of facilities are provided. There is a popular, well equipped leisure centre, a new conservatory restaurant and a cosy lounge.
ROOMS: 23 en suite (2 fmly) No smoking in 7 bedrooms s fr £39.95; d fr £67.50 (incl. bkfst) * LB **FACILITIES:** Indoor swimming (H) Squash Sauna Solarium Gym Aerobics & Steps classes Swimming lessons entertainment Xmas **CONF:** Thtr 200 Class 150 Board 100 Del from £57.95 * **PARKING:** 60 **NOTES:** No dogs (ex guide dogs) Civ Wed 200 **CARDS:**

REIGATE, Surrey

Map 04 TQ25

★★★65% Bridge House

Reigate Hill RH2 9RP
☎ 01737 246801 & 244821 Fax 01737 223756
Dir: *on A217 between M25 and Reigate*

High on Reigate Hill, this established hotel has panoramic views over surrounding countryside. Bedrooms, many with balconies, are thoughtfully equipped. Lanni's restaurant offers a high standard of cooking with a strong Mediterranean influence, and features live music and dancing most nights.

ROOMS: 39 en suite (3 fmly) s £58; d £80-£130 * **FACILITIES:** STV entertainment Xmas **CONF:** Thtr 100 Class 70 Board 60 Del £136 * **PARKING:** 110 **NOTES:** No dogs (ex guide dogs) RS Bank Holidays **CARDS:**

See advert on this page

★★★65% Reigate Manor Hotel

Reigate Hill RH2 9PF
☎ 01737 240125 Fax 01737 223883
e-mail: hotel@reigatemanor.btinternet.com
Dir: *on A217, 1m S of junct 8 on M25*

Best Western

Located close to the town on Reigate Hill, this Georgian mansion is clean and well maintained. Good-sized bedrooms are well appointed and equipped and public areas inviting and comfortable. The hotel is a popular venue for both business meetings and social functions.

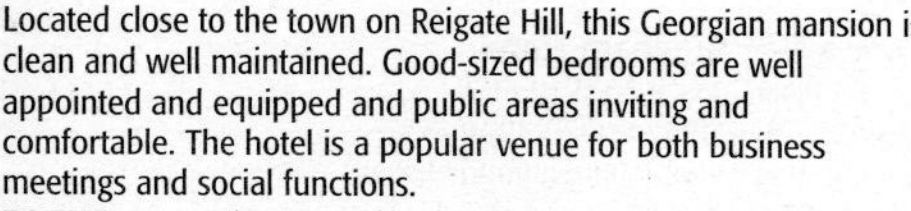

ROOMS: 50 en suite No smoking in 30 bedrooms s £95-£115; d £115-£135 * LB **FACILITIES:** STV Sauna Solarium Gym **CONF:** Thtr 200 Class 80 Board 50 Del from £130 * **PARKING:** 130 **NOTES:** No dogs (ex guide dogs) No smoking in restaurant Civ Wed 210 **CARDS:**

RENISHAW, Derbyshire

Map 08 SK47

★★★62% *Sitwell Arms*

Station Rd S21 3WF
☎ 01246 435226 Fax 01246 433915
Dir: *on A6135 to Sheffield, W of junct 30 of M1*

This stone-built hotel, parts of which date back to the 18th century, is conveniently situated close to the M1 and offers good value accommodation. Bedrooms are of a comfortable size, and offer the expected range of facilities and appointments. The public rooms offer a choice of bars and a restaurant, which provides a range of popular dishes and grills.

ROOMS: 30 en suite (6 fmly) No smoking in 10 bedrooms **CONF:** Thtr 160 Class 60 Board 60 **PARKING:** 150 **NOTES:** No dogs (ex guide dogs) **CARDS:**

See advert under SHEFFIELD

RICHMOND, North Yorkshire

Map 07 NZ10

★★68% King's Head

Market Place DL10 4HS
☎ 01748 850220 Fax 01748 850635
e-mail: res@kingsheadrichmond.co.uk
Dir: *in Richmond Market Place, 5m from A1/A66 at Scotch Corner on the A6108*

Best Western

Conveniently located in the historic market square, The Kings Head offers well equipped, modern bedrooms, and its lounges, furnished with deep sofas, display an interesting collection of antique clocks. Afternoon tea is worth sampling, whilst the restaurant offers a good choice for dinner.

ROOMS: 26 en suite 4 annexe en suite (1 fmly) No smoking in 11 bedrooms s £59-£79; d £89-£115 (incl. bkfst) * LB **FACILITIES:** STV Xmas **CONF:** Thtr 180 Class 80 Board 50 **PARKING:** 25 **NOTES:** No smoking in restaurant **CARDS:**

RICHMOND, continued

★★62% Frenchgate
59-61 Frenchgate DL10 7AE
☎ 01748 822087 📠 01748 823596
Dir: *turn off at Scotch Corner on the A6108 Richmond. Through Richmond to New Queens Road rdbt, turn left into Dundas St and left again into Frenchgate*
This small, personally run hotel offers a warm welcome to both leisure and business guests. The public rooms include a lounge bar and a cosy dining room. The majority of bedrooms have recently been stylishly refurbished and provide all the expected facilities.
ROOMS: 10 en suite 1 annexe en suite (1 fmly) No smoking in all bedrooms s £37; d £60 (incl. bkfst) * LB **FACILITIES:** Xmas **PARKING:** 9 **NOTES:** No smoking in restaurant
CARDS:

RICHMOND UPON THAMES, Greater London
See LONDON SECTION plan 1 C2

★★★★74% ❀❀ Richmond Gate
Richmond Hill TW10 6RP
corus
☎ 020 8940 0061 📠 020 8332 0354
e-mail: richmondgate@corus.co.uk
Dir: *from Richmond head to the top of Richmond hill and the hotel on left opposite the Star & Garter home at Richmond gate exit*

A stylish Georgian country ideal for both the leisure and corporate guest. Stylish bedrooms are equipped to a very high standard and include luxury doubles, spacious suites and smaller, more compact garden wing rooms. The Park Restaurant provides the highlight of any visit with bold contemporary cooking very much to the fore; enthusiasts of this style of cooking can join the hotels dining club! Cedars health and leisure club offers wide selection of fitness equipment and a large indoor pool.
ROOMS: 68 en suite (2 fmly) No smoking in 11 bedrooms s £139; d £165 (incl. bkfst) * LB **FACILITIES:** STV Indoor swimming (H) Sauna Solarium Gym Jacuzzi/spa Health & beauty suite Steam room entertainment Xmas **CONF:** Thtr 50 Class 25 Board 30 **PARKING:** 50 **NOTES:** No dogs (ex guide dogs) No smoking in restaurant Civ Wed 70
CARDS:

★★★69% Richmond Hill
Richmond Hill TW10 6RW
corus
☎ 020 8940 2247 & 8940 5466
📠 020 8940 5424
Dir: *located at the top of Richmond Hill on B321*
An imposing Georgian Manor house built in 1726 on Richmond Hill, nearby are views of the Thames and open parkland. Rooms come in a variety of sizes and styles. The restaurant offers a fixed price menu and an impressive array of dishes on its carte. The stylish, well designed health club with large pool is shared with sister hotel the Richmond Gate.

ROOMS: 138 en suite (9 fmly) No smoking in 48 bedrooms s £130-£140; d £150-£160 * LB **FACILITIES:** STV Indoor swimming (H) Sauna Solarium Gym Jacuzzi/spa Steam room Health & beauty suite entertainment Xmas **CONF:** Thtr 180 Class 150 Board 50 Del from £195 * **SERVICES:** Lift **PARKING:** 150 **NOTES:** Civ Wed 200
CARDS:

★★★60% Bingham Hotel
61-63 Petersham Rd TW10 6UT
☎ 020 8940 0902 📠 020 8948 8737
e-mail: reservation@binghamhotel.co.uk
Dir: *on A307*
Limited car-parking is a bonus at this Georgian period building within walking distance of the town centre. Bedrooms vary in size and style and some have wonderful river views.
ROOMS: 23 en suite **CONF:** Thtr 35 Class 14 Board 18 **PARKING:** 8
CARDS:

RINGWOOD, Hampshire — Map 04 SU10

★★★69% *Tyrrells Ford Country House*
Avon BH23 7BH
☎ 01425 672646 📠 01425 672262
Dir: *turn off A31 to Ringwood. Follow B3347, Hotel 3m S on left at Avon*
This friendly hotel is peacefully situated in 10 acres of grounds and woodland. There is a wide choice of menus available, whether guests wish to eat in the bar or the restaurant. Bedrooms are comfortably furnished and well equipped.
ROOMS: 16 en suite **CONF:** Thtr 40 Class 20 Board 20 **PARKING:** 100 **NOTES:** No dogs (ex guide dogs) No smoking in restaurant
CARDS:

★★71% ❀ Moortown Lodge Hotel
244 Christchurch Rd BH24 3AS
THE CIRCLE
Selected Individual Hotels
GREAT BRITAIN
☎ 01425 471404 📠 01425 476052
e-mail: hotel@burrows-jones.freeserve.co.uk
Dir: *off A31 onto B3347. Hotel 1.5m S on right*
This delightful little hotel is personally run by Jilly and Bob Burrows-Jones, who provide a warm welcome to their guests. The attractively decorated bedrooms are cosy, well maintained and have several thoughtful, extra features. Each evening, Jilly cooks an excellent fixed price menu, featuring honest cooking using local produce wherever possible.
ROOMS: 6 rms (5 en suite) (1 fmly) No smoking in 3 bedrooms s £50-£65; d £60-£85 (incl. bkfst) * LB **PARKING:** 8 **NOTES:** No dogs No smoking in restaurant Closed 24 Dec-mid Jan
CARDS:

★★64% Candlesticks Inn
136 Christchurch Rd BH24 3AP
☎ 01425 472587 📠 01425 471600
e-mail: roycoway@hotmail.com
Dir: *from M27/A31,take B3347 towards Christchurch, hotel on right hand side approx 0.5m from intersection/flyover*
This pretty 15th-century thatched inn, a consistent 'Ringwood in Bloom' winner, is situated on the edge of the town, conveniently located for the New Forest and major routes to the West Country and the coast. The well equipped bedrooms are located in a modern lodge to the rear, and include ground-floor rooms and one equipped for disabled guests. There is a bright conservatory bar-lounge where snacks can be taken, and a cosy beamed restaurant serving a more extensive menu.
ROOMS: 8 en suite (1 fmly) s fr £37; d fr £54 (incl. bkfst) * LB
PARKING: 45 **NOTES:** No dogs No children 2yrs Closed 23 Dec-9 Jan
CARDS:

RIPON, North Yorkshire Map 08 SE37

★★★69% Ripon Spa
Park St HG4 2BU
☎ 01765 602172 📠 01765 690770
e-mail: spahotel@bronco.co.uk
Dir: *follow signs to the B6265, at T junct to join this road, turn right back towards Ripon, hotel on this section of B6265*

Best Western

Situated in acres of attractive gardens, including well manicured croquet lawns, this traditional hotel, only a short walk from the city centre, provides comfortable and modern accommodation in a pleasant and relaxing environment. Many of the staff are long standing and traditional values are manifest in the hospitality and service provided. There are comfortable lounges, a terrace overlooking the gardens and the popular Turf Tavern. Traditional English cooking is served in the elegant main restaurant.
ROOMS: 40 en suite (5 fmly) s £73-£85; d £84-£102 (incl. bkfst) * LB
FACILITIES: STV Croquet lawn Xmas **CONF:** Thtr 150 Class 35 Board 40 Del £100 * **SERVICES:** Lift **PARKING:** 60 **NOTES:** Civ Wed 150
CARDS:

See advert under HARROGATE

★★63% Unicorn
Market Place HG4 1BP
☎ 01765 602202 📠 01765 690734
e-mail: info@unicorn-hotel.co.uk
Dir: *on south east corner of Market Place, 4m from A1 on A61*
There is plenty of history surrounding this hotel overlooking the market square. It offers pretty spacious, well furnished bedrooms, and public rooms include a popular bar with excellent murals depicting Ripon. There is a cosy rear dining room where a good range of dishes is available.
ROOMS: 33 en suite (4 fmly) s £47; d £67 (incl. bkfst) * LB
FACILITIES: STV entertainment **CONF:** Thtr 60 Class 10 Board 26 Del £72 * **PARKING:** 20 **NOTES:** Closed 24-25 Dec
CARDS:

RISLEY, Derbyshire Map 08 SK43

★★★72% Risley Hall
Derby Rd DE72 3SS
☎ 01159 399000 📠 01159 397766
Dir: *off junct 25 on M1, Sandiacre exit, left at T junct, 0.5m on left*
This impressive manor house, dating from the 11th century, is set in beautiful listed gardens. Relaxing areas include a choice of bars, morning room, private dining rooms and a grand baronial hall. Many of the individually styled bedrooms boast antique furnishings, exposed beams and wall timbers. An interesting menu is served, supplemented by daily dishes.
ROOMS: 16 en suite (8 fmly) s £85-£105; d £105-£115 * LB
FACILITIES: STV Indoor swimming (H) Snooker Gym Croquet lawn Jacuzzi/spa Archery Xmas **CONF:** Thtr 150 Class 80 Board 60 Del £145 * **SERVICES:** Lift **PARKING:** 100 **NOTES:** No dogs (ex guide dogs) No smoking in restaurant Civ Wed 120
CARDS:

See advert under DERBY

ROCHDALE, Greater Manchester Map 07 SD81

★★★★64% Norton Grange
Manchester Rd, Castleton OL11 2XZ
☎ 01706 630788 📠 01706 649313
Dir: *junct 20 of M62 follow signs for A627 (M) Oldham then A664 Middleton/Manchester then follow signs for Castleton on A664 on left*

MACDONALD HOTELS

Situated in nine acres of grounds this Victorian house provides modern standards of comfort. The well equipped bedrooms are in the process of refurbishment. Public areas include the Pickwick Bistro and Bar and a smart restaurant.
ROOMS: 51 en suite (28 fmly) No smoking in 25 bedrooms
FACILITIES: STV **CONF:** Thtr 250 Class 80 Board 60 **SERVICES:** Lift
PARKING: 150 **NOTES:** No smoking in restaurant
CARDS:

ROCHESTER, Kent Map 05 TQ76

★★★65% Posthouse Rochester
Maidstone Rd ME5 9SF
☎ 0870 400 9069 📠 01634 684512
Dir: *on A229 1m N of M2 jnct 3-from A229 head straight on over rdbt. Hotel and airport are signposted 100yds on the left*

Posthouse

Suitable for both the business and leisure traveller, this conveniently located hotel provides modern, well laid out bedrooms.
ROOMS: 145 en suite (45 fmly) No smoking in 93 bedrooms
FACILITIES: Indoor swimming (H) Sauna Solarium Gym Pool table Jacuzzi/spa Steam room Beautician available at charge **CONF:** Thtr 110 Class 48 Board 40 **SERVICES:** Lift **PARKING:** 250
CARDS:

R

ROCHESTER, continued

★68% Royal Victoria & Bull Hotel

16-18 High St ME1 1PX
☎ 01634 846266 📠 01634 832312
e-mail: reservations@ruandb.co.uk
Dir: *from M25 or London follow A2 into Rochester. Take second right after large bridge (over Medway River) then first right. Hotel located on the left*
A historic coaching inn, at the top end of the High Street, the Royal Victoria was visited by the Queen, its namesake, and features in some of Charles Dickens' novels. Its restaurant serves Italian food, and there is a popular bar. Bedrooms are smartly furnished.
ROOMS: 28 rms (24 en suite) (2 fmly) **FACILITIES:** STV Jacuzzi/spa **CONF:** Thtr 100 Class 60 Board 40 Del from £90 * **PARKING:** 25 **NOTES:** Closed 24 Dec-4 Jan **CARDS:**

ROCHFORD, Essex — Map 05 TQ89

★★★68% Hotel Renouf

Bradley Way SS4 1BU
☎ 01702 541334 📠 01702 549563
e-mail: reception@hotelrenouf.fsnet.co.uk
Dir: *turn off A127 onto B1013 to Rochford, at 3rd mini-rdbt turn right & keep right*

A smart establishment in the centre of Rochford, the Renouf is family owned and run. There is a comfortable bar filled with cricket and sporting memorabilia. The attractive French restaurant overlooks the garden and offers set-price and carte menus. Bedrooms are spacious and modern in style.
ROOMS: 24 en suite (2 fmly) **FACILITIES:** STV **CONF:** Thtr 30 Class 30 Board 20 **PARKING:** 25 **NOTES:** No smoking in restaurant Closed 26-31 Dec **CARDS:**

See advert on opposite page

ROMALDKIRK, Co Durham — Map 12 NY92

★★78% Rose & Crown

DL12 9EB
☎ 01833 650213 📠 01833 650828
e-mail: hotel@rose-and-crown.co.uk
Dir: *6m NW from Barnard Castle on B6277*

Located in a small village, this splendid Jacobean inn retains much of its original charm and character. It boasts a cosy pub with great bar food, a smart restaurant and a cosy lounge with lots to read. Stylish accommodation, all with luxurious bathrooms, includes refurbished bedrooms, two suites, and a stone-built row of spacious chalet-style rooms.
ROOMS: 7 en suite 5 annexe en suite (1 fmly) s £62; d £86 (incl. cont bkfst) * LB **FACILITIES:** STV **PARKING:** 20 **NOTES:** No smoking in restaurant Closed 24-26 Dec **CARDS:**

ROMFORD, Greater London — Map 05 TQ58

Premier Lodge

Whalebone Ln North, Chadwell Heath RM6 6QU
☎ 0870 700 1378 📠 0870 700 1379
PREMIER LODGE THE BEST. REST ASSURED.
Premier Lodge offers modern, well equipped, en suite accommodation suitable for both business and leisure travellers. Meals can be taken at the adjacent popular restaurant and bar which is fully licensed. For further details, consult the Hotel Groups page.
ROOMS: 40 en suite d £42 *

ROMSEY, Hampshire — Map 04 SU32

★★★67% Potters Heron

Winchester Rd, Ampfield SO51 9ZF
☎ 023 8026 6611 📠 023 8025 1359
corus
Dir: *M3 junct 12 follow signs for Chandlers Ford at rdbt take 2nd exit, follow signs for Ampfield, go over crossrds, hotel is on left hand side after 1m*

This distinctive thatched hotel retains many original features. Extensive refurbishment has taken place to offer a good standard of accommodation and public areas, all are comfortably and attractively furnished. The re-styled pub and restaurant operation offers an interesting range of dishes at dinner.
ROOMS: 54 en suite (4 fmly) No smoking in 32 bedrooms s fr £90; d fr £100 (incl. bkfst) * LB **FACILITIES:** STV Sauna entertainment Xmas **CONF:** Thtr 150 Class 70 Board 45 Del from £89.25 * **SERVICES:** Lift **PARKING:** 150 **NOTES:** No smoking in restaurant Civ Wed 60 **CARDS:**

★★★58% The White Horse

Market Place SO51 8ZJ
☎ 0870 400 8123 📠 01794 517485
HERITAGE HOTELS
Dir: *from M27 junct 3, follow A3057 to Romsey, then signs to town centre. Hotel can be seen on left, car park found on next turn on in Latimer St*
Set in the heart of this historic town, the White Horse dates back to Elizabethan times. Bedrooms, which are gradually being refurbished, are attractively furnished and equipped with modern amenities. Public areas include a large restaurant, separate bar and cosy lounge.

continued

ROOMS: 33 en suite (7 fmly) No smoking in 11 bedrooms s £60-£70; d £85-£90 * LB **FACILITIES:** Free use of nearby leisure facilities Xmas **CONF:** Thtr 40 Class 20 Board 20 Del from £80 * **PARKING:** 60 **NOTES:** No smoking in restaurant **CARDS:**

Premier Lodge (Southampton)
Romsey Rd, Ower SO51 6ZJ
☎ 0870 700 1542 ▯ 0870 700 1543

PREMIER LODGE

Premier Lodge offers modern, well equipped, en suite accommodation suitable for both business and leisure travellers. Meals can be taken at the adjacent popular restaurant and bar which is fully licensed. For further details, consult the Hotel Groups page.
ROOMS: 50 en suite d £46 *

ROSEDALE ABBEY, North Yorkshire — Map 08 SE79

★★★68% **Blacksmith's Country Inn**
Hartoft End YO18 8EN
☎ 01751 417331 ▯ 01751 417167
e-mail: blacksmiths.rosedale@virgin.net
Dir: *A64 from York turn off for Pickering A169. In Pickering turn left for Thirsk A170. Turn left at Wrelton sign post to Hartoft 5m*

This welcoming hotel enjoys a wonderful setting amongst the wooded valleys and hillsides of the Yorkshire Moors. The former farmhouse has a charming inn-like atmosphere, but with the expected hotel facilities and services. It offers a choice of bars and cosy lounges, plus the main feature, the popular dining room.
ROOMS: 18 en suite (1 fmly) **FACILITIES:** Pool table **PARKING:** 60 **NOTES:** No smoking in restaurant **CARDS:**

See advert on this page

★★72% **Milburn Arms**
YO18 8RA
☎ 01751 417312 ▯ 01751 417312
e-mail: info@milburnarms.com
Dir: *7m N off A170 from Wrelton village*
Set in the centre of a village on the North Yorkshire Moors, this welcoming hotel dates in parts back to the 16th century. The well equipped bedrooms vary in style between traditional and modern, there is a delightful bar, a comfortable lounge, and the Priory Restaurant for good food.
ROOMS: 3 en suite 8 annexe en suite (2 fmly) s £41.50-£45.50; d £64-£76 (incl. bkfst) * LB **CONF:** Thtr 48 Board 16 Del from £85 * **PARKING:** 35 **NOTES:** No children 8yrs No smoking in restaurant Closed 23-27 Dec & 12-29 Jan Civ Wed 65 **CARDS:**

Popped the question? Hotels with Civ Wed in their entry are licensed for civil wedding ceremonies. Maximum numbers for the ceremony only are shown, e.g. Civ Wed 50

ROSEDALE ABBEY, continued

★★65% White Horse Farm

YO18 8SE
☎ 01751 417239 01751 417781
e-mail: sarah@midnorth.fsnet.co.uk
Dir: *turn off A170, follow signs to Rosedale for approx 7m, hotel sign points up steep hill out of village, hotel 300yds on left*

From its position above the village, this hotel enjoys lovely views over the moors. Bedrooms, whether in the main house or an adjoining building in the gardens, are individually and attractively decorated. Meals are served in the bar or in the restaurant, and there is also a residents' lounge.

ROOMS: 11 en suite 4 annexe en suite (3 fmly) s £43-£47.50; d £66-£87 (incl. bkfst) * LB **FACILITIES:** Xmas **PARKING:** 100 **NOTES:** No smoking in restaurant **CARDS:**

ROSSINGTON, South Yorkshire Map 08 SK69

★★★72% Mount Pleasant

Best Western

Great North Rd DN11 0HW
☎ 01302 868696 & 868219 01302 865130
e-mail: mountpleasant@fax.co.uk
Dir: *on A638 Great North Rd between Bawtry and Doncaster*

This charming house dates back to the 18th-century and stands in 100 acres of wooded parkland. Bedrooms have been thoughtfully equipped and pleasantly furnished, the new Premier bedrooms being particularly spacious. There are comfortable lounges, a small bar and a traditionally styled restaurant.

ROOMS: 42 en suite (15 fmly) No smoking in all bedrooms s £57-£82; d £72-£98 (incl. bkfst) * LB **CONF:** Thtr 100 Class 50 Board 50 Del £105 * **PARKING:** 100 **NOTES:** No dogs (ex guide dogs) No smoking in restaurant Closed 25 Dec Civ Wed 110
CARDS:

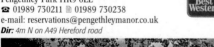

ROSS-ON-WYE, Herefordshire Map 03 SO62
see also Goodrich and Symonds Yat

★★★77% Pengethley Manor

Best Western

Pengethley Park HR9 6LL
☎ 01989 730211 01989 730238
e-mail: reservations@pengethleymanor.co.uk
Dir: *4m N on A49 Hereford road*

This fine Georgian mansion is set in extensive grounds with two vineyards. The accommodation is tastefully appointed and there is a wide variety of bedroom styles, all similarly well equipped. The elegant public rooms are furnished in a style sympathetic to the character of the house.

ROOMS: 11 en suite 14 annexe en suite (3 fmly) **FACILITIES:** Outdoor swimming (H) Golf 9 Fishing Snooker Croquet lawn Golf improvement course **CONF:** Thtr 50 Class 25 Board 28 Del from £105 *
PARKING: 70 **NOTES:** No smoking in restaurant Civ Wed 70
CARDS:

See advert on opposite page

★★★70% *Hunsdon Manor*

Gloucester Rd, Weston under Penyard HR9 7PE
☎ 01989 562748 & 563376 & 768348 01989 768348
Dir: *two miles east of M50 on the A40 road to Gloucester*

Hunsdon Manor is built of mellow local sandstone and dates back to Elizabethan times. Set in extensive grounds, it stands in the village of Weston under Penyard and offers accommodation ranging from rooms large enough for family use, to some with four-posters, and some on the ground and first floors of cleverly converted buildings near the main house. Public rooms include a pleasant bar and a very attractive restaurant.

ROOMS: 12 en suite 13 annexe en suite (3 fmly) **CONF:** Thtr 60 Class 46 Board 36 **PARKING:** 55 **CARDS:**

See advert on opposite page

★★★69% Chase

Gloucester Rd HR9 5LH
☎ 01989 763161 01989 768330
e-mail: info@chasehotel.co.uk
Dir: *leave M50 at junct 4, 1st left exit towards rdbt, left at rdbt towards A40. Right at 2nd rdbt towards Ross-on-Wye town centre, hotel 0.5m on left*

This Regency mansion is set in extensive grounds and gardens within easy reach of the town centre. Bedrooms vary in size, all have modern furnishings and are well equipped. Four-poster rooms are available. Public rooms include an attractive restaurant, a pleasant bar and lounge. Other facilities include conference rooms and a large function suite. The hotel is a popular venue for wedding receptions.

ROOMS: 36 en suite (1 fmly) No smoking in 10 bedrooms s £60-£85; d £75-£100 (incl. bkfst) * LB **FACILITIES:** STV leisure facilities available outside hotel with transport provided **CONF:** Thtr 300 Class 100 Board 50 **PARKING:** 200 **NOTES:** No dogs (ex guide dogs) No children 12yrs No smoking in restaurant Closed 26-30 Dec Civ Wed 100
CARDS:

TV dinner? Room service at three stars and above.

R

R

ROSS-ON-WYE, continued

★★★68% Pencraig Court

Pencraig HR9 6HR
☎ 01989 770306 01989 770040
e-mail: mike@pencraig-court.co.uk
Dir: *off A40, 4m S of Ross-on-Wye*
A large Georgian house, standing in extensive grounds and gardens, with impressive views of the River Wye. Personally run, it provides well equipped, traditionally furnished accommodation, including family rooms and a room with a four-poster. There is no bar, but drinks are dispensed in both lounges and the restaurant.
ROOMS: 11 en suite (1 fmly) **FACILITIES:** Fishing Riding Croquet lawn ch fac **CONF:** Board 20 **PARKING:** 20 **NOTES:** No smoking in restaurant **CARDS:**

See advert on page 467

★★★66% The Royal

Palace Pound HR9 5HZ
☎ 01989 565105 01989 768058
Dir: *at end of M50 take A40 'Monmouth'. At 3rd rdbt, take left to Ross, over bridge and take road signed 'The Royal Hotel' after left hand bend*

A new owner took over this hotel at the beginning of 2000 and at the time of our last inspection, he had made a lot of improvements to the public areas and bedrooms. The hotel enjoys a delightful location overlooking the River Wye and just a few minutes walk from the town centre. In addition to the comfortable lounge and attractively appointed restaurant, facilities here include a lovely garden and a choice of rooms for functions and conferences.
ROOMS: 40 en suite (3 fmly) No smoking in 11 bedrooms s £60-£65; d £80-£100 (incl. bkfst) * LB **FACILITIES:** STV Xmas **CONF:** Thtr 80 Class 50 Board 30 Del from £100 * **PARKING:** 38 **NOTES:** No smoking in restaurant Civ Wed **CARDS:**

R

★★74% Glewstone Court

Glewstone HR9 6AW
☎ 01989 770367 01989 770282
e-mail: glewstone@aol.com
Dir: *from Ross Market Place take A40/A49 Monmouth/Hereford, over Wilton Bridge to rdbt, turn left onto A40 to Monmouth, after 1m turn right for Glewstone*

Surrounded by three acres of mature grounds, this country house hotel offers a friendly and relaxed environment for both leisure and business guests. Informal service is delivered enthusiastically with owner Bill Reeve-Tucker leading from the front. The kitchen is the domain of Christine Reeve-Tucker who offers an extensive menu of well executed dishes. Throughout, the hotel is decorated and furnished with great flair.
ROOMS: 8 en suite (2 fmly) s £45-£62; d £92-£108 (incl. bkfst) * LB **FACILITIES:** Croquet lawn **CONF:** Thtr 35 Board 16 **PARKING:** 25 **NOTES:** Closed 25-27 Dec **CARDS:**

★★68% King's Head

8 High St HR9 5HL
☎ 01989 763174 01989 769578
e-mail: enquires@kingshead.co.uk
Dir: *near Ancient Town Centre on the High St*
Located in the town centre, this 14th-century coaching inn provides well-equipped accommodation, including some in a converted stable block. The traditionally-furnished dining room serves a good choice of popular dishes, while the bar has much charm and character and there is a comfortable coffee lounge.
ROOMS: 14 en suite 11 annexe en suite (6 fmly) s £43.50; d £75 (incl. bkfst) * LB **FACILITIES:** Xmas **PARKING:** 26 **NOTES:** No smoking in restaurant Closed 24-26 Dec **CARDS:**

★★66% Bridge House

Wilton HR9 6AA
☎ 01989 562655 01989 567652
Dir: *0.5m N of Ross-on-Wye, at joining of A40/A49 is a rdbt at Wilton, hotel 200yds from rdbt, towards Ross, at end of Wilton Bridge*
This Georgian house has a large garden extending to the bank of the River Wye. The privately owned and personally run hotel has a well deserved reputation for friendliness. Modern equipped accommodation includes several spacious rooms, and one with a four-poster bed.
ROOMS: 8 en suite (1 fmly) s £36-£37; d £55 (incl. bkfst) * LB **FACILITIES:** Xmas **PARKING:** 14 **NOTES:** No smoking in restaurant **CARDS:**

★★65% Castle Lodge Hotel

Wilton HR9 6AD
☎ 01989 562234 01989 768322
e-mail: carlos@castlelodge.co.uk
Dir: *on rdbt at junct of A40/A49, 0.5m from centre of Ross-on-Wye*
Dating back to the 16th century, with exposed timbers, this friendly hotel provides pleasant bedrooms, most of them

continued

pine-furnished. A good range of bar meals is offered, together with a varied restaurant menu, served in the cane-furnished restaurant. A large function room is available.
ROOMS: 10 en suite (3 fmly) s fr £40; d fr £53 (incl. bkfst) * LB
CONF: Thtr 100 Class 80 Board 60 **PARKING:** 40
CARDS:

★★65% Chasedale

Walford Rd HR9 5PQ
☎ 01989 562423 01989 567900
e-mail: chasedale@supanet.com
Dir: *from Ross-on-Wye town centre head south on B4234, hotel 0.5m on left*
A large, mid-Victorian country house in extensive gardens, the privately owned and personally run Chasedale provides well equipped accommodation, including ground-floor and family rooms. There is a spacious lounge and a restaurant with a good selection of wholesome food.
ROOMS: 10 en suite (2 fmly) No smoking in 1 bedroom s £32.50-£33; d £65-£66 (incl. bkfst) * LB **FACILITIES:** Xmas **CONF:** Thtr 40 Class 30 Board 25 **PARKING:** 14 **NOTES:** No smoking in restaurant
CARDS:

★★65% Orles Barn

THE CIRCLE
Selected Individual Hotels
GREAT BRITAIN

Wilton HR9 6AE
☎ 01989 562155 01989 768470
e-mail: orles.barn@clara.net
Dir: *off junct A40/A49*
This privately owned and personally run hotel stands in extensive gardens, which have an outdoor heated swimming pool. Bedrooms are well maintained and equipped and the owners' South African heritage is reflected in the menus.
ROOMS: 9 en suite (1 fmly) s £40-£45; d £45-£55 * LB
FACILITIES: Outdoor swimming (H) Fishing **CONF:** Board 16 Del from £50 * **PARKING:** 16 **NOTES:** No smoking in restaurant
CARDS:

ROSTHWAITE, Cumbria — Map 11 NY21

see also Borrowdale

★★63% *Scafell*

CA12 5XB
☎ 017687 77208 017687 77280
e-mail: scafellhotel@aol.com
Dir: *6m S of Keswick on B5289*

An established hotel run by an experienced and friendly team. A wide ranging menu of imaginative dishes is presented in the spacious dining room, or you can enjoy supper in the cocktail bar and the less formal 'Walkers Inn' pub. There is a wide choice of accommodation with the most sylish rooms in the main house.
ROOMS: 24 en suite (3 fmly) **PARKING:** 50 **NOTES:** No smoking in restaurant **CARDS:**

★69% Royal Oak

CA12 5XB
☎ 017687 77214 017687 77214
e-mail: royaloak@ukgateway.net
Set in a village in one of Lakeland's most picturesque valleys, this family-run hotel offers friendly and obliging service. A variety of accommodation styles are available, with particularly impressive rooms located in a converted barn across the courtyard. There is a choice of lounges and a cosy bar. A set home-cooked dinner is served at 7pm.
ROOMS: 11 rms (8 en suite) 4 annexe en suite (6 fmly) s £34-£50; d £60-£90 (incl. bkfst & dinner) * LB **PARKING:** 15 **NOTES:** No smoking in restaurant Closed 7-18 Jan & 2-27 Dec
CARDS:

ROTHERHAM, South Yorkshire — Map 08 SK49

★★★★63% Hellaby Hall

PARAMOUNT
GROUP OF HOTELS

Old Hellaby Ln, Hellaby S66 8SN
☎ 01709 702701 01709 700979
e-mail: hellabyhallreservations@paramount-hotels.co.uk
Dir: *1m off junct 1 of the M18 on the A631 towards Bawtry from Rotherham, in village of Hellaby*
This 17th-century hotel was built according to a Flemish design with high, beamed ceilings of grand proportions, and staircases which lead off to the private meeting rooms and a series of oak-panelled lounges. Bedrooms are all decorated in a similarly elegant style. Guests can dine in the formal Attic Restaurant, or Rizzio's informal restaurant/bar.

continued

R

ROTHERHAM, continued

ROOMS: 52 en suite (4 fmly) No smoking in 15 bedrooms s fr £90; d fr £105 * LB **FACILITIES:** STV Indoor swimming (H) Sauna Solarium Gym Croquet lawn Putting green Jacuzzi/spa Petanque Outdoor skittles Health Club entertainment Xmas **CONF:** Thtr 140 Class 75 Board 40 Del £130 * **SERVICES:** Lift **PARKING:** 235 **NOTES:** No smoking in restaurant Civ Wed 100 **CARDS:**

★★★71% Consort

Brampton Rd, Thurcroft S66 9JA
☎ 01709 530022 🖹 01709 531529
e-mail: info@consorthotel.com

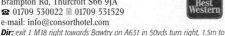

Dir: *exit 1 M18 right towards Bawtry on A631 in 50yds turn right, 1.5m to crossroads hotel opposite*

Bedrooms at this friendly modern hotel are comfortable and attractively decorated, with the added benefit of air conditioning. A wide range of dishes is offered in the bar and restaurant area. A quiet comfortable foyer lounge is also available. Excellent conference and function facilities include one suite catering for up to 300 people.

ROOMS: 27 en suite (2 fmly) No smoking in 6 bedrooms s £40-£70; d £60-£80 (incl. bkfst) * LB **FACILITIES:** STV **CONF:** Thtr 300 Class 120 Board 50 Del £100 * **PARKING:** 90 **NOTES:** No dogs (ex guide dogs) **CARDS:**

★★★68% Swallow

West Bawtry Rd S60 4NA
☎ 01709 830630 🖹 01709 830549
e-mail: info@swallowhotelseurope.com

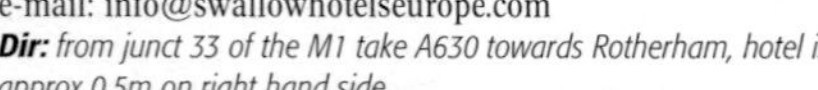

Dir: *from junct 33 of the M1 take A630 towards Rotherham, hotel is approx 0.5m on right hand side*

This large modern hotel is well situated for the motorway and the town centre. The bedrooms are spacious and well equipped. A good standard of cooking is provided in the restaurant and an interesting range of snacks is also offered.

ROOMS: 100 en suite (5 fmly) No smoking in 47 bedrooms s £44-£95; d £88-£120 (incl. bkfst) * LB **FACILITIES:** STV Indoor swimming (H) Solarium Gym Jacuzzi/spa Steam room Childrens pool Xmas **CONF:** Thtr 300 Class 120 Board 40 Del from £120 * **SERVICES:** Lift **PARKING:** 222 **NOTES:** Civ Wed 100 **CARDS:**

★★★67% Elton

Main St, Bramley S66 2SF
☎ 01709 545681 🖹 01709 549100
e-mail: bestwestern.eltonhotel@btinternet.com

Dir: *0.5m E A631, from M18 junct 1 follow A631 Rotherham, turn right to Ravenfield, hotel at end Bramley village*

Within easy reach of the M18, this welcoming, stone-built hotel with well tended gardens offers good accommodation. The larger rooms in the outbuilding are particularily comfortable and well equipped. A civil licence is held for wedding ceremonies and conference rooms are available.

ROOMS: 13 en suite 16 annexe en suite (4 fmly) No smoking in 5 bedrooms s £56-£72; d £80 * LB **FACILITIES:** STV **CONF:** Thtr 50 Class 24 Board 26 Del from £85 * **PARKING:** 48 **NOTES:** Civ Wed 50 **CARDS:**

★★★61% Carlton Park

102/104 Moorgate Rd S60 2BG
☎ 01709 849955 🖹 01709 368960
e-mail: 114317.2341@compuserve.com

Dir: *M1 junct 33, turn right onto A631 (Bawtry) and left onto A618. Hotel 800yds past Rotherham General Hospital*

This modern hotel is situated in a pleasant residential area of the town close to the District General Hospital. Bedrooms are furnished in a modern style and three have separate sitting rooms. The "Nelsons" Restaurant and Bar provides a lively atmosphere.

ROOMS: 76 en suite (6 fmly) No smoking in 33 bedrooms d £75 * LB **FACILITIES:** STV Sauna Solarium Gym Jacuzzi/spa entertainment Xmas **CONF:** Thtr 250 Class 160 Board 60 Del from £85 * **SERVICES:** Lift **PARKING:** 95 **NOTES:** Civ Wed 100 **CARDS:**

Campanile

Hellaby Industrial Estate, Lowton Way, Denby Way S66 8RY
☎ 01709 700255 🖹 01709 545169

Dir: *junct 1 of M18. Follow directions to Maltby off rdbt. At traffic lights turn left and take 2nd road on left*

This modern building offers accommodation in smart well equipped bedrooms, all with en suite bathrooms. Refreshments may be taken at the informal Bistro. For further details and the Campanile phone number, consult the Hotel Groups page.

ROOMS: 50 en suite **CONF:** Thtr 35 Class 18 Board 20

Early start? Hotels at all star levels should provide in-room alarm clocks and/or alarm calls.

⌂ Express by Holiday Inn Rotherham
Moorhead Way, Bramley S66 1YY
☎ 01709 730333 📠 730444
e-mail: rotherham@premierhotels.co.uk
Dir: *M18 J1. Left at rdbt. Left At 1st lights. Next to supermarket*

A modern budget hotel offering comfortable accommodation in refreshing, spacious and comprehensively-equipped bedrooms, en suite bathrooms with power showers. Suitable for business travellers or families. For further details consult Hotel Groups page.
ROOMS: 86 en suite (incl. cont bkfst) d £49.50 * **CONF:** Thtr 40 Class 12 Board 20 Del £80 *

ROTHERWICK, Hampshire — Map 04 SU75

Premier Collection

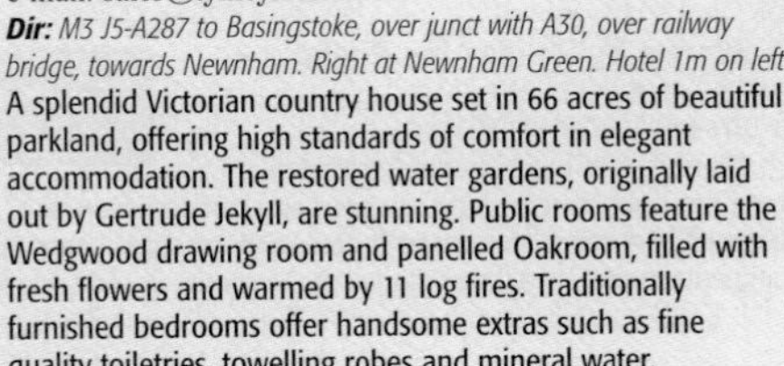

★★★★ Tylney Hall
RG27 9AZ
☎ 01256 764881 📠 01256 768141
e-mail: sales@tylneyhall.com
Dir: *M3 J5-A287 to Basingstoke, over junct with A30, over railway bridge, towards Newnham. Right at Newnham Green. Hotel 1m on left*
A splendid Victorian country house set in 66 acres of beautiful parkland, offering high standards of comfort in elegant accommodation. The restored water gardens, originally laid out by Gertrude Jekyll, are stunning. Public rooms feature the Wedgwood drawing room and panelled Oakroom, filled with fresh flowers and warmed by 11 log fires. Traditionally furnished bedrooms offer handsome extras such as fine quality toiletries, towelling robes and mineral water.
ROOMS: 35 en suite 75 annexe en suite (1 fmly) s £120-£299; d £152-£330 (incl. bkfst) * LB **FACILITIES:** STV Indoor swimming (H) Outdoor swimming (H) Tennis (hard) Snooker Sauna Gym Croquet lawn Jacuzzi/spa Clay pigeon shooting Archery Falconry Xmas **CONF:** Thtr 110 Class 70 Board 40 Del from £215 * **PARKING:** 120 **NOTES:** No dogs (ex guide dogs) No smoking in restaurant Civ Wed 100 **CARDS:**

See advert under BASINGSTOKE

ROTHLEY, Leicestershire — Map 08 SK51

★★★60% Rothley Court
Westfield Ln LE7 7LG
☎ 0116 237 4141 📠 0116 237 4483
Dir: *on B5328*
In places dating back to the 11th century, Rothley Court stands in six acres of gardens edged by the river and rolling hills. The public areas are impressive, dominated by a chapel of the Knights Templar, and full of original features and historical charm, even a suit of armour. Accommodation is offered either in the traditionally furnished rooms of the main house, or modern garden annexe bedrooms.
ROOMS: 13 en suite 21 annexe en suite No smoking in 14 bedrooms **CONF:** Thtr 100 Class 35 Board 35 **PARKING:** 100 **NOTES:** No smoking in restaurant **CARDS:**

★★72% The Limes
35 Mountsorrel Ln LE7 7PS
☎ 0116 230 2531
Dir: *turn of old A6, Hotel off village green*
The Limes, just beyond the village green, is owned and run by Mr and Mrs Soper. Public areas offer a comfortable lounge bar and a smart restaurant. The well maintained accommodation is equipped for the needs of the predominantly business clientele, with excellent facilities and comfortable executive swivel chairs.
ROOMS: 11 en suite s £42.50-£49.50; d £55-£65 (incl. bkfst) * **FACILITIES:** STV **SERVICES:** air con **PARKING:** 15 **NOTES:** No dogs (ex guide dogs) No children 14yrs No smoking in restaurant Closed 23 Dec-2 Jan **CARDS:**

ROWSLEY, Derbyshire — Map 08 SK26

★★★74% East Lodge Country House
DE4 2EF
☎ 01629 734474 📠 01629 733949
e-mail: info@eastlodge.com
Dir: *A6, Rowsley Village, 3m from Bakewell, 5m from Matlock*

A delightful country house hotel situated in ten acres of attractive grounds and gardens just off the A6 in the village of Rowsley. Public areas and most bedrooms have been refurbished to a very comfortable standard and a new conservatory lounge has been added to the front of the hotel. Bedrooms are individually furnished and decorated, one has a four poster bed and another, on the ground floor, is equipped for disabled persons. The main restaurant, which is well known for the quality of its cuisine, is open for lunch and dinner whilst lighter meals are available in the lounges. Traditional Sunday lunch is very much a feature and "Derbyshire Cream Teas" are also available.
ROOMS: 15 en suite (2 fmly) s £75-£90; d £95-£125 (incl. bkfst) * LB **FACILITIES:** Croquet lawn Xmas **CONF:** Thtr 75 Class 20 Board 22 Del from £105 * **PARKING:** 25 **NOTES:** No dogs No smoking in restaurant Civ Wed 74 **CARDS:**

See advert under BAKEWELL

RUAN HIGH LANES, Cornwall & Isles of Scilly Map 02 SW93

★★75% Hundred House
TR2 5JR
☎ 01872 501336 01872 501151
Dir: *from A390, 4m W of St Austell turn left onto B3287 to Tregony/St Mawes, turn left onto A3078 to St Mawes, hotel 4m along on right*
This Edwardian house on the Roseland Peninsula lies in one of the prettiest parts of Cornwall. The grounds and gardens are beautifully kept and include a croquet lawn. The house is tastefully furnished with fine antiques and pictures, and the bedrooms offer modern comforts and facilities. Guests meet in the bar before enjoying the award-winning cuisine in the restaurant.
ROOMS: 10 en suite No smoking in all bedrooms s £65-£73; d £130-£146 (incl. bkfst & dinner) * LB **FACILITIES:** Croquet lawn
PARKING: 15 **NOTES:** No children 8yrs No smoking in restaurant Closed Nov-Feb **CARDS:**

RUGBY, Warwickshire Map 04 SP57

★★★67% Brownsover Hall
REGAL
Brownsover Ln, Old Brownsover CV21 1HU
☎ 01788 546100 01788 579241
Dir: *come off M6 junct 1 and follow signs to Rugby A426, follow dual carriageway for 0.5m until slip road to right, follow for 400m, hotel on right*

A mock-Gothic hall in seven acres of wooded parkland. Bedrooms are spacious and well equipped, sixteen new rooms are being created in the converted stable block. The former chapel makes a stylish restaurant with mullion windows and stately chandeliers. For a less formal meal or a relaxing drink, the rugby themed bar is popular.
ROOMS: 27 en suite 20 annexe en suite (3 fmly) No smoking in 31 bedrooms s £70-£99; d £80-£130 * LB **FACILITIES:** STV Xmas
CONF: Thtr 70 Class 36 Board 35 Del from £110 * **PARKING:** 100
NOTES: No smoking in restaurant Civ Wed 56
CARDS:

★★★66% *Posthouse Northampton/ Rugby*
Posthouse
NN6 7XR
☎ 0870 400 9059 01788 823955
(For full entry see Crick)

★★65% Grosvenor Hotel Rugby
81-87 Clifton Rd CV21 3QQ
☎ 01788 535686 01788 541297
Dir: *M6 junct 1, turn right on to A426 towards Rugby centre, at first rdbt turn left continue to T junct and turn right onto B5414 hotel in 2m on right*
Close to the town centre, this family owned hotel is popular with both business and leisure guests. Bedrooms come in a variety of styles and sizes, including several new rooms. The public rooms are cosy, inviting and pleasantly furnished and service is both friendly and attentive.
ROOMS: 26 en suite (3 fmly) s £45-£74.50; d £58-£84.50 * LB
FACILITIES: Indoor swimming (H) Sauna Solarium Jacuzzi/spa Xmas
CONF: Thtr 30 Class 20 Board 30 Del from £102 * **PARKING:** 50
NOTES: No dogs (ex guide dogs) **CARDS:**

★★65% Hillmorton Manor
78 High St, Hillmorton CV21 4EE
☎ 01788 565533 & 572403 01788 540027
Dir: *leave M1 junct 18 & onto A428 to Rugby*
A Victorian manor house on the outskirts of Rugby. Public rooms are very inviting, and include a pleasant lounge bar and attractive restaurant, a good range of well prepared food is served. There is a wide choice of bedroom sizes; all rooms are well equipped.
ROOMS: 11 en suite (1 fmly) **CONF:** Class 30 Board 65 **PARKING:** 40
NOTES: No smoking in restaurant **CARDS:**

★★63% *Whitefields Hotel Golf & Country Club*
MINOTEL Great Britain
Coventry Rd, Thurlaston CV23 9JR
☎ 01788 521800 & 522393 01788 521695
Dir: *4m SW close to junc 1 M45*
A purpose built hotel situated on an 18-hole golf course. Bedrooms come in varying styles and sizes, with ground floor rooms being generally more spacious; a new wing of bedrooms was nearing completion at the time of our last visit. An open plan bar and lounge offers comfortable seating, and there are several well equipped conference suites available; public areas are shared with golf club members.
ROOMS: 34 en suite (2 fmly) No smoking in all bedrooms
FACILITIES: STV Golf 18 Fishing Putting green Driving range
CONF: Thtr 80 Class 50 Board 45 **PARKING:** 150 **NOTES:** No dogs (ex guide dogs) **CARDS:**

Express by Holiday Inn Rugby
Express by Holiday Inn
Brownsover Rd CV21 1HL
☎ 01788 550333 01788 550666
A modern budget hotel offering comfortable accommodation in refreshing, spacious and comprehensively-equipped bedrooms, en suite bathrooms with power showers and continental buffet breakfast included in the room rate. Suitable for

continued

business travellers or families. For further details and the Express by Holiday Inn phone number, consult the Hotel Groups page.
ROOMS: 49 en suite (incl. cont bkfst) d £49.95 * **CONF:** Thtr 30 Class 12 Board 16

RUGELEY, Staffordshire

Map 07 SK01

⌂ *Travelodge*

Travelodge

Western Springs Rd WS15 2AS
☎ 01889 570096 Fax 01889 570096
Dir: *on A51/B5013*
This modern building offers accommodation in smart, spacious and well equipped bedrooms, all with en suite bathrooms. Refreshments may be taken at the nearby family restaurant. For further details and the Travelodge phone number, consult the Hotel Groups page.
ROOMS: 32 en suite

RUISLIP, Greater London

See LONDON SECTION plan 1 *A5*

★★★62% Barn Hotel
West End Rd HA4 6JB
☎ 01895 636057 Fax 01895 638379
Dir: *take A4180 (Polish War Memorial) exit off the A40 to Ruislip, 2m to hotel entrance off a mini rdbt before Ruislip Underground Station*

The oldest parts of this sympathetically extended hotel date back to 1628. Today, there is a mixture of older rooms, with beams and uneven floors, and recently added modern rooms. All are comfortable and feature a good range of extra facilities. Snacks are served in the informal bar or meals can be taken in the Leaning Barn Restaurant.
ROOMS: 57 en suite (3 fmly) No smoking in 3 bedrooms s £88-£94; d £94-£100 (incl. bkfst) * LB **FACILITIES:** STV Xmas **CONF:** Thtr 100 Class 50 Board 40 Del from £145 * **PARKING:** 60 **NOTES:** No smoking in restaurant Civ Wed 50 **CARDS:**

See advert on this page

RUNCORN, Cheshire

Map 07 SJ58

★★★66% *Posthouse Warrington/ Runcorn*

Posthouse

Wood Ln, Beechwood WA7 3HA
☎ 0870 400 9070 Fax 01928 714611
Dir: *off M56 junc 12, turn left at roundabout then 100 yards on left turn into Halton Station Road under a railway bridge and continue into Wood Lane*
A modern hotel, conveniently situated just off junction 12 of the M56. Ample parking and spacious, comfortable, public areas make it an ideal venue for impromptu meetings as well as more formal gatherings. Bedrooms have every modern facilities and are shortly to be upgraded. The spacious Seasons restaurant is open for lunch and dinner and an all day menu is provided in the lounge and bar. 24 hour room service is also available. There are excellent conference and meeting facilities and a very well equipped leisure club which includes an indoor heated swimming pool.
ROOMS: 135 en suite No smoking in 86 bedrooms **FACILITIES:** Indoor swimming (H) Sauna Solarium Gym Pool table Jacuzzi/spa Beauty therapy Steam room **CONF:** Thtr 500 Class 60 Board 36 **SERVICES:** Lift **PARKING:** 210 **CARDS:**

⌂ Campanile

Campanile

Lowlands Rd WA7 5TP
☎ 01928 581771 Fax 01928 581730
Dir: *leave M56 at junct 12, take A557, then follow signs for Runcorn railway station*
This modern building offers accommodation in smart well equipped bedrooms, all with en suite bathrooms. Refreshments

continued

R

RUNCORN, continued

Campanile, Runcorn

may be taken at the informal Bistro. For further details and the Campanile phone number, consult the Hotel Groups page.
ROOMS: 53 en suite **CONF:** Thtr 35 Class 28 Board 20

RUSHDEN, Northamptonshire Map 04 SP96

Travelodge

Travelodge

Saunders Lodge NN10 9AP
☎ 01933 57008 01933 57008
Dir: *on A45, eastbound*
This modern building offers accommodation in smart, spacious and well equipped bedrooms, all with en suite bathrooms. Refreshments may be taken at the nearby family restaurant. For further details and the Travelodge phone number, consult the Hotel Groups page.
ROOMS: 40 en suite

RUSHYFORD, Co Durham Map 08 NZ22

★★★69% *Swallow Eden Arms*

DL17 0LL
☎ 01388 720541 01388 721871
e-mail: info@swallowhotels.com
Dir: *follow A689 to Rushyford rbt. Hotel on opposite side of rbt*

Tastefully constructed around the original 17th-century foundations, this modern styled hotel offers comfortable and attractively furnished bedrooms that have benefited from a stylish refurbishment. Service is friendly and willingly provided. A choice of dining is available, with lighter snacks in the conservatory, overlooking the leisure centre, or more formal dining in the spacious main restaurant.
ROOMS: 45 en suite (4 fmly) No smoking in 20 bedrooms
FACILITIES: STV Indoor swimming (H) Sauna Solarium Gym Pool table Jacuzzi/spa Steam room Plunge Pool **CONF:** Thtr 100 Class 40 Board 50
PARKING: 200 **CARDS:**

RUSTINGTON, West Sussex Map 04 TQ00

Travelodge

Travelodge

Worthing Rd BN17 6JN
☎ 01903 733150 01903 733150
Dir: *on A259, 1m E of Littlehampton*
This modern building offers accommodation in smart, spacious and well equipped bedrooms, all with en suite bathrooms. Refreshments may be taken at the nearby family restaurant. For further details and the Travelodge phone number, consult the Hotel Groups page.
ROOMS: 36 en suite

RYDE See Wight, Isle of

RYE, East Sussex Map 05 TQ92

★★★69% Mermaid Inn

Mermaid St TN31 7EY
☎ 01797 223065 & 223788 01797 225069
e-mail: mermaidinrye@btclick.com
Dir: *A259, follow signposts to town centre then up Mermaid St*
In business for over 150 years by the time Elizabeth I came to the throne, this famous smugglers' inn is steeped in history. The interior has ancient beamed ceilings and huge fireplaces. The public rooms include several lounge areas and the restaurant. Bedrooms vary considerably in size and shape.
ROOMS: 31 en suite (5 fmly) s £68-£72; d £136-£154 (incl. bkfst) *
FACILITIES: Xmas **CONF:** Thtr 80 Class 50 Board 40 Del from £125 *
PARKING: 25 **NOTES:** No dogs No smoking in restaurant
CARDS:

★★★61% *The George*

OLD ENGLISH INNS & HOTELS

High St TN31 7JP
☎ 01797 222114 01797 224065
Right in the heart of this historic town, near the myriad of small specialist shops, The George is full of character with cosy public rooms reflecting the period of the building. The majority of bedrooms have been sympathetically modernised and are well equipped. Although the restaurant is small, it blends in well with the architecture and style of the building.
ROOMS: 22 en suite No smoking in 5 bedrooms **CONF:** Thtr 100 Class 40 Board 40 **PARKING:** 7 **NOTES:** No smoking in restaurant
CARDS:

★★71% *Broomhill Lodge*

Rye Foreign TN31 7UN
☎ 01797 280421 01797 280402
Dir: *1.5m N on A268*
Built in the 1820s and set in its own grounds of three acres, this guest house is within easy reach of the historic Cinque Port town of Rye. Bedrooms are individually decorated, comfortably furnished and well equipped. There are two lounges and a bright restaurant.
ROOMS: 12 en suite **FACILITIES:** Sauna Mini gym **CONF:** Thtr 60 Class 60 Board 30 **PARKING:** 20 **NOTES:** No dogs No smoking in restaurant
CARDS:

Late for dinner? Quality Standards star rating means that last orders for dinner should be no earlier than:
★ 6.30pm ★★ 7.00pm ★★★ 8.00pm
★★★★ 9.00pm ★★★★★ 10.00pm

R

ST AGNES, Cornwall & Isles of Scilly Map 02 SW75

★★★70% Rose in Vale Country House
Rose in Vale, Mithian TR5 0QD
☎ 01872 552202 01872 552700
e-mail: reception@rose-in-vale-hotel.co.uk
Dir: *Turn right off A30 onto B3284 signposted Perranporth, cross A3075, 3/4ml 3rd left signposted Rose-in-Vale, hotel 1/2ml on left*

Peacefully located in a wooded valley, this Georgian manor house is set in spacious gardens including a pond with waterfowl and an area for croquet. The majority of rooms overlook the gardens, accommodation varies in size and style; several rooms are situated on the ground floor. Each evening in the spacious restaurant, an imaginative fixed price menu and a carte are offered. A warm welcome is assured to guests by the resident proprietors and their loyal team of staff.
ROOMS: 18 en suite (4 fmly) s £50.50; d £89-£109 (incl. bkfst) * LB
FACILITIES: Outdoor swimming (H) Sauna Solarium Croquet lawn Jacuzzi/spa Badminton Table tennis Billiards Scenic flights in hotel's own aeroplane Xmas **CONF:** Thtr 50 Class 50 Board 50 **PARKING:** 40
NOTES: No smoking in restaurant Closed Jan-Feb Civ Wed 75
CARDS:

See advert on this page

★★69% Rosemundy House
Rosemundy Hill TR5 0UF
☎ 01872 552101 01872 554000
e-mail: info@rosemundy.co.uk
Dir: *turn off A30 to St Agnes continue for approx 3m on entering village take 1st turning on the right signposted Rosemundy, hotel is at foot of the hill*

Sympathetically extended to provide comfortable accommodation, this elegant Queen Anne house is quietly located within well maintained gardens. Within 100 metres of the main street, the hotel has a secluded position and attracts a loyal and regular clientele. Guests can be assured of friendly and relaxed service from the mainly local staff. In the restaurant a short, fixed price menu is served, using fresh local produce.

continued on p476

S

ST AGNES, continued

ROOMS: 46 en suite (12 fmly) s £36-£48; d £72-£96 (incl. bkfst & dinner) * LB **FACILITIES:** Outdoor swimming (H) Squash Pool table Croquet lawn Putting green Xmas **PARKING:** 50 **NOTES:** No dogs (ex guide dogs) No smoking in restaurant **CARDS:**

★★69% *Sunholme*

Goonvrea Rd TR5 0NW
☎ 01872 552318
Dir: *on B3277, museum on left at mini rdbt, follow brown & white signs*
Enjoying spectacular views over the surrounding countryside to the sea, this personally run hotel is set in attractive grounds on the southern slopes of St Agnes Beacon. Guests are assured a friendly welcome, and many return on a regular basis. The bedrooms are well equipped and furnished, most having been upgraded to an excellent standard. The intimate bar is an ideal venue for guests to meet before dinner and in addition a choice of comfortable, inter-connecting lounges is provided.
ROOMS: 10 en suite (2 fmly) **PARKING:** 12 **NOTES:** No children 7yrs No smoking in restaurant Closed Nov-Mar **CARDS:**

ST ALBANS, Hertfordshire

Map 04 TL10

★★★★74% *Sopwell House Hotel & Country Club*

Best Western

Cottonmill Ln, Sopwell AL1 2HQ
☎ 01727 864477 01727 844741/845636
Dir: *follow St Albans sign to M10 rbt then take A414, first left and follow Sopwell signs*

The house and the surrounding land were once owned by the Mountbatten family. The public areas are impressive and include the Magnolia Restaurant, an informal brasserie and an impressive health spa. Bedrooms are furnished and decorated to a high standard and for long stay guests there are several self contained apartments.
ROOMS: 122 en suite 16 annexe en suite (6 fmly) **FACILITIES:** STV Indoor swimming (H) Snooker Sauna Solarium Gym Jacuzzi/spa Health & beauty spa Hairdressing salon **CONF:** Thtr 400 Class 220 Board 90 **SERVICES:** Lift **PARKING:** 360 **NOTES:** No smoking in restaurant Closed 31 Dec-1 Jan **CARDS:**

See advert on opposite page

★★★76% St Michael's Manor

Pride of Britain Member

Fishpool St AL3 4RY
☎ 01727 864444 01727 848909
e-mail: smmanor@globalnet.co.uk
Dir: *from St Albans Abbey follow Fishpool Street toward St Michael's village. Hotel located 0.5m on left hand side*
Fishpool Street boasts one of the finest selections of listed buildings, mills and ancient inns in England. This is where "a historic street meets a secret garden", which is five acres of hotel grounds, complete with lake and river. The hotel is furnished and decorated to a very high standard throughout, creating a real sense of luxury.
ROOMS: 23 en suite No smoking in 3 bedrooms s £110-£225; d £145-£295 (incl. bkfst) * LB **FACILITIES:** STV Croquet lawn Xmas **CONF:** Thtr 30 Class 18 Board 20 **PARKING:** 70 **NOTES:** No dogs (ex guide dogs) **CARDS:**

See advert on opposite page

★★67% Apples Hotel

The Independents

133 London Rd AL1 1TA
☎ 01727 844111 01727 861100
Dir: *sited on the main A1081, 0.5m from city centre*
A small hotel that is well located for access to the mainline station and local motorway network. The bedrooms are thoughtfully laid out and offer a comprehensive range of extra facilities. Guests have the use of a quiet residents lounge, a small bar overlooking the attractive garden and an outdoor swimming pool in the summer months.
ROOMS: 9 en suite (1 fmly) No smoking in 2 bedrooms s fr £50; d fr £70.50 (incl. bkfst) * LB **FACILITIES:** Outdoor swimming (H) **PARKING:** 9 **NOTES:** No smoking in restaurant
CARDS:

Express by Holiday Inn St Albans

London Rd, Flamstead AL3 8HT
☎ 01582 841332

A modern budget hotel offering comfortable accommodation in refreshing, spacious and comprehensively-equipped bedrooms, en suite bathrooms with power showers and continental buffet breakfast included in the room rate. Suitable for business travellers or families. For further details and the Express by Holiday Inn phone number, consult the Hotel Groups page.
ROOMS: 75 en suite (incl. cont bkfst) d £52.50 * **CONF:** Thtr 30 Class 16 Board 12

ST ANNES See Lytham St Annes

ST AUSTELL, Cornwall & Isles of Scilly

Map 02 SX05

★★★★74% Carlyon Bay

Brend Hotels

Sea Rd, Carlyon Bay PL25 3RD
☎ 01726 812304 01726 814938
e-mail: info@carlyonbay.co.uk
Dir: *from St Austell, follow signs for Charlestown Carlyon Bay is signposted on left, hotel lies at end of Sea Road*
Set in 250 acres of grounds and renowned for its leisure facilities, Carlyon Bay Hotel has established a loyal following. It is especially suited to the leisure visitor but can also cater for small conferences and business guests. Sea-facing rooms are always in demand for their marvellous views of St Austell Bay and fresh fruit and flowers are provided in the best bedrooms. There is a choice of lounges and bars.

continued

S

ROOMS: 73 en suite (14 fmly) s £72-£93; d £146-£220 (incl. bkfst) * LB **FACILITIES:** STV Indoor swimming (H) Outdoor swimming (H) Golf 18 Tennis (hard) Snooker Sauna Solarium Putting green Jacuzzi/spa Table tennis 9-hole approach course entertainment ch fac Xmas **CONF:** Thtr 100 **SERVICES:** Lift **PARKING:** 101 **NOTES:** No dogs (ex guide dogs) Civ Wed **CARDS:**

See advert on this page

★★★65% **Cliff Head**
Sea Rd, Carlyon Bay PL25 3RB
☎ 01726 812345 01726 815511
***Dir:** 2m E off A390*
Set in extensive grounds the hotel faces south and enjoys views over Carlyon Bay. A choice of lounges is provided and entertainment is available during the season. A range of menus is offered in 'Expressions' restaurant, featuring an interesting selection of dishes.

continued on p478

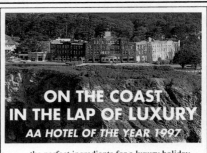

ST AUSTELL, continued

ROOMS: 60 rms (59 en suite) (2 fmly) s £45-£55; d £75-£85 (incl. bkfst) * LB **FACILITIES:** Outdoor swimming (H) Sauna Solarium Gym Pool table Xmas **CONF:** Thtr 150 Class 130 Board 170 Del £65 * **PARKING:** 60 **NOTES:** No dogs (ex guide dogs) No smoking in restaurant **CARDS:**

★★★64% Porth Avallen

Sea Rd, Carlyon Bay PL25 3SG
☎ 01726 812802 01726 817097
e-mail: nmarkis@aol.com
***Dir:** leave A30 onto A391. Follow signs to St Austell and then Charlestown and then Carlyon Bay. Turn right into Sea Rd*

This traditional hotel boasts panoramic views over the rugged Cornish coastline and Carlyon Bay. A comprehensive refurbishment programme is underway, including upgrading of the spacious bedrooms, many of which benefit from the wonderful outlook. The atmosphere here is friendly and welcoming and both the oak panelled lounge and conservatory are ideal for quiet relaxation. In addition to the convivial bar area, a function room is also available for private parties. Both fixed price and carte menus are offered each evening in the dining room.
ROOMS: 24 en suite (5 fmly) No smoking in 3 bedrooms s £61.50-£66.50; d £95-£115 (incl. bkfst) * LB **FACILITIES:** STV N **CONF:** Thtr 82 Class 82 Board 82 Del £87 * **NOTES:** No dogs (ex guide dogs) No smoking in restaurant Closed 23 Dec-4 Jan
CARDS:

See advert on opposite page

★★78% Boscundle Manor

Tregrehan PL25 3RL
☎ 01726 813557 01726 814997
e-mail: stay@boscundlemanor.co.uk
***Dir:** 2m E on A390 200yds up road signposted 'Tregrehan'*

This handsome 18th century stone-built mansion house offers very comfortable, well equipped bedrooms. The beautiful grounds extend to over ten acres and include lots of secluded corners, ponds and woodland. There is also a games room. The daily menu uses fresh produce to create traditional dishes to satisfy the appetite.
ROOMS: 9 en suite 3 annexe en suite (1 fmly) s £65-£85; d £110-£130 (incl. bkfst) * **FACILITIES:** Indoor swimming (H) Outdoor swimming (H) Snooker Gym Croquet lawn Golf practice area Table Tennis Badminton **PARKING:** 15 **NOTES:** No smoking in restaurant Closed end Oct-mid Mar RS Sun **CARDS:**

S

★★70% Pier House

Harbour Front, Charlestown PL25 3NJ
☎ 01726 67955 01726 69246
***Dir:** follow A390 to St Austell, Mt Charles rdbt turn left down Charlestown Road*

Formerly two cottages, built in 1794 and overlooking the working port, this friendly and relaxed hotel is situated on the picturesque harbour at Charlestown. Bedrooms, many of which have sea views, continue to be upgraded and improved and provide comfortable accommodation of a good standard. The public bar is popular with locals and tourists alike, and guests have their own lounge in addition to the restaurant where locally caught fish regularly features on the varied and interesting menu.
ROOMS: 26 en suite (4 fmly) No smoking in 5 bedrooms s £38-£40; d £63-£75 (incl. bkfst) * LB **PARKING:** 56 **NOTES:** No dogs (ex guide dogs) No smoking in restaurant Closed 24-25 Dec
CARDS:

★★67% Victoria Inn & Lodge

Victoria, Roche PL26 8LQ
☎ 01726 890207 01726 891233
e-mail: victorian@talk21.com
***Dir:** 6m W of Bodmin on A30. Turn 1st left after garage, Victoria Inn approx 500yds on right*

Situated on the A30, midway between Bodmin and Newquay, this is a convenient choice for both the business and leisure traveller. Purpose built, lodge-style bedrooms are both well-equipped and comfortable. Guests have a choice of dining options with the conviviality of the inn environment, or the more formal surroundings of the carte restaurant.
ROOMS: 28 en suite (7 fmly) No smoking in all bedrooms d £40 * LB **FACILITIES:** STV Pool table Xmas **CONF:** Thtr 32 Class 32 Board 24 Del from £75 * **PARKING:** 100 **NOTES:** No dogs (ex guide dogs) No smoking in restaurant **CARDS:**

★★63% *White Hart*

Church St PL25 4AT
☎ 01726 72100 01726 74705

Situated in the town centre, this 18th-century, stone-built inn is popular with visitors and locals alike. A choice of bars is available, both offering a lively atmosphere and range of local ales. Alternative seating is available in the foyer lounge, where cream teas may be taken. Meals are available at the bar or from a fixed price menu in the restaurant.
ROOMS: 18 en suite **FACILITIES:** STV **CONF:** Thtr 50 Board 20 **NOTES:** No dogs (ex guide dogs) Closed 25 & 26 Dec
CARDS:

ST HELENS, Merseyside Map 07 SJ59
see also Rainhill

★★★66% *Posthouse Haydock*

Posthouse

Lodge Ln WA12 OJG
☎ 0870 400 9039 01942 718419
(For full entry see Haydock)

⇧ Premier Lodge

PREMIER LODGE

Garswood Old Rd, East Lancs Rd WA11 9AB
☎ 0870 700 1544 0870 700 1545

Premier Lodge offers modern, well equipped, en suite accommodation suitable for both business and leisure travellers. Meals can be taken at the adjacent popular restaurant and bar which is fully licensed. For further details, consult the Hotel Groups page.
ROOMS: 43 en suite d £46 *

ST IVES, Cambridgeshire Map 04 TL37

★★★69% Olivers Lodge

Needingworth Rd PE17 4JP
☎ 01480 463252 01480 461150
e-mail: reception@oliverslodge.co.uk
***Dir:** follow A14 towards Huntingdon/Cambridge, take B1040 to St Ives, cross 1st rdbt, left at 2nd then 1st right. Hotel 500m on right*

Olivers Lodge is a popular and well run hotel, set in quiet residential surroundings on the edge of St Ives. The welcoming public rooms include an attractive conservatory dining area and breakfast room, a lounge bar and an air-conditioned restaurant. There are bedrooms in both the main house and an adjoining wing, housing modern appointments and a good range of useful facilities.

continued

ROOMS: 12 en suite 5 annexe en suite (3 fmly) No smoking in 1 bedroom s £65-£72; d £65-£85 (incl. bkfst) * LB **FACILITIES:** STV Croquet lawn Motor cruiser for hire Free use of local health club inc swimming, sauna, gym entertainment **CONF:** Thtr 65 Class 45 Board 40 Del £105 * **PARKING:** 30 **NOTES:** Civ Wed 85
CARDS:

★★★67% Slepe Hall

Ramsey Rd PE17 4RB
☎ 01480 463122 📠 01480 300706
e-mail: mail@slepehall.co.uk
Dir: *leave A14 on A1096 & follow by-pass signed Huntingdon towards St Ives, turn into Ramsey Rd at set of traffic lights by Toyota and Ford garages*

A pleasant hotel with a warm atmosphere close to the town centre. The spacious public rooms are intimate and welcoming. A wide range of food is offered, from lighter meals in the bar to a choice of menus in the more formal restaurant. Bedroom styles range between traditional in the main house and modern in the new wing, but all rooms offer good accommodation.
ROOMS: 16 en suite (1 fmly) s £50-£75; d £65-£100 (incl. bkfst) * LB **FACILITIES:** STV **CONF:** Thtr 200 Class 80 Board 60 Del from £95 * **PARKING:** 70 **NOTES:** No smoking in restaurant Closed 26-30 Dec Civ Wed 60 **CARDS:**

★★★65% Dolphin

London Rd PE17 4EP
☎ 01480 466966 & 497497 📠 01480 495597
Dir: *leave A14 between Huntingdon & Cambridge on A1096 towards St Ives. Left at first rdbt & immediately left and Hotel is on left after about 0.5m*

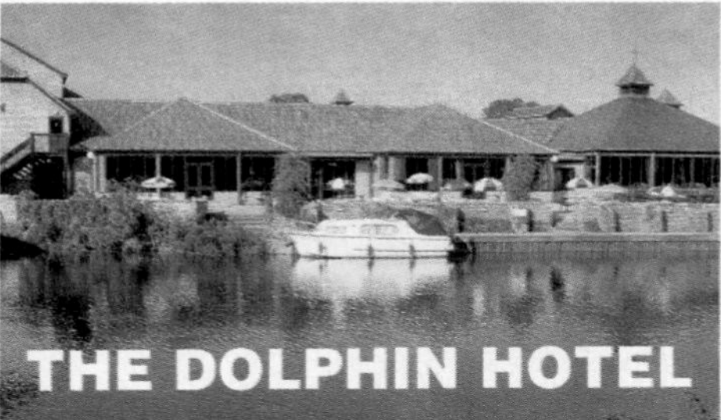

A modern hotel with views of the River Ouse, a pedestrian bridge leads to the market town centre. Open-plan public rooms include a choice of bars and a pleasant restaurant offering enjoyable cuisine. Bedrooms are divided between the hotel and adjacent wing. There are modern conference and function suites, and secure parking is available.
ROOMS: 31 en suite 36 annexe en suite (4 fmly) No smoking in 20 bedrooms s fr £70; d fr £90 (incl. bkfst) * LB **FACILITIES:** STV Fishing Sauna Gym **CONF:** Thtr 150 Class 50 Board 50 Del from £98 * **PARKING:** 400 **NOTES:** No dogs (ex guide dogs) RS 25-31 Dec Civ Wed 60 **CARDS:**

See advert on this page

ST IVES, Cornwall & Isles of Scilly — Map 02 SW54

★★★73% Carbis Bay

Carbis Bay TR26 2NP
☎ 01736 795311 📠 01736 797677
e-mail: carbisbayhotel@talk21.com
Dir: *from A30 turn right onto A3074 for 2m, then right again opposite Spar Shop*

This established, professionally run hotel enjoys a superb location with wonderful views overlooking its own sandy beach. The hotel

continued on p480

ST IVES, continued

Carbis Bay, St Ives

has spacious, newly furnished public rooms. Upgraded bedrooms provide comfort, quality and modern facilities; the attentive, natural hospitality is an attraction.

ROOMS: 35 en suite (9 fmly) No smoking in 5 bedrooms s £45-£75; d £90-£150 (incl. bkfst) * LB **FACILITIES:** Outdoor swimming (H) Fishing Snooker Pool table Private beach entertainment **CONF:** Thtr 120 Class 100 Board 100 **PARKING:** 200 **NOTES:** No smoking in restaurant Closed Jan Civ Wed 120 **CARDS:**

See advert on opposite page

★★★71% Porthminster

The Terrace TR26 2BN
☎ 01736 795221 📠 01736 797043
e-mail: reception@porthminster-hotel.co.uk

Dir: *on A3074*

With its enviable position overlooking the sandy beach, this long established hotel continues to provide excellent hospitality together with facilities for all the family, including both an indoor and outdoor pool. The loyal team of staff offer a warm welcome to guests, many of whom holiday at the hotel on a regular basis. Bedrooms are both comfortable and well equipped and all have been upgraded to meet modern demands. Public rooms are spacious and benefit from the spectacular views over the bay.

ROOMS: 43 en suite (14 fmly) s £44-£60; d £88-£120 (incl. bkfst) * LB **FACILITIES:** Indoor swimming (H) Outdoor swimming (H) Sauna Solarium Gym Pool table Jacuzzi/spa Xmas **CONF:** Thtr 130 Board 35 **SERVICES:** Lift **PARKING:** 43 **NOTES:** Closed 2-12 Jan Civ Wed 130 **CARDS:**

See advert on opposite page

★★★67% Garrack

Burthallan Ln, Higher Ayr TR26 3AA
☎ 01736 796199 📠 01736 798955
e-mail: garrack@accuk.co.uk

Dir: *turn off A30 for St Ives. Follow yellow holiday route signs on B3311. In St Ives, hotel is signposted from first mini rdbt*

The Garrack provides superb views over Porthmeor beach and stands in extensive grounds. Bedrooms are available in both the modern wing and in the original building; all are well equipped and comfortably furnished. The restaurant offers fixed price and carte menus featuring skilfully prepared dishes, making good use of home grown produce and local seafood.

ROOMS: 16 en suite (2 fmly) s £62-£65; d £124-£130 (incl. bkfst) * LB **FACILITIES:** Indoor swimming (H) Sauna Solarium Gym Jacuzzi/spa Xmas **CONF:** Thtr 30 Board 16 **PARKING:** 30 **NOTES:** No smoking in restaurant **CARDS:**

See advert on opposite page

★★★67% Tregenna Castle Hotel

Best Western

TR26 2DE
☎ 01736 795254 📠 01736 796066
e-mail: tregenna-castle@demon.co.uk

Dir: *main A30 from Exeter to Penzance, at Lelant just west of Hayle take A3074 to St Ives, through Carbis Bay, signposted main entrance on left*

The Tregenna Castle has spectacular views of St Ives and its beaches, sitting at the top of the town in beautiful landscaped gardens. Bedrooms are generally spacious with super views. A carte menu or carvery buffet are offered in the restaurant, there is also an Italian bistro adjacent to the golf course.

ROOMS: 84 en suite (12 fmly) No smoking in 49 bedrooms s £35-£72; d £70-£144 (incl. bkfst) * **FACILITIES:** STV Indoor swimming (H) Outdoor swimming (H) Golf 18 Tennis (hard) Squash Snooker Sauna Solarium Gym Pool table Jacuzzi/spa Health spa Steam room ch fac Xmas **CONF:** Thtr 400 Class 200 Board 50 Del from £75 * **SERVICES:** Lift **PARKING:** 200 **NOTES:** No dogs (ex guide dogs) No smoking in restaurant Civ Wed 130

CARDS:

★★73% Pedn-Olva

West Porthminster Beach TR26 2EA
☎ 01736 796222 📠 01736 797710

Dir: *take A30 to Hayle, then A3074 to St Ives. At St Ives turn sharp right at Bus Station into Railway Station car park, go down steps into Hotel*

Perched on the water's edge, this professionally managed hotel is currently being upgraded. The majority of the comfortably furnished bedrooms have glorious views across the bay, while the public rooms have vast picture windows to take advantage of its unique location. In the restaurant, an imaginative, fixed-price menu is offered; while during the summer lighter meals are available on the terraces.

ROOMS: 29 en suite 4 annexe en suite (4 fmly) No smoking in 12 bedrooms d £42-£51 (incl. bkfst) * LB **FACILITIES:** STV Outdoor swimming (H) Xmas **CONF:** Thtr 25 Class 20 Board 16 Del from £68 * **PARKING:** 17 **NOTES:** No dogs (ex guide dogs)

CARDS:

See advert on opposite page

★★70% Chy-an-Albany

Albany Ter TR26 2BS
☎ 01736 796759 📠 01736 795584
e-mail: info@chy-an-albanyhtl.demon.co.uk

Dir: *turn of A30 onto A3074 signposted St Ives, hotel on left just before junction*

Refurbished to a high standard throughout, this hotel benefits from spectacular views over St Ives Bay and Porthminster Beach. The comfortable bedrooms are well furnished and equipped, and the rooms with sea views are always popular. A fixed-price menu is offered in the attractive dining room, adjacent to the comfortable lounges and intimate bar.

ROOMS: 40 en suite (11 fmly) No smoking in all bedrooms s £35-£55; d £70-£110 (incl. bkfst) * LB **FACILITIES:** entertainment Xmas **CONF:** Class 60 Board 60 **SERVICES:** Lift **PARKING:** 37 **NOTES:** No dogs (ex guide dogs) No smoking in restaurant Civ Wed 90

CARDS:

★★69% Chy-an-Dour

Trelyon Av TR26 2AD
☎ 01736 796436 📠 01736 795772
e-mail: chyndour@aol.com

Dir: *turn off A30 onto A3074, follow signs to St Ives for approx 3m, hotel on the right just past Ford garage*

Built in 1890, this delightful family-owned hotel has inspiring views over St Ives, the harbour and Porthminster Beach. Good home cooking is provided in the restaurant at both dinner and breakfast.

continued on p482

S

AA ★★★ & Restaurant

The Garrack Hotel

Burthallan Lane, St. Ives, Cornwall TR26 3AA
Tel: 01736 796199 Fax: 01736 798955
Email: garrack@accuk.co.uk

- ☆ Rosetted Restaurant
- ☆ Secluded Position
- ☆ Fabulous Sea Views
- ☆ Small Leisure Centre
- ☆ 18 En Suite Rooms
- ☆ Extensive Wine List
- ☆ Highly Recommended
- ☆ Ample Car Parking

Freephone 08000 197393

★★★

THE CARBIS BAY HOTEL

CARBIS BAY
ST IVES
CORNWALL
TR26 2NP
Tel: 01736-795311
Fax: 01736-797677

Set in one of the most prestigious locations in the country; this award winning hotel boasts magnificent views across its own sandy beach and St Ives Bay.
Beautifully sited restaurant serving excellent English and Continental rosette awarded cuisine.
Heated swimming pool set amidst tropical surroundings with sun terrace.
Sea view holiday flats also available.

Please write or telephone for colour brochure and tariff.

The PEDN-OLVA HOTEL and 'LOOKOUT' Restaurant & Bar

WEST PORTHMINSTER BEACH
ST. IVES · CORNWALL · TR26 2EA
Tel: 01736 796222 · Fax: 01736 797710
Email: pednolvahotel@cornwall-county.com

Situated on rocks extending out into St. Ives Bay, the hotel is literally on the water's edge.

All bedrooms, public areas and patios have stunning views over the bay and harbour. The superb food is prepared from local produce and complemented by attentive friendly service.

Stay awhile and enjoy our style !

In or out of season you can enjoy our full comfort, superb cuisine and exceptional location. We offer sub-tropical gardens, direct access to the beach and horizon clear sea views, 43 en-suite bedrooms, passenger lift, indoor leisure pool complex, outdoor heated pool (June-Sept), direct dial telephones, 4 channel TV with video and a level of service that is second to none. Short breaks are available out of season.

PORTHMINSTER HOTEL

St. Ives, Cornwall TR26 2BN
Tel: 01736 795221 Fax: 01736 797043
Email: reception@porthminster-hotel.co.uk
Website: www.porthminster-hotel.co.uk

ST IVES, continued

The four-course dinner menu changes daily, often using fresh local produce. Most of the bedrooms enjoy the splendid views, and all the rooms are well equipped.
ROOMS: 23 en suite (2 fmly) No smoking in all bedrooms s £50-£61; d £70-£92 (incl. bkfst) * LB **SERVICES:** Lift **PARKING:** 23 **NOTES:** No dogs (ex guide dogs) No children 5yrs No smoking in restaurant
CARDS:

★★68% *Skidden House*
Skidden Hill TR26 2DU
☎ 01736 796899 01736 798619
e-mail: skiddenhouse@msn.com

THE CIRCLE
Selected Individual Hotels
GREAT BRITAIN

***Dir:** turn off A30 at St Erth rdbt, follow road sign A3074 to St Ives & railway station 1st right after rail/bus station*
Situated in the town centre, Skidden House is said to be the oldest hotel in St Ives. Its cosy bedrooms are well equipped with modern facilities. In the bistro-style dining room both fixed-price and carte menus are offered, often using fresh local produce. There is also a cosy bar and lounge.
ROOMS: 7 en suite No smoking in 2 bedrooms **PARKING:** 7
CARDS:

★★66% Hotel St Eia
Trelyon Av TR26 2AA
☎ 01736 795531 01736 793591
***Dir:** turn off A30 onto A3074, follow signs to St Ives, when approaching St Ives, the hotel is prominently on the right hand side*
This conveniently located hotel offers a warm welcome and spectacular views over St Ives, the harbour and Porthminster Beach. Guests can relax with a drink from the well stocked bar before dining in the attractive restaurant. A roof top terrace is also available, which boasts one of the best views in town!
ROOMS: 18 en suite s fr £36.50; d fr £73 (incl. bkfst) * **PARKING:** 16 **NOTES:** No dogs (ex guide dogs) No children 5yrs No smoking in restaurant Closed Dec-Jan **CARDS:**

★★64% Boskerris
Boskerris Rd, Carbis Bay TR26 2NQ
☎ 01736 795295 01736 798632
e-mail: Boskerris.Hotel@btinternet.com
***Dir:** upon entering Carbis Bay take 3rd turning right after garage*
With magnificent views over Carbis Bay, Boskerris Hotel is set in an acre and a half of gardens, in a quiet area. Comfortable lounge areas and an attractive dining room are provided, and there is also an outdoor swimming pool. Bedrooms vary in size and style, each being well decorated and equipped.
ROOMS: 18 rms (16 en suite) (2 fmly) No smoking in 4 bedrooms s £65-£75; d £80-£100 (incl. bkfst) * LB **FACILITIES:** Outdoor swimming (H) Putting green Table tennis **PARKING:** 20 **NOTES:** No smoking in restaurant Closed Nov-Etr **CARDS:**

★64% Dunmar
Pednolver Ter TR26 2EL
☎ 01736 796117 & 0500 131218 01736 796117
e-mail: dunmarhotel@btconnect.com
***Dir:** take A3074 and fork left at the Porthminster Hotel into Albert Road. Hotel is 200yds along at junction of Pednolver and Porthminster Terrace*
In an elevated position above the town and close to the centre, this popular hotel offers a warm welcome to all. Bedrooms are comfortable and most have sea views. Traditional English food is served in the dining room and the attractive lounge bar enjoys views over St Ives and the ocean.
ROOMS: 15 en suite (3 fmly) s £25-£32; d £50-£64 (incl. bkfst) * LB **FACILITIES:** Xmas **PARKING:** 20 **NOTES:** No smoking in restaurant Closed Jan **CARDS:**

ST KEYNE, Cornwall & Isles of Scilly Map 02 SX26

★★70% Old Rectory House
PL14 4RL
☎ 01579 342617 01579 342293
***Dir:** turn off A38 at Liskeard, take B3254 following signs to St Keyne, pass church on left, hotel is 500yds on left*
In a secluded location, surrounded by three acres of grounds and gardens, this delightful old house was built in 1820. Bedrooms are soundly maintained and include rooms with four-poster beds. There is a comfortable lounge and an attractively appointed dining room.
ROOMS: 6 en suite No smoking in all bedrooms s £85; d £85-£120 (incl. bkfst) * LB **PARKING:** 30 **NOTES:** No dogs (ex guide dogs) No children 15yrs No smoking in restaurant Closed Xmas & New Year
CARDS:

See advert under LISKEARD

ST LAWRENCE See Wight, Isle of

ST LEONARDS-ON-SEA See Hastings & St Leonards

ST MARTIN'S See Scilly, Isles of

ST MARY CHURCH See Torquay

ST MARY'S See Scilly, Isles of

ST MAWES, Cornwall & Isles of Scilly Map 02 SW83

★★★77% Idle Rocks
Harbour Side TR2 5AN
☎ 01326 270771 01326 270062
e-mail: idlerocks@richardsonhotels.co.uk
***Dir:** A30, A39, A3078*
Overlooking the quayside and to the sea beyond, this smart friendly hotel offers wonderful views from many of its bedrooms and its popular waterfront terrace. Bedrooms are individually styled and tastefully furnished to a high standard; the rooms in nearby Bohella House and the waterside cottage are particularly spacious. Cuisine is impressive and guests have a choice of dining options; either the fixed price dinner menu with its selection of innovative dishes or a lighter brasserie style menu.
ROOMS: 17 en suite 11 annexe en suite (6 fmly) s £56-£99; d £112-£198 (incl. bkfst & dinner) * LB **FACILITIES:** Xmas **CONF:** Thtr 30 Class 20 Board 20 Del from £45 * **PARKING:** 5 **NOTES:** No smoking in restaurant **CARDS:**

See advert on opposite page

★★70% Rising Sun
TR2 5DJ
☎ 01326 270233 01326 270198
***Dir:** from A39 take A3078 signposted St Mawes, hotel is in centre of village*
The haunt of artists for decades and popular with the yachting fraternity, the pretty harbour of St Mawes is the setting for this charming and convivial hotel. The bar is a focal point of village life, and the new brasserie and lounge bar offer imaginative cooking featuring local seafood. The stylish bedrooms are individually decorated and display a number of specially commissioned watercolours by local artists.
ROOMS: 9 en suite (1 fmly) **PARKING:** 6 **NOTES:** No smoking in restaurant **CARDS:**

Bad hair day? Hairdryers in all rooms three stars and above.

ST MELLION, Cornwall & Isles of Scilly Map 02 SX36

★★★72% St Mellion International
PL12 6SD
☎ 01579 351351 01579 350537
e-mail: stmellion@americangolf.uk.com
Dir: *from M5/A38 towards Plymouth & Saltash. St Mellion is located off A38 on A388 towards Callington and Launceston*
This purpose built hotel, golfing and leisure complex is surrounded by 450 acres of land with two 18 hole golf courses. The bedrooms generally have views over the courses, but with the vast array of leisure facilities on offer, most guests spend little time in their rooms! Public areas include a choice of bars and eating options. Other facilities include function suites for up to 180 people.
ROOMS: 39 annexe en suite (15 fmly) s £69-£80; d £88-£154 (incl. bkfst) * LB **FACILITIES:** Indoor swimming (H) Golf 36 Tennis (hard) Squash Snooker Sauna Solarium Gym Putting green Jacuzzi/spa Steam room Skincare & Spa centre ch fac Xmas **CONF:** Thtr 350 Class 150 Board 50 Del from £96 * **SERVICES:** Lift **PARKING:** 400 **NOTES:** No dogs (ex guide dogs) No smoking in restaurant Civ Wed 120
CARDS:

ST NEOTS, Cambridgeshire Map 04 TL16

★★69% Abbotsley Golf Hotel
Potton Rd, Eynesbury Hardwicke PE19 4XN
☎ 01480 474000 01480 471018
Dir: *leave A1 at junct with A428 to Cambridge. Take 1st left at 2nd rdbt and then last exit at next rdbt. Left after 300 yds and 1st right*
This purpose-built hotel caters well for its many avid golfing guests with a 250-acre estate encompassing two courses, a Golf School and leisure complex. A major refurbishment programme is adding

continued on p484

S

ST NEOTS, continued

more rooms, upgrading the existing ones and revamping public areas. The bedrooms are generally spacious and surround a pleasing courtyard garden with a putting green. Public rooms overlook the adjacent greens.
ROOMS: 42 en suite (2 fmly) s £47-£57; d £79-£89 (incl. bkfst) * LB **FACILITIES:** Golf 36 Squash Solarium Gym Pool table Putting green Holistic Health & Beauty Salon Xmas **CONF:** Thtr 40 Class 40 Board 40 Del £85 * **PARKING:** 80 **CARDS:**

Premier Lodge

Great North Rd, Eaton Socon PE19 3EN
☎ 0870 700 1368 📠 0870 700 1369
Premier Lodge offers modern, well equipped, en suite accommodation suitable for both business and leisure travellers. Meals can be taken at the adjacent popular restaurant and bar which is fully licensed. For further details, consult the Hotel Groups page.
ROOMS: 63 en suite d £42 *

SALCOMBE, Devon Map 03 SX73
see also Hope Cove, Kingsbridge & Thurlestone

★★★★72% Thurlestone Hotel

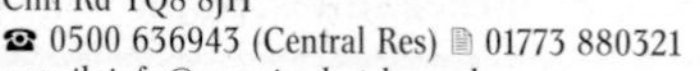

TQ7 3NN
☎ 01548 560382 📠 01548 561069
e-mail: enquires@thurlestone.co.uk
(For full entry see Thurlestone and advert opposite)

★★★★67% Menzies Marine

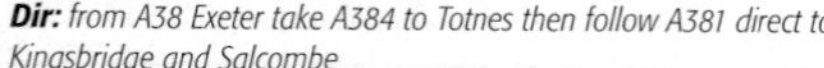

Cliff Rd TQ8 8JH
☎ 0500 636943 (Central Res) 📠 01773 880321
e-mail: info@menzies-hotels.co.uk
Dir: *from A38 Exeter take A384 to Totnes then follow A381 direct to Kingsbridge and Salcombe*
This splendid hotel enjoys a wonderful waterside location with stunning views of the estuary from all its public areas. It appeals particularly to guests wanting to escape and enjoy peace and tranquillity and perhaps a little exercise within the excellent leisure complex! All the bedrooms are well equipped and stylishly furnished, many having balconies. The restaurant serves appetising food with locally caught fish often featuring.
ROOMS: 53 en suite (10 fmly) s £120-£150; d £150-£180 (incl. bkfst) * LB **FACILITIES:** STV Indoor swimming (H) Sauna Solarium Gym Jacuzzi/spa Xmas **SERVICES:** Lift **PARKING:** 50 **NOTES:** No smoking in restaurant Civ Wed 70 **CARDS:**

S

★★★82% Soar Mill Cove

Soar Mill Cove, Malborough TQ7 3DS
☎ 01548 561566 📠 01548 561223
e-mail: info@makepeacehotels.co.uk
Dir: *3m W of town off A381 at Malborough. Follow signs 'Soar'*

continued

The hotel is set in extensive grounds, overlooking the bay, and has been run by the same family for more than 20 years. All the spacious bedrooms are well equipped, with either sea or garden views, and have private balconies or patios. The dining room has an excellent reputation for its cuisine.
ROOMS: 21 en suite (5 fmly) No smoking in all bedrooms s £69-£127; d £138-£170 (incl. bkfst) * LB **FACILITIES:** Indoor swimming (H) Outdoor swimming (H) Tennis (grass) Putting green Table tennis Large childrens games room & outdoor play area ch fac Xmas **CONF:** Board 25 Del from £100 * **PARKING:** 30 **NOTES:** No smoking in restaurant Closed 2 Jan-8 Feb **CARDS:**

See advert on page 483

★★★80% Tides Reach

South Sands TQ8 8LJ
☎ 01548 843466 📠 01548 843954
e-mail: enquire@tidesreach.com
Dir: *turn off the A38 at Buckfastleigh towards Totnes. At Totnes join A381 then into Salcombe follow signs to South Sands*
This personally run hotel has a delightful waterside location and staff are both professional and friendly. Many of the spacious bedrooms have balconies and the Garden Room restaurant offers high quality cuisine and pleasant views. Particularly comfortable public areas include both a leisure complex and a hair and beauty salon.
ROOMS: 35 en suite (7 fmly) No smoking in 2 bedrooms s £83-£113; d £146-£230 (incl. bkfst & dinner) * LB **FACILITIES:** Indoor swimming (H) Squash Snooker Sauna Solarium Gym Jacuzzi/spa Windsurfing Dingy sailing Water skiing entertainment Xmas **SERVICES:** Lift **PARKING:** 100 **NOTES:** No children 8yrs No smoking in restaurant Closed Jan-early Feb **CARDS:**

See advert on page 487

★★★77% Bolt Head

TQ8 8LL
☎ 01548 843751 📠 01548 843061
e-mail: info@bolthead-salcombe.co.uk
Dir: *follow signs to South Sands*

Built in 1901, the hotel is at the entrance to the National Trust-owned Sharpitor and enjoys magnificent views of Salcombe estuary. Public rooms are comfortable and the restaurant has a local reputation for seafood and fish. Pine furniture and well chosen colour schemes make the bedrooms attractive.
ROOMS: 28 en suite (6 fmly) s £49-£75; d £98-£150 * LB **FACILITIES:** Outdoor swimming (H) Pool table **PARKING:** 30 **NOTES:** No smoking in restaurant Closed mid Nov-mid Mar **CARDS:**

See advert on opposite page

Fancy a Singapore Sling? Bar staff in five star hotels should be skilled cocktail mixers.

AA ★★★ 77% ❀

BOLT HEAD HOTEL

Sharpitor, Salcombe, Devon TQ8 8LL
Te: 01548 843751 Fax: 01548 843061
E-mail: info@boltheadhotel.com
www.boltheadhotel.com

Magnificently situated with panoramic views over Salcombe Estuary, the sea and surrounding coastline. The hotel adjoins National Trust Property incorporating Overbecks Gardens & Museum and miles of unspoilt coastal paths for breathtaking walks. Our warm, friendly hotel is only two minutes from a lovely sheltered sandy beach, or you can have a swim in our heated pool. There are lots of interesting places to visit, or you can simply relax and enjoy the views.

Thurlestone Hotel

AA ★★★★

ENGLISH TOURISM COUNCIL ★★★★ HOTEL

'A world of its own'

Escape to a location of outstanding natural beauty on the spectacular & unspoilt South Devon coast near Salcombe, with miles of National Trust coastline to explore.

- Family owned for over 100 years
- Experienced & friendly staff
- Elegant & luxurious surroundings
- Fabulous leisure & sports facilities
- Rosetted restaurant - mouthwatering cuisine

Welcome, Relax, Indulge & Unwind

Telephone:
01548 560382

Thurlestone,
Near Kingsbridge, South Devon, TQ7 3NN
www.thurlestone.co.uk

WCTB Hotel of the Year 99 Winner
GOLD AWARD 1999
Egon Ronay Recommended AA Rosette for Cuisine

S

SALCOMBE, continued

★★★69% South Sands
South Sands TQ8 8LL
☎ 01548 843741 📠 01548 842112
e-mail: enquire@southsands.com
Dir: *off A38 at Buckfastleigh, travel to Totnes and follow A381 to Salcombe, then follow signs to South Sands*
A popular family hotel on the Salcombe estuary, the atmosphere is relaxed and informal, facilities include an indoor swimming pool and children's playroom. Bedrooms are comfortably furnished and equipped, many with superb views. The waterside dining room offers a range of interesting dishes, the beachside Terrace bar is a more informal setting.
ROOMS: 30 en suite (10 fmly) s £60-£90; d £110-£190 (incl. bkfst & dinner) * LB **FACILITIES:** STV Indoor swimming (H) Jacuzzi/spa ch fac **PARKING:** 50 **NOTES:** No smoking in restaurant Closed Nov-Mar **CARDS:**

See advert on page 485

★★71% Grafton Towers
Moult Rd TQ8 8LG
☎ 01548 842882 📠 01548 842857
e-mail: graftontowers.salcombe@virgin.net
Dir: *approach Salcombe from Kingsbridge, follow signs for South Sands, look for Hotel sign*
Enjoying superb views over the estuary, and standing in gardens, this family owned hotel offers bright, cheerful accommodation. Comfortable public rooms include a lounge and separate bar as well as a dining room.
ROOMS: 12 en suite s £45.50-£49; d £98-£108 (incl. bkfst & dinner) * LB **FACILITIES:** Croquet lawn **PARKING:** 13 **NOTES:** No children 14yrs No smoking in restaurant Closed Nov-Feb **CARDS:**

★★67% Sunny Cliff
Cliff Rd TQ8 8JX
☎ 01548 842207 📠 01548 843388
e-mail: The SunnyC@aol.com
Dir: *A381 into Salcombe follow road down hill, sharp left to South Sands, hotel 150m on left*
This small, friendly hotel enjoys an enviable elevated position above the water's edge. The bar-lounge has been moved to the ground floor and has marvellous views, shared by the dining room and all the bedrooms. The gardens lead down to the outdoor heated pool and the hotel's six private moorings. Bedrooms are generally spacious with light decor and modern facilities.
ROOMS: 9 en suite 4 annexe en suite (6 fmly) s £40-£73; d £80-£98 (incl. bkfst) * LB **FACILITIES:** Outdoor swimming (H) Fishing Moorings and Landing stage Xmas **PARKING:** 17 **NOTES:** No smoking in restaurant Closed Jan RS Nov-Mar **CARDS:**

SALE, Greater Manchester — Map 07 SJ79

★★★★74% Belmore Hotel
143 Brooklands Rd M33 3QN
☎ 0161 973 2538 📠 0161 973 2665
e-mail: belmore-hotel@hotmail.com
Dir: *from A56 turn onto A6144. At traffic lights (Brooklands Station on right) turn right into Brooklands Road*
This Victorian building, now a luxurious privately-owned hotel set in attractive gardens, dates back to 1875. Rooms, including two suites, are spacious, tastefully decorated and offer excellent facilities. There is a cocktail bar, a comfortable lounge with a real fire, a fine dining restaurant and an elegant banqueting suite. Staff are welcoming and attentive.

continued

ROOMS: 23 en suite (2 fmly) s £80-£180; d £90-£200 (incl. bkfst) * **FACILITIES:** STV Free access to local Health Club Xmas **CONF:** Thtr 80 Class 50 Board 40 Del from £115 * **PARKING:** 38 **NOTES:** No smoking in restaurant Civ Wed 60 **CARDS:**

SALISBURY, Wiltshire — Map 04 SU12

★★★74% Milford Hall
206 Castle St SP1 3TE
☎ 01722 417411 📠 01722 419444
e-mail: milfordhallhotel@compuserve.com
Dir: *hotel is a few hundred yds from the conjunction of Castle St, the A30 ring road and the A345 Amesbury Rd. It is 0.5m from Market Sq*
The hotel is quietly situated, within easy walking distance of the city centre and with a reputation for good hospitality. Bedrooms fall into two categories, traditional rooms in the original Georgian house and spacious, refurbished, modern rooms; all are well equipped. The smartly appointed restaurant is popular with guests and locals alike.
ROOMS: 35 en suite (1 fmly) No smoking in 6 bedrooms s £90-£120; d £100-£130 (incl. bkfst) * LB **FACILITIES:** STV Free facilities at local leisure centre **CONF:** Thtr 90 Class 70 Board 40 **PARKING:** 60 **NOTES:** No smoking in restaurant Civ Wed 50 **CARDS:**

★★★70% Red Lion
Milford St SP1 2AN
☎ 01722 323334 📠 01722 325756
e-mail: reception@the-redlion.co.uk
Dir: *in city centre off Market Sq*

Enjoying a central location this 13th-century coaching inn is one of the oldest buildings in Salisbury. Bedrooms and public areas offer modern levels of comfort, and decor styles keep to the traditional. Dining options include the restaurant and the lounge which is popular for lunches. The Frothblowers Arms is a recent addition to the hotel.

continued

ROOMS: 52 en suite (2 fmly) No smoking in 36 bedrooms s £81.50-£94; d £101.50-£119.50 * LB **CONF:** Thtr 100 Class 50 Board 40 Del from £98 * **SERVICES:** Lift **PARKING:** 10 **NOTES:** No dogs (ex guide dogs) No smoking in restaurant **CARDS:**

See advert on this page

★★★70% The White Hart

St John St SP1 2SD
☎ 0870 400 8125 📠 01722 412761
e-mail: heritagehotels_salisbury.white_hart @forte-hotels.com

Dir: *from M3 junct 7 take A3, A338 for Salisbury and follow signs for city centre. Hotel on Exeter St, parking at rear*

Dating in parts from the 16th century, this character hotel is directly opposite the cathedral precinct. Bedrooms vary in size, but all are tastefully decorated, bright and inviting. The traditional bar and lounge are popular for morning coffee and afternoon tea.

ROOMS: 68 en suite (7 fmly) No smoking in 28 bedrooms s £85-£105; d £115-£140 * LB **FACILITIES:** STV Xmas **CONF:** Thtr 80 Class 40 Board 40 Del from £99 * **PARKING:** 90 **NOTES:** No smoking in restaurant Civ Wed 80 **CARDS:**

★★★68% Rose & Crown

REGAL

Harnham Rd, Harnham SP2 8JQ
☎ 01722 399955 📠 01722 339816

Dir: *M3 junct 8 to A303 then A30 to centre of Salisbury*

A charming hotel on the banks of the river Avon, with views of the cathedral. Bedrooms, in the main house or new wing, are well designed and smartly furnished. The Pavilions restaurant is virtually on the water's edge, an evening fixed price menu is

continued on p488

SALISBURY, continued

Rose & Crown, Salisbury

offered. Public areas are cosy and attractively furnished, the two bars have log fires.
ROOMS: 28 en suite (5 fmly) No smoking in 4 bedrooms s fr £105; d fr £130 * LB **FACILITIES:** STV Fishing Xmas **CONF:** Thtr 80 Class 40 Board 40 Del from £100 * **PARKING:** 42 **NOTES:** No smoking in restaurant Civ Wed **CARDS:**

★★★66% Grasmere House

MINOTEL Great Britain

Harnhan Rd SP2 8JN
☎ 01722 338388 01722 333710
e-mail: grasmerehotel@mistral.co.uk
Dir: *on A3094 on S side of Salisbury next to All Saints Church in Harnham*
This Victorian house has gardens which run down to the River Nadder, and views towards the cathedral. Public areas include a spacious conservatory, traditionally furnished lounge, and cosy bar. In the restaurant, the daily changing menu offers an appetizing range of dishes. Bedrooms are tastefully furnished.
ROOMS: 4 en suite 16 annexe en suite (2 fmly) No smoking in 4 bedrooms s £72.50-£75.50; d £115-£155 (incl. bkfst) * LB **FACILITIES:** Fishing Croquet lawn Xmas **CONF:** Thtr 85 Class 65 Board 45 Del from £105.50 * **PARKING:** 36 **NOTES:** Civ Wed 120
CARDS:

See advert on opposite page

Premier Collection

★★ Howard's House

Teffont Evias SP3 5RJ
☎ 01722 716392 01722 716820
e-mail: paul.firmin@virgin.net
Dir: *turn off B3089 at Teffont Magna follow signs to Howards House*

This charming hotel is located in the quintessential English village of Teffont Evias. Spacious bedrooms are comfortably furnished, with thoughtful extras like fresh fruit, home-made biscuits and magazines. The cooking continues to prove popular - the culmination of excellent ingredients and experienced culinary skills.
ROOMS: 9 en suite (1 fmly) s £70-£75; d £95-£145 (incl. bkfst) * LB **FACILITIES:** Croquet lawn **CONF:** Class 20 Board 12 **PARKING:** 23 **NOTES:** No smoking in restaurant Closed 24-27 Dec **CARDS:**

○ Cathedral Hotel

Milford Place, 7-9 Milford St SP1 2AJ
☎ 01722 343700
Situated close to the shops and Cathedral Close, this hotel dates from the 1700s. It has a lively public bar, grill-type restaurant and first floor lounge; bedrooms are simply furnished and have some modern facilities.
NOTES: Open

SALTASH, Cornwall & Isles of Scilly Map 02 SX45

★★★67% China Fleet Country Club

North Pill PL12 6LJ
☎ 01752 848668 01752 848456
e-mail: sales@china-fleet.co.uk
This popular country hotel is set in 180 acres of countryside by the river Tamar. Accommodation is provided in a range of apartments, all of which are well equipped and comfortably furnished. A choice of dining options is available with the 'Farmhouse' restaurant. The club has a tremendous range of leisure activities.
ROOMS: 40 en suite No smoking in 6 bedrooms s fr £45; d £55-£70 * **FACILITIES:** STV Indoor swimming (H) Sauna Solarium Gym Pool table Putting green Jacuzzi/spa Badminton Floodlit driving range Health & beauty Indoor bowls ch fac Xmas **CONF:** Thtr 400 Class 150 Board 50 Del £71 * **SERVICES:** Lift **PARKING:** 400 **NOTES:** No dogs (ex guide dogs) **CARDS:**

⌂ *Travelodge*

Travelodge

Callington Rd, Carkeel PL12 6LF
☎ Central Res 0800 850950 01752 849028
Dir: *on A38 Saltash By-Pass - 1m from Tamar Bridge*
This modern building offers accommodation in smart, spacious and well equipped bedrooms, all with en suite bathrooms. Refreshments may be taken at the nearby family restaurant. For further details and the Travelodge phone number, consult the Hotel Groups page.
ROOMS: 31 en suite **CONF:** Thtr 25 Class 15 Board 12

SAMPFORD PEVERELL, Devon Map 03 ST01

★★62% Parkway House

32 Lower Town EX16 7BJ
☎ 01884 820255 01884 820780
Dir: *exit M5 junct 27. Proceed towards Tiverton and after 0.25m take road to Sampford Peverell. Follow into village, hotel is large white bldg on right*
Lying in landscaped gardens, just two minutes from J27 of the M5, this is an ideal choice for business and leisure travellers. On the edge of the village, the hotel benefits from extensive views across the Culm Valley. Bedrooms are smartly presented, offering high levels of equipment and include two family rooms. A tempting menu is served in Cezanne's Restaurant which provides a light and airy atmopshere. Additional facilities include a choice of function rooms.
ROOMS: 10 en suite (2 fmly) s £35-£45; d £50-£60 (incl. bkfst) * LB **FACILITIES:** STV ch fac **CONF:** Thtr 120 Class 40 Board 40 Del from £47.50 * **PARKING:** 100 **NOTES:** No dogs (ex guide dogs) No smoking in restaurant Civ Wed **CARDS:**

S

⇧ *Travelodge*

Sampford Peverell Service Area EX16 7HD

☎ 01884 821087

Dir: *junc 27, M5*

This modern building offers accommodation in smart, spacious and well equipped bedrooms, all with en suite bathrooms. Refreshments may be taken at the nearby family restaurant. For further details and the Travelodge phone number, consult the Hotel Groups page.

ROOMS: 40 en suite

SANDBACH, Cheshire — Map 07 SJ76

★★★66% Chimney House

Congleton Rd CW11 4ST

☎ 01270 764141 ⎙ 01270 768916

Dir: *on A534, 1m from M6 junct 17 heading for Congleton*

Set in eight acres of attractive grounds, this half-timbered Tudor style building is conveniently located close to junction 17 of the M6 motorway. Bedrooms are bright, modern and well equipped with more spacious rooms being located in the older wing. Dinner is served in the attractive Patio restaurant. Meeting and function suites are available, together with a sauna and spa bath.

ROOMS: 49 en suite (6 fmly) No smoking in 33 bedrooms s £80-£95; d £90-£105 * LB **FACILITIES:** STV Sauna Putting green entertainment **CONF:** Thtr 120 Class 40 Board 40 Del from £95 * **PARKING:** 110 **NOTES:** No dogs (ex guide dogs) No smoking in restaurant Civ Wed 40 **CARDS:**

SANDBANKS See Poole

SANDIACRE, Derbyshire — Map 08 SK43

★★★67% *Posthouse Nottingham/Derby*

Bostocks Ln NG10 5NJ

Posthouse

☎ 0870 400 9062 ⎙ 0115 9490469

Dir: *M1 J25 follow exit to Sandiacre, hotel on right*

This modern hotel is conveniently situated just off junction 25 of the M1 motorway. Bedrooms offer a good standard of contemporary furnishings and are well equipped, whilst public areas, including the refurbished Traders restaurant, are well maintained and comfortable. Staff are friendly and helpful, and an all day lounge menu and 24 hour room service are available. There are numerous conference rooms and ample parking.

ROOMS: 93 en suite (6 fmly) No smoking in 50 bedrooms **FACILITIES:** Pool table Day membership to David Lloyd Leisure **CONF:** Thtr 60 Class 26 Board 28 **PARKING:** 180 **CARDS:**

Bad hair day? Hairdryers in all rooms three stars and above.

S

SANDIWAY, Cheshire Map 07 SJ67

Premier Collection

★★★ Nunsmere Hall Country House

Tarporley Rd CW8 2ES
☎ 01606 889100 📠 01606 889055
e-mail: reservations@nunsmere.co.uk
Dir: *from Chester follow A51, A556-Manchester, reach intersection at A49 turn right to Whitchurch, Nunsmere Hall is 1m on left hand side*
This impeccably maintained, lakeside house dates back to 1900. The bedrooms are individually styled, tastefully appointed to a very high standard and thoughtfully equipped. Guests can relax in a choice of elegant lounges, the library or the oak-panelled bar. In the restaurant, the menu offers a cosmopolitan range of dishes.
ROOMS: 36 en suite No smoking in 10 bedrooms s £117.50-£137.50; d £160-£185 * LB **FACILITIES:** Snooker Croquet lawn Putting green Archery Air Rifle Shooting Falconry Clay pigeon shooting entertainment Xmas **CONF:** Thtr 50 Class 24 Board 32 Del £190 * **SERVICES:** Lift **PARKING:** 80 **NOTES:** No dogs (ex guide dogs) No smoking in restaurant RS Sun Civ Wed 70
CARDS:

SANDOWN See Wight, Isle of

SANDWICH, Kent Map 05 TR35

★★65% The Blazing Donkey Country Hotel & Inn

Hay Hill, Ham CT14 0ED
☎ 01304 617362 📠 01304 615264
e-mail: info@blazingdonkey.co.uk
Dir: *turn off A256 at Eastry into the village, turn right at the Five Bells public house, hotel is 0.75m along the lane situated on the left*

The Blazing Donkey is set in the heart of Kentish farmland. A former labourer's cottage and barn, it is now a distinctive inn of character. The atmosphere is convivial and informal. Bedrooms are big and arranged around a courtyard. Ideal for golfers the hotel is close to Royal St George's.
ROOMS: 19 en suite (2 fmly) No smoking in 5 bedrooms s £65; d £79.50 (incl. cont bkfst) * LB **FACILITIES:** Croquet lawn Putting green Childrens playground Xmas **SERVICES:** air con **PARKING:** 108 **NOTES:** No smoking in restaurant Civ Wed 350
CARDS:

SAUNDERTON, Buckinghamshire Map 04 SP70

★★63% Rose & Crown

Wycombe Rd HP27 9NP
☎ 01844 345299 📠 01844 343140
e-mail: rose.crown@btinternet.com
Dir: *on A4010, 6m from Exit4 M40*
This family run hotel has been offering hospitality to travellers for over a century and is conveniently situated between High Wycombe and Aylesbury. Rooms are comfortable and offer a good range of extra facilities. The bar, with its log fire, is the focal point of the hotel. Guests may choose dinner from an extensive blackboard menu, with meals taken in the bar or the more secluded restaurant which features a number of oil paintings by local artists.
ROOMS: 15 en suite s £65-£78.45; d £78-£88 (incl. bkfst) * LB **CONF:** Thtr 30 Board 15 **PARKING:** 50 **NOTES:** No dogs (ex guide dogs) No smoking in restaurant Closed 25 Dec-1 Jan
CARDS:

SAUNTON, Devon Map 02 SS43

★★★★70% Saunton Sands

EX33 1LQ
☎ 01271 890212 📠 01271 890145
e-mail: info@sauntonsands.co.uk
Dir: *turn off A361 at Braunton, signposted Croyde B3231 hotel 2m on left*

With direct access to five miles of sandy beach, this popular hotel enjoys stunning sea views. Bedrooms vary in size, several have private balconies and a number are especially suited for family occupation. All of the public areas benefit from the splendid views. A choice of comfortable lounges is provided with regular entertainment arranged on certain evenings. Extensive leisure facilities are available, including both indoor and outdoor swimming pools and a supervised nursery.
ROOMS: 92 en suite (39 fmly) s £68-£98; d £132-£210 (incl. bkfst) * LB **FACILITIES:** STV Indoor swimming (H) Outdoor swimming (H) Tennis (hard) Squash Snooker Sauna Solarium Gym Pool table Putting green Jacuzzi/spa Table tennis entertainment ch fac Xmas **CONF:** Thtr 150 **SERVICES:** Lift **PARKING:** 142 **NOTES:** No dogs (ex guide dogs) Civ Wed **CARDS:**

See advert on page 489

S

★★74% Preston House
EX33 1LG
☎ 01271 890472 01271 890555
e-mail: prestonhouse-saunton@zoom.co.uk
This delightful south-facing property, built during the reign of Queen Victoria as a summer retreat, occupies a stunning elevated position overlooking Barnstaple Bay. Now a small privately run hotel, complete with heated outdoor pool and terraced gardens, Preston House has direct access to Saunton beach and its four miles of golden sand. The bedrooms are equipped with modern comforts and most benefit from the best of the views. Public areas include an elegant sitting room, a sunny conservatory where breakfast is served and an impressive dining room where guests can sample imaginative dishes prepared from good quality, and wherever possible, local ingredients.
ROOMS: 12 en suite No smoking in all bedrooms s £55-£70; d £90-£130 (incl. bkfst) * LB **FACILITIES:** Outdoor swimming (H) Sauna Jacuzzi/spa **PARKING:** 16 **NOTES:** No dogs (ex guide dogs) No children 12yrs No smoking in restaurant Closed 21 Dec-Jan **CARDS:**

SCARBOROUGH, North Yorkshire Map 08 TA08

★★★71% Ox Pasture Hall Country Hotel
Lady Ediths Dr, Raincliffe Woods YO12 5TD
☎ 01723 365295 01723 355156
e-mail: hawksmoor@oxpasture.freeserve.co.uk
Dir: *A171 out of Scarborough, after passing hospital, follow tourist sign for "Forge Valley & Raincliffe Woods" turn left, hotel 1.5m on right*

This delightful country hotel is a lovely conversion of a farmhouse in the North Riding Forest Park. Three bedrooms are in the main house and the others around an attractive garden courtyard. Public areas include a split-level bar, a quiet lounge, and attractive restaurant offering both a carte and a fixed-price menu.
ROOMS: 23 en suite (4 fmly) No smoking in 4 bedrooms s £40.50-£53.50; d £65-£91 (incl. bkfst) * LB **FACILITIES:** Fishing Croquet lawn Putting green Xmas **PARKING:** 30 **NOTES:** No smoking in restaurant
CARDS:

See advert on this page

★★★70% Wrea Head Country Hotel
Scalby YO13 0PB
☎ 01723 378211 01723 371780
e-mail: wreahead@englishrosehotels.co.uk
Dir: *from Scarborough follow A171 until hotel signpost on left, turn into Barmoor Lane, hotel drive is on left*
Wrea Head Country Hotel is an elegant Victorian country house, standing in 14 acres of well tended grounds and gardens close to the National Park. The house has been delightfully furnished throughout and includes a cosy well stocked library and a comfortable bar. Bedrooms vary in size and all are thoughtfully equipped to a high standard. Service is professional and friendly.
continued

ROOMS: 20 en suite (2 fmly) s £57.50-£70; d £115-£185 (incl. bkfst) * LB **FACILITIES:** STV Croquet lawn Putting green Xmas **CONF:** Thtr 30 Class 16 Board 20 **PARKING:** 50 **NOTES:** No dogs (ex guide dogs) No smoking in restaurant Civ Wed 60
CARDS:

See advert on page 495

★★★65% Esplanade
Belmont Rd YO11 2AA
☎ 01723 360382 01723 376137
Dir: *from Scarborough town centre cross Valley Bridge, left after bridge then immediate right onto Belmont Rd, hotel 100mtrs on right*
This large hotel enjoys a superb position overlooking South Bay and the harbour. Both the terrace leading off the lounge bar, and the restaurant, with its striking oriel window, benefit from these views. Bedrooms are well furnished to a stylish modern standard and are well equipped.
ROOMS: 73 en suite (9 fmly) **FACILITIES:** Pool table Darts Table tennis **CONF:** Thtr 140 Class 100 Board 40 Del from £45 * **SERVICES:** Lift **PARKING:** 20 **NOTES:** No smoking in restaurant
CARDS:

★★★64% Ambassador
Centre of the Esplanade YO11 2AY
☎ 01723 362841 01723 366166
Dir: *A64, right at 1st small rdbt opposite, then right at next small rdbt, take immediate left down Avenue Victoria to the Cliff Top*
Standing on the South Cliff with excellent views over the bay, this friendly hotel offers well equipped bedrooms together with pleasantly decorated public rooms. A 40' indoor pool is available together with a sauna and solarium and entertainment is provided during the season.
continued on p492

S

SCARBOROUGH, continued

ROOMS: 59 en suite (10 fmly) s fr £30; d fr £60 (incl. bkfst) * LB **FACILITIES:** STV Indoor swimming (H) Solarium Jacuzzi/spa Steam room Games room available at Crown Hotel entertainment Xmas **CONF:** Thtr 140 Class 90 Board 60 Del from £50 * **SERVICES:** Lift **NOTES:** No smoking in restaurant **CARDS:**

See advert on opposite page

★★★ 64% Palm Court

St Nicholas Cliff YO11 2ES
☎ 01723 368161 01723 371547
Dir: *follow signs for Town Centre and Town Hall, hotel is on route to Town Hall situated on right hand side*

The public rooms are spacious and comfortable at this modern town centre hotel and the bedrooms are well equipped. Traditional cooking is provided in the attractive restaurant while staff are friendly and helpful.
ROOMS: 46 en suite (7 fmly) s £40-£45; d £74-£84 (incl. bkfst) * LB **FACILITIES:** Indoor swimming (H) Table tennis entertainment Xmas **CONF:** Thtr 200 Class 100 Board 60 Del from £48 * **SERVICES:** Lift **PARKING:** 80 **NOTES:** No dogs (ex guide dogs) **CARDS:**

See advert on opposite page

★★★ 64% Hotel St Nicholas

St Nicholas Cliff YO11 2EU
☎ 01723 364101 01723 500538
Dir: *in town centre, railway station on right, turn right at traffic lights, left at next set, follow road along, across rdbt, take next left*

A splendid Victorian hotel with fine views over the sea and with easy access to the town. Bedrooms are well equipped and there is a wide choice in room size. There are good lounge and bar facilities as well as a leisure club. Traditional food is served in the restaurant and there is also a themed pub.
ROOMS: 144 en suite s £35-£60; d £50-£95 (incl. bkfst) * LB **FACILITIES:** STV Indoor swimming (H) Snooker Sauna Solarium Gym entertainment Xmas **CONF:** Thtr 400 Class 100 Board 50 **SERVICES:** Lift **PARKING:** 5 **NOTES:** Civ Wed **CARDS:**

★★★ 63% Crown

Esplanade YO11 2AG
☎ 01723 373491 01723 362271
e-mail: reservations@scarboroughhotel.com
Dir: *On A64 follow town centre signs to traffic lights opposite railway station, turn r go across Valley Bridge 1st l then r up Belmont Rd to cliff top*

Occupying a prime position on the South Cliff, this elegant hotel overlooks the sea and is only a short walk from the town centre. Several bedrooms enjoy spectacular views over Scarborough Bay and there is a comfortable lounge and good conference and meeting facilities.
ROOMS: 83 en suite (7 fmly) s £43-£65; d £66-£80 (incl. bkfst) * LB **FACILITIES:** Snooker Pool table (Free use of indoor leisure facilities at the Ambassador Hotel) Xmas **CONF:** Thtr 180 Class 100 Board 100 Del from £55 * **SERVICES:** Lift **NOTES:** No smoking in restaurant **CARDS:**

★★★ 61% Clifton

Queens Pde, North Cliff YO12 7HX
☎ 01723 375691 01723 364203
e-mail: clifton@englishrosehotels.co.uk
Dir: *on entering the town centre, follow signs for North Bay*
Standing in an impressive position overlooking the bay, this large holiday hotel is convenient for Peasholm Park and other local leisure attractions. Bedrooms are pleasant and entertainment is provided in the spacious public rooms during the season.
ROOMS: 71 en suite (11 fmly) s £40-£55 (incl. bkfst) * LB **FACILITIES:** Sauna Solarium Pool table Xmas **CONF:** Thtr 120 Class 50 Board 50 Del from £55 * **SERVICES:** Lift **PARKING:** 45 **NOTES:** No dogs (ex guide dogs) No smoking in restaurant **CARDS:**

See advert on page 495

★★ 74% Gridley's Crescent

The Crescent YO11 2PP
☎ 01723 360929 & 507507 01723 354126
e-mail: reception@crescent-hotel.co.uk
Dir: *on entering Scarborough travel towards railway station then follow signs to Brunswick Pavilion, at traffic lights turn into Crescent*
This listed building sits just a short distance from the town centre. The accommodation is attractively decorated and well appointed, equipped with a useful range of facilities. A choice of dining options and bars is another bonus. There is an elegant restaurant serving a set price menu and carte, with the carvery offering a less formal option. Service is friendly and attentive.
ROOMS: 20 en suite No smoking in 7 bedrooms s £45; d £80 (incl. bkfst) * LB **CONF:** Thtr 40 Board 15 Del from £72.50 * **SERVICES:** Lift **NOTES:** No dogs (ex guide dogs) No children 6yrs No smoking in restaurant **CARDS:**

TV dinner? Room service at three stars and above.

S

★ ★ ★

Raven Hall

COUNTRY HOUSE HOTEL & GOLF COURSE

Half way between Scarborough and Whitby, this historic country house hotel is situated in 100 acres of award winning gardens and battlements.

★ 52 en-suite bedrooms ★ Private cliff top golf course ★ Tennis ★ Croquet ★ Putting ★ Crown Bowls ★ Swimming Pools - outdoor and indoor ★ Snooker ★ Hair & Beauty Salon ★ Sauna ★ Conference facilities ★ Medieval Banqueting Hall ★ Children welcome ★ Parking for 200 cars . . . and an enviable reputation for good food & warm hospitality

Tel: (01723) 870353 Fax: (01723) 870072
Ravenscar, North Yorkshire YO13 0ET
Email: enquiries@ravenhall.co.uk
Web: www.ravenhall.co.uk

Prime clifftop gracious and individual award winning AA/ETB 3-star sea view Victorian hotel, above spa entertainment/conference centre, offering friendly professional service and fine cuisine • 59 en-suite bedrooms with full facilities, satellite TV, lift, panoramic bay views • Conference facilities for the discerning delegate • 40ft indoor heated swimming pool, spa and steam room • Tasteful entertainment • Opposite famous Italian rose gardens • Cliff lift to beach and town • Free street parking and much more!

AMBASSADOR LEISURE HOTEL

Centre of the Esplanade
Scarborough, North Yorkshire YO11 2AY
Tel: 01723 362841 Fax: 01723 366166
www.ambassador-hotel.co.uk

The Mount Hotel

A FIRST CLASS, 50 BEDROOM HOTEL SITUATED IN A COMMANDING POSITION OVERLOOKING THE SOUTH BAY, ADJACENT TO THE SPA, AND IS IN CLOSE PROXIMITY TO THE SOUTH SANDS SHOPS, AND ALL PLACES OF AMUSEMENT.

AA ★ ★

- **A FULL RESIDENTIAL LICENCE**
- **A LIFT TO ALL FLOORS**
- **ALL ROOMS WITH PRIVATE BATHROOMS/SHOWERS, COLOUR TV, AND TELEPHONE**
- **GARAGE & REASONABLE PARKING WITHIN A FEW YARDS WALK**

SCARBOROUGH
Tel (01723) 360961
Fax (01723) 375850
CLIFF BRIDGE TERRACE, ST. NICHOLAS CLIFF SCARBOROUGH

PALM COURT HOTEL

St. Nicholas Cliff
Scarborough
YO11 2ES
telephone
01723 368161
facsimile
01723 371547

Superb central location with guaranteed free covered car parking and indoor heated swimming pool, minutes to the beach, town centre, theatres and spa. All 46 bedrooms en-suite with colour television. Ideal for the discerning conference delegate offering in-house conference facilities.

Weekend, midweek and weekly breaks all year.

Open Christmas and New Year.

AA ★ ★ ★

S

SCARBOROUGH, continued

★★71% *The Mount*

Cliff Bridge Ter, Saint Nicholas Cliff YO11 2HA
☎ 01723 360961 Fax 01723 360961
Standing in a fine, elevated position enjoying superb views of the bay, this elegant Regency hotel is personally owned and run to a high standard. The richly furnished and comfortable public rooms are inviting, and the well equipped bedrooms have been attractively decorated. The suites are especially comfortable.
ROOMS: 50 en suite (5 fmly) No smoking in 2 bedrooms **FACILITIES:** **SERVICES:** Lift **NOTES:** Closed Jan-mid Mar **CARDS:**

See advert on page 493

★★65% Bradley Court Hotel

Filey Rd, South Cliff YO11 2SE
☎ 01723 360476 Fax 01723 376661
e-mail: bradley@yorkshirecoast.co.uk
Dir: *from A64 enter Scarborough Town limits, at 1st rdbt turn right signposted Filey & South Cliff, at next rdbt turn left, hotel 50yds on left*
This generally modern hotel is only a short walk from both the town centre and the South Cliff. Bedrooms are well equipped and there are spacious public rooms which include a bar lounge and a large and modern function room.
ROOMS: 40 en suite (4 fmly) No smoking in 6 bedrooms s £30-£35; d £60-£70 (incl. bkfst) * LB **FACILITIES:** Pool table Xmas **CONF:** Thtr 160 Class 100 Board 60 Del from £49 * **SERVICES:** Lift **PARKING:** 20 **NOTES:** No dogs No smoking in restaurant
CARDS:

★★65% La Baia Hotel

24 Blenheim Ter YO12 7HD
☎ 01723 370780
e-mail: la.baia.hotel@talk21.com
Dir: *A64 to centre of town, left at railway station, 1st right Victoria Rd/ Castle Rd, left St Peters Church onto Blenheim St and left into Blenheim Ter*
This family owned hotel offers fine hospitality and enjoys superb views over the bay. Bedrooms are pleasantly furnished and have been thoughtfully equipped. A friendly bar and cosy dining room are also provided and a good range of home cooking is served each evening.
ROOMS: 12 en suite (2 fmly) s £26; d £44-£52 (incl. bkfst) **NOTES:** No dogs No smoking in restaurant Closed 27 Oct-28 Feb
CARDS:

S

★★65% Red Lea

Prince of Wales Ter YO11 2AJ
☎ 01723 362431 Fax 01723 371230
e-mail: redlea@globalnet.co.uk
Dir: *follow signs for South Cliff, Prince of Wales Terrace leads off the esplanade opp the cliff lift*
This family-owned hotel on the South Cliff provides very good value for money. It offers well equipped bedrooms and public areas, with an indoor pool. A good value five-course dinner is served in the spacious dining room while staff are friendly and attentive.
ROOMS: 67 en suite (7 fmly) s £34-£36; d £68-£72 (incl. bkfst) * LB **FACILITIES:** Indoor swimming (H) Sauna Solarium Gym Pool table Xmas **CONF:** Thtr 40 Class 25 Board 25 Del from £60 * **SERVICES:** Lift **NOTES:** No dogs (ex guide dogs) No smoking in restaurant
CARDS:

Read all about it! Newspapers delivered to bedrooms in four and five star hotels.

★★63% Southlands

15 West St, South Cliff YO11 2QW
☎ 01723 361461 Fax 01723 376035
e-mail: sales@southlandshotel.co.uk
Dir: *in Scarborough, follow town centre signs, turn right at railway station, at 2nd set of traffic lights turn left, car park is 200yds on left*
Situated in a quiet area close to the South Cliff, this hotel is popular with tour groups and offers spacious bedrooms and well proportioned public areas. Friendly and attentive service is provided by a pleasant and well managed team.
ROOMS: 58 en suite (8 fmly) No smoking in 2 bedrooms d £70-£92 (incl. bkfst) * LB **FACILITIES:** Xmas **CONF:** Thtr 150 Class 100 Board 20 Del from £80 * **SERVICES:** Lift **PARKING:** 35 **NOTES:** No smoking in restaurant **CARDS:**

★★61% Manor Heath Hotel

67 Northstead Manor Dr YO12 6AF
☎ 01723 365720 Fax 01723 365720
e-mail: enquiries@manorheath.freeserve.co.uk
Dir: *follow signs for North Bay and Peasholme Park*
A warm welcome is offered at this pleasant traditional private hotel, situated on the North Bay beside Peasholm Park. Public areas include a cosy bar, comfortable lounge together with a relaxing dining room. The bedrooms are modern and bright, offering all the expected comforts.
ROOMS: 14 en suite (6 fmly) s £23; d £46 (incl. bkfst) * LB **PARKING:** 16 **NOTES:** No smoking in restaurant Closed Dec-1 Jan
CARDS:

★★60% Brooklands

Esplanade Gardens, South Cliff YO11 2AW
☎ 01723 376576 Fax 01723 376576
Dir: *from A64 York turn left at B&Q rdbt, right at next mini rdbt then 1st left onto Victoria Av, at the end turn left then 2nd left*

The Brooklands is a traditional family owned and run seaside hotel, successfully catering for tours and offering sound value for money. It stands on the South Cliff overlooking a small park and is close to the sea. There are ample lounges and wholesome home cooking.
ROOMS: 63 rms (62 en suite) (11 fmly) s £33; d £66 (incl. bkfst) * LB **FACILITIES:** Riding Pool table Xmas **CONF:** Thtr 120 Class 80 Board 30 **SERVICES:** Lift **PARKING:** 1 **NOTES:** No dogs (ex guide dogs) No smoking in restaurant Closed Jan **CARDS:**

Late for dinner? Quality Standards star rating means that last orders for dinner should be no earlier than:
★ 6.30pm ★★ 7.00pm ★★★ 8.00pm
★★★★ 9.00pm ★★★★★ 10.00pm

ENGLISH ROSE HOTELS

WREA HEAD

COUNTRY HOUSE HOTEL

Sample the delights of this beautifully restored Victorian Country House set in acres of glorious gardens and park lands at the edge of the North York Moors National Park. Twenty individually styled bedrooms. Award winning Four Seasons restaurant offers superb cuisine using fresh local produce. Ample free car parking. Situated three miles north of Scarborough – a perfect base for touring the heritage coast. Meeting facilities for up to 20 persons in privacy and seclusion.

For details ring 01723 378211
Barmoor Lane, Scalby
Scarborough YO13 0PB
Fax: 01723 355936

AA ★★★

HACKNESS GRANGE COUNTRY HOTEL

AA ★★★

North Yorkshire Moors National Park
nr Scarborough YO13 0JW

Situated on the outskirts of Scarborough, this gracious Country House is set in acres of beautiful gardens and grounds beside the River Derwent, within the North York Moors National Park. Excellent leisure choices - indoor heated swimming pool with jacuzzi, tennis court, trout fishing (in season), croquet and nine hole pitch 'n putt. 33 delightful en-suite bedrooms, many with scenic country views, and award winning restaurant renowned for good food. Some ground floor rooms available. Perfect location for Board Meetings and available for exclusive use for corporated events and activities.

See entry under Hackness

Tel: 01723 882345 Fax: 01723 882391

THE CLIFTON HOTEL

QUEENS PARADE, NORTH SHORE
SCARBOROUGH YO12 7HX
Tel: 01723 375691 Fax: 01723 364203

AA ★★★

The finest location on Scarborough's North Shore with many of the 71 en-suite bedrooms having panoramic sea views over the Bay and Scarborough Castle headland.
Excellent food with good old fashioned Yorkshire portions! Free private car parking.
Adjacent to Alexander Bowls Centre and Scarborough Cricket Ground.

ENGLISH ROSE HOTELS

SCILLY, ISLES OF — Map 02

BRYHER — Map 02

★★★70% ❀ Hell Bay Hotel

TR23 0PR
☎ 01720 422947 🖷 01720 423004
e-mail: hellbay@aol.com
Dir: *island location means it is only accessible by helicopter from Penzance, ship from Penzance or plane from Bristol, Exeter, Plymouth or Land's End*

This friendly hotel is located on the smallest of the inhabited Scilly islands. Each of the comfortable bedrooms has its own sitting room and access to the garden; many have marvellous sea views. There is a choice of comfortable lounges, a restaurant and a bar.
ROOMS: 17 en suite (3 fmly) d £136-£180 (incl. bkfst & dinner) * LB **FACILITIES:** Croquet lawn Putting green Boules **NOTES:** No dogs (ex guide dogs) No smoking in restaurant Closed 29 Oct-12 Mar
CARDS:

ST MARTIN'S — Map 02

Premier Collection

★★★❀❀❀ St Martin's on the Isle

Lower Town TR25 0QW
☎ 01720 422090 🖷 01720 422298
e-mail: stay@stmartinshotel.co.uk
Dir: *20 minute helicopter flight to St Marys, then 20 minute launch to St Martins*

This island hideaway is ideal for those seeking tranquillity. The hotel has its own beach, jetty and yacht, and enjoys an unrivalled panorama. Bedrooms are individually decorated and furnished. Public rooms are cleverly designed and the restaurant serves award winning cuisine.
ROOMS: 30 en suite (10 fmly) d £230-£270 (incl. bkfst & dinner) * LB **FACILITIES:** Indoor swimming (H) Tennis (hard) Snooker Clay pigeon shooting ch fac **CONF:** Thtr 50 Class 50 Board 50
NOTES: No smoking in restaurant Closed Nov-Mar
CARDS:

ST MARY'S — Map 02

★★★71% ❀❀ Star Castle

The Garrison TR21 0JA
☎ 01720 422317 & 423342 🖷 01720 422343
e-mail: recep@starcastlescilly.demon.co.uk
Dir: *overlooking the Harbour.*

Built in 1593 as a fortress, this historic landmark now houses a comfortable hotel complete with modern facilities and panoramic views over St Mary's and the surrounding islands. Bedrooms vary in style and size, and most have sea views. The garden apartments are the most spacious whilst the castle rooms include four-poster beds and oak beamed ceilings. The cuisine is a strong feature of the hotel, and guests can choose between a bar meal on the ramparts, a seafood extravaganza in the garden conservatory or a traditional dinner from the carte menu in the castle restaurant.
ROOMS: 10 en suite 23 annexe en suite (17 fmly) s £62.50-£73; d £105-£190 (incl. bkfst) * LB **FACILITIES:** Indoor swimming (H) Tennis (grass) Pool table Games room **PARKING:** 6 **NOTES:** No smoking in restaurant Closed end Oct-Feb **CARDS:**

★★75% Tregarthens

Hugh Town TR21 0PP
☎ 01720 422540 🖷 01720 422089
e-mail: reception@tregarthens-hotel.co.uk
Dir: *100yds from the quay*

This well established, privately owned hotel was first opened in 1848 by Captain Tregarthen, a steam packet owner. It overlooks St Mary's harbour and some of the many islands, including Tresco and Bryher. The professional staff offer a warm and natural welcome to guests either staying for the first time, or to their many repeat visitors. The majority of bedrooms benefit from marvellous views out to sea; all are well equipped and neatly furnished. Traditional cuisine, with some wonderful home made desserts, is served in the restaurant, many tables here also enjoying the unique views.
ROOMS: 32 en suite 1 annexe en suite (5 fmly) s £71-£79; d £126-£176 (incl. bkfst & dinner) * LB **NOTES:** No dogs No smoking in restaurant Closed late Oct-mid Mar **CARDS:**

See advert on opposite page

TRESCO — Map 02

★★★78% ❀ The Island

TR24 0PU
☎ 01720 422883 🖷 01720 423008
e-mail: islandhotel@tresco.co.uk
Dir: *helicopter service Penzance to Tresco, hotel on north east side of island*

The magnificent island setting and stunning gardens are only the first impressions of this splendid hotel. Sunny public rooms include a popular lounge and bar, together with a quiet library for residents. Bedroom accommodation has been designed to make the best of the sea views. Local fish and shellfish are staples on the regularly-changing menus.
ROOMS: 48 en suite (27 fmly) s £90-£120; d £127-£175 (incl. bkfst & dinner) * LB **FACILITIES:** Outdoor swimming (H) Tennis (hard) Fishing Pool table Croquet lawn Boating Table tennis Bowls ch fac **NOTES:** No dogs (ex guide dogs) Closed Nov-Feb **CARDS:**

★★76% ❀ New Inn

TR24 0QQ
☎ 01720 422844 🖷 01720 423200
e-mail: newinn@tresco.co.uk
Dir: *by New Grimsby Quay*

One of the few hostelries on the island but it provides good cheer, a warm welcome and comfortable surroundings in good measure. The restaurant and the bar provide a good range of tasty meals. Bedrooms are well maintained, smart and well suited to the clientele's needs.
ROOMS: 14 en suite s £65-£97; d £156-£184 (incl. bkfst & dinner) * LB **FACILITIES:** Outdoor swimming (H) Tennis (hard) Pool table Sea fishing Xmas **NOTES:** No dogs No smoking in restaurant
CARDS:

> Arriving late? Four and five star hotels have night porters to assist with your luggage; and 24hr room service.

S

SCOTCH CORNER (NEAR RICHMOND), North Yorkshire Map 08 NZ20

★★★65% Quality Hotel, Scotch Corner
DL10 6NR
☎ 01748 850900 🖷 01748 825417
e-mail: admin@gb609.u-net.com
Dir: *at A1/A66 junct turn off towards Penrith*
Attractive decor characterises the spacious lounges, conference facilities and a smart leisure club while bedrooms fall into two well equipped and comfortable categories: Standard and Premier Plus. Food is served all day in the lounges and the restaurant, where there is a choice of evening menus.
ROOMS: 90 en suite (5 fmly) No smoking in 45 bedrooms s £61-£71; d £65-£83 (incl. bkfst) * LB **FACILITIES:** STV Indoor swimming (H) Sauna Solarium Gym Jacuzzi/spa Beauty therapist Hairdressers Xmas **CONF:** Thtr 280 Class 110 Board 40 Del from £80 * **SERVICES:** Lift **PARKING:** 200 **NOTES:** No smoking in restaurant Civ Wed 200
CARDS:

Travelodge
Skeeby DL10 5EQ
☎ 01748 823768 🖷 01748 823768
Dir: *0.5m S on A1*
This modern building offers accommodation in smart, spacious and well equipped bedrooms, all with en suite bathrooms. Refreshments may be taken at the nearby family restaurant. For further details and the Travelodge phone number, consult the Hotel Groups page.
ROOMS: 40 en suite

Travelodge
Middleton Tyas Ln DL10 6PQ
☎ 01325 377177 🖷 01325 377890
Dir: *A1/A66*
This modern building offers accommodation in smart, spacious and well equipped bedrooms, all with en suite bathrooms. Refreshments may be taken at the nearby family restaurant. For further details and the Travelodge phone number, consult the Hotel Groups page.
ROOMS: 50 en suite

SCUNTHORPE, Lincolnshire Map 08 SE81

★★★★69% Forest Pines Hotel
Ermine St, Broughton DN20 0AQ
☎ 01652 650770 🖷 01652 650495
e-mail: enquiries@forestpines.co.uk
Dir: *200yds from junct 4 on the M180, on the Brigg-Scunthorpe rdbt*
This modern hotel boasts a championship golf course, and an extensive leisure complex. The buttery, open all day, offers a range of snacks and meals in addition to the more formal and recently extended restaurant. The bars often feature live entertainment, and bedrooms are spacious, well equipped and very comfortable.
ROOMS: 86 en suite (40 fmly) No smoking in 50 bedrooms s fr £86; d fr £94 (incl. bkfst) * LB **FACILITIES:** STV Indoor swimming (H) Golf 27 Sauna Gym Putting green Jacuzzi/spa Golf practice nets Driving range Mountain bikes Jogging track entertainment ch fac Xmas **CONF:** Thtr 250 Class 120 Board 60 Del from £116 * **SERVICES:** Lift **PARKING:** 300 **NOTES:** No dogs (ex guide dogs) No smoking in restaurant Civ Wed 180 **CARDS:**

Early start? Hotels at all star levels should provide in-room alarm clocks and/or alarm calls.

★★★67% Menzies Royal
Doncaster Rd DN15 7DE
☎ 0500 636943 (Central Res) 🖷 01773 880321
e-mail: info@menzies-hotels.co.uk
Dir: *from M181, follow A18 to Scunthorpe centre, hotel is on left at a crossroads*
Standing on the A18 approach to the town, this hotel provides modern, freshly decorated bedrooms and attentive service. There is an extensive range of conference and banqueting facilities.
ROOMS: 33 en suite (1 fmly) No smoking in 10 bedrooms s £69.50-£79.50; d £79.50-£89.50 * LB **FACILITIES:** Gym Xmas **CONF:** Thtr 240 Class 200 Board 100 Del from £70 * **PARKING:** 33 **NOTES:** No smoking in restaurant Civ Wed 240
CARDS:

★★★66% Wortley House
Rowland Rd DN16 1SU
☎ 01724 842223 🖷 01724 280646
e-mail: wortley.hotel@virgin.net
Dir: *leave M181 at junct 3 and take A18. At 1st rdbt turn right, at 2nd take 3rd exit, take 2nd left over rdbt, hotel 200mtrs on right*
Catering mainly for the commercial trade, this friendly hotel is near the railway station on the southern edge of town. It has cheerfully decorated public rooms, informal bar meals are very popular, alternatively the bistro-style dining room offers daily and carte menu choices. Bedrooms are pleasantly furnished and well equipped.
ROOMS: 38 en suite (3 fmly) No smoking in 18 bedrooms s £79.50-£82; d £85.50-£90 (incl. bkfst) * LB **FACILITIES:** STV Xmas **CONF:** Thtr 300 Class 120 Board 80 Del from £95 * **PARKING:** 100
NOTES: Civ Wed 240 **CARDS:**

S

SEAHOUSES, Northumberland Map 12 NU23

★★73% Olde Ship
NE68 7RD
☎ 01665 720200 01665 721383
e-mail: theoldeship@seahouses.co.uk
Dir: *lower end of main street above harbour*
Just a stone's throw from the harbour, this friendly family-run hotel has tremendous character with its cosy public areas and corridors adorned with nautical memorabilia. Residents have their own lounge and there is a cabin bar as well as the popular saloon bar. Bedrooms are cosy, well equipped and furnished to a high standard; two four-poster rooms are available.
ROOMS: 12 en suite 7 annexe en suite s fr £37; d fr £74 (incl. bkfst) * LB **FACILITIES:** STV Putting green **PARKING:** 19 **NOTES:** No dogs No children 10yrs No smoking in restaurant Closed Dec-Jan
CARDS:

★★68% Bamburgh Castle
NE68 7SQ
☎ 01665 720283 01665 720848
Dir: *from A1 follow signs for Seahouses*
This holiday hotel overlooks the harbour, with views of Bamburgh Castle, the Farne Islands and Lindisfarne. You can watch the fishing boats from the restaurant or relax in one of the lounges. There is a wide choice of bedroom sizes; all rooms are well equipped and have comfortable seating.
ROOMS: 20 en suite (3 fmly) No smoking in 5 bedrooms s £39.95-£43.95; d £72.95-£84 (incl. bkfst) * LB **FACILITIES:** Putting green Small exercise room Outdoor table tennis **CONF:** Thtr 40 Class 20 Board 25 **PARKING:** 30 **NOTES:** Closed 24-26 Dec & 2wks mid Jan

★★68% Beach House
Sea Front NE68 7SR
☎ 01665 720337 01665 720921
e-mail: beach.house.hotel.seahouses@tinyonline.co.uk
Dir: *Seahouses signposted from A1 between Alnwick and Berwick*
This tourist hotel enjoys fine views out to sea towards the Farne Islands, and has a friendly and welcoming atmosphere. There is now a residents bar to complement the comfortable lounge. Both dinner and breakfast place emphasis on freshly cooked dishes using local produce. This is a non smoking establishment.
ROOMS: 14 en suite (5 fmly) No smoking in all bedrooms s £30-£35; d £60-£70 (incl. bkfst) * **PARKING:** 16 **NOTES:** No dogs No smoking in restaurant Closed Jan **CARDS:**

SEATON, Devon Map 03 SY29

★★69% Seaton Heights Hotel
Seaton Down Hill EX12 2TF
☎ 01297 20932 01297 24839
e-mail: seatonheightshotel@eclipse.co.uk
Dir: *located on A3052 at Tower Cross, Seaton*
With glorious views over the Axe Valley, the town of Seaton and a panoramic expanse of Lyme Bay, Seaton Heights Hotel has a relaxed and friendly atmosphere. Each of the well equipped bedrooms benefits from the splendid views, particularly those on the first floor. In the restaurant, imaginative cooking is the order of the day, with the use of fresh, local ingredients wherever possible. A diverse range of facilities is provided in the Sports Hall.
ROOMS: 26 en suite (8 fmly) s £35-£52; d £70-£82 (incl. bkfst) * LB **FACILITIES:** Outdoor swimming (H) Squash Sauna Solarium Gym Pool table Croquet lawn entertainment Xmas **CONF:** Thtr 600 Class 40 Board 30 Del from £45 * **PARKING:** 200 **NOTES:** No smoking in restaurant **CARDS:**

SEATON BURN, Tyne & Wear Map 12 NZ27

★★★★63% *Holiday Inn*
Great North Rd NE13 6BF
☎ 0191 201 9988 0191 236 8091
Dir: *3m W of Tyne Tunnel towards Morpeth*
This purpose-built hotel with its smart foyer lounge is popular with business guests. Many bedrooms have been refurbished; executive rooms are more modern with useful extras. Public areas have been smartly upgraded. The hotel offers a good range of conference and banqueting facilities.
ROOMS: 150 en suite (77 fmly) No smoking in 74 bedrooms **FACILITIES:** Indoor swimming (H) Sauna Solarium Gym Pool table Putting green Jacuzzi/spa Games room entertainment **CONF:** Thtr 400 Class 200 Board 100 **SERVICES:** air con **PARKING:** 300
CARDS:

⌂ *Travelodge (Newcastle North)*
Front St NE13 6ED
☎ 0191 217 0107
This modern building offers accommodation in smart, spacious and well equipped bedrooms, all with en suite bathrooms. Refreshments may be taken at the nearby family restaurant. For further details and the Travelodge phone number, consult the Hotel Groups page.
ROOMS: 40 en suite

SEAVIEW See Wight, Isle of

SEDGEFIELD, Co Durham Map 08 NZ32

★★★65% *Hardwick Hall*
TS21 2EH
☎ 01740 620253 01740 622771
Dir: *off A1M junct 60 towards Sedgefield, left at 1st rdbt hotel 400m on left*
Standing in extensive parkland with a country park nearby, this mansion house makes an ideal venue for weddings and functions. Bedrooms are all individually decorated and thoughtfully equipped. Guests can dine in the elegant restaurant or in the comfortable bar which offer extensive menus.
ROOMS: 17 en suite (2 fmly) **FACILITIES:** STV **CONF:** Thtr 80 Class 30 Board 40 **PARKING:** 200 **NOTES:** No dogs (ex guide dogs)
CARDS:

⌂ *Travelodge*
TS21 2JX
☎ 01740 623399 01740 623399
Dir: *on A689, 3m E of junct A1M*
This modern building offers accommodation in smart, spacious and well equipped bedrooms, all with en suite bathrooms. Refreshments may be taken at the nearby family restaurant. For further details and the Travelodge phone number, consult the Hotel Groups page.
ROOMS: 40 en suite

SEDGEMOOR MOTORWAY SERVICE AREA (M5), Somerset Map 03 ST35

⌂ Days Inn
BS24 0JL
☎ 01934 750831 01934 750808
Dir: *between junct 22 & 23 M5 northbound*
Fully refurbished, Days Inn offers well equipped, brightly appointed, modern accommodation with smart en suite

continued

bathrooms. There is a fully staffed reception; continental breakfast is available and other refreshments may be taken at the nearby family restaurant.
ROOMS: 40 en suite d fr £45 *

SEDLESCOMBE, East Sussex Map 05 TQ71

★★★67% Brickwall
The Green TN33 0QA
☎ 01424 870253 01424 870785
e-mail: reception@brickwallhotel.totalserve.co.uk
Dir: *off A21 on B2244 at top of Sedlescombe Green*
Dating in part from 1597, the original house here retains its Tudor character and a sympathetic extension houses modern bedrooms. The attractive wood-panelled and oak-beamed restaurant and lounge bar offer a fixed-price four-course menu of traditionally cooked food.
ROOMS: 26 en suite (2 fmly) No smoking in 9 bedrooms s £50-£55; d £70-£80 (incl. bkfst) * LB **FACILITIES:** STV Outdoor swimming (H) Xmas **CONF:** Thtr 30 Class 40 Board 30 **PARKING:** 50 **NOTES:** No smoking in restaurant **CARDS:**

SELBY, North Yorkshire Map 08 SE63

★★64% *Owl*
Main Rd YO8 9JH
☎ 01757 228374 01757 228125
(For full entry see Hambleton (4m W A63))

SENNEN, Cornwall & Isles of Scilly Map 02 SW32

★★65% Old Success Inn
Sennen Cove TR19 7DG
☎ 01736 871232 01736 871457
Dir: *turn right off the A30 approx 1mile before Land's End, signposted Sennen Cove. The Hotel is situated on the left at the bottom of the hill*
Situated on a well known cove, popular with surfers and walkers, this 17th-century inn offers a number of rooms with marvellous sea views. There is a comfortable lounge and a bar around which village and hotel life revolves and where bar meals are served. The restaurant offers traditional dishes and fish specialities.
ROOMS: 12 en suite (1 fmly) s £38-£42; d £65-£80 (incl. bkfst) * LB **FACILITIES:** STV entertainment Xmas **PARKING:** 12 **NOTES:** No smoking in restaurant **CARDS:**

SEVENOAKS, Kent Map 05 TQ55

★★★67% *Donnington Manor*
London Rd, Dunton Green TN13 2TD
☎ 01732 462681 01732 458116
Set in the Weald, near Sevenoaks, the hotel centres on a 15th-century manor with modern extensions. The attractive oak-beamed restaurant keeps its historic character, and the smart well equipped bedrooms are housed in the extension. The small leisure complex has squash courts.
ROOMS: 62 en suite No smoking in 20 bedrooms **FACILITIES:** Indoor swimming (H) Squash Sauna Gym Jacuzzi/spa **CONF:** Thtr 180 Class 60 Board 60 **PARKING:** 120 **NOTES:** No dogs (ex guide dogs)

★★★63% Royal Oak
Upper High St TN13 1HY
☎ 01732 451109 01732 740187
Dir: *on A225, through Town Centre on the right, opposite Sevenoaks School*
Situated in the centre of Sevenoaks this flint-fronted hotel dates back to the 17th century and provides a good base from which to visit the local area. Bedrooms, which are divided between the main building and an adjacent annexe, are all traditionally furnished and well equipped. Public areas include a refurbished bar and brasserie style restaurant which offers an interesting range of carefully prepared dishes.
ROOMS: 21 en suite 16 annexe en suite (2 fmly) No smoking in 6 bedrooms s fr £90; d fr £100 * LB **FACILITIES:** STV Tennis (hard) Xmas **CONF:** Thtr 35 Class 14 Board 20 Del from £115 * **PARKING:** 50 **CARDS:**

SEVERN STOKE, Worcestershire Map 03 SO84

★★67% *Old School House Hotel & Restaurant*
WR8 9JA
☎ 01905 371368 & 371464 01905 371591
Dir: *midway beween Worcester and Tewkesbury - just off the A38*
Situated in a quiet village, this timber-framed property was originally a farm, then, until the sixties, the village school. Bedrooms are comfortably furnished with modern facilities. Open-plan public areas are informally designed around the bar and restaurant.
ROOMS: 13 en suite (1 fmly) No smoking in 3 bedrooms
FACILITIES: Outdoor swimming (H) Fishing Boat for charter Clay pigeon shooting **CONF:** Thtr 100 Class 40 Board 40 **PARKING:** 80 **NOTES:** No smoking in restaurant **CARDS:**

SEVERN VIEW MOTORWAY SERVICE AREA (M4), Gloucestershire Map 03 ST58

Travelodge
M48 Motorway, Severn Bridge BS12 3BH
☎ 0800 850950 01454 632482
Dir: *junct 21 M48*
This modern building offers accommodation in smart, spacious and well equipped bedrooms, all with en suite bathrooms. Refreshments may be taken at the nearby family restaurant. For further details and the Travelodge phone number, consult the Hotel Groups page.
ROOMS: 51 en suite

SHAFTESBURY, Dorset Map 03 ST82

★★★72% Royal Chase
Royal Chase Roundabout SP7 8DB
☎ 01747 853355 01747 851969
e-mail: royalchasehotel@btinternet.com
Dir: *take A303 to within 7m of town and then A350 signposted Blandford Forum. Avoid town centre and follow road to second rdbt*
A well known local landmark, this personally managed hotel is a popular place to stay for both leisure and business guests. There are two categories of bedroom - standard and 'crown'. There are also good conference and leisure facilities.
ROOMS: 35 en suite (13 fmly) No smoking in 10 bedrooms s £58.50-£95; d £89.50-£115 * LB **FACILITIES:** STV Indoor swimming (H) Sauna Turkish steam bath Xmas **CONF:** Thtr 140 Class 90 Board 50 Del from £95 * **PARKING:** 100 **NOTES:** No smoking in restaurant Civ Wed 78 **CARDS:**

SHALDON See Teignmouth

SHANKLIN See Wight, Isle of

Fancy a Singapore Sling? Bar staff in five star hotels should be skilled cocktail mixers.

SHAP, Cumbria Map 12 NY51

★★★65% Shap Wells

CA10 3QU
☎ 01931 716628 🖷 01931 716377
e-mail: manager@shepwells.com
Dir: *from M6 junct 39, follow signs for Kendal, turn left at A6, after approx 1m turn left into hotel drive, hotel is situated about 1m down*

Minutes from the M6 in a secluded valley, this hotel was built in 1833 as a therapeutic spa, and the hotel has been popular with vistors ever since. There is a variety of sizes and styles in the bedrooms which are traditionally furnished. There is a choice of comfortable lounges. Extensive conference and banqueting facilities are available.
ROOMS: 90 en suite 6 annexe en suite (10 fmly) s £55; d £80 (incl. bkfst) * LB **FACILITIES:** Tennis (hard) Snooker Pool table Games room **CONF:** Thtr 200 Class 100 Board 50 Del from £65 * **SERVICES:** Lift **PARKING:** 200 **NOTES:** Closed 23 Dec-20 Feb Civ Wed 150
CARDS:

See advert under KENDAL

SHAPWICK, Somerset Map 03 ST43

★★66% ❀ Shapwick House

Monks Dr TA7 9NL
☎ 01458 210321 🖷 01458 210729
e-mail: keith@shapwickhouse.free-on-line.co.uk
Dir: *from M5 junct 23 turn left heading towards Glastonbury. Left again at junct onto A39 still heading Glastonbury. After 5m hotel signposted on left*
This 16th-century stone manor house, originally built for the Lord Chief Justice of England, has a relaxing atmosphere. The main hall, with its splendid fireplace, provides comfortable seating. Bedrooms are spacious and well equipped, and the restaurant offers an imaginative, fixed-price menu accompanied by a good wine list.
ROOMS: 10 en suite No smoking in all bedrooms s £42.50; d £60-£100 (incl. bkfst) * LB **FACILITIES:** Sauna Gym **CONF:** Thtr 25 Board 14 Del from £100 * **PARKING:** 40 **NOTES:** No children 10yrs RS Xmas day-New Years day **CARDS:**

SHEDFIELD, Hampshire Map 04 SU51

★★★★70% Marriott Meon Valley Hotel & Country Club

Marriott HOTELS·RESORTS·SUITES

Sandy Ln SO32 2HQ
☎ 01329 833455 🖷 01329 834411
Dir: *from W, M27 junct7 take A334 then towards Wickham and Botley. Sandy Lane is on left 2m from Botley*
This very smartly appointed hotel and country club with golf course provides spacious, modern bedrooms, extensive leisure/fitness facilities and a choice of restaurants and bars. Ideally placed for conferences, the Marriot also has a strong weekend leisure market.

continued

ROOMS: 113 en suite No smoking in 80 bedrooms d £86-£88 * LB **FACILITIES:** STV Indoor swimming (H) Golf 27 Tennis (hard) Sauna Solarium Gym Putting green Jacuzzi/spa Cardio-Vascular suite Aerobics studio Health & Beauty salon Xmas **CONF:** Thtr 110 Class 60 Board 40 Del from £135 * **SERVICES:** Lift **PARKING:** 320 **NOTES:** No dogs (ex guide dogs) No smoking in restaurant Civ Wed 80
CARDS:

SHEFFIELD, South Yorkshire Map 08 SK38

★★★★65% Swallow

Kenwood Rd S7 1NQ
☎ 0114 258 3811
🖷 0114 250 0138/0114 255 4744
e-mail: info@swallowhotels.com
Dir: *2m from Sheffield city centre*

Set in eleven acres of gardens and parkland, the hotel is conveniently located in a quiet residential area. Bedrooms range from spacious rooms with private balconies overlooking the ornamental lake, to refurbished rooms with much character in the original house. An extensive range of leisure and meeting facilities are available.
ROOMS: 116 en suite (33 fmly) No smoking in 75 bedrooms s fr £95; d fr £115 (incl. bkfst) * LB **FACILITIES:** STV Indoor swimming (H) Fishing Sauna Solarium Gym Jacuzzi/spa Steam room Xmas **CONF:** Thtr 200 Class 100 Board 60 Del £145 * **SERVICES:** Lift **PARKING:** 200 **NOTES:** No smoking in restaurant Civ Wed 120
CARDS:

★★★72% Beauchief

corus

161 Abbeydale Rd South S7 2QW
☎ 0114 262 0500 🖷 0114 235 0197
Dir: *from City Centre 2m on A621 signed Bakewell*
This comfortable and relaxing hotel is situated in well-tended gardens and grounds, with a stream running though the middle, three miles from the city centre. The bedrooms are very well appointed and include two with four-poster beds; the new Corus brand bedrooms are particularly appealing and well equipped.

continued

The Beauchief Restaurant and Merchants Bar have recently been refurbished and upgraded, offering a good combination of formal and light dining arrangements in cheerfully decorated surroundings. A friendly staff provide a cheerful and attentive service.

ROOMS: 50 en suite No smoking in 30 bedrooms s £80; d £90 * LB **FACILITIES:** STV Pool table entertainment **CONF:** Thtr 100 Class 50 Board 50 Del £115 * **PARKING:** 200 **NOTES:** No smoking in restaurant Civ Wed 120 **CARDS:**

★★★69% Charnwood

10 Sharrow Ln S11 8AA
☎ 0114 258 9411 Fax 0114 255 5107
e-mail: king@charnwood.force9.co.uk
Dir: *Sharrow Lane is near London Rd/Abbeydale Rd junction, on A621, 1.5m SW of city centre*

The Charnwood is within walking distance of the city centre, just off the London Road. It was once a Georgian mansion house owned by a Master Cutler. The bedrooms are well equipped; lounges and bars are ample and comfortable. Leo's Brasserie is an informal restaurant serving freshly cooked and interesting meals.
ROOMS: 22 en suite No smoking in 16 bedrooms s fr £75; d fr £90 (incl. bkfst) * LB **CONF:** Thtr 90 Class 40 Board 35 Del £95 * **PARKING:** 22 **NOTES:** No dogs (ex guide dogs) Closed 24-31 Dec Civ Wed 100 **CARDS:**

★★★68% Whitley Hall

Elliott Ln, Grenoside S35 8NR
☎ 0114 245 4444 Fax 0114 245 5414
Dir: *A61 past football ground and 2m further, turn right just before Norfolk Arms, turn left at bottom of hill. Hotel is on left*

This 16th-century house sits in 30 acres of quiet landscaped grounds and gardens. Public rooms are full of character, with an impressive gallery, and oak panelled restaurant, bar and lounge. Bedrooms are individually furnished in a style sympathetic to this country house setting; each room is equipped with a range of modern facilities and useful extras.
ROOMS: 19 en suite (1 fmly) s £70-£80; d £90-£100 (incl. bkfst) * LB **FACILITIES:** Croquet lawn Putting green **CONF:** Thtr 70 Class 50 Board 40 Del from £120 * **PARKING:** 100 **NOTES:** No smoking in restaurant RS Sat - No lunch Civ Wed 80 **CARDS:**

★★★67% Novotel

NOVOTEL

50 Arundel Gate S1 2PR
☎ 0114 278 1781 Fax 0114 278 7744
e-mail: h1348@accor-hotels.com
Dir: *between Registry Office and Crucible/Lyceum Theatres, follow signs to Town Hall/Theatres & Hallam University*

A modern hotel situated in the centre of the city close to the Lyceum and Crucible theatres. Bedrooms are well proportioned

continued

SHEFFIELD, continued

and suitable for families as well as being appropriately equipped for business guests. Public areas are spaciously designed and include an attractive restaurant, banqueting and meeting rooms and an indoor heated swimming pool.
ROOMS: 144 en suite (40 fmly) No smoking in 108 bedrooms d £79-£83 * LB **FACILITIES:** STV Indoor swimming (H) Gym Pool table Gym is not owned by hotel, but is free for residents use **CONF:** Thtr 200 Class 30 Board 100 Del from £85 * **SERVICES:** Lift **PARKING:** 44 **NOTES:** RS 24 Dec-2 Jan **CARDS:**

★★★66% The Regency

High St, Ecclesfield S35 9XB
☎ 0114 246 7703 🖷 0114 240 0081
Dir: *A629 to Chapeltown, turn left onto Nether Ln, straight across traffic lights, left into Church St, turn left opp church, left again, hotel on right*
This thoughtfully extended mansion house stands in the centre of Ecclesfield to the north of Sheffield. The restaurant serves a wide range of popular dishes and is locally popular. Bedrooms offer good comfort and are well equipped.
ROOMS: 19 en suite (1 fmly) s £66; d £80 (incl. bkfst) * LB **FACILITIES:** STV **CONF:** Thtr 250 Class 120 Board 40 Del £85 * **PARKING:** 80 **NOTES:** No dogs (ex guide dogs) Closed 25-26 Dec, 1 Jan Civ Wed 180 **CARDS:**

★★★65% ❀ Mosborough Hall

High St, Mosborough S20 5EA
☎ 0114 248 4353 🖷 0114 247 7042
Dir: *after leaving M1 at junct 30, travel 7m SE on A6135*
This 16th-century manor house, a Grade II listed building, is set in its own gardens not far from the M1 and convenient for the centre of the city. Bedrooms vary from modern to characterful, and some of them are very spacious. Apart from the galleried bar, there is a conservatory lounge, and freshly prepared dishes are served in the brightly furnished dining room.
ROOMS: 23 en suite (1 fmly) s £50-£75; d £56-£83 * LB **FACILITIES:** Pool table **CONF:** Thtr 50 Class 40 Board 40 Del from £89 * **PARKING:** 100 **NOTES:** Civ Wed 60
CARDS:

★★★62% Menzies Rutland

452 Glossop Rd, Broomhill S10 2PY
☎ 0500 636943 (Central Res) 🖷 01773 880321
e-mail: info@menzies-hotels.co.uk
Dir: *on A57, located next to the Royal Hallamshire Hospital*
This friendly hotel, close to the university, has been created from a cluster of seven Victorian houses, all but one interconnected. Bedrooms vary in size and shape, but all are comfortable. There is a choice of lounges and a restaurant with a conservatory overlooking the garden.
ROOMS: 63 en suite 13 annexe en suite (5 fmly) No smoking in 10 bedrooms s £69.50-£79.50; d £79.50-£89.50 * LB **FACILITIES:** STV Xmas **CONF:** Thtr 100 Class 40 Board 40 **SERVICES:** Lift **PARKING:** 80 **NOTES:** Civ Wed 100 **CARDS:**

★★★61% *Staindrop Hotel & Restaurant*

Ln End, Chapeltown S35 3UH
☎ 0114 284 6727 🖷 0114 284 6783
e-mail: staindrop@obelus.co.uk
Dir: *M1 junct 35, take A629 for 1m straight over 1st rdbt, right at 2nd rdbt, hotel is situated about 0.5m on right*
This small long established hotel is just a mile from the M1. Rooms are spacious and well equipped. An attractive function room and gardens make this a popular wedding venue.
continued

ROOMS: 13 en suite (1 fmly) **CONF:** Thtr 90 Class 60 Board 40 **PARKING:** 70 **NOTES:** No dogs (ex guide dogs) No smoking in restaurant **CARDS:**

★★★58% *Posthouse Sheffield*

Manchester Rd, Broomhill S10 5DX
☎ 0870 400 9071 🖷 0114 268 2620
Dir: *M1 J23, follow signs to city centre, then A57 Glossop. Hotel on L after 2.5 miles*
A high rise hotel that dominates the skyline west of the city centre where the majority of the bedrooms have fine views. It is situated in a residential area that is within easy reach of central Sheffield. The hotel features a Spa Leisure Club, the Hallam Banqueting Suite and a range of meeting and conference rooms. The Junction Restaurant is open for lunch and dinner, and there is an all day lounge menu plus 24-hour room service.
ROOMS: 136 en suite No smoking in 70 bedrooms **FACILITIES:** Indoor swimming (H) Sauna Solarium Gym Jacuzzi/spa Health & fitness centre **CONF:** Thtr 300 Class 130 Board 80 **SERVICES:** Lift **PARKING:** 120 **CARDS:**

★★65% Cutlers Hotel

George St S1 2PF
☎ 0114 273 9939 🖷 0114 276 8332
e-mail: enquiries@cutlershotel.co.uk
Dir: *city centre adjacent to Crucible Theatre*
Situated close to the Crucible Theatre in the city centre, this hotel offers accommodation in well equipped bedrooms, extras including hairdryers, trouser presses and business facilities. Public areas include a lower ground floor bistro although room service is available if required. Small meeting rooms are also available. Free overnight parking is provided in the nearby public car park.
ROOMS: 50 en suite No smoking in 5 bedrooms s fr £48.50; d fr £59.50 (incl. bkfst) * LB **CONF:** Thtr 25 Board 20 Del from £70 * **SERVICES:** Lift **NOTES:** No dogs (ex guide dogs) Closed 24 Dec-3 Jan **CARDS:**

⌂ Hotel Ibis Sheffield

Shude Hill S1 2AR
☎ 0114 241 9600 🖷 0114 241 9610
e-mail: H2891@accor-hotels.com
Modern, budget hotel offering comfortable accommodation in bright and practical bedrooms. Breakfast is self-service and dinner is available in the restaurant. For further details, consult the Hotel Groups page.
ROOMS: 95 en suite s £42; d £42 *

⌂ *Travelodge*

340 Prince of Wales Rd S2 1FF
☎ 0114 253 0935 🖷 0114 253 0935
Dir: *follow A630, take turn off for ring road & services*
This modern building offers accommodation in smart, spacious and well equipped bedrooms, all with en suite bathrooms. Refreshments may be taken at the nearby family restaurant. For further details and the Travelodge phone number, consult the Hotel Groups page.
ROOMS: 60 en suite **CONF:** Thtr 30 Board 20

○ Nether Edge

21-23 Montgomery Rd S7 1LN
☎ 0114 255 4363
Two converted and joined Victorian houses situated in a quiet residential area of the city. Public areas have been totally refurbished and include a comfortable lounge and bar, a games room and an attractively appointed restaurant. Toilet facilities for disabled persons are also a feature of the newly designed areas.
continued

Some bedrooms have new furniture; others are in the process of being upgraded. All have en suite facilities. There is a private car park at the rear.
ROOMS: 28 rms

○ *Premier Lodge*
Sheffield Rd, Meadowhall
☎ 0870 700 1540 🖷 0870 7001541

SHEPTON MALLET, Somerset Map 03 ST64

Premier Collection

★★★❀❀❀ Charlton House
Charlton Rd BA4 4PR
☎ 01749 342008 🖷 01749 346362
e-mail: reservations-charltonhouse@btinternet.com
Dir: *on A361, 1m beyond Shepton Mallet Town Centre, travelling towards Frome*
Situated just outside the town in landscaped grounds, this delightful country house dates back in parts to the 1500s. The bedrooms and public areas are a perfect setting for high quality fabrics and furnishings; the staff are friendly and professional and the surroundings conducive to relaxing and being pampered. The restaurant provides some very accomplished and distinctive cooking, with a focus on high quality local ingredients.
ROOMS: 12 en suite 5 annexe en suite (1 fmly) s £105-£135; d £140-£300 (incl. cont bkfst) * LB **FACILITIES:** STV Indoor swimming (H) Tennis (hard) Fishing Sauna Croquet lawn Archery Clay pigeon shooting Hot air ballooning Xmas **CONF:** Thtr 50 Class 18 Board 20 Del £150 * **PARKING:** 41 **NOTES:** No dogs (ex guide dogs) No smoking in restaurant Civ Wed 75
CARDS:

★★71% Shrubbery
Commercial Rd BA4 5BU
☎ 01749 346671 🖷 01749 346581
Dir: *turn off A37 at Shepton Mallet onto A371 Wells Rd, hotel 50mtrs past traffic lights in town centre*
This attractive town centre hotel is an elegant and thoroughly charming place of relaxation and fine food. The bedrooms have rich fabrics and co-ordinating colour schemes. The intimate restaurant overlooks a delightful garden and offers a varied choice of dishes in the modern style, often with Mediterranean influences.
ROOMS: 8 en suite (1 fmly) s £52.50; d £75-£79 (incl. bkfst) * LB **FACILITIES:** Xmas **CONF:** Thtr 36 Class 30 Board 24 **PARKING:** 20 **NOTES:** RS Sundays evenings **CARDS:**

SHERBORNE, Dorset Map 03 ST61

★★★69% ❀ Eastbury
Long St DT9 3BY
☎ 01935 813131 🖷 01935 817296
Dir: *turn left off A30, westbound, into Sherborne high street, at the bottom turn left 800yds along on the right is the Eastbury hotel*
A quiet and charming hotel close to the centre of Sherborne. Bedrooms are comfortable and have many thoughtful extras including bathrobes, fresh flowers and mineral water. The lounge is very elegant and the bar and restaurant are an ideal spot in which to enjoy award winning cuisine overlooking the lovely, walled garden.
ROOMS: 15 en suite (1 fmly) No smoking in 3 bedrooms s £45-£65; d £80-£100 (incl. bkfst) * LB **FACILITIES:** STV Croquet lawn Xmas **CONF:** Thtr 60 Class 40 Board 28 Del from £95 * **PARKING:** 50 **NOTES:** No dogs (ex guide dogs) Civ Wed 120
CARDS:

★★★63% The Sherborne
Horsecastles Ln DT9 6BB
☎ 01935 813191 🖷 01935 816493
Dir: *close to A30 on W outskirts of Sherborne*
Set in grounds, the hotel is within walking distance of the town centre. The public rooms have picturesque views. Bedrooms are well equipped and functional, all have been refurbished. Staff are friendly with prompt services delivered by a willing team.
ROOMS: 59 en suite (11 fmly) No smoking in 30 bedrooms d £49.50-£59.50 * LB **FACILITIES:** Croquet lawn Putting green Mini driving range Xmas **CONF:** Thtr 80 Class 30 Board 30 Del from £75 * **SERVICES:** air con **PARKING:** 100 **NOTES:** No smoking in restaurant Civ Wed 75
CARDS:

★★★60% Antelope
Greenhill DT9 4EP
☎ 01935 812077 🖷 01935 816473
THE CIRCLE *Selected Individual Hotels* GREAT BRITAIN
Dir: *stay on the A30 into Sherborne, hotel is located at the top of town with parking at rear*
Centrally located in Sherborne, this 18th-century coaching inn is an ideal base for exploring Hardy country. Many bedrooms have retained their original beams and fireplaces; some have their own access from the courtyard. The bar is popular with residents and locals alike. The formal restaurant offers a range of dishes in a smart environment.
ROOMS: 19 en suite (1 fmly) No smoking in 1 bedroom s £44-£60; d £49.95-£80 (incl. bkfst) * LB **FACILITIES:** Xmas **CONF:** Thtr 80 Class 60 Board 40 Del from £65 * **PARKING:** 22 **NOTES:** No smoking in restaurant **CARDS:**

S

★★71% ❀ The Grange Hotel & Restaurant
Oborne DT9 4LA
☎ 01935 813463 🖷 01935 817464
Dir: *turn of the A30. 1m out of Sherborne (heading East). At Oborne hotel is clearly marked by road sign*
This 200 year old country house has an idyllic setting in a quiet hamlet. Bedrooms are spacious and many overlook the beautiful gardens. The popular restaurant has a varied menu with plenty to suit all tastes.

continued

SHERBORNE, continued

The Grange Hotel & Restaurant, Sherborne

ROOMS: 10 en suite (2 fmly) No smoking in 7 bedrooms s £55-£65; d £75-£95 (incl. bkfst) * LB **FACILITIES:** STV **CONF:** Thtr 30 Class 20 Board 18 **PARKING:** 30 **NOTES:** No dogs (ex guide dogs) No smoking in restaurant Closed 26 Dec-12 Jan RS Sun evening (no dinner)
CARDS:

SHERINGHAM, Norfolk Map 09 TG14

★★70% Beaumaris

South St NR26 8LL
☎ 01263 822370 01263 821421
e-mail: beauhotel@aol.com
Dir: *turn off A148, turn left at rdbt, 1st right over railway bridge, 1st left by church, 1st left into South Street*
This very pleasant hotel is well established and its many loyal guests regularly return to enjoy the friendly hospitality. In quiet residential surroundings with well kept gardens, it is just five minutes' walk from the seafront, town centre and the golf course. Public rooms include two quiet lounges, an inviting bar, and a spacious dining room.
ROOMS: 21 en suite (5 fmly) s £40-£45; d £80-£90 (incl. bkfst) * LB **PARKING:** 25 **NOTES:** No smoking in restaurant Closed mid Dec-1 Mar
CARDS:

★★68% Southlands

South St NR26 8LL
☎ 01263 822679 01263 822679
Dir: *from A1082, turn left at rdbt. Take 1st right & then 1st left at St Peters Church. Then 1st left again & hotel is on the left*
This pleasant and homely hotel attracts many loyal regulars. A short walk from the town centre, it offers well maintained and attractively decorated accommodation. The large downstairs rooms include open plan lounges and several dining areas. A short but appetising menu is offered.
ROOMS: 17 en suite (3 fmly) s £32.50-£35; d £65-£70 (incl. bkfst) * **PARKING:** 20 **NOTES:** No smoking in restaurant Closed Oct-Etr
CARDS:

SHIFNAL, Shropshire Map 07 SJ70

★★★★63% Park House

Park St TF11 9BA
☎ 01952 460128 01952 461658
Dir: *leave M54 at junct 4 follow A464 Wolverhampton Rd for approx 2m, under railway bridge and hotel is 100yds on left*

MACDONALD HOTELS

Service is friendly at this sympathetically extended hotel. Originally two separate 17th-century houses, the hotel sits on the edge of this historic market town, within easy reach of M54(J4). Accommodation is spacious and well appointed. Elegant public areas include a good choice of meeting facilities, as well as a health club.

ROOMS: 38 en suite 16 annexe en suite (4 fmly) No smoking in 10 bedrooms s £113; d £134 * LB **FACILITIES:** STV Indoor swimming (H) Sauna Solarium Jacuzzi/spa Xmas **CONF:** Thtr 180 Class 100 Board 40 Del £155 * **SERVICES:** Lift **PARKING:** 200 **NOTES:** No smoking in restaurant Civ Wed 130 **CARDS:**

SHIPDHAM, Norfolk Map 05 TF90

★★62% Pound Green Hotel

Pound Green Ln IP25 7LS
☎ 01362 820940 01362 821253
e-mail: poundgreen@aol.com
Dir: *from A11, follow A1075 through Shipdham. Hotel on right beyond village green*
Situated in a quiet residential area in the village of Shipdham between Dereham and Watton. This small privately owned hotel offers spacious, soundly maintained and well equipped bedrooms throughout. Public areas include a popular lounge bar and a large restaurant offering a small carte menu. There is also a function room available.
ROOMS: 10 rms (8 en suite) (1 fmly) s £25-£35; d fr £45 (incl. bkfst) * LB **FACILITIES:** STV Snooker Xmas **CONF:** Thtr 30 Class 30 Board 100 Del £40 * **PARKING:** 41 **NOTES:** No smoking in restaurant
CARDS:

SHIPHAM, Somerset Map 03 ST45

★★★73% Daneswood House

Cuck Hill BS25 1RD
☎ 01934 843145 & 843945 01934 843824
e-mail: daneswoodhousehotel@compuserve.com
Dir: *turn off A38 towards Cheddar, travel through village, hotel on left*
This charming Edwardian hotel, set within its own grounds, offers wonderful views across the Bristol Channel towards Wales. Bedrooms, including five recent additions, are individually decorated and well equipped. There are also several cottage suites with private lounges. The spacious public areas include a breakfast conservatory and popular restaurant offering a daily fixed-price menu using quality local ingredients.
ROOMS: 14 en suite 3 annexe en suite (3 fmly) No smoking in 4 bedrooms s £79.50-£95; d £79.50-£135 (incl. bkfst) * LB **CONF:** Thtr 40 Board 20 Del from £130 * **PARKING:** 27 **NOTES:** No dogs (ex guide dogs) No smoking in restaurant RS 24 Dec-6 Jan
CARDS:

Early start? Hotels at all star levels should provide in-room alarm clocks and/or alarm calls.

S

SHIPLEY, West Yorkshire Map 07 SE13

★★★★70% Marriott Hollins Hall Hotel

Hollins Hill, Baildon BD17 7QW
☎ 01274 530053 📠 01274 530187
Dir: *from A650 follow signs to Salt Mill. At lights in Shipley take A6038. Hotel is 3m on left*

Some smartly appointed new bedrooms have been added to this attractive hotel overlooking the Esholt Valley. There are extensive leisure facilities, function suites and a formal restaurant, Heathcliff's.
ROOMS: 122 en suite (6 fmly) No smoking in 75 bedrooms s £89-£109 * LB **FACILITIES:** STV Indoor swimming (H) Golf 18 Sauna Solarium Gym Croquet lawn Putting green Jacuzzi/spa Creche Health Spa Xmas **CONF:** Thtr 200 Class 90 Board 60 **SERVICES:** Lift **PARKING:** 260 **NOTES:** No dogs (ex guide dogs) Civ Wed 120
CARDS:

Express by Holiday Inn Shipley

Salt Mill Rd BD18 3TT
☎ 01274 589333 📠 01274 589444
e-mail: bradford@premierhotels-8.demon.co.uk
Dir: *Follow tourist signs all the way for Salts Mill. Pick up A650 signs through & out of Bradford for approx 5m to Shipley. Hotel on Salts Mill Rd*

A modern budget hotel offering comfortable accommodation in refreshing, spacious and comprehensively-equipped bedrooms, en suite bathrooms with power showers and continental buffet breakfast included in the room rate. Suitable for business travellers or families. For further details and the Express by Holiday Inn phone number, consult the Hotel Groups page.
ROOMS: 78 en suite (incl. cont bkfst) d £52.50 * **CONF:** Thtr 35 Class 20 Board 20 Del £85 *

Read all about it! Newspapers delivered to bedrooms in four and five star hotels.

SHIPSTON ON STOUR, Warwickshire Map 04 SP24

★★60% The Red Lion

Main St, Long Compton CV36 5JS
☎ 01608 684221 📠 01608 684221
e-mail: redlionhot@aol.com
Dir: *on A3400 between Shipston on Stour/Chipping Norton*
A friendly inn that offers a very warm welcome to all its guests. The public rooms are charming, the focal point being the taproom with its friendly atmosphere and selection of real ales. Bedrooms, decorated in pretty pastel colours, vary in size and layout, and each has a useful range of facilities.
ROOMS: 5 en suite (1 fmly) s £30; d £50 (incl. bkfst) * LB
FACILITIES: Pool table **PARKING:** 60 **NOTES:** No smoking in restaurant
CARDS:

SHREWSBURY, Shropshire Map 07 SJ41
see also Church Stretton & Nesscliffe

★★★★63% Albrighton Hall

Albrighton SY4 3AG
☎ 01939 291000 📠 01939 291123
e-mail: info@albrightonmacdonaldhotels.co.uk
Dir: *2.5m N on A528*

Set in 14 acres of grounds, this 17th-century country house has elegant public rooms with beautiful oak panelling. Bedrooms in the main house are mostly spacious and have been refurbished; several have four-poster beds and the attic rooms are popular for their sloping beams. There is also a leisure centre and extensive conference facilities.
ROOMS: 29 en suite 42 annexe en suite (2 fmly) No smoking in 30 bedrooms s £77-£110; d £87-£120 (incl. bkfst) * LB **FACILITIES:** STV Indoor swimming (H) Squash Snooker Sauna Solarium Gym Pool table Croquet lawn Jacuzzi/spa Beauty treatment rooms Xmas **CONF:** Thtr 400 Class 120 Board 60 Del from £125 * **SERVICES:** Lift **PARKING:** 120 **NOTES:** No smoking in restaurant Civ Wed 200
CARDS:

★★★77% Albright Hussey

Ellesmere Rd SY4 3AF
☎ 01939 290571 & 290523 📠 01939 291143
e-mail: abbhotel@aol.com
Dir: *2.5m N of Shrewsbury on A528, follow signs for Ellesmere*
Converted from a classic farmhouse, this timber-framed Tudor building offers a choice of accommodation, with spacious and lavishly furnished bedrooms in the older part of the building and well equipped modern rooms in a new wing; many look out on to the four acres of mature landscaped gardens. Dinner is taken in the fine, beamed restaurant. A comfortable cocktail bar and lounge are separated from the new function suite, furnished to create a marquee effect.

continued

S

SHREWSBURY, continued

ROOMS: 14 en suite (4 fmly) No smoking in 3 bedrooms s £65-£79; d £85-£148.50 (incl. bkfst) * LB **FACILITIES:** Croquet lawn Jacuzzi/spa Xmas **CONF:** Thtr 250 Class 180 Board 80 Del from £110 * **PARKING:** 85 **NOTES:** No children 3yrs No smoking in restaurant Civ Wed 100 **CARDS:**

★★★73% Rowton Castle Hotel

Halfway House SY5 9EP
☎ 01743 884044 01743 884949
e-mail: rowtoncastle@go2.co.uk
Dir: 8m W off A458 Shrewsbury to Welshpool road

Rowton Castle stands in 17 acres of grounds on the site of a Roman Fort. The present building dates from 1696 but several additions have been made since then. Many original features remain including the oak-panelled restaurant and a magnificent 17th-century carved oak fireplace. Most of the bedrooms are spacious and all are equipped with modern facilities. The hotel has lovely formal gardens.

ROOMS: 19 en suite (3 fmly) s fr £59; d fr £79 (incl. bkfst) * LB **FACILITIES:** Fishing Croquet lawn Xmas **CONF:** Thtr 80 Class 40 Board 40 Del from £115 * **PARKING:** 100 **NOTES:** No dogs (ex guide dogs) No smoking in restaurant Civ Wed 110
CARDS:

★★★71% Prince Rupert

Butcher Row SY1 1UQ
☎ 01743 499955 01743 357306
e-mail: post@prince-rupert-hotel.co.uk
Dir: follow signs to Town Centre, drive over English Bridge and Wyle Cop Hill. Turn right into Fish St and continue for 200 yds till hotel is in view

This popular town centre hotel dates back, in parts, to medieval times. Many bedrooms have exposed beams and attractive wood panelling. In addition to the main 'Royalist' restaurant, diners can eat in 'Chambers' bar-bistro. The refurbished bedrooms include four luxury suites, family rooms and rooms with four-poster beds. The hotel's car parking service is recommended.
ROOMS: 70 en suite (4 fmly) s £75; d £95-£160 * LB **FACILITIES:** Snooker Sauna Gym Jacuzzi/spa Weight training room Beauty Salon Xmas **CONF:** Thtr 120 Class 80 Board 20 Del from £105 * **SERVICES:** Lift **PARKING:** 70 **CARDS:**

See advert on opposite page

★★★66% Lord Hill

Abbey Foregate SY2 6AX
☎ 01743 232601 01743 369734
e-mail: reservations@lordhill.u-net.com
Dir: from M54 take A5, at 1st rdbt left then right into London Rd. At next rdbt (Lord Hill Column) take 3rd exit for hotel on left

A pleasant and attractively appointed hotel close to the town centre. Most of the bedrooms are located in a purpose-built, separate building but those in the main building include one with a four-poster and a newly created suite. There is also a conservatory restaurant and large function suite.
ROOMS: 12 en suite 24 annexe en suite (1 fmly) No smoking in 18 bedrooms s £55-£63.50; d £73-£82 (incl. bkfst) * LB **FACILITIES:** Xmas **CONF:** Thtr 300 Class 120 Board 150 Del from £85 * **PARKING:** 120 **NOTES:** Civ Wed 100 **CARDS:**

★★★64% The Lion

REGAL

Wyle Cop SY1 1UY
☎ 01743 353107 01743 352744
Dir: from S: cross English Bridge, take right fork, hotel at top of hill on left. From N: to town centre, follow Castle St into Dogpole, hotel is ahead

Charles Dickens and other famous people have stayed at this 14th-century coaching inn. Public areas are elegant and comfortable, particularly the Tapestry Lounge. Bedrooms have modern equipment and are decorated and furnished to a good standard.
ROOMS: 59 en suite (3 fmly) No smoking in 30 bedrooms **CONF:** Thtr 200 Class 80 Board 60 **SERVICES:** Lift **PARKING:** 70 **NOTES:** No smoking in restaurant **CARDS:**

★★69% *Radbrook Hall*

SCOTTISH NEWCASTLE hotels

Radbrook Rd SY3 9BQ
☎ 01743 236676 01743 359194
Dir: from A5 take A488 to Shrewsbury. Hotel 1.5m on left

Parts of this hotel date back to the 15th century, but most of it was built more recently. It is surrounded by spacious grounds. The well equipped accommodation is suitable for both leisure and business guests. Public areas feature a pleasant lounge bar and an attractive and popular family restaurant.
ROOMS: 22 en suite (6 fmly) **FACILITIES:** Squash Sauna Solarium Gym Jacuzzi/spa ch fac **CONF:** Thtr 360 Class 60 Board 80 **PARKING:** 230 **NOTES:** No smoking in restaurant
CARDS:

★★65% Lion & Pheasant
49-50 Wyle Cop SY1 1XJ
☎ 01743 236288 📠 01743 244475
Dir: *town centre, by English Bridge, 2m from M54 motorway link*

Now a personally-run hotel, this 16th-century former coaching inn stands close to the town centre, near the English Bridge crossing of the River Severn. The accommodation is well equipped for both business and leisure guests. The public areas are full of character, with original features such as exposed beams and wall timbers.
ROOMS: 19 rms (17 en suite) (1 fmly) s fr £35; d £60 (incl. bkfst) * **CONF:** Thtr 25 Class 20 Board 16 **PARKING:** 20 **NOTES:** No smoking in restaurant Closed 24-30 Dec **CARDS:**

See advert on this page

TV dinner? Room service at three stars and above.

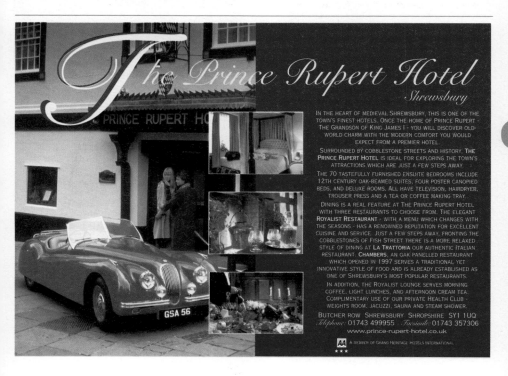

SHREWSBURY, continued

★★64% *Shelton Hall*
Shelton SY3 8BH
☎ 01743 343982 🖷 01743 241515
A large country house surrounded by extensive and mature gardens, thought to date back to around 1650 and a hotel since 1977. The bedrooms vary in size and style, but are equipped to suit all the possible needs of guests.
ROOMS: 9 en suite (2 fmly) **CONF:** Thtr 50 Class 24 Board 24
PARKING: 50 **NOTES:** No dogs **CARDS:**

★★63% Abbots Mead
9 St Julian's Friars SY1 1XL
☎ 01743 235281 🖷 01743 369133
e-mail: res@abbotsmeadhotel.co.uk
Dir: *first left after English Bridge coming into Shrewsbury from S*
This neatly maintained Georgian town house lies in a quiet cul-de-sac near the English Bridge, close to both the river and town centre. Bedrooms are compact but neatly decorated and well equipped. The hotel also has a bright dining room, overlooking the garden, and a bar with walls adorned by horse racing pictures.
ROOMS: 14 en suite s £39-£45; d £52-£56 (incl. bkfst) * LB
PARKING: 10 **NOTES:** No smoking in restaurant
CARDS:

★★63% Mytton & Mermaid Hotel
Atcham SY5 6QG
☎ 01743 761220 🖷 01743 761292
Dir: *from Shrewsbury cross old bridge in Atcham. Hotel beside River Severn opposite main entrance to Attingham Park*
Just three miles east of Shrewsbury, this ivy-clad former coaching inn enjoys a pleasant location beside the River Severn. Some bedrooms, including family suites, are in a converted stable block adjacent to the hotel whilst those in the main building, although varying in size, are freshly decorated and comfortable. The large lounge bar leads into an entertainment room, and there is also a brasserie and cosy guest lounge.
ROOMS: 8 en suite 7 annexe en suite (1 fmly) s fr £40; d fr £50 (incl. bkfst) * LB **FACILITIES:** Fishing Xmas **CONF:** Thtr 70 Class 24 Board 28 Del from £79.95 * **PARKING:** 54 **NOTES:** No dogs (ex guide dogs) Civ Wed 50 **CARDS:**

⇧ *Travelodge*
Travelodge
Bayston Hill Services SY3 0DA
☎ 01743 874256 🖷 01743 874256
Dir: *A5/A49 junct*
This modern building offers accommodation in smart, spacious and well equipped bedrooms, all with en suite bathrooms. Refreshments may be taken at the nearby family restaurant. For further details and the Travelodge phone number, consult the Hotel Groups page.
ROOMS: 40 en suite

SIDMOUTH, Devon — Map 03 SY18

★★★★72% ❁ Riviera
The Esplanade EX10 8AY
☎ 01395 515201 🖷 01395 577775
e-mail: enquiries@hotelriviera.co.uk
Dir: *leave M5 junc 30 & follow A3052*
Situated in a prime location, overlooking the sea, the Riviera is a fine Regency building, offering a high standard of service and stylishly furnished bedrooms with modern facilities. There is a good restaurant menu, supported by very good room service.
continued

ROOMS: 27 en suite (6 fmly) s £87-£113; d £154-£206 (incl. bkfst & dinner) * LB **FACILITIES:** STV entertainment Xmas **CONF:** Thtr 85 Class 60 Board 30 **SERVICES:** Lift **PARKING:** 26
CARDS:

See advert on opposite page

★★★★72% ❁ Victoria
The Esplanade EX10 8RY
☎ 01395 512651 🖷 01395 579154
e-mail: info@victoriahotel.co.uk
Dir: *on Sidmouth seafront*

Completed around the turn of the last century, this imposing building, set within its own manicured gardens, occupies the prime position on the esplanade. Fine sea views are enjoyed by many of the comfortable bedrooms and elegant public areas. Carefully prepared meals are served, in a professional yet friendly way, in the refurbished air-conditioned restaurant.
ROOMS: 61 en suite (18 fmly) s £71-£104; d £130-£226 (incl. bkfst) * LB **FACILITIES:** STV Indoor swimming (H) Outdoor swimming (H) Tennis (hard) Snooker Sauna Solarium Pool table Putting green Jacuzzi/spa entertainment ch fac Xmas **CONF:** Thtr 60 **SERVICES:** Lift **PARKING:** 104 **NOTES:** No dogs (ex guide dogs) No smoking in restaurant **CARDS:**

See advert on opposite page

★★★★69% Belmont
Brend Hotels
The Esplanade EX10 8RX
☎ 01395 512555 🖷 01395 579101
e-mail: info@belmont-hotel.co.uk
Dir: *on Sidmouth seafront*
Prominently positioned on the sea front, within a few minutes walk from the town centre, this traditional hotel continues to retain a regular following. A choice of comfortable lounges is offered and in the air conditioned restaurant, a pianist plays while guests dine. Bedrooms are attractively furnished and many enjoy fine views over the esplanade. Leisure facilities are available to residents at the sister hotel adjacent, the Victoria.

continued on p510

S

SIDMOUTH, continued

Belmont, Sidmouth

ROOMS: 54 en suite (10 fmly) s £59-£104; d £108-£218 (incl. bkfst) * LB **FACILITIES:** STV Putting green entertainment ch fac Xmas **CONF:** Thtr 50 **SERVICES:** Lift **PARKING:** 45 **NOTES:** No dogs (ex guide dogs) Civ Wed **CARDS:**

★★★79% Westcliff

Manor Rd EX10 8RU
☎ 01395 513252 01395 578203
e-mail: stay@westcliffhotel.co.uk
Dir: *turn off A3052 to Sidmouth and proceed to the seafront and esplanade, turn right, hotel is directly ahead*

This charming hotel is in walking distance of the Promenade and has been run by the same family for more than 30 years. Elegant lounges and the cocktail bar open onto a terrace leading to the pool and croquet lawn. Bedrooms are spacious, some with balconies, and the restaurant offers a good choice of dishes.
ROOMS: 40 en suite (4 fmly) No smoking in 4 bedrooms s £87-£98; d £148-£214 (incl. bkfst & dinner) * LB **FACILITIES:** STV Outdoor swimming (H) Gym Pool table Croquet lawn Putting green Jacuzzi/spa Mini tennis entertainment **SERVICES:** Lift **PARKING:** 40 **NOTES:** No dogs No children 5yrs No smoking in restaurant Closed Nov-Mar **CARDS:**

See advert on opposite page

★★★69% Salcombe Hill House

Beatlands Rd EX10 8JQ
☎ 01395 514697 & 514398 01395 578310
Dir: *At Radway Cinema in town centre turn left, go over bridge, turn sharp right then left into Beatlands Road. Hotel is 50yds on left*
Just a short walk from the seafront, this family run hotel stands in large gardens and has lovely views. It is south-facing, so the lounge and patio get the best of the sun; bedrooms are bright and spacious, and served by a lift.
ROOMS: 28 en suite (7 fmly) s £62-£64; d £124-£128 (incl. bkfst & dinner) * **FACILITIES:** Outdoor swimming (H) Tennis (grass) Putting green Games room **SERVICES:** Lift **PARKING:** 39 **NOTES:** No smoking in restaurant Closed 20 Nov-1 Mar **CARDS:**

★★★64% Royal Glen

Glen Rd EX10 8RW
☎ 01395 513221 & 513456 01395 514922
e-mail: sidmouthroyalglen.hotel@virgin.net
Dir: *take A303 to Honiton, turn onto A375 to Sidford, then onto the A175 to Sidmouth, follow seafront signs, turn right onto esplanade, turn right at end*
This historic, family owned, 19th-century hotel has associations with the then Duke of Kent and Queen Victoria. The connection is emphasised in the names of the comfortable bedrooms which are furnished in period. Day rooms include a 'smoking room' with open fire, and a dining room serving well prepared food. A heated indoor pool is also available for guests.
ROOMS: 32 en suite (4 fmly) s £36-£43; d £72-£86 (incl. bkfst) * LB **FACILITIES:** Indoor swimming (H) **PARKING:** 24 **NOTES:** No smoking in restaurant RS 2-31 Jan **CARDS:**

★★★61% *Fortfield*

Station Rd EX10 8NU
☎ 01395 512403 01395 512403
e-mail: reservations@fortfield-hotel.demon.co.uk
Just a short walk from the town centre, the hotel offers good standards of service, hospitality and cuisine. There are spacious lounges and a bar with a maritime theme. Some of the comfortable bedrooms have sea views.
ROOMS: 52 en suite 3 annexe en suite (7 fmly) **FACILITIES:** Indoor swimming (H) Sauna Solarium Health & beauty salon entertainment **CONF:** Thtr 70 Class 40 Board 20 **SERVICES:** Lift **PARKING:** 60 **NOTES:** No smoking in restaurant **CARDS:**

★★77% Brownlands

Sid Rd EX10 9AG
☎ 01395 513053 01395 513053
e-mail: brownlands.hotel@virgin.net
Dir: *turn off A3052 at Sidford, at Fortescue/Sidford sign, hotel 1m on left*
This fine Victorian country hotel, set peacefully on the wooded slopes of Salcombe Hill, has superb views to the town and sea. The smartly decorated bedrooms are well equipped, and guests have a choice of comfortable sitting rooms and a separate bar. Five-course dinner is served in the dining room which is spacious and enjoys the best of the view.
ROOMS: 14 en suite s £65-£68; d £55-£136 (incl. bkfst & dinner) * LB **FACILITIES:** Tennis (hard) Putting green Xmas **PARKING:** 25 **NOTES:** No children 8yrs No smoking in restaurant Closed Nov-mid Mar RS Dec

★★75% *Kingswood*

The Esplanade EX10 8AX
☎ 01395 516367 01395 513185
e-mail: enquiries@kingswood-hotel.co.uk
Dir: *in the centre of the Esplanade*
Kingswood is a family run hotel. All bedrooms have modern facilities and many have marvellous sea views. The two lounges offer comfort and space and the attractive dining room offers good traditional cooking.
ROOMS: 26 rms (25 en suite) (7 fmly) No smoking in all bedrooms **SERVICES:** Lift **PARKING:** 17 **NOTES:** No smoking in restaurant Closed Dec-25 Feb **CARDS:**

★★73% Royal York & Faulkner

The Esplanade EX10 8AZ
☎ 01395 513043 & 0800 220714 (Freephone) 01395 577472
e-mail: yorkhotel@eclipse.co.uk
Dir: *from M5 take A3052, travel 10m to Sidmouth, the hotel is on the esplanade in the centre*
This fine Regency building, facing the sea on the esplanade, has been owned and operated by the Hook family for generations.

continued

S

Bedrooms vary in size and style, some have balconies and sea views and all have modern facilities. A selection of traditional dishes make up the five course dinner menu served in the restaurant. A wide range of leisure facilities is also available.
ROOMS: 68 en suite (8 fmly) s £37.50-£56.50; d £75-£113 (incl. bkfst & dinner) * LB **FACILITIES:** Snooker Sauna Solarium Gym Jacuzzi/spa Indoor short mat bowls Free swimming at local indoor pool(200yds away) entertainment Xmas **SERVICES:** Lift **PARKING:** 20 **NOTES:** No smoking in restaurant Closed Jan **CARDS:**

★★72% Mount Pleasant

Salcombe Rd EX10 8JA
☎ 01395 514694
Dir: *turn off A3052 at Sidford x-rds after one & quarter miles turn left into Salcombe Rd, hotel opposite Radway Cinema*
A sympathetically modernised Georgian hotel, a short walk from the town centre and sea front, offering comfortable accommodation and a relaxed atmosphere. The dining room features a short fixed-price menu of home-cooked dishes, special requests are willingly catered for.
ROOMS: 16 en suite (2 fmly) No smoking in 12 bedrooms s £41-£47; d £82-£94 (incl. bkfst & dinner) * LB **FACILITIES:** Putting green **PARKING:** 20 **NOTES:** No children 8yrs Closed Nov-Feb

★★71% Devoran

Esplanade EX10 8AU
☎ 01395 513151 & 0800 317171 01395 579929
e-mail: devoran@cosmic.org.uk
Dir: *turn off B3052 at Bowd Inn follow Sidmouth sign for approx 2m turn left onto sea front, hotel is 50yds along at the centre of Esplanade*

The Devoran has comfortable and attractively decorated bedrooms, some with their own balconies and sea views. Well maintained public rooms include a large dining room, where guests can enjoy a five-course dinner, and a comfortable lounge and bar.
ROOMS: 23 en suite (4 fmly) No smoking in all bedrooms s £32-£45; d £64-£90 (incl. bkfst) * LB **SERVICES:** Lift **PARKING:** 4 **NOTES:** No smoking in restaurant Closed mid Nov-mid Mar RS Dec-Mar
CARDS:

★★67% Hunters Moon

Sid Rd EX10 9AA
☎ 01395 513380 01395 514270
e-mail: huntersmoon.hotel@virgin.net
Dir: *from A3052 to Sidford, pass Blue Ball Pub, then next turn on right at Fortescue, hotel 1 mile from turning*
This personally owned and run Georgian manor house is set in three acres of grounds, close to the town centre. Accommodation is comfortable, facilities are modern, and the restaurant serves enjoyable meals.

continued

ROOMS: 21 en suite (6 fmly) No smoking in all bedrooms d £47-£50 (incl. bkfst & dinner) * **FACILITIES:** Putting green Xmas **PARKING:** 20 **NOTES:** No smoking in restaurant Closed Jan-Feb (ex Xmas) RS Dec
CARDS:

★★65% Westbourne

Manor Rd EX10 8RR
☎ 01395 513774 01395 512231
Dir: *200yds from Connaught Gardens*
Quietly situated, this family owned and run hotel is convenient for the town centre and the seafront. Set in well tended gardens, the hotel offers an elegant drawing room and a spacious dining room, where both a daily menu and carte are available. Bedrooms vary in size and style, most benefiting from views over the town and surrounding countryside.
ROOMS: 11 rms (9 en suite) (1 fmly) d £42-£47 (incl. bkfst & dinner) * LB **FACILITIES:** Croquet lawn Garden with sun terrace **PARKING:** 16 **NOTES:** No smoking in restaurant Closed Nov-Feb

SIDMOUTH, continued

★★62% *Sidmount*
Station Rd EX10 8XJ
☎ 01395 513432
Dir: *on B3176, 0.50m from esplanade*
This fine Georgian house is set in gardens with views over the town to the sea. The comfortably furnished bedrooms vary in size and style, with some on the ground floor. The restaurant offers buffet service and looks out on the gardens.
ROOMS: 16 en suite (1 fmly) No smoking in 14 bedrooms
PARKING: 17 **NOTES:** No dogs No children 9yrs No smoking in restaurant Closed Nov-Feb

See advert on opposite page

SILCHESTER, Hampshire — Map 04 SU66

★★★74% ❀ Romans
Little London Rd RG7 2PN
☎ 0118 970 0421 🖷 0118 970 0691
e-mail: romanhotel@hotmail.com
Dir: *A340 Basingstoke to Reading, hotel is signposted*

Best Western

This privately owned Lutyens style manor house, set in three acres of attractive grounds, is about 15 minutes from the M3 and M4. Bedrooms are in both the main house and a separate wing. Public rooms include a number of function rooms, a comfortable lounge and a pleasant restaurant. Service is friendly and efficient.
ROOMS: 11 en suite 14 annexe en suite (1 fmly) No smoking in 2 bedrooms s fr £95; d fr £105 (incl. bkfst) * LB **FACILITIES:** STV Outdoor swimming (H) Sauna Gym Xmas **CONF:** Thtr 60 Class 15 Board 24 Del from £120 * **PARKING:** 60 **NOTES:** No smoking in restaurant Closed 1-7 Jan Civ Wed 65
CARDS:

See advert under BASINGSTOKE

SILLOTH, Cumbria — Map 11 NY15

★★★61% The Skinburness
CA5 4QY
☎ 016973 32332 🖷 016973 32549
Dir: *M6 junct 41, take B5305 to Wigton, then B5302 to Silloth. M6 junct 44, take A595 to Carlisle then on to Wigton, then the B5302 to Silloth*
Standing on the peaceful Solway Estuary, close to sandy beaches and coastal walks, this hotel provides traditionally furnished bedrooms, with a host of modern facilities. There is also a leisure complex with pool and spa. Good meals are available in the Mediterranean styled bar and the pleasing hotel restaurant.
ROOMS: 33 en suite (2 fmly) No smoking in 6 bedrooms s £58-£70; d £80-£90 (incl. bkfst) * LB **FACILITIES:** STV Indoor swimming (H) Fishing Sauna Solarium Gym Pool table Croquet lawn Jacuzzi/spa Xmas **CONF:** Thtr 120 Class 100 Board 60 Del from £42 *
PARKING: 120 **CARDS:**

★62% *Golf Hotel*
Criffel St CA5 4AB
☎ 016973 31438 🖷 016973 32582
Dir: *off B5302, in Silloth at T-junct turn left hotel overlooks the corner of the green*
This smartly presented hotel lies in the centre of the town and is handy for the pebbled beach just a short stroll away. Bedrooms are mainly well proportioned, and all are bright and fresh. There is a cosy restaurant, and one can dine equally well in the lounge bar.
ROOMS: 22 en suite (4 fmly) **FACILITIES:** Snooker Pool table ch fac
CONF: Thtr 100 Class 40 Board 40 **NOTES:** Closed 25 Dec
CARDS:

SIMONSBATH, Somerset — Map 03 SS73

★★76% Simonsbath House
TA24 7SH
☎ 01643 831259 🖷 01643 831557
e-mail: simonsbath@talk21.com
Dir: *situated in the village of Simonsbath on the B3223*
Said to be the first house to be built in the forest of Exmoor, Simonsbath House dates back to the 17th century. Bedrooms are equipped with modern facilities and there is a choice of delightful lounges with original features like wood panelling and ornate fireplaces.
ROOMS: 7 en suite s £50-£55; d £80-£90 (incl. bkfst) *
FACILITIES: Xmas **PARKING:** 40 **NOTES:** No children 10yrs No smoking in restaurant **CARDS:**

SIX MILE BOTTOM, Cambridgeshire — Map 05 TL55

★★★73% ❀ Swynford Paddocks
CB8 0UE
☎ 01638 570234 🖷 01638 570283
e-mail: info@swynfordpaddocks.com
Dir: *M11 junct 9, take A11 towards Newmarket, turn onto the A1304 to Newmarket, hotel is on left 0.75m along*
Ideally situated amidst its own attractive gardens is this pleasant country house which sits between Newmarket and Cambridge. The relaxing accommodation comes in a variety of shapes and styles, ranging from comfortably appointed quarters to regal bedrooms, with several offering four poster beds. The hotel restaurant provides an excellent choice of modern dishes in elegant surroundings.
ROOMS: 15 en suite s £110-£140; d £135-£195 (incl. bkfst) * LB
FACILITIES: STV Tennis (hard) Croquet lawn Putting green ch fac
CONF: Thtr 40 Class 12 Board 22 Del from £135 * **PARKING:** 180
NOTES: No smoking in restaurant Civ Wed 58
CARDS:

See advert under NEWMARKET

SKEGNESS, Lincolnshire — Map 09 TF56

★★★63% *Crown*
Drummond Rd, Seacroft PE25 3AB
☎ 01754 610760 🖷 01754 610847
Dir: *take A52 to town centre, hotel 1m from clock tower*
Ideally situated just a short walk from the seafront and town centre is this popular resort hotel. The bedrooms are attractively decorated, well maintained and thoughtfully equipped. A wide selection of enjoyable dishes is available either in the attractive modern bar or in the more formal restaurant.
ROOMS: 27 en suite (7 fmly) **FACILITIES:** STV Indoor swimming (H)
CONF: Thtr 120 Class 130 Board 120 **SERVICES:** Lift **PARKING:** 90
NOTES: No dogs (ex guide dogs) **CARDS:**

See advert on opposite page

S

★★65% North Shore
North Shore Rd PE25 1DN
☎ 01754 763298 ▯ 01754 761902
e-mail: golfotel@aol.com
Dir: *1m N of town centre on right of A52 towards Mablethorpe*
North Shore Golf Hotel is part of a championship course complex. There are ample public rooms including a superb conservatory and busy bar where simple informal fare is offered. The restaurant offers a carte and daily changing set menus. The bedrooms vary in size and style but all are smartly decorated and well equipped.
ROOMS: 33 en suite 3 annexe en suite (4 fmly) s £38-£55; d £76-£110 (incl. bkfst & dinner) * LB **FACILITIES:** Golf 18 Snooker Pool table Putting green Xmas **CONF:** Thtr 220 Class 160 Board 60 Del from £75 * **PARKING:** 200 **NOTES:** No dogs (ex guide dogs) No smoking in restaurant Civ Wed 200 **CARDS:**

★★65% Vine Hotel
Vine Rd, Seacroft PE25 3DB
☎ 01754 763018 & 610611 ▯ 01754 769845
Dir: *A52 to Skegness, head S towards Gibraltar Point, hotel is approx 1m from the clocktower*
Owned by the local brewery, it is reputedly the second oldest building in Skegness. Recently refurbished to modern standards, it has spacious, comfortable bedrooms. There are two bars, the Tennyson Lounge (the poet wrote some of his works in the garden), and the Oak Room with open fire and excellent beers. Freshly prepared dishes are served in the bar and restaurant.
ROOMS: 20 en suite (6 fmly) s £50-£60; d £70-£80 (incl. bkfst) * LB **FACILITIES:** Bowling green Xmas **CONF:** Thtr 100 Class 80 Board 50 **PARKING:** 50 **CARDS:**

SKIPTON, North Yorkshire

Map 07 SD95

★★★68% Coniston Hall Lodge

Coniston Cold BD23 4EB
☎ 01756 748080 01756 749487
e-mail: conistonhall@clara.net
Dir: *on A65, 5m NW of Skipton*

Coniston Hall Lodge is part of a 1,200 acre Yorkshire Dales estate. The grounds are dominated by the vast 24 acre lake, a relaxing venue for trout fly fishing. The cuisine at the hotel is highly skilled and offers a wide selection of dishes which continue to be popular. The richly decorated Macleod's Bar and the neighbouring buttery both offer all day meals. The modern bedrooms are spacious and comfortable, most with king size beds and baths.
ROOMS: 40 en suite (4 fmly) d £40-£72 * LB **FACILITIES:** STV Fishing 4 wheel drive Clay pigeon shooting Paintball Falconry Archery Xmas **CONF:** Thtr 100 Class 50 Board 20 Del from £85 * **PARKING:** 120 **NOTES:** Civ Wed 50
CARDS:

See advert on opposite page

★★★67% Hanover International

Keighley Rd BD23 2TA
☎ 01756 700100 01756 700107
Dir: *on A629, 1m from town*

This large, modern hotel, situated on the edge of the town, beside a canal and overlooking hills, offers spacious, well equipped bedrooms. There is a restaurant, and comfortable lounges on both the ground and first floors. In addition, the hotel has a children's nursery available to residents, and comprehensive business and leisure facilities.
ROOMS: 75 en suite (10 fmly) No smoking in 14 bedrooms s £80; d £90 * LB **FACILITIES:** STV Indoor swimming (H) Squash Sauna Solarium Gym Pool table Jacuzzi/spa Whirlpool spa Steam room ch fac Xmas **CONF:** Thtr 400 Class 180 Board 120 Del from £70 * **SERVICES:** Lift **PARKING:** 150 **NOTES:** No smoking in restaurant Civ Wed 200 **CARDS:**

★★66% Herriots

Broughton Rd BD23 1RT
☎ 01756 792781 01756 792781
Dir: *off A59, opposite railway station*
Close to the centre of the town and on the doorstep of the Yorkshire Dales National Park, this pleasant hotel offers brightly decorated and spacious bedrooms. The stylish open plan brasserie is a relaxing area in which to dine from the varied menu, with meals and snacks also available in the bar. Entertainment is normally provided on Sunday evenings. Service is friendly and helpful.
ROOMS: 13 en suite (2 fmly) No smoking in 8 bedrooms s £50-£55; d £65-£70 (incl. bkfst) * LB **FACILITIES:** Bar Billiards entertainment **CONF:** Thtr 20 Class 15 Board 14 **PARKING:** 26 **NOTES:** No smoking in restaurant **CARDS:**

★★63% Unicorn Hotel

Devonshire Place, Keighley Rd BD23 2LP
☎ 01756 794146 01756 793376
e-mail: christine@unicornhotel.freeserve.co.uk
Dir: *on A625, opposite the bus station*
This town centre hotel is found on two levels above a row of shops and has ample parking nearby. The hotel is pleasantly furnished throughout and has spacious and well equipped bedrooms. Home cooked dishes are served in cosy dining room and a small lounge is also provided.
ROOMS: 9 en suite (1 fmly) s £40-£44; d £51-£61 (incl. bkfst) * LB
CARDS:

⇧ *Travelodge*

Travelodge

Gargrave Rd BD23 1UD
☎ 01756 798091 01756 798091
Dir: *A65/A59 roundabout*
This modern building offers accommodation in smart, spacious and well equipped bedrooms, all with en suite bathrooms. Refreshments may be taken at the nearby family restaurant. For further details and the Travelodge phone number, consult the Hotel Groups page.
ROOMS: 32 en suite

SLEAFORD, Lincolnshire

Map 08 TF04

★★68% *Carre Arms*

1 Mareham Ln NG34 7JP
☎ 01529 303156 01529 303139
Dir: *take A153 to Sleaford, hotel on right at level crossing*
This welcoming hotel is situated close to the railway station and offers well equipped bedrooms. A good range of well produced food is offered in the smartly restyled Brasserie; bar food is also available. Whilst there is no lounge, the bars are comfortable and the spacious conservatory is a riot of colour during the summertime.
ROOMS: 13 en suite (1 fmly) **CONF:** Thtr 50 Class 20 Board 30 **PARKING:** 100 **NOTES:** No dogs (ex guide dogs)
CARDS:

Popped the question? Hotels with Civ Wed in their entry are licensed for civil wedding ceremonies. Maximum numbers for the ceremony only are shown, e.g. Civ Wed 50

⌂ *Travelodge*

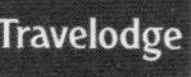

Holdingham NG34 8NP
☎ 01529 414752 🖹 01529 414752
Dir: *1m N, at roundabout A17/A15*
This modern building offers accommodation in smart, spacious and well equipped bedrooms, all with en suite bathrooms. Refreshments may be taken at the nearby family restaurant. For further details and the Travelodge phone number, consult the Hotel Groups page.
ROOMS: 40 en suite

SLOUGH, Berkshire — Map 04 SU97

★★★★68% Copthorne Slough/Windsor

COPTHORNE

400 Cippenham Ln SL1 2YE
☎ 01753 516222 🖹 01753 516237
Dir: *leave M4 junct 6 & follow A355 to Slough at next rdbt turn left & left again for hotel entrance*
This modern, purpose-built hotel offers well equipped bedrooms with the business person in mind. The main concourse and bar are ideal areas to rendezvous and the brasserie style restaurant boasts an interesting menu based on contemporary dishes.
ROOMS: 219 en suite d fr £160 * **FACILITIES:** STV Indoor swimming (H) Sauna Gym Jacuzzi/spa **CONF:** Thtr 250 Class 160 Board 60 Del from £135 * **SERVICES:** Lift air con **PARKING:** 300 **NOTES:** No dogs (ex guide dogs) No smoking in restaurant
CARDS:

★★★68% Courtyard by Marriott Slough/Windsor

COURTYARD

Church St SL1 2NH
☎ 01753 551551 🖹 01753 553333
Dir: *from junct 6 of M4 follow A355 to rdbt, turn right hotel approx 50 yds on right*
Location is a benefit for this modern hotel, with Heathrow Airport and local motorway networks easily accessible by car. Bedrooms feature a comprehensive range of facilities. The public areas are lively, modern and have an informal atmosphere.
ROOMS: 150 en suite (74 fmly) No smoking in 108 bedrooms d £115-£125 * LB **FACILITIES:** STV **CONF:** Thtr 45 Class 24 Board 24 Del from £149 * **SERVICES:** Lift air con **PARKING:** 162 **NOTES:** No dogs (ex guide dogs) **CARDS:**

○ Comfort Inn Heathrow

CHOICE HOTELS EUROPE

Sheppiston Ln, Hayes UB3 1LP
☎ 020 857 36162
ROOMS: 184 rms **NOTES:** Open

○ *Premier Lodge*

PREMIER LODGE

76 Uxbridge Rd SL1 1SU
☎ 0870 700 1502 🖹 0870 700 1503

○ Quality Hotel Heathrow

London Rd, Brands Hill SL3 8QB
☎ 01753 684001 🖹 01753 685767
ROOMS: 123 rms **NOTES:** No dogs Open

Late for dinner? Quality Standards star rating means that last orders for dinner should be no earlier than:
★ 6.30pm ★★ 7.00pm ★★★ 8.00pm
★★★★ 9.00pm ★★★★★ 10.00pm

S

SOLIHULL, West Midlands
Map 07 SP17

see also Dorridge

★★★★64% Swallow St John's

651 Warwick Rd B91 1AT
☎ 0121 711 3000 📠 0121 705 6629
e-mail: solihull@swallow-hotels.co.uk

Dir: *leave M42 junct 5 & follow signs for Solihull centre. At rdbt 2nd left - Warwick Rd. At Barley Mow Pub on left, 2nd left at rdbt, hotel on right*

This hotel has easy access to main arterial routes and is convenient for the NEC and airport. An attractive modern hotel, with bright, spacious reception rooms, it is popular with business guests. There are excellent leisure, conference and in room facilities.

ROOMS: 178 en suite (6 fmly) No smoking in 78 bedrooms s fr £150; d fr £165 (incl. bkfst) * LB **FACILITIES:** STV Indoor swimming (H) Sauna Solarium Gym Jacuzzi/spa Beauty therapist entertainment Xmas **CONF:** Thtr 700 Class 350 Board 60 Del from £90 * **SERVICES:** Lift **PARKING:** 380 **NOTES:** Civ Wed 100 **CARDS:**

★★★66% Regency

Stratford Rd, Shirley B90 4EB
☎ 0121 745 6119 📠 0121 733 3801

Dir: *beside A34, 0.5m from junct 4 of M42*

Convenient for the motorways, NEC and city centre, this popular hotel provides bedrooms in a range of styles, some of which are very smart indeed. Public areas include a restaurant and choice of bars; Morrissey's Irish Bar provides a lively venue with music.

ROOMS: 112 en suite (10 fmly) No smoking in 17 bedrooms **FACILITIES:** STV Indoor swimming (H) Sauna Solarium Gym Jacuzzi/spa Beauty health salon entertainment **CONF:** Thtr 180 Class 80 Board 60 **SERVICES:** Lift **PARKING:** 275 **NOTES:** No smoking in restaurant **CARDS:**

★★63% Flemings

141 Warwick Rd, Olton B92 7HW
☎ 0121 706 0371 📠 0121 706 4494
e-mail: reservations@flemingshotel.co.uk

Dir: *on A41, near Olton Station*

This privately owned hotel close to Olton railway station offers convenient access to the M42, the NEC and Birmingham International Airport. The accommodation is sensibly equipped with business travellers in mind. There are some ground-floor rooms, and some suitable for family use. Facilities include a small bistro adjacent to the bar, as an alternative to the main restaurant, and a snooker room.

ROOMS: 77 en suite (6 fmly) No smoking in 4 bedrooms s £25-£45; d £45-£56 (incl. bkfst) * LB **FACILITIES:** Snooker **CONF:** Thtr 40 Class 40 Board 22 **PARKING:** 80 **NOTES:** No smoking in restaurant Closed 24-28 Dec **CARDS:**

★★63% Richmond House Hotel

47 Richmond Rd, Olton B92 7RP
☎ 0121 707 9746 📠 0121 707 9746
e-mail: RichmondHouse@freeserve.co.uk

Set in a residential suburb and convenient for the NEC, this family-run hotel offers a cosy residents bar and a restaurant serving a good choice of British and European dishes.

ROOMS: 10 en suite No smoking in all bedrooms s fr £63; d fr £73 (incl. bkfst) * **FACILITIES:** Tennis (grass) Pool table **CONF:** Thtr 60 Class 60 Board 30 **PARKING:** 40 **NOTES:** No smoking in restaurant **CARDS:**

SONNING, Berkshire
Map 04 SU77

★★★77% 🏵🏵 French Horn

PRIDE OF BRITAIN MEMBER

RG4 6TN
☎ 0118 969 2204 📠 0118 944 2210
e-mail: thefrenchhorn@compuserve.com

Dir: *turn left off A4 into Sonning follow road through village over bridge, hotel on right, car park on left*

This long established Thames-side restaurant with rooms has a lovely village setting and retains the traditions of classical hotel-keeping. The restaurant is a particular attraction where the signature dish is duck, spit-roasted in front of the fire in the bar, and carved at the table. Bedrooms are spacious and comfortable, many offering stunning views over the river. There are also four cottage suites. A private board room and dining facilities are attractive to corporate guests.

ROOMS: 12 en suite 8 annexe en suite s £100-£140; d £120-£165 (incl. bkfst) * **FACILITIES:** Fishing **CONF:** Board 20 Del from £200 * **PARKING:** 40 **NOTES:** No dogs (ex guide dogs) Closed 26 Dec-2 Jan & Good Fri **CARDS:**

SOURTON, Devon
Map 02 SX59

★★71% *Collaven Manor*

EX20 4HH
☎ 01837 861522 📠 01837 861614

Dir: *turn off A30 onto A386 to Tavistock hotel 2m on right*

Set in five acres of well tended gardens on the edge of Dartmoor, this delightful 15th-century manor house benefits from stunning rural views to Cornwall in the distance. The comfortable bedrooms are individually designed and are exceptionally well equipped. Stone walls, old beams and inglenook fireplaces enhance the character of the cosy sitting rooms; one of which has a well stocked bar. Each evening an imaginative, fixed price menu is offered, using fresh local produce, featuring home grown vegetables wherever possible.

ROOMS: 9 en suite (1 fmly) **FACILITIES:** Croquet lawn Bowls Badminton **CONF:** Thtr 30 Class 20 Board 16 **PARKING:** 50 **NOTES:** No smoking in restaurant **CARDS:**

S

SOURTON CROSS, Devon
Map 02 SX59

Travelodge
EX20 4LY
☎ 01837 52124 Fax 01837 52124
***Dir:** 4m W, at junct of A30/A386*

Travelodge

This modern building offers accommodation in smart, spacious and well equipped bedrooms, all with en suite bathrooms. Refreshments may be taken at the nearby family restaurant. For further details and the Travelodge phone number, consult the Hotel Groups page.
ROOMS: 42 en suite

SOUTHAMPTON, Hampshire
Map 04 SU41

see also Shedfield

★★★★★59% De Vere Grand Harbour
West Quay Rd SO15 1AG
☎ 023 8063 3033 Fax 023 8063 3066
e-mail: grandharbour@devere-hotels.com
***Dir:** leave M27 junc 3 or M3 junc 13 follow Waterfront signs to West Quay Rd*

Located in West Quay, this impressive modern hotel is ideally placed for the city's business district, shopping centres, waterfront, and tourist attractions. Bedrooms and suites, some with balconies, are both comfortably furnished and thoughtfully equipped. A superb leisure centre, with its own bar and restaurant stands in a glass pyramid and guests also have a choice between two further restaurants. The hotel also provides an extensive range of banqueting and conference facilities.
ROOMS: 172 en suite No smoking in 139 bedrooms s £150-£175; d £170-£195 (incl. bkfst) * LB **FACILITIES:** STV Indoor swimming (H) Snooker Sauna Solarium Gym Jacuzzi/spa Steam room Beauty treatments Xmas **CONF:** Thtr 500 Class 270 Board 48 Del from £125 * **SERVICES:** Lift air con **PARKING:** 200 **NOTES:** No dogs (ex guide dogs) **CARDS:**

★★★71% Botleigh Grange
Hedge End SO30 2GA
☎ 01489 787700 Fax 01489 788535
e-mail: enquiries@botleighgrangehotel.co.uk
***Dir:** follow A334 to Botley & hotel is on the left just before Botley*

Best Western

A much extended mansion set in grounds and a popular venue for weddings. Spacious bedrooms are very comfortably furnished and well equipped. Public areas include a large bar, elegant lounge and attractive dining room, offering interesting, carefully prepared dishes. The hotel has a choice of function and conference rooms.
ROOMS: 57 en suite (4 fmly) No smoking in 10 bedrooms s £75-£100; d £99-£145 (incl. bkfst) * LB **FACILITIES:** STV Fishing Putting green Coarse fishing Xmas **CONF:** Thtr 500 Class 175 Board 60 Del £125 * **SERVICES:** Lift **PARKING:** 200 **NOTES:** No dogs (ex guide dogs) No smoking in restaurant Civ Wed 200
CARDS:

See advert on this page

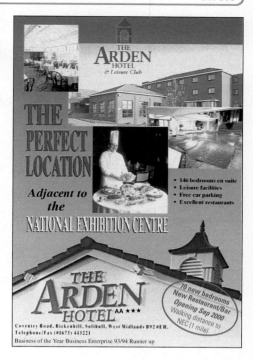

S

SOUTHAMPTON, continued

★★★70% The Woodlands Lodge
Bartley Rd, Woodlands SO40 7GN
☎ 023 8029 2257 📠 023 8029 3090
e-mail: woodlands_lodge@nortels.ltd.uk
Dir: *take A326 towards Fawley. 2nd rdbt turn right, after 0.25m turn left by White Horse PH. In 1.5m cross cattle grid, hotel is 70mtrs on left*
This beautifully restored 18th-century hunting lodge is set in four acres of attractive grounds on the edge of the New Forest. Bedrooms are furnished and decorated to a high standard, and there are a pleasant lounge and bar, both opening onto the gardens.
ROOMS: 16 en suite (1 fmly) No smoking in 2 bedrooms s £65-£75; d £118-£178 (incl. bkfst) * LB **FACILITIES:** Jacuzzi/spa Xmas **CONF:** Thtr 55 Class 16 Board 20 Del £116 * **PARKING:** 31 **NOTES:** No smoking in restaurant Civ Wed 60
CARDS:

★★★65% Novotel

1 West Quay Rd SO15 1RA
☎ 023 8033 0550 📠 023 8022 2158
e-mail: H1073@accor-hotels.com
Dir: *from M27 junct 3 follow for City Centre (A33). After 1m take right hand lane for 'Old Town' & 'Dock Gates 4-10'. Hotel entrance on right*
This modern, purpose built hotel is conveniently located in the heart of the new city centre, close to both the railway station and road network. The spacious bedrooms are brightly appointed and ideal for both families and business guests. Public areas include the garden brasserie and bar which is open throughout the day, a leisure complex, and extensive conference and banqueting facilities.
ROOMS: 121 en suite (50 fmly) No smoking in 71 bedrooms d £75-£79 * LB **FACILITIES:** STV Indoor swimming (H) Sauna Gym **CONF:** Thtr 500 Class 300 Board 150 **SERVICES:** Lift air con **PARKING:** 300
CARDS:

★★★64% *Posthouse Southampton*
Posthouse

Herbert Walker Av SO15 1HJ
☎ 0870 400 9073 📠 023 80332510
Dir: *from M27 follow signs for 'Western Docks 1-10'. Posthouse situated next to Dock Gate 8*
Conveniently located for both the port and the town centre, this modern hotel is popular with all types of guests. The well equipped bedrooms are comfortably furnished and modern in style. Public areas include an informal lounge bar and the Traders Restaurant which offers an extensive range of popular dishes. Conference facilities are available.
ROOMS: 128 en suite (14 fmly) No smoking in 75 bedrooms **FACILITIES:** Indoor swimming (H) Sauna Solarium Gym Jacuzzi/spa Beauty therapy room **CONF:** Thtr 250 Class 80 Board 50 **SERVICES:** Lift **PARKING:** 250 **CARDS:**

★★★64% Southampton Park
Forestdale Hotels

Cumberland Place SO15 2WY
☎ 023 8034 3343 📠 023 8033 2538
Dir: *hotel at northern end of the Inner Ring Rd opposite Watts Park & Civic Centre*

Located in the heart of the city opposite Watts Park, this modern hotel provides well equipped, smartly appointed bedrooms with comfortable furnishings. The public areas include a good leisure centre, spacious bar and lounge, and a choice of eating options. Parking is available in the multi-storey car park behind the hotel.
ROOMS: 72 en suite (10 fmly) No smoking in 20 bedrooms d fr £100 (incl. bkfst & dinner) * LB **FACILITIES:** STV Indoor swimming (H) Sauna Solarium Gym Jacuzzi/spa Massage Jet Steam room **CONF:** Thtr 200 Class 60 Board 70 Del from £100 * **SERVICES:** Lift **PARKING:** 8 **NOTES:** Closed 25 & 26 Dec nights **CARDS:**

★★★61% Highfield House
ZOFFANY HOTELS

Highfield Ln, Portswood SO17 1AQ
☎ 023 8035 9955 📠 023 8058 3910
e-mail: highfield@zoffanyhotels.co.uk
Dir: *from M27 junct 5 take A335 to city centre. Follow for Portswood/University, hotel on right after traffic lights at Portswood*
Close to the university and within easy reach of the motorway, this hotel remains a popular choice with all guests. New owners have initiated a major refurbishment programme. Bedrooms and public areas have all been upgraded.
ROOMS: 66 en suite (6 fmly) No smoking in 30 bedrooms s £85-£90; d £90-£100 (incl. bkfst) * LB **FACILITIES:** STV Sauna Gym Xmas **CONF:** Thtr 200 Class 100 Board 60 Del from £85 * **PARKING:** 80
CARDS:

★★67% *Busketts Lawn*
174 Woodlands Rd, Woodlands SO40 7GL
☎ 023 8029 2272 & 8029 2077 📠 023 8029 2487
Dir: *A35 W of city through Ashurst, over railway bridge, sharp right into Woodlands Road*
In a tranquil setting, on the edge of the New Forest, this charming hotel is family run. Bedrooms vary in size and are attractively furnished with many thoughtful extras. There is a cosy lounge, small separate bar and a dining room, where home cooked meals are served. The hotel is a popular venue for weddings.
ROOMS: 14 en suite (3 fmly) **FACILITIES:** Outdoor swimming (H) Croquet lawn Putting green Football **CONF:** Thtr 150 Class 75 Board 40 **PARKING:** 50 **NOTES:** No smoking in restaurant
CARDS:

★★64% Elizabeth House
43-44 The Avenue SO17 1XP
☎ 023 8022 4327 📠 023 8022 4327
e-mail: enquiries@elizabethhousehotel.com
Dir: *on the A33, left hand side travelling towards city centre, after Southampton Common, before main traffic lights*
Bedrooms are comfortably appointed and thoughtfully equipped. Guests can take dinner in the dining room or the popular, informal Cellar Bar. The hotel is equipped with a smart meeting room.
ROOMS: 21 rms (20 en suite) (3 fmly) s fr £47.50; d fr £57.50 (incl. bkfst) * **CONF:** Thtr 40 Class 24 Board 24 Del from £77.50 * **PARKING:** 23 **NOTES:** No smoking in restaurant
CARDS:

★★63% Rosida Garden
25-27 Hill Ln SO15 5AB
☎ 023 8022 8501 📠 023 8063 5501
e-mail: enquiries@rosidagarden.co.uk
Dir: *M3, A33 exit, rdbt 2nd exit, next rdbt 2nd exit, 1st exit next rdbt, straight across mini rdbt, 1.5m ahead, hotel on left*
Situated close to the city centre, this hotel is conveniently located for both the docks and ferry ports. The bedrooms are comfortably furnished, and guests can enjoy hearty home-cooked food in the well presented dining room. There is also a TV lounge and a licensed bar.
ROOMS: 27 en suite (6 fmly) s fr £49; d fr £61 (incl. bkfst) * LB **FACILITIES:** Outdoor swimming (H) **CONF:** Thtr 35 Class 20 Board 20 **PARKING:** 50 **CARDS:**

> Fancy a Singapore Sling? Bar staff in five star hotels should be skilled cocktail mixers.

S

★★63% The Star Hotel & Restaurant
26 High St SO14 2NA
☎ 023 8033 9939 ▯ 023 8033 5291
Dir: *enter city from A33 follow signs for city centre at Isle of Wight ferry terminal turn into High St, hotel on right just beyond zebra crossing*
This friendly city centre hotel continues to grow in stature. The bedrooms are bright and comfortably furnished. Public areas include a popular bar, smart reception area and dining room. There are several function rooms including a self-contained conference suite, secure parking is available.
ROOMS: 43 rms (37 en suite) (2 fmly) No smoking in 7 bedrooms s £52-£65; d £70-£80 (incl. bkfst) * LB **CONF:** Thtr 75 Class 25 Board 35 **SERVICES:** Lift **PARKING:** 30 **NOTES:** Closed 24 Dec-1 Jan
CARDS:

⌂ *Travelodge*
Lodge Rd SO17 1XS
☎ 023 8022 9023
This modern building offers accommodation in smart, spacious and well equipped bedrooms, all with en suite bathrooms. Refreshments may be taken at the nearby family restaurant. For further details and the Travelodge phone number, consult the Hotel Groups page.
ROOMS: 48 en suite

⌂ *Hotel Ibis*
West Quay Rd, Western Esplanade SO15 1RA
☎ 023 8063 4463 ▯ 023 8022 3273
e-mail: H1039@accor-hotels.com
Dir: *leave M27 junct 3 joining M271. Turn left to Southampton City. At 2nd set of traffic lights turn right*
Modern, budget hotel offering comfortable accommodation in bright and practical bedrooms. Breakfast is self-service and dinner is available in the restaurant. For further details, consult the Hotel Groups page.
ROOMS: 93 en suite **CONF:** Thtr 70 Class 40 Board 28

○ Express by Holiday Inn

Adanac Park, Redbridge Ln, Nursling SO16
☎ 0800 897121
ROOMS: 105 rms **NOTES:** Opening Autumn 2000

SOUTH BRENT, Devon
Map 03 SX66

★★75% Brookdale House Restaurant & Hotel
North Huish TQ10 9NR
☎ 01548 821661 ▯ 01548 821606
e-mail: Brookdalehouse@yahoo.com
Dir: *from A38 follow Avonwich signs, turn right at Avon Inn, next left at telephone box then right at hotel sign to bottom of valley*
This charming Tudor-style residence stands next to the river, with sloping gardens and a tumbling waterfall. Bedrooms are individually named and appointed, with predominantly antique furnishings. Extra touches include mineral water and fresh flowers. An interesting collection of fine artwork features in the public areas, while enjoyable cuisine is served in the restaurant.
ROOMS: 6 en suite 2 annexe en suite No smoking in 2 bedrooms
CONF: Thtr 50 Class 30 Board 30 Del from £90 * **NOTES:** No children 12yrs Civ Wed 120 **CARDS:**

SOUTH CAVE, East Riding of Yorkshire
Map 08 SE93

⌂ *Travelodge*
Beacon Service Area HU15 1RZ
☎ 01430 424455 ▯ 01430 424455
Dir: *A63 eastbound*
This modern building offers accommodation in smart, spacious and well equipped bedrooms, all with en suite bathrooms. Refreshments may be taken at the nearby family restaurant. For further details and the Travelodge phone number, consult the Hotel Groups page.
ROOMS: 40 en suite

SOUTHEND-ON-SEA, Essex
Map 05 TQ88

★★★64% Roslin Hotel
Thorpe Esplanade SS1 3BG
☎ 01702 586375 ▯ 01702 586663
e-mail: roslinhtl@aol.com
This is a small, attractive, family-run hotel located on the seafront. Accommodation is furnished and decorated in traditional style and offers a useful range of extra facilities. The public areas consist of a comfortable lounge/bar and a restaurant with sea views.

continued

S

SOUTHEND-ON-SEA, continued

Roslin Hotel, Southend-on-Sea

ROOMS: 39 rms (35 en suite) (4 fmly) s £36-£62; d £65-£78 (incl. bkfst) * LB **FACILITIES:** STV Temporary membership of local sports centre **CONF:** Thtr 30 Class 30 Board 28 **PARKING:** 34
CARDS:

★★★60% County Hotel Southend

REGAL

Aviation Way SS2 6UN
☎ 01702 279955 📠 01702 541961
e-mail: enquiries@countysouthend.co.uk
Dir: *turn off A127 at Tesco rdbt follow signs for Aviation Way, turn right at next rdbt straight over rdbt & then left at mini-rdbt, hotel on right*

This purpose built hotel is conveniently located for Southend Airport and only ten minutes from the town centre. The spacious accommodation is comfortable and well appointed. There is limited lounge seating available, a cosy bar with wide screen TV and an informal brasserie style restaurant.
ROOMS: 18 en suite 47 annexe en suite (65 fmly) No smoking in 22 bedrooms s £70-£75; d £80-£85 * LB **CONF:** Thtr 200 Class 120 Board 60 Del from £75 * **PARKING:** 200 **NOTES:** No smoking in restaurant Civ Wed 200 **CARDS:**

★★70% Balmoral

34 Valkyrie Rd, Westcliffe-on-Sea SS0 8BU
☎ 01702 342947 📠 01702 337828
e-mail: balmoralhotel@netscapeonline.co.uk
Dir: *off A13*
This delightful hotel is conveniently located for the local train station, the seafront and is a short distance from the town centre. The spacious and well kept bedrooms have been tastefully decorated and offer a good range of extra facilities. Public areas consist of a restaurant, small cocktail bar and a small seating area near the reception.
ROOMS: 29 en suite (4 fmly) s £49-£80; d £65-£100 (incl. bkfst) * LB **FACILITIES:** STV Arrangement with nearby health club **PARKING:** 23 **NOTES:** No smoking in restaurant **CARDS:**

★★70% Camelia

178 Eastern Esplanade, Thorpe Bay SS1 3AA
☎ 01702 587917 📠 01702 585704
e-mail: cameliahotel@fsbdial.co.uk
Dir: *from A13 or A127 follow signs to Southend seafront, on seafront turn left, hotel 1m east of the pier*
This small, privately owned hotel benefits from its location on the seafront, many rooms enjoying excellent sea views. The accommodation is well kept, smartly furnished and equipped with modern facilities. The air conditioned public areas consist of a cosy lounge/bar area and an informal restaurant.
ROOMS: 21 en suite (1 fmly) No smoking in 19 bedrooms s £46-£65; d £60-£90 (incl. bkfst) * LB **FACILITIES:** STV Jacuzzi/spa Cycle hire and local cycle tours arranged entertainment **PARKING:** 102 **NOTES:** No dogs (ex guide dogs) No smoking in restaurant
CARDS:

★★57% *Tower Hotel & Restaurant*

146 Alexandra Rd SS1 1HE
☎ 01702 348635 📠 01702 433044
Dir: *off A13 Cricketers Inn into Milton road, then left into Cambridge road and take 3rd turn right into Wilson Rd.*
This Victorian house, distinguished by its turrets, is situated in the conservation area just a short walk from the cliff top. There is a popular bar and accommodation is split between the main building and annexe across the road.
ROOMS: 15 rms (14 en suite) 17 annexe en suite (4 fmly)
FACILITIES: Residents Membership of local sports club. **PARKING:** 4
CARDS:

SOUTH MIMMS, Hertfordshire — Map 04 TL20

★★★65% *Posthouse South Mimms*

Posthouse

EN6 3NH
☎ 0870 400 9072 📠 01707 646728
Dir: *junc 23 on M25 & A1 take services exit off main rdbt then 1st left & follow hotel signs*
Within easy reach of local motorways, this hotel offers a range of conference and meeting rooms, meeting the needs of its clientele. Bedrooms vary, with the new millennium bedrooms being particularly smart and modern, all feature a good range of in room facilities. Guests have the use of two bars and a small, but well equipped leisure centre.
ROOMS: 143 en suite (25 fmly) No smoking in 70 bedrooms
FACILITIES: Indoor swimming (H) Sauna Solarium Gym Pool table Jacuzzi/spa Outdoor childrens play area **CONF:** Thtr 170 Class 85 Board 40 **PARKING:** 200 **CARDS:**

⇧ Days Inn

DAYS INN

South Mimms Service Area, Bignells Corner
EN6 3QQ
☎ 01707 665440 📠 01707 660189
Dir: *junct 23 on M25*
Fully refurbished, Days Inn offers well equipped, brightly appointed, modern accommodation with smart en suite bathrooms. There is a fully staffed reception; continental breakfast is available and other refreshments may be taken at the nearby family restaurant.
ROOMS: 74 en suite d fr £59 *

TV dinner? Room service at three stars and above.

S

SOUTH MOLTON, Devon
Map 03 SS72

★★76% Marsh Hall Country House
EX36 3HQ
☎ 01769 572666 01769 574230
Dir: *1.25m N towards North Molton off A361*
This personally owned hotel stands in large grounds within easy reach of Exmoor and the coast. Dating from the 17th century, it was built by the local squire for his mistress. Bedrooms are furnished in keeping with the elegance of the house, and there are two comfortable sitting rooms, one with a bar.
ROOMS: 7 en suite s £55-£80; d £85-£110 (incl. bkfst) * LB **FACILITIES:** Xmas **PARKING:** 20 **NOTES:** No dogs (ex guide dogs) No children 12yrs No smoking in restaurant **CARDS:**

★★70% The George Hotel
1 Broad St EX36 3AB
☎ 01769 572514 01769 572514
e-mail: george@s-molton.freeserve.co.uk
Dir: *turn off A361 at road island signposted 'South Molton 1.5m' to town centre, hotel is in square*
This charming 17th-century hotel has a long tradition of hospitality and has recently been very well restored. It stands in the town centre and attracts both business and leisure guests. Service is friendly and informal and there is a good selection of food in the bar as well as in the restaurant.
ROOMS: 7 en suite (2 fmly) s £40-£45; d £56-£60 (incl. bkfst) * LB **CONF:** Thtr 100 Class 16 Board 20 **PARKING:** 12 **NOTES:** No dogs (ex guide dogs) **CARDS:**

SOUTH NORMANTON, Derbyshire
Map 08 SK45

★★★★67% Swallow
SWALLOW HOTELS
Carter Ln East DE55 2EH
☎ 01773 812000 01773 580032
e-mail: info@swallowhotels.com
Dir: *situated on the E side of M1 junct 28 on A38 to Mansfield*

This smart hotel is just off junction 28 of the M1. All the spacious bedrooms have modern facilities and comfortable furnishings. There are two eating options: Chatterleys, and the more formal Pavilion.
ROOMS: 160 en suite (7 fmly) No smoking in 100 bedrooms s fr £115; d fr £130 (incl. bkfst) * LB **FACILITIES:** STV Indoor swimming (H) Sauna Solarium Gym Jacuzzi/spa Whirlpool Steam room Xmas **CONF:** Thtr 220 Class 100 Board 60 Del £140 * **PARKING:** 220 **NOTES:** Civ Wed 180 **CARDS:**

Arriving late? Four and five star hotels have night porters to assist with your luggage; and 24hr room service.

SOUTHPORT, Merseyside
Map 07 SD31
see also Formby

★★★68% Royal Clifton
Promenade PR8 1RB
☎ 01704 533771 01704 500657
e-mail: sales@royalclifton.co.uk
Dir: *hotel on Promenade adjacent to Marine Lake*
In a prime position on the promenade, this large hotel offers comfortable, modern bedrooms. A range of popular meals and snacks is available in the lively conservatory bar, and more formal dining can be had in the Pavilion Restaurant.
ROOMS: 106 en suite (22 fmly) No smoking in 10 bedrooms s fr £75; d fr £99 (incl. bkfst) * LB **FACILITIES:** STV Indoor swimming (H) Sauna Solarium Gym Jacuzzi/spa Hair & beauty salon Steam room entertainment Xmas **CONF:** Thtr 300 Class 170 Board 80 Del from £92.83 * **SERVICES:** Lift **PARKING:** 60 **NOTES:** No dogs (ex guide dogs) Civ Wed 100 **CARDS:**

★★★68% Stutelea Hotel & Leisure Club
Best Western
Alexandra Rd PR9 0NB
☎ 01704 544220 01704 500232
e-mail: info@stutelea.co.uk
Dir: *off the promenade near town & Hesketh Park*
A fully equipped leisure centre is one of the attractions at this popular family run hotel, situated not far from the Marine Lake. Nicely furnished bedrooms include family suites and rooms on the ground floor, as well as some having balconies overlooking the award winning garden. Carefully prepared evening meals are served in generous portions and snacks can also be had in the Garden bar.

continued

S

SOUTHPORT, continued

Stutelea Hotel & Leisure Club, Southport

ROOMS: 20 en suite (4 fmly) s £65-£68; d £90-£95 (incl. bkfst) * LB **FACILITIES:** STV Indoor swimming (H) Sauna Solarium Gym Pool table Jacuzzi/spa Games room Keep fit classes Steam room Xmas **SERVICES:** Lift **PARKING:** 18 **NOTES:** No dogs (ex guide dogs) **CARDS:**

See advert on opposite page

★★★67% Scarisbrick

Lord St PR8 1NZ
☎ 01704 543000 🖷 01704 533335
e-mail: scarisbrickhotel@talk21.com
Dir: *from South: M6 junct 26, M58 to Ormskirk then onto Southport. from North: A59 from Preston, well signposted. Also junct 26 M6, then M58 junct A570*

Sitting in the centre of Lord Street, this privately owned hotel offers attractively furnished bedrooms. A wide range of eating options is available, from the bistro style of Maloneys Kitchen to the more formal Knightsbridge restaurant.

ROOMS: 90 en suite (5 fmly) s £50-£77; d £70-£99 (incl. bkfst) * LB **FACILITIES:** STV Indoor swimming (H) Sauna Solarium Gym Pool table Jacuzzi/spa Use of private leisure centre entertainment Xmas **CONF:** Thtr 200 Class 100 Board 80 Del from £80 * **SERVICES:** Lift **PARKING:** 73 **NOTES:** No smoking in restaurant Civ Wed 170 **CARDS:**

★★71% Balmoral Lodge

41 Queens Rd PR9 9EX
☎ 01704 544298 & 530751 🖷 01704 501224
e-mail: balmorallg@aol.com
Dir: *edge of town on A565 Preston road*

Situated in a quiet residential area close to Lord Street, the atmosphere at this hotel is warm and friendly. Rooms are nicely furnished and well equipped, some with private patios overlooking the attractive rear gardens. There is a cosy bar and a comfortable residents lounge. The restaurant offers good, freshly cooked food.

ROOMS: 15 en suite (1 fmly) s £30-£52; d £56-£62 (incl. bkfst) * LB **FACILITIES:** STV Sauna **PARKING:** 12 **NOTES:** No dogs No smoking in restaurant **CARDS:**

★★67% *Bold*

585 Lord St PR9 0BE
☎ 01704 532578 🖷 01704 532528
Dir: *near M57 & M58, at the top end of Lord Street near the Casino*

This hotel offers easy access to the seafront and all the main attractions of the town. Bedrooms, a number of which are suitable for families, are generally spacious and well equipped. Downstairs, there is a nightclub (open at weekends only) and a popular bar and bistro, where the menu, ranging from snacks to full meals, is available all day.

continued

ROOMS: 23 rms (20 en suite) (4 fmly) **FACILITIES:** Special rates for local squash club entertainment **CONF:** Thtr 40 Class 40 Board 11 **SERVICES:** air con **PARKING:** 15 **NOTES:** No dogs (ex guide dogs) **CARDS:**

See advert on opposite page

★★65% Metropole

Portland St PR8 1LL
☎ 01704 536836 🖷 01704 549041
e-mail: metropole.southport@btinternet.com
Dir: *turn left off Lord St after Prince of Wales Hotel & Metropole is directly behind Prince of Wales*

This family-run hotel is located just 100 yards from the famous Lord Street and offers bright and modern bedrooms, with family rooms available. There is a choice of lounges, in addition to the bar-lounge, and a selection of freshly prepared dishes is offered in the restaurant.

ROOMS: 23 en suite (4 fmly) s £30-£35; d £52-£60 (incl. bkfst) * LB **FACILITIES:** Snooker Golf can be arranged at 8 local courses including Royal Birkdale Xmas **PARKING:** 12 **CARDS:**

★★65% *Shelbourne*

1 Lord St West PR8 2BH
☎ 01704 541252 & 530278 🖷 01704 501293
e-mail: shelbourne@mail.cybase.co.uk
Dir: *on A565, Lord St signposted from motorway*

Situated at the head of Lord Street, this family-run hotel offers spacious, brightly furnished bedrooms. There is a bar lounge and a sun terrace. Staff provide friendly service.

ROOMS: 20 en suite (1 fmly) No smoking in 4 bedrooms **CONF:** Thtr 150 Class 75 Board 50 **PARKING:** 20 **CARDS:**

SOUTHSEA See Portsmouth & Southsea

SOUTH SHIELDS, Tyne & Wear — Map 12 NZ36

★★★64% Sea

Best Western

Sea Rd NE33 2LD
☎ 0191 427 0999 🖷 0191 454 0500
e-mail: seahotel@fsmail.net
Dir: *on A183*

Situated on the promenade overlooking the River Tyne, this long-established hotel was originally built in the 1930s. Now a popular business hotel, the atmosphere is relaxed and the staff friendly. The restaurant and bar serve a good range of generously portioned dishes.

ROOMS: 33 en suite (2 fmly) s £49-£59; d £59-£100 (incl. bkfst) * **FACILITIES:** STV **CONF:** Thtr 200 Class 100 Board 50 Del from £77.50 * **PARKING:** 70 **CARDS:**

SOUTHWAITE MOTORWAY SERVICE AREA (M6), Cumbria — Map 12 NY44

⌂ *Travelodge*

Travelodge

Broadfield Site CA4 0NT
☎ Central Res 0800 850950 🖷 01525 878450
Dir: *on M6 junc 41/42*

This modern building offers accommodation in smart, spacious and well equipped bedrooms, all with en suite bathrooms. Refreshments may be taken at the nearby family restaurant. For further details and the Travelodge phone number, consult the Hotel Groups page.

ROOMS: 39 en suite

SOUTH WALSHAM, Norfolk — Map 09 TG31

★★★64% South Walsham Hall
The Street NR13 6DQ
☎ 01603 270378 & 270591 Fax 01603 270519
e-mail: Alex.Suss@btinternet.com
Dir: *E of Norwich on B1140 towards Acle*
This imposing hall dates back to Elizabethan times (with Victorian extensions) and is surrounded by the Fairhaven Trust gardens. There is a wide choice of bedroom style and size, all of which are well appointed with some excellent furnishings and a fresh colour scheme. There is a spacious bar-lounge and an intimate dining room.
ROOMS: 10 en suite 6 annexe en suite (1 fmly) **FACILITIES:** Outdoor swimming (H) Tennis (hard) Fishing 50 acres of woodland-water gardens ch fac **CONF:** Thtr 25 Class 15 Board 15 Del from £75 *
PARKING: 100 **NOTES:** Civ Wed 60
CARDS:

SOUTH WITHAM, Lincolnshire — Map 08 SK91

Travelodge
New Fox NG33 5LN
☎ 01572 767586 Fax 01572 767586
Dir: *on A1, northbound*
This modern building offers accommodation in smart, spacious and well equipped bedrooms, all with en suite bathrooms. Refreshments may be taken at the nearby family restaurant. For further details and the Travelodge phone number, consult the Hotel Groups page.
ROOMS: 32 en suite

S

SOUTHWOLD, Suffolk
Map 05 TM57

★★★71% Swan
Market Place IP18 6EG
☎ 01502 722186 Fax 01502 724800
Dir: *take A1095 to Southwold, hotel is located in the centre of town, parking is via an archway to the left of the building*
Overlooking the market place in the heart of town is this stylish hotel. The public areas include a drawing room, lounge and an intimate bar. In the elegant restaurant guests can choose from a selection of imaginative dishes, as well as an excellent wine list. The comfortable accommodation is equipped to a high standard.
ROOMS: 26 rms (25 en suite) 17 annexe en suite (2 fmly)
FACILITIES: Croquet lawn **CONF:** Thtr 50 Class 32 Board 12
SERVICES: Lift **PARKING:** 35 **NOTES:** No smoking in restaurant RS Nov-Mar **CARDS:**

★★69% The Crown
90 High St IP18 6DP
☎ 01502 722275 Fax 01502 727263
Dir: *off A12 take A1094 to Southwold, stay on main road into town centre, hotel on left in High St*
This old posting inn is an unusual combination of pub, wine bar, restaurant and hotel. The popular wine bar offers light meals featuring cosmopolitan cooking. The intimate restaurant serves a similarly modern style of cuisine. At the back of the inn, a locals' snug bar is the focal point for gossip and Adnams beers.
ROOMS: 12 rms (9 en suite) (1 fmly) **CONF:** Thtr 40 Class 20 Board 20
PARKING: 23 **NOTES:** No dogs (ex guide dogs) No smoking in restaurant Closed 1st or 2nd wk Jan **CARDS:**

★★64% The Blythe
Station Rd IP18 6AY
☎ 01502 722632 Fax 01502 722632
Dir: *turn off A12 at Southwold sign. Hotel 4m on by mini-rdbt at entrance to town*
On the outskirts of this upmarket seaside town, the Pier Avenue is quickly earning a good reputation for its lovely seafood cuisine. The downstairs rooms include two different bar areas with the local Adnams ales. Upstairs the bedrooms make the best use of the buildings original charm, and come in a variety of styles and sizes.
ROOMS: 12 en suite (4 fmly) **PARKING:** 10 **NOTES:** No smoking in restaurant **CARDS:**

S

SOUTH ZEAL, Devon
Map 03 SX69

★★67% Oxenham Arms
EX20 2JT
☎ 01837 840244 & 840577 Fax 01837 840791
e-mail: jhenry1928@aol.com
Dir: *just off A30 4m E of Okehampton in centre of village*
Dating back to the 12th century, the creeper-clad Oxenham Arms features an even more ancient standing stone, in the family/TV lounge. Beams, low door ways and flag-stoned floors, all add to the character and charm of this popular inn. In the comfortable lounge a welcoming open fire greets guests during cooler months, while in the restaurant and bar a varied choice of dishes is served. The individually furnished and decorated bedrooms are equipped with modern facilities.
ROOMS: 8 rms (7 en suite) (3 fmly) s £40-£45; d £50-£60 (incl. bkfst) * LB **FACILITIES:** Xmas **PARKING:** 8 **NOTES:** No smoking in restaurant
CARDS:

SPALDING, Lincolnshire
Map 08 TF22

★★65% Cley Hall
22 High St PE11 1TX
☎ 01775 725157 Fax 01775 710785
e-mail: cleyhall@enterprise.net
Dir: *remain on A16 to B1165, take 1st turning on rdbt across mini-rdbt to river turn left*
A Georgian house situated overlooking the River Welland which once belonged to the Cley family from Cockley Cley in Norfolk, hence the name. The refurbished bedrooms are very smart and offer high standards of comfort. Guests have a choice of places in which to dine. Theo's Bistro is beginning to gain a reputation locally for its food.
ROOMS: 4 en suite 8 annexe en suite (4 fmly) s £35-£65; d £65-£85 (incl. bkfst & dinner) * **FACILITIES:** STV ch fac **CONF:** Thtr 40 Class 23 Board 20 **PARKING:** 20 **NOTES:** No smoking in restaurant
CARDS:

SPENNYMOOR, Co Durham
Map 08 NZ23

★★★76% Whitworth Hall
Best Western

Stanners Ln DL16 7QX
☎ 01388 811772 Fax 01388 818669
e-mail: hotel@whithall.freeserve.co.uk
The house dates back to Norman times and is located in the centre of a deer park. The stylish bedrooms are spacious and well equipped whilst the public rooms include a separate pub, several comfortable lounges and an elegant dining room. A Georgian church in the grounds is popular for weddings.
ROOMS: 29 en suite (3 fmly) No smoking in all bedrooms s £70-£90; d £90-£120 (incl. bkfst) * LB **FACILITIES:** STV Fishing Xmas
CONF: Thtr 100 Class 40 Board 40 Del from £120 * **PARKING:** 100
NOTES: No smoking in restaurant Civ Wed 90
CARDS:

See advert on opposite page

STAFFORD, Staffordshire
Map 07 SJ92

★★★66% Tillington Hall
Best Western

Eccleshall Rd ST16 1JJ
☎ 01785 253531 Fax 01785 259223
Dir: *exit M6 junc 14 take A5013 to Stafford*
This large, privately owned hotel is situated close to M6(J14). The well equipped accommodation includes bedrooms on ground floor level, no smoking bedrooms, family bedded rooms and rooms which interconnect. It offers a selection of rooms for functions and conferences.
ROOMS: 91 en suite (31 fmly) No smoking in 37 bedrooms s £50-£70; d £80-£110 * LB **FACILITIES:** STV Indoor swimming (H) Tennis (hard) Sauna Solarium Gym Pool table Jacuzzi/spa Xmas **CONF:** Thtr 200 Class 80 Board 40 Del from £90 * **SERVICES:** Lift **PARKING:** 200
NOTES: No smoking in restaurant **CARDS:**

★★★65% Garth
REGAL

Wolverhampton Rd, Moss Pit ST17 9JR
☎ 01785 256124 Fax 01785 255152
Dir: *exit M6 at Junc 13 take A449*
Conveniently located between the town and junction 13 of the M6, this hotel complex has been developed from what was originally the home of an Edwardian industrialist. It is situated in pleasant gardens. Recently refurbished bedrooms are comfortable, well equipped and attractively furnished. Light meals and snacks are served in the popular bar, a range of real ales is also available. More substantial fare can be had in the light and airy restaurant.

continued

ROOMS: 60 en suite (4 fmly) No smoking in 28 bedrooms s £77; d £87 * LB **FACILITIES:** STV ch fac Xmas **CONF:** Thtr 120 Class 30 Board 48 Del from £105 * **PARKING:** 175 **NOTES:** No smoking in restaurant RS 25-26 Dec Civ Wed 100 **CARDS:**

★★67% **Abbey**
65-68 Lichfield Rd ST17 4LW
☎ 01785 258531 📠 01785 246875
Dir: *from M6 junct 13 towards Stafford. Turn right at Esso garage continue to mini-rdbt, then follow Silkmore Lane until 2nd rdbt, hotel 0.25 on right*
Family-run, this hotel has a friendly and relaxed atmosphere. The inviting public areas include a cosy bar and attractive restaurant, whilst bedrooms come in a variety of styles and sizes.
ROOMS: 17 en suite (3 fmly) s £35-£45; d £49.50-£60 (incl. bkfst) * LB **PARKING:** 25 **NOTES:** No dogs (ex guide dogs) No smoking in restaurant Closed 22 Dec-7 Jan **CARDS:**

★★63% ***Swan Hotel***
Greengate St ST16 2JA
☎ 01785 258142 📠 01785 223372
Dir: *south along A449 from north follow A34 access via Mill Street in town centre*
This former coaching inn is over 400 years old and was built on the site of monastic college buildings. Situated in the centre of the town, it has an enclosed car park at the rear. Oak beams and oak panelling in the restaurant are just some of its many features. The Romany Bar is open all day and is popular with younger customers. The well-equipped modern bedrooms have been tastefully decorated and include some rooms with four-poster beds and some family-bedded rooms.
ROOMS: 32 en suite (4 fmly) No smoking in 5 bedrooms
FACILITIES: STV **CONF:** Thtr 30 Class 20 Board 20 **PARKING:** 80
NOTES: No dogs (ex guide dogs) **CARDS:**

★★60% ***Vine***
Salter St ST16 2JU
☎ 01785 244112 📠 01785 246612
Dir: *located in the centre of town*
This 17th-century coaching inn offers comfortable, very well equipped bedrooms. Public areas are open plan and the exposed beams and timbers add character to the attractive dining area and bar lounges, which are used as a meeting place by a number of local people.
ROOMS: 25 en suite (1 fmly) **PARKING:** 20 **NOTES:** No dogs (ex guide dogs) No smoking in restaurant **CARDS:**

Read all about it! Newspapers delivered to bedrooms in four and five star hotels.

Whitworth Hall, Spennymoor

STAFFORD, continued

Express by Holiday Inn Stafford

Stafford South, Alton Gate, Alton Court ST18 9AR
☎ 01785 212244 🖷 01785 212277
e-mail: express_stafford@ingramhotels.co.uk
Dir: *M6 junct13. Hotel is situated just off junct on A449 to Stafford*

A modern budget hotel offering comfortable accommodation in refreshing, spacious and comprehensively-equipped bedrooms, en suite bathrooms with power showers and continental buffet breakfast included in the room rate. Suitable for business travellers or families. For further details and the Express by Holiday Inn phone number, consult the Hotel Groups page.
ROOMS: 103 en suite (incl. cont bkfst) d £49.95 * **CONF:** Thtr 40 Del from £75 *

STAINES, Surrey — Map 04 TQ07

★★★69% The Thames Lodge

Thames St TW18 4SF
☎ 0870 400 8121 🖷 01784 454858
e-mail: HeritageHotels_Staines.Thames_Lodge@Forte-Hotels.com
Dir: *follow signs A30 Staines town centre, bus station on right, hotel straight ahead*
Close to the centre of Staines and by the river, the Thames Lodge has its own mooring jetty and outdoor terrace. Public areas have been enhanced, there are new function suites and 32 new bedrooms. The brasserie with river views has been given a contemporary look. Services are willingly provided by a friendly team of staff.
ROOMS: 79 en suite (16 fmly) No smoking in 49 bedrooms s £125; d £145-£180 * LB **FACILITIES:** STV Xmas **CONF:** Thtr 40 Class 20 Board 20 Del from £160 * **PARKING:** 40 **NOTES:** No smoking in restaurant **CARDS:**

STALHAM, Norfolk — Map 09 TG32

★★69% *Kingfisher*

High St NR12 9AN
☎ 01692 581974 🖷 01692 582544
Dir: *Stalham is by-passed by A149 between Gt Yarmouth & North Walsham, hotel is located just off High St at west end*
In the heart of the Norfolk Broadlands, the hotel is a focal point for this bustling market town. Bedrooms are spacious and bright. The large bar is popular with locals and residents alike for its wide menu. In the more intimate restaurant, fixed price and carte menus offer an interesting choice of dishes.
ROOMS: 18 en suite (2 fmly) **CONF:** Thtr 100 Class 40 Board 30 **PARKING:** 40 **NOTES:** No smoking in restaurant **CARDS:**

STALLINGBOROUGH, Lincolnshire — Map 08 TA11

★★★65% Stallingborough Grange Hotel

Riby Rd DN41 8BU
☎ 01469 561302 🖷 01469 561338
e-mail: grange.hot@virgin.net
Dir: *from A180 take signs for Stallingborough Ind Est and then through the village, from rdbt take A1173 Caistor, hotel 1m on left just past windmill*
Originally an 18th-century country house, Stallingborough Grange is just outside the village. It has now developed into a popular business hotel, family-run and offering two different styles of food. The Tavern provides a good range of bar meals while the restaurant is the place to eat for a more serious dinner. Bedrooms provide good facilities and service is both attentive and friendly.
ROOMS: 32 en suite (2 fmly) No smoking in all bedrooms s £62-£68; d £74-£80 (incl. bkfst) * LB **FACILITIES:** STV **CONF:** Thtr 60 Class 40 Board 28 Del £98 * **PARKING:** 100 **NOTES:** No dogs (ex guide dogs) No smoking in restaurant Civ Wed 65
CARDS:

STAMFORD, Lincolnshire — Map 08 TF00

★★★75% The George of Stamford

71 St Martins PE9 2LB
☎ 01780 750750 & 750700 (Res) 🖷 01780 750701
e-mail: reservations@georgehotelofstamford.com
Dir: *turn off A1 onto B1081, 1m on left*
A charming coaching inn dating back hundreds of years, The George exudes quality and comfort. Staff are friendly, the atmosphere relaxed, bedrooms are decorated to a very high standard with lots of extras. Guests have a choice of dining options; and the cobbled courtyard is the ideal place to dine in the summer months.
ROOMS: 47 en suite (2 fmly) No smoking in 3 bedrooms s £78-£105; d £103-£220 (incl. bkfst) * LB **FACILITIES:** STV Croquet lawn Xmas **CONF:** Thtr 50 Class 25 Board 25 Del £130 * **PARKING:** 120 **NOTES:** Civ Wed 50 **CARDS:**

★★★65% Garden House

St Martin's PE9 2LP
☎ 01780 763359 🖷 01780 763339
e-mail: gardenhousehotel@stamford60.freeserve.co.uk
Dir: *A1 to South Stamford, B1081, signposted Stamford and Burghley House, Hotel on left on entering the town*
Situated within a few minutes walk of the town centre, this sympathetically transformed 18th-century house provides pleasant accommodation throughout. Bedrooms are well equipped, attractively furnished and offer good levels of comfort. The public rooms include a charming lounge bar and a conservatory. In addition there is a smartly furnished dining room.
ROOMS: 20 en suite (1 fmly) No smoking in 4 bedrooms s £50-£60; d £78-£85 (incl. bkfst) * LB **FACILITIES:** STV Xmas **CONF:** Thtr 40 Class 20 Board 20 Del from £70 * **PARKING:** 30
CARDS:

★★65% Crown

All Saints Place PE9 2AG
☎ 01780 763136 🖷 01780 756111
e-mail: thecrownhotel@excite.com
Dir: *off A1 onto A43, straight through town until Red Lion Sq, hotel is behind All Saints church in the square*
This small privately owned hotel is ideally situated in the town centre, behind the church in the main square. Bedrooms are suitably spacious and well equipped, some with four poster beds. Public areas include a smart breakfast room and spacious lounge

continued

bar where snacks are available. There is also an attractive restaurant offering a good cooked meals.

ROOMS: 17 en suite (2 fmly) s £50; d £65-£75 (incl. bkfst) * LB **FACILITIES:** STV **CONF:** Thtr 50 Class 40 Board 35 **PARKING:** 40 **NOTES:** No dogs (ex guide dogs) **CARDS:**

STANDISH, Greater Manchester Map 07 SD51

Premier Lodge

Almond Brook Rd WN6 0SS
☎ 0870 700 1574 ☐ 0870 700 1575

Premier Lodge offers modern, well equipped, en suite accommodation suitable for both business and leisure travellers. Meals can be taken at the adjacent popular restaurant and bar which is fully licensed. For further details, consult the Hotel Groups page.

ROOMS: 36 en suite d £42 *

STANSTEAD ABBOTS, Hertfordshire Map 05 TL31

★★★★60% Briggens House

Stanstead Rd SG12 8LD
☎ 01279 829955 ☐ 01279 793685

REGAL

Dir: *form M11 take the A414 to Hertford, after 10th rdbt look for left hand turn signposted Briggens Park, this is the hotel*

Enjoying views of the 80-acre estate in which it is set, Briggens House dates back to the 17th century and was formerly the home of Lord Aldenham. Conferences are often held here and there is a good range of meeting rooms. The bedroom refurbishment continues and the completed rooms are very smart. Outdoor attractions include an arboretum, swimming pool and golf.

ROOMS: 54 en suite (3 fmly) s £90-£100; d £95-£128 * LB **FACILITIES:** Outdoor swimming (H) Golf 9 Tennis (hard) Croquet lawn Putting green Xmas **CONF:** Thtr 120 Class 50 Board 50 Del from £130 * **SERVICES:** Lift **PARKING:** 100 **NOTES:** No smoking in restaurant Civ Wed 100 **CARDS:**

STANSTED AIRPORT, Essex Map 05 TL52

★★★74% Whitehall

Church End CM6 2BZ
☎ 01279 850603 ☐ 01279 850385
e-mail: sales@whitehallhotel.co.uk

Dir: *leave M11 J8, follow signs to Stansted Airport, then hotel signs to Broxted village*

This friendly hotel dates back to the Tudor period and boasts good-sized, well equipped bedrooms. The character of the original building is reflected in the timber-vaulted restaurant where guests can enjoy soundly prepared dishes. The walled garden shelters the landscaped lawns and yew trees.

ROOMS: 25 en suite (3 fmly) s £95-£195; d £120-£220 * LB **CONF:** Thtr 120 Class 80 Board 48 Del £165 * **PARKING:** 35 **NOTES:** No dogs (ex guide dogs) Closed 26-30 Dec Civ Wed 60 **CARDS:**

Days Inn

Birchanger Green, Old Dunmow Rd CM23 5QZ
☎ 01279 656477 ☐ 01279 656590

Dir: *M11 junct 8*

Fully refurbished, Days Inn offers well equipped, brightly appointed, modern accommodation with smart en suite bathrooms. There is a fully staffed reception; continental breakfast is available and other refreshments may be taken at the nearby family restaurant.

ROOMS: 60 en suite d fr £59 *

STANTON ST QUINTIN, Wiltshire Map 03 ST97

★★★68% Stanton Manor Country House Hotel

SN14 6DQ
☎ 01666 837552 ☐ 01666 837022
e-mail: reception@stantonmanor.co.uk

Dir: *leave M4 junc 17 onto A429 Malmesbury/Cirencester within 200yds turn 1st left signed Stanton St Quintin entrance to hotel on left just after church*

Set in seven acres of lovely gardens with a nine hole golf course, this charming Cotswold stone manor house offers easy access to J17 of the M4. Every bedroom and all the delightful public areas have been totally refurbished and Stanton Manor offers all the comforts expected of a quality hotel. In the restaurant a short carte of imaginative dishes is supported by a selection of interesting wines.

ROOMS: 13 en suite (2 fmly) No smoking in 3 bedrooms s £75-£95; d £95-£125 (incl. bkfst) * LB **FACILITIES:** Croquet lawn 9 hole pitch & putt **CONF:** Thtr 60 Class 50 Board 30 Del from £125 * **PARKING:** 40 **NOTES:** No smoking in restaurant **CARDS:**

STAVERTON, Devon Map 03 SX76

★★67% Sea Trout Inn
TQ9 6PA
☎ 01803 762274 01803 762506
Dir: *turn off A38 onto A384 at Buckfastleigh, follow signs to Staverton*
Dating back to the 15th century, the public bars have lots of character. Set high up in the Dart Valley, the surrounding countryside is superb. Bedrooms offer a high level of comfort and bathrooms are smart. In addition to well cooked bar meals, fine cuisine is served in the pretty conservatory-style restaurant.
ROOMS: 10 en suite (1 fmly) s £35-£49; d £58-£78 (incl. bkfst) * LB **FACILITIES:** Pool table **CONF:** Board 14 **PARKING:** 48 **NOTES:** No smoking in restaurant **CARDS:**

STEEPLE ASTON, Oxfordshire Map 04 SP42

★★★68% The Holt Hotel
Oxford Rd OX6 3QQ
☎ 01869 340259 01869 340865
e-mail: info@holthotel.oxford.co.uk
Dir: *junct of B4030/A4260*
This attractive stone-built hotel offers well presented conference facilities and smart, spacious and comfortable public areas. Bedrooms, which are being steadily upgraded, are comfortably furnished and well equipped for the business guest. Well presented cooking is provided in Duvals restaurant.
ROOMS: 86 en suite (19 fmly) No smoking in 16 bedrooms s fr £79; d fr £116 (incl. bkfst) * LB **FACILITIES:** STV Pool table Xmas **CONF:** Thtr 150 Class 70 Board 40 Del from £120 * **PARKING:** 200 **NOTES:** No smoking in restaurant Civ Wed 80
CARDS:

STEVENAGE, Hertfordshire Map 04 TL22

★★★64% Novotel
Knebworth Park SG1 2AX
☎ 01438 346100 01438 723872
e-mail: h0992@accor-hotels.com
Dir: *off junct 7 of A1(M), at entrance to Knebworth Park*
Pleasantly located in a Green Belt site, this modern red-brick building is only moments from the A1(M), which makes it a popular meeting and conference venue. The informal bar and restaurant are set up to deal with this kind of business. All the large bedrooms are well appointed for both business guests and families.
ROOMS: 100 en suite (20 fmly) No smoking in 75 bedrooms d fr £85 * **FACILITIES:** STV Outdoor swimming (H) Pool table **CONF:** Thtr 150 Class 80 Board 70 Del from £125 * **SERVICES:** Lift **PARKING:** 100
CARDS:

★★★62% Cromwell
High St, Old Town SG1 3AZ
☎ 01438 779954 01438 742169
e-mail: 114501.3425@compuserve.com
Dir: *leave A1(M1) junct 8. Follow signs for town centre, over 2 rdbts. Join one-way system. Turn off into Old Town. Hotel is on the left after mini rdbt*
Easily accessible from the nearby A1(M), this High Street hotel has retained much of its historic charm, and offers many useful facilities for business and leisure guests alike. The attractive bedrooms are well equipped, and some are more modern in style than others. Amongst the range of public areas, there are two bars and large meeting rooms.

continued

ROOMS: 76 en suite No smoking in 33 bedrooms s £98-£118; d £113-£133 * LB **FACILITIES:** STV Xmas **CONF:** Thtr 200 Class 60 Board 60 Del from £90 * **PARKING:** 70 **NOTES:** RS 25-31 Dec
CARDS:

★★★61% *Posthouse Stevenage*
Old London Rd, Broadwater SG2 8DS
☎ 0870 400 9076 01438 741308
Dir: *off B1970*
Suitable for both the business and leisure traveller, this hotel provides spacious accommodation in well equipped bedrooms. There is some character to the older part of the building which contains the bar and restaurant.
ROOMS: 54 en suite No smoking in 27 bedrooms **CONF:** Thtr 60 Class 20 Board 30 **PARKING:** 80 **CARDS:**

⌂ *Ibis*
Danestrete SG1 1EJ
☎ 01438 779955 01438 741880
Dir: *in town centre adjacent to BHS & Westgate Multi-Store*
ROOMS: 98 en suite **CONF:** Thtr 200 Class 80 Board 60

STEYNING, West Sussex Map 04 TQ11

★★★69% The Old Tollgate
The Street BN44 3WE
☎ 01903 879494 01903 813399
e-mail: otr@fastnet.co.uk
Dir: *on A283 at Steyning rdbt, turn off to Bramber, the hotel is situated approx 200yds along on the right*
A well presented hotel on the site of the old Toll-House. Bedrooms are spacious, smartly designed and furnished to a high standard. An extensive choice of dishes are offered in the popular carvery style restaurant. The hotel has adaptable function rooms for weddings and conferences.
ROOMS: 11 en suite 20 annexe en suite (5 fmly) d £69-£95 * LB **FACILITIES:** STV **CONF:** Thtr 50 Class 32 Board 26 Del £86.95 * **SERVICES:** Lift **PARKING:** 60 **NOTES:** No dogs (ex guide dogs) Civ Wed 40 **CARDS:**

STILTON, Cambridgeshire Map 04 TL18

★★★69% Bell Inn
Great North Rd PE7 3RA
☎ 01733 241066 01733 245173
e-mail: reception@thebellstitton.co.uk
Dir: *turn off A1(M) at junct 16 then follow signs for Stilton, hotel is situated on the main road in centre of village*
A wealth of original rural features makes the Bell a charming place to stay. Now even easier to get to, despite its lovely village setting, with the A1(M) motorway just minutes away. With its beamed ceilings and open log fires, the village bar is full of character, as is

continued

S

the galleried restaurant above, which offers an interesting menu that mixes modern and traditional influences to good effect. A recent refurbishment programme to bedrooms, which are built around the old courtyard, has seen the introduction of individual styling to all rooms, with colourful soft furnishings creating a pleasing effect; deluxe rooms offer four-poster beds and whirlpool baths.

ROOMS: 19 en suite (1 fmly) No smoking in 7 bedrooms s £62-£89.50; d £82-£109.50 (incl. bkfst) * **FACILITIES:** STV **CONF:** Thtr 100 Class 46 Board 50 Del from £98.50 * **PARKING:** 30 **NOTES:** No dogs (ex guide dogs) Closed 25 Dec RS 26 Dec Civ Wed 80
CARDS:

STOCKPORT, Greater Manchester — Map 07 SJ88

see also Manchester Airport & Marple

★★★67% Bredbury Hall Hotel & Country Club

Goyt Valley SK6 2DH
☎ 0161 430 7421 ⎙ 0161 430 5079
e-mail: reservations@bredburyhallhotel.co.uk
Dir: *M60 J25 signposted Bredbury, right at traffic lights, left onto Osbourne St, hotel 500mtrs on right*

With views over open countryside, this large modern hotel is near the M60. Bedrooms offer space and comfort and the restaurant serves a range of freshly prepared dishes. There is a popular nightclub next door to the hotel and a leisure centre is under construction.

ROOMS: 120 en suite (2 fmly) s fr £49.50; d fr £64.50 *
FACILITIES: STV Fishing Snooker Pool table Night club entertainment Xmas **CONF:** Thtr 160 Class 90 Board 70 Del from £95 *
PARKING: 400 **NOTES:** No dogs (ex guide dogs) Civ Wed 150
CARDS:

★★★64% County Hotel Bramhall

REGAL

Bramhall Ln South SK7 2EB
☎ 0161 455 9988 ⎙ 0161 440 8071
(For full entry see Bramhall)

★★70% Springfield

Station Rd SK6 6PA
☎ 0161 449 0721 ⎙ 0161 449 0766
(For full entry see Marple)

★★68% *Saxon Holme*

230 Wellington Rd SK4 2QN
☎ 0161 432 2335 ⎙ 0161 431 8076
Dir: *N, beside A6*

This well run and comfortable hotel is situated outside the town. Bedrooms, including a number on the ground floor, have modern facilities, and reception rooms are elegant, with ornately decorated plaster ceilings. A good range of well produced food is available.

continued

ROOMS: 33 en suite (3 fmly) No smoking in 11 bedrooms
FACILITIES: STV Pool table **CONF:** Thtr 70 Class 10 Board 20
SERVICES: Lift **PARKING:** 40 **NOTES:** No dogs (ex guide dogs) No smoking in restaurant **CARDS:**

★★67% Wycliffe

74 Edgeley Rd, Edgeley SK3 9NQ
☎ 0161 477 5395 ⎙ 0161 476 3219
Dir: *from M60 junct 2 follow A560 for Stockport, at 1st lights turn right, hotel half a mile on left*

This family run, welcoming hotel has immaculately maintained and well equipped bedrooms. There is popular restaurant and well a stocked bar with the menu having an Italian bias.

ROOMS: 20 en suite s fr £46; d fr £58 (incl. bkfst) * **FACILITIES:** STV Xmas **CONF:** Thtr 20 Class 20 Board 20 Del from £116 * **PARKING:** 46
NOTES: No dogs (ex guide dogs) **CARDS:**

⌂ Premier Lodge

PREMIER LODGE
THE BEST, BEST ASSURED.

Churchgate SK1 1YG
☎ 0870 700 1484 ⎙ 0870 700 1485

Premier Lodge offers modern, well equipped, en suite accommodation suitable for both business and leisure travellers. Meals can be taken at the adjacent popular restaurant and bar which is fully licensed. For further details, consult the Hotel Groups page.

ROOMS: 46 en suite d £46 *

⌂ *Travelodge*

Travelodge

London Rd South SK12 4NA
☎ 01625 875292 ⎙ 01625 875292
Dir: *on A523*

This modern building offers accommodation in smart, spacious and well equipped bedrooms, all with en suite bathrooms. Refreshments may be taken at the nearby family restaurant. For further details and the Travelodge phone number, consult the Hotel Groups page.

ROOMS: 32 en suite

STOCKTON-ON-TEES, Co Durham — Map 08 NZ41

★★★★61% Swallow

SWALLOW HOTELS

John Walker Square TS18 1AQ
☎ 01642 679721 0800 7317549 ⎙ 01642 601714
e-mail: stockton@swallow-hotels.co.uk
Dir: *from A1(M) follow A177 to Town Centre cont along Riverside Road to Castlegate Car Park*

Easily recognisable as the tallest building in town, this hotel forms part of a shopping development and has direct access to a multi-storey car park. Bedrooms are smart and well equipped, and guests have the choice of two restaurants to eat in. Friendly staff provide attentive service.

ROOMS: 125 en suite (12 fmly) No smoking in 77 bedrooms s £95-£115; d £110-£120 (incl. bkfst) * LB **FACILITIES:** STV Indoor swimming (H) Sauna Solarium Gym Jacuzzi/spa Tanning booth Xmas **CONF:** Thtr 300 Class 150 Board 40 Del from £105 * **SERVICES:** Lift **PARKING:** 400
NOTES: Civ Wed 250 **CARDS:**

★★★71% ❀ Parkmore

Best Western

636 Yarm Rd, Eaglescliffe TS16 0DH
☎ 01642 786815 ⎙ 01642 790485
e-mail: enquiries@parkmorehotel.co.uk
Dir: *turn off A19 at Crathorne, follow A67 to Yarm. Through Yarm bear right onto A135 to Stockton. Hotel approx. 1m from Yarm on left*

In this Victorian house hotel, bedrooms are well equipped and have modern fittings, public rooms are comfortable and inviting. Extensive menus are available in the 'Reeds at six three six'

continued

S

STOCKTON-ON-TEES, continued

restaurant with inventive combinations of flavours used in the cuisine. There is a well equipped leisure centre and good conference facilities.

ROOMS: 55 en suite (8 fmly) No smoking in 30 bedrooms s £58-£60; d £74-£88 * LB **FACILITIES:** STV Indoor swimming (H) Sauna Solarium Gym Jacuzzi/spa Beauty salon Badminton Aerobics studio **CONF:** Thtr 140 Class 40 Board 40 Del from £85 * **PARKING:** 120 **NOTES:** No smoking in restaurant Civ Wed 90 **CARDS:**

★★★66% *Posthouse Teeside*

Posthouse

low Ln, Stainton Village, Thornaby TS17 9LW
☎ 0870 400 9081 🖷 01642 594989

Dir: *off A19 onto A174, then B1380 towards Stainton Village, 2nd exit at rdbt towards Stainton Village again, hotel is on right*

A large modern hotel situated in spacious open grounds on the south east of the town. Bedrooms are of a particularly good standard and include several Millennium style as well as executive and family rooms. The menu in Seasons restaurant provides a good choice of dishes.

ROOMS: 136 en suite (10 fmly) No smoking in 87 bedrooms **CONF:** Thtr 120 Class 60 Board 70 **PARKING:** 250 **CARDS:**

★★67% Claireville

519 Yarm Rd, Eaglescliffe TS16 9BG
☎ 01642 780378 🖷 01642 784109
e-mail: reception@clairev.demon.co.uk

Dir: *on A135 adjacent to Eaglescliffe Golf Course, between Stockton-on-Tees and Yarm*

A family-run hotel with comfortable, pleasantly furnished bedrooms. There is a cosy bar/lounge and attractive dining room which offers a reasonably priced carte. A delightful conservatory has been added to the rear, providing extra function and lounge facilities.

ROOMS: 18 en suite (2 fmly) No smoking in 4 bedrooms s £39.50-£48; d £48.50-£60 (incl. bkfst) * **FACILITIES:** STV **CONF:** Thtr 40 Class 20 Board 25 **PARKING:** 30 **NOTES:** No smoking in restaurant RS Xmas & New Year **CARDS:**

⇧ Express by Holiday Inn Stockton

Junction A19 & A 689,Coal Ln, Wynyard Park Services, Wolviston TS22 5PZ
☎ 01740 644000 🖷 644111

Dir: *located at the junct of A19 & A689*

A modern budget hotel offering comfortable accommodation in refreshing, spacious and comprehensively-equipped bedrooms, en suite bathrooms with power showers and continental buffet breakfast included in the room rate. Suitable for business travellers or families. For further details and the Express by Holiday Inn phone number, consult the Hotel Groups page.

ROOMS: 49 en suite (incl. cont bkfst) d £49.95 *

STOKE D'ABERNON, Surrey Map 04 TQ15

★★★★67% ❀ Woodlands Park

ARCADIAN HOTELS Distinctly Different

Woodlands Ln KT11 3QB
☎ 01372 843933 🖷 01372 842704
e-mail: info@woodlandspark.co.uk

Dir: *from A3 towards London, exit at Cobham. Through town centre & Stoke D'Abernon, left at garden centre into Woodlands Ln, hotel 0.5m on right*

Conveniently close to the motorway network, this Victorian mansion enjoys an attractive parkland setting. Bedrooms are traditionally furnished and well equipped. There are two dining options, Quotes Bar & Brasserie, and the Oak Room Restaurant.

ROOMS: 59 en suite (4 fmly) No smoking in 9 bedrooms s £120-£215; d £140-£245 * LB **FACILITIES:** STV Tennis (hard) Croquet lawn Xmas **CONF:** Thtr 280 Class 100 Board 50 **SERVICES:** Lift **PARKING:** 150 **NOTES:** No dogs (ex guide dogs) **CARDS:**

See advert on opposite page

STOKE GABRIEL, Devon Map 03 SX85

★★★71% Gabriel Court

TQ9 6SF
☎ 01803 782206 🖷 01803 782333
e-mail: obeacom@aol.com

Dir: *off A38 down the A384 onto the A385 towards Paignton, turn right by the Parkers Arms, follow road down until reaching Stoke Gabriel*

This charming old house, mainly Victorian in character and set in lovely gardens, is a comfortable, civilised hotel with elegant reception rooms. Individually designed bedrooms retain a sense of period.

ROOMS: 19 en suite s fr £55; d fr £80 (incl. bkfst) * **FACILITIES:** Outdoor swimming (H) Tennis (grass) Croquet lawn ch fac Xmas **CONF:** Thtr 20 Board 20 Del from £115 * **PARKING:** 20 **NOTES:** No smoking in restaurant **CARDS:**

STOKENCHURCH, Buckinghamshire Map 04 SU79

★★★68% The Kings Arms

Oxford Rd HP12 3TA
☎ 01494 609090 🖷 01494 484582

Dir: *junct 5 of M40 turn right over motorway bridge, hotel 600yds on the left*

Rooms are attractively decorated and well equipped for the business guest. Public areas include a busy bar offering an extensive range of hot and cold dishes throughout the day, and a more formal restaurant. There are several smart air-conditioned conference rooms.

ROOMS: 43 en suite (3 fmly) No smoking in 22 bedrooms s £99-£119; d £109-£129 (incl. bkfst) * LB **FACILITIES:** STV Xmas **CONF:** Thtr 150 Class 80 Board 50 Del from £145 * **SERVICES:** Lift air con **PARKING:** 95 **NOTES:** No dogs (ex guide dogs) Civ Wed 200 **CARDS:**

STOKE-ON-TRENT, Staffordshire Map 07 SJ84
see also Newcastle-under-Lyme

★★★73% ❀❀ Manor House

Audley Rd ST7 2QQ
☎ 01270 884000 🖷 01270 882483
e-mail: manres@compasshotels.co.uk
(For full entry see Alsager)

Read all about it! Newspapers delivered to bedrooms in four and five star hotels.

★★★69% George
Swan Square, Burslem ST6 2AE
☎ 01782 577544 01782 837496
e-mail: georgestoke@btinternet.com
Dir: *take A53 towards Leek, turn left at 1st set of traffic lights onto A50, follow road to Burslem centre, George hotel is on right*
This privately owned, friendly hotel stands in the centre of Burslem, close to the Royal Doulton factory. It provides well equipped modern accommodation, which is equally suitable for business people and tourists. A good choice of dishes is available in the elegant restaurant. In addition to the spacious lounge bar, there is a comfortable lounge for residents, a choice of function rooms, plus a large ballroom.
ROOMS: 39 en suite (5 fmly) s £65-£75; d £85-£95 (incl. bkfst) * LB **FACILITIES:** entertainment **CONF:** Thtr 180 Class 150 Board 60 Del from £80 * **SERVICES:** Lift **PARKING:** 28 **NOTES:** No dogs (ex guide dogs) **CARDS:**

★★★68% North Stafford

Station Rd, Winton Square ST4 2AE
☎ 01782 744477 01782 744580
e-mail: Reservations.NorthStafford@PrincipalHotels.co.uk
Dir: *follow signs for Railway Station and hotel is directly opposite*
This modernised Victorian hotel stands opposite the railway station. Bedrooms retain much of their historic character. The Clayhanger Bar, named after one of Arnold Bennett's famous novels, displays memorabilia of the pottery industry, and there is also a pleasant restaurant.
ROOMS: 80 en suite (8 fmly) s £95-£105; d £105-£115 * LB **FACILITIES:** STV Pool table Xmas **CONF:** Thtr 450 Class 150 Board 85 Del from £95 * **SERVICES:** Lift **PARKING:** 120 **NOTES:** No smoking in restaurant Civ Wed **CARDS:**

★★★66% Haydon House
MINOTEL Great Britain
Haydon St, Basford ST4 6JD
☎ 01782 711311 01782 717470
Dir: *from M6 junct 15 A500 to Stoke-on-Trent, turn onto A53 Hanley/Newcastle, at rdbt take 1st exit, go up hill, take 2nd left at top of hill*
A Victorian property close to the junction of the A53 and A500, within easy reach of Newcastle-under-Lyme town centre. The public rooms are furnished in a style befitting the age and character of the house. The bedrooms all have modern furnishings, several rooms are located in a separate house across the road. The hotel has a good reputation for its food and is popular with local diners. Function and conference rooms are available, and the hotel can accommodate marriage ceremonies.
ROOMS: 17 en suite 6 annexe en suite (4 fmly) s fr £62; d fr £79 (incl. bkfst) * **CONF:** Thtr 80 Class 25 Board 30 Del from £79 * **PARKING:** 52 **NOTES:** Civ Wed 40 **CARDS:**

Express by Holiday Inn
Express by Holiday Inn
Stanley Matthews Way ST4 4EG
☎ 01782 377000 01782 377037
Dir: *from M6 junct15, follow signs for Uttoxeter/Derby which leads to A50. Hotel is located alongside Brittanic Stadium on the A50*
A modern budget hotel offering comfortable accommodation in refreshing, spacious and comprehensively-equipped bedrooms, en suite bathrooms with power showers and continental buffet breakfast included in the room rate. Suitable for business

continued on p532

S

STOKE-ON-TRENT, continued

Express by Holiday Inn, Stoke-on-Trent

travellers or families. For further details and the Express by Holiday Inn phone number, consult the Hotel Groups page.
ROOMS: 123 en suite (incl. cont bkfst) d £52 * **CONF:** Thtr 30 Class 20 Board 18

STONE, Staffordshire Map 07 SJ93

★★★67% Stone House

Stafford Rd ST15 0BQ
☎ 01785 815531 🖷 01785 814764
Dir: *beside A34, 0.5m S of town centre*

corus

Set in attractively landscaped gardens and grounds, this former country house has been sympathetically extended to appeal to both leisure and business guests. Public areas are stylish and comfortable and the restaurant overlooks the gardens.
ROOMS: 50 en suite (1 fmly) No smoking in 33 bedrooms s fr £85; d fr £95 * LB **FACILITIES:** STV Indoor swimming (H) Tennis (hard) Sauna Solarium Gym Putting green Xmas **CONF:** Thtr 190 Class 60 Board 50 Del from £95 * **SERVICES:** Lift **PARKING:** 120 **NOTES:** No dogs RS Sat Civ Wed 120 **CARDS:**

⇧ *Travelodge*

Eccleshall Rd ST15 0EU
☎ 01785 811188
Dir: *between junc 14&15 M6 northbound only*

Travelodge

This modern building offers accommodation in smart, spacious and well equipped bedrooms, all with en suite bathrooms. Refreshments may be taken at the nearby family restaurant. For further details and the Travelodge phone number, consult the Hotel Groups page.
ROOMS: 49 en suite

Fancy a Singapore Sling? Bar staff in five star hotels should be skilled cocktail mixers.

STON EASTON, Somerset Map 03 ST65

Premier Collection

★★★★ *Ston Easton Park*

BA3 4DF
☎ 01761 241631 🖷 01761 241377
e-mail: stoneastonpark@stoneaston.co.uk
Dir: *turn off A37 onto A39, hotel is one mile from junction in village of Ston Easton*

RELAIS & CHATEAUX.

This Palladian mansion is set in extensive grounds with a river and man-made lake. The interior includes a saloon and cosy library. Food is taken seriously, from the breakfast croissants to the excellent afternoon teas. Dinner offers a balanced menu of mainly traditional British dishes.
ROOMS: 18 en suite 2 annexe en suite **FACILITIES:** Tennis (hard) Snooker Croquet lawn Hot air ballooning Archery Clay Shooting Horse riding **CONF:** Thtr 50 Class 25 Board 26 **PARKING:** 52 **NOTES:** No dogs (ex guide dogs) No children 7yrs No smoking in restaurant **CARDS:**

STONEHOUSE, Gloucestershire Map 03 SO80

★★★72% *Stonehouse Court*

GL10 3RA
☎ 01453 825155 🖷 01453 824611
e-mail: stonehouse.court@pageant.co.uk
Dir: *off M5 at J13, follow signs for Stonehouse, hotel is on right hand side approx 0.25m after 2nd rdbt*

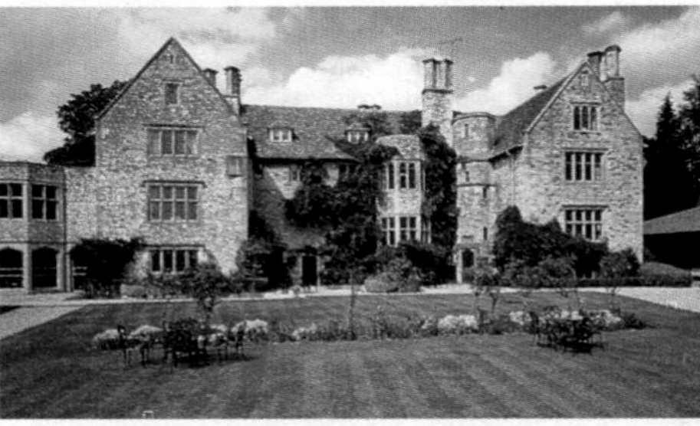

This Grade II listed manor house dates from 1601, but has been considerably extended. Bedrooms offer modern comforts, and two of them have four-poster beds. Public rooms include a lounge with panelled walls, a bar and a restaurant.
ROOMS: 9 en suite 27 annexe en suite (1 fmly) No smoking in 4 bedrooms **FACILITIES:** STV Fishing Pool table Croquet lawn Bowls **CONF:** Thtr 150 Class 75 Board 50 **PARKING:** 150 **NOTES:** No smoking in restaurant **CARDS:**

See advert under GLOUCESTER

STONELEIGH, Warwickshire — Map 04 SP37

Stoneleigh Park Lodge

MARSTON HOTELS

The NAC Stoneleigh Park CV8 2LZ
☎ 024 7669 0123 Fax 024 7669 0789
e-mail: stoneleighpark@marstonhotels.co.uk
This brand new lodge is situated in the centre of the National Agricultural Centre, and is conveniently close to Warwick, Coventry and Leamington Spa. Rooms are spacious, comfortable and attractively presented.
ROOMS: 58 en suite

STONOR, Oxfordshire — Map 04 SU78

★★★73% Stonor Arms Hotel

RG9 6HE
☎ 01491 638866 Fax 01491 638863
e-mail: stonorarms.hotel@virgin.net
Dir: *off A4130 onto B480, hotel 3m on right in Stonor village*

Picturesque scenery and a pretty village set the scene for this hotel overflowing with historic charm. The spacious bedrooms are well furnished and comfortable, they enjoy views over the well tended gardens and surrounding countryside. Public areas include a lounge where tea and pre-dinner drinks can be served, and also a bar with a boating theme. Dinner can be enjoyed either in the conservatory or a more formal dining room. The pretty gardens make this a popular choice for weddings.
ROOMS: 10 en suite No smoking in 4 bedrooms s £99-£125; d £125-£155 (incl. bkfst) * LB **FACILITIES:** Xmas **CONF:** Thtr 20 Board 12 Del £150 * **PARKING:** 27 **NOTES:** No smoking in restaurant Civ Wed 80
CARDS:

STOURPORT-ON-SEVERN, Worcestershire — Map 07 SO87

★★★★69% Menzies Stourport Manor

MENZIES HOTELS

Hartlebury Rd DY13 9LT
☎ 0500 636943 (Central Res) Fax 01773 880321
e-mail: info@menzies-hotels.co.uk
Dir: *E, off B4193*
Once the home of former Prime Minister Sir Stanley Baldwin, today Stourport Manor is a busy hotel offering modern equipped bedrooms and suites. Public areas include extensive lounge facilities and hotel cuisine is of good quality.
ROOMS: 68 en suite (4 fmly) No smoking in 25 bedrooms s £95-£140; d £115-£140 * LB **FACILITIES:** STV Indoor swimming (H) Outdoor swimming (H) Tennis (hard) Squash Sauna Solarium Gym Pool table Putting green Xmas **CONF:** Thtr 420 Class 120 Board 80 Del from £95 * **PARKING:** 200 **NOTES:** No dogs (ex guide dogs) Civ Wed 350
CARDS:

Bad hair day? Hairdryers in all rooms three stars and above.

STOW CUM QUY, Cambridgeshire — Map 05 TL56

★★★73% Cambridge Quy Mill Hotel

Best Western

Newmarket Rd CB5 9AG
☎ 01223 293383 Fax 01223 293770
e-mail: cambridgequy@bestwestern.co.uk
Dir: *turn off A14 at junct east of Cambridge onto B1102 for 50yds, hotel entrance opposite church*
Convenient for Cambridge city centre, this 19th-century former watermill is set in water meadows. Well designed public areas include several spacious bar and lounge areas and there are informal and formal eating areas. Bedrooms are smartly appointed and brightly decorated.
ROOMS: 24 en suite (2 fmly) s £75-£95; d £90-£140 * LB **FACILITIES:** STV Fishing Clay pigeon shooting **CONF:** Thtr 80 Class 24 Board 24 Del from £110 * **PARKING:** 100 **NOTES:** No dogs (ex guide dogs) Closed 26-30 Dec **CARDS:**

STOWMARKET, Suffolk — Map 05 TM05

★★65% Cedars

The Independents

Needham Rd IP14 2AJ
☎ 01449 612668 Fax 01449 674704
e-mail: info@cedarshotel.co.uk
Dir: *A1308 1m outside Stowmarket on road to Needham Market, close to junction with A1120*
About a mile from the town centre, this convivial hotel combines historic charm in the public areas with modern facilities in its comfortable accommodation, located in purpose-built extensions or in the original main house. The spacious restaurant and bar both offer a wide choice of appetising dishes, served by a friendly team.
ROOMS: 25 en suite (4 fmly) s fr £44; d fr £50 (incl. bkfst) * LB **FACILITIES:** STV **CONF:** Thtr 160 Class 60 Board 60 Del from £65 * **PARKING:** 75 **NOTES:** No smoking in restaurant Closed 25 Dec-1 Jan
CARDS:

Travelodge

Travelodge

IP14 3PY
☎ 01449 615347 Fax 01449 615347
Dir: *on A14 westbound*
This modern building offers accommodation in smart, spacious and well equipped bedrooms, all with en suite bathrooms. Refreshments may be taken at the nearby family restaurant. For further details and the Travelodge phone number, consult the Hotel Groups page.
ROOMS: 40 en suite

STOW-ON-THE-WOLD, Gloucestershire — Map 04 SP12

★★★★71% Wyck Hill House

Burford Rd GL54 1HY
☎ 01451 831936 Fax 01451 832243
e-mail: wyckhill@wrensgroup.com
Dir: *3m SE on A424 towards Burford & Swindon*
Set amidst 100 acres of woodlands and gardens, this delightful 18th-century house enjoys superb views across the Windrush Valley and is ideally positioned for a relaxing weekend exploring the Cotswolds, or for a quiet business meeting. The spacious and thoughtfully equipped bedrooms have been refurbished to a high standard and are divided between the main house and the original coach house. An open fire burns in the magnificent front hall and there is a cosy bar in the restaurant.
ROOMS: 16 en suite 16 annexe en suite (1 fmly) s £110-£175; d £155-£275 (incl. bkfst) * LB **FACILITIES:** STV Croquet lawn Archery Clay pigeon shooting Ballooning Honda pilots Xmas **CONF:** Thtr 40 Class 20 Board 20 Del from £158 * **SERVICES:** Lift **PARKING:** 100
NOTES: No smoking in restaurant Civ Wed 80
CARDS:

S

STOW-ON-THE-WOLD, continued

★★★74% Fosse Manor

GL54 1JX
☎ 01451 830354 01451 832486
e-mail: fossemanor@bestwestern.co.uk
Dir: *1m S on A429, 300yds past junction with A424*

Situated on the outskirts of Stow on the Wold, Fosse Manor nestles peacefully in the English countryside. Bedrooms are tastefully decorated, with good levels of comfort. Guests can enjoy a relaxing lounge, cosy bar serving a wide range of meals, and a restaurant offering imaginative cooking. Croquet, giant chess, a golf driving range, function room and beauty salon are also available.

ROOMS: 14 en suite 6 annexe en suite (3 fmly) s £55-£75; d £98-£130 (incl. bkfst) * LB **FACILITIES:** Croquet lawn Beautician Golf practice net ch fac **CONF:** Thtr 40 Class 20 Board 20 Del from £135 * **PARKING:** 40 **NOTES:** No smoking in restaurant Closed 23 Dec-4 Jan Civ Wed **CARDS:**

★★★70% Grapevine

Sheep St GL54 1AU
☎ 01451 830344 01451 832278
e-mail: enquiries@vines.co.uk
Dir: *on A436 towards Chipping Norton. 150 yds on right, facing green*

This delightful 17th-century hotel is situated in the centre of town, and retains much of its original charm and character. The bedrooms vary in size, and are thoughtfully equipped with charming furnishings. Accomplished cooking is offered in the Conservatory Restaurant, with a more informal brasserie-style menu available at lunch.

ROOMS: 12 en suite 10 annexe en suite (2 fmly) No smoking in all bedrooms s £74-£94; d £110-£130 (incl. bkfst) * LB **FACILITIES:** Xmas **CONF:** Thtr 30 Class 18 Board 20 Del from £135 * **PARKING:** 23 **NOTES:** No dogs (ex guide dogs) No smoking in restaurant Civ Wed 60 **CARDS:**

★★★68% The Unicorn

Sheep St GL54 1HQ
☎ 01451 830257 01451 831090
e-mail: bookings@cotswold-inns-hotels.co.uk
Dir: *situated at the junct of A429 & A436*

A friendly hotel that retains much of its original 17th-century character, while offering accommodation equipped to modern standards of comfort; bedrooms are individual in style, and brightly decorated. Public areas are inviting and smartly presented.

ROOMS: 20 en suite No smoking in 6 bedrooms s £60-£70; d £105-£120 (incl. bkfst) * LB **FACILITIES:** Xmas **CONF:** Thtr 50 Board 24 Del from £110 * **PARKING:** 60 **NOTES:** No smoking in restaurant Civ Wed 45 **CARDS:**

★★★66% Stow Lodge

The Square GL54 1AB
☎ 01451 830485 01451 831671
e-mail: enquiries@stowlodge.com
Dir: *in town centre*

Set in large grounds, this family-run hotel has direct access to the market square. It offers comfortable accommodation in traditionally styled bedrooms, some in a converted coach house, and good home cooking.

ROOMS: 11 en suite 10 annexe en suite (1 fmly) No smoking in all bedrooms s £60-£110; d £70-£120 (incl. bkfst) * LB **PARKING:** 30 **NOTES:** No dogs No children 5yrs No smoking in restaurant Closed Xmas-end Jan **CARDS:**

★★70% Old Stocks

The Square GL54 1AF
☎ 01451 830666 01451 870014
Dir: *turn off A429 to town centre. Hotel is facing Village Green*

This Grade II listed hotel built of mellow Cotswold stone is situated in the heart of the old market square. Original charm and character is in abundance with its stone walls and oak beams. The lounge, restaurant and bar are tastefully furnished, offering attractive, comfortable areas in which to relax, and the bedrooms are well maintained.

ROOMS: 15 en suite 3 annexe en suite (1 fmly) No smoking in 10 bedrooms s £40-£80; d £80-£90 (incl. bkfst) * LB **FACILITIES:** ch fac Xmas **PARKING:** 14 **NOTES:** No smoking in restaurant Closed 18-27 Dec **CARDS:**

★★67% *The Royalist at Stow-on-the-Wold*

Digbeth St GL54 1BN
☎ 01451 830670 01451 870048
Dir: *turn off A429 onto A436*

Featured in the Guinness Book of Records as the 'oldest inn in England', this friendly hotel has a wealth of history and character. Public areas and the charming bedrooms are bright and cheerful. Meals can be enjoyed in either the bar or the restaurant.

ROOMS: 8 en suite 4 annexe en suite (2 fmly) No smoking in 6 bedrooms **CONF:** Board 10 **PARKING:** 12 **NOTES:** No smoking in restaurant **CARDS:**

STRATFIELD TURGIS, Hampshire Map 04 SU65

★★★65% Wellington Arms

RG27 0AS
☎ 01256 882214 01256 882934
e-mail: Wellington.Arms@Virgin.net
Dir: *A33 between Basingstoke & Reading*

Situated at one of the entrances to the ancestral home of the Duke of Wellington, the white Georgian facade is a familiar landmark. The bar-lounge offers seating around a log fire. The majority of bedrooms are located in the Garden Wing and offer every modern convenience. Rooms in the original building have a more period feel to them.

ROOMS: 35 en suite (2 fmly) No smoking in 3 bedrooms s £90-£125; d £95-£125 (incl. bkfst) * LB **CONF:** Thtr 160 Class 40 Board 50 Del from £150.50 * **PARKING:** 150 **CARDS:**

Popped the question? Hotels with Civ Wed in their entry are licensed for civil wedding ceremonies. Maximum numbers for the ceremony only are shown, e.g. Civ Wed 50

STRATFORD-UPON-AVON, Warwickshire Map 04 SP25

★★★★74% Welcombe Hotel and Golf Course

Warwick Rd CV37 0NR
☎ 01789 295252 Fax 01789 414666
e-mail: sales@welcombe.co.uk
Dir: 1.5m NE of Stratford on A439

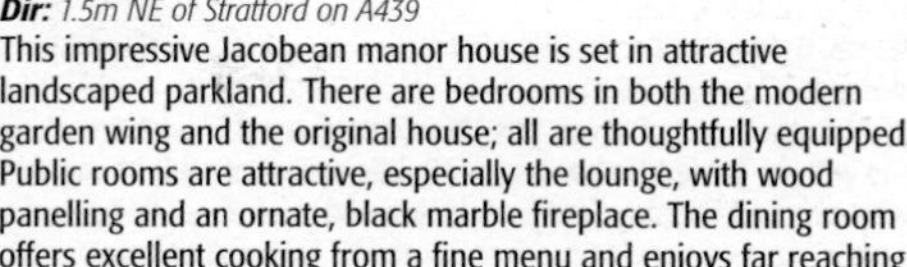

This impressive Jacobean manor house is set in attractive landscaped parkland. There are bedrooms in both the modern garden wing and the original house; all are thoughtfully equipped. Public rooms are attractive, especially the lounge, with wood panelling and an ornate, black marble fireplace. The dining room offers excellent cooking from a fine menu and enjoys far reaching views of the countryside.

ROOMS: 64 en suite (2 fmly) s £115-£295; d £150-£750 (incl. bkfst) * LB **FACILITIES:** STV Golf 18 Tennis (hard) Fishing Snooker Solarium Gym Putting green Table tennis Xmas **CONF:** Thtr 120 Class 55 Board 26 Del from £145 * **PARKING:** 210 **NOTES:** No dogs (ex guide dogs) No smoking in restaurant Civ Wed 45
CARDS:

See advert on this page

★★★★69% Billesley Manor

Billesley, Alcester B49 6NF
☎ 01789 279955 Fax 01789 764145
e-mail: enquires@billesleymanor.co.uk
Dir: Turn off A46 then 200yds on right

This 16th-century manor is set in peaceful grounds and park land with a delightful topiary garden. The spacious bedrooms and suites, most in traditional country house style, are thoughtfully designed and well equipped. The public areas retain many original

continued on p536

STRATFORD-UPON-AVON, continued

Billesley Manor, Stratford-upon-Avon

features, such as oak panelling, exposed stone, and fireplaces.
ROOMS: 41 en suite (8 fmly) s £125-£170; d £180-£240 * LB **FACILITIES:** Indoor swimming (H) Tennis (hard) Croquet lawn Putting green Xmas **CONF:** Thtr 100 Class 60 Board 50 Del from £170 * **PARKING:** 85 **NOTES:** No dogs (ex guide dogs) No smoking in restaurant RS Sat **CARDS:**

See advert on opposite page

★★★★68% Stratford Manor

MARSTON HOTELS

Warwick Rd CV37 0PY
☎ 01789 731173 01789 731131
e-mail: stratfordmanor@marstonhotels.co.uk
Dir: *3m N of Stratford town centre on A439, or leave M40 junct 15, take Stratford-upon-Avon road, hotel is 2m on left*
Just outside Stratford, this smart modern hotel is set in extensive well-manicured grounds. Bedrooms are spacious, comfortably furnished and well equipped. Public areas include a split level restaurant and an open plan lounge bar.
ROOMS: 104 en suite (8 fmly) No smoking in 52 bedrooms s £97-£107; d £115-£135 * LB **FACILITIES:** STV Indoor swimming (H) Tennis (hard) Sauna Solarium Gym Pool table Jacuzzi/spa ch fac Xmas **CONF:** Thtr 360 Class 200 Board 100 Del from £180 * **SERVICES:** Lift **PARKING:** 220 **NOTES:** No smoking in restaurant Civ Wed **CARDS:**

★★★★68% Stratford Victoria

MARSTON HOTELS

Arden St CV37 6QQ
☎ 01789 271000 01789 271001
e-mail: stratfordvictoria@compuserve.com
Dir: *A439 into Stratford, in town follow A3400 Birmingham, at traffic light junct turn left into Arden St, the hotel is 150yds on right hand side*

A new hotel with enthusiastic staff and a welcoming atmosphere, open plan public areas include a lounge and a restaurant. Bedrooms are spacious and comfortably equipped.

continued

ROOMS: 100 en suite (35 fmly) No smoking in 40 bedrooms s £89.50-£95; d £109-£129.50 (incl. bkfst) * LB **FACILITIES:** STV Gym Jacuzzi/spa Beauty Salon **CONF:** Thtr 110 Class 66 Board 54 Del from £125 * **SERVICES:** Lift **PARKING:** 96 **NOTES:** No smoking in restaurant **CARDS:**

★★★★66% The Shakespeare

Chapel St CV37 6ER
☎ 0870 400 8182 01789 415411
Dir: *adjoining town hall*
Right in the heart of town, this 18th-century hotel is a landmark site with its gabled timber façade. Public rooms are full of charm with exposed beams, classic staircases and open fires. Bedrooms vary in size but provide modern comforts. The quality hotel cuisine combines traditional and modern influences through an interesting carte; informal dining is also available in the hotel bistro.
ROOMS: 74 en suite No smoking in 20 bedrooms s fr £125; d £170-£265 * LB **FACILITIES:** Xmas **CONF:** Thtr 120 Class 50 Board 40 Del from £150 * **SERVICES:** Lift **PARKING:** 34 **NOTES:** No smoking in restaurant Civ Wed 50 **CARDS:**

★★★★65% The Alveston Manor

Clopton Bridge CV37 7HP
☎ 0870 400 8181 01789 414095
Dir: *S of Clopton Bridge*
A striking red brick and wooden façade, well tended grounds, and a giant cedar tree all contribute to the charm of this well established hotel. Bedrooms vary in size and character, but all provide modern comforts - the recent conversion of a coach house offers an impressive mix of comfortable full and junior suites. The Manor Grill restaurant offers menus based on popular traditional choices, whilst in summer months a terrace food operation offers Mediterranean style grills.
ROOMS: 114 en suite No smoking in 30 bedrooms s fr £120; d £160-£265 * LB **FACILITIES:** STV Xmas **CONF:** Thtr 140 Class 80 Board 40 Del from £150 * **PARKING:** 200 **NOTES:** No smoking in restaurant Civ Wed 36 **CARDS:**

★★★75% Salford Hall

Best Western

WR11 5UT
☎ 01386 871300 01386 871301
e-mail: reception@salfordhall.co.uk
(For full entry see Abbot's Salford)

★★★69% Grosvenor House

Warwick Rd CV37 6YT
☎ 01789 269213 01789 266087
e-mail: sales@patenhotels.freeserve.co.uk
Dir: *turn off jct 15 on M40 follow Stratford signs to A439 Warwick Rd, hotel is 7m from jct on town centre one way system*
Grosvenor House is a short distance from the town centre and many of the historic attractions. Staff are both friendly and efficient, and useful services, such as an all-day menu of refreshments in the lounge, and room service, are available. The Garden Room restaurant offers a choice of interesting modern dishes from set priced and carte menus. Bedroom styles and sizes vary; the most recent wing of new rooms are spacious and cheerfully appointed, with smart modern bathrooms.
ROOMS: 67 en suite (1 fmly) No smoking in 25 bedrooms s £79; d £90 * LB **FACILITIES:** Xmas **CONF:** Thtr 100 Class 50 Board 40 **PARKING:** 53 **NOTES:** No dogs (ex guide dogs) No smoking in restaurant Civ Wed 80 **CARDS:**

★★★66% The Falcon

Chapel St CV37 6HA

☎ 01789 279953 🖷 01789 414260
Dir: *town centre-opposite Guild Chapel and Nash House*

Situated in the heart of the town this traditional inn provides a choice of bars, a sun lounge, pretty gardens and a modern brasserie style restaurant. Well equipped bedrooms vary in style; the older, beamed rooms in the original section are smaller but have their own charm.
ROOMS: 73 en suite 11 annexe en suite (13 fmly) No smoking in 38 bedrooms s £80-£114; d £115-£130 * LB **FACILITIES:** Xmas **CONF:** Thtr 200 Class 110 Board 40 Del £140 * **SERVICES:** Lift **PARKING:** 124 **NOTES:** No smoking in restaurant
CARDS:

★★★66% The Swan's Nest

Bridgefoot CV37 7LT
☎ 0870 400 8183 🖷 01789 414547
e-mail: heritage-hotelsstratforduponavon.swansnest@forte-hotels.com
Dir: *from M40 junct 15, A46 to Stratford, leave at 1st rdbt A439 to town centre, entering town follow one way system left over river bridge hotel by river*
Partly dating back to the 17th century and with its own river frontage, this hotel is a short walk from The Royal Shakespeare Theatre and town centre. Most bedrooms are in a modern wing and several are in the Posthouse's new millennium design. The Cygnet restaurant has been restyled and offers an improved dining choice. Both the lounge and room service supplement these menu choices. The courtyard garden is ideal for weddings.
ROOMS: 68 en suite (3 fmly) No smoking in 30 bedrooms d £95-£115 * LB **FACILITIES:** STV Xmas **CONF:** Thtr 150 Class 80 Board 50 Del from £120 * **PARKING:** 72 **NOTES:** Civ Wed 50
CARDS:

★★★63% Charlecote Pheasant

Charlecote CV35 9EW
REGAL
☎ 01789 279954 🖷 01789 470222
Dir: *leave M40 junc15, take A429 towards Cirencester through Barford village after 2m turn right into Charlecote, hotel opp Charlecote Manor Park*
Located just outside Stratford, this large complex is set in extensive grounds. There is a distinctly rustic feel to the public rooms, restaurant and bars. Bedrooms are well equipped and range from functional to quite luxurious.

continued on p538

S

STRATFORD-UPON-AVON, continued

Charlecote Pheasant, Stratford-upon-Avon

ROOMS: 70 en suite (2 fmly) No smoking in 26 bedrooms s £80-£95; d £100-£130 * LB **FACILITIES:** Outdoor swimming (H) Tennis (hard) Pool table Childrens Play area Xmas **CONF:** Thtr 160 Class 90 Board 50 Del from £110 * **PARKING:** 100 **NOTES:** No dogs (ex guide dogs) No smoking in restaurant RS 27-31 Dec Civ Wed 120
CARDS:

★★★61% The White Swan

Rother St CV37 6NH
☎ 01789 297022 📠 01789 268773
Dir: *leave M40 junct15 signposted Stratford on Avon. Hotel is in the Market Square*
Right in the heart of the town, this half-timbered building has retained many of its original features and offers cosy, traditionally styled public areas. Bedrooms come in a variety of shapes and sizes; all are well equipped, and a few boast beamed ceilings.
ROOMS: 41 en suite (3 fmly) No smoking in 16 bedrooms s fr £70; d fr £85 * LB **FACILITIES:** entertainment Xmas **CONF:** Thtr 30 Class 10 Board 20 Del from £95 * **PARKING:** 10 **NOTES:** No smoking in restaurant **CARDS:**

See advert on opposite page

★★73% Stratford Court

Avenue Rd CV37 6UX
☎ 01789 297799 📠 01789 262449
e-mail: stratfordcourt@easynet.co.uk
Dir: *Stratford town centre: follow one way system taking A439, 1st left after one way system into Welcombe Rd, continue to top. Stratford Court on right*
A relaxed and friendly environment exists within this delightful Edwardian property, which sits in a quiet residential area close to the theatres and town centre. Bedrooms have all been furnished and equipped to a very high standard with dramatic fabrics and furnishings; period pieces of furniture live in harmony with modern extras. The comfortable and tastefully furnished lounge and cosy bar are conducive to socialising.
ROOMS: 13 en suite (2 fmly) s £65-£75; d £95-£160 (incl. bkfst) * **PARKING:** 20 **NOTES:** No children 14yrs No smoking in restaurant
CARDS:

★★65% The Coach House Hotel

THE CIRCLE Selected Individual Hotels GREAT BRITAIN

16-17 Warwick Rd CV37 6YW
☎ 01789 204109 📠 01789 415916
e-mail: kiwiavon@aol.com
Dir: *leave M40 junct 15. Follow A46 - Stratford. Exit next rdbt onto A439 - Town Centre. Hotel on the right, just after St Gregory's church*
Convenient for the town centre, this popular hotel provides well equipped bedrooms in both the main house and a nearby wing.

continued

There is a small lounge, a cellar bar and a restaurant. Residents have free use of the leisure centre just a few minutes' walk away.
ROOMS: 10 en suite 11 annexe en suite (1 fmly) No smoking in 14 bedrooms s £39-£65; d £55-£109 (incl. bkfst) * LB
FACILITIES: Whirlpool bath (2 rms) Local Leisure centre free to guests (2 mins walk) entertainment Xmas **PARKING:** 30 **NOTES:** No dogs (ex guide dogs) No smoking in restaurant
CARDS:

★★65% The New Inn Hotel & Restaurant

Clifford Chambers CV37 8HR
☎ 01789 293402 📠 01789 292716
e-mail: thenewinn65@aol.com
Dir: *Turn off A3400 onto B4632 , follow signs to shire horse centre, hotel 200yds on left*
A welcoming, family-run hotel in a pretty village. The bar has an open log fire and, together with the restaurant, offers a choice of dining options. Bedrooms, especially those in the new wing, are appealing; four-poster and disabled rooms are available. A courtesy car can be arranged to/from Stratford or for local tours.
ROOMS: 12 en suite (2 fmly) No smoking in all bedrooms s £27.50-£57.50; d £55-£57.50 (incl. bkfst) * LB **CONF:** Class 50 Del from £50 * **PARKING:** 40 **NOTES:** No dogs No smoking in restaurant
CARDS:

STREATLEY, Berkshire — Map 04 SU58

★★★★70% Swan Diplomat

High St RG8 9HR
☎ 01491 878800 📠 01491 872554
e-mail: sales@swan-diplomat.co.uk
Dir: *M4 junct12 towards Theale, at 2nd rdbt A340 to Pangbourne, A329 to Streatley. Right at 1st traffic lights, hotel 200yds on left, before bridge*
This stylish hotel provides the perfect riverside location for the quintessential English summer's day. Comfortable lounges and restaurants all look onto the superb gardens and river. Bedrooms are spacious and thoughtfully equipped, most enjoying the lovely views. The hotel is well suited to both leisure and business guests with several conference rooms and a modern leisure suite.
ROOMS: 46 en suite No smoking in 8 bedrooms s £99-£128; d £138-£155 * LB **FACILITIES:** STV Indoor swimming (H) Sauna Solarium Gym Croquet lawn Jacuzzi/spa Boat hire Steam room Xmas **CONF:** Thtr 90 Class 50 Board 40 Del from £165 * **PARKING:** 135
NOTES: Civ Wed 90 **CARDS:**

See advert on opposite page

STREET, Somerset — Map 03 ST43

★★★62% Wessex

High St BA16 0EF
☎ 01458 443383 📠 01458 446589
e-mail: Wessex@hotel.street.freeserve.co.uk
Dir: *from A303 follow road B3151 to Somerton and Street*
A purpose built hotel in the centre of town with ample parking, a short walk from Clarks village. Spacious bedrooms are equipped with modern facilities. Public areas include function rooms, a cosy bar, and a comfortable restaurant offering a fixed price menu and popular carvery.
ROOMS: 50 en suite (2 fmly) No smoking in 24 bedrooms s £40-£50; d £50-£60 * LB **FACILITIES:** STV Xmas **CONF:** Thtr 250 Class 150 Board 50 Del £80 * **SERVICES:** Lift **PARKING:** 90 **NOTES:** No smoking in restaurant **CARDS:**

Packed in a hurry? Ironing facilities should be available at all star levels, either in rooms or on request.

STRETTON, Rutland Map 08 SK91

★★71% ❀ Ram Jam Inn
Great North Rd LE15 7QX
☎ 01780 410776 Fax 01780 410361
e-mail: rji@rutnet.co.uk
Dir: *on Nbound carriageway of A1 past the B1668 turn off, thru service station into hotel carpark. Sbound take A668 - Oakham & follow signs under A1*
The delightful Ram Jam has always been a landmark on the long haul up the A1, and its informal but stylish ambience is very pleasant, much like a cafe bar and bistro with rooms. The combination between English country house and continental decoration in the public areas compliment each other well. The spacious high quality bedrooms have cheerful soft furnishings and most overlook the rear garden and orchard.
ROOMS: 7 en suite (1 fmly) s £45; d £55 * **CONF:** Thtr 60 Class 40 Board 40 Del from £72.50 * **PARKING:** 64 **NOTES:** Closed 25 Dec
CARDS:

STROUD, Gloucestershire Map 03 SO80

★★★70% ❀ The Bear of Rodborough
Rodborough Common GL5 5DE
☎ 01453 878522 Fax 01453 872523
e-mail: bookings@cotswold-inns-hotels.co.uk
Dir: *1m S on A46, turn left to Rodborough Common*
Situated high above Stroud, and set in acres of National Trust Parkland, stands this imposing 17th-century former coaching Inn. The character of the Bear speaks volumes with lounges, cocktail bar and elegant Mulberry restaurant epitomising the inherent charm of the building. Bedrooms offer comfort and style with a good selection of extra touches. There is also a traditional and popular public bar. Food is good, and based where possible on local produce.
ROOMS: 46 en suite (2 fmly) No smoking in 23 bedrooms s £65-£75; d £110-£150 (incl. bkfst) * LB **FACILITIES:** Croquet lawn Xmas **CONF:** Thtr 60 Class 30 Board 30 Del from £115 * **PARKING:** 122 **NOTES:** No smoking in restaurant Civ Wed 100
CARDS:

★★★69% ❀ Burleigh Court
Minchinhampton GL5 2PF
☎ 01453 883804 Fax 01453 886870
e-mail: burleighcourthotel@talk21.com
Dir: *0.75m off A419 E of Stroud*
A charming manor house set in attractive grounds. Spacious public areas include a panelled bar, pleasant lounge and attractive restaurant serving well prepared, interesting food. Bedrooms are individually decorated, well equipped and split between the main house and adjoining coach house.
ROOMS: 11 en suite 7 annexe en suite (2 fmly) No smoking in 4 bedrooms s £67.50-£87.50; d £90-£110 (incl. bkfst & dinner) * LB **FACILITIES:** Outdoor swimming Putting green Xmas **CONF:** Thtr 60 Board 16 **PARKING:** 41 **NOTES:** No smoking in restaurant
CARDS:

★★64% The Bell
Wallbridge GL5 3J5
☎ 01453 763556 Fax 01453 758611
Dir: *at junct of A419/A46, outside Stroud Town Centre*
This one time public house, dating back to the Victorian era, offers well equipped and comfortable accommodation. Facilities include a room for meetings, a lounge bar, pleasant restaurant and convenient parking all in a central location.

continued on p540

S

STROUD, continued

ROOMS: 12 en suite (2 fmly) s £35-£45; d £45-£70 (incl. bkfst) * LB **FACILITIES:** STV Pool table ch fac Xmas **CONF:** Thtr 35 Class 20 Board 16 **PARKING:** 15 **NOTES:** No smoking in restaurant
CARDS:

Premier Lodge
Stratford Lodge GL5 4AF
☎ 0870 700 1548 🖷 0870 700 1549
Premier Lodge offers modern, well equipped, en suite accommodation suitable for both business and leisure travellers. Meals can be taken at the adjacent popular restaurant and bar which is fully licensed. For further details, consult the Hotel Groups page.
ROOMS: 30 en suite d £42 *

Travelodge
A 419 Easington, Stonehouse GL10 3SQ
☎ 01962 760779
This modern building offers accommodation in smart, spacious and well equipped bedrooms, all with en suite bathrooms. Refreshments may be taken at the nearby family restaurant. For further details and the Travelodge phone number, consult the Hotel Groups page.
ROOMS: 40 en suite

STUDLAND, Dorset — Map 04 SZ08

★★68% Manor House
BH19 3AU
☎ 01929 450288 🖷 01929 450288
Dir: *from Bournemouth, follow signs to Sandbanks/Sandbanks ferry, over ferry, then 3m to Studland*
Views over Studland Bay are delightful and can be enjoyed from many of the hotel's bedrooms, the dining room and lounge. Rooms are mostly spacious, all are individually decorated and some have four-poster beds. Downstairs, the lounge has a lovely open fire for the winter months and the panelled dining room has a baronial feel. Twenty acres of secluded gardens surround the hotel, including a tennis court for residents' use. There is also a lovely conservatory style dining room and separate bar.
ROOMS: 20 en suite (9 fmly) d £110-£170 (incl. bkfst & dinner) * LB **FACILITIES:** Tennis (hard) Croquet lawn **CONF:** Class 25 **PARKING:** 80 **NOTES:** No children 5yrs No smoking in restaurant Closed 20 Dec-13 Jan
CARDS:

STURMINSTER NEWTON, Dorset — Map 03 ST71

★★★71% Plumber Manor
Hazelbury Bryan Rd DT10 2AF
☎ 01258 472507 🖷 01258 473370
e-mail: book@plumbermanor.com
Dir: *1.5m SW of Sturminster Newton, off A357 towards Hazelbury Bryan*

continued

This beautiful Jacobean manor is set in extensive, lovingly tended grounds. Bedrooms in the main house retain much character, where those in the converted barns opposite tend to be more spacious and modern in style. The restaurant is very much the centre of the operation, and has an excellent reputation for good traditional cooking.
ROOMS: 6 en suite 10 annexe en suite s £80-£90; d £95-£145 (incl. bkfst) * LB **FACILITIES:** Tennis (hard) Croquet lawn **CONF:** Thtr 25 Board 12 Del from £135 * **PARKING:** 30 **NOTES:** Closed Feb
CARDS:

SUDBURY, Derbyshire — Map 07 SK13

★★★68% *The Boars Head*
Lichfield Rd DE6 5GX
☎ 01283 820344 🖷 01283 820075
e-mail: boars@derbys14.freeserve.co.uk
Dir: *Turn off A50 onto A515 towards Lichfield, hotel 1m on right close to railway crossing*

This roadside inn offers comfortable accommodation in well equipped bedrooms. There is a relaxed atmosphere in the public rooms, which offer a choice of bars and dining options. The refurbished beamed lounge bar provides informal dining while the restaurant and cocktail bar offer a more formal environment.
ROOMS: 22 en suite 1 annexe en suite (1 fmly) **FACILITIES:** STV **CONF:** Thtr 35 Class 45 Board 25 **PARKING:** 85
CARDS:

See advert under BURTON ON TRENT

SUDBURY, Suffolk — Map 05 TL84

★★★69% Mill
Walnut Tree Ln CO10 1BD
☎ 01787 375544 🖷 01787 373027
Dir: *from Colchester take A134 to Sudbury, follow signs for Chelmsford after town square take 2nd right*
Located on the outskirts of the town, overlooking open pastures and the River Stour, this hotel has its own mill pond and retains charming features from the building's three century history including open fires, exposed beams and a working waterwheel. Bedrooms vary in size and most enjoy a view of the river or mill pond.
ROOMS: 52 en suite (2 fmly) s £59; d £69 * LB **FACILITIES:** STV Xmas **CONF:** Thtr 90 Class 50 Board 40 Del from £75 * **PARKING:** 60
CARDS:

Late for dinner? Quality Standards star rating means that last orders for dinner should be no earlier than:
★ 6.30pm ★★ 7.00pm ★★★ 8.00pm
★★★★ 9.00pm ★★★★★ 10.00pm

SUNDERLAND, Tyne & Wear

Map 12 NZ35

★★★★67% Swallow

Queen's Pde, Seaburn SR6 8DB
☎ 0191 529 2041 🖷 0191 529 3843
e-mail: info@swallowhotels.com
Dir: *off A19 to Sunderland N on A1231, at traffic lights follow A183 for approx 3m to seafront, where hotel is situated*

Occupying a seafront position overlooking the promenade, this hotel now boasts a fine extension providing 33 impressive bedrooms and a secure covered car park. Stylish public areas include a comfortable foyer lounge and lounge bar. The Promenade Restaurant features a unique Victorian 'bandstand' where a pianist plays at dinner.
ROOMS: 98 en suite (3 fmly) No smoking in 37 bedrooms s £50-£125; d £65-£180 (incl. bkfst) * LB **FACILITIES:** STV Indoor swimming (H) Sauna Solarium Gym Jacuzzi/spa Steam room entertainment Xmas **CONF:** Thtr 300 Class 120 Board 90 Del from £99 * **SERVICES:** Lift **PARKING:** 130 **NOTES:** No smoking in restaurant
CARDS:

★★★68% Quality Friendly Hotel

Witney Way, Boldon NE35 9PE
☎ 0191 519 1999 🖷 0191 519 0655
e-mail: admin@gb621.u-net.com
Dir: *junct A19/A184*
Situated in the business park (turn into Witney Way), this modern purpose-built hotel focuses well on the needs of the business person. It offers spacious, very well equipped bedrooms, while public areas include a leisure centre and a variety of meeting rooms. Dinner offers a good choice of menu options.
ROOMS: 82 en suite (10 fmly) No smoking in 42 bedrooms s £83; d £109 * LB **FACILITIES:** STV Indoor swimming (H) Sauna Solarium Gym Jacuzzi/spa ch fac Xmas **CONF:** Thtr 200 Class 100 Board 75 Del £115 * **PARKING:** 150 **NOTES:** Civ Wed 300
CARDS:

★★68% *Roker*

Roker Ter SR6 0PH
☎ 0191 567 1786 🖷 0191 510 0289
Dir: *1m N of Sunderland town centre on the sea front, follow signs to Roker A183*
This seafront business hotel provides well equipped bedrooms, a stylish bar and smart new themed restaurant with a good selection of popular dishes. There is secure undercover parking with direct assess to and from the hotel.
ROOMS: 45 en suite (8 fmly) **FACILITIES:** STV Pool table **CONF:** Thtr 350 Class 100 Board 50 **PARKING:** 140 **NOTES:** No dogs (ex guide dogs) **CARDS:**

Premier Lodge

Timber Beach Rd, Off Chessington Way, Castletown SR5 3XG
☎ 0870 700 1550 🖷 0870 700 1551
Premier Lodge offers modern, well equipped, en suite accommodation suitable for both business and leisure travellers. Meals can be taken at the adjacent popular restaurant and bar which is fully licensed. For further details, consult the Hotel Groups page.
ROOMS: 63 en suite d £46 *

SUTTON, Greater London

Map 04 TQ26

★★63% Thatched House

135 Cheam Rd SM1 2BN
☎ 020 8642 3131 🖷 020 8770 0684
Dir: *junct 8 of M25, follow A217 to London until reaching A232, turn right onto A232, hotel is half a minute's drive on the right*
As its name suggests, this is a thatched, cottage-style hotel on the Epsom/Croydon road. Bedrooms, either in the main building or a separate extension, are neatly decorated and well equipped. Public rooms include a lounge, a bar and a dining room overlooking the garden.
ROOMS: 32 rms (29 en suite) 5 annexe rms **CONF:** Thtr 50 Class 30 Board 26 **PARKING:** 26 **NOTES:** No smoking in restaurant
CARDS:

SUTTON COLDFIELD, West Midlands

Map 07 SP19

Premier Collection

★★★★ New Hall

Walmley Rd B76 1QX
☎ 0121 378 2442 🖷 0121 378 4637
e-mail: new.hall@thistle.co.uk
Dir: *follow A38 'Lichfield' until B4148 'Walmley'. 2.5m on B4148, at 2nd rdbt turn left and then right into Walmley Road. Hotel is on left*
Set in immaculate grounds and gardens, this hotel is reputedly the oldest moated manor house in England. The day rooms are delightful. Divided between a purpose-built wing and the main house, the bedrooms vary in size but all are furnished and decorated to a high standard. The restaurant offers imaginative dishes of a consistently high quality.
ROOMS: 60 en suite No smoking in 54 bedrooms s £145-£195; d £170-£425 * LB **FACILITIES:** STV Golf 9 Fishing Croquet lawn Putting green Golf driving net Xmas **CONF:** Thtr 50 Class 30 Board 30 Del from £184 * **PARKING:** 70 **NOTES:** No dogs (ex guide dogs) No smoking in restaurant RS Sat Civ Wed 70
CARDS:

S

SUTTON COLDFIELD, continued

★★★72% Moor Hall

Moor Hall Dr, Four Oaks B75 6LN
☎ 0121 308 3751 🖷 0121 308 8974
e-mail: mail@moorhallhotel.co.uk

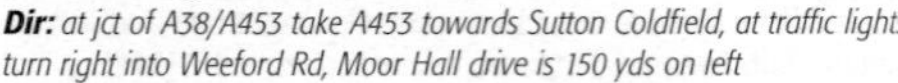

Dir: *at jct of A38/A453 take A453 towards Sutton Coldfield, at traffic lights turn right into Weeford Rd, Moor Hall drive is 150 yds on left*

Although only a short distance from the city centre and 15 minutes from the NEC and the motorway network, this hotel enjoys a peaceful setting, overlooking extensive grounds and an adjacent golf course. Bedrooms are well equipped and the executive rooms particularly spacious. In the evenings, there are two choices for dinner: a formal restaurant, the Oak Room, and the informal Country Kitchen, offering a carvery and blackboard specials.
ROOMS: 74 en suite (5 fmly) No smoking in 36 bedrooms s £100-£110; d £115-£125 (incl. bkfst) * LB **FACILITIES:** STV Indoor swimming (H) Sauna Solarium Gym Jacuzzi/spa Steam room **CONF:** Thtr 250 Class 120 Board 45 Del £136 * **SERVICES:** Lift **PARKING:** 164 **NOTES:** Civ Wed 120 **CARDS:**

See advert under BIRMINGHAM

★★★65% *Marston Farm*

Bodymoor Heath B76 9JD
☎ 01827 872133 🖷 01827 875043
e-mail: brook@brook-hotels.demon.co.uk
Dir: *take A4091 in direction of Tamworth and turn right for Bodymoor Heath. Turn right after humpback bridge*

Situated close to Birmingham city centre, the NEC and the airport, this 17th-century farmhouse provides attractive and well equipped accommodation to both leisure and business markets. Features of the hotel include the courtyard restaurant, permanent marquee, conference rooms and ample car parking.
ROOMS: 37 en suite No smoking in 5 bedrooms **FACILITIES:** STV Tennis (hard) Fishing Croquet lawn Boules Golf practice net Mountain bikes **CONF:** Thtr 150 Class 80 Board 50 **PARKING:** 150 **NOTES:** No smoking in restaurant **CARDS:**

★★★64% Quality Hotel Sutton Court

60-66 Lichfield Rd B74 2NA
☎ 0121 354 4991 🖷 0121 355 0083
e-mail: reservations@sutton-court-hotel.co.uk
Dir: *take M42 junct 9, then A446 to Lichfield. At rdbt take A453 to Sutton Coldfield. Hotel is at 2nd set of traffic lights at junct of A5127/A453*

A privately-owned hotel, close to the town centre, providing modern and well equipped bedrooms with some ladies bedrooms available. Public rooms are comfortable and there are a good range of conference and function facilities. There is also a deep south American-styled bar and restaurant called Savanaghs.
ROOMS: 56 en suite 8 annexe en suite (9 fmly) No smoking in 40 bedrooms s £40-£95; d £55-£118 (incl. bkfst) * LB **FACILITIES:** STV Free use of local leisure centre entertainment Xmas **CONF:** Thtr 90 Class 70 Board 50 Del from £65 * **PARKING:** 90 **NOTES:** Civ Wed 130 **CARDS:**

See advert under BIRMINGHAM

★★65% *Royal*

High St B72 1UD
☎ 0121 355 8222 🖷 0121 355 1837
Dir: *from A38/A453 to Sutton Coldfield turn left at 2nd set of traffic lights, hotel 400metres on right hand side*

Dating back to the 18th century and close to the airport and NEC, stands this town centre hotel. Bedrooms are attractively furnished, some with four-posters, and well equipped. There is also a varied selection of meals available from the bar and restaurant.
ROOMS: 22 en suite (3 fmly) **FACILITIES:** STV **CONF:** Thtr 60 Class 40 Board 30 **PARKING:** 80 **NOTES:** No dogs (ex guide dogs) **CARDS:**

⌂ Premier Lodge (Birmingham North)

Whitehouse Common Rd B75 6HD
☎ 0870 700 1322 🖷 0870 700 1323

Premier Lodge offers modern, well equipped, en suite accommodation suitable for both business and leisure travellers. Meals can be taken at the adjacent popular restaurant and bar which is fully licensed. For further details, consult the Hotel Groups page.
ROOMS: 42 en suite d £46 *

⌂ *Travelodge*

Boldmere Rd B73 5UP
☎ 0121 355 0017 🖷 0121 355 0017
Dir: *2m S, on B4142*

This modern building offers accommodation in smart, spacious and well equipped bedrooms, all with en suite bathrooms. Refreshments may be taken at the nearby family restaurant. For further details and the Travelodge phone number, consult the Hotel Groups page.
ROOMS: 32 en suite

SUTTON IN THE ELMS, Leicestershire — Map 04 SP59

★★61% Mill On The Soar

Coventry Rd LE9 6QD
☎ 01455 282419 🖷 01455 285937
Dir: *SE of Leicester, on B4114*

The Mill On The Soar is a busy roadside inn which caters well for family dining. The accommodation is housed in a separate wing and offers pleasing colour co-ordinated bedrooms that are very well equipped and fully en suite. The public areas centre around the open-plan bar where there is an extensive range of bar meals, informally served. The gardens to the rear lead to a falconry centre, play area, river and small well stocked lake.
ROOMS: 25 en suite (10 fmly) d £40 * **FACILITIES:** Fishing Falconry centre **CONF:** Thtr 50 Class 20 Board 15 Del from £75 * **PARKING:** 200 **NOTES:** No dogs (ex guide dogs) **CARDS:**

See advert on opposite page

SUTTON ON SEA, Lincolnshire — Map 09 TF58

★★★66% Grange & Links

Sea Ln, Sandilands LN12 2RA
☎ 01507 441334 🖷 01507 443033
e-mail: grangelinks@ic24.net
Dir: *A1111 to Sutton-on-Sea, follow signs to Sandilands*

Close to the beach in five acres of grounds, this friendly family run hotel is popular with golfers. Delightful public rooms include an attractive bar together with ample lounge areas. Good home cooking is served in the traditional style dining room and most of the bedrooms have been well equipped and pleasantly furnished.

continued

ROOMS: 23 en suite (10 fmly) s fr £59.50; d fr £71.50 (incl. bkfst) * LB **FACILITIES:** Golf 18 Tennis (hard) Snooker Gym Croquet lawn Putting green Bowls Xmas **CONF:** Thtr 200 Board 100 **PARKING:** 60 **NOTES:** No dogs (ex guide dogs) Civ Wed 500
CARDS:

SUTTON SCOTNEY, Hampshire — Map 04 SU43

Travelodge (North)
SO21 3JY
☎ 01962 761016
Dir: *on A34 northbound*
This modern building offers accommodation in smart, spacious and well equipped bedrooms, all with en suite bathrooms. Refreshments may be taken at the nearby family restaurant. For further details and the Travelodge phone number, consult the Hotel Groups page.
ROOMS: 30 en suite

Travelodge

Travelodge (South)
SO21 3JY
☎ 01962 760779
Dir: *on A34 southbound*
This modern building offers accommodation in smart, spacious and well equipped bedrooms, all with en suite bathrooms. Refreshments may be taken at the nearby family restaurant. For further details and the Travelodge phone number, consult the Hotel Groups page.
ROOMS: 40 en suite

Travelodge

SUTTON UPON DERWENT, East Riding of Yorkshire — Map 08 SE74

★★65% Old Rectory
Sandhill Ln YO41 4BX
☎ 01904 608548 ▤ 01904 608548
Dir: *off A1079 at Grimston Bar rdbt onto B1228 for Howden, through Elvington to Sutton-upon-Derwent, the hotel is situated on left opposite tennis courts*
This former rectory stands close to the village centre and overlooks the Derwent valley. The house provides spacious bedrooms together with a separate bar and lounge. Home cooking is served in the traditional-style dining room, and service is friendly and polite.
ROOMS: 6 rms (5 en suite) (2 fmly) s fr £30; d fr £52 (incl. bkfst) * LB **FACILITIES:** STV **PARKING:** 30 **NOTES:** Closed 2 wks Xmas
CARDS:

SWAFFHAM, Norfolk — Map 05 TF80

★★★65% George
Station Rd PE37 7LJ
☎ 01760 721238 ▤ 01760 725333
Dir: *turn off A47 signposted Swaffham, hotel opposite the church of St Peter & St Paul*
Situated in the bustling town of Swaffham adjacent to the market square is this popular family run coaching inn. The well equipped bedrooms are located in the main house and a modern wing. There is a busy bar serving a range of snacks and a more formal restaurant offering a carte menu. There is also a building opposite where several function/conference rooms are available.
ROOMS: 29 en suite (1 fmly) s £50-£60; d £60-£75 (incl. bkfst) * LB **FACILITIES:** STV Xmas **CONF:** Thtr 150 Class 70 Board 70 Del from £60 * **PARKING:** 100 **NOTES:** No smoking in restaurant
CARDS:

Best Western

SWALLOWFIELD, Berkshire — Map 04 SU76

★★68% The Mill House
Old Basingstoke Rd, Swallowfield RG7 1PY
☎ 0118 988 3124 ▤ 0118 988 5550
e-mail: info@themillhousehotel.co.uk
Dir: *M4 junct 11, S on A33, left at 1st rdbt onto B3349. Approx 1m after signpost for Three Mile Cross and Spencer's Wood, hotel is on right*
This friendly small hotel is conveniently located in a rural setting between the M3 and M4. Bedrooms are quiet, spacious and well equipped, with attractive decor. The restaurant offers a well prepared, popular menu and has some pretty views onto the large garden.
ROOMS: 10 en suite (2 fmly) No smoking in 2 bedrooms s fr £67.50; d fr £80 (incl. bkfst) * LB **FACILITIES:** STV Croquet lawn **CONF:** Thtr 250 Class 100 Board 60 Del from £115 * **PARKING:** 60 **NOTES:** No smoking in restaurant Closed 24 Dec-4 Jan RS Sun evenings Civ Wed 125
CARDS:

SWANAGE, Dorset — Map 04 SZ07

★★★67% The Pines
Burlington Rd BH19 1LT
☎ 01929 425211 ▤ 01929 422075
e-mail: reservations@pineshotel.co.uk
Dir: *follow A351 to seafront, turn left then take second right and continue to end of road*
A popular family hotel, The Pines enjoys a superb location with spectacular views to the Isle of Wight in the distance. The cheerful bedrooms offer a good level of comfort. Public areas include two comfortable lounges. The restaurant offers good value home-cooked food and a less formal option is available in the bar.

continued

SWANAGE, continued

The Pines, Swanage

ROOMS: 49 en suite (26 fmly) s £42.50-£56; d £85-£112 (incl. bkfst) * LB **FACILITIES:** Xmas **CONF:** Thtr 60 Class 60 Board 30 **SERVICES:** Lift **PARKING:** 60 **NOTES:** No smoking in restaurant **CARDS:**

★★★67% Purbeck House

91 High St BH19 2LZ
☎ 01929 422872 01929 421194
e-mail: purbeckhouse@easynet.co.uk
Dir: *A351 to Swanage via Wareham, turn right into Shore Road and on into Institute Road, right into High Street*

Located close to the town centre, this former convent is set in well tended grounds. The bedrooms are tastefully decorated and appointed with old pine furnishings. Smartly presented public areas have some stunning features, such as painted ceilings, wood panelling and fine tiled floors.

ROOMS: 18 en suite (5 fmly) No smoking in 3 bedrooms s £40-£52; d £80-£104 (incl. bkfst) * LB **FACILITIES:** STV Pool table Croquet lawn Xmas **CONF:** Thtr 100 Class 70 Board 70 **PARKING:** 42 **NOTES:** No smoking in restaurant **CARDS:**

See advert on opposite page

★★★64% Grand

Best Western

Burlington Rd BH19 1LU
☎ 01929 423353 01929 427068
e-mail: grandhotel@bournemouth-net.co.uk
Dir: *via Sandbanks Toll Ferry from Bournemouth, follow signs to Swanage, at 2nd town centre sign take 4th left into Burlington Rd*

Spectacular views across Swanage Bay can be enjoyed from this hotel, which has access to a private beach. A sunny conservatory, a bar and well tended gardens are available for guests' use. Bedrooms vary in size, but all are smartly decorated. An imaginative menu is offered in the restaurant.

ROOMS: 30 en suite (2 fmly) No smoking in 3 bedrooms s £55-£59; d £110-£138 (incl. bkfst & dinner) * LB **FACILITIES:** STV Indoor swimming (H) Fishing Sauna Solarium Gym Jacuzzi/spa Table tennis Xmas **SERVICES:** Lift **PARKING:** 15 **NOTES:** No dogs No smoking in restaurant **CARDS:**

See advert on opposite page

★★66% Havenhurst

Cranborne Rd BH19 1EA
☎ 01929 424224 01929 422173

This personally run small hotel offers a friendly welcome to guests. A comfortable lounge is provided in addition to the popular bar. Each evening, home cooked meals are served, featuring an enormous range of home made desserts. Bedrooms are bright and sunny.

ROOMS: 17 en suite (4 fmly) s £22-£35; d £44-£70 (incl. bkfst) * LB **PARKING:** 20 **NOTES:** No dogs No smoking in restaurant **CARDS:**

SWANWICK See Alfreton

SWAVESEY, Cambridgeshire Map 05 TL36

Travelodge

Travelodge

Cambridge Rd CB4 5QA
☎ 01954 789113 01954 789113
Dir: *on eastbound carriageway of the A14*

This modern building offers accommodation in smart, spacious and well equipped bedrooms, all with en suite bathrooms. Refreshments may be taken at the nearby family restaurant. For further details and the Travelodge phone number, consult the Hotel Groups page.

ROOMS: 36 en suite

SWAY, Hampshire Map 04 SZ29

★★★65% String of Horses

Mead End Rd SO41 6EH
☎ 01590 682631 01590 682911
e-mail: relax@stringofhorses.co.uk
Dir: *A337 Lyndhurst/Brockenhurst, right opposite Carey's Manor Hotel onto B3055 to Sway, right onto Stn Rd, 2nd left,after railway station 350m on left*

A well maintained hotel in peaceful, mature grounds adjoining the New Forest. The majority of the well presented bedrooms are equipped with large spa baths, and all feature thoughtful extras such as dressing gowns. There is a cosy bar, separate breakfast room and comfortable lounge overlooking the pool and garden.

ROOMS: 8 en suite s £65-£70; d £98-£118 (incl. bkfst) * LB **FACILITIES:** STV Outdoor swimming (H) Croquet lawn Jacuzzi/spa Xmas **CONF:** Thtr 40 Board 30 Del from £106.75 * **PARKING:** 32 **NOTES:** No dogs No children 16yrs No smoking in restaurant **CARDS:**

★★66% White Rose

Station Rd SO41 6BA
☎ 01590 682754 01590 682955
Dir: *turn off B3055 Brockenhurst/New Milton road into Sway village centre*

Situated in the heart of the village, this spacious Victorian house is set in well tended gardens complete with outdoor pool. Bedrooms are equipped and decorated to a very comfortable standard. There is also a large dining room and lounge with views over the garden.

ROOMS: 15 en suite (3 fmly) **FACILITIES:** Outdoor swimming **SERVICES:** Lift **PARKING:** 50 **NOTES:** No smoking in restaurant **CARDS:**

Popped the question? Hotels with Civ Wed in their entry are licensed for civil wedding ceremonies. Maximum numbers for the ceremony only are shown, e.g. Civ Wed 50

SWINDON, Wiltshire Map 04 SU18
see also Wootton Bassett

★★★★72% ❀ Blunsdon House Hotel & Leisure Club

Blunsdon SN26 7AS
☎ 01793 721701 🖷 01793 721056
e-mail: info@blunsdonhouse.co.uk
Dir: *3m N off A419*

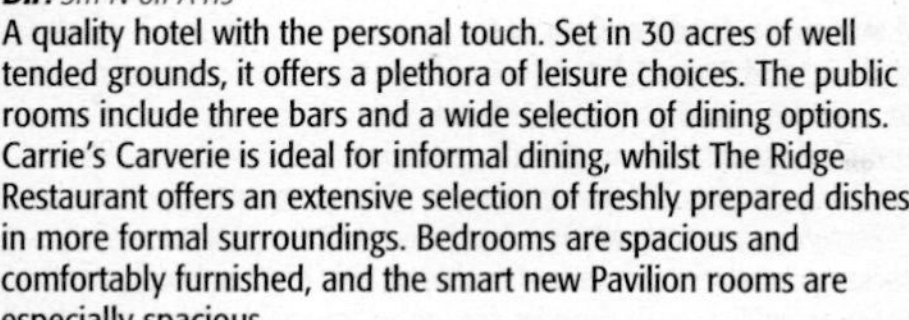

A quality hotel with the personal touch. Set in 30 acres of well tended grounds, it offers a plethora of leisure choices. The public rooms include three bars and a wide selection of dining options. Carrie's Carverie is ideal for informal dining, whilst The Ridge Restaurant offers an extensive selection of freshly prepared dishes in more formal surroundings. Bedrooms are spacious and comfortably furnished, and the smart new Pavilion rooms are especially spacious.

ROOMS: 120 en suite (14 fmly) No smoking in 77 bedrooms s £94-£124; d £122-£152 (incl. bkfst) * LB **FACILITIES:** STV Indoor swimming (H) Golf 9 Tennis (hard) Squash Sauna Solarium Gym Pool table Putting green Jacuzzi/spa Beauty therapy Woodland walk ch fac Xmas **CONF:** Thtr 300 Class 200 Board 40 Del from £100 * **SERVICES:** Lift **PARKING:** 300 **NOTES:** No dogs (ex guide dogs) Civ Wed 100 **CARDS:**

Early start? Hotels at all star levels should provide in-room alarm clocks and/or alarm calls.

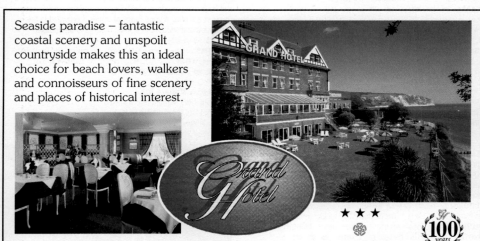

SWINDON, continued

★★★★71% De Vere
Shaw Ridge Leisure Park, Whitehill Way
SN5 7DW
☎ 01793 878785 01793 877822
e-mail: devere.swindon@airtime.co.uk
***Dir:** M4 junct 16, signs for Swindon off 1st rdbt, 2nd rdbt follow signs for Link Centre over next 2 rdbts, 2nd left at 3rd rdbt, left onto slip road*
This modern, purpose built hotel is located to the west of town, adjacent to an entertainment park (offering ten-pin bowling and a multiplex cinema). Bedrooms are smartly appointed and offer a good level of modern comfort. There are a range of eating options including an impressive new bar and brasserie.
ROOMS: 154 en suite (10 fmly) No smoking in 77 bedrooms d £115-£130 (incl. bkfst) * LB **FACILITIES:** STV Indoor swimming (H) Sauna Solarium Gym Jacuzzi/spa Health & beauty treatment rooms Xmas **CONF:** Thtr 400 Class 168 Board 80 Del from £130 * **SERVICES:** Lift **PARKING:** 170 **NOTES:** No smoking in restaurant Civ Wed 60
CARDS:

★★★★65% Swindon Marriott
Pipers Way SN3 1SH
☎ 01793 512121 01793 513114
***Dir:** from junct 15 of M4 follow A419, then A4259 to Coate roundabout and B4006 signed 'Old Town'*

A busy, modern hotel, suitable for business and leisure travellers. Public areas include a selection of conference facilities and a smartly refurbished leisure club. Service is attentive.
ROOMS: 153 en suite (42 fmly) No smoking in 86 bedrooms d £102 * LB **FACILITIES:** STV Indoor swimming (H) Tennis (hard) Sauna Solarium Gym Jacuzzi/spa Hair Salon Steam Room Health & Beauty Xmas **CONF:** Thtr 250 Class 100 Board 40 Del from £130 * **SERVICES:** Lift air con **PARKING:** 185 **NOTES:** Civ Wed
CARDS:

★★★78% The Pear Tree at Purton
Church End SN5 9ED
☎ 01793 772100 01793 772369
e-mail: stay@peartreepurton.co.uk
(For full entry see Purton)

★★★70% Chiseldon House
New Rd, Chiseldon SN4 0NE
☎ 01793 741010 01793 741059
***Dir:** M4 junct 15, onto A346 signposted Marlborough, at brow of hill turn right by Esso garage onto B4005 into New Rd, hotel is 200yds along on right*
Chiseldon is a traditional country house near Swindon that provides an excellent venue for a peaceful and comfortable stay. Quiet bedrooms, most of which are very spacious, are tastefully decorated with many thoughtful extras. There is also the Orangery Restaurant, a comfortable lounge and well kept gardens.
ROOMS: 21 en suite (4 fmly) No smoking in 6 bedrooms s fr £75; d £95-£110 (incl. bkfst) * **FACILITIES:** STV Outdoor swimming (H) **CONF:** Thtr 40 Class 40 Board 35 Del from £140 * **PARKING:** 50 **NOTES:** Closed 26 Dec Civ Wed 120 **CARDS:**

★★★67% *Stanton House*
The Avenue, Stanton Fitzwarren SN6 7SD
☎ 01793 861777 01793 861857
***Dir:** off A419 onto A361 towards Highworth, pass Honda factory and turn left towards Stanton Fitzwarren about 600yds past business park, hotel is on left*
Extensive grounds surround this Cotswold stone manor house. Bedrooms are smart and well maintained. There are lovely public areas, including: a games room; a lounge; a bar; conference facilities; and the super gardens. The restaurant specialises in traditional Japanese dishes, but equally good European cuisine is also available.
ROOMS: 86 en suite No smoking in 3 bedrooms **FACILITIES:** STV Tennis (hard) Table tennis Darts Mah Jong **CONF:** Thtr 110 Class 70 Board 40 **SERVICES:** Lift air con **PARKING:** 110 **NOTES:** No dogs (ex guide dogs) **CARDS:**

See advert on opposite page

★★★65% Goddard Arms
High St, Old Town SN1 3EG
☎ 01793 692313 01793 512984
e-mail: thegoddardarms@zoffanyhotels.co.uk
***Dir:** M4 junct 15, go along A419 towards Cirencester, at 1st rdbt take a left, go straight across 2nd and 3rd rdbts, hotel is on the right hand side*
Backing onto acres of natural parkland, this historic hotel is in the heart of Old Town. Bedrooms are in the original building and two wings, all are recently refurbished. Public areas include the vaults cellar bar, a charming restaurant with food to suit all palates, and extensive conference facilities.
ROOMS: 18 en suite 47 annexe en suite (3 fmly) No smoking in 31 bedrooms s £90; d £95 (incl. bkfst) * LB **FACILITIES:** STV **CONF:** Thtr 180 Class 100 Board 40 Del £99 * **PARKING:** 90 **NOTES:** No dogs (ex guide dogs) No smoking in restaurant Civ Wed 180
CARDS:

See advert on opposite page

★★★65% *Posthouse Swindon*
Marlborough Rd SN3 6AQ
☎ 0870 400 9079 01793 512887
***Dir:** off A419 for Swindon at rdbt, onto A4259. Continue for 1m, hotel is on right opposite Coate Water Country Park*
This smart hotel provides good accommodation close to the Town Centre and major road networks. Bedrooms are well decorated and have many modern, useful facilities and the small leisure complex is a plus. A good range of dishes is provided in the Restaurant and snacks can also be ordered in the lounge.
ROOMS: 98 en suite (30 fmly) No smoking in 65 bedrooms **FACILITIES:** Indoor swimming (H) Sauna Solarium Gym Pool table Jacuzzi/spa **CONF:** Thtr 70 Class 30 Board 30 **PARKING:** 200
CARDS:

★★★63% Villiers Inn
Moormead Rd, Wroughton SN4 9BY
☎ 01793 814744 01793 814119
e-mail: villiers.inn@villiers-hotels.demon.co.uk
***Dir:** 1m S of Swindon, on A4361*

An attractive period property with accommodation in a purpose built extension. Bedrooms are well equipped while public areas include a comfortable library lounge and a spacious conservatory. The Pig on the Wall bar and bistro offers an interesting range of dishes. Conference and function facilities are also available.

continued on p548

S

SWINDON, continued

ROOMS: 33 en suite No smoking in 10 bedrooms s £49-£69; d £69-£89 (incl. bkfst) * LB **FACILITIES:** STV Xmas **CONF:** Thtr 80 Class 30 Board 32 Del from £115 * **PARKING:** 60 **NOTES:** Civ Wed 120 **CARDS:**

See advert on page 547

Premier Lodge

Ermin St, Blunsdon SN2 4DJ
☎ 0870 700 1554 ▯ 0870 700 1555

PREMIER LODGE

Premier Lodge offers modern, well equipped, en suite accommodation suitable for both business and leisure travellers. Meals can be taken at the adjacent popular restaurant and bar which is fully licensed. For further details, consult the Hotel Groups page.

ROOMS: 40 en suite d £42 *

Hotel Ibis Swindon

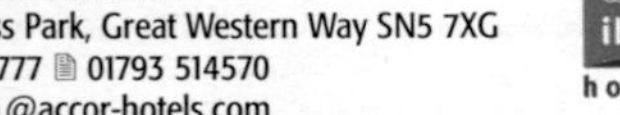

Delta Business Park, Great Western Way SN5 7XG
☎ 01793 514777 ▯ 01793 514570
e-mail: H1041@accor-hotels.com

ibis hotel

***Dir:** A3102 to Swindon, straight over rdbt, slip road onto Delta Business Park and turn left*

Modern, budget hotel offering comfortable accommodation in bright and practical bedrooms. Breakfast is self-service and dinner is available in the restaurant. For further details, consult the Hotel Groups page.

ROOMS: 120 en suite d fr £42 * **CONF:** Thtr 80 Class 40 Board 40 Del from £90 *

SWINTON, Greater Manchester — Map 07 SD70

Premier Lodge (Manchester West)

East Lancs Rd M27 8AA
☎ 0870 700 1472 ▯ 0870 700 1473

Premier Lodge offers modern, well equipped, en suite accommodation suitable for both business and leisure travellers. Meals can be taken at the adjacent popular restaurant and bar which is fully licensed. For further details, consult the Hotel Groups page.

ROOMS: 27 en suite d £46 *

SYMONDS YAT (EAST), Herefordshire — Map 03 SO51

★★65% Forest View Hotel

HR9 6JL
☎ 01600 890210 ▯ 01600 891147

***Dir:** from A40 Ross to Monmouth road take B4229 towards Goodrich & follow signs for Symonds Yat East*

This privately-owned and personally-run hotel occupies an idyllic location in a popular beauty spot. Fronted by its own delightful garden, it enjoys impressive views of the River Wye. The accommodation is very well equipped and includes rooms on ground floor level as well as two self-contained luxury suites with their own kitchens.

ROOMS: 10 en suite No smoking in all bedrooms s fr £35; d fr £70 (incl. bkfst) * LB **FACILITIES:** STV Fishing Xmas **PARKING:** 15 **NOTES:** No dogs (ex guide dogs) No children 14yrs No smoking in restaurant Closed Dec-Feb (ex Xmas & New Year) **CARDS:**

> Fancy a Singapore Sling? Bar staff in five star hotels should be skilled cocktail mixers.

★★65% Saracens Head

HR9 6JL
☎ 01600 890435 ▯ 01600 890034
e-mail: bookings@saracenshead.com

***Dir:** A40 Monmouth/Ross-on-Wye, turn off at Little Chef, signpost Goodrich & Symonds. 0.5m turn right, 1m fork right alongside river Wye to hotel*

This family owned hostelry stands alongside the River Wye, at the heart of a renowned beauty spot. It provides traditionally furnished but well equipped accommodation, the majority of the bedrooms having river views. In addition to the cosy residents' lounge, there is a very attractive dining room and a popular bar full of character.

ROOMS: 9 en suite (1 fmly) s £35-£40; d £56 (incl. bkfst) * LB **FACILITIES:** Fishing Pool table Canoeing Mountain bike hire Walking Climbing Horse riding **PARKING:** 15 **NOTES:** No dogs (ex guide dogs) No smoking in restaurant **CARDS:**

See advert on opposite page

★★58% Royal

HR9 6JL
☎ 01600 890238 ▯ 01600 890777

***Dir:** off A40 onto B4229 to Goodrich and Symonds Yat East. Continue through village to car park at end of road*

At the foot of a wooded cliff overlooking the River Wye, this hotel offers mainly spacious bedrooms, including some four-posters. All are well equipped, although there is no TV as reception is too poor. Most have either river or garden views, as does the attractive restaurant. In chilly weather, welcoming fires burn in the bar and lounge.

ROOMS: 21 en suite (1 fmly) s £33-£48; d £66-£86 (incl. bkfst) * LB **FACILITIES:** Fishing **CONF:** Thtr 70 Class 25 Board 30 Del from £85 * **PARKING:** 80 **CARDS:**

TADCASTER, North Yorkshire — Map 08 SE44

★★★75% Hazlewood Castle

Paradise Ln, Hazlewood LS24 9NJ
☎ 01937 535353 ▯ 01937 530630
e-mail: info@hazlewood-castle.co.uk

***Dir:** signposted off the A64, W of Tadcaster & before the A1/M1 link road*

Mentioned in the Domesday Book, this castle, set in 77 acres of parkland, opened in the spring of 1998 as a luxurious hotel. Hospitality and service are of the highest order. Bedrooms, many of them with private sitting rooms, are split between the main house and other buildings in the courtyard.

ROOMS: 9 en suite 12 annexe en suite s £95-£195; d £125-£300 (incl. bkfst) * LB **FACILITIES:** STV Croquet lawn ch fac Xmas **CONF:** Thtr 150 Class 60 Board 36 Del £160 * **PARKING:** 150 **NOTES:** No smoking in restaurant **CARDS:**

TADWORTH, Surrey
Map 04 TQ25

⌂ Premier Lodge

Brighton Rd, Burgh Heath KT20 6BW
☎ 0870 700 1438 Fax 0870 700 1439

Premier Lodge offers modern, well equipped, en suite accommodation suitable for both business and leisure travellers. Meals can be taken at the adjacent popular restaurant and bar which is fully licensed. For further details, consult the Hotel Groups page.

ROOMS: 75 en suite d £49.50 *

TALKE, Staffordshire
Map 07 SJ85

⌂ *Travelodge*

Travelodge

Newcastle Rd ST7 1UP
☎ 01782 777000 Fax 01782 777000

Dir: *at junct of A34/A500*

This modern building offers accommodation in smart, spacious and well equipped bedrooms, all with en suite bathrooms. Refreshments may be taken at the nearby family restaurant. For further details and the Travelodge phone number, consult the Hotel Groups page.

ROOMS: 62 en suite **CONF:** Thtr 50 Class 25 Board 32

TAMWORTH, Staffordshire
Map 07 SK20

★★66% Drayton Court Hotel

65 Coleshill St, Fazeley B78 3RG
☎ 01827 285805 Fax 01827 284842

Dir: *from M42 junct 9 then A446 to Litchfield at next rdbt turn right onto A4091 after 2m Drayton Manor Park on left hotel further along on right*

The Drayton Court Hotel dates back to the 18th century and retains much of its original charm and character. The recently refurbished bedrooms are all well equipped, attractive and individually styled. Public rooms include a cosy bar with panelled walls, comfortable lounge and spacious restaurant. A convenient car park is situated at the rear and service is friendly.

ROOMS: 19 en suite (3 fmly) s £40-£130; d £70-£155 (incl. bkfst) * LB
PARKING: 22 **NOTES:** Closed 24-27 Dec **CARDS:**

★★65% Globe Inn

Lower Gungate B79 7AW
☎ 01827 60455 Fax 01827 63575

Dir: *follow signs Lower Gungate car park and shops, Hotel is adjacent to car park*

Located in the centre of Tamworth, this popular inn provides well equipped and modern accommodation. The recently refurbished public areas feature a spacious lounge bar and a relaxed dining area where a varied selection of dishes is available. There is a function room for up to 100 delegates and public parking adjacent to the hotel.

continued on p550

T

TAMWORTH, continued

ROOMS: 18 en suite (2 fmly) No smoking in 2 bedrooms **FACILITIES:** STV **CONF:** Class 90 Board 90 **NOTES:** No dogs (ex guide dogs) No smoking in restaurant **CARDS:**

Travelodge

Travelodge

Green Ln B77 5PS
☎ Central Res 0800 850950 01525 878450
Dir: *A5/M42 junct 10*
This modern building offers accommodation in smart, spacious and well equipped bedrooms. Refreshments may be taken at the nearby family restaurant. For further details and the Travelodge phone number, consult the Hotel Groups page.
ROOMS: 62 en suite

TANKERSLEY, South Yorkshire — Map 08 SK39

★★★69% Tankersley Manor

Church Ln S75 3DQ
☎ 01226 744700 01226 745405
Dir: *from M1 junct 36 take A61 Sheffield road. Hotel 0.5m on left*
This stone-built hotel, originally a farmhouse, offers modern, attractive bedrooms. An adjoining building provides additional bedrooms and meeting rooms. Public areas include a spacious restaurant and a popular pub; a good range of meals is available.
ROOMS: 70 en suite (2 fmly) No smoking in all bedrooms s £75-£105; d £85-£115 (incl. bkfst) * **FACILITIES:** STV Golf 18 **CONF:** Thtr 400 Class 200 Board 50 Del from £95 * **PARKING:** 300 **NOTES:** No dogs (ex guide dogs) No smoking in restaurant Civ Wed 120
CARDS:

See advert on page 549

TAPLOW, Buckinghamshire — Map 04 SU98

Premier Collection

★★★★★ *Cliveden*

SL6 0JF
☎ 01628 668561 01628 661837
Cliveden Hotel is approached through a 375-acre National Trust managed estate. Visitors are treated as house guests and staff recapture the country house tradition of fine hospitality and service. Bedrooms are steeped in quality and individual style. Guests can dine in the Terrace Restaurant with views across the parterre, or in the discreet luxury of Waldo's Restaurant.
ROOMS: 32 en suite 7 annexe en suite No smoking in 13 bedrooms **FACILITIES:** STV Indoor swimming (H) Outdoor swimming (H) Tennis (hard) Fishing Squash Riding Snooker Sauna Solarium Gym Jacuzzi/spa Indoor tennis/Turkish bath/massage entertainment **CONF:** Thtr 42 Class 70 Board 28 **SERVICES:** Lift **PARKING:** 63 **NOTES:** No smoking in restaurant **CARDS:**

★★★74% Taplow House Hotel

Berry Hill SL6 0DA
☎ 01628 670056 01628 773625
e-mail: taplow@wrensgroup.com
Dir: *turn off A4 onto Berry Hill, hotel 0.5m on right*
Dating from 1598, this elegant Georgian manor has been beautifully restored and offers a high standard of accommodation. It boasts several air conditioned conference rooms, an elegant restaurant and a comfortable drawing room with an oak bar.
ROOMS: 32 en suite (4 fmly) No smoking in all bedrooms s fr £140; d fr £175 * LB **FACILITIES:** STV Croquet lawn Putting green Xmas **CONF:** Thtr 100 Class 50 Board 40 Del from £155 * **SERVICES:** air con **PARKING:** 100 **NOTES:** No dogs (ex guide dogs) Civ Wed 95
CARDS:

TARPORLEY, Cheshire — Map 07 SJ56

★★★62% *The Wild Boar*

Whitchurch Rd, Beeston CW6 9NW
☎ 01829 260309 01829 261081
Dir: *turn off A51 Nantwich/Chester rd onto A49 to Whitchurch at Red Fox pub traffic lights, hotel on left at brow of hill after about 1.5m*
A black and white half-timbered Grade II listed building built in the 17th century as a hunting lodge. Later extensions have resulted in spacious and comfortably furnished bedrooms, stylish bar and lounge areas and a warm and intimate restaurant.
ROOMS: 37 en suite (10 fmly) No smoking in 10 bedrooms **FACILITIES:** STV **CONF:** Thtr 150 Class 33 Board 36 **PARKING:** 80
CARDS:

TAUNTON, Somerset — Map 03 ST22

Premier Collection

★★★ Castle

Castle Green TA1 1NF
☎ 01823 272671 01823 336066
e-mail: reception@the-castle-hotel.com
Dir: *from M5 junct 25/26 follow town centre and signs to Hotel*
This long standing hotel, owned and run by the same family for many years, occupies an enviable position in the heart of town. Instantly recognisable by its wisteria-covered front, the hotel has delightful bedrooms and public rooms, which offer every creature comfort. The kitchen team create excellent British dishes and there is a stunning brasserie.
ROOMS: 44 en suite d fr £145 (incl. bkfst) * LB **FACILITIES:** STV Xmas **CONF:** Thtr 100 Class 40 Board 40 Del from £135 * **SERVICES:** Lift **PARKING:** 40 **NOTES:** No smoking in restaurant
CARDS:

★★★75% The Mount Somerset
Henlade TA3 5NB
☎ 01823 442500 Fax 01823 442900
Dir: *turn off M5 at junct 25, take A358 towards Chard/Ilminster, at Henlade right into Stoke Rd, left at T-junct at end Stoke Rd then right into drive*
This splendid Georgian house stands high on the Blackdown Hills with wonderful views of the Somerset countryside. Public rooms are a blend of elegance, style and intimacy with sumptuous sofas beside a crackling log fire. Bedrooms are well appointed with rich fabrics and some wonderful beds and bathrooms. A pleasing, daily changing menu is served in the dining room.
ROOMS: 11 en suite No smoking in 6 bedrooms s £100-£125; d £120-£170 (incl. bkfst) * LB **FACILITIES:** Arrangement with health club adjacent entertainment Xmas **CONF:** Thtr 50 Class 30 Board 20 Del from £110 * **SERVICES:** Lift **PARKING:** 100 **NOTES:** No dogs
CARDS:

See advert on this page

★★★71% Rumwell Manor
Rumwell TA4 1EL
Best Western
☎ 01823 461902 Fax 01823 254861
e-mail: rumhotel@aol.com
Dir: *leave M5 junct 26 follow signs to Wellington, turn onto A38 to Taunton, hotel is 2.5m on right*
Situated in mellow Somerset countryside, Rumwell Manor offers easy access to the centre of Taunton and the M5. Bedrooms vary, with those in the main house offering greater space and character. In the candlelit restaurant an interesting selection of freshly prepared dishes is offered. A cosy bar and adjacent lounge are available for guests.
ROOMS: 10 en suite 10 annexe en suite (3 fmly) No smoking in 2 bedrooms s £57-£67; d £77-£97 * LB **FACILITIES:** Xmas **CONF:** Thtr 40 Class 24 Board 26 Del from £94 * **PARKING:** 40 **NOTES:** No smoking in restaurant Civ Wed 50 **CARDS:**

★★★63% *Posthouse Taunton*
Deane Gate Av TA1 2UA
Posthouse
☎ 0870 400 9080 Fax 01823 332266
Dir: *adjacent to junct 25 on M5*
Situated at Junction 25 of the M5, this newly refurbished hotel is suitable for both business and leisure travellers. In addition to a range of meeting rooms and good leisure facilities, this bright establishment provides smart modern accommodation in well equipped bedrooms with en suite bathrooms.
ROOMS: 99 en suite (68 fmly) No smoking in 55 bedrooms **FACILITIES:** Gym Pool table ch fac **CONF:** Thtr 300 Class 110 Board 105 **SERVICES:** Lift **PARKING:** 300 **CARDS:**

★★73% Farthings Hotel & Restaurant
Hatch Beauchamp TA3 6SG
☎ 01823 480664 Fax 01823 481118
e-mail: farthing1@aol.com
Dir: *from A358, between Taunton and Ilminster turn into Hatch Beauchamp for hotel in village centre*
In a quiet village location, this attractive Georgian hotel offers tastefully furnished and decorated bedrooms. In addition to the lounge bar, a comfortable sitting room is available for guests. A well balanced choice of dishes is served in the dining rooms. A separate cottage is also available to rent.

continued on p552

TAUNTON, continued

Farthings Hotel & Restaurant, Taunton

ROOMS: 9 en suite (2 fmly) No smoking in all bedrooms s £59-£69; d £87-£97 (incl. bkfst) * LB **FACILITIES:** Croquet lawn Xmas **CONF:** Thtr 24 Class 18 Board 16 Del from £90 * **PARKING:** 22 **NOTES:** No dogs (ex guide dogs) No smoking in restaurant Civ Wed 61 **CARDS:**

★★66% Corner House Hotel

Park St TA1 4DQ
☎ 01823 284683 01823 323464
e-mail: res@corner-house.co.uk
Dir: *0.3m from centre of Taunton (5 mins walk). Hotel on junction of Park Street & A38 Wellington Road*

This Victorian house retains much of its character and many period features. A friendly team of staff create a relaxed atmosphere for guests. Accommodation is of a high standard with comfortable rooms with modern fittings. A choice of freshly prepared dishes is offered in the cosy bar and the more formal surroundings of the restaurant.

ROOMS: 33 rms (27 en suite) (4 fmly) s fr £42.50; d fr £49 * LB **CONF:** Thtr 60 Class 60 Board 35 Del from £75 * **PARKING:** 42 **NOTES:** No dogs (ex guide dogs) No smoking in restaurant **CARDS:**

See advert on opposite page

★★61% Falcon

Henlade TA3 5DH
☎ 01823 442502 01823 442670
Dir: *M5 junct 25 1m E of A358 Taunton to Yeovil Road*

Conveniently located on the eastern side of the town, minutes from the M5, this Victorian hotel provides bedrooms of varying sizes, equipped with all modern comforts. The convivial bar is a popular meeting place for residents.

ROOMS: 11 en suite (2 fmly) No smoking in 3 bedrooms **FACILITIES:** STV **CONF:** Thtr 65 Class 40 Board 40 Del from £80 * **PARKING:** 25 **NOTES:** No smoking in restaurant Closed 25 Dec **CARDS:**

⇧ Express by Holiday Inn Taunton

Express by Holiday Inn

Blackbrook Park Av TA1 2RW
☎ 01823 624000 01823 624024
Dir: *M5 junct25. Follow signs for Blackbrook Business Park. 100yds down on the right, just off rdbt at junct25*

A modern budget hotel offering comfortable accommodation in refreshing, spacious and comprehensively-equipped bedrooms, en suite bathrooms with power showers and continental buffet breakfast included in the room rate. Suitable for business

continued

travellers or families. For further details and the Express by Holiday Inn phone number, consult the Hotel Groups page.

ROOMS: 92 en suite (incl. cont bkfst) d £43-£49.50 * **CONF:** Thtr 30 Class 15 Board 20

⇧ Premier Lodge

PREMIER LODGE
THE BEST. REST ASSURED.

Ilminster Rd, Rushton TA3 5LU
☎ 0870 700 1558 0870 700 1559

Premier Lodge offers modern, well equipped, en suite accommodation suitable for both business and leisure travellers. Meals can be taken at the adjacent popular restaurant and bar which is fully licensed. For further details, consult the Hotel Groups page.

ROOMS: 38 en suite d £42 *

⇧ *Travelodge*

Travelodge

Riverside Retail Park, Hankridge Farm TA1 2LR
☎ 01823 444702
Dir: *M5 junc25*

This modern building offers accommodation in smart, spacious and well equipped bedrooms, all with en suite bathrooms. Refreshments may be taken at the nearby family restaurant. For further details and the Travelodge phone number, consult the Hotel Groups page.

ROOMS: 48 en suite

TAVISTOCK, Devon Map 02 SX47

★★★68% Bedford

1 Plymouth Rd PL19 8BB
☎ 01822 613221 01822 618034
Dir: *leave M5 junct 31 - Launceston/Okehampton A30. Take A386 - Tavistock. On entering Tavistock follow signs for town centre. Hotel opposite church*

Built on the site of a Benedictine Abbey in 1820, the Bedford Hotel is an impressive, castellated building, situated in the town centre.

continued

The refurbished bedrooms are ideally equipped for both business and leisure guests, and public areas combine comfort with the hotel's abundant character. In the Woburn Restaurant, an imaginative and innovative, fixed-price menu is served, gaining a popular following locally.
ROOMS: 30 en suite (1 fmly) No smoking in 11 bedrooms s £35-£45; d fr £70 (incl. bkfst) * LB **FACILITIES:** Xmas **CONF:** Thtr 70 Class 45 Board 25 Del from £72 * **PARKING:** 50 **NOTES:** No smoking in restaurant **CARDS:**

TEBAY, Cumbria — Map 12 NY60

★★★71%
Westmorland Hotel & Bretherdale Restaurant
Orton CA10 3SB
☎ 015396 24351 015396 24354
Dir: *next to Westmorland's Tebay Services on the M6, easily reached from the southbound carriageway using the road linking the two service areas between*

This modern family-owned hotel enjoys stunning views of the central Cumbrian moors whilst enjoying convenient access from the M6 at the Westmorland services. The stylish bedrooms and refurbished public rooms reflect a cosmopolitan approach with pleasing interior design used to good effect. Staff are keen to please and a pleasant menu is offered in the open-plan Bretherdale restaurant.
ROOMS: 53 en suite (30 fmly) No smoking in 20 bedrooms s fr £49; d fr £59 * LB **FACILITIES:** STV Xmas **CONF:** Thtr 80 Class 40 Board 30 Del from £80 * **SERVICES:** Lift **PARKING:** 100 **NOTES:** No smoking in restaurant Civ Wed 100
CARDS:

See advert on this page

TEES-SIDE AIRPORT, Co Durham — Map 08 NZ31

★★★64% **The St George**
Middleton St George, Darlington DL2 1RH
☎ 01325 332631 01325 333851
e-mail: bookings@stgeorgehotel.net.
Dir: *turn off A67 by pass directly into Airport grounds*
This former wartime officers' mess is conveniently situated within walking distance of the airport terminal building. Bedrooms, having been refurbished, are modern and well equipped. Staff throughout are friendly and professional and there are also versatile banqueting and conference facilities.
ROOMS: 59 en suite No smoking in 14 bedrooms s fr £62.50; d fr £72.50 (incl. bkfst) * **FACILITIES:** STV Sauna Solarium Xmas **CONF:** Thtr 160 Class 60 Board 50 **PARKING:** 100
CARDS: 

Corner House Hotel, Taunton

TEIGNMOUTH, Devon Map 03 SX97

★★70% Ness House
Marine Dr, Shaldon TQ14 0HP
☎ 01626 873480 🖷 01626 873486
Dir: *from M5 take A380 turn onto A381 to Teignmouth, cross bridge to Shaldon, hotel 0.5m on left on Torquay Rd*
Overlooking the Teign Estuary, this Georgian house has kept its original character as a nobleman's summer residence. As an alternative to formal dining in the elegant restaurant, meals are also served in the bar and conservatory. Bedrooms are well equipped, spacious and comfortable, many including a balcony and sea view.
ROOMS: 7 en suite 5 annexe en suite (2 fmly) No smoking in 4 bedrooms s £45-£69; d £79-£99 (incl. bkfst) * LB **FACILITIES:** STV ch fac Xmas **PARKING:** 20 **NOTES:** No dogs (ex guide dogs) No smoking in restaurant Closed 24 & 25 Dec **CARDS:**

TELFORD, Shropshire Map 07 SJ60
see also Worfield

★★★★64% *Buckatree Hall*
The Wrekin, Wellington TF6 5AL
☎ 01952 641821 🖷 01952 247540
Dir: *exit 7 of M54, turn left and left again for 1m*

Dating from 1820, this former hunting lodge is located in an extensive wooded estate on the slopes of the Wrekin. Bedrooms are well equipped and have been furnished to a high standard. A suite is available, some rooms are inter-connecting, and some have balconies. Public rooms include function and conference facilities.
ROOMS: 60 en suite (3 fmly) No smoking in 4 bedrooms **FACILITIES:** STV Pool table entertainment **CONF:** Thtr 200 Class 100 Board 60 **SERVICES:** Lift **PARKING:** 100 **NOTES:** No smoking in restaurant **CARDS:**

★★★67% Clarion Hotel Madely Court
Castlefields Way, Madeley TF7 5DW
☎ 01952 680068 🖷 01952 684275
e-mail: admin@gb068.u-net.com
Dir: *M54 junct 4, A4169 Telford, A442 at 2nd rdbt signs for Kidderminster, continue along (ignore sign to Madeley & Kidderminster) 1st left off rdbt*

A delightful 16th-century manor house with a lakeside setting. Panelled walls, large fireplaces and a solid oak spiral staircase give character to the original house, where the historic bedrooms have fine antique furnishings. The modern adjacent wing has, appropriately, more modern style bedrooms.
ROOMS: 29 en suite 18 annexe en suite (1 fmly) No smoking in 6 bedrooms s £90-£98; d £110-£120 * LB **FACILITIES:** Fishing Archery Horse riding arranged Xmas **CONF:** Thtr 220 Class 150 Board 50 Del from £130 * **PARKING:** 180 **NOTES:** Civ Wed 190
CARDS:

★★★67% Valley
TF8 7DW
☎ 01952 432247 🖷 01952 432308
e-mail: valley.hotel@ironbridge.fsnet.co.uk
Dir: *M6, M54 junct 6 onto A5223 to Ironbridge*
Best Western
A personally run hotel situated in attractive gardens and close to the famous iron bridge at Coalbrookdale. Bedrooms vary in size and are split between the main house and an attractive mews development. A wide range of dishes is offered in the restaurant, including a selection of healthier options and vegetarian meals.
ROOMS: 35 en suite s £95; d £110 (incl. bkfst) * LB **FACILITIES:** STV ch fac **CONF:** Thtr 250 Class 100 Board 50 Del £120 * **PARKING:** 100 **NOTES:** No dogs (ex guide dogs) No smoking in restaurant Civ Wed 200
CARDS:

★★★66% Telford Golf & Country Club
Great Hay Dr, Sutton Hill TF7 4DT
☎ 01952 429977 🖷 01952 586602
Dir: *M54 junct 4, A442 - Kidderminster, follow signs for Telford Golf Club*
REGAL

A modern and much extended former farmhouse situated in an elevated position overlooking Ironbridge Gorge. The well equipped bedrooms are located in several different wings some with fine views over the gorge and others looking out over the golf course. The Ironbridge Restaurant offers carvery and carte menus, and Darby's Pantry provides light meals in a more informal setting. The many facilities include an 18-hole golf course and driving range, a large indoor swimming pool, squash courts, a gymnasium and a billiards room.
ROOMS: 96 en suite (16 fmly) No smoking in 36 bedrooms d £85-£115 * LB **FACILITIES:** Indoor swimming (H) Golf 18 Squash Snooker Sauna Solarium Gym Pool table Putting green Jacuzzi/spa Health & Beauty Driving range Xmas **CONF:** Thtr 200 Class 140 Board 60 Del £119 * **PARKING:** 200 **NOTES:** No smoking in restaurant
CARDS:

★★68% White House
Wellington Rd, Muxton TF2 8NG
☎ 01952 604276 & 603603 🖷 01952 670336
e-mail: james@whhotel.co.uk
Dir: *off A518 Telford-Stafford road*
The White House is a friendly family-run hotel which provides well equipped modern accommodation. The attractive public areas offer a choice of bars and a very pleasant restaurant, where a wide range of dishes is available. There is also a small lounge for residents and a beer garden.
ROOMS: 32 en suite (3 fmly) s £50-£62; d £65-£75 (incl. bkfst) * LB **PARKING:** 100 **NOTES:** No dogs (ex guide dogs)
CARDS:

Bad hair day? Hairdryers in all rooms three stars and above.

T

★★65% *Oaks Hotel & Restaurant*

Redhill, St Georges TF2 9NZ
☎ 01952 620126 ▯ 01952 620257
Dir: *M54 junct 4, A5 Cannock 1.5 miles*

The Oaks is a family-run hotel, popular with both commercial visitors and tourists. It provides well equipped accommodation, including family rooms. There is a pleasant bar, beer garden, function room, and an attractively appointed restaurant serving a good choice of popular dishes. The hotel is located on the A5, just east of Telford and can best be found by following signs for the Crematorium.

ROOMS: 12 en suite (4 fmly) **CONF:** Thtr 40 Class 40 Board 25 **PARKING:** 36 **NOTES:** No dogs (ex guide dogs) **CARDS:**

★★62% Arleston Inn

Arleston Ln, Wellington TF1 2LA
☎ 01952 501881 ▯ 01952 506429
Dir: *from M54 junct 6 take A5223 Ironbridge road, 4th exit at next rdbt past Lawley School right into Arleston Lane*

This small privately owned and personally run hotel has a lot of charm and character and was once a coaching inn. It is conveniently located for access to the M54 motorway and Telford centre. The well maintained accommodation has modern furnishings and equipment. Apart from the bar, there is a conservatory lounge which overlooks the lovely garden, and a popular restaurant where a good choice of dishes is available.

ROOMS: 7 en suite s fr £40; d fr £50 (incl. bkfst) * **FACILITIES:** Xmas **PARKING:** 40 **NOTES:** No dogs (ex guide dogs) No smoking in restaurant **CARDS:**

⌂ *Travelodge*

Travelodge

Whitchurch Dr, Shawbirch TF1 3QA
☎ 01952 251244 ▯ 01952 251244
Dir: *1m NW, on A5223*

This modern building offers accommodation in smart, spacious and well equipped bedrooms, all with en suite bathrooms. Refreshments may be taken at the nearby family restaurant. For further details and the Travelodge phone number, consult the Hotel Groups page.

ROOMS: 40 en suite

TEMPLE SOWERBY, Cumbria — Map 12 NY62

★★★71% ❀ Temple Sowerby House

CA10 1RZ
☎ 017683 61578 ▯ 017683 61958
Dir: *midway between Penrith and Appleby, 7m from M6 junct 40*

This delightful former Cumbrian farmhouse has a relaxed country house atmosphere. The bedrooms are quite individual with both traditional and modern furnishings, and the restaurant is a particularly pleasant venue for dinner.

ROOMS: 9 en suite 4 annexe en suite (2 fmly) s fr £68; d fr £96 (incl. bkfst) * LB **FACILITIES:** Fishing Croquet lawn Xmas **CONF:** Thtr 30 Class 20 Board 20 Del from £95 * **PARKING:** 15 **NOTES:** No smoking in restaurant **CARDS:**

Late for dinner? Quality Standards star rating means that last orders for dinner should be no earlier than:
★ 6.30pm ★★ 7.00pm ★★★ 8.00pm
★★★★ 9.00pm ★★★★★ 10.00pm

TENBURY WELLS, Worcestershire — Map 07 SO56

★★66% *Cadmore Lodge*

Berrington Green, St Michaels WR15 8TQ
☎ 01584 810044 ▯ 01584 810044
e-mail: info@cadmorelodge.demon.co.uk
Dir: *on A4112 from Tenbury Wells to Leominster, turn right at St Michaels Church, signposted to Cadmore Lodge, hotel 0.75m on left*

This modern hotel is situated a short distance from Tenbury Wells in a secluded location on a 70-acre private estate that features a 9-hole golf course, two fishing lakes and indoor leisure facilities. The traditionally furnished bedrooms have modern facilities and a large function room, with lake views, is a popular venue.

ROOMS: 14 en suite (1 fmly) No smoking in all bedrooms **FACILITIES:** Indoor swimming (H) Golf 9 Tennis (hard) Fishing Gym Pool table Jacuzzi/spa Bowling green Steam room **CONF:** Thtr 100 Class 40 Board 30 **PARKING:** 60 **NOTES:** No dogs No smoking in restaurant **CARDS:**

See advert on this page

TETBURY, Gloucestershire Map 03 ST89

Premier Collection

★★★ ❀❀ **Calcot Manor**
Calcot GL8 8YJ
☎ 01666 890391 🖷 01666 890394
e-mail: reception@calcotmanor.co.uk
Dir: *4m West of Tetbuty W at junct A4135/A46*
Originally farmed by Cistercian monks, Calcot Manor has a 14th-century tithe barn amongst its outbuildings. Retaining much of its original charm, this beautiful country house offers high standards of accommodation. In the elegant and relaxing sitting rooms log fires burn in the winter, and a bright and stylish restaurant extends into a conservatory. The cooking is imaginative with a Mediterranean bias and good robust flavours. Children are made welcome with some specially designed family rooms and a superb playroom. The Gumstool bar offers informal dining in a country pub atmosphere.
ROOMS: 8 en suite 20 annexe en suite (10 fmly) s fr £115; d £130-£175 (incl. bkfst) * LB **FACILITIES:** Outdoor swimming (H) Croquet lawn Clay pigeon shooting ch fac Xmas **CONF:** Thtr 60 Class 40 Board 30 Del from £150 * **PARKING:** 150 **NOTES:** No dogs (ex guide dogs) No smoking in restaurant Civ Wed 90
CARDS:

★★★ 77% ❀❀❀ **Close**
8 Long St GL8 8AQ
☎ 01666 502272 🖷 01666 504401
Dir: *in the centre of Tetbury, from M4 junct 17 onto A429 to Malmesbury, Tetbury signposted from here. M5 junct 14 onto B4509 follow signs to Tetbury*
Set in the heart of this pretty Cotswold town, this special hotel has a genuine country house feel to it. Bedrooms are decorated and furnished with an air of luxury and include many thoughtful touches. The public rooms provide a range of relaxing areas to sit and take refreshment, including the terrace in the lovely walled garden. As well as the brasserie, the main restaurant is the venue for some impressive, modern British cooking.
ROOMS: 15 en suite s £50-£85; d £75-£140 (incl. bkfst) * LB **FACILITIES:** STV Croquet lawn Xmas **CONF:** Thtr 50 Board 22 Del from £130 * **PARKING:** 22 **NOTES:** No smoking in restaurant Civ Wed 50
CARDS:

★★★ 74% ❀ **Snooty Fox**
Market Place GL8 8DD
☎ 01666 502436 🖷 01666 503479
e-mail: res@snooty-fox.co.uk
Dir: *in the centre of the town, by market place*
Situated in the picturesque market town of Tetbury this former 16th-century coaching Inn provides high levels of comfort and quality. In recent years bedrooms and public areas have been transformed to a high standard. The charming bar and restaurant areas are the focal point, serving good wholesome cooking. Meeting rooms are available and there is a comfortable lounge.
ROOMS: 12 en suite s £67.50-£95; d £90-£145 (incl. bkfst) * LB **FACILITIES:** STV Xmas **CONF:** Thtr 30 Board 15 **NOTES:** No dogs (ex guide dogs) No smoking in restaurant
CARDS:

★★★ 70% ***Hare & Hounds***
Westonbirt GL8 8QL
☎ 01666 880233 🖷 01666 880241
Dir: *2.5m SW of Tetbury on A433*

This impressive country house lies close to Westonbirt Arboretum. The public areas are spacious and welcoming. Bedrooms are generally of a good size and are furnished in the character of the building. Some are located in the coach house with their own entrances.
ROOMS: 24 en suite 7 annexe en suite (3 fmly) No smoking in 12 bedrooms **FACILITIES:** Tennis (hard) Squash Pool table Croquet lawn Table tennis **CONF:** Thtr 120 Class 80 Board 30 **PARKING:** 85 **NOTES:** No smoking in restaurant **CARDS:**

★★★ 67% ***Priory Inn***
London Rd GL8 8JJ
☎ 01666 502251 🖷 01666 503534
Dir: *on A433, Cirencester/Tetbury road 200yds from High St*
This modern hotel offers a good all-round standard of comfort, and parts of the house have an interesting theatrical theme. Bedrooms are attractive, with well chosen fabrics and decor, and the lounge has an airy 'colonial' style.
ROOMS: 14 en suite (1 fmly) No smoking in 3 bedrooms **FACILITIES:** STV entertainment **CONF:** Thtr 70 Class 25 Board 35 **PARKING:** 40 **CARDS:**

TEWKESBURY, Gloucestershire Map 03 SO83

★★★ 68% **Tewkesbury Park Hotel**
Lincoln Green Ln GL20 7DN
☎ 01684 295405 🖷 01684 292386
REGAL
Dir: *M5 junct 9 take A438 through Tewkesbury onto A38 passing Abbey on left, turn right into Lincoln Green Lane before Esso Station*
An extended 18th-century mansion with fine views over the Vale of Evesham and River Severn. There is a fully equipped leisure centre and an 18-hole golf course in the grounds. A choice of dining areas and a number of function rooms are available.
ROOMS: 78 en suite (12 fmly) No smoking in 35 bedrooms s £71-£85; d fr £72 (incl. bkfst) * LB **FACILITIES:** STV Indoor swimming (H) Golf 18 Tennis (hard) Squash Sauna Solarium Gym Putting green Jacuzzi/spa Activity field Xmas **CONF:** Thtr 160 Class 90 Board 60 Del £140 * **PARKING:** 200 **CARDS:**

★★★ 65% ***Bell***
57 Church St GL20 5SA
☎ 01684 293293 🖷 01684 295938
Dir: *on A38 in town centre opposite Abbey*
This former 14th century coaching house is on the edge of town, opposite the Norman Abbey. Bedrooms are comfortably furnished and feature thoughtful extras such as sherry. Open plan public areas are bright and inviting and include a popular restaurant where cuisine continues to show much promise.
ROOMS: 25 en suite (1 fmly) No smoking in 5 bedrooms **CONF:** Thtr 40 Class 15 Board 20 **PARKING:** 35 **NOTES:** No smoking in restaurant RS 25 Dec & 1 Jan **CARDS:**

★★★59% Royal Hop Pole
Church St GL20 5RT
☎ 01684 293236 🖷 01684 296680
Dir: *M5 junct 9 head for Tewkesbury approx 1.5m. At War Memorial rdbt straight across Hotel is on the right*
Situated in the heart of the picturesque town of Tewkesbury stands the Royal Hop Pole Hotel. This former coaching Inn dating back to the 14th century retains many of its original features including sloping floors and exposed beams. Bedrooms vary in size and decor and one has a four poster bed. Additional features include a comfortable lounge, cosy bar, meeting rooms, restaurant and convenient car park.
ROOMS: 24 en suite 5 annexe en suite (1 fmly) No smoking in 14 bedrooms s £74; d £84 * LB **FACILITIES:** Xmas **CONF:** Thtr 50 Class 25 Board 20 Del from £99 * **PARKING:** 30 **NOTES:** No smoking in restaurant **CARDS:**

THAME, Oxfordshire — Map 04 SP70

★★★76% Spread Eagle
Cornmarket OX9 2BW
☎ 01844 213661 🖷 01844 261380
e-mail: enquiries@spreadeaglehotel.fsnet.co.uk
Dir: *town centre on A418 Oxford to Aylesbury Road, exit 6 M40 south exit 8 north*
Expect a warm, friendly welcome from the hosts and their professional team of staff at this popular hotel, situated in the bustling market town of Thame and within easy reach of Oxford city centre. The accommodation varies in size and style and ranges from the spacious new rooms in an extension, to bedrooms in the main building offering traditional period charm. There are extensive banqueting facilities and the traditional restaurant offers a wide selection of interesting dishes.
ROOMS: 33 en suite (1 fmly) s £89.95-£104.95; d £104.95-£122.95 (incl. cont bkfst) * LB **FACILITIES:** Xmas **CONF:** Thtr 250 Class 100 Board 50 Del £144.95 * **PARKING:** 80 **NOTES:** No dogs (ex guide dogs) Closed 28-30 Dec Civ Wed 200 **CARDS:**

Travelodge
OX9 3XD
☎ 01844 218740 🖷 01844 218740
Dir: *A418/B4011*
This modern building offers accommodation in smart, spacious and well equipped bedrooms, all with en suite bathrooms. Refreshments may be taken at the nearby family restaurant. For further details and the Travelodge phone number, consult the Hotel Groups page.
ROOMS: 31 en suite

THAXTED, Essex — Map 05 TL63

★★70% Four Seasons
Walden Rd CM6 2RE
☎ 01371 830129 🖷 01371 830835
Dir: *0.5m N on the B184 at the junction with the B1051 Gt Sampford/Haverhill road*
Set in two acres of its own grounds, this lovely, privately owned hotel is noted for its courteous service. Bedrooms are tastefully decorated, well laid out and feature a thoughtful range of extra facilities. Guests may choose to dine in the informal Grill Room, or the more formal Restaurant. There is also a quiet first floor residents lounge in which guests can relax. An added advantage for guests using Stansted Airport is free parking for 14 days.
ROOMS: 9 en suite No smoking in all bedrooms s £55-£65; d £65-£75 * LB **CONF:** Thtr 70 Class 60 Board 40 **PARKING:** 100 **NOTES:** No dogs No children 12yrs No smoking in restaurant
CARDS:

THEALE, Berkshire — Map 04 SU67

Travelodge (Westbound)
Burghfield RG30 3UQ
☎ 0118 956 6966
Dir: *M4 between junc 11&12*
This modern building offers accommodation in smart, spacious and well equipped bedrooms, all with en suite bathrooms. Refreshments may be taken at the nearby family restaurant. For further details and the Travelodge phone number, consult the Hotel Groups page.
ROOMS: 40 en suite

THETFORD, Norfolk — Map 05 TL88

see also Brandon (Suffolk)

★★65% The Thomas Paine Hotel
White Hart St IP24 1AA
☎ 01842 755631 🖷 01842 766505
e-mail: thomaspainehotel@hotmail.com
Dir: *heading N on the A11, at rdbt immediately before Thetford take A1075, the hotel is on the right hand side as you approach the town*
Close to the town centre, this popular hotel extends a friendly welcome and offers spacious public rooms and a choice of eating options in the open-plan bar and more formal restaurant. The bedrooms vary in size but all offer character and comfort.
ROOMS: 13 en suite (1 fmly) s £50-£53; d £62-£66 (incl. bkfst) * LB **FACILITIES:** Xmas **CONF:** Thtr 70 Class 35 Board 30 Del from £60 * **PARKING:** 30 **NOTES:** No smoking in restaurant
CARDS: 

THETFORD, continued

★★63% The Anchor Hotel
Bridge St IP24 3AE
☎ 01842 763925 🖷 01842 766873
e-mail: anchor@norfolk-hotels.co.uk
Dir: *leave A11 at Bury St Edmunds turn. Cross traffic lights, then left into Bridge Street. Hotel on right*
In a riverside setting within walking distance of the town centre, The Anchor is a popular venue for locals to enjoy a drink in one of the bars or a meal in the spacious restaurant. The bedrooms come in a range of shapes and styles, but all offer expected comforts.
ROOMS: 16 en suite s fr £42; d fr £54 (incl. bkfst) * **FACILITIES:** entertainment **CONF:** Thtr 180 Class 120 Board 60 **PARKING:** 60 **NOTES:** No dogs (ex guide dogs) RS 24-25 Dec **CARDS:**

THIRLSPOT, Cumbria — Map 11 NY31

★★★69% Kings Head Hotel & Inn
CA12 4TN
☎ 017687 72393 🖷 017687 72309
e-mail: kings@lakelandsheart.demon.co.uk
Dir: *from M6 junct 40 take A66 to Keswick, then A591 towards Grasmere to hotel in 4m*

Located just south of Keswick, this welcoming Jacobean inn provides a warm welcome. The bedrooms vary in size and style but all are furnished with attractive soft furnishings and quality pine furniture. Many enjoy delightful mountain views. Comfortable public rooms include an elegant restaurant, restful lounge and a more informal pub.
ROOMS: 17 en suite No smoking in 10 bedrooms s £29-£34; d £58-£64 (incl. bkfst) * **FACILITIES:** STV Pool table Free use of local Leisure Centre entertainment Xmas **CONF:** Thtr 100 Class 40 Board 20 Del from £60 * **PARKING:** 60 **NOTES:** No smoking in restaurant **CARDS:**

T

THIRSK, North Yorkshire — Map 08 SE48

★★71% Sheppard's
Church Farm, Front St, Sowerby YO7 1JF
☎ 01845 523655 🖷 01845 524720
e-mail: sheppards@thirskny.freeserve.co.uk
Dir: *take A61 Ripon road from Market Sq, at mini rdbt turn left towards Sowerby. Hotel on right 0.25m along Sowerby road*
Set in the village suburb of Sowerby, this former farm has evolved from the original granary and stables, grouped around the yard. Attractive bedrooms are decorated in cottage style with stripped pine, and are thoughtfully equipped. Public areas include a cheery bistro with a glass domed conservatory, and a more intimate restaurant.
ROOMS: 8 en suite No smoking in all bedrooms s £62; d £84 (incl. bkfst) * LB **CONF:** Thtr 80 Class 40 Board 30 **PARKING:** 30 **NOTES:** No dogs No children 10yrs Closed 1st wk Jan **CARDS:**

★★69% Golden Fleece
Best Western
42 Market Place YO7 1LL
☎ 01845 523108 🖷 01845 523996
Dir: *off A19 at the Thirsk turn off, proceed to the town centre, Hotel is situated on the southern edge of Market Place*
This delightful old coaching inn, once the haunt of Dick Turpin, lies behind a Queen Anne facade in the market square. It offers modern well equipped bedrooms, a cosy bar and a restaurant which provides a good choice of dishes. Friendly and attentive service is provided by a dedicated staff.
ROOMS: 18 en suite (3 fmly) s £65-£75; d £85-£110 * LB **FACILITIES:** ch fac Xmas **CONF:** Thtr 100 Class 40 Board 40 Del from £85 * **PARKING:** 50 **NOTES:** No smoking in restaurant Civ Wed 100 **CARDS:**

★★62% Three Tuns Hotel
Market Place YO7 1LH
☎ 01845 523124 🖷 01845 526126
e-mail: threetuns@talk21.com
Dir: *directly on A19, A61, 6m from A1 on A168 & A61*
This Georgian hotel stands in the corner of the Market Square and offers pleasantly furnished bedrooms. There is also a wide range of well produced food available.
ROOMS: 10 en suite (3 fmly) No smoking in all bedrooms s £40-£45; d £60-£65 (incl. bkfst) * LB **CONF:** Thtr 50 Board 35 **PARKING:** 52 **NOTES:** No smoking in restaurant **CARDS:**

THORNBURY, Gloucestershire — Map 03 ST69

Premier Collection

★★★ Thornbury Castle
Pride of Britain Member
Castle St BS35 1HH
☎ 01454 281182 🖷 01454 416188
e-mail: thornburycastle@compuserve.com
Dir: *on A38 travelling N from Bristol take the first turning to Thornbury. At end of the High St left into Castle St, entrance to Castle on left*
Located in its own splendid grounds, guests at this Tudor castle have included Henry VIII, Anne Boleyn and Mary Tudor, and modern day visitors have the unrivalled opportunity to sleep in the same historic rooms. Now a fine country house hotel, its sumptuous handmade furnishings combine with modern comforts to create a truly luxurious atmosphere. Service is professional yet approachable, and the galleried dining rooms make a memorable setting for some enjoyable meals.
ROOMS: 20 en suite s £105-£165; d £130-£350 (incl. cont bkfst) * LB **FACILITIES:** STV Croquet lawn Hot air ballooning Archery Xmas **CONF:** Thtr 36 Class 12 Board 24 Del from £190 * **PARKING:** 40 **NOTES:** No dogs (ex guide dogs) No smoking in restaurant Closed 4 days Jan Civ Wed 50 **CARDS:**

See advert under BRISTOL

★★67% Thornbury Golf Lodge
Bristol Rd BS35 3XL
☎ 01454 281144 📠 01454 281177
Dir: *from junct of M4/M5 take A38 N. At traffic lights (Berkeley Vale Motors) take left. Entrance 1m on left*
The old farmhouse exterior of Thornbury Golf Lodge disguises a completely refurbished interior with spacious and comfortable bedrooms, all well equipped and attractively decorated. Many include pleasant views over the Centre's two golf courses or towards the Severn estuary. Meals are taken in the adjacent golf clubhouse which features a full bar and a range of hot and cold food served all day.
ROOMS: 11 en suite d £45 * LB **FACILITIES:** STV Golf 36 Putting green **CONF:** Thtr 80 Class 20 Board 60 Del from £65 * **PARKING:** 150 **NOTES:** No dogs (ex guide dogs) No children 1yr **CARDS:**

THORNE, South Yorkshire — Map 08 SE61

★★70% Belmont
Horsefair Green DN8 5EE
☎ 01405 812320 📠 01405 740508
e-mail: belmonthotel@compuserve.com
Dir: *M18 exit 6 A614 signed Thorne. Hotel is on the right of the Market Place*
Standing in the centre of Thorne, this very friendly and well managed hotel features a delightful bar and well furnished restaurant offering a wide choice of dishes; there is also a small bistro. The bedrooms are modern, well equipped and have been delightfully furnished in pine.
ROOMS: 23 en suite (3 fmly) No smoking in 5 bedrooms s £59.95-£65.95; d £75.95-£98.95 (incl. bkfst) * LB **FACILITIES:** STV Xmas **CONF:** Thtr 60 Class 20 Board 25 Del from £69.95 * **PARKING:** 30 **NOTES:** Civ Wed **CARDS:**

THORNHAM, Norfolk — Map 09 TF74

★★65% Lifeboat Inn
Ship Ln PE36 6LT
☎ 01485 512236 📠 01485 512323
e-mail: reception@lifeboatinn.co.uk
Dir: *follow coast road from Hunstanton A149 for approx 6m and take first left after Thornham sign*
This 16th century ale house combines historic charm with 20th century comforts. The relaxing views over the open meadows lead to the distant horizon of Thornham Harbour and the sea. The attractive bedrooms are well equipped and suitably furnished. The popular bar and restaurant provide a wide choice of tempting meals.
ROOMS: 13 en suite (3 fmly) No smoking in all bedrooms s £40-£77; d £77-£84 (incl. bkfst) * LB **FACILITIES:** Xmas **CONF:** Thtr 50 Class 30 Board 30 **PARKING:** 120 **CARDS:**

THORNTON HOUGH, Merseyside — Map 07 SJ38

★★★70% Thornton Hall
Neston Rd CH63 1JF
☎ 0151 336 3938 📠 0151 336 7864
e-mail: thorntonhallhotel@btinternet.com
Dir: *M53 junct 4 take B5151 Neston onto B5136 to Thornton Hough*
Lying in several acres of mature grounds in the delightful village of Thornton Hough, this country house was built in the 18th century by a shipping magnate. The hall still features original stained glass windows and impressive oak panelling. Bedrooms are spacious with good facilities. An impressive leisure centre, which includes a 20m pool, is now part of the complex.

continued

ROOMS: 5 en suite 58 annexe en suite (6 fmly) **FACILITIES:** STV Indoor swimming (H) Tennis (grass) Sauna Solarium Gym Croquet lawn Jacuzzi/spa Hot tub Beauty Spa **CONF:** Thtr 200 Class 80 Board 40 Del from £105 * **PARKING:** 250 **NOTES:** Civ Wed 200
CARDS:

THORNTON WATLASS, North Yorkshire — Map 08 SE28

★69% Buck Inn
HG4 4AH
☎ 01677 422461 📠 01677 422447
Dir: *A684 towards Bedale, B6268 towards Masham, after 2m turn right at crossroads to Thornton Watlass, the hotel is situated by the Cricket Green*
This welcoming country inn, renowned for its food, is situated on the edge of the village green overlooking the cricket pitch, with part of the inn wall forming the boundary on match days. Cricket prints and old photographs are a feature of the small dining room and an open fire in the bar adds to the warm and intimate atmosphere. Lunch and dinners are served in the bar or dining room everyday and there is an excellent choice of dishes from an extensive menu. Bedrooms are brightly decorated, some overlook the green, others the sheltered garden at the back.
ROOMS: 7 rms (5 en suite) (1 fmly) s £32-£38; d £52-£58 (incl. bkfst) * LB **FACILITIES:** Fishing Pool table Quoits Childrens play area entertainment **CONF:** Thtr 70 Class 40 Board 30 Del from £60 * **PARKING:** 10 **NOTES:** No smoking in restaurant
CARDS:

THORPE (DOVEDALE), Derbyshire — Map 07 SK15

★★★71% Izaak Walton
DE6 2AY
☎ 01335 350555 📠 01335 350539
e-mail: reception@izaakwalton-hotel.com
Dir: *leave A515 on B5054, follow road to Thorpe village, continue straight through over cattle grids & 2 small bridges, take 1st right & sharp left*
This hotel is ideally situated in a peaceful spot with magnificent views over Thorpe Cloud. Many of the bedrooms have lovely views, and 'executive' rooms are particularly spacious. Meals are served in the bar area, with more formal dining in the Haddon restaurant, which also has splendid outlook. Fishing on the River Dove can be arranged.
ROOMS: 30 en suite (4 fmly) No smoking in 24 bedrooms s £83; d £108-£138 (incl. bkfst) * LB **FACILITIES:** Fishing Fly fishing Xmas **CONF:** Thtr 50 Class 40 Board 30 Del from £115 * **PARKING:** 80 **NOTES:** No smoking in restaurant Civ Wed 70
CARDS:

★★★64% The Peveril of the Peak
DE6 2AW
☎ 0870 400 8109 📠 01335 350507
Dir: *from M1 junct25, A52 towards Ashbourne then A515 towards Buxton for 1m to Thorpe. From M6 junct15/16, A50 to Stoke then A515 to Ashbourne and Thorpe*
Situated in the beautiful scenery of Dovedale, this hotel is named after one of Sir Walter Scott's heroic novels. Most of the bedrooms have doors opening on to the gardens, while the rest have individual patios. Some rooms have been adapted for disabled guests. There is a cosy cocktail bar, a comfortable lounge and an attractive restaurant which overlooks the gardens. Conference and meeting rooms are also available.
ROOMS: 46 en suite (2 fmly) No smoking in 20 bedrooms d £59-£72 (incl. bkfst & dinner) * LB **FACILITIES:** Tennis (hard) Xmas **CONF:** Thtr 70 Class 30 Board 36 Del from £87 * **PARKING:** 65 **NOTES:** No smoking in restaurant **CARDS:**

T

THORPE MARKET, Norfolk — Map 09 TG23

★★73% Elderton Lodge

Gunton Park NR11 8TZ
☎ 01263 833547 Fax 01263 834673
e-mail: enquiries@eldertonlodge.co.uk
Dir: *at N Walsham take A149 towards Cromer, the hotel is approx. 3m out of North Walsham on left, just prior to entering Thorpe Market village*
Once frequented by King Edward the VII, Elderton Lodge was originally a shooting lodge. The sporting heritage has been maintained with lots of field-sport paintings and prints. A wealth of local seasonal game is offered on the menu. The bedrooms are attractively decorated, equipped with many useful extras and come in a variety of styles.
ROOMS: 11 en suite (2 fmly) No smoking in 3 bedrooms s £57-£65; d £90-£105 (incl. bkfst) * LB **FACILITIES:** Fishing Croquet lawn Shooting by arrangement Xmas **CONF:** Thtr 30 Class 30 Board 16 Del from £65 * **PARKING:** 30 **NOTES:** No children 10yrs No smoking in restaurant Closed 8-26 Jan **CARDS:**

THRAPSTON, Northamptonshire — Map 04 SP97

Travelodge

Thrapston Bypass NN14 4UR
☎ 01832 735199 Fax 01832 735199
Dir: *on A14 link road A1/M1*
This modern building offers accommodation in smart, spacious and well equipped bedrooms, all with en suite bathrooms. Refreshments may be taken at the nearby family restaurant. For further details and the Travelodge phone number, consult the Hotel Groups page.
ROOMS: 40 en suite

THRUSSINGTON, Leicestershire — Map 08 SK61

Travelodge

LE7 8TF
☎ 01664 424525 Fax 01664 424525
Dir: *on A46, southbound*
This modern building offers accommodation in smart, spacious and well equipped bedrooms, all with en suite bathrooms. Refreshments may be taken at the nearby family restaurant. For further details and the Travelodge phone number, consult the Hotel Groups page.
ROOMS: 32 en suite

THURLESTONE, Devon — Map 03 SX64

★★★★72% Thurlestone

TQ7 3NN
☎ 01548 560382 Fax 01548 561069
e-mail: enquires@thurlestone.co.uk
Dir: *A38 take A384 into Totnes, A381 towards Kingsbridge, onto A379 towards Churchstow, onto B3197 turn into lane signposted to Thurlestone*
This family-owned hotel affords fabulous views of the South Devon coast from its stunning location in beautifully kept grounds. Superb leisure facilities are among the hotel's many attractions, in addition to entertainment, which is provided during the summer months. Bedrooms, all very well equipped, now include many popular suites. The majority benefit from sea views, some have balconies. Stylish public rooms include a no smoking lounge and great outdoor bar terrace.

continued

ROOMS: 64 en suite (20 fmly) s £61-£96; d £122-£192 (incl. bkfst & dinner) * LB **FACILITIES:** Indoor swimming (H) Outdoor swimming (H) Golf 9 Tennis (hard) Squash Snooker Sauna Solarium Gym Croquet lawn Putting green Jacuzzi/spa Games room Badminton ch fac Xmas **CONF:** Thtr 140 Class 100 Board 40 Del from £90 * **SERVICES:** Lift **PARKING:** 119 **NOTES:** No smoking in restaurant
CARDS:

See advert under SALCOMBE

★★★63% Heron House

Thurlestone Sands TQ7 3JY
☎ 01548 561308 & 561600 Fax 01548 560180
Dir: *take A381 off A38. Take Salcombe road & approx. 2m on turn right to S Milton. Turn left to 'Thurslestone Rock', Hotel 1.5m on beach road*
Standing on the coast close to Thurlestone Sands, guests will feel like they have got away from it all here. Bedrooms vary in size and some have superb views of the sea. Public areas are spacious with a lovely open plan lounge, a smaller first floor lounge overlooking the swimming pool, and a games rooms. The friendly team of staff ensure guests feel welcome.
ROOMS: 16 en suite (3 fmly) No smoking in 6 bedrooms s £60-£85; d fr £110 (incl. bkfst) * LB **FACILITIES:** Outdoor swimming (H) Pool table Golf breaks Xmas **PARKING:** 50 **NOTES:** No smoking in restaurant **CARDS:**

TICEHURST, East Sussex — Map 05 TQ63

★★★★67% Dale Hill Hotel & Golf Club

TN5 7DQ
☎ 01580 200112 Fax 01580 201249
e-mail: info@dalehill.co.uk
Dir: *situated on B2087 1.25m off A21*
This impressive modern hotel offers spacious bedrooms, good leisure facilities, and elegantly furnished public areas. The brasserie serves light meals all day, and the formal restaurant overlooks the 18th green. Hotel guests can enjoy the the clubby atmosphere of Spikes Bar.
ROOMS: 26 en suite (6 fmly) **FACILITIES:** STV Indoor swimming (H) Golf 36 Sauna Gym Pool table Putting green **CONF:** Thtr 60 Class 40 Board 40 Del from £120 * **SERVICES:** Lift **PARKING:** 220 **NOTES:** Civ Wed 100 **CARDS:**

TINTAGEL, Cornwall & Isles of Scilly — Map 02 SX08

★★78% Trebrea Lodge

Trenale PL34 0HR
☎ 01840 770410 Fax 01840 770092
Dir: *from A39 take Tintagel sign about 1m before Tintagel turn into Trenale*
With stunning views over Tintagel to the Cornish coastline in the distance, this charming property is decorated and furnished in keeping with the period in which it was built. Set in four acres of grounds, mainly at the rear of the property, Trebrea Lodge is personally run by the resident proprietors. Bedrooms are individually decorated with thoughtful extras. There is an elegant, first-floor drawing room and a popular snug with a log fire and honesty bar. Set dinners in the panelled dining room continue to prove popular with residents.

continued

ROOMS: 6 en suite 1 annexe en suite No smoking in all bedrooms s £62-£67.50; d £86-£96 (incl. bkfst) * LB **PARKING:** 12 **NOTES:** No children 12yrs No smoking in restaurant Closed Jan
CARDS:

★★65% Bossiney House
Bossiney PL34 0AX
☎ 01840 770240 01840 770501
e-mail: bossineyhh@eclipse.co.uk
Dir: *from A39 take B3263 into Tintagel, then Boscastle road for 0.5m to hotel on left*
Located on the outskirts of the village, Bossiney House is family run, with a relaxed and friendly atmosphere. The well stocked lounge bar overlooks the putting green and a cosy lounge is also available. An attractive, Scandinavian style log cabin in the grounds houses the majority of the leisure facilities.
ROOMS: 19 en suite (1 fmly) s £28-£44; d £58-£68 (incl. bkfst) LB
FACILITIES: Indoor swimming (H) Sauna Solarium Putting green
PARKING: 30 **NOTES:** No smoking in restaurant Closed Nov-Jan
CARDS:

★★65% *The Wootons Country Hotel*
Fore St PL34 0DD
☎ 01840 770170 01840 770978
Dir: *Follow A30 until sign for N Cornwall, then right onto A395. Continue & then turn right onto B3314 go straight over x-rds onto B3263 to Tintagel*
This hotel offers exceptionally well equipped bedrooms, suitable for all requirements. Located in the main street of this much visited village, the bar proves a popular venue for locals and visitors alike. An extensive range of bar meals is available, while in the restaurant a carte menu is offered. There are also glorious country views.
ROOMS: 11 en suite **FACILITIES:** Snooker Pool table ch fac
PARKING: 35 **NOTES:** No dogs (ex guide dogs)
CARDS:

★★62% Atlantic View
Treknow PL34 0EJ
☎ 01840 770221 01840 770995
e-mail: atlantic-view@eclipse.co.uk
Dir: *B3263 to Tregatta turn left into Treknow, hotel in situated on road to Trebarwith Strand Beach*
With coastal views, and convenient for all the attractions of Tintagel, this hotel is family run and has a relaxed atmosphere. Public areas include a bar, comfortable lounge and TV/games room. Some of the spacious bedrooms have distant sea views.
ROOMS: 9 en suite (1 fmly) No smoking in 3 bedrooms
FACILITIES: Indoor swimming (H) Pool table **PARKING:** 10 **NOTES:** No smoking in restaurant Closed Nov-Jan **CARDS:**

TITCHWELL, Norfolk
Map 09 TF74

★★73% Titchwell Manor
PE31 8BB
☎ 01485 210221 01485 210104
e-mail: margaret@titchwellmanor.co.uk
Dir: *on A149 between Brancaster and Thornham on A149 coast road*
A charming hotel in an unspoilt coastal location, Titchwell Manor makes the best use of the wealth of local produce, specialising in fish and shellfish, either in the seafood bar or the Garden Restaurant. The hotel is attractively decorated, with bold colour schemes throughout the comfortable public areas and a lighter floral style through the well appointed bedrooms.
ROOMS: 11 rms (7 en suite) 4 annexe en suite (2 fmly) No smoking in 5 bedrooms s £45-£70; d £70-£110 (incl. bkfst) * LB
FACILITIES: entertainment ch fac **CONF:** Thtr 20 Class 35 Board 25
PARKING: 50 **NOTES:** No smoking in restaurant Closed 18-31 Jan
CARDS:

See advert on this page

★★70% Briarfields
Main St PE31 8BB
☎ 01485 210742 01485 210933
e-mail: briarfields@norfolk-hotels.co.uk
Dir: *A149 coastal road towards Wells-next-Sea, Titchwell is the 3rd village & 7m from Hunstanton, hotel is situated on left of main road into village*
Situated close to the Titchwell RSPB reserve is this relaxing country hotel. The comfortable public rooms feature two eating areas, a smart restaurant and a bar serving meals. The accommodation is attractively decorated, quite spacious and has comfy seating.

continued

T

TITCHWELL, continued

Some rooms are located out of the main building with private terrace doors.
ROOMS: 18 en suite (2 fmly) No smoking in 15 bedrooms s £47.50; d fr £75 (incl. bkfst) * LB **FACILITIES:** Xmas **CONF:** Thtr 25 Class 12 Board 16 **PARKING:** 50 **NOTES:** No smoking in restaurant
CARDS:

See advert under HUNSTANTON

TIVERTON, Devon Map 03 SS91

★★★65% Tiverton

Blundells Rd EX16 4DB
☎ 01884 256120 01884 258101
e-mail: tiverton@devonhotels.com
Dir: *M5 junct 27, go onto dual carriageway A361 N Devon link road, Tiverton exit 7m W. Hotel on Blundells Rd next to business park*
Situated on the outskirts of Tiverton, this hotel has a comfortable and relaxed atmosphere. The bedrooms are spacious and well equipped. Additional features include 24 hour room service and ample car parking. In the restaurant there is a choice from the carvery and carte menu, or a more informal option is available in the bar.
ROOMS: 74 en suite (10 fmly) No smoking in 54 bedrooms s £45-£52; d £85 (incl. bkfst & dinner) * LB **FACILITIES:** STV Xmas **CONF:** Thtr 300 Class 140 Board 70 Del from £65 * **PARKING:** 130 **NOTES:** No smoking in restaurant Civ Wed 170
CARDS:

TIVETSHALL ST MARY, Norfolk Map 05 TM18

★★72% The Old Ram Coaching Inn

Ipswich Rd NR15 2DE
☎ 01379 676794 01379 608399
e-mail: theoldram@btinternet.com
Dir: *on A140 15m S of Norwich*

The Old Ram dates back to the 17th century as a staging post on the main Norwich to London road. Log fires, exposed brick and original timbers feature in the popular bar-restaurant eating areas. Upstairs, the very high quality and well equipped bedrooms come in two types: the old split level suites and family rooms; and the modern executive rooms.
ROOMS: 11 en suite (1 fmly) s £45; d £57 * LB **FACILITIES:** STV **CONF:** Thtr 30 Class 20 Board 20 Del £83.95 * **PARKING:** 150 **NOTES:** No dogs (ex guide dogs) Closed 25 & 26 Dec

Read all about it! Newspapers delivered to bedrooms in four and five star hotels.

CARDS:

TODDINGTON MOTORWAY SERVICE AREA (M1), Bedfordshire Map 04 TL02

Travelodge

LU5 6HR
☎ Central Res 0800 850950 01525 878452
Dir: *between junct 11 & 12 M1*
This modern building offers accommodation in smart, spacious and well equipped bedrooms, all with en suite bathrooms. Refreshments may be taken at the nearby family restaurant. For further details and the Travelodge phone number, consult the Hotel Groups page.
ROOMS: 66 en suite

TOLLESHUNT KNIGHTS, Essex Map 05 TL91

★★★★72% Five Lakes Country House

Colchester Rd CM9 8HX
☎ 01621 868888 01621 869696
e-mail: enquiries@fivelakes.co.uk
Dir: *exit A12 follow signs to Tiptree, over staggered x-rds past Wilkin's Jam Factory, fork left to Salcott, at x-rds turn right, 500 metres on right*
A truly stunning hotel, set in over 300 acres of countryside. Bedrooms are furnished and equipped to a very high standard and feature an excellent range of extra facilities. The hotel also boasts an exceptional range of leisure facilities: there are five bars, an informal brasserie and the more formal Camelot Restaurant.
ROOMS: 114 en suite (7 fmly) No smoking in 11 bedrooms s £99-£125; d £145-£210 * LB **FACILITIES:** STV Indoor swimming (H) Golf 36 Tennis (hard) Squash Snooker Sauna Solarium Gym Pool table Putting green Jacuzzi/spa Steam room Health & Beauty Spa Aerobics Xmas **CONF:** Thtr 3000 Class 1000 Board 50 Del from £119 * **SERVICES:** Lift **PARKING:** 700 **NOTES:** No smoking in restaurant RS 30 Dec-3 Jan Civ Wed 350 **CARDS:**

TONBRIDGE, Kent Map 05 TQ54

★★★65% The Langley

18-20 London Rd TN10 3DA
☎ 01732 353311 01732 771471
e-mail: the.langley@virgin.net
Dir: *turn off A21 signposted Tonbridge N on B245, hotel 500 metres on left beyond Oast Theatre*
Set in the heart of Kent, the Langley Hotel offers good access to the county's historical attractions. The atmosphere is relaxed and friendly. Bedrooms are spacious and attractive, with high levels of comfort. The restaurant offers a varied menu of carefully prepared fresh produce and there is a popular bar.
ROOMS: 34 en suite (3 fmly) No smoking in 12 bedrooms s £70; d £70-£90 (incl. bkfst) * **FACILITIES:** STV **CONF:** Thtr 25 Class 15 Board 18 Del from £100 * **SERVICES:** Lift **PARKING:** 50 **NOTES:** No dogs (ex guide dogs) No smoking in restaurant Civ Wed 80
CARDS:

★★★64% Rose & Crown

THE CIRCLE
Selected Individual Hotels
GREAT BRITAIN

125 High St TN9 1DD
☎ 01732 357966 01732 357194
Dir: *take A21 to Hastings. At 2nd interchange take B245 through Hildenbouough. Continue to Tonbridge. At 1st t/lights right, over next set. Hotel on left*
An attractive 15th century coaching inn, located opposite the ruins of the old Norman castle. The hotel offers all the character of the period, combined with modern comforts. Accommodation is divided between the new extension at the rear of the hotel and

continued

the main building. The bar is equally popular with locals and residents and is known for its cricket memorabilia.
ROOMS: 49 en suite (1 fmly) No smoking in 23 bedrooms s fr £80; d fr £90 * **FACILITIES:** Xmas **CONF:** Thtr 80 Class 30 Board 35 Del from £95 * **PARKING:** 39 **NOTES:** No dogs (ex guide dogs)
CARDS:

⌂ Premier Lodge (Tunbridge Wells)
Pembury Rd TN11 0NA
☎ 0870 700 1560 🖷 0870 700 1561
Dir: S off A21
Premier Lodge offers modern, well equipped, en suite accommodation suitable for both business and leisure travellers. Meals can be taken at the adjacent popular restaurant and bar which is fully licensed. For further details, consult the Hotel Groups page.
ROOMS: 38 en suite d £46 * **CONF:** Thtr 30 Class 16 Board 20

TOPCLIFFE, North Yorkshire — Map 08 SE47

★★ 69% The Angel Inn
Long St YO7 3RW
☎ 01845 577237 🖷 01845 578000
Dir: turn off the A168 link road (between A1(M) & A19) & the Angel Inn is situated in the centre of Topcliffe
At the heart of Topcliffe, this attractive inn is very popular for its country-style cooking using high quality local produce. Pleasant bars lead through to a fine pub water garden. The bedrooms are well equipped and very comfortable. Staff are friendly, and wedding's can now be carried out at the hotel.
ROOMS: 15 en suite (1 fmly) s £44.50-£50; d £60 (incl. bkfst) * LB **FACILITIES:** STV Fishing Pool table **CONF:** Thtr 150 Class 60 Board 50 Del from £79.95 * **PARKING:** 150 **NOTES:** No dogs (ex guide dogs) Civ Wed 150 **CARDS:**

TORBAY See under Brixham, Paignton & Torquay

TORCROSS, Devon — Map 03 SX84

★ 70% Grey Homes
TQ7 2TH
☎ 01548 580220 🖷 01548 580832
e-mail: howard@greyhomeshotel.co.uk
Dir: take A379 to village square, then take right fork and second turning on left
Built in the 1920s by the grandfather of the present owner, this delightful hotel enjoys spectacular views over Start Bay and Slapton Ley Nature Reserve. Public rooms retain much of the elegant character of the original period, and bedrooms have modern facilities.
ROOMS: 6 en suite (1 fmly) s £34-£36; d £56-£60 (incl. bkfst) * LB **FACILITIES:** Tennis (hard) **PARKING:** 15 **NOTES:** No children 4yrs No smoking in restaurant Closed Nov-Mar **CARDS:**

TORMARTON, Gloucestershire — Map 03 ST77

★★ 70% Compass Inn
GL9 1JB
☎ 01454 218242 & 218577 🖷 01454 218741
e-mail: info@compass-inn.co.uk
Dir: 0.5m from junct 18, M4
This friendly 18th-century coaching inn is set in a tranquil setting, and features good facilities for business, leisure and conferences. Many of the bedrooms are in a modern extension, with the bars and public rooms concentrated in the main building.
ROOMS: 26 en suite (7 fmly) s £74.50-£84.50; d £84.50-£94.50 * LB **FACILITIES:** STV **CONF:** Thtr 100 Class 30 Board 34 Del from £92.50 * **PARKING:** 160 **NOTES:** Closed 24-26 Dec
CARDS:

TORPOINT, Cornwall & Isles of Scilly — Map 02 SX45

★ 71% *Whitsand Bay Hotel, Golf & Country Club*
Portwrinkle PL11 3BU
☎ 01503 230276 🖷 01503 230329
e-mail: earlehotels@btconnect.com
Dir: 5m W, off B3247. Turn off A30 at Trevlefoot rdbt on A374 to Crafthole, then take turn for Portwrinkle
An imposing Victorian stone building with oak panelling, stained glass windows and a sweeping staircase. Bedrooms range from family rooms and a suite with balcony to children's rooms named after pirates. Facilities include an 18-hole cliff-top golf course. The fixed price menu offers an interesting selection of dishes; light meals and snacks are served in the bar.
ROOMS: 39 rms (37 en suite) (15 fmly) **FACILITIES:** Indoor swimming (H) Golf 18 Sauna Solarium Gym Pool table Putting green Beauty salon Steam room Hairdressers Games room ch fac **CONF:** Thtr 100 Class 100 Board 40 **PARKING:** 60 **CARDS:**

TORQUAY, Devon — Map 03 SX96

★★★★★ 70% The Imperial
Park Hill Rd TQ1 2DG
☎ 01803 294301 🖷 01803 298293
e-mail: imperialtorquay@paramount-hotels.co.uk
Dir: from A380, when in town, head towards the seafront. Turn left and follow the road to the harbour, at clocktower turn right. Hotel 300yrds on right

This well established hotel can legitimately claim to offer some of the best views in town. Elegant public areas include the Sundeck brasserie, a large lounge and meeting rooms. The Regatta Restaurant serves a choice of menus and features superb fresh local fish. Bedrooms vary in style, many have balconies and sea views. Service is welcoming and professional.

continued

T

TORQUAY, continued

ROOMS: 153 en suite (7 fmly) No smoking in 26 bedrooms s fr £95; d fr £170 * LB **FACILITIES:** STV Indoor swimming (H) Outdoor swimming (H) Tennis (hard) Squash Snooker Sauna Solarium Gym Pool table Jacuzzi/spa Beauty salon Hairdresser entertainment Xmas **CONF:** Thtr 350 Class 200 Board 30 Del from £135 * **SERVICES:** Lift **PARKING:** 140 **NOTES:** No smoking in restaurant Civ Wed 200 **CARDS:**

★★★★70% Grand

Sea Front TQ2 6NT
☎ 01803 296677 01803 213462
e-mail: grandhotel@netsite.co.uk
Dir: *from M5, A380 to Torquay. At sea front turn right, then first right. Hotel is on corner, entrance is in the first turning on left*

Overlooking the bay, this Edwardian hotel offers friendly service and modern facilities. Many bedrooms and various suites have sea views and balconies; all are very well equipped. Boaters Bar also benefits from the hotel's stunning position. In the evening guests enjoy the more formal atmosphere of the Gainsborough Restaurant.
ROOMS: 110 en suite (30 fmly) No smoking in 30 bedrooms s £60-£95; d £140-£240 (incl. bkfst) * LB **FACILITIES:** STV Indoor swimming (H) Outdoor swimming (H) Tennis (hard) Snooker Sauna Solarium Gym Pool table Jacuzzi/spa Hairdressers Beauty clinic entertainment ch fac Xmas **CONF:** Thtr 350 Class 100 Board 60 Del from £115 * **SERVICES:** Lift **PARKING:** 55 **NOTES:** No smoking in restaurant **CARDS:**

See advert on opposite page

★★★★68% Palace

Babbacombe Rd TQ1 3TG
☎ 01803 200200 01803 299899
e-mail: mail6@palacetorquay.co.uk
Dir: *on entering Torquay, head for the harbour, turn left by the clocktower into Babbacombe Rd, hotel on right after about 1m*

The hotel was formerly the summer residence of the Bishop of Exeter. Bedrooms are attractively decorated and offer many modern amenities. Public areas include a choice of lounges, a cocktail bar, and leisure facilities. The restaurant offers traditional cuisine in a formal atmosphere.
ROOMS: 141 en suite (20 fmly) No smoking in 18 bedrooms s £71-£81; d £162-£300 (incl. bkfst & dinner) * LB **FACILITIES:** Indoor swimming (H) Outdoor swimming (H) Golf 9 Tennis (hard) Squash Snooker Sauna Gym Pool table Croquet lawn Putting green Fitness suite Table tennis entertainment ch fac Xmas **CONF:** Thtr 1000 Class 150 Board 40 Del from £110 * **SERVICES:** Lift **PARKING:** 180 **NOTES:** No dogs (ex guide dogs) No smoking in restaurant
CARDS:

See advert on opposite page

★★★75% The Osborne

Hesketh Crescent, Meadfoot TQ1 2LL
☎ 01803 213311 01803 296788
e-mail: enq@osborne-torquay.co.uk
Dir: *A380 via Newton Abbot, follow signs to seafront, follow road, A3022, down and turn left, turn onto B3199 and follow road up to hotel*
Forming the centrepiece of an elegant Regency terrace, The Osborne commands superb views over the beach and Torbay. Set in five acres of well-tended gardens leading down to the sea, the hotel offers friendly and attentive standards of service and a host of leisure facilities. Bedrooms are smartly appointed and many benefit from fine sea views. The restyled public areas include an informal brasserie offering all-day service, while the restaurant provides a more formal eating option.
ROOMS: 29 en suite (2 fmly) s £68-£100; d £136-£200 (incl. bkfst & dinner) * LB **FACILITIES:** STV Indoor swimming (H) Outdoor swimming (H) Tennis (hard) Snooker Sauna Solarium Gym Putting green Plunge pool Xmas **CONF:** Thtr 30 Class 28 Board 30 Del from £82 * **SERVICES:** Lift **PARKING:** 90 **NOTES:** No dogs (ex guide dogs) No smoking in restaurant **CARDS:**

See advert on page 567

★★★74% Corbyn Head Hotel & Orchid Restaurant

Torquay Rd, Sea Front, Livermead TQ2 6RH
☎ 01803 213611 01803 296152
e-mail: rewhotels@aol.com
Dir: *follow signs to Torquay seafront, turn right on seafront. Hotel situated on right hand side of seafront with green canopies*

Situated in a prime position overlooking Tor Bay, and within easy walking distance of the town centre and harbour, Corbyn Head offers affordable luxury and traditional hospitality. A relaxed atmosphere pervades with staff all committed to ensuring guests receive high standards of service. The quality of cuisine is high, accommodation is carefully designed, and all furnishings are well co-ordinated. Many bedrooms benefit from wonderful sea views with ground floor rooms also available. Facilities include an outdoor pool and a choice of restaurants.

continued on p566

T

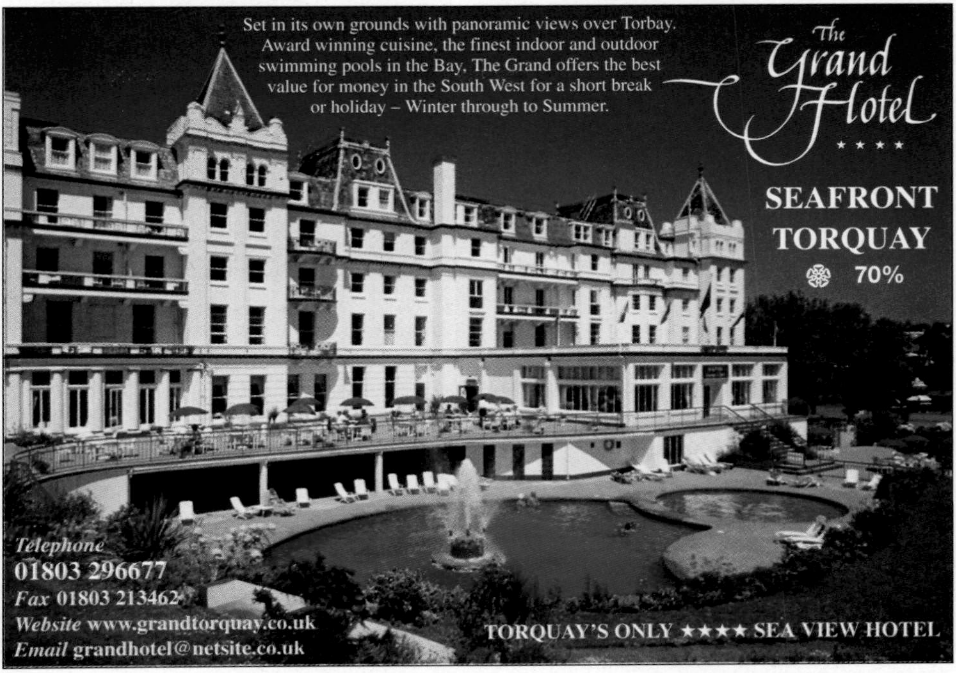

T

TORQUAY, continued

ROOMS: 51 en suite (4 fmly) No smoking in 3 bedrooms s £48-£73; d £96-£146 (incl. bkfst & dinner) * LB **FACILITIES:** Outdoor swimming (H) entertainment Xmas **CONF:** Thtr 30 Class 20 Board 20 Del from £45 * **PARKING:** 50 **NOTES:** No smoking in restaurant
CARDS:

★★★73% Livermead Cliff

Torbay Rd TQ2 6RQ
☎ 01803 299666 & 292881 01803 294496
e-mail: enquiries@livermeadcliff.co.uk
Dir: *take A380 towards Newton Abbot, at Penn Inn rdbt, take A380/3022 to Torquay seafront, turn right, Livermead Cliff is 600yds on left*
Situated on the edge of the bay, the hotel provides warm hospitality and attentive service in addition to the superb sea views which may be enjoyed from many of the bedrooms. The comfortable lounges and bar are spacious and tastefully decorated. The elegant restaurant offers carefully prepared enjoyable cuisine.
ROOMS: 64 en suite (21 fmly) s £42.50-£66; d £79-£129 (incl. bkfst) * LB **FACILITIES:** Outdoor swimming (H) Fishing Solarium Sun terrace Xmas **CONF:** Thtr 100 Class 40 Board 30 Del from £53.50 * **SERVICES:** Lift **PARKING:** 72 **NOTES:** No smoking in restaurant
CARDS:

★★★71% *Lincombe Hall*

Meadfoot Rd TQ1 2JX
☎ 01803 213361 01803 211485
e-mail: lincombehall@lineone.net
Set in five acres of grounds, close to the centre, this hotel has views over Torquay. Bedrooms are tastefully furnished and vary in size, the Sutherland rooms being the most spacious and in demand. There are comfortable lounges and Harleys restaurant offers a comprehensive choice of menu and wine.
ROOMS: 42 en suite (8 fmly) **FACILITIES:** STV Outdoor swimming (H) Tennis (hard) Sauna Solarium Gym Pool table Putting green Jacuzzi/spa Play area Crazy golf **CONF:** Thtr 50 Class 30 Board 20 **PARKING:** 40 **NOTES:** No smoking in restaurant **CARDS:**

★★★70% The Grosvenor

Belgrave Rd TQ2 5HG
☎ 01803 294373 01803 291032
e-mail: raylott@grosvenor-torquay.co.uk
Dir: *hotel on first left, just off main beach/seafront road*
Close to the seafront and the main attractions of the bay, The Grosvenor Hotel offers spacious and attractively furnished bedrooms. Guests can choose to dine in the restaurant, coffee shop or the award winning Mima's Bistro. Many leisure facilities are available.
ROOMS: 46 en suite (8 fmly) s fr £55; d fr £110 (incl. bkfst) * LB **FACILITIES:** STV Indoor swimming (H) Outdoor swimming (H) Tennis Sauna Solarium Gym Pool table Jacuzzi/spa entertainment Xmas **CONF:** Thtr 150 Class 100 Board 40 **PARKING:** 40 **NOTES:** No dogs (ex guide dogs) No smoking in restaurant Civ Wed 400
CARDS:

See advert on opposite page

★★★69% Livermead House

Torbay Rd TQ2 6QJ
☎ 01803 294361 01803 200758
e-mail: rewhotels@aol.com
Dir: *from seafront turn right, follow A379 towards Paignton and Livermead, the hotel is opposite Institute beach*
Situated on the waterfront, Livermead House was built in the 1820s and is where Charles Kingsley wrote *The Water Babies*. Bedrooms have been refurbished to a high standard, and the excellent public rooms are popular for private parties, functions

and meetings. A range of leisure facilities is provided and the attractive restaurant offers views of the bay.
ROOMS: 66 en suite (6 fmly) No smoking in 12 bedrooms s £50-£55; d £100-£130 (incl. bkfst & dinner) * LB **FACILITIES:** Outdoor swimming (H) Squash Snooker Sauna Solarium Gym entertainment Xmas **CONF:** Thtr 320 Class 175 Board 80 Del from £45 * **SERVICES:** Lift **PARKING:** 131 **NOTES:** No smoking in restaurant
CARDS:

See advert on page 569

★★★69% *Toorak*

Chestnut Av TQ2 5JS
☎ 01803 291444 01803 291666
Dir: *opposite Riviera Conference Centre*
The Toorak hotel offers many facilities here and in 'sister' hotels. Conference rooms are popular and there are a number of lounges. Bedrooms have modern facilities, superior 'Terrace' bedrooms are very spacious and well decorated. A fixed price menu and international buffet are available in the restaurant.
ROOMS: 92 en suite (29 fmly) **FACILITIES:** Indoor swimming (H) Outdoor swimming (H) Tennis (hard) Snooker Sauna Solarium Pool table Croquet lawn Jacuzzi/spa Childrens play area Indoor Games Arena **CONF:** Thtr 200 Class 150 Board 80 **SERVICES:** Lift **PARKING:** 90 **NOTES:** No dogs (ex guide dogs) **CARDS:**

See advert on opposite page

★★★67% Belgrave

Seafront TQ2 5HE
☎ 01803 296666 01803 211308
Dir: *turn off A38 onto the A380 then onto A3022 for 4m head for seafront*
With a choice of two bars and spacious lounges, all taking full advantage of the hotel's prime, seafront position, the Belgrave Hotel continues to prove popular. There is an impressive ballroom, and a restaurant serving a daily table d'hôte menu, in addition to lunch-time snacks. The bedrooms all offer modern facilities.
ROOMS: 68 en suite (16 fmly) No smoking in 20 bedrooms s £42-£58; d £84-£116 (incl. bkfst) * LB **FACILITIES:** Outdoor swimming (H) Pool table Xmas **CONF:** Thtr 150 Class 70 Board 50 Del from £59 * **SERVICES:** Lift **PARKING:** 86 **NOTES:** No smoking in restaurant
CARDS:

★★73% Oscars Hotel & Restaurant

56 Belgrave Rd TQ2 5HY
☎ 01803 293563 01803 296685
e-mail: reservations@oscars-hotel.com
Dir: *from A3022 into Torquay turn left, then right at next set of lights, head down hill towards seafront, hotel is at the junction with Falkland Rd*
This attractive hotel is close to the shops and seafront. It offers comfortable, smartly decorated and furnished bedrooms. The bistro-style restaurant offers an extensive range of enjoyable dishes.
ROOMS: 13 en suite (2 fmly) s £26.55-£38.50; d £47.30-£70 (incl. bkfst) * LB **PARKING:** 4 **NOTES:** No children 10yrs
CARDS:

AA ★★★

"Traditional hospitality, excellent facilities, friendly personal attention, perfect for every occasion"

Belgrave Road, Torquay, Devon TQ2 5HG
Tel 01803 294373 Fax 01803 291032
Email: @grosvenor-torquay.co.uk
Internet: http://www.grosvenor-torquay.co.uk/

★★★ 75%

THE OSBORNE HOTEL AND LANGTRY'S

A 29 bedroomed hotel, which is the centrepiece of an elegant Regency crescent, overlooks Meadfoot Beach and is 'probably' Torquay's most romantic hotel. Having recently achieved the Courtesy & Care Award, this 3-star AA rated hotel offers a friendly ambience complemented by superior standards of comfort and service. Facilities include five acres of lovely gardens, indoor and outdoor pools, tennis court, putting green, Hesketh's Health Club, The Brasserie and Langtry's guide-acclaimed restaurant, one of the foremost restaurants on the English Riviera.

Hesketh Crescent, Meadfoot, nr Torquay TQ1 2LL
Tel: 01803 213311 Fax: 01803 296788

BUTE COURT HOTEL

Run by the same family for 50 years, the hotel is situated in its own grounds with garden, swimming pool and car park, overlooking Torbay.
All 45 bedrooms are ensuite. Lift, bar, spacious lounges and games rooms.
Off season mini-breaks.

BELGRAVE ROAD
TORQUAY TQ2 5HQ
Tel: 01803 213055 Fax: 01803 213429
www.bute-court-hotel.co.uk

the Toorak hotel

69% AA ★★★

CHESTNUT AVENUE · TORQUAY
DEVON TQ2 5JS
TELEPHONE 01803 400400

For pure quality, attentive service, fine dining and elegant ambience, you'll go a long way to find better than the Toorak Hotel.
Comfortable lounges. Renowned restaurant.
All inclusive golf packages available.
Explore Torquay and the beautiful surrounding countryside, or relax and enjoy our wide range of leisure facilities, including luxury indoor pool complex.

T

TORQUAY, continued

★★72% Albaston House
27 St Marychurch Rd TQ1 3JF
☎ 01803 296758 📠 01803 211509
Albaston House is situated between the town centre, historic St Marychurch and the beaches of Babbacombe. Standards of housekeeping, hospitality and service are high and accommodation is smartly decorated, offering modern comforts.
ROOMS: 13 en suite (4 fmly) s £35-£40; d £70-£80 (incl. bkfst) * LB **PARKING:** 12 **NOTES:** No smoking in restaurant Closed Jan
CARDS:

★★71% Bute Court
Belgrave Rd TQ2 5HQ
☎ 01803 293771 📠 01803 213429
Dir: *take A380 to Torquay, continue until traffic lights, bear right past police station, straight across at traffic lights, hotel 200yds on right*
A short walk from the seafront, this popular hotel (once home to Lord Bute) has been owned by the same family since 1940. The recently refurbished bedrooms are comfortably furnished with modern facilities and helpful extras. Spacious public rooms, night-time entertainment and leisure facilities are all added attractions.
ROOMS: 45 en suite (10 fmly) s £32-£40; d £64-£80 (incl. bkfst & dinner) * LB **FACILITIES:** Outdoor swimming (H) Snooker Table tennis Darts Xmas **CONF:** Class 40 Del from £25 * **SERVICES:** Lift **PARKING:** 37 **CARDS:**

See advert on page 567

★★70% *Hotel Sydore*
Meadfoot Rd TQ1 2JP
☎ 01803 294758 📠 01803 294489
e-mail: john@sydore.co.uk
Dir: *A380 to Harbour, left at clock tower 40 metres to traffic lights, right into Meadfoot Rd hotel 100 metres on left*
A charming Georgian villa set in smart, well tended gardens. The hotel is full of character and individuality matched by the owners' charismatic approach to hospitality. It offers traditional cuisine in the attractive restaurant, adjacent to the cosy bar and lounge. Bedrooms are individual in style and decor.
ROOMS: 13 en suite (5 fmly) No smoking in 11 bedrooms **FACILITIES:** Croquet lawn Bar billiards Table tennis **PARKING:** 16 **NOTES:** No smoking in restaurant **CARDS:**

★★69% *Rawlyn House*
Rawlyn Rd, Chelston TQ2 6PL
☎ 01803 605208
Surrounded by large gardens, this delightful hotel is in a quiet area, but within easy reach of the centre. Bedrooms are individual in style and have the expected modern facilities. Meals are freshly prepared, with a range of bar meals on offer at lunchtime.
ROOMS: 14 rms (12 en suite) 2 annexe en suite (2 fmly) No smoking in all bedrooms **FACILITIES:** Outdoor swimming (H) Pool table Badminton Table tennis **PARKING:** 16 **NOTES:** No dogs No smoking in restaurant Closed Nov-Apr **CARDS:**

★★68% The Berburry
64 Bampfylde Rd TQ2 5AY
☎ 01803 297494
e-mail: bsellick@berburry.co.uk
Dir: *at Torre railway station lights bear right into Avenue Rd signposted seafront.Hotel 50yds before 2nd lights,300yds from seafront*
Overlooking the Torre valley, the hotel is a short level stroll from the seafront and Torre Abbey gardens. The bedrooms, including several on the ground floor, are comfortably furnished and well equipped. The enjoyable home cooking and friendly atmosphere enhance your stay.

continued

ROOMS: 10 en suite 5 annexe en suite (2 fmly) No smoking in all bedrooms s £26-£35; d £52-£70 (incl. bkfst) LB **PARKING:** 14 **NOTES:** No dogs No children 8yrs Closed Dec ex Xmas RS 2wks Nov/Dec & 2 wks Feb

★★68% *Carlton*
Falkland Rd TQ2 5JJ
☎ 01803 400300 📠 01803 400130
Dir: *take A380 into Torquay, follow signs to seafront, at traffic light junction on Belgrave Rd turn right into Falkland Rd hotel is 100yds on left*
Centrally positioned, this popular holiday hotel is conveniently close to beaches and other amenities. Guests can use the extensive leisure facilities here and at the adjacent hotels in the same group. The individually styled bedrooms are equipped to a good, modern standard. In the spacious ballroom, regular entertainment is staged.
ROOMS: 47 en suite (26 fmly) **FACILITIES:** Indoor swimming (H) Outdoor swimming (H) Tennis (hard) Snooker Sauna Solarium Gym Childrens playden & Adventure playground Ten-Pin Bowling entertainment **CONF:** Thtr 120 Class 60 Board 25 **SERVICES:** Lift **PARKING:** 28 **NOTES:** No dogs (ex guide dogs) No smoking in restaurant
CARDS:

★★68% Frognel Hall
Higher Woodfield Rd TQ1 2LD
☎ 01803 298339 📠 01803 215115
e-mail: frognel@btinternet.com
Dir: *follow signs to seafront, then follow esplanade to harbour, left to Babbacombe, right at lights towards Meadfoot beach, 3rd left, Hotel on left*
In an elevated position with fine views over Torquay, the hotel has comfortable bedrooms with modern facilities and a newly installed lift. The owners and their friendly staff ensure a pleasant stay. The traditional English food includes many vegetarian dishes.
ROOMS: 28 rms (27 en suite) (4 fmly) s £25-£29; d £50-£58 (incl. bkfst) * LB **FACILITIES:** Sauna Pool table Croquet lawn Putting green Games room Exercise equipment entertainment Xmas **CONF:** Thtr 50 Class 30 Board 15 Del from £33 * **SERVICES:** Lift **PARKING:** 25 **NOTES:** No smoking in restaurant **CARDS:**

★★68% Red House
Rousdown Rd, Chelston TQ2 6PB
☎ 01803 607811 📠 01803 200592
e-mail: stay@redhouse-hotel.co.uk
Dir: *head for seafront/Chelston, turn into Avenue Rd, 1st set of lights turn right. Follow road past shops and church, take next left. Hotel on right*

Situated in the quiet residential area of Chelston, this relaxing hotel provides comfortable accommodation. The hotel has both a restaurant and a new all-day, informal 'coffee shop' with an extensive menu. The bedrooms are comfortable, varying in size and style, and all offer modern facilities and amenities.

continued on p570

TORQUAY, continued

ROOMS: 10 en suite (5 fmly) s £20-£31; d £40-£62 (incl. bkfst) * **FACILITIES:** Indoor swimming (H) Outdoor swimming (H) Sauna Solarium Gym Pool table Jacuzzi/spa Games room Table tennis Beauty salon Xmas **CONF:** Thtr 20 Class 20 Board 16 **PARKING:** 10 **NOTES:** No smoking in restaurant **CARDS:**

See advert on opposite page

★★67% Ansteys Cove

327 Babbacombe Rd TQ1 3TB
☎ 0800 0284953 📠 01803 211150
e-mail: info@ansteyscove.co.uk
Dir: *turn off A380 Torquay to A3022 turn left onto the B3199. At Babbacombe turn right onto Babbacombe Rd hotel 1m on right opposite Place Hotel*

A family run hotel located close to the beaches and the Coastal Footpath. The hotel is homely, providing comfortable and well equipped bedrooms. An attractive dining room and a relaxing bar lounge are also available to guests.

ROOMS: 11 en suite (1 fmly) No smoking in all bedrooms s £26-£32; d £42-£58 (incl. bkfst) * LB **FACILITIES:** STV Xmas **PARKING:** 12 **NOTES:** No dogs (ex guide dogs) No smoking in restaurant **CARDS:**

★★67% Ansteys Lea

Babbacombe Rd, Wellswood TQ1 2QJ
☎ 01803 294843 📠 01803 214333
e-mail: stay@ansteys-lea.com
Dir: *from Torquay Harbour take the Babbacombe road, hotel approx 0.75m towards Babbacombe*

This friendly hotel is a short walk from Ansteys Cove. Bedrooms offer comfortable, well furnished accommodation with a good range of facilities. There is an attractive lounge/TV room overlooking the garden and a heated outdoor pool. The set five-course dinner menu offers a choice of home-cooked dishes.

ROOMS: 24 en suite (4 fmly) s £25-£31; d £50-£62 (incl. bkfst) * LB **FACILITIES:** Outdoor swimming (H) Sauna Gym Pool table Putting green Table tennis Xmas **SERVICES:** air con **PARKING:** 18 **NOTES:** No smoking in restaurant Closed 3 Jan-13 Feb **CARDS:**

★★67% Dunstone Hall

Lower Warberry Rd TQ1 1QS
☎ 01803 293185 📠 01803 201180
e-mail: info@dunstonehall.com

An imposing mansion overlooking Torbay. Comfortable bedrooms are equipped with modern facilities. Public areas include a choice of lounges, and a magnificent wooden staircase and gallery. The Victorian conservatory has been refurbished to provide an intimate restaurant where evening dinner may be enjoyed while taking in the panoramic views of the bay.

continued

ROOMS: 13 en suite (3 fmly) s £30-£40; d £60-£80 (incl. bkfst) * LB **FACILITIES:** Outdoor swimming (H) Pool table Arrangement with nearby Health Club Xmas **CONF:** Thtr 30 Class 30 Board 24 Del from £58 * **PARKING:** 18 **NOTES:** No dogs (ex guide dogs) No smoking in restaurant **CARDS:**

★★66% Ashley Court

107 Abbey Rd TQ2 5NP
☎ 01803 292417 & 292541 📠 01803 215035
e-mail: reception@ashleycourt.demon.co.uk
Dir: *A380 onto seafront, left to Sheddon Hill to traffic lights, hotel opposite*

Close to the seafront, local amenities and attractions, this hotel has been in the same family for over three decades. The friendly staff are committed to ensuring a relaxed, comfortable stay for all guests. Bedrooms are well maintained, an outdoor pool and patio are provided as well as live entertainment in the attractive lounge.

ROOMS: 53 en suite (5 fmly) s £20-£30; d £40-£60 (incl. bkfst) * LB **FACILITIES:** Outdoor swimming (H) entertainment Xmas **SERVICES:** Lift **PARKING:** 28 **NOTES:** No smoking in restaurant Closed 2 Jan-13 Feb **CARDS:**

★★66% *Hotel Balmoral*

Meadfoot Sea Rd TQ1 2LQ
☎ 01803 293381 & 299224 📠 01803 299224
Dir: *at Torquay harbour go left at Clock Tower towards Babbacombe, after 100yds right at lghts. Follow the rd to Meadfoot beach. Hotel on right*

Superbly situated just two minutes' stroll from Meadfoot Beach with views to the sea, the Balmoral is a friendly, well run hotel with modern well equipped bedrooms and bathrooms. The spacious lounges and bar offer guests every comfort. The daily menu provides a good selection of traditional home cooking in the bright, attractive dining room, with pleasant views over the well tended gardens.

ROOMS: 24 en suite (7 fmly) **FACILITIES:** entertainment ch fac **PARKING:** 18 **NOTES:** No smoking in restaurant **CARDS:**

★★66% Bancourt

Avenue Rd TQ2 5LG
☎ 01803 295077 📠 01803 201114
Dir: *on A38 straight into Torquay, when you reach Torre Station and Halford superstore, stay in right-hand lane through the lights, hotel is on left*

A lively hotel, popular with business guests and coach parties, offers comfortable bedrooms and spacious public rooms, where entertainment is regularly provided. There is also an indoor pool and pretty gardens.

ROOMS: 52 en suite (11 fmly) s £30-£35; d £60-£80 (incl. bkfst) * LB **FACILITIES:** Indoor swimming (H) Pool table Games room entertainment Xmas **CONF:** Thtr 80 Del from £40 * **SERVICES:** Lift **PARKING:** 50 **NOTES:** No smoking in restaurant **CARDS:**

See advert on opposite page

★★66% Gresham Court

Babbacombe Rd TQ1 1HG
☎ 01803 293007 & 293658 📠 01803 215951
e-mail: trevor@thrropelodge.freeserve.co.uk
Dir: *proceed along The Strand/Harbourside & bear left into Torwood St. Cross set of lights into Babbacombe Road. Hotel is on left*

Situated close to the harbour and shops, this well run family hotel offers high levels of hospitality. In the dining room, the fixed price menu offers a varied choice of food. The bedrooms are comfortable and vary in style and size.

ROOMS: 30 en suite (6 fmly) s £32-£37; d £64-£74 (incl. bkfst & dinner) * LB **FACILITIES:** Pool table entertainment **SERVICES:** Lift **PARKING:** 14 **NOTES:** No smoking in restaurant Closed Dec-Feb **CARDS:**

★★66% *Shelley Court*
Croft Rd TQ2 5UD
☎ 01803 295642 Fax 01803 215793
Dir: *A380 from Newton Abbot, then onto A3022 to seafront, hotel is 250yds turning off Shedden Hill into Croft Rd*
This popular hotel is close to the town and beach. Entertainment is provided three nights a week. All rooms are bright and well appointed with many modern facilities. The refurbished lounge, together with some of the bedrooms, benefit from attractive sea views. The dining room offers a selection of home-cooked, traditional cuisine.
ROOMS: 27 en suite (3 fmly) **FACILITIES:** entertainment **PARKING:** 20 **NOTES:** No dogs No smoking in restaurant Closed 21 Dec-Jan
CARDS:

★★66% Torcroft
Croft Rd TQ2 5UE
☎ 01803 298292 Fax 01803 291799
Dir: *follow signs to seafront & town centre, at traffic lights junct turn left, take 1st right into Croft Rd, hotel is 200yds along on left*
A Grade II listed Victorian property, convenient for the town centre, shops and sea front. The quiet location also has the benefit of a small patio with seating which overlooks the well maintained garden. Bedrooms are well decorated and furnished and include some on the ground floor. A friendly and relaxed atmosphere is created by the proprietors.
ROOMS: 15 en suite (2 fmly) s £29-£39; d £58-£78 (incl. bkfst) * **FACILITIES:** Xmas **CONF:** Class 20 Board 26 **PARKING:** 16 **NOTES:** No dogs (ex guide dogs) No children 3yrs No smoking in restaurant
CARDS:

★★65% Burlington
462-466 Babbacombe Rd TQ1 1HN
☎ 01803 210950 Fax 01803 200189
e-mail: burlington.hotel@virgin.net
Dir: *A380 to Torquay, follow signs to seafront, left at harbour, left at clock tower, the hotel is 0.5m on right hand side*
Providing a convenient base to enjoy the attractions of Torbay, the Burlington is a short walk from the harbour and shops of Torquay. Public areas include a pool room, entertainment room, leisure facilities and a popular bar. Traditional dishes are served in the spacious dining room by the friendly team of staff. Bedrooms are comfortable and available in a variety of sizes.
ROOMS: 55 en suite (7 fmly) s £34-£37; d £54-£60 (incl. bkfst) * LB **FACILITIES:** Indoor swimming (H) Sauna Solarium Pool table Jacuzzi/spa Games room Games machines Table tennis Pinball entertainment Xmas **PARKING:** 20 **NOTES:** No smoking in restaurant
CARDS:

★★65% *Coppice*
Babbacombe Rd TQ1 2QJ
☎ 01803 297786 Fax 01803 211085
The Coppice, conveniently situated just off the Babbacombe Road and within walking distance of the beaches and shops, is a friendly and comfortable hotel. Bedrooms are bright and airy with modern amenities. Evening entertainment is often available in the spacious and attractive bar.
ROOMS: 39 en suite (16 fmly) **FACILITIES:** Indoor swimming (H) Outdoor swimming (H) Sauna Solarium Gym Pool table Putting green Jacuzzi/spa **PARKING:** 36 **NOTES:** Closed 1 Dec-31 Jan

Early start? Hotels at all star levels should provide in-room alarm clocks and/or alarm calls.

TORQUAY, continued

★★65% Elmington Hotel

St Agnes Ln, Chelston TQ2 6QE
☎ 01803 605192 📠 01803 690488
e-mail: mail@elmington.co.uk
Dir: to thr rear of Torquay station
Lovingly restored, this splendid Victorian villa has Art Deco additions and is set in sub-tropical gardens in a quiet residential area, close to the centre and harbour. Guest comfort here is of the utmost importance. Comfortable bedrooms are attractively decorated. There is a spacious lounge, bar and dining room with wonderful views over the bay.
ROOMS: 22 rms (19 en suite) (5 fmly) No smoking in all bedrooms s fr £32; d fr £54 (incl. bkfst) * **FACILITIES:** Outdoor swimming (H) Pool table Croquet lawn ch fac Xmas **PARKING:** 18 **NOTES:** No dogs (ex guide dogs) No smoking in restaurant
CARDS:

★★64% *Maycliffe*

St Lukes Rd North TQ2 5DP
☎ 01803 294964 📠 01803 201167
Dir: left from Kings Dr, along sea front keep left lane, next lights (Belgrave Rd) proceed up Shedden Hill, 2nd right into St Lukes Rd then 1st left
In a quiet locatation with views over Torbay from some bedrooms. Rooms are individual in design and decor and have modern facilities. There is a comfortable lounge and attractive bar with cabaret three nights a week. Good home cooked food is served in the pretty dining room.
ROOMS: 28 en suite (1 fmly) No smoking in 9 bedrooms
FACILITIES: entertainment **SERVICES:** Lift **PARKING:** 10 **NOTES:** No dogs No children 10yrs No smoking in restaurant Closed 2 Jan-12 Feb
CARDS:

★★63% Anchorage Hotel

Cary Park, Aveland Rd TQ1 3NQ
☎ 01803 326175 📠 01803 316439
e-mail: landlin@aol.com

The Anchorage is quietly situated in a residential part of town and offers a very friendly welcome. A lift serves most of the bedrooms, and there are also some on the ground floor. The fixed-price dinner menu offers a wide choice. Evening entertainment is sometimes provided in the large comfortable lounge.
ROOMS: 53 en suite (5 fmly) No smoking in all bedrooms s £17-£24; d £34-£48 (incl. bkfst) * LB **FACILITIES:** Outdoor swimming (H) entertainment Xmas **CONF:** Thtr 50 Class 20 Board 24 **SERVICES:** Lift **PARKING:** 26 **NOTES:** No smoking in restaurant
CARDS:

Arriving late? Four and five star hotels have night porters to assist with your luggage; and 24hr room service.

★★62% Norcliffe

7 Babbacombe Downs Rd, Babbacombe TQ1 3LF
☎ 01803 328456 📠 01803 328023
Dir: from M5, take A380, after Sainsburys turn left at lights, across rdbt, left next at lights into Manor road, from Babbacombe Rd turn left
Situated on the Babbacombe Downs, with marvellous views across Lyme Bay, the Norcliffe is convenient for visitors to St Marychurch or nearby Oddicombe Beach. All bedrooms are comfortable, varying in style and size. Relaxing public areas include an indoor swimming pool.
ROOMS: 27 en suite (3 fmly) s £18-£36; d £36-£72 (incl. bkfst) * LB **FACILITIES:** Indoor swimming (H) Sauna 3/4 size snooker table ch fac Xmas **SERVICES:** Lift **PARKING:** 20 **NOTES:** No smoking in restaurant
CARDS:

★★59% Roseland

Warren Rd TQ2 5TT
☎ 01803 213829 📠 01803 291266
e-mail: burlington.hotel@virgin.net
Dir: at sea front turn left, up Sheddon Hill and turn right at Warren Road
The former home of Lord Lytton, Viceroy of India, this hotel enjoys fine views over Torbay. Bedrooms are simply furnished with modern facilities, some with patios and sea views. There is entertainment in the bar-lounge throughout the season, and a small leisure complex.
ROOMS: 39 en suite 1 annexe en suite (8 fmly) s £34-£42; d £54-£70 (incl. bkfst) * LB **FACILITIES:** Indoor swimming (H) Sauna Solarium Pool table Jacuzzi/spa Games room entertainment ch fac Xmas
SERVICES: Lift **NOTES:** No smoking in restaurant
CARDS:

★★59% *Seascape*

8-10 Tor Church Rd TQ2 5UT
☎ 01803 292617 📠 01803 292617
Dir: take A380 Torquay, at Torre station turn R, at 2nd traffic lights turn L, go through 1 set of lights, hotel is 100yds on right after lights
This hotel offers splendid panoramic views and is only a short stroll from the town centre. Bedrooms are well furnished and equipped. Meals are served in the bright, cheerful dining room.
ROOMS: 60 en suite (14 fmly) **FACILITIES:** STV Sauna Solarium Gym Pool table Table tennis Darts entertainment **SERVICES:** Lift
PARKING: 27 **NOTES:** No dogs No smoking in restaurant Closed Jan-Feb **CARDS:**

★69% Westwood

111 Abbey Rd TQ2 5NP
☎ 01803 293818 📠 01803 293818
e-mail: reception@westwoodhotel.co.uk
Dir: on A380 follow for Seafront. At lights turn into Hand Lane & up Sheddon Hill. At lights at top of hill, turn left into Abbey Rd, hotel is on right
A small family-run hotel within walking distance of the town centre. The owners offer an enthusiastic and friendly welcome. Regular guests enjoy the informal atmosphere, particularly in the comfortable bar. Bedrooms are tastefully decorated, offering many modern facilities.
ROOMS: 26 en suite (6 fmly) s £20-£27; d £48-£54 (incl. bkfst) * LB **FACILITIES:** Xmas **PARKING:** 12 **NOTES:** No dogs (ex guide dogs) No smoking in restaurant RS Oct-Mar **CARDS:**

Popped the question? Hotels with Civ Wed in their entry are licensed for civil wedding ceremonies. Maximum numbers for the ceremony only are shown, e.g. Civ Wed 50

★62% Villa Marina
Cockington Ln, Livermead TQ2 6QU
☎ 01803 605440 01803 605440
e-mail: villamarina@demon.co.uk
Dir: *from main seafront head towards Paignton, turn right towards Cockington Village. Hotel 70yds on left*
A warm welcome awaits visitors to this family owned hotel, conveniently located just a short walk from the seafront. From its elevated position, wonderful sea views across Torbay can be enjoyed from both public rooms and a number of bedrooms. Live entertainment is provided during the high season and a heated outdoor pool is also available.
ROOMS: 25 en suite (5 fmly) No smoking in all bedrooms s £17-£25.50; d £34-£51 (incl. bkfst) * LB **FACILITIES:** Outdoor swimming (H) Pool table Xmas **PARKING:** 20 **NOTES:** No dogs (ex guide dogs) No smoking in restaurant Closed 3-30 Jan **CARDS:**

TOTLAND BAY See Wight, Isle of

TOTNES, Devon
Map 03 SX86
see also Staverton

★★65% Royal Seven Stars
The Plains TQ9 5DD
☎ 01803 862125 & 863241 01803 867925
Dir: *A38 Devon Expressway, exit Buckfastleigh turn off onto A384, follow the signs to Totnes town centre*
Situated in the heart of the town, the Royal Seven Stars Hotel is popular with locals and residents alike. Seventeenth-century charm is successfully combined with comfortable accommodation, and traditional cuisine is provided in the bar or restaurant.
ROOMS: 16 rms (14 en suite) (2 fmly) s £49-£59; d £62-£69 (incl. bkfst) * LB **FACILITIES:** Xmas **CONF:** Thtr 70 Class 20 Board 20 **PARKING:** 20 **CARDS:**

TOWCESTER, Northamptonshire
Map 04 SP64

⌂ *Travelodge*
Travelodge
NN12 6TQ
☎ 01327 359105 01327 359105
Dir: *A43 East Towcester by-pass*
This modern building offers accommodation in smart, spacious and well equipped bedrooms, all with en suite bathrooms. Refreshments may be taken at the nearby family restaurant. For further details and the Travelodge phone number, consult the Hotel Groups page.
ROOMS: 33 en suite

TRESCO See Scilly, Isles of

TREYARNON BAY, Cornwall & Isles of Scilly
Map 02 SW87

★★67% Waterbeach
PL28 8JW
☎ 01841 520292 01841 521102
e-mail: waterbeach@aol.com
Dir: *from A389 take B3276 signed Newquay, after 2.5m straight across St Merryn X-rds, 3rd turning on right signed Treyarnon then 1st right and 1st left*
Set in grounds three miles south of Padstow, the Waterbeach is a popular coastal hotel. Bedrooms of varying size are all equipped to a high standard. Cottage rooms are especially suited for families. Public areas are comfortable and well proportioned. Each evening, home-cooked six-course dinners are served.
ROOMS: 11 en suite 6 annexe en suite (9 fmly) s £41-£50; d £82-£100 (incl. bkfst & dinner) * **FACILITIES:** Tennis (hard) Pool table Putting green **PARKING:** 20 **NOTES:** No smoking in restaurant Closed Nov-Etr **CARDS:**

TRING, Hertfordshire
Map 04 SP91

★★★★65% Pendley Manor
Cow Ln HP23 5QY
☎ 01442 891891 01442 890687
e-mail: info@pendley-manor.co.uk
Dir: *M25 junct 20. Take A41 leaving at Tring exit. At rdbt take exit for Berkhamsted & London. Take 1st left signposted Tring Station & Pendley Manor*
This impressive Victorian mansion is set in extensive and mature landscaped grounds. Bedrooms are located in the manor house or in the newer wing. All rooms are equipped with a useful range of extra facilities, including fax machines, and many have four poster beds. Public areas include a traditional bar with armchairs and sofas, making this an ideal venue to relax before dinner in the Oak Restaurant.
ROOMS: 74 en suite (4 fmly) s fr £100; d fr £120 (incl. bkfst) * LB **FACILITIES:** STV Tennis (hard) Snooker Gym Pool table Croquet lawn Games room Archery Laser shooting Hot Air balloon rides Xmas **CONF:** Thtr 180 Class 80 Board 40 Del from £190 * **SERVICES:** Lift **PARKING:** 250 **NOTES:** No smoking in restaurant Civ Wed 140 **CARDS:**

See advert on this page

Early start? Hotels at all star levels should provide in-room alarm clocks and/or alarm calls.

T

TROUTBECK (NEAR WINDERMERE), Cumbria Map 07 NY40

★★★ 72% Broadoaks Country House

Bridge Ln, Troutbeck LA23 1LA
☎ 015394 45566
e-mail: broadoaks.com@virgin.net
Dir: *A591 towards Ambleside turn right at Troutbeck Bridge follow signs to Troutbeck & youth hostel*

This restored Victorian country residence is quietly situated in the Troutbeck valley. Public areas include a music room complete with Bechstein piano and barrel vaulted ceiling, as well as the dining room, where fresh local produce is used. Individually designed bedrooms follow a Victorian theme, but have all the comforts expected by today's guest.
ROOMS: 9 en suite 3 annexe en suite (1 fmly) No smoking in all bedrooms s £65-£130; d £110-£210 (incl. bkfst) * LB **FACILITIES:** STV Fishing Pool table Croquet lawn Putting green Xmas **CONF:** Del from £120 * **PARKING:** 42 **NOTES:** No children 5yrs No smoking in restaurant **CARDS:**

See advert on opposite page

★★ 70% Mortal Man

LA23 1PL
☎ 015394 33193 ▤ 015394 31261
e-mail: the-mortalman@btinternet.com
Dir: *2.5m N from junct of A591/A592, turn left before church into village, right at T junction, hotel 800m on right*
Nestling in an idyllic Lakeland hamlet, the Mortal Man combines the character of a village inn with the style of a country-house hotel. Day rooms include a comfortable lounge, and a bar featuring an open fire and old beams. The dining room looks out onto the valley and the well equipped, attractively decorated bedrooms also enjoy views of the countryside.
ROOMS: 12 en suite s £65-£85; d £80-£90 (incl. bkfst) * LB **FACILITIES:** entertainment Xmas **PARKING:** 20 **NOTES:** No smoking in restaurant **CARDS:**

TROWBRIDGE, Wiltshire Map 03 ST85

★★ 64% Fieldways Hotel & Health Club

Hilperton Rd BA14 7JP
☎ 01225 768336 ▤ 01225 753649
Dir: *last property on left leaving Trowbridge on A361 towards Melksham/Chippenham/Devizes*
Fieldways Hotel and Health Club is quietly set in well kept grounds and forms part of a property reputed to be Trowbridge's finest Victorian mansion. The hotel provides a pleasant combination of spacious, comfortably furnished bedrooms, an impressive wood panelled dining room and a considerable range of indoor leisure facilities.

continued

ROOMS: 7 en suite 5 annexe en suite (1 fmly) s £45-£55; d £60-£75 (incl. bkfst) * LB **FACILITIES:** Indoor swimming (H) Sauna Solarium Gym Pool table Jacuzzi/spa Beauty treatment **CONF:** Thtr 70 Class 50 Board 14 Del from £70 * **PARKING:** 70 **NOTES:** No dogs (ex guide dogs) No smoking in restaurant **CARDS:**

TROWELL MOTORWAY SERVICE AREA (M1), Nottinghamshire Map 08 SK44

Travelodge

Travelodge

NG9 3PL
☎ 01159 320291
Dir: *M1 junc 25/26 northbound*
This modern building offers accommodation in smart, spacious and well equipped bedrooms, all with en suite bathrooms. Refreshments may be taken at the nearby family restaurant. For further details and the Travelodge phone number, consult the Hotel Groups page.
ROOMS: 35 en suite

TRURO, Cornwall & Isles of Scilly Map 02 SW84

★★★ 74% Royal

Lemon St TR1 2QB
☎ 01872 270345 ▤ 01872 242453
e-mail: recception@royalhotelcornwall.co.uk
Dir: *follow A30 to Carland Cross then Truro. Follow brown tourists signs to hotel in city centre. Drive up to barrier to obtain a pass from reception*
Perfectly situated in the centre of Truro, The Royal Hotel has extremely impressive bedrooms. These comfortable rooms are complemented by some 'executive' rooms complete with fax machines, CD players and work stations. Mannings Brasserie offers interesting modern, ethnic and classical dishes in an informal atmosphere.
ROOMS: 35 en suite (4 fmly) No smoking in 22 bedrooms s £67; d £85 (incl. cont bkfst) LB **FACILITIES:** STV Snooker Fitness area **PARKING:** 40 **NOTES:** No dogs (ex guide dogs) Closed 25 & 26 Dec **CARDS:**

See advert on opposite page

★★★ 72% Alverton Manor

Tregolls Rd TR1 1ZQ
☎ 01872 276633 ▤ 01872 222989
e-mail: alverton@connexions.co.uk
Dir: *from at Carland Cross take A39 to Truro.*
Formerly a convent, this impressive sandstone property stands in six acres of grounds, within walking distance of the city centre. Alverton Manor provides a wide range of smart bedrooms. Stylish public areas include the library and the former chapel, now a striking function room, licensed for wedding ceremonies. Both a carte and fixed price menu are offered in the candlelit restaurant, and dishes are innovative and highly enjoyable.
ROOMS: 34 en suite s fr £67; d fr £99 (incl. bkfst) * LB **FACILITIES:** STV Golf 18 Snooker Xmas **CONF:** Thtr 370 Class 178 Board 136 Del from £95 * **SERVICES:** Lift **PARKING:** 120 **NOTES:** No smoking in restaurant Civ Wed 120 **CARDS:**

See advert on opposite page

★★ 63% Carlton

Falmouth Rd TR1 2HL
☎ 01872 272450 ▤ 01872 223938
Dir: *just off A390 towards city centre*
This family-run hotel is within walking distance of Truro city centre. Bedrooms, some recently refurbished, vary in size and style, but all are well equipped and suited to the hotel's mainly business clientele. Guests can enjoy drinks in the attractive lounge

continued on p576

T

TRURO, continued

bar. The restaurant, useful for functions, serves a wide selection of home cooked food.
ROOMS: 29 en suite (4 fmly) No smoking in 12 bedrooms s £34.50-£39.50; d £47.50 (incl. bkfst) * LB **FACILITIES:** Sauna Jacuzzi/spa **CONF:** Thtr 70 Class 24 Board 36 **PARKING:** 31 **NOTES:** Closed 20 Dec-3 Jan **CARDS:**

See advert on opposite page

TUNBRIDGE WELLS (ROYAL), Kent — Map 05 TQ53

★★★76% The Spa
Mount Ephraim TN4 8XJ
☎ 01892 520331 01892 510575
e-mail: info@spahotel.co.uk
Dir: *follow signposts to A264 East Grinstead, hotel is on right hand side*

Set in 15 acres of parkland, with ponds and floodlit tennis courts, this 18th-century country house retains much of its original character. Bedrooms, many of which overlook the attractive gardens, are smartly furnished. Wood-panelled public rooms include a comfortable lobby lounge, a bar and a grand restaurant which serves a fixed-price menu and an interesting carte.
ROOMS: 71 en suite (10 fmly) No smoking in 13 bedrooms s £82-£92; d £99-£155 * LB **FACILITIES:** STV Indoor swimming (H) Tennis (hard) Riding Sauna Gym Croquet lawn Dance studio Steam room Beauty Salon entertainment Xmas **CONF:** Thtr 300 Class 93 Board 90 Del from £120 * **SERVICES:** Lift **PARKING:** 120 **NOTES:** Civ Wed 100
CARDS:

See advert on opposite page

★★★72% *Royal Wells Inn*
Best Western
Mount Ephraim TN4 8BE
☎ 01892 511188 01892 511908
e-mail: info@royalwells.co.uk
Dir: *turn off A21 onto A26 then into Tunbridge Wells avoiding town centre, at junct of A264 take right fork, Inn is 150mtrs on right*

This delightful family-run hotel is situated high above the town with stunning views. The accommodation is being continually upgraded, and all rooms are stylishly and comfortably furnished. There are two eating options, The Brasserie with its extensive blackboard menu, and the refurbished Conservatory with a full carte and daily menu. The dishes are interesting and carefully prepared from fresh local produce. The wine list is well chosen and offers a range of reasonably priced selections to complement the menu. The staff provide relaxed and cheerful service.
ROOMS: 19 en suite (2 fmly) **FACILITIES:** STV entertainment **CONF:** Thtr 100 Class 40 Board 40 Del from £97.50 * **SERVICES:** Lift **PARKING:** 31 **NOTES:** Closed 25-26 Dec
CARDS:

See advert on opposite page

★★64% Russell
80 London Rd TN1 1DZ
☎ 01892 544833 01892 515846
e-mail: Sales@Russell-Hotel.com
Dir: *at junct A26/A264 uphill onto A26, hotel on right*
A bustling, friendly Victorian hotel, The Russell is very close to the town centre. Bedrooms are spacious and well equipped, and there is 24-hour room service. A separate building houses self-contained luxury suites. Enjoyable meals are served in the restaurant and there is a popular bar.
ROOMS: 19 en suite 5 annexe en suite (2 fmly) No smoking in 10 bedrooms s £48-£68; d £58-£82 (incl. bkfst) * LB **FACILITIES:** STV **CONF:** Thtr 50 Class 20 Board 32 Del £80 * **PARKING:** 15 **NOTES:** No dogs (ex guide dogs) **CARDS:**

Town House

★★★★ Hotel Du Vin & Bistro
Crescent Rd TN1 2LY
☎ 01892 526455 01892 512044
e-mail: reception@tunbridgewells.hotelduvin.co.uk
Dir: *follow town centre to main intersection of Mount Pleasant Rd & Crescent Rd/Church Rd. Hotel 150yds along Crescent Rd on R just past Phillips House*
An old-fashioned hotel offering simple but spacious accommodation. Many of the rooms have pleasant views over the rear gardens. It is conveniently located for the centre of the town.
ROOMS: 32 en suite s fr £75; d fr £85 * **FACILITIES:** STV Snooker Pool table **CONF:** Thtr 40 Board 25 Del from £145 * **SERVICES:** Lift **PARKING:** 40 **NOTES:** No dogs (ex guide dogs) No smoking in restaurant **CARDS:**

TURNERS HILL, West Sussex — Map 04 TQ33

Premier Collection

★★★ Alexander House
East St RH10 4QD
☎ 01342 714914 01342 717328
e-mail: info@alexanderhouse.co.uk
Dir: *on B2110 between Turners Hill and East Grinstead, 6m from junct 10 on M23*
Dating in part from the 17th century, this fine house is set in 135 acres of grounds. Reception rooms include the sunny south drawing room, and the oak-panelled library. Individually decorated bedrooms include some full suites, one with a four-poster bed believed to have been made for Napoleon. The restaurant offers confident modern British cooking.

continued

T

ROOMS: 15 en suite (5 fmly) s fr £129; d £158-£295 (incl. bkfst) * LB **FACILITIES:** STV Tennis (hard) Snooker Croquet lawn Clay pigeon shooting Archery by arrangement entertainment Xmas **CONF:** Thtr 70 Class 24 Board 24 Del £225 * **SERVICES:** Lift **PARKING:** 50 **NOTES:** No dogs (ex guide dogs) No smoking in restaurant Civ Wed 60 **CARDS:**

See advert under GATWICK AIRPORT (LONDON)

TUTBURY, Staffordshire Map 08 SK22

★★★68% Ye Olde Dog & Partridge

High St DE13 9LS

☎ 01283 813030 ☎ 01283 813178

Dir: *exit A50 between Burton-on-Trent and Uttoxeter, signposted off A50 as A511*

Dating in parts from the 15th century, this pleasant village hotel lies within easy access of the road network. Public rooms have

continued on p578

TUTBURY, continued

been extended and refurbished, offering a further dining option in the form of a vibrant Brasserie that provides modern cooking; a strikingly refurbished bar complements. Alternatively, informal dining is provided within a very popular carvery restaurant. Bedrooms, which vary in size and style, are available in the main hotel or an adjacent Georgian building. Six deluxe bedrooms are individually and tastefully appointed, exceptionally well equipped and comfortably furnished.
ROOMS: 6 en suite 14 annexe en suite (1 fmly) No smoking in 6 bedrooms s £45-£75; d £50-£99 (incl. bkfst) * LB **FACILITIES:** STV Full Leisure pass to Branston Golf & Country Club entertainment **PARKING:** 150 **NOTES:** RS evenings 25 & 26 Dec & 1 Jan **CARDS:**

See advert on opposite page

TWICKENHAM, Greater London
See LONDON SECTION plan 1 *B2*

Premier Lodge

Chertsey Rd, Whitton TW2 6LS
☎ 0870 700 1440 📠 0870 700 1441

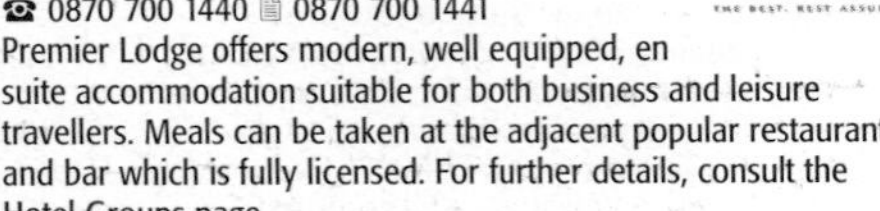

Premier Lodge offers modern, well equipped, en suite accommodation suitable for both business and leisure travellers. Meals can be taken at the adjacent popular restaurant and bar which is fully licensed. For further details, consult the Hotel Groups page.
ROOMS: 30 en suite d £42 *

TWO BRIDGES, Devon
Map 02 SX67

★★78% Prince Hall

PL20 6SA
☎ 01822 890403 📠 01822 890676
e-mail: bookings@princehall.freeserve.co.uk
Dir: *on B3357 1m E of Two Bridges road junct*

Set in the heart of Dartmoor National Park, Prince Hall offers spectacular views. Each of the spacious bedrooms is named after one of the tors. Public areas include a bar-lounge and a sitting room. The impressive, but short, fixed-price menu changes daily. Breakfast is equally memorable.
ROOMS: 8 en suite (1 fmly) s £65-£100; d £137-£170 (incl. bkfst & dinner) * LB **FACILITIES:** Fishing Croquet lawn **PARKING:** 13 **NOTES:** No children 10yrs No smoking in restaurant Closed Jan **CARDS:**

See advert under DARTMOOR

★★71% Two Bridges Hotel

PL20 6SW
☎ 01822 890581 📠 01822 890575
Dir: *junc of B3212 & B3357*
Surrounded by the natural splendour of Dartmoor National Park, this is a comfortable hotel for all seasons. Traditional bar food is found in the Saracen's Bar, and the restaurant provides more formal dining with a choice of menus featuring locally sourced produce, cooked with style and flair. Three standards of bedrooms are available.

ROOMS: 29 en suite (2 fmly) No smoking in 21 bedrooms s £37.50-£47.50; d fr £75 (incl. bkfst) * LB **FACILITIES:** STV Fishing Xmas **CONF:** Thtr 150 Class 58 Board 40 **PARKING:** 100 **NOTES:** No smoking in restaurant **CARDS:**

See advert on opposite page

TYNEMOUTH, Tyne & Wear
Map 12 NZ36

★★★68% Grand

Grand Pde NE30 4ER
☎ 0191 293 6666 📠 0191 293 6665
e-mail: info@grand-hotel.demon.co.uk
Dir: *A1058 for Tynemouth, when reach coastline rdbt turn right. The Grand Hotel is on right approx 0.5m along road*
Standing on the seafront and with fine views from many of its rooms, this classic Victorian resort hotel has been completely upgraded to attract the modern traveller. Public rooms retain their former elegance with an imposing reception lobby and grand staircase setting the scene. There is a choice of bars, whilst bedrooms are smartly furnished and have impressive bathrooms.
ROOMS: 45 annexe en suite (13 fmly) s £90; d £60-£160 (incl. bkfst) * **FACILITIES:** STV entertainment Xmas **CONF:** Thtr 130 Class 40 Board 40 Del from £80 * **SERVICES:** Lift **PARKING:** 18 **NOTES:** No dogs (ex guide dogs) Civ Wed 100 **CARDS:**

UCKFIELD, East Sussex
Map 05 TQ42

★★★★70%
Buxted Park Country House Hotel

Buxted TN22 4AY
☎ 01825 732711 📠 01825 732770
Dir: *on A272. Turn off the A22, A26, or A267 on to the A27 towards Heathfield then Buxted*
A Georgian mansion set in 300 acres of beautiful countryside, offering a grand country house atmosphere and retaining many original features. Bedrooms, mostly in the modern Garden Wing, are stylish and well equipped. The original Victorian Orangery serves good cuisine from an interesting menu.
ROOMS: 44 en suite (6 fmly) No smoking in 16 bedrooms s £65-£105; d £110-£130 (incl. bkfst) * LB **FACILITIES:** STV Outdoor swimming (H) Fishing Snooker Sauna Solarium Gym Croquet lawn Putting green Jacuzzi/spa Beauty salon Clay pigeon shooting Archery Xmas **CONF:** Thtr 150 Class 60 Board 40 Del from £130 * **PARKING:** 150 **NOTES:** No dogs (ex guide dogs) No smoking in restaurant Civ Wed 80
CARDS:

★★★ 77% Horsted Place

Little Horsted TN22 5TS
☎ 01825 750581 01825 750459
e-mail: hotel@horstedplace.co.uk
Dir: *2m S on A26 towards Lewes*

One of Britain's finest examples of Gothic revivalist architecture, Horsted Place is surrounded by its own estate which includes a golf club. Inside there are many fine architectural features, including a splendid Pugin staircase. Bedrooms are notably spacious and well appointed, many are suites.

ROOMS: 17 en suite (5 fmly) d £110-£145 (incl. bkfst) * LB **FACILITIES:** STV Indoor swimming (H) Golf 36 Tennis (hard) Croquet lawn entertainment Xmas **CONF:** Thtr 100 Class 50 Board 40 **SERVICES:** Lift **PARKING:** 36 **NOTES:** No dogs (ex guide dogs) No smoking in restaurant Civ Wed 50
CARDS:

ULLESTHORPE, Leicestershire — Map 04 SP58

★★★ 67% Ullesthorpe Court Hotel & Golf Club

Frolesworth Rd LE17 5BZ
☎ 01455 209023 01455 202537
e-mail: reservations@ullesthorpe-court.freeserve.co.uk
Dir: *from junct 20 of M1 head towards Lutterworth then follow brown tourist signs*

This impressive hotel, golf and country club complex has extensive grounds and is near the motorway network, the NEC and Birmingham Airport. Public areas include a choice of restaurants and offer a good range of leisure facilities and pursuits. Bedrooms are spacious and well equipped.

ROOMS: 38 en suite (1 fmly) No smoking in 20 bedrooms s £80; d £105 (incl. bkfst) * LB **FACILITIES:** STV Indoor swimming (H) Golf 18 Tennis (hard) Snooker Sauna Solarium Gym Pool table Putting green Jacuzzi/spa Beauty room **CONF:** Thtr 70 Class 40 Board 30 Del from £95 * **PARKING:** 500 **NOTES:** RS 25 & 26 Dec
CARDS:

ULLINGSWICK, Herefordshire — Map 03 SO54

★★ 75% *The Steppes Country House*

HR1 3JG
☎ 01432 820424 01432 820042
Dir: *off A417, 1.5m NW of junct with A465, signposted 'Ullingswick'*

Parts of this charming country house date back to 1380, though much of it is 17th century. It has a wealth of character, with beamed ceilings, stone flagged and tiled floors, as well as antique furnishings. Surrounded by pleasant gardens, the comfortable and well equipped bedrooms are located in delightfully converted buildings, including a beautifully restored timber framed barn. The award winning cook produces some imaginative dishes.

ROOMS: 6 annexe en suite No smoking in all bedrooms **PARKING:** 8 **NOTES:** No children 12yrs No smoking in restaurant Closed early Dec-late Jan **CARDS:**

U

ULLSWATER See Glenridding, Patterdale, & Watermillock

UMBERLEIGH, Devon Map 02 SS62

★★69% Rising Sun Inn
EX37 9DU
☎ 01769 560447 01769 560764
e-mail: risingsuninn@btinternet.com
Dir: *situated at Umberleigh Bridge on the A377, Exeter/Barnstaple road, at the junct of the B3227*
This charming inn has long been a popular haunt for fishermen, and overlooks the river. Extensively renovated without sacrificing character, the Rising Sun provides comfortable, well equipped bedrooms. The bar features an inglenook fireplace and fishing memorabilia. An interesting range of dishes feature on both the table d'hôte menu and blackboard specials.
ROOMS: 6 en suite 3 annexe en suite (1 fmly) No smoking in all bedrooms s £40; d £77 (incl. bkfst) * LB **FACILITIES:** Fishing entertainment Xmas **CONF:** Thtr 50 Board 24 **PARKING:** 35 **NOTES:** No smoking in restaurant **CARDS:**
See advert under BARNSTAPLE

UPHOLLAND, Lancashire Map 07 SD50

★★★63% Quality Hotel Skelmersdale
Prescott Rd WN8 9PU
☎ 01695 720401 01695 50953
e-mail: admin@gb656.u-net.com
CHOICE HOTELS EUROPE
Dir: *exit M6 junct 26 to M58. Leave at junct 5 for 'Pimbo' & turn left at rdbt follow into Prescott Road. Hotel situated on right*
This friendly hotel has attractive grounds and a magnificent Great Hall, dating back to 1580, now restored and used primarily for banquets and weddings. The modern bedrooms are well equipped, and include facilities for disabled persons. One room also has a four-poster bed. Bare stone walls in the bar and restaurant give character to the public areas.
ROOMS: 55 en suite (3 fmly) No smoking in 32 bedrooms s £71-£85; d £83-£90 * LB **FACILITIES:** STV Xmas **CONF:** Thtr 200 Class 125 Board 70 Del from £87 * **PARKING:** 200 **NOTES:** No smoking in restaurant Civ Wed 200 **CARDS:**

UPPER SLAUGHTER, Gloucestershire Map 04 SP12

Premier Collection

★★★ Lords of the Manor
GL54 2JD
☎ 01451 820243 01451 820696
e-mail: lordsofthemanor@btinternet.com
Dir: *2m W of A429. Turn off A40 onto A429, take 'The Slaughters' turning. Continue through Lower Slaughter for 1m until Upper Slaughter-hotel on right*
This 17th-century country manor house hotel sits in eight acres of gardens and parkland. Spacious and deeply comfortable lounges and the luxuriously appointed restaurant look over the front lawn and the formal rear garden. The restaurant offers cuisine that combines modern British and classical French styles in some impressive, well judged
continued

dishes, supplemented by an excellent wine list. The bedrooms vary in size, but are all appointed to a very high standard, with some ground floor rooms available.

ROOMS: 27 en suite s £99; d £145-£295 (incl. bkfst) * LB **FACILITIES:** STV Fishing Croquet lawn Xmas **CONF:** Thtr 30 Class 20 Board 20 Del £150 * **PARKING:** 40 **NOTES:** No dogs (ex guide dogs) No smoking in restaurant Civ Wed 50
CARDS:

UPPINGHAM, Rutland Map 04 SP89

★★73% Lake Isle
High St East LE15 9PZ
☎ 01572 822951 01572 822951
Dir: *in the centre of Uppingham via Queen street*
Developed from the original restaurant, this town house hotel has bedrooms in the main house and adjacent converted cottages; all are attractively decorated and well equipped with thoughtful extras and useful facilities. The ground floor public rooms are dominated by the hotel restaurant. Guests can also use the comfortably appointed first floor lounge.
ROOMS: 10 en suite 2 annexe en suite s fr £52; d fr £69 (incl. bkfst) * LB **FACILITIES:** Xmas **PARKING:** 7 **NOTES:** No smoking in restaurant **CARDS:**

UPTON UPON SEVERN, Worcestershire Map 03 SO84

★★★66% White Lion
21 High St WR8 0HJ
☎ 01684 592551 01684 593333
e-mail: reservations@whitelionhotel.demon.co.uk
MINOTEL Great Britain
Dir: *from A422 take A38 towards Tewkesbury. In 8m take B4104 and after 1m cross bridge, turn left to hotel around bend on left*

Despite its Georgian façade, this town centre inn dates back to 1510, and is famous for being the inn depicted in Henry Fielding's novel *Tom Jones*. The public areas have a lot of character,
continued

including exposed beams. The hotel is earning a well deserved reputation for the quality of its food.
ROOMS: 10 en suite s £53; d £77 (incl. bkfst) * LB **CONF:** Thtr 24 Board 12 **PARKING:** 20 **NOTES:** No smoking in restaurant
CARDS:

UTTOXETER, Staffordshire Map 07 SK03

Travelodge
Ashbourne Rd ST14 5AA
☎ 01889 562043 01889 562043
Dir: *on A50/A5030*
This modern building offers accommodation in smart, spacious and well equipped bedrooms, all with en suite bathrooms. Refreshments may be taken at the nearby family restaurant. For further details and the Travelodge phone number, consult the Hotel Groups page.
ROOMS: 32 en suite

VENTNOR See Wight, Isle of

VERYAN, Cornwall & Isles of Scilly Map 02 SW93

★★★★77% **Nare**
Carne Beach TR2 5PF
☎ 01872 501111 01872 501856
e-mail: office@narehotel.co.uk
Dir: *from Tregony follow A3078 for approx 1.5m turn left at signpost Veryan, drive straight through village towards sea and hotel*
This delightful property offers country house care and courtesy in a seaside setting. Many of the bedrooms have balconies. Fresh flowers and antiques add to the warm atmosphere, and a choice of restaurants offers a wide range of food from light snacks to superb local seafood.
ROOMS: 38 en suite (4 fmly) s £82-£161; d £164-£214 (incl. bkfst & dinner) * LB **FACILITIES:** STV Indoor swimming (H) Outdoor swimming (H) Tennis (hard) Snooker Sauna Gym Croquet lawn Jacuzzi/spa Windsurfing Health & Beauty clinic Hotel Boat Xmas
SERVICES: Lift **PARKING:** 80 **NOTES:** No smoking in restaurant
CARDS:

See advert on this page

VIRGINIA WATER, Surrey Map 04 TQ06

★★70% ***The Wheatsheaf***
London Rd GU25 4QF
☎ 01344 842057 01344 842932
Conveniently located on the A30, this friendly hotel is popular with both business and leisure guests. Bedrooms have been furnished to a high standard and are well equipped. Food is available all day and evening in the attractive Chef and Brewer style bar/restaurant.

WADEBRIDGE, Cornwall & Isles of Scilly Map 02 SW97

★★65% **Molesworth Arms**
Molesworth St PL27 7DP
☎ 01208 812055 01208 814254
e-mail: sarah@molesworth.ision.co.uk
Dir: *A30 to Bodmin town centre and follow directions to Wadebridge. Over old bridge turn right and then 1st left*
Situated in a pedestrian area of the town, this 16th-century former coaching inn is an ideal base for exploring the area. The comfortable bedrooms have been decorated to retain their original character and charm. In addition to the wide range of snacks and meals served in the beamed bar, the Courtyard Restaurant offers a comprehensive carte.
ROOMS: 16 rms (14 en suite) (2 fmly) s fr £35; d fr £55 (incl. bkfst) * LB **FACILITIES:** STV **CONF:** Thtr 60 Class 50 Board 40 Del from £45 * **PARKING:** 16 **NOTES:** No smoking in restaurant
CARDS:

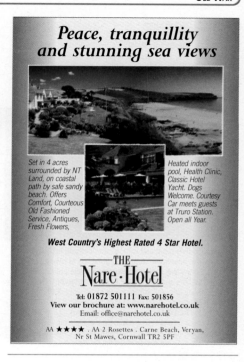

WAKEFIELD, West Yorkshire Map 08 SE32

★★★73% **St Pierre**
Barnsley Rd, Newmillerdam WF2 6QG
☎ 01924 255596 01924 252746
e-mail: sales@hotelstpierre.co.uk
Dir: *A636 to Wakefield, 3rd exit at rdbt, across 2 mini rdbts, right lane at lights follow signs Barnsley(A61). Pass Newmillerdam hotel 500yds on left*
This well furnished hotel lies three miles to the south of Wakefield. The interior of the modern building has much charm, with comfortable and thoughtfully equipped bedrooms and an elegantly furnished and intimate restaurant. The public areas also include a range of conference rooms and a gymnasium. Staff are friendly and helpful.
ROOMS: 54 en suite (3 fmly) No smoking in 33 bedrooms d £46-£100 * LB **FACILITIES:** STV Gym Xmas **CONF:** Thtr 130 Class 70 Board 50 Del from £70 * **SERVICES:** Lift **PARKING:** 70 **NOTES:** Civ Wed 60
CARDS:

Bad hair day? Hairdryers in all rooms three stars and above.

WAKEFIELD, continued

★★★72% **Waterton Park**

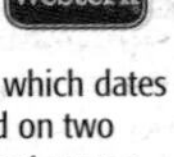

Walton Hall, The Balk, Walton WF2 6PW
☎ 01924 257911 & 249800 🖷 01924 240082
Dir: *3m SE off B6378 - off M1 at junct 39 towards Wakefield. At rdbt take right for Crofton. At the second set of traffic lights turn right follow signs*

Surrounded by a moat and with its own lake and extensive grounds, this impressive stone built hotel has its own golf course. There are attractive, modern bedrooms and the public rooms include two bars and a delightful beamed restaurant. The spacious and appealing annexe bedrooms are particularly desirable.
ROOMS: 25 en suite 35 annexe en suite s £70-£95; d £110-£130 (incl. bkfst) * LB **FACILITIES:** STV Indoor swimming (H) Golf 18 Fishing Snooker Sauna Solarium Gym Jacuzzi/spa Steam room Xmas
CONF: Thtr 180 Class 80 Board 60 **PARKING:** 180 **NOTES:** No dogs (ex guide dogs) No smoking in restaurant Civ Wed 60
CARDS:

★★★68% ***Posthouse Wakefield***

Posthouse

Queen's Dr, Ossett WF5 9BE
☎ 0870 400 9082 🖷 01924 276437
e-mail: gm1231@forte-hotels.com
Dir: *exit M1 at junct 40 following signs for Wakefield. Hotel is on the right after 200yrds*
This modern hotel provides a good standard of accommodation. Bedrooms are smartly decorated, many in the new 'Millennium' style. Traders' Restaurant offers a full menu, and refreshments are served all day in the lounge. 24-hour room service is also available. Several new conference suites enhance meeting room options.
ROOMS: 99 en suite (27 fmly) No smoking in 71 bedrooms **CONF:** Thtr 160 Class 70 Board 100 **SERVICES:** Lift **PARKING:** 130
CARDS:

★★★65% **Chasley Hotel**

Queen St WF1 1JU
☎ 01924 372111 🖷 01924 383648
Dir: *leave M1 junct 39 & follow signs for town centre. Queen St is on the left*
Situated in the centre of the city and close to the cathedral, this modern multi-storey hotel offers well equipped and pleasantly furnished bedrooms. There is a comfortable bar lounge next to the spacious restaurant where a set price menu with is offered. Conference facilities are also available.
ROOMS: 64 en suite (4 fmly) No smoking in 16 bedrooms s fr £75; d fr £90 * **FACILITIES:** STV Xmas **CONF:** Thtr 250 Class 90 Board 54 **SERVICES:** Lift **PARKING:** 30 **NOTES:** No smoking in restaurant Civ Wed **CARDS:**

W

★★★61% ***Stoneleigh***

Doncaster Rd WF1 5HA
☎ 01924 369461 🖷 01924 201041
Dir: *1.5m S from Wakefield on A638*
This hotel is a conversion of a Victorian stone terrace which dates back to 1870. The modern style bedrooms are located on two floors with a lift available. The well decorated restaurant serves good value menus that are popular with the local community. Guests have complimentary use of a nearby health club and gymnasium.
ROOMS: 32 en suite **FACILITIES:** STV Free use of adjacent Private Health Club for all residents **CONF:** Thtr 200 Class 100 Board 100
SERVICES: Lift **PARKING:** 80 **NOTES:** No dogs (ex guide dogs) Closed New Years day **CARDS:**

⌂ **Campanile**

Campanile

Monckton Rd WF2 7AL
☎ 01924 201054 🖷 01924 201055
Dir: *M1 junct 39, 1m towards Wakefield, left onto Monckton Road, hotel on left*

This modern building offers accommodation in smart well equipped bedrooms, all with en suite bathrooms. Refreshments may be taken at the informal Bistro. For further details and the Campanile phone number, consult the Hotel Groups page.
ROOMS: 77 annexe en suite **CONF:** Thtr 35 Class 18 Board 20

⌂ ***Travelodge***

Travelodge

M1 Service Area, West Bretton WF4 4LQ
☎ Central Res 0800 850950
(For full entry see Woolley Edge)

WALLASEY, Merseyside Map 07 SJ29

★★72% ***Grove House***

Grove Rd L45 3HF
☎ 0151 639 3947 & 0151 630 4558 🖷 0151 639 0028
Dir: *M53 junct 1, follow A544*
An immaculately maintained family owned hotel. Many bedrooms enjoy a view over attractive gardens to the rear, all are comfortably furnished and particularly well equipped. The bar lounge provides a venue for drinks before dinner in the oak panelled restaurant.
ROOMS: 14 en suite (3 fmly) **FACILITIES:** STV **CONF:** Thtr 60 Class 40 Board 50 **PARKING:** 28 **NOTES:** No dogs (ex guide dogs)
CARDS:

Read all about it! Newspapers delivered to bedrooms in four and five star hotels.

WALLINGFORD, Oxfordshire

Map 04 SU68

★★★72% Springs

Wallingford Rd, North Stoke OX10 6BE
☎ 01491 836687 🖷 01491 836877
e-mail: info@thespringshotel.co.uk
Dir: *turn off the A4074 Oxford-Reading Rd onto the B4009 - Goring. The Springs and Golf club is approx. 1m on the right hand side*

The Springs Hotel is set in the heart of the Thames Valley, and has its own 18 hole golf course. The house dates back to 1874 and offers spacious and well equipped bedrooms, many with balconies. The restaurant enjoys splendid views over the lake and grounds and other public rooms include a cosy lounge with a log fire as well as several dining rooms.

ROOMS: 31 en suite (3 fmly) s fr £90; d fr £100 (incl. bkfst) * LB **FACILITIES:** STV Outdoor swimming (H) Golf 18 Fishing Sauna Croquet lawn Putting green Xmas **CONF:** Thtr 50 Class 16 Board 26 Del from £160 * **PARKING:** 120 **NOTES:** No smoking in restaurant Civ Wed **CARDS:**

★★★66% The George

High St OX10 0BS
☎ 01491 836665 🖷 01491 825359
Dir: *E side of A329 on N entry to town*

PEEL HOTELS

The main building of this hotel is believed to date back to the 16th century, and has all the delightful features to match. Bedrooms in the main building have lots of character and comfort. A purpose-built wing houses the majority of the bedrooms which are all well equipped. Public areas include Wealh's restaurant, the popular public bar offering a range of light snacks, and the brasserie bar serving light refreshments all day.

ROOMS: 39 en suite (1 fmly) No smoking in 9 bedrooms s £85-£95; d £99-£120 * LB **FACILITIES:** STV Xmas **CONF:** Thtr 120 Class 60 Board 40 Del from £119 * **PARKING:** 60 **NOTES:** No smoking in restaurant **CARDS:**

★★★65% Shillingford Bridge

Shillingford OX10 8LZ
☎ 01865 858567 🖷 01865 858636
Dir: *from M4 junct 10 follow A329 through Wallingford towards Thame. From M40 junct 6 join B4009. Take A4074 then turn left on to A329 to Wallingford*

Forestdale Hotels

This popular hotel, situated on the banks of the Thames, has its own moorings and a waterside open-air swimming pool. The public areas make good use of the view from the large picture windows, where guests can relax or enjoy a meal in the restaurant. Bedrooms are well equipped and furnished with comfort in mind.

ROOMS: 34 en suite 8 annexe en suite (6 fmly) No smoking in 5 bedrooms s fr £60; d fr £120 (incl. bkfst & dinner) * LB **FACILITIES:** Outdoor swimming (H) Fishing Squash Xmas **CONF:** Thtr 80 Class 36 Board 26 Del from £125 * **PARKING:** 100 **CARDS:**

WALSALL, West Midlands

Map 07 SP09

★★★★66% Menzies Baron's Court

Walsall Rd, Walsall Wood WS9 9AH
☎ 0500 636943 (Central Res) 🖷 01773 880321
e-mail: info@menzies-hotels.co.uk
Dir: *3m NE A461*

MENZIES HOTELS

The Baron's Court Hotel is ideally situated for both leisure and business requirements in the heart of the Midlands. Refurbishment has seen significant improvements to bedrooms, public areas and the stylish brasserie. Additional features of the hotel include a leisure complex and conference facilities.

continued

ROOMS: 95 en suite (2 fmly) No smoking in 19 bedrooms s £85; d £85-£105 * LB **FACILITIES:** STV Indoor swimming (H) Sauna Solarium Gym Pool table Jacuzzi/spa entertainment Xmas **CONF:** Thtr 200 Class 100 Board 100 Del from £85 * **SERVICES:** Lift **PARKING:** 200 **NOTES:** No smoking in restaurant Civ Wed 200 **CARDS:**

★★★76% The Fairlawns at Aldridge

178 Little Aston Rd, Aldridge WS9 0NU
☎ 01922 455122 🖷 01922 743210
e-mail: welcome@fairlawns.co.uk
Dir: *off A452 towards Aldridge at crossroads with A454, Hotel 600 yards on right*

An attractive red brick building that retains the charm of a smaller hotel. There is a smart leisure club and comfortable and well equipped accommodation. The kitchen continues to provide quality food from an imaginative modern British menu. Service is professional, attentive and friendly.

ROOMS: 50 en suite (8 fmly) No smoking in 20 bedrooms s £39.50-£95; d £72.50-£125 (incl. bkfst) * LB **FACILITIES:** STV Indoor swimming (H) Tennis (hard) Sauna Solarium Gym Croquet lawn Putting green Jacuzzi/spa Dance studio Hair and Beauty Salon Petanque **CONF:** Thtr 80 Class 40 Board 30 Del from £107.50 * **PARKING:** 140 **NOTES:** No smoking in restaurant RS 23 Dec-2 Jan Civ Wed 90 **CARDS:**

★★★66% Beverley

58 Lichfield Rd WS4 2DJ
☎ 01922 614967 & 622999 🖷 01922 724187
Dir: *1m N of Walsall town centre on A461 to Lichfield*

A privately owned hotel that offers a warm welcome to all its guests. Bedrooms, though varying in size, are thoughtfully equipped, tastefully appointed and pleasantly decorated. The public rooms include a lounge bar with a conservatory extension, which opens onto an attractive patio terrace. The restaurant is pleasantly appointed and serves daily-changing and carte menus; there is also a wide range of meeting rooms available.

ROOMS: 40 en suite (2 fmly) No smoking in 2 bedrooms s £58-£70; d £70-£85 (incl. bkfst) * LB **FACILITIES:** Pool table Games room **CONF:** Thtr 60 Class 30 Board 30 Del from £80 * **PARKING:** 68 **NOTES:** No dogs (ex guide dogs) No smoking in restaurant **CARDS:**

★★★65% Quality Hotel & Suites Walsall

20 Wolverhampton Rd West, Bentley WS2 0BS
☎ 01922 724444 🖷 01922 723148
e-mail: admin@gb622.u-net.com
Dir: *situated on the rdbt at junct 10, M6*

CHOICE HOTELS EUROPE

Clearly signed from the M6 at junction 10, the hotel offers easy access to the city. All the accommodation is well equipped, including air conditioned suites with a personal fax and a kitchen with microwave and fridge. There is an extensive all day menu, room service and carvery restaurant.

ROOMS: 154 en suite (120 fmly) No smoking in 64 bedrooms s £45-£115; d £60-£125 * LB **FACILITIES:** STV Indoor swimming (H) Sauna Gym Jacuzzi/spa **CONF:** Thtr 180 Class 70 Board 80 Del from £90 * **PARKING:** 160 **NOTES:** No dogs (ex guide dogs) Civ Wed 120 **CARDS:**

Fancy a Singapore Sling? Bar staff in five star hotels should be skilled cocktail mixers.

WALSALL, continued

★★★60% The Boundary

Birmingham Rd WS5 3AB
☎ 01922 633609 01922 612034
e-mail: boundaryhotel@talk21.com
Dir: *off M6 at junc 7, A34 to Walsall. Hotel 2m on left*

This modern, purpose-built hotel is located within easy reach of junctions 7 and 9 of the M6. Facilities include convenient parking, bar, lounge and restaurant.

ROOMS: 96 en suite (3 fmly) No smoking in 53 bedrooms d fr £75 * LB **FACILITIES:** STV Tennis (hard) Pool table entertainment **CONF:** Thtr 65 Class 35 Board 30 Del from £104 * **SERVICES:** Lift **PARKING:** 250 **NOTES:** No smoking in restaurant RS 25-30 Dec
CARDS:

★★62% Bescot

87 Bescot Rd WS2 9DG
☎ 01922 622447 01922 630256
Dir: *from junct 9 M6 take Walsall road. Hotel 100mtrs on right*

The Bescot is a privately owned and business focused hotel. Public rooms are comfortable and freshly furnished, including a large function suite and a spacious restaurant. Bedrooms have a good range of facilities and the annexe rooms are spacious, especially the two ground floor courtyard rooms. The new owners have positive plans for major refurbishment.

ROOMS: 22 en suite 11 annexe en suite (4 fmly) s £35-£40; d £45-£50 (incl. bkfst) * LB **FACILITIES:** STV **CONF:** Thtr 70 Class 50 Board 40 Del from £60 * **PARKING:** 55 **NOTES:** No dogs (ex guide dogs)
CARDS:

WALTERSTONE, Herefordshire — Map 03 SO32

★★★67% *Allt-yr-Ynys Country House Hotel*

HR2 0DU
☎ 01873 890307 01873 890539
e-mail: allthotel@compuserve.com
Dir: *take A465 N of Abergavenny. After 5m turn left at Old Pandy Inn in Pandy. After 300 yrds turn right and hotel is 300yds on the right*

This lovely house dates back to around 1550 and Queen Elizabeth I is reputed to have been a guest here. Most of the modern equipped bedrooms are located in separate single storey stone buildings. Public rooms, which include a comfortable lounge with an ornate ceiling, are contained within the main house.

ROOMS: 1 en suite 18 annexe en suite (2 fmly) No smoking in 6 bedrooms **FACILITIES:** Indoor swimming (H) Fishing Sauna Jacuzzi/spa Clay pigeon range **CONF:** Thtr 100 Class 30 Board 40 **PARKING:** 100 **NOTES:** No smoking in restaurant **CARDS:**

WALTHAM ABBEY, Essex — Map 05 TL30

★★★★64% Swallow

Old Shire Ln EN9 3LX
☎ 01992 717170 01992 711841
e-mail: info@swallowhotels.com
Dir: *off junct 26 of M25*

Near the M25, this modern hotel gives easy access to London. Useful facilities include extensive meeting rooms, a leisure club, modern restaurant, and a bus shuttle to nearby transport links. Bedrooms are comfortable and well equipped.

ROOMS: 163 en suite (14 fmly) No smoking in 132 bedrooms s £120; d £145 (incl. bkfst) * **FACILITIES:** STV Indoor swimming (H) Sauna Solarium Gym Jacuzzi/spa Steam room Beauty Salon entertainment Xmas **CONF:** Thtr 250 Class 120 Board 50 Del from £125 * **PARKING:** 240 **NOTES:** No smoking in restaurant
CARDS:

WALTON UPON THAMES See Weybridge

WANSFORD, Cambridgeshire — Map 04 TL09

★★★74% The Haycock Hotel

PE8 6JA
☎ 01780 782223 01780 783031
Dir: *at junct of A47/A1*

Situated just off the A1, this 17th-century hotel has welcomed travellers for many years. Attractive stone buildings have been restored to provide well equipped bedrooms with thoughtful extras. Guests can dine in the main restaurant or in the Orchards conservatory brasserie. Lounges with log fires and an inviting bar form the hub of the hotel.

ROOMS: 50 en suite (3 fmly) No smoking in 6 bedrooms d £80-£100 * LB **FACILITIES:** STV Fishing Petanque Xmas **CONF:** Thtr 250 Class 100 Board 40 Del from £130 * **PARKING:** 300 **NOTES:** No smoking in restaurant **CARDS:**

W

WARDLEY, Tyne & Wear — Map 12 NZ36

Travelodge

Travelodge

Leam Ln, Whitemare Pool NE10 8YB
☎ 0191 438 3333 📠 0191 438 3333
Dir: *at junc of A194M/A184*

This modern building offers accommodation in smart, spacious and well equipped bedrooms, all with en suite bathrooms. Refreshments may be taken at the nearby family restaurant. For further details and the Travelodge phone number, consult the Hotel Groups page.

ROOMS: 71 en suite

WARE, Hertfordshire — Map 05 TL31

★★★★★70% Marriott Hanbury Manor

Marriott HOTELS·RESORTS·SUITES

SG12 0SD
☎ 01920 487722 📠 01920 487692
Dir: *on A10 12m N of junc 25 of M25*

The range of leisure facilities at this impressive Jacobean-style mansion is outstanding. Set in 200 acres of grounds and wonderful gardens, this hotel offers a golf course of growing international reputation, together with excellent indoor leisure facilities. Bedrooms, both in the main building and in the separate stable wing, are comfortably furnished in the country house-style and have smart marbled bathrooms. The extensive public areas feature fine wood panelling, crystal chandeliers, antique furniture and open fires. There are a number of options for food and refreshment, of which the Zodiac Restaurant is renowned for its high standards of cooking.

ROOMS: 69 en suite 27 annexe en suite No smoking in 10 bedrooms d £130-£160 * LB **FACILITIES:** STV Indoor swimming (H) Golf 18 Tennis (hard) Snooker Sauna Solarium Gym Pool table Croquet lawn Putting green Jacuzzi/spa Health & beauty treatments Aerobics ch fac Xmas **CONF:** Thtr 150 Class 72 Board 42 Del from £195 * **SERVICES:** Lift **PARKING:** 200 **NOTES:** No smoking in restaurant Civ Wed 160 **CARDS:**

★★★60% *Roebuck*

ZOFFANY HOTELS

Baldock St SG12 9DR
☎ 01920 409955 📠 01920 468016
e-mail: roebuck@zoffanyhotels.co.uk
Dir: *turn off A10 onto B1001 turn left at rdbt first left behind Fire Station*

Close to the town centre, this popular modern hotel offers a range of versatile conference rooms, a giant screen satellite TV and a bar with pool table. Bedrooms are spacious and well equipped, some are suitable for disabled guests.

ROOMS: 50 en suite (1 fmly) No smoking in 16 bedrooms **FACILITIES:** Pool table **CONF:** Thtr 175 Class 75 Board 60 **SERVICES:** Lift **PARKING:** 64 **NOTES:** No dogs (ex guide dogs) No smoking in restaurant **CARDS:**

WAREHAM, Dorset — Map 03 SY98

Premier Collection

★★★ Priory

Church Green BH20 4ND
☎ 01929 551666 📠 01929 554519
e-mail: reception@theprioryhotel.co.uk
Dir: *A351 at Station rdbt take North Causeway/North St, left into East St at lights, 1st right into Church St, hotel between church and river*

Set amidst four acres of well tended gardens on the banks of the River Frome, this historic former priory balances true professionalism with friendliness. A choice of comfortable lounges is available, enhanced by log fires during cooler weather. Bedrooms are luxurious and full of character, especially those in the adjacent boathouse, which are particularly spacious. At dinner, both carte and set menus are offered in the vaulted, stone cellar Restaurant, while during the week lunches are served in the Garden Room.

ROOMS: 15 en suite 4 annexe en suite s £80-£125; d £100-£240 (incl. bkfst) * LB **FACILITIES:** STV Fishing Croquet lawn Sailing Moorings for guests entertainment Xmas **CONF:** Board 20 **PARKING:** 25 **NOTES:** No dogs (ex guide dogs) No children 8yrs No smoking in restaurant **CARDS:**

★★★71% Springfield Country Hotel & Leisure Club

Grange Rd BH20 5AL
☎ 01929 552177 📠 01929 551862
Dir: *from Wareham take Stoborough road then first right in village to join by-pass. Turn left and take first turn immediately on right for hotel*

Situated in attractive countryside, this smart hotel is notable for its extensive leisure and conference facilities. Bedrooms vary in style from the main house to newer rooms, however, all are smart and well furnished.

ROOMS: 48 en suite (7 fmly) s £70-£80; d £110-£130 (incl. bkfst) * LB **FACILITIES:** Indoor swimming (H) Outdoor swimming (H) Tennis (hard) Squash Snooker Sauna Gym Pool table Jacuzzi/spa Steam room Table tennis Beauty treatment ch fac **CONF:** Thtr 200 Class 50 Board 60 Del from £80 * **SERVICES:** Lift **PARKING:** 150 **NOTES:** No smoking in restaurant **CARDS:**

★★69% Kemps Country House

East Stoke BH20 6AL
☎ 01929 462563 📠 01929 405287
Dir: *mid-way between Wareham/Wool on A352*

A relaxing family-owned hotel with views over the Purbeck Hills in the distance. Bedrooms are spacious, garden rooms being more modern in style. There are two comfortable lounges and an adjoining bar. An extensive choice is available from the imaginative and innovative set menu and carte, with bar meals being available at lunch time.

continued

WAREHAM, continued

ROOMS: 5 rms (4 en suite) 10 annexe en suite (4 fmly) s £63; d £90-£94 (incl. bkfst) * LB **FACILITIES:** Xmas **CONF:** Thtr 50 Class 20 Board 20 Del from £95.95 * **PARKING:** 50 **NOTES:** No dogs (ex guide dogs) No smoking in restaurant **CARDS:**

★★ 65% *Worgret Manor*

Worgret Rd BH20 6AB
☎ 01929 552957 01929 554804
e-mail: worgretmanorhotel@btinternet.com
Dir: *on A352 from Wareham to Wool-0.5m from Wareham rdbt*

On the edge of Wareham, with easy access to major routes, this privately owned hotel has a friendly, cheerful atmosphere. The bedrooms come in a variety of sizes. Day rooms comprise a popular bar, a quiet lounge and a restaurant where good, home cooked meals are served.

ROOMS: 13 rms (11 en suite) (1 fmly) No smoking in 4 bedrooms **FACILITIES:** Free use of local sports centre **CONF:** Thtr 90 **PARKING:** 25 **NOTES:** No smoking in restaurant **CARDS:**

WARMINSTER, Wiltshire — Map 03 ST84

★★★★ 73% Bishopstrow House

BA12 9HH
☎ 01985 212312 01985 216769
e-mail: reservations@bishopstrow.co.uk
Dir: *A303, A36, B3414, premises 2m on right*

A classical Georgian house set in 27 acres of grounds. Comfortably furnished with English antiques, 19th-century paintings and log fires, the atmosphere is luxurious yet relaxed. An impressive range of facilities is available to guests. Bedrooms are individually furnished and equipped with many thoughtful extras. The Mulberry Restaurant and the Wilton Room offer traditional English fare with flair, and afternoon tea is served in one of several lounges.

ROOMS: 32 en suite (3 fmly) No smoking in 1 bedroom s £90-£99; d £170-£195 (incl. cont bkfst) * LB **FACILITIES:** STV Indoor swimming (H) Outdoor swimming (H) Tennis (hard) Fishing Sauna Gym Croquet lawn Clay pigeon shooting Archery Cycling entertainment ch fac Xmas **CONF:** Thtr 65 Class 32 Board 36 Del from £165 * **PARKING:** 60 **NOTES:** No smoking in restaurant Civ Wed 70 **CARDS:**

Travelodge

A36 Bath Rd BA12 7RU
☎ Central Res 0800 850950 01525 878450
Dir: *junc A350/A36*

This modern building offers accommodation in smart, spacious and well equipped bedrooms, all with en suite bathrooms. Refreshments may be taken at the nearby family restaurant. For further details and the Travelodge phone number, consult the Hotel Groups page.

ROOMS: 31 en suite

WARRINGTON, Cheshire — Map 07 SJ68

★★★★ 74% Park Royal International Hotel

Stretton Rd, Stretton WA4 4NS
☎ 01925 730706 01925 730740
e-mail: hotel@park-royal-int.co.uk
Dir: *off M56 junc 10, A49 to Warrington, at traffic lights turn right to Appleton Thorn, hotel 200 yards on right*

Situated between Warrington and the M56, this large modern hotel still enjoys a peaceful location. Spacious bedrooms are comfortable and attractive. Meals in the Harlequin Restaurant are carefully prepared and enjoyable. The hotel has good function suites and leisure facilities, including outdoor tennis courts.

ROOMS: 140 en suite (15 fmly) No smoking in 54 bedrooms s £59-£110.75; d £69-£130 (incl. bkfst) * LB **FACILITIES:** STV Indoor swimming (H) Tennis (hard) Sauna Solarium Gym Jacuzzi/spa Retreat Beauty centre with beauty rooms,including Hydrotherapy bath & Solarium Xmas **CONF:** Thtr 400 Class 250 Board 90 Del £147 * **SERVICES:** Lift **PARKING:** 400 **NOTES:** Civ Wed 400 **CARDS:**

See advert on opposite page

★★★★ 73% Daresbury Park

Chester Rd, Daresbury WA4 4BB
☎ 01925 267331 01925 265615
e-mail: daresburyparksalesmanager@devere-hotels.com
Dir: *entrance off junction 11 rdbt*

A £10.5 million redevelopment has completely transformed this well positioned hotel. Superb public areas include a magnificent glass rotunda, two new restaurants, a wide range of meeting rooms and extensive leisure facilities. All the existing bedrooms have been refurbished to a very high standard and newly built rooms include a number of superbly appointed and equipped suites.

ROOMS: 181 en suite (14 fmly) No smoking in 114 bedrooms s £120-£195; d £140-£205 (incl. bkfst) * LB **FACILITIES:** STV Indoor swimming (H) Squash Snooker Sauna Solarium Gym Jacuzzi/spa Steam room Beautician Hairdresser ch fac Xmas **CONF:** Thtr 500 Class 240 Board 100 Del from £125 * **SERVICES:** Lift **PARKING:** 400 **NOTES:** Civ Wed 300 **CARDS:**

★★★ 69% *Fir Grove*

Knutsford Old Rd WA4 2LD
☎ 01925 267471 01925 601092
Dir: *turn off M6 at junc 20, follow signs for A50, at Warrington before the swing bridge over canal, turn right, and right again*

Situated in a quiet residential area, conveniently located between the centre of town and junction 20 of the M6. Comfortable, smart bedrooms are set around an attractive garden courtyard, and offer some excellent extra facilities including play-stations and CD players. There is a choice of bars, a neatly appointed restaurant and excellent function and meeting facilities.

ROOMS: 40 en suite No smoking in 4 bedrooms **FACILITIES:** STV **CONF:** Thtr 200 Class 80 Board 40 **PARKING:** 100 **CARDS:**

> Late for dinner? Quality Standards star rating means that last orders for dinner should be no earlier than:
> ★ 6.30pm ★★ 7.00pm ★★★ 8.00pm
> ★★★★ 9.00pm ★★★★★ 10.00pm

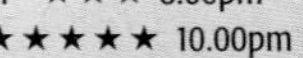

★★75% Rockfield
Alexandra Rd, Grappenhall WA4 2EL
☎ 01925 262898 Fax 01925 263343
Dir: from M6 take A50 to Warrington, continue over lights & at junct A50/A56 take side road into Victoria Road, then 1st right into Alexandra Road

This friendly private hotel is situated in a leafy, residential part of town. The proprietor's native Swiss cuisine, served in the restaurant, is renowned in the area. Bedrooms, some in an adjacent house, are well equipped with all modern comforts. The hotel benefits from a pretty garden and a welcoming lounge and bar.

ROOMS: 6 en suite 6 annexe en suite s £51-£54; d £61-£65 (incl. bkfst) * LB **FACILITIES:** STV ch fac Xmas **CONF:** Thtr 60 Class 40 Board 28 Del from £84 * **PARKING:** 25 **NOTES:** No dogs (ex guide dogs) Civ Wed 60 **CARDS:**

★★63% Paddington House
514 Old Manchester Rd WA1 3TZ
☎ 01925 816767 Fax 01925 816651
e-mail: hotel@paddingtonhouse.co.uk
Dir: located 1m from junct 21 M6 off the A57, 2 miles from Warrington town centre

MINOTEL Great Britain

Just over a mile from junction 21 of the M6, Paddington House Hotel is a vibrant commercial venue. The bedrooms are attractively furnished, with four-poster rooms available and some on the ground floor. Diners can eat in the wood-panelled Padgate restaurant in the cosy bar.

ROOMS: 37 en suite (9 fmly) No smoking in 16 bedrooms s £57.50-£67.50; d £65-£75 (incl. bkfst) * LB **CONF:** Thtr 200 Class 100 Board 40 Del from £95 * **SERVICES:** Lift **PARKING:** 50 **NOTES:** No smoking in restaurant Civ Wed 150 **CARDS:**

⇧ Premier Lodge (Warrington North)
Golbourne Rd, Winwick WA2 8LF
☎ 0870 700 1562 Fax 0870 700 1563

PREMIER LODGE

Premier Lodge offers modern, well equipped, en suite accommodation suitable for both business and leisure travellers. Meals can be taken at the adjacent popular restaurant and bar which is fully licensed. For further details, consult the Hotel Groups page.

ROOMS: 42 en suite d £42 *

⇧ Premier Lodge (Warrington South)
Tarporley Rd, Stretton WA4 4NB
☎ 0870 700 1564 Fax 0870 700 1565

PREMIER LODGE

Premier Lodge offers modern, well equipped, en suite accommodation suitable for both business and leisure travellers. Meals can be taken at the adjacent popular restaurant and bar which is fully licensed. For further details, consult the Hotel Groups page.

ROOMS: 29 en suite d £42 *

WARWICK, Warwickshire — Map 04 SP26
see also Claverdon, Honiley & Leamington Spa (Royal)

★★★68% Ardencote Manor Hotel & Country Club
Lye Green Rd CV35 8LS
☎ 01926 843111 Fax 01926 842646
e-mail: hotel@ardencote.com
(For full entry see Claverdon & advert on page 589)

Bad hair day? Hairdryers in all rooms three stars and above.

WARWICK, continued

★★★63% *Lord Leycester*
Jury St CV34 4EJ
☎ 01926 491481 01926 491561
This historic Grade II building is just a short walk from the famous castle. Upgraded bedrooms and public rooms provide comfortable accommodation. A choice of eating options is available in either the Squires Buttery, or the Knights Restaurant.

ROOMS: 52 en suite (3 fmly) **CONF:** Thtr 250 Class 100 Board 60
SERVICES: Lift **PARKING:** 40 **CARDS:**

★★65% Warwick Arms
17 High St CV34 4AT
☎ 01926 492759 01926 410587
Dir: *off M40 junc 15, main road into Warwick, premises 100 yards past Lord Leycester Hospital*
A relaxed and friendly hotel in the heart of Warwick, close to the castle walls. Public rooms offer a cosy bar and comfortable foyer lounge area, and a good choice of meals is served in the restaurant from a daily set priced menu and carte; light snacks and informal meals are available in the bar. Bedrooms vary in style and size, each has a good range of facilities.
ROOMS: 35 en suite (4 fmly) s £55-£60; d £65-£70 (incl. bkfst) *
FACILITIES: Xmas **CONF:** Thtr 110 Class 50 Board 50 Del from £75 *
PARKING: 21 **CARDS:**

⌂ Express by Holiday Inn Warwick

Stratford Rd CV34 6TW
☎ 01926 483000 01926 483033
Dir: *M40 junct15, follow signs A429 to Warwick. Take 1st turning on right*

A modern budget hotel offering comfortable accommodation in refreshing, spacious and comprehensively-equipped bedrooms, en suite bathrooms with power showers and continental buffet breakfast included in the room rate. Suitable for business travellers or families. For further details and the Express by Holiday Inn phone number, consult the Hotel Groups page.
ROOMS: 117 en suite d £60 (incl. cont bkfst) * **CONF:** Thtr 24 Class 20

WARWICK MOTORWAY SERVICE AREA, Warwickshire — Map 04 SP35

⌂ Days Inn

Warwick Services, M40 Northbound, Banbury Rd CV35 0AA
☎ 01926 651681 01926 651634
Dir: *M40 northbound between junct 12 & 13*
Fully refurbished, Days Inn offers well equipped, brightly appointed, modern accommodation with smart en suite bathrooms. There is a fully staffed reception; continental breakfast is available and other refreshments may be taken at the nearby family restaurant.
ROOMS: 54 en suite d fr £45 *

⌂ Days Inn

Warwick Services, M40 Southbound, Banbury Rd CV35 0AA
☎ 01926 650168 01926 651601
Dir: *M40 southbound between junct 13 & 12*
Fully refurbished, Days Inn offers well equipped, brightly appointed, modern accommodation with smart en suite bathrooms. There is a fully staffed reception; continental breakfast is available and other refreshments may be taken at the nearby family restaurant.
ROOMS: 40 en suite d fr £45 *

WASHINGTON, Tyne & Wear — Map 12 NZ35

★★★67% *Posthouse Washington*
Posthouse
Emerson District 5 NE37 1LB
☎ 0870 400 9084 0191 415 3371
Dir: *off A1 (M) exit A195-take left hand sliproad signposted district 5. Turn left at rdbt and hotel is on the left*
Lying close to the A1(M), this purpose-built hotel is popular with business travellers. Bedrooms are comfortable and well equipped and include a number of 'superior' rooms in contemporary design. The Junction Restaurant offers a full menu and there is also a wide-ranging lounge menu and 24-hour room service.
ROOMS: 138 en suite (7 fmly) No smoking in 89 bedrooms
FACILITIES: Pitch & putt **CONF:** Thtr 100 Class 40 Board 50
SERVICES: Lift **PARKING:** 198 **CARDS:**

★★★65% George Washington Golf & Country Club
REGAL
Stone Cellar Rd, District 12, High Usworth NE37 1PH
☎ 0191 402 9988 0191 415 1166
e-mail: reservations@corushotels.com
Dir: *off A1 (M), follow signs for District 12 and Golf Course*

Surrounded by its own 18-hole golf course, this popular, purpose-built hotel offers smart well equipped accommodation, including

continued

some suites and family rooms. A leisure club and business centre form part of the hotel's many facilities.
ROOMS: 103 en suite (9 fmly) No smoking in 44 bedrooms s £90-£110; d £90-£150 * LB **FACILITIES:** Indoor swimming (H) Golf 18 Squash Sauna Solarium Gym Pool table Putting green Jacuzzi/spa Golf driving range Pitch and putt **CONF:** Thtr 200 Class 100 Board 80 Del from £85 * **PARKING:** 200 **NOTES:** No smoking in restaurant Civ Wed 35
CARDS:

Campanile

Emerson Rd NE37 1LE
☎ 0191 416 5010 🖷 0191 416 5023
Dir: *turn off A1 at junct 64, A195 to Washington, first left at rdbt into Emerson Road, Hotel 800yds on left*

This modern building offers accommodation in smart well equipped bedrooms, all with en suite bathrooms. Refreshments may be taken at the informal Bistro. For further details and the Campanile phone number, consult the Hotel Groups page.
ROOMS: 77 annexe en suite **CONF:** Thtr 35 Class 18 Board 20

WASHINGTON SERVICE AREA, Tyne & Wear — Map 12 NZ25

Travelodge (North)

Travelodge

Motorway Service Area, Portobello DH3 2SJ
☎ 01914 103436
Dir: *northbound carriageway of A1(M)*
This modern building offers accommodation in smart, spacious and well equipped bedrooms, all with en suite bathrooms. Refreshments may be taken at the nearby family restaurant. For further details and the Travelodge phone number, consult the Hotel Groups page.
ROOMS: 31 en suite

Travelodge (South)

Travelodge

Portobello DH3 2SJ
☎ 01914 103436
Dir: *A1M*
This modern building offers accommodation in smart, spacious and well equipped bedrooms, all with en suite bathrooms. Refreshments may be taken at the nearby family restaurant. For further details and the Travelodge phone number, consult the Hotel Groups page.
ROOMS: 36 en suite

Late for dinner? Quality Standards star rating means that last orders for dinner should be no earlier than:
★ 6.30pm ★★ 7.00pm ★★★ 8.00pm
★★★★ 9.00pm ★★★★★ 10.00pm

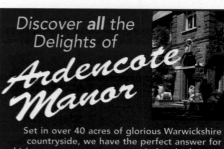

WATCHET, Somerset — Map 03 ST04

★★70% Downfield Hotel

16 St Decuman's Rd TA23 0HR
☎ 01984 631267 🖷 01984 634369
Dir: *from A39 1.5m out of Williton onto B3190, ignore signs to town ctr 200m past Railway St turn right at jct into St Decuman's Rd, hotel 200m on right*
Overlooking the harbour this substantial Victorian house stands in large, well kept gardens. The bedrooms range from spacious in the main house, to more compact in the Coach House. In the dining room, with its splendid chandelier, freshly prepared dinners are provided using local produce wherever possible. A comfortable sitting room is also available.
ROOMS: 5 en suite 2 annexe en suite (1 fmly) No smoking in all bedrooms s £39-£43; d £54-£62 (incl. bkfst) * **PARKING:** 14
NOTES: No smoking in restaurant **CARDS:**

WATERGATE BAY, Cornwall & Isles of Scilly — Map 02 SW86

★67% *Tregurrian*

TR8 4AB
☎ 01637 860540 🖷 01637 860280
Dir: *on B3276, 3m from Newquay*
Conveniently located for easy access to the famous beach, this relaxed and friendly hotel is ideal for walkers of the coastal path and families alike. The well maintained bedrooms are comfortable and vary in size. In the dining room, both breakfast and dinner are buffet style, with hearty portions served and good use of fresh ingredients.
ROOMS: 27 rms (22 en suite) (8 fmly) **FACILITIES:** Outdoor swimming (H) Sauna Solarium Pool table Jacuzzi/spa Games room **PARKING:** 26
NOTES: No dogs (ex guide dogs) Closed Nov-Feb
CARDS:

WATERHOUSES, Staffordshire Map 07 SK05

Premier Collection

★★ Old Beams Restaurant with Rooms
Leek Rd ST10 3HW
☎ 01538 308254 01538 308157
Dir: *on A523 Leek to Ashbourne Road*
The dedicated proprietors are now in their 20th year at The Old Beams, a mid-18th-century property in a village setting on the edge of the Staffordshire Moorlands, between Leek and Ashbourne. During their time here they have transformed the simple cottage-style premises into a charming restaurant characterised by its low beamed ceilings and the conservatory extension which overlooks the lovely rear garden. For those who wish to extend their stay, a separate building has been converted to provide five tastefully appointed, luxurious bedrooms. The warmth, friendliness and attentiveness of the service never falters. Only the best available fresh produce is used for frequently changing set price menus. Vegetarian dishes do not generally feature but can always be provided on request.
ROOMS: 5 annexe en suite s fr £65; d £75-£120 (incl. cont bkfst) * **PARKING:** 22 **NOTES:** No dogs (ex guide dogs) No smoking in restaurant Closed January RS Sun eve & Mon
CARDS:

WATERINGBURY, Kent Map 05 TQ65

Premier Lodge (Maidstone)
Tonbridge Rd ME18 5NS
☎ 0870 700 1468 0870 700 1469
PREMIER LODGE
Premier Lodge offers modern, well equipped, en suite accommodation suitable for both business and leisure travellers. Meals can be taken at the adjacent popular restaurant and bar which is fully licensed. For further details, consult the Hotel Groups page.
ROOMS: 40 en suite d £46 *

WATERMILLOCK, Cumbria Map 12 NY42

★★★ 79% Rampsbeck Country House
CA11 0LP
☎ 017684 86442 & 86688 017684 86688
e-mail: enquiries@rampsbeck.fsnet.co.uk
Dir: *leave M6 at junct 40, follow signs for A592 to Ullswater, at T-junct with lake in front, turn right, hotel is 1.5m along lake's edge*
This fine country house lies in 18 acres of parkland and gardens on the shores of Lake Ullswater. Hospitality and service are splendid and food is excellent. Public rooms include three delightful lounges, an elegant restaurant and traditional bar. There are three styles of bedrooms. The spacious front-facing rooms - some with lounges and balconies - overlook the lake, but others are equally characterful and also enjoy good views.
ROOMS: 20 en suite No smoking in 2 bedrooms s fr £60; d fr £100 (incl. bkfst) * LB **FACILITIES:** Fishing Croquet lawn Xmas **PARKING:** 30 **NOTES:** No smoking in restaurant Closed end Jan-early Feb **CARDS:**

★★★ 73% Leeming House
CA11 0JJ
☎ 0870 400 8131 017684 86443
e-mail: HeritageHotels_Ullswater.Leeming_House@Forte-hotels.com
Dir: *exit junct 40 M6 and take A66 to Keswick. Turn left after 1m (to Ullswater). Continue for 5m until T-junct and turn right. Hotel on left (3m)*
This country house hotel is situated in extensive grounds that run down to the shores of Lake Ullswater. The stylish and comfortable bedrooms are thoughtfully equipped and many have their own balcony or patio. The lounge and library boast real fires in winter.
ROOMS: 40 en suite No smoking in 11 bedrooms s £69-£99; d £138-£178 (incl. bkfst) * LB **FACILITIES:** STV Fishing Croquet lawn Xmas **CONF:** Thtr 35 Board 20 Del from £120 * **PARKING:** 50 **NOTES:** No smoking in restaurant Civ Wed 30
CARDS:

Premier Collection

★ Old Church
Old Church Bay CA11 0JN
☎ 017684 86204 017684 86368
e-mail: info@oldchurch.co.uk
Dir: *7m from junc 40 M6, 2.50m S of Pooley Bridge on A592*
This comfortable, well-equipped hotel is set in an idyllic location. The bedrooms at the front enjoy views of the lake and mountains. The two lounges, one of which is a bar in the evening, and fireside seating in the lobby offer a choice of quiet places for contemplation. Board games and reading material are provided for guests' use and a soft furnishings course is often run at the hotel.
ROOMS: 10 en suite s £59-£99; d £90-£135 (incl. bkfst) * LB **FACILITIES:** Fishing Boat hire Moorings/fishing **PARKING:** 20 **NOTES:** No dogs (ex guide dogs) No smoking in restaurant Closed Dec-Feb & Sun & Mon Mar-Nov **CARDS:**

Popped the question? Hotels with Civ Wed in their entry are licensed for civil wedding ceremonies. Maximum numbers for the ceremony only are shown, e.g. Civ Wed 50

WATFORD, Hertfordshire Map 04 TQ19

★★★64% The White House

Upton Rd WD1 7EL
☎ 01923 237316 📠 01923 233109
e-mail: info@whitehousehotel.co.uk
Dir: *main Watford centre ring road goes into Exchange Rd, Upton Rd left turn off, hotel can be seen on left*

This is a well located and popular commercial hotel. Bedrooms are practically furnished and decorated and offer a good range of in room facilities. The public areas are open plan in style and comprise a lounge/bar area and an attractive conservatory restaurant. The availability of off street parking opposite the hotel is an advantage for car users.
ROOMS: 60 en suite 26 annexe en suite (1 fmly) No smoking in 9 bedrooms s £79-£119; d £99-£145 * LB **FACILITIES:** STV **CONF:** Thtr 250 Class 80 Board 50 **SERVICES:** Lift **PARKING:** 40 **NOTES:** No smoking in restaurant **CARDS:**

See advert on this page

WATFORD GAP MOTORWAY SERVICE AREA (M1), Northamptonshire Map 04 SP66

WATTON, Norfolk Map 05 TF90

★★63% Broom Hall Country Hotel

Richmond Rd, Saham Toney IP25 7EX
☎ 01953 882125 📠 01953 882125
e-mail: enquiries@broomhallhotel.co.uk
Dir: *leave A11 at Thetford on A1075 to Watton (12m) B1108 to Swaffham, in 0.5m at rdbt take B1077 to Saham Toney, hotel 0.5m on the left*

Broom Hall is a privately owned Victorian country house situated in the Norfolk village of Saham Toney amidst 15 acres of garden and parkland. The hotel makes an excellent base for guests wishing to explore East Anglia and local tourist attractions. Guests can enjoy facilities such as an indoor swimming pool, a full size snooker table or during the winter just sit and relax by the open fire in the large lounge.
ROOMS: 9 en suite (3 fmly) No smoking in all bedrooms s £39-£52; d £64-£100 (incl. bkfst) * LB **FACILITIES:** Indoor swimming (H) Snooker **CONF:** Class 20 Board 16 **PARKING:** 60 **NOTES:** No dogs (ex guide dogs) No smoking in restaurant Closed 24 Dec-4 Jan Civ Wed 30 **CARDS:**

See advert under THETFORD

WEEDON, Northamptonshire Map 04 SP65

★★64% Globe

High St NN7 4QD
☎ 01327 340336 📠 01327 349058
e-mail: 11ct@tinyworld.co.uk
Dir: *at crossroads of A5/A45*

This friendly coaching inn, just three miles from the M1 is very popular with all types of guests. There is a charming family atmosphere and excellent service. Bedrooms are all pleasantly decorated and well equipped, and a number of rooms offer four-poster beds.

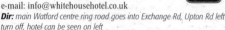

ROOMS: 15 en suite 3 annexe en suite (3 fmly) No smoking in 2 bedrooms s £45-£50; d £55-£60 (incl. bkfst) * LB **FACILITIES:** STV entertainment **CONF:** Thtr 30 Board 16 Del from £90 * **PARKING:** 22 **NOTES:** No smoking in restaurant **CARDS:**

Premier Lodge (Daventry)

PREMIER LODGE

High St NN7 4PX
☎ 0870 700 1520 📠 0870 700 1521
Dir: *at A5/A45 crossroads*

Premier Lodge offers modern, well equipped, en suite accommodation suitable for both business and leisure travellers. Meals can be taken at the adjacent popular restaurant and bar which is fully licensed. For further details, consult the Hotel Groups page.
ROOMS: 45 en suite d £46 *

WELLINGBOROUGH, Northamptonshire Map 04 SP86

★★★65% Menzies Hind

Sheep St NN8 1BY
☎ 0500 636943 (Central Res) 🖹 01773 880321
e-mail: info@menzies-hotels.co.uk
Dir: *on A509 in town centre*
Dating back to Jacobean times, this central hotel provides a good base for visiting the town. The all-day coffee shop is a smart meeting place for locals. There are extensive function and meeting rooms, bedrooms are mainly spacious and well designed. A wide range of food is available in the restaurant.
ROOMS: 34 en suite (2 fmly) No smoking in 5 bedrooms s £75-£85; d £85-£95 * LB **FACILITIES:** Xmas **CONF:** Thtr 130 Class 60 Board 50 **PARKING:** 15 **NOTES:** No smoking in restaurant Civ Wed 120
CARDS:

★★65% Columbia

19-31 Northampton Rd NN8 3HG
☎ 01933 229333 🖹 01933 440418
e-mail: SimonRobson@connectfree.co.uk
Dir: *access from town centre via Oxford Street*
A friendly hotel in the centre of town, the Columbia offers comfortable bedrooms equipped with modern facilities. There is a pleasant restaurant and also a room available for meetings or private dining.
ROOMS: 29 en suite (5 fmly) s £40-£50; d £50-£65 (incl. bkfst) * LB **FACILITIES:** STV Xmas **CONF:** Thtr 30 Class 30 Board 20 Del from £70 * **PARKING:** 20 **NOTES:** No smoking in restaurant
CARDS:

★★64% High View

156 Midland Rd NN8 1NG
☎ 01933 278733 🖹 01933 225948
e-mail: highviewhotel@supanet.com
Dir: *turn off A45 onto B573, follow sign post to rail station, at Midland road T-junct turn left towards town centre, hotel approx 100yds on left*
This small hotel is close to the centre of town and offers a warm welcome to all its guests. Bedrooms are spacious and have all the expected facilities, home-cooked food is also available.
ROOMS: 14 en suite (2 fmly) s £34-£45; d £45-£56 (incl. bkfst) * **PARKING:** 8 **NOTES:** No dogs No children 3yrs No smoking in restaurant Closed 25 Dec-1 Jan **CARDS:**

⌂ Express by Holiday Inn Wellingborough

Express by Holiday Inn

Enstone Court NN8 2DR
☎ 01933 228333 🖹 01933 228444
Dir: *located on junct of A45 & A509 towards Kettering on the SW edge of Wellingborough*

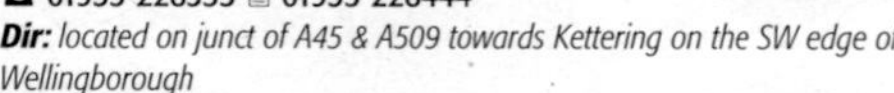

A modern budget hotel offering comfortable accommodation in refreshing, spacious and comprehensively-equipped bedrooms, en suite bathrooms with power showers and continental buffet breakfast included in the room rate. Suitable for business travellers or families. For further details and the Express by Holiday Inn phone number, consult the Hotel Groups page.
ROOMS: 78 en suite (incl. cont bkfst) d fr £49.50 *

WELLINGTON See Telford (Shropshire)

WELLINGTON, Somerset Map 03 ST12

★★★78% ❀❀ Bindon Country House Hotel & Restaurant

PRIDE OF BRITAIN MEMBER

Langford Budville TA21 0RU
☎ 01823 400070 🖹 01823 400071
e-mail: bindonhouse@msn.com
Dir: *from Wellington B3187 to Langford Budville, through village, right towards Wiveliscombe, right at junct, pass Bindon Farm, right after 450yds*

Mentioned in the Domesday Book, this delightful country retreat is set in seven acres of formal and woodland gardens. Each bedroom is named after a battle fought by the Duke of Wellington, and is decorated with sumptuous fabrics and equipped with every modern facility. The public rooms are equally stunning, with original features such as a tiled floors, stairwells and fireplaces. Dinner is a delight, prepared with flair and innovation from the best of fresh ingredients.
ROOMS: 12 en suite (2 fmly) No smoking in all bedrooms s £85-£95; d £95-£185 (incl. bkfst) * LB **FACILITIES:** Outdoor swimming (H) Tennis (hard) Croquet lawn entertainment Xmas **CONF:** Thtr 50 Class 30 Board 20 Del from £125 * **PARKING:** 30 **NOTES:** No smoking in restaurant Civ Wed 50 **CARDS:**

See advert under TAUNTON

★★★62% The Cleve Country House Hotel

Mantle St TA21 8SN
☎ 01823 662033 🖹 01823 660874
Dir: *from M5 junct 26 follow signs to Wellington, then left before Elf Petrol Station in town*
Offering comfortable bedrooms and public areas, The Cleve Hotel is quietly located in an elevated position above the town of Wellington. The atmosphere is relaxed and guests can enjoy dining in the open plan restaurant. Two full size snooker tables are available for guest use.
ROOMS: 15 en suite (5 fmly) No smoking in 12 bedrooms s £47.50-£57.50; d £59.50-£69.50 (incl. bkfst) * LB **FACILITIES:** Snooker Sauna Solarium **CONF:** Thtr 150 Class 70 Board 50 Del from £54.50 * **PARKING:** 60 **NOTES:** No smoking in restaurant Civ Wed 120
CARDS:

> Packed in a hurry? Ironing facilities should be available at all star levels, either in rooms or on request.

★★64% Beambridge
Sampford Arundel TA21 0HB
☎ 01823 672223 📠 01823 673100
Dir: *1.5m W on A38 between junct 26 & 27 of M5*

The Beambridge offers value for money; a relaxed and friendly hotel, ideally located at the gateway to the West Country. The dedicated team provide a smooth service, ensuring a stress free stay for all guests. A wide range of bar food is served, with the option of a more formal restaurant. The comfortable bedrooms are well equipped and decorated, suiting all needs.

ROOMS: 9 en suite (1 fmly) s £39; d £47 (incl. bkfst) * **CONF:** Thtr 100 Class 100 Board 50 **PARKING:** 100 **NOTES:** No dogs (ex guide dogs) No smoking in restaurant Closed 25-26 Dec
CARDS:

WELLS, Somerset
Map 03 ST54

★★★70% ❀ The Market Place
One Market Place BA5 2RW
☎ 01749 672616 📠 01749 679670
e-mail: marketplace@bhere.co.uk
Dir: *A39, A371 - in City Centre (Market Place) along one way system*

In the centre of the city of Wells, this unique hotel combines modern style and elegance with the character and appeal of a building built over 500 years ago. In the restaurant the chefs produce award-winning cuisine. All bedrooms, whether in the main house or annexe, are comfortable and well furnished.

ROOMS: 24 en suite 10 annexe en suite (4 fmly) s £75-£85; d £99.50-£119.50 (incl. bkfst) * LB **FACILITIES:** Xmas **CONF:** Thtr 150 Class 75 Board 75 Del from £99 * **PARKING:** 30 **NOTES:** No smoking in restaurant Closed 28-31 Dec **CARDS:**

★★★69% Swan

Sadler St BA5 2RX
☎ 01749 678877 📠 01749 677647
e-mail: swan@bhere.co.uk
Dir: *A39, A371, opp cathedral*

The Swan is a former coaching inn, and has one of the best views of the West Front of Wells cathedral. The individually decorated bedrooms vary in size and style; a third of the rooms have four-poster beds, nicely complementing the 15th-century architecture. A fixed-price menu is served in the dining room, with the added bonus of a roast trolley.

ROOMS: 38 en suite (2 fmly) s £79.50-£84.50; d £99.50-£119.50 (incl. bkfst) * LB **FACILITIES:** Xmas **CONF:** Thtr 100 Class 30 Board 30 Del from £99 * **PARKING:** 30 **NOTES:** No smoking in restaurant Civ Wed 80 **CARDS:**

★★69% White Hart
Sadler St BA5 2RR
☎ 01749 672056 📠 01749 672056
e-mail: whitehart@wells.demon.co.uk
Dir: *Sadler St is the start of the one-way system. Hotel opposite the cathedral*

Situated just a short stroll from the cathedral, this former coaching inn dates back to the 15th century. The bedrooms, many located in a nearby former stable block, offer comfortable, modern accommodation. Public areas include a spacious bar-lounge, a cosy landing lounge for residents and a beamed restaurant. Guests can choose between the formal fixed-price menu or the brasserie-style menu.

ROOMS: 13 en suite (1 fmly) No smoking in 5 bedrooms s £52.50-£57.50; d £70-£80 (incl. bkfst) * LB **FACILITIES:** STV Xmas **CONF:** Thtr 80 Class 40 Board 35 Del from £65 * **PARKING:** 17
CARDS:

★69% ❀ Ancient Gate House
20 Sadler St BA5 2RR
☎ 01749 672029 📠 01749 670319
Dir: *first hotel on left situated on the Cathedral Green, overlooking the West Front of the Cathedral*

A charming family-run hotel where guests are treated to good old fashioned hospitality in a friendly informal atmosphere. Bedrooms, many of which boast unrivalled cathedral views and four poster beds, are furnished in keeping with the age of the building, but have the advantage of modern facilities. The hotel's Rugantino Restaurant offers a typically Italian menu.

ROOMS: 9 rms (7 en suite) (1 fmly) s £40-£55; d £60-£70 (incl. bkfst) * LB **NOTES:** No smoking in restaurant Closed 25-26 Dec
CARDS:

W

Late for dinner? Quality Standards star rating means that last orders for dinner should be no earlier than:
★ 6.30pm ★★ 7.00pm ★★★ 8.00pm
★★★★ 9.00pm ★★★★★ 10.00pm

WELWYN, Hertfordshire Map 04 TL21

★★★64% Quality Hotel Welwyn

The Link AL6 9XA
☎ 01438 716911 📠 01438 714065
e-mail: admin@gb623.u-net.com

CHOICE HOTELS EUROPE

***Dir:** exit A1(M) junct 6 follow for A1000 Welwyn. Follow A1(M) Stevenage towards motorway again but at 3rd rdbt take first left and turn into hotel*

The hotel is well located for access to the nearby motorway and offers a versatile range of conference and meeting rooms, making it popular with business guests. Bedrooms are suitably appointed and offer a useful range of in room facilities and amenities. Guests have the choice of two informal dining rooms and a comfortable bar in which to relax.

ROOMS: 96 en suite (6 fmly) No smoking in 47 bedrooms s £75; d £83 * LB **FACILITIES:** STV Gym Xmas **CONF:** Thtr 250 Class 60 Board 50 Del from £87.50 * **PARKING:** 150 **NOTES:** Civ Wed 100
CARDS:

WELWYN GARDEN CITY, Hertfordshire Map 04 TL21

★★★65% The Homestead Court Hotel

Homestead Ln AL7 4LX
☎ 01707 324336 📠 01707 326447

corus

***Dir:** turn off A1000 into Woodhall Lane and left at Pear Tree public house into Cole Green Lane. After 2 mini-rdbts turn right into Homestead Lane*

Ideally located this hotel, only 15 miles north of London, is within easy reach of road and rail networks. Bedrooms are smart, modern and well equipped. Public areas include the Terrace Bar and Restaurant and a versatile range of conference rooms.

ROOMS: 58 en suite No smoking in 25 bedrooms s £65-£85; d £70-£95 * LB **FACILITIES:** STV Xmas **CONF:** Thtr 80 Class 45 Board 40 Del from £100 * **SERVICES:** Lift **PARKING:** 80 **NOTES:** No smoking in restaurant **CARDS:**

WEMBLEY, Greater London
See LONDON SECTION plan 1 C4

○ *Premier Lodge (London Wembley)*

151 Wembley Park Dr HA9 8HQ
☎ 0870 700 1446 📠 0870 700 0447

PREMIER LODGE

WENTBRIDGE (NEAR PONTEFRACT), West Yorkshire Map 08 SE41

★★★70% ❀ Wentbridge House

WF8 3JJ
☎ 01977 620444 📠 01977 620148

***Dir:** Wentbridge is 0.5m off A1 and 4m S of the M62/A1 interchange*

An established hotel in 15 acres of landscaped gardens, offering spacious, well equipped bedrooms, and a choice of two bars. Service in the Fleur de Lys restaurant is polished and there is a varied menu of traditional dishes.

ROOMS: 15 en suite 4 annexe en suite s £72-£98; d £82-£108 (incl. bkfst) * LB **CONF:** Thtr 120 Class 60 Board 50 Del from £86 * **PARKING:** 100 **NOTES:** No dogs (ex guide dogs) Closed 25 Dec-evening only Civ Wed 130 **CARDS:**

WEOBLEY, Herefordshire Map 03 SO45

★★73% ❀❀ Salutation Inn

Market Pitch HR4 8SJ
☎ 01544 318443 📠 01544 318216
e-mail: info@salutation.com

***Dir:** Weobley is 12m NW of Hereford, on the A4112, The Old Salutation Inn is in the village centre, facing Broad Street*

A delightful timber-framed property in the centre of the medieval village, dating back over 500 years. It has a good reputation for hospitality and food. The well equipped, traditionally furnished accommodation includes a family room, and a room with a four-poster bed.

ROOMS: 4 en suite No smoking in all bedrooms s £44-£50; d £68-£74 (incl. bkfst) * LB **FACILITIES:** STV Gym **PARKING:** 14 **NOTES:** No children 14yrs No smoking in restaurant
CARDS:

WEST AUCKLAND, Co Durham Map 12 NZ12

★★★70% ❀ The Manor House

The Green DL14 9HW
☎ 01388 834834 📠 01388 833566

***Dir:** A1(M) junct 58, then A68 to West Auckland*

This historic manor house has been sympathetically extended and still retains all its original character and charm. The hotel offers a wide range and standard of facilities that meet modern expectations. Flagstone floors in the bar lead to the stylish restaurant offering artistically presented dishes. The bedrooms in the main house are particularly large.

continued

ROOMS: 25 en suite 11 annexe en suite (8 fmly) s £60-£70; d £85-£105 (incl. bkfst) * LB **FACILITIES:** Indoor swimming (H) Sauna Solarium Gym Pool table Jacuzzi/spa Beauty treatment Xmas **CONF:** Thtr 100 Class 80 Board 50 Del from £85 * **PARKING:** 200
CARDS:

WEST BAY See Bridport

WEST BEXINGTON, Dorset
Map 03 SY58

★★70% Manor
Beach Rd DT2 9DF
☎ 01308 897616 📠 01308 897035
e-mail: themanorhotel@btconnect.com
This hotel stands in the scenic splendour of the tranquil village of West Bexington. The hotel itself is south facing and enjoys uninterrupted sea views. Each bedroom has its own unique charm and a number of thoughtful extras. The Cellar Bar provides a range of meals, and an imaginative selection of dishes is offered in the restaurant.
ROOMS: 13 rms (12 en suite) (1 fmly) d fr £100 (incl. bkfst) * LB **CONF:** Thtr 50 Class 60 Board 30 **PARKING:** 28 **NOTES:** No dogs Civ Wed 45 **CARDS:**

WESTBURY, Wiltshire
Map 03 ST85

★★66% The Cedar
Warminster Rd BA13 3PR
☎ 01373 822753 📠 01373 858423
e-mail: mail@cedarhotel.co.uk
Dir: *on A350, 0.5m from Westbury towards Warminster*
This 18th century hotel offers attractive accommodation in well equipped bedrooms which are individually decorated with cheerful extras. On the edge of Westbury, the hotel provides a base for exploring Bath and the surrounding area. A variety of meals is available in both the bar lounge and conservatory, whilst the Regency restaurant is popular for more formal dining.
ROOMS: 8 en suite 8 annexe en suite (4 fmly) s £50-£55; d £60-£80 (incl. bkfst) * LB **FACILITIES:** STV ch fac **CONF:** Thtr 40 Class 30 Board 20 **PARKING:** 35 **NOTES:** No smoking in restaurant Closed 27-29 Dec **CARDS:**

WEST CHILTINGTON, West Sussex
Map 04 TQ01

★★★65% *Roundabout*
Monkmead Ln RH20 2PF
☎ 01798 813838 📠 01798 812962
e-mail: roundabouthotelltd@btinternet.com
Dir: *A24 onto A283 turn right at mini rdbt in Storrington, left at hill top. After 1m bear left*

This well established hotel enjoys a most peaceful setting, surrounded by gardens deep in the Sussex countryside. Mock Tudor in style, the hotel exudes character. Bedrooms are comfortably furnished and well equipped. Public areas include a spacious lounge and bar and neatly appointed restaurant where guests are offered an extensive range of dishes.
ROOMS: 23 en suite (4 fmly) No smoking in 2 bedrooms
FACILITIES: STV **CONF:** Thtr 60 Class 20 Board 26 **PARKING:** 46
NOTES: No children 3yrs No smoking in restaurant
CARDS:

See advert on this page

WESTCLIFF-ON-SEA, Essex
Map 05 TQ88

★★★66% *Westcliff*
Westcliff Pde, Westcliff-on-Sea SS0 7QW
☎ 01702 345247 📠 01702 431814
Dir: *M25 J29, A127 towards Southend, follow signs for Cliffs Pavillion when approaching town centre*

Built in 1891, this grade II listed Victorian building enjoys views over the cliffs, gardens and Thames Estuary. Bedrooms are

continued

WESTCLIFF-ON-SEA, continued

spacious and tastefully decorated, offering a useful range of extra facilities. The public areas include a restaurant with sea views, a modern bar and spacious lounge. There is also a versatile range of function rooms.
ROOMS: 55 en suite (3 fmly) No smoking in 7 bedrooms
FACILITIES: STV entertainment **CONF:** Thtr 225 Class 90 Board 64
SERVICES: Lift **NOTES:** No dogs (ex guide dogs) No smoking in restaurant **CARDS:**

See advert under SOUTHEND-ON-SEA

★★★61% *Erlsmere*
24/32 Pembury Rd SS0 8DS
☎ 01702 349025 🖷 01702 337724

Quietly located in a residential area just off the seafront, this hotel offers well equipped bedrooms. The Restaurant serves a short fixed-price menu, and guests can relax in the Wellington Bar at the rear of the building. Service is friendly.
ROOMS: 30 en suite 2 annexe en suite (2 fmly) **CONF:** Thtr 100 Class 40 Board 45 Del from £65 * **PARKING:** 12 **NOTES:** No dogs (ex guide dogs) **CARDS:**

WEST DRAYTON Hotels are listed under Heathrow Airport

WESTLETON, Suffolk Map 05 TM46

★★75% ❁ *Westleton Crown*
IP17 3AD
☎ 0800 328 6001 🖷 01728 648239
e-mail: reception@westletoncrown.com
Dir: *turn off A12 just beyond Yoxford, northbound, and follow AA signs for 2m*
Ideally situated just off the A12 in a quiet village location is this delightful inn which continues to charm its many valued guests. The excellent hospitality together with attentive service make this an ideal place to visit. Guests can dine in the main restaurant with its appealing menus which include vegetarian and seafood specialities. For more informal fare try the bar with its range of real ales, blazing fire and vast array of malt whiskies. Although the bedrooms vary in size and style they are all smartly decorated and equipped with many useful extras.
ROOMS: 10 en suite 9 annexe en suite (2 fmly) No smoking in all bedrooms **CONF:** Thtr 60 Class 40 Board 30 **PARKING:** 40 **NOTES:** RS 24-26 Dec (Meals only) **CARDS:**

> Popped the question? Hotels with Civ Wed in their entry are licensed for civil wedding ceremonies. Maximum numbers for the ceremony only are shown, e.g. Civ Wed 50

W

WEST LULWORTH, Dorset Map 03 SY88

★★70% Shirley
Main Rd BH20 5RL
☎ 01929 400358 🖷 01929 400167
e-mail: durdle@aol.com
Dir: *on B3070 in centre of village*
Many guests return regularly to this attractive, family-run hotel with warm hospitality. The smart bedrooms are attractively decorated with modern facilities, and public areas include an indoor pool and two comfortable lounges. Each evening in the restaurant, guests enjoy an ample choice of good wholesome cooking.
ROOMS: 15 en suite (2 fmly) s £35-£45; d £70-£90 (incl. bkfst) * LB
FACILITIES: Indoor swimming (H) Jacuzzi/spa Giant chess
PARKING: 20 **NOTES:** No smoking in restaurant Closed mid Nov-mid Feb **CARDS:**

★★64% *Cromwell House*
Lulworth Cove BH20 5RJ
☎ 01929 400253 & 400332 🖷 01929 400566
e-mail: alastair@lds.co.uk
Dir: *200 yds beyond end of West Lulworth village, turn left at Lulworth Lodge, Cromwell House 100yds on left*
With spectacular elevated views across the sea and countryside, this family-run hotel offers guests an ideal base from which to explore the area. Built in 1881 by the mayor of Weymouth, specifically as a guest house, the bedrooms are bright and attractive with co-ordinated fabrics and modern facilities. There is a traditionally furnished dining room serving home-cooked meals, and popular cream teas.
ROOMS: 17 en suite (3 fmly) **FACILITIES:** Outdoor swimming (H)
PARKING: 15 **NOTES:** No smoking in restaurant Closed 22 Dec-3 Jan
CARDS:

WESTON-ON-THE-GREEN, Oxfordshire Map 04 SP51

★★★67% ❁❁ *Weston Manor*
OX6 8QL
☎ 01869 350621 🖷 01869 350901
Dir: *M40 junct 9 towards Oxford (A34), leave A34 at 1st exit, turn right at rdbt (B4030), hotel is 100yds on the left*
This splendid manor house has a wealth of history. Public rooms include a foyer lounge and a magnificent vaulted restaurant with minstrels' gallery and original panelling. Bedrooms are available in the main house and a tastefully converted coach house, and though they may vary in size, each room is particularly well equipped.
ROOMS: 16 en suite 20 annexe en suite (5 fmly) No smoking in 6 bedrooms **FACILITIES:** Outdoor swimming (H) Squash Croquet lawn
CONF: Thtr 40 Class 20 Board 25 **PARKING:** 100 **NOTES:** No dogs (ex guide dogs) No smoking in restaurant **CARDS:**

WESTON-SUPER-MARE, Somerset Map 03 ST36

★★★66% Beachlands
17 Uphill Rd North BS23 4NG
☎ 01934 621401 🖷 01934 621966
e-mail: beachlands@wsmare96.freeserve.co.uk
Dir: *follow tourist signs for Tropicana from M5 junct 21, hotel overlooks golf course, it is situated 6.5m away from motorway, before reaching Tropicana*
This delightful hotel has the added bonus of a 10 metre indoor pool and sauna. It is very close to the 18-hole links course and a short walk from the sea front. Elegantly decorated public areas include a bar, a choice of lounges and a bright dining room,

continued

offering a fixed price daily changing menu. Bedrooms vary in size and comfort but are well equipped.

ROOMS: 24 en suite (4 fmly) s fr £45; d fr £79 (incl. bkfst) * LB **FACILITIES:** Indoor swimming (H) Sauna **CONF:** Thtr 80 Class 30 Board 36 **PARKING:** 28 **NOTES:** No smoking in restaurant Closed 23 Dec-2 Jan Civ Wed 85 **CARDS:**

★★★62% The Grand Atlantic

Beach Rd BS23 1BA
☎ 01934 626543 📠 01934 415048
Dir: *M5 junct 21, follow signs for town centre, drive through town to the Grand Pier, turn left onto seafront, hotel is 500yds along on the left*

An imposing building on the famous promenade, this traditional seafront hotel retains much of its historic charm, with high ceilings, sweeping stairwells and some delightful plasterwork. The refurbished banqueting and conference suites are popular locally, and friendly staff provide efficient service.
ROOMS: 74 en suite (5 fmly) No smoking in 22 bedrooms s fr £64; d fr £79 * LB **FACILITIES:** Tennis Xmas **CONF:** Thtr 180 Class 80 Board 70 Del from £75 * **SERVICES:** Lift **PARKING:** 100 **NOTES:** No smoking in restaurant **CARDS:**

★★★62% *The Old Colonial Hotel*

30 Knightstone Rd BS23 2AN
☎ 01934 620739 📠 01934 642725
Dir: *follow 'Seafront' signs. Hotel 0.5m N of Pier*
Formerly the Melrose Hotel, The Old Colonial has undergone major refurbishment to create an unusual hotel in a prime sea-front location. Most of the bedrooms benefit from excellent views across Weston Bay. The downstairs bar/restaurant offers a wide range of freshly cooked meals served in pleasantly relaxed surroundings.
ROOMS: 10 en suite (3 fmly) **FACILITIES:** STV **PARKING:** 20 **NOTES:** No dogs Closed 24-27 Dec **CARDS:**

TV dinner? Room service at three stars and above.

W

WESTON-SUPER-MARE, continued

★★74% Madeira Cove Hotel
32-34 Birnbeck Rd BS23 2BX
☎ 01934 626707 📠 01934 624882
Dir: *Follow signs to western seafront, pass Grand Pier, hotel on right*
Within easy walking distance of the town centre, Madeira Cove Hotel enjoys an ideal location overlooking the sea. It has been upgraded throughout to provide comfortable and thoughtfully equipped accommodation. A good range of food is available in the well appointed restaurant, and the pleasant lounge-bar is the ideal place in which to enjoy a pre-dinner drink.
ROOMS: 19 en suite 4 annexe en suite (1 fmly) No smoking in 3 bedrooms s £25-£28; d £50-£60 (incl. bkfst) * LB **SERVICES:** Lift **PARKING:** 10 **NOTES:** No children 7yrs Closed 25 Dec-31 Jan
CARDS:

★★65% *Royal*
South Pde BS23 1JN
☎ 01934 623601 📠 01934 415135
Dir: *on the seafront, adjacent to the Winter Gardens*
This hotel is situated on the promenade overlooking Weston Bay and is within close proximity of the town centre. Bedrooms are bright, nicely co-ordinated and well equipped. Public rooms include a ballroom, pleasant family restaurant and choice of bars, including the adjacent O'Malley's Bar which has a lively, local following.
ROOMS: 37 en suite (8 fmly) No smoking in 16 bedrooms **FACILITIES:** entertainment **CONF:** Thtr 250 Class 60 Board 40 **SERVICES:** Lift **PARKING:** 150 **NOTES:** No dogs (ex guide dogs)
CARDS:

★66% *Timbertop Aparthotel*
8 Victoria Park BS23 2HZ
☎ 01934 631178 📠 01934 414716
e-mail: francesca@timbertop.freeserve.co.uk
Dir: *follow signs to pier, then 1st right (with Winter Gardens on right), 1st left Lower Church Road. Bear left then turn right to hotel*

Located in a leafy cul-de-sac close to the seafront and Winter Gardens, the homely Timbertop Aparthotel offers a warm and personal welcome to all guests. Bedrooms have a bright fresh appearance and many pine furnishings. In addition to a small bar, the hotel offers a choice of two relaxing guest lounges. Substantial home-cooked dinners are provided with the emphasis on fresh ingredients.
ROOMS: 8 rms (7 en suite) 4 annexe en suite (2 fmly) **FACILITIES:** STV **PARKING:** 15 **NOTES:** No dogs (ex guide dogs) No smoking in restaurant **CARDS:**

> Packed in a hurry? Ironing facilities should be available at all star levels, either in rooms or on request.

WEST THURROCK, Essex — Map 05 TQ57

Hotel Ibis London Thurrock
Weston Av RM20 3JQ
☎ 01708 686000 📠 01708 680525
e-mail: H2176@accor-hotels.com
Modern, budget hotel offering comfortable accommodation in bright and practical bedrooms. Breakfast is self-service and dinner is available in the restaurant. For further details, consult the Hotel Groups page.
ROOMS: 102 en suite d £52 *

Travelodge
Arterial Rd RM16 3BG
☎ 01708 891111 Central Res 0800 850950
📠 01525 878450
Dir: *off A1306 Arterial Rd*
This modern building offers accommodation in smart, spacious and well equipped bedrooms, all with en suite bathrooms. Refreshments may be taken at the nearby family restaurant. For further details and the Travelodge phone number, consult the Hotel Groups page.
ROOMS: 44 en suite

WEST WITTON, North Yorkshire — Map 07 SE08

★★70% Wensleydale Heifer Inn
DL8 4LS
☎ 01969 622322 📠 01969 624183
e-mail: heifer@daelnet.co.uk
Dir: *A684, at west end of village*
This historic inn has been a landmark in the village since the 17th century; its original character still remains in the cosy lounge and atmospheric bar. It has a good reputation for comfortable accommodation, friendly service and excellent cuisine. Bedrooms are located in the inn or in a stone-built house just across the road.
ROOMS: 9 en suite 5 annexe en suite (1 fmly) s £60; d £80 (incl. bkfst) * LB **FACILITIES:** Beer garden Xmas **PARKING:** 40
CARDS:

WETHERBY, West Yorkshire — Map 08 SE44

★★★75% Wood Hall
Trip Ln, Linton LS22 4JA
☎ 01937 587271 📠 01937 584353
Dir: *from Wetherby town centre take Harrogate road N from market place and turn left to Linton, hotel is then signposted*

A striking Georgian hall in 100 acres of parkland. Conference and banqueting facilities are stylish, the leisure club has a beauty room, pool and gym. Day rooms include a smart drawing room with open fire, and an oak-panelled bar. Food is imaginative and well prepared.

continued

ROOMS: 36 en suite 6 annexe en suite d £80-£125 * LB **FACILITIES:** STV Indoor swimming (H) Fishing Snooker Solarium Gym Jacuzzi/spa Treatment room for massage and facials Steam room Xmas **CONF:** Thtr 150 Class 70 Board 30 Del from £118 * **SERVICES:** Lift **PARKING:** 120 **NOTES:** No smoking in restaurant RS Sat Civ Wed 110 **CARDS:**

★★★67% Linton Springs

Sicklinghall Rd LS22 4AF
☎ 01937 585353 01937 587579
e-mail: info@lintonsprings.co.uk

A gracious 18th-century former shooting lodge set in 14 acres of park and woodland. Spacious oak panelled bedrooms are attractive and well equipped. Helpful staff are an asset and the open plan reception, lounge and cocktail bar are very welcoming. The Gun Room restaurant and adjoining conservatory serves both traditional and modern British cooking.

ROOMS: 12 en suite (2 fmly) s £75-£95; d £95-£115 (incl. bkfst) * **FACILITIES:** STV Tennis (hard) Croquet lawn golf driving range **CONF:** Thtr 80 Class 50 Board 30 Del £120 * **PARKING:** 70 **NOTES:** No dogs (ex guide dogs) Closed 1 Jan **CARDS:**

★★★61% The Bridge Inn

Walshford LS22 5HS
☎ 01937 580115 01937 580556
e-mail: bridge.walshford@virgin.net

Conveniently located adjacent to the A1, this hotel offers a choice of bars and a spacious, beamed, open-plan restaurant. Bedrooms are comfortable and well equipped. The good range of conference

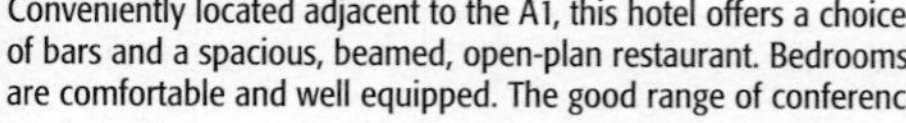

and banqueting suites are popular, especially with wedding parties, which have use of the Italian courtyard.

ROOMS: 30 en suite (1 fmly) s £45-£59.50; d £65-£79.50 (incl. bkfst) * LB **FACILITIES:** STV Pool table Xmas **CONF:** Thtr 130 Class 50 Board 50 Del from £85 * **PARKING:** 90 **CARDS:**

WEYBRIDGE, Surrey

See LONDON SECTION plan 1 *A1*

★★★★70% Oatlands Park

146 Oatlands Dr KT13 9HB
☎ 01932 847242 01932 842252
e-mail: oatlandspark@btinternet.com

Dir: *through Weybridge High Street to top of Monument Hill. Hotel third of a mile on left*

Set in 10 acres of parkland once owned by Henry VIII this impressive building has the advantage of a countryside location. The glass covered atrium and marble-pillared lounge lead into a comfortable bar. The Broadwater Restaurant is spacious and well appointed, with candlelit tables popular for celebrations. Bedrooms include a number of suites, and several comfortable single rooms. Leisure time may be spent playing tennis, golf or working out in the fitness centre.

ROOMS: 134 en suite (5 fmly) No smoking in 20 bedrooms s fr £105; d fr £140 * LB **FACILITIES:** STV Golf 9 Tennis (hard) Gym Croquet lawn Jogging course Fitness suite entertainment **CONF:** Thtr 300 Class 200 Board 70 Del from £185 * **SERVICES:** Lift **PARKING:** 140 **NOTES:** Civ Wed 200 **CARDS:**

Arriving late? Four and five star hotels have night porters to assist with your luggage; and 24hr room service.

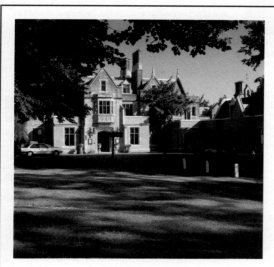

W

WEYBRIDGE, continued

★★★67% The Ship

Monument Green KT13 8BQ
☎ 01932 848364 🖷 01932 857153

PEEL HOTELS

Dir: *turn off M25 junc 11, A317, at third rdbt turn left into the High Street, hotel on left*

The Ship is a spacious, comfortable hotel which is in a great location for visitors to the town. Bedrooms have been designed with consideration for both business and leisure guests needs. The restaurant, lounge and bar are all spacious. Car parking is available.

ROOMS: 39 en suite No smoking in 10 bedrooms s fr £115; d fr £135 * LB **FACILITIES:** STV entertainment **CONF:** Thtr 140 Class 70 Board 60 Del from £145 * **PARKING:** 75 **NOTES:** No dogs (ex guide dogs) No smoking in restaurant **CARDS:**

WEYMOUTH, Dorset Map 03 SY67

★★★75% Moonfleet Manor

Fleet DT3 4ED
☎ 01305 786948 🖷 01305 774395

Dir: *A354 to Weymouth; turn right on B3157 to Bridport. At Chickerell turn left at mini rdbt to Fleet*

Moonfleet Manor is an enchanting hideaway near to Chesil Beach. The hotel is furnished with style and panache. Bedrooms are well equipped, spacious and comfortable. Accomplished cuisine is served in the beautiful restaurant.

ROOMS: 33 en suite 6 annexe en suite (26 fmly) s fr £75; d £95-£220 (incl. bkfst) * LB **FACILITIES:** STV Indoor swimming (H) Tennis (hard) Squash Snooker Sauna Solarium Pool table Croquet lawn Childrens nursery ch fac Xmas **CONF:** Thtr 50 Class 18 Board 26 Del from £120 * **SERVICES:** Lift **PARKING:** 50 **NOTES:** No smoking in restaurant **CARDS:**

See advert on opposite page

★★★62% Hotel Rembrandt

12-18 Dorchester Rd DT4 7JU
☎ 01305 764000 🖷 01305 764022
e-mail: reception@hotelrembrandt.co.uk

Dir: *0.75m on left after Manor rdbt on A354 from Dorchester*

A good restaurant, bar and leisure facilities are key features at this hotel. Bedrooms too have modern facilities and many of them have also recently been refurbished. The hotel is located on the road to Dorchester, and is not far from the town centre or beach.

ROOMS: 74 en suite (5 fmly) No smoking in 30 bedrooms s £55-£74; d £70-£98 (incl. bkfst) * LB **FACILITIES:** STV Indoor swimming (H) Sauna Solarium Gym Jacuzzi/spa Steam room Xmas **CONF:** Thtr 200 Class 100 Board 50 Del from £90 * **SERVICES:** Lift **PARKING:** 80 **NOTES:** No smoking in restaurant Civ Wed 100 **CARDS:**

★★★61% Hotel Rex

29 The Esplanade DT4 8DN
☎ 01305 760400 🖷 01305 760500
e-mail: rex@kingshotels.f9.co.uk

Dir: *on seafront opposite Alexandra Gardens*

Originally built as a summer residence for the Duke of Clarence, this hotel has superb views across Weymouth Bay. Bedrooms are well equipped and vary in outlook. The restaurant serves a wide range of dishes and there is also a well stocked bar. A comfortably furnished lounge is provided.

ROOMS: 31 en suite (5 fmly) s £48.50-£56; d £78-£99 (incl. bkfst) LB **FACILITIES:** STV entertainment **CONF:** Thtr 40 Class 30 Board 25 Del from £64 * **SERVICES:** Lift **PARKING:** 6 **NOTES:** Closed Xmas **CARDS:**

★★68% Glenburn

42 Preston Rd DT3 6PZ
☎ 01305 832353 🖷 01305 835610

Dir: *on A353 1.5m E of town centre*

A warm welcome is assured at this small hotel, which is just a short, level walk from the seafront. Bedrooms and public areas now offer good standards of comfort. The restaurant offers an interesting selection of dishes from both fixed-price and carte menus.

ROOMS: 13 en suite (2 fmly) No smoking in 8 bedrooms s £35-£43; d £55-£70 (incl. bkfst) * **FACILITIES:** Jacuzzi/spa **PARKING:** 15 **NOTES:** No dogs (ex guide dogs) No smoking in restaurant **CARDS:**

★★66% Hotel Prince Regent

139 The Esplanade DT4 7NR
☎ 01305 771313 🖷 01305 778100
e-mail: hprwey@aol.com

Best Western

Dir: *from A354 follow signs for Seafront. At Jubilee Clock turn left along Seafront, for 0.25m*

Overlooking Weymouth Bay, this welcoming resort hotel, dating from 1855, is conveniently close to the town centre, beaches and the harbour. Bedrooms come in a range of styles and sizes, with sea-facing rooms being generally the most desirable. The restaurant offers a choice of menus, and entertainment is regularly provided in the ballroom in season.

ROOMS: 50 en suite (21 fmly) No smoking in 6 bedrooms s £55-£65; d £75-£85 (incl. bkfst) * LB **FACILITIES:** STV Pool table Table tennis **CONF:** Thtr 200 Class 150 Board 150 Del from £59 * **SERVICES:** Lift **PARKING:** 18 **NOTES:** No dogs (ex guide dogs) No smoking in restaurant Closed 24 Dec-8 Jan **CARDS:**

Early start? Hotels at all star levels should provide in-room alarm clocks and/or alarm calls.

★★63% Crown
51-53 St Thomas St DT4 8EQ
☎ 01305 760800 📠 01305 760300
e-mail: crown@kingshotels.f9.co.uk
Dir: *turn off A35 at Dorchester, take A354 to Weymouth, pass over second bridge, premises on left*
Situated close to the harbour, beach and town amenities, this popular tourist hotel provides comfortable accommodation. The public areas include a spacious ballroom, a first-floor lounge and a brightly decorated bar. Guests can eat either in the restaurant or the bar.
ROOMS: 86 en suite (11 fmly) s £33-£35; d £58-£64 (incl. bkfst) LB **FACILITIES:** STV **CONF:** Class 140 Board 80 **SERVICES:** Lift **PARKING:** 12 **NOTES:** No dogs (ex guide dogs) Closed 25-26 Dec **CARDS:**

WHATTON, Nottinghamshire — Map 08 SK73

★★61% The Haven
Grantham Rd NG13 9EU
☎ 01949 850800 📠 01949 851454
Dir: *off A52, take turning to Redmile/Belvoir Castle*
This welcoming, family-run hotel offers a large public bar and dining room in which a good range of popular dishes are available. The bedrooms have a modern outlook, and are furnished with pleasing colour schemes and useful facilities.
ROOMS: 33 en suite (5 fmly) s £37.50; d £49.50 (incl. bkfst) * LB **FACILITIES:** STV Pool table **CONF:** Thtr 100 Class 20 Board 60 Del from £85 * **PARKING:** 70 **CARDS:**

WHEDDON CROSS, Somerset — Map 03 SS93

★★70% Raleigh Manor
TA24 7BB
☎ 01643 841484 📠 01643 841484
Dir: *at Wheddon Cross, turn right on A396 for Dunster. Private drive to Raleigh Manor on left. Raleigh Manor on right if coming from A39*
Set in Exmoor National Park, this Victorian country house enjoys views over Snowdrop Valley. The individually decorated bedrooms are comfortably furnished and equipped. The relaxing lounge, snug library and conservatory all take full advantage of the lovely views. The dining room offers a choice of carefully prepared, quality dishes.
ROOMS: 7 en suite No smoking in all bedrooms s £31-£46; d £62-£74 (incl. bkfst) * LB **PARKING:** 10 **NOTES:** No dogs No children 12yrs No smoking in restaurant Closed Dec-Feb **CARDS:**

WHICKHAM, Tyne & Wear — Map 12 NZ26

★★★69% Gibside Arms
Front St NE16 4JG
☎ 0191 488 9292 📠 0191 488 8000
e-mail: gibsidehotel@btclick.com
Dir: *turn off A1M towards Whickham on the B6317, B6317 leads onto Whickham Front Street, 2m on right*
This modern hotel in the old village centre enjoys spectacular views over the Tyne Valley towards Newcastle. Its well equipped bedrooms are modern and smartly decorated. Public rooms include a cocktail lounge and restaurant, and a bar offering food throughout the day. There is secure garage parking.
ROOMS: 45 en suite (2 fmly) No smoking in 10 bedrooms s £57.50; d £69 * LB **FACILITIES:** STV entertainment Xmas **CONF:** Thtr 100 Class 50 Board 50 Del from £74 * **SERVICES:** Lift **PARKING:** 28 **CARDS:**

WHITBY, North Yorkshire — Map 08 NZ81

★★★70% Dunsley Hall
Dunsley YO21 3TL
☎ 01947 893437 📠 01947 893505
e-mail: reception@dunsleyhall.com
Dir: *3m N of Whitby, signposted off the A171*

Good hospitality is a strong feature of this country house situated just outside of town in four acres of well tended gardens. Oak panelling, carved fireplaces and mullioned windows all add to the character of the house, which offers a well appointed restaurant and a popular bar. Spacious bedrooms are bright, comfortable and beautifully furnished.
ROOMS: 18 en suite (2 fmly) No smoking in 4 bedrooms **FACILITIES:** Indoor swimming (H) Tennis (hard) Sauna Solarium Gym Croquet lawn Putting green **CONF:** Thtr 60 Class 30 Board 30 **PARKING:** 20 **NOTES:** No dogs (ex guide dogs) No smoking in restaurant Civ Wed **CARDS:**

WHITBY, continued

★★72% Saxonville
Ladysmith Av, Argyle Rd YO21 3HX
☎ 01947 602631 🖷 01947 820523
e-mail: saxonville@onyxnet.co.uk
Dir: *A174 on to North Promenade. Turn inland at large four towered building visable on West Cliff into Argyle Road, then first turning on right*
This comfortable holiday hotel provides bedrooms that are nicely presented in modern style and offer all the expected amenities: refurbished bedrooms are particularly appealing. Public areas include a choice of lounges, a small bar, and an attractive restaurant; an extensive range of carefully prepared English dishes are offered here.
ROOMS: 22 en suite (2 fmly) No smoking in all bedrooms s £38-£40; d £76-£80 (incl. bkfst) * LB **CONF:** Thtr 100 Class 64 Board 56 Del from £56 * **PARKING:** 20 **NOTES:** No dogs (ex guide dogs) No smoking in restaurant Closed mid Oct-Etr **CARDS:**

See advert on opposite page

★★68% Stakesby Manor
Manor Close, High Stakesby YO21 1HL
☎ 01947 602773 🖷 01947 602140
e-mail: rod@stakesby-manor.co.uk

MINOTEL Great Britain

Dir: *at rdbt junct of A171/B1416 take road for West Cliff. Third turning on right*
Situated in a residential area, this Georgian mansion is becoming a very popular hotel. There is a wide choice in bedroom sizes and style, and all rooms are well maintained and neatly presented. Quality cooking is served in the oak panelled dining room, and there is a cosy lounge upstairs in addition to the lounge bar.
ROOMS: 13 en suite (2 fmly) No smoking in 6 bedrooms s £54; d £74-£80 (incl. bkfst) * LB **CONF:** Thtr 100 Class 46 Board 40 Del £67.50 * **PARKING:** 40 **NOTES:** No dogs (ex guide dogs) No smoking in restaurant Closed 24-30 Dec **CARDS:**

★★67% White House
Upgang Ln, West Cliff YO21 3JJ
☎ 01947 600469 🖷 01947 821600
e-mail: 101745.1440@compuserve.com
Dir: *on A174 beside the golf course*
This family-run hotel is on the north side of town and overlooks the golf course at Sandsend Bay. Attractively appointed bedrooms vary in size, and there is a choice of two bars where locals and visitors mingle. The bars and dining room offer a varied selection of dishes including fresh local fish.
ROOMS: 10 en suite (3 fmly) **PARKING:** 50
CARDS:

★★66% Cliffemount Hotel
Runswick Bay TS13 5HU
☎ 01947 840103 🖷 01947 841025
e-mail: cliffemount@runswickbay.fsnet.co.uk
Dir: *turn off A174 N of Whitby, follow road 1m to dead end where hotel is situated on clifftop*
Standing in a delightful elevated position, overlooking the pretty village and with splendid views over the bay, this family run hotel offers good hospitality together with a wide range of quality home cooking. The bedrooms, some of which have balconies, are well equipped and comfortable.
ROOMS: 12 en suite s £28-£38; d £56.50-£75 (incl. bkfst) LB **PARKING:** 30 **NOTES:** Closed 25-26 Dec **CARDS:**

Bad hair day? Hairdryers in all rooms three stars and above.

★★62% Old West Cliff Hotel
42 Crescent Av YO21 3EQ
☎ 01947 603292 🖷 01947 821716
Dir: *leave A171, follow signs for West Cliff, approach spa complex. Hotel 100yds from centre off Crescent Gardens*
This family owned and run hotel is close to the sea and convenient for the town centre. It provides well equipped bedrooms, a cosy lounge and separate bar. A good range of food is served in the cosy basement restaurant.
ROOMS: 12 en suite (6 fmly) s £31.50; d £52 (incl. bkfst) * **NOTES:** No dogs (ex guide dogs) No smoking in restaurant Closed 24 Dec-31 Jan **CARDS:**

WHITLEY BAY, Tyne & Wear — Map 12 NZ37

★★★63% Windsor
South Pde NE26 2RF
☎ 0191 251 8888 🖷 0191 297 0272
e-mail: info@windsor-hotel.demon.co.uk
Dir: *from A19 Tyne Tunnel follow for A1058 to Tynemouth. At coast rdbt turn left to Whitley Bay. After 2m turn left at Rex Hotel, Windsor on left*
A popular business hotel set between the town centre and the seafront. Accommodation is modern and well equipped, and the public areas are pleasant and comfortable.
ROOMS: 70 en suite (24 fmly) s £40-£59; d £50-£60 (incl. bkfst) * LB **FACILITIES:** STV **CONF:** Thtr 20 Class 10 Board 10 Del from £80 * **SERVICES:** Lift **PARKING:** 46 **NOTES:** RS 25 Dec
CARDS:

★★65% High Point
The Promenade NE26 2NJ
☎ 0191 251 7782 🖷 0191 251 6318
e-mail: highpointhotel@aol.com
Dir: *from A1058 follow signs for Tynemouth, then seafront, turn left at Sealife Centre, follow rd for 1.5m, hotel on left going into Whitley Bay*
This friendly hotel offers a pleasing standard of comfort; the rooms are generally spacious and many enjoy sea views. Meals are served in the attractive little restaurant or the lounge bar. Meals on Sunday evening are more modest.
ROOMS: 14 en suite (3 fmly) s £45.50-£49.50; d £55-£58 (incl. bkfst) * LB **FACILITIES:** STV Pool table entertainment **PARKING:** 20 **NOTES:** No dogs (ex guide dogs) **CARDS:**

WHITNEY-ON-WYE, Herefordshire — Map 03 SO24

★★73% The Rhydspence Inn
HR3 6EU
☎ 01497 831262 🖷 01497 831751
Dir: *Hotel located 1m W of Whitney-on-Wye on A438 Hereford to Brecon road*

This former manor house dates back in part to 1380. Privately owned and personally run in a warm and friendly manner, it

continued

provides well equipped accommodation, including a room with a four-poster bed. Public areas, which include an elegant restaurant, have a wealth of charm and character, which is enhanced by features such as exposed beams, timber framed walls and welcoming log fires. A blackboard selection supplements a large bar meal choice and the restaurant serves from an extensive carte menu. The quality of its food attracts a large local following.
ROOMS: 7 en suite s £32.50-£42.50; d £65-£75 (incl. bkfst) * LB **PARKING:** 30 **NOTES:** No dogs (ex guide dogs) No smoking in restaurant Closed 2wks Jan **CARDS:**

WICKHAM, Hampshire Map 04 SU51

★★67% Old House
The Square PO17 5JG
☎ 01329 833049 01329 833672
e-mail: eng@theoldhousehotel.co.uk
Dir: *2m N of Fareham off A32*
Situated in the charming Georgian village of Wickham, close to the M27. Individually decorated, spacious bedrooms have much character and are well equipped with extras. There is a choice of lounges, a small bar and a popular restaurant. Off-street parking is plentiful.
ROOMS: 9 en suite (1 fmly) s £60-£75; d £65-£80 (incl. cont bkfst) * LB **PARKING:** 12 **NOTES:** No dogs (ex guide dogs) No smoking in restaurant Closed 10 days Xmas RS Mon-Sat
CARDS:

WIDNES, Cheshire Map 07 SJ58

★★★64% Everglades Park
Best Western
Derby Rd WA8 3UJ
☎ 0151 495 2040 0151 424 6536
Dir: *from M62 junct follow A557 for Widnes, take first exit signed Widnes N A5080, right at rdbt, left at 2nd rdbt onto A5080 hotel 200mts on right*
Bedrooms are nicely spacious at this modern hotel and offer good levels of comfort, with executive suites and family rooms also being available. A wide choice of snacks and bar meals is served in the recently refurbished Glades bar, as well as a full menu in the restaurant which overlooks the swimming pool.
ROOMS: 65 en suite (4 fmly) No smoking in 20 bedrooms **FACILITIES:** Indoor swimming (H) Pool table Croquet lawn **CONF:** Thtr 200 Class 90 Board 50 **SERVICES:** air con **PARKING:** 200 **NOTES:** No dogs (ex guide dogs) **CARDS:**

★★★64% Hill Crest
REGAL
75 Cronton Ln WA8 9AR
☎ 0151 424 1616 0151 495 1348
Dir: *take A5080 Cronton to traffic lights turn right and drive for 0.75m, right at T-junct, follow A5080 for 500yds. Hotel on right*

This modern hotel is situated within easy reach of the M62 motorway to the north west of town. All bedrooms are comfortable and well equipped, particularly the executive rooms. Suites with four poster or canopy beds and spa baths are also available. Public areas include extensive conference facilities, Palms restaurant and bar, as well as Nelsons public bar.
ROOMS: 50 en suite (5 fmly) No smoking in 20 bedrooms s £44-£77; d £59-£87 (incl. bkfst) * LB **FACILITIES:** STV entertainment Xmas **CONF:** Thtr 140 Class 80 Board 40 **SERVICES:** Lift **PARKING:** 150 **CARDS:**

Travelodge
Travelodge
Fiddlers Ferry Rd WA8 2NR
☎ 0800 850950
Dir: *on A562*
This modern building offers accommodation in smart, spacious and well equipped bedrooms, all with en suite bathrooms. Refreshments may be taken at the nearby family restaurant. For further details and the Travelodge phone number, consult the Hotel Groups page.
ROOMS: 32 en suite

WIGAN, Greater Manchester Map 07 SD50

★★★★64% Kilhey Court
MACDONALD HOTELS
Chorley Rd, Standish WN1 2XN
☎ 01257 472100 01257 422401
e-mail: reservations@kilhey.co.uk
Dir: *on A5106 1.5m N of A49/A5106 junct*
This extended Victorian mansion, set in ten acres of grounds overlooking the Worthington lakes, offers well appointed accommodation, including a number of magnificent suites. There are two restaurants, the casual Peligrino's, and a more formal one featuring a Victorian conservatory.

continued

W

WIGAN, continued

Kilhey Court, Wigan

ROOMS: 62 en suite (3 fmly) No smoking in 38 bedrooms **FACILITIES:** STV Indoor swimming (H) Fishing Sauna Solarium Gym Jacuzzi/spa **CONF:** Thtr 180 Class 60 Board 60 **SERVICES:** Lift **PARKING:** 400 **NOTES:** No smoking in restaurant
CARDS:

★★★73% *Wrightington Hotel & Restaurant*

Moss Ln, Wrightington WN6 9PB
☎ 01257 425803 🖷 01257 425830
e-mail: 100631.3514@compuserve.com
Dir: *M6 junct 27, 0.25m W, hotel situated on right after church*

This privately owned, modern hotel is situated in open countryside. It provides well equipped accommodation and has an excellent leisure centre and a high reputation for service and cuisine.
ROOMS: 47 en suite (4 fmly) No smoking in 12 bedrooms **FACILITIES:** STV Indoor swimming (H) Squash Sauna Solarium Gym Jacuzzi/spa Sports Injuries Clinic Health & Beauty clinic Hairdresser **CONF:** Thtr 200 Class 120 Board 40 **PARKING:** 170
CARDS:

See advert on opposite page

★★★65% Quality Hotel Wigan

CHOICE HOTELS EUROPE

Riverway WN1 3SS
☎ 01942 826888 🖷 01942 825800
e-mail: admin@gb058.u-net.com
Dir: *from A49 take B5238 from rdbt, continue for 1.5m through traffic lights, through 3 more sets of lights, at 4th set turn right and take first left*
Close to the centre of the town this modern hotel offers spacious and well equipped bedrooms. The open plan public areas include a comfortable lounge bar, adjacent to the popular restaurant which serves a good range of dishes.
ROOMS: 88 en suite No smoking in 35 bedrooms **FACILITIES:** STV **CONF:** Thtr 200 Class 90 Board 60 **SERVICES:** Lift **PARKING:** 100
CARDS:

★★★62% *Bellingham*

141-149 Wigan Ln WN1 2NB
☎ 01942 243893 🖷 01942 821027
Dir: *hotel is situated on the A49 Wigan Lane approximately 0.5m out of Wigan town centre heading North, directly opposite Wigan Infirmary*

The Bellingham provides well equipped, modern accommodation. The pleasant public areas offer a choice of bars and a selection of function rooms, the largest of which can accommodate up to 180 people.
ROOMS: 32 en suite (4 fmly) No smoking in 2 bedrooms **FACILITIES:** STV Pool table **CONF:** Thtr 150 Class 50 Board 40 **SERVICES:** Lift **PARKING:** 40 **NOTES:** No smoking in restaurant
CARDS:

★★63% Bel-Air

236 Wigan Ln WN1 2NU
☎ 01942 241410 🖷 01942 243967
e-mail: belair@hotelwigan.freeserve.co.uk
Dir: *M6 junct 27, follow signs for Standish. In Standish turn right at traffic lights towards A49. Hotel is on right, 1.5m from Standish towards Wigan*
This family-run hotel is just to the north of the town. Bedrooms are well equipped and maintained, there is a pleasant bar and the Gaslight Restaurant offers a range of carefully prepared meals.
ROOMS: 11 en suite (1 fmly) s fr £39.50; d fr £49.50 (incl. bkfst) * **CONF:** Thtr 30 Board 8 **PARKING:** 10 **NOTES:** No dogs (ex guide dogs)
CARDS:

⇧ Premier Lodge

PREMIER LODGE
THE BEST. REST ASSURED.

53 Warrington Rd, Ashton-in-Makerfield WN4 9PJ
☎ 0870 700 1572 🖷 0870 700 1573
Premier Lodge offers modern, well equipped, en suite accommodation suitable for both business and leisure travellers. Meals can be taken at the adjacent popular restaurant and bar which is fully licensed. For further details, consult the Hotel Groups page.
ROOMS: 28 en suite d £42 *

WIGHT, ISLE OF

BONCHURCH See Ventnor

CHALE Map 04 SZ47

★★69% *Clarendon Hotel & Wight Mouse Inn*

PO38 2HA
☎ 01983 730431 🖷 01983 730431
Dir: *on B3099 main coast road junct of B3055*
A charming 17th-century former coaching inn offering comfortable accommodation. Bedrooms include three well equipped suites. Guests can enjoy freshly prepared food in the smart Clarendon Restaurant or dine more informally at the inn.
ROOMS: 13 en suite (9 fmly) **FACILITIES:** Riding Pool table entertainment ch fac **PARKING:** 200 **CARDS:**

COWES

Map 04 SZ49

★★★66% *New Holmwood*

Queens Rd, Egypt Point PO31 8BW
☎ 01983 292508 📠 01983 295020
Dir: *from Cowes Parade turn right by Royal Yacht Squadron*

A superbly located hotel, only meters from Cowes Esplanade and superb Solent views. Public rooms include a cosy bar, sea facing restaurant with adjoining sun terrace and lounge with board games and books. Bedrooms are well equipped all with bath and shower. Ongoing improvements ensure attractive surroundings with good levels of comfort.
ROOMS: 25 en suite **FACILITIES:** Outdoor swimming (H) **CONF:** Thtr 120 Class 50 Board 32 **PARKING:** 17 **CARDS:**

See advert on this page

W

COWES, continued

★62% Duke of York
Mill Hill Rd PO31 7BT
☎ 01983 295171 🖷 01983 295047
This family-run inn is in a quiet situation close to the town centre. Bedrooms are split between the main building and a nearby annexe, and are neatly appointed. There is a well stocked bar and a pleasant restaurant offering a range of popular dishes.
ROOMS: 8 rms (7 en suite) (2 fmly) No smoking in 4 bedrooms s fr £35; d fr £49 (incl. bkfst) * **PARKING:**
CARDS:

RYDE Map 04 SZ59

★★★64% Appley Manor
Appley Rd PO33 1PH
☎ 01983 564777 🖷 01983 564704
e-mail: appleymanor@lineone.net
Dir: *on B3330*
Originally a Victorian Manor House, Appley is located just five minutes from the Town Centre in very peaceful surroundings. The spacious bedrooms are well furnished, with all the expected, modern facilities. There is a residents' lounge and breakfast room overlooking the gardens, and the popular Manor Inn provides a range of well cooked meals.
ROOMS: 12 en suite (2 fmly) No smoking in 3 bedrooms s £35-£37; d £45-£47 * **PARKING:** 60 **NOTES:** No dogs (ex guide dogs)
CARDS:

★★70% Biskra Beach Hotel & Restaurant
17 Saint Thomas's St PO33 2DL
☎ 01983 567913 🖷 01983 616976
e-mail: info@biskra-hotel.com
Dir: *Ryde Esplanade to West End follow St. Thomas's Street, approx. 2 mins on right*
Refurbished in a contemporary style, Biskra House has bucked the more traditional trends. The result is a light airy hotel with spacious bedrooms and well lit bathrooms. Public areas convey a stylish, light colonial feel with a spacious bar and very popular restaurant.
ROOMS: 14 en suite (2 fmly) d £70-£120 (incl. bkfst) * LB
FACILITIES: Exterior Canadian hot tub Seasonal moorings with water taxi service **CONF:** Thtr 30 Class 30 Board 25 **PARKING:** 12
NOTES: Civ Wed 60 **CARDS:**

See advert on opposite page

★★61% Yelf's
Union St PO33 2LG
☎ 01983 564062 🖷 01983 563937
e-mail: yelfs.hotel@virgin.net
Dir: *from Ryde Esplanande, turn into Union St, Hotel is on right hand side*
This former coaching inn is undergoing refurbishment, under new ownership. Public areas are smartly appointed and include a busy bar, separate lounge and attractive dining room. Bedrooms, being upgraded, are comfortably furnished and well equipped.
ROOMS: 21 en suite (2 fmly) s fr £49; d fr £65.50 (incl. bkfst) *
CONF: Thtr 70 Class 10 Board 20 **CARDS:**

Late for dinner? Quality Standards star rating means that last orders for dinner should be no earlier than:
★ 6.30pm ★★ 7.00pm ★★★ 8.00pm
★★★★ 9.00pm ★★★★★ 10.00pm

ST LAWRENCE Map 04 SZ57

★★69% *Rocklands*
PO38 1XH
☎ 01983 852964 🖷 01983 852964
Dir: *A3055 from Ventnor to Niton, pass botanical gardens, Rare Breeds, & St Lawrence Church, hotel is 200m on right*
A friendly welcome is assured from the team at Rocklands. The hotel is located in peaceful surroundings with ample gardens. Public rooms convey much of the original character of the building with a bar, elegant dining room and comfortable lounge. Bedrooms are neatly decorated and thoughtfully equipped. The interesting range of evening meals make use of local fresh produce.

ROOMS: 15 en suite 4 annexe en suite (6 fmly) **FACILITIES:** Outdoor swimming (H) Snooker Sauna Solarium Croquet lawn Table tennis Games room entertainment ch fac **CONF:** Class 50 Board 40 **PARKING:** 20
NOTES: No dogs (ex guide dogs) No smoking in restaurant May-Oct

SANDOWN Map 04 SZ58

★★67% *Cygnet Hotel*
58 Carter St PO36 8DQ
☎ 01983 402930 🖷 01983 405112
e-mail: cyghotel@aol.com
Dir: *situated on the corner of Broadway - A3055 and the corner of Carter St*
Popular with tour groups, this family run hotel offers bedrooms that are mostly spacious, comfortably furnished and well equipped. Public areas include two lounge areas and a large bar which regularly stages live entertainment.
ROOMS: 45 rms (44 en suite) (9 fmly) **FACILITIES:** Indoor swimming (H) Outdoor swimming (H) Sauna Solarium Pool table Jacuzzi/spa
SERVICES: Lift **PARKING:** 30 **NOTES:** No dogs (ex guide dogs) No smoking in restaurant

SEAVIEW Map 04 SZ69

★★★78% Seaview Hotel & Restaurant
High St PO34 5EX
☎ 01983 612711 🖷 01983 613729
e-mail: reception@seaviewhotel.co.uk
Dir: *B3330 Ryde-Seaview rd, turn left via Puckpool along seafront Duver Rd, hotel is situated on left hand side*
This is a charming hotel in a quiet seaside village. Bedrooms vary in size and style, all are decorated with flair and comfort in mind. A quiet residents lounge with magazines is on the first floor, two bars and a separate, two-roomed restaurant complete public areas. All are decorated in a nautical theme with loads of memorabilia to study.
ROOMS: 16 en suite (1 fmly) No smoking in 2 bedrooms s fr £55; d fr £70 (incl. bkfst) * LB **FACILITIES:** Sailing lessons Painting breaks Special arrangement with local sports club **CONF:** Thtr 30 Class 15 Board 16 Del from £97 * **PARKING:** 12 **NOTES:** Closed 24-27 Dec
CARDS:

W

★★★75% Priory Bay
Priory Dr PO34 5BU
☎ 01983 613146 01983 616539
e-mail: reception@priorybay.co.uk
Dir: *B3330 towards Seaview, through Nettlestone. Do not take Seaview turning, instead continue 0.5m until sign for The Priory Bay Hotel becomes visible*

This hotel with its own stretch of beach has re-opened following extensive refurbishment. Public areas are comfortable as are the upgraded bedrooms. The kitchen creates interesting and imaginative dishes, using local produce as much as possible.
ROOMS: 19 en suite 15 annexe en suite (17 fmly) s £50-£94; d £88-£138 (incl. bkfst) * LB **FACILITIES:** Outdoor swimming Golf 9 Tennis (hard) Croquet lawn Private beach Xmas **CONF:** Thtr 80 Class 60 Board 30 Del from £100 * **PARKING:** 65 **NOTES:** Civ Wed 50
CARDS:

★★64% *Springvale Hotel*
Springvale PO34 5AN
☎ 01983 612533
A friendly hotel in a quiet beach front location with views across the Solent. Bedrooms, varying in shape and size, are attractive and well equipped. Public areas are traditionally furnished and include a cosy bar, dining room and small separate lounge.
ROOMS: 13 en suite (2 fmly) **FACILITIES:** Tennis (grass) Jacuzzi/spa Sailing dinghy hire & tuition **CONF:** Class 30 Board 20 Del £120 * **PARKING:** 1 **NOTES:** No dogs (ex guide dogs) No smoking in restaurant
CARDS:

SHANKLIN

Map 04 SZ58

★★★65% Keats Green
3 Queens Rd PO37 6AN
☎ 01983 862742 01983 868572
e-mail: keatsgreen@netguides.co.uk
Dir: *on A3055 follow signs Old Village/Ventnor, avoiding town centre, hotel on left past St Saviors church*
This well established hotel enjoys a super location overlooking Keats Green and Sandown Bay. Bedrooms are attractively decorated and pine furnished. Public rooms include a comfortable bar/lounge and a smartly appointed dining room.
ROOMS: 33 en suite (7 fmly) s £32-£40; d £64-£80 (incl. bkfst & dinner) * LB **FACILITIES:** Outdoor swimming (H) **PARKING:** 34 **NOTES:** No smoking in restaurant Closed Nov-Mar
CARDS:

★★★62% Brunswick
Queens Rd PO37 6AN
☎ 01983 863245 01983 868398
e-mail: enquires@brunswick-hotel.co.uk
This established hotel, on the cliff-top path known as Keat's Green, has lovely sea views. Bedrooms are comfortably furnished, with well chosen colour schemes. Public rooms include a spacious lounge/bar, attractive restaurant and choice of swimming pools.
ROOMS: 27 en suite 8 annexe en suite (9 fmly) s £37-£52; d £74-£104 (incl. bkfst) * LB **FACILITIES:** Indoor swimming (H) Outdoor swimming (H) Sauna Pool table Jacuzzi/spa Xmas **PARKING:** 30 **NOTES:** No smoking in restaurant Closed Dec & Jan **CARDS:**

★★★62% *Holliers Hotel*
5 Church Rd, Old Village PO37 6NU
☎ 01983 862764 01983 867134
A popular 18th-century hotel in the heart of the old village. Bedrooms are comfortably appointed and equipped with modern amenities. Public areas include a quiet first floor lounge, a smart bar with live entertainment and a spacious, brightly decorated restaurant with a comprehensive dinner menu.
ROOMS: 30 en suite (6 fmly) **FACILITIES:** STV Indoor swimming (H) Outdoor swimming (H) Sauna Pool table Jacuzzi/spa **PARKING:** 50 **NOTES:** No dogs (ex guide dogs) **CARDS:**

★★67% Fernbank
Highfield Rd PO37 6PP
☎ 01983 862790 01983 864412
e-mail: fern.bankhotel@virgin.net
Dir: *at Shanklin's old village traffic lights turn onto Victoria Ave, take 3rd left into Highfield Rd*
An established hotel in a peaceful location minutes from the old village. Bedrooms are comfortably appointed and equipped with modern facilities. Guests enjoy the sheltered lawns and leisure facilities. The smartly presented dining room overlooks gardens and countryside.

continued

W

SHANKLIN, continued

ROOMS: 19 en suite 5 annexe en suite (8 fmly) s fr £30; d fr £60 (incl. bkfst) * LB **FACILITIES:** Indoor swimming (H) Sauna Pool table Jacuzzi/spa Petanque **PARKING:** 22 **NOTES:** No children 7yrs No smoking in restaurant Closed Xmas & New Year
CARDS:

★★67% Luccombe Hall

Luccombe Rd PO37 6RL
☎ 01983 862719 📠 01983 863082
e-mail: reservations@luccombehall.co.uk
Dir: *take A3055 to Shanklin, through old village then 1st left into Priory Rd, left into Popham Rd, 1st right into Luccombe Rd. Hotel on right*
This hotel was originally built as a summer home for the Bishop of Portsmouth in 1870. Enjoying a peaceful clifftop location the property benefits from sea views and direct access to the beach. Bedrooms are comfortably furnished and well equipped.
ROOMS: 30 en suite (19 fmly) **FACILITIES:** Indoor swimming (H) Outdoor swimming (H) Tennis (grass) Squash Sauna Solarium Gym Pool table Jacuzzi/spa Games room entertainment **PARKING:** 20
CARDS:

★★65% Hambledon

Queens Rd PO37 6AW
☎ 01983 862403 & 863651 📠 01983 867894
e-mail: hambledonhotel@aol.com
Dir: *off A3055 turn left into Queens Rd at lights at the foot of Arthurs Hill*
The Hambledon specialises in walking holidays which the proprietors arrange for guests. Bedrooms are comfortable, nicely furnished and feature modern shower facilities. There is a cosy bar, adjacent lounge and a smartly appointed dining room.
ROOMS: 10 en suite (3 fmly) No smoking in all bedrooms s £24-£25; d £48-£50 (incl. bkfst) * LB **FACILITIES:** Free use of nearby indoor leisure facilities **PARKING:** 8 **NOTES:** No dogs No smoking in restaurant Closed 1 Dec-15 Jan **CARDS:**

★★64% Malton House

8 Park Rd PO37 6AY
☎ 01983 865007 📠 01983 865576
e-mail: christos@excite.co.uk
Dir: *from Hope Road traffic lights go straight up the hill then turn left on the third road*
A well kept Victorian hotel in a quiet location. Recently refurbished bedrooms are brightly appointed. Public rooms include a small comfortable lounge, bar and dining room. The hotel is conveniently located for cliff top walks and the public lift down to the promenade.
ROOMS: 15 en suite (3 fmly) s £24-£26; d £44-£48 (incl. bkfst) * **FACILITIES:** Xmas **PARKING:** 12 **NOTES:** No dogs No smoking in restaurant **CARDS:**

★★63% Melbourne Ardenlea

Queen's Rd PO37 6AP
☎ 01983 862283 📠 01983 862865
Dir: *turn left at Fiveways Crossroads, off A3055, hotel on right 150yds past the tall spired church*
Conveniently located for both the town centre and the lift down to the promenade, this friendly hotel continues to successfully cater for coach parties. Spacious public areas are smartly presented, bedrooms are traditionally furnished.
ROOMS: 55 en suite (9 fmly) s £30-£45; d £60-£90 (incl. bkfst & dinner) * LB **FACILITIES:** Indoor swimming (H) Sauna Solarium Pool table Jacuzzi/spa Pool Table tennis **SERVICES:** Lift **PARKING:** 28 **NOTES:** Closed mid Dec-mid Feb RS Nov-mid Dec & mid Feb-Mar
CARDS:

TOTLAND BAY

★★★66% *Sentry Mead*

Madeira Rd PO39 0BJ
☎ 01983 753212 📠 01983 753212
e-mail: sentry_mead@netguides.co.uk
Dir: *turn off A3054 at Totland war memorial rdbt, 300yds on right just before going to beach*
Just two minutes from the sea at Totland Bay, this well kept Victorian villa includes a comfortable lounge and separate bar as well as a conservatory overlooking the garden. Bedrooms feature co-ordinated soft furnishings and extras like mineral water, biscuits and pot-pourri.
ROOMS: 14 en suite (4 fmly) **FACILITIES:** Putting green **PARKING:** 10 **NOTES:** No smoking in restaurant Closed 22 Dec-2 Jan
CARDS:

VENTNOR

Map 04 SZ57

★★★★70% The Royal Hotel

Belgrave Rd PO38 1JJ
☎ 01983 852186 📠 01983 855395
e-mail: royalhotel@zetnet.co.uk
Dir: *A3055 main coastal road, into Ventnor follow one way system around Town, after traffic lights turn left into Belgrave road, Hotel is on right*
The Royal has been refitted to provide good quality accommodation. Bedrooms are available in different styles. Public areas include a sunny conservatory and restful lounge. The restaurant provides an appropriate setting for good cooking from modern, eclectic menus.
ROOMS: 55 en suite (7 fmly) No smoking in 2 bedrooms s £55-£120; d £110-£170 (incl. bkfst) * LB **FACILITIES:** STV Outdoor swimming (H) Croquet lawn Xmas **CONF:** Thtr 100 Class 80 Board 50 Del from £100 * **SERVICES:** Lift **PARKING:** 56 **NOTES:** No dogs (ex guide dogs) No smoking in restaurant **CARDS:**

See advert on opposite page

★★★65% Burlington

Bellevue Rd PO38 1DB
☎ 01983 852113 📠 01983 853862
Eight of the attractively decorated bedrooms have balconies, three ground floor rooms have french doors into the garden. There is a cosy bar, comfortable lounge and a dining room where home-made bread rolls accompany the five-course dinners. Service is both friendly and attentive.
ROOMS: 24 en suite (8 fmly) s £46-£49; d £92-£98 (incl. bkfst & dinner) * LB **FACILITIES:** Outdoor swimming (H) Pool table **PARKING:** 20 **NOTES:** No dogs No children 3yrs No smoking in restaurant Closed Nov-Etr **CARDS:**

★★★65% *Ventnor Towers*

Best Western

Madeira Rd PO38 1QT
☎ 01983 852277 📠 01983 855536
e-mail: ventnor@inc.co.uk
Dir: *first left after Trinity church, follow road for 0.25m*
This mid-Victorian hotel set in spacious grounds (from which a path leads down to the shore) is high above the bay and enjoys some splendid sea views. Lots of potted plants and fresh flowers grace day rooms which include two lounges and a roomy bar. Bedrooms include two four-posters and some with their own balconies.
ROOMS: 27 en suite (4 fmly) **FACILITIES:** Outdoor swimming (H) Tennis (hard) Pool table Croquet lawn Putting green Games room entertainment ch fac **CONF:** Thtr 80 Class 50 Board 35 **PARKING:** 26
CARDS:

★★★64% Eversley
Park Av PO38 1LB
☎ 01983 852244 Fax 01983 853948
e-mail: eversleyhotel@fsbdial.co.uk
Dir: *on A3055 west of Ventnor*
Conveniently located to the west of town by Ventnor Park. Bedrooms which are generally spacious are comfortably appointed and quiet. Public areas include a choice of lounges, bright dining room and a separate bar with a terrace overlooking a lawn and pool.
ROOMS: 30 en suite (8 fmly) **FACILITIES:** Outdoor swimming (H) Tennis (hard) Pool table **CONF:** Class 40 Board 20 Del from £45 * **PARKING:** 23 **NOTES:** No smoking in restaurant Closed 16 Nov-22 Dec & 2 Jan-15 Feb **CARDS:**

★★67% Hillside Hotel
Mitchell Av PO38 1DR
☎ 01983 852271 Fax 01983 852271
e-mail: aa@hillside-hotel.co.uk
Dir: *turn off A3055 onto B3327. Hotel 0.5m on right behind tennis courts*
Built in 1801 and enjoying an elevated position above the town, this popular hotel offers bedrooms which are smartly appointed, and equipped with modern facilities. Public rooms include a lounge, conservatory and dining room where guests can enjoy home cooking featuring good vegetarian options.
ROOMS: 12 rms (11 en suite) (1 fmly) No smoking in all bedrooms s £33-£35; d £66-£70 (incl. bkfst & dinner) LB **PARKING:** 12 **NOTES:** No children 5yrs No smoking in restaurant
CARDS:

★★67% *St Maur Hotel*
Castle Rd PO38 1LG
☎ 01983 852570 & 853645 Fax 01983 852306
Dir: *W of Ventnor off main A3055 (Park Avenue)*
Guests will find a warm welcome awaits them at this hotel, where six course home cooked dinners are on offer. The well equipped bedrooms are traditionally decorated. In addition to a spacious lounge the hotel benefits from a cosy residents' bar.
ROOMS: 14 en suite (2 fmly) **FACILITIES:** STV **PARKING:** 12 **NOTES:** No dogs No children 5yrs No smoking in restaurant Closed Dec
CARDS:

YARMOUTH — Map 04 SZ38

Premier Collection

★★★ George Hotel
Quay St PO41 0PE
☎ 01983 760331 Fax 01983 760425
e-mail: res@thegeorge.co.uk
Dir: *between the castle and the pier*
Superbly located between the quay and the castle, in this picturesque yachting town the George offers great character and quality throughout. Bedrooms have been individually decorated with great taste and style. The elegant restaurant offers excellent cooking, and the bright brasserie offers a less formal setting.

continued

ROOMS: 16 en suite No smoking in 4 bedrooms s £85-£165; d £145-£192 (incl. bkfst) * **FACILITIES:** STV Xmas **CONF:** Thtr 40 Class 20 Board 20 Del from £170 * **NOTES:** No children 10yrs Civ Wed 60 **CARDS:**

WILLERBY, East Riding of Yorkshire — Map 08 TA03

★★★71% Willerby Manor

Well Ln HU10 6ER
☎ 01482 652616 Fax 01482 653901
e-mail: info@willerbymanor.co.uk
Dir: *turn off A63, signposted Humber Bridge. Follow road, take right at rdbt by Safeway. At next rdbt hotel is signposted*
Surrounded by well tended gardens, this hotel was originally the home of Sir Henry Salmon, an Edwardian shipping merchant. It has been thoughtfully extended to provide tasteful bedrooms

continued

W

WILLERBY, continued

equipped with many useful extras. The wide choice of public areas include the Lafite Restaurant and excellent leisure facilities.
ROOMS: 51 en suite No smoking in 26 bedrooms s £73.50; d £84-£89 * LB **FACILITIES:** STV Indoor swimming (H) Sauna Solarium Gym Croquet lawn Jacuzzi/spa Steam room Beauty therapist Aerobic classes entertainment **CONF:** Thtr 500 Class 200 Board 100 Del £95 * **PARKING:** 300 **NOTES:** No dogs (ex guide dogs) RS 24-26 Dec Civ Wed 300 **CARDS:**

WILLINGTON, Co Durham — Map 12 NZ13

★★66% Kensington Hall
Kensington Ter DL15 0PJ
☎ 01388 745071 📠 01388 745800
e-mail: kensingtonhall@cs.com
Dir: *off A690*
This friendly family-run business and tourist hotel is also a popular venue for local weddings. The comfortable, well equipped bedrooms are attractively furnished, and public areas include a choice of smart bars and a cosy restaurant.
ROOMS: 10 en suite (3 fmly) No smoking in 2 bedrooms s £38-£40; d £48-£50 (incl. bkfst) * LB **CONF:** Class 80 Board 50 Del from £50 * **PARKING:** 40 **NOTES:** No dogs (ex guide dogs)
CARDS:

WILLITON, Somerset — Map 03 ST04

★★73% Curdon Mill
Vellow TA4 4LS
☎ 01984 656522 📠 01984 656197
e-mail: curdonmill@compuserve.com
Dir: *1m SE off A358*
Outstanding hospitality and good food are the strengths of this charming hotel. Bedrooms are compact and designed to make the best use of space. The restaurant incorporates original machinery from the water mill, providing an atmospheric environment in which to enjoy a menu enriched by high quality local produce and home-grown vegetables.
ROOMS: 8 rms (6 en suite) No smoking in all bedrooms s £40-£55; d £60-£80 (incl. bkfst) * LB **FACILITIES:** Outdoor swimming (H) Tennis Fishing Riding Croquet lawn Xmas **CONF:** Thtr 50 Class 50 Board 20 **PARKING:** 100 **NOTES:** No dogs (ex guide dogs) No children 8yrs No smoking in restaurant Civ Wed 300 **CARDS:**

★★72% White House
Long St TA4 4QW
☎ 01984 632306 & 632777
Dir: *on A39 in the centre of the village*
A wonderfully relaxed and easy going atmosphere is the hallmark of this charming little Georgian hotel. Bedrooms vary in size, those in the main building being rather more spacious, but all are well equipped with those extra touches that make this delightful place more of a home than a hotel.
ROOMS: 6 rms (5 en suite) 4 annexe en suite (1 fmly) s £52-£69; d £90-£110 (incl. bkfst) * LB **PARKING:** 12 **NOTES:** No smoking in restaurant Closed Nov-mid May

> Late for dinner? Quality Standards star rating means that last orders for dinner should be no earlier than:
> ★ 6.30pm ★★ 7.00pm ★★★ 8.00pm
> ★★★★ 9.00pm ★★★★★ 10.00pm

WILMSLOW, Cheshire — Map 07 SJ88
see also Manchester Airport

★★★★68% Mottram Hall
Wilmslow Rd, Mottram St Andrew, Prestbury SK10 4QT
De Vere Hotels
☎ 01625 828135 📠 01625 828950
e-mail: dmh.sales@devere-hotels.com
This extremely popular hotel lies in attractive grounds in the heart of the Cheshire countyside, yet is very conveniently located for Manchester airport and the motorway network. With extensive leisure and meeting facilities, including a magnificent golf course, and a new restaurant - Nathaniel's - this makes for a well rounded product.
ROOMS: 132 en suite (6 fmly) No smoking in 26 bedrooms s £145; d £170 (incl. bkfst) * LB **FACILITIES:** STV Indoor swimming (H) Golf 18 Tennis (hard & grass) Squash Snooker Sauna Solarium Gym Croquet lawn Putting green Jacuzzi/spa Beautician & Nail Salon Xmas **CONF:** Thtr 275 Class 140 Board 110 Del from £140 * **SERVICES:** Lift **PARKING:** 400 **NOTES:** No smoking in restaurant
CARDS:

Premier Lodge
Racecourse Rd SK9 5LR
PREMIER LODGE
☎ 0870 700 1578 📠 0870 700 1579
Premier Lodge offers modern, well equipped, en suite accommodation suitable for both business and leisure travellers. Meals can be taken at the adjacent popular restaurant and bar which is fully licensed. For further details, consult the Hotel Groups page.
ROOMS: 37 en suite d £46 *

WIMBORNE MINSTER, Dorset — Map 04 SZ09

★★75% Beechleas
17 Poole Rd BH21 1QA
☎ 01202 841684 📠 01202 849344
e-mail: hotelbeechleas@hotmail.com
Dir: *on A349*
Furnished to a high standard, the spacious bedrooms at this elegant Georgian town house are well equipped and individually styled. The lounge is very comfortable and the conservatory restaurant bright and airy. Dinner menus provide honest food; many ingredients are sourced from a local organic farm.
ROOMS: 5 en suite 4 annexe en suite No smoking in all bedrooms s £69-£89; d £79-£99 (incl. bkfst) * LB **FACILITIES:** Sailing on Hotel's yacht from Poole Harbour **CONF:** Thtr 20 Class 20 Board 14 Del from £129 * **PARKING:** 11 **NOTES:** No smoking in restaurant Closed 25 Dec-11 Jan **CARDS:**

WINCANTON, Somerset — Map 03 ST72

★★★68% Holbrook House
Holbrook BA9 8BS
☎ 01963 32377 📠 01963 32681
e-mail: holbrookhotel@compuserve.com
Dir: *from A303 at Wincanton, turn left on A371 towards Castle Cary and Shepton Mallet*
This charming country house is set in pretty grounds with mature trees and clipped box hedges. The comfortable lounges have log fires and deep armchairs, whilst skilfully prepared and imaginative dishes are offered in the elegant dining room. Hotel service is professional and informal and well suited to both business and leisure use. Should romance develop during your stay, the hotel holds a licence for civil weddings!

continued on p612

W

W

WINCANTON, continued

ROOMS: 15 en suite (2 fmly) s £80-£130; d £100-£150 (incl. cont bkfst) * LB **FACILITIES:** Indoor swimming (H) Outdoor swimming (H) Tennis (hard & grass) Sauna Gym Croquet lawn Jacuzzi/spa Beauty treatment ch fac Xmas **CONF:** Thtr 200 Class 50 Board 55 Del from £120 * **PARKING:** 100 **NOTES:** No dogs (ex guide dogs) No smoking in restaurant Civ Wed 80 **CARDS:**

WINCHESTER, Hampshire Map 04 SU42

★★★★73% Lainston House

Sparsholt SO21 2LT

☎ 01962 863588 01962 776672

e-mail: enquiries@lainstonhouse.com

Dir: *2m NW off B3049 towards Stockbridge*

This hotel embodies the fine traditions of a quality British country house. Rooms vary from spacious and well equipped rooms in Chudleigh Court to spectacular suites in the main house. The cuisine combines fresh clear flavours with imaginative presentation.

ROOMS: 41 en suite (2 fmly) s fr £95; d £145-£285 * LB **FACILITIES:** STV Tennis (hard) Fishing Gym Croquet lawn Archery Clay pigeon shooting entertainment Xmas **CONF:** Thtr 80 Class 50 Board 40 Del from £150 * **PARKING:** 150 **NOTES:** No smoking in restaurant Civ Wed 120 **CARDS:**

See advert on page 611

★★★★65% The Wessex

Paternoster Row SO23 9LQ

☎ 0870 400 8126 01962 841503

e-mail: heritagehotels_winchester.wessex@forte-hotels.com

Dir: *from M3 follow signs for town centre, at rdbt by King Alfred's statue proceed past the Guildhall and take the next left, hotel on right*

This large modern hotel is ideally positioned, tucked away in the heart of the city, and boasting unrestricted cathedral views from the public rooms and a good number of bedrooms. Designed with the business and leisure guest in mind the bedrooms are smart, comfortable and well equipped.

ROOMS: 94 en suite No smoking in 61 bedrooms s £127; d £155 (incl. bkfst) * LB **FACILITIES:** STV entertainment Xmas **CONF:** Thtr 100 Class 60 Board 60 Del from £135 * **SERVICES:** Lift **PARKING:** 60 **NOTES:** No smoking in restaurant Civ Wed 100

CARDS:

★★★70% *Royal*

Saint Peter St SO23 8BS

☎ 01962 840840 01962 841582

Once a convent and located in a quiet position right in the city centre, this hotel continues to be a popular choice. Bedrooms are split between the main house and a modern wing, the latter being slightly smaller and less opulent. Guests have use of the smartly appointed lounge and bar. The air-conditioned restaurant offers an interesting menu using fresh ingredients.

ROOMS: 75 en suite No smoking in 25 bedrooms **FACILITIES:** STV **CONF:** Thtr 150 Class 50 Board 40 **PARKING:** 80 **NOTES:** No smoking in restaurant **CARDS:**

See advert on page 611

★★★63% Marwell

Thompson Ln, Colden Common, Marwell SO21 1JY

☎ 01962 777681 01962 777625

Dir: *on B2177 opposite Marwell Zoological Park*

This modern hotel, well suited to both business and leisure guests, is situated in a unique location, built on stilts and set in the grounds of Marwell Zoological Park. Breakfast and dinner are served in the colonial style La Bambouserie Restaurant, and a good snack menu is available either in the lounge or the spacious well equipped bedrooms.

ROOMS: 68 en suite (35 fmly) No smoking in 47 bedrooms s £72.50-£90; d £80-£105 (incl. bkfst) * LB **FACILITIES:** STV Indoor swimming (H) Sauna Solarium Gym Pool table Jacuzzi/spa Xmas **CONF:** Thtr 160 Class 60 Board 60 Del from £75 * **PARKING:** 85 **NOTES:** No smoking in restaurant RS Sat Civ Wed 150 **CARDS:**

Town House

★★★★ Hotel du Vin & Bistro

14 Southgate St SO23 9EF

☎ 01962 841414 01962 842458

e-mail: admin@winchester.hotelduvin.co.uk

Dir: *M3 junct 11 towards Winchester, follow all signs. Hotel du Vin is situated approx 2m from junct 11 on left hand side just past cinema*

Relaxed, charming and unpretentious are the key words to describe this centrally located town house, which maintains a high profile amongst the locals. The individually decorated bedrooms, each sponsored by a different wine house, show considerable originality of style. The bistro serves imaginative and enjoyable food from a daily changing menu. The wine list has been selected by a master hand, offering a great choice from around the world.

ROOMS: 23 en suite (1 fmly) d £89-£185 * **FACILITIES:** STV Xmas **CONF:** Thtr 40 Class 30 Board 25 Del from £145 * **PARKING:** 45 **NOTES:** No dogs (ex guide dogs)

CARDS:

WINDERMERE, Cumbria Map 07 SD49

see also Crosthwaite

Premier Collection

★★★ Gilpin Lodge Country House Hotel & Restaurant

Crook Rd LA23 3NE

☎ 015394 88818 015394 88058

e-mail: hotel@gilpin-lodge.co.uk

Dir: *M6 junct 36, take A590/A591 to rdbt North of Kendal, take B5284, hotel is 5m on the right*

Gilpin Lodge is an attractive Victorian residence set in picturesque woodlands, moors and gardens. The public rooms are furnished with antiques and offer the perfect place to unwind. Some of the comfortable individually styled bedrooms have four-poster beds and private sun terraces. Imaginative and exciting food is served in one of three dining rooms.

continued

ROOMS: 14 en suite s £120-£125; d £140-£250 (incl. bkfst & dinner) * LB **FACILITIES:** Croquet lawn Free membership of local private Leisure Club Xmas **CONF:** Board 12 Del from £140 * **PARKING:** 30 **NOTES:** No dogs No children 7yrs No smoking in restaurant **CARDS:**

Premier Collection

★★★ Holbeck Ghyll Country House
Holbeck Ln LA23 1LU
☎ 015394 32375 015394 34743
e-mail: accommodation@holbeck-ghyll.co.uk
Dir: *3m North of Windermere on A591, turn right into Holbeck Lane (sign Troutbeck), hotel is 0.5m along on left*
In an area not short of dramatic views, Holbeck Ghyll still manages to stand out. Panoramic vistas stretch across Windermere Lake to the magnificent Langdale Fells beyond. The gently sloping grounds house a tennis court, and further leisure facilities have recently been added to include a health spa. Bedrooms, each individually furnished to the same high standard, are thoughtfully equipped and some have private balconies. Some rooms are in a separate cottage.
ROOMS: 14 en suite 6 annexe en suite (1 fmly) No smoking in 6 bedrooms s £95-£175; d £170-£300 (incl. bkfst & dinner) * LB **FACILITIES:** STV Tennis (hard) Sauna Gym Croquet lawn Putting green Jacuzzi/spa Beautician Steam room Xmas **CONF:** Thtr 45 Class 25 Board 25 **PARKING:** 30 **NOTES:** No smoking in restaurant Civ Wed 65 **CARDS:**

Courtesy & Care Award

★★★81% Linthwaite House Hotel
Crook Rd LA23 3JA
☎ 015394 88600 015394 88601
e-mail: admin@linthwaite.com
Dir: *A591 towards the lakes for 8m to large rdbt, take 1st exit (B5284), continue for 6m, hotel is on left hand side 1m past Windermere golf club*
Linthwaite House lies in delightful gardens. Formerly an Edwardian residence, this country house has its own tarn for fishing and swimming. The restaurant and bedrooms re-create the colonial 'Raffles' style. The lounges are furnished with deep cushioned armchairs and sofas and are warmed by open fires. The team at Linthwaite House hold the Courtesy & Care Award for England 2000-2001.

continued

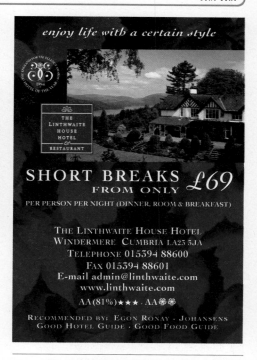

ROOMS: 26 en suite (1 fmly) No smoking in 19 bedrooms s £85-£110; d £115-£260 (incl. bkfst) * LB **FACILITIES:** STV Fishing Croquet lawn Putting green Free use of nearby leisure spa Xmas **CONF:** Thtr 47 Class 19 Board 22 Del from £150 * **PARKING:** 40 **NOTES:** No dogs (ex guide dogs) No smoking in restaurant Civ Wed 60 **CARDS:**

See advert on this page

★★★76% Storrs Hall
Storrs Park LA23 3LG
☎ 015394 47111 015394 47555
e-mail: reception@storrshall.co.uk
Dir: *on the A592 2m S of Bowness on the Newby Bridge road*
This is a faithfully restored Georgian mansion set on a peninsula of Lake Windermere with magnificent views to three sides. Imaginatively restored bedrooms are furnished with wonderful fine arts and antiques. The public areas are comfortable with deep

continued

W

WINDERMERE, continued

Storrs Hall, Windermere

cushioned sofas. The atmosphere is relaxed, the hospitality is warm and the food is good.

ROOMS: 18 en suite s £125-£155; d £215-£360 (incl. bkfst & dinner) * LB **FACILITIES:** Fishing Sailing Water skiing Xmas **CONF:** Board 20 Del from £180 * **PARKING:** 50 **NOTES:** No dogs (ex guide dogs) No children 12yrs No smoking in restaurant Closed 2 Jan-2 Feb **CARDS:**

★★★75% Lindeth Howe Country House

Lindeth Dr, Longtail Hill LA23 3JF
☎ 015394 45759 📠 015394 46368
e-mail: lindeth.howe@kencomp.net

Dir: *turn off A592 onto B5284 (Longtail Hill), hotel is the last driveway on the right hand side*

This delightful house, once the home of Beatrix Potter, is set in secluded woodlands and gardens, enjoying views over Lake Windermere. Major development has resulted in spacious, attractively furnished bedrooms. There is a choice of comfortable lounges, as well as an indoor leisure area. The restaurant is light and airy, the good value menu featuring carefully prepared local produce.

ROOMS: 36 en suite (3 fmly) No smoking in 28 bedrooms s £43-£82; d £85-£160 (incl. bkfst) * LB **FACILITIES:** STV Indoor swimming (H) Sauna Solarium Gym Xmas **CONF:** Thtr 30 Class 20 Board 18 Del from £100 * **PARKING:** 50 **NOTES:** No dogs (ex guide dogs) No smoking in restaurant **CARDS:**

★★★73% *Beech Hill*

Best Western

Newby Bridge Rd LA23 3LR
☎ 015394 42137 📠 015394 43745
e-mail: beechhill@talk21.com

Dir: *A591 towards Windermere, turn onto A590 to Newby Bridge, then take A592 toward Bowness, hotel is on left hand side 4m S from Bowness*

This stylish, modern hotel stands on the lakeside to the south of Bowness. Public rooms are very comfortable and bedrooms, which are being continually upgraded, are well equipped and generally very spacious. There is an indoor heated swimming pool and lake activities can be arranged. Imaginative dishes can be sampled in the restaurant, or alternatively a light lunch/snack menu is served in the smart lounge.

ROOMS: 57 en suite (4 fmly) **FACILITIES:** Indoor swimming (H) Fishing Sauna Solarium entertainment **CONF:** Thtr 80 Class 50 Board 40 **PARKING:** 70 **NOTES:** No smoking in restaurant **CARDS:**

TV dinner? Room service at three stars and above.

★★★72% Burn How Garden House Hotel

Best Western

Back Belsfield Rd, Bowness LA23 3HH
☎ 015394 46226 📠 015394 47000
e-mail: burnhowhotel@btinternet.com

Dir: *on entering Bowness, carry on past main lake piers on right, take first left to Hotel entrance*

Just a stroll from the lakeside and town centre, this hotel nestles in leafy woodland. Accommodation is spacious, well furnished and soundly equipped. Rooms are available in a nearby Victorian house or chalet-style rooms along the main drive. The attractive open plan lounges, bar, and elegant restaurant offer splendid views of the area.

ROOMS: 26 annexe en suite (10 fmly) No smoking in 2 bedrooms s £60-£75; d £70-£110 (incl. bkfst) * LB **FACILITIES:** Water sports entertainment Xmas **PARKING:** 30 **NOTES:** No dogs (ex guide dogs) No smoking in restaurant Closed 3-18 Jan **CARDS:**

See advert on opposite page

★★★70% Fayrer Garden House

THE CIRCLE Selected Individual Hotels GREAT BRITAIN

Lyth Valley Rd, Bowness on Windermere LA23 3JP
☎ 015394 88195 📠 015394 45986
e-mail: lakescene@fayrergarden.com

Dir: *on A5074 1m from Bowness Bay*

Located high above the lake and away from the hubbub of Bowness, this turn-of-the-century residence continues to be a popular destination for discerning guests. Elegant public rooms include a panelled hall leading into a cosy sitting room and a richly furnished conservatory restaurant. The appealing bedrooms are stylishly furnished.

ROOMS: 18 en suite (3 fmly) s £62.50-£85; d £115.50-£198 (incl. bkfst & dinner) * LB **FACILITIES:** STV Fishing Free membership of leisure club Xmas **PARKING:** 25 **NOTES:** No dogs (ex guide dogs) No smoking in restaurant **CARDS:**

★★★68% Burnside

Kendal Rd, Bowness LA23 3EP
☎ 015394 42211 015394 43824
Dir: *from M6 junct 36 follow A590 signs to Lakeside Steamers or follow A591 for Bowness and Ambleside. Hotel is 300 yds past steamer pier on the left*

A contemporary complex with well-tended gardens and views to the lake. At its heart is a Victorian house, extended to include comfortably furnished lounges, restaurants and spacious modern bedrooms. There is a wide range of conference and leisure facilities.

ROOMS: 57 en suite (15 fmly) No smoking in 18 bedrooms s fr £73; d fr £106 (incl. bkfst) * LB **FACILITIES:** STV Indoor swimming (H) Squash Snooker Sauna Solarium Gym Jacuzzi/spa Steam room Badminton Beauty salon entertainment Xmas **CONF:** Thtr 100 Class 70 Board 38 Del from £68.15 * **SERVICES:** Lift **PARKING:** 100 **NOTES:** Civ Wed 120 **CARDS:**

★★★68% *Langdale Chase*

Langdale Chase LA23 1LW
☎ 015394 32201 015394 32604
Dir: *2m S of Ambleside and 3m N of Windermere*

This grand country mansion nestles within colourful terraced gardens running down to the lake. Inside, the public areas have carved fireplaces, oak panelling, and a unique galleried staircase. The atmospheric lounges, the restaurant and most of the spacious bedrooms offer superb views. Dinner provides modern, imaginative dishes, cooked with flair.

ROOMS: 29 en suite (1 fmly) **FACILITIES:** Tennis (grass) Fishing Croquet lawn Putting green Sailing boats **CONF:** Thtr 25 Class 16 Board 20 **PARKING:** 50 **NOTES:** No smoking in restaurant **CARDS:**

★★★67% Wild Boar

Crook LA23 3NF
☎ 015394 45225 015394 42498
e-mail: wildboar@ehl.co.uk
Dir: *2.5m S of Windermere on B5284 Crook road. From rdbt where A591, A5284 & B5284 intersect take B5284 to Crook. Continue for 3.5m, hotel is on right*

Enjoying a rural location in the Gilpin Valley between Kendal and Windermere, this welcoming hotel, a former coaching inn, has been considerably extended to provide modern day comforts and facilities. Bedrooms are bright and airy and come with a good range of amenities. Public areas have a more traditional feel with many of the original features sympathetically retained. The lounge invites relaxation while the rustic bar is stocked with a tempting range of refreshments. Adjacent, the heavily beamed split-level restaurant provides an appropriate setting for the enjoyable fare which is based on local produce and traditional British recipes. The wine list is extensive and carefully chosen.

continued

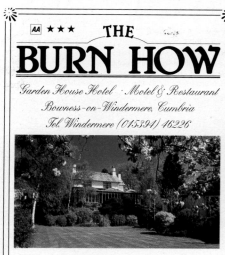

ROOMS: 36 en suite (3 fmly) No smoking in 6 bedrooms **FACILITIES:** STV Use of leisure facilities at sister hotel whilst in residence. **CONF:** Thtr 40 Class 20 Board 26 Del from £65 * **PARKING:** 60 **NOTES:** No smoking in restaurant **CARDS:**

★★★66% *Craig Manor*

Lake Rd LA23 3AR
☎ 015394 88877 015394 88878
Dir: *A590 to Windermere, then A591 into Windermere, turn left at Windermere hotel go through village, pass Magistrates court, hotel is on left*

Just north of Bowness town centre, and five minutes walk from the lake, the hotel is a converted Victorian house with smartly furnished bedrooms and stylish day rooms, consisting of a restaurant, lounge bar and a choice of sitting rooms with splendid Lakeland views.

ROOMS: 16 en suite **FACILITIES:** Pool table Table tennis **PARKING:** 70 **NOTES:** No smoking in restaurant **CARDS:**

★★★65% The Old England

Church St, Bowness LA23 3DF
☎ 0870 400 8130 015394 43432
Dir: *M6 junct 36- follow signs for Windermere. Continue through Windermere town centre to Bowness. Hotel is behind St Martins Church near pier*

An elegant Georgian country house with lake-front views and instant access to Bowness and the lake. Stylish, comfortable bedrooms have modern facilities. The Vinand Restaurant is noted for imaginative cuisine, with a pianist some evenings. There is an outdoor heated swimming pool, banqueting and function suites.

ROOMS: 76 en suite (8 fmly) No smoking in 26 bedrooms s £70-£110; d £140-£220 (incl. bkfst & dinner) * LB **FACILITIES:** Outdoor swimming (H) Snooker entertainment Xmas **CONF:** Thtr 140 Class 50 Board 42 Del from £75 * **SERVICES:** Lift **PARKING:** 82 **NOTES:** No smoking in restaurant Civ Wed 60 **CARDS:**

W

WINDERMERE, continued

★★★64% Belsfield
Kendal Rd, Bowness LA23 3EL
☎ 015394 42448 📠 015394 46397
e-mail: belsfield@regalhotels.co.uk
Dir: from M6 junct 36 follow Windermere signs take 1st left into Windermere follow Bowness signs & the lake. In Bowness take 1st left after Royal Hotel

REGAL

The hotel stands in six acres of gardens, many of its rooms look over a lake. Bedrooms are comfortable and guests have a choice of lounges. Meals are served in the Chandelier Restaurant and there are good leisure facilities.
ROOMS: 64 en suite (6 fmly) No smoking in 17 bedrooms s £44-£57; d £88-£114 (incl. bkfst & dinner) * LB **FACILITIES:** Indoor swimming (H) Snooker Sauna Solarium Putting green Mini golf - Pitch & Putt 9 holes entertainment Xmas **CONF:** Thtr 130 Class 60 Board 50 Del from £85 * **SERVICES:** Lift **PARKING:** 64 **NOTES:** No smoking in restaurant Civ Wed 80 **CARDS:**

★★★64% *Low Wood*
LA23 1LP
☎ 015394 33338 📠 015394 34072
e-mail: lowwood@elh.co.uk
Dir: M6 junct 36, follow A590 then A591 to Windermere, continue along A591 for 3m towards Ambleside, hotel is situated on the right hand side
Enjoying broad market appeal this popular hotel enjoys a splendid outlook over Lake Windermere to the Langdale Pikes beyond. Added attractions include a well equipped leisure club, a Watersports Centre, and good conference facilities. Bedrooms come in mixed sizes and styles and offer the expected comforts and facilities. Public areas include a choice of contrasting bars, a relaxing lounge, and spacious dining room where the fine dining menu offers a good example of traditional English cooking.
ROOMS: 117 en suite (13 fmly) No smoking in 18 bedrooms **FACILITIES:** STV Indoor swimming (H) Fishing Squash Snooker Sauna Solarium Gym Pool table Croquet lawn Putting green Jacuzzi/spa Water skiing Sub aqua diving Windsurfing Canoeing Laser clay pigeon shooting entertainment **CONF:** Thtr 340 Class 180 Board 150 **SERVICES:** Lift **PARKING:** 200 **NOTES:** No smoking in restaurant
CARDS:

Premier Collection

★★ Miller Howe
Rayrigg Rd LA23 1EY
☎ 015394 42536 📠 015394 45664
e-mail: lakeview@millerhowe.com
Dir: on A592 between Bowness & Windermere
A popular hotel with a real flavour of the Lake District. The stunning views of Windermere from the sumptuous public rooms are unrivalled. Bedrooms are both elegant and stylish and offer many thoughtful extras. Dinner remains a highlight

of any visit and the previous set menu has now been extended to offer a good choice of imaginative dishes.
ROOMS: 12 en suite **FACILITIES:** entertainment **PARKING:** 40 **NOTES:** No children 8yrs No smoking in restaurant Closed 3 Jan-10 Feb **CARDS:**

★★77% Lindeth Fell
Lyth Valley Rd, Bowness-on-Windermere LA23 3JP
☎ 015394 43286 & 44287 📠 015394 47455
e-mail: kennedy@lindethfell.co.uk
Dir: 1m South of Bowness on A5074
Enjoying delightful views over the lake and fells, this smart Edwardian residence stands in glorious gardens just a short walk from the town. The comfortable bedrooms vary in style and size, while skilfully prepared dinners are served in the dining room.
ROOMS: 14 en suite (2 fmly) s £52-£69; d £104-£138 (incl. bkfst) * LB **FACILITIES:** Tennis Fishing Croquet lawn Putting green Bowling green Pitch & putt Xmas **PARKING:** 20 **NOTES:** No dogs No smoking in restaurant Closed 3 Jan-14 Feb **CARDS:**
See advert on opposite page

★★76% Cedar Manor Hotel & Restaurant
Ambleside Rd LA23 1AX
☎ 015394 43192 📠 015394 45970
e-mail: cedarmanor@fsbdial.co.uk
Dir: 0.25m N on A591 by St Marys Church
This friendly, privately owned hotel enjoys an attractive location. Bedrooms, some in an adjacent cottage, are tastefully appointed. There is a comfortable lounge, a cosy bar and a dining room where an interesting range of dishes is offered.
ROOMS: 10 en suite 2 annexe en suite (4 fmly) s £32-£42; d £64-£84 (incl. bkfst) * LB **FACILITIES:** Private arrangements nearby free of charge to guests eg pool, sauna, solarium **PARKING:** 15 **NOTES:** No smoking in restaurant **CARDS:**

★★68% Glenburn
New Rd LA23 2EE
☎ 015394 42649 📠 015394 88998
Dir: M6 junct 36, 16m to Windermere A591, through Windermere village, go past shops and the hotel is 500yds along on the left hand side
Located between Windermere and Bowness, this family-run hotel is set in attractive surroundings. The stylish bedrooms come in a variety of sizes and are well equipped. A smart new reception has enhanced the interior. Dinner in the attractive dining room is available from 6.30pm.
ROOMS: 16 en suite (4 fmly) No smoking in all bedrooms d £50-£80 (incl. bkfst) * LB **PARKING:** 17 **NOTES:** No dogs (ex guide dogs) No children 5yrs No smoking in restaurant **CARDS:**

★★67% **Hideaway**
Phoenix Way LA23 1DB
☎ 015394 43070 📠 015394 48664
Dir: *turn left off A591 at the Ravensworth Hotel into Phoenix Way. Hideaway Hotel is situated 100yds down the hill on the right hand side*

This welcoming family run hotel has a secluded location a short walk from the town centre. Bedrooms, some in a separate building across the courtyard, are individually furnished, with four poster and family rooms available. Good home cooked meals are served in the dining room, there is a cosy bar and inviting lounge.
ROOMS: 10 en suite 5 annexe en suite (3 fmly) s £30-£45; d £50-£100 (incl. bkfst) * LB **FACILITIES:** Free use of nearby leisure facilities Xmas **PARKING:** 16 **NOTES:** No smoking in restaurant Closed 3-31 Jan
CARDS:

See advert on this page

W

WINDERMERE, continued

★★67% Ravensworth
Ambleside Rd LA23 1BA
☎ 015394 43747 015394 43670
e-mail: ravenswth@aol.com
Dir: *M6 junct 36, take A590/A591 and travel for 16m into Windermere, hotel is on the left hand side of road*
This well kept Victorian hotel is located on the edge of the village. The bedrooms are all neatly appointed and include both family and four-poster rooms. Public areas feature a cosy bar, comfortable lounge and an attractive conservatory dining room. This is a no smoking establishment.
ROOMS: 12 en suite 2 annexe en suite (1 fmly) No smoking in all bedrooms s £23.50-£46.50; d £47-£73 (incl. bkfst) * LB
FACILITIES: Available at local Leisure Club (charged) Xmas **PARKING:** 17
NOTES: No smoking in restaurant **CARDS:**

See advert on page 617

★★64% Cranleigh
Kendal Rd, Bowness on Windermere LA23 3EW
☎ 015394 43293 015394 47283
e-mail: mike@thecranleigh.com
Dir: *off Lake Road, opp St Martin's church and along Kendal Rd 150m*
Within walking distance of the town centre, this welcoming, traditional hotel offers a choice of lounges and an attractive dining room which serves a tempting dinner menu. The bedrooms are very pleasant with a few rooms located in a nearby building.
ROOMS: 9 en suite 6 annexe en suite (3 fmly) s £40-£72; d £50-£120 (incl. bkfst) * LB **FACILITIES:** Free membership of leisure club
PARKING: 15 **NOTES:** No dogs (ex guide dogs) No smoking in restaurant **CARDS:**

★65% Willowsmere
Ambleside Rd LA23 1ES
☎ 015394 43575 & 44962 015394 44962
e-mail: willowsmerehotel@hotmail.com
Dir: *stay on A591, just past St Marys Church*
Guests can expect a warm welcome at this family-run hotel. Bedrooms, which vary in shape and size, are traditionally furnished. There are two comfortable lounges and an attractive dining room.
ROOMS: 13 en suite (7 fmly) s £25-£30; d £50-£60 (incl. bkfst) * LB
PARKING: 20 **NOTES:** No smoking in restaurant Closed Nov-Feb RS Dec-Jan **CARDS:**

WINDSOR, Berkshire Map 04 SU97

★★★★73% Oakley Court
Windsor Rd, Water Oakley SL4 5UR
☎ 01753 609988 01628 637011
e-mail: sales.oakleycourt@queensmoat.co.uk
Dir: *leave M4 junct 6, head for Windsor, then right onto A308 Maidenhead. Pass racecourse & hotel is 2.5m on right*

Built in 1859, this splendid Victorian Gothic mansion is enviably situated in extensive grounds leading down to the Thames. All rooms are spacious, beautifully furnished and many enjoy river views. The Oakleaf restaurant offers a range of carefully prepared dishes. The hotel offers a small nine hole golf course, and boat trips can be easily arranged.
ROOMS: 63 en suite 52 annexe en suite No smoking in 45 bedrooms s fr £185; d fr £215 * LB **FACILITIES:** STV Indoor swimming (H) Golf 9 Fishing Snooker Sauna Solarium Gym Croquet lawn Jacuzzi/spa Boating Xmas **CONF:** Thtr 160 Class 100 Board 48 Del £280 *
PARKING: 120 **NOTES:** No dogs (ex guide dogs) No smoking in restaurant Civ Wed 180 **CARDS:**

★★★75% Sir Christopher Wren's House Hotel
Thames St SL4 1PX
☎ 01753 861354 01753 860172
Dir: *M4 junct 6, continue along A332, left at rdbt, left at next rdbt, 0.5m on left signposted Eton Bridge*
This historic hotel occupies an idyllic position on the banks of the Thames near the footbridge to Eton. Diners in the restaurant benefit from these lovely views and enjoy a range of complex yet inventive dishes. The hotel offers a variety of bedrooms, from single rooms to self contained apartments, all rooms however feature fine furnishings, tasteful decor and a thoughtful range of extra facilities.
ROOMS: 70 en suite (11 fmly) No smoking in 22 bedrooms s £125-£235; d £135-£235 * LB **FACILITIES:** STV Xmas **CONF:** Thtr 120 Class 70 Board 50 Del from £195 * **PARKING:** 30 **NOTES:** No dogs (ex guide dogs) Civ Wed 100 **CARDS:**

★★★69% Christopher Hotel
110 High St, Eton SL4 6AN
☎ 01753 852359 & 811677 01753 830914
e-mail: sales@christopher-hotel.co.uk
Originally dating from 1511, this old coaching inn enjoyed a racy reputation and was a major attraction for the boys of Eton College. Today, the hotel provides modern accommodation for its guests, located in the main building or in the courtyard rooms. The public areas consist of a traditional pub and a modern French-style Bistro.
ROOMS: 11 en suite 22 annexe en suite No smoking in 21 bedrooms s £100-£120; d £110-£120 * LB **FACILITIES:** Xmas **CONF:** Thtr 40 Class 30 Board 28 Del from £135 * **PARKING:** 23 **NOTES:** No smoking in restaurant **CARDS:**

★★★67% The Castle
18 High St SL4 1LJ
☎ 0870 400 8300 01753 830244
e-mail: heritagehotels_windsor.castle@forte-hotels.com
Dir: *M4 junct 6/M25 junct 15-follow signs to Windsor town centre and castle. Hotel located at the top of hill by the castle opposite the Guildhall*
This popular hotel lies right next to Windsor Castle. Bedrooms are smartly appointed, ranging from the traditionally furnished to the deluxe executive rooms. Public areas include an attractive lounge, small open-plan bar and a choice of eating options: the Castle restaurant; and the less formal Freshfields.
ROOMS: 41 en suite 70 annexe en suite (18 fmly) No smoking in 50 bedrooms s fr £150; d £175-£265 * LB **FACILITIES:** STV **CONF:** Thtr 370 Class 155 Board 80 Del from £145 * **SERVICES:** Lift
PARKING: 100 **CARDS:**

Early start? Hotels at all star levels should provide in-room alarm clocks and/or alarm calls.

★★★67% Royal Adelaide

46 Kings Rd SL4 2AG
☎ 01753 863916 01753 830682
e-mail: royaladelaide@meridianleisure.com

Dir: *from M4 junct 6 A322 to Windsor. Take 1st left off 1st rdbt into Clarence Rd. At 4th set of lights turn right into Sheet St, Hotel is on right*

In an ideal location, close to Windsor Castle, this recently renovated Georgian style hotel offers tastefully furnished and comfortable bedrooms, a range of meeting rooms, bar and restaurant. The hotel is well suited to the needs of both business and leisure travellers.

ROOMS: 38 en suite 4 annexe en suite (5 fmly) s fr £85; d fr £95 (incl. bkfst) * LB **FACILITIES:** Xmas **CONF:** Thtr 75 Class 50 Board 40 Del from £120 * **PARKING:** 20 **NOTES:** No smoking in restaurant Civ Wed 100 **CARDS:**

See advert on this page

★★★65% *Ye Harte & Garter*

High St SL4 1PH
☎ 01753 863426 01753 830527

Dir: *in town centre opposite front entrance to Windsor Castle*

Situated in the heart of this historic town, the hotel has been carefully restored to combine traditional Victorian elegance with all the modern comforts. Bedrooms vary in size, but offer a useful range of facilities and many have enviable views of the castle, Eton College or the Thames. There is also a café bar, two restaurants and a traditional pub.

ROOMS: 42 en suite (4 fmly) **FACILITIES:** STV Pool table entertainment **CONF:** Thtr 300 Class 150 Board 80 **SERVICES:** Lift **NOTES:** No dogs (ex guide dogs) **CARDS:**

WINDERMERE, continued

★★72% Aurora Garden
Bolton Av SL4 3JF
☎ 01753 868686 01753 831394
Dir: take junct 6 M4 onto the A332 for Windsor. At first rdbt, second exit towards Staines. At third rdbt third exit for 500yds. Hotel is on right
Located half a mile from the centre of this historic town and close to Windsor Great Park, this privately run hotel is noted for its warm and friendly atmosphere. The restaurant overlooks the landscaped water gardens and serves a wide choice of dishes at breakfast and dinner. Bedrooms are individually appointed and offer many extras.
ROOMS: 19 en suite (7 fmly) s fr £80; d fr £100 (incl. bkfst) * LB
FACILITIES: STV **CONF:** Thtr 90 Class 30 Board 25 Del from £135 *
PARKING: 25 **NOTES:** No smoking in restaurant Civ Wed 120
CARDS:

See advert on page 619

WINSCOMBE, Somerset Map 03 ST45

Premier Lodge
Bridgwater Rd BS25 1NN
☎ 0870 700 1340 0870 700 1341
Premier Lodge offers modern, well equipped, en suite accommodation suitable for both business and leisure travellers. Meals can be taken at the adjacent popular restaurant and bar which is fully licensed. For further details, consult the Hotel Groups page.
ROOMS: 31 en suite d £46 *

WINSFORD, Somerset Map 03 SS93

★★★70% Royal Oak Inn
Exmoor National Park TA24 7JE
☎ 01643 851455 01643 851009
e-mail: enquiries@royaloak-somerset.co.uk
Dir: N from Tiverton on A396 for 15m then left to Winsford. First turning left on entering village

This 12th-century thatched inn has comfortable lounges for guests to relax in. The restored bedrooms in the main building, retain the character of the building, while those in the courtyard have more of a cottage style. In the beamed bars a selection of meals are available. A carte menu of traditional old English cuisine is served in the hotel's restaurant.
ROOMS: 8 en suite 6 annexe en suite (1 fmly) s £65-£85; d £75-£145 (incl. bkfst) * LB **FACILITIES:** Fishing Hunting Shooting Xmas
PARKING: 23 **CARDS:**

Arriving late? Four and five star hotels have night porters to assist with your luggage; and 24hr room service.

WINTERINGHAM, Lincolnshire Map 08 SE92

Premier Collection

★★ Winteringham Fields
DN15 9PF
☎ 01724 733096 01724 733898
e-mail: wintfields@aol.com
Dir: in the centre of the village at the X-roads
This is a fine restaurant with rooms, quietly situated in a small village. Bedrooms vary in size, and are comfortably decorated and furnished. Public areas are comfortable and inviting but it is the quality of the cooking that is the main draw, combining Swiss recipes with fine local produce to provide memorable meals.
ROOMS: 4 en suite 6 annexe en suite No smoking in all bedrooms s £75-£110; d £90-£155 (incl. cont bkfst) * **PARKING:** 17
NOTES: No children 8yrs No smoking in restaurant Closed Sun, Mon & BH/2wks Xmas/Aug/late Mar **CARDS:**

WISBECH, Cambridgeshire Map 05 TF40

★★72% Crown Lodge
Downham Rd, Outwell PE14 8SE
☎ 01945 773391 & 772206 01945 772668
e-mail: crownlodgehotel@hotmail.com
Dir: on A1122/A1101 approx 5m from Wisbech and 7m from Downham Market
A popular hotel, situated on the banks of Well Creek in the village of Outwell and just a short drive from Wisbech. Bedrooms are modern and well equipped, with good levels of space and comfort. A wide selection of food is available in the popular restaurant which has a loyal following.
ROOMS: 10 en suite s £45-£50; d £60-£65 (incl. bkfst) * LB
FACILITIES: Squash Snooker Solarium **CONF:** Thtr 40 Class 30 Board 20 **PARKING:** 57 **CARDS:**

★★63% ***Rose & Crown Hotel***
Market Place PE13 1DG
☎ 01945 589800 01945 474610
Dir: in centre of Wisbech, access from A47 & A1101
For over 500 years this former hostelry has provided hospitality for adventurers and travellers. The wide range of spacious public rooms includes the Tidnams Tipple Inn, the coffee shop/delicatessen, the traditional Rose Restaurant and several function rooms. Accommodation is modern and comfortable.
ROOMS: 20 en suite (1 fmly) **CONF:** Thtr 100 Class 60 Board 60
PARKING: 20 **NOTES:** Closed 25-26 Dec
CARDS:

WISHAW, Warwickshire Map 07 SP19

★★★★74% ֍֍ The De Vere Belfry

B76 9PR

☎ 01675 470301 🖹 01675 470256

e-mail: enquiries@thebelfry.com

Dir: *take junct 9 off M42 and follow A446 towards Lichfield, the Belfry is 1m on right*

DE VERE HOTELS

Hotels of character, run with pride.

Well known as a venue for the Ryder Cup, The Belfry offers three golf courses amongst the many leisure facilities. The well equipped leisure club includes squash courts and snooker tables, whilst there is also a jogging trail to burn off some of the calories from any of the five restaurants. The dedicated team of staff are friendly and welcoming. Bedrooms vary in size, the best having fine views over the golf course, and a wide range of conference suites and a nightclub complete the package at this busy resort hotel.

ROOMS: 324 en suite (133 fmly) No smoking in 124 bedrooms s fr £160; d £185-£425 (incl. bkfst) * LB **FACILITIES:** STV Indoor swimming (H) Golf 36 Tennis (hard) Squash Snooker Sauna Solarium Gym Pool table Putting green Jacuzzi/spa Bel Air night club in grounds Driving range Xmas **CONF:** Thtr 400 Class 220 Board 60 Del from £99 * **SERVICES:** Lift **PARKING:** 1000 **NOTES:** No dogs (ex guide dogs) Civ Wed 250 **CARDS:**

WITHERSLACK, Cumbria Map 07 SD48

★★74% ֍ Old Vicarage Country House

Church Rd LA11 6RS

☎ 015395 52381 🖹 015395 52373

e-mail: hotel@oldvicarage.com

Dir: *from A590 turn into Witherslack, take left after phone box signposted to the church, continue straight on for 0.75m*

This delightful Georgian house is peacefully situated in attractive natural gardens. Bedrooms in the main house are attractively furnished, with some fine antique pieces, whilst the larger rooms in Orchard House have a more modern feel. Good use is made of local produce on the daily changing menu and there are two inviting lounges.

ROOMS: 8 en suite 5 annexe en suite (1 fmly) s £65-£75; d £98-£138 (incl. bkfst) * LB **FACILITIES:** Tennis (hard) Arrangement with local leisure club Xmas **PARKING:** 25 **NOTES:** No smoking in restaurant **CARDS:**

See advert on this page

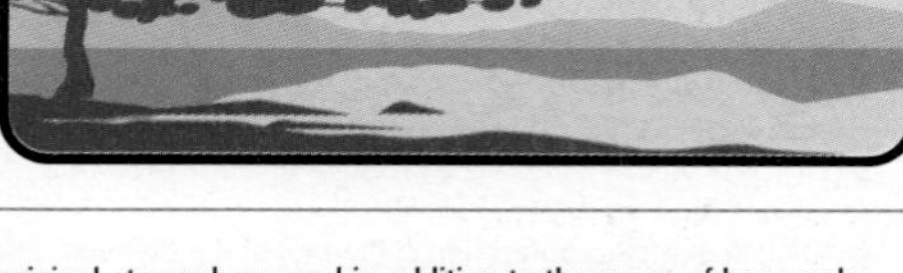

WITHYPOOL, Somerset Map 03 SS83

★★74% ֍ Royal Oak Inn

TA24 7QP

☎ 01643 831506 🖹 01643 831659

Dir: *7m N of Dulverton, off B3223*

This hotel combines the character and charm of an old village inn with high standards of service and comfort. The bars retain there original atmosphere, and in addition to the range of bar meals, guests have the choice of either a fixed-price menu or a short carte. Bedrooms are well equipped and comfortable.

ROOMS: 8 rms (7 en suite) s £55; d £82-£92 (incl. bkfst) * **FACILITIES:** Riding Shooting **PARKING:** 20 **NOTES:** No smoking in restaurant **CARDS:**

WITNEY, Oxfordshire Map 04 SP30

★★★70% Witney Four Pillars Hotel

Ducklington Ln OX8 7TJ

☎ 01993 779777 🖹 01993 703467

e-mail: enquiries@four-pillars.co.uk

Dir: *M40 off junc 9, A34 to A40, exit A415 Witney/Abingdon, Hotel on left, second exit for Witney*

FOUR PILLARS HOTELS

This smart modern hotel offers well equipped rooms. There is a popular restaurant which operates a carvery on certain evenings. Facilities include a swimming pool, gym and sauna.

continued

W

WITNEY, continued

ROOMS: 83 en suite (16 fmly) No smoking in 30 bedrooms s £55-£90; d £80-£115 * LB **FACILITIES:** STV Indoor swimming (H) Sauna Solarium Gym Pool table Jacuzzi/spa Whirlpool spa entertainment Xmas **CONF:** Thtr 160 Class 80 Board 46 Del from £120 * **SERVICES:** air con **PARKING:** 170
CARDS:

WIVELISCOMBE, Somerset Map 03 ST02

Premier Collection

★★ Langley House

Langley Marsh TA4 2UF
☎ 01984 623318 01984 624573
e-mail: user@langley.in2home.co.uk
Dir: *follow signs to Wiveliscombe town centre, turn right at town centre. Hotel 0.5m on right*

Nestling in peaceful countryside at the foot of the Brendon Hills, parts of Langley House date back to the 16th century, although it is predominantly Georgian. There are deep armchairs and comfortable sofas in the sitting room where a log fire burns on colder evenings. Bedrooms vary in size and design, but all have thoughtful touches. Hospitality is warm and service is attentive. The award winning cuisine should not be missed.
ROOMS: 8 en suite (1 fmly) No smoking in 2 bedrooms s £77.50-£82.50; d £97-£127.50 (incl. bkfst) * LB **FACILITIES:** Croquet lawn ch fac Xmas **PARKING:** 20 **NOTES:** No smoking in restaurant
CARDS:

WOKINGHAM, Berkshire Map 04 SU86

★★★63% Edward Court Hotel

Wellington Rd RG40 2AN
☎ 0118 977 5886 0118 977 2018
Dir: *from Wokingham follow A329 towards Reading. Left at mini-rdbt signed Railway Station/Arborfield. Next left before level crossing. Hotel on right*

Close to the town's station and with excellent parking the Edward Court is in an ideal location for business visitors. Bedrooms are spacious with plenty of desk space. The bar and restaurant, with comfortable seating and a friendly atmosphere, offer an excellent range of dishes that are skilfully presented.

continued

ROOMS: 27 en suite No smoking in 14 bedrooms s £78; d £101-£106 (incl. bkfst) * **FACILITIES:** Xmas **CONF:** Thtr 50 Class 36 Board 24 Del £147 * **PARKING:** 45 **NOTES:** No dogs (ex guide dogs)
CARDS:

WOLVERHAMPTON, West Midlands Map 07 SO99
see also Himley & Worfield

★★★68% Park Hall Hotel

Best Western

Park Dr, Goldthorn Park WV4 5AJ
☎ 01902 331121 01902 344760
e-mail: enquiries@parkhallhotel.co.uk
Dir: *turn off A4039 towards Penn and Wombourne, take 2nd road on left (Ednam Road) hotel is at end of road*

This 18th-century house stands in extensive grounds and gardens, a short drive from the town centre. Bedrooms vary in style, but all are well equipped. The Terrace restaurant offers a carvery buffet and both set price and à la carte menus.
ROOMS: 57 en suite (4 fmly) No smoking in 4 bedrooms s £59-£64; d £64-£69 (incl. bkfst) * LB **FACILITIES:** STV Pool table Croquet lawn Table tennis **CONF:** Thtr 450 Class 250 Board 100 Del from £95 * **PARKING:** 250 **NOTES:** No dogs (ex guide dogs) No smoking in restaurant **CARDS:**

★★★65% Novotel

NOVOTEL

Union St WV1 3JN
☎ 01902 871100 01902 870054
Dir: *6m from jct10 of M6. Following Black Country route. Take A454 to Wolverhampton. Hotel is situated on the main ring road*

This large, modern and purpose built hotel stands close to the town centre and ring road. It provides spacious, smartly presented and well equipped accommodation, all of which contain convertible bed settees for family occupancy. In addition to the open plan lounge and bar area, there is an attractive brasserie style restaurant, which overlooks the small outdoor swimming pool.
ROOMS: 132 en suite (10 fmly) No smoking in 88 bedrooms d £70-£85 * LB **FACILITIES:** STV Outdoor swimming (H) Pool table **CONF:** Thtr 200 Class 100 Board 80 Del from £105 * **SERVICES:** Lift **PARKING:** 120 **CARDS:**

★★★65% Quality Hotel Wolverhampton

CHOICE HOTELS EUROPE

Penn Rd WV3 0ER
☎ 01902 429216 01902 710419
e-mail: admin@gb069.u-net.com
Dir: *on A449, Wolverhampton to Kidderminster, 0.25m from ring road on right, opposite Safeway super market*

The original Victorian house has been considerably extended to create a large, busy and popular hotel. Ornately carved woodwork and ceilings still remain in the original building. All the bedrooms are well equipped. The pleasant public areas have a lot of character and offer a choice of bars.

continued

ROOMS: 66 en suite 26 annexe en suite (1 fmly) No smoking in 48 bedrooms s fr £81; d fr £97 (incl. bkfst) * LB **FACILITIES:** STV Indoor swimming (H) Sauna Gym Steam room Xmas **CONF:** Thtr 140 Class 70 Board 40 Del £128 * **PARKING:** 120 **NOTES:** No dogs (ex guide dogs) No smoking in restaurant Civ Wed 100
CARDS:

★★69% *Ely House*

MINOTEL Great Britain

53 Tettenhall Rd WV3 9NB
☎ 01902 311311 01902 421098
Dir: *take A41 towards Whitchurch from town centre-ring road. 200yds on left hand side after traffic lights*

This delightful property dates back to 1742 and has been tastefully converted into a charming hotel. Bedrooms are all spacious, comfortably furnished, with some rooms on the ground floor, which can be easily reached from the secure car park. There is a pleasant dining room and spacious lounge bar.

ROOMS: 18 en suite **PARKING:** 20 **NOTES:** No dogs (ex guide dogs) No children 7yrs Closed 24-26 Dec **CARDS:**

★★59% Fox Hotel International

118 School St WV3 0NR
☎ 01902 421680 01902 711654
e-mail: sales@foxhotel.co.uk
Dir: *in town centre on ring road junction with A449*

This privately owned, purpose-built hotel is situated on the inner ring road, close to the town centre. Its modern, well equipped bedrooms are popular with business guests. There is a choice of bars and good meeting and function rooms.

ROOMS: 33 en suite (1 fmly) No smoking in 5 bedrooms s £35-£39; d £55-£59 (incl. bkfst) * LB **FACILITIES:** STV Jacuzzi/spa entertainment ch fac Xmas **CONF:** Thtr 60 Class 60 Board 40 **PARKING:** 20 **NOTES:** No dogs (ex guide dogs) **CARDS:**

WOOBURN COMMON, Buckinghamshire Map 04 SU98

★★68% *Chequers Inn*

Kiln Ln, Wooburn HP10 0JQ
☎ 01628 529575 01628 850124
e-mail: info@chequers-inn.com
Dir: *from M40 junct 2 take A40 through Beaconsfield Old Town towards High Wycombe. 2m outside town turn left into Broad Lane. Hotel is 2.5m along road*

This 17th-century inn enjoys a peaceful, rural location, right by the common. Bedrooms feature stripped pine furniture, co-ordinated fabrics and an excellent range of extra facilities. The bar, with its massive oak post, beams and flagstone floor is very much the focal point of the hotel and enjoys a loyal local trade.

ROOMS: 17 en suite **FACILITIES:** STV **CONF:** Thtr 50 Class 30 Board 20 **PARKING:** 60 **NOTES:** No dogs (ex guide dogs)
CARDS:

See advert on this page

W

WOODALL, South Yorkshire Map 08 SK48

Days Inn

S31 8XR

☎ 0114 248 7992 Fax 0114 248 5634

Dir: situated on the southbound side of the M1 at Woodall services between jct31/jct31

Fully refurbished, Days Inn offers well equipped, brightly appointed, modern accommodation with smart en suite bathrooms. There is a fully staffed reception; continental breakfast is available and other refreshments may be taken at the nearby family restaurant.

ROOMS: 38 en suite d fr £45 *

WOODBRIDGE, Suffolk Map 05 TM24

★★★75% Seckford Hall

IP13 6NU

☎ 01394 385678 Fax 01394 380610

e-mail: reception@seckford.co.uk

Dir: signposted on A12 (Woodbridge bypass). Do not follow signs for town centre

Seckford Hall is an attractive manor house that was reputed to be the court of Queen Elizabeth I. In addition to the splendid pannelled lounge, the elegant restaurant offers an interesting choice of dishes, and a lighter selection is provided in the courtyard brasserie. The spacious bedrooms retain much of the original character of the building.

ROOMS: 22 en suite 10 annexe en suite (4 fmly) s £79-£130; d £110-£165 (incl. bkfst) * LB **FACILITIES:** STV Indoor swimming (H) Golf 18 Fishing Solarium Gym Putting green Jacuzzi/spa Xmas **CONF:** Thtr 100 Class 46 Board 40 Del £140 * **PARKING:** 200 **NOTES:** No smoking in restaurant Closed 25 Dec Civ Wed 125

CARDS:

★★★70% Ufford Park Hotel Golf & Leisure

Yarmouth Rd, Ufford IP12 1QW

☎ 01394 383555 Fax 01394 383582

e-mail: uffordparkltd@btinternet.com

Dir: A12 N to A1152, in Melton turn left at traffic lights, premises 1m on right

Set amidst the rolling Suffolk countryside is this golf and leisure complex with a challenging 18 hole course. The public rooms feature an array of lounge areas as well as popular meeting and banqueting suites. The smart new Vista restaurant offers a carte menu or guests can chose to dine in the carvery or informal bar area. The accommodation is modern and well appointed, and many of the rooms overlook the golf course.

ROOMS: 42 en suite 8 annexe en suite (20 fmly) No smoking in 20 bedrooms s £49-£79; d £69-£119 * LB **FACILITIES:** Indoor swimming (H) Golf 18 Sauna Solarium Gym Pool table Putting green Jacuzzi/spa Beautician Dance studio Games room Hair stylist Xmas **CONF:** Thtr 200 Class 80 Board 80 Del from £93.50 * **PARKING:** 160 **NOTES:** No dogs (ex guide dogs) No smoking in restaurant Civ Wed 200

CARDS:

WOODFORD BRIDGE, Greater London See LONDON SECTION plan 1 *H6*

★★★★62% Menzies Prince Regent

Manor Rd IG8 8AE

☎ 0500 636943 (Central Res)

Fax 01773 880321

e-mail: info@menzies-hotels.co.uk

Situated on the edge of Woodford Bridge and Chingford, this hotel offers easy access to London and the M25. There are a range of well equipped bedrooms and good conference and banqueting rooms, in addition to a smart bistro style restaurant.

ROOMS: 61 en suite No smoking in 10 bedrooms s £110-£130; d £130-£175 * LB **FACILITIES:** STV Xmas **CONF:** Thtr 500 Class 150 Board 120 **SERVICES:** Lift **PARKING:** 60 **NOTES:** Civ Wed 400

CARDS:

WOODFORD GREEN, Greater London See LONDON SECTION plan 1 *G6*

★★★66% County Hotel Epping Forest

30 Oak Hill IG8 9NY

☎ 020 8787 9988 Fax 020 8506 0941

e-mail: eppingcounty@compuserve.com

Dir: from A406 take first exit left onto A104 towards Woodford. At rdbt keep right then take first left turn into Oakhill

In a residential area on the edge of Epping Forest, this modern hotel is convenient for both the North Circular and M11. Bedrooms have been decorated and equipped to a good standard, and business guests will appreciate the business centre. Public areas include an informal brasserie.

ROOMS: 99 en suite (16 fmly) No smoking in 25 bedrooms s £90-£100; d £100-£110 * LB **FACILITIES:** STV Pool table Xmas **CONF:** Thtr 150 Class 80 Board 40 Del from £100 * **SERVICES:** Lift **PARKING:** 100 **NOTES:** No dogs (ex guide dogs) No smoking in restaurant

CARDS:

WOODHALL SPA, Lincolnshire Map 08 TF16

★★★67% Petwood

Stixwould Rd LN10 6QF

☎ 01526 352411 Fax 01526 353473

Dir: from Sleaford take A153 (signposted Skegness). At Tattershall turn left on B1192. Hotel is signposted from the village

Standing in thirty acres of mature woodlands and gardens, is this lovely Edwardian house. Originally built for Lady Weignall on a site chosen by her in the area of her favourite 'pet wood', the hotel is furnished in the character of the period, with original features retained in the elegantly proportioned public rooms and bedrooms.

ROOMS: 50 en suite No smoking in 9 bedrooms s £75-£85; d £100-£110 (incl. bkfst) * LB **FACILITIES:** Snooker Croquet lawn Putting green Complimentary pass to leisure centre Xmas **CONF:** Thtr 160 Class 60 Board 50 Del £90 * **SERVICES:** Lift **PARKING:** 80 **NOTES:** No smoking in restaurant Civ Wed 100

CARDS:

> Fancy a Singapore Sling? Bar staff in five star hotels should be skilled cocktail mixers.

★★★63% Golf Hotel

The Broadway LN10 6SG
☎ 01526 353535 📠 01526 353096
Dir: *from A158 Lincoln-Horncastle turn onto B1191 towards Woodhall Spa. Hotel is located in the village centre just past Woodhall Spa Golf Club*

Famous for its golf course and ideally situated in the centre of the village this traditional hotel offers sound accommodation throughout. The bedrooms come in a variety of sizes and include several 'Club' style rooms. Meals are available in the Wentworth Restaurant or the Sunningdale Bar with its blackboard menu.

ROOMS: 50 en suite (4 fmly) s £65-£75; d £85-£95 (incl. bkfst) * LB **FACILITIES:** STV Tennis (hard) Pool table Croquet lawn Xmas **CONF:** Thtr 150 Class 45 Board 50 Del from £85 * **PARKING:** 100 **NOTES:** No smoking in restaurant Civ Wed 120 **CARDS:**

★★60% Eagle Lodge

The Broadway LN10 6ST
☎ 01526 353231 📠 01526 352797
Dir: *in the centre of Woodhall Spa*

Family owned and run, this hotel is located in the town centre, providing soundly appointed accommodation together with comfortable public rooms. A good choice of food is available, including daily blackboard specials, which are served in the bar or the dining room.

ROOMS: 23 en suite (2 fmly) s £45; d £70 (incl. bkfst) * LB **FACILITIES:** STV entertainment Xmas **CONF:** Thtr 100 Class 50 Board 50 **PARKING:** 70 **CARDS:**

WOODSTOCK, Oxfordshire — Map 04 SP41

★★★79% ❀❀❀ Feathers

Market St OX20 1SX
☎ 01993 812291 📠 01993 813158
e-mail: enquiries@feathers.co.uk
Dir: *from Oxford take A44 to Woodstock, after traffic lights take first left, the hotel is on the left*

In the centre of Woodstock, the Feathers combines high standards of service and professionalism with an easy-going and cheerful approach. The warren of rooms include a number of areas to relax and take refreshment and use of a pretty garden in the summer months. Bedrooms all have their individual character and are thoughtfully appointed with a number of thoughtful extra comforts. Hotel cuisine is of very high quality and guarantees satisfaction.

ROOMS: 21 en suite (4 fmly) s £105-£170; d £130-£290 (incl. bkfst) * LB **FACILITIES:** STV Xmas **CONF:** Thtr 20 Board 25 Del £160 * **NOTES:** No smoking in restaurant **CARDS:**

★★★67% ❀❀ The Bear

Park St OX20 1SZ
☎ 0870 400 8202 📠 01993 813380
Dir: *M 40 junct 8 onto A40 to Oxford/M40 junct 9 onto A34 S to Oxf'd. Take A44 into Woodstock. Turn left to town centre hotel on left opp town hall*

This former 13th-century coaching inn has exposed stone walls, heavily beamed ceilings and log fires. Bedrooms have been refurbished and provide a good standard of accommodation. The attractive restaurant offers imaginative rosette worthy cuisine, with a menu of traditional and contemporary dishes that is changed seasonally.

ROOMS: 32 en suite 12 annexe en suite (2 fmly) No smoking in 15 bedrooms **CONF:** Thtr 40 Class 12 Board 24 **PARKING:** 30 **NOTES:** No smoking in restaurant **CARDS:**

★★70% Kings Arms

19 Market St OX20 1SU
☎ 01993 813636 📠 01993 813737
Dir: *located on the corner of Market St and the A44 Oxford Road in the centre of Woodstock*

Situated in the centre of town just a short walk from Blenheim Palace is this appealing hotel. The spacious public areas feature an attractive bistro style restaurant and a smart bar. Bedrooms are comfortably furnished, equipped with many useful extras and have stylish decor.

ROOMS: 9 en suite No smoking in all bedrooms s £50-£60; d £75-£90 (incl. bkfst) * **CONF:** Class 40 Board 20 **NOTES:** No dogs (ex guide dogs) No smoking in restaurant **CARDS:**

WOODY BAY, Devon — Map 03 SS64

★★63% *Woody Bay Hotel*

EX31 4QX
☎ 01598 763264 📠 01598 763563

Popular with walkers, this hotel has commanding sweeping views over Woody Bay to the sea beyond. Bedrooms vary in style and size, with the majority benefiting from stunning views. Guests have a choice of dining options, either from the imaginative fixed price menu in the restaurant or the simple bar menu.

ROOMS: 10 en suite (1 fmly) **PARKING:** 10 **NOTES:** Closed Jan RS Nov, Dec & Feb **CARDS:**

WOOLACOMBE, Devon — Map 02 SS44

see also Mortehoe

★★★75% ❀ Watersmeet

Mortehoe EX34 7EB
☎ 01271 870333 📠 01271 870890
e-mail: watersmeethotel@compuserve.com
Dir: *follow B3343 into Woolacombe, turn right onto the esplanade, hotel is situated 0.75m on left*

With magnificent views over the bay, this popular hotel provides professional and attentive service. Bedrooms vary in size, sea-facing rooms always being in demand, particularly those with private balconies. The public areas all benefit from the hotel's stunning position, especially the attractive restaurant. Each evening, an imaginative and innovative range of dishes is offered from a fixed price menu.

ROOMS: 22 en suite (3 fmly) s £71-£125; d £116-£220 (incl. bkfst & dinner) * **FACILITIES:** STV Indoor swimming (H) Outdoor swimming (H) Tennis (grass) Pool table Croquet lawn Jacuzzi/spa entertainment Xmas **CONF:** Thtr 40 Class 25 Board 25 **PARKING:** 30 **NOTES:** No dogs (ex guide dogs) No smoking in restaurant Closed 4 Jan-10 Feb **CARDS:**

See advert on page 627

WOOLACOMBE, continued

★★★74% Woolacombe Bay
South St EX34 7BN
☎ 01271 870388 🖷 01271 870613
e-mail: woolacombe-bayhotel@btinternet.com
Dir: *from M5 junct 27 follow A361 to Mullacot Cross. Take first left onto B3343 to Woolacombe. Hotel in centre of village on the left*

This family oriented hotel is adjacent to the beach and the village centre. The public areas are spacious and comfortable. Many of the well equipped bedrooms have the benefit of a balcony with splendid views over the bay. In addition to the fixed price menu served in the formal restaurant, Maxwell's bistro offers an informal alternative.
ROOMS: 65 en suite (27 fmly) s £94-£109; d £188-£218 (incl. bkfst & dinner) * LB **FACILITIES:** STV Indoor swimming (H) Outdoor swimming (H) Golf 9 Tennis (hard) Squash Snooker Sauna Solarium Gym Pool table Croquet lawn Jacuzzi/spa Table tennis Beautician Children's Club Aerobics Classes entertainment ch fac Xmas **CONF:** Thtr 200 Class 150 Board 150 Del from £65 * **SERVICES:** Lift **PARKING:** 150 **NOTES:** No dogs No smoking in restaurant Closed 1st week Jan-mid Feb **CARDS:**

★★75% Little Beach
The Esplanade EX34 7DJ
☎ 01271 870398
Dir: *A361 at Barnstaple turn onto B3343 to Woolacombe*
With splendid views over Morte Bay, the Little Beach Hotel was built as a gentleman's residence in 1900. Sympathetically restored, with many of the original features retained, the hotel offers a relaxed atmosphere and friendly service. The individually furnished and decorated bedrooms are light and airy, some have their own balconies.
ROOMS: 9 en suite (1 fmly) No smoking in all bedrooms d £26-£48 (incl. bkfst) * **PARKING:** 10 **NOTES:** No children 6yrs No smoking in restaurant Closed Nov-Feb **CARDS:**

★★63% *The Royal Hotel*
Beach Rd EX34 7AB
☎ 01271 870001 🖷 01271 870701
Dir: *turn off A361 at Mullacott Cross rdbt on to B3343. Follow the main road into Woolacombe, hotel on the right*
From its elevated position high above Woolacombe Bay, this family hotel offers comfortable bedrooms and an extensive range of leisure and recreational facilities. In the Lundy Restaurant, meals cater for all tastes, with the majority being on a self service basis.
ROOMS: 95 en suite (40 fmly) **FACILITIES:** Indoor swimming (H) Squash Snooker Sauna Solarium Pool table entertainment **SERVICES:** Lift **PARKING:** 80 **NOTES:** No dogs (ex guide dogs) No smoking in restaurant Closed 15-23 Dec & 2-15 Jan
CARDS:

★72% Crossways
The Esplanade EX34 7DJ
☎ 01271 870395 🖷 01271 870395
Dir: *M5 junc27 onto A361 to Barnstaple, follow signs for Ilfracombe, then Woolacombe. At sea-front turn right onto esplanade, hotel 0.5m on right*
Overlooking Combesgate Beach, Crossways Hotel offers a relaxed atmosphere and has access to National Trust moorland at the rear. Bedrooms are attractively decorated, many enjoying dramatic sea views. Public areas include a lounge, bar and spacious dining room where friendly resident proprietors provide natural hospitality.
ROOMS: 9 rms (7 en suite) (3 fmly) s £33-£36; d £66-£72 (incl. bkfst & dinner) * LB **PARKING:** 9 **NOTES:** No smoking in restaurant Closed last Sat in Oct-1st Sat in Mar

WOOLER, Northumberland — Map 12 NT92

★★64% *Tankerville Arms*
Cottage Rd NE71 6AD
☎ 01668 281581 🖷 01668 281387
e-mail: enquiries@tankervillehotel.co.uk
Dir: *on A697*
This charming Inn provides a friendly destination for those seeking peace and tranquillity in traditional surroundings. The cosy bar and restaurant boast open fires, and wide ranging menus provide choice to suit all. Well equipped bedrooms comes in a variety of styles with one family suite being especially popular.
ROOMS: 15 en suite (2 fmly) **CONF:** Thtr 60 Class 60 Board 30 **PARKING:** 100 **NOTES:** No smoking in restaurant Closed 22-28 Dec
CARDS:

WOOLLEY EDGE MOTORWAY SERVICE AREA (M1), West Yorkshire — Map 08 SE31

⌂ *Travelodge*
Travelodge

M1 Service Area, West Bretton WF4 4LQ
☎ Central Res 0800 850950
Dir: *between junct 38/39, adj to service area*
This modern building offers accommodation in smart, spacious and well equipped bedrooms, all with en suite bathrooms. Refreshments may be taken at the nearby family restaurant. For further details and the Travelodge phone number, consult the Hotel Groups page.
ROOMS: 32 en suite

WOOTTON BASSETT, Wiltshire — Map 04 SU08

★★★74% Marsh Farm
Coped Hall SN4 8ER
☎ 01793 848044 🖷 01793 851528
e-mail: marshfarmhotel@btconnect.com
Dir: *take A3102 from M4, go straight on at first rdbt, at next rdbt (with garage on the left) turn right. Hotel is 200 yds on the left*
Originally a Victorian farmhouse this hotel, a short drive from the motorway, combines charm and elegance with modern facilities. Bedrooms, including superior rooms, are decorated to a high standard. Formal carte and modern bistro style menus are served in the atmospheric Rawlings Restaurant. Staff are helpful and attentive.
ROOMS: 11 en suite 27 annexe en suite (1 fmly) No smoking in 11 bedrooms s fr £100; d fr £120 (incl. bkfst) * LB **FACILITIES:** STV **CONF:** Thtr 120 Class 50 Board 35 **PARKING:** 150 **NOTES:** No dogs (ex guide dogs) No smoking in restaurant RS 26-30 Dec Civ Wed 100
CARDS:

See advert under SWINDON

★★ 72% Noremarsh Manor Hotel

Noremarsh Rd SN4 8BW
☎ 01793 849333 🖷 01793 849555
e-mail: noremarsh@aol.com
Dir: *M4 junct 16 head for Wootton Bassett. Left at sign for Stoneover Rd, then right at mini-rdbt into Noremarsh Road to hotel 50yds on right*

Dating from the late 17th Century, this Grade II listed William and Mary house has unique charm. Located on the outskirts of town, the hotel provides quick and easy access to the M4. Quality and character are evident throughout with the well equipped bedrooms offering high standards of comfort. An interesting choice of dishes is served in the intimate dining room, after which guests may like to relax in the well appointed lounge.

ROOMS: 4 en suite 6 annexe en suite No smoking in 8 bedrooms s £70-£100; d £75-£100 (incl. bkfst) * LB **PARKING:** 20 **NOTES:** No dogs (ex guide dogs) No smoking in restaurant Closed 24 Dec-2 Jan
CARDS:

WORCESTER, Worcestershire — Map 03 SO85

★★★ 75% Pear Tree Inn & Country Hotel

Smite WR3 8SY
☎ 01905 756565 🖷 01905 756777
e-mail: thepeartreeuk@aol.com
Dir: *from M5 junct 6 take Droitwich road after 300yds turn 1st right into small country lane over canal bridge, up a hill, hotel on left*

Situated within easy reach of M5, Worcester and Droitwich stands this traditional English Inn and country hotel. Bedrooms are spacious with attractive colour schemes and good facilities. Guests can enjoy good food and drink in a warm and relaxed surroundings, with an excellent range of conference/function rooms and convenient car parking.

ROOMS: 24 en suite (2 fmly) No smoking in 6 bedrooms s £75-£95; d £95-£110 (incl. bkfst) * LB **FACILITIES:** STV **CONF:** Thtr 280 Class 40 Board 30 Del £120.50 * **PARKING:** 200 **NOTES:** No dogs (ex guide dogs) **CARDS:**

★★★ 68% *Bank House Hotel Golf & Country Club*

Best Western

Hereford Rd, Bransford WR6 5JD
☎ 01886 833551 🖷 01886 832461
Dir: *M5 junct 7 follow signs to Worcester West, pick up signs for Hereford on A4440 then the A4103 Hereford Rd. Turn left, hotel approx. 2m on left*

Partly dating back to the 17th century, Bank House is set in 123 acres overlooking the Malvern Hills, three miles west of Worcester. There is a good choice of function and conference suites, and the bedrooms are classically appointed. Fixed price menus are offered in the attractive first-floor Farthings Restaurant. The hotel has an outdoor swimming pool and an 18-hole golf course on site.

ROOMS: 68 en suite (20 fmly) No smoking in 15 bedrooms
FACILITIES: Outdoor swimming Golf 18 Sauna Solarium Gym Putting green Jacuzzi/spa **CONF:** Thtr 400 Class 150 Board 70 **PARKING:** 350 **NOTES:** No smoking in restaurant **CARDS:**

★★★ 63% Star

REGAL

Foregate St WR1 1EA
☎ 01905 24308 🖷 01905 23440
Dir: *take A44 to city centre, right at lights into City Walls Road. Straight on at rdbt, left at lights then right at lights, follow signs for A38*

Set in the heart of Worcester stands this busy Hotel. A popular bar and coffee shop are focal points and attract much local and passing trade. Bedrooms are well equipped, comfortable and smartly presented. Other features include a restaurant, cosy residents bar, meeting rooms and secure car park.

ROOMS: 45 en suite (2 fmly) No smoking in 9 bedrooms s £65; d £75 * LB **FACILITIES:** STV Xmas **CONF:** Thtr 125 Class 50 Board 50 Del £89 * **SERVICES:** Lift **PARKING:** 55
CARDS:

Bad hair day? Hairdryers in all rooms three stars and above.

W

WORCESTER, continued

★★★61% The Gifford
High St WR1 2QR
☎ 01905 726262 🖹 01905 723458
e-mail: gm12402@forte-hotels.com
Dir: *leave M5 at junct 7 and follow signs for city centre. Hotel opp Worcester Cathedral*
This popular city centre hotel provides all the services today's traveller could need. Bedrooms vary, but all have modern facilities, with some of the larger rooms being suitable for families. A choice of bars and restaurants cater for a mixture of tastes.
ROOMS: 103 en suite (3 fmly) No smoking in 50 bedrooms s £75; d £85 * LB **FACILITIES:** Xmas **CONF:** Thtr 150 Class 100 Board 40 Del from £90 * **SERVICES:** Lift **CARDS:**

WORFIELD, Shropshire Map 07 SO79

Premier Collection

★★★ Old Vicarage
WV15 5JZ
☎ 01746 716497 & 0800 0968010
🖹 01746 716552
e-mail: admin@the-old-vicarage.demon.co.uk
Dir: *off A454 between Bridgnorth & Wolverhampton*
This delightful hotel was an Edwardian vicarage. The bedrooms are thoughtfully furnished and well equipped. There is a lounge and a restaurant where the cuisine receives great acclaim.
ROOMS: 10 en suite 4 annexe en suite (1 fmly) No smoking in all bedrooms s £75-£110; d £115.50-£175 (incl. bkfst) * LB **FACILITIES:** Croquet lawn Xmas **CONF:** Thtr 30 Class 30 Board 20 **PARKING:** 30 **NOTES:** No smoking in restaurant
CARDS:

WORKINGTON, Cumbria Map 11 NY02

★★★78% Washington Central
Washington St CA14 3AY
☎ 01900 65772 🖹 01900 68770
Dir: *M6 junct 40 towards Keswick, follow to Workington. At traffic lights at the bottom of Ramsey Brow, turn right and follow signs for hotel*
Located in the centre of the town, this impressive, modern hotel provides comfortable, well equipped accommodation. Day rooms include two stylish lounges and an attractive first floor bar. Staff are very friendly.

continued

ROOMS: 46 en suite (4 fmly) No smoking in 10 bedrooms s £69.95-£89.95; d £104.95-£149.95 (incl. bkfst) * LB **FACILITIES:** STV Indoor swimming (H) Sauna Solarium Gym Jacuzzi/spa Mountain biking Nightclub ch fac Xmas **CONF:** Thtr 300 Class 250 Board 150 Del from £99.95 * **SERVICES:** Lift **PARKING:** 20 **NOTES:** No dogs (ex guide dogs) No smoking in restaurant Civ Wed 300
CARDS:

★★★66% *Hunday Manor Country House*
Hunday, Winscales CA14 4JF
☎ 01900 61798 🖹 01900 601202
e-mail: hundaymanorhotel@lineone.net
Dir: *turn off A66 onto A595 towards Whitehaven, hotel is 3m along on right hand side, signposted*
Delightfully situated and enjoying distant views of the Solway Firth, this charming hotel has comfortable rooms that are well furnished. Some of the spacious rooms have been refurbished to a high standard. The open plan bar and foyer lounge boast welcoming open fires, and the attractive restaurant overlooks the woodland gardens.
ROOMS: 13 en suite **FACILITIES:** STV Tennis (grass) **CONF:** Thtr 25 Class 15 Board 20 **PARKING:** 50 **NOTES:** No smoking in restaurant
CARDS:

WORKSOP, Nottinghamshire Map 08 SK57

★★★68% Clumber Park
Clumber Park S80 3PA
☎ 01623 835333 🖹 01623 835525
Dir: *M1 junct 30/31 follow signs for Worksop. A1 fiveways rdbt onto A614 5m NE*

REGAL

With easy access to the A1, this hotel is situated in open countryside, edging on to Sherwood Forest and Clumber Park. Bedrooms are comfortably furnished and well equipped to meet travellers needs, while public areas include a choice of two restaurants. The recently refurbished Dukes Tavern is lively and informal, whilst the Restaurant offers a more traditional style of service.
ROOMS: 48 en suite (6 fmly) No smoking in 31 bedrooms s fr £72; d fr £85 * LB **FACILITIES:** STV Xmas **CONF:** Thtr 270 Class 150 Board 90 Del from £85 * **PARKING:** 200 **NOTES:** No smoking in restaurant Civ Wed 150 **CARDS:**

★★★65% Lion
112 Bridge St S80 1HT
☎ 01909 477925 🖹 01909 479038
e-mail: lionhotel@hotmail.com
Dir: *A57 to town centre, turn at Walkers Garage on right and follow road to Norfolk Arms and turn left*

Best Western

This former coaching inn, dating from the 16th century, has been extended to offer spacious and comfortable accommodation, including a number of suites. It is conveniently situated on the

continued

edge of the main shopping and business area of Worksop, and the bar and restaurant are popular with locals as well as visitors. There is a car park behind the hotel.
ROOMS: 32 en suite (3 fmly) No smoking in 7 bedrooms s £57-£77; d £67-£77 (incl. bkfst) * LB **FACILITIES:** STV Sauna Solarium Gym Xmas **CONF:** Thtr 60 Class 60 Board 60 Del from £75 * **PARKING:** 50 **NOTES:** Civ Wed 120 **CARDS:**

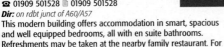

⌂ *Travelodge*
St Anne's Dr, Dukeries Dr S80 3QD
☎ 01909 501528 🖷 01909 501528
Dir: *on rdbt junct of A60/A57*
This modern building offers accommodation in smart, spacious and well equipped bedrooms, all with en suite bathrooms. Refreshments may be taken at the nearby family restaurant. For further details and the Travelodge phone number, consult the Hotel Groups page.
ROOMS: 40 en suite

WORSLEY, Greater Manchester — Map 07 SD70

★★★66% Novotel
Worsley Brow M28 4YA
☎ 0161 799 3535 🖷 0161 703 8207
e-mail: h0907@accor-hotels.com
Dir: *adjacent to M60 junc 13*
This modern hotel stands in its own mature grounds. It provides well equipped, spacious and comfortable accommodation. The open plan public areas include a pleasant restaurant, a bar and lounge area.
ROOMS: 119 en suite (5 fmly) No smoking in 72 bedrooms d £75 * LB **FACILITIES:** STV Outdoor swimming (H) Pool table **CONF:** Thtr 220 Class 140 Board 50 Del £119 * **SERVICES:** Lift **PARKING:** 133 **CARDS:**

WORTHING, West Sussex — Map 04 TQ10

★★★71% Ardington
Steyne Gardens BN11 3DZ
☎ 01903 230451 🖷 01903 526526
Dir: *A27 - turn off at Lancing Leisure centre rdbt to seafront. Follow coast rd to right. Turn left at 1st Church into Steyne Gardens*
Run with professionalism and commitment, the Ardington continues to provide excellent accommodation. Bedrooms are modern in style, very well equipped and feature smartly appointed bathrooms. Public rooms include a comfortable bar-lounge and an attractive restaurant where an interesting range of dishes is served. Service is excellent and includes a 24-hour room service menu.
ROOMS: 45 en suite (4 fmly) No smoking in 10 bedrooms s £57-£79; d £80-£95 (incl. bkfst) * LB **FACILITIES:** STV ch fac **CONF:** Thtr 140 Class 60 Board 35 Del from £65 * **PARKING:** 25 **NOTES:** Closed 25 Dec-4 Jan **CARDS:**

★★★68% Beach
Marine Pde BN11 3QJ
☎ 01903 234001 🖷 01903 234567
e-mail: thebeachhotel@btinternet.com
Dir: *W of town centre, about 1 third of a mile from pier*
This well established hotel, with its impressive 1930s frontage continues to be popular. Bedrooms, some which have sea views and balconies, are traditionally furnished and fully equipped with modern amenities. Public areas are spacious and comfortable, with the restaurant offering a wide choice of popular dishes. The hotel has secure parking.

continued

ROOMS: 80 en suite (8 fmly) No smoking in 6 bedrooms s fr £67; d £93-£98 (incl. bkfst) * LB **FACILITIES:** STV Pool table Xmas **CONF:** Thtr 200 Class 40 Board 12 Del from £60 * **SERVICES:** Lift **PARKING:** 55 **NOTES:** No dogs (ex guide dogs) Closed 30 Dec-3 Jan **CARDS:**

★★★68% Berkeley
86-95 Marine Pde BN11 3QD
☎ 01903 820000 🖷 01903 821333
e-mail: berkeley@wakefordhotels.co.uk
Dir: *follow signs to Worthing seafront, the hotel is 0.5m West from pier*
Located on the seafront and only a few minutes walk from the town centre, the Berkeley goes from strength to strength. Public areas are smartly appointed and include a comfortable cocktail bar and spacious restaurant. Bedrooms are modern, furnished to a good standard and well equipped. Attentive service is provided by the professional team of staff.
ROOMS: 84 en suite (3 fmly) No smoking in 29 bedrooms s £68.50-£93; d £94-£105 (incl. bkfst) * LB **FACILITIES:** STV Xmas **CONF:** Thtr 150 Class 50 Board 50 Del from £80 * **SERVICES:** Lift **PARKING:** 25 **NOTES:** No dogs (ex guide dogs) No smoking in restaurant Civ Wed 60 **CARDS:**

★★★67% Kingsway
Marine Pde BN11 3QQ
☎ 01903 237542 🖷 01903 204173
Dir: *A24 to seafront, turn West past pier and lido*
Ideally located on the seafront and close to the town centre, the Kingsway continues to provide warm hospitality to guests. Bedrooms which are gradually being upgraded are comfortably furnished and equipped with modern facilities. Day rooms include two comfortable lounge areas, a bar offering a good range of meals and a well appointed restaurant.
ROOMS: 29 en suite 7 annexe en suite (2 fmly) No smoking in 13 bedrooms s £58-£63; d £90-£120 (incl. bkfst) * LB **FACILITIES:** STV Xmas **CONF:** Thtr 50 Class 20 Board 30 Del £68 * **SERVICES:** Lift **PARKING:** 12 **NOTES:** No smoking in restaurant **CARDS:**

★★★67% *Windsor House*
14/20 Windsor Rd BN11 2LX
☎ 01903 239655 🖷 01903 210763
e-mail: windsorhouse@compuserve.com
Dir: *A259 from Brighton, 2nd right past Half Brick Pub*
Popular with business guests for its good service and relaxed atmosphere, this well maintained hotel stands in a quiet road near the seafront. Rooms are attractively decorated and equipped to a good standard. Public areas include a smart bar, well appointed restaurant and appealing conservatory/reception area.
ROOMS: 30 en suite (4 fmly) No smoking in 5 bedrooms **FACILITIES:** STV Pool table **CONF:** Thtr 120 Class 48 Board 40 **PARKING:** 18 **NOTES:** No dogs (ex guide dogs) No smoking in restaurant Closed 24-25 Dec **CARDS:**

★★★62% Chatsworth
Steyne BN11 3DU
☎ 01903 236103 🖷 01903 823726
e-mail: chatsworth@wakefordhotels.co.uk
Dir: *A24 to Worthing town centre, left at rdbt by Blockbuster Video, follow signs to seafront. Hotel 200yds E of pier, adjacent to Promenade*
Distinguished by an imposing creeper-clad frontage, the Chatsworth has a prime position overlooking a garden square close to the pier and the town centre. Public areas include a lounge bar and a games room. Bedrooms are equipped with the

continued

WORTHING, continued

usual modern facilities. Guests have a preferential rate at a car park across the square.
ROOMS: 107 en suite (5 fmly) s £55-£59; d £84-£92 (incl. bkfst) * LB **FACILITIES:** STV Snooker Pool table Games room Xmas **CONF:** Thtr 150 Class 60 Board 40 Del from £60 * **SERVICES:** Lift **NOTES:** No smoking in restaurant Civ Wed **CARDS:**

★★64% Cavendish

115 Marine Pde BN11 3QG
☎ 01903 236767 🖹 01903 823840
e-mail: thecavendish@mistral.co.uk
Dir: *on Worthing seafront 600yds west of pier*
This small popular hotel enjoys a sea front location. Bedrooms are neatly decorated, comfortably furnished and well equipped. Dining options are extensive with bar snacks in the traditional bar-lounge or a carte menu in the attractive restaurant. Limited parking is available at the rear.
ROOMS: 17 en suite (4 fmly) No smoking in 3 bedrooms s £40-£45; d £65-£75 (incl. bkfst) * LB **FACILITIES:** STV **CONF:** Thtr 30 Class 20 Board 16 **SERVICES:** air con **PARKING:** 5
CARDS:

WROTHAM, Kent — Map 05 TQ65

★★★66% *Posthouse Maidstone/ Sevenoaks*

Posthouse

London Rd, Wrotham Heath TN15 7RS
☎ 0870 400 9054 🖹 01732 885850
Conveniently situated just off the M26 at Wrotham Heath, this is a busy, popular hotel. Bedrooms are comfortably appointed and well equipped. Public areas include an open plan lounge/bar, attractive restaurant and a health and fitness club.
ROOMS: 106 en suite (15 fmly) No smoking in 42 bedrooms **FACILITIES:** Indoor swimming (H) Sauna Solarium Gym Jacuzzi/spa Health & fitness centre ch fac **CONF:** Thtr 60 Class 30 Board 30 **PARKING:** 110 **CARDS:**

WROXHAM, Norfolk — Map 09 TG21

★★67% Hotel Wroxham

The Bridge NR12 8AJ
☎ 01603 782061 🖹 01603 784279

Situated overlooking Wroxham Broads in the heart of the bustling town centre, this private hotel offers well equipped accommodation. Many rooms have balconies with views of the busy waterways. There is a restaurant serving an extensive carte menu, a carvery and a popular riverside bar.
ROOMS: 18 en suite **FACILITIES:** Fishing Boating facilities (by arrangement) entertainment **CONF:** Thtr 200 Board 20 **PARKING:** 45 **NOTES:** No dogs (ex guide dogs) No smoking in restaurant
CARDS:

★★60% *Kings Head*

Station Rd NR12 8UR
☎ 01603 782429 🖹 01603 784622
Dir: *in centre of village*
This popular hotel has a large local clientele, and being in the heart of Wroxham makes it popular with tourists holidaying on the Norfolk Broads. Day rooms open out onto the hotel's river frontage and gardens; the carvery restaurant specialises in traditional food. Bedrooms are attractive and comfortable.
ROOMS: 8 en suite (2 fmly) No smoking in all bedrooms **FACILITIES:** Fishing Pool table **PARKING:** 45 **NOTES:** No dogs (ex guide dogs) No smoking in restaurant
CARDS:

WYMONDHAM, Norfolk — Map 05 TG10

★★72% Wymondham Consort Hotel

28 Market St NR18 0BB
☎ 01953 606721 🖹 01953 601361
e-mail: wymondham@bestwestern.co.uk
Dir: *off A11 (M11) Thetford to Norwich road, turn left at traffic lights and left again*

This pleasant hotel is situated in the heart of this bustling market town. Although the bedrooms vary in size and character they are all well maintained and equipped with many thoughtful extras that include fresh fruit and mineral water. The public areas feature an intimate restaurant offering freshly prepared meals and a cosy lounge bar.
ROOMS: 20 en suite (1 fmly) No smoking in 10 bedrooms s £55-£60; d £68-£75 (incl. bkfst) * LB **FACILITIES:** STV **PARKING:** 18 **NOTES:** No smoking in restaurant **CARDS:**

★★70% Abbey

10 Church St NR18 0PH
☎ 01953 602148 🖹 01953 606247
e-mail: paulconnor@theabbeyhotel.freeserve.co.uk
Dir: *from A11 follow Wymondham sign. At traffic lights left and first left into one-way system. Continue and left into Church St*

continued

Hospitality is the keyword at this delightful hotel, close to the historic abbey. Its origins go back to the 16th century, and it has kept much of its character, although the bedrooms have modern comforts. There is a pleasant ambience in the public areas, with a convivial lounge and a cosy bar in which pre-dinner drinks can be enjoyed.
ROOMS: 22 en suite 1 annexe en suite (3 fmly) s £58-£65; d £65-£79 (incl. bkfst) * LB **FACILITIES:** Xmas **SERVICES:** Lift **PARKING:** 4 **NOTES:** No smoking in restaurant **CARDS:**

See advert under NORWICH

YARCOMBE, Devon Map 03 ST20

★★ 72% The Belfry Country Hotel

MINOTEL Great Britain

EX14 9BD
☎ 01404 861234 🖷 01404 861579
Dir: *on A30, 7m E of Honiton, 5m W of Chard, 10m S of M5 junct 25 at Taunton*
This hotel is based on a converted Victorian school house, where some of the attractively decorated bedrooms retain the original arched windows. Home cooked dishes are offered in the panelled bar/restaurant but please note that this is a no smoking establishment.
ROOMS: 6 en suite (1 fmly) No smoking in all bedrooms s £40-£45; d £60-£72 (incl. bkfst) * LB **FACILITIES:** Xmas **PARKING:** 10 **NOTES:** No dogs (ex guide dogs) No children 12yrs No smoking in restaurant **CARDS:**

YARM, North Yorkshire Map 08 NZ41

★★★ 75% Judges Hotel

Kirklevington TS15 9LW
☎ 01642 789000 🖷 01642 782878
Dir: *located 1.5m from A19. At A67 junct, follow the Yarm road and hotel is clearly visible on the left hand side*

Set in beautiful gardens and parkland, this imposing country mansion was once a judge's lodgings. Elegant day rooms include an attractive restaurant leading into a conservatory, and there is to be a separate function suite. Bedrooms are all impressively well furnished in individual style.
ROOMS: 21 en suite (3 fmly) s fr £132; d fr £167 (incl. bkfst) * LB **FACILITIES:** STV Croquet lawn Xmas **CONF:** Thtr 200 Class 80 Board 50 Del £150 * **PARKING:** 102 **NOTES:** No dogs (ex guide dogs) No smoking in restaurant Closed 31 Dec-8 Jan Civ Wed 200
CARDS:

YARMOUTH See Wight, Isle of

Read all about it! Newspapers delivered to bedrooms in four and five star hotels.

YATTENDON, Berkshire Map 04 SU57

★★ 71% Royal Oak

REGAL

The Square RG18 0UG
☎ 01635 201325 🖷 01635 201926
Dir: *M4 junct 12 follow A4-Newbury & at 2nd rdbt 3rd exit to Pangbourne, then left to Yattendon*
The quintessential English country inn, which has welcomed guests for 300 years; a veritable little haven with wisteria-clad walls and an attractive garden. Public rooms are cosy and congenial, while the stylishly furnished bedrooms have smart bathrooms. The imaginative 'brasserie style' menu is served in the bar and restaurant, offering guests a great choice of modern and traditional dishes.
ROOMS: 5 en suite s fr £95; d fr £115 * LB **FACILITIES:** STV Croquet lawn Xmas **CONF:** Thtr 30 Class 18 Board 22 Del from £165 * **PARKING:** 20 **NOTES:** No smoking in restaurant
CARDS:

YELVERTON, Devon Map 02 SX56

★★★ 71% Moorland Links

Forestdale Hotels

PL20 6DA
☎ 01822 852245 🖷 01822 855004
Dir: *from A38 dual carriageway from Exeter to Plymouth, take the A386 towards Tavistock. Continue for 5m onto open moorland, hotel is 1m on the left*

Standing in nine acres of well kept grounds in the Dartmoor National Park, this hotel has a regular and loyal following. Rooms range from well equipped standard to stylish executive rooms, many of which have balconies. The restaurant looks out over lovely gardens and the hotel also has a number of meeting rooms.
ROOMS: 45 en suite (4 fmly) No smoking in 21 bedrooms s fr £60; d fr £120 (incl. bkfst & dinner) * LB **FACILITIES:** Tennis (hard) Xmas **CONF:** Thtr 120 Class 60 Board 60 Del from £115 * **PARKING:** 120 **NOTES:** No smoking in restaurant Civ Wed
CARDS:

See advert under PLYMOUTH

YEOVIL, Somerset Map 03 ST51
see also Martock

Y

★★★ 72% Yeovil Court

West Coker Rd BA20 2HE
☎ 01935 863746 🖷 01935 863990
e-mail: verne@yeovilcourt.freeserve.co.uk
Dir: *2.5m W of town centre on the A30 (Exeter)*
This comfortable, family-run hotel benefits from a very friendly and relaxed atmosphere. All bedrooms are well furnished and equipped, some of them are located at ground floor level in a new adjacent building. Public areas consist of a smart lounge, a popular bar and an attractive restaurant. An extensive selection of dishes is available to suit all tastes and budgets.

continued

YEOVIL, continued

ROOMS: 15 en suite 15 annexe en suite (4 fmly) s fr £66.50; d fr £75 (incl. bkfst) * LB **FACILITIES:** Xmas **CONF:** Thtr 44 Class 20 Board 28 **PARKING:** 65 **NOTES:** No smoking in restaurant RS Sat-Sun (restaurant) **CARDS:**

See advert on opposite page

Premier Collection

★ Little Barwick House

Barwick Village BA22 9TD

☎ 01935 423902 01935 420908

Dir: *turn left off A37, Yeovil/Dorchester road, at first rdbt. Through village, take 1st left, Hotel 0.25m on left*

This delightful listed Georgian dower house, situated in a quiet hamlet on the edge of Yeovil, is an ideal retreat for those seeking peaceful surroundings and good food. Guests can enjoy the informal atmosphere of a private home combined with the facilities and comforts of a modern hotel. The bedrooms are individually decorated and each has its own character and a range of thoughtful touches. The restaurant is but one of the highlights of a stay here.

ROOMS: 6 en suite **CONF:** Thtr 50 Board 26 Del £100 * **PARKING:** 30 **NOTES:** No smoking in restaurant Civ Wed 40 **CARDS:**

★62% Preston

64 Preston Rd BA20 2DL

☎ 01935 474400 01935 410142

Dir: *from A30 (hospital rdbt) head north on A37 Bristol road for 0.25m. At rdbt take first exit for Preston Road*

This family run hotel, situated on the outskirts of Yeovil, is popular both with all types of guests. Many of the rooms have been adapted for family purposes, in particular the family suite. A relaxed, friendly and informal atmosphere can be expected here.

ROOMS: 6 en suite 8 annexe en suite (7 fmly) s £39-£45; d £49-£67 (incl. bkfst) * **PARKING:** 19 **NOTES:** No smoking in restaurant **CARDS:**

Y

YORK, North Yorkshire

Map 08 SE65

see also Aldwark, Escrick & Pocklington

★★★★64% Swallow

SWALLOW HOTELS

Tadcaster Rd YO24 1QQ

☎ 01904 701000 01904 702308

e-mail: york@swallow-hotels.co.uk

Dir: *heading E turn off A64 at York 'West' onto A1036, hotel is on right after church and traffic lights*

Situated less than a mile from the city walls and overlooking the Knavesmire and the racecourse, The Swallow offers smartly presented public areas and a wide range of leisure and meeting facilities. Bedrooms many of which have been recently refurbished, are spacious, comfortable and well equipped; the best have balconies over-looking the racecourse. The hotel also has its own purpose built, self-contained training centre and extensive parking.

ROOMS: 112 en suite (14 fmly) No smoking in 40 bedrooms s fr £115; d fr £140 (incl. bkfst) * LB **FACILITIES:** STV Indoor swimming (H) Tennis (hard) Sauna Solarium Gym Pool table Croquet lawn Putting green Jacuzzi/spa Beauty treatment Golf practice Xmas **CONF:** Thtr 170 Class 90 Board 40 Del from £145 * **SERVICES:** Lift **PARKING:** 200 **NOTES:** No smoking in restaurant Civ Wed **CARDS:**

★★★★63% Royal York

PRINCIPAL HOTELS

Station Rd YO24 2AA

☎ 01904 653681 01904 653271

Dir: *adjacent to railway station*

This magnificent Victorian hotel, with its own private gardens, is close to the city walls, the railway station, and five minutes walk from the Minster. Its attractive, well equipped bedrooms are divided between the main building and the garden mews. Guests have a choice of eating options: Tiles Bar, room service, or the main Rose Room restaurant. Extensive refurbishment is underway and a well equipped leisure centre is being added.

ROOMS: 166 en suite (10 fmly) s fr £120; d £140-£180 * LB **FACILITIES:** STV Indoor swimming (H) Sauna Solarium Gym Pool table Croquet lawn Jacuzzi/spa Steam room Xmas **CONF:** Thtr 410 Class 250 Board 80 Del from £150 * **SERVICES:** Lift **PARKING:** 130 **NOTES:** No smoking in restaurant Civ Wed 100 **CARDS:**

See advert on opposite page

Premier Collection

★★★ The Grange

1 Clifton YO30 6AA

☎ 01904 644744 01904 612453

e-mail: info@grangehotel.co.uk

Dir: *on A19 York/Thirsk road, approx 500 yds from city centre*

This bustling Regency town house is just a few minutes' walk from York's centre. The individually designed bedrooms have been thoughtfully equipped for both business and leisure guests. Public rooms are comfortable and have been tastefully furnished for leisure guests; conference and wedding facilities are also available. There are two dining options, The Brasserie in the cellar offering an informal, relaxed atmosphere; and The Ivy with its impressive marquee trompe l'oeil and fine dining menu.

continued

ROOMS: 30 en suite s £99-£160; d £125-£215 (incl. bkfst) * LB **FACILITIES:** STV Xmas **CONF:** Thtr 50 Class 20 Board 24 Del £140 * **PARKING:** 26 **CARDS:**

Premier Collection

★★★ Middlethorpe Hall

Bishopthorpe Rd, Middlethorpe YO23 2GB
☎ 01904 641241 📠 01904 620176
e-mail: info@middlethorpe.com

RELAIS & CHATEAUX.

Dir: *from A1036 signed York (west), follow signs to Bishopthorpe and racecourse. Hotel is on right just before racecourse*

This splendid country house overlooks the racecourse. The elegant drawing room is impressive and enjoys views of the beautiful garden. The kitchen offers a fine cuisine from a seasonal menu in the wood panelled dining room. Individually furnished bedrooms are split between the main house and a nearby courtyard. A new spa includes a pool, small gym and beauty treatment rooms.

ROOMS: 30 en suite s £105-£130; d £155-£260 * LB **FACILITIES:** Indoor swimming (H) Sauna Solarium Gym Croquet lawn Jacuzzi/spa Leisure Spa Xmas **CONF:** Thtr 56 Class 30 Board 25 Del from £160 * **SERVICES:** Lift **PARKING:** 70 **NOTES:** No dogs No children 8yrs No smoking in restaurant RS 25 & 31 Dec **CARDS:**

★★★75% Dean Court

Duncombe Place YO1 7EF
☎ 01904 625082 📠 01904 620305
e-mail: info@deancourt-york.co.uk

Best Western

Dir: *city centre opposite York Minster*

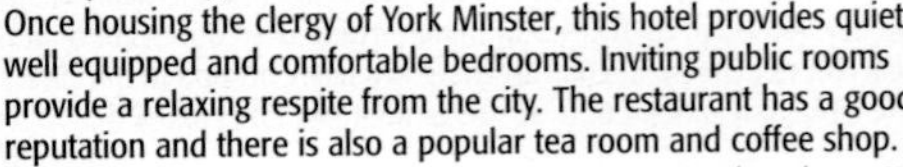

Once housing the clergy of York Minster, this hotel provides quiet, well equipped and comfortable bedrooms. Inviting public rooms provide a relaxing respite from the city. The restaurant has a good reputation and there is also a popular tea room and coffee shop.

continued on p634

YORK, continued

ROOMS: 39 en suite (2 fmly) No smoking in 12 bedrooms s £80-£100; d £100-£170 (incl. bkfst) * LB **FACILITIES:** Xmas **CONF:** Thtr 60 Class 24 Board 32 Del from £95 * **SERVICES:** Lift **PARKING:** 30 **NOTES:** No dogs (ex guide dogs) No smoking in restaurant RS 25 Dec evening Civ Wed 70 **CARDS:**

★★★ 75% Parsonage Country House

York Rd YO19 6LF
☎ 01904 728111 📠 01904 728151
e-mail: reservations@parsonagehotel.co.uk
(For full entry see Escrick)

★★★ 73% Mount Royale

The Mount YO24 1GU
☎ 01904 628856 📠 01904 611171
e-mail: reservations@mountroyale.co.uk
Dir: *W on A1036, towards racecourse*

This friendly hotel offers comfortable bedrooms in a variety of styles, several of which lead into the delightful gardens. Public rooms include a relaxing lounge, a cosy bar, and separate cocktail lounge which overlooks the garden. A separate bistro called Oxos has been added this year. Freshly prepared food is presented on the daily-changing menus.

ROOMS: 23 en suite (2 fmly) s £85-£105; d £95-£140 (incl. bkfst) * LB **FACILITIES:** STV Outdoor swimming (H) Snooker Sauna Solarium Beauty treatment centre **CONF:** Thtr 25 Board 16 Del £120 * **PARKING:** 18 **NOTES:** No smoking in restaurant RS Rest closed & hotel B&B only on 31/12/99 **CARDS:**

★★★ 72% *York Pavilion*

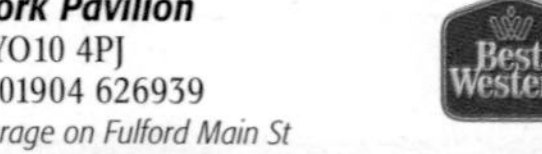

45 Main St, Fulford YO10 4PJ
☎ 01904 622099 📠 01904 626939
Dir: *on A19, opposite garage on Fulford Main St*

An attractive Georgian hotel situated in its own gardens and grounds to the south of the city. The individually designed and well equipped bedrooms are situated in the main house and the converted stables. There is a comfortable lounge, a conference centre and an inviting Brasserie-style restaurant, where the regularly changing menu features many daily specials.

ROOMS: 44 en suite (2 fmly) No smoking in 3 bedrooms **FACILITIES:** STV **CONF:** Thtr 150 Class 75 Board 50 **PARKING:** 72 **NOTES:** No dogs (ex guide dogs) No smoking in restaurant **CARDS:**

See advert on opposite page

> Fancy a Singapore Sling? Bar staff in five star hotels should be skilled cocktail mixers.

★★★ 69% Aldwark Manor Hotel, Golf & Country Club

YO61 1UF
☎ 01347 838146 & 838251 📠 01347 838867
e-mail: reception@aldwarkmanor.co.uk
Dir: *from A1, A59 towards Green Hammerton, then B6265 towards Little Ouseburn & follow signs Aldwark Bridge/Manor. A19 through Linton on Ouse to Aldwark*

Surrounded by a well designed golf course, this 19th-century manor house offers spacious bedrooms and public rooms furnished in period style. There is a bar and the brasserie serves a range of light meals and snacks. The restaurant offers imaginative dishes in a more formal setting.

ROOMS: 25 en suite 3 annexe rms (2 en suite) (2 fmly) s fr £65; d £100-£120 (incl. bkfst) * LB **FACILITIES:** STV Indoor swimming (H) Golf 18 Fishing Sauna Solarium Gym Putting green Jacuzzi/spa Coarse fishing Xmas **CONF:** Thtr 80 Class 40 Board 30 **PARKING:** 150 **NOTES:** No smoking in restaurant Civ Wed 100 **CARDS:**

★★★ 68% Ambassador

123 The Mount YO24 1DU
☎ 01904 641316 📠 01904 640259
e-mail: stay@ambassadorhotel.co.uk
Dir: *from A1036 York/Bishopthorpe, follow city centre signs along Tadcaster Road. Hotel is located on the right 300yds after the racecourse*

An elegant Georgian house which offers a quiet and relaxing atmosphere. The well-equipped bedrooms are mostly spacious with the larger ones generally overlooking the attractive and secluded gardens to the rear. The spacious and richly furnished Grays Restaurant is a delightful setting in which to enjoy well produced dishes.

ROOMS: 25 en suite (2 fmly) s £85-£98; d £85-£120 (incl. bkfst) * LB **FACILITIES:** STV entertainment Xmas **CONF:** Thtr 60 Class 24 Board 30 Del from £98 * **SERVICES:** Lift **PARKING:** 35 **NOTES:** No dogs (ex guide dogs) No smoking in restaurant Civ Wed 50 **CARDS:**

See advert on opposite page

★★★ 67% The Judges Lodging

9 Lendal YO1 8AQ
☎ 01904 638733 📠 01904 679947
e-mail: judgeshotel@aol.com
Dir: *from West Door York Minster, 250yds towards Lendal bridge. Turn left into Lendal*

This 18th-century listed building with many Georgian features has been thoughtfully renovated and is situated right in the heart of the city. Although at the hub of things, inside is an atmosphere of peaceful relaxation. In contrast there is a lively basement bar or one can enjoy a drink outside under the trees and survey the

continued

scene while the bedrooms complement the character of the house and include two suites.

ROOMS: 14 en suite (2 fmly) No smoking in all bedrooms s £75-£85; d £100-£150 (incl. bkfst) * **FACILITIES:** STV Xmas **PARKING:** 16 **NOTES:** No dogs (ex guide dogs) **CARDS:**

★★★67% Monkbar
St Maurices Rd YO31 7JA
☎ 01904 638086 🖷 01904 629195

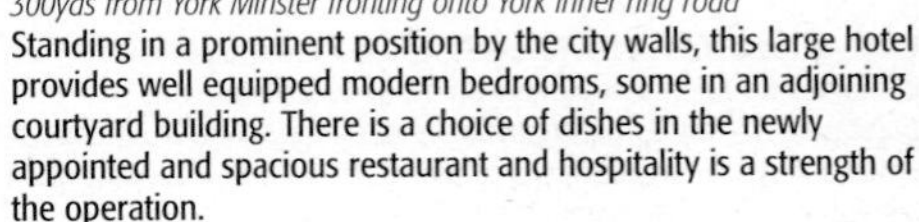

***Dir:** situated overlooking City Walls and Monkbar, 300yds from York Minster fronting onto York inner ring road*
Standing in a prominent position by the city walls, this large hotel provides well equipped modern bedrooms, some in an adjoining courtyard building. There is a choice of dishes in the newly appointed and spacious restaurant and hospitality is a strength of the operation.

continued on p636

Y

YORK, continued

ROOMS: 99 en suite (3 fmly) No smoking in 45 bedrooms s £65-£85; d £125-£175 (incl. bkfst) * LB **FACILITIES:** Xmas **CONF:** Thtr 200 Class 80 Board 50 Del from £110 * **SERVICES:** Lift **PARKING:** 80 **NOTES:** No dogs No smoking in restaurant Civ Wed 60
CARDS:

See advert on page 635

★★★66% *Posthouse York*

Posthouse

Tadcaster Rd YO24 1QF
☎ 0870 400 9085 🖹 01904 702804
Dir: *from A1(M) take A64 towards York. Continue for 7m, then take A106 to York. Straight over at rdbt to York city centre. Hotel 0.5m on right*

A modern hotel situated on the main western approach to the city centre and close to the famous racecourse, which can be seen from several of the comfortable bedrooms. Public rooms include a popular bar and grill. There are good facilities for meetings, and a large car park.
ROOMS: 143 en suite (37 fmly) No smoking in 83 bedrooms **FACILITIES:** Childrens mini-golf **CONF:** Thtr 100 Class 40 Board 40 **SERVICES:** Lift **PARKING:** 137 **CARDS:**

★★★63% *Kexby Bridge*

THE CIRCLE Selected Individual Hotels GREAT BRITAIN

Hull Rd, Kexby YO41 5LD
☎ 01759 388223 & 388154 🖹 01759 388822
e-mail: kexby@btconnect.com
Dir: *Turn off A64 onto A1079, travel 3 miles away from York A1079-Hull hotel on left hand side of main road*

This family-run hotel backs onto extensive gardens. Its spacious bedrooms meet modern standards of comfort, its restaurant serves enjoyable food and it has a pleasant bar lounge.
ROOMS: 32 en suite No smoking in 8 bedrooms **FACILITIES:** Fishing **CONF:** Thtr 30 Class 30 Board 30 **PARKING:** 60 **NOTES:** No dogs (ex guide dogs) **CARDS:**

★★★63% Novotel

NOVOTEL

Fishergate YO10 4FD
☎ 01904 611660 🖹 01904 610925
e-mail: h0949@accor-hotels.com
Dir: *S off A19*

This smart modern hotel is just outside the city walls, and offers well equipped accommodation. The spacious bedrooms are all identical, but are ideal for both the business guest and families. Guests can dine from the extensive room-service menu, or in the garden brasserie until midnight.
ROOMS: 124 en suite (124 fmly) No smoking in 93 bedrooms s £86; d £99 (incl. bkfst) * LB **FACILITIES:** STV Indoor swimming (H) Playstations Juke Box Games machines Internet use Childrens play area ch fac Xmas **CONF:** Thtr 210 Class 80 Board 60 **SERVICES:** Lift **PARKING:** 150 **CARDS:**

★★71% Clifton Bridge

Water End YO30 6LL
☎ 01904 610510 🖹 01904 640208
e-mail: enq@cliftonbridgehotel.co.uk
Dir: *NW side of city between A19 & A59*

Standing between Clifton Green and the River Ouse and within walking distance of the city this hotel offers good hospitality and attentive service. The house is well furnished and features oak panelled walls in the public rooms, while the modern bedrooms are attractively decorated and thoughtfully equipped. Good home cooking is served in the cosy dining room from a pleasing menu.

continued

ROOMS: 14 en suite (1 fmly) s £35-£44; d £55-£72 (incl. bkfst) * LB **CONF:** Thtr 20 Board 16 Del from £50 * **PARKING:** 14 **NOTES:** No smoking in restaurant Closed 24-25 Dec
CARDS:

★★70% Ashcroft

MINOTEL Great Britain

294 Bishopthorpe Rd YO23 1LH
☎ 01904 659286 🖹 01904 640107
Dir: *turn off A64 on to A1036 and follow signs to Bishopthorpe, turn left in village and take road to York, hotel is 1.5m on right*

Close to the banks of the River Ouse, this Victorian mansion combines traditional heritage with modern facilities. The pleasantly decorated bedrooms have been thoughtfully equipped while a very inviting lounge is provided. Good home cooking is served in the stylish restaurant and service is friendly and attentive.
ROOMS: 11 en suite 4 annexe en suite (3 fmly) s £45-£50; d £50-£85 (incl. bkfst) * LB **FACILITIES:** River moorings **PARKING:** 40 **NOTES:** No children 5yrs No smoking in restaurant Closed 24-30 Dec
CARDS:

★★70% Heworth Court

76 Heworth Green YO31 7TQ
☎ 01904 425156 🖹 01904 415290
e-mail: hotel@heworth.co.uk
Dir: *drive around the outer ring road towards Scarborough rdbt on NE side of York, exit onto A1036 Malton Rd, hotel is on left*

Friendly and attentive service is provided at this family owned hotel, situated within walking distance of the city. Public rooms are comfortable, and the well furnished bedrooms are thoughtfully equipped. An extensive range of freshly prepared food is served in the Lamp Light restaurant.
ROOMS: 15 en suite 10 annexe en suite (5 fmly) No smoking in 8 bedrooms s £46-£81; d £90-£105 (incl. bkfst) * LB **FACILITIES:** STV Whisky bar Xmas **CONF:** Thtr 22 Class 12 Board 16 **PARKING:** 27 **NOTES:** No dogs (ex guide dogs) No smoking in restaurant
CARDS:

See advert on opposite page

'You deserve a break'

COMFORTABLE BEDROOMS

A comfortable, highly recommended, family-run hotel with private car park and friendly, helpful staff.

WHISKY BAR

We are conveniently situated on a main route into York and only 3/4 of a mile from York Minster. Our Lamplight Restaurant serves freshly cooked food. Homemade bread and sweets!

HEWORTH COURT HOTEL

76 HEWORTH GREEN, YORK, ENGLAND

All twenty-five of our en-suite bedrooms have their own individual character – the most luxurious of which being our beautifully appointed 4-poster bedrooms.

http://www.visityork.com
Email: hotel@heworth.co.uk

LAMPLIGHT RESTAURANT

AA ★★

All major credit cards accepted. Please phone for a free brochure and details of special breaks.

4-POSTER ROOMS

(01904) 425156 www.visityork.com

Y

YORK, continued

★★ 69% Beechwood Close

19 Shipton Rd, Clifton YO30 5RE
☎ 01904 658378 📠 01904 647124
e-mail: bch@dial.pipex.com
Dir: *the hotel is situated on the A19 (Thirsk Rd, between ring rd and city centre) on the right hand side when entering the 30mph zone*

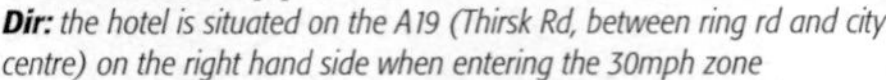

Just a mile north of the city centre, this family owned hotel offers spacious, well equipped bedrooms. Public areas are maintained to a high standard and enjoyable food is served by friendly staff in the traditionally furnished dining room.
ROOMS: 14 en suite (2 fmly) s £40-£47; d £60-£79 (incl. bkfst) * LB **FACILITIES:** STV **CONF:** Thtr 60 Class 35 Board 42 Del from £58 * **PARKING:** 36 **NOTES:** No dogs Closed 25 Dec
CARDS:

★★ 69% Knavesmire Manor

302 Tadcaster Rd YO2 2HE
☎ 01904 702941 📠 01904 709274
e-mail: knavesmire@easynet.co.uk
Dir: *follow signs for York (West) A1036*

Standing opposite the Racecourse this well furnished hotel offers bedrooms either in the main house or garden rooms to the rear. All are well equipped whilst the public rooms offer very good comforts. Quality cooking is served in the bistro style dining room.
ROOMS: 12 en suite 9 annexe en suite (2 fmly) s £45-£69; d £59-£85 (incl. bkfst) * LB **FACILITIES:** STV Indoor swimming (H) Sauna Xmas **CONF:** Thtr 36 Class 30 Board 28 **SERVICES:** Lift **PARKING:** 27 **NOTES:** No smoking in restaurant Civ Wed 60
CARDS:

See advert on opposite page

★★ 68% Hudsons

60 Bootham YO30 7BZ
☎ 01904 621267 📠 01904 654719
Dir: *situated on the A19 which runs from the north of the city into city centre, just after Bootham Park and before city walls*

A careful conversion of two large Victorian houses, Hudsons sits within easy walking distance of the city centre; an archway leads to a secured car park and a modern mews development of purpose-built bedrooms. Many of the bedrooms in the original building retain a period style, as does the elegant dining room. Downstairs there is a refurbished cosy bar as well as a bistro featuring flagstone floors and a menu of traditional cooking.
ROOMS: 31 en suite No smoking in 17 bedrooms s £70-£80; d £90-£115 (incl. bkfst) * LB **FACILITIES:** STV Xmas **CONF:** Thtr 80 Class 30 Board 25 Del from £100.95 * **SERVICES:** Lift **PARKING:** 34 **NOTES:** No dogs (ex guide dogs) **CARDS:**

See advert on opposite page

★★ 67% Alhambra Court

31 St Mary's, Bootham YO30 7DD
☎ 01904 628474 📠 01904 610690
Dir: *off Bootham A19*

In a quiet side road within easy walking distance of the city, this attractive Georgian building is pleasantly furnished and offers well equipped accommodation. The hotel has a car park, service is cheerful and attentive, and good home cooking is a feature.
ROOMS: 24 en suite (5 fmly) No smoking in 14 bedrooms s £35-£47.50; d £47-£75 (incl. bkfst) * LB **SERVICES:** Lift **PARKING:** 25 **NOTES:** No dogs (ex guide dogs) No smoking in restaurant Closed 24-31 Dec & 1-7 Jan **CARDS:**

★★ 67% *Cottage*

3 Clifton Green YO30 6LH
☎ 01904 643711 📠 01904 611230

Overlooking Clifton Green, this well furnished and comfortable hotel is within easy walking distance of the city. Bedrooms, some of which are located in the rear courtyard, are all well equipped. The public rooms are cosy and pleasantly appointed, and there is a good range of food available.
ROOMS: 16 en suite 3 annexe en suite (3 fmly) **FACILITIES:** STV **PARKING:** 10 **NOTES:** Closed 24-26 Dec **CARDS:**

★★ 67% Kilima Hotel

129 Holgate Rd YO24 4AZ
☎ 01904 625787 📠 01904 612083
Dir: *on A59, on W outskirts*

A well furnished and comfortable hotel, the Kilima is within walking distance of the City centre. There is a relaxed and friendly atmosphere in the hotel, with a young staff providing an attentive service. There is a ground floor lounge, a lower ground floor bar and restaurant. Bedrooms are well equipped, comfortably appointed and all have en suite bathrooms.
ROOMS: 15 en suite (1 fmly) s fr £58; d £86-£98 (incl. bkfst) * LB **FACILITIES:** Xmas **CONF:** Thtr 25 Board 14 Del from £84.50 * **PARKING:** 20 **NOTES:** No smoking in restaurant
CARDS:

★★65% Jacobean Lodge
Plainville Ln, Wigginton YO32 2RG
☎ 01904 762749 🖷 01904 768403
Dir: *from A64-A1237-A19 signed Thirsk 0.75m take A19 to Skelton. Right at Blacksmith Arm, 2m to Jacobean*
This comfortable hotel stands in open countryside and is within easy driving distance of the city. Bedrooms are modern and well equipped, and a good range of home cooked meals is available in the pleasant bars or the cosy restaurant. The hotel is family owned and run, and is set in extensive gardens.
ROOMS: 8 en suite 6 annexe en suite (2 fmly) s fr £37.50; d £60-£66 (incl. bkfst) * LB **FACILITIES:** Giant chess Childrens play area entertainment **CONF:** Thtr 40 Class 30 Board 30 **PARKING:** 52 **NOTES:** No smoking in restaurant **CARDS:**

See advert on this page

★★65% Lady Anne Middletons Hotel
Skeldergate YO1 6DS

☎ 01904 611570 🖷 01904 613043
e-mail: bookings@ladyannes.co.uk
Dir: *from A1036 towards City Centre. Right at City Walls lights, keep left, 1st left before bridge, then 1st left into Cromwell Rd. Hotel on right*
This well furnished city-centre hotel has been created from several listed buildings. Among its amenities are a bar lounge and a dining room where a satisfying range of dishes is served. A leisure club is also attached.
ROOMS: 37 en suite 15 annexe en suite (3 fmly) No smoking in 15 bedrooms s £80; d £115 (incl. bkfst) * LB **FACILITIES:** Indoor swimming (H) Sauna Solarium Gym No leisure facilities for under 16yrs **CONF:** Thtr 100 Class 30 Board 30 Del from £95 * **PARKING:** 56 **NOTES:** No smoking in restaurant Closed 24-29 Dec **CARDS:**

Knavesmire Manor AA ★★ HOTEL & RESTAURANT

302 TADCASTER ROAD, YORK, YO24 1HE

Telephone: 01904 702941
Fax: 709274

This late Regency villa (c.1833) was once a Rowntree family home and overlooks York Racecourse whilst close to the city centre. The house became affectionately known as 'a place of friendliness refreshment and peace' and it is in this same tradition of hospitality that guests are welcomed today. The Manor retains many original features, the Oak Room Bar providing added relaxation together with a private indoor swimming pool and spa with sauna, housed in a Victorian style conservatory • Hotel and Motel accommodation • Arnold's Brasserie Restaurant (Red Rosette award) • Conferences and meetings (2-40 delegates) • Walled gardens and car park

All major credit cards accepted

Jacobean Lodge Hotel

WIGGINTON, YORK YO3 3RG
Tel: 01904 762749 Fax: 01904 768403
AA ★★

Converted 17th century detached farmhouse situated in rural surroundings four miles north of York.
Fourteen tastefully decorated and well equipped bedrooms including four-posters.
In winter, relax by open fires in the oak beamed bars – while in summer enjoy 'al fresco' on the patio in our 1½ acre gardens.

★★ *Hudson's* HOTEL

60 BOOTHAM YORK YO30 7BZ
Tel: 01904 621267
Fax: 01904 654719
Only two minutes from York Minster.
Victorian styled Restaurant and Bar.
Secure Car Park.
Conference facilities.

YORK, continued

★★65% Savages
St Peters Grove, Clifton YO30 6AQ
☎ 01904 610818 📠 01904 627729
Dir: *off A19 at Clifton*

Standing in a quiet side road and within easy walking distance of the city and the Minster this pleasant and well run hotel offers a good standard of both accommodation and service. Good honest home cooking is served in the dining room and the bedrooms are well equipped.
ROOMS: 21 en suite (4 fmly) No smoking in 2 bedrooms s £27-£42; d £54-£94 (incl. bkfst & dinner) * LB **PARKING:** 14 **NOTES:** No dogs (ex guide dogs) No smoking in restaurant Closed 25 & 26 Dec
CARDS:

★★63% Abbots' Mews
6 Marygate Ln, Bootham YO30 7DE
☎ 01904 634866 📠 01904 612848
Dir: *overlooking Marygate car park, 1st left along Bootham from York art gallery*
This Victorian cottage and other nearby buildings have been converted into a comfortable hotel. It provides modern bedrooms together with cosy public rooms overlooking a floodlit garden. A good range of food is available in the spacious restaurant.
ROOMS: 12 en suite 35 annexe en suite (8 fmly) s £37-£40; d £64-£70 (incl. bkfst) * LB **FACILITIES:** Xmas **CONF:** Thtr 30 Class 30 Board 20 Del from £60 * **PARKING:** 30 **NOTES:** No dogs (ex guide dogs)
CARDS:

See advert on opposite page

★★62% Elliotts
Sycamore Place, Bootham YO30 7DW
☎ 01904 623333 📠 01904 654908
e-mail: elliottshotel@aol.com
Dir: *A19 Thirsk follow road to York centre under footbridge, 2nd turning on right alongside railway lines, hotel at the bottom*
This delightful Victorian house has a friendly and relaxing atmosphere and offers good accommodation together with freshly prepared meals in both bar and restaurant. It is set in a quiet side road and there are ongoing improvements to the bedrooms.
ROOMS: 18 en suite (2 fmly) No smoking in 1 bedroom s £30-£50; d £50-£66 (incl. bkfst) * LB **FACILITIES:** Xmas **PARKING:** 14 **NOTES:** No dogs (ex guide dogs) **CARDS:**

★★62% *Orchard Court Hotel*
4 St Peters Grove, Bootham YO30 6AQ
☎ 01904 653964
Situated in a quiet side road and within easy walking distance of the city, this family run hotel provides modern and comfortable accommodation. A range of home cooked dishes are available at dinner and staff are polite and friendly.
ROOMS: 14 en suite 4 annexe en suite

⌂ Express by Holiday Inn York
Malton Rd YO3 9TE
☎ 01904 438660
📠 01904 438560

A modern budget hotel offering comfortable accommodation in refreshing, spacious and comprehensively-equipped bedrooms, en suite bathrooms with power showers and continental buffet breakfast included in the room rate. Suitable for business travellers or families. For further details and the Express by Holiday Inn phone number, consult the Hotel Groups page.
ROOMS: 49 en suite (incl. cont bkfst) d £49.95 * **CONF:** Thtr 36 Class 25 Board 20

⌂ Express by Holiday Inn York Clifton
Clifton Business Park, Shipton Rd YO3 6RD
☎ 01904 659992
📠 01904 659994

Express
by Holiday Inn

A modern budget hotel offering comfortable accommodation in refreshing, spacious and comprehensively-equipped bedrooms, en suite bathrooms with power showers and continental buffet breakfast included in the room rate. Suitable for business travellers or families. For further details and the Express by Holiday Inn phone number, consult the Hotel Groups page.
ROOMS: 49 en suite (incl. cont bkfst) d £49.95 * **CONF:** Thtr 16 Class 16 Board 20

○ *Premier Lodge (City Centre)*
20 Blossom St YO24 1AJ
☎ 0870 700 1584 📠 0870 700 1585

Late for dinner? Quality Standards star rating means that last orders for dinner should be no earlier than:
★ 6.30pm ★★ 7.00pm ★★★ 8.00pm
★★★★ 9.00pm ★★★★★ 10.00pm

YOXFORD, Suffolk Map 05 TM36

★★72% Satis House
IP17 3EX
☎ 01728 668418 01728 668640
e-mail: yblackmore@aol.com
Dir: *set back from A12 midway between Ipswich & Lowestoft*
An 18th century grade II listed house once frequented by Charles Dickens. Satis means "whoever lives here could wish for nothing more" this is the explanation given in the book *Great Expectations.* East really does meet West here the elegant public rooms combine English character with Oriental charm. Bedrooms vary in size but all are individually decorated and tastefully furnished. The Malaysian cuisine is a real treat particularly the Kenduri banquet which is well worth a try.
ROOMS: 8 en suite s £55-£65; d £80-£95 (incl. bkfst) * LB
FACILITIES: Tennis (hard) Sauna Jacuzzi/spa **CONF:** Thtr 26 Class 20 Board 14 Del from £105 * **PARKING:** 30 **NOTES:** No dogs No children 7yrs No smoking in restaurant **CARDS:**

Bad hair day? Hairdryers in all rooms three stars and above.

Y

Channel Islands

Directory of establishments in alphabetical order of location.

Guernsey

CHANNEL ISLANDS

Map 16

GUERNSEY

CATEL

★★★75% Cobo Bay
Cobo GY5 7HB
☎ 01481 257102 01481 254542
e-mail: info@cobobay.guernsey.net
Dir: *on main coast road*
This very popular hotel, overlooking Cobo Bay, offers modern, tastefully decorated accommodation. Bedrooms at the front have balconies and there is a secluded sun terrace. Guests can enjoy the candle-lit restaurant and the Chesterfield bar with its leather sofas and armchairs. The Cobo Suite is available for private parties.
ROOMS: 36 en suite (4 fmly) s £39-£69; d £58-£98 (incl. bkfst) * LB **FACILITIES:** STV Snooker Sauna Solarium Pool table Jacuzzi/spa **CONF:** Thtr 50 Class 30 Board 30 **SERVICES:** Lift **PARKING:** 60 **NOTES:** No dogs (ex guide dogs) Closed 2 Jan-6 Mar
CARDS:

★★75% Hotel Hougue du Pommier
Hougue Du Pommier Rd GY5 7FQ
☎ 01481 256531 01481 256260
e-mail: hotel@houguedupommier.guernsey.net

Dating from the 18th century, this private, well run hotel retains much of its original charm, combined with modern comforts. Spacious, well equipped bedrooms are furnished to a high standard. There is a large restaurant, popular bar and an outdoor pool with sun deck.
ROOMS: 43 en suite (5 fmly) No smoking in all bedrooms s £45-£55; d £90-£110 (incl. bkfst) * LB **FACILITIES:** STV Outdoor swimming (H) Golf 10 Sauna Putting green Xmas **PARKING:** 87 **NOTES:** No smoking in restaurant **CARDS:**

FERMAIN BAY

★★★75% *La Favorita*
GY4 6SD
☎ 01481 235666 01481 235413
e-mail: admin@favorita.com
Dir: *at the junct of Fort Road, Sausmarez Road and Fermain Lane take the road (Fermain Lane) signposted to La Favorita Hotel and Fermain Bay*
This charming hotel is on the side of a wooded valley in walking distance of Fermain Bay. Bedrooms are smartly decorated, comfortably furnished and well equipped. Spacious public areas include a choice of lounges, bar, restaurant and a café/brasserie, open all day.

ROOMS: 37 en suite (6 fmly) No smoking in all bedrooms **FACILITIES:** Indoor swimming (H) Sauna Jacuzzi/spa ch fac **CONF:** Thtr 70 Class 30 Board 30 **SERVICES:** Lift **PARKING:** 40 **NOTES:** No dogs No smoking in restaurant Closed 20 Dec-1 Mar
CARDS:

See advert on opposite page

★★★68% Le Chalet
GY4 6SD
☎ 01481 235716 01481 235718
e-mail: chalet@sarniahotels.com
Dir: *from airport turn left, heading towards St Martins village. At filter turn right to Sausmarez Rd then follow sign for Fermain bay & Le Chalet hotel*
Nestling in the wooded valley above the bay, this family-run hotel has a spectacular location on the island. Bedrooms, all well equipped, are tastefully furnished and decorated. There is a wood panelled lounge, bar area, restaurant and a sheltered sun terrace.
ROOMS: 41 en suite (5 fmly) s £50.50-£62.50; d £83-£101 (incl. bkfst) * LB **FACILITIES:** Indoor swimming (H) Sauna Solarium Jacuzzi/spa **PARKING:** 35 **NOTES:** Closed mid Oct-mid Apr
CARDS:

FOREST

★★★64% The Mallard
La Villiaze GY8 0HG
☎ 01481 264164 01481 265732
e-mail: jimgillespie@guernseyholidays.co.uk
Over the years this hotel has been developed into a leisure complex and now boasts a cinema, health club, outdoor swimming pool and themed All Stars Restaurant. Accommodation is modern, tastefully decorated and well equipped. The self-contained apartments are popular with families.
ROOMS: 44 en suite (9 fmly) d £49.50-£69.50 * LB **FACILITIES:** Outdoor swimming (H) Tennis (hard) Sauna Solarium Gym Putting green Jacuzzi/spa **CONF:** Board 25 **PARKING:** 200 **NOTES:** Closed Nov-Mar **CARDS:**

★★67% Le Chene
Forest Rd GY8 0AH
☎ 01481 235566 01481 239456
e-mail: lechenehotel@strayduck.co.uk
Within easy reach of the coast, this Victorian manor house is well located for guests wishing to explore Guernsey's spectacular south

continued

coast. The building has been skilfully extended to house a range of well equipped, modern bedrooms and most recently two popular, self catering apartments. There is a swimming pool, a cosy cellar bar and an informal restaurant.
ROOMS: 26 en suite (2 fmly) s £34-£48; d £48-£76 (incl. bkfst) * **FACILITIES:** Outdoor swimming (H) **PARKING:** 21 **NOTES:** No dogs No children 12yrs No smoking in restaurant Closed 11 Oct-2 May
CARDS:

PERELLE

★★★ 73% L'Atlantique
Perelle Bay GY7 9NA
☎ 01481 264056 01481 263800
e-mail: enquiries@perellebay.com
Dir: *exit Guernsey airport, turn right and continue on this route until you reach the sea. Turn right and follow the coast road for 1.5m*
Set in its own landscaped grounds beside the bay on the west coast, the hotel is within sight, and sound, of the sea. Accommodation varies, rooms with sea view have balconies and there are suites suitable for family accommodation. There are two eating options, the restaurant and the less formal Victorian Bar.
ROOMS: 23 rms (21 en suite) (4 fmly) No smoking in 12 bedrooms s £45-£53.50; d £77-£94 (incl. bkfst) * LB **FACILITIES:** STV Outdoor swimming (H) Tariff prices include car hire ch fac **PARKING:** 80 **NOTES:** No dogs (ex guide dogs) Closed Nov-Feb
CARDS:

ST MARTIN

★★★ 72% La Barbarie
Saints Rd, Saints Bay GY4 6ES
☎ 01481 235217 01481 235208
e-mail: barbarie@guernsey.net
Dating from the 17th century, this former priory enjoys a peaceful setting. The character and charm of the original building has been retained and carefully combined with modern facilities. The bedrooms are tastefully decorated and the beamed restaurant offers a wide range of interesting dishes. There is also a bar menu that features fresh fish.
ROOMS: 23 en suite (4 fmly) s £27-£54; d £54-£84 (incl. bkfst) * LB **FACILITIES:** Outdoor swimming (H) **PARKING:** 50 **NOTES:** No dogs
CARDS:

★★★ 69% Bella Luce Hotel & Restaurant
La Fosse GY4 6EB
☎ 01481 238764 01481 239561
e-mail: info@bellalucehotel.guernsey.net
Dir: *from airport, turn left to St Martins. At second set of traffic lights contiue 30yds and turn right, straight on to hotel*
This 12th-century manor house, set in pleasant and well kept gardens, offers attractive and comfortable accommodation. The bar, lounge and dining room have retained much of their original character. Bar lunches are popular and the restaurant provides a more formal dining option.
ROOMS: 31 en suite (5 fmly) s fr £54; d fr £103 (incl. bkfst) * LB **FACILITIES:** STV Outdoor swimming (H) Sauna Solarium ch fac Xmas **PARKING:** 60 **CARDS:**

See advert on this page

★★★ 69% St Margaret's Lodge
Forest Rd GY4 6UE
☎ 01481 235757 01481 237594
e-mail: smlhotel@gtonline.net
Dir: *1m W at airport turn left into Forest Road, 0.5m ahead*
Equally suited to both leisure and business guests, this well

continued on p644

S

ST MARTIN, continued

presented hotel continues to be popular. Bedrooms vary in size and shape; three spacious suites on the top floor are available. In the modern bar and adjoining conservatory, a range of lighter meals and snacks are provided throughout the day, while in the hotel's restaurant an imaginative selection of dishes is offered at dinner.

St Margaret's Lodge, St Martin

ROOMS: 47 en suite (2 fmly) s £28-£33; d £56-£66 (incl. bkfst) * LB **FACILITIES:** STV Outdoor swimming (H) Fishing Sauna Pool table Table tennis entertainment Xmas **CONF:** Thtr 120 Class 80 Board 20 Del £27.50 * **SERVICES:** Lift **PARKING:** 100 **NOTES:** No dogs No smoking in restaurant Civ Wed 150 **CARDS:**

★★★68% Green Acres

Les Hubits GY4 6LS
☎ 01481 235711 🖹 01481 235978
e-mail: greenacres@guernsey.net
Dir: *behind parish church, 2m from airport*
Within walking distance of Fermain Bay and St Peter Port which is about one mile away, Green Acres Hotel is in a peaceful, country setting. Bedrooms are neatly furnished and decorated, some of the ground floor rooms have the benefit of patio doors straight onto the terrace and pool area. Public areas include a spacious, comfortable lounge, a bar-lounge featuring an interesting menu; while in the formal restaurant a fixed price menu is offered.
ROOMS: 47 en suite (3 fmly) **FACILITIES:** Outdoor swimming (H) **CONF:** Thtr 30 Class 20 Board 20 Del from £65 * **PARKING:** 75 **NOTES:** No dogs (ex guide dogs) No smoking in restaurant Closed Nov-Mar **CARDS:**

S

★★★68% Hotel Bon Port

Moulin Huet Bay GY4 6EW
☎ 01481 239249 🖹 01481 239596
e-mail: mail@bonport.com
Dir: *exit airport turn left into St Martins village, at final traffic lights turn right, follow signs from here*
From its peaceful cliff-top location, this well maintained hotel, boasts spectacular views over Moulin Huet Bay, the famous Peastacks and Saints Bay. The comfortable, well equipped bedrooms vary in size, those with sea-facing balconies being the most sought-after. In addition to the spacious lounge, cosy bar and adjoining sun terraces, in the smartly appointed restaurant an imaginative range of food is served by courteous staff.
ROOMS: 18 en suite (2 fmly) **FACILITIES:** STV Outdoor swimming (H) Sauna Gym Croquet lawn Putting green **PARKING:** 30 **NOTES:** No dogs (ex guide dogs) No smoking in restaurant
CARDS:

See advert on opposite page

★★★68% Idlerocks

Jerbourg Point GY4 6BJ
☎ 01481 237711 🖹 01481 235592
e-mail: info@idlerocks.com
From its cliff top location, this family run hotel enjoys sea views towards the other islands and French coast in the far distance. The well equipped, individually decorated bedrooms varying in shape and size. Delightful terraces and a cosy lounge provide ample areas for guests to relax. A choice of dining options is provided, either from the fixed price menu in Admirals Restaurant or more informally in Raffles lounge bar.
ROOMS: 28 en suite (4 fmly) No smoking in 11 bedrooms s £18-£58; d £36-£116 (incl. bkfst) * LB **FACILITIES:** STV Outdoor swimming (H) Xmas **CONF:** Board 30 **PARKING:** 100
CARDS:

★★★67% Hotel Jerbourg

Jerbourg Point GY4 6BJ
☎ 01481 238826 🖹 01481 238238
e-mail: hjerb8765@aol.com
Dir: *from airport turn left and follow rd to St Martins village, then right onto filter road then straight on at lights, hotel at end of the rd on right*
A cliff top hotel at the end of a quiet lane, with excellent sea views. Smartly appointed public areas include an extensive bar/lounge and bright conservatory-style restaurant. Bedrooms are all well furnished, and newer luxury Bay rooms are more spacious.
ROOMS: 32 en suite (4 fmly) No smoking in all bedrooms s £20-£55; d £35-£135 (incl. bkfst) * LB **FACILITIES:** STV Outdoor swimming (H) Xmas **CONF:** Thtr 50 Class 50 Board 50 **PARKING:** 50 **NOTES:** No dogs (ex guide dogs) **CARDS:**

★★★64% La Trelade

Forest Rd GY4 6UB
☎ 01481 235454 🖹 01481 237855
e-mail: latrelade@guernsey.net
Dir: *3m out of St Peter Port, 1m from airport*
Set in attractive gardens, with a pool at the rear of the hotel, this hotel is conveniently located for easy access to the many attractions the island has to offer. Bedrooms are tastefully decorated and equipped with modern comforts. In addition to a choice of lounges, a range of light meals and snacks is offered in the popular bar; an interesting, fixed price menu being served in the hotel's restaurant.
ROOMS: 45 en suite (3 fmly) s £30-£57; d £60-£114 (incl. cont bkfst) * LB **FACILITIES:** STV Outdoor swimming (H) Xmas **CONF:** Thtr 120 Class 48 Board 40 Del from £55 * **SERVICES:** Lift **PARKING:** 120 **NOTES:** No smoking in restaurant Closed 28 Dec-Feb
CARDS:

See advert on opposite page

★★73% La Michele
Les Hubits GY4 6NB
☎ 01481 238065 01481 239492
e-mail: lamichelehotel@ukgateway.net
Dir: *located in a quiet country lane, about 10 minutes walk from Fermain Bay, about 1.5m from St Peter Port*
This delightful family-run hotel enjoys a peaceful location. Bedrooms are neatly presented, comfortably furnished and very well equipped. Public areas include a conservatory and restaurant which overlook the attractive garden.
ROOMS: 16 en suite (3 fmly) s £32-£43; d £64-£86 (incl. bkfst & dinner) * LB **FACILITIES:** Outdoor swimming (H) **PARKING:** 16 **NOTES:** No dogs (ex guide dogs) No children 8yrs No smoking in restaurant Closed Nov-Mar **CARDS:**

★★69% La Villette
GY4 6QG
☎ 01481 235292 01481 237699
e-mail: reservations@lavillettehotel.co.uk
Peacefully located in spacious grounds, this Georgian property has been extended over the years. Family-run, the hotel has a friendly and relaxed atmosphere. Bedrooms are decorated in a modern style and are well equipped. A range of light meals and snacks are served in the large bar, where live music is a regular feature, while in the separate restaurant a fixed price menu is provided. A superb, professionally supervised leisure complex, is the hotel's latest addition, available for hotel guests to use as well as its own private membership.
ROOMS: 41 en suite 1 annexe rms (13 fmly) d £54-£72 (incl. bkfst) * LB **FACILITIES:** Indoor swimming (H) Outdoor swimming (H) Solarium Jacuzzi/spa Steam room Petanque Xmas **PARKING:** 50 **NOTES:** No smoking in restaurant **CARDS:**

ST MARTIN, continued

★★66% *Carlton*

Les Caches, Forest Rd GY4 6PR
☎ 01481 235678 📠 01481 236590
Dir: *on road from airport to main town of St Peter Port*

The Carlton is performing well in its early days, having re-opened after extensive refurbishment. The public areas are smart and inviting, particularly the dining room. There is a public bar where snacks are available, and a residents' lounge.
ROOMS: 45 en suite 2 annexe en suite (4 fmly) **FACILITIES:** STV Pool table entertainment ch fac **NOTES:** No dogs (ex guide dogs) No smoking in restaurant **CARDS:**

See advert on page 645

ST PETER PORT

★★★★70% Old Government House Hotel

Ann's Place GY1 4AZ
☎ 01481 724921 📠 01481 724429
e-mail: ogh@guernsey.net
Dir: *from airport hotel is located in centre of St Peter Port, overlooking harbour and neighbouring islands of Alderney, Sark and Jersey*
Furbished to a very high standard, the affectionately known OGH is a leading hotel. Bedrooms are comfortable and offer high quality accommodation. The restaurant overlooks the town and neighbouring islands, and offers fine dining; snacks are available in the Centenary bar.
ROOMS: 68 en suite s £60-£75; d £92-£115 (incl. bkfst) * LB **FACILITIES:** STV Outdoor swimming (H) Xmas **CONF:** Thtr 180 Class 150 Board 90 Del from £112.25 * **SERVICES:** Lift **PARKING:** 24 **NOTES:** No dogs (ex guide dogs) **CARDS:**

S

★★★★68% St Pierre Park

Rohais GY1 1FD
☎ 01481 728282 📠 01481 712041
e-mail: stppark@itl.net
Dir: *10 minutes from airport*
Located just outside St Peter Port, this attractive, purpose built hotel is set in 45 acres of parkland. The well appointed bedrooms all have either balcony or terrace. Guests have a choice of two dining options, the casual Café Renoir, or the more formal Victor Hugo restaurant. The lounge bar with spacious terrace, overlooks an elegant water feature.
ROOMS: 132 en suite (4 fmly) No smoking in 17 bedrooms s £130; d £170 (incl. bkfst) * LB **FACILITIES:** STV Indoor swimming (H) Golf 9 Tennis (hard) Snooker Sauna Solarium Gym Pool table Croquet lawn Putting green Jacuzzi/spa Bird watching Trim trail Child playground Crazy golf ch fac Xmas **CONF:** Thtr 200 Class 100 Board 30 Del from £140 * **SERVICES:** Lift **PARKING:** 150 **NOTES:** No dogs (ex guide dogs) **CARDS:**

★★★73% Hotel de Havelet

Best Western

Havelet GY1 1BA
☎ 01481 722199 📠 01481 714057
e-mail: havelet@sarniahotels.com
Dir: *from Guernsey airport follow signs for St Peter Port through St. Martins. At bottom of 'Val de Terres' hill turn left into Havelet*
This extended Georgian hotel looks over the harbour to Castle Cornet. Many of the well equipped bedrooms are set around a pretty colonial-style courtyard. Day rooms in the original building have period elegance, the restaurant and bar are on the other side of the car park in a converted stables.
ROOMS: 34 en suite (4 fmly) s £54-£84; d £93-£116 (incl. bkfst) * LB **FACILITIES:** STV Indoor swimming (H) Sauna Jacuzzi/spa Xmas **CONF:** Thtr 40 Class 24 Board 26 Del from £85 * **PARKING:** 40 **NOTES:** No dogs (ex guide dogs) **CARDS:**

★★★72% La Fregate

Les Cotils GY1 1UT
☎ 01481 724624 📠 01481 720443
e-mail: lafregate@guernsey.net

La Fregate enjoys splendid views from its elevated position. However, it can be difficult to locate and it is wise to ask for detailed directions. Bedrooms are comfortably furnished and well equipped, and many have balconies. The bar and restaurant are popular with both residents and locals.
ROOMS: 13 en suite s £63; d £78-£105 (incl. bkfst) * **FACILITIES:** STV **CONF:** Board 18 **PARKING:** 25 **NOTES:** No dogs No children 14yrs **CARDS:**

See advert on opposite page

★★★70% Moore's

Best Western

Pollet GY1 1WH
☎ 01481 724452 📠 01481 714037
e-mail: moores@sarniahotels.com
Dir: *left at airport, follow signs to St Peter Port, Fort Road to sea front, straight on, turn right before rdbt, continue up to hotel*
The hotel, dating in parts from the 18th century, is set just back from the harbour, but still in the heart of St Peter Port. It has kept much of its original character, combined with such modern amenities as the Sanctuary health suite. Bedrooms are comfortably appointed and well equipped. Attractive public areas include an Austrian Patisserie, conservatory restaurant, library bar and carvery. Service is both attentive and friendly.
ROOMS: 46 en suite 3 annexe en suite (8 fmly) s £63-£75; d £82-£102 (incl. bkfst) * LB **FACILITIES:** STV Sauna Solarium Gym Jacuzzi/spa Xmas **CONF:** Thtr 35 Class 20 Board 15 Del from £95 * **SERVICES:** Lift **NOTES:** No dogs (ex guide dogs) **CARDS:**

Read all about it! Newspapers delivered to bedrooms in four and five star hotels.

★★ 69% Sunnycroft
5 Constitution Steps GY1 2PN
☎ 01481 723008 🖷 01481 712225

This small hotel has glorious views of the neighbouring islands of Herm, Jethou and Sark. Bedrooms are freshly decorated, many have balconies and all are equipped with modern facilities. The public rooms include a bar/lounge, a sitting room, a reading room and an attractive dining room.
ROOMS: 12 en suite s £46-£50; d £72-£80 (incl. bkfst) *
FACILITIES: STV **PARKING:** 3 **NOTES:** No dogs (ex guide dogs) No children 12yrs No smoking in restaurant Closed Nov-22 Mar
CARDS:

See advert on this page

Arriving late? Four and five star hotels have night porters to assist with your luggage; and 24hr room service.

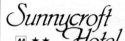

ST PETER PORT, continued

★★62% Duke of Normandie

Lefebvre St GY1 2JP
☎ 01481 721431 🖷 01481 711763
e-mail: dukeofnormandie@gtonline.net
***Dir:** From harbour r/about up St Julians Ave, 3rd left after lights, continue to right up hill, then left into Lefebvre St, archway on right*

Dating back to the 18th Century, this modernised hotel is perfectly located if you wish to be just a stroll from the harbour of St Peter Port or adjacent to the High Street. Well-equipped en suite accommodation is set around a courtyard, which also provides guest parking. Public areas include the busy bar, now restored with beams and open fireplace.

ROOMS: 20 en suite 17 annexe en suite (1 fmly) s £29.50-£41; d £59-£82 (incl. bkfst) LB **FACILITIES:** STV Xmas **PARKING:** 15 **NOTES:** No dogs (ex guide dogs) No smoking in restaurant **CARDS:**

VALE

★★★64% Pembroke Bay

Pembroke Bay GY3 5BY
☎ 01481 247573 🖷 01481 248838
e-mail: pembroke@guernsey.net

This family-run hotel is situated between one of the best bathing beaches on the island and the local golf course. Modern bedrooms, all with garden or sea views, are tastefully furnished and decorated. Guests can enjoy the bar, restaurant and lounge areas.

ROOMS: 12 en suite (2 fmly) No smoking in all bedrooms d £85-£98 (incl. bkfst) * **FACILITIES:** STV Outdoor swimming (H) Tennis (hard) Sailing Surfing Bicycle hire **NOTES:** Closed Oct-early Apr
CARDS:

★★★63% Peninsula

Les Dicqs GY6 8JP
☎ 01481 248400 🖷 01481 248706
e-mail: peninsula@guernsey.net

Adjacent to a sandy beach and set in five acres of grounds, this modern hotel provides comfortable accommodation. The recently refurbished bedrooms all have additional sofa beds to suit families and good work space for the business traveller. Both fixed price and an à la carte menus are served in the restaurant, while guests may eat more informally in the bar.

ROOMS: 99 en suite (99 fmly) No smoking in 18 bedrooms
FACILITIES: STV Outdoor swimming (H) Croquet lawn Putting green Petanque Playground **CONF:** Thtr 250 Class 140 Board 105 Del from £65 * **SERVICES:** Lift **PARKING:** 120 **NOTES:** No smoking in restaurant
CARDS:

S

HERM

★★75% White House

GY1 3HR
☎ 01481 722159 🖷 01481 710066
e-mail: hotel@herm-island.com
***Dir:** hotel located close to harbour*

Just a twenty minute boat trip from Guernsey, this attractive island hotel enjoys a unique setting on the harbour, offering superb sea views. Set in well tended gardens, the hotel offers neatly decorated bedrooms, located in either the main house or adjacent cottages. Guests can relax in one of several comfortable lounges, enjoy a drink in one of two bars and choose from the imaginative and ambitious in the Conservatory Restaurant or more informally from the Captain's Table menu in the Ship Inn.

ROOMS: 16 en suite 22 annexe en suite (12 fmly) s £57-£74; d £114-£148 (incl. bkfst & dinner) * LB **FACILITIES:** Outdoor swimming (H) Tennis (hard) Croquet lawn **NOTES:** No dogs (ex guide dogs) No smoking in restaurant Closed 9 Oct-5 Apr
CARDS:

See advert on opposite page

JERSEY

BEAUMONT

★★65% Hotel L'Hermitage

JE3 7BR
☎ 01534 733314 & 758272 🖷 01534 721207
e-mail: lhermitage@jerseymail.co.uk
***Dir:** on N12, from airport-B36-A12 Beaumont, on left past crossroad*

L'Hermitage is based on a fine period house, many bedrooms open directly onto a lawned 'Piazza' to the rear. Rooms are generally spacious with bright fresh decor. Public rooms include a comfortable bar, non-smoking lounge and large dining room which features regular after dinner entertainment. Sandy beaches are two minutes away.

ROOMS: 43 en suite 65 annexe rms (64 en suite) s £43.50; d £83 (incl. bkfst & dinner) * **FACILITIES:** Indoor swimming (H) Outdoor swimming (H) Sauna Solarium Jacuzzi/spa entertainment **PARKING:** 100 **NOTES:** No dogs (ex guide dogs) No children 14yrs No smoking in restaurant Closed mid Oct-mid Apr **CARDS:**

GOREY

★★★66% *The Moorings*

Gorey Pier JE3 6EW
☎ 01534 853633 🖷 01534 857618
e-mail: casino@itl.net
***Dir:** Situated beneath Mont Orgueil Castle, Gorey Pier overlooking the sandy beach of Grouville*

The Moorings enjoys an enviable position down by the harbour and is somewhat of an institution with both locals and visitors. A well-appointed restaurant, featuring local seafood, is at the heart of public areas that include a cosy bar, with a log fire in winter, and comfortable first-floor residents' lounge. Attractive bedrooms are all en suite and have recently been fully refurbished. Rooms at the front have a fine view of the harbour and three have access to a balcony.

ROOMS: 16 en suite **CONF:** Thtr 20 Class 20 Board 20
CARDS:

★★★66% Old Court House

JE3 9FS
☎ 01534 854444 🖷 01534 853587
e-mail: ochhotel@itl.net

A short walk from the beaches of the island's east coast, this long established hotel is popular with locals as well as visitors. Some bedrooms have balconies which overlook the gardens. Spacious public areas include a restaurant, a large bar with a dance floor and a comfortable lounge.

ROOMS: 58 en suite (4 fmly) s £41-£60; d £82-£120 (incl. bkfst & dinner) * LB **FACILITIES:** STV Outdoor swimming (H) Sauna entertainment **SERVICES:** Lift **PARKING:** 40 **NOTES:** Closed Nov-Mar
CARDS:

ROZEL BAY

Premier Collection

★★★ **Château la Chaire**

Rozel Bay JE3 6AJ

☎ 01534 863354 01534 865137

e-mail: res@chateau-la-chaire.co.uk

Dir: *from direction of St Helier on B38 turn left in village by the Rozel Bay Inn, hotel 100yds on right*

High up over Rozel Bay, Château la Chaire is positioned on the side of a wooded valley and surrounded by five acres of terraced gardens. Close to the village of Rozel and its beaches. Built as a gentleman's residence in 1843, the Château retains much of the atmosphere of a private country house, including some exquisite decorative plaster work in the drawing room. The oak-panelled dining room, with an conservatory extension, is a fine setting for some skilful and consistent cooking which feature imaginative menus using the best of local produce and introduce many contemporary trends. Individually-styled bedrooms feature a host of comforting extras.

ROOMS: 14 en suite (1 fmly) s £80-£130; d £105-£240 (incl. bkfst) * LB **FACILITIES:** STV entertainment Xmas **CONF:** Board 20 **PARKING:** 30 **NOTES:** No dogs (ex guide dogs) No children 7yrs **CARDS:**

smart. Bedrooms vary in style and a number of superior rooms offer higher levels of luxury.

ROOMS: 59 rms (58 en suite) (7 fmly) **FACILITIES:** STV Outdoor swimming (H) entertainment **CONF:** Thtr 40 Class 25 Board 30 **SERVICES:** Lift **PARKING:** 40 **NOTES:** No dogs No children 4yrs Closed 2 Jan-10 Feb **CARDS:**

See advert on page 651

ST AUBIN

★★★72% **Somerville**

Mont du Boulevard JE3 8AD

☎ 01534 741226 01534 746621

e-mail: somerville@dolanhotel.com

Dir: *from village, follow harbour then take Mont du Boulevard and second right hand bend*

This friendly hotel, enjoying spectacular views of St Aubin's Bay, is popular with the leisure traveller. Bedrooms and public areas are

ST BRELADE

★★★★78% **The Atlantic**

Le Mont de la Pulente JE3 8HE

☎ 01534 744101 01534 744102

e-mail: atlantic@itl.net

Recently reopened after a £3.5 million refit this luxury property has 42 modern refurbished bedrooms. Quality and comfort aspects are high, heated mirrors in bathrooms, king size beds with fine cotton linen in bedrooms. First and second floor rooms have

continued

Jersey

ST BRELADE, continued

great views of the sea and the La Moye golf course. Cuisine remains a focus here with an interesting range of dishes.
ROOMS: 50 en suite s £125-£165; d £160-£240 (incl. bkfst) * LB **FACILITIES:** STV Indoor swimming (H) Outdoor swimming (H) Tennis (hard) Sauna Solarium Gym Jacuzzi/spa Xmas **CONF:** Thtr 60 Class 40 Board 20 Del from £190 * **SERVICES:** Lift **PARKING:** 60 **NOTES:** No dogs (ex guide dogs) Closed Jan-Feb
CARDS:

★★★★ 78% Hotel L'Horizon

St Brelade's Bay JE3 8EF
☎ 01534 743101 01534 746269
e-mail: lhorizon@hotellhorizon.com
Dir: *3m from airport. 6m from harbour*

One of the most popular hotels on the island, superbly located on the golden sands of St Brelade's Bay, offering a friendly welcome and great facilities. Bedrooms are all well equipped, many stylishly decorated with a seashore theme and some with great views. Public areas are bright and spacious, including a choice of three eating options. The Grill, decorated in art deco style, makes very good use of fresh seafood.
ROOMS: 107 en suite (7 fmly) s £90-£160; d £160-£240 (incl. bkfst) * LB **FACILITIES:** STV Indoor swimming (H) Sauna Gym Jacuzzi/spa Windsurfing Water skiing entertainment Xmas **CONF:** Thtr 250 Class 58 Board 40 Del from £140 * **SERVICES:** Lift **PARKING:** 125 **NOTES:** No dogs (ex guide dogs) **CARDS:**

★★★★ 70% Hotel La Place

Route du Coin, La Haule JE3 8BT
☎ 01534 744261 01534 745164
e-mail: hotlaplace@aol.com
Dir: *turn off main St Helier/St Aubin coast rd at La Haule Manor (B25). Up hill, 2nd Left (to Redhouses), 1st R. Hotel 100m on R*

Created around a 17th-century farmhouse in a rural part of the island, the hotel offers a range of bedrooms, some designed for the business traveller, and all equipped to a good modern standard. Day rooms include a beamed lounge, a cocktail bar and Knights Restaurant, where the decor follows a medieval theme. The sheltered pool area and terrace make a great sun trap, landscaped gardens offer a quieter alternative for an afternoon snooze.
ROOMS: 43 en suite (1 fmly) No smoking in 25 bedrooms s £92; d £142-£188 (incl. bkfst) * LB **FACILITIES:** STV Outdoor swimming (H) Sauna Xmas **CONF:** Thtr 120 Class 40 Board 40 Del from £110 * **PARKING:** 100 **NOTES:** No smoking in restaurant
CARDS:

See advert on opposite page

★★★★ 69% St Brelade's Bay

JE3 8EF
☎ 01534 746141 01534 747278
Dir: *SW corner of the island*

Overlooking St Brelade's Bay this well run family hotel has both long standing guests and staff. Attractions include terraced gardens with a choice of pools, easy access to the beach, children's rooms and the latest new addition, a small gym and sauna. Bedrooms have now all been refurbished, most offering king size beds, many rooms have a children's room within the unit. Morning and afternoon tea are included in the tariff.
ROOMS: 72 en suite (50 fmly) s £56-£98; d £86-£202 (incl. bkfst) * **FACILITIES:** STV Outdoor swimming (H) Tennis (hard & grass) Snooker Sauna Solarium Pool table Croquet lawn Putting green Petanque Mini-gym entertainment **SERVICES:** Lift **PARKING:** 60 **NOTES:** No dogs (ex guide dogs) No smoking in restaurant Closed 12 Oct-21 Apr
CARDS:

★★★ 73% Sea Crest Hotel & Restaurant

La Route Du Petit Port JE3 8HH
☎ 01534 746353 01534 747316
e-mail: seacrest@super.net.uk
Dir: *from Red Houses follow 'Route Orange' A13 to hotel on right at the bottom of a dip*

The sea can not only be seen but also heard from this welcoming hotel situated on the picturesque bay of Petit Port. The restaurant has a good local reputation. All bedrooms have views of the bay, and among the hotel's amenities are a sun lounge, terrace and pool.
ROOMS: 7 rms (6 en suite) s £80-£85; d £120-£130 (incl. bkfst) * **FACILITIES:** Outdoor swimming **PARKING:** 70 **NOTES:** No dogs (ex guide dogs) Closed Jan RS Rest closed Mon & Sun eve out of season
CARDS:

See advert on opposite page

★★★ 70% *Château Valeuse*

Rue de Valeuse, St Brelade's Bay JE3 8EE
☎ 01534 746281 01534 747110

Expect a friendly welcome here, and high levels of service. Château Valeuse stands in lovely gardens, just above St Brelades, with views of the bay from some of the comfortable bedrooms. Public areas include a spacious lounge, separate bar and sun terrace. The restaurant offers a good choice of dishes.
ROOMS: 34 en suite (1 fmly) **FACILITIES:** Outdoor swimming (H) Putting green **PARKING:** 50 **NOTES:** No dogs No children 5yrs Closed Nov-Mar **CARDS:**

★★★ 69% Golden Sands

St Brelade's Bay JE3 8EF
☎ 01534 741241 01534 499366
e-mail: goldensands@dolanhotels.com

Centrally located in the popular area of St Brelade's Bay the hotel enjoys direct access to the beach. Several different styles of bedroom are offered with the majority sea-facing and equipped with balconies. All rooms provide good levels of space and comfort, and are furnished to a high standard. Public areas

continued on p652

S

SEA CREST

HOTEL & RESTAURANT

LA ROUTE DU PETIT PORT
ST. BRELADE
JERSEY JE3 8HH

TEL: (01534) 746353
FAX: (01534) 747316

The Sea Crest Hotel and Restaurant maintains a very high standard of decor, service and attention to detail in all areas.

•

The sophisticated surroundings of the restaurant are complimented by the extensive collection of 20th century pictures from the owner's private collection.

•

The food is strongly influenced by local seafood and Jersey fresh produce is used whenever possible.

•

The stunning sunsets can be enjoyed from the bedrooms, the restaurant and the swimming pool terrace.

Hotel La Place

AA ★★★★

ST BRELADE, JERSEY

★ Rural location close to St Aubin's Bay
★ Superb cuisine, service and hospitality
★ Swimming pool, sauna, gardens
★ Short Breaks, holidays and special rates available year round

Telephone: 01534 744261
Email: HotLaPlace@aol.com
www.jersey.co.uk/hotels/laplace

THE Somerville HOTEL

Overlooking the yachting harbour of St. Aubin. The hotel stands in its own award winning gardens with heated pool and lawns.
Superb sea view restaurant.
Evening entertainment.

Cocktail and lounge bars. All bedrooms have private facilities, satellite TV. Car park and courtesy minibus to St. Helier and St. Brelade.

Children under 4 not accepted.

St. Aubin

Tel: 01534 741226 Fax: 01534 746621
Email: somerville@dolanhotels.com
Website: www.dolanhotels.com

Golden Sands HOTEL

The hotel enjoys direct access to the beach and is close to the lovely gardens of the bay. Attractive sea view dining room, bar and lounge entertainment. All bedrooms have private facilities, satellite TV, tea/coffee tray. Supervised children's creche at meal times. Lift. Courtesy minibus to St. Helier and St. Aubin.

St. Brelade's Bay

Tel: 01534 741241 Fax: 01534 499366
Email: goldensands@dolanhotels.com
Website: www.dolanhotels.com

HOTEL Cristina

From its hillside position the hotel boasts one of the finest views in Jersey. Overlooking St. Aubin's Bay, historic Elizabeth Castle and St. Aubin's Fort, this peaceful location is only 1½ miles from St. Helier and a few minutes walk from the golden beach of St. Aubin's Bay. Two sea view restaurants and bars, entertainment, heated pool, sun terrace.
Free minibus to St. Helier, St. Aubin and St. Brelade.

St. Aubin's Bay

Tel: 01534 758024 Fax: 01534 758028
Email: christina@dolanhotels.com
Website: www.dolanhotels.com

ST BRELADE, continued

include a smart reception foyer, separate lounge and spacious bar and restaurant which overlook the bay. Staff provide friendly and attentive service.

Golden Sands, St Brelade

ROOMS: 62 en suite (5 fmly) s £42-£92.75; d £54-£120 (incl. bkfst) * **FACILITIES:** STV Childrens play room ch fac **SERVICES:** Lift **NOTES:** No dogs No smoking in restaurant Closed Nov-mid Apr
CARDS:

★★★69% Silver Springs

La Route des Genets JE3 8DB
☎ 01534 746401 🖷 01534 746823
e-mail: silver@itl.net
Dir: *turn right from leaving Airport onto B36 till you reach traffic lights. Turn left onto A13 & Hotel is 0.5m along this road.*
This well presented hotel set in seven acres of beautiful gardens and private woodland continues to be very popular with leisure guests, in particular families. Public areas are spacious with separate lounges, a smart bar and a restaurant that overlook a wooded valley. Bedrooms are neatly decorated and comfortably furnished, some equipped with balconies.
ROOMS: 88 en suite (14 fmly) s fr £36; d fr £72 (incl. bkfst) * **FACILITIES:** STV Outdoor swimming (H) Tennis (hard) Pool table Croquet lawn Putting green Boules Children's pool & playground Table tennis entertainment ch fac **PARKING:** 50 **NOTES:** No dogs (ex guide dogs) No smoking in restaurant Closed 25 Oct-23 Apr
CARDS:

See advert on opposite page

S

★★71% Beau Rivage

St Brelade's Bay JE3 8EF
☎ 01534 745983 🖷 01534 747127
e-mail: beaurivage@jerseyweb.demon.co.uk
Dir: *seaward side of coast rd in centre of bay, 1.5m S of airport*
Almost on the beach this hotel has an enviable location. The majority of bedrooms are sea facing and nine have large, furnished balconies. The bar boasts various games machines and a juke box. There is also live music most nights during the season.
ROOMS: 27 en suite (9 fmly) No smoking in 1 bedroom s £57-£75; d £84-£119 (incl. bkfst) * LB **FACILITIES:** STV Pool table Sunbathing terrace Video games entertainment **SERVICES:** Lift **PARKING:** 16 **NOTES:** No dogs No smoking in restaurant Closed 29 Oct-6 Apr
CARDS:

ST HELIER

★★★★69% The Grand

De Vere Hotels

The Esplanade JE4 8WD
☎ 01534 722301 🖷 01534 737815
e-mail: grand.jersey@devere-hotels.com
This hotel, centrally located for the town and beaches, has lovely views from front bedrooms and public areas. Bedrooms, all well equipped, vary in size and outlook. Staff are friendly, dedicated and smartly dressed. There are two restaurants, Victoria's, and the more relaxed Regency.

ROOMS: 116 en suite No smoking in 22 bedrooms d £150 (incl. bkfst) * LB **FACILITIES:** STV Indoor swimming (H) Snooker Sauna Solarium Gym Jacuzzi/spa Beauty therapy Massage parlour entertainment Xmas **CONF:** Thtr 180 Class 100 Board 40 Del from £130 * **SERVICES:** Lift **PARKING:** 27 **NOTES:** No dogs (ex guide dogs)
CARDS:

★★★70% Pomme d'Or

Liberation Square JE1 3UF
☎ 01534 880110 🖷 01534 737781
e-mail: pomme@seymour-hotels-jersey.com
Dir: *opposite the harbour*
Overlooking Liberation Square and the marina, this established hotel offers comfortably furnished and well equipped bedrooms with modern amenities and 24 hour room service. Public areas include extensive conference facilities and a choice of two restaurants and coffee shop. Car parking is close at hand in the Esplanade car park.
ROOMS: 141 en suite (3 fmly) No smoking in 72 bedrooms s £77.50-£135; d £125-£185 (incl. bkfst) * LB **FACILITIES:** STV Use of Aquadome at Merton Hotel Xmas **CONF:** Thtr 220 Class 100 Board 50 Del from £78.50 * **SERVICES:** Lift **NOTES:** No dogs (ex guide dogs)
CARDS:

★★★69% Royal

David Place JE2 4TD
☎ 01534 726521 🖷 01534 724035
e-mail: royalhot@4.net

Centrally located, the Royal is ideal for both business and leisure guests and offers comfortable bedrooms, some of which are particularly smart. The elegant public areas consist of a very comfortable lounge, No 27 bar and brasserie, a lounge bar, and a stylish restaurant. The hotel also boasts one of the largest conference rooms on the island.

continued

ROOMS: 88 en suite (39 fmly) s £65-£77; d £110-£128 (incl. bkfst) * LB **FACILITIES:** entertainment Xmas **CONF:** Thtr 400 Class 150 Board 30 Del from £110 * **SERVICES:** Lift **PARKING:** 15
CARDS:

See advert on this page

★★★68% Apollo

St Saviours Rd JE2 4GJ
☎ 01534 725441 01534 722120
e-mail: huggler@psilink.co.je
Dir: *on St Saviours Road at its junct with La Motte Street. 5 mins walk from Town Centre*

Conveniently located in the centre of the town, this popular hotel is equally suited to both the leisure and business user. Public areas have benefited from recent refurbishment including the smartly appointed front foyer and main restaurant. All bedrooms are en-suite and attractively furnished. Service is professional and

continued on p654

S

ST HELIER, continued

attentive from the dedicated team of staff. Plenty of parking and both indoor and outdoor pools area are two key attractions.
ROOMS: 85 en suite (5 fmly) s £50.50-£69.50; d £93-£103 (incl. bkfst) * LB **FACILITIES:** STV Indoor swimming (H) Outdoor swimming (H) Sauna Solarium Gym Jacuzzi/spa Xmas **CONF:** Thtr 150 Class 100 Board 80 Del £85 * **SERVICES:** Lift **PARKING:** 50 **NOTES:** No dogs (ex guide dogs) **CARDS:**

See advert on opposite page

★★★ 67% Beaufort

Green St JE2 4UH
☎ 01534 732471 01534 720371
e-mail: huggler@psilink.co.je
Dir: *located on Green Street, 5 mins walk from main shopping centre*

Within walking distance of the main business and shopping areas, the Beaufort is in a convenient location. All bedrooms are spacious and have excellent facilities. Public areas include a sun terrace.
ROOMS: 54 en suite (4 fmly) s £65; d £90-£115 (incl. bkfst) * LB **FACILITIES:** STV Indoor swimming (H) Outdoor swimming (H) Jacuzzi/spa Xmas **CONF:** Thtr 160 Class 140 Del £89 * **SERVICES:** Lift **PARKING:** 30 **NOTES:** No dogs **CARDS:**

See advert on opposite page

★★★ 67% *Royal Yacht*

The Weighbridge JE2 3NF
☎ 01534 720511 01534 767729
e-mail: casino@itl.net
Dir: *Situated in town centre, opposite the Marina and harbour, 0.5 mile from beach*
Enjoying a central location overlooking the harbour and marina, the Royal Yacht is thought be the oldest established hotel on the island. Bedrooms are comfortably furnished, soundproofed and well equipped. Public areas include several bars and a grill room in addition to the main first-floor restaurant.
ROOMS: 45 en suite **FACILITIES:** STV Sauna ch fac **CONF:** Thtr 20 Class 20 Board 20 **SERVICES:** Lift **CARDS:**

★★★ 66% Hotel Revere

Kensington Place JE2 3PA
☎ 01534 611111 01534 611116
e-mail: reservations@revere.co.uk
Located on the west side of town this 17th-century building retains many of its original features. Bedrooms are individually decorated and have high quality bedding. Public areas include several cosy lounges, three eating options and a sun terrace.
ROOMS: 58 en suite (4 fmly) No smoking in 14 bedrooms **FACILITIES:** STV Outdoor swimming (H) **NOTES:** No dogs (ex guide dogs) **CARDS:**

★★ 69% Sarum Hotel

19-21 New St Johns Rd JE2 3LD
☎ 01534 758163 01534 731340
e-mail: sarum@jerseyweb.demon.co.uk
Dir: *W side of St Helier, 0.5m from Town Centre*
Situated in a residential area just five minutes walk from the town centre and beaches, the Sarum is suitable for guests who like to have everything close by. All bedrooms are neatly decorated and comfortably furnished, some with small kitchens.
ROOMS: 47 en suite s £44-£54; d £72-£92 (incl. bkfst) * LB **FACILITIES:** STV Outdoor swimming (H) Video games **SERVICES:** Lift **PARKING:** 11 **NOTES:** No dogs (ex guide dogs) No children No smoking in restaurant Closed 29 Oct-6 Apr
CARDS:

★★ 68% Uplands

St John's Rd JE2 3LE
☎ 01534 730151 01534 639899
e-mail: morfanho@itl.net
Dir: *turn off main esplanade (A1) onto Pierson Rd by Grand Hotel, follow ring road for 200mtrs, third on left into St Johns Rd, hotel in 0.5m*
Based around the granite buildings of a former dairy farm and dating back to the 17th century, Uplands Hotel is set in twelve acres of farmland and yet only one mile from the centre of St Helier. The bedrooms are modern, spacious and comfortable, some overlooking the swimming pool, some with country views. Twelve self catering cottages are available. Plenty of parking and spacious public areas add to the attraction.
ROOMS: 43 en suite (3 fmly) s £26-£39; d £52-£78 (incl. bkfst) * **FACILITIES:** STV Outdoor swimming (H) Xmas **PARKING:** 44 **NOTES:** No dogs (ex guide dogs) No children 3yrs No smoking in restaurant **CARDS:**

ST LAWRENCE

★★★ 68% Hotel Cristina

Mont Feland JE3 1JA
☎ 01534 758024 01534 758028
e-mail: cristina@dolanhotels.com
Dir: *turn off the A10 on to Mont Felard, hotel on the left*

In prime position above St Aubin's bay the Cristina has unrivalled views of the bay. Another advantage is the peace and quiet from the rural location, although only five minutes walk from the sea. Bedrooms all have bath and shower, most have super views and balconies. Two bars, dining room with panoramic views and heated pool are other attractions.
ROOMS: 62 en suite d £68-£96 (incl. bkfst) * **FACILITIES:** STV Outdoor swimming (H) entertainment **PARKING:** 80 **NOTES:** No dogs No children 4yrs No smoking in restaurant Closed Nov-Mar
CARDS:

See advert on page 651

S

Apollo Hotel

St. Saviour's Rd, St. Helier, Jersey, JE2 4GJ, Channel Islands
Telephone: (01534) 725441 Fax: (01534) 722120
www.huggler.com
Email: huggler@psilink.co.je

45' OUTDOOR HEATED POOL WITH 35' WATER CHUTE

Modern 3 Star Hotel with an Indoor Leisure Centre, built around a quiet courtyard in the middle of St. Helier.

85 rooms with bathroom en suite, colour TV with satellite link, direct dial telephone, tea and coffee making facilities, hair dryers and trouser press.

Indoor swimming pool, jacuzzi, saunas, sun beds, gymnasium and games room.

'The Coffee Grove' overlooking the Pool.

'Le Petit Jardin' for aperitifs and fine cuisine.
'Chaplins Bar'- our newest bar with VAT free drinks.

CENTRALLY HEATED THROUGHOUT
AMPLE CAR PARKING OPEN ALL YEAR

AA ★★★ A Huggler Hotel

Beaufort Hotel

St. Helier, Jersey, JE2 4UH, Channel Islands
Telephone: (01534) 732471 Fax: (01534) 720371
www.huggler.com

INDOOR SWIMMING POOL AND SPA

Modern 3 Star Hotel well situated for shopping, business or beach in St. Helier's centre. The Beaufort has been designed to offer every amenity for today's traveller. Brummels Bar for aperitifs. The Rib Room for fine cuisine. Ample car parking. New outdoor pool with waterfall.

All Bedrooms are equipped with:

- ★ FULL BATHROOM AND SHOWER
- ★ HAIRDRYER AND TROUSER PRESS
- ★ TEA AND COFFEE MAKING FACILITIES
- ★ 2 DIRECT DIAL TELEPHONES
- ★ COLOUR TELEVISION WITH SATELLITE CHANNELS
- ★ FULL LOUNGE ARMCHAIRS
- ★ WRITING DESK
- ★ MINI BAR

AA ★★★ A Huggler Hotel

S

ST LAWRENCE, continued

★★67% Hotel White Heather

Rue de Haut, Millbrook JE3 1JZ
☎ 01534 720978 Fax 01534 720968
Dir: *from A11 turn right at school, follow road, hotel on right*

Tucked away in a quiet residential area within walking distance of the beach, White Heather has many regular guests. Most bedrooms have balconies with sun beds, all are brightly decorated. Public areas are similarly comfortable and well presented.

ROOMS: 33 en suite (3 fmly) s £24.50-£38.50; d £42-£64 (incl. bkfst) * LB **FACILITIES:** STV Indoor swimming (H) **PARKING:** 11 **NOTES:** No dogs (ex guide dogs) No smoking in restaurant Closed Nov-Mar
CARDS:

ST PETER

★★★69% Mermaid

JE3 7BN
☎ 01534 741255 Fax 01534 745826
e-mail: huggler@psilink.co.je

Packed with leisure facilities and a caring team of staff are two reasons why guests like the Mermaid. Leisure includes, indoor and outdoor pools, putting green, driving range and tennis court. The hotel is close to the airport so is convenient to the business visitor. Almost every well equipped bedroom has its own furnished balcony overlooking the lake in the hotel grounds.

ROOMS: 68 en suite s £43-£64.75; d £72-£99.50 (incl. bkfst) * LB **FACILITIES:** STV Indoor swimming (H) Outdoor swimming (H) Tennis (hard) Sauna Solarium Gym Croquet lawn Putting green Jacuzzi/spa Xmas **CONF:** Thtr 100 Class 60 Board 50 Del £92 * **PARKING:** 250 **NOTES:** No dogs (ex guide dogs) **CARDS:**

See advert on opposite page

ST SAVIOUR

Premier Collection

★★★★ Longueville Manor

JE2 7WF
☎ 01534 725501 Fax 01534 731613
e-mail: longman@itl.net
Dir: *take A3 E from St Helier towards Gorey. Hotel 1m on left hand side*

RELAIS & CHATEAUX.

Dating back in part to the 13th century, Longueville Manor is set in 17 acres of well-kept grounds that include many fine specimen trees along with a lake, swimming pool and tennis court. The various day rooms give guests an ideal excuse to enjoy a sumptuous afternoon tea or quiet hour with a book, comfort and style being paramount. Antique-furnished bedrooms are individually decorated in great style with ornaments and fresh flowers providing the personal touch along with fine embroidered bed linen and all sorts of cosseting extras. The twin dining rooms, one with ancient, heavily carved oak panelling, are appointed to the highest standard and provide an appropriate setting for some fine cooking. Good use is made of produce from the hotel's extensive kitchen garden in the sophisticated dishes to be found on the well balanced menus.

ROOMS: 32 en suite s £150-£195; d £180-£270 (incl. bkfst) * LB **FACILITIES:** STV Outdoor swimming (H) Tennis (hard) Croquet lawn Xmas **CONF:** Thtr 40 Class 30 Board 30 Del from £190 * **SERVICES:** Lift **PARKING:** 40 **CARDS:**

TRINITY

★★★68% Highfield Country

Route d'Ebenezer JE3 5DT
☎ 01534 862194 Fax 01534 865342
e-mail: highfield@jersey.net.je

Highfield is situated in the north east of the island, which is favoured for its walks. Bedrooms are spacious and some have kitchenettes. Guests can relax in the conservatory and adjacent bar or the quiet lounge. The table d'hôte dinner menu offers good value for money.

ROOMS: 38 en suite (32 fmly) s £52.50; d £94 (incl. bkfst) * **FACILITIES:** Indoor swimming (H) Outdoor swimming Sauna Solarium Gym Pool table Petanque **SERVICES:** Lift **PARKING:** 41 **NOTES:** No dogs No smoking in restaurant Closed Nov-Mar
CARDS:

S

SARK

★★69% Dixcart
Dixcart Valley GY9 0SD
☎ 01481 832015 01481 832164
e-mail: dixcart@itl.net
Dir: *ten minutes S of village, following signed footpath*

Dixcart offers a friendly welcome with all the comforts of home. Log fires burn, even in summer, two cosy lounges offer seclusion and the gardens beckon on a sunny day. Two eating options are available, the restaurant or the bar. Bedrooms come in a variety of shapes and sizes.
ROOMS: 15 en suite (5 fmly) **FACILITIES:** Horse-drawn carriage tours available ch fac **CONF:** Thtr 60 Class 20 Board 10
CARDS:

S

Isle of Man

Directory of establishments in alphabetical order of location.

C

MAN, ISLE OF — Map 06

CASTLETOWN — Map 06 SC26

★★★68% Castletown Golf Links

Best Western

Fort Island IM9 1UA
☎ 01624 822201 📠 01624 824633
e-mail: fowlds@enterprise.net
Dir: *A1 south of airport, turn left then left again*
With the sea on three sides and adjoining a championship golf course, this hotel has much to offer those who look for traditional and friendly service in a relaxing environment. The accommodation is modern and well equipped; ground floor rooms, family bedded rooms and full suites are all available. Function and conference facilities, together with the hotel's proximity to the airport, make it a popular business venue.
ROOMS: 58 en suite (3 fmly) s £45-£85; d £80-£110 (incl. bkfst) * LB **FACILITIES:** STV Indoor swimming (H) Golf 18 Snooker Sauna Solarium Putting green Xmas **CONF:** Thtr 200 Class 50 Board 20 Del from £85 * **PARKING:** 200 **CARDS:**

DOUGLAS — Map 06 SC37

★★★★67% Mount Murray

Santon IM4 2HT
☎ 01624 661111 📠 01624 611116
e-mail: hotel@enterprise.net
Dir: *from Douglas head towards airport. Hotel is signposted on the road 4m from Douglas, just before Stanton*

This purpose built, modern hotel and country club offers a wide range of sporting and leisure facilities, and a health and beauty salon. The extensive and attractively appointed public areas give a choice of bars and eating options. The spacious bedrooms are well equipped and many enjoy fine views. There is a very large function suite.
ROOMS: 90 en suite (4 fmly) No smoking in 12 bedrooms s £49.50-£79; d £69.50-£99 (incl. bkfst) * LB **FACILITIES:** STV Indoor swimming (H) Golf 18 Tennis (hard) Squash Snooker Sauna Solarium Gym Putting green Bowling green Driving range Sports hall Xmas **CONF:** Thtr 300 Class 260 Board 100 Del from £75 * **SERVICES:** Lift **PARKING:** 400 **CARDS:**

★★★★67% Sefton

Harris Promenade IM1 2RW
☎ 01624 645500 📠 01624 676004
e-mail: info@seftonhotel.co.im
Dir: *500yds from the Ferry Dock on Douglas promenade*
This large Victorian hotel is centrally situated and dominates the promenade area. Many bedrooms have balconies overlooking the internal courtyard and water garden. The public areas offer a choice of comfortable lounges and bars as well as a range of eating options.
ROOMS: 104 en suite No smoking in 22 bedrooms s £67-£79; d £84-£96 (incl. bkfst) * **FACILITIES:** STV Indoor swimming (H) Sauna Solarium Gym Jacuzzi/spa Cycle hire **CONF:** Thtr 180 Class 40 Board 20 Del from £110 * **SERVICES:** Lift **PARKING:** 40 **NOTES:** No dogs (ex guide dogs) RS 26 Dec-14 Jan **CARDS:**

★★★68% *Ascot Hotel*

7/8 Empire Ter IM2 4LE
☎ 01624 675081 📠 01624 661512
e-mail: ascot@mc6.net
This friendly, family-run hotel is conveniently situated close to the sea front, shops and theatre. It provides soundly maintained, modern-furnished accommodation.
ROOMS: 40 en suite (4 fmly) **FACILITIES:** STV **SERVICES:** Lift **NOTES:** No dogs **CARDS:**

★★★68% Welbeck Hotel

13/15 Mona Dr IM2 4LF
☎ 01624 675663 📠 01624 661545
e-mail: welbeck@isle-of-man.com
Dir: *at the crossroads of Mona & Empress Drive off Central Promenade*
Welbeck Hotel offers its guests a friendly welcome and a choice of attractive accommodation, from well equipped bedrooms to six newly-constructed luxury apartments, each with its own lounge and small kitchen. The hotel is family-run and located within easy reach of the sea front.
ROOMS: 27 en suite (7 fmly) s £44-£60; d £70-£85 (incl. bkfst) * **FACILITIES:** STV **CONF:** Thtr 60 Class 36 Board 30 **SERVICES:** Lift **NOTES:** No dogs (ex guide dogs) **CARDS:**

★★★67% *Empress*

BROOK HOTELS

Central Promenade IM2 4RA
☎ 01624 661155 📠 01624 673554
A large Victorian hotel on the central promenade, overlooking Douglas Bay. Well equipped, modern bedrooms include suites and rooms with sea views. A pianist entertains in the lounge bar most evenings, and there is a lounge, a sun lounge and a brasserie-style restaurant.
ROOMS: 102 en suite No smoking in 6 bedrooms **FACILITIES:** STV Indoor swimming (H) Sauna Solarium Gym Jacuzzi/spa entertainment **CONF:** Thtr 200 Class 150 Board 50 **SERVICES:** Lift **NOTES:** No dogs (ex guide dogs) **CARDS:**

See advert on opposite page

★★67% Sea View
13/15 Empress Dr IM2 4LQ
☎ 01624 674090 & 670845 🖷 01624 670846
e-mail: enquiries@seaview.co.im
This friendly, family owned and personally run hotel is conveniently situated just off the promenade. It provides well equipped accommodation suitable for business travellers and holidaymakers. Some family rooms are available.
ROOMS: 20 en suite s £24-£27; d £48 (incl. bkfst) * **FACILITIES:** Pool table **NOTES:** No dogs **CARDS:**

PEEL

Map 06 SC28

★★69% Ballacallin House
Dalby Village IM5 3BT
☎ 01624 841100 🖷 01624 845055
e-mail: ballacallin@advsys.co.uk

MINOTEL Great Britain

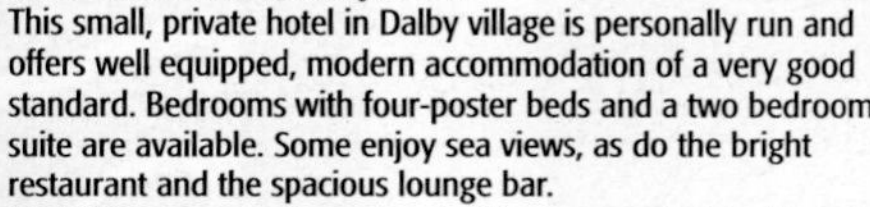

This small, private hotel in Dalby village is personally run and offers well equipped, modern accommodation of a very good standard. Bedrooms with four-poster beds and a two bedroom suite are available. Some enjoy sea views, as do the bright restaurant and the spacious lounge bar.
ROOMS: 10 en suite No smoking in all bedrooms s fr £45; d £65-£75 (incl. bkfst) * **PARKING:** 70

PORT ERIN

Map 06 SC16

★★★67% Cherry Orchard
Bridson St IM9 6AN
☎ 01624 833811 🖷 01624 833583
e-mail: enquiries@cherry-orchard.com
Dir: *from Seaport/Airport take main road south past Castletown to Port Erin*
The comfortable bedrooms at this modern hotel are well equipped and attractively furnished, with a room available for less able guests. Self-catering apartments are located within the same complex, allowing visitors to use the public areas, which include a well appointed restaurant, cosy lounge bar and leisure centre; there is also a choice of function rooms.
ROOMS: 32 en suite (12 fmly) s £50-£54; d £70-£78 (incl. bkfst) * LB **FACILITIES:** STV Indoor swimming (H) Sauna Solarium Gym Pool table Croquet lawn Jacuzzi/spa Games room ch fac Xmas **CONF:** Thtr 200 Class 120 Board 70 Del from £70 * **SERVICES:** Lift **PARKING:** 80 **NOTES:** No dogs (ex guide dogs) No smoking in restaurant **CARDS:**

Late for dinner? Quality Standards star rating means that last orders for dinner should be no earlier than:
★ 6.30pm ★★ 7.00pm ★★★ 8.00pm
★★★★ 9.00pm ★★★★★ 10.00pm

P

Hotel of the Year, Scotland

The Macdonald Holyrood Hotel, Edinburgh

ABERDEEN, Aberdeen City Map 15 NJ90
see also Aberdeen Airport

★★★★75% The Marcliffe at Pitfodels

North Deeside Rd AB15 9YA
☎ 01224 861000 📠 01224 868860
e-mail: enquiries@marcliffe.com
Dir: *turn off A90 onto A93 signposted Braemar. 1m on right after turn off at traffic lights*

This hotel stands in eight acres of landscaped grounds in the west end. Well cooked local produce is offered in the informal atmosphere of the conservatory restaurant while more formal dining is available in the elegant Invery Room. There is a range of bedrooms, all of which are decorated to a high standard and furnished in the elegant character of the house.
ROOMS: 42 en suite (4 fmly) No smoking in 10 bedrooms s £115-£175; d £145-£195 (incl. bkfst) * LB **FACILITIES:** STV Snooker Croquet lawn Putting green Xmas **CONF:** Thtr 500 Class 300 Board 24 Del from £150 * **SERVICES:** Lift **PARKING:** 160 **NOTES:** Civ Wed 360
CARDS:

See advert on this page

★★★★73% ❀❀ Ardoe House

South Deeside Rd, Blairs AB12 5YP
☎ 01224 860600 📠 01224 861283
e-mail: info@ardoe.macdonald.hotels.co.uk
Dir: *4m W of city off B9077*

Set amid extensive grounds, this impressive mansion house offers comfortable, traditional bedrooms in the main house and smart, modern accommodation in the newer wing. Many original features of the house have been retained in the delightful drawing room and the choice of contrasting bars and restaurants. The Garden Room provides an appropriate setting for a fine dining experience.
ROOMS: 112 en suite (3 fmly) No smoking in 81 bedrooms s £70-£150; d £100-£170 * LB **FACILITIES:** STV Indoor swimming (H) Sauna Solarium Gym Croquet lawn Putting green Jacuzzi/spa Petanque Xmas **CONF:** Thtr 500 Class 250 Board 100 Del from £140 * **SERVICES:** Lift **PARKING:** 200 **NOTES:** No smoking in restaurant
CARDS:

★★★★67% Patio
Beach Boulevard AB24 5EF
☎ 01224 633339 📠 01224 638833
e-mail: patioab@globalnet.co.uk
Dir: *from the A90 follow signs for city centre, then for sea beach. On Beach Boulevard, turn left at traffic lights and hotel is on right*

Close to the seafront and within easy reach of central amenities, this purpose-built hotel appeals to visiting businessmen. The Premier Club rooms are tastefully appointed, while the original standard rooms retain a lighter airy feel. Public areas include an open plan lounge, continental style café/bar, and a choice of restaurants.
ROOMS: 124 en suite (8 fmly) No smoking in 58 bedrooms d £117-£137 * LB **FACILITIES:** STV Indoor swimming (H) Sauna Solarium Gym Jacuzzi/spa Steam room, Treatment Room **CONF:** Thtr 150 Class 80 Board 50 **SERVICES:** Lift **PARKING:** 196
CARDS:

ABERDEEN, continued

★★★★65% **Copthorne Aberdeen**

COPTHORNE

122 Huntly St AB10 1SU
☎ 01224 630404 🖷 01224 640573
e-mail: reservations.aberdeen@mill-cop.com
Dir: *W of city centre, off Union Street, up Rose Street, hotel quarter of a mile on right on corner with Huntly Street*
The smart bedrooms are comfortably modern in style and thoughtfully equipped. Guests will appreciate the added enhancement provided in the Connoisseur rooms. Mac's bar offers a relaxed atmosphere where the guest can enjoy a refreshment or dine informally. Adjacent, the tastefully appointed Poachers Restaurant offers a more formal dining experience.
ROOMS: 89 en suite (15 fmly) No smoking in 37 bedrooms d £50-£145 * LB **FACILITIES:** STV entertainment **CONF:** Thtr 220 Class 100 Board 80 Del from £130 * **SERVICES:** Lift **PARKING:** 20 **NOTES:** Civ Wed 80
CARDS:

★★★74% **Simpsons**

59 Queens Rd AB15 4YP
☎ 01224 327777 🖷 01224 327700
e-mail: address@simpsonshotel.com
Dir: *turn off ring road (A90) at Earls Court rbt & drive down Queens Road. Hotel 700yds on left*
Two granite town houses have been linked to create this exciting hotel. One part contains smart modern bedrooms with warm Mediterranean colour schemes. The other house contains the lively split-level bar and brasserie where Moroccan columns support a colonnade of arches, and competently prepared modern dishes are served from the innovative menus.
ROOMS: 37 en suite (8 fmly) No smoking in all bedrooms s £90-£145; d £125-£145 (incl. bkfst) * **FACILITIES:** STV Complimentary use of Health Club **CONF:** Thtr 25 Class 12 Board 20 **SERVICES:** Lift air con **PARKING:** 102 **NOTES:** Closed 1 Jan Civ Wed 25
CARDS:

★★★73% **Atholl**

54 Kings Gate AB15 4YN
☎ 01224 323505 🖷 01224 321555
e-mail: info@atholl-aberdeen.co.uk
Dir: *in West End 400yds from Anderson Drive, the main ring road*
This popular, suburban business hotel is within easy reach of central amenities and the ring route. The smart bedrooms with pleasing colour schemes are comfortably modern in style. Public areas include a foyer lounge, well stocked bar and restaurant which offers competitively priced dishes from the carte.
ROOMS: 35 en suite (1 fmly) No smoking in all bedrooms s £71-£81; d £89 (incl. bkfst) * LB **FACILITIES:** STV **CONF:** Thtr 60 Class 25 Board 25 **PARKING:** 60 **NOTES:** No dogs (ex guide dogs)
CARDS:

See advert on opposite page

★★★70% **Queens Hotel**

51-53 Queens Rd AB15 4YP
☎ 01224 209999 🖷 01224 209009
e-mail: enquires@vagabond-hotels.com
This comfortable business hotel is also a popular venue for local functions. A programme of bedroom enhancement has recently been completed to provide every modern comfort and amenity in both the executive and standard accommodation. Nicely presented public areas include a bright foyer lounge, a spacious and well stocked bar, and a smart restaurant.
ROOMS: 27 en suite (3 fmly) No smoking in 4 bedrooms s £65-£75; d £75-£85 (incl. bkfst) * **FACILITIES:** STV **CONF:** Thtr 400 Class 150 Board 60 **PARKING:** 80 **NOTES:** No dogs (ex guide dogs) No smoking in restaurant Closed 25-26 Dec & 1-2 Jan **CARDS:**

★★★68% **Westhill**

Best Western

Westhill AB32 6TT
☎ 01224 740388 🖷 01224 744354
e-mail: info@westhillhotel.co.uk
Dir: *follow A944 West of the city towards Alford, Westhill is 6m out of centre on the right*
The city centre and airport are within a 15 minute drive from this comfortable modern business hotel in the Garden suburb of Westhill. The nicely presented public areas include a choice of three contrasting bars, a split-level restaurant, banqueting facilities, and a smart new fitness centre. Bedrooms are comfortably modern in appointment and offer a good range of amenities.
ROOMS: 38 en suite (2 fmly) No smoking in 8 bedrooms s £40-£65; d £54-£86 (incl. bkfst) * LB **FACILITIES:** STV Sauna Solarium Gym Pool table entertainment Xmas **CONF:** Thtr 300 Class 200 Board 200 Del from £70 * **SERVICES:** Lift **PARKING:** 250 **NOTES:** Civ Wed 150
CARDS:

★★★67% **The Craighaar**

Waterton Rd, Bankhead AB21 9HS
☎ 01224 712275 🖷 01224 716362
e-mail: info@craighaar.co.uk
Dir: *NW near the airport off A947*
Situated in a residential area convenient for the airport this smart modern hotel has a welcoming atmosphere. Bedrooms range from comfortable gallery suites and executive rooms, to the smaller standard rooms. Public areas include a restaurant, a popular bar, and various sitting areas.
ROOMS: 55 en suite (2 fmly) No smoking in 13 bedrooms s £49-£109; d £59-£119 (incl. bkfst) * LB **FACILITIES:** STV **CONF:** Thtr 90 Class 35 Board 30 Del from £110 * **PARKING:** 80 **NOTES:** No smoking in restaurant Closed 26 Dec & 1-2 Jan **CARDS:**

★★★67% **Norwood Hall**

Garthdee Rd, Cults AB15 9FX
☎ 01224 868951 🖷 01224 869868
e-mail: info@norwood-hall.co.uk
Dir: *off the A90, at 1st rdbt cross Bridge of Dee and turn left at the rdbt onto Garthdee Rd (B&Q and Sainsbury on the left) continue until hotel sign*

This extended Victorian mansion has particular appeal for business travellers and is a popular venue for conferences and functions. Many of the original features such as beautiful panelling, stained glass windows, ornate plaster work and fireplaces and gold leaf wall coverings have been retained in the day rooms. The refined restaurant offers a fine dining experience. The larger bedrooms with antique furnishings are in the main house, and those in the newer wing are comfortably modern. Staff are friendly and willing to please.
ROOMS: 21 en suite (3 fmly) No smoking in 8 bedrooms s £89-£109; d £129-£149 (incl. bkfst) * LB **FACILITIES:** Xmas **CONF:** Thtr 200 Class 80 Board 40 Del from £138 * **PARKING:** 80 **NOTES:** No dogs (ex guide dogs) No smoking in restaurant **CARDS:**

★★★66% Palm Court
81 Seafield Rd AB15 7YU
☎ 01224 310351 🖷 01224 312707
e-mail: info@palmcourt.co.uk.
Dir: *take A92 to the Seafield rdbt, drive up Seafield Rd and Hotel is on left hand side*

Situated with convenient access to the ring road and central amenities, this smart modern hotel has particular appeal for the visiting businessman. Bedrooms are comfortably modern and include a choice of executive and standard rooms. Public areas centre around the open-plan conservatory bar and brasserie restaurant.

ROOMS: 24 en suite (1 fmly) No smoking in 9 bedrooms s £79-£89; d £89-£99 (incl. bkfst) * LB **FACILITIES:** STV **CONF:** Thtr 110 Class 80 Board 80 Del £110 * **PARKING:** 65 **NOTES:** No smoking in restaurant Closed 26 Dec & 1-2 Jan Civ Wed 110 **CARDS:**

★★★65% *Grampian*
Stirling St AB11 6JU
☎ 01224 589101 🖷 01224 574288

This impressive Victorian hotel, reputed to be the oldest hotel in Aberdeen, is located close to the railway station and central amenities. Bedrooms, with pleasing colour schemes, have been comfortably refurbished in the modern style. Public areas include a library style lounge, well stocked bar, and a popular brasserie restaurant.

ROOMS: 108 en suite (3 fmly) **SERVICES:** Lift **CARDS:**

★★★65% Maryculter House Hotel
South Deeside Rd, Maryculter AB12 5GB
☎ 01224 732124 🖷 01224 733510
e-mail: maryculter.house.hotel@dial.pipex.com
Dir: *turn off A90 on S side of Aberdeen, onto B9077. Hotel located 8m along on right hand side, 0.5m beyond Templars Park*

This popular hotel is set amid five acres of woodland and landscaped gardens on the banks of the River Dee. The cocktail bar with its vaulted ceiling is particularly impressive and contrasts with the more relaxed atmosphere of the Poachers bar which serves light meals. Fine dining and Scottish specialities are available in the tasteful Priory Restaurant. Bedrooms are generally spacious and are well equipped.

ROOMS: 23 en suite (1 fmly) No smoking in 17 bedrooms s fr £85; d fr £110 (incl. bkfst) * LB **FACILITIES:** STV Fishing Clay pigeon shooting Xmas **CONF:** Thtr 250 Class 120 Board 40 Del from £110 * **PARKING:** 150 **NOTES:** No smoking in restaurant Civ Wed 120 **CARDS:**

See advert on this page

Early start? Hotels at all star levels should provide in-room alarm clocks and/or alarm calls.

ABERDEEN, continued

A

★★★64% *Posthouse Aberdeen*

Claymore Dr, Bridge of Don AB23 8BL

Posthouse

☎ 0870 400 9046 ▤ 01224 823923

Dir: *follow signs for Peterhead and Aberdeen Exhibition Conference Centre hotel is adjacent to AECC*

Situated on the north side of the city, this purpose-built modern hotel is popular with all types of guest. Bedrooms, with attractive colour schemes, are comfortably modern in style and offer a good range of amenities. Public areas are of the open-plan style, and contained within the bright foyer area.

ROOMS: 123 en suite (23 fmly) No smoking in 49 bedrooms **FACILITIES:** ch fac **SERVICES:** Lift **PARKING:** 200 **CARDS:**

★★73% *Craiglynn Hotel*

36 Fonthill Rd AB11 6UJ

THE CIRCLE Selected Individual Hotels GREAT BRITAIN

☎ 01224 584050 ▤ 01224 212225

e-mail: craiglynn@compuserve.com

Dir: *from S (A90) cross River Dee via King George VI Bridge, then Gt. Southern Road to Whinhill and forward to Bon Accord Street & hotel car park*

This small hotel provides personal attention in a friendly and relaxed environment. A fine Victorian granite stone house, it lies in a residential area just south of the city centre. It offers a choice of lounges, where drinks are served (there is no bar). It is worth dining in to enjoy home-cooked dinners, chosen from a short selection and served at 7pm.

ROOMS: 9 rms (7 en suite) (1 fmly) No smoking in all bedrooms **PARKING:** 9 **NOTES:** No dogs No smoking in restaurant Closed 25-26 Dec **CARDS:**

★★68% Mariner

349 Great Western Rd AB10 6NW

☎ 01224 588901 ▤ 01224 571621

e-mail: enquiries@vagabond-hotels.com

Dir: *turn off Anderson Drive at Great Western Road. Hotel on right on the corner of Gray Street*

Within easy reach of central amenities, this comfortable hotel has a particular appeal for the visiting businessman. Public areas which have an interesting nautical theme, include a well stocked bar and the conservatory restaurant. Bedrooms with pleasing colour schemes are comfortably modern in style and equipped with a wide range of amenities.

ROOMS: 14 en suite 8 annexe en suite s £60-£70; d £85-£95 (incl. bkfst) * **FACILITIES:** STV Xmas **PARKING:** 48 **NOTES:** No dogs (ex guide dogs) **CARDS:**

★★66% Dunavon House

60 Victoria St, Dyce AB21 7EE

☎ 01224 722483 & 772496 ▤ 01224 772721

e-mail: info@dunavon-hotel.com

Dir: *from A96 follow A947 into Victoria St, Dyce. Hotel 500yds on right*

This Victorian villa is now a pleasant hotel with a relaxed atmosphere. Bedrooms are well appointed and there is a traditional lounge bar and restaurant, both offering a wide range of dishes with international appeal.

ROOMS: 17 en suite No smoking in 5 bedrooms s £55-£65; d £62-£65 (incl. bkfst) * LB **FACILITIES:** STV **PARKING:** 23 **NOTES:** No dogs (ex guide dogs) No smoking in restaurant Closed 25 Dec-4 Jan **CARDS:**

⌂ Premier Lodge (Aberdeen West)

North Anderson Dr AB15 6DW

PREMIER LODGE THE BEST. BEST ASSURED.

☎ 0870 700 1300 ▤ 0870 7001301

Premier Lodge offers modern, well equipped, en suite accommodation suitable for both business and leisure travellers. Meals can be taken at the adjacent popular restaurant and bar which is fully licensed. For further details, consult the Hotel Groups page.

ROOMS: 60 en suite d £42 *

⌂ *Travelodge*

9 Bridge St AB11 6JL

Travelodge

☎ 01224 584555 ▤ 01224 584587

This modern building offers accommodation in smart, spacious and well equipped bedrooms, all with en suite bathrooms. Refreshments may be taken at the nearby family restaurant. For further details and the Travelodge phone number, consult the Hotel Groups page.

ROOMS: 95 en suite

○ *Premier Lodge (Aberdeen City Centre)*

Invelair House, West North St

PREMIER LODGE THE BEST. BEST ASSURED.

☎ 0870 700 1304 ▤ 0870 700 1305

ABERDEEN AIRPORT, Aberdeen City — Map 15 NJ81

★★★★69% Aberdeen Marriott

Overton Circle, Dyce AB21 7AZ

Marriott HOTELS · RESORTS · SUITES

☎ 01224 770011 ▤ 01224 722347

Dir: *follow A96 to Bucksburn village, turn right at the rdbt onto the A947. After 2m you will see the hotel at the second rdbt*

This comfortable hotel is in the suburb of Dyce, just a short drive from the airport. Attractive public areas include a choice of bars, a comfortable foyer lounge, and a tastefully appointed split-level restaurant. Bedrooms, some of which are generously sized, offer comfortable modern appointments along with a good range of accessories.

ROOMS: 155 en suite (68 fmly) No smoking in 88 bedrooms d £105-£130 (incl. bkfst) * LB **FACILITIES:** STV Indoor swimming (H) Sauna Solarium Gym Jacuzzi/spa Xmas **CONF:** Thtr 400 Class 200 Board 60 Del from £120 * **SERVICES:** air con **PARKING:** 180 **NOTES:** No dogs (ex guide dogs) Civ Wed 320 **CARDS:**

ABERDOUR, Fife — Map 11 NT18

★★68% *Woodside*

High St KY3 0SW

☎ 01383 860328 ▤ 01383 860920

e-mail: reception@woodside-hotel.demon.co.uk

Dir: *E of Forth Road Bridge, across rbt into town, hotel on left after garage*

This long-established hotel can be recognised by its palms and in summer a colourful flower display. Smart public areas include a welcoming foyer lounge, a tastefully appointed restaurant and a lounge bar.

ROOMS: 20 en suite (1 fmly) **CONF:** Thtr 25 Class 40 Board 25 **PARKING:** 30 **CARDS:**

See advert on opposite page

A

★★62% The Aberdour Hotel

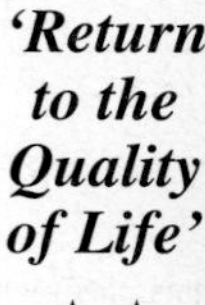

38 High St KY3 0SW
☎ 01383 860325 Fax 01383 860808
e-mail: reception@aberdourhotel.co.uk
Dir: *take exit 1 off M90 and travel E on A291 for 5m. Hotel is located in the centre of the village opposite the post office*
This small hotel offers a relaxed and welcoming atmosphere. Real ales feature in the cosy bar and good value home cooked fare is offered in the beamed dining room. Bedrooms, including those in the converted stable block, offer mixed styles of appointment together with a good range of amenities.
ROOMS: 16 en suite (4 fmly) s £41.50-£45; d £52-£60 (incl. bkfst) * LB
FACILITIES: STV **PARKING:** 8 **CARDS:**

ABERFELDY, Perth & Kinross — Map 14 NN84

★★72% Guinach House
"By The Birks", Urlar Rd PH15 2ET
☎ 01887 820251 Fax 01887 829607
Dir: *access off A826 Crieff road*
A charming small hotel on the southern edge of town. The elegant restaurant is an appropriate setting for the fine dining experience, and there is also a relaxing lounge where refreshments are served. Bedrooms are well presented in both modern and traditional styles.
ROOMS: 7 en suite No smoking in all bedrooms s £45.50; d £91 (incl. bkfst) * **PARKING:** 12 **NOTES:** No smoking in restaurant Closed 4 days Xmas **CARDS:**

Bad hair day? Hairdryers in all rooms three stars and above.

'Return to the Quality of Life'

★★

The Udny Arms Hotel Newburgh

Main Street, Newburgh
Aberdeenshire AB41 6BL

This popular award-winning family-run hotel – only 20 minutes from the centre of Aberdeen, overlooking the Ythan Estuary – offers a perfect location for business people, golfers, fishermen and nature lovers alike. Telephone today and let one of our friendly staff help you with your enquiry.

For more information
Tel: 01358 789444 Fax: 01358 789012
Email: enquiry@udny·demon.co.uk
Website: www.udny·com

THE
WOODSIDE HOTEL
AA ★★

High Street · Aberdour · Fife

Award winning chef - superb food. Situated in the heart of an historic conservation village - a short distance from Edinburgh by train or car. Golf can be arranged on our spectacular seaside course, or enjoy glorious woodland and coastal walks. The Woodside has a unique bar taken from the steamship Orantes at the turn of the century.

Conveniently located for Edinburgh, Perth, Dunfermline and St Andrews.

Tel: 01383 860328 Fax: 01383 860920

AA ★★ 67%

BANCHORY

Situated on the A93, only 18 miles from central Aberdeen. Ideally suited for visiting the city and industrial estates, or touring the North East and Royal Deeside. Sixteen en-suite bedrooms, lounge and public bar, restaurant, function and conference suite.

For reservations contact:
THE BURNETT ARMS HOTEL, BANCHORY
ABERDEENSHIRE AB31 5TD
Tel: 01330 824944 Fax: 01330 825553
See gazetteer listing under Banchory

ABERFELDY, continued

★★70% The Weem
Weem PH15 2LD
☎ 01887 820381 🖹 01887 829720
e-mail: weem@compuserve.com
Dir: *1m NW B846*
There is a wonderfully relaxed and welcoming atmosphere at this historic roadside inn. Some of the bedrooms can be adapted for self catering use, while others are tastefully decorated and equipped with a good range of accessories. The homely public areas are full of character with natural stone walls and panelling. The 'den' is a cosy retreat and a range of interesting dishes are served in the Trencherman Restaurant and Bar.
ROOMS: 12 en suite (4 fmly) No smoking in 4 bedrooms s £29.50-£49.50; d £55-£85 (incl. bkfst) * LB **FACILITIES:** Shooting Fishing Golf (can be arranged) **CONF:** Thtr 60 Class 30 Board 30 **PARKING:** 20 **NOTES:** No smoking in restaurant RS Dec-Jan
CARDS:

ABERFOYLE, Stirling Map 11 NN50

★★★★65% Forest Hills
Kinlochard FK8 3TL
☎ 01877 387277 🖹 01877 387307
Dir: *3m W on B829*
Part of a resort complex, this is a pleasant and popular hotel. Bedrooms are comfortably furnished, and those to the front enjoy loch views. Dining takes place in the Garden restaurant or less formal Bonspiel, and there are lounges to relax in after dinner.
ROOMS: 56 en suite (16 fmly) No smoking in 26 bedrooms **FACILITIES:** Indoor swimming (H) Tennis (hard) Fishing Squash Riding Snooker Sauna Solarium Gym Pool table Putting green Jacuzzi/spa Bowls Curling entertainment ch fac **CONF:** Thtr 150 Class 60 Board 45 **PARKING:** 80 **CARDS:**

ABERLADY, East Lothian Map 12 NT47

★★66% Kilspindie House
Main St EH32 0RE
☎ 01875 870682 🖹 01875 870504
e-mail: khh@stones.com
Dir: *on A198 - centre of village on main street, from Edinburgh take A1 S then A198 signed to North Berwick, from S A1 then A6137*
This long-established family-run hotel lies close to some excellent golf courses and is within thirty minutes drive of Edinburgh. Staff are friendly and attentive and the atmosphere relaxed. The bright, cheerful bedrooms are well equipped.
ROOMS: 26 en suite s £40-£44; d £30-£78 (incl. bkfst) * LB **FACILITIES:** Xmas **CONF:** Thtr 60 Class 40 Board 8 Del from £60 * **PARKING:** 30 **NOTES:** No smoking in restaurant
CARDS:

ABERLOUR See Archiestown

ABINGTON, South Lanarkshire Map 11 NS92

⇧ Days Inn
ML12 6RE
☎ 01864 502782 🖹 01864 502759
Dir: *off junct 13 of M74, accessible from northbound and southbound carriageways*
Fully refurbished, Days Inn offers well equipped, brightly appointed, modern accommodation with smart en suite bathrooms. There is a fully staffed reception; continental breakfast is available and other refreshments may be taken at the nearby family restaurant.
ROOMS: 56 en suite d fr £45 *

ACHNASHEEN, Highland Map 14 NH15

★★★65% Ledgowan Lodge
IV22 2EJ
☎ 01445 720252 🖹 01445 720240
e-mail: garymillard@ledgowan.freeserve.co.uk
Dir: *0.25m on A890 to Kyle of Lochalsh - from Achnasheen*
This highland hotel is well situated for exploring Western Ross. Relaxing public areas include an interesting aquarium and collection of whisky artefacts in the hall, as well as a lounge, a cosy bar and coffee shop serving meals and snacks all day. The attractive dining room offers an extensive carte. Bedrooms are comfortable and traditional.
ROOMS: 11 en suite (2 fmly) s £25-£29; d £50-£58 * **FACILITIES:** STV **PARKING:** 25 **NOTES:** No dogs No smoking in restaurant Closed Jan-Mar & Nov-Dec RS Apr & Oct **CARDS:**

ANNAN, Dumfries & Galloway Map 11 NY16

★★62% Queensberry Arms
47 High St DG12 6AD
☎ 01461 202024 🖹 01461 205998
Dir: *located on left of main street, 1.5m from A75*
Formerly a coaching inn, the Queensberry Arms with its distinctive black and white facade, sits conveniently in the town centre. A variety of lounges are available hosting popular morning coffees and afternoon teas. The attractive upstairs restaurant, which has a nautical theme, serves a good range of popular dishes.
ROOMS: 24 en suite (3 fmly) s £54.50; d £64.50 (incl. bkfst) * LB **FACILITIES:** STV Tennis (hard & grass) Xmas **CONF:** Thtr 70 Class 40 Board 40 Del from £45 * **PARKING:** 30 **NOTES:** Civ Wed 70
CARDS:

ANSTRUTHER, Fife Map 12 NO50

★★64% Smugglers Inn
High St East KY10 3DQ
☎ 01333 310506 🖹 01333 312706
e-mail: smugglers@norscot.idps.co.uk
Dir: *on High Street East A719 after bridge*
This welcoming inn in the centre of the village is said to be steeped in Jacobean history. In the bedrooms, attractive co-ordinated fabrics have been used to good effect to enhance the pretty colour schemes and comfortable furnishings. There is a choice of contrasting bars, a cosy lounge, and a beamed dining room.
ROOMS: 9 en suite (1 fmly) s £32.50-£36; d £55-£62 (incl. bkfst) * LB **FACILITIES:** Pool table **PARKING:** 14 **NOTES:** No dogs (ex guide dogs) No smoking in restaurant **CARDS:**

ARBROATH, Angus Map 12 NO64

★★★★64% The Letham Grange Mansion House Hotel
Colliston DD11 4RL
☎ 01241 890373 🖹 01241 890725
e-mail: lethamgrange@sol.co.uk
Dir: *leave A92 onto A933 to Brechin, Letham Grange signposted at village of Colliston*
Situated in the heart of the Angus countryside, this impressive Victorian mansion house boasts two challenging golf courses, a curling rink and attractive, comfortable bedrooms. The inviting

continued

public areas feature ornate ceilings, beautiful panelling and fine paintings, and include a relaxing drawing room, bar, conservatory and elegant dining room serving Scottish and international dishes.
ROOMS: 19 en suite 22 annexe en suite (1 fmly) No smoking in 2 bedrooms s fr £100; d fr £145 (incl. bkfst) * LB **FACILITIES:** STV Golf 36 Croquet lawn Putting green Curling rink Xmas **CONF:** Thtr 700 Class 300 Board 20 Del from £125 * **PARKING:** 150 **NOTES:** No smoking in restaurant **CARDS:**

★★64% Hotel Seaforth

Dundee Rd DD11 1QF
☎ 01241 872232 01241 877473
Dir: *on southern outskirts, on A92*

This long established commercial hotel is situated on the west side of town. The well equipped bedrooms are comfortable. Public areas include a restaurant, a well stocked bar, as well as leisure and function facilities.
ROOMS: 19 en suite (4 fmly) s £45-£65; d £58-£85 (incl. bkfst) * LB **FACILITIES:** Indoor swimming (H) Snooker Sauna Gym Jacuzzi/spa Steam room Xmas **CONF:** Thtr 120 Class 60 Board 40 Del from £65 * **PARKING:** 60 **NOTES:** No smoking in restaurant
CARDS:

ARCHIESTOWN, Moray — Map 15 NJ24

★★75% Archiestown

AB38 7QL
☎ 01340 810218 01340 810239
Dir: *on B9102, 5m SW of Craigellachie*
As ever, anglers have a particular 'soft spot' for this welcoming hotel, but the touring holidaymaker is equally at home. The well presented public areas include a choice of inviting and relaxing lounges, and two dining rooms. The pleasantly decorated bedrooms are comfortably furnished.
ROOMS: 8 rms (7 en suite) s £37.50-£45; d £90 (incl. bkfst) * **PARKING:** 20 **NOTES:** Closed Oct-9 Feb **CARDS:**

ARDBEG See Bute, Isle of

ARDELVE, Highland — Map 14 NG82

★68% Loch Duich

IV40 8DY
☎ 01599 555213 01599 555214
Dir: *from Inverness A82 towards Fort William, turn right at Invermoriston on to A887 then A87 towards Kyle of Lochalsh and Ardelve*
This welcoming tourist hotel is a former drovers inn beside the Road to the Isles. Many bedrooms have been individually refurbished. Relaxing public areas include a choice of lounges and a cosy dining room, serving the same good food as available in the popular Duich Pub.
ROOMS: 11 rms (9 en suite) (1 fmly) s £31.50; d £63 (incl. bkfst) * LB **FACILITIES:** Fishing Shooting Sailing **CONF:** Board 40 Del from £39.50 * **PARKING:** 41 **NOTES:** No smoking in restaurant Closed 4 Jan-1 Mar & 19-28 Dec RS Nov-18 Dec Civ Wed 40 **CARDS:**

ARDUAINE, Argyll & Bute — Map 10 NM71

★★★76% Loch Melfort

Scotland's Hotels of Distinction

PA34 4XG
☎ 01852 200233 01852 200214
e-mail: lmhotel@aol.com
Dir: *on A816, midway between Oban and Lochgilphead*

A delightful, welcoming hotel which overlooks Loch Asknish Bay mid way between Oban and Lochgilphead. There is a cosy library lounge, a cocktail bar and the popular Skerry Bistro. The elegant restaurant overlooking the loch offers a fine dining experience, where the emphasis remains on delicious fresh seafood. Most of the comfortable bedrooms enjoy splendid sea views, with those in the adjacent cedar wing having either a patio or balcony.
ROOMS: 7 en suite 20 annexe en suite (2 fmly) s £40-£75; d £60-£110 (incl. bkfst) * LB **FACILITIES:** Xmas **CONF:** Thtr 50 Board 24 **PARKING:** 65 **NOTES:** No smoking in restaurant Closed 4 Jan-15 Feb
CARDS:

ARDVASAR See Skye, Isle of

Popped the question? Hotels with Civ Wed in their entry are licensed for civil wedding ceremonies. Maximum numbers for the ceremony only are shown, e.g. Civ Wed 50

ARISAIG, Highland

Map 13 NM68

Premier Collection

★★★ Arisaig House

Beasdale PH39 4NR

☎ 01687 450622 01687 450626

e-mail: ArisaiGHse@aol.com

Dir: *3m E A830*

This splendid Scottish mansion stands peacefully amid extensive woodland and carefully tended gardens with beautiful azaleas and rhododendrons. Bedrooms include some Prime Rooms and many of the bathrooms are luxurious. Inviting day rooms include a choice of wonderfully relaxing sitting rooms, enhanced by fine furnishings, fresh floral displays, and on colder evenings welcoming open fires. The elegant panelled dining room provides an appropriate setting for creative cooking. The finest ingredients are used and natural flavours are allowed to shine through.

ROOMS: 12 en suite s fr £125; d £160-£290 (incl. bkfst) * LB **FACILITIES:** Snooker Croquet lawn **PARKING:** 16 **NOTES:** No dogs (ex guide dogs) No children 10yrs No smoking in restaurant Closed Nov-Mar Civ Wed 30 **CARDS:**

★★68% Arisaig

PH39 4NH

☎ 01687 450210 01687 450310

e-mail: arisaighotel@dial.pipex.com

Dir: *on A830 opposite the harbour*

This roadside hotel occupies an enviable position on the shores of Loch Nan Ceal with fine sea views towards the islands of Rhum, Eigg, Muck and Skye. The smartly appointed and thoughtfully equipped bedrooms are now all en suite and some enjoy the marvellous views across the bay. The comfortable public areas include a choice of lounges and bars, and a children's playroom. The atmosphere is very friendly and relaxed.

ROOMS: 13 en suite (2 fmly) s £32-£40; d £64-£80 (incl. bkfst) * LB **FACILITIES:** Pool table ch fac **PARKING:** 30 **NOTES:** No smoking in restaurant Closed 24-26 Dec **CARDS:**

Late for dinner? Quality Standards star rating means that last orders for dinner should be no earlier than:
★ 6.30pm ★★ 7.00pm ★★★ 8.00pm
★★★★ 9.00pm ★★★★★ 10.00pm

ARRAN, ISLE OF, North Ayrshire

Map 10

BRODICK

Map 10 NS03

★★★75% Auchrannie Country House

KA27 8BZ

☎ 01770 302234 01770 302812

e-mail: info@auchrannie.co.uk

Dir: *turn right from Brodick Ferry terminal, through Brodick village, turn second left after Brodick Golf Course clubhouse, 300yds to Hotel*

Genuine hospitality and extensive leisure facilities are all part of the appeal at this Victorian mansion, which stands in six acres of landscaped grounds. Bedrooms are well equipped, those in the newer wing being particularly spacious. There is a choice of relaxing lounges, a bistro and the Garden Restaurant with its conservatory extension, where the daily changing fixed-price menu has earned a Rosette award for quality cooking.

ROOMS: 28 en suite (3 fmly) s £44-£55; d £68-£90 (incl. bkfst) * LB **FACILITIES:** STV Indoor swimming (H) Snooker Sauna Solarium Gym Jacuzzi/spa Hair salon Aromatherapy Shiatsu Xmas **CONF:** Thtr 120 Board 30 **PARKING:** 50 **NOTES:** No dogs (ex guide dogs) No smoking in restaurant **CARDS:**

Premier Collection

★★ Kilmichael Country House

Glen Cloy KA27 8BY

☎ 01770 302219 01770 302068

Dir: *from Brodick Ferry Terminal follow northbound (Lochranza) road for 1m. At golf course turn left inland between sports field & church, follow signs*

Believed to be the oldest house on the island, Kilmichael is a friendly haven of elegance and luxury. The house nestles in a peaceful glen with well tended gardens. Bedrooms are stylishly decorated, well equipped and furnished in traditional country house style; those in the converted barns being particularly elegant. Dinner in the smart restaurant is a treat and the recipes make excellent use of fresh, seasonal, local produce.

ROOMS: 5 en suite 3 annexe en suite No smoking in all bedrooms s £65; d £88-£150 (incl. bkfst) * LB **FACILITIES:** Jacuzzi/spa **PARKING:** 12 **NOTES:** No children 12yrs No smoking in restaurant Closed Nov-Feb (ex for prior bookings) **CARDS:**

Read all about it! Newspapers delivered to bedrooms in four and five star hotels.

AUCHENCAIRN, Dumfries & Galloway Map 11 NX75

★★★70% Balcary Bay

DG7 1QZ
☎ 01556 640217 & 640311 01556 640272
e-mail: reservations@balcary-bay-hotel.co.uk
Dir: *on coast 2m from village*

A comfortable 17th-century hotel with a fascinating history, standing in a delightful location overlooking Balcary Bay, with lawns running down to the water's edge. Many of the larger bedrooms have views over the bay whilst others have garden views; each room is individually designed and equipped with every modern facility. The dining room is much acclaimed and offers many local delicacies along with an impressive selection of wines.

ROOMS: 17 en suite (1 fmly) s £60; d £108-£120 (incl. bkfst) LB **PARKING:** 50 **NOTES:** No smoking in restaurant Closed Dec-Feb **CARDS:**

AUCHTERARDER, Perth & Kinross Map 11 NN91

Premier Collection

★★★★★ The Gleneagles Hotel

PH3 1NF
☎ 01764 662231 01764 662134
e-mail: resort.sales@gleneagles.com
Dir: *on A823*

With its wealth of sporting activities, including the famous golf courses, falconry, angling, shooting and cycling, as well as the equestrian centre and indoor leisure club, this renowned hotel has something to suit most sporting guests. Set in beautiful countryside, it also offers a peaceful retreat for visitors who want to relax and unwind. Restyled bedrooms provide a choice between traditional comfort and a more contemporary theme. Afternoon tea is a feature of the smart lounge. Among the choice of eating areas, the Strathearn restaurant is the fine dining option; service is professional and diners are entertained by a pianist.

ROOMS: 222 en suite No smoking in 118 bedrooms s £200; d £290-£410 (incl. bkfst) * LB **FACILITIES:** STV Indoor swimming (H) Golf 36 Tennis (hard & grass) Fishing Squash Riding Snooker Sauna Solarium Gym Pool table Croquet lawn Putting green Jacuzzi/spa Bowls Shooting Falconry Esquestrian Off-Road Driving ch fac Xmas **CONF:** Thtr 360 Class 240 Board 70 Del from £269 * **SERVICES:** Lift **PARKING:** 200 **NOTES:** Civ Wed **CARDS:**

Arriving late? Four and five star hotels have night porters to assist with your luggage; and 24hr room service.

★★★77% Auchterarder House

PH3 1DZ
☎ 01764 663646 01764 662939
e-mail: auchterarder@wrensgroup.com
Dir: *NW off B8062 1.2m from village*

This imposing manor house stands in 17 acres of wooded grounds and landscaped gardens. The Victorian interior is enhanced by oak panelling, ornate ceilings, and lovely fireplaces. Bedrooms range from well proportioned superior rooms with fine antique furnishings and luxurious bathrooms, to modern rooms in the Turret wing which are more compact. The restaurant offers prime Scottish produce cooked with flair and imagination.

ROOMS: 15 en suite (3 fmly) s £125-£275; d £195-£350 (incl. bkfst) * LB **FACILITIES:** STV Croquet lawn Putting green Xmas **CONF:** Thtr 50 Class 20 Board 25 Del from £120 * **PARKING:** 30 **NOTES:** No children 12yrs No smoking in restaurant RS Sat Civ Wed 70 **CARDS:**

See advert on this page

★★★75% Duchally House Hotel

PH3 1PN
☎ 01764 663071 01764 662464
Dir: *leave A9 at the A823 Gleneagles exit for hotel 2m SW off A823 Dunfermline road*

A major refurbishment programme has been completed at this welcoming Victorian mansion house. Bedrooms, some of which are generously proportioned, are sympathetic to the character of the house. Inviting public areas include a relaxing panelled lounge with open fire and a bar. The adjacent stylish restaurant provides an appropriate setting for the fine dining experience on offer.

continued

AUCHTERARDER, continued

Duchally House Hotel, Auchterarder

ROOMS: 13 en suite (3 fmly) s £65; d £85-£110 (incl. bkfst) * LB **FACILITIES:** STV Xmas **PARKING:** 30 **NOTES:** No dogs (ex guide dogs) No smoking in restaurant Civ Wed 40 **CARDS:**

★★77% ❀❀ Cairn Lodge

Orchil Rd PH3 1LX
☎ 01764 662634 & 662431 ▤ 01764 664866
e-mail: email@cairnlodge.co.uk
Dir: *from the A9 take A824 into Auchterarder then A823 signposted Crieff & Gleneagles in approx 200yds hotel on the Y junct*

This charming, small hotel stands in wooded, landscaped grounds on the edge of the village. Bedrooms are generously proportioned and beautifully appointed, two of which are suitable for disabled visitors. Public areas include a relaxing lounge, and a spacious bar which offers informal food. Formal meals are served in the elegant Capercaille Restaurant.

ROOMS: 11 en suite (6 fmly) No smoking in 4 bedrooms s £60-£110; d £110-£180 (incl. bkfst) * LB **FACILITIES:** Putting green Xmas **CONF:** Thtr 20 Class 20 Board 20 Del from £95 * **PARKING:** 40 **NOTES:** No dogs No smoking in restaurant **CARDS:**

AUCHTERHOUSE, Angus — Map 11 NO33

★★★77% ❀❀ Old Mansion House

DD3 0QN
☎ 01382 320366 ▤ 01382 320400
e-mail: oldmansionhouse@netscapeonline.co.uk
Dir: *take A923 off Kingsway ringroad, Dundee to Birkhill then B954 for 2m, hotel is on left*

This charming country house hotel is an impressive baronial mansion peacefully set in 12 acres of landscaped and wooded gardens. The house has historic connections with Sir William Wallace and Glamis Castle. Most of the delightful bedrooms are well proportioned and are comfortably traditional in style. All the expected amenities are provided along with thoughtful personal touches. Public areas include some splendid examples of beautiful ornate plaster ceilings and some wonderful fireplaces. The Library bar invites comfortable relaxation while the Courtyard Bistro offers a useful informal food option. The serious food is served in the grand dining room. Both fixed price and carte menus are available, the latter concentrating on Taste of Scotland specialities.

ROOMS: 5 en suite 2 annexe en suite (1 fmly) s £70-£85; d £95-£110 (incl. bkfst) * LB **FACILITIES:** Outdoor swimming (H) Tennis (grass) Squash Croquet lawn Clay pidgeon shooting Xmas **CONF:** Thtr 30 Class 30 Board 20 Del from £85 * **PARKING:** 50 **NOTES:** No smoking in restaurant **CARDS:**

AVIEMORE, Highland — Map 14 NH81

★★★66% Aviemore Highlands

Aviemore Mountain Resort PH22 1PJ
☎ 01479 810771 ▤ 01479 811473
e-mail: sales@aviehighlands.demon.co.uk
Dir: *off A9 signed Aviemore B9152, turn left opposite railway station around Ring road Hotel is 2nd on left*

From its position in the Aviemore centre, this modern hotel enjoys lovely views of the Cairngorms. Public areas are spread over two floors with an informal bar and lounge being located at ground level, while upstairs is where you will find the more formal bar and spacious restaurant. Bedrooms, with pleasing colour schemes, are comfortably modern in appointment.

ROOMS: 103 en suite (37 fmly) s fr £85; d fr £95 * LB **FACILITIES:** Pool table ch fac Xmas **CONF:** Thtr 140 Class 80 Board 60 Del from £75 * **SERVICES:** Lift **PARKING:** 140 **NOTES:** No smoking in restaurant **CARDS:**

★★★58% Freedom Inn

Aviemore Centre PH22 1PF
☎ 01479 810781 ▤ 01479 811167
e-mail: freedom.inn@avicentre.fsnet.co.uk
Dir: *from A9 follow directions to Aviemore, hotel is in the Leisure Centre*

PEEL HOTELS

Situated in the Aviemore Centre this purpose built hotel remains a popular base for visiting tour groups. Bedrooms feature small kitchens and come with mixed modern appointments and offer the expected amenities. Public areas include a spacious bar where the atmosphere is lively, and a large restaurant.

ROOMS: 94 en suite (85 fmly) No smoking in 6 bedrooms s fr £30; d fr £60 (incl. bkfst) * LB **FACILITIES:** entertainment Xmas **CONF:** Thtr 100 Class 60 Board 50 Del from £70 * **SERVICES:** Lift **PARKING:** 94 **CARDS:**

AYR, South Ayrshire — Map 10 NS32

★★★★67% ❀ Fairfield House

12 Fairfield Rd KA7 2AR
☎ 01292 267461 ▤ 01292 261456
e-mail: reservations@fairfieldhotel.co.uk
Dir: *from A77 head for Ayr South (A30). Follow signs for the town centre, down Miller Road and turn left then right into Fairfield Road*

This peaceful Victorian mansion has unrestricted views across the promenade towards the Firth of Clyde. Stylish and elegant public areas include a smart restaurant, and club style lounges. More informal dinner and drinks are available in the conservatory bar/brasserie. Bedrooms offer a choice of styles, from splendid spacious rooms furnished in period style to the attractive modern rooms in the new extension.

continued

ROOMS: 41 rms (39 en suite) 4 annexe en suite (3 fmly) No smoking in 7 bedrooms **FACILITIES:** STV Indoor swimming (H) Sauna Solarium Gym Jacuzzi/spa **CONF:** Thtr 150 Class 60 Board 60 Del from £120 * **SERVICES:** Lift **PARKING:** 52 **NOTES:** No smoking in restaurant Civ Wed 110 **CARDS:**

★★★70% Savoy Park

16 Racecourse Rd KA7 2UT
☎ 01292 266112 📠 01292 611488
e-mail: mail@savoypark.com
Dir: *from A77 follow Holmston Road(A70)for 2m, go through Parkhouse Street and turn left into Beresford Terrace, take first right onto Bellevue Road*

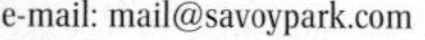

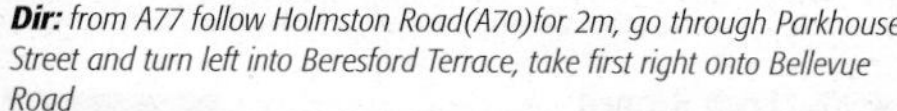

This is a well established hotel that still retains many of its traditional values. Public rooms feature impressive panelled walls, ornate ceilings and open fires. The restaurant is reminiscent of a Highland shooting lodge. Bedrooms and bathrooms are all contemporary in style with colourful decor and fabrics.
ROOMS: 15 en suite (3 fmly) No smoking in all bedrooms s £65-£75; d £80-£100 (incl. bkfst) * LB **FACILITIES:** Xmas **CONF:** Thtr 50 Class 40 Board 30 Del from £65 * **PARKING:** 60 **NOTES:** No smoking in restaurant **CARDS:**

See advert on this page

★★★58% Quality Hotel Ayr

Burns Statue Square KA7 3AT
☎ 01292 263268 📠 01292 262293
e-mail: admin@gb624.u-net.com
Dir: *A70 from South/A77 from North*
This Victorian railway hotel sits right by the station in the centre of town. Bedrooms are spacious, with high ceilings and large windows; all have modern amenities and the Premier Rooms are particularly well equipped.
ROOMS: 75 en suite (18 fmly) No smoking in 26 bedrooms s £71-£83; d £83-£96 * LB **FACILITIES:** STV Sauna Solarium Gym Jacuzzi/spa Xmas **CONF:** Thtr 250 Class 120 Board 100 Del £87 * **SERVICES:** Lift **PARKING:** 50 **CARDS:**

CHOICE HOTELS EUROPE

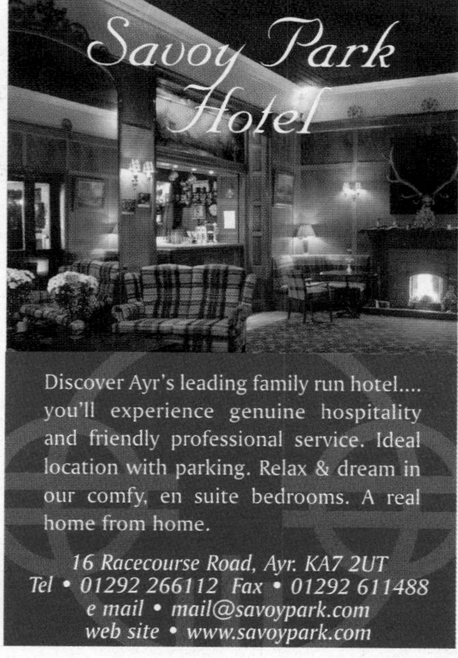

★★ Ladyburn

KA19 7SG
☎ 01655 740585 📠 01655 740580
e-mail: jhdh@ladyburn.freeserve.co.uk
(For full entry see Maybole)

★★71% *Grange*

37 Carrick Rd KA7 2RD
☎ 01292 265679 📠 01292 285061
Dir: *0.5m from rail station & city centre, turn off A77 at A713 into Ayr, straight through rdbt 0.25m to Chalmers Rd, at the end turn right hotel 100yds*
Located in a residential area, within walking distance of both the town centre and the seafront, this hotel offers friendly and attentive service. Bedrooms are individually styled, and public areas include an open plan lounge/bar and dining area. Well presented meals regularly feature local seafood.
ROOMS: 8 en suite (2 fmly) **CONF:** Thtr 100 Class 50 Board 24 **PARKING:** 25 **CARDS:**

★★66% Carrick Lodge

46 Carrick Rd KA7 2RE
☎ 01292 262846 📠 01292 611101
e-mail: ian@carricklodgehotel.co.uk
Dir: *from A77, take A79 until T-junct, then right, hotel on left*
This hotel, lying south of Ayr, has bright, cheerful bedrooms, including several that are suitable for families. The popular bar is divided into two areas, one attractively wood-panelled, and both are ideal for enjoying the freshly cooked meals. The more formal dining room has a carte menu and there is a separate suite for private functions.

continued

AYR, continued

ROOMS: 8 en suite (3 fmly) s £38-£45; d £50-£60 (incl. bkfst) * LB **FACILITIES:** Xmas **CONF:** Thtr 50 Class 50 Board 50 Del from £50 * **PARKING:** 25 **NOTES:** No dogs No smoking in restaurant **CARDS:**

BALLACHULISH, Highland — Map 14 NN05

★★★71% Ballachulish Hotel
PH49 4JY
☎ 01855 811606 📠 01855 821463
e-mail: reservations@freedomglen.co.uk
Dir: *on A828, Fort William-Oban road 3m N of Glencoe*

This long established Highland holiday hotel is situated in the shadow of the bridge and has a smart new bedroom wing where all rooms enjoy glorious views of Loch Linnhe. The public areas include a spacious and comfortable lounge, a supper room and a modern cocktail bar adjacent to the dramatic and attractive restaurant.

ROOMS: 54 en suite (4 fmly) s £64.50-£72; d £129-£170 (incl. bkfst & dinner) * LB **FACILITIES:** Pool table Complimentary Membership of Leisure Club at nearby Sister Hotel entertainment ch fac Xmas **CONF:** Thtr 100 Class 50 Board 30 Del from £75 * **PARKING:** 54 **NOTES:** No smoking in restaurant Closed 12-23 Dec & 9-23 Jan **CARDS:**

See advert on opposite page

BALLANTRAE, South Ayrshire — Map 10 NX08

○ Glenapp Castle
KA26 0NZ
☎ 01465 831212 📠 01465 831000
e-mail: castle@glenapp.demon.co.uk
ROOMS: 17 rms **NOTES:** Open

BALLATER, Aberdeenshire — Map 15 NO39

★★★74% ❀❀❀ Darroch Learg
Braemar Rd AB35 5UX
☎ 013397 55443 📠 013397 55252
e-mail: nigel@darroch-learg.demon.co.uk
Dir: *hotel situated on the A93, at western edge of Ballater*

This charming hotel stands in four acres of wooded grounds and enjoys a superb outlook. Public rooms are particularly comfortable and include an inviting drawing room and separate smoke room. The main focal point is the attractive conservatory restaurant where innovative modern Scottish cuisine is served. Some of the bedrooms have four-poster beds; all are comfortable and individual in style.

ROOMS: 13 en suite 5 annexe en suite No smoking in 4 bedrooms s £82-£90; d £164-£210 (incl. bkfst) LB **FACILITIES:** Xmas **CONF:** Thtr 25 Board 12 Del from £85 * **PARKING:** 25 **NOTES:** No smoking in restaurant Closed Xmas & Jan (ex New Year) **CARDS:**

Premier Collection

★★❀❀ Balgonie Country House
Scotland's Hotels of Distinction
Braemar Place AB35 5NQ
☎ 013397 55482 📠 013397 55482
Dir: *turn off A93 [Aberdeen - Perth] on western outskirts of village of Ballater, hotel is sign-posted*

This charming Edwardian style country house is a peaceful haven set in secluded gardens, with views of Glen Muick. A short walk from the village, the house is impeccably maintained and has a friendly atmosphere. Comfortable bedrooms come in two styles, period or more contemporary. There is a cosy bar with an adjoining lounge. Food is foremost at Balgonie, from the excellent breakfasts to the scrumptious afternoon teas and daily-changing four course dinners. Service is exemplary.

ROOMS: 9 en suite s £69-£75; d £118-£125 (incl. bkfst) * LB **FACILITIES:** Croquet lawn Xmas **PARKING:** 12 **NOTES:** No dogs (ex guide dogs) No smoking in restaurant Closed 6 Jan-Feb **CARDS:**

★★70% Loch Kinord
MINOTEL Great Britain
Ballater Rd, Dinnet AB34 5JY
☎ 013398 85229 📠 013398 87007
e-mail: info@lochkinord.com
Dir: *on A93, in the village of Dinnet*

A Victorian hotel, situated between Aboyne and Ballater, well located for leisure and sporting pursuits. Bedrooms are comfortable and well equipped. There is a cosy bar and a lounge where good meals are available. Carte dinners are served in the elegant, formal dining room.

ROOMS: 11 rms (9 en suite) (3 fmly) **FACILITIES:** Sauna Pool table Jacuzzi/spa ch fac **CONF:** Thtr 30 Class 20 Board 20 **PARKING:** 20 **NOTES:** No smoking in restaurant **CARDS:**

BALLOCH, West Dunbartonshire — Map 10 NS38

★★★★★72% ❀❀❀ Cameron House Hotel
De Vere Hotels
G83 8QZ
☎ 01389 755565 📠 01389 759522
e-mail: devere.cameron@airtime.co.uk
Dir: *from M8 (W) junct 30 for Erskine Bridge. Then A82 for Crainlarich. After 14m, at rdbt signed Luss straight on towards Luss, hotel on right*

This impressive mansion house, which has been sympathetically extended, enjoys a glorious setting beside the picturesque shore of Loch Lomond. Reception rooms are spacious and comfortable with a good choice of bar and food options available. More serious food is served in the elegant and formal Georgian Room. Bedrooms range from luxury suites to the standard rooms, all tasteful in appointment and comfortably furnished.

ROOMS: 96 en suite (9 fmly) No smoking in all bedrooms s £160-£170; d £225-£235 (incl. bkfst) * LB **FACILITIES:** STV Indoor swimming (H) Golf 9 Tennis (hard) Fishing Squash Snooker Sauna Solarium Gym Pool table Croquet lawn Jacuzzi/spa Quad Bikes Watersports Laser shooting ch fac Xmas **CONF:** Thtr 300 Class 80 Board 80 Del from £170 * **SERVICES:** Lift **PARKING:** 250 **NOTES:** No dogs (ex guide dogs) Civ Wed 180 **CARDS:**

See advert under LOCH LOMOND

BALQUHIDDER, Stirling
Map 11 NN52

★★71% ❀❀ Monachyle Mhor
FK19 8PQ
☎ 01877 384622 🖷 01877 384305
e-mail: monachylemhorhotel@balquidder.freeserve.co.uk
Dir: *11m N of Callander on A84, turn right at Kingshouse Hotel this road takes you under the A84 towards Balquhidder, the hotel is 6m on the right*
Many guests return to this charming country hotel where a truly warm welcome and delicious food are assured. Set amid a 2000 acre estate, the hotel is in the heart of the picturesque Braes of Balquhidder. Public areas include a cosy snug bar and a relaxing sitting room, each warmed by welcoming open fires. The adjacent conservatory restaurant provides an appropriate setting for the innovative fixed-price menu. Bedrooms, including those in the rear courtyard wing, combine traditional styles with modern day amenities.
ROOMS: 5 en suite 5 annexe en suite No smoking in all bedrooms s £50-£70; d £70-£95 (incl. bkfst) **FACILITIES:** Fishing Xmas **PARKING:** 20 **NOTES:** No dogs (ex guide dogs) No children 12yrs No smoking in restaurant **CARDS:**

See advert on this page

BANCHORY, Aberdeenshire
Map 15 NO69

★★★78% ❀ Tor-na-Coille
AB31 4AB
☎ 01330 822242 🖷 01330 824012
e-mail: tornacoille@btinternet.com
Dir: *on the main A93 Aberdeen/Braemar road, 0.5m west of Banchory town centre, opposite golf course*
This charming ivy-clad Victorian house set in landscaped and wooded grounds offers pretty bedrooms comfortably furnished in mixed styles with thoughtful extras such as fresh fruit and flowers. Smart public areas include a lovely sitting room which boasts a welcoming log fire. There is also a well stocked bar and in the adjacent Watson's Restaurant a tempting range of 'Taste of Scotland' specialities are served.
ROOMS: 23 en suite (4 fmly) No smoking in 17 bedrooms s £55-£75; d £95-£120 (incl. bkfst) * LB **FACILITIES:** Croquet lawn entertainment ch fac Xmas **CONF:** Thtr 90 Class 60 Board 30 Del from £95 * **SERVICES:** Lift **PARKING:** 130 **NOTES:** No smoking in restaurant Closed 25-28 Dec Civ Wed 95 **CARDS:**

★★★75% ❀❀ Raemoir House
Scotland's Hotels of Distinction
Raemoir AB31 4ED
☎ 01330 824884 🖷 01330 822171
e-mail: raemoirhse@aol.com
Dir: *take the A93 to Banchory turn right onto the A980, to Torphins, main drive is 2m ahead at T-junct*

This country house forms part of a 3,500 acre estate. The public rooms include a choice of sitting rooms, a bar and a Georgian

continued on p674

BANCHORY, continued

dining room. These rooms have tapestry-covered walls, open fires, and fine antiques. The bedrooms are individual in style, the 'master' rooms being furnished in period.
ROOMS: 14 en suite 6 annexe en suite (1 fmly) s £50-£70; d £90-£120 (incl. bkfst) * LB **FACILITIES:** Golf 9 Tennis (hard) Croquet lawn Putting green Shooting Stalking **CONF:** Thtr 40 Class 50 Board 30 Del from £95.50 * **PARKING:** 100 **NOTES:** No smoking in restaurant
CARDS:

★★★74% Banchory Lodge
AB31 5HS
☎ 01330 822625 01330 825019
e-mail: banchorylodgeht@btconnect.com
Dir: *off A93 13m west of Aberdeen*
This delightful hotel stands in carefully tended grounds beside the River Dee. Victorian furnishings feature in the attractive dining room where the menu offers a range of dishes carefully prepared from fresh local ingredients. Bedrooms, with pleasing colour schemes, are comfortably furnished in both modern and traditional styles.
ROOMS: 22 en suite (11 fmly) s £55-£75; d £45-£110 (incl. bkfst) * LB **FACILITIES:** Fishing Sauna Pool table Xmas **CONF:** Thtr 30 Class 30 Board 28 Del from £90 * **PARKING:** 50 **NOTES:** Civ Wed 50
CARDS:

★★67% Burnett Arms
25 High St AB31 5TD
☎ 01330 824944 01330 825553
e-mail: TheBurnett@email.msn.com
Dir: *town centre on north side of A93, 18m from centre of Aberdeen*

Best Western

This popular, town centre hotel offers comfortably modern bedrooms with attractive colour schemes. Nicely presented public areas include a choice of contrasting bars, foyer lounge, while the smart dining room offers good value high teas and table d'hôte dinner.
ROOMS: 16 en suite s £40-£56; d £56-£76 (incl. bkfst) * LB **FACILITIES:** STV Pool table Xmas **CONF:** Thtr 100 Class 50 Board 50 Del from £65 * **PARKING:** 40 **NOTES:** No smoking in restaurant Civ Wed 100 **CARDS:**

See advert under ABERDEEN

BANFF, Aberdeenshire Map 15 NJ66

★★★67% *Banff Springs*
Golden Knowes Rd AB45 2JE
☎ 01261 812881 01261 815546
Dir: *western outskirts of the town overlooking the beach on the A98 Banff to Inverness road*
A welcoming atmosphere prevails at this modern purpose-built business and tourist hotel on the eastern edge of town. Bedrooms, which have benefited from refurbishment in recent years, are comfortably modern in appointment. Public areas include a bright foyer lounge, spacious well stocked bar, a restaurant and good function facilities.
ROOMS: 31 en suite **FACILITIES:** STV Gym **CONF:** Thtr 400 Class 100 Board 40 **PARKING:** 200 **NOTES:** No smoking in restaurant Closed 25 Dec **CARDS:**

BARRA, ISLE OF, Western Isles Map 13

TANGASDALE Map 13 NF60

★★68% Isle of Barra
Tangasdale Beach HS9 5XW
☎ 01871 810383 01871 810385
e-mail: barrahotel@aol.com
Dir: *turn left after leaving ferry terminal on to the A888, hotel is 2m on the left*
This hotel occupies a stunning position overlooking the white sands of the crescent shaped Halaman Bay and the Atlantic Ocean beyond. The public areas are comfortable and optimise the views, as do most of the pleasant bedrooms. An attractive table d'hôte dinner is served and it is worth the supplement to savour the local scallops.
ROOMS: 30 en suite (2 fmly) s £44-£47; d £78-£84 (incl. bkfst) * LB **FACILITIES:** STV Pool table Xmas **CONF:** Class 70 Board 60 Del from £48 * **PARKING:** 50 **NOTES:** No smoking in restaurant Closed mid Oct-Mar exc Xmas & New Year **CARDS:**

BARRHEAD, East Renfrewshire Map 11 NS45

★★★69% Dalmeny Park Country House
Lochlibo Rd G78 1LG
☎ 0141 881 9211 0141 881 9214
e-mail: enquires@maksu-group.co.uk
Dir: *on A736 towards Glasgow*
This hotel lies on the outskirts of town in seven acres of well tended gardens. Bedrooms offer good levels of comfort and quality with many thoughtful extras. The hotel is well equipped for both business and leisure markets and is also popular as a wedding venue.
ROOMS: 20 en suite (2 fmly) No smoking in 2 bedrooms s £69-£120; d £80-£175 (incl. bkfst) * **FACILITIES:** STV Jacuzzi/spa Xmas **CONF:** Thtr 250 Class 100 Board 60 Del from £95 * **PARKING:** 150 **NOTES:** Civ Wed 200 **CARDS:**

BATHGATE, West Lothian Map 11 NS96

★★★67% Cairn Hotel
Blackburn Rd EH48 2EL
☎ 01506 633366 01506 633444
Dir: *M8 exit 3A, at rdbt 1st left, next rdbt 1st left, small rdbt straight on then 1st slip rd signed Blackburn, at T-junct turn right, hotel next right*
Smart stylish public areas with ample comfortable seating, plus an attractive restaurant, are features of this modern business hotel. Bedrooms, though not large, reflect a similar standard and are well equipped. There are also several meeting rooms.
ROOMS: 61 en suite (2 fmly) No smoking in 49 bedrooms s fr £70; d fr £90 (incl. bkfst) * LB **FACILITIES:** STV Xmas **CONF:** Thtr 250 Class 100 Board 50 Del from £80 * **SERVICES:** Lift **PARKING:** 150 **NOTES:** No smoking in restaurant Civ Wed 200
CARDS:

Packed in a hurry? Ironing facilities should be available at all star levels, either in rooms or on request.

B

⌂ Express by Holiday Inn Livingston
Starlaw Rd EH48 1LQ
☎ 01506 650650 📠 01506 650651
Dir: *M8 junct3A. Follow sliproad to 1st rdbt, take 1st exit (Bathgate). Continue on road, over bridge. At 2nd rdbt take 1st exit & hotel 200yrds on left*

A modern budget hotel offering comfortable accommodation in refreshing, spacious and comprehensively-equipped bedrooms, en suite bathrooms with power showers and continental buffet breakfast included in the room rate. Suitable for business travellers or families. For further details and the Express by Holiday Inn phone number, consult the Hotel Groups page.
ROOMS: 74 en suite (incl. cont bkfst) d £49.95 * **CONF:** Thtr 25 Class 18 Board 20

BEARSDEN, East Dunbartonshire — Map 11 NS57

○ *Premier Lodge (Glasgow North)*
Milngavie Rd G61 3TA
☎ 0870 700 1400 📠 0870 700 1401

BEAULY, Highland — Map 14 NH54

★★★70% Priory
The Square IV4 7BX
☎ 01463 782309 📠 01463 782531
e-mail: reservations@priory-hotel.com
Dir: *signposted from A832, into village of Beauly, hotel in village square on left*
Occupying a prime position in the village square, this popular and friendly business and tourist hotel continues to improve, with new, more spacious and non-smoking bedrooms complementing the existing rooms, all of which offer good levels of comfort with a wide range of amenities. The attractive open plan public areas include a comfortable foyer lounge and a spacious split-level restaurant.
ROOMS: 36 en suite (3 fmly) No smoking in 6 bedrooms s £39.50-£47; d £79-£90 (incl. bkfst) * LB **FACILITIES:** STV Snooker Pool table ch fac Xmas **CONF:** Thtr 40 Class 40 Board 30 Del from £65 * **SERVICES:** Lift **PARKING:** 20 **NOTES:** No smoking in restaurant
CARDS:

BIGGAR, South Lanarkshire — Map 11 NT03

★★★69% ❀❀ Shieldhill Castle
Quothquan ML12 6NA
☎ 01899 220035 📠 01899 221092
e-mail: enquires@shieldhill.co.uk
Dir: *turn off A702 onto B7016 Biggar to Carnwath rd in the middle of Biggar, after 2m turn left into Shieldhill rd, Hotel 1.5m on right*
Dating in parts back to 1199, with a 'new' wing built in 1826, this fortified mansion house and grounds has peaceful views of rolling countryside. Bedrooms are generally spacious, including a number of large suites with luxurious comfort. An oak panelled lounge leads into the equally comfortable Chancellor restaurant where fresh local ingredients form the basis of meals worthy of our rosette award.
ROOMS: 16 en suite No smoking in all bedrooms s fr £90; d fr £134 (incl. bkfst) * LB **FACILITIES:** Croquet lawn Cycling Clay shoot Hot air ballooning ch fac Xmas **CONF:** Thtr 500 Class 200 Board 250 **PARKING:** 25 **NOTES:** No smoking in restaurant Civ Wed 250
CARDS:

BIRNAM, Perth & Kinross — Map 11 NO04

★★65% Birnam House
PH8 0BQ
☎ 01350 727462 📠 01350 728979
e-mail: RaeJ@birnamhouse.co.uk
Dir: *off A9*
Situated in the centre of the village, this substantial Victorian hotel remains a popular base for visiting tour groups. Public areas include a choice of contrasting bars, a foyer lounge, and attractive restaurant. Bedrooms vary in size and in style and offer a good range of amenities.
ROOMS: 30 en suite (6 fmly) No smoking in 7 bedrooms s £41-£48; d £62-£76 (incl. bkfst) * LB **FACILITIES:** STV Pool table Xmas **CONF:** Thtr 150 Class 60 Board 60 Del £85 * **SERVICES:** Lift **PARKING:** 50 **NOTES:** No smoking in restaurant
CARDS:

See advert on page 693

BLAIR ATHOLL, Perth & Kinross — Map 14 NN86

★★68% *Atholl Arms*
PH18 5SG
☎ 01796 481205 📠 01796 481550
Dir: *off main A9 to B8079, 1m into Blair Atholl, hotel is situated in the village near entrance to Blair Castle*
A popular base for tour groups, this well established hotel is close to the famous castle and railway station. Day rooms are impressive and include a choice of bars and lounges, as well as a splendid baronial-style dining room with a minstrels' gallery. Rooms come in mixed sizes and styles and provide all the expected amenities.
ROOMS: 30 en suite (3 fmly) **FACILITIES:** Fishing Pool table Rough shooting, fishing **PARKING:** 103 **NOTES:** No smoking in restaurant
CARDS:

★★59% Bridge of Tilt
Bridge of Tilt PH18 5SU
☎ 01796 481333 📠 01796 481335
Dir: *turn off A9 onto B8079, hotel is three quarters of a mile on left, with wishing well in front*
Situated close to Blair Castle, this long established Highland hotel in the centre of the village is a popular base for visiting tour groups. There is a wide choice of bedroom sizes, and all rooms are modern and offer useful amenities. Public areas include a spacious and well stocked bar, a lounge, and the dining room.
ROOMS: 20 en suite 7 annexe en suite (7 fmly) d £60-£80 (incl. bkfst) * LB **FACILITIES:** Fishing Pool table Jacuzzi/spa Xmas **PARKING:** 40 **NOTES:** No smoking in restaurant Closed Jan
CARDS:

> Arriving late? Four and five star hotels have night porters to assist with your luggage; and 24hr room service.

BLAIRGOWRIE, Perth & Kinross — Map 15 NO14

see also Coupar Angus

Premier Collection

★★★ Kinloch House

PH10 6SG
☎ 01250 884237 📠 01250 884333
e-mail: enquires@kinlochhouse.com
Dir: *3m W on A923*

This country house hotel stands in 25 acres of wood and parkland. The bar, with its conservatory extension and extensive range of malt whiskies, is the ideal place to relax and unwind. Adjacent, the elegant dining room is the appropriate setting for fine dining. Main house bedrooms are individual in style while the spacious wing rooms have a more modern feel and boast luxurious bathrooms.

ROOMS: 20 en suite s £90-£160; d £205-£270 (incl. bkfst & dinner) LB **FACILITIES:** Indoor swimming (H) Fishing Sauna Gym Croquet lawn Jacuzzi/spa Sailing Cycling Xmas **PARKING:** 40 **NOTES:** No smoking in restaurant Closed 18-29 Dec
CARDS:

★★★61% Angus

46 Wellmeadow PH10 6NQ
☎ 01250 872455 📠 01250 875615
e-mail: info@theangus.freeserve.co.uk
Dir: *on the main A93 Perth/Blairgowrie Rd overlooking the Wellmeadow in the town centre*

In recent years, major improvements have taken place at this long established town centre hotel which remains popular with visiting tour groups. Although variable in size, the bedrooms are comfortably modern. The bar is spacious and includes a non-smoking area, and the refurbished restaurant offers a good value fixed price menu plus a short carte. Leisure facilities are also available.

ROOMS: 81 en suite (4 fmly) s £45-£60; d £90-£120 (incl. bkfst) LB **FACILITIES:** Indoor swimming (H) Sauna Solarium Jacuzzi/spa entertainment Xmas **CONF:** Thtr 200 Class 60 Board 40 Del from £40 * **SERVICES:** Lift **PARKING:** 62 **NOTES:** No smoking in restaurant
CARDS:

★★70% Altamount House Hotel

Coupar Angus Rd PH10 6JN
☎ 01250 873512 📠 01250 876200
e-mail: althotel@netcomuk.co.uk
Dir: *on entering Blairgowrie on A93 turn right onto Golf Course Rd, after one and a half miles at t-junct turn left, hotel 1m on left*

This delightful, small hotel, is a converted Georgian house set in six acres of landscaped and wooded grounds. Public areas include a well stocked bar, a choice of comfortable lounges, and an elegant restaurant which provides a fine dining experience. Bedrooms vary in size, and most of them are furnished in a traditional style.

ROOMS: 7 en suite (2 fmly) s £40-£55; d £80-£110 (incl. bkfst) * LB **CONF:** Thtr 150 Class 40 Board 60 **PARKING:** 60 **NOTES:** No dogs (ex guide dogs) No smoking in restaurant Closed 2-14 Jan Civ Wed 130
CARDS:

BOAT OF GARTEN, Highland — Map 14 NH91

★★★70% Boat

PH24 3BH
☎ 01479 831258 📠 01479 831414
e-mail: holidays@boathotel.co.uk
Dir: *turn off A9 N of Aviemore onto A95 & follow signposts to Boat of Garten*

This is a long established Highland Hotel that now also offers special golfing packages. Public areas include a bar, a smart new library lounge, and an attractive restaurant where fine dining based on quality fresh ingredients is offered on the daily changing menu. The bedrooms offer all the expected amenities.

ROOMS: 32 en suite (1 fmly) s £75-£85; d £130-£150 (incl. bkfst & dinner) * LB **FACILITIES:** Pool table Xmas **CONF:** Thtr 50 Class 35 Board 25 Del from £65 * **PARKING:** 36 **NOTES:** No smoking in restaurant Civ Wed 60 **CARDS:**

BOTHWELL, South Lanarkshire — Map 11 NS75

★★★67% *Bothwell Bridge*

89 Main St G71 8EU
☎ 01698 852246 📠 01698 854686
Dir: *turn off M74 at junct 5 & follow signs to Uddingston, turn right at mini-rndabt. Hotel located just past shops on left*

This red sandstone mansion house is a popular business, function and conference centre. The bedrooms are mostly spacious and all are well equipped. The conservatory drawing room provides comfortable seating and a versatile, informal, bar/meal operation.

continued

A more formal dining experience is offered in the restaurant, which has a strong Italian influence.
ROOMS: 90 en suite (14 fmly) No smoking in 14 bedrooms
FACILITIES: STV entertainment **CONF:** Thtr 200 Class 80 Board 350
SERVICES: Lift **PARKING:** 125 **NOTES:** No dogs (ex guide dogs)
CARDS:

See advert on this page

BOWMORE See Islay, Isle of

BRAEMAR, Aberdeenshire — Map 15 NO19

★★★66% The Invercauld Arms

AB35 5YR
☎ 013397 41605 Fax 013397 41428
PEEL HOTELS
Dir: *on the A93 equidistant between Perth and Aberdeen*
Colourful flowering baskets adorn the facade of this impressive Victorian hotel on the eastern edge of the village. Spacious public areas are comfortably traditional in style and include a choice of inviting lounges, a well stocked tartan themed bar, and an attractive dining room which offers a table d'hôte menu. Bedrooms, with solid furnishings, come in mixed sizes and are equipped with the expected amenities. Staff are friendly and willing to please.
ROOMS: 68 en suite (11 fmly) No smoking in 18 bedrooms s £42-£85; d £84-£110 (incl. bkfst) * LB **FACILITIES:** STV Xmas **CONF:** Thtr 60 Class 20 Board 24 Del from £65 * **SERVICES:** Lift **PARKING:** 80
NOTES: No smoking in restaurant **CARDS:**

★★72% *Braemar Lodge*

Glenshee Rd AB35 5YQ
☎ 013397 41627 Fax 013397 41627
Dir: *on the A93 south approach to Braemar*
This welcoming small hotel stands in its own well tended garden on the north side of the village. Bedrooms are bright and airy with pleasing colour schemes and comfortable furnishings. Welcoming log fires burn on the cooler evenings in the well stocked bar and in the adjacent lounge. Carefully prepared and substantial meals are served in the attractive restaurant.
ROOMS: 7 rms (6 en suite) (2 fmly) No smoking in all bedrooms
PARKING: 16 **NOTES:** No smoking in restaurant
CARDS:

BRECHIN, Angus — Map 15 NO66

★★63% Northern

2/4 Clerk St DD9 6AE
☎ 01356 625505 Fax 01356 622714
e-mail: northernhotel@uku.co.uk
Dir: *hotel 1m from St Annes junction (north) on A90 Trunk Road, and 1.5m from Keithock junction A90 (south)*
This long established commercial hotel is conveniently situated in the centre of town. The bedrooms are comfortable and well appointed. Public areas include a choice of contrasting bars and a smart restaurant where the menus offer a varied choice at competitive prices.
ROOMS: 16 en suite (1 fmly) No smoking in 10 bedrooms s £40-£45; d £60-£65 (incl. bkfst) * LB **FACILITIES:** Pool table Xmas **CONF:** Thtr 120 Class 80 Board 40 Del from £50 * **PARKING:** 20 **NOTES:** No smoking in restaurant **CARDS:**

BRIDGEND See Islay, Isle of

Bad hair day? Hairdryers in all rooms three stars and above.

B

BRIDGE OF ALLAN, Stirling Map 11 NS79

★★★65% ❀ Royal
Henderson St FK9 4HG
☎ 01786 832284 🖷 01786 834377
e-mail: stay@royal-stirling.co.uk
Dir: *at the end of the M9 turn right at the rbt for Bridge of Allan. Hotel is in the centre of Bridge of Allan on the left hand side*

This impressive Victorian hotel offers a welcoming atmosphere together with a fine dining experience. Though variable in size, the bedrooms are comfortably modern in style and offer a good range of amenities. Public areas include a relaxing oak panelled lounge, well stocked bar, and an elegant restaurant offering innovative Scottish fare from both the carte and fixed price menus.
ROOMS: 32 en suite (2 fmly) s £70-£85; d £90-£118 (incl. bkfst) * LB **FACILITIES:** STV Xmas **CONF:** Thtr 150 Class 60 Board 50 Del from £105 * **SERVICES:** Lift **PARKING:** 40 **NOTES:** No dogs (ex guide dogs) No smoking in restaurant Civ Wed 100 **CARDS:**

See advert under STIRLING

BRIDGE OF ORCHY, Argyll & Bute Map 10 NN23

★★76% ❀❀ *Bridge of Orchy Hotel*
PA36 4AD
☎ 01838 400208 🖷 01838 400313
e-mail: bridgeoforchy@onyxnet.co.uk
Dir: *located on main A82 6m N of Tydrum*

Situated amid spectacular Highland scenery this completely refurbished tourist hotel provides a welcoming atmosphere together with good food and modern comforts. The non-smoking bedrooms with pretty colour schemes are comfortably furnished in mixed modern styles and offer a range of thoughtful extras. Public areas include a spacious and inviting lounge and a well stocked bar. The elegant restaurant provides the appropriate setting for the carefully prepared Scottish fare.
ROOMS: 10 en suite (2 fmly) No smoking in all bedrooms **FACILITIES:** STV Fishing **CONF:** Thtr 40 Class 30 Board 20 **PARKING:** 50 **NOTES:** No dogs (ex guide dogs) No smoking in restaurant Closed 1 Dec-1 Jan **CARDS:**

BROADFORD See Skye, Isle of

BRODICK See Arran, Isle of

BRORA, Highland Map 14 NC90

★★★72% ❀ Royal Marine
Golf Rd KW9 6QS
☎ 01408 621252 🖷 01408 621181
e-mail: highlandescape@btinternet.com
Dir: *turn off A9 in village toward beach and golf course*
This distinctive house, built in 1913 by Scottish architect, Sir Robert Latimer has been transformed under the ownership of Robert Powell. An attractive bedroom wing has been added and the swimming pool renewed. The leisure centre has full curling facilities. Both the restaurant and the bar enjoy busy trade, and the Garden Room provides a more leisurely environment where bistro style food can be enjoyed.
ROOMS: 22 en suite (1 fmly) s fr £65; d fr £98 (incl. bkfst) * LB **FACILITIES:** STV Indoor swimming (H) Golf 18 Tennis (hard) Fishing Snooker Sauna Solarium Gym Pool table Croquet lawn Putting green Jacuzzi/spa Ice curling rink in season Table Tennis Xmas **CONF:** Thtr 70 Class 40 Board 40 Del from £105 * **PARKING:** 40 **NOTES:** No smoking in restaurant RS Dec-Jan **CARDS:**

★★★66% The Links
Golf Rd KW9 6QS
☎ 01408 621225 🖷 01408 621383
e-mail: highlandescape@btinternet.com
Dir: *turn off A9 in village of Brora towards beach and golf course, hotel overlooks golf course*
Owned and personally run by The Powell family, this hotel occupies an enviable position overlooking the golf course towards the North Sea. The attractive bedrooms include a number of family rooms and suites. Guests can enjoy the marvellous view from the lounges and restaurant, where a choice of interesting dishes are available from the carte and table d'hote menus. Nearby, the Royal Marine Hotel, under the same ownership, offers good leisure facilities.
ROOMS: 23 en suite (2 fmly) s £65; d fr £98 (incl. bkfst) * LB **FACILITIES:** Indoor swimming (H) Fishing Snooker Sauna Solarium Gym Croquet lawn Putting green Jacuzzi/spa Xmas **CONF:** Thtr 100 Class 40 Board 20 Del from £105 * **PARKING:** 55 **NOTES:** No smoking in restaurant Closed 31 Oct-Mar RS Apr/Oct (dinner may be in sister hotel) **CARDS:**

BROUGHTY FERRY, Dundee City Map 12 NO43

⇧ Premier Lodge (Dundee East)
115-117 Lawers Dr, Panmurefield DD5 3TS
☎ 0870 700 1360 🖷 0870 770 1361
Premier Lodge offers modern, well equipped, en suite accommodation suitable for both business and leisure travellers. Meals can be taken at the adjacent popular restaurant and bar which is fully licensed. For further details, consult the Hotel Groups page.
ROOMS: 60 en suite d £42 *

BUCKIE, Moray Map 15 NJ46

★★67% Mill House
Tynet AB56 5HJ
☎ 01542 850233 🖷 01542 850331
e-mail: george@millhouse98.freeserve.co.uk
Dir: *on A98 between Buckie and Fochabers*
Situated between Fochabers and Buckie, this popular business and

continued

tourist hotel has been created by conversion and extension of a former mill. Bedrooms are appointed in the modern style and offer the expected amenities. Public areas include the entrance lobby where the original water wheel machinery has been retained and adjacent is the attractive restaurant. The well stocked bar is located upstairs on the first floor. Staff are friendly and willing to please.
ROOMS: 15 en suite (2 fmly) s fr £37; d fr £57 (incl. bkfst) * LB **CONF:** Thtr 100 Class 60 Board 30 **PARKING:** 101 **NOTES:** No smoking in restaurant **CARDS:**

BUNESSAN See Mull, Isle of

BURNTISLAND, Fife Map 11 NT28

★★64% Inchview Hotel

THE CIRCLE Selected Individual Hotels GREAT BRITAIN

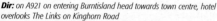

69 Kinghorn Rd KY3 9EB
☎ 01592 872239 01592 874866
e-mail: inchview@msn.com
Dir: *on A921 on entering Burntisland head towards town centre, hotel overlooks The Links on Kinghorn Road*
A welcoming atmosphere prevails at this family-run hotel, a listed Georgian terraced house, which looks out over the links to the Firth of Forth. Bedrooms, which vary in size and in style, offer modern comforts together with the expected amenities. The well stocked bar offers a varied selection of meals, and in the restaurant more adventurous fare is provided.
ROOMS: 12 en suite (1 fmly) No smoking in 4 bedrooms s £39.50-£52.50; d £69.50-£79.50 (incl. bkfst) * LB **FACILITIES:** Xmas **CONF:** Thtr 80 Class 40 Board 30 Del from £79.95 * **PARKING:** 15 **CARDS:**

BUTE, ISLE OF, Argyll & Bute

ARDBEG Map 10 NS06

★★77% Ardmory House Hotel & Restaurant

Ardmory Rd PA20 0PG
☎ 01700 502346 01700 505596
e-mail: ardmory.house.hotel@dial.pipex.com
Dir: *N from Rothesay on A844, 1m turn left up Ardmory Road, hotel 300mtrs on left*
Genuine hospitality together with good food are the hallmarks of this welcoming hotel which stands on a hillside above the bay. Although variable in size, the non-smoking bedrooms are comfortable furnished and provide a good range of accessories. Relaxing public areas include a well stocked bar with conservatory extension, and the attractive restaurant provides the appropriate setting for enjoyable meals.
ROOMS: 5 en suite (1 fmly) No smoking in all bedrooms s £47.50; d £75 (incl. bkfst) * **CONF:** Thtr 60 Class 30 Board 30 **PARKING:** 12 **NOTES:** No smoking in restaurant Closed 21 Oct-5 Nov & 2 weeks Feb **CARDS:**

CAIRNDOW, Argyll & Bute Map 10 NN11

★★67% Cairndow Stagecoach Inn

THE CIRCLE Selected Individual Hotels GREAT BRITAIN

PA26 8BN
☎ 01499 600286 01499 600220
e-mail: cairndinn@aol.com
Dir: *from Tarbet take A83 pass Dunoon Junction to Cairndow village*
This comfortable 18th-century inn stands beside the shore of Loch Fyne. Old beams are a feature of the comfortable lounge, the bar serves food throughout the day and there is a more formal restaurant with a conservatory extension. Bedrooms are smartly decorated and there are two 'superior' rooms with large spa baths.

ROOMS: 13 en suite (2 fmly) No smoking in 3 bedrooms s £30-£45; d £50-£64 (incl. bkfst) * LB **FACILITIES:** Sauna Solarium Gym Pool table Xmas **PARKING:** 32 **CARDS:**

CALLANDER, Stirling Map 11 NN60

★★★74% Roman Camp Country House

FK17 8BG
☎ 01877 330003 01877 331533
e-mail: mail@roman-camp-hotel.co.uk
Dir: *heading north on the A84 turn left at the east end of Callander High street, down a 300 yard driveway into the hotel grounds*
A warm welcome is assured at this comfortable country hotel, peacefully set beside the River Teith. Day rooms include charming lounges and an elegant tapestry-hung dining room. The innovative

continued

CALLANDER, continued

menu offers highly accomplished, modern cooking. Bedrooms are individual in style and offer many thoughtful extras.
ROOMS: 14 en suite (3 fmly) s fr £90; d £110-£165 (incl. bkfst) LB **FACILITIES:** Fishing Xmas **CONF:** Thtr 100 Class 40 Board 20 Del from £145 * **PARKING:** 80 **NOTES:** No smoking in restaurant
CARDS:

See advert on page 679

★★72% Lubnaig
Leny Feus FK17 8AS
☎ 01877 330376 🖷 01877 330376
Dir: *travelling W on the A84 through main street of Callander to the W outskirts, turn right into Leny Feus, just after Poppies sign*
A welcoming and secluded hotel set in well tended gardens with an atmosphere of warmth and relaxtion. Three lounges and a delightful dining room look out over the garden. The hotel's menu provides a good choice of dishes prepared from fine Scottish produce, complimented by a wide range of malt whiskies. Bedrooms are very well appointed; ground floor rooms are available.
ROOMS: 6 en suite 4 annexe en suite d £64-£76 (incl. bkfst) * LB **PARKING:** 10 **NOTES:** No dogs No children 7yrs No smoking in restaurant Closed Nov-Etr RS Apr (B&B only) **CARDS:**

★★64% Bridgend House
Bridgend FK17 8AH
☎ 01877 330130 🖷 01877 331512
e-mail: bridgendhotel@hotmail.com
Dir: *proceed down Callander main street, turn onto A81 (Aberfoyle rd) over red sandstone bridge, hotel on right*
Easily recognised by its black and white façade, this is a welcoming hotel alongside the River Teith. Public areas include a popular bar, comfortable lounge, and a dining room that overlooks the garden. The bedrooms, two with four posters, have good quality furnishings and all the expected amenities.
ROOMS: 6 rms (5 en suite) s £29.50-£39.50; d £55-£59 (incl. bkfst) * LB **FACILITIES:** STV Pool table entertainment Xmas **CONF:** Thtr 100 Board 20 **PARKING:** 30 **CARDS:**

★★64% *Dalgair House*
113-115 Main St FK17 8BQ
☎ 01877 330283 🖷 01877 331114
Dir: *300 metres beyond access road to golf course on main street*

A relaxed atmosphere prevails at this family-run hotel in the main street. Public areas are quite informal and include a front dining area and popular bar to the rear of the house. Bedrooms, most of which have benefited from refurbishment, are brightly decorated and comfortably furnished in pine.
ROOMS: 8 en suite (1 fmly) **FACILITIES:** STV **PARKING:** 12
CARDS:

CAMPBELTOWN, Argyll & Bute — Map 10 NR72

★★68% Seafield
Kilkerran Rd PA28 6JL
☎ 01586 554385 🖷 01586 552741
A welcoming atmosphere prevails at this comfortable family-run hotel which, from its position close to the harbour, enjoys lovely views of the bay. Bedrooms, some in the garden annexe, come in various sizes and offer modern appointments along with a good range of amenities. There is a bright and comfortable open-plan foyer lounge and bar, and an extensive range of home cooked dishes are available in the attractive restaurant.
ROOMS: 3 en suite 6 annexe en suite s £40-£50; d £60-£75 (incl. bkfst) * LB **PARKING:** 11 **NOTES:** No children 14yrs No smoking in restaurant
CARDS:

CARNOUSTIE, Angus — Map 12 NO53

★★★★66% Carnoustie Golf Resort & Spa
The Links DD7 7JE
☎ 01241 411999
Dir: *Right turn into Carnoustie from A92, follow golf course signs*
Opened early in 1999 this imposing hotel beside the Championship Course, offers guests the facility to book tee times on the three links courses. Bedrooms, all appointed to a high standard, range from opulent suites to superior and regular rooms, while the reception areas radiate from the smart foyer and include a restaurant overlooking the course. Other facilities include a golf shop as well as banqueting and leisure facilities.
ROOMS: 85 en suite (12 fmly) d £130-£160 (incl. bkfst) * LB **FACILITIES:** STV Indoor swimming (H) Golf 18 Gym Putting green Jacuzzi/spa entertainment **CONF:** Thtr 400 Class 200 Board 20 Del from £165 * **SERVICES:** Lift **PARKING:** 2000 **NOTES:** No smoking in restaurant RS Xmas **CARDS:**

★★68% Carnoustie Links
Links Pde DD7 7JF
☎ 01241 853273 🖷 01241 853319
e-mail: enquiries@carnoustielinks.com
Dir: *off A92, adjoining Golf Course*
This relaxed hotel, from its position opposite the 18th green of the championship course, has particular appeal for the visiting golfer. Bedrooms have attractive colour schemes and offer comfortable modern appointments. Relaxing public areas include a golf themed bar, lounge, restaurant and a popular golf shop.
ROOMS: 7 en suite (4 fmly) s fr £40; d fr £60 (incl. bkfst) * LB **PARKING:** 10 **NOTES:** No smoking in restaurant **CARDS:**

★★67% Carlogie House Hotel
Carlogie Rd DD7 6LD
☎ 01241 853185 🖷 01241 856528
e-mail: carlogie@lineone.net
Dir: *take A92 from Dundee to Arbroath, turn right at Pambride/West Haven continue to junct with A930, then turn sharp right. Hotel 300 yrds on right*
This comfortable hotel on the north side of town is popular with visiting golfers. Although variable in size, main house bedrooms are modern in style and offer a wide range of amenities. Adjacent, a former stable block has been converted to provide accommodation for the disabled traveller. The adventure playground in the garden is a big hit with the children.
ROOMS: 12 en suite 4 annexe en suite (2 fmly) s £55; d £75-£85 (incl. bkfst) * LB **FACILITIES:** STV Use of facilities at local leisure centre **CONF:** Thtr 25 Class 25 Board 25 **PARKING:** 40 **NOTES:** Closed 1-3 Jan **CARDS:**

CARRBRIDGE, Highland Map 14 NH92

★★★68% Dalrachney Lodge

PH23 3AT
☎ 01479 841252 01479 841383
e-mail: stay@dalrachney.co.uk
Dir: *follow Carrbridge signs off main A9. Located at the N end of the village on the A938*

A warm welcome is assured at this comfortable family-run Highland hotel on the edge of the village. The well maintained bedrooms are generally spacious and are comfortably furnished in period style. The smartly presented public areas include a comfortable and relaxing sitting room, a well stocked bar, and attractive dining room.

ROOMS: 11 en suite (3 fmly) No smoking in 4 bedrooms s £55; d £110 (incl. bkfst) * LB **FACILITIES:** STV Fishing Xmas **PARKING:** 40 **NOTES:** No smoking in restaurant **CARDS:**

★★70% Fairwinds

THE CIRCLE Selected Individual Hotels GREAT BRITAIN

PH23 3AA
☎ 01479 841240 01479 841240
e-mail: fairwindsinfo@tesco.net
Dir: *turn off A9 1m N of Aviemore. Follow A95 signposted Carrbridge for 3m then onto B9153, hotel on left side of main road*

Bedrooms are comfortable and modern in style with a good range of amenities. Public areas include a smart conservatory restaurant and lounge. There are self-catering chalets in the grounds. There is also an honesty bar in the lounge for guest use.

ROOMS: 5 en suite No smoking in all bedrooms s £34; d £64-£68 (incl. bkfst) * LB **FACILITIES:** Xmas **PARKING:** 6 **NOTES:** No dogs (ex guide dogs) No smoking in restaurant **CARDS:**

CARRUTHERSTOWN, Dumfries & Galloway Map 11 NY17

★★★67% *Hetland Hall*

Best Western

DG1 4JX
☎ 01387 840201 01387 840211
e-mail: hetlandhallhotel@ic24.net
Dir: *midway between Annan & Dumfries on A75*

This hotel is set in extensive parkland just off the A75. Appealing to a wide market, including weddings and conferences, it offers well equipped bedrooms in variety of styles and sizes, all enhanced by attractive fabrics.

ROOMS: 30 en suite (4 fmly) No smoking in 6 bedrooms **FACILITIES:** STV Indoor swimming (H) Fishing Snooker Sauna Solarium Gym Putting green ch fac **CONF:** Thtr 200 Class 100 Board 100 **PARKING:** 60 **NOTES:** No smoking in restaurant **CARDS:**

See advert under DUMFRIES

CASTLE DOUGLAS, Dumfries & Galloway Map 11 NX76

★★70% Douglas Arms

King St DG7 1DB
☎ 01556 502231 01556 504000
e-mail: doughot@aol.com
Dir: *in centre of town, adjacent to Clock Tower*

Friendly service is guaranteed at this former coaching inn situated in the centre of the town. The lounge bar is popular for meals, or guests can eat in the stylish little restaurant. Bedrooms are very well equipped.

ROOMS: 24 en suite (1 fmly) No smoking in 8 bedrooms s £37.50; d £68.50 (incl. bkfst) * LB **FACILITIES:** STV Pool table Xmas **CONF:** Thtr 150 Class 40 Board 40 Del from £52.50 * **PARKING:** 16 **NOTES:** No smoking in restaurant Civ Wed 100 **CARDS:**

★★68% Urr Valley

Ernespie Rd DG7 3JG
☎ 01556 502188 01556 504055
Dir: *off A75 towards Castle Douglas, turn left at 1st rdbt, hotel entrance approx 1m on left*

Reached by a long drive, this country house is set in 14 acres of woodland a mile from town. Public areas include a wood panelled foyer lounge, bar and restaurant. Bedrooms are well equipped and in the main spacious.

ROOMS: 19 rms (17 en suite) (5 fmly) s £39.50-£49.50; d £65-£75 (incl. bkfst) * LB **FACILITIES:** STV Xmas **CONF:** Thtr 200 Class 100 Board 50 Del from £50 * **PARKING:** 100 **CARDS:**

★★65% Imperial

35 King St DG7 1AA
☎ 01556 502086 01556 503009
e-mail: david@thegolfhotel.co.uk
Dir: *turn off A75 at sign for Castle Douglas go down main street hotel opposite the town library*

Situated in the main street, this former coaching inn, popular with golfers, offers well equipped and cheerfully decorated bedrooms. There is a choice of bars, and good meals are served either in the foyer bar or the upstairs dining room.

ROOMS: 12 en suite (1 fmly) No smoking in 6 bedrooms s £35-£43.50; d £54-£56 (incl. bkfst) * LB **FACILITIES:** Pool table **CONF:** Thtr 40 Class 20 Board 20 Del from £40 * **PARKING:** 29 **NOTES:** No smoking in restaurant **CARDS:**

★★64% King's Arms

St Andrew's St DG7 1EL
☎ 01556 502626 01556 502097
e-mail: david@galloway-golf.co.uk
Dir: *through main street, left at town clock, hotel situated on corner site*

This former coaching inn has a characterful interior which includes a choice of cosy bar areas and a restaurant overlooking an ivy clad courtyard. Both the bar and the restaurant offer a good choice of menus.

ROOMS: 10 rms (9 en suite) (2 fmly) No smoking in 2 bedrooms s £35; d £56 (incl. bkfst) * LB **FACILITIES:** Pool table ch fac **CONF:** Thtr 35 Class 20 Board 25 Del from £43.50 * **PARKING:** 15 **NOTES:** No smoking in restaurant Closed 25-26 Dec & 1-2 Jan **CARDS:**

TV dinner? Room service at three stars and above.

C

CLACHAN-SEIL, Argyll & Bute — Map 10 NM71

★★72% Willowburn
PA34 4TJ
☎ 01852 300276 01852 300597
e-mail: willowburn.hotel@virgin.net
Dir: *0.5m from Atlantic Bridge, on left*
This welcoming holiday hotel enjoys a peaceful outlook over Clachan Sound and lies 14 miles south of Oban. Peace and quiet along with fine food are the keys to this hotel's success. There is a small bar, a formal dining room and a comfortable inviting lounge. The attractive non smoking bedrooms have pine furnishings and are thoughtfully equipped.
ROOMS: 7 en suite No smoking in all bedrooms **PARKING:** 36
NOTES: No smoking in restaurant Closed Jan-Feb
CARDS:

CLUANIE INN, Highland — Map 14 NH01

★★64% Cluanie Inn
Glenmoriston IV63 7YW
☎ 01320 340238 01320 340293
e-mail: claunie@ecosse.net
Set in splendid isolation at the western end of Loch Cluanie and surrounded by mountains, this roadside inn is a haven for climbers and a welcoming stop for travellers to and from Skye. Sympathetically extended and upgraded, it provides accommodation in smart pine-furnished bedrooms. No TV or radio reception here, but each room has a VCR and there is a video library, or bring your own.
ROOMS: 15 en suite **PARKING:** 10 **CARDS:**

CLYDEBANK, West Dunbartonshire — Map 11 NS56

★★★★66% Beardmore
Best Western
Beardmore St G81 4SA
☎ 0141 951 6000 0141 951 6018
e-mail: beardmore.hotel@hci.co.uk
Dir: *M8 junct 19 follow the A814 towards Dumbarton then follow tourist signs. Turn left onto Beardsmore St and follow signs*
Beside the River Clyde, near the Erskine Bridge, this impressive modern hotel is well placed for business guests and holidaymakers. Bedrooms are attractive and some are of 'executive' standard. Business and conference facilities are very extensive and the Citrus Restaurant serves tempting modern dishes at dinner, whilst the Café-Bar offers a more informal alternative.
ROOMS: 168 en suite No smoking in 112 bedrooms **FACILITIES:** STV Indoor swimming (H) Sauna Solarium Gym Jacuzzi/spa Beauty treatment **CONF:** Thtr 170 Class 40 Board 30 **SERVICES:** Lift air con **PARKING:** 150 **CARDS:**

★★★64% Patio
1 South Av, Clydebank Business Park G81 2RW
☎ 0141 951 1133 0141 952 3713
e-mail: patiocly@golbalnet.co.uk
Situated in the local business park, this modern hotel is a popular conference and function venue. Public areas are contemporary in style and the restaurant offers a range of menus at lunch and dinner. Bedrooms have interesting lacquer and marble furniture.
ROOMS: 82 en suite No smoking in 16 bedrooms s £39-£69; d £49-£79 * LB **FACILITIES:** STV **CONF:** Thtr 150 Class 30 Board 30 **SERVICES:** Lift **PARKING:** 120 **CARDS:**

COLONSAY, ISLE OF, Argyll & Bute — Map 10

SCALASAIG — Map 10 NR39

★★70% Colonsay
PA61 7YP
☎ 01951 200316 01951 200353
e-mail: colonsay.hotel@pipemedia.co.uk
Dir: *400mtrs W of Ferry Pier*
The Island of Colonsay, which is accessed by ferry from the mainland every other day, is the ideal place to escape the pressures of modern day living. The hotel combines modern amenities with traditional comforts and offers a wonderfully relaxed atmosphere. Bedrooms are comfortably furnished and public areas include a choice of relaxing lounges, well stocked bars, and a traditional wood-clad dining room where fresh produce features on the short daily changing fixed price menu. The coffee and craft shops are located in an adjoining building.
ROOMS: 11 rms (9 en suite) (2 fmly) s £66-£80; d £132-£160 (incl. bkfst & dinner) * LB **FACILITIES:** Xmas **PARKING:** 8 **NOTES:** No smoking in restaurant **CARDS:**

COLVEND, Dumfries & Galloway — Map 11 NX85

★★64% Clonyard House
DG5 4QW
☎ 01556 630372 01556 630422
e-mail: nickthompson@clara.net
Dir: *through Dalbeattie and turn left onto A710 for about 4m*
This family run hotel is set in seven acres of grounds, which include a childrens' play area and an 'enchanted tree'. Most of the spacious, comfortable bedrooms are housed in a purpose-built extension. Meals are served in the bar lounge or in the restaurant proper.
ROOMS: 15 en suite (2 fmly) s fr £40; d fr £70 (incl. bkfst) * LB **CONF:** Class 35 Board 20 Del from £25 * **PARKING:** 40
CARDS:

COMRIE, Perth & Kinross — Map 11 NN72

★★★70% *Royal*
Melville Square PH6 2DW
☎ 01764 679200 01764 679219
e-mail: reception@royalhotel.co.uk
Dir: *situated on the main square in Comrie, which the A85 runs through*
Guests are warmly welcomed to this inviting hotel. Bedrooms are comfortably furnished in traditional style and offer modern amenities. Relaxing public areas include a comfortable library/lounge, a choice of contrasting bars, as well as a brasserie and formal dining room where the emphasis is on Taste of Scotland dishes.
ROOMS: 11 en suite **FACILITIES:** STV Fishing Pool table Croquet lawn **PARKING:** 8 **NOTES:** No dogs (ex guide dogs) No children 5yrs
CARDS:

See advert on opposite page

CONNEL, Argyll & Bute — Map 10 NM93

★★70% Falls of Lora
PA37 1PB
☎ 01631 710483 01631 710694
Dir: *off A85, overlooking Loch Etive, 5m from Oban*
Personally run and welcoming, this long established holiday hotel beside the A85 enjoys fine views over Loch Etive. The pleasant public areas include a comfortable traditional lounge, a well stocked bar with a popular bistro adjoining, and a formal dining

continued

room. Bedrooms offer a variety of styles and standards which range from spacious luxury rooms to the standard cabin rooms.
ROOMS: 30 en suite (4 fmly) s £35.50-£53.50; d £43-£111 (incl. bkfst) * LB **CONF:** Thtr 45 Class 20 Board 15 **PARKING:** 40 **NOTES:** Closed mid Dec & Jan **CARDS:**

See advert under OBAN

CONTIN, Highland Map 14 NH45

★★★74% Coul House

IV14 9EY
☎ 01997 421487 01997 421945
Dir: *from South by passing Inverness continue on A9 over Moray Firth bridge, after 5m take 2nd exit at rdbt on to A835 follow to Contin*

Hospitable attention is provided at this lovely Victorian country house. Individually decorated bedrooms have good amenities. A log fire invites relaxation in the foyer lounge in contrast with the more refined atmosphere of the octagonal drawing room. The elegant dining room offers an enjoyable range of Taste of Scotland specialities, with more informal meals available in the new Bistro or the Kitchen Bar.
ROOMS: 20 en suite (3 fmly) s £70; d £110-£122 (incl. bkfst) * LB
FACILITIES: STV Pool table Putting green Pitch & putt Xmas
CONF: Thtr 50 Class 30 Board 30 Del from £56.25 * **PARKING:** 40
NOTES: No smoking in restaurant **CARDS:**

★★70% *Achilty*

IV14 9EG
☎ 01997 421355 01997 421923
Dir: *on A835, at the northern edge of Contin*

This hotel offers a choice of comfortable lounges with plenty of reading material and some games. A good value carte menu is served in The Steading lounge bar, where rough-cut stone walls add to the character. Well equipped bedrooms, four with external access, are bright and modern in style.
ROOMS: 12 en suite (3 fmly) No smoking in 6 bedrooms **CONF:** Thtr 50 Class 50 Board 30 **PARKING:** 150 **NOTES:** No smoking in restaurant
CARDS:

COUPAR ANGUS, Perth & Kinross Map 11 NO23

★★★71% Moorfield House

Myreriggs Rd PH13 9HS
☎ 01828 627303 01828 627339
Dir: *from Perth turn off A94 onto B923, Blairgowrie road, In 2m cross the Isla Bridge, hotel off A923 on the right*

This delightful country house hotel, in splendid gardens, has a welcoming and relaxed atmosphere. The bedrooms have pretty colour schemes and the public areas are nicely presented and comfortable. The spacious bar provides a popular informal food option. The elegant restaurant offers a fine dining experience, with a short fixed-price menu.

continued

Moorfield House, Coupar Angus

ROOMS: 12 en suite No smoking in 5 bedrooms s fr £50; d £78-£94 (incl. bkfst) * LB **FACILITIES:** Xmas **CONF:** Thtr 140 Class 80 Board 40 Del from £65 * **PARKING:** 100 **NOTES:** Closed 23 Dec-7 Jan
CARDS:

See advert under BLAIRGOWRIE

CRAIGELLACHIE, Moray Map 15 NJ24

★★★76% *Craigellachie*

AB38 9SR
☎ 01340 881204 01340 881253
e-mail: sales@craigellachie.com
Dir: *on the A95 in Craigellachie, 300yds from the A95/A941 crossing*

Accommodation at this Victorian hotel ranges from impressive suites and master bedrooms, to comfortable and individually decorated standard rooms. Public areas include a choice of relaxing lounges, meeting rooms, and bars. There are

continued

CRAIGELLACHIE, continued

Craigellachie Hotel, Craigellachie

also three dining rooms offering excellent dishes prepared from fresh Scottish produce.
ROOMS: 26 en suite (1 fmly) **FACILITIES:** Gym Pool table **CONF:** Thtr 60 Class 36 Board 24 **PARKING:** 50 **NOTES:** No smoking in restaurant **CARDS:**

See advert on opposite page

CRAIL, Fife Map 12 NO60

★★68% Balcomie Links

Balcomie Rd KY10 3TN
☎ 01333 450237 📠 01333 450540
e-mail: joemcgachy@aol.com
Dir: *take A917, on approaching Crail follow road for golf course, hotel last large building on left*
Especially popular with visiting golfers, this welcoming family-run hotel on the east side of the village represents good value for money in a relaxing atmosphere. Well maintained bedrooms come in a variety of sizes and styles and offer all the expected amenities. There is a contrasting choice of well stocked bars and an attractive restaurant.
ROOMS: 15 en suite (2 fmly) No smoking in 3 bedrooms s £30-£35; d £60-£70 (incl. bkfst) * LB **FACILITIES:** STV Pool table Games room entertainment Xmas **PARKING:** 40 **CARDS:**

★65% *Croma*

Nethergate KY10 3TU
☎ 01333 450239
Dir: *take A917 to Crail*
This comfortable small hotel has particular appeal for families and visiting golfers. Public areas include a cosy bar and traditional style dining room. Bedrooms, which are modern in style, are due to benefit from a rolling programme of refurbishment.
ROOMS: 8 rms (6 en suite) (6 fmly) **PARKING:** 6 **NOTES:** No smoking in restaurant Closed Dec-Mar

CRIEFF, Perth & Kinross Map 11 NN82

★★★73% ❀ Crieff Hydro

Best Western

Ferntower Rd PH7 3LQ
☎ 01764 655555 📠 01764 653087
e-mail: enquires@crieffhydro.com
Dir: *from Perth first right up Connaught Terrace, first right again*
Known for its excellent leisure and sporting facilities, the Crieff Hydro maintains a traditional standard of service and hospitality. Rooms, ranging from 'standard' to 'executive' and opulent suites, have every modern comfort, and families will find that children are well catered for. There is a large restaurant and also an informal brasserie which takes its cooking seriously.

continued

ROOMS: 203 en suite 6 annexe en suite (67 fmly) s £59-£87; d £118-£174 (incl. bkfst) * LB **FACILITIES:** Indoor swimming (H) Golf 9 Tennis (hard) Fishing Squash Riding Snooker Sauna Solarium Gym Pool table Croquet lawn Putting green Jacuzzi/spa Bowling Off-road Football pitch Adventure playground Water ski-ing Cinema entertainment ch fac Xmas **CONF:** Thtr 335 Class 125 Board 68 Del £125 * **SERVICES:** Lift **PARKING:** 205 **NOTES:** No dogs (ex guide dogs) No smoking in restaurant Civ Wed 150 **CARDS:**

★★69% *Murraypark*

Connaught Ter PH7 3DJ
☎ 01764 653731 📠 01764 655311
Dir: *off A85 to Perth, near Crieff Golf Club*
Now operated by the owners of Crieff Hydro, this well established resort hotel has been considerably upgraded, with most bedrooms now being very smartly appointed with the public rooms being bright and comfortable. The dining room is formally set and offers an enjoyable table d'hôte menu. Quietly located in a residential area close to the golf course.
ROOMS: 11 en suite 8 annexe en suite (1 fmly) **CONF:** Thtr 30 Class 20 Board 16 Del from £75 * **PARKING:** 40 **NOTES:** No smoking in restaurant **CARDS:**

★★64% Lockes Acre

7 Comrie Rd PH7 4BP
☎ 01764 652526 📠 01764 652526
Dir: *take A9/M9 for Perth, turn off at A822 Crieff, once in Crieff take A85 Comrie/Lochearnhead Rd, hotel on right hand side of A85 just outside Crieff*
A comfortable holiday hotel, situated at the west side of town overlooking the surrounding hills. Bedrooms, though variable in size, are comfortably modern in style and offer all the expected amenities. Public areas include a conservatory lounge, and enjoyable home cooked fare is served in either the bar or dining room.
ROOMS: 7 rms (4 en suite) (1 fmly) s £28-£36; d £50-£58 (incl. bkfst) * **PARKING:** 35 **NOTES:** No dogs (ex guide dogs) No smoking in restaurant **CARDS:**

★★61% *Crieff*

49 East High St PH7 3HY
☎ 01764 652632 & 653854 📠 01764 655019
Dir: *M80 to Stirling then A9 to Dunblane, leave A9 at Braco and follow A82 to A822 into Crieff, go through town centre to East High St hotel on right*
A relaxed informal atmosphere prevails at this welcoming family-run hotel, in the centre of town. Public areas include a choice of well stocked bars, a small restaurant, and a beauty & hair salon. The well equipped bedrooms vary in size and in style.
ROOMS: 10 rms (9 en suite) (1 fmly) **FACILITIES:** Solarium Pool table Hair & beauty salon Beauty therapist **PARKING:** 9 **CARDS:**

★★61% The Drummond Arms
James Square PH7 3HX
☎ 01764 652151 📠 01764 655222
e-mail: drummondarmshotel@btinternet.com
In 1745 Bonnie Prince Charlie and his generals held a Council of War at the Drummond Arms. The brightly decorated bedrooms come in mixed sizes and are furnished in both modern and traditional styles. The main public rooms are located on the first floor and include a well stocked cocktail bar with the smart restaurant adjacent.
ROOMS: 30 rms (29 en suite) 7 annexe en suite (3 fmly) s fr £28; d fr £56 (incl. bkfst) * LB **FACILITIES:** Pool table Xmas **CONF:** Thtr 120 Class 60 Board 30 Del from £54 * **SERVICES:** Lift **PARKING:** 30
CARDS:

CRUDEN BAY, Aberdeenshire — Map 15 NK03

★★65% Red House
Aulton Rd AB42 0NJ
☎ 01779 812215 📠 01779 812320
e-mail: ian@redhousehotel7.freeserve.co.uk
Dir: *turn off A952 Aberdeen/Peterhead road at Little Chef onto the A975 towards Cruden Bay, hotel opposite golf course*
This personally run small hotel is situated opposite the golf course. The smartly decorated bedrooms are modern in style and offer a good range of amenities. Inviting public areas include a choice of bars, a foyer lounge and attractive dining room. Varied menus offer a wide range of reasonably priced dishes.
ROOMS: 6 rms (5 en suite) (1 fmly) **FACILITIES:** STV Pool table **CONF:** Board 180 **PARKING:** 40 **CARDS:**

CUMBERNAULD, North Lanarkshire — Map 11 NS77

★★★★60% *Westerwood Hotel Golf & Country Club*
1 St Andrews Dr, Westerwood G68 0EW
☎ 01236 457171 📠 01236 738478
e-mail: westerwoodhotels@btinternet.com
Dir: *A80 exit after passing Oki factory signposted Wardpark/Castlecary second left at Old Inns rdbt then right at mini rdbt*
The 18-hole golf course, designed by Seve Ballesteros, together with the range of leisure, conference and function facilities, are major attractions at this modern business hotel. There is a wide choice of accommodation, all rooms are smartly furnished. The Tipsy Laird restaurant offers a modern style of cooking using the best local ingredients.
ROOMS: 49 en suite (20 fmly) No smoking in 19 bedrooms
FACILITIES: STV Indoor swimming (H) Golf 18 Tennis (hard) Snooker Solarium Gym Pool table Putting green Jacuzzi/spa Steam room Bowling green Driving range **CONF:** Thtr 300 Class 160 Board 40 **SERVICES:** Lift air con **PARKING:** 204 **NOTES:** No dogs (ex guide dogs) No smoking in restaurant **CARDS:**

CUPAR, Fife — Map 11 NO31

★★69% Eden House
2 Pitscottie Rd KY15 4HF
☎ 01334 652510 📠 01334 652277
e-mail: lv@eden.u-net.com
Dir: *overlooking Haugh Park, Cupar on A91, 8m W of St.Andrews*
The tastefully decorated bedrooms are comfortably furnished and come with a good range of accessories. Public areas include a well stocked bar which also provides a popular informal food option. The candle lit conservatory restaurant is a relaxed setting for the fine dining experience offered by the seasonal changing carte and fixed price menus.

continued

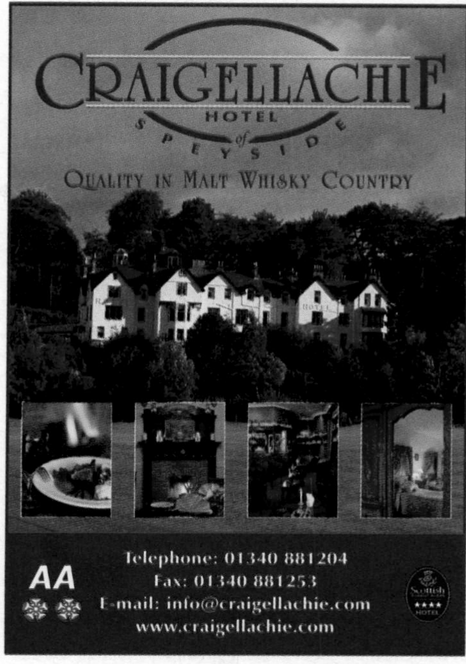

CRAIGELLACHIE
HOTEL
of
SPEYSIDE
QUALITY IN MALT WHISKY COUNTRY
AA
Telephone: 01340 881204
Fax: 01340 881253
E-mail: info@craigellachie.com
www.craigellachie.com

ROOMS: 9 en suite 2 annexe en suite (3 fmly) s £50-£57; d £76-£86 (incl. bkfst) * LB **FACILITIES:** STV **CONF:** Thtr 40 Class 40 Board 40 **PARKING:** 18 **NOTES:** No dogs (ex guide dogs)
CARDS:

DERVAIG See Mull, Isle of

DINGWALL, Highland — Map 14 NH55

★★76% Kinkell House
Easter Kinkell, Conon Bridge IV7 8HY
☎ 01349 861270 📠 01349 865902
e-mail: kinkell@aol.com
Dir: *10m N of Inverness turn off A9 onto B9169 for 1m*
Kinkell House is a 19th-century farmhouse, restored and extended to create a delightful small country house hotel and restaurant, with splendid views over the Cromarty Firth. There are three comfortable lounges, one of which is a conservatory, and a tempting dinner menu which changes daily.
ROOMS: 9 en suite (1 fmly) No smoking in all bedrooms s £45-£60; d £80-£100 (incl. bkfst) * LB **FACILITIES:** Croquet lawn **PARKING:** 20 **NOTES:** No smoking in restaurant Civ Wed 70 **CARDS:**

DIRLETON, East Lothian — Map 12 NT58

★★★68% The Open Arms
EH39 5EG
☎ 01620 850241 📠 01620 850570
e-mail: openarms@clara.co.uk
Dir: *from A1 take signs for North Berwick, pass through Gullane, 2m on left*
This long-established hotel sits by the village green and looks across to Dirleton Castle. It has the ambience of a country house,

continued

DIRLETON, continued

with friendly service to match. Public areas include an inviting lounge and a cosy bar, a smart brasserie and intimate restaurant. Bedrooms come in a variety of sizes.
ROOMS: 10 en suite s £90-£90; d £140-£180 (incl. bkfst) * LB **FACILITIES:** Xmas **CONF:** Thtr 200 Class 150 Board 100 **PARKING:** 30 **NOTES:** No smoking in restaurant **CARDS:**

DORNIE, Highland Map 14 NG82

★★62% Dornie

Francis St IV40 8DT
☎ 01599 555205 📠 01599 555429
e-mail: dornie@madasafish.com
Dir: *turn off A87, signposted to the village of Dornie, hotel situated in centre of village on right*

A warm welcome awaits guests at this small hotel by the shore of Loch Duich. Bedrooms have comfortable modern appointments. Public areas include a comfortable lounge, a popular bar and an attractive restaurant.
ROOMS: 13 rms (7 en suite) (3 fmly) s fr £35; d fr £70 (incl. bkfst) * LB **FACILITIES:** Pool table Xmas **PARKING:** 16 **NOTES:** No smoking in restaurant **CARDS:**

DORNOCH, Highland Map 14 NH78

★★★64% Royal Golf Hotel

The First Tee, Grange Rd IV25 3LG
☎ 01862 810283 📠 01862 810923
e-mail: royalgolf@morton-hotels.com
Dir: *from A9, turn right to Dornoch and continue through main street. Straight ahead at cross roads then hotel is 200yds on the right*
Situated beside the Royal Dornoch Golf Club and overlooking the first tee and the Dornoch Firth, this well established hotel attracts golfers from all around the world. Accommodation includes two fine suites on the top floor. The sun lounge is a popular venue for watching the course.
ROOMS: 25 en suite 8 annexe rms (2 fmly) s £83-£98; d £102-£225 (incl. bkfst) * LB **FACILITIES:** Tennis (hard) Fishing ch fac Xmas **CONF:** Thtr 120 Class 50 Board 50 **PARKING:** 20 **NOTES:** No smoking in restaurant Closed Jan-Feb RS Nov, Dec & Mar
CARDS:

★★70% *Dornoch Castle*

Castle St IV25 3SD
☎ 01862 810216 📠 01862 810981
Dir: *2m North of Dornoch Firth Bridge on A9, turn right onto A949*
Once the Palace of the Bishops of Caithness, dating back to the 16th century, this welcoming family run hotel is popular with tourists and golfers. The comfortable lounge, overlooking the well tended gardens, offers a relaxing environment, and the cocktail bar, with its panelled and natural stone walls, reflects the original character of the house. Main house bedrooms tend to be more spacious and traditional than those in the wing. The Green Room offers an more informal eating option to the dining room.
ROOMS: 4 en suite 13 annexe en suite (4 fmly) **SERVICES:** Lift **PARKING:** 16 **NOTES:** Closed Nov-Mar **CARDS:**

★★65% *Burghfield House*

IV25 3HN
☎ 01862 810212 📠 01862 810404
Dir: *turn off A9 at Evelix junct then travel 1m into Dornoch. Just before War Memorial turn left and follow road up hill to tower in the trees*
This extended Victorian mansion stands in well kept gardens and is under new ownership for the first time in over 50 years. Bedrooms are located either in the main house or in the Garden Wing annexe, with varying styles of decor. Public areas, including a large comfortable lounge, are enhanced with antiques, fresh flowers and real fires, while the bright dining room features an interesting table d'hôte menu
ROOMS: 13 en suite 15 annexe en suite **FACILITIES:** Sauna Putting green **CONF:** Thtr 100 Board 80 **PARKING:** 62
CARDS:

DRUMNADROCHIT, Highland Map 14 NH53

★★★67% Polmaily House

IV63 6XT
☎ 01456 450343 📠 01456 450813
e-mail: polmaily@BTinternet.com
Dir: *in Drumnadrochit turn onto A831 signposted to Cannich, hotel is 2m on right. 1.5m from Loch Ness*
Standing in 18 acres of lawns and woods, a child-friendly environment is created with facilities such as a popular pets' corner. The informal conservatory bar is accessed through the inviting drawing room, while the upstairs library is a quiet retreat. The elegant dining room provides a pleasant setting for the four-course dinner.
ROOMS: 10 en suite (6 fmly) s £64-£75; d £128-£150 (incl. bkfst) * LB **FACILITIES:** Indoor swimming (H) Tennis (hard) Fishing Riding Croquet lawn Indoor/outdoor childs play area Boating Pony rides Beauty/massage Pets corner ch fac Xmas **CONF:** Thtr 16 Class 8 Board 14 **PARKING:** 20 **NOTES:** No smoking in restaurant Closed 31 Oct-30 Dec & 2 Jan-Mar Civ Wed **CARDS:**

DRYMEN, Stirling Map 11 NS48

★★★67% *Buchanan Arms*

23 Main St G63 0BQ
☎ 01360 660588 📠 01360 660943
Dir: *travelling N from Glasgow on the A81 take the turn off onto the A811, the hotel is situated at the S end of Main Street*
This former coaching inn has been extended and modernised to provide a wide range of facilities. Well equipped bedrooms are attractively decorated and the bar has wooden flooring and oak beams. There is also a spacious lounge and conservatory, and a very popular restaurant.
ROOMS: 52 en suite (3 fmly) No smoking in 6 bedrooms **FACILITIES:** STV Indoor swimming (H) Squash Sauna Solarium Gym Jacuzzi/spa **CONF:** Thtr 150 Class 60 Board 60 **PARKING:** 100 **NOTES:** No smoking in restaurant **CARDS:**

★★★64% Winnock

Best Western

The Square G63 0BL
☎ 01360 660245 📠 01360 660267
Dir: *from S follow M74 onto M8 through Glasgow. Exit junct 16B, follow A809 to Aberfoyle*
Prominently situated by the village green, this welcoming 17th-

continued

century inn has been extensively modernised. The bar, with stucco walls and beamed ceiling is a popular rendezvous, whilst the restaurant offers Scottish fare.

ROOMS: 48 en suite (12 fmly) No smoking in 17 bedrooms s £49-£59; d £39-£46 (incl. bkfst) * LB **FACILITIES:** Petanque entertainment ch fac Xmas **CONF:** Thtr 140 Class 60 Board 70 Del from £49 * **PARKING:** 60 **NOTES:** No smoking in restaurant Civ Wed 120 **CARDS:**

DULNAIN BRIDGE, Highland — Map 14 NH92

★★★71% *Muckrach Lodge*

PH26 3LY
☎ 01479 851257 Fax 01479 851325
e-mail: muckrach.lodge@sol.co.uk
Dir: *from A95 Dulain Bridge exit follow A938 towards Carrbridge. Hotel 500mtrs on right*

Muckrach is a Victorian shooting lodge, quietly situated in neatly tended and attractive grounds. Bedrooms, including two suites and some rooms located in the Coach House, are comfortably appointed. The recently refurbished bar leads into a comfortable lounge. Some meals are served in the bar, while a more formal option is offered in the conservatory restaurant.

ROOMS: 9 en suite 4 annexe en suite (2 fmly) **FACILITIES:** Beauty & aroma therapy ch fac **CONF:** Thtr 80 Class 20 Board 24 **PARKING:** 53 **NOTES:** No dogs (ex guide dogs) No smoking in restaurant **CARDS:**

DUMBARTON, West Dunbartonshire — Map 10 NS37

Travelodge

Travelodge

Milton G82 2TY
☎ 01389 765202 Fax 01389 765202
Dir: *1m E, on A82 westbound*

This modern building offers accommodation in smart, spacious and well equipped bedrooms, all with en suite bathrooms. Refreshments may be taken at the nearby family restaurant. For further details and the Travelodge phone number, consult the Hotel Groups page.

ROOMS: 32 en suite

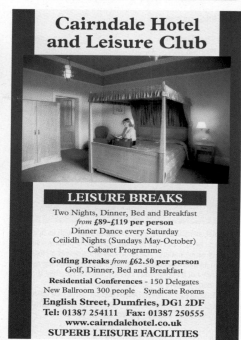

DUMFRIES, Dumfries & Galloway — Map 11 NX97

see also Carrutherstown

★★★69% Cairndale Hotel & Leisure Club

English St DG1 2DF
☎ 01387 254111 Fax 01387 250555
e-mail: sales@cairndale.fsnet.co.uk
Dir: *from S turn off M6 onto A75 to Dumfries, left at first rdbt, cross railway bridge, continue to traffic lights, hotel is 1st building on left*

Within walking distance of the town centre, this hotel provides a wide range of amenities, including extensive leisure facilities and an impressive new conference and entertainment centre. Bedrooms range from stylish new suites to cosy singles. Restaurants and a coffee shop offer everything from a full dinner to a quick snack.

ROOMS: 91 en suite (22 fmly) No smoking in 40 bedrooms s £65-£85; d £105 (incl. bkfst) * LB **FACILITIES:** STV Indoor swimming (H) Sauna Solarium Gym Jacuzzi/spa Steam room entertainment Xmas **CONF:** Thtr 300 Class 150 Board 50 Del from £95 * **SERVICES:** Lift **PARKING:** 70 **NOTES:** Civ Wed 300 **CARDS:**

See advert on this page

DUMFRIES, continued

★★★68% Station

49 Lovers Walk DG1 1LT
☎ 01387 254316 📠 01387 250388
Dir: *from A75 follow signs to Dumfries town centre, hotel is opposite the railway station*

This hotel, sympathetically modernised to blend with its fine Victorian characteristics, offers well equipped bedrooms and a choice of eating options. The Courtyard Bistro serves an extensive menu in an informal atmosphere and the Pullman dining room, which may not be open every evening, offers a carefully chosen dinner menu in more relaxed surroundings.
ROOMS: 32 en suite (2 fmly) **FACILITIES:** STV Jacuzzi/spa **CONF:** Thtr 60 Class 20 Board 30 Del from £70 * **SERVICES:** Lift **PARKING:** 40 **NOTES:** Civ Wed 60 **CARDS:**

See advert on opposite page

⌂ *Travelodge*

Annan Rd, Collin DG1 3SE
☎ 01387 750658 📠 01387 750658
Dir: *on A75*
This modern building offers accommodation in smart, spacious and well equipped bedrooms, all with en suite bathrooms. Refreshments may be taken at the nearby family restaurant. For further details and the Travelodge phone number, consult the Hotel Groups page.
ROOMS: 40 en suite

DUNBAR, East Lothian — Map 12 NT67

★★65% Bayswell

Bayswell Park EH42 1AE
☎ 01368 862225 📠 01368 862225
Dir: *off A1 into Dunbar High St, turn left and follow road to left then take first right into Bayswell Park*
There is a friendly and informal atmosphere at this family-run hotel, which enjoys panoramic views over the Firth of Forth from its striking clifftop position. Bedrooms offer mixed modern appointments. As well as the cosy ground floor bar, there is a residents' bar adjacent to the restaurant.
ROOMS: 13 en suite (4 fmly) s £49.50-£59.50; d £69-£79 (incl. bkfst) * LB **FACILITIES:** STV Petanque entertainment Xmas **PARKING:** 20 **CARDS:**

> Popped the question? Hotels with Civ Wed in their entry are licensed for civil wedding ceremonies. Maximum numbers for the ceremony only are shown, e.g. Civ Wed 50

DUNBLANE, Stirling — Map 11 NN70

Premier Collection

★★★ *Cromlix House*

Kinbuck FK15 9JT
☎ 01786 822125 📠 01786 825450
e-mail: reservations@cromlixhousehotel.com
Dir: *off the A9 N of Dunblane. Exit B8033 to Kinbuck Village cross narrow bridge drive 200yds on left*
This fine Edwardian mansion lies amidst neatly tended gardens in a 3000 acre estate. Bedrooms, many of them having a private sitting room, have the real character of a country house and are comfortably furnished. There is a choice of sitting rooms, both the drawing room and library heated by log fires during the cooler months, whilst dinner, using local ingredients wherever possible, is served in one of two elegant dining rooms. Breakfast is taken in the conservatory overlooking the gardens.
ROOMS: 14 en suite **FACILITIES:** Tennis (hard) Fishing Croquet lawn Clay pigeon shooting Falconry **CONF:** Thtr 40 Class 30 Board 22 **PARKING:** 51 **NOTES:** No smoking in restaurant Closed 2-29 Jan RS Oct-Apr **CARDS:**

DUNDEE, Dundee City — Map 11 NO43

see also Auchterhouse

★★★70% Swallow

Kingsway West, Invergowrie DD2 5JT
☎ 01382 641122 📠 01382 631201
e-mail: info@swallowhotels.com
Dir: *turn off from A90/A929 rdbt following sign for Denhead of Gray, hotel on left*
Conveniently situated just off the Dundee bypass, this extended Victorian mansion, is set amid landscaped gardens. The comfortable and well equipped bedrooms range from attractive suites and executive rooms to smaller standard rooms. Public areas include a bright foyer lounge, well stocked bar, an attractive restaurant and the leisure and conference centres.
ROOMS: 107 en suite (11 fmly) No smoking in 60 bedrooms s £95-£105; d £115-£150 (incl. bkfst) * LB **FACILITIES:** STV Indoor swimming (H) Sauna Solarium Gym Putting green Jacuzzi/spa Trim trail Mountain bike hire Xmas **CONF:** Thtr 100 Class 36 Board 50 Del from £108 * **PARKING:** 140 **NOTES:** No smoking in restaurant Civ Wed 120 **CARDS:**

> Early start? Hotels at all star levels should provide in-room alarm clocks and/or alarm calls.

★★★68% Sandford Hotel

Newport Hill, Wormit DD6 8RG
☎ 01382 541802 🖹 01382 542136
e-mail: sandford.hotel@btinternet.com
Dir: *Hotel located 4m S of the Tay Bridge at the junction with A914/B946*
Built around the turn of the century, Sandford Hotel is now a most comfortable country house. Bedrooms with pleasing colour schemes are comfortably furnished and offer the expected amenities. You can unwind in front of a log fire in the wonderfully relaxing Minstrels' Gallery. There is also a well stocked bar and an elegant restaurant which offers a varied menu. Staff are friendly and willing to please.
ROOMS: 16 en suite (1 fmly) **FACILITIES:** STV **CONF:** Thtr 45 Class 24 Board 28 **PARKING:** 30 **CARDS:**

★★★67% Invercarse
371 Perth Rd DD2 1PG
☎ 01382 669231 🖹 01382 644112
Dir: *from the A90 Perth to Aberdeen Road take the A85 (Taybridge) then follow signs*
This comfortable hotel, a former mansion house with its own grounds in the west end, is a popular base for visiting businessmen. The variable sized bedrooms are comfortable in appointment, and offer a good range of amenities. Inviting public areas include a choice of bars and a smart restaurant.
ROOMS: 42 en suite No smoking in 29 bedrooms s £37.50-£68; d £64-£80 (incl. bkfst) * LB **FACILITIES:** STV **CONF:** Thtr 300 Class 100 Board 50 Del from £69 * **PARKING:** 119 **NOTES:** No smoking in restaurant Closed 24-26 Dec & 31 Dec-2 Jan
CARDS:

★★70% *The Shaftesbury*
1 Hyndford St DD2 1HQ
☎ 01382 669216 🖹 01382 641598
e-mail: reservations@shaftesbury-hotel.co.uk
Dir: *from Perth follow signs to Airport, take first left at circle then turn right, follow Perth Road and turn right*
A comfortable, welcoming family-run hotel in the west end, this impressive Victorian house has been sympathetically converted. Public areas include a small relaxing lounge, a well stocked bar and separate restaurant where the menu offers a range of light and substantial dishes prepared from quality fresh ingredients. Staff are friendly and willing to please.
ROOMS: 12 en suite (2 fmly) **NOTES:** No smoking in restaurant
CARDS:

⌂ Premier Lodge (Dundee North)

Dayton Dr, Camberdown Leisure Park, Kingsway DD2 3SQ
☎ 0870 700 1362 🖹 0870 700 1363
Premier Lodge offers modern, well equipped, en suite accommodation suitable for both business and leisure travellers. Meals can be taken at the adjacent popular restaurant and bar which is fully licensed. For further details, consult the Hotel Groups page.
ROOMS: 80 en suite d £42 *

⌂ *Travelodge*
A90 Kingsway DD2 4TD
☎ 0800 850950
Dir: *on A90*
This modern building offers accommodation in smart, spacious and well equipped bedrooms, all with en suite bathrooms. Refreshments may be taken at the nearby family restaurant. For further details and the Travelodge phone number, consult the Hotel Groups page.
ROOMS: 30 en suite

DUNDONNELL, Highland Map 14 NH08

★★★74% Dundonnell

Little Loch Broom IV23 2QR
☎ 01854 633204 01854 633366
e-mail: selbie@dundonnellhotel.co.uk
Dir: *turn off A835 at Braemore junct on to A832*

Situated by the roadside at the head of Little Loch Broom, this hospitable hotel has been extensively developed over 25 years by the Florence family as a haven of relaxation and good food. The bedrooms are well equipped and most enjoy fine views.

ROOMS: 28 en suite (2 fmly) s £55-£67.50; d £100-£110 (incl. bkfst) * LB **FACILITIES:** Pool table Xmas **CONF:** Thtr 70 Class 50 Board 40 Del from £69.50 * **PARKING:** 60 **NOTES:** No smoking in restaurant Closed 22 Nov-Feb (ex Xmas/New Year) **CARDS:**

DUNFERMLINE, Fife Map 11 NT08

★★★72% Keavil House

Crossford KY12 8QW
☎ 01383 736258 01383 621600
e-mail: keavil@queensferry-hotels.co.uk
Dir: *2m W of Dunfermline on A994*

This hotel is a former manor house in the village of Crossford. Inviting public areas include a choice of contrasting bars, a comfortable lounge and a smart Conservatory Restaurant which specialises in carefully prepared Taste of Scotland specialities. Bedrooms, with pleasing colour schemes are comfortably modern in style.

ROOMS: 47 en suite (4 fmly) No smoking in 26 bedrooms s £75-£78; d £90-£105 * LB **FACILITIES:** STV Indoor swimming (H) Sauna Solarium Gym Jacuzzi/spa Aerobics studio Steam room Xmas **CONF:** Thtr 200 Class 60 Board 50 Del from £99 * **PARKING:** 150 **NOTES:** No dogs (ex guide dogs) No smoking in restaurant **CARDS:**

See advert on opposite page

★★★70% Garvock House Hotel

St John's Dr, Transy KY12 7TU
☎ 01383 621067 01383 621168
e-mail: sales@garvock.co.uk
Dir: *from M90 junct 3 take A907 into Dunfermline. After football stadium turn left into Garvock Hill, then 1st right St John's Drive, hotel on right*

A welcoming atmosphere prevails at this handsome Georgian house which stands in its own grounds on the east side of town near the football stadium. The spacious bedrooms are modern in style and offer a good range of amenities. Much of the original character of the house has been carefully retained in the attractive public areas. Two relaxing lounges are serviced by a small bar and fresh produce features on the short menu in the elegant dining room.

continued

ROOMS: 11 en suite (1 fmly) No smoking in all bedrooms s fr £65; d fr £95 (incl. bkfst) * LB **FACILITIES:** Xmas **CONF:** Thtr 25 Class 25 Board 25 Del from £109 * **PARKING:** 38 **NOTES:** No smoking in restaurant **CARDS:**

★★★69% Elgin

Charlestown KY11 3EE
☎ 01383 872257 01383 873044
e-mail: Enquiries@elgin-hotel.co.uk
Dir: *3m W of M90, junct 1, on loop road off A985, signposted Limekilns & Charlestown*

A comfortable, welcoming hotel overlooking the Firth of Forth to the Pentland Hills beyond. All the comfortable bedrooms offer a good range of accessories. A new extension provides a lounge and a small chapel. The Tavern bar is relaxed and informal, and a wide range of competitively priced dishes are available in the adjacent restaurant. Golfing packages are available.

ROOMS: 12 en suite (3 fmly) No smoking in 6 bedrooms s £52-£58.50; d £70-£90 (incl. bkfst) * LB **FACILITIES:** STV Xmas **CONF:** Thtr 150 Class 80 Board 50 Del from £70 * **PARKING:** 70 **NOTES:** No smoking in restaurant Civ Wed 160 **CARDS:**

★★★67% Pitbauchlie House

Aberdour Rd KY11 4PB
☎ 01383 722282 01383 620738
e-mail: info@pitbauchlie.com
Dir: *leave M90 at junct 2, continue onto A823, turn onto B916. Hotel situated 0.5m on right*

A comfortable business and tourist hotel, Pitbauchlie House is set in wooded grounds. Public areas are bright and modern with a choice of bars, a foyer lounge, and a restaurant which overlooks the garden. Bedrooms range in size.

ROOMS: 50 en suite (2 fmly) s £66-£82; d £83-£99 (incl. bkfst) * LB **FACILITIES:** STV Gym **CONF:** Thtr 150 Class 80 Board 60 Del from £103 * **PARKING:** 80 **NOTES:** No smoking in restaurant **CARDS:**

★★★65% King Malcolm
Queensferry Rd KY11 8DS
☎ 01383 722611 🖷 01383 730865

Dir: *on A823, S of town*
This popular business hotel is located on the east side of town. The top floor bedrooms have been considerably enhanced and all rooms now offer comfortable modern appointments. Public areas include a choice of bars, one with a bright conservatory extension, a foyer lunge, restaurant, and a range of banqueting facilities.
ROOMS: 48 en suite (2 fmly) No smoking in 12 bedrooms s £80-£90; d £110-£120 * **FACILITIES:** STV Pool table Xmas **CONF:** Thtr 150 Class 60 Board 50 Del from £80 * **PARKING:** 60 **NOTES:** No smoking in restaurant Civ Wed 70 **CARDS:**

★★★61% Pitfirrane Arms
Main St, Crossford KY12 8NJ
☎ 01383 736132 🖷 01383 621760
e-mail: info@scothotels.com
Dir: *from Kincardine-follow the A985 at large rdbt take the A994 to Dunfermline, Crossford is the second village from the rdbt, hotel on right*
Situated in the village of Crossford west of town, this long-established business hotel offers good value accommodation. Bedrooms, which are compact and practical in appointment, have benefitted from cosmetic enhancement. Public areas include a smart restaurant and a choice of contrasting bars.
ROOMS: 40 en suite (1 fmly) **FACILITIES:** STV **CONF:** Thtr 90 Class 60 Board 40 **PARKING:** 72 **NOTES:** No smoking in restaurant
CARDS:

★★66% The Hideaway Lodge & Restaurant
Kingseat Rd, Halbeath KY12 0UB
☎ 01383 725474 🖷 01383 622428
e-mail: enquiries@thehideaway.co.uk
Dir: *from M90 junct 3 follow signs for Dunfermline. At mini-rdbt turn right. Hotel 800yds on right over level crossing*
A relaxed and informal atmosphere prevails at this family-run establishment on the east side of town. The original lodge is comprised of a bar and restaurant where the carte menu, available in both areas, offers an extensive range of dishes. The lodge contains the comfortable new bedrooms with smart appointments and a range of amenities.
ROOMS: 8 en suite d £45 * LB **FACILITIES:** ch fac **PARKING:** 30 **NOTES:** No dogs (ex guide dogs) **CARDS:**

DUNKELD, Perth & Kinross — Map 11 NO04

Premier Collection

★★★ Kinnaird
Kinnaird Estate PH8 0LB
☎ 01796 482440 🖷 01796 482289
e-mail: enquiry@kinnairdestate.com
RELAIS & CHATEAUX
Dir: *from Perth, A9 towards Inverness until Dunkeld but do not enter, continue N for 2m then B898 on left*
Part of a 9000 acre estate in the heart of the Perthshire countryside this Edwardian mansion provides a very warm welcome. There are several inviting sitting rooms and a snooker room warmed by open fires. Innovative cooking is offered in one of the two dining rooms. Bedrooms are generously proportioned and luxurious in appointment; living flame gas fires are a unique characteristic.

ROOMS: 9 en suite s £300-£395; d £345-£440 (incl. bkfst & dinner) * LB **FACILITIES:** STV Tennis (hard) Fishing Snooker Croquet lawn Shooting **CONF:** Thtr 25 Class 10 Board 15 **SERVICES:** Lift **PARKING:** 22 **NOTES:** No dogs No children 12yrs No smoking in restaurant RS Jan-Mar (closed Mon-Wed)
CARDS:

★★65% Atholl Arms
Bridgehead PH8 0AQ
☎ 01350 727219 & 727759 🖷 01350 727219
e-mail: cdarbishire@aol.com
Dir: *12m N of Perth, turn off A9 into Dunkeld, the hotel will be found on the right overlooking the bridge and the River Tay*
This long established family-run hotel, is a former coaching inn situated close to the River Tay. Bedrooms, with the expected amenities, are comfortably traditional in style and some overlook the river. Public areas include a choice of contrasting bars and

continued

DUNKELD, continued

enjoyable home prepared fare is offered in the dining room or homely foyer.
ROOMS: 13 en suite (1 fmly) No smoking in 12 bedrooms s £45-£50; d £60-£65 (incl. bkfst) * LB **FACILITIES:** Pool table Xmas **CONF:** Thtr 40 Board 30 **PARKING:** 21 **NOTES:** No children 8yrs
CARDS:

D

DUNOON, Argyll & Bute Map 10 NS17

★★76% Enmore

Marine Pde, Kirn PA23 8HH
☎ 01369 702230 01369 702148
e-mail: enmorehotel@btinternet.com
Dir: *on coastal route between two ferries, 1m N of Dunoon*

This comfortable seafront hotel enjoys a wonderful outlook over the Firth of Clyde. Inviting public areas, enhanced by fresh floral displays, include a comfortable and relaxing lounge. The attractive dining room provides the setting for carefully prepared Taste of Scotland dishes. Some of the attractive bedrooms have four-poster beds, others are comfortably furnished in mixed styles.
ROOMS: 10 en suite (2 fmly) s fr £35; d £99-£150 (incl. bkfst) * LB **FACILITIES:** Squash Xmas **PARKING:** 20 **NOTES:** No smoking in restaurant Closed 2-12 Jan RS Nov-Feb **CARDS:**

★★68% Royal Marine

Hunters Quay PA23 8HJ
☎ 01369 705810 01369 702329
e-mail: rmhotel@sol.co.uk
Dir: *on A815 opposite Western Ferries terminal*

Situated opposite the Hunters Quay Ferry Terminal and enjoying lovely views over the Firth of Clyde, this family run hotel provides a welcoming atmosphere. Bedrooms, including those in the adjacent annexe, are comfortably modern in style and offer the expected amenities. Public areas include a spacious lounge on the first floor, and the new Ghillies café/bar provides an informal setting for the extensive range of dishes offered from the varied menus.
ROOMS: 28 en suite 10 annexe en suite (3 fmly) s fr £40; d fr £60 (incl. bkfst) * LB **FACILITIES:** Xmas **CONF:** Thtr 80 Class 30 Board 30 Del from £60 * **PARKING:** 30 **NOTES:** No dogs (ex guide dogs) No smoking in restaurant **CARDS:**

★★66% Esplanade Hotel

West Bay PA23 7HU
☎ 01369 704070 01369 702129
e-mail: togwells@ehd.co.uk
Dir: *in town centre pass main pier and continue up hill, then first left and left again at the bottom of the Avenue*

This long established family run hotel in the West Bay enjoys a lovely outlook over the Firth of Clyde and offers a genuinely warm welcome to all its guests. The nicely presented public areas include a choice of comfortable lounges at ground and first floor levels. Bedrooms range from tastefully appointed superior and premier rooms to the smaller standard rooms.
ROOMS: 60 en suite 5 annexe rms (4 en suite) (4 fmly) No smoking in 3 bedrooms s £32.50-£45; d £60-£83 (incl. bkfst) * LB **FACILITIES:** Putting green entertainment **SERVICES:** Lift **PARKING:** 20 **NOTES:** No dogs (ex guide dogs) No smoking in restaurant Closed 21 Oct-20 Apr **CARDS:**

★70% Lyall Cliff

141 Alexandra Pde, East Bay PA23 8AW
☎ 01369 702041 01369 702041
e-mail: lyallcliff@talk21.com
Dir: *on A815 between Kirn and Dunoon on sea front, between the ferry terminals at Dunoon amd Hunters Quay*

This comfortable small hotel stands in its own well tended garden on the seafront enjoying views of the Firth of Clyde. The smartly decorated bedrooms, mostly non-smoking, come with mixed modern furnishings and the expected amenities. Public areas include a comfortable lounge and small library adjacent. Enjoyable home cooked fare is provided in the dining room. Musical themed weekend breaks during winter, spring and autumn are popular.
ROOMS: 10 en suite (3 fmly) No smoking in 8 bedrooms s £27-£37; d £46-£64 (incl. bkfst) LB **CONF:** Board 22 **PARKING:** 9 **NOTES:** No smoking in restaurant RS Jan-Mar **CARDS:**

EAST KILBRIDE, South Lanarkshire Map 11 NS65

★★★★70% Crutherland Country House Hotel

MACDONALD HOTELS

Strathaven Rd G75 0QZ
☎ 01355 577000 01355 220855
e-mail: info@crutherland.macdonald-hotels.co.uk
Dir: *off A725, in East Kilbride follow signs for Strathaven A726, approx 1.5m on A726 through Torrance rdbt and Crutherland House is on left in 150 yds*

This renovated mansion is set in 37 acres of landscaped grounds, two miles from the town centre. Behind the Georgian façade is a very spacious and comfortable hotel with extensive banqueting and leisure facilities. The bedrooms are all spacious and comfortable.
ROOMS: 76 en suite (26 fmly) No smoking in 62 bedrooms s fr £85; d fr £105 * LB **FACILITIES:** STV Indoor swimming (H) Sauna Solarium Gym Steam room Technogym Xmas **CONF:** Thtr 500 Class 100 Board 100 **SERVICES:** Lift **PARKING:** 150 **NOTES:** No dogs (ex guide dogs) No smoking in restaurant Civ Wed 150
CARDS:

Early start? Hotels at all star levels should provide in-room alarm clocks and/or alarm calls.

★★★69% Bruce Hotel
Cornwall St G74 1AF
☎ 01355 229771 🖹 01355 242216
e-mail: enquiries@maksu-group.co.uk
***Dir:** leave M74 at junct 5 on to A725 and follow to East Kilbride, follow town centre signs and turn right into Cornwall St, hotel 200yds on left*
Situated in the centre of East Kilbride and forming part of the main shopping centre, this purpose-built hotel offers a variety of rooms. The elegant lounge bar and formal restaurant serve a variety of excellent dishes, and secure car parking is available.
ROOMS: 65 en suite No smoking in 10 bedrooms s £55-£75; d £75-£95 (incl. bkfst) * **FACILITIES:** STV entertainment Xmas **CONF:** Thtr 600 Class 150 Board 100 Del from £85 * **SERVICES:** Lift **PARKING:** 30 **NOTES:** Civ Wed 300 **CARDS:**

★★★63% Stuart
2 Cornwall Way, Town Centre G74 1JR
☎ 013552 21161 🖹 013552 64410
***Dir:** 6m from junct 5 off M74, head for town centre, hotel on rdbt*
This business, conference and function hotel is convenient for the central shopping area. The spacious lounge bar is complemented by a split-level cocktail bar. Jellowickis, an informal and popular American Western diner, offers a varied good value menu. Executive rooms provide the best accommodation.
ROOMS: 38 en suite (1 fmly) No smoking in 4 bedrooms s £65-£75; d £80-£90 (incl. bkfst) * LB **FACILITIES:** STV **CONF:** Thtr 200 Class 80 Board 60 Del from £99 * **SERVICES:** Lift **NOTES:** No dogs (ex guide dogs) RS Christmas & New Year's Day **CARDS:**

⌂ Premier Lodge
Eaglesham Rd G75 8LW
☎ 0870 700 1398 🖹 0870 7001399

Premier Lodge offers modern, well equipped, en suite accommodation suitable for both business and leisure travellers. Meals can be taken at the adjacent popular restaurant and bar which is fully licensed. For further details, consult the Hotel Groups page.
ROOMS: 40 en suite d £42 *

EDINBURGH, City of Edinburgh — Map 11 NT27

★★★★★69% ❀❀❀ Sheraton Grand
1 Festival Square EH3 9SR
☎ 0131 229 9131 🖹 0131 228 4510
e-mail: sue_finlay@sheraton.com

***Dir:** follow City Centre signs(A8). Pass through Shandwick, right at lights into Lethian Rd. Right at next lights. Hotel on left at next lights*
This striking modern building forms part of an evolving development to be known as Exchange Square. Public rooms include a marble entrance hall with grand central staircase leading up to the popular Lobby Bar. The Terrace restaurant enjoys floodlit views of the Usher Hall and the historic castle beyond. The Grill Room is a discreet fine-dining restaurant suited to executive lunches. Bedrooms are mostly well proportioned.
ROOMS: 260 en suite (27 fmly) No smoking in 123 bedrooms s £175-£240; d £215-£280 * LB **FACILITIES:** STV Indoor swimming (H) Sauna Solarium Gym Jacuzzi/spa entertainment Xmas **CONF:** Thtr 485 Class 350 Board 120 Del from £160 * **SERVICES:** Lift air con **PARKING:** 80 **NOTES:** No dogs (ex guide dogs) Civ Wed 480
CARDS:

★★★★★65% ❀❀ Balmoral
1 Princes St EH2 2EQ
☎ 0131 556 2414 🖹 0131 557 8740
e-mail: reservations@balmoral-rf.demon.co.uk
***Dir:** the east end of Princes Street. Corner of North Bridge*
This classic Edwardian building dominates the east end of Princes

continued

Street. The elegant bedrooms are tastefully decorated, while the public areas include the Palm Court, a popular meeting place, particularly for the traditionally served afternoon teas. Guests can dine in 'Hadrians' restaurant or at the gourmet 'No.1' restaurant.
ROOMS: 186 en suite No smoking in 82 bedrooms **FACILITIES:** STV Indoor swimming (H) Sauna Solarium Gym Beauty salon Aromatherapy massage Hairdressers entertainment **CONF:** Thtr 380 Class 180 Board 40 **SERVICES:** Lift air con **PARKING:** 100 **CARDS:**

Hotel of the Year

★★★★77% ❀❀ Holyrood Hotel
Holyrood Rd EH8 6AE
☎ 0131 550 4500 🖹 0131 550 4545
e-mail: info@holyrood.macdonald-hotels.co.uk

MACDONALD HOTELS

***Dir:** the hotel is parallel to the Royal Mile, and near the Holyrood Palace and Dynamic Earth within Edinburgh city centre*
Chosen as Hotel of the Year for Scotland, this impressive and immensely stylish new building sits beside the Scottish Parliament, within a stone's throw of Holyrood Palace. The air-conditioned bedrooms and suites include a special Butler's Club floor and lounge. The hotel boasts many extra services such as valet parking and evening turndown, as well as a spa and leisure facility.
ROOMS: 157 en suite (10 fmly) No smoking in 140 bedrooms s £99; d £150-£220 * LB **FACILITIES:** STV Indoor swimming (H) Sauna Solarium Gym Jacuzzi/spa Beauty treatment rooms **CONF:** Thtr 300 Class 80 Board 80 Del from £150 * **SERVICES:** Lift air con **PARKING:** 80 **NOTES:** No smoking in restaurant **CARDS:**

EDINBURGH, continued

★★★★72% Marriott Dalmahoy

Kirknewton EH27 8EB
☎ 0131 333 1845 📠 0131 333 1433
Dir: *7m W of Edinburgh on the A71*

Set in extensive parkland with glorious views and convenient for the airport and city centre, this converted and extended Adam House attracts many returning guests. Bedrooms in the main house are comfortably traditional in style. Accommodation in the wing is bright, modern and well suited to the needs of business guests. Public areas include a choice of bars, informal and formal eating options. Serious eating takes place in the elegant Pentland Restaurant.
ROOMS: 43 en suite 172 annexe en suite (59 fmly) No smoking in 136 bedrooms d £79-£145 * LB **FACILITIES:** STV Indoor swimming (H) Golf 18 Tennis (hard) Sauna Solarium Gym Putting green Jacuzzi/spa Health & beauty treatments Steam room Dance Studio Driving range Xmas **CONF:** Thtr 350 Class 150 Board 90 Del from £139 * **SERVICES:** Lift **PARKING:** 350 **NOTES:** No dogs (ex guide dogs) No smoking in restaurant **CARDS:**

★★★★70% Roxburghe

MACDONALD HOTELS

38 Charlotte Square EH2 4HG
☎ 0131 240 5500 📠 0131 240 5555
e-mail: info@roxburghe.macdonald-hotels.co.uk
Dir: *located in central Edinburgh, on corner of Charlotte st & George st*

In the heart of the city, overlooking Charlotte Square Gardens, this long-established hotel has been upgraded and extended. Stylish areas include relaxing lounges and a choice of bars and restaurants. Smart bedrooms come in classic or contemporary style. Parking/setting down can be tricky but friendly obliging staff will assist.
ROOMS: 197 en suite (20 fmly) No smoking in 167 bedrooms s £85-£130; d £105-£155 (incl. cont bkfst) * LB **FACILITIES:** Indoor swimming (H) Sauna Solarium Gym Dance studio Spa treatment rooms Xmas **CONF:** Thtr 300 Class 120 Board 80 Del from £125 * **SERVICES:** Lift **PARKING:** 20 **NOTES:** No smoking in restaurant
CARDS:

★★★★69% George Inter-Continental

INTER-CONTINENTAL HOTELS AND RESORTS

19-21 George St EH2 2PB
☎ 0131 225 1251 📠 0131 226 5644
e-mail: edinburgh@interconti.com
Dir: *city centre, E side parallel to Princes Street*

A short walk from Princes Street, this stylish hotel, as its name suggests, attracts an international clientele. Original architectural features include an impressive marble-floored foyer, a welcoming bar, and a choice of restaurants, of which Le Chambertin offers fine dining. Bedrooms come in a variety of sizes, but all are comfortable and well equipped.
ROOMS: 195 en suite No smoking in 73 bedrooms s £99-£170; d £125-£190 * LB **FACILITIES:** STV Complimentary Fitness club nearby Xmas **CONF:** Thtr 200 Class 80 Board 80 Del from £125 * **SERVICES:** Lift **PARKING:** 24 **NOTES:** No dogs (ex guide dogs) Civ Wed 100
CARDS:

★★★★66% Carlton

PARAMOUNT GROUP OF HOTELS

North Bridge EH1 1SD
☎ 0131 472 3000 📠 0131 556 2691
e-mail: carlton@paramount-hotels.co.uk
Dir: *on North Bridge which links Princes St to the Royal Mile*

It's all happening at this hotel which occupies a prime position in the heart of the city close to the Royal Mile and railway station. A refurbishment of all bedrooms is scheduled for completion by the end of 2000, with public areas to follow.
ROOMS: 185 en suite (20 fmly) No smoking in 56 bedrooms s £125; d £193 * LB **FACILITIES:** STV Indoor swimming (H) Tennis (hard & grass) Squash Sauna Solarium Gym Jacuzzi/spa Table tennis Dance studio Creche entertainment ch fac Xmas **CONF:** Thtr 300 Class 160 Board 60 Del from £95 * **SERVICES:** Lift air con **NOTES:** No dogs (ex guide dogs) Civ Wed 150 **CARDS:**

★★★★64% Royal Terrace

PRINCIPAL HOTELS

18 Royal Ter EH7 5AQ
☎ 0131 557 3222 📠 0131 557 5334
Dir: *from A1 - follow sign into city centre, turn left at the end of London Road into Bleinheim Place continuing onto Royal Terrace*

Close to Princes Street, and forming part of a quiet Georgian terrace, this attractive hotel offers a variety of styles of bedroom, some lofty and spacious, with four-poster beds. All look out, either over the Forth, or over the gardens at the back of the hotel. Service is attentive.
ROOMS: 108 en suite (19 fmly) s £95-£125; d £130-£195 * LB **FACILITIES:** STV Indoor swimming (H) Sauna Solarium Gym Jacuzzi/spa Beauty salon Giant Chess Xmas **CONF:** Thtr 100 Class 36 Board 40 Del from £110 * **SERVICES:** Lift **NOTES:** No dogs (ex guide dogs) Civ Wed 70 **CARDS:**

See advert on opposite page

★★★★62% Swallow Royal Scot

111 Glasgow Rd EH12 8NF
☎ 0131 334 9191 📠 0131 316 4507
e-mail: info@swallowhotels.com
Dir: *on A8 on western outskirts of city*

From its position in the city's western fringes, close to the bypass and convenient for the airport, showground and business park, this purpose-built hotel attracts an international clientele. The bedrooms are contained in two wings, one offering executive rooms, the other housing the smaller standard rooms. Public areas radiate from the attractive marbled foyer and include two bars, a hairdressers and conference facilities able to accommodate large corporate groups.
ROOMS: 259 en suite (17 fmly) No smoking in 160 bedrooms s fr £115; d fr £145 (incl. bkfst) * LB **FACILITIES:** STV Indoor swimming (H) Sauna Solarium Gym Jacuzzi/spa Steam room Xmas **CONF:** Thtr 300 Class 120 Board 45 Del from £115 * **SERVICES:** Lift **PARKING:** 300 **NOTES:** No smoking in restaurant Civ Wed 80
CARDS:

★★★76% Norton House

Ingliston EH28 8LX
☎ 0131 333 1275 🖹 0131 333 5305
e-mail: hotel.reservations@virgin.co.uk
Dir: *off A8, 5m W of city centre*

Situated close to the airport on the west side of the city, this extended Victorian mansion lies in 55 acres of parkland and attracts the business and corporate market to its variety of meeting rooms. Bedrooms come in two styles, the quietly elegant ones in the main house and the more modern ones in an adjoining wing. The Gathering, in the grounds, is a popular meeting place for an informal meal. Fine dining is found in the Conservatory Restaurant.

ROOMS: 47 en suite (2 fmly) No smoking in 27 bedrooms s fr £125; d fr £150 (incl. bkfst) * LB **FACILITIES:** STV Archery Laser Clay pigeon shooting Xmas **CONF:** Thtr 300 Class 100 Board 60 Del from £145 * **PARKING:** 200 **CARDS:**

★★★74% Bruntsfield

69/74 Bruntsfield Place EH10 4HH
☎ 0131 229 1393 🖹 0131 229 5634
e-mail: bruntsfield@queensferry-hotels.co.uk
Dir: *from S enter Edinburgh on A702. Hotel is located overlooking Bruntsfield Links Park. 1m S of the W end of Princes Street*

Overlooking Bruntsfield Links, this smart hotel has stylish public rooms including relaxing lounge areas; a lively pub; and a conservatory restaurant with adjoining bar. Bedrooms come in a variety of sizes and are well equipped. Imaginative dinner menus and hearty Scottish breakfasts are served in the bright 'Potting Shed' conservatory restaurant.

ROOMS: 75 en suite (5 fmly) No smoking in 49 bedrooms
FACILITIES: STV **CONF:** Thtr 75 Class 30 Board 30 Del from £115 *
SERVICES: Lift **PARKING:** 25 **NOTES:** Civ Wed 70
CARDS:

See advert on this page

★★★73% *Posthouse Edinburgh*

Posthouse

Corstorphine Rd EH12 6UA
☎ 0870 400 9026 🖹 0131 334 9237
Dir: *adjacent to Edinburgh Zoo*

Lying right next to Edinburgh zoo and enjoying superb views over the city, this modern hotel has undergone extensive refurbishment and provides smart well equipped accommodation. There is an impressive business meeting room complex 'The Academy', and in addition to the main restaurant and popular bar, there is the exciting 'Sampans' where a range of Oriental dishes can be sampled.

ROOMS: 303 en suite (35 fmly) No smoking in 176 bedrooms
CONF: Thtr 110 Class 70 Board 50 **SERVICES:** Lift **PARKING:** 100
NOTES: No smoking in restaurant **CARDS:**

EDINBURGH, continued

★★★71% *Dalhousie Castle Hotel*

Bonnyrigg EH19 3JB
☎ 01875 820153 🖹 01875 821936
e-mail: res@dalhousiecastle.co.uk
Dir: *take A7 S from Edinburgh through Lasswade & Newtongrange, turn right at Shell Garage onto B704, hotel 0.5m from junction*

This imposing 13th-century castle sits in a delightful position by the River South Esk. It offers a peaceful retreat from the bustle of Edinburgh, just a 20-minute drive away. While there is no bar, drinks are served in the two lounges and meals in the vaulted dungeon restaurant. Accommodation ranges from grand period rooms to cottage-style rooms in a quiet house in the grounds. The castle's own chapel makes it a popular wedding venue.
ROOMS: 34 en suite (5 fmly) No smoking in 2 bedrooms **FACILITIES:** STV Fishing Clay pigeon shooting, Archery, Falconry ch fac **CONF:** Thtr 120 Class 60 Board 40 **PARKING:** 110 **NOTES:** No smoking in restaurant Closed 10-26 Jan **CARDS:**

★★★71% Malmaison

One Tower Place EH6 7DB
☎ 0131 468 5000 🖹 0131 468 5002
e-mail: edinburgh@malmaison.com
Dir: *A900 from city centre towards Leith, at end of Leith Walk continue over lights through 2 more sets of lights, left into Tower St-hotel on right*
This former Seaman's Mission stands on the quayside in this rejuvenated part of the city. Bedrooms are a key feature throughout the group, with striking decor as well as CD players, mini bars and a number of individual welcoming touches. In addition to the fashionable café bar, there is a brasserie serving a mix of modern and traditional dishes. The service is both friendly and attentive.
ROOMS: 60 en suite (6 fmly) d £105 * LB **FACILITIES:** STV Gym **CONF:** Thtr 50 Class 16 Board 26 Del £146 * **SERVICES:** Lift **PARKING:** 50 **CARDS:**

★★★70% Braid Hills

134 Braid Rd EH10 6JD
☎ 0131 447 8888 🖹 0131 452 8477
e-mail: bookings@braidhillshotel.co.uk
Dir: *2.5m S A702, opposite Braid Burn Park*
This long-established hotel enjoys splendid panoramic views of the city from its elevated position on the south side. Bedrooms are smart, stylish and well equipped, though varied in size. The public areas are comfortable and inviting, and one can eat in the restaurant or bistro.

continued

ROOMS: 68 en suite (6 fmly) No smoking in 8 bedrooms s £80; d £135 (incl. bkfst) * LB **FACILITIES:** STV Xmas **CONF:** Thtr 100 Class 50 Board 30 Del from £95 * **PARKING:** 38 **NOTES:** No dogs (ex guide dogs) No smoking in restaurant Civ Wed 170
CARDS:

See advert on opposite page

★★★69% Apex International

31/35 Grassmarket EH1 2HS
☎ 0131 300 3456 🖹 0131 220 5345
e-mail: international@apexhotels.co.uk
Dir: *turn into Lothian Rd at the West End of Princes Street, then turn 1st left along King Stables Rd. This leads onto the Grassmarket Square*
This modern hotel enjoys a superb city centre location, lying in an historic square in the shadow of Edinburgh Castle. It has an impressive business and conference centre, and the bedrooms are spacious and well equipped. The restaurant boasts stunning views of the Castle whilst providing a wide ranging menu to satisfy all tastes.
ROOMS: 175 en suite (99 fmly) No smoking in 100 bedrooms d £120-£160 * LB **FACILITIES:** STV Xmas **CONF:** Thtr 225 Class 120 Board 50 Del from £95 * **SERVICES:** Lift **PARKING:** 60 **NOTES:** No dogs (ex guide dogs) Civ Wed **CARDS:**

★★★68% *Prestonfield House*

Priestfield Rd EH16 5UT
☎ 0131 668 3346 🖹 668 3976
e-mail: prestonfield_house@compuserve.com
Dir: *A720 City Bypass exit Sherrifhall rdbt A7 into Edinburgh, right after 3m onto Priestfield Rd, 400 metres on left*
Built in 1687, Prestonfield House is set in thirteen acres of gardens and parkland, with a golf course on its doorstep and Arthur's Seat as a backdrop. Smartly appointed and thoughtfully equipped bedrooms are housed in an extension. The public rooms still hold much of their charm from the days when this was a private house; the Tapestry, Leather and Italian rooms all contain their original late 17th and 18th-century decorative schemes.
ROOMS: 31 rms (30 en suite) No smoking in 16 bedrooms **FACILITIES:** STV Golf 18 **CONF:** Thtr 800 Class 350 Board 30 **SERVICES:** Lift **PARKING:** 200 **CARDS:**

★★★67% Jurys Inn Edinburgh

43 Jeffrey St EH1 1DG
☎ 0131 200 3300 🖹 0131 200 0400
e-mail: info@jurys.com
Dir: *A8/M8 onto Princes Street - 1m turn right at the Waverley Station, next left*
Located next to Waverley Station and close to key attractions, this inexpensive hotel is ideal for anyone who wants to explore the delights of Edinburgh. Eating options include the Inn Pub and the

continued

Arches Restaurant, while the rooms are brand new and contain the majority of the essentials.
ROOMS: 186 en suite (68 fmly) No smoking in 121 bedrooms d £61-£110 * **FACILITIES:** STV entertainment **CONF:** Thtr 50 Class 35 Board 30 Del from £100 * **SERVICES:** Lift **NOTES:** No dogs (ex guide dogs)
CARDS:

★★★66% Apex European

90 Haymarket Ter EH12 5LQ
☎ 0131 474 3456 📠 0131 474 3400
e-mail: european@apexhotels.co.uk
Within easy reach of Haymarket Station and the Conference Centre, this smart modern hotel is ideal for business guests. The comfortable, well equipped bedrooms have a bright contemporary feel, as does Tabu, the brasserie which will encourage guests to dine in.
ROOMS: 67 en suite No smoking in 51 bedrooms d £90-£120 * **FACILITIES:** STV **CONF:** Thtr 100 Class 60 Board 40 Del from £90 * **SERVICES:** Lift **PARKING:** 17 **NOTES:** No dogs (ex guide dogs)
CARDS:

★★★66% Greens Hotel

24 Eglinton Crescent EH12 5BY
☎ 0131 337 1565 📠 0131 346 2990

Four Georgian houses have been converted to create this comfortable hotel in the west end. Bedrooms are smartly furnished and well equipped, superior rooms are particularly spacious. Public rooms include a cosy panelled bar adjacent to the Club Room Bistro offering an appealing alternative to the main restaurant.
ROOMS: 55 en suite (5 fmly) No smoking in 10 bedrooms s £35-£65; d £50-£95 (incl. bkfst) * LB **FACILITIES:** Xmas **CONF:** Thtr 50 Class 14 Board 20 **SERVICES:** Lift **NOTES:** No dogs (ex guide dogs) No smoking in restaurant **CARDS:**

★★★65% Grange Hotel

MINOTEL Great Britain

8 Whitehouse Ter EH9 2EU
☎ 0131 667 5681 📠 0131 668 3300
e-mail: grange-hotel@talk21.com

Dir: *turn off A702 (Morningside Road) onto Newbattle Terrace which lead into Whitehouse Terrace*

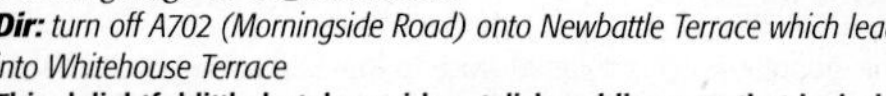

This delightful little hotel provides stylish public areas that include a small library lounge, a well stocked bar, and a bright conservatory restaurant offering modern cooking from an imaginative seasonal menu. The bedrooms vary in size and style but all boast attractive fabrics and are suitably equipped.
ROOMS: 13 en suite 2 annexe en suite (3 fmly) s £80-£90; d £135-£160 (incl. bkfst) * LB **FACILITIES:** Putting green **CONF:** Thtr 40 Class 16 Board 22 **PARKING:** 25 **NOTES:** No dogs No smoking in restaurant
CARDS:

EDINBURGH, continued

★★★65% Kings Manor

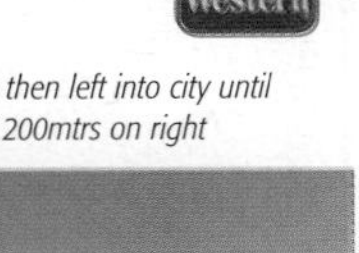

100 Milton Rd East EH15 2NP
☎ 0131 669 0444 🖷 0131 669 6650
e-mail: info@kingsmanor.com
Dir: *follow A720 E until Old Craighall Junction then left into city until turning right at the A1/A199 intersection, hotel 200mtrs on right*

Lying on the east side of the city, this hotel is popular with business guests, conferences and tour groups. It now boasts a fine leisure complex and a bright modern bistro which complements the more traditional restaurant.
ROOMS: 69 en suite (8 fmly) No smoking in 22 bedrooms s £64-£90; d £80-£135 (incl. cont bkfst) * LB **FACILITIES:** STV Indoor swimming (H) Tennis (hard) Sauna Solarium Gym Jacuzzi/spa Hairdressing Health & beauty salon Xmas **CONF:** Thtr 140 Class 70 Board 50 Del from £85 * **SERVICES:** Lift **PARKING:** 100 **CARDS:**

See advert on page 697

★★★63% The Barnton

Queensferry Rd, Barnton EH4 6AS
☎ 0131 339 1144 🖷 0131 339 5521
PEEL HOTELS
Dir: *cross Forth Road Bridge towards Edinburgh, follow A90, 4m on left by rdbt*
This long-established business hotel is ideally positioned on the A90, four miles from the city centre, the Forth Road Bridge and the airport. It offers a choice of smart executive and standard bedrooms, a restaurant and conference facilities.
ROOMS: 50 en suite (9 fmly) No smoking in 25 bedrooms s £89-£109; d £99-£119 * LB **FACILITIES:** STV Sauna entertainment Xmas **CONF:** Thtr 150 Class 60 Board 50 Del from £95 * **SERVICES:** Lift **PARKING:** 100 **NOTES:** No dogs (ex guide dogs) Civ Wed 100
CARDS:

★★★62% Carlton Greens Hotel

2 Carlton Ter EH7 5DD
☎ 0131 556 6570 🖷 0131 557 6680

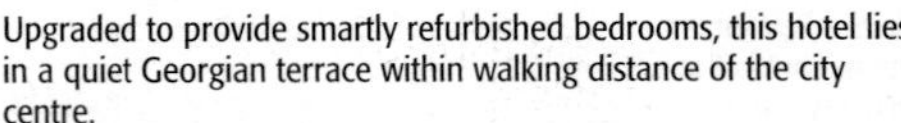

Upgraded to provide smartly refurbished bedrooms, this hotel lies in a quiet Georgian terrace within walking distance of the city centre.
ROOMS: 26 en suite s £35-£60; d £70-£90 (incl. bkfst) * LB **FACILITIES:** Xmas **CONF:** Thtr 20 Class 10 Board 20 **NOTES:** No dogs (ex guide dogs) No smoking in restaurant **CARDS:**

★★★61% Old Waverley

43 Princes St EH2 2BY
☎ 0131 556 4648 🖷 0131 557 6316
PARAMOUNT GROUP OF HOTELS
e-mail: waverley@paramount-hotels.co.uk
Dir: *in the centre of city, opposite the Scott Monument, Waverley Station and Jenners*
Positioned on Princes Street right in the heart of the city, this long-established hotel enjoys views of the city skyline, as well as the Scott Monument and the Castle behind. Sharing these are the front-facing bedrooms, as well as public rooms, all of which are at first floor level and add a striking contemporary decor style to a traditional environment.
ROOMS: 66 en suite (8 fmly) No smoking in 12 bedrooms s £40-£99; d £70-£160 * LB **FACILITIES:** STV Xmas **CONF:** Thtr 70 Class 30 Board 26 Del from £99 * **SERVICES:** Lift **NOTES:** No smoking in restaurant **CARDS:**

★★★58% Quality Hotel

Edinburgh Airport, Ingliston EH28 8NF
☎ 0131 333 4331 🖷 0131 333 4124
CHOICE HOTELS EUROPE
Situated right next to the Royal Showground at Ingliston this modern hotel is also convenient for the airport. The spacious executive bedrooms are the pick of the accommodation, and there is a café restaurant offering a range of contemporary dishes.
ROOMS: 95 en suite No smoking in 64 bedrooms d fr £55 * **FACILITIES:** STV **CONF:** Thtr 70 Class 24 Board 24 **SERVICES:** Lift **PARKING:** 100 **NOTES:** No smoking in restaurant
CARDS:

★★68% *Allison House*

15/17 Mayfield Gardens EH9 2AX
☎ 0131 667 8049 🖷 0131 667 5001
e-mail: dh007ljh@msn.com
Dir: *1m S of city centre on A701*
This family-run hotel has inviting public areas which include an attractive restaurant with a good range of dishes, and a lounge with a small residents' dispense bar. Bedrooms come in a variety of sizes, but all are well equipped and complemented by tasteful fabrics and smart decor.
ROOMS: 23 rms (21 en suite) (5 fmly) **FACILITIES:** ch fac **CONF:** Thtr 25 Class 12 Board 16 **PARKING:** 12 **NOTES:** No smoking in restaurant
CARDS:

★★67% *Murrayfield*

18 Corstophine Rd EH12 6HN
☎ 0131 337 1844 🖷 0131 346 8159
This popular hotel is situated close to the national rugby stadium. The smart restaurant is accompanied by a spacious bar. There is a wide choice of well equipped bedrooms of varying sizes and styles, both in the main building and in a converted mansion nearby.
ROOMS: 23 en suite 10 annexe en suite (1 fmly) **CONF:** Thtr 30 Class 12 Board 20 **PARKING:** 30 **NOTES:** Closed 2 days Xmas & 2 days New Year **CARDS:**

Bad hair day? Hairdryers in all rooms three stars and above.

★★67% Salisbury View Hotel

64 Dalkeith Rd EH16 5AE
☎ 0131 667 1133 🖷 0131 667 1133
e-mail: enquiries@salisburyviewhotel.co.uk
Dir: *on the A7, approx 1m to the south of the city centre, adjacent to Holyrood Park*

This intimate Georgian hotel provides a relaxed atmosphere, a cosy bar lounge (residents and diners only) and an attractive restaurant suitably named Potters Fine Dining. Dishes are well presented and there is an emphasis on utilising regional Scottish produce. Bedrooms are smart and well equipped.
ROOMS: 8 en suite (1 fmly) s £32-£59; d £64-£99 (incl. bkfst) LB **FACILITIES:** STV **PARKING:** 8 **NOTES:** No dogs (ex guide dogs) No smoking in restaurant Closed 23-26 Dec **CARDS:**

★★66% Orwell Lodge

29 Polwarth Ter EH11 1NH
☎ 0131 229 1044 🖷 0131 228 9492
Dir: *From A702 turn into Gilmore Place (opposite King's theatre) hotel 1m on the left*
Friendly staff offer attentive service at this hotel, a sympathetic conversion and extension of an elegant Victorian mansion. Bedrooms are comfortable, smartly furnished and well equipped. The spacious bar is a focal point, providing food in addition to the dining room upstairs.
ROOMS: 10 en suite No smoking in all bedrooms s £45-£55; d £70-£85 (incl. bkfst) * LB **FACILITIES:** entertainment **CONF:** Thtr 250 Class 120 Board 80 **PARKING:** 40 **NOTES:** No dogs (ex guide dogs) No smoking in restaurant Closed 25 Dec Civ Wed 200 **CARDS:**

★★64% Iona

Strathearn Place EH9 2AL
☎ 0131 447 6264 & 0131 447 5050 🖷 0131 452 8574
e-mail: ronald.pugh@dial.pipex.com
Dir: *from Morningside Rd (main access into Edinburgh) turn left at lights into Chamberlain Rd, turn right at the end of the road, at junction turn left*
This hotel lies in a leafy suburb on the south side of the city. It offers comfortable, well equipped accommodation, and a bar which is popular with local residents. Good value meals are served both there and in the restaurant.
ROOMS: 17 en suite (3 fmly) s £30-£65; d £60-£95 (incl. bkfst) * LB **FACILITIES:** entertainment **CONF:** Thtr 40 Board 22 **PARKING:** 20 **CARDS:**

Late for dinner? Quality Standards star rating means that last orders for dinner should be no earlier than:
★ 6.30pm ★★ 7.00pm ★★★ 8.00pm
★★★★ 9.00pm ★★★★★ 10.00pm

Roslin Glen Hotel

AA ★★ STB

Situated seven miles south of Edinburgh's Princes Street in the quiet conservation village of Roslin, with Rosslyn Chapel, Castle and Glen within easy walking distance. The Roslin Glen Hotel is the ideal base for the Edinburgh visitor who enjoys the tranquility of the countryside, yet would like easy access to the many major attractions in Scotland's capital (15 minutes by car). Pleasant rooms, all en-suite, well equipped with telephone, tea/coffee making equipment, TV, satellite and in-house video. For formal or casual dining, our restaurant and lounge bar provide and imaginative menu using fresh, top quality local ingredients, prepared by our experienced chefs.

Stay with confidence at
Roslin Glen Hotel, 2 Penicuik Road
Roslin, Midlothian EH25 9LH
Tel: 0131 440 2029 Fax: 0131 440 2229

★★61% Thrums Private Hotel

14 Minto St EH9 1RQ
☎ 0131 667 5545 & 667 8545 🖷 0131 667 8707
Dir: *off A701 follow city bypass - Edinburgh South - Newington/A7 - A701*
Two Georgian houses have been converted to create this family-run hotel. Informal public areas include a lounge where drinks are available, and a smart restaurant. Bedrooms, which are well equipped, are available in a variety of sizes leading up to several spacious rooms with period furnishings.
ROOMS: 6 en suite 8 annexe en suite (5 fmly) s £35-£55; d £55-£85 (incl. bkfst) * LB **PARKING:** 10 **NOTES:** Closed Xmas **CARDS:**

Fancy a Singapore Sling? Bar staff in five star hotels should be skilled cocktail mixers.

EDINBURGH, continued

Premier Collection

★★★★ 🏵🏵 🏠 **The Howard**
34 Great King St EH3 6QH
☎ 0131 315 2220 & 557 3500 🖷 0131 557 6515
e-mail: reserve@thehoward.com
Dir: *travelling E on Queen St, take 2nd left, Hanover St. Continue through 3 sets of lights, turn right & hotel on left*

Comfortable and inviting bedrooms, including some half and full suites, are a feature of this town house, made up of three linked Georgian houses. Ornate chandeliers and lavish drapes characterise the drawing room, whilst the adjacent restaurant, 36, has much more of a contemporary feel. Service is professional and, above all, friendly and caring.

ROOMS: 15 en suite s £135-£165; d £245-£325 (incl. bkfst) * LB **FACILITIES:** STV **CONF:** Thtr 20 Board 18 **SERVICES:** Lift **PARKING:** 10 **NOTES:** No dogs (ex guide dogs) No smoking in restaurant Closed 22-28 Dec **CARDS:**

Town House

★★★★ 🏵🏵 🏠 **Channings**
South Learmonth Gardens EH4 1EZ
☎ 0131 332 3232 & 315 2225 🖷 0131 332 9631
e-mail: reserve@channings.co.uk
Dir: *approach Edinburgh on the A90 from Forth Road Bridge, follow signs for city centre*

Originally five Edwardian terraced houses, recent refurbishment has resulted in comfortable and attractively furnished bedrooms, equipped to meet the needs of tourists and business visitors alike. Ground floor lounges, split into a number of separate areas, have a club-like feel to them, whilst the wine bar and conservatory restaurant are definitely modern in design, providing a suitable backdrop to the carefully prepared and imaginative cuisine offered.

continued

ROOMS: 46 en suite (1 fmly) No smoking in 30 bedrooms s £125-£150; d £170-£260 (incl. bkfst) * LB **FACILITIES:** STV **CONF:** Thtr 60 Board 34 Del from £125 * **SERVICES:** Lift **NOTES:** No dogs (ex guide dogs) No smoking in restaurant Closed 24-28 Dec Civ Wed 80 **CARDS:**

Town House

★★★★ 🏵 🏠 **The Bonham**
35 Drumsheugh Gardens EH3 7RN
☎ 0131 623 6060 & 226 6050 🖷 0131 226 6080
e-mail: reserve@thebonham.com
Dir: *located close to West End & Princes St*

A previous winner of the Hotel of the Year award for Scotland, this imaginative conversion of former university accommodation combines many of the original Victorian features with a more contemporary style. Comfortable and practical bedrooms offer up-to-the-minute technology, with a number of stylish suites also available. Modern cuisine is served in the brasserie dining area. Service is professional and friendly.

ROOMS: 48 en suite No smoking in 24 bedrooms s £135-£155; d £165-£295 (incl. cont bkfst) * LB **FACILITIES:** STV **CONF:** Thtr 50 Board 24 **SERVICES:** Lift **NOTES:** No dogs (ex guide dogs) Closed 24-28 Dec **CARDS:**

⌂ **Express by Holiday Inn Edinburgh Leith**
Britannia Way, Ocean Dr, Leith EH6 6LA
☎ 0131 555 4422 🖷 555 4646
e-mail: info@hiex-edinburgh.com
Dir: *follow signs for Royal Yacht Britannia. Hotel is located just before Britannia on the right*

A modern budget hotel offering comfortable accommodation in refreshing, spacious and comprehensively-equipped bedrooms, en suite bathrooms with power showers and continental buffet

continued

breakfast included in the room rate. Suitable for business travellers or families. For further details and the Express by Holiday Inn phone number, consult the Hotel Groups page.
ROOMS: 102 en suite (incl. cont bkfst) d £57.50-£77.50 * **CONF:** Thtr 60 Class 30 Board 30

⇧ Premier Lodge (City Centre)

Grassmarket EH1 2JF
☎ 0870 700 1370 ▤ 0870 700 1371
Premier Lodge offers modern, well equipped, en suite accommodation suitable for both business and leisure travellers. Meals can be taken at the adjacent popular restaurant and bar which is fully licensed. For further details, consult the Hotel Groups page.
ROOMS: 45 en suite d £46 *

⇧ *Travelodge*

33 St Marys St ED1 1TA
☎ 0113 557 6281
This modern building offers accommodation in smart, spacious and well equipped bedrooms, all with en suite bathrooms. Refreshments may be taken at the nearby family restaurant. For further details and the Travelodge phone number, consult the Hotel Groups page.

⇧ *Travelodge*
Old Craighall EH21 8RE
☎ 0131 653 6070
Dir: *off A1, 2m from eastern outskirts Edinburgh*
This modern building offers accommodation in smart, spacious and well equipped bedrooms, all with en suite bathrooms. Refreshments may be taken at the nearby family restaurant. For further details and the Travelodge phone number, consult the Hotel Groups page.
ROOMS: 45 en suite

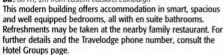

⇧ *Travelodge*

46 Dreghorn Link EH13 9QR
☎ 0131 441 4296 ▤ 0131 441 4296
Dir: *6m S, A720 Ring Rd South*
This modern building offers accommodation in smart, spacious and well equipped bedrooms, all with en suite bathrooms. Refreshments may be taken at the nearby family restaurant. For further details and the Travelodge phone number, consult the Hotel Groups page.
ROOMS: 40 en suite

⇧ *Hotel Ibis*

6 Hunter Square, (off The Royal Mile) EH1 1QW
☎ 0131 240 7000 ▤ 0131 240 7007
e-mail: H2039@accor-hotels.com
Dir: *from Queen St (M8/M9) or Waterloo Pl (A1) crossover North Bridge (A7) & High St, take 1st right off South Bridge, this is Hunter Sq*
Modern, budget hotel offering comfortable accommodation in bright and practical bedrooms. Breakfast is self-service and dinner is available in the restaurant. For further details, consult the Hotel Groups page.
ROOMS: 99 en suite

○ Parliament House Hotel

15 Carlton Hill EH1 3BJ
☎ 0131 478 4000
NOTES: Open

○ *Premier Lodge (City Centre South)*

Lauriston Place, Lady Lawson St
☎ 0870 700 1374 ▤ 0870 700 1375

○ *Premier Lodge (Edinburgh East)*

City Bypass, Newcraighall
☎ 0870 700 1372 ▤ 0870 700 1373

EDZELL, Angus — Map 15 NO66

★★★64% Glenesk
High St DD9 7TF
☎ 01356 648319 ▤ 01356 647333
e-mail: glenskhotel@btconnect.com
Dir: *off A90 just after Brechin Bypass*

This long established family-run hotel is situated at the south end of the village beside the golf course. The bedrooms vary in size and have been refurbished to offer modern appointments. Comfortable public areas include a choice of relaxing lounges, contrasting bars, a dining room overlooking the garden, and a well equipped leisure centre.
ROOMS: 24 en suite (5 fmly) s fr £55; d fr £90 (incl. bkfst) * LB
FACILITIES: Indoor swimming (H) Snooker Sauna Solarium Gym Pool table Croquet lawn Jacuzzi/spa Xmas **CONF:** Board 30 **PARKING:** 81
NOTES: No smoking in restaurant **CARDS:**

ELGIN, Moray — Map 15 NJ26

★★★76% ❀ Mansion House
The Haugh IV30 1AW
☎ 01343 548811 ▤ 01343 547916
e-mail: reception@mhelgin.co.uk
Dir: *in Elgin turn off the A96 into Haugh Rd, hotel at the end of the road by the river*
A baronial-style mansion close to the River Lossie. Bedrooms are individual in size and style with a wide range of amenities and many have four poster beds. Attractive public areas include a lounge, bar, billiard room, and a leisure club. The popular Bistro is an informal alternative to the elegant restaurant where fine cooking is offered.
ROOMS: 23 en suite (3 fmly) s £75-£95; d £120-£150 (incl. bkfst) * LB
FACILITIES: STV Indoor swimming (H) Snooker Sauna Solarium Gym Jacuzzi/spa Hairdresser Beauty therapist Steam room Xmas **CONF:** Thtr 200 Class 150 Board 50 Del from £110 * **PARKING:** 150 **NOTES:** No dogs (ex guide dogs) No smoking in restaurant Civ Wed 180
CARDS:

★★★67% Laichmoray
Maisondieu Rd IV30 1QR
☎ 01343 540045 ▤ 01343 540055
e-mail: enquiries@laichmorayhotel.co.uk
Dir: *opposite the railway station*
Centrally situated, friendly family hotel on the south side of town. It offers well equipped bedrooms in a variety of styles. A range of

continued

ELGIN, continued

Laichmoray, Elgin

bar meals is available in the lounge and conservatory and carte dining and high teas are served in the restaurant.
ROOMS: 35 rms (34 en suite) (5 fmly) No smoking in 4 bedrooms s £42-£52; d £60-£78 (incl. bkfst) * LB **FACILITIES:** Pool table Darts ch fac Xmas **CONF:** Thtr 200 Class 160 Board 40 Del from £55.50 * **PARKING:** 60 **NOTES:** Civ Wed 120 **CARDS:**

ELIE, Fife — Map 12 NO40

★★★65% Golf Hotel
Bank St KY9 1EF
☎ 01333 330209 01333 330381
e-mail: golf@standrews.co.uk
Dir: *on entering Elie turn right off A917 at T-junct, hotel 100mtrs on right*

This welcoming family-run hotel, situated beside the splendid links course, has particular appeal for visiting golfers. The attractive restaurant offers enjoyable fare prepared from fresh local ingredients and there is also a spacious bar.
ROOMS: 22 en suite (2 fmly) **FACILITIES:** Golf 27 **CONF:** Thtr 120 Class 60 Board 40 **PARKING:** 50 **NOTES:** No smoking in restaurant Civ Wed 120 **CARDS:**

ERISKA, Argyll & Bute — Map 10 NM94

Premier Collection

★★★★ Isle of Eriska
Eriska, Ledaig PA37 1SD
☎ 01631 720371 01631 720531
e-mail: office@eriska-hotel.co.uk
Dir: *leave A85 at Conneland join A828 and follow for 4m, then follow signs from north of Benderloch*
This Victorian mansion house is situated on a private island approached by a small bridge. Guests are encouraged to explore the island, visiting the beaches, woodland and natural gardens. Spacious bedrooms provide good levels of comfort and boast some fine antique pieces. Public areas include a choice of different lounges as well as the part wood-panelled dining room. Here, local seafood features prominently in the carefully prepared meals.

ROOMS: 17 en suite **FACILITIES:** Indoor swimming (H) Golf 6 Tennis (hard) Fishing Sauna Gym Croquet lawn Putting green Jacuzzi/spa Steam room Skeet shooting Nature trails **CONF:** Thtr 30 Class 30 Board 30 Del from £140 * **PARKING:** 40 **NOTES:** No smoking in restaurant Closed Jan **CARDS:**

ERSKINE, Renfrewshire — Map 11 NS47

★★★65% *The Erskine Bridge Hotel*
North Barr PA8 6AN
☎ 0870 400 9033 0141 812 7642
Dir: *M8 junct 30 and take A726 to Erskine. At 1st rndbt turn right 2nd straight through 3rd turn left*
Located on the banks of the River Clyde within sight of Erskine Bridge, this bright, modern hotel offers well equipped bedrooms. Function facilities are extensive and there is a good leisure centre.
ROOMS: 177 en suite (3 fmly) No smoking in 77 bedrooms **FACILITIES:** Indoor swimming (H) Sauna Gym Pool table Jacuzzi/spa **CONF:** Thtr 600 Class 400 Board 40 **SERVICES:** Lift **PARKING:** 200 **CARDS:**

FALKIRK, Falkirk — Map 11 NS88

★★★69% *Park Lodge Hotel*
Camelon Rd FK1 5RY
☎ 01324 628331 01324 611593
e-mail: park@queensferry-hotels.co.uk
Dir: *from M8 take A803 into Falkirk, hotel 1m beyond Mariner Leisure Ctr, opposite Dollar Park. From M9, A803 through Falkirk follow signs Dollar Park*

This popular corporate and banqueting hotel is located on the west side of town. Bedrooms are comfortable, modern in style and offer a good range of amenities. Public areas include a

continued

spacious lounge/bar, and the new La Bonne Auberge Brasserie where the varied menus offer something to suit everyone.
ROOMS: 55 en suite (3 fmly) No smoking in 32 bedrooms **FACILITIES:** STV **CONF:** Thtr 300 Class 180 Board 80 **SERVICES:** Lift **PARKING:** 160 **NOTES:** No dogs (ex guide dogs) No smoking in restaurant **CARDS:**

See advert on this page

Premier Lodge

Bellsdyke Rd, Larbert FK5 4EG
☎ 0870 700 1386 📠 0870 7001387

PREMIER LODGE
THE BEST. REST ASSURED.

Premier Lodge offers modern, well equipped, en suite accommodation suitable for both business and leisure travellers. Meals can be taken at the adjacent popular restaurant and bar which is fully licensed. For further details, consult the Hotel Groups page.
ROOMS: 60 en suite d £42 *

FENWICK, East Ayrshire — Map 11 NS44

★★★67% Fenwick

Ayr Rd KA3 6AU
☎ 01560 600478 📠 01560 600334

e-mail: fenwick@bestwestern.co.uk

Dir: *2nd Fenwick junct on A77*
Situated by the A77 and convenient for both Glasgow and the Ayrshire coast, this hotel has been expanded and upgraded to provide a bright reception foyer, restaurant, comfortable lounge bar and a wing of smart modern bedrooms. It is the hospitality and the refreshingly good cooking that makes this a hotel worth seeking out. Seafood and game feature regularly on the menu.
ROOMS: 31 en suite (2 fmly) No smoking in 4 bedrooms s £55-£72; d £75-£92 (incl. bkfst) * LB **FACILITIES:** Clay pigeon Quad bike ch fac Xmas **CONF:** Thtr 160 Class 60 Board 18 Del from £73 * **PARKING:** 80 **NOTES:** Civ Wed 100 **CARDS:**

FORFAR, Angus — Map 15 NO45

★★★67% Idvies House

Letham DD8 2QJ
☎ 01307 818787 📠 01307 818933
e-mail: idvies@mail.com
Dir: *from Forfar B9128 signed Carnoustie, 2m left at fork Letham & Arbroath. 1.5m to T-junct, ignore Letham signs, left towards Arbroath, hotel on left*
Peacefully set amid wooded grounds, this comfortable Victorian country house offers a relaxed and welcoming atmosphere. Bedrooms, with all the expected amenities, are furnished with attractive period pieces. Public areas include a well stocked bar with a small study adjacent, and two dining rooms.
ROOMS: 11 en suite (1 fmly) s £40-£50; d £65-£75 (incl. bkfst) * LB **FACILITIES:** STV Squash Snooker **CONF:** Thtr 50 Class 30 Board 30 Del from £39.50 * **PARKING:** 60 **NOTES:** No smoking in restaurant Closed 25 Dec-2 Jan Civ Wed 40 **CARDS:**

Late for dinner? Quality Standards star rating means that last orders for dinner should be no earlier than:
★ 6.30pm ★★ 7.00pm ★★★ 8.00pm
★★★★ 9.00pm ★★★★★ 10.00pm

FORRES, Moray — Map 14 NJ05

★★★74% Knockomie

Grantown Rd IV36 2SG
☎ 01309 673146 📠 01309 673290
e-mail: stay@knockomie.co.uk
Dir: *S on A940 towards Grantown*

Genuine hospitality and good food feature at this charming country house. Bedrooms range from Grand Master rooms to the slightly smaller standard rooms. Inviting public rooms include a choice of lounges and a cocktail bar. A bistro provides an alternative to the restaurant and there is the Party Room for additional informal dining.
ROOMS: 15 en suite (1 fmly) No smoking in 3 bedrooms s £74-£115; d £115-£150 (incl. bkfst) * LB **FACILITIES:** STV Putting green Xmas **CONF:** Thtr 40 Class 20 Board 20 Del from £124 * **PARKING:** 45 **NOTES:** No smoking in restaurant Closed 24 Dec-27 Dec & 5-10 Jan **CARDS:**

FORRES, continued

★★★66% Ramnee

Victoria Rd IV36 3BN
☎ 01309 672410 📠 01309 673392
e-mail: ramneehotel@btconnect.com
Dir: *turn off A96 at rdbt on eastern side of Forres, hotel 200yds on right*

Situated in two acres of gardens, the Ramnee Hotel was built in 1907 as a private residence and has been transformed into a country house-style hotel. Public areas are inviting and the lively lounge bar is very popular for meals.
ROOMS: 20 en suite (4 fmly) s £55-£67.50; d £65-£90 (incl. bkfst) * LB **FACILITIES:** STV **CONF:** Thtr 100 Class 30 Board 45 Del £99.50 * **PARKING:** 50 **NOTES:** No smoking in restaurant RS Xmas day 1-3 Jan **CARDS:**

See advert on opposite page

FORT WILLIAM, Highland — Map 14 NN17

Premier Collection

★★★★ Inverlochy Castle

Torlundy PH33 6SN
☎ 01397 702177 📠 01397 702953
e-mail: info@inverlochy.co.uk
Dir: *accessible from either A82 Glasgow-Fort William or A9 Edinburgh-Dalwhinnie. Hotel 3m N of Fort William on A82, in Torlundy*

RELAIS & CHATEAUX.

Set amidst glorious scenery this impressive Victorian building has 500 acres of grounds. Bedrooms are lavishly appointed and spacious, some facing Ben Nevis. Private dining rooms are available, but the main dining room, adjacent to the elegant drawing room, has stunning loch and mountain views. Top quality ingredients are carefully cooked.
ROOMS: 17 en suite s £180-£255; d £250-£480 (incl. bkfst) * **FACILITIES:** STV Tennis (hard) Fishing Snooker entertainment Xmas **PARKING:** 18 **NOTES:** No dogs (ex guide dogs) No smoking in restaurant Closed 5 Jan-12 Feb Civ Wed 40 **CARDS:**

★★★71% Moorings

Banavie PH33 7LY
☎ 01397 772797 📠 01397 772441
e-mail: reservations@moorings-fortwilliam.co.uk
Dir: *3m N of Fort William off A830. Take A830 for approx 1m, cross the Caledonian canal and take first right*

This modern hotel west of Fort William is beside 'Neptune's Staircase' of the Caledonian Canal with views of Ben Nevis on clear days. Interesting meals are available as a two or four course fixed price menu in the Jacobean-style dining room, or as bar food in the Upper Deck lounge bar or popular Mariners Bar. Bedrooms have fresh decor and good facilities.
ROOMS: 21 en suite (1 fmly) No smoking in 4 bedrooms s £46-£60; d £72-£100 (incl. bkfst) * LB **FACILITIES:** STV Xmas **CONF:** Thtr 120 Class 40 Board 30 Del from £66 * **PARKING:** 60 **NOTES:** No smoking in restaurant Civ Wed 90 **CARDS:**

See advert on opposite page

★★70% Nevis Bank

Belford Rd PH33 6BY
☎ 01397 705721 📠 01397 706275
e-mail: enquiries@nevisbankhotel.co.uk
Dir: *on A82, at junct to Glen Nevis*

Situated at the northern end of the town at the junction of the access road to Ben Nevis, this privately owned hotel offers traditional highland hospitality, with the welcoming staff being both attentive and friendly. Bedrooms are well equipped and many have recently been enhanced with co-ordinating fabrics. There is a choice of two popular bars.
ROOMS: 31 en suite 8 annexe en suite (3 fmly) s £40-£50; d £60-£70 (incl. bkfst) * LB **FACILITIES:** Sauna Solarium Gym Pool table Xmas **CONF:** Thtr 40 Class 20 Board 20 **PARKING:** 50 **NOTES:** No smoking in restaurant **CARDS:**

★★69% *Imperial*

Best Western

Fraser's Square PH33 6DW
☎ 01397 702040 & 703921 📠 01397 706277
Dir: *from town centre travel along Middle St approx 400mtrs from junction with A82*

This well established friendly family-run hotel in the town centre provides comfortable standards throughout, including an attractive cocktail bar as well as a busier lounge bar. There is a quiet first floor lounge and an adjacent conference room. Bedrooms feature a good range of facilities.
ROOMS: 32 en suite (3 fmly) **FACILITIES:** Pool table **CONF:** Thtr 60 Class 30 Board 30 **PARKING:** 15 **NOTES:** No smoking in restaurant **CARDS:**

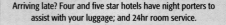

Arriving late? Four and five star hotels have night porters to assist with your luggage; and 24hr room service.

FORT WILLIAM, continued

★★68% Grand
Gordon Square PH33 6DX
☎ 01397 702928 📠 01397 702928
e-mail: enquiries@grandhotel-scotland.co.uk
Dir: *on A82 at W end of High St*
Considerable improvements have taken place at this friendly family run hotel at the south end of the pedestrianised High Street. Most bedrooms are refurbished and bathrooms continue to be enhanced. Public areas include comfortable non smoking lounges, a spacious bar where tasty freshly prepared bar meals are a feature, and an attractive formal dining room.
ROOMS: 33 en suite (4 fmly) s £25-£42.50; d £44-£65 (incl. bkfst) * LB **CONF:** Thtr 110 Class 60 Board 20 **PARKING:** 20 **NOTES:** No smoking in restaurant Closed Jan Civ Wed 80
CARDS:

See advert on opposite page

★★68% *Milton Hotel & Leisure Club*
North Rd PH33 6TG
☎ 01397 702331 📠 01397 700132
e-mail: sales@miltonhotels.com
Dir: *N of town, on A82*
A popular base for visiting tour groups and families, attracted by the smart new leisure centre. Refurbishment has enhanced the comfortable foyer lounge and large dining room. Bedrooms range from spacious executive rooms to smaller, practical standard rooms.
ROOMS: 52 en suite 67 annexe en suite (14 fmly) **FACILITIES:** Indoor swimming (H) Sauna Solarium Gym Pool table Jacuzzi/spa Beauty salon entertainment **CONF:** Thtr 220 Class 70 Board 60 **PARKING:** 140
NOTES: No smoking in restaurant **CARDS:**

★★65% *Alexandra*
The Parade PH33 6AZ
☎ 01397 702241 📠 01397 705554
e-mail: sales@miltonhotels.com
Dir: *North end of town centre*
Situated at the north end of the High Street, this long established and welcoming Victorian hotel remains a popular base for visiting tour groups. The best bedrooms are the executive rooms on the top floor which contrast with the smaller and more practical standard rooms on the other levels. Meals are available all day in the coffee shop. Leisure facilities are available to guests at the nearby sister hotel.
ROOMS: 97 en suite (14 fmly) **FACILITIES:** Free use of nearby leisure club entertainment **CONF:** Thtr 140 Class 40 Board 26 **SERVICES:** Lift
PARKING: 65 **NOTES:** No smoking in restaurant
CARDS:

★★63% The Caledonian
Achintore Rd PH33 6RW
☎ 01397 703117 📠 01397 700550
PEEL HOTELS
Dir: *on A 82, just south of Fort William centre*
Popular with tour groups, this modern hotel enjoys views over Loch Linnhe from its position south of town. The loch can also be seen from the open plan public areas.
ROOMS: 86 en suite (12 fmly) s £20-£75; d £40-£95 (incl. bkfst) * LB
FACILITIES: Sauna Pool table entertainment Xmas **CONF:** Thtr 60 Class 40 Board 30 Del from £40 * **SERVICES:** Lift **PARKING:** 60
NOTES: No smoking in restaurant **CARDS:**

> Packed in a hurry? Ironing facilities should be available at all star levels, either in rooms or on request.

FREUCHIE, Fife — Map 11 NO20

★★67% Lomond Hills
Parliament Square KY15 7EY
☎ 01337 857329 & 857498 📠 01337 858180
e-mail: lomond_foresthotels@hotmail.com
Dir: *in centre of village off A92 2m north of Glenrothes*
A former coaching inn has been considerably extended to create this welcoming tourist and business hotel in the centre of the village. Bedrooms come in mixed sizes and styles, but all are comfortable and offer a good range of amenities. Public areas offer all the expected facilities with the popular leisure centre being an added attraction.
ROOMS: 25 en suite (3 fmly) No smoking in 3 bedrooms s £50-£54; d £75-£78 (incl. bkfst) * LB **FACILITIES:** STV Indoor swimming (H) Sauna Solarium Gym Jacuzzi/spa Xmas **CONF:** Thtr 200 Class 100 Board 80 Del from £50 * **PARKING:** 21
CARDS:

GAIRLOCH, Highland — Map 14 NG87

★★★67% Creag Mor Hotel
Charleston IV21 2AH
☎ 01445 712068 📠 01445 712044
e-mail: enquiries@creagmor-hotel.co.uk
Dir: *A9 to Inverness, then A832 following signs to Ullapool, pass through village of Garve and follow signs for Gairloch, hotel 1st on right*
Situated in the highland scenery of Wester Ross, bedrooms at this comfortable hotel are pleasantly decorated and offer every modern convenience. Tranquil public areas include an inviting split level gallery bar/lounge from which views of the harbour can be enjoyed. Local produce features strongly in the dining room and there is also an all-day menu. There are separate restaurants for both smokers and non-smokers.
ROOMS: 17 en suite (1 fmly) s £35-£62.50; d £70-£110 (incl. bkfst) * LB **FACILITIES:** Fishing Pool table **CONF:** Class 40 **PARKING:** 29
NOTES: Closed 6 Nov-Feb **CARDS:**

See advert on opposite page

★★70% Myrtle Bank
Low Rd IV21 2BS
☎ 01445 712004 📠 01445 712214
e-mail: myrtlebank@msn.com
Dir: *off B8012 Melvaig road*
A warm welcome is assured at this hotel by the shore of Loch Gairloch. The bedrooms are comfortably furnished and several enjoy views over the loch to the Skye hills. Day rooms consist of a lounge, conservatory, and a bar and dining room, both serving enjoyable food.
ROOMS: 12 en suite (2 fmly) s £35-£44; d £70-£88 (incl. bkfst) *
FACILITIES: Pool table **PARKING:** 20 **NOTES:** No smoking in restaurant
CARDS:

GALASHIELS, Scottish Borders — Map 12 NT43

★★★66% Kingsknowes
Selkirk Rd TD1 3HY
☎ 01896 758375 📠 01896 750377
e-mail: sylvia@kingsknowes.co.uk
Dir: *off A7 at Galashiels/ Selkirk rdbt*
A friendly and informal atmosphere can be enjoyed at this family-run hotel, which stands in its own grounds south of the town, close to the River Tweed. A Victorian turreted mansion, its public areas feature a marble entrance and imposing staircase, whilst there is a choice of bars, one offering a good range of bar meals

continued

to complement the restaurant. Bedrooms are tastefully furnished and several on the first floor are massive.
ROOMS: 11 en suite (3 fmly) s £49; d £74 (incl. bkfst) * LB
FACILITIES: Xmas **CONF:** Thtr 65 Class 45 Board 30 Del from £70 *
PARKING: 72 **NOTES:** No smoking in restaurant Civ Wed 100
CARDS:

★★★62% Woodlands House Hotel & Restaurants

Windyknowe Rd TD1 1RG
☎ 01896 754722 📠 01896 754892
e-mail: woodlands.uk@virgin.net
Dir: *A7 into Galashiels, take A72 towards Peebles, take the 1st left into Hall St, then 2nd road on right to hotel*

Quietly situated in two acres of grounds, this fine Victorian Gothic mansion lies above the town, within easy walking distance of the centre. Bedrooms are generally spacious, many having views over the gardens, whilst the ground floor offers a high ceilinged bar and nicely furnished restaurant, both featuring fine period architecture.
ROOMS: 10 en suite (1 fmly) s £51-£55; d £72-£96 (incl. bkfst) * LB
FACILITIES: Xmas **CONF:** Thtr 50 Class 30 Board 24 **PARKING:** 35
NOTES: No smoking in restaurant Civ Wed 54 **CARDS:**

★★65% *King's*

56 Market St TD1 3AN
☎ 01896 755497 📠 01896 755497
e-mail: kingsgala@aol.com
Dir: *adjacent to southbound A7 in town centre*
A welcoming atmosphere is offered at this family-run hotel close to the town centre. The en suite bedrooms are equipped with a good range of amenities. Freshly prepared meals are provided in the dining room and bar while home baking accompanies the morning coffees and afternoon teas.
ROOMS: 7 en suite (2 fmly) **FACILITIES:** ch fac **CONF:** Thtr 80 Class 30 Board 40 **NOTES:** No dogs (ex guide dogs) Closed 1-3 Jan
CARDS:

★★62% Abbotsford Arms

63 Stirling St TD1 1BY
☎ 01896 752517 📠 01896 750744
Dir: *turn off A7 down Ladhope Vale, turn left opposite bus station*
A friendly and informal hotel, the Abbotsford Arms lies just off the inner ring road within walking distance of the town centre. It serves food throughout the day, and is very popular for its good range of dishes and generous portions, both in the bar and restaurant.
ROOMS: 14 en suite (2 fmly) s £38-£40; d £58-£60 (incl. bkfst) * LB
FACILITIES: STV **CONF:** Thtr 150 Class 100 Board 100 **PARKING:** 10
NOTES: No dogs (ex guide dogs) Closed 24-25 & 31 Dec & 1 Jan
CARDS:

GATEHOUSE OF FLEET, Dumfries & Galloway Map 11 NX55

★★★★67% *Cally Palace*

DG7 2DL
☎ 01557 814341 📠 01557 814522
e-mail: cally@mcmhotel.demon.co.uk
Dir: *1m from Gatehouse. From M6 & A74, follow signs for Dumfries and then A75 Stranraer*

Few hotels can claim to be a palace, but this grand 17th-century building, set in 500 acres of forest and parkland, meets all the criteria. The hotel boasts extensive leisure facilities, and the public rooms include a new conservatory bar. There are several suites and bedrooms with separate sitting areas. All rooms are spacious, and offer extras such as bathrobes and complimentary sherry. The short dinner menu places emphasis on freshly prepared dishes.

ROOMS: 56 en suite (7 fmly) **FACILITIES:** STV Indoor swimming (H) Golf 18 Tennis (hard) Fishing Snooker Sauna Solarium Pool table Croquet lawn Putting green Jacuzzi/spa Table tennis Practice fairway **CONF:** Thtr 80 Class 40 Board 35 **SERVICES:** Lift **PARKING:** 100 **NOTES:** No dogs (ex guide dogs) No smoking in restaurant Closed 3 Jan-3 Feb RS Feb **CARDS:**

★★★64% Murray Arms

DG7 2HY
☎ 01557 814207 📠 01557 814370
Dir: *off A75, hotel at edge of town, near clock tower*

A relaxed and welcoming atmosphere prevails at this family-run hotel, a former coaching inn at the north end of the main street. Public areas retain a comfortable traditional feel and include a choice of lounges, a snug bar, and the popular Lunky Hole restaurant where all day food is available from the varied menu. Bedrooms provide modern comforts and amenities.

ROOMS: 12 en suite 1 annexe en suite (3 fmly) s £45-£50; d £89-£99 (incl. bkfst) * LB **FACILITIES:** Tennis (hard) Croquet lawn Xmas **CONF:** Thtr 120 Class 50 Board 30 Del from £50 * **PARKING:** 50 **CARDS:**

GIFFNOCK, East Renfrewshire Map 11 NS55

★★★67% The Macdonald

Eastwood Toll G46 6RA
☎ 0141 638 2225 📠 0141 638 6231
Dir: *on A77 Kilmarnock/Ayr Rd at Eastwood Toll, Giffnock - take 1st exit onto A726 East Kilbride, then 1st right to hotel*

A well established, friendly comfortable hotel, conveniently situated for both the city centre and the Ayrshire coast. The bedrooms are neat and well equipped, with four comfortable suites. The public rooms include a choice of bars and modern Scottish cuisine is served in generous portions in the elegant Oscar's Restaurant.

ROOMS: 56 en suite (4 fmly) No smoking in 12 bedrooms s £85-£95; d £95-£105 * LB **FACILITIES:** STV Sauna Solarium Pool table Xmas **CONF:** Thtr 160 Class 60 Board 35 Del from £105 * **PARKING:** 130 **NOTES:** Civ Wed 130 **CARDS:**

★★65% *The Redhurst*

Eastwoodmains Rd G46 6QE
☎ 0141 638 6465 📠 0141 620 0419
Dir: *on A726 main Paisley route, from city centre take M77/M8 follow signs for A77/A726 to East Kilbride*

This popular hotel is situated in a suburb south of the city, which is easily accessible via the nearby M77. Bedrooms are decorated nicley and equipped well. The attractively furbished bar and restaurant offers a popular menu that suits all.

continued

ROOMS: 19 en suite (2 fmly) **FACILITIES:** entertainment **CONF:** Thtr 200 Class 150 Board 40 **PARKING:** 50 **NOTES:** No dogs (ex guide dogs) **CARDS:**

GLASGOW, City of Glasgow Map 11 NS56
see also Clydebank & Uplawmoor

★★★★69% Glasgow Marriott

500 Argyle St, Anderston G3 8RR
☎ 0141 226 5577 📠 0141 221 7676
Dir: *off junct 19 of M8, turn left at lights, then left into hotel*

The Glasgow Marriott is a well-established and conveniently located hotel that has been refurbished to provide a smart ground floor with a bar/lounge, informal café, and attractive restaurant. The hotel boasts its own leisure club, which includes a gym and pool. High quality, well-equipped bedrooms benefit from air conditioning and generous beds; the suites are particularly comfortable.

ROOMS: 300 en suite (89 fmly) No smoking in 212 bedrooms d £88-£145 * LB **FACILITIES:** STV Indoor swimming (H) Sauna Solarium Gym Jacuzzi/spa Heated whirlpool Beautician Xmas **CONF:** Thtr 650 Class 350 Board 40 Del from £145 * **SERVICES:** Lift air con **PARKING:** 250 **NOTES:** Civ Wed 250 **CARDS:**

★★★★66% Beardmore

Beardmore St G81 4SA
☎ 0141 951 6000 📠 0141 951 6018
e-mail: beardmore.hotel@hci.co.uk
(For full entry see Clydebank)

★★★★64% Millennium Hotel Glasgow

George Square G2 1DS
☎ 0141 332 6711 📠 0141 332 4264
e-mail: sales.glasgow@mill-cop.com
Dir: *take junct 15 from M8 follow signs City Centre/George Sq, travel along Cathedral St past Strathclyde University, turn left into Hanover St*

This Victorian building overlooking George Square in the heart of the city was undergoing a major and exciting redevelopment programme at the time of our last inspection. Guests can look forward to an elegant reception hall with cocktail bar and a smart new restaurant and bar.

ROOMS: 117 en suite (16 fmly) No smoking in 55 bedrooms s £80-£145; d £100-£165 * LB **FACILITIES:** STV Gym Xmas **CONF:** Thtr 400 Class 15 Board 40 Del from £120 * **SERVICES:** Lift air con **NOTES:** No dogs (ex guide dogs) **CARDS:**

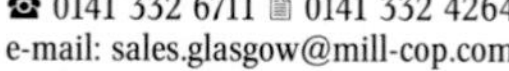

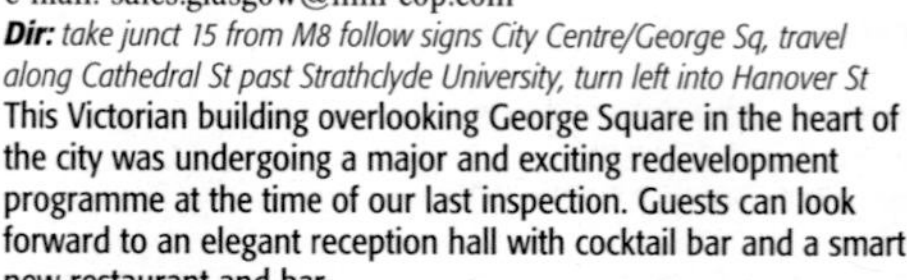

Read all about it! Newspapers delivered to bedrooms in four and five star hotels.

Premier Collection

★★★ One Devonshire Gardens
1 Devonshire Gardens G12 0UX
☎ 0141 339 2001 🖷 0141 337 1663
e-mail: markcalpin@btconnect.com
Dir: *M8 junct 17, follow signs for A82, after 1.5m turn left into Hyndland Rd, 1st right, right at mini rdbt, right at end then continue to end*
Three town houses form this highly individual hotel. Luxurious bedrooms follow an individual and distinctive decorative theme. One house has a stylish drawing room, and there is a cocktail bar and restaurant in another, where guests can enjoy classic dishes with a modern touch.
ROOMS: 27 en suite (3 fmly) **FACILITIES:** STV **CONF:** Thtr 40 Class 20 Board 26 **PARKING:** 12 **NOTES:** No smoking in restaurant
CARDS:

★★★77%
The Devonshire Hotel of Glasgow
5 Devonshire Gardens G12 0UX
☎ 0141 339 7878 🖷 0141 339 3980
e-mail: devonshire@aol.com
Dir: *M8 junct 17. Right at slip road lights on to A82. Continue 1.5m. Over 1st lights, left at 2nd. 1st right, right at mini rdbt. Hotel at end of road*
Standing on the corner of an imposing tree-lined Victorian terrace, the Devonshire is one of the city's most stylish hotels. The sumptuously furnished drawing room is the focal point of the day rooms, with all the elegance and comfort expected in such a grand house. An imaginatively prepared Scottish menu is served in the small dining room and there is extensive 24-hour room service. Spacious bedrooms are richly furnished and equipped with many luxuries.
ROOMS: 14 en suite (3 fmly) s £110-£140; d £120-£175 * LB
FACILITIES: STV Xmas **CONF:** Thtr 50 Class 30 Board 30
NOTES: Civ Wed 50 **CARDS:**

★★★73% **Malmaison**
278 West George St G2 4LL
☎ 0141 572 1000 🖷 0141 572 1002
e-mail: glasgow@malmaison.com
Dir: *from South/East-M8 Junction 18 (Charing Cross), from West/North-M8 City Centre Glasgow*
The original Malmaison, a concept now successfully transferred south of the border as well, is built around a former church, the brasserie being situated in the crypt. The comfortable bedrooms are strikingly decorated and include split-level suites. All are equipped with CD players, mini bars and ISDN telephone lines. The all-day Café Mal provides lighter fare than the brasserie, and there is also a small gym to work off the extra calories.
continued

ROOMS: 72 en suite (4 fmly) No smoking in 20 bedrooms d £105 * LB
FACILITIES: STV Gym **CONF:** Thtr 35 Class 20 Board 20 Del £146 *
SERVICES: Lift **NOTES:** No dogs (ex guide dogs)
CARDS:

★★★68% **Holiday Inn**
161 West Nile St G1 2RL
☎ 0141 352 8300 🖷 0141 332 7447
Dir: *M8 jnct 16, follow signs for Royal Concert Hall, hotel is opposite*
Purpose built on a corner site close to the Theatre Royal and the Concert Hall, this contemporary hotel features the popular Bonne Auberge French restaurant, a bar area and conservatory. Bedrooms are well equipped and comfortable with suites available. Staff are friendly and attentive.
ROOMS: 113 en suite (24 fmly) No smoking in 78 bedrooms d £89-£105 * **FACILITIES:** STV Xmas **CONF:** Thtr 130 Class 80 Board 80 Del £115 * **SERVICES:** Lift **NOTES:** No dogs (ex guide dogs) Civ Wed 120
CARDS:

★★★68% **Jurys Glasgow**
Great Western Rd G12 0XP
☎ 0141 334 8161 🖷 0141 334 3846
e-mail: glasgow_hotel@jurys.com
Dir: *M8 junct 17. Take A82 signs. Continue on rd through 2 sets of lights. At 3rd set turn left, just before BP garage. Then right follow rd to hotel*
This friendly business and leisure hotel is situated in the west end beside the A82. All bedrooms have benefited from refurbishment. Inviting public areas include a choice of contrasting bars, a well equipped leisure club, conference and banqueting facilities, and an attractive split-level restaurant offering both carte and fixed-price menus as well as the good value carvery.
continued

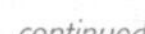

GLASGOW, continued

ROOMS: 136 en suite (12 fmly) No smoking in 100 bedrooms s £60-£80; d £70-£90 (incl. bkfst) * LB **FACILITIES:** STV Indoor swimming (H) Sauna Solarium Gym Jacuzzi/spa entertainment Xmas **CONF:** Thtr 140 Class 80 Board 40 Del from £105 * **SERVICES:** Lift **PARKING:** 300 **CARDS:**

★★★67% Ewington

Balmoral Ter, 132 Queens Dr, Queens Park G42 8QW
☎ 0141 423 1152 🖷 0141 422 2030
e-mail: ewington@aol.com
Dir: *M8 junct 20 onto A77, go trough 8 sets of traffic lights, at crossroads the hotel is on 2nd left after crossroads*

Part of a Victorian terrace on the south side opposite Queens Park, this is a stylish town house hotel. Dedicated staff provide friendly service. The public areas include an inviting foyer lounge, a smart restaurant and comfortable cocktail lounge. Bedrooms range in size and style and include spacious executive rooms.
ROOMS: 41 en suite (4 fmly) No smoking in 6 bedrooms s £50-£93; d £60-£130 * LB **FACILITIES:** STV Internet terminal Xmas **CONF:** Thtr 70 Class 20 Board 30 Del from £80 * **SERVICES:** Lift **PARKING:** 16 **NOTES:** Civ Wed 60 **CARDS:**

See advert on page 709

★★★67% Swallow

517 Paisley Rd West G51 1RW
☎ 0141 427 3146 🖷 0141 427 4059
e-mail: info@swallowhotels.com
Dir: *off junc 23 of M8, from S M6/M8 off junct 24 of M8, from W M8*

Conveniently situated for both the city centre and the airport. Bedrooms, the majority of which have been refurbished, are comfortable and equipped to meet the needs of all travellers. Spacious lounges and Readers restaurant are complemented by the popular leisure club.
ROOMS: 117 en suite (11 fmly) No smoking in 63 bedrooms s £54.50-£99; d £79-£130 (incl. bkfst) * LB **FACILITIES:** STV Indoor swimming (H) Sauna Solarium Gym Jacuzzi/spa Steam room Xmas **CONF:** Thtr 300 Class 150 Board 30 Del from £90 * **SERVICES:** Lift **PARKING:** 150 **NOTES:** No smoking in restaurant
CARDS:

★★★66% *Posthouse Glasgow City*

Bothwell St G2 7EN
☎ 0870 400 9032 🖷 0141 221 8986
This large, modern city centre hotel offers two eating outlets in the form of a Traditional Carvery and Jules restaurant, with its range of international dishes. Bedroom styles vary; the smart Millennium rooms offer the highest standards, but all accommodation is very well equipped. Extra services include a concierge and all-day room service. There is limited parking, but extra free parking is offered in the nearby NCP.

continued

ROOMS: 247 en suite (28 fmly) No smoking in 102 bedrooms **CONF:** Thtr 850 Class 450 Board 100 **SERVICES:** Lift air con **CARDS:**

★★★65% Sherbrooke Castle

11 Sherbrooke Av, Pollokshields G41 4PG
☎ 0141 427 4227 🖷 0141 427 5685
e-mail: mail@sherbrooke.co.uk
Dir: *from M8 junct 23 left to Dumbreck Rd, then 2nd left Nithsdale Rd at lights. Hotel 0.5m on right*

Built in 1896 this impressive, turreted red-sandstone hotel is located in a residential area south of the city with convenient access to the M77. Nicely presented public areas include a well stocked bar and popular function suite. The elegant restaurant offers fine dining from a short fixed-price menu. Bedrooms have attractive colour schemes and are comfortably furnished.
ROOMS: 10 en suite 9 annexe en suite (2 fmly) No smoking in 6 bedrooms s £65-£95; d £85-£150 (incl. bkfst) * LB **FACILITIES:** STV Xmas **CONF:** Thtr 200 Class 100 Board 50 Del from £135 * **PARKING:** 80 **NOTES:** No smoking in restaurant
CARDS:

★★★64% Quality Hotel Glasgow

99 Gordon St G1 3SF
☎ 0141 221 9680 🖷 0141 226 3948
e-mail: admin@gb627.u-net.com
Dir: *exit 19 of M8, left into Argyle St and left into Hope St*
A splendid Victorian railway hotel, forming part of Central Station. It retains much original charm yet has modern facilities. Public rooms are impressive and continue to be upgraded and improved. Bedrooms are well equipped and mostly spacious. Guests can eat informally in the Coffee Shop or in the main restaurant.
ROOMS: 222 en suite (8 fmly) No smoking in 70 bedrooms s £75-£83; d £90-£108 * LB **FACILITIES:** STV Indoor swimming (H) Sauna Solarium Gym Jacuzzi/spa Hair & beauty salon Steamroom Xmas **CONF:** Thtr 600 Class 170 Board 40 Del from £90 * **SERVICES:** Lift **NOTES:** No smoking in restaurant **CARDS:**

★★★64% The Tinto Firs

470 Kilmarnock Rd G43 2BB
☎ 0141 637 2353 🖷 0141 633 1340
Dir: *4m S of Glasgow City Centre on the A77*
This modern, purpose-built hotel is four miles south of the city centre and convenient for the airport and the Burrell Collection. Comfortably furnished public areas include a choice of bars, an attractive restaurant and a smart boardroom. Bedrooms are mostly cosy studio singles which are very well equipped.
ROOMS: 27 en suite (4 fmly) No smoking in 10 bedrooms s £85-£95; d £95-£105 * LB **FACILITIES:** STV Xmas **CONF:** Thtr 150 Class 50 Board 50 Del from £105 * **PARKING:** 46 **NOTES:** Civ Wed 130
CARDS:

★★★63% Kings Park
Mill St G73 2LX
☎ 0141 647 5491 📠 0141 613 3022
e-mail: enquiries@maksu-group.co.uk
Dir: *on A730 East Kilbride road*

This modern refurbished hotel is convenient for Glasgow city centre and East Kilbride. Bedrooms are suitably equipped and feature comfortable furnishings and fittings. Particularly noteworthy are the conference and banqueting suites.
ROOMS: 26 en suite (4 fmly) No smoking in 4 bedrooms s £50-£75; d £70-£95 (incl. bkfst) * **FACILITIES:** STV Pool table Jacuzzi/spa Xmas **CONF:** Thtr 250 Class 80 Board 50 Del from £90 * **PARKING:** 150 **NOTES:** Civ Wed 200 **CARDS:**

★★★60% Carrick
REGAL
377 Argyle St G2 8LL
☎ 0141 248 2355 📠 0141 221 1014
Dir: *junct 19 M8 bear left onto Argyle St, hotel opposite Cadogan Square 200m on right*

A modern hotel at the west end of one of the city's best known streets. The compact but well equipped bedrooms have all the essential facilities. The restaurant, lounge bar and a number of meeting rooms are on the first floor. Free overnight car parking is available nearby.
ROOMS: 121 en suite No smoking in 79 bedrooms s £30-£70; d £35-£85 * LB **FACILITIES:** Xmas **CONF:** Thtr 80 Class 40 Board 24 Del from £65 * **SERVICES:** Lift **NOTES:** No smoking in restaurant
CARDS:

★★★60% Kelvin Park Lorne
REGAL
923 Sauchiehall St G3 7TE
☎ 0141 314 9955 📠 0141 337 1659

This popular hotel is five minutes' walk from the S.E.C. and art galleries. It offers mixed styles of smart, attractive accommodation. Guests can eat informally in the bar, from the room service menu or in the smart restaurant. There is a private car park beneath the hotel and conference facilities in a separate wing.

continued

ROOMS: 100 en suite (7 fmly) No smoking in 20 bedrooms s £40-£75; d £50-£120 * LB **FACILITIES:** Xmas **CONF:** Thtr 300 Class 100 Board 80 Del £97.50 * **SERVICES:** Lift **PARKING:** 25 **NOTES:** No dogs (ex guide dogs) Civ Wed 200 **CARDS:**

⇧ *Travelodge*
Travelodge
251 Paisley Rd G5 8RA
☎ 0141 420 3882
Dir: *0.5m from city centre just off junc 20 M8 from south/junc 21 M8 from north. Behind Harry Ramsden's*

This modern building offers accommodation in smart, spacious and well equipped bedrooms, all with en suite bathrooms. Refreshments may be taken at the nearby family restaurant. For further details and the Travelodge phone number, consult the Hotel Groups page.
ROOMS: 100 en suite

⇧ Premier Lodge (Glasgow North East)
PREMIER LODGE
Cumbernauld Rd, Muirhead, Chryston G69 9BJ
☎ 0870 700 1396 📠 0870 700 1397

Premier Lodge offers modern, well equipped, en suite accommodation suitable for both business and leisure travellers. Meals can be taken at the adjacent popular restaurant and bar which is fully licensed. For further details, consult the Hotel Groups page.
ROOMS: 38 en suite d £42 *

⇧ Express by Holiday Inn Glasgow City Centre

112 Stockwell St G1 4LT
☎ 0141 548 5000 📠 0141 548 5048

A modern budget hotel offering comfortable accommodation in refreshing, spacious and comprehensively-equipped bedrooms, en suite bathrooms with power showers and continental buffet breakfast included in the room rate. Suitable for business travellers or families. For further details and the Express by Holiday Inn phone number, consult the Hotel Groups page.
ROOMS: 128 en suite (incl. cont bkfst) d £56-£58 * **CONF:** Thtr 30 Class 30 Board 14

⇧ Express by Holiday Inn Theatreland
Express by Holiday Inn
165 West Nile St G1 2RL
☎ 0141 331 6800 📠 0141 331 6828
e-mail: express@holidayinn.demon.co.uk
Dir: *follow signs to Royal Concert Hall*

A modern budget hotel offering comfortable accommodation in refreshing, spacious and comprehensively-equipped bedrooms, en suite bathrooms with power showers and continental buffet

continued

GLASGOW, continued

Express by Holiday Inn Theatreland, Glasgow

breakfast included in the room rate. Suitable for business travellers or families. For further details and the Express by Holiday Inn phone number, consult the Hotel Groups page.
ROOMS: 88 en suite (incl. cont bkfst) d fr £56.95 *

⇧ Premier Lodge (City Centre)

PREMIER LODGE

10 Elmbank Gardens G2 4PP
☎ 0870 700 1394 🖷 0870 700 1395
Premier Lodge offers modern, well equipped, en suite accommodation suitable for both business and leisure travellers. Meals can be taken at the adjacent popular restaurant and bar which is fully licensed. For further details, consult the Hotel Groups page.
ROOMS: 278 en suite d £46 *

⇧ *Travelodge*

Travelodge

9 Hill St G3 6PR
☎ 0141 333 1515
This modern building offers accommodation in smart, spacious and well equipped bedrooms, all with en suite bathrooms. Refreshments may be taken at the nearby family restaurant. For further details and the Travelodge phone number, consult the Hotel Groups page.
ROOMS: 93 en suite

○ Novotel Glasgow

181 Pitt St
☎ 020 828 34500
ROOMS: 137 rms **NOTES:** Open November 2000

GLASGOW AIRPORT, Renfrewshire — Map 11 NS46

see also Howwood

★★★70% *Posthouse Glasgow Airport*

Posthouse

Abbotsinch PA3 2TR
☎ 0870 400 9031 🖷 0141 887 3738
e-mail: gm1791@forte-hotels.com
Dir: *from E M8 J28 signs for Hotel; from W M8 J29 follow airport slip rd to Hotel*
This Posthouse is situated opposite the arrivals/departure hall of the airport. It offers modern accommodation, including smartly decorated 'Millennium' bedrooms, as well as good public areas and a comfortable restaurant and bar.
ROOMS: 298 en suite (9 fmly) No smoking in 158 bedrooms
FACILITIES: Solarium **CONF:** Thtr 250 Class 120 Board 20
SERVICES: Lift air con **PARKING:** 60 **CARDS:**

★★★69% Dalmeny Park Country House

Lochlibo Rd G78 1LG
☎ 0141 881 9211 🖷 0141 881 9214
e-mail: enquires@maksu-group.co.uk
(For full entry see Barrhead)

★★★69% *Glynhill Hotel & Leisure Club*

Paisley Rd PA4 8XB
☎ 0141 886 5555 & 885 1111 🖷 0141 885 2838
e-mail: glynhillleisurehotel@msn.com
Dir: *on M8 towards Glasgow airport,turn off at junct 27,take A741 towards Renfrew cross small rdbt approx 300yds from motorway exit Hotel on right*
A smart and welcoming hotel with bedrooms that range from spacious executive rooms to smaller standard rooms which are tastefully appointed with a good range of amenities. The hotel boasts a luxurious leisure complex and extensive conference facilities; the choice of contrasting bars and restaurants should suit most tastes and budgets.
ROOMS: 125 en suite (25 fmly) No smoking in 51 bedrooms
FACILITIES: STV Indoor swimming (H) Snooker Sauna Solarium Gym Jacuzzi/spa entertainment **CONF:** Thtr 450 Class 240 Board 60
PARKING: 230 **NOTES:** No dogs (ex guide dogs)
CARDS:

★★★69% Lynnhurst

Park Rd PA5 8LS
☎ 01505 324331 & 324600 🖷 01505 324219
e-mail: enquiries@lynnhurst.co.uk
Dir: *past airport, take slip road (A737). Continue 2m & take B789 road. At slip road left into Johnstone. 1st main lights right then 1st left. 1st right*
Genuine hospitality together with high standards of guest care are the hallmarks of this family run hotel convenient for Glasgow Airport. Although variable in size, bedrooms are comfortably modern and offer a good range of amenities. Public areas present well and include a spacious bar, conservatory lounge, and an attractive panelled restaurant where fixed price and carte menus are available.
ROOMS: 21 en suite (2 fmly) s £40-£55; d £70-£80 (incl. bkfst) *
FACILITIES: STV Arrangement with local leisure centre **CONF:** Thtr 160 Class 160 Board 20 Del from £65 * **PARKING:** 100 **NOTES:** No dogs (ex guide dogs) Closed 1-3 Jan **CARDS:**

See advert on opposite page

★★★63% *Dean Park*

91 Glasgow Rd PA4 8YB
☎ 0141 304 9955 🖷 0141 885 0681
Dir: *3m NE A8 - turn off M8 at junct 26 onto A8 for Renfrew, follow road for 600yds, hotel is on the left*
Situated close to the airport and with convenient access to the M8, this modern purpose-built hotel attracts both the business and leisure traveller and is also a popular venue for local functions. Although not expansive, bedrooms are comfortable and well equipped. Public areas include a well stocked split-level bar, an attractive restaurant offering both fixed price and carte menus, and a comfortable foyer lounge.
ROOMS: 118 en suite (6 fmly) **FACILITIES:** Snooker Beautician & arrangement with leisure club **CONF:** Thtr 350 Class 150 Board 100
PARKING: 200 **CARDS:**

○ Express by Holiday Inn

St Andrews Dr PA3 2TJ
☎ 0141 842 1100 🖷 0141 842 1122
NOTES: Open

GLENCOE, Highland
Map 14 NN15

★★68% Glencoe
PA39 4HW
☎ 01855 811245 Fax 01855 811687
Dir: *on A82 in Glencoe village, 15m S of Fort William*
Beside the A82 this family-run holiday hotel offers a relaxed welcoming atmosphere. The bedrooms have pleasing colour schemes together with modern furnishings and all the expected amenities. Loch views can be enjoyed from the attractive restaurant, while the well stocked bar remains popular with non residents for the good value informal dining; the Grotto bar is also popular.
ROOMS: 15 en suite (4 fmly) s £36-£48; d £48-£72 (incl. bkfst) * LB **FACILITIES:** STV Pool table Games room Xmas **CONF:** Thtr 100 **PARKING:** 30 **NOTES:** No smoking in restaurant
CARDS:

GLENEAGLES See Auchterarder

GLENFARG, Perth & Kinross
Map 11 NO11

★★65% Glenfarg
Main St PH2 9NU
☎ 01577 830241 Fax 01577 830665
e-mail: info@glenfarghotel.co.uk
THE CIRCLE Selected Individual Hotels GREAT BRITAIN
Dir: *travelling S on M90, off at junc 9, turn left, Hotel 5m; travelling N on M90, off at junc 8, second left, Hotel 2m*
Situated in the centre of Glenfarg, this hotel has a relaxed, informal atmosphere. Bedrooms come in a variety of sizes, and rooms for families are provided. The outside adventure playground also proves a big hit with children. The restaurant offers enjoyable food, but the popular bar is well worth considering as an informal alternative.
ROOMS: 16 rms (15 en suite) (4 fmly) No smoking in all bedrooms s £39; d £66 (incl. bkfst) * LB **FACILITIES:** STV Pool table entertainment ch fac Xmas **CONF:** Thtr 60 Class 60 Board 30 Del from £60 * **PARKING:** 20 **NOTES:** No smoking in restaurant Civ Wed 60
CARDS:

GLENFINNAN, Highland
Map 14 NM98

★★76% *The Princes House*
PH37 4LT
☎ 01397 722246 Fax 01397 722307
e-mail: princeshouse@glenfinnan.co.uk
Dir: *15m W of Fort William on A830, 0.5m on right past monument*
Genuine hospitality and fine food are part of the appeal of this charming hotel, which stands close to historic site where Bonnie Prince Charlie raised the Jacobite standard. With its light, natural wood, the Pretender's Bar is a cosy place to unwind and enjoy a casual meal. Flora's Restaurant offers an interesting menu within a more formal environment. Attractive fabrics have been used to good effect in the well equipped bedrooms.
ROOMS: 9 en suite (1 fmly) No smoking in all bedrooms **FACILITIES:** Fishing Mountain bike hire **CONF:** Thtr 40 Class 20 **PARKING:** 20 **NOTES:** No children 5yrs No smoking in restaurant Closed Dec-Feb RS Feb, Mar, Nov & Dec
CARDS:

GLENLUCE, Dumfries & Galloway
Map 10 NX15

★★66% Kelvin House Hotel
53 Main St DG8 0PP
☎ 01581 300303 Fax 01581 300303
e-mail: kelvinhouse@lineone.net
Dir: *midway between Newton Stewart & Stranraer, just off the A75.*
This small privately run hotel is in the centre of a village in unspoilt countryside. The bedrooms are bright and spacious and

continued

GLENLUCE, continued

there is a comfortable residents' lounge. Meals are served either in the popular bar or the separate restaurant overlooking the garden.
ROOMS: 6 rms (5 en suite) (3 fmly) No smoking in 3 bedrooms s £25-£30; d £45-£53 (incl. bkfst) * LB **FACILITIES:** ch fac Xmas **CONF:** Thtr 50 Class 20 Board 20 Del from £51 * **CARDS:**

GLENROTHES, Fife Map 11 NO20

★★★62% Balgeddie House

Balgeddie Way KY6 3ET
☎ 01592 742511 01592 621702
e-mail: balgeddie@easynet.co.uk
Dir: *from A911 E of Leslie follow the signs to the hotel*
Enthusiastic owners look forward to welcoming you to their comfortable hotel, which stands in landscaped grounds. Bedrooms have attractive colour schemes and the most spacious are on the first floor. Public areas include a lounge, cocktail bar and restaurant.
ROOMS: 19 en suite (2 fmly) s £65; d £50-£85 (incl. bkfst) * LB **FACILITIES:** STV Riding Pool table Croquet lawn entertainment ch fac Xmas **CONF:** Thtr 140 Class 80 Board 60 Del from £85 * **PARKING:** 80 **NOTES:** No dogs (ex guide dogs) No smoking in restaurant Civ Wed 150 **CARDS:**

★★75% *Rescobie*

6 Valley Dr, Leslie KY6 3BQ
☎ 01592 749555 01592 620231
e-mail: rescobiehotel@compuserve.com
Dir: *turn off A92 at Glenrothes onto A911, through Leslie. End of high street follow straight ahead. Left at Zak Yule hairdressing salon. Hotel 1st left*

This delightful small hotel has taken on a new lease of life. The house has been completely refurbished and guests are assured of a warm welcome. Bedrooms are tasteful and comfortable. Public areas include an inviting lounge where refreshments are willingly served. Adjacent, the elegant restaurant provides the setting for an innovative short fixed price menu.
ROOMS: 10 en suite **PARKING:** 12 **NOTES:** No dogs (ex guide dogs) No children 12yrs No smoking in restaurant
CARDS:

See advert on opposite page

⌂ Express by Holiday Inn Glenrothes

Leslie Roundabout, Leslie Rd KY7 6XX
☎ 01592 745509 01592 743377
Dir: *turn off A92 onto A911. Straight over 4 rdbts. Hotel is on the left*
A modern budget hotel offering comfortable accommodation in refreshing, spacious and comprehensively-equipped bedrooms, en suite bathrooms with power showers and continental buffet breakfast included in the room rate. Suitable for business

continued

travellers or families. For further details and the Express by Holiday Inn phone number, consult the Hotel Groups page.
ROOMS: 49 en suite (incl. cont bkfst) d fr £47.50 * **CONF:** Thtr 30 Board 20

GLENSHEE (SPITTAL OF), Perth & Kinross Map 15 NO16

★★69% Dalmunzie House

PH10 7QG
☎ 01250 885224 01250 885225
e-mail: dalmunzie@aol.com
Dir: *on the A93 at Spittal of Glenshee, follow signs to hotel*

A welcoming atmosphere prevails at this impressive turreted house which is peacefully set amid a 6,500-acre estate. The comfortable bedrooms vary in size and are individually furnished, offering a good range of amenities. The restaurant serves carefully prepared fare based on quality local ingredients. A nine-hole golf course is available.
ROOMS: 18 rms (16 en suite) s £53-£61; d £84-£110 (incl. bkfst) * LB **FACILITIES:** Golf 9 Tennis (hard) Fishing Croquet lawn Clay pigeon shooting Deer stalking Mountain bikes Xmas **CONF:** Thtr 20 Class 20 Board 20 Del from £73 * **SERVICES:** Lift **PARKING:** 32 **NOTES:** No smoking in restaurant Closed end Nov-28 Dec
CARDS:

GRANGEMOUTH, Falkirk Map 11 NS98

★★★71% *Grange Manor*

Glensburgh FK3 8XJ
☎ 01324 474836 01324 665861
e-mail: info@grangemanor.co.uk
Dir: *travelling E; off M9 at junc 6, Hotel 200m to right. Travelling W; off M9 at junc 5, A905 for 2m*
Situated in the south side of town within easy reach of the M9 this hotel offers high quality spacious accommodation with superb bathrooms. The smart foyer area includes a comfortable lounge, and there is also an original bar and restaurant. Enjoyable modern Scottish fare features on both the fixed price and carte menus.

continued

ROOMS: 7 en suite 30 annexe en suite (6 fmly) No smoking in 16 bedrooms **FACILITIES:** STV **CONF:** Thtr 150 Class 68 Board 40 **PARKING:** 154 **NOTES:** No dogs (ex guide dogs) **CARDS:**

GRANTOWN-ON-SPEY, Highland Map 14 NJ02

★★77% Culdearn House Hotel

Woodlands Ter PH26 3JU
☎ 01479 872106 01479 873641
e-mail: culdearn@globalnet.co.uk

THE CIRCLE Selected Individual Hotels GREAT BRITAIN

***Dir:** enter Grantown on the A95 from SW and turn at 30mph sign*

Many guests return time and time again to this charming small hotel on the south side of town. The immaculate bedrooms have pleasing colour schemes and are comfortably furnished in mixed modern styles. The elegant dining room offers a fine dining experience which is based on careful treatment of quality raw ingredients. Service is excellent.

ROOMS: 9 en suite No smoking in 3 bedrooms s £65-£75; d £130-£150 (incl. bkfst & dinner) * LB **PARKING:** 12 **NOTES:** No dogs (ex guide dogs) No children 10yrs No smoking in restaurant Closed 30 Oct-28 Feb **CARDS:**

GRETNA (WITH GRETNA GREEN), Dumfries & Galloway Map 11 NY36

★★★65% *Garden House*

Sarkfoot Rd DG16 5EP
☎ 01461 337621 01461 337692

***Dir:** just off junct 45 on the M6 at Gretna*

From its position close to the famous blacksmith's shop, this purpose-built modern hotel is especially popular for wedding receptions, but corporate and leisure guests are equally well catered for. Bedrooms, including several honeymoon suites, are spacious and modern in style. Public areas include a large open-plan foyer where you will find the lounge and restaurant with a small bar adjacent. The leisure centre is an added attraction.

ROOMS: 21 en suite (2 fmly) **FACILITIES:** STV Indoor swimming (H) Jacuzzi/spa **CONF:** Thtr 100 Class 80 Board 40 **PARKING:** 105 **NOTES:** No dogs (ex guide dogs) **CARDS:**

See advert on this page

★★70% Gretna Chase

DG16 5JB
☎ 01461 337517 01461 337766

***Dir:** off A74 onto B7076, left at top of slip road, hotel 400yds on right*

A favourite venue for wedding parties, this hotel is seemingly situated in "no man's land" between the signs for Scotland and England, yet surrounded by delightful gardens. The well equipped bedrooms are comfortable and full of character. The dining room

continued on p716

G

GRETNA, continued

can accommodate functions and the lounge bar is a popular retreat.
ROOMS: 9 en suite (4 fmly) No smoking in 3 bedrooms s £55-£75; d £79.50-£125 (incl. bkfst) * **FACILITIES:** Jacuzzi/spa **CONF:** Thtr 50 Class 30 Board 20 **PARKING:** 40 **NOTES:** No dogs (ex guide dogs) Closed 1st 2 weeks in Jan **CARDS:**

★★68% Solway Lodge

Annan Rd DG16 5DN
☎ 01461 338266 🖷 01461 337791
e-mail: j.welsh@btconnect.com
Dir: *A74(M), take Gretna/Longtown exit, turn left at top of road past Welcome to Scotland sign, BP petrol stn turn left for town centre 250 yds on right*

Close to the blacksmith's shop, this friendly family run hotel offers a choice of accommodation. There are two honeymoon suites in the main house, and the chalet block rooms are ideal for overnight stops. A range of home-made meals is offered in the restaurant and lounge bar.
ROOMS: 3 en suite 7 annexe en suite s £40-£50; d £60-£80 (incl. bkfst) * **PARKING:** 25 **NOTES:** No smoking in restaurant Closed 25 & 26 Dec RS 10 Oct-Mar **CARDS:**

Days Inn

Gretna Green, A74M Trunk Rd DG16 5HQ
☎ 01461 337566 🖷 01461 337823
Dir: *situated at the Welcome Break service area Gretna Green on A74 - Accessible from both Northbound & Southbound carriageway*

Fully refurbished, Days Inn offers well equipped, brightly appointed, modern accommodation with smart en suite bathrooms. There is a fully staffed reception; continental breakfast is available and other refreshments may be taken at the nearby family restaurant.
ROOMS: 64 en suite d fr £45 *

GULLANE, East Lothian — Map 12 NT48

Premier Collection

★★★ Greywalls

Muirfield EH31 2EG
☎ 01620 842144 🖷 01620 842241
e-mail: hotel@greywalls.co.uk
Dir: *A198, hotel is signposted at E end of village*

Designed by Lutyens, and with gardens created by Gertrude Jekyll, Greywalls overlooks the famous Muirfield Golf Course and guests may find themselves sleeping in the bedrooms occupied by many of the game's greats in the past. Public areas include a library with a log fire and grand piano, and a lovely sun lounge. At dinner a simple cooking style allows top quality ingredients to shine through. Bedrooms are furnished in period style and are exceptionally well equipped and smart.
ROOMS: 17 en suite 5 annexe en suite s £105-£180; d £180-£210 (incl. bkfst) * LB **FACILITIES:** STV Tennis (hard & grass) Croquet lawn Putting green **CONF:** Thtr 30 Class 20 Board 20 **PARKING:** 40 **NOTES:** No smoking in restaurant Closed Nov-Mar **CARDS:**

HALKIRK, Highland — Map 15 ND15

★★63% Ulbster Arms

Bridge St KW12 6XY
☎ 01847 831206 & 831641 🖷 01847 831206
Dir: *A9 to Thurso from Perth, 3m after village of Spittal turn Left*

Situated adjacent to the River Thurso, this long-established Highland hotel is particularly popular with the sporting clientele. Public areas include an attractive dining room, a quiet lounge and a lively lounge bar, which is popular for bar meals. Bedrooms vary in size and style and all have the expected facilities, with larger rooms in the main house. The simpler chalet rooms at the rear have their own entrances.
ROOMS: 10 en suite 16 annexe en suite s £37-£43; d £61-£76 (incl. bkfst & dinner) * **FACILITIES:** Fishing entertainment **PARKING:** 36 **CARDS:**

HAMILTON, South Lanarkshire — Map 11 NS75
see also Bothwell

Express by Holiday Inn Strathclyde

ML1 3RB
☎ 01698 858585 🖷 01698 852375
Dir: *junct 5 off M74 follow signs for Strathclyde Country park*

A modern budget hotel offering comfortable accommodation in refreshing, spacious and comprehensively-equipped bedrooms, en suite bathrooms with power showers and continental buffet breakfast included in the room rate. Suitable for business travellers or families. For further details and the Express by Holiday Inn phone number, consult the Hotel Groups page.
ROOMS: 120 en suite (incl. cont bkfst) d £55-£60 * **CONF:** Thtr 30 Class 10 Board 15 Del from £80 *

Early start? Hotels at all star levels should provide in-room alarm clocks and/or alarm calls.

HAWICK, Scottish Borders — Map 12 NT51

★★66% Kirklands

West Stewart Place TD9 8BH
☎ 01450 372263 Fax 01450 370404
Dir: *0.5m N from Hawick High St, 200yds W of A7*
This fine Victorian house lies in gardens in a quiet residential area north of the town centre. The hotel has a cosy lounge bar, popular restaurant and comfortable well equipped bedrooms.
ROOMS: 5 en suite 4 annexe en suite **FACILITIES:** Snooker Pool table ch fac **CONF:** Thtr 20 Board 12 **PARKING:** 20
CARDS:

HELENSBURGH, Argyll & Bute — Map 10 NS28

★★★63% Rosslea Hall Country House

Ferry Rd G84 8NF
☎ 01436 439955 Fax 01436 820897
Dir: *on A814, opposite church*
This early Victorian mansion stands in its own grounds by the shore of Gareloch. The comfortable rear bar provides an informal eating alternative to the main restaurant, an attractive Italian style dining environment. The well equipped bedrooms are gradually being upgraded.
ROOMS: 29 en suite 5 annexe en suite (2 fmly) No smoking in 5 bedrooms **FACILITIES:** STV Pool table **CONF:** Thtr 100 Class 40 Board 50 **PARKING:** 60 **NOTES:** No smoking in restaurant
CARDS:

HOWWOOD, Renfrewshire — Map 10 NS36

★★★67% Bowfield Hotel & Country Club

PA9 1DB
☎ 01505 705225 Fax 01505 705230
Dir: *M8, A737 for 6m, left onto B787, right after 2m, follow road for 1m to hotel*
This former textile mill now houses a popular hotel which has become a convenient stop-over for travellers using Glasgow Airport. Extensive leisure facilities are a major attraction. Public areas have beamed ceilings, brick and white painted walls, and welcoming open fires. Bedrooms are housed in a separate wing and offer good modern comforts and facilities.
ROOMS: 23 en suite (3 fmly) **FACILITIES:** Indoor swimming (H) Squash Snooker Sauna Solarium Gym Pool table Jacuzzi/spa Health & beauty studio entertainment **CONF:** Thtr 80 Class 60 Board 20 **PARKING:** 100 **NOTES:** No dogs (ex guide dogs) No smoking in restaurant
CARDS:

See advert on this page

HUMBIE, East Lothian — Map 12 NT46

★★★63% The Johnstounburn House

PEEL HOTELS

EH36 5PL
☎ 01875 833696 Fax 01875 833626
Dir: *A68, B6368, 1.5m S of Humbie village is the hotel*
Surrounded by acres of gardens and the rolling farmland of the Lammermuir Hills, this 17th-century country house provides friendly and relaxed service in a peaceful atmosphere. Bedrooms, some of which are in a converted coach house five minutes' walk through the gardens, are furnished in keeping with the style of the house. Public areas have open fires, fine wood panelling and stone stairs.
ROOMS: 11 rms (10 en suite) 9 annexe en suite (5 fmly) s £115-£140; d £150-£185 (incl. bkfst) * LB **FACILITIES:** STV Fishing Croquet lawn Clay pigeon shooting All terrain vehicle off rd driving Xmas **CONF:** Thtr 50 Class 24 Board 30 Del from £145 * **PARKING:** 100 **NOTES:** No smoking in restaurant **CARDS:**

HUNTLY, Aberdeenshire — Map 15 NJ53

★★61% Gordon Arms Hotel

The Square AB54 8AF
☎ 01466 792288 Fax 01466 794556
e-mail: reception@gordonarms.demon.co.uk
A relaxed, welcoming atmosphere prevails at this family-run, commercial hotel in the central square. Best use has been made of available space in the well equipped bedrooms. Public areas include a choice of contrasting bars and there is a traditional style dining room upstairs on the first floor.
ROOMS: 14 en suite (3 fmly) s £35; d £45 (incl. bkfst) * LB **FACILITIES:** Pool table entertainment Xmas **CONF:** Thtr 180 Class 120 Board 120 **CARDS:**

INVERARAY, Argyll & Bute — Map 10 NN00

★★★68% The Argyll

Best Western

Front St PA32 8XB
☎ 01499 302466 Fax 01499 302389
e-mail: argyll@bestwestern.co.uk
Located beside The Arch, enjoying views of Loch Fyne, this hotel offers smartly refurbished bedrooms that are comfortable and well equipped. Four executive bedrooms are available and facilities include a choice of bars, foyer lounge and conservatory. The attractive restaurant features carefully prepared fare based on quality Scottish ingredients.
ROOMS: 35 en suite (7 fmly) s £51-£63; d £62-£86 (incl. bkfst) * **FACILITIES:** Pool table **CONF:** Thtr 120 Class 80 Board 50 Del from £91 * **PARKING:** 25 **NOTES:** No dogs (ex guide dogs) No smoking in restaurant Closed 25-26 Dec **CARDS:**

INVERARAY, continued

★★★68% Loch Fyne Hotel

PA32 8XT
☎ 01499 302148 01499 302348

This long established hotel enjoys lovely views over Loch Fyne. Sympathetically refurbished and extended, the hotel offers comfortable and well equipped bedrooms of a good size. Inviting public areas include a well stocked bar with loch views, a Bistro serving informal meals, and a restaurant providing fine cuisine on both carte and fixed price menus.
ROOMS: 80 en suite No smoking in 10 bedrooms s £35-£60; d £50-£95 (incl. bkfst) * LB **FACILITIES:** Indoor swimming (H) Sauna Solarium Jacuzzi/spa Xmas **CONF:** Thtr 30 Class 15 Board 24 **SERVICES:** Lift **PARKING:** 30 **NOTES:** No dogs (ex guide dogs) No smoking in restaurant **CARDS:**

INVERGARRY, Highland — Map 14 NH30

★★★69% Glengarry Castle

PH35 4HW
☎ 01809 501254 01809 501207
e-mail: castle@glengarry.net
Dir: *on A82 beside Loch Oich, 0.5m from A82/A87 junction*

Standing in 50 acres of grounds near Loch Oich, this fine hotel has been run by the same family for many years. Bedrooms range from smart and comfortable 'standard' rooms to de luxe 'superior' rooms, some with four-poster or half-tester beds. Public areas include a panelled reception hall and two comfortable sitting rooms. The dining room offers a traditional menu.
ROOMS: 26 en suite (2 fmly) No smoking in 6 bedrooms s £55-£75; d £90-£140 (incl. bkfst) **FACILITIES:** Tennis (hard) Fishing **PARKING:** 32 **NOTES:** No smoking in restaurant Closed early Nov-late Mar **CARDS:**

See advert on opposite page

INVERKEITHING, Fife — Map 11 NT18

★★★63% Queensferry Lodge

corus

St Margaret's Head, North Queensferry KY11 1HP
☎ 01383 410000 01383 419708
Dir: *from M90 junct 1 left onto A921, right thru Inverkeithing, at rdbt head under m'way follow signs Deep Sea World- hotel 0.5m on left*
From its position on the north side of the river this smart modern hotel enjoys fine views of famous road and rail bridges. Bright modern public areas include a comfortable foyer lounge and bar, a smart restaurant, and a good range of banqueting facilities. Bedrooms are comfortably modern in style and offer a good range of amenities.
ROOMS: 77 en suite (4 fmly) No smoking in 46 bedrooms s £85; d £105 * LB **FACILITIES:** STV Xmas **CONF:** Thtr 150 Class 60 Board 45 Del from £85 * **SERVICES:** Lift **PARKING:** 165
CARDS:

INVERMORISTON, Highland — Map 14 NH41

★★74% Glenmoriston Arms Hotel & Restaurant

IV63 7YA
☎ 01320 351206 01320 351308
e-mail: scott@lochness-glenmoriston.co.uk
Dir: *at the junct of A82/A877*
A warm welcome awaits at this friendly family-run hotel close to Loch Ness. Comfortable, well equipped bedrooms include a four-poster room with a spa bath. There is an attractive bar, and the refurbished restaurant offers a range of Taste of Scotland dishes.
ROOMS: 8 en suite s £55-£65; d £70-£90 (incl. bkfst) * LB **FACILITIES:** Fishing Stalking Shooting Xmas **PARKING:** 24 **NOTES:** No smoking in restaurant Closed early Jan-end Feb **CARDS:**

INVERNESS, Highland — Map 14 NH64
see also Kirkhill

★★★★76% Culloden House

Culloden IV2 7BZ
☎ 01463 790461 01463 792181
e-mail: reserv@cullodenhouse.co.uk
Dir: *take A96 from town and turn right for Culloden. After 1m, turn left at White Church after second traffic lights*

This fine Adam-style Georgian mansion is set in 40 acres of grounds, from where Bonnie Prince Charlie left for the battle of Culloden. Day rooms with chandeliers, marble fireplaces and ornate plasterwork include an inviting drawing room, clubby bar and the refined Adam dining room. Bedrooms range from opulent period suites and master rooms to comfortable contemporary refurbished rooms. No-smoking suites are in a separate mansion house in the grounds, suitable for small seminars.

continued

ROOMS: 23 en suite 5 annexe en suite (1 fmly) No smoking in 8 bedrooms s fr £145; d £190-£270 (incl. bkfst) * LB **FACILITIES:** STV Tennis (hard) Sauna Croquet lawn Boules Badminton entertainment Xmas **CONF:** Thtr 60 Class 40 Board 30 Del from £110 * **PARKING:** 50 **NOTES:** No smoking in restaurant Civ Wed 60 **CARDS:**

See advert on this page

★★★★71% Inverness Marriott

Culcabock Rd IV2 3LP

☎ 01463 237166 🖷 01463 225208

Marriott HOTELS · RESORTS · SUITES

Dir: *from A9 S, exit Culduthel/Kingsmills 5th exit at rdbt, follow rd 0.5m, over mini-rdbt pass golf club, hotel on left after traffic lights*

Set in four acres of gardens on the south side of town, this long established hotel provides a warm welcome to the Highland capital. Public areas include a choice of relaxing lounges, a well stocked bar, and a bright and spacious conservatory. The Inglis restaurant specialises in dishes using fine Scottish ingredients. The spacious bedrooms are well equipped and comfortable, and range from impressive executive rooms to standard rooms, several of which overlook the gardens.

ROOMS: 76 en suite 6 annexe en suite (11 fmly) No smoking in 29 bedrooms **FACILITIES:** STV Indoor swimming (H) Sauna Solarium Gym Putting green Jacuzzi/spa Hair & beauty salon Steam room **CONF:** Thtr 100 Class 28 Board 40 Del from £110 * **SERVICES:** Lift **PARKING:** 120 **NOTES:** No smoking in restaurant **CARDS:**

★★★75% Craigmonie

9 Annfield Rd IV2 3HX

☎ 01463 231649 🖷 01463 233720

e-mail: info@craigmonie.com

Dir: *off A9/A96 follow signs Hilton, Culcabock pass golf course second road on right*

Bedrooms at this welcoming hotel range from the attractive poolside suites with spa bath and balcony, to standard rooms. Public areas include a lounge and bar with a conservatory extension where light meals are served. Guests can also dine in the restaurant.

ROOMS: 35 en suite (3 fmly) No smoking in 10 bedrooms s £75-£88; d £95-£115 (incl. bkfst) * LB **FACILITIES:** STV Indoor swimming (H) Sauna Gym Jacuzzi/spa **CONF:** Thtr 180 Class 70 Board 50 Del from £115 * **SERVICES:** Lift **PARKING:** 60 **NOTES:** No smoking in restaurant **CARDS:**

★★★74% ❀❀ Glenmoriston Town House Hotel

20 Ness Bank IV2 4SF

☎ 01463 223777 🖷 01463 712378

e-mail: glenmoriston@cali.co.uk

Dir: *located on riverside opposite theatre, 5 minutes from town centre*

This popular hotel is situated on the north bank of the River Ness overlooking the cathedral and Eden Court. Bedrooms have pretty colour schemes and smart modern furnishings. Public areas are

continued on p720

INVERNESS, continued

Glenmoriston Town House Hotel, Inverness

nicely presented. The restaurant menu offers a tempting range of Mediterranean influenced cuisine.
ROOMS: 15 en suite (1 fmly) s £82-£93; d £104-£138 (incl. bkfst) * LB **FACILITIES:** STV Xmas **CONF:** Thtr 50 Class 50 Board 30 Del from £100 * **PARKING:** 40 **NOTES:** No dogs (ex guide dogs)
CARDS:

★★★72% Bunchrew House
Bunchrew IV3 8TA
☎ 01463 234917 01463 710620
e-mail: welcome@bunchrew-inverness.co.uk
Dir: *leave Inverness heading W on the A862 along the shore of the Beauly Firth. Hotel on right of road 2m after crossing canal*

A lovely 17th-century mansion set in 20 acres of wooded grounds right on the shore of the Beauly Firth. Public areas have many original features, a relaxing atmosphere, natural fires and lots of reading material. Bedrooms are all individual and graced with thoughtful touches. The dinner menu provides a good choice of enjoyable dishes featuring local produce.
ROOMS: 11 en suite (2 fmly) **FACILITIES:** Fishing **CONF:** Thtr 80 Class 30 Board 30 Del from £102.50 * **PARKING:** 40 **NOTES:** No smoking in restaurant Civ Wed 120 **CARDS:**

★★★67% Lochardil House
Stratherrick Rd IV2 4LF
☎ 01463 235995 01463 713394
e-mail: lochardil@ukonline.co.uk
Dir: *follow Island Bank Road for 1m, fork left into Drummond Crescent, into Stratherrick Road, 0.5m hotel on left*
A castellated Victorian house, with attractive gardens and a friendly atmosphere. Bedrooms are comfortable and modern. There is a function suite, cocktail bar and a popular conservatory restaurant which offers a wide range of dishes at lunch and dinner.
ROOMS: 12 en suite s £75-£85; d £95-£115 (incl. bkfst) * LB **FACILITIES:** STV **CONF:** Thtr 120 Class 100 Board 60 **PARKING:** 123 **NOTES:** No dogs (ex guide dogs) **CARDS:**

★★★66% Loch Ness House

Glenurquhart Rd IV3 8JL
☎ 01463 231248 01463 239327
e-mail: lnhhchris@aol.com
Dir: *1.5m from town centre, overlooking Tomnahurich Bridge on canal. From A9 turn L at Longman rdbt, follow signs for A82 for 2.5miles*
Close to the Caledonian Canal, this popular, family-run hotel provides welcoming public areas and modern bedrooms which vary in size. The restaurant features Scottish fare and fresh seafood, while lighter meals are served in the bars.
ROOMS: 22 en suite (3 fmly) No smoking in 6 bedrooms s £60-£80; d £101-£110 (incl. bkfst) * LB **FACILITIES:** STV Xmas **CONF:** Thtr 150 Class 60 Board 40 Del from £75 * **PARKING:** 60 **NOTES:** No smoking in restaurant **CARDS:**

★★★65% Crown Court Hotel
25 Southside Rd IV2 3BG
☎ 01463 234816 01463 714900
e-mail: reception@crowncourt.co.uk
Dir: *from A9 at Travel Inn take right at large rdbt then cross small rdbt. Pass golf course on left then right to Annfield Rd, at lights hotel on right*
This friendly family run hotel is conveniently located on the southern approach to the town centre, which is just five minutes' walk away. The many returning business guests enjoy the restaurant with its attractive menu and the adjoining bar which provides a relaxed environment. Bedrooms are all carefully co-ordinated, comfortable and well equipped.
ROOMS: 9 en suite (2 fmly) No smoking in all bedrooms s £69-£75; d £85-£95 (incl. bkfst) * LB **FACILITIES:** STV Xmas **CONF:** Thtr 200 Class 100 Board 50 **PARKING:** 36 **NOTES:** No smoking in restaurant
CARDS:

★★★61% Palace Milton
8 Ness Walk IV3 5NE
☎ 01463 223243 01463 236865
Dir: *town centre on banks of River Ness*
Located beside the river with views of the castle, this well run hotel remains a popular base for visiting tour groups. Public areas enjoy views of the river and include a foyer lounge, well stocked bar and a formal dining room. Most bedrooms have been upgraded and the new leisure centre is a popular attraction.
ROOMS: 88 en suite (12 fmly) No smoking in 6 bedrooms s £47-£75; d £70-£95 (incl. bkfst) * LB **FACILITIES:** STV Indoor swimming (H) Sauna Solarium Gym Jacuzzi/spa Beauty salon entertainment Xmas **CONF:** Thtr 100 Class 40 Board 40 Del from £90 * **SERVICES:** Lift **PARKING:** 20 **NOTES:** No smoking in restaurant
CARDS:

★★62% *Windsor Town House*
22 Ness Bank IV2 4SF
☎ 01463 715535 01463 713262
e-mail: info@windsor-inverness.co.uk
Dir: *follow signs Dores/Holm Mills-rd B862, hotel below castle along riverside*
This friendly town house hotel is situated close to the castle and overlooks the river towards the Eden Court theatre. A light evening menu is served in the Conservatory. The cosy lounge is a quiet place to relax and guests have access to an honesty bar. Most bedrooms are non-smoking and have been furnished with pine and pretty fabrics and all the expected amenities.
ROOMS: 18 en suite (5 fmly) No smoking in 16 bedrooms **FACILITIES:** STV **CONF:** Class 30 **PARKING:** 14 **NOTES:** No dogs (ex guide dogs) No smoking in restaurant Closed 23 Dec-4 Jan RS 1 Nov-15 May **CARDS:**

★★56% Smithton
Smithton IV1 2NL
☎ 01463 791999 🖹 01463 794559
e-mail: smithhotel@aol.com
Dir: *A96, 2m turn first right, 2m to Smithton Hotel*
This purpose-built hotel is in the centre of the village of Smithton. Bedrooms are attractively furnished in pine and offer good amenities. The spacious family room has very fine views. Both the lounge bar and public bar are popular with the locals.
ROOMS: 16 en suite (2 fmly) s fr £35; d fr £52 (incl. bkfst) * LB **FACILITIES:** STV Snooker Pool table entertainment **CONF:** Board 20 Del £55 * **PARKING:** 60 **NOTES:** No dogs (ex guide dogs) Civ Wed 40 **CARDS:**

⌂ Express by Holiday Inn
Stoneyfield IV2 7PA
☎ 01463 732700 🖹 01463 732732

A modern budget hotel offering comfortable accommodation in refreshing, spacious and comprehensively-equipped bedrooms, en suite bathrooms with power showers and continental buffet breakfast included in the room rate. Suitable for business travellers or families. For further details and the Express by Holiday Inn phone number, consult the Hotel Groups page.
ROOMS: 94 en suite (incl. cont bkfst) d £49.50 * **CONF:** Thtr 35 Class 15 Board 16

INVERURIE, Aberdeenshire — Map 15 NJ72

★★★★67% ❀❀ Thainstone House Hotel and Country Club
AB51 5NT
☎ 01467 621643 🖹 01467 625084
e-mail: info@thainstone.macdonald-hotels.co.uk
Dir: *A96 from Aberdeen, past Kintore, entrance to hotel at first rdbt to Thainstone, take left then immediate right to hotel*

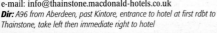

MACDONALD HOTELS ★★★★

Set in 40 acres of mature grounds, this impressive mansion house has particular appeal for the corporate guest and is popular for conference and banqueting events. Attractive public areas include a choice of inviting lounges, contrasting bars, and an elegant Georgian-style restaurant which provides the appropriate setting for the fine dining experience offered by the talented kitchen team. Bedrooms are tasteful in appointment and provide the expected amenities.
ROOMS: 48 en suite (3 fmly) No smoking in 32 bedrooms
FACILITIES: STV Indoor swimming (H) Snooker Gym Jacuzzi/spa Archery Shooting Grass Karts Quad Bikes **CONF:** Thtr 300 Class 100 Board 40 Del from £120 * **SERVICES:** Lift **PARKING:** 100 **NOTES:** No dogs (ex guide dogs) No smoking in restaurant Civ Wed 130
CARDS:

★★★69% Strathburn
Burghmuir Dr AB51 4GY
☎ 01467 624422 🖹 01467 625133
e-mail: strathburn@btconnect.com
Dir: *at Blackhall rbt into Blackhall Rd for 100yds then into Burghmuir Drive*
A welcoming atmosphere prevails at this personally-run modern hotel on the west side of town. Inviting public areas include an attractive split-level foyer lounge, a spacious well stocked bar, and a tastefully appointed restaurant. Bedrooms come in mixed sizes and offer comfortable modern styles along with a good range of amenities.
ROOMS: 25 en suite (2 fmly) No smoking in 18 bedrooms s £65-£85; d £85-£100 (incl. bkfst) * LB **FACILITIES:** STV **CONF:** Thtr 30 Class 24 Board 16 Del from £85.75 * **PARKING:** 40 **NOTES:** No dogs (ex guide dogs) No smoking in restaurant **CARDS:**

IRVINE, North Ayrshire — Map 10 NS33

★★★64% Annfield House
6 Castle St KA12 8RJ
☎ 01294 278903 🖹 01294 278904
e-mail: annfield@tinyonline.co.uk
Dir: *follow signs to Irvine. Once in the town follow signs to Bridgegate which lead to Castle Street where the hotel is located*

Set within a quiet residential area close to the town centre and harbour, this friendly, fully restored 19th-century gentleman's residence retains many of its original features and benefits from well tended gardens. Good wholesome food is prepared from fresh ingredients and an elegant first-floor lounge provides quiet and comfort. Bedrooms are mostly spacious and attractively decorated.
ROOMS: 9 en suite s £49.50-£59; d £70-£80 (incl. bkfst) *
FACILITIES: STV ch fac **PARKING:** 28
CARDS:

Read all about it! Newspapers delivered to bedrooms in four and five star hotels.

ISLAY, ISLE OF, Argyll & Bute — Map 10

BOWMORE — Map 10 NR35

★★60% Lochside
19 Shore St PA43 7LB
☎ 01496 810244 🖷 01496 810390
e-mail: ask@lochsidehotel.co.uk
Dir: *on A846, 100yds from main village square on shore side of road*
Lovely views over Loch Indaal can be enjoyed from the rear of this family run hotel on the main street. Bedrooms, though compact, are modern in style and offer a wide range of amenities. In the small dining room, seafood specialities feature strongly on the varied menu, and the cosy bar has a wide range of malt whiskies.
ROOMS: 8 en suite (1 fmly) s £30-£39; d £45-£69 (incl. bkfst) * LB
FACILITIES: Pool table **CONF:** Class 20 Board 12
CARDS:

BRIDGEND — Map 10 NR36

★★69% *Bridgend*
PA44 7PQ
☎ 01496 810212 🖷 01496 810960
A warm welcome is assured at this Victorian hotel, positioned in the heart of the island. Bedrooms vary in size and are comfortably furnished in mixed styles, with a wide range of amenities. There is a quiet first floor lounge and a choice of bars, the attractive dining room features island produce on the dinner menu.
ROOMS: 10 rms (9 en suite) (3 fmly) **FACILITIES:** Fishing Bowls
PARKING: 30 **NOTES:** No smoking in restaurant
CARDS:

PORT ASKAIG — Map 10 NR46

★★63% Port Askaig
PA46 7RD
☎ 01496 840245 🖷 01496 840295
e-mail: hotel@portaskaig.co.uk
Dir: *at Ferry Terminal*
From its position beside the ferry terminal, this welcoming family-run hotel enjoys glorious views over the Sound of Islay to Jura, and provides traditional hospitality and comforts along with modern amenities. Inviting public areas include a snug bar, a dining room and a quiet first-floor lounge. Bedrooms are modern in design and come in a variety of sizes. A range of home-cooked food is served in the bar or the cosy dining room.
ROOMS: 8 rms (6 en suite) (1 fmly) s £30-£40; d £60-£72 (incl. bkfst) * LB **PARKING:** 21 **NOTES:** No children 5yrs No smoking in restaurant
CARDS:

ISLE OF

Placenames incorporating the words 'Isle' or 'Isle of' will be found under the actual name, eg Isle of Arran is under Arran, Isle of.

ISLE ORNSAY See Skye, Isle of

JEDBURGH, Scottish Borders — Map 12 NT62

★★★74% Jedforest Hotel
Camptown TD8 6PJ
☎ 01835 840222 🖷 01835 840226
e-mail: mail@jedforesthotel.freeserve.co.uk
Dir: *3m S of Jedburgh off A68*
A charming country house hotel in 35 acres of grounds, Jedforest was completely refurbished in 1999. Immaculately presented throughout, it offers an attractive and stylish restaurant and a relaxing lounge with open fire. The bedrooms are very smart, with the larger ones being particularly impressive. Service is very attentive.

ROOMS: 8 en suite (1 fmly) No smoking in all bedrooms s £65-£75; d £105-£115 (incl. bkfst) * LB **FACILITIES:** Fishing Xmas **CONF:** Class 40 Board 25 **PARKING:** 20 **NOTES:** No dogs No smoking in restaurant
CARDS:

JOHN O'GROATS See Halkirk and Lybster

KELSO, Scottish Borders — Map 12 NT73

★★★74% The Roxburghe Hotel & Golf Course
Heiton TD5 8JZ
☎ 01573 450331 🖷 01573 450611
e-mail: hotel@roxburghe.net
Dir: *from A68 Jedburgh join A698 to Heiton, 3m SW of Kelso*
Owned by the Duke of Roxburghe, this impressive Jacobean mansion is in a peaceful location among acres of parkland close to the River Teviot. Sporting guests predominate, attracted by the shooting, fishing and golf, but other guests will appreciate the individually designed and attractive bedrooms, some of which have real fires. In addition to the library bar there is also a comfortable drawing room, and a dining area.
ROOMS: 16 en suite 6 annexe en suite (3 fmly) No smoking in 1 bedroom s fr £120; d £150-£255 (incl. bkfst) * LB **FACILITIES:** STV Golf 18 Tennis (hard) Fishing Croquet lawn Putting green Clay shooting Health & Beauty Salon **CONF:** Thtr 40 Class 20 Board 20 Del from £130 * **PARKING:** 150 **NOTES:** No smoking in restaurant Closed 23-29 Dec Civ Wed 50 **CARDS:**

★★★66% Ednam House
Bridge St TD5 7HT
☎ 01573 224168 🖷 01573 226319
This fine Georgian mansion overlooks the River Tweed and proves popular with salmon fishermen. Bedrooms range from standard to grand, and there are several lounges, two bars and a dining room offering wholesome British cooking. Service at the hotel is helpful and attentive.
ROOMS: 32 en suite (2 fmly) No smoking in 3 bedrooms
FACILITIES: Croquet lawn Free access to Abbey Fitness Centre
CONF: Thtr 250 Board 200 **PARKING:** 100 **NOTES:** Closed 25 Dec-10 Jan **CARDS:**

★★★63% Cross Keys
36-37 The Square TD5 7HL
☎ 01573 223303 🖷 01573 225792
e-mail: cross-keys-hotel@easynet.co.uk
Dir: *on approaching Kelso, follow signs for town centre. The hotel is located in main square*
Originally a coaching inn, this family-run hotel overlooks Kelso's fine cobbled square and its window boxes provide a mass of

continued

colour in summer. Bedrooms offer a choice of superior or standard, whilst the spacious lounge bar and restaurant are supplemented by the Oak Room bar/bistro.
ROOMS: 27 en suite (5 fmly) No smoking in 12 bedrooms s £44-£49; d £60-£72 (incl. bkfst) * LB **FACILITIES:** STV Xmas **CONF:** Thtr 280 Class 220 Board 70 Del from £68 * **SERVICES:** Lift air con **NOTES:** Civ Wed 270 **CARDS:**

KENTALLEN, Highland Map 14 NN05

★★73% Holly Tree
Kentallen Pier PA38 4BY
☎ 01631 740292 01631 740345
e-mail: reception@hollytreehotel.co.uk
Dir: *3m S of Ballachulish on A828*

THE CIRCLE
Selected Individual Hotels

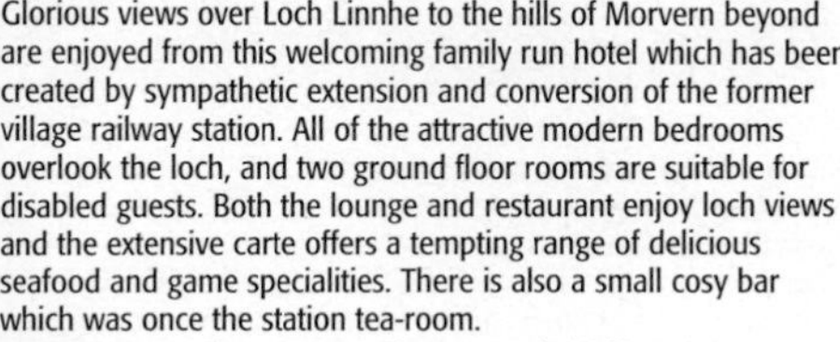

Glorious views over Loch Linnhe to the hills of Morvern beyond are enjoyed from this welcoming family run hotel which has been created by sympathetic extension and conversion of the former village railway station. All of the attractive modern bedrooms overlook the loch, and two ground floor rooms are suitable for disabled guests. Both the lounge and restaurant enjoy loch views and the extensive carte offers a tempting range of delicious seafood and game specialities. There is also a small cosy bar which was once the station tea-room.
ROOMS: 10 en suite s £30-£76; d £60-£119 (incl. bkfst) * LB **FACILITIES:** Fishing **CONF:** Class 20 **PARKING:** 30 **NOTES:** No smoking in restaurant Closed Dec-Jan **CARDS:**

KILCHRENAN, Argyll & Bute Map 10 NN02

★★★77% Taychreggan
PA35 1HQ
☎ 01866 833211 & 833366 01866 833244
e-mail: taychreggan@btinternet.com
Dir: *W from Glasgow A82 to Crianlarich, W from Crianlarich on A85 to Taynuilt, S for 7m on B845 to Kilchrenan and Taychreggan*

Scotland's Hotels of Distinction

Superb hospitality and fine dining are the hallmarks of this delightful hotel, a former drovers inn built around a cobbled courtyard. Add to this the wonderful romantic setting beside the shoreline of Loch Awe, and it is easy to understand why so many guests return. There is a choice of comfortable lounges which invite peaceful relaxation, and the bar boasts a tempting range of malt whiskies. The restaurant serves excellent fare, supported by an impressive list of fine wines. Bedrooms, with individual colour schemes, come in modern and traditional styles and include several four-poster rooms in the original part of house.
ROOMS: 19 en suite No smoking in 3 bedrooms s £99; d £165-£250 (incl. bkfst & dinner) * LB **FACILITIES:** Fishing Snooker Xmas **CONF:** Class 15 Board 20 Del from £155 * **PARKING:** 40 **NOTES:** No children 14yrs No smoking in restaurant
CARDS:

KILLIECHRONAN See Mull, Isle of

KILLIECRANKIE, Perth & Kinross Map 14 NN96

★★76% Killiecrankie
PH16 5LG
☎ 01796 473220 01796 472451
e-mail: killiecrankie.hotel@btinternet.com
Dir: *turn off A9 at Killiecrankie, hotel is 3m along B8079 on right*
This charming holiday hotel is set in mature grounds close to the historic Pass of Killiecrankie. The bedrooms have pretty colour schemes and are thoughtfully equipped. There is a relaxing lounge, a cosy well stocked bar with adjacent sun lounge and an attractive dining room providing a fine dining experience.
continued

ROOMS: 10 en suite (1 fmly) No smoking in 1 bedroom s fr £92; d fr £184 (incl. bkfst & dinner) * LB **FACILITIES:** Croquet lawn Putting green Xmas **PARKING:** 30 **NOTES:** No children 5yrs No smoking in restaurant Closed 3 Jan-4 Feb & 10 days early Dec
CARDS:

KILLIN, Stirling Map 11 NN53

★★★65% Dall Lodge Country House
Main St FK21 8TN
☎ 01567 820217 01567 820726
e-mail: wilson@dalllodgehotel.co.uk
Dir: *from M9 at Stirling turn left A84-Crianlarich, 3m after Lochearnhead turn right onto A827-Killin*

This charming small hotel stands in well kept grounds by the main road on the north side of the village. The smartly decorated bedrooms are comfortably modern in appointment. Public areas include an inviting conservatory lounge which features some
continued

K

KILLIN, continued

interesting oriental furnishings. Enjoyable fare is provided in the attractive restaurant.
ROOMS: 10 en suite (2 fmly) s £42.50-£49.50; d £65-£79 (incl. bkfst) * LB **FACILITIES:** Tennis (grass) Pool table **CONF:** Thtr 20 Class 16 Board 10 **PARKING:** 20 **NOTES:** No smoking in restaurant Closed Nov-Feb **CARDS:**

See advert on page 723

KILMARNOCK, East Ayrshire Map 10 NS43

Travelodge

Travelodge

Kilmarnock By Pass KA1 5LQ
☎ 01563 573810 📠 01563 573810
Dir: *at Bellfield Interchange just off A77*
This modern building offers accommodation in smart, spacious and well equipped bedrooms, all with en suite bathrooms. Refreshments may be taken at the nearby family restaurant. For further details and the Travelodge phone number, consult the Hotel Groups page.
ROOMS: 40 en suite

KILWINNING, North Ayrshire Map 10 NS34

★★★74% Montgreenan Mansion House

Best Western

Montgreenan Estate KA13 7QZ
☎ 01294 557733 📠 01294 850397
e-mail: info@montgreenanhotel.com
Dir: *4m N of Irvine on A736*
Set in 48 acres of parkland and woods, this 19th-century mansion offers a peaceful atmosphere. Gracious day rooms retain many original features such as ornate ceilings and marble fireplaces and include a splendid drawing room, library and a club-style bar. The restaurant offers a five-course, fixed-price menu, and a small carte. Bedrooms are well equipped and come in a variety of sizes.
ROOMS: 21 en suite s fr £80; d £115-£175 (incl. bkfst) * LB **FACILITIES:** STV Golf 5 Tennis (hard) Snooker Croquet lawn Putting green Jacuzzi/spa Clay pigeon shooting Xmas **CONF:** Thtr 110 Class 60 Board 60 Del from £115 * **SERVICES:** Lift **PARKING:** 50 **NOTES:** No smoking in restaurant Civ Wed 110 **CARDS:**

KINCLAVEN, Perth & Kinross Map 11 NO13

★★★79% Ballathie House

PH1 4QN
☎ 01250 883268 📠 01250 883396
e-mail: email@ballathiehousehotel.com
Dir: *from A9 2m north of Perth, B9099 through Stanley & signposted or off A93 at Beech Hedge follow signs for Ballathie 2.5m*
Set in the heart of the Perthshire countryside overlooking the River Tay, this splendid Scottish mansion house combines the grandeur of a former age with every modern comfort. The elegant restaurant overlooking the river is a great setting in which to enjoy the fine dining experience offered. Bedrooms range from well proportioned Master rooms to the more varied sized standard rooms. All rooms are individual in style, feature stylish fabrics and most are furnished with antiques.
ROOMS: 27 en suite (2 fmly) s £95-£100; d £150-£160 (incl. bkfst) LB **FACILITIES:** STV Fishing Croquet lawn Putting green Xmas **CONF:** Thtr 50 Class 20 Board 26 Del from £120 * **PARKING:** 50 **NOTES:** No smoking in restaurant Civ Wed 200 **CARDS:**

Bad hair day? Hairdryers in all rooms three stars and above.

KINGUSSIE, Highland Map 14 NH70

Premier Collection

★★ The Cross

Tweed Mill Brae, Ardbroilach Rd PH21 1TC
☎ 01540 661166 📠 01540 661080
e-mail: relax@thecross.co.uk
Dir: *from traffic lights in centre of Kingussie, travel uphill along Ardbroilach Rd for 300mtrs, turn left into Tweed Mill Brae*
A former tweed mill, this delightful restaurant with rooms provides high standards of comfort, excellent hospitality and refined service. Bedrooms combine contemporary fittings with traditional furnishings and there is an attractive lounge with ample reading material. Imaginative cooking at dinner and an impressive wine list are offered in the stylish, stone walled dining room.
ROOMS: 9 en suite No smoking in all bedrooms d £150 (incl. bkfst) LB **PARKING:** 12 **NOTES:** No dogs (ex guide dogs) No children 12yrs No smoking in restaurant Closed Dec-Mar RS Tuesdays **CARDS:**

★★75% Osprey

Ruthven Rd PH21 1EN
☎ 01540 661510 📠 01540 661510
e-mail: aileen@ospreyhotel.freeserve.co.uk
Dir: *S end of Kingussie High St*
This delightful small hotel stands beside the Memorial Gardens. The nicely presented public areas include a choice of inviting and comfortable lounges. In the dining room, the menu offers an interesting choice of carefully prepared specialities. Attractive fabrics are used to good effect in the bright and comfortable bedrooms which are traditional in style.
ROOMS: 8 en suite No smoking in 6 bedrooms s £50-£55; d £90-£102 (incl. bkfst & dinner) * LB **PARKING:** 6 **NOTES:** No smoking in restaurant **CARDS:**

★★74% The Scot House

Newtonmore Rd PH21 1HE
☎ 01540 661351 📠 01540 661111
e-mail: shh@sirocco.globalnet.co.uk
Dir: *from A9 trunk road, take Kingussie exit, hotel is approx 0.50m at S end of village main street*
The warmly welcoming atmosphere together with good food are the hallmarks of this comfortable Highland hotel on the south side of town. Throughout, the house is decorated to a high standard and inviting public areas include a relaxing lounge, a well stocked bar, and the attractive restaurant provides interesting and wholesome Scottish fare from carte and fixed price menus. Bedrooms with smart modern furnishings present well and offer a good range of amenities.

continued

ROOMS: 9 en suite (1 fmly) s £40; d £67 (incl. bkfst) * LB **FACILITIES:** Xmas **PARKING:** 30 **NOTES:** No smoking in restaurant Closed 6-31 Jan **CARDS:**

See advert on this page

KINNESSWOOD, Perth & Kinross Map 11 NO10

★★65% Lomond Country Inn
Main St KY13 9HN
☎ 01592 840253 01592 840693
e-mail: the.lomond@dial.pipex.com
Dir: *M90 junct 5, follow signs for Glenrothes then Scotlandwell, Kinnesswood next village*

THE CIRCLE
Selected Individual Hotels
GREAT BRITAIN

A welcoming atmosphere prevails at this unpretentious small, country hotel overlooking Loch Leven. Bedrooms come in various sizes and offer modern appointments and amenities. Public areas include a cosy, well-stocked bar with real ales and open fires, a small sitting room, and an attractive dining room where the emphasis is on uncomplicated treatment of fresh Scottish fare.
ROOMS: 4 en suite 8 annexe en suite (2 fmly) s £40-£50; d £64-£70 (incl. bkfst) * LB **FACILITIES:** Xmas **PARKING:** 50 **NOTES:** No smoking in restaurant **CARDS:**

KINROSS, Perth & Kinross Map 11 NO10
see also Powmill

★★★73% Green
2 The Muirs KY13 8AS
☎ 01577 863467 01577 863180
e-mail: reservations@green-hotel.com
Dir: *M90 junct 6 follow signs for Kinross, turn onto A922, the hotel is situated on this road*

Most of the comfortable bedrooms are generously proportioned, in pleasing colour schemes with smart modern furnishings. Public areas include relaxing lounges, a choice of contrasting bars, an attractive restaurant and well stocked gift shop. Other facilities include two 18 hole golf courses, a leisure centre, squash and tennis courts, and a curling rink.
ROOMS: 47 en suite (4 fmly) s £75-£100; d £130-£155 (incl. bkfst) * LB **FACILITIES:** STV Indoor swimming (H) Golf 36 Fishing Squash Sauna Solarium Gym Pool table Croquet lawn Putting green Curling in season Xmas **CONF:** Thtr 140 Class 100 Board 60 Del from £100 * **PARKING:** 60 **CARDS:**

See advert on this page

Late for dinner? Quality Standards star rating means that last orders for dinner should be no earlier than:
★ 6.30pm ★★ 7.00pm ★★★ 8.00pm
★★★★ 9.00pm ★★★★★ 10.00pm

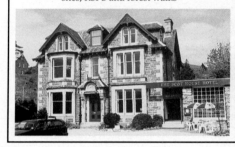

KINROSS, continued

★★★69% Windlestrae Hotel Business & Leisure Centre

REGAL

The Muirs KY13 8AS
☎ 01577 863217 ▤ 01577 864733
Dir: *leave M90 junct 6 turn E into Kinross, stop at mini rdbt turn left in approx 350yds Windlestrae on right*

Situated off the main road at the north end of town, this comfortable modern hotel combines a welcoming atmosphere with impressive leisure and conference facilities. Bedrooms, most of which are spacious, offer comfortable modern appointments together with a good range of amenities. Public areas include a well stocked split-level bar, a spacious foyer lounge, and a smart restaurant.
ROOMS: 45 en suite (5 fmly) No smoking in 15 bedrooms s £80-£100; d £100-£120 (incl. bkfst) * LB **FACILITIES:** STV Indoor swimming (H) Snooker Sauna Solarium Gym Jacuzzi/spa Beautician Steam room Toning tables Xmas **CONF:** Thtr 250 Class 100 Board 80 Del from £90 * **SERVICES:** air con **PARKING:** 80 **NOTES:** No smoking in restaurant Civ Wed 100 **CARDS:**

★★68% Kirklands

MINOTEL Great Britain

20 High St KY13 8AN
☎ 01577 863313 ▤ 01577 863313
e-mail: info.kirklandshotel@virgin.net
Dir: *M90 junc 6, into Kinross, at mini-rdbt turn left. Hotel is 80yds on left*
A welcoming atmosphere prevails at this popular family-run hotel, a former coaching inn which has been completely modernised and refurbished. The variable sized bedrooms are tastefully decorated and well equipped. Public areas include a choice of contrasting and well stocked bars, an attractive restaurant, and coffee lounge.
ROOMS: 9 rms (8 en suite) (1 fmly) s £39; d £68 (incl. bkfst) * **FACILITIES:** STV Xmas **PARKING:** 30 **NOTES:** No dogs (ex guide dogs) No smoking in restaurant **CARDS:**

⌂ *Travelodge*

Travelodge

Kincardine Rd KY13 7NQ
☎ Central Res 0800 850950 ▤ 01577 864108
Dir: *on A977, off junct 6 of M90 Turfhills Tourist Centre*
This modern building offers accommodation in smart, spacious and well equipped bedrooms, all with en suite bathrooms. Refreshments may be taken at the nearby family restaurant. For further details and the Travelodge phone number, consult the Hotel Groups page.
ROOMS: 35 en suite

> Early start? Hotels at all star levels should provide in-room alarm clocks and/or alarm calls.

KINTORE, Aberdeenshire — Map 15 NJ71

★★66% *Torryburn*
School Rd AB51 0XP
☎ 01467 632269 ▤ 01467 632271
Dir: *travelling north from Aberdeen leave dual carriageway for the village of Kintore. Hotel on the corner of Dunecht Rd*
This welcoming family-run hotel features a children's play area within its walled grounds. There is a smart conservatory restaurant with lounge area adjacent, a well stocked bar and supper room. Menus in both the restaurant and the supper room are varied and offer a wide range of enjoyable fare at competitive prices. Tastefully decorated bedrooms offer a good range of amenities.
ROOMS: 9 rms (8 en suite) (1 fmly) No smoking in all bedrooms **FACILITIES:** STV Tennis (hard) Fishing Snooker Shooting **CONF:** Class 50 Board 50 **PARKING:** 30 **NOTES:** Closed 1 Jan
CARDS:

KIRKBEAN, Dumfries & Galloway — Map 11 NX95

★★70% Cavens
DG2 8AA
☎ 01387 880234 ▤ 01387 880467
e-mail: enquiries@cavens.com
Dir: *on entering village of Kirkbean on A710, hotel signed*
Dating back to 1752, Cavens has been home to many notable worthies. Guests will enjoy the comfort and tranquillity of this country house, set in six acres of parkland gardens. A set four course dinner menu, using local produce, provides good value.
ROOMS: 8 en suite No smoking in all bedrooms s £35; d £60 (incl. bkfst) * LB **FACILITIES:** Xmas **CONF:** Thtr 30 Board 20 Del from £65 * **PARKING:** 12 **NOTES:** No smoking in restaurant
CARDS:

KIRKCALDY, Fife — Map 11 NT29

★★★ Dunnikier House Hotel
Dunnikier Park KY1 3LP
☎ 01592 268393 ▤ 01592 642340
e-mail: recp@dunnikier-house-hotel.co.uk
Dir: *turn off A92 at Kirkcaldy West, then 3rd exit on rdbt signed 'Hospital/Crematorium'. First left past school*

A friendly atmosphere prevails at this privately-owned hotel, an 18th-century mansion house set in parkland beside Dunnikier Golf Course. Bedrooms, which are variable in size and in style, are benefiting from an ongoing refurbishment programme. Original features such as beautifully carved fireplaces and ornate plasterwork have been retained in the inviting public areas. Views over the parkland can be enjoyed from the comfortable lounge and the adjacent bar offers a wide selection of whisky. The elegant Oswald restaurant provides an appropriate setting for the fine dining experience which features carefully prepared fresh produce from Scotland's larder.

continued

ROOMS: 14 en suite s fr £60; d fr £85 (incl. bkfst) * **FACILITIES:** Xmas **CONF:** Thtr 75 Class 30 Board 40 Del from £70 * **PARKING:** 100 **NOTES:** No smoking in restaurant Civ Wed 40 **CARDS:**

★★★65% Dean Park

Chapel Level KY2 6QW
☎ 01592 261635 📠 01592 261371
Dir: *signposted from A92, Kirkcaldy West junc*

A smart and constantly improving business hotel at the northern edge of town, the Dean Park is also a popular venue for local conferences and functions. Bedrooms vary in size and in style, but all are comfortable, modern, and offer the expected amenities. Public areas include a well stocked bar and an attractive restaurant.

ROOMS: 34 en suite 12 annexe en suite (2 fmly) No smoking in 3 bedrooms s £49.50-£69; d £65-£105 (incl. bkfst) * **FACILITIES:** STV **CONF:** Thtr 250 Class 125 Board 54 **SERVICES:** Lift **PARKING:** 250 **NOTES:** No dogs (ex guide dogs) Civ Wed 250 **CARDS:**

★★66% The Belvedere

Coxstool, West Wemyss KY1 4SL
☎ 01592 654167 📠 01592 655279
e-mail: info@thebelvederehotel.com
Dir: *A92 from M90 junct 3, at Kirkaldy East take A915, 1m NE turn right to Coaltown, at T-junct turn right then left, hotel 1st building in village*

Wonderful views over the Firth of Forth can be enjoyed from this welcoming hotel in the picturesque village of Coxstool. The bright, airy bedrooms are smartly decorated and offer comfortable modern furnishings. Public areas include a cosy bar and tastefully appointed restaurant.

ROOMS: 5 en suite 15 annexe en suite (2 fmly) s £57.50-£70; d £70-£90 (incl. bkfst) * LB **FACILITIES:** STV **PARKING:** 50 **NOTES:** No dogs (ex guide dogs) **CARDS:**

KIRKCUDBRIGHT, Dumfries & Galloway — Map 11 NX65

★★★71% Selkirk Arms

Old High St DG6 4JG
☎ 01557 330402 📠 01557 331639
e-mail: reception@selkirkarmshotel.co.uk
Dir: *turn off A75 5m W of Castle Douglas onto A711, 5m to Kirkcudbright in centre of town*

Originally a hostelry frequented by Robert Burns, the Selkirk Arms is now a smart hotel. Service is friendly and attentive and one can eat well in either the attractive restaurant - where the food has achieved our rosettes award - or the bistro and comfortable lounge bar. Bedrooms are modern and well equipped.

ROOMS: 13 en suite 3 annexe en suite (2 fmly) No smoking in 6 bedrooms s fr £60; d fr £90 (incl. bkfst) * LB **FACILITIES:** STV Xmas **CONF:** Thtr 70 Class 60 Board 40 Del from £87.95 * **PARKING:** 9 **NOTES:** No smoking in restaurant **CARDS:**

★★61% Arden House Hotel

Tongland Rd DG6 4UU
☎ 01557 330544
Dir: *turn off A57 Euro route (Stranraer), 4m W of Castle Douglas onto A711. Take signs for Kirkcudbright, crossing Telford Bridge. Hotel 400metres on left*

Set well back from the main road in extensive grounds on the north east side of town, this well maintained hotel offers attractive bedrooms, a lounge bar and adjoining conservatory serving a range of popular dishes, also available in the dining room. It boasts an impressive function suite in its grounds.

continued

ROOMS: 9 rms (8 en suite) (7 fmly) s fr £30; d fr £56 (incl. bkfst) * **FACILITIES:** Pool table **CONF:** Class 250 Board 100 Del from £55 * **PARKING:** 70

★★58% Royal

St Cuthbert St DG6 4DY
☎ 01557 331213 📠 01557 331513
e-mail: royal@pheasanthotel.co.uk
Dir: *turn off A75 onto A711 hotel is in the centre of Kirkcudbright, on the corner at crossroads*

Refurbishment has enhanced the accommodation at this conveniently situated, town centre tourist and commercial hotel. Rooms have en suite facilities and include colour television and direct-dial telephones. There is a ground floor bar, popular with hotel guests and locals alike, and a residents lounge is located on the first floor.

ROOMS: 17 en suite (7 fmly) s £25-£30; d £38-£50 (incl. bkfst) * LB **FACILITIES:** entertainment **CONF:** Thtr 120 Class 60 Board 60 **CARDS:**

KIRKHILL, Highland — Map 14 NH54

★★65% *Bogroy Inn*

IV5 7PX
☎ 01463 831296 📠 01463 831296
Dir: *at junct A862/B9164*

In the 16th century the inn was closely associated with whisky smuggling; it is now a small, friendly hotel. The neat bedrooms are nicely presented in modern style with good facilities. Public areas include a choice of bars and a pleasant dining room offering wholesome fare.

ROOMS: 7 en suite (3 fmly) **FACILITIES:** Pool table **PARKING:** 40 **NOTES:** No dogs (ex guide dogs) No smoking in restaurant **CARDS:**

KYLE OF LOCHALSH, Highland
Map 13 NG72

★★★64% Lochalsh

Ferry Rd IV40 8AF
☎ 01599 534202 🖷 01599 534881
e-mail: mdmacrae@lochalsh-hotel.demon.co.uk
Dir: *turn off A82 onto A87*

Almost next to the new Skye Bridge, this established hotel has a prominent position by the former ferry slip. The modern bedrooms vary in size and are brightly decorated. Fine views are enjoyed from public areas and the formal restaurant serves interesting modern food from a short carte.

ROOMS: 38 en suite (8 fmly) s £55-£70; d £85-£130 (incl. cont bkfst) LB **FACILITIES:** STV Xmas **CONF:** Thtr 20 Class 20 Board 20 **SERVICES:** Lift **PARKING:** 50 **NOTES:** No smoking in restaurant
CARDS:

See advert on page 727

LADYBANK, Fife
Map 11 NO30

★★★65% Fernie Castle

Letham KY15 7RU
☎ 01337 810381 🖷 01337 810422
e-mail: mail@ferniecastle.demon.co.uk
Dir: *from M90 junct 6 take A91 east (Tay Bridge/St Andrews) to Melville Lodges rdbt. Left onto A92 signed Tay Bridge. Hotel 1.2m on right*

This turreted castle is set amid 17 acres of wooded grounds in the heart of Fife. Bedrooms range from King and Queen rooms, to the more standard sized Squire and Lady rooms. Formal dining can be enjoyed in the elegant Auld Alliance Restaurant. The Keep Bar is also available, serving less formal meals, and there is a choice of relaxing lounges.

ROOMS: 20 en suite (2 fmly) No smoking in 12 bedrooms s £85-£95; d £170-£190 (incl. bkfst & dinner) * LB **FACILITIES:** Croquet lawn Putting green 17 acres woodland with loch entertainment Xmas **CONF:** Thtr 120 Class 120 Board 25 Del from £100 * **PARKING:** 80 **NOTES:** No smoking in restaurant Civ Wed 180
CARDS:

LAIRG, Highland
Map 14 NC50

★★67% Overscaig

Loch Shin IV27 4NY
☎ 01549 431203
Dir: *on A838*

For pure isolation it is hard to beat this idyllic Highland holiday and fishing hotel, beside the picturesque shore of Loch Shin. Bedrooms are cheerfully decorated and have comfortable modern furnishings. Public rooms include the bar with pool room, a coffee lounge for snacks, a quiet lounge and a smart dining room which enjoys panoramic views of the loch. Fishing rights are provided for the loch, along with boats.

ROOMS: 9 en suite (2 fmly) s £25-£35; d £50-£70 (incl. bkfst) * **FACILITIES:** Fishing Pool table Xmas **PARKING:** 30 **NOTES:** No dogs (ex guide dogs) No smoking in restaurant

LANARK, South Lanarkshire
Map 11 NS84

see also Biggar

★★★65% *Cartland Bridge*

Glasgow Rd ML11 9UF
☎ 01555 664426 🖷 01555 663773
Dir: *follow A73 through Lanark towards Carluke. Hotel 1.25m on right*

This Grade I listed mansion lies in wooded grounds just north of Lanark. A popular hotel with business people, its public areas feature splendid wood panelling and fireplaces. Food is served in the restaurant or the bar and there is also a small cocktail lounge. Bedrooms vary in size; the larger master bedrooms are particularly attractive.

ROOMS: 18 en suite (2 fmly) No smoking in 9 bedrooms **FACILITIES:** STV **CONF:** Thtr 350 Class 100 Board 80 **PARKING:** 120 **NOTES:** No smoking in restaurant **CARDS:**

LANGBANK, Renfrewshire
Map 10 NS37

★★★★67% Gleddoch House

PA14 6YE
☎ 01475 540711 🖷 01475 540201
e-mail: gleddochhouse@ukonline.co.uk
Dir: *signposted from B789 at Langbank rdbt*

Set above Langbank, this regal mansion house enjoys spectacular views over the River Clyde. The elegant restaurant is the setting for innovative fare, offered from both the carte and fixed price menus. Bedrooms come in a range of styles, those in the main part of the house keep much of the original character, and the wings are more modern in style.

ROOMS: 39 en suite (4 fmly) No smoking in 6 bedrooms s fr £99; d fr £150 (incl. bkfst) * LB **FACILITIES:** STV Golf 18 Fishing Squash Riding Putting green Clay pigeon shooting Xmas **CONF:** Thtr 100 Class 60 Board 40 Del from £130 * **PARKING:** 200
CARDS:

LARGS, North Ayrshire
Map 10 NS25

★★★73% Brisbane House

14 Greenock Rd, Esplanade KA30 8NF
☎ 01475 687200 🖷 01475 676295
e-mail: enquiries@maksu-group.co.uk
Dir: *on A78 midway between Greenock and Irvine, on seafront*

Friendly staff offer a high level of hospitality and attentive service at this modernised Georgian house, looking out over the promenade to the Isle of Cumbrae. There is a choice of bars and eating options. The conservatory adjoining the lounge bar offers informal dining, and the elegant restaurant has its own conservatory cocktail bar. Bedrooms come in a variety of sizes and are well equipped.

ROOMS: 23 en suite (2 fmly) No smoking in 5 bedrooms s £75-£120; d £95-£150 (incl. bkfst) * LB **FACILITIES:** STV Jacuzzi/spa entertainment Xmas **CONF:** Thtr 120 Class 60 Board 50 Del from £95 * **PARKING:** 60 **NOTES:** Civ Wed 120
CARDS:

> Fancy a Singapore Sling? Bar staff in five star hotels should be skilled cocktail mixers.

★★★72% ***Priory House***
Broomfields KA30 8DR
☎ 01475 686460 ⎙ 01475 689070
e-mail: enquiries@maksu-group.co.uk
Dir: *on A78 midway between Greenock and Irvine, hotel on seafront*
Standing on the seafront looking out across the Firth of Clyde, this hotel boasts a fine conservatory in which to relax and take in the views. Food is available in the restaurant, or in the bar with its own dining conservatory and extensive menu. The friendly staff provide attentive service throughout. Bedrooms vary in size, but all are thoughtfully equipped.
ROOMS: 21 en suite (2 fmly) No smoking in 5 bedrooms
FACILITIES: STV Jacuzzi/spa **CONF:** Thtr 100 Class 50 Board 50
PARKING: 50 **CARDS:**

★★68% **Willowbank**
96 Greenock Rd KA30 8PG
☎ 01475 672311 ⎙ 01475 672311
Dir: *on A77*
A relaxed, friendly atmosphere prevails at this well maintained hotel. The well decorated bedrooms tend to be spacious and offer comfortable modern appointments, while public areas include a large, well stocked bar, a lounge and dining room. Attractive floral baskets hanging outside are a feature during summer.
ROOMS: 30 en suite (4 fmly) s £60-£80; d £80-£120 (incl. bkfst) LB
FACILITIES: entertainment Xmas **CONF:** Thtr 200 Class 100 Board 40 Del from £80 * **PARKING:** 40 **CARDS:**

LAUDER, Scottish Borders — Map 12 NT54

★★66% **Lauderdale**
1 Edinburgh Rd TD2 6TW
☎ 01578 722231 ⎙ 01578 718642
e-mail: enquiries@lauderdale-hotel.co.uk
Dir: *on A68 from S, drive through centre of Lauder, hotel is on right. From Edinburgh, hotel is on left at first bend after passing sign for Lauder*
Set on the main road on the north side of town, this friendly hotel provides good value meals in both the bar and cosy dining room. The well equipped bedrooms are comfortable and well kept.
ROOMS: 9 en suite (1 fmly) No smoking in 3 bedrooms s £37-£40; d £56-£60 (incl. bkfst) * LB **FACILITIES:** STV **PARKING:** 50
NOTES: No dogs (ex guide dogs) No smoking in restaurant
CARDS:

LERWICK See Shetland

LETTERFINLAY, Highland — Map 14 NN29

★★67% **Letterfinlay Lodge**
PH34 4DZ
☎ 01397 712622
Dir: *7m N of Spean Bridge, on A82 beside Loch Lochy*
The hotel is set in grounds and enjoys a spectacular outlook over Loch Lochy. Relaxing public areas include a choice of lounges, one of which is popular for bar meals, a snug bar with a pool table, and an attractive dining room. Bedrooms vary in size and offer modern and traditional appointments.
ROOMS: 13 rms (11 en suite) (5 fmly) s £28.50-£39.50; d £57-£79 (incl. bkfst) * LB **FACILITIES:** Fishing **PARKING:** 100 **NOTES:** No smoking in restaurant Closed Nov-Feb (ex New Year)
CARDS:

Read all about it! Newspapers delivered to bedrooms in four and five star hotels.

LEUCHARS, Fife — Map 11 NO42

★★★69% **Drumoig Golf Hotel**
Drumoig KY16 OBE
☎ 01382 541800 ⎙ 01382 542211
e-mail: drumoig@sol.co.uk
Dir: *M90 to Tay Bridge turn off, then A92 Taybridge/Dundee at the Forgan rdbt turn right to Leuchars/St Andrews, hotel at bottom of the hill on the left*

Opposite the Scottish National Golf Centre, this smart hotel is especially popular with visiting golfers. Most of the modern bedrooms are contained in three separate lodges but five new luxury bedrooms have been created in the main house. Public areas include a well stocked bar and attractive restaurant both of which overlook the golf course.
ROOMS: 5 en suite 24 annexe en suite No smoking in 17 bedrooms s £57.50-£77.50; d £80-£120 (incl. bkfst) * LB **FACILITIES:** STV Golf 18 Fishing Gym Putting green Home of Scottish National golf centre Xmas
CONF: Thtr 50 Class 15 Board 24 Del from £65 * **PARKING:** 120
NOTES: No dogs (ex guide dogs) No smoking in restaurant
CARDS:

LEWIS, ISLE OF, Western Isles — Map 13

STORNOWAY — Map 13 NB43

★★★66% **Cabarfeidh**
HS1 2EU
☎ 01851 702604 ⎙ 01851 705572
Dir: *1m from town centre on main road to Tarbert, turn left at rdbt and take first turn on right*
Situated on the edge of town, this comfortable modern hotel is a popular venue for local functions and conferences. The attractive foyer lounge is a comfortable place to relax and there is a choice of bars as well as a smart restaurant. Bedrooms are mostly well proportioned with modern facilities. Staff offer friendly, obliging service.
ROOMS: 46 en suite (36 fmly) No smoking in 12 bedrooms s £72-£75; d £92-£95 (incl. bkfst) * LB **FACILITIES:** STV **CONF:** Thtr 350 Class 100 Board 35 **SERVICES:** Lift air con **PARKING:** 100 **NOTES:** No smoking in restaurant **CARDS:**

LOCHCARRON, Highland — Map 14 NG83

★★68% **Lochcarron**
Main St IV54 8YS
☎ 01520 722226 ⎙ 01520 722612
Dir: *take A9 N from Inverness, then A835 at Tore rdbt for Ullapool, then A890 Kyle of Lochalsh, hotel is in E end of village on Lochcarron*
A friendly hotel with a touch of Irish hospitality. Bedrooms, two with private sitting rooms, follow a modern decorative scheme.

THE CIRCLE
Selected Individual Hotels
GREAT BRITAIN

continued

LOCHCARRON, continued

Meals and light snacks are available all day in the bar. In the dining room the emphasis is on fresh local seafood. Both bar and restaurant look out on the loch.
ROOMS: 10 rms (9 en suite) (2 fmly) No smoking in 2 bedrooms
FACILITIES: Pool table Hunting Shooting Fishing **PARKING:** 40
NOTES: No smoking in restaurant **CARDS:**

See advert on opposite page

LOCHEARNHEAD, Stirling Map 11 NN52

★67% Lochearnhead
Lochside FK19 8PU
☎ 01567 830229 01567 830364
e-mail: gus@lochhot.freeserve.co.uk
Dir: *from A84 follow signs Crianlarich/Callander for Lochearnhead where turn right at T-junct, hotel is 500 mtrs ahead*
This friendly hotel overlooks Loch Earn, a popular resort for visitors attracted by the extensive range of water pursuits. Lovely loch views can be enjoyed from all the public rooms and there is a choice of bedrooms. The varied menus offer a good range of home-cooked dishes in both the bar and restaurant.
ROOMS: 12 rms (8 en suite) s £30-£40; d £48-£62 (incl. bkfst) * LB
FACILITIES: STV Fishing Water skiing Windsurfing Sailing **PARKING:** 82
NOTES: Closed Dec-Mar **CARDS:**

LOCHGILPHEAD, Argyll & Bute Map 10 NR88

★★★68% Cairnbaan
Crinan Canal, Cairnbaan PA31 8SJ
☎ 01546 603668 01546 606045
e-mail: cairnbaanhotel@virgin.net
Dir: *2m N, A816 from Lochgilphead, hotel off B841*
This wonderfully relaxing hotel, beside lock five on the Crinan Canal, boasts comfortable lounges, a bar area and a delightful patio where many guests dine informally. The menu offered in the attractive, formal restaurant features traditional Scottish dishes carefully prepared from quality local ingredients.
ROOMS: 12 en suite No smoking in all bedrooms s fr £65; d fr £90 (incl. bkfst) * **PARKING: CARDS:**

★★62% *The Stag*
Argyll St PA31 8NE
☎ 01546 602496 01546 603549
Dir: *from central Scotland A82 then A38, follow rd to Inveraray, turn right at mini rdbt into main st, hotel is large black/white turreted building*
This long-established, family-run hotel is centrally located and offers good value accommodation. It boasts a smart dining room, a bar and a first floor lounge. Bedrooms, although quite compact, are well equipped.
ROOMS: 17 en suite **FACILITIES:** STV Pool table **CONF:** Thtr 50 Class 20 Board 30 **CARDS:**

LOCHINVER, Highland Map 14 NC02

★★★80% Inver Lodge
IV27 4LU
☎ 01571 844496 01571 844395
e-mail: stay@inverlodge.com
Dir: *A835 to Lochinver continue through village and turn left after village hall, follow private road for 0.50m*
This smart, modern purpose-built hotel, on a hillside above the village with a backdrop of unspoilt wilderness and mountains, enjoys spectacular views of the harbour and bay. There is a choice of lounges and a restaurant. Bedrooms are stylish and comfortable. Staff are friendly and obliging.

continued

ROOMS: 20 en suite s £80-£170; d £130-£200 (incl. bkfst) * LB
FACILITIES: STV Fishing Snooker Sauna Solarium **CONF:** Thtr 30 Board 20 Del from £60 * **PARKING:** 30 **NOTES:** No smoking in restaurant Closed Dec-Etr **CARDS:**

LOCH LOMOND
See Balloch & Luss and advert on opposite page

LOCHMADDY See North Uist, Isle of

LOCKERBIE, Dumfries & Galloway Map 11 NY18

★★★67% Dryfesdale
DG11 2SF
☎ 01576 202427 01576 204187
e-mail: reception@dryfesdalehotel.co.uk
Dir: *from A74 take 'Lockerbie North' junct, 3rd left at 1st rdbt, 1st exit left at 2nd rdbt, hotel is 200yds on left hand side*
This relaxing hotel is only five minutes' drive from the motorway, yet tucked away behind a shield of trees. Bedrooms vary in size, and all are equipped comfortably. Dinner is served in the light, airy restaurant overlooking the gardens.
ROOMS: 9 en suite 6 annexe en suite (1 fmly) s £55-£60; d £84-£87 (incl. bkfst) * LB **FACILITIES:** Xmas **CONF:** Thtr 80 Class 20 Board 20 Del from £71 * **PARKING:** 50 **NOTES:** No smoking in restaurant Closed 26 Dec Civ Wed 84 **CARDS:**

★★70% *Somerton House*
35 Carlisle Rd DG11 2DR
THE CIRCLE Selected Individual Hotels GREAT BRITAIN
☎ 01576 202583/202384 01576 204218
Dir: *off A74*
This fine Victorian mansion - a friendly family-run hotel - has been well preserved and features beautiful woodwork, particularly in the restaurant. An attractive conservatory adds a new dimension and is equally popular for bar meals.
ROOMS: 7 en suite 4 annexe en suite (2 fmly) No smoking in 4 bedrooms **CONF:** Thtr 25 Class 15 Board 15 **PARKING:** 100
NOTES: No smoking in restaurant **CARDS:**

★★64% Kings Arms Hotel
High St DG11 2JL
☎ 01576 202410 01576 202410
e-mail: reception@kingsarmshotel.co.uk
Dir: *A74M, 0.5m into town centre, hotel is opposite Town Hall*
Reputedly one of the oldest hotels in the town, this friendly hotel has hosted both Bonnie Prince Charlie and Sir Walter Scott in its time. Today it attracts custom to its inviting bars, restaurant and well equipped bedrooms.
ROOMS: 14 rms (12 en suite) (1 fmly) s £30-£35; d £50-£60 (incl. bkfst) *
FACILITIES: Xmas **CONF:** Thtr 90 Class 50 Board 40 Del from £39.50 *
PARKING: 8 **CARDS:**

★66% Ravenshill House
12 Dumfries Rd DG11 2EF
☎ 01576 202882 01576 202882
e-mail: ravenshillhouse.hotel@virgin.net
Dir: *on A709 which is signed from the A74M Lockerbie junct, travel W of town centre. Hotel is 0.5m on right*
Cheerful and attentive service plus good value home cooked meals feature at this friendly family-run hotel, set in its own gardens on the edge of the town. It also boasts well equipped bedrooms, most of which are of a good size.
ROOMS: 8 rms (7 en suite) (1 fmly) s £25-£35; d £40-£50 (incl. bkfst) * LB **CONF:** Thtr 30 Class 20 Board 12 **PARKING:** 35 **NOTES:** No smoking in restaurant **CARDS:**

L

LUNDIN LINKS, Fife Map 12 NO40

★★★74% ❀❀ Old Manor

Leven Rd KY8 6AJ
☎ 01333 320368 🖷 01333 320911
e-mail: enquiries@oldmanorhotel.co.uk
Dir: *1m E of Leven on A915 Kirkaldy-St Andrews Rd*

Situated on the western edge of the village overlooking the golf course to the Firth of Forth, this hotel provides good food with high standards of guest care. The nicely presented public areas invite comfortable relaxation. Bedrooms, with pretty colour schemes, are comfortably modern in style and offer the expected amenities.

ROOMS: 24 en suite (3 fmly) No smoking in 4 bedrooms s £60-£80; d £120-£180 (incl. bkfst) * LB **FACILITIES:** Complimentary membership of Lundin Sports Club Xmas **CONF:** Thtr 140 Class 70 Board 50 **PARKING:** 100 **NOTES:** No smoking in restaurant Civ Wed 100 **CARDS:**

See advert on page 731

LUSS, Argyll & Bute Map 10 NS39

★★★70% The Lodge on Loch Lomond

G83 8PA
☎ 01436 860201 🖷 01436 860203
e-mail: lusslomond@aol.com
Dir: *turn off A82, follow sign for hotel*

Wonderful views over Loch Lomond can be enjoyed from this modern purpose-built hotel beside the village of Luss. Public areas include a spacious open-plan split-level bar and restaurant overlooking the loch. Bedrooms, which are fully pine furnished, range from spacious executive rooms to the smaller standard rooms, all with good amenities.

ROOMS: 29 en suite (20 fmly) d £105-£165 (incl. bkfst) * LB **FACILITIES:** STV Sauna fishing, boating Xmas **CONF:** Thtr 35 Class 18 Board 25 Del from £150 * **PARKING:** 82 **CARDS:**

MALLAIG, Highland Map 13 NM69

★★67% Marine

PH41 4PY
☎ 01687 462217 🖷 01687 462821
e-mail: marinehotel@theinternet.com
Dir: *adjacent to railway terminal, first hotel on right off A830*

This welcoming, family-run hotel beside the railway station is also convenient both for the ferry terminal and the harbour. Bedrooms are equipped with all modern comforts. Day rooms, on the first floor, consist of a popular lounge bar which has a small sitting area adjacent. The restaurant offers a varied menu with local seafood a particular attraction.

ROOMS: 19 en suite (2 fmly) s £35-£40; d £64-£70 (incl. bkfst) * LB **PARKING:** 6 **NOTES:** No smoking in restaurant RS Nov-Mar **CARDS:**

★★63% West Highland

PH41 4QZ
☎ 01687 462210 🖷 01687 462130
e-mail: westhighland.hotel@virgin.net
Dir: *from Fort William turn right at rdbt then 1st right up hill, from ferry left at rdbt then 1st right uphill*

Lovely views of the Isle of Skye are a memorable feature of a stay in this popular holiday hotel which has good facilities for tour groups. Bedrooms are up-to-date and come in a range of sizes and styles. There are attractive public areas and well prepared bar meals are served.

ROOMS: 34 en suite (6 fmly) No smoking in 6 bedrooms s £25-£36; d £50-£72 (incl. bkfst) * LB **FACILITIES:** entertainment **CONF:** Thtr 100 Class 80 Board 100 **PARKING:** 40 **NOTES:** No smoking in restaurant Closed Nov-15 Mar RS 16 Mar-1 Apr **CARDS:**

MARKINCH, Fife Map 11 NO20

Premier Collection

★★★★❀❀ Balbirnie House

Balbirnie Park KY7 6NE
☎ 01592 610066 🖷 01592 610529
e-mail: balbirnie@breathemail.net
Dir: *turn off A92 onto B9130, entrance 0.5m on left*

This luxury hotel has been lovingly restored to provide well equipped, spacious accommodation. Opulent day rooms furnished with antiques include three sitting rooms, one of which has a well stocked bar. A stylish new conservatory restaurant provides an elegant venue in which guests can enjoy the imaginative cooking.

ROOMS: 30 en suite (9 fmly) s £125-£160; d £185-£245 (incl. bkfst) * LB **FACILITIES:** STV Golf 18 Pool table Croquet lawn Putting green Xmas **CONF:** Thtr 220 Class 100 Board 60 Del from £152 * **PARKING:** 120 **NOTES:** No smoking in restaurant Civ Wed 200 **CARDS:**

MAYBOLE, South Ayrshire

Map 10 NS20

Premier Collection

★★❀ Ladyburn
KA19 7SG
☎ 01655 740585 📠 01655 740580
e-mail: jhdh@ladyburn.freeserve.co.uk
This charming country house is ideally situated in open countryside and surrounded by an attractive natural garden. Comfortable bedrooms are complemented by a choice of sitting areas, the drawing room and library, whilst dinner comprises a carefully cooked three course set menu, discussed beforehand with alternatives available. The genuine warmth of welcome is a particular feature and services are provided willingly.
ROOMS: 8 rms (7 en suite) No smoking in 7 bedrooms s £100-£115; d £145-£175 (incl. bkfst) * LB **FACILITIES:** Croquet lawn Boules **PARKING:** 12 **NOTES:** No dogs (ex guide dogs) No children 16yrs RS Nov-Dec 2 weeks, Jan/Mar 4 weeks Civ Wed 250
CARDS:

MELROSE, Scottish Borders

Map 12 NT53

★★68% *Bon Accord*
Market Square TD6 9PQ
☎ 01896 822645 📠 01896 823474
Dir: *from A68 into Melrose, hotel in centre of square*
Colourful window boxes adorn the facade of this friendly hotel in the Market Square. Bedrooms are brightly decorated, offer comfortable modern furnishings and a wide range of amenities. Attractive public areas include contrasting bars and a smart split-level dining room.
ROOMS: 10 en suite (1 fmly) **FACILITIES:** STV **CONF:** Thtr 100 Class 60 Board 50 **NOTES:** No dogs (ex guide dogs) No children 12yrs Closed 25 Dec **CARDS:**

★★66% ❀❀ Burt's
The Square TD6 9PL
☎ 01896 822285 📠 01896 822870
e-mail: burtshotel@aol.com
Dir: *A6091, 2m from A68 3m S of Earlston*
Set in the market square, this family-run hotel continues to offer traditional hospitality in a welcoming environment. The well stocked bar, with its open fire, is popular for informal lunches and suppers. The elegant restaurant provides formal meals artistically presented in the modern style.

continued

ROOMS: 20 en suite No smoking in all bedrooms s £50; d £88 (incl. bkfst) * LB **FACILITIES:** Shooting Salmon Fishing **CONF:** Thtr 38 Class 20 Board 20 Del from £78 * **PARKING:** 40 **NOTES:** No smoking in restaurant Closed 24-26 Dec **CARDS:**

★★66% *George & Abbotsford*
High St TD6 9PD
☎ 01896 822308 📠 01896 823363
Best Western
Dir: *from A68 or A7 take A6091 to Melrose, hotel is in middle of High St*
Standing in the town centre, this substantial 18th-century former coaching inn enjoys a mixed trade from business persons, holiday makers and tours. It has a lounge bar which complements the dining room by serving a good range of bar meals.
ROOMS: 30 en suite (3 fmly) **FACILITIES:** STV Fishing **CONF:** Thtr 130 Class 60 Board 30 **PARKING:** 102
CARDS:

M

MEY, Highland

Map 15 ND27

★★65% Castle Arms
KW14 8XH
☎ 01847 851244 📠 01847 851244
Dir: *on A836*
A modernised 19th-century coaching inn with uninterrupted views over the Pentland Firth to Orkney. Public areas include a well stocked lounge bar and adjoining dining room, offering a choice of light meals. There is an interesting photographic gallery of the Royal Family. Most bedrooms are in a modern extension at the rear of the hotel, all are bright and airy.
ROOMS: 3 en suite 5 annexe en suite (1 fmly) s £30-£39; d £48-£58 (incl. bkfst) * **FACILITIES:** Fishing Pool table **PARKING:** 30 **NOTES:** RS Oct-Mar **CARDS:**

MOFFAT, Dumfries & Galloway

Map 11 NT00

★★★71% Moffat House
High St DG10 9HL
☎ 01683 220039 📠 01683 221288
e-mail: moffat@talk21.com
Best Western
Dir: *from M74 at Beattock (junct 15) take the A701 in 1m hotel at end of High St*
This inviting Adam style mansion enjoys extensive gardens to the rear and is situated in the centre of the town. The public rooms include a number of relaxing lounges to suit all moods while the bedrooms, including some in the tastefully converted coaching house are attractively decorated and offer a stylish and comfortable environment. The ambitious menus can be sampled both in the bar or in the more formal restaurant. Staff are friendly and keen to please.

continued

MOFFAT, continued

Moffat House, Moffat

ROOMS: 21 en suite (2 fmly) No smoking in 6 bedrooms s £50-£60; d £70-£90 (incl. bkfst) * LB **FACILITIES:** ch fac Xmas **CONF:** Thtr 70 Class 50 Board 40 Del from £67.50 * **PARKING:** 61 **NOTES:** No smoking in restaurant Civ Wed 110 **CARDS:**

★★★70% Auchen Castle

Best Western

Beattock DG10 9SH
☎ 01683 300407 01683 300667
e-mail: reservations@auchen-castle-hotel.co.uk
Dir: *1m N of Moffat village access from M74, then onto B7076*

Situated close to the motorway, but separated from it by extensive grounds, terraced gardens and a lake stocked with brown trout, this impressive mansion dates back to 1849. Public rooms include a comfortable drawing room as well as a light and airy dining room. Bedrooms vary in size and price, and have all been attractively furnished.

ROOMS: 15 en suite 10 annexe en suite (1 fmly) No smoking in 8 bedrooms s £50-£65; d £60-£110 (incl. bkfst) * LB **FACILITIES:** STV Fishing Clay pigeon shooting **CONF:** Thtr 70 Class 40 Board 28 Del from £75 * **PARKING:** 37 **NOTES:** No smoking in restaurant Closed 3 wks Xmas-New Year **CARDS:**

★★74% Beechwood Country House

Harthope Place DG10 9RS
☎ 01683 220210 01683 220889
e-mail: info@beechwoodhousehotel.co.uk
Dir: *at north end of town. Turn right at St Marys Church into Harthope Place and follow the 'Hotel' sign*

A delightful country house in attractive gardens, a short walk from the town. There are two comfortable lounges, one with a small bar. Bedrooms are named after local rivers. The kitchen continues to delight guests with imaginative cooking.

ROOMS: 7 en suite (1 fmly) s £50-£54; d £72-£76 (incl. bkfst) * LB **FACILITIES:** Xmas **PARKING:** 15 **NOTES:** No smoking in restaurant Closed 2 Jan-14 Feb **CARDS:**

See advert on opposite page

★★66% The Star

44 High St DG10 9EF
☎ 01683 220156 01683 221524
e-mail: tim@famousstarhotel.com
Dir: *M74 Moffat, hotel is 2m from junct first hotel on right in High Street*

Smart, modern and well equipped bedrooms plus enjoyable food, served either in the bar or the restaurant, are just some of the virtues of this friendly hotel. Its claim to be the world's narrowest hotel is a novel conversation point.

ROOMS: 8 en suite (1 fmly) s £40; d £56-£65 (incl. bkfst) * LB **FACILITIES:** STV Pool table **NOTES:** No dogs (ex guide dogs) No smoking in restaurant **CARDS:**

Premier Collection

★ Well View

THE CIRCLE
Selected Individual Hotels

Ballplay Rd DG10 9JU
☎ 01683 220184 01683 220088
e-mail: info@wellview.co.uk
Dir: *on A708 from Moffat, pass fire station and first left*

Located on a quiet road within walking distance of town, Well View Hotel retains many of its original Victorian features. Individually furnished bedrooms are comfortable and thoughtfully equipped. Dinner is a six-course affair, using fine ingredients which are locally sourced whenever possible.

ROOMS: 6 en suite No smoking in all bedrooms s £53-£65; d £72-£110 (incl. bkfst) * LB **FACILITIES:** Xmas **PARKING:** 8 **NOTES:** No smoking in restaurant Closed 2wk Jan & 1wk Nov **CARDS:**

MONTROSE, Angus Map 15 NO75

★★★67% Links Hotel

Mid Links DD10 8RL
☎ 01674 671000 01674 672698
e-mail: reception@linkshotel.com
Dir: *turn off A90 at Brechin, take A935 to Montrose, 10m turn right at Lochside junct, left at swimming pool right by tennis courts hotel 200yds*

This hotel is a former Edwardian townhouse with distinctive architecture and has been fully refurbished and restored. It is situated close to recreational facilities and central amenities. Main house bedrooms are tastefully decorated and offer comfortable pine furnishings. Wing rooms are being enhanced. Public areas include a well stocked bar, attractive restaurant, and a popular coffee shop where all day food is available.

continued

ROOMS: 25 en suite (12 fmly) No smoking in 11 bedrooms s £48-£74; d £64-£96 (incl. bkfst) * LB **FACILITIES:** STV Xmas **CONF:** Thtr 160 Class 70 Board 55 Del from £98 * **PARKING:** 30 **NOTES:** No smoking in restaurant Civ Wed **CARDS:**

See advert on this page

★★★65% Montrose Park Hotel & Golf Lodges

61 John St DD10 8RJ
☎ 01674 663400 📠 01674 677091
e-mail: recep@montrosepark.co.uk
Dir: *from A90 turn off at A935 to A92, from A92 turn off Montrose High Street into John Street*

A welcoming hotel which, from its position on the mid links, offers convenient access to central and recreational facilities. Smart public areas include a bright foyer lounge, a popular bar and brasserie, and a tasteful, split-level restaurant.

continued on p736

MONTROSE, continued

ROOMS: 53 en suite 5 annexe en suite (4 fmly) No smoking in 16 bedrooms **FACILITIES:** STV **CONF:** Thtr 200 Class 80 Board 80 **PARKING:** 50 **NOTES:** No smoking in restaurant Civ Wed 220 **CARDS:**

See advert on page 735

MORAR, Highland — Map 13 NM69

★★64% Morar

PH40 4PA
☎ 01687 462346 Fax 01687 462212
e-mail: agmacleod@morarhotel.freeserve.co.uk
Dir: *in the village of Morar on the A830 "Road to the Isle". The hotel overlooks the silver sands of Morar*

Situated beside the scenic West Highland Railway, with wonderful views over the bay, this welcoming family-run hotel caters equally well for individuals and tour groups. There is a good range of accommodation, open plan reception areas, and a separate dining room overlooking the sea which serves good value meals.
ROOMS: 27 en suite (3 fmly) s £30-£35; d £60-£70 (incl. bkfst) * LB **FACILITIES:** Fishing entertainment **CONF:** Board 100 **PARKING:** 50 **NOTES:** No smoking in restaurant Closed 22 Oct-Mar **CARDS:**

MUIR OF ORD, Highland — Map 14 NH55

★★67% Ord House

THE CIRCLE Selected Individual Hotels GREAT BRITAIN

IV6 7UH
☎ 01463 870492 Fax 01463 870492
e-mail: eliza@ord-house.com
Dir: *turn off A9 at Tore rdbt onto A832. Follow for 5m into Muir of Ord. Turn left outside Muir of Ord, to Ullapool still on A832. Hotel 0.5m on left*

Dating back to 1637, this former laird's house lies secluded in wooded grounds. Now a country house hotel, it offers simply furnished but well proportioned accommodation. Public areas reflect the character of the house, with inviting lounges, a cosy rustic bar and a dining room serving fine country cooking.
ROOMS: 11 en suite s £37; d £94 (incl. bkfst) * **FACILITIES:** Croquet lawn Putting green Clay pigeon shooting **PARKING:** 30 **NOTES:** Closed Nov-Feb **CARDS:**

Premier Collection

★ The Dower House

Highfield IV6 7XN
☎ 01463 870090 Fax 01463 870090
e-mail: aa@thedowerhouse.co.uk
Dir: *on Dingwall rd A862, 1m from town on left*

This small and charming hotel in four acres of secluded grounds has a splendid sitting room featuring an open fire and plenty to read. The bedrooms offer quality and comfort; the house is full of thoughtful touches and fresh flowers. Set dinners and hearty breakfasts are prepared with much care using fresh herbs and seasonal produce.
ROOMS: 5 en suite 2 annexe en suite No smoking in all bedrooms s £45-£85; d £110-£150 (incl. bkfst) * LB **FACILITIES:** Croquet lawn **PARKING:** 20 **NOTES:** No dogs (ex guide dogs) No smoking in restaurant Closed Xmas day & 1wk Mar **CARDS:**

MULL, ISLE OF, Argyll & Bute — Map 10

BUNESSAN — Map 10 NM32

★★74% Assapol House

PA67 6DW
☎ 01681 700258 Fax 01681 700445
e-mail: alex@assapolhouse.demon.co.uk
Dir: *turn left off A849 100mtrs after Bunessan School and follow signpost for 1m on minor road*

Many guests return time and time again to this delightful small country house hotel which enjoys a tranquil setting beside the shore of Loch Assapol. Bedrooms are decorated to a high standard and are furnished with comfort in mind. Public areas include a choice of relaxing lounges and an attractive dining room where delicious home-cooked meals are served at individual tables. The daily changing menu is a four-course affair.
ROOMS: 5 rms (4 en suite) No smoking in all bedrooms s £54-£58; d £136-£146 (incl. bkfst & dinner) LB **FACILITIES:** Fishing **PARKING:** 8 **NOTES:** No dogs No children 10yrs No smoking in restaurant Closed Nov-Mar **CARDS:**

DERVAIG — Map 13 NM45

★★76% Druimard Country House

PA75 6QW
☎ 01688 400345 & 400291 Fax 01688 400345
Dir: *from Craignure ferry terminal turn right towards Tobermory, go through Salen Village, after 1.5m turn left to Dervaig, hotel on right*

A charming Victorian country house on the edge of the village beside the Mull Little Theatre. Attractive colour schemes feature in the variable sized bedrooms, which are comfortably furnished and thoughtfully equipped. There is a relaxing lounge and conservatory bar, but the real focal point is the dining room, where tempting five-course dinners attract high praise.
ROOMS: 5 en suite 2 annexe en suite (2 fmly) s £75-£85; d £120-£150 (incl. bkfst & dinner) * **FACILITIES:** Mull Little Theatre within grounds **PARKING:** 20 **NOTES:** No smoking in restaurant Closed Nov-Mar **CARDS:**

KILLIECHRONAN — Map 10 NM54

Premier Collection

★★ Killiechronan House

Killiechronan Estate PA72 6JU
☎ 01680 300403 Fax 01680 300463
Dir: *leaving ferry turn right to Tobermory A849, in Salen (12m) turn left onto B8035, after 2m turn right to Ulva ferry B8073, hotel on right*

This delightful small country house provides an ideal base for exploring Mull. There are two inviting sitting rooms and guests can enjoy carefully prepared five-course dinners in the elegant dining room. Individually styled bedrooms are attractive and comfortable. Dedicated staff provide a high level of care.

continued

ROOMS: 6 en suite No smoking in all bedrooms s fr £85; d fr £170 (incl. bkfst & dinner) * LB **FACILITIES:** Fishing Riding **PARKING:** 10 **NOTES:** No children 12yrs No smoking in restaurant Closed Nov-Feb **CARDS:**

TOBERMORY

Map 13 NM55

★★★74% Western Isles

PA75 6PR
☎ 01688 302012 📠 01688 302297
e-mail: wihotel@aol.com
Dir: *Glasgow to Oban, ferry to Isle of Mull, after leaving ferry turn right to Tobermory*

From its elevated position above the pier, this elegant Victorian hotel enjoys a spectacular outlook over the bay and Calve Island to the hills of Morvern beyond. Public areas include a comfortable and relaxing lounge, beyond which is the bright airy conservatory bar which provides an informal food option in contrast to the more formal atmosphere found in the tasteful dining room. The patio, which overlooks the bay, is a popular feature. Accommodation ranges from an impressive suite to generously proportioned deluxe and master rooms, as well as standard rooms, all with delightful colour schemes and furnished with comfort in mind. Staff are friendly and willing to please.
ROOMS: 28 en suite (2 fmly) s £41-£45; d £82-£190 (incl. bkfst) * LB **FACILITIES:** Xmas **CONF:** Board 30 Del £120 * **PARKING:** 20 **NOTES:** No smoking in restaurant Closed 17-28 Dec Civ Wed 70 **CARDS:**

★★77% Highland Cottage

Breadalbane St PA75 6PD
☎ 01688 302030 📠 01688 302727
e-mail: davidandjo@highlandcottage.co.uk
Dir: *A848 Craignure/Fishnish ferry terminal, pass Tobermory signs, ahead at mini rdbt across narrow bridge turn right. Hotel on right opp Fire Station*
Visitors are assured of a warm personal welcome at this charming cottage-style hotel which is situated in the conservation part of upper Tobermory. Bedrooms, with an island theme, are appointed to a high standard and feature antique beds as well as a range of thoughtful extras. Public areas include a relaxing first floor lounge where an honesty bar has been added, while the ground floor has a smart conservatory. Adjacent, the elegant dining room is the appropriate setting in which to enjoy praiseworthy cuisine which is based on careful treatment of quality raw ingredients.

ROOMS: 6 en suite (1 fmly) No smoking in all bedrooms s £45-£54; d £79-£90 (incl. bkfst) * LB **FACILITIES:** STV **PARKING:** 4 **NOTES:** No smoking in restaurant Closed 4wks mid Oct/mid Nov RS Oct-early Feb **CARDS:**

★★72% Ulva House

PA75 6PR
☎ 01688 302044 📠 01688 302044
e-mail: info@ulvahousehotel.co.uk
Dir: *on waterfront take only left hand turn. Within 100m sharp turn sharp right then hotel sign on left*
A small welcoming hotel, standing above the town overlooking the bay, offering a high level of personal care. Bedrooms are comfortable and tastefully decorated. There is a relaxing lounge, a residents bar and an attractive dining room, where enjoyable home-cooked fare is served. The proprietor's wildlife tours of the island are an added attraction.
ROOMS: 6 rms (4 en suite) No smoking in all bedrooms s £47.50-£64.50; d £95-£109 (incl. bkfst & dinner) * LB **FACILITIES:** Landrover wildlife expeditions ch fac **PARKING:** 8 **NOTES:** No smoking in restaurant Closed Nov-Mar

NAIRN, Highland

Map 14 NH85

★★★★67% Golf View

Seabank Rd IV12 4HD
☎ 01667 452301 📠 01667 455267
e-mail: golfview@morton-hotels.com
Dir: *turn off A96 into Seabank Rd, follow road to end hotel on right*
The leisure centre is a major attraction at this business and tourist hotel. The conservatory provides an informal alternative to the more traditional restaurant. The bedrooms are steadily being enhanced and offer very pleasant accommodation.
ROOMS: 48 en suite (3 fmly) No smoking in 8 bedrooms s £83-£220; d £102-£225 (incl. bkfst) * LB **FACILITIES:** STV Indoor swimming (H) Tennis (hard) Sauna Solarium Gym Putting green Jacuzzi/spa Cycle hire ch fac Xmas **CONF:** Thtr 120 Class 50 Board 40 Del from £129 * **SERVICES:** Lift **PARKING:** 40 **NOTES:** No smoking in restaurant **CARDS:**

> Late for dinner? Quality Standards star rating means that last orders for dinner should be no earlier than:
> ★ 6.30pm ★★ 7.00pm ★★★ 8.00pm
> ★★★★ 9.00pm ★★★★★ 10.00pm

NAIRN, continued

★★★★67% Newton
Inverness Rd IV12 4RX
☎ 01667 453144 01667 454026
e-mail: info@morton-hotels.co.uk
Dir: *15m from Inverness on A96, turn left into tree lined driveway*

Looking towards the Moray Firth, this hotel is an impressive combination of Georgian and Scottish baronial architecture. Guests may use the leisure facilities at the nearby Golf View Hotel.
ROOMS: 57 en suite (2 fmly) No smoking in 15 bedrooms s £95-£130; d £135-£220 (incl. bkfst) * LB **FACILITIES:** STV Tennis (hard) Fishing Use of leisure club at sister hotel "The Golf View Hotel" Xmas **CONF:** Thtr 400 Class 250 Board 50 **SERVICES:** Lift **PARKING:** 80 **NOTES:** No smoking in restaurant **CARDS:**

★★★73% Boath House
Auldearn IV12 5TE
☎ 01667 454896 01667 455469
e-mail: wendy@boath-house.demon.co.uk
Dir: *2m past Nairn on A96 driving east towards Forres, signposted on main road*
This splendid Georgian mansion, set amidst 20 acres of mature wooded grounds, has been lovingly restored. A choice of inviting lounges feature open fires and an impressive display of Highland art, whilst carefully prepared meals are served in the airy dining room overlooking the lake. Bedrooms are comfortable and include many fine antique pieces.
ROOMS: 6 en suite 1 annexe en suite (1 fmly) No smoking in all bedrooms d £110-£175 (incl. bkfst) * LB **FACILITIES:** STV Fishing Sauna Gym Croquet lawn Jacuzzi/spa Beauty & Hair salon Xmas **PARKING:** 30 **NOTES:** No smoking in restaurant Civ Wed 200 **CARDS:**

★★★68% Claymore House
45 Seabank Rd IV12 4EY
☎ 01667 453731 & 453705 01667 455290
e-mail: claymorenairnscotland@compuserve.com
Dir: *turn into Seabank Rd from the A96 at the parish church. Hotel is halfway down on the right hand side*
Popular with all kinds of guests - from sporting enthusiasts to business people and holidaymakers. There are comfortable, modern bedrooms, four have direct access to the garden. Public areas include a lively bar serving a popular range of food, a conservatory lounge and adjoining restaurant. Golfing breaks can be arranged.
ROOMS: 14 en suite (2 fmly) No smoking in 4 bedrooms s £42.50-£60; d fr £85 (incl. bkfst) * LB **FACILITIES:** entertainment ch fac Xmas **CONF:** Thtr 50 Class 35 Board 35 Del from £52.50 * **PARKING:** 30 **NOTES:** No smoking in restaurant **CARDS:**

★★65% *Alton Burn*
Alton Burn Rd IV12 5ND
☎ 01667 452051 01667 456697
Dir: *follow signs from A96 via Sandown Farm Lane*
This hotel was originally built as a school around 1900. It lies to the west of the town with views across the Moray Firth. Bedrooms are practically furnished, and enhanced with colourful fabrics. Public areas include a sun lounge and dining room.
ROOMS: 19 rms (17 en suite) 7 annexe en suite (6 fmly) **FACILITIES:** Outdoor swimming (H) Tennis (hard) Putting green Games room ch fac **CONF:** Thtr 70 Class 30 Board 30 **PARKING:** 30 **NOTES:** RS Nov-Mar **CARDS:**

NEWBURGH, Aberdeenshire Map 15 NJ92

★★71% Udny Arms
Main St AB41 6BL
☎ 01358 789444 01358 789012
e-mail: enquiry@udny.demon.co.uk
Dir: *turn off A92 at sign marked Newburgh, hotel 2m, in centre of village right hand side*

This comfortable, family-run hotel stands in the centre of the village overlooking the golf course to the Ythan estuary. The variable sized bedrooms are comfortably furnished in the traditional style and offer a good range of modern amenities. Public areas offer a choice of rustic country bars, a relaxing lounge, and a split-level bistro restaurant.
ROOMS: 26 en suite (1 fmly) No smoking in all bedrooms s £45-£66; d £60-£82 (incl. bkfst) * LB **FACILITIES:** Fishing Petanque **CONF:** Thtr 100 Class 30 Board 30 Del £100 * **PARKING:** 100 **NOTES:** No smoking in restaurant **CARDS:**

See advert under ABERDEEN

NEW LANARK, South Lanarkshire Map 11 NS84

★★★70% New Lanark Mill Hotel
Mill One, New Lanark Mills ML11 9DB
☎ 01555 667200 01555 667222
e-mail: hotel@newlanark.org
Dir: *signposted from all major roads, M74 junct 7 also signed from M8*
This hotel occupies an impressively restored 18th-century cotton mill and is part of a heritage village nestling in the Clyde river valley. Inside, a bright modern style is balanced with features from the original mill; there is a comfortable foyer lounge with a galleried restaurant above. Views of the valley from the upper floors are wonderful.

continued

ROOMS: 38 en suite (2 fmly) No smoking in 28 bedrooms s £57.50; d £75 (incl. bkfst) * LB **FACILITIES:** Fishing Access to Wildlife Reserve Xmas **CONF:** Thtr 200 Class 50 Board 50 Del from £75 * **SERVICES:** Lift **PARKING:** 75 **NOTES:** No smoking in restaurant **CARDS:**

NEWTON STEWART, Dumfries & Galloway Map 10 NX46

Premier Collection

★★★ Kirroughtree House

Minnigaff DG8 6AN
☎ 01671 402141 01671 402425
e-mail: kirroughtree@n-stewart.demon.co.uk
Dir: *from A75 take A712, New Galloway rd, for hotel on left*

Standing in eight acres of landscaped gardens on the edge of Galloway Forest park, this 17th-centry mansion offers guests comfort and elegance in impressive surroundings. Lounges have deep sofas and antique furniture. Spacious bedrooms are individually decorated with many personal touches. The hotel is justly proud of its high levels of hospitality. Dinners are a highlight, served in the formal dining rooms.

ROOMS: 17 en suite s £75-£100; d £120-£170 (incl. bkfst) * LB **FACILITIES:** STV Tennis (grass) Croquet lawn Pitch and putt Xmas **CONF:** Thtr 30 Class 20 Board 20 **PARKING:** 50 **NOTES:** No children 10yrs No smoking in restaurant Closed 4 Jan-10 Feb **CARDS:**

★★★64% Bruce

88 Queen St DG8 6JL
☎ 01671 402294 01671 402294
Dir: *leave A75 at Newton Stewart rdbt, hotel 600mtrs on right past filling station, at junction*

A family run hotel, named after Robert the Bruce, just a short distance from the A75. Guests will enjoy the choice of dishes offered either from the lounge bar menu, or the more formal restaurant menu. The accommodation is well appointed and features one room with a four-poster bed and others for family use, containing separate bedrooms for children. There is a comfortable, spacious lounge on the first floor and private parking at the rear.

ROOMS: 18 en suite (2 fmly) No smoking in 6 bedrooms **CONF:** Thtr 60 **PARKING:** 20 **NOTES:** No smoking in restaurant **CARDS:**

★★72% Creebridge House

DG8 6NP
☎ 01671 402121 01671 403258
e-mail: creebridge.hotel@daelnet.co.uk
Dir: *off A75*

This former shooting lodge lies secluded in attractive gardens. A comfortable drawing room and restaurant are supplemented by a traditional bar/bistro offering an interesting and wide selection of dishes. The smart bedrooms come in a variety of styles and include some family suites.

ROOMS: 19 en suite (3 fmly) s £59; d £98 (incl. bkfst) * LB **FACILITIES:** STV Fishing Croquet lawn Putting green Xmas **CONF:** Thtr 70 Class 20 Board 30 Del from £80 * **PARKING:** 50 **NOTES:** No smoking in restaurant RS Nov-Mar **CARDS:**

NORTH BALLACHULISH, Highland Map 14 NN06

★★64% *Loch Leven*

Onich PH33 6SA
☎ 01855 821236 01855 821550
Dir: *1st turning on right after crossing Ballachulish Bridge from S*

A welcoming Highland hostelry by the north shore of Loch Leven. A relaxed and friendly atmosphere prevails in the public areas, which include a choice of bars. Meals are served in a pleasant, informal dining area next to one of the bars.

ROOMS: 10 en suite (7 fmly) **FACILITIES:** Pool table Local fishing or shooting trips can be arranged **PARKING:** 60 **CARDS:**

NORTH BERWICK, East Lothian Map 12 NT58

★★★65% The Marine

Cromwell Rd EH39 4LZ
☎ 0870 400 8129 01620 894480
e-mail: HeritageHotels_North_Berwick.Marine @forte-hotels.com
Dir: *from A198 turn into Hamilton Rd at traffic lights then take 2nd right*

This imposing leisure and conference hotel commands stunning views across the golf course to the Firth of Forth. The well proportioned public areas and many of the bedrooms enjoy the view. The bedrooms come in a variety of sizes, some are impressively large.

ROOMS: 83 en suite No smoking in 20 bedrooms s £65-£110; d £90-£130 (incl. bkfst) * LB **FACILITIES:** STV Outdoor swimming (H) Tennis (hard) Snooker Sauna Solarium Putting green Childrens playground ch fac Xmas **CONF:** Thtr 300 Class 150 Board 100 Del from £85 * **SERVICES:** Lift **PARKING:** 202 **NOTES:** No smoking in restaurant Civ Wed 200 **CARDS:**

N

NORTH BERWICK, continued

★★63% Nether Abbey

20 Dirleton Av EH39 4BQ
☎ 01620 892802 🖹 01620 895298
e-mail: bookings@netherabbey.co.uk
Dir: *at junct with A198, leave A1 and continue S to rdbt, take B6371 to N Berwick, hotel is second on left when entering town*
Popular with golfers, this hotel boasts stylish and well equipped bedrooms. Downstairs the focus remains on its lively bar/bistro where a good range of tasty home cooked dishes are on offer.
ROOMS: 14 en suite (4 fmly) s £35-£55; d £70-£85 (incl. bkfst) * LB **FACILITIES:** Xmas **CONF:** Thtr 80 Class 50 Board 30 **PARKING:** 40
CARDS:

NORTH UIST, ISLE OF, Western Isles — Map 13

LOCHMADDY — Map 13 NF96

★★66% Lochmaddy

HS6 5AA
☎ 01876 500331 & 500332 🖹 01876 500210
Dir: *100yds from Lochmaddy ferry terminal*
A welcoming, long-established hotel beside the ferry terminal, Lochmaddy is especially popular with anglers, but other country activities can be arranged. There is a cosy lounge, sometimes with a peat fire, a new bistro near the bar, both of which are popular for bar meals, and a formal dining room which offers a good value daily menu. Several of the bedrooms have fine sea views.
ROOMS: 15 en suite (1 fmly) s £40; d £80 (incl. bkfst) * LB **FACILITIES:** Fishing Pool table **PARKING:** 30 **NOTES:** No smoking in restaurant **CARDS:**

N

OBAN, Argyll & Bute — Map 10 NM83

★★★62% Columba

North Pier PA34 5QD
☎ 01631 562183 🖹 01631 564683
Dir: *A85 to Oban, first set of lights in town, turn right. The Columba Hotel is facing you*

Situated by the North Pier, many of the comfortable bedrooms at this popular tourist hotel overlook the bay. The public areas include a choice of contrasting bars and an attractive restaurant. Guests are welcome to use the leisure facilities at the sister hotel, The Alexandra.
ROOMS: 48 en suite (6 fmly) s £49-£59; d £75-£95 (incl. bkfst) * LB **FACILITIES:** Xmas **CONF:** Thtr 70 Class 30 Board 20 **SERVICES:** Lift **PARKING:** 8 **NOTES:** No smoking in restaurant
CARDS:

See advert on opposite page

★★★61% Alexandra

Corran Esplanade PA34 5AA
☎ 01631 562381 🖹 01631 564497
Dir: *arrive Oban on A85, descend Hill, turn right at first rdbt, hotel 200yds further on seaside*

This holiday hotel on the Esplanade enjoys wonderful views over the bay. Bedrooms are modern in style and include two ground-floor suites. There is a comfortable lounge, a well stocked bar, and a spacious dining room.
ROOMS: 64 en suite (6 fmly) **FACILITIES:** Indoor swimming (H) Snooker Sauna Solarium Gym Steam room Games room Golf practice nets entertainment **CONF:** Class 60 Board 60 **SERVICES:** Lift **PARKING:** 80 **NOTES:** No smoking in restaurant
CARDS:

★★74% ❀ Manor House

Gallanach Rd PA34 4LS
☎ 01631 562087 🖹 01631 563053
Dir: *Follow signs MacBrayne Ferries and pass ferry entrance for hotel on right*

The welcoming atmosphere, well motivated staff and good food are all part of the appeal of this charming small hotel, a former Georgian dower house. Wonderful views over Oban Bay and islands can be enjoyed. The public rooms are delightful, and a daily-changing dinner menu using good quality local produce is a feature of the intimate dining room. The non-smoking bedrooms, with attractive colour schemes, have been thoughtfully equipped and are comfortably furnished.
ROOMS: 11 en suite No smoking in all bedrooms s fr £80; d fr £160 (incl. bkfst & dinner) * LB **FACILITIES:** Xmas **PARKING:** 20 **NOTES:** No children 12yrs No smoking in restaurant RS Nov-Feb
CARDS:

Read all about it! Newspapers delivered to bedrooms in four and five star hotels.

★★72% Willowburn
PA34 4TJ
☎ 01852 300276 300597
e-mail: willowburn.hotel@virgin.net
(For full entry see Clachan-Seil)

★★70% **Falls of Lora**
PA37 1PB
☎ 01631 710483 01631 710694
(For full entry see Connel)

★★70% ***Foxholes***
Cologin, Lerags PA34 4SE
☎ 01631 564982
Dir: *3m S of Oban*
A charming small country hotel, set in a quiet glen just south of Oban. The no-smoking bedrooms are decorated in attractive colour schemes with modern furnishings. There is a small dispense bar in the relaxing lounge.
ROOMS: 7 en suite **PARKING:** 8 **NOTES:** No dogs No smoking in restaurant Closed 31 Oct-Mar **CARDS:**

★★66% **Dungallan House Hotel**
Gallanach Rd PA34 4PD
☎ 01631 563799 01631 566711
e-mail: welcome@dungallanhotel-oban.co.uk
Dir: *at Argyll Square in town centre follow signs for Gallanch, hotel 0.5m from square*
From its elevated position set in attractive gardens, this friendly and relaxing hotel commands splendid views of Oban Bay. Public areas are comfortable and bedrooms well proportioned. Good home-cooked dinners invariably feature fish, seafood and beef, whilst breakfasts are equally enjoyable.
ROOMS: 13 rms (11 en suite) (2 fmly) s £40-£48; d £88-£96 (incl. bkfst) * LB **FACILITIES:** Xmas **CONF:** Board 35 **PARKING:** 20 **NOTES:** No smoking in restaurant Closed Nov & Feb **CARDS:**

★★61% ***Caledonian***
Station Square PA34 5RT
☎ 01631 563133 01631 562998
e-mail: sales@miltonhotels.com
Dir: *opposite railway station at edge of Oban Bay*
Situated opposite the railway station and ferry terminal, this large Victorian hotel, overlooking Oban Bay, has a spacious bar and choice of eating options. Bedrooms range from the comfortable modern executive and superior rooms to the smaller standards, which are more practical in appointment.
ROOMS: 70 en suite (10 fmly) **CONF:** Thtr 120 Class 60 Board 40 **SERVICES:** Lift **PARKING:** 6 **NOTES:** No smoking in restaurant **CARDS:**

★★61% **Lancaster**
Corran Esplanade PA34 5AD
☎ 01631 562587 01631 562587
e-mail: john@lancasterhotel.freeserve.co.uk
Dir: *on seafront near St Columba's Cathedral*
Lovely views over the bay towards the Isle of Mull can be enjoyed from this welcoming family-run hotel on the Esplanade. Bedrooms, although variable in size and in style, are comfortable and offer a good range of amenities. Public areas include a choice of contrasting lounges and bars and the swimming pool is an added attraction.

continued on p742

O

OBAN, continued

Lancaster Hotel, Oban

ROOMS: 27 rms (24 en suite) (3 fmly) s £27.50-£33; d £60 (incl. bkfst) * LB **FACILITIES:** STV Indoor swimming (H) Sauna Solarium Pool table Jacuzzi/spa Steam room **CONF:** Thtr 30 Class 30 Board 20 **PARKING:** 20 **CARDS:**

OLDMELDRUM, Aberdeenshire Map 15 NJ82

★★62% Meldrum Arms
The Square AB51 0DS
☎ 01651 872238 🖹 01651 872238
Dir: *off the B947, in centre of village*
From its position in the centre of the village, this family-run hotel combines a welcoming atmosphere with good value for money. Bedrooms, although compact, are modern in style and come with all the expected facilities. Public areas include a well stocked bar and separate restaurant with a wide range of food being offered in both areas.
ROOMS: 7 en suite 4 annexe rms (1 fmly) s £25-£38; d £58 (incl. bkfst) * **FACILITIES:** Pool table **CONF:** Thtr 80 Board 40 **PARKING:** 25 **NOTES:** No dogs (ex guide dogs) **CARDS:**

O

OLD RAYNE, Aberdeenshire Map 15 NJ62

★★62% Lodge
AB52 6RY
☎ 01464 851205 🖹 01464 851205
Dir: *A96 turn off Pitmachie, hotel on the right*
A relaxed and welcoming atmosphere is offered at this small family-run hotel, situated just off the A96. There is a cosy bar/lounge and smart dining room. Bedrooms are located in the main house and in the cedar annexe.
ROOMS: 6 annexe en suite (2 fmly) s fr £40; d fr £56 (incl. bkfst) * LB **FACILITIES:** Pool table **PARKING:** 60
CARDS:

ONICH, Highland Map 14 NN06

★★★70% ❀ Onich
PH33 6RY
☎ 01855 821214 🖹 01855 821484
e-mail: reservations@onich-fortwilliam.co.uk
Dir: *beside A82, 2m N of Ballachulish Bridge*
With well-tended gardens sweeping down to the picturesque shore of Loch Linnhe, this friendly hotel is an ideal base for the touring holidaymaker. Public areas include a choice of comfortable bars and relaxing lounges, and the attractive restaurant offers interesting Scottish fare. Bedrooms, many with loch views, offer comfortable modern appointments together with the expected amenities.

continued

ROOMS: 25 en suite (6 fmly) s £46-£60; d £72-£100 (incl. bkfst) * LB **FACILITIES:** STV Pool table Jacuzzi/spa Games room Xmas **CONF:** Class 20 Board 20 Del from £48.50 * **PARKING:** 50 **NOTES:** No smoking in restaurant **CARDS:**

See advert under FORT WILLIAM

★★★68% ❀❀ Allt-nan-Ros
PH33 6RY
☎ 01855 821210 🖹 01855 821462
e-mail: allt-nan-ros@zetnet.co.uk
Dir: *1.5m N of Ballachulish Bridge on A82*
Highland hospitality and good food are part of the appeal of this comfortable hotel, overlooking Loch Linnhe. Bedrooms are variable in size and modern in style. Inviting public areas include a well-stocked bar and pleasant south-facing lounge. House guests and diners will enjoy the relaxed yet formal style of attention, along with the splendid views.
ROOMS: 20 en suite (2 fmly) s £79.50; d £159 (incl. bkfst & dinner) * LB **FACILITIES:** Xmas **PARKING:** 30 **NOTES:** No smoking in restaurant **CARDS:**

See advert on opposite page

★★★67% Lodge on the Loch
PH33 6RY
☎ 01855 821237 🖹 01855 821463
e-mail: reservations@freedomglen.co.uk
Dir: *beside A82 - 5m N of Glencoe, 10m S of Fort William*
Palm trees grow in the attractive grounds of this friendly holiday hotel, which enjoys a panoramic outlook over Loch Linnhe. Public areas have a relaxing aura and include a comfortable lounge, a tastefully appointed restaurant with fine food and a snug canopy-draped bar. There are some smart new bedrooms to complement the range of accommodation available.
ROOMS: 18 rms (16 en suite) (1 fmly) s £69.50-£77; d £139-£199 (incl. bkfst & dinner) * LB **FACILITIES:** Leisure facilities at sister hotel entertainment Xmas **CONF:** Thtr 50 Class 30 Board 30 Del from £79 * **PARKING:** 25 **NOTES:** No children 12yrs No smoking in restaurant Closed Jan-Mar & Nov-23 Dec **CARDS:**

See advert under GLENCOE

★★66% *Creag Mhor*
PH33 6RY
☎ 01855 821379 🖹 01855 821579
Dir: *beside A82*
The genial owner welcomes guests old and new to his comfortable hotel overlooking Loch Linnhe. The bar is comfortably appointed and is popular for its good value meals. There are loch views from the spacious front-facing bedrooms. Rear rooms tend to be smaller and more practical in appointment.
ROOMS: 14 en suite (3 fmly) **PARKING:** 35 **NOTES:** No smoking in restaurant Closed last 3 wks Nov & first 2 wks Dec RS Late Nov-17 Jan (open Xmas & New Year) **CARDS:**

PAISLEY Hotels are listed under Glasgow Airport.

PEAT INN, Fife Map 12 NO40

Premier Collection

★★ Peat Inn
KY15 5LH
☎ 01334 840206 01334 840530
e-mail: reception@thepeatinn.co.uk
Dir: *6m SW of St Andrews at junct B940/B941*
Just six miles from St Andrews, this popular restaurant with rooms was originally a coaching inn. The creative cooking is of a consistently high quality, based mainly on local produce. Although a cooked breakfast is not served, superb continental trays are served in the bedrooms. The luxuriously appointed, split level bedroom suites offer a host of thoughtful extras including smart bathrooms adorned with Italian marble.
ROOMS: 8 en suite (2 fmly) s fr £95; d fr £145 (incl. cont bkfst) * LB **PARKING:** 24 **NOTES:** No smoking in restaurant Closed Sun, Mon, Xmas day & New Years day **CARDS:**

PEEBLES, Scottish Borders Map 11 NT24

★★★79% **Cringletie House**
EH45 8PL
☎ 01721 730233 01721 730244
e-mail: enquiries@cringletie.com
Dir: *2m N on A703*
Set in 28 acres of grounds, this immaculately maintained baronial mansion features a superb walled garden that provides much of the kitchen's produce during the summer. Delightful public rooms include a cocktail lounge with adjoining conservatory, and a small library. The refurbished bedrooms are very comfortable and service throughout is excellent.
ROOMS: 14 en suite (2 fmly) s £75-£90; d £150-£180 (incl. bkfst) * LB **FACILITIES:** STV Tennis (hard) Fishing Croquet lawn Putting green Xmas **CONF:** Thtr 60 Class 30 Board 20 Del from £110 * **PARKING:** 30 **NOTES:** No smoking in restaurant **CARDS:**

See advert on this page

★★★71% **Peebles Hydro**
EH45 8LX
☎ 01721 720602 01721 722999
e-mail: reservations@peebleshotelhydro.co.uk
Dir: *on A702, one third mile out of town*
This hotel commands magnificent views across the valley from its hillside position on the eastern approach to Peebles. The well equipped bedrooms come in a variety of styles and sizes and include two-roomed family units. The range of leisure activities, both indoors and out, are second to none; there's also a lively brasserie open during the day.

continued on p744

PEEBLES, continued

ROOMS: 133 en suite (24 fmly) s £94-£102; d £149.50-£204 (incl. bkfst & dinner) * LB **FACILITIES:** STV Indoor swimming (H) Tennis (hard) Riding Snooker Sauna Solarium Gym Pool table Croquet lawn Putting green Jacuzzi/spa Badminton Beautician Hairdressing entertainment ch fac Xmas **CONF:** Thtr 450 Class 200 Board 74 Del from £123 * **SERVICES:** Lift **PARKING:** 200 **NOTES:** No dogs (ex guide dogs) Civ Wed 250 **CARDS:**

See advert on opposite page

★★★69% Castle Venlaw

Edinburgh Rd EH45 8QG
☎ 01721 720384 01721 724066
e-mail: enquiries@venlaw.co.uk
Dir: *off A703 Peebles/Edinburgh road, 0.75m from Peebles*

A splendid turreted mansion in four acres of grounds and gardens, set high above the town. Most of the bedrooms are very spacious and command fine views, three have an adjoining turret room. Light meals and pre-dinner drinks are served in the oak panelled Library Bar. More formal meals can be enjoyed in the attractive restaurant.

ROOMS: 12 en suite (3 fmly) No smoking in 5 bedrooms s £55-£80; d £90-£130 (incl. bkfst) LB **FACILITIES:** STV Croquet lawn Xmas **CONF:** Thtr 40 Class 20 Board 24 Del from £75 * **PARKING:** 30 **NOTES:** No smoking in restaurant **CARDS:**

See advert on opposite page

★★★68% Park

Innerleithen Rd EH45 8BA
☎ 01721 720451 01721 723510
e-mail: reserve@parkpeebles.co.uk
Dir: *in centre of Peebles opposite filling station*

The Park Hotel is little sister to the larger Hydro; guests can use the Hydro's extensive leisure facilities and yet enjoy the comfort of a smaller hotel. Public areas enjoy views of the gardens and include an attractive tartan-clad bar, a relaxing lounge and a well proportioned wood-panelled restaurant. Well equipped bedrooms vary in size, those in the original house are very spacious.

ROOMS: 24 en suite s £64-£92; d £116-£160 (incl. bkfst & dinner) * LB **FACILITIES:** Putting green Access to leisure facilities of Peebles Hotel Hydro Xmas **PARKING:** 50 **CARDS:**

★★68% Kingsmuir

Springhill Rd EH45 9EP
☎ 01721 720151 01721 721795
e-mail: chrisburn@kingsmuir.scotborder.co.uk
Dir: *cross Tweed Bridge from High St, then straight ahead up Springhill Rd, hotel is 300 yds on right hand side*

Located in a residential area on the south side of the River Tweed, this hotel offers friendly service and well equipped accommodation. There is a choice of lounges and good value home-cooked meals are available in the dining room and the bar.

ROOMS: 10 en suite (2 fmly) No smoking in 5 bedrooms **CONF:** Thtr 40 Class 20 Board 20 **PARKING:** 35 **NOTES:** No smoking in restaurant **CARDS:**

PERTH, Perth & Kinross — Map 11 NO12

★★★80% Kinfauns Castle

Kinfauns PH2 7JZ
☎ 01738 620777 01738 620778
e-mail: email@kinfaunscastle.co.uk
Dir: *2m beyond Perth on the A90 Perth/Dundee road*

A distinctive hotel retaining many fine architectural features, such as ornate ceilings and marble fireplaces, combined with a range of Far Eastern artefacts. Good food prepared from quality produce is offered in the beautiful panelled restaurant. Bedrooms range from first class suites to master and standard rooms, all with high quality furnishings and luxurious bathrooms.

ROOMS: 16 en suite s £110-£170; d £180-£300 (incl. bkfst) * **FACILITIES:** STV Fishing Croquet lawn Putting green Xmas **CONF:** Thtr 60 Class 50 Board 24 Del from £150 * **PARKING:** 40 **NOTES:** No children 8yrs No smoking in restaurant Civ Wed 60 **CARDS:**

★★★75% Huntingtower

Crieff Rd PH1 3JT
☎ 01738 583771 01738 583777
e-mail: reception@piersland@talk21.com
Dir: *3m W off A85*

A delightful Edwardian house set in attractive landscaped grounds. The stylish bedrooms are generally spacious and provide a host of modern facilities. The elegant, traditional day rooms include a cosy lounge, a well stocked bar, a bright conservatory extension, and a restaurant offering an imaginative menu based on classic, modern and ethnic dishes.

ROOMS: 31 en suite 3 annexe en suite (2 fmly) s fr £89.50; d fr £110 (incl. bkfst) * LB **FACILITIES:** STV Xmas **CONF:** Thtr 200 Class 140 Board 30 Del from £103 * **SERVICES:** Lift **PARKING:** 100 **NOTES:** No smoking in restaurant Civ Wed 100 **CARDS:**

See advert on opposite page

★★★75% Murrayshall Country House Hotel & Golf Course

New Scone PH2 7PH
☎ 01738 551171 01738 552595
Dir: *from Perth take A94 towards Coupar Angus, 1m from Perth turn right to Murrayshall just before New Scone*

Corporate visitors and golfers are attracted to this impressive mansion house which is set amid 300 acres of parkland and boasts its own challenging golf course; a second course was due to open after our press date. Bedrooms, which are comfortably appointed and well equipped, range from superior suites and executive rooms, to standard rooms. On the cooler evenings, a welcoming log fire warms the well stocked bar. Adjacent, the Old Masters' restaurant provides an appropriate setting for the fine dining experience offered by the talented kitchen team. Staff are friendly and willing to please.

ROOMS: 27 en suite 14 annexe en suite (3 fmly) No smoking in 1 bedroom s £98-£128; d £146-£176 (incl. bkfst & dinner) * LB **FACILITIES:** STV Golf 36 Tennis (hard) Sauna Gym Putting green Jacuzzi/spa Driving range Xmas **CONF:** Thtr 180 Class 30 Board 30 Del from £96 * **PARKING:** 80 **CARDS:**

★★★67% Lovat

90 Glasgow Rd PH2 0LT
☎ 01738 636555 01738 643123
e-mail: e-mail@lovat.co.uk
Dir: *from M90 follow signs for Stirling to rdbt, then turn right into Glasgow Rd, hotel situated 1.50m on right*

A welcoming atmosphere prevails at this popular business and tourist hotel which is situated beside the Glasgow Road. The smartly decorated bedrooms are comfortably modern in style and offer a good range of amenities. In the public areas there is an attractive conservatory lounge, and a spacious bar where a range of bistro/bar meals is offered. A formal fixed price menu is provided in the smart restaurant.

ROOMS: 30 en suite (1 fmly) No smoking in 12 bedrooms s £87-£104; d £99-£133 (incl. bkfst) * LB **FACILITIES:** STV Pool table Xmas **CONF:** Thtr 200 Class 70 Board 70 Del from £72.50 * **PARKING:** 40 **NOTES:** No dogs (ex guide dogs) No smoking in restaurant **CARDS:**

See advert on opposite page

The Peebles Hydro and its sister hotel the Park, just 700 yards away, offer friendly comfort, fine food, a stunning Borders location and a range of indoor and outdoor activities you have to see to believe.

For a day or two, or a week or two, there's something for everyone – *see our listings under Peebles*

THE PEEBLES HOTEL HYDRO
PEEBLES EH45 8LX, SCOTLAND
Tel: 01721 720602 Fax: 01721 722999

This family run hotel is situated only ½ mile from the city centre. All bedrooms are en-suite with hospitality tray, hairdryer & satellite TV etc. Ladies, non-smoking and family rooms available. There is a beautiful Conservatory, large bistro bar with a small intimate restaurant for more formal dining.

Glasgow Road, Perth PH2 0LT
t. 01738 636555 f. 01738 643123
E-mail: e-mail@lovat.co.uk
Web site: www.scotlandshotels.co.uk

CASTLE VENLAW HOTEL

Edinburgh Road, Peebles EH45 8QG
Telephone: 01721 720384
Email: enquiries@venlaw.co.uk

Built in 1782 and now fully refurbished, this magnificent castle stands atop Venlaw Hill enjoying panoramic views over Peebles, the River Tweed and surrounding countryside. The Castle has retained its old character whilst skillfully adding modern touches so important to today's traveller. Peebles is the ideal centre for touring, sporting or relaxing with such attractions as Traquair House close by. It is also an ideal base for visiting Edinburgh.

PERTH, continued

★★★67% Queens Hotel

Leonard St PH2 8HB
☎ 01738 442222 🖷 01738 638496
e-mail: e-mail@queensperth.co.uk

Close to the railway and bus stations and within easy reach of central amenities, this popular business and tourist hotel offers a welcoming atmosphere and good levels of guest care. Public areas include a bright foyer lounge, well stocked bar, and an attractive first floor restaurant. Bedrooms, which include both superior and standard rooms, are smartly decorated and offer comfortable modern furnishings. Leisure and banqueting facilities are added attractions.

ROOMS: 51 en suite (6 fmly) No smoking in 16 bedrooms s fr £89.50; d fr £52 (incl. bkfst) * LB **FACILITIES:** STV Indoor swimming (H) Sauna Gym Pool table Jacuzzi/spa Steam room Xmas **CONF:** Thtr 270 Class 120 Board 70 Del from £67.50 * **SERVICES:** Lift **PARKING:** 50 **NOTES:** No dogs (ex guide dogs) **CARDS:**

★★★60% Quality Hotel Perth

Leonard St PH2 8HE
☎ 01738 624141 🖷 01738 639912
e-mail: admin@gb628.u-net.com

Dir: *from A9 head for city centre & pass Perth Leisure Pool on right. Turn right & continue for 300yds*

Situated beside the railway station this substantial Victorian hotel is also conveniently positioned to give easy access to central amenities. Spacious public areas with lofty ceilings include a choice of bars and lounge areas. The Premier Plus bedrooms offer more space and have extra facilities than the more varied standard rooms.

ROOMS: 70 en suite (4 fmly) No smoking in 25 bedrooms s fr £71; d fr £83 * LB **FACILITIES:** STV Gym Mini-gym Golf simulator entertainment ch fac Xmas **CONF:** Thtr 300 Class 150 Board 30 Del from £55 * **SERVICES:** Lift **PARKING:** 100 **NOTES:** No smoking in restaurant Civ Wed 300 **CARDS:**

★★64% *The New County Hotel*

26 County Place PH2 8EE
☎ 01738 623355 🖷 01738 628969
e-mail: info@countyhotel.co.uk

In a central location, this friendly hotel provides comfortable, modern bedrooms. The restaurant offers a good selection of well cooked dishes and food is also available throughout the day in the popular bar.

ROOMS: 23 en suite (4 fmly) **CONF:** Thtr 110 Class 60 Board 40 **PARKING:** 10 **NOTES:** No smoking in restaurant Closed 25 Dec **CARDS:**

> Fancy a Singapore Sling? Bar staff in five star hotels should be skilled cocktail mixers.

★65% Woodlea

23 York Place PH2 8EP
☎ 01738 621744 🖷 01738 621744

Dir: *take A9 into Perth city centre, hotel is on left next to church & opposite library*

A relaxed and friendly atmosphere prevails at this small family-run hotel close to central amenities. The bright airy bedrooms make best use of available space and offer modern facilities. Public areas include a cosy lounge and the high tea menu is a popular feature in the dining room.

ROOMS: 13 rms (11 en suite) (2 fmly) s £30-£40; d £46-£50 (incl. bkfst) * **PARKING:** 4 **NOTES:** No dogs (ex guide dogs) No smoking in restaurant

Express by Holiday Inn

200 Dunkeld Rd, Inveralmond PH1 3AQ
☎ 01738 636666 🖷 01738 633363

Dir: *turn off A9 Inverness to Stirling Rd at Inveralmond rdbt onto A912 signposted Perth. Turn right at 1st rdbt & follow signs for hotel*

A modern budget hotel offering comfortable accommodation in refreshing, spacious and comprehensively-equipped bedrooms, en suite bathrooms with power showers and continental buffet breakfast included in the room rate. Suitable for business travellers or families. For further details and the Express by Holiday Inn phone number, consult the Hotel Groups page.

ROOMS: 81 en suite (incl. cont bkfst) d £52.50-£55 * **CONF:** Thtr 60 Class 20 Board 20 Del £74.50 *

PETERHEAD, Aberdeenshire — Map 15 NK14

★★★★68% Waterside Inn

Fraserburgh Rd AB42 3BN
☎ 01779 471121 🖷 01779 470670
e-mail: info@waterside.macdonald-hotels.co.uk

Dir: *from Aberdeen A90, 1st rdbt turn left signed Fraserburgh, cross small rdbt, hotel at end of rd*

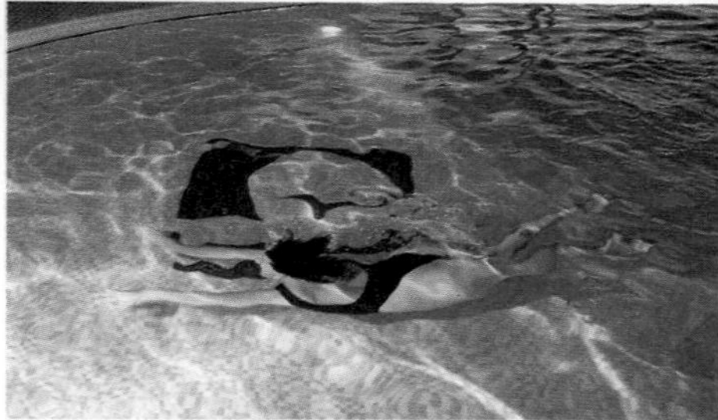

The atmosphere is welcoming at this business and tourist hotel. The attractive public areas include a choice of bars and a lounge.

continued

Accommodation ranges from executive rooms and suites to studio rooms, and all are well equipped.
ROOMS: 69 en suite 40 annexe en suite (15 fmly) No smoking in 55 bedrooms **FACILITIES:** STV Indoor swimming (H) Snooker Sauna Solarium Gym Jacuzzi/spa Steam room Childrens play area Sunbeds entertainment ch fac **CONF:** Thtr 250 Class 100 Board 50 **PARKING:** 250 **NOTES:** No smoking in restaurant Civ Wed 250
CARDS:

★★★65% *Palace*

Prince St AB42 1PL
☎ 01779 474821 🖷 01779 476119
Dir: *from Aberdeen, take the A90 and follow signs to Peterhead, on entering Peterhead, turn into Prince Street, then right into main car park*

From its position close to central amenities, this comfortable hotel has particular appeal for the visiting businessman and is also a popular venue for local functions. A lively atmosphere prevails in the spacious split-level café/bar, while the ambience in the comfortable cocktail bar and adjacent Brasserie restaurant is more formal. Bedrooms, with modern appointments, range from spacious executive rooms to the smaller standard rooms.
ROOMS: 66 en suite (2 fmly) No smoking in 8 bedrooms **FACILITIES:** STV Snooker Pool table entertainment **CONF:** Thtr 280 Class 100 Board 30 **SERVICES:** Lift **PARKING:** 90
CARDS:

PITLOCHRY, Perth & Kinross

Map 14 NN95

★★★76% ❀❀ *Pine Trees*

Strathview Ter PH16 5QR
☎ 01796 472121 🖷 01796 472460
e-mail: info@pinetrees-hotel.demon.co.uk
Dir: *along main street (Atholl Road), turn into Larchwood Road, follow signs for hotel*

This impressive Victorian mansion is set in 14 acres of mature grounds. Day rooms are decorated in the original style of the house. Features include wood panelling, ornate ceilings, and a wonderful marbled staircase with stained glass windows.

continued

PITLOCHRY, continued

Bedrooms are variable in size and are appointed to a sound standard.
ROOMS: 19 en suite No smoking in all bedrooms **FACILITIES:** Putting green entertainment **PARKING:** 20 **NOTES:** No smoking in restaurant
CARDS:

See advert on page 747

★★★72% Green Park
Clunie Bridge Rd PH16 5JY
☎ 01796 473248 01796 473520
e-mail: bookings@thegreenpark.co.uk
Dir: *turn off A9 at Pitlochry, follow signs 0.25m through town, hotel on banks of Loch Faskally*

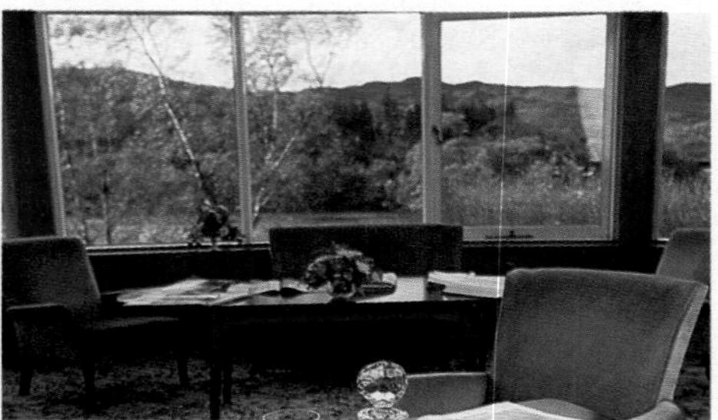

Lovely views over Loch Faskally can be enjoyed from this delightful and welcoming holiday hotel. Inviting public areas include a well stocked bar, a spacious lounge, and an attractive dining room in which to enjoy carefully prepared fare. Most of the comfortable bedrooms overlook the garden and loch. This is a non-smoking hotel.
ROOMS: 39 en suite No smoking in all bedrooms s £40-£65; d £80-£130 (incl. bkfst & dinner) * LB **FACILITIES:** Putting green Xmas
PARKING: 40 **NOTES:** No smoking in restaurant **CARDS:**

See advert on page 747

★★★68% Dundarach
Perth Rd PH16 5DJ
☎ 01796 472862 01796 473024
e-mail: hotel.pitlochry@btinternet.com
Dir: *S of town centre on main route*
Ongoing improvements have been taking place at this welcoming family run holiday hotel which stands in mature grounds at the south end of town. Many of the original architectural features have been carefully retained in the inviting public areas which include a choice of relaxing lounges, a well stocked bar, and an attractive conservatory restaurant. Bedrooms are comfortably modern in style and offer all the expected amenities.
ROOMS: 20 en suite 19 annexe en suite (7 fmly) No smoking in 8 bedrooms s £62; d £90 (incl. bkfst) * LB **FACILITIES:** STV Pool table Xmas **CONF:** Thtr 60 Class 40 Board 40 Del from £95 * **PARKING:** 39 **NOTES:** No dogs (ex guide dogs) No smoking in restaurant Closed Jan RS Dec-early Feb **CARDS:**

Best Western

★★★67% Scotland's
40 Bonnethill Rd PH16 5BT
☎ 01796 472292 01796 473284
e-mail: stay@scotlandshotel.co.uk
This long established tourist hotel is conveniently located in the centre of town and boasts a well equipped leisure centre. Public areas include a choice of eating options, foyer lounge, and a well stocked bar. Bedrooms vary in size and in style, however they are all comfortably appointed and furnished.

continued

ROOMS: 75 en suite (18 fmly) No smoking in 21 bedrooms s £42-£75; d £70-£125 (incl. bkfst) * LB **FACILITIES:** Indoor swimming (H) Sauna Solarium Gym Jacuzzi/spa Therapy treatments entertainment Xmas **CONF:** Thtr 200 Class 100 Board 30 Del from £85 * **SERVICES:** Lift **PARKING:** 87 **NOTES:** No dogs (ex guide dogs) No smoking in restaurant **CARDS:**

★★75% Knockendarroch House
Higher Oakfield PH16 5HT
☎ 01796 473473 01796 474068
e-mail: info@knockendarroch.co.uk
Dir: *turn off A9 going N at Pitlochry sign. After railway bridge, take 1st right, then 2nd left*
A friendly and relaxed atmosphere prevails at this delightful Victorian mansion, which stands in mature grounds with fine views over the Tummel Valley. There is no bar, but guests can enjoy a drink in the inviting lounges while perusing the daily fixed-price menu of freshly prepared dishes. Bedrooms are very comfortable and well equipped.
ROOMS: 12 en suite No smoking in all bedrooms s £73-£77; d £110-£118 (incl. bkfst & dinner) * LB **FACILITIES:** Leisure facilities at nearby hotel **PARKING:** 30 **NOTES:** No dogs (ex guide dogs) No children 10yrs No smoking in restaurant Closed Dec-Feb RS Nov
CARDS:

★★72% Acarsaid
8 Atholl Rd PH16 5BX
☎ 01796 472389 01796 473952
e-mail: acarsaid@msn.com
Dir: *take main road from A9 Perth to Inverness to Pitlochry, hotel on right hand side as you enter town*

This comfortable hotel stands in its own garden beside the main road on the east side of town. The well maintained bedrooms come in mixed sizes and styles and offer a good range of amenities. Inviting public areas include a choice of relaxing lounges and a spacious dining room. A courtesy coach is available to transport guests to the Festival Theatre.

continued

ROOMS: 19 en suite (1 fmly) No smoking in 15 bedrooms s £30-£40; d £60-£80 (incl. bkfst) * LB **FACILITIES:** Xmas **PARKING:** 20 **NOTES:** No dogs (ex guide dogs) No children 10yrs No smoking in restaurant Closed 3 Jan-10 Mar **CARDS:**

★★71% Westlands of Pitlochry

160 Atholl Rd PH16 5AR
☎ 01796 472266 🖹 01796 473994
e-mail: info@westlandshotel.co.uk
Dir: *turn off A9 into centre of Pitlochry, hotel situated at N end of town*

Many guests return regularly to this welcoming family-run hotel which, from its position beside the main road at the north end of town, is an ideal base for touring the surrounding countryside. Nicely presented public areas include a comfortable lounge for relaxation, a well stocked bar, and a smart restaurant where the varied menus focus of Taste of Scotland specialities. The comfortable bedrooms are modern in appointment and offer a good range of amenities.

ROOMS: 15 en suite (2 fmly) s £44-£59; d £78-£98 (incl. bkfst) * LB **FACILITIES:** Fishing Xmas **CONF:** Thtr 35 Class 24 Board 20 **PARKING:** 28 **NOTES:** No smoking in restaurant **CARDS:**

★★70% Balrobin

Higher Oakfield PH16 5HT
☎ 01796 472901 🖹 01796 474200
e-mail: balrobin@globalnet.co.uk
Dir: *leave A9 at Pitlochry junct, continue to town centre and follow brown tourists signs to hotel*

A welcoming atmosphere prevails at this comfortable family-run holiday hotel which, from its position above the town, enjoys views of the surrounding countryside. Public areas include a relaxing lounge, well stocked bar, and an attractive restaurant offering traditional home cooked fare. The well maintained bedrooms are comfortably modern in appointment.

ROOMS: 15 en suite (2 fmly) s £39.50-£42.50; d £68-£79 (incl. bkfst) * LB **PARKING:** 15 **NOTES:** No children 5yrs No smoking in restaurant Closed Nov-Feb **CARDS:**

★★69% Claymore

162 Atholl Rd PH16 5AR
☎ 01796 472888 🖹 01796 474037
Dir: *turn off A9 into Pitlochry, hotel last on right hand side after passing through town centre - heading north*

This comfortable hotel stands in its own well tended garden on the north side of town. Public areas include a comfortable lounge; a cosy bar which has an attractive conservatory extension; and a smart restaurant for more formal dining. Bedrooms, with attractive decor and pretty co-ordinated fabrics, are modern and come with the expected amenities.

ROOMS: 7 en suite 4 annexe en suite (1 fmly) No smoking in 7 bedrooms **PARKING:** 25 **NOTES:** No smoking in restaurant Closed 3 Jan-14 Feb **CARDS:**

★★69% Craigvrack

West Moulin Rd PH16 5EQ
☎ 01796 472399 🖹 01796 473990
e-mail: irene@craigvrack-hotel.demon.co.uk
Dir: *from the main street, turn into West Moulin Road, Craigvrack has three large flagpoles on the lawn and is illuminated at night*

This welcoming family run holiday hotel has lovely views. Bedrooms, though variable in size, offer pretty co-ordinated colour schemes and comfortable modern furnishings. Inviting public areas include a choice of relaxing lounges, a well stocked bar and an attractive restaurant offering varied menus.

continued

ROOMS: 16 en suite (2 fmly) s £28-£47; d £56-£70 (incl. bkfst) * LB **FACILITIES:** Xmas **CONF:** Thtr 30 Class 32 Board 16 Del from £59.95 * **PARKING:** 20 **NOTES:** No smoking in restaurant **CARDS:**

★★69% Moulin Hotel

11-13 Kirkmichael Rd, Moulin PH16 5EW
☎ 01796 472196 🖹 01796 474098
e-mail: hotel@moulin.u-net.com
Dir: *turn off A9 into Pitlochry in centre of town take A924 signed Braemar. Moulin village 0.75m outside Pitlochry*

At this hotel, guests can relax in the comfort of the residents lounge and bar, or in the original Moulin Inn bar, which dates back to 1695 and is worth a visit to sample the home-brewed beer. Enjoyable home cooked fare is served in the attractive restaurant. Bedrooms, with pleasing colour schemes, are comfortably modern in style.

ROOMS: 15 en suite (3 fmly) s £40-£60; d £50-£75 (incl. bkfst) * LB **FACILITIES:** Pool table entertainment **PARKING:** 30 **NOTES:** No smoking in restaurant **CARDS:**

★★68% Birchwood

THE CIRCLE
Selected Individual Hotels
GREAT BRITAIN

2 East Moulin Rd PH16 5DW
☎ 01796 472477 🖹 01796 473951
e-mail: viv@birchwoodhotel.co.uk
Dir: *signposted from Atholl Rd on South side of town*

This comfortable and well maintained hotel stands in four acres of mature grounds at the east end of Pitlochry. Inviting public areas include a relaxing lounge where refreshments are served from a dispense bar, and a smart dining room which offers wholesome cooking. Bedrooms are attractively decorated and thoughtfully equipped.

ROOMS: 12 en suite No smoking in all bedrooms s £39; d £78 (incl. bkfst) * LB **FACILITIES:** Xmas **PARKING:** 25 **NOTES:** No dogs (ex guide dogs) No smoking in restaurant Closed Jan-mid Mar **CARDS:**

★★63% *Pitlochry Hydro*

Knockard Rd PH16 5JH
☎ 01796 472666 🖹 01796 472238
Dir: *turn off A9, proceed to town centre and turn right onto A924 Braemar Rd. Hotel is 0.5m on right*

From its position above the town, this substantial hotel enjoys a lovely outlook over the surrounding countryside, and remains a popular base for visiting tour groups. Bedrooms are comfortably modern in style and offer a good range of amenities. Live entertainment features regularly in the public areas and the leisure centre is an added attraction.

ROOMS: 64 en suite (6 fmly) **FACILITIES:** STV Indoor swimming (H) Snooker Sauna Solarium Gym Croquet lawn Putting green Jacuzzi/spa **CONF:** Thtr 120 Class 40 Board 40 **SERVICES:** Lift **PARKING:** 100 **NOTES:** No smoking in restaurant Closed Jan **CARDS:**

P

PLOCKTON, Highland

Map 14 NG83

★★73% Haven

Innes St IV52 8TW

☎ 01599 544334 & 544223 Fax 01599 544467

Dir: *turn off A87 just before Kyle of Lochalsh, after Balmacara there is a signpost to Plockton, hotel on main road just before lochside*

Set in the picturesque conservation village of Plockton, well known as the location for the TV series 'Hamish Macbeth', the Haven lies close to the harbour and bay. The comfortable well equipped bedrooms include two splendid suites, but it is the quality of the food which attracts both visitors and locals. The spacious restaurant is complemented by two lounges and a cosy bar.

ROOMS: 15 en suite s £36-£39; d £72-£78 (incl. bkfst) * LB **PARKING:** 7 **NOTES:** No children 7yrs No smoking in restaurant Closed 20 Dec-1 Feb **CARDS:**

POLMONT, Falkirk

Map 11 NS97

★★★★70% Inchyra Grange

Grange Rd FK2 0YB

☎ 01324 711911 Fax 01324 716134

Dir: *just beyond BP Social Club*

This former manor house is ideally located near to the M9. Public areas are bright and modern, and include a choice of eating options. Peligrinos offers a range of Italian specialities in an informal atmosphere. The Priory Restaurant provides a fine, formal dining experience. Bedrooms are mostly spacious with comfortable modern appointments.

ROOMS: 109 en suite (5 fmly) No smoking in 57 bedrooms **FACILITIES:** STV Indoor swimming (H) Tennis (hard) Sauna Solarium Gym Jacuzzi/spa Steam room Beauty therapy room Aerobics studio Aromatherapist **CONF:** Thtr 600 Class 250 Board 80 **SERVICES:** Lift **PARKING:** 400 **NOTES:** No smoking in restaurant **CARDS:**

POOLEWE, Highland

Map 14 NG88

★★★65% Pool House Hotel

IV22 2LD

☎ 01445 781272 Fax 01445 781403

e-mail: poolhouse@inverewe.co.uk

Dir: *6m N of Gairloch on the A832. Located in the middle of Poolewe village, next to the bridge at the edge of the sea*

In a lovely waterside position at the head of Loch Ewe, this friendly hotel commands stunning sea views across the loch towards the famous Inverewe gardens. The pretty bedrooms are well equipped and the public rooms are comfortable. The chef produces a range of food that can be enjoyed in the lounge bar or the traditional dining room.

continued

ROOMS: 9 en suite No smoking in all bedrooms s £65; d £50-£125 (incl. bkfst) * LB **FACILITIES:** Xmas **PARKING:** 20 **NOTES:** No dogs (ex guide dogs) No children 14yrs No smoking in restaurant Closed Jan-Feb **CARDS:**

PORT APPIN, Argyll & Bute

Map 14 NM94

Premier Collection

★★★ Airds

PA38 4DF

☎ 01631 730236 Fax 01631 730535

e-mail: airds@airds-hotel.com

Dir: *16m S of Ballachulish Bridge turn off A828 and drive for 2m*

Overlooking Loch Linnhe, this is a relaxing destination. Bedrooms are furnished with flair, and the lounges offer an environment in which to unwind totally. There is also an enclosed sun porch from which to take in the stunning views. In the kitchen, top quality ingredients are prepared with a light touch.

ROOMS: 12 en suite d fr £272 (incl. bkfst & dinner) * LB **FACILITIES:** Fishing Xmas **PARKING:** 15 **NOTES:** No smoking in restaurant Closed 23-27 Dec & 6-26 Jan **CARDS:**

PORT ASKAIG See Islay, Isle of

PORTMAHOMACK, Highland

Map 14 NH98

★★65% Caledonian

Main St IV20 1YS

☎ 01862 871345 Fax 01862 871757

e-mail: info@caleyhotel.co.uk

Dir: *from S A9 to Nigg rdbt then B9165 for 10m to village. From N travel through Tain, turn off for Portmahomack after 0.5m*

Situated in the centre of this pretty village, the Caledonian overlooks a sandy beach across the Dornoch Firth to the Sutherland hills. Hotel service is friendly and attentive. A popular range of food is available from the bar and dining room menus.

ROOMS: 15 en suite (5 fmly) s £25-£33; d £45-£57 (incl. bkfst) * LB **FACILITIES:** Pool table entertainment **PARKING:** 16 **NOTES:** No smoking in restaurant **CARDS:**

PORT OF MENTEITH, Stirling

Map 11 NN50

★★72% Lake of Menteith

FK8 3RA

☎ 01877 385258 Fax 01877 385671

Dir: *just off A81, beside village church 200yds on right*

This is a charming holiday hotel. The inviting sitting room and conservatory enjoy stunning views over the lake. Comfortable bedrooms range from spacious superior rooms to cosy standard

continued

rooms; all are tastefully decorated and offer many thoughtful extras.
ROOMS: 16 en suite No smoking in all bedrooms s £35-£75; d £70-£150 (incl. bkfst) * LB **FACILITIES:** Xmas **CONF:** Thtr 30 Board 20 **PARKING:** 35 **NOTES:** No children 8yrs No smoking in restaurant RS Nov-Feb **CARDS:**

PORTPATRICK, Dumfries & Galloway Map 10 NX05

★★★73% Fernhill

Heugh Rd DG9 8TD
☎ 01776 810220 01776 810596
e-mail: fernhill@portpatrick.demon.co.uk
Dir: *from Stranraer A77 to Portpatrick, 100yds past Portpatrick village sign, turn right before war memorial. Hotel is 1st on left*
Commanding panoramic views over the harbour and the Irish Sea this friendly hotel is ideally situated for access to the many activities in the area. Bedrooms are comfortable, some with balconies overlooking the harbour. The conservatory restaurant is an ideal location for a relaxing breakfast or dinner.
ROOMS: 14 en suite 9 annexe en suite (2 fmly) s £58-£90; d £85-£110 (incl. bkfst) * LB **FACILITIES:** STV Leisure facilities available at sister hotel in Stranraer Xmas **CONF:** Thtr 24 Class 12 Board 12 **PARKING:** 32 **CARDS:**

Premier Collection

★★ Knockinaam Lodge

DG9 9AD
☎ 01776 810471 01776 810435
Dir: *from A77 or A75 follow signs to Portpatrick. 2m W of Lochans watch for hotel sign on the right, take next left and follow signs to hotel*
This idyllically situated hotel, next to its own beach and surrounded by cliffs on three sides, offers the perfect 'get away from it all' environment. Bedrooms are very comfortable with extras such as current novels and magazines by the bedside. There is a drawing room and bar offering an extensive range of malt whiskies. The set four course dinner and comprehensive wine list are a highlight of any stay.
ROOMS: 10 en suite (6 fmly) s £100-£135; d £160-£320 (incl. bkfst & dinner) * LB **FACILITIES:** STV Croquet lawn ch fac Xmas **CONF:** Board 20 **PARKING:** 20 **NOTES:** No smoking in restaurant Civ Wed 45 **CARDS:**

PORTREE See Skye, Isle of

Early start? Hotels at all star levels should provide in-room alarm clocks and/or alarm calls.

PORT WILLIAM, Dumfries & Galloway Map 10 NX34

★★★65% *Corsemalzie House*

DG8 9RL
☎ 01988 860254 01988 860213
e-mail: corsemalzie@ndirect.co.uk
Dir: *From A75 turn left at Newton Stewart rdbt onto A714, by passing Wigtown: turn right after crossing bridge at Bladnoch onto B7005 for Corsemalzie*
This 19th-century Scottish country mansion is set in 40 acres of woodland gardens and offers a comfortable retreat for those keen on outdoor pursuits. A good level of hospitality is provided by friendly and attentive staff.
ROOMS: 14 en suite (1 fmly) No smoking in 3 bedrooms **FACILITIES:** Fishing Croquet lawn Putting green Game shooting **PARKING:** 31 **NOTES:** No smoking in restaurant Closed 21 Jan-5 Mar & Xmas **CARDS:**

POWFOOT, Dumfries & Galloway Map 11 NY16

★★70% Golf

Links Av DG12 5PN
☎ 01461 700254 01461 700288
e-mail: info@powfoothotel.co.uk
Dir: *turn off M74 at Gretna onto A75 round Annan bypass, hotel sign 2m on turn left onto B724 and follow sign to Powfoot village*
Popular with golfers and providing a retreat for business people, this hotel sits next to the local golf course at the end of the village and enjoys panoramic views across the Solway Firth. Bedrooms and public areas are comfortable and service is friendly and obliging.
ROOMS: 18 en suite s fr £55; d fr £74 (incl. bkfst) * LB **FACILITIES:** Pool table Xmas **CONF:** Thtr 150 Class 70 Board 70 Del from £85 * **SERVICES:** air con **PARKING:** 60 **CARDS:**

POWMILL, Perth & Kinross Map 11 NT09

★★★66% Gartwhinzean Hotel

FK14 7NW
☎ 01577 840595 01577 840779
Dir: *from M90 junct 6 take A977 Kincardine Bridge Road, in approx 8m the village of Powmill, hotel at end of village*
A welcoming atmosphere prevails at this family-run country inn, which stands in its own garden beside the A997 on the west side of the village. Bedrooms are contained in a modern wing and the majority are generously proportioned with attractive decor and comfortable pine furnishings. Public areas have a more traditional feel and include a panelled lounge, choice of contrasting bars, as well as a bistro and restaurant which are quite rustic in style.
ROOMS: 23 en suite (6 fmly) No smoking in 6 bedrooms s £55-£60; d £85-£95 (incl. bkfst) * LB **FACILITIES:** Pool table **CONF:** Thtr 250 Class 80 Board 30 Del from £75 * **PARKING:** 150 **NOTES:** No dogs (ex guide dogs) No smoking in restaurant Civ Wed 100 **CARDS:**

PRESTWICK, South Ayrshire Map 10 NS32

★★★66% Parkstone

Esplanade KA9 1QN
☎ 01292 477286 01292 477671
e-mail: info@parkstonehotel.co.uk
Dir: *from Prestwick Main St (A79) turn west to seafront - hotel 600yds*
Situated on the sea front in a quiet residential area, this family-run hotel caters for business visitors as well as golfers. There is a wing of smart new bedrooms and the original rooms are furnished to a

continued

PRESTWICK, continued

similar standard. In addition to the enjoyable and good value restaurant meals, one can eat well from the lounge bar menu.
ROOMS: 22 en suite (2 fmly) s £41-£48; d £66-£72 (incl. bkfst) * LB **CONF:** Thtr 100 **PARKING:** 34 **NOTES:** No dogs No smoking in restaurant **CARDS:**

RENFREW For hotels see Glasgow Airport

ROSEBANK, South Lanarkshire Map 11 NS84

★★★71% Popinjay
Lanark Rd ML8 5QB
☎ 01555 860441 01555 860204
e-mail: sales@popinjayhotel.co.uk
Dir: *on A72 between Hamilton & Lanark*

Best Western

This well established hotel with Tudor style facade has grounds that extend to the banks of the River Clyde. Public areas include a panelled bar with open fireplaces and the elegant restaurant looking towards the river is a fitting venue to enjoy the fine cuisine. Functions, especially weddings, are popular (the gardens provide a lovely backdrop). The well equipped bedrooms vary in size.
ROOMS: 40 en suite 5 annexe en suite (2 fmly) No smoking in 19 bedrooms s fr £59; d fr £75 (incl. bkfst) * LB **FACILITIES:** STV Fishing Xmas **CONF:** Thtr 250 Class 120 Board 60 **PARKING:** 300 **CARDS:**

See advert on opposite page

ROSLIN, Midlothian Map 11 NT26

★★63% Roslin Glen
2 Penicuik Rd EH25 9LH
☎ 0131 440 2029 0131 440 2229
e-mail: roslinglen@aol.com
Dir: *in the village of Roslin 1m from the A701 Edinburgh/Peebles Rd. 2m S of Edinburgh City bypass*

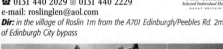

THE CIRCLE Selected Individual Hotels GREAT BRITAIN

This family-run hotel provides a relaxed, welcoming atmosphere. The bright, cheery bedrooms come in a variety of sizes, and a popular choice of dishes is available in the bar and cosy restaurant.
ROOMS: 7 en suite (3 fmly) **FACILITIES:** STV Pool table **CONF:** Class 50 Board 50 **PARKING:** 6 **NOTES:** No smoking in restaurant **CARDS:**

See advert under EDINBURGH

Read all about it! Newspapers delivered to bedrooms in four and five star hotels.

ROSYTH, Fife Map 11 NT18

★★63% Gladyer Inn
Heath Rd, Ridley Dr KY11 2BT
☎ 01383 419977 01383 411728
e-mail: gladyer@aol.com
Dir: *from junct 1 of M90 travel along Admiralty Road, past rdbt then first road on the left*

Within easy reach of the dockyard and Forth Bridge, this purpose-built hotel is a popular base for the visiting businessman. Although compact, the bedrooms are modern in style and offer a wide range of amenities. Public areas include a choice of contrasting bars and a smart restaurant, where both fixed-price and carte menus are available.
ROOMS: 21 en suite (3 fmly) s fr £39.50; d fr £55 (incl. bkfst) * LB **FACILITIES:** STV Pool table entertainment **CONF:** Thtr 100 Class 70 Board 80 Del from £50 * **PARKING:** 81 **NOTES:** No dogs (ex guide dogs) **CARDS:**

ROY BRIDGE, Highland Map 14 NN28

★★★69% Glenspean Lodge Hotel
PH31 4AW
☎ 01397 712223 01397 712660
e-mail: wdgsl@aol.com
Dir: *2m E of Roy Bridge, turn right off A82 at Spean Bridge onto A86*

Best Western

Lovely views over the glen and Nevis mountains can be enjoyed from this delightful country house hotel which is set amid carefully landscaped gardens. Inviting public areas include a relaxing lounge, a spacious well stocked bar, and attractive restaurant where the carte provides a selection of carefully prepared Scottish dishes. The variable sized bedrooms with pleasing colour schemes are comfortably furnished in pine.
ROOMS: 15 en suite s £49-£75; d £80-£130 (incl. bkfst) * LB **FACILITIES:** Xmas **CONF:** Thtr 50 Class 25 Board 25 **PARKING:** 50 **NOTES:** No dogs (ex guide dogs) No smoking in restaurant Closed Nov-Feb Civ Wed 65 **CARDS:**

See advert under FORT WILLIAM

★★64% *Stronlossit*
PH31 4AG
☎ 01397 712253

THE CIRCLE Selected Individual Hotels GREAT BRITAIN

A relaxed informal atmosphere prevails at this family-run holiday hotel which is situated at the east end of the village. Bedrooms, though variable in size, are comfortably modern in style and offer the expected amenities. Public areas include a homely bar, small lounge and an attractive restaurant where the carte offers a range of dishes at competitive prices.
ROOMS: 9 en suite (2 fmly) **PARKING:** 30 **NOTES:** Closed 10 Nov-10 Dec & Jan **CARDS:**

ST ANDREWS, Fife

Map 12 NO51

see also Leuchars

★★★★★70% *The Old Course Hotel*
KY16 9SP
☎ 01334 474371 Fax 01334 477668
e-mail: sales@oldcoursehotel.co.uk
Dir: *close to the A91 on the outskirts of the city*
Set beside the 17th hole of the famous championship course and enjoying stunning sea views, this hotel attracts golfers from all over the world. Bedrooms are provided in a variety of sizes and styles with a new block of suites set for completion as we went to press. Dining options include the traditional Road Hole Grill or the Pacific Rim influenced 'Sands' serving international, imaginative cuisine. Smart public areas include the cosy lounges, bright conservatory, a range of golf shops and the well equipped spa. The informal Jigger Inn next to the hotel provides a relaxed and intimate venue in which guests can relax after a day of golf.
ROOMS: 125 en suite (6 fmly) **FACILITIES:** STV Indoor swimming (H) Golf 18 Sauna Solarium Gym Jacuzzi/spa Health spa Steam room **CONF:** Thtr 300 Class 150 Board 60 **SERVICES:** Lift **PARKING:** 150 **NOTES:** No smoking in restaurant Closed 24-28 Dec
CARDS:

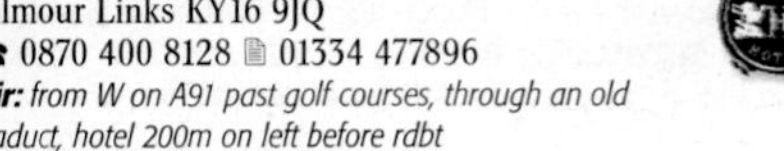

★★★★74% Rusacks
Pilmour Links KY16 9JQ
☎ 0870 400 8128 Fax 01334 477896
Dir: *from W on A91 past golf courses, through an old viaduct, hotel 200m on left before rdbt*

This long standing and well managed hotel continues to go from strength to strength. A number of smart new rooms, with unrivalled views and balconies, are being added to the already excellent and very comfortable bedrooms. In addition, an enviable position with the most stunning views, friendly staff and good food, make for a very well rounded hotel.
ROOMS: 68 en suite **FACILITIES:** STV Sauna Solarium Golf Mgr to organise golf **CONF:** Thtr 90 Class 40 Board 20 **SERVICES:** Lift **PARKING:** 21 **NOTES:** No smoking in restaurant
CARDS:

ST ANDREWS, continued

Premier Collection

★★★ Rufflets Country House

Strathkinness Low Rd KY16 9TX
☎ 01334 472594 01334 478703
e-mail: reservations@rufflets.co.uk
Dir: *1.5m W on B939*

The committed team at Rufflets Country House have nurtured and maintained an ethos of top class hotelkeeping and fine hospitality. The success of this approach is clear in the number of guests who return time and again. A choice of welcoming and individually furnished lounges, overlooking the award winning gardens, is complemented by a comfortable restaurant, where imaginative Scottish cuisine is served and a separate, popular brasserie. Thoughtfully equipped bedrooms, many with striking colour schemes, complete the package.

ROOMS: 19 en suite 3 annexe en suite (1 fmly) No smoking in 13 bedrooms s £95-£130; d £170-£220 (incl. bkfst) * LB **FACILITIES:** STV Putting green Jacuzzi/spa Golf driving net Xmas **CONF:** Thtr 50 Class 30 Board 25 Del from £117.50 * **PARKING:** 52 **NOTES:** No dogs (ex guide dogs) No smoking in restaurant **CARDS:**

★★★77% St Andrews Golf

40 The Scores KY16 9AS
☎ 01334 472611 01334 472188
e-mail: thegolfhotel@standrews.co.uk
Dir: *follow signs 'Golf Course' into Golf Place and in 200yds right into The Scores*

This stylish Victorian hotel overlooks the bay and many of the rooms have fine views over the coastline and nearby golf course. Comfortable bedrooms are attractively furnished, the lounges are relaxing and the restaurant provides carefully prepared meals, which make good use of local ingredients.

continued

ROOMS: 22 en suite (9 fmly) s £88-£96; d £145-£185 (incl. bkfst) * LB **FACILITIES:** STV Xmas **CONF:** Thtr 200 Class 50 Board 20 **SERVICES:** Lift **PARKING:** 6 **NOTES:** No smoking in restaurant **CARDS:**

★★★69% Drumoig Golf Hotel

Drumoig KY16 OBE
☎ 01382 541800 01382 542211
e-mail: drumoig@sol.co.uk
(For full entry see Leuchars)

★★★66% *Scores*

76 The Scores KY16 9BB
☎ 01334 472451 01334 473947
Dir: *on entering St Andrews follow signs to West Sands and Sea Life Centre, premises facing the sea diagonally opposite the Royal & Ancient Clubhouse*

Best Western

This comfortable hotel enjoys views over St Andrews Bay and is situated only a few yards from the first tee of the famous Old Course. Public areas include a choice of well stocked bars, an all day coffee shop, and an attractive restaurant where seafood specials predominate. The variable sized bedrooms come with mixed appointments and a good range of amenities.

ROOMS: 30 en suite (1 fmly) **FACILITIES:** STV **CONF:** Thtr 150 Class 60 Board 40 **SERVICES:** Lift **PARKING:** 10 **NOTES:** No dogs (ex guide dogs) No smoking in restaurant **CARDS:**

See advert on page 753

★★72% *The Inn at Lathones*

Largoward KY9 1JE
☎ 01334 840494 01334 840694
e-mail: lathones@theinn.co.uk
Dir: *situated 5m S of St Andrews on A915, 0.5m before the village of Largoward on left hand side of the road, just after the hidden dip*

MINOTEL Great Britain

This delightful small country inn, parts of which date back over 400 years, combines a welcoming atmosphere with delicious food, and attracts visitors from around the world. Bedrooms, all of which have been upgraded, are accessed externally and offer

continued

comfortable modern appointments and are thoughtfully equipped. The oldest part is The Stables bar, which has stone walls, brick floor and a log burning stove. In the cosy restaurant the creative carte offers a tempting selection of dishes based on fresh Scottish ingredients and treated with a strong French influence.
ROOMS: 14 annexe en suite (2 fmly) **FACILITIES:** ch fac **CONF:** Thtr 30 Class 10 Board 20 Del £95 * **PARKING:** 35 **NOTES:** No smoking in restaurant Closed 25-26 Dec & 3-23 Jan RS 24 Dec
CARDS:

★★68% Russell Hotel
26 The Scores KY16 9AS
☎ 01334 473447 01334 478279
e-mail: russellhotel@talk21.com
Dir: *A91-St Andrews turn right at 2nd rdbt into Golf Place, turn right again after 200yds into The Scores, hotel in 300yds on the left*
Enjoying lovely sea views, this family-run hotel lies near to the famous Old Course. A small lounge is provided on the first floor and the bar remains a popular rendezvous. An extensive range of dishes is offered here and in the adjoining Supper Room. The bedrooms are comfortably modern in style.
ROOMS: 10 en suite (3 fmly) s £65-£85; d £92-£98 (incl. bkfst) * LB **FACILITIES:** STV **NOTES:** No dogs (ex guide dogs) No smoking in restaurant **CARDS:**

★★63% *Ardgowan*
2 Playfair Ter KY16 9HX
☎ 01334 472970 01334 478380
Dir: *follow A91 straight into town, past first rdbt & then a mini rdbt, hotel 200 metres on left*
A relaxed friendly atmosphere prevails at this family-run hotel close to the Old Course and the seafront. Enjoyable meals are served in the bar and restaurant. Best use has been made of space in the carefully designed bedrooms.
ROOMS: 12 en suite (2 fmly) **NOTES:** Closed 25-26 Dec 1-2 Jan
CARDS:

★★60% *Parkland Hotel & Restaurant*
Kinburn Castle, Double Dykes Rd KY16 9DS
☎ 01334 473620 01334 473620
Dir: *opposite Kinburn Park and Museum*
Located opposite Kinburn Park, this friendly hotel appeals to golfers, tourists and business guests. Bedrooms vary in size and style and offer all the expected modern amenities. The attractive dining room is a focal point.
ROOMS: 9 rms (7 en suite) (2 fmly) **PARKING:** 9 **NOTES:** No dogs (ex guide dogs) No smoking in restaurant Closed Xmas/New Year
CARDS:

ST BOSWELLS, Scottish Borders — Map 12 NT53

★★★76% *Dryburgh Abbey*
TD6 0RQ
☎ 01835 822261 01835 823945
e-mail: enquiries@dryburgh.co.uk
Dir: *at St Boswells turn onto B6404 & through village. Continue 2m, then turn left B6356 Scott's View. Through Clintmains village, hotel 1.8m*
An impressive red sandstone mansion, with stylish public areas, a choice of inviting lounges and a well stocked bar. In the restaurant a carefully selected wine list complements fresh local produce on the daily changing menu. Thoughtfully equipped bedrooms vary in size with suites and deluxe rooms available; there is smart accommodation in a new wing.

Scotland's Hotels of Distinction

continued

ROOMS: 37 en suite 1 annexe en suite (5 fmly) **FACILITIES:** Indoor swimming (H) Fishing Putting green **CONF:** Thtr 120 Class 90 Board 70 **SERVICES:** Lift **PARKING:** 103 **NOTES:** No smoking in restaurant
CARDS:

★★69% Buccleuch Arms
The Green TD6 0EW
☎ 01835 822243 01835 823965
e-mail: bucchotel@aol.com
Dir: *on A68, 8m N of Jedburgh*
Formerly a coaching inn, this charming hotel stands opposite the village green and beside the local cricket pitch. It offers a good range of meals in the hotel bar and stylish restaurant. Morning coffees and afternoon teas are served in the attractive lounge with its open fire. The well equipped bedrooms come in a variety of sizes.
ROOMS: 19 en suite (2 fmly) s £30-£47; d £60-£75 (incl. bkfst) * LB **FACILITIES:** Putting green Xmas **CONF:** Thtr 100 Class 40 Board 30 **PARKING:** 52 **NOTES:** No smoking in restaurant Closed 25 Dec
CARDS:

ST FILLANS, Perth & Kinross — Map 11 NN62

★★★67% The Four Seasons Hotel
Loch Earn PH6 2NF
☎ 01764 685333 01764 685444
e-mail: info@thefourseasonshotel.co.uk
Dir: *on A85, towards W of village facing Loch*

A welcoming holiday hotel enjoying spectacular views over Loch Earn. Refurbished bedrooms are comfortable and modern. Public areas overlook the loch and include a snug bar, lounge and the Tarken Bar, an informal food option. The Meall Raemhar Restaurant offers fine dining with a tempting contemporary Scottish menu.
ROOMS: 12 en suite 6 annexe en suite s £32-£64; d £64-£88 (incl. bkfst) * LB **FACILITIES:** STV Xmas **CONF:** Thtr 95 Class 45 Board 38 Del from £63.90 * **PARKING:** 40 **NOTES:** No smoking in restaurant Closed 15 Jan-15 Mar **CARDS:**

★★72% Achray House
Loch Earn PH6 2NF
☎ 01764 685231 01764 685320
e-mail: achrayhotelsltd@btinternet.com
Dir: *on A85 12 miles from Crieff*
This delightful holiday hotel overlooking the picturesque Loch Earn offers a warm welcome. Bedrooms are decorated to a high standard providing comfortable modern furnishings. There is a bar with a conservatory for informal meals. A formal menu is served in the smart dining room.
ROOMS: 9 rms (8 en suite) (1 fmly) s fr £46.50; d fr £69 (incl. bkfst) * LB **FACILITIES:** Xmas **CONF:** Class 20 Board 20 Del from £52 * **PARKING:** 30 **NOTES:** No dogs (ex guide dogs) No smoking in restaurant Closed 4 Jan-2 Feb **CARDS:**

S

SANQUHAR, Dumfries & Galloway Map 11 NS70

★★67% *Blackaddie House*
Blackaddie Rd DG4 6JJ
☎ 01659 50270 01659 50270
Dir: *turn off A76 just N of Sanquhar at Burnside Service Station. Private road to hotel 300mtrs on right*
This former rectory, which dates back to 1540, is now under the care and direction of enthusiastic new owners and old and new guests alike are assured of a warm welcome. The variable sized bedrooms are comfortably modern in style and offer all the expected amenities. Public areas include an inviting lounge, a cosy bar with adjacent bistro, and carte restaurant.
ROOMS: 10 en suite (2 fmly) **FACILITIES:** Fishing Riding Game shooting Gold panning Bike hire ch fac **CONF:** Thtr 50 Class 20 Board 20 **PARKING:** 20 **NOTES:** No dogs (ex guide dogs) No smoking in restaurant **CARDS:**

SCALASAIG See Colonsay, Isle of

SCOURIE, Highland Map 14 NC14

★★70% Eddrachilles
Badcall Bay IV27 4TH
☎ 01971 502080 01971 502477
e-mail: enq@eddrachilles.com
Dir: *2m S on A894, 7m N of Kylesku Bridge*
An appealing holiday hotel in woodland beside the Badcall Bay, with sea views. There are inviting lounges and a popular conservatory overlooking the bay. The dining room, with its natural stone walls and flagstone floor, offers fixed-price and carte menus. The well equipped bedrooms are smartly refurbished.
ROOMS: 11 en suite (1 fmly) s £47.70-£53.50; d £75.40-£87 (incl. bkfst) * LB **FACILITIES:** Fishing Boats for hire **PARKING:** 25 **NOTES:** No dogs (ex guide dogs) No children 3yrs Closed Nov-Feb
CARDS:

★★68% Scourie
IV27 4SX
☎ 01971 502396 01971 502423
e-mail: patrick@scourie-hotel.co.uk
Dir: *situated on A894 in the village of Scourie*
An angler's paradise, with extensive fishing rights available on a 25,000-acre estate. Public areas include a choice of comfortable lounges, a cosy bar and a smart dining room offering wholesome fare. There is a relaxed and friendly atmosphere.
ROOMS: 18 rms (17 en suite) 2 annexe en suite (2 fmly) s £34-£46; d £58-£80 (incl. bkfst) * LB **FACILITIES:** Fishing Pool table **PARKING:** 30 **NOTES:** No smoking in restaurant Closed mid Oct -end Mar **CARDS:**

SHETLAND Map 16

LERWICK Map 16 HU44

★★★69% ❀ Shetland
Holmsgarth Rd ZE1 0PW
☎ 01595 695515 01595 695828
e-mail: reception@shetlandhotel.co.uk
Dir: *opposite P&O ferry terminal, on main route north from town centre*
This modern hotel stands directly opposite the main ferry terminal. Public areas include a comfortable open plan bar/lounge and two dining options, Oasis Bistro and the more formal Ninian Restaurant. Bedrooms are well proportioned and comfortable.
continued

ROOMS: 64 en suite (4 fmly) No smoking in 14 bedrooms s £76.95; d £92 (incl. bkfst) * LB **FACILITIES:** STV **CONF:** Thtr 320 Class 75 Board 50 **SERVICES:** Lift **PARKING:** 150 **NOTES:** No dogs (ex guide dogs) No smoking in restaurant **CARDS:**

★★★68% Lerwick
15 South Rd ZE1 0RB
☎ 01595 692166 01595 694419
e-mail: lerwickhotel@mes.co.uk
Dir: *near town centre, on main road southwards to/from airport. 25m from main airport, located in central Lerwick*
This popular hotel has lovely views over Breiwick Bay to Bressay and Breiwick Islands. The variably sized bedrooms have modern facilities. The public areas consist of an attractive foyer lounge, a pleasant Brasserie which is open for lunch and dinner and a more formal restaurant with sea views, open for dinner with a menu based on fine local produce.
ROOMS: 35 en suite (3 fmly) s fr £73; d fr £90 (incl. bkfst) * LB **FACILITIES:** STV **CONF:** Thtr 60 Class 40 Board 20 **PARKING:** 50 **NOTES:** No dogs (ex guide dogs) Civ Wed 100
CARDS:

UNST Map 16 HP60

★★63% The Baltasound
ZE2 9DS
☎ 01957 711334 01957 711358
e-mail: balta.hotel@zetnet.co.uk
Dir: *from ferry from Lerwick, follow the main road north. Hotel is in Baltasound close to the pier.*
This family-run hotel is the most northerly hotel in the British Isles. Apart from the separate breakfast room, public areas are open plan, with a comfortable lounge, bar and dining room flowing through an L-shaped space. Some bedrooms are in the main building, but most are in pleasant log cabins dispersed around the grounds.
ROOMS: 8 rms (5 en suite) 17 annexe en suite (17 fmly) s fr £40; d fr £59 (incl. bkfst) * **FACILITIES:** Fishing Pool table **PARKING:** 20 **NOTES:** No smoking in restaurant **CARDS:**

SHIELDAIG, Highland Map 14 NG85

★73% ❀ Tigh an Eilean
IV54 8XN
☎ 01520 755251 01520 755321
e-mail: tighaneileanhotel@shieldaig.fsnet.co.uk
Dir: *turn off A896 onto village road signposted Shieldaig,hotel in centre of village on loch front just along from small jetty*
The 'house of the island' looks out on the bay and is surrounded by whitewashed crofts and fishermen's cottages, sheltered by pine trees. Bedrooms are well maintained, and there is a bar and three comfortable lounges.
ROOMS: 11 en suite (1 fmly) s fr £48.55; d fr £107.60 (incl. bkfst) * LB **PARKING:** 15 **NOTES:** No smoking in restaurant Closed mid Oct- mid Mar **CARDS:**

SKYE, ISLE OF, Highland Map 13

ARDVASAR Map 13 NG60

★★67% Ardvasar Hotel
Sleat IV45 8RS
☎ 01471 844223 01471 844495
e-mail: christine@ardvasar-hotel.demon.co.uk
Dir: *leave ferry, drive 50yds & turn left*
Many improvements have been undertaken by the hotel's
continued

S

enthusiastic owners. The bedrooms in particular have benefited from refurbishment and are smartly decorated and equipped to modern standards. Public areas include an inviting lounge, a separate dining room and a bar where enjoyable food is also served.

ROOMS: 10 en suite (4 fmly) s fr £45; d fr £80 (incl. bkfst) * LB **FACILITIES:** Pool table entertainment Xmas **CONF:** Thtr 50 Board 24 **PARKING:** 30 **NOTES:** No smoking in restaurant
CARDS:

BROADFORD Map 13 NG62

★★64% Dunollie Hotel

IV49 9AE
☎ 01471 822253 🖷 01471 822060

Situated by the water's edge, this spacious tourist hotel gives fine views from the dining room across the bay toward the mountains of Torridon. The spacious foyer/lounge and bar is often the venue for lively evening entertainment. Bedrooms are freshly decorated and have good facilities.
ROOMS: 84 en suite s £35-£60; d £50-£95 (incl. bkfst) * LB **PARKING:** 6 **NOTES:** No smoking in restaurant Closed Nov-9 Mar
CARDS:

COLBOST Map 13 NG24

Premier Collection

Three Chimneys Restaurant & House Over-By

IV55 8ZT
☎ 01470 511258 🖷 01470 511358
e-mail: eatandstay@threechimneys.co.uk
Dir: *from Dunvegan take B884 to Glendale. Colbost 4.5m from main road turn off*
The House Over-By provides accommodation par excellence in spacious split-level rooms - all individually designed in harmony with the environment. An outstanding Scottish cold breakfast, featuring fresh fruits, locally smoked meats and fish, and other regional produce, is served in a bright room overlooking the sea loch. In the cottage-style Three Chimneys Restaurant visitors are enchanted by flavoursome cooking and unfussy treatment of prime Scottish ingredients. Put this on your 'can't miss' list for your next visit to Scotland.

ROOMS: 6 en suite (1 fmly) No smoking in all bedrooms s £120; d £140 (incl. cont bkfst) * LB **FACILITIES:** Xmas **CONF:** Thtr 28 Class 24 Board 18 **PARKING:** 8 **NOTES:** No dogs (ex guide dogs) No smoking in restaurant Closed 3 weeks in Jan RS Sun
CARDS:

Popped the question? Hotels with Civ Wed in their entry are licensed for civil wedding ceremonies. Maximum numbers for the ceremony only are shown, e.g. Civ Wed 50

ISLE ORNSAY

Map 13 NG61

★★★68% ❀❀ Duisdale Hotel

Sleat IV43 8QW
☎ 01471 833202 📠 01471 833404
e-mail: marie@duisdalehotel.demon.co.uk
Dir: *on A851 Armadale to Broadford road, just north of the village of Isle Ornsay*

This delightful country house hotel stands in its own gardens and wooded grounds with lovely views over the Sound of Sleat. The nicely presented public rooms include an inviting sitting room with sun lounge adjacent. There is also a cosy bar and the attractive restaurant which provides an appropriate setting for the five course menu featuring local game and fish. Refurbished bedrooms provide all the expected amenities.

ROOMS: 17 en suite 2 annexe en suite (3 fmly) No smoking in 7 bedrooms s £60-£70; d £80-£130 (incl. bkfst) * LB **FACILITIES:** Fishing Croquet lawn Putting green **PARKING:** 20 **NOTES:** No dogs No smoking in restaurant Closed Nov-Feb (Prebooking possible)
CARDS:

See advert on page 757

★★75% ❀❀ Kinloch Lodge

IV43 8QY
☎ 01471 833214 & 833333 📠 01471 833277
e-mail: kinloch@dial.pipex.com
Dir: *6m S of Broadford on A851, 10m N of Armadale on A851*

At the end of a bumpy forest track, which replaces the former drive because of a damaged bridge, is the fine home of Lord and Lady Macdonald where guests are made to feel like friends by the owners and their charming staff. Some rooms have views over Loch Na Dal, and bedrooms are priced according to their size and location in the building. The two drawing rooms have log fires and comfortable settees; family portraits and photos are displayed throughout, and the elegant dining room complements Lady Claire's renowned cuisine. The latest development of a house in the grounds is now complete and contains five splendid new bedrooms, a homely lounge and Lady Claire's magnificent demonstration kitchen.

ROOMS: 9 en suite 5 annexe en suite No smoking in all bedrooms s £60-£120; d £100-£180 (incl. bkfst) * LB **FACILITIES:** Fishing Deer Stalking Cooking demonstrations Xmas **PARKING:** 18 **NOTES:** No smoking in restaurant Closed 22 Dec-28 Dec **CARDS:**

★★71% ❀ Hotel Eilean Iarmain

THE CIRCLE
Selected Individual Hotels
GREAT BRITAIN

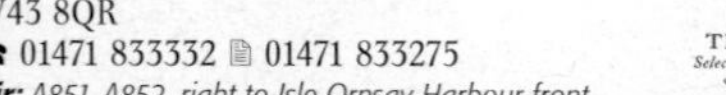

IV43 8QR
☎ 01471 833332 📠 01471 833275
Dir: *A851, A852, right to Isle Ornsay Harbour front*

This 19th-century island inn provides traditional values of hospitality from the friendly Gaelic-speaking staff. Bedrooms, including those in the Garden House opposite the main building, are traditional in style and most have lovely views. The cosy sitting room has been extended and the timber-clad pub often features impromptu ceilidhs. The attractive candlelit dining room, also extended, offers innovative Scottish fare.

ROOMS: 6 en suite 10 annexe en suite No smoking in 10 bedrooms s £90-£120; d £120-£200 (incl. bkfst) * LB **FACILITIES:** Fishing Shooting entertainment ch fac Xmas **CONF:** Thtr 50 Class 30 Board 25 **PARKING:** 40 **NOTES:** No smoking in restaurant
CARDS:

See advert on opposite page

PORTREE

Map 13 NG44

★★★76% ❀ Cuillin Hills

IV51 9QU
☎ 01478 612003 📠 01478 613092
e-mail: office@cuillinhills.demon.co.uk
Dir: *turn right 0.25m N of Portree off the A855 and follow signs for hotel*

Improvements continue at this popular hotel overlooking the bay towards the Cuillin Mountains. There is a new elegant split level restaurant, where fine dining can be enjoyed; the comfortable bar offers more informal meals. The new bedrooms are most attractively finished, with plans to upgrade more bedrooms.

ROOMS: 21 en suite 9 annexe en suite (2 fmly) No smoking in 7 bedrooms s £38-£60; d £76-£150 (incl. bkfst) * LB **FACILITIES:** STV Xmas **CONF:** Thtr 100 Class 60 Board 30 Del from £70 * **PARKING:** 56 **NOTES:** No smoking in restaurant
CARDS:

See advert on opposite page

★★73% ❀ Rosedale

Beaumont Crescent IV51 9DB
☎ 01478 613131 📠 01478 612531
Dir: *follow the directions to the Village Centre and Harbour, hotel is on the waterfront of Portree Harbourside*

A charming hotel overlooking the bay, run by enthusiastic owners. Public areas, spread over different levels, and linked by an artery of corridors and stairs, include a well stocked bar, comfortable lounge, and a coffee shop. A lovely view of the bay can also be enjoyed from the attractive restaurant, where the short fixed-price

continued on p760

Hotel Eilean Iarmain

AA ★★ *(Isle Ornsay Hotel)* 71%

Award winning 19th century inn. Built in 1888, owned by Sir Iain and Lady Noble. Retains its Victorian charm and old world character. Log fires in an idyllic location by the sea amongst breathtaking scenery, tranquil surroundings, in the most magical and truly romantic setting with magnificent picturesque panoramic sea views. Twelve bedrooms plus four luxurious suites. All en-suite, with hospitality trays, hair dryers, dressing robes, toiletries and telephones. AA Rosette for the restaurant, specialising in local seafood and fresh produce from estate. Extensive wine list. Open all year.

General manager: Morag MacDonald.

Macallan Taste of Scotland Award
Runner up of the Year 1997
AA Courtesy & Care Award 1995

Hotel Eilean Iarmain
Sleat, Isle of Skye IV43 8QR
Tel: 01471 833332 Fax: 01471 833275

THE ROYAL HOTEL ★★★

A beautifully restored Victorian Hotel with an excellent reputation for fine cuisine.

BRIDGE OF ALLAN
STIRLING · SCOTLAND

Tel:
01786 · 832284
Fax:
01786 · 834377
Email:
stay@royal-stirling.co.uk
Website:
www.royal-stirling.co.uk

The Isle of Skye

Set in its own grounds overlooking Portree Bay with spectacular views of the Cuillin mountains. Enjoy the peace and tranquillity of Skye from the Cuillin Hills Hotel where high standards of comfort and service and award-winning cuisine combine with the warmth of Highland hospitality.

★★★

Cuillin Hills Hotel, Portree,
Isle of Skye IV51 9QU.
Tel: 01478 612003
Fax: 01478 613092

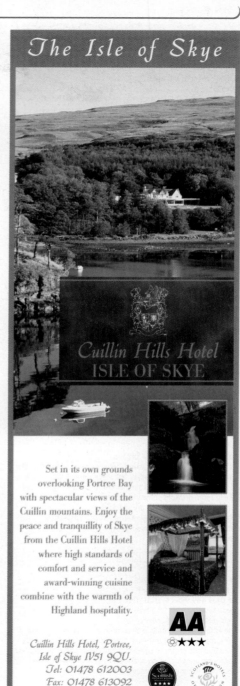

PORTREE, continued

menu offers a range of Taste of Scotland specialities. Bedrooms have pleasing colour schemes and offer the expected amenities. Staff are friendly and willing to please.
ROOMS: 20 en suite 3 annexe en suite (1 fmly) s £40-£46; d £68-£98 (incl. bkfst) * LB **FACILITIES:** Xmas **PARKING:** 10 **NOTES:** No smoking in restaurant Closed Nov-Mar **CARDS:**

★★72% *Bosville*
Bosville Ter IV51 9DG
☎ 01478 612846 01478 613434
e-mail: bosville@macleodhotels.co.uk
Close to the town centre, this well established family hotel has been completely refurbished to provide attractive and well equipped accommodation. The restaurant offers two distinctive styles of cuisine.
ROOMS: 15 en suite (2 fmly) No smoking in 10 bedrooms
FACILITIES: STV **PARKING:** 14 **NOTES:** No dogs (ex guide dogs)
CARDS:

See advert on opposite page

★★67% Royal
IV51 9BU
☎ 01478 612525 01478 613198
e-mail: info@royal-hotel.demon.co.uk
Dir: *turn off A850 on to A855, hotel is on corner overlooking the harbour*
This established hotel overlooks the picturesque harbour and has a well-equipped leisure centre. The bistro, lounge and bars are attractively decorated. In the high season, live entertainment is provided in the Ceilidh Room. Bedrooms offer a good standard of comfort.
ROOMS: 21 en suite No smoking in 14 bedrooms s £44-£54; d £70-£88 (incl. bkfst) * LB **FACILITIES:** Sauna Solarium Gym Pool table Jacuzzi/spa entertainment Xmas **CONF:** Thtr 130 Board 40 Del from £60 * **PARKING:** 14 **CARDS:**

UIG — Map 13 NG36

★★70% *Uig*
IV51 9YE
☎ 01470 542205 01470 542308
An established hotel overlooking the bay and ferry terminal. The welcoming residents' bar offers fine views as well as a good range of tasty bar food, there is a simpler bar to the rear. The formal dining room provides some interesting and innovative dishes locally sourced. Bedrooms are spacious.
ROOMS: 10 en suite 7 annexe en suite (2 fmly) **FACILITIES:** Riding
PARKING: 20 **NOTES:** No smoking in restaurant RS Nov-Mar
CARDS:

S

SOUTH QUEENSFERRY, City of Edinburgh — Map 11 NT17

★★★61% Forth Bridges
REGAL
1 Ferrymuir Gait EH30 9SF
☎ 0131 469 9955 0131 319 1733
Dir: *adjacent to Forth Road Bridge on south side, follow signs - M90 then A8000, hotel on left*
The Firth of Forth with its famous bridges provides a breathtaking backdrop for this purpose-built hotel situated only 20 minutes from both the centre of Edinburgh and the airport. The river-facing bedrooms are particularly spacious, while the upstairs restaurant also takes maximum advantage of the panoramic views.

continued

ROOMS: 108 en suite (19 fmly) No smoking in 35 bedrooms s £95-£115; d £115-£135 * LB **FACILITIES:** Indoor swimming (H) Squash Sauna Solarium Gym Jacuzzi/spa Dance studio Xmas **CONF:** Thtr 200 Class 90 Board 60 Del from £70 * **SERVICES:** Lift **PARKING:** 200
CARDS:

STIRLING, Stirling — Map 11 NS79

★★★★66% Stirling Highland
PARAMOUNT GROUP OF HOTELS
Spittal St FK8 1DU
☎ 01786 272727 01786 272829
e-mail: stirling@paramount-hotels.co.uk
Dir: *take A84 into Stirling and follow signs to Stirling Castle until you reach the Albert Hall. Turn left and left again, following signs to Castle*
Dating back to 1854 and once the town's High School, this impressive hotel is close to the famous castle. Guests can relax with a refreshment in the comfort of the Headmasters Study before moving through to the elegant Scholars Restaurant to enjoy the innovative cuisine. The comfortably appointed bedrooms are well equipped and maintained.
ROOMS: 94 en suite (4 fmly) No smoking in 56 bedrooms s £107-£110; d £144-£150 * LB **FACILITIES:** STV Indoor swimming (H) Squash Snooker Sauna Solarium Gym Jacuzzi/spa Steam room Dance Studio Beauty therapist Xmas **CONF:** Thtr 120 Class 80 Board 45 Del from £125 * **SERVICES:** Lift **PARKING:** 96 **NOTES:** No smoking in restaurant
CARDS:

★★69% Terraces
Best Western
4 Melville Ter FK8 2ND
☎ 01786 472268 01786 450314
e-mail: terraceshotel@compuserve.com
Dir: *from A872 1st left at 2nd rdbt. At lights onto Melville Terrace (inside lane) parallel to main rd on left. Hotel at bottom*
Situated in the centre of town this popular hotel, an elegant Georgian building, provides a welcoming atmosphere to its business and leisure customers. Public areas include a well stocked bar and a carte restaurant adjacent. Though variable in size, the bedrooms are comfortably modern in style and offer a wide range of amenities.
ROOMS: 17 en suite (3 fmly) s £56-£69; d £80-£82 (incl. bkfst) * LB **FACILITIES:** STV Xmas **CONF:** Thtr 120 Class 60 Board 48 Del from £62.50 * **PARKING:** 25 **NOTES:** No smoking in restaurant
CARDS:

⌂ *Travelodge*
Travelodge
Pirnhall Roundabout, Snabhead FK7 8EU
☎ Central Res 8000 555300 01525 878450
Dir: *junct M9/M80*
This modern building offers accommodation in smart, spacious and well equipped bedrooms, all with en suite bathrooms. Refreshments may be taken at the nearby family restaurant. For further details and the Travelodge phone number, consult the Hotel Groups page.
ROOMS: 37 en suite

⇧ Express by Holiday Inn Stirling

Springkerse Business Park FK7 7XH
☎ 01786 449922 ▯ 01786 449932
e-mail: info@hiex-stirling.com
Dir: *M9/M80 jct 9. Take A91 Stirling/St Andrews exit. Keep on rd for 2.8m. Hotel located on 4th rdbt. Take 2nd exit to sports stadium & then 3rd to hotel*

A modern budget hotel offering comfortable accommodation in refreshing, spacious and comprehensively-equipped bedrooms, en suite bathrooms with power showers and continental buffet breakfast included in the room rate. Suitable for business travellers or families. For further details and the Express by Holiday Inn phone number, consult the Hotel Groups page.
ROOMS: 80 en suite (incl. cont bkfst) d £52.50-£55 * **CONF:** Thtr 35 Class 18 Board 18 Del £75 *

STONEHAVEN, Aberdeenshire — Map 15 NO88

★★66% County Hotel & Leisure Club

Arduthie Rd AB39 2EH
☎ 01569 764386 ▯ 01569 762214
Dir: *off A90, opposite railway station*

This welcoming hotel sits on the outskirts of town close to the railway station. The variable sized bedrooms have been freshly decorated and offer mixed styles of furnishings. Public areas include a choice of well stocked bars and an attractive restaurant featuring a fascinating collection of prints of celebrities.
ROOMS: 14 en suite (1 fmly) s £40-£46; d £50-£60 (incl. bkfst) * LB **FACILITIES:** Squash Sauna Gym Table tennis **CONF:** Thtr 150 Class 60 Board 32 **PARKING:** 40 **NOTES:** No dogs (ex guide dogs) Civ Wed 180
CARDS:

STORNOWAY See Lewis, Isle of

STRACHUR, Argyll & Bute — Map 10 NN00

★★★67% *Creggans Inn*

PA27 8BX
☎ 01369 860279 ▯ 01369 860637
e-mail: info@creggans-inn.co.uk
Dir: *follow A82/A83 Loch Lomond road to Arrochar. Continue on A83 then take A815 Strachur*

This long established roadside inn enjoys spectacular views of Loch Fyne and surrounding mountains. Charm and character prevail throughout. Inviting public areas include a choice of lounges, contrasting bars and a shop/café, as well as a stylish dining room. Bedrooms are smartly decorated and enhanced by attractive fabrics.
ROOMS: 17 en suite **FACILITIES:** Fishing Pool table Clay pigeon shooting Archery Off road driving **CONF:** Thtr 25 Class 25 Board 25 **PARKING:** 50 **NOTES:** No smoking in restaurant
CARDS:

STRANRAER, Dumfries & Galloway
Map 10 NX06

★★★★68% North West Castle
DG9 8EH
☎ 01776 704413 🖷 01776 702646
e-mail: mcmhotel@mcmhotel.demon.co.uk
Dir: *on seafront, close to Stena ferry terminal*
This popular hotel overlooks the bay and ferry terminal. Public areas include an elegant dining room where a pianist plays during dinner, and an adjoining lounge with large leather armchairs and blazing fire in season. Bedrooms are well equipped and many are very spacious.
ROOMS: 70 en suite 3 annexe en suite (22 fmly) **FACILITIES:** STV Indoor swimming (H) Snooker Sauna Solarium Gym Pool table Jacuzzi/spa Curling (Oct-Apr) Games room **CONF:** Thtr 150 Class 60 Board 40 **SERVICES:** Lift **PARKING:** 100 **NOTES:** No dogs (ex guide dogs) No smoking in restaurant **CARDS:**

STRATHAVEN, South Lanarkshire
Map 11 NS74

★★★68% Strathaven

Hamilton Rd ML10 6SZ
☎ 01357 521778 🖷 01357 520789
e-mail: sthotel@globalnet.co.uk
This Robert Adam designed mansion house on the outskirts of town is a popular venue for functions. A wing of smart new bedrooms has been added, which are all well equipped. Public areas include a comfortable lounge, dining room and attractive bar/lounge.
ROOMS: 22 en suite No smoking in 12 bedrooms s fr £69; d fr £85 (incl. bkfst) * LB **FACILITIES:** STV Xmas **CONF:** Thtr 180 Class 120 Board 30 Del from £100 * **PARKING:** 80 **NOTES:** No dogs (ex guide dogs) No smoking in restaurant Civ Wed 110
CARDS:

STRATHBLANE, Stirling
Map 11 NS57

★★★71% Country Club Hotel
Milngavie Rd G63 9EH
☎ 01360 770491 🖷 01360 770345
Dir: *From Glasgow follow A81 through Strathblane. Turn left after leaving the village*
This country house, set in 15 acres of grounds, offers mostly spacious bedrooms, all of which are attractively and comfortably furnished. Guests can enjoy a choice of lounge areas and a popular brasserie. The classically presented dining room attracts a discerning clientele.
ROOMS: 10 en suite No smoking in all bedrooms **CONF:** Thtr 120 Class 60 Board 40 **SERVICES:** Lift **PARKING:** 100 **NOTES:** No smoking in restaurant **CARDS:**

STRATHYRE, Stirling
Map 11 NN51

Premier Collection

★ Creagan House
FK18 8ND
☎ 01877 384638 🖷 01877 384319
e-mail: mail@creaganhouse.fsnet.co.uk
Dir: *0.25m N of Strathyre on A84*
A cosy hotel of distinction, with a lovely friendly atmosphere, this restored 17th century farmhouse lies just outside the village and is backed by forest walks within the Queen Elizabeth Park. Carefully chosen pieces furnish the attractive bedrooms which are thoughtfully equipped to include excellent CD/radio sets; TVs are available on request. The little lounge is inviting and refreshments are served here before and after an enjoyable meal in the impressive baronial-style dining room. The cuisine is bold, imaginative, and two different menus are provided to tempt guests. Breakfasts will also be remembered.

ROOMS: 5 en suite (1 fmly) No smoking in all bedrooms s £52.50; d £85 (incl. bkfst) LB **FACILITIES:** Xmas **CONF:** Thtr 35 Class 12 Board 35 **PARKING:** 26 **NOTES:** No smoking in restaurant Closed 28 Jan-2 Mar **CARDS:**

STRONTIAN, Highland
Map 14 NM86

Courtesy & Care Award

★★80% Kilcamb Lodge
PH36 4HY
☎ 01967 402257 🖷 01967 402041
e-mail: kilcamblodge@aol.com
Dir: *off A861*
This sympathetically modernised former hunting lodge with loch views offers open fires, deep cushioned sofas, flowers, books and magazines in the elegant public rooms. The delightfully furnished bedrooms are thoughtfully equipped with items such as bathrobes. A short choice of well prepared dishes are complemented by a carefully selected wine list. Kilcamb Lodge has been awarded the AA Courtesy & Care Award for Scotland 2000-2001.
ROOMS: 11 en suite (1 fmly) No smoking in all bedrooms s £60-£90; d £80-£130 * LB **FACILITIES:** Fishing Mountain bike & Fishing rod hire & trips Moorings ch fac Xmas **CONF:** Class 30 Board 20 **PARKING:** 20 **NOTES:** No smoking in restaurant Closed Dec-Feb (ex NY) **CARDS:**

TAIN, Highland Map 14 NH78

★★★75% Mansfield House
Scotsburn Rd IV19 1PR
☎ 01862 892052 01862 892260
e-mail: mansfield@cali.co.uk
Dir: *A9 from S, ignore 1st exit signed Tain and take the 2nd exit signed police station*
An impressive mansion house, in grounds opposite the Royal Academy. Inviting public areas include a comfortable bar and formal dining rooms. Innovative dishes are found on the fixed-priced daily dinner menu and the bar menu. Bedrooms range from tastefully appointed de luxe rooms, furnished in period style, to pleasantly redecorated rooms in the wing.
ROOMS: 8 en suite 10 annexe en suite (6 fmly) No smoking in 4 bedrooms s £65-£85; d £100-£150 (incl. bkfst) * LB
FACILITIES: Croquet lawn Beauty salon Xmas **CONF:** Thtr 40 Class 20 Board 20 Del from £85 * **PARKING:** 100 **NOTES:** No smoking in restaurant Civ Wed 70 **CARDS:**

★★★72% Morangie House
Morangie Rd IV19 1PY
☎ 01862 892281 01862 892872
e-mail: wynne@morangiehotel.com
Dir: *turn right off A9 northwards*
This welcoming family-run hotel gives fine views of the Dornoch Firth. Attractive bedrooms in the newer wing are comfortably modern whilst those in the main house are more traditional; all are well equipped with useful accessories. An extensive range of dishes is available in the formal dining room and smart Garden Restaurant.
ROOMS: 26 en suite (1 fmly) No smoking in 4 bedrooms s £60-£75; d £80-£95 (incl. bkfst) * LB **FACILITIES:** STV **CONF:** Thtr 40 Class 40 Board 24 **PARKING:** 40 **CARDS:**

TANGASDALE See Barra, Isle of

TARBERT LOCH FYNE, Argyll & Bute Map 10 NR86

★★★69% *Stonefield Castle*
PA29 6YJ
☎ 01880 820836 01880 820929
Dir: *signed off A83, 2m N of Tarbert*
An impressive baronial mansion, set in 60 acres of wooded gardens. Ornate ceilings, marble fireplaces and old family portraits add interest to the delightful day rooms, which include a choice of lounges, a bar, and a spacious restaurant, overlooking Loch Fyne. Most bedrooms are in a modern wing and are contemporary in style.
ROOMS: 33 en suite (1 fmly) **FACILITIES:** Fishing Snooker Sauna Solarium **CONF:** Thtr 180 Class 100 Board 60 **SERVICES:** Lift **PARKING:** 50 **NOTES:** No smoking in restaurant
CARDS:

See advert on this page

★★69% The Columba Hotel
East Pier Rd PA29 6UF
☎ 01880 820808 01880 820808
e-mail: columbahotel@fsbdial.co.uk
Dir: *turn off A83 into Tarbert village. Keep loch on left and continue to hotel in 0.5m*
The enthusiastic owners look forward to welcoming guests to their delightful Victorian hotel that overlooks the harbour approach and Loch Fyne. The comfortable, traditional style bedrooms range from well proportioned superior rooms to smaller, standard accommodation. The bar, with its welcoming log fire, is full of character reflecting the heritage of the village. Adjacent, the elegant restaurant provides the appropriate setting for the enjoyable French-influenced Scottish fare.
ROOMS: 10 en suite (3 fmly) s £34.95-£49.95; d £69.90-£83.90 (incl. bkfst) * LB **FACILITIES:** Sauna Gym **PARKING:** 10 **NOTES:** No smoking in restaurant Closed 24-26 Dec
CARDS:

TAYNUILT, Argyll & Bute Map 10 NN03

★★60% Polfearn
PA35 1JQ
☎ 01866 822251 01866 822251
Dir: *turn N off A85, continue 1.5m through village down to Loch Shore*
Ongoing improvements are continuing at this family owned hotel which stands one mile north of the village close to the shore of Loch Etive. It enjoys delightful all round views and offers friendly and informal service. A good range of food is available either in the bar or the dining room and the bedrooms come in several different styles.
ROOMS: 16 rms (14 en suite) (2 fmly) s £25-£35; d £50-£70 (incl. bkfst) * LB **FACILITIES:** Xmas **CONF:** Board 70 **PARKING:** 21 **NOTES:** No smoking in restaurant RS end of January **CARDS:**

THORNHILL, Dumfries & Galloway Map 11 NX89

★★73% Trigony House
Closeburn DG3 5EZ
☎ 01848 331211 01848 331303
Dir: *off A76 between Thornhill & Closeburn on the left hand side, clearly signed*
A friendly and relaxed atmosphere prevails at this Edwardian hunting lodge, set in four acres of gardens and grounds south of

continued

THORNHILL, continued

the village. Meals, which can be had either in the cosy bar or comfortable dining room, feature all fresh produce, organically grown when available. Bedrooms come in a variety of sizes, some are quite spacious.
ROOMS: 8 en suite s fr £47.50; d fr £75 (incl. bkfst) * LB
FACILITIES: Fishing **CONF:** Class 30 Board 30 **PARKING:** 20
NOTES: No children 8yrs No smoking in restaurant
CARDS:

THURSO, Highland Map 15 ND16

★★★63% Royal
Traill St KW14 8EH
☎ 01847 893191 🖷 01847 895338

Set in the town centre, this traditional hotel attracts a mixed market including tours. It has been completely refurbished inside, offering comfortable lounges and a trendy bar appealing to business residents.
ROOMS: 102 en suite s £35-£60; d £50-£95 (incl. bkfst) * LB
SERVICES: Lift **CARDS:**

★★70% Park Hotel
KW14 8RE
☎ 01847 893251 🖷 01847 893252
e-mail: reception@parkhotelthurso.co.uk
Dir: *situated on the right hand side of the A9, on approach to Thurso town centre*
A family run hotel on the southern approach to the town. The conservatory extension has enhanced the convivial lounge bar where enjoyable bar meals are served, and the more formal dining room where an attractive carte menu is offered. Bedrooms are bright and well equipped, most are suitable for families.
ROOMS: 11 en suite (8 fmly) s £35-£47; d £65 (incl. bkfst) * LB
FACILITIES: Pool table **CONF:** Thtr 100 Class 20 Board 40
PARKING: 40 **NOTES:** No smoking in restaurant Closed 1-3 Jan RS 25 Dec **CARDS:**

TIGHNABRUAICH, Argyll & Bute Map 10 NR97

★★73% Royal Hotel
Shore Rd PA21 2BE
☎ 01700 811239 🖷 01700 811300
e-mail: royalhotel@btinternet.com
Dir: *from Stachur on A886 turn right onto the A8003 to Tighnabruaich. Hotel is located on the right at the bottom of the hill, at the 'T' junct*
Enthusiastic owners have transformed this established hotel overlooking the Kyles of Bute. All the refurbished non smoking bedrooms have pleasing colour schemes and are comfortably furnished in traditional style. Public areas include contrasting bars, one has a popular brasserie providing informal food. Two other dining areas feature seafood and game.

continued

ROOMS: 11 en suite (1 fmly) No smoking in all bedrooms s £77; d £94 (incl. bkfst) * LB **CONF:** Class 20 Board 10 Del from £65 *
PARKING: 20 **NOTES:** No smoking in restaurant Closed 25-26 Dec
CARDS:

TOBERMORY See Mull, Isle of

TOMINTOUL, Moray Map 15 NJ11

★★★68% The Gordon Hotel & Cromdales Restaurant

The Square AB37 9ET
☎ 01807 580206 🖷 01807 580488

A popular base for tour groups and private holidaymakers, this friendly hotel overlooks the village square. Public areas are well presented and include a choice of contrasting bars and dining rooms. Bedrooms are bright and airy with comfortable modern furnishings and offer a good range of accessories.
ROOMS: 29 en suite (2 fmly) s fr £25; d fr £50 (incl. bkfst) *
FACILITIES: Fishing Pool table Xmas **CONF:** Thtr 100 Class 120 Board 10 **PARKING:** 14 **NOTES:** No smoking in restaurant
CARDS:

TONGUE, Highland Map 14 NC55

★★71% Ben Loyal
Main St IV27 4XE
☎ 01847 611216 🖷 01847 611212
e-mail: Thebenloyalhotel@btinternet.com
Dir: *Tongue lies at the intersection of the A838/A836, hotel is in the centre of village, next door to The Royal Bank of Scotland*
This friendly and informal hotel enjoys a splendid view of the Kyle of Tongue and ruins of Varrich Castle. Bedrooms are smartly furnished in pine, whilst both the comfortable lounge and adjoining dining room take full advantage of the views. The latter offers a five-course dinner menu featuring freshly prepared dishes using local produce, with lobsters and oysters when available.
ROOMS: 11 en suite s fr £35; d fr £70 (incl. bkfst) * LB
FACILITIES: Fishing Pool table Fly fishing tuition entertainment
PARKING: 20 **NOTES:** No smoking in restaurant Closed 25-26 Dec & 1-3 Jan RS Oct-Apr **CARDS:**

TORRIDON, Highland Map 14 NG95

★★★79% Loch Torridon Country House Hotel
IV22 2EY
☎ 01445 791242 🖷 01445 791296
e-mail: enquiries@lochtorridonhotel.com
Dir: *from A832 at Kinlochewe, take the A896 towards Torridon, do not turn into village carry on for 1m, hotel is on right*
This fine hotel with friendly and attentive service is set amidst

continued

spectacular scenery overlooking the loch, with the mountains providing a dramatic backdrop. Bedrooms are generally spacious, comfortable, and attractively furnished, many with fine antique furniture. The entrance hall leads into a welcoming lounge and there is also a wood panelled bar offering a great range of 250 malt whiskies. Hotel cuisine uses good quality ingredients from the kitchen garden to produce memorable meals.
ROOMS: 20 en suite (1 fmly) No smoking in all bedrooms s £50-£90; d £90-£260 (incl. bkfst) * LB **FACILITIES:** STV Fishing Pool table Croquet lawn Stalking Pony trekking Mountain biking Xmas
SERVICES: Lift **PARKING:** 30 **NOTES:** No dogs (ex guide dogs) No smoking in restaurant Civ Wed 38
CARDS:

TROON, South Ayrshire

Map 10 NS33

★★★★66% Marine

Crosbie Rd KA10 6HE
☎ 01292 314444 01292 316922
e-mail: marine@paramount-hotels.co.uk

PARAMOUNT GROUP OF HOTELS

Dir: *from A77 to A78, then A79 onto B749. Hotel on left passed the Municipal Golf Course*

This hotel has a fine position overlooking the 18th fairway of Royal Troon Golf Course and enjoying panoramic views of the Firth of Clyde, across to the Isle of Arran. Immaculate staff provide a notable level of hospitality and service, whilst smart public rooms include a choice of restaurants. Fairways restaurant (open just for dinner) serves award-winning cuisine, or one can eat less formally in Rizzios. Bedrooms range from spacious suites to cosy standard rooms.
ROOMS: 74 en suite (7 fmly) No smoking in 12 bedrooms s £94-£98; d £152-£158 * LB **FACILITIES:** STV Indoor swimming (H) Squash Sauna Solarium Gym Putting green Jacuzzi/spa Aerobics Beautician Steam room entertainment Xmas **CONF:** Thtr 220 Class 120 Board 60 Del from £129 * **SERVICES:** Lift **PARKING:** 200 **NOTES:** Civ Wed 50
CARDS:

Premier Collection

★★★ Lochgreen House

Monktonhill Rd, Southwood KA10 7EN
☎ 01292 313343 01292 318661
e-mail: lochgreen@costley-hotels.co.uk

Dir: *from A77 follow signs for Prestwick airport, 0.5m before airport take B749 to Troon. Hotel 1m on left*

Lochgreen is situated in 30 acres of wooded and landscaped gardens enjoying views over the Royal Troon golf course to the Clyde. Inside, the house offers the charm and elegance of past eras with antique furnishings and wood panelling. Bedrooms are well proportioned, stylish and very comfortable. Public areas include two sumptuously furnished sitting rooms, one of which contains the bar and malt whisky collection. The restaurant is unique in design; its high ceilings and tapestried walls lend a baronial feel to the surroundings.
ROOMS: 7 en suite 8 annexe en suite **FACILITIES:** Tennis (hard)
CONF: Thtr 40 Class 16 Board 16 Del from £127.50 *
PARKING: 50 **NOTES:** No dogs (ex guide dogs) No smoking in restaurant **CARDS:**

★★★74% *Highgrove House*

Old Loans Rd KA10 7HL
☎ 01292 312511 01292 318228

This stylish hotel enjoys magnificent panoramic views over the Firth of Clyde, and its guests are welcomed by a friendly and efficient team. The attractive split-level restaurant provides the ideal setting for impressively presented contemporary style cooking, whether from the good value lunch menu and evening brasserie selection, or the more sophisticated dinner dishes. Booking is almost essential to ensure a seat in either the restaurant or the bar. Bedrooms come in a variety of sizes and are all well equipped and smartly presented.
ROOMS: 9 en suite (2 fmly) **PARKING:** 50 **NOTES:** No dogs (ex guide dogs) **CARDS:**

★★★74% Piersland House

Craigend Rd KA10 6HD
☎ 01292 314747 01292 315613
e-mail: reception.piersland@talk21.com

SCOTLAND'S HOTELS OF DISTINCTION

Dir: *just off A77 on the B749 opposite Royal Troon Golf Club*

Close to the championship golf course, this fine hotel has been much extended over the years and is a popular venue for business trade, tourists and locals. Public rooms feature delightful oak panelling and large open fires in season. The lounge bar offers an

continued on p766

TROON, continued

extensive menu, whilst fine dining is par for the course in the elegant restaurant, with its relaxing cocktail lounge adjoining. Residents can choose from three styles of bedroom, cottage suites situated in a row to the rear of the hotel, large superior rooms in the main house, or smaller standard rooms. Whatever the choice, all are very well equipped.

ROOMS: 15 en suite 13 annexe en suite (2 fmly) s £82.50-£90; d £119-£165 (incl. bkfst) * LB **FACILITIES:** STV Croquet lawn Xmas **CONF:** Thtr 100 Class 60 Board 30 Del from £90 * **PARKING:** 150 **NOTES:** No smoking in restaurant Civ Wed 75 **CARDS:**

See advert on page 765

TURNBERRY, South Ayrshire — Map 10 NS20

Premier Collection

★★★★★ ֍֍
Turnberry Hotel, Golf Courses & Spa

KA26 9LT
☎ 01655 331000 Fax 01655 331706
Dir: *from Glasgow take the A77/M77 S towards Stranraer, 2m past Kirkoswald, follow signs for A719 Turnberry Village, hotel 500m on right*

This world-famous hotel enjoys tremendous views over to the Isle of Arran, the Mull of Kintyre and Ailsa Craig, as well as the adjoining golf courses, home to the Open Championship on several occasions. New for 2001 is the excellent Colin Montgomerie Golf Academy and accommodation in the new lodges. Spacious bedrooms and suites in the main hotel are equipped to high standards. The main restaurant offers classical cuisine in a traditional setting, whilst the brasserie has a modern more informal style; light meals are also served in the Golf Club house.

ROOMS: 132 en suite **FACILITIES:** STV Indoor swimming (H) Golf 18 Tennis (hard) Squash Riding Snooker Sauna Solarium Gym Putting green Jacuzzi/spa Health spa **CONF:** Thtr 160 Class 115 Board 50 **SERVICES:** Lift **PARKING:** 200 **CARDS:**

★★★77% ֍֍ **Malin Court**

Best Western

KA26 9PB
☎ 01655 331457 Fax 01655 331072
e-mail: info@malincourt.co.uk
Dir: *on A74 take Ayr exit. From Ayr take the A719 to Turnberry and Maidens*

This comfortable hotel enjoys lovely views over the Firth of Clyde and Turnberry golf courses. Public areas include a choice of lounges, plus a cocktail lounge adjoining the attractive restaurant. The restaurant serves light lunches and formal dinners.

continued

Standard and executive rooms are available, all equipped to a high standard.

ROOMS: 18 en suite (9 fmly) s £72-£82; d £104-£124 (incl. bkfst) * LB **FACILITIES:** STV Tennis (grass) Putting green Pitch & putt Childrens play area Xmas **CONF:** Thtr 200 Class 60 Board 30 Del from £65.50 * **SERVICES:** Lift **PARKING:** 110 **NOTES:** Civ Wed 120 **CARDS:**

See advert on opposite page

TYNDRUM, Stirling — Map 10 NN33

★62% **Invervey**
FK20 8RY
☎ 01838 400219 Fax 01838 400 280
Dir: *In the centre of Tyndrum beside the road, A82/85*

This welcoming family-run hotel, located in the village centre, has an informal atmosphere. Bedrooms are well equipped and the smallest rooms are in the chalet accommodation. There is a choice of lounges and bars, one with a smart conservatory extension. Food is served all day and the evening menu offers a good choice of dishes.

ROOMS: 21 rms (18 en suite) (3 fmly) s £25-£35; d £50 (incl. bkfst) * LB **FACILITIES:** Pool table Games room ch fac Xmas **CONF:** Class 15 **PARKING:** 50 **NOTES:** RS Nov-Apr **CARDS:**

UDDINGSTON, South Lanarkshire — Map 11 NS66

★★68% **Redstones**
8-10 Glasgow Rd G71 7AS
☎ 01698 813774 & 814843 Fax 01698 815319
e-mail: info@morris-inns.com
Dir: *1m along A721, opposite Uddingston railway station*

This friendly hotel comprises two linked sandstone Victorian villas. Public areas have all been attractively refurbished with the elegant Papillon restaurant offering interesting menus. The Brooklands lounge and dining room is more informal. Bedrooms, two of which have four-posters, offer mixed modern appointments and a good range of amenities.

ROOMS: 14 en suite (2 fmly) s fr £52; d fr £65 (incl. bkfst) * LB **FACILITIES:** STV Xmas **CONF:** Board 20 Del from £52 * **PARKING:** 27 **CARDS:**

UIG See Skye, Isle of

UNST See Shetland

Late for dinner? Quality Standards star rating means that last orders for dinner should be no earlier than:
★ 6.30pm ★★ 7.00pm ★★★ 8.00pm
★★★★ 9.00pm ★★★★★ 10.00pm

UPHALL, West Lothian
Map 11 NT07

★★★★67% ❀❀ Houstoun House
EH52 6JS
☎ 01506 853831 🖹 01506 854220
e-mail: info@houstoun.macdonaldhotels.co.uk
Dir: *from M8 junct 3 follow signs for Broxburn, go straight over rdbt then at mini-rdbt turn right heading for Uphall, hotel is 1m on right*

An impressive house set in 20 acres of grounds, handy for Livingston and the airport. Tastefully extended, it has a smart new Country Club with stylish Italian bistro. In the original house, a stone staircase leads from the vaulted cocktail bar to three elegant dining areas. Bedrooms, particularly the 'executive' rooms, are inviting.
ROOMS: 25 en suite 47 annexe en suite (30 fmly) No smoking in 63 bedrooms s fr £89; d fr £109 * LB **FACILITIES:** STV Indoor swimming (H) Sauna Solarium Gym Steam room Dance studio Beauty therapy room Xmas **CONF:** Thtr 350 Class 120 Board 70 Del from £145 * **PARKING:** 200 **NOTES:** No dogs (ex guide dogs) No smoking in restaurant **CARDS:**

UPLAWMOOR, East Renfrewshire
Map 11 NS45

★★71% Uplawmoor Hotel
Neilston Rd G78 4AF
☎ 01505 850565 🖹 01505 850689
e-mail: enquiries@uplawmoor.co.uk
Dir: *exit at junct 2 of M77, take A736 signposted to Barrhead and Irvine. Hotel located 4m beyond Barrhead*
Set in a village off the Glasgow to Irvine road, this friendly hotel has restaurant featuring imaginative dishes. There is a cocktail lounge adjacent, and a separate lounge bar serving food. The modern bedrooms are comfortable and well equipped.
ROOMS: 14 en suite (1 fmly) No smoking in 3 bedrooms s £47.50; d £70 (incl. bkfst) * **FACILITIES:** STV Pool table **PARKING:** 40 **NOTES:** No dogs No smoking in restaurant **CARDS:**

WESTHILL, Aberdeenshire
Map 15 NJ80

○ *Premier Lodge (Aberdeen South West)*
☎ 0870 700 1302 🖹 0870 700 1303
NOTES: Open Autumn 2000

TV dinner? Room service at three stars and above.

Popped the question? Hotels with Civ Wed in their entry are licensed for civil wedding ceremonies. Maximum numbers for the ceremony only are shown, e.g. Civ Wed 50

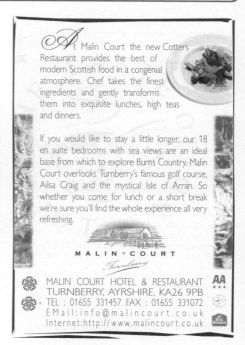

WHITBURN, West Lothian
Map 11 NS96

★★★65% The Hilcroft
East Main St EH47 0JU
☎ 01501 740818 🖹 01501 744013
e-mail: hilcroft@bestwestern.co.uk
Dir: *turn off M8 junct 4 follow signs for Whitburn, hotel 0.5m on left from junct*
This popular business hotel is in easy reach of the M8. Public areas have a bright contemporary style, with food served all day in the split-level bar and Bistro restaurant. All bedrooms are well equipped, but it is worth asking for one of the excellent executive rooms.
ROOMS: 31 en suite (7 fmly) No smoking in 12 bedrooms s £51-£59; d £64-£76 (incl. bkfst) * LB **FACILITIES:** STV Free use of Balbardie Sports Centre **CONF:** Thtr 200 Class 50 Board 30 Del from £75 * **PARKING:** 80 **NOTES:** No dogs (ex guide dogs) Civ Wed 200
CARDS:

WHITEBRIDGE, Highland

Map 14 NH41

Premier Collection

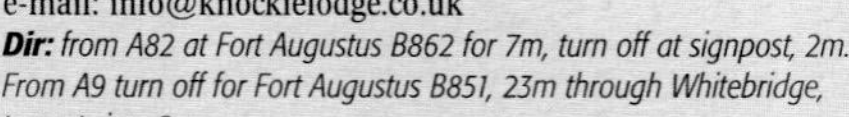

★★ Knockie Lodge

IV2 6UP

☎ 01456 486276 01456 486389

e-mail: info@knockielodge.co.uk

Dir: *from A82 at Fort Augustus B862 for 7m, turn off at signpost, 2m. From A9 turn off for Fort Augustus B851, 23m through Whitebridge, turn at sign, 2m*

Built as a shooting lodge over 200 years ago by the chief of Clan Fraser, Knockie Lodge enjoys a peaceful yet dramatic setting overlooking Loch nan Lann. After enjoying the great outdoors, guests can relax in the conservatory or enjoy afternoon tea in the comfortable lounge, with its log fire and honesty bar. The tempting but informal five-course set dinners are preceded by mouth-watering canapés in the lounge. There is a wide choice of bedroom sizes, with many thoughtful touches; do not expect televisions.

ROOMS: 10 en suite s £75-£138; d £120-£185 (incl. bkfst) * **FACILITIES:** Fishing Snooker Sailing **PARKING:** 10 **NOTES:** No children 10yrs No smoking in restaurant Closed Nov-Apr **CARDS:**

★★66% Whitebridge

IV2 6UN

☎ 01456 486226 & 486272 01456 486413

e-mail: whitebridgehotel@southlochness.demon.co.uk

Dir: *turn off A9 onto B851, follow signs to Fort Augustus*

On the south eastern side of Loch Ness, this family-run Highland hotel has a relaxed and welcoming atmosphere. The bedrooms are pleasant. Public areas include a choice of bars, a sitting room, and a dining room offering home-cooked fare.

ROOMS: 12 rms (10 en suite) (3 fmly) s £25-£30; d £48-£52 (incl. bkfst) * LB **FACILITIES:** Fishing Pool table **CONF:** Class 30 Board 25 **PARKING:** 32 **NOTES:** Closed 21 Dec-Feb **CARDS:**

WICK, Highland

Map 15 ND35

★★67% Mackay's

Union St KW1 5ED

☎ 01955 602323 01955 605930

e-mail: mackays.hotel@caithness_mm.co.uk

Dir: *opposite Caithness General Hospital*

This well established family-run hotel, standing on the south shore of the River Wick and close to the town centre, offers friendly and informal service. Many guests choose to eat in Ebenezers bar.

ROOMS: 27 rms (19 en suite) (4 fmly) **FACILITIES:** STV entertainment **CONF:** Thtr 100 Class 100 Board 60 **SERVICES:** Lift **NOTES:** No smoking in restaurant Closed 1-2 Jan **CARDS:**

Hotel of the Year, Wales

The Celtic Manor Resort,
Newport

A

ABERCRAF, Powys
Map 03 SN81

★★75% *Maes-Y-Gwernen*
School Rd SA9 1XD
☎ 01639 730218 01639 730765
e-mail: maesyg@globalnet.co.uk
On the edge of the Brecon Beacons, this hotel, surrounded by gardens and lawns, contains two annexe rooms and a building with gym equipment, sunbed and spa bath. Bedrooms are well appointed and an extensive menu is served in the spacious restaurant. An attractive conservatory and lounge offer pleasant areas in which to relax.
ROOMS: 10 en suite No smoking in 1 bedroom **FACILITIES:** STV Sauna Solarium Gym Jacuzzi/spa ch fac **PARKING:** 20 **NOTES:** No smoking in restaurant **CARDS:**

ABERDYFI, Gwynedd
Map 06 SN69

★★★71% Trefeddian
LL35 0SB
☎ 01654 767213 01654 767777
e-mail: tref@saqnet.co.uk
Dir: *0.5m N off A493*

A holiday hotel overlooking the local golf course, surrounded by grounds and gardens. It provides sound modern accommodation with well equipped bedrooms and bathrooms. Eight new luxury rooms with balconies and sea views are due to open in March 2001. Public areas include elegantly furnished lounges, indoor swimming pool and pitch-and-putt golf green. Children are welcome and recreation areas are provided.
ROOMS: 48 en suite (7 fmly) No smoking in 46 bedrooms s £58-£67; d £116-£134 (incl. bkfst & dinner) * LB **FACILITIES:** Indoor swimming (H) Tennis (hard) Snooker Solarium Pool table Putting green Table tennis Play area ch fac Xmas **SERVICES:** Lift **PARKING:** 68 **NOTES:** No smoking in restaurant Closed 4 Jan-5 Mar **CARDS:**

See advert on opposite page

★★★66% *Plas Penhelig Country House*
LL35 0NA
☎ 01654 767676 01654 767783
e-mail: contact@plaspenhelig.co.uk
An impressive country house in 14 acres of beautiful grounds and public gardens which overlook the Dyfi estuary. Bedrooms are bright and fresh, with modern facilities. The magnificent wood-panelled hall and adjacent lounge have log fires. Fish, game and other meats feature on the daily menu, which continues to maintain high standards.

continued

ROOMS: 11 en suite **FACILITIES:** Croquet lawn Putting green **CONF:** Thtr 40 Class 20 Board 22 **PARKING:** 40 **NOTES:** No children 10yrs No smoking in restaurant Closed Jan & Feb
CARDS:

See advert on opposite page

★★72% Penhelig Arms Hotel & Restaurant
LL35 0LT
☎ 01654 767215 01654 767690
e-mail: penheligarms@saqnet.co.uk
Dir: *take A493 coastal road, hotel faces Penhelig harbour*
This delightful 18th-century hotel stands opposite the old harbour overlooking the Dyfi Estuary to the mountains beyond. The bedrooms are well maintained, furnishings and fittings are of excellent quality, and there are good modern facilities. The public bar retains its original character and is much loved by locals who enjoy the bar food, particularly the fish and seafood, and real ale selections.
ROOMS: 10 en suite No smoking in all bedrooms s £39.50; d £69-£79 (incl. bkfst) LB **PARKING:** 12 **NOTES:** No smoking in restaurant Closed 25 & 26 Dec **CARDS:**

★★70% Harbour
LL35 0EB
☎ 01654 767250 01654 767792
e-mail: john.darcy@hemscott.net
Dir: *on the A493 coastal road between Dolgellau & Machynlleth*
This delightful hotel looks out towards the sand dunes of Ynyslas. Many of the tastefully decorated bedrooms enjoy the views and several family suites are provided. The elegant public areas are particularly attractive. There are three restaurants, but their availability is seasonal. A wine bar opens every evening and provides an extensive range of meals, there is an all-day coffee shop and the hotel restaurant serves fixed-price menus. There is a first floor residents' lounge and bar.
ROOMS: 9 en suite (3 fmly) No smoking in 3 bedrooms s £35-£64.50; d £70-£99 (incl. bkfst) * **FACILITIES:** ch fac **CONF:** Thtr 30 Class 12 Board 12 Del from £45 * **NOTES:** RS 30 Oct-Mar
CARDS:

ABERGAVENNY, Monmouthshire
Map 03 SO21

★★★67% *Allt-yr-Ynys Country House Hotel*
HR2 0DU
☎ 01873 890307 01873 890539
e-mail: allthotel@compuserve.com
(For full entry see Walterstone (Herefordshire))

Read all about it! Newspapers delivered to bedrooms in four and five star hotels.

★★★66% ❀❀ Llansantffraed Court

Llanvihangel Gobion NP7 9BA

☎ 01873 840678 🖷 01873 840674

e-mail: reception@llch.co.uk

Dir: *at A465/A40 Abergavenny intersection take B4598 signposted to Usk (do not join A40). Continue towards Raglan and hotel on left after 4.5m*

Set in extensive grounds, this imposing red brick country house enjoys views of the Brecon Beacons. The elegant ground floor public areas include an Italianate lobby and bar with a large lounge and spacious restaurant. Bedrooms are comfortably furnished with modern facilities.

ROOMS: 21 en suite (3 fmly) No smoking in 7 bedrooms s £70-£88; d £82-£155 (incl. bkfst) * LB **FACILITIES:** STV Fishing Croquet lawn Putting green Ornamental trout lake **CONF:** Thtr 220 Class 120 Board 100 Del from £115 * **SERVICES:** Lift **PARKING:** 250 **NOTES:** No smoking in restaurant Civ Wed 150

CARDS:

A

ABERGAVENNY, continued

★★70% ❀ *Llanwenarth Arms*
Brecon Rd NP8 1EP
☎ 01873 810550 ▯ 01873 811880
e-mail: mcgregor@netmatters.co.uk
Dir: *on A40 midway between Abergavenny and Crickhowell beside River Usk*
Standing on the A40 and sandwiched between the River Usk and the Sugar Loaf mountain, panoramic views of beautiful countryside are guaranteed at this privately owned hotel. The main building dates back to the 16th century, with a purpose-built annexe housing the attractively furnished and well equipped bedrooms. All but three bedrooms overlook river views and many have balconies. The traditional restaurant and bright conservatory lounge make the most of the riverside setting, and are complemented by a cosy bar. The restaurant menu makes extensive use of quality fresh produce and has a strong local flavour. Guests may also take advantage of the two stretches of trout and salmon fishing available to the hotel.
ROOMS: 18 en suite (2 fmly) **FACILITIES:** Fishing **PARKING:** 60 **NOTES:** No dogs (ex guide dogs) **CARDS:**

ABERGELE, Conwy Map 06 SH97

★★★65% Kinmel Manor
St Georges Rd LL22 9AS
☎ 01745 832014 ▯ 01745 832014
Dir: *at Abergele exit on A55*
Set in several acres of grounds, this 16th-century manor house provides several function suites and a fully equipped leisure centre. Many original features have been retained, including superb fireplaces in the restaurant and the hall. Several family rooms are available and all bedrooms are equipped with modern amenities.
ROOMS: 51 en suite (3 fmly) No smoking in 12 bedrooms s £52; d £72 (incl. bkfst) * LB **FACILITIES:** STV Indoor swimming (H) Sauna Solarium Gym Jacuzzi/spa Steam room Xmas **CONF:** Thtr 250 Class 100 Board 70 Del £69.50 * **PARKING:** 120 **NOTES:** Civ Wed 250
CARDS:

ABERPORTH, Ceredigion Map 02 SN25

★★★69% Hotel Penrallt
SA43 2BS
☎ 01239 810227 ▯ 01239 811375
Dir: *take B4333 signed Aberporth. Hotel 1m on the right*
This impeccably maintained Edwardian mansion, is now a privately owned and personally run hotel. It stands in extensive, well maintained grounds, complete with tennis courts, a swimming pool and a children's play area. Inside, original features such as carved ceiling beams and a splendid stained glass window are among the attractions in the smart public areas that include an inviting restaurant and a popular bar. The bedrooms are generally spacious, with balcony, and family rooms both available.
ROOMS: 16 en suite (2 fmly) s fr £60; d fr £95 (incl. bkfst) * LB
FACILITIES: Indoor swimming (H) Outdoor swimming (H) Tennis (hard) Sauna Solarium Gym Pool table Croquet lawn Putting green ch fac
CONF: Class 60 Board 30 **PARKING:** 100 **NOTES:** No smoking in restaurant Closed 23-31 Dec **CARDS:**

★★75% ❀ Penbontbren Farm
Glynarthen SA44 6PE
☎ 01239 810248 ▯ 01239 811129
Dir: *3.5m SE off Cardigan A487*
A genuine farm-house with 90 acres of land, which has a truly Welsh flavour as the caring staff are native speakers and the bilingual menus are based mainly around Welsh cuisine. Courtyard style bedrooms are located in classical farm buildings, all of which are well equipped and decorated. Public areas include a pine-furnished restaurant and a spacious lounge; there is also a games room, a farm museum and a nature trail.
ROOMS: 10 annexe en suite (6 fmly) No smoking in 2 bedrooms s £49; d £86 (incl. bkfst) * LB **FACILITIES:** Fishing Pool table Farm trail
CONF: Thtr 50 Class 25 Board 30 Del £60.50 * **PARKING:** 35
NOTES: No smoking in restaurant Closed 24-28 Dec
CARDS:

★★62% Highcliffe
SA43 2DA
☎ 01239 810534 ▯ 01239 810534
Dir: *off B4333*
A coastal hotel enjoying an elevated position above Cardigan Bay, with the sandy beaches close at hand. Hospitality is jovial and service is relaxed and informal. A wide range of meals is offered at good prices in the bar and restaurant. Bedrooms are comfortable and equipped with modern facilities.
ROOMS: 9 rms (8 en suite) 6 annexe en suite (4 fmly) s £30-£36; d £37-£55 (incl. bkfst) * LB **FACILITIES:** Xmas **PARKING:** 18
NOTES: No smoking in restaurant **CARDS:**

ABERSOCH, Gwynedd Map 06 SH32

★★★76% ❀ Neigwl
Lon Sarn Bach LL53 7DY
☎ 01758 712363 ▯ 01758 712544
e-mail: neigwl.hotel@which.net
Dir: *on A499, drive through Abersoch, hotel on the left overlooking the sea*
This delightful, small, family run hotel is conveniently located for access to the town, harbour and beach. It has a well deserved high reputation for its food and warm hospitality. Both the attractive restaurant and very pleasant lounge bar overlook sea views, as do several of the tastefully appointed bedrooms.
ROOMS: 7 en suite 2 annexe en suite (3 fmly) s £36-£71; d £56-£113 (incl. bkfst) * LB **FACILITIES:** ch fac **PARKING:** 30 **NOTES:** No dogs (ex guide dogs) **CARDS:**

★★★73% ❀❀ Porth Tocyn
Bwlch Tocyn LL53 7BU
☎ 01758 713303 ▯ 01758 713538
e-mail: porthtocyn.hotel@virgin.net
Dir: *2.5m S follow signs 'Porth Tocyn' and Brown Highway signs marked 'Gwesty/Hotel'*
Located above Cardigan Bay with fine views over the area, set in attractive gardens. Several elegantly furnished sitting rooms are provided and bedrooms are comfortably furnished. Children are especially welcome and have a play room. Fine food earns the restaurant a prestigious two-rosette award.
ROOMS: 17 en suite (1 fmly) s £49-£64; d £65.50-£119 (incl. cont bkfst) * LB **FACILITIES:** Outdoor swimming (H) Tennis (hard) **PARKING:** 50
NOTES: No smoking in restaurant Closed mid Nov-wk before Etr
CARDS:

See advert on opposite page

★★★68% ❀ White House
LL53 7AG
☎ 01758 713427 ▯ 01758 713512
e-mail: whitehousehotel@btinternet.com
Dir: *on A499 from Pwllheli hotel is on the right just before entering Abersoch village*
This well maintained, privately owned and personally run hotel stands in an elevated position on the outskirts of Abersoch, overlooking Cardigan Bay. The modern equipped and tastefully appointed accommodation includes bedrooms for non

continued

smokers. Public areas include a choice of lounges, a bright and spacious restaurant and a lounge bar with sea views.
ROOMS: 13 en suite (1 fmly) No smoking in 6 bedrooms s £37.50-£57.50; d £75-£85 (incl. bkfst) * LB **FACILITIES:** Xmas **CONF:** Thtr 90 Class 60 Board 40 **PARKING:** 100 **NOTES:** No smoking in restaurant
CARDS:

★★65% Deucoch

LL53 7LD
☎ 01758 712680 01758 712670
e-mail: deucoch@supanet.com
Dir: *through Abersoch village following signs for Sarn Bach. At cross roads in Sarn Bach (approx 1m from village centre) turn right, hotel on top of hill*
This hotel sits in an elevated position above the village and enjoys lovely views. There is a choice of bars and food options. The regular carvery provides excellent value and has a large following, so booking is essential. Pretty bedrooms are equipped with satellite television and other modern amenities. The hotel specialises in golfing packages.
ROOMS: 10 rms (9 en suite) (2 fmly) s £29.50; d £60 (incl. bkfst) * LB **FACILITIES:** Xmas **PARKING:** 30 **NOTES:** No smoking in restaurant
CARDS:

ABERYSTWYTH, Ceredigion — Map 06 SN58

★★★73% Conrah

Ffosrhydygaled, Chancery SY23 4DF
☎ 01970 617941 01970 624546
e-mail: hotel@conrah.freeserve.co.uk
Dir: *on A487, 3.5m S*

This country house hotel stands in 22 acres of mature grounds, three and a half miles south of Aberystwyth. The elegantly furnished public rooms include a choice of comfortable lounges with welcoming open fires. Conference and leisure facilities are available, while the cuisine which is French with modern influences, continues to achieve very high standards. Rooms are available in both the country house and a nearby annexe, and are well equipped and tastefully furnished.

continued

ROOMS: 11 en suite 6 annexe en suite (1 fmly) s £68-£90; d £90-£130 (incl. bkfst) LB **FACILITIES:** Indoor swimming (H) Sauna Croquet lawn Table tennis **CONF:** Thtr 40 Class 20 Board 20 Del from £120 * **SERVICES:** Lift **PARKING:** 60 **NOTES:** No dogs No children 5yrs No smoking in restaurant Closed 23 Dec-2 Jan Civ Wed 65
CARDS:

★★★69% *Belle Vue Royal*

Marine Ter SY23 2BA
☎ 01970 617558 01970 612190
Dir: *near the Pier*

Dating back more than 170 years, this family owned hotel stands on the promenade, a short walk from the shops. Family and sea-view rooms are available, and all are well equipped. Public areas include extensive function rooms and a choice of bars. Food options include bar meals and more formal restaurant dining, where fresh local produce always satisfies the appetite of the guests.

continued

ABERYSTWYTH, continued

ROOMS: 34 en suite (6 fmly) No smoking in 10 bedrooms
FACILITIES: STV **CONF:** Thtr 70 Class 20 Board 28 **PARKING:** 15
NOTES: No dogs (ex guide dogs) Closed 24-26 Dec
CARDS:

See advert on opposite page

★★68% Four Seasons
50-54 Portland St SY23 2DX
☎ 01970 612120 🖹 01970 627458
e-mail: info@fourseasonshotel.demon.co.uk
Dir: *in town centre, car park entrance in Bath Street*
Conveniently located between the town centre and the seafront, the Four Seasons is a well maintained and friendly hotel, which can also cater for small meetings. A cosy lounge is provided, plus a separate bar. A wide choice of food is available, and there is an enclosed rear car park. The bedrooms are attractive and well equipped.
ROOMS: 14 rms (13 en suite) (1 fmly) No smoking in 7 bedrooms s £55; d £82 (incl. bkfst) * LB **CONF:** Thtr 25 Class 15 **PARKING:** 10 **NOTES:** No dogs (ex guide dogs) No smoking in restaurant Closed 25-31 Dec **CARDS:**

★★68% *Richmond*
44-45 Marine Ter SY23 2BX
☎ 01970 612201 🖹 01970 626706
Dir: *on entering town follow signs for Promenade*
This hotel lies in the centre of the promenade with good sea views from the public areas and from many of the bedrooms. The public areas and bedrooms are comfortably furnished and family rooms are available. An attractive dining room and comfortable lounge with a bar are provided. There is also a suite available for local functions.
ROOMS: 15 en suite (6 fmly) **FACILITIES:** STV **CONF:** Thtr 60 Class 22 Board 28 **PARKING:** 20 **NOTES:** No dogs (ex guide dogs) No smoking in restaurant Closed 20 Dec-3 Jan **CARDS:**

★★64% *Groves*
MINOTEL Great Britain
44-46 North Pde SY23 2NF
☎ 01970 617623 🖹 01970 627068
e-mail: info@ghotel.force9.co.uk
Dir: *N on A487, in town centre*
Conveniently located just a few minutes walk from the shopping area and the sea front, the Groves Hotel is both a friendly and popular hotel. Functions and meetings of up to 50 people can be accommodated and the bar and cafe-style restaurant offer a good range of eating options. Bedrooms are well equipped with modern facilities.
ROOMS: 9 en suite (1 fmly) No smoking in 2 bedrooms **CONF:** Thtr 50 **PARKING:** 4 **NOTES:** No dogs (ex guide dogs) No smoking in restaurant **CARDS:**

★★62% Marine Hotel
The Promenade SY23 2BX
☎ 01970 612444 🖹 01970 617435
Dir: *from W on A44. From north or south Wales on A487. On sea front west of pier*
Situated on the promenade overlooking Cardigan Bay the hotel is also close to the centre of town with its many attractions. Bedrooms have been tastefully decorated, some have four poster beds and many have sea views. The recently refurbished reception rooms are comfortable and relaxing and meals are served in the elegant dining room or the bar. Wedding and conference facilities are also available.

continued

ROOMS: 44 en suite (7 fmly) No smoking in 1 bedroom s £38-£58; d £55-£89 (incl. bkfst) * LB **FACILITIES:** Sauna Solarium Gym Pool table Jacuzzi/spa Xmas **CONF:** Thtr 250 Class 180 Board 120 Del from £65 * **SERVICES:** Lift **PARKING:** 15
CARDS:

AMLWCH See Anglesey, Isle of

AMMANFORD, Carmarthenshire — Map 03 SN61

★★68% *Mill at Glynhir*
Glyn-Hir, Llandybie SA18 2TE
☎ 01269 850672 🖹 01269 850672
e-mail: tgittins@aol.com
Dir: *turn off A483 Llandybie signposted Golf Course*
Nestling in beautiful countryside, this former water mill is situated adjacent to the local golf course. Popular with golfers and walkers, accommodation comprises restful and well equipped bedrooms around the mill. The bar/lounge and restaurant make up the public areas which also include a heated indoor swimming pool.
ROOMS: 11 en suite **FACILITIES:** Indoor swimming (H) Golf 18 Fishing **PARKING:** 20 **NOTES:** No children 11yrs No smoking in restaurant Closed Xmas RS 24-30 Dec **CARDS:**

ANGLESEY, ISLE OF, Isle of Anglesey

AMLWCH — Map 06 SH49

★★69% Lastra Farm
Penrhyd LL68 9TF
☎ 01407 830906 🖹 01407 832522
e-mail: booking@lastra-hotel.com
Dir: *after 'Welcome to Amlwch' sign turn left. Straight across main road, left at T-junct on to Rhosgoch road*
This former 17th-century farmhouse offers pine-furnished, colourfully decorated bedrooms, some of which are in the newly converted lodge a short distance from the hotel. There is also a comfortable lounge and a cosy bar. A wide range of good-value food is available. The hotel can cater for functions and banquets in a nearby hall.
ROOMS: 5 en suite 3 annexe en suite (1 fmly) s fr £32; d fr £53.50 (incl. bkfst) * LB **CONF:** Thtr 100 Class 80 Board 30 Del from £50 * **PARKING:** 40 **NOTES:** No smoking in restaurant Civ Wed 85
CARDS:

★★66% *Trecastell*
Bull Bay LL68 9SA
☎ 01407 830651 🖹 01407 832114
e-mail: trecastell.hotel@nol.co.uk
Dir: *1m N on A5025, adjacent to Golf Club*
Near the local golf course, this traditional hotel overlooks Bull Bay. The popular bar serves a range of food, with formal dining in the

continued

attractive restaurant. Refurbished bedrooms are well equipped, family and sea view rooms are available. There is a games room and cosy lounge.
ROOMS: 13 rms (11 en suite) (3 fmly) **FACILITIES:** Pool table **CONF:** Thtr 20 Class 10 Board 10 **PARKING:** 60 **NOTES:** No smoking in restaurant **CARDS:**

BEAUMARIS
Map 06 SH67

★★75% ❀❀ Ye Olde Bulls Head Inn
Castle St LL58 8AP
☎ 01248 810329 🖷 01248 811294
e-mail: info@bullsheadinn.co.uk
Dir: *from Britannia road bridge follow A545, located in town centre*
Charles Dickens and Samuel Johnson were regular visitors to this inn. Features include exposed beams, fireplaces and antique weaponry. Richly decorated bedrooms are well equipped. There is a spacious lounge, meetings and small functions are catered for. Food continues to attract praise in the restaurant and brasserie.
ROOMS: 14 en suite 1 annexe en suite No smoking in 4 bedrooms s £53-£55; d £83-£85 (incl. bkfst) LB **CONF:** Thtr 25 Board 16 **PARKING:** 11 **NOTES:** No dogs (ex guide dogs) No smoking in restaurant Closed 25-26 Dec & 1 Jan **CARDS:**

★★71% Bishopsgate House
54 Castle St LL58 8BB
☎ 01248 810302 🖷 01248 810166
e-mail: hazel@johnson-ollier.freeserve.co.uk
Dir: *turn off in Menai Bridge onto A545. Follow the only road into Beaumaris, hotel is on the left in the main street*
Dating back to 1760, this immaculately maintained small hotel features fine examples of wood panelling and a Chinese Chippendale staircase. Well equipped bedrooms are attractively decorated and two have four-poster beds.
ROOMS: 9 en suite s £40-£50; d £65-£75 (incl. bkfst) * LB **PARKING:** 8 **NOTES:** No smoking in restaurant Closed 31 Dec-10 Jan
CARDS:

★★67% *Bulkeley Arms*
Best Western
Castle St LL58 8AW
☎ 01248 810415 🖷 01248 810146
e-mail: consorthotels@compuserve.com
Dir: *leave the A5 and follow signs for Menai Bridge. Take A545 from bridge to Beaumaris. Hotel in centre of town opposite pier overlooking waterfront*
A Grade I listed hotel built in 1831 to celebrate a visit by Princess Victoria, it has fine views from many rooms. Well equipped bedrooms are generally spacious with pretty fabrics and wallpapers. There is a choice of bars, an all-day coffee lounge and health club. Regular jazz evenings, a resident pianist and friendly staff create a relaxed atmosphere.
ROOMS: 41 rms (40 en suite) (4 fmly) **FACILITIES:** Sauna Solarium Gym Climbing wall entertainment **CONF:** Thtr 200 Class 180 Board 40 **SERVICES:** Lift **PARKING:** 30 **NOTES:** No smoking in restaurant
CARDS:

HOLYHEAD
Map 06 SH28

★★66% Boathouse Hotel
Newry Promenade, Newry Beach LL65 1YF
☎ 01407 762094 🖷 01407 764898
Dir: *follow signs for Maring. Hotel is situated at end of Promenade*
Situated in a prominent position overlooking the harbour and the Holyhead Mountains, the hotel makes an ideal ferry stop. Rooms are en suite, attractively decorated to a high standard and well equipped. Downstairs the attractive lounge bar offers a wide range of home cooked food and there is a separate breakfast room.
continued

ROOMS: 17 en suite (1 fmly) No smoking in 15 bedrooms s £45-£47; d £65-£70 (incl. bkfst) * LB **CONF:** Thtr 40 Class 30 Board 30 Del from £68 * **PARKING:** 40 **NOTES:** No smoking in restaurant
CARDS:

★★61% Bull
London Rd, Valley LL65 3DP
☎ 01407 740351 🖷 01407 742328
Dir: *3.5m from ferry terminal, on A5 near junct with A5025*
A busy hotel on the approach to Holyhead. Its popular bars offer good-value food and host local quizzes and other functions. There is a choice of bedroom location, either in the main building or nearby annexe; all rooms are well equipped with modern amenities and family rooms are available.
ROOMS: 9 en suite 5 annexe en suite (4 fmly) s £37; d £50 (incl. bkfst) * LB **PARKING:** 130 **NOTES:** No dogs (ex guide dogs)
CARDS:

LLANFAIRPWLLGWYNGYLL
Map 06 SH57

★★★64% Carreg Bran Country Hotel
Church Ln LL61 5YH
☎ 01248 714224 🖷 01248 715983
Dir: *from Holyhead 1st junct for Llanfairpwll. Through village then 1st right before dual carriageway and bridge*
A family-run hotel close to the banks of the Menai Straits. Rooms are prettily decorated, spacious and well equipped. The restaurant is attractively decorated and food has a local flavour. There is a choice of bars and a large function room, popular for weddings and business meetings.
ROOMS: 29 en suite (3 fmly) No smoking in 7 bedrooms s fr £50; d fr £69 (incl. bkfst) * LB **FACILITIES:** Pool table Xmas **CONF:** Thtr 130 Class 120 Board 100 **PARKING:** 120 **NOTES:** No smoking in restaurant Civ Wed **CARDS:**

A

MENAI BRIDGE — Map 06 SH57

★★66% *Anglesey Arms*
LL59 5EA
☎ 01248 712305 01248 712076
Dir: *on left after Menai Bridge*
This popular hotel next to the Menai Suspension bridge sits in well maintained, pretty gardens. The hotel provides smart, well equipped accommodation. Bedrooms are attractively furnished in pine and equipped with thoughtful extras. There is a choice of bars and an excellent selection of meals.
ROOMS: 16 en suite (2 fmly) **CONF:** Thtr 60 Class 40 Board 40 **PARKING:** 60 **NOTES:** No dogs (ex guide dogs)
CARDS:

★★60% *Victoria Hotel*
Telford Rd LL59 5DR
☎ 01248 712309 01248 716774
Dir: *cross Menai Bridge, turn right at rdbt and continue 100yds to hotel*
This family run hotel is situated in Menai Bridge and with panoramic views of the Menai Straits and Britannia bridge and is an ideal base for touring Anglesey or Snowdonia. Many rooms have their own balconies and overlook the Straits. Downstairs there are two character bars where meals are available and there is also a more formal conservatory dining room. The hotel also holds a civil marriage licence.
ROOMS: 14 en suite 3 annexe en suite **FACILITIES:** Pool table Childrens playground **PARKING:** 40 **CARDS:**

TREARDDUR BAY — Map 06 SH27

★★★70% Trearddur Bay
LL65 2UN
☎ 01407 860301 01407 861181
e-mail: mark@markdglil.demon.co.uk
Dir: *from A5 turn left at lights in Valley on the B4545 toward Trearddur Bay, at Power garage on right, turn left opposite garage, hotel on right*
Facilities at this fine modern hotel include extensive function and conference rooms, an indoor swimming pool and a games room. Bedrooms are well equipped, many have sea views and suites are available. An all-day bar serves a wide range of snacks and lighter meals, supplemented by a cocktail bar and the more formal hotel restaurant.
ROOMS: 37 en suite (7 fmly) No smoking in 1 bedroom
FACILITIES: STV Indoor swimming (H) Croquet lawn **CONF:** Thtr 120 Class 60 Board 40 **PARKING:** 300 **NOTES:** No smoking in restaurant Civ Wed **CARDS:**

★★★64% Beach
Lon St Ffraid LL65 2YT
☎ 01407 860332 01407 861140
Dir: *from mainland follow A5 to Valley Crossroads. Left at lights, follow B4545 for 2.5m, hotel on right*
The refurbished leisure centre at this busy commercial hotel provides some excellent facilities, including a supervised play-centre for children. Light meals and snacks are available from the London Road bar and more formal dining is available in the main restaurant. Bedrooms are all equipped with modern facilities.
ROOMS: 27 en suite (3 fmly) s £39.50-£44.50; d £65-£70 (incl. bkfst) * LB **FACILITIES:** Snooker Pool table ch fac Xmas **CONF:** Thtr 70 Class 70 Board 40 Del from £42.50 * **PARKING:** 100
CARDS:

Bad hair day? Hairdryers in all rooms three stars and above.

BALA, Gwynedd — Map 06 SH93

★★★75% Pale Hall Country House
Llandderfel LL23 7PS
☎ 01678 530285 01678 530220
e-mail: palehall@fsbdial.co.uk
Dir: *off the B4401 Corwen/Bala road 4m from Llandrillo*
This enchanting mansion was built in 1870 and overlooks extensive grounds and beautiful woodland. The fine entrance hall, with vaulted ceiling and galleried oak staircase leads off to the library bar, two elegant lounges and the smart dining room. The standard of cooking remains high and is complemented by fine wines. The spacious bedrooms are furnished to the highest standards with many thoughtful extras.
ROOMS: 17 en suite (1 fmly) No smoking in 7 bedrooms s £69-£120; d £95-£155 (incl. bkfst) * LB **FACILITIES:** Fishing Clay pigeon/Game shooting Xmas **CONF:** Board 22 **PARKING:** 60 **NOTES:** No dogs No smoking in restaurant Civ Wed 100 **CARDS:**

See advert on opposite page

★★65% *Plas Coch*
High St LL23 7AB
☎ 01678 520309 01678 521135
Dir: *on A494*
A focal point for the bustling town, this 18th-century coaching inn is popular with locals and guests alike. The spacious public areas include a pleasant reception lounge, separate bistro-style restaurant, and the public and lounge bars. Bedrooms are comfortable and pleasantly decorated.
ROOMS: 10 en suite (4 fmly) **FACILITIES:** Windsurfing Canoeing Sailing **PARKING:** 20 **NOTES:** No dogs (ex guide dogs) No smoking in restaurant Closed 25 Dec **CARDS:**

BANGOR, Gwynedd — Map 06 SH57

Travelodge
Llys-y-Gwynt LL57 4BG
☎ 01248 370345 01248 370345

Travelodge

Dir: *junc A5/A55*
This modern building offers accommodation in smart, spacious and well equipped bedrooms, all with en suite bathrooms. Refreshments may be taken at the nearby family restaurant. For further details and the Travelodge phone number, consult the Hotel Groups page.
ROOMS: 62 en suite

BARMOUTH, Gwynedd — Map 06 SH61

★★69% Wavecrest Hotel
8 Marine Pde LL42 1NA
☎ 01341 280330 01341 280330
Dir: *turn left over level-crossing, then immediately right onto Marine Parade*
This delightful hotel on the promenade has superb views from many rooms over Cardigan Bay towards the Cader Idris mountains. Bedrooms are attractively decorated and several rooms are suitable for families. The bar and restaurant are open plan and there is also a small seating area on the first-floor. Hotel cuisine is excellent and often uses local produce.
ROOMS: 9 en suite (4 fmly) No smoking in all bedrooms s £23-£37; d £40-£54 (incl. bkfst) LB **PARKING:** 2 **NOTES:** No smoking in restaurant Closed Nov-Mar **CARDS:**

Packed in a hurry? Ironing facilities should be available at all star levels, either in rooms or on request.

★★66% Ty'r Graig Castle Hotel
Llanaber Rd LL42 1YN
☎ 01341 280470 01341 281260
e-mail: tyrgraig.castle@btinternet.com
Dir: *0.75m from Barmouth on the Harlech road, Seaward side*
An unusual Gothic-style hotel with impressive stained glass windows and wood-panelled walls. There is a comfortable lounge and a modern conservatory bar with ocean views. Bedrooms are modern and well equipped, four are in rounded towers with views over Cardigan Bay. Food is of good quality, and enjoyed in a friendly and relaxed atmosphere.
ROOMS: 12 en suite No smoking in 1 bedroom s £42; d £65-£75 (incl. bkfst) * LB **FACILITIES:** STV **CONF:** Thtr 50 Class 30 Board 20 **PARKING:** 15 **NOTES:** No smoking in restaurant Closed 25 Dec-1 Feb
CARDS:

★★65% Bryn Melyn
Panorama Rd LL42 1DQ
☎ 01341 280556 01341 280342
e-mail: bryn.melyn@virgin.net
Dir: *off A496, 0.25m on left - Panorama Road - leaving Barmouth for Dolgellau*
This family-run hotel has superb views over the Mawddach Estuary to the Cader Idris mountains. Bedrooms are decorated with pretty wallpapers and fabrics and equipped with modern facilities. Public areas include a comfortable lounge and a cane-furnished conservatory. Good home cooking is on offer and vegetarians are well looked after.
ROOMS: 9 rms (8 en suite) (1 fmly) s £29-£39; d £44-£68 (incl. bkfst) * LB **FACILITIES:** Xmas **PARKING:** 10 **NOTES:** No smoking in restaurant **CARDS:**

BARRY, Vale of Glamorgan — Map 03 ST16

★★★77% Egerton Grey Country House
Porthkerry CF62 3BZ
☎ 01446 711666 01446 711690
e-mail: info@egertongrey.co.uk
Dir: *from junct 33 of M4 follow signs for airport and turn left at rdbt for Porthkerry, after 500yds turn left down lane between thatched cottages*

An elegant country house that offers warm hospitality and attentive service. The charming public areas are very relaxing; period furnishings adorn the restaurant, lounge and library. Spacious bedrooms are tastefully appointed, some wonderful original bathroom furniture. Cuisine is taken seriously at both breakfast and dinner with a menu which includes wonderful Glamorgan sausages.
ROOMS: 10 en suite (4 fmly) s £89.50-£110; d £95-£130 (incl. bkfst) * LB **FACILITIES:** STV Tennis Croquet lawn Croquet Xmas **CONF:** Thtr 30 Class 30 Board 22 Del from £120 * **PARKING:** 41 **NOTES:** No smoking in restaurant Civ Wed 120
CARDS:

See advert under CARDIFF

B

BARRY, continued

★★★65% Mount Sorrel

Porthkerry Rd CF62 7XY
☎ 01446 740069 🖷 01446 746600
e-mail: res@mountsorrel.co.uk
Dir: *from M4 junct 33 on A4232. Follow signs for A4050 through Barry. Upon reaching mini rdbt with church opposite turn left, hotel 300mtrs on the left*
Situated in an elevated position above the town centre this is an extended Victorian property, offering comfortable accommodation. The public areas include a choice of conference rooms, restaurant and bar, together with leisure facilities.
ROOMS: 43 en suite (3 fmly) s £55-£75; d £75-£95 (incl. bkfst) * LB **FACILITIES:** STV Indoor swimming (H) Sauna Gym Xmas **CONF:** Thtr 150 Class 100 Board 50 Del £90 * **PARKING:** 17 **NOTES:** No smoking in restaurant Civ Wed 150 **CARDS:**

BEAUMARIS See Anglesey, Isle of

BEDDGELERT, Gwynedd — Map 06 SH54

★★★66% *Royal Goat*

LL55 4YE
☎ 01766 890224 & 890343 🖷 01766 890422
Dir: *off A498*
A privately owned hotel built over 200 years ago. Modern bedrooms are pretty and well equipped. Public areas include a choice of bars, a comfortable lounge, meeting and function rooms. Friendly staff are mostly Welsh speaking.
ROOMS: 32 en suite (3 fmly) No smoking in 10 bedrooms **FACILITIES:** STV Fishing Pool table **CONF:** Thtr 80 Class 70 Board 70 **SERVICES:** Lift **PARKING:** 100 **NOTES:** No smoking in restaurant **CARDS:**

★★71% Tanronnen Inn

LL55 4YB
☎ 01766 890347 🖷 01766 890606
Dir: *in the centre of village*
This delightful small hotel offers comfortable and well appointed bedrooms and a range of attractive and relaxing public areas. The wide range of bar food is popular with tourists, more formal meals are served in the restaurant. Staff are friendly and helpful, there is a peaceful atmosphere. Beddgelert has won the 'Britain in Bloom' competition for many years.
ROOMS: 7 en suite (3 fmly) s £40; d £78 (incl. bkfst) * LB **FACILITIES:** STV Xmas **PARKING:** 15 **NOTES:** No dogs **CARDS:**

BETWS-Y-COED, Conwy — Map 06 SH75

see also Llanrwst

★★★70% Royal Oak

Holyhead Rd LL24 0AY
☎ 01690 710219 🖷 01690 710603
e-mail: royal-oak@betws-y-coed.co.uk
Dir: *on main A5 in centre of town, next to St Mary's church*
This fine hotel started life as a coaching inn, and now provides smart bedrooms and a wide range of public areas. Food is available in the bistro and in Stables Bar, a Grill Room for snacks, while more formal eating is available in the main dining room.
ROOMS: 26 en suite (3 fmly) No smoking in 6 bedrooms s £50; d £70-£92 (incl. bkfst) * LB **FACILITIES:** STV Pool table entertainment Xmas **CONF:** Thtr 20 Class 20 Board 20 **PARKING:** 90 **NOTES:** No dogs (ex guide dogs) Closed 25-26 Dec Civ Wed 100
CARDS:

See advert on opposite page

★★★69% *Waterloo*

LL24 0AR
☎ 01690 710411 🖷 01690 710666
e-mail: reservations
@waterloohotel.infotrade.co.uk
Dir: *close to A5, near Waterloo Bridge*
This long established hotel named after the nearby Waterloo bridge is ideally located for touring Snowdonia. Accommodation is split between rooms in the main hotel as well as modern, cottage style rooms located in buildings to the rear. Public areas include the attractive Snowdonia Restaurant, offering traditional Welsh specialities, the Wellington Bar, offering light meals and snacks, and a well equipped leisure and spa complex.
ROOMS: 40 en suite **FACILITIES:** Indoor swimming (H) Sauna Solarium Gym Pool table Jacuzzi/spa Steam room **CONF:** Thtr 75 Class 50 Board 25 **PARKING:** 200 **NOTES:** Closed 30 Dec-8 Jan
CARDS:

★★★64% Craig-y-Dderwen Country House Hotel

LL24 0AS
☎ 01690 710293 🖷 01690 710362
e-mail: craig-y-dderwen@betws-y-coed.co.uk
Dir: *A5 to town, cross Waterloo Bridge and take first left*
This Victorian country house hotel in well maintained grounds, lies alongside the River Conwy at the end of a tree-lined drive. Very pleasing views can are enjoyed from many rooms. Comfortable lounges are provided, and two of the bedrooms have four-posters. The atmosphere is tranquil and relaxing.
ROOMS: 16 en suite (5 fmly) d £55-£87.50 (incl. bkfst) * LB **FACILITIES:** Badminton,Golf driving range,Volleyball **CONF:** Thtr 50 Class 25 Board 12 Del from £60 * **PARKING:** 50 **NOTES:** No smoking in restaurant Closed Dec-1 Feb **CARDS:**

★★★64% Glan Aber

Holyhead Rd LL24 0AB
☎ 01690 710325 🖷 01690 710700
e-mail: glanaber@hotmail.com
Dir: *turn off A5 onto the Waterloo Bridge and proceed a quarter mile. Hotel on left next to HSBC Bank*
Glan Aber is located in the heart of the mountain resort and provides modern, well equipped bedrooms and comfortable public areas. A large menu is offered, supplemented by a good range of bar meals. There is a choice of bars, a separate pool room, and a secure car park. A first floor lounge is provided, and there is a spa bath and sun-bed.
ROOMS: 25 en suite (3 fmly) s £24.50-£27.50; d £49-£55 (incl. bkfst) * LB **FACILITIES:** STV Fishing Sauna Solarium Pool table Jacuzzi/spa **CONF:** Thtr 30 Class 30 Board 20 **SERVICES:** Lift **PARKING:** 21 **NOTES:** Closed 24-25 Dec **CARDS:**

See advert on opposite page

Premier Collection

★★ Tan-y-Foel Country House

Capel Garmon LL26 0RE
☎ 01690 710507 🖷 01690 710681
e-mail: tanyfoel@wiss.co.uk
Dir: *off A5 at Betws-y-Coed onto A470, travel 2m N sign marked Capel Garmon on right, take this turning towards Capel Garmon for 1.5m hotel sign on left*
Perched on a wooded hillside overlooking the Conwy Valley and the town below Tan Y Foel appears the archetypal country house. The 16th century stone built house leaves some traditions at the front door whilst valuing those of

continued

comfort, service and hospitality. The interior design and colour schemes are both bold and modern -the lounge is furnished and decorated using earthy tones whilst the restaurant is verdant and cosy warmed by a wood burning stove and the breakfast room has stunning lighting effects. Bedrooms typically are individually designed with brighter colour effects. The cooking is also vibrant and modern using organic produce where possible to great effect.

ROOMS: 5 en suite 2 annexe en suite No smoking in all bedrooms s £70-£90; d £90-£150 (incl. bkfst) * LB **PARKING:** 9 **NOTES:** No dogs (ex guide dogs) No children 7yrs No smoking in restaurant Closed mid-27 Dec RS Jan **CARDS:**

Arriving late? Four and five star hotels have night porters to assist with your luggage; and 24hr room service.

B

BETWS-Y-COED, continued

★★67% Park Hill
Llanrwst Rd LL24 0HD
☎ 01690 710540 01690 710540
e-mail: parkhill.hotel@virgin.net
Dir: *0.5m N of Betws-y-Coed on A470 Llanrwst road*
This friendly hotel benefits from a peaceful location overlooking the village. Comfortable bedrooms come in a wide range of sizes and are well equipped. There is a choice of lounges, seating in the covered entrance porch and a heated swimming pool is available to residents.
ROOMS: 9 en suite (2 fmly) s £35-£50; d £55-£75 (incl. bkfst) * LB **FACILITIES:** Indoor swimming (H) Sauna Jacuzzi/spa Xmas **PARKING:** 11 **NOTES:** No dogs (ex guide dogs) No children 6yrs No smoking in restaurant **CARDS:**

★68% Fairy Glen
LL24 0SH
☎ 01690 710269 01690 710269
Dir: *turn off A5 onto A470 Southbound (Dolwyddelan Road.) Hotel 0.5m on left by Beaver bridge*
Dating back over 300 years, this former coaching inn is near the Fairy Glen beauty spot. It provides modern accommodation with good facilities and very friendly service. There is a cosy bar and separate lounge, good home cooking is served.
ROOMS: 8 rms (6 en suite) (2 fmly) s £21-£36; d £42-£48 (incl. bkfst) * LB **PARKING:** 10 **NOTES:** No smoking in restaurant Closed Nov-Jan **CARDS:**

BIRCHGROVE, Swansea Map 03 SS79

★★62% *Oak Tree Parc*
Birchgrove Rd SA7 9JR
☎ 01792 817781 01792 814542
Dir: *300yds from M4 junc 44*
A large Victorian house standing in its own grounds which provides a variety of accommodation including family-bedded rooms. The public areas comprise a lounge bar and a restaurant serving an extensive range of varied dishes.
ROOMS: 10 en suite (2 fmly) **CONF:** Thtr 40 Class 25 Board 20 **PARKING:** 40 **NOTES:** Closed 25-31 Dec **CARDS:**

BLACKWOOD, Caerphilly Map 03 ST19

★★★67% Maes Manor
NP12 0AG
☎ 01495 224551 & 220011 01495 228217
Dir: *A4048 to Tredega. At Pontllanfraith left at rdbt,through Blackwood High St. After 1.25m left at Rack Inn. Hotel 400yds on left*
Standing high above the town, this 19th-century manor house is set in nine acres of gardens and woodland. Bedrooms are attractively decorated with co-ordinated furnishings. The restaurant is supplemented by a choice of bars with a lounge/lobby area and a large function room, which is regularly the setting for live enertainment.
ROOMS: 8 en suite 14 annexe en suite (2 fmly) s £57.50-£75; d £75-£85 (incl. bkfst) * LB **CONF:** Thtr 200 Class 200 Board 100 Del from £75 * **PARKING:** 100 **CARDS:**

Early start? Hotels at all star levels should provide in-room alarm clocks and/or alarm calls.

BLAENAU FFESTINIOG, Gwynedd Map 06 SH74

★★68% Queens Hotel
1 High St LL41 3ES
☎ 01766 830055 01766 830046
e-mail: cathy@queensffestiniog.freeserve.co.uk
Dir: *on A470 adjacent to Ffestiniog railway, between Betws-y-Coed & Dolgellau*
A flourishing hotel with an all-day bistro serving popular meals and snacks, with more formal dining in the evening. A large function room is available for weddings and other events, and business meetings can be accommodated. Bedrooms are well equipped, attractively decorated and furnished; family rooms are available. The hotel lies at the northern end of the famous Ffestiniog narrow gauge railway line.
ROOMS: 12 en suite (4 fmly) s £40-£60; d £55-£80 (incl. bkfst) * LB **FACILITIES:** STV entertainment **CONF:** Thtr 100 Class 60 Board 40 **NOTES:** No dogs (ex guide dogs) No smoking in restaurant Closed 25 Dec **CARDS:**

BONTDDU, Gwynedd Map 06 SH61

★★★71% Bontddu Hall
LL40 2UF
☎ 01341 430661 01341 430284
e-mail: reservations@bontdduhall.fsnet.co.uk
Dir: *located in Bontddu village , turn off A470 N of Dolgellau heading towards Barmouth. Halfway between Dolgellau and Barmouth on the A496*

Overlooking the beautiful Mawddach Estuary, this 19th century house was once the country retreat of the Lord Mayor of Birmingham. Bedrooms are spacious and well equipped. Elegant public areas include lounges and an attractive bar. In addition to the formal dinner menu, there is a lighter brasserie-style option.
ROOMS: 15 en suite 5 annexe en suite (6 fmly) s fr £62.50; d fr £110 (incl. bkfst) * LB **FACILITIES:** 14 acres of gardens/woodland **PARKING:** 50 **NOTES:** No children 3yrs No smoking in restaurant Closed Nov-Mar Civ Wed 150 **CARDS:**
See advert under BARMOUTH

BRECHFA, Carmarthenshire Map 02 SN53

★★73% Ty Mawr Country Hotel
SA32 7RA
☎ 01267 202332 01267 202437
Dir: *off B4310 in centre of village*
Ty Mawr (the Big House), with the River Marlais flowing through its grounds, dates back some 450 years. The accommodation is well maintained and public areas have both charm and character. Privately owned and personally run, the hotel is establishing a firm reputation for its friendly hospitality and good food.
ROOMS: 5 rms (4 en suite) (1 fmly) No smoking in all bedrooms s £52-£75; d £84-£130 (incl. bkfst) * LB **PARKING:** 45 **NOTES:** No smoking in restaurant **CARDS:**

BRECON, Powys Map 03 SO02

★★★74% ❀ Nant Ddu Lodge
Cwm Taf, Nant Ddu CF48 2HY
☎ 01685 379111 ▤ 01685 377088
e-mail: enquiries@nant-ddu-lodge.co.uk
(For full entry see Nant-Ddu)

★★★73% Peterstone Court
Llanhamlech LD3 7YB
☎ 01874 665387 ▤ 01874 665376
Dir: *A40 towards Abergavenny, hotel in approximately 4m, on the right hand side*
This impressive 18th-century house, located less than four miles east of Brecon on the A40, makes a relaxing centre from which to tour what is a remote and beautiful corner of Wales. The stone built court is surrounded by the Brecon Beacons and stands in an elevated position over-looking the River Usk. Spacious bedrooms are equipped with plenty of antiques, comfortable armchairs and thoughtful extras such as heavy towelling robes. There is an elegant drawing room with some fine paintings and a library filled with leather and highly polished wood. Leisure facilities include a basement health club and an outdoor heated swimming pool located in the extensive terraced garden. Other facilities include a choice of rooms for functions and meetings.
ROOMS: 8 en suite 4 annexe en suite (1 fmly) s £85-£115; d £95-£115 (incl. bkfst) * LB **FACILITIES:** STV Outdoor swimming (H) Fishing Sauna Solarium Gym Pool table Croquet lawn Jacuzzi/spa Xmas **CONF:** Thtr 200 Class 100 Board 30 Del from £125 * **PARKING:** 90 **CARDS:**

BRECON, continued

★★70% ❀
Best Western Castle of Brecon
Castle Square LD3 9DB
☎ 01874 624611 📠 01874 623737
e-mail: hotel@breconcastle.co.uk
Dir: *follow signs to Town Centre. Turn opposite The Boars Head, towards Cradoc*
Standing next to the ruins of Brecon Castle, this early 19th century coaching inn has impressive views of the Usk Valley and the Brecon Beacons National Park. The public rooms include a choice of two bars and a separate lounge in addition to a large restaurant that is the venue for some imaginative cooking of quality produce. The bedrooms are modern and include a number of extra facilities. Conference and function rooms are also available.
ROOMS: 30 en suite 12 annexe en suite (4 fmly) s £45-£59; d £59-£79 (incl. bkfst) * LB **FACILITIES:** STV **CONF:** Thtr 170 Class 150 Board 80 Del from £59 * **PARKING:** 30 **NOTES:** No smoking in restaurant Closed 23-25 Dec Civ Wed **CARDS:**

★★70% **Lansdowne Hotel & Restaurant**
The Watton LD3 7EG
☎ 01874 623321 📠 01874 610438
e-mail: reception@lansdownehotel.co.uk
Dir: *turn off A40/A470 onto the B4601, hotel in town centre*
A family-run hotel close to the town centre, it provides good value accommodation and friendly hospitality. The bedrooms are all well equipped, and ground floor and family rooms are available. Facilities include a traditionally furnished lounge, a split level dining room with original stone fireplace, and a bar.
ROOMS: 9 en suite (2 fmly) s £27.50; d £47.50 (incl. bkfst) * LB **FACILITIES:** Xmas **NOTES:** No dogs (ex guide dogs) No children 5yrs **CARDS:**

BRIDGEND, Bridgend — Map 03 SS97
see also Porthcawl

Courtesy & Care Award

★★★76% ❀ **Coed-y-Mwstwr**
Coychurch CF35 6AF
☎ 01656 860621 📠 01656 863122
e-mail: anything@coed-y-mwstwr.com
Dir: *leave A473 at Coychurch and turn right at petrol station. Follow signs at top of hill*
Set in seventeen acres of grounds, just a few miles from the centre of Bridgend, this is a tranquil setting for both business and leisure guests. The hotel retains many of its original features, including an impressive domed ceiling in what is now the elegantly appointed restaurant. The spacious bedrooms, which include two full suites, offer a good range of extra facilities. A variety of meeting rooms is also available, as well as a large function suite. The hotel also boasts an outdoor heated swimming pool and tennis court.
ROOMS: 23 en suite (2 fmly) No smoking in 10 bedrooms s £95; d £135 (incl. bkfst) * LB **FACILITIES:** STV Outdoor swimming (H) Golf 9 Tennis (hard) Croquet lawn Xmas **CONF:** Thtr 225 Class 75 Board 60 **SERVICES:** Lift **PARKING:** 100 **NOTES:** No dogs (ex guide dogs) Civ Wed 200 **CARDS:**

★★★75% ❀ **The Great House Restaurant & Hotel**
Laleston CF32 0HP
☎ 01656 657644 📠 01656 668892
e-mail: greathse1@aol.com
Dir: *at side of A473, 400yds from its junction with A48*
A hotel housed in a Grade II listed building, dating back to 1550. Original features such as mullioned windows, flagstone floors, oak beams and inglenook fireplaces add character, especially the great stone arch over the fireplace in the bar. The restaurant offers a wide range of dishes. Bedrooms are located in the original building and a purpose built annexe, and decorated with rich colours and fabrics.
ROOMS: 8 en suite 8 annexe en suite No smoking in 4 bedrooms s £55-£85; d £80-£120 (incl. bkfst) * LB **FACILITIES:** STV Sauna Gym Croquet lawn Jacuzzi/spa Health suite **CONF:** Thtr 40 Class 40 Board 20 Del from £99 * **PARKING:** 40 **NOTES:** No dogs (ex guide dogs) No smoking in restaurant Closed 25 Dec-2 Jan
CARDS:

★★★69% ***Heronston***
Ewenny Rd CF35 5AW
☎ 01656 668811 📠 01656 767391
Dir: *exit M4 at junc 35, follow signs for Porthcawl, at fourth rdbt turn left towards Ogmore-by-Sea (B4265) hotel 200yds on left*
Situated close to the town centre and the M4, this large modern hotel offers spacious well-equipped accommodation. Public areas which have recently been refurbished include an open plan lounge/bar, attractive restaurant, a smart leisure club complete with a new gym. The hotel is also equipped with a variety of conference rooms.
ROOMS: 69 en suite 6 annexe en suite (4 fmly) No smoking in 12 bedrooms **FACILITIES:** STV Indoor swimming (H) Outdoor swimming (H) Sauna Solarium Jacuzzi/spa Steamroom Residential Aromatherapist and Masseur **CONF:** Thtr 200 Class 80 Board 60 **SERVICES:** Lift **PARKING:** 250 **NOTES:** RS 25-26 Dec
CARDS:

⌂ **Days Inn**
Sarn Park Services, M4 CF32 9RW
☎ 01656 659218 📠 01656 768665
Dir: *M4 junct 36*
Fully refurbished, Days Inn offers well equipped, brightly appointed, modern accommodation with smart en suite bathrooms. There is a fully staffed reception; continental breakfast is available and other refreshments may be taken at the nearby family restaurant.
ROOMS: 40 en suite d fr £40 *

BUILTH WELLS, Powys — Map 03 SO05

★★★71% ❀ **Caer Beris Manor**
LD2 3NP
☎ 01982 552601 📠 01982 552586
e-mail: caerberismanor@btinternet.com
Dir: *SW on A483*
There is some excellent fishing at this 19th-century country house, but you don't have to fish to appreciate the River Irfon that runs

through the grounds. Many improvements have been made to the public areas and bedrooms, all benefiting from elegant decoration. Meals can be taken in the oak-panelled dining room or in the less formal conservatory.
ROOMS: 23 en suite (1 fmly) s £51-£61; d £82-£102 (incl. bkfst) * LB **FACILITIES:** STV Fishing Riding Sauna Gym Clay pigeon shooting Xmas **CONF:** Thtr 100 Class 75 Board 50 Del from £59.95 * **PARKING:** 32 **NOTES:** No smoking in restaurant Civ Wed 100 **CARDS:**

★★68% Pencerrig Gardens
Llandrindod Rd LD2 3TF
☎ 01982 553226 🖷 01982 552347
e-mail: pencerrig@travers-hotels.co.uk
Dir: *2m N on A483 towards Llandrindod Wells*

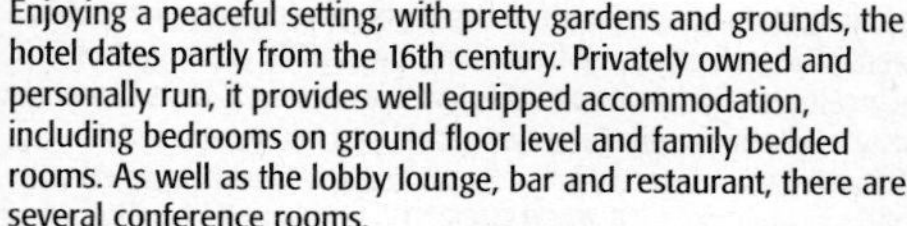

Enjoying a peaceful setting, with pretty gardens and grounds, the hotel dates partly from the 16th century. Privately owned and personally run, it provides well equipped accommodation, including bedrooms on ground floor level and family bedded rooms. As well as the lobby lounge, bar and restaurant, there are several conference rooms.
ROOMS: 20 en suite (3 fmly) s £30-£60; d £50-£80 (incl. bkfst) * LB **FACILITIES:** Croquet lawn Xmas **CONF:** Thtr 75 Class 40 Board 30 Del from £70 * **PARKING:** 40 **NOTES:** No smoking in restaurant **CARDS:**

BURTON, Pembrokeshire — Map 02 SM90

★★66% Beggars Reach
SA73 1PD
☎ 01646 600700 🖷 01646 600560
e-mail: stay@beggars-reach.com
Dir: *8m S of Haverfordwest, off A477*
This privately owned and personally run hotel was once a Georgian rectory. It stands in 4 acres of grounds and is peacefully located close to the village of Burton, to the south of Haverfordwest. Milford Haven and the ferry terminal at Pembroke Dock are both within easy reach. It provides modern equipped accommodation, which is suitable for both business people and tourists. Two of the bedrooms are located in former stables, which date back to the 14th century.
ROOMS: 10 en suite 2 annexe en suite (4 fmly) No smoking in 3 bedrooms s £32.50-£62.50; d £52.50-£62.50 (incl. bkfst) * LB **FACILITIES:** STV Xmas **PARKING:** 50 **CARDS:**

CAERNARFON, Gwynedd — Map 06 SH46

★★★79% Seiont Manor
Llanrug LL55 2AQ
☎ 01286 673366 🖷 01286 672840
Dir: *E on A4086, 2.5m from Caernarfon*
This splendid hotel, set in tranquil countryside near to Snowdonia, was created from authentic rural buildings. Individually decorated bedrooms are well equipped and include luxurious extra touches. Public rooms are cosy and comfortable, furnished in a country house style. The hotel cuisine often features regional specialities.
ROOMS: 28 en suite (7 fmly) No smoking in 8 bedrooms s £95-£150; d £140-£180 (incl. bkfst) * LB **FACILITIES:** STV Indoor swimming (H) Fishing Sauna Solarium Gym Jacuzzi/spa Xmas **CONF:** Thtr 100 Class 40 Board 40 Del from £135 * **PARKING:** 150 **NOTES:** No smoking in restaurant Civ Wed 100 **CARDS:**

★★★65% Celtic Royal Hotel
Bangor St LL55 1AY
☎ 01286 674477 🖷 01286 674139
Dir: *7m off A55 Expressway at Bangor*
This well known hotel, close to the centre of the town, offers generally spacious and attractively furnished bedrooms. The lounge bar, serving snacks at lunchtime and in the evening, features regular local entertainment. The restaurant offers good freshly prepared meals.
ROOMS: 110 en suite s £55-£64; d £80-£90 (incl. bkfst) * LB **FACILITIES:** STV Indoor swimming (H) Sauna Gym Jacuzzi/spa Aerobics Xmas **CONF:** Thtr 300 Class 170 Board 125 **SERVICES:** Lift **PARKING:** 180 **NOTES:** Civ Wed 200 **CARDS:**

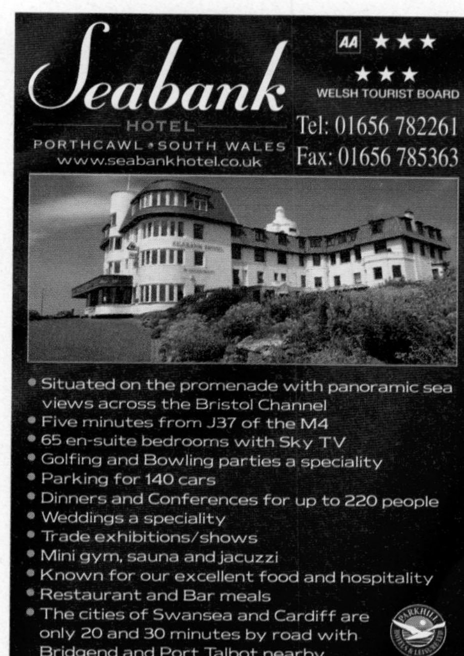

★★74% Ty'n Rhos Country Hotel & Restaurant
Llanddeiniolen LL55 3AE
☎ 01248 670489 🖷 01248 670079
e-mail: enquiries@tynrhos.co.uk
Dir: *situated in the hamlet of Seion between B4366 and B4547*
Ty'n Rhos is a peaceful converted farmhouse, set in lovely countryside between Snowdon and the Menai Straits. The lounge, with its slate inglenook fireplace, is elegantly furnished and there is a small bar for pre-dinner drinks. The conservatory offers a comfortable vantage point from which to admire the views and the gardens.
ROOMS: 11 en suite 3 annexe en suite No smoking in all bedrooms s £55-£75; d £80-£110 (incl. bkfst) LB **FACILITIES:** Croquet lawn **CONF:** Board 20 **PARKING:** 14 **NOTES:** No dogs (ex guide dogs) No children 6yrs No smoking in restaurant Closed 24-30 Dec, RS Sun evening (rest closed to non-res) **CARDS:**

★★65% Menai Bank
North Rd LL55 1BD
☎ 01286 673297 🖷 01286 673297
e-mail: menaibankhotel@tesco.net
Dir: *on A487 towards Bangor, on rdbt opposite Safeways foodmarket*
Built at the turn of the century as a private residence, this hotel provides bright, modern accommodation. It features original

continued

CAERNARFON, continued

stained glass windows and tiled fireplaces. A comfortable lounge is provided for residents and there is a small bar.
ROOMS: 16 en suite (6 fmly) No smoking in 5 bedrooms s £32-£41; d £50-£62 (incl. bkfst) LB **FACILITIES:** Pool table **PARKING:** 10
NOTES: No smoking in restaurant **CARDS:**

C

★★65% Stables
Llanwnda LL54 5SD
☎ 01286 830711 & 830935 01286 830413
Dir: *3m S of Caernarfon, on A499*
A pleasing rural hotel complex in North Wales. The bar and tempting restaurant reside in converted stables, with the rest of the facilities in a modern annexe, which include a breakfast room, and reception area. Bedrooms are brightly decorated and many have four poster beds.
ROOMS: 22 annexe en suite (8 fmly) s £39-£48; d £59-£68 (incl. bkfst) * LB **FACILITIES:** Outdoor swimming Guests may bring own horse to stables Xmas **CONF:** Thtr 50 Class 30 Board 30 Del £69.95 *
PARKING: 40 **CARDS:**

CAERPHILLY, Caerphilly — Map 03 ST18

Premier Lodge
Corbetts Ln CF83 3HX
☎ 0870 700 1346 0870 700 1347
Premier Lodge offers modern, well equipped, en suite accommodation suitable for both business and leisure travellers. Meals can be taken at the adjacent popular restaurant and bar which is fully licensed. For further details, consult the Hotel Groups page.
ROOMS: 40 en suite d £42 *

PREMIER LODGE

CAPEL CURIG, Conwy — Map 06 SH75

★★64% Cobdens
LL24 0EE
☎ 01690 720243 01690 720354
e-mail: info@cobdens.co.uk
Dir: *on A5, 4m W of Betws-y-Coed*
For over 200 years this hotel at Moel Siabod in the heart of Snowdonia has been a centre for outdoor pursuits. The bedrooms are modern and well equipped, and many enjoy the lovely views. There are two bars, one with an impressive, exposed rock face. The hotel is run by a friendly team and offers a full range of good-value meals.
ROOMS: 16 en suite (2 fmly) s £29.50; d £59 (incl. bkfst) *
FACILITIES: Fishing Pool table Xmas **CONF:** Thtr 40 Class 30 Board 25 Del £55 * **PARKING:** 60 **NOTES:** No smoking in restaurant
CARDS:

THE CIRCLE Selected Individual Hotels GREAT BRITAIN

CARDIFF, Cardiff — Map 03 ST17
see also Barry

★★★★★71% St David's Hotel & Spa
Havannah St, Cardiff Bay CF10 5SD
☎ 029 2045 4045 029 2048 7056
e-mail: reservations@fivestar-htl-wales.com
This stunning hotel has quickly become a destination in itself. All the stylish bedrooms in this imaginatively designed building have outside terraces and views over Cardiff Bay. Rooms are equipped to a high standard and comfortably furnished. Public areas are equally impressive, the seven story atrium towers above the lobby. The spa offers an impressive range of facilities and treatments. The Tides restaurant serves accomplished cooking.

continued

ROOMS: 136 en suite (10 fmly) No smoking in 50 bedrooms s £130; d £160 * LB **FACILITIES:** STV Indoor swimming (H) Sauna Solarium Gym Jacuzzi/spa entertainment Xmas **CONF:** Thtr 270 Class 110 Board 110 Del from £140 * **SERVICES:** Lift air con **PARKING:** 80
NOTES: No dogs (ex guide dogs) No smoking in restaurant Civ Wed 150
CARDS:

★★★★71% Copthorne Cardiff-Caerdydd
Copthorne Way, Culverhouse Cross CF5 6DH
☎ 029 2059 9100 029 2059 9080
e-mail: sales.cardiff@mill-cop.com
Dir: *exit at junct 33 of M4 and take A4232 for 2.5m in direction of Cardiff West and then A48*
Conveniently located for the city and airport, the Copthorne is a comfortable, popular, modern hotel with bright open-plan public areas. The well equipped bedrooms are smartly presented with rich colours and fabrics and comfortable seating. Guests can enjoy tasty meals in the restaurant overlooking a lake.
ROOMS: 135 en suite (10 fmly) No smoking in 78 bedrooms s £120-£140; d £140-£160 * LB **FACILITIES:** STV Indoor swimming (H) Snooker Sauna Gym Jacuzzi/spa Steam room Xmas **CONF:** Thtr 300 Class 140 Board 80 Del £140 * **SERVICES:** Lift **PARKING:** 225
NOTES: No smoking in restaurant **CARDS:**

COPTHORNE

★★★★66% Cardiff Marriott
Mill Ln CF10 1EZ
☎ 029 2039 9944 029 2039 5578
Dir: *from M4 junct 29 follow signs City Centre. Turn left into High Street opposite Castle, then 2nd left, at bottom of High St into Mill Lane*
Ideally located in the heart of the city, this large modern hotel boasts smart new public areas and a good range of services. Eating options include Chats café bar and the contemporary Mediterrano restaurant. The well equipped bedrooms are comfortable and are furnished to a high standard, with the bonus of air-conditioning. On site parking is also useful.
ROOMS: 182 en suite (58 fmly) No smoking in 124 bedrooms d £104-£135 * LB **FACILITIES:** STV Indoor swimming (H) Sauna Solarium Gym Jacuzzi/spa Steam room Xmas **CONF:** Thtr 300 Class 200 Board 100 Del from £115 * **SERVICES:** Lift air con **PARKING:** 110
NOTES: No dogs (ex guide dogs) Civ Wed 120
CARDS:

Marriott HOTELS · RESORTS · SUITES

★★★★65% Jurys Cardiff
Mary Ann St CF10 2JH
☎ 029 2034 1441 029 2022 3742
e-mail: info@jurys.com
Dir: *next to Ice Rink, opposite Cardiff International Arena*
A stylish city centre hotel located directly opposite the Cardiff International Arena. The comfortable, well-equipped bedrooms are situated around an impressive central atrium which gives access to the restaurant and Kavanagh's Irish theme bar. Extensive conference and function facilities are available in addition to a business centre and a fitness room.
ROOMS: 146 en suite (6 fmly) No smoking in 24 bedrooms d £70-£125 * LB **FACILITIES:** STV **CONF:** Thtr 200 Class 80 Board 50 Del from £100 * **SERVICES:** Lift **PARKING:** 55 **NOTES:** No dogs (ex guide dogs)
CARDS:

JURYS HOTEL GROUP

Popped the question? Hotels with Civ Wed in their entry are licensed for civil wedding ceremonies. Maximum numbers for the ceremony only are shown, e.g. Civ Wed 50

★★★★64% Cardiff Bay
Schooner Way, Atlantic Wharf CF10 4RT
☎ 029 2047 5000 Fax 029 2048 1491
e-mail: gwyn.jones@awhotels.com
Dir: *leave M4 junct 33 follow signs to Cardiff Bay A4232, then to Atlantic Wharf & Cardiff Bay Hotel. Hotel at Schooner Way & Tyndall St junct*
Situated in the heart of Cardiff's exciting new Bay development area, this is a smart modern hotel. A new wing of bedrooms complements existing rooms which have been upgraded. Halyard's restaurant is the primary eating option, and lighter meals are available in two of the bars. Lounge areas are provided, as well as conference and leisure facilities.
ROOMS: 156 en suite (6 fmly) No smoking in 50 bedrooms s £110; d £130 (incl. bkfst) * LB **FACILITIES:** STV Indoor swimming (H) Snooker Sauna Solarium Gym Pool table Jacuzzi/spa Xmas **CONF:** Thtr 250 Class 90 Board 40 Del from £105 * **SERVICES:** Lift **PARKING:** 150 **NOTES:** No smoking in restaurant Civ Wed 180
CARDS:

★★★★61% Angel Hotel
Castle St CF10 1SZ
☎ 029 2023 2633 Fax 029 2039 6212
e-mail: angel@paramount-hotels.co.uk
Dir: *opposite Cardiff Castle*
This well established hotel is ideally placed in the heart of the city overlooking the castle. Bedrooms all featuring air conditioning are decorated and furnished to a high standard. Public areas include an impressive lobby, a modern restaurant and a selection of conference rooms.
ROOMS: 102 en suite (4 fmly) No smoking in 32 bedrooms s £60-£105; d £78-£120 * LB **FACILITIES:** STV Xmas **CONF:** Thtr 300 Class 180 Board 80 Del from £85 * **SERVICES:** Lift air con **PARKING:** 60 **NOTES:** No smoking in restaurant **CARDS:**

PARAMOUNT GROUP OF HOTELS

★★★74% New House
Thornhill CF14 9UA
☎ 029 2052 0280 Fax 029 2052 0324
e-mail: newhousecountry@bestwestern.co.uk
Dir: *on A469*
Standing on the Cardiff side of Caerphilly mountain, the New House enjoys tranquil rural surroundings with panoramic views of the city centre. There is a country house feel to the public areas, which comprise a lounge and bar with deep cushioned seating and an elegant restaurant. The bedrooms are primarily located in a nearby annexe and all are spacious, well appointed and imaginatively decorated.
ROOMS: 36 en suite (3 fmly) No smoking in 3 bedrooms s £87.50-£102; d £112.50-£165 (incl. bkfst) * LB **FACILITIES:** STV Outdoor swimming (H) Xmas **CONF:** Thtr 200 Class 150 Board 200 Del from £103 * **PARKING:** 100 **NOTES:** No dogs (ex guide dogs) Civ Wed 200
CARDS:

Best Western

★★★73% Manor Parc Country Hotel & Restaurant
Thornhill Rd, Thornhill CF14 9UA
☎ 029 2069 3723 Fax 029 2061 4624
Dir: *on A469*
On the northern suburban edge of Cardiff, this hotel is located in pleasingly leafy grounds. There is a warm welcome and professional service delivered by smartly attired staff. The bedrooms are spacious and thoughtfully furnished and include a luxury suite. The public rooms offer a comfortable lounge and a restaurant with a magnificent lantern ceiling.
ROOMS: 12 en suite (2 fmly) **FACILITIES:** STV Tennis (hard) **CONF:** Thtr 120 Class 80 Board 50 **PARKING:** 70 **NOTES:** No dogs (ex guide dogs) Closed 24-26 Dec & 1 Jan Civ Wed 100
CARDS:

CARDIFF, continued

★★★72% Quality

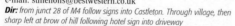

Merthyr Rd, Tongwynlais CF15 7LD
☎ 029 2052 9988 🖷 029 2052 9977
e-mail: admin@gb629.u-net.com
Dir: *M4 junct 32, take exit for Tongwynlais A4054 off large rdbt, hotel situated on right hand side*

In a prime location on the major interchange between Cardiff and the M4 motorway, this modern hotel provides very well-equipped, comfortable bedrooms together with bright open-plan public areas and leisure facilities. A good range of meeting rooms and extensive car parking make it a popular conference venue.

ROOMS: 95 en suite (6 fmly) No smoking in 47 bedrooms s £83; d £108 * LB **FACILITIES:** STV Indoor swimming (H) Sauna Solarium Gym Jacuzzi/spa ch fac Xmas **CONF:** Thtr 200 Class 80 Board 80 Del £104 * **SERVICES:** Lift **PARKING:** 100 **NOTES:** No smoking in restaurant Civ Wed 180 **CARDS:**

★★★72% St Mellons Hotel & Country Club

Castleton CF3 2XR
☎ 01633 680355 🖷 01633 680399
e-mail: stmellons@bestwestern.co.uk
Dir: *from junct 28 of M4 follow signs into Castleton. Through village, then sharp left at brow of hill following hotel sign into driveway*

In a quiet location on the Western edge of Cardiff, this country house style hotel offers quality accommodation with excellent leisure facilities. The bedrooms are located in nearby wings and are spacious and well appointed. The main house offers relaxing lounges, a bar and an elegant restaurant.

ROOMS: 21 en suite 20 annexe en suite (9 fmly) s £90-£120; d £100-£130 (incl. bkfst) * LB **FACILITIES:** Indoor swimming (H) Tennis (hard) Squash Sauna Solarium Gym Jacuzzi/spa Beauty salon Xmas **CONF:** Thtr 220 Class 70 Board 40 Del from £120 * **PARKING:** 90 **NOTES:** No smoking in restaurant Civ Wed 160 **CARDS:**

★★★70% *Posthouse Cardiff*

Pentwyn Rd, Pentwyn CF2 7XA
☎ 0870 400 8141 🖷 029 2054 9147
Dir: *leave M4 Jct29, onto A48M, take 2nd exit (Pentwyn) 3rd exit off the rdbt. Hotel is located on the R.H.S, past the Mercedes garage*

Suitable for both the business and leisure traveller, this bright hotel provides modern accommodation in well equipped bedrooms with en suite bathrooms.

ROOMS: 142 en suite (50 fmly) No smoking in 55 bedrooms **FACILITIES:** Indoor swimming (H) Sauna Solarium Gym Pool table Jacuzzi/spa Childrens play area ch fac **CONF:** Thtr 140 Class 70 Board 40 **SERVICES:** Lift **PARKING:** 300 **NOTES:** No smoking in restaurant **CARDS:**

★★★66% *Posthouse Cardiff City*

Castle St CF1 2XB
☎ 0870 400 8140 🖷 029 2023 1482

A large modern hotel with a wide range of services and amenities, designed particularly for the business traveller. Some bedrooms look out over the River Taff and the new National Stadium. Bedrooms are smart, comfortable and well equipped.

ROOMS: 155 en suite No smoking in 102 bedrooms **FACILITIES:** STV Pool table **CONF:** Thtr 170 Class 65 Board 50 **SERVICES:** Lift **PARKING:** 130 **CARDS:**

★★67% Sandringham

21 St Mary St CF10 1PL
☎ 029 2023 2161 🖷 029 2038 3998
Dir: *access via junct 29 on M4, follow 'City Centre' signs. Opposite the castle turn into High Street which leads to St Mary St*

Located in Cardiff city centre, the Sandringham offers convenient shopping and a friendly atmosphere. A smart restaurant and bar, 'Café Jazz' complements the hotel; as the name suggests live jazz is on offer several nights a week. The hotel also has a separate bar and a breakfast room. The bedrooms are well equipped with modern facilities and furnishings.

ROOMS: 28 en suite (1 fmly) No smoking in 2 bedrooms s £45-£65; d £55-£70 (incl. bkfst) * LB **FACILITIES:** entertainment **CONF:** Thtr 100 Class 70 Board 60 **PARKING:** 6 **NOTES:** No dogs (ex guide dogs) **CARDS:**

⌂ Express by Holiday Inn Cardiff

Malthouse Av, Cardiff Gate Business Park, Pontprennau CF23 8RA
☎ 029 2073 3222 🖷 029 2073 4222
Dir: *M4 junct30, take slip road signed Cardiff Service Station. Hotel located on left hand side*

A modern budget hotel offering comfortable accommodation in refreshing, spacious and comprehensively-equipped bedrooms, en suite bathrooms with power showers and continental buffet breakfast included in the room rate. Suitable for business travellers or families. For further details and the Express by Holiday Inn phone number, consult the Hotel Groups page.

ROOMS: 78 en suite (incl. cont bkfst) d fr £52.50 * **CONF:** Thtr 35 Class 30 Board 20

⌂ Express by Holiday Inn Cardiff Bay

Schooner Way, Atlantic Wharf CF10 5EQ
☎ 029 2044 9000 🖷 029 2048 8922
e-mail: sarah@cdfba.freeserve.co.uk
Dir: *From M4 junct33, take A4232 & follow rd to end. Left at 1st rdbt & left again past the Country Hall on right. Take 1st right & hotel is on the right*

A modern budget hotel offering comfortable accommodation in

continued

refreshing, spacious and comprehensively-equipped bedrooms, en suite bathrooms with power showers and continental buffet breakfast included in the room rate. Suitable for business travellers or families. For further details and the Express by Holiday Inn phone number, consult the Hotel Groups page.
ROOMS: 87 en suite (incl. cont bkfst) d £50-£59.50 * **CONF:** Thtr 30 Class 30 Board 20 Del £87.50 *

⌂ *Hotel Ibis Cardiff*
Churchill Way CF1 4JH
☎ 029 2064 9250
Modern, budget hotel offering comfortable accommodation in bright and practical bedrooms. Breakfast is self-service and dinner is available in the restaurant. For further details, consult the Hotel Groups page.

⌂ Campanile
Caxton Place, Pentwyn CF2 7HA
☎ 029 2054 9044 🖷 029 2054 9900

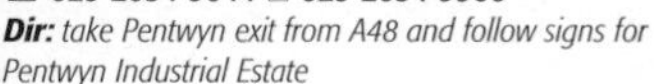
Dir: *take Pentwyn exit from A48 and follow signs for Pentwyn Industrial Estate*

This modern building offers accommodation in smart well equipped bedrooms, all with en suite bathrooms. Refreshments may be taken at the informal Bistro. For further details and the Campanile phone number, consult the Hotel Groups page.
ROOMS: 50 annexe en suite **CONF:** Thtr 35 Class 18 Board 20

⌂ *Travelodge*
Circle Way East, Llanedeyrn CF3 7ND
☎ 029 2054 9564 🖷 029 2054 9564
Dir: *M4 junc30, take A4232 to North Pentwyn Interchange. A48 & signs for Cardiff East & Docks. 3rd exit at Llanedeyrn Interchange, follow Circle Way East*
This modern building offers accommodation in smart, spacious and well equipped bedrooms, all with en suite bathrooms. Refreshments may be taken at the nearby family restaurant. For further details and the Travelodge phone number, consult the Hotel Groups page.
ROOMS: 32 en suite

⌂ *Travelodge*
Granada Service Area M4, Pontyclun CF72 8SA

☎ 029 2089 1141 🖷 029 2089 2497
Dir: *M4, junct 33/A4232*
This modern building offers accommodation in smart, spacious and well equipped bedrooms, all with en suite bathrooms. Refreshments may be taken at the nearby family restaurant. For further details and the Travelodge phone number, consult the Hotel Groups page.
ROOMS: 50 en suite **CONF:** Thtr 45 Board 34

CARDIGAN See Gwbert-on-Sea

CARMARTHEN, Carmarthenshire — Map 02 SN42

★★63% *Falcon*
Lammas St SA31 3AP
☎ 01267 234959 & 237152 🖷 01267 221277
Dir: *in town centre opposite Monument*

Located in the centre of Carmarthen, this delightfully cosy hotel provides smart modern accommodation. There is a comfortable foyer, lounge and bar (which serves tea and coffee). The restaurant serves commendable meals using fresh local produce, and also caters for functions. Bedrooms are well equipped, some have four-poster beds.
ROOMS: 14 en suite (1 fmly) **CONF:** Thtr 100 Class 50 Board 40
PARKING: 38 **NOTES:** Closed 25-26 Dec RS Sun
CARDS:

CHEPSTOW, Monmouthshire — Map 03 ST59

★★★★69% Marriott St Pierre
St Pierre Park NP16 6YA
☎ 01291 625261 🖷 01291 629975

Dir: *leave M48 junct 2. At rdbt on slip road take A466 Chepstow. At next rdbt take 1st exit Caerwent A48. Hotel approx 2m on left*

Situated either in the main house, at the Lakeside, or in the adjacent cottage suites, the bedrooms are well equipped and inviting. The hotel benefits from extensive leisure and conference facilities. Guests have the option of either dining formally in the Orangery Restaurant or less formally in the Long Weekend Café/bar. A willing team of enthusiastic young staff provide a high level of hospitality.
ROOMS: 148 en suite No smoking in 74 bedrooms s fr £99; d fr £109 (incl. bkfst) * LB **FACILITIES:** STV Indoor swimming (H) Golf 36 Tennis (hard) Sauna Solarium Gym Croquet lawn Putting green Jacuzzi/spa Health spa Xmas **CONF:** Thtr 240 Class 120 Board 90 Del from £130 *
PARKING: 430 **NOTES:** No dogs (ex guide dogs) No smoking in restaurant Civ Wed **CARDS:**

CHEPSTOW, continued

★★★61% The Old Course

Newport Rd NP16 5PR
☎ 01291 626261 📠 01291 626263
e-mail: bookings@oldcoursechepstow.co.uk
Dir: *leave M48 junct 2, follow signs to Chepstow, A466 & A48 into town, hotel is on the left*

Convenient for both the M4 and the M48, this privately owned hotel lies just south of the town centre. The public areas include a spacious lounge bar, a comfortable lounge and an attractively appointed restaurant. There is a choice of conference rooms and a large ballroom.
ROOMS: 31 en suite (4 fmly) s £39.50-£45.50; d £42.50-£49.50 * LB **FACILITIES:** STV Xmas **CONF:** Thtr 240 Class 70 Board 70 Del from £82.50 * **SERVICES:** Lift **PARKING:** 180 **NOTES:** No smoking in restaurant **CARDS:**

See advert on opposite page

★★68% Castle View

16 Bridge St NP6 5EZ
☎ 01291 620349 📠 01291 627397
e-mail: mart@castview.demon.co.uk
Dir: *opposite the castle*
This 300-year-old building looks out onto the impressive Norman castle. The bedrooms, two of which are situated in a building at the end of the attractive garden, offer comfortable accommodation. The restaurant is supplemented by a bar and residents' lounge.
ROOMS: 9 en suite 4 annexe en suite (7 fmly) s £36.95-£46.95; d £50.95-£59.95 * LB **FACILITIES:** STV **NOTES:** No smoking in restaurant **CARDS:**

See advert on opposite page

★★67% George

Moor St NP16 5DB
☎ 01291 625363 📠 01291 627418
Dir: *M48, junct 2, follow signs for town centre, hotel adjacent to 16th century town gate*
This former posting house retains a good deal of historic character. Located next to the 16th-century town gate, The George has a cosy, stylish bar and lounge, popular with locals and an informal, bistro-style restaurant. Well-equipped bedrooms are a good size and are smartly decorated in dark wood and traditional fabrics.

continued

ROOMS: 14 en suite No smoking in 7 bedrooms s fr £70; d fr £80 * LB **FACILITIES:** Xmas **CONF:** Thtr 40 Class 20 Board 26 Del from £85 * **PARKING:** 20 **NOTES:** No smoking in restaurant Civ Wed **CARDS:**

★★66% Beaufort

Beaufort Square NP6 5EP
☎ 01291 622497 📠 01291 627389
e-mail: info@beauforthotelchepstow.com
Dir: *off A48, at St Mary's church turn left and left again at end of public car park into Nelson St. Hotel car park 100yds on right*
Located in the town centre, this 16th-century coaching inn is now a popular hotel. The bedrooms, including ground-floor and family rooms, are furnished and equipped in a modern style. Public areas comprise a busy bar and a restaurant offering a wide choice of dishes including steaks and pasta.
ROOMS: 18 en suite (2 fmly) s £39.50; d £49.50 * LB **FACILITIES:** STV **CONF:** Thtr 40 Class 25 Board 20 Del from £60 * **PARKING:** 14 **CARDS:**

CHIRK, Wrexham Map 07 SJ23

★★★64% *Hand*

Church St LL14 5EY
☎ 01691 773472 📠 01691 772479
Dir: *in the centre of Chirk on the B5070*
A Grade II listed coaching house in the centre of Chirk. The hotel provides modern accommodation, which includes a family bedroom and a room with a four-poster bed. Public areas include a number of lounges and bars, as well as a choice of eating options, one of which is the smartly appointed Regency restaurant. Other facilities include a beer garden with a play area for children.
ROOMS: 16 en suite (1 fmly) **FACILITIES:** STV Sauna Solarium Gym Pool table **CONF:** Thtr 250 Class 225 Board 200 **PARKING:** 50 **CARDS:**

COLWYN BAY, Conwy Map 06 SH87

★★★65% Norfolk House

39 Princes Dr LL29 8PF
☎ 01492 531757 📠 01492 533781
Dir: *from A55 at Colwyn Bay exit into right lane of slip road right at traffic lights pass station continue,hotel almost opposite filling station*
Norfolk House is a family-run hotel with a warm, friendly atmosphere, within easy walking distance of the seafront, town centre and railway station. The accommodation is well equipped, comfortable and relaxing. Bedrooms are prettily decorated with family suites offered. There are several lounges, a popular bar, and conference facilities available.
ROOMS: 20 rms (13 en suite) 1 annexe en suite (4 fmly) No smoking in 2 bedrooms s £35-£45; d £57 (incl. bkfst) * LB **FACILITIES:** STV ch fac **CONF:** Thtr 35 Class 30 Board 20 **SERVICES:** Lift **PARKING:** 30 **NOTES:** No smoking in restaurant **CARDS:**

See advert on opposite page

★★★64% Hopeside
63-67 Prince's Dr, West End LL29 8PW
☎ 01492 533244 Fax 01492 532850
e-mail: hopesidecb@aol.com
Dir: *turn off A55 at Rhos-on-Sea exit, turn left at lights, hotel 50yds on right*
The promenade and town centre are within easy walking distance of this friendly hotel. The restaurant offers a good choice, and bar food and blackboard specials are also available. Bedrooms are mostly pine-furnished and all are attractively decorated. The hotel also holds a licence for civil marriage ceremonies.
ROOMS: 18 en suite (2 fmly) No smoking in 9 bedrooms s £49; d £59 (incl. bkfst) * LB **FACILITIES:** STV **CONF:** Thtr 45 Class 45 Board 28 **PARKING:** 14 **NOTES:** Civ Wed **CARDS:**

★★65% Marine
West Promenade LL28 4BP
☎ 01492 530295 Fax 0870 168 9400
e-mail: reservations@marinehotel.co.uk
Dir: *turn off A55 at Old Colwyn to seafront. Turn left, and after pier turn left just before traffic lights, car park on corner*
This cheerful seaside hotel is close to the sea front and not far from town. Bedrooms are decorated attractively with modern facilities and many enjoy good views. There is a cosy bar and separate lounge and tasty home cooking is available.
ROOMS: 14 rms (12 en suite) (4 fmly) No smoking in 9 bedrooms s £27-£28; d £44-£46 (incl. bkfst) * LB **PARKING:** 11 **NOTES:** No smoking in restaurant Closed mid Oct-mid Apr
CARDS:

COLWYN BAY, continued

★★60% Lyndale
410 Abergele Rd, Old Colwyn LL29 9AB
☎ 01492 515429 🖷 01492 518805
Dir: *exit A55 Old Colwyn, turn left. At rdbt through village continue for 1m on A547*
Located at Old Colwyn this family-run hotel offers a range of comfortable accommodation including family suites and a four-poster room. There is a cosy bar and a comfortable foyer lounge. Weddings and other functions can be accommodated and there are facilities for business meetings.
ROOMS: 14 en suite (3 fmly) No smoking in 3 bedrooms s £25-£35; d £40-£60 (incl. bkfst) * LB **FACILITIES:** Xmas **CONF:** Thtr 40 Class 20 Board 20 Del from £35 * **PARKING:** 20 **CARDS:**

CONWY, Conwy — Map 06 SH77

★★★71% Groes Inn
Tyn-y-Groes LL32 8TN
☎ 01492 650545 🖷 01492 650855
Dir: *leave A55 at Conwy turn off, cross Old Conwy Bridge, 1st left through Castle Walls on B5106 Trefriew road, follow for approx 2m, hotel on right*

The original inn dates back to at least the 16th century and has charming features such as low beamed ceilings, log fires, period furniture and an abundance of bric-a-brac. It offers a choice of bars and has a beautifully appointed restaurant, with a conservatory extension opening onto the lovely rear garden. The comfortable, well equipped bedrooms are contained in a separate building; some have balconies or private terraces.
ROOMS: 14 en suite (1 fmly) No smoking in 6 bedrooms s £64-£95; d £81-£115 (incl. bkfst) * LB **FACILITIES:** Xmas **CONF:** Thtr 25 Class 15 Board 15 **PARKING:** 100 **NOTES:** No smoking in restaurant
CARDS:

★★★64% The Castle
High St LL32 8DB
☎ 01492 592324 🖷 01492 583351
Dir: *within town walls, on A55*

Centrally situated and convenient for the castle and quay this hotel dates back to 1500 and is one of Conway's distinguished historic buildings. Refurbishment of several bedrooms has considerably improved the accommodation, but guests will also enjoy the warm and hospitable atmosphere. Fine paintings by a local artist are featured in the public areas which are also enhanced by the presence of fresh flowers for most of the year.
ROOMS: 29 en suite (2 fmly) No smoking in 16 bedrooms s £60; d £80 (incl. bkfst) * LB **FACILITIES:** Xmas **CONF:** Thtr 35 Class 20 Board 20 Del £80 * **PARKING:** 30 **NOTES:** No smoking in restaurant
CARDS:

Premier Collection

★★ The Old Rectory Country House
Llanrwst Rd, Llansanffraid Glan Conwy LL28 5LF
☎ 01492 580611 🖷 01492 584555
e-mail: info@oldrectorycountryhouse.co.uk
Dir: *0.5m S from A470/A55 junct on left hand side*
A charming hotel with delightful terraced gardens overlooking the Conwy Estuary and Snowdonia beyond. Inside, the intimate public rooms are complemented by classical interior design and antique pieces. Bedrooms, most of which have sea or estuary views, are tastefully furnished in keeping with the building, and many thoughtful extra comforts are provided. Two bedrooms are located in the grounds and can be used as a family suite. The cuisine is excellent with well selected ingredients carefully put together in appealing yet reassuring combinations on the Anglo-French menu. The warm and caring hospitality is also outstanding.
ROOMS: 4 en suite 2 annexe en suite No smoking in 4 bedrooms s £109-£129; d £129-£149 (incl. bkfst) * LB **PARKING:** 10
NOTES: No children 5yrs No smoking in restaurant Closed Dec-Jan
CARDS:

★★67% Castle Bank
Mount Pleasant LL32 8NY
☎ 01492 593888 🖷 01492 596466
e-mail: castlebank@bwn.com
Dir: *turn off A55 expressway at Conwy. Hotel is accessed through public car park on Mount Pleasant, adjacent to the Bangor Archway in town wall*
This small friendly hotel lies near the old town walls and is well located for touring the surrounding countryside and attractions. Bedrooms are bright, freshly decorated and well equipped. There is a spacious dining room with a bar, and a comfortably furnished guests' lounge.
ROOMS: 9 en suite (2 fmly) s £35-£40; d £55-£59 (incl. bkfst) * LB **FACILITIES:** Xmas **PARKING:** 12 **NOTES:** No dogs (ex guide dogs) No smoking in restaurant **CARDS:**

C

★★66% Tir-y-Coed Country House

Rowen LL32 8TP
☎ 01492 650219 Fax 01492 650219
Dir: *turn off B5106 into unclassified road signposted Rowen, hotel is on fringe of village about 60mtrs N of Post Office*

Located in the Conwy valley, this small and relaxing hotel is at the edge of Conwy. Bedrooms are bright and freshly decorated with family rooms available. There is a small cocktail bar and a comfortable lounge. Freshly-cooked meals are served in the dining room.

ROOMS: 7 en suite 1 annexe en suite (1 fmly) s £28-£32; d £51-£59 (incl. bkfst) * LB **FACILITIES:** ch fac **PARKING:** 8 **NOTES:** No smoking in restaurant Closed Xmas & New Year RS Nov-Feb **CARDS:**

Read all about it! Newspapers delivered to bedrooms in four and five star hotels.

CRICCIETH, Gwynedd Map 06 SH43

★★★68% Bron Eifion Country House

LL52 0SA
☎ 01766 522385 Fax 01766 522003
e-mail: broneifion@criccieth.co.uk
Dir: *0.5m outside Criccieth on A497 towards Pwllheli*

A fine country house in well maintained grounds west of Criccieth. Bedrooms are nicely decorated and most are equipped with period and antique furniture. Several rooms have four-poster beds or attractive canopies. The central hall features a minstrel's gallery. Several comfortable lounges are provided and the restaurant overlooks the gardens.

ROOMS: 19 en suite (2 fmly) s £62-£71; d £92-£130 (incl. bkfst) * LB **FACILITIES:** Croquet lawn Putting green Xmas **CONF:** Thtr 30 Class 25 Board 25 Del from £85 * **PARKING:** 80 **NOTES:** No smoking in restaurant **CARDS:** 

CRICCIETH, continued

★★69% Caerwylan

LL52 0HW
☎ 01766 522547
A long established holiday hotel above the seafront; many rooms have fine views of the castle and Cardigan Bay. Comfortably furnished lounges are available for residents and the five-course menu changes daily. Bedrooms are smart, modern, and several have their own private sitting areas. The enjoyable atmosphere ensures many guests return year after year.
ROOMS: 25 en suite s £20-£25; d £40-£50 (incl. bkfst) * LB
SERVICES: Lift **PARKING:** 9 **NOTES:** No smoking in restaurant Closed Nov-Etr **CARDS:**

★★68% Parciau Mawr

High St LL52 0RP
☎ 01766 522368
Dir: *off the A497 off the high street, on the Pwllheli side of the village*
The original part of this hotel dates back more than 300 years and is set in several acres of attractive grounds. The restaurant is in a converted barn forming part of the main building. There is a choice of sitting rooms and bedrooms are bright and fresh, including several pine-furnished rooms in nearby outbuildings.
ROOMS: 6 en suite 6 annexe en suite (1 fmly) s fr £31.50; d £53-£60 (incl. bkfst) * LB **PARKING:** 30 **NOTES:** No children 5yrs No smoking in restaurant Closed Nov-Mar **CARDS:**

★★67% Gwyndy

Llanystumdwy LL52 0SP
☎ 01766 522720 ⎙ 01766 522720
Dir: *turn off A497 into village of Llanystumdwy follow road for 0.25m, hotel is next to church*
A popular hotel with a 17th-century cottage and a nearby purpose-built bedroom complex. The original cottage contains the lounge, bar and restaurant, which are comfortably furnished. Exposed timbers feature and there are several stone fireplaces. Bedrooms are spacious and relaxing.
ROOMS: 10 annexe en suite (5 fmly) s £30; d £50 (incl. bkfst) *
FACILITIES: Fishing **PARKING:** 20 **NOTES:** No smoking in restaurant Closed Nov-Mar

★★66% Lion

Y Maes LL52 0AA
☎ 01766 522460 ⎙ 01766 523075
e-mail: info@lionhotelcriccieth.co.uk
Dir: *turn off A497 in the centre of Criccieth on to village green north, hotel located on green*
This hotel lies just a short walk from Criccieth castle and seafront, with fine views from many rooms. The bars enjoy a good local following and staff are friendly and welcoming. Bedrooms are well decorated and furnished, spread between the main building and nearby annexe. Regular live entertainment is held during the summer.
ROOMS: 34 en suite 12 annexe en suite (8 fmly) s £30.50-£35; d £55-£62.50 (incl. bkfst) * LB **FACILITIES:** Pool table entertainment Xmas
SERVICES: Lift **PARKING:** 30 **NOTES:** No smoking in restaurant RS Nov-Mar **CARDS:**

CRICKHOWELL, Powys — Map 03 SO21

★★★73% ❀❀ *Bear*

NP8 1BW
☎ 01873 810408 ⎙ 01873 811696
e-mail: bearhotel@aol.com
Dir: *on A40 between Abergavenny and Breen*
Offering impressive accommodation and cuisine, the character and friendliness of this 15th-century coaching inn are renowned.

The bar and restaurant areas are furnished in keeping with the building. The hotel uses quality, local produce for its cuisine and provides excellent restaurant and bar food.
ROOMS: 13 en suite 13 annexe en suite (6 fmly) **CONF:** Thtr 60 Class 30 Board 20 **PARKING:** 38 **CARDS:**

See advert on page 791

★★★71% ❀❀ Gliffaes Country House Hotel

NP8 1RH
☎ 01874 730371 & 0800 146719 (Freephone) ⎙ 01874 730463
e-mail: calls@gliffaeshotel.com
Dir: *1m from A40 - 2.5m W of Crickhowell*
This impressive country house was built in 1885. It stands in 33 acres of gardens and wooded grounds by the River Usk. Now a family owned and personally run hotel, it provides recently refurbished, good quality accommodation and has comfortable public rooms with a wealth of charm and character. The hotel has a well deserved high reputation for its food, which is complemented by willing, friendly and attentive service.
ROOMS: 19 en suite 3 annexe en suite (3 fmly) s £52-£120; d £63-£133 (incl. bkfst) * LB **FACILITIES:** Tennis (hard) Fishing Snooker Croquet lawn Putting green Golf practice net Cycling Birdwatching Walking ch fac
CONF: Thtr 40 Class 16 Board 16 **PARKING:** 34 **NOTES:** No dogs (ex guide dogs) No smoking in restaurant Civ Wed
CARDS:

★★★70% ❀ Manor

Brecon Rd NP8 1SE
☎ 01873 810212 ⎙ 01873 811938
Dir: *on A40, Crickhowell/Brecon, 0.5m from Crickhowell*

In a stunning location on a hillside of the Usk Valley way above Crickhowell, this impressive manor house was the birthplace of Sir George Everest. The bedrooms and public areas retain an elegant yet relaxed atmosphere, and there are extensive leisure facilities. The restaurant has panoramic views and is the setting for exciting modern cooking. Guests can also dine in the informal atmosphere of the nearby Nantyffin Cider Mill, the hotel's sister operation.

continued

ROOMS: 20 en suite (1 fmly) No smoking in 8 bedrooms s £50-£60; d £70-£95 (incl. cont bkfst) * LB **FACILITIES:** Indoor swimming (H) Sauna Solarium Gym Jacuzzi/spa Fitness assessment Sunbed Xmas **CONF:** Thtr 400 Class 300 Board 300 Del from £90 * **PARKING:** 200 **CARDS:**

See advert on this page

★★73% Ty Croeso
The Dardy, Llangattock NP8 1PU
☎ 01873 810573 01873 810573
e-mail: tycroeso@ty-croeso-hotel.freeserve.co.uk
Dir: *at Shell garage on A40 take opposite road, down hill over river bridge. Turn right, after 0.5m turn left, up hill over canal, hotel signed*
Ty Croeso, meaning 'House of Welcome' lives up to its name. In the restaurant an interesting carte and a Taste of Wales fixed price menu are available. Glamorgan Sausages and laverbread are available at breakfast. Public areas are comfortable, with log fires. Bedrooms are decorated with pretty fabrics and all have good facilities.
ROOMS: 8 en suite (1 fmly) s £35-£50; d £60-£75 (incl. bkfst) * LB **PARKING:** 20 **NOTES:** No smoking in restaurant RS 24-26 Dec **CARDS:**

CROSS HANDS, Carmarthenshire Map 02 SN51

Travelodge
SA14 6NW
☎ 01269 845700 01269 845700
Dir: *on A48, westbound*
This modern building offers accommodation in smart, spacious and well equipped bedrooms, all with en suite bathrooms. Refreshments may be taken at the nearby family restaurant. For further details and the Travelodge phone number, consult the Hotel Groups page.
ROOMS: 32 en suite

C

CRUGYBAR, Carmarthenshire
Map 03 SN63

★★72% Glanrannell Park
SA19 8SA
☎ 01558 685230 01558 685784
e-mail: glanparkhotel@btinternet.com
Dir: *from A40 take A482 to Lampeter after 5.5m follow signs to hotel. From Llandeilo take B4302 for 10.5m , hotel is signposted*
This fine country house is surrounded by 23 acres of mature grounds, fronted by a lake where birds of prey are regular visitors. The hotel has a number of loyal guests who return year after year. Bedrooms are immaculately maintained and there is a bar and several comfortable sitting rooms. Good home cooking is offered from a fixed-price menu.
ROOMS: 8 en suite (2 fmly) s £40-£43; d £66-£76 (incl. bkfst) * LB **FACILITIES:** Fishing **PARKING:** 33 **NOTES:** No smoking in restaurant Closed Nov-Mar **CARDS:**

CWMBRAN, Torfaen
Map 03 ST29

★★★★65% Parkway
Cwmbran Dr NP44 3UW
☎ 01633 871199 01633 869160
e-mail: user@parkwayhotel.freeserve.co.uk
Best Western
Dir: *from M4 take A4051 for Cwmbran until you see signs for Cwmbran-Llantarnam Park. Turn right at rdbt then right for Hotel*
With easy access to the M4, this purpose built hotel complex includes a spacious lounge/bar which doubles as a coffee shop during the day time, with light snacks on offer. Both carvery and carte menus are available for guests in Ravellos, providing a formal dining option. Extensive leisure facilities are provided, which hotel residents use alongside the members. Several thoughtful extras are provided in the bedrooms.
ROOMS: 70 en suite (4 fmly) No smoking in 24 bedrooms s £76-£93.70; d £88.20-£105.85 * LB **FACILITIES:** STV Indoor swimming (H) Sauna Solarium Gym Jacuzzi/spa Steam room Xmas **CONF:** Thtr 500 Class 240 Board 100 Del from £115 * **PARKING:** 300 **NOTES:** Closed 24-31 Dec Civ Wed 90 **CARDS:**

See advert on page 793

DEVIL'S BRIDGE, Ceredigion
Map 06 SN77

★★68% Hafod Arms
SY23 3JL
☎ 01970 890232 01970 890 394
e-mail: enquiries@hafordarms.co.uk
Dir: *turn off the A44 Trunk Road a Ponterwyd. Hotel is then 5m along A4120, 11m E of Aberystwyth*
This stone-built former hunting lodge dates back to the 17th century and is now a family owned and run hotel providing accommodation suitable for both business people and tourists. Family bedded rooms and a four-poster room are available. In addition to the dining area and lounge, there are tea rooms, a secure car park and six acres of grounds.
ROOMS: 15 rms (11 en suite) (1 fmly) s £35; d £56-£80 (incl. bkfst) * **CONF:** Board 25 **PARKING:** 70 **NOTES:** No children 12yrs No smoking in restaurant Closed 15 Dec-Jan **CARDS:**

DOLGELLAU, Gwynedd
Map 06 SH71

★★★72% Penmaenuchaf Hall
Penmaenpool LL40 1YB
☎ 01341 422129 01341 422787
e-mail: relax@penhall.co.uk
Dir: *off A470 onto A493 to Tywyn. Hotel entrance is approx. 1m on the left*
Built in 1860, this impressive hall stands in 20 acres of woodland and enjoys magnificent views. Careful restoration has created a comfortable and welcoming hotel which provides elegant public areas and attractive bedrooms. The wood-panelled restaurant serves fresh produce cooked in modern English style.
ROOMS: 14 en suite (2 fmly) No smoking in 5 bedrooms s £70-£110; d £100-£160 (incl. bkfst) LB **FACILITIES:** Fishing Snooker Croquet lawn Xmas **CONF:** Thtr 50 Class 30 Board 22 Del from £99 * **PARKING:** 30 **NOTES:** No children 6yrs No smoking in restaurant Civ Wed 50
CARDS:

★★★71% Plas Dolmelynllyn
Ganllwyd LL40 2HP
☎ 01341 440273 01341 440640
e-mail: info@dolly-hotel.co.uk
Dir: *5m N of Dolgellau on A470*
Surrounded by three acres of gardens and National Trust land, this fine house dates back to the 16th-century. Spacious bedrooms are attractively furnished and offer comfortable seating as well as many thoughtful extras. Dinner is served in the comfortable dining room, adjacent to the conservatory bar.
ROOMS: 10 en suite No smoking in all bedrooms s £50-£62.50; d £85-£120 (incl. bkfst) * LB **FACILITIES:** STV Fishing Mountain walking Mountain Bike riding **CONF:** Thtr 20 Class 20 Board 20 **PARKING:** 20 **NOTES:** No smoking in restaurant Closed Nov-Feb
CARDS:

★★72% Dolserau Hall
LL40 2AG
☎ 01341 422522 01341 422400
e-mail: aa@dolserau.co.uk
Dir: *1.5m outside town between A494 to Bala and A470 to Dinas Mawddwy*
This hospitable hotel lies in attractive grounds extending to the river and surrounded by green fields. Several comfortable lounges are provided with warming log fires. The hotel cuisine is excellent, serving rosette-worthy dishes. The smart bedrooms are well equipped and have comfortable seating.
ROOMS: 15 en suite (3 fmly) s £48-£61; d £88-£114 (incl. bkfst & dinner) * LB **FACILITIES:** STV Xmas **SERVICES:** Lift **PARKING:** 70 **NOTES:** No children 6yrs No smoking in restaurant Closed mid Nov-mid Feb (ex Xmas & New Year) **CARDS:**

★★70% George III Hotel
Penmaenpool LL40 1YD
☎ 01341 422525 01341 423565
e-mail: reception@george-3rd.co.uk
Dir: *turn left off A470 towards Tywyn, approx. 2m, turn right for toll bridge then 1st left for hotel*
Idyllically located on the banks of the Mawddach Estuary, this delightful small hotel started life as an inn and a chandlers to the local boat yard. A nearby building, that now houses several bedrooms, was the local railway station. There is a choice of bars providing a wide range of food with more formal dining available in the restaurant.
ROOMS: 6 en suite 5 annexe en suite s £40-£55; d £70-£94 (incl. bkfst) * LB **FACILITIES:** Fishing Free fishing permits Mountain bike hire **PARKING:** 60 **NOTES:** No smoking in restaurant
CARDS:

★★66% *Fronoleu Farm*
Tabor LL40 2PS
☎ 01341 422361 & 422197 01341 422023
Dir: *at junct of the A487 from Machynlleth with the A470. Take road signed Tabor opposite Cross Foxes and continue for 1.25m*
This 16th-century farmhouse lies under the shadow of Cader Idris. Carefully extended over recent years, it retains many original features. The bar and lounge are both located in the old building

continued

where there are exposed timbers and open fires. Most of the bedrooms are in a modern extension and these are spacious and well equipped. The wide range of food on offer attracts a large local following to the restaurant. There is also a recently opened cellar bar.
ROOMS: 11 rms (7 en suite) (3 fmly) No smoking in 6 bedrooms **FACILITIES:** Fishing Pool table **CONF:** Thtr 150 Class 80 Board 80 **PARKING:** 60 **CARDS:**

★67% Royal Ship

Queens Square LL40 1AR
☎ 01341 422209 01341 421027
Dir: *located in the centre of the town*
The Royal Ship dates from 1813 when it was a coaching inn. There are three bars and several lounges, all most comfortably furnished and appointed. It is very much the centre of local activities and a wide range of food is available. Bedrooms are tastefully decorated and fitted with modern amenities.
ROOMS: 24 rms (18 en suite) (4 fmly) s £25-£35; d £40-£60 (incl. bkfst) * LB **FACILITIES:** STV Pool table Xmas **CONF:** Thtr 80 Class 60 Board 60 **PARKING:** 12 **NOTES:** No dogs (ex guide dogs) No smoking in restaurant **CARDS:**

See advert on this page

DOLWYDDELAN, Conwy — Map 06 SH75

★★65% Elen's Castle

LL25 0EJ
☎ 01690 750207 01690 750207
e-mail: elens98@aol.com
Dir: *on A470, 5m S of Betws-y-Coed*
This hotel is small and very friendly and was operated as a beer house in the 18th century. The original bar, complete with a slab floor and pot-belly stove, remains and two cosy sitting rooms have open fires and exposed timbers. Bedrooms are being upgraded and pretty fabrics are used to good effect. Two rooms have four-poster beds and families can be accommodated. A good range of bar and restaurant food is provided and staff and owners are friendly and welcoming.
ROOMS: 9 rms (8 en suite) (2 fmly) No smoking in 2 bedrooms s £17-£37; d £34-£74 (incl. bkfst) * LB **FACILITIES:** STV Fishing Xmas **CONF:** Class 20 **PARKING:** 40 **NOTES:** No dogs No smoking in restaurant **CARDS:**

EGLWYSFACH, Ceredigion — Map 06 SN69

Premier Collection

★★★ Ynyshir Hall

SY20 8TA
☎ 01654 781209 01654 781366
e-mail: info@ynyshir-hall.co.uk
Dir: *off A487, 5.5m S of Machynlleth, signposted from the main road*
This fine country house hotel is set in 12 acres of scenic gardens. The bedrooms vary in size and are all are individually designed, furnished with antiques, and equipped with a range of thoughtful extras. Both the bar and the drawing room are adorned with striking paintings of local scenes, and excellent cuisine is served in the smart dining room.

continued

ROOMS: 8 en suite 2 annexe en suite No smoking in all bedrooms s £95-£135; d £120-£195 (incl. bkfst) * LB **FACILITIES:** Croquet lawn Xmas **CONF:** Thtr 25 Class 20 Board 18 Del from £170 * **PARKING:** 20 **NOTES:** No children 9yrs No smoking in restaurant Closed 5-23 Jan **CARDS:**

EWLOE, Flintshire — Map 07 SJ36

★★★★70% De Vere St David's Park

De Vere Hotels

St Davids Park CH5 3YB
☎ 01244 520800 01244 520930
e-mail: reservations@st.davidspark.co.uk
Dir: *take A494 Queensferry to Mold for 4m, then take left slip road B5127 towards Buckley*
This is a fine modern hotel providing well equipped and comfortable bedrooms. Suites are also available, and some have

continued

EWLOE, continued

four-posters. The restaurant offers a full range of eating options and the large team of staff are friendly and welcoming.
ROOMS: 145 en suite (26 fmly) No smoking in 54 bedrooms d £109-£154 * LB **FACILITIES:** Indoor swimming (H) Golf 18 Tennis (hard) Snooker Sauna Solarium Gym Pool table Putting green Jacuzzi/spa Steam bath Beauty Therapist Playroom Xmas **CONF:** Thtr 270 Class 150 Board 40 Del from £139 * **SERVICES:** Lift **PARKING:** 240 **NOTES:** No smoking in restaurant Civ Wed **CARDS:**

FISHGUARD, Pembrokeshire Map 02 SM93

E

★★69% *Cartref*

15-19 High St SA65 9AW
☎ 01348 872430 📠 01348 873664
Dir: *on A40 in town centre*
This personally run and friendly hotel is close to the town centre and is convenient for access to the ferry terminal. The well maintained and modern equipped accommodation includes family bedded rooms. A limited number of secure garage spaces are available.
ROOMS: 10 en suite (2 fmly) **PARKING:** 4 **NOTES:** No smoking in restaurant **CARDS:**

★★60% *Abergwaun*

The Market Square SA65 9HA
☎ 01348 872077 📠 01348 875412
Dir: *on A40 in the centre of town*
Originally an 18th-century coaching inn, this privately owned and run hotel stands in the main square of the town, within easy reach of the ferry terminal. Upgraded bedrooms are comfortable and smartly furnished in pine. A comfortable bar serves a good range of meals and the restaurant offers a selection of more substantial dishes.
ROOMS: 11 rms (7 en suite) (2 fmly) **FACILITIES:** Pool table
CONF: Thtr 50 Class 20 Board 24 **PARKING:** 3
CARDS:

FLINT, Flintshire Map 07 SJ27

★★★61% Mountain Park Hotel

Northop Rd, Flint Mountain CH6 5QG
☎ 01352 736000 & 730972 📠 01352 736010
Dir: *Turn off A55 for Flint onto A5119,hotel 1 mile on left*

This farm house has modern, well equipped bedrooms and is conveniently situated close to the motorway. Facilities include: Sevens Brasserie Restaurant serving delectable modern cuisine; a comfortable lounge bar offering a range of bar meals; an attractively designed function room; a children's play area; and ample parking.
ROOMS: 21 annexe en suite (1 fmly) No smoking in 11 bedrooms s £45.50 (incl. bkfst) * LB **FACILITIES:** Golf 9 Jacuzzi/spa ch fac Xmas
CONF: Del from £65.25 * **SERVICES:** air con **PARKING:** 94
NOTES: No dogs (ex guide dogs) No smoking in restaurant
CARDS:

GLYN CEIRIOG, Wrexham Map 07 SJ23

★★★64% Golden Pheasant

LL20 7BB
☎ 01691 718281 📠 01691 718479
Dir: *take B4500 at Chirk, continue along this road for 5m, follow hotel signs*
This privately-owned 18th-century hostelry is on the edge of the village surrounded by hills and countryside. There is a choice of bars, as well as a lounge and a restaurant. To the rear is a courtyard with shrub and flower beds. One of its main features is an aviary containing exotic birds. Bedrooms include four-posters and family rooms.
ROOMS: 19 en suite (5 fmly) s £35-£45; d £59-£79 (incl. bkfst) * LB
FACILITIES: Xmas **CONF:** Thtr 60 Board 10 Del from £62 *
PARKING: 45 **CARDS:**

GWBERT-ON-SEA, Ceredigion Map 02 SN15

★★★67% ❀ *Cliff*

SA43 1PP
☎ 01239 613241 📠 01239 615391

This privately owned hotel sits on the cliff tops at Gwbert on Sea, just north of Cardigan. Most of the spacious and comfortable public rooms have superb sea views, as do many of the modern equipped bedrooms. Apart from conference and function facilities, the hotel has a wide range of leisure activities, including an outdoor swimming pool and 9 hole golf course, in its 30 acres of grounds.
ROOMS: 70 en suite (4 fmly) No smoking in 10 bedrooms
FACILITIES: Outdoor swimming (H) Golf 9 Fishing Squash Snooker Sauna Solarium Gym Pool table Putting green Sea fishing **CONF:** Thtr 200 Class 100 Board 64 **SERVICES:** Lift **PARKING:** 100 **NOTES:** Closed 25-26 Dec **CARDS:**

HALKYN, Flintshire Map 07 SJ27

⌂ *Travelodge*

Travelodge

CH8 8RF
☎ 01352 780952 📠 01352 780952
Dir: *on A55, westbound*
This modern building offers accommodation in smart, spacious and well equipped bedrooms, all with en suite bathrooms. Refreshments may be taken at the nearby family restaurant. For further details and the Travelodge phone number, consult the Hotel Groups page.
ROOMS: 31 en suite

HARLECH See Talsarnau

HAVERFORDWEST, Pembrokeshire Map 02 SM91
see also Burton

★★67% Hotel Mariners

MINOTEL Great Britain

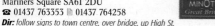

Mariners Square SA61 2DU
☎ 01437 763353 01437 764258
Dir: *follow signs to town centre, over bridge, up High St, take 1st turning on the right Dark St hotel at the end*
Located just out of the town centre, this privately owned, friendly hotel dates back to 1625. The bedrooms are equipped with modern facilities and are well maintained. Family bedded rooms are available. The popular bar is a focus for the town and offers a good range of food in addition to that available in the more formal restaurant.
ROOMS: 28 en suite (5 fmly) No smoking in 3 bedrooms s £51.50-£59.75; d £71.50-£77.50 (incl. bkfst) * LB **FACILITIES:** STV Short mat bowls **CONF:** Thtr 50 Class 28 Board 28 **PARKING:** 50 **NOTES:** Closed 26-27 Dec & 1 Jan **CARDS:**

★★66% Wilton House

6 Quay St SA61 1BG
☎ 01437 760033 01437 760297
e-mail: phil@wiltonhouse.co.uk
This friendly family-run hotel lies in a quiet area next to the River Cleddau. Ground floor areas include several shops as well as a lounge bar/bistro style restaurant serving authentic home-made dishes. Spacious bedrooms are attractively decorated with pretty papers and good furnishings; Family rooms are also available.
ROOMS: 10 en suite (3 fmly) s £39.50-£42.50; d £59.50-£65 (incl. bkfst) * **FACILITIES:** Outdoor swimming (H) Solarium **PARKING:** 6
NOTES: No dogs (ex guide dogs) No smoking in restaurant
CARDS:

★★59% Castle

Castle Square SA61 2AA
☎ 01437 769322 01437 769493
Dir: *from the main rdbt into Haverfordwest take the town centre turn off, follow the road for approx 200yds, hotel on right hand side*
This 19th-century inn overlooks the castle square in the town centre. The spacious bar is popular with locals for its lively ambience and evening entertainment. The bedrooms are modern and comfortably furnished, and include one with a four-poster bed.
ROOMS: 9 en suite (1 fmly) s £32.50-£40; d £40-£55 (incl. bkfst) * LB
NOTES: No dogs (ex guide dogs) **CARDS:**

HAY-ON-WYE, Powys Map 03 SO24

★★★66% *The Swan-at-Hay*

Church St HR3 5DQ
☎ 01497 821188 01497 821424
Dir: *enter Hay-on-Wye on B4350 from Brecon, hotel on left. From any other route follow signs for Brecon & just before leaving town hotel on right*
A coaching inn built in 1821, close to the town centre. Well equipped accommodation includes rooms in converted cottages across the courtyard car park. Facilities include a large function room, a room for smaller meetings, a choice of bars, a comfortable lounge and a bright and pleasant restaurant.
ROOMS: 16 en suite 3 annexe en suite (1 fmly) **FACILITIES:** Fishing Pool table **CONF:** Thtr 140 Class 60 Board 50 **PARKING:** 18
NOTES: No smoking in restaurant **CARDS:**

★★67% *Kilverts*

The Bull Ring HR3 5AG
☎ 01497 821042 & 820564 01497 821580
Dir: *from Brecon on B4350, on entering Hay-on-Wye take 1st right after Cinema Bookshop. Then 1st left and hotel is on right after 40yds*
This converted Victorian house provides well equipped bedrooms and has bustling public areas with both character and charm. Facilities include a spacious and attractive beer garden. Imaginative cooking using good quality fresh produce is available in both the bar, and 'Colin's Restaurant'.
ROOMS: 11 en suite (1 fmly) **FACILITIES:** Croquet lawn **PARKING:** 15
NOTES: Closed 25 Dec **CARDS:**

★★66% Old Black Lion

26 Lion St HR3 5AD
☎ 01497 820841
Dir: *from TIC car park turn right along Oxford Rd pass Nat West bank, next left (Lion St), hotel 20yds on right*
With a history stretching back over several centuries, this fine old coaching inn was occupied by Oliver Cromwell during the siege of Hay Castle. Privately owned and personally run, it provides cosy and well equipped bedrooms. Some are located in an adjacent building. A wide range of food is provided and service is friendly.
ROOMS: 6 rms (5 en suite) 4 annexe en suite (1 fmly) No smoking in all bedrooms s £28; d £58.90-£60 (incl. bkfst) * LB **FACILITIES:** Fishing Xmas **PARKING:** 16 **NOTES:** No children 5yrs No smoking in restaurant
CARDS:

★65% Baskerville Arms

Clyro HR3 5RZ
☎ 01497 820670 01497 821609
e-mail: arms@baskerville.com
Dir: *from Hereford follow Brecon A438 into Clyro. Hotel signposted*
This large, Georgian, former coaching inn was originally called The Swan and featured as such in Kilvert's Diaries. The accommodation includes no smoking bedrooms and family bedded rooms. The restaurant menu and bar meal operation, give good choice and variety.
ROOMS: 11 rms (8 en suite) (2 fmly) No smoking in 3 bedrooms s £20-£35; d £45-£55 (incl. bkfst) * LB **FACILITIES:** Pool table Games room **CONF:** Thtr 65 Class 40 Board 36 **PARKING:** 12 **NOTES:** No dogs (ex guide dogs) No smoking in restaurant
CARDS:

HIRWAUN, Rhondda Cynon Taff Map 03 SN90

★★★62% Ty Newydd Country Hotel

Penderyn Rd CF44 9SX
☎ 01685 813433 01685 813139
Dir: *off A4059, close to A465*
This country mansion set in 2.3 acres of woodland has been carefully restored and extended. The older bedrooms have antique furnishings and most rooms are spacious, well equipped and comfortable. All are non-smoking. There is a pleasant panelled bar, an attractive restaurant and comfortable lounges, where welcoming log fires are lit in cold weather.
ROOMS: 27 en suite (2 fmly) s £51-£59.75; d £71-£90 (incl. bkfst) * LB **FACILITIES:** Xmas **CONF:** Thtr 300 Class 100 Board 40 Del from £77 * **PARKING:** 100 **NOTES:** No dogs No smoking in restaurant Civ Wed 160 **CARDS:**

HOLYHEAD See Anglesey, Isle of

H

HOLYWELL, Flintshire Map 07 SJ17

★★64% Stamford Gate
Halkyn Rd CH8 7SJ
☎ 01352 712942 🖹 01352 713309
Dir: *take Holywell turn off A55 on to A5026, hotel 1m on right*
This busy hotel provides well equipped bedrooms and spacious public areas. The bar and restaurant are both popular locally and there is a wide range of food options. Extensive function and conference facilities are provided and staff are friendly and welcoming.
ROOMS: 12 en suite **FACILITIES:** STV entertainment **CONF:** Thtr 60 Class 30 Board 30 **PARKING:** 100 **NOTES:** No dogs (ex guide dogs) **CARDS:**

ISLE OF
Placenames incorporating the words 'Isle' or 'Isle of' will be found under the actual name, eg Isle of Anglesey is under Anglesey, Isle of.

KNIGHTON, Powys Map 07 SO27

★★★62% The Knighton Hotel
Broad St LD7 1BL
☎ 01547 520530 🖹 01547 520529
e-mail: knightonhotel@freeserve.co.uk
The impressive free-standing staircase at the centre of this market town hotel is reputedly the largest in Europe. The hotel is an amalgamation of a 16th-century coaching inn and a 19th-century manor house. The public areas include a bar, lounge, steak bar and a spacious restaurant.
ROOMS: 15 en suite s £45-£65; d £65-£90 (incl. bkfst) * LB **FACILITIES:** Pool table **CONF:** Thtr 150 Class 75 Board 90 Del from £50 * **SERVICES:** Lift **PARKING:** 15 **NOTES:** No children 12yrs No smoking in restaurant Civ Wed 120 **CARDS:**

MINOTEL Great Britain

★★77% Milebrook House
Milebrook LD7 1LT
☎ 01547 528632 🖹 01547 520509
e-mail: hotel@milebrook.kc3ltd.co.uk
Dir: *2m E, on A4113*
Set in 3 acres of grounds in the Teme Valley 2 miles east of Knighton, this charming house dates back to 1760. In 1987 it was extended and converted into an hotel by owners Rodney & Beryl Marsden. Since then it has acquired a well deserved reputation for its warm and friendly hospitality, the comfort and quality of the accommodation and the quality of the food. The bedrooms which include rooms on ground floor level, are well equipped. Public rooms are tastefully appointed and comfortably furnished.
ROOMS: 10 en suite (2 fmly) No smoking in 6 bedrooms s £51-£55; d £75.50-£83.50 (incl. bkfst) * LB **FACILITIES:** Fishing Croquet lawn Badminton Xmas **CONF:** Class 30 **PARKING:** 20 **NOTES:** No dogs No children 8yrs No smoking in restaurant RS Mon
CARDS:

TV dinner? Room service at three stars and above.

Late for dinner? Quality Standards star rating means that last orders for dinner should be no earlier than:
★ 6.30pm ★★ 7.00pm ★★★ 8.00pm
★★★★ 9.00pm ★★★★★ 10.00pm

LAMPETER, Ceredigion Map 02 SN54
see also Crugybar

★★★68% Falcondale Mansion
SA48 7RX
☎ 01570 422910 🖹 01570 423559
Dir: *800yds W of Lampeter High Street A475 or 1.5m NW of Lampeter A482*

This charming Victorian property is set in extensive grounds and beautiful park land. Bedrooms are generally spacious, well equipped and smartly presented. Bars and lounges are comfortable with additional facilities including conservatory and function rooms.
ROOMS: 19 en suite (8 fmly) s £55-£57.50; d £75-£85 (incl. bkfst) * LB **FACILITIES:** Tennis (hard) Fishing Putting green Xmas **CONF:** Thtr 60 Class 15 Board 30 **SERVICES:** Lift **PARKING:** 80 **NOTES:** No dogs No smoking in restaurant **CARDS:**

See advert on opposite page

LAMPHEY See Pembroke

LANGLAND BAY, Swansea Map 02 SS68

★★★70% Langland Court
Langland Court Rd SA3 4TD
☎ 01792 361545 🖹 01792 362302
Dir: *take B4593 towards Langland and turn left at St Peter's church*

A large, friendly, personally run Victorian property with lots of original character. Particularly impressive are the oak panelled public areas and the imposing stairway. Bedrooms are generally spacious, with some family rooms, and an annexe with ground floor access. There is a formal restaurant supplemented by the more relaxed surroundings of Polly's wine bar.
ROOMS: 14 en suite 5 annexe en suite (5 fmly) No smoking in 2 bedrooms s £61-£71; d £82-£94 (incl. bkfst) * LB **FACILITIES:** STV **CONF:** Thtr 150 Class 60 Board 40 Del from £81 * **PARKING:** 45 **NOTES:** No dogs (ex guide dogs) No smoking in restaurant Civ Wed 100 **CARDS:**

See advert under SWANSEA

★★67% Wittemberg

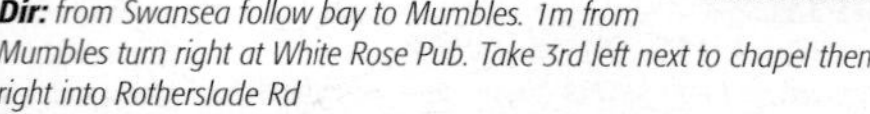

Rotherslade Rd SA3 4QN
☎ 01792 369696 🖷 01792 366995
Dir: *from Swansea follow bay to Mumbles. 1m from Mumbles turn right at White Rose Pub. Take 3rd left next to chapel then right into Rotherslade Rd*

Just a short walk from the beaches of Langland Bay, this friendly small hotel is close to the Mumbles, Swansea and the Gower peninsular. The public areas include a bar, lounge and a restaurant which is the venue for good wholesome cooking. Bedrooms are well maintained, comfortable and have modern facilities.

ROOMS: 11 en suite (2 fmly) **FACILITIES:** Jacuzzi/spa **PARKING:** 12 **NOTES:** No smoking in restaurant Closed Jan **CARDS:**

LLANARMON DYFFRYN CEIRIOG, Wrexham — Map 07 SJ13

★★70% ❀ West Arms

LL20 7LD
☎ 01691 600665 🖷 01691 600622
e-mail: gowestarms@aol.com
Dir: *turn off A483/A5 at Chirk, in Chirk take B4500 to Ceiriog Valley, Llanarmon is 11m at the end of B4500*

Set in the beautiful Ceiriog Valley, this fine hotel features an abundance of exposed beams. There is a particularly impressive entrance hall with a log fire and comfortable armchairs, a sitting room, and two bars where a wide range of meals is available; there is also a restaurant offering a short fixed-price menu of enjoyable, freshly cooked dishes. Bedrooms vary, having a mixture of modern and period furnishings, but all are attractively decorated.

ROOMS: 12 en suite 3 annexe en suite (1 fmly) s £44.50-£54.50; d £78-£99 (incl. bkfst) * LB **FACILITIES:** Fishing Xmas **CONF:** Thtr 60 Class 50 Board 50 Del £99 * **PARKING:** 22 **NOTES:** No smoking in restaurant Civ Wed 80 **CARDS:**

See advert on this page

LLANBEDR, Gwynedd — Map 06 SH52

★★65% Cae Nest Hall Country House

LL45 2NL
☎ 01341 241349 🖷 01341 241349
e-mail: cae-nest@uk2.so-net.com
Dir: *turn off A496 at Victoria Pub, turn left at the War Memorial (100yds from pub) then straight ahead to hotel approx 300yds*

A delightful small country house, the hotel dates back to the 15th century and lies in pleasant grounds. Original features include flagstone floors in the bar and an old black stove in the dining room. Bedrooms have been completely modernised over the last few years, pretty papers and fabrics are used to good effect and other modern facilities are provided.

ROOMS: 10 en suite (3 fmly) No smoking in all bedrooms s £39.50-£49.50; d £59-£74 (incl. bkfst) * LB **PARKING:** 10 **NOTES:** No dogs No smoking in restaurant

LLANBEDR, continued

★★63% Ty Mawr
LL45 2NH
☎ 01341 241440 ▤ 01341 241440
Dir: *travelling from Barmouth, turn right after the bridge in the village, hotel 50yds on left, brown tourist signs on junction to direct the way*

Located in a picturesque village, this family-run hotel lies in pleasant grounds opposite the River Artro - known for its trout and salmon. The grounds are popular as a beer garden during better weather. The bar is attractively cane-furnished and a good choice of real ales is always available. There is a blackboard selection for bar food and a more formal offering in the restaurant. Bedrooms are smart and brightly decorated. Owners and staff are welcoming and friendly, there is a relaxed atmosphere throughout.
ROOMS: 10 en suite (2 fmly) No smoking in 3 bedrooms s £30-£35; d £58 (incl. bkfst) * LB **FACILITIES:** STV ch fac **CONF:** Class 25 Del from £45 * **PARKING:** 30 **NOTES:** No smoking in restaurant Closed 24-26 Dec **CARDS:**

L

LLANBERIS, Gwynedd — Map 06 SH56

★★★66% Royal Victoria
LL55 4TY
☎ 01286 870253 ▤ 01286 870149
e-mail: info@royalvictoria.fsnet.co.uk
Dir: *on A4086 Caernarfon to Llanberis road, directly opposite Snowdon Mountain railway*
An established hotel near the foot of Snowdon, between the Peris and Padarn lakes. Pretty gardens and grounds are an attractive backdrop for the many weddings held there. Bedrooms have been refurbished and modernised in recent years and are well equipped. There are spacious lounges and bars, and a large dining room with a conservatory overlooking the lakes.
ROOMS: 111 en suite (4 fmly) s £29.50-£47.50; d £59-£95 (incl. bkfst) * LB **FACILITIES:** STV Pool table Mountaineering entertainment Xmas **CONF:** Thtr 130 Class 50 Board 40 Del from £56.50 * **SERVICES:** Lift **PARKING:** 300 **NOTES:** No smoking in restaurant Civ Wed 120 **CARDS:**

See advert on opposite page

★★66% Lake View
Tan-y-Pant LL55 4EL
☎ 01286 870422 ▤ 01286 872591
Dir: *1m from Llanberis on A4086 towards Caernarfon*
The lake itself is impossible to miss, as the vast expanse of water is just across the road from the hotel. Dramatic landscapes are all around, with Snowdon itself only a short distance away. The bar, restaurant and comfortable lounge have an appealing, country inn character. The bedrooms have modern facilities and are well maintained.
ROOMS: 10 rms (9 en suite) (3 fmly) s £31.95; d £45 (incl. bkfst) * **PARKING:** 20 **CARDS:**

LLANDEGLA, Denbighshire — Map 07 SJ25

★★★71% *Bodidris Hall*
LL11 3AL
☎ 01978 790434 ▤ 01978 790335
Dir: *in village take A5104 at Crown pub towards Corwen. Hotel 1m on left*
This impressive old manor house, surrounded by ornamental gardens and mature woodlands, still retains its character in the original oak beams and inglenook fireplaces. Bedrooms are furnished with antique pieces and some have four-poster beds. Dining at Bodidris is an enjoyable experience; the food is cooked with flair and stylishly presented. Provision can be made for weddings and business meetings.
ROOMS: 9 en suite 2 annexe en suite (2 fmly) No smoking in 4 bedrooms **FACILITIES:** Fishing Clay pigeon & Driven shooting Falconry **CONF:** Thtr 50 Class 25 Board 20 **PARKING:** 80 **NOTES:** No smoking in restaurant **CARDS:**

LLANDEILO, Carmarthenshire — Map 03 SN62

★★★70% *The Plough Inn*
Rhosmaen SA19 6NP
☎ 01558 823431 ▤ 01558 823969
e-mail: theploughinn@rhosmaen.demon.co.uk
Dir: *1m N, on A40*
This pleasing inn, situated in gardens, provides well equipped modern accommodation including bedrooms on ground floor level and a room for disabled guests. Public areas comprise an attractively appointed restaurant and a cosy bar. Conference and leisure facilities are availiable.
ROOMS: 12 en suite **FACILITIES:** STV Sauna Gym **CONF:** Thtr 45 Class 24 Board 24 **PARKING:** 70 **NOTES:** No dogs Closed 25 Dec RS Sun **CARDS:**

See advert on opposite page

★★★66% Cawdor Arms
Rhosmaen St SA19 6EN
☎ 01558 823500 ▤ 01558 822399
e-mail: cawdor.arms@btinternet.com
Dir: *centre of Llandeilo town, 20 mins from M4 junc 49. Follow signs to Llandeilo*
A warm welcome is offered to guests at this impressive Georgian hotel in the centre of Llandeilo. The hotel has elegantly furnished public rooms and bedrooms, some with four poster beds. An impressive menu is offered that is highly regarded locally.
ROOMS: 17 en suite (2 fmly) No smoking in 9 bedrooms s £45; d £60 (incl. bkfst) * LB **FACILITIES:** entertainment Xmas **CONF:** Thtr 60 Class 40 Board 26 **PARKING:** 7 **NOTES:** No smoking in restaurant **CARDS:**

★62% White Hart Inn
36 Carmarthen Rd SA19 6RS
☎ 01558 823419 ▤ 01558 823089
e-mail: therese@whitehartinn.fsnet.co.uk
Dir: *Turn off A40 onto A483, hotel 200yds on left*
This privately owned roadside hostelry is situated on the outskirts of Llandeilo. It provides accommodation equipped with all modern comforts. Facilities include a meetings room and a large function room.
ROOMS: 11 rms (8 en suite) (2 fmly) s £26-£40; d £40-£60 (incl. bkfst) * **FACILITIES:** STV **CONF:** Thtr 70 Class 45 Board 40 Del from £57 * **PARKING:** 50 **NOTES:** No dogs (ex guide dogs) **CARDS:**

Arriving late? Four and five star hotels have night porters to assist with your luggage; and 24hr room service.

LLANDRILLO, Denbighshire Map 06 SJ03

Premier Collection

★★ Tyddyn Llan Country Hotel & Restaurant
LL21 0ST
☎ 01490 440264 01490 440414
e-mail: tyddynllanhotel@compuserve.com
Dir: *on B4401, Corwen-Bala road*

Set in landscaped gardens amongst fine scenery, this Georgian house has been carefully restored to provide an idyllic, comfortable country retreat. Individually styled bedrooms are tastefully and thoughtfully furnished and the delightful lounges are warmed by roaring log fires during winter months. The elegant restaurant serves an imaginative selection of excellent dishes, created from quality local produce.

ROOMS: 10 en suite (2 fmly) s £67.50-£85; d £105-£140 (incl. bkfst) * LB **FACILITIES:** Fishing Croquet lawn Xmas **CONF:** Thtr 30 Class 30 Board 20 Del from £120 * **PARKING:** 30 **NOTES:** No smoking in restaurant Civ Wed 30
CARDS:

LLANDRINDOD WELLS, Powys Map 03 SO06
see also Penybont

★★★69% Hotel Metropole
Temple St LD1 5DY
☎ 01597 823700 01597 824828
e-mail: info@metropole.co.uk
Dir: *on A483 in centre of town*

Best Western

The centre of the famous spa town is dominated by this Victorian hotel. The lobby leads to a choice of bars, elegant lounge and an extensive restaurant. Bedrooms vary in style, and all are spacious and well equipped. Additional facilities include a leisure centre, conference rooms and shop.

ROOMS: 121 en suite (2 fmly) No smoking in 10 bedrooms s £55-£69; d £72-£92 (incl. bkfst) LB **FACILITIES:** Indoor swimming (H) Sauna Solarium Jacuzzi/spa Beauty salon Rowing & Cycling machines ch fac Xmas **CONF:** Thtr 300 Class 200 Board 80 Del from £74 * **SERVICES:** Lift **PARKING:** 150 **NOTES:** No smoking in restaurant Civ Wed 250 **CARDS:**

★★65% Greenway Manor Hotel
Crossgates LD1 6RF
☎ 01597 851230 01597 851912
Dir: *0.25m from Crossgate village island, on A44 towards Rhayader*

This friendly, family run hotel is a mock Tudor building set in 12 acres and has a mile of private fishing. It is located 3 miles from the spa town of Llandridnod Well and close to the Elan Valley and is an ideal base for country pursuits or touring the area. Rooms

continued on p802

LLANDRINDOD, continued

are tastefully decorated and well equipped and there is a bridal suite with a four poster bed. Downstairs there is an attractive bar and elegant restaurant as well as a comfortable lounge.
ROOMS: 12 en suite (1 fmly) No smoking in 4 bedrooms s £35; d £55 (incl. bkfst) * LB **FACILITIES:** STV Fishing **CONF:** Thtr 40 Class 36 Board 26 Del from £70 * **PARKING:** 30 **NOTES:** No dogs (ex guide dogs) No smoking in restaurant Closed 24 Dec-1 Jan Civ Wed 60
CARDS:

LLANDUDNO, Conwy Map 06 SH78

Premier Collection

★★★ Bodysgallen Hall

LL30 1RS
☎ 01492 584466 01492 582519
e-mail: info@bodysgallen.com

RELAIS & CHATEAUX.

Dir: *take A55 to intersection with A470, then follow A470 towards Llandudno. Hotel 1m on right*

From its elevated position on the outskirts of Llandudno, this 17th-century country house set in 200 acres of parkland and superb gardens, enjoys views of Conwy Castle and Snowdonia. Charm and character are displayed in the wood panelled walls adorned with Old Masters, elegant furnishings, and open fires. Spacious bedrooms include many thoughtful extras. Some rooms are in converted cottages. The restaurant offers imaginative cooking using the finest local ingredients. A high level of customer care is provided by a friendly and dedicated team.
ROOMS: 19 en suite 16 annexe en suite (2 fmly) No smoking in 3 bedrooms s £104-£170; d £140-£235 * LB **FACILITIES:** STV Indoor swimming (H) Tennis (hard) Sauna Solarium Gym Croquet lawn Jacuzzi/spa Beauty salons Steam room Club room entertainment Xmas **CONF:** Thtr 50 Class 30 Board 24 Del from £145 * **PARKING:** 50 **NOTES:** No children 8yrs No smoking in restaurant
CARDS:

★★★75% Empire

Church Walks LL30 2HE
☎ 01492 860555 01492 860791
e-mail: emphotel@aol.com

Dir: *A55 from Chester - Leave at intersection for Llandudno (A470). Follow signs for town centre - Hotel is at end & facing main street*

Professionally run by the same family for over 50 years, the Empire is very much a leader in the hotel industry of North Wales. Bedrooms offer every modern facility and are luxuriously appointed. The nearby 'Number 72' bedrooms are even more sumptuously appointed. There is an indoor swimming pool, overlooked by an all-day restaurant, and a further outdoor pool and roof garden. The Watkins restaurant offers a daily changing fixed-price menu.

continued

ROOMS: 50 en suite 8 annexe en suite (3 fmly) s £57.50-£72.50; d £85-£110 (incl. bkfst) * LB **FACILITIES:** STV Indoor swimming (H) Outdoor swimming (H) Sauna Jacuzzi/spa Beauty treatments entertainment **CONF:** Thtr 36 Class 20 Board 20 Del from £85 * **SERVICES:** Lift **PARKING:** 40 **NOTES:** No dogs (ex guide dogs) Closed 16-28 Dec
CARDS:

See advert on opposite page

★★★68% Imperial

The Promenade LL30 1AP
☎ 01492 877466 01492 878043
e-mail: imphotel@btinternet.com

A large traditional seaside hotel. Many of the bedrooms have views over the bay and there are also several suites available. The elegant Chantrey restaurant offers a fixed-price menu which changes monthly and uses local produce. There is a fully equipped leisure club and extensive conference and banqueting facilities.
ROOMS: 100 en suite (10 fmly) **FACILITIES:** STV Indoor swimming (H) Sauna Solarium Gym Jacuzzi/spa Beauty therapist Hairdressing **CONF:** Thtr 150 Class 50 Board 50 **SERVICES:** Lift **PARKING:** 40 **NOTES:** No smoking in restaurant **CARDS:**

See advert on opposite page

★★★65% St George's

The Promenade LL30 2LG
☎ 01492 877544 01492 877788

Dir: *A55-A470, follow the road to the promenade, 0.25m, the hotel is on the corner, overlooking the sweep of Llandudno Bay*

This popular seafront hotel was the first to be built in the town and still retains many Victorian features including the splendidly ornate Wedgwood Room. The main lounges overlook the bay and incorporate a Coffee Shop serving hot and cold snacks. There is a wide variety of room sizes available and several have fine views over the sea and some also have balconies. Hotel staff are friendly and helpful.

continued

ROOMS: 84 en suite (4 fmly) No smoking in 12 bedrooms s £60-£70; d £90-£110 (incl. bkfst) * LB **FACILITIES:** STV Sauna Solarium Jacuzzi/spa Hairdressing Health & beauty salon Xmas **CONF:** Thtr 250 Class 200 Board 45 Del £90 * **SERVICES:** Lift **PARKING:** 36
NOTES: No dogs (ex guide dogs) No smoking in restaurant Civ Wed 100
CARDS:

★★★ 62% *Gogarth Abbey Hotel*
West Shore LL30 2QY
☎ 01492 876211 📠 01492 875805
Dir: *A55 from Chester turn off rdbt signed Llandudno Junction continue to Llandudno turn left onto West Shore*
It was at this Victorian house that Charles Dodgson (Lewis Carroll) was inspired to write "Alice in Wonderland". Accommodation here is suitable for both business people and holiday makers, and public areas include several lounges, a restaurant and a lounge bar.
ROOMS: 39 en suite (4 fmly) **FACILITIES:** STV Indoor swimming (H) Sauna Solarium Gym Pool table Croquet lawn Putting green Table tennis Boules **CONF:** Thtr 40 Class 30 Board 30 **PARKING:** 40
NOTES: No smoking in restaurant **CARDS:**

★★★ 60% Risboro
Clement Av LL30 2ED
☎ 01492 876343 📠 01492 879881
e-mail: colin.irving@easynet.co.uk
Dir: *A55 to Llandudno, follow A470 into town centre, at large roundabout turn left then take 3rd right*
Situated close to the base of the Great Orme, this popular family hotel provides agreeably furnished bedrooms. Amongst the extensive public areas are a comfortable lounge with a small terrace and a large restaurant overlooking the pool.
ROOMS: 65 en suite (7 fmly) **FACILITIES:** STV Indoor swimming (H) Squash Riding Sauna Solarium Gym Jacuzzi/spa Table tennis
CONF: Thtr 150 Class 100 Board 80 **SERVICES:** Lift **PARKING:** 40
NOTES: No smoking in restaurant **CARDS:**

★★★ 59% *Chatsworth House*
Central Promenade LL30 2XS
☎ 01492 860788 📠 01492 871417
This traditional family-run Victorian hotel occupies a central position on the promenade and caters for many families and groups. There is an indoor swimming pool, separate paddling pool, sauna and solarium. Modern bedrooms, some of them quite spacious, are complemented by well maintained public areas, where a varied entertainment programme is laid on in the summer months.
ROOMS: 72 en suite (19 fmly) **FACILITIES:** Indoor swimming (H) Sauna Jacuzzi/spa **SERVICES:** Lift **PARKING:** 9 **CARDS:**

LLANDUDNO, continued

Premier Collection

★★❀❀❀ St Tudno
Promenade LL30 2LP
☎ 01492 874411 📠 01492 860407
e-mail: sttudnohotel@btinternet.com
Dir: *on reaching Promenade drive towards the pier, hotel is opposite pier entrance & gardens*

A high quality resort hotel which although not the place for buckets and spades, will receive toddlers as warmly as adults. Bedrooms, some with sea views, offer a wide choice of sizes and individual styles, so discuss exact requirements at the time of booking. Public rooms include a no-smoking lounge, a convivial bar-lounge, and a small indoor pool. The air-conditioned Garden Room Restaurant is the focal point for enjoyable cuisine using good local produce.

ROOMS: 19 en suite (2 fmly) No smoking in 3 bedrooms s £78-£150; d £95-£190 (incl. bkfst) * LB **FACILITIES:** STV Indoor swimming (H) entertainment Xmas **CONF:** Thtr 40 Class 25 Board 20 Del from £135 * **SERVICES:** Lift **PARKING:** 12 **NOTES:** No smoking in restaurant **CARDS:**

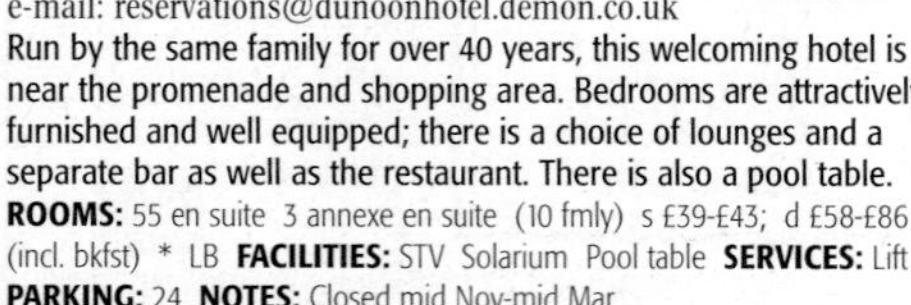

★★72% Dunoon
Gloddaeth St LL30 2DW
☎ 01492 860787 📠 01492 860031
e-mail: reservations@dunoonhotel.demon.co.uk

Run by the same family for over 40 years, this welcoming hotel is near the promenade and shopping area. Bedrooms are attractively furnished and well equipped; there is a choice of lounges and a separate bar as well as the restaurant. There is also a pool table.

ROOMS: 55 en suite 3 annexe en suite (10 fmly) s £39-£43; d £58-£86 (incl. bkfst) * LB **FACILITIES:** STV Solarium Pool table **SERVICES:** Lift **PARKING:** 24 **NOTES:** Closed mid Nov-mid Mar
CARDS:

★★71% Epperstone
15 Abbey Rd LL30 2EE
☎ 01492 878746 📠 01492 871223
Dir: *A55-A470 to Mostyn Street. At rdbt turn left, take 4th right into York Road. Hotel on junction of York road and Abbey Road*

A delightful hotel with wonderful gardens located in a residential part of town, within easy walking distance of the seafront and shopping area. Bedrooms are attractively decorated and thoughtfully equipped. Two lounges are available, a comfortable no-smoking room and a Victorian-style conservatory. A daily changing menu is offered in the bright dining room.

ROOMS: 8 en suite (5 fmly) No smoking in 6 bedrooms s £39-£42; d £78-£84 (incl. bkfst & dinner) * LB **FACILITIES:** STV Xmas **PARKING:** 8 **NOTES:** No smoking in restaurant
CARDS:

★★71% Tan-Lan
Great Orme's Rd, West Shore LL30 2AR
☎ 01492 860221 📠 01492 870219
e-mail: info@tanlanhotel.co.uk
Dir: *turn off A55 onto A546 signposted Deganwy. Straight over 2 rdbts, approx 3m from A55, hotel on left just over mini rdbt*

Located under the Great Orme on the West Shore, a warm welcome is certain at this well presented small hotel. Bedrooms, many on the ground floor, are brightly decorated and well equipped. There is a cosy bar and a comfortable lounge, separated by the attractive restaurant, where freshly prepared meals are served in generous portions.

ROOMS: 17 en suite (3 fmly) No smoking in 2 bedrooms s £25-£37; d £50-£54 (incl. bkfst) * LB **FACILITIES:** Xmas **PARKING:** 12 **NOTES:** No smoking in restaurant Closed 2 Jan-10 Feb & 11 Nov-24 Dec
CARDS:

★★71% *Toldy's Hotel & Bistro Restaurant*
67 Church Walks LL30 2HG
☎ 01492 877200 📠 01492 877200
e-mail: toldyshotel@llandudno67.freeserve.co.uk
Dir: *from A470 follow signs into Llandudno and take Mostyn St, then Upper Mostyn St and turn left at top of hill. Hotel 100yds on right*

This elegant hotel, conveniently situated, has been elegantly restored to create a unique Victorian atmosphere. All rooms are individually styled with luxurious drapes and antiques and have many extras. Run by the friendly Toldi family the hotel is relaxed and informal. Guests can dine either in Gothic-style bistro or the Mediterranean conservatory where a wide selection of dishes is offered.

ROOMS: 8 rms (7 en suite) (3 fmly) No smoking in all bedrooms **PARKING:** 8 **NOTES:** No dogs (ex guide dogs) Closed Jan
CARDS:

★★70% Sandringham
West Pde LL30 2BD
☎ 01492 876513 & 876447 📠 01492 872753
e-mail: sandringham@which.net
Dir: *enter Llandudno on A470 follow signs for West Shore, hotel is located in centre of West Shore Promenade*

This holiday hotel on the West Shore has superb views over the Conwy Estuary towards Snowdonia. There are two restaurants and a full range of bar food. Bedrooms are tastefully decorated with matching fabrics, some at ground floor level and others suitable for families.

ROOMS: 18 en suite (3 fmly) s £28-£31; d £56-£60 (incl. bkfst) * LB **FACILITIES:** STV Xmas **CONF:** Thtr 70 Class 60 Board 30 **PARKING:** 6 **NOTES:** No dogs No smoking in restaurant RS 25 & 26 Dec
CARDS:

★★68% Tynedale
Central Promenade LL30 2XS
☎ 01492 877426 📠 01492 871213
Dir: *on promenade opposite bandstand*

Tour groups are well catered for at Tynedale, and regular live entertainment is a feature. Public areas include good lounge facilities and an attractive patio overlooking the bay. Bedrooms are fresh and well equipped, many have good views over the sea front and the Great Orme.

ROOMS: 56 en suite (4 fmly) s £33-£42; d £66-£84 (incl. bkfst) * LB **FACILITIES:** Xmas **SERVICES:** Lift **PARKING:** 30 **NOTES:** No dogs (ex guide dogs) No smoking in restaurant **CARDS:**

Packed in a hurry? Ironing facilities should be available at all star levels, either in rooms or on request.

★★68% Wilton
South Pde LL30 2LN
☎ 01492 878343 📠 01492 876086
e-mail: info@wiltonhotel.com
Dir: *from A470 head towards promenade, Pier & Great Orme. At Pier turn left before cenataph - Prince Edwards Sq. Hotel last on left before rdbt*
A well maintained hotel, just off the promenade with the main shopping centre nearby. It has very pretty bedrooms, and most have four-poster beds; modern amenities are provided. There is a comfortable lounge bar for residents and good value meals are available.
ROOMS: 14 en suite (7 fmly) No smoking in 4 bedrooms s £26-£36; d £52 (incl. bkfst) * LB **FACILITIES:** STV **PARKING:** 3 **NOTES:** No smoking in restaurant Closed 28 Nov-6 Feb RS early & late season
CARDS:

★★67% Belle Vue
26 North Pde LL30 2LP
☎ 01492 879547 📠 01492 870001
Dir: *follow the promenade towards the pier, as the road bends the Belle Vue Hotel is on the left*
This peaceful and relaxing hotel under the Great Orme is within easy distance of Llandudno town centre and boasts stunning views across the bay. The well equipped bedrooms are comfortable and include video players and a large film library. A comfortable bar and separate lounge is provided for guests and the small daily menu offers good traditional cooking.
ROOMS: 15 en suite (3 fmly) No smoking in all bedrooms s £31-£37; d £52-£68 (incl. bkfst) LB **FACILITIES:** Xmas **SERVICES:** Lift **PARKING:** 12 **NOTES:** No smoking in restaurant
CARDS:

★★67% Sunnymede
West Pde LL30 2BD
☎ 01492 877130 📠 01492 871824
Dir: *from A55 follow signs for Llandudno & Deganwy. At 1st rdbt after Deganwy take 1st exit towards the sea. At corner turn left & follow rd for 400yds*
The Sunnymede is a friendly family-run hotel lying on Llandudno's West Shore. Many rooms have views over the Conwy Estuary and Snowdonia. Modern bedrooms are decorated with pretty wallpapers. Lounge areas are particularly comfortable and attractive.
ROOMS: 16 rms (15 en suite) (3 fmly) s £37-£39; d £74-£78 (incl. bkfst & dinner) * LB **FACILITIES:** Xmas **PARKING:** 18 **NOTES:** No smoking in restaurant Closed Jan-Feb **CARDS:**

★★66% Bedford
Promenade LL30 1BN
☎ 01492 876647 📠 01492 860185
e-mail: thebedford@netscape.net
Dir: *at intersection of A55/A470, take exit for Llandudno (A470) and continue until 4th rdbt. Take exit for Craig-y-Don (B115) and turn right*
This hotel is located on the eastern approach to Llandudno at Craig-y-Don. Many of the well equipped bedrooms are suitable for families and enjoy fine views over the bay towards Great Orme. The hotel's Italian restaurant and pizzeria has a local following and supplements the traditional hotel restaurant. There is a comfortable lounge for residents.
ROOMS: 27 en suite (2 fmly) No smoking in 3 bedrooms s £28-£35; d £42-£50 (incl. bkfst) * LB **FACILITIES:** STV Xmas **CONF:** Thtr 30 Class 20 Board 20 Del from £42 * **SERVICES:** Lift **PARKING:** 21
CARDS:

★★66% *Esplanade*
Glan-y-Mor Pde, Promenade LL30 2LL
☎ 0800 318688 (freephone) & 01492 860300 📠 01492 860418
e-mail: info@esplanadehotel.co.uk
Dir: *turn off A55 at Llandudno junct & proceed on A470*
One of the first hotels in Llandudno and popular for weekend and golfing breaks, the family run Esplanade Hotel is located in the centre of the promenade with the main shopping area nearby. Many bedrooms have superb views over the bay, and are all thoughtfully equipped. An all-day buttery serves light snacks and refreshments.
ROOMS: 59 en suite (20 fmly) **FACILITIES:** entertainment **CONF:** Thtr 90 Class 40 Board 40 **SERVICES:** Lift **PARKING:** 30
CARDS:

★★66% Leamore
40 Lloyd St LL30 2YG
☎ 01492 875552 📠 01492 879386
Dir: *300 mtrs on seafront, opposite life boat station*
This hotel is conveniently located for access to the town centre, the promenade and other amenities. It provides warm and friendly hospitality and well equipped accommodation. Nadege James is a talented singer who frequently entertains her guests.
ROOMS: 12 rms (8 en suite) (4 fmly) No smoking in all bedrooms d fr £36 (incl. bkfst) * LB **FACILITIES:** entertainment **PARKING:** 6
NOTES: No dogs (ex guide dogs) No smoking in restaurant Closed Dec

★★66% Somerset
St Georges Crescent, Promenade LL30 2LF
☎ 01492 876540 📠 01492 863700
Dir: *on the Promenade*
With its sister hotel, The Wavecrest, this cheerful holiday hotel occupies an ideal location on the central promenade and there are superb views over the bay from many rooms. Regular entertainment is provided as well as a range of bar and lounge areas. Bedrooms are well decorated and modern facilities are provided.
ROOMS: 37 en suite (4 fmly) **FACILITIES:** Pool table Games room **SERVICES:** Lift **PARKING:** 20 **NOTES:** No smoking in restaurant Closed Nov-Feb **CARDS:**

★★66% Stratford
8 Craig-y-Don Pde, Promenade LL30 1BG
☎ 01492 877962 📠 01492 877962
Dir: *from A55 take A470 to Llandudno at 4th rdbt take Craig-y-Don sign to Promenade*
A pleasant holiday hotel on the Craig-y-Don promenade. The Conference Centre and theatre are nearby, with the local shops only a short walk away. The comfortable bedrooms include many canopied beds. A daily changing menu provides generously priced home cooking. Guests have a comfortable lounge, separate bar and an inviting patio overlooking the sea.
ROOMS: 10 en suite (4 fmly) s £21-£27; d £38-£50 (incl. bkfst) * LB **FACILITIES:** STV ch fac **NOTES:** No smoking in restaurant Closed Dec-Feb **CARDS:**

★★66% White Lodge
9 Neville Crescent, Central Promenade LL30 1AT
☎ 01492 877713
Dir: *A55 then A470, then onto the B5115*
This friendly and relaxing hotel is located on the promenade with all local amenities within easy walking distance. Many bedrooms enjoy good seafront views and have pretty canopies over the beds. Good value food is on offer and guests have use of a lounge and separate bar.
ROOMS: 12 en suite (4 fmly) s £34-£38; d £54-£64 (incl. bkfst) * LB **PARKING:** 12 **NOTES:** No dogs (ex guide dogs) No children 5yrs No smoking in restaurant Closed Nov-Mar **CARDS:**

L

LLANDUDNO, continued

★★65% Wavecrest
St Georges Crescent, Central Promenade LL30 2LF
☎ 01492 860615 📠 01492 863700
Dir: *on promenade behind Marks & Spencer*
The Wavecrest is the sister hotel of the adjoining Somerset, and public areas are shared. It lies on the central promenade and most bedrooms have lovely sea views. Lounge and bar areas are comfortably furnished and a games room is available. Staff are friendly and regular entertainment is staged.
ROOMS: 41 en suite (7 fmly) **FACILITIES:** Pool table **CONF:** Class 70 **SERVICES:** Lift **PARKING:** 12 **NOTES:** No smoking in restaurant Closed Nov-Mar **CARDS:**

★★64% *Evans*
Charlton St LL30 2AA
☎ 01492 860784 📠 01492 860784
This friendly, privately owned hotel provides comfortable, well appointed bedrooms including some family rooms. Spacious public areas include a well equipped games room and comfortable lounge bar, where regular live evening entertainment is held. Dinner is served until 7pm and a non-cooked supper can be provided for later arrivals.
ROOMS: 50 en suite (4 fmly) **FACILITIES:** STV Snooker Solarium Pool table entertainment **SERVICES:** Lift **NOTES:** No dogs (ex guide dogs) No smoking in restaurant Closed Jan

L

★★64% Royal
Church Walks LL30 2HW
☎ 01492 876476 📠 01492 870210
e-mail: royal@northwales.uk.com
Dir: *exit A55 for A470 to Llandudno. Follow through town to T-jct, then left into Church Walks. Hotel 200yds on left, almost opp. Great Orme tram station*
A long established hotel lying under the Great Orme within easy reach of the promenade, town centre and other amenities. Bedrooms are furnished in a modern style, and many have views over the town and seafront. There is a bar and a spacious dining room, and seasonal live entertainment.
ROOMS: 38 rms (36 en suite) (7 fmly) s fr £35; d fr £70 (incl. bkfst) * LB **FACILITIES:** Pool table Putting green Xmas **CONF:** Class 50 Del from £50 * **SERVICES:** Lift **PARKING:** 20 **NOTES:** No dogs (ex guide dogs) No smoking in restaurant **CARDS:**

★★63% Ambassador Hotel
Grand Promenade LL30 2NR
☎ 01492 876886 📠 01492 876347
Dir: *turn off A55 onto A470. Take turn to Promenade, then left towards pier*
This friendly, family hotel is situated on the sea front and close to the centre of town. Rooms are tastefully decorated and many have sea views. Downstairs there is an attractive bar where snacks are available at lunch time and breakfast and dinner are served in the restaurant. There is also a choice of comfortable lounges to relax in.
ROOMS: 57 en suite (8 fmly) s £29-£47; d £58-£94 (incl. bkfst) * LB **FACILITIES:** entertainment Xmas **CONF:** Thtr 40 Class 18 Board 18 **SERVICES:** Lift **PARKING:** 11 **NOTES:** No dogs (ex guide dogs) No smoking in restaurant **CARDS:**

★★63% *Headlands*
Hill Ter LL30 2LS
☎ 01492 877485
Lovely views over the town and seafront are enjoyed from the public areas and many bedrooms of this resort hotel, at the foot of the great Orme. Bedrooms with four-posters are available. There is a range of comfortable sitting areas and the hotel staff are friendly and welcoming.
ROOMS: 17 rms (15 en suite) (4 fmly) **PARKING:** 7 **NOTES:** No children 5yrs Closed Jan-Feb **CARDS:**

★★63% Oak Alyn
2 Deganwy Av LL30 2YB
☎ 01492 860320 📠 01492 860320
Dir: *situated in the centre of Llandudno, 200 yards from the Town Hall, opposite the Catholic Church*
This is a friendly resort hotel that lies in a residential part of Llandudno, near to the main shopping area and the seafront. Bedrooms are fresh and bright and all are equipped with modern facilities. There is a comfortable lounge for residents and a separate bar.
ROOMS: 12 en suite (2 fmly) s £22-£28; d £44-£48 (incl. bkfst) * LB **FACILITIES:** Xmas **PARKING:** 16 **NOTES:** No smoking in restaurant Closed 22-31 Dec **CARDS:**

★★63% Ormescliffe
East Pde LL30 1BE
☎ 01492 877191 📠 01492 860311
e-mail: ormescliffe@clara.net
This family-run hotel lies at the eastern end of the promenade and is convenient for the theatre and conference centre. Bedrooms are modern and well equipped, several are suitable for families and most have superb views over the seafront and Great Orme. Comfortable bars and lounges are provided and there is a ballroom with regular live entertainment. The atmosphere is warm and relaxing.
ROOMS: 61 en suite (7 fmly) No smoking in 6 bedrooms s £35-£42; d £70-£84 (incl. bkfst) * LB **FACILITIES:** Snooker Table tennis Xmas **CONF:** Thtr 120 Class 120 Board 80 **SERVICES:** Lift **PARKING:** 15 **NOTES:** No smoking in restaurant Closed 2 Jan-2 Feb **CARDS:**

★★63% Ravenhurst
West Pde LL30 2BB
☎ 01492 875525 📠 01248 681143
Dir: *on West Shore, opposite boating pool*
This comfortable hotel lies on Llandudno's West Shore with lovely views from many rooms over the Conwy Estuary towards Snowdonia. Smart accommodation includes several family suites. Two lounges and a small bar are provided, the dining room offers a daily fixed-price menu.
ROOMS: 25 en suite (3 fmly) s £27; d £54 (incl. bkfst) * LB **FACILITIES:** Xmas **PARKING:** 15 **NOTES:** No smoking in restaurant Closed Dec-Feb **CARDS:**

★63% Min-y-Don
North Pde LL30 2LP
☎ 01492 876511 📠 01492 878169
Dir: *leave A55 Expressway Llandudno junct taking A470. Through Martyn St, turn right at rdbt then left North Parade*
This is a cheerful family-run hotel located under the Great Orme and close to the pier. Bedrooms include several suitable for families and many have lovely views over the bay. Regular entertainment is held and there are comfortable lounge and bar areas.
ROOMS: 28 rms (19 en suite) (12 fmly) **FACILITIES:** **SERVICES:** air con **PARKING:** 7 **NOTES:** No dogs Closed Jan-Feb **CARDS:**

LLANELLI, Carmarthenshire Map 02 SN50

★★★66% Diplomat Hotel
Felinfoel SA15 3PJ
☎ 01554 756156 📠 01554 751649
Dir: *from M4 exit junct 48 onto A4138 then B4303 hotel in 0.75m on the right*
Best Western
A Victorian mansion in several acres of mature grounds. Public

continued

rooms include good lounge and bar areas, a large function suite and fully equipped leisure centre. Bedrooms are well appointed and available in the mansion and the nearby coach house.
ROOMS: 23 en suite 8 annexe en suite (2 fmly) s £65-£75; d £85-£95 (incl. bkfst) * LB **FACILITIES:** Indoor swimming (H) Sauna Solarium Gym Jacuzzi/spa entertainment Xmas **CONF:** Thtr 250 Class 100 Board 100 Del £88 * **SERVICES:** Lift **PARKING:** 250 **NOTES:** Civ Wed 200
CARDS:

★★66% Ashburnham

Ashburnham Rd, Pembrey SA16 0TH
☎ 01554 834343 & 834455 📠 01554 834483
Dir: *M4 junct 48, A4138 to Llanelli, A484 West to Pembrey, look out for road sign as entering village*
A friendly hotel in Pembrey with nineteenth century architecture, to the west of Llanelli. Amelia Earhart stayed here at the end of her historic Atlantic flight of 1928, and doubtless enjoyed her stay. Today, the bright bar and restaurant serve bar meals and a carte menu. Bedrooms have modern furnishings and facilities, family rooms are also available.
ROOMS: 12 en suite (2 fmly) s £50; d £68 (incl. bkfst) * LB
FACILITIES: STV Pool table **CONF:** Thtr 150 Class 150 Board 80 Del £65 * **PARKING:** 100 **NOTES:** No smoking in restaurant RS 25 Dec Civ Wed 120 **CARDS:**

★★65% Miramar

158 Station Rd SA15 1YU
☎ 01554 754726 & 773607 📠 01554 772454
e-mail: hotel-miramar@lineone.net
Dir: *take junct 48 on M4. Follow road to Llanelli. In Llanelli follow railway station signs. Hotel is adjacent to the station*
A family-run hotel located opposite the railway station and conveniently near the town centre. Accommodation is well maintained and comfortable with modern facilities. There is a cheerful bar and two restaurants with an extensive choice of dishes, including a number of Portuguese specialities. Secure car-parking is an additional asset.
ROOMS: 12 en suite (2 fmly) s fr £22; d fr £36 (incl. bkfst) *
PARKING: 10 **NOTES:** No dogs (ex guide dogs)
CARDS:

LLANFAIRPWLLGWYNGYLL See Anglesey, Isle of

LLANFYLLIN, Powys — Map 06 SJ11

★★67% Cain Valley

High St SY22 5AQ
☎ 01691 648366 📠 01691 648307
Dir: *at the end of A490 - Llanfillin, 12m from Welshpool. Hotel is situated in the centre of town on the square, car park at the rear*
A family run, Grade II listed coaching inn with exposed beams and a Jacobean staircase. The comfortable accommodation includes family rooms. Public areas include a choice of bars where a range of food is available. Alternatively, diners can choose from the extensive restaurant carte.
ROOMS: 13 en suite (3 fmly) s £36-£40; d £59-£66 (incl. bkfst) * LB
PARKING: 12 **NOTES:** No smoking in restaurant Closed 24-25 Dec
CARDS:

> Popped the question? Hotels with Civ Wed in their entry are licensed for civil wedding ceremonies. Maximum numbers for the ceremony only are shown, e.g. Civ Wed 50

LLANGAMMARCH WELLS, Powys — Map 03 SN94

Premier Collection

★★★ Lake Country House

LD4 4BS
☎ 01591 620202 & 620474 📠 01591 620457
e-mail: info@lakecountryhouse.co.uk
Dir: *from Builth Wells head W on A483 to Garth (6m approx) turn left for Llangammarch Wells follow signs for hotel*
This Victorian country house hotel comes complete with a golf course, lake, wooded grounds and river. Bedrooms are individually decorated and furnished with designer fabrics and with many extra comforts as standard. Great afternoon teas are served in the lounge in front of a log fire. In addition to the elegant restaurant there is a separate bar and billiard room. The kitchen produces a good standard of cuisine.
ROOMS: 19 en suite (1 fmly) No smoking in 6 bedrooms d £130-£215 (incl. bkfst) * **FACILITIES:** Golf 9 Tennis (hard) Fishing Snooker Croquet lawn Putting green Clay pigeon shooting
CONF: Thtr 80 Class 30 Board 25 **PARKING:** 72 **NOTES:** No smoking in restaurant **CARDS:**

LLANGOLLEN, Denbighshire — Map 07 SJ24

see also Glyn Ceiriog

★★★70% The Wild Pheasant Hotel & Restaurant

Berwyn Rd LL20 8AD
☎ 01978 860629 📠 01978 861837
e-mail: wild.pheasant@talk21.com
Dir: *hotel situated 0.5m from town centre on the left hand side of the main A5 towards Betws-y-Coed/Holyhead*

A professionally run hotel providing smart, modern accommodation. Bedrooms, several with four-posters, are well equipped. The reception area, resembling an old village square, has comfortable seating areas. There is a choice of bars and a

continued

LLANGOLLEN, continued

range of eating options including a formal restaurant. A self-contained function suite is available.
ROOMS: 34 en suite (2 fmly) No smoking in 6 bedrooms s fr £53; d fr £86 (incl. bkfst) * LB **FACILITIES:** Golf Laser pigeon shooting Xmas **CONF:** Thtr 140 Class 70 Board 50 **PARKING:** 100 **NOTES:** No smoking in restaurant Civ Wed 140 **CARDS:**

★★★66% Bryn Howel
LL20 7UW
☎ 01978 860331 01978 860119
e-mail: hotel@brynhowel.demon.co.uk
Best Western
Dir: *follow signs for Llangollen on A539. Pass through Acrefair & Trevor, continue for 2m & hotel is on left*
Built in 1896, this carefully extended house stands in well tended gardens with magnificent views across the Vale of Llangollen. The restaurant overlooks the well tended gardens with a backdrop of mountains beyond, and there are comfortable lounges for relaxation after dinner. Accommodation is attractive, modern, and thoughtfully equipped.
ROOMS: 36 en suite s £75-£125; d £95-£145 * LB **FACILITIES:** STV Fishing Sauna Solarium Pool table Croquet lawn Xmas **CONF:** Thtr 250 Class 60 Board 50 Del from £88.13 * **SERVICES:** Lift **PARKING:** 200 **NOTES:** No dogs (ex guide dogs) No smoking in restaurant Civ Wed 300 **CARDS:**

L

★★★61% The Royal
Bridge St LL20 8PG
REGAL
☎ 01978 860202 01978 861824
Dir: *from A5 to Llangollen. Turn right into Castle St. Hotel is on junct with Bridge St. From Wrexham take A539 Llangollen, turn left across Bridge*

This traditional hotel, where Queen Victoria once stayed, is situated in the centre of the town overlooking the River Dee. The most recently refurbished bedrooms are comfortable and have been attractively decorated. All rooms have modern facilities and several have river views. The restaurant also overlooks the river as does the comfortable lounge. There are two bars, one in a modern theme, the other more in character with the age of the hotel. Staff are friendly and guests are assured of a warm welcome. The hotel has its own car park, opposite.
ROOMS: 33 en suite (3 fmly) No smoking in 8 bedrooms s £27-£37; d £54-£74 (incl. bkfst) * LB **FACILITIES:** Fishing Pool table Xmas **CONF:** Thtr 70 Class 30 Board 20 Del £70 * **PARKING:** 20 **NOTES:** No smoking in restaurant **CARDS:**

★★★59% Hand
Bridge St LL20 8PL
☎ 01978 860303 01978 861277
PEEL HOTELS
Dir: *from A539, turn right over bridge, drive up Castle St, at lights turn left onto A5 towards Oswestry, hotel car park is 2nd turning on left hand side*
Situated close to the town centre this 18th-century former coaching inn has gardens which lead down to the River Dee, on which the hotel has fishing rights. The bedrooms are well appointed, several to a very high standard. Good cuisine is provided in the restaurant, which has river views. Lighter meals are available in the hotel bar.
ROOMS: 58 en suite (3 fmly) No smoking in 11 bedrooms s £65-£70; d £80-£90 (incl. bkfst) * LB **FACILITIES:** Fishing entertainment Xmas **CONF:** Thtr 100 Class 50 Board 50 Del from £47 * **PARKING:** 40 **NOTES:** No smoking in restaurant **CARDS:**

★★64% *Chain Bridge Hotel*
Berwyn LL20 8BS
☎ 01978 860215
The hotel is situated in an idyllic location on the banks of the river Dee and takes its name from the bridge which spans the river. The historic town of Llangollen is about two miles away and the Shropshire Union canal runs nearby. Rooms are comfortably furnished and some are suitable for families. Downstairs the restaurant overlooks the river and meals are also available in the Tudor bar. Function facilities are also available.

★★63% Abbey Grange Hotel
LL20 8DD
☎ 01978 860753 01978 869070
e-mail: enquiries@abbey-grange-hotel.co.uk
The hotel is situated close to Llangollen and is a good base for exploring Offa's Dyke and the surrounding countryside. Rooms are spacious and well equipped, some of which are suitable for families. Guests can dine in the restaurant or the bar, and outside there is a sun patio and large children's play area.
ROOMS: 8 en suite (3 fmly) s fr £30; d fr £50 (incl. bkfst) * LB **FACILITIES:** Pool table Xmas **PARKING:** 40 **CARDS:**

LLANGYBI, Monmouthshire — Map 03 ST39

★★★★70% Cwrt Bleddyn Hotel & Country Club
NP5 1PG
☎ 01633 450521 01633 450220
Dir: *from M4 junct 25 follow signs Caerleon and around 1-way system, straight over mini-rdbt, follow country road for 4m, hotel on left*

Cwrt Bleddyn is an attractive Victorian building set in parkland in the Welsh Borders. Most of the bedrooms are smartly modernised; some have four-posters and carved oak furniture, and four are in a separate cottage, but all have many little extras to cosset guests. There is a fine leisure complex, and Jesters restaurant is a colourful setting for a range of dishes making the most of local produce.
ROOMS: 29 en suite 4 annexe en suite No smoking in 9 bedrooms s £75-£105; d £95-£125 (incl. bkfst) * LB **FACILITIES:** STV Indoor swimming (H) Tennis (hard) Squash Sauna Solarium Gym Jacuzzi/spa Beauty salon Xmas **CONF:** Thtr 200 Class 60 Board 40 Del from £111 * **PARKING:** 100 **NOTES:** No dogs (ex guide dogs) No smoking in restaurant **CARDS:**

LLANRWST, Conwy Map 06 SH76
see also Betws-y-Coed

★★★62% *Maenan Abbey*
Maenan LL26 0UL
☎ 01492 660247 📠 01492 660734
Dir: *3m N on A470*
Built as an abbey in 1850 on the site of a 13th-century monastery, now a popular venue for weddings. The grounds and magnificent galleried staircase make an ideal backdrop for photographs. Bedrooms are equipped with modern facilities, and a wide range of food is served in the hotel's two bars.
ROOMS: 12 en suite (2 fmly) **FACILITIES:** Fishing Clay pigeon shooting entertainment **CONF:** Class 50 Board 50 **PARKING:** 60
CARDS:

★★66% *Meadowsweet*
Station Rd LL26 0DS
☎ 01492 642111 📠 01492 642111
e-mail: dolydd@globalnet.co.uk
Dir: *on the main A470 through Llanrwst*
The Meadowsweet is a small friendly hotel on the northern outskirts of the town, convenient for many local attractions such as Snowdonia National Park, Bodnant Gardens, Conwy and Llandudno. Rooms are spacious and have modern facilities. There is also a pleasant bar with an open fire. The attractive dining room offers both fixed-price and carte menus.
ROOMS: 10 en suite (3 fmly) **PARKING:** 9
CARDS:

LLANWDDYN, Powys Map 06 SJ01

★★★73% Lake Vyrnwy
Lake Vyrnwy SY10 0LY
☎ 01691 870692 📠 01691 870259
e-mail: res@lakevyrnwy.com
Dir: *on A4393, 200yds past dam*
This fine country house hotel lies in 26,000 acres of woodland above Lake Vyrnwy. It provides a wide range of bedrooms, most with superb views and many with four-poster beds and balconies. The extensive public rooms are elegantly furnished and include a choice of bars. The Tavern bar serves meals while the main restaurant offers more formal dining.
ROOMS: 35 en suite (4 fmly) s £100-£145; d £146-£210 (incl. bkfst & dinner) LB **FACILITIES:** STV Tennis (hard) Fishing Riding Game/Clay shooting Sailing Cycling Archery Quad trekking Xmas **CONF:** Thtr 120 Class 60 Board 40 Del from £150 * **PARKING:** 70 **NOTES:** No smoking in restaurant Civ Wed 90 **CARDS:**

LLANWRTYD WELLS, Powys Map 03 SN84

★★73% Carlton House
Dolycoed Rd LD5 4RA
☎ 01591 610248 📠 01591 610242
e-mail: info@carltonrestaurant.co.uk
Dir: *centre of town*
Carlton House stands in a beautiful and unspoilt area of Wales, which is reputed to be the smallest rural town in Britain. The bedrooms are striking in their style, each being decorated with a different theme with high levels of comfort. The communal areas are pleasing with warm, fresh colours and period furniture. The hotel cuisine is rated very highly in the region, and is perfectly complimented by a very well chosen wine list.
ROOMS: 7 rms (5 en suite) (2 fmly) s £30-£40; d £60-£75 (incl. bkfst) * LB **FACILITIES:** Pony trekking Mountain biking **NOTES:** No smoking in restaurant RS 15-30 Dec **CARDS:**

★★68% Lasswade Country House Hotel
Station Rd LD5 4RW
☎ 01591 6105150 📠 01591 610611
e-mail: lasswade.kencarol@virgin.net
Dir: *turn off A483 toward station Llangammarch Well, 200yds on right*
An Edwardian country house set on the edge of town, Lasswade commands enriching countryside views. Bedrooms are comfortably furnished with thoughtful extra facilities. Dinner can be taken in the elegant dining room or in the bright conservatory. Guests can relax and take drinks in the lounge. Also on offer are rough shooting and trout fishing. The hotel is non-smoking throughout.
ROOMS: 8 en suite No smoking in all bedrooms **FACILITIES:** STV Sauna **PARKING:** 10 **NOTES:** No dogs No children 14yrs No smoking in restaurant **CARDS:**

LLYSWEN, Powys Map 03 SO13

Premier Collection

★★★★ Llangoed Hall
LD3 0YP
☎ 01874 754525 📠 01874 754545
e-mail: llangoed_hall_co_wales_uk@compuserve.com
Dir: *follow A470 through village of Llyswen for 2m. Hotel drive on right hand side*
Set amidst beautiful countryside this imposing country house offers an exterior remodelled by Clough Williams-Ellis (of Portmeirion fame). Inside there is a splendid balance between comfort, grandeur and interest with wood-burning open fires, deep-cushioned sofas, and a range of artwork and artefacts. Bedrooms are furnished with a pleasing mix of antiques and Laura Ashley designs together with smart bathrooms. The hotel cuisine complements the opulent surroundings with accomplished, imaginative cooking.
ROOMS: 23 en suite s £105-£305; d £135-£335 (incl. bkfst) * LB **FACILITIES:** STV Tennis (hard) Fishing Croquet lawn Mazes Clay pigeon shooting Xmas **CONF:** Thtr 60 Class 30 Board 28 Del from £150 * **PARKING:** 85 **NOTES:** No dogs (ex guide dogs) No children 8yrs No smoking in restaurant Civ Wed 50
CARDS:

★★70% Griffin Inn
LD3 0UR
☎ 01874 754241 📠 01874 754592
e-mail: info@griffin-inn.freeserve.co.uk
Dir: *on A470*
A true country inn with log fires in the bar and a hearty menu of local game and other produce. A warm welcome is guaranteed and the Griffin has established a loyal following. The bedrooms

continued

LLYSWEN, continued

vary in size, all are prettily decorated and sympathetically furnished.
ROOMS: 8 rms (7 en suite) s £45-£55; d £70-£80 (incl. bkfst) * LB
FACILITIES: Fishing **PARKING:** 14 **NOTES:** No smoking in restaurant
CARDS:

MACHYNLLETH, Powys Map 06 SH70
see also Eglwysfach

★★66% Wynnstay
Maengwyn St SY20 8AE
☎ 01654 702941 📠 01654 703884
e-mail: wynnstay@btinternet.com
Dir: *at junct of A487/A489*
Long established, this hotel lies in the centre of historic Machynlleth. Bedrooms are pleasing and provide modern facilities. Its bars are popular locally and a good range of food is available. The restaurant is home to more formal dining; guests can choose from a sizeable fixed price menu.
ROOMS: 23 en suite (3 fmly) No smoking in 7 bedrooms s £45; d £70-£96 (incl. bkfst) * LB **FACILITIES:** Xmas **CONF:** Thtr 40 Class 20 Board 24 Del from £70 * **PARKING:** 30 **NOTES:** No smoking in restaurant **CARDS:**
See advert on opposite page

MANORBIER, Pembrokeshire Map 02 SS09

★★65% Castle Mead Hotel
SA70 7TA
☎ 01834 871358 📠 01834 871358

THE CIRCLE
Selected Individual Hotels
GREAT BRITAIN

Dir: *A4139 towards Pembroke from Tenby, turn onto B4585 into village and follow signs to beach and castle. Hotel on left above beach*
The hotel benefits from a superb location overlooking the bay, a Norman church and Manorbier Castle. This family-run establishment has a friendly style and public areas that include a sea view restaurant, bar and residents lounge, together with extensive gardens. The bedrooms are generally quite spacious and offer modern facilities throughout.
ROOMS: 5 en suite 3 annexe en suite (2 fmly) No smoking in 2 bedrooms s fr £33; d fr £65 (incl. bkfst) * LB **PARKING:** 20
NOTES: Closed Nov-Feb **CARDS:**

MENAI BRIDGE See Anglesey, Isle of

MERTHYR TYDFIL, Merthyr Tydfil Map 03 SO00
see also Nant-Ddu

★★★69% Tregenna
Park Ter CF47 8RF
☎ 01685 723627 & 382055 📠 01685 721951
e-mail: reception@tregenna.co.uk
Quiet surroundings and a warm welcome give guests a relaxing start to any visit here whether it be business or pleasure. This family-run hotel is situated just north of the town centre and has plenty of parking. Bedrooms are well equipped; half the rooms are housed in a purpose-built annexe. Ground floor public areas include a traditionally furnished restaurant and bar which serves a good selection of meals.
ROOMS: 24 en suite (9 fmly) No smoking in 4 bedrooms s £44-£48; d £55-£60 (incl. bkfst) * LB **FACILITIES:** STV Xmas **CONF:** Thtr 70 Class 70 Board 30 **PARKING:** 60 **CARDS:**

MISKIN, Rhondda Cynon Taff Map 03 ST08

★★★★69% ❀ Miskin Manor
Groes Faen, Pontyclun CF72 8ND
☎ 01443 224204 📠 01443 237606
e-mail: info@miskin-manor.co.uk
Dir: *leave M4 at junct 34 & follow hotel signs - 300yds on left*
This manor house is set in 20 acres of grounds, only minutes away from the M4 Motorway. Public areas are spacious and comfortable and include a variety of function rooms. Bedrooms are furnished to a high standard and include some located in converted stables and cottages. Frederick's health club has leisure facilities and a bar/bistro.
ROOMS: 35 en suite 11 annexe en suite s £94; d £126 (incl. bkfst) * LB **FACILITIES:** STV Indoor swimming (H) Squash Sauna Solarium Gym Croquet lawn Jacuzzi/spa Xmas **CONF:** Thtr 160 Class 80 Board 65 Del from £135 * **PARKING:** 200 **NOTES:** No smoking in restaurant Civ Wed 200 **CARDS:**
See advert under CARDIFF

MOLD, Flintshire Map 07 SJ26
see also Northop Hall

★★★64% Beaufort Park Hotel
Alltami Rd, New Brighton CH7 6RQ
☎ 01352 758646 📠 01352 757132
e-mail: bph@beaufortparkhotel.co.uk
Dir: *A55 - take Mold slip road, A494. Through Alltami traffic lights. Over mini rdbt by petrol station towards Mold, A5119. Hotel 100yds on right*
With the North Wales Expressway just a short drive away, this large hotel attracts a business and holiday clientele. Accommodation is spacious and modern, and there are plenty of meeting and function rooms. There is a wide range of eating options and several popular bars.
ROOMS: 106 en suite (4 fmly) No smoking in 25 bedrooms s fr £70; d fr £85 (incl. bkfst) * LB **FACILITIES:** Squash Pool table Jacuzzi/spa Darts Games Room entertainment Xmas **CONF:** Thtr 250 Class 120 Board 50 Del £95 * **PARKING:** 200 **NOTES:** Civ Wed 80
CARDS:

★★64% Bryn Awel
Denbigh Rd CH7 1BL
☎ 01352 758622 📠 01352 758625
e-mail: bryn@awel.fsbusiness.co.uk
Dir: *NW edge of town, on A541*
This small privately run hotel is in easy reach of the town centre. It provides well equipped modern accommodation. Some bedrooms are in a purpose built annexe. Public areas comprise a spacious lounge bar and attractive restaurant, a good choice is offered from the carte menu and an extensive selection of bar meals.
ROOMS: 7 en suite 10 annexe en suite No smoking in 5 bedrooms s fr £38; d fr £50 (incl. bkfst) * LB **CONF:** Thtr 35 Class 20 Board 20 Del from £59 * **PARKING:** 44 **NOTES:** No smoking in restaurant
CARDS:

MONMOUTH, Monmouthshire Map 03 SO51
see also Whitebrook

★★70% Riverside
Cinderhill St NP25 5EY
☎ 01600 715577 & 713236 📠 01600 712668

MINOTEL
Great Britain

Dir: *leave A40 signposted Rockfield & Monmouth hotel on left beyond garage & before rdbt*
Close to the famous 13th century bridge, this privately owned hotel offers comfortable accommodation and a relaxed and informal atmosphere. The well equipped bedrooms, include one

continued

ground floor room, with its own access. Facilities include an attractive restaurant providing a fixed price menu and a short carte, a pleasant bar and a conservatory lounge at the rear of the property.

ROOMS: 17 en suite (2 fmly) No smoking in 2 bedrooms s £48; d £68 (incl. bkfst) * LB **FACILITIES:** STV Pool table Xmas **CONF:** Thtr 200 Class 100 Board 80 **PARKING:** 30 **NOTES:** No smoking in restaurant **CARDS:**

MONTGOMERY, Powys Map 07 SO29

★★70% Dragon

MINOTEL Great Britain

SY15 6PA
☎ 01686 668359 01686 668287
e-mail: reception@dragonhotel.com
Dir: *behind the Town Hall*

This fine 17th-century coaching inn stands in the centre of Montgomery. Beams and timbers from the nearby castle, which was destroyed by Cromwell, are visible in the lounge and bar. A wide choice of soundly prepared, wholesome food is available in both the restaurant and bar. Bedrooms are well equipped and family rooms are available.

ROOMS: 20 en suite (6 fmly) No smoking in 5 bedrooms s £44-£54; d £74 (incl. bkfst) * LB **FACILITIES:** Indoor swimming (H) Sauna entertainment Xmas **CONF:** Thtr 40 Class 30 Board 25 **PARKING:** 21 **CARDS:**

MUMBLES (NEAR SWANSEA), Swansea Map 02 SS68

★★67% St Anne's

Western Ln SA3 4EY
☎ 01792 369147 01792 360537
e-mail: pcs.cardiff@btinternet.com
Dir: *follow A483/A4067 along coastal rd to Mumbles, on reaching village drive straight over mini rdbt and cont along rd, Western Lane is 3rd right*

Standing on a hillside above Swansea, this former convent school, dating in places back to 1823, enjoys some superb views over Swansea Bay. The accommodation is modern and bedrooms are well maintained with good facilities. Many rooms overlook the sea as do the public areas that include a spacious lounge with a large picture window.

ROOMS: 33 en suite (3 fmly) No smoking in 7 bedrooms s £52-£60; d £69.50 (incl. bkfst) * LB **FACILITIES:** STV **CONF:** Thtr 100 Class 50 Board 50 Del from £65 * **PARKING:** 50 **NOTES:** No smoking in restaurant **CARDS:**

See advert under SWANSEA

Fancy a Singapore Sling? Bar staff in five star hotels should be skilled cocktail mixers.

N

NANT-DDU (NEAR MERTHYR TYDFIL), Powys Map 03 SO01

★★★74% Nant Ddu Lodge

Cwm Taf, Nant Ddu CF48 2HY
☎ 01685 379111 01685 377088
e-mail: enquiries@nant-ddu-lodge.co.uk
Dir: *6m N of Merthyr Tydfil on main A470 between Merthyr and Brecon*

This 19th Century Georgian hotel is situated in the picturesque Brecon Beacons, a stones throw away from Nant Ddu (Black Stream). Bedrooms are attractively furnished with a good range of facilities. The charming bar and bistro areas are the focal point, serving imaginative good food. Meeting rooms are available and there is a comfortable lounge.

ROOMS: 12 en suite 10 annexe en suite (3 fmly) s £55-£67.50; d £69.50-£89.50 (incl. bkfst) * LB **CONF:** Thtr 30 Class 15 Board 16 **PARKING:** 60 **NOTES:** No smoking in restaurant RS 24-30 Dec **CARDS:**

See advert under BRECON

NEATH, Neath Port Talbot Map 03 SS79

★★65% Castle Hotel

The Parade SA11 1RB
☎ 01639 641119 & 643581 🖷 01639 641624
Dir: *M4 junct43, follow signs for Neath town centre, 500yds past railway station hotel is situated on right hand side*
The Castle hotel is an old coaching inn situated in the heart of Neath. Reputedly frequented by Lord Nelson; it is also where the Welsh Rugby Union was founded over a century ago. The bars and restaurant are popular local venues and there are function and conference rooms available. The bedrooms are well equipped and generally spacious.
ROOMS: 29 en suite (3 fmly) No smoking in 4 bedrooms s £55-£65; d £65-£75 (incl. bkfst) * LB **FACILITIES:** STV **CONF:** Thtr 120 Class 75 Board 50 **PARKING:** 26 **NOTES:** No dogs (ex guide dogs)
CARDS:

NEVERN, Pembrokeshire Map 02 SN03

★★68% Trewern Arms

SA42 0NB
☎ 01239 820395 🖷 01834 811 679
Dir: *off A487 coast road - midway between Cardigan and Fishguard*
This ivy clad 16th-century inn has a wealth of charm and character. It stands alongside the River Nevern, just off the A487, nine miles north-east of Fishguard. Original features include stone flagged floors, exposed stone walls and beamed ceilings in the two bars and the attractively appointed restaurant. The modern bedrooms are spacious and comfortable and include family bedded rooms. A function area caters for up to 100 people.
ROOMS: 10 en suite (4 fmly) s fr £35; d fr £50 (incl. bkfst) *
FACILITIES: Fishing Riding Pool table Xmas **PARKING:** 100
NOTES: No dogs **CARDS:**

N

NEWPORT, Newport Map 03 ST38

Hotel of the Year

★★★★★77% The Celtic Manor Resort

Coldra Woods NP18 1HQ
☎ 01633 413000 🖷 01633 412910
e-mail: postbox@celtic-manor.com
Dir: *leave M4 at junct 24, take A48 towards Newport town centre. Celtic Manor is 1st right turn past Newbridge Networks*
A destination in itself, this international-scale hotel, awarded Hotel of the Year for Wales, offers some of the most impressive and wide-ranging facilities in the UK. Four golf courses, two leisure clubs (with spa and beauty treatments) are coupled with enormous conference facilities and luxurious bedrooms and suites. A cavernous atrium makes a striking first impression of the hotel, leading onto smart lounges and restaurants. Owen's offers fine dining with a modern Celtic bent and the Olive Tree provides a lighter Mediterranean option. Roof gardens, an art gallery and shops are further features of this awe-inspiring operation. Much of the hotel overlooks golf courses and the open countryside, but the M4 and Severn Bridge are just minutes away.
ROOMS: 400 en suite (28 fmly) No smoking in 167 bedrooms d £153-£177 * LB **FACILITIES:** STV Indoor swimming (H) Golf 54 Snooker Sauna Solarium Gym Putting green Jacuzzi/spa Golf Academy Spa with beauty treatments entertainment Xmas
CONF: Thtr 1500 Class 300 Board 50 Del from £155 *
SERVICES: Lift air con **PARKING:** 1300 **NOTES:** No dogs (ex guide dogs) **CARDS:**

★★★67% Newport Lodge

Bryn Bevan, Brynglas Rd NP20 5QN
☎ 01633 821818 🖷 01633 856360
e-mail: info@newportlodgehotel.co.uk
Dir: *off M4 at junct 26 follow signs Newport Town centre. Turn left after 0.5m onto Malpal Road, up hill for 0.5m to hotel*
On the edge of the town centre, close to junction 26 of the M4, this is a purpose-built, friendly hotel. Public areas include a bistro-style restaurant which offers a wide range of freshly prepared dishes. The bedrooms are well maintained, have modern facilities and are well presented. A room with a four-poster bed is available.
ROOMS: 27 en suite No smoking in 3 bedrooms s £60-£65; d £75-£85 (incl. bkfst) * LB **CONF:** Thtr 25 Class 20 Board 20 **PARKING:** 63
NOTES: No children 14yrs **CARDS:**

★★★64% Kings

High St NP20 1QU
☎ 01633 842020 🖷 01633 244667
e-mail: kingshotels.wales@netscapeonline.co.uk
Dir: *from town centre, take left hand road (not flyover) right hand lane to next rdbt, 3rd exit off across front of hotel then left for carpark*
Situated right in the town centre, this privately owned hotel offers comfortable bedroom accommodation and bright spacious public areas. The hotel's main dining room is supplemented by a separate, Chinese restaurant. There are also two bars, function rooms and a ballroom where live music features once a month.
ROOMS: 61 en suite (15 fmly) No smoking in 20 bedrooms s £60-£70; d £80-£110 * LB **FACILITIES:** STV entertainment Xmas **CONF:** Thtr 150 Class 70 Board 50 Del £95 * **SERVICES:** Lift **PARKING:** 50
NOTES: No dogs (ex guide dogs) Closed 26 Dec-4 Jan
CARDS:

See advert on opposite page

NEWTOWN, Powys Map 06 SO19

★★64% Elephant & Castle

Broad St SY16 2BQ
☎ 01686 626271 🖷 01686 622123
e-mail: anyone@theelephant.prestel.co.uk
Dir: *turn for Newtown town centre at traffic lights by St Davids Church, this road meets main street, the hotel is opposite the junct next to river*
Located beside the River Severn and near the town centre, this privately owned hotel is busy and popular. Bedrooms are well equipped; several rooms are located across the hotel car park. There is a choice of bars, a range of food options and extensive function facilities. A fitness centre is also provided.
ROOMS: 23 en suite 11 annexe en suite (2 fmly) No smoking in 11 bedrooms s £39; d £58 (incl. bkfst) * LB **FACILITIES:** STV Solarium Gym **CONF:** Thtr 200 Class 100 Board 25 Del from £50 *
PARKING: 15 **NOTES:** No dogs (ex guide dogs) No smoking in restaurant RS 24-26 Dec Civ Wed 30
CARDS:

NORTHOP, Flintshire Map 07 SJ26

★★★77% Soughton Hall
CH7 6AB
☎ 01352 840811 01352 840382
Dir: *A55-B5126, after 500mtrs turn left for Northop, left at traffic lights (A5119-Mold). After 0.5m look for signs on left for the hall*

Built as a Bishop's Palace in 1714, this is a truly elegant country house, set in its own magnificent grounds. Bedrooms are individually decorated and furnished with fine antiques and rich fabrics. There are several spacious day rooms furnished in keeping with the style of the house. The bustling, trendy, adjacent Stables bar and restaurant offers a contrast to fine dining in the main hotel.

ROOMS: 14 en suite (2 fmly) s fr £70; d £110-£170 (incl. bkfst) * LB
FACILITIES: Golf 18 Tennis (hard) Riding Croquet lawn Xmas
CONF: Thtr 60 Class 30 Board 20 Del from £128 * **PARKING:** 100
NOTES: No dogs (ex guide dogs) No smoking in restaurant Civ Wed 150
CARDS:

NORTHOP HALL, Flintshire Map 07 SJ26

Travelodge
CH7 6HB
☎ 01244 816473 01244 816473
Dir: *on A55, eastbound*

This modern building offers accommodation in smart, spacious and well equipped bedrooms, all with en suite bathrooms. Refreshments may be taken at the nearby family restaurant. For further details and the Travelodge phone number, consult the Hotel Groups page.

ROOMS: 40 en suite

PEMBROKE, Pembrokeshire Map 02 SM90

★★★74% Court
Lamphey SA71 5NT
☎ 01646 672273 01646 672480
e-mail: enquiries@lampheycourt.co.uk
Dir: *take A477 to Pembroke. Turn left at Village Milton. In Lamphey village hotel on right*

This fine Georgian mansion lies in several acres of mature grounds and landscaped gardens. Bedrooms are well equipped and include several family suites, some located in a nearby converted coach house. Public areas include function and conference rooms and a modern conservatory.

ROOMS: 26 en suite 11 annexe en suite (15 fmly) s £69-£83; d £85-£110 (incl. bkfst) * LB **FACILITIES:** STV Indoor swimming (H) Tennis (hard) Sauna Solarium Gym Jacuzzi/spa Yacht charter Xmas
CONF: Thtr 80 Class 60 Board 40 Del from £99.50 * **PARKING:** 50
NOTES: No dogs No smoking in restaurant Civ Wed 70
CARDS:

See advert on this page

P

PEMBROKE, continued

★★73% Bethwaite's Lamphey Hall
Lamphey SA71 5NR
☎ 01646 672394 01646 672369
Dir: *on A4139 Pembroke/Tenby Road in centre of village, opposite parish church*
This welcoming hotel is set in the pretty village of Lamphey. The two popular restaurants, one of which is an informal bistro, are at the hub of the operation. Bedrooms are smart and modern and include some ground-floor and family rooms. Residents have use of a lounge and bar.
ROOMS: 10 en suite (2 fmly) No smoking in 1 bedroom s £40-£50; d £50-£80 (incl. bkfst) * LB **PARKING:** 32 **NOTES:** No dogs
CARDS:

★★61% *Old Kings Arms*
Main St SA71 4JS
☎ 01646 683611 01646 682335
Dir: *situated in Main Street. Approach from Carmarthen, Tenby or Pembroke Dock*
A former coaching inn, now a bustling town centre hotel which is very much the heart of local activities. The bars are a locally popular venue and the restaurant offers good wholesome fare. Surroundings are traditional with stone walls, flagged floors and roaring log fires.
ROOMS: 21 en suite **PARKING:** 21 **NOTES:** Closed 25-26 Dec & 1 Jan
CARDS:

PEMBROKE DOCK, Pembrokeshire Map 02 SM90

★★★67% Cleddau Bridge
Essex Rd SA72 6EG
☎ 01646 685961 & 0800 279 4055 01646 685746
e-mail: information@cleddaubridgehotel.co.uk
Dir: *M4 to Camarthen A40 to St Clears A477 to Pembroke Dock at rdbt 2nd exit for Haverfordwest via the toll bridge take left before the toll bridge*
This purpose built hotel is situated at the Pembroke Dock end of the Cleddau Bridge, from where it overlooks impressive views of the river. It provides modern well equipped accommodation including suites, all located on ground level. The hotel is a very popular venue for weddings and other functions. Facilities include an outdoor heated swimming pool.
ROOMS: 24 en suite (2 fmly) No smoking in 12 bedrooms s £37.50-£55; d £55.50-£69.50 (incl. bkfst) * LB **FACILITIES:** STV Outdoor swimming (H) Xmas **CONF:** Thtr 160 Class 60 Board 60 Del from £65 *
PARKING: 140 **CARDS:**

PENARTH, Vale of Glamorgan Map 03 ST17

★67% *Walton House*
37 Victoria Rd CF64 3HY
☎ 029 2070 7782 029 2071 1012
Dir: *from M4 junct 33 into Penarth, 3rd left off rdbt at town center, through traffic lights, over railway bridge next left Victoria Rd, hotel 500yds*
Located in a quiet residential area, this attractive Victorian house is set in well tended gardens. Bedrooms vary in size, there is a pleasant lounge/bar and a traditionally furnished restaurant and breakfast room.
ROOMS: 13 rms (11 en suite) (7 fmly) **CONF:** Class 30 **PARKING:** 13
CARDS:

PENCOED, Bridgend Map 03 SS98

★★★73%
St Mary's Hotel & Country Club
St Marys Golf Club CF35 5EA
☎ 01656 861100 & 860280 01656 863400
e-mail: stmaryshotel@hotmail.com
Dir: *just off junct 35 of M4, on A473*

The stone buildings that comprise this modern hotel and golf course were formerly a 16th-century farmhouse. The two golf courses, 9 and 18 hole, surround the hotel buildings and form a pleasant backdrop to the public areas and bedrooms, many of which look out over the fairways. Inside, there is a choice of bars and Rafters Restaurant with its stone walls and exposed beams. The bedrooms are generous in size and benefit from good quality furnishings.
ROOMS: 24 en suite (19 fmly) s £72-£89; d £92-£99 (incl. bkfst) * LB
FACILITIES: STV Golf 27 Tennis (hard) Putting green Jacuzzi/spa Floodlit driving range Xmas **CONF:** Thtr 120 Class 60 Board 40 Del from £100 * **PARKING:** 140 **NOTES:** No dogs (ex guide dogs)
CARDS:

See advert on page 781

⌂ *Travelodge*
Old Mill, Felindre Rd CF35 5HU
☎ 01656 864404 01656 864404
Dir: *on A473*
Travelodge
This modern building offers accommodation in smart, spacious and well equipped bedrooms, all with en suite bathrooms. Refreshments may be taken at the nearby family restaurant. For further details and the Travelodge phone number, consult the Hotel Groups page.
ROOMS: 40 en suite

PENYBONT, Powys Map 03 SO16

★★67% *Severn Arms*
LD1 5UA
☎ 01597 851224 & 851344 01597 851693
Dir: *5m from LLandrindod Wells on A44 at junct with A488*
An early 19th-century coaching inn, this friendly, family-run hotel lies in the centre of Penybont. There is a choice of bars, a beamed restaurant and a first floor lounge for residents. Bedrooms have modern facilities and period furnishings, which add to the traditional character. Each room has a welcoming sherry decanter and even stamped postcards are provided. A full range of bar food is available and the restaurant offers fixed-price and carte menus.
ROOMS: 10 en suite (6 fmly) **FACILITIES:** Fishing Pool table
PARKING: 62 **CARDS:**

P

PONTERWYD, Ceredigion
Map 06 SN78

★★62% The George Borrow Hotel
SY23 3AD
☎ 01970 890230 🖷 01970 890587
e-mail: georgeborrow@clara.net
Dir: *on A44 Aberystwyth-Llangurig road. Aberystwyth side of village*

THE CIRCLE Selected Individual Hotels GREAT BRITAIN

This friendly family hotel nestles in the foothills of the Cambrian Mountains about 12 miles from the university town of Aberystwyth. The hotel provides an ideal base for walking, fishing and bird watching (the red kite abounds) and is an excellent base for touring mid Wales. Rooms are comfortable with their own facilities and downstairs there are two character bars and a restaurant where a good range of meals is available.
ROOMS: 9 en suite (2 fmly) s £22-£25; d £44-£50 (incl. bkfst) * LB **FACILITIES:** Pool table **CONF:** Thtr 40 Class 35 Board 30 **PARKING:** 54 **NOTES:** No smoking in restaurant **CARDS:**

PONTYCLUN, Rhondda Cynon Taff
Map 03 ST08

○ Vale of Glamorgan Hotel Golf & Country Club
Hensol Park CF72 8JY
☎ 01443 667800
ROOMS: 143 rms **NOTES:** Open

PONTYPOOL, Torfaen
Map 03 SO20

○ Express by Holiday Inn
Little Mill, Ty-rfelin NP4 0RH
☎ 0800 897121
ROOMS: 49 rms **NOTES:** Opening September 2000

Early start? Hotels at all star levels should provide in-room alarm clocks and/or alarm calls.

PONTYPRIDD, Rhondda Cynon Taff
Map 03 ST08

★★★69% *Llechwen Hall*
Llanfabon CF37 4HP
☎ 01443 742050 & 740305 🖷 01443 742189
Dir: *A470 N towards Merthyr Tydfil, at rdbt turn right towards Nelson, at next rdbt right onto A4054, left next to factory and follow hotel signs*
Dating back to the 17th century this country house hotel enjoys a stunning mountain top location. Bedrooms are divided between the main house and a smart new coach house. There is a choice of two restaurants, both offer a range of popular dishes.

ROOMS: 12 en suite 8 annexe en suite (4 fmly) No smoking in 8 bedrooms **FACILITIES:** STV **CONF:** Thtr 80 Class 30 Board 40 **PARKING:** 100 **CARDS:**

★★★67% Heritage Park
Coed Cae Rd, Trehafod CF37 2NP
☎ 01443 687057 🖷 01443 687060
Dir: *off A4058, follow signs to the Rhondda Heritage Park*
Adjacent to the Rhondda Heritage Park, this privately owned, modern hotel is suitable for all types of guest. The spacious bedrooms include ground floor and interconnecting rooms, and a room equipped for less able guests. Meals can be taken in the attractive, wood-beamed, "Loft Restaurant".
ROOMS: 44 en suite (4 fmly) No smoking in 19 bedrooms s £55-£70; d £69.50-£80 (incl. bkfst) * LB **FACILITIES:** STV Indoor swimming (H) Sauna Solarium Gym Jacuzzi/spa Xmas **CONF:** Thtr 220 Class 60 Board 60 Del from £85 * **PARKING:** 150 **NOTES:** No smoking in restaurant Civ Wed 220 **CARDS:**

PORT EINON, Swansea
Map 02 SS48

★★63% *Culver House*
SA3 1NN
☎ 01792 390755
Dir: *in village continue past church turn right at post office, 50yds on turn left, hotel a further 100yds on left*
This privately owned and personally run small hotel is just a few hundred yards from the shoreline, and is ideal for those visiting the Gower peninsular. Many of the modern bedrooms have sea views. The restaurant serves home cooking meals and is supplemented by a bar and lounge.
ROOMS: 10 rms (8 en suite) (3 fmly) No smoking in all bedrooms **PARKING:** 8 **NOTES:** No smoking in restaurant Closed 1-30 Nov
CARDS:

Late for dinner? Quality Standards star rating means that last orders for dinner should be no earlier than:
★ 6.30pm ★★ 7.00pm ★★★ 8.00pm
★★★★ 9.00pm ★★★★★ 10.00pm

P

PORTHCAWL, Bridgend

Map 03 SS87

★★★68% Atlantic

West Dr CF36 3LT
☎ 01656 785011 📠 01656 771877
e-mail: enquiries@atlantichotelporthcawl.co.uk
Dir: *leave M4 junct 35 or 37, follow signs for Porthcawl, on entering Porthcawl follow signs for Seafront/Promenade, hotel on seafront*

This privately owned and personally run, friendly hotel is a short walk from the town centre. Guests can enjoy sea views from the sun terrace, bright conservatory and some of the bedrooms. Bedrooms are well maintained and decorated, and feature good levels of equipment.

ROOMS: 18 en suite (2 fmly) s £59-£69; d £80-£90 (incl. bkfst) LB **FACILITIES:** STV Xmas **CONF:** Thtr 50 Class 50 Board 25 Del from £65 * **SERVICES:** Lift **PARKING:** 20 **NOTES:** No dogs (ex guide dogs) **CARDS:**

★★★64% Seabank

The Promenade CF36 3LU
☎ 01656 782261 📠 01656 785363
Dir: *turn off junct 37 M4, follow A4229 to sea front, hotel is located on the promenade*

This large privately owned hotel stands on the promenade and overlooks the sea. The well equipped accommodation includes rooms with four-poster beds, and most enjoy sea views. There is a spacious restaurant, a lounge bar and a choice of lounges.

ROOMS: 65 en suite (2 fmly) No smoking in 15 bedrooms s £59.50; d £80 (incl. bkfst) * LB **FACILITIES:** STV Sauna Gym Pool table Jacuzzi/spa entertainment Xmas **CONF:** Thtr 200 Class 90 Board 70 Del £89 * **SERVICES:** Lift **PARKING:** 140 **NOTES:** No dogs (ex guide dogs) **CARDS:**

See advert under BRIDGEND and on opposite page

★★62% *Glenaub*

50 Mary St CF36 3YA
☎ 01656 788242 & 788846 📠 01656 773649
Dir: *leave M4 junct 37 follow signs for Porthcawl town centre, turn left before Somerfield supermarket, 1st right into carpark*

Located just a short walk from the town centre and the seafront, this personally run hotel offers comfortable accommodation and a warm welcome. The lounge bar has an attractive conservatory extension and there is a traditionally furnished dining room.

ROOMS: 18 en suite **FACILITIES:** STV **PARKING:** 12 **NOTES:** No dogs (ex guide dogs) **CARDS:**

Early start? Hotels at all star levels should provide in-room alarm clocks and/or alarm calls.

★★62% *Rose & Crown*

SCOTTISH NEWCASTLE hotels

Heol-y-Capel, Nottage CF36 3ST
☎ 01656 784850 📠 01656 772345
Dir: *take A4229 towards Porthcawl and Nottage*

A popular and friendly traditional inn situated in the pretty village of Nottage on the outskirts of Porthcawl. The bedrooms are attractively decorated, with pine furnishings and modern facilities. The public areas include a choice of bars, a television lounge and a restaurant which also offers a carvery.

ROOMS: 8 en suite **PARKING:** 15 **NOTES:** No dogs (ex guide dogs) No smoking in restaurant **CARDS:**

PORTMEIRION, Gwynedd

Map 06 SH53

★★★77% ✿✿ The Hotel Portmeirion

LL48 6ET
☎ 01766 770000 📠 01766 771331
e-mail: hotel@portmeirion-village.com
Dir: *2m W, Portmeirion village is S off A487*

Nestling under the wooded slopes of the famous Italianate village, (as featured in the cult 1960s series,'The Prisoner') and looking out over the sandy estuary towards Snowdonia, this hotel has one of the finest settings in Wales. Many rooms have balconies and private sitting rooms and most are located within the village and command spectacular views. Public areas are elegantly furnished and mostly Welsh-speaking staff offer warm hospitality.

ROOMS: 14 en suite 25 annexe en suite (4 fmly) s £90; d £110-£155 * LB **FACILITIES:** STV Outdoor swimming (H) Tennis (hard) Xmas **CONF:** Thtr 100 **PARKING:** 40 **NOTES:** No dogs No smoking in restaurant Civ Wed 100 **CARDS:**

See advert on opposite page

PORT TALBOT, Neath Port Talbot

Map 03 SS79

★★★67% Aberavon Beach

Best Western

SA12 6QP
☎ 01639 884949 📠 01639 897885
Dir: *M4 junct 41 (A48) and follow signs for Aberavon Beach & Hollywood Park*

Enjoying a seafront location with views across Swansea bay, this privately owned hotel continues to benefit from a gradual programme of refurbishment of bedrooms and public areas. The bedrooms are comfortably appointed with modern furnishings and include family rooms. Public areas include a leisure suite, open plan bar and restaurant, and a selection of function rooms.

ROOMS: 52 en suite (6 fmly) s £80; d £85 (incl. bkfst) * LB **FACILITIES:** Indoor swimming (H) Sauna Jacuzzi/spa All weather leisure centre entertainment Xmas **CONF:** Thtr 300 Class 200 Board 50 Del £99 * **SERVICES:** Lift **PARKING:** 150 **NOTES:** No smoking in restaurant Civ Wed 300 **CARDS:**

See advert under SWANSEA

P

PRESTATYN, Denbighshire

Map 06 SJ08

★★66% Traeth Ganol Hotel

41 Beach Rd West LL19 7LL
☎ 01745 853594 01745 886687
e-mail: hotel@dnetw.co.uk
Dir: *from A55 follow brown tourist signs to Nova Centre & Beachs. Hotel beyond Nova, fourth property from end of cul-de-sac*

This small friendly, family run hotel is close to the sea front and is less that a mile away from the town centre. Prestatyn's championship golf course is just a few minutes away and the Nova Leisure Complex is also nearby. The bedrooms are spacious, freshly decorated and well equipped. Downstairs there is a cosy bar and restaurant as well as a comfortable guests lounge.

ROOMS: 9 en suite (6 fmly) No smoking in all bedrooms s £39-£54; d £56-£62 (incl. bkfst) LB **FACILITIES:** Xmas **PARKING:** 9 **NOTES:** No dogs (ex guide dogs) No smoking in restaurant
CARDS:

PRESTEIGNE, Powys

Map 03 SO36

★★★65% Radnorshire Arms

High St LD8 2BE
☎ 01544 267406 01544 260418
Dir: *A456 from Birmingham pass through Kidderminster, Bewdley and Tenbury Wells, through to Wooferton near Ludlow then change to the B4362 to Presteigne*

This delightful 17th-century timbered coaching inn features original panelling and real fires in the public rooms. Bedrooms are split between the main building and an annexe across the pretty garden; most are spacious with a full range of facilities.

ROOMS: 8 en suite 8 annexe en suite (6 fmly) No smoking in 5 bedrooms s £59.50-£64; d £79-£82 (incl. bkfst) * LB **FACILITIES:** Xmas **CONF:** Thtr 60 Class 15 Board 30 Del from £85 * **PARKING:** 54 **NOTES:** No smoking in restaurant Civ Wed 50
CARDS:

PWLLHELI, Gwynedd

Map 06 SH33

★★78% ❀❀❀ *Plas Bodegroes*

Nefyn Rd LL53 5TH
☎ 01758 612363 01758 701247
e-mail: gunna@bodegroes.co.uk
Dir: *on the A497, 1.5m W on Nefyn road*

This fine Georgian house is peacefully situated amidst colourful gardens, including an impressive avenue of mature beech trees. Individually furnished bedrooms display a great deal of style, as do the comfortable public rooms, including the dining room where Chris Chown and his team make good use of the fine produce available locally.

ROOMS: 9 en suite 2 annexe en suite No smoking in all bedrooms **PARKING:** 15 **NOTES:** No smoking in restaurant Closed Dec-Feb & Mon
CARDS:

RAGLAN, Monmouthshire

Map 03 SO40

⇧ *Travelodge*

Travelodge

Granada Services A40, Nr Monmouth NP5 4BB
☎ 01600 740444
Dir: *on A40 near junct with A449*

This modern building offers accommodation in smart, spacious and well equipped bedrooms, all with en suite bathrooms. Refreshments may be taken at the nearby family restaurant. For further details and the Travelodge phone number, consult the Hotel Groups page.

ROOMS: 42 en suite

R

REYNOLDSTON, Swansea Map 02 SS48

Premier Collection

★★❀❀❀ **Fairyhill**
SA3 1BS
☎ 01792 390139 01792 391358
e-mail: postbox@fairyhill.net
Dir: *just outside Reynoldston off the A4118 from Swansea in the middle of the Gower Peninsula*
Set in 24 acres of grounds, this impressive stone-built 18th-century mansion benefits from a tranquil location in the heart of the Gower peninsular. Bedrooms are individually decorated and furnished with style. There is a choice of comfortable seating areas, with log fires contributing to the warm and relaxed atmosphere. The cuisine is imaginative and accomplished, and features many local specialities.
ROOMS: 8 en suite s £95-£175; d £110-£190 (incl. bkfst) * LB
FACILITIES: Croquet lawn **CONF:** Thtr 40 Class 20 Board 26
PARKING: 50 **NOTES:** No dogs (ex guide dogs) No children 8yrs No smoking in restaurant Closed 24-29 Dec
CARDS:

RHAYADER, Powys Map 03 SN96

★★64% **Brynafon Country House**
South St LD6 5BL
☎ 01597 810735 01597 810111
e-mail: info@brynafon.co.uk
Dir: *0.5m from Rhayader on the main A470 road to Builth Wells*
This imposing stone built building dates back to 1878 and stands in its own pleasant garden, on the A470, half a mile south of the town. It served as a workhouse until 1932. Now a privately owned and personally run hotel, it provides well equipped accommodation and has public areas with lots of charm and character. Facilities include rooms for meetings or small conferences.
ROOMS: 16 en suite 2 annexe en suite No smoking in 2 bedrooms s £35-£45; d £50-£75 (incl. bkfst) * LB **CONF:** Thtr 40 Class 20 Board 20 Del from £70 * **PARKING:** 40 **NOTES:** No smoking in restaurant Closed 18-27 Dec **CARDS:**

RHOSSILI, Swansea Map 02 SS48

★★61% **Worms Head**
SA3 1PP
☎ 01792 390512 01792 391115
Dir: *from Swansea take A4118 to Scurlage. Turn right onto B4247 to Rhossili. Drive through village until car park on left, and hotel is opposite*
Named after the famous point which is a short walk away, this hotel caters to the many visitors who enjoy the peace and space of the Gower peninsular. Most bedrooms and public areas have superb cliff top views. Bedrooms are comfortably furnished with convenient extras. The hotel has two bars and a restaurant.

ROOMS: 19 rms (17 en suite) (5 fmly) No smoking in 10 bedrooms
FACILITIES: STV Pool table ch fac **CONF:** Thtr 80 Class 40 Board 20
NOTES: No smoking in restaurant **CARDS:**

RHYL, Denbighshire Map 06 SJ08

★★60% **Marina**
Marine Dr LL18 3AU
☎ 01745 342371 01745 342371
This old established holiday hotel is located on the seafront, and the town centre and Rhyl's many amenities are just a short walk away. Several function suites are provided and there is a choice of bars. Live entertainment is regularly held. Bedrooms include several suitable for families and many have fine sea views.
ROOMS: 29 en suite (6 fmly) s £39.50; d £49.50 (incl. bkfst) * LB
FACILITIES: Pool table entertainment Xmas **CONF:** Class 300 Del from £30 * **SERVICES:** Lift **PARKING:** 75 **NOTES:** No dogs (ex guide dogs) No smoking in restaurant **CARDS:**

ROSSETT, Wrexham Map 07 SJ35

★★★72% **Llyndir Hall**
Llyndir Ln LL12 0AY
☎ 01244 571648 01244 571258
e-mail: llyndir.hall@pageant.co.uk
Dir: *5m S of Chester follow signs for Pulford on B5445. On entering Rossett hotel is set back off road*

Located on the English/Welsh border, this is a comfortable, modern hotel, that lies in several acres of mature grounds and is a popular conference venue. Bedrooms are spacious and the lounges are elegantly furnished. The Redwood brasserie and bar serves a wide selection of interesting dishes and light snacks and the leisure facilities are popular with guests. The hotel also holds a civil wedding licence.

continued

R

ROOMS: 38 en suite (3 fmly) No smoking in 12 bedrooms s £70-£80; d £80-£85 (incl. bkfst) * LB **FACILITIES:** STV Indoor swimming (H) Solarium Gym Croquet lawn Jacuzzi/spa Steam room Xmas **CONF:** Thtr 140 Class 60 Board 40 Del from £105 * **PARKING:** 80 **NOTES:** No smoking in restaurant Civ Wed 120 **CARDS:**

★★★69% ❀ Rossett Hall Hotel

Chester Rd LL12 0DE
☎ 01244 571000 ▯ 01244 571505
Dir: *from the M56 take the M53 which becomes A55. Take Wrexham/Chester exit & head to Wrexham. Onto B5445 & Hotel entrance in Rossett village*

Best Western

This hotel, which in places dates back to 1750, lies in several acres of mature gardens in the lovely Welsh border country. Pretty bedrooms are generally spacious and are well equipped and furnished. A comfortable foyer lounge is provided and Oscar's bistro serves a wide range of dishes. Extensive function and conference facilities are available.
ROOMS: 30 en suite (2 fmly) No smoking in 10 bedrooms s £70-£80; d £90-£125 * LB **FACILITIES:** STV Xmas **CONF:** Thtr 120 Class 50 Board 50 Del from £83.20 * **PARKING:** 120 **NOTES:** No dogs (ex guide dogs) Civ Wed 120 **CARDS:**

RUTHIN, Denbighshire — Map 06 SJ15

★★★66% *Ruthin Castle*

LL15 2NU
☎ 01824 702664 ▯ 01824 705978
e-mail: reservations@ruthincastle.co.uk

Best Western

The main part of this impressive castle was built in the early 19th-century but there are many ruins in the impressive grounds that date back much further. Inside the elegantly panelled castle the public areas include a restaurant and bar along with a medieval banqueting hall. Many of the bedrooms are spacious and furnished with fine period pieces.
ROOMS: 58 en suite (6 fmly) **FACILITIES:** Fishing Snooker entertainment **CONF:** Thtr 150 Class 100 Board 30 **SERVICES:** Lift **PARKING:** 200 **NOTES:** No dogs (ex guide dogs)
CARDS:

★★68% ❀ Ye Olde Anchor Inn

Rhos St LL15 1DY
☎ 01824 702813 ▯ 01824 703050
e-mail: hotel@anchorinn.co.uk
Dir: *on the junction of the A494 and A525 within Ruthin*
Originally an 18th-century drovers inn, this hotel retains much of its character. The accommodation is attractively furnished and inter-connecting rooms are available for families. The bar provides a happy mix of locals and visitors, as does the restaurant which offers a selection of freshly prepared and substantial meals.
ROOMS: 26 en suite (4 fmly) No smoking in 6 bedrooms s £39.50; d £49 (incl. bkfst) * LB **FACILITIES:** STV Xmas **CONF:** Thtr 40 Class 40 Board 30 Del from £50 * **PARKING:** 20 **NOTES:** No smoking in restaurant **CARDS:**

ST ASAPH, Denbighshire — Map 06 SJ07

★★★64% Oriel House

Upper Denbigh Rd LL17 0LW
☎ 01745 582716 ▯ 01745 585208
Dir: *turn off A55 on to A525, left at cathedral 1m along A525 on right hand side*
Set in several acres of mature grounds south of St Asaph. Extensive function facilities are provided, catering for business meetings and weddings. Several bars are available and the Fountain Restaurant serves a wide choice of meals. Bedrooms are generally spacious and staff are friendly and hospitable.
ROOMS: 19 en suite (1 fmly) **FACILITIES:** STV Fishing Snooker **CONF:** Thtr 250 Class 150 Board 50 **PARKING:** 200 **NOTES:** Closed 26 Dec **CARDS:**

★★65% Plas Elwy Hotel & Restaurant

The Roe LL17 0LT
☎ 01745 582263 & 582089 ▯ 01745 583864
Dir: *turn left off A55 at junct A525 signposted Rhyl/St Asaph. On left opposite petrol station*
This hotel dates back to 1850 and much original character has been preserved. Spacious bedrooms are provided in a purpose-built extension, one with a four-poster bed. Equally well equipped bedrooms are in the main building. Public rooms are smart and comfortably furnished, a range of food options is provided in the attractive restaurant.
ROOMS: 7 en suite 6 annexe en suite (2 fmly) s £40-£46; d £58-£68 (incl. bkfst) * LB **PARKING:** 28 **NOTES:** No dogs (ex guide dogs) No smoking in restaurant Closed 26-30 Dec
CARDS:

ST CLEARS, Carmarthenshire — Map 02 SN21

★★67% Forge

SA33 4NA
☎ 01994 230300 ▯ 01994 231577
Dir: *1m E, beside A40*
This family owned business has developed over the last 45 years into a modern motel complex with adjoining leisure centre. The bedrooms are in modern buildings, which are spacious and furnished to high standards. Another building houses an all-day restaurant and bar, and also includes a function suite.
ROOMS: 18 annexe en suite (8 fmly) s £44-£54; d £60 (incl. bkfst) * **FACILITIES:** Indoor swimming (H) Sauna Gym **CONF:** Thtr 80 Class 80 Board 80 **PARKING:** 80 **NOTES:** Closed 25 & 26 Dec Civ Wed 120
CARDS:

ST DAVID'S, Pembrokeshire — Map 02 SM72

★★★77% ❀❀ Warpool Court

SA62 6BN
☎ 01437 720300 ▯ 01437 720676
e-mail: warpool@enterprise.net
Dir: *from Cross Square bear left beside Cartref Restaurant down Goat Street. Pass Farmers Arms on right, follow road to left and signposted at fork*
Originally the cathedral choir school, Warpool Court Hotel is set in landscaped gardens looking out to sea. The lounges are spacious and comfortable. Bedrooms are well furnished and equipped with modern facilities. Gastronomic delights feature in the restaurant.

continued on p820

S

ST DAVID'S, continued

Warpool Court, St David's

ROOMS: 25 en suite (4 fmly) s fr £61; d fr £120 (incl. bkfst) * LB **FACILITIES:** Indoor swimming (H) Tennis (hard) Sauna Gym Pool table Croquet lawn Childrens play area ch fac Xmas **CONF:** Thtr 40 Class 25 Board 25 Del from £85 * **PARKING:** 100 **NOTES:** No smoking in restaurant Closed Jan Civ Wed 100
CARDS:

★★71% St Non's Hotel

Catherine St SA62 6RJ
☎ 01437 720239 01437 721839
e-mail: stnons@enterprise.net
Dir: *from Cross Square in St Davids bear left between Midland Bank and Cartref Restaurant, follow road for 700yds, hotel on the left*
The hotel is situated close to the cathedral and the 14th-century Bishops' Palace. Well equipped modern accommodation includes ground floor rooms. The spacious restaurant offers a range of tempting dishes.
ROOMS: 21 en suite (4 fmly) s £44-£52; d £68-£86 (incl. bkfst) * LB **CONF:** Thtr 32 Class 32 Board 32 Del from £67 * **PARKING:** 40 **NOTES:** No smoking in restaurant Closed Dec & Nov
CARDS:

★★70% Old Cross

Cross Square SA62 6SP
☎ 01437 720387 01437 720394
e-mail: oldcross@stdavids.co.uk
Dir: *right in centre of St David's facing Cross Square*
This privately owned and friendly hotel is located in the centre of historic St David's. Parts of the property date back to the 18th century. The famous cathedral is just a short walk away. The bedrooms are generally spacious with good facilities and some are suitable for families. There is a choice of comfortable lounges along with a bar and a restaurant.
ROOMS: 16 en suite (1 fmly) No smoking in 5 bedrooms s £39-£48; d £71.50-£82 (incl. bkfst) * LB **PARKING:** 18 **NOTES:** No smoking in restaurant Closed Xmas-1 Mar **CARDS:**

★★61% Grove Hotel

High St SA62 6SB
☎ 01437 720341 01437 720770
e-mail: ggpengelly@aol.com
Dir: *follow A487 from Haverfordwest to St Davids, hotel on right opposite new Tourist Information Centre, at top of High St*
This small personally run hotel is a good base for exploring St David's and the West Wales coast. A lively bar is supplemented by a restaurant with some good home cooking. Bedrooms vary in size and style.

continued

ROOMS: 10 rms (9 en suite) No smoking in all bedrooms s £32-£36; d £34-£72 (incl. bkfst) * LB **FACILITIES:** Pool table ch fac **PARKING:** 30 **NOTES:** No smoking in restaurant RS 25 Dec
CARDS:

SAUNDERSFOOT, Pembrokeshire — Map 02 SN10

★★★67% *St Brides*

St Brides Hill SA69 9NH
☎ 01834 812304 01834 813303
e-mail: lanbell@cipality.u-net.com
Dir: *on Tenby road, overlooking the harbour*

High above the town with superb views of the coastline, this hotel offers bedrooms in a variety of sizes and styles. There is a comfortable bar in addition to the restaurant. The garden is well tended and there is a heated outdoor pool.
ROOMS: 43 en suite (2 fmly) No smoking in 6 bedrooms **FACILITIES:** STV Outdoor swimming (H) entertainment **CONF:** Thtr 150 Class 80 Board 60 **PARKING:** 70 **NOTES:** Closed 1-20 Jan
CARDS:

See advert on opposite page

★★65% Jalna

Stammers Rd SA69 9HH
☎ 01834 812282 01834 812166
e-mail: jalnahtl@aol.com
Dir: *turn off A478 at Pentlepoir onto B4316 into Saundersfoot, take 1st junction on the right leaving the village for Tenby, hotel is on the right*
This small and friendly hotel lies just 200 yards from the harbour. Bedrooms are well equipped, with modern amenities. A cosy lounge is available as well as a bar, and a daily fixed-price menu that offers good value food.
ROOMS: 13 en suite (7 fmly) No smoking in 6 bedrooms s £30-£40; d £50-£60 (incl. bkfst) * LB **PARKING:** 14 **NOTES:** No smoking in restaurant **CARDS:**

★★65% Rhodewood House

St Brides Hill SA69 9NU
☎ 01834 812200 01834 811863
e-mail: relax@rhodewood.co.uk
Dir: *from St Clears, take A477 to Kilgetty, then A478 to Tenby, turn left onto B4316 signposted Saundersfoot*
This well established privately owned and personally run hotel is just a short walk from the town centre and the harbour. It is popular with coach tour groups. Live entertainment is regularly provided for guests. Bedrooms are equipped with modern amenities and many useful extras. Rooms on ground floor level are available. Facilities include a spacious bar, separate function room and a snooker room
ROOMS: 45 en suite (13 fmly) No smoking in 6 bedrooms s £28-£35; d £46-£50 (incl. bkfst) * LB **FACILITIES:** STV entertainment Xmas **CONF:** Thtr 100 Board 100 **PARKING:** 70 **NOTES:** No dogs (ex guide dogs) Closed 4-29 Jan **CARDS:**

S

★★64% Merlewood
St Brides Hill SA69 9NP
☎ 01834 812421 & 813295 ▤ 01834 814886
e-mail: merlewood@saundersfoot.freeserve.co.uk
Dir: *turn off A477 onto A4316, hotel on other side of village on St Brides Hill*

A purpose-built resort-style hotel, Merlewood is popular with more mature guests, as it offers ground floor and family rooms among its modern equipped accommodation. Public areas include a bright dining room, a large lounge bar and a mini-launderette; outside is a lovely garden.

ROOMS: 29 en suite (8 fmly) No smoking in all bedrooms d £46-£54 (incl. bkfst) * LB **FACILITIES:** Outdoor swimming (H) Pool table Putting green Children's swings & slide Table tennis entertainment ch fac Xmas **CONF:** Thtr 70 Class 100 **PARKING:** 34 **NOTES:** No dogs (ex guide dogs) No smoking in restaurant Closed Nov-Etr RS Etr-May & Oct
CARDS:

SENNYBRIDGE, Powys — Map 03 SN92

★★67% The White House Inn
LD3 8RP
☎ 01874 636396 ▤ 01874 636680
e-mail: hotel@the-white-house-inn.co.uk
Dir: *on the A40, 8m W of Brecon just before Sennybridge*

A Georgian property located just 8 miles south-west of Brecon. Privately owned and personally run, it provides warm and friendly hospitality and well equipped modern accommodation, including family bedded rooms. The hotel has a excellent reputation for the extensive choice and variety of its soundly prepared food.

ROOMS: 7 en suite (3 fmly) s £27-£35; d £50 (incl. bkfst) * LB
PARKING: 40 **NOTES:** No dogs (ex guide dogs)
CARDS:

SWANSEA, Swansea — Map 03 SS69
see also Port Talbot

★★★★66% Swansea Marriott
The Maritime Quarter SA1 3SS
☎ 01792 642020 ▤ 01792 650345

Dir: *M4 junct 42, follow A483 to the City Centre past Leisure Centre, then follow signs to Maritime Quarter*

This smart property is well situated on the marina, enjoying glorious views over the bay. Large and bustling, the hotel provides an ideal base for both business and leisure visitors. The well equipped bedrooms are spacious and benefit from large beds, in addition to such extra facilities as satellite TV and trouser press. The hotel has a number of meeting rooms, and a popular leisure club.

ROOMS: 117 en suite (49 fmly) No smoking in 85 bedrooms s £93; d £108 * LB **FACILITIES:** STV Indoor swimming (H) Sauna Gym Jacuzzi/spa **CONF:** Thtr 250 Class 120 Board 30 Del from £89 * **SERVICES:** Lift air con **PARKING:** 122 **NOTES:** No dogs (ex guide dogs) No smoking in restaurant Civ Wed 250
CARDS:

★★★65% *Posthouse Swansea*
The Kingsway Circle SA1 5LS
Posthouse
☎ 0870 400 9078 ▤ 01792 456044
Dir: *M4 junct 42, A483 Swansea exit. Signs for city centre W. At lights after Sainsbury's, right along Wind St then left at lights, hotel ahead at rdbt*

In the centre of town, this Posthouse offers comfortable accommodation and useful amenities, including a good Spa leisure club. Guests can eat in the lounge, The Junction restaurant or the new Mongolian Barbecue. Refurbishment of a number of bedrooms was imminent at the time of our last inspection.

continued

S

SWANSEA, continued

ROOMS: 99 en suite (12 fmly) No smoking in 66 bedrooms **FACILITIES:** Indoor swimming (H) Sauna Solarium Gym **CONF:** Thtr 230 Class 120 Board 60 **SERVICES:** Lift **PARKING:** 42
CARDS:

★★ Fairyhill

SA3 1BS
☎ 01792 390139 01792 391358
e-mail: postbox@fairyhill.net
(For full entry see Reynoldston)

★★74% *Beaumont*

72-73 Walter Rd SA1 4QA
☎ 01792 643956 01792 643044
Dir: *M4 junct 42 - A483 to Swansea. Right on Oystermouth Rd to Kingsway R/A then left & 1st right to junct A4118 & turn left. Hotel 400yds on left*

A family-run hotel offering cheerful hospitality. The public areas and the bedrooms have been furnished and decorated with an eye for quality and an emphasis on guest comfort. The conservatory restaurant is the bright and airy venue for a range of popular home-cooked dishes.
ROOMS: 17 en suite No smoking in 1 bedroom **PARKING:** 10
NOTES: Closed 23 Dec-2 Jan **CARDS:**

See advert on opposite page

★★74% Windsor Lodge

Mount Pleasant SA1 6EG
☎ 01792 642158 & 652744 01792 648996
Dir: *M4 exit 42 onto A483, turn right at lights past Sainsburys, turn left at station, turn right immediately after 2nd set of lights*
Just a short walk from the city centre, this is a welcoming family-run hotel. Both bedrooms and public areas are attractively decorated with a choice of lounge areas and a deservedly popular restaurant.
ROOMS: 18 en suite (2 fmly) s £50-£55; d £55-£70 (incl. bkfst) * LB **CONF:** Thtr 30 Class 15 Board 24 Del from £65 * **PARKING:** 26
NOTES: No smoking in restaurant Closed 25-26 Dec
CARDS:

★★62% *Oak Tree Parc*

Birchgrove Rd SA7 9JR
☎ 01792 817781 01792 814542
(For full entry see Birchgrove)

★★61% Worms Head

SA3 1PP
☎ 01792 390512 01792 391115
(For full entry see Rhossili)

Travelodge

Penllergaer SA4 1GT
☎ 01792 896222 01792 898806
Dir: *M4 junct 47*

Travelodge

This modern building offers accommodation in smart, spacious and well equipped bedrooms, all with en suite bathrooms. Refreshments may be taken at the nearby family restaurant. For further details and the Travelodge phone number, consult the Hotel Groups page.
ROOMS: 50 en suite **CONF:** Thtr 25 Class 32 Board 20

TALSARNAU, Gwynedd Map 06 SH63

Premier Collection

★★ Maes y Neuadd

LL47 6YA
☎ 01766 780200 01766 780211
e-mail: maes@neuadd.com
Dir: *3m NE of Harlech, signposted on an unclassed road off B4573*
Dating back to the 14th century in parts, various additions over the intervening centuries have resulted in a substantial stone-built house enjoying fine views over the mountains and across the bay to the Llyn Peninsula. Bedrooms, some in an adjacent coach house, are individually furnished and many have fine antique pieces. Public areas display a similar welcoming character, including the restaurant where the team make good use of locally sourced ingredients to produce fine meals.
ROOMS: 12 en suite 4 annexe en suite s £124-£175; d £169-£230 (incl. bkfst & dinner) * LB **FACILITIES:** Croquet lawn Xmas
CONF: Thtr 20 Class 20 Board 16 Del from £140 * **PARKING:** 50
NOTES: No smoking in restaurant Civ Wed 65
CARDS:

★★66% Estuary Motel

LL47 6TA
☎ 01766 771155 01766 771697
Dir: *4m N of Harlech, on the A496*
At the edge of the village against wooded slopes, this family-run hotel has been renovated over recent years to provide modern accommodation. Bedrooms are spacious and well equipped and there is a small lounge. The restaurant serves a carte menu of popular dishes and offers good value for money.
ROOMS: 10 en suite (2 fmly) No smoking in 4 bedrooms s £36; d £47-£52 (incl. bkfst) * LB **PARKING:** 30 **NOTES:** No smoking in restaurant
CARDS:

TV dinner? Room service at three stars and above.

S

★★ 64% *Tregwylan*
LL47 6YG
☎ 01766 770424 📠 01766 771317
Dir: *off A496, 0.5m N of Talsarnau and 4m N of Harlech*
Located above the bay and enjoying superb views, this family-run hotel offers genuine Welsh hospitality. The bedrooms are prettily decorated and there is an attractive restaurant and a cosy bar. Pretty grounds surround the hotel.
ROOMS: 10 en suite (3 fmly) **PARKING:** 20 **NOTES:** No dogs (ex guide dogs) No smoking in restaurant Closed Jan-mid Feb
CARDS:

TAL-Y-BONT (NEAR CONWY), Gwynedd Map 06 SH76

★★ 69% *Lodge*

LL32 8YX
☎ 01492 660766 📠 01492 660534
e-mail: b.baldon@lodgehotel.co.uk
Dir: *on B5106, hotel on right hand side of the road when entering village*
Situated in a beautiful part of the Conwy Valleys, the Lodge Hotel has modern bedrooms, some of which are suitable for families. A welcoming log fire burns in the bar lounge during the winter months while diners peruse the daily changing menu. Much of the produce comes from the hotel's gardens and home-cooked meals are served in generous portions.
ROOMS: 14 annexe en suite **PARKING:** 50 **NOTES:** No smoking in restaurant RS Winter **CARDS:**

Fancy a Singapore Sling? Bar staff in five star hotels should be skilled cocktail mixers.

TAL-Y-LLYN, Gwynedd

Map 06 SH70

★★70% Minffordd

LL36 9AJ
☎ 01654 761665 01654 761517
e-mail: hotel@minffordd.com

Dir: *at junct of A487/B4405 midway between Dolgellau and Machynlleth*

Located in spectacular countryside below Cader Idris, this delightful former drovers' inn is a haven of peace and relaxation. Exposed timbers and thick stone walls remain but bedrooms are smart, modern and well equipped. Residents have use of an elegantly furnished lounge and bar and a further sun lounge. The character restaurant uses local produce where possible. The hotel is non-smoking throughout.

ROOMS: 7 en suite No smoking in all bedrooms s fr £37; d fr £74 * LB **PARKING:** 18 **NOTES:** No children 13yrs No smoking in restaurant Closed 30 Nov-1 Mar **CARDS:**

TENBY, Pembrokeshire

Map 02 SN10

★★★77% Penally Abbey Country House

Penally SA70 7PY
☎ 01834 843033 01834 844714
e-mail: penally.abbey@btinternet.com

Dir: *1.5m from Tenby, off A4139, overlooking golf course, close to Penally village green & Carmarthen Bay*

This fine old country house has a wealth of charm and character. Standing in 5 acres of gardens and woodland, from its elevated position above the village of Penally, it overlooks Tenby golf course to Carmarthen Bay. All the bedrooms are spacious, comfortable and have thoughtful decoration and superior furnishings. On the ground floor the drawing room, bar, elegant restaurant and conservatory are all stylishly appointed.

ROOMS: 8 en suite 4 annexe en suite (3 fmly) s £124; d £136 (incl. bkfst & dinner) * LB **FACILITIES:** Indoor swimming (H) Snooker Xmas **PARKING:** 14 **NOTES:** No dogs (ex guide dogs) No smoking in restaurant Civ Wed 50 **CARDS:**

★★★73% Atlantic

The Esplanade SA70 7DU
☎ 01834 842881 & 844176 01834 842881 ex 256

Dir: *take A478 into Tenby & follow signs to town centre, keep town walls on left then turn right at Esplanade, hotel half way along on right*

The Atlantic Hotel over looks the beautiful Isle of Caldy and south Welsh coastline. Bedrooms are tastefully decorated and well equipped with modern facilities. The public rooms include cocktail bar, the Cellar Bistro restaurant and comfortable lounge, with the added facilities of swimming pool and solarium.

ROOMS: 42 en suite (11 fmly) No smoking in 2 bedrooms s £60-£65; d £84-£130 (incl. bkfst) **FACILITIES:** STV Indoor swimming (H) Solarium Jacuzzi/spa Steam room **SERVICES:** Lift **PARKING:** 30 **NOTES:** Closed 17 Dec-21 Jan **CARDS:**

★★★68% Heywood Mount

Heywood Ln SA70 8DA
☎ 01834 842087 01834 842087
e-mail: reception@heywoodmount.co.uk

Dir: *follow signs for Wild Life Park when entering Tenby this will lead into Heywood Lane, Heywood Mount is the third hotel on the left*

This privately owned and personally run hotel is situated in a peaceful residential area, but within easy reach of Tenby's beaches and town centre. The well maintained 18th-century house is surrounded by extensive, mature and attractive gardens. The ground floor public areas include a comfortable lounge, bar and restaurant. Several of the nicely appointed bedrooms are on ground floor level. Service is willing, friendly and attentive.

continued

ROOMS: 21 en suite (4 fmly) No smoking in 11 bedrooms s £26-£30; d £52-£60 (incl. bkfst) * LB **FACILITIES:** Xmas **CONF:** Class 50 Board 30 **PARKING:** 25 **NOTES:** No dogs (ex guide dogs) No smoking in restaurant **CARDS:**

★★★66% Fourcroft

North Beach SA70 8AP
☎ 01834 842886 01834 842888
e-mail: hospitality@fourcroft-hotel.co.uk

Dir: *from A478, after "Welcome to Tenby" sign bear left towards North Beach & walled town. On reaching sea front turn sharp left. Hotel on left*

This friendly, family-run hotel offers a beach-front location together with a number of extra leisure facilities that make it particularly suitable for families with children. Guests have direct access to the beach through the hotel's own cliff-top gardens which also provide terraced gardens where refreshments can be taken. The bedrooms are all of a good size with modern facilities and are smartly decorated. No smoking rooms, family bedded rooms and rooms with sea views are all available. Besides the bar, lounge and restaurant the public areas include an outdoor pool, jacuzzi, games room and play area.

ROOMS: 45 en suite (10 fmly) No smoking in 29 bedrooms s £31-£49; d £62-£98 (incl. bkfst) * LB **FACILITIES:** Outdoor swimming (H) Snooker Sauna Pool table Jacuzzi/spa Table tennis Indoor bowls Giant chess Human Gyroscope ch fac Xmas **CONF:** Thtr 80 Class 50 Board 40 Del from £80 * **SERVICES:** Lift **PARKING:** 6 **NOTES:** No smoking in restaurant Civ Wed 100 **CARDS:**

★★72% Panorama Hotel & Restaurant

The Esplanade SA70 7DU
☎ 01834 844976 01834 844976
e-mail: mail@panoramahotel.f9.co.uk

Dir: *from A478 follow 'South Beach' & 'Town Centre' signs. Sharp left under railway arches, up Greenhill Road, onto South Parade then Esplanade*

This charming little hotel is part of a Victorian terrace, overlooking the South Beach and Caldy Island. Privately owned and personally run, it provides a variety of sizes and styles of non smoking bedrooms, all of which are well equipped. Rooms with sea views and family bedded rooms are available. Facilities include a cosy bar and an elegantly appointed restaurant, where a good choice of skilfully prepared dishes are available.

ROOMS: 7 en suite (2 fmly) No smoking in all bedrooms s £30-£35; d £60-£70 (incl. bkfst) * LB **NOTES:** No dogs (ex guide dogs) No smoking in restaurant **CARDS:**

★★69% Hammonds Park

Narberth Rd SA70 8HT
☎ 01834 842696 01834 844295
e-mail: bryndraper@compuserve.com

Dir: *take left turn off A478 into Narberth Rd leading to North Beach & Bus Park, look for white sign with hotel name in red*

Situated on a hill just north of Tenby, this is a cosy family-run hotel. The no smoking bedrooms are all well equipped and have modern facilities; family bedded, four-poster, and ground floor rooms are all available. Many of the dining tables are situated in the bright conservatory which leads into a cosy bar.

ROOMS: 14 en suite (5 fmly) No smoking in all bedrooms s £39-£43; d £50-£64 (incl. bkfst) * LB **FACILITIES:** Gym Jacuzzi/spa Natural Therapy clinic ch fac **PARKING:** 14 **NOTES:** No dogs (ex guide dogs) No smoking in restaurant **CARDS:**

Read all about it! Newspapers delivered to bedrooms in four and five star hotels.

★★67% Tenby House Hotel
Tudor Square SA70 7AJ
☎ 01834 842000 📠 01834 844647
e-mail: tenbyhouse@virgin.net
Dir: *in town centre pass St Mary's Church on right into Tudor Square. Hotel on right at end of Square*
This privately owned and personally run hotel is conveniently located in the town centre, just a few minutes walk from the harbour, beach and other amenities. The accommodation has been recently upgraded to a good standard and is well equipped. Facilities include a pleasant bar which has tremendous character and a separate bistro style restaurant. Garage parking is available nearby.
ROOMS: 18 en suite No smoking in all bedrooms s £55-£60; d £75-£90 (incl. bkfst) * LB **FACILITIES:** Pool table Games room entertainment Xmas **PARKING:** 14 **NOTES:** No dogs (ex guide dogs)
CARDS:

THREE COCKS, Powys — Map 03 SO13

★★73% Three Cocks
LD3 0SL
☎ 01497 847215 📠 01497 847339
Dir: *on A438, between Brecon & Hereford*
A unique 15th century inn surrounded by the rugged countryside of the Brecon Beacons National Park. Stone and timber abound in the public rooms which include the restaurant, bar and separate lounge. The impeccably kept bedrooms are modestly decorated and do not have televisions. The cuisine is tempting, with many speciality dishes from Belgium.
ROOMS: 7 rms (6 en suite) (2 fmly) s £40-£121; d £67-£121 (incl. bkfst) * LB **PARKING:** 40 **NOTES:** No dogs (ex guide dogs) Closed Dec & Jan RS Tue **CARDS:**

TINTERN, Monmouthshire — Map 03 SO50

★★73% Parva Farmhouse Hotel & Restaurant
THE CIRCLE
Selected Individual Hotels
GREAT BRITAIN
NP6 6SQ
☎ 01291 689411 & 689511 📠 01291 689557
Dir: *leave junct 2 M48, N of village on A466*
On the banks of the River Wye, this 17th-Century farmhouse retains many original features and a wealth of character. The lounge is comfortable and the bedrooms are tastefully furnished. Wholesome and delicious home cooking is served in the dining room.
ROOMS: 9 en suite (3 fmly) s fr £48; d fr £72 (incl. bkfst) * LB **FACILITIES:** Cycle hire **PARKING:** 10 **NOTES:** No smoking in restaurant
CARDS:

★★70% Royal George
Best Western
NP16 6SF
☎ 01291 689205 📠 01291 689448
e-mail: royalgeorgetintern@hotmail.com
Dir: *turn off M48 on to A466, 4m along this road into Tintern 2nd on left*
This delightful hotel provides comfortably equipped and spacious accommodation, including bedrooms with balconies overlooking the well tended garden. Family bedded rooms and rooms on the ground floor level are available. The public areas include a choice of bars, and a large function room.
ROOMS: 2 en suite 14 annexe en suite (13 fmly) No smoking in 9 bedrooms s £62-£68; d £88-£98 (incl. bkfst) * LB **CONF:** Thtr 120 Class 40 Board 50 Del £90 * **PARKING:** 50 **NOTES:** No smoking in restaurant **CARDS:**

TREARDDUR BAY See Anglesey, Isle of

TREFRIW, Conwy — Map 06 SH76

★★70% Hafod Country Hotel
LL27 0RQ
☎ 01492 640029 📠 01492 641351
e-mail: haford@breathemail.net
Dir: *on B5106 - between A5 at Betws-y-Coed and A55 at Conwy, on the southern edge of the village of Trefriw*

This former farmhouse has been turned into a fine modern hotel. It is located in the picturesque Conwy Valley and many of the bedrooms have private balconies that take advantage of the views. The tastefully appointed bedrooms contain much period furniture and are provided with many thoughtful extras including baskets of fresh fruit. There is a comfortable, character sitting room and a cosy bar for residents. The fixed-price menu is imaginative and makes good use of fresh and local produce.
ROOMS: 6 en suite No smoking in all bedrooms s £50.50-£72.50; d £91-£115 (incl. bkfst & dinner) * LB **FACILITIES:** Xmas **PARKING:** 14 **NOTES:** No dogs (ex guide dogs) No children 11yrs No smoking in restaurant Closed early Jan-mid Feb **CARDS:**

★★65% *Princes Arms*
LL27 0JP
☎ 01492 640592 📠 01492 640559
e-mail: princes.arms@easynet.co.uk
Dir: *take A470 to Llanrwst left onto B5106 over bridge & follow to Trefriw, hotel just through village on left*

Located in the Conwy Valley, this hotel offers superb views from many bedrooms. Bedrooms are pleasingly decorated, and modern facilities are provided. The main restaurant is attractive and provides excellent food. There is also the newly opened Kings Brasserie which offers comfortable surroundings with log fires and a wide range of innovative dishes.
ROOMS: 14 en suite (5 fmly) **FACILITIES:** STV **CONF:** Class 60 Board 10 **PARKING:** 40 **NOTES:** No dogs (ex guide dogs) No smoking in restaurant **CARDS:**

See advert under BETWS-Y-COED

T

TYWYN, Gwynedd
Map 06 SH50

★62% Greenfield
High St LL36 9AD
☎ 01654 710354 01654 710354
e-mail: greentywyn@aol.com
Dir: *on A493, opposite leisure centre*
In the middle of a small seaside town, this family-run hotel also operates a busy restaurant offering a good range of inexpensive meals. Bedrooms are plainly furnished but all are fresh and bright. Each has modern facilities and several are suitable for families.
ROOMS: 8 rms (6 en suite) (2 fmly) s £17-£19.50; d £30-£37 (incl. bkfst) * **NOTES:** No dogs (ex guide dogs) No smoking in restaurant Closed Jan-Feb RS Nov-Mar **CARDS:**

USK, Monmouthshire
Map 03 SO30

★★★74% Three Salmons
Porthycarne St NP15 1RY
☎ 01291 672133 01291 673979
Dir: *turn off A449, 1m into Usk, hotel on the corner of Porthycarne St, B4598*
A former coaching inn dating back to the 17th century. Bedrooms are spacious, comfortably furnished and well maintained, with some rooms in a nearby annexe. Ostlers restaurant offers carefully prepared dishes. The bar serves an extensive range of meals and there is a pleasant rear garden.
ROOMS: 10 en suite 14 annexe en suite (1 fmly) **FACILITIES:** STV **CONF:** Thtr 100 Class 40 Board 50 **PARKING:** 38 **NOTES:** No dogs (ex guide dogs) **CARDS:**

See advert on opposite page

★★★69% Glen-yr-Afon House
Pontypool Rd NP15 1SY
☎ 01291 672302 & 673202 01291 672597
e-mail: enquiries@glen-yr-afon.co.uk
Dir: *A472 through Usk High St, over river bridge following main rd around to the right hotel is 200yds on the left*
This large Victorian property stands in well maintained grounds and gardens. The young team of staff provide attentive and friendly service. Bedrooms are in the original house and a new wing. Public areas consist of a comfortable lounge, a bar and a traditionally furnished restaurant.
ROOMS: 28 en suite (2 fmly) No smoking in 14 bedrooms s fr £59.28; d fr £88.13 (incl. bkfst) * LB **FACILITIES:** STV Croquet lawn Xmas **CONF:** Thtr 100 Class 200 Board 30 **SERVICES:** Lift **PARKING:** 101 **NOTES:** No smoking in restaurant Civ Wed 200
CARDS:

WELSHPOOL, Powys
Map 07 SJ20

★★★68% Royal Oak
SY21 7DG
☎ 01938 552217 01938 556652
e-mail: oakwpool@.aol.com
Dir: *by traffic lights at junct of A483/A458*
A traditional market town hotel that dates back over 350 years. It provides well equipped bedrooms, a choice of bars and extensive function facilities. The 'cafe bar style' restaurant provides a good choice of popular dishes throughout the day and evening.
ROOMS: 24 en suite (2 fmly) No smoking in 10 bedrooms s £45-£58.50; d £75-£95 (incl. bkfst) * LB **FACILITIES:** STV **CONF:** Thtr 120 Class 60 Board 80 Del from £75 * **PARKING:** 40 **NOTES:** Civ Wed 100
CARDS:

★★71% Golfa Hall
Llanfair Rd SY21 9AF
☎ 01938 553399 01938 554777
e-mail: golfahall@welshpool.sagehost.co.uk
Dir: *1.5m W of Welshpool on the A458 to Dolgellau*
Set on the Powys Castle estate, this fine modern hotel was originally a farmhouse. Some of the well equipped bedrooms are particularly suitable for families. Elegant day rooms include a meeting room and a comfortable non-smoking lounge.
ROOMS: 10 en suite 4 annexe en suite (4 fmly) s £45-£60; d £65-£85 (incl. bkfst) * LB **FACILITIES:** Xmas **CONF:** Class 10 Board 15 Del from £45 * **PARKING:** 26 **NOTES:** No dogs (ex guide dogs) No smoking in restaurant **CARDS:**

WHITEBROOK, Monmouthshire
Map 03 SO50

★★70% Crown at Whitebrook
NP25 4TX
☎ 01600 860254 01600 860607
e-mail: crown@whitebrook.demon.co.uk
Dir: *turn W off A466, 50yds S of Bigsweir Bridge*
This privately owned hotel is quietly located in a wooded valley at Whitebrook. Most of the well equipped bedrooms enjoy views of the valley or the country garden. The hotel cuisine makes good use of quality local ingredients in a seasonal fixed-price menu, which is complemented by a well-chosen wine list.
ROOMS: 10 en suite s fr £50; d fr £80 (incl. bkfst) * LB
FACILITIES: Jacuzzi/spa **PARKING:** 40 **NOTES:** No children 12yrs No smoking in restaurant Closed 2 wks Jan & 2 wks Aug
CARDS:

WOLF'S CASTLE, Pembrokeshire
Map 02 SM92

★★73% Wolfscastle Country Hotel
SA62 5LZ
☎ 01437 741688 & 741225 01437 741383
e-mail: andy741225@aol.com
Dir: *on the A40 in the village of Wolf's Castle, at top of the hill left hand side, 6m N of Haverfordwest*
This large, stone-built house dates back to the mid-19th century. The well maintained and equipped accommodation includes a room with a four-poster bed and a family room. There is a pleasant bar, plus an attractive restaurant, where a good range of carefully prepared dishes is available.
ROOMS: 20 en suite 4 annexe en suite (2 fmly) s £39-£43; d fr £77 (incl. bkfst) * LB **FACILITIES:** STV entertainment **CONF:** Thtr 100 Class 100 Board 30 Del from £75 * **PARKING:** 60 **NOTES:** No smoking in restaurant Closed 24-26 Dec RS Sun nights Civ Wed 60
CARDS:

WREXHAM, Wrexham
Map 07 SJ35

★★★67% Cross Lanes Hotel & Restaurant
Cross Lanes, Bangor Rd, Marchwiel LL13 0TF
☎ 01978 780555 01978 780568
e-mail: guestservices@crosslanes.co.uk
Dir: *3m SE of Wrexham, on A525*
This privately owned hotel was built as a private house in 1890. Bedrooms, which include two with four-poster beds, are well equipped and meet the needs of today's traveller. "Kagan's Brasserie" restaurant offers a fine selection of well produced food. The hotel caters for conferences, weddings and other functions.

continued

ROOMS: 16 en suite (1 fmly) s £68-£72; d £74-£110 * LB
FACILITIES: Sauna Croquet lawn Putting green Fishing rights Xmas
CONF: Thtr 120 Class 60 Board 40 Del from £100 * **PARKING:** 80
NOTES: Closed 25 Dec (night) & 26 Dec Civ Wed 120
CARDS:

See advert under CHESTER

★★★66% Llwyn Onn Hall

Cefn Rd LL13 0NY
☎ 01978 261225 Fax 01978 363233
Dir: *between A525 Wrexham-Whitchurch road & A534 Wrexham-Nantwich road. Easy access Wrexham Ind Estate, 2m off main Wrexham-Chester A483*

Surrounded by open countryside this is a fine, ivy-clad, 17th-century manor house set in several acres of mature grounds. Exposed timbers remain, and the original oak staircase is still in use. Weddings and other functions are catered for. Bedrooms are equipped with modern facilities and one room has a four-poster bed which Bonnie Prince Charlie was once supposed to have slept in.

ROOMS: 13 en suite (1 fmly) No smoking in 4 bedrooms s £64-£72; d £84-£94 (incl. bkfst) * LB **CONF:** Thtr 60 Class 40 Board 12 Del £113.70 * **PARKING:** 40 **NOTES:** No dogs (ex guide dogs) No smoking in restaurant **CARDS:**

See advert on this page

★★★64% Wynnstay Arms

Yorke St LL13 8LP
☎ 01978 291010 Fax 01978 362138
e-mail: jeanroberts@wynnstayarms.fsnet.co.uk
Dir: *off A483 towards Wrexham. Right onto St Giles Rd at lights. Turn left at end of new road link, left again until pub and turn right,car park on left*

This large commercial hotel offers extensive function and conference facilities and a choice of bars. Bedrooms are well appointed and equipped with modern amenities. The restaurant serves both a set menu and carte, and bar snacks are served through the day.

ROOMS: 67 en suite (7 fmly) No smoking in 4 bedrooms **CONF:** Thtr 50 Class 10 Board 20 **SERVICES:** Lift air con **PARKING:** 70
NOTES: No dogs (ex guide dogs) No smoking in restaurant
CARDS:

Travelodge

Travelodge

Wrexham By Pass, Rhostyllen LL14 4EJ
☎ 01978 365705 Fax 01978 365705
Dir: *2m S, A483/A5152 roundabout*

This modern building offers accommodation in smart, spacious and well equipped bedrooms, all with en suite bathrooms. Refreshments may be taken at the nearby family restaurant. For further details and the Travelodge phone number, consult the Hotel Groups page.

ROOMS: 32 en suite

Llwyn Onn Hall Hotel, Wrexham

Hotel of the Year, Ireland

The Merrion Hotel,
Dublin

ABBEYLEIX, Co Laois
Map 01 C3

★★★64% Abbeyleix Manor Hotel
☎ 0502 30111 📠 0502 30220
e-mail: info@abbeyleixmanorhotel.com
Dir: *hotel situated on N8 (main Dublin-Cork road) just S of Abbeyleix Town*
This attractive hotel, on the outskirts of Abbeyleix heritage town, is ideal for those travelling on the National Route. Relaxing areas include a themed bar which serves snacks all day, an inviting foyer lounge and a conservatory. Fine dining is available in Knaptons restaurant. Spacious and comfortable bedrooms are furnished with locally crafted wood.
ROOMS: 23 en suite (2 fmly) s IR£40; d IR£70 (incl. bkfst) * **SERVICES:** air con **PARKING:** 270 **NOTES:** No dogs (ex guide dogs) No smoking in restaurant Closed 25-26 Dec **CARDS:**

ADARE, Co Limerick
Map 01 B3

★★★77% ❀❀❀ Dunraven Arms
☎ 061 396633 📠 061 396541
e-mail: dunraven@iol.ie
Dir: *first building as you enter the village*
This lovely, traditional country inn dates from 1792, and lies in one of Ireland's prettiest villages. The comfortable bedrooms are equipped with all modern facilities and the pleasant restaurant serves award-winning cuisine.
ROOMS: 75 en suite (1 fmly) s IR£95-IR£108; d IR£120-IR£147 LB **FACILITIES:** STV Indoor swimming (H) Fishing Riding Sauna Gym Pool table Jacuzzi/spa **CONF:** Thtr 300 Class 200 Board 50 **SERVICES:** Lift **PARKING:** 90 **NOTES:** No smoking in restaurant
CARDS:

★★★59%
Fitzgeralds Woodlands House Hotel
Knockanes
☎ 061 605100 📠 061 396073
e-mail: reception@woodlands-hotel.ie
Dir: *turn left at Lantern Lodge on N21 S of Limerick. Hotel 0.5m on right*
Set in 44 acres of woodland on the outskirts of Adare, this family-run hotel is friendly and welcoming. Comfortable bedrooms are all well appointed and are available in three styles, the newest featuring extras such as jacuzzis. The hotel specialises in golf break holidays.
ROOMS: 92 en suite (36 fmly) s IR£60-IR£70; d IR£90-IR£110 (incl. bkfst) * LB **FACILITIES:** STV Indoor swimming (H) Sauna Solarium Gym Jacuzzi/spa Health & beauty salon Thermal spa entertainment **CONF:** Thtr 400 Class 200 Board 50 Del IR£84 * **PARKING:** 290 **NOTES:** No dogs (ex guide dogs) No children 6wks Closed 24-25 Dec
CARDS:

AGHADOWEY, Co Londonderry
Map 01 C6

★★67% Brown Trout Golf & Country Inn
209 Agivey Rd BT51 4AD
☎ 028 7086 8209 📠 028 7086 8878
e-mail: bill@browntroutinn.com
Dir: *on intersection of A54/B66 on main road to Coleraine*
On the banks of the Agivey River, this friendly inn is popular with golfers. A courtyard area houses cheerfully decorated and spacious bedrooms. The restaurant serves hearty home-cooked fare and food is also available in the lounge bar.

continued

ROOMS: 17 en suite (11 fmly) s £50-£60; d £60-£85 (incl. bkfst) * LB **FACILITIES:** Golf 9 Fishing Gym Putting green Game fishing river entertainment Xmas **CONF:** Thtr 40 Class 24 Board 28 Del from £50 * **PARKING:** 80 **NOTES:** No smoking in restaurant
CARDS:

AHERLOW, Co Tipperary
Map 01 B3

★★★62% Aherlow House
☎ 062 56153 📠 062 56212
e-mail: aherlow@iol.ie
Dir: *6km from Tipperary, coming from Limerick turn right at the trafic lights, follow sign posts for hotel*
Located in a coniferous forest with superb views of the Galtee Mountains, this Tudor-style house offers comfortable public rooms, including a relaxing drawing room, a spacious lounge bar and a restaurant. Accommodation is well equipped and an additional wing has been added. The attentive staff create a warm and friendly atmosphere.
ROOMS: 29 en suite (23 fmly) s fr IR£57; d fr IR£94 (incl. bkfst) * LB **FACILITIES:** STV entertainment Xmas **CONF:** Thtr 250 Class 150 Board 20 Del from IR£85 * **PARKING:** 200 **NOTES:** No dogs (ex guide dogs) Closed 6 Jan-30 Mar(excl weekends) Civ Wed 300
CARDS:

ARDARA, Co Donegal
Map 01 B5

★★★60% Nesbitt Arms
☎ 075 41103 📠 075 41895
e-mail: nesbitta@indigo.ie
Dir: *from Donegal town, take N56, turning N for Ardara as signposted*
This hotel, built in 1838, is situated in the centre of Ardara heritage town. Bedrooms, contemporary in style, vary in size. There is a comfortable, spacious foyer lounge featuring an open fire and a traditional style bar and bistro serves food all day. Breakfast and dinner are served in Weavers restaurant.
ROOMS: 19 en suite (4 fmly) s IR£50-IR£57.50; d IR£63-IR£78 (incl. bkfst) * LB **FACILITIES:** entertainment Xmas **CONF:** Thtr 200 Class 100 **NOTES:** No dogs No smoking in restaurant **CARDS:**

ARDMORE, Co Waterford
Map 01 C2

★62% Round Tower
☎ 024 94494 & 94382 📠 024 94254
e-mail: rth@eircom.net
Dir: *Ardmore is located off the main N25 Rosslare-Cork route. Turn off onto Route R673. Hotel is situated in centre of village*
A large country house set in its own grounds in a pretty fishing village, boasting a blue flag beach, lovely marked cliff walks and much of early monastic interest. The atmosphere is friendly and there is a comfortable lounge, panelled bar and a conservatory, where bar food is served. A carte menu is available in the restaurant, featuring 'catch of the day' seafood.
ROOMS: 12 en suite (4 fmly) s IR£33; d IR£60 (incl. bkfst) * **CONF:** Thtr 50 Class 25 Board 30 **SERVICES:** air con **PARKING:** 40 **NOTES:** RS Oct-Apr **CARDS:**

ARTHURSTOWN, Co Wexford
Map 01 C2

★★★77% ❀❀
Dunbrody Country House Hotel & Restaurant
☎ 051 389600 📠 051 389601
e-mail: dunbrody@indigo.ie
Dir: *From N11 follow signs for Duncannon & Ballyhack (R733). Hotel is 20m on from turn off. Turn left at gate lodge on approaching Arthurstown*
Surrounded by peaceful parkland, this elegant Georgian manor

continued

ARTHURSTOWN, continued

house lies near the coast. The priorities here are tranquillity, generous hospitality and award-winning cuisine. The attractive bedrooms are all individually styled with marbled bathrooms. Activities nearby include walking, golf and horse riding.
ROOMS: 20 en suite (4 fmly) No smoking in 2 bedrooms **FACILITIES:** Riding Croquet lawn clay pigeon shooting **CONF:** Thtr 200 Class 100 Board 100 **PARKING:** 40 **NOTES:** No dogs (ex guide dogs) Closed 24-26 Dec **CARDS:**

ASHFORD, Co Wicklow Map 01 D3

★★ 66% *The Chester Beatty Inn*

☎ 0404 40682 🖷 0404 49003
e-mail: hotelchesterbeatty@tinet.ie
Dir: *in centre of Ashford village route N11 Rosslare to Dublin*
Well located for touring County Wicklow and convenient for the ferryport, guests are assured a warm welcome at this hotel. A restaurant and a lounge bar are available. Bedrooms are attractive.
ROOMS: 12 en suite (10 fmly) No smoking in 8 bedrooms **FACILITIES:** STV Snooker **PARKING:** 52 **NOTES:** No dogs Closed 25 Dec **CARDS:**

★★ 63% Cullenmore Hotel

☎ 0404 40187 🖷 0404 40471
e-mail: cullenmore@eircom.net
Dir: *located N of Ashford on the N11 main Dublin/Wexford Rosslaire Road, 32km S of Dublin*
This hotel is in a very convenient location for golfers, with numerous courses nearby and it is only a 45 minute drive from Dublin. It offers a smart lounge, adjoining the bar, where good value bar food is available, in addition to the fixed price menu served in the restaurant. There is also a conference/banqueting suite.
ROOMS: 17 en suite (4 fmly) s fr IR£45; d fr IR£70 (incl. bkfst) * LB **FACILITIES:** STV **CONF:** Board 30 **PARKING:** 100 **NOTES:** No dogs (ex guide dogs) Closed 24-27 Dec **CARDS:**

ATHLONE, Co Westmeath Map 01 C4

★★★ 69% ❀❀ Hodson Bay

Hodson Bay
☎ 0902 92444 🖷 0902 80520
e-mail: info@hodsonbayhotel.com
Dir: *from N6 take N61 to Roscommon. Take right turn - hotel situated 1km on Lough Ree*

Close to the River Shannon and right on the shore of Lough Ree, this historic hotel has been reconstructed and extended to provide comfortable accommodation. With a golf course to the rear and a marina to the front, most of the rooms have excellent views.
continued

ROOMS: 133 en suite (23 fmly) No smoking in 3 bedrooms s IR£78-IR£98; d IR£103-IR£122 * LB **FACILITIES:** STV Indoor swimming (H) Golf 18 Fishing Sauna Solarium Gym Steam room entertainment Xmas **CONF:** Thtr 1000 Class 300 Board 300 Del from IR£87 * **SERVICES:** Lift **PARKING:** 300 **NOTES:** No dogs (ex guide dogs) **CARDS:**

See advert on opposite page

★★★ 64% ❀ *Prince of Wales*

☎ 0902 72626 🖷 0902 75658
Dir: *in centre of town, opposite Bank of Ireland*
Situated in the centre of Athlone, this modern hotel offers comfortable, well equipped bedrooms. Its spacious restaurant and lounge bar are comfortable and pleasantly furnished.
ROOMS: 73 en suite (15 fmly) No smoking in 10 bedrooms **FACILITIES:** STV entertainment **CONF:** Thtr 270 Class 140 Board 50 **PARKING:** 35 **NOTES:** No dogs (ex guide dogs) RS 24-25 Dec **CARDS:**

★★ 68% *Royal Hoey*

Mardyke St
☎ 0902 72924 & 75395 🖷 0902 75194

Upholding a tradition of warm hospitality is the priority at this family-run hotel. Located in the centre of town, it has a comfortable foyer lounge bar and restaurant and the coffee shop serves snacks all day. Bedrooms are carefully maintained and well appointed.
ROOMS: 38 en suite (8 fmly) No smoking in 10 bedrooms **FACILITIES:** STV entertainment **CONF:** Thtr 250 Class 130 Board 40 **SERVICES:** Lift air con **PARKING:** 50 **NOTES:** No dogs (ex guide dogs) No smoking in restaurant Closed 25-27 Dec **CARDS:**

BALLINASLOE, Co Galway Map 01 B4

★★★ 72% Haydens Gateway Hotel

☎ 065 68 23000 🖷 065 68 23759
e-mail: cro@lynchotels.com
Dir: *located on the main Dublin/Galway road N6*
Built around 1803, this fine hotel offers excellent service. Meals are served throughout the day, either in the Gorbally Restaurant, with its extensive carte menu or the award-winning coffee shop which serves full meals, snacks and home-baking.
ROOMS: 48 en suite (8 fmly) s IR£40-IR£71.50; d IR£60-IR£113 * LB **FACILITIES:** STV entertainment Xmas **CONF:** Thtr 300 Class 160 Board 50 Del from IR£66 * **SERVICES:** Lift **PARKING:** 100 **NOTES:** No dogs (ex guide dogs) Civ Wed 300 **CARDS:**

Early start? Hotels at all star levels should provide in-room alarm clocks and/or alarm calls.

BALLON, Co Carlow

Map 01 C3

★★★63% Ballykealey House

☎ 0503 59288 & 59212 0503 59297
e-mail: bh@iol.ie

Dir: *take N80 out of Carlow town, hotel approx. 12m on right hand side, 1m before Ballon village*

This house, set in seven acres of parkland, was built in the 1830s and features Tudor chimney stacks, battlements, ornate plasterwork and fine oak reception room doors. Public areas include a pleasant lounge and lounge bar, banqueting suite and restaurant, serving good cuisine. Individually styled bedrooms are mostly spacious.

ROOMS: 12 en suite No smoking in 2 bedrooms s IR£40-IR£45; d IR£80-IR£90 (incl. bkfst) * LB **CONF:** Thtr 200 Class 100 Board 100 **PARKING:** 100 **NOTES:** No dogs No children 12yrs Closed 1 Dec-31 Mar **CARDS:**

BALLYBOFEY, Co Donegal

Map 01 C5

★★★70% *Kee's*

Stranorlar
☎ 074 31018 074 31917

Dir: *2km NE on N15, in Stranorlar village*

This former coaching inn is today a very comfortable hotel. Bedrooms are well furnished and offer good facilities. There is a Bistro as well as the conservatory lounge and popular Restaurant.

ROOMS: 53 en suite (10 fmly) **FACILITIES:** STV Indoor swimming (H) Sauna Solarium Gym Jacuzzi/spa Mountain bikes for hire entertainment **CONF:** Thtr 250 Class 100 Board 30 **SERVICES:** Lift **PARKING:** 90 **CARDS:**

BALLYCONNELL, Co Cavan

Map 01 C4

★★★★63% Slieve Russell Hotel Golf & Country Club

☎ 049 9526 444 049 9526 474
e-mail: slieve-russell@quinn-hotels.com

Dir: *from Cavan head for Enniskillen, at Butlersbridge turn left towards Belturbet. Through village towards Ballyconnell, hotel is on left after 5 miles*

This imposing hotel stands in 300 acres, which also accommodate a championship golf course. Public areas include a range of lounges, a restaurant and brasserie and a leisure centre. Bedrooms are tastefully furnished and equipped to a high standard.

ROOMS: 151 en suite (74 fmly) s IR£90-IR£95; d IR£150-IR£160 (incl. bkfst) * LB **FACILITIES:** STV Indoor swimming (H) Golf 18 Tennis (hard) Squash Snooker Sauna Solarium Gym Pool table Jacuzzi/spa Steam Room Hair & Beauty Salon entertainment Xmas **CONF:** Thtr 800 Class 450 Board 40 **SERVICES:** Lift **PARKING:** 600 **NOTES:** No dogs (ex guide dogs) **CARDS:**

BALLYCOTTON, Co Cork

Map 01 C2

★★★73% Bay View

☎ 021 646746 021 646075
e-mail: bayhotel@iol.ie

MANOR HOUSE

Dir: *turn off N25 at Castlemartyr and follow signs to Ballycotton*

The Bay View Hotel offers a mixture of past and present with its classic gabled exterior and modern interior, providing many comforts and facilities. Public areas are spacious and bedrooms are comfortable, some with superb views over Ballycotton Bay. Staff are friendly and efficient.

continued on p832

BALLYCOTTON, continued

ROOMS: 35 en suite s IR£87; d IR£135 (incl. bkfst) * LB **FACILITIES:** STV Hillwalking Horse riding Fishing Golf entertainment **CONF:** Thtr 60 Class 30 Board 24 Del from IR£95 * **SERVICES:** Lift air con **PARKING:** 40 **NOTES:** No dogs (ex guide dogs) Closed Nov-Apr Civ Wed 80 **CARDS:**

See advert on page 831

BALLYHEIGE, Co Kerry — Map 01 A2

★★★65% The White Sands
☎ 066 7133 102 📠 066 7133 357
e-mail: culv@indigo.ie
Dir: *18km from Tralee town on coast road in North Kerry, the hotel is situated on left on main street*
This seaside hotel, in a village near Tralee, has warm attractive colour schemes, a good restaurant, two cosy bars, and very pleasant staff.
ROOMS: 81 en suite **FACILITIES:** STV entertainment **SERVICES:** Lift air con **PARKING:** 40 **NOTES:** Closed Nov-Feb **CARDS:**

BALLYLICKEY, Co Cork — Map 01 B2

★★★75% Sea View
☎ 027 50073 & 50462 📠 027 51555
e-mail: seaviewhousehotel@eircom.net
Dir: *5km from Bantry, 11km from Glengarriff on N71*
Irish hospitality awaits at this delightful country house, overlooking Bantry Bay. Set in well tended gardens, it has cosy lounges with turf fires and comfortable, pleasantly decorated bedrooms. The hotel caters for the fishing and golfing enthusiast and is also a good touring base for West Cork and Kerry.
ROOMS: 17 en suite (3 fmly) s IR£45-IR£70; d IR£90-IR£100 (incl. bkfst) * LB **FACILITIES:** STV **PARKING:** 32 **NOTES:** No smoking in restaurant Closed mid Nov-mid Mar **CARDS:**

BALLYMENA, Co Antrim — Map 01 D5

★★★★72% Galgorm Manor
BT42 1EA
☎ 028 2588 1001 📠 028 2588 0080
e-mail: mail@galgorm.com
Dir: *1m outside Ballymena on A42, between Galgorm & Cullybackey*
This 19th-century mansion by the River Maine has an 85 acre estate, with an equestrian centre and grand banqueting/conference hall. Public areas include a library lounge, comfortable cocktail bar and elegant restaurant. Gillies Irish bar has a lively atmosphere. Bedrooms are well proportioned and modern in style.
ROOMS: 24 en suite (6 fmly) s fr £99; d fr £119 (incl. bkfst) * LB **FACILITIES:** STV Fishing Riding Clay pigeon shooting,Archery,Water skiing entertainment Xmas **CONF:** Thtr 500 Class 200 Board 12 Del from £110 * **PARKING:** 170 **NOTES:** No dogs (ex guide dogs) RS 25-26 Dec **CARDS:**

★★★66% Adair Arms
1 Ballymoney Rd BT43 5BS
☎ 028 2565 3674 📠 028 2564 0436
e-mail: reservations@adairarms.com
This hotel offers comfortable and well equipped bedrooms. Public areas are spacious and well presented. Lounges are inviting, the bar well stocked, and the restaurant offers a good choice from the carte and fixed price menus. Lighter meals are available in the Lanyon Grill.

continued

ROOMS: 44 en suite (3 fmly) s fr £59.50; d fr £85 (incl. bkfst) * LB **FACILITIES:** STV entertainment Xmas **CONF:** Thtr 250 Class 150 Board 60 **SERVICES:** air con **PARKING:** 50 **NOTES:** No dogs (ex guide dogs) Closed 25 Dec **CARDS:**

See advert on opposite page

BALLYNAHINCH, Co Galway — Map 01 A4

★★★★74% Ballynahinch Castle
☎ 095 31006 & 31086 📠 095 31085
e-mail: bhinch@iol.ie
Dir: *W from Galway on N59 direction Clifden. After village of Recess take Roundstone turn, 4km from turn off*
At the foot of Ben Lettery, this hotel stands on the banks of the famous salmon river, the Ballynahinch. Bedrooms are spacious, individually designed and comfortably equipped. There is a marvellous atmosphere in the Castle Bar. Game and fresh local produce are a treat in the charming restaurant.
ROOMS: 40 en suite No smoking in 4 bedrooms s IR£85-IR£115; d IR£130-IR£190 (incl. bkfst) * LB **FACILITIES:** STV Tennis (hard) Fishing Croquet lawn River & Lakeside walks entertainment Xmas **CONF:** Thtr 30 Class 20 Board 20 **PARKING:** 55 **NOTES:** No dogs (ex guide dogs) Closed Feb & 20-26 Dec **CARDS:**

BALLYVAUGHAN, Co Clare — Map 01 B3

Premier Collection

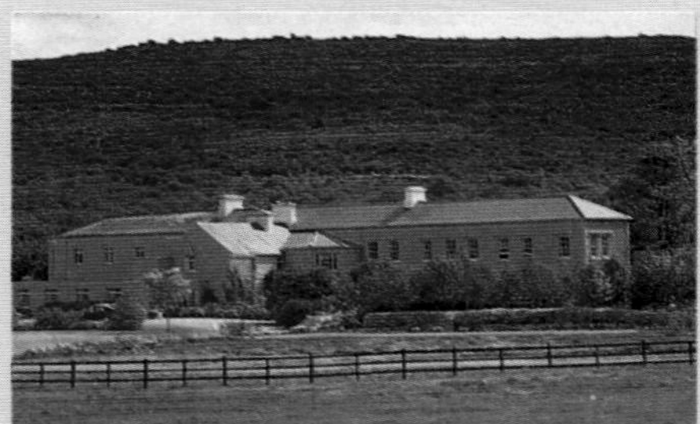

★★★ Gregans Castle
☎ 065 7077 005 📠 065 7077 111
e-mail: res@gregans.ie
Dir: *3.5miles S of the village of Ballyvaughan on the road N67*
Standing at the foot of Corkscrew Hill, with dramatic views over Galway Bay, this hotel is situated in an area which is rich in archaeological, geological and botanical interest. A high level of personal service and hospitality has earned the hotel special commendations in recent years and the welcoming staff fulfill their reputation. The cuisine is also excellent with the emphasis placed on good food, using fresh local produce.
ROOMS: 22 en suite **FACILITIES:** Croquet lawn **PARKING:** 25 **NOTES:** No dogs Closed 18 Oct-31 Mar **CARDS:**

★★★62% Hyland's Hotel

☎ 065 7077037 📠 065 7077131
e-mail: hylands@tinet.ie
Dir: *From Dublin take N6 to Craughwell, then follow N67 to Ballyvaughn village*
The proprietors have been restoring this cheerful 18th-century hotel and there are now extra 'superior' bedrooms which, as the category suggests, offer more space and comfort than the 'standard' rooms - although these are well equipped also. The

continued

hotel is the focal point of a charming village, with good food served in the restaurant and in the bar where sometimes the Seanchai, or storyteller, drops in in the evening to entertain customers with stories in the old Irish tradition.
ROOMS: 30 en suite (2 fmly) No smoking in 10 bedrooms s IR£36.50-IR£65; d IR£70-IR£93 (incl. bkfst) * LB **FACILITIES:** Riding entertainment **PARKING:** 50 **NOTES:** No dogs Closed Dec-Jan RS Oct-Dec & Feb-May **CARDS:**

BALTIMORE, Co Cork
Map 01 B1

★★★61%
Baltimore Harbour Resort Hotel & Leisure Ctr
☎ 028 20361 🖷 028 20466
e-mail: info@bhrhotel.ie
Dir: *S from Cork city N71 to Skibbereen, continue on R595 13km to Baltimore*
This smart, friendly hotel is set in a delightful position, overlooking the harbour. It has spacious, linked public areas, the restful lounge has deep sofas and a turf fire, and the bar and garden room open out onto the patio and gardens. Fresh local ingredients are served in the dining room. Bedrooms are well appointed, all have sea views.
ROOMS: 64 en suite (30 fmly) s IR£51-IR£70; d IR£72-IR£100 (incl. bkfst) * LB **FACILITIES:** Indoor swimming (H) Sauna Gym Pool table Croquet lawn Jacuzzi/spa Table Tennis, In-house video channel entertainment Xmas **CONF:** Thtr 120 Class 100 Board 30 Del from IR£80 * **SERVICES:** Lift **PARKING:** 80 **NOTES:** No dogs (ex guide dogs) No smoking in restaurant Closed Jan-mid Feb
CARDS:

★★★59% Casey's of Baltimore
☎ 028 20197 🖷 028 20509
e-mail: caseys@eircom.net
Dir: *Take the N71 from Cork to Skibbereen, follow R595 from Skibbereen*
Set in an elevated position, overlooking the harbour, this warm and friendly hotel offers attractive, comfortable bedrooms. Both the lounge and the restaurant enjoy superb views. The restaurant features seafood dishes and there is a traditional pub. Ferry trips to nearby islands are popular.
ROOMS: 14 en suite (1 fmly) **FACILITIES:** STV entertainment
PARKING: 50 **NOTES:** No dogs Closed 19-26 Feb,5-18 Nov & 21-27 Dec
CARDS:

BANGOR, Co Down
Map 01 D5

★★★72% Clandeboye Lodge
10 Estate Rd, Clandeboye BT19 1UR
☎ 028 9185 2500 🖷 028 9185 2772
e-mail: info@clandeboyelodge.com
Dir: *from Belfast on A2 turn right at signpost. 500yds down Ballygallagh Road turn left and take Crawfords Burn road. Hotel is 200yds on left.*
Three miles west of Bangor, Clandeboye Lodge stands in landscaped and wooded grounds. The hotel offers warm hospitality, attentive service and a high quality of accommodation. Public areas include a bright open-plan foyer bar and lounge. The restaurant serves carefully prepared cuisine.
ROOMS: 43 en suite (2 fmly) No smoking in 13 bedrooms s fr £75; d fr £75 * LB **FACILITIES:** STV Petanque court **CONF:** Thtr 350 Class 110 Board 50 Del from £68.50 * **SERVICES:** Lift **PARKING:** 250
NOTES: No dogs (ex guide dogs) Closed 24-26 Dec
CARDS:

BANGOR, continued

★★★67% Marine Court
The Marina BT20 5ED
☎ 028 9145 1100 ▯ 028 9145 1200
e-mail: marine.court@dial.pipex.com
On Bangor seafront, the Marine Court offers a good range of conference and leisure facilities. Extensive public areas include the first floor restaurant and cocktail bar. Alternatively, the popular Lord Nelson's Bistro/Bar is more relaxed and there is also a lively bar called Callico Jack's.
ROOMS: 52 en suite (11 fmly) No smoking in 16 bedrooms s £80-£90; d £90-£100 (incl. bkfst) * LB **FACILITIES:** STV Indoor swimming (H) Solarium Gym Jacuzzi/spa Steam room entertainment **CONF:** Thtr 350 Class 100 Board 20 Del from £110 * **SERVICES:** Lift **PARKING:** 30 **NOTES:** No dogs (ex guide dogs) RS 25 Dec Civ Wed 300
CARDS:

★★★60% Royal
Seafront BT20 5ED
☎ 028 9127 1866 ▯ 028 9146 7810
e-mail: theroyalhotel@compuserve.com
Dir: *take A2 from Belfast. Proceed through Bangor town centre to seafront. Turn right-Hotel 300 yards overlooking Marina*
This substantial Victorian hotel overlooks the marina and offers bedrooms that are comfortable and modern in style. Public areas are traditional and include a choice of contrasting bars and a popular brasserie. The Quays restaurant provides a more formal dining experience.
ROOMS: 50 en suite s £65-£75; d £80-£90 (incl. bkfst) LB **FACILITIES:** STV entertainment **CONF:** Thtr 80 Class 60 Board 40 Del from £90 * **SERVICES:** Lift **NOTES:** No dogs (ex guide dogs) Closed 25 Dec **CARDS:**

BANTRY, Co Cork — Map 01 B2

★★★61% Westlodge
☎ 027 50360 ▯ 027 50438
This modern, busy hotel has a popular leisure centre. It is set in its own grounds, on the outskirts of the town, overlooking the bay.
ROOMS: 90 en suite (20 fmly) s fr IR£67.50; d fr IR£115 (incl. bkfst) * LB **FACILITIES:** Indoor swimming (H) Tennis (hard) Squash Snooker Sauna Solarium Gym Pool table Putting green Jacuzzi/spa Pitch & Putt,wooded walks entertainment **CONF:** Thtr 400 Class 200 Board 24 **SERVICES:** air con **PARKING:** 400 **NOTES:** No dogs (ex guide dogs) Closed 23-27 Dec **CARDS:**

BELFAST — Map 01 D5

★★★★61% The McCausland Hotel
34-38 Victoria St BT1 3GH
☎ 028 9022 0200 ▯ 028 9022 0220
e-mail: info@mccauslandhotel.com
Dir: *Victoria St is one way, hotel next to First Trust building*

This exciting hotel has been created from the conversion of two warehouses built in 1850, with the original Italianate facade being retained. The bedrooms are very well equipped. Refined dining is on offer in the restaurant, or there is a continental style cafe.
ROOMS: 60 en suite (8 fmly) No smoking in 30 bedrooms s £120-£200; d £150-£200 * LB **FACILITIES:** STV entertainment **CONF:** Thtr 60 Class 30 Board 30 Del from £165 * **SERVICES:** Lift **PARKING:** 8 **NOTES:** No dogs (ex guide dogs) Closed 24-27 Dec
CARDS:

★★★67% *Jurys Belfast Inn*

Fisherwick Place, Great Victoria St BT2 7AP
☎ 028 9053 3500 ▯ 028 9053 3511
e-mail: info@jurys.com
Dir: *at the intersection of Grosvenor Road and Great Victoria St, beside the Opera House*
In the heart of Belfast, this smart hotel is well equipped for business guests. Public areas are contemporary in style and include a foyer lounge, a bar and a smart restaurant. Bedrooms are spacious with pretty fabrics and offer a good range of amenities.
ROOMS: 190 en suite No smoking in 76 bedrooms **FACILITIES:** STV entertainment **CONF:** Thtr 35 Class 20 Board 20 **SERVICES:** Lift **NOTES:** No dogs (ex guide dogs) Closed 24-26 Dec
CARDS:

★★★65% The Crescent Townhouse
13 Lower Crescent BT7 1NR
☎ 028 9032 3349 ▯ 028 9032 0646
e-mail: info@crescenttownhouse.com
Dir: *S towards Queens University, hotel is on Botanic Avenue opposite Botanic Train Station*
A fashionable Regency town house, situated next to the botanic gardens station. The popular Bar Twelve and Metro Brasserie are on the ground floor and the reception and bedrooms are situated on the upper floors. Bedrooms are smartly furnished in a country house style.
ROOMS: 11 en suite No smoking in 2 bedrooms s fr £80; d fr £100 (incl. bkfst) * **NOTES:** No dogs Closed 25-27 Dec & 11-13 Jul
CARDS:

★★★64% Lansdowne Court
657 Antrim Rd BT15 4EF
☎ 028 9077 3317 ▯ 028 9037 0125
Dir: *3m N of Belfast City Centre on the main Antrim road*
This bright, modern hotel is situated north of the city centre, beside the A6 and close to Belfast Castle. Bedrooms are tastefully decorated, well equipped and offer smart furnishings. Public areas include a spacious, lively bar and a themed restaurant.
ROOMS: 25 en suite (3 fmly) s fr £60 (incl. bkfst) * LB **FACILITIES:** STV entertainment **CONF:** Thtr 250 Class 60 Board 40 **PARKING:** 50 **NOTES:** No dogs (ex guide dogs) Closed 25 Dec
CARDS:

★★★62% ❀ Malone Lodge
60 Eglantine Av BT9 6DY
☎ 028 9038 8000 ▯ 028 9038 8088
e-mail: info@malonelodgehotel.com
Dir: *At Hospital r/about exit towards Bouchar Rd,left at 1st r/about,right at lights at top,1st left is Eglantine Ave*
Popular with business guests, this smart, modern hotel is close to the university and city centre. Public areas include an inviting foyer lounge, a tastefully appointed split-level restaurant and a bar. Bedrooms, varying in size, are comfortable, modern and well equipped.

continued

ROOMS: 51 en suite (5 fmly) s £55-£85; d £70-£105 (incl. bkfst) LB **FACILITIES:** STV Sauna Gym **CONF:** Thtr 220 Class 100 Board 20 **SERVICES:** Lift **PARKING:** 45 **NOTES:** No dogs (ex guide dogs) **CARDS:**

★★ 58% *Balmoral*

Blacks Rd, Dunmurry BT10 0ND
☎ 028 9030 1234 028 9060 1455
Dir: *take M1, 3m exit at Suffolk slip road, turn right and hotel is approx 300 yards*

This modern hotel lies south of Belfast in the village of Dunmurry and is popular with business guests. Bedrooms vary in size and offer practical furnishings and amenities. There is a choice of contrasting bars, one of which provides an informal alternative to the main restaurant.
ROOMS: 44 en suite **FACILITIES:** STV **CONF:** Thtr 150 Class 100 Board 80 **SERVICES:** air con **PARKING:** 300 **NOTES:** Closed 25 Dec **CARDS:**

⇧ Holiday Inn Express Belfast

Express by Holiday Inn

106a University St BT7 1HP
☎ 028 9031 1909 028 9031 1910
e-mail: express@holidayinn-ireland.com
Dir: *behind Queens University. Turn left at lights on Botanic Ave onto University St. Holiday Inn on left, 500yds down street*

A modern budget hotel offering comfortable accommodation in refreshing, spacious and comprehensively-equipped bedrooms, en suite bathrooms with power showers and continental buffet breakfast included in the room rate. Suitable for business travellers or families. For further details and the Express by Holiday Inn phone number, consult the Hotel Groups page.
ROOMS: 116 en suite (incl. cont bkfst) d fr £64.95 * **CONF:** Thtr 200 Class 100 Board 70 Del from £125 *

⇧ *Travelodge*

Travelodge

15 Brunswick St BT2 7GE
☎ 028 9033 3555 028 9023 2999
Dir: *from M2 follow city centre signs to Oxford St turn right to May St, Brunswick St is 4th on left*
This modern building offers accommodation in smart, spacious and well equipped bedrooms, all with en suite bathrooms. Refreshments may be taken at the nearby family restaurant. For further details and the Travelodge phone number, consult the Hotel Groups page.
ROOMS: 76 en suite **CONF:** Thtr 65 Class 50 Board 34

BETTYSTOWN, Co Meath — Map 01 D4

★★★★ 63% Neptune Beach Hotel & Leisure Club

☎ 041 9827107 041 9827412
e-mail: info@neptunebeach.ie
Dir: *Bettystown is located just off the main Dublin/Belfast road N1*
This hotel, overlooking the sea, has access to a sandy beach. Public areas include an inviting lounge and an attractive Winter Garden. Many bedrooms enjoy sea views and there is a leisure club with pool, gym and jacuzzi.
ROOMS: 38 en suite No smoking in 14 bedrooms s IR£85-IR£110; d IR£110-IR£140 (incl. bkfst) * LB **FACILITIES:** STV Indoor swimming (H) Sauna Solarium Gym Jacuzzi/spa Steam room Kiddies pool entertainment Xmas **CONF:** Thtr 250 Class 150 **SERVICES:** Lift **PARKING:** 60 **NOTES:** No dogs (ex guide dogs) No smoking in restaurant **CARDS:**

BIRR, Co Offaly — Map 01 C3

★★★ 61% *Dooley's*

Emmet Square
☎ 0509 20032 0509 21332
This hotel dates back to the era of the horse-drawn Bianconi carriages, when it was used as a staging post. Located in Emmet Square in the centre of this historic town, the hotel enjoys an excellent reputation for hospitality and cuisine. Birr is full of interest for visitors and Birr Castle Demesne, with its great telescope, is just a short walk away.
ROOMS: 18 en suite (4 fmly) **FACILITIES:** STV entertainment **CONF:** Thtr 400 Class 200 Board 30 **NOTES:** No dogs (ex guide dogs) RS 25-26 Dec **CARDS:**

★★★ 60% *County Arms*

☎ 0509 20791 0509 21234
e-mail: countyarmshotel@tinet.ie
Dir: *take N7 from Dublin to Roscrea, N62 to Birr, hotel on right before the church*
This fine Georgian house has comfortable bedrooms, all furnished and decorated to a very high standard. The rooms overlook the meticulously kept Victorian walled gardens which supply the fruit, vegetables and herbs to the hotel kitchens. There is a choice of two restaurants, a bar and a comfortable lounge.
ROOMS: 24 en suite (4 fmly) No smoking in 2 bedrooms **FACILITIES:** STV entertainment **CONF:** Thtr 250 Class 250 Board 150 **PARKING:** 150 **NOTES:** No dogs (ex guide dogs) RS 25 Dec **CARDS:**

B

BLARNEY, Co Cork
Map 01 B2

★★★70% Blarney Park
☎ 021 385281 021 381506
e-mail: info@blarneypark.com
Dir: *located in the village of Blarney, just 10 minutes from Cork city on the N20 between Cork and Limerick*
Standing in 10 acres of gardens beneath the woods of Blarney Castle, this hotel offers comfortable lounges, a smart bistro, and a convivial bar. There is also an excellent leisure centre, featuring a pool with a 40-metre slide and there are good facilities for children, with plenty of play space in the grounds.
ROOMS: 91 en suite (20 fmly) No smoking in 2 bedrooms s fr IR£77; d fr IR£124 (incl. bkfst) * LB **FACILITIES:** STV Indoor swimming (H) Tennis (hard) Sauna Gym Pool table Steam room Childrens pool & playroom entertainment ch fac Xmas **CONF:** Thtr 300 Class 130 Board 80 Del from IR£65 * **SERVICES:** Lift **PARKING:** 100 **NOTES:** No dogs (ex guide dogs) **CARDS:**

★★★68% *Christy's*
☎ 021 385011 021 385350
e-mail: christys@blarney.ie
Dir: *N20, exit at the Blarney sign, at the R617 5km from Cork city*
Part of the famous Blarney Woollen Mills and skilfully converted into a hotel, Christy's stands within sight of the historic castle. Staff are pleasantly attentive and the restaurant and library have a relaxing atmosphere. Adjacent to the hotel is an interesting shopping complex including Christy's Pub and self-service restaurant.
ROOMS: 49 en suite (2 fmly) No smoking in 10 bedrooms **FACILITIES:** Squash Sauna Solarium Gym Fitness classes **CONF:** Thtr 300 Class 100 Board 20 **SERVICES:** Lift **PARKING:** 200 **NOTES:** No dogs (ex guide dogs) Closed 24-26 Dec RS Good Friday
CARDS:

BLESSINGTON, Co Wicklow
Map 01 D3

★★★61% Downshire House
☎ 045 865199 045 865335
e-mail: info@downshirehouse.com
Dir: *on N81*
This family-run Georgian house is renowned for its friendly atmosphere. Bedrooms are comfortable and come in a variety of sizes, while the public areas are relaxing and inviting. Cooking is in traditional country house style. The hotel is located in the main street in the village, near to the Wicklow hills, amid some lovely scenery.
ROOMS: 14 en suite 11 annexe en suite **FACILITIES:** Tennis (hard) Croquet lawn Table tennis **CONF:** Thtr 40 Class 20 Board 20 **PARKING:** 30 **NOTES:** No dogs (ex guide dogs) Closed 22 Dec-6 Jan
CARDS:

BOYLE, Co Roscommon
Map 01 B4

★★64% *Royal*
☎ 079 62016 079 62016
Dir: *turn off N4 Dublin-Sligo road for Boyle, adjacent to bridge in town centre*
Beside the river, in the town centre, this hotel is comfortable and family-run, offering good accommodation. Public areas are cosy and attractively furnished. Bedrooms are spacious and well maintained. Beautifully prepared meals are served and food is also available from the bar and self-service buffet.
ROOMS: 16 en suite (6 fmly) **FACILITIES:** STV ch fac **CONF:** Thtr 80 Class 35 Board 35 **PARKING:** 120 **NOTES:** Closed 25-26 Dec
CARDS:

BRAY, Co Wicklow
Map 01 D4

★★★63% *Royal*
Main St
☎ 01 2862935 01 2867373
Dir: *from N11, First exit for Bray, 2nd exit from rdbt, through 2 sets traffic lights across bridge, hotel on the left side*
The Royal Hotel stands on the main street, near to the seafront, just a few miles from the Dun Laoghaire ferryport. The hotel has a well equipped leisure centre.
ROOMS: 91 en suite (3 fmly) **FACILITIES:** Indoor swimming (H) Sauna Solarium Gym Jacuzzi/spa Children's pool Whirlpool spa Creche Massage and beauty clinic entertainment **CONF:** Thtr 450 Class 300 Board 100 **SERVICES:** Lift **PARKING:** 100 **NOTES:** No dogs (ex guide dogs) No smoking in restaurant **CARDS:**

★★★60% Woodland Court
Southern Cross
☎ 01 276 0258 01 276 0298
e-mail: info@woodlandscourthotel.ie
Situated opposite Kilruddery House, this new hotel is comfortable and attractively appointed throughout. Most bedrooms are spacious and all have modern facilities. The large lobby lounge has a bar and access to the grounds. There are conference facilities and a large car park.
ROOMS: 65 en suite (4 fmly) s fr IR£65; d fr IR£75 * LB **CONF:** Thtr 60 Class 30 Board 20 Del from IR£100 * **SERVICES:** Lift **PARKING:** 70 **NOTES:** No dogs (ex guide dogs) No smoking in restaurant Closed 24-26 Dec **CARDS:**

BUNBEG, Co Donegal
Map 01 B6

★★★68% Ostan Gweedore
☎ 075 31177 & 31188 075 31726
e-mail: boylec@iol.ie
Dir: *1km up coast from Bunbeg crossroads - first road left down to sea*
This hotel offers spacious and well equipped bedrooms. Day rooms are designed to take full advantage of the ever-changing seascape and run the length of the hotel. Fresh seafood features daily on the carefully prepared menus.
ROOMS: 39 en suite (6 fmly) s IR£50-IR£55; d IR£90-IR£130 (incl. bkfst) * LB **FACILITIES:** STV Indoor swimming (H) Sauna Solarium Gym Jacuzzi/spa entertainment Xmas **CONF:** Thtr 250 Class 150 **PARKING:** 80 **NOTES:** No dogs (ex guide dogs) Closed Dec-Jan RS Oct, Nov, Dec, Feb & Mar **CARDS:**

BUNRATTY, Co Clare
Map 01 B3

★★★65% *Fitzpatrick Bunratty*
☎ 061 361177 061 471252
e-mail: info@fitzpatrick.com
Dir: *take Bunratty by-pass, exit off Limerick/Shannon dual carriageway*
Situated in the picturesque village of Bunratty, famous for its medieval castle, this modern ranch-style building is surrounded by lawns and flower beds. Bedrooms and public rooms are richly timbered, and there is a helipad in the grounds.
ROOMS: 115 en suite (7 fmly) No smoking in 7 bedrooms **FACILITIES:** STV Indoor swimming (H) Sauna Gym Jacuzzi/spa Steam room entertainment **CONF:** Thtr 1000 Class 550 Board 100 **PARKING:** 150 **NOTES:** No dogs (ex guide dogs) RS 24-25 Dec
CARDS:

Arriving late? Four and five star hotels have night porters to assist with your luggage; and 24hr room service.

C

BUSHMILLS, Co Antrim
Map 01 C6

★★68% *Beach House*
The Sea Front, 61 Beach Rd, Portballintrae BT57 8RT
☎ 028 2073 1214 🖷 028 2073 1664
e-mail: info@beachhousehotel.com
This resort hotel enjoys spectacular sea views towards Donegal and is close to the Giants Causeway and Bushmills distillery. Public areas include a choice of lounges, a bar with a nautical theme and a spacious dining room staffed by a welcoming team. Bedrooms offer modern comforts and amenities. Golf packages for tourists are a special feature.
ROOMS: 32 en suite (2 fmly) **FACILITIES:** STV entertainment **CONF:** Thtr 100 Class 40 Board 40 **PARKING:** 55 **NOTES:** No dogs (ex guide dogs) **CARDS:**

CAHERCIVEEN, Co Kerry
Map 01 A2

★★60% Caherciveen Park Hotel
Valentia Rd
☎ 066 9472543 🖷 066 9472893
e-mail: chp@cahedaniel.net
Dir: *hotel located on the main ring road in Caherciveen Town (Waterville end of town)*
In one of the villages on the Ring of Kerry, this pleasant hotel is near to the coast and many places of interest. There is an inviting bar and restaurant. The hotel is well located for trips to the nearby islands, which are well worth a visit.
ROOMS: 24 en suite (4 fmly) No smoking in 12 bedrooms s IR£35-IR£70; d IR£70-IR£140 (incl. bkfst) * LB **FACILITIES:** STV Pool table dancing room Games room entertainment **CONF:** Class 25 Board 60 Del from IR£30 * **PARKING:** 100 **NOTES:** No dogs (ex guide dogs) Closed 25 Dec Civ Wed 700 **CARDS:**

CAHERDANIEL, Co Kerry
Map 01 A2

★★★63% Derrynane
Best Western
☎ 066 9475136 🖷 066 9475160
e-mail: info@derrynane.com
Dir: *hotel is just off the main road. 2mins walking distance*
Halfway around the famous Ring of Kerry, this modern hotel, overlooking the sea, offers a relaxed and friendly atmosphere. The gardens and some of the bedrooms take advantage of the spectacular sea views. The area is ideal for touring and enjoying the scenery and there are plenty of quiet beaches.
ROOMS: 74 en suite (30 fmly) s IR£53.50; d IR£77-IR£98 (incl. bkfst) * LB **FACILITIES:** STV Outdoor swimming (H) Tennis (hard) Sauna Solarium Gym Pool table Steam room entertainment **PARKING:** 60 **NOTES:** No smoking in restaurant Closed 4 Oct-15 Apr **CARDS:**

CAHIR, Co Tipperary
Map 01 C3

★★★67% Cahir House
The Square
☎ 52 42727 🖷 52 42727
e-mail: cahirhousehotel@tinet.ie
Dir: *travelling S on N8 turn off at Cahir by-pass follow N24 to town, hotel on square in centre of town, car park at rear*
In the centre of Cahir, this hotel has been extending hospitality to visitors since the days of the famous Bianconi horse-drawn coaches. It offers modern comforts in well equipped and tastefully furnished rooms and maintains traditional standards of welcome and cuisine. The hotel is an ideal base from which to explore.
continued

ROOMS: 31 en suite (3 fmly) No smoking in 17 bedrooms **FACILITIES:** STV entertainment **CONF:** Thtr 500 Class 300 Board 80 **PARKING:** 80 **NOTES:** No dogs (ex guide dogs) Closed 25 Dec RS 24-26 Dec & Good Fri **CARDS:**

CARLOW, Co Carlow
Map 01 C3

★★★72% Dolmen
Kilkenny Rd
☎ 0503 42002 🖷 0503 42375
e-mail: reservations@dolmenhotel.ie
Dir: *approx 1m outside Corlow town on the main Kilkenny-Waterford road. Approx 0.5m on right past The Institute of Technology*
In 20 acres of landscaped grounds, this hotel nestles in a peaceful riverside location. Guests can relax in the grounds or take advantage of the free coarse fishing. There is a spacious reception and foyer, a large bar and restaurant, and a luxurious boardroom, which doubles as an additional lounge, overlooking the river. Bedrooms are all well equipped and comfortable.
ROOMS: 40 en suite 12 annexe en suite (1 fmly) s IR£50-IR£60; d IR£75-IR£110 (incl. bkfst) * LB **FACILITIES:** STV Fishing Xmas **CONF:** Thtr 1000 Class 300 Board 50 Del IR£75 * **SERVICES:** air con **PARKING:** 300 **NOTES:** No dogs (ex guide dogs) **CARDS:**

See advert on this page

★★★65% *Seven Oaks*
Athy Rd
☎ 0503 31308 🖷 0503 32155
e-mail: sevenoak@tinet.ie
Near to Carlow town centre, this hotel has a modern interior and the majority of rooms are contemporary in style and well
continued

CARLOW, continued

equipped. Public areas are comfortable and there are separate function facilities, catering for a wide range of events.
ROOMS: 32 en suite (3 fmly) **FACILITIES:** STV Fishing entertainment **CONF:** Thtr 400 Class 150 Board 80 **SERVICES:** Lift air con **PARKING:** 165 **NOTES:** No dogs (ex guide dogs) Closed 25 Dec & Good Friday **CARDS:**

C

CARNA, Co Galway — Map 01 A4

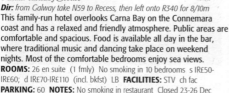

★★★61% Carna Bay Hotel
☎ 095 32255 📠 095 32530
e-mail: carnaby@iol.ie
Dir: *from Galway take N59 to Recess, then left onto R340 for 8/10m*
This family-run hotel overlooks Carna Bay on the Connemara coast and has a relaxed and friendly atmosphere. Public areas are comfortable and spacious. Food is available all day in the bar, where traditional music and dancing take place on weekend nights. Most of the comfortable bedrooms enjoy sea views.
ROOMS: 26 en suite (1 fmly) No smoking in 10 bedrooms s IR£50-IR£60; d IR£70-IR£110 (incl. bkfst) LB **FACILITIES:** STV ch fac **PARKING:** 60 **NOTES:** No smoking in restaurant Closed 23-26 Dec **CARDS:**

CARNLOUGH, Co Antrim — Map 01 D6

★★★64% ❀ *Londonderry Arms*
20 Harbour Rd BT44 0EU
☎ 028 2888 5255 📠 028 2888 5263
Dir: *14m N from Larne on the coast road*
Genuine Irish hospitality is the hallmark of this comfortable hotel, close to the small harbour. Public areas include a choice of cosy lounges and well stocked bars; the restaurant offers a varied selection of wholesome Antrim fare.
ROOMS: 35 en suite (5 fmly) **FACILITIES:** STV Fishing Cycles available **CONF:** Thtr 100 Class 50 Board 50 **SERVICES:** Lift **PARKING:** 50 **NOTES:** No dogs **CARDS:**

CARRICKFERGUS, Co Antrim — Map 01 D5

★★66% Dobbins Inn
6-8 High St BT38 7AP
☎ 028 9335 1905 📠 028 9335 1905
e-mail: info@dobbinsinnhotel.co.uk
Dir: *from Belfast take M2, keep right at rdbt follow A2 to Carrickfergus, turn left opp castle*
Colourful window boxes adorn the front of this popular inn, near the ancient castle and other attractions. Public areas are furnished to a modern standard without compromising the inn's original character. Bedrooms are comfortable and well equipped.
ROOMS: 15 en suite (2 fmly) s £35-£44; d £50-£62 (incl. bkfst) * LB **FACILITIES:** entertainment **NOTES:** Closed 25-26 Dec & 1 Jan RS Good Friday **CARDS:**

CARRICKMACROSS, Co Monaghan — Map 01 C4

★★★★75% ❀❀ Nuremore
☎ 042 9661438 📠 042 9661853
e-mail: nuremore@eircom.net
Dir: *3km S of Carrickmacross, on main Dublin/Derry road*
Overlooking a lake and 18-hole golf course, this hotel is a quiet retreat with excellent facilities. This Victorian mansion has spacious public areas and a wide variety of indoor and outdoor leisure and sporting facilities for the energetic. A very good restaurant serves imaginative dishes. A dedicated team ensures a pleasant visit to this friendly hotel.

continued

ROOMS: 72 en suite No smoking in 11 bedrooms s IR£100-IR£125; d IR£150-IR£200 (incl. bkfst) * LB **FACILITIES:** STV Indoor swimming (H) Golf 18 Tennis (grass) Fishing Squash Snooker Sauna Solarium Gym Putting green Jacuzzi/spa Beauty treatments Aromatherapy Xmas **CONF:** Thtr 250 Class 55 Board 30 Del from IR£115 * **SERVICES:** Lift air con **PARKING:** 200 **NOTES:** No dogs (ex guide dogs) **CARDS:**

CASHEL, Co Galway — Map 01 A4

Premier Collection

★★★❀❀ Cashel House
☎ 095 31001 📠 095 31077
e-mail: info@cashel-house-hotel.com
Dir: *turn S off N59, hotel 1.5km W of Recess*
Award-winning gardens are the setting for this gracious country house hotel. The comfortable lounges have turf fires and antique furnishings. The restaurant offers local produce such as Connemara lamb. Bedrooms are appealing and luxury suites are available.
ROOMS: 32 en suite (4 fmly) s IR£60.75-IR£90; d IR£121.50-IR£180 (incl. bkfst) * LB **FACILITIES:** STV Outdoor swimming Tennis (hard) Fishing Riding Xmas **PARKING:** 40 **NOTES:** No children 5yrs Closed 4 Jan-4 Feb **CARDS:**

★★★77% ❀❀ *Zetland Country House*
Cashel Bay
☎ 095 31111 📠 095 31117
e-mail: zetland@iol.ie
Dir: *N59 from Galway towards Clifden, turn right after recess onto R340, after approx 4m turn left onto R341, hotel is 1m ahead on right*
Set in very attractive gardens featuring unusual rock formations, flowers, shrubs and woodland, this peaceful country house overlooks Cashel Bay. Public areas include a fine lounge and reading room as well as a smart cocktail bar. Many of the bedrooms have sea or garden views. Warm hospitality is matched by good food and service.
ROOMS: 19 en suite (10 fmly) **FACILITIES:** STV Tennis (hard) Fishing Snooker Croquet lawn **CONF:** Board 20 **PARKING:** 32 **NOTES:** No smoking in restaurant Closed Nov-9 Apr **CARDS:**

CASHEL, Co Tipperary — Map 01 C3

★★★70% Cashel Palace Hotel
☎ 062 62707 📠 062 61521
e-mail: reception@cashel-palace.ie
Dir: *in centre of Cashel town*
The Rock of Cashel, floodlit at night, forms a dramatic backdrop to this fascinating hotel which was originally built in the 18th century as a bishop's palace. An enchanting drawing room leads to the

continued

gardens, which marks the start of a private walk to the Rock of Cashel. There is a cosy library and a bar adjoining the Buttery Restaurant. Bedrooms are all comfortable.
ROOMS: 13 en suite 10 annexe en suite (8 fmly) No smoking in 5 bedrooms s IR£90-IR£105; d IR£110-IR£225 (incl. bkfst) * LB **FACILITIES:** STV Fishing Private path walk to the Rock of Cashel ch fac Xmas **CONF:** Thtr 80 Class 45 Board 40 **SERVICES:** Lift **PARKING:** 35 **NOTES:** No dogs (ex guide dogs) **CARDS:**

CASTLEBAR, Co Mayo — Map 01 B4

★★★67% Breaffy House

☎ 094 22033 Fax 094 22276
e-mail: breaffyhotel@anu.ie
Dir: *on N60 in direction of Tuam and Galway*
This 19th-century manor house stands in 100 acres of leafy woodlands. Inside there are several lounges and a wing of luxuriously appointed bedrooms, which are an equal match for the attractively decorated rooms in the original house. Other facilities include a restaurant, a choice of bars and conference suites.
ROOMS: 59 en suite (3 fmly) s IR£74-IR£87; d IR£116-IR£137 (incl. bkfst) * LB **FACILITIES:** STV Gym Croquet lawn Crazy golf **CONF:** Thtr 250 Class 150 Board 50 Del from IR£90 * **SERVICES:** Lift **PARKING:** 300 **NOTES:** No dogs (ex guide dogs) Closed 23-26 Dec Civ Wed 250 **CARDS:**

See advert on this page

★★67% *Welcome Inn*

☎ 094 22288 & 22054 Fax 094 21766
e-mail: cb.welcome@mayo-ireland.ie
Dir: *take N5 to Castlebar situated near the town centre via ring road & rdbts passed the Church of the Holy Rosary*
This town centre hotel offers a range of modern facilities behind its Tudor frontage, including a banqueting/conference centre. Bedrooms are well equipped and there is a night club with disco on some evenings, as well as traditional music nights in the summer.
ROOMS: 40 en suite (5 fmly) **FACILITIES:** STV entertainment **CONF:** Thtr 500 Class 350 **SERVICES:** Lift **PARKING:** 100 **NOTES:** No dogs (ex guide dogs) Closed 23-25 Dec **CARDS:**

CASTLECONNELL, Co Limerick — Map 01 B3

★★★66% ❁ Castle Oaks House

☎ 061 377666 Fax 061 377717
e-mail: info@castle-oaks.com
Dir: *turn off N7 8km outside Limerick City. Hotel is 3km on left*
A fine old Georgian house with grounds reaching down to the River Shannon, set in the tiny village of Castleconnell. The hotel has been upgraded and guests can enjoy first class comfort in well equipped modern bedrooms. Facilities include river walks, good fishing and free use of a leisure centre.
ROOMS: 20 en suite (9 fmly) No smoking in 1 bedroom s IR£55-IR£64.90; d IR£72.60-IR£88 (incl. bkfst) * LB **FACILITIES:** STV Indoor swimming (H) Golf 9 Tennis (hard) Fishing Snooker Sauna Solarium Gym Jacuzzi/spa Angling centre entertainment **CONF:** Thtr 350 Class 95 Board 40 **PARKING:** 200 **NOTES:** No dogs (ex guide dogs) Closed 24-26 Dec **CARDS:**

CAVAN, Co Cavan — Map 01 C4

Popped the question? Hotels with Civ Wed in their entry are licensed for civil wedding ceremonies. Maximum numbers for the ceremony only are shown, e.g. Civ Wed 50

★★★65% ❁ Kilmore

Dublin Rd
☎ 049 4332288 Fax 049 4332458
e-mail: kilmore@quinn-hotels.com
Dir: *approx 3km from Cavan on N3*
Set on a hillside on the outskirts of Cavan, easily accessible from the main N3 route, this comfortable hotel features spacious public areas. Good food is served in the Annalee Restaurant, which is always appreciated by guests returning from fishing, golf, windsurfing or boating, all available nearby.
ROOMS: 39 en suite (17 fmly) s IR£38-IR£49; d IR£66-IR£78 (incl. bkfst) * LB **FACILITIES:** STV entertainment Xmas **CONF:** Thtr 300 Class 200 Board 60 **SERVICES:** air con **PARKING:** 450 **NOTES:** No dogs (ex guide dogs) **CARDS:**

CLIFDEN, Co Galway — Map 01 A4

C

Courtesy & Care Award

★★★77% ✿✿

Rock Glen Country House Hotel

MANOR HOUSE HOTELS

☎ 095 21035 & 21393 📠 095 21737
e-mail: rockglen@iol.ie
Dir: *N6 from Dublin to Galway, N57 from Galway to Clifden*
A comfortable, converted 18th-century shooting lodge set in lovely grounds and gardens. Elegance abounds throughout the gracious drawing room, cocktail bar and restaurant. The admirable hosts and attentive staff hold the Courtesy and Care Award for Ireland 2000-2001, and the experience of good company and food make this peaceful retreat beguiling.
ROOMS: 26 en suite (2 fmly) s IR£100; d IR£135 (incl. bkfst) * LB **FACILITIES:** STV Tennis (hard) Snooker Croquet lawn Putting green entertainment **PARKING:** 50 **NOTES:** No smoking in restaurant Closed 21 Nov-14 Mar **CARDS:**

★★★76% ✿✿ *Abbeyglen Castle*

MANOR HOUSE HOTELS

Sky Rd
☎ 095 21201 📠 095 21797
e-mail: info@abbeyglen.ie
Dir: *take N59 from Galway to Clifden. Hotel is 1km from Clifden on the Sky Road*
Set in its own grounds with panoramic views over Clifden Bay, this friendly family-run hotel gives high priority to hospitality and good food. Musical evenings are held regularly in the cosy bar, with turf fires. Extensive grounds include a helipad.
ROOMS: 36 en suite No smoking in 10 bedrooms **FACILITIES:** STV Outdoor swimming (H) Tennis (hard) Snooker Sauna Putting green Jacuzzi/spa entertainment **CONF:** Thtr 100 Class 50 Board 40 **SERVICES:** Lift **PARKING:** 40 **NOTES:** Closed 11 Jan-1 Feb
CARDS:

★★★69% ✿✿ Ardagh

Ballyconneely Rd
☎ 095 21384 📠 095 21314
e-mail: ardaghhotel@eircom.net
Dir: *N59 Galway to Clifden, signposted for Ballyconneely*
A family-run hotel in a quiet location, the Ardagh is just over a mile from Clifden. The restaurant overlooks the bay and serves impressive food. Fine lounges take full advantage of the views of Ardbear Bay.
ROOMS: 21 en suite (2 fmly) s IR£65-IR£85; d IR£105-IR£115 (incl. bkfst) * LB **FACILITIES:** Pool table **PARKING:** 35 **NOTES:** No dogs Closed Nov-Mar **CARDS:**

★★★62% ✿ Alcock & Brown Hotel

☎ 095 21206 & 21086 📠 095 21842
e-mail: alcockandbrown@eircom.net
Dir: *Take N59 from Galway via Oughterard, hotel in centre of Clifden*
A comfortable town centre hotel. The bar and restaurant are inviting with particularly pleasant decor. The menu offers a wide range of good food with many fish specialities. The friendly, attentive staff offer good service.
ROOMS: 20 en suite s IR£45-IR£53; d IR£62-IR£78 (incl. bkfst) * LB **FACILITIES:** entertainment **NOTES:** No dogs (ex guide dogs) Closed 23-25 Dec **CARDS:**

CLONAKILTY, Co Cork — Map 01 B2

★★★★75% ✿✿
The Lodge & Spa at Inchydoney Island

☎ 023 33143 📠 023 35229
e-mail: reservations@inchydoneyisland.com
Dir: *follow N71 West Cork road to Clonakilty, at entry rdbt in Clonakilty take 2nd exit and follow signs to Lodge and Spa*
A former winner of Hotel of the Year for Ireland this luxurious hotel enjoys a stunning location on the coastline, with steps down to a sandy beach. Bedrooms are furnished in a warm, contemporary style, most have sea views. The lounge is superb and there is a cocktail bar with a patio and also a library. The restaurant serves an imaginative menu.
ROOMS: 67 en suite (24 fmly) No smoking in 17 bedrooms s IR£100-IR£110; d IR£160-IR£180 * LB **FACILITIES:** STV Indoor swimming (H) Fishing Riding Snooker Sauna Gym Pool table Jacuzzi/spa Thalassotherapy spa Xmas **CONF:** Thtr 300 Class 150 Board 100 Del from IR£125 * **SERVICES:** Lift **PARKING:** 200 **NOTES:** No dogs
CARDS:

CLONMEL, Co Tipperary — Map 01 C2

★★★73% *Minella*

☎ 052 22388 📠 052 24381
e-mail: hotelminella@tinet.ie
This family-run hotel, set in nine acres of well kept grounds on the banks of the river Suir, offers comfort and courteous service. Facilities include a cocktail bar and lounge overlooking the gardens and a leisure centre and putting greens. Bedrooms are all tastefully decorated and well equipped, some have jacuzzis.
ROOMS: 70 en suite (8 fmly) No smoking in 16 bedrooms
FACILITIES: STV Indoor swimming (H) Outdoor swimming (H) Tennis (hard) Fishing Sauna Gym Croquet lawn Putting green Jacuzzi/spa Aerobics room **CONF:** Thtr 500 Class 300 Board 20 **PARKING:** 100 **NOTES:** No dogs Closed 24-26 Dec **CARDS:**

COBH, Co Cork — Map 01 B2

★★★67% Watersedge

Yacht Club Quay
☎ 021 815566 📠 021 812011
e-mail: watersedge@eircom.net
Dir: *follow road signs for Cobh Heritage Centre*
This delightful property is situated on the waterfront beside the Heritage Centre and railway station. Guests can enjoy spectacular views of the harbour from the restaurant. Spacious bedrooms are furnished to a high standard and four ground floor rooms have their own balconies.
ROOMS: 19 en suite (6 fmly) No smoking in 6 bedrooms s IR£45-IR£55; d IR£70-IR£130 (incl. bkfst) * LB **PARKING:** 25 **NOTES:** No dogs
CARDS:

COLLOONEY, Co Sligo
Map 01 B5

★★★62% Markree Castle
☎ 071 67800 071 67840
e-mail: markree@iol.ie
Dir: *turn off N4 at Collooney rdbt, take R290 towards Dromahaire. Just north of junct with N17, 11km S of Sligo, hotel gates on right hand side after 1km*
This magnificent castle dates back to 1640 and has all the grandeur expected in such a great building. Considerable restoration work has taken place to transform this historic building into a hotel and the imposing Knockmuldowney Restaurant gives a taste of the style.
ROOMS: 30 en suite (2 fmly) s IR£65-IR£75; d IR£111-IR£121 (incl. bkfst) * LB **FACILITIES:** Riding Croquet lawn **CONF:** Thtr 50 Class 30 Board 20 **SERVICES:** Lift **PARKING:** 60 **NOTES:** No smoking in restaurant Closed 24-26 Dec **CARDS:**

CORK, Co Cork
Map 01 B2

Premier Collection

★★★★ Hayfield Manor
Perrott Av, College Rd
☎ 021 315600 021 316839
e-mail: enquiries@hayfieldmanor.ie
Dir: *1m W of Cork city centre-head for N22 to Killarney, turn left at University Gates off Western Rd. Turn right into College Rd, left into Perrott Ave*
Hayfield Manor offers privacy and seclusion, within a mile of Cork city centre. This fine hotel is part of a grand two acre estate and gardens and has every modern comfort. It maintains an atmosphere of tranquillity and the bedrooms are spacious, containing many thoughtful extras. Guests also have access to the exclusive health club. Public rooms feature elegant architecture, carefully combined with fine furnishings and real fires to create an atmosphere of intimacy. The Manor Room restaurant serves dishes from the interesting carte.
ROOMS: 87 en suite No smoking in 25 bedrooms s IR£140-IR£180; d IR£180-IR£280 (incl. bkfst) LB **FACILITIES:** STV Indoor swimming (H) Gym Jacuzzi/spa Steam room entertainment Xmas
CONF: Thtr 100 Class 60 Board 40 Del from IR£175 *
SERVICES: Lift air con **PARKING:** 100 **NOTES:** No dogs (ex guide dogs) **CARDS:**

See advert on this page

Early start? Hotels at all star levels should provide in-room alarm clocks and/or alarm calls.

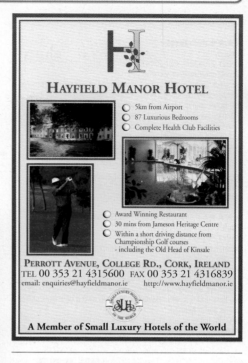

★★★★76% The Kingsley Hotel
Victoria Cross
☎ 021 4800500 021 4800527
e-mail: resv@kingsleyhotel.com
Situated on the banks of the river Lee, the Kingsley is a luxurious hotel with good facilities. Bedrooms are excellent and feature several thoughtful extra touches. Guests have use of a comfortable lounge and library. Contemporary and informal trends are evident in the bar and restaurant.
ROOMS: 69 en suite No smoking in 36 bedrooms s IR£95-IR£120; d IR£180-IR£300 (incl. bkfst) * LB **FACILITIES:** STV Indoor swimming (H) Fishing Sauna Solarium Gym Jacuzzi/spa **CONF:** Thtr 80 Class 50 Board 32 **SERVICES:** Lift air con **PARKING:** 250
CARDS:

★★★★70% Rochestown Park Hotel
Rochestown Rd, Douglas
☎ 021 892233 021 892178
e-mail: info@rochestownpark.com
Dir: *from Lee Tunnel, 2nd exit left off dual carriageway. Continue for 400mtrs, then first left and right at small rdbt. Hotel 600mtrs on right*
Set amongst chestnut trees in mature gardens, this hotel has much to offer, including an excellent Conference & Exhibition Centre. Staff are pleasant and professional and a variety of room styles are available including suites. Peacefully set in lovely gardens on the south side of the city, yet also convenient for the airport and ferries.
ROOMS: 115 en suite (17 fmly) s IR£70.88-IR£90; d IR£101.25-IR£123.75 (incl. bkfst) * **FACILITIES:** STV Indoor swimming (H) Sauna Solarium Gym Jacuzzi/spa Thalasso therapy & beauty centre **CONF:** Thtr 800 Class 360 Board 100 Del from IR£103 * **SERVICES:** Lift **PARKING:** 600
NOTES: No dogs Closed 25-26 Dec **CARDS:**

CORK, continued

★★★★ 69% Jurys

Western Rd
☎ 021 276622 🖷 021 274477
e-mail: enquires@jurys.com
Dir: *close to city centre, on main Killarney road as you exit Cork, past the court-house on the right hand side, situated 500yrds on the left*
This hotel enjoys a riverside setting near to the University and within walking distance of the city centre. The public areas have a fresh outlook, with a comfortable library lounge, in addition to leisure and conference facilities. Bedrooms are well equipped.
ROOMS: 185 en suite (23 fmly) No smoking in 48 bedrooms s IR£82-IR£125; d IR£95-IR£145 * LB **FACILITIES:** STV Indoor swimming (H) Outdoor swimming (H) Squash Sauna Gym Jacuzzi/spa ch fac Xmas **CONF:** Thtr 700 Class 400 Board 150 **SERVICES:** Lift **PARKING:** 231 **NOTES:** No dogs (ex guide dogs) Closed 25-27 Dec
CARDS:

★★★★ 65% *Fitzpatrick Silver Springs*

Tivoli
☎ 021 507533 🖷 021 507641
Dir: *from N8 south-bound take Silver Springs exit. Turn right across overpass - hotel is on right*
Overlooking the River Lee, this hotel has excellent convention facilities and a fully equipped indoor leisure centre. The public areas have all been refurbished and include a spacious lounge, two bars and a stylish restaurant. There is also a nine-hole golf course and a helipad.
ROOMS: 109 en suite (50 fmly) No smoking in 4 bedrooms
FACILITIES: STV Indoor swimming (H) Golf 9 Tennis (hard) Squash Snooker Sauna Gym Pool table Jacuzzi/spa Aerobics classes entertainment **CONF:** Thtr 800 Class 500 Board 50 **SERVICES:** Lift **PARKING:** 450 **NOTES:** Closed 24-25 Dec **CARDS:**

★★★ 69% *Imperial Hotel*

South Mall
☎ 021 274040 🖷 021 275375
This fine hotel has a hospitable and welcoming atmosphere. The reception rooms are on a grand scale, particularly the foyer, with its beautiful crystal chandelier and paintings. Bedrooms are of a high standard and Clouds Restaurant is earning a reputation for good food.
ROOMS: 98 en suite (12 fmly) **FACILITIES:** STV entertainment **CONF:** Thtr 400 Class 200 Board 150 **SERVICES:** Lift **PARKING:** 40 **NOTES:** No dogs (ex guide dogs) Closed 24 Dec-2 Jan
CARDS:

★★★ 67% Ambassador

Military Hill, St Lukes
☎ 021 4551996 🖷 021 4551997
e-mail: reservations@ambassadorhotel.ie
Dir: *city centre, just off Wellington Road*
Many pleasing features distinguish this sandstone and granite building which dates from the 19th century. Today it is a fine hotel with commanding views of the city and a feeling of space throughout. Some bedrooms have balconies, all are well equipped. Public areas include a cocktail lounge, bar and restaurant.
ROOMS: 60 en suite (8 fmly) No smoking in 8 bedrooms s IR£65-IR£80; d IR£85-IR£100 (incl. bkfst) **FACILITIES:** STV entertainment **CONF:** Thtr 80 Class 40 Board 35 **SERVICES:** Lift **PARKING:** 60 **NOTES:** Closed 24-25 Dec **CARDS:**

★★★ 65% *Arbutus Lodge*

Middle Glanmire Rd, Montenotte
☎ 021 501237 🖷 021 502893
e-mail: arbutus@iol.ie
This family-run period house, set above terraced gardens, overlooks the city. Facilities include comfortable lounges, a bar, an elegant restaurant, a pub and a banqueting suite. Guests can also enjoy the patio terrace and tennis courts.
ROOMS: 16 en suite **FACILITIES:** STV Tennis (hard) **CONF:** Thtr 100 Class 60 Board 30 **PARKING:** 36 **NOTES:** No dogs (ex guide dogs) Closed 24-28 Dec RS Sun **CARDS:**

★★★ 65% *Metropole Hotel & Leisure Centre*

MacCurtain St
☎ 021 508122 🖷 021 506450
e-mail: enq@metropoleh.com
Dir: *hotel is in the city centre located on MacCurtain St - leading to N25 main Dublin Rd*

This city centre hotel benefits from its comfortable and relaxing lounges and bar. Bedrooms vary in size and are well equipped and comfortable. There is a leisure centre which includes a supervised creche.
ROOMS: 98 en suite (3 fmly) No smoking in 6 bedrooms
FACILITIES: STV Indoor swimming (H) Snooker Sauna Solarium Gym Jacuzzi/spa entertainment **CONF:** Thtr 500 Class 180 Board 60 **SERVICES:** Lift **PARKING:** 254 **NOTES:** No dogs (ex guide dogs)
CARDS:

★★★ 58% Jurys Inn

Anderson's Quay
☎ 021 276444 🖷 021 276144
e-mail: enquiry@jurys.com
Dir: *Located in the city centre, on river beside eastern approach to the city from Dublin and South link road to airport*
Attractively decorated in a modern style, this hotel overlooks the River Lee and is just a short walk from the main street. Rooms can accommodate three adults or two adults and two children. The restaurant is informal in style and there is also a lively pub.
ROOMS: 133 en suite No smoking in 32 bedrooms s IR£60-IR£89; d IR£60-IR£89 * **FACILITIES:** STV entertainment **CONF:** Thtr 35 Class 20 Board 20 **SERVICES:** Lift **PARKING:** 22 **NOTES:** No dogs (ex guide dogs) Closed 24-26 Dec **CARDS:**

★★ 60% *Hotel Ibis*

Lee Tunnel Roundabout, Dunkettle
☎ 021 354354 🖷 021 354202
e-mail: H0580@accor-hotels.com
Dir: *situated off the N8 at Lee Tunnel rdbt, turn left in direction Waterford, at next rdbt turn left, hotel on left*
This hotel is furnished to well established group standards which

continued

offer comfortable, modern facilities at very affordable prices. The 24 hour snack service is a popular feature.
ROOMS: 100 en suite **FACILITIES:** STV **CONF:** Thtr 70 Class 40 Board 35 **SERVICES:** Lift **PARKING:** 100 **CARDS:**

Travelodge
Blackash
☎ 01 21310722 01 21310707
Dir: *at rdbt junc of South Ring Road/Kinsale Rd R600*

Travelodge

This modern building offers accommodation in smart, spacious and well equipped bedrooms, all with en suite bathrooms. Refreshments may be taken at the nearby family restaurant. For further details and the Travelodge phone number, consult the Hotel Groups page.
ROOMS: 40 en suite

COURTMACSHERRY, Co Cork Map 01 B2

★★64% Courtmacsherry
☎ 023 46198 023 46137
e-mail: cmv@indigo.ie
Dir: *take M71 to Bandon, R602 to Timoleague. From Timoleague head for Courtmacsherry, hotel is by the beach at the far end of the town*
This Georgian house is set in attractive grounds near the beach. The hotel is family-run, and its main selling points are the good quality meals served in the kitchen and a riding school available to all ages. Fishing and tennis are also available.
ROOMS: 12 rms (10 en suite) (1 fmly) s IR£25-IR£40; d IR£50-IR£70 (incl. bkfst) * LB **FACILITIES:** STV Tennis (hard & grass) Riding Shore fishing from hotel beach **PARKING:** 60 **NOTES:** Closed Oct-Mar
CARDS:

COURTOWN HARBOUR, Co Wexford Map 01 D3

★★68% *Courtown*
☎ 055 25210 & 25108 055 25304
Dir: *8km off N11*
Situated in the town centre, near to the beach and an 18 hole golf course, this refurbished hotel offers relaxing public areas including a comfortable lounge and spacious bar on two levels. Facilities include a restaurant and an indoor swimming pool.
ROOMS: 21 en suite (4 fmly) **FACILITIES:** Indoor swimming (H) Golf 18 Tennis (hard & grass) Fishing Squash Riding Sauna Solarium Gym Jacuzzi/spa Steam room Massage Crazy golf entertainment ch fac
PARKING: 10 **NOTES:** No dogs (ex guide dogs) Closed Nov-16 Mar
CARDS:

★★65% *Bay View*
☎ 055 25307 055 25576
e-mail: bayview@iol.ie
Overlooking the beach and harbour, this family-run hotel complex offers a range of leisure facilities. Many of the bedrooms have sea views.
ROOMS: 17 en suite (12 fmly) **FACILITIES:** Tennis (hard) Squash
PARKING: 30 **NOTES:** No dogs (ex guide dogs) Closed Nov-14 Mar
CARDS:

CRAWFORDSBURN, Co Down Map 01 D5

★★★71% *Old Inn*
15 Main St BT19 1JH
☎ 028 91853255 028 91852775
Dir: *A2, passing Belfast Airport and Holywood, 3m past Holywood sign for The Old Inn, 100yds turn L at lights, follow rd into village, hotel is on left*
Enjoying a quiet rural setting not far from Belfast, the Old Inn is reputed to date back to 1614. Much original character has been retained in the public areas which include bars, a bistro and a restaurant. Bedrooms vary in size and in style, and include a range of deluxe rooms.
ROOMS: 33 en suite **FACILITIES:** STV **CONF:** Thtr 120 Class 27 Board 40 **PARKING:** 65 **NOTES:** No dogs (ex guide dogs)
CARDS:

CROSSHAVEN, Co Cork Map 01 B2

★★65% *Whispering Pines Hotel*
☎ 021 831843 & 831448 021 831679
There is something inviting about this comfortable hotel with its sun lounge and bar overlooking the river. The hospitality is warming and the kitchen caters well for all its guests, particularly anglers, for whom fishing boats and equipment are available for hire. Transfers from Cork Airport can be arranged if required.
ROOMS: 15 en suite (6 fmly) **FACILITIES:** STV Own angling boats fish daily **PARKING:** 40 **NOTES:** No dogs (ex guide dogs)
CARDS:

DINGLE, Co Kerry Map 01 A2

★★★72% *Dingle Skellig Hotel*
☎ 066 51144 066 51501
e-mail: dsk@iol.ie
On the outskirts of the town, overlooking the bay, this modern hotel has bright, airy bedrooms and pleasant public areas, making it an excellent base for holidaymakers.
ROOMS: 115 en suite **FACILITIES:** STV Indoor swimming (H) Tennis (hard) Solarium Gym Pool table Jacuzzi/spa entertainment ch fac
CONF: Thtr 250 Class 140 Board 80 **SERVICES:** Lift **NOTES:** No dogs (ex guide dogs) Closed Jan-mid Feb **CARDS:**

DONEGAL, Co Donegal Map 01 B5

★★★74% *Harvey's Point Country*
Lough Eske
☎ 073 22208 073 22352
Dir: *from Donegal, take N56 then 1st right signposted Loch Eske/Harvey's Point. Hotel is approx 10 mins drive*
This modern hotel is in a superb lakeside location on Lough Eske, and was built with guests' peace and comfort in mind. There are spacious public rooms, excellent cuisine and a wide range of facilities.
ROOMS: 20 en suite 12 annexe en suite **FACILITIES:** STV Tennis (hard) Fishing entertainment **CONF:** Thtr 400 Class 400 Board 50
PARKING: 200 **NOTES:** No children 10yrs Closed weekdays Nov-Mar
CARDS:

★★★63% *Abbey*
The Diamond
☎ 073 21014 073 21014
Dir: *located in centre of Donegal Down - N15 from Sligo*
This friendly hotel is situated in the centre of the town overlooking the square. The Abbey Restaurant is an inviting place to eat lunch and dinner and hot food is available all day in the coffee shop. The lounge bar has a patio adjoining and there is nightly entertainment. Bedrooms are comfortable and well appointed.
ROOMS: 49 en suite (5 fmly) **FACILITIES:** STV **SERVICES:** Lift air con
PARKING: 40 **NOTES:** Closed 25-27 Dec **CARDS:**

TV dinner? Room service at three stars and above.

DOOLIN, Co Clare
Map 01 B3

★★★64% Aran View House
Coast Rd
☎ 065 7074061 & 7074420 065 7074540
e-mail: aranview@gofree.indigo.ie
Situated in 100 acres of rolling farmland and commanding panoramic views of the Aran Islands, this hotel offers attractive and comfortably furnished accommodation. Staff are welcoming, the atmosphere is convivial, and there is traditional music and song in the bar three times a week.
ROOMS: 13 en suite 6 annexe en suite (1 fmly) s IR£45-IR£50; d IR£70-IR£80 (incl. bkfst) * LB **FACILITIES:** entertainment **PARKING:** 40 **NOTES:** Closed 1 Nov-1 Apr **CARDS:**

See advert on opposite page

DROGHEDA, Co Louth
Map 01 D4

★★★61% *Boyne Valley Hotel & Country Club*
Stameen, Dublin Rd
☎ 041 9837737 041 9839188
Dir: *N1 towards Belfast, north of Dublin Airport on right - up Avenue before town of Droghedah*
This historic mansion stands in 16 acres of gardens and woodlands on the outskirts of Drogheda. Much emphasis is placed here on good food and attentive service and all the accommodation is well furnished and provides high standards of comfort. There are extensive amenities including a leisure centre.
ROOMS: 35 en suite (4 fmly) **FACILITIES:** STV Indoor swimming (H) Tennis (hard) Sauna Solarium Gym Putting green Jacuzzi/spa Pitch & putt entertainment **CONF:** Thtr 150 Class 100 Board 25 **PARKING:** 200 **NOTES:** No dogs (ex guide dogs) **CARDS:**

DUBLIN, Co Dublin
Map 01 D4
see also Portmarnock

Hotel of the Year

★★★★★79% The Merrion Hotel
Upper Merrion St 21
☎ 01 6030600 01 6030700
e-mail: info@merrionhotel.com
Dir: *situated at the top of Upper Merrion Street on the left hand side, beyond Government buildings which are on the right hand side*
The understated façade of four Grade I listed Georgian town houses belies the splendid interiors of this gracious city centre hotel, chosen as Hotel of the Year for Ireland. The garden suite bedrooms encircle the 18th-century style gardens. Luxurious surroundings, fine attention to detail, good cuisine and service, and friendly, efficient staff contribute to what makes the Merrion a hotel with a special ambience. There are two bars and two restaurants. The Mornington Brasserie offers both traditional and contemporary cuisine and an excellent gourmet restaurant provides a memorable dining occasion, early reservations advised. Additional features include conference/banqueting suites, tethra spa, beauty salons and valet parking.
ROOMS: 145 en suite No smoking in 65 bedrooms s IR£210-IR£250; d IR£250-IR£275 * LB **FACILITIES:** STV Indoor swimming (H) Sauna Gym **CONF:** Thtr 60 Class 25 Board 25 Del IR£275 * **SERVICES:** Lift air con **PARKING:** 60 **NOTES:** No dogs (ex guide dogs) **CARDS:**

★★★★★68% *Radisson SAS St Helen's Hotel*
Stillorgan Rd, Blackrock
☎ 01 2186000 01 2186010
Dir: *from city centre take N11 due S, Hotel 4km on left hand side of dual carriageway*
A fine 18th-century mansion, with many period features, including a magnificent Italian marble fireplace in the lounge. The Orangerie is popular for drinks and there are two restaurants. Many bedrooms have views of the lovely terraced gardens and suites and penthouse suites are available, as well as rooms for disabled guests.
ROOMS: 151 en suite No smoking in 39 bedrooms **FACILITIES:** STV Snooker Gym Croquet lawn Beauty salon entertainment **CONF:** Thtr 350 Class 210 Board 70 **SERVICES:** Lift air con **PARKING:** 230 **NOTES:** No dogs (ex guide dogs) **CARDS:**

Premier Collection

★★★★ The Clarence
6-8 Wellington Quay
☎ 01 4070800 01 4070820
e-mail: reservations@theclarence.ie
Dir: *from O'Connell Bridge, drive westwards along quays, through the 1st set of traffic lights (at the Ha'penny Bridge) the hotel is 500mtrs further on*
The Clarence is an individual and very tasteful hotel offering richly furnished bedrooms. For sheer luxury, the two bedroom penthouse suite is outstanding. Public areas include a long gallery with luxurious sofas. The bar is smart and the restaurant serves fine cuisine.
ROOMS: 50 en suite d IR£195-IR£210 * **FACILITIES:** STV **CONF:** Thtr 50 Class 24 Board 30 **SERVICES:** Lift **NOTES:** No dogs (ex guide dogs) **CARDS:**

Fancy a Singapore Sling? Bar staff in five star hotels should be skilled cocktail mixers.

★★★★75% Conrad International

Earlsfort Ter
☎ 01 6765555 01 6765424
e-mail: info@conrad-international.ie
Dir: *just off St.Stephen's Green*

The National Concert Hall stands opposite this hotel in central Dublin. Facilities include two restaurants, the Alexandra and a less formal brasserie which offers good value menus. The Alfie Byrnes Dublin Pub and the lobby lounge are popular. Bedrooms are spacious, especially the suites.

ROOMS: 191 en suite No smoking in 60 bedrooms s fr IR£205; d fr IR£230 * LB **FACILITIES:** STV Gym Xmas **CONF:** Thtr 320 Class 150 Board 75 **SERVICES:** Lift air con **PARKING:** 80 **NOTES:** No dogs (ex guide dogs) **CARDS:**

★★★★74% The Herbert Park Hotel

Ballsbridge
☎ 01 6672200 01 6672595
e-mail: reservations@herbertparkhotel.ie
Dir: *2m from city centre Dublin*

Contemporary style bedrooms have extras such as air-conditioning, mini-bars and safes. The marble tiled foyer leads to the Terrace Lounge, restaurant and bar. The Mezzanine lounge is for residents only and the Pavilion restaurant has views of the park. Executive suites and rooms, conference facilities and a fitness suite are also available.

ROOMS: 153 en suite (4 fmly) No smoking in 30 bedrooms s fr IR£160; d fr IR£195 * LB **FACILITIES:** STV Gym Located off Herbert Park entertainment **CONF:** Thtr 100 Class 55 Board 50 Del from IR£205 * **SERVICES:** Lift air con **PARKING:** 80 **NOTES:** No dogs (ex guide dogs) **CARDS:**

★★★★72% The Fitzwilliam

St Stephen's Green
☎ 01 4787000 01 4787878
e-mail: enq@fitzwilliamh.com
Dir: *located in city centre on St Stephen's Green, adjacent to the top of Grafton Street*

Contemporary, elegant, Conran designed luxury hotel, overlooking St Stephen's Green. The hotel features a distinctive foyer lounge, bar and award-winning restaurant. Stylish bedrooms, with excellent bathrooms, are equipped with modern facilities and some have park views and balconies. Staff are friendly, professional and helpful.

ROOMS: 130 en suite No smoking in 31 bedrooms s IR£195-IR£325; d IR£220-IR£475 * LB **FACILITIES:** STV Xmas **CONF:** Thtr 80 Class 50 Board 35 Del from IR£270 * **SERVICES:** Lift **PARKING:** 85 **NOTES:** No dogs (ex guide dogs) **CARDS:**

★★★★72% ***Jurys Hotel Dublin***

Pembroke Rd, Ballsbridge
☎ 01 6605000 01 6605540
e-mail: bookings@jurys.com
Dir: *from Dun Laighaire, follow signs for city to Merrion Rd, Ballsbridge & Pembroke Rd, hotel is at intersection of Pembroke Rd and Northumberland Rd*

This establishment has two identities: Jurys Hotel and The Towers at Jurys. The first is large and popular, boasting several restaurants and bars, as well as good conference and leisure facilities. The Towers specialises in discreet luxury, with spacious bedrooms and private suites. The complex is the flagship of the Jurys chain.

ROOMS: 294 en suite (27 fmly) No smoking in 150 bedrooms **FACILITIES:** Indoor swimming (H) Outdoor swimming (H) Sauna Gym Jacuzzi/spa Hairdresser Beauty Salon with Masseuse **CONF:** Thtr 850 Class 450 Board 100 **SERVICES:** Lift **PARKING:** 280 **NOTES:** No dogs (ex guide dogs) **CARDS:**

DUBLIN, continued

★★★★ 71%

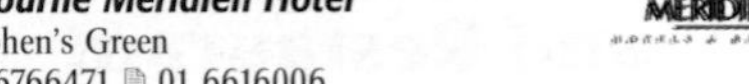

Shelbourne Meridien Hotel

St Stephen's Green
☎ 01 6766471 🖷 01 6616006
Dir: *in city centre*

A Dublin landmark since 1824, with strong literary and historical links, this elegant Georgian hotel boasts gracious reception rooms, a choice of restaurants, a leisure centre and popular bars. Bedrooms are smart, well appointed and comfortable.
ROOMS: 164 en suite (3 fmly) No smoking in 9 bedrooms
FACILITIES: Beauty Salon **CONF:** Thtr 400 Class 180 Board 60
SERVICES: Lift **PARKING:** 36 **CARDS:**

See advert on opposite page

★★★★ 69% Gresham

O'Connel St
☎ 01 8746881 🖷 01 8787175
e-mail: ryan@indigo.ie
Dir: *on O'Connel St, just off M1 close to the GPO*

A commitment to traditional standards of hotel keeping is evident at the Gresham Hotel. Bedrooms are well equipped and there is a foyer lounge serving snacks and afternoon teas. There is also the Aberdeen restaurant and 24-hour room service.
ROOMS: 288 en suite (4 fmly) No smoking in 26 bedrooms s IR£110-IR£200; d IR£130-IR£200 * LB **FACILITIES:** STV Gym Xmas
CONF: Thtr 350 Class 200 Board 100 Del from IR£180 * **SERVICES:** Lift air con **PARKING:** 150 **NOTES:** No dogs (ex guide dogs)
CARDS:

See advert on opposite page

★★★★ 68% *Burlington*

Upper Leeson St
☎ 01 6605222 🖷 01 6603172
Close to the city, this comfortable hotel features well appointed bedrooms, with some superior executive rooms available. Public areas include the smart Diplomat restaurant and a residents bar, in addition to the popular Buck Mulligan's Dublin pub.

continued

ROOMS: 526 en suite (6 fmly) No smoking in 95 bedrooms
FACILITIES: STV Use of facilities at fitness club **CONF:** Thtr 1500 Class 650 Board 40 **SERVICES:** Lift **PARKING:** 400 **NOTES:** No dogs (ex guide dogs) **CARDS:**

★★★★ 64% The Plaza Hotel

Belgard Rd, Tallaght 24
☎ 01 4624200 🖷 01 4624600
e-mail: reservations@plazahotel.ie
Dir: *6m from city centre, at S end of M50 motorway*
Contemporary in design, the Plaza is bright and spacious. The lounge and restaurant enjoy distant views of the Dublin mountains. Comfortable bedrooms are well equipped and include modem points. There is a roof garden, a traditional Irish pub and carvery and a sports-themed bar. Irish, French and Mediterranean influences are found in the Olive Tree restaurant.
ROOMS: 122 en suite (2 fmly) No smoking in 61 bedrooms s IR£70-IR£90; d IR£70-IR£90 * LB **FACILITIES:** STV entertainment **CONF:** Thtr 200 Class 150 Board 50 **SERVICES:** Lift air con **PARKING:** 520
NOTES: No dogs (ex guide dogs) Closed 24-29 Dec
CARDS:

★★★★ 64% Red Cow Morans

Red Cow Complex, Naas Rd
☎ 01 4593650 🖷 01 4591588
e-mail: reservations@morangroup.ie
Dir: *at junction of M50 & N7 Naas road on the city side of the motorway*
This smart hotel complex centres on the original Red Cow Inn, and its purpose-built extensions provide excellent conference facilities. Public areas are well furnished and strikingly decorated. Bedrooms are spacious, smartly presented and well equipped.
ROOMS: 123 en suite (5 fmly) No smoking in 44 bedrooms s IR£90-IR£115; d IR£140-IR£190 (incl. bkfst) * LB **FACILITIES:** STV entertainment **CONF:** Thtr 700 Class 520 Board 150 Del from IR£105 * **SERVICES:** Lift air con **PARKING:** 700 **NOTES:** No dogs (ex guide dogs) **CARDS:**

★★★★ 60% Clontarf Castle Hotel

Castle Av, Clontarf
☎ 01 8332321 🖷 01 8330418
e-mail: info@clontarfcastle.ie
Dir: *M1 towards town centre, right at whitehall church, left at T-junc, straight on at lights, right onto Castle Avenue, hotel entrance on right at roundabout*
Dating back to the 12th century, this Castle has been refurbished, and many of the features of previous eras have been combined with contemporary styled bedrooms, all well equipped and comfortable. Extensive banquet and conference facilities are available and a popular caberet runs from May to October. Modern cuisine is served in Templars Bistro.
ROOMS: 110 en suite (4 fmly) No smoking in 30 bedrooms s IR£100-IR£135; d IR£100-IR£160 * LB **FACILITIES:** STV Gym Xmas
CONF: Thtr 600 Class 250 Board 60 **SERVICES:** Lift **PARKING:** 130
NOTES: No dogs (ex guide dogs) Closed 24-25 Dec
CARDS:

★★★★ 60% Stillorgan Park

Stillorgan Rd
☎ 01 2881621 🖷 01 2831610
e-mail: sales@stillorganpark.com
Attractive decor and strong design are features of this recently rebuilt hotel. Comfortable public areas include a contemporary restaurant as well as conference and banqueting facilities. Staff are very friendly and helpful, and bedrooms are well equipped and have air conditioning.

continued

ROOMS: 100 en suite (12 fmly) No smoking in 16 bedrooms s IR£90-IR£105; d IR£110-IR£130 (incl. bkfst) * LB **FACILITIES:** STV Special rates for residents at Westwood Leisure Centre entertainment Xmas **CONF:** Thtr 180 Class 110 Board 50 Del from IR£105 * **SERVICES:** Lift air con **PARKING:** 350 **NOTES:** No dogs (ex guide dogs) **CARDS:**

★★★77% The Hibernian
Eastmoreland Place, Ballsbridge
☎ 01 6687666 01 6602655
e-mail: info@hibernianhotel.com
Dir: *turn right from Mespil Rd onto Baggot St Upper, then take 1st left into Eastmorelad Place/St Mary's Rd, the hotel is at the end on the left*

A previous winner of the AA Courtesy and Care Award, this hotel, an imposing building of magnificient architectural style, prides itself on the warmth of service it offers to guests. Real comfort and extra touches feature in the bedrooms and a country house ambience is abundant throughout. The Patrick Kavanagh

continued on p848

D

DUBLIN, continued

Restaurant serves high quality food and there is also a conservatory, a library and a cocktail lounge.
ROOMS: 40 en suite No smoking in 14 bedrooms s IR£120-IR£185; d IR£150-IR£185 * LB **FACILITIES:** STV **CONF:** Board 20 **SERVICES:** Lift **PARKING:** 18 **NOTES:** No dogs (ex guide dogs) Closed 24-27 Dec **CARDS:**

★★★70% Marine
Sutton Cross
☎ 01 8390000 01 8390442
Dir: *take rd from M1 towards Dublin City Centre, take second exit for Coolock, continue untilT-junct and turn left, after 1m hotel on right*
On the north shore of Dublin Bay, this hotel is situated in attractive gardens. The restaurant specialises in seafood. Bedrooms are attractively decorated and well equipped, and there is also a business centre. Public areas are comfortable and the hotel is only a 25 minute drive from Dublin airport.
ROOMS: 51 en suite (2 fmly) No smoking in 7 bedrooms s IR£110-IR£125; d IR£165-IR£180 (incl. bkfst) * LB **FACILITIES:** STV Indoor swimming (H) Sauna **CONF:** Thtr 220 Class 140 Board 40 Del from IR£115 * **SERVICES:** Lift **PARKING:** 150 **NOTES:** No dogs (ex guide dogs) Closed 25-27 Dec **CARDS:**

★★★70% *The Schoolhouse Hotel*
2-8 Northumberland Rd
☎ 01 6675014 01 6675015
e-mail: school@schoolhousehotel.iol.ie
Dir: *from N11 turn right at Lesson St Bridge, Avis on right. Through 2 sets of lights, pass Mespil Hotel, & turn left. Hotel 100yds on right*
A period red-brick building, dating from 1861, this hotel retains many original features. Satchels Restaurant and the Inkwell Bar continue the school theme. Bedrooms are inviting and feature custom-made oak furniture, which is very comfortable.
ROOMS: 31 en suite No smoking in 10 bedrooms **FACILITIES:** STV **CONF:** Class 15 Board 20 **SERVICES:** Lift air con **PARKING:** 21 **NOTES:** No dogs Closed 24-28 Dec **CARDS:**

★★★69% Longfield's Hotel
MANOR HOUSE HOTELS

Fitzwilliam St
☎ 01 6761367 01 6761542
e-mail: lfields@indigo.ie
Dir: *take Shelbourne Hotel exit from St Stephens Green, continue down Baggot St for 400m, turn left at Fitzwilliam St junct and Longfields is on the left*
This intimate town house hotel lies close to the city centre. Here, guests can enjoy good food and a relaxed atmosphere. An emphasis is placed on good service and hospitality.
ROOMS: 24 en suite s IR£70-IR£95; d IR£110-IR£160 (incl. bkfst) * LB **FACILITIES:** STV **SERVICES:** Lift **NOTES:** No dogs (ex guide dogs) RS 23-27 Dec **CARDS:**

See advert on opposite page

★★★69% *Posthouse Dublin*
Posthouse

Dublin Airport
☎ 01 8080500 01 8446002
e-mail: gm1767@forte-hotels.com
Dir: *the Hotel entrance is 1000yrds from main road entrance to Dublin airport, on the right hand side*
A large, modern hotel with a wide range of services and amenities, designed particularly for the business traveller. Bedrooms are smart, comfortable and well equipped.
ROOMS: 249 en suite (3 fmly) No smoking in 100 bedrooms **FACILITIES:** STV Free use of nearby sports club-ALSAA entertainment **CONF:** Thtr 130 Class 50 Board 40 **PARKING:** 250 **NOTES:** No dogs (ex guide dogs) Closed 24-25 Dec RS 31 Dec **CARDS:**

★★★68% Clarion Stephen's Hall All-Suite Hotel
CHOICE HOTELS EUROPE

The Earlsfort Centre, Lower Leeson St
☎ 01 6381111 01 6381122
e-mail: stephens@premgroup.ie
Dir: *from N11 into Dublin, hotel is on left after Hatch St junction, before St Stephens Green*
Adjacent to St Stephen's Green, this hotel offers a wide range of accommodation including penthouses, town houses, suites and studios, all with comfortable lounges and fully fitted kitchens. Some rooms include PCs with ISDN connections. There are also office facilities, room service and an inviting bistro.
ROOMS: 37 en suite (9 fmly) s fr IR£145; d fr IR£175 * LB **FACILITIES:** STV **CONF:** Thtr 30 Class 15 Board 20 **SERVICES:** Lift **PARKING:** 40 **NOTES:** No dogs (ex guide dogs) RS 24 Dec-4 Jan **CARDS:**

See advert on opposite page

★★★68% *Jurys Montrose*
Stillorgan Rd
☎ 01 2693311 01 2691164
Close to the campus of University College, this hotel offers smartly decorated, comfortable bedrooms. The public areas include good lounge space, a carvery bar and a more formal restaurant. The hotel is situated in a quiet suburb, a short distance from the city centre.
ROOMS: 179 en suite (6 fmly) No smoking in 12 bedrooms **FACILITIES:** STV entertainment **CONF:** Thtr 80 Class 40 Board 40 **SERVICES:** Lift **PARKING:** 150 **NOTES:** No dogs (ex guide dogs) **CARDS:**

★★★68% Jurys Tara Hotel
Merrion Rd 4
☎ 01 2694666 01 2691027
e-mail: michelle-bernie@jurys.com
Dir: *After RTE Studios on N11 turn right, turn right at St Vincents hospital, after St Marys home the hotel is on the right.*
The well equipped bedrooms of this hotel enjoy spectacular views of Dublin Bay and Howth Head. Attractively decorated public areas include a comfortable and relaxing foyer lounge, PJ Branagans Pub and a split-level conservatory restaurant.
ROOMS: 113 en suite (2 fmly) s fr IR£69 * **FACILITIES:** STV **CONF:** Thtr 300 Class 100 Board 40 **SERVICES:** Lift **PARKING:** 140 **NOTES:** No dogs (ex guide dogs) **CARDS:**

★★★67% Bewley's Hotel Ballsbridge
Merrion Rd, Ballsbridge
☎ 01 6681111 01 6681999
e-mail: res@bewleyshotel.com
Very conveniently located beside the RDS Showgrounds, this friendly hotel offers comfortable and good value accommodation. The informal restaurant is relaxed and serves interesting dishes, and there is a patio for summer dining.
ROOMS: 220 en suite (25 fmly) No smoking in 140 bedrooms s IR£69; d IR£69 * **FACILITIES:** STV **SERVICES:** Lift **PARKING:** 240 **NOTES:** No dogs Closed 24-26 Dec **CARDS:**

★★★67% Jurys Green Isle
Naas Rd
☎ 01 4593406 01 4592178
Dir: *on N7, 10km SW of the city centre*
The Green Isle Hotel lies on the southern outskirts of Dublin. Bedrooms, both standard and executive, are generously proportioned and stylishly furnished. Public areas include the Tower Restaurant, a spacious lobby, and Rosie O'Gradys Bar.

continued on p850

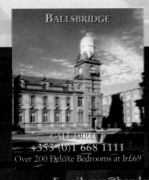

Longfield's Hotel, Dublin

DUBLIN, continued

ROOMS: 90 en suite s IR£66; d IR£66 * LB **FACILITIES:** STV **CONF:** Thtr 300 Class 100 Board 100 Del from IR£116 * **SERVICES:** Lift **PARKING:** 250 **NOTES:** No dogs (ex guide dogs) **CARDS:**

★★★67% *Jurys Skylon*

Drumcondra Rd
☎ 01 8379121 📠 01 8372778
In a convenient location, with easy access to the city centre, this hotel offers very well appointed bedrooms. There is a spacious lobby lounge and a comfortable bar. Good value dishes are served in the restaurant.
ROOMS: 92 en suite (10 fmly) **CONF:** Thtr 35 Class 20 Board 20 **SERVICES:** Lift **NOTES:** No dogs **CARDS:**

★★★66% Temple Bar

Fleet St, Temple Bar
☎ 01 6773333 📠 01 6773088
e-mail: templeb@iol.ie
Dir: *from Trinity College, head for O'Connell Bridge & take the 1st left onto Fleet St & the hotel is on the left hand side*
This stylish hotel lies in the heart of old Dublin and is ideally situated for experiencing the cultural life of the city. Comfortable, well equipped bedrooms are competitively priced, and good food is served throughout the day.
ROOMS: 129 en suite (6 fmly) No smoking in 10 bedrooms s IR£65-IR£100; d IR£80-IR£135 (incl. bkfst) * LB **FACILITIES:** STV **CONF:** Thtr 40 Class 40 Board 80 **SERVICES:** Lift **NOTES:** No dogs (ex guide dogs) Closed 24 & 25 Dec **CARDS:**

★★★65% *Bewley's Hotel Newlands Cross*

Newlands Cross, Naas Rd
☎ 01 464 0140 📠 01 464 0900
e-mail: res@bewleyshotels.com
Dir: *from M50 junct 9 take N7 Naas road, hotel is short distance from junc of N7 with Belgard Rd at Newlands Cross*

This hotel, on the outskirts of Dublin, has a bright and airy atmosphere. A spacious lobby and a residents' lounge are provided and there is a restaurant serving snacks during the day and more formal evening meals. Bedrooms are competitively priced and are furnished to a high standard.
ROOMS: 260 en suite (260 fmly) No smoking in 165 bedrooms **FACILITIES:** STV **CONF:** Board 20 **SERVICES:** Lift **PARKING:** 200 **NOTES:** No dogs (ex guide dogs) Closed 24-26 Dec
CARDS:

See advert on page 849

★★★65% ❀ Buswells

23-27 Molesworth St
☎ 01 6146500 📠 01 6762090
e-mail: quinn-hotels@sqgroup.com
Dir: *located on the corner of Molesworth St & Kildare St opposite Dail Eireann (Government Buildings)*
A popular rendezvous, Buswells is convenient for Dublin's main shopping and cultural attractions. Bedrooms are well equipped and attractively decorated. The club-style bar is the focal point and there are two restaurants.
ROOMS: 69 en suite (17 fmly) No smoking in 6 bedrooms s IR£101-IR£120; d IR£165 (incl. bkfst) * LB **FACILITIES:** Consession at nearby fitness club Complementary overnight parking **CONF:** Thtr 84 Class 30 Board 24 Del IR£145 * **SERVICES:** Lift **NOTES:** No dogs (ex guide dogs) Closed 25 & 26 Dec RS 24 Dec **CARDS:**

★★★64% Abberley Court

Belgard Rd, Tallaght
☎ 01 4596000 📠 01 4621000
e-mail: abberley@iol.ie
Dir: *opposite the Square town centre at the junction of the Belgard Rd and the Tallaght by-pass (N81)*
Located beside an excellent complex of shops, restaurants and a cinema, this hotel is very smartly furnished. Public areas include a lounge bar that serves food all day and the first floor Court Restaurant. There are sports facilities available nearby.
ROOMS: 40 en suite (34 fmly) No smoking in 2 bedrooms s IR£55-IR£79; d IR£70-IR£98 (incl. bkfst) * LB **CONF:** Thtr 200 Class 70 Board 70 **SERVICES:** Lift **PARKING:** 450 **NOTES:** No dogs (ex guide dogs) Closed 25 Dec **CARDS:**

★★★62% The Mercer Hotel

Mercer St Lower 2
☎ 01 4782179 📠 01 4780328
e-mail: tay@mercerhotel.ie
Dir: *St Stephens Green, at the shopping centre turn left down King Street, then left at end of road, hotel is 22m on the left*
A team of friendly staff create a pleasant atmosphere at this city centre hotel. Bedrooms are attractively decorated and well equipped, with fridges and CD players, as well as the usual amenities. Public areas include an inviting lounge with cocktail bar and a restaurant.
ROOMS: 21 en suite (1 fmly) No smoking in 4 bedrooms s IR£85-IR£120; d IR£105-IR£160 (incl. cont bkfst) * LB **FACILITIES:** STV **CONF:** Thtr 100 Class 80 Board 60 **SERVICES:** Lift air con **PARKING:** 21 **NOTES:** No dogs Civ Wed 60 **CARDS:**

★★★62% Mount Herbert Hotel

Herbert Rd, Lansdowne Rd 4
☎ 01 6684321 📠 01 6607077
e-mail: info@mountherberthotel.ie
Dir: *close Lansdowne Road Rugby Stadium, 220mtrs from Dart Rail Station*
Conveniently located near to local places of interest, this hotel offers comfortable public rooms, well equipped bedrooms and a friendly atmosphere. There is a spacious lounge, a TV room, a cocktail bar and a lovely restaurant, overlooking the floodit gardens, which serves good value cuisine. There is also a children's playground and conference rooms.
ROOMS: 175 en suite 10 annexe en suite (15 fmly) s IR£59-IR£69; d IR£85-IR£89 (incl. bkfst) * **FACILITIES:** STV Sauna Solarium Childrens playground Badminton court Xmas **CONF:** Thtr 80 Class 60 Board 40 **SERVICES:** Lift **PARKING:** 90 **NOTES:** No dogs (ex guide dogs) **CARDS:**

Packed in a hurry? Ironing facilities should be available at all star levels, either in rooms or on request.

★★★61% Quality Charville Hotel & Suites
Lower Rathmines Rd
☎ 01 4066100 📠 01 4066200
e-mail: info@charvillehotel.ie
Dir: *From M50 turn left to town centre, continue 3 mile through Terenure, Lathgar and into Rathminesvillage, hotel on left side of village*
This modern style hotel is within walking distance of the town centre and offers comfortable and well appointed, mainly suite, accommodation. There is a cocktail bar attached to the bistro style Carmines restaurant on the first floor. The TramCo theme bar is next door and serves snacks all day.
ROOMS: 51 en suite (2 fmly) No smoking in 9 bedrooms s fr IR£125; d fr IR£150 * **FACILITIES:** STV **CONF:** Thtr 20 Class 12 Board 10 Del from IR£102 * **SERVICES:** Lift **PARKING:** 35 **NOTES:** No dogs (ex guide dogs) Closed 24-27 Dec **CARDS:**

★★★59% Jurys Christchurch Inn
Christchurch Place
☎ 01 4540000 📠 01 4540012
e-mail: info@jurys.com
Dir: *N7 onto Nass Rd, follow signs for city centre upto O'Connell St, cont past Trinity College turn R onto Dame St upto Lord Edward St. Hotel is on left*
Centrally located opposite the 12th-century cathedral, this hotel is close to the Temple Bar and all the city amenities. The foyer lounge and pub are popular meeting places and there is also an informal restaurant. The bedrooms are well appointed and can accommodate families.
ROOMS: 182 en suite No smoking in 37 bedrooms s IR£66-IR£130; d IR£66-IR£130 * **SERVICES:** Lift **NOTES:** No dogs (ex guide dogs) Closed 24-26 Dec **CARDS:**

★★★59% Jurys Custom House Inn
Custom House Quay 8
☎ 01 6075000 📠 01 8290400
Overlooking the River Liffey, this hotel is situated less than ten minutes' walk away from the city's main shopping and tourist areas. Family rooms offer good value for money and facilities for business guests are excellent.
ROOMS: 239 en suite No smoking in 140 bedrooms s IR£66-IR£130; d IR£66-IR£130 * **FACILITIES:** STV **CONF:** Thtr 90 Class 52 Board 40 **SERVICES:** Lift **NOTES:** No dogs (ex guide dogs) Closed 25-26 Dec **CARDS:**

★★★56% The Parliament Hotel
Lord Edward St
☎ 01 6708777 📠 01 6708787
e-mail: info@regencyhotels.com
Dir: *adjacent to Dublin Castle in the Temple Bar area*
An attractive hotel, near to the Temple Bar area and Dublin Castle, offering a friendly welcome to all its guests. It provides well furnished bedrooms, decorated in a modern style. There is also a popular bar and a separate restaurant.
ROOMS: 63 en suite (8 fmly) No smoking in 22 bedrooms s IR£90; d IR£130 (incl. bkfst) * LB **FACILITIES:** STV **CONF:** Thtr 20 Board 10 **SERVICES:** Lift **NOTES:** No dogs (ex guide dogs) No smoking in restaurant **CARDS:**

★★64% Harding
Copper Alley, Fishamble St, Christchurch
☎ 01 6796500 📠 01 6796504
e-mail: harding.hotel@usitworld.com
Dir: *located at the top of Dame St beside Christchurch cathedral, on the edge of Dublin's Temple Bar area*
At the heart of the fascinating Temple Bar area of Dublin, this purpose-built hotel has a friendly atmosphere and offers good-value accommodation. Its Peruvian-style bar and Fitzers Restaurant are popular meeting places. There are plenty of shops, bars and restaurants in the area.
ROOMS: 53 en suite (14 fmly) s IR£45-IR£65; d IR£69-IR£110 * **FACILITIES:** STV entertainment **SERVICES:** Lift **NOTES:** No dogs (ex guide dogs) Closed 23-26 Dec **CARDS:**

★★60% *Hotel Ibis*
Monastery Rd, Clondalkin
☎ 01 4641480 📠 01 4641484
e-mail: H0595@accor-hotels.com
Dir: *off the M50, N7 turn off, in the direction of Naas, hotel is on the right, turn right into Monastery road, then next right again*
Close to Dublin airport and the M50, this hotel is modern in style. Bedrooms have contemporary furnishings including large desks. Public rooms include a restaurant and a lounge. Breakfast is self-service and a 24-hour snack service is also available.
ROOMS: 150 en suite No smoking in 33 bedrooms **FACILITIES:** STV **CONF:** Thtr 30 Class 18 Board 18 **SERVICES:** Lift **PARKING:** 180 **CARDS:**

⌂ *Travelodge*
Swords By Pass
☎ 01 8409233 📠 01 8409257
Dir: *on N1 Dublin/Belfast road*
This modern building offers accommodation in smart, spacious and well equipped bedrooms, all with en suite bathrooms. Refreshments may be taken at the nearby family restaurant. For further details and the Travelodge phone number, consult the Hotel Groups page.
ROOMS: 40 en suite

⌂ *Travelodge Castleknock*
Auburn Av Roundabout, Navan Rd
☎ 01 8202626
This modern building offers accommodation in smart, spacious and well equipped bedrooms, all with en suite bathrooms. Refreshments may be taken at the nearby family restaurant. For further details and the Travelodge phone number, consult the Hotel Groups page.

DUNDALK, Co Louth — Map 01 D4

★★★69% Ballymascanlon House
☎ 042 9371124 📠 042 9371598
e-mail: ifo@ballymascanlon
Dir: *N of Dundalk take T62 to Carlingford. Hotel is approx 1km*
This Victorian mansion is set in 130 acres of gardens and woodlands, which include an 18-hole golf course. Inside there is an elegant restaurant, a spacious and relaxing lounge, a modern wing of luxurious bedrooms and a highly equipped leisure club. Conference and banqueting facilities are also available.
ROOMS: 43 en suite (11 fmly) s IR£65-IR£72; d IR£90-IR£105 (incl. bkfst) * LB **FACILITIES:** STV Indoor swimming (H) Golf 18 Tennis (hard) Sauna Gym Jacuzzi/spa **CONF:** Thtr 300 Class 160 **SERVICES:** Lift **PARKING:** 250 **NOTES:** No dogs (ex guide dogs) Closed 24-26 Dec **CARDS:**

★★★61% Fairways Hotel & Leisure Centre
Dublin Rd
☎ 042 9321500 📠 042 9321511
e-mail: info@fairways.ie
Dir: *on N1 3km S of Dundalk*
Situated south of Dundalk, on the main Dublin/Belfast route, this modern family-run hotel offers well decorated, comfortable bedrooms. A wide range of food is available all day and golf can

continued

DUNDALK, continued

be organised, by the hotel, on a choice of nearby local golf courses.
ROOMS: 48 en suite (2 fmly) s IR£65-IR£70; d IR£95-IR£100 (incl. bkfst) * LB **FACILITIES:** STV Indoor swimming (H) Tennis (hard) Squash Snooker Sauna Solarium Gym Jacuzzi/spa Badminton court Steam room Sports therapist entertainment **CONF:** Thtr 350 Class 250 **PARKING:** 300 **NOTES:** No dogs (ex guide dogs) Closed 25 Dec **CARDS:**

D

★★65% Imperial
Park St
☎ 042 9332241 📠 042 9337909
A welcoming hotel in Dundalk town centre. The majority of the comfortable bedrooms are attractively decorated and have cherrywood furnishings. The coffee shop is open all day and there is also a restaurant and a bar.
ROOMS: 47 en suite (47 fmly) s IR£55-IR£65; d IR£80-IR£90 (incl. bkfst) * LB **FACILITIES:** STV **CONF:** Thtr 400 Class 125 Board 50 Del from IR£80 * **SERVICES:** Lift **PARKING:** 25 **NOTES:** Closed 25 Dec **CARDS:**

DUNFANAGHY, Co Donegal — Map 01 C6

★★★65% Arnold's
☎ 074 36208 📠 074 36352
e-mail: arnoldshotel@eircom.net
Dir: *on N56 from Letterkenny hotel is on left entering the village*
On the coast, with miles of sandy beaches close at hand. Public areas offer comfortable seating, and facilities include two restaurants and two bars. There is a choice of bedrooms, from well equipped standard rooms to larger ones with sofas.
ROOMS: 30 en suite (10 fmly) s IR£60-IR£70; d IR£80-IR£100 (incl. bkfst) * LB **FACILITIES:** STV Tennis (hard) Fishing Riding Croquet lawn Putting green entertainment **PARKING:** 60 **NOTES:** No dogs (ex guide dogs) Closed weekends Nov-mid Mar **CARDS:**

DUNGANNON, Co Tyrone — Map 01 C5

⌂ Cohannon Inn
212 Ballynakilly Rd BT71 6HJ
☎ 028 8772 4488 📠 028 8775 2217
e-mail: enquiries@cohannon-inn.com
Dir: *400yds from junct 14 on M1*
The Cohannon Inn offers competitive prices and well maintained accommodation. Rooms are located behind the Inn complex in a purpose-built block. Public areas are smartly furnished and good food is served all day.
ROOMS: 50 en suite **CONF:** Thtr 150 Class 150 Board 100

DUNGARVAN, Co Waterford — Map 01 C2

★★★56% *Lawlors*
☎ 058 41122 & 41056 📠 058 41000
Dir: *off N25*
An ideal base for touring the local area, this friendly family-run hotel caters for both business and leisure guests.
ROOMS: 89 en suite (8 fmly) **FACILITIES:** entertainment **CONF:** Thtr 420 Class 215 Board 420 **SERVICES:** Lift **NOTES:** Closed 25 Dec **CARDS:**

Fancy a Singapore Sling? Bar staff in five star hotels should be skilled cocktail mixers.

DUN LAOGHAIRE, Co Dublin — Map 01 D4

★★★65% *Royal Marine*
Marine Rd
☎ 01 2801911 📠 01 2801089
e-mail: ryan@indigo.ie
Dir: *follow signs for 'Car Ferry'*

Set in four acres, overlooking Dun Laoghaire harbour, the Victorian Royal Marine is a local landmark. The hotel has a range of contemporary facilities including a restaurant, bars, the popular Bay Lounge and attractive gardens. The hotel has easy access to the city centre.
ROOMS: 103 en suite No smoking in 10 bedrooms **FACILITIES:** STV Gym entertainment **CONF:** Thtr 500 Class 300 **SERVICES:** Lift **PARKING:** 300 **NOTES:** No dogs **CARDS:**

ENNIS, Co Clare — Map 01 B3

★★★★70% Woodstock
Shannaway Rd
☎ 065 684 6600 📠 065 684 6611
e-mail: info@woodstockhotel.com

Set in mature woodland, this newly built luxurious hotel overlooks Woodstock Championship Golf Course. The impressive lobby has comfortable lounge areas and leads into the drawing room and library. Spikes Brasserie serves contemporary dishes and enjoys spectacular views. Spacious bedrooms offer comfort and individuality, and the Spa offers a full range of leisure facilities including jacuzzi and sauna.
ROOMS: 67 en suite (16 fmly) No smoking in 45 bedrooms s IR£92.50-IR£175; d IR£135-IR£175 * LB **FACILITIES:** STV Indoor swimming (H) Golf 18 Sauna Solarium Gym Jacuzzi/spa steam room ch fac Xmas **CONF:** Thtr 200 Class 100 Board 70 Del from IR£124.75 * **SERVICES:** Lift **NOTES:** No dogs (ex guide dogs) **CARDS:**

★★★68% Temple Gate
The Square
☎ 065 6823300 065 6823322
e-mail: templegh@iol.ie
Dir: *from Ennis follow signs for Temple Gate*
A smart hotel in the centre of Ennis. Incorporating a 19th-century gothic style building, public areas are carefully planned and include a comfortable lounge library, Preachers Pub and Le Bistro Restaurant. Bedrooms are well equipped and attractively decorated.
ROOMS: 73 en suite (3 fmly) No smoking in 11 bedrooms s IR£55-IR£67.50; d IR£80-IR£95 (incl. bkfst) * LB **FACILITIES:** STV entertainment **CONF:** Thtr 90 Class 50 Board 35 **SERVICES:** Lift **PARKING:** 52 **NOTES:** No dogs (ex guide dogs) Closed 25 Dec
CARDS:

★★★66% West Country Hotel
Best Western
Clare Rd
☎ 065 6823000 065 6823759
e-mail: cro@lynchotels.com
Dir: *Located on the Limerick to Galway Road N18, 10 mins walk to Ennis town, next to St Flannans college*
This hotel offers a comfortable lounge which provides the ideal spot to relax in, or alternatively there is the spacious foyer lounge. The bedrooms are modern and include a wide range of facilities. The conference centre has all the latest equipment for business needs.
ROOMS: 152 en suite (56 fmly) No smoking in 4 bedrooms s IR£55-IR£90; d IR£80-IR£132 * LB **FACILITIES:** STV Indoor swimming (H) Sauna Solarium Gym Pool table Jacuzzi/spa Beauty treatments Kidsplus programme entertainment ch fac Xmas **CONF:** Thtr 1650 Class 1120 Board 50 Del from IR£103 * **SERVICES:** Lift **PARKING:** 370 **NOTES:** No dogs (ex guide dogs) Civ Wed 1000
CARDS:

★★64% Magowna House
Inch, Kilmaley
☎ 065 6839009 065 6839258
e-mail: Magowna@iol.ie
Dir: *on R474 off N18 pass golf course, and after approx 5km, hotel is signposted off to right, 300mtrs from junction*
This small family-run hotel, stands in 14 acres of grounds just off the R474 road to Ennis Golf Club and Kilmaley at Inch. The hotel provides a good standard of comfort and enjoyable meals. Good local fishing, boats for hire and a golf practice area are among the activities in the neighbourhood.
ROOMS: 10 en suite (3 fmly) No smoking in 4 bedrooms s IR£37-IR£43; d IR£56-IR£68 (incl. bkfst) * LB **FACILITIES:** 3 Boats for hire **CONF:** Thtr 350 Class 200 Board 20 **PARKING:** 60 **NOTES:** Closed 24-26 Dec **CARDS:**

ENNISCORTHY, Co Wexford — Map 01 D3

★★★69% *Riverside Park Hotel*
The Promenade
☎ 054 37800 054 37900
Dir: *0.5km from New Bridge, centre of Enniscorthy town, N11 Dublin/Rosslare Road*
Situated in a picturesque position beside the River Slaney, this hotel is easily distinguished by its terracotta and blue colour scheme. The foyer is equally dramatic and the public areas all take full advantage of the riverside views, including the Mill House pub. The spacious, attractively decorated bedrooms have every modern comfort.

continued

ROOMS: 60 en suite (50 fmly) No smoking in 6 bedrooms **FACILITIES:** STV entertainment **CONF:** Thtr 800 Class 500 Board 100 **SERVICES:** Lift **NOTES:** No dogs (ex guide dogs)
CARDS:

★60% *Murphy-Flood's*
Market Square
☎ 054 33413 054 33413
Dir: *follow signs to hotel in the town centre*
A family-run hotel in the centre of a lively market town, Murphy-Flood's has a comfortable bar where carvery lunches, grills and snacks are served throughout the day. Accommodation is pleasing and comfortable.
ROOMS: 21 rms (18 en suite) (2 fmly) No smoking in 2 bedrooms **FACILITIES:** entertainment **CONF:** Thtr 200 Class 100 Board 60 **NOTES:** No dogs (ex guide dogs) Closed 25 Dec
CARDS:

F

ENNISKILLEN, Co Fermanagh — Map 01 C5

★★★69% Killyhevlin
BT74 6RW
☎ 028 6632 3481 028 6632 4726
e-mail: info@killyhevlin.com
Dir: *2m S, off A4*
The Killyhevlin commands wonderful views over Lough Erne, visible from the hotel's comfortable public rooms. Attractive fabrics have been used to good effect in the smart bedrooms which are comfortable and modern in style.
ROOMS: 43 en suite (32 fmly) s £62.50-£65; d £95-£100 (incl. bkfst) * LB **FACILITIES:** STV Fishing ch fac **CONF:** Thtr 600 Class 350 Del from £77.50 * **PARKING:** 500 **NOTES:** No dogs (ex guide dogs)
CARDS:

FERMOY, Co Cork — Map 01 B2

★★★65% Castlehyde Hotel
Castlehyde
☎ 025 31865 025 31485
e-mail: cashyde@iol.ie
Dir: *turn off N8 just outside Fermoy onto N72 Fermoy-Mallow. Hotel in 2m*
Carefully restored 18th-century courtyard buildings, where old meets new sympathetically and comfortably. Individually styled bedrooms are attractively decorated and include five cottage suites. The welcoming lobby lounge features an open fire and there is a stylish restaurant overlooking the gardens and woodland.
ROOMS: 24 en suite (5 fmly) No smoking in 10 bedrooms s IR£85-IR£110; d IR£115-IR£150 (incl. bkfst) * LB **FACILITIES:** STV Outdoor swimming (H) entertainment Xmas **CONF:** Thtr 30 Class 18 Board 14 **PARKING:** 35 **NOTES:** No dogs (ex guide dogs) No smoking in restaurant RS Feb **CARDS:**

GALWAY, Co Galway Map 01 B4

Premier Collection

★★★★ **_Glenlo Abbey_**
Bushypark
☎ 091 526666 📠 091 527800
e-mail: glenlo@iol.ie
***Dir:** 4km from Galway City Centre on the N59*
Standing in a landscaped 134-acre estate, this restored 18th-century abbey overlooks a beautiful loch. The original building houses a boardroom, business centre, conference and banqueting facilities. The bedrooms are in a modern wing along with a library, restaurants, cocktail and cellar bars.
ROOMS: 45 en suite No smoking in 10 bedrooms **FACILITIES:** STV Golf 18 Fishing Putting green Boating Clay pigeon shooting entertainment **CONF:** Thtr 80 Class 60 Board 40 **SERVICES:** Lift **PARKING:** 150 **NOTES:** No dogs (ex guide dogs)
CARDS:

★★★★68% **Ardilaun Conference & Leisure Centre**
Taylor's Hill
☎ 091 521433 📠 091 521546
e-mail: ardilaun@iol.ie
***Dir:** take 4th left after 4th rdbt leading from main Dublin road*
Formerly a country mansion this hotel has comfortable lounges and the dining room overlooks beautiful gardens. Bedrooms are spacious, well furnished and individually decorated. Guests can enjoy extensive leisure facilities.
ROOMS: 90 en suite (16 fmly) No smoking in 6 bedrooms s IR£95; d IR£150 (incl. bkfst) * LB **FACILITIES:** STV Indoor swimming (H) Snooker Sauna Solarium Gym Jacuzzi/spa Treatment & Analysis Rooms Xmas **CONF:** Thtr 450 Class 200 Board 40 **SERVICES:** Lift **PARKING:** 220 **NOTES:** Closed 23-28 Dec **CARDS:**

★★★★65% **Westwood House Hotel**
Dangan, Upper Newcastle
☎ 091 521442 📠 091 521400
e-mail: westwoodhotel@eircom.net
***Dir:** from N6 enter Galway, continue on N6 following signs for Clifden (N59) once on Clifden Rd the Westwood House Hotel is on left*
Close to the university on the edge of the city, this hotel is luxuriously appointed. The public rooms include a themed bar, a restaurant and lounges. Bedrooms are comfortable and well equipped.
ROOMS: 58 en suite (10 fmly) No smoking in 17 bedrooms s IR£75-IR£99; d IR£108-IR£149 (incl. bkfst) * LB **FACILITIES:** STV Kingfisher Health and Leisure club ch fac **CONF:** Thtr 350 Class 275 Board 15 Del from IR£99.95 * **SERVICES:** Lift air con **PARKING:** 130 **NOTES:** No dogs (ex guide dogs) Closed 25-26 Dec Civ Wed 275
CARDS:

★★★★62%
Galway Bay Hotel Conference & Leisure Centre
The Promenade, Salthill
☎ 091 520520 📠 091 520530
e-mail: info@galwaybayhotel.net
***Dir:** on the promenade in Salthill on the coast road to Connemara. Follow signs to Salthill from all major routes*

Commanding lovely views from its seafront setting, the Galway Bay is a plush and peaceful hotel. The conservatory lounge and patio are the perfect setting in which to relax and enjoy the scenery. Dining options include the Lobster Pot restaurant, the Cafe Lido or a traditional Irish pub. Bedrooms are attractive and comfortable.
ROOMS: 153 en suite (10 fmly) No smoking in 24 bedrooms s IR£95-IR£105; d IR£135-IR£150 (incl. bkfst) LB **FACILITIES:** STV Indoor swimming (H) Sauna Gym Steam room entertainment Xmas **CONF:** Thtr 1100 Class 325 Del from IR£83 * **SERVICES:** Lift **PARKING:** 300 **NOTES:** No dogs (ex guide dogs)
CARDS:

See advert on opposite page

★★★★58%
Park House Hotel & Eyre House Restaurants
Forster St, Eyre Square
☎ 091 564924 📠 091 569219
e-mail: parkhousehotel@tinet.ie
***Dir:** in view of Eyre Square, city centre, Galway*
Easily accessible, this hotel offers bedrooms, all well decorated and furnished, which vary in size. Public rooms include comfortable lounges, a spacious dining room and a carvery bar.
ROOMS: 57 en suite s IR£60-IR£155; d IR£80-IR£155 (incl. bkfst) * **FACILITIES:** STV entertainment **CONF:** Thtr 50 Class 30 Board 30 **SERVICES:** Lift **PARKING:** 26 **NOTES:** No dogs (ex guide dogs) Closed 24-26 Dec **CARDS:**

★★★65% **_Galway Ryan_**
Dublin Rd
☎ 091 753181 📠 091 753187
e-mail: ryan@indigo.ie
***Dir:** follow signs to Galway West off N7*
This modern hotel offers a spacious, pleasantly decorated and furnished lounge and a leisure club. Accommodation is comfortable and well equipped.

continued

ROOMS: 96 en suite (96 fmly) No smoking in 6 bedrooms **FACILITIES:** STV Indoor swimming (H) Tennis (hard) Sauna Gym Sports hall Steam rooms entertainment **CONF:** Thtr 80 Class 110 Board 30 **SERVICES:** Lift **PARKING:** 100 **NOTES:** No dogs Closed 25 Dec **CARDS:**

★★★61% Menlo Park Hotel

Terryland
☎ 091 761122 Fax 091 761222
e-mail: menlopkh@iol.ie
Dir: *located at Terryland rdbt off N6 and N84 (Castlebar Rd)*
ROOMS: 44 en suite (6 fmly) No smoking in 10 bedrooms s IR£49-IR£95; d IR£75-IR£105 (incl. bkfst) * LB **FACILITIES:** STV **CONF:** Thtr 200 Class 100 Board 40 **SERVICES:** Lift air con **PARKING:** 100 **NOTES:** No dogs (ex guide dogs) Closed 24-25 Dec **CARDS:**

★★★59% Jurys Galway Inn

JURYS HOTEL GROUP

Quay St
☎ 091 566444 Fax 091 568415
e-mail: enquiry@jurys.com
Dir: *N6 follow signs for Docks. On arrival at Docks take Salthill Rd for 2-3 minutes*
This modern hotel stands at the heart of the city opposite the famous Spanish Arch. The hotel has an attractive patio and a garden bounded by the river. The 'one price' room rate and comfortable bedrooms ensure its popularity and this is an ideal base to tour the area.
ROOMS: 128 en suite (6 fmly) No smoking in 39 bedrooms s IR£54-IR£69; d IR£108-IR£138 * **FACILITIES:** STV entertainment **CONF:** Thtr 40 Class 40 Board 40 **SERVICES:** Lift **NOTES:** No dogs (ex guide dogs) Closed 24-26 Dec **CARDS:**

★★★59% Lochlurgain

22 Monksfield, Upper Salthill
☎ 091 529595 Fax 091 522399
e-mail: lochlurgain@eircom.net
Dir: *off R336 behind Bank of Ireland beside RC church*
This small family-run hotel stands in a quiet street, at Salthill, beside the Roman Catholic church. Service is of a very good standard and the bedrooms are comfortable, extras include electric blankets in season. Public rooms are attractively decorated.
ROOMS: 13 en suite (3 fmly) s IR£35-IR£65; d IR£60-IR£90 (incl. bkfst) * LB **FACILITIES:** STV **PARKING:** 8 **NOTES:** No dogs (ex guide dogs) No smoking in restaurant Closed 26 Oct-13 Mar **CARDS:**

★★★58% *Victoria*

Victoria Place, Eyre Square
☎ 091 567433 Fax 091 565880
e-mail: bookings@victoriahotel.ie
Dir: *off Eyre Sq on Victoria Place, Beside the rail station*
This city-centre hotel lies off Eyre Square. Bedrooms are well equipped and other facilities include 24-hour room service, a good bar and a pleasant restaurant. The atmosphere is relaxing and staff are friendly and attentive.
ROOMS: 57 en suite (20 fmly) No smoking in 1 bedroom **FACILITIES:** STV **CONF:** Thtr 50 Class 30 Board 25 **SERVICES:** Lift **NOTES:** No dogs (ex guide dogs) Closed 25 Dec **CARDS:**

★★58% *Hotel Ibis*

Headford Rd
☎ 091 771166 Fax 091 771646
e-mail: H0596@accor-hotels.com
Dir: *off rdbt at junct of N84 and N6*
On the outskirts of Galway, this modern hotel offers good value accommodation in well equipped bedrooms. Open-plan public areas include a lounge and informal restaurant. Refreshments and a 24-hour light snack service are available.
ROOMS: 100 en suite (50 fmly) No smoking in 23 bedrooms **FACILITIES:** STV **CONF:** Thtr 65 Class 40 Board 40 **SERVICES:** Lift **PARKING:** 110 **CARDS:**

GARRYVOE, Co Cork — Map 01 C2

★★67% Garryvoe

☎ 021 646718 Fax 021 646824
Dir: *turn off N25 onto L72 at Castlemartyr between Midleton and Youghal and continue for 6km*
A comfortable, family-run hotel with caring staff, the Garryvoe has been upgraded. It stands in a delightful position facing a sandy beach and the first floor lounge overlooks the sea. There is a hotel bar and also a public bar.
ROOMS: 19 en suite (2 fmly) s IR£30-IR£35; d IR£60-IR£70 (incl. bkfst) * LB **FACILITIES:** Tennis (hard) Putting green **CONF:** Thtr 400 Class 250 **PARKING:** 25 **NOTES:** No dogs (ex guide dogs) Closed 25 Dec **CARDS:**

GLENDALOUGH, Co Wicklow Map 01 D3

★★★64% *The Glendalough*

☎ 0404 45135 📠 0404 45142

Forest and mountains provide the setting for this long-established hotel, beside the famous monastic site. The hotel has been refurbished and additional bedrooms, many with lovely views, are now available. Bar food is available and the charming restaurant overlooks the river and forest. The whole area is ideal for walking, golf and trout fishing.

ROOMS: 44 en suite (3 fmly) **FACILITIES:** STV Fishing Pool table entertainment **CONF:** Thtr 200 Class 150 Board 50 **SERVICES:** Lift **PARKING:** 100 **NOTES:** No dogs (ex guide dogs) Closed 1 Dec-Jan **CARDS:**

GOREY, Co Wexford Map 01 D3

Premier Collection

★★★ Marlfield House

☎ 055 21124 📠 055 21572

e-mail: info@marlfieldhouse.ie

Dir: *1.5km outside Gorey on the Courtown Harbour road*

RELAIS & CHATEAUX

This distinctive Regency house was once the residence of the Earl of Courtown. The current hotel retains an atmosphere of elegance and luxury throughout. Public areas include a library, drawing room and dining room leading into a conservatory which overlooks the grounds and a wildlife preserve. Bedrooms are in keeping with the style of the downstairs rooms and there are some superb suites. Druids Glen and several other golf courses are nearby.

ROOMS: 19 en suite (3 fmly) s IR£85-IR£95; d IR£180-IR£520 (incl. bkfst) * LB **FACILITIES:** STV Tennis (hard) Sauna Croquet lawn **CONF:** Thtr 60 Board 20 **PARKING:** 50 **NOTES:** No smoking in restaurant Closed 15 Dec-30 Jan **CARDS:**

GOUGANE BARRA, Co Cork Map 01 B2

★★62% *Gougane Barra*

☎ 026 47069 📠 026 47226

e-mail: gouganbarrahotel@tinet.ie

Dir: *off N22*

Right on the shore of the lake, the Gougane Barra Hotel is very popular. Refurbishments have improved the restaurant, bedrooms and bathrooms, all of which have lovely views. Guests can be met from their train, boat or plane by prior arrangement.

ROOMS: 28 en suite **FACILITIES:** STV Fishing **PARKING:** 25 **NOTES:** No dogs (ex guide dogs) No smoking in restaurant Closed 15 Oct-21 Apr **CARDS:**

HILLSBOROUGH, Co Down Map 01 D5

★★★66% White Gables

14 Dromore Rd BT26 6HS

☎ 028 9268 2755 📠 028 9268 9532

Dir: *join M2 (Belfast) then M1 west, join A1 at junct 7 to Dublin. Take Hillsborough turn, go through village, hotel is on right hand side*

A comfortable, modern hotel appealing to business guests. Bedrooms range from executive rooms to standard rooms. All rooms are comfortably modern in style, with extra touches. Smart public areas include a bright foyer lounge, attractive split-level restaurant and an all-day coffee shop.

ROOMS: 31 en suite No smoking in 8 bedrooms s £69.50-£95; d £90-£115 * **FACILITIES:** STV Xmas **CONF:** Thtr 120 Class 40 Board 25 **PARKING:** 120 **NOTES:** No dogs (ex guide dogs) Closed 24-25 Dec RS Sun (residents only before 7pm) **CARDS:**

INISHANNON, Co Cork Map 01 B2

★★★68% *Inishannon House*

☎ 021 775121 📠 021 775609

Dir: *off N71 at eastern end of village*

MANOR HOUSE HOTELS

A charming hotel, the River Bandon flows by this eye-catching country house, complemented by attractive walks and gardens. Good food is prepared from the freshest ingredients, with seafood dishes a speciality.

ROOMS: 12 en suite 1 annexe en suite (4 fmly) **FACILITIES:** STV Fishing entertainment **CONF:** Thtr 200 Class 80 Board 50 **PARKING:** 100 **NOTES:** Closed 15 Jan-15 Mar **CARDS:**

IRVINESTOWN, Co Fermanagh Map 01 C5

★★66% Mahons

Mill St BT74 1GS

☎ 028 6862 1656 📠 028 6862 8344

e-mail: mahonshotel@lakeland.net

Dir: *on A32 midway between Enniskillen and Omagh - beside town clock in centre of Irvinestown*

A family-run hotel which has offered warm hospitality for over 100 years. Public areas, especially the bar, are filled with a collection of curiosities. In the restaurant, the extensive carte offers a wide range of dishes. Bedrooms come in a variety of sizes and have pretty decor.

ROOMS: 18 en suite (4 fmly) s £35-£37; d £60-£70 (incl. bkfst) * LB **FACILITIES:** STV Tennis (hard) Riding Solarium Pool table entertainment **CONF:** Thtr 450 Class 200 Del from £45 * **PARKING:** 40 **NOTES:** Closed 25 Dec **CARDS:**

KENMARE, Co Kerry Map 01 B2

Premier Collection

★★★★ Park Hotel Kenmare

☎ 064 41200 📠 064 41402

e-mail: phkenmare@iol.ie

Dir: *on R569 beside golf course*

The Park is a luxurious country house hotel on the famous Ring of Kerry. The hotel stands above terraced gardens which overlook the estuary of the Kenmare River, with a glorious mountain backdrop. Warm hospitality and professional excellence are provided. The restaurant offers very good food and fine wines.

continued

ROOMS: 49 en suite (2 fmly) No smoking in 5 bedrooms s IR£149-IR£168; d IR£264-IR£524 (incl. bkfst) * LB **FACILITIES:** STV Golf 18 Tennis (hard) Snooker Gym Pool table Croquet lawn Putting green entertainment Xmas **CONF:** Thtr 60 Class 40 Board 28 **SERVICES:** Lift **PARKING:** 60 **NOTES:** No dogs (ex guide dogs) No smoking in restaurant Closed 3 Jan-13 Apr & 29 Oct-23 Dec **CARDS:**

Premier Collection

★★★★ Sheen Falls Lodge

☎ 064 41600 064 41386
e-mail: info@sheenfallslodge.ie

RELAIS & CHATEAUX.

Dir: *from Kenmare take N71 to Glengarriff over the suspension bridge, take the first turn left*

This beautiful hotel, beside the Sheen River, is surrounded by stunning lakes and mountains. The cascading Sheen Falls are floodlit at night, creating a magical atmosphere which can be enjoyed from the the restaurant. A luxurious lounge, library, billiards room and cocktail bar complete the public rooms and there are three grades of comfortable bedrooms.

ROOMS: 61 en suite (14 fmly) No smoking in 10 bedrooms d IR£168-IR£258 * LB **FACILITIES:** STV Indoor swimming (H) Tennis (hard) Fishing Riding Snooker Sauna Solarium Gym Croquet lawn Jacuzzi/spa Table tennis Steam room Clay pigeon shooting Massage Seaweed therapy Cycling entertainment ch fac Xmas **CONF:** Thtr 150 Class 65 Board 50 **SERVICES:** Lift **PARKING:** 76 **NOTES:** No dogs (ex guide dogs) Closed 3-23 Dec & 2 Jan-2 Feb **CARDS:**

Read all about it! Newspapers delivered to bedrooms in four and five star hotels.

★★★68% Dromquinna Manor

Blackwater Bridge
☎ 064 41657 064 41791
e-mail: info@dromquinna.com

Dir: *take road to Kenmare, take the N70 towards Sneem (ring of Kerry Rd). Hotel 3m down on the left*

A lovely hotel, standing on the Ring of Kerry, in 42 acres of grounds on the banks of the river Kenmare. Public areas include a Great Hall, pleasant sitting rooms, and a welcoming bar. Bedrooms vary in size and there is a unique and much sought-after treehouse suite. On the riverside are the bistro, play areas for children and a marina with facilities for sailing, fishing and watersports.

ROOMS: 28 en suite 18 annexe en suite (6 fmly) s fr IR£75; d fr IR£110 (incl. bkfst) * LB **FACILITIES:** Outdoor swimming Tennis (hard) Fishing Riding Pool table Croquet lawn Table tennis Xmas **CONF:** Del from IR£80 * **PARKING:** 80 **NOTES:** No dogs (ex guide dogs) **CARDS:**

See advert on page 859

★★★65% *Riversdale House*

☎ 064 41299 064 41075

This hotel has wonderful views and nestles on the shores of Kenmare Bay, close to the town centre. In the bedrooms, floor-length window alcoves take advantage of the clarity of light for which Kenmare is famous, and on the top floor are four recommended mini-suites with balconies.

ROOMS: 64 en suite **FACILITIES:** STV entertainment **CONF:** Thtr 300 Class 250 Board 50 **SERVICES:** Lift **PARKING:** 200 **NOTES:** Closed Nov-Mar **CARDS:**

KILDARE, Co Kildare — Map 01 C3

★★63% Curragh Lodge

Dublin Rd
☎ 045 522144 521136 045 521274
e-mail: clhotel@iol.ie

Dir: *travelling from Dublin City Centre, follow signs for S or N7 motorway. Hotel 28m from City Centre, on left when entering Kildare town*

Curragh Lodge is located in Kildare town and within walking distance of the Irish National Stud and Japanese Gardens. There is a cosy lounge and a modern open-plan bar and restaurant. Bedrooms are comfortable and well equipped.

ROOMS: 21 en suite (3 fmly) No smoking in 4 bedrooms s IR£35-IR£45; d IR£70-IR£90 (incl. bkfst) * LB **FACILITIES:** STV entertainment **PARKING:** 30 **CARDS:**

KILKEE, Co Clare — Map 01 B3

★★★61% Ocean Cove Golf & Leisure Hotel

☎ 065 6823000 065 6823759
e-mail: clo@lynchotels.com

Dir: *from Ennis take N68 to Kilrush, turn right. Proceed through Kilkee until reaching the sea. Hotel is situated on right, overlooking the bay*

On an elevated site overlooking the seafront and beach in a popular seaside resort. Comfortable bedrooms are attractively decorated, and two are adapted for disabled guests. Leisure facilities include a children's play room, and the lounge, restaurant and bar all enjoy sea views.

ROOMS: 50 en suite (8 fmly) No smoking in 13 bedrooms s IR£45-IR£65; d IR£80-IR£110 (incl. bkfst) * LB **FACILITIES:** STV Gym Pool table entertainment Xmas **CONF:** Thtr 100 Class 60 Board 40 Del from IR£69 * **SERVICES:** Lift **PARKING:** 150 **NOTES:** No dogs (ex guide dogs) **CARDS:**

KILKEE, continued

★★64% *Halpin's*
Erin St
☎ 065 56032 065 56317
The finest tradition of hotel service is offered at this family-run hotel which has a commanding view over the old Victorian town. The attractive bedrooms are comfortable.
ROOMS: 12 en suite (6 fmly) No smoking in 4 bedrooms **FACILITIES:** STV Tennis (hard) **CONF:** Thtr 60 Board 30 **SERVICES:** air con **NOTES:** No dogs Closed 3 Jan-15 Mar **CARDS:**

KILKENNY, Co Kilkenny Map 01 C3

★★★★62% Kilkenny Ormonde
Ormonde St
☎ 056 23900 056 23977
e-mail: info@kilkennyormonde.com
Dir: *located in Kilkenny Town Centre off Patricks St. Hotel opposite multi-story car park*
This new contemporary styled hotel has a large lounge and reception area, a bar and a choice of two restaurants. Comfortable bedrooms are attractive, and facilities include data ports. There are conference and banqueting facilities, and a leisure club.
ROOMS: 118 en suite (6 fmly) No smoking in 70 bedrooms s IR£85; d IR£135 (incl. bkfst) * LB **FACILITIES:** STV Indoor swimming (H) Sauna Solarium Gym Jacuzzi/spa entertainment ch fac Xmas **CONF:** Thtr 420 Class 200 Board 36 Del from IR£98 * **SERVICES:** Lift air con **NOTES:** No dogs (ex guide dogs) **CARDS:**

★★★★62% Kilkenny River Court Hotel
The Bridge, John St
☎ 056 23388 056 23389
e-mail: krch@iol.ie
Dir: *at the bridge in the town centre, just opposite Kilkenny Castle*
Situated in a private courtyard, accessed through an arched entrance beside the river. Many rooms, in particular the restaurant and bar, have views of Kilkenny Castle, which is floodlit at night. Staff are pleasant and efficient.
ROOMS: 90 en suite (4 fmly) No smoking in 20 bedrooms s fr IR£85 (incl. bkfst) * LB **FACILITIES:** STV Indoor swimming (H) Sauna Gym Jacuzzi/spa Xmas **CONF:** Thtr 240 Class 180 Board 4 **SERVICES:** Lift **PARKING:** 84 **NOTES:** No dogs (ex guide dogs) **CARDS:**

★★★71% Newpark
☎ 056 22122 056 61111
e-mail: info@newparkhotel.com
A friendly hotel with an impressive foyer lounge, a bar/bistro and conference suites. A purpose-built bedroom wing offers a choice of rooms, decorated and equipped to a high standard.
ROOMS: 111 en suite (42 fmly) No smoking in 8 bedrooms s IR£59-IR£79; d IR£85-IR£109 * LB **FACILITIES:** STV Indoor swimming (H) Sauna Solarium Gym Jacuzzi/spa Plunge pool Xmas **CONF:** Thtr 600 Class 300 Board 50 Del from IR£85 * **PARKING:** 350 **NOTES:** No dogs (ex guide dogs) **CARDS:**

★★★63% Langton House
69 John St
☎ 056 65133 056 63693
Dir: *take N9 & N10 from Dublin follow signs for city centre at outskirts of Kilkenny turn to left Langtons 500 metres on left after 1st set of lights*
The exterior of this period town house hotel belies its internal size, which is large enough to include a ballroom. No expense has been spared in refurbishing the hotel. Lovely fabrics enhance the richness of specially designed mahogany furniture in the comfortable bedrooms, where marble tiled bathrooms also gleam. The well-known restaurant and pub are both very popular.

continued

ROOMS: 10 en suite 16 annexe en suite No smoking in 4 bedrooms s fr IR£70; d fr IR£110 (incl. bkfst) * LB **FACILITIES:** STV entertainment **PARKING:** 60 **NOTES:** No dogs (ex guide dogs) Closed 25 Dec **CARDS:**

★★59% Club House
Patrick St
☎ 056 21994 056 71920
e-mail: clubhse@iol.ie
Dir: *city centre, near Kilkenny castle*
This 200 year old hotel is located in the city centre and offers pleasant bedrooms. There is a lounge bar with an open fire, a Georgian dining room and a function suite. This is a comfortable and friendly hotel.
ROOMS: 28 en suite (3 fmly) s IR£37-IR£70; d IR£66-IR£100 (incl. bkfst) * LB **FACILITIES:** STV Gym **CONF:** Thtr 100 Class 75 Board 35 **PARKING:** 80 **CARDS:**

KILL, Co Kildare Map 01 D4

★★★63% *Ambassador*
☎ 045 886700 045 886777
e-mail: quinn-hotels@sqgroup.com
Dir: *Close to Dublin centre on the N7 to the south and south west*
Set beside the N7, 16 miles from Dublin the Ambassador offers comfortable and well appointed accommodation. The Ambassador Lounge carvery and the Diplomat Restaurant both offer tempting dishes, and there is also a bar.
ROOMS: 36 en suite (36 fmly) **FACILITIES:** STV entertainment **CONF:** Thtr 260 Class 140 Board 60 **PARKING:** 150 **NOTES:** No dogs (ex guide dogs) **CARDS:**

KILLARNEY, Co Kerry Map 01 B2

★★★★79% ❀❀❀ Aghadoe Heights
☎ 064 31766 064 31345
e-mail: aghadoeheights@eircom.net
Dir: *16km S of Kerry Airport and 5km N of Killarney. Signposted off the N22 Tralee road*
Superbly located overlooking Loch Lein, this hotel has been extensively refurbished to a very high standard. On the first floor Fredericks restaurant enjoys panoramic views, also shared by the stylish, air conditioned bedrooms which have their own decks. There is a spacious lounge, a cocktail bar and a banqueting/conference suite.
ROOMS: 75 en suite (5 fmly) **FACILITIES:** STV Indoor swimming (H) Tennis (hard) Fishing Sauna Solarium Gym Jacuzzi/spa Steam room Plunge pool **PARKING:** 120 **NOTES:** No dogs Closed Nov-1 Apr **CARDS:**

★★★★78% ❀ Killarney Park
Kenmare Place
☎ 064 35555 064 35266
e-mail: kph@iol.ie
Dir: *N22 from Cork to Killarney. At 1st rdbt take 1st exit to Town Centre and at 2nd rdbt take 1st exit. Hotel is 2nd entrance on the left*
On the edge of town, this charming purpose-built hotel combines elegance with comfort. The hotel has a warm atmosphere with rich colours and fabrics, open fires, and welcoming staff. Public rooms and bedrooms are very comfortable indeed.
ROOMS: 76 en suite (4 fmly) No smoking in 33 bedrooms d IR£240-IR£500 (incl. bkfst) * LB **FACILITIES:** STV Indoor swimming (H) Snooker Sauna Gym Pool table Jacuzzi/spa Outdoor Canadian hot-tub Plunge pool Xmas **CONF:** Thtr 150 Class 70 Board 35 **SERVICES:** Lift air con **PARKING:** 70 **NOTES:** No dogs (ex guide dogs) Closed 24-26 Dec **CARDS:**

★★★★64% Muckross Park Hotel
Muckross Village
☎ 064 31938 📠 064 31965
e-mail: muckrossparkhotel@tinet.ie
Dir: *from Killarney take road to Kenmare, hotel 4km on left, adjacent to National Park, Muckross House & Gardens*
An 18th century hotel set in the heart of the Killarney National Park. Relaxing lounge areas feature comfortable furniture, warm colour schemes and chandeliers. Bedrooms are attractively decorated and well equipped. Good food is served in the Bluepool restaurant, as well as the adjacent thatched pub, Molly Darcys, which offers live entertainment.
ROOMS: 27 en suite (2 fmly) No smoking in 2 bedrooms s IR£85; d IR£130 (incl. bkfst) * LB **FACILITIES:** STV **CONF:** Thtr 200 Class 80 Board 40 **PARKING:** 250 **NOTES:** No dogs (ex guide dogs) No smoking in restaurant Closed Dec-Feb **CARDS:**
See advert on this page

★★★76% *Cahernane*
MANOR HOUSE HOTELS
Muckross Rd
☎ 064 31895 📠 064 34340
e-mail: cahernane@tinet.ie
This fine old country mansion with a magnificent mountain backdrop enjoys panoramic views from its setting beside the lake. Elegant period furnishings, fresh flowers and the glow of silver combine to create a welcoming atmosphere. Service is attentive but unobtrusive, and cuisine is of a high standard.
ROOMS: 14 en suite 33 annexe en suite **FACILITIES:** Tennis (hard) Fishing Croquet lawn entertainment **PARKING:** 50 **NOTES:** No dogs (ex guide dogs) No smoking in restaurant Closed 2 Nov-Mar
CARDS:

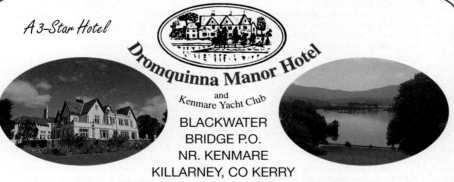

KILLARNEY, continued

★★★68% *Gleneagle*

☎ 064 31870 🖹 064 32646
e-mail: gleneagl@iol.ie
Dir: *1m outside Killarney town on the Kenmare Road - N71*

Excellent facilities for both leisure and corporate guests are offered in this family run hotel. The impressive new Events Centre is one of the largest in the country with a 2000 delegate capacity. Public areas are spacious, and the dedicated owners personally oversee the day to day running of the hotel.

ROOMS: 213 en suite (35 fmly) No smoking in 20 bedrooms **FACILITIES:** STV Indoor swimming (H) Tennis (hard) Fishing Squash Snooker Sauna Solarium Gym Pool table Jacuzzi/spa Pitch & Putt Table tennis Steam room Beauty therapist entertainment **CONF:** Thtr 1000 Class 400 Board 70 **SERVICES:** Lift **PARKING:** 500 **CARDS:**

★★★67% *Castlerosse*

☎ 064 31144 🖹 064 31031
Dir: *from Killarney town take R562 for Killorglin and The Ring of Kerry, hotel is 1.5km from town on the left hand side*

Set in 6,000 acres of land overlooking Lough Leane, this beautiful hotel offers warm hospitality and good food, as well as special facilities on the adjoining championship golf courses. Boating and fishing trips are available on nearby lakes.

ROOMS: 110 en suite (27 fmly) No smoking in 4 bedrooms **FACILITIES:** Indoor swimming (H) Tennis (hard) Snooker Sauna Gym Jacuzzi/spa Golfing & riding arranged entertainment **CONF:** Thtr 200 Class 100 **SERVICES:** Lift **PARKING:** 100 **NOTES:** No dogs (ex guide dogs) Closed Dec-Feb **CARDS:**

★★★67% *Lake*

Muckross Rd
☎ 064 31035 🖹 064 31902
e-mail: lakehotel@tinet.ie
Dir: *Kenmare road out of Killarney*

Approached by a wooded drive, this former mansion stands in lovely countryside with lake and mountain views, and woodland walks. Bedrooms are well equipped and some have balconies and four-poster beds. Public rooms are spacious and the lounge has kept an atmosphere of traditional comfort.

ROOMS: 65 en suite (10 fmly) **FACILITIES:** STV Tennis (hard) Fishing Pool table Putting green entertainment **CONF:** Thtr 80 Class 60 Board 40 **SERVICES:** Lift air con **PARKING:** 143 **NOTES:** No dogs (ex guide dogs) Closed 3 Dec-11 Feb **CARDS:**

★★★66% *Killarney Ryan*

Cork Rd
☎ 064 31555 🖹 064 32438
e-mail: ryan@indigo.ie
Dir: *on N22 route*

On the outskirts of Killarney, this hotel offers good standards of comfort. Public rooms include a large lounge, a restaurant and lounge bar opening on to the gardens. Many of the bedrooms can accommodate families, and the Ryan Group offer an all-inclusive summer holiday rate which can be good value.

ROOMS: 168 en suite (168 fmly) No smoking in 20 bedrooms **FACILITIES:** STV Indoor swimming (H) Tennis (hard) Sauna Jacuzzi/spa Steam room Crazy golf entertainment ch fac **SERVICES:** Lift **PARKING:** 180 **NOTES:** No dogs Closed Dec & Jan **CARDS:**

★★★65% International

Kenmare Pl
☎ 064 31816 🖹 064 31837
e-mail: inter@iol.ie
Dir: *town centre*

This hotel offers quality bedrooms with modern comforts. Hannigan's Bar and the lounge are popular and bar snacks are available. There is a more intimate dining room, where soft candlelight glows against mahogany panelling. There is a library, snooker room and a keen interest is taken in golfing guests - tee times can be arranged at any of the many courses in the area.

ROOMS: 75 en suite (6 fmly) **FACILITIES:** STV Pool table entertainment **CONF:** Thtr 200 Class 100 Board 25 **SERVICES:** Lift **NOTES:** Closed 23-27 Dec **CARDS:**

★★★63% *Killarney Court Hotel*

Tralee Rd
☎ 064 37070 🖹 064 37060
e-mail: stay@irishcourthotels.com
Dir: *Travelling from Tralee on the main Tralee Rd, the 1st rdbt towards Killarney, hotel on left*

Purpose built to a high standard, this new stone-fronted hotel has spacious public areas, an inviting pub and a contemporary restaurant offering a mix of transatlantic influences and traditional cuisine. The large bedrooms are attractively furnished and very comfortable. Bar food is served all day, as well as a carvery lunch.

ROOMS: 96 en suite (8 fmly) No smoking in 6 bedrooms **FACILITIES:** STV Sauna Gym Jacuzzi/spa Steam room **CONF:** Thtr 120 Class 70 Board 60 **SERVICES:** Lift **PARKING:** 130 **NOTES:** Closed 25 Dec **CARDS:**

★★★62% *White Gates*

Muckross Rd
☎ 064 31164 🖹 064 34850
Dir: *1km from Killarney town on Muckross road on left*

Distinctive blue and ochre paintwork draws the eye to this hotel. The same flair for colour combinations is evident throughout the interior and bedrooms are particularly attractive. The natural harmony of wood and stone is a feature of the well designed lounge bar and the restaurant, with its conservatory front, is filled with light. There is also a very comfortable lounge.

ROOMS: 27 en suite **FACILITIES:** STV entertainment **CONF:** Class 50 **PARKING:** 50 **NOTES:** No dogs (ex guide dogs) Closed 21-29 Dec **CARDS:**

★★★59% *Scotts Garden Hotel*
College St
☎ 064 31060 🖹 064 31582
Located in the town centre, this hotel offers pleasant bedrooms, a bar and a patio garden. Special concessions are available at the sister Gleneagles Hotel's leisure facilities.
FACILITIES: CARDS:

★★66% *Arbutus*
College St
☎ 064 31037 🖹 064 34033
e-mail: arbutushotel@tinet.ie

This attractive hotel has been completely renovated and its entrance now features a fine foyer lounge and a second lounge adjoining the bar. There is a good restaurant, serving freshly prepared dishes based on local Irish produce. Bedrooms are comfortable with modern facilities.
ROOMS: 39 en suite (4 fmly) **FACILITIES:** STV **NOTES:** No dogs (ex guide dogs) Closed 19-30 Dec **CARDS:**

See advert on this page

★★63% *Darby O'Gills*
Lissivigeen, Mallow Rd
☎ 064 34168 & 34919 🖹 064 36794
A modern country house, offering smart, spacious and well-equipped bedrooms. Dinner is served in the restaurant, and bar food in the comfortable lounge bar. There is also a traditional Irish pub.
ROOMS: 13 en suite (3 fmly) **FACILITIES:** STV entertainment **CONF:** Thtr 250 Class 150 Board 60 **SERVICES:** air con **PARKING:** 150 **NOTES:** No dogs (ex guide dogs) Closed 25 Dec
CARDS:

KILLASHEE, Co Kildare — Map 01 D3

○ Killashee House
☎ 045 879277 🖹 045 879266
ROOMS: 84 en suite **NOTES:** Opening November 2000

KILLINEY, Co Dublin — Map 01 D4

★★★65% Court
☎ 01 2851622 🖹 01 2852085
e-mail: book@killineycourt.ie
Dir: *from Dublin-N11 via Donnybrook and Stillorgan, turn left off dual carriageway at traffic lights 1.6km after Cabinteely, right at next traffic lights*
Overlooking the breathtaking Killiney Bay, this Victorian mansion with pleasing grounds is only 12 miles from Dublin with excellent train links. The International Conference facilities include translating equipment.

continued

ROOMS: 86 en suite (29 fmly) No smoking in 8 bedrooms s IR£75-IR£90; d IR£95-IR£115 (incl. bkfst) * LB **FACILITIES:** Beach in front of hotel Xmas **CONF:** Thtr 300 Class 180 Board 60 Del IR£100 * **SERVICES:** Lift **PARKING:** 200 **NOTES:** No dogs (ex guide dogs) **CARDS:**

★★★64% *Fitzpatrick Castle*
☎ 01 2840700 🖹 01 2850207
e-mail: info@fitzpatricks.com
This converted castle with modern extensions is set in its own attractive gardens and grounds with views over Dublin Bay. There is a helipad, and a courtesy coach is available for transfers to and from the airport.
ROOMS: 113 en suite (40 fmly) No smoking in 18 bedrooms **FACILITIES:** Indoor swimming (H) Sauna Gym Beauty/hairdressing salon Steam room entertainment **CONF:** Thtr 500 Class 240 Board 80 **SERVICES:** Lift **PARKING:** 300 **NOTES:** No dogs (ex guide dogs) **CARDS:**

KILTIMAGH, Co Mayo — Map 01 B4

★★65% Cill Aod-in Hotel
Main St
☎ 094 81761 🖹 094 81838
e-mail: cillaodain@tinet.com
Dir: *located in Kiltimagh Town Centre*
Situated in the heart of historic Kiltimagh, this hotel offers comfortable public areas and enjoyable cuisine. Guests are made to feel very welcome at this home from home. Easy on-and off-street parking is available opposite the hotel.
ROOMS: 19 en suite (4 fmly) No smoking in 4 bedrooms s IR£47.50-IR£55; d IR£58-IR£73 (incl. bkfst) * LB **FACILITIES:** STV Riding Xmas **NOTES:** No dogs (ex guide dogs) **CARDS:**

KINGSCOURT, Co Cavan Map 01 C4

★★★65% *Cabra Castle*
☎ 042 9667030 🖷 042 9667039
e-mail: cabrach@iol.ie

Rebuilt in 1808, the Castle stands in 100 acres of parkland and is part of a national park. The staff are friendly and welcoming. The main reception rooms are elegant and invite relaxation and there are some courtyard bedrooms. The pleasant bar leads out onto a patio garden. There is free golf to residents and fishing and archery nearby.

ROOMS: 20 en suite 46 annexe en suite (5 fmly) **FACILITIES:** Golf 9 Riding entertainment **CONF:** Thtr 300 Class 100 Board 50 **PARKING:** 200 **NOTES:** Closed 25-27 Dec **CARDS:**

KINSALE, Co Cork Map 01 B2

★★★73% Actons
Pier Rd
☎ 021 4772135 🖷 021 4772231
e-mail: actonsh@indigo.ie
Dir: *hotel is located in the Town Centre area facing Kinsale Harbour, 500 yards from Yacht Club Marina*

The location of this hotel, set in gardens overlooking the waterfront and marina, is ideal. The hotel has a bar and bistro and the Captain's Table restaurant, which continues to offer enjoyable food. The luxurious lounge is comfortable and bedrooms are all of a good standard. Friendly and attentive staff contribute greatly towards the enjoyment of a visit.

ROOMS: 76 en suite (20 fmly) s IR£70-IR£100; d IR£90-IR£130 (incl. bkfst) * LB **FACILITIES:** STV Indoor swimming (H) Sauna Solarium Gym entertainment Xmas **CONF:** Thtr 350 Class 200 Board 100 Del from IR£90 * **SERVICES:** Lift **PARKING:** 70 **NOTES:** No dogs (ex guide dogs) Closed 7 Jan-8 Feb **CARDS:**

★★★68% Trident
Worlds End
☎ 021 4772301 🖷 021 4774173
e-mail: info@tridenthotel
Dir: *take R600 from Cork city to Kinsale, drive along the Kinsale waterfront, the hotel is located just beyond the pier, on the waterfront*

Located at the harbour's edge, the Trident Hotel has its own marina with boats for hire. Many of the bedrooms have superb views and two have balconies. The restaurant and lounge both overlook the harbour and pleasant staff provide hospitable service.

ROOMS: 58 en suite (2 fmly) s IR£75-IR£95; d IR£110-IR£140 (incl. bkfst) * LB **FACILITIES:** STV Sauna Gym Jacuzzi/spa Steam room Xmas **CONF:** Thtr 250 Class 170 Board 60 Del from IR£100 * **SERVICES:** Lift **PARKING:** 60 **NOTES:** No dogs (ex guide dogs) Closed 25-26 Dec **CARDS:**

KNOCK, Co Mayo Map 01 B4

★★★65% Knock House
Ballyhaunis Rd
☎ 094 88088 🖷 094 88044
e-mail: hotel@knock-shrive.ie
Dir: *The hotel is located on the Ballyhaunis Road,1/2km from Knock village*

Adjacent to the Marian shrine and basilica, set in landscaped gardens, this creatively designed hotel features extensive use of limestone and natural wood finishes. Facilities include two spacious lounges, restaurant, dispense bar and conference centre. Contemporary bedrooms are decorated in soft colours, six rooms are suitable for disabled guests. There is a medical assessment centre for guests who require special care.

continued

ROOMS: 68 en suite (12 fmly) s IR£55; d IR£86 (incl. bkfst) LB **FACILITIES:** ch fac Xmas **CONF:** Thtr 150 Class 90 Board 45 **SERVICES:** Lift **PARKING:** 150 **NOTES:** No dogs (ex guide dogs) **CARDS:**

★★★59% Belmont
☎ 094 88122 🖷 094 88532
e-mail: belmonthotel@tinet.ie
Dir: *on the N17, Galway side of Knock Village. Turn right at Burke's supermarket & Pub. Hotel 150yards on right*

ROOMS: 64 en suite (6 fmly) No smoking in 3 bedrooms s IR£38-IR£52; d IR£58-IR£80 (incl. bkfst) * LB **FACILITIES:** Solarium Gym Jacuzzi/spa Steamroom Natural health therapies entertainment **CONF:** Thtr 500 Class 100 Board 20 **SERVICES:** Lift air con **PARKING:** 110 **NOTES:** No dogs (ex guide dogs) No smoking in restaurant Closed 25 & 26 Dec **CARDS:**

LAHINCH, Co Clare Map 01 B3

★★★59% *Aberdeen Arms*
☎ 065 81100 🖷 065 81228
e-mail: aberdeen@websters.ie
Dir: *56km from Shannon airport, N18 to Ennis, N85 to Ennistymon, turn left, approx 3km to Lahinch, turn left at top of Main St*

A popular and recently modernised hotel offering very comfortable day rooms where guests can expect to mingle with the golfing fraternity playing the famous Lahinch Links Course. Bedrooms are furnished in a popular style and well equipped.

ROOMS: 55 en suite **FACILITIES:** STV Snooker Sauna Pool table Jacuzzi/spa **CONF:** Thtr 200 Class 100 Board 50 **PARKING:** 85 **NOTES:** No dogs (ex guide dogs) **CARDS:**

LEIXLIP, Co Kildare Map 01 D4

★★★76% Leixlip House
Captains Hill
☎ 01 6242268 🖷 01 6244177
e-mail: manager@leixliphouse.com
Dir: *from Leixlip motorway junct continue into village. Turn right at lights and continue up hill*

This lovely stone-built country house dates from the 18th century and retains many of its original features. Accommodation is of high quality, as is the service, and the restaurant serves enjoyable meals.

ROOMS: 19 en suite (2 fmly) s IR£95-IR£115; d IR£130-IR£150 (incl. bkfst) * LB **FACILITIES:** STV **CONF:** Thtr 130 Class 60 Board 40 **PARKING:** 64 **NOTES:** No dogs **CARDS:**

LIMAVADY, Co Londonderry Map 01 C6

★★★★67% Radisson Roe Park Hotel & Golf Resort
BT49 9LB
☎ 028 7772 2222 🖷 028 7772 2313
e-mail: reservations@radissonroepark.com
Dir: *on the A2 Londonderry/Limavady road, 16m from Londonderry, 1m from Limavady*

In a stunning location just outside the town, this country house complex offers a superb range of sporting, leisure and business facilities. Public areas include lounges, a restaurant, brasserie, and a bar edging the colourful courtyard. The bedrooms are spacious and modern.

ROOMS: 64 en suite (15 fmly) No smoking in 16 bedrooms s £90-£115; d £130-£155 (incl. bkfst) * LB **FACILITIES:** STV Indoor swimming (H) Golf 18 Fishing Sauna Solarium Gym Pool table Croquet lawn Putting green Jacuzzi/spa Floodlit driving range practice area,otuside tees,golf training academy. Xmas **CONF:** Thtr 450 Class 180 Board 100 Del from £85 * **SERVICES:** Lift **PARKING:** 300 **NOTES:** No dogs (ex guide dogs) **CARDS:**

LIMERICK, Co Limerick Map 01 B3

★★★★71% Castletroy Park

Dublin Rd
☎ 061 335566 061 331117
e-mail: sales@castletroy-park.ie
Dir: *on N7, 5km from Limerick*
Encircled by gardens close to the University of Limerick, this hotel feels light and airy, and combines modern comforts with attractive decor. Fax and computer points in the bedrooms are popular with business guests while McLaughlin's Restaurant serves good food and is a popular meeting place.
ROOMS: 107 en suite (78 fmly) No smoking in 30 bedrooms s IR£90-IR£140; d IR£94-IR£160 (incl. bkfst) * LB **FACILITIES:** STV Indoor swimming (H) Sauna Gym Jacuzzi/spa Running track Steam room entertainment **CONF:** Thtr 450 Class 270 Board 100 Del from IR£109 * **SERVICES:** Lift **PARKING:** 160 **NOTES:** No dogs (ex guide dogs) Closed 24-26 Dec **CARDS:**

★★★72% Jurys

Ennis Rd
☎ 061 327777 061 326400
e-mail: bookings@jurys.com
Dir: *located at junction of Ennis Rd, O'Callaghan Strand and Sarsfield Bridge*
This hotel, standing in four acres of riverside grounds, offers excellent corporate and leisure facilities, including an indoor swimming pool. Bedrooms come in two styles, executive or standard and there is also a bar and restaurant.
ROOMS: 95 en suite (22 fmly) No smoking in 16 bedrooms s fr IR£107; d fr IR£134 * LB **FACILITIES:** STV Indoor swimming (H) Tennis (hard) Sauna Gym Jacuzzi/spa Steam room Plunge pool **CONF:** Thtr 200 Class 90 Board 45 **PARKING:** 200 **NOTES:** No dogs (ex guide dogs) Closed 24-27 Dec **CARDS:**

★★★72% *Limerick Ryan*

Ennis Rd
☎ 061 453922 061 326333
e-mail: ryan@indigo.ie
Dir: *on N18, Ennis road*

Close to the city, in its own grounds, the Limerick Ryan has smart public areas located in the original part of this classic house, including lounges and restaurants, a cocktail bar with a fire, sofas and a pianist. The well equipped bedrooms are located in a modern extension with 24-hour room service. Other facilities include conference suites, a business centre and patio gardens.
ROOMS: 181 en suite (181 fmly) No smoking in 19 bedrooms **FACILITIES:** STV Gym Gym nearby available free to guests entertainment **CONF:** Thtr 130 Class 60 Board 40 **SERVICES:** Lift **PARKING:** 180 **NOTES:** No dogs **CARDS:**

★★★64% South Court Business & Leisure Hotel

Adare Rd, Raheen
☎ 065 6823000 065 6823759
e-mail: cro@lynchotels.com
A pleasant purpose-built hotel, suitable for both leisure and business guests. The latter will appreciate the well-equipped executive rooms, where fax machines, ISDN lines and laptop computers are available. All the rooms are very comfortable and there is a restaurant and a pub/bistro. Secretarial services are provided in the Business Centre.
ROOMS: 65 en suite (65 fmly) No smoking in 6 bedrooms s fr IR£140; d fr IR£240 * LB **FACILITIES:** STV Sauna Solarium Gym Steam room (leisure centre due 2000) entertainment Xmas **CONF:** Thtr 200 Class 120 Board 50 Del from IR£50 * **SERVICES:** Lift air con **PARKING:** 250 **NOTES:** No dogs (ex guide dogs) Civ Wed 110 **CARDS:**

★★★62% *Greenhills*

Caherdavin
☎ 061 453033 061 453307
Dir: *situated on the N18, approx 2m from City Centre*
Set in 3.5 acres of lovely landscaped gardens, this hotel offers a range of large, comfortable and well appointed bedrooms. Along with tempting cuisine, the hotel also has superb conference and leisure facilities.
ROOMS: 58 en suite (4 fmly) **FACILITIES:** STV Indoor swimming (H) Tennis (hard) Sauna Solarium Gym Jacuzzi/spa Beauty parlour Massage **CONF:** Thtr 500 Class 200 Board 50 **PARKING:** 150 **NOTES:** No dogs **CARDS:**

★★★62% *Two Mile Inn*

Ennis Rd
☎ 061 326255 061 453783
Dir: *on N22, near Bunratty Castle & airport*
On the outskirts of Limerick city near Bunratty Castle and Shannon Airport, the Two Mile Inn has a new pub and restaurant, as well as a spacious lounge and comfortable bedrooms.
ROOMS: 123 en suite (30 fmly) No smoking in 67 bedrooms **FACILITIES:** STV **CONF:** Thtr 350 Class 200 Board 40 **PARKING:** 300 **NOTES:** No dogs (ex guide dogs) **CARDS:**

★★★60% Jurys Inn Limerick

Lower Mallow St
☎ 061 207000 061 400966
e-mail: info@jurys.com
Dir: *from N7 follow signs for City Centre into O'Connell St, turn off at N18 (Shannon/Galway), hotel is off O'Connell St*
A smartly decorated new hotel on the city side of the river, convenient for the shopping and business areas. Facilities include a spacious foyer, bar and restaurant, a board room for meetings and an elevator to all floors. Bedrooms are well equipped and offer good value, especially the family rooms. Staff are friendly and enthusiastic.
ROOMS: 151 en suite (108 fmly) No smoking in 56 bedrooms d IR£106 * **FACILITIES:** STV entertainment **CONF:** Thtr 50 Class 25 Board 18 **SERVICES:** Lift **NOTES:** No dogs (ex guide dogs) Closed 24-26 Dec **CARDS:**

★★70% Woodfield House

Ennis Rd
☎ 061 453022 061 326755
e-mail: woodfieldhotel@eircom.net
Dir: *on outskirts of city on main Shannon road*
This intimate hotel stands on the N18, a short distance from the city centre. The smart bedrooms are comfortable and well appointed. There is a dining room, and the bar serves food all day.

continued

LIMERICK, continued

ROOMS: 26 en suite (3 fmly) s IR£55-IR£59; d IR£85-IR£95 (incl. bkfst) * LB **FACILITIES:** STV Tennis (hard) **CONF:** Thtr 130 Class 60 Board 60 **SERVICES:** air con **PARKING:** 80 **NOTES:** No dogs (ex guide dogs) Closed 24-25 Dec **CARDS:**

LISDOONVARNA, Co Clare — Map 01 B3

★★70%

Sheedy's Restaurant & Hotel

village inn HOTELS

☎ 065 7074026 📠 065 7074555
e-mail: sheedys@gofree.indigo.ie

This well run family hotel provides warm hospitality, comfort, and good food from its award-winning restaurant. The hotel is situated beside a spa complex in well tended gardens in a fascinating region for tourists.

ROOMS: 11 en suite s IR£45-IR£55; d IR£65-IR£70 (incl. bkfst) * LB **PARKING:** 42 **NOTES:** No dogs (ex guide dogs) No smoking in restaurant Closed mid Oct-Etr **CARDS:**

LISMORE, Co Waterford — Map 01 C2

★★64% *Ballyrafter House*

☎ 058 54002 📠 058 53050
Dir: *1km from Lismore opposite Lismore Castle*

A welcoming country house, set in its own grounds opposite Lismore Castle. Inside, most of the bedrooms are pleasantly furnished in pine. The bar and conservatory are where guests, anglers and locals meet to discuss the day's events. The hotel has its own salmon fishing on the River Blackwater.

ROOMS: 10 en suite (1 fmly) **FACILITIES:** Fishing Riding Putting green **PARKING:** 20 **NOTES:** No dogs (ex guide dogs) Closed Nov-Feb **CARDS:**

LONDONDERRY, Co Londonderry — Map 01 C5

★★★71% Beech Hill Country House Hotel

MANOR HOUSE HOTELS

32 Ardmore Rd BT47 3QP
☎ 028 7134 9279 📠 028 7134 5366
e-mail: info@beech-hill.com
Dir: *From A6 Londonderry-Belfast take Faughan Bridge turning and continue 1m to hotel opposite Ardmore Chapel*

Dating back to 1729, Beech Hill is an impressive mansion, standing in 32 acres of woodlands, waterfalls and gardens. Public areas are comfortable and attractive, and the splendid bedroom wing provides spacious, well equipped rooms, in addition to those in the main house.

ROOMS: 17 en suite 10 annexe en suite (4 fmly) s £60-£80; d £80-£120 (incl. bkfst) * LB **FACILITIES:** Tennis (hard) Sauna Gym Jacuzzi/spa **CONF:** Thtr 100 Class 50 Board 30 Del from £85 * **SERVICES:** Lift **PARKING:** 75 **NOTES:** No dogs (ex guide dogs) No smoking in restaurant Closed 24-25 Dec **CARDS:**

★★★69% Trinity Hotel

22-24 Strand Rd BT48 7AB
☎ 028 7127 1271 📠 028 7127 1277
e-mail: ifo@thetrinityhotel.com
Dir: *to get to Derry City Centre cross River Foyle, follow signs for city centre, hotel is approx 0.5m from Guildhall adjecent to shopping centre/cinema*

The interior design at this modern hotel is contemporary and has created a good deal of interest. Public areas include a continental-style café bar and the former snug has been converted into a bar-bistro. The panelled restaurant provides a more formal dining option.

continued

ROOMS: 40 en suite (17 fmly) s £65-£75; d £85-£90 (incl. bkfst) * LB **FACILITIES:** STV Conservatory & roof garden entertainment **CONF:** Thtr 160 Class 80 Board 60 Del from £55 * **SERVICES:** Lift air con **PARKING:** 30 **NOTES:** No dogs (ex guide dogs) **CARDS:**

LUCAN, Co Dublin — Map 01 D4

★★★70%

Finnstown Country House Hotel & Golf Course

Newcastle Rd
☎ 01 6280644 📠 01 6281088
e-mail: manager@finnstown-hotel.ie
Dir: *from M1 take 1st exit onto M50 S/bound. 1st exit after Toll Bridge. At rdbt take 3rd left (N4 W). Left at t/lights. Over next 2 rdbt. Hotel on right*

Set in 45 acres of wooded grounds, Finnstown is a calm and peaceful country house. There is a wide choice of bedroom styles and the garden suites are particularly good. Reception rooms are inviting and furnished in period style.

ROOMS: 25 en suite 26 annexe en suite No smoking in 27 bedrooms s fr IR£95; d fr IR£160 (incl. bkfst) * LB **FACILITIES:** STV Indoor swimming (H) Tennis (hard & grass) Solarium Gym Pool table Croquet lawn Putting green Turkish bath Table tennis Massage Xmas **CONF:** Thtr 100 Class 60 Board 30 Del from IR£137 * **PARKING:** 90 **CARDS:**

See advert under DUBLIN

★★★64% Lucan Spa

☎ 01 6280495 & 6280497 📠 01 6280841
Dir: *hotel is located on N4, approx 11km from city centre, approx 20 mins from Dublin airport*

Set in its own grounds, the Lucan Spa is a fine Georgian house. Guests have complimentary use of Lucan Golf Course, adjacent to the hotel. A conference centre with facilities for 600 delegates is also available.

ROOMS: 71 rms (61 en suite) (15 fmly) No smoking in 21 bedrooms s fr IR£50; d fr IR£85 (incl. bkfst) * LB **FACILITIES:** STV Golf 18 entertainment **CONF:** Thtr 600 Class 250 Board 80 **SERVICES:** Lift air con **PARKING:** 90 **NOTES:** No dogs (ex guide dogs) Closed 25 Dec **CARDS:**

See advert on opposite page

MACREDDIN, Co Wicklow — Map 01 D3

★★★★71% *Brooklodge at MacCreddin*

Macreddin Village
☎ 0402 36444 📠 0402 36580
e-mail: brooklodge@macreddin.ie

MACROOM, Co Cork — Map 01 B2

★★72% Castle

village inn HOTELS

Main St
☎ 026 41074 📠 026 41505
e-mail: castlehotel@tinet.ie
Dir: *on N22*

The Castle Hotel contains a new leisure centre and some fine bedrooms. The hotel service is excellent and guests feel very much at home. There is a pleasant lounge and a function room, while the food in the restaurant and the bar is well cooked and imaginatively presented.

ROOMS: 42 en suite (5 fmly) s IR£50-IR£59; d IR£64-IR£78 (incl. bkfst) * LB **FACILITIES:** STV Indoor swimming (H) Sauna Gym Jacuzzi/spa **CONF:** Board 20 **SERVICES:** air con **PARKING:** 30 **NOTES:** No dogs Closed 25-27 Dec **CARDS:**

See advert on opposite page

MALLOW, Co Cork Map 01 B2

Premier Collection

★★★🏵🏵🏵 **Longueville House**

☎ 022 47156 & 47306 📠 022 47459

e-mail: info@longuevillehouse.ie

Dir: 3 miles west of Mallow via N72 Road 15 Killarney

Set in a wooded estate, this 18th-century Georgian mansion has many fine features. The comfortable bedrooms overlook the river valley and the courtyard maze. The two elegant sitting rooms have fine examples of Italian plasterwork and an Adams mantlepiece graces the Presidents Restaurant. Cuisine in the hotel restaurant is exciting and inventive, and makes good use of excellent fresh produce.

ROOMS: 22 en suite (5 fmly) No smoking in 5 bedrooms s IR£60-IR£200; d IR£120-IR£130 (incl. bkfst) * LB **FACILITIES:** STV Fishing Croquet lawn Country Walks on estate **CONF:** Thtr 50 Class 30 Board 30 Del from IR£130 * **PARKING:** 30 **NOTES:** No dogs (ex guide dogs) No smoking in restaurant Closed 17 Dec-2 Mar **CARDS:**

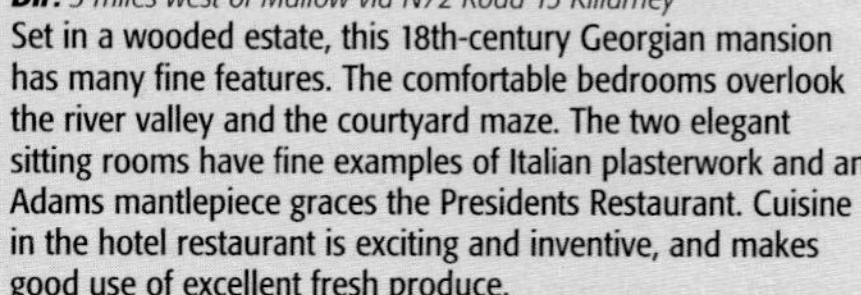

★★★63% **Springfort Hall Hotel**

☎ 022 21278 📠 022 21557

e-mail: stay@springfort-hall.com

Dir: on Mallow/Limerick road N20, right turn off at 2 Pot House R581, hotel 500mtrs on right sign over gate

This 18th century country manor is tucked away amid tranquil woodlands. There is an attractive oval dining room, as well as a drawing room and lounge bar. The comfortable bedrooms are mainly in the new wing and are spacious and well appointed, with superb country views.

ROOMS: 50 en suite (4 fmly) s IR£45-IR£60; d IR£80-IR£100 (incl. bkfst) * LB **FACILITIES:** STV entertainment **CONF:** Thtr 300 Class 200 Board 50 Del from IR£100 * **PARKING:** 200 **NOTES:** No dogs (ex guide dogs) Closed 23 Dec-2 Jan Civ Wed 250 **CARDS:**

MAYNOOTH, Co Kildare Map 01 C4

★★★74% 🏵🏵 **Moyglare Manor**

Moyglare

☎ 01 6286351 📠 01 6285405

e-mail: moyglare@iol.ie

Dir: turn off N4 at Maynooth/Naas, then right to Maynooth town. Keep right at St Marys Church and continue 2m then left at X-roads

This elegant 18th-century house is a haven of calm, set in its own grounds in rich pasture land. Guests arrive along an imposing avenue and are greeted with genuine hospitality. Bedrooms are beautifully furnished in keeping with the Georgian style of the house, and there are several peaceful lounges and a convivial bar. The hotel cuisine has a justified high reputation.

continued on p866

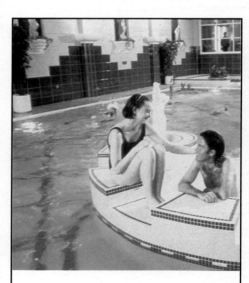

MAYNOOTH, continued

ROOMS: 17 en suite (1 fmly) No smoking in 5 bedrooms **FACILITIES:** STV Tennis **CONF:** Thtr 30 Board 20 **PARKING:** 120 **NOTES:** No dogs (ex guide dogs) No children 12yrs No smoking in restaurant Closed 24-26 Dec **CARDS:**

MIDLETON, Co Cork Map 01 C2

★★★66% Midleton Park

☎ 021 631767 021 631605
e-mail: info@midletonparkhotel.ie
***Dir:** from Cork, turn off N25 hotel on right hand side. From Waterford, turn off N25, over bridge until T-junct, turn right, hotel on right*
This purpose-built hotel, situated in an area of great interest, is just off the N25 Cork/Rosslare route, ten miles from Cork. The hotel features fine, spacious and well appointed bedrooms and the comfortable restaurant offers good food and attentive service. Conference and banqueting facilities are available.
ROOMS: 40 en suite (12 fmly) No smoking in 6 bedrooms s IR£60-IR£80; d IR£80-IR£130 * LB **FACILITIES:** STV **CONF:** Thtr 400 Class 200 Board 40 Del from IR£63.95 * **SERVICES:** air con **PARKING:** 500 **NOTES:** No dogs (ex guide dogs) Closed 25 Dec
CARDS:

MONAGHAN, Co Monaghan Map 01 C5

★★★★62% Hillgrove

Old Armagh Rd
☎ 047 81288 047 84951
e-mail: hillgrove@gmequinn-hotels.com
***Dir:** off N2 at Cathedral, cont for 400 mtrs, left just beyond Cathedral*
ROOMS: 44 en suite (2 fmly) s IR£48; d IR£78 (incl. bkfst) * LB **FACILITIES:** STV Jacuzzi/spa entertainment Xmas **CONF:** Thtr 1200 Class 600 Board 200 Del from IR£92 * **SERVICES:** Lift air con **PARKING:** 430 **NOTES:** No dogs (ex guide dogs)
CARDS:

NAVAN, Co Meath Map 01 C4

★★★62% Ardboyne Hotel

Dublin Rd
☎ 046 23119 046 22355
e-mail: ardboyne@quinn-hotels.com
***Dir:** From Dublin-N3 north through Blanchards Town to Navan, hotel is on left hand side on N3*
This welcoming hotel is situated on the edge of Navan. Bedrooms are comfortably furnished and freshly decorated, and overlook pretty gardens. Public areas are smartly furnished and include an inviting lounge warmed by an open fire, a well appointed dining room and a saloon style bar. Conference suites are available.
ROOMS: 29 en suite (25 fmly) No smoking in 10 bedrooms s IR£46-IR£56; d IR£72-IR£80 (incl. bkfst) * LB **FACILITIES:** STV entertainment **CONF:** Thtr 400 Class 200 Board 150 **PARKING:** 186 **NOTES:** No dogs Closed 24-26 Dec **CARDS:**

NENAGH, Co Tipperary Map 01 B3

★★★68% Nenagh Abbey Court Hotel

Dublin Rd
☎ 067 41111 067 41022
e-mail: abycourt@indigo.ie
***Dir:** Hotel 2 mins from O'Connor's Shopping Centre on Dublin side of Nenagh*
ROOMS: 46 en suite (3 fmly) No smoking in 10 bedrooms s fr IR£49; d fr IR£78 (incl. bkfst) * LB **FACILITIES:** STV entertainment **CONF:** Thtr 600 Class 150 Board 60 Del from IR£78 * **SERVICES:** Lift air con **PARKING:** 200 **NOTES:** No dogs (ex guide dogs) Closed 25 Dec
CARDS:

NEWBRIDGE, Co Kildare Map 01 C3

★★★73% Keadeen

☎ 045 431666 045 434402
e-mail: keadeen@iol.ie
***Dir:** M7 junct 10, (Newbridge, Curragh) at rdbt follow round to right and go in direction of Newbridge, hotel is on left 1km from rdbt*
This family-owned hotel is set in eight acres of landscaped gardens, and has good leisure facilities. Comfortable public areas include a spacious drawing room, reception foyer and two bars. The hotel is well placed for Dublin Airport and the Mondello racing circuit.
ROOMS: 55 en suite (4 fmly) s IR£95-IR£200; d IR£140-IR£200 (incl. bkfst) * LB **FACILITIES:** STV Indoor swimming (H) Sauna Solarium Gym Jacuzzi/spa Aerobics studio Treatment room Massage entertainment Xmas **CONF:** Thtr 800 Class 300 Board 40 Del from IR£109 * **PARKING:** 200 **NOTES:** No dogs (ex guide dogs) Closed 24 Dec-3 Jan RS low season **CARDS:**

NEWCASTLE, Co Down Map 01 D5

★★64% *Enniskeen House*

98 Bryansford Rd BT33 0LF
☎ 028 4372 2392 028 4372 4084
e-mail: enniskeen-hotel@demon.co.uk
***Dir:** from Newcastle town centre follow signs for Tollymore Forest Park, hotel 1m on left*
For 38 years now this hotel has been run by the same family and they continue to welcome guests into their peaceful hotel, which enjoys a superb location in the shadow of the Mountains of Mourne. Public areas and bedrooms are all traditional in style. Wholesome fare is offered in the two dining areas.
ROOMS: 12 en suite (1 fmly) No smoking in 3 bedrooms **CONF:** Thtr 60 Class 24 **SERVICES:** Lift **PARKING:** 45 **NOTES:** No dogs No smoking in restaurant Closed 12 Nov-14 Mar
CARDS:

NEWMARKET-ON-FERGUS, Co Clare Map 01 B3

★★★★★73% *Dromoland Castle*

☎ 061 368144 061 363355
e-mail: sales@dromoland.ie
Described as a "very large, early eighteenth century, gothic revival, castellated, irregular, multi-towered ashlar castle" Dromoland offers superbly appointed accommodation and facilities. The spacious, thoughtfully equipped and richly decorated bedrooms offer excellent levels of comfort. The magnificent public areas, warmed by log fires, are no less impressive. The hotel has two restaurants including the more formal Earl of Thomond. There are also immaculately maintained grounds and excellent leisure and meeting facilities.
ROOMS: 75 en suite (20 fmly) **FACILITIES:** STV Golf 18 Tennis (hard) Fishing Snooker Sauna Solarium Gym Putting green entertainment **CONF:** Thtr 450 Class 320 Board 80 **PARKING:** 120 **NOTES:** No dogs No smoking in restaurant **CARDS:**

★★★63% Clare Inn Golf & Leisure Hotel

☎ 065 6823000 065 6823759
e-mail: cro@lynchotels.com
***Dir:** on N18, 14km from Shannon International Airport*
The Clare Inn is set in open countryside next to an 18-hole golf course just 10 minutes from Shannon Airport. It is a comfortable hotel with excellent leisure facilities and friendly staff to ensure an enjoyable stay.

continued

ROOMS: 182 en suite (20 fmly) No smoking in 4 bedrooms s IR£55-IR£90; d IR£80-IR£132 * LB **FACILITIES:** STV Indoor swimming (H) Golf 18 Tennis (hard) Sauna Solarium Gym Pool table Croquet lawn Putting green Jacuzzi/spa Programme for children Crazy golf Horse riding Pitch and putt entertainment ch fac Xmas **CONF:** Thtr 400 Class 250 Board 100 Del from IR£115 * **SERVICES:** Lift **PARKING:** 300 **NOTES:** No dogs (ex guide dogs) Civ Wed 300 **CARDS:**

NEW ROSS, Co Wexford — Map 01 C3

★★★63% Clarion Brandon House Hotel

Wexford Rd
☎ 051 421703 Fax 051 421567
e-mail: brandonhouse@eircom.net
Dir: *Drive down the quays on Rosslake Road N25, hotel gates on the left 1.5km from the quays*

Set in its own grounds, this Victorian manor house has been refurbished, with the addition of a bedroom wing and extensive leisure centre. Public rooms include a library with open fire, a comfortable lounge bar and an attractive restaurant. Bedrooms are spacious and well appointed and the front rooms enjoy lovely views.

ROOMS: 61 en suite s IR£60-IR£70; d IR£90-IR£110 (incl. bkfst) * LB **FACILITIES:** STV Indoor swimming (H) Sauna Solarium Gym Jacuzzi/spa Beauty treatment rooms entertainment Xmas **CONF:** Thtr 300 Class 200 Board 100 Del from IR£78.50 * **PARKING:** 250 **NOTES:** No dogs (ex guide dogs) **CARDS:**

★★59% The Old Rectory

Rosbercon
☎ 051 421719 Fax 051 422974
e-mail: newrossoldrectoryhot@eircom.net
Dir: *in New Ross cross the bridge, turn right and continue for 200mtrs up hill, hotel is on the right*

A small and cosy hotel set in two and a half acres of lovely gardens. The hotel commands wonderful views over New Ross and the River Barrow from its elevated position. A warm welcome is assured for all guests along with a pleasant stay.

ROOMS: 12 en suite s IR£35-IR£40; d IR£65-IR£75 (incl. bkfst) * LB **FACILITIES:** STV entertainment **CONF:** Thtr 80 Class 48 Board 20 **PARKING:** 37 **NOTES:** No dogs (ex guide dogs) Closed Nov-Jan **CARDS:**

ORANMORE, Co Galway — Map 01 B3

★★★69% *Galway Bay Golf & Country Club Hotel*

☎ 091 790500 Fax 091 790510
e-mail: gbay.golf@iol.ie
Dir: *follow signs from Oranmore for 3km entrance beside the Galway Bay Sailing Club*

A stylish and friendly hotel, overlooking the golf course on the Penville Peninsula. This championship course was designed by Christie O'Connor Jnr and there is a grandstand view of the first fairway from the smart lounge. The bedrooms, all well equipped, range from executive suites, with their own sitting rooms, to standard rooms. The hotel cuisine is of a consistently high standard.

ROOMS: 90 en suite **FACILITIES:** STV Golf 18 Putting green Golf practice range Parkland walks **CONF:** Thtr 160 Class 100 Board 30 **SERVICES:** Lift **PARKING:** 200 **NOTES:** No dogs (ex guide dogs) Closed 24-26 Dec **CARDS:**

OUGHTERARD, Co Galway — Map 01 B4

★★★66% Ross Lake House

Rosscahill
☎ 091 550109 & 550154 Fax 091 550184
e-mail: rosslake@iol.ie
Dir: *22km from Galway City on N59, Galway - Clifden road. Turn left after village of Rosscahill*

Set in a peaceful woodland estate, this personally-run Georgian house offers a warm welcome. Good food is a feature, and carefully chosen produce includes Connemara lamb and fresh fish. Golf, lake fishing and boating are all near by.

ROOMS: 13 en suite s IR£62-IR£73; d IR£90-IR£113 (incl. bkfst) * LB **FACILITIES:** STV Tennis (hard) **PARKING:** 150 **NOTES:** No smoking in restaurant Closed Nov-mid Mar **CARDS:**

PARKNASILLA, Co Kerry — Map 01 A2

★★★★79% *Great Southern*

☎ 064 45122 Fax 064 45323
e-mail: res@parknasilla.gsh.ie
Dir: *on Kenmare road 3km from Sneem village*

The Great Southern on Kenmare Bay has fine sea views from many of its bedrooms. There are spacious, comfortable lounges, the excellent Pygmalion Retaurant and an impressive range of leisure facilities. Service is delightfully warm and welcoming.

continued

P

PARKNASILLA, continued

Great Southern, Parknasilla

ROOMS: 26 en suite 59 annexe en suite (6 fmly) No smoking in 11 bedrooms **FACILITIES:** STV Indoor swimming (H) Golf 9 Tennis (hard) Fishing Riding Snooker Sauna Pool table Croquet lawn Jacuzzi/spa Bike hire Windsurfing Clay pigeon shooting Archery entertainment **CONF:** Thtr 100 Class 80 Board 20 **SERVICES:** Lift **PARKING:** 60 **NOTES:** No dogs (ex guide dogs) **CARDS:**

See advert on page 867

PORTAFERRY, Co Down — Map 01 D5

★★★66% *Portaferry*

10 The Strand BT22 1PE
☎ 028 4272 8231 🖹 028 4272 8999
e-mail: portaferry@iol.ie
Dir: *situated on Lough Shore opposite ferry terminal*

This charming hotel enjoys spectacular views over Strangford Lough. Public areas include a choice of inviting lounges, a well stocked bar, and a smart restaurant which serves enjoyable cuisine. Bedrooms are comfortable and many have Lough views.

ROOMS: 14 en suite **FACILITIES:** STV **PARKING:** 6 **NOTES:** No dogs (ex guide dogs) Closed 24-25 Dec **CARDS:**

P

PORTMARNOCK, Co Dublin — Map 01 D4

★★★★77% Portmarnock Hotel & Golf Links

Strand Rd
☎ 01 8460611 🖹 01 8462442
e-mail: marketing@portmarnock.com
Dir: *Dublin Airport-N1, rdbt 1st exit, 2nd rdbt 2nd exit, next rdbt 3rd exit, T-junct turn left, over crossrds and cont, hotel is left past the Strand*

Enjoying a superb location overlooking the sea and the PGA Championship Golf Links, this 19th century former home of the Jameson whiskey family is now a smart hotel. Bedrooms are modern, while the public areas are furnished with period style. The Osborne Restaurant comes highly recommended.

ROOMS: 103 en suite No smoking in 6 bedrooms s IR£110-IR£140; d IR£160-IR£205 (incl. bkfst) * LB **FACILITIES:** STV Golf 18 Putting green Xmas **CONF:** Thtr 300 Class 110 Board 80 Del from IR£145 * **SERVICES:** Lift **PARKING:** 200 **NOTES:** No dogs (ex guide dogs) **CARDS:**

See advert on page 845

PORTRUSH, Co Antrim — Map 01 C6

★★★68% The Royal Court

233 Ballybogey Rd BT56 8NF
☎ 028 7082 2236 🖹 028 7082 3176
e-mail: royalcourthotel@aol.com
Dir: *from Ballymena head N on M2 which joins Ballymoney rdbt. Take 3rd exit to Portrush on B62. Hotel situated at end of road*

Situated east of the town in a dramatic position overlooking the East Strand beach with views towards Donegal and Scottish Islands. The hotel is modern, with comfortable public areas and provides a good range of meals. Bedrooms are spacious, and some have balconies giving superb views.

ROOMS: 18 en suite (10 fmly) s £55-£65; d £90-£100 (incl. bkfst) * LB **FACILITIES:** STV Xmas **CONF:** Thtr 100 Class 70 Board 50 Del from £56.45 * **PARKING:** 200 **NOTES:** No dogs (ex guide dogs) Closed 26 Dec **CARDS:**

★★★62% *Causeway Coast*

36 Ballyreagh Rd BT56 8LR
☎ 028 70822435 🖹 028 70824495
e-mail: info@causewaycoast.com
Dir: *on A2 between Portrush & Portstewart, opposite Ballyreagh Golf Course*

A purpose-built hotel and conference centre overlooking Ballyreagh golf course to the sea. Improvements include the addition of 20 more bedrooms and the creation of a leisure centre. Public areas are pleasing and decorated in a modern style.

ROOMS: 21 en suite (2 fmly) **FACILITIES:** entertainment **CONF:** Thtr 500 Class 170 **SERVICES:** Lift **PARKING:** 172 **NOTES:** No dogs (ex guide dogs) Closed 25 Dec **CARDS:**

PORTUMNA, Co Galway — Map 01 B3

★★★65% Shannon Oaks Hotel & Country Club

☎ 0509 41777 🖹 0509 41357
e-mail: sales@shannonoaks.ie

Situated in 8 acres of grounds on the edge of Portumna National Forest, this recently rebuilt hotel has a comfortable lounge, restaurant and bar where live entertainment takes place regularly. Spacious bedrooms are air conditioned and well equipped. There is an indoor pool, fitness centre, and conference and banqueting facilities, as well as extensive car parking.

ROOMS: 63 en suite s IR£87-IR£97; d IR£112-IR£121 (incl. bkfst) * LB **FACILITIES:** STV Indoor swimming (H) Tennis (hard) Sauna Solarium Gym Jacuzzi/spa entertainment Xmas **CONF:** Thtr 600 Class 380 Board 15 **SERVICES:** Lift air con **PARKING:** 360 **NOTES:** No dogs (ex guide dogs) **CARDS:**

RATHMULLAN, Co Donegal — Map 01 C6

★★★73% Fort Royal

MANOR HOUSE HOTELS

Fort Royal
☎ 074 58100 🖹 074 58103
e-mail: fortroyal@eircom.net
Dir: *take R245 from Letterkenny, through Rathmullan village, hotel is signposted*

On the shores of Lough Swilly, this period house stands in 18 acres of grounds and has private access to a secluded beach. The sitting room is a restful place overlooking the sea. Enjoyable meals

continued

are served in the restaurant, and the bar is inviting. Bedrooms are attractively decorated.
ROOMS: 11 en suite 4 annexe en suite (3 fmly) s IR£60-IR£75; d IR£95-IR£115 (incl. bkfst) * LB **FACILITIES:** Golf 9 Tennis (hard) Squash **PARKING:** 40 **NOTES:** No smoking in restaurant Closed Nov-Etr
CARDS:

★59% *Pier*

☎ 074 58178 & 58115 🖷 074 58115
Dir: *on sea front, near harbour*
This pleasant hotel stands directly opposite a sandy beach on the western shores of Lough Swilly. There is a comfortable lounge, a dining room and a bar. A good angling centre and golf course are available nearby.
ROOMS: 10 en suite (2 fmly) **FACILITIES:** entertainment **NOTES:** No dogs (ex guide dogs) Closed Nov-May RS Apr-May & Oct
CARDS:

RATHNEW, Co Wicklow — Map 01 D3

Premier Collection

★★★

Tinakilly Country House & Restaurant

☎ 0404 69274 🖷 0404 67806
e-mail: jandrpower@tinakally.ie
Dir: *follow the N11/M11 to Rathnew village, cont on R750 towards Wicklow. Entrance to hotel is approx 500mtrs from the village on left*
Built in 1870, this elegant house is set in seven acres of 19th century gardens with breathtaking views of the sea. The highest standards of accommodation and hospitality are offered and the bedrooms are tastefully decorated with period furnishings and some four-poster beds. Country house cuisine is served, including fresh fish, game and home-grown vegetables.
ROOMS: 52 en suite s IR£116-IR£124; d IR£136-IR£152 (incl. bkfst) * LB **FACILITIES:** STV Tennis (hard) Gym Croquet lawn Putting green 7 acres of gardens mapped for walking Xmas **CONF:** Thtr 80 Class 60 Board 40 **SERVICES:** Lift **PARKING:** 60 **NOTES:** No dogs (ex guide dogs) RS 24-26 Dec & 31 Dec-2 Jan
CARDS:

★★★67% *Hunter's*

☎ 0404 40106 🖷 0404 40338
Dir: *1.5km from village off N11*
A delightful hotel which is one of Ireland's oldest coaching inns. Noted for its prize-winning gardens bordering the River Vartry, the introduction of modern facilities has not detracted from the character of the original hotel. The restaurant has a good reputation for carefully prepared dishes which make the best use of high quality local produce. An ideal centre for touring, golf, and also commercial trade.
ROOMS: 16 en suite (2 fmly) **CONF:** Class 40 Board 16 **PARKING:** 50 **NOTES:** No dogs (ex guide dogs) Closed 24-26 Dec
CARDS:

RECESS, Co Galway — Map 01 A4

★★★77% Lough Inagh Lodge

Inagh Valley
☎ 095 34706 & 34694 🖷 095 34708
e-mail: inagh@iol.ie
Dir: *after Recess take R344 towards Kylemore through Inagh valley, hotel is in middle of valley*
A luxurious hotel, formerly a 19th century hunting lodge. Its setting, fronted by a good fishing lake, includes lovely mountain views. Large lounges and an oak-lined bar provide warmth and comfort, and the spacious bedrooms are beautifully furnished. The food is a highlight of any stay here.
ROOMS: 12 en suite s IR£72-IR£95; d IR£110-IR£132 (incl. bkfst) * LB **FACILITIES:** Fishing Hill walking, **CONF:** Thtr 20 Class 20 Board 20 **SERVICES:** air con **PARKING:** 16 **NOTES:** Closed 15 Dec-15 Mar
CARDS:

RENVYLE, Co Galway — Map 01 A4

★★★66% Renvyle House Hotel

☎ 095 43511 🖷 095 43515
e-mail: renvyle@iol.ie
Dir: *N59 west of Galway towards Clifden Pass through Oughterard & Maam Cross, at Recess turn right, Keymore turn left, Letterfrack turn right, hotel 5m*
This historic country house nestles between the mountains and the ocean on the unspoilt coast of Connemara. Spacious comfortable lounges and turf fires combined with friendly staff make a stay here relaxing and memorable. Bedrooms vary in size and are well equipped with spectacular views. Good leisure facilities include hard tennis courts, snooker room, outdoor pool, and a 9-hole golf course.
ROOMS: 65 en suite (8 fmly) s IR£50-IR£90; d IR£80-IR£140 (incl. bkfst) * LB **FACILITIES:** STV Outdoor swimming (H) Golf 9 Tennis (hard) Fishing Riding Snooker Croquet lawn ch fac Xmas **CONF:** Thtr 200 Class 80 Board 80 Del from IR£60 **PARKING:** 60 **NOTES:** Closed 2 Jan-28 Feb **CARDS:**

ROSCOMMON, Co Roscommon — Map 01 B4

★★★64% Abbey

Galway Rd
☎ 0903 26240 & 26505 🖷 0903 26021
Dir: *on N63 opposite railway station*
Set in its own grounds just outside Roscommon, this fine manor house dates back over 100 years. The bedrooms are well decorated, with a choice of period style rooms in the original part of the house, while those in the newer wing are more contemporary. Service is attentive and the hotel has a friendly atmosphere.
ROOMS: 25 en suite No smoking in 2 bedrooms s IR£65-IR£75; d IR£95-IR£120 (incl. bkfst) * LB **FACILITIES:** STV **CONF:** Thtr 300 Class 200 Board 25 **PARKING:** 100 **NOTES:** No dogs Closed 25-26 Dec
CARDS:

Arriving late? Four and five star hotels have night porters to assist with your luggage; and 24hr room service.

R

ROSCREA, Co Tipperary Map 01 C3

★★★67% Grant's
Castle St
☎ 0505 23300 0505 23209
e-mail: grantshotel@line7.ie
Dir: *off main N7 (Dublin/Limerick Road). Turn off for town centre and follow sign posts to hotel, opposite Roscrea Castle*
This attractive and inviting hotel stands opposite the 13th century castle and Heritage Centre. Bedrooms are pleasantly furnished in warm colours and there is an excellent, oak-panelled foyer lounge with deep leather armchairs and sofas. There is a choice of two restaurants, the Lemon Tree and the Bistro, as well as an informal pub with a cafe-bar area, Kitty's Tavern.
ROOMS: 25 en suite (3 fmly) **FACILITIES:** STV **CONF:** Thtr 600 Class 300 Board 30 **PARKING:** 30 **NOTES:** Civ Wed 300
CARDS:

ROSSCARBERY, Co Cork Map 01 B2

★★★69% Celtic Ross
☎ 023 48722 023 48723
e-mail: info@celticrosshotel.com
Dir: *on N71*

Overlooking a lagoon, on the edge of a peaceful village this hotel is a striking landmark on the West Cork coastline. The spacious public areas are luxuriously appointed with rich fabrics and polished Irish elm, yew bog oakwood and cherrywood. There is a cocktail bar and an Irish pub where a lunchtime carvery is on offer. The restaurant specialises in seafood dishes. One bedroom is fully adapted for the disabled.
ROOMS: 67 en suite (30 fmly) No smoking in 10 bedrooms **FACILITIES:** STV Indoor swimming (H) Sauna Gym Jacuzzi/spa Steam room entertainment **CONF:** Thtr 250 Class 80 Board 80 **SERVICES:** Lift air con **PARKING:** 200 **NOTES:** No dogs (ex guide dogs)
CARDS:

ROSSLARE, Co Wexford Map 01 D2

★★★★78% *Kelly's Resort*
☎ 053 32114 053 32222
e-mail: kellyhot@iol.ie
The range of facilities on offer is extensive at this popular seafront hotel, and include a leisure centre, health treatments, indoor and outdoor tennis courts, a children's crèche and spacious gardens. La Marine Bistro is the setting for good modern cuisine, while the main restaurant continues to produce award-winning food. Public rooms are adorned with contemporary Irish art.

continued

ROOMS: 99 annexe en suite (15 fmly) **FACILITIES:** STV Indoor swimming (H) Tennis (hard) Squash Snooker Sauna Solarium Gym Pool table Croquet lawn Jacuzzi/spa Bowls Plunge pool Badminton Crazy golf Outdoor Canadian hot tub entertainment ch fac **CONF:** Thtr 30 Class 30 Board 20 **SERVICES:** Lift **PARKING:** 99 **NOTES:** No dogs Closed mid Dec-late Feb **CARDS:**

ROSSLARE HARBOUR, Co Wexford Map 01 D2

★★65% *Danby Lodge Hotel*
Killinick
☎ 053 58191
This hotel is attached to the house of 18th-century landscape painter Francis Danby. Conveniently situated for the ferry terminal at Rosslare, it offers well equipped, stylish accommodation, including three annexe rooms in the restored stone built coach house. The cosy bar and dining room look out over a pretty garden.
ROOMS: 14 en suite

ROSSNOWLAGH, Co Donegal Map 01 B5

★★★77% Sand House
☎ 072 51777 072 52100
e-mail: info@sandhouse-hotel.ie
Dir: *on coast road from Ballyshannon in the centre of Donegal Bay*
MANOR HOUSE
Set in a crescent of golden sands five miles north of Ballyshannon, this hotel is well known for its hospitality, good cuisine and service. Many rooms have sea views and a conservatory lounge provides a relaxing retreat.
ROOMS: 46 en suite (6 fmly) s IR£60-IR£80; d IR£95-IR£130 (incl. bkfst) * LB **FACILITIES:** STV Tennis (hard) Croquet lawn Putting green Mini-golf Surfing Canoeing Sailing entertainment **CONF:** Thtr 60 Class 40 Board 30 Del from IR£75 * **PARKING:** 42 **NOTES:** No smoking in restaurant Closed mid Oct-Etr **CARDS:**

ROUNDSTONE, Co Galway Map 01 A4

★★70% *Eldons*
☎ 095 35933 & 35942 095 35871
Dir: *off N59 through Toombedla then lt to village*
This distinctive building stands on the main street of a picturesque fishing village. Guests are assured a warm welcome at this hotel along with good service. The seafood restaurant, Bedla, serves a good choice of dishes.
ROOMS: 13 en suite 6 annexe en suite (2 fmly)
FACILITIES: entertainment **SERVICES:** Lift **NOTES:** No dogs Closed 4 Nov-16 Mar **CARDS:**

SALTHILLSee Galway

SHANNON, Co Clare

Map 01 B3

★★★60% Quality Shannon Hotel

Ballycasey
☎ 061 364588 📠 061 364045
e-mail: sales@qualityshannon.com
Dir: *3m from Shannon International Airport*

This friendly hotel, conveniently situated just three miles from Shannon Airport, is close to Bunnatty Castle and multinational companies in the Shannon Free Zone. It offers contemporary styled bedrooms, the Old Lodge bar, an all day carvery, a steak house restaurant and meeting rooms.

ROOMS: 54 en suite (3 fmly) No smoking in 10 bedrooms s IR£59-IR£69; d IR£69-IR£79 * LB **FACILITIES:** STV entertainment **CONF:** Thtr 20 Class 12 Board 12 Del IR£78 * **SERVICES:** Lift **PARKING:** 130 **NOTES:** No dogs (ex guide dogs) Closed 24-25 Dec **CARDS:**

SKIBBEREEN, Co Cork

Map 01 B2

★★65% Eldon

Bridge St
☎ 028 22000 📠 028 22191
e-mail: welcome@eldon-hotel.ie
Dir: *On the N71 west*

Good food, good drink and good company can all be found here. The atmosphere at this family run hotel is friendly, there is a comfortable bar with patio gardens, and car parking to the rear of the hotel.

ROOMS: 19 en suite No smoking in 4 bedrooms s IR£28-IR£57; d IR£56-IR£70 (incl. bkfst) LB **FACILITIES:** Fishing use of local leisure centre entertainment **PARKING:** 40 **NOTES:** Closed 24-27 Dec **CARDS:**

SLANE, Co Meath

Map 01 D4

★★★61% *Conyngham Arms*

☎ 041 24155 📠 041 24205
Dir: *from N2 turn onto N51, hotel is 20mtrs on the left*

village inn HOTELS

Situated in a picturesque village near the famous prehistoric tombs of New Grange, this hotel has very comfortable public rooms including the unique Estate Agent's Restaurant. There are attractive gardens and this is an ideal location from which to explore the historic area including Tara and the Boyne Valley. Bedrooms are well presented.

ROOMS: 16 rms (15 en suite) (4 fmly) **FACILITIES:** STV **CONF:** Thtr 150 Class 120 **PARKING:** 12 **NOTES:** No dogs (ex guide dogs) Closed Good Fri & Xmas **CARDS:**

SLIGO, Co Sligo

Map 01 B5

★★★71% Sligo Park

Pearse Rd
☎ 071 60291 📠 071 69556
e-mail: sligopk@leehotels.ie
Dir: *on N4 1 mile from Sligo on Dublin Road also on Salway Road*

Set in seven acres of parkland on the southern edge of Sligo, this hotel is an ideal touring centre for the many attractions of Yeats country. The bedrooms offer good modern facilities, in particular the excellent 'executive' rooms. The restaurant is particularly attractive and inviting. A comprehensive leisure centre is an added attraction, and there are good beaches close at hand.

continued

ROOMS: 110 en suite No smoking in 4 bedrooms s IR£56-IR£61; d IR£99-IR£109 * LB **FACILITIES:** Indoor swimming (H) Tennis (hard) Snooker Sauna Solarium Gym Jacuzzi/spa Steam room Plunge pool entertainment Xmas **CONF:** Thtr 520 Class 350 Board 50 Del from IR£92 * **PARKING:** 200 **NOTES:** No dogs (ex guide dogs) RS 24-26 & 31 Dec **CARDS:**

★★★65% *Tower*

Quay St
☎ 071 44000 📠 071 46888
e-mail: towersl@iol.ie
Dir: *in the centre of Sligo*

Pleasantly located beside the quay, this attractively furnished hotel is right in the town centre. There is a smart foyer lounge, a pleasant restaurant and bar; the bedrooms are comfortable and well equipped. Guests have access to the local leisure and fitness centre at reduced rates.

ROOMS: 58 en suite No smoking in 12 bedrooms **CONF:** Thtr 200 Class 60 Board 50 **SERVICES:** Lift air con **PARKING:** 20 **NOTES:** No dogs (ex guide dogs) No smoking in restaurant Closed 21-30 Dec **CARDS:**

★★63% *Ocean View Hotel*

Strandhill
☎ 071 68115

village inn HOTELS

This family-run hotel, situated in a seaside village to the west of Sligo town, is close to a sandy beach, golf courses and an equestrian centre. Bedrooms are attractively decorated and facilities include a comfortable bar, a restaurant and residents' lounge.

★★61% *Silver Swan*

☎ 071 43231 📠 071 42232
Dir: *situated on the banks of the Garavogue River in the town centre beside G.P.O. and on the junction of N4, N15, N16*

Family-owned, this hotel stands beside the Garavogue River in the heart of Sligo. The bedrooms are well furnished and comfortable with good bathrooms, some with aero-spa baths. The Horseshoe Bar is a popular spot for snacks and drinks.

ROOMS: 29 en suite **FACILITIES:** entertainment **CONF:** Thtr 100 Class 60 Board 30 **PARKING:** 40 **NOTES:** No dogs (ex guide dogs) No smoking in restaurant Closed 25 & 26 Dec **CARDS:**

S

STRAFFAN, Co Kildare Map 01 D4

Premier Collection

★★★★★

The Kildare Hotel & Country Club

☎ 01 6017200 📠 01 6017299
e-mail: hotel@kclub.ie/golf@kclub.ie
Dir: *from Dublin take N4, take exit for R406 hotel entrance is on right in Straffan*

A luxurious hotel set in 330 acres of park and woodland, with a golf course designed by Arnold Palmer - the venue for the 2005 Ryder Cup. Opulent reception rooms include the Chinese Drawing Room, overlooking the gardens and the River Liffey. Richly furnished bedrooms are most comfortable and extremely well equipped. Staff are very attentive, and there are extensive leisure and conference facilities.

ROOMS: 36 en suite 9 annexe en suite (10 fmly) **FACILITIES:** STV Indoor swimming (H) Golf 18 Tennis (hard) Fishing Squash Snooker Sauna Solarium Gym Pool table Croquet lawn Putting green Jacuzzi/spa Beauty salon Driving range Golf tuition Fishing tuition entertainment **CONF:** Thtr 160 Class 60 Board 40 **SERVICES:** Lift **PARKING:** 205 **NOTES:** No dogs
CARDS:

★★★76% *Barberstown Castle*

☎ 01 6288157 📠 01 6277027
e-mail: castleir@iol.ie

Dating from the 13th century, this castle houses a hotel which provides the highest standards of comfort. Inviting public rooms range from the original castle keep, now housing one of the two restaurants, to the soft warmth of the drawing room and cocktail bar. Bedrooms are well equipped and appointed.

ROOMS: 22 en suite **FACILITIES:** STV entertainment **CONF:** Thtr 50 Class 40 Board 30 **PARKING:** 200 **NOTES:** No dogs No children 12yrs No smoking in restaurant Closed 24-26 Dec & 2-16 Jan
CARDS:

TEMPLEGLANTINE, Co Limerick Map 01 B2

★★★59% *The Devon Inn*

☎ 069 84122 📠 069 84255
Dir: *midway between Limerick City and Killarney on N21*

A hotel with a smart reception area, comfortable foyer lounge, and all-day bar and restaurant. Bedrooms offer spacious accommodation with good quality wood finishes and thoughtful extras. Salmon and trout fishing are available, along with golf.

ROOMS: 59 en suite (20 fmly) **FACILITIES:** STV Pool table **CONF:** Thtr 400 Class 200 Board 30 **PARKING:** 200 **NOTES:** Closed 24-25 Dec
CARDS:

THOMASTOWN, Co Kilkenny Map 01 C3

Premier Collection

★★★★ Mount Juliet

☎ 056 73000 📠 056 73019
e-mail: info@mountjuliet.ie
Dir: *take M7 from Dublin, N9 towards Waterford then to the Mount Juliet on the N9 via Carlow and Gowran*

Set in 1500 acres of parkland, including a Jack Nicklaus designed golf course where the Irish Opens were played in 1993 and 1994, this beautiful Palladian mansion is now a very special hotel. The elegant and spacious public rooms retain much of the original architectural features, including ornate plasterwork and fine Adam fireplaces in the cocktail bar, restaurant and drawing room.

ROOMS: 32 en suite 27 annexe en suite No smoking in 1 bedroom s IR£120-IR£160; d IR£160-IR£250 * LB **FACILITIES:** STV Indoor swimming (H) Golf 18 Tennis (hard) Fishing Riding Snooker Sauna Gym Pool table Croquet lawn Putting green Beauty salon Archery Clay pigeon shooting Cycling Golf tuition Putting course Xmas **CONF:** Thtr 200 Class 80 Board 50 Del from IR£120 * **PARKING:** 200 **NOTES:** No dogs (ex guide dogs) No smoking in restaurant **CARDS:**

TRALEE, Co Kerry Map 01 A2

★★★69% Meadowlands Hotel

Oakpark
☎ 066 7180444 📠 066 7180964
e-mail: medlands@iol.ie
Dir: *1km from Tralee town centre on N69*

This smart new hotel has been built to a high standard and is within walking distance of the town centre. There is stylish use of colour, tile and timber throughout, and the tastefully decorated bedrooms are comfortable and fitted with locally crafted pine furniture.

ROOMS: 27 en suite (3 fmly) s IR£75; d IR£120 (incl. bkfst) * LB **FACILITIES:** STV entertainment **CONF:** Thtr 40 Class 40 Board 20 **SERVICES:** Lift air con **PARKING:** 120 **NOTES:** No dogs (ex guide dogs) Closed 24-26 Dec **CARDS:**

★★★67% The Brandon

Princes St
☎ 066 7123333 📠 066 7125019
e-mail: info@brandon
Dir: *Turn off Dingle Road T68 at the aquadrome, to the right and continue 500mts,the hotel is on the left*

This modern hotel, completely refurbished, is situated in the town centre. It has excellent leisure facilities and is a golfer's paradise, within 30 minutes' of six superb courses.

continued

ROOMS: 185 en suite (4 fmly) s IR£58-IR£110; d IR£70-IR£110 (incl. bkfst) * LB **FACILITIES:** STV Indoor swimming (H) Sauna Solarium Gym Jacuzzi/spa Concessionary Green fees entertainment Xmas **CONF:** Thtr 1200 Class 600 Board 30 Del from IR£105 * **SERVICES:** Lift **PARKING:** 300 **NOTES:** No dogs (ex guide dogs) Closed 23-28 Dec **CARDS:**

★★★64% Abbey Gate

Maine St
☎ 066 7129888 🖷 066 7129821
e-mail: abbeygat@iol.ie
Dir: *in town centre*

The Abbey Gate is a smartly appointed town centre hotel. The well equipped bedrooms include some suitable for those with mobility problems. Public areas include a spacious foyer and lounge area with attractive decor, a traditional pub, 'The Old Market Place' where carvery lunches are served, a cocktail bar, the Vineyard Restaurant and banqueting and conference suites.

ROOMS: 100 en suite (4 fmly) s IR£45-IR£95; d IR£70-IR£100 (incl. bkfst) * LB **FACILITIES:** STV Xmas **CONF:** Thtr 350 Class 250 Board 25 **SERVICES:** Lift **PARKING:** 20 **NOTES:** No dogs (ex guide dogs) Closed 25 Dec **CARDS:**

★★★60% *Tralee Court*

Castle St
☎ 066 7121877 🖷 066 7122273
Dir: *on N22*

ROOMS: 45 en suite **FACILITIES:** entertainment **SERVICES:** Lift air con **PARKING:** 15 **NOTES:** No dogs (ex guide dogs) Closed 25 Dec **CARDS:**

TRAMORE, Co Waterford — Map 01 C2

★★★63% *Majestic*

☎ 051 381761 🖷 051 381766
Dir: *turn off N25 through Waterford onto R675 to Tramore*

A warm welcome awaits at this hotel, overlooking Tramore Bay and 10kms from Waterford City. All bedrooms are well equipped. The restaurant specialises in local fresh seafood and steak dishes. Full leisure facilities are available to residents at Splashworld Health & Fitness Club across the road from the hotel.

ROOMS: 57 en suite (4 fmly) No smoking in 5 bedrooms **FACILITIES:** STV Outdoor swimming (H) **SERVICES:** Lift **PARKING:** 10 **NOTES:** No dogs (ex guide dogs) **CARDS:**

VIRGINIA, Co Cavan — Map 01 C4

★★66% ❀ *The Park*

Virginia Park
☎ 049 8547235

A charming hotel, built in 1750 and the summer retreat of the Marquis of Headford, situated at the end of a beach avenue. There is a golf course and mature gardens and walks. Public rooms are furnished in keeping with the style of the house and bedrooms vary in size. Dinner is served in the Marquis dining room, overlooking Lough Ramor.

ROOMS: 18 en suite

WATERFORD, Co Waterford — Map 01 C2

★★★★74% ❀❀ Waterford Castle

The Island
☎ 051 878203 🖷 051 879316
e-mail: info@waterfordcastle.com
Dir: *Waterford city centre, turn onto Dunmore East Rd, continue for 1.5ml, pass hospital, 0.5m left after lights, ferry at bottom of road*

Picturesque and enchanting, this historic castle which dates back to Norman times, is a former home of the Fitzgerald clan. Reached by a chain link ferry, just a short distance from the mainland, the castle has a grand entrance hall boasting Elizabethan panelling and a cavernous fireplace. Enjoyable cuisine is served in the Munster Room, where table d'hôte and carte menus are complemented by a good wine list. Bedrooms, all comfortable, include The Presidential Suite.

ROOMS: 19 en suite (2 fmly) **FACILITIES:** STV Indoor swimming (H) Golf 18 Tennis (hard) Croquet lawn Putting green Clay pigeon shooting entertainment ch fac **CONF:** Thtr 30 Board 15 **SERVICES:** Lift **PARKING:** 50 **NOTES:** No dogs No smoking in restaurant **CARDS:**

★★★71% Granville

The Quay
☎ 051 305555 🖷 051 305566
e-mail: stay@granville-hotel.ie
Dir: *take the N25 to the waterfront, city centre , opposite the Clock Tower*

Best Western

Situated on the quayside, this charming old hotel has been extensively refurbished to a high standard, while still retaining its original character. Bedrooms, in a choice of standard or executive rooms, are comfortable. The public areas and the restaurant are all appointed to a very high standard.

ROOMS: 100 en suite (5 fmly) No smoking in 20 bedrooms s IR£60-IR£150; d IR£110-IR£180 (incl. bkfst) * LB **FACILITIES:** STV **CONF:** Thtr 200 Class 150 Board 30 **SERVICES:** Lift **PARKING:** 300 **NOTES:** No dogs (ex guide dogs) Closed 25-26 Dec **CARDS:**

★★★66% Dooley's

30 The Quay
☎ 051 873531 🖷 051 870262
e-mail: hotel@iol.ie
Dir: *on N25*

Situated in the heart of Waterford overlooking the quayside, Dooley's is a comfortable family-run hotel. The smart public areas and bedrooms offer comfortable and stylish accommodation, and there is an elevator to all floors. Guests are very well cared for in a warm and friendly atmosphere.

ROOMS: 113 en suite (3 fmly) No smoking in 17 bedrooms **FACILITIES:** STV entertainment **CONF:** Thtr 260 Class 180 Board 100 **SERVICES:** Lift **NOTES:** No dogs (ex guide dogs) Closed 25-27 Dec **CARDS:**

★★★66% Tower

The Mall
☎ 051 875801 🖷 051 870129
e-mail: towerw@iol.ie
Dir: *opposite Reginald's Tower in the centre of town hotel located at end of quay in Waterford on N25 the Cork Road*

The Tower Hotel offers a full range of banqueting, conference and leisure facilities. Also included is an attractive restaurant and a pleasant bar overlooking the river. Helpful, friendly staff provide good service throughout.

ROOMS: 142 en suite (10 fmly) s IR£56-IR£90; d IR£89-IR£132 (incl. bkfst) * LB **FACILITIES:** Indoor swimming (H) Sauna Solarium Gym Jacuzzi/spa entertainment ch fac Xmas **CONF:** Thtr 650 Class 300 Board 100 Del from IR£68 * **SERVICES:** Lift **PARKING:** 90 **NOTES:** No dogs (ex guide dogs) Closed 24-28 Dec **CARDS:**

★★★65% *Waterford Manor*

Killotteran, Butlerstown
☎ 051 377814 🖷 051 354545

A period residence set in 180 acres of mature grounds on the outskirts of Waterford. Refurbishment has taken place here, and facilities now include lounges, restaurant, and a new bar bistro which overlooks the gardens. The new business centre and exhibition hall are due to open in October 2000.

ROOMS: 10 en suite (3 fmly) No smoking in 6 bedrooms

W

WATERFORD, continued

★★★62% Bridge Hotel

1 The Quay
☎ 051 877222 📠 051 877229
e-mail: bridgehotel@treacyhotelsgroup.com
Dir: *the Hotel is located opposite the Waterford City Bridge when following the N25*

This busy hotel stands near the City Bridge, convenient for the shops and local amenities. The bedrooms are well furnished and really comfortable. Public areas include a country-style bistro, a restaurant, a traditional Irish pub and a relaxing lounge bar.

ROOMS: 100 en suite (20 fmly) No smoking in 4 bedrooms s IR£40-IR£60; d IR£70-IR£90 (incl. bkfst) * LB **FACILITIES:** STV entertainment **CONF:** Thtr 400 Class 300 Board 70 **SERVICES:** Lift air con **NOTES:** No dogs Closed 25 Dec **CARDS:**

★★★62% Jurys

Ferrybank
☎ 051 832111 📠 051 832863
e-mail: michaelwalsh@jurys.com
Dir: *on N25 1km from City Centre*

Situated in parkland overlooking the city, this large modern hotel has spacious public rooms and caters for tourists and business guests.

ROOMS: 98 en suite (20 fmly) No smoking in 4 bedrooms s IR£55-IR£87; d IR£79-IR£117 * LB **FACILITIES:** Indoor swimming (H) Tennis (hard) Sauna Solarium Gym Pool table Jacuzzi/spa Steam room Plunge pool Jacuzzi entertainment Xmas **CONF:** Thtr 700 Class 400 Board 100 Del from IR£55 * **SERVICES:** Lift **PARKING:** 300 **NOTES:** No dogs (ex guide dogs) Closed 24-27 Dec **CARDS:**

★★60% Ivory's Hotel

Tramore Rd
☎ 051 358888 📠 051 358899
e-mail: ivoryhotel@voyager.ie
Dir: *from Waterford city centre take the N25 to Cork. After 600yds take exit to Tramore R675. Hotel is on right hand side*

This distinctive modern hotel near the Waterford Glass factory, is just south-west of the city. It offers good value accommodation, with family rooms as well as standard rooms, all are furnished with writing desks, as well as the usual amenities. The restaurant, with its 'Catch of the Day' selection of fresh seafood dishes is very popular. The hotel is close to six golf courses, where golfing packages can be arranged.

ROOMS: 40 en suite (20 fmly) No smoking in 20 bedrooms s IR£49.50-IR£69.50; d IR£39-IR£95 (incl. bkfst) * LB **FACILITIES:** STV ch fac Xmas **PARKING:** 120 **CARDS:**

⇧ *Travelodge*

Cork Rd
☎ 051 358885 📠 051 358890
Dir: *On N25, 1km from Waterford Glass Visitors Centre*

This modern building offers accommodation in smart, spacious and well equipped bedrooms, all with en suite bathrooms. Refreshments may be taken at the nearby family restaurant. For further details and the Travelodge phone number, consult the Hotel Groups page.

ROOMS: 32 en suite

> Popped the question? Hotels with Civ Wed in their entry are licensed for civil wedding ceremonies. Maximum numbers for the ceremony only are shown, e.g. Civ Wed 50

WATERVILLE, Co Kerry — Map 01 A2

★★★72% Butler Arms

☎ 066 9474144 📠 066 9474520
e-mail: butarms@iol.ie
Dir: *centre of Waterville village on seafront. N70 Ring of Kerry*

Standing on the Ring of Kerry overlooking the ocean, the Butlers Arms offers traditional high standards of service. Most of the bedrooms have marble bathrooms and enjoy sea views, whilst public areas include spacious lounges and a billiards room. An 18-hole championship golf course is situated opposite.

ROOMS: 30 en suite (1 fmly) s fr IR£87.50; d fr IR£125 (incl. bkfst) * LB **FACILITIES:** STV Tennis (hard) Fishing Snooker **PARKING:** 30 **NOTES:** No dogs (ex guide dogs) Closed Jan-Apr & Oct-Dec **CARDS:**

WESTPORT, Co Mayo — Map 01 B4

★★★★65% Knockranny House Hotel

☎ 098 28600 📠 098 28611
e-mail: info@khh.ie
Dir: *on the main Westport/Castlebar Road (N5) close to town of Westport*

Overlooking Westport with Clew Bay in the distance, the reception rooms of this family-run hotel take full advantage of the lovely views. The luxurious furnishings create an inviting and relaxing atmosphere throughout the lounge, bar and restaurant which are all located on the first floor. All types of rooms are well appointed. There is a helicopter landing area.

ROOMS: 54 en suite (4 fmly) No smoking in 4 bedrooms s IR£95-IR£165; d IR£140-IR£210 (incl. bkfst) LB **FACILITIES:** STV Tennis (hard) Jacuzzi/spa Full Leisure centre free to all guests, at associated hotel 3mins away entertainment **CONF:** Thtr 700 Class 400 Board 40 Del from IR£130 * **SERVICES:** Lift **PARKING:** 120 **NOTES:** No dogs (ex guide dogs) Closed 24-26 Dec **CARDS:**

★★★70% *Ardmore Country House*

The Quay
☎ 098 25994 📠 098 27795

A charming country house hotel, elevated over the quay, within walking distance of the town centre. The attractive restaurant and relaxing lounges overlook Clew Bay, with Croagh Patrick in the background. Individually styled bedrooms are spacious and comfortable, most have spectacular sea views.

★★★70% Hotel Westport

The Demesne, Newport Rd
☎ 098 25122 📠 098 26739
e-mail: sales@hotelwestport.co.uk
Dir: *N5 to Westport, at end of Castlebar St turn right, first right, first left, follow road to end*

Opposite the grounds of Westport House, this hotel offers welcoming accommodation comprising a reception foyer, lounge, spacious restaurant and comfortable bedrooms including six suites. The hotel has much to offer the leisure and business guest, with a swimming pool, sauna and gym, and new conference and syndicate rooms.

ROOMS: 129 en suite (36 fmly) s IR£73-IR£85; d IR£60-IR£70 (incl. bkfst) * LB **FACILITIES:** STV Indoor swimming (H) Sauna Solarium Gym Jacuzzi/spa Steam room Lounger pool & childrens pool Jet stream entertainment ch fac Xmas **CONF:** Thtr 500 Class 150 Board 60 Del from IR£120 * **SERVICES:** Lift **PARKING:** 220 **NOTES:** No dogs (ex guide dogs) No smoking in restaurant **CARDS:**

★★72% ❀ ***The Olde Railway***
The Mall
☎ 098 25166 & 25605 🖷 098 25090
e-mail: railway@anu.ie
Dir: *overlooking the Carrowbeg River in the town centre*
Set on a tree-lined mall overlooking the river, this classic coaching inn offers a welcoming atmosphere with blazing turf fires. There is a variety of bedroom sizes, including some very spacious rooms, all are well equipped. Communal areas include an attractively furnished bar, a comfortable lounge and a Conservatory Restaurant with access to the patio and barbecue area.
ROOMS: 24 en suite (2 fmly) **FACILITIES:** STV Fishing & Shooting arranged entertainment **PARKING:** 34 **NOTES:** No dogs (ex guide dogs) No smoking in restaurant **CARDS:**

See advert on this page

★★65% **Clew Bay Hotel**
James St
☎ 098 28088 🖷 098 25783
e-mail: clewbay@anu.ie
Dir: *At the bottom of James St, which is parallel to the main street. Two doors away from the tourist office*
ROOMS: 35 en suite (3 fmly) No smoking in 5 bedrooms
FACILITIES: STV entertainment **NOTES:** Closed Xmas & New Year
CARDS:

village inn HOTELS

WEXFORD, Co Wexford   Map 01 D3

★★★★67% ❀❀ **Ferrycarrig**
Ferrycarrig
☎ 053 20999 🖷 053 20982
e-mail: ferrycarrig@griffingroup.ie
Dir: *on N11 by Slaney Estuary, beside Ferrycarrig Castle*
Set in one of the most inspiring locations in Ireland, this lovely hotel has sweeping views across the estuary. The public rooms curve round the waterfront and include a fine leisure centre. The bedrooms are freshly furbished with particularly good rooms available in the new extension. Both restaurants are at the water's edge, the lively bistro offers a wide menu, while Tides restaurant offers gourmet cuisine.
ROOMS: 103 en suite (3 fmly) No smoking in 45 bedrooms s IR£75-IR£85; d IR£130-IR£150 (incl. bkfst) * LB **FACILITIES:** STV Indoor swimming (H) Sauna Solarium Gym Jacuzzi/spa Aerobics Beauty treatments on request entertainment Xmas **CONF:** Thtr 400 Class 250 Board 60 Del from IR£90 * **SERVICES:** Lift **PARKING:** 235 **NOTES:** No dogs (ex guide dogs) **CARDS:**

★★★72% ❀ **Talbot**
Trinity St
☎ 053 22566 🖷 053 23377
e-mail: talbotwx@eircom.net
Dir: *from Rosslare, take N11 & follow the signs for Wexford, hotel on the right hand side of the Quays - 12miles*
Centrally situated on the quayside, this hotel has been extensively refurbished. All the well equipped bedrooms offer custom-made oak furniture and attractive decor. Day rooms include a spacious foyer, comfortable lounge, and a bar with an open fireplace. The attractive restaurant serves interesting food, and there are good leisure facilities.
ROOMS: 100 en suite (12 fmly) No smoking in 10 bedrooms s IR£59-IR£65; d IR£90-IR£102 (incl. bkfst) * LB **FACILITIES:** STV Indoor swimming (H) Sauna Solarium Gym Jacuzzi/spa Childrens room Beauty Salon entertainment Xmas **CONF:** Thtr 600 Class 300 Board 110 Del from IR£83 * **SERVICES:** Lift **PARKING:** 100 **NOTES:** No dogs (ex guide dogs) **CARDS:**

Olde Railway Hotel, Westport

★★★70% ❀ **Whitford House**
New Line Rd
☎ 053 43444 & 43845 🖷 053 46399
e-mail: whitford@indigo.ie
Dir: *located left off second rdbt on main Dublin to Rosslare road, (N11)*
A family run hotel on the edge of Wexford with a choice of lounges, a spacious bar and a restaurant offering a good value menu with a variety of seafood dishes. The comfortable bedrooms are equipped with modern facilities, and de-luxe patio rooms are available. Additional guest facilities include an indoor swimming pool, tennis courts and a children's playground.
ROOMS: 36 en suite (28 fmly) s IR£41-IR£49; d IR£68-IR£85 (incl. bkfst) * LB **FACILITIES:** STV Indoor swimming (H) Tennis (hard) Childrens playground entertainment **CONF:** Board 50 **PARKING:** 140 **NOTES:** No dogs Closed 23 Dec-13 Jan RS 24 Dec-Jan **CARDS:**

★★★63% **River Bank House Hotel**
☎ 053 23611 🖷 053 23342
e-mail: river@indigo.ie
Dir: *beside Wexford Bridge on R741*
As its name suggests, this hotel overlooks the River Slaney. Public areas include a very smart foyer, attractively decorated dining room and a Victorian style bar where food is served all day. Bedrooms are comfortable and well equipped.
ROOMS: 24 en suite s IR£58-IR£65; d IR£90-IR£110 (incl. bkfst) * LB **FACILITIES:** STV **PARKING:** 40 **NOTES:** No dogs (ex guide dogs) Closed 24-25 Dec **CARDS:**

Packed in a hurry? Ironing facilities should be available at all star levels, either in rooms or on request.

W

★★★62% White's Hotel

George St
☎ 053 22311 🖷 053 45000
e-mail: info@whiteshotel.iol.ie
Dir: *on entering Wexford Town from the N11 or N25 follow directional signs for White's Hotel*

Best Western

This historic former coaching inn provides comfortable modern facilities while retaining much of its charm. The entrance is through a modern extension, and entertainment is provided in the converted saddlery and forge.

ROOMS: 76 en suite 6 annexe en suite (1 fmly) s IR£35-IR£45; d IR£70-IR£90 (incl. bkfst) * LB **FACILITIES:** STV Sauna Gym Jacuzzi/spa Disco Bar entertainment Xmas **CONF:** Thtr 400 Class 250 Board 100 **SERVICES:** Lift **PARKING:** 100 **NOTES:** No dogs (ex guide dogs) **CARDS:**

WICKLOW See Rathnew

Late for dinner? Quality Standards star rating means that last orders for dinner should be no earlier than:
★ 6.30pm ★★ 7.00pm ★★★ 8.00pm
★★★★ 9.00pm ★★★★★ 10.00pm

WOODENBRIDGE, Co Wicklow Map 01 D3

★★★64% ❀ Woodenbridge

☎ 0402 35146 🖷 0402 35573
e-mail: wbhote@iol.ie
Dir: *between Avoca & Arklow*

This comfortable hotel in the Vale of Avoca, under an hour's drive from the ferry ports of Dun Laoghaire and Rosslaire, and close to the N11, continues to thrive. With new bedrooms and a modern conference and banqueting suite the hotel facilities are excellent. Hospitality and good food is assured, golf and fishing are on the doorstep.

ROOMS: 23 en suite (13 fmly) s IR£43-IR£57; d IR£76-IR£100 (incl. bkfst) * LB **FACILITIES:** STV Pool table Xmas **CONF:** Thtr 200 Class 200 Board 200 **PARKING:** 100 **NOTES:** No dogs **CARDS:**

YOUGHAL, Co Cork Map 01 C2

★★66% ❀ *Devonshire Arms*

Pearse Square
☎ 024 92827 & 92018 🖷 024 92900

This 19th-century hotel has been restored with considerable care and attention to detail. It offers good food in both the restaurant and the bar.

ROOMS: 10 en suite (3 fmly) **CONF:** Class 150 **PARKING:** 20 **NOTES:** No dogs (ex guide dogs) Closed Xmas
CARDS:

W

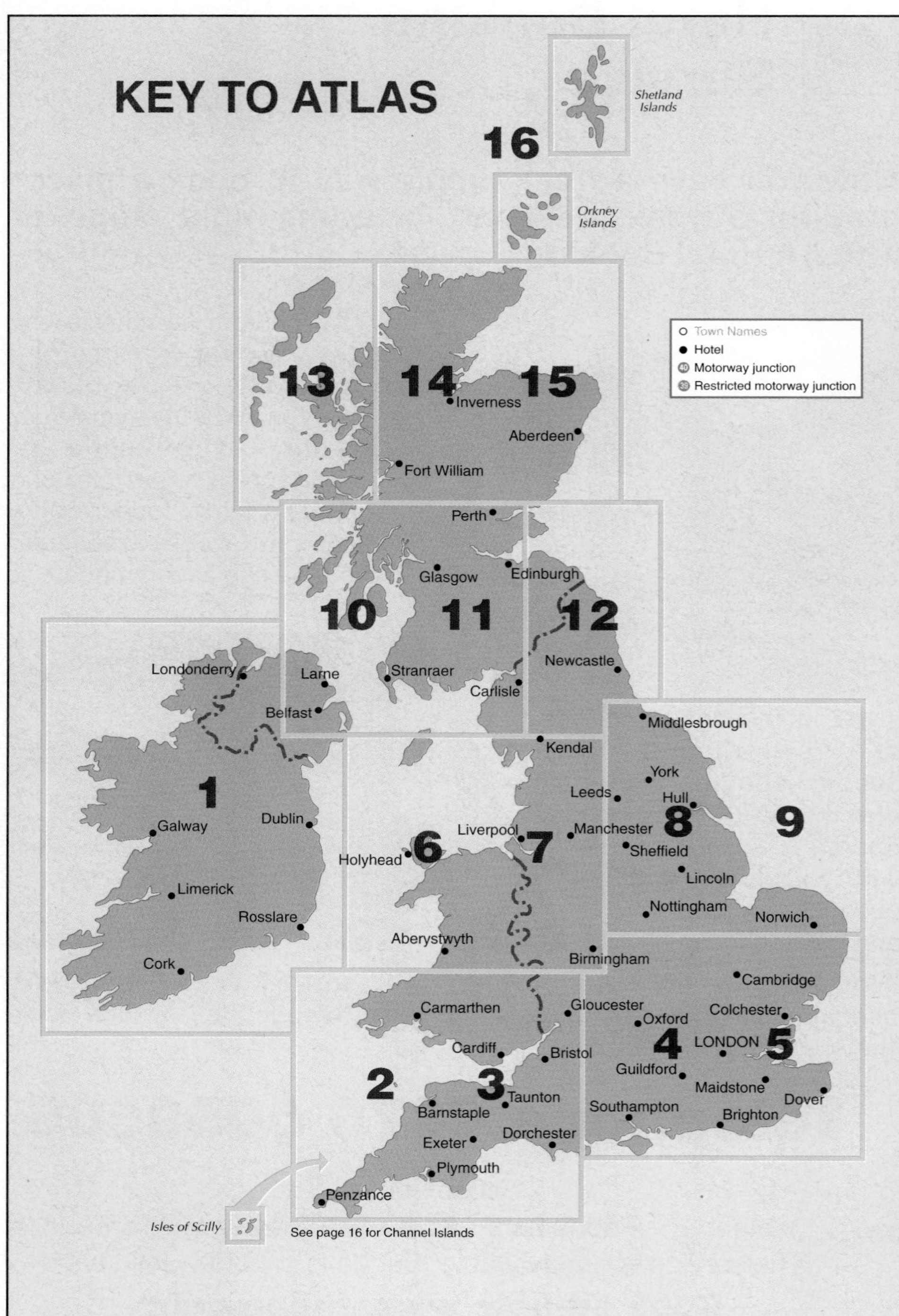
KEY TO ATLAS
16
Shetland Islands
Orkney Islands
13
14
15
Inverness
Aberdeen
Fort William
Town Names
Hotel
Motorway junction
Restricted motorway junction
Perth
Glasgow
Edinburgh
10
11
12
Londonderry
Larne
Stranraer
Newcastle
Belfast
Carlisle
Middlesbrough
Kendal
York
1
Leeds
Hull
Galway
Dublin
Liverpool
Manchester
8
9
6
7
Holyhead
Sheffield
Lincoln
Limerick
Nottingham
Rosslare
Norwich
Aberystwyth
Cork
Birmingham
Cambridge
Carmarthen
Gloucester
Colchester
Oxford
4
LONDON
5
Cardiff
Bristol
Guildford
2
3
Maidstone
Taunton
Dover
Barnstaple
Southampton
Brighton
Exeter
Dorchester
Plymouth
Penzance
Isles of Scilly
See page 16 for Channel Islands

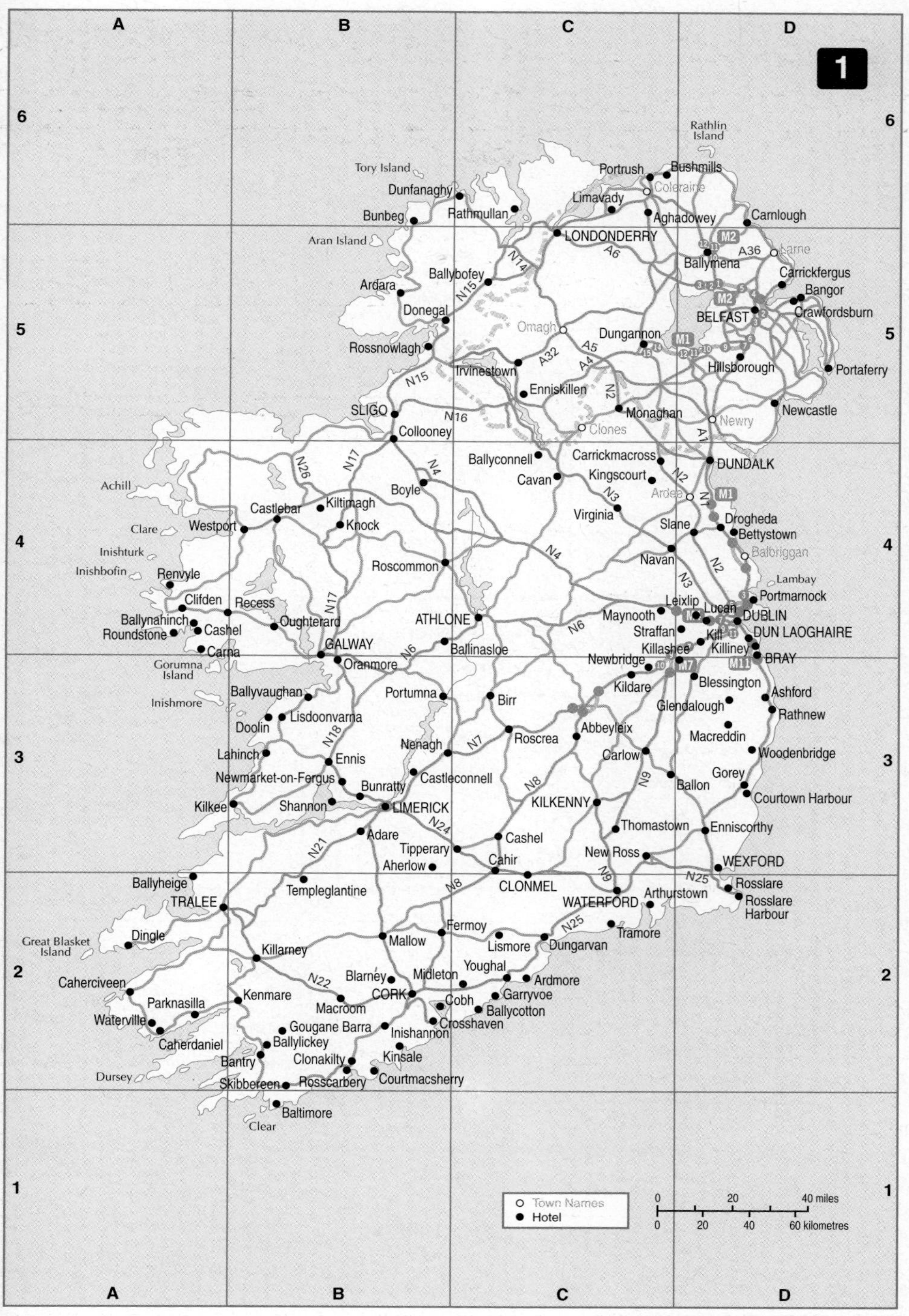

1
A
B
C
D
6
5
4
3
2
1
Rathlin Island
Tory Island
Portrush
Bushmills
Coleraine
Dunfanaghy
Limavady
Bunbeg
Rathmullan
Aghadowey
Carnlough
Aran Island
LONDONDERRY
Ballymena
Larne
Ballybofey
Carrickfergus
Ardara
Bangor
Donegal
BELFAST
Crawfordsburn
Omagh
Dungannon
Rossnowlagh
Irvinestown
Hillsborough
Portaferry
Enniskillen
SLIGO
Monaghan
Newcastle
Collooney
Clones
Newry
Ballyconnell
Carrickmacross
DUNDALK
Achill
Cavan
Kingscourt
Boyle
Ardee
Castlebar
Kiltimagh
Virginia
Drogheda
Clare
Westport
Knock
Slane
Bettystown
Inishturk
Balbriggan
Inishbofin
Renvyle
Roscommon
Navan
Lambay
Clifden
Recess
Portmarnock
Ballynahinch
Oughterard
ATHLONE
Maynooth
Leixlip
Lucan
DUBLIN
Roundstone
Cashel
Straffan
Kill
DUN LAOGHAIRE
Carna
GALWAY
Ballinasloe
Killashee
Killiney
Gorumna Island
Oranmore
Newbridge
BRAY
Blessington
Kildare
Ballyvaughan
Portumna
Birr
Ashford
Inishmore
Glendalough
Lisdoonvarna
Rathnew
Doolin
Abbeyleix
Roscrea
Macreddin
Nenagh
Lahinch
Carlow
Woodenbridge
Ennis
Castleconnell
Gorey
Newmarket-on-Fergus
Bunratty
Ballon
KILKENNY
Courtown Harbour
Kilkee
Shannon
LIMERICK
Thomastown
Adare
Enniscorthy
Cashel
Tipperary
New Ross
Cahir
WEXFORD
Aherlow
Ballyheigue
Templeglantine
CLONMEL
Rosslare
TRALEE
WATERFORD
Arthurstown
Rosslare Harbour
Fermoy
Tramore
Dingle
Great Blasket Island
Mallow
Lismore
Dungarvan
Killarney
Youghal
Caherciveen
Blarney
Midleton
Ardmore
Kenmare
CORK
Garryvoe
Parknasilla
Macroom
Cobh
Waterville
Ballycotton
Crosshaven
Gougane Barra
Caherdaniel
Ballylickey
Inishannon
Bantry
Clonakilty
Kinsale
Dursey
Skibbereen
Rosscarbery
Courtmacsherry
Baltimore
Clear
Town Names
Hotel
0
20
40 miles
0
20
40
60 kilometres

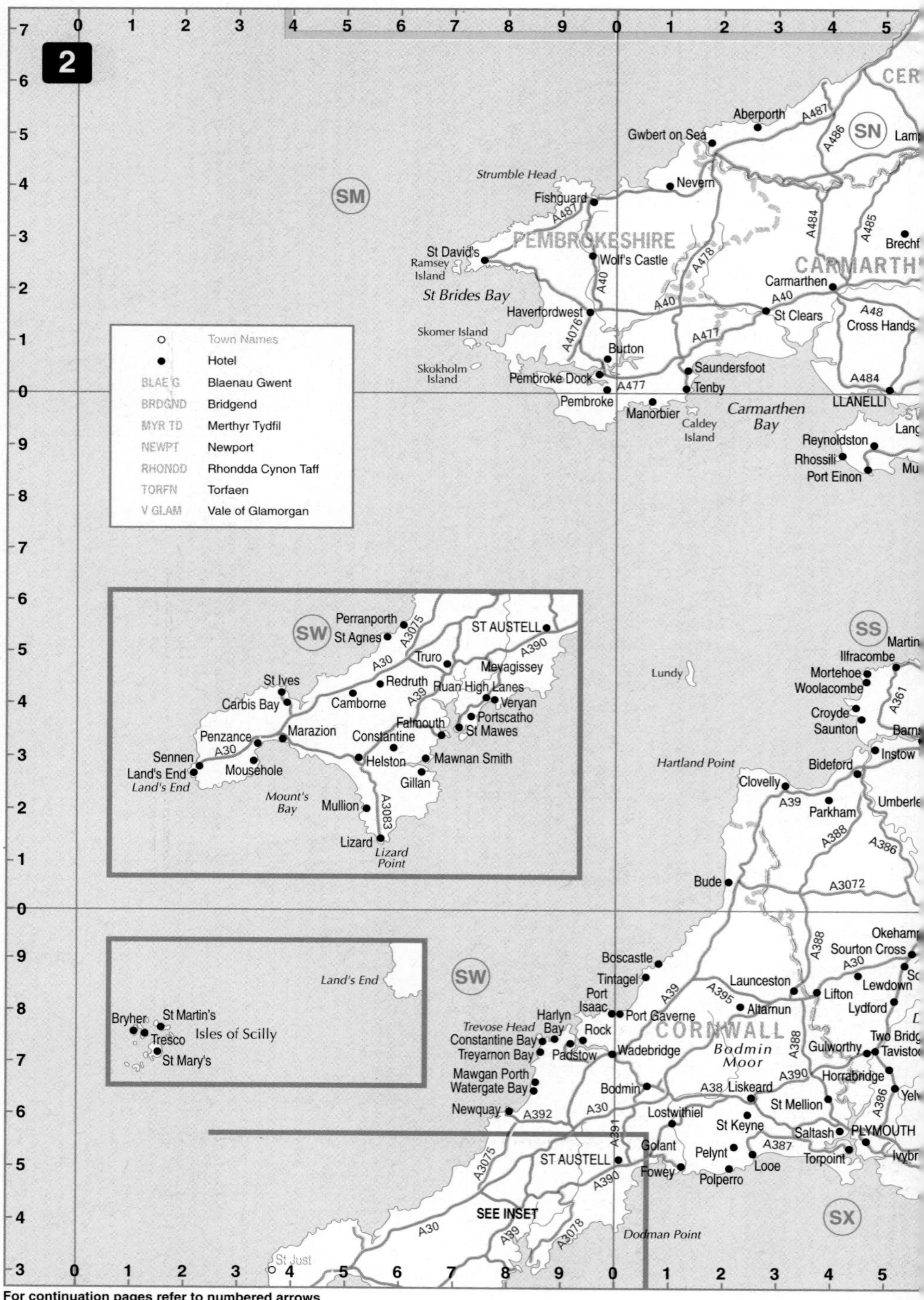

For continuation pages refer to numbered arrows

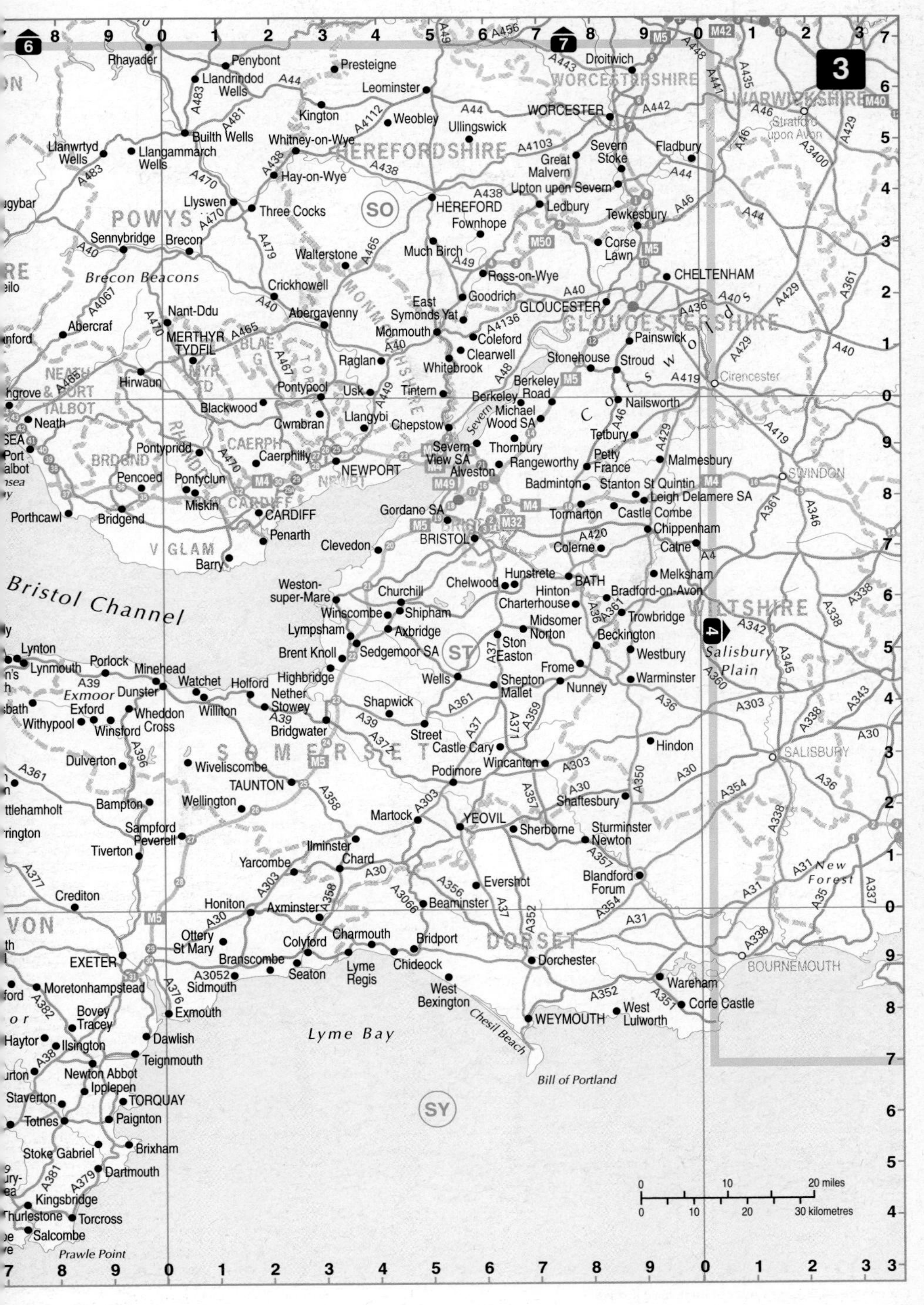

6
7
WORCESTERSHIRE
WARWICKSHIRE
HEREFORDSHIRE
POWYS
GLOUCESTERSHIRE
Cotswold
Brecon Beacons
SO
ST
SY
Bristol Channel
Exmoor
SOMERSET
WILTSHIRE
Salisbury Plain
DORSET
DEVON
New Forest
Lyme Bay
Chesil Beach
Bill of Portland
Prawle Point
Severn
NEATH & PORT TALBOT
BRDGND
CAERPH
RHONDDA
V GLAM
CARDIFF
NEWPT
BLAE G
MYR TD
TORFAEN
MONMOUTHSHIRE
4
Rhayader
Penybont
Presteigne
Llandrindod Wells
Leominster
Droitwich
Kington
Weobley
Ullingswick
WORCESTER
Stratford upon Avon
Builth Wells
Llanwrtyd Wells
Llangammarch Wells
Whitney-on-Wye
Severn Stoke
Great Malvern
Fladbury
Hay-on-Wye
Upton upon Severn
Llyswen
Three Cocks
HEREFORD
Ledbury
Fownhope
Tewkesbury
Sennybridge
Brecon
Walterstone
Much Birch
Corse Lawn
CHELTENHAM
Ross-on-Wye
Crickhowell
Goodrich
East
Symonds Yat
GLOUCESTER
Nant-Ddu
Abergavenny
Abercraf
MERTHYR TYDFIL
Monmouth
Coleford
Painswick
Clearwell
Raglan
Whitebrook
Stonehouse
Stroud
Hirwaun
Pontypool
Usk
Tintern
Berkeley Road
Berkeley
Cirencester
Blackwood
Michael Wood SA
Nailsworth
Neath
Cwmbran
Llangybi
Chepstow
Tetbury
Pontypridd
Caerphilly
Severn View SA
Thornbury
Malmesbury
Rangeworthy
Petty France
NEWPORT
Alveston
Badminton
Stanton St Quintin
SWINDON
Pencoed
Pontyclun
Leigh Delamere SA
Miskin
CARDIFF
Porthcawl
Bridgend
Gordano SA
Tormarton
Castle Combe
BRISTOL
Penarth
Chippenham
Clevedon
Colerne
Calne
Barry
Hunstrete
BATH
Melksham
Weston-super-Mare
Churchill
Chelwood
Hinton Charterhouse
Bradford-on-Avon
Winscombe
Shipham
Trowbridge
Midsomer Norton
Lympsham
Axbridge
Beckington
Ston Easton
Lynton
Lynmouth
Porlock
Brent Knoll
Sedgemoor SA
Westbury
Minehead
Highbridge
Frome
Watchet
Holford
Dunster
Wells
Shepton Mallet
Nunney
Warminster
Nether Stowey
Williton
Exford
Wheddon Cross
Shapwick
Withypool
Winsford
Bridgwater
Street
Hindon
Castle Cary
Dulverton
Wiveliscombe
Wincanton
SALISBURY
Podimore
TAUNTON
Shaftesbury
Wellington
Bampton
Martock
YEOVIL
Sherborne
Sturminster Newton
Sampford Peverell
Tiverton
Ilminster
Chard
Yarcombe
Blandford Forum
Evershot
Crediton
Honiton
Axminster
Beaminster
Ottery St Mary
Colyford
Charmouth
Bridport
EXETER
Branscombe
Seaton
Lyme Regis
Chideock
Dorchester
BOURNEMOUTH
Sidmouth
Moretonhampstead
West Bexington
Wareham
Corfe Castle
Exmouth
West Lulworth
Bovey Tracey
WEYMOUTH
Dawlish
Haytor
Ilsington
Teignmouth
Newton Abbot
Ipplepen
TORQUAY
Staverton
Totnes
Paignton
Brixham
Stoke Gabriel
Dartmouth
Kingsbridge
Thurlestone
Torcross
Salcombe
M5
M4
M50
M32
M49
M42
M40
A44
A49
A456
A443
A448
A441
A435
A46
A442
A429
A4112
A4103
A3400
A483
A481
A438
A470
A479
A465
A40
A4067
A4136
A436
A419
A361
A48
A449
A467
A4061
A4119
A420
A4
A342
A345
A338
A350
A37
A39
A371
A359
A303
A36
A360
A343
A30
A354
A357
A358
A3066
A356
A352
A35
A31
A337
A3052
A376
A382
A38
A381
A379
A396
A377
A372
0 10 20 miles
0 10 20 30 kilometres
8 9 0 1 2 3 4 5 6 7 8 9 0 1 2 3
7 8 9 0 1 2 3 4 5 6 7 8 9 0 1 2 3 3
7 6 5 4 3 2 1 0 9 8 7 6 5 4 3 2 1 0 9 8 7 6 5 4 3

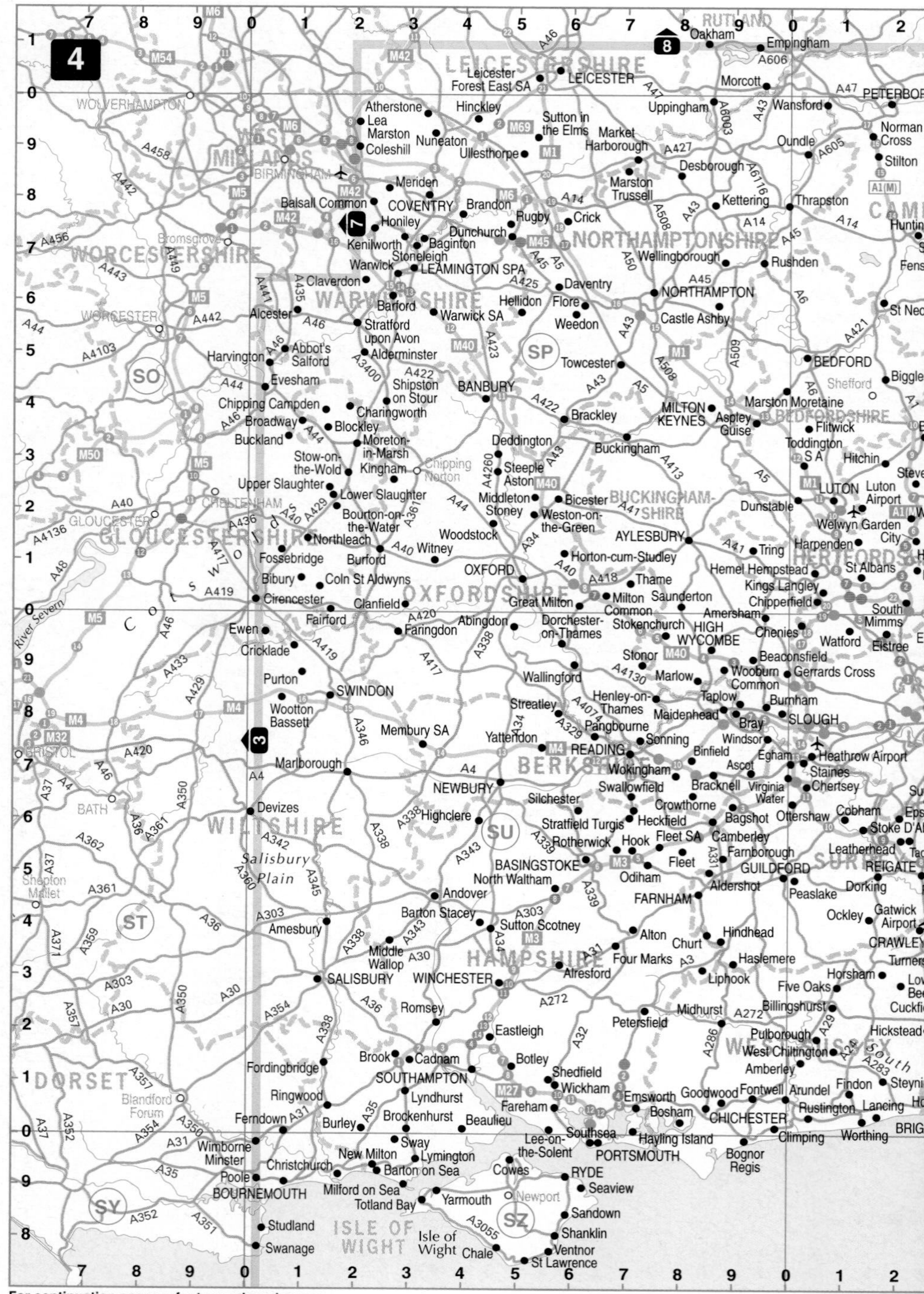

For continuation pages refer to numbered arrows

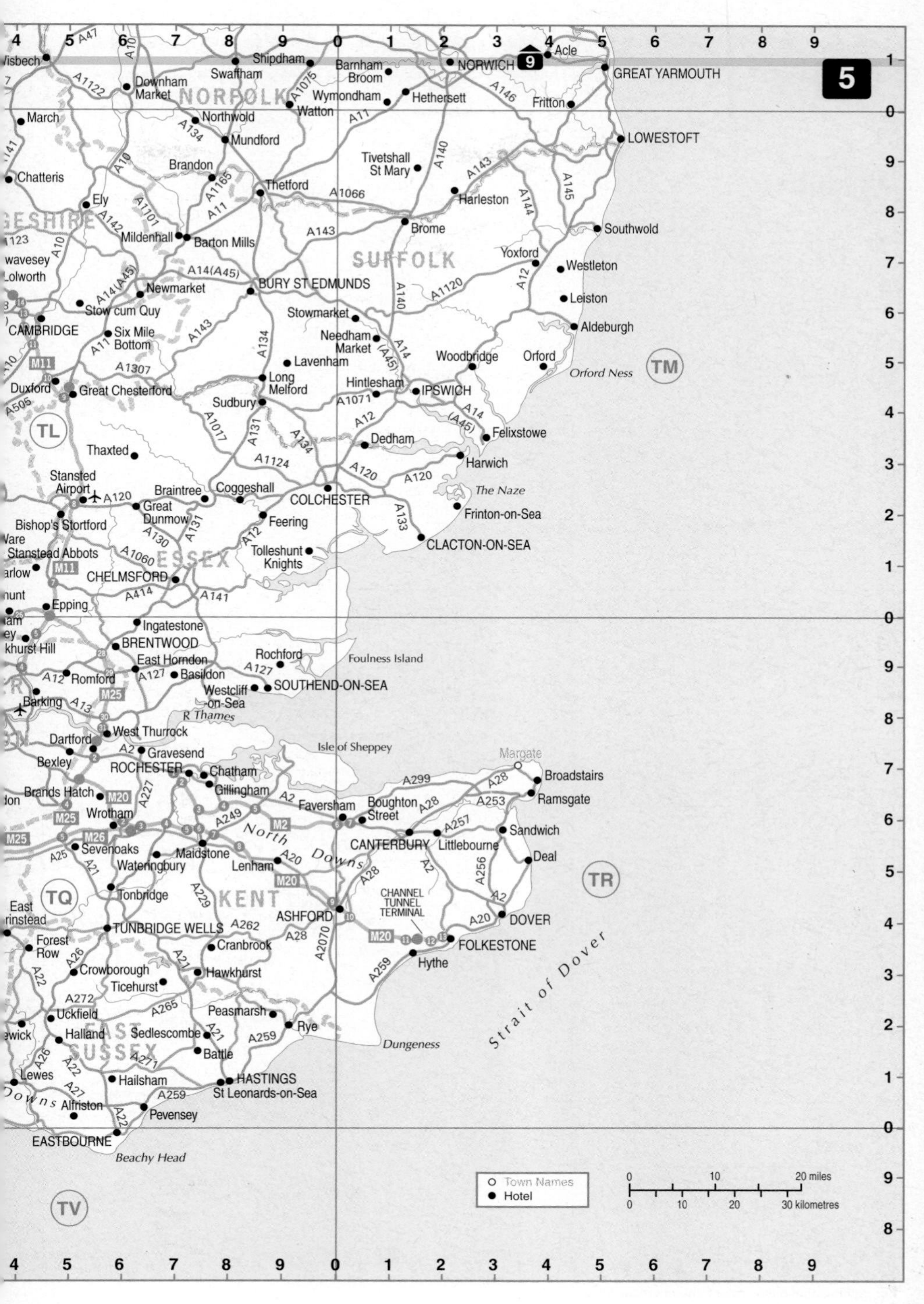
5
NORFOLK
SUFFOLK
ESSEX
KENT
EAST SUSSEX
Norwich
Great Yarmouth
Lowestoft
Thetford
Bury St Edmunds
Ipswich
Felixstowe
Harwich
Colchester
Clacton-on-Sea
Chelmsford
Southend-on-Sea
Rochester
Canterbury
Ashford
Dover
Folkestone
Hastings
Eastbourne
Tunbridge Wells
Cambridge
Strait of Dover
TL
TM
TQ
TR
TV
Town Names
Hotel
20 miles
30 kilometres

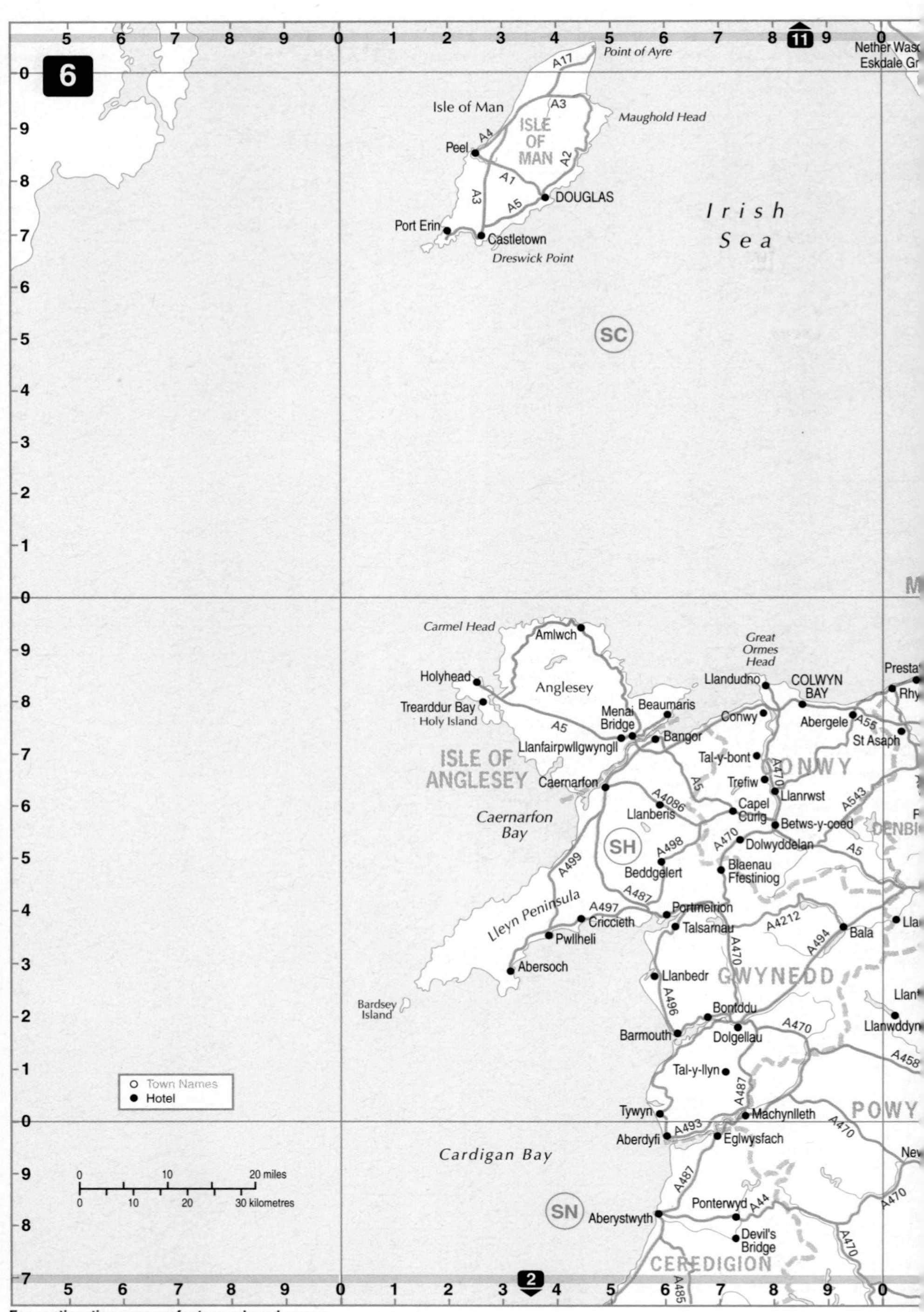

For continuation pages refer to numbered arrows

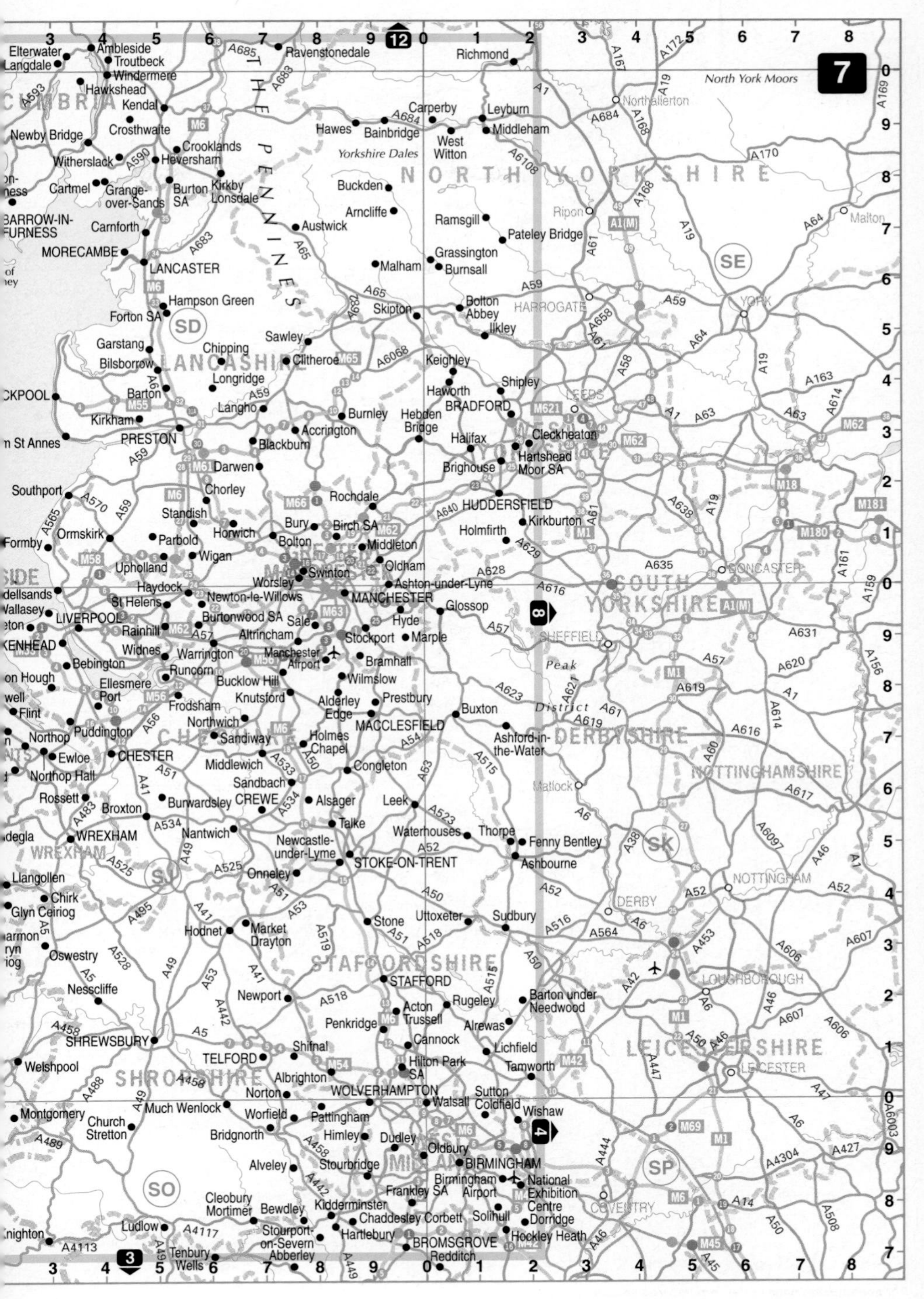

7
12
8
4
3
North York Moors
Yorkshire Dales
CUMBRIA
THE PENNINES
NORTH YORKSHIRE
LANCASHIRE
WEST YORKSHIRE
SOUTH YORKSHIRE
CHESHIRE
DERBYSHIRE
NOTTINGHAMSHIRE
STAFFORDSHIRE
LEICESTERSHIRE
SHROPSHIRE
WREXHAM
Peak District
SD
SE
SJ
SK
SO
SP
Elterwater
Langdale
Ambleside
Troutbeck
Windermere
Hawkshead
Kendal
Newby Bridge
Crosthwaite
Witherslack
Heversham
Crooklands
Cartmel
Grange-over-Sands
Burton SA
Kirkby Lonsdale
BARROW-IN-FURNESS
Carnforth
MORECAMBE
LANCASTER
Hampson Green
Forton SA
Garstang
Bilsborrow
Chipping
Longridge
Barton
Kirkham
PRESTON
Langho
Clitheroe
Sawley
Ravenstonedale
Richmond
Hawes
Bainbridge
Carperby
Leyburn
Middleham
West Witton
Buckden
Arncliffe
Austwick
Ramsgill
Pateley Bridge
Grassington
Burnsall
Malham
Skipton
Bolton Abbey
Ilkley
Keighley
Haworth
Shipley
BRADFORD
Hebden Bridge
Halifax
Brighouse
Cleckheaton
Hartshead Moor SA
HUDDERSFIELD
Holmfirth
Kirkburton
Northallerton
Ripon
HARROGATE
LEEDS
Malton
YORK
DONCASTER
SHEFFIELD
Matlock
NOTTINGHAM
DERBY
LOUGHBOROUGH
LEICESTER
COVENTRY
Southport
Ormskirk
Formby
Parbold
Upholland
Wigan
Standish
Horwich
Chorley
Darwen
Blackburn
Accrington
Burnley
Rochdale
Bury
Birch SA
Bolton
Middleton
Oldham
Swinton
Worsley
Haydock
St Helens
Newton-le-Willows
MANCHESTER
Ashton-under-Lyne
Glossop
Hyde
Marple
Stockport
Sale
Burtonwood SA
Altrincham
LIVERPOOL
Rainhill
Widnes
Warrington
Manchester Airport
Bramhall
Runcorn
Bucklow Hill
Wilmslow
Bebington
Ellesmere Port
Frodsham
Knutsford
Alderley Edge
Prestbury
MACCLESFIELD
Buxton
Ashford-in-the-Water
Flint
Northop
Puddington
Northwich
Sandiway
Holmes Chapel
Ewloe
CHESTER
Northop Hall
Middlewich
Congleton
Sandbach
Rossett
Broxton
Burwardsley
CREWE
Alsager
Leek
WREXHAM
Nantwich
Talke
Waterhouses
Thorpe
Fenny Bentley
Ashbourne
Newcastle-under-Lyme
STOKE-ON-TRENT
Llangollen
Onneley
Chirk
Glyn Ceiriog
Oswestry
Hodnet
Market Drayton
Stone
Uttoxeter
Sudbury
STAFFORD
Nesscliffe
Newport
Rugeley
Barton under Needwood
Acton Trussell
Penkridge
Alrewas
SHREWSBURY
Shifnal
Cannock
Lichfield
Welshpool
TELFORD
Hilton Park SA
Tamworth
Albrighton
WOLVERHAMPTON
Norton
Walsall
Sutton Coldfield
Wishaw
Montgomery
Church Stretton
Much Wenlock
Worfield
Pattingham
Bridgnorth
Himley
Dudley
Oldbury
Alveley
Stourbridge
BIRMINGHAM
Birmingham Airport
National Exhibition Centre
Frankley SA
Cleobury Mortimer
Bewdley
Kidderminster
Chaddesley Corbett
Solihull
Dorridge
Ludlow
Stourport-on-Severn
Hartlebury
BROMSGROVE
Hockley Heath
Knighton
Tenbury Wells
Abberley
Redditch

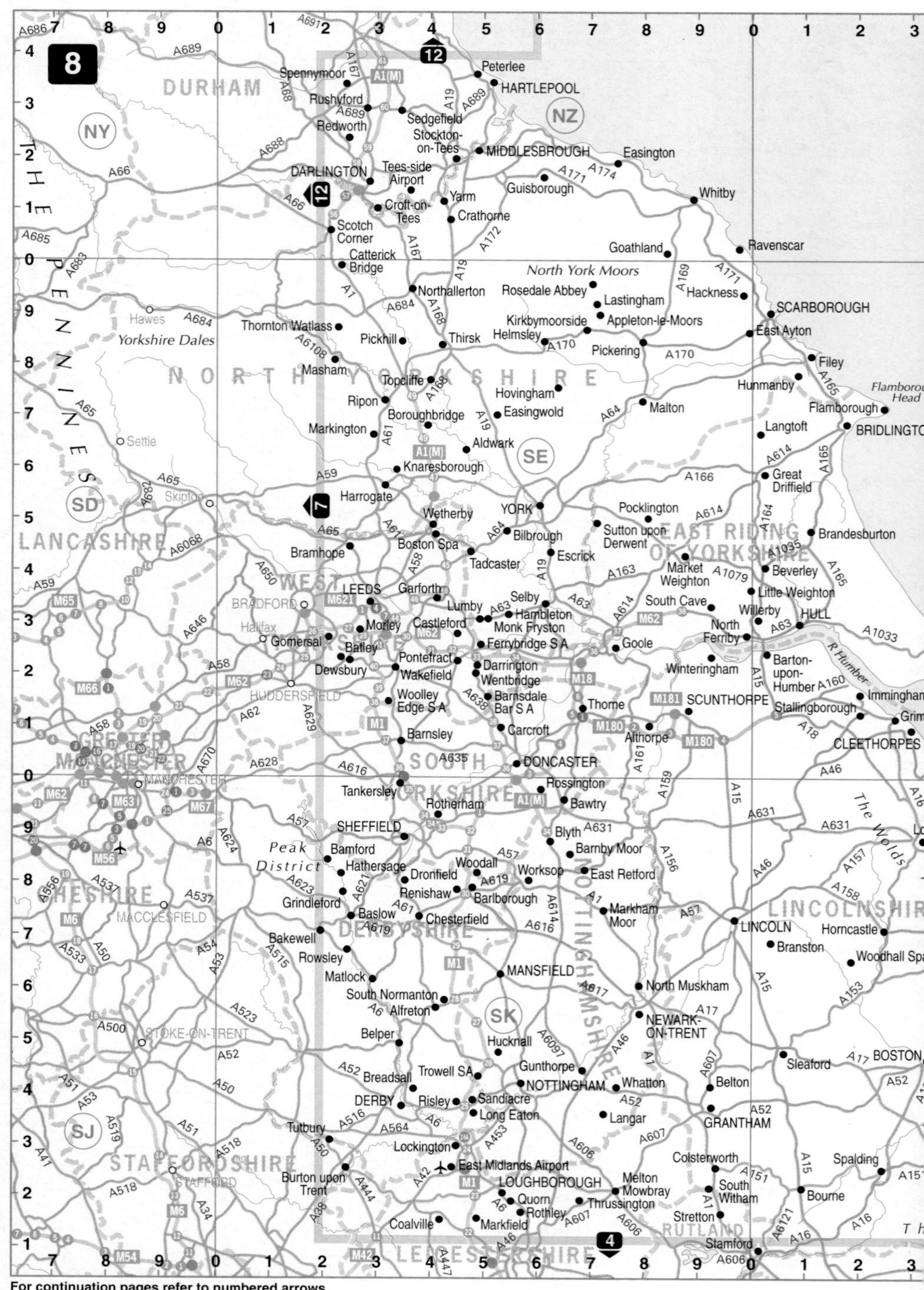

For continuation pages refer to numbered arrows

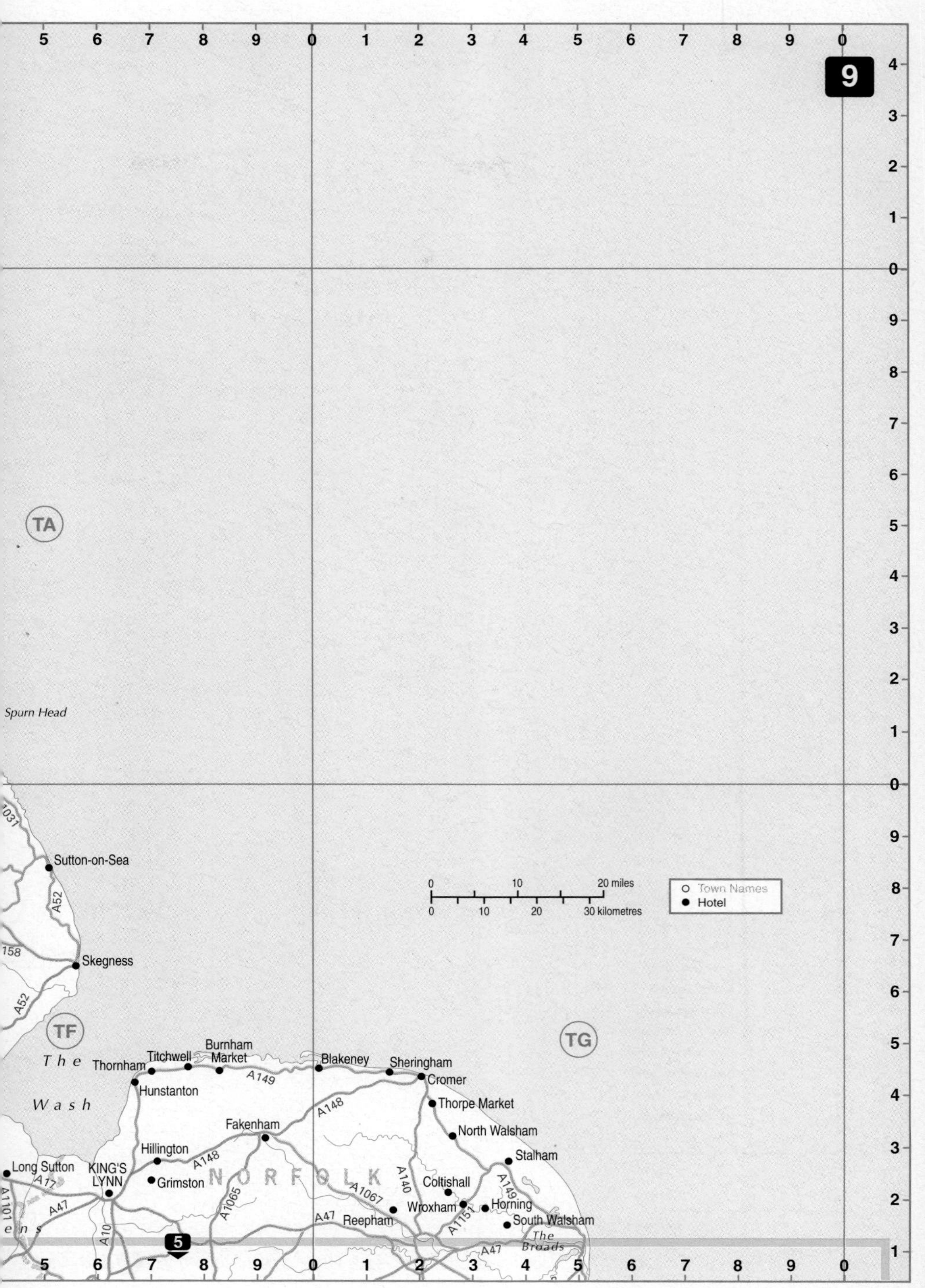
9
TA
Spurn Head
Sutton-on-Sea
Skegness
TF
The Wash
Thornham
Titchwell
Burnham Market
Hunstanton
Blakeney
Sheringham
Cromer
Thorpe Market
North Walsham
Fakenham
Hillington
Long Sutton
KING'S LYNN
Grimston
NORFOLK
Stalham
Coltishall
Wroxham
Horning
Reepham
South Walsham
The Broads
TG
5
0 10 20 miles
0 10 20 30 kilometres
Town Names
Hotel

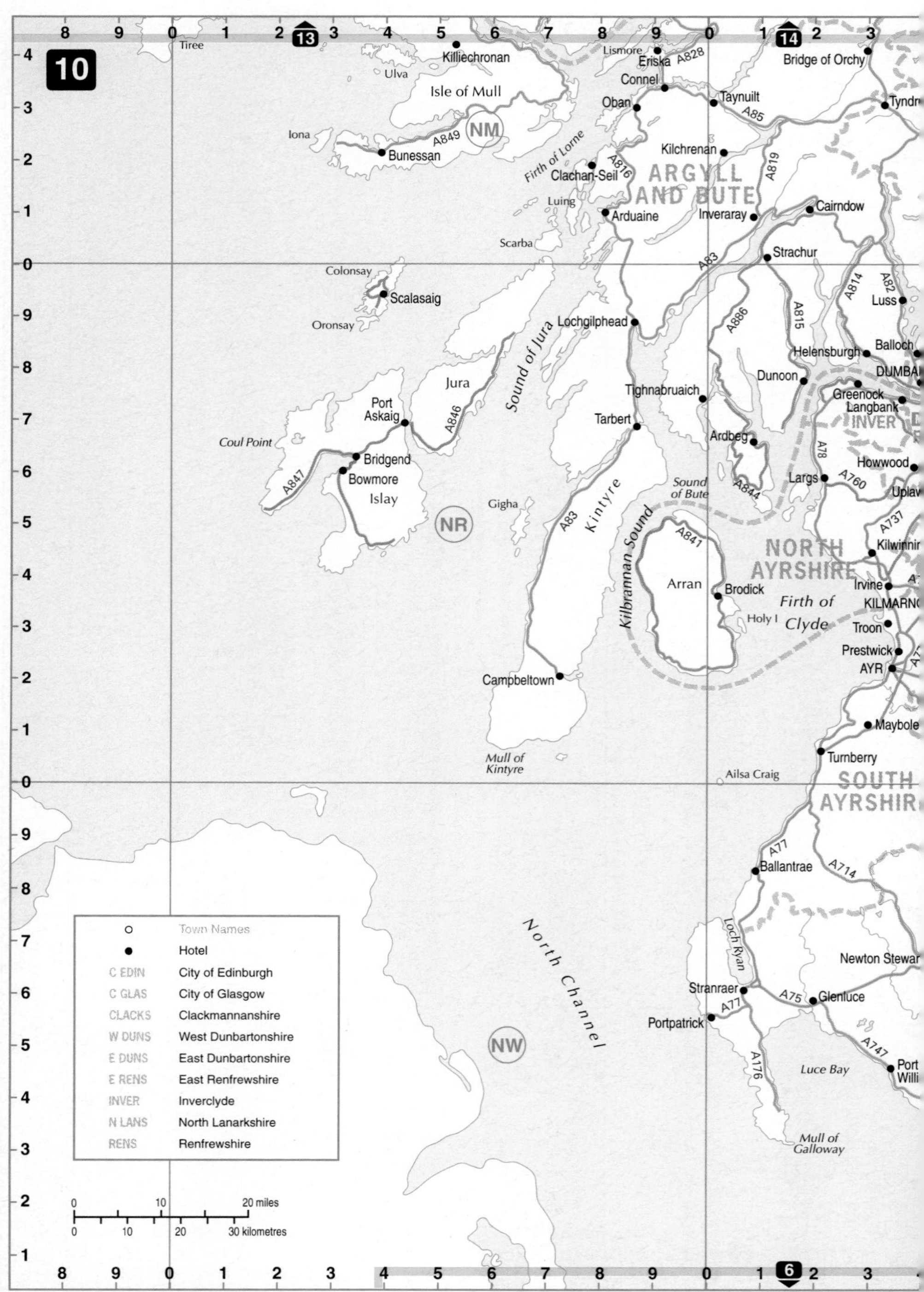

For continuation pages refer to numbered arrows

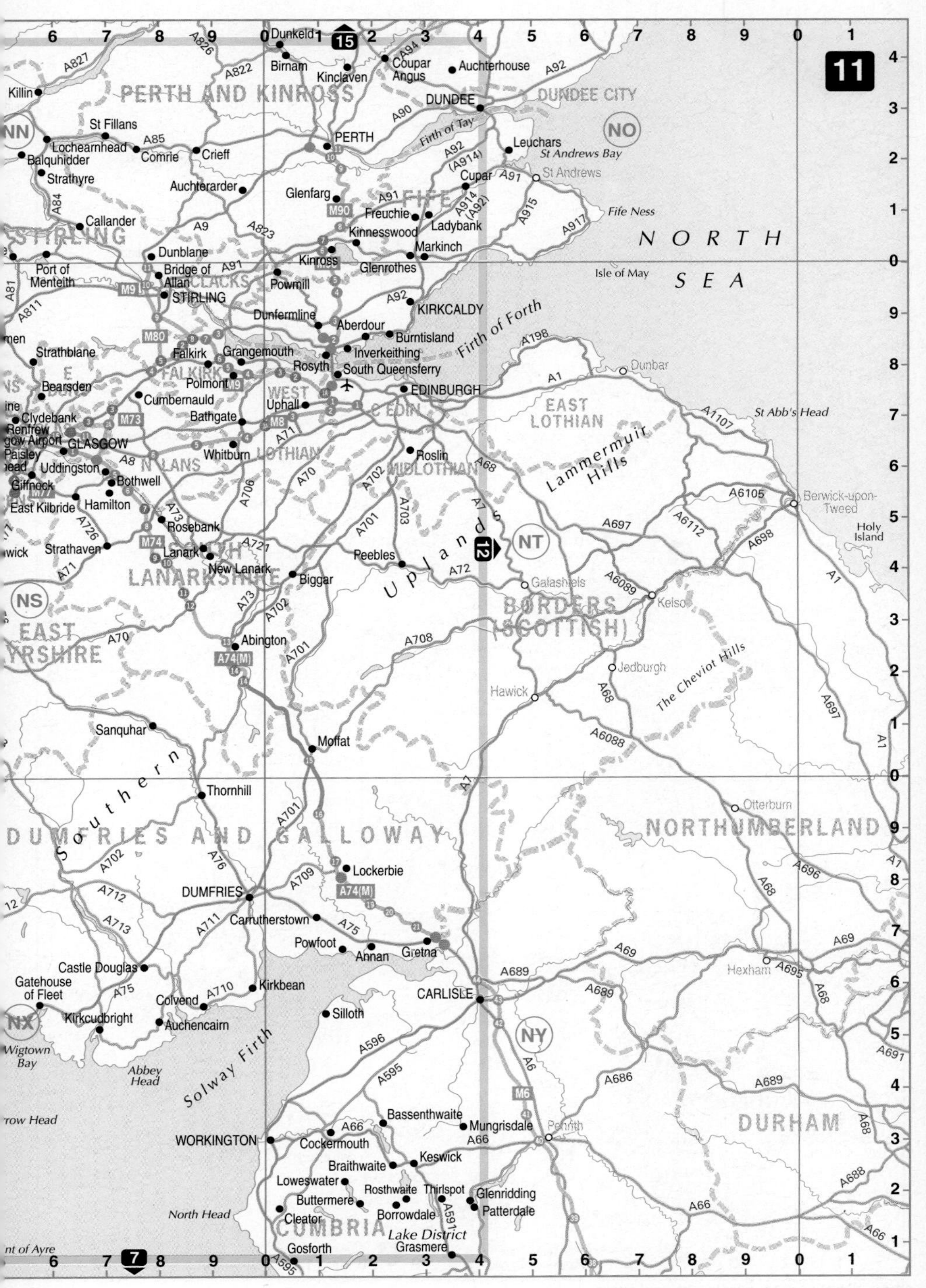

PERTH AND KINROSS
DUNDEE CITY
Dunkeld
Birnam
Kinclaven
Coupar Angus
Auchterhouse
Killin
DUNDEE
Firth of Tay
NN
NO
St Fillans
Lochearnhead
Balquhidder
Comrie
Crieff
PERTH
Leuchars
St Andrews Bay
St Andrews
Strathyre
Auchterarder
Glenfarg
Cupar
FIFE
Freuchie
Ladybank
Fife Ness
Callander
STIRLING
Kinnesswood
Markinch
NORTH SEA
Dunblane
Kinross
Glenrothes
Isle of May
Port of Menteith
Bridge of Allan
CLACKS
Powmill
STIRLING
KIRKCALDY
Dunfermline
Aberdour
Burntisland
Firth of Forth
Strathblane
Falkirk
Grangemouth
Inverkeithing
Rosyth
South Queensferry
Dunbar
FALKIRK
Polmont
Bearsden
WEST LOTHIAN
EDINBURGH
Cumbernauld
Uphall
C EDIN
EAST LOTHIAN
St Abb's Head
Clydebank
Renfrew
Glasgow Airport
GLASGOW
Bathgate
Paisley
Whitburn
Roslin
MIDLOTHIAN
Lammermuir Hills
Uddingston
N LANS
Giffnock
Bothwell
East Kilbride
Hamilton
Berwick-upon-Tweed
Rosebank
NT
Holy Island
Strathaven
Lanark
SOUTH LANARKSHIRE
New Lanark
Peebles
Uplands
Biggar
Galashiels
NS
BORDERS (SCOTTISH)
Kelso
EAST AYRSHIRE
Abington
Jedburgh
The Cheviot Hills
Hawick
Sanquhar
Moffat
Southern
Thornhill
Otterburn
DUMFRIES AND GALLOWAY
NORTHUMBERLAND
Lockerbie
DUMFRIES
Carrutherstown
Powfoot
Annan
Gretna
Hexham
Castle Douglas
Gatehouse of Fleet
Kirkbean
Colvend
CARLISLE
NX
Kirkcudbright
Auchencairn
Silloth
NY
Wigtown Bay
Abbey Head
Solway Firth
Bassenthwaite
Mungrisdale
DURHAM
WORKINGTON
Cockermouth
Penrith
Braithwaite
Keswick
Loweswater
Rosthwaite
Thirlspot
Glenridding
Buttermere
Borrowdale
Patterdale
North Head
Cleator
CUMBRIA
Lake District
Gosforth
Grasmere

For continuation pages refer to numbered arrows

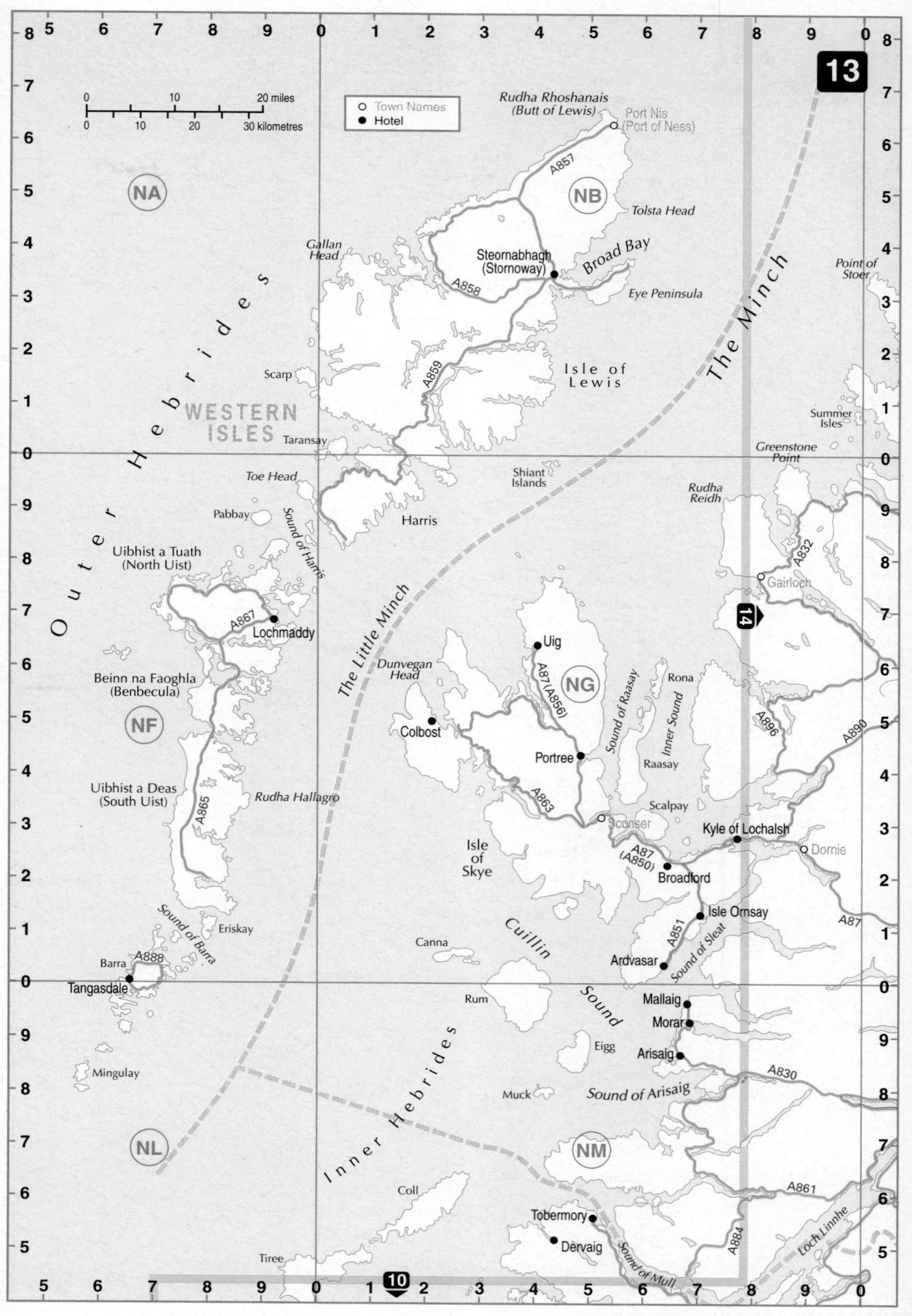

13
Town Names
Hotel
0 10 20 miles
0 10 20 30 kilometres
Rudha Rhoshanais (Butt of Lewis)
Port Nis (Port of Ness)
A857
NA
NB
Tolsta Head
Gallan Head
Steornabhagh (Stornoway)
Broad Bay
A858
Eye Peninsula
Point of Stoer
The Minch
Outer Hebrides
A859
Isle of Lewis
Scarp
WESTERN ISLES
Taransay
Summer Isles
Greenstone Point
Toe Head
Shiant Islands
Rudha Reidh
Pabbay
Sound of Harris
Harris
Uibhist a Tuath (North Uist)
A832
Gairloch
A867
Lochmaddy
The Little Minch
14
Uig
Beinn na Faoghla (Benbecula)
Dunvegan Head
NG
A87 (A856)
Sound of Raasay
Rona
Inner Sound
NF
Colbost
A896
A890
Portree
Uibhist a Deas (South Uist)
Raasay
A865
Rudha Hallagro
A863
Scalpay
Sconser
Kyle of Lochalsh
Isle of Skye
A87 (A850)
Dornie
Broadford
Isle Ornsay
A87
Sound of Barra
Eriskay
Cuillin
Canna
A851
Barra
A888
Ardvasar
Sound of Sleat
Tangasdale
Rum
Sound
Mallaig
Morar
Eigg
Arisaig
Mingulay
A830
Muck
Sound of Arisaig
Inner Hebrides
NL
NM
A861
Coll
Tobermory
Loch Linnhe
Dervaig
A884
Sound of Mull
Tiree
10

For continuation pages refer to numbered arrows

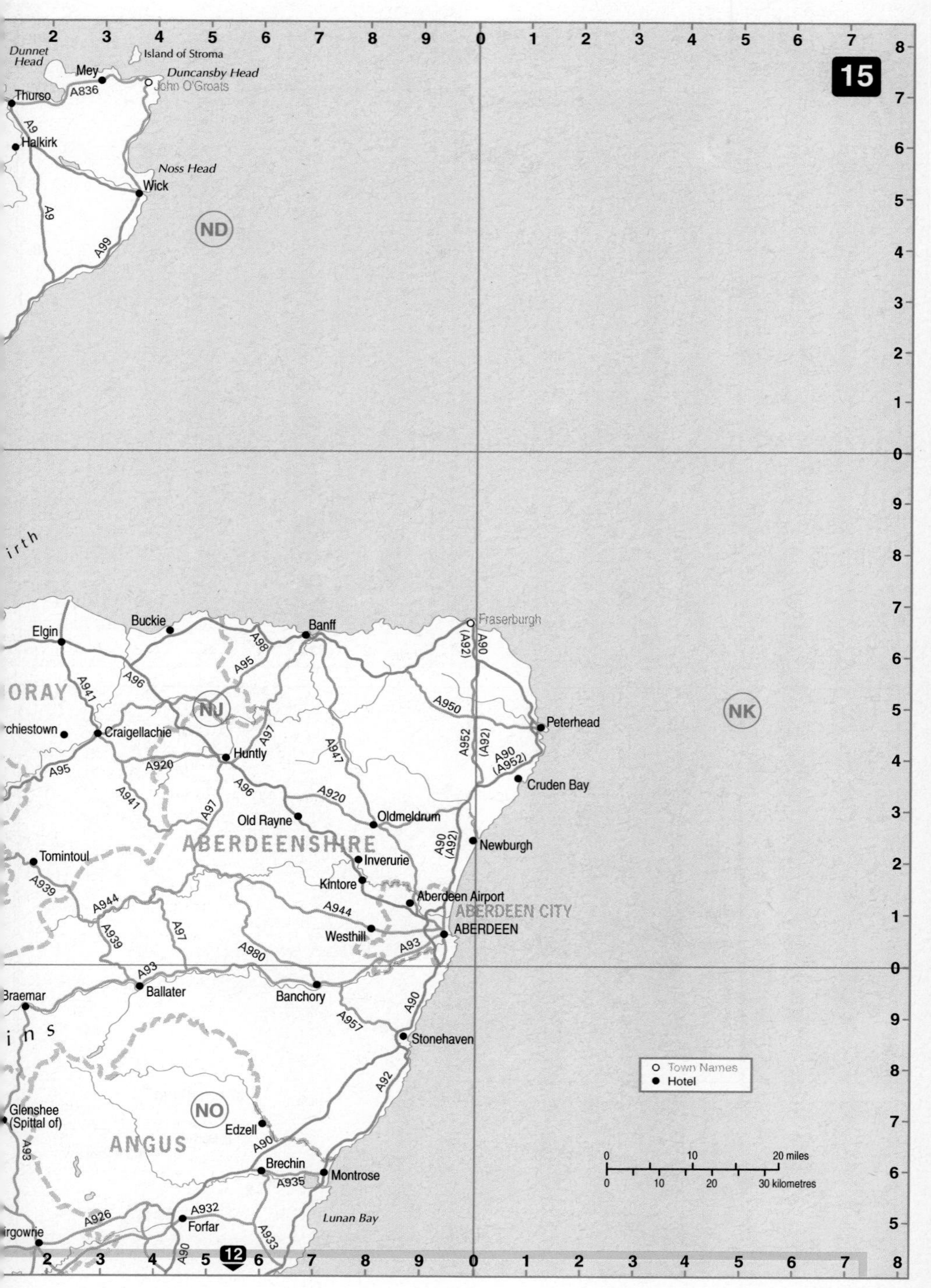

15
Dunnet Head
Island of Stroma
Mey
Duncansby Head
John O'Groats
Thurso
A836
A9
Halkirk
Noss Head
Wick
A9
A99
ND
irth
Elgin
Buckie
Banff
Fraserburgh
A98
A95
A96
A941
A92
A90
ORAY
NJ
A950
Peterhead
NK
rchiestown
Craigellachie
A97
A947
A952
(A92)
Huntly
A95
A920
A96
A90
(A952)
Cruden Bay
A941
A920
A97
Old Rayne
Oldmeldrum
A90
(A92)
Newburgh
ABERDEENSHIRE
Tomintoul
Inverurie
A939
Kintore
A944
Aberdeen Airport
A944
ABERDEEN CITY
A939
A97
Westhill
ABERDEEN
A980
A93
A93
Braemar
Ballater
Banchory
A90
A957
ins
Stonehaven
Town Names
Hotel
A92
Glenshee (Spittal of)
NO
Edzell
A93
ANGUS
A90
0
10
20 miles
Brechin
Montrose
A935
0
10
20
30 kilometres
A926
A932
Lunan Bay
Forfar
irgowrie
A933
A90
12

16

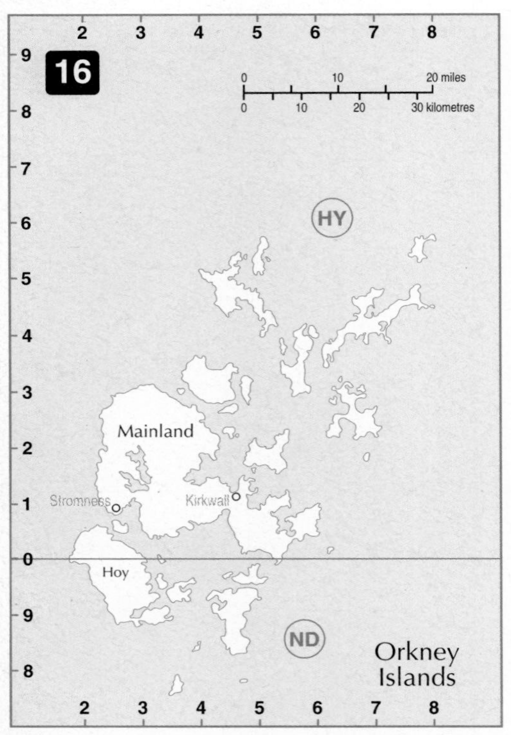

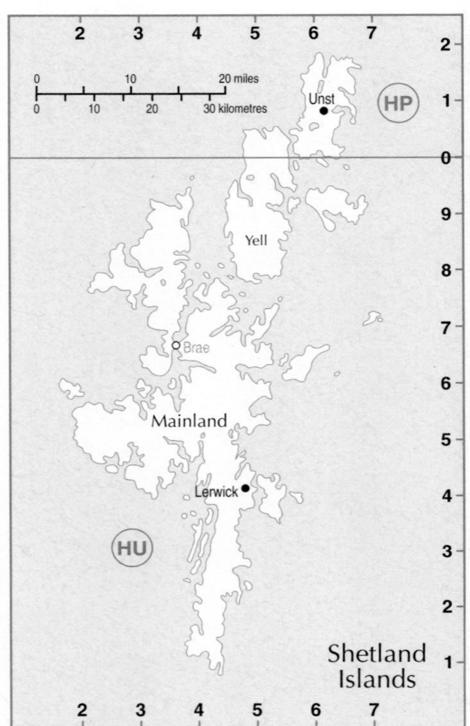

Jersey

0 1 2 3 miles
0 1 2 3 4 kilometres

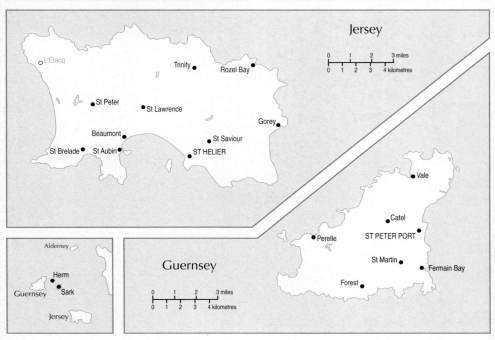

L'Etacq
Trinity
Rozel Bay
St Peter
St Lawrence
Gorey
Beaumont
St Saviour
St Brelade
St Aubin
ST HELIER

Alderney
Herm
Sark
Guernsey
Jersey

Guernsey

0 1 2 3 miles
0 1 2 3 4 kilometres

Vale
Catel
Perelle
ST PETER PORT
St Martin
Fermain Bay
Forest

Civil Wedding Venues

CIVIL WEDDING VENUES

Hotels holding a civil wedding licence are listed here alphabetically by town. The figure following the telephone number indicates the number of guests the hotel can accommodate for the ceremony, (e.g. ***C.50***). Where no number is given, please telephone the hotel for details. Also, note that in Scotland a licence is not required for religious ceremonies at any location.

ENGLAND

ABBOT'S SALFORD
Salford Hall Hotel
☎ 01386 871300 ***C:50***
ABINGDON
Abingdon Four Pillars Hotel
☎ 01235 553456 ***C:60***
ACCRINGTON Sparth House Hotel
☎ 01254 872263 ***C:100***
ACTON TRUSSELL
The Moat House
☎ 01785 712217 ***C:150***
ALBRIGHTON Lea Manor Hotel
☎ 01902 373266 ***C:60***
ALDERLEY EDGE
Alderley Edge Hotel
☎ 01625 583033 ***C:100***
ALDWARK Aldwark Manor Hotel, Golf & Country Club
☎ 01347 838146 ***C:100***
ALFRISTON Deans Place
☎ 01323 870248 ***C:150***
ALNWICK White Swan Hotel
☎ 01665 602109 ***C:120***
ALSAGER Manor House Hotel
☎ 01270 884000 ***C:50***
ALSTON Lovelady Shield Country House Hotel
☎ 01434 381203 ***C:100***
ALTON Alton Grange Hotel
☎ 01420 86565 ***C:100***
ALTON Alton House Hotel
☎ 01420 80033 ***C:75***
ALTRINCHAM
Woodland Park Hotel
☎ 0161 928 8631 ***C:80***
ALVELEY Mill Hotel & Restaurant
☎ 01746 780437 ***C:200***
ALVESTON Alveston House Hotel
☎ 01454 415050 ***C:75***
AMBERLEY Amberley Castle
☎ 01798 831992 ***C:48***
ANDOVER Esseborne Manor
☎ 01264 736444 ***C:120***
ANDOVER Quality Hotel Andover
☎ 01264 369111 ***C:85***
APPLEBY-IN-WESTMORLAND
Tufton Arms Hotel
☎ 017683 51593 ***C:100***

ARUNDEL Norfolk Arms Hotel
☎ 01903 882101
ASCOT The Berystede
☎ 0870 400 8111 ***C:60***
ASHBOURNE Hanover International Hotel
☎ 01335 346666
ASHFORD Eastwell Manor
☎ 01233 213000 ***C:250***
ASHFORD-IN-THE-WATER
Riverside House Hotel
☎ 01629 814275 ***C:30***
ASHTON-UNDER-LYNE
York House Hotel
☎ 0161 330 9000 ***C:50***
ASPLEY GUISE Moore Place Hotel
☎ 01908 282000 ***C:80***
BAGSHOT Pennyhill Park Hotel & Country Club
☎ 01276 471774 ***C:160***
BAKEWELL Hassop Hall Hotel
☎ 01629 640488 ***C:120***
BALSALL COMMON Nailcote Hall
☎ 024 7646 6174 ***C:120***
BANBURY Whately Hall
☎ 0870 400 8104 ***C:100***
BANBURY Wroxton House Hotel
☎ 01295 730777 ***C:60***
BAR HILL
Cambridgeshire Moat House
☎ 01954 249988 ***C:180***
BARNARD CASTLE Morritt Arms Hotel & Restaurant
☎ 01833 627232
BARNHAM BROOM Barnham Broom Hotel
☎ 01603 759393 ***C:200***
BARNSTAPLE Barnstaple Hotel
☎ 01271 376221
BARTON Barton Grange Hotel
☎ 01772 862551 ***C:120***
BASINGSTOKE
Basingstoke Country Hotel
☎ 01256 764161
BASINGSTOKE Ringway Hotel
☎ 01256 796700 ***C:200***
BASLOW Fischer's Baslow Hall
☎ 01246 583259 ***C:40***
BASSENTHWAITE
Armathwaite Hall
☎ 017687 76551 ***C:100***

BASSENTHWAITE Castle Inn Hotel
☎ 017687 76401 ***C:120***
BATH Cliffe Hotel
☎ 01225 723226 ***C:50***
BATH Combe Grove Manor Hotel & Country Club
☎ 01225 834644 ***C:50***
BATH The Bath Spa Hotel
☎ 0870 400 8222 ***C:140***
BATH The Old Mill Hotel
☎ 01225 858476 ***C:40***
BATH The Royal Crescent Hotel
☎ 01225 823333 ***C:90***
BATLEY Alder House Hotel
☎ 01924 444777 ***C:100***
BATTLE Powder Mills Hotel
☎ 01424 775511 ***C:100***
BAWTRY The Crown Hotel
☎ 01302 710341 ***C:100***
BEAULIEU Beaulieu Hotel
☎ 023 8029 3344 ***C:80***
BEDFORD The Barns Hotel
☎ 01234 270044 ***C:100***
BEDFORD
Woodlands Manor Hotel
☎ 01234 363281 ***C:50***
BELPER Makeney Hall Country House Hotel
☎ 01332 842999 ***C:150***
BELTON Belton Woods Hotel
☎ 01476 593200 ***C:60***
BEVERLEY Tickton Grange Hotel
☎ 01964 543666 ***C:150***
BEXLEYHEATH
Bexleyheath Marriott
☎ 020 8298 1000 ***C:50***
BIDEFORD Royal Hotel
☎ 01237 472005 ***C:100***
BIRKENHEAD Bowler Hat Hotel
☎ 0151 652 4931 ***C:90***
BIRMINGHAM Birmingham Grand Moat House
☎ 0121 607 9988 ***C:150***
BIRMINGHAM The Westley Hotel
☎ 0121 706 4312 ***C:70***
BIRMINGHAM Westmead Hotel & Restaurant
☎ 0121 445 1202 ***C:120***
BLACKBURN Clarion Hotel & Suites Foxfields
☎ 01254 822556 ***C:200***

BLACKPOOL De Vere Hotel
☎ 01253 838866 ***C:600***
BLACKPOOL Savoy Hotel
☎ 01253 352561 ***C:200***
BLANCHLAND
Lord Crewe Arms Hotel
☎ 01434 675251 ***C:65***
BLANDFORD FORUM
Crown Hotel
☎ 01258 456626 ***C:140***
BLUNDELLSANDS
The Blundellsands Hotel
☎ 0151 924 6515 ***C:80***
BLYTH Charnwood Hotel
☎ 01909 591610 ***C:120***
BOGNOR REGIS The Inglenook
☎ 01243 262495 ***C:120***
BOLTON Bolton Moat House
☎ 01204 879988 ***C:200***
BOREHAMWOOD
Elstree Moat House
☎ 020 8214 9988
BOROUGHBRIDGE Crown Hotel
☎ 01423 322328 ***C:70***
BOSHAM The Millstream Hotel & Restaurant
☎ 01243 573234 ***C:90***
BOURNEMOUTH
Durley Hall Hotel
☎ 01202 751000 ***C:85***
BOURNEMOUTH
Heathlands Hotel
☎ 01202 553336
BOURNEMOUTH Hotel Miramar
☎ 01202 556581 ***C:130***
BOURNEMOUTH
Marsham Court Hotel
☎ 01202 552111 ***C:200***
BOURNEMOUTH
Menzies Anglo-Swiss
☎ 0500 636943 ***C:150***
BOURNEMOUTH Menzies Carlton
☎ 0500 636943 ***C:140***
BOURNEMOUTH
Menzies East Cliff Court
☎ 0500 636943 ***C:150***
BOURNEMOUTH
Swallow Highcliff Hotel
☎ 01202 557702 ***C:100***
BRACKNELL Coppid Beech
☎ 01344 303333 ***C:150***
BRADFORD
Cedar Court Hotel Bradford
☎ 01274 406606 ***C:600***

Looking for an intimate setting in period surroundings? Look no further than Waterford House in Middleham, with just 24 guests for the ceremony you can keep it simple. Typical wedding parties here are small family groups looking for a stress-free experience. The informal setting for the ceremony is a converted dining room or lounge, with a delightful walled garden for photographs.

BRADFORD Courtyard by Marriott Leeds/Bradford
☎ 0113 285 4646
BRADFORD Guide Post Hotel
☎ 01274 607866 ***C:100***
BRAINTREE White Hart Hotel
☎ 01376 321401 ***C:60***
BRAMHALL
County Hotel Bramhall
☎ 0161 455 9988 ***C:140***
BRANDON The Brandon Hall
☎ 0870 400 8150 ***C:90***
BRANDS HATCH
Brandshatch Place
☎ 01474 872239 ***C:80***
BRANSTON Branston Hall Hotel
☎ 01522 793305 ***C:120***
BRAY Chauntry House Hotel & Restaurant
☎ 01628 673991 ***C:55***
BREADSALL Marriott Breadsall Priory Hotel/Country Club
☎ 01332 832235 ***C:100***
BRENT KNOLL
Battleborough Grange Hotel
☎ 01278 760208 ***C:80***
BRENTWOOD Marygreen Manor
☎ 01277 225252 ***C:60***
BRIGHTON Queens Hotel
☎ 01273 321222
BRIGHTON The Grand
☎ 01273 224300 ***C:400***
BRISTOL Aztec Hotel
☎ 01454 201090 ***C:250***
BRISTOL
Bristol Marriott City Centre
☎ 0117 929 4281 ***C:500***
BRISTOL The Avon Gorge
☎ 0117 973 8955 ***C:100***
BRIXHAM Berryhead Hotel
☎ 01803 853225 ***C:200***
BROADWAY Dormy House Hotel
☎ 01386 852711 ***C:170***
BROADWAY The Broadway Hotel
☎ 01386 852401 ***C:50***
BROADWAY The Lygon Arms
☎ 01386 852255 ***C:80***
BROCKENHURST
Careys Manor Hotel
☎ 01590 623551 ***C:110***
BROCKENHURST Cloud Hotel
☎ 01590 622165 ***C:40***

BROCKENHURST
Forest Park Hotel
☎ 01590 622844
BROCKENHURST
New Park Manor
☎ 01590 623467 ***C:50***
BROCKENHURST
Rhinefield House
☎ 01590 622922 ***C:80***
BROMLEY Bromley Court Hotel
☎ 020 8464 5011 ***C:50***
BROXTON
De Vere Carden Park Hotel
☎ 01829 731000 ***C:100***
BROXTON Frogg Manor
☎ 01829 782629 ***C:60***
BUCKHURST HILL Roebuck Hotel
☎ 020 8505 4636 ***C:120***
BUCKLERS HARD
Master Builders House Hotel
☎ 01590 616253
BURFORD The Bay Tree
☎ 01993 822791 ***C:70***
BURLEY Burley Manor
☎ 01425 403522
BURNHAM Burnham Beeches
☎ 01628 429955 ***C:120***
BURNHAM Grovefield Hotel
☎ 01628 603131 ***C:200***
BURNLEY Oaks Hotel
☎ 01282 414141 ***C:150***
BURNLEY Rosehill House Hotel
☎ 01282 453931 ***C:100***
BURNSALL Red Lion Hotel
☎ 01756 720204 ***C:50***
BURRINGTON Northcote Manor
☎ 01769 560501 ***C:40***
BURY ST EDMUNDS Angel Hotel
☎ 01284 741000 ***C:100***
BURY ST EDMUNDS
Ravenwood Hall Hotel
☎ 01359 270345 ***C:200***
BUXTON
Best Western Lee Wood Hotel
☎ 01298 23002 ***C:160***
CADNAM Bartley Lodge
☎ 023 80812248 ***C:100***
CAMBERLEY Frimley Hall
☎ 0870 400 8224 ***C:120***
CAMBRIDGE Cambridge Garden House Moat House
☎ 01223 259988 ***C:250***
CAMBRIDGE
Royal Cambridge Hotel
☎ 01223 351631 ***C:100***
CAMBRIDGE
University Arms Hotel
☎ 01223 351241 ***C:200***
CANNOCK Roman Way Hotel
☎ 01543 572121
CANTERBURY The Chaucer
☎ 0870 400 8106 ***C:100***

CARLISLE Crown Hotel
☎ 01228 561888
CARLISLE Swallow Hilltop Hotel
☎ 01228 529255 ***C:300***
CARNFORTH Royal Station Hotel
☎ 01524 732033 ***C:50***
CASTLE ASHBY Falcon Hotel
☎ 01604 696200 ***C:60***
CASTLE COMBE
Manor House Hotel
☎ 01249 782206 ***C:90***
CASTLE DONINGTON
Donington Manor Hotel
☎ 01332 810253 ***C:120***
CASTLE DONINGTON The Priest House on the River
☎ 01332 810649
CHAGFORD Mill End Hotel
☎ 01647 432282 ***C:60***
CHARD Lordleaze Hotel
☎ 01460 61066 ***C:110***
CHARINGWORTH
Charingworth Manor
☎ 01386 593555 ***C:50***
CHATHAM
Bridgewood Manor Hotel
☎ 01634 201333 ***C:120***
CHELTENHAM
Cheltenham Park Hotel
☎ 01242 222021 ***C:300***

CHELTENHAM
Cheltenham/Gloucester Moat House
☎ 01452 519988 ***C:180***
CHELTENHAM The Greenway
☎ 01242 862352 ***C:45***
CHELTENHAM The Prestbury House Hotel & Restaurant
☎ 01242 529533 ***C:60***
CHELTENHAM The Queen's
☎ 0870 400 8107 ***C:50***
CHELTENHAM White House Hotel
☎ 01452 713226 ***C:180***
CHESHUNT
Cheshunt Marriott Hotel
☎ 01992 451245 ***C:120***
CHESTER Chester Moat House
☎ 01244 899988 ***C:150***
CHESTER Crabwall Manor Hotel
☎ 01244 851666 ***C:90***
CHESTER Grosvenor Pulford Hotel
☎ 01244 570560 ***C:250***
CHESTER Hoole Hall
☎ 01244 408800 ***C:140***
CHESTER
Mollington Banastre Hotel
☎ 01244 851471
CHESTER Queen Hotel
☎ 01244 305000 ***C:250***
CHESTER
The Chester Grosvenor Hotel
☎ 01244 324024

CHIPPENHAM Angel Hotel
☎ 01249 652615 ***C:100***
CHIPPING
The Gibbon Bridge Hotel
☎ 01995 61456 ***C:180***
CHIPPING CAMPDEN
Cotswold House
☎ 01386 840330 ***C:40***
CHIPPING CAMPDEN
Noel Arms Hotel
☎ 01386 840317 ***C:70***
CHIPPING CAMPDEN
Seymour House Hotel
☎ 01386 840429 ***C:65***
CHIPPING CAMPDEN
Three Ways House
☎ 01386 438429 ***C:80***
CHOLLERFORD
Swallow George Hotel
☎ 01434 681611 ***C:80***
CHORLEY Shaw Hill Hotel Golf & Country Club
☎ 01257 269221 ***C:200***
CHRISTCHURCH The Avonmouth
☎ 0870 400 8120 ***C:70***
CLACTON-ON-SEA
Esplanade Hotel
☎ 01255 220450 ***C:70***
CLIMPING Bailiffscourt Hotel
☎ 01903 723511 ***C:70***
CLITHEROE Shireburn Arms Hotel
☎ 01254 826518 ***C:80***

COALVILLE
Charnwood Arms Hotel
☎ 01530 813644
COCKERMOUTH
Broughton Craggs Hotel
☎ 01900 824400 ***C:150***
COCKERMOUTH The Trout Hotel
☎ 01900 823591 ***C:60***
COLCHESTER Marks Tey Hotel
☎ 01206 210001 ***C:160***
COLEFORD The Speech House
☎ 01594 822607
COLERNE Lucknam Park
☎ 01225 742777 ***C:64***
COLESHILL Grimstock Country House Hotel
☎ 01675 462121 ***C:90***
CONSETT Raven Country Hotel
☎ 01207 562562 ***C:140***
COPTHORNE
Copthorne Effingham Park
☎ 01342 714994
COPTHORNE
Copthorne London Gatwick
☎ 01342 348800
CORNHILL-ON-TWEED Tillmouth Park Country House Hotel
☎ 01890 882255
CORSE LAWN
Corse Lawn House Hotel
☎ 01452 780479 ***C:75***
COVENTRY Allesley Hotel
☎ 024 7640 3272 ***C:350***
COVENTRY Aston Court Hotel
☎ 024 7625 8585 ***C:60***
COVENTRY Courtyard by Marriott Coventry
☎ 024 7630 1585 ***C:112***
COVENTRY Menzies Leofric Hotel
☎ 0500 636943 ***C:500***
COVENTRY The Chace Hotel
☎ 024 7630 3398 ***C:60***
CRATHORNE Crathorne Hall Hotel
☎ 01642 700398 ***C:132***
CREDITON
Coombe House Country Hotel
☎ 01363 84487 ***C:80***
CREWE Crewe Hall
☎ 01270 253333 ***C:220***
CREWE Hunters Lodge Hotel
☎ 01270 583440 ***C:130***
CREWE White Lion Hotel
☎ 01270 587011 ***C:65***
CRICKLADE Cricklade Hotel
☎ 01793 750751 ***C:120***
CROOKLANDS Crooklands Hotel
☎ 015395 67432
CROWBOROUGH
Winston Manor Hotel
☎ 01892 652772 ***C:45***
CROYDON Coulsdon Manor
☎ 020 8668 0414 ***C:60***
CROYDON Selsdon Park Hotel
☎ 020 8657 8811 ***C:100***
CUCKFIELD Ockenden Manor
☎ 01444 416111 ***C:75***
DARLINGTON Blackwell Grange
☎ 01325 509955 ***C:200***
DARLINGTON Hall Garth Golf and Country Club Hotel
☎ 01325 300400 ***C:170***
DARLINGTON Headlam Hall Hotel
☎ 01325 730238 ***C:150***
DARTFORD
Rowhill Grange Hotel & Spa
☎ 01322 615136 ***C:60***
DARWEN Whitehall Hotel
☎ 01254 701595 ***C:120***
DAVENTRY Fawsley Hall
☎ 01327 892000 ***C:140***
DAVENTRY Hanover International Hotel & Club Daventry
☎ 01327 301777 ***C:200***
DAWLISH Langstone Cliff Hotel
☎ 01626 868000 ***C:400***
DEAL Royal Hotel
☎ 01304 375555 ***C:30***
DEDDINGTON
Holcombe Hotel & Restaurant
☎ 01869 338274
DEDHAM Maison Talbooth
☎ 01206 322367
DERBY Aston Court Hotel
☎ 01332 342716 ***C:60***
DERBY International Hotel
☎ 01332 369321 ***C:100***
DERBY Menzies Mickleover Court
☎ 0500 636943 ***C:200***
DERBY Midland Hotel
☎ 01332 345894 ***C:100***
DEWSBURY Heath Cottage Hotel & Restaurant
☎ 01924 465399 ***C:100***
DONCASTER Danum Hotel
☎ 01302 342261 ***C:250***
DONCASTER
Doncaster Moat House
☎ 01302 799988 ***C:250***
DONCASTER Grand St Leger
☎ 01302 364111 ***C:60***
DOVER The Churchill
☎ 01304 203633 ***C:80***
DRIFFIELD (GREAT)
Bell Hotel
☎ 01377 256661 ***C:100***
DULVERTON
Carnarvon Arms Hotel
☎ 01398 323302
EAST GRINSTEAD
Woodbury House Hotel
☎ 01342 313657 ***C:80***
EASTBOURNE Chatsworth Hotel
☎ 01323 411016 ***C:140***
EASTBOURNE Grand Hotel
☎ 01323 412345 ***C:200***
EASTBOURNE Hydro Hotel
☎ 01323 720643 ***C:100***
EASTBOURNE York House Hotel
☎ 01323 412918 ***C:40***
EGHAM Runnymede Hotel & Spa
☎ 01784 436171 ***C:150***
ELLESMERE PORT
Quality Hotel Chester
☎ 0151 339 5121
ELSTREE Edgwarebury Hotel
☎ 020 8953 8227
ENFIELD Royal Chace Hotel
☎ 020 8884 8181 ***C:220***
ESCRICK The Parsonage Country House Hotel
☎ 01904 728111 ***C:50***
ESKDALE GREEN
Bower House Inn
☎ 019467 23244 ***C:60***
EVESHAM Wood Norton Hall
☎ 01386 420007 ***C:60***
EXETER Devon Hotel
☎ 01392 259268 ***C:100***
EXETER Gipsy Hill Hotel
☎ 01392 465252 ***C:120***
EXETER Royal Clarence
☎ 01392 319955 ***C:50***
EXETER The Southgate
☎ 0870 400 8333 ***C:80***
EXMOUTH Royal Beacon Hotel
☎ 01395 264886 ***C:150***
FAKENHAM Sculthorpe Mill
☎ 01328 856161 ***C:120***
FALMOUTH Falmouth Beach Resort Hotel
☎ 01326 318084 ***C:300***
FALMOUTH Falmouth Hotel
☎ 01326 312671 ***C:250***
FALMOUTH Penmere Manor
☎ 01326 211411 ***C:80***
FALMOUTH Royal Duchy Hotel
☎ 01326 313042
FALMOUTH
St Michaels of Falmouth
☎ 01326 312707 ***C:100***
FAREHAM Lysses House Hotel
☎ 01329 822622 ***C:95***
FAREHAM Solent Hotel
☎ 01489 880000 ***C:250***
FARNHAM Farnham House Hotel
☎ 01252 716908 ***C:70***
FARNHAM The Bush Hotel
☎ 0870 400 8225 ***C:90***
FIR TREE Helme Park Hall Hotel
☎ 01388 730970 ***C:150***
FLEET Lismoyne Hotel
☎ 01252 628555 ***C:200***
FLITWICK Menzies Flitwick Manor
☎ 0500 636943 ***C:50***

FLORE Courtyard by Marriott Daventry
☎ 01327 349022 ***C:100***
FORDINGBRIDGE Ashburn Hotel & Restaurant
☎ 01425 652060 ***C:180***
FOREST ROW Ashdown Park Hotel
☎ 01342 824988 ***C:140***
FOSSEBRIDGE Fossebridge Inn
☎ 01285 720721 ***C:75***
FOWEY Fowey Hall
☎ 01726 833866 ***C:40***
GARSTANG Pickering Park Country House
☎ 01995 600999 ***C:60***
GATESHEAD Eslington Villa Hotel
☎ 0191 487 6017
GATESHEAD Newcastle Marriott City Centre
☎ 0191 493 2233 ***C:100***
GATWICK AIRPORT Le Meridien London Gatwick
☎ 0870 4008494 ***C:250***
GERRARDS CROSS Bull Hotel
☎ 01753 885995 ***C:200***
GISBURN Stirk House Hotel
☎ 01200 445581 ***C:150***
GLENRIDDING Glenridding Hotel
☎ 017684 82228 ***C:60***
GLOUCESTER Hatherley Manor Hotel
☎ 01452 730217 ***C:300***
GLOUCESTER Hatton Court
☎ 01452 617412 ***C:80***
GOMERSAL Gomersal Park Hotel
☎ 01274 869386 ***C:200***
GOODWOOD Marriott Goodwood Park Hotel & Country Club
☎ 01243 775537 ***C:120***
GRANGE-OVER-SANDS Netherwood Hotel
☎ 015395 32552 ***C:150***
GRASMERE Michael's Nook Country House Hotel & Rest.
015394 35496 ***C:30***
GRASMERE Wordsworth Hotel
☎ 015394 35592 ***C:120***
GRAYS Lakeside Moat House
☎ 01708 719988 ***C:120***
GREAT CHESTERFORD The Crown House
☎ 01799 530515 ***C:40***
GREAT MILTON Le Manoir Aux Quat' Saisons
☎ 01844 278881 ***C:55***
GREAT YARMOUTH Cliff Hotel
☎ 01493 662179
GREAT YARMOUTH Knights Court Hotel
☎ 01493 843089

GREAT YARMOUTH Regency Dolphin Hotel
☎ 01493 855070 ***C:140***
GRIMSTON Congham Hall Country House Hotel
☎ 01485 600250 ***C:40***
GRINDLEFORD Maynard Arms Hotel
☎ 01433 630321 ***C:120***
GUILDFORD The Manor
☎ 01483 222624 ***C:120***
GULWORTHY The Horn of Plenty
☎ 01822 832528 ***C:120***
HADLEY WOOD West Lodge Park Hotel
☎ 020 8216 3900 ***C:40***
HAILSHAM Boship Farm Hotel
☎ 01323 844826
HALIFAX Holdsworth House Hotel
☎ 01422 240024 ***C:118***
HALIFAX Rock Inn Hotel & Churchills
☎ 01422 379721 ***C:200***
HALIFAX The Imperial Crown
☎ 01422 342342 ***C:200***
HAMPSON GREEN Hampson House Hotel
☎ 01524 751158 ***C:70***
HAMPTON COURT Menzies Liongate
☎ 0500 636943 ***C:60***
HANDFORTH Belfry House Hotel
☎ 0161 437 0511 ***C:60***
HARLOW Harlow/Stansted Moat House
☎ 01279 829988
HARLOW Swallow Churchgate Hotel
☎ 01279 420246
HARPENDEN Glen Eagle Hotel
☎ 01582 760271 ***C:120***
HARROGATE Old Swan Hotel
☎ 01423 500055 ***C:450***
HARROGATE Rudding Park House & Hotel
☎ 01423 871350
HARROGATE Swallow St George Hotel
☎ 01423 561431 ***C:140***
HARROGATE The Crown
☎ 01423 567755 ***C:400***
HARROGATE The Majestic
☎ 01423 700300 ***C:450***
HARROGATE The White House
☎ 01423 501388 ***C:60***
HARROW Quality Harrow Hotel
☎ 020 8427 3435 ***C:120***
HARTLEPOOL The Grand Hotel
☎ 01429 266345 ***C:200***
HARWICH The Pier at Harwich
☎ 01255 241212

HASLEMERE Lythe Hill Hotel
☎ 01428 651251 ***C:128***
HASTINGS & ST LEONARDS Beauport Park Hotel
☎ 01424 851222 ***C:65***
HAWES Simonstone Hall Hotel
☎ 01969 667255 ***C:120***
HAYES Sheraton Skyline Hotel & Conference Centre
☎ 020 8759 2535 ***C:360***
HEBDEN BRIDGE Carlton Hotel
☎ 01422 844400 ***C:90***
HECKFIELD New Inn
☎ 0118 932 6374
HELMSLEY The Carlton Lodge Hotel
☎ 01439 770557 ***C:160***
HEMEL HEMPSTEAD Watermill Hotel
☎ 01442 349955 ***C:100***
HEREFORD Belmont Lodge & Golf Course
☎ 01432 352666
HEREFORD Three Counties Hotel
☎ 01432 299955
HEXHAM Langley Castle Hotel
☎ 01434 688888 ***C:120***
HINCKLEY Hanover International Hotel & Club Hinckley
☎ 01455 631122 ***C:250***
HINCKLEY Kings Hotel & Restaurant
☎ 01455 637193 ***C:60***
HINCKLEY Sketchley Grange Hotel
☎ 01455 251133 ***C:250***
HINTLESHAM Hintlesham Hall Hotel
☎ 01473 652334 ***C:120***
HINTON CHARTERHOUSE Homewood Park Hotel
☎ 01225 723731 ***C:80***
HOCKLEY HEATH Nuthurst Grange Country House Hotel
☎ 01564 783972 ***C:100***
HODNET Bear Hotel
☎ 01630 685214 ***C:70***
HOLMES CHAPEL Holly Lodge Hotel & Truffles Restaurant
☎ 01477 537033 ***C:140***
HONILEY Honiley Court Hotel
☎ 01926 484234 ***C:146***
HONITON Combe House Hotel at Gittisham
☎ 01404 540400 ***C:100***
HORLEY Langshott Manor
☎ 01293 786680 ***C:60***
HORLEY Stanhill Court Hotel
☎ 01293 862166 ***C:160***
HORTON-CUM-STUDLEY Studley Priory Hotel
☎ 01865 351203 ***C:50***

HOUNSLOW The Renaissance London Heathrow Hotel
☎ 020 8897 6363 ***C:400***
HOVE Princes Marine
☎ 01273 207660
HOVINGHAM
The Worsley Arms Hotel
☎ 01653 628234 ***C:90***
HOWTOWN Sharrow Bay Country House Hotel
☎ 017684 86301 ***C:35***
HUDDERSFIELD Bagden Hall
☎ 01484 865330 ***C:76***
HUDDERSFIELD Briar Court Hotel
☎ 01484 519902 ***C:150***
HUDDERSFIELD
Old Golf House Hotel
☎ 01422 379311 ***C:180***
HUDDERSFIELD
Pennine Manor Hotel
☎ 01484 642368 ***C:100***
HUDDERSFIELD The George Hotel
☎ 01484 515444 ***C:150***
HULL Quality Hotel Hull
☎ 01482 325087 ***C:450***
HUNSTANTON
Le Strange Arms Hotel
☎ 01485 534411 ***C:150***
HUNSTRETE
Hunstrete House Hotel
☎ 01761 490490 ***C:50***
HUNTINGDON
Huntingdon Marriott
☎ 01480 446000 ***C:250***
HUNTINGDON
The Old Bridge Hotel
☎ 01480 424300 ***C:80***
HYTHE The Hythe Imperial Hotel
☎ 01303 267441 ***C:200***
ILKLEY
Rombalds Hotel & Restaurant
☎ 01943 603201 ***C:70***
ILMINSTER Shrubbery Hotel
☎ 01460 52108 ***C:200***
INGATESTONE
The Heybridge Hotel
☎ 01277 355355 ***C:200***
IPSWICH County Hotel Ipswich
☎ 01473 209988 ***C:120***
IPSWICH Courtyard by Marriott Ipswich
☎ 01473 272244
IPSWICH Marlborough Hotel
☎ 01473 257677 ***C:120***
IPSWICH
Swallow Belstead Brook Hotel
☎ 01473 684241 ***C:130***
KEGWORTH Yew Lodge Hotel & Conference Centre
☎ 01509 672518 ***C:150***
KENDAL The Castle Green Hotel in Kendal
☎ 01539 734000 ***C:300***
KENILWORTH
Chesford Grange Hotel
☎ 01926 859331 ***C:80***
KENILWORTH
Clarendon House Hotel
☎ 01926 857668 ***C:150***
KESWICK
Keswick Country House Hotel
☎ 017687 72020 ***C:130***
KETTERING Kettering Park Hotel
☎ 01536 416666 ***C:200***
KIDDERMINSTER
Stone Manor Hotel
☎ 01562 777555 ***C:50***
KING'S LYNN Knights Hill Hotel
☎ 01553 675566 ***C:75***
KING'S LYNN The Duke's Head
☎ 01553 774996 ***C:100***
KINGSBRIDGE
Buckland-Tout-Saints
☎ 01548 853055 ***C:130***
KIRKBURTON Hanover International Hotel
☎ 01484 607788 ***C:80***
KNUTSFORD Cottons Hotel
☎ 01565 650333
LANCASTER
Menzies Royal Kings Arms
☎ 0500 636943 ***C:100***
LANGAR Langar Hall
☎ 01949 860559 ***C:40***
LANGHO Northcote Manor
☎ 01254 240555 ***C:40***
LAVENHAM The Swan
☎ 0870 400 8116 ***C:40***
LEATHERHEAD
Bookham Grange Hotel
☎ 01372 452742 ***C:100***
LEDBURY Feathers Hotel
☎ 01531 635266 ***C:90***
LEEDS Crowne Plaza Leeds
☎ 0113 244 2200 ***C:150***
LEEDS Haley's Hotel & Restaurant
☎ 0113 278 4446 ***C:136***
LEEDS Leeds Marriott Hotel
☎ 0113 236 6366 ***C:280***
LEEDS Queen's Hotel
☎ 0113 243 1323 ***C:400***
LEEDS The Metropole
☎ 0113 245 0841
LEICESTER Belmont House Hotel
☎ 0116 254 4773 ***C:100***
LEICESTER Charnwood Hotel
☎ 0116 286 2218 ***C:150***
LEICESTER Hermitage Hotel
☎ 0116 256 9955 ***C:200***
LEICESTER Leicester Stage Hotel
☎ 0116 288 6161 ***C:300***
LEICESTER
Time Out Hotel & Leisure
☎ 0116 278 7898 ***C:90***
LENHAM Chilston Park Hotel
☎ 01622 859803 ***C:80***
LEOMINSTER Talbot Hotel
☎ 01568 616347 ***C:150***
LEWDOWN Lewtrenchard Manor
☎ 01566 783256
& 783222 ***C:100***
LEWES Shelleys Hotel
☎ 01273 472361 ***C:50***
LICHFIELD Little Barrow Hotel
☎ 01543 414500 ***C:80***
LIFTON Arundell Arms
☎ 01566 784666 ***C:100***
LINCOLN The Bentley Hotel & Leisure Club
☎ 01522 878000 ***C:120***
LINCOLN The White Hart
☎ 0870 400 8117 ***C:120***
LIPHOOK Old Thorns Hotel, Golf & Country Club
☎ 01428 724555 ***C:80***
LITTLE WEIGHTON
The Rowley Manor Hotel
☎ 01482 848248 ***C:100***
LIVERPOOL
Liverpool Marriott City Centre
☎ 0151 476 8000 ***C:250***
LIVERPOOL
Liverpool Moat House Hotel
☎ 0151 471 9988 ***C:200***
LONDON N10 Raglan Hall Hotel
☎ 020 8883 9836 ***C:100***
LONDON NW1 Landmark Hotel
☎ 020 7631 8000 ***C:300***
LONDON NW3 London Marriott Hotel Regents Park
☎ 020 7722 7711 ***C:250***
LONDON SE1
London Marriott County Hall
☎ 020 7928 5200 ***C:85***
LONDON SE3 Clarendon Hotel
☎ 020 8318 4321 ***C:50***
LONDON SW1 Goring Hotel
☎ 020 7396 9000 ***C:50***

Hundreds of friends and relatives? Fear not - our survey showed that the Hotel Inter-Continental London has the largest capacity for guests at a civil ceremony in London, taking a maximum of 750 guests. Nothing is too much trouble, with a dedicated events co-ordinator to help plan your big day, from choosing the cake and flowers to a preview of the band.

LONDON SW1
Hyatt Carlton Tower Hotel
☎ 020 7235 1234 ***C:360***
LONDON SW1
Mandarin Oriental Hyde Park
☎ 020 7235 2000 ***C:400***
LONDON SW1 The Berkeley
☎ 020 7235 6000 ***C:160***
LONDON SW1 The Stafford
☎ 020 7493 0111 ***C:60***
LONDON SW19 Cannizaro House
☎ 020 8879 1464 ***C:60***
LONDON SW7 The Millennium Gloucester Hotel
☎ 020 7373 6030 ***C:300***
LONDON W1 Athenaeum Hotel & Apartments
☎ 020 7499 3464 ***C:55***
LONDON W1
Churchill Inter-Continental
☎ 020 7486 5800 ***C:180***
LONDON W1 Claridge's
☎ 020 7629 8860 ***C:240***
LONDON W1 Four Seasons Hotel
☎ 020 7499 0888 ***C:500***
LONDON W1 Grosvenor House
☎ 0870 400 8500 ***C:100***
LONDON W1 Hotel Inter-Continental London
☎ 020 7409 3131 ***C:750***
LONDON W1
Le Meridien Piccadilly
☎ 0870 400 8400 ***C:200***
LONDON W1 Mayfair Inter-Continental London
☎ 020 7629 7777 ***C:250***
LONDON W1
Millennium Britannia Mayfair
☎ 020 7629 9400 ***C:400***
LONDON W1
Radisson SAS Portman Hotel
☎ 020 7208 6000 ***C:450***
LONDON W1
Sheraton Park Lane Hotel
☎ 020 499 6321 ***C:600***
LONDON W1 The Berners Hotel
☎ 020 7666 2000
LONDON W1
The Chesterfield Hotel
☎ 020 7491 2622 ***C:100***
LONDON W1 The Dorchester
☎ 020 7629 8888 ***C:500***
LONDON W1 The Montcalm-Hotel Nikko London
☎ 020 7402 4288 ***C:100***
LONDON W1 The Ritz
☎ 020 7493 8181 ***C:50***
LONDON W11 Halcyon Hotel
☎ 020 7727 7288 ***C:120***
LONDON W8 Royal Garden Hotel
☎ 020 7937 8000 ***C:400***

LONDON WC2 One Aldwych
☎ 020 7300 1000 ***C:60***
LONG MELFORD The Bull
☎ 01787 378494 ***C:50***
LONGRIDGE
Ferrari's Country House
☎ 01772 783148 ***C:120***
LOOE Hannafore Point Hotel
☎ 01503 263273 ***C:160***
LOUGHBOROUGH Quality Hotel
☎ 01509 211800 ***C:80***
LOUTH Kenwick Park Hotel
☎ 01507 608806 ***C:92***
LOWER BEEDING
South Lodge Hotel
☎ 01403 891711 ***C:65***
LOWESTOFT Hotel Hatfield
☎ 01502 565337 ***C:200***
LUDLOW The Feathers at Ludlow
☎ 01584 875261 ***C:80***
LYMINGTON Stanwell House Hotel
☎ 01590 677123 ***C:60***
LYMPSHAM Batch Country Hotel
☎ 01934 750371 ***C:120***
LYNDHURST Crown Hotel
☎ 023 8028 2922 ***C:30***
LYNDHURST Forest Lodge Hotel
☎ 023 8028 3677 ***C:100***
LYNDHURST Le Poussin at Parkhill
☎ 023 8028 2944
LYNDHURST Lyndhurst Park Hotel
☎ 023 8028 3923
LYTHAM ST ANNES Bedford Hotel
☎ 01253 724636 ***C:120***
MACCLESFIELD
Belgrade Hotel & Restaurant
☎ 01625 573246 ***C:50***
MACCLESFIELD Shrigley Hall Hotel Golf & Country Club
☎ 01625 575757 ***C:220***
MAIDENHEAD Elva Lodge Hotel
☎ 01628 622948 ***C:60***
MAIDENHEAD Fredrick's Hotel
☎ 01628 581000 ***C:120***
MAIDSTONE Marriott Tudor Park Hotel & Country Club
☎ 01622 734334 ***C:180***
MALVERN The Abbey Hotel
☎ 01684 892332 ***C:300***
MANCHESTER Le Meridien Victoria & Albert
☎ 0870 400 8585 ***C:200***
MANCHESTER Manchester Marriott Worsley Park Hotel & Country Club
☎ 0161 975 2000
MANCHESTER Palace Hotel
☎ 0161 288 1111 ***C:100***
MANCHESTER Royals Hotel
☎ 0161 998 9011 ***C:100***

MANCHESTER AIRPORT Etrop Grange Hotel & Restaurant
☎ 0161 499 0500 ***C:90***
MANCHESTER AIRPORT Swallow Four Seasons Hotel
☎ 0161 904 0301 ***C:100***
MANSFIELD Portland Hall Hotel
☎ 01623 452525 ***C:150***
MARKET DRAYTON
Goldstone Hall
☎ 01630 661202 ***C:60***
MARKET DRAYTON
Rosehill Manor
☎ 01630 638532 ***C:90***
MARKET HARBOROUGH
Menzies Angel Hotel
☎ 0500 636943 ***C:75***
MARKET HARBOROUGH
Three Swans Hotel
☎ 01858 466644 ***C:200***
MARLOW Danesfield House
☎ 01628 891010 ***C:170***
MARLOW The Compleat Angler
☎ 0870 400 8100
MATLOCK Riber Hall
☎ 01629 582795 ***C:45***
MATLOCK BATH New Bath Hotel
☎ 0870 400 8119
MAWNAN SMITH Budock Vean-The Hotel on the River
☎ 01326 252100 ***C:100***
MERIDEN Marriott Forest of Arden Hotel & Country Club
☎ 01676 522335 ***C:150***
MIDDLEHAM Waterford House
☎ 01969 622090 ***C:24***
MIDHURST Angel Hotel
☎ 01730 812421 ***C:40***
MIDHURST
Southdowns Country Hotel
☎ 01730 821521 ***C:100***
MIDHURST Spread Eagle Hotel and Health Spa
☎ 01730 816911 ***C:120***
MIDSOMER NORTON
Centurion Hotel
☎ 01761 417711 ***C:80***
MILFORD ON SEA
Westover Hall Hotel
☎ 01590 643044 ***C:100***
MILTON COMMON
The Oxford Belfry
☎ 01844 279381 ***C:250***
MILTON KEYNES Quality Hotel & Suites Milton Keynes
☎ 01908 561666 ***C:90***
MILTON KEYNES
Swan Revived Hotel
☎ 01908 610565 ***C:75***
MORECAMBE Elms Hotel
☎ 01524 411501 ***C:100***

MORECAMBE Strathmore Hotel
☎ 01524 421234 ***C:100***
MORETON Leasowe Castle Hotel
☎ 0151 606 9191 ***C:120***
MORETONHAMPSTEAD
Manor House Hotel
☎ 01647 440355 ***C:100***
MUNDFORD Lynford Hall Hotel
☎ 01842 878351 ***C:550***
NANTWICH
Crown Hotel & Restaurant
☎ 01270 625283 ***C:150***
NEW MILTON Chewton Glen Hotel
☎ 01425 275341 ***C:120***
NEWBURY Donnington Valley Hotel & Golf Course
☎ 01635 551199 ***C:85***
NEWBURY
The Vineyard at Stockcross
☎ 01635 528770
NEWBY BRIDGE Lakeside Hotel
☎ 015395 31207 ***C:140***
NEWBY BRIDGE The Swan Hotel
☎ 015395 31681 ***C:80***

NEWBY BRIDGE Whitewater Hotel
☎ 015395 31133 ***C:100***
NEWCASTLE UPON TYNE
Cairn Hotel
☎ 0191 281 1358
NEWCASTLE UPON TYNE Swallow Imperial Hotel
☎ 0191 281 5511 ***C:135***
NEWCASTLE-UNDER-LYME
Comfort Inn
☎ 01782 717000
NEWICK
Newick Park Country Estate
☎ 01825 723633 ***C:70***
NEWMARKET Heath Court Hotel
☎ 01638 667171 ***C:80***
NEWQUAY Barrowfield Hotel
☎ 01637 878878 ***C:150***
NEWQUAY Glendorgal Hotel
☎ 01637 874937 ***C:100***
NEWQUAY Headland Hotel
☎ 01637 872211 ***C:250***
NEWQUAY Hotel Riviera
☎ 01637 874251 ***C:200***

NEWQUAY Kilbirnie Hotel
☎ 01637 875155
NORTHALLERTON
Solberge Hall Hotel
☎ 01609 779191 ***C:100***
NORTHALLERTON
The Golden Lion
☎ 01609 777411 ***C:70***
NORTHAMPTON
Northampton Marriott
☎ 01604 768700 ***C:80***
NORTHAMPTON
Quality Hotel Northampton
☎ 01604 739955 ***C:150***
NORTHWICH
Quality Hotel Northwich
☎ 01606 44443 ***C:80***
NORTHWOLD
Comfort Inn - Thetford
☎ 01366 728888
NORWICH Maids Head Hotel
☎ 01603 209955 ***C:100***
NORWICH Quality Hotel
☎ 01603 741161 ***C:70***
NOTTINGHAM Nottingham Royal Moat House
☎ 0115 936 9988 ***C:400***
OAKHAM Barnsdale Hall Hotel & Country Club
☎ 01572 757901 ***C:120***
OAKHAM Barnsdale Lodge Hotel
☎ 01572 724678 ***C:100***
OAKHAM Hambleton Hall
☎ 01572 756991 ***C:60***
OAKHAM Whipper-in Hotel
☎ 01572 756971 ***C:65***
OCKLEY Gatton Manor Hotel Golf & Country Club
☎ 01306 627555 ***C:50***
OLDHAM Menzies Avant Hotel
☎ 0500 636943 ***C:200***
ORMSKIRK Beaufort Hotel
☎ 01704 892655 ***C:50***
OSWESTRY Wynnstay Hotel
☎ 01691 655261 ***C:90***
OXFORD Fallowfields Country House Hotel
☎ 01865 820416 ***C:100***
OXFORD Hawkwell House
☎ 01865 749988 ***C:200***
OXFORD Linton Lodge Hotel
☎ 01865 553461 ***C:80***
OXFORD Oxford Thames Four Pillars Hotel
☎ 01865 334444 ***C:140***
PAIGNTON Redcliffe Hotel
☎ 01803 526397 ***C:150***
PAINSWICK Painswick Hotel
☎ 01452 812160 ***C:100***
PANGBOURNE The Copper Inn Hotel & Restaurant
☎ 0118 984 2244 ***C:80***

PATTERDALE Patterdale Hotel
☎ 017684 82231 ***C:110***
PATTINGHAM Patshull Park Hotel Golf & Country Club
☎ 01902 700100 ***C:100***
PEASMARSH Flackley Ash Hotel
☎ 01797 230651 ***C:120***
PENKRIDGE Quality Hotel Stafford
☎ 01785 712459 ***C:70***
PENRITH North Lakes Hotel
☎ 01768 868111 ***C:200***
PENZANCE Queen's Hotel
☎ 01736 362371 ***C:180***
PETERBOROUGH Peterborough Moat House
☎ 01733 289988 ***C:100***
PETERLEE Hardwicke Hall Manor Hotel
☎ 01429 836326 ***C:110***
PETERSFIELD Langrish House
☎ 01730 266941 ***C:60***
PETTY FRANCE Petty France Hotel
☎ 01454 238361
PICKERING Forest & Vale Hotel
☎ 01751 472722 ***C:100***
PLYMOUTH Copthorne Plymouth
☎ 01752 224161 ***C:100***
PLYMOUTH Duke of Cornwall Hotel
☎ 01752 275850 ***C:120***
PLYMOUTH Kitley House Hotel
☎ 01752 881555 ***C:80***
PLYMOUTH Langdon Court Hotel
☎ 01752 862358 ***C:75***
PLYMOUTH New Continental Hotel
☎ 01752 220782 ***C:130***
PONTEFRACT Rogerthorpe Manor Hotel
☎ 01977 643839 ***C:300***
POOLE Haven Hotel
☎ 01202 707333 ***C:80***
POOLE Mansion House Hotel
☎ 01202 685666 ***C:35***
POOLE Salterns Hotel
☎ 01202 707321 ***C:120***
PORTSMOUTH & SOUTHSEA Portsmouth Marriott
☎ 023 9238 3151 ***C:100***
PORTSMOUTH & SOUTHSEA Sandringham Hotel
☎ 023 9282 6969 ***C:130***
PRESTBURY Bridge Hotel
☎ 01625 829326 ***C:100***
PRESTON Mill Hotel
☎ 01772 600110 ***C:70***
PRESTON Pines Hotel
☎ 01772 338551 ***C:150***
PRESTON Preston Marriott
☎ 01772 864087 ***C:180***
PRESTON Tickled Trout
☎ 01772 877671 ***C:120***
PUDDINGTON Craxton Wood
☎ 0151 347 4000 ***C:400***
PURTON The Pear Tree at Purton
☎ 01793 772100 ***C:50***
QUORN Quorn Country Hotel
☎ 01509 415050 ***C:100***
RANGEWORTHY Rangeworthy Court Hotel
☎ 01454 228347 ***C:60***
READING Courtyard by Marriott Reading
☎ 0118 971 4411 ***C:120***
READING Holiday Inn
☎ 0118 925 9988 ***C:35***
READING The Mill House Hotel
☎ 0118 988 3124 ***C:125***
REDDITCH Quality Hotel
☎ 01527 541511 ***C:100***
REDHILL Nutfield Priory
☎ 01737 824400 ***C:60***
REDRUTH Penventon Hotel
☎ 01209 203000 ***C:200***
REDWORTH Redworth Hall Hotel & Country Club
☎ 01388 770600 ***C:220***
REEPHAM The Old Brewery House Hotel
☎ 01603 870881 ***C:200***
REIGATE Reigate Manor Hotel
☎ 01737 240125 ***C:210***
RICHMOND UPON THAMES Richmond Gate Hotel
☎ 020 8940 0061 ***C:70***
RICHMOND UPON THAMES Richmond Hill
☎ 020 8940 2247 ***C:200***
RIPON Ripon Spa Hotel
☎ 01765 602172 ***C:150***
RISLEY Risley Hall Hotel
☎ 01159 399000 ***C:120***
ROMSEY Potters Heron Hotel
☎ 023 8026 6611 ***C:60***
ROSEDALE ABBEY Milburn Arms Hotel
☎ 01751 417312 ***C:65***
ROSS-ON-WYE Chase Hotel
☎ 01989 763161 ***C:100***
ROSS-ON-WYE Pengethley Manor
☎ 01989 730211 ***C:70***
ROSS-ON-WYE The Royal
☎ 01989 565105
ROSSINGTON Mount Pleasant Hotel
☎ 01302 868696 ***C:110***
ROSTHWAITE Scafell Hotel
☎ 017687 77208 ***C:75***
ROTHERHAM Carlton Park Hotel
☎ 01709 849955 ***C:100***
ROTHERHAM Elton Hotel
☎ 01709 545681 ***C:50***
ROTHERHAM Hellaby Hall Hotel
☎ 01709 702701 ***C:100***
ROTHERHAM Swallow Hotel
☎ 01709 830630 ***C:100***
ROTHERWICK Tylney Hall Hotel
☎ 01256 764881 ***C:100***
ROWSLEY East Lodge Country House Hotel
☎ 01629 734474 ***C:74***
ROYAL LEAMINGTON SPA Falstaff Hotel
☎ 01926 312044
ROYAL LEAMINGTON SPA Mallory Court Hotel
☎ 01926 330214 ***C:35***
ROYAL LEAMINGTON SPA Manor House Hotel
☎ 01926 423251 ***C:96***
ROYAL LEAMINGTON SPA The Leamington Hotel & Bistro
☎ 01926 883777 ***C:40***
ROYAL TUNBRIDGE WELLS The Spa Hotel
☎ 01892 520331 ***C:100***
RUGBY Brownsover Hall Hotel
☎ 01788 546100 ***C:56***
RUISLIP Barn Hotel
☎ 01895 636057 ***C:50***
RYDE Biskra Beach Hotel & Restaurant
☎ 01983 567913 ***C:60***
SALCOMBE Menzies Marine
☎ 0500 636943 ***C:70***
SALE Belmore Hotel
☎ 0161 973 2538 ***C:60***
SALISBURY Grasmere House Hotel
☎ 01722 338388 ***C:120***
SALISBURY Milford Hall Hotel
☎ 01722 417411 ***C:50***
SALISBURY Rose & Crown Hotel
☎ 01722 399955
SALISBURY The White Hart
☎ 0870 400 8125 ***C:80***
SAMPFORD PEVERELL Parkway House Hotel
☎ 01884 820255
SANDBACH Chimney House Hotel
☎ 01270 764141 ***C:40***
SANDIWAY Nunsmere Hall Country House Hotel
☎ 01606 889100 ***C:70***
SANDWICH The Blazing Donkey Country Hotel & Inn
☎ 01304 617362 ***C:350***
SAUNTON Saunton Sands Hotel
☎ 01271 890212
SCARBOROUGH Hotel St Nicholas
☎ 01723 364101
SCARBOROUGH Wrea Head Country Hotel
☎ 01723 378211 ***C:60***

Last minute rush? Bookings at Waterford House in Middleham are generally made six months in advance, but some as late as one month before the big day. With about one wedding each month the hotel can give you personal attention, whether it's booking the photographer or finding a local florist.

SCOTCH CORNER
Quality Hotel Scotch Corner
☎ 01748 850900 ***C:200***
SCUNTHORPE Forest Pines Hotel
☎ 01652 650770 ***C:180***
SCUNTHORPE
Menzies Royal Hotel
☎ 0500 636943 ***C:240***
SCUNTHORPE
Wortley House Hotel
☎ 01724 842223 ***C:240***
SEAVIEW Priory Bay Hotel
☎ 01983 613146 ***C:50***
SHAFTESBURY Royal Chase Hotel
☎ 01747 853355 ***C:78***
SHAP Shap Wells Hotel
☎ 01931 716628 ***C:150***
SHEDFIELD Marriott Meon Valley Hotel & Country Club
☎ 01329 833455 ***C:80***
SHEFFIELD Beauchief Hotel
☎ 0114 262 0500 ***C:120***
SHEFFIELD Charnwood Hotel
☎ 0114 258 9411 ***C:100***
SHEFFIELD
Menzies Rutland Hotel
☎ 0500 636943 ***C:100***
SHEFFIELD
Mosborough Hall Hotel
☎ 0114 248 4353 ***C:60***
SHEFFIELD Sheffield Moat House
☎ 0114 282 9988 ***C:400***
SHEFFIELD Swallow Hotel
☎ 0114 258 3811 ***C:120***
SHEFFIELD The Regency
☎ 0114 246 7703 ***C:180***
SHEFFIELD Whitley Hall Hotel
☎ 0114 245 4444 ***C:80***
SHEPPERTON Shepperton Moat House Hotel
☎ 01932 899988 ***C:300***
SHEPTON MALLET
Charlton House
☎ 01749 342008 ***C:75***
SHERBORNE Eastbury Hotel
☎ 01935 813131 ***C:120***
SHERBORNE The Sherborne Hotel
☎ 01935 813191 ***C:75***
SHIFNAL Park House Hotel
☎ 01952 460128 ***C:130***
SHIPLEY Marriott Hollins Hall Hotel and Country Club
☎ 01274 530053 ***C:120***
SHREWSBURY
Albright Hussey Hotel
☎ 01939 290571 ***C:100***
SHREWSBURY
Albrighton Hall Hotel
☎ 01939 291000 ***C:200***
SHREWSBURY Lord Hill Hotel
☎ 01743 232601 ***C:100***

SHREWSBURY
Mytton & Mermaid Hotel
☎ 01743 761220 ***C:50***
SHREWSBURY
Rowton Castle Hotel
☎ 01743 884044 ***C:110***
SIDMOUTH Belmont Hotel
☎ 01395 512555
SILCHESTER
Romans Country House Hotel
☎ 0118 970 0421 ***C:65***
SIX MILE BOTTOM
Swynford Paddocks Hotel
☎ 01638 570234 ***C:58***
SKEGNESS North Shore Hotel & Golf Course
☎ 01754 763298 ***C:200***
SKIPTON Coniston Hall Lodge
☎ 01756 748080 ***C:50***
SKIPTON Hanover International Hotel & Club
☎ 01756 700100 ***C:200***
SOLIHULL Solihull Moat House
☎ 0121 623 9988 ***C:50***
SOLIHULL Swallow St John's Hotel
☎ 0121 711 3000 ***C:100***
SOUTH BRENT Brookdale House Restaurant & Hotel
☎ 01548 821661 ***C:120***
SOUTH NORMANTON
Swallow Hotel
☎ 01773 812000 ***C:180***
SOUTH WALSHAM
South Walsham Hall Hotel
☎ 01603 270378 ***C:60***
SOUTHAMPTON
Botleigh Grange Hotel
☎ 01489 787700 ***C:200***
SOUTHAMPTON
The Woodlands Lodge Hotel
☎ 023 8029 2257 ***C:60***
SOUTHEND-ON-SEA
County Hotel Southend
☎ 01702 279955 ***C:200***
SOUTHPORT Royal Clifton Hotel
☎ 01704 533771 ***C:100***
SOUTHPORT Scarisbrick Hotel
☎ 01704 543000 ***C:170***
SPENNYMOOR Whitworth Hall
☎ 01388 811772 ***C:90***
ST AGNES Rose in Vale Country House Hotel
☎ 01872 552202 ***C:75***
ST AUSTELL Carlyon Bay Hotel
☎ 01726 812304

ST IVES Carbis Bay Hotel
☎ 01736 795311 ***C:120***
ST IVES Chy-an-Albany Hotel
☎ 01736 796759 ***C:90***
ST IVES Olivers Lodge Hotel
☎ 01480 463252 ***C:85***
ST IVES Porthminster Hotel
☎ 01736 795221 ***C:130***
ST IVES Slepe Hall Hotel
☎ 01480 463122 ***C:60***
ST IVES The Dolphin Hotel
☎ 01480 466966 ***C:60***
ST IVES Tregenna Castle Hotel
☎ 01736 795254 ***C:130***
ST MELLION
St Mellion International
☎ 01579 351351 ***C:120***
STAFFORD Garth Hotel
☎ 01785 256124 ***C:100***
STALLINGBOROUGH
Stallingborough Grange Hotel
☎ 01469 561302 ***C:65***
STAMFORD
The George of Stamford
☎ 01780 750750 ***C:50***
STANSTEAD ABBOTS
Briggens House Hotel
☎ 01279 829955 ***C:100***
STANSTED Whitehall Hotel
☎ 01279 850603 ***C:60***
STEEPLE ASTON The Holt Hotel
☎ 01869 340259 ***C:80***
STEYNING The Old Tollgate Restaurant & Hotel
☎ 01903 879494 ***C:40***
STILTON Bell Inn Hotel
☎ 01733 241066 ***C:80***
STOCKPORT Bredbury Hall Hotel & Country Club
☎ 0161 430 7421 ***C:150***
STOCKTON-ON-TEES
Parkmore Hotel
☎ 01642 786815 ***C:90***
STOCKTON-ON-TEES
Swallow Hotel
☎ 01642 679721 ***C:250***
STOKE-ON-TRENT
Haydon House Hotel
☎ 01782 711311 ***C:40***
STOKE-ON-TRENT
North Stafford Hotel
☎ 01782 744477
STOKE-ON-TRENT
Stoke-on-Trent Moat House
☎ 01782 609988 ***C:600***

STOKENCHURCH The Kings Arms
☎ 01494 609090 ***C:200***
STONE Stone House Hotel
☎ 01785 815531 ***C:120***
STONOR The Stonor Arms Hotel
☎ 01491 638866 ***C:80***
STOURPORT-ON-SEVERN Menzies Stourport Manor
☎ 0500 636943 ***C:350***
STOW-ON-THE-WOLD Fosse Manor
☎ 01451 830354
STOW-ON-THE-WOLD Grapevine Hotel
☎ 01451 830344 ***C:60***
STOW-ON-THE-WOLD The Unicorn
☎ 01451 830257 ***C:45***
STOW-ON-THE-WOLD Wyck Hill House Hotel
☎ 01451 831936 ***C:80***
STRATFORD-UPON-AVON Charlecote Pheasant
☎ 01789 279954 ***C:120***
STRATFORD-UPON-AVON Grosvenor Hotel
☎ 01789 269213 ***C:80***

STRATFORD-UPON-AVON Stratford Manor
☎ 01789 731173
STRATFORD-UPON-AVON The Alveston Manor
☎ 0870 400 8181 ***C:36***
STRATFORD-UPON-AVON The Shakespeare
☎ 0870 400 8182 ***C:50***
STRATFORD-UPON-AVON The Swan's Nest
☎ 0870 400 8183 ***C:50***
STRATFORD-UPON-AVON Welcombe Hotel and Golf Course
☎ 01789 295252 ***C:45***
STREATLEY The Swan Diplomat Hotel
☎ 01491 878800 ***C:90***
STROUD The Bear of Rodborough
☎ 01453 878522 ***C:100***
SUNDERLAND Quality Hotel
☎ 0191 519 1999 ***C:300***
SUTTON COLDFIELD Moor Hall Hotel
☎ 0121 308 3751 ***C:120***
SUTTON COLDFIELD New Hall
☎ 0121 378 2442 ***C:70***

SUTTON COLDFIELD Quality Hotel Sutton Court
☎ 0121 354 4991 ***C:130***
SUTTON ON SEA Grange & Links Hotel
☎ 01507 441334 ***C:500***
SWINDON Blunsdon House Hotel & Leisure Club
☎ 01793 721701 ***C:100***
SWINDON Chiseldon House Hotel
☎ 01793 741010 ***C:120***
SWINDON De Vere Hotel
☎ 01793 878785 ***C:60***
SWINDON Swindon Marriott
☎ 01793 512121
SWINDON The Goddard Arms Hotel
☎ 01793 692313 ***C:180***
SWINDON Villiers Inn
☎ 01793 814744 ***C:120***
TANKERSLEY Tankersley Manor
☎ 01226 744700 ***C:120***
TAPLOW Cliveden
☎ 01628 668561 ***C:120***
TAPLOW Taplow House Hotel
☎ 01628 670056 ***C:95***
TAUNTON Farthings Hotel and Restaurant
☎ 01823 480664 ***C:61***

TAUNTON Rumwell Manor Hotel
☎ 01823 461902 ***C:50***
TEBAY Westmorland Hotel & Bretherdale Restaurant
☎ 015396 24351 ***C:100***
TELFORD
Clarion Hotel Madeley Court
☎ 01952 680068 ***C:190***
TELFORD Valley Hotel
☎ 01952 432247 ***C:200***
TETBURY Calcot Manor
☎ 01666 890391 ***C:90***
TETBURY The Close Hotel
☎ 01666 502272 ***C:50***
THAME Spread Eagle Hotel
☎ 01844 213661 ***C:200***
THIRSK Golden Fleece Hotel
☎ 01845 523108 ***C:100***
THORNBURY Thornbury Castle
☎ 01454 281182 ***C:50***
THORNE Belmont Hotel
☎ 01405 812320
THORNTON HOUGH
Thornton Hall Hotel
☎ 0151 336 3938 ***C:200***
THORPE Izaak Walton Hotel
☎ 01335 350555 ***C:70***
TICEHURST
Dale Hill Hotel & Golf Club
☎ 01580 200112 ***C:100***
TIVERTON The Tiverton Hotel
☎ 01884 256120 ***C:170***
TOLLESHUNT KNIGHTS Five Lakes Hotel, Golf, Country Club & Spa
☎ 01621 868888 ***C:350***
TONBRIDGE The Langley Hotel
☎ 01732 353311 ***C:80***
TOPCLIFFE The Angel Inn
☎ 01845 577237 ***C:150***
TORQUAY The Grosvenor Hotel
☎ 01803 294373 ***C:400***
TORQUAY The Imperial
☎ 01803 294301 ***C:200***
TRING Pendley Manor
☎ 01442 891891 ***C:140***
TRURO Alverton Manor
☎ 01872 276633 ***C:120***
TURNERS HILL Alexander House
☎ 01342 714914 ***C:60***
TYNEMOUTH Grand Hotel
☎ 0191 293 6666 ***C:100***
UCKFIELD Buxted Park Country House Hotel
☎ 01825 732711 ***C:80***
UCKFIELD Horsted Place
☎ 01825 750581 ***C:50***
UPHOLLAND
Quality Hotel Skelmersdale
☎ 01695 720401 ***C:200***
UPPER SLAUGHTER
Lords of the Manor
☎ 01451 820243 ***C:50***
WAKEFIELD Chasley Hotel
☎ 01924 372111
WAKEFIELD Hotel St Pierre
☎ 01924 255596 ***C:60***
WAKEFIELD Waterton Park Hotel
☎ 01924 257911 ***C:60***
WALLINGFORD Springs Hotel
☎ 01491 836687
WALSALL Menzies Baron's Court
☎ 0500 636943 ***C:200***
WALSALL
Quality Hotel & Suites Walsall
☎ 01922 724444 ***C:120***
WALSALL
The Fairlawns at Aldridge
☎ 01922 455122 ***C:90***
WARE Marriott Hanbury Manor Hotel & Country Club
☎ 01920 487722 ***C:160***
WARMINSTER Bishopstrow House
☎ 01985 212312 ***C:70***
WARRINGTON
Daresbury Park Hotel
☎ 01925 267331 ***C:300***
WARRINGTON
Paddington House Hotel
☎ 01925 816767 ***C:150***
WARRINGTON Park Royal International Hotel
☎ 01925 730706 ***C:400***
WARRINGTON Rockfield Hotel
☎ 01925 262898 ***C:60***
WARWICK Ardencote Manor Hotel & Country Club
☎ 01926 843111 ***C:150***
WASHINGTON George Washington Golf & Country Club
☎ 0191 402 9988 ***C:35***
WATERMILLOCK Leeming House
☎ 0870 400 8131 ***C:30***
WATFORD Watford Moat House
☎ 01923 429988 ***C:200***
WATTON
Broom Hall Country Hotel
☎ 01953 882125 ***C:30***
WELLINGBOROUGH
Menzies Hind Hotel
☎ 0500 636943 ***C:120***
WELLINGTON Bindon Country House Hotel & Restaurant
☎ 01823 400070 ***C:50***
WELLINGTON The Cleve Country House Hotel
☎ 01823 662033 ***C:120***
WELLS Swan Hotel
☎ 01749 678877 ***C:80***
WELWYN Quality Hotel Welwyn
☎ 01438 716911 ***C:100***
WENTBRIDGE
Wentbridge House Hotel
☎ 01977 620444 ***C:130***
WEST BEXINGTON Manor Hotel
☎ 01308 897616 ***C:45***
WEST BROMWICH
Birmingham/West Bromwich Moat House
☎ 0121 609 9988 ***C:180***
WEST DRAYTON Le Meridien Excelsior Heathrow
☎ 0870 400 8899
WESTON-SUPER-MARE Beachlands Hotel
☎ 01934 621401 ***C:85***
WETHERBY Wood Hall Hotel
☎ 01937 587271 ***C:110***
WEYBRIDGE Oatlands Park Hotel
☎ 01932 847242 ***C:200***
WEYMOUTH Hotel Rembrandt
☎ 01305 764000 ***C:100***
WHITBY Dunsley Hall
☎ 01947 893437
WILLERBY Willerby Manor Hotel
☎ 01482 652616 ***C:300***
WILLITON Curdon Mill
☎ 01984 656522 ***C:300***
WILMSLOW Stanneylands Hotel
☎ 01625 525225 ***C:80***
WINCANTON
Holbrook House Hotel
☎ 01963 32377 ***C:80***
WINCHESTER
Lainston House Hotel
☎ 01962 863588 ***C:120***
WINCHESTER Marwell Hotel & Conference Centre
☎ 01962 777681 ***C:150***
WINCHESTER The Wessex
☎ 0870 400 8126 ***C:100***
WINDERMERE Belsfield Hotel
☎ 015394 42448 ***C:80***
WINDERMERE Burnside Hotel
☎ 015394 42211 ***C:120***
WINDERMERE Holbeck Ghyll Country House Hotel
☎ 015394 32375 ***C:65***
WINDERMERE Linthwaite House Hotel & Restaurant
☎ 015394 88600 ***C:60***
WINDERMERE The Old England
☎ 0870 400 8130 ***C:60***
WINDSOR Aurora Garden Hotel
☎ 01753 868686 ***C:120***
WINDSOR Oakley Court Hotel
☎ 01753 609988 ***C:180***
WINDSOR Royal Adelaide Hotel
☎ 01753 863916 ***C:100***
WINDSOR Sir Christopher Wren's House Hotel
☎ 01753 861354 ***C:100***

WISHAW The De Vere Belfry
☎ 01675 470301 ***C:250***
WOLVERHAMPTON Quality Hotel Wolverhampton
☎ 01902 429216 ***C:100***
WOODBRIDGE Seckford Hall Hotel
☎ 01394 385678 ***C:125***
WOODBRIDGE Ufford Park Hotel Golf & Leisure
☎ 01394 383555 ***C:200***
WOODFORD BRIDGE Menzies Prince Regent
☎ 0500 636943 ***C:400***
WOODHALL SPA Golf Hotel
☎ 01526 353535 ***C:120***
WOODHALL SPA Petwood Hotel
☎ 01526 352411 ***C:100***
WOOTTON BASSETT Marsh Farm Hotel
☎ 01793 848044 ***C:100***
WORKINGTON Washington Central Hotel
☎ 01900 65772 ***C:300***
WORKSOP Clumber Park Hotel
☎ 01623 835333 ***C:150***
WORKSOP Lion Hotel
☎ 01909 477925 ***C:120***
WORTHING Berkeley Hotel
☎ 01903 820000 ***C:60***
WORTHING Chatsworth Hotel
☎ 01903 236103
YARM Judges Hotel
☎ 01642 789000 ***C:200***
YARMOUTH George Hotel
☎ 01983 760331 ***C:60***
YELVERTON Moorland Links Hotel
☎ 01822 852245
YEOVIL Little Barwick House
☎ 01935 423902 ***C:40***
YORK Ambassador Hotel
☎ 01904 641316 ***C:50***
YORK Dean Court Hotel
☎ 01904 625082 ***C:70***
YORK Knavesmire Manor Hotel
☎ 01904 702941 ***C:60***
YORK Monkbar Hotel
☎ 01904 638086 ***C:60***
YORK Swallow Hotel
☎ 01904 701000
YORK The Royal York Hotel & Conference Centre
☎ 01904 653681 ***C:100***
YORK York Moat House
☎ 01904 459988 ***C:80***

CHANNEL ISLANDS

ST MARTIN St Margaret's Lodge Hotel
☎ 01481 235757 ***C:150***

NORTHERN IRELAND

BANGOR Marine Court Hotel
☎ 028 9145 1100 ***C:300***

REPUBLIC OF IRELAND

AHERLOW Aherlow House
☎ 062 56153 ***C:300***
BALLINASLOE Haydens Gateway Business, Leisure Hotel
☎ 065 68 23000 ***C:300***
BALLYCOTTON Bay View Hotel
☎ 021 646746 ***C:80***
CAHERCIVEEN Caherciveen Park Hotel
☎ 066 9472543 ***C:700***
CASTLEBAR Breaffy House Hotel
☎ 094 22033 ***C:250***
CORK Ambassador Hotel
☎ 021 4551996 ***C:60***
DUBLIN The Mercer Hotel
☎ 01 4782179 ***C:60***
ENNIS West County Conference, Leisure Hotel
☎ 065 6823000 ***C:100***
GALWAY Westwood House Hotel
☎ 091 521442 ***C:275***
LIMERICK South Court Business & Leisure Hotel
☎ 065 6823000 ***C:110***
MALLOW Springfort Hall Hotel
☎ 022 21278 ***C:250***
NEWMARKET-ON-FERGUS Clare Inn Golf and Leisure Hotel
☎ 065 6823000 ***C:300***
ROSCREA Grant's Hotel
☎ 0505 23300 ***C:300***

SCOTLAND

ABERDEEN Aberdeen Marriott
☎ 01224 770011 ***C:320***
ABERDEEN Copthorne Aberdeen
☎ 01224 630404 ***C:80***
ABERDEEN Maryculter House Hotel
☎ 01224 732124 ***C:120***
ABERDEEN Palm Court
☎ 01224 310351 ***C:110***
ABERDEEN Simpsons Hotel
☎ 01224 327777 ***C:25***
ABERDEEN The Marcliffe at Pitfodels
☎ 01224 861000 ***C:360***
ABERDEEN Westhill Hotel
☎ 01224 740388 ***C:150***
ANNAN Queensberry Arms Hotel
☎ 01461 202024 ***C:70***
ARDELVE Loch Duich Hotel
☎ 01599 555213 ***C:40***
ARISAIG Arisaig House
☎ 01687 450622 ***C:30***
AUCHTERARDER Auchterarder House
☎ 01764 663646 ***C:70***
AUCHTERARDER Duchally Country Estate
☎ 01764 663071 ***C:40***
AUCHTERARDER The Gleneagles Hotel
☎ 01764 662231
AYR Fairfield House Hotel
☎ 01292 267461 ***C:110***
BALLOCH Cameron House Hotel
☎ 01389 755565 ***C:180***
BANCHORY Banchory Lodge Hotel
☎ 01330 822625 ***C:50***
BANCHORY Burnett Arms Hotel
☎ 01330 824944 ***C:100***
BANCHORY Tor-na-Coille Hotel
☎ 01330 822242 ***C:95***
BARRHEAD Dalmeny Park Country House Hotel
☎ 0141 881 9211 ***C:200***
BATHGATE Cairn Hotel
☎ 01506 633366 ***C:200***
BIGGAR Shieldhill Castle
☎ 01899 220035 ***C:250***
BLAIRGOWRIE Altamount House Hotel
☎ 01250 873512 ***C:130***
BOAT OF GARTEN Boat Hotel
☎ 01479 831258 ***C:60***
BRIDGE OF ALLAN Royal Hotel
☎ 01786 832284 ***C:100***
CASTLE DOUGLAS Douglas Arms
☎ 01556 502231 ***C:100***
CRIEFF Crieff Hydro
☎ 01764 655555 ***C:150***
DINGWALL Kinkell House
☎ 01349 861270 ***C:70***
DRUMNADROCHIT Polmaily House Hotel
☎ 01456 450343
DRYMEN Winnock Hotel
☎ 01360 660245 ***C:120***
DUMFRIES Cairndale Hotel & Leisure Club
☎ 01387 254111 ***C:300***

If you are planning a wedding in the capital, the Hotel Inter-Continental London takes bookings up to two years in advance. May to September are the busiest periods with around three in every four Sundays booked for weddings.

DUMFRIES Station Hotel
☎ 01387 254316 ***C:60***
DUNDEE Swallow Hotel
☎ 01382 641122 ***C:120***
DUNFERMLINE
Elgin Hotel and Restaurants
☎ 01383 872257 ***C:160***
DUNFERMLINE King Malcolm
☎ 01383 722611 ***C:70***
EAST KILBRIDE Bruce Hotel
☎ 01355 229771 ***C:300***
EAST KILBRIDE Crutherland Country House Hotel
☎ 01355 577000 ***C:150***
EDINBURGH
Apex International Hotel
☎ 0131 300 3456
EDINBURGH Braid Hills Hotel
☎ 0131 447 8888 ***C:170***
EDINBURGH Bruntsfield Hotel
☎ 0131 229 1393 ***C:70***
EDINBURGH Carlton Hotel
☎ 0131 472 3000 ***C:150***
EDINBURGH Channings
☎ 0131 332 3232 ***C:80***
EDINBURGH Edinburgh Capital Moat House
☎ 0131 535 9988 ***C:250***
EDINBURGH
George Inter-Continental
☎ 0131 225 1251 ***C:100***
EDINBURGH Orwell Lodge Hotel
☎ 0131 229 1044 ***C:200***
EDINBURGH Royal Terrace
☎ 0131 557 3222 ***C:70***
EDINBURGH
Swallow Royal Scot Hotel
☎ 0131 334 9191 ***C:80***
EDINBURGH The Barnton
☎ 0131 339 1144 ***C:100***
EDINBURGH
The Sheraton Grand Hotel
☎ 0131 229 9131 ***C:480***
ELGIN Laichmoray Hotel
☎ 01343 540045 ***C:120***
ELGIN Mansion House Hotel
☎ 01343 548811 ***C:180***
ELIE The Golf Hotel
☎ 01333 330209 ***C:120***
FENWICK Fenwick Hotel
☎ 01560 600478 ***C:100***
FORFAR Idvies House Hotel
☎ 01307 818787 ***C:40***
FORT WILLIAM Grand Hotel
☎ 01397 702928 ***C:80***
FORT WILLIAM
Inverlochy Castle Hotel
☎ 01397 702177 ***C:40***
FORT WILLIAM Moorings Hotel
☎ 01397 772797 ***C:90***
GALASHIELS Kingsknowes Hotel
☎ 01896 758375 ***C:100***

GALASHIELS Woodlands House Hotel & Restaurants
☎ 01896 754722 ***C:54***
GIFFNOCK The Macdonald
☎ 0141 638 2225 ***C:130***
GLASGOW Glasgow Marriott
☎ 0141 226 5577 ***C:250***
GLASGOW Holiday Inn
☎ 0141 352 8300 ***C:120***
GLASGOW Kelvin Park Lorne
☎ 0141 314 9955 ***C:200***
GLASGOW Kings Park Hotel
☎ 0141 647 5491 ***C:200***
GLASGOW The Devonshire Hotel of Glasgow
☎ 0141 339 7878 ***C:50***
GLASGOW The Ewington
☎ 0141 423 1152 ***C:60***
GLASGOW The Tinto Firs
☎ 0141 637 2353 ***C:130***
GLENFARG The Glenfarg Hotel & Restaurant
☎ 01577 830241 ***C:60***
GLENROTHES
Balgeddie House Hotel
☎ 01592 742511 ***C:150***
INVERNESS
Bunchrew House Hotel
☎ 01463 234917 ***C:120***
INVERNESS Culloden House Hotel
☎ 01463 790461 ***C:60***
INVERNESS Smithton Hotel
☎ 01463 791999 ***C:40***
INVERURIE Thainstone House Hotel and Country Club
☎ 01467 621643 ***C:130***
KELSO Cross Keys Hotel
☎ 01573 223303 ***C:270***
KELSO The Roxburghe Hotel & Golf Course
☎ 01573 450331 ***C:50***
KILWINNING Montgreenan Mansion House Hotel
☎ 01294 557733 ***C:110***
KINCLAVEN Ballathie House Hotel
☎ 01250 883268 ***C:200***
KINROSS Windlestrae Hotel Business & Leisure Centre
☎ 01577 863217 ***C:100***
KIRKCALDY Dean Park Hotel
☎ 01592 261635 ***C:250***
KIRKCALDY
Dunnikier House Hotel
☎ 01592 268393 ***C:40***
LADYBANK Fernie Castle
☎ 01337 810381 ***C:180***
LARGS Brisbane House
☎ 01475 687200 ***C:120***
LERWICK Lerwick Hotel
☎ 01595 692166 ***C:100***

LOCKERBIE The Dryfesdale Country House Hotel
☎ 01576 202427 ***C:84***
LUNDIN LINKS Old Manor Hotel
☎ 01333 320368 ***C:100***
MARKINCH Balbirnie House
☎ 01592 610066 ***C:200***
MAYBOLE Ladyburn
☎ 01655 740585 ***C:250***
MOFFAT Moffat House Hotel
☎ 01683 220039 ***C:110***
MONTROSE Links Hotel
☎ 01674 671000
MONTROSE Montrose Park Hotel and Golf Lodges
☎ 01674 663400 ***C:220***
NAIRN Boath House
☎ 01667 454896 ***C:200***
NORTH BERWICK The Marine
☎ 0870 400 8129 ***C:200***
PEEBLES Peebles Hydro Hotel
☎ 01721 720602 ***C:250***
PERTH Huntingtower Hotel
☎ 01738 583771 ***C:100***
PERTH Kinfauns Castle
☎ 01738 620777 ***C:60***
PERTH Quality Hotel Perth
☎ 01738 624141 ***C:300***
PETERHEAD Waterside Inn
☎ 01779 471121 ***C:250***
PORTPATRICK
Knockinaam Lodge Hotel
☎ 01776 810471 ***C:45***
POWMILL Gartwhinzean Hotel
☎ 01577 840595 ***C:100***
ROY BRIDGE
Glenspean Lodge Hotel
☎ 01397 712223 ***C:65***
STONEHAVEN
County Hotel & Leisure Club
☎ 01569 764386 ***C:180***
STRATHAVEN Strathaven Hotel
☎ 01357 521778 ***C:110***
TAIN Mansfield House Hotel
☎ 01862 892052 ***C:70***
TOBERMORY Western Isles Hotel
☎ 01688 302012 ***C:70***
TORRIDON Loch Torridon Country House Hotel
☎ 01445 791242 ***C:38***
TROON Marine Hotel
☎ 01292 314444 ***C:50***
TROON Piersland House Hotel
☎ 01292 314747 ***C:75***
TURNBERRY Malin Court
☎ 01655 331457 ***C:120***
WHITBURN The Hilcroft Hotel
☎ 01501 740818 ***C:200***

WALES

ABERDYFI Plas Penhelig Country House Hotel
☎ 01654 767676 ***C:60***

ABERGAVENNY
Llansantffraed Court Hotel
☎ 01873 840678 ***C:150***

ABERGELE Kinmel Manor Hotel
☎ 01745 832014 ***C:250***

ABERYSTWYTH Conrah Hotel
☎ 01970 617941 ***C:65***

AMLWCH Lastra Farm Hotel
☎ 01407 830906 ***C:85***

BALA Pale Hall Country House Hotel
☎ 01678 530285 ***C:100***

BARRY Egerton Grey Country House Hotel
☎ 01446 711666 ***C:120***

BARRY Mount Sorrel Hotel
☎ 01446 740069 ***C:150***

BETWS-Y-COED
The Royal Oak Hotel
☎ 01690 710219 ***C:100***

BONTDDU Bontddu Hall Hotel
☎ 01341 430661 ***C:150***

BRECON Best Western Castle of Brecon Hotel
☎ 01874 624611

BRIDGEND Coed-Y-Mwstwr Hotel
☎ 01656 860621 ***C:200***

BUILTH WELLS
Caer Beris Manor Hotel
☎ 01982 552601 ***C:100***

CAERNARFON Celtic Royal Hotel
☎ 01286 674477 ***C:200***

CAERNARFON
Seiont Manor Hotel
☎ 01286 673366 ***C:100***

CARDIFF Cardiff Bay Hotel
☎ 029 2047 5000 ***C:180***

CARDIFF Cardiff Marriott
☎ 029 2039 9944 ***C:120***

CARDIFF Manor Parc Country Hotel & Restaurant
☎ 029 2069 3723 ***C:100***

CARDIFF
New House Country Hotel
☎ 029 2052 0280 ***C:200***

CARDIFF Quality Hotel
☎ 029 2052 9988 ***C:180***

CARDIFF St Mellons Hotel & Country Club
☎ 01633 680355 ***C:160***

CARDIFF
The St David's Hotel & Spa
☎ 029 2045 4045 ***C:150***

CHEPSTOW George Hotel
☎ 01291 625363

CHEPSTOW Marriott St Pierre Hotel & Country Club
☎ 01291 625261

COLWYN BAY Hopeside Hotel
☎ 01492 533244

CRICKHOWELL
Gliffaes Country House Hotel
☎ 01874 730371

CWMBRAN Parkway Hotel
☎ 01633 871199 ***C:90***

DOLGELLAU
Penmaenuchaf Hall Hotel
☎ 01341 422129 ***C:50***

EWLOE De Vere St Davids Park
☎ 01244 520800

HAVERFORDWEST
Wolfscastle Country Hotel
☎ 01437 741688 ***C:60***

HIRWAUN
Ty Newydd Country Hotel
☎ 01685 813433 ***C:160***

KNIGHTON The Knighton Hotel
☎ 01547 520530 ***C:120***

LANGLAND BAY Langland Court
☎ 01792 361545 ***C:100***

LLANARMON DYFFRYN CEIRIOG
West Arms Hotel
☎ 01691 600665 ***C:80***

LLANBERIS Royal Victoria Hotel
☎ 01286 870253 ***C:120***

LLANDRILLO Tyddyn Llan Country Hotel & Restaurant
☎ 01490 440264 ***C:30***

LLANDRINDOD WELLS
Greenway Manor Hotel
☎ 01597 851230 ***C:60***

LLANDRINDOD WELLS
Hotel Metropole
☎ 01597 823700 ***C:250***

LLANDUDNO St George's Hotel
☎ 01492 877544 ***C:100***

LLANELLI Ashburnham Hotel
☎ 01554 834343 ***C:120***

LLANELLI Diplomat Hotel
☎ 01554 756156 ***C:200***

LLANFAIRPWLLGWYNGYLL Carreg Bran Country Hotel
☎ 01248 714224

LLANGOLLEN Bryn Howel Hotel & Restaurant
☎ 01978 860331 ***C:300***

LLANGOLLEN The Wild Pheasant Hotel & Restaurant
☎ 01978 860629 ***C:140***

LLANWDDYN Lake Vyrnwy Hotel
☎ 01691 870692 ***C:90***

LLYSWEN Llangoed Hall
☎ 01874 754525 ***C:50***

MISKIN Miskin Manor Hotel
☎ 01443 224204 ***C:200***

MOLD Beaufort Park Hotel
☎ 01352 758646 ***C:80***

NEWTOWN Elephant & Castle
☎ 01686 626271 ***C:30***

NORTHOP Soughton Hall Hotel
☎ 01352 840811 ***C:150***

PEMBROKE Court Hotel
☎ 01646 672273 ***C:70***

PONTYPRIDD Heritage Park Hotel
☎ 01443 687057 ***C:220***

PORT TALBOT
Aberavon Beach Hotel
☎ 01639 884949 ***C:300***

PORTMEIRION
The Hotel Portmeirion
☎ 01766 770000 ***C:100***

PRESTEIGNE
Radnorshire Arms Hotel
☎ 01544 267406 ***C:50***

ROSSETT Llyndir Hall Hotel
☎ 01244 571648 ***C:120***

ROSSETT Rossett Hall Hotel
☎ 01244 571000 ***C:120***

ST CLEARS
Forge Restaurant & Lodge
☎ 01994 230300 ***C:120***

ST DAVID'S Warpool Court Hotel
☎ 01437 720300 ***C:100***

SWANSEA Swansea Marriott
☎ 01792 642020 ***C:250***

TALSARNAU Hotel Maes y Neuadd
☎ 01766 780200 ***C:65***

TENBY Fourcroft Hotel
☎ 01834 842886 ***C:100***

TENBY
Penally Abbey Country House
☎ 01834 843033 ***C:50***

TREARDDUR BAY
Trearddur Bay Hotel
☎ 01407 860301

USK Glen-yr-Afon House Hotel
☎ 01291 672302 ***C:200***

WELSHPOOL Royal Oak Hotel
☎ 01938 552217 ***C:100***

WREXHAM Cross Lanes Hotel & Restaurant
☎ 01978 780555 ***C:120***

Photograph Credits

Permission for the use of photographs in the preliminary pages of this guide was kindly given by the following establishments:

Capital Hotel, London
Inverlochy Castle, Fort William
Lainston House, Winchester
The Lanesborough, London
Radisson Edwardian Hotels
Rookery Hall, Nantwich
The Savoy, London
Swynford Paddocks Hotel, Six Mile Bottom
Thornbury Castle, Thornbury
Tregenna Castle Hotel, St Ives
Ynyshir Hall, Eglwysfach

Other photographs used with the kind permission of the AA Photo Library are as follows:

All main pictures are held in the Automobile Association's own library (AA PHOTOLIBRARY) and were taken by M BIRKITT 32, 33a, 33b, 33c, 33d.

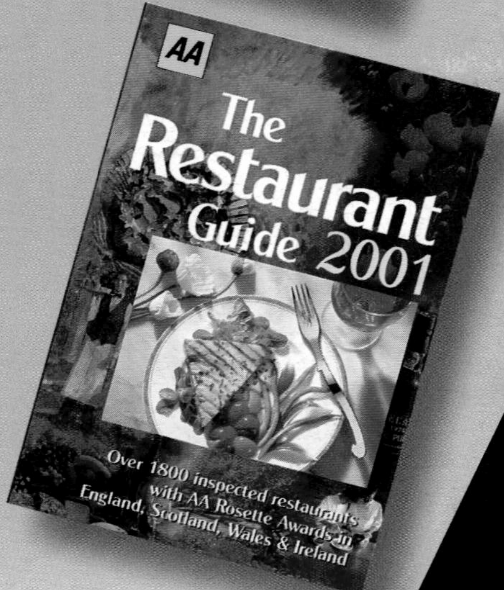